About the Author

MICHAEL GRAY is a distinguished critic, writer and broadcaster. He graduated in History & English Literature at York University, England, in the 1960s, where he studied under the controversial, brilliant critic Dr. F.R. Leavis, and where as a student journalist he interviewed, among others, the eminent British historian A.J.P. Taylor and the legendary American guitarist Jimi Hendrix. His pioneering study of Bob Dylan's work, *Song & Dance Man*, first published in the 1970s in Britain, America and Japan, was the first full-length critical study of this crucial 20th century cultural figure. It is now recognised as a classic in its field. A selection of pieces on Dylan, *All Across the Telegraph: A Bob Dylan Handbook*, published in 1987, was co-edited by Gray and included work by several distinguished academics in the fields of English & American Literature and Music. In 1996, Michael Gray co-authored *The Elvis Atlas: A Journey Through Elvis Presley's America*, published in hardback in New York by Henry Holt. The massive *Song & Dance Man III: The Art of Bob Dylan* was published by Continuum in March 2000. A special reprint appeared in the US in April 2001, when Gray delivered talks at a number of US universities; a fourth reprint was published in New York and London in 2002 and a fifth in 2004. Michael Gray is recognised as a world authority on the work of Bob Dylan and is an expert on rock'n'roll history and the blues, with a special interest in pre-war blues.

FROM REVIEWS OF
SONG & DANCE MAN III: THE ART OF BOB DYLAN
by Michael Gray

GREIL MARCUS:
'Extraordinarily useful . . . I have always admired Gray's reach, tone, and acuity but the research here is just amazing.'

ANDREW MOTION, British Poet Laureate, *The Observer*, London:
'One of my three best books of the year. . . . The best book there is on Dylan, now better than ever.'

THE NEWS & OBSERVER, US:
'Notably, there is a fat, new edition of Michael Gray's huge and wonderful critical work, *Song & Dance Man*. . . . Gray's book proves that scholarship can be fun to read.'

ROLLING STONE:
'Monumental, endlessly illuminating.'

BLOOMSBURY REVIEW, US:
'An engaging, intellectual discussion of the passion, pain and trends that have poured out of Bob Dylan . . . anyone who is interested in the artistic impact of music on an intellectual level will jump at the chance to have a truly highbrow discussion about rock'n'roll.'

CHRISTOPHER RICKS:
'Immense and immensely illuminating. . . . It is wonderfully comic and serious and sharp. I am enjoying it hugely and learning from every page.'

THE TIMES, London:
'In examining the influences that shaped Dylan into one of the most influential post-war artists, Gray draws on everyone from Elvis to Eliot, Robert Johnson to Rimbaud . . . This huge work is overwhelming. . . . "It's all been written in the book," sang Bob Dylan. Now it really has.'

NEWSDAY, US:
'Illuminating, wry and exhaustive.'

DER BUND, Switzerland:
'Gray's monumental study . . . dissects Dylan's songs to reveal their literary and musical origins . . . provides insight into Dylan's methodology and reveals hidden layers . . . His precision identifies the essence of Dylan. . . . Michael Gray writes exuberantly, critically and is never lost for a judgment. . . . His evaluations are refreshing and accurate.'

UNCUT, London:
'Now comes the third (and allegedly final) edition of Michael Gray's pioneering tome, which helped launch the Zimmerman book industry. It runs to a colossal 900 pages and confirms once again Gray's position as the doyen of Dylan scholars . . . even in its initial modest form, [it] was profoundly significant . . . a revelation . . . thrilling. . . . His book invented a new school of rock criticism which made most of the writing that had gone before seem superficial, irrelevant and trivial. . . . The third edition of Gray's lifetime study displays an almost insane degree of scholarship . . . a quite dazzlingly brilliant essay on Dylan's use of imagery borrowed from

old blues songs. A similar essay on the use of nursery rhyme and fairy tale . . . [and] the final chapter is an intellectual tour de force. . . . Of course there will always be those who prefer simply to enjoy the songs rather than to analyse them. But anyone who is remotely curious about the richness of the man's extraordinary imagination will find Gray's work an essential companion. ***** '

STEPHEN SCOBIE, University of Victoria, Canada & author of *Alias Bob Dylan*:
'Indispensable. . . . His research is formidable, and his knowledge encyclopedic . . . great cogency, confidence and authority . . . a quite splendid critic. . . . Gray can explain *how* the text [of a song] works poetically. It's a rare gift: . . . [his] expositions of "Every Grain of Sand", "Angelina", "Jokerman" and "Under the Red Sky" are utterly definitive . . . at the heart of this book is some of the finest critical writing ever done about Bob Dylan.'

BRYAN APPLEYARD, *Sunday Times*, London:
'Serious Dylan criticism . . . intricate analyses . . . monumental.'

AUSTIN CHRONICLE, US:
'A startling piece of scholarship. By scrutinizing Dylan's canon, Gray achieves a fresh read of his life. . . . *Song & Dance Man III* overshadows others' accounts of secret marriages and mythic motorcycle crashes, and it entirely outdoes other analyses . . . frank, insightful, unassailably excellent.'

RECORD COLLECTOR, London:
'The original *Song & Dance Man* was a pioneering piece of rock scholarship. . . . Written with great intelligence and passion . . . the result was the first important book about a rock artist's output, not just their life. . . . But these 250 pages are merely a fragment of the 900-page monster which Gray has [now] unleashed . . . magnificent . . . soaked in insight.'

DAVID HAJDU, author of *Positively 4th Street*:
'It is the most penetrating and clear-headed work on his work ever done—a monumental achievement.'

FOLK ROOTS, London:
'This major update of a seminal work deserves to be read and studied by anyone with even the slightest interest in song lyrics and it's essential as a storehouse of knowledge on folk, country and blues records.'

BLUEPRINT, British blues magazine:
'Fascinating, scholarly and very readable. . . . The longest and most relevant chapter for *Blueprint* readers ["Even Post-Structuralists Oughta Have the Pre-War Blues"] is . . . packed solid with informative and enthralling reading. I cannot congratulate Gray enough for this outstanding chapter . . . [a] very important study. A thoroughly enjoyable and informative book by an author who writes knowledgeably, with style and with great insight—very highly recommended to all.'

Q, London:
'This book is an event . . . delivering prodigious analyses of Dylan's artistry and his polymath sources in pre-war blues, nursery rhymes, fairy tales and Hollywood movie dialogue. . . . Gray maintains a ruthless integrity regarding Dylan himself. ***** '

EVENING STANDARD, London:
'The definitive critical work.'

THE OBSERVER, London:
'Paperback of the Week. A mammoth work of scholarship, often enthralling and never less than illuminating. His chapter on Dylan's sources in the blues . . . is almost worth the price of admission alone. . . . This is trenchant and thought-provoking stuff, and pretty much characterises Gray's style and his approach to a subject who has suffered more than most at the hands of lesser, and less well-informed, critics. A must for anyone interested in the great adventure that is Bob Dylan's work.'

BOSTON GLOBE:
'Michael Gray's *Song & Dance Man* . . . has grown across three decades and as many editions into a comprehensive critical companion.'

LONDON REVIEW OF BOOKS:
'The last word on Dylan is neither possible nor desirable . . . perhaps the closest that anyone has come . . . is Michael Gray in his awesome and encyclopedic *Song & Dance Man*, currently in its third, extensively revised edition.'

SALON.COM:
'. . . to study some of the finest work found in American song . . . requires someone with the boldness and the breadth of knowledge shown by Michael Gray, whose hefty study . . . puts the bulk of rock-crit writing about Dylan to shame.'

NEW YORK REVIEW OF BOOKS:
'Michael Gray . . . probably Dylan's single most assiduous critic.'

THE BOB DYLAN ENCYCLOPEDIA

MICHAEL GRAY

NEW YORK • LONDON

2006

The Continuum International Publishing Group Inc
80 Maiden Lane, New York, NY 10038

The Continuum International Publishing Group Ltd
The Tower Building, 11 York Road, London SE1 7NX

www.continuumbooks.com

This book is printed in the United Kingdom at CPI Bath

Cover art by Stefan Killen Design

Library of Congress Cataloging-in-Publication Data
Gray, Michael, 1946–
The Bob Dylan encyclopedia / Michael Gray.
p. cm.
Includes bibliographical references and index.
ISBN 0-8264-6933-7 (leatherbound hardcover : alk. paper)
1. Dylan, Bob, 1941—Encyclopedias. I. Title.
ML420.D98G68 2006
782.42164092–dc22
[b]
2006012728

to Magdalena

Contents

Thanks and Acknowledgements

SPECIAL THANKS TO

Sarah Beattie; John Baldwin; Alan Balfour; David Barker; Derek Barker; Glen Dundas; Dave Engel; the Council, SCR & Library of Girton College, Cambridge, and especially Dr. Alastair Reid; Terry Kelly; Andrew Muir; Gabriella Page-Fort and Tony Russell.

THANKS TO

Jerome B. Abrams, Bill Aikins, Russell Alexander, Rhonda Allende, Audre John & Mose Allison, Karl Erik Andersen, Suzanne Ashley, Lillian Baharestani, Helen Bailey, Gordon Ball, Tracy Barker, Dylan Beattie, Zuleika Benitez, Toby Berger, Olof Björner, Terence Blacker, Simon Blackley, Judy Brown at Denver Public Library, Chris Bucklen, Gary Burke, Hanns Peter Bushoff, Jane Butler, Larry Campbell, Eric Campos, Anne Cartwright, Flo Castner, Lynn Castner, Rick Clark, Jim Clements, Andy Cohen, Chris Cooper, Neal Cooper, Michael Corcoran, Neil Corcoran, Jonathan Cott, Chris Coughlan-Smith, Ben Covington, Jan Cox, Richard Crooks, Adam Crothers, Jones Cullinan, Arline Cunningham, Jenny Curtis, Andrew Darke, Aidan Day, Mary Dean, Adrian Deevoy, Nick Dodd, Jim Dring, Robert L. Drew, Tim Dunn, Hans Eisenbeis, David Evans, Robert Forryan, Alan Fraser, Denny Freeman, Frances Gandy, Paul Garon, Jeffrey Gaskill, Karl Gedlicka, Charlie Gillett, Toby Gleason, Tony Glover, Rob Goetz, Steven Goldberg, Lily Goodwin, Barbara Ribakove Gordon, Al Gorgoni, Robert Gover, Mike Gray, Mark Greenberg, Greyhound Soul & Duane, Michael Gross, Malcolm Guite, David Hajdu, Si Halley, Peter Hues Harrison, Mary Amelia Cummins Harvey, Todd Harvey, Nicholas Hawthorne, April C. Hayes, John Herdman, Carolyn Hester, Clinton Heylin, John Hinchey, Terri Hinte, Nigel Hinton, Historic Waco Foundation, Jan Høiberg, John Hopkins, Barney Hoskyns, Duncan Hume, Patrick Humphries, Don Hunstein, Ira Ingber, A.J. Iriarte, John Jackson, Elana James, Craig Jamieson, Peter Jesperson, Janet Joyce, Ric Kangas, Daniel Karlin, Larry Keenan, Roy Kelly, Mark Kidel, Kaitlin King, Malcolm Kirton, Freddy Koella, Robert Köhler, Sandy Konikoff, Daniel Kramer, Michael Krogsgaard, Jeff Laine, Jon Landau, Bruce Langhorne, Jonathan Lauer, Eric LaBlanc, C.P. Lee, Bob

Levinson, Dan Levy, John Lindley, Dennis Lloyd, Charlie McCoy, Regina McCrary, Brian McMahon, Dave Madeloni, Toby Manners, Marc at Double M Management, Greil Marcus, Mike Marqusee, Kathy Mattea, John May, Jesse Meehl, Vince Melamed, Pat Missin, Dave Morton, Wayne Moss, Geoff Muldaur & Mary, Joy Munsey, Michele Murino, Rab Noakes, Tanya Nolan, Brendan O'Brien, Brendan O'Dwyer, Joe Offer, Robert Oermann, Eric Oliver, Eric Olsen, Hoyle Osborne, Eyolf Østrem, Bill Pagel, Jon Pankake, Alan Pasqua, Faith Petric, Sue Phelps, David Pichaske, Michel Pomarède, Andy Prevezer, Darrell Redmond, Sy Ribakove, Amadee Ricketts, Alan Rinzler, John Roberts, BA Robertson, Christopher Rollason, Jahanara Romney, Jeff Rosen, Fred Rothwell, Howard Rutman, Barbara Sandlin at Waco-McLennan County Library, Mala Sharma, Jerry Schatzberg, Burkhard Schleser, Sandra Hale Schulman, Cameron Sclater, Stephen Scobie, Carl Sealove, Joel Selvin, Brad Shipp, Neil Slaven, Larry Sloman, Chris Smith, Howard Sounes, Minton Sparks, Leyla Spencer, Wes Stace, Lucas Stensland, Rob Stoner, Marilyn Strathern, Bryan Styble, Ed Suthon, Gregg Sutton, Christer Svensson, David Tedeschi, Happy Traum, Rainer Vesely, Vin Vincent, Peter Viney, Paolo Vites, Elijah Wald, Melanie Watson, Winston A. Watson, Lisa Mattioni Weber, Miriam Weissman, Dave Whitaker, Sean Wilentz, Ruth Williams, Nigel Williamson, Val Wilmer, Terry Winston, Stefan Wirz, Richard Wissolik, Robin Witting, Daniel Wolfe, John Wraith, Bob Yellin, Richard Younger, Zimmy's proprietors Bob & Linda, Matthew Zuckerman.

ACKNOWLEDGEMENTS

The author and the publishers wish to express their thanks to the undermentioned copyright owners for the use of material written and composed by Bob Dylan. Quotations are taken from Bob Dylan recordings and may in some cases differ slightly from the printed sheet-music versions and/or the anthology *Bob Dylan: Lyrics: 1962–2001*:

(a) Copyright by Duchess Music (now MCA Music): **Song to Woody**, © 1962, renewed 1990; **Talking New York**, © 1962, renewed 1990; **Talking Bear Mountain Picnic Massacre Blues**, © 1962, renewed 1990.

(b) Copyright by Dwarf Music: **Rainy Day Women # 12 and 35**, © 1966, renewed 1994; **Pledging My Time**, © 1966, renewed 1994; **Visions of Johanna**, © 1966, renewed 1994; **Stuck Inside of Mobile with the Memphis Blues Again**, © 1966, renewed 1994; **Leopard-Skin Pill-Box Hat**, © 1966, renewed 1994; **Just Like a Woman**, © 1966, renewed 1994; **Absolutely Sweet Marie**, © 1966, renewed 1994; **Temporary Like Achilles**, © 1966, renewed 1994; **4th Time Around**, © 1966, renewed 1994; **Sad-Eyed Lady of the Lowlands**, © 1966, renewed 1994; **Too Much of Nothing**, © 1967, renewed 1995; **Please, Mrs. Henry**, © 1967, renewed 1995; **Down in the Flood**, © 1967, renewed 1995; **You Ain't Goin' Nowhere**, © 1967, renewed 1995; **Tears of Rage** (Words by Bob Dylan, Music by Richard Manuel), © 1968, renewed 1996; **This Wheel's on Fire** (Words & Music by Bob Dylan & Rick Danko), © 1967; renewed 1995; **Open the Door, Homer**, © 1968, renewed 1996; **John Wesley Harding**, © 1968, renewed 1996; **All Along the Watchtower**, © 1968, renewed 1996; **The Ballad of Frankie Lee and Judas Priest**, © 1968, renewed 1996; **I Dreamed I Saw St. Augustine**, © 1968, renewed 1996; **Drifter's Escape**, © 1968, renewed 1996; **I Pity the Poor Immigrant**, © 1968, renewed 1996; **I Shall Be Released**, © 1967; **Nothing Was Delivered**, © 1968, renewed 1996; **I'll Be Your Baby Tonight**, © 1968, renewed 1996; **She's Your Lover Now**, © 1971; **I Wanna Be Your Lover**, © 1971, 1976.

(c) Copyright by Big Sky Music: **I Threw It All Away**, © 1969, renewed 1997; **Lay, Lady, Lay**, © 1969, renewed 1997; **One More Night**, © 1969, renewed 1997; **Country Pie**, © 1969, renewed 1997; **Tonight I'll Be Staying Here With You**, © 1969, renewed 1997; **Minstrel Boy**, © 1970; **In Search of Little Sadie**, © 1970; **All the Tired Horses**, © 1970; **Day of the Locusts**, © 1970; **Time Passes Slowly**, © 1970; **Went to See the Gypsy**, © 1970; **Winterlude**, © 1970; **New Morning**, © 1970; **Sign on the Window**, © 1970; **One More Weekend**, © 1970; **The Man in Me**, © 1970; **Three Angels**, © 1970; **Father of Night**, © 1970; **Watching the River Flow**, © 1971; **When I Paint My Masterpiece**, © 1971, 1972.

(d) Copyright by Ram's Horn Music: **George Jackson**, © 1971; **Going, Going, Gone**, © 1973, 1974; **Tough Mama**, © 1973, 1974; **Hazel**, © 1973, 1974; **Something There Is About You**, © 1973, 1974; **Dirge**, © 1973, 1974; **You Angel You**, © 1973, 1974; **Never Say Goodbye**, © 1973, 1974; **Wedding Song**, © 1973, 1974; *Planet Waves* sleevenote © 1973, 1974; **Nobody 'Cept You**, © 1973, 1976; **You're Gonna Make Me Lonesome When You Go**, © 1974, 1975; **You're a Big Girl Now**, © 1974, 1975; **Tangled Up in Blue**, © 1974, 1975; **Shelter from the Storm**, © 1974, 1975; **Idiot Wind**, © 1974, 1975; **If You See Her, Say Hello**, © 1974; **Buckets of Rain**, © 1974, 1975; **Call Letter Blues**, © 1974; **Hurricane** (words written with Jacques levy), © 1975; **Isis** (written with Jacques Levy), © 1975, 1976; **Oh, Sister** (written with Jacques Levy), © 1975, 1976; **Joey** (written with Jacques Levy), © 1975, 1976; **Romance in Durango** (written with Jacques Levy), © 1975, 1976; **Sara**, © 1975, 1976; **Rita May** (words written with Jacques Levy), © 1975, 1976; **Abandoned Love**, © 1975, 1976; **Sign Language**, © 1976.

(e) Copyright by Warner Bros. Music and renewed by Special Rider Music: **Blowin' in the Wind**, © 1962, renewed 1990; **Let Me Die in My Footsteps**, © 1963, 1965, renewed 1991, 1993; **Girl of the North Country**, © 1963, renewed 1991; **Tomorrow Is a Long Time**, © 1963, renewed 1991; **I Shall Be Free**, © 1963, renewed 1991; **Down the Highway**, © 1963, renewed 1991; **With God on Our Side**, © 1963, renewed 1991; **Ballad of Hollis Brown**, © 1963, renewed 1991; **When the Ship Comes In**, © 1963, renewed 1991; **Don't Think Twice, It's All Right**, © 1963, renewed 1991; **Masters of War**, © 1963, renewed 1991; **The Times They Are a-Changin'**, © 1963, renewed 1991; **Only a Pawn In Their Game**, © 1963, renewed 1991; **Bob Dylan's Dream**, © 1963, renewed 1991; **Walls of Red Wing**, © 1963, renewed 1991; **Eternal Circle**, © 1963, renewed 1991; **Hero Blues**, © 1963, renewed 1991; **Quit Your Low Down Ways**, © 1963, 1964, renewed 1991, 1992; **Whatcha Gonna Do**, © 1963, 1966, renewed 1991, 1994; **Percy's Song**, © 1964, renewed 1992; **It Ain't Me, Babe**, © 1964, renewed 1992; **My Back Pages**, © 1964, renewed 1992; **Restless Farewell**, © 1964, renewed 1992; **To Ramona**, © 1964, renewed 1992; **Motorpsycho Nightmare**, © 1964, renewed 1992; **Chimes of Freedom**, © 1964, renewed 1992; **Black Crow Blues**, © 1964, renewed 1992; **Spanish Harlem Incident**, © 1964, renewed 1992; **Ballad in Plain D**, © 1964, renewed 1992; **One Too Many Mornings**, © 1964, renewed 1992; **I Don't Believe You (She Acts Like We Never Have Met)**, © 1964, renewed 1992; **Lay Down Your Weary Tune**, © 1964, renewed 1992; **Mr. Tambourine Man**, © 1964, renewed 1992; **Positively 4th Street**, © 1965, renewed 1993; **Gates of Eden**, © 1965, renewed 1993; **Subterranean Homesick Blues**, © 1965, renewed 1993; **Outlaw Blues**, © 1965, renewed 1993; **She Belongs to Me**, © 1965, renewed 1993; **Love Minus Zero/No Limit**, © 1965, renewed 1993; **Bob Dylan's 115th Dream**, © 1965, renewed 1993; **It's All Over Now, Baby Blue**, © 1965, renewed 1993; **It's Alright, Ma (I'm Only Bleeding)**, © 1965, renewed 1993; **Farewell Angelina**, © 1965, renewed 1993; **Desolation Row**, © 1965, renewed 1993; **Just Like Tom Thumb's Blues**, © 1965, renewed 1993; **Ballad of a Thin Man**, © 1965, renewed 1993; **It Takes a Lot to Laugh, It Takes a Train to Cry**, © 1965, renewed 1993; **Queen Jane Approximately**, © 1965, renewed 1993; **Can** *You* Please Crawl Out **Your Window?**, © 1965, renewed 1993; **Highway 61 Revisited**, © 1965, renewed 1993; **Like a Rolling Stone**, © 1965, renewed 1993; **From a Buick 6**, © 1965, renewed 1993; **Sign on the Cross**, © 1971, renewed 1999; **California**, © 1972, renewed 2000.

(f) Copyright by Special Rider Music: **11 Outlined Epitaphs**, © 1964, renewed 1992; **Advice to Geraldine on Her Miscellaneous Birthday**, © 1964, renewed 1992; **Talkin' John Birch Paranoid Blues** © 1970; **I Shall Be Free No. 10**, © 1971; **Last Thoughts on Woody Guthrie**, © 1973; **My Life in a Stolen Moment**, © 1973; **Some Other Kinds of Songs . . .** , © 1973; **Ain't Gonna Go to Hell for Anybody**, © 1980; **Ain't No Man Righteous, No Not One**, © 1981; **Angelina**, © 1981; **Legionnaire's Disease**, © 1981; **You Changed My Life**, © 1982; **Band of the Hand**, © 1986; **Biograph** interview, © 1985; **Bringing It All Back Home** sleevenotes, © 1965, renewed 1993; **Where Are You Tonight? (Journey Through Dark Heat)**, © 1978; **Changing of the Guards**, © 1978; **No Time to Think**, © 1978; **True Love Tends to Forget**, © 1978; **Is Your Love in Vain?**, © 1978; **Senor (Tales of Yankee Power)**, © 1978; **Baby, Stop Crying**, © 1978; **New Pony**, © 1978; **Do Right to Me Baby (Do Unto Others)**, © 1979; **When He Returns**, © 1979; **Precious Angel**, © 1979; **Man Gave Names to All the Animals**, © 1979; **Gotta Serve Somebody**, © 1979; **I Believe in You**, © 1979; **Gonna Change My Way of Thinking**, © 1979; **Slow Train Coming**, © 1979; **Trouble in Mind**, © 1979; **Saving Grace**, © 1980; **Solid Rock**, © 1980; **In the Garden**, © 1980; **What Can I Do for You?**, © 1980; **Covenant Woman**, © 1980; **Saved**, © 1980; **Lenny Bruce**, © 1981; **Every Grain of Sand**, © 1981; **The Groom's Still Waiting at the Altar**, © 1981; **Let's Keep It Between Us**, © 1982; **Need a Woman**, © 1982; **Jokerman**, © 1983; **Sweetheart Like You**, © 1983; **Man of Peace**, © 1983; **Don't Fall Apart on Me Tonight**, © 1983; **I and I**, © 1983; **Blind Willie McTell**, © 1983; **Foot of Pride**, © 1983; **Lord Protect My Child**, © 1983; **Someone's Got a Hold of My Heart**, © 1983; **Clean-Cut Kid**, © 1984; **Tight Connection to My**

Heart (Has Anybody Seen My Love), © 1985; **I'll Remember You**, © 1985; **Never Gonna Be the Same Again**, © 1985; **Seeing the Real You at Last**, © 1985; **When the Night Comes Falling from the Sky**, © 1985; **Emotionally Yours**, © 1985; **Something's Burning, Baby**, © 1985; **Dark Eyes**, © 1985; **Caribbean Wind**, © 1985; **Driftin' Too Far from Shore**, © 1986; **Maybe Someday**, © 1986; **Brownsville Girl** (lyrics co-written with Sam Shepard), © 1986; **Had a Dream About You, Baby**, © 1987; **Where Teardrops Fall**, © 1989; **Man in the Long Black Coat**, © 1989; **Most of the Time**, © 1989; **Ring Them Bells**, © 1989; **What Was It You Wanted**, © 1989; **Shooting Star**, © 1989; **Dignity**, © 1989; **Wiggle Wiggle**, © 1990; **Under the Red Sky**, © 1990; **Unbelievable**, © 1990; **10,000 Men**, © 1990; **Handy Dandy**, © 1990; **Cat's in the Well**, © 1990; **World Gone Wrong** sleevenotes, © 1993; **Love Sick**, © 1997; **Standing in the Doorway**, © 1997; **Million Miles**, © 1997; **Tryin' to Get to Heaven**, © 1997; **Not Dark Yet**, © 1997; **Highlands**, © 1997; **Mississippi**, © 1997; **Things Have Changed**, © 1999; **Lonesome Day Blues**, © 2001; **Floater (Too Much to Ask)**, © 2001; **Po' Boy**, © 2001. **Under Your Spell** (co-written with Carol Bayer Sager), © 1986 Special Rider Music & Carol Bayer Sager Music. **Silvio** (co-written with Robert Hunter), © 1988 Special Rider Music & Ice Nine Music.

The author is once again grateful to Jeff Rosen at Special Rider Music for his cooperation, and to Bob Dylan for consenting to the quoting of so much from his extraordinary body of work.

The author and publishers also wish to thank the following for permission to quote from copyright works: to Thames & Hudson for permission to quote from *The Uses of Enchantment* by Bruno Bettelheim, © Bruno Bettelheim, 1976; to HarperCollins Publishers Ltd. and Houghton Mifflin Company for permission to quote from *The Lord of the Rings* by J.R.R. Tolkien, © 1954–55; *The Land where the Blues Began* by Alan Lomax, © Alan Lomax, 1993, reprinted by permission of Pantheon Books, a division of Random House Inc. For permission to quote from an interview with Bob Dylan by Jann Wenner in *Rolling Stone*, November 29, 1969, © by Straight Arrow Publishers Inc., 1969, all rights reserved, reprinted by permission; quotation from *The Oxford Dictionary of Nursery Rhymes*, by Iona and Peter Opie, 1951 revised edition, © Iona and Peter Opie, 1951, by permission of Oxford University Press; from '23rd Street Runs Into Heaven' by Kenneth Patchen, from *The Collected Poems of Kenneth Patchen*, copyright © 1957 by New directions Publishing Corp., reprinted by permission of New Directions Publishing Corp.; 'Bob Dylan: Genius or Commodity' by David Horowitz, © 1964, quoted by kind permission of *Peace News*, London; 'Sounds Authentic: Black Music, Ethnicity and the Challenge of a Changing Same' by Paul Gilroy, © 1991, quoted by kind permission of Paul Gilroy; 'From Refrain to Rave: the Decline of Figure and the Rise of Ground' by Philip Tagg © 1993, quoted by kind permission of Philip Tagg; and 'Bob Dylan and the Poetry of Salvation' by Steven Goldberg, used with permission.

Finally, the author wishes to thank those who commissioned articles from him from which small amounts of published and unpublished material have been revised within the present work, from fragments of an October 1967 article in *OZ* through to observations on Meridian MS made possible by the commissioning of the article on trains in Mississippi by the *Weekend Telegraph*, September 25, 2004. In between, the author thanks in particular commissioning editors at *Melody Maker* in the 1970s, the *Telegraph* fanzine and *The Independent* in the 1980s, *Homer, the slut* and *Isis* fanzines, *The Times* and *Daily Telegraph* and the part-work *The Blues Collection* plus Germinal Verlag, the publishers of the book *Bob Dylan: Funfzig Jahre . . .* in the 1990s, and *Judas!*, *Uncut*, the *Weekend Telegraph* and the *Observer Music Monthly* in the 2000s.

Preface

This is essentially the book of a critic. It was prompted by a number of people being kind enough to urge that material 'hidden' within the long and discursive chapters of my critical study *Song & Dance Man III: The Art of Bob Dylan*, including the fruits of a great deal of research undertaken for that work, should be made available in a more accessible, more reference-based way. But as the present book grew, and ever greater amounts of non-*Song & Dance Man* material demanded inclusion, it seemed more fun and more interesting to base the entries on *people*, where possible, rather than on, say, tours or even songs. I hope that what emerges, as well as a gathering together of much disparate information in one place, is a sense of the boundless, obdurate creativity of large numbers of people, coming and going and bumping into the world of Bob Dylan in their greatly differing ways en route.

What I hope emerges too is a proper sense that to burrow into Dylan's art at length and in detail is not to shut the door on the wider world in pursuit of a narrow obsession but rather to open up that wider world, to be sent down a thousand boulevards, to hear different musics and read other authors, and to listen out for the myriad voices of the clamorous past: not least the voices of those who did not make records or write books but whose lives and labours have helped inform our own.

Bob Dylan's reach is too wide, too deep and too long for any book about him to cover it all. He's a senior citizen. His career spans 45 years of American history, and that history has intersected with his prolific songwriting, recording, touring, acting, filmmaking, TV appearances and interviews. He has published a novel and a book of drawings, composed for film soundtracks and written a best-selling first volume of memoirs. He has found a place in the world of literature and academic study as well as in popular music. He is important to the history of the times, having given voice to a generation at a time of huge social change and political struggle; his songs are enmeshed in the story of the US civil rights movement as well as the Folk Revival movement. His busy life has embraced everything from bohemian excess to being Born Again.

His work has revolutionised song, reaching into every area of popular music from folk to blues to rock to gospel. He has met and worked with untold hundreds of musicians, politicians, celebrities, singers, poets, writers, painters, film-makers, actors and activists. He has released several dozen albums, written many hundreds of songs, in many cases adapting them from older folk and blues material, and recorded songs by many other composers. He has been the subject of an enormous number of books, academic conference papers, showbiz stories, essays and concert reviews. He has attracted more fanzine enthusiasm, and inspired more websites, than almost anyone in the world.

In order to resist the forces of infinity pushing the book beyond all bounds, in principle I have omitted background business people such as concert promoters, accountants, lawyers, managers, music publishers, booking agents, film producers and so on. No doubt a scrutiny of these would make an interesting book but this is not it. I have also omitted most photographers, album-cover designers and magazine editors, though a very few photographers whose Dylan shots are iconic are included. I have also omitted people whose only connection with Dylan is that they have made cover versions of his songs.

The different kinds of entry that *are* here include: some key moments from Dylan's career and life; singers, musicians, songwriters and composers who have influenced Dylan and/or worked with him; writers, poets and other non-musical cultural figures who have impacted on Dylan's work and/or who are mentioned within it, in each case delineating the sometimes surprising ways in which they connect to Dylan's work; critical assessments and factual details (including place and date of recording, date of release and original catalogue numbers) for all Dylan's albums and for individual songs from all through Dylan's decades of work; critical assessments and factual details on Dylan's own books and films; relevant music critics, authors of books and major websites on Dylan; and topics like artists v. critics, angels, Dylan interpeters, the co-option of real music by advertising, early 1960s pop music, Beat poetry, rock'n'roll, country blues, pre-20th century American poetry, Dylan fanzines, cowboy heroes, the use of film dialogue in Dylan's lyrics and many more.

In other words, there are entries about songs and about albums, about famous and 'obscure' individuals, about ideas and history.

Naturally, though, it is Bob Dylan's art that is the heart of the book: it is his art that has got inside our heads, has changed the world around us and justifies his being paid so much attention. If in 100 years' time Dylan's art goes unheard and discounted, well, in 200 years' time it may bounce back. If not, *The Bob Dylan Encyclopedia* might help some scholar of the future to sift through the rusted nuts and bolts of our mistaken enthusiasm. We can't know. But this book is my own large bet that we were on the right track all along.

How to Read This Book

Like the instructions on how to play a perfectly simple board game, what follows sounds far more complicated than the actual practice it tries to explain. If, therefore, the explanation below makes you want to throw the book across the room, please remember that the book is very heavy; also that you can of course read it how you like, and without referring to this guidance ever again.

Song titles, essay/article titles and television programmes and series are given inside single quotation marks; album titles, book titles and film titles are given in italics. Short quotations from other works and other people are given within single quotation marks; longer quoted passages are given as inset paragraphs.

For most entries, there is a main text and then, inside square brackets and in smaller print, some endnotes. Each main text is complete in itself, and you need feel no duty to wade through the endnotes at all. But should you demand to know publication details of the particular sources drawn upon for the facts offered in the entry, or for particular books or articles quoted, or discographical details of records mentioned, this is where those details will be, so that you don't have to go backwards and forwards between the entry and somewhere else hundreds of pages away in the process.

Within the main text, the appearance of CAPITALS or *ITALIC CAPITALS* inside an entry indicates that the topic receives an entry of its own—with the exception of works of Dylan himself, in order to avoid an unnecessary blizzard of capitals.

If an entry relates to a person, the entry heading will include the year of birth for that person, where known, and the year of death if known and applicable. If the entry relates to a work—a song, an album, a film—never officially released, or released only in a much later retrospective collection, the entry heading will include the year that piece of work was created; if the entry relates to an officially issued work, the date will be the year of its first *release.*

Within the endnotes, publication details will follow convention. That is, details about a book will be author, title, place of publication, name of publisher, year of publication. There may be additional information. Example:

> Levon Helm (with Stephen Davis), *This Wheel's on Fire: Levon Helm and the Story of The Band*, New York: William Morrow, 1993 & Chicago: A Capella Books, 2000.

Details given about an article will be author, title, name of journal, issue number and date, place of publication, date. Example:

> Brian Walden, 'Questionnaire: John Lee Hooker', *Q* no.85, London, Oct 1993.

Details given about an online source will be author where stated, nature or title of text where stated, date of composition where stated, URL and when accessed online. The URL as given begins by including 'http://' only when this is *not* followed by 'www'. Example:

> Jim Keltner quoted from interview by Don Zulaica, seen online 6 Jan 2006 on the Drummerworld website at *www.drummerworld.com/drummers/Jim_Keltner.html.*

Film details given will be the title, the director's name, the production company or companies, country of origin and year of release. Additional information may be given. Example:

> *Heaven's Gate*, dir. & written Michael Cimino; Partisan Productions/UA, US, 1980.

Discographical data: the amount of discographical information offered varies. At its fullest it will give, in this order:

name of artist
name of track or album
place and date of recording
label and catalogue number for release
city or country of issue
year of issue

but recording data is not always included. If place and date of recording *are* given, they always appear ahead of the name of the record label. Example:

> Fats Domino: 'The Fat Man', New Orleans, 10 Dec 1949, Imperial 5058, LA, 1950.

This indicates that Domino's record 'The Fat Man' was recorded in New Orleans on December 10, 1949, and was released as a single on Imperial Records, catalogue no. 5058, and issued from Los Angeles, the label's HQ, in 1950. Sometimes the track will only have been issued on an album, and therefore the information will proceed like this:

> Bo Diddley: 'Hey, Red Riding Hood', Chicago, 25 Jul 1965, *500% More Man*, Checker LP(S) 2996, Chicago, 1965.

However, if no recording information were given, the example above would go straight from the title to the release information, like so:

> Bo Diddley: 'Hey, Red Riding Hood', *500% More Man*, Checker LP(S) 2996, Chicago, 1965.

Sometimes, when information ought to be there but is not known, the letters *nia* (meaning *no information available*) are inserted in place of the missing data—e.g. here, where the catalogue no. of the album is not known:

> Merle Haggard: *Strangers*, Hollywood, 1965, Capitol, *nia*, US, 1965.

NB. In this example, where the record referred to is the whole album, rather than a specific track, the place and date of recording come after the album title; but as ever, this information still precedes the naming of the record label. It should therefore be clear that 'Hollywood 1965' is place and date of *recording*, and that 'US, 1965' is place and date of *release*.

In the case of pre-war recordings, the release data will relate to its first release *on vinyl*—the purpose of this being to clarify when it would most likely have first become accessible to the post-war listener. Example:

> Frank Hutchison: 'Stack a Lee', NY, 28 Jan 1927, *American Folk Music*, Folkways FP 251–253, NY, 1952.

Sometimes CD-reissue information is also given, and again this will normally be data on the *first* CD reissue, unless otherwise stated.

A

Aaronson, Kenny [1952 -] Kenny Aaronson was born on April 14, 1952 in Brooklyn, New York. After playing drums, he switched to bass (the bass line to THE BYRDS' 'Mr. Tambourine Man' was learnt very early); he dropped out of high school to play in a group called Dust, which cut two albums, and then joined Stories and played on 'Brother Louie', which became a US no.1 hit in 1973. The band shriveled away, Aaronson toured with Hall & Oates, who were the support to LOU REED; then with Leslie West, then—and this was for three years and six albums—with Rick Derringer, mostly touring as support to mega-groups like Aerosmith, Foreigner, Boston and Led Zeppelin. In the 1980s it was Edgar Winter, Billy Squier, Foghat, Sammy Hagar, Brian Setzer and then Billy Idol. An impressive list of the truly dreadful.

From there he joined Bob Dylan, to be the first bass player on what would later be known as the Never-Ending Tour, starting on June 7, 1988 in Concord, California, and completing a total of 70 more concerts by the end of the year. He was great, too: he sounded punk and funky, and he looked fabulously skinny and modern. In 1989, after Dylan finished recording *Oh Mercy* in New Orleans and went back on the road, Aaronson was there again, rehearsing in New York in mid-May and then beginning the concerts on May 27 in Andarum, Sweden. After Stockholm came Helsinki, Dublin, Glasgow, Birmingham and London, but Aaronson was unable to play the first of the two nights in Dublin on June 3—his friend TONY GARNIER stepped in—and had to drop out again after the London concert on June 8.

He was suffering from skin cancer, and left to return to the US for surgery, believing he'd been reassured that he could come back in when he was ready. In the meantime, Tony Garnier replaced him. The tour continued through Holland, Belgium, France, Spain, Italy and Greece, where the band played Athens on June 28. Three days later they opened in the States, beginning in Peoria, Illinois, and playing a further 43 concerts by the end of August.

Aaronson came back in the middle of this run—he turned up, and played in place of Garnier, at Wantagh, New York, on July 23: but Dylan wouldn't take him back after all, and this was the last time he played. Notoriously, Dylan is reported to have told him: 'I don't give a shit who plays bass.' Inertia kept the less interesting player in the band instead. Kenny Aaronson had played at a total of some 75 Dylan concerts.

Since then he's gone back to his old ways: Dave Edmunds, Joan Jett . . .

Abrams, Harvey [1938 -] Harvey Alan Abrams was born in Hennepin County, Minnesota, on June 18, 1938. He was a student near a contemporary of Dylan's in Minneapolis in 1960—and he's the one who gave ROBERT SHELTON that great quote, 'Dylan was the purest of the pure. He had to get the oldest record and, if possible, the Library of Congress record, or go find the original people who knew the original song.'

Abrams met Dylan in the summer of 1960, and told Shelton that by that point Dylan 'had already written a couple of beautiful songs, like "The Klan"' (in fact Dylan hadn't written this song at all; he'd picked it up from WALT CONLEY in Colorado).

Dylan, Abrams added, 'was playing weekends at the [10 O'Clock] Scholar, earning five dollars a night.' Abrams and a friend rented an old house to turn into a coffee-house, which they called the Bastille. (Dylan mentions it in *Chronicles Volume One* as the place he first met FLO CASTNER.) At some point he, Dylan and another friend, DAVE MORTON, shared an apartment at 714 15th Avenue SE. Abrams, like DAVE WHITAKER, tried to educate Dylan about politics, and says Dylan 'got a lot of exuberance about it from us', but that Dylan never did deal well with political dogma: 'he probably just identifies with the underdog'.

By 1966, when Dylan was changing the world, Abrams was a social worker, and, according to Shelton, 'bright, tough, articulate'. No update on him could be found for this entry, except that he's believed to be living in Florida.

[Harvey Abrams, quoted in Robert Shelton, *No Direction Home: The Music and Life of Bob Dylan*, London: Penguin edn., 1987, pp. 68–69. Other data from the Minnesota Births Index 1935–2002, file no. 1938-MN-019893.]

Ace, Johnny [1929 - 1954] The death, by Russian roulette, of R&B singer and pianist Johnny Ace, backstage in Houston, Texas, in December 1954, is better known now than at the time, though Ace had scored many R&B hits in his brief recording career. Signed to Duke Records in 1952, the following year saw his first hit, 'My Song', after which came eight hits in a row, including 'Cross My Heart', 'Please Forgive Me' and 'Never Let Me Go'.

Born John Marshall Alexander Jr. in Memphis on June 29, 1929, Johnny Ace shot himself on December 24 during a break in the show he was a part of, and died on Christmas Day. 'Pledging My Love' became, posthumously, his biggest hit, in 1955.

His 'Never Let Me Go' was performed as a duet by Dylan and JOAN BAEZ at 21 of 1975's Rolling Thunder Revue shows.

[Johnny Ace: 'Never Let Me Go', Houston, 1954, Duke 132, Houston, 1954.]

Acuff, Roy [1903 - 1992] Roy Acuff was born in miniscule Maynardville, Tennessee, on September 15, 1903, though his family later moved to Knoxville. He grew up wanting to be a sportsman but after suffering from a severe sunstroke that precipitated a nervous breakdown he turned instead to music, learning violin, joining a medicine show and then the Tennessee Crackjacks, who had a radio outlet on WROL in Knoxville.

Acuff's first session, as by Roy Acuff & His Crazy Tennesseeans, yielded him a big hit with an old gospel song, 'Great Speckle Bird' (cut in Chicago in 1936), and he went on to record 120 pre-war sides, including 'Wabash Cannonball'. When he sang 'Bird' on the Grand Ole Opry in 1938 it was a sensation all over again, clinching him a regular slot (on condition that the group change its name to the Smoky Mountain Boys) and launched his climb to huge stardom. He swiftly became so big a cultural figure that when Japanese troops went into battle at Okinawa in WWII, reputedly they shouted 'To hell with Roosevelt, to hell with Babe Ruth, to hell with Roy Acuff!' as they charged. Postwar Acuff flourished but chose to concentrate more on touring than recording. (He released no singles between 1947 and 1958.) In 1962 he became the first living person to be inducted into the Country Music Hall of Fame.

One of Acuff's pre-war recordings was of the popular song 'Drifting Too Far from the Shore', also recorded pre-war by the Monroe Brothers (and by country acts the Carolina Gospel Singers, Arty Hall and Judie & Julie). Dylan re-used the title, though nothing else in the song, in his own *Knocked Out Loaded* number 'Driftin' Too Far from Shore'. In the MARTIN SCORSESE film *No Direction Home* the era of country music Dylan heard on the radio when he was growing up, and the kind of 78rpm records people had in their homes up in Hibbing, Minnesota, are suggested by the playing of a post-war recording of the Acuff song by Bill Monroe & the Blue Grass Boys . . . which is problematic, to say the least, because Bill Monroe & the Blue Grass Boys didn't record the song till 1962, and then only released it on an LP; so it was never a 78 and didn't exist when Dylan was growing up. Nor is the version played in *No Direction Home* the pre-war Monroe Brothers recording—though that *was* a 78rpm record, recorded at their first session back in 1936, so it's possible that's what should have been illustrated in the film.

Dylan sings a version of Roy Acuff's 'Freight Train Blues' (one of Acuff's earliest hits) on his first album. It is not widely known that the vocal on Acuff's version was not by him but by band member Sam 'Dynamite' Natcher; Acuff's are the train whistle effects. Dylan also says in *Chronicles Volume One* that his own 'Let Me Die in My Footsteps' is based on an old Acuff ballad—though he doesn't say which, and it's hard to think of *any* relevant Acuff song. Dylan also remembers that Acuff, always introduced as the 'King of Country Music', was MC on the *Grand Ole Opry* the first time he heard HANK WILLIAMS.

One more song strongly associated with Acuff, 'Wait for the Light to Shine', was introduced to Dylan's concert repertoire at Spokane, Washington, on October 5, 2001. Between then and the end of the year, he performed it 22 more times, adding a further seven renditions in 2002.

Acuff co-founded the Acuff-Rose music publishing company with Fred Rose in 1942, and among other achievements nurtured the career of Hank Willams. Acuff-Rose sold recently for 100 million dollars. Roy Acuff died in Nashville on November 23, 1992, aged 89.

[Roy Acuff: 'Drifting Too Far from the Shore', Memphis, 6 Jul 1939; 'Freight Train Blues' Chicago, 21 Oct 1936; 'Wait for the Light to Shine', Chicago or Nashville, Dec 1944. Bill Monroe & His Blue Grass Boys: 'Drifting Too Far from the Shore', Nashville, 16 May 1962, *I'll Meet You in Church Sunday Morning*, Decca DL 4537, NY, 1962; Monroe Brothers: 'Drifting Too Far from the Shore', Charlotte, NC, 17 Feb 1936. Bob Dylan, *Chronicles Volume One*, pp.270 & 95.]

Aikins, Bill [1940 -] Bill Aikins was born on July 16, 1940 in Glen Ridge, New Jersey, but his place in history is that he played keyboards on the *Blonde on Blonde* session of February 14, 1966 in Nashville. His overriding memory of the session is that 'Dylan would sit there at the piano for hours with the Bible, and then he'd come and say "OK. I'm ready"'. That day they laid down, if you include fragments, a total of 38 takes, including 13 fruitless takes of 'Leopard-Skin Pill-Box Hat' and 19 failed takes of '4th Time Around'—but in this case with take 20 they achieved the version released on the album *and*, after hardly any takes at all, the album version of 'Visions of Johanna'. Not a bad day's work. After which it seems ludicrous to mention that Bill Aikins also did sessions for ex-Joy of Cooking women Toni & Terry's 1973 album *Cross Country* (produced by WAYNE MOSS) and for Area Code 615 stalwart Mac Gayden's 1976 album *Hymn to the Seeker*, and, more interestingly perhaps, also played on Bobby Darin's 1969 pseudo-hip album *Commitment*, which included Dylanesque harmonica on the track 'Mr. & Mrs. Hohner', while another track was called, er, 'Hey Magic Man'. Aikins was, in fact, Darin's Musical Director and conductor, from March 1969 until Darin's death in December 1973. He also played on the SIMON & Garfunkel sessions that yielded 'I Am a Rock'.

These days, Bill Aikins works as a Worship Leader in a Praise and Worship band at a Las Vegas branch of the California-based Church of the Foursquare Gospel.

[Background detail and quote re Dylan from Bill Aikins, phone call to this writer 12 Apr 2006.]

Alarm, the The Alarm began in 1978 as a band called Seventeen in Rhyl, North Wales, comprising Mike Peters, Nigel Twist, Dave Sharp and Eddie MacDonald. Then they became Alarm Alarm, and then the Alarm. They moved to London at the start of the 1980s, found a manager, Ian Wilson, and got a record deal with IRS. BONO saw them live and offered them a U2 support slot in the US in 1983, which led to a small headline tour of their own. Then they had hits, opened for the Pretenders' 1985 world tour, had more hits, met Elliot Roberts, sometime Bob Dylan manager, dumped Ian Wilson in Roberts' favour, made friends with NEIL YOUNG, went on another huge tour behind their album *Eye of the Hurricane* and in June 1988 found themselves as Dylan's support act: the first support act of the Never-Ending Tour. On August 4, at his concert in Hollywood, Dylan brought them on to augment his own band for the last encore number of the night, 'Knockin' on Heaven's Door'. Peters, Twist and MacDonald shared vocals, and Dave Sharp played guitar. The same thing happened again on August 7 in Santa Barbara, the Alarm's last night with Dylan. They had played 40 shows. It did them no good—they were disintegrating anyway, and within a couple of years had broken up—and it's doubtful it did Bob Dylan any good either. Dave Sharp subsequently made two solo albums, *Hard Travelin'* (1991) and *Downtown America* (1994), produced by ex-Dylan producer BOB JOHNSTON.

[The Alarm's non-Dylan history potted from the unused liner notes intended for the 1998 album *The Best of the Alarm and Mike Peters* by Steve Fulton, seen online 27 Oct 2005 at *www.thealarm.com*.]

'Alberta' [1970] The song 'Alberta', which Dylan sings twice on *Self Portrait*—as 'Alberta No.1' and then as the not very different 'Alberta No.2', seems first to have come together as a DOC WATSON rag doll of traditional black and white lyric off-cuts, pinned and dressed up with a few arty chords, with Doc sounding not unlike Jim Reeves. It was issued on his LP *Southbound* in 1966. Dylan scraps the arty chords and some of the words, and tacks in some others. The results, though casually reminiscent of 'Corrina Corrina', 'Baby Let Me Follow You Down' and 'Girl of the North Country', are dull, but not as dull as Doc's.

[Doc Watson: 'Alberta', *Southbound*, Vanguard VSD-79213, NY (Fontana TFL 6074, London), 1966, CD-reissued Vanguard VMD 79213-2, NY, 1988 (London, 1995). His 'Alberta' was also reissued on *The Essential Doc Watson, nia*, 1973 (Vanguard 45/46, London, 1976), CD-reissued *The Essential Doc Watson Vol.1*, Vanguard VMCD 7308, NY, 1987.]

Alexander, Arthur [1940 - 1993] Arthur Alexander was born on May 10, 1940 in Florence, Alabama, just five miles from Sheffield and Muscle Shoals. His father played gospel slide guitar (using the neck of a whiskey bottle); his mother and sister sang in a local church choir.

Dylan covers Arthur Alexander's début single, 'Sally Sue Brown', made in 1959 and released under his nickname June Alexander (short for Junior), on his *Down in the Groove* album. You can't say he pays tribute to Alexander with this, because he makes such a poor job of reviving it. (See also **recording quality and cynicism**.)

It was really with 'You Better Move On' that Arthur Alexander made himself an indispensable artist. He wrote this exquisite classic while working as a bell-hop in the Muscle Shoals Hotel. And then he made a perfect record out of it, produced by Rick Hall at his original Fame studio (an acronym for Florence, Alabama Music Enterprises), which was an old tobacco barn out on Wilson Dam Highway. Leased to Dot Records in 1961, 'You Better Move On' was a hit and helped Hall to build his bigger Fame Studio, which later attracted the likes of Aretha Franklin and Wilson Pickett. In 1969 Fame's studio musicians opened their own independent studio, Muscle Shoals Sound, where Dylan would later make his gospel albums *Slow Train Coming* and *Saved*.

Despite this hit and its influence on other artists, however, while an EP of his work was highly sought-after in the UK, Arthur Alexander was generally received with indifference by the US public, and his career stagnated. After years of personal struggle with drugs and health problems (he was hospitalized several times in the mid-1960s, sometimes at his own request, in a mental health facility in southern Alabama), he returned in the 1970s, first with an album on Warner Brothers and then with a minor hit single in 1975, 'Every Day I Have to Cry Some'.

One of Arthur Alexander's innovations as a songwriter was the simple use of the word 'girl' for the addressee in his songs. When he first used it, it had a function: it was a statement of directness, it instantly implied a relationship; but soon, passed down through LENNON and McCARTNEY to every 1964 beat-group in existence, it became a meaningless suffix, a rhyme to be paired off with 'world' as automatically as 'baby' with 'maybe'. This couldn't impair the precision with which Arthur Alexander wrote, the moral scrupulousness, the distinctive, careful way that he delineated the dilemmas in eternal-triangle songs with such finesse and economy. All this sung in his unique, restrained, deeply affecting voice. Rarely has moral probity sounded so appealing, so human, as in his work. Listen not only to 'You Better Move

On' but to the equally impeccable 'Anna' and 'Go Home Girl' and the funkier but still characteristic 'The Other Woman'.

Arthur Alexander is also one of the many R&B artists whose work was happy to incorporate children's song, as so much of Dylan's work does (most especially, of course, the album *Under the Red Sky* in 1990). Alexander's 1966 single 'For You' incorporates the title line and the next from the children's rhyming prayer 'Now I lay me down to sleep' (the next line is 'And pray the Lord my soul to keep'), which first appeared in print in Thomas Fleet's *The New-England Primer* in 1737.

The ROLLING STONES covered 'You Better Move On'; THE BEATLES covered 'Anna'; and it was after Arthur Alexander cut Dennis Linde's song 'Burning Love' in 1972 that ELVIS PRESLEY covered that one. Add to that the fact that Dylan covered 'Sally Sue Brown', and you have a pretty extraordinary level of coverage for an artist who remains so far from a household name.

After his 1975 hit, he went back on the road briefly but didn't enjoy it; he felt he'd received no money from the record's success and meanwhile he 'had found religion and got myself completely straight', so he quit the music business and moved north. By the 1980s he was driving a bus for a social services agency in Cleveland, Ohio, when, to his surprise, Ace Records issued its collection of his early classics, *A Shot of Rhythm and Soul*—which included reissue of that first (and by now super-rare) single, 'Sally Sue Brown'. His attempt at another comeback, in the early 1990s, yielded an appearance at the Bottom Line in New York City, another in Austin, Texas, and the Nonesuch album *Lonely Just Like Me*, which included several re-recordings. 'Sally Sue Brown' was one of them. As on the original 'You Better Move On', the musicians included SPOONER OLDHAM.

It all came too late. Arthur Alexander died of a heart attack in Nashville on June 9, 1993. A few months earlier, on February 20, his biographer, Richard Younger, went to interview him, at a Cleveland Holiday Inn. 'He told me,' wrote Younger, that 'he had no old photos of himself, nor any of his old records, and had never even heard many of the cover versions of his songs. I had anticipated this and brought along a copy of Bob Dylan's version of "Sally Sue Brown". With the headphones pressed to his ears, Arthur moved back and forth in his seat. "Bob's really rocking," he said.' It was a generous verdict.

[Arthur Alexander: 'Sally Sue Brown', Sheffield, AL, 1959, Judd 1020, US, 1960; 'You Better Move On' c/w 'A Shot of Rhythm and Blues', Muscle Shoals, AL, 2 Oct 1961, Dot 16309, US, 1962; 'Anna', Nashville, Jul 1962, Dot 16387, 1962; 'Go Home Girl', Nashville, c.Sep 1962, Dot 16425, 1963; '(Baby) For You' c/w 'The Other Woman', Nashville, 29 Oct 1965, Sound Stage 7 2556, US, 1965; 'Burning Love', Memphis, Aug 1971, on *Arthur Alexander*, Warner Bros. 2592, US, 1972; 'Every Day I Have to Cry Some', Muscle Shoals, Jul 1975, Buddah 492, US, 1975; *A Shot of Rhythm and Soul*, Ace CH66, London, 1982; Nashville, 12–17 Feb 1992, *Lonely Just Like Me*, Elektra Nonesuch 7559-61475-2, 1993. Special thanks for input and detail to Richard Younger, author of *Get a Shot of Rhythm & Blues: The Arthur Alexander Story*, Tuscaloosa, AL: University of Alabama Press, 2000; quote is p.168.]

Alk, Howard [1930 - 1982] Howard Alk was born on October 25, 1930 in Chicago. He was described as a great 'bear of a man' not only by LARRY SLOMAN, who encountered him on the Rolling Thunder Revue in 1975, but by Bernard Sahlins, who remembered Alk from Chicago in the 1950s.

Sahlins and Alk plus director Paul Sills were the three founders of the theatre company the Second City, which took premises on the corner of Wells Street and Lincoln Avenue and opened its first production on December 16, 1959. All three were graduates of the University of Chicago; Sills was already a theatre director, Sahlins an enthusiast who had sold his shares in a tape-recorder factory to pursue the theatrical life, and Howard Alk was their 'pipeline to the counterculture'. This was crucial, since what they were attempting with the Second City was less a conventional theatre than a coffee-house type of environment, since Chicago then entirely lacked any center or focus for Beat bohemian culture.

Alk 'couldn't act, play the guitar or sing, but he managed to do all those things convincingly', Sahlins recalled. Alk 'had a highly developed sense of irony, a voracious appetite for high-level gossip and a well-developed nose for trends and fakery . . . his incisive knowledge of young, avant-garde thinking was invaluable at the start.' He checked the others' tendency 'to be awed by the intellectual and was quick with the witty analysis of life's contradictions. It was he who defined a Freudian slip as "meaning to say one thing and saying a mother."' Alk's ex-wife Jones Cullinan remembers him from this period as a great reciter of pretend-Latin and inventor of satiric comic characters: 'He made a great Superjew!'

Alk stayed with the Second City company only a few months; he quickly tired of acting, was replaced by Alan Arkin and went on to other things. By this time he had already worked as film editor on a short black and white movie, *Cry of Jazz*, directed by Edward Bland and co-written by Bland and Nelam Hill, released in 1959 and described as a 'Discussion of jazz and the role of African-Americans in the United States'.

By early 1963 Alk was opening and running a music venue, the Bear. That other bear-like figure, ALBERT GROSSMAN, booked Bob Dylan to appear there that April. Grossman and Alk had met in New York a year or two earlier. Dylan did two unpaid performances at the Bear 'for the exposure', and he and Howard Alk promptly developed a friendship that lasted the rest of Alk's life.

Accounts vary greatly as to the importance of the work of Howard and Jones Alk (they had married in Chicago on the last day of 1964) in the making of the Dylan movie *Don't Look Back*, and how they were brought into it in the first place. In summary, the D.A. PENNEBAKER version is that the Alks were brought in to assist because, being friends of Dylan's, they'd be cheap to employ. 'Howard Alk,' he said later, 'was kind of helping out. I think I had a camera for Howard'; he calls it 'a fallback camera'. But this is to denigrate Alk's contribution, though he wasn't primarily a cameraman but an editor. The Alk version is that they were brought in *before* Pennebaker and that though it became the latter's film, they were crucial throughout. This seems essentially correct. (For more detail see separate entry on the film.)

At any rate, the following year, when the same team of people filmed Dylan on tour in the UK again for *Eat the Document*, their rôles were very different. This time Pennebaker wasn't the auteur director but, like Alk, the hired hand working on what was emphatically Dylan's film. Alk now had more clout. Pennebaker wasn't impressed; he thought Dylan was 'very influenced by Howard's film ideas, which didn't interest me much, frankly, at the time, and they still don't.'

This was the core of it: as well as doing more of the filming this time around, Alk duly became the film editor, working alongside (and perhaps advising) Dylan. They started work on the film in June 1966 but were interrupted by Dylan's motorcycle crash that July. They resumed work on what was originally intended as a one-hour television film (it had been commissioned by ABC-TV), worked on it in fits and starts through much of 1967 and worked on it again in 1968.

In the end, Dylan came to feel that the footage was hopeless—how wrong he was can be seen from MARTIN SCORSESE's use of it in *No Direction Home*—though this was mostly because Dylan had lost whatever small interest he'd ever had in the concert footage (strange but true) and was mainly interested in the tiresome little staged scenes of stoned, amateur acting that took place in hotel rooms and 'on the road' as the tour progressed. *Eat the Document* was released minimally; it was premiered at an art-house cinema in New York City on February 8, 1971 and has rarely seen the official light of day since (though it has circulated on bootleg videos and DVDs).

As CLINTON HEYLIN notes, however, what came of it was 'an idea for a film to be directed by Dylan, with Alk advising. The product of this resolve was realized years later in the making of *Renaldo & Clara*. That this epic film was an eventual result of the months of labour on *Eat the Document* is evident from many parallels of style, structure and symbolism in the two films.'

In the interim, Howard Alk worked on other films. He worked as editor on Murray Lerner's magnificent musical documentary film *Festival* (starring everyone from JOAN BAEZ to Cousin Emmy and from SON HOUSE to HOWLIN' WOLF), and he was in Woodstock, New York, in 1967, when Dylan and THE BAND were there, editing the avant-garde footage that would become *You Are What You Eat*, starring Peter Yarrow of PETER, PAUL & MARY, plus The Band's about-to-be producer, John Simon, plus Tiny Tim, PAUL BUTTERFIELD, Barry MacGuire, DAVID CROSBY and JOHN HERALD. This film was shot and directed by Alk's friend Barry Feinstein, who was also a photographer: his is the cover shot on Dylan's *Bootleg Series Vol. 7: No Direction Home* 2-CD set. *You Are What You Eat* came out in 1968, and was about as widely seen as *Eat the Document*.

Alk then made two politically radical films with Mike Gray, a founder of the Chicago-based production company the Film Group and later the story and screenplay writer on the prophetic movie *The China Syndrome*. Alk had been a political radical all along, but like so many, he became more politicised in the second half of the 1960s as the US raged with the turmoil of ghetto riots, war protests and murderous repression by government forces. (By 1978 writer Gerald Peary was asserting that to speak of Alk in other than political terms was 'to misrepresent him' and that he often expressed his 'total support for the programs of the Black Panther Party'.)

The first of the political films, 1969's *American Revolution 2*, focused on the infamous 1968 Democratic Party Convention in Alk's hometown, Chicago; the second was *The Murder of Fred Hampton*, released in 1971. Gray says (correcting the credits given on the *www.imdb.com* website database) that 'Howard directed both films and I was director of photography and producer.' He gives this account of how it all happened:

'Howard came back to Chicago in late September of 1968 at my request. He had been working in New York with Dylan on *Eat the Document*. I had shot footage of the Democratic Convention in August and that fall we collaborated on the film. . . . We finished shooting in January 1969 and immediately shifted our focus to Fred Hampton, whom we followed for what turned out to be the last nine months of his life.' Jones says: 'Howard's great idea was to make films *with* people instead of *about* people. That's what made these films so good.'

In 1971 the Alks went to India, encouraged by Albert Grossman's wife Sally's enthusiasm after their own trip. Howard made a film there too, having connected with the musicians Grossman had brought over to Woodstock years earlier, the Bauls of Bengal, who can be seen on the front cover of Dylan's album *John Wesley Harding*. Alk's film was a 50-minute feature, *Bauls of Bengal: Luxman Baul's*

Movie shot on video in Birbhum District, Bengal, in Bengali and English (with English subtitles). The finished film had Sally Grossman as narrator and producer; Alk was its director and editor.

Howard Alk came back from India; Jones Alk stayed out there and then flew to Europe for another prolonged trip. This was the end of their marriage. Howard went out to the West Coast and worked as editor on the Hollywood movie *A Safe Place*, directed by Henry Jaglom and starring Orson Welles and Tuesday Weld. Alk, brought in by producer Bert Schneider, goes uncredited because of problems over union recognition.

In 1974, Alk released his posthumous film about Janis Joplin, *Janis*, co-directed by Seaton Findlay, and the following year turned his attention back to Dylan, rejoining him to start shooting the 1975 Rolling Thunder Revue and its circus of performers for what became *Renaldo & Clara*.

Alk and Dylan, working together again, started editing their substantial concert footage and their 80-plus hours of non-concert footage, at the beginning of 1976. It took months, was interrupted by the second Rolling Thunder Revue, and, within it, the filming of the 'Hard Rain' TV Special at Fort Collins, Colorado, on May 23, again made by Howard Alk (see separate entry). He was almost certainly involved too, in the shelved alternative film from Clearwater, Florida, that April 22. A further concentrated six months of work on *Renaldo & Clara* took place in 1977.

Released in 1978, it showed clear signs of Alk's input, especially, as Heylin put it, in 'one major, sustained sequence—the brilliantly rendered series of street interviews about HURRICANE CARTER', a sequence that 'shows both his political solidarity with black America (and his commitment to using the camera to let the disenfranchised speak for themselves) and his trademark of cutting from conversation to music and back again to emphasize points and set contexts.'

Heylin suggests too that Alk's interest in the Black Panthers would have been what prompted Dylan to the fruitless meeting that 'supposedly took place between Dylan and Huey Newton and David Hilliard' in 1970. Alk commented years later that 'Bob Dylan is by nature not a political person'. In more recent years too, people have lined up to say that Dylan was apolitical. But this may be misleading, granted how strong his instinct for the underdog and for liberty has always been. The Dylan who stays quiet about his reluctant meeting with the Panthers stays so about many things, mistrusts organisations and orthodoxy ('There is only up wing and down wing') and will have understood his own inevitable irrelevance to the Panther programme. And just as the *power* of Alk's politics derives not from dogma but from his trust in those 'who have been stepped on and victimised', so there is nothing apolitical in Dylan's consistent and similar solidarity with the pawns in society's game. While Alk made *The Murder of Fred Hampton*, Dylan had made 'The Lonesome Death of Hattie Carroll'. The unsatisfactory Panthers meeting didn't put Dylan off visiting Hurricane Carter in jail five years later (however misguidedly); and in the same era in which Alk made his political films, Dylan came out with the record 'George Jackson'.

Alk's influence may have been marked but he surely didn't insert politics into *Renaldo & Clara* despite Dylan. The 'Hurricane' sequence is clearly a co-production. Whatever the film achieves or doesn't, it offers a survey of North America—and while TV reportage deliberately keeps non-WASP America invisible, the special strength of *Renaldo & Clara*'s survey is the high visibility it insists on giving to this other America. Two things about this are clear: it makes for a politically radical act, and it reflects Bob Dylan's vision as much as Howard Alk's.

Before they saw how badly it was received upon its release in 1978, Alk and Dylan planned to make further films. Alk announced: 'You can believe that Bob is fully committed to filmmaking. That we are discussing the next *two* films.'

These didn't happen, but Alk's association with Dylan continued. He took the front and back cover photographs of Dylan used on the *Street Legal* album of 1978 and all the photos in the songbook for the 1981 album *Shot of Love*, and he filmed at least two of that year's Dylan concerts (Avignon on July 25 and Boston on October 21) and attended most of the rest. The fall tour began with two nights in Milwaukee (a bizarre place to launch a tour, Jones teased Bob), and Howard Alk was using a new camera to film Dylan, CLYDIE KING and others in the hotel after the first concert, that October 16.

Alk was still with the Dylan tour in Bethlehem, Pennsylvania, that October 25 when he turned 51 and Dylan sang him 'Happy Birthday' during the encore. That the two men had remained close friends all through the long years of working together is also suggested by it being Howard Alk who was around to take the most informal pictures of Dylan shown in the booklet inside the 1985 *Biograph* box set, including the delicately intimate pictures of Dylan and Clydie King from 1980–81.

Alk also had time in 1981 to appear in a small acting rôle: as a party guest in the car-racing drama, Noel Nosseck's *King of the Mountain*. By this time, however, he is alleged to have become a heroin addict; re-married, he had separated from his current wife and on December 31, hanging out at Dylan's old stomping ground, Santa Monica's Rundown Studios, he was desperately low and was trying to phone people to say he was going to kill himself. This depression was the flipside to his tremendously energetic engagement with people. One of those he called was ex-wife Jones, who happened to be home changing between parties. It was New Year's Eve. It was also their wedding anniversary, he reminded her. She said no it wasn't, because they weren't married anymore. She said she'd ring round to try to get someone nearby to come and see him, but everyone was out, including Dylan, and Howard gave her the wrong number to call back. He went ahead and killed himself; he was found dead at the studio on New Year's Day 1982.

'Howard was one of a kind,' says Mike Gray: 'He deserves an entry in every encyclopedia.'

[Bernard Sahlins: *Days and Nights at the Second City: A Memoir*, Chicago: Ivan R. Dee, 2002, quoted online 29 Oct 2005 at *http://sctvguide.ca/features/sahlins.htm*. Clinton Heylin, 'A Profile of Howard Alk' in *All Across the Telegraph: A Bob Dylan Handbook*, eds. Michael Gray & John Bauldie, London: Futura edn., 1988, pp.146 & 150. Gerald Peary quoted from ditto, p.149; Alk quoted ditto p.152. Mike Gray, e-mail to this writer 30 Oct 2005. Other information from Jones Cullinan, phone interview with this writer, 1 Nov 2005.]

'All Along the Watchtower' [1968] Recorded on November 6, 1967, this spare, dark song came out of the *John Wesley Harding* sessions that yielded such a stark rebuke to the 'summer of love' and such a contrast to Dylan's previous mid-1960s work.

The nature of the language in this song, as it struck us when it was new, was a sort of impressionism revisited, but no longer reflecting summer tension in the city, as did *Blonde on Blonde*, and instead reflecting winter time in the psyche (helped by having an allusion within it to T.S. ELIOT's *The Waste Land*: 'all the women came and went', sings Dylan, echoing Eliot's 'the women come and go').

How does it end, this stark song? There used to be two alternatives. Either it was experienced as circular, drawing an added element of menace from the very endlessness of the nightmare vision offered, with the song going round and round, so that the helpless cry 'There must be some way out of here' *recurs after* 'The wind began to howl'. Or else, if it were not experienced as circular in that way, then it was felt to end, as Richard Goldstein argued in a *Village Voice* review, on an emphatic full-stop—indeed, a terrifying full-stop. Just three clean, razor-sharp verses, with an end that signifies the end of *everything*: 'Outside in the distance / A wild cat did growl / Two riders were approaching / The wind began to howl.' As Goldstein says, the suggestion of menace in these lines is far too ominous and powerful for them to be concluded with a series of dots.

Dylan, though, has other ideas, and in the last few years he has been performing the song in concert in such a way as to give it a third ending. In this version 'There must be some way out of here' *does* recur after 'The wind began to howl': but not because the song never ends. Rather, because Dylan chooses to finish in a way that at once reduces its apocalyptic import and hugely cranks up its emphasis on the artist's own centrality. Repeating the first stanza as the last means that Dylan now ends with this: 'Businessmen they drink my wine / Plowmen dig my earth / None of them along the line / Know what any of it is worth' (and this is sung with a prolonged, dark linger on that word 'worth'). It's a lesser ending—but an audacious hijacking of his own song.

The first live performance of 'All Along the Watchtower' was on the opening night of the 'comeback tour' of 1974, in Chicago on January 3, and it was, from the outset, the JIMI HENDRIX version of the song that Dylan offered: heavy rock, rather than the album's eerie acoustic minimalism. It became the most performed of all Dylan songs: one might say the most over-performed. It was eventually given a sustained rest in 1997, after being played at 40 out of 40 concerts in 1974, 110 out of 114 concerts in 1978, 10 out of 19 of 1980's semi-secular concerts, 35 out of 54 shows in 1981, all 27 of 1984's concerts, 11 out of 60 in 1986, 8 out of 36 in 1987, 39 out of 71 in 1988, 63 out of 99 in 1989, 81 out of 92 in 1990, 89 out of 101 in 1991 and 86 out of 92 concerts in 1992.

From August 20, 1992 until August 3, 1997 it became the third song in *every* Bob Dylan concert. For five years! That last night it came fourth, was then dropped for a few days, reintroduced on August 12th and then dropped properly until resuscitated as the opening number at his 43rd concert of 1998. Thus it had been performed a further 76 times in 1993, 109 times in 1994, 118 times in 1995, 86 times in 1996 and 38 times in 1997. By the end of 1998 this had already totaled a numbing 1,033 performances in 25 years, 690 of them in the 1990s alone. By the end of 2003 the total had reached 1,393. Nothing could be more dramatic, effective or welcome than if he were to come on stage with an acoustic guitar and try to sing it as he'd heard and recorded it in the first place, in late 1967, before Jimi Hendrix.

(Re 'Outside in the distance / A wildcat did growl', see also **'Call Letter Blues'**.)

['All Along the Watchtower', Nashville, TN, 6 Nov 1967. Live versions have been included on the albums *Before the Flood*, *Bob Dylan at Budokan*, *Biograph* (the *Before the Flood* version), *Dylan and the Dead* and *Unplugged*.]

Allen, Colin [1938 -] Colin Allen was born in Bournemouth, England, on May 9, 1938. Mainly keen on modern jazz, he took up drums at age 18, while working as an apprentice aircraft fitter. He moved to London on the first day of 1964, along with fellow local-jazzer Andy Summers (later of the Police), becoming a professional musician and founder member of Zoot Money's Big Roll Band, which played with many visiting American blues legends including MEMPHIS SLIM, JOHN LEE HOOKER and SONNY BOY WILLIAMSON, and was the opening act for Otis Redding in England and for James Brown in France. Three years later the band split, and Colin Allen became the drummer with JOHN MAYALL's Bluesbreakers in summer 1968, playing in Europe and touring the US.

In 1969 he joined the recently formed British group Stone the Crows (which featured singer Maggie Bell), and played on all their albums. The group also toured the US twice, once as support act to Joe Cocker's 'Mad Dogs & Englishmen'. In 1974 he became a member of that essentially Dutch band Focus, toured the States with them, contributed to their albums *Hamburg Concerto* and *Ship of Memories* but soon quit because there were so many tensions within the group. By the early 1980s he had re-located to Los Angeles, and re-joined John Mayall for several more tours. The other band members were MICK TAYLOR and the Fleetwood Mac bass player John McVie.

Allen has also played on over 50 albums, including Rod Stewart's *Foolish Behaviour*. He is also a lyric writer, and more than 60 of his songs have been recorded by other people, among them Wings, Fleetwood Mac and MICK RONSON.

More to the point for present purposes he was the drummer on Bob Dylan's 1984 tour of Europe—rehearsing in Los Angeles in May, playing the first concert on May 28 in Verona, Italy, and running through to Slane Castle in Ireland on July 8. Allen played a total of 27 concerts, and inevitably appears on the largely uninspiring album *Real Live*.

In 1985 Colin Allen moved to Stockholm, Sweden, where he still lives and continues to play. In September 2005 he played with the British Blues All Stars (along with the legendary Peter Green and others) at the Orkney Blues Festival in the Outer Hebrides.

Allen, Woody [1935 -] See ***Annie Hall*, dismissal of Dylan in.**

Allison, Mose [1927 -] Mose Allison was born on November 11, 1927 in tiny Tippo, Mississippi, learnt piano as a child, played in the US Army Band, attended first the University of Mississippi and then gained a BA in English and Philosophy at Louisiana State University, Baton Rouge, in 1952. He moved to New York City in 1956, where he played with jazz names like Stan Getz, Zoot Sims and Charlie Byrd, and from 1957 quickly moved record labels from Prestige to Columbia to Atlantic but then stayed with this once-indie label for decades. He was quick at making albums, too: he made eight LPs for Prestige in a three-year period.

Allison was not at all your archetypal blues man, though he did wander towards the blues rather than simply play jazz. He was a sophisticat with an unemotional keyboard style combined with a knowing vocal flippancy, but while he certainly trademarked this finger-snap jazz side to his style—such an unfortunate influence on VAN MORRISON—nevertheless the down-home blues was his basic inspiration and he was a popular Greenwich Village performer whom Dylan certainly encountered. One of the things SUZE ROTOLO emphasises in her testimony is that the Village was explored in its every facet—that she and Dylan, like many others, would try out all kinds of events and venues and genres and art forms.

As she says it: 'You were young, you'd be hanging out, there'd be musicians with you, so you'd go from place to place . . . and people did different things. So it wasn't just to hear folk music. I went to jazz clubs all the time . . . and by the end of the night we'd go down to Chinatown to have some food. . . . there was a lot of stuff going on, culturally going on, and a lot of different ideas through this music, and through the poetry, the jazz, the stand-up, the folk, the whatever.'

Mose Allison's version of 'Baby Please Don't Go' was a fixture of Village musical life, as was his uptown jazz re-interpretation of BUKKA WHITE's 'Parchman Farm', in which Allison paired the line 'Way down on Parchman Farm' with 'The place was loaded with rustic charm'. Though Bob Dylan would never have written such a pay-off line, the act of respecting source material and smiling at it at the same time is something we might recognise as Dylanesque.

Allison was introduced to Dylan by Bill Cosby outside the Village Gate, where Allison was working at the time. He tended to work a month at a time there, plus two or three nights a year as opening act for other people at the Village Vanguard. Cosby told Allison as he introduced Dylan: 'He's into WOODY GUTHRIE'. Mose Allison had no interest in Guthrie whatsoever, but somebody gave him Dylan's début album and he liked it. He thought 'it was different, the sound and the tunes. And I liked the humor: I liked "Talkin' New York".'

A few weeks later Dylan and JOHN HAMMOND JR. came to one of his shows at the Village Vanguard, and later still, when he was back working at the Gate, Allison remembers driving Dylan around in his car one time, and an evening 'sitting at a table with Bob, telling him about a record I had just heard and thought was good, "Rise to Fall", by Edgar Winter. Minutes later Edgar Winter walked in the place. That's the last time I ever saw Bob except on TV.'

Mose Allison is still up and running, with a youthful speaking voice belied by his looking strikingly similar to LAWRENCE FERLINGHETTI. In 2001 he was a 'special guest' in the movie *The Score*, directed by Frank Oz and starring Robert de Niro and Marlon Brando. He still performs, and in 2005 the BBC filmed a documentary about him.

He dropped 'Parchman Farm' from his repertoire many years ago.

[Mose Allison quotes: e-mail to & phone-call with this writer, 10 & 12 Nov 2005.]

Alvin, Dave [1955 -] David Alvin was born in Downey, California, on November 11, 1955, younger brother of Phil, with whom he formed the Blasters in 1979. He had learnt guitar in 1970 from T-Bone Walker, one of the creators of modern blues and an electric guitar pioneer whose own earliest tuition had come from BLIND LEMON JEFFERSON, thus providing Alvin with a link right back to the beginnings of the music he loved. The aptly named Blasters gained a huge international cult following, and BRUCE SPRINGSTEEN singled them out as 'a major influence'; but a cult they remained. They made the albums *American Music* (1980), *Blasters* (1981), *Over There* (1982), *Non Fiction* (1983) and *Hard Line* (1985); but Dave Alvin, dissatisfied, quit the group in 1986. He promptly joined X as lead guitarist but left again soon after the sessions for their *See How We Are* album the same year. Several members of X, including Alvin, had also been in a country-music side band named the Knitters, who made the 1985 album *Poor Little Critter on the Road.*

Alvin then went solo (though he toured with the Blasters in 1987 too), producing a large number of albums starting with 1987's *Romeo's Escape* (renamed *Every Night About This Time* in the UK), after which he switched labels. He toured with Mojo Nixon and Country Dick Montana as the Pleasure Barons and did a large amount of session work. His 2000 album *Public Domain: Songs from the Wild Land*, traditional folk and blues numbers, won him a Grammy as Best Contemporary Folk Album (the same award Dylan had won with *Time Out of Mind* in 1997).

Alvin's session work included playing on Dylan's 'Driftin' Too Far from Shore'. The basic track was recorded in New York at early sessions for the *Empire Burlesque* album but left off it; Alvin was one of those brought in to studios at Topanga Park, California, on April 28, 1986 to overdub guitar; the track was issued on that year's *Knocked Out Loaded* album. Alvin also played guitar that day on Dylan's first attempt at 'You'll Never Walk Alone'; this has not circulated. A year later, in Hollywood studios, Alvin played guitar on similarly unheard versions of 'Look on Yonder Wall', 'Rollin' and Tumblin'', 'Red Cadillac and a Black Mustache' and two takes of 'Rock with Me Baby'. Fifteen years after that, during a Never-Ending Tour concert, Dave Alvin replaced band member CHARLIE SEXTON on 'To Be Alone with You' and 'Lay Lady Lay', consecutive numbers in the middle of Dylan's set of August 31, 2002 at Grand Junction, Colorado. Dylan was reportedly overheard to ask: 'Dave, when are you and Phil getting back together? Man, that stuff was magic!'

In 2005 Alvin was still working with the Knitters, and recording their second album, *The Modern Sounds of the Knitters*, 20 years after the first. He is also in the Guilty Men. He has not abandoned his solo career.

'Am I Your Stepchild?' [1978] & blues accusation-laments Dylan introduced this song—one of his own compositions—on the first night of the North American leg of the 1978 tour, on September 15 at Augusta, Maine, and played it at a further 52 out of 64 concerts before the tour's end. There were lyric variations every time Dylan sang it, but the live recording from the Oakland, CA, concert of November 13 was used as a Special Rider music-publishing demo. Dylan's final performance of the song was on the tour's last night, December 16 in Hollywood, Florida. He has never performed it since.

'Am I Your Stepchild?' may be an obscure item in Dylan's canon—it is omitted from the official lyrics books and from the list of his songs at *www.bobdylan.com*—but its lyric tells us something about his interest in blues lyric poetry. It is what Stanley Booth calls 'a blues in the familiar accusation-lament pattern', as is, for example, BLIND WILLIE McTELL's 'Death Cell Blues', from the early 1930s: 'They got me 'cused for murder, and I haven't harmed a man / They got me charged for burglarin', I haven't even raised my hand . . . / They got me 'cused for forging, and I can' even write my name' (in which the pathos is not reliant upon our knowing that the singer is blind), and LONNIE JOHNSON's fastidiously mordant 'I Have to Do My Time', in which 'The judge say I was guilty and he couldn't explain / Charged me with forgery an' I cain't even sign my name.'

Dylan's 1978 song can't match these; but there is a piece of his writing much earlier and more successful than 'Am I Your Stepchild?' into which he imports an echo of such songs, and that is the poem 'My Life in a Stolen Moment': suggesting that even when any persecution he suffered was largely the fantasy-stuff of the middle-class post-adolescent, his affinity for the blues world (and his familiarity with its poetry) ran deep. His poem includes these lines: 'Got jailed for suspicion of armed robbery / Got held four hours on a murder rap / Got busted for looking like I do / An' I never done none a them things.'

Such alert writing. The blues echo is especially clear in that last line, with its perfectly mimicked appeasing cadence, while Dylan good-humouredly acknowledges his myth-making, his inexperience of such outward oppression, with a series of deft disclaimers. That 'four hours' makes something slighter and more acceptable of what would otherwise be the over-the-top, too easily refutable (and too self-aggrandising) claim 'Got held on a murder rap'. Then there's the double-joke of the last line itself: it's a nifty audacity that he can claim never to have looked like he does; and, in the context of the whole fabricated autobiography the poem offers, it's funny that it ends with the laughing admission that it has *all* been made up.

[Bob Dylan: 'My Life in a Stolen Moment', first published in the program for the New York Town Hall concert, 12 Apr 1963. Blind Willie McTell: 'Death Cell Blues', NY, 19 Sep 1933, *The Atlanta Blues*, RBF RF15, NY, 1966; CD-reissued *The Definitive Blind Willie McTell*, Columbia Legacy Roots N' Blues 53234, NY, 1994. Lonnie Johnson: 'I Have to Do My Time', NY, 5 Aug 1930, unissued until the CD *Lonnie Johnson Complete Recorded Works Vol. 6*, Document DOCD-5068, Vienna, 1991; CD-reissued *Roots N' Blues Retrospective*, Columbia Legacy Roots N' Blues 47911, NY, 1992.]

American Civil War in *World Gone Wrong*, the A main feature of the 1993 solo acoustic album *World Gone Wrong* is its evocation of the American Civil War: all its psychic divides, its North-South, its then-now and its slave-abolitionist flames that have never been extinguished, defeat being still so real and fundamentally defining in the South that it might have happened in the 1990s rather than the 1860s. The modern plaque at the campus entrance to the University of Georgia in Athens, home to 30,000 students and hometown of R.E.M. and the B52s, refers not to the American Civil War but to 'the War for Southern Independence'. Except for the veterans and their families directly involved, the Vietnam War seems longer ago and harder to remember.

It is with 'Two Soldiers' and 'Jack-a-Roe' that Dylan invokes the Civil War's foment. In many versions of 'Jack-a-Roe', not only does the disguised heroine claim that she *could* 'see ten thousand fall', she participates in the warfare, so that there is much more common ground—common battleground—shared by the two songs than Dylan's version of the latter suggests.

There is a stirring conjunction between these two adjacently placed songs and the eloquent memorial to the defeated Confederate Army in Columbia, state capital of South Carolina—the state that led the breakaway from the Union—about which V.S. Naipaul writes:

'On one side of the monument was engraved: "To South Carolina's dead of the Confederate Army 1861–1865." On another side it said: "Erected by the Women of South Carolina. Unveiled May 13, 1879." There was rhetoric in that reference to women; monuments of grief and revenge, or grief and piety, are most unsettling when they depict women bowed in grief.' (Again, another sub-text of such monuments can be the message that the Civil War matters far more than any other. In BLIND WILLIE McTELL's place of burial, Thomson, Georgia, the town's memorial statue plinth reads 'In Memory of the Women of the Sixties . . .' Everyone understands that this means the 1860s.)

The Columbia memorial reads: 'This monument perpetuates the memory of those who, true to the instincts of their birth, faithful to the teachings of their fathers, constant in their love for the state, died in the performance of their duty: who have glorified a fallen cause by the simple manhood of their lives, the patient endurance of suffering, and the heroism of death, and who, in the dark hours of imprisonment, in the hopelessness of the hospital, in the short, sharp agony of the field, found support and consolation in the belief that at home they would not be forgotten.'

The first half of this, up to 'the heroism of death', is the predictable clamour of patriotism and (white) male supremacy: but how striking, how enlivening for its candour and compassion, is the passage this official monumentese slides into, as into a confession: you don't expect a war memorial to meditate upon 'the dark hours of imprisonment . . . the hopelessness of the hospital' (that phrase seems especially subversive) and 'the short, sharp agony of the field'. It is this humane and feminine second half of the inscription that converges upon 'Two Soldiers' (and that the 'Two Soldiers' are blue-eyed Boston boys of the Yankee army only serves to make the common humanity of both sides reverberate the more poignantly) and 'Jack-a-Roe'.

In the latter, the disguised woman, having claimed that it wouldn't faze her 'to see ten thousand fall', finds her lover 'among the dead and dying': among those, indeed, 'in the short, sharp agony of the field'. In the version Dylan sings, it is nicely ambiguous as to whether she finds her lover a wounded survivor among the dead and dying, or whether he too is truly 'among the dead and dying', after which the doctor tends his wounds but can do nothing to countermand their mortal effect, so that the marriage with which the song then ends is the death-bed marriage: the kind Barbara Allen is too late with her change of heart to offer Sweet William in the version Dylan sings of *that* ballad.

In 'Two Soldiers'—'a battle song extraordinaire, some dragoon officer's epaulettes laying liquid in the mud, physical plunge into Limitationville. . . . America when Mother was the queen of Her heart,' as Dylan puts it with sumptuous muscularity in the album's unexpected sleevenotes—the soldiers are indeed preoccupied with seeking 'consolation in the belief that at home they should not be forgotten' by the women who do stay and wait.

In this case they wait in vain, for both soldiers turn out to be 'among the dead', not among 'those whom death and doom had spared'. It is also in this simple phrase 'among the dead' and its extension 'and dying', omitted but implicit here, that the two songs come together. There are not only common concerns but common-stock elements in each song, and that this is one they share is shown by those versions of 'Two Soldiers' brought together under varying titles in G. Malcolm Laws' standard work *Native American Balladry*. In 'The Drummer Boy of Shiloh', 'On Shiloh's dark and bloody ground / The dead and wounded lay around'; in 'A Soldier from Missouri' (aka 'The Kansas Line'), 'A soldier from Missouri / In early manhood's prime / Lay with the dead an' dyin' / In Mississippi's clime'. Yet 'Two Soldiers' ends not with their deaths per se but with the bleakness of their leaving a silence behind, with 'no-one to write' to the women left stranded at home. They are the women who might have paid to raise such a memorial as the one to be found in South Carolina.

Its inscription's end—envisaging that the dying soldiers would find 'consolation in the belief that at home they would not be forgotten'—is itself the lonely consolation of the women. The sensibility of these songs is such as to offer a sisterhood to these disruptive human whispers from within the carved stone: a fluid, oral guardianship of the past running alongside the fixity of its official text.

In the 19-verse version of 'Jack-a-Roe' called 'Jackie Frazier', collected in A.L. Lloyd's *Folk Songs of the Americas*, her lover unambiguously recovers, and the far less reverberative moral of the story is 'So parents let your children get married as they please' (or, as someone else put it, 'your sons and your daughters are beyond your command'). But as Roscoe Holcomb refashions the story in his tour de force recording 'Across the Rocky Mountain'—a title surely echoed by Dylan's own most recent Civil War song ''Cross the Green Mountain'—the song ends with the callous boast of the heroine, the subsequent discovery of her lover and the pared-down ambiguity of a frantic dash to the doctor, its outcome left unclear. The words duplicate those of 'Jack-a-Roe': 'My cheeks are not too rosy, my fingers not too small / No they would not change my conscience to see ten thousand fall / . . . She's walking through the battlefield a-searching up and down / It's all among the dead and wounded her darling Jack she found / . . . She picked him up all in her arms, she carried him to the town / She took him to the doctor for to quickly heal the wound.'

That we cannot assume a happy ending from the mere invocation of the doctor is also pressed upon us by recalling that the same line—about the doctor, the healing and the wound—is an ingredient in the 'Unfortunate Rake' series of songs, in which despite the physician's attention, the outcome is death. With the happy ending refused, in both the Holcomb and the Dylan versions of the 'Jackie Frazier' song, we're left to question the consolation the heroine receives for having refused to wait passively at home for news from the war, as wives and mothers and sisters more usually must.

Consolation was small either way. The American Civil War was the biggest in the western world in the hundred years between the end of the Napoleonic Wars and the start of World War I. It cost more American lives than the two world wars, Korea and Vietnam combined. On a single day in the wet spring of 1864, May 12, almost 13,000 men died fighting for a patch of ground abandoned within days afterwards. It also introduced the special horrors of 'modern' warfare: the trenches, the prisoner-of-war camp, the first American conscription, ironclad ships, aerial observation, the Gatling gun and propaganda.

'Two Soldiers' focuses upon the Battle of Fredericksburg (the song is sometimes known as 'The Battle of Fredericksburg' and also as 'The Last Fierce Charge'), which took place on December 13, 1862, demoralised the North and heartened the South yet proved the latter's last significant victory (and was largely by default at that). The North lost over 12,000 men and the Confederate South had 5,000 killed or wounded. It was this battle too that brought home to people on both sides the sense that the war might be a remorseless, continuing conflict with no end ever in sight.

Bob Dylan's richly concentrated, somber and ineffably tender version of 'Two Soldiers' draws out of the song every last sorrowful morsel of its skilful encapsulation of this vast, doomed slaughter into the story of two individual doomed innocents and the repercussions of grief and silence that follow from their deaths. It works affectingly despite its historical inaccuracy—there was, for instance, no cavalry engagement at the Battle of Fredericksburg. And even though it is so very difficult to hear all the words as Dylan sings them, you feel when you listen that he sings them extraordinarily well!

Dylan's liner notes say that JERRY GARCIA showed him 'Two Soldiers' and that 'Jack-a-Roe' is a TOM PALEY ballad. 'Two Soldiers' was published in *Sing Out!* in July 1964. 'Jackaroe' is also released on the fourth JOAN BAEZ album—the one for which Dylan contributed a sleevenote poem; Dylan's 'Jack-a-Roe', 30 years later, uses the Baez version of the text.

Dylan's live début of 'Jack-a-Roe' was at the New York Supper Club (2nd Show) on November 16, 1993, within three weeks of the release of *World Gone Wrong*; more surprisingly, he débuted his live version of 'Two Soldiers' (with insignificant small variations in the lyric from the album version) five years *before* he included it on the album: at Sacramento on June 9, 1988, the second concert of the Never-Ending Tour.

(See also **''Cross the Green Mountain'**.)

[V.S. Naipaul, *A Turn in the South*, New York: Knopf, 1989. G. Malcolm Laws Jr., *Native American Balladry*, Philadelphia: American Folklore Society, revised edn., 1964. A.L. Lloyd, *Folk Songs of the Americas*, London:

Novello, 1965. Roscoe Holcomb: 'Across the Rocky Mountain', Daisy, VA, 1959, *Mountain Music of Kentucky*, Folkways FA 2317, NY, 1960; CD-reissued (as 2-CD set with extra tracks) Smithsonian-Folkways SFCD 40077, Washington, D.C., 1996. *Sing Out!* vol.14, no.3, New York, July 1964. 'Jack Monroe' quoted from *The Greig-Duncan Folk Song Collection, Vol.1*, ed. Patrick Shuldham-Shaw & Emily B. Lyle, Aberdeen, UK: Aberdeen University Press, 1981. Joan Baez: 'Jackaroe', *Joan Baez in Concert, Part 2*, Vanguard VRS-9113, NY, 1964. This account has leant on Douglas Welsh, *American Civil War: A Complete Military History*, London: Bison, 1981 and William Least Heat-Moon, *Blue Highways: A Journey into America*, London: Picador, 1984 (US 1st edition 1983). Athens & Thomson, GA, inscriptions seen firsthand.]

***American Folk Music* [1952, 1997]** HARRY SMITH's groundbreaking, essential 6-LP anthology of pre-war white and black recordings was issued in 1952 on Folkways Records under the title *American Folk Music* (and is therefore so called here). However, it has long been commonly referred to as the *Anthology of American Folk Music*, a title eventually made official by the CD-reissue of 1997.

When the set was released originally it was the first collection to put black and white American folk musics together instead of keeping them separate, and it provided crucial source material for the whole revivalist scene that was to thrive in Greenwich Village and Boston by the end of that decade.

DAVE VAN RONK wrote in 1991 that the anthology had been its bible. 'We all knew every word of every song on it, including the ones we hated.'

The six LPs came with Harry Smith's notes, which are terrific, not least for their summarising the story-lines of the songs almost in tabloid headline style. For instance, re 'Ommie Wise': 'GREEDY GIRL GOES TO ADAM SPRINGS WITH LIAR: LIVES JUST LONG ENOUGH TO REGRET IT'.

It was an eerie work of archeology altogether. As Luc Santé writes in the CD box-set reissue booklet: 'In 1952, when its contents were only twenty or twenty-five years old, they must have already seemed ancient.'

This pioneering compilation was certainly crucial to Dylan from very early in his career. Of this set's 84 recordings, at least 30 have a Bob Dylan connection: and he had already taped performances of ten of them, and rewritten another two, by the end of 1961.

The ten were 'The House Carpenter' (the anthology's 3rd track is CLARENCE ASHLEY's 1930 recording); 'The Butcher's Boy (The Railroad Boy)' (the anthology's 6th track, by Buell Kazee from 1928); 'The Wagoner's Lad' (7th track, ditto); 'Ommie Wise' (13th: Grayson & Whitter, 1927); 'John the Revelator' (52nd: BLIND WILLIE JOHNSON, 1930); 'The Coo-Coo Bird' (57th: Clarence Ashley again, 1929); 'East Virginia' (58th: Buell Kazee again, 1927 [though Smith says 1929]); 'James Alley Blues' (61st: RICHARD RABBIT BROWN, 1927); 'K.C. Moan' (81st: MEMPHIS JUG BAND, 1929); and 'See That My Grave Is Kept Clean' (76th: BLIND LEMON JEFFERSON, 1928).

Dylan also turned the collection's song 'Down on Penny's Farm' (25th: the Bently Boys, 1929: one of the mere two tracks they ever recorded) into his own song 'Hard Times in New York Town', and had turned 'A Lazy Farmer Boy', known also as 'The Young Man Who Wouldn't Hoe Corn' (11th: Buster Carter & Preston Young, 1931 [though Smith says 1930]), into his own 'Man on the Street'.

Further references to material from this collection, and to Dylan's use of it, will be found throughout this encyclopedia.

Before the flurry of commentary on Smith's anthology that came with, and was prompted by, its CD reissue, a distinctive voice on the subject was Robert Cantwell's, in a sometimes mystical essay 'Smith's Memory Theater', first published in 1991. More conventionally, as GREIL MARCUS writes in 'The Old, Weird America', his essay in the CD-reissue package (adapted from his book *Invisible Republic: Bob Dylan's Basement Tapes*, itself aka *The Old Weird America*), we can say in summary that the *American Folk Music* anthology was 'the founding document of the American folk revival'. But don't hold that against it.

[Harry Smith, compiler & sleevenote writer: *American Folk Music* (6-LP set), Folkways FP251-253, NY, 1952; CD-reissued as *Anthology of American Folk Music* (6-CD box set) with copious notes by many hands and a CD-ROM of extras, Smithsonian Folkways SRW 40090, Washington, D.C., 1997.

Clarence Ashley: 'The House Carpenter', Atlanta, 14 Apr 1930 & 'The Coo-Coo Bird', Johnson City, TN, 23 Oct 1929. Buell Kazee: 'The Butcher's Boy (The Railroad Boy)', NY, Jan 16, 1928, 'The Wagoner's Lad (Loving Nancy)', NY, 18 Jan 1928 & 'East Virginia', NY, 20 Apr 1927. Grayson & Whitter: 'Ommie Wise', Atlanta, 18 Oct 1927. Blind Willie Johnson: 'John the Revelator', Atlanta, 20 Apr 1930. Richard Rabbit Brown: 'James Alley Blues', New Orleans, 11 Mar 1927. Memphis Jug Band: 'K.C. Moan', Memphis, 4 Oct 1929. Blind Lemon Jefferson: 'See That My Grave Is Kept Clean', Chicago, c.Feb 1928. The Bently Boys: 'Down on Penny's Farm', Johnson City, TN, 23 Oct 1929. Buster Carter & Preston Young: 'A Lazy Farmer Boy', NY, 26 Jun 1931.

Robert Cantwell: 'Smith's Memory Theater', *New England Review*, Middlebury, VT, spring/summer 1991, republished as Ch.6 in Cantwell: *When We Were Good: The Folk Revival*, Cambridge, MA: Harvard University Press, 1996.]

Andersen, Karl Erik [1948 -] Karl Erik Andersen runs one of the most extraordinary, copious Dylan websites of all the hundreds that are out there in cyberspace: *http://expectingrain.com*, which he updates *twice daily* in order to post the URL of every web page that mentions Bob Dylan's name (and a number of extra ones that he thinks will interest people keen enough to be regular visitors to the site 'and even maybe the man himself').

Andersen was born in Mosjøen, Sweden, on July 15, 1948. The first Dylan album he bought was *Bringing It All Back Home* but it was 30 years on before he attended a Dylan concert (Oslo, July 1995). He has never published any work of his own and never encountered any bootlegs or fanzines until he started the website, which was in 1994: 'Year Zero of the World Wide Web'. At first his idea was to assemble the information resources he found posted on the newsgroup *http://rec.music.dylan*; when webserver software became available he found it fun to allow others to access the same resources. The first items of content he published online were stills from the 'Jokerman' video and the online Bob Dylan Atlas and Dylan Who's Who pages. As media interest in Dylan grew it seemed useful to gather links to relevant stories on the net, and updating these daily began in February 2000. In the summer of 2005 the still-burgeoning amount of material prompted him to update twice daily instead.

Karl Erik Andersen was a teacher for 11 years but since 1992 he has been curator of the broadcasting archive at the branch of the Swedish National Library in his hometown, Mo i Rana. His goal?: 'To see Bob Dylan play in Mo i Rana.'

'Angelina' [1981] Recorded at the *Shot of Love* sessions in 1981, 'Angelina' remained unissued until the box set the *Bootleg Series Vols. 1–3* a decade later.

'Angelina' is romantically entangled in the visionary fever of the Book of Revelation—and of EZEKIEL, the Old Testament book that the writer of Revelation seems to have had continually in mind. This is familiar territory in Dylan's work, a backdrop to songs from 'Blowin' in the Wind' to 'Dignity'. With 'Angelina' he is here again: and here as if for the first time, since the narrative seems that of someone wandering lost in a perilous landscape. The recording takes us on a long road, as through a trance or a dream, in which, as they are wont to do in dreams, time and place shift and a different logic prevails. If this parallels perfectly the experience of reading the long, strange biblical passages to which it refers, it also makes 'Angelina' a difficult song to comprehend. It is hard because of the disconnectedness, the impossible images, the general air of smudging which clings to it, and the collision of the narrative into different genres as it passes.

As ever, the way into the song is from the performance. It begins thrillingly, holding out infinite promise (which is of course impossible to deliver), shimmering into being like the gorgeous solo version of 'Spanish Is the Loving Tongue', with piano and voice. The first words are these: 'Well it's always been my nature to take chances / My right hand drawing back while my left hand advances.' This is doubly striking. First, the character of the opening line is surely unique in Dylan's work. Many Bob Dylan songs begin with that direct conversational tone but there is no other in which its content appears candidly self-defining. Bob Dylan is not a man who writes 'I'm a man who . . .' It's never been his nature to define his nature.

Second, Dylan then structures his second line to stress the 'drawing back'—and it's the right hand 'drawing back' while the weaker, sinister hand 'advances'. This is a tantalising, provoking line, never quite satisfying but not dismissible either. There's an ellipse in here: a stage in the logic of exposition has been squeezed unspoken into the crack between Dylan's first line and his second. The result is that the two lines themselves enact what they describe: Dylan has set up a tugging back and forth between them. It isn't comfortable but it is poetry.

Nor is there any carelessness in the structure of the song. Each verse is of eight lines, rhyming AAABCCCB, each last line being (with one deliberate exception, considered below) simply the title word 'Angelina'. After each verse comes a single line of refrain, acting as a simple echo ('Oh—— Angelina! Oh—— Angelina!'). There are no half-rhymes: the shape Dylan has chosen, with those clusters of three adjacent rhyming lines, only works if it delivers the pleasure of repetition, and it cannot deliver that if the rhymes are inexact. The 'echo' must be simple here too. Dylan knows not to settle for less.

If the AAA and CCC rhymes in the verses must be straight, there is opportunity galore in the B rhymes, the 'Angelina' rhymes, for the flamboyant and extravagant. And Dylan seizes it. There are no half-rhymes here either, nor any demure, quietening rhymes designed to pass unnoticed: no Anglican words like 'cleaner', no innocuous phrase like 'have you seen her?' Every one Dylan sings chimes its ding-dong, two-tone bell, its Latin and Latin-American bell, as ostentatiously as possible: concertina, hyena, subpoena, Argentina, arena. This engineering precision, the sturdy carriages of the five verses built to one blueprint, the ringing iron certainty of the rails of rhyme—these are sufficient to propel us through all the swirling mists and past all the looming vague shapes of the song's narrative landscape.

The declaration that there is such a journey comes at the start of the second verse, with the deft line 'Blood dryin' in my yellow hair as I go from shore to shore.' This sets the tone; it establishes the vague generality, the grand sweep, of the song's journey—and simultaneously supplies those specific details, the blood drying in the yellow hair: details which, far from clarifying, only serve to clinch how little we are to be left to feel we know. The 'yellow hair' tells us that the narrator's persona isn't Bob Dylan; the 'blood drying', while detailed, is wholly unexplained. The line that follows, 'I know what it is that has drawn me to your door', only serves to tell us that we *don't* know what it is, after which comes an immediate confession that much is unknown to the singer too: 'But whatever could it be, makes you think you seen me before / Angelina?'

Yet 'Blood dryin' in my yellow hair as I go from shore to shore' yields more than so far allowed. This blood flows from no ordinary wound: blood doesn't go on drying all through the lengthy travail of going from shore to shore. Continual drying suggests continual flow behind it. The aura here is of stigmata, of those favourite phenomena of the Catholic Church, statues that weep and effigies that bleed. 'Yellow' is less curious as a hair-colour on a plaster saint than a real person. There's an atmosphere here that hints of those countries in which there are many Angelinas and where the more lurid mysticisms of Catholic paraphernalia most nearly make sense: the southern Mediterranean and the Americas. In other words, this line suggests itself as the song's first tentative breath of the air of magic realism.

'Argentina' is named, later in the song, inside a question as rhetorical as that just quoted: 'Tell me, tall man, where would you like to be overthrown: / In Jerusalem or Argentina?' Comically audacious rhetoric it is too, of course: no 'tall man' would like to be overthrown anywhere. Singular or plural, dictator or junta, here Dylan adds in the presence of political violence that permeates everyday life (the realism) and is as much a part of the genre as the acceptance of the fantastical (the magic). What unites the two is the feeling that anything can happen. For the ordinary peasant populace, no outrage, no violent act, no bizarre rumour, no lurid superstition, no horror, no miracle, can confidently be ruled beyond the realms of possibility. (When Dylan gave concerts in South America in the early 1990s, he was described by a São Paolo journalist in a phrase entirely characteristic of this sensibility: he called Dylan 'the white monster of three decades.')

In 'Angelina', the ingredient of menace has been located already, at the beginning of the 'tall man' verse, in the deliciously sinister line 'There's a black Mercedes rollin' through the combat zone.' In this part of the world the powerless see the Mercedes as the symbol of northern, capitalist corruption. Dylan's line evokes the hushed purposiveness (that luxury auto's self-confident 'rollin''), the invulnerability that comes from being the power behind the fighting ('rollin' through the combat zone'), the unaccountability of the sheltered occupant inside the cold, black machine. Its windows are surely as black as its body-work (we cannot see through this glass darkly), and its fat black tyres glide over the dust. This is also the USA's territorial back yard: a place 'where the stars and stripes explode' but the CIA determines 'the combat zone'. And in a compelling double-image of soldiers in battle, suggestive both of pawns in the game and of hacked-up horror, we 'see pieces of men marching'. These elements of the song are companion pieces to that part of 'The Groom's Still Waiting at the Altar' in which 'They're killing nuns and soldiers / There's fighting on the border.'

There are many other vapours from this magic realist world in 'Angelina'. All these lines and phrases, these touches and details, accord with this Latin-American milieu: 'the monkey dances / To the tune of a concertina'; 'just step into the arena'; those 'spiral staircases'. This is also a land of blood-feud and revenge, a culture in which it might be par for the course to find that 'She was stolen from her mother when she was three days old', and in which the inevitable follow-up report must be that 'Now her vengeance has been satisfied . . .' In the same climate, the overheated idolatry of a lurid Catholicism has people worshipping 'surrounded by God's angels', readily seeing or believing in a 'tree of smoke' and an 'angel with four faces', and 'Begging God for mercy and weeping in unholy places'. Oh Angelina, oh Angelina . . . As the very noises of the recording whisper into the listener's mind, 'Spanish is the loving tongue'.

Dylan is drawn to this southern, Spanish door recurrently in his work, from romancing the breathy gypsy gal of 'Spanish Harlem Incident' to consulting the wise peasant-Christ in 'Señor', and from the horse ride across the Mexican desert with Magdalena in 'Romance in Durango' to the portrait of the peasant father in 'One More Cup of Coffee'. There has even been an earlier Bob Dylan song with an Angelina in the title, 1965's 'Farewell Angelina'. And when Dylan sang about turning the other cheek before, in 'Queen Jane Approximately', the song's heroine was envisaged as turning that other cheek to 'bandits' who would then lay down their 'bandanas'.

Perhaps there is a precedent too for Dylan's being drawn to this world's magic realism. Dylan remarks to Nat Hentoff in the 1966 *Playboy* interview that '. . . traditional music is too unreal to die', and so yields 'all these songs about roses growing out of people's brains and lovers who are really geese and swans who turn into angels'. There may be compelling parallels between this 'unrealism' in the traditional folksong of neo-medieval rural Britain and Ireland and the 'magic realism' pinned down in the heavily folk-cultured fiction of modern South American writers like Gabriel García Márquez. When, therefore, Bob Dylan experiments, in 'Angelina', with the evocative poetic effects of this magic realism, it's likely that he finds these effects attractive in the same way as he finds attractive 'roses growing out of people's brains' and 'lovers who are really geese'. Dylan's taste in narrative ballads has always been either for those of mystery or else for tales of horses and daughters and hangings, exile and injustice. In 'Angelina' he creates a narrative, though not a ballad, in which most of these elements co-exist.

But 'Angelina' is a song which seems to pass through several different worlds. If the vaporous postmodernism of magic realism is one, Ancient Egypt, as filtered by Bob Dylan's imagination, seems to be another. Idolatry is heavily present in this world too. Egyptian gods appear predominantly with the forms of animals. Horus is depicted as a sparrow-hawk, Khunm as a ram. Anubis has a hyena-like head, and so does Seth. Depicted so superbly on the walls and in the tombs of an architecture that almost defies time, the idols of Ancient Egypt can readily be imagined to include, as Dylan's second verse has it, '. . . a god with the body of a woman well endowed / And the head of a hyena.' Equally, the vivid and tough first line of this verse, describing a man's face rather than a god's, does so in terms distinctively in tune with, even seeming to summarise, the Ancient Egyptian style, linear and clear: 'His eyes were two slits, make any snake proud.'

In this context, several other lines and phrases resonate, including one or two that function quite differently in the song's other worlds. That phrase 'pieces of men marching' is one. Co-existing with its effectiveness in the Latin-American magic realist context it has another life in this one. Here we can make sense of it as describing how those rows of soldiers are rendered, parading everywhere that Ancient Egyptian carving and drawing survives: cartoon-like, each figure half-hidden by the next, each fitting into the next like jigsaw pieces. Those who are conquered enemies–and these are regularly depicted: the triumphalism of the conqueror demands it–become slaves, put to work building the architectural glories of kings who decree themselves gods and build as if to conquer eternity: in some cases building pyramids in the attempt both to pierce the sky and to decipher the stars. This is indeed 'trying to take heaven by force.'

This is a culture of ritual sacrifices and power-struggles, high priests and god-kings, incest and intrigue, in which, by the time of the Ptolemaic dynasties, a young man might indeed have to 'just step into the arena'. Dylan sets this world 'In the valley of the giants where the stars and stripes explode.' The 'Valley of the Giants' acts as his fictional addition to, or perhaps his summarising retitling of, the Valley of the Kings, the Valley of the Queens, the Valley of the Nobles and the Valley of the Workmen. This vast time and place, this trying to take heaven by force, is 'where the stars and stripes explode' in the sense that here one great, crumbled empire mocks the claims of another. As he sings in another song of the early 1980s, the fairly awful 'Neighborhood Bully', 'Every empire . . . is gone / Egypt and Rome, even the great Babylon.'

Two further wisps of Ancient Egyptian air thread their way around 'Angelina'. One, unsurprising, is evoked by the mention of 'milk and honey'; the other, surprisingly, floats up from the phrase 'When you cease to exist . . .' Both bring us to meeting-points with the other world of the song, that of the Bible story. Merely by using the phrase 'milk and honey', Dylan reminds us that the children of Israel escaped from Ancient Egypt, embarking upon their own long journey and crossing the Red Sea from shore to shore to gain the promised land.

The other point of contact lies in what the Ancient Egyptian and Judaeo-Christian belief systems had in common. Here is a song about worshipping gods, a song in which, so far, all the stress has been on idolatry and the worship of many different figures. When we reach the terrain of apocalypse, we can expect a contrasting emphasis on the legitimacy of just one god, the God whose judgement day shall come, and whose son Jesus Christ shall usher in a new heaven and a new earth: a new Jerusalem. Yet in fact the contrast between the multiple gods of the one and the monotheism of the other is not so certain or straightforward. The Ancient Egyptians too believed in monotheism: in one God of Gods, creator of all things, a God who, in the attractive phrase of the guidebook *Egypt*, edited by Giovanni Magi, 'is one and primordial'. In the holy books of the Ancient Egyptians too one finds the concepts of original sin and of redemption, the promise of a redeeming god and the resurrection of the flesh at the end of time. This God of gods is Osiris, who 'married Isis', to quote another Dylan song, and he, deified, ruled over the supreme court for the judgement of the souls of the dead.

Dylan seems aware of this belief system–seems to allude to it within one of the song's sudden rhetorical questions. As with 'Tell me, tall men, where would you like to be overthrown . . . ?', we suddenly come upon this in mid-song: 'When you cease to exist, who will you blame?'

This might seem a random interjection–yet it makes a specific sense in the context of Ancient Egyptian belief about the after-life or lack of it: about what happens to those who beg God for mercy and are saved and what happens to those who beg God for mercy and are not saved. As Magi summarises this belief, it was as follows:

'If the dead person had done more good than evil they became one of the "true of voice" and thus a part of the mystical body of the god Osiris. If this was not so, the heart was eaten by an animal with the head of a crocodile and the body of a hippopotamus and *ceased to exist* in the other world' [emphasis added]. So Dylan's rhetoric translates, on this level, as 'When you are judged and not saved, who will you blame?': a meaning that sits happily with the implicit allusion to the devil, just two lines later, in the claim 'Your best friend and my worst enemy is one and the same.' So we are back once again, as so often in Dylan's work, to the question of ultimate salvation, of where we all end up at the end of the world. It's where we end up at the end of the song, guided by the Old Testament book of Ezekiel and the New Testament book of Revelation.

The long night's journey into day happens as follows: after 430 years under the Ancient Egyptians, the children of Israel escape, led by Moses, who brings them to the promised land (though Moses himself dies just before they reach it). They are not good children. Even before they arrive, they give a lot of trouble, not least in their sneaking fondness for the old Egyptian idols. When they run amok at the very moment Moses is up on the mountain receiving the Ten Commandments, God wants to wipe out the lot of them then and there, and is only dissuaded by Moses. Spared, they gain the promised land and build Jerusalem. Life goes on and they relapse, the worship of false idols again a prominent part of their transgression.

God calls on a priest, Ezekiel, who is living in exile in Babylon, and commands him to take on the rôle of prophet, return to Jerusalem and warn the people that, as in Moses' time, next time they see Him coming they'd better run: if they don't change their ways, He's going to kill them all. (In the *Good News Bible*, God's crossness is unintentionally funny. He comes across like a thwarted small-time hood: 'The Lord spoke to me. "Mortal man," he said, "this is what I, the Sovereign Lord, am saying to the land of Israel: This is the end for the whole land! Israel, the end has come. . . . One disaster after another is coming on you. It's all over. This is the end. You are finished. The end is coming for you people . . ."'.)

Ezekiel is guided by his visions, the first of which Dylan alludes to in 'Angelina's' magnificent and stately final verse, when he sings of journeying that must 'pass the angel with four faces'. Ezekiel Chapter 1, from verse 5 onwards, describes this vision of 'four living creatures' emerging from the midst of a fire: 'And every one had four faces. . . . As for the likeness of their faces, they four had the face of a man, and the face of a lion, on the right side: and they four had the face of an ox on the left side; they four also had the face of an eagle.' Adam Clarke, writing a note about this in his *Commentary on the Bible* that, for our purposes, links the angel with four faces to the 'god with a body of a woman well-endowed and the face of a hyena', notes that many such 'compound images appear in the Asiatic idols . . . some with the head and feet of a monkey, with the body, arms and legs of a man. Others with the head of the dog; body, arms and legs human. . . . The head of a lion and the head of a cock, the whole body human, and the legs terminating in snakes.'

The irony here, then, is that the inspirational vision of Ezekiel calls up creatures reminiscent of the very idols his God deplores; it's a strength of Bob Dylan's song that, unfettered by editorialising, these resemblances can float through the lyric heeded or unheeded. As noted earlier, this is a song about worshipping gods. You might say that 'Angelina' is a chimera about chimera.

Ezekiel tells God he can't do much because people always complain that he speaks in riddles. As in the past, God relents a little; but He remains so furious at His people's continued worship of false idols that He allows Jerusalem to fall to the Babylonians (in 586 BC). Ezekiel's last vision is an architecturally detailed one of how a new Jerusalem will be when the people restore themselves to righteousness.

This vision of the 12-gated city, and the earlier vision of the four angels with four faces riding around upon fiery wheels within wheels, are invoked more than half a millenium later in the Revelation of St. John the Divine, or the Revelation to John: the revelation by Jesus Christ in heaven to his faithful, persecuted followers below that a day shall finally come when through him, God's enemies, including Satan, shall be defeated and the faithful rewarded with a new heaven and a new earth: a new Jerusalem. Revelation is no straightforward read, but memorably within its turbid prose arise the four horsemen of the apocalypse:

'And I saw, and behold a white horse; and he that sat upon him had a bow; and a crown was given unto him: and he went forth conquering; and to conquer.' This horseman is supposedly Christ, preaching the purity of the gospel and sending the darts of conviction into the hearts of sinners. Next 'there went out another horse that was red: and power was given to him that sat thereon to take peace from the earth . . . and there was given unto him a great sword.' The red horse's rider, then, is War. Next comes the black horse, Famine. '. . . And I looked, and behold, a pale horse; and his name that sat on him was Death, and Hell followed with him' (from 6:2–8).

In 'Angelina', then, when Dylan alludes to this passage, singing 'I can see the unknown rider, I can see the pale white horse', he fuses, with a quiet and clever touch, the 'pale horse' and the 'white horse'; and because he cannot say which he is seeing, he sees an 'unknown' rider. He is asking: is it Christ or is it Death that faces me? This is a question Bob Dylan often asks, and often urges us to ask ourselves.

As for 'the angel with four faces', this phrase is not only inspired by the biblical text but in detail—in its rhythm, shape, length and tone—it stays faithful to it, echoing very precisely the Revelation phrase 'the sharp sword with two edges' (2:12).

The 'tree of smoke' is another quiet and clever poetic touch: it's a phrase Dylan invents to cover a great deal of spiritual territory. As so often, he seems to take the inherent poetry of the passage he's using, and to set it free in his imagination. Chapters 8 and 9 of Revelation (both very short) go on to describe the destructions to be visited on those not saved—those without seals on their foreheads—and these visions encompass burning trees and several sorts of smoke: 'the smoke of the incense, which came with the prayers of the saints' (8:4) and, in contrast (9:1–4), the smoke from the bottomless pit:

> 'And the fifth angel sounded, and I saw a star fall from heaven unto the earth: and to him was given the key of the bottomless pit. And he opened the bottomless pit; and there arose a smoke out of the pit, as the smoke of a great furnace; and the sun and the air were darkened by reason of the smoke of the pit. And there came out of the smoke locusts upon the earth . . .'

(The locusts appear like horses with 'crowns like gold, faces of men, hair of women, heads and teeth of lions, tails like scorpions', and so on. Here yet again we contemplate images constructed as if by genetic pick'n'mixing.) Then comes a different army of horses, 'and out of their mouths issued fire and smoke and brimstone. By these three was the third part of men killed, by the fire, and by the smoke, and by the brimstone, which issued out of their mouths.'

There is lots more smoke later: 'And the smoke of their torment ascendeth up for ever and ever: and they have no rest day or night, who worship the beast . . .' This contrasts with 'And the temple was filled with smoke from the glory of God, and from his power . . .' When Babylon falls, we get yet another smoke—the smoke of her burning: 'And the kings of the earth, who have committed fornication and lived deliciously with her, shall bewail her, and lament for her, when they shall see the smoke of her burning' (the phrase 'the smoke of her burning' is repeated). Then in the next chapter we get 'And her smoke rose up for ever and ever'—which Dylan uses more directly in 'Ain't Gonna Go to Hell for Anybody', in which the melodically lovely bridge begins with 'Smoke it rises for ever / On a one-way ticket to burn' (while, in 'Saved', drawing on Revelation 12, the singer's saviour has 'Freed me from the pit, / Full of emptiness and wrath / And the fire that burns in it / I've been saved / By the blood of the lamb').

So the image Dylan invents in 'Angelina', 'the tree of smoke', seems entirely apt: a scripturally alert emblem, characterising the enormous sweep of turmoil that must unfold before the establishment of the new heaven and the new earth. A 'tree of smoke' seems especially apt since when the new Jerusalem is built, 'Blessed are they that do his commandments, that they may have right to the tree of life . . .' (Revelation 22:14). It's not the least of Dylan's achievements that while 'the tree of smoke' sounds so *right* as a feature of the magic realist landscape—it could be drifting up from the pages of *One Hundred Years of Solitude*—it sounds just as accurately honed as a phrase compressing so much of Revelation.

The looser phrase 'surrounded by God's angels' enjoys a similar double-life. Encountered already as evoking a peasant culture's panting religiosity, now it re-imprints itself as part of a genuinely visionary picture: a brushstroke in Dylan's painting of the apocalypse. In this particular too we've shifted from Argentina to Jerusalem. Likewise 'I see pieces of men marching, trying to take heaven by force' acts now as another series of brushstrokes on this swirling canvas of an overcrowded sky thronging and exploding with fires and angels, armies and horsemen, the quick and the dead, the Lord and His heavenly hosts. Milton's *Paradise Lost* has much on Satan's legions trying to take heaven by force. The phrase echoes too the calmer text of Matthew 11:12: 'And from the days of John the Baptist until now the kingdom of heaven suffereth violence, and the violent take it by force.'

A renewal of meaning is given too to that small phrase 'them spiral staircases': it becomes a figurative expression of the circling motion of ascent as the beholder of such visions feels body and soul rise up, up, up (like smoke) into that thrashing heaven. Beat a path of retreat from sin; choose Christ not Death; choose between the part of oneself that draws back and the part that advances; climb '. . . up them spiral staircases, / Pass the tree of smoke, pass the angel with four faces, / Begging God for mercy and weeping in unholy places, / Angelina.'

Cutting across these general themes of worship and salvation, and recurring in amongst these shifts from world to world, there is also present in 'Angelina' the more personal cutting and shifting of a man-woman dialogue. Fragments of this dialogue seem to fall within our hearing, like parts of a loudly whispered, fitful conversation overheard on a moving train. The terrain outside the windows keeps changing; the lovers' quarrel runs through the middle of it all, as a series of one-liners, occasionally calmly resigned ('I've tried my best to love you but I cannot play this game') but mostly seething with reproach and the malice of the hurt.

Yet these lines and phrases rarely turn out to be unconnected with the terrain around them. We've seen how one line which sounds to be part of the lovers' quarrel, the hissing 'When you cease to exist, who will you blame?', touches upon one of the song's big themes, salvation, and has a special resonance of meaning in one of the song's locations, the world of Ancient Egypt. Similarly, the memorable core of this personal dialogue leads a double-life, its other one lived within the world of contemporary political menace. These are the lines: 'Do I need your permission to turn the other cheek? / If you can read my mind why must I speak? / No, I have heard nothing about the man that you seek . . .' This is admirably captured quarrelsome rhetoric, authentic in its conversational tone, in which belligerence is barely concealed beneath the sweetly reasonable, unanswerable questions and hot jealousy hisses around the sides of an insistent disinterest.

Attractively snappy, quotable stuff, this is clearly from the same pen, 15 years on, as lines like 'And you, you just sit around and ask for ashtrays: can't you reach?' (from the quintessential 'She's Your Lover Now', 1966). But you can hear these same lines altogether differently. They speak from the tortured to the torturer in the South American jail cell, calling out at once hapless and defiant from those unholy places where anything can happen: 'Do I need your permission to turn the other cheek? / If you can read my mind why must I speak? / No, I have heard nothing about the man that you seek . . .' And there is a response, half a verse later: the voice of the other side, mouthing the classic mitigating plea of the torturer and sadistic jailer everywhere: 'I was only following instructions . . .' Less in extremis, this is the excuse of the jobsworth the world over, the excuse of the minion who enjoys his little exercise of power on behalf of the authorities. In this instance 'I was only following instructions when the judge sent me down the road / With your subpoena.'

That 'subpoena' is offered with a smile, acknowledging its own disruptive ostentation. Indeed Dylan maximises its impact by the deliberate abruptness of the line that disgorges it. Every other verse has a fourth line of eight to ten syllables (not counting the extra syllables of filigree that Dylan's voice draws out of these '-ina' words). 'With your subpoena' is a brusquely foreshortened five-syllable line, and Dylan emphasises its brevity by his phrasing, so that 'subpoena' not only jumps out at us but jumps out early.

Gavin Selerie has pointed out an extraordinary possible source for this rhyme—indeed for the whole process of rhyming words with the name Angelina: 'Dylan's song echoes the opening chorus of Gilbert & Sullivan's *Trial By Jury*, which contains the lines: "For to-day in this arena / Summoned by a stern subpoena / Edwin, sued by Angelina, / Shortly will appear." . . . Later in the operetta, Angelina is summoned . . . with the echoing recitative: "Oh, Angelina! Come thou into Court! Angelina! Angelina!"' (As Selerie adds, these names come from Oliver Goldsmith's ballad 'The Hermit, Or Edwin and Angelina'.)

There is one other juncture at which Dylan deliberately abandons the orderly pattern of his lines. Again, the effect is to surprise for a specific purpose. As mentioned, the last line of each verse is the one word 'Angelina', except in the penultimate verse where we live vividly in the moment in the lovers' quarrel by hearing what is, in content, a blurted interjection ('But so are you') delivered as a blurted interjection in form too. Instead of what we expect, we get '. . . and she's wearin' a blindfold / But so are you, Angelina.' It is a clear, small illustration of a general truth often asserted in the arts, that only those who have mastered the rules can break them successfully.

Not that 'Angelina' is wholly a success. Dylan's cut-up narrative, whereby phrase by phrase the flow of logic is defeated, and lines and half-lines fail to connect with those nearest them, but rather call out to others half the song away, while the 'me' and 'you' and 'she' and 'he' refuse identification: in the end, it fails to satisfy. We drink in the riches of ellipse and leaps of imagination, the compressed layering of meaning and powerful air of mystery that such a method achieves . . . and still we thirst for narrative clarity.

Yet what a compelling, grand failure 'Angelina' remains. Not mere smoke but a tree of smoke. This song about angels with many faces and gods made from more than one animal achieves the same multiplicity itself. Its lines and phrases often have several faces—are frequently more than one kind of creature themselves. It may lack narrative clarity, but it has in abundance that other quality we demand of a complex work: it has unity.

This is partly achieved by its series of inner pairings, which extend far beyond the obvious—right hand, left hand; best friend, worst enemy; body of woman, head of hyena; Jerusalem or Argentina; vengeance satisfied, possessions sold; he's this and she's that; to love versus to play a game; rider and horse; tree and angel; the other cheek. As well as all these, which are all pairings placed in proximity, we can discern a further set more distantly placed: that 'right hand drawing back' at the beginning and that 'path of retreat' at the end; 'pieces of men' and body of this, head of that; the ambiguity of 'pieces of men marching' paralleled by that of 'Your servants are half dead'; 'tall men' and 'giants'; 'his eyes were two slits' and 'she's wearin' a blindfold'; the combat zone and the arena. This satisfying inner cohesion, this sense of balance, is augmented by Dylan's reliance upon one Old and one New Testament book—and since both look forward to the second coming of Christ, it is apt that Christ's first coming also has a presence in 'Angelina'.

This presence is evoked by another pairing: in this case a pair of allusions to Christ's words to the apostles from the Sermon on the Mount (Matthew 5–8 and Luke 6 & 11). For 'Do I need your permission to turn the other cheek?' not only operates as personal dialogue and political drama, as noted. It carries further resonance by alluding to Christ's dictum '. . . resist not evil: but whoever shall smite thee on thy right cheek, turn to him the other also' (from Matthew 5:39), or 'And unto him that smiteth thee on the one cheek offer also the other . . .' (from Luke 6:29).

In turn, to remember that this derives from the Sermon on the Mount is to hear as a back-echo something else in 'Angelina', from the very start of the song, that Dylan draws from the same well: that right hand drawing back while the left hand advances. We come to recognise that this notion of having our hands acting independently of each other is also from a dictum of Christ's (from Matthew 6:3): '. . . let not thy left hand know what thy right hand doeth.'

Here, then, another of the song's inner matches is made. Not only Ezekiel balanced by Revelation but Revelation balanced by the Gospels. Counterbalancing the boiling incomprehensibility of Christ's visionary 'Revelation' from heaven to his apostle John, here is a glimpse of his calm, strong presence on earth, as he gives clear, kind guidance to all his apostles.

Dylan's performance, which is the other great strength of 'Angelina', enhances this sense of Christ's earthly presence. He sings the line 'If you can read my mind, why must I speak?' with such quiet simplicity that you can hear it anew in this context, hearing not the lover's anger disguised by sweet reasonableness, nor the defiance of the political victim, but the mode of address we associate with Jesus when he's teaching: a mode of piercing but patient questioning.

The exquisite intelligence of Bob Dylan's performance throughout 'Angelina' is easy to disregard, since it works with self-deprecating quietness; but all through the song his voice draws out its multiplicities of meaning and lights up its detail as no other artist could hope to do. And always it rises to the occasion: when the writing is at its best, the singing informs it with genius. Verse two begins with this idiosyncratic, fresh and playful line: 'His eyes were two slits, make any snake proud'—and Dylan sings 'twoooo slits' as two long, equal syllables. *Anyone* else would, less alertly, give an automatic greater length to 'slits' than to 'two', but Dylan sings them as if he has all the time in the world, and sings them not to achieve a belaboured hissing on 'slits', not to illustrate a sound at all but to illustrate a picture: drawing out the 'two slits' as if actually drawing them, or etching them with a knife.

He passes over the internal rhyme of 'make' and 'snake' without the slightest stress, and passes nonchalantly over the three internal chimes of the next line, in which 'face' is half-echoed by 'painter' and 'paint', knowing that the way 'face' is only half-echoed rescues the repetition of 'painter would paint' from its potential troublesomeness. In case this is still problematic on the ear, the next line is quick to yield its own contrasting internal rhyme, sounding a different vowel: 'Worshipping a *god* with the *body* of a woman well endowed'—and Dylan, fully alert to this, renders it perfectly, lingering on these syllables with measured sagacity. There is no excess of stress: he gives it just enough attention to make it always pleasing to hear. Bound in with this come two instances of that other dangerous kind of chiming, so easy to overdo: alliteration. '*W*orshipping a god with the body of a *w*oman *w*ell endowed / And the *h*ead of a *h*yena.'

Such muscular writing and impeccable execution. The '*w*oman *w*ell' can afford to toll emphatically because it precedes the third consecutive strong line-end rhyme, the third consecutive AAA rhyme, and since these have a cumulative effect upon the ear, the third one must sound so inevitable, necessary, firm and set that you can get away with more or less any degree of insistent alliteration on the way to it. As for 'And the head of a hyena', the small pause before 'hyena' and the sense of wariness achieved in that word's delivery (which would make any hyena proud): these are the brushstrokes of genius.

As JOHN BAULDIE puts it in the *Bootleg Series Vols. 1–3* booklet, Dylan has a 'facility to make his voice reflect the meanings of the words he's singing'. He notes how in 'Someone's Got a Hold of My Heart' Dylan's voice 'seems to wind around the words "wind around", or be as wide as "wide" or as easy as "easy".' In 'Angelina', comparably, Dylan sings 'Do I need your permission to turn the other cheek?' such that on the word 'turn' his voice enacts a turning: the sound pivots around inside his mouth. He gives us the full sense of the moment's drama—of the way that to turn the other cheek is actually to take strong, challenging, even aggressive, *action*.

This attention to detail, which always avoids reductive predictability in favour of intuitive flash, stays with us throughout the song's long journey. It gives us the dying breath with which Dylan appears to expire on the long-drawn-out end of 'arena———' and then the final climb up the melodic steps which begin with 'up them spiral staircases' (no-one else could sing that phrase at all, let alone with the sumptuous sadness and humane modesty Dylan brings to it) and which keep ascending, words and melody perfectly at one, till the last cathartic incantation of the song title itself.

[Bob Dylan: 'Angelina', Santa Monica, CA, 26 Mar 1981, the *Bootleg Series Vols. 1–3*, 1991. Dylan quotes: 'The Playboy Interview: Bob Dylan: A Candid Conversation with the Iconoclastic Idol of the Folk-Rock Set', *Playboy*, Chicago, Mar 1966; & *Dallas Times-Herald*, Dallas, TX, 6 Nov 1983. *Good News Bible: Today's English Version* quote from Ezekiel 7:1–7, London: Bible Societies / Collins / Fontana, 1976. Adam Clarke, *Commentary on the Bible*, London: Thomas Tegg, 1844 (7 vols.).

'Chimera, or chimaera . . . : 1. Greek myth: a fire-breathing monster with the head of a lion, body of a goat and tail of a serpent. 2. a fabulous beast made up of parts taken from various animals. 3. a wild and unrealistic dream . . .': from *Collins English Dictionary*, Glasgow: HarperCollins, 1994.

Giovanni Magi, ed., *Egypt*, Florence: Casa Editrice Bonechi, 1993. Gabriel García Márquez, *One Hundred Years of Solitude*, 1st UK edn., London: Jonathan Cape, 1970. John Milton, *Paradise Lost*, 1667 (revised edn. 1674). Gavin Selerie: 'Tricks and Training: Some Dylan Sources and Analogues' *Telegraph* no.50, UK, winter 1994. Oliver Goldsmith, 'The Hermit, Or Edwin and Angelina', written c.1762, published 1766.]

angels The word 'angel' comes from the Greek 'angelos', meaning messenger. But angels, says the Bible, are sent from God to guide and/or protect us (much like good fairies in fairy-tales). Traditional Catholic belief is that every person has a guardian angel. Pope John Paul II re-asserted the existence of angels in 1986. They are defined attractively in Paul's Epistle to the Hebrews (in a passage that also yields the well-known phrase 'a little lower than the angels'): 'Are they not all ministering spirits, sent forth to minister for them who shall be heirs to salvation?' (Hebrews 1:14). Paul is saying that Christ, 'Being made so much better than the angels, as he hath by inheritance obtained a more excellent name than they' (1:4), has all the same been sent to earth in the form of a man, 'a little lower than the angels', for our sake: 'But we see Jesus, who was made a little lower than the angels for the suffering of death, crowned with glory and honour; that he by the grace of God should taste death for every man' (Hebrews 2:9). 'For verily he took not on him the nature of angels; but he took on him the seed of Abraham' (2:16).

In the Christian hierarchy, nine orders of supernatural beings lie between God and people: seraphim, cherubim and thrones (contemplating God and reflecting His glory); dominations, virtues and powers (regulators of the universe); and principalities, archangels and angels (ministering to humanity). In a passage that transcends these risible delineations, Paul passionately lists some of these orders out of sheer exuberance: 'For I am persuaded, that neither death, nor life, nor angels, nor principalities, nor powers, nor things present, nor things to come, Nor height, nor depth, nor any other creature, shall be able to separate us from the love of God, which is in Christ Jesus our Lord' (Romans, 8:38–39).

Angels in the Bible are always male: only in modern times have they become feminised and sexualised, by a process of colloquialisation, into women with 'heavenly bodies'. This transformation may have come in stages, via Florence Nightingale (1820–1910), who organised, for the first time, a nursing service, taking a team of nurses to tend the copious wounded of the Crimean War in 1854 (and reducing the war hospital death rate from 42 to 2 per cent): these were readily thought 'ministering angels'.

In 'Precious Angel', then, Dylan is punning on 'angel': i.e. so calling the song's addressee because she has been sent by God to guide him to the Lord, and calling her 'angel' secularly because she has become his beloved sexual partner: she has to be a human creature for this union to be blessed, as the singer believes it is. Hence his line 'What God has given to us no man can take away.' This is taken straight from Matthew 19:5–6: '. . . they twain shall be one flesh. . . . What therefore God hath joined together, let not man put asunder' (repeated verbatim in Mark 10:9) and echoes the equivalent verse in the Marriage Service in the Church of England's *Book of Common Prayer*: 'Those whom God hath joined together let no man put asunder.' Dylan reconfirms that his 'precious angel' has this double function in the song's last verse, which begins: 'You're the queen of my flesh, girl. . . . You're the lamp of my soul'.

As he puns on 'angel', so he does on 'sun' (making for a pun-packed opening phrase: 'Precious angel, under the sun . . .'). It's part of Dylan's greatness that in the best of these Christian songs, he can press into service so much scriptural moment, yet keep his lines sounding so casual, so conversational, so expressively relaxed. 'Under the sun', of course, has come into common currency, or at least been continually recirculated there, by its repeated incantation in memorably famous passages of the brief but hugely influential ECCLESIASTES (upon which Dylan draws in many songs, from 'It's Alright Ma [I'm Only Bleeding]' to 'Pressing On' and from 'Jokerman' to 'Tell Me'): '. . . and there is no new thing under the sun' (from Ecclesiastes 1:9); '. . . wise under the sun' (2:19); '. . . vanity under the sun' (4:7) etc.

In this usage, 'under the sun' is conventional; yet Dylan's 'precious angel' is also 'under the sun' in the sense of being 'under the Son', a messenger of the Lord—and this is exactly how the pun is used in one of the very last verses of the Old Testament: 'But unto you that fear my name shall the Sun of righteousness arise with healing in his wings . . .' (from Malachi 4:2). We're likely to infer a further hint of angels flying around here too, by that 'healing in his wings', and to be reminded, in turn, that Dylan has visited this terrain, and wittily, before: 'You angel you / You got me under your wing', as he sings in 'You Angel You' on *Planet Waves*.

An angel or angels also occur in the following Dylan songs: 'Three Angels', 'Winterlude', 'Angelina', 'From a Buick 6', 'Tough Mama', 'Dirge', 'Political World', 'Just Like Tom Thumb's Blues', 'Changing of the Guards', 'Gates of Eden', 'Sara', 'Dignity', 'Jokerman' and 'Sad-Eyed Lady of the Lowlands'. In only five of these are they clearly secularly meant allusions; in at least seven they appear to be angels in the Christian or spiritual sense.

[Bob Dylan: 'Precious Angel', single taken from Dylan's first 'evangelical' album, 1979's *Slow Train Coming*, Sheffield, Alabama, 30 Apr–4 May (+ over-dubs 11 May) 1979, Columbia FC-36120, NY (CBS 86095, UK), 28 Aug 1979.]

Animals, the The Animals were an early-60s British rock group from Newcastle. They arose after keyboard player ALAN PRICE quit local group the Kansas City Five (which included drummer John Steel) to join the Kontours (which included bassist Chas Chandler, later to be the man who brought JIMI HENDRIX to Britain and stardom) and singer Eric Burdon quit to seek his fortune in London. The Kontours eventually became the Alan Price R& B Combo, with Steel coming in, Burdon returning early in 1963 and guitarist Hilton Valentine augmenting the line-up and prompting the name change to the Animals.

They were Newcastle's best beat group, playing raw and exciting music; their sound was distinguished by Burdon's voice, Price's exceptional keyboard playing and the sometimes lyrical lead guitar-work of Hilton Valentine. Given a record-deal with a major label (the British Columbia label—part of the EMI group and unconnected with the US Columbia label, to which Dylan was signed) as the hunt for new talent spread beyond Merseybeat to the other big cities of the United Kingdom, in February 1964 they recorded a variant on the traditional song 'Baby Let Me Follow You Down' / 'Baby Don't You Tear My Clothes', which they re-worked as the tamer and more pop-normal-sounding 'Baby Let Me Take You Home', which they probably adapted after hearing the version on Dylan's first album—and then they put out a rock version of 'House of the Rising Sun', which was also a cleaned-up re-working of the version of the song on Dylan's album. (It was 'revealed', many years later, that they had picked up both songs not from Dylan but from Josh White—which might have been true but wouldn't have been helpful to say at the time.)

'House of the Rising Sun' captured the virtues of the group's live act on record (something that eluded many of the best of the British beat groups of the day), and was an inspired fusion of traditional folk words and rock. It is the record that disputes the claim that THE BYRDS created folk rock—though it did *not* kick off the folk rock movement as the Byrds' 'Tambourine Man' and Dylan himself did, mostly because when first released it was too early for that—it was instead heard as part of another movement: in the UK as part of the beat-group boom and in the US as 'the British invasion'. It reached no.1 in the US and the British charts, and on the back of it the Animals toured America and met Bob Dylan (briefly). They had much subsequent chart success, including with a very respectable version, based on Nina Simone's, of 'Don't Let Me Be Misunderstood'.

In another way too their 'House of the Rising Sun' was ahead of its time: long before 'Like a Rolling Stone', it broke the three-minute rule for singles: and by a long way. It ran to 4:30. It was also the first British-made US no.1 since 1962 not written by LENNON & McCARTNEY.

[The Animals: 'House of the Rising Sun', *nia*, Columbia DB 7301, London (MGM USA 1STP, US), 1964.]

***Annie Hall*, dismissal of Dylan in** The chorus of 'Just Like a Woman' ends with '. . . she aches just like a woman / But she breaks just like a little girl.' This non-statement doesn't describe an individual characteristic, doesn't say anything fresh about a universal one yet pretends to do both. What parades as reflective wisdom ('. . . woman but . . . girl') is really maudlin platitude. It hasn't even engaged Dylan's skill in minimising the badness. It would be less bad if the 'But' of the pay-off line was an 'And'—for at least we would then be spared so blatantly lame and predictable a 'paradox'.

This is exactly the 'lameness' honed in on in Woody Allen's 1977 film *Annie Hall*, in which a vacuous hippie character played by the wonderful Shelley Duvall recites the lines just quoted as if they're far-out and profound, and the character played by Allen (the usual character played by Allen), pulls a face that means he fails to see in them anything less empty-headed than their admirer.

In *Chronicles Volume One*, 2004, Dylan recalls (without comment) that Woody Allen was one of the comedians performing at the Café Wha at the start of the 1960s.

[*Annie Hall*, dir. Woody Allen, United Artists, USA, 1977. Dylan: *Chronicles Volume One*, p.11.]

***Another Side of Bob Dylan* [1964]** The fourth album, and recorded in a day. The title was not of Dylan's choosing; it would be the last time that someone other than the artist decided what to name the work. The Dave Spart section of his constituency declared that this was an unwelcome side of Bob Dylan and the album was a sell-out—just as more people were to feel later when he 'went electric', again when he 'went country' and yet again when he was 'Born Again'. This fourth album was much the same stark, solo performance as on the preceding three (though Dylan added piano and somehow more space and colour in the sound) but with the exception of the long 'Chimes of Freedom' there wasn't a protest song or any overtly political theme anywhere on the record: and even 'Chimes of Freedom' was, for many, uncomfortably close to blurry impressionism rather than activist clarity.

They were love songs—and many people felt betrayed. It must be hard now to understand how this album could have angered so many; but it did. Yet it was clear to plenty of people at the time, and is all the more so looking back, that the love songs Dylan offered on this album were more true and real—and ultimately more radical—than protest songs. 'All I Really Want to Do' and 'It Ain't Me Babe' are historically important songs: they questioned the common assumptions of true love and the male-female relationship; they not only avoided possessiveness and macho strut but explained why as well. This was years before any of us understood that 'love' and politics weren't opposites—that there was such a thing as sexual politics. And among the ways Dylan mounted these challenges to love-song convention was by his irreverent upending of pop cliché in general, and in particular in his playful, tack-sharp response to the ubiquitous presence of THE BEATLES. Everyone else was rolling over and submitting to the Beatles Invasion. Not Dylan. (So his 'no, no, no,' in 'It Ain't Me, Babe' is a discreet riposte to their 'yeah, yeah, yeah' in 'She Loves You'.) This album also contained Dylan's specific recantation of the protest phase. 'My Back Pages' did this, and had the celebrated chorus line 'Ah but I was so much older then / I'm younger than that now.' This permanently beguiling claim was enacted by Dylan's voice, which sounds far younger than on his earlier work. Here he has thrown off his self-imposed obligation to seek gravitas in sounding as old as the hills, and begun to rejoice in his youthfulness. If you could have only about five Bob Dylan albums, it wouldn't be crazy if this were one of them. His writing and control of atmosphere on songs like 'To Ramona' and 'Spanish Harlem Incident' come across as early flashes of the creative explosion that he was to go through in 1965–66. A great minor album, and his last solo album until the 1990s.

[Recorded NY, 9 Jun 1964; released as Columbia CL 2193 (mono) and CS 8993 (stereo), 8 Aug 1964. In UK, CBS BPG 62429 (mono), SBPG 62429 (stereo).]

***Anthology of American Folk Music* [1952, 1997]** See *American Folk Music* [1952, 1997] and **Smith, Harry**.

Armstrong, Gillian [1950 -] Gillian Armstrong was born on December 18, 1950 in Melbourne, Australia. Regarded as part of the self-exporting Australian New Wave (like Mel Gibson) she learnt filmcraft first as an editor on educational films, won scholarship to the Australian Film, Television & Radio School just outside Sydney, directed shorts and documentaries and began her feature-film directorial career with the brilliant *My Brilliant Career* in 1979, made in Australia. After that came *Starstruck*, a musical, then a move to Hollywood for the dull *Mrs. Soffel*, starring Diane Keaton and Mel Gibson in 1984.

When this bombed she returned to Australia, and in early 1986, in Sydney, agreed to film Bob Dylan backed by TOM PETTY & THE HEARTBREAKERS to make a concert film for distribution straight to HBO and video release. She directed the filming at his Sydney concerts of February 24 & 25, 1986, and came away with beautifully shot footage edited into a ten-song mixed-repertoire concoction, *Hard to Handle*, that makes everyone involved look and sound better than they deserved.

Armstrong remained in Australia long enough to re-unite with Judy Davis (who had achieved stardom via *My Brilliant Career*); they made the less successful 1987 film *High Tide*. Since then Armstrong has continued to veer back and forth between the US and her native land, where she made the fine 1992 film *The Last Days of Chez Nous* before finally achieving a happy result in Hollywood with her 1994 version of the Louisa May Alcott novel *Little Women*. Her 1997 film *Oscar and Lucinda* was a more complex film, handled imaginatively and adroitly.

She had not abandoned the documentary, however; she made a long-term commitment to following the lives of three 14-year-old working-class Australian girls in a series of three films made between 1975 and 1988 (*Smoke and Lollies*, 1975, *Fourteen's Good, Eighteen's Better*, 1980 and *Bingo, Bridesmaids and Braces*, 1988), and in 1996 reshaped the footage into an award-winning feature-length film, *Not Fourteen Again*.

Granted that, more generally, she has always been keen to explore the lives of women, and with distinctive success ('Gillian Armstrong cuts closer to the core of women's divided yearnings than any other director', in Molly Haskell's comment), it was perhaps an odd partnership, but a welcome one, when she and Bob Dylan got together.

Arnold, Jerome [1936 -] Jerome Arnold, a year younger than his more famous harmonica-playing brother Billy Boy Arnold, was born in Chicago in 1936. He was playing bass guitar in the city in the 1950s and from around 1957 played in HOWLIN' WOLF's band (though he didn't play on Wolf's records till the 1962 session that yielded 'Tail Dragger', to which the lyric of Dylan's 1990 blues 'Cat's in the Well' slyly alludes). He and SAM LAY were poached from Wolf in 1963 by PAUL BUTTERFIELD, who was forming the pioneering Paul Butterfield Blues Band. Arnold and Lay were the bi-racial band's black members, and the authentic Chicago blues rhythm section on which the band's white soloists built. Arnold kept things solid when MIKE BLOOMFIELD introduced Indian music into the band on their second album, *East-West*, yet while reportedly uneasy with the 'progressive' organ-playing of Mark Naftalin (who joined in 1964), he was more than capable of laying down jazz-rooted bass lines flowing around behind Bloomfield on the eight-minute-long 'Work Song', which emerged on the Bloomfield compilation *Don't Say That I Ain't Your Man: Essential Blues 1964–1969*. He continued to play on Howlin' Wolf records after joining the Butterfield outfit.

Arnold, described by Butterfield Blues Band enthusiast Charles Sawyer as 'quiet and unassuming; a conservative dresser given to double knits and loafers', was nevertheless one of those who played behind Dylan—with Bloomfield, AL KOOPER, BARRY GOLDBERG and Sam Lay—at Dylan's controversial electric début at the 1965 NEWPORT FOLK FESTIVAL. It was the only time he played behind Dylan; he continued with the Paul Butterfield Blues Band, which Butterfield disbanded in 1972.

By 1978 he had changed his name to Julio Finn and moved to London. Now playing more harmonica than bass, he played with jazz acts, including Archie Shepp (for instance on the album *Black Gipsy*) and the Art Ensemble of Chicago (*Certain Blacks*, recorded in Paris in 1970). On the 1970 eponymously titled album by Archie Shepp and Philly Joe Jones, Finn is credited as composer of the 21-minute-long 'Howling in the Silence', on which he contributes vocals as well as harmonica.

In 1981 he was asked to write the sleevenotes for the UK label Charley's album *Crying and Pleading*, by his brother Billy Boy Arnold. He agreed, mentioned their relationship in his notes but still signed as Julio Finn. Interested in gay rights and in black history, he wrote the 1986 book *The Blues Man: The Musical Heritage of Black Men and Women in the Americas*, which was published in London by Quartet Books.

Finn/Arnold still keeps open his playing and academic options, and still ranges widely without abandoning the blues. In 1998 he played harmonica on the Linton Kwesi Johnson album *Independent Intavenshan*; in 2000 he was the respondent at a panel discussion on 'The Blues as Individual and Collective History' at a conference on 'The Blues Tradition' at Penn State University.

[Bob Dylan with Jerome Arnold et al: 'Maggie's Farm', 'Like a Rolling Stone' & 'It Takes a Lot to Laugh, It Takes a Train to Cry', Newport, RI, 25 Jul 1965. Charles Sawyer quote from 'Blues With a Feeling: A Biography of the Paul Butterfield Blues Band', 1994, online 2 Jul 2005 at *www.people.fas.harvard.edu/~sawyer/bwf.html*.]

Aronowitz, Al [1928 - 2005] Al Aronowitz was born in Bordentown, NJ, on May 20, 1928, and grew up in nearby Linden and Roselle. He became a professional journalist in 1950 (editor of the *Daily Times* in Lakewood, New Jersey) and was a music columnist for the *New York Post* in the 1960s to early 70s. He wrote a well-regarded long piece on Beatlemania for the *Saturday Evening Post* in 1964. Latterly a freelance writer (mostly on the internet) living in Elizabeth, NJ, and calling himself 'the Blacklisted Journalist', he died of cancer there on August 1, 2005.

Aronowitz claimed: 'The 60s wouldn't have been the same without me.' This was because he famously brought Dylan and THE BEATLES together for the first time, and introduced the Beatles to marijuana, at the Hotel Delmonico, Park Avenue, NY, on August 28, 1964. He also said that Dylan wrote 'Mr. Tambourine Man' in his kitchen (after listening to Marvin Gaye's 'Can I Get a Witness' all night), and that he drove Dylan over to buy the famous Triumph motorcycle. He was around Dylan a lot in the Woodstock days, and was also in the backstage posse when Dylan and his wife SARA arrived at the Isle of Wight for the 1969 festival appearance. He is 'the friend' in this brief 1967 Woodstock anecdote he tells (against himself):

> 'Do you like that song?' Dylan asked a friend. 'I think it's great,' the friend said. 'I don't like that song,' Dylan said. The friend was crestfallen. Later, Dylan sang another new song. 'I like that one better than the other one,' the friend said. Dylan turned to Jaime [ROBBIE] ROBERTSON. 'See,' Dylan said, 'we shouldn't keep any music critics around here. We just lost another song.'

Aronowitz was also a hanger-on/hanger-out with many people with Dylan associations, including ALLEN GINSBERG, THE BAND and GEORGE HARRISON, as well as with a number of jazz and BEAT people. (He wrote a 12-part series on the Beat Poets in the *New York Post* in 1960.) A selection of his (mostly retrospective) music columns was self-published as *Bob Dylan and the Beatles, Volume One of the Best of the Blacklisted Journalist*, 2004.

Artes, Mary Alice [1948 -] It was the black American actor Mary Alice Artes, born on May 19, 1948, who helped bring Dylan to Christianity, allegedly after refusing to continue living with him after converting to Christ herself (or re-converting; it's been suggested that she had strayed from the faith of her upbringing). She is first mentioned by Dylan on the cover of the *Street Legal* LP, where her namecheck comes immediately below those of the album's producers, and reads 'Queen Bee—Mary Alice Artes'. She is also surely the subject of 'Precious Angel' on *Slow Train Coming* and 'Covenant Woman' on *Saved*. And as JOHN BAULDIE wrote: 'Dylan reportedly bought her an engagement ring in early 1980; later that year he wrote relevant versions of "Groom's Still Waiting at the Altar" and "Caribbean Wind".'

The New Testament text, 'But if we walk in the light, as he is in the light, we have fellowship one with another, and the blood of Jesus Christ his Son cleanseth us from all sin' (I John 1:7) is a core text for 'Precious Angel', and drawn upon in those great lines in which Dylan, the Jewish American descendant of Moses, and his 'precious angel', the black American descendant of slaves, are envisaged walking in fellowship: 'We are covered in blood, girl, you know our forefathers were slaves / . . . But there's violence in the eyes, girl, so let us not be enticed / On our way out of Egypt, through Ethiopia, to the judgment hall of Christ.'

Dylan achieves a concentration of three meanings into that 'covered in blood': blood as in one's family and racial history (blood thicker than water); blood as in carrying the stain of people's inherent violence and sin; and blood as in 'the blood of Jesus Christ' that 'covers us' by cleansing us all from sin. He also manages, with these lines, to invoke the whole story of the exodus from Egypt under Moses (Exodus) and by taking that exodus 'through Ethiopia' he not only emphasises that his 'precious angel' is an African-American, but echoes the specific scriptural detail remembered not in Exodus itself but in the fourth book of Moses, Numbers: '. . . for he [Moses] had married an Ethiopian woman' (Numbers 12:1).

Thus Dylan indicates the biographical parallel with his own story, and that of Mary Alice Artes.

Artes, aka Mary Akins, played the character 'Faith' in an episode of the TV series 'The Beverly Hillbillies', 'Three-Day Reprieve', in 1970 and appeared in a spectacularly dreadful low-budget western movie called *She Came to the Valley*, aka *Texas in Flames*, filmed in 1977 and released in 1979, the same year as *Slow Train Coming*, in which she played a very small part, that of Fanny. The film featured RONEE BLAKLEY in the lead female rôle.

[John Bauldie: 'Four and Twenty Windows and a Woman's Face in Every One: Significant Women in Bob Dylan's Life and Art', in *All Across the Telegraph: A Bob Dylan Handbook*, ed. Michael Gray & John Bauldie, London: Futura paperback edn., 1988, p.270. Mary Alice Artes: 'Three-Day Reprieve', 'The Beverly Hillbillies' episode 8.20, screened 4 Feb 1970; *She Came to the Valley*, dir. Albert Band, RGV Pictures, US, 1979.]

'Arthur McBride' [song, 1992] See **Brady, Paul.**

artists v. critics Dylan's antipathy and contempt for critics, however distinguished, has almost been matched by his extravagance of reverence for artists, however undistinguished. But 'artists v. critics' is a false distinction. There's many a major creative writer who has also functioned as a critic. The 19th century American poet and writer EDGAR ALLAN POE also published much acute, lively criticism. T.S. ELIOT's criticism was a significant part of his work in the world, as was that of ROBERT GRAVES, while it was a critical book by D.H. Lawrence, his *Studies in Classic American Literature*, published in 1923, that rescued WALT WHITMAN's poetry from the neglect and contempt into which it had fallen since the poet's death. So while Dylan's hostility to 'interpreters' is one thing (see **Dylan interpreters**), his antagonism to critics, as if on principle—as if to be pro-artist must mean to be anti-critic—is misplaced.

Asch, Moses [1905 - 1986] Moses Asch was born in Poland in 1905, the son of Sholem Asch (1880–1957), a Yiddish novelist and dramatist whose trilogy *Farn Mabul* (1929–31) translates as *Before the Flood* and may thus have given Dylan the title of one of his albums. As a child Moses Asch moved to Paris and then emigrated to the US, living with his family in Brooklyn. In the 1920s he studied electronics in Germany but was back in the US by 1926 and later, drawn to folk music, left-wing politics and outsiders, had the idea of founding a record label for artists the majors deemed insufficiently commercial. As he explained later:

> 'The depression helped me understand folk music . . . the songs of the people made more sense to me than the popular songs of the 20s with their Wall Street slant. The depression made me go into business for myself. . . . At this time the price of phonograph records was cut so drastically that stores dumped their unsold stocks. This gave me a chance to buy thousands of folk music records for 5 to 10 cents a piece. These formed the basis later for the *Anthology of American Folk Song* series.'

He started the Asch and Disc labels, both of which failed—though not before he had recorded WOODY GUTHRIE and LEADBELLY. He founded the far more successful Folkways label in 1947 and ran it until his death almost 40 years later, making available more Guthrie and Leadbelly plus the work of PETE SEEGER, the NEW LOST CITY RAMBLERS, PAUL CLAYTON and many others, including an album Dylan says 'knocked me out', the compilation *Foc'sle Songs and Shanties*. It was also Asch's Folkways label that issued, as mentioned above, HARRY SMITH's invaluable and historic 6-LP set, the anthology *American Folk Song*. In 1987, the Smithsonian Institute in Washington, D.C., bought out Folkways and undertook to keep all 2,200 Folkways albums in print.

That's the Moses Asch legacy. Its influence, therefore, on the young Bob Dylan might be said to be huge. In *Chronicles Volume One* Dylan writes of his earliest days in New York City: 'I envisioned myself recording for Folkways Records. That was the label I wanted to be on. That was the label that put out all the great records.' He adds: 'It would have been a dream come true if Moe would have signed me to the label.'

[Moses Asch quoted from 'Folk Music—A Personal Statement', *Sing Out!*, NY, Feb–Mar 1961, reprinted online 7 Jun 2005 at *www.radiohazak.com/Asch.html*. Dylan quoted from *Chronicles Volume One*, 2004, p.239, 15 & 72. Paul Clayton & the Foc'scle Singers: *Foc'sle Songs and Shanties*, Folkways FA 2429, 1959. Harry Smith: *American Folk Music*, Folkways FP251-253, NY, 1952, CD-reissued as *Anthology of American*

Library of Congress

Roy Acuff, 1948

Johnny Ace

Bob Yellin / Smithsonian

Clarence Ashley

Library of Congress

Harry Belafonte at Brown v. Board of Education rally in New York, 1960

Photography by Sherry Rayn Barnett

Chuck Berry

David Bromberg

Kurtis Blow

Folk Music (6-CD box set) with copious notes by many hands and a CD-ROM of extras, Smithsonian Folkways SRW 40090, Washington, D.C., 1997.]

Ashley, Clarence [1895 - 1967] Clarence Earl McCurry, known by adulthood as, variously, Thomas Clarence Ashley, Thomas C. Ashley McCurry, Tom McCurry Ashley and rather later as Clarence Ashley, was born in Bristol, TN, on September 29, 1895. Meeting his bigamous father for the first time at age 39, Tom/Clarence elicited this response from his parent: 'My God, how can a man get that ugly in 39 years?' By this time he had long been an accomplished country banjo player and guitarist with a rich repertoire of old songs (many learnt from more accessible relatives). He had joined a medicine show at 16, playing mostly in Tennessee and Virginia, and stayed with it every summer from 1911 to 1943, by which time his recording début was also long behind him. He had first recorded as Thomas C. Ashley (vocal and guitar) accompanied by banjoist Dwight Bell in 1928; then with Byrd Moore and his Hot Shots; and later as part of the Blue Ridge Mountain Entertainers. On October 23, 1929, at the end of a Columbia session by the former, Ashley recorded four solo numbers—'Dark Holler Blues', 'The Coo-Coo Bird', 'Little Sadie' and 'Naomi Wise'. These were issued on two 78s. He also recorded with the Carolina Tar Heels for Victor, and with Gwen Foster for Vocalion. After 1933, his next recordings were in 1960, after a chance meeting with RALPH RINZLER at a fiddlers' convention in North Carolina led to a reluctant Ashley singing, but not playing, for Folkways Records. After this—and after more than a decade of not playing—he resumed banjo-playing in his mid-60s and began an active new career in the Folk Revival boom years, heading a group that brought DOC WATSON to people's attention and with 'The Coo-Coo Bird' a highlight of their set. Ashley died of cancer on June 2, 1967.

There is every reason to feel that Dylan's 'In Search of Little Sadie' and 'Little Sadie', both on *Self Portrait*, were prompted by his knowing the song as by Ashley. *Sing Out!* magazine (Vol.14, no.6, NY, January 1964) published 'Little Sadie' (along with 'Copper Kettle', which is also on *Self Portrait*, and Dylan's own 'All I Really Want to Do') with this introduction:

> 'Woody Guthrie called it "Bad Lee Brown" and others have titled it "Sadie", "Late One Night", "Chain Gang Blues", "Out Last Night" and "Penitentiary Blues". Clarence Ashley calls it "Little Sadie", and it is his version we print here. According to [the eminent folklorist] D.K. Wilgus, the song seems to be an example of a "blues ballad", which he describes as "a loose, shifting, emotional narrative that celebrates and comments on an event instead of presenting a straightforward, detailed account." "Little Sadie", in all its various titles, has enjoyed wide currency among both Negro and white singers.'

Dylan was well aware of Ashley as a conduit of folksong: Ashley's pre-war recordings of 'The House Carpenter' and 'The Coo-Coo Bird' are on (and his 'Naomi Wise' & 'Dark Holler Blues' cited in) the 1952 HARRY SMITH 6-LP anthology *AMERICAN FOLK MUSIC*, which Dylan certainly knew by May 1961. Equally, Dylan was well aware of *Sing Out!* as a source of material. It is no surprise, then, to find that Dylan's 'Little Sadie' is nigh word for word the same as the lyric *Sing Out!* publishes as Ashley's.

In *Chronicles Volume One* Dylan also recalls having seen Ashley in person as one of the people 'hanging around' in IZZY YOUNG's Folklore Center, and perhaps also hearing him perform at one or more of ALAN LOMAX's twice-monthly 3rd Street 'soirées'.

Dylan cut 'House Carpenter' in 1961, at his first LP sessions (it was finally issued 30 years later on the *Bootleg Series Vols. 1–3*) and performed 'Naomi Wise' at Riverside Church Saturday of Folk Music in New York City that July. Dylan put 'Naomi Wise' on tape again that December in Minneapolis. 'Dark Holler Blues' is related to 'East Virginia Blues', which Dylan recorded in the *Self Portrait* period, i.e. with EARL SCRUGGS in 1970.

[Clarence Ashley: 'Naomi Wise' c/w 'Little Sadie', and 'Dark Holler Blues' c/w 'The Coo-Coo Bird', Johnson City, TN, 23 Oct 1929. 'Little Sadie', Chicago, Feb 1962, *Old-Time Music at Clarence Ashley's, Volume 2*, Folkways FA 2359, NY, 1963; 'The House Carpenter', Atlanta, 14 Apr 1930 & 'The Coo-Coo Bird' (1929 version), *American Folk Music*, Folkways FP251-253, NY, 1952, CD-reissued as *Anthology of American Folk Music* (6-CD box set), Smithsonian Folkways SRW 40090, Washington, D.C., 1997.

Bob Dylan: 'House Carpenter', NY, 20 Nov 1961; 'Naomi Wise', NY, 29 Jul 1961 (broadcast WRVR-FM, NY, same day) and Minneapolis, 22 Dec 1961; 'East Virginia Blues' (with Earl Scruggs), Carmel, Dec 1970, broadcast NET TV, US, Jan 1971, issued *Festival of Music* video, New Line Cinema 2015, NY. *Chronicles Volume One*, 2004, p.19 & 70.

Much Ashley biographical data from *www.clarenceashley.com*, online 5 Aug 2005, but with recording data corrected using Tony Russell's monumental and authoritative *Country Music Records: A Discography, 1921–1942*.]

Auden, W.H. [1907 - 1973] Wystan Hugh Auden was born in York on February 21, 1907, growing up first in Birmingham and then at Surrey and Norfolk boarding schools. After Oxford he spent a year in Weimar Berlin before returning to Britain, where he wrote his early love poems. He moved to the US in 1939, as World War II was beginning, and became a naturalized citizen in 1946. He was living on West 4th Street in Greenwich Village when Dylan was there in 1962, and though there's no evidence that he was aware of Dylan in particular, he was responsible for directing PHILIP SAVILLE's attention to the nearby bohemian folk clubs, as a result of which Saville saw Dylan perform and brought him over to London in late 1962 to appear in the TV drama *The Madhouse on Castle Street*. Auden was Poetry Professor at Oxford 1955–61 and died in Vienna September 29, 1973.

As Gavin Selerie points out, there are strong, particular similarities between Auden's poem/ ballad 'Victor', 1937, and Dylan's 'Lily, Rosemary & the Jack of Hearts', 1975. The Auden verses include, for example, 'Anna was sitting at table / Waiting for her husband to come back. / It wasn't the Jack of Diamonds / Nor the Joker she drew at first; / It wasn't the King or the Queen of Hearts / But the Ace of Spades reversed. / Victor stood in the doorway, / He didn't utter a word. / She said: "What's the matter, darling?" / He behaved as if he hadn't heard.'

[Gavin Selerie: 'Tricks and Training: Some Dylan Sources and Analogues', *Telegraph* no.50, Richmond, UK, winter 1994. W.H. Auden: 'Victor', in *The English Auden*, ed. E. Mendelson, 1977, p.221.]

audience members performing with Dylan There was a brief period during the Never-Ending Tour when instead of staying put or being violently repulsed by hired psychotics in tight yellow t-shirts bearing the word 'SECURITY', members of the audience at Dylan concerts were allowed to clamber on stage and dance, or even join in a song performance. On May 2, 1992, at Santa Rosa, California, an unidentified girl came up from the audience and sang most of 'Mr. Tambourine Man', the 11th number of an 18-song set. (Dylan stood back to indulge this.) On February 17, 1993 at Eindhoven in the Netherlands, a young woman named Liz Souissi shared the task with Dylan of singing 'The Times They Are a-Changin'', the 14th song of the set. And some years later on May 11, 2000 in Cologne, Germany, a fan with a guitar, one Dagmar Mueller, brought it on stage with him and augmented the band on 'Like a Rolling Stone'.

[As so often in the present work, information here has been gleaned from Glen Dundas' invaluable listings book *Tangled*, Thunder Bay: SMA Services, 2004.]

Aufray, Hugues [1929 -] Hugues Auffray [sic] was born in an agreeable suburb of Paris on August 18, 1929, but when his family fled the German occupation of the city in 1940 he was sent away to a Dominican monastery school in the Tarn, in south-west France. In 1945 his divorced father moved him to a school in Madrid. He returned to Paris in 1948, hoping to become a painter but busking for money either side of military conscription in 1949 (in the Alps). On his return to Paris he married a dancer, had children and for almost ten years worked only by singing in local bars and cabaret. In 1959, pushed into entering a radio competition, he won a record deal and found immediate popularity. In 1962 he visited New York City, encountered the excitement of the Greenwich Village folk-revival movement and met Bob Dylan. The two formed a personal bond and Aufray was inspired by the young American's songs. On Aufray's return to France he introduced the acoustic folk style to French pop (which, God knows, would have been improved by almost anything), and toured to great acclaim performing a number of Dylan's songs.

In the spring of 1964, just before returning to the States to record *Another Side of Bob Dylan*, Dylan visited France and stayed with Hugues Aufray in Paris. Aufray began working (with Pierre Delance and Jean-Pierre Sabar) on translating an album of Dylan songs into French. This famous album, *Aufray chante Dylan*, duly appeared in 1965 to widespread European and French-Canadian acclaim (and was also issued in the UK). The songs, refreshed by their French-language titles, were: 'La fille du nord', 'Ce que je veux surtout' ('All I Really Want to Do'), 'Ce n'était pas moi', 'Oxford Town', 'Corrina Corrina', 'Cauchemar psychomoteur', 'Les temps changent', 'La ballade de Hollis Brown', 'La mort solitaire de Hattie Carroll', 'Dieu est a nos côtés' and 'Le jour où le bâteau viendra'. When CD-reissued in the 1990s it came with the extra tracks 'L'homme orchestre' ('Mr. Tambourine Man') and 'N'y pense plus tout est bien' plus a live 1964 cut of the latter and four live 1966 tracks: 'Les temps changent', 'La fille du nord', 'L' homme orchestre' and 'Cauchemar psychomoteur'.

In another lifetime, 30 years later, Aufray released a 2-CD set, *Aufray trans Dylan*, the first disc comprising re-recordings of more or less the original album's worth of Dylan songs, and the second new translations (all his own work) of newer material. This was still mostly drawn from the 1960s but did include a 'Mais qu'est-ce que tu voulais?' ('What Was It You Wanted?') and an 'Au coeur de mon pays' ('Heartland', the Bob Dylan-WILLIE NELSON song). A year later, on the live 2-CD set *Au Casino de Paris*, 17 of its 27 songs were by Dylan and included 'Comme des pierres qui roulent' ('Like a Rolling Stone') and the song Dylan himself had had an English-language hit with in France, 'Man Gave Names to All the Animals', or as Aufray had it, 'L'homme dota d'un nom chaque animal'.

In the summer of 1984, Aufray made surprise appearances on stage with Dylan—at Bob's Paris concert of July 1 and then two nights later in Grenoble—in each case playing guitar and sharing vocals with Dylan on 'Les temps changent'.

Aufray has remained a law unto himself, often disappearing from public view to his farm or his ranch for long periods, sometimes not giving the French public what it thinks it wants, touring Africa and generally espousing rural and ecological causes like a decent human being.

[Hugues Aufray: *Aufray chante Dylan*, *nia*, Barclay 80.289S (mono) & BB106 SS (stereo), Paris, 1965; Fontana TL 5329, UK; Barclay CBLP 2076, B-8019 & 45503, Canada; CD-reissue Dial 900 2217, France 1992 & Barclay 519 9 308-2 (with only 2 'bonus tracks'), Paris, 1993 (the 1997 & 2000 reissues have no extra tracks); *Aufray trans Dylan*, *nia*, Arcade 3006762 (2-LP version Arcade 3006766), Paris, 1995; *Au Casino de Paris*, Paris, Feb 1996, 2-CD set Arcade 3032272, Paris, 1997.]

Augustine, St. [354 - 430] St. Augustine of Hippo (now Annaba, Algeria) studied and lectured in Carthage before converting to Christianity in the 380s. His *Confessions* is a spiritual autobiography. He died in Hippo in 430 as the Vandals were taking the handles. He features (as you might expect) in Dylan's marvellous 'I Dreamed I Saw St. Augustine', from *John Wesley Harding* (a song that, alarmingly, Dylan decided to perform in the midst of his wretched 2005 US concerts). See also Augustine's appearance in **Eliot, T.S.**

Austrian Bob Dylan Convention, the annual The annual Austrian Bob Dylan Convention was founded by ROBERT KÖHLER in 1992 and, except for two Vienna-based festivals at the end of the 1990s (organised by RAINER VESELY), Köhler has continued to organise and oversee this venerable event. It has usually been held at the amazing Castle Plankenstein, spread over several days each May (or thereabouts) and providing a unique venue and an occasion for people to come together over and over again down the years. While it has attracted foreign speakers including MICHAEL GRAY, STEPHEN SCOBIE and PAUL WILLIAMS, it has been at heart a German-speaking Austro-German and Eastern European rendezvous in and around the courtyard of this medieval castle in the hills, encompassing the playing of rare video, audio and live music, merchandise stalls and the consumption of huge amounts of beer.

'Baby Let Me Follow You Down' [1962] Although on his first album Dylan credits 'Baby Let Me Follow You Down' as learnt from (E)RIC VON SCHMIDT, saying with lovely timing and wit on the spoken intro to the track that he'd 'met him one day in the green pastures of Harvard University' (a track laid down on his first day in the studios as an artist in his own right), he was aware that it could be traced back through the REV. GARY DAVIS' 'Baby, Let Me Lay It on You' and back beyond that all the way to MEMPHIS MINNIE and her second husband, Joe McCoy.

B

They may have been the first to record this song, but their 1930 version is actually a vocal duet, with McCoy doing the asking and her the spurning, so that the whole nature of the song is different. That is, before it becomes the familiar song of implicitly successful seduction, it is an inconsequential chat-up novelty item, a sort of early 'Come Outside'. It is impossible to say whose street-singing or fish-fry live version developed first or from where, but the pattern of the song's early committal to record in its various guises seems to run like this:

Memphis Minnie (with Joe McCoy): 'Can I Do It for You—Part 1' and 'Can I Do It for You—Part 2', Memphis, February 21, 1930; The State Street Boys (i.e. BIG BILL BROONZY and others): 'Don't Tear My Clothes', Chicago, January 10, 1935; Walter Coleman: 'Mama Let Me Lay It on You', Chicago, February 8, 1936 (re-cut in Chicago, June 3, 1936); Sheik Johnson: 'Baby Let Me Lay It on You', Chicago, March 27, 1936; BLIND BOY FULLER: 'Mama Let Me Lay It on You', NY, April 29, 1936; Georgia White: 'Daddy Let Me Lay It on You', Chicago, May 11, 1936; Washboard Sam: 'Don't Tear My Clothes', Chicago, June 26, 1936; Chicago Black Swans (i.e. again, Bill Broonzy and others): 'Don't Tear My Clothes No. 2', Chicago, January 26, 1937; State Street Swingers: 'Don't Tear My Clothes No. 2', also Chicago, January 26, 1937.

In the 1950s it became popular with New Orleans-based artists, including Professor Longhair, who recorded it in 1957, and Snooks Eaglin, who revived it in 1959 in its Big Bill Broonzy form as '(Mama) Don't You Tear My Clothes'—at which point its line 'You can rock me all night long . . . but don't you tear my clothes' is likely to have sounded as if it were pinching ideas from CARL PERKINS' then-recent 'Blue Suede Shoes'. Two years after Snooks Eaglin, Dylan recorded it as 'Baby Let Me Follow You Down'. The version he put on his début album is his earliest-known extant performance of it.

Three days later, however, Dylan was taped performing the song solo at the New York City home of friends Eve and 'Mac' MacKenzie; the same applied a month later in Minneapolis. He performed it live on the Billy Faier radio show on WBAI-FM in October 1962—and then, as if remembering it anew and deciding he'd written it himself, he recorded it as a Witmark music-publishing demo in January 1964. After 'going electric', Dylan then reintroduced the song to his set in concert, though not straight away: the earliest extant concert tape to include it comes from Hartford, Connecticut, on October 30, 1965. By February 1966 it had gained a regular position as the tenth song in the turbulent set Dylan & THE HAWKS took across the States and Australia and Europe; the Manchester, UK, version of this beautifully deranged reinvention of the song, from May 1966, can be heard on the *Bootleg Series Vol. 4*.

The song took a decade's rest after that, reappearing unexpectedly, though not especially beguilingly, at THE BAND's farewell concert in November 1976 (later issued as part of *The Last Waltz* album set and film). Again this was followed by a long gap: of over 11 years, before 'Baby Let Me Follow You Down' resurfaced at the second-ever Never-Ending Tour concert, Sacramento on June 9, 1988. There were three revisits in 1989—and the third, at Costa Mesa, California, that September 8, has (as of October 2005) proved to be the last time Dylan played the song in public.

For all this, the versions on Dylan's début album, and the live 1966 versions, are the ones that matter. They could hardly be more different from each other, or more perfect.

[Bob Dylan: 'Baby Let Me Follow You Down', NY, 20 Nov 1961, *Bob Dylan*.

Professor Longhair, 'Baby Let Me Hold Your Hand', New Orleans, 1957; *Mardi Gras in New Orleans 1949–1957*, Nighthawk 108, *nia*. Snooks Eaglin: 'Don't You Tear My Clothes', New Orleans, 1959; *Snooks Eaglin's New Orleans Blues*, Heritage EP 301, *nia*; re-recorded with 12-string guitar at same sessions as 'Mama Don't You Tear My Clothes', New Orleans, 1959; *That's All Right*, Bluesville BVLP 1046, *nia*.]

Baez, Joan [1941 -] Joan Chandos Baez was born on Staten Island, New York City, on January 9, 1941. She and her prettier, less talented sister MIMI both grew up to be folksingers. They, plus Bob Dylan and Mimi's husband RICHARD FARIÑA are the subjects of the book *Positively 4th Street* by DAVID HAJDU, published in 2001. He cuts to one core when he writes, brusquely but tellingly, that 'In folk circles . . . [amid] down-home characters groaning in and out of tune, Joan Baez seemed like the spirit of a child-queen, floating in off the moors.' Her pure voice was exactly what Dylan didn't like about her.

In one of those autobiographical poems of his that got into print from time to time on the back of LP covers and in old underground magazines—in this case on the back of her album *Joan Baez in Concert Part 2* (an album on which Baez sings the traditional 'Jackaroe' with the same set of lyrics Dylan uses thirty years later for the version on *World Gone Wrong*)—he uses the railroad remembered from his 'youngest years' as an axis round which to spin ideas of what is real. The 'iron bars an' rattlin' wheels' are real, the nightingale sound of Joan Baez's voice an alien, smooth opposite: 'A girl I met on common ground / Who like me strummed lonesome tunes / With a "lovely voice" so I first heard / "A thing a beauty" people said / "Wondrous sounds" writers wrote / "I hate that kind a sound" said I / "The only beauty's ugly, man / The crackin' shakin' breakin' sounds're / The only beauty I understand" . . .'

He suggests that he changes his mind. Not everybody does. Some of us hear those early duets, as at Newport, and can't but wince at the strident gauchery of her rigid delivery, the irritating way she's lost the moment he improvises, and her martyred suffering of these challenges she's privileged to have him throw at her.

But Baez, awful though she is in many ways (specially when she tries to dance on stage), should not be discounted as a conduit of traditional material to Bob Dylan. Once he accepted her voice and listened to her, she might have drawn his ever-curious attention to more than one or two of the songs with which we can now associate him. He could have heard them all from any number of other sources, and might well have done, but Joan Baez's early recordings happen to assemble quite a few of them conveniently together. In *Chronicles Volume One* he writes that he was struck straight away by what her first album contained: 'The Vanguard record was no phony baloney. It was almost frightening—an impeccable repertoire of songs, all hard-core traditional.'

Her first album includes 'East Virginia', 'Fare Thee Well', 'House of the Rising Sun' and 'Little Moses', her second 'Wagoner's Lad', 'The Lily of the West', 'Barbara Allen' and 'Railroad Boy', while 'The Trees They Do Grow High' is an alternative title for 'Young But Daily Growing'. On the third Baez album comes 'Copper Kettle', 'House Carpenter' and 'Pretty Boy Floyd', and in among the four Bob Dylan songs on the sixth album, *Farewell Angelina*, we find 'Will Ye Go, Laddie, Go' and 'Satisfied Mind' (which he gets around to on *Saved* in 1980).

Many further connections and comparisons arise on the same albums. Baez's first album's 'John Riley', a broadside ballad collected by G. Malcolm Laws Jr., belongs with 'Belle Isle' in telling of a soldier or sailor returning in disguise to test his lover's fidelity, while 'Rake and Rambling Boy' has a final verse that melds together the 'I'm Riding Old Paint' format discussed elsewhere ('when I die, don't bury me at all / Place my bones in alcohol') and the ending of 'Railroad Boy' ('at my feet place a white snow dove / To tell the world I died for love'). This last formulation is found widely—as for instance in the Lincolnshire folk song 'Died for Love (I Wish My Baby It Was Born)', which not only ends the same way ('Dig me my grave long, wide and deep / Put a marble stone at my head and feet / But a turtle white dove put over above / For to let the world know that I died for love') but also offers this recognisable prefiguring of a portion of 'Bob Dylan's Dream': 'I wish, I wish, but it's all in vain / I wish I was a maid again'.

The third album's 'Matty Groves', a CHILD ballad, shares its theme with that other Child ballad 'Blackjack Davey', while 'Geordie', a part-Child and part-broadside ballad, reminds us of both 'Blackjack Davey' and Dylan's own 'Seven Curses': 'Ah my Geordie will be hanged . . . / Go bridle me my milk white steed / Go bridle me my pony / I will ride to London's court / To plead for the life of Geordie . . . / The judge looked over his left shoulder / He said fair maid I'm sorry'.

Quite apart from all that, Baez comes into the Dylan story recurrently, of course. They hung around together, he took up with her, she helped spread his name around when she was a star and he wasn't (her second, third and fourth albums all went gold, she made the covers of upscale New York magazines, her concerts were reviewed by JOHN UPDIKE: she was the acceptable face and voice of folk music), she duetted with Dylan at the NEWPORT FOLK FESTIVAL in July 1963—during her own set—and the following month warbled away behind him, as if to validate his presence, at the March on Washington. She gave him a significant slot on her own shows when she was a bigger name than him. In 1965 she accompanied him and his retinue to England (where, that year, she enjoyed a top 10 hit with her single of his song 'Farewell Angelina') for his last set of solo concerts before he 'went electric', expecting him to reciprocate. He didn't. Her pain is there for all to feel embarrassed by in D.A. PENNEBAKER's film of the tour, *Don't Look Back*.

She continued with her political activism: campaigning, giving benefit concerts, visiting Vietnam and helping to establish Amnesty International in the United States—and she has continued her good works ever since, visiting trouble spots with great persistence, though people have occasionally questioned the quality of her commitment. Terry Castle, reminiscing not altogether fondly about her late mistress Susan Sontag, revealed that Baez was an especial bugbear to the great critic:

> '. . . she regaled me—for the umpteenth time—about the siege of Sarajevo, the falling bombs, and

how the pitiful Joan Baez had been too terrified to come out of her hotel room. Sontag flapped her arms and shook her big mannish hair—inevitably described in the press as a "mane"—contemptuously. *That woman is a fake! She tried to fly back to California the next day! I was there for months. Through all of the bombardment, of course, Terry.* Then she ruminated. Had I ever met Baez? Was she a secret lesbian? I confessed that I'd once waited in line behind the folk singer at my cash machine (Baez lives near Stanford) and had taken the opportunity to inspect the hairs on the back of her neck. Sontag, who sensed a rival, considered this non-event for a moment, but after further inquiries, was reassured . . .'

Meanwhile, back in the 1960s, Baez was widely assumed to have been the subject of Dylan's song 'She Belongs to Me': the woman with the Egyptian ring (though the song can just as well be 'about' the US, rather than any individual). She also somewhere suggested herself as the 'Johanna' in his *Blonde on Blonde* song 'Visions of Johanna'. More certain is that earlier, when things between them were at their most productive, it was at her house outside Big Sur that he wrote his magnificent 'Lay Down Your Weary Tune'. If she had done nothing else, we'd be in Joan Baez's debt for helping that song come into being.

Less vitally, she also became a conduit for his songs as a performer: not only scattering many of them around her albums but devoting entire albums to them. *Any Day Now—Songs of Bob Dylan* came out in 1968, was CD-reissued in 1987 and then reissued again in 2005 with two 'bonus tracks' taken from her 1967 *Live in Japan* album. There were various extra such projects in Europe—a 2-LP set in Holland in 1975, for instance—and then in 1988 came the retrospective US release of material from 1963–68, *Baez Sings Dylan*. Of more importance to Dylan collectors, a couple of official Baez releases include performances by the two of them, and offer the only non-bootleg way to acquire these. 'Troubled and I Don't Know Why', sung live at Forest Hills, NY, in August 1963 was released on the Baez 3-CD box set *Rare, Live & Classic* in 1994; her *Live at Newport* CD, compiled and released by Vanguard in 1997 offers their previously unreleased duet of 'It Ain't Me Babe' from July 24, 1964, plus their 'With God on Our Side' from two nights later. (A slightly different edit of this 'It Ain't Me Babe', with Baez introducing Dylan as 'George Washington', and with an outtro, was released in 1998 on the various artists CD *Vanguard Sessions: Folk Duets*.)

A slattern for punishment, Baez returned within the Dylan orb for his Rolling Thunder Revues of 1975–76. Musically, these yielded by far their best collaborations, as can be seen and heard in the movie *Renaldo & Clara*, filmed during the 1975 Revue, and in the 'Hard Rain' TV Special, filmed the following year. On the JOHNNY ACE song 'Never Let Me Go', and especially on WOODY GUTHRIE's 'Deportees' (its lovely melody was written by a schoolteacher, Martin Hoffman), their duets are so good you don't even want her to not be there. (On the other hand that dancing, on Dylan's splendidly flamencoid reinvention of 'I Pity the Poor Immigrant', is excruciating.)

Yet it seems to have been another personal humiliation. What we see, in the end, in *Renaldo & Clara*, is Baez asking Dylan aloud what he thought would have happened if they had married, parading around in a gypsy wedding dress, trying to square off against SARA DYLAN in a doomed, unsavory way and, within the fictional-storyline portion of the film, being traded for a horse.

On June 6, 1982 they came together on another public platform, for a 'Peace Sunday' concert in Pasadena. Photographs taken at this brief, three-song meeting are rare, but show Dylan and Baez standing at the microphone looking dignified and well-attuned (and looking, for the 1980s, pretty good). They performed 'With God on Our Side' and 'Blowin' in the Wind', but between these came the surprise of a Jimmy Buffett song, 'A Pirate Looks at Forty'.

In 1984, unbelievably, Baez consented to come along on yet another Dylan tour, his tour of European stadiums with SANTANA—only to storm off before the end and write about how horrid Bob was in her second attempt at autobiography, 1988's *And a Voice to Sing With*. (In her first, *Daybreak*, 20 years earlier, she had written about him admiringly, and called him 'the Dada King'.)

At least twice she made him the subject of her own songs, too. First there was the ill-advised 'To Bobby', in 1972, remonstrating with him for deserting the right-on political troops and imploring him to return to the head of their raggedly righteous phalanxes. The chorus went: 'Do you hear the voices in the night, Bobby? / They're crying for you / See the children in the morning light, Bobby / They're dying.' (Not quite 'They're dying for you', but close.)

This did not go down well: and not merely on aesthetic grounds; Dylan was still muttering about it over 30 years later in *Chronicles Volume One*: 'Joan Baez recorded a protest song about me that was getting big play, challenging me to get with it—come out and take charge, lead the masses—be an advocate, lead the crusade. The song called out to me from the radio like a public service announcement.'

Yet three years later, she wrote and recorded a song as good as 'To Bobby' was gruesomely bad. 'Diamonds and Rust' is immeasurably better than anything else Joan Baez has ever written (which might not prove, in itself, ardent recommendation): it was a superb love song, full of ebb and flow, a well-judged mix of vivid detail and warm feeling. It managed to be mature but fresh, quirky and direct. It was also Baez being *dignified* and open, with absolutely no sulks or martyrdom, about her relationship with and feelings for Bob Dylan. The lyric is so self- confident, too: it can include 'As I remember your eyes / Were bluer than robin's eggs / My poetry was lousy, you said', this deft, witty pay-off line sung without rancour or reproach, enacting that acknowledgement within those lines while the broader sweep of 'Diamonds and Rust' was its own refutation of such a judgment. It also includes these acute lines: lines that pin down part of Dylan, as man and as artist, with fond aplomb but great clear-sightedness: 'Now you're telling me / You're not nostalgic: / Well give me another word for it / You who're so good with words / And at keeping things vague.'

In *Chronicles Volume One* Dylan rewrites his first reactions to the Baez voice. He forgets that initial clinging to the feeling that 'the only beauty's ugly'; he says of seeing her for the first time on TV, when he was still in Minnesota: 'I couldn't stop looking at her, didn't want to blink. . . . The sight of her made me sigh. All that and then there was the voice. A voice that drove out bad spirits . . . she sang in a voice straight to God. . . . Nothing she did didn't work.' He adds that 'also she was an exceptionally good instrumentalist.' This last, unelaborated observation accords with what he says in the interview in the film *No Direction Home*, where he stresses that she was 'an excellent guitar player.' She gives an interview for the film too, the bile of the late 1980s gone: but with a sub-text of gentle, not so subtle cutting down to size going on. In contrast, the last things he writes about her in *Chronicles Volume One* are of unmitigated respect for her artistry.

> 'The singer has to make you believe what you are hearing and Joan did that. . . . Soon I was rolling through the snowy Wisconsin prairie fields, the looming shadows of Baez and ELLIOTT were not far from my heels. The world I was heading into . . . was really the world of Jack Elliott and Joan Baez.'

[Joan Baez: *Joan Baez*, Vanguard VRS-9078, NY, 1960; *Joan Baez, Vol. 2*, Vanguard VRS-9094, NY, 1961; *Joan Baez in Concert*, Vanguard VRS-9112, NY, 1962; *Joan Baez in Concert, Part 2*, Vanguard VRS-9113, NY, 1964; *Farewell Angelina*, Vanguard VRS-9200 (stereo VSD-79200), NY, 1965. All these are CD-reissued on, respectively, Vanguard VMD 79078-2, 1995; VMD 79094-2, 1995; VMD 79112-2, 1996; VMD 79113-2, 1996; & VMD 79200-2, 1995. All these songs are published in *British Ballads and Folk Songs from the Joan Baez Songbook* (with illustrations by ERIC VON SCHMIDT), 1964 & 1967. Joan Baez: *Any Day Now—Songs of Bob Dylan*, Vanguard VSD-79306/7, US (SVRL 19037/8, UK), 1968; CD-reissued VSD-79306/7, US, 1987; CD-reissue with bonus tracks 79747-2, US, 2005; 'To Bobby', *nia*, *Come from the Shadows*, A&M 3103, 1972; 'Diamonds and Rust', LA, 17–29 Jan 1975, A&M SP 3233, LA (AMLH 64527, London), 1975; *Baez Sings Dylan*, Vanguard 79512-2, US, 1988. Joan Baez & Bob Dylan: 'With God on Our Side', Newport, RI, 28 Jul 1963, Various Artists LP *Newport Broadside*, Vanguard VRS-9144 (mono) / VSD 79144, NY, 1964, CD-reissued VCD 770003-2, NY, 1997; 'Troubled and I Don't Know Why', Forest Hills, NY, 17 Aug 1963, *Rare, Live & Classic*, Vanguard VCD 125/27-2, NY, 1994; 'It Ain't Me Babe', Newport, RI, 24 Jul & 'With God on Our Side' 26 Jul 1964, *Live at Newport* Vanguard 77015-2, NY, 1997; 'It Ain't Me Babe', ditto (different edit), *Vanguard Sessions: Folk Duets*, Vanguard 79511 2, 1998.

Bob Dylan: 'Joan Baez in Concert, Part 2' (poem; in *Lyrics 1962–85* it is copyrighted 1973: almost a decade after its publication on the back of the Baez album); *Chronicles Volume One*, 2004, pp.119, 254–57.

'Died for Love (I Wish My Baby It Was Born)' in the pamphlet *Twenty-one Lincolnshire Folk Songs*, the Percy Grainger collection, ed. Patrick O'Shaughnessy, Lincolnshire & Humberside Arts, UK, 2nd edn., 1983. (Incidentally, Percy Grainger died in New York City in the midst of the folk revival in 1961.) Terry Castle: 'Desperately Seeking Susan', *London Review of Books*, 17 Mar 2005.]

Baker, Arthur [1955 -] Arthur Baker was born in Boston, Massachusetts, on April 22, 1955. His music-biz career began as a Boston club DJ. He produced for a local label, moved to New York, produced there with no special success, returned to Boston, produced some more, moved back to New York City and there, for Tommy Boy Records, co-produced Afrika Bambaataa's 1982 single 'Jazzy Sensation', an update of Gwen McCrae's 'Funky Sensation', with Shep Pettibone. This was well-regarded (by those who like that sort of thing) and led to his producing the group's 'Planet Rock', a record that was an early hip hop landmark yet had been inspired by Kraftwerk. In 1984 Baker made dance remixes of big-name rock artists' tracks, first revamping Cyndi Lauper's 'Girls Just Wanna Have Fun' and then BRUCE SPRINGSTEEN's 'Dancing in the Dark'. Baker also produced Manchester group New Order's track 'Confusion', which became a crossover hit on the US dance charts. All this set the precedent for rock acts to make dance remixes of their records.

In *Chronicles Volume One* Dylan credits Arthur Baker with having 'helped' him 'produce the album *Empire Burlesque*'. Most people would say the opposite: that when Dylan latched onto Baker and this re-mix guru was invited to go through these recordings discoing them up (or down), the vapid, inhuman drumbeat Baker imposed, and the concrete stadium acoustics he threw over everything, were no more capable of injecting real life into these tracks than could Frankenstein into his dead metal monster.

Dylan reportedly told Baker: 'I want to make a record like Madonna or Prince. I want to sell a lot of records.' But dragging Arthur Baker into his arena in order to tart up *Empire Burlesque* delivered Dylan the worst of both worlds: it convinced neither the market that turns corporate rock into platinum nor those whose ear and mind is on the lookout for an alternative to the mainstream. If you use your position in the evil empire of the music business to send someone out to buy you disco clothes, you'll end up in the clothes of the emperor. And shopping for modishness is still shopping.

Specifically, though, Dylan credits Baker with having persuaded him that he needed an acoustic track to complete the album. How right this was is doubtful, granted the dodginess of the song Dylan went back and wrote that night at the Plaza Hotel, New York ('Dark Eyes'), and granted too how uncomfortably it sits with the mechanistic bedlam of the other tracks as remixed by Arthur Baker.

Baker has continued to work with New Order and still works as both a producer and DJ, though he is modish no more. In the 1990s he moved to London and opened a chain of Elbow Room bars and restaurants in Brixton and Notting Hill.

The failure of the *Empire Burleseque* album even from Baker's point of view, in commercial and artistic terms, is more than hinted at by the fact that almost every website biography of him omits Bob Dylan's name.

[Bob Dylan: *Chronicles Volume One*, 2004, pp.209–210; quote re cf. Madonna & Prince: Nigel Williamson, *The Rough Guide to Bob Dylan*, London: Rough Guides, 2004, p.154.]

Baldwin, John [1948–] John Baldwin was born on Christmas Eve 1948 in Bermondsey, London, amid the slums and dereliction left over from World War II. After leaving school he entered the pharmaceutical industry and remained in its employ for 27 years but is now an independent consultant in drug safety evaluation.

He first showed an interest in Dylan's work at age 17. In 1996 he self-published the first of six volumes of *The Fiddler Now Upspoke*, a series that collates all known interviews with Dylan with adequate indexing and cross-referencing. He also founded and edited the bi-monthly fanzine *Dignity*, which has run to 31 issues but is now in a rather lengthy temporary abeyance. Though founded to provide serious analytical discussion, in which it never succeeded, it found a niche as a more friendly discussion forum for fans, and for fans to see their work in print 'without unwarranted criticism'.

John Baldwin also runs the Desolation Row Information Service, keeping people up to date with Dylan-related news. It began after JOHN BAULDIE's death in 1996, as a replacement for the latter's telephone hotline service. (More of a 'warmline', really.) This still exists but widespread internet access means that the main form of communication is now by regular e-mailings to 'subscribers, friends and other strangers'. Courtesy of his Desolation Row Promotions, for nearly a decade now John Baldwin has run the 'fan club' ticket allocation for all Dylan's UK concerts.

At the time of writing John and his daughter Mary-Anne are about to self-publish a new book focussing on Dylan's *Desire* song 'Isis', titled *On the Fifth Day of May*.

[John Baldwin: *The Fiddler Now Upspoke*, Welwyn Garden City & Campton, UK; Desolation Row Promotions, *www.desolation-row.co.uk*. John & Mary-Anne Baldwin, *On the Fifth Day of May*, Campton: Desolation Row Promotions, 2006.]

Ball, Gordon [1944–] Gordon Victor Ball Jr., born in Paterson, New Jersey, on December 30, 1944, is an underground filmmaker turned Colonel and Professor of Literature at the Virginia Military Institute, and is the man who has nominated Dylan for the Nobel Prize for Literature annually since 1996.

He first took an interest in Dylan's work in 1965, but his first published article about it was a review of *Renaldo & Clara*. Some early listenings to Dylan are recounted in his book *'66 Frames: A Memoir*, published in 1999.

In 1968 he was hired as ALLEN GINSBERG's farm manager, later editing the poet's early writings. His book *Allen Verbatim: Lectures on Poetry, Politics, Consciousness* was nominated for a Pulitzer Prize. He wrote Ginsberg's entry in the *Encyclopaedia of American Literature* and JACK KEROUAC's entry for the *Dictionary of American Biography*. At the Caen University Dylan Colloquium of March 2005 he delivered a paper on 'Dylan and the Nobel'.

GREIL MARCUS probably speaks for many when, asked if he thinks Dylan will 'ever get the Nobel Prize for Literature', replies:

> 'I hope not. There are thousands of novelists more deserving than he is. It's a prize for literature; he's a songwriter, he's a singer, he's a performer. Anyway, Bob Dylan's won lots of awards, he doesn't need this one. There are plenty of people who need the money, need the readers.'

[Gordon Ball: Review Notes and a Community Proposal, *North Carolina Anvil*, vol. 12, no. 567, Durham, NC, 5 May 1978, p.8; *'66 Frames: A Memoir*, Minneapolis, MN: Coffee House Press, 1999; *Allen Verbatim: Lectures on Poetry, Politics, Consciousness*, New York: McGraw-Hill, 1974. Greil Marcus: interviewed by Thomas Storch, *Isis* no.122, Bedworth, UK, Sep–Oct 2005, pp.47–49.]

Band, The The very name The Band was, as Barney Hoskyns wrote, 'born of a beguiling mixture of humility and arrogance. They were not just "the band" but they were THE band.' And they were so called only at the very last minute before the 1968 issue of their début album, the great *Music from Big Pink*. Their record contract signed them as the Crackers. Then the US promo single of 'The Weight', taken from the finished album, was billed not as by The Band but as by Jaime ROBBIE ROBERTSON, RICK DANKO, RICHARD MANUEL, GARTH HUDSON, LEVON HELM. Even on the label of the British LP itself it doesn't say The Band; it says 'Rick Danko, Levon Helm, Garth Hudson, Richard Manuel, Jaime Robbie Robertson'.

They had begun as the backing band to Arkansas' mediocre rocker and charmer RONNIE HAWKINS, with Levon Helm the first to be recruited and the only American in the group. All the others came from southern Ontario, Canada.

Toronto-based soon after Helm joined, Hawkins & the Hawks were signed to Roulette Records and had two immediate hits, 'Forty Days' and 'Mary Lou', before the other members of what would become The Band were gradually brought into the group: Jaime Robbie Robertson as guitarist, Richard Manuel as pianist, Rick Danko as bass player and Garth Hudson on organ.

After splitting with Hawkins the group went out as Levon & the Hawks, then briefly as the Canadian Squires, and then as the Hawks again. But writer Peter Viney suggests that our notion of these five musos working as a team for eight or nine years before meeting success is mistaken: this was a myth created by the predatory ALBERT GROSSMAN after he stepped in as their manager.

Viney points out that when they were working with Hawkins, the group was a changeable unit, using extra horn players at their longer Ontario residencies but with a smaller core unit when they traveled around; that Hudson, for example, came into the group far later than Helm and Robertson: he doesn't appear on a Hawks recording until 1963; and that even when they left Hawkins, Jerry Penfound was still a member, on horns, while initially the group had also included a vocalist named Bruce Bruno. In other words, as Viney notes, 'They didn't coalesce as a solid unit of five until very late in 1964.'

They met up with Bob Dylan in 1965. Only Helm and Robertson played the early electric gigs that followed the NEWPORT FOLK FESTIVAL electric début, starting at Forest Hills, New York, that August 28. The rest of Dylan's band at this point were AL KOOPER on organ and Harvey Brooks (aka HARVEY GOLDSTEIN) on bass. This unit lasted only a short time, and after a Hollywood Bowl concert on September 3, Dylan got together with Helm, Robertson, Danko, Hudson and Manuel to rehearse in Woodstock, New York, for further live gigs. That same month, according to Robertson's often wilfully inaccurate notes, Helm and the others were still active as Levon & the Hawks, and they recorded Robertson's songs 'He Don't Love You (And He'll Break Your Heart)' and 'The Stones I Throw' plus the traditional 'Go Go Liza Jane' in New York City some time that September and duly released on two Levon & the Hawks singles on the Atlantic Records subsidiary label Atco. But on October 5 they went into the studio with Dylan for the first time, followed by more live concerts and a second studio stint on November 30 (from which comes the single 'Can You Please Crawl Out Your Window?'). This session has also now yielded the version of 'Visions of Johanna' released on the *Bootleg Series Vol. 7*, 2005.

At this point, Helm quit; he couldn't stand the booing at Dylan's electric performances. By December 4, at Berkeley, the rest of the Hawks were still in there but Levon had been replaced by BOBBY GREGG. Back in the studio again on January 21–22, it was SANDY KONIKOFF on drums along with the Hawks minus Levon.

The whole of the amazing 1966 tour thus took place without Levon Helm. On the early North American dates, from February 5 at White Plains, NY, through to March 26 in Vancouver, Canada, the drummer was Sandy Konikoff; after that, and so for all the tumultuous Australian and European dates, including the historic Manchester Free Trade Hall concert in May, the drummer was MICKEY JONES.

Drummer aside, however, this blazing, transcendent music was by the Hawks, which is to say The-Band-in-waiting. So loud and badly reproduced in the halls, so smudgily filmed yet mercifully so well recorded, this was the most radical, oceanic and storming electric music ever played live. How was it that Dylan, a solo performer who hadn't played live with a group since he was a schoolboy, and the Hawks, whose earlier music was undistinguished bar-room blowing, coalesced so incandescently well, that they could go on stage in Liverpool in May 1966—the city that had so recently been the centre of the musical universe—and hurl at their audience rock music a thousand times more sublime, challenging, multi-layered and exciting than anything Liverpudlians had ever heard before? Impossible to say, but easy to prove. Play that night's 'Just Like Tom Thumb's Blues'. By this point Dylan's cawing voice and searing harmonica were both perfectly integrated instruments in amongst those of the Hawks, whose hard-won knowledge of each other's playing freed them all to ride each moment in a ceaseless interchange of fiery, creative levitation.

In extraordinary contrast, in the calm of the countryside and after Dylan's long post-motorcycle crash unwinding, their next co-operative project was the informal Basement Tapes sessions. But what about all the time in between the two—between the end of May 1966 and the spring of 1967? The group, supposedly such a hard-working, on-the-road unit, played not a single live date that anyone has been able to discover.

What's more, Levon Helm was out of the picture all that time, and indeed was still missing when the Basement sessions began. Exactly when that was remains in doubt. It's been suggested (by Helm, who wasn't around) that they began as early as March '67, but more certain is that in June 1967 they assembled at Dylan's house in Woodstock, and at that point the group and Dylan were recorded by Garth Hudson on primitive machinery. These June sessions yielded 20 tracks that have circulated, including a wealth of traditional material and old songs like 'Rock Salt and Nails', 'I Don't Hurt Anymore' and 'Be Careful of Stones That You Throw': material that only came to light in the 1980s and 1990s. Over that summer, partly at Dylan's house but mostly at 'Big Pink', the group's house at nearby West Saugerties–in *the* basement: a room only about 12 foot square–another 67 tracks plus seven further fragments were recorded, including nine Dylan tracks that emerged in 1975 on the official *The Basement Tapes* double-LP and two ('Santa Fe' and 'I Shall Be Released') that emerged in 1991 on the *Bootleg Series Volumes 1–3*.

Across all these tracks the four Helm-less band members spread themselves out into the multi-instrumentalism for which they would later become famous and admired. Here we got, in addition to their primary instruments, Robertson playing drums, Manuel on drums (they needed someone on drums, after all) and harmonica, Danko on fiddle and mandolin and Hudson on accordion, tenor sax, piano and clavinette.

Further sessions followed in September–October and in October–November, all at 'Big Pink', with Levon Helm arriving in October, better late than never. These sessions yielded 29 more tracks, among them Dylan's 'Tears of Rage', 'Clothes Line Saga', 'Goin' to Acapulco' and, like the marathon June-to-August sessions, other high-spot Dylan items that saw official release only on *The Basement Tapes* in 1975 but were circulated as song demos in London very soon after their recording.

The tracks by The Band on this album are highly suspect. 'Bessie Smith' was actually an outtake from the fourth Band album, *Cahoots*, and the others were almost as dubious. As CLINTON HEYLIN comments:

> 'Intermingling eight songs by The Band supposedly cut in the fall of 1967, Robertson sought to imply that the alliance between Dylan and The Band was far more equal than it was: "Hey, we were writing all these songs, doing our own thing, oh and Bob would sometimes come around and we'd swap a few tunes." In fact, the so-called Band basement tapes have nothing to do with the Dylan/Band sessions . . . [and] Richard Manuel compositions recorded at Big Pink in 1967 . . . were omitted from the set possibly because they highlighted how Manuel, not Robertson, was the first to pen original Band material. Though revealing in their own right, the Band tracks only pollute the official set and reduce its stature. Dylan's songs, fully sprung from his reactivated muse, are the work of an artist at the pinnacle of his powers. The Band's songs are signposts along the way, notes detailing the search for an independent voice so magically realized on *Music from Big Pink*. No more, no less.'

When Dylan made his first public appearance for 20 months in January 1968 at the WOODY GUTHRIE Memorial Concerts, the Hawks (or the Crackers) played behind him, and Levon Helm was among them for the first time in over two years. But the group was reaching its own maturity, emerging into the light as a unique creative unit. It was becoming The Band.

Their recording deal and their management was now courtesy of Dylan's manager, Albert Grossman. They were signed to Capitol Records as the Crackers in February 1968, but they had already begun recording the first album in New York in January, and then completed it in Los Angeles in February.

Given their shared management and their very distinguished musical relationship, it was unsurprising that *Music from Big Pink* drew on Dylan's support: one of his paintings comprised its front cover, and the songs inside included three of his that were attracting attention at the time because they were famed products of the legendary yet still-recent Basement Tapes sessions: 'Tears of Rage' co-written by Dylan and Manuel, 'This Wheel's on Fire' by Dylan and Danko, and Dylan's own 'I Shall Be Released'. (On the original LP issues, all three songs were credited to Dylan alone.) No officially released Dylan versions of these great songs existed when *Music from Big Pink* burst upon the world.

Yet though these songs were powerful and would have grabbed any listener's attention, to suggest that the album's mesmeric quality and success are due to Dylan would be unreasonable. It was The Band, not Dylan, and it was like no other record. Strongly affecting, touching, sad, eerie and shining almost too brightly, it melded beautifully primitive soulful singing, ultra-vivid sound and production, and music that was at once hillbilly, gospel, rock'n'roll and gothic ghostliness. Understatement and subtlety held their own against the exciting phantasmagoric organ excesses of 'Chest Fever'; the slow-motion fruit-machining of who was taking lead vocals, the plaintive echoey quality that offset the neatly crude plainness of instrumentation; the mix of song type and of songwriter. It was an absolute triumph. As William Ruhlmann writes in the online All Music Guide:

> 'At first . . . the group seemed to affect the sound of a loose jam session, alternating emphasis on different instruments, while the lead and harmony vocals passed back and forth as if the singers were making up their blend on the spot. In retrospect . . . [it all] seemed far more considered and crafted to support a group of songs that took family, faith, and rural life as their subjects and proceeded to imbue their values with uncertainty . . . the points were made musically

> as much as lyrically. Tenor Richard Manuel's haunting, lonely voice gave the album much of its frightening aspect, while Rick Danko and Levon Helm's rough-hewn styles reinforced the songs' rustic fervor. The dominant instrument was Garth Hudson's often icy and majestic organ, while Robbie Robertson's unusual guitar work further destabilized the sound. The result was an album that reflected the turmoil of the late 60s in a way that emphasized the tragedy inherent in the conflicts. *Music from Big Pink* came off as a shockingly divergent musical statement only a year after the ornate productions of *Sgt. Pepper* . . . the album and the group made their own impact, influencing a movement toward roots styles and country elements in rock. Over time, *Music from Big Pink* came to be regarded as a watershed work in the history of rock, one that introduced new tones and approaches . . .'

The album was released in July 1968.

It was truly a collaborative work. On 'Tears of Rage', 'In a Station', 'Chest Fever', 'Lonesome Suzie' and 'I Shall Be Released' the lead vocalist was Manuel; on 'Caledonia Mission', 'Long Black Veil' and 'This Wheel's on Fire', it was Danko; on 'To Kingdom Come' it was Robertson and Manuel; on 'The Weight' it was Helm and Danko; on 'We Can Talk' it was Manuel, Helm and Danko, appearing to throw the vocals around between them as if by spontaneous instinct (and using stereo placement with ingenious apparent abandon, which in a later era somehow became prohibited). And while Robertson wrote 'To Kingdom Come', 'Caledonia Mission', 'The Weight' and 'Chest Fever', Manuel wrote 'In a Station', 'We Can Talk' and 'Lonesome Suzie'.

There was almost a sixth member of the group, too, in producer John Simon, whom they had met through film-maker HOWARD ALK. Not only was Simon's production fresh and resourceful but he also played tenor sax on 'Tears of Rage', piano on 'Caledonia Mission' and baritone sax on 'Chest Fever'.

The problem of that traditionally difficult second album was brilliantly solved by their simply titled follow-up, *The Band*, which from its dark brown textured packaging incorporating black and white photos of the group that might have been taken during the American Civil War, to its corresponding, defiantly unmodish stance and its unity of sound, came across like a concept album without any of the preciousness that might imply. The songs—this time eight by Robertson, three by Manuel & Robertson and one by Helm & Robertson—flowed one into another like the movements of one work. If there was less pain there was a more dignified foreboding. This was timeless American music. In an era of hipness in which parents were part of an old, foolish, evil order to be abolished and replaced by new, revolutionary enlightenment, here were these strong dissenting voices from the backwoods, singing their connections, not so much reaching back into the past as seeing it right there among them and allowing its chords to sound. If the Basement Tapes sessions had explored these old strengths in muffled form and mostly through Bob Dylan's eyes, here we had The Band in neighboring territory but standing firm on their own homestead, this second album their masterpiece.

If this was partly because Robertson's lyrics had matured into thoughtfulness, and found a way to specify seeing the past as the present without being didactic—'The Night They Drove Old Dixie Down', with its 'in the winter of sixty-five' hovering naturally over two centuries' '65s—it was in greater part because the group had reached new heights of wholly co-operative work. Again here was each musician's multi-instrumental dexterity: Hudson on organ, clavinette, piano, accordion, soprano sax, tenor sax, baritone sax and trumpet; Manuel on piano, drums, baritone sax and harmonica; Danko on bass, violin and trombone; Helm on drums, mandolin and guitar; Robertson on guitar and engineering. Plus producer John Simon on tuba, electric piano and tenor horn. And again the lead vocals shift across the tracks, from Manuel to Helm to Danko to combinations of the three. And while Robertson had written so much of the material, he sang lead on none of it.

The album was released in 1969 and had real impact on rock consciousness: perhaps more so than Dylan's *John Wesley Harding* had done, because it was a more accessible work with a far richer sound; both pushed youth culture to recognise its own shallowness, to admit that contemporary experience could range far beyond a modish obsession with underground culture or the grooviness of the spacey and new; that we all have roots. And they brought this message to a different part of Woodstock, the instant new hippie center of the universe that was Woodstock Nation, where on the last night, August 17, 1969, they were headliners.

Exactly two weeks later, The Band accompanied Dylan again at his Isle of Wight Festival appearance (on August 31). In turn, at their 1971 New Year's Eve concert in New York City, Dylan came on in the early hours of January 1, 1972 and as well as singing 'Down in the Flood', 'When I Paint My Masterpiece' and 'Like a Rolling Stone', he also played guitar behind Helm on 'Don't Ya Tell Henry'.

In the interim The Band had released their third and fourth albums, the disappointing *Stage Fright* (1970) and *Cahoots* (1971), the best thing on the latter being their version of another obscure new Dylan song, the gorgeous 'When I Paint My Masterpiece'—a version that included, unlike Dylan's own, the high comedy of the bridge couplet 'Sailing round the world in a dirty gondola / Oh to be back in the land of Coca-Cola'. Producer John

Simon had not been used on these albums, and Robertson's songwriting was at once growing anaemic and shoving Richard Manuel's out of the way. You could say that there was a simple equation here: teamwork gave way to Robertson's ego and domination; The Band went downhill. Their 'maturity' just sounded like tiredness.

Moondog Matinee, in 1973, was an album of oldies at a time when people like CHUCK BERRY were regarded as long-gone irrelevancies from an era so superficial that it had enjoyed two-minute singles instead of long concept albums; but like JOHN LENNON'S album *Rock 'n' Roll* two years later, it seemed pointless as well as not good enough.

In 1974 The Band rejoined Dylan for his mega so-called Come-Back Tour of North America, from which came the double-LP billed as by Bob Dylan & The Band, *Before the Flood*, which followed their working together one more time in the studio, on Dylan's *Planet Waves*. At the time, the album was underrated and the tour overrated—and live, The Band seemed keener when backing Dylan than when playing their own considerable material.

In 1975 they produced *Northern Lights—Southern Cross*. It was their first studio album of new material in four years. As a comeback, it didn't make it. Their self-produced sound was thin, every song was by Robertson alone, and you had to work hard to pick up the gems from among self-imitative pearls like 'Ophelia' and 'Forbidden Fruit'. The gems were the exceptionally lovely vocal by Richard Manuel on 'Hobo Jungle', the searing heartbreak Rick Danko brings to his vocal on 'It Makes No Difference' and the standout 'Acadian Driftwood': so good it could have been on *The Band*. Which says it all.

The end of The Band was in sight, and it came with the concert at the Winterland Palace in San Francisco on November 25, 1976, filmed by MARTIN SCORSESE (using great cinematographers Michael Chapman, Vilmos Zsigmond and Laszlo Kovacs) as the rather glorious *The Last Waltz*—glorious as a film, but not as an album. Three LPs was too much (and now, as four CDs, it's worse yet still has things missing), and as the Rev. Al Friston points out: 'Dylan's stuff is no less hot-airish than most of *Before the Flood*.'

One last studio album, the insipid *Islands*, was issued in 1977, but The Band had left the building.

All the classic Band albums have now been CD-reissued with unnecessary 'bonus' tracks of out-takes and the like. This is a clear case of 'more means less'. It's no service at all to a new listener to be given a version of *Music from Big Pink* that fails to come to rest at the perfect end of 'I Shall Be Released' but instead putters and bumps along with a series of tracks of dodgy provenance that are nothing whatever to do with the unimprovable original album. The same applies to *The Band*; the extras here are less irrelevant—but who needs them? The original album is unsurpassable. Out-takes clutter. De trops = to detract. And the latest, most overblown of these rewritings of history is the five CDs plus a DVD package, *The Band: A Musical History*, Robbie Robertson's newest opportunity to lie about what was recorded then, and to remaster things his way.

The Band reformed in a partial sort of way, with Earl Cate of the Cate Brothers and without Robbie Robertson, in 1983; but Richard Manuel committed suicide in 1986. A dismayingly enfeebled version of The Band tottered onto the stage at Dylan's so-called 30th Anniversary Concert in New York City in 1992 and flailed their way through 'When I Paint My Masterpiece'.

Yet soon afterwards the trio of original members who were left recorded and released a new Band album, *Jericho* (1993), which included a version of Dylan's song 'Blind Willie McTell': and when Dylan took to performing it in concert later, he followed The Band's way of doing it rather than his own.

Further albums followed, *High on the Hog* in 1996 and two years later, celebrating their 30th anniversary, came *Jubilation*. The last line-up of The Band had comprised Randy Ciarlante, Jim Weider, Levon Helm, Garth Hudson, Richard Bell and Rick Danko. The death of Danko at the end of 1999 meant that of the five classic members, 'then there were two'. It sounded a sad death knell for a once truly great group.

How much Dylan owed The Band is an interesting question, and less discussed than how much they had owed him. He surely gained plenty. The long slog of the 1966 tour gave him priceless support, and for long enough to confirm for him that with the right back-up, the choice to go electric and play live with a group was absolutely the right decision in spite of the booing. The long cathartic Big Pink and Woodstock months brought him the benefit of a sustained informality in his working relationship with a bunch of resourceful musicians: and daily, casual exchange is what builds the deepest kind of intimacy in the easiest possible way. Perhaps too, Dylan learned something about singing with someone else. True, he had harmonised with various folkies in earlier years, and most especially with JOAN BAEZ. But folk wasn't rock, and Baez's voice and Dylan's were worlds apart. With Rick Danko, he found a surer kind of vocal partner and in a group setting: and he must surely have felt this, since he brought Danko forward to become his chosen partner. More generally, we can say that The Band gave Dylan every possible kind of solidity through his most perilous period; it's hard to imagine that any other unit could have served him better.

More generally still, The Band influenced everyone. THE GRATEFUL DEAD were pointed towards *Workingman's Dead* by The Band; ERIC CLAPTON was turning away from Blind Faith for the simple life of Derek & the Dominoes; CROSBY, Stills, Nash & YOUNG's *Déjà Vu* paid tribute to *The Band* even by copying its sleeve; and at the sessions for *Let It Be*, THE BEATLES played 'To Kingdom Come' and 'I Shall Be Released' and HARRISON and Lennon urged George Martin to make them sound like The Band. That, of course, was asking too much. But their legacy was everywhere. They had shown the possibilities of co-operation, of multi-instrumental and vocal flexibility, in a rock scene that had previously stressed the figurehead lead singer and the lone lead-guitar genius; they had brought their own model of 'the invisible republic' into public consciousness; they had helped bring us out of the city of alienation.

[Ronnie Hawkins & the Hawks: see **Hawkins, Ronnie**. The Canadian Squires: 'Uh-Uh-Uh' c/w 'Leave Me Alone' 1964, Ware 6002, NY, 1964 & Apex 76964, Toronto, 1965. Levon & the Hawks: 'The Stones I Throw' c/w 'He Don't Love You (And He'll Break Your Heart)', NY, 1965, Atco 6383, NY, 1965; 'Go Go, Liza Jane' c/w 'He Don't Love You (And He'll Break Your Heart)', NY, 1965, Atco 6625, 1968. Jaime Robbie Robertson, Rick Danko, Richard Manuel, Garth Hudson, Levon Helm: 'The Weight', NY, 12 Jan 1968, Capitol 2269 (promo single), NY, 1968. The Band: *Music from Big Pink*, NY Jan & LA Feb 1968, Capitol SKAO-2955, NY (ST 2955, London), 1968; *The Band*, Hollywood Mar–Apr & NY May–Jun 1969, Capitol STAO-132, NY (E-ST 132, London), 1969; *Stage Fright*, NY Jun & Woodstock Jun–Jul 1970, Capitol SW-425, NY (GO 2003, London), 1970; *Cahoots*, Bearsville, NY, Jul–Aug 1971, Capitol ST-651, NY (& London), 1971; *Rock of Ages*, NY, 28 Dec 1971–1 Jan 1972, Capitol SABB-11045, 1972; *Moondog Matinee*, Bearsville & LA, 1972–73, Capitol SW-112, 1973; *Northern Lights—Southern Cross*, Malibu & LA, Jun 1975, Capitol ST-11440, 1975; *Islands*, Malibu & NY, 1976, Capitol SO-11602, 1977; *The Last Waltz*, San Francisco, 25 Nov 1976 (up to a point), Warner Bros. 3WB-3146, NY, 1978: remastered 4-CD reissue with bonus tracks (incl. Dylan's 'Hazel'), Rhino/Warner Bros. 78278, US, 2002; *Jericho*, *nia*, Pyramid R2 71564, US, 1993; *High on the Hog*, Rhino/Pyramid 72404 US (Transatlantic TRA CD 228, Europe), 1996; *Jubilation*, Woodstock, spring 1998, River North Records CD 51416 1420 2, US, 1998; *The Band: A Musical History*, 5-CD + DVD set, EMI/Capitol CAP 77409, NY, 2005. (This includes a remastered Dylan & the Hawks: 'Just Like Tom Thumb's Blues' live in Liverpool, 14 May 1966.) *The Last Waltz* film, dir. Martin Scorsese, US, 1978; DVD remixed remastered issue with extras, MGM, US, 2002.

Barney Hoskyns, *Across the Great Divide: The Band & America*, London: Viking-Penguin, 1993 & New York: Hyperion, 1993 (the 'revised' update, London: Pimlico, 2003, is updated very little and its discography not at all). Size of basement from John Simon, interviewed by Lee Gabites, posted online on the crucial, all-encompassing and excellent unofficial Band website *http://theband.hiof.no*, to which the entry above is much indebted. Clinton Heylin, *Bob Dylan: The Complete Recording Sessions: 1960–1994*, New York: St. Martin's Press, pp.67–68. William Ruhlmann, on *www.allmusic.com*, quoted from *http://theband.hiof.no*. The Rev. Al Friston: 'The Night They Put The Band to Rest: *The Last Waltz* Revisited', Rock's Backpages (*www.rocksbackpages.com*), 26 Apr 2002. Thanks also to Peter Viney for much feedback to enquiries; quoted from e-mail to the present writer 18 Sep 2005.]

Bangs, Lester, the Black Panthers & Bob The *Desire* song 'Sara' includes 'Stayin' up for days in the Chelsea Hotel / Writin' "Sad-Eyed Lady of the Lowlands" for you'. The subject was memorably polemicised by rock critic Lester Bangs (1948–82) in a funny, wrong-headed froth of a review of *Desire*: '. . . if he really did spend days on end sitting up in the Chelsea sweating over lines like "your streetcar visions which you place on the grass", then he is stupider than we ever gave him credit for.'

This was from a piece titled 'Bob Dylan's Dalliance with Mafia Chic', from 1976. Bangs' phrase 'Mafia chic' picks up the coinage of Tom Wolfe from his book *Radical Chic and Mau-Mauing the Flak-Catchers*, 1970, in which he excoriated New York socialites for their dalliance with Black Power, focussing on the appearance of prominent Black Panthers at a Leonard Bernstein party.

Bangs, likewise, duly excoriates Bob Dylan. An alleged meeting in 1970 between Bob Dylan and Black Panthers Huey Newton and David Hilliard had been mooted by Dylan's first biographer, ANTHONY SCADUTO, in the *New York Times* in 1971, and discussed in 'A Profile of HOWARD ALK' by Dylan's third biographer, CLINTON HEYLIN (with research assistance by George Webber), in *All Across the Telegraph: A Bob Dylan Handbook*, 1987.

Leslie Conway Bangs, born in Escondido, California, on December 14, 1948, began writing freelance in 1969, starting with *Rolling Stone* but later for other music magazines, for the *Village Voice*, and for *Playboy* and *Penthouse*; his main influences were BEAT authors (though he often comes close to sounding like HUNTER S. THOMPSON). In 1973 he was banned from *Rolling Stone* by JANN WENNER for being 'disrespectful to musicians'. He died of an overdose on April 30, 1982.

[Lester Bangs: 'Bob Dylan's Dalliance with Mafia Chic', *Creem* no.7, Birmingham, MI, Apr 1976; republished Thomson & Gutman: *The Dylan Companion*, 1990. Anthony Scaduto: 'Won't You Listen to the Lambs, Bob Dylan?', *New York Times*, 28 Nov 1971. (Tom Wolfe's later essay on the same period, 'Funky Chic', is collected in *Mauve Gloves & Madmen, Clutter & Vine*, 1976.)]

Barker, Derek [1954 -] & Tracy [1963 -] Derek Gordon Barker was born in Tarporley, Cheshire, UK, on July 31, 1954. His wife Tracy was born in Coventry on March 29, 1963. Derek first noticed Dylan's work in the late 1960s but only became 'obsessive from 1978 on'. Tracy didn't become interested in Dylan till 1992. Between them, they run the longest-running extant Dylan fanzine, *Isis*, which began in September 1985 and has now published well over 120 issues, always under Derek Barker's editorship. Tracy started working with *Isis* in 1993. She handles the subscriptions, helps design, edit and lay out the magazine and she designs and maintains its website.

The first 17 issues were published as free photocopied newsletters, and though the magazine offers a variety of kinds of work its purpose has traditionally been to find and give out information rather than to offer critical assessment. Since February 1989, *Isis* has incorporated IAN WOODWARD's *The Wicked Messenger*, which acts as a near-daily log of Dylan news and rumour as it arrives. Because of the large-format size of the fanzine, and in its more recent incarnations its glossy paper, it is also an excellent outlet for Dylan photographs, though all too often squandering its photo pages on gruesome recent concert shots of dubious quality that capture Dylan looking like an aged Norman Vaughn. Though also notorious for its misspellings and misplaced apostrophes, *Isis* has in recent years expanded the breadth and depth of its writing, and Derek Barker himself has become a more than competent, articulate commentator.

As the level of interest in Dylan has increased, especially since 1996–97, the range of *Isis* activity has increased too, offering not only an active website but also starting to participate in CD releases and edit best-of anthologies. The magazine itself is sold through bookstores and record shops as well as direct to subscribers in over 30 countries.

Derek Barker edited *ISIS: A Bob Dylan Anthology* in 2001, with a revised edition appearing in 2004, the year before *Bob Dylan Anthology Volume 2: 20 Years of ISIS*. He has also been interviewed on TV and radio, has promoted two Dylan conventions and co-promoted four others, and now advises Christie's auction house in London and New York on the authenticity of Dylan memorabilia items. Derek and Tracy live in Warwickshire, England.

[Derek & Tracy Barker: *Isis*, Bedworth, UK & *www.bobdylanisis.com.* Derek Barker: *ISIS: A Bob Dylan Anthology*, London, Helter Skelter Publishing, 2001 & 2004; *Bob Dylan Anthology Volume 2: 20 Years of ISIS*, New Malden, UK: Chrome Dreams, 2005.]

***Basement Tapes, The* [1975]** This 17th album, a double-LP, marked the first official release of a version of the world's most bootlegged bootleg: material cut by Dylan and the Crackers / THE BAND up near Woodstock in 1967 during the long silence between *Blonde on Blonde* (and Dylan's motorcycle crash) in 1966 and *John Wesley Harding* in 1968. The core Dylan songs from these sessions actually do form a clear link between these two utterly different albums. They evince the same highly serious, precarious quest for a personal and universal salvation which marked out the *John Wesley Harding* collection–yet they are soaked in the same blocked confusion and turmoil as *Blonde on Blonde*.

'Tears of Rage', for example, is a halfway house between, say, 'One of Us Must Know (Sooner or Later)' and 'I Dreamed I Saw St. Augustine'. There is also a unique, radical corpus of spacey yet exuberant music here, as on 'Crash on the Levee (Down in the Flood)', 'Please Mrs. Henry' and 'Million Dollar Bash'. Essential stuff, badly compiled.

The interspersed tracks by The Band alone disrupt the unity of Dylan material, much more of which should have been here. Indeed The Band's tracks are thoroughly dodgy, even including one, 'Bessie Smith', which wasn't recorded in this period at all but was an outtake from four years later, from their 1971 album *Cahoots*.

The authentic 1967 sessions had also included a wealth of traditional material revisited, the existence of which was far less known at the time of this release than became apparent in the 1990s, when it was widely circulated and became the main subject of GREIL MARCUS' book *Invisible Republic*, 1997.

Key Dylan-composed items missing include 'I Shall Be Released' and 'This Wheel's on Fire'. And having kept all these 1967 recordings unreleased all through the aeons from 1967 to the mid-1970s, this album was then issued curiously swiftly after the release of *Blood on the Tracks*. There was also something disquieting about the specially posed cover photos (by Reid Miles, in the basement of the YMCA in LA), which seemed to reduce jostling figures of myth and imagination to a callow am-dram tableau–a suggestion here that Dylan was at once packaging and repackaging his own myth. As well as Dylan, The Band and people dressed as song 'characters', others on camera include NEIL YOUNG and DAVID BLUE.

The double-album received fine reviews; John Rockwell in the *New York Times* declared it 'The greatest album in the history of popular American music.' But it wasn't, and for all the riches within it, all of which are presented out of context, it was a shamefully poor representation of an astonishingly creative, important period in this great artist's working life.

[Recorded West Saugerties, NY (& possibly Woodstock, NY), Jun–Aug & Sep–Nov 1967; released as stereo 2-LP set, Columbia C2 33682 (CBS 88147 in UK), 26 Jun or 1 Jul 1975. *New York Times* review quoted in Robert Shelton, *No Direction Home: The Life and Music of Bob Dylan*, 1986, Penguin edn., p.383.]

Baudelaire, Charles [1821 - 1867] Charles Baudelaire was born in Paris on April 9, 1821. The first great poet of the modern city, he spent almost his entire adult life in Paris on inherited money, producing the enormously influential poetry collection *Les Fleurs du Mal* (*Flowers of Evil*) in 1857, plus other works including the autobiographical novella *La Fanfarlo*, 1847, and the essays collection *Les Paradis Artificiels*, 1860.

Along with the verse of EDGAR ALLAN POE, Baudelaire's poetry, especially his sonnet 'Correspondances', was an important precursor of the symbolist movement, initiated by VERLAINE and Mallarmé, which used symbols to explore and evoke cross-currents and 'illogical' affinities, especially between the senses.

Drugs commonly make this sense-mingling prevalent and vivid. As Kenneth Allsop noted, Baudelaire 'cherished a particular trick of hashish, familiar in mechanised form to the audiences of today's electronic acid rock: the infusion of the senses one with another.' He notes that 'Baudelaire started experimenting with opium while a Sorbonne student, emulating Poe's saturation of his work with the fumes and furies of opium—the "épouvantable mariage de l'homme avec lui-même" was a constant theme of Poe's which Baudelaire found enthralling.'

Compare this with Bob Dylan's 1966 interview comments: 'I wouldn't advise anyone to use drugs. . . . But opium and hash and pot—now, those things aren't drugs; they just bend your mind a little. I think *everybody's* mind should be bent once in a while.' (Oddly, he went on to say this: 'Not by LSD, though. LSD is medicine—a different kind of medicine. It makes you aware of the universe so to speak; you realize how foolish *objects* are. But LSD is not for groovy people; it's for mad, hateful people who want revenge. . . . They ought to use it at the Geneva Convention.')

Dylan's mention of Baudelaire on the terrific sleevenotes to *Planet Waves* (see ***Planet Waves*, the disappearing sleevenotes**) implies that he was struck by the poet very early on: 'Duluth—where Baudelaire Lived and Goya cashed in his Chips, where Joshua brought the house down!', though in the interviews for his *Biograph* box set, he says that 'Suzie Rotolo, a girlfriend of mine in New York, later turned me on to all the French poets . . .'

WISSOLIK & McGRATH's *Bob Dylan's Words*, 1994, suggests a direct parallel between lines in 'Idiot Wind'—'One day you'll be in the ditch, flies buzzin' around your eyes / Blood on your saddle . . . blowing through the flowers on your tomb'—and a passage from Baudelaire's *Les Fleurs du Mal* poem 'The Carcass', in which two lovers see the rotting corpse of an animal in the road: 'The flies buzzed and hissed on these filthy guts . . . / And you, in your turn, will be rotten as this . . . / under the weeds / under blossoming grass'. Wissolik & McGrath suggest too a direct correspondence between lines from Dylan's '11 Outlined Epitaphs'—'cats across the roof / mad in love / scream into the drainpipes'—and a passage from Baudelaire's 'Spleen LXXVII': 'My cat . . . wails in the rain-spouts like a swollen ghost.' (These translations may or may not be taken from *An Anthology of French Poetry from Nerval to Valery*, ed. Angel Flores, 1958, which Wissolik & McGrath suggest as the volume Dylan 'probably used in the early 1960s'.)

In *Chronicles Volume One*, the only mention of Baudelaire comes in a description of DANIEL LANOIS, the record producer Dylan was working with for the first time in the late 1980s, in New Orleans; here he reports without comment that 'Dan . . . said that he'd hung around in Texas libraries reading RIMBAUD and Baudelaire to get his language down.'

Baudelaire moved from Paris to Brussels in search of a publisher in 1863 and while there suffered a series of strokes. He returned to Paris in 1867 and died there eight weeks later, in his mother's arms, on August 31.

[Kenneth Allsop, 'The Technicolor Wasteland: on Drugs and Literature', *Encounter*, vol.32, no.3, US, Mar 1969. Bob Dylan: 'The Playboy Interview: Bob Dylan: A Candid Conversation with the Iconoclastic Idol of the Folk-Rock Set', *Playboy*, Chicago, Mar 1966; *Chronicles Volume One*, p.182.]

Bauldie, John [1949 - 1996] John Stewart Bauldie was born on August 23, 1949. He is best known as the founder and editor of *The Telegraph*, the finest Dylan fanzine there's ever been, and one of the earliest and longest running. It was the best because of the vision of what it could be, which Bauldie kept in his head, and constantly extended, and conjured into reality, starting from a stapled booklet of typed print on cheap paper, all black and white, totalling 20 small pages, in November 1981, and becoming a professional-looking, authoritative but quirky, properly bound quarterly in full colour.

Early on, though, *The Telegraph* became more than a publication: it became an essential part of the Dylan follower's world. This happened before the internet and the mobile phone—indeed in a world that had only recently acquired the fax machine. Dylan's 1978 European tour, his first for 12 years, was a great stimulus to a renewed need for aficionados to build means of contact and camaraderie. And then a first Bob Dylan Convention took place, in Manchester (conveniently close to Bauldie's home) in 1979.

John Bauldie's immense contribution began in the wake of these events, though he had been listening to Dylan since 1964 and had started collecting taped rarities from late 1969, stimulated by an article by GREIL MARCUS in *Rolling Stone* that opened John's eyes to the existence of such things. He wrote to Marcus, who sent him a tape of Dylan's 1966 Liverpool concert to start him off collecting. He was aided by 'two good friends, Rob Griffith and MICHAEL KROGSGAARD' and encouraged by coming across the first American fanzine,

Talkin' Bob Zimmerman Blues, run by BRYAN STYBLE. It folded in 1979, just when that first Dylan convention was happening. As John put it: 'Here were 600 people whose interest had brought them from all over the world: here were writers and critics who didn't have a forum; here were fans who were not kept informed by an increasingly negligent music press.'

Bauldie's founding idea was thus to create a distribution network to circulate news and exchange information, and to sneak a quality Dylan journal into existence on the back of it. This outfit became Wanted Man, The Bob Dylan Information Service, involving a number of fans in north-west England, and it was this outfit that published *The Telegraph*, offered a telephone hotline and distributed IAN WOODWARD's incessant logging of Dylan news and rumour, *The Wicked Messenger*. In the early years, CLINTON HEYLIN was its news editor. For a while, too, there was a Dylan mail-order bookselling unit, the Wanted Man Bookshelf, but this was eventually replaced by a similar but separate enterprise, My Back Pages, run by Dave Heath and Dave Dingle. For some time the latter also took over editorial control of an annual summer issue of *The Telegraph* while John Bauldie holidayed in Greece; these issues always emphasised how crucial Bauldie himself was to its character. His achievement as editor was multi-skilled but at its core was an ability to keep the whole thing sharp and sane—sane in spite of the necessary fanaticism.

He was not, himself, interested solely in Bob Dylan. He was also keen on PHIL OCHS, DAVID BLUE, NEIL YOUNG, BRUCE SPRINGSTEEN, ROGER McGUINN and a number of other singer-songwriters, and was himself an amateur guitarist and songwriter. He was also a football devotee with a life-long loyalty to the romantically named Bolton Wanderers. A well-educated man, he had been a lecturer in English Literature at a higher-education college in the north of England.

John Bauldie's own writing, as well as his editing, was a vital part of his Dylan enterprise and in the magazine's quest for an ever-improving quality of contribution, he led by example, with work that was witty and generous-minded yet rigorous and brightly acute, whether it was essays about Dylan's work, investigations into events like the 1966 motorcycle crash or pieces that fused the two, as for instance with a scrutiny of the *Desire* album collaboration between Dylan and JACQUES LEVY.

Around the time of the filming of the *Hearts of Fire* movie, John and the magazine moved to London and he took a job working on the editorial side of *Q* magazine, becoming its Hi-Fi Editor before leaving, shortly before his death, to move across to another national glossy magazine, *House and Garden*.

By this point, he was also the author and editor of a number of Dylan books and booklets, the first of which had been booklet no.2 in his own Wanted Man Study Series, an essay on *Bob Dylan and* Desire. In 1987 he co-edited with MICHAEL GRAY the first best-of selection from the magazine, *All Across the Telegraph: A Bob Dylan Handbook*, and later came the second volume, edited by Bauldie alone, *Wanted Man: In Search of Bob Dylan*. In 1991, with veteran British music journalist PATRICK HUMPHRIES, he produced the postmodernly titled *Oh No! Not Another Bob Dylan Book*, renamed *Absolutely Dylan: An Illustrated Biography* for the US market. A worthier work, though disappointing in its design and print quality, was the fascinating and important self-published limited-edition hardback *The Ghost of Electricity*, 1988, about the Dylan of the 1966 tour (republished in smaller-format paperback in 1993). There was also a collection of John's on-the-road pieces into the small-print-run 90-page book *Diary of a Bobcat*, 1995.

Finally, however, Bauldie became the first Dylan writer honoured with recognition by Dylan's own office when he was asked to produce—under near-impossible conditions—a booklet of liner-notes for the first of the official Bootleg Series of Dylan record releases, the *Bootleg Series Vols. 1–3*: resulting in the work of his that will have been by far the most widely read, and which almost won him a Grammy. It can still be accessed on the Dylan website, *www.bobdylan.com*.

John Bauldie was killed with four others in a helicopter crash late on the evening of October 22, 1996 while traveling back to London from a football match in which his beloved Bolton Wanderers had just beaten Chelsea, whose Vice-Chairman had chartered the helicopter that killed them. An inquest returned a verdict of accidental death on February 25, 1998—by which time the UK civil aviation authorities had already put in place extra safety rules for helicopter flights, prompted by this crash. John Bauldie was 47. The ownership of his literary estate is still in doubt.

See also ***Bridge, The***.

[John Bauldie: *Bob Dylan and* Desire, Wanted Man Study Series no.2 (Bury, UK: 1983); *The Ghost of Electricity* (Romford, UK: self-published, 1988); *Wanted Man: In Search of Bob Dylan* (London: Black Spring Press, 1990); liner-notes, the *Bootleg Series Vols. 1–3*, Columbia Legacy, NY, 1991; *Diary of a Bobcat* (Romford: Wanted Man, 1995). Co-editor with Michael Gray: *All Across the Telegraph: A Bob Dylan Handbook* (London: W.H. Allen, 1987); and co-author with Patrick Humphries: *Oh No! Not Another Bob Dylan Book* (UK: Square One Books, 1991), aka *Absolutely Dylan: An Illustrated Biography* (New York: Viking Studio Books, 1991). Editor of *The Telegraph*, first from Bury and then Romford, UK, 1981–96. The quotes from John Bauldie above are taken from his article 'Introduction: All Across the What?', intended for inclusion in *All Across the Telegraph*, ibid, but unused. A contents list of each issue of *The Telegraph* is still online at *www.expecting*

rain.com/dok/div/telegraph/pasttishes.html, though its hyperlinks no longer work.]

Baxter, Bucky [1955 -] William Baxter was born in Melbourne, Florida, in 1955, went to junior high in Philadelphia (where he played in his first band in 1968); he could already play oboe, clarinet and guitar, but it was hearing JIMI HENDRIX that prompted him to take music seriously as a career, and after hearing NEIL YOUNG's *After the Gold Rush* he took pedal steel lessons from Ernest Tubb's steel man Buddy Carlton. Eventually, after mixed success and much sticking at it, he joined the Steve Earle Band, first recording with them on Earle's 1986 début album, *Guitar Town*. He also played on the 1988 R.E.M. album *Green*, among other things, but remained with Steve Earle–and was still in Earle's band when it was support act to Dylan for part of the summer 1989 leg of the Never-Ending Tour. Baxter was asked on stage towards the end of Dylan's set in Springfield, Illinois, that August 19 and played pedal steel on 'I Shall Be Released' and 'Like a Rolling Stone'. Six nights later he returned for the first of four consecutive Dylan sets in New Orleans, Texas and New Mexico (August 25, 26, 27 and 29), playing on four songs each time.

Dylan eventually lured him into his own band, in which he débuted in Perth, Australia, on March 18, 1992. His last Dylan concert was in Munich, Germany, on May 2, 1999: the last date before a month's break and the start of Dylan's touring with PAUL SIMON. Between 1992 and 1999, Baxter played behind Dylan a formidable 730 times (739, if you count non-NET occasions too, including the *MTV Unplugged* débacle of 1995). He also played dobro and pedal steel on the album *Time Out of Mind*.

Asked afterwards by *ON THE TRACKS* whether he had been 'buddies' with Bob, he answered: 'No, I didn't really try to be. I just worked for him. And we had a good working relationship . . . but I never went to his house for Thanksgiving, or anything. I think that's why I lasted so long–I conducted myself professionally and let him be.' It could be said that he did more than that. He certainly added colour to the band's sound, and though his pedal steel playing was flexible enough to accommodate many kinds of song, he was really the first to tip the Never-Ending Tour Band towards the kind of country emphasis it has retained ever since. Not everyone feels unmitigated enthusiasm for that.

Baxter remains a producer. His studio is out in the woods around Nashville, thanks partly to one of his artists, Welsh ex-Catatonia singer Cerys Matthews. 'When I ended up on his doorstep,' she says, 'all he had was a little portable four-track, which wasn't what I had in mind. Then he started building a pond. I said to him: "What about the studio?" He said, "You just write some songs, and give me a hand with this." I thought I was going to a nice studio in the woods. I didn't realise I would be helping to build it.'

[Baxter quote from interview by Scott Marshall, *On the Tracks* no.20, *nia*, seen online 14 Jul 2005 at *www.b-dylan.com/pages/samples/buckybaxter.html*. Cerys Matthews quote from Will Hodgkinson interview, *The Guardian*, London, 13 Jun 2003.]

Bayer Sager, Carole [1947 -] Carole Bayer Sager was born on March 8, 1947 (though 1946 is sometimes suggested) in New York City, where she grew up, becoming a hit songwriter (mostly a lyricist) who straddles the divide between musicals and pop. Her first music-publishing deal was gained while she was still a schoolgirl and her first hit was the co-written 'A Groovy Kind of Love', a moronically simple and horribly catchy song by British group the Mindbenders (who couldn't have bent a note, let alone anybody's mind). When she was given a record deal and made her début album in 1977, *Carole Bayer Sager*, it went platinum, thanks to its inclusion of 'You're Moving Out Today', an international no.1 hit. She also wrote a Leo Sayer transatlantic no.1, 'When I Need You', and co-wrote Melissa Manchester's 'Midnight Blue'. It all seems a long time ago.

After being married to Marvin Hamlisch–with whom she wrote 'Nobody Does It Better', Carly Simon's stentorian but sinuous hit from the 1977 James Bond movie *The Spy Who Loved Me*–she married Burt Bacharach instead, and with him wrote another mega-seller by various artists, 'That's What Friends Are For', which became a significant fund-raiser for AIDS research when covered in 1985 by the terrifying team of Dionne Warwick, Gladys Knight, ELTON JOHN and STEVIE WONDER. Carole Bager Sayer's songs have also been recorded by everyone from Michael Jackson to FRANK SINATRA and from BETTE MIDLER to the Doobie Brothers. She and Bacharach divorced in 1991, though not before he *and* Marvin Hamlisch had worked on her album *Sometimes Late at Night*. She is now married to a former Warner Brothers chairperson with baseball-team connections, and lives in LA.

In 1986 she and Bob Dylan wrote one song together, 'Under Your Spell'–although 'together' is hardly the word. She told biographer HOWARD SOUNES that he strummed the guitar and she wrote in a notepad, but added: 'Although it was really exciting, it was probably one of the least collaborative experiences I had with anybody. It was kind of like going back to grade school when you are given a test and you put your hand over your work so nobody would copy it.' Dylan recorded and released it on that year's *Knocked Out Loaded*, and Sounes writes that it was only 'when she received an advance copy of the song that Bayer Sager found out which of her ideas Bob had used. Aside from the title . . . virtually none of the lyrics were hers. Yet Bob said he would never have written the song without her.'

It was immaculately sung but shifty pop, and it includes the line that gives the album its title, 'I was knocked out and loaded in the naked night.' It also includes a line that only Dylan could have written. Anyone else would have offered 'You'll never get rid of me as long as I'm alive'; Dylan has the delightfully more arrogant touch of 'You'll never get rid of me as long as you're alive'.

[Carole Bayer Sager: *Carole Bayer Sager*, Elektra K 52059, US, 1977; 'You're Moving Out Today', Elektra 45422, US, 1977; *Sometimes Late at Night*, Boardwalk FW 37069, US, 1981. The Mindbenders: 'Groovy Kind of Love', Fontana TF644, UK, 1966. Melissa Manchester: 'Midnight Blue', Arista 0116, US, 1975. Leo Sayer: 'When I Need You', Warner Bros. 8332, US, 1977. Carly Simon: 'Nobody Does It Better', Elektra 45413, 1977. Dionne Warwick, Gladys Knight, Elton John & Stevie Wonder: 'That's What Friends Are For', Arista AS1-9422, US, 1985. Howard Sounes, *Down the Highway: A Life of Bob Dylan*, New York: Grove Press, 2001, Chapter 9, manuscript p.444.]

Beatles, the A pop group. See **Harrison, George**; **Lennon, John**; **McCartney, Paul**; and **Starr, Ringo**. See also **Aronowitz, Al**.

Beats, the KENNETH PATCHEN, JACK KEROUAC, LAWRENCE FERLINGHETTI, ALLEN GINSBERG and those like them and around them constructed (drawing heavily on influences like WILLIAM CARLOS WILLIAMS and **e.e. cummings**) the genre of the Beat Poets—indeed they became known as the Beat Generation. It was more than poetry: it was a way of life. Hence, here, the more general name 'the Beats'. Anyone could join.

It was an artistic storm that Dylan, some years later, seemed so avant-garde in visiting upon a mass market and a new generation. The Dylan of 1965–66 swims in a milieu taken from these men and their contemporaries. In a way all Dylan did with it was to put it up on stage with a guitar. His greatness lies in the way he did that, the cohesive, individual voice with which he re-presented it and the brilliance of his timing in doing so. There was also the intelligence with which he allowed the influence of the Beats to jostle along, contemporaneously, with a torrent of other 20th century artistic influences.

In 1985 he made it clear that he was well aware of how all this played together inside his life and his art. With *Biograph*'s release came a warm memorialising (on the sleevenotes) of all these influences:

> 'Minneapolis . . . I came out of the wilderness and just naturally fell in with the beat scene, the Bohemian, BeBop crowd, it was all pretty much connected . . . people just passed through, really, carrying horns, guitars, suitcases, whatever, just like the stories you hear, free love, wine, poetry, nobody had any money anyway . . . there were a lot of house parties. . . . There were always a lot of poems recited—"Into the room people come and go talking of Michelangelo, measuring their lives in coffee spoons" . . . "What I'd like to know is what do you think of your blue-eyed boy now, Mr. Death". T.S. ELIOT, e.e. cummings. It was sort of like that and it woke me up. . . . Jack Kerouac, Ginsberg, CORSO and Ferlinghetti—'Gasoline', 'Coney Island of the Mind', . . . oh man, it was wild—"I saw the best minds of my generation destroyed by madness": that said more to me than any of the stuff I'd been raised on . . . whatever was happening of any real value was . . . sort of hidden from view and it would be years before the media would be able to recognize it and choke-hold it and reduce it to silliness. Anyway, I got in at the tail-end of that and it was magic . . . it had just as big an impact on me as ELVIS PRESLEY. POUND, Camus, T.S. Eliot, e.e. cummings, mostly expatriate Americans who were off in Paris and Tangiers. Burroughs, "Nova Express", John Rechy, Gary Snyder, Ferlinghetti, "Pictures From the Gone World", the newer poets and folk music, jazz, Monk, Coltrane, SONNY and BROWNIE, BIG BILL BROONZY, Charlie Christian . . . it all left the rest of everything in the dust . . .'

In *Chronicles Volume One*, 2004, Dylan adds footnotes, as it were, noting that folk songs 'automatically went up against the grain' of all the things the Beats regarded as 'the devil . . . bourgeois conventionality, social artificiality and the man in the gray flannel suit.' He also notes of the Beats' musical preferences that they 'tolerated folk music, but they really didn't like it. They listened exclusively to modern jazz, bebop.'

Very interesting to re-encounter what DAVE VAN RONK told ROBERT SHELTON about Dylan: 'Bobby is very much a product of the beat generation. . . . You are not going to see any more like him. Bobby came into beat poetry just at the very tail end. He towers above all of them, except perhaps Ginsberg.'

[*Gasoline* is by Gregory Corso, 1958. 'I saw the best minds of my generation destroyed by madness' is the most frequently quoted line (it is the main part of the opening line) from Ginsberg's *Howl*; *Nova Express* is by William Burroughs, 1964; *Pictures from the Gone World* is Ferlinghetti's first book of poetry, 1955. It is incorporated into his *A Coney Island of the Mind*, 1958. Bob Dylan: *Chronicles Volume One*, pp.247–48 & p.48. Robert Shelton, *No Direction Home: The Life and Music of Bob Dylan*, 1986, Penguin edn., p.99.]

Beckett, Barry [1943 -] Barry Beckett was born in Birmingham, Alabama, on February 4, 1943. He started his musical life as a pianist for a dancing school, but moved on to become a keyboards session player and eventually a record producer. He first became involved with Rick Hall's Fame studio, on a session for James & Bobby Purify, and then replaced SPOONER OLDHAM in the Muscle Shoals band. He co-produced Mel & Tim and his later production credits include work with JOAN BAEZ, Joe Cocker, Etta James, JOHN PRINE, Delbert McClinton, Alabama, the STAPLE SINGERS and McGUINN-Hillman.

Beckett was co-producing with JERRY WEXLER when, in 1979, Dylan called on Wexler to produce the *Slow Train Coming* sessions in the Muscle Shoals studio in Sheffield, Alabama. Beckett not only co-produced the album but played piano and organ throughout. He did not go on the road as a gospel tour musician behind Dylan, but he was back in the studio with him in February 1980 to co-produce, again with Wexler, the album *Saved*, on which he was replaced on keyboards by Spooner Oldham and TERRY YOUNG after the session of February 12, 1980 and so does not play on 'Saving Grace', 'Pressing On', 'In the Garden', 'Are You Ready?' or 'Covenant Woman', but does play on the album's title track and on 'Solid Rock', 'What Can I Do for You?' and 'Satisfied Mind'. On the album liner notes Beckett is billed as co-producer and as 'special guest artist'.

In 1985 Beckett moved to Nashville, working with Warner Brothers' A&R department before running an independent production company. He is also a partner in BTM Records. He has never worked with Dylan again since the *Saved* sessions.

Beecher, Bonnie [1941 -] See **Romney, Jahanara.**

***Before the Flood* [1974]** From Dylan's huge 1974 North American 'come-back tour' with THE BAND, on which it seemed a surprise, at the time, that he revisited a large number of his old songs, this album, Dylan's 15th, was his first 'live' album. (It was also the second and last for David Geffen's Asylum label.) The title is said to be the English translation of the Yiddish phrase 'Farn Mabul', the title of a trilogy of novels by Sholem Asch (1880–1957), published 1929–31 and translated into English as *Three Cities*, 1933. Asch was the father of MOSES ASCH, founder of Folkways Records.

Before the Flood was a double-LP of confident, brash rock'n'roll Dylan: a record of an artist exhilarated by being back on stage after a long absence, and in the process largely ignoring the differences between one song and another. There is an over-speedy, break-neck quality here that does little justice to the lyrics and has Dylan mainly just throwing back his head and yelling. It has never been a favourite of anyone keen on Bob Dylan, and he has himself bad-mouthed the atmosphere that obtained on the tour itself, which he recognised accorded a questionable primacy to energy. Don't look to this album for any of the subtlety, nuance or understatement which have always been hallmarks of Dylan's genius.

[Recorded at concerts in NY, 30 Jan and Inglewood, CA, 13 & 14 Feb 1974; released as 2-LP set, Asylum AB 201 (Island IDBD 1 in UK), 20 Jun 1974.]

being unable to die 'Can you imagine the darkness that will fall from on high,' asks Dylan, clearly enjoying imagining it himself, especially the torture, 'when men will pray to God to kill them and they won't be able to die?'

This dark scenario, on 'Precious Angel', on the 1979 'Born Again' album *Slow Train Coming*, is laid out in both the Old Testament and the New. Job 3:20–22 speaks of those '. . . bitter in soul; Which long for death, but it cometh not; and dig for it more than for hid treasures; Which rejoice exceedingly, and are glad, when they can find the grave . . .'; and Revelation 9:6 looks forward (like Dylan) to a time of squirming: 'And in those days shall men seek death, and shall not find it; and shall desire to die, and death shall flee from them.'

This is a prospect Dylan refers to 16 years earlier, in 'Seven Curses', and again in 1965 on 'Gates of Eden', though with a healthier detachment on this occasion, when he sings of 'Leaving men wholly, totally free / To do anything they wish to do but die / And there are no trials inside the gates of Eden.'

Belafonte, Harry [1927 -] Harold George Belafonte was born on March 1, 1927 in Harlem, New York City, though his father was from Martinique and his mother from Jamaica. At the age of eight he and his brother Dennis were sent to school in Jamaica (reports vary as to whether their mother went with them or sent them away to boarding school). He returned to the US to attend high school but dropped out at 17 and served in the US Navy during World War II.

First returning to civilian life as a maintenance man, he became a highly distinguished and politicised musician and actor. His first RCA album, in 1954, was *Mark Twain and Other Folk Favorites*; his third, *Calypso* in 1956, was the first album to sell over a million copies, spent 31 weeks at the top of the *Billboard* charts, started the calypso craze and made him forever associated with 'Day-O', aka 'The Banana Boat Song'. His first film rôle was in 1953's goody-goody movie *Bright Road*, but 1959's *Odds Against Tomorrow*, which he co-produced, was the real thing, and the first American film noir to star a noir American.

He was an early supporter of Martin Luther King Jr. and the civil rights movement, and grew more radical, rather than less, as he aged, despite being festooned with awards and official appointments (like being made a UNICEF goodwill ambassador in 1987). On the syndicated daily radio and TV news program 'Democracy Now!', he once quoted Malcolm X on modern slave equivalents: 'There was two kinds of slaves. There was the house Negro and the field Negro. The house Negroes, they lived in the house with master, they dressed pretty good, they ate good 'cause they ate his food and what he left. . . . In those days he was called a "house nigger". And that's what we call him today, because we've still got some house niggers running around here.' And on a San Diego radio station in October 2002, Belafonte called Colin Powell and Condoleezza Rice 'house slaves' serving war-mongering master George W. Bush. Accepting the Human Rights Award for 2004 from the San Francisco-based group Global Exchange, he said in his acceptance speech: 'We have got to bring Corporate America to its knees, not just in defeat but perhaps in prayer. To understand that we can come together, we can make a difference, a world that is filled with people who are nourished, a world that is filled with people who can read and write and debate and have exchange and dialogue.'

In 2005 he compared the Bush administration to the Third Reich. Three years earlier he said of his United Nations work: 'I go to places where enormous upheaval and pain and anguish exist. And a lot of it exists based upon American policy. Whom we support, whom we support as heads of state, what countries we've helped to overthrow, what leaders we've helped to diminish because they did not fit the mold we think they should fit, no matter how ill advised that thought may be.'

Belafonte also heads a group called the Urban Peace Movement, and 20 per cent of his income goes to the Belafonte Foundation of Music and Art, which helps young blacks study for careers in the arts.

Dylan fans used to believe that Bob played harmonica on only one track (the title track, as it happened) of the Belafonte album *Midnight Special* because all the re-takes drove him to impatient despair; the assumption was that Dylan found Belafonte tedious, ponderous, over-polished, too showbiz: a mainstream drag for whom he had no respect. It's hard to pin down a source for this belief, but it was widespread for many years. In *Chronicles Volume One*, Dylan blew this rumour out of the water with a surprisingly long and strong tribute to Belafonte, as folk artist, actor and human being. He wrote:

> 'Harry was the best balladeer in the land and everybody knew it. He was a fantastic artist, sang about lovers and slaves—chain gang workers, saints and sinners and children. His repertoire was full of old folk songs . . . all arranged in a way that appealed to a wide audience, much wider than the Kingston Trio. Harry had learned songs directly from LEADBELLY and WOODY GUTHRIE . . . one of his records, *Belafonte Sings of the Caribbean*, had even sold a million copies. He was a movie star, too . . . an authentic tough guy . . . dramatic and intense on the screen. . . . In the movie *Odds Against Tomorrow*, you forget he's an actor, you forget he's Harry Belafonte. His presence and magnitude was so wide. . . . As a performer, he broke all attendance records. He could play to a packed house at Carnegie Hall and then the next day he might appear at a garment center union rally. To Harry, it didn't make any difference. People were people. He had ideals and made you feel you're a part of the human race. There never was a performer who crossed so many lines as Harry. He appealed to everybody, whether they were steelworkers or symphony patrons or bobby-soxers, even children—everybody. He had that rare ability. Somewhere he had said that he didn't like to go on television, because he didn't think his music could be represented well on a small screen, and he was probably right. Everything about him was gigantic. The folk purists had a problem with him, but Harry—who could have kicked the shit out of all of them—couldn't be bothered, said that all folksingers were interpreters, said it in a public way as if someone had summoned him to set the record straight. . . . I could identify with Harry in all kinds of ways. Sometime in the past, he had been barred from the door of the world famous nightclub the Copacabana because of his color, and then later he'd be headlining the joint. You've got to wonder how that would make somebody feel emotionally. Astoundingly . . . I'd be making my professional recording début with Harry, playing harmonica on one of his albums. . . . With Belafonte I felt like I'd become anointed in some kind of way. . . . Harry was that rare type of character that radiates greatness, and you hope that some of it rubs off on you. The man commands respect. You know he never took the easy path, though he could have.'

Despite Dylan's comments, Belafonte was not always averse to TV. When he became the first black American to win an Emmy award, it was for his first TV special, 'Tonight with Harry Belafonte'.

Belafonte and Dylan came together again after a gap of over 20 years when both appeared on Live Aid and sang on the fund-raising single 'We Are the World' in 1985.

[Harry Belafonte: 'Day-O', NY, 20 Oct 1955, *Calypso*, RCA LPM1150, NY, 1956; 'Midnight Special' (w/ Dylan on harmonica; 20 takes; 1 on LP), NY, 2 Feb 1962, *Midnight Special*, RCA LMP 2449 (mono) & LSP 2449, NY, Mar 1962. *Bright Road*, dir. Gerald Mayer, MGM, US, 1953; *Odds Against Tomorrow*, dir. William Wise, co-prod. Harry Belafonte, United Artists, US, 1959. Bob Dylan: *Chronicles Volume One*, pp.68–69. Sources include the African American Registry; Wikipedia, online 23 Oct 2005 at *http://en.wikipedia.org/wiki/Harry_Belafonte*; the Democracy Now! report *www.democracynow.org/article.pl?sid=04/06/15/1410245*, online ditto, and the 'Harry Belafonte & Friends' discography online ditto at *www.akh.se/harbel/index.htm*.]

'Belle Isle' 'Belle Isle' is a terrific traditional song, probably Celtic in origin, that is, not untypically, 'a model of non-linear narrative', in Bill Damon's phrase—and it may be the highlight of the *Self Portrait* album. Its land of origin may be uncertain but as CHRISTER SVENSSON pointed out in a fanzine in 1983, Dylan probably first came across the song in *Sing Out!* magazine's booklet *Reprints from* Sing Out! *Volume 9*, New York, 1966; this also includes 'Copper Kettle', 'It Hurts Me Too' (here titled 'When Things Go Wrong with You') and 'Little Sadie', all also on *Self Portrait*.

In Dylan's canon it also rubs shoulders with the much earlier, beautiful and self-penned 'Boots of Spanish Leather'. They are both love *dialogues*, the latter ending with an estrangement and 'Belle Isle' ending as if its sequel, with an imagined spiritual reconciliation: a neatening-up of existential history. Yet 'Belle Isle' is also self-sufficient and self-contained. Like an island, in fact.

The tune flows out lightly and gracefully, like the gown billowing out around the maiden in the story; but the accompanying strings are sombre: more so than any appropriate Celtic mist would demand. Dylan treats the subject and the tradition it springs from with respect and a sympathetic mockery simultaneously; yet there is also a tone in his voice that takes up that foreboding suggestion in the strings: a darker presence around the edges of this Romance.

This disperses for a little while near the end (before the strings impinge to bring it back again) when the full sunshine of Dylan's comic delivery bursts through: 'Young maiden I wish not to banter / 'Tis true I come here in disguise / I came here to fulfil my last promise / And hoped to give you a surprise! / I own you're a maid I love dearly / And you've been in my heart all the while . . .'

Dylan singing these archaisms is the aural equivalent of 'A Sight to Be Seen'. The second line, with its force falling so gleefully on 'disguise', makes it radiantly clear how far into the Celtic story-world Dylan is taking us, while the third line has a well-contrived calming influence—its words float down in a gentle spiral—so that the imminent absurdity of what follows doesn't overbalance and come too soon. The fourth line brings the fall: that ludicrously bad distribution of syllables, the awfulness of the rhyme and the bathos of the hope expressed (itself accentuated by the rush of syllables given over to its expression). It has all been perfectly timed. It is brilliant clowning, like that unbalanced line from 'Leopard-Skin Pill-Box Hat', 'You know it balances on your head just like a mattress balances on a bottle of wine'. With the lines that follow, all is restored. That 'I own' enacts the first flourish towards a restoration, as Dylan's voice gently hams up a bewildered search for the right note; the hush through 'you're a maid I' begins to get it back; the slowing-down on 'love' gives the necessary foothold; 'de-e-ear-ly' acts as one last wobble; 'And you've bin in my heart' is oh-so-nearly back in balance; and the eventual resolve of the voice's note with the music, at the end of 'all the while', announces the firm restoration of the balance. So then, as the emphasised beat comes down on 'me' in the line that follows—'For me there is no other damsel' (where the voice and the music are precisely synchronised)—Dylan resets the tone of the song, right there at the end. In the music that follows to close over the song, Dylan draws all its elements together: the sombre quality, the humour and the traditional Romance.

The sum of these parts is, in 'Belle Isle', mystery. And mystery, as Dylan said in 1966, 'is a fact, a traditional fact . . . traditional music is too unreal to die. It doesn't need to be protected. Nobody's going to hurt it. . . . All these songs about roses growing out of people's brains and lovers who are really geese and swans who turn into angels—they're not going to die.'

[Bill Damon, 'Herewith, a Second Look at *Self Portrait*', *Rolling Stone*, 3 Sep 1970, San Francisco. For a full discussion of the song's origins, see Michael Gray, 'Back to Belle Isle', *Telegraph* no. 29, Romford, UK, spring 1988 & follow-up correspondence in subsequent issues, or Michael Gray, 'Grubbing for a Moderate Jewel: In Search of the Blooming Bright Star of Belle Isle', *Canadian Folklore canadien* (Journal of the Folklore Studies Association of Canada) vol.8, 1-2, officially 1986 but in fact published 1989. Christer Svensson: 'Stealin', Stealin', Pretty Mama Don't You Tell on Me', *Endless Road* no.4, Hull, UK, 1983. Bob Dylan, 'The Playboy Interview: A Candid Conversation with the Iconoclastic Idol of the Folk Rock Set', *Playboy*, Chicago, Mar 1966.]

Berry, Chuck [1926 -] Born Charles Edward Anderson Berry in San Jose, CA, on January 15, or October 18 or 26, 1926, but growing up in St. Louis, Chuck Berry was rock'n'roll's first black guitar-hero and first poet.

His first song, the often misspelt 'Maybellene', began life as 'country music', by which Berry meant country blues, but revamped, on the great post-war Chicago label Chess in 1955, it was not only rock'n'roll but the perfect indicator of just what riches its singer-songwriter would bring to this emergent genre. Berry, never wild but always savvy, introduced the welcome flash of electric guitar-work and piquant comic tales, starting with a race between a Cadillac and a Ford, told from the Ford owner's, and therefore the underdog's, viewpoint. This became one of the most famous opening verses in popular music: 'As I was motorvatin' over the hill / I saw Maybellene in a Coup de Ville.' Here, out of nowhere, was the enticing combination of an instantly recognisable, fresh guitar ('just like a-ringin' the bell,' as he would soon put it), an insistent tune and a highly distinctive lyric that celebrated with deft wit and loving detail the glories of 1950s US teen consumerism.

Even so distinctive a lyricist as Chuck Berry has specific forbears from the pre-war blues world: within that rich, under-familiar terrain are records full of comic wit about domestic detail and city life, and even several on which singers ask phone-operators to call their girlfriends, stating the numbers and sometimes the romantic purpose of their calls. Nonetheless Berry was way ahead of his time, offering an urban slang-sophistication slicker than any bluesman before him.

He offered a bold and captivating use of cars, planes, highways, refrigerators and skyscrapers, and also the accompanying details: seat-belts, bus conductors, ginger ale and terminal gates. And he brought all this into his love songs. He put love in an everyday metropolis, fast and cluttered, as no-one had done before him. In Chuck Berry's cities, real people—individuals—struggled and fretted and gave vent to ironic perceptions. Chuck Berry also specialized in place-names, as no one before him or since has done. He releases the power of romance in each one, and thereby flies with relish through a part of the American dream. The blow-by-blow narrative, the brand-name detail, and a slyly innocent joy at being so *au fait* with such detail, is the hallmark of almost all Berry's best work.

So is the seamless match of words to melodic line. This unrivalled technical panache was itself part of his humour. Take the opening lines of 'Nadine' (1964): 'As I got on a city bus and found a vacant seat / I thought I saw my future bride walkin' up the street / I shouted to the driver, "Hey conductor! you must / Slow down, I think I see her: please, let me off this bus!" / "Nadine! Honey, is that you?! . . ."' The lively, perfect fit of street-talk to music avoids mere automatic chug-a-chug-a-chug, showing off the true poet's touch as the rhythm *enacts* the plea that 'you must [pause] slow down . . .'

Here, right from rock'n'roll's outset, was an artist who injected it with wit, the very quality supposed to belong only to the music rock'n'roll displaced. And unlike the Cole Porters, Berry never paraded cleverness for its own sake but always in energetic celebration of life. 'Maybellene' was an instant success, and his guitar-driven classics in the prolific years that followed were the anthems every local group played every weekend ever after. They included 'Roll Over Beethoven', 'Too Much Monkey Business', 'Oh Baby Doll', 'Rock & Roll Music', 'Sweet Little Sixteen', 'Johnny B. Goode', 'Carol', 'Little Queenie', 'Back in the USA', 'Bye Bye Johnny', 'Come On', 'No Particular Place to Go' and 'The Promised Land'. THE EVERLY BROTHERS would master teenage-bedroom angst; but Chuck proclaimed the upside of modern adolescence—which was odd, because he was already 19 by the end of World War II, and turned 30 by the time he began to sing of high-school romance.

In doing so, Berry was also curiously colour-neutral. Before him, black singers invoking schoolgirls somehow always made clear that they moved within black terrain. Chuck elected himself poet of the whole of US high school life. His music was, Tom Zito observed, 'Not so much black as American'. Yet stories like 'Maybellene' were certainly in the spirit of Stagger Lee and the other speedy superheroes of black folksong, while 'Brown-Eyed Handsome Man' (1956) avowed that Black Is Beautiful ahead of its time—the title's understatement adroitly set against the extravagant wordplay of the verses: 'de Milo's Venus was a beautiful lass / She had the world in the palm of her hand / But she lost both her arms in a wrestling match / To get a brown-eyed handsome man.'

Berry's songs ranged far beyond adolescence. 'Havana Moon' (1956) is a vivid drama of lovers' lost opportunity, as affecting as *Brief Encounter* but funky and told in three minutes; 'You Never Can Tell' (1964) smiles at newly-weds, as do 'the old folks' inside the song; 'Memphis, Tennessee' (1959) laments the pain of divorce as the narrator sings of missing six-year-old daughter Marie, last seen 'with hurry home drops on her cheeks that trickled from her eye'. And Berry was pioneering all this at a time when most people were either singing 'Rock, baby, rock', or 'I love you when you do the—'.

In the midst of the hits, Berry was imprisoned. At 18 he'd been jailed for three years for petty robbery, and in 1959 held for trying to date a white woman in Mississippi. In 1960, now married with four children, he was found guilty of taking a 14-year-old girl across a state line. Berry protested that she only went to the police after he fired her from his nightclub, and that anyway he'd thought she was 20—this from the writer of the line 'She's too cute to be a minute over seventeen'. He was jailed till late 1963. He served his time honing his songwriting, and his records of 1964 are at least as good as the earlier hits. Of no other rock'n'roller is this remotely true.

But in 1972 came the artistic shame of 'My Ding-a-Ling', a smutty song wholly lacking Berry's wit (and written, surprisingly, by FATS DOMINO's great bandleader and co-writer Dave Bartholomew), with which Chuck topped the charts at last, at the age of 46. By then his eulogies of Americana ('I'm so glad I'm living in the USA / Where hamburgers sizzle on an open griddle night and day / Anything you want they got it right here in the USA') had long been deeply unfashionable, as the Beatles had noted with their sardonic 'Back in the USSR'.

Yet Berry's huge influence remained tangible throughout the 1960s and beyond, both generally and in particular, as upon the Beach Boys ('Surfing USA'), Merseybeat, the BEATLES ('Get Back'), the STONES ('Come On' was their first single), Bob Dylan—and right on through to rap.

The fine 1987 documentary film *Chuck Berry Hail! Hail! Rock'n'Roll!* showed a Berry still slim, still obliging with his trademark duck-walk and still coaxing those lazily bent notes from his beautiful scarlet Gibson guitar. He retained an alert grace; and, as with Dylan, indifferent concerts were the price paid for genuinely spontaneous performance that on other nights yielded magical reinvention and creative musicianship.

(KEITH RICHARDS complains in the film that Berry tried to change key on him when Keith was 'helping' him on stage; on the evidence of Bob Dylan at Live Aid, though, Keith's help is best avoided.)

Dylan learnt a lot from Chuck Berry: from his music and his words. It is Berry's distinctive, driving cameos, tight-knit and self-sufficient, that inspire most of the rock side of Dylan's *Bringing It All Back Home* and much of *Highway 61 Revisited* and many other cuts, including, in slow-motion, 'Sittin' on a Barbed Wire Fence'. It isn't old ELVIS records that these albums update: it's Chuck Berry's.

The urban slickness, precision and irony are there in many Dylan songs, including 'On the Road Again'—which is, with its wild domestic detail, 'You Never Can Tell' turning sour. Dylan uses the same Berry qualities on 'Bob Dylan's 115th Dream', 'From a Buick 6', 'Highway 61 Revisited', 'Memphis Blues Again', 'Visions of Johanna' and so on. Dylan also takes over Berry's manipulation of objects and the details and ad-man phrases that surround them. Dylan could never have written 'Tombstone Blues' without Chuck Berry; nor, especially, could 'Subterranean Homesick Blues' have come into being without him, either in its musical format or its words. It needed Berry's 'Too Much Monkey Business' first.

The Berry song's technique is to pile up, like a list, the pressures that are on the story's narrator, and to suggest their unreasonableness by their phrased sharpness and multiplicity. The last verse runs: 'Workin' in the fillin' station / Too many tasks / Wipe the windows / Check the tyres / Check the oil / Dollar gas?!' Dylan, taking this up, makes it serve in a far more complex capacity. He widens the context and the predicament of the man under pressure. Chuck Berry might have a nasty job but Dylan has to fight off the whole of society: 'Ah, get born, keep warm, / Short pants, romance, learn to dance, / Get dressed, get blessed, / Try to be a success, / Please her, please him, buy gifts, / Don't steal, don't lift, / Twenty years of schoolin' an' they put you on the day shift. / Look out kid . . .'

Dylan and LEVON HELM performed 'Nadine' during Helm's Lone Star Café gig, New York City, May 29, 1988, and Dylan sang it live in concert in Berry's hometown, St. Louis, June 17, 1988. He played saxophone(!) while LARRY KEGAN sang Berry's 'No Money Down' live in Merrillville, Indiana, on October 19, 1981 and in Boston two days later, and Dylan uses the song's title inside the lyric of his own 'Maybe Someday' on *Knocked Out Loaded* (1986). He also performed Berry's 'Around and Around' in concert in Leysin, Switzerland, July 10, 1992. Things do indeed come around and around.

[Chuck Berry: 'Maybellene', Chicago, 21 May 1955, Chess 1604, Chicago, 1955; 'Nadine (Is That You?)', Chicago, 15 Nov 1963, Chess 1883 (Pye International 7N 25236, London), 1964; 'Roll Over Beethoven', Chicago, 16 Apr 1956, Chess 1626, 1956 (London-American HLU 8428, London, 1957); 'Too Much Monkey Business' c/w 'Brown-Eyed Handsome Man', Chicago, 16 Apr 1956, Chess 1635, 1956; 'Oh Baby Doll', Chicago, 6 May 1957, Chess 1664, 1957; 'Rock & Roll Music', Chicago, 6 May 1957, Chess 1671 (London-American HLM 8531), 1957; 'Sweet Little Sixteen' (c/w 'Reelin' and Rockin'), Chicago, 29 Dec 1957, Chess 1683 (London-American HLM 8585), 1958. ('Reelin' and Rockin'' was a UK top 20 hit 15 years later, Chess Records 6145 020, 1973); 'Johnny B. Goode', Chicago, 30 Dec 1957 c/w 'Around and Around', Chicago, 28 Feb 1958, Chess 1691, 1958; 'Carol', Chicago, 12 Jun 1958, Chess 1700 (London-American HL-8712), 1958; 'Little Queenie', Chicago, 19 Nov 1958, Chess 1722 (London-American HLM 8853), 1959; 'Memphis (Tennessee)', St. Louis, July 1958, c/w 'Back in the USA', Chicago, 17 Feb 1959, Chess 1729, 1959 (this was a belated UK top 10 hit in 1963, c/w 'Let It Rock', Chicago, 29 Jul 1959, Pye International 7N 25218, 1963); 'Bye Bye Johnny', Chicago, 12 Feb 1960, Chess 1754 (London-American HLM 9159), 1960; 'Come On', Chicago, 29 Jul 1961, Chess 1799, 1961 (Pye International 7N 25209, London, 1963); 'No Particular Place to Go', Chicago, 26 Mar 1964, Chess 1898 (Pye International 7 25242), 1964; 'Promised Land', Chicago, 25 Feb 1964, Chess 1916 (Pye Intnl. 7N 25285), 1964; 'Havana Moon', Chicago, 29 Oct 1956, Chess 1645, 1956 (London-American HLN 8375, 1957); 'You Never Can Tell', Chicago, 15 Nov 1963, Chess 1906 (Pye Intnl 7N 25257), 1964; 'My Ding-a-Ling', Coventry, UK, 3 Feb 1972, Chess CH-2131 (Chess 6145 019), 1972. (Most discographical information from Michael Gray, *Song & Dance Man III: The Art of Bob Dylan*, but for additional detail and corrections Fred Rothwell and his paperback book *Long Distance Information—Chuck Berry's Recorded Legacy*, York, UK: Music Mentor Books, 2001, have been valuable.) *Chuck Berry Hail! Hail! Rock'n'-Roll!*, prod. Stephanie Bennett & Keith Richards, dir. Taylor Hackford, US, 1987.]

***Best of Bob Dylan, The* [version 1: 1997]** An unnecessary UK-and-Australia-only compilation album, especially since it came so soon after *Greatest Hits Volume 3*, contrived by the record company's TV-advertising division with no thought for how it cut across Dylan's catalogue and certainly with no thought of contributing usefully to it. Worse, for all this CD's claims of digital remastering and Super Bit Mapping™, the versions here of early material like 'Blowin' in the Wind' give an alarmingly poor idea of how these originally sounded. This represents a disquieting form of rewriting audio history. It has one previously unreleased track: an unexceptional outtake of 'Shelter from the Storm' from the *Blood on the Tracks* sessions, as used in the overrated Tom Cruise film *Jerry Maguire* (and also released on the soundtrack album *Jerry Maguire: Music from the Motion Picture*, Epic Soundtrax EK 67910, 10 Dec 1996).

Not very cleverly, another album with the same title but different tracks was issued in the US in 2005.

[Released as Columbia SONYTV28CD, UK; Columbia 31-487924-10, Australia, 2 Jun 1997.]

***Best of Bob Dylan, The* [version 2: 2005]** Burdened with exactly the same title as a different compilation issued in the UK and Australia eight years earlier, this compilation was issued in the US and Japan only, and promoted as the first single CD to span Dylan's whole career. Rather a lot to ask of 16 tracks. They are: 'Blowin' in the Wind', 'The Times They Are a-Changin', 'Mr. Tambourine Man', 'Like a Rolling Stone', 'Rainy Day Women # 12 & 35', 'All Along the Watchtower', 'Lay Lady Lay', 'Knockin' on Heaven's Door', 'Tangled Up in Blue', 'Hurricane', 'Forever Young' (disrupting the chronology, since this is from the *Planet Waves* album, pre-dating 'Tangled Up in Blue' on *Blood on the Tracks* and 'Hurricane' on *Desire*), 'Gotta Serve Somebody', 'Jokerman', 'Not Dark Yet', 'Things Have Changed' and 'Summer Days'. Since these are absolutely the most obvious tracks you could have thought of, this was clearly an album designed for the Christmas market and for people who only like Bob Dylan a bit.

[Released as SONCD675013, US & Japan, 15 Nov 2005.]

***Best of Bob Dylan Vol. 2, The* [2000]** A more interesting selection than the earlier volume, partly for beginning not at the chronological beginning but with what was then the most recent studio recording, 'Things Have Changed', a single and a track from the soundtrack of the film *Wonder Boys*, recorded on July 26, 1999. Then the chronology kicks in and ranges from 'A Hard Rain's a-Gonna Fall' from 1963 through to 'Not Dark Yet' from 1997's *Time Out of Mind* album, and runs along very much in parallel to its predecessor: 'Hard Rain' and 'It Ain't Me Babe' instead of 'Blowin' in the Wind' and 'The Times They Are a-Changin'; 'Subterranean Homesick Blues' from *Bringing It All Back Home* instead of 'Mr. Tambourine Man'; 'Highway 61 Revisited' instead of 'Like a Rolling Stone'; 'I Want You' instead of 'Just Like a Woman'; 'I'll Be Your Baby Tonight' instead of 'All Along the Watchtower'; the 1970 'Quinn the Eskimo' instead of the 1971 'I Shall Be Released'; 'Simple Twist of Fate' instead of 'Tangled Up in Blue'; 'Hurricane' instead of 'Oh Sister'; 'License to Kill' instead of 'Jokerman'. But it's by no means an exact parallel. This time there's nothing from the third album, nothing from *Planet Waves* and nothing from *Slow Train Coming*. From *Oh Mercy* there's an outtake of 'Dignity' rather than an album track; but *Street Legal* is represented, by 'Changing of the Guards', and, ignoring the claim in the collection's title, so is *Down in the Groove*, with 'Silvio'. More usefully, we also get that great single 'Positively 4th Street'.

As with the earlier volume's offering of 'Blowin' in the Wind', though, the audio quality on 'A Hard Rain's a-Gonna Fall' here is hopeless: a pallid, lo-fi version of what was to be found on the *Freewheelin'* album. To find this replicated decently on CD you need the CD/SACD (Super Audio CD) reissue of the album from 2003. Meanwhile, it would surely be asking only for competence to expect 'Subterranean' here not to be misspelt 'Subterannean', as happens on the back cover and the insert. But this collection gives us the unadulterated version of 'Dignity': the incomparably best version.

As a 'limited edition bonus' the collection was first released with an extra CD containing two live tracks from a concert in Santa Cruz on March 16, 2000—i.e. a concert that took place less than two months before this release. The two are: a fair 'Highlands', Dylan's voice at times too struttingly boastful (a mannerism he often falls into in recent years) but more often alertly responsive, with moments of great delicacy on the choruses; and an execrable 'Blowin' in the Wind' that is nothing but overblown pose. It is the perfect audio argument for his abandoning altogether a song that seems meaningless to him. Once, his direct, intelligent communication set his version apart from the glossier, flossier cover versions of others. Here, he sounds like one of them.

[Released as Columbia 498361-2 (limited edn. version with bonus disc 498361-9), Europe, 8 May 2000.]

Betts, Dickie [1943 -] Forrest Richard Betts was born in West Palm Beach, Florida, on December 12, 1943.

After fronting the psychedelic Jacksonville, Florida, band the Second Coming, he was a co-founder of the Allman Brothers Band in 1969 and one of its crucial guitarists; he composed their crucial songs 'Rambling Man', 'In Memory of Elizabeth Reed,' 'Blue Sky', 'Southbound' and 'Jessica.' One of the survivors of all the road deaths the band managed to chalk up, he took over Duane Allman's leadership rôle after Duane's death (while they were still working on their great album *Eat a Peach*).

Because of his alcohol problems, but officially 'due to creative differences with Greg Allman', Betts was fired from the Allman Brothers Band in May 2000—fired by fax after 31 years in the group—and immediately hit the road, first fronting the Dickey Betts Band and later his current outfit, Dickey Betts & Great Southern (re-using the name he'd claimed on his own records during the Allman Brothers' long vacation of 1976 to 1978, in which time he released *Dickie Betts* and *Atlanta's Burning Down*). Dickey Betts & Great Southern have released two CDs, *Let's Get Together* (2001) and *The Collectors, Vol. 1* (2003).

His public connections with Dylan are brief. When the Never-Ending Tour came to Sarasota, Florida (where his old acquaintance ERIC VON SCHMIDT had a home), on November 9, 1992, Dylan brought Dickie Betts on stage in mid-set to play guitar behind him and the rest of the band on 'Cat's in the Well'; a few months later, at the New Orleans Jazz & Heritage Festival on April 23, 1993, Betts again came on in Dylan's set and again played only on 'Cat's in the Well'. He contributed more at their third and (so far) final encounter, when Dylan's 1995 tour reached Tampa, Florida, on the last day of that September. This time Dickie Betts shared vocals with Dylan as well as played guitar on an unexpected performance of Betts' own 'Rambling Man'; and played guitar on five other numbers: 'Seeing the Real You at Last', 'She Belongs to Me', 'Obviously 5 Believers', 'Highway 61 Revisited' and the final encore number, 'Rainy Day Women # 12 & 35'. Thus the audience were treated to both Betts' fluid guitar-work and his curiously strangulated vocals. On the album *The Songs of JIMMIE RODGERS—A Tribute*, finally issued on Dylan's Egyptian Records label in 1997, Betts offers a decent performance of Rodgers' great song 'Waiting for a Train'.

[Dickie Betts: *Dickie Betts*, 1977, CD-reissued Razor & Tie 82141, US, 1997; *Atlanta's Burning Down*, 1978, CD-reissued Razor & Tie 82142, 1997; 'Waiting for a Train', *nia*, *The Songs of Jimmie Rodgers—A Tribute*, Various Artists, Egyptian/Columbia Records 485189 2, NY, 1997. Dickie Betts & Great Southern: *Let's Get Together*, Free Falls Ent., US, 2001. Allman Brothers: *Eat a Peach*, 1971, Capricorn, US, 1972.]

biblical text, Dylan's capacity for modernising See 'What Can I Do for You?'.

Bikel, Theodore [1924 -] Meir Bikel was born in Vienna, Austria, on May 2, 1924. His family fled the Nazis in the late 1930s, and he lived in Palestine from 1938 to 1945, moving to the UK in 1946 and finally settling in the US in 1954. Bikel claims to have been fluent in Hebrew, Yiddish and German and, modestly, to have had only 'a respectable command of English and French' by this point. He has since learned many other languages. He had joined the Habimah Theatre in 1943 as an apprentice actor and in 1944 became one of the co-founders of the Israeli Chamber Theatre. On arriving in London in 1946, he enrolled at the Royal Academy of Dramatic Art, graduating two years later while starting to develop 'a serious interest in the guitar and folk music'. Hence he became a decent character actor as well as a rather laboured folk singer specialising in Jewish folksong. Laurence Olivier gave him the rôle of Mitch in his London production of *A Streetcar Named Desire*.

He had already worked in the US by the time he settled there in 1954; he made his Hollywood acting début in *The African Queen* in 1951, in which he played a German naval officer. He created the part of Baron von Trapp in the first Broadway cast of *The Sound of Music*, and later starred in the equally remorseless *Fiddler on the Roof*. Other films included *The Defiant Ones* (1958), *My Fair Lady* (1964) and *The Russians Are Coming, The Russians Are Coming* in 1965. In FRANK ZAPPA's *200 Motels* (1971) he played a game show host and the Devil.

Bikel was signed to Elektra by the indefatigable Jac Holzman in 1958, who proceeded to record him on a vast number of those awful LPs offering ponderous geographical tours of folksongs from around the world, country by country, sometimes partnered by others, including CYNTHIA GOODING. He not only plays guitar but also mandolin, balalaika and harmonica.

'One night in the summer of 1962,' ROBERT SHELTON reports first-hand, 'Bikel . . . threw a party at his Washington Square Village apartment. Dylan . . . more than a bit stoned', gatecrashed it and 'careened around the room in his top hat'; Bikel was 'gently bemused'. The following summer, they almost worked together; certainly they travelled together. On July 6, 1963, Bikel and Dylan flew down to the deep south to meet up with THE FREEDOM SINGERS, LEN CHANDLER and PETE SEEGER, and to take part in a voter registration rally in Greenwood, Mississippi. Bikel paid Dylan's fare, and watched the emergent young star closely—and found Dylan a watcher too. 'I saw Bob observing everything down there. He was also watching the reaction to himself. He was very humble to the farmers . . .' This is where Dylan performed 'Only a Pawn in Their Game' to black workers in a field outside Greenwood.

At the time, Bikel was a regular on the weekly TV show 'Hootenanny', which had an audience of around 11 million. Since then, he has continued to appear, if his vainglorious website is to be believed, in almost every play, film, television drama and opera that was ever a success. His autobiography, *Theo*, was re-published in 2002. No doubt it elaborates upon his online claims, which include these: that he is 'One of the world's best-known folk singers'; 'a founder in 1961 of the NEWPORT FOLK FESTIVAL'; 'a multi-faceted entertainer' who gives 'some 50 to 60 concerts per year, performing alone or with large symphony orchestras'; he was 'active for many years in the civil rights movement', 'an elected delegate to the 1968 Democratic Convention in Chicago', President of the Actors' Equity Association (1973–82), a Vice President of the International Federation of Actors (1981–91), a Board Member of Amnesty International (USA), and, 'by Presidential appointment' a member of the National Council on the Arts (1977–82).

'An American citizen since 1961, Theodore Bikel divides his time between California and Connecticut, where he resides with his wife Rita.' What's more, 'Theodore Bikel is a Renaissance Man, a concerned human being who works in the arts', who is not a 'specialist but a general practitioner in the world of the arts.' 'This is reflected in his multiplicity of talents: Bikel the actor on stage, screen and television; Bikel the folksinger and guitarist; Bikel the author, lecturer and raconteur; and Bikel the activist and arts advocate.' And just possibly Bikel the bighead.

[Theodore Bikel, *Theo*, 2nd edn., Madison, WI: University of Wisconsin Press, 2002. His website is at *www.bikel.com*. Robert Shelton, *No Direction Home: The Life and Music of Bob Dylan*, London, Penguin edn., 1987, pp.152, 170–79.]

***Biograph* [1985]** A 5-LP box set retrospective of Dylan's work from 1962–81, packaged with an unprecedented collection of personal and rare photographs and equally unprecedented interview comments by Dylan about the songs themselves, plus other interview material ranging over many topics in which Dylan, sometimes surly but more often open, remains unpredictable and spikey. Though criticised (inevitably) by some collectors, it is a fine if quirky selection of previously issued album tracks plus a significant number of previously unreleased recordings: a different take of 'Mixed-Up Confusion' (1962); 'Baby, I'm in the Mood for You' (1962); the exquisitely performed 'protest' number 'Percy's Song' (1963); the incomparable 'Lay Down Your Weary Tune' (1963); by no means the best take of 'I'll Keep It with Mine' (1965); a fragment, previously unknown even to avid collectors, from the *Highway 61 Revisited* sessions, 'Jet Pilot' (1965); the wonderful 'I Wanna Be Your Lover' (1965); live cuts from the 1966 tour—the electric 'I Don't Believe You' and the acoustic solo 'Visions of Johanna' and 'It's All Over Now Baby Blue'; the belated release of take 2 of the original 1967 Dylan & the Crackers takes of 'Quinn the Eskimo (The Mighty Quinn)'—though take 1 had long circulated unofficially; a publisher's office demo solo of 'Forever Young' (1973); the original studio cut of 'You're a Big Girl Now' and the *Blood on the Tracks* outtake 'Up to Me'(1974); the lovely *Desire* outtake 'Abandoned Love' (1975); excellent live recordings of two other *Desire* songs, 'Isis' and 'Romance in Durango', from the first Rolling Thunder Revue (1975); a major song from the *Shot of Love* sessions, 'Caribbean Wind' (1981), and a live 'Heart of Mine' (1981). An affirmation of the astonishing variety as well as richness of Dylan's corpus, the collection was well-received by the public and went some way to reviving that fickle thing, Dylan's critical reputation.

[Released as Columbia C5X 38830 (CBS 20-66509 in UK), 28 Oct or 7 Nov 1985.]

Björner, Olof [1942 -] Olof Edvard Björner was born on November 26, 1942, in Stockholm, Sweden. He first took an interest in Dylan's work in 1963. Gaining a computer science degree in 1967, Olof became a computer consultant and later a management consultant working on IT strategies for health care. In 2003 he and his wife Agneta bought a bookshop in the Swedish country town of Filipstad.

His first publication was the now very rare booklet *Words Fill My Head, Written, Spoken, Sung by Bob Dylan*, self-published in 1989, which compiled some of the material written by Dylan yet excluded from the official book *Bob Dylan Lyrics 1962–1985*. Around the same time, Björner started to distribute update pages to MICHAEL KROGSGAARD's enormous log of Dylan recording sessions, *Master of the Tracks*, published in 1988. He was also very active in the early days of the internet discussion group *http://rec.music.dylan*. He soon started to complement these update pages with yearly chronicles—which duly became far too costly to keep on distributing on paper. In 1999 he decided to make them all available on the internet and at the same time to expand vastly his chronicling of Dylan's work and career activity.

The result is the enormous and invaluable website *www.bjorner.com*, which (so far) offers a detailed run-down on every Dylan year from 1958 to 2002: offering a catalogue of his recording sessions, his concert performances—listing every song performed in every concert—plus his record releases, books published by and about him, tapes newly coming into circulation, and more besides. The detail is extraordinary, and the level of accuracy phenomenal. There's also a section of Olof's site with transcriptions of Dylan interviews from the 1960s to the 1990s, a vast listing of cover versions of Dylan songs by other artists (accessible by song or by artist) *and* an online version of *Words Fill My Head*. And more besides. Truly a gigantic undertaking, maintained to a very high standard indeed.

Some of the annual chronicles are also becoming available in book form, for those with a good deal of money to spend. *Olof's Files: A Bob Dylan Performance Guide*, in fourteen volumes including an index volume, each priced at almost $50, are being issued by the quaintly named small UK publishing house Hardinge Simpole, from *Volume One: 1958–1969* through to *Volume Thirteen: 2003–2004*.

As you can tell, Olof Björner is some kind of hero.

[Olof Björner: *Olof's Files: A Bob Dylan Performance Guide*, Aylesbeare, Devon, UK: Hardinge Simpole, 2002; or online free at *www.bjorner.com*.]

Blackwell, Chuck [1940 -] Charles Edward Blackwell (not to be confused with the black drummer of that name) was born in Oklahoma City on August 19, 1940. He grew up in Tulsa and became an LA-based drummer around 1958, touring behind LITTLE RICHARD, JERRY LEE LEWIS and THE EVERLY BROTHERS, before playing with Delaney Bramlett, Don Preston, JAMES BURTON and Glen D. Hardin in the Shindogs and the Pebbles, and becoming a long-time collaborator with LEON RUSSELL. Hence he was part of Joe Cocker's Mad Dogs and Englishmen tour (as were those other drummers with a Dylan connection, JIM KELTNER and SANDY KONIKOFF). Hence too when Leon Russell produced Dylan's sessions at New York City's Blue Rock Studios on March 16–19, 1971, Blackwell was the drummer. He can be heard, therefore, on the lovely 'When I Paint My Masterpiece' and heard to more advantage on the 1971 single of 'Watching the River Flow'. (But see **Keltner, Jim**.)

Blackwell continued to play sessions, including for Freddie King and on many a Taj Mahal album. Today, having survived cancer a decade ago, Chuck owns Blackwell's Stained Glass & Doors Inc., a shop in Broken Arrow, Oklahoma, where he and his wife moved around 1980.

Blade, Brian [1970 -] Brian Blade, younger brother of Brady Blade Jr. (see **musical accompanists to Dylan, other**), was born in Shreveport, Louisiana, in 1970 into a gospel-enthusiast family and started playing drums in church at age 13. He worked in a Shreveport record store before going to college in New Orleans, where he became a professional drummer, mostly of a jazz persuasion, and got to know DANIEL LANOIS, with whom he has recorded, as he has on EMMYLOU HARRIS' album *Wrecking Ball*. A fan of John Coltrane and Miles Davis in his youth, he was given a copy of JONI MITCHELL's 1976 album *Hejira* when he was 16, let it seep into his soul and, many years later, was thrilled to find himself in her band. He plays on albums including her *Taming the Tiger* and was on the short West Coast tour of May 1998 that sandwiched her set between those by VAN MORRISON and Dylan—by which time he had been one of the drummers on Dylan's Lanois-produced album *Time Out of Mind*. He plays on 'Love Sick', 'Standing in the Doorway', 'Million Miles', ''Til I Fell in Love With You', 'Not Dark Yet' and 'Can't Wait'.

On his PR portrait Blade is poised meditatively at the drumkit, looking like a young Arthur Ashe. In 1998 he formed the Brian Blade Fellowship—a musical rather than religious group, and an unusual jazz combo in featuring a steel guitar. They have made two CDs, *The Brian Blade Fellowship* (1998) and *Perceptual* (2000), both produced by Lanois, who also plays on both. Joni Mitchell plays on 'Steadfast' on the latter. Blade has also taken to playing with Wayne Shorter's quartet and with an outfit called Directions in Music, which exists to pay homage to his early heroes, Coltrane and Davis, and in whose ranks lurks another big-name jazz musician, Herbie Hancock.

Not, in other words, Bob Dylan's usual sort of musician at all.

[The Brian Blade Fellowship: *The Brian Blade Fellowship*, Blue Note 59417, US (8594172, UK), 1998; *Perceptual*, Blue Note 23571, US, 2000.]

Blake, Norman [1938 -] Norman Blake was born in Chattanooga, Tennessee, on March 10, 1938, grew up in north-west Georgia and became a Nashville session musician. He has now been playing traditional bluegrass and old-time music for almost half a century. A singer and songwriter but primarily a multi-instrumentalist, he plays guitar, mandolin, fiddle, banjo and Dobro, though he is specially noted for flat-picking fiddle tunes on guitar with speed and precision. He has toured and/or recorded with June Carter, JOHNNY CASH, the Nitty Gritty Dirt Band, KRIS KRISTOFFERSON, DOC WATSON and numerous others, played on the JOAN BAEZ record of 'The Night They Drove Old Dixie Down' and more recently played prominently on the soundtrack for the film *O Brother, Where Art Thou*.

In February 1969 he became one of the studio musicians for Dylan's *Nashville Skyline* sessions, playing guitar on all tracks, including all the outtakes and the duets with Johnny Cash. That album was released in April 1969, and later that month Blake returned to the studios with Dylan. He doesn't seem to have been there for the first of these *Self Portrait* sessions but he was there on the second day, April 26, at which 'Take Me as I Am', 'I Forgot More (Thank You'll Ever Know)' and 'Let It Be Me' were recorded, and on May 3 for 'Take A Message to Mary' and 'Blue Moon'. This means that he was also a contributor to the track 'A Fool Such as I' on the album *Dylan*.

Today, Norman Blake frequently performs and records with his singer-musician wife Nancy Short. They returned to live in Dade County, Georgia, in the early 1970s, and there Blake launched a successful independent recording career with *Back Home in Sulphur Springs* in 1972. He has now released over two dozen solo albums, as well as guitar and mandolin instruction sets.

Blake, William [1757 - 1827] Blakeian influence on Dylan can be apparent as a question of 'thought': that is, in a labour of thought that achieves a concentrated economy of language and a tone almost of disinterestedness about what is actually experienced with intense emotion by the writer. In Blake we see this, for instance, in 'The Sick Rose'. In Dylan we see it in the make-up of the *John Wesley Harding* album (especially in 'I Dreamed I Saw St Augustine') and in individual songs throughout his repertoire, including 'Love Minus Zero/No Limit', a song that shares with 'The Sick Rose' the theme of possessiveness destroying love.

A difficult and central early work of Dylan's, 'Gates of Eden', also begs to be considered in relation to Blake. Its general themes could not be more Blakeian; and nor could their treatment. Dylan is treating balances of opposites—of material wealth and spiritual; of earthly reality and the imaginatively real; of the body and soul; of false gods and true vision; of self-gratification and salvation; of mortal ambitions and the celestial city; of sins and forgiveness; of evil and good. Not only are these Blake's themes, but they receive directly comparable handling. Both artists address themselves, as Max Plowman phrased it, 'not to common sense, but to individual senses.'

But it is in 'Every Grain of Sand', on 1981's album *Shot of Love*, that Dylan draws on Blake most and best. Blake, rewriting the Bible in his own unique way, hovers all around Dylan's song, in its themes, its language and in the rhythms of that language, though there is little conjunction of philosophy. Blake's philosophy, as Yeats claimed, brings him '. . . at last to forget good and evil in an absorbing vision of the happy and the unhappy.' The ideas Dylan takes from the Judeao-Christian religion are far more orthodox—though it happens that when Blake reaches his forties he comes to accept, like Dylan, a degree of Christian orthodoxy previously refused: as Peter Ackroyd notes in *Blake* (1995), it is in 1797's *Vala or the Four Zoas*, the great epic poem of Blake's middle age, that he first uses the word 'saviour' and the phrase 'the Lamb of God'. Blake's interest in taking biblical text and flying it to mystical heights is evident everywhere in his own work, and Dylan's interest in the work of this mystic predecessor is never more evident than here.

'Auguries of Innocence'—a single, 133-line poem written in or shortly before 1803 and not part of the *Songs of Innocence*—begins with the well-known first stanza 'To see a World in a Grain of Sand / And a Heaven in a Wild Flower / Hold Infinity in the palm of your hand / And Eternity in an hour': but though a Dylan remark of 1976, 'I can see God in a daisy', directly parallels Blake here, and is clearly re-echoed in Dylan's 'I can see the Master's hand / In every leaf that trembles, in every grain of sand', what Blake suggests by 'To see a World in a Grain of Sand' is something more complex than merely that the fact of the grain of sand reveals God's presence. Blake presses the idea that there is a world to be seen *within* a grain of sand, if our 'doors of perception' (this phrase too is Blake's) could be 'cleansed'. He insists on this idea many times over, as here in *Vala*: 'Then Eno, a daughter of Beulah, took a Moment of Time / And drew it out to seven thousand years with much care & affliction / And many tears, & in every year made windows into Eden. / She also took an atom of space & opened its centre / Into Infinitude . . .'

Blake's vision embraces every possible sense in which every grain of sand is bound up with man's destiny and God's all-caring universe; the boundaries of Dylan's vision in his song are smaller and more modest.

But that Dylan intends his embrace of Blake in 'Every Grain of Sand' is indicated by the echoes of Blake in Dylan's 'the ancient footsteps', of Blake's line 'While he keeps onwards in his wondrous journey on the earth' (from *Milton*, 1804–08) in Dylan's own 'onward in my journey' and in the half-echoes of Blake in Dylan's Bible-derived 'sparrow falling', the numbering of every hair and every grain of sand, and in the striking sun-steps-time combination in Dylan's majestic line 'The sun beat down upon the steps of time to light the way': the same sun-steps-time combination at the heart of 'Ah! Sun-Flower', from *Songs of Experience*.

More tellingly, Dylan declares that his embrace of Blake is crucial to his own song by his use not just of Blake's language and of some commonality of theme but by his insistent use of Blake's rhythms.

The rhythmic correspondence is concise and unmistakeable. The whole song is built upon the heptameter, or septenarius, the seven-foot or seven-beat line, which is rare in English-language poetry but is one of Blake's principal trademarks, starting with 'Tiriel' (written about 1786), in which we find 'A worm of sixty winters creeping on the dusky ground.' This distinctive metre recurs throughout Blake's work, as here in *The Book of Thel*: 'Why fade these children of the spring? born but to smile & fall' and 'Thou seest me the meanest thing, and so I am indeed; / My bosom of itself is cold and of itself is dark'. This seven-beat line is the distinctive foundation upon which Dylan builds the whole of 'Every Grain of Sand'.

You cannot read Blake without noticing the particular words and constructions he likes a lot and returns to often—and some of these Blakeian words and word-patterns are taken up and re-sung in hugely varying works by Bob Dylan.

Put crudely, there are two Blake modes of poetic writing: the sublimely simple mode of the *Songs of Innocence & Experience*, and the hyperactive complexity of the declamatory epic poems; and clearly Dylan's work reflects both kinds of Blake. But in 'Every Grain of Sand' Blake's presence is indicated by Dylan's use of specific Blakeian ingredients, rather than merely because Blake has been a major influence upon Dylan's work.

Many of Dylan's most Blakeian lines are of the long visionary kind that Blake would punctuate with scattered capital letters and might end with an exclamation-mark, as for instance in these disparate examples (respectively from 'Precious Angel', 1979, and 'Visions of Johanna', 1966, appropriately repunctuated): 'On the way out of Egypt, thro' Ethiopia to the Judgment Hall of Christ' and 'The Ghost of Electricity howls in the Bones of her Face!'

In fact 'howl' is one of Blake's very favourite words. He also likes 'Golden Loom' and 'the rolling thunder'—and, to bring us back directly to 'Every Grain of Sand', that distinctive little word 'wintry', which Dylan deploys towards the end of the song.

Blake uses 'wintry' all the time, as in the final verse of an untitled poem from about 1793, found in Blake's notebook, which has become titled after its first line, 'Let The Brothels Of Paris Be Opened': 'O, who would smile on the wintry seas, / & Pity the stormy roar? / Or who will exchange his new born child / For the dog at the wintry door?' 'The Dog at the wintry door' is re-used for Plate 25 of *The First Book of Urizen* (1794), and again, almost identically, in *Vala*—'It is an easy thing. . . . To hear the dog howl at the wintry door'—a poem that also offers 'To listen to the hungry raven's cry in wintry season', 'then sleep the wintry days . . . & prepare for a wintry grave', 'rugged wintry rocks' and 'the wintry blast / . . . or the summer pestilence'. We find 'the myriads of Angelic hosts / Fell thro' the wintry skies' in *Europe, a Prophecy* (1794); 'Thro' the wintry hail & rain' is a line from the 1800–1803 notebook—and in a poem etched on a cancelled plate for *America, a Prophecy* (1793) we get the exact prefiguring of Dylan's usage, in '. . . & his white garments cast a wintry light.'

The other specifically Blakeian characteristic of 'Every Grain of Sand' is the formally ordered 'poetic' structural motif, insistently repeated throughout the song, that piles up 'the flowers of indulgence', 'the weeds of yesteryear', 'the breath of conscience', 'the broken mirror of innocence' and so on. Dylan can't be said to use this construction as skilfully as Blake, whose best equivalents are far more vivid, fresh and original. These wipe the floor with Dylan's: 'in the dark delusions of repentance', 'shoes of indolence', 'Clouds of Learning' and, famously, 'the horses of instruction' (as, come to that, does the King James Bible version of Psalm 40 verse 3 with its 'thou hast made us drink the wine of astonishment.').

The contrast in vividness between Blake's and Dylan's phrases here is a matter of vigour of language and of meaning. That 'shoes of indolence' works by its soft-footed surrealism, its striking originality and the beguiling surprise of the image, but also because that image actively illuminates the idea it offers: there's a suggestion that indolence may or may not fit, that it can be stepped out of and discarded, that it isn't a part of the naked self—and so on. These hints about the nature of 'indolence' come directly from the imaginative choice of 'shoes'. The 'Clouds of Learning', more simply and obviously, suggests that 'Learning' may not clarify (à la 'your useless and pointless knowledge', perhaps). It is different with the 'dark delusions of repentance'. This offers the oddity of neither quite yielding an image nor being quite matter-of-fact, so that the word-effect itself, the sheer physique of the cadence, predominates. It has a gorgeous hammering muscularity, a rhythm in which you can certainly hear a master's hand, and as it ends on that rat-tat and hiss, it recharges 'repentance', giving it an almost onomatopoeic eloquence. Blake does not make it 'poetic'; he makes it poetry.

In 'Every Grain of Sand' Dylan's equivalents never quite keep the right side of the gap between the two. He manages it brilliantly in all manner of ways in all manner of songs throughout his repertoire, showing again and again the creative imagination and the judgment for equivalents of 'shoes of indolence' and for muscularity of writing that can stand alongside 'the dark delusions of repentance'—but he doesn't manage it via this form of construction in this song.

His image-carrying phrases are intermingled with echoing phrases that don't present images (matter-of-fact ones like 'time of my confession', 'memory of decay' and 'pain of idleness') so that there is variety in this usage throughout; yet he doesn't quite carry it off. By the midway point, you already feel that there have been too many of these phrases. Their vigour and illuminative power is not enough to stop the device itself obtruding: and once it obtrudes, you start to check on whether each of these constructions is really authentic.

That 'broken mirror of innocence', for instance: you might be able to work out how this image is an apt one (or you might not: to begin with, is innocence the mirror or the broken mirror?)—but it certainly doesn't succeed by any direct, free appeal to the imagination, like the 'shoes of indolence'. It's too careful, too self-consciously writerly, too constructed.

Finally, we can say that Dylan and Blake share also the desire to fight off public assumptions about their abnormality. Blake found it astonishing and perplexing that people should have considered him and his work deliberately puzzling and peculiar; in 1966 Dylan told *Playboy*: 'people actually have the gall to think that I have some kind of fantastic imagination. It gets very lonesome.'

This commonly felt sense of isolation might not be worth claiming as any special linkage between Blake and Dylan except that it seems to have provoked such strikingly similar expressions of defiance in the two artists. Compare Blake's 'Island in the Moon' (written around 1784–85) and Dylan's liner-notes for *Highway 61 Revisited* (1965):

Blake:

> '. . . in a great hurry, Inflammable Gass the Windfinder enter'd. They seem' d to rise & salute each other. Etruscan Column & Inflammable Gass fix'd their eyes on each other; their tongues went in question and answer, but their thoughts were otherwise employ'd. "I don't like his eyes," said Etruscan Column. "He's a foolish puppy," said Inflammable Gass, smiling on him. The 3 Philosophers—the Cynic smiling, the Epicurean seeming

studying the flame of the candle, & the Pythagorean playing with the cat–listen'd with open mouths. . . . Then Quid call' d upon Obtuse Angle for a song, & he, wiping his face & looking on the corner of the ceiling, sang: To be or not to be / Of great capacity / Like Sir Isaac Newton, / Or Locke, or Doctor South . . .'

Dylan:

'Savage Rose & Openly are bravely blowing kisses to the Jade Hexagram–Carnaby Street & To all of the mysterious juveniles & the Cream Judge is writing a book on the true meaning of a pear–last year, he wrote one on famous dogs of the Civil War & now he has false teeth and no children . . . when the Cream met Savage Rose & Openly, he was introduced to them by none other than Lifelessness–Lifelessness is the Great Enemy & always wears a hipguard–he is very hipguard. . . . Lifelessness said when introducing everybody "go save the world" & "involvement! that's the issue" & things like that & Savage Rose winked at Openly & the Cream went off with his arm in a sling singing "so much for yesterday" . . . the clown appears–puts a gag over Autumn's mouth & says "there are two kinds of people–simple people & normal people" this usually gets a big laugh from the sandpit & White Heap sneezes–passes out & wakes up & rips open Autumn's gag & says "What do you mean you're Autumn and without you there'd be no Spring! you fool! without Spring, there'd be no you! what do you think of that???" then Savage Rose & Openly come by & kick him in the brains & colour him pink for being a phony philosopher–then the clown comes by . . . & some college kid who's read all about Nietzsche comes by & says "Nietzsche never wore an umpire's suit" . . .'

See also the entry below, plus **Ginsberg, Allen** (re Blakeian influence on Dylan that may have come via Ginsberg) and **'Every Grain of Sand', non-Blake elements**. Blake's 'If the doors of perception were cleansed every thing would appear to man as it is, infinite. For man has closed himself up, till he sees all things thro' narrow chinks of his cavern': from 'A Memorable Fancy' in *The Marriage of Heaven and Hell*, c.1790–93 is also (inevitably) drawn upon in various entries about creativity and drugs.

[William Blake: 'The Sick Rose', *Songs of Experience* (1794), published together with *Songs of Innocence* (1789) as *Songs of Innocence and Songs of Experience: Shewing the Two Contrary States of the Human Soul* in 1794. *The Book of Thel*, 1789. 'Island in the Moon' was left untitled and unpublished by Blake; first publication was in E. J. Ellis: *The Real Blake*, 1907. This work was a product of the co-editorship of Blake's work by Ellis and W.B. Yeats–'Blake's first proper editors', as Peter Ackroyd says in *Blake*. Yeats's editorial work on Blake was done in 1893; his essay 'William Blake' was republished in W.B. Yeats: *Essays*, 1924. (There is an entry on Dylan's possible use of Yeats' poem 'VACILLATION'.)

Max Plowman: *An Introduction to the Study of Blake*, 1st edn., 1927, p.26. The greatest contemporary Blake scholar is perhaps poet and critic Kathleen Raine, who published the 2-volume *Blake and Tradition*, 1968, and the illustrated *William Blake*, 1970. Quotations from Blake above are taken from *Blake: Complete Writings*, ed. Geoffrey Keynes, London, 1969, and the Dover Thrift Edition of *Songs of Innocence and Songs of Experience*, 1992. Dylan's remark re God in a daisy is quoted in the booklet of notes for the *Bootleg Series Vols. 1–3* box set, 1991.

Dylan's use of Blake in 'Every Grain of Sand' is examined at length in Michael Gray: *Song & Dance Man III: The Art of Bob Dylan*, 1999, Ch. 12 (drawn on above). There is also an interesting essay by J.R. Stokes on Blake's presence within Dylan's *New Morning* album, 'Waking Up to a New Morning (And linking arms in the Universal Brotherhood)', *Judas!* no.14, Huntingdon, UK, July 2005.

Set to music by Mike Westbrook, Adrian Mitchell's arrangement of some Blake text (Mitchell calls it '*Let the Slave*, incorporating *The Price of Experience*'), is performed by VAN MORRISON on *A Sense of Wonder* (1984). The section Mitchell calls 'The Price of Experience' is lines 397–418 of the Second Night portion of *Vala*. The poetry called 'Let the Slave' on the Morrison album comprises lines 670–676 and 825–826 of the Ninth Night portion of *Vala*, the last line of the 'Song of Liberty' that ends *The Marriage of Heaven and Hell* (also used in *America: A Prophecy*) and half of line 366 from the Second Night portion of *Vala*, which Morrison says four times over. PATTI SMITH performed her musical interpretation of *Songs of Innocence* 18 Jun 2005 at the Meltdown Festival, London Royal Festival Hall.]

Blake, William, beat/hippie revival of 20th century social poets such as Peter Porter have recoiled from the beat/hippie revival of Blake, either disliking per se exactly those mystical qualities for which he is a New Age hero, or else simply objecting to his appropriation. 'William Blake, William / Blake, William Blake, William Blake, / say it and feel new!', sneers a verse of Porter's poem 'Japanese Jokes'. Poet and critic Fred Grubb's misremembrance of this salvo, offered inside a book review, is pithier: 'Blake! Blake! Blake! Say it and feel good'. Porter's attack may have beat poet ALLEN GINSBERG in mind–a Blake fan who was almost certainly one conduit for Dylan's absorption of Blake.

Porter and his friends are complaining as if there were just one warping of Blake's otherwise correct and static reputation. It's never been like that. Max Plowman, writing his irrepressible *Introduction to the Study of Blake* in the 1920s, felt that at last 'the day seems to be not far distant when . . . apologies will be unnecessary and the complete Blake will be no longer regarded as a narcotic for numbskulls, but will stare every university undergraduate full in the face.'

[Peter Porter: 'Japanese Jokes', *Last of England*, 1970. Fred Grubb: 'Mountaineer', *London Magazine*, Dec 1989–Jan 1990. Max Plowman, *Introduction to the Study of Blake*, London: Dent, 1927, p.2.]

Blakley, Ronee [1945 -] Ronee Blakley was born on August 24, 1945 in Stanley, Idaho, but grew up in nearby Caldwell, the daughter of a civil engineer. She became an actor as well as a singer-songwriter and pianist. Her film début had been a fleeting appearance in Tom McGowan's *Wilbur and the Baby Factory* in 1970, but her most prominent rôle was in her second movie, the great Robert Altman's masterpiece *Nashville*, made in 1975 and released a year later, in which she played Barbara Jean, a country star allegedly modelled on Loretta Lynn. She appeared in many other films, but never bettered this performance, and never became a star.

As a singer she could perform powerfully, and after singing duets with Dylan at the end of a DAVID BLUE gig in the Village on October 22, 1975, as he was putting together the Rolling Thunder Revue, she became one of its featured singers, performing songs at each concert and being filmed giving a dramatic rendition at the piano of her own song 'Need a New Sun Rising' in *Renaldo & Clara*, released in 1978, in which, inevitably, she takes part in some of the improvised acting scenes. Part of her job in the film was to be one of the several dark-haired beauties of a certain type (Dylan's type, clearly) who all looked a bit like JOAN BAEZ and a bit like SARA DYLAN.

'Need a New Sun Rising' was one of the tracks on her 1975 album *Welcome*, on which she had played guitar as well as keyboards. She had earlier been a performer on the experimental 1970 album *First Moog Quartet*, devised by Gershon Kingsley; and had made her own début album, *Ronee Blakley*, in 1972.

In 1979 she married the European auteur film director Wim Wenders (and directed *him* in her own film *I Played It for You*) but they remained married only until 1981. She continued to appear in films, including Nicholas Ray's last picture, *Lightning Over Water* in 1979, and *Nightmare on Elm Street* in 1984, but hasn't made a film since Paul Leder's *Murder by Numbers* in 1990. She and Dylan don't seem to have crossed professional paths since the 1970s.

[*Nashville*, dir. Robert Altman, ABC / Paramount, US, 1976. *Renaldo & Clara*, dir. Bob Dylan, Circuit Films, US, 1978. *I Played It for You*, dir. Ronee Blakley, US, 1985.]

Blind Blake [c.1890 - c.1935] Probably born Arthur Blake in Jacksonville, Florida, around 1890, he became an immensely popular recording artist in the 1920s, less for his voice than his phenomenally good guitar playing, while remaining a deeply undocumented figure. He was almost as big a name as BLIND LEMON JEFFERSON, and almost as influential on other performers, especially the guitarists of Georgia and the Carolinas. His playing was *the* main influence on the creator of 'Step It Up & Go', BLIND BOY FULLER.

Blind Blake is the man in the main picture on the cover of Paul Oliver's book *The Story of the Blues* (with a smaller shot of BLIND WILLIE McTELL, whom Blake influenced, stuck on the corner). He had a light, swinging guitar technique and a touchingly rueful way of singing, though this was balanced by a rough-edged quality (Ma Rainey liked him as an accompanist for this reason). His style suited dances and rags, and he was a prominent early transmitter of 19th century rags into the 20th century blues repertoire. Tony Russell describes him as having an 'unequalled command of rag and blues guitar-playing, displayed both in songs and, unusually for the time, in effervescent and technically demanding instrumentals'. Among much else he played guitar for GUS CANNON on 'Poor Boy', recorded 'Hastings Street' (which is in Detroit) with Charlie Spand and recorded with the writers of Bessie Smith's 'Gimme a Pigfoot', Leola B. Wilson and Welsey 'Kid Sox' Wilson. Josh White acted as Blind Blake's 'eyes' at one time. He had moved to Chicago at some point in the 1920s, signed to Paramount Records and cut dozens of sides for them in his own right, starting with 'Early Morning Blues' and 'West Coast Blues' in the summer of 1926.

His best-known and most popular sides included 'That Will Never Happen No More', 'You Gonna Quit Me Blues', 'He's in the Jailhouse Now' and 'Police Dog Blues' (which includes the 'Dylanesque' lines 'Got a police dog craving for a fight / His name is Rambler, and when he gets a chance / He leaves his mark on ev'ybody's pants'). His 'Georgia Bound', recorded the same day, offers an unusual expression of regret at having migrated to the cold northern city: 'I got the Georgia Blues / For the plow and hoe.' The graceful, rueing heart of the old country blues has never been better voiced than in the brilliant ellipse of the opening line of his 'One Time Blues' from 1927: 'Ah the rising sun going down'. His 'Southern Rag' was so well-known and of such lasting appeal that even musical ingenue ALLEN GINSBERG knew of Blind Blake as well as William: Ginsberg's 'Tear Gas Rag', about an anti-Vietnam War demo in Colorado in 1972, is based on what he calls Blake's 'Old Southern Rag'.

Bob Dylan recorded the eight-bar blues 'You Gonna Quit Me' on his first solo acoustic album of the 1990s, *Good as I Been to You*, and the song's oft-repeated line supplies Dylan with his album title. (The line 'The day you quit me baby: that's the day you die' is used almost verbatim by Blind Blake as the ending to his earlier 'Early Morning Blues', and the same line recurs at the end of Barbecue Bob's 'Easy Rider Don't Deny My Name' from 1927.) Dylan introduced 'You Gonna Quit Me' to his concert repertoire with 28 performances on the summer 1993 leg of the Never-Ending Tour; its début was as the first song performed that August 22 at Vancouver, and it stayed in that slot, with one exception, in every concert through to the last of the leg, on October 9 in Mountain View, California. The song was then dropped until 1999, when it was re-performed a further three times.

Blind Blake is believed to have died back in Florida around 1935.

[Blind Blake: 'You Gonna Quit Me Blues', Chicago, c.Oct 1927; 'Police Dog Blues' & 'Georgia Bound', Richmond, IN, 17 Aug 1929, vinyl-issued respectively on *The Georgia Blues*, Yazoo L-1012, NY, 1968 and *Blind Blake: Blues in Chicago*, Riverside RLP8804, Holland, 1960s; 'Early Morning Blues' (2 takes, NY, c.Sep 1926; one issued *No Dough Blues: Blind Blake, Vol. 3*, Biograph BLP-12031, Canaan, NY, 1971, the other on *Rope Stretchin' Blues: Blind Blake, Vol. 4, 1926–31*, Biograph BLP-12037, Canaan, NY, 1972); 'Southern Rag', Chicago, c.Oct 1927, *Blind Blake: Foremost Fingerpicker*, Yazoo L-1068, US, 1984, now CD-reissued.

Barbecue Bob: 'Easy Rider Don't Deny My Name', NY, 16 Jun 1927; *The Atlanta Blues*, RBF RF-15, NY, 1966. Tony Russell, *The Blues from Robert Johnson to Robert Cray*, London: Carlton, 1997, p.33. Allen Ginsberg: 'Tear Gas Rag', in *First Blues / Rags, Ballads & Harmonium Songs 1971–1974*, New York: Full Court Press, 1975.]

'Blind Willie McTell' [song, 1983] The English ballad 'The Unfortunate Rake'; its many variants, including the cowboy ballad 'The Streets of Laredo'; the black standard 'St. James Infirmary'; and BLIND WILLIE McTELL's 'The Dyin' Crapshooter's Blues': all these related songs end up wondrously transmuted into Dylan's 1980s masterpiece 'Blind Willie McTell'.

What all these songs do is allow some articulation of a fundamental human problem: how to face death. The use of two narrators allows an interplay, or balancing, between different strategies. In the early versions, the dying hero or heroine is often preoccupied with a sense of shame or unworthiness, while the person who comes upon them, and tells us their story, is confronting imminent loss, the impermanence of comradeship, the responsibility of bearing witness to death. Later versions mediate between these feelings of tenderness, sorrow and grief for another, and the dying person's own need to banish the fear of death by making light of it.

This duality is especially heightened in McTell's 'Dyin' Crapshooter's Blues', which begins (in the 1956 version) with a long and attentive spoken account of caring for the dying friend, of the daily care over a period of weeks, the ambulance ride, the father on hand, the sorting out of practicalities—followed by the reductive mythologising of those practicalities by the careless victim ('Let a deck of cards be my tombstone. . . . Life been a doggone curse'), and culminates in the first narrator's submission to the second's show of indifference: 'Throw my buddy Jesse in the hoodoo wagon / Come here mama with that can of booze . . . / With the Dyin' Crapshooter's Blues.'

This is a very similar ending to the conventional one for 'St. James' Infirmary': 'Well now you've heard my story / Have another shot of booze / And if anyone should happen to ask you / I got the St. James Infirmary Blues.' What makes 'St. James' Infirmary' different is that it almost has *three* narrators. That is, the first narrator meets not a dying second narrator but a healthy one, who is in turn contemplating the death of a third character (his lover). Because death has already arrived in this construction, though only just, the lover doesn't get to speak, but the effect is to make the second narrator meditate upon his own mortality much like the dying second narrators of all the other songs.

The question of how many elements of the 'Rake' cycle Dylan imports into (it's tempting to say 'retains in') 'Blind Willie McTell' is only one of its aspects, but it's a starting point: it stresses their shared central purpose. Dylan's rich and complex song, with a melody that winds across the path of the 'St. James' Infirmary' tune, is also about the problem of how to face death, extended onto the grandest of scales. While implicitly it mourns the death of McTell, it struggles with the problem of how to face, to witness, to confront, the world's death rather than an individual one.

Like the 'Rake' songs, there are two narrators, and for the same reason, to summon more than one strategy in the face of death. In the Dylan song we find a first narrator who witnesses and a second who, says the first, could witness better. The opening verse parallels the beginning of the 'Rake' songs at once. Where they see a doomed comrade wrapped in white linen and cold as the clay, Dylan sees the same thing on the grand scale: he has '. . . seen the arrow on the doorpost / Sayin' this land is condemned / All the way from New Orleans to Jerusalem.' In the next lines, he pluralises coming upon 'one of my comrades', remembering that 'many martyrs fell', and expressing a sympathy with other unwilling recruits whose presence is felt in this pageant of suffering and struggle: the tribes conscripted from Africa as slaves, the chain-gangs forced to build the highways, the rebels forced to fight. And between 'All the way from New Orleans to Jerusalem' and 'I travelled through East Texas' he sets up echoes of 'The Streets of Laredo', in which the narrator 'born in South East Texas' says 'I've trailed from Canadee down to old Mexico'. Instead of a crowd round the bedside and people 'to sing a song', here 'I heard that hoot-owl singin' / As they were takin' down the tents / The stars above the barren trees was his only audience.' In parallel with 'the women from Atlanta', 'them flash-girls', or 'pretty maidens', here 'Them charcoal gypsy maidens / Can strut their feathers well.' The flowers are here too. The

'Rake' songs have 'green laurel', 'white roses', 'red roses', 'wild roses', 'green roses' and 'those sweet-smellin' roses'; they also have, in 'The Streets of Laredo', a southern setting in which 'the jimson weed and the lilac does bloom'. In 'Blind Willie McTell' we see a southern setting in which we 'smell that sweet magnolia bloom'. Dylan's 'With some fine young handsome man' matches the 'St. James Hospital' variant's 'with them handsome young ladies' and 'The Unfortunate Rake's' 'some handsome young woman', while Dylan unites the 'Hamilton Hotel' of McTell's narrative with the conventional 'St. James' Infirmary' in his own, perfectly placed 'St. James Hotel'. Dylan also uses 'the window', from the James Baker/DOC WATSON variant. This begins with the window: 'It was early one morning I passed St. James' Hospital / . . . I looked in the window . . .' and Dylan ends with it: 'I am gazin' out the window', which reverses the old Texan version and places Dylan as the dying inmate, quietly appropriate to the theme that we are all facing imminent death.

Dylan can also use the same language as the 'Rake' cycle but undermine its meaning. That 'fine young handsome man' is 'dressed up like a squire, bootleg whiskey in his hand', which throws a shadow across his fine and handsome aspect: 'dressed up like' suggests both the counterfeit, weighted down by that 'bootleg whiskey', and the vain, fluffed up by the resonance of the earlier, matching 'strut'. Even the 'sweet magnolia' sounds quite unlike the 'sweet-smellin' roses' of the earlier songs. Dylan adds nothing more beyond the phrase itself, yet we smell it as overripe and sickly. Where once the flowers were there to cover the smell of corruption, in Dylan's song they give off the smell of corruption themselves.

Falsity, vanity and corruption compound cruelty and pain. Everywhere people are fallen, in chains, under the whip in this maelstrom of history. Though it's been said that 'Blind Willie McTell' rolls backwards through America's past, in truth it offers no such consistent reverse chronology, and its vision is not limited to American terrain, though it returns to it time and again, not least by the device of McTell's omnipresence.

This may disappoint the need for neatness but it is a strength of the song that most of its images evoke more than one era: more than one time *and* place, while pressing upon us, time and again, a running analogy between Old Testament and New World.

It begins at the beginning. The 'arrow on the doorpost / Sayin' this land is condemned' flickers with a picture of the marking out of Jewish houses in the pogroms of the 1930s, and with the daubing of the doors of plague-victims in medieval Europe, but it harks back, as both these later scenes must, to the first occasion to yield such an image: the time of the Passover, when the first-born in Egypt were slain in the night by God, after the people of Moses were instructed to mark a sign on their doorposts in lamb's blood so that death might pass over and spare their children: '. . . take of the blood, and strike it on the two side posts and on the upper door post of the houses', as God instructs Moses in Exodus 12:7.

What's so striking in Bob Dylan's lyric, what gives us the sense that poetry is at work, is that Dylan can use this as the opening of a song that holds out no hope that anyone shall be spared the destruction coming in *our* night. There may be a sign on the doorpost but whose first-born—whose future—is to be spared this time, now that the land has been '. . . condemned / All the way from New Orleans to Jerusalem'?

We reach America explicitly enough, of course, when we get to 'East Texas, where many martyrs fell'. Across the border from New Orleans, Louisiana, it sticks in the memory as a stronghold of the Ku Klux Klan: a place where black victims were untold martyrs, and where the same racist attitudes linger still. Yet 'martyrs' has other, primarily religious, connotations. The word is thrown in like a spanner, to wobble us off our course of easy assumption about the focus of the song. The word 'fell' has a distracting quality here too, somehow calling attention to itself by its declamatory vagueness.

'Takin' down the tents' gives us another glimmer of the Israelites, now on their way out of Egypt, but suggests too the medicine shows, the carnival tents that lingered into the 20th century from an older America. McTell and Dylan both claim a bit of tent-cred in their early days—and for someone whose experience of it was mostly in the mind, Dylan wrote of it in thrillingly energetic detail in 'Dusty Old Fairgrounds', where we feel the setting down and pulling up of the tents as a routine, an activity, a part of life, all through the song. He claims a similar intimacy with this life when he discusses his own (now-lost) poem 'Won't You Buy a Postcard?' on CYNTHIA GOODING's radio show in New York in 1962. THE HAWKS had medicine show experience; ELVIS' manager, Colonel Parker, was an old carnie trooper. Even as recent a figure as the contemporary blues singer Robert Cray recalls that in the early days he and his musicians hit the road in an old truck and camped overnight in tents as they travelled (roaming the country like 'charcoal gypsy maidens'). But 'them charcoal gypsy maidens' also conjures up nubile black girls in 1920s cabaret routines, shimmying through the floor-shows of smokey night-clubs in black and white movies: the sort in which the blues singers never get a look in, because 'sophisticated' jazz combos deliver slicker, jollier routines more compatible with Hollywood sensibilities.

There is *almost* nothing ambiguous about time or place in the next section of the song, in which time is running backwards from *Gone with the Wind* to *Roots*: yet the word 'tribes' arrives strikingly here: it has a rigour that cuts across the assemblage of shorthand images of the Antebellum South: it dislocates the expected chain of words as 'martyrs' does earlier.

Aptly, 'them tribes' come pouring in across the very centre of the song: aptly because the analogy clutched in this double image, the analogy between the twelve tribes of Israel and the African tribes brought over on the slavery ships, is the central analogy Dylan draws all through the song. It is, moreover, the classic analogy drawn by the oppressed American blacks themselves, all the way through till at least Blind Willie McTell's generation, as they compensated themselves for the miseries of this life by looking forward to justice in the next, and reading the Bible's accounts of the struggles of the Israelites in order to voice their own aspirations. We shall overcome some day. That's why I'm sending up my timber. And I know no-one can sing them hymns like Blind Willie McTell.

The 'woman by the river' might equally be biblical or Mississippian. She's timeless. The 'squire' suggests the 17th or 18th century, but 'dressed up like a squire' adds in all those 19th century Southern landowners striding their estates in high boots and frilly shirts while the blacks, almost invisible, worked the land. The 'bootleg whiskey in his hand' can equally smell of the stills in the hills (where they ain't paid no whiskey tax since 1792) or of Prohibition Chicago, another milieu the old blues singers lived and worked in. The 'chain-gang on the highway' must keep us in that recent past but the 'rebels', whoever else they may be, insist on yelling to us from the American Civil War.

This multi-layering of the pageant takes its cue from the opening verse: crucially to our whole understanding of the song, 'All the way from New Orleans to Jerusalem' must be capable of pitching us both backwards and forwards—back from the New Orleans of now or of McTell's generation, the New Orleans where you might say black American music found its feet, to the Jerusalem of Bible days; and forward to the new Jerusalem dreamed of but now doomed not to be: dreamed of but 'condemned'.

One of Dylan's inspired touches here, in that nigh-perfect penultimate stanza, is to underscore his tolling of doomsday by alluding to, and then contorting, those well-known lines of optimism and hope, 'God's in His heaven—All's right with the world.' (For detail see **Browning, Robert**.)

While Dylan sounds the undertaker's bell, the song itself never shrivels: it moves but it certainly doesn't depress. It examines the problem of how to face death but it tingles with life. The black girls, in that lovely, eccentric construction, strut their feathers. The song presses a sense of our senses upon us. *Blind* Willie McTell, his other senses heightened, is never far away. Yet true to McTell's uncanny visualising spirit, *seeing* is insisted upon. In one verse alone we see, hear, smell and see again. The first word of the song is 'seen'; the end of the song finds him 'gazing'. All through, spooky as the plangent, coiling music, Dylan's sixth sense emits its vibrant, probing beam.

Out of death, life arises. Out of bodily pain, the triumph of the spirit (pain sure brings out the best in people, doesn't it?). Out of singing the blues, compensation: even joy. Dylan celebrates, in this song—as Blind Willie McTell does in 'The Dyin' Crapshooter's Blues'. The work of art, as ever with Bob Dylan, is the recording, not the words on the page: but the words on the page demand from Dylan, and receive, two of his most focussed performances: paying tribute to McTell's artistry, he rises to the occasion with the excellence of his own.

This is the spookiest important record since 'Heartbreak Hotel', and is built upon the perfect interweaving of guitar, piano, voice and silence—an interweaving that has space for the lovely clarity of single notes: a guitar string stroking the air here, a piano note pushing back the distance there. And if anything, the still-unreleased performance is even better, for its more original melody (less dependent upon the conventional 'St. James' Infirmary' structure) and its incandescent vocal, which soars to possess the heights of reverie and inspiration. No-one can sing the blues like Blind Willie McTell, but no-one can write or sing a blues like 'Blind Willie McTell' like Bob Dylan.

Spookily, too, perhaps, Dylan's recording of 'Blind Willie McTell' manages to commemorate not only the death of McTell but his birthday also. McTell was almost certainly born in 1903, and the only specific birthdate ever mooted has been May 5. Either by eerie coincidence, or because Dylan is a walking blues encyclopedia, when he came to record 'Blind Willie McTell' in 1983, he did so on May 5.

Aptly, in view of their subject matter, there is even a further correspondence between McTell's masterpiece 'The Dyin' Crapshooter's Blues' and Dylan's masterpiece 'Blind Willie McTell'—these two great songs about appropriate leave-taking—in the tiny detailing of how they take their leave of us. A *doubled rhyme* is one way to signal the end of a song, as CHRISTOPHER RICKS points out à propos of 'Señor (Tales of Yankee Power)', which ends with 'Can you tell me what we're waiting *for*, Señ*or*?' Ricks calls this 'making a conclusive ending, that your conclusions can be more drastic,' adding that this is 'exactly what Andrew Marvell did in the greatest political poem in the English language: that is, the "Horatian Ode". . .'

Nowhere this side of Marvell will you find more effective use of such extra emphasis of rhyme as a signing-off device at song's end than when McTell ends 'The Dyin' Crapshooter's Blues'. He sings the final phrase as 'It's the dyin' crap-*shoo-doo's blues*': putting equal and emphatic weight on each of these last sounds. As you might expect, Dylan finds a neatly equivalent little thing for the end of 'Blind Willie McTell'. In fact Ricks makes a generalisation in 1980 about Dylan's work which is prophetically accurate about this 1983 song: '. . . he's obsessed with two things. One is human situations which you can't imagine ever really coming to an end, and the other is the simple technical question of how if you're singing a song you do something intuitive and imaginative to let people know that it really is the end.' In this case, paralleling 'The Dyin' Crapshooter's Blues', Dylan finds a solution to this 'simple technical question' that is an intuitive touch of tribute to McTell. Instead of a rhyme like those that conclude his other verses—'bell/McTell', and so on—his last verse simply doubles that subliminal 'tell', pairing 'I am gazing out the window of the St. James Ho*tel*' with 'And I know no-one can sing the blues like Blind Willie Mc*Tell*.'

The very phrase 'sing the blues' re-expresses in colloquial terms the ancient Hebrew custom of making *lamentations*, or mourning songs, 'upon the death of great men . . . and upon any occasion of public miseries and calamities,' in Adam Clarke's phrase. In the Old Testament book Lamentations (short for the Lamentations of Jeremiah), Jeremiah composes a lamentation on the death of Josiah the King, but also a lamentation upon the desolations of Jerusalem, which are visited on the Jews by God for their worship of false idols. In 'Blind Willie McTell' Dylan achieves a lamentation that serves to commemorate both public calamity *and* individual demise: to deal with the envisaged desolations to come, 'all the way from New Orleans to Jerusalem', *and* the death of Blind Willie McTell.

In concert, Dylan waited until 1997 before singing 'Blind Willie McTell' at all (its début was in Montreal that August 5th and he has performed it a further 94 times since), and even then, he chose to duplicate the inferior, re-shaped version recorded by THE BAND. This decision, combined with a tendency to easy posturing in his delivery, has meant that in concert it has never received its due: never been quite the fitting tribute it should be, to either McTell or to his own masterly song.

[Bob Dylan: 'Blind Willie McTell', NY, 5 May 1983; 1 take issued the *Bootleg Series Vols. 1–3*, 1991; 2nd take unreleased but circulated. Dylan to Cynthia Gooding, 'Folksinger's Choice', WBAI Radio, NY, prob. 13 Jan 1962 & prob. broadcast 11 Mar 1962.

For the English ballad cluster, try *The Unfortunate Rake: A Study in the Evolution of a Ballad*, various versions by various artists, compiled & edited by Kenneth Goldstein, Folkways FS3805, NY, 1960. Doc Watson: 'St. James' Hospital', *nia*, reissued *The Essential Doc Watson Vol. 1*, Vanguard 5308, NY, 1973, CD-reissued Vanguard VMCD 7308, NY, 1987.

Blind Willie McTell: 'Dyin' Crapshooter's Blues, Atlanta, Sep 1956; *Blind Willie McTell: Last Session*, Prestige Bluesville 1040, Bergenfield, NJ, 1961, reissued Prestige PR 7809, Bergenfield, 1966 (& in the UK first then, as *Blind Willie McTell: Last Session*, Transatlantic PR1040, London, 1966); CD-reissued Prestige Bluesville Original Blues Classics OBCCD-517-2 (BV-1040), Berkeley, CA, 1992.

Christopher Ricks: radio broadcast in Australia, *nia*, 1980. Andrew Marvell: 'An Horatian Ode Upon Cromwell's Return from Ireland', 1650. Adam Clarke, *Clarke's Commentary on the Bible, Old Testament* Vol. 4, London: Thomas Tegg, 1844 edn.]

***Blonde on Blonde* [1966]** The seventh album and Dylan's first double-album. To have followed up one masterpiece with another was Dylan's history-making achievement here. It aims, perhaps, at a more limited canvas than *Highway 61 Revisited* but evokes a much richer, more multi-layered, synapse-jumping consciousness. Where *Highway 61 Revisited* has Dylan exposing and confronting like a laser-beam in surgery, descending from outside the sickness, *Blonde on Blonde* offers a persona awash inside the chaos and speaking to others who are acceptedly in the same boat and on the same ocean. We're tossed from song to song, and they all move into each other. The feel and the music are on a grand scale, truly oceanic, and the language and delivery is a unique mixture of the visionary and the colloquial, the warm and the alert. Dylan dances like his own 'Mr. Tambourine Man' through these songs, even though tossed and blown by disorientating, desperate forces. It seems against the spirit of the double-album's cumulative effect to single out particular songs, but they include 'Visions of Johanna', 'Pledging My Time', 'Memphis Blues Again' and 'Sad-Eyed Lady of the Lowlands'.

[Recorded NY, 25 Jan; Nashville, TN, 14–17 Feb & 8–10 Mar 1966; released as 2-LP set, Columbia C2S 841 (stereo) & C2L 41 (mono), Jun 1966. (An official US release date of 16 May has been noted but was theoretical at best. Late Jun/early Jul was the earliest it was really available.) In the UK CBS SDDP 66012 & CS 9316-9317 (stereo), & CBS DDP 66012/CL 2516-2517 (mono), Aug 1966.]

***Blood on the Tracks* [1975]** In stunning, total contrast to the previous album, *Before the Flood*, this 16th Dylan album triumphantly shows more subtlety and nuance than anything he'd ever done, and as honed a use of understatement as on *John Wesley Harding*. At the time this was the most unexpected leap of Dylan's career. After years of comparatively second-rate work and a considerable decline in his reputation, here was an album to stand with *Highway 61 Revisited* and *Blonde on Blonde*. As EYOLF ØSTREM puts it: 'A unique combination of a new interest in open tunings (inspired by JONI MITCHELL), a new perspective on writing and time (inspired by the mysterious art-teacher NORMAN RAEBEN), and a broken heart (inspired by SARA [DYLAN]), brought about a burst of creative energy comparable only to the making of his mid-sixties trilogy.'

It was an album of genius—of powerful emotional complexity, unerring fresh insight and the kind of maturity that manifests itself not remotely as grown-up tiredness but as pure, strong intelligence. Yet the point is that while it compared with the mid-60s 'trilogy' in quality, it was not a creature of the 1960s at all. With *Blood on the Tracks* Dylan's progress suddenly showed through in a tremendous, unexpected leap forwards and upwards. One of his very best, it gave us, on a whole new plateau, a successfully attained, fresh language that achieved the new simplicity he'd been striving for ever since *John Wesley Harding*—and in which, as ever in the best of Dylan's work, simplicity was deceptive, communicating more by being able confidently to say less.

Blood on the Tracks gave us, also, Dylan's scorching urgency at its very best, and utterly free from the chains of the 1960s. This was *the* best album of the 1970s.

For this reason alone, its historical importance is immense. When it was first released, in 1975, its effect was colossal. An adjustment was needed, critically, to the fact that Dylan had so dramatically broken free of the decade with which he was deeply associated by virtue of having so profoundly affected it. Some adjustment was necessary to Dylan's generation's consciousness, from the fact that with *Blood on the Tracks* it was Bob Dylan who had produced the most strikingly intelligent, apposite and entirely contemporary album of the 1970s.

Most people had assumed that, in effect, Dylan's decline at the end of the decade he had made his own, the 1960s, had frozen seminal work—*Highway 61 Revisited*, *Blonde on Blonde*, the basement tapes, *John Wesley Harding*—into an historical religious object that one had to choose, by the mid-70s, either to put away in the attic or else to revere perhaps at the expense of more contemporary artists. Instead, *Blood on the Tracks* legitimised Dylan's claim to a creative prowess—a power capable of being directed at us effectively for perhaps another 30 or 40 years.

The common conception of how rock music moves forward needed to be adjusted too. That conception had always been that artists come and go in relatively short time-spans, with careers peaking early. *Blood on the Tracks* challenged that idea. Here was a masterpiece fully ten years after Dylan's first major 'peak', *Highway 61 Revisited*—and one as different and as fresh as it possibly could have been. It addressed the post-1960s world, and our darkness within, with a whole arsenal of weapons.

Its creative genius is still very much an undiminished thing of the present. It has as much sheer freshness as Dylan's, or anyone else's, first album; as much genuine urge to communicate; as much zest. Yet it combines them all with a sharp wit and corrosive intelligence, and an impeccable judgement, so that the sum of these parts is a greater whole than any of Dylan's other achievements.

Like *Planet Waves*, *Blood on the Tracks* deals, among much else, with the overlaying of the past upon the present—but gone, utterly, is any element of Dylan's myopic early-70s insistence on eternal love and its wholesome cocoon. In its place is a profoundly felt understanding of our fragile impermanence of control, so that in dealing with the overlay of past upon present, Dylan is dealing also (unlike *Planet Waves*) with the inexorable disintegration of relationships, and with the dignity of keeping on trying to reintegrate them against all odds.

'Tangled Up in Blue', tackling all this head on, opens the album at a high level of intensity and brilliance. (See separate entry.) 'Simple Twist of Fate' carves out its own indelible impression on the mind, and 'You're a Big Girl Now' presses on still further with the unsparing examination of whether a decaying relationship can withstand the strains of time and other lovers; and then with 'Idiot Wind' we return to these themes again but with a yet greater intensity.

Seen first as a sort of 'Positively 4th Street Revisited', the version Dylan chose to release is not the album's most successful song. The too-personal bone-scraping jars: 'Someone's got it in for me / They're planting stories in the press . . . / I haven't known peace and quiet / For so long I can't remember what it's like . . . / You'll find out when you reach the top / You're on the bottom . . .' It also produces, in Dylan, a need to step back from that extra-personal quality somehow: and he does so in the wrong way, by stylizing his delivery of the anger, so that his voice at those points comes across with a faked-sounding passion. (The original version, which Dylan got cold feet about releasing, needed no exaggerated delivery; its angry eloquence is genuinely personal, and all the more thrilling for being so scrupulously sotto voce.) Yet this is a small element in the song. It deepens into one of infinitely greater emotional range than a 'Positively 4th Street'. The idiot wind that blows is the whole conglomeration of things that assail our integrity and of love that renders us hapless and out of control. The song locks us in a fight to the death, in a contemporary graveyard landscape of skulls and dust and changing seasons. Destruction and survival again.

The preoccupation with this just-possible survival one must fight for is urged most eloquently in this tremendous, evocative stanza: 'There's a lone soldier on the cross / Smoke pourin' out of a box-car door / You didn't know it, you didn't think it could be done: / In the final end he won the war / After losing every battle . . .'

That is matched, later in the song, by the extraordinary tugging wildness of this—a triumph of poetic strength: 'The priest wore black on the seventh day / And sat stone-faced while the building burned / I waited for you on the runnin' boards / 'Neath the cypress tree while the springtime turned / Slowly into autumn: / Idiot wind / Blowin' like a circle around my skull / From the Grand Coulee Dam to the Capitol . . .' (And what a rhyme!)

Then, in total contrast, we have the lightly sketched humane straightforwardness of 'You're Gonna Make Me Lonesome When You Go', another fully fledged success for Dylan's new simplicity of language and a conscious reversing of all those Dylan songs where the singer leaves his lover for the road. This time, she leaves him for the road—though there is a fine 'live' version of the song by Shawn Colvin which strongly evokes a sense that the person going is departing this life altogether. ('I'll see you in the sky above / In the tall grass and the ones I love'.) The strength of the song lies in its tone of lively philosophic acceptance: there is no self-absorption, much less self-pity. His love for her comes through from the way in which he accepts that she must go and so tells her his feelings unreprovingly: 'I've seen love go by my door / Never bin this close before . . .'

Much of the song is thus delivered, so lightly as to suggest that it's in brackets, with the same sparkling, generous humour. Astonishing that a man who, by the time he made this album, had been monstrously famous for over a decade and had been acclaimed as a genius before he was 25, could have the down-to-earth self-knowledge to throw out, in this song, so ordinarily humorous and puckish a phrase as the one that ends this stanza: 'You're gonna make me wonder what I'm doin' / Stayin' far behind without you / You're gonna make me wonder what I'm sayin'— / You're gonna make me give myself a good talkin' to . . .'

Again, as ever on this unsurpassed album, the simplicity of language represents the opposite of a dullness of emotion. Throughout, from the deft movie-script of 'Lily, Rosemary and the Jack of Hearts' to the scrupulously checked-in intensity of 'If You See Her, Say Hello' (a marvellous re-write of 'Girl of the North Country', with the earlier song's line 'See for me if . . .' echoed in the later's 'Say for me that . . .') and from the flawless blues of 'Meet Me in the Morning' to the barbed sanity of 'Buckets of Rain', *Blood on the Tracks* is the work of an artist who has never been of sharper intelligence nor more genuinely preoccupied with the inner struggles and complexities of human nature. Dylan's sensibility here is 100 per cent intact. He is also an artist who has lost, on *Blood on the Tracks*, not one iota of his devotion to, nor expertise with, a wide range of American music.

[Recorded NY, 16–17, 19 Sep, and Minneapolis, MN, 27 & 30 Dec 1974; released as Columbia PC 33235 (CBS 69097 in UK), 17 Jan 1975. Eyolf Østrem: 'Tangled Up in "Tangled Up in Blue"', online 7 Jun 2005 at *www.dylanchords.com/index.htm*. Shawn Colvin: 'You're Gonna Make Me Lonesome When You Go', NY, 5–6 Aug 1993, *Cover Girl*, Columbia 477240 2, NY, 1994.]

Bloomfield, Mike [1944 - 1981] Michael Bloomfield was born in Chicago on July 28, 1944, hung around the city's blues clubs from a very young age and by the time he hit adulthood was already one of the great white blues guitarists and one of the earliest blues-rock virtuosos: an influence on all the rest and a pioneer of the extended solo. He learnt from, and sat in with, many blues greats, including BIG JOE WILLIAMS, who once tried to stab him. His short memoir, *Me and Big Joe*, 1980, describes not only Williams himself but also going with him to visit Tampa Red, SONNY BOY WILLIAMSON, Tommy McClennan, Kokomo Arnold and others.

Bloomfield joined the PAUL BUTTERFIELD Blues Band in late 1964 (in time to play much-admired solos on their 1965 début album) and increasingly influenced the adventurousness of the group's subsequent work, flying off in exploratory ways while relying on the Chicago blues-band anchor of Butterfield and his rhythm section. He brought an Indian influence into the group's second album, *East-West*, after exploring Indian music on a series of acid trips.

After a first meeting in Chicago in early 1963, Bloomfield's working relationship with Bob Dylan began, as for so many musicians Dylan has locked onto down the years, with a phone call out of the blue. Would he like to fly to New York and play on this song? Dylan specified only this: 'None of that B.B. King shit': and however you feel about B.B. King, you know what Dylan meant. He wanted the pioneering rock-blues side of Bloomfield, and he got it. Bloomfield took the flight, his guitar on the seat next to him; he didn't own a guitar-case. The sessions began on June 15, 1965. They started with 'It Takes a Lot to Laugh, It Takes a Train to Cry', didn't get the take they wanted, moved on to the more obscure 'Sitting on a Barbed Wire Fence' (the third take of which was issued in 1991 on the *Bootleg Series Vols. 1–3*), and then, without success, tried 'Like a Rolling Stone'.

Next day they went back to it, and the session's fifth take was *it*. A few weeks later, with AL KOOPER, BARRY GOLDBERG, JEROME ARNOLD and SAM LAY, Mike Bloomfield was up there with Dylan facing the partially hostile crowd at the NEWPORT FOLK FESTIVAL, and back in the studio four days after that, cutting more of *Highway 61 Revisited*. On July 29, they pinned down 'Tombstone Blues', 'It Takes a Lot to Laugh, It Takes a Train to Cry' and the 'Positively 4th Street' single. July 30 secured 'From a Buick 6' and the version of 'Can You Please Crawl Out Your Window?' that, also labeled 'Positively 4th Street', was issued by mistake. On August 2, the highly productive penultimate day, they cut the album's title track, 'Just Like Tom Thumb's Blues', 'Queen Jane Approximately' and 'Ballad of a Thin Man'.

Bloomfield bowed out and went back to his other life. He left the Paul Butterfield Blues Band early in 1967 and on the West Coast formed the Electric Flag, with his old friends Nick Gravenites and Barry Goldberg, plus Buddy Miles on drums and a brass section. Their first recordings were for the soundtrack of the cult film *The Trip*, followed by a first album, *A Long Time Comin'*, in spring 1968. Mike Bloomfield left the group that summer, before Buddy Miles prompted them to make a second album (*The Electric Flag*). The group disbanded in 1969.

Bloomfield had moved on to join Stephen Stills and Al Kooper for an album on which they're billed as, er, Stills-Kooper-Bloomfield. *Supersession* includes a very odd treatment of 'It Takes a Lot to Laugh, It Takes a Train to Cry', typifying in its strain after effect that period immediately after the heyday of Angst Bards, when, as this album's title implies, rock groups suddenly produced superstars: a new term, then, signifying a new breed of people so stratospheric that they could hardly play their instruments at all any more. Quitting their original successful groups, they tried to join forces, generally for one-off gigs in front of massive rock-festival audiences; but excesses of money, alcohol, drugs and ego made it impossible for these titans even to speak to each other, much less work productively. Kooper and Bloomfield were not in the same league, superstar-wise, as Stephen Stills, and perhaps their lesser status is what keeps their collaboration from falling apart altogether.

Bloomfield managed a series of solo albums, uninhibited by the fact that he didn't know what he wanted to say and was lost outside the framing of a band. In 1973 another not-very-supergroup was attempted, joining Bloomfield with Dr. John and JOHN HAMMOND JR., calling itself Triumvirate and redirecting Bloomfield back towards the blues. It was no success at all. In 1974 Bloomfield contributed to an Electric Flag reunion album produced by JERRY WEXLER, *The Band Kept Playing*. It didn't.

He also wrote for 'underground' movies other than *The Trip*, and made appearances in several too. He wrote all the original music for that important 1960s independent film *Medium Cool*, directed and written by Haskell Wexler in 1969. He appears as himself in *Bongo Wolf's Revenge*, 1970, directed by WARHOL hanger-on Tom Baker, and wrote its original music, and gets credits as musician and lyricist on 1973's archetypal 1970s movie *Steelyard Blues*, directed by Alan Myerson and starring Donald Sutherland, Peter Boyle and Jane Fonda. In 1977 he wrote the music for *Andy Warhol's Bad*, directed by Jed Johnson.

A decent sampler of Bloomfield's real work in the 1960s is the compilation *Don't Say That I Ain't Your Man: Essential Blues 1964–1969*. His 1970s solo albums include *Try It Before You Buy* (1973) and *Analine* (1977). The same year's *If You Love These Blues, Play 'Em as You Please* attracted more attention but by this time Bloomfield was a long-term heroin user and hostile to the idea of touring (though in summer 1980 he toured Italy with classical guitarist Woody Harris and cellist Maggie Edmondson). By the late 1970s much of his modest income was earned from creating the music scores for porn movies, a gig that had been at its best in the much-praised semi-overground porn of *Sodom and Gomorrah*, made by the Mitchell Brothers in 1975.

Fifteen years after their historic 1965 collaboration, when Dylan was playing 12 nights at the Fox-Warfield in San Francisco in November 1980, mounting a series of golden concerts that marked his first semi-return to the secular world after the adamantly all-gospel tours of 1979 and spring 1980, he went round one day to Mike Bloomfield's house, not knowing in what condition he'd find the guitarist, and had to climb in through a window to get to see him. They talked, Dylan urging Bloomfield to come to one of the concerts and play with him again. A couple of nights later (on November 15), friends took Bloomfield along, though he was so sceptical of Dylan's really wanting him to play that he wore his slippers. But Dylan called him on stage, giving him time to adjust to the rather scary situation and much reassurance, by offering the audience a long, affectionate and generous speech on who Mike Bloomfield was. Then they did 'Like a Rolling Stone', with Bloomfield delivering a biting, triumphant guitar-part, matched by a second contribution towards the end of the concert, on a glittering, epic ride through 'Groom's Still Waiting at the Altar'.

Three months later to the day, Mike Bloomfield took a drug overdose and was found dead in his car. He was 36.

[Mike Bloomfield, with S. Summerville: *Me and Big Joe*, San Francisco: Re/Search Productions, 1980. Mike Bloomfield: *Analine*, Takoma B-1059, US, 1977; *If You Love These Blues, Play 'Em as You Please*, Guitar Player KT 5006, 1977; 'Tomorrow Night', *nia*, unreleased till the CD version of his 1973 LP *Try It Before You Buy*, One Way A21265, NY, c.1990. Paul Butterfield Blues Band: *Paul Butterfield Blues Band*, Elektra 7294, NY, 1975; *East-West*, Elektra 7315, NY, 1976. Electric Flag: *The Trip* soundtrack; *Long Time Comin'*; *The Band Kept Playing*, Atlantic 18112, US, 1974.

Bob Dylan (with Bloomfield & others): 'Can *You* Please Crawl Out Your Window?', NY, 30 Jul 1965, issued mistitled 'Positively 4th Street' & with its catalogue number (Columbia 4-43389), NY, 1965. B.B. King quote from Bloomfield, article in *Hit Parader*, US, Jun 1968; republished (but last word given as 'stuff') in Mike Bloomfield: 'Impressions of Bob

Dylan', *On the Tracks* no.10, Grand Junction, CO, 1997.]

Blow, Kurtis [1959 -] Kurtis Walker was born in Harlem, New York City, on August 9, 1959. From mid-1970s breakdancing he moved across to being a DJ (Kool DJ Kurt) and then *the* pioneer of rap. He was a club sensation in the late 1970s; his début album, *Kurtis Blow*, 1980, was the first rap album on a major label; and he proved the first commercially successful rapper and a giant figure in the history of hip-hop. His second single, 'The Breaks', was a huge hit and in the early 1980s he also produced and talent-spotted other artists, not least the Fat Boys. His own albums included *Deuce* (1981), *Tough* (1982), *Ego Trip* and *Rapper in Town* (both 1984). He appeared in the film *Krush Groove*, performing 'If I Ruled the World', his biggest hit single since 'The Breaks'. The album *America* was issued in 1985.

By 1986 he was so thoroughly passé that Bob Dylan had picked up on him, and on April 1, 1986 went in the studio and overdubbed vocals on one verse of 'Street Rock', which was duly released on the next Blow album, *Kingdom Blow*, later that year. In his memoir *Chronicles Volume One*, Dylan writes that Blow had asked him to be on one of his records, and that 'he familiarized me with that stuff, Ice-T, Public Enemy, N.W.A., Run-D.M.C. . . . They were all poets and knew what was going on. . . . The music that Danny [LANOIS] and I were making was archaic.'

But 'time will tell who has fell and who's been left behind', and Kurtis Blow sounds at least as archaic now. 'The Breaks' sounds like nothing so much as Ian Dury's 'Hit Me With Your Rhythm Stick'; in exactly the same corny comic way as Dury, Kurtis here intones 'If your woman steps out with another man / And she runs off with him to Japan . . . / And Ma Bell sends you a whopping bill / For 18 phone calls to Brazil'. In other words, this pioneering rap sounds just like vaudeville. Blow's fans sound quaintly old-fashioned too. One posted this comment to Amazon.com as a review of *Kurtis Blow Presents the History of Rap* (a venerable-sounding title in itself): 'I have been a fan of curtis blow far many years. This is a must for the old school.'

[Kurtis Blow (with Bob Dylan): 'Street Rock', NY, 1 Apr 1986, *Kingdom Blow*, Mercury 8360-215-1, US, Sep 1986. Bob Dylan: *Chronicles Volume One*, 2004, p.219. Fan comment seen online 4 Sep 2005 at *www.amazon .com/exec/obidos/tg/detail/-/B00000343F/002-9914338-585 9204?v=glance*. Various Artists: *Kurtis Blow Presents the History of Rap*, Rhino/WEA 72852, US, 1997; this includes Blow's 'The Breaks'.]

'Blowin' in the Wind' GIL TURNER was hosting the Monday-night hootenannies at Gerde's Folk City when Dylan, accompanied by DAVID BLUE, brought Gil a song he'd just written. David Blue tells the story like this:

'Bob was nervous and he was doing his Chaplin shuffle as he caught Gil's attention. "I got a song you should hear, man," Bob said, grinning from ear to ear. "Sure thing, Bob," Gil said. He moved closer to hear better. A crowd sort of circled the two of them. Bob sang it out with great passion. When he finished there was silence all around. Gil Turner was stunned. "I've got to do that song myself," he said. "Now!" "Sure, Gil, that's great. You want to do it tonight?" "Yes," said Turner, picking up his guitar, "teach it to me now."

'Bob showed him the chords and Gil roughly learned the words. He took the copy Bob made for him and went upstairs. We followed, excited by the magic that was beginning to spread. Gil mounted the stage and taped the words on to the mike stand. "Ladies and gentlemen," he said, "I'd like to sing a new song by one of our great songwriters. It's hot off the pencil and here it goes."

'He sang the song, sometimes straining to read the words off the paper. When he was through, the entire audience stood on its feet and cheered. Bob was leaning against the bar near the back smiling and laughing.'

Naturally, Dylan started performing 'Blowin' in the Wind' in Greenwich Village clubs himself by late that April and it was one of three songs he sang at the '*Broadside* Reunion' show in May 1962, but it was July 9th before he recorded it—on one of the many session days for his second album, *The Freewheelin' Bob Dylan* (though the same month he also recorded it as a Witmark song demo)—and its release would come almost a year later than this.

In the interim, his manager ALBERT GROSSMAN gave an acetate of the song (plus 'Tomorrow Is a Long Time') to Milt Okun, who worked with PETER, PAUL & MARY, the Brothers Four and the Chad Mitchell Trio. Okun allocated 'Blowin' in the Wind' to the Mitchells, who started to perform it and recorded it for a new album. Thus the first record release of 'Blowin' in the Wind' was on *The Chad Mitchell Trio in Action* (Kapp Records 3313) in March 1963.

Warner Bros. released Peter, Paul & Mary's version June 18, 1963. *Billboard* heard 'this slick ditty' as 'a sailor's lament, sung softly and tenderly.' It sold 320,000 copies in eight days: the fastest-selling single in Warners' five-year history. Charting June 29, it peaked Aug 17 at no.2. William Ruhlmann notes, 1996, that it 'remains the most successful single recording of a Bob Dylan song on the Hot 100. Though never certified by the Record Industry Association of America, it is reported to have sold two million copies. It would win Peter, Paul & Mary Grammy Awards for Best Performance by a Vocal Group and Best Folk recording'.

Dylan's own version saw release on May 27, 1963: three days after his 22nd birthday, and the night after performing it triumphantly at the 1963 NEWPORT FOLK FESTIVAL. About 80 versions were released within two years, as the song's hit potential and cultural impact was recognised. These included, apart from the predictable folkies' versions, recordings by Marlene Dietrich, Eddy Arnold, Bobby Darin, Stan Getz, Duke Ellington and Johnny Tillotson. By 2002 at least 375 recordings had been made of the song (far more than of any other Dylan composition), including by ELVIS PRESLEY, NEIL YOUNG, Sebastian Cabot, Ace Cannon, SAM COOKE, Mahalia Jackson, the Four Seasons, Trini Lopez, Cliff Richard (on the 1966 LP *Kinda Latin*) and Johnny Nash.

Dylan himself eschewed the song within eight months of its Newport performance and didn't reintroduce it to his repertoire until, after recording 15 studio takes of it in New York City in June 1970 (all still uncirculated), he performed it at the afternoon and evening Concerts for Bangladesh on August 1, 1971. (Ahead of these performances, it was said that GEORGE HARRISON had asked Dylan if he were going to sing it and that Dylan had replied: 'Why? Are you going to sing "She Loves You"?')

On the 1974 North American 'comeback tour', it was not performed until the 25th concert (Madison Square Garden, NYC); but since then Dylan has performed the song ad nauseam. The gospel versions of the Born Again period were often effective, and once or twice the song has befitted a particular occasion—e.g. the Martin Luther King Birthday concert at Washington, D.C., on January 20, 1986, when Dylan sang it with Peter, Paul & Mary; but overall it has degenerated into a meaningless Greatest Hit, sung with predictable inattentiveness and overblown or cheesy music. Nastiest so far have been the versions performed with horrendous vocal back-ups by Never-Ending Tour musicians LARRY CAMPBELL and CHARLIE SEXTON in and beyond the last days of the 20th century. (On this tour alone, from its beginning in mid-1988 to the end of 2000, 'Blowin' in the Wind' was performed 407 times. The career-long total number of times Dylan had performed it by the end of 2003 was 935.)

The lyric is an early example of Dylan's quiet incorporation of Biblical rhetoric into his own. A particular rhetorical format deployed time and again in the New Testament and founded upon a text from the Old Testament book of Ezekiel (12:1–2) is: 'The word of the Lord also came unto me, saying, Son of man, thou dwellest in the midst of a rebellious house, which have eyes to see, and see not; they have ears to hear, and hear not . . .' In 'Blowin' in the Wind' this is redeployed as 'Yes' n' how many ears must one man have . . . ?' and 'Yes' n' how many times must a man turn his head / Pretending he just doesn't see?'

(In the New Testament the Ezekiel passage is cited by Christ in Matthew 13:43 ['. . . Who hath ears to hear, let him hear'] and repeatedly by Christ and others in Mark and Revelation: 'And he said unto them, He that hath ears to hear, let him hear' [Mark 4:9]; 'If any man have ears to hear, let him hear' [Mark 4:23]; 'If any man have ears to hear, let him hear' [Mark 7:16]; 'Having eyes, see ye not? and having ears, hear ye not? . . .' [Mark 8:18]; and 'He that hath an ear, let him hear . . .' [Revelation 2:7, 11 & 29; 3:6, 13 & 22]. Dylan returns to the same rhetoric in the lyric of 'When He Returns', on the *Slow Train Coming* album of 1979. See also **'Angelina'** for more on Revelation's use of Ezekiel and echoes of these in Dylan's lyrics.)

Dylan's own early, perhaps disingenuous, comments about the song suggest that he saw it as an altogether simpler creation. This is what he says in June 1962, when the lyric is published in *Sing Out!* magazine:

> 'There ain't too much I can say about this song except that the answer is blowing in the wind. It ain't in no book or movie or TV show or discussion group. Man, it's in the wind—and it's blowing in the wind. Too many of these hip people are telling me where the answer is but oh I won't believe that. I still say it's in the wind and just like a restless piece of paper it's got to come down some time. . . . But the only trouble is that no one picks up the answer when it comes down so not too many people get to see and know it . . . and then it flies away again. . . . I still say that some of the biggest criminals are those that turn their heads away when they see wrong and know it's wrong. I'm only 21 years old and I know that there's been too many wars. . . . You people over 21, you're older and smarter.'

[Bob Dylan: 'Blowin' in the Wind', prob. Gerde's Folk City, prob. late Apr 1962; at the '*Broadside* Reunion' show, May 1962, broadcast WBAI-FM, NY, Fall 1962; and Witmark demo, NY, Jul 1962. David Blue quoted from Robbie Woliver, *Hoot! A 25-Year History of the Greenwich Village Music Scene*, New York: 1986, pp. 83–84, seen online 12 Sep 2004 at *www.fortunecity.com/tinpan/parton/2/blowin.html*. (Blue dates this as Apr 16; Ian Woodward dates it as Apr 9.) Much other factual secular information here is taken from William Ruhlmann's research, published *Goldmine*, 12 Apr 1996, excerpted on the History pages of *www.peterpaulmary.com*, including the quote from *Billboard*, 22 Jun 1963. The list of covers also draws on *www.bjorner.com/covers.htm*, online 29 Jul 2005. Dylan's June 1962 comments, *Sing Out!*, New York, Oct–Nov 1962 issue; reprinted in liner notes to *Broadside Ballads*, Broadside BR 301, NY, Oct 1963.]

Blue, David [1941 - 1982] Stuart David Cohen was born in Pawtucket, Rhode Island, on February 18, 1941. He had a difficult relationship with his parents, joined the Navy, got kicked out, found Greenwich Village and took a job washing dishes at the Gaslight. He wanted to be an actor first, and then said he was a poet, but mostly he was a hanger-on in the Village, a singer-songwriter whose work no-one much appreciated except, it's said, PHIL OCHS, whom he used to cheat out of the dope he was selling him, by supplying it and then filching it back after collecting the money. LEONARD COHEN (no relation) liked him as a person, and JONI MITCHELL spent years trying to help him, not least with recurrent payments of money. Dylan gave him the nickname 'David Blue' and he took it.

Nervous, strenuously determined to be cool, he naturally gravitated towards Dylan over and above other people. Marc Eliot said David 'was a character. He would be offended if someone told him he looked like Dylan, yet he looked like that on purpose.' It's said that Dylan treated him badly, but Blue himself said Dylan had encouraged his songwriting, enthusing about it and urging him to work at it. They were very friendly—'tight', in the Village jargon—at one point, and he became another figure a bit like BOBBY NEUWIRTH, but earlier. He was with Dylan when he wrote 'Blowin' in the Wind' and took it round to play to GIL TURNER in April 1962.

After contributing three tracks under the name David Cohen to a compilation album on Elektra, *The Singer/Songwriter Project* in 1965, he made a handful of albums as David Blue—*David Blue* (1966, which was said to be very *Bringing It All Back Home*), *These 23 Days in September* (1968), *Stories* (1971), *Nice Baby & the Angel* (1973, produced by Graham Nash), *Com'n Back for More* (1975) and *Cupid's Arrow* (1976)—on which an extraordinary array of star names gave musical support, including Joni Mitchell. In 1969 he threw in another, *Me*, under the name S. David Cohen.

They all sold so badly that he's one of the only people in the world whose LPs have mostly not been CD-reissued. One of them, when in 1966–67 he was fronting the band American Patrol, wasn't even released on vinyl in the first place. On *Com'n Back for More*, his star contributors included Bob Dylan, who dropped into a Los Angeles studio in the summer of 1975 to play harmonica on one track, Blue's composition 'Who Love (If Not You Love)'. Even this didn't achieve real sales. He never got over getting nowhere while those around him prospered and became stars.

That same year, 1975, Blue kept dropping in on the Rolling Thunder Revue. SAM SHEPARD described him: 'Blue gangster suit, bleary eyed, hoarse throat, wrinkled scarf . . .' and he's to be seen in *Renaldo & Clara*, playing a pinball machine in a rather neurotic, fretful way while delivering a long, self-consciously hip reminiscence about the old days in Greenwich Village. He also appeared in Wim Wenders' *The American Friend* (1977) and the TV movie *The Ordeal of Patty Hearst*, directed by Paul Wendkos (1979), and although he is uncredited, allegedly he was somewhere in NEIL YOUNG and Dean Stockwell's 1982 film *Human Highway*. That year he also sang and danced in a Broadway production, starred in *American Days* at the Manhattan Theatre Club and made an appearance on a soap opera, 'All My Children'. He also started work on a new album.

On December 2, 1982, David Blue died of a massive heart attack while keeping fit in Washington Square Park, back in the Village.

[David Cohen & others: *The Singer/Songwriter Project*, Elektra EKS 7299, NY, 1965. S. David Cohen: *Me*, Reprise RS 6375, US, 1969. David Blue: *David Blue*, Elektra EKS 74003, NY, 1966; *David Blue & American Patrol*, Elektra, unreleased; *These 23 Days in September*, Reprise RS 6296, US, 1968; *Stories*, Asylum SD 5052, US, 1971; *Nice Baby & the Angel*, Asylum SD 5066, US, 1973; *Com'n Back for More*, Asylum 7E 1043, 1975; *Cupid's Arrow*, Asylum 7E 1077, 1976. There's a detailed website re David Blue at *http://folk.uio.no/alfs/blue.html*.]

blues, external signals of Dylan's interest in
That the old blues have been seminal all through his career, Dylan has made plain in a series of signals, though we have not always paid attention. The early signals were that he was listening to LEADBELLY and ODETTA by 1959; he was performing blues songs as early as 1960; by June 1961 he was sufficiently confident of his blues harmonica playing to get himself taken on as session player for HARRY BELAFONTE's recording of 'Midnight Special', a traditional blues song that had been a key item in BLIND BOY FULLER's repertoire; he was writing blues songs himself by January 1962; by March of that year he was proficient enough, and keen enough, to play harmonica on sessions with BIG JOE WILLIAMS for VICTORIA SPIVEY.

The original title planned for his second album was *Bob Dylan's Blues*, reflecting the number of blues songs he recorded at the sessions for the album in April, July and October–December 1962; and there is a telling outtake of 'Ballad of Hollis Brown' from 1962 (which despite its title is a blues-structured song) on which Dylan includes the stanza 'There's bedbugs on your baby's bed, there's chinches on your wife / Gangrene snuck in your side, it's cuttin' you like a knife'. Dylan probably put in the bedbugs and chinches for extra 'realism', and was aware of them because they pop up commonly in the old blues—and he dropped them again probably because he couldn't quite make them an authentic fit: not least because in the blues they are mostly objects of humorous exaggeration and not of solemn complaint such as Dylan is stuck with by the nature of his song.

However, the signals kept on coming after that early period, and have continued ever since. 1965's album *Bringing It All Back Home* cites SLEEPY JOHN ESTES in its sleevenotes right up there at the beginning—'I'm standing there watching the parade / feeling combiniation of sleepy john estes. jayne mansfield. humphrey bogart . . .'—and contains within its front-cover picture the front cover of the all-important first reissue album of ROBERT JOHNSON recordings, Columbia's *King of the Delta*

Blues Singers. For the making of the radical three-minute-format-breaking rock anthem 'Like a Rolling Stone' later the same year, Dylan flew in the *blues* guitarist MIKE BLOOMFIELD.

Indeed the album title *Highway 61 Revisited* announces that we are in for a long revisit, since it is such a long, blues-travelled highway. Many bluesmen had been there before him, all recording versions of a blues called 'Highway 61'. That world is exactly what the album declares that it *revisits*. And of course the previous album title *also* suggests that Dylan was referring us *back* to older music. We didn't want to know. His originality, his revolutionary newness, was the point then. Yet Dylan could not have chosen a more apt and accurate route, a better set of songs to allude to or a finer emblem for his own musical journey. (See separate entry **Highway 61**.)

All through Dylan's white-heat hip period in the mid-sixties, when his creative greatness was in symbiosis with the foment of the times, he stayed rooted in the blues. He continued to put the word 'Blues' (like the word 'Ballad') into song titles when no-one else in rock did: indeed most people at the time thought Dylan's was deliberate ironic usage of a passé term. Even his constant use of the word 'mama' in the songs of this period is imported from the blues—in rock, few people used it (though one of Dylan's old favourites, GENE VINCENT, commonly did), and in white folksong it really does mean 'mother': but in the blues, as Michael Taft's invaluable *Blues Lyric Poetry: A Concordance* tells us, 'mother' as addressed to a lover, or a prospective one, occurs more frequently even than words like 'if' and 'when'. In 1966 Dylan opened the electric-début second half of each of his concerts with a bluesy, deranged rock song called 'Tell Me Momma'; 'Tell Me Mama' is the title of a song ROBERT JOHNSON wrote but didn't record. (It was recorded by Johnny Shines.)

This is not the only blues title Dylan used directly in this period. While his 1965 song-title 'On the Road Again' might be taken as a reference to JACK KEROUAC's novel 'On the Road', it is also a well-known track by his old friends THE MEMPHIS JUG BAND. 'Long-Distance Operator', another Dylan song from 1965, which he sung in concerts that year, takes its title straight from a blues single, now rather scarce, by Little Milton, made in 1959, while his basement tapes rock song 'Odds and Ends' is the title of a prominent 1957 JIMMY REED record (prominent for the splendidly named Remo Biondi 'playing the electric violin'). And while the 1966 on-stage Dylan was using that Robert Johnson title 'Tell Me Momma', off stage he could be found, as the fragmentary film of that tour, *Eat the Document*, revealed, playing a song that didn't sound like a blues at all from the delicate, faltering way that he explored it—yet 'What Kind of Friend Is This?'—copyrighted as Dylan's by Dwarf Music in 1978!—duplicated a 1964 blues record by Koko Taylor, cut at her début session, called 'What Kind of Man Is This?'

(GLEN DUNDAS' *Tangled* credits Dylan's version 'Willie Dixon, adapted Bob Dylan', but Dixon's 1989 autobiography, *I Am the Blues: The Willie Dixon Story*, does not include it in the list of 500-plus songs he claims to have written, and MICHAEL KROGSGAARD's *Positively Bob Dylan* credits it to Koko Taylor herself. Whoever may claim the song, it is merely adapted from a gospel song, also called 'What Kind of Man Is This?': a title founded in turn upon a phrase in the biblical story of Christ calming the storm when He and the disciples are on the sea: 'What manner of man is this, that even the winds and the sea obey him!' they ask themselves in Matthew 8:27; in Mark 4:41 they ask, very similarly, 'What manner of man is this, that even the wind and the sea obey him?"; and in Luke 8:25, 'What manner of man is this! for he commandeth even the winds and water, and they obey him.')

At the end of the 1960s, when Dylan was said to be looking to found his own record label, its proposed name was Ashes and Sand: an ellipse of the blues expression 'ashes to ashes and sand to sand' (a far rarer cousin to the Bible's 'ashes to ashes and dust to dust'), which BLIND WILLIE McTELL sings in his 1931 song 'Southern Can Is Mine', and which Geeshie Wiley and Elvie Thomas had sung in their earlier 'Over to My House' ('I cried ashes to ashes, said sand to sand / Every married woman got a back-door man').

Likewise, when Dylan named his own main music-publishing outfit, he called it Special Rider Music, borrowing another piece of old country-blues idiom: 'Special rider' conventionally means favourite lover, which makes it a telling way for Dylan to choose to refer to his muse. He likes the poetry of the term, the elegance of which comes from an understatement achieved by everyday vocabulary (as with so much of the blues): a term that intimates affection and sex while also suggesting a magic journeying. Dylan finds it more sympathetic than the etiolated, twee ways the Muse is referred to (the word 'muse' itself sounds precious—very luvvies—and the worse for the capital M) in mainstream white western culture, where its personification tends towards Greco-Roman lyre-playing women with wispy hair and long nylon dresses.

'Rider' itself is one of the 250 most frequently occurring words in the Taft concordance: so often used that it ranks ahead of 'feet', 'mother', 'help', 'stand', 'might', 'things', 'thinking', 'pay', 'jail', 'thought' and 'sleep'. But '*Special* rider' is more special: it seems to occur in only four pre-war songs and by implication—'Ain't got no special, got no trifling kind'—in a fifth (though it may have occurred in some unrecorded songs, and may occur more frequently in post-war blues). The four are: 'Special Rider Blues' by SKIP JAMES and by

SON HOUSE, 'No Special Rider Blues' by Eurreal Little Brother Montgomery and 'Mean Old Frisco Blues' by ARTHUR CRUDUP; the implicit fifth is Ishman Bracey's 'Left Alone Blues'.

Then when Dylan came to issue his first box set retrospective collection, in 1985, he called it after one of the main blues-reissue labels, *Biograph*: a label that specialised in the 1960s and 1970s in releasing work by BLIND LEMON JEFFERSON, Ma Rainey, BLIND BLAKE, SKIP JAMES, Leroy Carr, Papa Charlie Jackson and other important figures. Other significant Biographs included *MISSISSIPPI JOHN HURT, 1928: His First Recordings* (1972), *Early Leadbelly, 1935–1940: Narrated by WOODY GUTHRIE* (1969) and a volume with Willie McTell's rare 1950 recordings for the independent Regal label on one side and on the other, cuts from the same label's 1949 Chicago session by MEMPHIS MINNIE, *Blind Willie McTell—Memphis Minnie, 1949 Love Changin' Blues*, issued around 1972.

When Dylan published his selected works *Writings and Drawings* in 1972, it was dedicated in part 'To the magnificent Woodie [sic] Guthrie and Robert Johnson who sparked it off'. When *Playboy* asked Dylan in 1977 what music he listened to—by implication challenging him as to whether he was keeping an ear on what was contemporary and popular: Steely Dan, perhaps, or the Jacksons—Dylan replied: 'I listen to Memphis Minnie a lot.'

The year that interview was published, 1978, is one during which Dylan draws especially deeply and recurrently from the waters of the blues. This is evident from that year's world tour—on which within 114 concerts he gave a total of 109 performances of six different blues songs by people from Tampa Red to Willie Dixon, as well as a remarkable Robert Johnsonised re-write of his own 'Going Going Gone'. It was just as evident from that year's album, *Street Legal*, which is at least as soaked in the blues as any of his work before or since.

Even writing a song named after a disease or an illness, like Dylan's late-1970s song 'Legionnaire's Disease' (copyrighted 1981), is in a blues tradition. It joins a waiting list that takes in Memphis Minnie's 'Meningitis Blues', TB songs by Leadbelly, Victoria Spivey and Sonny Boy Williamson I, Blind Lemon Jefferson's 'Pneumonia Blues', Blind Blake's 'Hookworm Blues' and 'Depression's Gone from Me Blues', Sylvester Weaver's 'Me and My Tapeworm', BUKKA WHITE's 'High Fever Blues', Vol Stevens' 'Baby Got the Rickets', Elder Curry's 'Memphis Flu', Champion Jack Dupree's 'Bad Health Blues', Josh White's 'Silicosis Is Killin' Me' and Buddy Moss' 'T.B.'s Killing Me', through GEORGIA TOM's 'Terrible Operation Blues' right on down to Blind Richard Yates' 'Sore Bunion Blues'. (Some such titles use illness as, yes you guessed it, a sexual metaphor. 'Terrible Operation Blues' is one of these.)

In 1983 Dylan wrote and recorded his own blues masterpiece 'Blind Willie McTell'. In 1986 when he titled his album 'Knocked Out Loaded' he was quoting a phrase from a song on the album, 'Under Your Spell' co-written with the pop artist CAROLE BAYER SAGER—but that Dylan lyric was itself quoting the phrase from 'Junko Partner', a 1940s semi-cajun blues that the deeply obscure New Orleans blues singer James Wayne recorded in Atlanta and which Dr. John, among others, revived in the early 1970s.

Those, then, are just some of the external signals. No wonder the inheritance of blues lyric poetry is everywhere in Dylan's work.

[Bob Dylan: 'What Kind of Friend Is This?', Glasgow hotel room, 18–19 May 1966. Dylan quote re Memphis Minnie, interview by Ron Rosenbaum, Burbank, CA, Nov 1977, *Playboy*, Chicago, Mar 1978.

Johnny Shines, 'Tell Me Mama', prob. NY, 1972; *Sitting on Top of the World*, Biograph 12044, Canaan, NY, c.1972. Memphis Jug Band: 'On the Road Again', Memphis, 11 Sep 1928. Little Milton: 'Long Distance Operator', St. Louis, MO, 1959, Bobbin 103, 1960, LP-issued *Raise a Little Sand*, Red Lightnin' RL0011, UK, 1975. Jimmy Reed: 'Odds and Ends', Chicago, 3 Apr 1957, Vee Jay 298, Chicago, 1957. (An 'Odds and Ends' was also cut by rockabilly artist Warren Smith, Hollywood, 17 Nov 1960, Liberty LRP 3199 / LST 7199 / LB 1181, Hollywood, 1961.)

Koko Taylor: 'What Kind of Man Is This?', Chicago, 30 Jun 1964, Checker 1092, Chicago, 1964. Blind Willie McTell: 'Southern Can Is Mine', Atlanta, 23 Oct 1931, *Blind Willie McTell: The Early Years (1927–1933)*, Yazoo L-1005, NY, 1968 & re-make 'Southern Can Mama', NY, 21 Sep 1933, *Blind Willie McTell, 1927–1935*, Yazoo L-1037, NY, 1973; both CD-reissued *The Definitive Blind Willie McTell*, Columbia Legacy Roots N' Blues Series C2K 53234, NY, 1994. Wiley & Thomas: 'Over to My House', Grafton, WI, c.Mar 1930, Going Away Blues", Yazoo L-1018, NY, 1969.

Skip James: 'Special Rider Blues', Grafton, WI, c.Feb 1931, *Mississippi Blues 1927–1941*, Yazoo L-1001, NY, 1968 & *Skip James: King of the Delta Blues Singers 1928–1964*, Biograph BLP-12029, Canaan, NY, 1971. Son House: 'Special Rider Blues' (1 fast & 1 slow take), Robinsonville, MI, 17 Jul 1942, *Negro Blues and Hollers*, AFS L 59, Washington, D.C., 1962, CD-reissued Rounder CD1501, Cambridge, MA, 1997 & *Son House: The Complete Library of Congress Sessions 1941–1942*, Travelin' Man TM CD 02, Crawley, UK, 1990. Eurreal Little Brother Montgomery: 'No Special Rider Blues', Grafton, WI, c.Sep 1930; may be issued on *Piano Blues 1927–1933*, Riverside RM8809, NY, 1966. Arthur Crudup: 'Mean Old Frisco Blues', Chicago, 15 Apr 1942, *The Rural Blues*, RBF RF-202, NY, 1964. Ishman Bracey: 'Left Alone Blues', Memphis, 4 Feb 1928, *The Famous 1928 Tommy Johnson—Ishman Bracey Session*, Roots RL-330, Vienna, 1970. *Mississippi John Hurt, 1928: His First Recordings*", Biograph BLP-C4, Canaan, NY, 1972; *Early Leadbelly, 1935–1940: Narrated by Woody Guthrie*, Biograph BLP-12013, NY, 1969; *Blind Willie McTell—Memphis Minnie, 1949 Love Changin' Blues*, Biograph BLP-12035, Canaan, NY, c.1972.

Memphis Minnie: 'Meningitis Blues', Memphis, 26 May 1930. Leadbelly: 'TB Woman Blues', NY, 23 Mar

1935. Victoria Spivey: 'TB's Got Me Blues', Chicago, 7 Jul 1936. Sonny Boy Williamson I: 'TB Blues', Chicago, 21 Jul 1939. Blind Lemon Jefferson: 'Pneumonia Blues', Richmond, IN, 24 Sep 1929. Blind Blake: 'Hookworm Blues', Richmond, IN, 20 Jul 1929 & 'Depression's Gone from Me Blues', Grafton, WI, c.Jun 1932. Sylvester Weaver: 'Me and My Tapeworm', NY, 27 Nov 1927 (but, cut for OKeh but left unissued & untitled, the title was assigned it only for its retrospective 1st issue, *Songs of Humor and Hilarity*, Library of Congress Folk Music of America series LBC 11, Washington, D.C., 1978).

Bukka White: 'High Fever Blues', Chicago, 8 Mar 1940. Vol Stevens: 'Baby Got the Rickets', Atlanta 20 Oct 1927. Elder Curry: 'Memphis Flu', Jackson, MI, 16 Dec 1930. Champion Jack Dupree: 'Bad Health Blues', Chicago, 23 Jan 1941. Pinewood Tom (Joshua White): 'Silicosis Is Killin' Me', NY, 26 Feb 1936. Buddy Moss: 'T.B.'s Killing Me', NY, 18 Jan 1933. Georgia Tom & Hannah May: 'Terrible Operation Blues', NY, 17 Sep 1930; Georgia Tom & Jane Lucas: 'Terrible Operation Blues', Richmond, IN 19 Nov 1930. Blind Richard Yates: 'Sore Bunion Blues', NY, c.9 Apr 1927.

James Wayne: 'Junko Partner', Atlanta, 1951, Ray Charles in R&B Greats (sic), Oriole Realm RM-101, UK 1963. Dr. John: 'Junko Partner', New Orleans 1972, *Gumbo*, Atlantic (K40384 in UK), reissued on Various Artists, *Let It Rock*, Atlantic K40455, UK, 1973. The Clash did a fine version, 'Junco Partner', *nia*, on *Sandinista!*, Epic CBS FSLN 1, UK, 1980. (A similar song by Champion Jack Dupree, 'Junker Blues', Chicago, 28 Jan 1941, became, cleaned up, FATS DOMINO's 'The Fat Man', New Orleans, 10 Dec 1949, Imperial 5058, LA, 1950, CD-reissued *Fats Domino: The Early Imperial Singles 1950–1952*, Ace CDCHD 597, London, 1996).

Michael Taft, *Blues Lyric Poetry: A Concordance*, 3 vols, New York: Garland, 1984 (for more detail, see the entry **'Call Letter Blues'**).]

blues, inequality of reward in The inequality of reward and credit as between the old black singer-songwriters and the newer white ones is a topic that arises unavoidably from any scrutiny of what Dylan has taken from the blues.

Four years after the beginning of Dylan's recording career, and already a superstar, he is visiting Tennessee, the state in which Memphis is located, to record the deeply blues-soaked album *Blonde on Blonde*. In Memphis itself, ELVIS PRESLEY is residing in decadent luxury, resting on the laurels of a career launched from the Sun studios on a cover-version of an ARTHUR CRUDUP blues at a time when Arthur Crudup wouldn't even have been allowed to ride alongside Presley on a public bus. (Not that Crudup was in Memphis; he'd migrated to Chicago, where to begin with he'd lived in a wooden crate under the 'L' station.)

While Dylan is recording 'Pledging My Time', and Elvis is playing games at Graceland, 40 miles south of Memphis on Highway 51, Mississippi Fred McDowell, that state's greatest living bluesman and a big influence on Ry Cooder and Bonnie Raitt, is working in a gas-station in Como, Mississippi. As Stanley Booth notes in his appealing book *Rythm Oil*, 'there is a telephone handy for when he gets calls to appear at places like the NEWPORT FOLK FESTIVAL.'

What can you say? Several things. Elvis had to live his whole adult life with the accusation that he'd somehow stolen this music, and had only succeeded at it because he was white. This is in every detail untrue. First, Elvis' early record producer, Sam Phillips, recorded Elvis singing blues because they both loved it; Phillips launched the careers of black artists (HOWLIN' WOLF included) as well as white, and willingly let each move on to bigger things than Sun could accommodate.

Against the wishes of his manager Colonel Parker, Elvis continued to record black material throughout his life, because his love for it remained undimmed when precious little else did. Rightly he credited its composers on his records and paid them songwriting royalties. That his own music-publishing outfits took hefty proportions was a corrupt practice endemic in the industry then and now, and applied equally to the white songwriters who hit the theoretical jackpot of having Presley record their material. Low royalty rates, and royalties flowing into the wrong pockets, were aspects of the business that applied without regard to race. ROY ORBISON recalled that he'd been signed to Sun Records for quite a while before he heard, from an older songwriter, that you were supposed to get paid when they played your songs on the radio—and when Orbison told CARL PERKINS, it was news to him too.

It's a myth too that Elvis stole 'Hound Dog' from Big Mama Thornton. White Jewish songwriters Leiber & Stoller wrote it, and offered it to Johnny Otis; he offered it to Thornton and stole the composer credit, which, as GREIL MARCUS wrote in his classic book *Mystery Train*, 'Leiber and Stoller had to fight to get back. Elvis heard the record, changed the song completely, from the tempo to the words, and cut Thornton's version to shreds.'

Elvis made this material his own; he did something special with all of it. He couldn't have ignited a revolution through unfair good luck. That's the essence of it. And Dylan too takes from the blues because he loves it, and then makes of it something his own. It's a creative process, and creativity deserves success.

That success doesn't always come, that life is essentially unfair, is also true, but beyond the capacity of a Presley or a Dylan to affect. Neither is its unfairness racially scrupulous. Consider the case of another old blues singer, FURRY LEWIS, about whom no black writer or singer has ever said a word but of whom white Stanley Booth writes at length. Like Hubert Sumlin, Furry Lewis came from Greenwood, Mississippi, but he moved to Memphis at the age of six, in 1899. At 23, he lost a leg trying to catch a freight train outside Du Quoin, Illinois. A protégé of W.C. Handy, he recorded four sessions in the 1920s but the depression killed off his career and he didn't record again till 1959. After the end of the 1920s he was never again a full-time pro. He isn't mentioned in Louis Cantor's history of Memphis-based WDIA, the first all-black radio station: 230 pages on how this wonderful station gave blacks their own voice and put the blues on the air—but no change for a bluesman of Lewis' generation: he was still excluded. So was FRANK STOKES, another giant of the early Memphis blues scene who was still alive and living in neglect in Memphis when Elvis made his first records there. Stokes died, aged 67, in 1955. 'Frank Stokes: Creator of the Memphis Blues', the reissue label Yazoo was calling him two decades later.

Then there are the salutary cases of the innovative Noah Lewis and of GUS CANNON, another towering Memphis figure. When Bob Dylan chose to open his performance at the 1996 Aarhus Festival, Denmark, with an approximation of THE GRATEFUL DEAD's 'New New Minglewood Blues', he's likely to have chosen it not because it's a Dead song but because it isn't: because, rather, it's based on 'New Minglewood Blues' by Noah Lewis's Jug Band from 1930, itself a re-modelling of 'Minglewood Blues' by Cannon's Jug Stompers (comprising, in this instance, Gus Cannon, Ashley Thompson and Noah Lewis) from 1928. The Dead's recording may well have reminded Dylan of the song, but there's no reason to suppose that he hadn't been familiar with the original Noah Lewis's Jug Band recording, since this had been vinyl-reissued in the early 1960s. The key figure here, then, is the pioneering and splendid harmonica-player Noah Lewis, whose work set new expressive standards in the pre-war period (and who is credited as the composer of 'Minglewood Blues' as well as of 'New Minglewood Blues': the two may share a tune but are otherwise dissimilar songs—different in lyrics, pace and mood). Lewis was long thought to have been murdered in 1937, but Swedish researcher Bent Olsson discovered that in fact he had retired to Ripley, Tennessee, in the 30s, where in his old age he got frostbite, had both legs amputated and in the process got blood-poisoning, from which he died in the winter of early 1961.

Cannon was by far the better-known figure by the time Bob Dylan reached Greenwich Village. He was one of the featured artists on both HARRY SMITH's 1952 anthology *AMERICAN FOLK MUSIC* and on the next crucial release of the period, SAM CHARTERS' 1959 compilation *Country Blues*. Cannon's track on the former, indeed, was 'Minglewood Blues' while on the latter was his 1929 cut 'Walk Right In', which was taken up by the Rooftop Singers, who topped the US charts with a single of the song, complete with beefy 12-string guitar sound, in 1963.

Cannon's own career was first 'revived' in 1956 when he was recorded, for the first time since 1930, by Folkways. They let him cut two tracks. Then in 1963, in the wake of the Rooftop Singers' success, Cannon cut an album issued by Stax (!) which featured 'Walk Right In' plus standards like 'Salty Dog', 'Boll-Weevil' and 'Make Me a Pallet on Your Floor'. He also made appearances at the Newport Folk Festival. He survived to the age of 96, living long enough to still be around in Memphis at the time of Elvis Presley's funeral there in 1977.

Despite his eminence and his 'rediscovery', Gus Cannon too suffered neglect, poverty and lack of respect. His situation is described eloquently by Jim Dickinson, the Memphis session-player who features on Dylan's *Time Out of Mind* album twenty years after Cannon's death:

> 'In the summer of 1960, a friend and I followed the trail that Charters left to Gus Cannon. . . . He was the yardman for an anthropology professor. Gus had told this family that he used to make records and he had been on RCA and they'd say, "Yeah Gus, sure: cut the grass." . . . He lived on the property, back over a garage, and he took us up into his room, and on the wall he had a certificate for sales from 'Walk Right In', for which of course he didn't get any money. And he had a copy of the record that Charters had made for Folkways, but he had no record-player. That was a real good introduction to the blues.'

Likewise, right through to the 1970s Furry Lewis remained a street-sweeper in Memphis. Now and then in the mid-1960s he'd play a set between rock acts at the Bitter Lemon coffee-house in East Memphis. Stanley Booth writes: 'Next morning he's back sweeping the streets. At the crack of dawn, on his way to work, he passes the Club Handy. On the door is a handbill that reads *Blues Spectacular, City Auditorium: JIMMY REED, JOHN LEE HOOKER, Howlin' Wolf . . .*'

Inequality of reward, like the blues itself, works on many levels.

blues lines smuggled into Dylan's lyrics In the course of his enormous body of work Dylan draws on blues lyric poetry in many ways, and moves through periods of greater and lesser exploratory debt to it. As is the process with that poetry itself, Dylan is sometimes leaning on a common cluster of song and sometimes on an individually created stanza. Likewise he is sometimes taking a common cluster or individual stanza only to turn it inside out or to twist it round, to make of it something new. It exemplifies his remarkable quiet ability to set himself unobtrusive creative goals and reach them—a side of his work inevitably overlooked inside a pop and media culture attuned only to notice and celebrate hugely dramatic artistic acts—that there is a pattern, though not a rigid one, to Dylan's uses of the blues. It is this: time and again when you come across these streams of blues consciousness in his work, the verbatim blues phrases, quoted either from the common stock or from specific writers, are found inside his *non*-blues songs, while his blues songs offer such phrases innovatively tweaked. These patterns, and the exceptions to them, were first noted in MICHAEL GRAY's *Song & Dance Man III: The Art of Bob Dylan*, in which they are examined in great detail.

[Michael Gray, *Song & Dance Man III: The Art of Bob Dylan*, London: Cassell Academic, 1999 & Continuum, 2000, and New York, Continuum, 2000.]

***Blues Project* [album, 1964]** See **Muldaur, Geoff.**

***Bob Dylan* [1962]** The first album, this features the 20-year-old Dylan, unique among the Greenwich Village folkies in having been signed to the huge Columbia label, which had missed out on rock'n'roll altogether. In staff-producer JOHN HAMMOND they had a man who'd been involved in Bessie Smith's recordings and those of many more great blues acts besides. He signed Dylan, spent less than $500 in the studio and came out with an album few people liked and that didn't sell. The record company was all for dropping him. This album is, in retrospect, terrific. It has such a young Dylan on it that he sounds about 85. Only two of the songs are his own: one dedicated to his early idol WOODY GUTHRIE ('Song to Woody') and the other owing its format and spirit to Guthrie's own work ('Talkin' New York'), though using a format, the talking blues, that goes further back than Guthrie. The other songs are mainly his own impressionistic arrangements of traditional songs and old blues songs by men like JESSE FULLER, BUKKA WHITE and BLIND LEMON JEFFERSON, performed without any gentility and with a voice that, far from suggesting a soul-mate for PETER, PAUL or MARY suggested some black octogenarian singing personal blues at the back of his shack. The blurb that went out on the album could quite plausibly call Dylan the newest voice in country blues.

Dylan comes across as obsessed with the romance of dying, but the speed, energy and attack in his guitar, harmonica and voice show how fresh and excellently 'unprofessional' he was. There are tracks that ring a little false. On Dylan's rendition of 'Gospel Plow', for instance, the death-wish of the young man may be genuine but the evocation is not: wrongly, it relies on a pretence at the experience of age to 'justify' that death-wish. So that what comes through is a clumsiness of understanding as to what the artist requires of himself.

Yet what comes through from the album as a whole is a remarkable skill and more than a hint of a highly distinctive vision. In the context of what was happening at the time—American folk culture all but obliterated and a stagnating 'folk' cult established as if in its place—Dylan's first album can hardly be faulted. It is a brilliant début, a performer's tour de force, and it served as a fine corrective for Greenwich Village: it was the opposite of effete. Dylan's recordings of folk material are very much more extensive than those officially released suggest, but this first official album is a unit, a fine collection that stands up by itself.

[Recorded NY, 20 & 22 Nov 1961; released as Columbia CL 1779 (mono) & CS 8579 (stereo), 19 Mar 1962. In UK CBS BPG 62022 (mono) & SBPG 62022 (stereo), Jun 1962.]

***Bob Dylan at Budokan* [1978]** Dylan's third 'live' album, all within a five-year period and revisiting many of the same songs. This double-LP was recorded live in concert in Japan, where Dylan began the tour with the band that appeared on the *Street Legal* studio album (the largest band he's ever used on stage). A good recording that includes re-workings of many Dylan classics, it is a pity it caught Dylan and the band before they reached the magical, incandescent form they hit later that year in Europe and North America.

The tour was remarkable in re-asserting Dylan's power and relevance in an entirely different decade from the one he had shaped so significantly. The album is a pale souvenir of what went down, yet the freshness of focus Dylan brings to these songs is especially dramatic: 'I Want You', 'Ballad of a Thin Man', 'Blowin' in the Wind', 'The Times They Are a-Changin'', 'Don't Think Twice, It's All Right' and 'All Along the Watchtower'. The album cover includes a cringemaking quote about leaving his heart in Kyoto (though the album was recorded in Tokyo) and on-stage photos of Dylan dressed up like ELVIS in Las Vegas.

Many bootlegs from the same tour outshine this release, as is always the case with official 'live' Dylan recordings. There is a fine 6-CD set, ranging right across the tour and the year, which among much else shows that the early Japanese concerts were altogether more alive and effervescent than *Budokan* has had us believe. The band was hot—and what generous expressiveness we get from Dylan. Lovely, heartfelt, instinctive vocal phrasings and filigrees pouring out of him all the way through. *Budokan* misses much of it.

[Recorded Tokyo, 28 Feb and 1 Mar 1978; released first in Japan as CBS/Sony 40AP 1100/01 (Japan), 21 Aug 1978. Columbia PC2-36067 (USA), CBS 96004 (UK), Apr 1979.]

***The Bob Dylan Scrapbook* [2005]** Drawing on material made available by his office for the unprecedented Bob Dylan Exhibition ('Bob Dylan: An American Journey 1956–1966') mounted at the Experience Music Project in Seattle in November 2004 and subsequently a touring exhibition, the expensive book *The Bob Dylan Scrapbook: An Ameri-*

can Journey 1956–1966 was published in autumn 2005, compiled by Bob Santelli, curator of the Seattle exhibition 'in association with Bob Dylan'. The hardcover 'scrapbook', a mere 64 pages but beautifully produced, contains replicas of handwritten song lyrics, rare photographs, facsimile pull-outs of concert programmes, tickets, publicity stickers and other memorabilia—not all of which are 100 per cent pukka, Dylan experts suspect—interviews with Dylan and various associates plus an audio CD of interviews: and even a pull-out, cardboard stand-up Bob.

In the UK it was published at the same time as the first paperback edition of *Chronicles Volume One*; in the US it was published a little later.

[*The Bob Dylan Scrapbook: An American Journey 1956–1966*, New York & London: Simon & Schuster, 2005.]

***Bob Dylan's Greatest Hits* [1967]** The title was offensive at the time; Dylan was no mere pop artist and his greatness had nothing to do with whether DJs loved his records or whether his singles ran up the charts. In fact never has so influential an artist had so few hit singles. More importantly, each of the previous albums had had its own unity. They'd never been collections of isolated tracks. So a 'greatest hits' collection made no sense at all except in money terms. The album was put out in what was considered the disastrously long silence from Dylan between *Blonde on Blonde* in 1966 and the next proper album a week before the start of 1968. In those days, everyone made two albums a year and a long gap was supposed to be career death. This was badly selected regurgitation and provided nothing new; nor did it give an accurate picture of Dylan's progress through the earlier recordings. The US and UK track selections differ slightly.

In some countries the album was titled *Subterranean Homesick Blues*.

[Released as Columbia KCS 9643 (stereo) & KCL 2663 (mono), 27 Mar 1967. In UK CBS 460907(stereo) & BGP 62847 (mono), 27 Mar 1967.]

***Bob Dylan's Greatest Hits Vol. II* [1971]** Like *Bob Dylan's Greatest Hits*, this is a collection that rides roughshod over both the real chronology of Dylan's career and the whole-album unities of most Dylan work, but at least here there are tracks not obtainable on other albums: the 1971 (hit) single 'Watching the River Flow'; the 1965 masterpiece of put-down 'Positively 4th Street' and five previously unissued tracks. If it sounds odd to have previously unissued material on a 'greatest hits' collection, it wasn't so odd in the light of what songs they were. 'When I Paint My Masterpiece' (recorded 1971) was already well-known from THE BAND's recording on their *Cahoots* album; 'Tomorrow Is a Long Time' (a nigh-perfect live performance from 1963) was a Dylan song that other people, including, to Dylan's delight, ELVIS PRESLEY, had recorded in the interim; and 'I Shall Be Released', 'Down in the Flood' and, with playfully different lyrics, 'You Ain't Goin' Nowhere' were newly recorded (1971), outrageously loose versions of three songs that had long been popular from bootlegs of the famed 1967 Basement Tapes. All this makes it an interesting album for collectors, although it would have been more valuable if it had rounded up his other previously only-on-singles tracks too. They could have had 'Mixed-Up Confusion' (1962), which had never had a UK release; 'If You Gotta Go, Go Now' (1965) ditto; the live-in-Liverpool cut of 'Just Like Tom Thumb's Blues' (1966), the best live song performance ever achieved by anyone yet issued only as the B-side of the 'I Want You' single; the gorgeous 1971 B-side 'Spanish Is the Loving Tongue'; the 1965 A-side 'Can You Please Crawl Out Your Window?'; and the 1971 single 'George Jackson', issued two weeks before this album. But record companies never do these things right.

[Released as 2-LP set, Columbia KG 31120, 17 Nov 1971. (The UK title was *More Bob Dylan Greatest Hits*, CBS S 67239, Dec 1971 and has a slightly different track-list. On CD re-releases, the US tracklist has superseded the UK vinyl list in both countries.)]

***Bob Dylan's Greatest Hits Volume 3* [1994]** Twenty-four years since the last 'greatest hits' package, and how remarkably seldom in this aeon had he had a hit of any sort. The last real hit Bob Dylan scored in Britain was in 1978, with 'Baby, Stop Crying'—and that's not included here. Plus ça change. Here instead is the previously unreleased track 'Dignity', an unfinished outtake from *Oh Mercy* put through the *in*dignity of a working-over by another modish-for-15-minutes hit-guru (BRENDAN O'BRIEN). 'Silvio' also seems to have been remixed, removing its posturing edge to re-present it as an amiable, light, poised little thing; it is still not worth including.

This is otherwise a well-planned selection, its non-chronological running order creating some neat meeting points: 'Ring Them Bells' (1989) is followed by 'Gotta Serve Somebody' from a decade earlier, emphasising similarities of theme and production; 'Series of Dreams' gives way to 'Brownsville Girl'. The inclusion of 'Under the Red Sky' is right and, admirably, the collection opens with a run of four long, demanding songs that stress, perhaps with some pride, Dylan's unrivalled weaponry of *words*: 'Tangled Up in Blue' (though this is the wrong song-choice from *Blood on the Tracks*: it has already been re-collected *and* an outtake issued, while the equally fine 'Simple Twist of Fate' has never been re-collected), 'Changing of the Guards' (a fine choice), 'The Groom's Still Waiting at the Altar' and 'Hurricane' (which comes out very strongly). The studio albums issued since

Greatest Hits II but unrepresented here are *Dylan*, *The Basement Tapes*, *Saved* and *Empire Burlesque*.

[Released as Columbia CK 66783 (Columbia 477805 2 in UK), 15 Nov 1994.]

Bono See **U2**.

book endorsements, unfortunate It was a new development in a reductive direction when, in the 1980s, Dylan tiptoed towards being one of those celebrities who endorse other people's work by giving them blurb quotes. This began reasonably enough with a book-jacket endorsement for ALLEN GINSBERG's *Collected Poems 1947–1980* (1985) but by the end of 1991 this had been joined by the dubious company of two gruesome and vacuous Dylan book blurbs for far less distinguished work. Here's Dylan on *Lazarus and the Hurricane* by Sam Chaiton & Terry Swinton: 'The first book [RUBIN HURRICANE CARTER's *The Sixteenth Round*, 1974] was a heartbreaker. This one is a mind-breaker, abolishing parts of the nervous system.' And on Minneapolis Rabbi Manis Friedman's book *Doesn't Anyone Blush Any More? Reclaiming Intimacy, Modesty and Sexuality in a Permissive Age*, there is this back-cover testimonial: 'Anyone who's either married or thinking of getting married would do well to read this book.' (Doesn't anyone blush any more?)

Is this an example of how Dylan keeps on doing the same thing but it comes across differently because he's grown older, or because the world has changed around him (as for instance you might argue is the case with Dylan's clothes: you could say that he's always had dodgy clothes but used to be young and beautiful enough to get away with them)? In the case of these endorsements, well, he endorsed Fender bass guitars in 1965, didn't he? And in that same decade, the decade of his greatest immaculacy, he wrote the sleevenotes for *JOAN BAEZ in Concert Part 2*, and for PETER, PAUL & MARY's album *In the Wind*.

But the Fender ads were discreet—they showed a photo of the 1965 leather-jacketed Dylan posing with a Fender electric bass guitar: an instrument everyone knew he didn't play—and Fenders were an honourable name in musical instrument-making, an honourable profession. And Dylan used those album sleevenotes as opportunities to publish 'some other kinds of songs', and to reach the large audiences of people who had already performed his work and therefore with whom he had some tangible artistic connection. He also did so in his own uncompromising style: they were sleevenotes unlike any other.

The more recent blurbs are the opposite. They are Dylan playing a conventional showbiz game, no differently from Bob Hope or Bob Roberts. As with pally music-biz tributes and mutually-presented awards to other celebs, which Dylan has also (after a lifetime's honorable opposition) begun to do, this seems merely demeaning—at least to those who admired his long-term contempt for such stuff.

(See also **co-option of real music by advertising, the**.)

[The Fender ads appeared in spring 1965 in the UK music papers, and Fender sponsored Dylan's 1965 and 1966 tours. Joan Baez: *Joan Baez in Concert Part 2*, Vanguard VRS-9113, NY , 1964. Peter, Paul & Mary: *In the Wind*, Warner Bros. WS1507, NY, 1963.]

Booker T [1944 -] Booker T Jones was born in Memphis on November 12, 1944 and grew up there learning a number of instruments in school. In 1960, aged 16, he began playing sax for Stax Records in Memphis; Booker T and the MGs were formed to be the Stax-Volt house band in 1962, with Steve Cropper of the Mar-Keys and Lee Steinberg, who was replaced by Donald 'Duck' Dunn, also an ex-Mar-Key, in 1964. The group claimed fame in its own right in 1962 with the funky instrumental classic 'Green Onions', but continued to play behind many others, creating the 'Memphis sound' behind Sam & Dave, Carla Thomas, Otis Redding and many more. In June 1967 they backed Otis Redding for his triumphant, gloriously unhippie performance at that year's Monterey International Pop Festival. Three years later they quit as Stax house band, and disbanded in 1972.

Jones moved to California to become a staff producer at A&M Records, recording Bill Withers and RITA COOLIDGE, whose sister Priscilla was his wife. With Priscilla he recorded three albums in the early 1970s, plus a solo album, *Evergreen*.

Dylan played harmonica on the track 'The Crippled Crow', probably recorded in Malibu, California, in February 1973, on *Chronicles*, one of the albums by Booker T and Priscilla—and in turn both contributed to a Dylan session that same month: the final session for the *Pat Garrett & Billy the Kid* soundtrack in Burbank. Booker T played bass; Priscilla sang backing vocals. The session yielded five of the album's tracks: 'Main Title Theme', 'Cantina Theme', 'Billy 1', 'River Theme' and 'Turkey Chase'.

Booker T & the MGs had planned a reunion when drummer Al Jackson was shot dead in Memphis in October 1975. After various experiments, Jones rejoined Steve Cropper and Duck Dunn to record (with others) as the RCO All-Stars—including *LEVON HELM and the RCO All Stars*, made in 1977 after the break-up of THE BAND. While Cropper & Dunn toured and recorded behind the Blues Brothers (and appeared in the 1980 hit movie *The Blues Brothers*), Jones produced the 1978 WILLIE NELSON album *Stardust* and played for RAY CHARLES. The 1981 hit 'I Want You' was not the Dylan song, but Booker T & the MGs did record 'Gotta Serve Somebody' and 'Lay Lady Lay'.

In 1992 a renewed Booker T & the MGs, including Anton Fig, became, with JIM KELTNER, the house band at the so-called Bob Dylan 30th Anniversary Concert Celebration at Madison Square Garden, NY, October 16, 1992, backing or augmenting the sound of most of the performers.

This inspired NEIL YOUNG to hire Booker T & the MGs and Keltner to play behind him on European and North American dates in 1993, and wrote of this experience: 'As I stood where Otis Redding, Wilson Pickett, Sam and Dave and so many great singers stood, and felt that groove surrounding me, I knew that I had found a place. It's something I can't forget. Something to return to again and again, like church or your hometown. A musical place where history surrounds you without getting in the way. The music of Booker T & the MGs will live forever.'

Booker T now runs two bands: the largely instrumental Booker T & the MGs, and what he describes as his 'solo band', the Booker T Band.

[Booker T (w Bob Dylan): 'The Crippled Crow', prob. Malibu, CA, Feb 1973; issued on Booker T: *Chronicles*, A&M ST-4413, NY, 1973. *Bob Dylan, The 30th Anniversary Concert Celebration*, 2-CD set, Columbia 474000 2, NY, 1993. *Levon Helm and the RCO All Stars*, ABC AA-1017, NY, 1977, CD-reissued Edsel EDCD 494, 1996. Booker T Jones quote online 17 Sep 2005 at *www.bookert.com/main/booking.html*. Neil Young quote online ditto at *www.fantasyjazz.com/html/bookert4424.html*, from notes to the 3-CD set *Booker T. & the MGs: Time Is Tight*, Stax 3SCD-4424-2, 1998, by Rob Bowman (author of *Soulsville, U.S.A.: The Story of Stax Records*, New York: Schirmer Books, 1997). This CD set includes Booker T & the MGs' 'Gotta Serve Somebody' and 'Lay Lady Lay'.]

***Bootleg Series Vols. 1–3* [1991]** A 3-CD (or, optionally in Europe, 5-LP) box set ranging over Dylan's career from 1961 to 1989, composed entirely of never-released material. Most artists couldn't muster a single outtake to hold alongside any of this; Dylan can provide 58 recordings almost every one of which is of numinous excellence. There are the perfectly controlled solo performances of the infinitely variegated pre-electric period ('Kingsport Town', 'Worried Blues', 'Walls of Red Wing', 'Moonshiner' and the unique 'Last Thoughts on WOODY GUTHRIE'); the electric acid glory of the fast 'It Takes a Lot to Laugh, It Takes a Train to Cry' and of 'She's Your Lover Now', a gleeful masterpiece more redolent of its era than most things that came out at the time; on through incomparable studio performances of 'Tangled Up in Blue' and 'Idiot Wind' and other, more fragile, faltering works from the 1970s; riches from the 1980s which it was madness to have left unissued: 'Need a Woman', 'Angelina', 'Someone's Got a Hold of My Heart', 'Lord Protect My Child', 'Foot of Pride' and 'Blind Willie McTell'; and finishing with an outtake from *Oh Mercy* perhaps as strong as anything on the album, the compelling 'Series of Dreams'. This well-received collection could, of itself, establish Dylan's place as the pre-eminent songwriter and performer of the age and as one of the great artists of the 20th century.

[Released as Columbia C3K 47382, 26 Mar 1991. In UK/Europe Columbia COL 468086 1 (5-LPs) or Columbia 468086 2 (3-CDs).

***Bootleg Series Vol. 4: Bob Dylan Live 1966—The "Royal Albert Hall" Concert* [1998]** (Snappy title!) The most enthralling, truthful, priceless concert performance ever issued by a great artist. Three decades afterwards, and in heart-stopping quality, came the complete concert from 1966 at last. Long thought to have been from the Royal Albert Hall, London (the early, incomplete bootlegs had claimed this), the concert was actually from the Manchester Free Trade Hall: the time-stopping, astonishing, riveting, synapse-crinkling acoustic solo half and, performed with THE HAWKS, the transcendant, revolutionary electric second half. Bob Dylan at the absolute lapidary peak of inspiration, just turned 25 years old and utterly dismissive of the received wisdom of showbiz. This concert also embraces that telling moment when someone in the audience shouts 'Judas!'.

The 2-CD set is extremely well packaged, with a generous supply of vivid, telling photographs and an exceptionally fine, thoughtful essay, informed by the writer's personal knowledge, by Dylan's old Minnesota friend and fellow musician TONY GLOVER, plus decent and straightforward information about the available officially recorded tour tapes and how they had been reprocessed for the release of this concert, 32 years after it happened.

[Recorded Manchester, UK, 17 May 1966; released as Columbia Legacy C2K 65759, 13 Oct 1998.]

***Bootleg Series Vol. 5: Bob Dylan Live 1975* [2002]** This 2-CD set offers a compilation of live recordings from the first Rolling Thunder Revue (the 1975 tour), taken from five different concerts but assembled so as to represent one complete performance—or rather, the Dylan part of a Rolling Thunder Revue evening. The general pattern of the concerts was that various individual members of the backing band GUAM opened each of these 'gyspy carnival' shows, and then Dylan came on, opening with a 'When I Paint My Masterpiece' on which he shared vocals with BOBBY NEUWIRTH and then delivering a set of around five songs before being joined by JOAN BAEZ for several duets, after which she would then perform her own set. Dylan would then return to perform a couple of acoustic solos before bringing Guam back on to play behind him on the final songs. On the usual penultimate song, 'Knockin' on Heaven's Door', ROGER McGUINN would join him, and on the final number, 'This Land Is Your Land', everyone, including ALLEN GINSBERG and RAMBLIN' JACK ELLIOTT, would provide a chorus of vocals.

The *Bootleg Series Vol. 5* release does not quite stick to this; if you prefer, it re-writes history a little, partly perhaps to idealise–and people will disagree as to track selection in any case, since the set was not identical each night and nor, of course, were Dylan's performances–but there was a technical consideration too. As the sleevenotes say, it was decided to limit the selections 'only to the 24 track recordings made by a professional sound truck in Worcester, Boston, Cambridge [all Massachusetts] and Montréal.' (The sleevenotes include a longish essay by LARRY SLOMAN.)

The set omits the opener, 'When I Paint My Masterpiece' and begins with the re-written 'Tonight I'll Be Staying Here With You': a neat opening statement but in fact not a song he had ever put in the second slot. And in the real show, after 'Isis' the curtain would fall, signalling the end of the first half, after which it would rise again to reveal Dylan and Baez standing there together–a theatrical touch that was heart-stopping for many of those in the crowd who had known the days of yore to which the sight harked back. And after Baez left the stage, then, in Larry Sloman's words, 'before the audience could even catch its collective breath, Dylan [would] amble . . . onstage alone' and solo on 'Mr. Tambourine Man'. On the 2-CD set, however, that solo 'Mr. Tambourine Man' comes straight after 'Isis' and before the Baez duets–which are themselves split up so that the fourth and last of them comes later than the rest, and so is placed on the other disc. Nevertheless, as the sleevenotes say, the aim was to compile best performances 'roughly the way they might have occurred once Bob Dylan stepped onto the stage', and with the slight bonus that we get 22 songs here: a couple more than Dylan offered most nights. (At Worcester and Cambridge it had been 19, at the Boston second show 20, but at Montréal he performed an exceptional 23 in all.)

Before this 2002 release, the only official issues from these shimmering, frequently magical shows–from, as it has turned out, one of the real 'dream periods' of Dylan's live work–had been the footage that could be gleaned from *Renaldo & Clara*, released in 1978, and the versions of 'Romance in Durango' and 'Isis' issued on the *Biograph* box set in 1985. Granted this, granted the exuberant fandango band that gives this blazing music such a fusion of shambles and precision, and granted the triumph of the spirit encapsulated in Dylan's electric performances and the committed yet nuanced acoustic ones, it was extraordinary how much carping went on among aficionados when they were finally able to acquire this beautifully packaged set, and in gorgeous sound. *And* if you bought the set promptly, a 'bonus DVD' was thrown in, comprising the riveting footage from *Renaldo & Clara* of Dylan and his hat performing 'Tangled Up in Blue' and 'Isis', plus an audio-only cut of another 'Isis'.

With or without this bonus, this release is too rich in gems to be able to select 'highlights'; but it is a special pleasure of this set to be able to hear songs from *Blood on the Tracks* performed when this was still his latest studio album, and to hear a generous supply of the songs that were to come on *Desire*, played to these audiences when they were utterly new, before the album had been released.

[Released as Columbia/Legacy 510140 2, US & Europe, 2002.]

***Bootleg Series Vol. 6: Bob Dylan Live 1964* [2004]** Forty years after it was recorded, here was Dylan's big-venue New York City concert at the Philharmonic Hall on Hallowe'en 1964, released as a 2-CD set, with excellent scene-setting, historical-context-setting notes by SEAN WILENTZ (who attended the concert at the age of 13). This is a brief early excerpt from his essay, which begins by reminding us that Dylan was 23 years old at the time, and in intoxicatedly relaxed mood:

> 'Many of the songs, although less than two years old, were so familiar that the crowd knew every word. Others were brand new and baffling. Dylan played his heart out on these new compositions, as he did on the older ones, but only after an introductory turn as the mischievous tease. "This is called 'A Sacrilegious Lullaby in D minor'," he announced, before beginning the second public performance ever of "Gates of Eden". He was the cynosure of hip, when hipness still wore pressed slacks and light-brown suede boots . . .
>
> 'Yet hipness was transforming right on stage. Dylan had already moved on, well beyond the most knowing New Yorkers in the hall, and he was singing about what he was finding. The show was in part a summation of past work and in part a summons to an explosion for which none of us, not even he, was fully prepared . . .
>
> 'The world seemed increasingly out of joint during the weeks before the concert. The trauma of John F. Kennedy's assassination less than a year earlier had barely abated. Over the summer, the murders in Mississippi of the civil rights workers James Chaney, Andrew Goodman, and Michael Schwerner had created traumas anew. President Lyndon Johnson managed to push a Civil Rights Bill through Congress in July 1964; by early autumn, it seemed as if he would trounce the arch-conservative Barry Goldwater in the coming election. But in August, Johnson received a congressional blank check to escalate American involvement in the Vietnam conflict. On a single day in mid-October, Soviet leader Nikita Krushchev was overthrown and Communist China exploded its first atomic bomb. A hopeful phase of the decade was quickly winding down, and a scarier phase loomed.'

Not only are some of the songs the 'old' ones—Dylan even includes a version of that once-troublesome comic 'protest' song 'Talkin' John Birch Paranoid Blues'—and some new—he sings five songs from his newest album, *Another Side of Bob Dylan*—but some are so new that they're destined to make it onto an album still in the future, *Bringing It All Back Home*—'Mr. Tambourine Man' and 'It's Alright Ma (I'm Only Bleeding)' as well as 'Gates of Eden'—and some, like 'If You Gotta Go, Go Now' and 'Mama You Been on My Mind' destined not to be on studio albums at all yet thrillingly new too in their radical exploration of contemporary sex and what could be said of it in song. Dylan's work was one of the things that made it a commonplace later, but here in the hall in October 1964, when Dylan sings lines like 'It's not that I'm asking for anything you never gave before / It's just that I'll be sleeping soon and it'll be too dark for you to find the door', it's a joyous relief to hear someone articulate such stuff, and from so ultra-modern and cool a stance. And in 'Mama You Been on My Mind', to hear someone sing 'It don't even matter where you're waking up tomorrow'—or, as he has it on the unreleased studio cut, 'I don't even mind who you'll be waking with tomorrow / Mama you're just on my mind': well! That level of unpossessive sangfroid took the breath away; in an era when more than a couple of dates with someone meant either owning or being owned by them, this was delirious libertarianism.

Some Dylan aficionados were surprised to find themselves disappointed by this concert when officially released—surprised to find Dylan's voice unappealingly harsh: not rough but piercing—while others, already content with their reasonable-quality bootleg copies, considered it 'a waste' of a *Bootleg Series* slot. (Others still tend to wince or reach for the skip button when JOAN BAEZ comes on. She duets with Dylan on 'Mama You Been on My Mind', 'With God on Our Side' and 'It Ain't Me, Babe', and Dylan plays harmonica as she sings 'Silver Dagger' alone.) Yet for most, this is a near-crucial addition to Dylan's officially released canon.

Specifically, the concert captures his *only* live performance of the splendid 'Spanish Harlem Incident' and the first live performance of 'If You Gotta Go, Go Now' (there were very few later, and none has been issued). More generally, it gives us a Dylan who disappeared almost immediately afterwards: the Dylan who almost abolished the divide between performer and audience, who chatted as if one-to-one with the crowd and with good-humoured, open, youthful exuberance. And there's one marvellous moment, caught here, when this abolition of the divide is made vivid and real. Dylan starts to sing one of the songs from the album issued that June, 'I Don't Believe You (She Acts Like We Never Have Met)' and as he's strumming away on the guitar, he forgets the opening words of the song. Eventually, breaking free of the showbiz rules inspiredly, he simply asks if anyone knows how it goes; a chorus of voices chants 'I can't understand, she let go of my hand!' and without breaking stride Dylan switches from a spoken 'Oh yeah' into singing the prompted words.

In one way, this intimate accord between Dylan and his listeners was illusory, and Dylan knew it. He was ahead of the rest of us in many ways. And this too was the concert at which he made his oft-quoted remark: 'I have my Bob Dylan mask on. I'm masquerading.'

As Sean Wilentz sums it up: '*Live 1964* brings back a Bob Dylan on the cusp. . . . It brings back a time between his scuffling sets at the downtown clubs and his arena-rock tours of the 1970s and after. It brings back a long gone era of intimacy between performer and audience, and the last strains of a self-aware New York bohemia before bohemia became diluted and mass marketed.'

[*Bootleg Series Vol. 6: Bob Dylan Live 1964*, Sony Legacy 512358 2, NY, 2004.]

***Bootleg Series Vol. 7—No Direction Home: The Soundtrack* [2005]** This 2-CD set's title claims to offer the soundtrack to what is the MARTIN SCORSESE film *No Direction Home: Bob Dylan*, 2005 (and at Scorsese's insistence the cover was changed to add his name under that title). But of course it doesn't. These CDs draw on some of the same material as the film, but offer complete tracks, in roughly chronological order, beginning with a previously unknown 1959 recording, 'When I Got Troubles', ending with 'Like a Rolling Stone' live from Manchester, 1966 (already released on the *Bootleg Series Vol. 4: Bob Dylan Live 1966—The "Royal Albert Hall" Concert*, 1998), but including, in between, outtakes from *Blonde on Blonde*, something never made available before—indeed something most people never thought they'd live to hear.

The rest of the collection is of varying rarity and value. That 1959 track 'When I Got Troubles', were it not by Bob Dylan, would be of no interest whatever: but it is. After that comes 'Rambler, Gambler', a track now said to be from August 1960 (accompanying booklet, p.19) or autumn 1960 (same booklet, p.50) and recorded at the University of Minnesota by one Cleve Petterson (though it sounds like a quality-upgraded version of a track on the so-called Minnesota Party Tape of 'Fall 1960' always said to have been recorded by BONNIE BEECHER).

Next is 'This Land Is Your Land', live from the 1961 Carnegie Chapter Hall concert, previously known about but uncirculating; 'Song to Woody'—unhappily, the first album version, rather than, as would have been more logical, the Carnegie Chapter Hall version; 'Dink's Song' and 'I Was Young

When I Left Home', both informally recorded in Minnesota in December 1961 and already widely circulated, with the latter also included on various 'official rarities'; and 'Sally Gal', an outtake from *The Freewheelin' Bob Dylan* not previously circulated (five takes are known to exist but only one—probably take 3—has previously been in circulation; the one released here is reported to be take 1).

Then comes a Witmark Music Publishing demo version of 'Don't Think Twice, It's Alright' from 1963, already circulating, and a 'Man of Constant Sorrow' taken from the TV show 'Folk Songs & More Folk Songs', Dylan's first US network TV appearance, made in New York City on March 4, 1963 (already circulating, as is video footage); then 'Blowin' in the Wind' from the important New York Town Hall concert of April 12, 1963, previously uncirculating; 'Masters of War' from the same concert (already circulating); 'A Hard Rain's a-Gonna Fall' from the Carnegie Hall concert of October 26, 1963 (previously known but uncirculating); 'When the Ship Comes In' from the same concert (already circulating); the early version of 'Mr. Tambourine Man' recorded with RAMBLIN' JACK ELLIOTT as part of the *Another Side of Bob Dylan* session of June 9, 1964 (already circulating); the wondrous 'Chimes of Freedom' performed live at the NEWPORT FOLK FESTIVAL on July 26, 1964 (already circulating); an outtake version of 'It's All Over Now, Baby Blue' from the *Bringing It All Back Home* sessions of January 1965; ditto for 'She Belongs to Me'; the historic début of 'Maggie's Farm' live at the Newport Folk Festival, 1965 (in circulation from the film soundtrack, but now released from the uncirculated Vanguard Records line recording); previously uncirculated outtake versions of 'It Takes a Lot to Laugh, It Takes a Train to Cry', 'Tombstone Blues' and 'Just Like Tom Thumb's Blues' from the *Highway 61 Revisited* sessions of June 1965; an outtake 'Desolation Row' from the same sessions but previously circulated; and a previously *un*circulated outtake of the same album's title track. Then we get to the never-circulated *Blonde on Blonde* outtakes: there's a beautifully slow, more conventionally bluesy 'Leopard-Skin Pill-Box Hat' with much variant lyrics; an experimental early version of 'Stuck Inside of Mobile with the Memphis Blues Again' on which he hasn't even decided, at the beginning, that the chorus formula will be 'Oh Mama, can this really be the end?'; and a 'Visions of Johanna' backed by THE BAND.

The set finishes with 'Ballad of a Thin Man' live in Edinburgh on May 20, 1966 (three days after the 'Judas!' moment in Manchester), which has circulated as an audience recording but not, as here, from the official line recording; plus, because it ties in with the *No Direction Home* film, the magnificent Manchester 'Like a Rolling Stone'.

With the set comes a booklet that includes the odd choice of an unimpressive essay by Andrew Loog Oldham, which strives harder to be eccentric than to justify its presence; a not wholly accurate track-by-track guide by Eddie Gorodetsky, a Dylan friend who appears in *Masked & Anonymous* and was a writer on 'DHARMA & GREG', the sitcom, when Dylan appeared on it in 1999; and a long, fine piece from AL KOOPER, full of detail both human and factual about the sessions for *Highway 61 Revisited* and for *Blonde on Blonde*.

Trivia: as well as adding 'A Martin Scorsese Picture' under the title, an alteration was made to the registration number of the car in the CD-set cover photograph by Barry Feinstein. Its real number, clearly shown as 540 CYN, has been changed to 1235 RD: a whimsical, quiet allusion to those rainy day women . . . but on the *inside*, they haven't changed it . . . and they haven't changed it on the cover of the *No Direction Home* DVD either. The car, a British-made Austin Princess, belonged to the ROLLING STONES. The man leaning on it was Dylan's filmmaker friend HOWARD ALK. They were awaiting the old Aust Ferry to take them across the River Severn from England to Wales, after the Bristol and before the Cardiff concerts. In the background, still under construction, is the Severn Bridge; it opened that September 8, replacing the ferry.

[Bob Dylan: *Bootleg Series Vol. 7—No Direction Home: The Soundtrack*, Columbia / Legacy C2K 93937, US (Columbia / Legacy 520358 2, Europe), 30 Aug 2005.]

'Born Again' period, the Dylan began to hint that he must have undergone some kind of conversion to Christian faith halfway through the North American (last) leg of his 1978 world tour, when *Street Legal* was his current album. This section of the tour ran from October 28 (Carbondale, Illinois) through to December 16 (Hollywood, Florida). On November 24 (Fort Worth, Texas) he wore a metal cross around his neck, which had been thrown onto the stage for him from the audience in San Diego on the 17th.

On the 26th (in Houston), he began to perform what became a series of re-writes of a passage in 'Tangled Up in Blue': instead of 'She opened up a book of poems and handed it to me / Written by an Italian poet from the thirteenth century', Dylan sang 'She opened up the Bible and started quotin' it to me / Gospel According to Matthew, verse 3, Chapter 33.' This was either a mistake or a tease: there is no Chapter 33; nor does it work the other way round: there is no verse 33 in Chapter 3. But at the next concert, two nights later, Dylan cited a passage that made a most pertinent sense, singing 'She opened up the Bible, started quotin' it to me / Jeremiah Chapter 31, verses 9–33.'

This passage states Jeremiah's prophecy of a new covenant. As Rod Anstee notes: 'As a Jew, Dylan understood this to mean a remaking, a renewal of the old covenant of Moses. But in 1978, when he read or was shown this passage his heart and mind was struck by the Christian interpretation of the passage, which is that it is a prophecy concerning the coming of Christ.' Its core is the verse Dylan would reproduce on the sleeve of his 1980 album *Saved*: 'Behold, the days come, saith the Lord, that I will make a new covenant with the house of Israel, and with the house of Judah' (31:31). This is repeated verbatim in the New Testament, in Paul's Epistle to the Hebrews 8:8.

Dylan's tour continued. On December 2nd, in Nashville, he sang an early version of 'Slow Train' at the pre-concert soundcheck, and then during the final concert, he débuted another song later to appear on the *Slow Train Coming* album, 'Do Right to Me Baby (Do Unto Others)'.

Dylan's move towards Christian faith was encouraged by at least three musicians in his band (though this was only possible if he were receptive to their persuasion). It may be that this process goes right back to the 1975 Rolling Thunder Revue, on which T-BONE BURNETT and STEVEN SOLES were guitarists and DAVID MANSFIELD played violin, mandolin and steel guitar. All three were Born Again Christians, and Soles and Mansfield were back in the band that toured with Dylan all through 1978. Most of the backing singers were members of conventional black churches, with strong faiths.

On a January Sunday in 1979, at Dylan's request, singer MARY ALICE ARTES (who was not in his 1978 band) asked a pastor attached to the very Californian VINEYARD CHRISTIAN FELLOWSHIP if someone could come to an apartment in Brentwood, West LA, to speak to her 'boyfriend'. She didn't name him. Dylan was duly drawn into both Bible study and worship. He spent the first months of 1979 attending Bible classes most weekday mornings, at the Reseda, California, office of the St. Paul's United Methodist Church of Tarzana (on the southern edge of the San Fernando Valley), a church that the Vineyard Fellowship used for evening services. He attended further classes at the home of songwriter Al Kasha in Beverly Hills.

Dylan's church attendance was soon curtailed by the influx of people drawn by knowledge of his presence—many of them wanting to get him to listen to their demo tapes—and by media attention; but though Pastor Larry Myers disputes this, Dylan appears to have been baptised, as Mary Alice Artes had been, in the swimming pool of Pastor Bill Dwyer in May 1979. (Swimming-pool baptism is not confined to the rich; in many US churches, black and white, where baptism by submersion is practised, the pool of the local motel is often borrowed by the congregation for this purpose.)

Starting on April 30, Dylan went into the Muscle Shoals studios down in Sheffield, Alabama—studios famed for producing great R&B music, including by the exceptional ARTHUR ALEXANDER—and with JERRY WEXLER as producer, began recording what would become the first 'Born Again' album, *Slow Train Coming*. The sessions concluded on May 4, and the album was released on August 18.

In the autumn, Dylan made what many found a surprising appearance on 'Saturday Night Live' on NBC-TV on October 20, performing three of the songs from the album, backed by five musicians and three female gospel singers (and looking, despite the fire-and-brimstone lyrics sung, strangely tame: almost domesticated). Then came the first gospel tour, beginning on November 1, launched with 14 concerts in 16 days, all at the Fox Warfield Theater in San Francisco, and then continuing for four nights in Santa Monica, two in Tempe, Arizona, two in San Diego, two in Albuquerque, New Mexico, and finishing on December 5 & 6 with concerts in Tucson, Arizona.

These were extraordinary concerts. They began by asking the audience to listen to *six* songs by the gospel singers with piano accompaniment, and then when Dylan came on he featured only gospel songs, and therefore no material from any album prior to *Slow Train Coming*. Many of the songs were not on that album either (and would mostly emerge the following year on the next album, *Saved*). In most places the audience response was mixed. The exception was Santa Monica, where all performances were benefit concerts for World Vision International, a non-denominational Christian charity. Elsewhere, there was less enthusiasm. Part of the crowd was now young Born Again youths in challenging, scripture-based t-shirts; but the normal Dylan part of the crowd was confused and troubled, with some people quietly dismayed and others hostile. Dylan responded with long sermons that included alarming mini-rants about homosexuals and muslims, but were mostly about the end of the world being nigh.

When he reached San Diego he recalled that this was where, the previous year, he had been given a small silver cross, and said this to the audience:

> 'Last time I was here in San Diego—I think about a year ago, I don't know—I was coming, coming from some place, and I was feeling real sick when I came through here and I was playing the show. . . . Anyway . . . just about towards the end of the show someone out in the, someone out in the crowd—they knew I wasn't feeling too well—I think they could see that, and they threw a silver cross on the stage.
>
> 'Now usually I don't pick things up in front of the stage. Once in a while I do, sometimes I don't but, ahh, I looked down at that cross, I said "I gotta pick that up". So I picked up the cross and I put it in my pocket. A little silver cross, I'd say maybe so high.
>
> 'And I put it—I brought it backstage and I brought it with me to the next town, which was out in Arizona. I think it was, uh, Phoenix. Any-

way, I got back there: I was feeling even worse than I'd felt when I was in San Diego. I said "Well I need something tonight". I didn't know what it was. I was used to all kinds of things. I said "I need something tonight that I didn't have before". And I looked in my pocket and I had this cross. So if that person is here tonight, I just wanna thank you for that cross.'

Dylan began 1980 with another similar tour, starting in Portland, Oregon, on January 11th, and running through Washington State, Colorado, Nebraska, Missouri, Tennessee and Alabama, and ending on February 9th in Charleston, West Virginia. The response was again mixed and ticket sales were poor. Two days later he was back in Muscle Shoals studios, recording *Saved*. These sessions lasted five consecutive days.

Later that month, Dylan was thrown a lifeline of worldly affirmation when he was presented with a Grammy by the National Academy of Recording Arts and Sciences in Los Angeles for 'Best Male Rock Vocal Performance of 1979' on 'Gotta Serve Somebody', the opening track of *Slow Train Coming*. The live CBS showing of this event was a feast for the eyes. Dylan, elegant in his tuxedo, took the opportunity of performing at the ceremony to hurl the chastising burn of his winning song at a glitzy audience which, having so clearly chosen to serve mammon, was satisfactorily discomfited by its lyric. Dylan accepted the Grammy with the words 'I didn't expect this and I want to thank the Lord for it. And most likely I want to thank Jerry Wexler, BARRY BECKETT, who believed in it. Thank you.'

The following month, in a Los Angeles studio, he played harmonica on one track by fellow Vineyarder KEITH GREEN, 'Pledge My Head to Heaven', which would appear on an album called *So You Wanna Go Back to Egypt* later in the year.

In mid-April, Dylan was back on tour, beginning with four consecutive nights in Toronto, the third and fourth nights being recorded, and the latter filmed, at Dylan's expense, to provide the material for a live album of his gospel material, to be called *Solid Rock*. These concerts were ferocious, mesmeric, shining—you might say inspired. They remain a favourite of many Dylan aficionados who are unconvinced by the religious message but appreciative of a great artist on one of the peaks of his form. The record company, more interested in sales than artistry, declined to issue the album, though one track, 'When He Returns', from the last night, was issued officially on the relatively obscure *Highway 61 Interactive* CD-Rom in 1995.

The tour—which was to be Dylan's last 100 per cent gospel tour—moved on from Toronto through four nights in Montréal, four in New York State, then Massachusetts, back into New York State, Connecticut, Maine and Rhode Island before heading to Pittsburgh and finally Akron, Columbus and Dayton, Ohio.

The tour's last night was May 21, 1980. A month later, the *Saved* album was released, to some of the poorest reviews of Dylan's career. It seemed the nearest thing he'd ever done to a follow-up album, and with a far less compelling collection of songs and perhaps too a slackening off in production values (a great production having been one of the unarguable strengths of *Slow Train Coming*). Few people appreciated songs that appeared to relish others' damnation—songs like the title track, in fact, that seemed to boil down to the message 'I'm saved, you're not, ha ha.'

In all this vengeful foment, it was easy to overlook the achievement of 'Pressing On', a really fine piece of hot-gospel songwriting with Dylan's usual deft deployment of biblical text—and thus a case of Dylan adding one more strand of American music to his work as, in his own later, clever phrase, 'a musical expeditionary': and not merely adding it but adding to it in the process.

Easy to overlook too the quiet strength of 'Saving Grace' and of the album's finest moment, the lovely 'What Can I Do for You?' (the stimulus to one of CHRISTOPHER RICKS' best song scrutinies, his short essay 'What He Can Do for You' in 1985). The harmonica solos alone, on this track, justify the album's place in Dylan's canon.

Dylan wrote other fine songs in this period—songs that didn't make it onto any album. The beguiling 'Trouble in Mind' was recorded the first day of the *Slow Train Coming* sessions, but issued only as the B-side of the single 'Precious Angel' (and with both tracks shortened); and the explanatory, scripturally careful 'Ain't No Man Righteous, No Not One' was recorded a day later. Best were the smouldering, menacing R&B strut that is 'Cover Down / Break Through' and the freewheelin' wit and melodious eloquence of the thoroughly likeable, anthemic 'Ain't Gonna Go to Hell for Anybody' (which would have made a *great* record). These last two went unrecorded but were both featured live on the April–May 1980 tour, and the latter featured again in further concerts that fall: concerts at which, supposedly under pressure from promoter Bill Graham, secular material returned to Dylan's repertoire.

This short tour, from November 9 through to December 4, began by defiantly re-occupying the Fox Warfield in San Francisco, where Dylan's gospel shows had proved so unpopular the previous year. This time he played 12 nights there, and for the first seven nights, he opened with 'Gotta Serve Somebody' and 'I Believe in You', immediately followed by 'Like a Rolling Stone'. On November 17, for one night only, he followed 'Gotta Serve Somebody' with 'Simple Twist of Fate' and 'All Along the Watchtower'; then came 'Like a Rolling Stone' followed by the *Slow Train Coming* song 'Man Gave Names to All the Animals'. The other nights reverted to the previous pattern.

What was common to all these concerts was the commitment and beauty of Dylan's vocal delivery, especially on newly introduced songs like the lovely traditional 'Mary from the Wild Moor', and 'Abraham Martin and John' (on both of which Dylan shared vocals with CLYDIE KING), and on his own great new secular songs 'Let's Keep It Between Us' and 'Caribbean Wind'. On November 13, CARLOS SANTANA was a guest guitarist on four consecutive songs in mid-set, 'Covenant Woman', 'Solid Rock', 'What Can I Do for You?' and the turbulent new half-secular song 'Groom's Still Waiting at the Altar'. The following night, MIKE BLOOMFIELD was brought on to play lead guitar on 'Like a Rolling Stone' and, incandescently, on 'Groom's Still Waiting at the Altar'. The night after, the guest guitarist was JERRY GARCIA, who played on 'To Ramona', 'Ain't Gonna Go to Hell for Anybody', 'Girl of the North Country' and 'Slow Train'. Three nights later, Dylan brought on MARIA MULDAUR (another avowedly Christian singer by this point) to sing 'Nobody's Fault but Mine'. And on the last night in San Francisco, the guest was ROGER McGUINN, who played guitar and shared vocals with Dylan on 'Mr. Tambourine Man' and 'Knockin' on Heaven's Door'.

From 17 Dylan song performances on the opening night, these concerts had lengthened to 25 songs before the end of the San Francisco run. From there the tour revisited other places on the first, controversial all-gospel tour of the previous year, stopping at Tucson, Arizona, and then San Diego—this time rewarded with a 26-song performance from Dylan—and then Seattle and finally Salem and Portland, Oregon. On the final night, the distinguished bluegrass mandolin player DAVID GRISMAN guested mid-set on 'To Ramona'.

March to May 1981 found Dylan recording the next album, *Shot of Love*, which seemed to offer a studio version of the religious-secular mix he had been offering in concert, but with new material. 'Groom Still Waiting at the Altar' and 'Caribbean Wind' were now recorded, though in the end neither ended up on the album as first released. ('Groom' was added when the album was CD-reissued.)

Before the album was released, in August 1981, Dylan had returned once again to the road, with four warm-up dates in the US preceding a large-venue tour of Europe, bringing his gospel-plus-secular repertoire to France, England, Sweden, Norway, Denmark, West Germany, Austria and Switzerland, finishing back in France on July 25. These were the first European dates since the highly-acclaimed, sell-out concerts of 1978; in London he returned to Earl's Court, the same vast hall he had played back then; again he did six nights there; yet there was no mistaking the downturn in the excitement he was generating, and no disguising the many empty seats. And in France this time, there were no Paris concerts at all.

The *Shot of Love* secular material amounted to 'Lenny Bruce' and 'Heart of Mine'; the rest could fairly be accounted Christian in theme and intent, though with the exception of the rather agitated 'Property of Jesus' the songs lack the evangelising of the *Slow Train Coming* and *Saved* material. Indeed, the evangelising Bob Dylan—his declamatory 'Born Again' period—was drawing to a close. Yet the new album's last track, the majestic 'Every Grain of Sand', made clear that while Dylan was in retreat from preaching, he remained steadfast in his faith. And in essence, that might still be said to be his position.

If you seek a confession of further retreat, the nearest thing (outside of forming your own judgments about how he comports himself in the world) is in remarks Dylan made to *Newsweek* in 1997: "I don't adhere to rabbis, preachers, evangelists, all of that. I've learned more from the songs than I've learned from any of this kind of entity. The songs are my lexicon. I believe in the songs.'

As for the work the 'Born Again' period produced, this has to be said: that at their worst Dylan's evangelical songs offer much dead language and a paucity of creative imagination, in contrast to so much of his earlier work. 'Are You Ready?' may express urgently the need to consider the imminent end of the world, but 'A Hard Rain's a-Gonna Fall' is an infinitely better song. At their worst, these songs catch a Dylan who has been satisfied to assert and argue and declaim but who has hardly bothered to fulfil the more important tasks of the artist: he has not created worlds here, he has only argued about them.

At their best, though, Dylan's sharp, deft attention to detail in his use of language, combined with a rich range of subject-matter, yield songs that can hold their own in any selection from his corpus. They often offer a strange bonus too, in their mesmerising special tension between text and recording. No other part of his output seems to work so well 'on the page'—perhaps because so much of the lyric content hinges upon close attention to use of language itself, as process, not least in Dylan's witty interaction with biblical text. Yet this work also contains within it the writer's focussing of an intensely felt array of belief, and this is brought alive most powerfully in some of his performances of these works, both in the studio and at such concerts as in Toronto in April 1980.

Moreover, whatever Dylan aficionados might feel about his Christian songs, the best of them surely comprise a body of work that brings to contemporary religious song something fresh yet well-grounded in traditional strengths, something passionate and full of an authentic saturation in biblical teaching and in the gospel music of the black church. Anyone can hear that it wipes the floor with all that awful Pat Boonery, that horrid, pallid, acoustic-guitar-and-tambourine sing-song modernism and those gruesome Age of Aquarius lasers-and-love productions offered to white worshippers over the last 30 years. Dylan's religious work has gravitas.

[Bob Dylan: 'Gotta Serve Somebody', 'I Believe in You' & 'When You Gonna Wake Up?', 'Saturday Night Live', NBC-TV, NY, 20 Oct 1979; remarks to San Diego crowd, 27 Nov 1979; 'Gotta Serve Somebody', Grammy Awards, LA, 27 Feb 1980; 'Trouble in Mind', Sheffield, AL, 30 Apr 1979, Columbia 1-11072, NY (S CBS 7828, London), 1979. Dylan quote, 'a musical expeditionary', *No Direction Home*, dir. Martin Scorsese, US, 2005; outstanding concert, Toronto, 20 Apr 1980. Keith Green (+ Bob Dylan): 'Pledge My Head to Heaven', *So You Wanna Go Back to Egypt*, Pretty Good PG1, US, 1980; quote re songs as his lexicon: *Newsweek*, NY, 6 Oct 1997. Rod Anstee quote, letter to this writer from Ottawa, 16 Dec 1981.]

'Born Again' period, a slow train coming to the Dylan has always given us songs that burned with a moral sense. This was true in 1962 when he was restating the morality of WOODY GUTHRIE on his own début album's song 'Talkin' New York', and it has remained crucial in Dylan's work ever since. He was happy to declare in 'Masters of War' that 'Even Jesus will never forgive what you do', and biblical quotations and allusions pour readily out of the early 'protest' songs: out of 'The Times They Are a-Changin'', 'A Hard Rain's a-Gonna Fall' and 'When the Ship Comes In'.

'Let Me Die in My Footsteps', written to deride the craze for fall-out shelters (not the happiest solution to the threat of nuclear war, a threat often felt to be imminent in the 1950s to early-60s, especially during the 'Cuba Crisis' of 1962), shows that the very young Dylan was already confidently using biblical text without missing a beat. The second verse, which begins 'There's been rumors of war and wars that have been / The meaning of life has been lost in the wind', takes its text, without nudging the listener toward noticing it, from the words of Christ given in Matthew 24:6 and Mark 13:7: 'And ye shall hear of wars and rumours of wars: see that ye be not troubled . . .' and 'And when ye shall hear of wars and rumours of wars, be ye not troubled . . .'

But it is in the work that burgeoned in the mid-60s that Dylan-the-moralist asserts himself forcefully with a new complexity people commonly mistook for amorality or a denial of moral judgment. The songs that included 'she knows too much to argue or to judge', 'there are no sins inside the gates of Eden', 'to live outside the law you must be honest', 'don't follow leaders' and so on—that favourite side of Bob Dylan was never urging on us the unimportance of moral clarity. He was arguing that to achieve that clarity, the individual must shake off the hand-me-down conventional moral codes, and the judgements we make thoughtlessly from them. He was pressing us to take the solo flight of responsibility for arriving at our own morality.

This is everywhere in Dylan's work from 1961 to 1978. When, in 1979, Dylan declared himself 'Born Again', the turnabout was in his acceptance, after all those years, of an outside, handed-down moral code—the Bible accepted as the authentic voice of God and Jesus embraced as the true son of God. It was a complete *volte face* from 'Don't follow leaders / Watch the parkin' meters' to 'there's only one authority / And that's the authority on high' (on 'Gonna Change My Way of Thinking', from *Slow Train Coming*, 1979).

It was not, however, a sudden change from the hip amoralist to the priest: Dylan had seized on a new code, but remained utterly consistent in his preoccupation with struggling *for* a code.

Along with this unfailing sense of the need for moral clarity, Dylan's work has also been consistently characterized by a yearning for salvation. The quest for salvation might well be the central theme of his entire output. To survive, you must attain that clarity of morality: you won't even get by without going that far; and then you must go beyond—get rescued from the chaos and purgatory and find some spiritual home.

This is the constant theme. It is as strong in the *Blonde on Blonde* period as in any other: 'And me, I sit so patiently / Waiting to find out what price / You have to pay to get out of / Going through all these things twice.' That is how 'Memphis Blues Again' ends; and the chorus of that song too emphasizes this felt need to pass from one place to another—from one quality of life to another: 'To be stuck inside of Mobile / With the Memphis Blues Again!'

Twelve years later, he is waiting and yearning again: 'This place don't make sense to me no more / Can you tell me what we're waiting for, Señor?' (from 'Señor: Tales of Yankee Power' on *Street Legal*, 1978)—and in the interim we've had the same quest for salvation echoed again and again, from 1967's 'I Shall Be Released' to 1974's *Planet Waves*: 'In this age of fiber-glass / I'm searching for a gem' (from 'Dirge'); 'My dreams are made of iron and steel / With a big bouquet / Of roses hanging down / From the heavens to the ground' ('Never Say Goodbye') and 'I was in a whirlwind / Now I'm in some better place' ('Something There Is About You'). The same quest for salvation permeates *John Wesley Harding* (1968) and *Blood on the Tracks* (1975) too.

It is the focus that shifts. Dylan's quest, as it is unfolded in the songs, has always been a struggle within him between the ideas of the flesh and the spirit, between love and a kind of religious asceticism—between woman as the saviour of his soul, and woman's love seen as part of what must be discarded in the self-denial process necessary to his salvation.

In the early days, woman's love was not enough; all those gotta-move-on songs resulted. By the beginning of the 1970s, Dylan was focusing in the other direction, following the tenets of the *Nashville Skyline* album: 'Love is all there is / It makes the world go round' (from 'I Threw It All Away'). By the time of 'Wedding Song' on *Planet Waves*, Dylan is even more specifically disavowing the asceticism of the *John Wesley Harding* collection, declaring a woman's love rather than religion as his path to salvation: 'What's lost is lost, we can't regain / What went down in the flood / But happiness to me is you / And I love you more than blood.' (More, that is, than the blood of the lamb on which, later, he is to become so keen.)

From *Blood on the Tracks*, Dylan shifts away from woman as saviour: and to trace this process is to hear his slow train in the distance—to find his quest for salvation refocussing itself into a quest for Christ.

On *Blood on the Tracks* and the next album, *Desire* (1976), Dylan is trying to do a balancing act—trying to fuse God and Woman: 'In a little hilltop village / They gambled for my clothes / I bargained for salvation / And they gimme a lethal dose / I offered up my innocence / Got repaid with scorn / Come in she said I'll give ya / Shelter from the storm . . . / If I could only turn back the clock / To when God and her were born / Come in she said I'll give ya / Shelter from the storm.'

The *Desire* album follows this through: 'Oh sister . . . / And is our purpose not the same on this earth: / To love and follow His direction? / We grew up together from the cradle to the grave / We died and were reborn and then mysteriously saved.'

The fact that it seems to have been so personal a journey—not simply an objective narrator (the Artist) musing on Woman versus God as Salvation in theoretical, philosophical terms—makes it more complex. The personal intensity adds other strands, which it is part of Dylan's struggle to try to interweave. Not only are we seeing Dylan-the-moralist move from the upholder of individual conscience to the priest passing on God's word; not only are we seeing a consistency in a Dylan whose songs have always been rich in biblical allusion and language; not only are we tracing Dylan's tussle between woman as sensual mystery and God; we are also seeing, as the albums of the 1970s unfold, Dylan's increased preoccupation with the idea of betrayal.

This strand begins to appear on *Planet Waves*—'I ain't a-haulin' any of my lambs to the marketplace anymore'—and it produces in Dylan's work something that at first comes across as an astonishing leap of arrogance: that is, that Dylan quite clearly starts to *identify* with Christ. He begins to do this not in the conventionally-taught sense—that of Jesus is my friend, sent by God to be human just like me—but in the sense of confusing himself with Christ.

From *Blood on the Tracks* onwards, we are given parallel after parallel between Dylan and Christ: both charismatic leaders, both message-bringers to their people, both martyrs because both *get betrayed*. In retrospect, it is as if Dylan eventually converts to Christianity because of the way he has identified with Christ and understood His struggles through his own. (In the period after his outburst of evangelism is over, in the early 1980s, he looks back at his Christ-Dylan parallels with an admirable rigour: one that avoids simplistic revisionist declarations. In particular he looks at these issues in the great 1984 song 'Jokerman', on *Infidels*.)

Dylan had had one eye on Jesus ever since the motorcycle crash of 1966 (or ever since, as he confessed in 'Sara', he had 'taken the cure' the same year). The unreleased 'Sign on the Cross' from the 1967 Basement Tapes declared: 'I know in my head / That we're all so misled / And it's that ol' sign on the cross / That worries me . . . / You might think you're weak / But I mean to say you're strong / Yes you are / If that sign on the cross / If it begins to worry you.' But from *Blood on the Tracks* Dylan's *identification* with Christ begins in earnest:

'I came in from the wilderness . . . / She walked up to me so gracefully / And took my crown of thorns'; 'In a little hilltop village / They gambled for my clothes . . .'

The placing of a crown of thorns on Jesus's head is cited in three of the four Apostles' accounts: Matthew 27:29; Mark 15:17; and John 19:2—texts Dylan revisits in the evangelical period in 'In the Garden' on *Saved*. The scriptural passage Dylan uses for 'In a little hilltop village, they gambled for my clothes / I bargained for salvation an' they gimme a lethal dose' occurs in all four: mentioned fleetingly in Mark 15:24 ('And when they had crucified him, they parted his garments, casting lots upon them, what every man should take') and yet more fleetingly in Luke 23:34 ('Then said Jesus, Father, forgive them; for they know not what they do. And they parted his raiment, and cast lots'), it is explained better in Matthew 27:35 and most fully in John, 19:23–24:

'Then the soldiers, when they had crucified Jesus, took his garments, and made four parts, to every soldier a part; and also his coat: now the coat was without seam, woven from the top throughout. They said therefore among themselves, Let us not rend it, but cast lots for it, whose it shall be: that the scripture might be fulfilled, which saith, They parted my raiment among them, and for my vesture they did cast lots. These things therefore the soldiers did.' That this happens 'that the scripture might be fulfilled' refers back to one of the Psalms of David, Psalm 22, which prophesies Christ and His suffering on the cross. It begins with a prefiguring of Christ's famous words 'My God, my God, why hast thou forsaken me?' (later spoken by Christ as reported in Matthew 27:46 and Mark 15:34) and it includes this passage:

'. . . the assembly of the wicked have inclosed me: they pierced my hands and my feet. I may tell all my bones: they look and stare upon me. They part my garments among them, and cast lots upon my vesture' (Psalm 22, 16–18).

Those lines from 'Shelter from the Storm' are matched, in 'Idiot Wind', by 'There's a lone soldier on the cross / Smoke pourin' out of a box-car door'—and the reference to that 'box-car door' prefigures the image Dylan is to choose later of the slow train coming while also reminding us that the links to his earliest influences are still there: Woody Guthrie's autobiography, *Bound for Glory*, is so titled to quote from the old song 'This Train' ('This train is bound for glory, this train'), and part of the soundtrack from Dylan's film *Renaldo & Clara* has him singing a song popularized by those other early idols of his, THE STAPLE SINGERS: 'People get ready / There's a train a-comin'' which uses the same train image to stand for the coming of the Lord.

There is another song, 'Abandoned Love', performed by Dylan first at an impromptu guest appearance during a JACK ELLIOTT set in New York in July 1975, and then recorded for, but not released on, *Desire*, that brings us back to Dylan's process of struggle for salvation as we begin to see it from *Blood on the Tracks* onwards. It includes this: 'I thought that you was righteous but it's vain / Somethin's tellin' me I wear a ball and chain . . . / I march in the parade of liberty / But as long as I love ya, I'm not free . . . / Let me feel your love one more time / Before I abandon it.'

This is the pivotal theme of all Dylan's major work of the 1970s: his journey from SARA to Jesus. The most interesting work falls in the middle, when Dylan is in the thick of the dilemma. After *Desire*, we come to the really central album in the journey from the 'Love is all there is' of *Nashville Skyline* to the core conclusion of *Saved*, which is that '. . . to search for love, that ain't no more than vanity: / As I look around this world, all that I'm finding / Is the saving grace that's over me.'

This truly central album is *Street Legal* (1978). It brings it all together: Dylan the consistent moralist, Dylan the writer who draws heavily on the Bible, Dylan caught in the struggle between the flesh and the spirit, Dylan ending his key relationship, Dylan the betrayed victim both of what he sees as love in vain and of all of us.

Consummately, Dylan pulls all these strands together on this album, both on its minor songs and its three outstanding major works, 'Changing of the Guards', 'No Time to Think' and 'Where Are You Tonight (Journey Through Dark Heat)?'.

'New Pony', the first minor song, is a farewell to the world of sensual pleasures, a fond goodbye to remind us that Dylan is not quitting the world because he can't cope with it but because it isn't enough. As the gospel chant in the background repeats, over and over, his feeling underneath is 'How much longer? / How much longer?' and that counterpointing of Dylan's sexy, sleazy blues voice by the gospel plea for deliverance is a brilliantly economic, forceful way of evoking the tussle between flesh and spirit.

Then there is 'Señor (Tales of Yankee Power)', in which the singer seeks guidance in the attempt to make the leap from worldly meaninglessness to a new higher ground. 'Let's overturn these tables' is the Christ-gesture, a swift allusion to the routing of the money-lenders in the temple (Matthew 21:12: 'And Jesus went into the temple of God . . . and overthrew the tables of the moneychangers . . .'; John 2:15: '. . . he drove them all out of the temple . . . and poured out the changers' money, and overthrew the tables'), to which Dylan adds that 'This place don't make sense to me no more'.

'Baby Stop Crying' re-presents the themes of betrayal and salvation. 'You been down to the bottom with a bad man, babe' is the dark, accusing opening line. The song goes on to try to reach the woman, despite the felt betrayal, urging her to join him down the new road to salvation, with the singer still loathe to walk that road alone: 'Go down to the river babe / Honey I will meet you there.' This plea that she understand the need for a new baptism and the need to renounce, that she accept his need for spiritual journeying, that she come along too, is developed in the album's major songs in writing as absorbing, complex and vivid as anything Dylan has given us.

It is in these songs too that the writer's comparisons between himself and Christ come thick and fast, as Dylan pulls all these themes and strands together and prepares the way unhesitatingly for the *Slow Train Coming* and *Saved* albums.

'Changing of the Guards' opens with Dylan reflecting on his own career: the time and energy spent; and at once we are back on the betrayal theme—but here it is betrayal by the world, not one woman. 'Sixteen years' is the opening line: as economic a statement of Dylan's career-span, and the weariness felt, as it would be possible to make. But the song ends with a gentle attempt to explain—and to urge acceptance of—what is to come from 'the new transition'. The times they are a-changing in a radically different way from before. To the world, to the 'gentlemen' of 'the organization', and to his lover too, he sings that the change must come now: 'Either get ready for elimination / Or else your hearts must have the courage / For the changing of the guards'. It can be all right in the end: 'Peace will come / With tranquility and splendor on the WHEELS OF FIRE' but there will be no worldly gain: no instant material dividend to be had from surrendering the old, false life. It must be done anyway: 'Peace will come . . . / But will offer no reward / When her false idols fall / And cruel death surrenders / With its pale ghost retreating / Between the king and the queen of swords'. The embattled lovers must stop their self-destruction and accept the new regime in which truth of spirit is its own reward.

'No Time to Think' has Dylan still on the merry-go-round: the noisy, mechanical going-nowhere of 'real life'. The hypnotic yet ridiculous waltz-rhythm underlines this, as do the incandescent jingle jangles of internal rhyme. Here we have the singer back on the edge, knowing he must make the leap, resist old love and old earthly niggling, yet with the disputatious voices of love and money, public and pleasure, politics and philosophy, all trying for his attention, leaving him no time to think. The song opens with the clear statement of his conviction that without a re-birth, we are among the walking dead: 'In death you face life with a charm and a wife / Who sleepwalks through your dreams into walls'—and 'walls' suggests both the wraithlike quality involved in walking through them *and* the restrictiveness of their presence. Voices call him back, with their bamboozling choices, their shallow temptations and abstractions.

Dylan is swift to summarise for himself the plain facts of the predicament he's been examining throughout the album: 'You know you can't keep her and the water gets deeper / It's leading you on to the brink . . . / You've murdered your vanity burdened your sanity / For pleasure you must now resist.' 'The bridge that you travel on goes to the Babylon / Girl with the rose in her hair'.

And in the last verse, there's a deft pun on 'receive' in these lines: 'Stripped of all virtue as you crawl through the dirt, / You can give but you cannot receive'. Both meanings of 'receive' refer us to biblical text. First, Dylan acknowledges Jesus' teaching, reported in Acts 20:35: '. . . remember the words of the Lord Jesus, how he said, It is more blessed to give than to receive.' Yet by twisting the line around, as if the giving were easy and the receiving more problematic—'You can give but you cannot receive'—Dylan uses the allusion to lament his lingering reluctance, at this point, to 'receive' Christ himself. On and on goes the struggle: but in prospect at last there is 'Starlight in the east, you're finally released'.

This final journey is the 'journey through dark heat' and out the other side that constitutes the album's final song, 'Where Are You Tonight?' The singer has asked his lover to make the pilgrimage alongside him; she has declined; he has gone on alone. As the song opens, he is *on* the slow train: 'There's a long-distance train rolling through the rain / Tears on the letter I write / There's a woman I long to touch and I'm missing her so much / But she's drifting like a satellite'. The second verse is a glancing reflection back to the old New York days. In 1965 we had that scathing song 'Positively 4th Street'; this time Greenwich Village's Elizabeth Street is used to place that finished camaraderie (and so to prefigure those lines on *Slow Train Coming*, 'My so-called friends have fallen under a spell').

The last verse of the song—and of the album—announces Dylan's final arrival at re-birth. He has made it at last. Yet what is striking here is the humanity, the generosity of feeling. There is no note of glee or superiority. There is only a gladness which Dylan admits to, while admitting also that it is lessened by the final loss of love: 'There's a new day at dawn and I've finally arrived / If I'm there in the morning baby, you'll know I've survived / I can't believe it! I can't believe I'm alive! / But without you it doesn't seem right / Oh! where are you tonight?!'

It is therefore only the *tone*, one of uncompromising certainty, that should surprise us on coming to the *Slow Train Coming* album, after all the struggle between his twin selves so brilliantly documented by *Street Legal*. The initial shock should properly be at the leap having *succeeded*—and at the tone of voice switching from the 'oh! but . . .' of *Street Legal* to the severe certainty of 'You either got faith or you got unbelief / And there ain't no neutral ground' on 'Precious Angel'.

The substance of what Dylan has to say on *Slow Train Coming* and *Saved*, tone of voice aside, is not so very different from what he's been saying before. The import of that last verse of 'Where Are You Tonight?'—'I've finally arrived . . . / I can't believe it! I can't believe I'm alive!', is restated on *Saved* in 'Saving Grace', which must stand as a direct, careful and courageous summary of his new position: 'By this time I'd-a thought that I would be sleeping / In a pine box for all eternity: / My faith keeps me alive.'

In 1962, as noted, he was writing about the need to conduct one's life in the light of one's expecting death: 'I will not go down under the ground / 'Cause somebody tells me that death's comin' round . . . / Let me die in my footsteps / Before I go down under the ground'; and even in the white heat of the mid-60s he was saying that you have to decide how you behave in the face of the certainty that you will die. (See **'Vacillation'** for specifics on this.)

His conversion to Christianity prompted what is essentially a re-statement of that earlier agnostic seriousness, re-approached as 'Prepare to Meet Thy Maker'. It is one of the basic, major themes of *Slow Train Coming* and *Saved*—and it is a message Dylan urges on us regardless of our religious tenets. It is a message about not wasting our time in this world, regardless (effectively) of whether we believe there is another world to come. For himself, in this period, he chooses to concentrate on this theme with a conventional Christian focus, but essentially it is a re-statement of the same conviction as to the dignity of life and the individual's responsibility for controlling its quality and worthiness as he was expressing in the 1960s.

[Bob Dylan: 'Let Me Die in My Footsteps', NY, 25 Apr 1962, was issued on the almost immediately withdrawn first version of *The Freewheelin' Bob Dylan*, 1963; with one verse excised it was finally issued on *Bootleg Series Vols. 1–3* box set, 1991; Dylan had played it privately to IZZY YOUNG at the Folklife Center 22 Feb 1962, performed it in public in Montréal, 2 Jul 1962, recorded it again as a Witmark song-publishing demo, NY, Dec 1962 and played guitar (as Blind Boy Grunt) behind HAPPY TRAUM on the latter's version, NY, 24 Jan 1963, *Broadside Ballads*, Broadside BR301, NY, 1963; 'Abandoned Love', the Other End, NY, 3 Jul 1975, & at the *Desire* sessions, NY, 31 Jul 1975, this version issued *Biograph* box set, 1985.

Woody Guthrie: *Bound for Glory*, 1943; the 1st paperback edn., which Dylan owned, was Garden City, NY: Dolphin, 1949. The Staple Singers: 'People Get Ready': see **'People Get Ready'**.]

Bowden, Betsy [1948 -] Elizabeth Ann Bowden (the Bow pronounced as in bow and arrow) was born in Grove City, Pennsylvania, on January 30, 1948. Now a Professor of English at Rutgers University in Camden, New Jersey, her first work on Dylan was her PhD dissertation, completed at the University of California at Berkeley in 1978. This work then mutated into her 1982 book *Performed Literature: Words and Music by Bob Dylan*, Chapter One of which was also published as 'Performed Literature: A Case Study of Bob Dylan's "Hard Rain"' in an academic journal in North Carolina.

The book was a pioneering attempt both to find an apt language for discussing in print the non-print parts of Dylan's art (whether the title phrase itself augurs success at this task will strike readers differently) and, in the process, to look at the importance of performance for song as a whole. She was touching here on concerns central to present-day folklore studies, the drift of which from the 1980s onwards was away from 'text' and towards 'performance'. *Performed Literature* was originally published by Indiana University Press; an edition modestly updated (with a new introduction, chronology, bibliography and appendix) came out from the University Press of America in April 2001.

Bowden's other work includes articles in learned journals–from 1979's 'The Art of Courtly Copulation', published in *Medievalia et Humanistica*, to 'A Modest Proposal, Relating Four Millennia of Proverb Collections to Chemistry within the Human Brain' in a 1996 edition of *Journal of American Folklore*. A specialist in Chaucer, medieval literature and folklore, she has published two books on Chaucer and edited the collection *Eighteenth-Century Modernizations from the Canterbury Tales*, published in 1991, and is now working on a project entitled *Beyond Textuality: The Audiovisual Wife of Bath, 1660–1810*, looking at verbal, visual and musical interpretations of this pilgrim between that of Richard Brathwaite in 1665 and WILLIAM BLAKE's in 1809.

Bowden has not entirely abandoned Bob Dylan studies. At the 2nd International Conference of the Lyrica Society for Word-Music Relations on the Mountain Campus of Northern Arizona University in Flagstaff in 1998, she delivered a paper entitled 'My Way or Yours? The Album as Aesthetic Unit in the Works of Bob Dylan and FRANK SINATRA', which looked in particular at Sinatra's 1957 album *Come Dance with Me* and Dylan's album of 40 years later, *Time Out of Mind*.

[Betsy Bowden: 'The Art of Courtly Copulation', *Medievalia et Humanistica* no. 9, 1979, Denton, TX, pp. 67–85; 'Performed Literature: A Case Study of Bob Dylan's "Hard Rain"', *Literature in Performance* vol.3, no.1, 1982, University of North Carolina at Chapel Hill; *Performed Literature: Words and Music by Bob Dylan*, Bloomington: Indiana University Press, 1982, 2nd ed., Lanham, MD: University Press of America, 2001; 'A Modest Proposal, Relating Four Millennia of Proverb Collections to Chemistry within the Human Brain', *Journal of American Folklore* 109, 1996, Champaign, IL, pp.440–49.]

Brady, Paul [1947 -] Born on May 19, 1947 in Strabane, County Tyrone, Northern Ireland, on the border with the Irish Republic, Brady grew up there, listening first to the swing, jazz and show tunes of his parents' generation, and then to 1950s rock'n'roll, 60s pop, Motown, blues, R&B and country music. He taught himself rock'n'roll piano before taking up the guitar at 11 and then developing as a singer while covering the RAY CHARLES and James Brown repertoires in a band called the Kult at college in Dublin in the mid-1960s, while all around him the city was witnessing a renewal of interest in Irish traditional music. One of the groups on this scene, perhaps the least famous, was the Johnstons. Brady joined and recorded seven albums with them.

The Johnstons, including Brady, moved to London in 1969 and then to New York City in 1972, but he quit and returned to Dublin in 1974 to join the much more famous Planxty, and then from 1976 to 1978 formed a duo with fellow ex-Planxty Andy Irvine, releasing the album *Andy Irvine and Paul Brady*, which clinched his popularity and reputation as one of the great Irish traditional song interpreters. He made an acclaimed solo folk album 'Welcome Here Kind Stranger' in 1978 and then changed direction, putting folksong on the back burner and boiling up widely praised self-composed rock music instead.

Brady is a singer Dylan much admires, calling him one of his 'secret heroes' in the *Biograph* box set interview in 1985. In Ireland in July 1984, at Dylan's request, Brady showed him how he played his guitar accompaniment to another old song, 'The Lakes of Ponchartrain', which Brady had included on that much-lauded solo album of 1978. Four years after receiving Brady's in-person tuition, Dylan began to perform 'The Lakes of Pontchartrain' in the acoustic section of his Never-Ending Tour concerts, introducing it at the very first one, on June 7, 1988 in Concord, California. (For an exposition of the rather complex route whereby 'The Lakes of Pontchartrain' came to Brady, see Gavin Selerie's 1995 article 'Tricks and Training: Some Dylan Sources and Analogues, Part 2', which includes excerpts from a letter from Brady to its author.)

It was also Brady who had tidied the old anti-militarist song 'Arthur McBride' into the order and exact shape Dylan recycles on his first return to a solo acoustic album in almost 30 years, 1992's *Good as I Been to You*. This great Irish folk number was A.L. Lloyd's favourite song—'that most good-natured, mettlesome and un-pacifistic of anti-militarist songs', he called it—and it passed from him into the repertoire of the 1960s English folk scene. It had been collected in Limerick from a Patrick W. Joyce in 1840, and, says Lloyd, 'around the same time George Petrie received a version from a Donegal correspondent. Sam Fone, the aging Dartmoor mason whom Baring-Gould found to be an inexhaustible fountain of songs, [who] remembered it as his father's favourite in Devon in the 1830s. . . . [The song] made its way to the Scottish north-east during the latter half of the century. . . . More recently, a singer from Walberswick, Suffolk, recorded it for the BBC early in 1939.'

The recruiting sergeant was one of the most hated figures in Irish and British life, especially since poverty gave many men little alternative but to join up, though of course in the case of the Irish, the army they were joining was not even their own. The roving recruiting sergeant encountered by Arthur McBride and his cousin had a function halfway between that of the earlier press gang and the modern recruiting office, which still pulls in those with least education and fewest opportunities.

Like 'Jim Jones', this makes for a song readily understood within Bob Dylan's repertoire—and is as good an anti-militarist song as 'John Brown' is a bad one, being alive, spanning many moods and full of individual detail instead of polemical and built upon lurid stereotypes to the exclusion of all real observation.

Paul Brady sang the song in Planxty and later as a solo performer, and his recording of it was on the duo album *Andy Irvine and Paul Brady*. Brady himself had been familiar with the song for many years, but he found a particular arrangement of it in a 1973 American book, *A Heritage of Songs: The Songs of Carrie Grover* (a Maine resident of Irish and Scottish ancestry), when living at the home of the 1960s folksinger Patrick Sky in Rhode Island, and this was the version he adapted for his own recording of it in 1976. There is no doubting that Dylan knew this recording, nor that his own performance of it on *Good as I Been to You* is close—word for word, and melodically—to Brady's.

How interesting it is then, that a specific part of the melody of 'Arthur McBride' is to be found in Dylan's much earlier 'Ballad in Plain D' (from *Another Side of Bob Dylan*: his *previous* solo album, as it happens, though from 1964). The tune of each verse's third line is the same in each song—so that 'Arthur McBride's' 'Now mark what followed and what did betide' can be overlaid, syllable for syllable and note for note, by the 'Ballad in Plain D' line 'Noticing not that I'd already slipped'—while the next line, the fourth line of each four-line verse, would also be the same in both songs except that in 'Arthur McBride' the line in question alternates verse by verse between ending on the resolved tonic, as 'Ballad in Plain D' always does, and ending on a half-resolve, to hang over, awaiting the start of the next. The upshot is that half of every second verse of 'McBride'—and the melody-line of the guitar intro too—has the same tune as 'Ballad in Plain D'. Thus, for example, these 'McBride' lines (comprising the second half of verse two)—'And a little wee drummer intending to camp / For the day being pleasant and charming'—can be replaced, so far as the tune is concerned, by these, the second half of 'Plain D's' verse: 'At the peak of the night, the king and the queen / Tumbled all down into pieces.'

It was Paul Brady who introduced these half-resolves on alternate verses. That Dylan follows him in doing so is one of the things that establishes how closely Dylan's version is modelled upon Brady's. If it were not for this, then the second half of *every* verse of 'McBride' would parallel those of 'Ballad in Plain D'.

This is hardly the whole story, however. Dylan brings his own knowledge and his own otherness to his 'McBride' recording. As Gavin Selerie puts it in a later article: 'I hear Brady's performance beneath Dylan's but there are other influences there as well . . . one can hear layers of musical experience in Dylan's work . . .' Moreover, Brady's phrasing and intonation may in turn owe something to Dylan: '. . . notably a charged casualness of reference and an elasticity of syllabic emphasis.' Playing in Dublin, London and New York in his formative musical years, Brady can hardly have failed to absorb Dylan influences.

Dylan's 'Arthur McBride', then, may be very close to Brady's but the voice is so strongly his own that he makes it seem an apt vehicle for expressing himself, and does so with a fond admiration for the song and a range of feeling that make this a highlight of the album.

Paul Brady has continued to make solo albums and to be a national hero on both sides of the border in Ireland. He has also, through the long reaches of his career, played on an unexpected list of other people's records, including playing mandolin on Tanita Tikaram's *Ancient Heart* and tin whistle on MARK KNOPFLER's *Golden Heart*, Mary Chapin Carpenter's *Stones in the Road* and Marianne Faithfull's cover of the PATTI SMITH song 'Ghost Dance', and sharing vocals with Bonnie Raitt on the title track (which he wrote) of her album *Luck of the Draw*, and on 'Our Little Angel' on the Roseanne Cash album *Retrospective*. Many others have recorded his compositions, including (co-written with Ronan Keating) a no.1 country hit for Brooks & Dunn, 'The Long Goodbye' in 2003. His album *Nobody Knows: The Best of Paul Brady*, 1999, includes 1990s re-recordings of 'The Lakes of Pontchartrain' and 'Arthur McBride'.

[Paul Brady: 'Arthur McBride', Wales, fall 1976, *Andy Irvine–Paul Brady*, Mulligan LUN 008, Dublin, 1976, CD-reissued LUNCD008, Dublin, 1990; 'The Lakes of Pontchartrain', Dublin, Mar–Apr 1978, *Welcome Here Kind Stranger*, Mulligan LUN 024, Dublin 1978. For career background this entry owes much to the online biog seen 2 Dec 2005 at *www.paulbrady.com/biog/default.asp*.

A.L. Lloyd, *Folk Song in England*, London: Penguin, 1967. Gavin Selerie: 'Tricks and Training: Some Dylan Sources and Analogues, Part 2', *The Telegraph* no.51, Romford, UK, spring 1995, and quoted from *The Telegraph* no.54, spring 1996.]

Brecht, Bertolt [1898 - 1956] Eugen Bertolt Brecht was born in Augsburg, Germany, on February 19, 1898, studied philosophy and medicine at the University of Munich and served as a medical orderly in a military hospital in World War I. He was only 20 at the end of that war. He became a socialist, a communist and a dramatist—forced to flee Nazi Germany in 1933 (living in exile in Denmark, Sweden, the Soviet Union and the US) and was prompted to flee the US after being hauled up before the House UnAmerican Activities Committee in 1947—though he gave a brilliant performance at the hearing, not least in that his interrogators failed to grasp his game-playing obfuscation; this drama was once compared to 'the cross-examination of a zoologist by apes'. He returned to Europe and entered the Soviet Bloc's East Germany, forming the Berliner Ensemble theatre company in 1949.

Brecht was, above all, a revolutionary dramatist, refuting the 'make-believe' of the traditional theatre in favour of 'epic theatre', in which ideas and didactic lessons are what is important, and all 'realism' is to be suppressed as distracting from the 'message' of the play. His earliest works as a playwright were written in post-WWI Germany: *Baal*, *Drums in the Night*, *Jungle of the Cities* and *A Man's a Man*. In 1927 he worked with composer Kurt Weill on his own adaptation of the 1728 play *The Beggar's Opera* by John Gay (which had been revived to great acclaim in London in 1920). Brecht's re-write was *die Dreigroschenoper*, or *The Threepenny Opera*, and mocked the Victorian bourgeoisie instead of Italian grand opera. This is the work that gave us 'Mack the Knife' and 'Pirate Jenny'; it also helped train a number of actors, including Lotte Lenya and Peter Lorre. The more demanding musical play *Rise and Fall of the City of Mahagonny*, again with songs composed by Kurt Weill, was completed in 1931.

Brecht's greatest plays were written in exile, in the late 1930s and early 40s: principally *Mother Courage* (1939), *The Good Man of Szechuan* and *The Resistible Rise of Arturo Ui* (1941) and *The Caucasian Chalk Circle* (1943). In Hollywood in this period he could get none of his screenplay writing accepted other than some work with the great Fritz Lang and John Wexley on the 1942–43 film *Hangmen Also Die*, which Lang directed (and in which Walter Brennan was cast improbably as a professor).

Like so many intellectuals, Brecht was unsuited to Hollywood, remarking that 'Svendborg was a world center' of ideas in comparison; yet post-World War II Berlin proved almost as far from ideal, and after forming the Berliner Ensemble he wrote only one new play while in East Germany. But Brecht was a poet as well as a playwright and his song lyrics were always arresting and vivid. Not all were written with Weill: in 1930 he worked with the composer Hanns Eisler (who was his almost exact contemporary and would later write the East German national anthem, 'Auferstanden aus Ruinen'), on *The Measure Taken*.

The songs, naturally, were part of the reason Dylan was so taken with Brecht when he first encountered his work in a Greenwich Village musical production SUZE ROTOLO was designing for, *Brecht on Brecht*. You could reasonably call them 'protest songs', and they were sometimes achieved, like early Dylan numbers, by reading of a specific injustice in a newspaper and crafting a song from that individual case. In *The Threepenny Opera* one of the main figures is a kitchen maid fantasising about liberation from those whom she serves. Another early Brecht song came out of a news story about another domestic servant, named as Marie Farrar. It isn't far from here to Dylan's early masterpiece 'The Lonesome Death of Hattie Carroll'. (Nor, in the simpler sense of a title and a phrase, is it far from *Brecht on Brecht* to *Blonde on Blonde*.)

Brecht would sing his own songs, too, with a guitar, in a 'raw, abrasive' voice. Unlike Dylan, he 'loved complicated chords that were difficult to finger: C-sharp minor or E-flat major chords,' as another playwright, Carl Zuckmayer, observed.

In an open letter to *Broadside* in August 1963, Dylan wrote: 'Hallelullah to you for puttin' Brecht in your same last issue. He should be as widely known as WOODY an' should be as widely read as Mickey Spillane . . .'; in *11 Outlined Epitaphs* he wrote: 'I stumble on lost cigars / of Bertolt Brecht' (indicating, beyond the singling out of the artist, that he knew something of the man too: Brecht smoked cigars copiously—and had done so as part of his performance at his HUAC interrogation). Years later, Dylan told ANTHONY SCADUTO that he 'was influenced by Brecht. Used to be Woody, but not any more'. And years later still, in *Chroni-*

cles Volume One, Dylan sets out in far more detail the basis of the pull of the songs (in which, as he rightly says, Weill's 'melodies were like a combination of opera and jazz'):

'I . . . was aroused straight away by the raw intensity of the songs', Dylan writes, and then lists some (including one with a title he used himself in the 1970s, 'Wedding Song'). 'Songs with tough language.' He describes the staging vividly, the characters singing—'thieves, scavengers or scallywags'—and the maid, her attitude 'so strong and burning' in 'a hideous netherworld'; and he stresses the special impact of 'Pirate Jenny':

> 'This is a wild song. Big medicine in the lyrics. Heavy action spread out. . . . It leaves you breathless. . . . This piece left you flat on your back and it demanded to be taken seriously. It lingered. Woody had never written a song like that. It wasn't a protest song or a topical song and there was no love for people in it.'

All this is a very short extract from Dylan's long and impassioned, very specific scrutiny, which includes a clear and direct description of the attempts at a particular kind of songwriting to which the Brecht song led him, and how he couldn't achieve this straight away. A few pages later he takes his leave of Brecht in the book with this:

> 'In a few years' time I'd write and sing songs like "It's Alright Ma (I'm Only Bleeding)", "Mr. Tambourine Man", "The Lonesome Death of Hattie Carroll", "Who Killed Davey Moore", "Only a Pawn in Their Game", "A Hard Rain's a-Gonna Fall" and some others like that. If I hadn't gone to the Theatre de Lys and heard the ballad "Pirate Jenny", it might not have dawned on me to write them, that songs like that could be written.'

The present entry gives only the merest skim across the surface of Brecht's overall pre-figuring of Dylan. The place to find it delineated properly is in the brilliant and refreshing essay by Esther Quin, 'The Brecht of the Electric Guitar'—one of the finest pieces about any aspect of Bob Dylan's work—published in the British fanzine *The Bridge* in 2004, and which Ms. Quin wrote before she could have known what Dylan himself would say in *Chronicles*. Only one of the gems in her essay – which draws from a longer work in progress, her PhD thesis on the influence of Brecht on Dylan, at the Victoria University of Wellington, New Zealand—is the 'discovery' of these lines in Brecht's 'Song of the Moldau', written in the US about Nazi-occupied Czechoslovakia:

> 'Times are a-changing. The mightiest scheming / Won't save the mighty. The bubble will burst. / Like bloody old peacocks they're strutting and screaming, / But, times are a-changing. The last shall be the first. / The last shall be the first.'

Bertolt Brecht died of a coronary thrombosis in East Berlin on August 14, 1956.

[*Hangmen Also Die*, dir. Fritz Lang, Arnold Pressburger Films, US, 1942. Bob Dylan, *Chronicles Volume One*, 2004, pp.272–275 & 287. Esther Quin: 'The Brecht of the Electric Guitar', *The Bridge* no.18, Gateshead, UK, spring 2004, pp. 49–68.]

Bremser, Ray [1934 - 1998] One of the lesser-known of THE BEATS, Bremser was born February 22, 1934 in Jersey City, NJ. He was a minor poet who served prison terms for armed robbery (often when he was only pretending to have a gun) and for drug offences between 1953 and 1965, when his *Poems of Madness* was published; in 1967 came the prose-poem *Angel*, with an introduction by FERLINGHETTI, and in 1968 *Drive Suite*. (Bremser's wife Bonnie published her *Troia: Mexican Memoirs* in 1969.) He was an acquaintance of GREGORY CORSO and ALLEN GINSBERG, and moved into Ginsberg's upstate New York farmhouse in 1970.

Barry Miles, in his excellent *Ginsberg: A Biography*, 1989, reports that when Ginsberg came to ask Dylan for $15,000 payment for his appearances in, and work on, the film *Renaldo & Clara*, he said he 'wanted a car and a stereo set and to give some money to Ray Bremser. The mention of Bremser, whom Dylan had heard read in New York in 1961, did the trick, and the money came through.'

Bremser's other poetry publications were *Black Is Black Blues* (1971), *Blowing Mouth* (1978), *The Conquerors* (1998) and the posthumous *The Dying of Children* (1999).

Dylan recalls the 'love songs of Allen Ginsberg / an' jail songs of Ray Bremser' in his poem sequence *11 Outlined Epitaphs*, on the sleevenotes of his third album. Bremser died of cancer in hospital in Utica, NY, November 3, 1998.

[A useful website is *www.cosmicbaseball.com/bremser9.html*, seen online 5 Aug 2005.]

***Bridge, The* [fanzine]** *The Bridge*, which began in 1998, was a delayed reaction to the inevitable closure of *The Telegraph* after the death of its founder and editor JOHN BAULDIE in 1996. Looking exactly like *The Telegraph*, *The Bridge* was founded by Mike Wyvill and JOHN WRAITH, who had run a regular column, 'Jotting Down Notes', logging new official releases with a Dylan connection, in the earlier journal and now transferred this to their own replacement publication. The first issue began by saying: 'It is with the strangest feeling that we write this introduction. As you will realise we would certainly rather not be doing it at all and that John was still writing . . . in *The Telegraph*.'

The Bridge, however, has not proved much of a substitute; it conspicuously lacks personality, vision and definition, and its editors never actually seem to come out and *say* anything—which is very different from John Bauldie's approach. Its small, glossy pages and its quarterliness are ideally suited to discursive essays and criticism rather than to news (which is bound to be a thousand miles behind) or song-performance lists (which take up far too much space) yet it has insisted on trying to offer all these things—with some issues largely given over to MICHAEL KROGSGAARD's interminable lists of Dylan sessions: invaluable in themselves but utterly unsuited to this magazine's pages, and every issue giving page upon page to listings of what Dylan has sung in dozens of consecutive recent concerts—recent, but not recent enough, since by the time *The Bridge* has been built and opened to its very small public, everyone interested has long since logged those concert lists from more immediate (mostly online) sources. Nor, when it comes to critical scrutiny, do the editors seem qualified to hold out for rigour or wit.

Nonetheless they are lucky enough to have amongst their contributors both ROY KELLY and TERRY KELLY (unrelated people), and their 20-plus issues have offered many individually interesting and valuable pieces, perhaps especially interviews with important and/or quirky people who have been tangled up in Bob down the years; it is able, too, to publish some tremendous rare photographs of Dylan (continuing John Bauldie's tradition of pairing, subtly and without saying so, photos taken years apart yet capturing the same pose or facial expression).

[*The Bridge* no.1, Gateshead, UK, summer 1998. Website: *www.two-riders.co.uk*.]

Bringing It All Back Home **[1965]** The fifth album—another breakthrough and another sudden jump to new ground. One side of the record is solo and has four long tracks, each of which has become a classic—'Mr. Tambourine Man'; the visionary 'Gates of Eden'; 'It's Alright Ma (I'm Only Bleeding)' and the beautiful 'It's All Over Now, Baby Blue'. This solo side of the album contained more than enough to justify Dylan's burgeoning popularity as a uniquely contemporary spokesman. But the other side was enough to gain him a new notoriety and to lose him even more devotees than his previous album had done. Unprecedentedly, here was this folk-singer committing the ultimate sacrilege of singing rock'n'roll songs with electric guitars behind him. Students—serious-minded young people unaware of the social upheavals about to happen—were appalled that Dylan should resort to such triviality. Mostly this side sounds pretty thin now, and a dress-rehearsal/prototype for what was to come next. But it was undeniably innovative and gives us yet another collection of stand-out Dylan songs, 'Subterranean Homesick Blues', 'She Belongs to Me', 'Love Minus Zero/No limit' and 'Maggie's Farm' among them.

[Recorded NY, 14–15 Jan 1965; released as Columbia CS 9128 (stereo) & CL 2328 (mono), 22 Mar 1965. In UK, CBS SBPG 62515 (stereo) & BPG 62515 (mono), May 1965.]

Bromberg, David [1945 -] David Bromberg was born in Philadelphia on September 19, 1945 but grew up in Tarrytown, New York. He began playing guitar at 13, after hearing PETE SEEGER. After high school he attended Columbia University and assumed he would become a musicologist, but dropped out to join the university of life in Greenwich Village, where he rapidly became a sought-after session musician because of his exceptional touch and feel as a picker on guitar and dobro. He may well be the only folkie who has played behind Chubby Checker.

He made an unscheduled appearance at the 1970 Isle of Wight Festival (the same year as JIMI HENDRIX's appearance, and the year after Bob Dylan's) and believes that it was this performance that gained him a contract for four solo albums with Columbia, on the first of which, *David Bromberg*, released in 1972, Dylan played harmonica on the final track, 'Sammy's Song' (recorded in New York on October 5, 1971).

By this time Bromberg had already played on two Dylan albums—*Self Portrait* and *New Morning*, both in 1970. On the first of these, Bromberg had played guitar, dobro and bass on the New York session of March 3, 1970, and guitar and dobro on March 4 and 5. Back in the studio three months later, he played guitar and dobro on the June 1 session that yielded the *Dylan* tracks 'Mr. Bojangles' and 'Mary Ann', and on June 3, which produced two more *Dylan* tracks, 'Can't Help Falling in Love' and 'Lily of the West' (plus the uncirculated 'Jamaica Farewell') and the *New Morning* track 'One More Weekend'. On June 4 Bromberg again played guitar and dobro, and thus also appears on the *Dylan* track 'Big Yellow Taxi' and the *New Morning* title track and 'Three Angels'. On June 5, still on guitar and dobro, Bromberg contributed to 'If Dogs Run Free', 'Went to See the Gypsy', 'Sign on the Window', 'The Man in Me', 'Father of Night' and 'Winterlude'. On June 30 he played guitar on the 15 attempted takes of 'Blowin' in the Wind' that Dylan recorded but which have never circulated. (Bromberg had played on the 1968 Jerry Jeff Walker album *Mr. Bojangles* and had recorded it himself on his own second album, *Demon in Disguise* in 1972—and on his third, *Wanted Dead or Alive*, he put Dylan's then-recent composition 'Wallflower', along with the BLIND WILLIE McTELL classic 'Statesboro Blues'. And on the live 1979 album *You Should See the Rest of the Band*, he is supported by GARTH HUDSON on two tracks.)

After *New Morning* and *David Bromberg*, Bromberg and Dylan next appeared together on the album *DOUG SAHM & Band*, recorded in New York in 1972 (which is where Bromberg picked up Dylan's 'Wallflower', of course); but after this they seem to have stayed out of professional contact for almost 20 years. After moving to California in 1977, Bromberg moved again in 1980, this time to Chicago, and he was still there in 1992 when, after Dylan had recorded his first solo album in three decades, *Good as I Been to You*, he asked Bromberg to produce what would have been an intriguing follow-up album: a follow-up in being another set of traditional folk songs and old blues, but this time backed by a number of musicians, including Bromberg's regular band and, on more than one track, by the renowned Chicago black gospel choir the Annettes (not a children's choir, as reported). Dylan was encouraged to turn to Bromberg after seeing him play, back in the Village that February. Dylan had been to NEIL YOUNG's concerts at the Beacon Theater (February 13–15, 1992) and one night he and Neil went on to the Bottom Line (not the Bitter End, as often stated) to catch a Bromberg performance there.

Dylan and Bromberg went into the studios in Chicago from June 4 to June 21, and reportedly recorded 12–26 songs in that time. In fact it was 30. The few that have circulated—and they didn't emerge at all for more than a decade after their recording—were the JIMMIE RODGERS song 'Miss the Mississippi and You', the traditional 'Polly Vaughn' (which Shirley Collins sang a good deal), the oddly spelt 'Kaatskill Serenade', which Bromberg had composed and which is on his 1977 double-album *How Late'll Ya Play 'Til?*, and a blues called 'Sloppy Drunk', which bears no resemblance to the Jimmy Rodgers song and may be the old Walter Davis number but was certainly also on the Bromberg double-album. The last of these Dylan tracks was a bit phlegm-driven 1990s Bob-on-automatic but the others were wonderful, especially 'Polly Vaughn'. Unfortunately, they have circulated only in poor quality.

The rest of the recorded tracks, which all remain unheard, comprise: 'Hey Joe'; 'Mobile Line'; 'Just Because'; 'Field of Stone (Would You Lay with Me)'; 'Annie's Song'; 'Jugband Song'; 'Rock Me Baby'; 'Send Me to the 'Lectric Chair'; 'Gotta Do My Time'; 'Su Su's Got a Mohawk'; 'Northeast Texas Women'; 'Sail On'; 'Can't Lose What You Never Had'; 'World of Fools'; 'Everybody's Crying Mercy'; 'Tennessee Blues'; 'Summer Wages'; 'Casey Jones'; 'Morning Blues'; 'Young Westley'; 'The Lady Came from Baltimore'; 'New Lee Highway Blues'; 'Rise Again'; 'Duncan and Brady'; 'The Main Street Moan'; and 'Nobody's Fault But Mine'.

It may be that 'Hey Joe' doesn't really exist, or if it does it's probably only a fragment, since this was merely a warm-up; when Dylan first arrived at the studio, he sat straight down at the piano and started performing it without a word to anyone. The tape wasn't rolling till some time had passed. But Dylan had performed Hendrix's 'Dolly Dagger' in concert in Australia earlier the same year, and would open his Juan-les-Pins concert with 'Hey Joe' that July.

'Mobile Line' is a song cut by the Holy Modal Rounders, JIM KWESKIN and Jimmie Dale Gilmore, but it's based on our old friend 'Hey Lawdy Mama—the France Blues', that great pre-war record by Papa Harvey Hull and Long Cleve Reed. 'Just Because' is probably the old country song written by the Shelton Brothers, recorded by them in 1942 and revived by ELVIS PRESLEY at Sun in 1954 (though unreleased till on RCA in 1956). 'Field of Stone' is a song by David Allan Coe but covered by, among others, JOHNNY CASH and Tanya Tucker; the only well-known 'Annie's Song' is, oh dear, John Denver's.

'Rock Me Baby' may be the B.B. King song revived by Hendrix at the 1967 Monterey Pop Festival—which is essentially the same thing as the earlier ARTHUR CRUDUP song 'Rock Me Mama', cut by Dylan at the *Pat Garrett & Billy the Kid* sessions almost 20 years earlier—and 'Gotta Do My Time' may be the 1950s Roy Moss song, or a number by FLATT & SCRUGGS also cut by Johnny Cash, but may equally be the bluegrass favourite 'Doin' My Time', by Jimmie Skinner. 'Can't Lose What You Never Had' is a MUDDY WATERS number. 'Everybody's Crying Mercy' is by Dylan's old Greenwich Village acquaintance MOSE ALLISON: it's on a 1968 album of his, *I've Been Doin' Some Thinkin'*, but had been revived by Bonnie Raitt in 1973 (and a couple of years after these Dylan-Bromberg sessions was revived again by ELVIS COSTELLO).

'Tennessee Blues' was a song Dylan had played harp on at the Doug Sahm sessions of 1972 (which Bromberg had also attended); 'Morning Blues' might prove to be the LIGHTNIN' HOPKINS song of that name, or LEADBELLY's 'Good Morning Blues', or the lovely Uncle Dave Macon number 'Mourning Blues'. 'Young Westley' was written by folksinger Mary McCaslin, and featured on her 1974 début album *Way Out West*. Tim Hardin wrote 'The Lady Came from Baltimore' (which Dylan went on to perform live in 1994: twice in the US in April and once in France in July).

The Dallas Holm gospel number 'Rise Again', which Dylan had sung 11 times in concert in 1980 and once in 1981, is the track reported to use the choir, but in fact this is more prominent on 'Nobody's Fault But Mine', the old blues gospel number by BLIND WILLIE JOHNSON (and which MARIA MULDAUR had sung at a 1981 Dylan concert). 'Casey Jones' and 'Duncan and Brady' are well-known traditional black ballads, and 'Sail On' is probably the 1934 Bumble Bee Slim hit 'Sail on Little Girl Sail On', covered widely in the 1930s—including by Leadbelly and Roosevelt Sykes—and many times since.

The provenance of 'Su Su's Got a Mohawk' has not been identified, despite its distinctive working title. 'Summer Wages' is a mid-1960s composition by Ian Tyson of IAN & SYLVIA. As for 'New Lee Highway Blues', this is based on 'Goin' Down the Lee Highway', written by G.B. Grayson of Grayson & Whitter, one of the founding success stories of recorded Old Timey music (and whom Dylan had encountered on the HARRY SMITH anthology *AMERICAN FOLK MUSIC*). Their 1929 recording led to its widespread adoption as a standard under the title 'Lee Highway Blues'; it was duly turned into 'New Lee Highway Blues' by Bromberg himself.

And that is the striking story of these sessions: that an almost absurd proportion of the songs recorded were Bromberg songs, whether written by him or not. As noted, he had written and recorded 'Kaatskill Serenade' and recorded 'Sloppy Drunk'. 'World of Fools' is also his, as is the rambunctious 'Northeast Texas Women' (not 'Woman', as often listed by Dylan discographers), a song from yet another Bromberg album, 1979's *Bandit in a Bathing Suit*. Additionally 'Jugband Song' is on his 1972 album *Demon in Disguise*; 'Send Me to the 'Lectric Chair' (originally by Bessie Smith in 1927), 'New Lee Highway Blues' and 'The Main Street Moan' are all on Bromberg's *Wanted Dead or Alive*; and 'Young Westley' and 'Summer Wages' are further tracks on the double-LP *How Late'll Ya Play 'Til?*.

This preponderance of old Bromberg material was apparently mostly at Dylan's insistence. At the time, casting around for songs, reportedly he kept saying, 'What about that one of yours . . .' Afterwards, of course, it was a different matter. Perhaps Dylan felt that it had turned into a David Bromberg album; perhaps not. But for whatever reason, having asked Bromberg to mix a few tracks–six or seven, apparently–he heard the mixes, hated them and promptly abandoned the entire album. And he reportedly ordered the tapes destroyed. They weren't, and Dylan is sitting on the masters. Yet to judge by the quality of 'Kaatskills Serenade' and 'Polly Vaughn', this really is the great lost Dylan album.

Five years later, Bromberg was still Chicago-based when Dylan's Never-Ending Tour came through the city on a wintry night–December 14, 1997–and Bromberg came on stage in the middle of Dylan's set and played guitar on the instrumental 'Ragtime Annie' (his own composition) and on 'It Takes a Lot to Laugh, It Takes a Train to Cry'. So far it's been their last connection.

Bromberg had spent his first Chicago years training at the Kenneth Warren School of Violin Making, and these days spends less time performing than making, selling and repairing these instruments (and their bows) from his store in Wilmington, Delaware (the town in which Dylan's first wife SARA grew up). He still plays music live, with Jay Ungar & Molly Mason and others–usually acoustic music, and covering, as he always has, an enormous sweep of different music, from jazz to rock to gospel to bluegrass. In 2005 he played over 40 gigs, including nine festival dates, sometimes with the David Bromberg Big Band, sometimes with the David Bromberg Quartet and sometimes as part of the Angel Band (comprising the Wilmington-based O'Byrne Family plus electric bassist Bob Taylor).

In 2003 he released a 'new' CD by the David Bromberg Quartet, confessing the age of its material by the title *Live New York City 1982* and issued on the somewhat defensively named label David's Private Collection.

[David Bromberg: *David Bromberg*, Columbia 31104, US, 1972; *Demon in Disguise*, Columbia KC31753, US, 1972; *Wanted Dead or Alive*, Columbia 32717, US, 1974. The David Bromberg Band: *Midnight on the Water*, Columbia CK33397, 1975; *How Late'll Ya Play 'Til?*, San Francisco, 18–19 Jun 1976, Fantasy, US, 1977; *Reckless Abandon*, Fantasy, US, 1987; *Bandit in a Bathing Suit*, Fantasy, US, 1979; *You Should See the Rest of the Band*, 1979, Fantasy F-9590, US, 1980, CD-reissued with *My Own House* (originally 1980 also) as *My Own House/You Should See the Rest of the Band*, Fantasy 24752, US, 1999 (on which Garth Hudson is credited as playing organ and accordion). The David Bromberg Quartet: *Live New York City 1982*, David's Private Collection, US, 2003.

Bob Dylan: 'Dolly Dagger', Perth, 18 Mar 1992; 'Lady Came from Baltimore', Davenport, IA, 6 Apr 1994, Peoria, IL, 13 Apr 1994 & Besançon, France, 4 Jul 1994; 'Rise Again' débuted San Francisco, 18 Nov 1980 & last played Clarkston, MI, 12 Jun 1981.]

Broonzy, Big Bill [prob. 1893 - 1958] William Lee Conley Broonzy was born in Scott, Mississippi, on June 26, 1893 or 1898. (He claimed the former; the latter is the date on his twin sister's birth certificate). He became one of the most famous, influential, versatile and retrospectively dismissed names in the history of the blues: a singer, songwriter, guitarist and teller of wholly unreliable tales, starting his career in the late 1920s and helping to set in motion in the late 1950s the folk revival movement that hit its peak soon after his death.

One of 21 children, he and his family moved to Arkansas to farm early in the 20th century; he served in France in World War I and moved to Chicago in 1920, where he was later recorded more frequently than any other single figure. He knew everyone, played with most and racked up huge sales, not least in partnership with Georgia Tom (later the gospel songwriter and music publisher THOMAS A. DORSEY) on a series of nudge-nudge records as by the Famous Hokum Boys. With the Boys' associate Hannah May (aka Jane Lucas), too, he made records like 1930's 'Pussy Cat, Pussy Cat', which begins with Ms Lucas singing the immortal 'You can play with my pussy but please don't dog it around / If you going to mistreat it, no pussy will be found', to which Big Bill, wittily bringing in nursery rhyme and combining it with the 'Corrina Corrina' format, ripostes: 'Pussy cat, pussy cat, where have you been so long?'

In the 1930s alone Broonzy played on more than 600 recorded sides (including accompanying rôles), defying the power of the Depression to shut him down. His feel-good guitar style and strong vocals were a shaping force in that decade and that city, but though he had an uncanny facility for changing styles, when fashion shifted more fundamentally in the late 1940s and MUDDY WATERS electrified Chicago, Broonzy felt the backlash, yet then found belated favour among white audiences interested in 'folk blues' and 'authenticity', and his last decade was spent pleasing concert audiences in Europe as well as in the US. In turn, after his death in 1958, and after the first release on vinyl of pre-war recordings by more uncompromising artists, Broonzy's name became almost a byword for middle-of-the-road Uncle Tom blues (despite his participation in the brave and daring conversation with MEMPHIS SLIM, SONNY BOY WILLIAMSON and Big Bill recorded by ALAN LOMAX in 1947 and released later as *Blues in the Mississippi Night*, in which they described the iniquities of the racial divide and the violence of life for blacks in the South, and despite his overt 'protest song' dating back at least to the start of the 1950s, 'Black, Brown and White').

Whatever was said of him, his influence was ubiquitous, as Dylan acknowledged. In the interview accompanying the *Biograph* box set in 1985, Dylan places Broonzy's cultural significance for those who had grown up in the white 1940s and for whom Big Bill was somehow an inevitable presence within the bohemian world: 'the newer poets and folk music, jazz, Monk, Coltrane, SONNY and BROWNIE, Big Bill Broonzy, Charlie Christian . . . it all left the rest of everything in the dust.'

One of Broonzy's stories is that in 1933 he lost a songwriting contest to MEMPHIS MINNIE when his 'Just a Dream (On My Mind)' was defeated by her 'Me and My Chauffeur Blues'. His contest loser is a terrific song in itself, and with strong 'Dylanesque' touches. You can easily hear him in your head singing these lines with relish and aplomb: 'I dreamed that I got married, raised up a family / I dreamed I had ten children and they all looked just like me / . . . I dreamed I had a million dollars, had a mermaid for a wife / I dreamed I won the Brooklyn Bridge on my knees shootin' dice.'

The songs with which Broonzy is associated include 'This Train Is Bound for Glory'; 'Key to the Highway', which he may not have written (pianist Charles Segar recorded it first) but he made it a 'classic' and it was one of the tracks released on SAM CHARTERS' highly influential 1959 LP *The Country Blues*; and 'When Did You Leave Heaven?'

Dylan's work grazes up against 'This Train Is Bound for Glory' in a number of ways (and it gives WOODY GUTHRIE the title for his autobiography); Dylan performs 'Key to the Highway' during the surprising sets delivered at Toad's Place in New Haven, Connecticut, on January 12, 1990, and again in concerts in Washington, D.C., on January 17, 1993 and in Fort Lauderdale, Florida, on September 23, 1995; and Dylan both performs and records 'When Did You Leave Heaven?' In concert he débuted the song in Stockholm on May 28, 1989 and sang it a further six times that year. This song too is included in the Toad's Place sets, and received two further outings in 1991—in Montevideo, Uruguay, that August 12 and in Rio de Janiero nine days later. Dylan's studio recording of 'When Did You Leave Heaven?', made in Hollywood probably in June 1987, is one of the better tracks on the 1989 album *Down in the Groove*.

Big Bill Broonzy died in Chicago on August 15, 1958. When news of his death reached Europe, an international collection was taken up for his widow. Embarrassingly, there was found to be more than one.

[Big Bill: 'Just a Dream (On My Mind)', Chicago, 5 Feb 1939; 'Just a Dream No.2', Chicago, 14 Sep 1939; 'Key to the Highway', Chicago, 2 May 1941, *The Country Blues*, RBF RF-1, NY, 1959. Jane Lucas & Big Bill: 'Pussy Cat, Pussy Cat' (aka 'Pussy Cat Blues'), NY, 15 Sep 1930, *Big Bill Broonzy 1928–1935: Do That Guitar Rag*, Yazoo L-1035, NY, 1973. Big Bill Broonzy: 'Black Brown and White', Paris 20 Sep 1951, Paris 7 Feb 1952, Antwerp, 29 Mar 1952 & Copenhagen, 4 May 1956; 'When Did You Leave Heaven?', Paris, 21 Sep 1951; 'This Train', Copenhagen, 4 May 1956; 'This Train Is Bound for Glory' (with Pete Seeger), *Big Bill Broonzy and Pete Seeger in Concert*, Verve Folkways FV 9008, US, 1963.

Blues in the Mississippi Night, Chicago, Mar 1947, 1st release United Artists, US, 1959; CD-reissued Rounder CDROUN1860 / 6 82161 1860 2 3, US, 2003. Broonzy's story re songs & Memphis Minnie is in his autobiography *Big Bill Blues* (as told to Yannick Bruynoghe), London: Cassell, 1955, re-told in Linda Dahl, *Stormy Weather: The Music and Lives of a Century of Jazz Women*, New York: Pantheon, 1984.]

Brown, Richard Rabbit [c.1880 - 1937] BONNIE BEECHER recalls that around 1960 Dylan and HARVEY ABRAMS sat around in the 10 O'Clock Scholar in the Dinkytown area of Minneapolis, mentioning obscure singers' names, and that she and Dylan met because she was able to join in. This was because she would go to Sam Goodys in New York to buy records, choosing 'any old record that looked like it had some kind of funky singer or blues singer . . . records by CAT IRON, Rabbit Brown . . .'

She's misremembering here: there was no such thing as a Richard Rabbit Brown record available at Sam Goodys, either then or since. Yet by May 1961, when he was recorded in Bonnie Beecher's own Minneapolis apartment, Dylan was already performing Rabbit Brown's great 'James Alley Blues'. He knew it, and Ms Beecher knew the name, from the HARRY SMITH anthology *AMERICAN FOLK MUSIC*, issued in 1952, on which it appears as track 61 of the overall 84.

'James Alley Blues' was the very first track Brown recorded at the only session he ever achieved, which was for Victor in a garage in New Orleans on Friday, March 11, 1927. It was the city he'd been born in, and into great poverty, over 40 years before he got to make his record. Jane's [sic] Alley was a noted rough-house, street-fighting area, the worst place in the patch known as 'the Battlefield', and no-go area to the police. Louis Armstrong came from Jane's Alley too. A street singer, Brown also worked as a singing boatman on Lake Pontchartrain. 'I done seen better days but I'm puttin' up with these . . .' he sang, in his voice of molten chocolate.

That's one of the lines from 'James Alley Blues', and if you mix together the Bob Dylan-SAM SHEPARD line from 'Brownsville Girl', 'I feel pretty good but that ain't sayin' much: I could feel a whole lot better', and the ROBERT HUNTER-Bob Dylan line from 'Silvio', 'Seen better days but who has not?', you're more or less back to Rabbit Brown's.

Brown's song also includes the common-stock couplet 'Sometime I think that you too sweet to die / Then another time I think you oughta be buried alive' (though there's nothing 'common' about it when Brown's voice shudders and resonates along his complex vowel-sounds as he lands on those words 'die' and 'alive'). Variants of this formulation can be traced in earlyish Dylan songs such as 'Black Crow Blues', with its 'Sometimes I'm thinkin' I'm too high to fall / Other times I'm thinkin' I'm so low I don't know if I can come up at all'.

Dylan, however, owes a more striking debt to Brown's 'James Alley Blues' than those above. Most of us used to think, hearing the formulation 'Well it's sugar for sugar and salt for salt', used on his 1967 song 'Down in the Flood', that this was Dylanesque playful weirdness (if not mysterious drug terminology), typical of the Basement Tapes material. Later, we might have assumed instead that it was Dylan quoting one of these formulaic blues phrases: another common-stock motif. In fact, it seems an individually created variant, actually appearing on only one extant record: Rabbit Brown's 'James Alley Blues'. Dylan adapts this but slightly, shifting it from 'I'll give you sugar for sugar, let you get salt for salt / And if you can't get along with me well it's your own fault' to include his own song title within it: 'Well it's sugar for sugar and salt for salt / If you go down in the flood it's gonna be your fault'.

Decades later, returning to the terrain of those floods on the *"Love and Theft"* album's majestic 'Mississippi', Dylan calls up the memory of Brown again, and of his transcendent voice, when he echoes yet another line of 'James Alley Blues'. Brown delivers the classic complaint 'Cos I was born in the country, she thinks I'm easy to rule / She try to hitch me to a wagon, she try to drive me like a mule.' Dylan sings two separate lines that reprise Brown's key words here. The words on which Brown's voice lands with its incomparable juddering emphasis are 'country' and 'mule'. In each case Dylan returns them to us with equivalent feeling as he too lands on them with heartfelt, dark-toned emphasis, on his own lines 'I was raised in the country, I been workin' in the town' and 'Well, the devil's in the alley, mule's in the stall'. In each case, the word is mid-line, not at its end; yet the expressiveness of that 'country' and that 'mule' as he sings of them takes us straight back to, and is wholly worthy of, Rabbit Brown himself.

Brown's other five recorded numbers, all done that same March day in 1927, were 'Great Northern Blues' (which was never issued), 'Never Let the Same Bee Sting You Twice', 'I'm Not Jealous', 'Mystery of the Dunbar Child' (about a local kidnapping) and 'Sinking of the Titanic', but he was also known to sing 'Gyp the Blood', about a murder, and his signature song on the street was 'Downfall of the Lion', about the far more famous murder of New Orleans police chief David C. Hennessey by a gang of men who ambushed him in the streets in 1890 (when Rabbit Brown was a child). It was a notorious case all across the States at the time. Brown never got to record it, but local blues guitarist Lemon Nash, who long outlived his old friend, recalled that one of the verses was this: 'I'm gonna tell you racketeers, something you can understand: / Don't let your tongues say nothin' that you head can't stand.' Which makes it sound as if it must have been another 'James Alley Blues'. We lost out there.

Richard Rabbit Brown is reported to have died, still in great poverty and still in New Orleans, in 1937. This has never been confirmed.

[Bonnie Beecher, aka Jahanara Romney, quoted in Markus Wittman, 'The Wanted Man Interview: Jahanara Romney', *Telegraph* no.36, Romford, UK, summer 1990.]

Browning, Robert [1812 - 1889] The dramatic monologue differs from the soliloquy, which it superficially resembles, in starting with an already established perspective, instead of searching for one as it runs its course. It looks outwards, so that self-revelation appears incidental. It takes the form of a one-sided conversation: half of a dialogue in which the imagined other participant gets only an implicit hearing. It is an open-ended excerpt from the mind of the speaker: it has, in Robert Langbaum's words, 'no necessary beginning and end but only arbitrary limits, limits which do not cut the action off from the events that precede and follow, but shade into those events, suggesting as much as possible of the speaker's whole life and experience'. The unity of the form is its singleness of viewpoint. Browning mastered the dramatic monologue as no one before him; Dylan has used it as no one else since.

They share a brand of irony and dramatic similarities of technique. Part of Browning's 'Bishop Blougram's Apology' (published in *Men and Women*, 1855) runs as follows: 'You Gigadibs, who, thirty years of age / Write statedly for Blackwood's Magazine / Believe you see two points in Hamlet's soul / Unseized by the Germans yet . . .' In 'Ballad of a Thin Man' Dylan sings: 'You've been with the professors and they've all liked your looks / With great lawyers you have discussed lepers and crooks / You've bin through all of F. Scott Fitzgerald's books / You're very well read, it's well known / But something is happening here and you don't know what it is, / Do you, Mr Jones?'

These two mockings, adopting much the same tone of voice, become identical in tone when addressing their silent interlocutors. 'You, Gigadibs.' 'Do you, Mr Jones?'

Not only do the techniques resemble each other—they are put to comparable uses. Both attack the complacency that makes men use their intellects as blindfolds. Bishop Blougram reproves Gigadibs for not being alive to the real world; Dylan derides the artificial safeness of vicarious living. The same song extends his attack (and with mathematical rhymes again, too): 'You have many contacts / Among the lumberjacks / To get you facts / When someone attacks / Your imagination.'

When Browning and Dylan address this theme of life versus nullity of experience, the results are comparable more than once. Here is Browning again: 'Lord so-and-so—his coat bedropped with wax / All Peter's chains about his waist, his back / Brave with the needlework of Noodledom / Believes!'—and here is Dylan: 'And Ezra Pound and T.S. Eliot / Fighting in the captain's tower, / While calypso singers laugh at them / And fishermen hold flowers. . . . And nobody has to think too much / About Desolation Row.' And Browning again: 'you know physics, something of geology, / Mathematics are your pastime; souls shall rise in their degree; / Butterflies may dread extinction,—you'll not die, it cannot be!'

In all this, Dylan's use of the dramatic monologue conforms to Browning's use of it. But Browning usually identifies the narrator and his environment explicitly; Dylan often fills in these details implicitly, frequently using a belated introduction of his persona's position to achieve a particular effect. In 'Desolation Row' this happens only in the final verse, where it is sprung upon the listener that the whole song has been communicating on a person-to-person, and intensely personal, level: 'When you asked me how I was doing / Was that some kind of joke?' In 'Gates of Eden', similarly, the last stanza gives us the narrator's reflection that 'At times I think there are no words / But these to tell what's true / And there are no truths outside the gates of Eden': so that the rest of the song is thrown back upon us, demanding an immediate reassessment.

Another difference is that whereas Browning projects varied fictional characters, Dylan, like other modern writers, often projects himself, so that it becomes difficult to distinguish the created character from the man. There is a consequent further divergence between Browning's conventions and Dylan's. With Browning, the silent interlocutor is not merely silent but actually unnecessary: a mere tip of the hat to Victorian expectations. In contrast, Dylan's 'silent' interlocutor is not merely eloquent in helping to draw out the narrator's mood and predicament, but in many cases has a felt presence the exploration of which is central to the song's purpose—as in 'Most Likely You Go Your Way (And I'll Go Mine)', 'One of Us Must Know (Sooner or Later)', 'Leopard-Skin Pill-Box Hat' and '4th Time Around' (where two women are portrayed in this extraordinarily implicatory way), all on *Blonde on Blonde*.

Perhaps most of all we encounter this in 'Positively 4th Street': 'You see me on the street, / You always act surprised; / You say How Are You?—Good Luck! / But you don't mean it / When you know as well as me / You'd rather see me paralysed: / Why don't you just come out once and scream it?'

The effect, in this passage, hardly depends at all on the 'How are you?' and 'Good Luck!' that the interlocutor is permitted to actually say: the force of his portrayal comes from that masterfully irregular last line. Its length and pent-up cadence half-echo, half-mimic the scream that is withheld. Yet here too Dylan returns this dramatic monologue to somewhere close to Browning's. To hear the song not as Dylan addressing a woman but as Dylan challenging the callow pigeon-holing and 'the dirt of gossip' (as he calls it elsewhere, in a phrase that might be Lawrence's) of those who see him on the street, is to place it in the footsteps of 'Bishop Blougram's Apology', in which the Bishop, falsely assumed to have grown worldly and corrupt, addresses 'an idealist. . . . [T]he Bishop proceeds . . . to expose the young man's affected pose . . . and charges that in any age he would merely echo fashionable ideas.' (The précis is from Roma A. King: *The Bow & The Lyre: The Art of Robert Browning*, 1957.)

Beyond the dramatic monologue, other corridors run between Dylan's work and Browning's. One reaches back to Browning the archetypal Victorian in experiencing (like Dorothea Brooke in George Eliot's *Middlemarch*, 1871–72) 'aspiration without an object': experiencing, that is, religious ardour without being able to focus it on traditional Christianity. Unable to worship God, George

Eliot consecrated duty. Faced with the same predicament, Browning idealized love. So did Dylan.

As Walter E. Houghton explains it in *The Victorian Frame of Mind* (p.385): 'In an age of transition in which crucial problems, both practical and theoretical, exercised the thinking mind at the expense of the sensibility, and in which baffled thought so often issued in a feeling of impotence and a mood of despair, the thinker could find in love a resolution of psychological tensions, and a religion . . . to take the place of Christianity.'

The first hint of this process at work in Dylan comes at the end of the *John Wesley Harding* album, where the agonized search for a more noble America ends in 'Close your eyes, close the door'. The Dylan of *Nashville Skyline* redirects his search towards fulfilment through love. As with the Victorians, that way lies salvation. 'Love is all there is'.

Then there's their equal relish for the blatantly grotesque. G.K. Chesterton, thinking of Behemoth in 'Job', wrote that '. . . the notion of the hippopotamus as a household pet is curiously in the spirit of the humour of Browning.' It has the appeal of incongruity, and this scatters itself throughout Browning's work, in rhymes, names, ludicrous alliteration (that 'needlework of Noodledom') and in a Puckish garlanding together of temperamental incompatibles, as in 'The Cardinal and the Dog' (1890). In this short poem, the Cardinal lies on his death-bed at Verona and cries out loud to try to stop 'a black Dog of vast bigness, eyes flaming' from jumping all over the sheets.

It is an area of humour Dylan enjoys as fully. His sense of the grotesque continually invades his visions both of carefree living ('Saddle me up a big white goose / Tie me on her and turn her loose') and of Apocalypse. There is the common circus imagery—camels, clowns, freaks, masked faces, organ-grinders, dwarfs—and people with their trousers down, from the President of the United States to Dylan himself ('They asked me for some collateral an' I pulled down my pants').

This Browning-like celebration of the incongruous is everywhere in Dylan's mid-1960s work. In 'Leopard-Skin Pill-Box Hat' it isn't only the panache of, say, 'you know it balances on your head just like a mattress balances on a bottle of wine' sung with appropriate top-heaviness (Chaplin on a tightrope) as just one line within a formal, 3-line, 12-bar framework. It's also the obvious pleasure taken in Dylan—prophet, visionary, seer—singing a whole song about a hat. (Not a pleasure appreciated by the antagonists at Dylan's 1966 concerts.) This same mood, Dylan as surreal Puck, figures beguilingly throughout the Basement Tapes, especially in songs like 'Million Dollar Bash'—where a Browning-like alliterative lunacy is much in evidence: 'Well that big dumb blonde / With her wheel gorged / And Turtle, that friend of theirs / With his cheques all forged / And his cheeks in a chunk . . .' The needlework of Noodledom lives indeed.

In different mood, Dylan returns us, in the 1980s, to the work of this predecessor in the marvellous 'Blind Willie McTell' (see entry). One of his inspired touches, in that song's nigh-perfect penultimate stanza, is to underscore his tolling of doomsday by contorting those well-known lines of optimism and hope, 'God's in His heaven—All's right with the world.' The twisting of this fresh-faced couplet into the brutish modernism of 'Well God is in His heaven / And we all want what's His' could hardly be bettered. Dylan uses the mugging energy of the bare greed he describes to give his lines a slashing economy, hitting us with the switch from the lost innocence of the original.

Those lines are by Browning—from the first section, 'Morning', of the dramatic poem 'Pippa Passes'—and Dylan's song takes from the poem more than just this one, expertly-handled, crude allusion. To know the context is to see that Dylan snatches away not just the gentleness, nor even primarily the reassuring stasis or apparent permanence of those often-quoted lines, when he replaces Browning's contentment with the bleakness of 'But power and greed and corruptible seed seem to be all that there is' but more especially Dylan contradicts Browning's vision of the world as fresh and pure because *young*, because purged by the coming of spring.

This is the context: 'The year's at the spring, / And day's at the morn; / Morning's at seven; / The hill-side's dew-pearled; / The lark's on the wing; / The snail's on the thorn; / God's in His heaven—/ All's right with the world.' Dylan's 'seed' deftly acknowledges this context, while shrivelling it away at once into the biblical rhetoric of 'corruptible seed': a latency that promises only further decay in a world already old and exhausted. Dylan turns morning into mourning, replacing the lark on the wing with the hoot-owl in the barren trees.

And if many an old song lies behind 'Blind Willie McTell' (see entry), Browning's verse too serves as a structural model. To the extent that Dylan's verses can be said to set themselves out in reverse order, to roll backwards through the panorama of North America's southern history, this follows Browning, who sets out his own scene backwards: 'The year's at the spring, / And day's at the morn; / Morning's at seven . . .'

Here's one last parallel. This is Browning, from 'Up at a Villa—Down in the City', also in *Men and Women*: 'Look, two and two go the priests, then the monks with cowls and sandals / And the penitents dressed in white shirts, a-holding the yellow candles / One, he carries a flag up straight, and another a cross with handles, / And the Duke's guard brings up the rear, for the better prevention of scandals.' And this is Dylan's 'Subterranean Homesick Blues': 'Better jump down a manhole / Light y'self a candle, / Don't wear sandals, / Try to avoid the scandals / Don't wanna be a bum / Y' better chew gum / The pump don't work / 'Cause the vandals / Took the handles.'

There is even more in the comparison than the startling duplication of ostentatious rhyming words. Read out Browning's verse in Dylan's *Blonde on Blonde* voice (relishing Dylanesque words like 'penitents') and you will find the two immaculately compatible. Sometimes Browning and Dylan sound like soulmates.

[Robert Browning: 'Pippa Passes' (Part 1, 'Morning') formed part of *Bells and Pomegranates* (a reference to Exodus 28:33–4), published in sections, London, 1841–1846. A useful collection is *Robert Browning: Poetical Works 1833–1864*, ed. Ian Jack, 1970. Robert Langbaum: *The Poetry of Experience: The Dramatic Monologue in Modern Literary Tradition*, 1957 (Langbaum has written extensively on Browning's work.) G.K. Chesterton: *Robert Browning*, 1903. The biblical text from which Dylan takes 'corruptible seed' is I Peter 1:23–24: 'Being born again, not of corruptible seed, but of incorruptible, by the word of God, which liveth and abideth for ever. For all flesh is as grass, and all the glory of man as the flower of grass. The grass withereth, and the flower thereof falleth away.']

'Brownsville Girl' [1986] This song, hidden away at the start of side 2 of the original LP of the deeply mediocre *Knocked Out Loaded*, was composed by Dylan but its lyric written jointly by Dylan and SAM SHEPARD. In the opinion of STEPHEN SCOBIE it is 'a masterpiece, a song that must rank among the five or six best songs Dylan has ever written.' NIGEL HINTON writes that 'When Dylan is working at this level of creativity—a level that puts him head and shoulders above everyone else—there's a magic evocativeness about everything he writes that gives the words enormous possibilities,' even though many of them are quite deliberately the words of Hollywood cliché. The best scrutiny of the song may be that by AIDAN DAY in his book *Jokerman: Reading the Lyrics of Bob Dylan*. Agreeing in effect with Stephen Scobie's explanation of the song's structural complexity—that it 'never develops a single, coherent narrative: rather it presents the fragments of several possible narratives, sometimes evoked and discarded within a line, whose relationship to each other remains unspecified . . .' but that these fragments are 'thematically congruent'—Day offers two main reasons why the song has been so structured that 'scraps of memory and thought mix with other scraps in an unstable temporal sequence.'

The first purpose of such a structure is that the lyric 'plays with tenses and perspectives as it enacts the lack of chronological structure in the inner life of the mind.' But—and this is Day's main theme—it is 'not only the fluidity of memory or mind which the lyric dips into. It is that throughout "Brownsville Girl" the mind's images and memories have only a questionably "real" status.' For this, he suggests, is a song about how cliché invades the memory and mind. He says that the opening two verses of this 17-verse song describe memories held by the narrator that are composed of 'the stock diction and conventions of a Western': 'He was shot down by a hungry kid tryin' to make a name for himself. / The townspeople wanted to crush that kid down and string him up by the neck. / Well the marshal, now he beat that kid to a bloody pulp. / As the dying gunfighter lay in the sun and gasped for his last breath: / "Turn him loose, let him go, let him say he outdrew me fair and square. / I want him to feel what it's like to every moment face his death."'

These *are* memories composed of 'the stock diction and conventions of a Western': they're a description of what's remembered from the film *The Gunfighter*. But as Aidan Day suggests, they are also stock Western ingredients. There's nothing described here that *sounds* unique to the particular film the song's narrator is describing. The opening moment is 'a man riding 'cross the desert'; the storyline of the renowned gunfighter always being challenged by some 'hungry kid tryin' to make a name for himself' and the dialogue quoted—these are familiar commonplaces of the cowboy film genre: you could say that it's their grinding familiarity on the screen that accounted for the death of the genre at the box-office.

Aidan Day argues that this cheap cliché is being emphasised, exposed, pointed out, by Dylan, and with regret and even disdain. This is the song that has him exclaim 'Oh! if there's an original thought out there I could use it right now!': a line that, says Day, 'reflects upon one of the fundamental preoccupations of the lyric. . . . It is when this crescendo of cliché has been reached in the last line of the second verse . . . that the recollections momentarily break and the speaker expresses his disdain for the formulae purveyed by the film. But disdain is accompanied by a recognition that such formulae are, inescapably, a part of the raw material of memory and mind.' And to illustrate this sense of what's being communicated by the song's narrator, Day quotes its next two lines, which are: 'Well I keep seeing this stuff and it just comes a-rolling in / And you know it blows right through me like a ball and chain.'

These lines suggest rueful acknowledgement that something of no special value, 'this stuff', continually invades the mind unbidden. This is brought acutely to life at the end. From similes of what's in the air, and therefore unavoidable—it comes 'a-rolling in' like the tide, it 'blows right through me' like the wind—Dylan makes an inspired switch and we find that it blows right through him with far greater invasive violence: 'like a ball and chain', like the very fabric of your house being demolished. And the sudden surprise of the switch to this image enacts the effect it describes.

At the same time, 'like a ball and chain' carries its other meaning into the song: the 'ball and chain' that ties the prisoner down, the effect of which is to underline that the narrator cannot escape 'this stuff' rolling in. The brilliant touch on Dylan's part here—the first of so many in this song—is that while 'ball and chain' is itself a cliché, the effect Dylan puts it to is anything but tired.

But is Dylan's emphasis really on the exhausted unoriginality of these Hollywood scenes? Just as people so often parody what they're most fond of, so Dylan's feeling for Hollywood images and filmgoer's memories here is surely 90 per cent affection and only 10 per cent challenge and demurral. Several things inside and outside the song itself suggest this. First, the words are not wholly weighted as Day suggests. The summary Dylan offers of *The Gunfighter*'s key points reveals a noticeably straightforward desire to communicate what's up on the screen in the film's dramatic action. In the earlier, unreleased version of the song, 'New Danville Girl', the equivalent passage is also scrupulous in saying at the outset that he remembers little about the film, yet that which is remembered is given clearly and in some detail. For a narrative so 'unstable', 'fragmented' and 'indeterminate', it starts out with an almost urgently expressed clarity.

Nor are words the sole evidence here. There is also the way Dylan says them. There is no demurral in his voice, no sneer at or apology for the clichéd nature of the scenes he describes in these first two verses, and when he steps back, to say how he keeps seeing 'this stuff', the change in his voice, far from adding distance, expresses ruefully acknowledged fondness. It's the same all through the song. Great affection, enthusiasm and yearning are expressed for the very scenes from 'his own life' that are described as if they too are scenes from movies: 'Ah but you were right: it was perfect as I got in behind the wheel'; 'Well we're drivin' this car and the sun is coming up over the Rockies'; 'It was the best acting I saw anybody do.'

Moreover, the narrative Dylan so carefully gives us at the beginning of 'Brownsville Girl' is the perfect articulation of Dylan's most perturbed feelings about his own dilemma as a celebrity. He identifies readily with the gunfighter who can't go anywhere without being stared at, measured up and challenged, perhaps lethally and by the very people who admire the skills on which that celebrity is based. Even the death that the gunfighter feels 'every moment' might indeed be hovering for Dylan in real life. Every 'star' has felt this since death came up on JOHN LENNON from a 'fan'. (Dylan speaks about this in the interview with CAMERON CROWE for *Biograph*.) *The Gunfighter* is a film about fame and how lethal it can be, and this is intensely interesting to Bob Dylan. When he hears 'this stuff' about wanting the hungry kid to feel what it's like for the weary hero, he doesn't hear stock convention and cliché: he identifies with it through and through.

Given all this, it's a central irony that the narrator in Dylan's song is himself a fan, of the Hollywood star Gregory Peck. The film was 'about a man riding 'cross the desert and it starred Gregory Peck,' he says without a pause, suggesting unrestrained keenness, right there in the song's second line; 'All I remember about it was it's Gregory Peck,' he says later; then he's 'standin' in line in the rain to see a movie starring Gregory Peck . . . I'll see him in anything'; later still, thinking of the first movie again, he says, like a shy fan confessing fan behaviour, 'I think I sat through it twice'. Then, rounding things off neatly at the end by returning to the beginning, he says two 'fan-like' things on the two final lines, punning on 'stars' in the second: 'All I remember about it was it starred Gregory Peck . . . / Seems like a long time ago, long before the stars were torn down.'

This irony is energised when we know that Dylan really is a fan of Gregory Peck. In 1971, the *Jerusalem Post* asked how Dylan had spent his 30th birthday: 'We went to see a Gregory Peck movie—I'm quite a fan of his,' he said.

In any case, the very point about *The Gunfighter* upon which critics and viewers are agreed is that it stood out from the run of the genre: it avoided the stock conventions and cliché and went to some trouble in the pursuit of authenticity of look and feel. It's an irony, then, that while the film goes all out for outer realism, Dylan's narrative both does the opposite and doesn't. On the one hand the song is *more* realistic than the film, because the film straightforwardly counterfeits authenticity whereas the song keeps its eye on the difficult matter of what's real and what is not, and on the invisible passageways that slip us between the real and the fictional, all the time. Yet the song refuses the realistic style of the film's narrative, as, in Aidan Day's phrase, it 'plays with tenses and perspectives as it enacts the lack of chronological structure in the inner life of the mind.'

Nonetheless the parallels present themselves insistently. The film's hero is no hero at all, but a man who lives by the gun and dies by it. He is a failure as an integrated human being: isolated, incapable of living with or protecting his family, roaming without purpose and without the nourishment of any sort of intimacy. In the song, the narrative and chronology may be unclear but here too the narrator's memories are of failed relationships, failed connections and the failure to protect either himself or those he loves. Unlike the stock Western hero, the song's narrator abandons women, or is abandoned by them, or both—'Way down in Mexico you went out to find a doctor and you never came back. / I would have gone after you but I didn't feel like letting my head get blown off' (a cowardice re-emphasised later when '. . . shots rang out. / I didn't know whether to duck or to run. So I ran')—or else he needs to be rescued by women instead of the other way round: 'You went out on a limb to testify for me. You said I was with you.' It heightens the contrast between the heroic cowboy archetype and the song's less-than-reliable narrator that the song sets his nebulous exploits in western terrain also. Stephen Scobie notes that 'Brownsville seems intended to unify the geographical references—San Anton[e], the Alamo, Amarillo, Corpus Christi—along the border area between Texas and Mexico that has fascinated Dylan from "Just Like Tom Thumb's Blues". . . . As a border town it stands between the various realms of history, fiction and myth . . .'

Border towns are also where people cross from one kind of place to another, yet where the conjunction of the two makes for an ill-defined, nebulous entity, and uncertain crossings of one sort or another are a recurrent motif in 'Brownsville Girl'. The first thing we see is a man crossing the desert—always a risky business, a place in which to lose your way. When the narrator steps into the action himself, he's 'too over the edge'. Then he crosses 'the panhandle'—the term for a narrow strip of land in one state that projects into another (in this case the Texas Panhandle): another place of nebulous boundaries. But there's also a frisson here of crossing a *moral* boundary: a stain that seeps in from the word's other meaning. To panhandle is to accost people and beg. When the song's travellers arrive 'where Henry Porter used to live', Ruby tells them they've crossed another invisible borderline: 'She said "Welcome to the land of the living dead."'

Next thing we know, with another switch of scene, the narrator feels vulnerable, violent danger seems to loom, even in the act of the smallest crossing: 'I was crossin' the street,' he says, 'when shots rang out.' Then, matching the earlier phrase 'too over the edge', the woman who saves him with an alibi goes 'out on a limb' in doing so. There is also 'somethin' about you baby' that belongs in another world, while the narrator has left a part of himself behind in another place of uncertain territorial identity and, these days, uncertain authenticity too, 'the French Quarter', way down yonder in New Orleans. The theme is stated most directly and concentratedly in the narrator's protestation that he's 'always been the kind of person that doesn't like to trespass, but sometimes you just find yourself over the line.'

Crossing is not only a recurrent theme *in* the song; the song itself eschews linear narrative the better to stand by its core: a series of memories and recollections crossing and re-crossing the narrator's mind. This tracking and tracing, in 'Brownsville Girl', of notions of how these realms blend or fuse or confuse with reality, can only communicate, in the end, one aspect of what's absorbing in the song and why it's so pleasurable and rich an item in Bob Dylan's body of work.

There is also the joy of his matchless delivery, timing and phrasing, the humour that runs through the song, and the skill in its language: a skill touched on in noting the unexpected brilliance of that 'ball and chain' in the third stanza.

There are features of the early version, 'New Danville Girl', in the writing and the performance, which it's a pity we have to lose in the transfer to 'Brownsville Girl': but not many, and it's clear why they are discarded. This is an unusually clear example of the recording chosen for release being superior to the unreleased, while a comparative look at the lyrics alone would tell which was the tentative early attempt and which the later, more realised success. We could tell it from Dylan's delivery too: there are detectable falterings all through 'New Danville Girl'; 'Brownsville Girl' has none.

A kind of music is abandoned when we move from the earlier to the later recording. In the earlier, there is an instrumental break after the first chorus, in which the lead instrument is an almost comically plaintive, wonky harmonica from Dylan, making strangely half-indecipherable noises; and after the third chorus comes a caressingly expressive electric guitar solo, at once soaring and dignified, impassioned and restrained, simple and imaginative, grungy and refined. There may be no better electric solo on any studio recording in Bob Dylan's work than this, by IRA INGBER—and it has to go, because the song must single-mindedly occupy the cowboy and western genre, not criss-cross in and out of rock music signifiers. On 'Brownsville Girl' these pauses after the choruses are mostly abolished, and we are propelled right out of the Hollywood-epic whoosh of the overblown, declamatory chorus music straight back into the narrative, with its more urgent, greater articulation of detail and its far longer lines that must be spoken fast to fit the musical frame. Thus we lose too the simpler, more appealing music on those choruses themselves, where you can hear the rock musicians playing and the vocal lines are sung with a sort of matching pop normalcy; instead we get an epic blare that might be from a full orchestra playing a movie score, with trumpet and sax, women singers and echo, and with the trumpet blurting out high above the rest with a distressingly stiff riff, a stentorian, martial oscillation between two uninteresting notes.

We also lose some of the greatest 'oohs' and 'ahs' in Dylan's entire repertoire, and there seems no good reason for this, beyond the fact that they do seem impelled by the need to fill in spaces, whereas in 'Brownsville Girl' it is words and more words that fill them in. The 'awh' that he has Ruby say in 'New Danville Girl', in the line 'awh, you know some babies never learn' is many-splendoured, and after the 'lost' line 'And everything he did in it reminded me of me' comes an 'ah-ah-ah!' of sublime seductive grace. At the end of the last verse—which offers the unquestionably inferior 'But that was a long time ago, and it was made in the shade' (much inferior, that is, to 'Seems like a long time ago, long before the stars were torn down') Dylan releases us by releasing a most exquisite, yearning 'Yeah—' And after the last chorus, Dylan returns to give one more benediction of really lovely long 'ohs' and 'ahs' that linger for us at the song's final end.

However, these consummately enunciated pseudo-words of exclamation, these most articulate of grunts, are dissipated by fill-ins. Too many times we get the sort of 'yes you are' or 'yes you do' that garrulous soul-singers cannot resist. Thus we get 'Yeah I feel pretty good but you know I could feel a whole lot better, *ah yes I could'*—and its effect in weakening the line is demonstrable. It is the tightened-up 'Brownsville Girl' version that sticks in the mind, even though in fact it's only one word shorter. It's more focussed, and its rhythm propels it more purposively along: 'You know I feel pretty good but that ain't sayin' much—I could feel a whole lot better'. That *is* a whole lot better.

The 'Brownsville Girl' version solves all such problems. The narrator who is no Gregory Peck loses the earlier song's tendency to petulant cod-philosophising and becomes a keenly realised individual, a wittily self-deprecating hopeless romantic who likes women and has heart. He's generous-minded. The key exchanges between him and 'you' have a radiant charm that exudes the narrator's awareness of how different the two of them are—how hopelessly boyish he is, and how maturely rooted she is. He delights in the way that what they say to each other comes in from such different starting points of personality, as if the two glance off each other in passing. When he exclaims 'You know I can't believe we've lived so long and are still so far apart', the tone is partly of genuine surprise (a tone echoed twice as he exclaims 'Strange how people who suffer together have stronger connections than people who are most content!' and 'You know it's funny how things never turn out the way you had 'em planned')—but also carries in its tone not rebuke or complaint but a relishing of difference. The gulf between their two approaches to life, hers so practical and his risibly romantic, is comically delineated more than once, and without representing her universe reductively, he makes it clear that his own, while riddled with impracticality and shameless bravado, nevertheless has virtues of its own: indomitable energy, cheeriness, spontaneity, inclusivity. He may be a sucker for the grand gestures of romanticism—he admits that both this 'you' and also Ruby with her 'some babies never learn' have a healthy scepticism towards the way that he flops about in the world—but the self-deprecation and warm susceptibility that shine through him have their validity too. And really, what's the point of living in this terrain, this border territory of history, fiction and myth, where every place name is soaked in romantic resonance—the Alamo, Amarillo, the Painted Desert, San Antone—if you're not a romantic?

Nor has Ruby's cynicism got her anywhere. She feels this literally, and is 'thinkin' of bummin' a ride back to from where she started'. So much for her connections with the man whose washing she is hanging on the line. And so much for her stoicism. This is flimsy, in any case: she changes the subject 'every time money comes up', but she initiates the topic of 'how times were tough'. She's thinking of bumming a ride back to where she came from, yet when she asks how far the narrator and his companion(s) are going, she is good-naturedly sceptical that *they* will really get anywhere. Her sense of feeling stuck may discolour her view of everything, or may be unsullied realism. We can hear her observation that 'even the swap-meets around here are getting pretty corrupt' either way. No-one has any monopoly on what's real or true in this song, any more than they can stake any claim to heroic qualities.

Meanwhile, their exchanges towards the end of the song resemble nothing so much as great fragments of movie dialogue. They could belong to Bogart and Bacall. The whole song offers the extra irony of being in itself like a half-remembered movie with its episodes and flashbacks and cuts, its panning camera eye and its widescreen pageant. A very vivid one it is too. We see Ruby so clearly out there in the dusty yard, hanging out that washing in the dry western air, where your eyes can follow the flat land way off in the distance. We feel the complexity of her character from the very few lines of dialogue we hear her speak. What a creation she is. Can anyone else create so much in so few frames?

Inside this rhetorical question is the particular question, can Sam Shepard? Of the two co-lyricists of this song, Shepard is the one who writes screenplays; but in the end this is a song, not a screenplay, and Bob Dylan is the one who writes songs. To put this question another way: who wrote what?

The comic interplay between the narrator's voice and the Greek-chorus grunts of the female backing singers, who tiptoe in in the song's 11th verse, seems an innovation: something new to Dylan's oeuvre, and therefore quite likely to be a dramatic element imported by Sam Shepard—it's plays that have Greek choruses, after all—but Dylan seems very comfortable with the innovation, embracing its comic potential with flair yet restraint, never allowing it to dominate or grow tiresome.

More fundamentally there is one striking difference between 'New Danville Girl' and 'Brownsville

Girl'. The first has a lot of short lines that seem to resemble the terse minimalism of Shepard's dialogue in, say, *Paris, Texas*, in which the monosyllable rules, and Dylan sounds as if he finds some of this inadequate and awkward to deliver; whereas 'Brownsville Girl' is delivered by someone so wholly in command of his material that perhaps it *is* rather more his material. On the other hand there are certain orders of detail that Dylan's own songs never show much interest in yet are prominent in some of the co-written ones–those co-written for *Desire* with JACQUES LEVY, in particular–which argues that they are the co-writer's babies. In the Dylan-Shepard collaboration, the sort of detail that seems unDylanesque includes 'your platform heels', 'her red hair tied back' and possibly 'the swap-meets' and 'the water moccasin'.

All that can be said with any certainty is that while 'Brownsville Girl' is a unique item in Dylan's work, there are *many* unique items in his work, part of his greatness being his extraordinary range, and there is nothing about 'Brownsville Girl' to make you feel that Bob Dylan couldn't have written it. Its themes and preoccupations are wholly in keeping with those he offers all through his writing; its fictional characters stand in line without any incongruity among the many others he's created; the interest in the silver screen has been evinced throughout his songwriting life, and never more so than in the mid-1980s (see **film dialogue in Dylan lyrics**); the 'unstable temporal sequence' of its narrative structure, and the shifting between 'you's' and other 'you's' and between 'you's' and 'she's', are all features familiar from earlier Bob Dylan songs; the wit and sense of humour are Dylan's; the very idea that a song can be that long is Dylan's.

Finally, when we come to the released version, 'Brownsville Girl', the masterly delivery by Dylan makes it his, whoever contributed what in the drafting of it. No-one in the world can deliver a talking song or a half-talking song as Dylan can. It's a facet of his genius he has remained in full control of, apparently from the first day he opened his mouth until now. This mastery, and his audible joy in it–a generous, sharing joy–is there right back in 1961 when he records 'Talkin' New York' on his first album, and when he produces the perfect mimickry of the voices on the unreleased 'Black Cross'; it's there in the faultless dumb-hick impersonation he gives us in 'Clothes Line Saga' on the Basement Tapes sessions of 1967; it's there when he preaches during the evangelical concerts of 1979; and it's there undiminished late in the 1990s on the final track on *Time Out of Mind*, the exalted 'Highlands'. The same genius is in command of every breath and pause, every unseen tilt of the head, every sung and every spoken syllable, every long line and every switch of mood in 'Brownsville Girl'.

One of the marks of its excellence as a performance, and a particularly important one granted the actorish subject matter of the song, is that there is never an adumbration of luvvieness in it. Dylan sounds so fully open to spontaneity of expression and unrehearsed conversational flow that he makes it sound easy *for him*. Yet to hold the printed-out lyric in your hand while playing the recording through headphones, and to mark which passages are spoken and which sung as it unfolds: this alone is enough to show you what unmitigated genius he brings to it. There are whole passages where he alternates a spoken with a sung line, one-two one-two one-two, without this ever striking you as a rigid pattern, or a technique, or something calculated; others where speech holds for several lines and then soars into singing in mid-line, again without ever sounding like set policy: without style ever seeming to take its leave of content; and others–for example 'dyin' gunfighter lay in the sun and gasped for his last breath'–where breath is so special that it is impossible to say if this is sung or not. There are lines that no-one else would decide to sing rather than speak; yet Dylan sings them as if to do so is the most natural thing in the world. In 'New Danville Girl' for instance he *sings* 'Way down in Mexico you went out to see a doctor and you never came back'. In 'Brownsville Girl', after the first chorus, there is a passage of ten consecutive spoken lines, and when the line after that breaks into song, the flow from one to the other is at once immersingly beautiful and unobtrusive. The least high-flown lines are sung with an exquisite, yearning caress that animates the desire and sense of loss behind the prosaic. Listen to this detailing in the superb way he sings lingeringly of 'your busted down Ford and your platform heels'. The word 'heels' has never been stroked so expressively in its life. (In 'New Danville Girl' he doesn't sing this line at all.)

Nor does Dylan overdo it when it comes to the more obviously strokeable. When we lose 'New Danville Girl's' 'fell out under the stars' to 'Brownsville Girl's' 'your skin was so tender and soft' the gain is in the sublimity of delivery rather than in the words. Dylan's voice enacts these words. There is nothing pejoratively soft, or easy, about the tenderly careful touch of his voice on the several syllables he carries us through on 'soft'.

Altogether, the delivery is astonishing. Not a false moment, not a foot wrong. Keeping up a curious tension between the very measured, slightly *too slow* musical accompaniment and the urgency of his voice, he gives a faultless performance, infinitely fluid and expressive, from beginning to end a plausible, intelligent and immensely humane persona and narrator, alert to the turbulent complexities of every moment. It's a long tour de force not a moment too long, and the Dylan who incandesces through it is the full Bob Dylan of genius and generous intelligence, fully engaged.

[Bob Dylan: 'New Danville Girl', LA, Dec 1984; 'Brownsville Girl', Topanga Park, CA, 30 Apr 1986, *Knocked Out Loaded*, US, 1986; 'Black Cross', Minneapolis, 22 Dec 1961, unissued; 'Clothes Line Saga', West Saugherties, NY, Sep–Oct 1967, unissued.

The Gunfighter, dir. Henry King, written William Bowers & William Sellers, 20th Century Fox, US, 1950. Stephen Scobie, *Alias Bob Dylan*, 1991, Red Deer, Alberta, Canada: Red Deer College Press, p.151. Nigel Hinton, 'Into the Future, Knocked Out and Loaded', *Telegraph* no.25, Bury, UK, autumn/winter 1986, but quoted here as collected in Michael Gray & John Bauldie, *All Across the Telegraph: A Bob Dylan Handbook*, London: W.H. Allen, 1987. All Aidan Day quotes are from the chapter 'That Enemy Within' in, *Jokerman: Reading the Lyrics of Bob Dylan*, Oxford: Blackwell, paperback edn., 1989. Catherine Rosenheimer, *Jerusalem Post* magazine, Jerusalem, 4 Jun 1971.]

Bruce, Jack [1943 -] John Symon Asher Bruce was born near Glasgow, Scotland, on May 14, 1943, received classical music training and gained a working understanding of bass parts from studying Bach; played string bass in the Graham Bond Organisation (as did Ginger Baker, with whom he was in constant dispute and by whom he was effectively fired), then played with JOHN MAYALL and Manfred Mann before rejoining his old enemy Baker and ERIC CLAPTON in 'the first supergroup', Cream. Bruce and wordsmith Pete Brown wrote the band's hits 'Sunshine of Your Love', 'White Room' and 'I Feel Free'. He was the Cream member left out when the others joined the short-lived Blind Faith. In 1969 he made the successful solo album *Songs for a Tailor*, named for Cream's fatal car-crash victim, a stage-clothes maker (and PHIL OCHS' cousin), on which he not only sang and played bass but also piano, organ, cellos and guitar (and which included a guest appearance by GEORGE HARRISON), joined the once-bedazzling guitar wizard Robin Trower, then formed West, Bruce and Laing with the ex-Mountain (but still mountainous) Leslie West and Corky Laing but also worked with jazz musicians, which was where his musical heart lay. In the 1970s he made a further five solo albums but only two in the 1980s and three in the 1990s.

Jack Bruce and Bob Dylan played together, probably to Bruce's distaste, at the Guitar Legends Festival in Seville, Spain, on October 17, 2001, at which Dylan was possibly the event's least proficient guitarist, technically, and at which Bruce played behind Bob on the latter's opening number of a five-song set, 'All Along the Watchtower' (with RICHARD THOMPSON and Phil Manzanera on guitars, Ray Cooper on percussion and Simon Phillips on drums), and on the ensemble number at evening's end, 'I Can't Turn You Loose', on which Dylan was merely one of many on guitar.

Liver cancer halted Jack Bruce's career at the beginning of the 21st century but a liver transplant in 2003, though initially almost fatal, was a success in the long term and he was able to play a series of London concerts as part of the temporarily re-formed Cream in May 2005.

[Jack Bruce: *Songs for a Tailor*, Polydor, UK (Atco, US), 1969. Guitar Legends Festival, Seville, 17 Oct 2001, shown live internationally on TV.]

Bruce, Lenny [1925 - 1966] Leonard Alfred Schneider was born in Mineola, New York, on October 13, 1925 and became the first really contemporary comedian, taking satire outside the bounds of light-entertainment rules and the gentle parodying of foibles to coruscate the unpleasant realities of American society and shocking the audiences—and more particularly the self-appointed moral guardians—of the day with long monologues of sometimes embarrassing autobiographical directness, 'foul language' and biting humour. He was also one of those who divided the world into the Jewish and the rest in a way that suggested that this was a matter of spirit and outlook rather than race: 'To me,' he once said, 'if you live in New York, you're Jewish. If you live in Butte, Montana, you're going to be goyish even if you're Jewish.'

He served in the US Navy and after his 1946 discharge studied acting in Hollywood, changing his name to Lenny Bruce in 1947, but was soon working in nightclubs in Brooklyn and Baltimore, coming to national attention in October 1948 on the Arthur Godfrey Talent Scouts Show, on which he launched into an unprecedented satirical probing of sacred-cow subjects, topics that made the average American nervous and with a previously unheard vituperative disrespect for the President and the privileged.

His club act prospered and he pushed the monologues further and further out onto an experimental limb—though the period when his routine still included worked-out short sketches too probably represents him at his funniest: as in his *Concert at Carnegie Hall*, recorded in 1961—but it was in 1961 that he suffered the first of a series of arrests and harrassments which came to be deliberate FBI policy against the man they described as 'the nightclub and stage performer widely known for his obscenity'. His arrest in Philadelphia on September 29, 1961 was for narcotics possession, though the charge was later dropped; five days later he was arrested at the San Francisco Jazz Workshop for using the word 'cocksucker' in his stage act (a violation of the California Obscenity Code), but later acquitted. In 1962 he was again arrested for narcotics possession (October 6) and for using the word 'motherfucker' on stage at the Hollywood Troubadour (October 24). Again Bruce was acquitted, this time after a landmark trial that helped uphold the citizen's right to free speech but cost

Bruce all his money and left him perceived as too big a risk for most clubs and theatre bookings. In 1963, by now addicted to heroin, Bruce was arrested and this time found guilty of narcotics possession, and in April 1964 he was arrested in New York and again convicted, on obscenity charges arising from his act at the Café au Go Go in Greenwich Village. He was defended by Norman Mailer and various New York intellectuals as a social satirist 'in the tradition of Swift, Rabelais and Twain', but the FBI didn't have them on file.

His autobiography, the sardonically titled *How to Talk Dirty and Influence People*, was serialised in *Playboy* from 1963 to 1965, before its publication in book form. And *Playboy* took the copyright.

Bob Dylan mentioned Lenny Bruce fleetingly several times in the latter's lifetime. In his poem 'Blowin' in the Wind', published in *Hootenanny* in December 1963, Dylan wrote that 'Junkies an flunkies line the wind along side ban-the-bomb demonstrators / Girls're hustlin for dollars on one side a the street an / Girls're sitting down for their rights on the other side a the street . . . / Lenny Bruce's talkin / an LORD BUCKLEY's memory still movin"; and in the marvellous incantatory memorialising offered by *11 Outlined Epitaphs*, published on the sleeve of *Another Side of Bob Dylan* two months after Bruce's Greenwich Village arrest, Dylan wrote: 'Lenny Bruce says there're no dirty / words . . . just dirty minds an' I say there're / no depressed words just depressed minds'.

Bruce gave his last performance on June 26, 1966 at the Fillmore in San Francisco and was found dead from a morphine overdose at his Hollywood home less than six weeks later, on August 3, 1966.

It was 15 years later that Dylan released his song 'Lenny Bruce', on the first post-gospel album, 1981's *Shot of Love*. (It was also issued as a single, in the UK only, and pre-release copies in a picture sleeve had to be recalled and replaced, because they managed to misspell its subject's name as 'Lennie'; in the mad world of collectors, of course, this is the rarer and thus more valued version of the record.)

ALLEN GINSBERG singled out the song, saying of it that he liked 'the rawness of the voice, and the directness, and the statement, and the kind of pathos.' But he also noted and admired Dylan's 'unexpected sympathy for Lenny Bruce at a time when he was supposed to be a Born Again moralist Christian . . . he was coming out for the injured and the insulted and the wounded and the supposedly damned.'

In lines of mixed success and skill, Dylan's song stresses, like so much writing about Bruce, his truth-telling and his victimisation. As with most accounts, Dylan mentions in passing that Lenny Bruce 'sure was funny' but this is never emphasised. How *funny* Bruce could be is what always seems omitted. That said, the Dylan song was a sincere tribute and an acute summary of at least part of what had been at stake in the struggle that was Lenny Bruce's life:

'He was an outlaw, that's for sure, / More of an outlaw than you ever were. / . . . . Never robbed any churches nor cut off any babies' heads, / He just took the folks in high places and he shined a light in their beds.' The song ends disarmingly: 'He fought a war on a battlefield where every victory hurts. / Lenny Bruce was bad, he was the brother that you never had.'

Introducing the song in concert in Nagoya, Japan, Dylan said this: 'Here's a song about recognition, or lack of recognition. Tennessee Williams, it was he who said "I don't ask for your pity, just your understanding–not even that, but just your recognition of me in you, and time, the enemy in us all." Tennessee Williams led a pretty drastic life. He died all by himself in a New York hotel room without a friend in the world. Another man died like that.'

[Lenny Bruce: *How to Talk Dirty and Influence People*, ed. Paul Krassner, *Playboy*, Chicago, 1963–65; *Carnegie Hall*, NY, early hours of 5 Feb 1961, United Artists UAS-9800, US, 1972. Bob Dylan: 'Lenny Bruce', 2 uncirculated takes attempted LA, 29 Apr 1981; album version LA, May 14, 1981; single release as 'Lennie Bruce' & 'Lenny Bruce', CBS A 1640, UK, 1981. Ginsberg quoted from interview by Wes Stace, Cambridge, UK, 27 Apr 1985, collected in Michael Gray & John Bauldie, eds, *All Across the Telegraph: A Bob Dylan Handbook*, London: Futura edn., 1988, p.173. Bruce's FBI file online at *www.fadetoblack.com/foi/lennybruce/fbi file.htm*.]

Brumley, Albert E. [1905 - 1977] Albert Edward Brumley was born on his parents' cotton farm in Spiro, Oklahoma, on October 29, 1905. He studied sacred music in Hartford, Arkansas, under Virgil O. Stamps and others, sang in the Hartford Quartet and became a peripatetic schools singing teacher. In 1929 he wrote 'I'll Fly Away', based on an older ballad, but only submitted it for publication in 1932. The Hartford Music Co., which accepted it and watched it become one of the most popular songs in America, hired him as an in-house writer. In the end he wrote around 800 songs, including 'Rank Stranger to Me' (his title has it in the singular), and bought out his employers.

Dylan plays harmonica on CAROLYN HESTER's 1961 recording of 'I'll Fly Away' and sings 'Rank Strangers to Me' on his own album *Down in the Groove*. He has also performed the latter a number of times in concert.

Brumley died on November 15, 1977 in tiny Powell, Missouri (right in the state's southwest corner, bordering Arkansas and Kansas), where he had lived for over 45 years and where his company, Albert E. Brumley & Sons, is still trading. Its subsidiary, the Hartford Music Co., is now based in Powell too.

Bruton, Stephen [1948 -] Turner Stephen Bruton was born in Wilmington, Delaware, on November 7, 1948 but brought up in Fort Worth, Texas, with a jazz-drummer father who ran a record store. A teenage friend of T-BONE BURNETT, he became a guitarist equally keen on bluegrass, blues and soul, as well as a songwriter. In 1970 he joined KRIS KRISTOFFERSON's band and stayed with him for well over ten years, though also touring with Bonnie Raitt and others. He moved to Austin, Texas, in the mid-1980s, producing other artists' records and having his songs covered by WILLIE NELSON, Waylon Jennings, JOHNNY CASH, Little Feat, Jimmy Buffett and others. Starting with Kristofferson's film *A Star Is Born*, Bruton has also built a Hollywood bit-part career and has appeared in *Convoy*, *Heaven's Gate*, *Miss Congeniality*, *Sweet Thing* and *The Alamo*. As a studio session musician he has played on the Kristofferson & RITA COOLIDGE album *Full Moon* (1973) and on records by Delbert McClinton, ELVIS COSTELLO, Carly Simon, THE WALLFLOWERS and many others.

More importantly, however, Stephen Bruton played guitar on the Mexico City session for Dylan's *Pat Garrett & Billy the Kid* album (on January 20, 1973), from which came the album track 'Billy 4', while a bit of the instrumental 'Billy Surrenders' was used in the film—and then 27 years later Bruton played guitar with Dylan's band for a few nights in 2000: August 19 in Victoria, British Columbia, Canada; August 20 in Vancouver; August 21 in Portland, Oregon; August 24 in Pueblo, California; August 26 in Des Moines, Iowa; August 27 & 28 in Merrillville, Indiana; and August 29 in St. Paul, Minnesota—and then he returned to play both guitar and mandolin on October 11 in Greenvale, New York, and October 12 in Springfield, Massachusetts.

'Buckets of Rain' [1975] The closing track on the *Blood on the Tracks* album, this is an immensely likeable, modest song of barbed sanity. A blues-structured work, it also neatly conflates other old song titles within its lyric, as when Dylan sings 'Little red wagon, little red bike / I ain't no monkey but I know what I like'. In a genre so riddled with sexual innuendo and double entendre as the blues, it's sometimes hard to know whether a phrase or a line belongs in the nursery or the porn shop, and this is a good example. One long-term Dylan collector was told years ago that the phrase 'little red bike' was a blues term for anal sex: which certainly puts a different perspective on Dylan's lyric. But it is not a *common* blues term: there isn't a single 'little red wagon' in Michael Taft's *Blues Lyric Poetry: A Concordance*. 'Little Red Wagon' is, however, a recording by the pre-war blues artist Georgia White, and by a happy coincidence the very next track she laid down at the same session is called 'Dan the Back Door Man'. On the other hand, 'Won't You Ride in My Little Red Wagon?' by Hank Penny & His Radio Cowboys (featuring a young Boudleaux Bryant) was a western swing recording from 1939, and songs about anal intercourse didn't usually make it onto radio shows. That wasn't the meaning of the term 'western swing'.

The Georgia White song would suggest that the phrase 'that's your (little) red wagon' means 'that's your preoccupation, not mine', or, to use a comparable expression, its metaphor also taken from the nursery, 'your hobbyhorse.' This meaning is confirmed by a 1945 recording by ARTHUR CRUDUP: 'That's Your Red Wagon'.

'Little Red Wagon' is in any case the title of a Woody Guthrie song (in a 1987 interview, Dylan mentions it as one he knew early on) and a well-known traditional phrase in children's song.

Then there's 'Little Red Monkey', which on the face of it might sound like another children's song but definitely isn't. NIGEL HINTON noted in *Judas!* that 'Little Red Monkey' was a hit for the Harmonicats and for Rosemary Clooney in 1953, and that Bob Dylan, then aged 12, would have heard it. In Britain it was a hit for Frank Chacksfield & His Orchestra, and was in the charts at the same time as Jo Stafford's 'You Belong to Me' (and Frankie Laine's 'I Believe'). In the US the version by Rose Murphy on London Records also got airplay.

Hinton says that it was used as the 'unsettling theme song' of a B-movie spy film, but this 1955 film, *The Little Red Monkey* (US title *The Case of the Red Monkey*), reworked a 1953 BBC television serial by Eric Maschwitz, 'The Little Red Monkey' (six half-hour episodes, shown January to February 1953, starring Donald Houston, Arthur Rigby and Honor Blackman), in which the title character is a midget Russian spy. The sheet music for the title song credits Jack Jordan as its composer.

'Buckets of Rain' ends with a particular touch of grace, unafraid to leave the listener with a moral: 'Life is sad, life is a bust / All you can do is do what you must / You do what you must do and you do it well.' Yet here there is a harking back too: Dylan gives us, in these concluding lines, what is effectively a re-write of an old blues couplet by Kid Wesley Wilson and Harry McDaniels (the words are probably Wilson's) from their 1929 record 'Do It Right', on which they sing: 'Whenever you do it, whatever you should / Just do your best to do it good.'

Dylan's only live performance of 'Buckets of Rain' has been in Detroit on November 18, 1990. Fifteen years before that, he had recorded a duet version, with a playfully altered lyric, with BETTE MIDLER.

[Georgia White: 'Little Red Wagon' & 'Dan the Back Door Man', Chicago, 7 Dec 1936. Hank Penny & His Radio Cowboys: 'Won't You Ride in My Little Red Wagon', Memphis, 4 Jul 1939; *Tobacco State Swing*, Rambler R 103, El Cerrito, CA, 1980. Arthur Crudup:

'That's Your Red Wagon', Chicago, 22 Oct 1945, not issued on LP until *Give Me a 32–20*, Crown Prince IG-403, Stockholm, 1983. The film *Little Red Monkey*, aka *The Case of the Red Monkey*, dir. Ken Hughes, Merton Park Studios, UK, 1955. Kid Wesley Wilson and Harry McDaniels (as Pigmeat Pete & Catjuice Charlie): 'Do It Right', NY, 5 Sep 1929, *Rare Blues, 1927–1930*, Historical HLP-5, Jersey City, NJ, c.1967.]

Bucklen, John [1941 -] John Charles Bucklen was born in Bemidji, Minnesota, on December 20, 1941, but soon afterwards moved the 100 miles or so east to Hibbing. There he became a good friend of Bob Dylan's, the one with whom he made the 1958 tape recording at Dylan's home featuring fragments of song and of conversation (see **earliest extant recordings, Dylan's**), and the one Dylan phoned up excitedly when he first heard the 78rpm records of LEADBELLY he'd been given, to shout down the phone: '*This* is the real thing! You gotta hear *this!*'

John Bucklen was younger than Bob by eight months and a high-school year below him, but he was, in his own words, 'a born follower'; Bob also liked the easier atmosphere in the impoverished Bucklen household, with its lesser emphasis on 'achievement' and 'discipline'. John's father was a disabled miner and a musician, his mother a seamstress, his sister Ruth a lively girl with a record player. Trying out the hipster language they learnt together off James Dean movies and the radio, Dylan told Bucklen: 'You are my main man.'

As they grew up, music held them together, and Bucklen, though without his friend's ambition, neverthless learnt guitar—playing it alongside Dylan's piano—and before long Bucklen was playing blues on the 1959 Gibson J-50 he still plays regularly today. (Dylan played an identical guitar in the late 1960s.)

Dylan told ROBERT SHELTON in the 1970s that Bucklen had really been his 'best buddy' back in Hibbing, and regretted having been 'terribly rushed, terribly busy' when they'd last met.

John Bucklen left Hibbing and became a DJ, first in the Twin Cities and then in Fond Du Lac in Wisconsin in the late 1960s. He and his first wife LaVonne had one child, Chris, now a Minnesota-based ambient folk guitarist. John moved on to DJ work in Superior, Wisconsin, in 1971 and then, with second wife Gracie (with whom he has three children), he moved again, though still within Wisconsin, in 1977. He has worked for the same radio station there ever since, claims never to have missed a day of work in 30 years and is, in son Chris' opinion, 'an excellent blues musician'.

[Information from Chris Bucklen, e-mails to this writer 16 & 20 Oct 2005; quotes from Robert Shelton, *No Direction Home: The Life and Music of Bob Dylan*, London: Penguin edn., 1987, pp.45, 49 & 16.]

Bunyan, John [1628 - 1688] There's a specific sense in which John Bunyan's achievement prefigures Bob Dylan's. Although he was the worst, the least Miltonic, kind of puritan, epitomising narrow sectarianism, Bunyan restored the strengths of popular culture to mainstream literary culture after the two had gone their largely separate ways. He was thus Elizabethan in spirit. Granted the new conditions, it is reasonable to say that what Bunyan did then, Dylan has done again: put the dynamics of folk culture back into sophisticated art, exalting the one to the level of the other's greatness.

The parallel between the two writers may take us further—to say which involves recognising that *Pilgrim's Progress* is, in the best sense, a classic. Overriding its reductive intention—to lacerate life with the stick of hellfire—it offers an enriching humanitarianism. Its humanity comes across with that biblical dignity of expression which graces the language of all folk culture. Bunyan's work is a reminder of the powerful influence of the various English-language translations of the Bible, from John Wyclif's first vernacular version to the Authorized of 1611—an influence that still operates powerfully on folk idiom both in England and America, as, indeed, Dylan's work testifies. The Authorized version has been the most important: has been, for hundreds of years, the countryman's only book. In imagery and rhythm, it is popular, not classical; it harks back to and reflects the language of medieval England, while influencing seminally the language of 20th century America, especially black America.

Bunyan therefore harks back also to the language of medieval England—and so does Dylan. It is not mere coincidence—it is a question of common roots: shared cultural history. As if to prove the point, Cecil Sharp (*English Folk-Songs from the Southern Appalachians*, ed. Maud Karpeles, 1932) discovered the popular culture Bunyan represented, not fossilised but vitally alive, in the remoter valleys of the southern Appalachians during the First World War.

Bunyan, then, is very much Dylan's forebear; and there are many noticeable similarities of language in their work. It is from Bunyan, and certainly not from any rock'n'roll vocabulary, that Dylan gets this great, and typical, phrase from Joey on the *Desire* album: 'God's in heaven, overlooking His preserve'. And isn't this, for example, instantly recognisable as a line from the Dylan of the *John Wesley Harding* album?: 'Pray who are your kindred there, if a man may be so bold?' But it is not Bob Dylan, it is Christian in *Pilgrim's Progress*. And doesn't this comply almost exactly in rhythm and vocabularitive tone?: 'Oh what dear daughter beneath the sun could treat a father so: / To wait upon him hand and foot and always answer no?' Thus Dylan's 'Tears of Rage' also illustrates, as do so many Dylan songs, its creator's concern for salvation. In terms of the parallels with Bunyan, this is the nearest to a merely coincidental one: and yet even here, coincidence is perhaps not the right word.

When Bunyan was writing, of course, God existed. To his contemporary pamphleteers, salvation was a narrowly Christian matter (either you got there or you didn't) and it was a wider thing to Bunyan himself in spite of, not because of, his Calvinism. Since then, God has been through many changes, all reducing His omnipotence. Yet the Dylan of the mid-60s to mid-70s showed us our world too plagued and helpless easily to countenance that God really was dead. We identified with the tortured vision of the medieval Hieronymus Bosch. There was a serious anguish behind our trivia: hence the power of a book like *Catch-22*. With *Slow Train Coming* and *Saved*, in 1979 and 1980, Dylan demands that we re-examine all this—and indeed that we re-examine Bunyan's vision and our notion of what our quest for salvation requires of us.

John Bunyan died in London on August 31, 1688. His immense popularity and impact on mainstream literature won him, after his death, few friends among the literary elite. As Raphael Samuel wrote: 'Bunyan's *literary* reputation was almost non-existent before the Romantics, even among those who recommended *The Pilgrim's Progress* for religious instruction. . . . Coleridge was one of the first literary voices raised in favour of Bunyan. Southey's 1830 edition of *The Pilgrim's Progress* . . . marked Bunyan's entry into the literary pantheon after a century and a half of well-bred putdowns.'

See also the entry on the Dylan song **'Dignity'**.

[John Bunyan: *The Pilgrim's Progress: From This World to That Which Is to Come*, Part I published 1678, Part II 1684. *The Life and Death of Mr. Badman* published 1680. Raphael Samuel, 'The Discovery of Puritanism, 1820–1914', reprinted in his *Island Stories: Unravelling Britain—Theatres of Memory Volume II*, 1998. This essay is a reminder of our shifting use and understanding of the term 'puritanism', and by extension of the unheeding way we bandy ideas in modish ways that we forget are merely modish, assuming them to have, instead, historical fixity.]

Burke, Gary [1948 -] Gary Burke was born in Troy, New York, on April 9, 1948. He was the percussionist in the backing band informally known as GUAM on the second Rolling Thunder Revue tour, which began with the RUBIN HURRICANE CARTER fund-raising concert in Houston on January 25, 1976 but really rolled as from April 18 in Lakeland, Florida, and ran through a further 22 dates, including the concert filmed but unreleased at Clearwater, Florida, on April 22 and the concert used instead at Fort Collins, Colorado, on May 23, which yielded both the 'Hard Rain' TV Special and the *Hard Rain* album. The tour's last night was in Salt Lake City on May 25.

Gary Burke replaced LUTHER RIX, who had been in the line-up for the 1975 Rolling Thunder Revue. He therefore appears not only on the *Hard Rain* album (and very briefly on camera in 'Hard Rain') but also on the track 'Seven Days' on the *Bootleg Series Vols. 1–3* (1991), recorded live in Tampa, Florida, on April 21, 1976.

The way that he came to be part of the band is, as he recounts it, 'a two-part story'. Part One:

> 'I was sitting out in front of Trude Heller's (a club in New York City at that time) at about 4am after a gig. I was just killing time before going home when I noticed Sue Evans walking down the street. I had just seen her perform on percussion, especially tympani (!), the week before at the Village Vanguard with the Gil Evans Orchestra. I introduced myself and told her I loved what she was doing with the band. We got talking and I told her what I was doing and she did the same, mentioning that she was just asked to replace Luther Rix on the Rolling Thunder gig. Luther was unavailable. . . . Sue said she didn't want to do the gig because she was afraid there might be a lot of drugs around and she didn't want to be around that. I said, "Well, if you don't want the gig I'll take it!" Sue said, "Alright, I'll recommend you." I thought to myself, "Yeah, right." Well, she did! I got a call from ROB STONER to get together and play, just the two of us, bass and drums. We jammed at my loft and he said, "You got the gig."'

Part Two:

> 'We were all scheduled to leave for Florida to begin rehearsals for the second part of the tour. There was a sort of going-away party at a hotel before we were to leave. Everybody in the band was there *but* Dylan and BOBBY NEUWIRTH. I noticed everyone was getting handed itineraries and what looked like contracts to sign except for me. I asked the road manager what was going on and how come I wasn't getting a contract as well. He implied that the rehearsal period was a kind of an audition for me. I told him that as far as I was concerned I already auditioned with Stoner and I had cancelled an album project to do this tour. I then proceeded to tell him that I'd better get a contract or I wasn't getting on the plane and they would also owe me $5,000 for the cancelled album recording. This caused quite a fuss and pretty soon the phone rang in the hotel room and it was Neuwirth. He got me on the line and said he was there with Bob and heard what was going on. He said, "I only have one question for you." I said, "What's that?" He said, "Do you like music?" I said, "No." There was a stunned silence. I said, "I *love* music." I was told to get on the plane.'

After dropping off Dylan's radar at the end of the Rolling Thunder Revue he played on Kinky Friedman's *Lasso from El Paso* album (1976), SCARLET RIVERA's *Scarlet Rivera* (1977), Jesse Winchester's *Talk Memphis* (1981) and others, and was the drummer with the Radio City Music Hall Orchestra for four years, before joining Joe Jackson's band, with which he toured, appearing on at least ten Jackson albums while still doing session work for Graham Parker and others, including Artie Traum (*Letters from Joubee*, 1993), RICK DANKO, on whose 2000 album *Times Like These* Burke played drums, and GARTH HUDSON, on whose 2001 album *The Sea to the North* he also played. (On the Rees Shad album *Anderson, Ohio* in 1996 he had done almost everything, being producer, editor, assistant engineer, horn arranger, strings arranger and player of percussion, drums, harmonium and keyboards.)

Since 2000 Gary Burke has been a member of the unit Professor Louie & the Crowmatrix, playing on their albums *Over the Edge* (2000), *Jam* (2001), *Flyin' High* (2002), the only half-truthfully titled *Live* (2003) and *Century of the Blues* (2005)—'Professor Louie' being latter-day BAND producer Aaron Hurwitz of Woodstock Records, and Gary Burke being a resident of the Woodstock, New York, area.

Some of his playing has earlier roots, however. In the 1970s, when he was playing xylophone with four mallets, he was apparently reviving an approach pioneered in the 1930s by the now-forgotten jazz multi-instrumentalist, band-leader and former child-prodigy Adrian Rollini (a one-man Rollini Thunder Revue).

[Gary Burke date & place of birth details, plus Rolling Thunder recruitment account, e-mails to this writer, 12 Jan 2006.]

Burnett, T-Bone [1948 -] Joseph Henry Burnett was born in St. Louis, Missouri, on January 14, 1948. He grew up in Fort Worth, Texas, an enthusiast for Tex-Mex music and BUDDY HOLLY, and he became a songwriter, guitarist, singer, studio engineer and record producer—and in the 21st century one of the highest-paid and most successful suppliers of soundtrack music to Hollywood.

He launched his career after finishing high school, playing in local blues bands (later calling himself T-Bone Burnett in tribute to blues-guitarist hero T-Bone Walker) and opening his own small Fort Worth studio, before moving to Los Angeles, producing records by Delbert McClinton and others and then, as J. Henry Burnett, releasing a début album of unusual overt moral rectitude, *The B-52 Band and the Fabulous Skylarks*, in 1972, the cover of which features a photograph of Burnett alone, bean-pole thin and very tall. SAM SHEPARD describes him as 'seven feet tall' in the *Rolling Thunder Logbook*. The band (unrelated to Athens, Georgia's legendary B52s) was a quirky five-piece unit featuring Burnett on guitar and vocals, Gary Montgomery as main vocalist, Rodney Dillard on dobro, Dean Parks on saxophone and Willie Leonard on trumpet. The Fabulous Skylarks were two female backing singers. The album, needless to say, required extra musicians to provide mundane things like a rhythm section.

Burnett was taken up by the temporarily modish white soul duo Delaney & Bonnie, with whom he toured, became friends with long-term Bob Dylan sidekick BOB NEUWIRTH and so eventually was brought into the group informally known as GUAM, who backed Dylan on the Rolling Thunder Revues of 1975 and 1976. Though Burnett seems to have arrived late on in the proceedings—he never appears over the summer of 1975 when ROB STONER, HOWIE WYETH and SCARLET RIVERA are already in place from their studio sessions for the *Desire* album and the TV appearance on the 'World of JOHN HAMMOND' tribute show—nonetheless he was there for both tours, appearing in a total of 56 concerts plus the film *Renaldo & Clara*, the TV special 'Hard Rain' and the albums *Hard Rain* and the *Bootleg Series Vol. 5*. On the first tour he played guitar, and relished the constructed but improvised acting scenes that *Renaldo & Clara* demanded. Sam Shepard remembers him warming up in New York, before they even set out on the road, 'disguised as a professional golfer, complete with golf bag and cap.' And then on tour, he 'often appeared on stage disguised as Merlin the Magician. Often roped ROGER McGUINN around the neck at the conclusion of . . . "Chestnut Mare"'. On the second tour, his on stage profile increased: he played both guitar and piano and he sang 'Silver Mantis' in the early part of every concert.

Burnett's overt Christianity hit Dylan at the right moment. Howie Wyeth told CLINTON HEYLIN specifically that 'T-Bone read Bob that line in the Bible that says if you listen to astrologers and people who are into the black arts . . . your family will be taken from you. And he'd just lost the battle [against SARA DYLAN for custody of his children] in court. . . . T-Bone told me that the thing that really nailed it was when he showed him, in the Bible, that quote.' Yet Jesus doesn't seem to bring much peace to T-Bone Burnett. 'He has a peculiar quality of craziness about him,' writes Sam Shepard. 'He's the only one on the tour I'm not sure has relative control over his violent dark side.' And he tells Shepard that it is Dylan who has given him 'reason to live'.

After the Revues, Burnett and fellow Guam Christians DAVID MANSFIELD and STEVE SOLES took themselves and their Bibles away and formed the Alpha Band, making three indifferent albums for an indifferent public, *The Alpha Band* (1976), *Spark in the Dark* (1977) and *Statue Makers of Hollywood* (1978). They disbanded, and in 1980 came a new solo album with the groan-inducingly bad punning title *Truth Decay*: exactly the sort of play on words that preachers and proselytising churches love and imagine to be captivating. It was followed by a 1982 EP, *Trap Door*, a big-name-guest-filled album, *Proof Through the Night*, in 1983 and another sort-of EP, *Behind the Trap Door*, in 1984. None of these records sold well, and nor did 1986's *T-Bone Burnett*. Nor did the single he and ELVIS COSTELLO issued under the name the Coward Brothers (Henry and Howard Coward), 'The People's Limousine', in 1985. But T-Bone had kept on producing other people's work in this period, including Marshall Crenshaw's *Downtown* album and two by Costello, *King of America* (1986) and *Spike* (1988), and had continued playing guitar on other people's albums.

One of these was *Knocked Out Loaded*, Dylan's 1986 album. T-Bone Burnett was one of those who reported for work at the Topanga Park, California, studio that May 1, and was set to work overdubbing on 'Brownsville Girl', as well as playing on still-uncirculated cuts of 'Without Love' and 'Unchain My Heart'. This work continued on May 2 but after that, according to the listings in GLEN DUNDAS' *Tangled*, Burnett's services don't seem to have been required. Yet on the album credits, Burnett is *not* listed as on 'Brownsville Girl' and *is* listed for 'You Wanna Ramble', the album's opening track, which was recorded on May 5.

More certainly, it was six years later that T-Bone Burnett played with Dylan again, and, so far, for the last time. On May 9, 1992, at a Never-Ending Tour concert at San Jose State University, Burnett came onstage late on in the set and played guitar on 'Cat's in the Well', 'Idiot Wind' and 'Highway 61 Revisited'. ('Idiot Wind' had been revived that year for the first time since the days when Burnett had been playing it all the time on the 1976 Rolling Thunder Revue. Perhaps he thought Dylan always played it.)

Burnett has since married, produced, written for and recorded with singer Sam Phillips (formerly 'Christian pop singer' Leslie Phillips; Burnett's first work with her was on her last pre-secular album, *The Turning*, 1986–87). His own subsequent solo albums have been *The Talking Animals* (1988) and *The Criminal Under My Own Hat* (1992).

More notably, in an involvement with ROY ORBISON that included producing his 1987 album *In Dreams* and his 1989 *Mystery Girl*, T-Bone was also musical director and producer of the 1987 Orbison show 'Black and White Night', a Cinemax TV special filmed in Los Angeles on September 30, 1987 and broadcast in 1988, which starred Orbison with support from Jackson Browne, Elvis Costello, kd lang, Bonnie Raitt, BRUCE SPRINGSTEEN, JENNIFER WARNES, Steven Soles and T-Bone himself, while the band Burnett had assembled also included JAMES BURTON and the Buddy Holly and ELVIS PRESLEY pianist Glen D. Hardin. Burnett also produced the album taken from the event, *A Black and White Night Live*. Against many odds, this is a worthy representation of Orbison live—indeed the only live album issued in his lifetime—and the re-creation of the *sounds* behind his hits is thrillingly more accurate than is usual with such projects.

Though first broadcast on HBO this became the biggest fund-raising programme in PBS history, which meant that Burnett, despite a lifetime of failing to sell his own records, was suddenly a music industry heavyweight. He had proved himself as an adroit and effective assembler of talent for 'serious' projects, and so began his big Hollywood years. After working as 'musical archivist' on the Coen Brothers' *The Big Lebowski* in 1998 he swiftly triumphed with his award-winning soundtrack for their mega-hit *O Brother, Where Art Thou?*, a film in which the music was omnipresent and crucial, and which led to a dramatic upswing in the popularity of traditional folk, bluegrass and general pre-1950s quirky music. He was therefore also a key part of the documentary about that film's music, *Down from the Mountain* (2000), which he co-produced with, among others, Bobby Neuwirth and D.A. PENNEBAKER. He has since been executive music producer for *Divine Secrets of the Ya-Ya Sisterhood* (2002), to which Dylan contributed the dreary new song 'Waitin' for You', and *Cold Mountain* (2003).

All this re-uniting with old cronies didn't stop there. In 1996–97 he had written new songs for a revival of a 1970s Sam Shepard play, *Tooth of Crime*, and in 2003, he was reunited with Shepard yet again in the documentary film *This So-Called Disaster: Sam Shepard Directs the Late Henry Moss*, directed by Michael Almereyda, in which both play themselves (at work on another Shepard play).

In 2005, coming full circle, Burnett stepped back into the world of southern rock'n'roll he had grown up with in the first place when he produced the soundtrack, wrote the score and trained actors for their singing rôles in the JOHNNY CASH biopic *Walk the Line*.

[J. Henry Burnett: *The B-52 Band and the Fabulous Skylarks*, Uni, US, 1972. The Alpha Band: *The Alpha Band*, Arista A 4102, US, 1976; *Spark in the Dark*, Arista AD-4145, US, 1977; *Statue Makes of Hollywood*, Arista AB-4179, US, 1978. T-Bone Burnett: *Truth Decay*, Takoma TAX7080, US, 1980; *Trap Door* (EP), Warner Bros. WB 23691, US, 1982; *Proof Through the Night*, Warner Bros. 23921-1, US, 1983; *Behind the Trap Door*, Demon VEX3, UK, 1984; *T-Bone Burnett, nia*, US, 1986. *The Talking Animals*, Columbia BFC 40792, US, 1988; *The Criminal Under My Own Hat*, Columbia 45213, US, 1992. The Coward Brothers: 'The People's Limousine', Imp IMP006, UK, 1985.

The Big Lebowski, dir. Joel Coen; PolyGram Filmed Entertainment / Working Title, US/UK, 1998. *O Brother, Where Art Thou?*, dir. Joel Coen; Buena Vista / Mike Zoss / Studio Canal / Touchstone / Universal / Working Title, US, 2000. *Down from the Mountain*, dir. Nick Doob, Chris Hegedus & D.A. Pennebaker; Mike Zoss / Pennebaker Hegedus, US, 2000. *This So-Called Disaster: Sam Shepard Directs the Late Henry Moss*, dir. Michael

Almereyda; IFC / Keep Your Head, US, 2003. *Walk the Line*, dir. James Mangold; Fox 2000 / Tree Line / Konrad / Catfish, US, 2005.

Sam Shepard, *Rolling Thunder Logbook*, London & New York: Penguin, 1978, pp.17 & 58. Howie Wyeth quote from Clinton Heylin, *Behind the Shades*, as seen online 26 Sep 2005 at *http://web.utk.edu/~wparr/HistChrDyl.html*.]

Burnette, Billy [1953 -] William Beau Burnette III was born on May 8, 1953 in Memphis, Tennessee, and grew up to be a rockabilly guitarist with an inexplicable fondness for the work of Fleetwood Mac and the kind of saturnine good looks that in any southern melodrama would signal inbred madness. He is the son and nephew respectively of those rockabilly pioneers the Burnette Brothers, Dorsey and Johnny, and cousin of singer Rocky Burnette. (Dorsey and Johnny were Golden Gloves boxing champions as well as rockabillies; Dorsey wrote many of RICKY NELSON's hits and died of a massive heart attack in California in 1979; Johnny had big international hit singles with 'Dreaming' and 'You're Sixteen' and drowned in a lake in California in 1964.)

Billy—who became great friends with Ricky Nelson, with whom he shared birthdays—first performed at age three, singing a doubtless outrageously cute 'Hound Dog' with the Rock N'Roll Trio, made his first single, 'Hey Daddy (I'm Gonna Tell Santa on You)', at age seven (with Ricky's band), recorded his first album at age 11 and was touring Japan and the Far East with Little Miss Dynamite, Brenda Lee, at age 13. He neglected to learn to play guitar until age 16.

Burnette grew up in Los Angeles but moved back to Memphis in 1969, where Chips Moman taught him studio engineering and encouraged his songwriting, to develop which he moved to Nashville in 1972. There he recorded a début album, *Billy Burnette*, for a small label and scored his first hit as a writer with 'Do I Ever Cross Your Mind?', a hit for Kin Vassy and later covered by Dolly Parton and RAY CHARLES. Burnette signed to Polydor in 1979 and made another album titled *Billy Burnette*, followed by *Between Friends*, which yielded the hit single 'What's a Little Love Between Friends?'

His career continued through the 1980s with New Wave Rockabilly albums for Columbia—the first one was called, yes, *Billy Burnette*—and MCA and hits written for others but in 1987 he joined old wave Fleetwood Mac, with whom he toured and recorded for nearly a decade. (He and Mick Fleetwood also had a band called Zoo.) Burnette wrote 'Dream You', one of the songs on ROY ORBISON's 1980s album *Mystery Girl*, and his work has also been recorded by JERRY LEE LEWIS, BOB WEIR, Cher, THE EVERLY BROTHERS and Gregg Allman (a pleasing juxtaposition of names). He returned to the fray of solo albums in 1993, with *Coming Home*; other albums include *All Night Long* (1999) and *Are You With Me Baby* (2000). He has also acted in films: *Saturday Night Special* (aka *Deadly Desire*—in which his character, all but inevitably called Travis, 'arrives like a hot wind on a steamy summer night') and *Caspar 3* (aka *Caspar Meets Wendy*).

In 2003 Billy Burnette became a very temporary guitarist and backing vocalist in Bob Dylan's band, replacing CHARLIE SEXTON and being replaced himself by the great FREDDY KOELLA on a tour of Australia and New Zealand. Billy's run of dates began in Canberra that February 6, Dylan's first date of the year, and ended in Christchurch on February 26, the last night of that leg of the Never-Ending Tour. Burnette had played a total of 11 dates.

[Billy Beau: 'Hey Daddy (I'm Gonna Tell Santa on You)' c/w 'Santa's Coffee', Dot 45-16281, US, 1961. Billy Burnette: *Billy Burnette*, Entrance Z 31228, US, 1972; *Billy Burnette*, Polydor PD-1-6187, US, 1979; *Between Friends*, Polydor PD-1-6242, US, 1979; *Billy Burnette*, Columbia NJC 36792 (CBS 84642, UK), 1980; *Coming Home*, Capricorn / WEA, US, 1993; *All Night Long*, Grand Avenue, US, 1999; *Are You With Me Baby*, Free Falls 7009, US, 2000. *Deadly Desire*, dir. Dan Golden, Concorde-New Horizons, US, 1994.]

Burton, James [1939 -] James Burton was born in Minden, Louisiana, on August 21, 1939, moved to Shreveport ten years later and became one of the defining stylists of electric rock'n'roll guitar, playing mainly a Fender Telecaster yet owning 200 other guitars. He worked his way through backing Slim Whitman and others on the Louisiana Hayride while still virtually a child, escaping into session work after playing a striking solo while still a young teenager on the 1957 Dale Hawkins hit 'Suzie Q'. It was on RICKY NELSON's records that he became widely noticed and admired, playing a series of discreet yet inventive, tantalisingly brief solos on Nelson's big hits. It's astonishing how short the instrumental breaks were on pop singles.

In 1969 he was asked to back ELVIS PRESLEY on his return to live performance, and stayed in service through all the numbing, demeaning tours until Presley's death, though he was never free to impose either his flair or his restraint on this overblown orchestral unit.

His credentials were better respected on albums by Hoyt Axton, JUDY COLLINS, Ry Cooder and others, and on the Gram Parsons albums *GP* and *Grievous Angel*. After Parsons' death he was a member of EMMYLOU HARRIS' Hot Band (between Elvis tours), touring and recording with her. He and the steel player Ralph Mooney made the duets album *Corn Pickin' and Slick Slidin'* in 1966 (CD-reissued in 2005), and five years later Burton made his only solo album, which suffered under the title *The Guitar Sounds of James Burton*, the sort of name normally associated with albums by middle-of-the-road hacks, and catches Burton trying haplessly to look early-1970s hip, in one of the world's nastiest shirts. This album was CD-reissued in 2001.

James Burton's connection with Dylan—aside from the mere rumour that Dylan had wanted Burton in his band when he first 'went electric' in 1965—is that when the Never-Ending Tour came through Shreveport on October 30, 1996, the veteran guitarist came on stage and played with Dylan and the band on five numbers: 'Seeing the Real You At Last', 'She Belongs to Me', 'Maggie's Farm', 'Like a Rolling Stone' and the final encore item, 'Rainy Day Women # 12 & 35'.

[James Burton: *The Guitar Sounds of James Burton*, A&M, US, 1971. James Burton & Ralph Mooney, *Corn Pickin' and Slick Slidin'*, Capitol T 2872, US, 1966.]

Butler, Keith [1945 - 2002] See 'Judas!' [shout].

Butterfield, Paul [1942 - 1987] Paul Butterfield was born in Chicago on December 17, 1942 and grew up in the city. He was exposed to jazz and was taught classical flute as a child. He learnt guitar and harmonica, dropped out of college to visit blues clubs and by 1961 he and Elvin Bishop were good enough players that they could sit in with HOWLIN' WOLF, Little Walter, MUDDY WATERS, Junior Wells and others in clubs where they were commonly the only white faces. In 1963 he formed the Butterfield Blues Band, with Bishop, the splendidly named Little Smokey Smothers, JEROME ARNOLD and SAM LAY. In 1964 out went Smothers, the word 'Paul' was added to the band's name and in came Mark Naftalin and MIKE BLOOMFIELD: a line-up that stayed steady until illness forced drummer Sam Lay's 1966 replacement by Billy Davenport. Butterfield led this extraordinary unit till 1972, when he disbanded it.

He was a remote individual but an adequate yet expressive vocalist and a superb harmonica player, and his achievement was to create and lead the band that 'slit the membrane between the two cultures', with a first album (*The Paul Butterfield Blues Band*, on Elektra) that was racially mixed, hard-driving, unapologetic blues that showed white enthusiasts how to play it instead of archiving it, and thus brought urban Chicago blues into the white mainstream. The band's appearance under its own name at the 1965 NEWPORT FOLK FESTIVAL was a revelation to those who heard it, taking this music to a whole new level of energy. It was as vividly remembered by the likes of MARIA MULDAUR as the Dylan controversy at the same festival.

For Dylan's appearance, Butterfield lent him his rhythm section and Mike Bloomfield but did not play himself. The only time he came together with Dylan on stage was at THE BAND's Farewell Concert at the Winterland in San Francisco on November 25, 1976, when he and others provided backing vocals on Dylan's performance of 'I Shall Be Released'.

Towards the end, the Paul Butterfield Blues Band nudged closer to rock, and the group he formed afterwards, Paul Butterfield's Better Days, reined in this trend but was never outstanding. In 1976 Butterfield made the solo album *Put It in Your Ear* (on which LEVON HELM and GARTH HUDSON both played), and five years later *North South*, but neither sold well. He moved to Los Angeles, did some session work and made one last album, *The Legendary Paul Butterfield Rides Again* in 1986—a decent album that includes a fine rendition of the Bob Dylan-HELENA SPRINGS song 'The Wandering Kind', on which he proved he could still play the harmonica searingly well.

Butterfield was by then a heroin addict and in poor health after years of heavy drinking and suffering from peritonitis. He died of drug-related heart failure in Hollywood on May 4, 1987. He was 44.

[Paul Butterfield Blues Band: *The Paul Butterfield Blues Band*, Elektra 7294, NY, 1965. Paul Butterfield: *Put It in Your Ear*, Bearsville, BR 6960, US, 1976; *The Legendary Paul Butterfield Rides Again*, Amherst, MA 1986 (CD-AMH 93305, 1990). The 'membrane' quote from Charles Sawyer, 'Blues With a Feeling: A Biography of the Paul Butterfield Blues Band', 1994, online 2 Jul 2005 at *www.people.fas.harvard.edu/~sawyer/bwf.html*.]

Buttrey, Kenny [1945 - 2004] Kenneth A. Buttrey was born in Nashville on April 1, 1945 and became one of the great drummers of the 1960s. Playing professionally by age 14, he joined CHARLIE McCOY & the Escorts, and played on ARTHUR ALEXANDER's great record 'Anna (Go to Him)'—the one THE BEATLES covered—in 1962. He was often a persuasive on-the-spot arranger whose creative touch made him invaluable in the studio. He played on dozens of big-name artists' albums including work by the Canadians RONNIE HAWKINS, GORDON LIGHTFOOT, IAN & SYLVIA and eventually NEIL YOUNG, whose Stray Gators he belonged to (he played on Young's *After the Gold Rush*, *Harvest* and *Tonight's the Night*), as well as playing on records by country stars like JERRY LEE LEWIS, ROY ORBISON, Waylon Jennings, WILLIE NELSON and Jimmy Buffett, and on albums by rock and folk artists from BOB SEGER and SIMON & Garfunkel to RAMBLIN' JACK ELLIOTT, Eric Andersen and JOAN BAEZ. Crucially, he played on the core Dylan albums *Blonde on Blonde* and *John Wesley Harding*, as well as on *Nashville Skyline* and *Self Portrait*.

For *Blonde on Blonde* he was there as soon as the sessions shifted from New York—where BOBBY GREGG played on 'One of Us Must Know (Sooner or Later)'—beginning on February 14, when they cut final takes of '4th Time Around' and 'Visions of Johanna'. Over the days that followed came 'Sad-Eyed Lady of the Lowlands', 'Stuck Inside of Mobile with the Memphis Blues Again', and in early March 'Absolutely Sweet Marie' and all the rest. Eighteen months later, Bob, Charley McCoy and Kenny Buttrey re-convened for Dylan's first studio session since *Blonde on Blonde*'s completion and the very different working environs of West Saugherties and the making of the Basement Tapes. It was October 17, 1967, and they laid down the three tracks for *John Wesley Harding*: 'Drifter's Escape', 'I Dreamed I Saw St. Augustine' and 'The Ballad of Frankie Lee and Judas Priest'. On November 6, they added 'All Along the Watchtower', 'John Wesley Harding', 'As I Went Out One Morning', 'I Pity the Poor Immigrant' and 'I Am a Lonesome Hobo'. Incredibly, one more session wrapped it up: November 30, yielding 'The Wicked Messenger', 'I'll Be Your Baby Tonight', 'Down Along the Cove' and 'Dear Landlord' (with PETE DRAKE on steel guitar for the middle two of the four).

On February 13, 1969—almost three years to the day since his first *Blonde on Blonde* session—Buttrey was back with Dylan, McCoy and others for the first *Nashville Skyline* session. He was the drummer on all tracks, and on outtakes that included the many duets between Dylan and JOHNNY CASH, and he played on Dylan's 'Johnny Cash TV Show' appearance that May 1. And by that time he'd played on the first of the *Self Portrait* sessions too, beginning on April 24 and 26 and then continuing on May 3. When Dylan returned to New York for further sessions in March 1970, Buttrey was less involved. Alvin Rogers played drums on the New York tracks early that month, but these were flown to Nashville for overdubs, on which Buttrey duly played drums on March 11 and 12, and contributed bongos and congas on March 13. At the beginning of May he was replaced as drummer by RUSS KUNKEL—but by then Kenny Buttrey had played on the *Dylan* album tracks 'Spanish Is the Loving Tongue' and 'A Fool Such as I' as well as on the *Self Portrait* tracks 'Living the Blues', 'Take Me as I Am', 'I Forgot More', 'Let It Be Me', 'Take a Message to Mary' and 'Blue Moon', and overdubs on others.

The *Village Voice* critic Robert Christgau once wrote that while 'Dylan has known great rhythm sections (in Muscle Shoals and, especially, THE BAND), his seminal rock records were cut with Nashville cats on drums—Kenny Buttrey when he was lucky, nonentities when he wasn't.' And in the end, the key point is this: Kenny Buttrey plays so beautifully on *Blonde on Blonde*, makes the drumming a defining part of every track. Think back to the sound of 'Just Like a Woman', 'I Want You', 'Pledging My Time' and so on: Buttrey's contribution, never attention-seeking, always *does* something. Here is a musician who could always be proud that he played on 'Visions of Johanna' and then on 'All Along the Watchtower' too.

Buttrey went on not only to work with Neil Young but to co-found Area Code 615 with Charley McCoy, WAYNE MOSS and others: a revered outfit in spite of poor sales for its only two LPs—sales that weren't helped by the group only playing once live and once on 'The Johnny Cash Show'. The first album, *Area Code 615*, included a version of 'Just Like a Woman'; the second, *Trip in the Country*—an emphatic term at the time, shouting the new hipness of a group with straitlaced Nashville roots – included the harmonica-centred instrumental track 'Stone Fox Chase', which became the theme tune for the long-running BBC-TV rock music series 'The Old Grey Whistle Test'.

Buttrey went on to reunite with McCoy in the less interesting but more prolific Barefoot Jerry, while continuing to hire out his talents to others in the studios, as on the Jimmy Buffett album that produced Buffett's hit 'Margaritaville', and on sessions in May 1971 for ELVIS PRESLEY (for whom he'd first worked in 1965, on the music for the gruesomely bad film *Harum Scarum*).

Kenny Buttrey died at his home in a Nashville suburb on September 12, 2004, after a long battle with cancer. He was 59.

[Area Code 615: *Area Code 615*, Polydor 24-4002, US (Polydor 583572, UK), 1969; *Trip in the Country*, Polydor 24 4025, US, 1970. Robert Christgau quote unattributed, seen online *nia*, 10 Jan 2006.]

Byatt, A.S. [1936 -] See **'Keats v. Dylan'**.

'Bye and Bye' [2001] See **Shakespeare in *"Love and Theft"*** and **'If Dogs Run Free'**.

Byrds, the The Byrds were the group with the best claim to have originated folk-rock, though were folk-rock not essentially an American sound, THE ANIMALS might dispute such a claim, having rocked up two traditional songs after hearing them by Dylan: 'Baby Let Me Follow You Down' and 'House of the Rising Sun', both on his first LP, and achieving a US no.1 with the latter.

The Byrds, though, were dubbed the American Beatles and in 1965 seemed to be everywhere. They were the group that 'electrified' Bob Dylan's work the most, beginning with 'Mr. Tambourine Man', a huge hit single and a record that thrilled Dylan himself and deserves the epithet 'a classic', with its joyous, gritty fusion of Dylan's celebratory lyrics and ROGER McGUINN's electric 12-string Rickenbacker guitar and his highly distinctive voice. In fact none of the rest of the band played on this single—though session men Hal Blaine, Larry Knetchel and LEON RUSSELL did.

The group began as a trio featuring McGuinn, Gene Clark and DAVID CROSBY, then added Chris Hillman and Michael Clarke to become the Jet Set in the summer of 1964—heavily influenced by THE BEATLES. Re-named the Beefeaters (do we detect the arrival of 'the British invasion' here?), they issued a Beatleised single that fall, 'Please Let Me Love You' on Elektra. After its failure they became the Byrds and concocted 'Mr. Tambourine Man'. When the post-folkie Bob Dylan came to the West

Coast in 1965, it was the groovy world of Hollywood club Ciro's, the milieu of hip rock groups, the home turf of the Byrds, to which he gravitated and allied himself—he even joined them on stage during their set once, not long after his electric début at the NEWPORT FOLK FESTIVAL that July. Dylan and the Byrds created a new zenith of hipness when they came together, and did so by leaning a little each upon the other.

The next Byrds single was 'All I Really Want to Do', by which time they found themselves competing with copyists like the Turtles and Sonny & Cher; their next, 'Turn! Turn! Turn!', restored them to the US no.1 slot. In the singles charts, their best days were over, and after 'My Back Pages' in 1967 they never again hit the US top 20. But their importance and influence was as an albums band, and through various personnel changes their albums flowed out in profusion all through the 1960s, and were undeniably part of the soundtrack of the age. After *Mr. Tambourine Man* (1965) came *Turn! Turn! Turn!* (1966) and *Fifth Dimension* (1966)—on which they shifted away from folk-rock and towards a little electronic experimentation (at McGuinn's prompting); this was intensified on *Younger Than Yesterday* (1967), after which came *The Notorious Byrd Brothers* (1968), and then their pioneering, marvellous album *Sweetheart of the Rodeo*, also 1968, which embraced country music before anyone else in rock had brought themselves to think of it as other than hopelessly reactionary and redneck. It did not go down well but it was a tremendous achievement. Having created folk-rock, the Byrds had now created country-rock too—and though Dylan's sign-off tracks on *John Wesley Harding*, 'Down Along the Cove' and 'I'll Be Your Baby Tonight', were recorded in 1967, and his own interest in country music clearly preceded all these releases, nonetheless *Sweetheart of the Rodeo* nudged hip rock in the direction of country and came before *Nashville Skyline*.

The later career of the Byrds is not important: all their innovations took place in the 1960s, McGuinn was launching a solo career by the early 1970s, and though a re-formed version of the Byrds finally performed a live 'Mr. Tambourine Man' with Dylan at the so-called 'ROY ORBISON Tribute Show' in LA on February 24, 1990 (McGuinn, David Crosby, Chris Hillman, John Jorgenson and Steve Duncan), this was hardly significant. And if the Byrds had merely made cover versions of Dylan songs, this would not be the place for an account of them—but they did not merely make cover versions: they created at least one genre in which Bob Dylan's own work got a new kind of hearing, and they provided the stimulus to radical change in that work itself.

[The Byrds: 'Mr. Tambourine Man', Columbia 43271, US 1965; 'All I Really Want to Do', Columbia 43332, US 1965; 'Turn! Turn! Turn!', Columbia 43424, US 1965; 'My Back Pages', Columbia 44504, US, 1967; *Mr. Tambourine Man*, Columbia CL-2372/CS-9172/CK-9172, US, 1965; *Turn! Turn! Turn!*, Columbia CL-2454/ CS-9254/CK-9254, US, 1965; *Fifth Dimension*, Columbia CL-2549/CS-9349/CK-9349, US, 1966; *Younger Than Yesterday*, Columbia CL-2642/CS-9442/CK-9442, 1967; *The Notorious Byrd Brothers*, Columbia CL-2775/CS-9575/ CK-9575, US, 1968; *Sweetheart of the Rodeo*, Columbia CS-9670/CK-9670, US, 1968.

Bob Dylan & the Byrds: 'Mr. Tambourine Man', LA, 24 Feb 1990, telecast Showtime Network, US, 30 Oct 1990 & released *The Byrds*, Columbia Legacy CK46773, US, 1990. The Beefeaters: 'Please Let Me Love You', Elektra 45013, US, 1964.]

Photography by Sherry Rayn Barnett

T-Bone Burnett

Charles Sawyer

Paul Butterfield

The Carter Family

Th Byrds & Bob Dylan promo shot, 1965

Arvhives of Traditoinal Music, Indiana University

Hoagy Carmichael

Cage, Buddy [1946 -] Buddy Cage was born in Toronto in 1946, where at age 11 he learnt Hawaiian guitar, shifting over to pedal steel after his tutor discovered 'Nashville tuning' in the late 1950s. He won talent shows and conventions galore and was an unrivalled Canadian player at 15. In Toronto he worked in a country band that made cover albums (George Jones covers, for example) and backed visiting Grand Ole Opry stars—which is how the youthful Cage got to play with LEFTY FRIZZELL near the end of that fine artist's life. (Cage was a fan. 'He was drunk, he kept forgetting words. . . . He'd say "I'm sorry, man," and I'd say "It's OK, Lefty."') Cage then played on Anne Murray's first five albums and for RONNIE HAWKINS, who, disappointingly, also required only straight country playing from him.

Cage has a black tattoo of Chinese lettering covering one whole side of his neck. 'Loosely translated,' he says, 'it means "insane musician."' He has not only always been the rebel type, in music and in daily life ('I was just a smart-ass punk-ass kid'), but more interestingly he places himself on the political Left, has always been hostile to the redneck culture he found in Nashville and is proud that it was 'stoned hippies' like him who effected much radical change in the late 1960s:

> 'We weren't country Nashville, redneck hillbilly guys, we were, you know, like in '68. . . . you know think of the time—the race riots, the racial injustice, the injustice to women, the war. All of that shit. We voted a crook out of office—the presidential office. We ended up changing the voting age to 18 by *three years* man, you know. We were involved in our time. What do you mean we were just a bunch of stoned hippies?!'

Cage is best known for his work with New Riders of the Purple Sage, into which he moved via the legendary 1968 band the Great Speckled Bird ('legendary' as in no-one listens to but everyone remembers the name).

He joined the third line-up of New Riders, which existed as from November 1971, and in the end played on ten of their albums and was with them for 11 years. The first album he's on is *Powerglide* (1972), followed by *Gypsy Cowboy* and *Panama Red* (1973), *Home on the Road* and *Brujo* (1974).

On *Brujo*, at producer BOB JOHNSTON's request, they cut a version of Dylan's 'You Angel You', and a Columbia exec and friend of Dylan's, Ellen Bernstein, gave Dylan the album—as a result of which Cage was invited to play on the original New York sessions for *Blood on the Tracks* in September 1974. Cage's account is colourful:

> 'Ostensibly he was supposed to listen to "You Angel You", but when he heard the other things that I was playing with the Fuzz Tone, he said "Oh, is he going to be around? I'm going to be doing some more sessions in New York . . ." So. . . . I came over, but it was one of those situations where I was alone out in the studio. The studio was *huge*, man, and it was this cavernous feeling of "Oh God, man . . .". So, he says Phil Ramone was on the board. For Christ's sake, I mean no production credit at all. Just to do the *engineering*! It was like holy fuck man! This is big time! I'm sitting here, Dylan is over there, Phil is sitting here and MICK JAGGER is behind me, just being an observer. And I'm thinking "*Man*, this better be good!"
>
> 'Then Dylan says "Uh, Phil, play him the tunes." Here was like 18 of the most incredible masterpieces of Dylan that you could hope to hear. . . . I looked at Dylan, and I looked at Ramone, and I said "What the fuck am I supposed to do with *those*?! They're masterpieces, they are finished!" Dylan went "Oh, thank you man, but I would like for you to get some stuff on there." I went [sigh] "I honestly don't know where to begin." He said "Phil, play them again: play him the tunes." 18 more fucking tunes! So finally I kind of bookmarked "Meet Me in the Morning" and a couple, three more is all.
>
> 'But the funny thing was, the way that I was used to recording was, I will record over everything. You start the tape and I will start and at the end of the tape I will give you two or three, four versions of it. You have extra tracks—till I burn out spiritually and then you could do whatever you want in the final mix. Dylan *hated* that, man. I did one take, then two takes, then I'm going to offer one more. Then I did like a third take and then there was like this *silence*. The red light would go off, end of the song, and I was sitting there, and *all fucking alone:* you had to see this place. . . . You could barely see through the glass: you could just see Ramone . . . with his head in his hands. Finally . . . Dylan . . . walks out and . . . sticks his boot tips under my pedal board and he says "*The first six verses are singing! You don't play! The last verse is playing! You play!*" Then he turns around and walks out.
>
> 'I was stunned. . . . I looked through the glass and I saw Phil and them go like this [waves his hand in the air]. Like, there he goes again, right? Just in that split second the old punk ass came out. Normally it wouldn't, but just in that situation I said, Fuck you, Jack. I *deserve* to be here you little son of a bitch. . . . I knew what he wanted, and so Phil hit the foldback and he said "Buddy, do you want to practice one out?" I said "No, hit the tape." . . . the little red light comes

on and I'm thinking you little motherfucker, you're not getting away with this. . . .

'I just played it just like he wanted it, I took the direction and stuff like that. Then when it came out to the end, I played the end in one take and I had the picks off and the bar down before the red light was off. I was walking out of the room, and I'm walking *hard* man, and I pushed open the fucking door and Dylan is sitting back in the control room and he leaned back and said "*Hah!*" . . . Dylan says to Phil "Play it man, it was *great!*" . . . after the playback . . . I said "Bob, that was the toughest three and half minutes of my life. . . . Not playing it but sitting here listening to it with you." He said "Can you go out and do some more?"'

So Cage overdubbed steel guitar onto 'Call Letter Blues' (released in 1991 on *Bootleg Series Vols. 1–3*), the backing track which was re-used for the released track 'Meet Me in the Morning'; and onto 'You're a Big Girl Now'. He played too on the session of September 18, when Dylan made a number of attempts at 'Buckets of Rain', none of which have circulated.

Cage resumed life with the New Riders of the Purple Sage, whose next album, *Oh What a Mighty Time* (1975), the last of their Columbia albums, included 'Farewell Angelina'. After that they switched to MCA and in 1978 Cage quit and co-formed the San Francisco All Stars, rejoined New Riders in 1980 and left again in '82 (though they reunited for a one-off in October 2001). He worked in a trio with RICK DANKO in 1987 and toured Australia with THE BAND in 1988, but he spent most of the 1980s swamped by an alcoholism far more incapacitating than the drugs habits of earlier years. Near the end of the decade he attended an AA meeting, and it saved his life. He's stayed sober ever since. 'One day at a time.'

[Buddy Cage: all quotes from the undated interview by J.B. Arnold, posted on Cage's website *www.buddycage.net/psga/interview.htm*, seen online 11 Jan 2006. New Riders of the Purple Sage: *Powerglide*, Columbia US (CBS 64843, UK), 1972; *Gypsy Cowboy*, Columbia (CBS 65008), 1973; *Panama Red*, Columbia (CBS 65687), 1973; *Home on the Road*, Columbia (CBS 80060), 1974; *Brujo*, Columbia, 1974; *Oh What a Mighty Time*, Columbia, 1975; *New Riders*, MCA, US, 1976; *Who Are Those Guys?*, MCA, 1977; *Marin County Line*, MCA, 1977; *Feelin' Alright*, A&M, US, 1980.]

'Call Letter Blues' & 'the shock of recognition' Chapter 9 of MICHAEL GRAY's *Song & Dance Man III: The Art of Bob Dylan* was called 'Even Post-Structuralists Oughta Have the Pre-War Blues' because its study of Dylan's use of the blues emphasised areas of connection between these relatively new and old topics. A useful way into this subject is the preface of Michael Taft's pioneering book *Blues Lyric Poetry: A Concordance*, in which he stresses the communality, open-endedness and multi-layered nature of the blues.

First, Taft explains that in constructing a folkloric, rather than a literary, concordance you have an *open-ended* and more or less infinite corpus of work to deal with, instead of a known, finite one; there are problems, in other words, in *defining the text*. This brings the Dylan scholar to the core of the divide between a literary and an oral culture and to Dylan's pertinence to these matters, as someone who straddles the oral folkloric cultures of the ballads and the blues *and* the literary culture, and who moves his own extraordinary fusion of it all forward into the *new* oral culture—the *non-linear, postmodernist* culture—of MARSHALL McLUHAN's global village; an artist who, almost at the very moment of 'going electric', proclaimed the death of the eye (book) and the re-emergence of the mouth (oral noise).

As we touch on these concerns of contemporary folklorists and issues raised by a concordance of *traditional* pre-World War II songs, what should hove into view but the *postmodernist* concerns (and the very language) of post-structuralism. For what NEIL CORCORAN wrote of 'Tangled Up in Blue' is as true of the whole culture of the old blues: 'it refuses the consolations of the finished in favour of a poetics of process, of constant renewal, of performance rather than publication.'

Taft brings these post-structuralist concerns yet closer, stressing one overriding point about the structure of blues lyrics and the functioning of the blues as an oral cultural form (and in making the point also explains the fundamental reason for having the concordance):

'. . . the essence of the blues is the blues couplet. Indeed, the nature of this type of song is such that one might very well define the genre as one big blues composed of a large but finite number of couplets, lines and formulaic phrases; each individual text is but a sub-text of these couplets . . . the concordance reveals formulaic and linguistic repetitions in the corpus.

'I came to realize that the blues singers employed a type of formulaic structure in the composition of [the lyrics of] their songs . . . somewhat similar to that of epic singers far removed in space and time from these Afro-American artists. . . . I had to re-order or "deconstruct" lines and phrases . . . the purpose of a concordance is to re-order a text so that the analyst might visualize it in a new way . . .'

From here Taft at once shows how the blues concordance and the concerns of current folklore studies yield special insights into the gist of lit-crit post-structuralism; thus the blues bring us right back to Dylan's post-structuralist critics, STEPHEN SCOBIE and AIDAN DAY. Taft writes: '. . . in the case of folklore this jumbling of the text also reveals the way the singer and his audience *see* the text . . .' [emphasis added] This converges directly with what Day says about how we *see* altogether: how our minds give us 'this jumbling of the text' of our past. Taft goes on:

> 'Because of the formulaic nature of the blues . . . when a singer sings a phrase or line, both he and his audience recognize that particular part of the song. Perhaps semi-consciously, they compare this specific singing of the phrase with other singings of that phrase and phrases similar to it. In an instant, the singer and his audience compare the way the sung phrase is juxtaposed with others, both in the song being sung and in other songs. . . . Thus, every phrase in the blues has the potential of a literary richness far beyond its specific usage in one song.'

Taft quotes from sleevenotes by Pete Welding, one of the few to have discussed this property of the blues lyric:

> 'The blues is most accurately seen as a music of re-composition. That is, the creative bluesman is the one who imaginatively handles traditional elements and who, by his realignment of commonplace elements, shocks us with the familiar. He makes the old newly meaningful to us . . . providing the listener with what critic Edmund Wilson described as "the shock of recognition", a pretty accurate description . . . of the process of re-shaping and re-focusing of traditional forms in which the blues artist engages.'

This 'process of re-shaping and re-focusing' was often a deliberate one on the part of the individual creative bluesman. In *For What Time I Am in This World*, Colin Linden describes visiting Tampa Red in a nursing home on Chicago's South Side: 'He said. . . . "When you make records, take some from me and some from everybody else to make it your own way"'. And BLIND WILLIE McTELL said that when writing 'The Dyin' Crapshooter's Blues' he 'had to steal music from every which way to get it—to get it to fit.'

As Taft adds:

> 'If one were to illustrate how the audience undergoes this "shock of recognition", how the mental processes of the listener bring about this shock, one would construct something like a concordance. Each word and each phrase would be lined up against all other words and phrases which are similar to it in all the songs in which the phrase occurred. By looking down a page in the concordance . . . one sees in an instant what must occur for the listener at the moment of "shock". Both the singer and his audience automatically re-order and deconstruct the text as it is being sung; that constitutes their method of appreciation and the basis of their understanding of the blues. . . . The computer concordance is simply a concrete representation of this intuitive process.'

How well all this relates to Dylan and his achievement—including Welding's description of the creative bluesman's way of working, which so aptly applies to Dylan himself: 'the creative bluesman is the one who imaginatively handles traditional elements and who, by his realignment of commonplace elements, shocks us with the familiar. He makes the old newly meaningful to us . . .'

In illustration of this, consider Dylan's 1970s 'Call Letter Blues', recorded at the *Blood on the Tracks* sessions, left off the album but issued on the *Bootleg Series Vols. 1–3* in 1991. This is the lyric: 'Well I walked all night long, hearin' them church bells tone / Yes I walked all night long, listenin' to them church bells tone / Either someone needing mercy or maybe be somethin' I done wrong. / When your friends come by for you, I don't know what to say / When your friends come by for you, I don't know what to say / I just can't face up to tell 'em, honey you just went away. / The children cry for mother, I tell 'em mother took a trip / Well the children cry for mother, I tell 'em mother took a trip / Well I walk on pins and needles—I hope my tongue don't slip. / Well I gaze at passing strangers in case I might see you / Yes I gaze at passing strangers in case I might see you / But the sun goes around the heavens, and another day just drives on through. / Way out in the distance, I know you're with some other man / Way out in the distance, I know you're with some other man / But that's alright, baby, you know I always understand. / Call-girls in the doorway all giving me the eye / Call-girls in the doorway all giving me the eye / But my heart's just not in it—I might as well pass right on by. / My ears are ringin', ringin' like empty shells / My ears are ringin', ringin' like empty shells / Well it can't be no guitar player; it must be convent bells.'

This is a blues of the highest order: carefully constructed, with real artistic detachment—to create what may be one of the most rawly autobiographical blues songs ever put on record. All through it, there is a tense and multi-layered struggle between a lashing out and a stepping back. It seethes with the vitriol of bitterness, the rage of betrayal, but in the midst of it, the singer fights for, and achieves, moments of wry equilibrium.

This warring of opposites is present everywhere. The neatly structured song may begin and end with bells, but there's slippage and disparity here, from the certainty of 'hearing them church bells' to the uneasy conjecture of 'it must be convent bells'. The song also begins and ends with an either/or. The opening verse's 'Either . . .' starts with the narrator's compassion for a vaguely envisaged 'someone needing', out there, before suddenly turning, with less compassion, on the self. The closing either/or of the song makes strongly contrasting intuitive leaps between the secular, mobile, sexually active associations of that 'guitar player' and the timeless austerity of those 'convent bells'.

In between, there's the beautiful simplicity of that line in which complete strangers might somehow include the intimately known 'you'. There's the quiet topsy-turvy joke of the narrator's not responding to the call-girls because his 'heart's just not in it'—the heart being, after all, exactly what *isn't* involved in such exchanges. There are the conflicts between all these people in their different rôles: the woman at the centre who is absent friend, absent mother, absent lover; the man who is the lover walking all night long, ears ringing 'like empty shells', the social diplomat handling the unknowingly intrusive enquiries of those 'friends', and the protective father.

Given this savage pull between the fury of betrayal and the galvanising of inner strength, it is a deft touch, psychologically right, that the song contains one of Dylan's characteristic bumpings-together of two clichés to produce something new: furious duty walks a razor's edge on the surreally painful, black-humorously vivid 'I walk on pins and needles—I hope my tongue don't slip'. In the same verse, there is the equal deftness of that ambiguous 'I tell 'em mother took a trip', which lets us hear the attempted reassurance to the children that their mother is only temporarily absent, yet gives us the very different message that he feels her 'trip' is into a kind of madness, of aberrational abandonment; and Dylan's vocal delivery, unstoppering all the narrator's raw fury the first time he hits that word 'trip', vividly brings to life the bitter ambiguity of this pun. And topping this with a further truth, he uses the opportunity afforded by the song's blues structure to re-sing this same line as if in a different mood, this time not in fury but resignedly, more mindful of the part of him that is the adult guardian than the part which is the spurned child-man.

It has always been a strength arising out of this 'limitation' of the form, in the hands of its best practitioners, to effect a change of feeling across the repeated line. When, here, Dylan traces this particular shift of feeling, he is also enacting precisely what the blues as a form can achieve at all times, since it is not a music for making people angry and miserable but for engendering resilience against anger and misery.

In achieving this complex surging of feeling, Dylan draws on the blues form itself yet more deeply. Its very familiarity, its commonality of language, woven in among those parts of the lyric that are Dylan's alone, allows him to allude to other blues, and other songs of his own, and so to bring other voices into the tumult, other reverberations. The upshot is that 'Call Letter Blues' demonstrates beautifully how 'the shock of recognition', always within reach in the blues, can be activated—in this case many times over—not only as random soundings in the deep pool of the listener's subconscious but consciously too, to specific, pointed effect.

Consider how one or two of these work, starting with a case where the resonance from a familiarity in the lyric can only be *un*conscious. It is impossible, now, to hear that 'I gaze at passing strangers' followed by those 'call-girls in the doorway . . . I might as well pass right on by' without hearing the echo, from underneath, of lines Bob Dylan didn't write until six or seven years later: the lines from 'Every Grain of Sand' in which, he sings, 'I gaze into the doorway of temptation's angry flame / And every time I pass that way I always hear my name'. This echo, unstriven for but par for the course, has the effect of emphasising as you listen to 'Call Letter Blues' that aspect of the narrator's plight common to both songs, which is the bleak gulf between him and the night-world he finds himself wandering, and between the distraction of temptation and the real quest for passion lost or to be worked for.

The most striking echo from other work of Dylan's comes from that 'Way out in the distance', which jangles with the presence of 'Way out in the wilderness a cold coyote calls', from 'The Ballad of Hollis Brown', and 'Outside in the distance a wildcat did growl', from 'All Along the Watchtower'. The effect is that behind the 'Call Letter Blues' line we feel that Hollis Brown bleakness, we feel that wind begin to howl, and the singer's attitude to that 'some other man' is coloured in for us by the parallel conjured out of the earlier songs—the parallel of the predator: 'Way out in the wilderness a cold coyote calls'; 'Outside in the distance a wildcat did growl'; 'Way out in the distance I know you're with some other man.'

We set it down on paper one line after the other, but as the 'shock of recognition' works, it all comes through at once, the echoes of the older lines deepening the meaning and resonance of the line being sung.

Different echoes are sounded at the start of the song. When Dylan sings in the opening line that he is 'hearin' them church bells tone', one of the things we might recognise him as hearing is the church bell tone that BLIND LEMON JEFFERSON imitates on the guitar in his performance of 'See That My Grave Is Kept Clean', which the young Bob Dylan had certainly been listening to. And in writing 'Call Letter Blues' in 1974, Bob Dylan may or may not remember that the similar phrase he uses to end the second line, 'listenin' to them church bells tone', is the last line of a song he wrote himself many years earlier, in 1961–62, 'Ballad for a Friend'. But whether he remembers this or not, it was already, back then, a line he knew he was picking up wholesale from the great common-stock storehouse of blues lyric poetry, and its chime, in every one of the old blues songs that shared it, is always the sound of death come around, or death nearby. By their very familiarity as a blues-song image, those toning church bells at the beginning of 'Call Letter Blues' (a title that is itself an echo: of the far more common blues title 'Death Letter Blues') help signal the presence of the fear of loss. So it is that the familiar in the blues can inform and intensify the new.

So it is too that in the process of recognising cross-currents in Dylan's own corpus, we deconstruct and re-order *his* 'text' in our minds. When Taft says that 'If one were to illustrate how the audience undergoes this "shock of recognition", how the mental processes of the listener bring about this shock, one would construct something like a concordance', with each word and each phrase lined up against all other words and phrases similar to it in all the songs in which the phrase occurred, we can get a sense of the truth of this simply by looking at the Index of Titles, First Lines and Key Lines at the back of Dylan's *Lyrics 1962–1985*. This acts like the fragments of a Dylan Concordance. Let your eye drift down these few pages and you'll get a sense of the process at work. But with or without a concordance, the deepest disturbance and the deepest pleasure yielded by those 'shocks of recognition' comes when they rise out of the music, as with 'Call Letter Blues'.

[Michael Taft: *Blues Lyric Poetry: A Concordance* (3 vols.), New York: Garland, 1984. Neil Corcoran: 'Going Barefoot: Thinking About Bob Dylan's Lyrics', *Telegraph* 27, Romford, UK, summer 1987. Pete Welding quoted in Taft from 'Big Joe and Sonny Boy: The Shock of Recognition', *Big Joe Williams and Sonny Boy Williamson*, Blues Classics BC-21, Berkeley, 1969. Colin Linden in Bill Usher, ed.: *For What Time I Am in This World*, London: Peter Martin, 1977. Blind Willie McTell: spoken intro to 'The Dyin' Crapshooter's Blues', Atlanta, Sep 1956, *Blind Willie McTell: Last Session*, Prestige Bluesville 1040, Bergenfield, NJ, 1961 (Transatlantic PR1040, UK, 1966), CD-reissued Prestige Bluesville Original Blues Classics OBCCD-517-2 (BV-1040), US, 1992. Blind Lemon Jefferson: 'See That My Grave Is Kept Clean', Chicago, c.Feb 1928, *American Folk Music*, Folkways FP251-253, NY, 1952.

Bob Dylan: 'Ballad for a Friend', NY, Jan 1962, unreleased music-publishing demo; 'Call Letter Blues', NY, 16 Sep 1974, the *Bootleg Series Vols. 1–3*, 1991.]

Campbell, Larry [1955 -] Larry Campbell is older than he looks. Born in New York City on February 21, 1955, he grew up in the city to become a near-ubiquitous multi-instrumentalist session player: an old friend of HAPPY TRAUM (he first plays on his album *Bright Morning Stars* in 1980), which gives him a connection to Dylan's folk years; a player on the 75th Anniversary album by the Dixie Hummingbirds, *Diamond Jubilation*, which connects him to BAND members LEVON HELM and GARTH HUDSON and so to both the Basement Tapes era of Dylan's career and to his gospel years (the album includes Dylan's song 'City of Gold'); he worked for a lengthy period with Kinky Friedman, and his first album as a session player was on ROB STONER's album *Patriotic Duty* in 1980, giving him two links to the Dylan era of the Rolling Thunder Revue.

But in fact Larry Campbell's own experience of Dylan events stretches back to within months of the Basement Tapes era. As performer Rick Robbins recounts: 'Larry and I were trading stories. I knew I had a good 10 years on him and I was telling him about the time I went to Carnegie Hall in 1968 with ARLO [GUTHRIE] for the Tribute to WOODY GUTHRIE. Bob Dylan had been out of public view for a long time, and that night he made a surprise appearance with The Band. I was going on about what a special show it was and who was there and all that, and Larry said, "Yeah, I know, I was there." I said—"Really!!?", and he said, "Yeah, I was in the audience with my parents. I was 9 years old."' (In fact, he was almost 13, but '9' makes a better story.)

He has also played on Shawn Colvin's excellent *Cover Girl* and Edie Brickell's début solo album *Perfect Picture Morning* (both 1994), Joan Osborne's 1995 *Relish* (which includes a 'Man in the Long Black Coat'), JUDY COLLINS' pointless 1998 album of re-recordings *Both Sides Now* (which includes 'Blowin' in the Wind' and 'The Times They Are a-Changin''), albums by Steve Forbert and a hundred others besides, right up to Happy Traum's 2005 album *I Walk the Road Again*. He plays too on WILLIE NELSON's version of Dylan's 'He Was a Friend of Mine', used on the soundtrack of the 2005 film *Brokeback Mountain*. He also produces albums, has made a solo album of his own (*Rooftops*, 2005) and generally impressed all who work with him. Musician Kenny Davis says this: 'Larry has always been better at everyone's else's instrument than they were; a fine blues singer, extraordinarily versatile, not only with the number of instruments, but the diversity of styles he plays. I'd say the one thing that set him apart from every other player I know from that time was that Larry was *always* practicing.'

That certainly sets him apart from Bob Dylan—but centrally, Larry Campbell became a long-serving and stalwart member of Dylan's Never-Ending Tour band, replacing JOHN JACKSON in 1997. Slow 'to settle in', as ANDREW MUIR notes, when he did he stuck it out right through till the last night of the last leg of 2004. He first played with the band on the night of Dylan's début in Newfoundland, at St. John's Memorial University on March 31, 1997, and he last played at Allston, Massachusetts, on November 21, 2004.

He arrived as lead guitarist (electric and acoustic) and then after playing violin early on in his time with the band expanded his range until by the end of 1999 he had also played pedal steel guitar, lap steel guitar, electric and acoustic slide guitar, dobro, bouzouki and mandolin, and by 2000 had added the cittern.

On record, he plays on the JOHNNY CASH song 'Train of Love', video'd and taped at an unknown location in March 1999 for inclusion on the Cash tribute album *Kindred Spirits* (unreleased on record until 2002 but the footage televised April 18, 1999 as part of TNT's 'All-Star Tribute to Johnny Cash' TV special); on 'Things Have Changed'; on *"Love and Theft"*; on the re-make of 'Gonna Change My Way of Thinking' made by Dylan and MAVIS STAPLES in 2002, issued on *Gotta Serve Somebody: The Gospel Songs of Bob Dylan* (2003); on Dylan's *Secrets of the Ya-Ya Sisterhood* track 'Waitin' for You'; on various live recordings like the CD singles of 'Love Sick', the Dylan Las Vegas performance from March 1, 1999 of 'Friend of the Devil', released on the various artists tribute album *Stolen Roses: Songs of the Grateful Dead* in 2000, and on Dylan's soundtrack item for the film *Gods and Generals*, ''Cross the Green Mountain', on the video for which Campbell can also be glimpsed plodding through the mud.

He played when Dylan performed with Joan Osborne on the TV show 'The '60s', on Hallowe'en 1998, from which their shared 'Chimes of Freedom' was released on the 1999 various artists album *The '60s—TV Soundtrack*; in May 2000 on 'Red Cadillac and a Black Moustache', Dylan's charming studio-recorded contribution to the rockabilly retrospective album *Good Rockin' Tonight—The Legacy of Sun Records* (released 2001); on 'Return to Me', the Dean Martin song Dylan recorded for 'THE SOPRANOS' and 'I Can't Get You Off of My Mind', the HANK WILLIAMS song he recorded for the tribute album *Timeless* (both issued 2001). He was also in the band for a live satellite-feed performance of 'Things Have Changed' from Australia broadcast at the Academy Awards show on March 26, 2001 and the live televised performance of 'Cry a While' at the Grammy Awards in LA on February 27, 2002. He also plays in the band on the 2003 film *Masked & Anonymous*, filmed in July 2002 (and on its soundtrack album).

In the end Larry Campbell played 852 concerts in Dylan's band and most people rated his contributions highly. He also lent an air of flowing-locked, bandit-moustachioed, gambling-man glamour to the look of the band while still managing to radiate easy-going good nature. Others found him just a little bit dull.

[Larry Campbell: *Rooftops*, Treasure, US, 2005. Various Artists: *The '60s—TV Soundtrack*, Mercury/Polygram 314 538 743-2, US, 1999. Bob Dylan & band: 'Friend of the Devil', Las Vegas, 1 Mar 1999, *Stolen Roses: Songs of the Grateful Dead*, Grateful Dead SDCD4073, US, 2000.]

Campbell, Mike [1950 -] Michael Campbell was born in Panama City, Florida, on February 1, 1950. He learnt the guitar and in 1970 dropped out of the University of Florida in Jacksonville to aim at a career in music. After forming a short-lived band named Dead or Alive, he joined TOM PETTY and BENMONT TENCH in Mudhutch, which got as far as a record deal with Shelter in LA, but the album they made in 1974 was shelved. Mudhutch mutated into TOM PETTY & THE HEARTBREAKERS in 1975. Campbell proved an adroit co-writer of songs with Petty, a competent producer (not only co-producing many of the group's albums but Petty's solo albums too) and above all one of 'only a handful of guitarists who can claim to have never wasted a note', as *Guitar World* magazine put it. He has a side-band called the Dirty Knobs (a name especially unalluring to British ears), and has written songs for JOHNNY CASH, ROGER McGUINN, Don Henley, Fleetwood Mac and others.

Mike Campbell's first working encounter with Dylan came long before the Tom Petty & the Heartbreakers tours of 1986 and '87. On April 27, 1981, he was brought in on studio sessions Dylan was working on in Los Angeles (Campbell's friend Benmont Tench had been at earlier sessions off and on all month), and played guitar on several takes each of new songs 'Need a Woman', 'Dead Man, Dead Man' and 'In the Summertime', and one of 'Watered-Down Love'. None made it onto the album that eventually emerged, *Shot of Love*, and no unissued material has circulated; but the fourth take of 'Need a Woman' was officially released ten years later on the *Bootleg Series Vols. 1–3*.

On December 6, 1984, in a studio in Hollywood, Campbell, Tench and Heartbreaker HOWIE EPSTEIN backed Dylan's attempts at 'New Danville Girl', 'Queen of Rock'n'Roll' (almost certainly a revival of an obscure slice of borderline rockabilly issued as a single by one Lewis Weber from 1959) and a song that might be called 'Look Yonder'. Their recording of 'New Danville Girl' may or may not be the one later overdubbed and turned into 'Brownsville Girl'. (Another version of 'New Danville Girl' was recorded with different musicians earlier the same day.) Eight days later Campbell, Tench and Epstein were back in the studio recording 'Something's Burning, Baby' and, somewhat surprisingly, 'The Girl I Left Behind' (a folk song Dylan had sung exquisitely on radio in October 1961). These were sessions for the album *Empire Burlesque*, and with later overdubs 'Something's Burning, Baby' was issued on that album. Campbell and Epstein (without Tench) cut another track, 'Seeing the Real You at Last' on January 28, 1985 and on February 5 added 'Trust Yourself' and 'I'll Remember You'. (They had another run at 'Queen of Rock'n'Roll' while they were at it, but this too remains unissued and uncirculated.) On February 14 they recorded various songs that didn't make it onto the album, including 'Straight A's in Love' and the marvellously sinister 'Waiting to Get Beat', plus another track that did make it, the awful 'Emotionally Yours'.

That fall they were reunited with Dylan as part of the backing group Tom Petty & the Heartbreakers provided for him at Farm Aid. Then came the group's tours with Dylan in 1986 and 1987, and 15 years later a couple of shared concerts in New Jersey in 2003.

Mike Campbell is still playing, writing and producing, working with and without Tom Petty & the Heartbreakers. The Dirty Knobs are still going too.

[Unspecified *Guitar World* quote from Wikipedia online; Lewis Weber: 'Queen of Rock'n'Roll', *nia*, Vim K8OW-4759/60 & Scottie 1304, US, 1959. Bob Dylan: 'The Girl I Left Behind', NY, 29 Oct 1961, live on WNYC Radio.]

'Can You Please Crawl Out Your Window?' [1965] Perhaps the first to truly mark the arrival of Dylan's fully realised new complex type of song was 'Can You Please Crawl Out Your Window?', which he recorded twice in 1965, once at *Highway 61 Revisited* sessions and once at *Blonde on Blonde* sessions, using different musicians each time. It literally was a pivotal song (but much ignored).

In a classic record-company cock-up, both versions were issued as a single (though with little commercial success). In July he recorded it with AL KOOPER on organ, MIKE BLOOMFIELD on guitar, HARVEY GOLDSTEIN (aka Harvey Brooks) or RUSS SAVAKUS on bass, PAUL GRIFFIN or an unknown on piano, and BOBBY GREGG on drums. This version was released, mistitled 'Positively 4th Street', and then withdrawn. In November, with either Al Kooper or GARTH HUDSON on organ but with ROBBIE ROBERTSON on guitar, RICHARD MANUEL on piano, RICK DANKO on bass and Bobby Gregg again on drums, Dylan recorded it again. This version was duly released properly.

In this song, the language flashes and sculpts, takes a hundred different photographs, captures a human possibility that comes across as always having been there, recurring and recurring, but never detected or seen in focus before. It needn't be a relationship we have been through for it to impress us as true—as accurately stated and real; and only the insensitive listener would feel a need to ask what the song 'means'. It almost stands up just as words on the page; and while the recordings are fine things, the language of the song is at least as interesting as its music.

Consider the phrase 'fist full of tacks'. Dylan uses that in at least three main ways. First, it gives us a visual image of sorts. It directs our awareness towards the man's hands: and these are kept before us implicitly when we come, later in the same verse, to his 'inventions' and again later when we come to 'hand him his chalk'. Second, 'fist full of tacks' gives us a vivid metaphor at the same time as yielding a neat juxtaposition—for in the first half of the relevant line we get the man and the sweep of the room and then we zoom down to the tiny contents of his closed hand. (The same happens in the comparable example of 'You walk into the room / With a pencil in your hand', from 'Ballad of a Thin Man': that too yields a visual incongruity by its juxtapositioning, and uses the 'pencil' as a symbol, so that the two lines give us not only the man's entrance as others see it but also his own attitude, because to come in 'with a pencil in your hand' is plainly to be unreceptive to real life—to wish to be an observer and not a participant.) These metaphors are characteristic of Dylan, and take us all the way back to 'Talkin' New York', on his very first album, where he says 'A lot of people don't have much food on their table / But they got a lot of forks 'n' knives / And they gotta cut somethin'.' Those lines are explaining why his initial New York audiences were hostile: it is a figurative explanation. 'Fist full of tacks' operates similarly. It could be swapped, in a prose précis, with the word 'aggressively', and yet it does a lot more than 'aggressively' could do.

The third way it works is in establishing a tone of verbal precision—it is an incisive, sharp phrase—which is important throughout the song. It influences the sound, later on in the song, of words like 'test' and 'inventions', 'righteous' and 'box', and links up, in effect, with that phrase 'little tin women' in the final verse. 'Little tin women' is of exactly corresponding brittleness and precision. This impression is enforced in the music, too, by the guitar-work and the insistent cymbal strikes in particular and by various xylophonic percussive effects in general.

(In *Lyrics 1962–1985*, the phrase is given as 'little ten women', but this is surely a mishearing by the transcriber. An alternative mishearing, 'lilting women', is listed in 'Pardon, Monsieur, Am I Hearing You Right?' in *All Across the Telegraph: A Bob Dylan Handbook*, 1987. Neither so well suits—indeed the second contradicts—the chinking sharpness Dylan is chipping in with in the verses of the song. 'Little tin women' is surely right: Dylan had already used the phrase 'little tin men' in his poem 'jack o'diamonds', 1964, one of the poems forming *Some Other Kinds of Songs*, published as sleevenotes to *Another Side of Bob Dylan*, 1964: 'jack o'diamonds / wrecked my hand / left me here t'stand / little tin men play / their drums now'.)

Dylan provides a contrast to all this 'tin-tack' atmosphere: it is beautifully contradicted by that gangling (and warm) chorus line 'Use your arms and legs, it won't ruin you', where the words enact the motion, so that the listener is actually a part of the flailing limbs swimming out of the window—where, in other words, the sounds and impressions are rounded instead of thin, and soft rather than sharp. The whole chorus takes part in this exercise of contrast: the qualities of 'crawl', 'use', 'ruin', 'haunt', and Dylan's long-drawn-out 'want' are all antithetical to the qualities of that initial 'fist full of tacks'.

Consider too the tremendous line 'With his businesslike anger and his bloodhounds that kneel'. Until we isolate that line, it doesn't occur to our visual response to have our murky, semi-existent bloodhounds actually *kneeling*. Dogs cannot easily kneel at all; yet in the sense that they are humble/faithful/servile etc., they are kneeling, figuratively, while they stand. We meet the Dylan phrase accordingly: we visualise the atmosphere that corresponds to silent, standing bloodhounds ranged around the man: ranged, in fact, around *his* knee. By one of those Dylan tricks of transference, it is the man's knees that comes into our picture, and not the dogs' knees at all.

Dylan has never performed this quintessential mid-1960s song in concert.

(See also **Hornby, Nick**.)

[Bob Dylan: 'Can You Please Crawl Out Your Window?': NY, 30 Jul 1965, one take issued in error as 'Positively 4th Street', Columbia 4-43389, 1965; and NY, 30 Nov 1965, issued as Columbia 4-43477, 1966.]

'Canadee-i-o' [1993] See **American Civil War in *World Gone Wrong*, the.**

Cannon, Gus [1883 - 1979] See **blues, inequality of reward in.**

Carl XVI Gustav of Sweden [1946 -] Carl XVI Gustav Folke Hubertus, King of Sweden, was born in Stockholm on April 30, 1946, the fifth child but the first son of the then-heir to the throne Gustaf Adolf and Princess Sibylla of Sachsen-Coburg-Gotha. Prince Gustaf Adolf died in an air crash in Copenhagen in 1947; a Gustaf VI Adolf acceded to the throne in 1950 following the death of Gustaf V, and our Carl Gustaf became Crown Prince. (Do pay attention.) Then when Gustaf VI Adolf died on September 15, 1973, Crown Prince Carl Gustaf became King Carl XVI Gustav at the age of 27.

(Because he is Carl XVI and his next name is Gustaf, that means he isn't called Carl Gustav XVI but Carl XVI Gustav. So there. Why isn't he just called Carl XVI? This would surely be an FAQ, if there were such a section, on the website *www.royalcourt.se*, but there isn't.)

Serendipitously, the new king took as his motto 'For Sweden–With the times'; on May 15, 2000, in Stockholm, he found himself presenting Bob Dylan with a Berwaldhallen Polar Music Prize, bestowed by the Royal Swedish Academy of Music. The rather nice citation read:

> 'Bob Dylan's influence, as a singer-songwriter, on the development of 20th Century popular music is indisputable. His achievements encompass almost four decades of constantly changing modes of creativity, always innovative, but always based on American musical traditions and roots. Starting with folk music and reaching the heights of critical and public fame, he set aside the rules of the day, appearing no longer alone with his acoustic guitar but in the company of a rock and roll band. It was a development that required both integrity and determination, a move that cemented his rôle as one of the greatest rock artists of our time.
>
> 'Bob Dylan's ability to combine poetry, harmony and melody in a meaningful, often provocative context, has captivated millions in all age groups, and in most cultures and societies. Through his modest, persuasive musical approach, he has demonstrated an impressive ability to question the most determined political forces, to fight all forms of prejudice and to offer unflinching support for the less fortunate. Even those who might not have shared his views would find it impossible to argue against Bob Dylan's musical and poetic brilliance.'

Dylan accepted the award from the king without saying a word.

Carmichael, Hoagy [1899 - 1981] Hoagy Carmichael was born Hoagland Howard Carmichael on November 22, 1899 and raised in Bloomington, Indiana. He grew up to be a singer and actor but primarily a popular songwriter. His very first composition was called 'Freewheeling', and he also wrote a song titled 'Things Have Changed'. More famously he wrote or co-wrote, among many, many others, 'Stardust' and 'Georgia on My Mind'.

Carmichael is one of the many improbable people whose work and persona Dylan admires, possibly just to be perverse. Hoagy's photo is pinned up on the wall of the shack behind him on the photo by DANIEL KRAMER planned for the US hardback of Dylan's *Tarantula* but rejected (it's reproduced in Kramer's book *Bob Dylan*) and in the *Empire Burlesque* song 'Tight Connection to My Heart' Dylan names a Hoagy Carmichael composition. Dylan sings: 'Well, they're not showing any lights tonight / And there's no moon. / There's just a hot-blooded singer / Singing "Memphis in June"'.

'Memphis in June' was composed by Carmichael with lyrics by Johnny Mercer (who also wrote the lyric to 'Moon River', which Dylan sang one night on the Never-Ending Tour in tribute to the late STEVIE RAY VAUGHAN). Dylan's 'hot-blooded singer' is a neat small joke about Hoagy, whose many assets include a calculatedly lizard-like presence. It was a joke Dylan had retained from an earlier version of the song, then called 'Someone's Got a Hold of My Heart', which he'd recorded at the sessions for *Infidels*, the album before *Empire Burlesque*. Several performances of this have floated around, but the one eventually released officially, on the *Bootleg Series Vols. 1–3* in 1991, offered these alternative lines: 'I hear the hot-blooded singer / On the bandstand croon / "September Song", "Memphis in June"'. Clearly Dylan was determined to retain Hoagy, whatever other changes he made. ('September Song' was written by Maxwell Anderson and composed by Kurt Weill for the 1938 Broadway play *Knickerbocker Holiday*.)

'Memphis' was written for the 1945 George Raft film *Johnny Angel*, in which Carmichael played a philosophical singing cab driver. ('After that I was mentioned for every picture in which a world-weary character in bad repair sat around and sang or leaned on a piano'). Subsequent film rôles included being the pianist who sings 'Hong Kong Blues' in the Bogart-Bacall film *To Have and Have Not*, one of Dylan's favourite hunting-grounds for lyrics in the *Empire Burlesque* period.

The least hot-blooded cover version of 'Memphis in June' may be by Matt Monro, from 1962; the best (and 'on a bandstand croonin'') may be by Lucy Ann Polk, cut in July 1957 in Hollywood. Hoagy himself recorded the song in 1947 with Billy May & His Orchestra and again in 1956 with a jazz ensemble that included Art Pepper. Carmichael and Mercer also wrote that great song 'Lazy Bones'—in twenty minutes, in 1933—which was revisited magnificently in the 1960s by soul singer James Ray (who made the original US hits of 'If You Gotta Make a Fool of Somebody' and 'Itty Bitty Pieces'; in the UK he was unlucky enough to find these savaged in unusually distressing ways, even by the standards of British cover versions of the time, by Freddie & the Dreamers and Brian Poole in the first case and by the Rockin' Berries and Chris Farlowe in the second).

Carmichael played ranch-hand Jonesey in the 1959–60 season of the TV series 'Laramie'. In 1972 he was given an Honorary Doctorate by Indiana University back in Bloomington (which is where BETSY BOWDEN got *her* doctorate for a study of Bob Dylan's performance art that became her book *Performed Literature*).

Hoagy Carmichael died two days after Christmas, 1981. When a retrospective 4-LP box set of his work, *The Classic Hoagy Carmichael*, was issued in 1988, with copious notes by John Edward Hasse, Curator of American Music at the Smithsonian Institution, it was released and published jointly by the Smithsonian and the Indiana Historical Society. (American hobbyists are so lucky: there are always plenty of places to go for funding. Imagine trying to get funds to research, compile and write an accompanying book about Billy Fury from the British Museum and the Birkenhead Historical Society.) The Carmichael box set notes say this, among much else, and might just remind you of someone else (not Billy Fury):

> 'At first listeners may be distracted by the flatness in much of Carmichael's singing, and turned off especially by his uncertain intonation. The singer himself said, "my native woodnote and often off-key voice is what I call 'Flatsy through the nose'". But . . . one becomes accustomed to these traits and grows to appreciate and admire other qualities of his vocal performances, specifically his phrasing . . . intimacy, inventiveness and sometimes even sheer audacity. Also, many . . . evidence spontaneous and extemporaneous qualities, two important ingredients in jazz.'

[Hoagy Carmichael: *The Classic Hoagy Carmichael*, 4-LP set compiled & annotated by John Edward Hasse; issued as 4 LPs or 3 CDs, BBC BBC 4000 and BBC CD3007, UK, 1988; *Johnny Angel*, dir. Edwin L. Marin, written Steve Fisher, RKO, US, 1945. Daniel Kramer: *Bob Dylan*, New York: Citadel Press edn., 1991, p.127. Betsy Bowden: *Performed Literature*, Bloomington: Indiana University Press, 1982.]

Carradine, William [c.1896 - c.1958] William Carradine, born in Garden City, Louisiana, around 1896, became a splendidly obscure street singer known as CAT-IRON. BONNIE BEECHER recalls that around 1960 Dylan and HARVEY ABRAMS sat around in the 10 O'Clock Scholar in the Dinkytown area of Minneapolis mentioning obscure singers' names, and that she and Dylan met because she was able to join in. This was because she would go to Sam Goodys in New York to buy records, choosing 'any old record that looked like it had some kind of funky singer or blues singer . . . records by Cat-Iron, Rabbit Brown . . .'

The Cat-Iron record mentioned can only have been a newish copy of his LP *Cat-Iron Sings Blues & Hymns*, recorded by Fred Ramsey in Natchez, Mississippi (probably in 1957), and released on Folkways in 1958. It was his only record, the fruit of his only recording session. The tracks were traditional and gospel songs, including 'Poor Boy a Long, Long Way from Home', 'Don't Your House Look Lonesome' and 'When I Lay My Burden Down'. In May 1957, Cat-Iron had been recorded on film in Natchez for an item in that year's new TV documentary series 'Seven Lively Arts'.

Cat-Iron / William Carradine is understood to have died in Natchez in 1958. His track 'Jimmy Bell' was included on the 2003 CD *Classic Blues from Smithsonian Folkways*, and he was still achieving airplay, at least on the Poughkeepsie, New York, radio station WVKR, in November 2005, 109 years after he was born.

[Cat-Iron: Natchez MS, c.1957; *Cat-Iron Sings Blues & Hymns*, Folkways LP2389, NY, 1958. Filmed in Natchez, 28 May 1957; footage shown 'Seven Lively Arts', CBS-TV, *nia*, 1957. Various Artists: *Classic Blues from Smithsonian Folkways*, CD Smithsonian Folkways 40134, Washington, D.C., 2003. Bonnie Beecher, aka Jahanara Romney, quoted in Markus Wittman, 'The Wanted Man Interview: Jahanara Romney', *Telegraph* no.36, Romford, UK, summer 1990.]

Carroll, Lewis [1832–1898], echoes of Dylan's work occasionally recalls that of Lewis Carroll, born Charles Lutwidge Dodgson in Daresbury,

Cheshire, UK, on January 27, 1832. The relevant Carroll works are *Alice's Adventures in Wonderland* (1865; originally titled *Alice's Adventures Under Ground*) and *Through the Looking-Glass* (1871; full title *Through the Looking-Glass and What Alice Found There*).

If a substantial portion of Dylan's 'The Drifter's Escape' seems to remind us vaguely of the pack-of-cards trial scene in *Wonderland*, this is principally because it echoes the knowingly preposterous tone (and the metre) of many of the Lewis Carroll verses. The Dylan lines begin with this: 'Well the judge he cast his robe aside / A tear came to his eye / "You fail to understand," he said / "Why must you even try?"' and *Wonderland*'s 'The Lobster-Quadrille' includes this: '"What matters it how far we go?" his scaly friend replied. / "There is another shore, you know, upon the other side . . ."'—which fits the Dylan tune as if purpose-built: as indeed it does the verses read as 'evidence' in the card-pack trial; and it's easy to imagine Dylan singing this one: 'He sent them word I had not gone / (We know it to be true): / If she should push the matter on / What would become of you?'

Resemblance extends also, in *Looking-Glass*, through much of the poem 'The Walrus and the Carpenter', and while that book's song about Tweedledum and Tweedledee ends with 'Just then flew down a monstrous crow / As black as a tar-barrel / Which frightened both the heroes so / They quite forgot their quarrel', Dylan's 'Drifter's Escape' ends like this: 'Just then a bolt of lightning / Struck the courthouse out of shape / And while everybody knelt to pray / The drifter did escape.' Over 33 years later, Dylan namechecked Tweedledee and Tweedledum on the opening track of the album *"Love and Theft"*, in a song that gives a vivid, dark portrait of two feuding men whose lives are locked so tight together that they may, or may as well, be twins.

Last, but perhaps not least direct as an echo, in *Wonderland*'s 'The Mock Turtle's Story' there is a line from the Duchess—she is herself quoting from a popular song of the period—that Dylan reproduces all but verbatim in 'I Threw It All Away', released the year after 'The Drifter's Escape': '"'Tis so," said the Duchess: "and the moral of that is—'Oh, 'tis love, 'tis love, that makes the world go round!'"'

Lewis Carroll died in Guildford, Surrey, on January 14, 1898.

[Antonio Iriarte notes (letter to this writer, 9 Oct 2000) that the popular song quoted by the Duchess, unidentified in Martin Gardner's *The Annotated Alice* (New York: Clarkson N. Potter, 1960), is also mentioned in Charles Dickens' *Our Mutual Friend* (serialised 1864–65), Part IV, Chap. 5, *in fine*. Iriarte suggests that 'it could well be "'Tis Love that Makes the World Go Round", by R.S. Ambrose, an English composer active in the mid-19th Century.' In fact though born in England, Robert Steele Ambrose lived and died in Canada (born Chelmsford, Essex, 7 Mar 1824; died Hamilton, Ontario, 30 Mar 1908).]

Carter Family, the Ralph Peer discovered both JIMMIE RODGERS and the Carter Family, encountering them in Bristol, Virginia in April 1927, and first recording them there on August 1st that year. Their début tracks were the cheerily titled 'Bury Me Under the Weeping Willow', 'Little Log Cabin by the Sea', 'The Poor Orphan Child' and 'The Storms Are on the Ocean'.

The Carter Family consisted then of Alvin Pleasant Delaney Carter (known as A.P., born at Maces Springs, Virginia, on April 15, 1891), mostly on harmony vocals, his wife Sara (born Sara Dougherty in Flat Woods, Virginia, on July 21, 1898) on autoharp and guitar, and Sara's cousin Maybelle (born Maybelle Addington in Nickelsville, Virginia, on May 10, 1909) on vocals and guitar. Their phenomenal popular success, along with that of Rodgers, kept the Victor record company afloat through the Depression.

The advertisements for their shows (using an approach that would not, today, encourage such success) proclaimed: 'THIS PROGRAM IS MORALLY GOOD'. Their repertoire was a mix of old-time ballads and A.P.'s own songs, and their importance in the history of old-timey and country music is vast. HARRY SMITH would write of them in 1952, on his compilation LP set *AMERICAN FOLK MUSIC*, that 'Their 1927 records . . . are among the very first electrical recordings. Using autoharp chords, played by Sara (who usually leads the singing) and a guitar melodic line (Maybelle), their instantly recognizable rhythm has influenced every folk musician for the past 25 years.'

Dylan probably first heard them in Minneapolis when he was played the Smith compilation, on which they feature four times—giving them an unrivalled prominence on this 84-track set. Track 17 is their 'John Hardy Was a Desperate Little Man' (summarised by Smith as 'JOHN HARDY HELD WITHOUT BAIL AFTER GUNPLAY, GIRLS IN RED AND BLUE VISIT JAIL, WIFE AT SCAFFOLD'). The song is credited to A.P. Carter and the lead vocal is by Sara. Track 23 is another song Pop Carter claimed, 'Engine One-Forty-Three' ('GEORGIE RUNS INTO ROCK AFTER MOTHER'S WARNING. DIES WITH THE ENGINE HE LOVES'), though Smith quotes John Harrington Cox (in his *Folk Songs of the South*, 1925) as noting of this real-life narrative that it was 'probably composed by a worker in the round house at Hinton, West Virginia.' Track 67 is 'Single Girl, Married Girl', another A.P. Carter number (though, as Smith says, it is 'of a type frequently represented by such songs as "When I Was Single", "Lord, I Wish I Was a Single Girl Again", "The Sporting Bachelor" etc.'). And more pertinently, Track 53 is one more Pop Carter composition (allegedly), the lovely 'Little Moses', which Dylan took to singing live, and with much benign and seemly gravity, in the early 1990s. He débuted the song in Adelaide, Australia, at the start of his tour there on March 21, 1992 and played it a further 95 times between then and Wantagh, New York, on September 11, 1993.

A decade later the scripted chat on the Dylan and MAVIS STAPLES re-write of 'Gonna Change My Way of Thinking', recorded in 2002 and released on the Various Artists album *Gotta Serve Somebody: The Gospel Songs of Bob Dylan* in 2003, is a knowing and in-jokey echo of that on the 1931 novelty record 'The Carter Family and Jimmie Rodgers in Texas'. Chris Rollason has detected several further Carter touches in the same Dylan record: 'The "welcome table" in stanza 2 was already laid out in "River of Jordan" . . . while stanza 6 ("There are storms on the ocean / Storms out on the mountain too . . . / Oh Lord / You know I have no friend without you") combines elements from "The Storms Are on the Ocean" . . . and "Can't Feel at Home".' Rollason adds that there are other 'Dylan links, too, scattered across' the Carters' recorded work, one of which is this: '. . . the song "Meet Me by the Moonlight, Alone" . . . is an obvious precedent for the title and refrain of Dylan's [*"Love and Theft"* track] "Moonlight" . . .' He might have added that one of the tracks known to have been recorded at Dylan's May 1993 sessions for *World Gone Wrong* but left off the album was a version of the Carter Family's lovely 1930s song 'Hello Stranger'.

More generally, though, the Carter Family was a prime influence on the work of WOODY GUTHRIE—indeed he builds many of his old dustbowl jalopies on the chassis of the Carter songbook. Their 'Can't Feel at Home' becomes Guthrie's 'I Ain't Got No Home', which Dylan performed very early on in his career and again with THE BAND in 1968. Then again, much of the Carter repertoire was taken from traditional song, including a number of adaptations of CHILD ballads, as with 'Who's Gonna Shoe Your Pretty Little Feet?', which passed from the Carters to Guthrie and on to Dylan, who was performing it as early as 1960.

The Carter Family was open to black influence also. They often travelled around on song-collecting trips, frequently taking along the black singer-guitarist Leslie Riddles (Riddles learnt the tunes; A.P. wrote down the words). It was from Riddles that Maybelle Carter 'picked up many of her instrumental ideas,' notes Tony Russell, who adds that Riddles also 'had a friend in BROWNIE McGHEE . . . and he too used to be visited by A.P. in search of songs.'

Sometimes this traffic moved the other way. The only black artist to record 'John Hardy', LEADBELLY, said that he learnt the song from Guthrie, who learnt it, of course, from the Carters. Neither, though, gave him one ingredient on his recording: what blues critic Chris Smith calls 'Leadbelly's mournfully funky accordion arrangement'.

The Carter Family also recorded 'My Clinch Mountain Home' (from which RALPH STANLEY doesn't take his group name, since he's from Clinch Mountain himself), 'Motherless Children', 'Wabash Cannonball', 'See That My Grave Is Kept Green' [sic], 'The Old Rugged Cross', 'The East Virginia Blues', 'The Girl on the Greenbriar Shore' (which Dylan performed in Gothenberg, Sweden, and Dunkirk, France, on June 28 & 30, 1992) and many others with degrees of Dylan reverberation. Further songs in their repertoire include 'Are You Lonesome Tonight?', memorably revived by ELVIS PRESLEY in 1960 and 'Diamonds in the Rough', memorably revived by JOHN PRINE aeons later, in the early 1970s. (The Carters' 'Are You Lonesome Tonight?', with lead vocal by A.P., sounds nothing like Presley's, which probably came to him from Al Jolson via the Ink Spots; A.P. makes it sound like a Carter Family song—singing it more or less to the tune Woody Guthrie used later for his own 'Reuben James'.)

The Carter family begat June Carter, who married JOHNNY CASH. More precisely, Maybelle Carter, wife of Eck Carter, gave birth to Valerie June Carter on June 23, 1929 at home in Maces Springs, Virginia. After the Carters disbanded, Mother Maybelle & the Carter Sisters replaced them: Maybelle performing with her daughters Helen, Anita and June as from 1943. They duly teamed up with Chet Atkins, joined the Grand Ole Opry, encountered HANK WILLIAMS and Elvis and thus moved into a more modern musical world, but one they had helped to form in the first place. Johnny Cash became June's third husband and she his second wife. June and first husband Carl Smith begat Carlene Carter; Johnny and first wife Vivian Liberto begat Roseanne Cash.

June and Johnny performed 'It Ain't Me Babe', and Roseanne Cash joined Shawn Colvin and Mary Chapin Carpenter to harmonise on 'You Ain't Goin' Nowhere', at the so-called Bob Dylan 30th Anniversary Concert Celebration at Madison Square Garden on October 16, 1992. This programme was morally not so good.

[Carter Family: 'John Hardy Was a Desperate Little Man', Camden, NJ, 10 May 1928; 'My Clinch Mountain Home' & 'Little Moses', Camden, 14 Feb 1929; 'Engine One-Forty-Three' & 'Diamonds in the Rough', Camden, 15 Feb 1929; 'Motherless Children', Atlanta, GA, 22 Nov 1929; 'Wabash Cannonball', Atlanta, 24 Nov 1929; 'Can't Feel at Home', Charlotte, NC, 26 May 1931; 'The Carter Family and Jimmie Rodgers in Texas', Louisville, KY, 12 Jun 1931; 'See That My Grave Is Kept Green' & 'The Old Rugged Cross', Camden, 17 Jun 1933; 'The East Virginia Blues', Camden, 8 May 1934; 'Single Girl, Married Girl', NY, 8 May 1935; 'Hello Stranger', NY, 17 Jun 1937; 'Are You Lonesome Tonight?', NY, 8 Jun 1936; 'The Girl on the Greenbriar Shore', NY, 14 Oct 1941.

Compilations include *Original & Essential Carter Family Vol. 1*, Country Music History CMH112, US, 1973; *The Original and Great Carter Family*, RCA Camden 586, UK, *nia*, which includes 'Little Moses' and

'Diamonds in the Rough'); and the 5-CD set *The Carter Family 1927–1934*, JSP JSPCD7701, UK, 2001, which contains 127 tracks (surely far more than anyone sane would wish to listen to). Leadbelly: 'John Hardy', NY, late 1943.

Christopher Rollason quoted from his online posting seen 11 Jan 2006 at the Bob Dylan Who's Who website at *www.expectingrain.com/dok/who/c/carter family.html*. Other sources include Tony Russell, *Blacks Whites and Blues*, London: Studio Vista, 1970, pp.15 & 41, and his *Country Music Records: A Discography, 1921–1942*, New York: Oxford University Press, 2004, pp.187–95. Chris Smith, e-mail to the pre-war blues discussion group at *pre-war-blues@yahoogroups.com*, 12 Jan 2006.]

Carter, Rubin 'Hurricane' [1937 -] Rubin Carter was born in Paterson, New Jersey, on May 6, 1937. At age nine he was placed on probation and at 11 sent to the Jamesburg State Home for Boys. He ran away in 1954 and though only 5′8″ he signed up for the US Army and joined the Paratroopers. He was discharged in 1956. From then until 1961 he spent much of his time in jail for various different crimes. The zenith of his boxing career came soon after this; he went from unranked in 1962 to no.3 in 1963 and 1964.

He never rose higher. There is no truth to Dylan's claim in the song 'Hurricane', on the *Desire* album, that if Carter hadn't been arrested for murder 'he could-a been / The champion of the world'. His career was already on the slide. In 1965 his ranking fell to no.5 and in 1966 he was unranked. *The Ring* magazine for April 1966, six months before he was arrested, made this assessment: 'Since his defeat at the hands of Dick Tiger in New York last May, Rubin has won three and lost four. His only victories during that period were over two little-known fighters . . . and the erratic McClure. His most recent defeats have dropped Carter from his once high rating and killed his hopes of a crack at Dick Tiger's middleweight crown.'

The song, and Carter's life, turned upon the murder of two men and a woman at the Lafayette Bar and Grill in Paterson on the night of June 17, 1966, and the story of how these murders were followed up. Carter and his friend John Artis were questioned by police that night but released. Resuming his boxing, he lost to Rocky Rivero on August 6. On October 14 local small-time criminal Alfred P. Bello said in a signed a statement that he had seen Carter and Artis at the murder scene. They were arrested and indicted. On May 27, 1967 an all-white jury convicted them; the prosecution sought the death penalty but the jury recommended mercy; they were sentenced to life terms and taken to Rahway State Prison (now the East Jersey State Prison) in Woodbridge, New Jersey. In 1971 riots broke out there and several inmates were killed.

On April 30, 1974 Carter was transferred to the brutal Vroom Readjustment Unit at Trenton State Psychiatric Hospital. That July Carter's federal suit against the state for inflicting 'cruel and unusual punishment' succeeded and he was released from the unit. In September his book *The Sixteenth Round* was published, and Alfred P. Bello and a second witness, Arthur P. Bradley, claimed that they had been bribed and pressured into making false statements and denied that they had in fact seen Carter and Artis at the murder scene. Carter sent Dylan a copy of his book.

Dylan eventually read *The Sixteenth Round* and in May 1975 visited Carter in prison. (The photograph of the two men standing talking with the prison bars between them was staged later, however.) 'I realized,' said Dylan, 'that the man's philosophy and my philosophy were running down the same road, and you don't meet too many people like that.' In July 1975 Dylan and JACQUES LEVY wrote the first version of 'Hurricane', and recorded three takes of it on July 28, at the second session for the *Desire* album. On July 30, two further takes were attempted. On September 10, Dylan performed the song in public for the first time, along with 'Oh Sister' and 'Simple Twist of Fate', at the telerecording of the tribute TV program 'The World of JOHN HAMMOND' in Chicago, shown that December 13 on PBS (and simulcast on FM radio).

CBS lawyers insisted on lyric changes, and the album version was re-recorded on October 24. Six days later Dylan & Co. launched into the first Rolling Thunder Revue, giving 31 concerts and finishing at Madison Square Garden on December 8. This final concert was a benefit for Carter, titled 'The Night of the Hurricane', which included an appearance from MUHAMMAD ALI, then heavyweight world champion (having beaten Joe Frazier in the Philippines less than six weeks earlier).

The previous night, a revue concert had taken place at the so-called Correctional Institution for Women at Clinton, New Jersey. You'd be wrong to assume that this held only women prisoners; it didn't, and its inmates now included Carter. It was a 'country club prison', worlds away from the Vroom Readjustment Unit, and there were no bars on inmates' rooms. A grate of bars used to close off a hallway served as a fake cell barrier for the photo opportunity staged by Carter and Dylan; the picture of their 'meeting' was duly published in *People* magazine. At the concert itself, prisoners mingled freely on the floor of the hall where the musicians played on a small raised stage. At the end, Carter was allowed to hold a press conference.

Dylan had sung 'Hurricane' at every Rolling Thunder concert, and had released it as a single that November. In January 1976 *Desire* was released, with 'Hurricane' the opening track, and in Houston, Texas, on the 25th a further benefit concert was held. Less than two months later, on

Ken Regan / Camera 5

The faked shot of Bob Dylan visiting Rubin 'Hurricane' Carter in prison, December 7, 1975

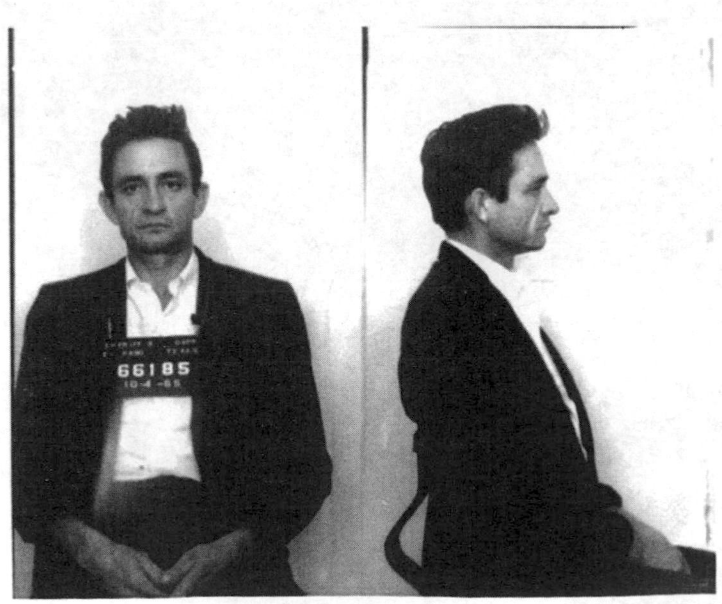

Johnny Cash, El Paso, TX, 1965

Library of Congress

The Clancy Brothers & Tommy Makem modelling knitwear, 1962

South Dakota State Historical Society-State Archives

Charles Badger Clark

March 17, the New Jersey Supreme Court overturned the convictions of Carter and Artis, ruling that the prosecution had withheld evidence that would have favoured the defence; but they ordered a retrial and released both men on bail.

On December 22, 1976, this retrial ended. The defence had argued that the first trial had been racially biased; but this time it was not an all-white jury, the prosecutor was Burrell Ives Humphreys, a black NAACP member and ex-civil rights activist; yet both men were found guilty again, sentenced again to life imprisonment and sent back to prison.

Exactly five years after the second trial ended, John Artis was released on parole; he had served a total of 15 years. Carter remained in prison. In July 1985 the New Jersey Federal District Court in Newark overturned the second trial's convictions, ruling them 'unsafe' because based on 'racism rather than reason and concealment rather than disclosure'. The prosecutors requested Carter's continued detention pending the result of the state's appeal but Judge H. Lee Sarokin ordered him set free, saying that 'human decency mandates his immediate release'. The US Court of Appeal upheld Sarokin's decision in August 1987, and on January 11, 1988 the US Supreme Court denied the state's appeal against it. The local Prosecutor's Office in Passaic County, New Jersey, decided against seeking a third trial.

This is not the same as establishing that Carter was innocent. Judge Sarokin only ruled that 'To permit convictions to stand which have as their foundation appeals to racial prejudice and the withholding of evidence critical to the defense is to commit a violation of the Constitution as heinous as the crimes for which these petitioners were tried and convicted.' Carter was not, and has never been, found 'not guilty'. Nor has he ever sued for false imprisonment. His history of violence includes beating up a black woman who had been prominent in campaigning for his release. Many of his claims, small and large, have been discredited. No instance of his claimed activism in the civil rights struggle has ever been specified.

Almost every line of Dylan's song is inaccurate, from its description of events and who was where when through to its depiction of Carter. Before his arrest he had not been sitting on horses but in bars, including the Nite Spot, where he spent so much time he's said to have had his own table. This was where he was on the night of the shooting; it was not 'far away on the other side of town', as Dylan sang, based on the claim in Carter's book; it was five blocks down the street from the Lafayette Grill, close enough that if you stand outside the one, you can see the other.

None of this makes any difference to 'Hurricane' as a creative achievement, any more than the facts of Pretty Boy Floyd's life can have any power over the life of the WOODY GUTHRIE song about him. Dylan's record has a blazing vivacity, a life-affirming generosity of sweep; it's a scintillating rendition of a skilful, affecting narrative crafted with great skill, not as a 'message' but as lines of song shaped as a series of cascades and sung with much verve, alertly expressive in its detailing, its ability to change mood and pace, and to dart in, paint a quick and vivid picture and move on. It's cinematic and celebratory.

The facts don't get in the way of a good song or a bad film. The Norman Jewison movie *Hurricane*, 1999, was based partly on *The Sixteenth Round* and partly on the later book by Sam Chaiton and Terry Swinton, *Lazarus and the Hurricane*. It managed the worst of both worlds: it took Carter's own account as gospel, muddied things further, played up the racism of individuals without scrutinising anything uncomfortable about the state's use of it, and threw in the usual quota of white liberal McGuffins.

Carter became a Canadian resident in the early 1990s. He has campaigned for, and is an executive director of, the Association in Defence of the Wrongly Convicted.

On November 17, 2005, boxing promoter Chris Sanigar presented 'An Evening with Former world title contender Rubin "Hurricane" Carter' in the Dolman Exhibition Hall at Ashton Gate Stadium, Bristol, south-west England; the 'support act' was four boxing bouts by local fighters.

When Dylan played a Toronto concert on October 29, 1998 (the 1,040th concert of the Never-Ending Tour) he said from the stage 'My friend Rubin Carter is here tonight'. But he didn't perform the song. He hasn't sung 'Hurricane' live since that second benefit concert on January 25, 1976.

[Rubin Carter: *The Sixteenth Round: From Number 1 Contender to #45472*, New York: Viking Press, 1974. Bob Dylan: 'Hurricane', NY, Oct 24, 1975. Boxing stats from *www.graphicwitness.com/carter/mov-boxing_a.html*, seen online Oct 2005; *The Ring*, April 1966, US, p.26; more generally see the fascinating, and mostly persuasive website *www.graphicwitness.com/carter/index.html* (though it wrongly dates the Carter Press Conference as 5 Dec and the concert preceding it as 6 Dec; both took place 7 Dec 1975). *People* magazine, US, 22 Dec 1975. Sam Chaiton & Terry Swinton, *Lazarus and the Hurricane*, London: Penguin, 1991. *Hurricane*, dir. Norman Jewison, Azoff / Beacon / Universal, US, 1999.]

Cartwright, Bert [1924 - 1996] Colbert Scott Cartwright was born in Coffeyville, Kansas, on August 7, 1924. From 1928 to 1940 his family lived in Chattanooga, Tennessee (on the Georgia border), and then moved to St Louis, Missouri, where Bert received his BA in 1946 before gaining Bachelor of Divinity and Master of Sacred Theology degrees from Yale in 1948 and 1950. He became an ordained minister of the Christian Church (Disciples of Christ), serving first in the ominously named Lynchburg, Virginia (1950–1953).

He is the writer of one of JOHN BAULDIE's Wanted Man Study Series of booklets, *The Bible in the Lyrics of Bob Dylan*, published in 1985, in which he divides Dylan's use of the Bible into five phases, the first three of which cover the 1960s and 1970s before the conversion to Christ.

First is a pre-motorcycle crash phase, drawing on the Bible as 'part of the poor white and black cultures of America with which he sought to identify', yet revealing that Dylan was already familiar with the Bible in some detail; second is a Woodstock and *John Wesley Harding* phase, in which 'at times a biblical perspective is clearly assumed though not personally claimed'; and third is the period from *Planet Waves* through till the late autumn of 1978, when the Bible is used 'as material for a sophisticated artist'. (Cartwright includes particularly interesting commentary on the Christ persona in songs such as 'I Pity the Poor Immigrant' and 'Oh Sister' from these second and third phases.)

Then comes the conversion. Cartwright quotes Dylan as telling Robert Hilburn: 'I had always read the Bible, but I only looked at it as literature. I was never really instructed in it in a way that was meaningful to me.'

By Cartwright's analysis, when we reach the beginning of the 1980s, we are in the midst of the fourth phase of Dylan's use of the Bible, the phase that 'reveals his unabashed acceptance of Jesus Christ as Lord and his desire to express in life and song what his fresh study of the Bible as a believer was telling him'. Cartwright designates the fifth phase, 'in which biblical faith [has] been internalized sufficiently for it to serve subtly as Dylan's worldview', as being signalled by the 1983 release of the *Infidels* album.

It can be argued, however, that a major change occurs *between* Cartwright's fourth and fifth phases: that what we begin to see after the *Saved* album of 1980 is Dylan's retreat from evangelism—not a recanting, but a move forward, away from the concern to preach to others and towards a more reflective interest in writing songs that examine the interplay in Dylan's own heart and mind between his Christian faith and other aspects of his life. This is a specially interesting period: it finds Dylan moving beyond insistence on the tenets of faith toward the pain of recognising that faith gets tested, that 'sometimes . . . there's someone there, other times it's only me' and that it's altogether a more complex business than is suggested by 'You either got faith or you got unbelief'.

The original booklet said of Cartwright that he 'first picked up on Bob Dylan in 1965 when a friend referred to young Dylan as a theologian. Curious, he went out and bought Dylan's albums. "Ever since, I have not only been fascinated by his artistic struggle to express through his lyrics and music what life means to him, but by his ability to create his own character out of his fertile imagination."'

Beyond that, his 1985 publication says only that Bert Cartwright was living in Fort Worth, Texas; was 'a Protestant minister' with 'two theological degrees from Yale University and an honorary theological doctorate from Texas Christian University' [in Fort Worth] and 'the author of several books on biblical themes'.

This showed a great deal of modesty on Cartwright's part—because in fact his career had included playing a striking and honourable rôle in the civil rights struggle in the 1950s. From 1953 to 1963 he was the minister at the Pulaski Heights Christian Church in Little Rock, Arkansas, throughout which time he went out on a limb to fight against segregation. After the US Supreme Court ruling of May 17, 1954 in the Brown v. Board of Education case, Cartwright immediately preached a sermon urging obedience to its desegregation ruling, published his sermon in the *Arkansas Gazette* and so went on record at once in support of the integration of schools. In 1955 he was a co-founder of the Arkansas Council on Human Relations and served on its board, chaired the committee to unite black and white ministries in Little Rock, and gave campaigning public speeches all over the state and more widely, at great personal risk to himself and to his career. In late 1957, 31 members of his church left it in protest at his stance; the church board responded by giving Cartwright a unanimous vote of confidence; new stained glass windows came from an anonymous donor in recognition of the minister's 'courage and conviction'.

Cartwright wrote articles on racial issues in many publications, including *The Christian Century*, *The Reporter*, *New South* and *Christianity and Crisis* (among them, in this last, 'Church, Race and the Arts of Government', in 1959), persuaded many other Little Rock ministers to come out in support of desegregation and to oppose obstructive state legislation, and throughout this period liaised between the white and black communities, endeavouring to keep the struggle moving forward nonviolently. In 1990 he allowed the University of Arkansas Libraries Special Collections to microfilm the 14 volumes of scrapbooks he had made between 1954 and 1963, documenting that tumultuous period in Little Rock's history.

None of this was known within the Dylan world. Nor was it known that as Colbert S. Cartwright he had moved on from Little Rock to churches in Youngstown, Ohio (1964–1970), and then Fort Worth, Texas (1971–1979). It was in 1976 that Texas Christian University awarded him the honorary doctorate. TCU is owned by the Christian Church (Disciples of Christ), Cartwright's semi-Baptist sect, which was founded as a breakaway from the Presbyterians in the early 19th century and in 1990 had 1,043,943 members, 4,105 congregations and 6,845 ministers; its headquarters is in Indianapolis.

Cartwright then served as his sect's area manager for the Southwest, from 1979 until he retired in 1989. The 'books on biblical themes' referred to in *The Bible in the Lyrics of Bob Dylan* and published under his fuller name Colbert S. Cartwright, were *He Taught Them Saying* (co-authored by Robert M. Platt, 1960), *People of the Chalice: Disciples of Christ in Faith and Practice* (1987) and *Candles of Grace: Disciples Worship in Perspective* (1992). He also self-published a number of other works, including *Disciples Worship: Heritage and Promise* (1988) and an autobiography, *Walking My Lonesome Valley* (as by Colbert Scott Cartwright, 1993). In 1992 he was the subject of a profile by one Roy Reed, 'Colbert S. Cartwright: God's Stranger' in *Sources of Inspiration*, an essays collection published in Kansas City.

As Bert Cartwright he continued to connect with *The Telegraph*, writing an investigative profile of 'Dylan's Mysterious Man Called NORMAN RAEBEN' in the spring 1987 issue and the updating article 'The Bible in the Lyrics of Bob Dylan 1985–1990' in the spring 1991 issue.

Cartwright also self-published, in 1989, *Annotated Dylan: A Critical Analysis of the Lyrics of Bob Dylan*, and in 1990 the 112-page large-format book, *Bob Dylan in Print*. In 1992 he self-published a revised, enlarged edition of *The Bible in the Lyrics of Bob Dylan* (both as by Colbert S. Cartwright). Then, at some point around early 1999, the US fanzine *On the Tracks* posted online, undated, an advertisement for a new book by Bert Cartwright and 'Jonathon Lauer' (elsewhere they spell it correctly as Jonathan), *The Dylan Song Companion: A Commentary with Annotations, Volume One*, with the following explanatory blurb: 'This in-depth song-by-song examination of Dylan songs up through *Blood on the Tracks* is one huge piece of work. Before well-known Dylan scholar Bert Cartwright passed on, one of his final wishes was that this book, which he'd been working on for a number of years, be completed by "a writer of similar mind." We contacted Jonathan Lauer—our first choice—and he agreed to finish the book.'

The Rolling Tomes organisation, which published *On the Tracks*, seems to have become defunct (despite maintaining its website) and at the time of the present volume's going to press no further information had emerged. Jonathan D. Lauer, Library Director of Messiah College in Grantham, Pennsylvania—a Christian but liberal arts college, absolutely nothing to do with the neo-con far right—confirms that he was indeed asked by Rolling Tomes to complete this new book by Bert Cartwright, after he'd published an article himself in *On the Tracks* in 1997 (the interesting 'Last Songs on Dylan Albums, 1974–1993').

Lauer was asked 'to edit Cartwright's manuscript and finish his song-by-song analysis of the last four or five songs on *Blood on the Tracks*, the last album Cartwright had considered at the time of his death. My son and I worked . . . on the manuscript. . . . Most of the work I did was to rationalise his system of notes and reference, to bring them into conformity with standard practise. There was a lot of bibliographic clean up and consistency to bring to a manuscript numbering about 320 pages. I probably added only about 15 pages. The general character of the book was a bit like TODD HARVEY's [*The Formative Dylan: Transmissions and Stylistic Influences, 1961–1963*] but without the musical expertise: dealing only with lyrics. It covered the first 12 studio albums, as it said, song by song.'

Lauer returned the finished manuscript to Rolling Tomes in late 1998. 'Over the next couple of years, it appeared in several of their catalogues, complete with a pre-publication order number. . . . I waited patiently. . . . Finally, in January of 2002 I was sent what I took to be galley proofs and asked to proof and correct them. About three days later I sent them back . . . with a number of corrections and a suggestion for updated acknowledgements. That is the last I heard of the project.'

Lauer never met Cartwright, but was given to understand that Bert had sent the manuscript to Rolling Tomes less than a month before he died, 'asking them to find someone to finish a near-completed project he knew he would not live to finish.' Lauer understood too that Cartwright's widow (whose name he was never told and whom he never met) had 'invested in getting this, his final project published.'

Bert Cartwright died in Fort Worth on April 13, 1996. The following year his widow Anne received on his behalf the Christian Board of Publication's Chalice Lifetime Achievement Award for 'significant contributions to the vital worship life' of the church.

It's a small irony that the writer of the article 'Dylan's Mysterious Man Called Norman Raeben' should have remained, within the Dylan world, a modest mystery man himself.

[Colbert S. Cartwright, 'Church, Race and the Arts of Government', *Christianity and Crisis* vol.19, no.2, US, 1959, pp.12–14; *People of the Chalice: Disciples of Christ in Faith and Practice*, St. Louis, MO: CBP Press, 1987; *Disciples Worship: Heritage and Promise*, Fort Worth, TX: Cartwright, 1988; *Candles of Grace: Disciples Worship in Perspective*, St. Louis, MO, CBP Press, 1992; *The Bible in the Lyrics of Bob Dylan*, revised & enlarged 2nd edn., *nia*, 1992. Colbert Scott Cartwright, *Walking my Lonesome Valley*, Fort Worth, TX: Cartwright, 1993. Bert Cartwright, *The Bible in the Lyrics of Bob Dylan*, The Wanted Man Study Series no. 4, Bury, UK, 1985; 'Dylan's Mysterious Man Called Norman Raeben', *Telegraph* no. 26, UK, spring 1987; *Bob Dylan in Print*, *nia*; 'The Bible in the Lyrics of Bob Dylan 1985–1990', *Telegraph* no. 38, UK, spring 1991. Colbert S. Cartwright &

Robert M. Platt, *He Taught Them Saying*, St. Louis, MO: Bethany Press, 1960). Bert Cartwright & Jonathan D. Lauer, *The Dylan Song Companion: A Commentary With Annotations, Volume One*, unpublished. Robert Hilburn quoted by Cartwright from *Los Angeles Times* Calendar, Jun 1980. Roy Reed: 'Colbert S. Cartwright: God's Stranger', *Sources of Inspiration*, Kansas City, MO: Sheed & Ward, 1992. Jonathan D. Lauer, 'Last Songs on Dylan Albums, 1974–1993', *On the Tracks* vol.5, no.1, 15 Jun 1997, Grand Junction, CO, pp.14–23. Quotes from Lauer, e-mails to & phone calls from this writer, 12 & 13 Jan 2006.

Main source for background information on Cartwright's life from Leon C. Miller's 1990 notes to Manuscript Collection MC 1026, Special Collections, University of Arkansas Libraries, seen online 12 Jan 2006 at *http://libinfo.uark.edu/specialcollections/finding aids/cartwrightaid.html*; main source for publication details of Cartwright's work from WorldCat and Epnet databases c/o Jonathan Lauer's Messiah College library. Sect statistics from J. Gordon Melton, *Encyclopedia of American Religions*, 6th edn., Detroit: Gale, 1999 (Section 11, 'Baptist Family,' entry no.900), p.499.]

Cash, Johnny [1932 - 2003] J.R. Cash (his given name) was born at Kingsland, Arkansas, on February 26, 1932, into a penurious cotton-farming family headed by an abusive, drunken preacher father. They were moved across the state to a farm at Dyess as part of a New Deal social program when J.R. was three, and he was picking cotton soon afterwards. His only formal education was at Dyess' local school. Disturbed for life by the mill accident that befell his brother Jack in 1944 (he was sliced almost in half and took many days to die), Cash grew up listening to gospel music, learning guitar and writing songs.

He served as a radio operator in the US Air Force till 1954, when he moved to Memphis and broke into the music business via Sun Records, on which he had minor rockabilly hits before hitting the country top five with 'Folsom Prison Blues' and crossover hit 'I Walk the Line'. (He appears, more briefly than the others, as one of the legendary 'Million Dollar Quartet' when he drops in at the Sun studio in December 1956 and finds JERRY LEE LEWIS and CARL PERKINS jamming with ELVIS, who had by then left the label but still lived in Memphis.)

Cash left Sun for Columbia, had more hits, fought the Nashville establishment, maintained his blue-collar following but opposed the Vietnam War, and grew to be a legend in his own lifetime, a dignified man battling his own demons and an artist ever more widely respected as he crossed over the lines of more and more genres.

He signally affected Dylan's career, first by using his own clout as a successful artist to defend him from Columbia executives who wanted Dylan dropped after the commercial failure of his first album, and secondly by endorsing Dylan when the latter 'went country' with *Nashville Skyline* in 1969—appearing on the album with him and writing its liner notes, and introducing Dylan as a guest on the network TV show Cash had from 1969 to 1971. In between, Cash had made the less necessary but telling gesture of defending Dylan in print to the folk-revival community when Dylan was under attack for 'abandoning' protest songs, writing the short piece 'Shut up and let him sing!' in the March 1964 issue of *Broadside*.

The two had listened to each other's work from early on. As Cash told it: 'I was deeply into folk music in the early 1960s, both the authentic songs from various periods and areas of American life and the new "folk revival" songs of the time, so I took note of Bob Dylan as soon as the *Bob Dylan* album came out in early '62 and listened almost constantly to *The Freewheelin' Bob Dylan* in '63. . . . I'd put on *Freewheelin'* backstage, then go out and do my show, then listen again as soon as I came off. After a while at that, I wrote Bob a letter telling him how much of a fan I was.'

He elaborated: 'I congratulated him on a fine country record. I could hear JIMMIE RODGERS in his record, and Vernon Dalhart from back in the twenties, the whole talking blues genre. I said, "You're about the best country singer I've heard in years". . . . He wrote back and seemed kind of flabbergasted. . . .' And: 'He wrote back almost immediately, saying he'd been following my music since "I Walk the Line", and so we began a correspondence. Mostly it was about music: what we ourselves were doing, what other people were doing, what I knew about so-and-so and he didn't and vice versa. He asked me about country people; I asked him about the circles he moved in.'

They first met backstage at the Gaslight in 1963 when Cash came to hear PETE LaFARGE (Cash would soon afterwards record LaFarge's 'The Ballad of Ira Hayes' and make a top three country hit of it; Dylan would record it himself in 1970). They next met when both were appearing at the NEWPORT FOLK FESTIVAL in 1964. In Cash's hotel room, according to TONY GLOVER, 'Dylan and Cash sat on the floor trading songs. JOAN [BAEZ] set up a little portable machine, and that's where Bob gave Johnny "It Ain't Me, Babe" and "Mama, You Been on My Mind". Johnny was there with June Carter, so shy and sweet and gentle, in a room full of freaks. Afterward, Johnny took Bob aside and gave him his guitar—an old country gesture of admiration.' This was not long after Dylan's *11 Outlined Epitaphs* had appeared on the back cover of his *Times They Are a-Changin'* album. In one of these poems Dylan rhapsodises about specific people who had affected him in his youthful New York City days; the penultimate line speaks of 'the beat visions of Johnny Cash'. When Cash's album *Orange Blossom Special* came out in 1965, it duly contained covers of 'It Ain't Me,

Babe', 'Mama, You Been on My Mind' *and* 'Don't Think Twice, It's All Right'.

They met a number of times in the mid-60s, not least when Cash visited Dylan backstage at the Capitol Theatre, Cardiff, on May 11, 1966, when Dylan was touring the UK. In *Eat the Document* there is an all-too-brief moment with Bob playing piano and trying to get Cash to join him in singing Cash's own 'I Still Miss Someone'; and in *No Direction Home* we find them, positions unchanged, tiptoeing towards a duet on HANK WILLIAMS' 'I'm So Lonesome I Could Cry'.

Then come the 1969 *Nashville Skyline* sessions, at which Cash appears on the third day, February 17, and the two sing a series of duets, on 'One Too Many Mornings', 'I Still Miss Someone' and a mix of the melodically very similar 'Don't Think Twice It's All Right' and Cash's 'Understand Your Man'. The next day they returned to the studio and laid down further duet cuts on 'One Too Many Mornings' (again), 'Mountain Dew', 'I Still Miss Someone' (again), 'Careless Love', 'Matchbox' (Carl Perkins was Cash's guitarist in this period), 'That's All Right', 'Mystery Train', 'Big River', 'Girl of the North Country', 'I Walk the Line', 'Five Feet High and Rising', 'You Are My Sunshine', 'Ring of Fire', 'Wanted Man', 'Guess Things Happen That Way', 'Amen' (?), 'Just a Closer Walk With Thee', 'Blue Yodel No.1' and 'Blue Yodel No.5'. Their hope for a joint album was disappointed, and these are largely indifferent performances (though they sound a lot less so in retrospect than at the time, when more was expected). Nonetheless, an album's worth of these have circulated, and a couple officially released: a sumptuously lovely take of 'Girl of the North Country' appears on *Nashville Skyline* and a take of 'One Too Many Mornings' was shown in the film *Johnny Cash, The Man and His Music* (1969, aka *Johnny Cash! The Man, His World, His Music*) and was also released 15 years later on the video *The Other Side of Nashville* (1984).

Dylan's album *Nashville Skyline* was released on April 9, 1969, and on May 1 he recorded his appearance on the ABC 'Johnny Cash TV Show', singing 'I Threw It All Away' and 'Living the Blues' and then sitting with Cash to sing and play guitars together on 'Girl of the North Country'. This was shown coast-to-coast that June 7.

Two days after the TV recording, Dylan was back in the studios for more of the sessions that eventually resulted in the albums *Self Portrait* and, less intentionally, *Dylan*. These sessions had begun on April 24 and 26; this May 3 session was the third. It yielded the *Self Portrait* cuts of 'Take a Message to Mary' and 'Blue Moon' but then moved on to never-issued Dylan renditions of two Cash classics, 'Ring of Fire' and 'Folsom Prison Blues'. Over 25 years later, in late February 1996, Dylan re-recorded 'Ring of Fire' for the soundtrack album of the film *Feeling Minnesota*—a version described by Amazon.com's official reviewer as 'pitiful' but which, by its sheer muted, struggling character, is an affecting treatment of a song easily made into a feeling-free singalong.

In 1985, for one of the better songs Dylan recorded and rejected for the *Empire Burlesque* album, he took the title (though not the rest) of a 1958 Johnny Cash record, cut soon after the latter had left Sun: 'Straight A's in Love'. Unlike the Cash song, Dylan's splendidly un-PC take on the dumb blonde (or brunette) includes in its detailing of the ignorance of the 'you' in the song the triumphantly funny one-liner 'You could confuse Geronimo with Johnny Appleseed.'

Early on the Never-Ending Tour, Dylan jumped on Cash warhorses again, débuting his maudlin 'Give My Love to Rose' in Canandaigua, New York, on June 28, 1988 and playing it again in Columbia, South Carolina, that September 16. (In 1989 this was the only Cash song played; it was performed at Christinehofs Slott, Skåne, Sweden, that May 27). 'Big River' was débuted in Santa Barbara on August 7, 1988.

Eleven years later, because of his own touring, Dylan was unable to join a cavalcade of stars paying live tribute to the ailing Cash in New York (an all-star cast that included Cash himself, to some surprise), but had arranged for JEFF ROSEN to film a contribution for showing at the performance; backed by his Never-Ending Tour Band of the day, he sang and played, for the first time in public, Cash's 'Train of Love'—a song Dylan had slyly name-dropped in the sleevenotes to his *World Gone Wrong* album of 1993. This was duly shown on the night of the tribute (April 18, 1999) and later included on the various artists audio CD *Kindred Spirits: A Tribute to the Songs of Johnny Cash*.

After fighting addiction in the early 1960s, getting religion, becoming a huge star, plunging in popularity in the mid-1970s, selling over a million copies of his (first) autobiography, *Man in Black*, getting more religion and making a Jesus film with Billy Graham, losing his major-label deals, winning acclaim as an actor, plunging back into addiction after relying on painkillers in the aftermath of being almost disembowelled by an ostrich (really), recovering from both, having heart surgery, diabetes, autonomic neuropathy and pneumonia, recording the modishly simple acoustic comeback album *American Recordings* in 1994, appearing at the Glastonbury Festival, recording anew with everyone from U2 to TOM PETTY and winning Grammies galore, Johnny Cash died in hospital in Nashville on September 12, 2003.

The standard, respectful story, therefore, is as above, augmented by this sort of assessment: that Cash was a rock'n'roll pioneer who recorded seminal, original music early on (not mere standard rockabilly), crossed many boundaries and remained creative from the folk blues of *Blood Sweat and Tears* on through the raw power of the prison albums and arrived, at the last, at the stripped down, uncannily personal *American Recordings*, an album comparable to Dylan's *World Gone Wrong* and offering a visionary and personal message through a collection of seemingly unconnected tunes.

Some, however, demur, noting the blatant way he marketed himself as the Man in Black and finding the image risible: it would have to be black, wouldn't it? And they suggest that you'd be hard pressed to think of a more cringe-inducing record than Johnny Cash's 'A Boy Named Sue'.

They note too that when Dylan and Cash are glimpsed together in those delicious moments caught on film in 1966, with Dylan at the piano being aptly inventive with the melody lines of both Cash's own 'I Still Miss Someone' and Hank Williams' 'I'm So Lonesome I Could Cry', Cash is visibly confounded: he can't cope with being asked to diverge from his own rigid way of doing them—even though Dylan is leading him gently along alternative melodic paths that make sense, instantly, to the ears of most listeners.

Similarly, in the film footage of their Nashville 1969 duet on 'One Too Many Mornings', when the camera cuts from their recording it to their hearing it back, it's a delight to see Dylan grinning behind his arm when they reach that moment when Cash had been settling in for a predictable ending on three swapped 'And a thousand' lines leading into a final shared extended 'miles— be— hind—': and Dylan hasn't let him get there: he's kept throwing in extra 'And a thousand's', forcing Cash to duplicate them still further. It is done playfully: there's no spite or competitive animus behind it at all, but again, Cash can only stand there in bovine perplexedness till Dylan rescues him. In any case, it might be said that through the main body of this performance, which is mostly not really a duet but an alternating of vocalists, verse by verse, Dylan sings in the most beautiful, spontaneous, inventive way, throwing himself fully on the mercy of the gods yet delivering a vocal that is judicious and discreet as well as fresh and free. Cash just plods through it being obvious and 'manly'. Some might add that to hear Cash's hit recording of 'It Ain't Me, Babe' is to encounter him at his most wooden: he declaims the 'No, no, no' in the recurrent 'No, no, no, it ain't me babe' with desperate, pompous rigidity: a manly man in black who can't understand what everyone else finds funny.

There's also something inherently suspect about the kind of tribute Cash gets paid by other stars. This isn't Cash's fault, or particular to him, but it would still be healthier to discount it. Dylan himself can say 'It's important to stay away from the celebrity trap', and this truth is partly to do with the innate unwholesomeness of schmoozing. What Dylan says about Cash once they're good ole buddies, fellow artistes and liggers at other celebrities' parties is probably less interesting than what he said about Cash when Bob was still in Hibbing, with impassioned and unfettered feelings about music, and Cash was already out there in the public sphere. And as it happens, we have on the tape made with his schoolfriend John Bucklen in 1958 exactly what Bob thought about Johnny then:

Bucklen: You think singing is just jumping around and screaming?
Dylan: You gotta have some kind of expression.
Bucklen: Johnny Cash has got expression.
Dylan: There's no expression! [sings imitation in slow monotone]: *'I met her at a dance St. Paul Minnesota . . . I walk the line, because you're mine, because you're mine . . .'*
Bucklen: You're doing it wrong, you're just—What's the best kind ofmusic?
Dylan: Rhythm & blues.
Bucklen: State your reason in no less than twenty-five minutes!
Dylan: Ah, rhythm & blues you see is something that you really can't quite explain see. When you hear a song rhythm & blues—when you hear it's a good rhythm & blues song, chills go up your spine . . .
Bucklen: Whoa-o-o!
Dylan: . . . when you hear a song like that. But when you hear a song like Johnny Cash, whaddaya wanna do? You wanna leave . . .'

It may be adolescent, and Dylan is entitled to have changed his mind (by 2004, in *Chronicles*, Dylan was saying that 'I Walk the Line' was 'a song I'd always considered to be up there at the top, one of the most mysterious and revolutionary of all time'), but his Hibbing comments reflect what many still find highly resistable about the style of Johnny Cash.

After his death, Dylan said this: 'Johnny was and is the North Star. You could guide your ship by him—the greatest of the greats then and now.' BONO, doubtless intending to praise him, in fact highlighted the intrinsic downside to the Cash mystique when his homage came out as this: 'Every man knows he's a sissy compared to Johnny Cash.' That's a recommendation?

[Johnny Cash: 'It Ain't Me, Babe', 'Don't Think Twice, It's All Right' & 'Mama, You Been on My Mind', *nia*, *Orange Blossom Special*, Columbia CL-2309, 1965; 'Straight A's In Love', Memphis, c.1956, Sun 334, Memphis (London-American HCSD 9070, UK), 1960; 'A Boy Named Sue', San Quentin, 24 Feb 1969. *Johnny Cash, The Man and His Music*, later re-titled *Johnny Cash! The Man, His World, His Music*, dir. Robert Elfstrom, Verité Production / WJRZ Radio, US, May 16, 1969; *The Other Side of Nashville*, dir. Etienne Mirlesse, MGM/UA Home Video UMV 10351, US, Aug 1984.

Bob Dylan: 'Straight A's In Love', Hollywood, 14 Feb 1985, unissued (2 takes circulated); 'Train of Love', *nia*, Mar 1999, on Various Artists: *Kindred Spirits: A Tribute to the Songs of Johnny Cash*, Lucky Dog CK86310, Sep 2002. 1st & 3rd Cash quotes from Johnny Cash (with Patrick Carr), *Cash: The Autobiogra-*

phy, San Francisco: Harper, 1996/7, pp.197–198; 2nd quote in Frye Gaillard, *Watermelon Wine—The Spirit of Country Music*, New York: 1978, p.61. Tony Glover, 'adden'dum', in Paul Nelson & Tony Glover, *The Festival Songbook*, New York: Amsco Music Publishing, 1973, p.35. The 'augmenting assessment' summarises posting by Mitch Rath, 29 Aug 1999, seen online 24 May 2005 at *www.expectingrain.com/dok/who/who.html.* Dylan-Bucklen transcript corrected from that online at *www.bjorner.com/DSN00003%201960.htm#DSN00003.* Bob Dylan, *Chronicles Volume One*, 2004, p.216.]

Castner, Flo [1939 -] & Lynn [1934 -] Florence Therese Castner (born Minneapolis, April 23, 1939) and Lynn Sumner Castner (Minneapolis, April 11, 1934) were the sister and brother from the Twin Cities of Minneapolis-St. Paul who between them introduced Dylan to WOODY GUTHRIE's records. When Dylan met them, Flo was an aspiring actress and her brother a graduate student at the university law school with a Dinkytown apartment and an interesting record collection. Dylan describes them both in *Chronicles Volume One* (misspelling Lynn as Lyn throughout), writing that Flo 'was an actress in the drama academy . . . odd looking but beautiful in a wacky way, had long red hair . . . dressed in black from head to foot. She had an uptown but folksy manner, was a mystic and a transcendentalist . . . [and] serious about reincarnation'; Lynn had 'thin, wispy hair, wore a bow tie and little James Joyce glasses. . . . he never said much and I never spoke to him.'

Flo took Dylan round to hear records, and it was then and there that Dylan first heard, on Lynn Castner's recommendation, the collection of 78s that made up the JOHN HAMMOND *Spirituals to Swing Concert at Carnegie Hall* releases from the late 1930s, and then a series of Woody Guthrie 78s that 'stunned' him, made his head spin and made him 'want to gasp'.

Yet as Dylan was to discover, Castner wasn't merely a man with a record collection: he'd been involved in Guthriesque Left Wing folkie music events for some years before Dylan came to Dinkytown: indeed for most of the 1950s. At 18, after his first undergraduate year in college in Minneapolis he went to the Bay Area of California, where he met folksinger Rolf Kahn and his wife Barbara Dane, and co-produced concerts with Kahn in and around San Francisco—co-producing the first ODETTA concert.

Castner returned to Minneapolis for a second college year, then went back to San Francisco, and so on. By the time Dylan met him he was a graduate law student and not yet the attorney Dylan describes him as being (and which he became only in 1963)—and while it may be true that Castner and Dylan had never spoken before the day of the record playing visit, they certainly spoke after that. Rolf Kahn came to Minneapolis and gave a concert, produced by Castner, at the Minneapolis Unitarian Society, which Dylan probably attended, and certainly Castner introduced Dylan to Kahn, they spent some time together and played at coffee-houses during the several days Kahn was in town—and when Dylan lit out for the East Coast, he had with him some contact details from Castner and Kahn for people in New York City.

Along with his early active engagement in the folk scene Lynn Castner developed a parallel interest in civil liberties issues—in people like Guthrie, of course, the two came together—and he became active in, and by 1965 the first full-time director of, the Minnesota Civil Liberties Union. In 1968 he was the attorney fighting on behalf of the Union against Minnesota's Attorney General, to assert the right of the Minnesota Communist Party's candidates to have their names on the ballot paper for the November 1968 presidential election. Castner's clients won their case and duly stood—they won only 415 Minnesotan votes but an important right, and ramifications took the case on up to the US Supreme Court in 1970.

Today Lynn's name heads that of the Minneapolis law firm Lynn S. Castner & Associates, specialising less loftily in Drunk Under the Influence cases, but he no longer runs the firm; he lives at Hilton Head Island, South Carolina, semi-retired at 72 years of age; he owns a small real-estate business, he uses his knowledge of the law in doing volunteer work and he still sits on the national council of the American Civil Liberties Union.

Flo was a theatre major at the university and was working with the internationally reputable Minnesota Dance Theater & School. She went on to become a founding member of the Minneapolis Children's Theater Company and a drama teacher. Around 1967 she left Minnesota when invited onto the faculty of the American branch of RADA (the London-based Royal Academy of Dramatic Arts), which had been established at Oakland University in Rochester, Michigan. At the end of the 1960s she was invited on a State Department sponsored tour of the Soviet Union with the mime artist Marcel Marceau, but because she refused to sign a passport application loyalty oath, she couldn't go. She returned to Minneapolis and set about a long and varied career acting, designing and directing, and at one point was pursuing two-pronged studies, into Shakespeare and post-graduate level constitutional law.

Dylan's depiction of her as a 'transcendentalist' was accurate on one level—she was 'exploring' the subject, studying informally with a visiting Indian practitioner of advanced yoga who was demonstrating mind-over-matter powers at the university at the time—yet she was also, obviously, a political activist, and has remained so. Like her brother before her, she was at one point an executive director of the Minnesota Civil Liberties Union and she remains, in her brother's phrase, 'a woman with many, many interests'. Today, disabled and living in community housing herself, she campaigns on affordable housing issues, including the problems low-income people have in accessing help with health and education as well as housing. Her answer-machine message says: 'Hi, you've reached go-with-the-Flo and the Hope Project.'

In 2002 she gave an interview to Minneapolis' *Rake* magazine that was used as part of a detailed profile of 'Dylan in Dinkytown 1959' reconstructed by writer Hans Eisenbeis. She made a point no other Dylan contemporary of the period seems to have made: that the University of Minneapolis into which Dylan arrived as a young freshman in 1959 was still in the grip of the McCarthyism of the mid-1950s (as was the wider world, and would remain so for many more years, to judge by the case her brother had to fight in 1968 and her own struggles with the State Department later still). Flo Castner told Eisenbeis:

> 'You've got to remember what McCarthyism did to individual freedom and independent academic research. All university research fell under the Defense Department, and everything was supposed to fit into our grand military and political schemes. Real research was dead. There were loyalty oaths. That was the climate."

She also recalled that Dylan 'hadn't found himself yet, hadn't developed that poetic vision. He was much more into pop and rock.' Even after she introduced him to her brother's Guthrie collection, she said that the poetic vision Dylan had 'was just a seed at that point, and hadn't rooted and flowered. . . . He was still bewildered and confused, stunned by what he was discovering.'

It had to happen somewhere, sometime, but in the event it fell to the Castners to have this small but crucial rôle in furthering Bob Dylan's musical education and, through Guthrie's stimulus, the first major phase of his creative development.

[Lynn S. Castner, phone call with this writer 16 Jan 2006; Flo Castner, phone call ditto 17 Jan 2006. Bob Dylan, *Chronicles Volume One*, pp.242, 243 & 244; Hans Eisenbeis, 'Dylan in Dinkytown 1959', *Rake*, Minneapolis, Apr 2002, seen online 15 Aug 2005 at *www.rake mag.com / stories / printable.aspx?itemID = 2210&catID = 146&SelectCat . . .*]

Cat-Iron See **Carradine, William**.

Chabad telethons Chabad 'To Life' telethons began in 1980 as a fund-raising and publicity device in support of the worldwide Chabad-Lubavitch movement, which claims to be 'the largest Jewish organization in the world today' and is certainly one of the largest groups within Hasidic Judaism.

'Chabad' is a Hebrew acronym for 'wisdom, understanding and knowledge' and Lubavitch, meaning 'brotherly love' in Russian, is the name of the Russian town where the movement was long based. Chabad was founded in 1772, and galvanised in its modern form from 1950 onwards by the leadership of Lubavitcher Rebbe Menachem Mendel Schneerson. Its Californian branches were founded in the 1960s. The organisation claims to espouse 'a philosophy of study, meditation, and social outreach that bridges rigorous academics 'with proactive community involvement', to offer a 'network of educational and nonsectarian social services' and to have benefitted 'people of all faiths'. Inevitably, perhaps, Chabad Lubavitch has been involved in much controversy, sometimes disquieting both more traditionalist and more liberal wings of Judaism and in recent years much criticised for its alleged 'messianic tendency'.

The annual telethons from California have raised many millions of dollars for the organisation, and on its website its list of the stars and celebrities who have appeared starts with Bob Dylan's name. (Others include Martin Sheen, Whoopi Goldberg, Anthony Hopkins, James Caan, Dick Van Dyke, Elliott Gould, NEIL DIAMOND and Jon Voight.)

Dylan has made three appearances, always amusing and usually bizarre, beginning in 1986, when he performed the song 'Thank God', written and composed by Fred Rose and once recorded by HANK WILLIAMS. Dylan's version, backed by TOM PETTY & THE HEARTBREAKERS, was filmed in San Francisco that August and shown on September 14. He also consented to deliver an 'anti-drug message' for the show (surely a bizarre decision in itself—on both sides), which was probably made in Wales while Dylan was filming *Hearts of Fire*. He found a circumspect, honourable route through, by saying this:

> 'This is Bob Dylan and I'm in England [sic] right now, working, so I can't be there tonight; but I'd like to say that Chabad is a worthy organisation helping people in need, helping to set them free from the misconceptions and devastation which is destroying their lives from within. Of course, this is a fierce battle, for those responsible for poisoning the minds and bodies of America's youth are reaping great profits. If you can help Chabad to help others who have fallen victim to the lies and deceits of those who are much more powerful, do it.'

Dylan's second appearance on a Chabad telethon was three years later, in the studios of KCOP-13 in LA, at which he gave one of his weirdest-ever performances, taking part in three songs with HARRY DEAN STANTON and Dylan's son-in-law PETER HIMMELMAN. (See the latter's entry for details.)

Two years on from this comes the further high comedy of his third (and so far final) telethon appearance, broadcast live on September 15, 1991, starting with the show's host, a Rabbi, urging Dylan to help them obtain the return of ancient holy books from Russia. Dylan asks, 'What do you want me to say?!' The Rabbi: 'Tell them to give back the books.' Dylan: 'Oh, yeah. Give back the books. And give plenty of money to Chabad. It's my favourite organisation in the whole world, really. They do nothing but good things with all the money, and the more you can give, the more it's going to help everybody.'

The Rabbi interjects: 'I want to say something, Bob, if I might. I think the people out there . . . that heard us talk about the cry of these books—these are books that have suffered for 70 years behind those bars of the Lenin Library. Mr. Gorbachev said he's going to give it back, Mr. Yeltsin says he's going to give it back, everybody says he's going to give it back. Bob, tell them to give it back!' Bob: 'Yeah, give it back. Give the books back.' Rabbi: 'If Bob Dylan says they'll give it back, they'll give it back.'

After this Dylan is seen scuttling out of sight as the young man standing alongside him starts to confess to a sinfully drug-taking past. When this ends, Dylan re-appears, and the Rabbi says: 'Please go to your phones and call and call and call. Bob, tell them what to do.' Dylan, in a refreshing acknowledgement that people who *do* phone in have a long and miserable time of it, concludes by saying this: 'Call and call and call some more until you get somebody to answer—and give what you can. And thanks for inviting me down here.' At another point in the show he plays guitar behind Kinky Friedman as Friedman performs 'Sold American'.

[Chabad Lubavitch quotes from its official US west coast website, seen online 12 Jan 2006 at *www.chabad.com/show_art.php?articleID=2*. All transcription of Dylan and others' telethon dialogue reprocessed from Glen Dundas, *Tangled*, Thunder Bay, Canada: SMA, 2004.]

Chandler, Len [1935 -] Leonard Hunt Chandler Jr. was born on May 27, 1935 in Akron, Ohio, and became one of the best-known black guitarists and folk singer-songwriters active in the early 1960s folk scene. He was trained in classical piano and oboe, joined the Akron Symphony Orchestra but was introduced to pre-war blues records by a professor and began performing converted folk songs with the New Jersey Symphony Orchestra before moving to New York City at the age of 15. Playing regularly at the Café Wha at the beginning of the 1960s, he told the then *New York Times* folk critic ROBERT SHELTON that 'he had thrown over his classical background to rediscover his people's music.' His best-known song is 'Keep Your Eyes on the Prize (Hold On)', a civil rights anthem which he performed, with Bob Dylan and JOAN BAEZ as back-up participants, at the momentous March on Washington performance at the Lincoln Memorial in D.C. on August 28, 1963, film of which can be seen in the MARTIN SCORSESE film *No Direction Home* (2005).

This marked the high point of Chandler's career, though Robert Shelton says he was still regarded as 'a rising figure' at the time of the 1964 NEWPORT FOLK FESTIVAL. On the evidence of the March on Washington footage he seems to have resembled an earnest schoolteacher (which is what he had wanted to be), far from charismatic as a performer. Yet Dylan says the opposite—'His personality overrode his repertoire'—and found him a compelling, audacious companion of some personal power, as he attests in *Chronicles Volume One*, where he writes of him warmly and recalls him as one of those who 'would play poker continuously through the night', stresses that he was 'one of the few' who wrote his own songs ('topical songs' that were 'pretty much accepted . . . because they used old melodies with new words'), who 'Besides being a songwriter . . . was also a daredevil', and who became a friend of Dylan's after sharing bills at the Gaslight:

> 'Len was educated and serious about life, was even working with his wife downtown to start a school for underprivileged children [St. Barnabas House]. . . . One of his most colorful songs had been about a negligent school bus driver in Colorado who accidentally drove a bus full of kids down a cliff. It had an original melody and because I liked the melody so much, I wrote my own set of lyrics to it. Len didn't seem to mind.'

This breathtaking ingenuousness tiptoes around the ethics of how Dylan stole the chords and tune of 'The Bus Driver', a song Chandler often performed but never recorded, about an incident in Greeley, Colorado, plucked from the newspapers, and turned it into the superior 'The Death of Emmett Till'. He was more straightforward when playing it for CYNTHIA GOODING in early 1962, saying then: 'I stole the melody from Len Chandler. . . . He uses a lot of funny chords, you know, when he plays, and he's always getting to, want me, to use some of these chords . . . trying to teach me new chords all the time. Well, he played me this one; said "Don't those chords sound nice?" An' I said they sure do, an so I stole it, stole the whole thing.' Playing the song on the Billy Faeir radio show on WBAI-FM that October he added informatively: 'Before I met him, I never sang one song in minor key.'

Eventually, Chandler retaliated. *Broadside* no.51 published his song 'Ain't No Use to Sit and Wonder Why, Chuck', which has the final line 'Don't think twice, we might fight.' This is not a knowing parody but a dreadful, ingenuous protest song of Chandler's own. Or rather, not.

Chandler was strongly involved with civil rights activity—and with *Broadside*, which he greatly helped. (The issue for November 5, 1963 got round to focussing on him, publishing several of his songs—'Secret Songs', 'To Be a Man' and 'Keep on Keeping On', plus two pages of biography, mainly about his anti-war efforts and civil rights activism.) He was married to JUDY COLLINS' sister in the mid-1960s and appeared at the Newport Folk Festival as late as 1969, still singing topical songs (this time notably 'Moon Men', about the moon landing by US astronauts). In 1971–72 he was one of the troupe that took the anti-Vietnam War show *F.T.A.* (officially 'Free the Army' but often understood to mean 'Fuck the Army') around the US West Coast and across the Pacific, playing as near as possible to US military bases; the show was a mix of satirical sketches and song, and the actors involved were principally Jane Fonda, Donald Sutherland and Peter Boyle; Len Chandler was its main folk star. The show was filmed and the result, *F.T.A.* (1972), contemporary re-release of which Fonda has allegedly squashed, provoked predictably mixed reactions.

The show's audiences were mainly servicemen and women, and at the time (and more so now) the film's power lies in the interviews with individual serving troops

> 'who openly question the purpose and planning of the American involvement in Vietnam. Most memorable here are the members of the *U.S.S. Coral Sea*, who presented a petition to their superiors demanding a halt to the bombing in Vietnam; African-American soldiers and marines who angrily decried racist attitudes among the white commanding officers at the U.S. military installations, usually with an upraised fist of the Black Power movement; women serving in the U.S. Air Force who talk unhappily about sexual harassment from their male counterparts; and soldiers who pointedly refer to the dictatorial government in South Vietnam which was being presented as the democracy which they were supposedly defending. The extraordinary air of dissent that rises out of *F.T.A.* provides a rare glimpse into a unhappy and demoralized fighting force stuck in a war which they did not believe in. . . . As for the F.T.A. show itself, it was actually a rather benign event full of soggy anti-war folks songs and silly military skits.'

So reports Phil Hall for the independent film review website Film Threat (re-circulated on that other independent film review website Rotten Tomatoes).

In the early 1970s too, Len Chandler formed the Alternative Chorus-Songwriters Showcase to promote new talent, as a direct result of which over 300 writers have been signed to recording and publishing contracts.

Eventually, despite two 1967 Columbia Records solo albums of his own (*To Be a Man*, produced by JOHN HAMMOND and *The Lovin' People*, on which he plays not only guitars but organ and 'English horn'), and despite his fine track record, he moved to the West Coast and worked in the field of education. At the same time, he became a co-founder and director of the Los Angeles Songwriters Showcase and a Senior Editor of something hideously called the *Songwriter Musepaper*.

[Len Chandler: 'The Bus Driver', unreleased; 'Ain't No Use to Sit and Wonder Why, Chuck', unreleased but published *Broadside* no.51, NY, 20 Oct, 1964. *To Be a Man*, Columbia CL 2459 / CS 9259, US (CBS BPG 62931, UK), 1967; *The Lovin' People*, Columbia CL 2753 / CS 9553, US, 1967. *Broadside* Chandler profile in no.34, NY, 5 Nov 1963. *F.T.A.*, dir. Francine Parker, Duque Films / Free Theater Associates, US, 1972; Phil Hall, review for *www.filmthreat.com/index.php*. Robert Shelton, *No Direction Home*, London: Penguin edn., 1987, pp.93 & 257. Bob Dylan, *Chronicles Volume One*, 2004, pp.260, 47, 91, 81–82. Dylan to Cynthia Gooding, NY, 13 Jan 1962, broadcast 'Folksinger's Choice', WBAI, 11 Mar 1962.]

Chapman, Tracy [1964 -] Tracy Chapman was born in Cleveland, Ohio, on March 20, 1964. She learnt piano, ukulele and guitar, and started writing songs while still a child. The Better Chance organisation awarded her a scholarship to attend the private Wooster School in Danbury, Connecticut, and from there she won a Minority Placement Scholarship to Tufts University in Boston, where she studied African culture and anthropology. She also began performing around Harvard Square, recorded some demo tapes and was signed to Elektra in 1987. She graduated before turning full-time to her music career and her début album was released in 1988; the single 'Fast Car' became an immediate top 10 hit on both sides of the Atlantic, followed by the further hits 'Talkin' 'Bout a Revolution' and 'Baby Can I Hold You?'.

That June 11, at London's Wembley Stadium (and live on television to six billion viewers worldwide) Tracy Chapman appeared as the new girl amid a ferocious array of mega-stars at the 70th Birthday Concert for Nelson Mandela—and wiped the floor with them all as her unique, rich voice, slightly shaky as if expressive of the effort of keeping passion contained, soared up from the huge stage. For many this was the first time they'd heard her or heard of her, and it was a rare experience to encounter such incontestably powerful talent as if out of nowhere. Her short dreadlocked hair and African gravity made her a striking figure; her record sales rose exponentially: the album went double-platinum and was a transatlantic no.1, despite its dark themes of political outrage, abuse and suffering.

At a time when Bob Dylan was dithering around offering albums like *Down in the Groove*, here was a contrastingly potent communicator, writing and performing songs of import and remonstration: a 'new Dylan' all the more interesting and contemporary for being a woman and being black.

Somehow, though, Tracy Chapman vanished almost as quickly as she had arrived. Her second album, *Crossroads* (1989), exemplified 'difficult-second-album' syndrome and though it went platinum, topped the UK charts and yielded another US top 10 single with its title track, it disappointed all who bought it and Ms. Chapman's career settled down as if back to the level of small gigs and coffee-house worthiness. The third album, *Matters of the Heart* (1992), did nothing to change this, though it scraped into the charts. Three years later and *New Beginning* almost was: its range was broader and it included at least two terrific tracks, 'Smoke and Ashes' and the genuinely funky, bluesy single 'Give Me One Reason', on which she is finally unafraid to loosen up and sound sexy and fun. It was her first huge US hit for six years. Since then she has kept on keeping on, with Amnesty appearances and the albums *Telling Stories* (2000), *Let It Rain* (2002) and *Where You Live* (2005).

On October 16, 1992 she made a brief solo appearance at the so-called Bob Dylan 30th Anniversary Concert Celebration, managing an odd mix of the powerful and cosy on an anthem with no obvious current applicability, 'The Times They Are a-Changin''; more interestingly, four years earlier, at the red-hot moment of her initial explosion onto the scene, she had played a series of dates on the same bill as Dylan, in August 1988. His Never-Ending Tour was then only two months old: these were exciting times. On August 21, in Vancouver, Canada, Tracy Chapman came on stage at the end of Dylan's own set to play guitar and share vocals with him on the encore number 'Knockin' on Heaven's Door'; at the next concert, on August 23 in Calgary, she did the same; and the following night they stood onstage together for the third and last time, again for 'Knockin' on Heaven's Door'. Hers was the more powerful voice those nights; but his had already proved resilient, and has proved the more so again since then. Now, suddenly, it's nearly 20 years since Tracy Chapman first emerged. That début album has sold over 10 million copies (far more than a Bob Dylan album ever has). Yet in spite of her rare talent and sumptuous, stand-alone voice, she's spent a long time being quiet.

[Tracy Chapman: *Tracy Chapman*, Elektra 60774, US, 1988; *Crossroads*, Elektra 60888, US, 1989; *Matters of the Heart*, Elektra 61216, 1992; *New Beginning*, Elektra 61850, 1996; *Telling Stories*, Elektra 62478, 2000; *Let It Rain*, Elektra 62803, 2002; *Where You Live*, Elektra *nia*, 2005. Sources include the *www.rockonthenet.com/artists-c/tracychapman_main.htm timeline*, Wikipedia and William R. Pringle's discography at *www.folklib.net/uwp/wrp_chapman_tracy.shtml*, all seen online 12 Jan 2006.]

Charles, Bobby [1938 -] Robert Charles Guidry, born February 21, 1938 in Abbeville, Louisiana, wrote, and recorded the original version of, Bill Haley's hit 'See You Later, Alligator', which THE BAND and Bob Dylan transmuted into 'See Ya Later, ALLEN GINSBERG' during the Basement Tapes sessions in West Saugerties, New York, June to August 1967. He also wrote FATS DOMINO's hit 'Walking to New Orleans' and wrote or co-wrote most of the lovely early 1960s hits by Clarence Frogman Henry, including the biggest, 'But I Do', using his real surname of Guidry.

Charles was later on the fringes of PAUL BUTTERFIELD's Better Days, and at The Band's farewell concert at the Winterland, San Francisco, on November 25, 1976 (filmed and recorded as *The Last Waltz*), he refused to sing 'See You Later Alligator' but followed a joyous rendition of JOHNNIE & JACK's 'Down South in New Orleans' with backing vocals on Dylan & The Band's performance of 'I Shall Be Released'.

[Bill Haley: 'See You Later Alligator', NY, 12 Dec 1955, Decca *Nia*, 1956; Clarence Frogman Henry: 'But I Do', New Orleans, c.Aug 1960; Argo 5378 (Pye International 7N 25078, UK), 1961. *The Last Waltz* soundtrack, Warner Brothers 3WS 3146, LA, 1978; film directed by Martin Scorsese.]

Charles, Larry [19?? -] Larry Charles was born in Brooklyn, New York, but seems very reluctant to state his date of birth. He is the director and co-writer with Dylan of his film *Masked & Anonymous*, 2003, initially with Charles credited as writer Rene Fontaine (and Dylan as Sergei Petrov). Charles' many claims for the film, and the partnership within it, include 'Shakespeare meets Cassavetes'. Interviewed about the 'experience' of meeting Bob Dylan, he said: 'It was the most life changing experience of my life.'

This eternal-hippie-in-Hollywood graduated from TV, where he made an unbilled appearance in the 'Seinfeld' TV series of 1992 as Stinky Man in the episode 'The Airport', having been Series Producer for 1990 and the writer of 18 episodes from 1991–94. He was also executive producer of series four of 'Curb Your Enthusiasm' and executive producer *and* a prolific writer of series like 'Mad About You' and 'Dilbert'. This qualified him to create an art movie with Bob Dylan?

[Larry Charles on Shakespeare & John Cassavetes, seen online 21 Aug 2005 at *www.trevgibb.co.uk/Masked/Director.htm*; on meeting Dylan, quoted from interview by Trev Gibb, ditto at *www.trevgibb.co.uk/Masked/riffing_larry.htm*.]

Charles, Ray [1930 - 2004] Ray Charles Robinson was born into rural poverty in Northern Louisiana on September 23, 1930 and went blind in childhood, a process that began soon after the accidental death of his younger brother. He was brought up by his mother. Taught piano informally, in the late 1940s he took a bus up to Seattle and got into music, meeting Quincy Jones and Lowell Fulson and joining the latter's band. Signed to Swingtime Records, his first recordings catch him as a Nat King Cole soundalike. Signed to Atlantic Records by Ahmet Ertegun in 1954, he found his own voice and made a series of mostly self-composed hit singles, fuelled in part by a flagrant and controversial secularisation of gospel songs (as with 'I Got a Woman', 'Leave My Woman Alone' and 'Hallelujah I Love Her So').

When his contract with Atlantic came up for renewal, Charles, a shrewd businessman, signed instead to ABC-Paramount, a major label, in a deal that gave the artist, unprecedentedly, ownership of his own master recordings. In the early 1960s he was banned from performing in the state of Georgia after refusing to play to segregated audiences; a state government ceremony, attended by Charles, gave him an official public apology in 1979. He died of cancer of the liver on June 10, 2004, aged 73.

The influence of his (mostly 1950s) R&B records on Dylan is one thing, and the influence of his seminal soul-country crossover work of the early 1960s is another.

First, Charles appears to be the source for a very early piece of near-plagiarism by Dylan. The fragment of a song called 'Blackjack Blues', which Dylan's first biographer, ANTHONY SCADUTO, says Dylan had told him was his 'first original folk song', comes almost verbatim from Charles' 1955 R&B-charting single 'Blackjack'. The Dylan lyric fragment is: 'Blackjack blues, yea yea yea / How unlucky can one man be? / Every quarter I make / Old Blackjack takes away from me.' Ray Charles' first verse ends with this: 'How unlucky can one man be? / Well, every quarter I get / Blackjack takes away from me.'

A later, less plagiaristic use of Ray Charles' R&B material by Dylan occurs in the mid-1960s. ROBERT SHELTON says that Dylan and PHIL SPECTOR were in an LA coffee-shop when they heard Charles' 'Let's Go Get Stoned' (written by Ashford & Simpson) on the jukebox, and were struck by the open upfrontery of the lyric. A few months later Dylan recorded 'Rainy Day Women Nos. 12 & 35', with its chorus of 'Everybody must get stoned'. As the webmaster of a 'Ray Charles Is God' website says of the song that inspired this (and what it says about Charles): 'He could be particularly pleasingly dark and wilful in his humor. Notably, he recorded "Let's Go Get Stoned" some scant few months after kicking a 20 year heroin addiction.' (He gives a better example: 'On *SNL* during the Carter administration, Ray waxed sentimental about their mutual Georgia roots, claiming to feel a special closeness to the president on the grounds that "his grandad used to own my grandad".')

It might also have been Ray Charles' late 1950s recording of the old blues song '(Night Time Is) The Right Time', included on his 1961 album *The Genius Sings the Blues*, that prompted Dylan's importing of the lines 'The night time is the right time / To be with the one you love' into his own *Nashville Skyline* song 'To Be Alone With You'.

Decades later, Dylan performed Ray Charles' 'What'd I Say' with TOM PETTY & THE HEARTBREAKERS at rehearsals for Farm Aid (LA, September 19, 1985) and then performed Ray Charles' Freddy Jones-penned 'Unchain My Heart', in US concerts in June and July 1986, soon after three attempts at recording it at early *Knocked Out Loaded* sessions that April and May—sessions at which he also twice attempted 'You'll Never Walk Alone', another song that many associate with Ray Charles, thanks to the memorably outrageous version he recorded in the early 1960s. (Britons find it hard not be hit over the head with renditions by the awful Gerry Marsden—he of Gerry & the Pacemakers—because he can always exploit a perverse fondness for it among crowds at football matches.)

Charles' R&B hit singles also almost foregrounded the back-up singers—he gave the Raelettes some of the lines in the lyrics, rather than just having them echo his own (again importing the devices of the gospel performance into the secular song). In London in June 1978, backstage at Earl's Court, Robert Shelton remarked to Dylan that a review of his warm-up dates in LA at the start of the month had said that his back-up singers sounded like the Supremes. Dylan retorted: 'Oh, no: not the Supremes—the Raelettes, maybe!' This was a shrewd remark: in retrospect, it's striking that many of Dylan's live 1978 song renditions had a distinctly Ray Charles flavour, both in his own exuberantly R&B phrasing and in his use of the back-up singers (his equivalent of the Raelettes), to whom he, like Charles, allocated a number of midsong lead vocal lines. A similar Ray Charles flavor can be detected on the tapes from Dylan's 1981 European tour, too.

Charles' crucial crossover album was *Modern Sounds in Country and Western*, released in 1962. Regarded as a 'sell-out' by R&B purists, but widely welcomed as bringing fresh life into country and pop, it was influential and immensely successful, as were a number of hit singles taken from it—one of which was the lovely 'You Don't Know Me', 1962. Dylan introduced this song into his concert repertoire, performing it with great affection in Andrarum, Sweden, May 27, 1989, and sang it at five further 1989 concerts and at five in 1991, including at South Bend, Indiana, November 6, 1991: an exceptional performance, managing to be both the ultimate prom band moment and an affecting tribute to Ray Charles.

('You Don't Know Me' was written by Eddie Arnold and Cindy Walker. As with Dylan's contribution to the WILLIE NELSON-Bob Dylan song 'Heartland', it is alleged that Arnold wrote only the title of 'You Don't Know Me' and his co-writer all the rest.)

The Ray Charles version of 'That Lucky Old Sun' also seems the prompt for Dylan's performances of this beguiling, neo-minstrel pop song, which he may have recorded in 1971 at the session that yielded the 'Watching the River Flow' single, and which he certainly offered in concert at Farm Aid, Champaign, Illinois, September 21, 1985, at 23 concerts in 1986, at Madison, Wisconsin, November 5, 1991, in Hollywood, May 19, 1992, and at the so-called 'free rehearsal' at Fort Lauderdale, September 23, 1995.

There is at least one further small connection between Ray and Bob. The main soloist in the Ray Charles band of the 1950s to early 1960s was Dave 'Fathead' Newman; he and Dylan play together behind DOUG SAHM on the track 'Me & Paul' on the fine album *Doug Sahm & Band*, 1972. Fathead is one of many long-suffering musicians in Ray Charles' band given sympathetic treatment in the vivid, old-fashioned biopic *Ray*.

[Ray Charles: 'Blackjack', Atlanta, 18 Nov 1954, Atlantic 1076, NY, 1955; 'The Right Time', NY, 28 Oct 1958, Atlantic 2010, NY, 1958, & on *The Genius Sings the Blues*, Atlantic 8052, 1961; 'What'd I Say', NY, Feb 1959, issued as 2-part single Atlantic 2031, NY, 1959 & on *What'd I Say*, Atlantic, NY, 1959; all reissued on the 3-CD set *Ray Charles: The Birth of Soul—The Complete Atlantic Rhythm & Blues Recordings, 1952–1959*, Atlantic & Atco Remasters Series, Atlantic 82310–2, NY, 1991. Ray Charles: 'Unchain My Heart', NY, May 1961, ABC-Paramount 10266, US, 1961; 'Let's Go Get Stoned', LA, late 1965, *Crying Time*, ABC-Paramount & then as single, ABC-Paramount 10808, US, 1966; 'You'll Never Walk Alone', *nia*, *Modern Sounds in Country and Western*, ABC-Paramount 410, Hollywood (HMV CLP 1580 & CSD 1451, London), 1962; 'You Don't Know Me', Hollywood, 15 Feb 1962, ABC-Paramount 10345 (HMV POP 1064), 1962; 'That Lucky Old Sun', Hollywood, 10 Jul 1963, ABC-Paramount 10509, 1963. The Ray Charles website is at *www.morethings.com/music/brother-ray/index.html*.

Bob Dylan: 'Unchain My Heart', Topanga Park, CA, 29 Apr, 1 May & 2 May 1986, all unreleased & uncirculated; 'You'll Never Walk Alone', Topanga Park, CA, 28 & 29 Apr 1986, unreleased & uncirculated; one version overdubbed with different bass player 28 May 1986, ditto. Dylan's remark re the Raelettes in this writer's presence, London, 17 Jun 1978; 'That Lucky Old Sun', reportedly recorded NY, 16–19 Mar 1971. Doug Sahm & Band: 'Me & Paul', NY, Oct 1972, *Doug Sahm & Band*, Atlantic SD-7254, NY, 1972. *Ray*, dir. Taylor Hackford, written Hackford & James L. White, Anvil / Baldwin / Bristol Bay, US, 2004.]

Charters, Samuel B. [1929 -] Samuel Barclay Charters was born in Pittsburgh on August 1, 1929. His family moved to Sacramento, California, in 1945 and three years later he began performing in jazz combos in the Bay Area. He began making field recordings by jazz and blues musicians in 1955, and while everyone else who was in Memphis in 1956 was excited by ELVIS PRESLEY, Charters was excited to find old blues singers from the pre-war era, still alive and functioning: 'GUS CANNON and Will Shade and everybody with the jug bands.'

When Charters found them, and recorded them again for the first time in over 20 years, it made him realise something simple and powerful: 'that these people weren't from another planet, they were part of our life and some of them were still alive.'

In November 1959, the New York publisher Rinehart published Sam Charters' book *The Country Blues*—and it proved one of those rare books that actually makes something happen out in the world. Effectively it kicked off the blues revival that became a shaping force within the whole burgeoning scene that encompassed the New Left, the civil rights movement, the Greenwich Village folk phenomenon, the rise of Bob Dylan and more.

The blues that Charters drew to people's attention, and which he invented the phrase 'country blues' to describe, was neither the vaudeville-jazz sort they'd heard by Bessie Smith nor the electric post-war blues of MUDDY WATERS, SONNY BOY WILLIAMSON and HOWLIN' WOLF. It was the great hidden mass of still largely unknown, pre-war, mostly down-home blues, southern and unamplified, and as richly diverse as life under the sea. *The Country Blues* was a revelation and an inspiration to many, and prompted young, white, urban aficionados to trawl the Deep South and 'find' a number of old, black, rural musicians, who duly appeared in the coffee-houses of Greenwich Village, Philadelphia, Cambridge and Washington, D.C.—among them many at whose feet Dylan was literally able to sit, soaking up some of the riches of their styles, techniques and musical heritage.

Charters' book didn't impress everybody. He pipped to the post the rather more precise and thorough-going, wide-ranging blues scholar and British architect Paul Oliver, whose book *Blues Fell This Morning* (in the US *The Meaning of the Blues*) arrived in 1960, as did American jazz writer Frederic Ramsey's *Been Here and Gone*, a richly photo-loaded account of travels through the 1950s South in search, as later editions said, 'of what might still remain of an original, authentic African American musical tradition'.

There was much carping too from some of those who felt that they already knew about all this music but hadn't troubled to write books about it. They felt that despite all the fieldwork Charters had done, in Alabama, New Orleans, Memphis and even the Bahamas, he didn't have a proper folklorist's interest in 'the tradition', but rather had the sort of flighty interest in 'originality' and 'creativity' that is just what you'd expect from a literary person with an inclination towards BEAT poetry.

Charters' critics also felt that there were far richer seams of pre-war blues than those he had mined: that many of the figures he championed were second-rate and that he gave too much attention to the light-weight, hokum end of the spectrum at the expense of the heavier, darker material born in the Mississippi delta.

In fact the LP issued as a companion to Charters' book contradicted this claim: it was deliberately wide-ranging but included tracks by BLIND LEMON JEFFERSON, BLIND WILLIE JOHNSON, SLEEPY JOHN ESTES, the very raw Tommy McClennan and ROBERT JOHNSON. It also included BLIND WILLIE McTELL's 1928 classic 'Statesboro Blues'—and after the HARRY SMITH compilation of 1952, *AMERICAN FOLK MUSIC*, the Charters record was the next most crucial release in the history of how pre-war music was regained.

Charters was subsequently responsible for 'discovering' the Bahamian songster Joseph Spence in 1958 (whose trademark rhythm Bob Dylan utilises on the faster, largely ignored version of 'Forever Young' on *Planet Waves*) and was active on the fringes of the Village scene in the early 1960s. Charters produced around 20 Folkways albums, recorded as part of the True Endeavor Jug Band, partnered HAPPY TRAUM's brother Artie in the New Strangers, was an A&R man for Prestige in 1963, oversaw many blues reissues and even produced early albums by Country Joe & the Fish. In the early 1970s he moved to Sweden and later that decade travelled in West Africa for his 1981 book *The Roots of the Blues: An African Search*.

Still alive, in 2000 Sam and his second wife, Beats-specialist literary scholar Ann Charters, established the Charters Archives of Blues and Vernacular African American Music at the University of Connecticut. But if he had done nothing else after *The Country Blues*, he would have earned his place in the history of the music, as a significant figure in bringing the pre-war blues world forward into the heart of the 1960s and right into the consciousness of Dylan's generation. And specifically, his LP *The Country Blues* almost certainly gave Bob Dylan his first hearing of the work of Blind Willie McTell.

[Samuel B. Charters, *The Country Blues*, New York: Rinehart, 1959; *The Roots of the Blues: An African Search*, New York: Marion Boyars, 1981. Various Artists: *The Country Blues*, RBR RF-1, NY, 1959. Charters' quotes, phone interview by this writer, 08 Aug 2002.]

Child, Francis James [1825 - 1896] Francis James Child was born in Boston, Massachusetts, on February 1, 1825. A Professor of English Literature at Harvard, he made a significant contribution to Chaucer studies (1863) and published a five-volume edition of Spenser (1885) but was also a pioneering collector of traditional (non-broadsheet) ballads, which he published in his *The English and Scottish Popular Ballads, 1882–98* [five volumes], a standard work. His numbering system for these ballads is the universally accepted way to identify them. He also argued for attention to be paid to children's game songs, writing that they are 'the last stage of many old ballads'.

Child Ballads that Dylan has bumped up against in one way or another include 'Blackjack Davey' and 'Love Henry'. 'Blackjack Davey', 'Gypsy Davey' and 'The Raggle-Taggle Gypsies' are all versions of Child no.200. 'Love Henry' is essentially Child no.68, 'Young Hunting', of which he gives 11 versions (all from Scotland) but which is offered with over 40 variants in Bronson's standard companion work *The Traditional Tunes of the Child Ballads—Vol. II* (1962, pp.60–82). Dylan sings Bronson Variant 19 almost word for word with the addition of one verse from elsewhere.

Child also collected a variant of the 'Scarborough Fair' song cluster, from an 1827 manuscript, that offers this verse: 'Did ye ever travel twixt Berwick and Lyne? / Sober and grave grows merry in time / There ye'll meet wi a handsome young dame / Ance she was a true love of mine'—which, though located on a different borderline (Berwick is the last English town before you reach Scotland, on the east coast), is very close to Dylan's lyric in 'Girl of the North Country'.

Child died in Boston on September 11, 1896.

***Chronicles* [album]** See Booker T.

***Chronicles Volume One* [2004]** The first long-rumoured and then long-awaited volume of a trilogy of books of memoirs by Dylan was published by Simon & Schuster on October 5, 2004 (having originally been described by them as 'the most-awaited book of 2002' and listed in their fall catalogue that year, though at 92 pages shorter than the 2004 version). An abridged audio book, with narration by Sean Penn, was issued simultaneously on CD and on cassette. (Penn, if it matters, had never read for an audio book before.)

Six weeks later, the book was no.5 on the *New York Times* Hardcover Non-Fiction best seller list, and Amazon.com and Barnesandnoble.com had it as their all-round no.2 best seller. It reached no.2 in the *New York Times* non-fiction best-seller list by late December, and was nominated for a National Book Award. Clearly, like many aspects of what might be seen as the official marketing of Bob Dylan Heritage (by Dylan, his office, his music-publishing and his record company, and extending into areas like films—especially the MARTIN SCORSESE film *No Direction Home*, 2005), a striking aspect of *Chronicles Volume One* is its dollar power.

Its success was aided by its receiving generally rapturous reviews, often by somewhat surprised reviewers impressed by its clarity and 'candor'. Its accuracy was noted even by some who had a more specialist knowledge to measure it against. Elijah Wald, co-author with DAVE VAN RONK of the latter's own memoir of the folk revival years, *The Mayor of MacDougal Street*, wrote this: 'The Dylan book is extraordinarily honest, straightforward and accurate, at least about his early New York days. There are some minor lapses and shifts of memory, as is inevitable after forty-plus years, but everyone I know who was on the scene at that time is blown away at how clear a picture he paints of it.' He adds: 'As for Dylan's picture of Van Ronk, it is largely accurate as well as highly complimentary.'

Likewise IZZY YOUNG, who ran the Folklore Center in Greenwich Village when Dylan was new there, writes this about the book: 'His description of the Folklore Center, and the same for Dave Van Ronk, is priceless, and, more importantly, correct. . . . I lived in the center of the folk music revival in America and Bob Dylan made it real for me forty years later.'

On the other hand, you didn't have to be a Dylan aficionado to detect errors. One correspondent to the publisher's website (Paul Baragona, from Raleigh, NC) complained: 'I noticed on page 8 that Bob Dylan claims to have initially traveled to New York in a 1957 Impala. . . . Impala was not introduced until 1958. Sorry to be so picky, but the body styles were totally different.'

Others had more fundamental qualms about the book's hard-to-measure but certainly odd relationship to truth. Many noted that this unexpectedly direct and detailed narrative, offered with such vivid zing, and certainly giving the lie to the old saw that 'if you can remember the 60s you weren't really there', nonetheless avoids most of the major events in Dylan's life and career—among them his marriages, their break-ups, his going electric, his partnership with THE BAND, the making of the Basement Tapes or of any of his greatest albums, or becoming a Born Again Christian. And some felt that beyond what was missing there was a slippery quality about what was there.

Perhaps with an artist like Dylan this was inevitable. To some extent, indeed, this might apply to anyone. As writer NIGEL HINTON has commented, 'People ask what in fiction draws on personal memory. But memory and invention are impossible to untangle. No memory is untouched by invention and no invention untainted by memory. And I think *Chronicles* operates like that. I don't believe most of the things Dylan tells us, but I think we know more about him from this invented memory than from any attempt to reconstruct perfectly a sequence of events. The essence, the pure spirit of how he is and how he sees the world comes through the fictionalised memory.'

A less charitable but most interesting near-instant assessment came from CLINTON HEYLIN, whose article 'I Don't Believe You—*Chronicles*, Thru the Eyes of a Critic' (though he might have made that 'Thru the Green Eyes of a Biographer') was published in the UK fanzine *Judas!* in January 2005. He notes the book's 'gaping chasms in chronology, even within the corset-tight remit [Dylan] imposes', coming from 'a self-conscious artist painting a flattering, self-serving portrait', in which 'its 300 pages contain not a single accurate date. I mean, not one.'

Heylin also recalls that Dylan mentioned, 'back in the spring of 1963, that he was writing an autobiography of sorts . . . "about somebody who has come to the end of one road, knows there's another road there but doesn't know exactly where it is" . . .', and that Dylan had also kept a diary of the 1974 tour. He concludes: '*Chronicles* confirms that he has been chronicling for many a year . . . this is no work of memory, even one that is working a lot better than others might previously have suspected.' Heylin is also perceptive on the detail of how many of Dylan's metaphors suggest by their clumsiness that they have been contributed by the contemporary Dylan rather than the more sure-footed younger man.

Complaint at all this 'circumspection and dissembling' is not always just: he claims it as typical that *Chronicles* produces 'the previously unknown FLO CASTNER', when in fact she is a prominent interviewee and witness to Dylan's Dinkytown period in the lengthy 2002 article 'Desire Revisited: Dylan in Dinkytown 1959' by Hans Eisenbeis; more generally Heylin refers to the book as 'Bob Dylan's 2004 autobiography' when it clearly *isn't* an autobiography but that lesser and more reasonably partial a thing, a memoir, and never claims to be more. Heylin concedes that despite everything, the book is 'still nail-hammeringly riveting', and argues reasonably that it could have been far better—'a genuine literary triumph'—had Dylan allowed an editor in on it.

An axe to grind, of course, differs from the inevitablitiy of 'fictionalised memory', and Dylan does offer both. Least impressive is the sour and dissembling poor-little-me rant about being abused by the special kind of fame that was his in the second half of the 1960s: 'A few years earlier Ronnie Gilbert, one of The Weavers, had introduced me at one of the NEWPORT FOLK FESTIVALS saying, "And here he is . . . take him, you know him, he's yours." I had failed to sense the ominous forebodings in the introduction. ELVIS had never been introduced like that.'

So far simply a bit petulant, plus a little disingenuous to suggest that Elvis had never been made to feel 'owned' by the burden of fame. But then we get this: '"Take him, he's yours!" What a crazy thing to say! Screw that.' This is not the great wordsmith at his judicious or graceful best. And he goes on to offer this embarrassing piece of sulky special pleading, in which he wants it both ways so shamelessly that it's comic: 'All I'd ever done was sing songs that were dead straight and expressed powerful new realities.' Oh is *that* all? As Jim Kunstler comments, this suggests 'someone strikingly peevish, given the fantastic advantages and emoluments of his position in life. But the book as a whole is a different matter.'

The book as a whole is a surprisingly vivid, detailed, intensive, unpredictable delight, and most of all an absolutely invaluable, rich and (mostly) existentially truthful memoir about the long-gone world of Greenwich Village at the start of the 1960s—at the start, that is, of everything.

[Bob Dylan, *Chronicles Volume One*, New York: Simon & Schuster, 2004 (poor-me rant p.115); Sean Penn, *Chronicles Volume One (Abridged)*, New York: Simon & Schuster Audio, 2004. Nigel Hinton quoted with permission from private e-mail to writer Sarah Beattie, 16 Jan 2005. Elijah Wald quoted with permission from e-mail to the Pre-War Blues online discussion group *pre-war-blues@yahoogroups.com*, 11 Aug 2005 & e-mail to this writer 16 Aug 2005. Izzy Young, 'Bob Dylan's Chronicles', *Judas!* no.14, Huntingdon, UK, Jul 2005. Clinton Heylin: 'I Don't Believe You—*Chronicles*, Thru the Eyes of a Critic', *Judas!* no.12, Jan 2005. Hans Eisenbeis: 'Desire Revisited: Dylan in Dinkytown 1959', *Rake*, Minneapolis, Apr 2002, seen online 15 Aug 2005 at *www.rakemag.com/stories/section_detail.aspx?itemID=2210&catID=146&SelectCatID=146*. Jim Kunstler, online book review at *www.kunstler.com/mags_dylan.html*, 4 Aug 2005.]

Clancy Brothers & Tommy Makem An influential and popular US-based Irish folk group from the end of the 1950s onwards: the musically respectable flipside of the Dubliners—despite, as Dylan noted when comparing them to Northern Ireland's McPeake Family, having 'that touch of commerciality to them: you didn't mind it, but it was still there', and despite looking, in photos, like ads for knitting patterns. They're to be seen proving the point in archive footage unearthed in the film *No Direction Home* (2005).

Paddy Clancy was born in Carrick-on-Suir, Ireland, in 1922; brother Tom was born there in 1923; Liam was born in 1936. The older two left Ireland for Canada in 1947, crossed illegally into the US in 1948, working first in Cleveland, Ohio, and then moving via Chicago to New York City. Tommy Makem, born in Keady, Northern Ireland, in 1932, first joined them in 1956 in Chicago, shortly before the move to New York, where Paddy helped Folkways and Elektra to record Irish music and set up his own label, Tradition, which issued LPs by the McPeakes, Josh White, ODETTA and, from 1959 onwards, by, er, the Clancy Brothers & Tommy Makem. They had wanted to be actors, not singers, and Tom Clancy had some success at this—even playing on Broadway in Orson Welles' *King Lear*—but the others struggled in small venues until they switched to singing, which was immediately more popular with audiences. Their first two LPs, *The Rising of the Moon* and *Come Fill Your Glass with Us*, were followed by a 1961 appearance on the 'Ed Sullivan' TV show that emblazoned their name at once on the American public mind. In the late 1960s, Paddy Clancy returned to Ireland to take up dairy farming, and Tommy Makem went solo in 1969.

In *Chronicles Volume One* (2004) Dylan recalls, while dismissing the concept 'protest songs' and endorsing the very different category of 'rebellion songs', that the Clancy Brothers 'and their buddy Tommy Makem' were crucial purveyors of 'rebellion songs'. He says that these 'really moved me' and that 'they sang them all the time', and that in the White Horse Bar on Hudson Street in the Village, where he befriended Liam, its clientele, 'mostly . . . guys from the old country . . . would sing drinking songs, country ballads and rousing rebel songs . . .' In *No Direction Home* Dylan calls the Clancy Brothers & Tommy Makem 'musketeers'.

But Dylan was enthusing about them long before this. He told interviewers David Hammond and Derek Bailey much the same things at Slane, Ireland, in 1984: 'The times I remember the Clancy Brothers most was not mostly in the clubs where we played [the Village Vanguard, the Village Gate and Gerde's Folk City] but in those bars . . . the White Horse bar . . . you could always go there, any time, and they'd be singing . . . Irish folk songs. Actually I learnt quite a few there myself. . . . Liam always sang those ballads which always would get to me—I'd never heard those kind of songs before, close up, you know. I'd heard them on record but I hadn't heard them close up. All the legendary people they used to sing about—Brennan on the Moor, or Roddy McCorley—I wasn't aware of them, when they existed—but it was as if they'd just existed yesterday.' In the televised part of this interview he also said: 'They just reached a lot of people, you know, with their exuberance and their attitude. They're all great singers. They're all so different, too, aren't they?'

He adds: 'I never heard a singer as good as Liam ever. He was just the best ballad singer I'd ever heard in my life. Still is, probably.'

Liam Clancy is also to be seen in *No Direction Home*, sat at that White Horse Tavern bar doing his Stage Irishman act (once an actor . . .) and saying highly interesting things: particularly about Dylan being one of that recognisable category of person the Irish have a term for—a 'shape-changer'; but he too was recorded talking about Bob Dylan two decades earlier, and talking too about what Dylan had told him he remembered about *him* from the White Horse days. He told PATRICK HUMPHRIES in October 1984:

> '. . . I was coming through La Guardia Airport about six months ago, and I had the bodhran on my back, and the guitars, and the next thing I felt this body behind me, and I got this great hairy kiss on the cheek. Now when that happens in New York you're going to turn round and belt whoever it is. So I turn around and it's Bob Dylan. We stood talking for a little while and suddenly the whole thing flooded back to me—what it was all like at that time. He says: "I love you guys. And I love [ROBERT] SHELTON for bringing me to your first concert in [New York] Town Hall. You know what I remember about that concert,

Liam? You sang a commercial about Donnelly's sausages!"'

In 2002 Liam Clancy published his autobiography, *The Mountain of the Women: Memoirs of an Irish Troubadour*, and in it he describes the importance of the White Horse bar not only to the Clancys but to the life of Greenwich Village in general: 'For us,' he writes at one point, 'the White Horse Tavern was the poetic, singing center of the Village.' But it was also where Dylan Thomas had committed suicide by whiskey in 1953, so it was on the tourist trail, and regulars sometimes perforce valued the back room more than the bar itself:

'Crowds of students would come on weekends to worship at the shrine. We, the locals, resented the invasion. This was our sanctuary: the back room was our singing place, the place where sea shanties, rebel songs, and raw love songs were exposed. This was where THEO BIKEL could cry over the beauty of his Old Testament recitals, where RICHARD FARIÑA could hold forth with snatches of his novel in progress' and 'where Jimmy [i.e. James] Baldwin could flaunt his homosexual intellectualism and snort scornfully at our ballsy shanties . . .' (Fariña was, according to Clancy, 'a regular' at the White Horse and a 'close friend', whom he calls 'the poet/singer/revolutionary'.)

In 1992, at the so-called Bob Dylan 30th Anniversary Concert Celebration in New York City, the Clancy Brothers and Robbie O'Connell with special guest Tommy Makem performed a gloriously unrockist, moving 'When the Ship Comes In' (with Paddy Clancy on harmonica and vocals, Liam on guitar and vocals, young whippersnapper Bobby Clancy on percussion and vocals, Tommy Makem on banjo and vocals, Robbie O'Connell on guitar and vocals, and G.E. SMITH on bass). Paddy came out of retirement for this concert—for the second time; they had re-formed in 1984 for a one-off concert and a new album, *Reunion*. For the party after the Dylan 'Celebration' concert, everyone repaired to Tommy Makem's club, the Irish Pavilion.

Liam wasn't happy with the sales figures of the 2-CD set of the concert. As HOWARD SOUNES recounted it, sales were good 'in the first few months and then . . . fell sharply. Artists who were on the CD received a percentage of royalties and were surprised to see how modest these were. "Some of the statements I got didn't read very well," [said] Liam Clancy. "You know, Denmark: two copies."'

In Patrick Humphries' 1984 interview with the Clancys, Paddy suddenly offers this odd little story about Dylan and his absorption of material back in the early days: 'You want to know where Dylan got his stuff? There was a little folk club here in London, down in the basement; we sang in it one night. . . . Anyway, AL GROSSMAN paid somebody and gave them a tape-recorder, and every folksinger that went up there was taped, and Bob Dylan got all those tapes . . .' And Liam agrees with this, adding: 'Yes, and the tune of "Farewell" [a song Dylan copyrighted in 1963 and is included in his official songbooks] . . . whoever was singing harmony was closer to the mike than the guy singing melody, and when [Dylan] wrote his version, he wrote it to the harmony not the melody line.'

The Clancys were carriers, not composers, of their material, so they have no cause to complain that Dylan took things from them (and generally they don't), but the songs he probably took specifically from hearing the Clancy Brothers & Tommy Makem performing live are: the traditional 'Brennan on the Moor', which becomes his 'Rambling Gambling Willie' (copyrighted 1962, and an outtake from *The Freewheelin' Bob Dylan*, 1963), the traditional 'The Parting Glass', which mutates into 'Restless Farewell' on *The Times They Are a-Changin'*, and the Appalachian song 'The Nightingale', whose tune Dominic Behan used for his song 'The Patriot Game', which the Clancys sang and from which Dylan in turn created 'With God on Our Side'.

Liam Clancy certainly recognised Dylan's artistic legitimacy: indeed he specifies the moment at which this really struck him, again in the interview with Patrick Humphries. He is recalling seeing Dylan at the 1965 NEWPORT FOLK FESTIVAL and reacting to the solo acoustic performance of 'Mr. Tambourine Man' that came *after* 'It's All Over Now, Baby Blue':

> 'I was actually filming at the Newport Festival that year. I was up a 12-foot platform filming with a telephoto lens, so I could zoom in close. And Dylan came out, and it was obvious that he was stoned, bobbing around the stage. Very Chaplinesque, actually. He broke into that "Tambourine Man" and I found myself standing there with tears streaming down my face, because—I saw the butterfly emerging from the caterpillar. I also saw, for the first time, the immense value of what the man was about. When he sang "my ancient empty street's too dead for dreaming", I knew it was Sullivan Street on a Sunday. So it was not only a street, it was *our* street. I suddenly realised that this kid, who had bugged us so often, had emerged into a very major artist.'

Tom died in Cork (Ireland) on November 7, 1990; Paddy died of cancer at home back in Carrick-on-Suir on November 10, 1998; Liam Clancy and Tommy Makem survive.

[Liam Clancy, *The Mountain of the Women: Memoirs of an Irish Troubadour*, New York: Doubleday, 2002, pp.250–51, 202. Bob Dylan, interview by Bono (who hadn't heard of the McPeake Family but liked the name), Slane, Ireland, Jul 1984, *Hot Press*, Dublin, *nia*, 1984; interview by David Hammond & Derek Bailey, Slane, 8 Jul 1984, partly broadcast RTE 2 TV, Dublin, Dec 1984 on 'It's a Long Way from Tipperary and Armagh: The Story of the Clancy Brothers and Tommy

Makem' (also broadcast Channel 4 TV, UK, 31 Dec 1985 & various US stations 1986); *Chronicles*, 2004, p.83 & 'Liam Clancy, by Bob Dylan', collected in Michael Gray & John Bauldie, eds., *All Across the Telegraph: A Bob Dylan Handbook*, London: Futura paperback edn., 1988, p.20; Patrick Humphries, 'Bob Dylan, by Liam Clancy', collected ditto, pp.20–21. The quotes re 'Farewell' & Albert Grossman, from same interview, first published with the rest in *The Telegraph* no.18, UK, winter 1984, pp.62–68, & collected in John Bauldie, ed, *Wanted Man: In Search of Bob Dylan*, London: Penguin rev. edn., 1992, pp.49–51. Reminder of specific song debts to the Clancys by seeing online 13 Jan 2006 Clancys section of *www.bobdylanroots.com*. Howard Sounes, *Down The Highway: A Life of Bob Dylan*, New York: Grove Press, 2001, Chapter 9, manuscript p.470.]

Clapton, Eric [1945 -] Eric Clapton was born at Ripley in the English Home Counties on April 30, 1945. He became a Rooster, then one of Casey Jones' Engineers, then a Yardbird, then quit when that fragile group became too pop for his taste—though the effect of his work would soon enough be to turn blues into rock. He joined JOHN MAYALL's Bluesbreakers and then, with Ginger Baker and JACK BRUCE, formed Cream (the first 'supergroup') in the unequalled summer of 1966. He was by now already spoken of as Britain's finest blues guitarist, and while Cream was a quintessential part of Swinging London (and more King's Road Chelsea than Carnaby Street) its repertoire included much pre-war as well as post-war blues material, albeit sometimes barely recognisable. The band split at the end of 1968, and Clapton, whose songwriting included collaboration with GEORGE HARRISON on Cream's hit single 'Badge', next tottered into new creation Blind Faith, with ex-Traffics Stevie Winwood and Rick Grech. Blind Faith recorded one album, with a front cover deemed more tasteless now than then, played their one obligatory free concert in June 1969 and then some big-money US dates, and promptly disintegrated.

Clapton was soon nicknamed 'God' but, caught between a recognition that JIMI HENDRIX was at least as Godlike and a terror at his own reputation, Clapton's work became muted and nervous; he also fell victim to heroin addiction. Yet he played with JOHN LENNON's Plastic Ono Band and Delaney & Bonnie and in 1970 released his first solo album, *Eric Clapton*, the first time he had dared be a lead singer. It yielded a placid hit version of J.J. Cale's song 'After Midnight', which itself served notice of how laid back and unguitar-star Clapton now intended to be, even though afterwards came the back-to-basics of the Derek & the Dominoes persona and some perkier playing on the album *Layla and Other Love Songs*.

He re-emerged, drug free, in 1973 and made a series of tediously mainstream rock albums, though some touching and poignantly-sung love songs came out of his widely publicised love-tussle with George Harrison and Patti Boyd in this period (especially on 1977's *Slowhand*) and his interest in the blues seemed given a fillip by his hearing its 1980s Texas reincarnation as personified by the Vaughan brothers, STEVIE RAY and JIMMIE. He returned to an older blues milieu with the styling of his mega-successful *Unplugged* album in 1992, and has been proselytising ROBERT JOHNSON into the ground ever since. For at least 20 years now he seems to have given annual multi-night concerts at London's beautiful Royal Albert Hall at which adoring fans still turn out dutifully for some of the world's most stultifyingly boring musical performances from a likeable man and ponderous artist who cannot but turn all he touches to the dullest gold, or more normally platinum. Since his heroin days, various other shootings-in-the-foot and personal tragedies have befallen him without discernible effect on his work.

It was inevitable that he and Dylan should come into working contact, for better and for worse. The main lines of their collaborations have been as follows. The first time Eric Clapton *didn't* play with Dylan was in London in 1965, when in the midst of the latter's last solo tour, he went into a small studio at his New York record company's behest to record a message for that year's annual Sales Convention: a message intended to gee up Columbia's rack-jobbers all over the world. The widely circulated tape of Dylan's predictably irreverent, but perhaps unpredictably gauche, doomed attempts is very funny. While he was at it, Dylan made an equally diffident but far more genuine attempt to lay down a cut of his still relatively new song 'If You Gotta Go, Go Now', playing piano and singing, backed by John Mayall's Bluesbreakers, who had been rounded up hastily for this brief and fruitless occasion. Eric Clapton was with the group and in the room at the time, but did not play. It was soon over, since Dylan proved himself too embarrassed to count the others in competently and the bemused British musos unable to get past this unprofessionalism or see the point of Bob Dylan at all.

At the Isle of Wight Concert in 1969, Clapton watched Dylan's performance and was far from bemused, observing shrewdly and at once that Dylan was 'being HANK WILLIAMS', even as most of the rest of us were fumbling in puzzlement at a Bob Dylan so uncannily different from the previous, 1966 version. Two years later, both artists took part in the *Concert for Bangla Desh*.

Clapton was one of the overfilled roomful of musicians (there were 20 others including vocalists: 21 others including Dylan) brought into Columbia's Studio E in New York City on July 28, 1975, for the second day of tentative sessions for the *Desire* album. Nonetheless, and undetectable though his contribution may be, Eric was present for that day's cut of 'Romance in Durango', which made it onto the album, and for a cut of 'Catfish' which later made it onto *Bootleg Series Vols. 1–3*.

In August 1975, Clapton released as a single a version of Dylan's 'Knockin' on Heaven's Door' that was at once ineffably dreary and an enormous hit—in both respects, therefore, being a worthy follow-up to his version of Bob Marley's 'I Shot the Sheriff'. Early the following year, when Clapton was making one of his plodding solo albums (*No Reason to Cry*) at THE BAND's studio in Malibu, California, and had brought in ROBBIE ROBERTSON and RICK DANKO, Dylan came too, and he wrote 'Sign Language', a modest song pleasing mostly for Dylan's rhyming of 'language' with 'sandwich' and, on the jointly sung recording, for a relaxed feel that owes more to Robertson's guitar-work than Clapton's and rightly has Dylan's voice higher than Eric's in the mix. It was included on the album. That March 30 (1976), the two of them spent further time in the studio, each performing behind the other but also sharing vocals on 'Adelita' and 'Big River', and with Clapton attempting Dylan's 'When the Ship Comes In'. None of these tracks has been released. Both artists took part in the concert that became *The Last Waltz* that November.

In the course of the European leg of Dylan's huge 1978 World Tour, Eric Clapton guested twice. At Nuremberg on July 1, Clapton was a support act, but returned to the stage for the encore of Dylan's set, to play lead guitar on 'I'll Be Your Baby Tonight' and stay for the final number, 'The Times They Are a-Changin''. On July 15, the last event of this leg of the tour, the gigantic gathering at Blackbushe Aerodrome in Southern England, Clapton was again a featured support act; but he came back on stage for the last Dylan number before the encore, and played on 'Forever Young'. And on that year's Clapton album *Backless* (nicknamed *Spineless*), he covered the Dylan-HELENA SPRINGS songs 'Walk Out in the Rain' and 'If I Don't Be There By Morning'.

On July 7, 1984, when Dylan and SANTANA played at London's huge Wembley Stadium, Eric Clapton joined Bob for a run of numbers at the end of his set, adding his guitar to 'Leopard-Skin Pill-Box Hat', 'It's All Over Now, Baby Blue', 'Tombstone Blues', 'Señor (Tales of Yankee Power)', 'The Times They Are a-Changin'', 'Blowin' in the Wind' and 'Knockin' on Heaven's Door'. Two years later, back in the studios in London on July 27–28, 1986 for a Dylan session intended to provide fresh material for his ill-advised film *Hearts of Fire*—material that Dylan had signally failed to compose—the musicians assembled behind him included Clapton on guitar, RON WOOD on bass and guitar and several others. They managed to get through some takes of John Hyatt's song 'The Usual', a 'Ride This Train', some stabs at Dylan's anyone-could-have-written-this-song 'Had a Dream About You Baby', some of Billy Joe Shaver's 'Old Five & Dimers Like Me', a 'To Fall in Love', a 'Night After Night' and a pleasant cut of Shel Silverstein and Dennis Locorriere's 'A Couple More Years'. Several of these made it onto the soundtrack album, several made it into the film, one made it onto *Down in the Groove* and one further cut even made it onto the Argentine *Down in the Groove* release.

Clapton was a distinguished guest at Live Aid in 1985, and seven years later a prominent figure at Dylan's so-called 30th Anniversary Concert Celebration at Madison Square Garden, New York, at which he was one of the inner circle of accompanists, with ROGER McGUINN, TOM PETTY, NEIL YOUNG and George Harrison. That October 15 when they rehearsed, Clapton and Dylan shared vocals on 'It Takes a Lot to Laugh It Takes a Train to Cry', and, with the others, on 'My Back Pages'. Clapton, naturally, also played guitar. At the event itself, before the ensemble finish, Clapton sang 'Love Minus Zero / No Limit' and gave a blistering version of 'Don't Think Twice, It's All Right', a real reoccupation of the song as a surging blues.

In the same hall, seven years further on, Dylan joined Clapton as a surprise guest at his Benefit for the Crossroads (in aid of a centre Clapton established in Antigua to help drug and alcohol addicts), and this time Bob performed 'Don't Think Twice It's All Right' and 'It Takes a Lot to Laugh, It Takes a Train to Cry' before he and Clapton shared vocals on the *Under the Red Sky* song 'Born in Time' (Clapton had covered this song on his 1998 album *Pilgrim*); Dylan then performed 'Leopard-Skin Pill-Box Hat' and 'Not Dark Yet' before Clapton rejoined him for further shared vocals on 'Crossroads'. Dylan finished off by playing behind Eric's lead vocals on 'Bright Lights, Big City'. The subsequent telecast and DVD included Dylan's 'Don't Think Twice' and their shared 'Crossroads'. Predictably, neither artist is at his best here; but then neither is ever at his best when the two get together.

[Eric Clapton (with Bob Dylan): 'Sign Language', *No Reason to Cry*, Polydor RSO RS1-3004, US, Sep 1976, CD-reissued 1996; Eric Clapton: *Backless*, RSO 3039, 1981; *Pilgrim*, Reprise / Wea 46577, US, 1998. *Eric Clapton: Benefit for the Crossroads*, VH-1 telecast 17 Jul 1999; DVD issued US, 26 Oct 1999. Bob Dylan: *Hearts of Fire* soundtrack album, Columbia SC40870, Oct 1987; *Hearts of Fire* film, dir. Richard Marquand, Lorimar / Warners, UK, 1987; *Down in the Groove*, Columbia 120.017, Argentina, 1988.]

Clark, Alan [1952 -] Alan Clark was born in Durham, north-east England, on March 5, 1952, lived in nearby Birtley and then the equally nearby Great Lumley, which overlooks Durham County Cricket ground and the River Wear. He learnt piano from age six but outplayed the manager of a local Hammond Organs shop on organ when hardly able to reach the pedals, and was earning money in clubs by age 13. He rejected a place at the Guildhall School of Music in London and spent 1971 playing on a cruise ship between Miami,

Haiti and Jamaica, where he encountered reggae music and lived a clubbing high life. From here he became a session musician whose trademark sound is 'to record two slightly different Hammond tracks and play them back together', which 'works particularly well on faster rock tracks.'

Early on he played in Splinter, a duo on GEORGE HARRISON's Dark Horse label, played in ERIC CLAPTON's band, recorded with Gallagher & Lyle in 1978–79 and toured with Lindisfarne in the same period. In late 1980 he had a glum week playing clubs with British Sinatra wannabe Matt Monro (it should have been glum, anyway) and then joined Dire Straits, which had formed in 1977 but never before had a keyboards player (though E Street Band pianist Roy Bittan played keyboards on the album *Making Movies*, recorded in summer 1980, shortly before Clark joined). Clark remained in Dire Straits right through till its disbandment in 1995.

One day in early 1983 he was in front man MARK KNOPFLER's Bank Street, Greenwich Village house when Bob Dylan called round to play demos of new songs. 'He appeared at the top of the stairs, the sun beaming through the open door behind him, like a superhero. Next thing you know, we're playing pool. He was quite good, but I won.'

Alan Clark duly played keyboards on the *Infidels* album, going into the studios in New York in 1983, starting on April 11 for five consecutive days, followed by a one-day gap and then another six consecutive studios days, then another four, and finally a last session on May 2. He plays, therefore, not only on the album but on the great tracks left unreleased until the 1991 box set the *Bootleg Series Vols. 1–3*, including 'Blind Willie McTell', on which he plays organ, and 'Foot of Pride'.

He returned to the studio for Dylan (though Dylan wasn't there) nearly two years after those sessions, on February 20 & 24 and March 4, 1985, for some overdubbing on *Empire Burlesque* tracks, and ended up putting synthesizers on 'Never Gonna Be the Same Again' and a number of unreleased tracks. Finally he found himself on *Down in the Groove* (misspelt as Alan Clarke) when an outtake from the *Infidels* sessions, the lugubrious 'Death Is Not the End', was placed, in desperation, on that 1988 album.

Since 1983, he and Dylan have '[run] into each other once or twice' but, he says, sounding a changed character from the old days in the northeast of England, Miami and Jamaica, 'I'm not one for turning up at people's gigs, less still for going backstage. Our paths will cross again.'

[Special thanks to Terry Kelly; all quotes from, and most facts re, Clark from Kelly's interview, *The Bridge* no.23, winter 2005, pp.6–15; birthplace & date c/o Kelly, e-mails to this writer, 26 & 27 Oct 2005; some Dire Straits detail from 'Mustafa Odabasi's Dire Straits Page . . . the first and the only Dire Straits page in Turkey', seen online 14 Jan 2006 at *www.ada.com.tr/~modabasi/ds.htm*.]

Clark, Charles Badger [1883 - 1957] See **'Spanish Is the Loving Tongue'**.

Clayton, Paul [1931 - 1967] Paul Clayton was a field-recorder, folksong collector, singer, guitarist and songwriter, and a well-known figure in folk revivalist circles. He was a friend of, and a major conduit of songs for, Bob Dylan.

He was born Paul Clayton Worthington in the old whaling port of New Bedford, Massachussets, on March 3, 1931, though part of his family came from Virginia. He field-recorded blues songster Pink Anderson in Charlottesville, Virginia, in 1950, first recorded as an artist himself in 1952 and had established himself as a singer-guitarist by 1956, when a whole flurry of his folksong albums was released on the Folkways, Riverside and Tradition labels. Further 1950s albums, of which there were many, included collections of broadside ballads, lumberjack songs, an album recorded with Jean Ritchie and one titled *Bobby Burns' Merry Muses of Caledonia*.

In the interview with Dylan by CAMERON CROWE, published within *Biograph*, 1985, Dylan says of him: 'Paul was just an incredible songwriter and singer. He must have known a thousand songs. I learned "Pay Day at Coal Creek" and a bunch of other songs from him.'

ROBERT SHELTON's *No Direction Home*, 1986, says that it was from Clayton's adaptation of the traditional 'Scarlet Ribbons for Her Hair' that Dylan took the melody for his 'Don't Think Twice, It's All Right', and he might have added that Dylan's lyric too owes something to Clayton's, which includes 'T'ain't no use to sit and wonder why, darlin,' and 'So I'm walkin' down that long, lonesome road, / You're the one that made me travel on . . .' This song, titled 'Who's Gonna Buy You Ribbons (When I'm Gone)', was first issued on a Monument Records single in 1959 and resurfaced on Clayton's 1961 album *Home-Made Songs and Ballads*.

In 1970 Dylan recorded Clayton's 'Gotta Travel On' for *Self Portrait*, and that album's record label duly credits Clayton as its composer (though GLEN DUNDAS' *Tangled Up in Tapes* 3rd edition, 1994, lists it as composed jointly by Clayton, Lazar, Ehrlich & Six–i.e. by Clayton plus David Lazar, Larry Ehrlich and Tom Six). In this case at least, however, Dylan knew the song before he knew Clayton. Robert Shelton's book dates their first meeting as in 1962, but the song is on the tape of Dylan made back in St. Paul, Minnesota, as early as May 1960. Perhaps Dylan knew the song then because Monument (the label for which ROY ORBISON had his run of mega-hits) had given the song to another artist on their roster, Billy Grammer, who in 1959 promptly had his first hit with it; Grammer's

'Gotta Travel On' reached the top five on the country charts and crossed over to the pop charts. Or perhaps Dylan knew the song because it had started out life as a 19th Century British melody that had been revived pre-Clayton by the Weavers—if 'revived' isn't too strong a word for it, in the case of the Weavers' insipid, repulsively winsome goody-two-shoes version.

Intriguingly, it's also likely that Dylan heard what must have been the far gutsier version performed live by BUDDY HOLLY, with which the latter certainly opened his final concert, at Clear Lake, Iowa, and which he therefore probably featured as the opener for the concert he gave at Duluth, Minnesota, which Dylan attended, two days earlier. And to complete a circle, it just may be that Holly himself knew the song from hearing Clayton perform it in the Village. As DAVID HAJDU reminds us in his book *Positively 4th Street*, Holly knew CAROLYN HESTER, who had recorded her first album with his producer Norman Petty, and Holly had attended those sessions. We know too that—perhaps prompted by Hester, or his own interest in her—Holly moved into a Greenwich Village apartment some time before his death. The enticing fact is, indeed, that had Holly lived a year or two longer, he and Dylan would probably have bumped into each other in the Village.

In any case, after the *Self Portrait* recording, Dylan also performed 'Gotta Travel On' at 16 of his 1976 Rolling Thunder Revue concerts.

Dylan is rumoured to have made a guest appearance at a Paul Clayton concert at the Showboat Lounge in Washington, D.C., as early as September 24, 1961. After their fortunes were swiftly reversed, Paul Clayton was a companion on Dylan's 1964 CAR-RIDE THROUGH AMERICA, and is warmly commemorated in Dylan's *Chronicles Volume One*, in which Dylan seems to say that he first encountered Clayton as 'a folksinger friend of [DAVE] VAN RONK' and describes him as 'good-natured, forlorn and melancholic', adding that he 'must have had at least thirty records out but was unknown to the American public—an intellectual, a scholar and a romantic with an encyclopedic knowledge of balladry'. He also says that Clayton would be one of those playing poker all night upstairs above the Gaslight, and remembers spending 'a week or so' in the cabin that Clayton retained in the mountains outside Charlottesville, Virginia. In the last *Chronicles* passage about Clayton, Dylan turns to the question of song sources, and claims that 'Paul got all his versions of songs by adapting transcriptions from old texts. He knew hundreds of songs and must have had a photographic memory. . . . I liked Clayton and I liked his friends.'

It has often been suggested that Clayton, who was gay, felt rather more for Dylan than that. Paul Clayton died in 1967, electrocuted in his bath. As Kristine Baggelaar and Donald Milton put it somewhat crassly and starkly in *Folk Music: More Than a Song*: 'After a history of a problem with pills, Paul Clayton took his life on March 30, 1967, and his death brought to light the fine tension between artistic creativity and insanity.'

[Paul Clayton: field recordings of blues songster Pink Anderson, Charlottesville, VA, 29 May 1950, issued on *Rev. Gary Davis and Pink Anderson: American Street Songs*, Riverside RLP 12-611, 1961. Paul Clayton: *Bill Clifton & Paul Clayton: The First Recordings: A Bluegrass Session, 1952*, Folk Variety FV 12004 (D), 1975 and Bear Family BF-15001, Vollersode, West Germany, 1979; *Jean Ritchie & Paul Clayton: American Folk Tales & Songs*, Tradition TLP 1011, 1950s; *Bobby Burns' Merry Muses of Caledonia*, Elektra EKL-155, NY, 1958; 'Pay Day at Coal Creek' and 'Gotta Travel On' issued on *Paul Clayton, Folk Singer!*, Monument MLP 8017, US, 1965. 'Who's Gonna Buy You Ribbons (When I'm Gone)', Monument 45-416, US, 1959; *Home-Made Songs & Ballads*, Monument M 4001, US, 1961. Paul Clayton & the Foc'scle Singers: *Foc'sle Songs and Shanties*, Folkways FA 2429, NY, 1959.

Billy Grammer: 'Gotta Travel On', Monument, US, 1959. The Weavers: 'Gotta Travel On', collected on *The Weavers' Greatest Hits*, Vanguard, NY, 1957. Glen Dundas, *Tangled Up in Tapes*, 3rd ed., 1994. David Hajdu, *Positively 4th Street*, p.32. Carolyn Hester's 1st album was *Scarlet Ribbons*, Coral 57143, 1958. Bob Dylan, *Chronicles Volume One*, 2004, pp.25–26, 46–47, 260–261. Kristine Baggelaar and Donald Milton, *Folk Music: More Than a Song*, New York: Thomas Y. Crowell, 1976.

An invaluable resource for this entry was Stefan Wirz's American Music website, specifically the page *www.wirz.de/music/claytfrm.htm*, seen online 6 Aug 2005.]

Clinch Mountain Boys, the See **Stanley, Ralph**.

Cohen, John [1932 -] John Cohen was born in New York City in 1932 to folk-dancing parents of Russian descent. At 14 he encountered gospel music, from the kitchen staff at summer camp, and at 16 he heard WOODY GUTHRIE's *Dust Bowl Ballads* and some LPs of hillbilly music that he seized upon as part of his anti-middle-class rebellion. By then in Long Island, NY, he learnt guitar while still at school (no-one else there did) and he was soon listening to Library of Congress field recordings, and records of old-time fiddlers, LEADBELLY, Hobart Smith, Texas Gladden and others. At Williams College he turned away from fraternity life, hiking mountain trails, drawing and learning banjo. Nevertheless he transferred to the school of art at Yale University in 1951.

At Yale he was inspired by art teacher Josef Albers but drawn to photography by strongly disturbing shots by Robert Frank—disturbing in showing Cohen that 'art could be personal, biographical, even sentimental at the same time it was surreal. . . . It suggested a sense of action where an artist might move through the world and make images from his own experience.'

Taking up photography, he was in the right places at the right time to record in his quiet, vivid photos the struggles of peasants in Patagonia, the penurious life of musicians and others in Kentucky–see his superb black and white portraits of the great Roscoe Holcomb–but also of THE BEATS and the coffee-house life of Greenwich Village during the late 1950s and early 1960s.

After a lengthy trip to Peru, Cohen returned to New York City in 1957, moved into a loft and began working as a freelance professional photographer. At the same time, he was also an undimmed music enthusiast and by 1952 had been hanging out with the REV. GARY DAVIS, documenting his music and escorting him to concerts. In 1958 he formed the revivalist group the NEW LOST CITY RAMBLERS, with TOM PALEY and MIKE SEEGER, and though it faltered from time to time in later decades (Paley dropped out in 1962), Cohen could claim by 2000 to have been playing with the group for more than 40 years.

It was a group Bob Dylan admired, and he and Cohen got on well. The pictures Cohen took around the Village include gorgeous early shots of the young Bob Dylan. And when Cohen tried out movie film, his first test roll was three minutes of silent footage of a playful Huck Finn Dylan on the roof of Cohen's 3rd Avenue apartment block. Yet Cohen writes of this period: 'In the loft I also photographed . . . ALAN LOMAX and the Kentucky singer Roscoe Holcomb. THE STANLEY BROTHERS and Woody Guthrie visited, along with a stream of other musicians and artists. Over the distance of time, those years . . . seem very exciting, but in reality it felt mostly desolate and run down.'

Cohen made fieldtrips to Kentucky where he 'discovered', recorded and filmed Holcomb, and later brought him to New York to record him in the studio. This alone would have indebted us to him. Cohen also coined the phrase 'that high lonesome sound', which has moved from its original function as a description of Holcomb's unique, keening, wondrous voice, and has now come to describe Appalachian music in general.

Five decades' worth of Cohen's photographs have been published in his great book *There Is No Eye: John Cohen Photographs*, 2001, including shots of Dylan (plus a wonderful shot of Red Grooms, the artist remembered so ardently in Dylan's *Chronicles* as having been his favourite contemporary painter in those Greenwich Village days: a shot of Grooms running across 3rd Avenue with a huge framed canvas wedged precariously in an old pram).

The book's title comes from Dylan, from near the end of the prose poem that forms the sleevenotes to the *Highway 61 Revisited* album of 1965: 'you are right john cohen–quazimodo was right–mozart was right. . . . I cannot say the word eye anymore . . . there is no eye–there is only a series of mouths–long live the mouths–your rooftop–if you don't already know–has been demolished. . . . eye is plasma & you are right about that too . . .'

Photographs *not* in Cohen's book include the colour shots of Dylan used on the covers of the *Self Portrait* album, and not used, but taken by Cohen in 1970, and the colour shots Dylan got him to take from a great distance–'bring one of those lenses like a telescope, so you can take pictures from a couple of blocks away'–while he walked on New York City streets unrecognised.

All these photographs *are* published, however, along with a wide selection of the 1962 black and white shots of Bob, in Cohen's 2003 volume *Young Bob: John Cohen's Early Photographs of Bob Dylan*.

Accompanying the earlier of these two books is a terrific, eclectic CD collection, *There Is No Eye: Music for Photographs*, conceived and supervised by Cohen and featuring rare recordings made by him and others, including a Holcomb version of 'Man of Constant Sorrow' and Dylan's 'Roll On, John' (for detail on this cut, see **Rinzler, Ralph**).

In June to July 1968 John Cohen and HAPPY TRAUM conducted the three interviews with Dylan that appeared as one feature, 'Conversations with Bob Dylan', in *Sing Out!* magazine that October, much to the surprise of many Dylan followers, who had perhaps never expected him to return to the pages of this folk scene magazine. Dylan also surprised Cohen, when he mentioned biblical parables. Cohen asks: 'When did you read the Bible parables?' and Dylan responds: 'I have always read the Bible, though not necessarily always the parables.' Cohen comments: 'I don't think you're the kind who goes to the hotel, where the Gideons leave a Bible, and you pick it up.' Dylan, resenting, as ever, people's assumptions about him, retorts quickly: 'Well, you never know.'

Many decades later, Cohen is himself an interviewee–a modest, perspicacious one–in MARTIN SCORSESE's 2005 film *No Direction Home*. He lives and works in Putnam Valley, New York.

As if all the above were not enough for one lifetime, Cohen's work is in the collections of the Museum of Modern Art, the Metropolitan Museum of Art in New York and many other places; from 1992 to 1997 Cohen was Professor of Visual Arts at the State University of New York in Purchase, NY, and one of his field recordings, of a young girl singing an Andean huayno in the Quechua language, is up there on the Voyager spacecraft, traveling beyond the solar system to the stars.

[John Cohen, *There Is No Eye: John Cohen Photographs*, New York: powerHouse Books, 2001; quote re desolation, p.83; *Young Bob: John Cohen's Early Photographs of Bob Dylan*, powerHouse Books, 2003; Dylan quote p.48. Various Artists: *There Is No Eye: Music for Photographs*, Smithsonian Folkways 4001, US, 2001. John Cohen & Happy Traum: 'Conversations with Bob Dylan', *Sing Out!* no.18, Oct–Nov 1968, New York, pp.6–23, 27.]

Cohen, Leonard [1934 -] Few people named Leonard Norman (or Cohen) are as cool as the poet, novelist and singer-songwriter born in Montreal, Quebec, on September 21, 1934. He learnt guitar as a teenager, co-founded a countryish folk group, attended McGill University, began his 50-year career by publishing his first poetry book in 1956 (*Let Us Compare Mythologies*), followed this in 1961 with *The Spice-Box of Earth*, moved to a Greek island, published his first novel *The Favorite Game* in 1963, the poetry volume *Flowers for Hitler* in 1964 and the novel *Beautiful Losers* in 1966. In 1967 he was signed to Columbia Records (Dylan's label) by JOHN HAMMOND (the man who'd signed Dylan) and made a début album whose influence seemed inversely proportionate to its commercial success.

Songs like 'Suzanne' and 'Hey That's No Way to Say Goodbye' conquered at once the world of bedsit suicide music, reshaping it with a lugubrious sang-froid that was easy to parody but hard to shut out. He changed the rules of noir with his almost expressionless monotone, remorselessly plinkety serenading guitar and eerily cheerful female vocal chorus, and divided people into those who adored, and those reduced to suffocating rage by, this music's handsome and intellectual creator. *The Songs of Leonard Cohen* (JUDY COLLINS had a hit with 'Suzanne' that managed to put it on the soundtrack of the summer of love) was followed by *Songs from a Room* (1969), which featured 'Bird on a Wire', and then *Songs of Love and Hate* (1971) and after *Live Songs* (1973) came *New Skin for the Old Ceremony* (1974).

Always more popular in Europe and Canada than the US, Cohen's career as a singer-songwriter was not helped by the 1977 album *Death of a Ladies' Man*, produced by a deranged, gun-toting PHIL SPECTOR, on which Bob Dylan and ALLEN GINSBERG were back-up vocalists on 'Don't Go Home with Your Hard-On', a song as uninteresting as its title is contrived. A volume of poetry the year after was titled *Death of a Lady's Man*. (Precious, moi?)

The 1984–85 album *Various Positions* included the song 'Hallelujah', which has proved compelling to many other artists, most notably Jeff Buckley (and least notably BONO). Dylan performed it with mixed success in concert (its 1988 début in Montreal was well wrought, its second and final outing of the year, in Hollywood, not so), and the two chatted about it in a café in Paris' 14th Arondissement some time afterwards. (The song had two endings; Dylan preferred the less bleak one: 'And even though it all went wrong / I'll stand before the Lord of Song / With nothing on my tongue but Hallelujah!' This was too cheerful for Jeff Buckley; the doomier ending is on his multi-million-selling album *Grace*.)

To ADRIAN DEEVOY Cohen reported the café conversation with Dylan as being 'a real good writers' shop talk. We really went into the stuff very technically. You couldn't meet two people who work more differently. He said, "I like this song you wrote called 'Hallelujah'." He said, "How long did that take you to write?" And I said, "Oh, the best part of two years." He said, "Two years?" Kinda shocked. And then we started talking about a song of his called "I and I" from *Infidels*. I said, "How long did you take to write that?" He said, "Oh, 15 minutes." I almost fell off my chair. Bob just laughed.'

This is, apart from anything else, illustrative of how much more willing Cohen is than Dylan to discuss the processes of his work straightforwardly—to give good 'shop talk'—in public. He does so with a lovely lucidity for German television in 1997, saying, among much else: 'I wish it didn't take so long to finish a song and to make a record . . . it seems to be a long process . . . it's trying to discover how I really feel about something. To move a song from a slogan to an authentic expression is really what the enterprise is about . . . discarding the lines that come too easy . . . waiting until something else bubbles up that is a little truer . . .'

He moves on, after elaborating on the writing stage, to the other stages: 'There's the writing of the song, which can be laborious and difficult; there's the recording of the song in the studio, which also takes a tremendous concentration . . . to materialize the songs. And then the third part of the process is singing the songs in front of other people.'

The monotone of the singing voice deepened as the years went by. The 1988 album *I'm Your Man* captured Cohen's 'new sound' perfectly: he still had the female chorus high in the mix, the same horribly catchy melody lines and the same showing off about their simplicity, but the voice now came as from the bottom of a well, the production values were higher, the synthesisers calmer, and as well as the title track and the near self-parody of 'Everybody Knows', there was the song Phil 'Wall of Sound' Spector could have wished he had produced, 'First We Take Manhattan'. The darker album *The Future* followed in 1992 and won him a Juno award for Best Male Vocalist. (He began his acceptance speech by saying: 'Only in Canada could somebody with a voice like mine win "Vocalist of the Year".')

Leonard Cohen once told ROBERT SHELTON that it was Dylan who had inspired him to sing his own poems. 'Dylan is not just a great poet, he's a great man,' Cohen added.

An early critical essay on similarities and differences between the two was Frank Davey's 'Leonard Cohen and Bob Dylan: Poetry and the Popular Song', published in 1969. Exactly 35 years later came the small book *Dylan & Cohen: Poets of Rock and Roll*, by an academic from Wales, David Boucher, whose Introduction manages to mistitle Cohen's 1977 album as *Death of a Lady's Man*; not a promising start. Cohen's poetry and prose is examined more attractively in STEPHEN SCOBIE's 1978 book *Leonard Cohen*.

Cohen said in 1997: 'The beautiful losers are still around, and I'm still with them.' In 2003 he was made a Companion of the Order of Canada, his country's highest civilian honour.

[Leonard Cohen: *The Songs of Leonard Cohen*, Columbia (CBS 63421, Canada & UK), 1967; *Songs from a Room*, Columbia (CBS 63587, Canada & UK), 1969; *Songs of Love and Hate*, Columbia (CBS 69004), 1971; *Live Songs*, Columbia (CBS 65224; short version CBS 63587), 1973. *New Skin for Old Ceremonies*, Columbia (CBS 69087), 1974; 'Don't Go Home with Your Hard-On', LA, Mar 1977, *Death of a Ladies' Man*, Warner Bros. BS-3125, 1977; *Various Positions*, Columbia (CBS 26222), 1984 & 1985. Quote on chat with Dylan: Adrian Deevoy: 'Brief Encounter: Leonard Cohen', *The Telegraph* no. 41 Romford, UK, winter 1991, p.30 (possibly reprinted from Q magazine, *n/a*); quote on accepting Juno from Wikipedia; quote re Dylan inspiring him: Robert Shelton, *No Direction Home: The Life and Music of Bob Dylan*, 1986, Penguin edn. p.230; other quotes: 'Leonard Cohen Special', Docklands TV, Germany, 1997. Bob Dylan: 'Hallelujah', Montreal, 8 Jul 1988 & Hollywood, 4 Aug, 1988.

Stephen Scobie, *Leonard Cohen*, Vancouver: Douglas & McIntyre, 1978. Frank Davey, 'Leonard Cohen and Bob Dylan: Poetry and the Popular Song' *Alphabet* no.17, London, Ontario, Dec 1969. David Boucher, *Dylan & Cohen: Poets of Rock and Roll*, New York: Continuum, 2004.]

Collins, Judy [1939 -] Judith Marjorie Collins was born in Seattle, Washington, on May 1, 1939, studied classical piano from the age of five and at 13 played at a public performance of Mozart's *Concerto for Two Pianos*. She was equally in a hurry about marrying her childhood sweetheart, and had a son when she was 19. She began folksinging to try to support him.

When the Exodus club opened in Denver in 1959, Collins became the regular opening act (alternating with WALT CONLEY) for national-name folk headliners like Josh White, Jimmy Driftwood and Bob Gibson. Collins and Conley both appear on the local Sky Lark label's 1959 album *Folk Song Festival at Exodus*, her songs being 'House of the Rising Sun', 'Tell Old Bill' and 'Two Sisters'—all of which Bob Dylan picked up on and was playing early on: in the case of 'Two Sisters' he was recorded performing it in a Minneapolis apartment as early as May 1960.

Back in Denver, Judy Collins performed at that year's Exodus Festival too, duly appearing on the equally obscure album *1960 Folk Festival at the Exodus*, on the Sight and Sound label, performing 'The Prickili Bush', 'Johnny Has Gone for a Soldier', 'Tim Evans', 'Boots and Stetsons and Sixguns' and 'This Land Is Your Land'. She became a popular performer throughout Colorado and then moved across to Chicago, where she played at the Gate of Horn.

Arriving in New York, Judy Collins became at least briefly a member of two groups with awful folk-revival period names, the Homesteaders and the Wanderin' Five. With the former she recorded the 1962 album *Railroad Bill* on Riverside (on which she is uncredited; other members seem to have been Ronnie Gilbert, Mike Settle and Walter Raim); with the latter she appears on the album *Hootenanny at the Limelight in the Village*, issued without identifying any of the group by the obscure Somerset label around 1963.

Perhaps she went uncredited on these dull excursions because she had already signed to Elektra Records, which had released her début album in 1961, *Maid of Constant Sorrow*, which as its title suggests, concentrated on traditional material. (It includes 'Wild Mountain Thyme' and 'Pretty Saro'.) She swiftly became the nearest thing to a JOAN BAEZ rival, with a voice less pure, more soulful and just as easy to recognise. It wouldn't be controversial to say that along with Baez and JONI MITCHELL, Collins was the third great female singer to emerge via folk in the 1960s. Though she was shy of writing her own material, she was quick to catch the winds blowing through the Village and early to broaden her repertoire to embrace the songs of new writers.

She recorded Dylan material in 1963, and was the first to record LEONARD COHEN's 'Suzanne', releasing the latter on her indomitable 1967 album *In My Life*, which also offered a calmly independent reading of Dylan's 'Just Like Tom Thumb's Blues' (called 'Tom Thumb's Blues' on the sleeve), Donovan's 'Sunny Goodge Street', Randy Newman's 'I Think It's Going to Rain Today' and tremendous, sinuously dramatic versions of Jacques Brel's 'La Colombe', the medley 'Marat/Sade' and the BRECHT & Weill masterpiece 'Pirate Jenny'—though she makes almost everything on the album sound like Brecht & Weill, aided and abetted by arranger Joshua Rifkin (who may have his merits but has less feel for down-home music than a dog, and hasn't a clue how to end a track, so that every one of them simply comes to a solemn concert-platform sort of a halt). Despite him it's a numinous album and for many was a crucial part of 1967's soundtrack—a useful corrective, even, to too much smudgy flower-power music.

Her follow-up later that year, *Wildflowers* (on which she first ventured a run of songs of her own, the best of which was 'Since You Asked'), could not match it, hampered as it was by over-the-top string arrangements and the comparative mediocrity of Collins' own compositions. Yet it contained early and beautiful versions of Joni Mitchell's 'Both Sides Now' and 'Michael from Mountains' and further covers of Leonard Cohen and Brel material, and her next album, *Who Knows Where the Time Goes*, which includes electric guitar by JAMES BURTON, was produced by Stephen Stills, with whom she was involved; hers were the 'Suite: Judy Blue Eyes' in the CROSBY, Stills & Nash song of that name. After that came *Whales and Nightingales* (1970) which, very much of its time, did indeed feature humpback whales 'singing', but also featured a very promptly seized-upon cover of Dylan's 'Time Passes Slowly', only released on *New Morning* that October.

By 1975 she had descended to Stephen Sondheim's wretchedly portentous 'Send in the Clowns', one of those items with the same capacity for cultural assault as 'My Way' or 'Feelings'.

Yet in the early 1960s she had been drawn to social activism and in 1964 was among those helping to register black voters in Mississippi. This interest in politics has, as with so many, shifted in more recent decades into a general willingness to do good works, and she is a UNICEF representative and a campaigner for suicide prevention (that son she had at 19 killed himself when he was 33 in 1992) and for the abolition of landmines. She deals with the struggle to recover from her son's suicide in a 2003 book, *Sanity & Grace: A Journey of Suicide, Survival and Strength*; in the 1980s she had battled to overcome her own alcoholism. In 1996 she married her longtime partner Louis Nelson, an industrial designer.

Judy Collins has also written a novel, *Shameless* (described by *Publishers Weekly* as a 'lackluster thriller set in the glamorous world of rock and roll'), and the autobiography *Trust Your Heart*; and as early as 1974 she produced and co-directed the Oscar-nominated documentary film *Antonia: A Portrait of the Woman*, a homage to the piano mentor she had been taught by when she was ten, the Dutch-born American conductor and pianist Antonia Brico.

Her career has only touched Bob Dylan's in that they were around together now and again down the years, starting in the unlikely setting of Colorado when both of them were teenagers (both also appeared in May 1961 at the Indian Neck Folk Festival in Branford, Connecticut), and she had often covered his material—and in that at least on one occasion, he built a song from one of hers.

Collins was almost certainly the conduit to Dylan of the song 'Anathea', which she was performing in 1963 and recorded (with musicians including Jim, later ROGER McGUINN) on *Judy Collins No. 3*, released in March 1964, and from which he created his wonderful 'Seven Curses', which Dylan first recorded as a Witmark song demo in May 1963. Collins credits 'Anathea' to Neil Roth and Lydia Wood, but it has strong traditional elements and a dramatic storyline, and many of these elements, and the same storyline, reverberate through 'Seven Curses', a Dylan song it is impossible to feel came to him out of nowhere and yet which is, on his recording, so quintessentially a display of his strengths as writer and as singer. Stories of corrupt judges can only be brought individually alive by narrative detail, and 'Seven Curses' is rich in it.

Judy Collins willingly stresses that Dylan, as man and artist, has been there for her through what seems to have been the near-permanent disarray of her own life. The sleevenotes to her 1993 album of Dylan covers (which harbours not only predictable 1960s choices but two *Slow Train Coming* songs, plus 'Sweetheart Like You' and 'Dark Eyes' from the 1980s), the repulsively titled *Just Like a Woman: Judy Collins Sings Dylan*, may be gushy but is sincere, telling and gives some interesting detail:

> 'Dear Bobby. This is a love letter to you, who called to me from the precipice, you with your wild hair and your thin bones and your silver-tipped black boots, a figure of my imagination, a fact of my life. When I was at the edge, when death was at my door with his raven look and his hour-glass—your words, like the point of a knife, cut to the bone of memory. You spoke to me of timelessness, of light, told me where I had been, helped me not to fear where I was going . . .
>
> 'You materialize in some city, we embrace, and you are always a gentleman, always kind. I remember that summer at Newport, boats bobbing out on the harbor, sun dancing on the water, crowds screaming, critics saying you were a traitor. All of us, singers, audience, loved you because you didn't care what the critics said, because they were fools, because we knew we were fools, too, children of an uncomfortable and unfathomable, disturbing age, an age of shattered dreams, and nightmares. You gave words to our journey, treaties to our wars of the heart and the head, and your music moved in our bones. . . . And I remember another summer in Woodstock . . . at ALBERT [GROSSMAN]'s house when I woke from dreams to hear your voice, sweet and haunting, singing a new, wonderful song. Deep in the basement behind a closed door you sang softly . . . and I climbed out of my high feather-pillowed bed and crept down the stairs to sit outside your door. When I knocked and asked you to sing the song again, you did. . . . it was "Mr. Tambourine Man." My life was in turmoil and your songs were solace.
>
> 'There was that first summer of '59. I was singing at the Gilded Garter, a bar in Central City, Colorado, three shows a night. . . . You were playing a honky-tonk mountain bar over in Cripple Creek, singing for miners and cowboys and summer people. I was barely nineteen, you were even younger.
>
> 'When I moved to New York I found you in a funky bar in the Village, a sloppy hat drawn over your forehead and the tops of your eyebrows, your elbows on the bar, a drink in front of you. On stage at Gerde's you bent over your guitar, muttering the lyrics of WOODY and CISCO [HOUSTON]. . . . VAN RONK and JACK ELLIOTT and Cisco showed up sometimes, and Joanie and

PAUL BUTTERFIELD. . . . We howled at the moon on Broadway, you sang the old blues and then you found your own voice, giving our fears and our triumphs faces and names. Somebody sent me a copy of "Blowin' in the Wind." I couldn't believe that rumpled guy, slumped in the shadows of Gerde's . . . could have written such a breathtaking song.

'I recorded "I'll Keep It With Mine," which you said you wrote for me and the years went by. . . . And then I lost the treasure, almost lost my mind. It is unbearable sometimes, what happens in life, and I needed comfort. I found you on the journey again. . . . I have a fantasy that back in Minnesota you had a high tenor voice as a child. Right behind the raspiness in your singing there is a sweetness that never got lost, the tone always true to our hearts and memories. As I sang these songs I looked for you. I found you. And I found me.'

Her latest book is *Morning, Noon, and Night: Living the Creative Life*, which takes the feel-good, self-improving theme much too far, and declares this sort of thing: 'Creativity is a voice that calls us from dreams, that peeks out the corners of our eyes when we think no one is looking.' Oh dear. A far more appealing voice calls for the Judy Collins of the 1960s instead.

[Judy Collins: 3 tracks on *Folk Song Festival at Exodus*, Sky Lark SK-1002 (mono), US, c.1959; 5 tracks on *1960 Folk Festival at the Exodus*, Sight and Sound SS-1002 (mono), US, c.1960; *Maid of Constant Sorrow*, Elektra EKL-209 (mono) & EKS-7209, US, 1961; *Judy Collins No. 3*, Elektra EKS 7243, US, 1964; *In My Life*, Elektra EKS-7320, US, 1967; *Wildflowers*, Elektra EKS-74012, US, 1967; *Who Knows Where the Time Goes*, Elektra EKS-74033, US, 1968; *Whales and Nightingales*, Elektra EKS-75010, US, 1970; *Just Like a Woman: Judy Collins Sings Dylan*, Geffen 2064 24612 2, US, 1993. The Homesteaders: *Railroad Bill*, Riverside RM 7537 (mono) & RS 97537, US, c.1962. The Wanderin' Five: *Hootenanny at the Limelight in the Village*, Somerset SF-19900, US, c.1963. *Antonia: A Portrait of the Woman*, dir. Jill Godmilow & Judy Collins; Direct Cinema / Rocky Mountain, US, 1974. Judy Collins, *Trust Your Heart: An Autobiography*, Boston: Houghton Mifflin, 1987; *Shameless, nia*, US reprint 1995; *Sanity & Grace: A Journey of Suicide, Survival and Strength*, New York: Putnam, 2003; *Morning, Noon, and Night: Living the Creative Life*, New York: Tarcher, 2005.

Some details re 'Anathea' c/o the discussion of it seen online 14 Jan 2006 at Manfred Helfert's website page *www.bobdylanroots.com/anathe.html*; other sources include T. Fennel Crenshaw's Collins interview for *Empire*, seen online 14 Jan 2006 at *www.empirezine.com/lyrics/4a.htm*, and the invaluable detailed discography by Richard L. Hess at *www.richardhess.com/judy/index2.htm*.]

'Columbus Stockade Blues' [1960] Written by Tom Darby and Jimmie Tarlton, and first recorded by them (as Darby & Tarlton) in 1927, at their second recording session, this song is one of the 27 numbers Dylan sings on the very early—May 1960—home-recording made at the apartment of one Karen Wallace in St. Paul, Minnesota.

The relevant Columbus is in Georgia, not Ohio—indeed an alternative title for the song is 'Georgia Stockade' (as for instance by the Kingston Trio). The stockade itself, built in the 1850s, comprised two brick buildings: a jail and police HQ, in use until 1906 and listed on the US National Register of Historic Places in 1980. Columbus, GA, was the birthplace of Tom Darby, in 1884. Tarlton (real name Johnny James Rimbert) was born in Chesterfield County, South Carolina, on May 8, 1892.

Darby and Tarlton were one of the great, crucial, traditional country acts of the mid-1920s to mid-1930s, Darby playing rhythm guitar and singing lead, Tarlton lead guitar and harmony vocals (including yodeling). Tarlton is recognised as having brought the steel guitar into country music. Together they recorded from 1927 to 1933, mostly for for Columbia and Victor, enjoying huge success. Their 'Columbus Stockade Blues', released on a 78rpm record coupled with 'Birmingham Jail', from the same session, was their biggest, career-launching hit. It sold over 200,000 copies, one of Columbia's biggest selling records. Unhappily, however, they had accepted a $75 flat fee instead of royalties.

The first track they ever recorded, 'Down in Florida on a Hog', is mentioned by Dylan in *Chronicles Volume One* as a record heard at somebody's father's house in St. Paul [probably in 1959]: 'I always thought "A-wop-bop-a-loo-lop [sic] a-lop-bamboo [sic]" had said it all until I heard Darby and Tarlton doing "Way Down in Florida on a Hog [sic]." Darby and Tarlton, too, were out of this world.'

Tom Darby also recorded three short sessions with Jesse Pitts as the Georgia Wildcats in 1931, though four of their six tracks remained unissued; Jimmie Tarlton cut thirteen sides under his own name in 1930 and 1932. Both gave up their music careers in 1935, but were 'rediscovered' during the folk revival at the beginning of the 1960s. Only Tarlton recorded again, though both gave live performances, separately and together. Tom Darby died in 1971, Jimmie Tarlton in 1979.

ELVIS PRESLEY sings a few lines of 'Columbus Stockade Blues' in 1973 at the start of take 4 of a recording of 'Promised Land', issued 25 years afterwards.

[Darby & Tarlton: 'Columbus Stockade Blues', Atlanta, GA, 10 Nov 1927. Bob Dylan: 'Columbus Stockade Blues', St. Paul, MN, May 1960; *Chronicles Volume One*, 2004, p.241. Elvis Presley: 'Promised Land', 15 Dec 1973, *Rhythm and Country: Essential Elvis Vol. 5*, RCA 07863676722, NY, 1998. The Kingston Trio: 'Georgia Stockade', *nia*, *Back in Town*, Capitol T/ST-2061, NY, *nia*.]

'Congratulations' A song Dylan composed, and on which he takes lead vocals, on the 1988 album *The Traveling Wilburys Volume 1*, though all songs are credited to the group. Not to be confused with the earlier song 'Congratulations', which was, as Andrew O'Hagan put it, 'sung by Cliff Richard to remind people that happiness is a feeling constantly under threat from the songs that celebrate it.'

['Congratulations', *Traveling Wilburys Volume 1*, LA, 7-16 May, 1988; Wilbury / Warner Brothers 9 25796-2, USA, 18 Oct 1988. Andrew O'Hagan, 'Four Funerals and a Wedding', *London Review of Books*, Vol.27, no.9, 5 May 2005.]

Conley, Walt [1929 - 2003] Walter Conley was born in Denver, Colorado, on May 20, 1929 but raised by adoptive parents 158 miles away in Scottsbluff, Nebraska (a depressingly long way from anywhere). He and his mother returned to Denver after his father's death, he won a football scholarship to junior college—where, as throughout his life, he was almost the only black person in the community—and worked summers on a Taos, New Mexico, dude ranch. In Taos he met the Weavers, and PETE SEEGER allegedly gave him a guitar and set him on the road to folk music.

After Korean War navy service and more college, he slid into a folk career, beginning with calypsos when HARRY BELAFONTE was in vogue, and singing in a deep, adequate baritone. When the Exodus club opened in Denver in 1959, he became the regular opening act (alternating with JUDY COLLINS) for national-name folk headliners like Josh White, Jimmy Driftwood and Bob Gibson. Conley and Collins both appear on the local Sky Lark label's 1959 album *Folk Song Festival at Exodus*. Conley's tracks, which open the LP, are: '900 Miles', 'Worried Man Blues', 'Passing Through' and 'John Henry'.

In the summer of 1959 or 1960, Dylan arrived to try his luck, hustle around and hang out. Walt Conley may or may not have been a performer whose repertoire offered Dylan material he wanted—Conley seems to have been playing whatever was popular, but is unlikely to have been any more up-to-date or wide-ranging than Dylan's musician friends back in Dinkytown, but ROBERT SHELTON reports that it was from Conley that Dylan picked up an anti-KKK song, 'The Klan'. When Dylan got back to Minneapolis, he let his friend HARVEY ABRAMS think it was his own.

What Dylan certainly got from Walt Conley was recorded repertoire and hospitality: Walt let him stay at his house on East 17th Avenue near Williams Street. Dylan repaid him by stealing a pile of his records. 'Yeah,' Dylan told Shelton, 'I was run out of Denver for robbing a cat's house.' Conley's friend Bob Turner told the *Rocky Mountain News* years later: 'I think Walt felt that when Dylan got big, he could have at least returned a few.'

In the early 1970s Conley moved to Hollywood and earned small rôles in TV hit series (The Rockford Files', 'The Six Million Dollar Man'), while doing voice-overs for ads and performing in Pasadena. He returned to Denver in 1983, opened his own club and booked in names like DAVE VAN RONK. In the 1990s, still performing himself, he formed an Irish folk band, Conley & Company, that proved highly popular. 'If U2 can sing American blues,' he said, 'I sure as hell can sing Irish folk songs!'

The 'founding father of the Denver folk scene' died in Denver aged 74 on November 16, 2003.

[Information in part from *http://waltconley.freeservers.com*, seen online 7 Oct 2005, and Robert Shelton, *No Direction Home: The Life and Music of Bob Dylan*, Penguin edn. pp.64 & (re Harvey Abrams) 68. Bob Turner quoted from Conley's obituary, *Rocky Mountain News*, Denver, CO, 19 Nov 2003. Conley & others: *Folk Song Festival at Exodus*, 1959, Sky Lark SK-1002 (mono), Denver, 1959.]

Cooke, Sam [1931 - 1964] Sam Cook was born January 22, 1931 in Clarksdale, Mississippi, but grew up in Chicago, one of eight children of a Baptist preacher; they formed the Singing Children when he was nine. Later he moved over to the Highway QCs and then replaced R.K. Harris as lead tenor of the Soul Stirrers. With this innovative and contemporary gospel group he began recording in 1951 (though his singing at this point is often overrated: his version of THOMAS DORSEY's great song 'Peace in the Valley', pallid and unmemorable, cannot compare with those by ELVIS PRESLEY and LITTLE RICHARD).

He 'went secular' in 1957, becoming Sam Cooke and starting a long and splendid run of hits, almost all his own compositions, many of which have been covered time and again by artists of the stature of VAN MORRISON. He was a consummate vocalist and a bright, lithe, sexy young man, whose TV appearances helped make black sexuality visible to young white America. He may have learnt his trade in gospel but church-going modesty was not his style.

Sam Cooke was very popular but never popular enough. Most of his work is of undimmed excellence: great records by a terrific songwriter and a masterful soul singer of panache, integrity and expressive generosity. In 1960–63 he was in his prime, not least in live performance (try *One Night Stand: Sam Cooke Live at the Harlem Square Club, 1963*).

By the end of 1963, Cooke had notched up 18 top 30 hits since 1957; but pop success was not enough. Earlier that year he had heard Bob Dylan's 'Blowin' in the Wind' and is reported to have felt shaken that it had been 'a white boy' who had written so potent a song—a song that eloquently, if implicitly, addressed the urgent issues of political struggle that so deeply involved his own race. He began performing the Dylan song himself (a version is captured on the album *Live at the Copacabana*, 1964), but his more profound response was to write the moving, thoughtful and dignified 'A Change Is Gonna Come' (originally called 'My Brother') which he recorded on January 30, 1964.

Despite the quality of the song and Cooke's recording of it, it was slipped out as an album track (on *Ain't That Good News*) and its release as a single was long delayed. On December 11, 1964, Cooke died after being shot in unclear circumstances in an LA motel. He was 33 years old. Two weeks later, and with one verse edited out, 'A Change Is Gonna Come' was released . . . as the B-side of 'Shake'.

Dylan mentions the song in *Chronicles Volume One*; the context is complex but this is what he writes: 'Sometimes you know things have to change, are going to change, but you can only feel it—like in that song of Sam Cooke's, "Change Is Gonna Come" . . .' And in an interview in 2001, he reveals an awareness of Cooke's early gospel group the Highway QCs, recalling that when he was '12 years old, listening to the radio . . . at midnight the gospel stuff would start, and so I got . . . to be acquainted with the Swan Silvertones and the Dixie Hummingbirds and, you know, Highway QCs . . .'

Dylan cut a version of Cooke's 'Cupid' with GEORGE HARRISON in a New York City studio in May 1970 (which would have been effective had Dylan remembered more than a handful of the words) and attempted Cooke's hit 'Chain Gang' at March and April 1987 studio sessions for the *Down in the Groove* album. (These remain uncirculated.)

'A Change Is Gonna Come' was revisited by THE BAND on their *Moondog Matinee* album of oldies in the 1970s, and on Dylan's 1978 world tour, on which various of his back-up singers were given solo spots (with Dylan and the band playing behind them). CAROLYN DENNIS sang 'A Change Is Gonna Come' in Hitler's old Zeppelinfeld stadium at Nuremberg that July 1 and again at Blackbushe Aerodrome in England two weeks later.

Matching song to venue with his usual quiet shrewdness, Dylan finally performed a respectful version of 'A Change Is Gonna Come' himself live at the home of early-60s R&B and black aspiration, the Apollo Theater in Harlem, NYC, on March 28, 2004, 40 years after the creation of the song for which his own work had been a catalyst.

In 2004, *Rolling Stone* magazine asked 172 prominent music-industry figures, including artists such as JONI MITCHELL, to vote for the 500 Greatest Songs of All Time. Sam Cooke's 'Change Is Gonna Come' came in at no.12—two places higher than 'Blowin' in the Wind'.

Dylan, however, was at no.1 with 'Like a Rolling Stone'.

[The Soul Stirrers: 'Peace in the Valley', *nia*, CD-reissued on *Sam Cooke: My Gospel Roots*, Xtra 26471, UK, 2005. Sam Cooke: *One Night Stand: Sam Cooke Live at the Harlem Square Club, 1963*, NY, 12–13 Jan 1963, RCA PL85181, Rome, 1985; 'Blowin' in the Wind', NY, 7–8 Jul 1964, *Live at the Copacabana*, Victor LPM /LSP-2970, NY, 1964; 'A Change Is Gonna Come', 30 Jan 1964, RCA 8486, NY, 1964. Bob Dylan: 'A Change Is Gonna Come', NY, 28 Mar 2004, broadcast on NBC-TV's program 'Apollo at 70: A Hot Night in Harlem', NY, 19 Jun 2004; *Chronicles Volume One*, 2004, p.61; interview for WTTW-TV, Chicago, 27 Oct 2001. The Band: 'A Change Is Gonna Come', Bearsville, NY, Mar–Jun 1973, *Moondog Matinee*, Capitol SW-11214, 1973. Bob Dylan, *Rolling Stone* poll seen online 7 Aug 2005 at *www.rollingstone.com/rs500moretext*.]

Coolidge, Rita [1944 -] Rita Coolidge was born on May 1, 1944 (some sources claim 1945) in Lafayette, just outside Nashville, Tennessee, part Cherokee but one of four children of a Baptist minister and schoolteacher. She and sisters Priscilla and Linda formed singing group the Coolidge Sisters, a local success, after which Rita took an art degree at Florida State University. While a student she sang on advertising jingles and made her first single, 'Turn Around and Love You', a regional hit on the West Coast, which brought her to the attention of the Mad Dogs & Englishmen stars Joe Cocker and LEON RUSSELL. (This 40-strong touring commune or circus was Cocker's 1970 US tour, and caught him in his prime.) Her beauty brought her to people's attention while she was standing on stages as a back-up singer for them on the tour; she thus appears in the important concert film of the same name in 1971 (reissued in wide screen, 1995), though her turgid solo number, 'Superstar', was cut from the original film release for contractual reasons. Leon Russell wrote the hit song 'Delta Lady' about her, and she was supposedly Stephen Stills' muse for three: 'Cherokee', 'The Raven' and a song called 'Sugar Babe'.

In November 1970 she met KRIS KRISTOFFERSON, whom she married on August 19, 1973; the same year she appeared in the film *Mad Dogs & Englishmen* she also appeared, uncredited, as a singer in *Vanishing Point*. In 1971 she signed a new solo deal with A&M records and made a number of indifferent-selling albums. Her first film as an actor was SAM PECKINPAH's *Pat Garrett & Billy the Kid*, in which she starred with Kristofferson, James Coburn and Bob Dylan. The only time she appears on the soundtrack album with Dylan is on 'Billy 4', the one issued track recorded in Mexico. It was recorded (along with much unreleased but circulated material) in Mexico City on January 20, 1973 and Coolidge and Kristofferson are backing singers.

After this project, she continued to pursue her fading solo career but also made duet albums with Kristofferson, notably *From the Bottle to the Bottom* in 1974 and *Lover Please* in 1976, the year she also appeared as herself in the Streisand-Kristofferson vehicle *A Star Is Born*. Coolidge was five months pregnant when, in May 1977, her baby suddenly died; she responded by concentrating on a new album, *Anytime . . . Anywhere*, which included a slowed-down re-make of Jackie Wilson's old hit 'Higher and Higher' that became her first and only platinum hit, after which came other inexplicable singles successes, all from the Karen Carpenter school of musical excitement, as with the Boz Scaggs song 'We're All Alone' and CAROLE BAYER SAGER's 'I'd Rather Leave While I'm in Love'. She and Kristofferson divorced in 1980.

Coolidge provided the voice of Melissa Raccoon in the TV hits 'The Christmas Raccoons' (1980) and 'The Raccoons on Ice' (1981) but after *Pat Garrett & Billy the Kid* her first movie acting rôle was over a quarter of a century later, in a comedy with a Native American setting, *Christmas in the Clouds*, a hit at film festivals in 2001.

Native American culture had increasingly interested Ms. Coolidge and in 1994 she and her sister Priscilla, plus Priscilla's daughter Laura Satterfield, were harmony singers on the Turner TV special 'The Native Americans'; on the soundtrack album *Music for the Native Americans*, by ROBBIE ROBERTSON & the Red Road Ensemble, they were featured upfront on 'The Cherokee Morning Song', using the group name Coolidge. This prompted them to record together more actively in their own right, and under the group name Walela (Cherokee for hummingbird) they have since recorded a number of CDs, starting with a self-titled album that includes a fine 'Amazing Grace' sung in the Cherokee language. Walela appeared, representing the US and the Cherokee Nation, at the opening ceremony for the 2002 Winter Olympics in Salt Lake City. A remastered 2-CD version of *Delta Lady: The Rita Coolidge Anthology* includes most of her hits (described very reasonably by *Village Voice* critic Robert Christgau as 'sultry cornpone' and less reasonably as 'Andy Williams with cleavage') and was released in 2004.

[Rita Coolidge: 'Turn Around and Love You', Pepper 443, US, 1969; *Anytime . . . Anywhere*, US, 1977; *Delta Lady: The Rita Coolidge Anthology* CD reissue, Hip-O, US, 2004. Rita Coolidge & Kris Kristofferson: *From the Bottle to the Bottom*, US, 1974; *Lover Please*, US, 1976. Coolidge: 'The Cherokee Morning Song' & other harmony vocals on Robbie Robertson's *Music for the Native Americans*, Capitol 28295, US, 1994. Walela: *nia* on original releases; all CDs reissued Triloka, US, 2002. *Mad Dogs & Englishmen*, dir. Robert Abel & Pierre Adidge; A&M Films / Creative Assocs., US, 1971. *Christmas in the Clouds*, dir. & written Kate Montgomery; Random Ventures / Stockbridge, US, 2001.]

Cooper, Ray [1942 -] Raymond Cooper was born on August 19, 1942 in Watford, Hertfordshire, southern England, and came to sudden visibility as a percussionist extraordinaire when he was part of ELTON JOHN's touring band starting at the beginning of the 1970s. On stage he brought dramatically to the forefront, and with good humoured panache, the previously lowly rôle of percussion player (always regarded as an optional extra person tinkling and swooshing away irrelevantly at the back). Thin as a whippet, balding and intense, his playing was ferocious and his theatrical sense assured.

In the same decade he also managed to play in a band called Alphalpha and in one of Britain's cheeriest and worst artificially constructed bands, the Wombles (designed to put music to a children's TV series about litter-collecting creatures in ill-fitting nylon-rug costumes, but which somehow escaped into the middle of the road and enjoyed enormous success with no less than six albums and many singles), while also bringing his session playing skills to albums by America, Harry Nilsson, Joan Armatrading, Carly Simon, Rick Wakeman, Donovan, THE ROLLING STONES, GEORGE HARRISON, the Who, Herbie Flowers, Elton John, Phil Manzanera, Bryan Ferry, Gallagher & Lyle, PAUL McCARTNEY & Wings, Colin Blunstone, Art Garfunkel and more besides.

After JOHN LENNON's death, the 17-year-old Julian Lennon dropped out of school and soon afterwards moved to London, where he stayed with Ray Cooper for a recuperative six months. In the 1980s Cooper continued to flourish, playing on sessions for several of the above all over again, plus Ian Dury, RINGO STARR, Pink Floyd, ERIC CLAPTON, INXS, MICK JAGGER, Ravi Shankar and others. He also worked in films, co-producing with George Harrison a number of George's Handmade films, including Terry Gilliam movies like *Brazil* (1985) and *The Adventures of Baron Munchausen* (1988) as well as Neil Jordan's stylish British thriller *Mona Lisa* (1986). Cooper also took small acting rôles (a technician in *Brazil*, for example) and composing music scores for other films, including, more recently, *Fear & Loathing in Las Vegas* in 1998. In 1992 he was very visible on Eric Clapton's *MTV Unplugged*.

Ray Cooper's work has bumped into Bob Dylan's several times. First, from May 7–16, 1988, he played percussion on all the tracks for *The Traveling Wilburys Volume 1* (except 'Handle with Care', recorded in April and without him) at DAVE STEWART's home studio in Los Angeles. In April 1990 in Bel Air, Cooper was on all the sessions for *Traveling Wilburys Volume 3*, including for the recording of the single of 'Runaway' and the Romanian orphan appeal fundraiser 'Nobody's Child'. Eighteen months later he was there in Seville, Spain, playing behind Dylan and the rest of the world on 'All Along the Watchtower' and 'I Can't Turn You Loose' at the October 17, 1991 concert that was part of the Guitar Legends Festival. Finally, on May 20–22, 1994, there he was in Nara, Japan, playing alongside the Tokyo New Philharmonic Orchestra, drummer JIM KELTNER and others at the Todaiji

Temple Great Music Experience extravaganza, all backing Bob Dylan as he delivered, in these unusual circumstances, versions of 'A Hard Rain's a-Gonna Fall', 'I Shall Be Released', 'Ring Them Bells' and a second, ensemble 'I Shall Be Released' each night. Thus Cooper also appears on the Dylan single release of 'A Hard Rain's a-Gonna Fall', recorded live on the last night of the three.

Coopers & Lybrand In the interview material Dylan provided for the retrospective *Biograph* box set in 1985, he rails against artists letting their work get used for adverts; he's rightly proud of having not joined in; and he's conscious of how perilous it is.

Subequently he has joined in—joined in the CO-OPTION OF REAL MUSIC BY ADVERTISING and the turning of his art into a tool for selling other things. On US television in the first week of January 1994, there appeared minute-long commercials for the mega-accountancy consulting agency Coopers & Lybrand, using a Richie Havens recording of 'The Times They Are a-Changin''.

If this were not shameful in itself, the fact is that Coopers & Lybrand was a deeply unsavory organisation that anyone with a serviceable moral radar would have known to avoid. They were investigated in Britain in the case of their auditing of the notorious swindler Robert Maxwell's business affairs. They were also, to quote British MP Frank Field, 'auditors of all the development companies by which the funds were lost' by the Church Commissioners, the money-handling division of the Church of England—and were then appointed to carry out the technical side of the report commissioned to investigate those losses! Field told the then Archbishop of Canterbury, Dr. George Carey, when Carey appeared before the House of Commons Social Services Select Committee in May 1994 that 'Some of us felt that Coopers & Lybrand should be investigated, not just the Commissioners.'

The Maxwell-related investigation began in 1993; in 1994 Coopers & Lybrand attempted, unsuccessfully, to have this investigation halted, and in February 1999, as a result of the investigation, it was announced that the company and four of its senior employees were to be fined a record amount: with costs, nearly £3.5 million (currently $6 million). The fine, detailed in a long-awaited report from the tribunal of the Accountants Joint Disciplinary Scheme, was accompanied by severe criticism of the firm.

So Dylan leases out a song to them: a song only heeded in the first place because of its political integrity, and only sought by the advertising industry for the kudos of this special credibility. Two years later, in October 1996, 'The Times They Are a-Changin'' was back on TV as a jingle, this time sung by a choir of children promoting the Bank of Montreal. PETE SEEGER may be an infinitely lesser talent than Bob Dylan, but his integrity is in better shape.

In 1998 Coopers & Lybrand completed a global merger with the similar firm Price Waterhouse, becoming PricewaterhouseCoopers. On July 30, 2002, PricewaterhouseCoopers Consulting was sold to IBM.

[Frank Field MP quoted from *Private Eye* no.847, London, 3 Jun 1994.]

co-option of real music by advertising, the By the mid-1980s rock'n'roll, once the music of the youthfully alive, had become overblown and encrusted with its own corruption; what was underground and radical had become corporate mega-product. Rock music was no more culturally separate from Reaganism than the Pentagon.

The music had become corporate rock in two senses: the music industry itself had become such big business that boardroom policy dictated who got signed and who got marketed; and the music itself had been gobbled up by mainstream commerce. Where once the music had been living outside the law and being honest—an outlaw on the opposite side from TV and musicals and soap operas and ads—by 1985 the co-option of real music by advertising and the whole squashy cottonwool entertainment mainstream had been achieved. In the 1950s, rock'n'roll had been shocking: condemned from the pulpit and thrillingly rebellious; in the late 1960s, rock was underground and radical: it was going to change the world and abolish the suits. By 1985 the empire had struck back. It owned the music and threw it back in people's faces.

In 1993 at a cultural studies conference Philip Tagg delivered this tirade about where rock had gone:

> 'What sort of socialisation strategy is encoded in . . . rock? It seems to me that we are hearing individuals who beat the fascinating but overbearing system by screaming louder than it, by roaring or chain-sawing their way through it. . . . Hence the heavy-metal audience's arm raised in a collective V-sign as the singer or lead guitarist rides away into another heroic urban sunset. Unfortunately, the emancipatory potential of this . . . strategy can degenerate into the vulgar entrepreneurial egoism of the Thatcher and Reagan era and into its musical equivalent—hyper-melodic pomp and its elevation to a hegemonic position . . . we have witnessed the obvious promotion of the corporeal from Youth Subcultural Division Four to the premier league of capitalist culture. Young US-Americans are not recruited into the marines by Sousa marches but by Van Halen . . . Vauxhalls [cars] are sold to the tune of "Layla", Fords to the ex-Queen guitarist Brian May's "Driven By You" . . .'

With *Empire Burlesque* Bob Dylan seemed to join this party. The album's writing, as well as its sound, seemed saturated in the shallow histrionics of this corporate rock. Yet that same year, in the interview within the *Biograph* box set, Dylan still seemed adamant about not caving in directly like the Van Halens and Brian Mays:

> 'Rock'n'roll, I don't know, rhythm and blues or whatever, I think it's gone. In its pure form. There are some guys true to it but it's so hard . . . everything is against it. I'd like to see CHARLIE SEXTON become a big star, but the whole machine would have to break down right now before that could happen . . . stock-broker rock, it's now a highly visible enterprise, big establishment thing. You know things go better with Coke because Aretha Franklin told you so and Maxwell House Coffee must be OK because RAY CHARLES is singing about it. Everybody's singing about ketchup or headache medicine or something. In the beginning it wasn't anything like that, had nothing to do with pantyhose and perfume and barbecue sauce . . . you were eligible to get busted for playing it. It's like Lyndon Johnson saying "we shall overcome" to a nation wide audience, ridiculous . . . there's an old saying, "If you want to defeat your enemy, sing his song" . . .'

Within a decade Dylan started selling his own music to TV ads (see **Coopers & Lybrand**). The year after that he was grubbing around on much lower levels of gratuitous commerce. On the back of the tickets for his Edinburgh concert of April 5, 1995 was a 'Special Offer' for McChicken Sandwiches™ . . .

How can it have come to this?—Bob Dylan promoting battery chickens. Don't say it's nothing to do with him. Would that stance suffice if the ad was from the British Nazi Party? All it takes is a simple clause in his contract with the promoter prohibiting these sordid commercial tie-ins.

In 1993, Dylan also discarded his life-long eschewal of political endorsement—a fastidiousness the young Bob Dylan had had the sense to maintain without a moment's hesitation—and threw one of his silliest hats into the ring to appear at the inaugural concert for President Clinton, singing so risibly incomprehensible a version of his magnificent 'Chimes of Freedom' that the whole First Family was smirking and fidgeting through it while the oleaginous Tony Bennett waited in the wings unable to believe his luck.

In February 1996, Dylan and his band were hired to give a private concert in Phoenix, Arizona, for 250 senior staff of something called Nomura Securities International. It was to be the first of several such demeaning occasions. The following September, looking about as comfortable as he should have done, Dylan performed three songs for Pope John Paul II: one of the most pro-actively right-wing popes of recent decades.

The 'pantyhose' soon followed. In 2004, an exclusive 9-track compilation CD of Dylan's work was sold at lingerie retailer Victoria's Secret—a division of Limited Brands Inc.—and that April Dylan himself appeared in their television ads. The CD, called *Lovesick*, included a remix of the track 'Love Sick' unavailable elsewhere (slightly longer, and with a clearer sound than the *Time Out of Mind* version), and its artwork offered three previously unpublished Dylan photos. It could be purchased for $10, but only with any Victoria's Secret item.

The year after, Dylan became the latest musician to sign up with the Starbucks Corporation in an exclusive CD deal. If, within the first 18 months of its release, you wanted to buy *Live at the Gaslight 1962*, with its previously unreleased tracks (long bootlegged but never circulated in this quality before), you had to go to the coffee shop equivalent of Burger King to buy it.

Dylan himself talks in the *Biograph* interview about how 'Sometimes you feel you're walking around in that movie *Invasion of the Bodysnatchers* and you wonder if it's got you yet, if you're still one of the few or are you "them" now.'

Well, yes.

[Bob Dylan: 'Chimes of Freedom', America's Reunion on the Mall, Lincoln Memorial, Washington, D.C., 17 Jan 1993; Namura Securities International private performance, Biltmore Hotel, Phoenix, 2 Feb 1996. Performance for Pope John Paul II at the World Eucharistic Congress, Bologna, Italy, 27 Sep 1997; *Lovesick*, Sony A72812, US, 2004; *Live at the Gaslight 1962*, NY, Oct 1962, Columbia/Legacy A 96016, US (COL 82876728622, Belgium), 2005.

Philip Tagg, 'From Refrain to Rave: The Decline of Figure and the Rise of Ground', paper delivered at the Convegno sulle culture del rock, Istituto Gramsci/La Repubblica, Bologna, Italy, May 1993.]

'Copper Kettle' 'Copper Kettle', of which Dylan released an odd but effectively atmospheric version on *Self Portrait*, is a traditional southern mountain song, much favoured around Greenwich Village in Dylan's time there. It is on JOAN BAEZ's third album, *Joan Baez in Concert*, and was published in the same issue of *Sing Out!* as 'Little Sadie' in 1964.

Dylan's recording, as with all the music he touches on *Self Portrait*, brings back to life the spirit of the age that the song is all about, and does it immeasurably better than those purists to whom his version is anathema. Dylan's has violins and women on it (and features the latter in a way that recalls the use of the back-up singers on the 1950s hit 'The Three Bells' by the Browns); but for an inspired example of his own unique expressiveness, hear the way his own voice enacts the sound of rotten wood snapping as he lands on 'rotten' in the line 'Don't use no green or rotten wood'.

Dylan has never performed this fine song in concert.

[Bob Dylan: 'Copper Kettle', NY, 3 Mar (+ overdubs without Dylan, 12, 17 & 30 Mar) 1970. *Joan Baez in Concert*, Vanguard VRS-9112, NY, 1962, CD-reissued Vanguard VDM 79112-2, NY & London, 1996. *Sing Out!* Vol.14, no.6, NY, Jan 1964. (The same magazine's booklet *Reprints from* Sing Out! *Volume 9*, NY, 1966, also includes 'Copper Kettle' & 'Little Sadie', along with 'It Hurts Me Too'—here titled 'When Things Go Wrong with You'—and 'Belle Isle'.) The Browns: 'The Three Bells', *n/a*, RCA Victor 20-7555, NY (RCA 1140, London), 1959.]

Corcoran, Neil [1948 -] Cornelius David Corcoran was born in Cork, Ireland, on September 23, 1948. He first took an interest in Dylan's work in 1964. An academic at the University of St. Andrews, Scotland, he has published many books on modern literature including critical works on David Jones, Seamus Heaney and Elizabeth Bowen. His writing on Dylan includes 'Going Barefoot: Thinking About Bob Dylan's Lyrics', published in *The Telegraph* in 1987 (see **'Tangled up in Blue'**) and he was editor of the rather poorly received book of essays *Do You Mr. Jones?: Bob Dylan with the Poets and Professors*, published in 2002, which includes his preface, an introduction to the book called 'Writing Aloud' and one essay, 'Death's Honesty'.

Neil Corcoran's real contribution to the Dylan world was to persuade the University of St. Andrews to award Bob an honorary doctorate in 2004, and to persuade Bob to accept it: the first such acceptance since Princeton in 1970.

The speech Corcoran gave at the ceremony, on the afternoon of Wednesday, June 23, 2004, was at once scrupulous and heartfelt, efficiently compressed yet warmly eloquent, and full of freshly specific ways to praise familiar virtues. He said this:

> 'Chancellor, it's my privilege to present Bob Dylan for the Degree of Doctor of Music, honoris causa.
>
> 'In one of his first concerts in New York in the 1960s Bob Dylan said that he'd recently been asked to contribute to a book about Woody Guthrie, the great folksinger, songwriter and political activist. He'd been asked to say 'What does Woody Guthrie mean to you in 25 words?', and Bob Dylan said, 'I couldn't do it'. So instead he read 'Last Thoughts on Woody Guthrie', a tender poem about Guthrie and the spirit of American idealism. I feel similarly incapable when I'm asked to say what Bob Dylan means to me in a few minutes. In fact, what I'm here to say isn't really what he means to me, but what he means to the University of St Andrews that we should have offered him the honour of a doctoral degree. It goes without saying that his acceptance of our invitation deeply honours us, and I really can't say what a great privilege and pleasure his presence here is today.
>
> 'Bob Dylan was born Robert Allen Zimmerman in Duluth, Minnesota, in 1941 and grew up in Hibbing, on the Canadian border. He briefly attended the University of Minnesota, and then made what's become an almost mythical trip to New York to visit the dying Woody Guthrie, and to begin the career, which he continues still—writing, singing, recording and performing his songs. Performing is what he'll be doing once more tonight; and not the least of Bob Dylan's claims on our attention is his mercurial, devoted and exceptional commitment to the constant renewal of his work that performance involves. It's as true now as it ever was that "no one sings Dylan like Dylan".
>
> 'Bob Dylan's life as writer and singer has the aspect of vocation, of calling, and his is an art of the most venturesome risk and the most patient endurance. He's spent a lifetime applying himself to such long-sanctioned forms of art as folk, blues, country and rock music. And, partly by transfusing them with various kinds of poetic art, he's reinvented them so radically that he's moved everything on to a place it had never expected to go and left the deepest imprint on human consciousness. Many members of my generation can't separate a sense of our own identity from his music and lyrics. He's been for us an extension of consciousness—a way of growing up, and a way of growing more alive. And his work acts like that for succeeding generations too—witness the eager younger people who attend his concerts, which still sell out as soon as they're advertised. Bob Dylan possesses, in several senses of the phrase, staying power. He keeps on keeping on.
>
> 'His magnificent songs will last as long as song itself does. There are the early songs of political engagement, songs like "The Lonesome Death of Hattie Carroll", songs inseparable from the history of the American civil rights movement. There are the revolutionary songs of the mid-1960s, songs that seem to well up out of nowhere, an electric nowhere of American turbulence, songs like "Subterranean Homesick Blues" and "Mr. Tambourine Man", "Desolation Row" and "Like a Rolling Stone"—songs that made their time as much as it made them. And then there are, always, the love songs—songs of longing and desire, of hope and hopelessness, songs like "Boots of Spanish Leather" and "Lay, Lady, Lay", "Tangled up in Blue" and "Lovesick"—songs that make Bob Dylan one of the great writers of the drama of human relationship.
>
> 'And there are so many other songs and other kinds of song: devotional songs like "Precious Angel" and "I Believe in You", and poignant songs of older age such as "Not Dark Yet", songs of resilience, songs of what it means to have come through. Truly, there is God's plenty in Bob Dylan's work; and something FRANZ KAFKA said about Charles Dickens seems to apply to him too—"his vast, instinctive prodigality": a kind of volatile superplus of creative energy and momentum. Bob Dylan's work has been one of the places where the English language has extended itself in our time.
>
> '"What are your songs about?" Bob Dylan was once asked. "Oh," he said, "some of them are about three minutes, some of them are about five minutes, and some of them, believe it or not,

are about eleven minutes". And songs are about time, about passing the time and filling the time, and doing these things well. Bob Dylan has passed our time very well.

'Our graduand has been given numerous awards, including France's highest cultural accolade, when he was made a Commander of the Order of Arts and Letters in 1990, and a Hollywood Oscar for his song "Things Have Changed" in 2001. But he's accepted only one honorary degree—from Princeton in 1970. It seems appropriate that his second such degree should come from Scotland's oldest university, since Scottish border ballads and folksongs have been the inspiration for some of his melodies, and his great song "Highlands" is an elaborate riff, or descant, on Robert Burns.

'Chancellor, in recognition of his incomparable contribution to musical and literary culture, I invite you to confer on Bob Dylan the Degree of Doctor of Music, honoris causa.'

[Neil Corcoran, 'Going Barefoot: Thinking About Bob Dylan's Lyrics', *The Telegraph* no.27, Romford, UK, summer 1987. *Do You Mr. Jones?: Bob Dylan with the Poets and Professors*, ed. Neil Corcoran, London: Chatto & Windus, 2002.]

Cordwell, John [1944 - 2001] See 'Judas!' [shout].

'Corrina Corrina' [1963] Dylan included a superbly performed version of this old song on *The Freewheelin' Bob Dylan* (accompanied by BRUCE LANGHORNE and others), and several outtakes have circulated, in which the variations—particularly of pace: a strikingly slower earlier take appeared on one of the first bootleg LPs—are interesting but don't improve upon the issued version nor illuminate anything to do with the song, which may have originated with Bo Chatmon (aka Chatman and aka Bo Carter) of the MISSISSIPPI SHEIKS, and which has been recorded by dozens of other artists, especially in the 1930s. As with Dylan's treatment of the Sheiks' 'Blood in My Eyes' on *World Gone Wrong*, 30 years after 'Corrina Corrina', he takes a lightweight, cheery little number and makes it new, in this case as something sexy, yearning and tender, rueful and contemplative. On *Freewheelin'* it served to confirm what 'Song to Woody' on Dylan's début album had suggested: that this very young man could bring an enviably mature, convincing detachment to songs of secular devotion, and utilise the strengths of old styles to create something memorable and fresh—including the delicate falsetto jump on 'plea-please', derived from Kokomo Arnold (perhaps via Josh White), and lyric phrases pulled from other old blues.

The song is also related to 'Alberta', which Dylan includes two versions of on *Self Portrait* in 1970 and to the standard 'C.C. Rider'. Bo Chatmon cut 'Corrine Corrina' at his début session in around December 1928 in New Orleans (more than a year before the first Mississippi Sheiks sides were made) and it was issued on 78rpm on Brunswick, Supertone and Vocalion, in each case with a B-side as by another artist, John Oscar. BLIND LEMON JEFFERSON had recorded a 'Corrina Blues' in Chicago around April 1926.

For an especially vituperative attack on Dylan's 'Corrina Corrina'—on his version, his motives and more besides—see 'Race/Music: Corrine Corrina, Bo Chatmon, and the Excluded Middle' by Christopher A. Waterman of the University of California in Los Angeles, posted online in 1998 before its appearance in *Music and the Racial Imagination*, a book edited by Ronald Radano and Philip V. Bohlman in 2000. Waterman concedes that Dylan's 'Corrina Corrina' gives the song its 'most radical transformation', but this is only to be deplored. It is a version 'in which the Greenwich Village *wunderkind* deconstructs and reassembles the song in accordance with the ideological norms of the urban folk revival, and the aesthetic contours of his own emergent *auteur*ship.' Dylan, he argues, is dishonestly trying to make Chatmon's work into 'a folk song', dishonestly trying to give it 'the authentication of a white subject *via* the black other', dishonestly throwing in a line from a ROBERT JOHNSON song—this was bad, you see, because it contributed to the white lauding of Johnson and didn't acknowledge that Johnson himself took from many sources—and dishonestly claiming composer royalties instead of giving them 'to Bo Chatmon and Mayo Williams'.

This is an argument that keeps on shooting itself in the foot. Among the many small points those less seething than Professor Waterman might like to make are these:

Is the line 'I got a bird that whistles, I got a bird that sings', which Waterman notes as coming from Johnson's 'Stones in My Passway', supposed to be original to Johnson or not? If yes, why not complain that Dylan is doing Johnson down instead of lauding him like a typical white folkie? If no, why mention Johnson at all, since Dylan doesn't? Further, why present Johnson's drawing on other people's work as a secret known only to Professor Waterman? It isn't. And why present it as deplorable? Chatmon didn't create everything he sang, either (except, apparently, in this case).

As for the royalties question, if Dylan's version is so horribly radical a transformation and so unfaithful to the Chatmon 'original', why should he not take some credit for it? And were Dylan's version sufficiently faithful to Chatmon's to satisfy even Professor Waterman, why should J. Mayo Williams receive half the royalties? As Waterman himself acknowledges, Williams was the producer, the talent scout, the record-company fixer, and taking half the composer credit on your artists' songs was merely the common industry scam. Everyone knew that. Bo Chatmon certainly did. No, Professor, at least let's agree to hold the Mayo.

Dylan would also have known the pop single version, a hit for Ray ('Tell Laura I Love Her') Peterson in 1961, in that style of the moment, a frothy white concoction of swooping strings and overwrought vocal cords, the latter giving way in the middle so that the strings can play the hopelessly perky melody in unison in place of a guitar solo. This was not one of producer PHIL SPECTOR's finest creations; it was Peterson's second and last top 10 hit. (He went country, then became a Baptist minister yet kept touring on the oldies circuit, and he died of cancer at the age of 69 on January 25, 2005.)

To switch from Ray Peterson's to Dylan's version is like turning from a mosquito's whine to Paul Robeson and a string quartet. The only extant live Dylan recording of the song is from Gerde's Folk City, probably in late April 1962. In the studio he cut it that April 24—two takes have circulated—and then he returned to it not at the next session, or the next, but on the one after that, on October 26, when seven takes were attempted, one of which was issued on a single and the other, only slightly different, became the more familiar *Freewheelin'* track. On August 11 Dylan had also been recorded performing it at DAVE WHITAKER's home in Minneapolis (though this remains uncirculated); there is no extant trace of his having ever recorded or performed it since—except that November, when he recorded it again as a Witmark music-publishing demo.

His claim to copyright is hard to pin down. The original *Freewheelin'* LP label gives the song credit as 'Adapted and Arranged by Bob Dylan', which was certainly true; the SACD reissue label says 'All songs written by B. Dylan except "Honey Just Allow Me One More Chance"'; and on the *www.bobdylan.com* website it just says 'arranged by Bob Dylan'.

[Bob Dylan: 'Corrina Corrina' (take 4), NY, 26 Oct 1962 (c/w 'Mixed-Up Confusion', NY, 14 Nov 1962), Columbia 4-42656, NY, Dec 1962; 'Corrina Corrina' (take 7), *The Freewheelin' Bob Dylan*, 1963.

Blind Lemon Jefferson; 'Corrina Blues', Chicago, c. Apr 1926; Bo Chatmon (as Bo Chatman): 'Corrine Corrina', New Orleans, c.Dec 1928. Ray Peterson: 'Corrina Corrina' c/w 'Be My Girl', 1961, Dunes 45-DU2002, US, 1961.

Christopher A. Waterman, 'Race/Music: Corrine Corrina, Bo Chatmon, and the Excluded Middle' (© 1998), in Ronald Radano & Philip V. Bohlman, eds, *Music and the Racial Imagination*, Urbana, IL: University of Chicago Press, 2000.]

Corso, Gregory [1930 - 2001] One of THE BEATS, Gregory Nunzio Corso was born in New York City on March 26, 1930. He served three years in prison for attempted robbery as a teenager. His first poetry collection was *The Vestal Lady of Brattle* (1955), and in 1961 he published a novel, *The American Express*. His better-known 1958 poetry collection *Gasoline* (with back-cover blurb by JACK KEROUAC) is cited by Dylan as an influence, and in *Chronicles Volume One* Dylan describes Corso as 'heavy' and 'hip, cool', and says that his poem 'Bomb' touched the spirit of the times.

We can also hear in this passage from his poem 'Marriage' (from *The Happy Birthday of Death*, 1960), something that will sound familiar for followers of Dylan's 1960s work: 'So much to do! like sneaking into Mr Jones' house late at night / and cover his golf clubs with 1920 Norwegian books / Like hanging a picture of RIMBAUD on the lawnmower'. It seems clear that Dylan moved Corso's work forward, making something more biting, multi-layered and consequential: less cautious, less anxious to please.

Corso, like ALLEN GINSBERG, attended Dylan's post-concert party after his 1964 Hallowe'en Concert at the Philharmonic Hall, NYC. Corso died in Minnesota on January 17, 2001. On May 5, his ashes were buried in Rome's 'English Cemetery', in a tomb in front of Shelley's grave (and near Keats'). The last thing thrown into the grave was the residue of a joint that had been ritually smoked over it.

[Dylan cites Corso's *Gasoline* in the interviews for *Biograph*, 1985, and mentions Corso in *Chronicles Volume One*, 2004, pp.47, 111 & 235.]

Costello, Elvis [1954 -] Declan Patrick MacManus was born on August 25, 1954, and emerged in the foment of the British punk scene of 1976–78 as its most talented singer-songwriter (though perish the term, back then). He took his grandmother's maiden name, Costello, and posed as someone who would have sold her with no hesitation; and he took the King's first name as an act of deflationary irreverent defiance (though the same gesture had been made before, by Reg Presley of the Troggs, and no-one had minded in any case). He was only four or five years younger than the 'old hippies' that he and his combative manager were going around saying should be lined up against a wall and shot, but he was sharp and adept at the whole punk stance, and looked as if his suppressed past had probably been more mod than rocker.

Signed to one of the new indy labels but under the umbrella of one of the old majors, Elvis Costello & the Attractions released *My Aim Is True* in 1977. He was an immediate hit on album and with a series of singles, all of which combined punk attitude with witty lyrics, immensely catchy tunes—'Alison', 'The Angels Wanna Wear My Red Shoes', '(I Don't Want to Go to) Chelsea', 'Watching the Detectives', 'Pump It Up'—and a beat-combo sound that was, endearingly, only slightly more dangerously modern than BUDDY HOLLY & the Crickets, to whom Costello owed a great deal. Live, they were less similar to the Sex Pistols, the Jam, the Clash or the Buzzcocks than to the early 1970s pub-rock acts like Ian Dury & the Blockheads (themselves updated equivalents of cockney music-hall acts.) Further albums followed–*This Year's Model, Armed Forces, Get Happy*–yielding more hit singles, including the lovely, anthemic 'Oliver's Army', which was richer in sound–more reminiscent of the Beach Boys' 'God Only Knows' than of the Crickets–and as Margaret Thatcher and the 1980s came in and punk faded from modishness, Costello grew in stature, concentrated more on albums and singer-songwriterliness, and to a melody by Clive Langer wrote the angry lyrics to 'Shipbuilding', a much-admired condemnation of Thatcher's Falklands War, that was briefly a hit for Robert Wyatt. He confessed his interest in old-fashioned country music, collaborated with George Jones, and later with a string ensemble, the Brodsky Quartet and even with PAUL McCARTNEY. *Goodbye Cruel World, Blood and Chocolate, Spike, Mighty Like a Rose, Brutal Youth*–the albums flowed on into the 1990s and beyond, and Costello settled into his niche as serious senior figure in the British musical establishment.

In the middle of Dylan's spring 1995 European tour leg, Elvis Costello was the support act, though only for five shows, and these not even consecutively. He played solo acoustic sets each time, and tried out new material. Half of Dylan's audience stayed in the bar.

Costello's first show was Paris on March 24. Then, avoiding Brighton and Cardiff, he played the three London Brixton nights (March 29–31), avoided Birmingham, Manchester, Edinburgh, Glasgow and Belfast, and played the support spot one last time in Dublin on April 11. On three out of the five, he also came on stage during Dylan's set. At the second London Brixton concert, on March 30, Costello came on for the last encore number, sharing vocals and playing guitar on 'I Shall Be Released'; the following night he was there for the same song, followed by a bonus (well, depending on point of view) 'Rainy Day Women # 12 & 35'–this time with Chrissie Hynde and CAROLE KING on backing vocals too. Finally, in Dublin, Costello and VAN MORRISON *both* joined Dylan at the end, for the same two songs as before. Four years later, in New York, Costello joined Dylan on stage once again, on July 26, 1999, to share vocals and play guitar on one more 'I Shall Be Released'.

When British punk exploded into being in 1976, and pursued its generally healthy reign of terror through till late 1978, its main enemy had been Progressive Rock. Before punk, it had got to the point where no-one in Britain dared to get on a stage, even in a pub, unless they had monstrous megawatt equipment and could play 15 chords. Punk saw this for the nonsense it was and did something about it–and the boom whereby hundreds of obscure singles of very primitive technical quality were issued on hundreds of tiny independent labels was a demonstration that when you feel you have something to say, the technology is not going to inhibit you. Now Bob Dylan had known that all along, and in spirit had always been on that side of things–but for other reasons, he was one of the enemy to the punk army: he was the 1960s; he was an old hippie. (According to DEREK BARKER, Dylan was physically attacked by Sex Pistol Sid Vicious back-stage at the Music Machine in Finchley on the night of June 14, 1978, while Dylan was in London for that year's extraordinary run of 'come-back concerts' there.) When Elvis Costello was 'new', he couldn't be caught praising Dylan; by the 1990s, he was happy to be his support act; and by the 2000s, he was readily going to extremes in praising Dylan's newest studio album, *"Love and Theft"*, as the best he'd ever made.

Like most people, he'd become one of the old farts he used to rage against. He was asked in a recent interview: 'Did you ever get people at record labels telling you, "Elvis, with all this genre-hopping, you're diluting the brand"?'–and Costello replied: 'But who would that person have been? That figure of extreme authority who's been on the job five years, or me who's been in the job 25 years? I rank everybody now. If Bob Dylan were to come up to me and say that, I might have a thought for it. But there's not too many people that have been doing what they do as long as I've been doing what I do.'

[Elvis Costello: *My Aim Is True*, Stiff SEEZ 3, UK, 1977; quote from 'Question & Answer with Elvis Costello' by Chris Willman, *Entertainment Weekly*, LA, 13 May 2002. Derek Barker, '1978 and All That', collected in *20 Years of Isis: Bob Dylan Anthology Volume 2*, New Malden: Chrome Dreams, 2005, p.231.]

Cott, Jonathan [1942 -] Jonathan Cott was born in New York City on December 24, 1942, and lives there still. His books include *Wandering Ghost: The Odyssey of Lafcadio Hearn, Conversations with Glenn Gould* and, in fall 2005, the extraordinary *On the Sea of Memory: A Journey from Forgetting to Remembering*, prompted by what happened to Cott at the end of the 1990s, when, after electroshock treatments for severe clinical depression, he could remember nothing he had experienced between 1985 and 2000. The book combines autobiography with a scrutiny of 'the mysteries of human memory' and the rôles played in our lives by both remembering and forgetting.

Cott first took an interest in Dylan when he saw him perform in a Greenwich Village café in 1963 and bought *The Freewheelin' Bob Dylan*. His first published work about him was an article/review of *Eat the Document* in *Rolling Stone* in 1971. He has also written one book about him and edited another. The first, *Dylan*, mixing criticism with biography and collecting terrific photographs, is from 1985; the second, *Dylan: The Essential Interviews*, is from 2006.

In 1978 Cott interviews Dylan himself—on a bus from Portland, Maine, to the airport, on the plane to New Haven, CT, and in his dressing room at the Veterans' Memorial Coliseum, on September 17, 1978. When he asks about the 1978 album *Street Legal*, a classic encounter between the interpreter and the artist ensues, as TERRY KELLY points up (albeit with a bad case of mixed metaphors): 'Cott fires an arsenal of quotations and references he finds relevant to "Changing of the Guards" at a typically taciturn Dylan. The loquacious Cott builds up to a tidal wave of feverish explication, peppered with Tarot card references, songwriting sub-codes and . . . subconscious images. . . . He tells a still-silent Dylan that he believes each floor of "the palace of mirrors" contains another significant image or level of awareness. . . . After what seems like a lifetime of silence, Dylan eventually puts Cott out of his misery. "I think," Dylan mumbles, "you might be in some areas I'm not too familiar with."'

[Jonathan Cott, *Dylan*, New York: Dolphin/Doubleday, 1985; *Dylan: The Essential Interviews*, New York: Wenner Books, 2006; *Eat the Document* review, *Rolling Stone* no.47, US, 4 Mar 1971; the 1978 interview, 17 Sep 1978, partly published *Rolling Stone* 16 Nov 1978; *On the Sea of Memory: A Journey from Forgetting to Remembering*, New York: Random House, 2005. Terry Kelly, 'All of F. Scott Fitzgerald's Books', *The Bridge* no. 14, UK, winter 2002.]

Cotten, Elizabeth [1895 - 1987] Elizabeth ('Libba') Cotten was born near Chapel Hill, North Carolina, on January 5, 1895 and started playing her older brother's banjo when she was a young girl. At 11, already playing a borrowed guitar 'upside down and backward' because she was left-handed, she started work as a domestic servant to save up for her own guitar. She acquired this eventually and started both playing and writing her own songs but, pressured out of performing by her local church, she resumed domestic work. In 1943, aged almost 50, she moved to Washington, D.C., to work as housekeeper to ethnomusicologist Charles Seeger (father of PETE). The Seegers encouraged her to resume performing music, and MIKE SEEGER produced her début album for Folkways in 1957.

This introduced her most successful composition, 'Freight Train', which by April 1957 was a hit for others, including, in both the US and skiffle-mad Britain, the Chas McDevitt Skiffle Group & Nancy Whiskey. ('Last Train to San Fernando' by Johnny Duncan & the Blue Grass Boys was to arrive just as Chas & Nancy were pulling out of the charts.)

This début album was reputedly among those 'borrowed' by Dylan from JON PANKAKE in Minneapolis, and its contents included 'Oh Babe It Ain't No Lie', which he performed over 30 years later at his unusual four-set appearance at Toad's Place in New Haven, Connecticut. In some of his 1996 concerts Dylan then included 'Sugaree', a JERRY GARCIA/GRATEFUL DEAD reworking of a song much associated with Elizabeth Cotten in the early 1960s, 'Shake Sugaree': indeed it was the title of another of her Folkways albums (and she may in fact have written this 'folksong'); and on his first tour-dates of 1997, in Japan, Dylan reintroduced 'Oh Babe It Ain't No Lie'. Altogether he has performed it 49 times in concerts across three continents, most recently in Little Rock, Arkansas, on August 14, 2001.

The blues critic Andrew M. Cohen writes of 'Freight Train' and the two songs covered by Dylan that they are the songs Elizabeth Cotten will always be associated with; that 'they are prime examples of Piedmont-style guitar playing and simple enough . . . for beginning guitarists. Since the late 1950s untold thousands of young folkies have used them . . .', while her début recording, because it was 'one of the very few recordings of . . . authentic black folk song . . . became one of the most influential, especially in college communities.'

Elizabeth Cotten performed at the NEWPORT FOLK FESTIVAL in 1964 (and is on the Vanguard release *Newport Folk Festival 1964 Blues II* from that event, singing 'Oh Babe' and 'Freight Train' again); she recorded another Folkways album in 1965–66 and played at the Mariposa Folk Festivals in 1970 and 1974. She performed at Carnegie Hall at the age of 76, and died in Syracuse, New York, on June 29, 1987, aged 92.

In a 1989 book by Brian Lanker and Barbara Summer, *I Dream a World: Portraits of Black Women Who Changed America*, Elizabeth Cotten was recognised as one of those women.

[Elizabeth Cotten: *Negro Folk Songs and Tunes*, Washington, D.C., 1957, Folkways FG3526, NY, 1957; 'Freight Train' & 'Oh Babe It Aint No Lie', live, Newport, RI, 23–26 Jul 1964, *Newport Folk Festival 1964 Blues II*, Vanguard LP 9181, NY, *nia*; 'Shake Sugaree', NY?, Feb 1965, *Shake Sugaree*, Folkways 1003, NY, c.1967. *Elizabeth Cotten Live!*, *nia*, Arhoolie LP 1089, El Cerrito CA, *nia.*, also includes 'Freight Train' & 'Babe, It Ain't No Lie'.

Bob Dylan: 'Oh Babe It Ain't No Lie', New Haven, CT, 12 Jan 1990 & as follows in Japan, 1997: Tokyo, 9–11 Feb; Kurashikim, 13 Feb; Fukuoka, 14 Feb; & Osaka, 17–18 Feb 1997; 'Sugaree', Berlin, 17 Jun 1996; Utrecht, 20 Jun 1996; Munster, 1 Jul 1996; Pistoia, Italy, 7 Jul 1996; Pori, Finland, 21 Jul 1996; Stockholm, 27 Jul 1996; Atlanta, GA, 3 Aug 1996; Atlanta, 1 Dec 1997.

Jerry Garcia: 'Sugaree', San Francisco, 1971, *Garcia*, Warner Brothers BS 2582, LA, 1972. (By the Grateful Dead it 1st appeared officially as: 'Sugaree', San Fran-

Leonard Cohen

Judy Collins

Sam Cooke

© Ray Santos, used courtesy of Bread & Roses

Elizabeth Cotten

Library of Congress

e.e. cummings

cisco, 1974, *Steal Your Face*, Grateful Dead GD LA620 J2GD 104, San Francisco, 1976 & had become the Dead's 25th most performed song by the end of 1993. Brian Lanker & Barbara Summer, *I Dream a World: Portraits of Black Women Who Changed America*, New York: Stewart, Tabori & Chang, 1989. Andrew M. Cohen quoted from his useful entry on Cotten in the *Encyclopedia of the Blues* vol.1, New York: Routledge, 2005, p.228.]

country music, Dylan's early interest in Dylan is known to have taken an interest in country music, on radio and on record, in the late 1940s to early 1950s—that is, pre-dating its re-energising by the EVERLY BROTHERS and others of the rock' n'roll generation, and dating from his own boyhood.

This is evident from, for example, the line 'An' my first idol was HANK WILLIAMS', offered in the sleevenote poem for *JOAN BAEZ in Concert, Part 2*, 1964, and from Dylan's much later comments on hearing songs like 'I Forgot More (Than You'll Ever Know)' on the radio when he was growing up. Performing it as a 1940s-style country harmony duet with TOM PETTY at 55 concerts in 1986, he introduced it at one of them by remarking: 'Very seldom do you hear a real song anymore. But we were lucky enough to grow up when you could hear 'em all the time. All you had to do was just switch on your radio . . .' Perhaps this reveals why he had chosen to include the song on *Self Portrait* in 1970—though you may also be reminded of the rather different assertion in those lines from 'Visions of Johanna' just four years (and an aeon) earlier: 'The country music station plays soft / But there's nothing, really nothing, to turn off.'

Notwithstanding that last, ROBERT SHELTON's biography *No Direction Home* reports: 'I had always found Dylan more aware of the country currents than most other city folk singers . . . [around 1961]. He often alluded to HANK SNOW, Hank Thompson, Bill Andersen. . . . He repeatedly told associates that he regarded country music as the coming thing, long before he cut *Nashville Skyline* . . .' And when Shelton, visiting Dylan's boyhood home in Hibbing, MN, in 1968, was shown the old records (78s and vinyl) left behind in his bedroom, he says they included 'a flood of Hank Williams's lonesome blues', some Webb Pierce and the LP *Hank Snow Sings JIMMIE RODGERS' Songs*. In more recent years Dylan has paid fulsome tribute, in interviews and the like, to the hillbilly-country-bluegrass influence of groups like the Delmore Brothers and the STANLEY BROTHERS.

[Dylan comments on 'I Forgot More', Sydney, Australia, 24 Feb 1986. *Joan Baez in Concert, Part 2*, Vanguard VRS-9113, NY, 1964. Hank Snow: *Hank Snow Sings Jimmie Rodgers' Songs*, RCA Victor LSP/LPM-2043, NY, 1959.]

'Covenant Woman' and 'Pretty Boy Floyd' Despite being one of the duller performances on the *Saved* album, 'Covenant Woman' was a significant song for Dylan himself. He put it on a single, and on the first gospel tour, months before *Saved* had even been recorded, he performed it live at all 26 concerts: and he always placed it first among those featured songs that were not drawn from *Slow Train Coming*. On the second gospel tour, in early 1980, he gave it the same prominence at all 24 concerts. Then he dropped it altogether for the April–May dates but brought it back in for that year's fall tour.

The song's significance for Dylan may come down to its being an address of private gratitude (made somewhat public by the lyric) to MARY ALICE ARTES, the woman who prayed that Dylan be brought to Christ and asked a VINEYARD CHRISTIAN FELLOWSHIP pastor to visit him (see also **'Born Again' period, the**) and whom he also seems to address in the *Slow Train Coming* song 'Precious Angel'. The chorus of 'Covenant Woman' includes the straightforward 'I just got to thank you / Once again / For making your prayers known / Unto heaven for me'.

Like 'Precious Angel', the verses of 'Covenant Woman' suggest a fusing of spiritual and earthly passion, but there's another detectable affection here too, as he lingers warmly along this gentle, eloquent line: 'You know that we are strangers in a land we're passing through'. His delivery seems to recall the younger Dylan's fondness for all those romance-of-the-road, leaving songs.

Scripturally, though, Dylan is bending an ear to God's recurrent exhortation to His people to treat strangers with kindness. This is no mere Gentle Jesusism, but a command insisted upon time and again in the Old Testament. The point is to remind people of their own ancestral suffering as captive strangers in Egypt:

'Thou shalt neither vex a stranger, nor oppress him: for ye were strangers in the land of Egypt' (Exodus 22:21). 'Also thou shalt not oppress a stranger: for ye know the heart of a stranger, seeing ye were strangers in the land of Egypt' (Exodus 23:9). 'And if a stranger sojourn with thee in your land, ye shall not vex him. But the stranger that dwelleth with you shall be unto you as one born among you, and thou shalt love him as thyself; for ye were strangers in the land of Egypt . . .' (Leviticus 19:33–34). '. . . as ye are, so shall the stranger be before the Lord. One law and one manner shall be for you, and for the stranger that sojourneth with you' (Numbers 15:16). 'Love ye therefore the stranger: for ye were strangers in the land of Egypt' (Deuteronomy 10:19).

In the New Testament, this theme is linked to the subject of angels. Hebrews 13:2 advises: 'Be not forgetful to entertain strangers; for thereby some have entertained angels unawares.'

This idea is paralleled by, and perhaps is the conscious inspiration for, part of the lyric of WOODY GUTHRIE's song 'Pretty Boy Floyd', which

Dylan got around to recording in 1987: 'And Pretty Boy found a welcome at every farmer's door. / Others tell you of a stranger that come to beg a meal / And underneath a napkin left a thousand-dollar bill.' (A few lines later, Guthrie adds a note 'from' Floyd, left with a gift of food: 'You say that I'm an outlaw, you say that I'm a thief / Well here's a Christmas dinner for the families on relief.' This dovetails into the argument of the song's most famous line: 'Some will rob you with a six-gun and some with a fountain-pen'—the line quoted by Dylan in his own early song 'Talkin' New York'—before the song ends with 'You won't never see an outlaw drive a family from their home.')

Dylan's first known extant recording of this song (an amateur recording, and unissued) has him contributing back-up vocals, guitar and harmonica behind RAMBLIN' JACK ELLIOTT, live at a club in Greenwich Village in July 1975—and his official 1987 recording is modelled on Elliott's two classic recordings of the song, one made in England in 1956 and the other in New York in 1960. Dylan also performed the song live at the Bridge School Benefit Concert in Oakland, California, on December 4, 1988.

The link between the biblical text and this quintessential Guthrie lyric tends to corroborate the notion that Dylan's lines from 'Covenant Woman', as delivered, still carry a residue of affection for the romantic songs of an earlier era.

[Bob Dylan: 'Solid Rock' c/w 'Covenant Woman', single, Muscle Schoals, AL, 15 Feb 1980, Columbia 1-11318, NY, 2 Jun 1980; 'Pretty Boy Floyd', back-up vocals, guitar & harmonica behind Ramblin' Jack Elliott, live NY, 3 Jul 1975; and LA, prob. Apr 1987, *Folkways: A Vision Shared*, Columbia OC 44034, NY (CBS 460905 1, London), 1988.

Woody Guthrie: 'Pretty Boy Floyd', 26 Apr 1939, reissued *Folkways: The Original Vision*, Smithsonian Folkways SF400001, Washington, D.C., 1988. Ramblin' Jack Elliott: 'Talking Miner's Blues' c/w 'Pretty Boy Floyd', London, c.1956, 78 rpm Topic TRC98, London, c.1956; and 'Pretty Boy Floyd', NY, Jun 1960, *Jack Elliott Sings the Songs of Woody Guthrie*, Prestige PR13016, Bergenfeld, NJ, 1960/61.]

Crackers, the See Band, The.

Crooks, Richard [1942 -] Richard Crooks, a longtime session drummer, who was born on January 16, 1942 in Chicago and grew up in Gilroy, California, played on the September 1974 New York sessions—that is, the original sessions—for *Blood on the Tracks*.

He has played drums on many Tom Chapin albums and albums as obscure as the Hitman Blues Band's *Angel in the Shadows*, but he has also recorded and played with many, many others, from Roy Buchanan to Jean Ritchie, and including Dr. John, JOHN SEBASTIAN, PAUL SIMON (he's on 'Mother and Child Reunion' and others of the period), MARIA MULDAUR, LEONARD COHEN (he's on *Various Positions*, and therefore on tracks like 'Dance Me to the End of Love', 1985), Loudon Wainwright III and Steve Forbert. He also plays on the Village People's 1979 album *Live and Sleazy* and plays spoons on BETTE MIDLER's *Bathhouse Betty* (1998). He is currently the drummer in the David Bromberg Band (2006). He lives in Bronxville, NY, in the summer months, but winters in Key West, Florida.

Crosby, David [1941 -] David Van Cortland Crosby was born in Los Angeles on August 14, 1941, a son of the cinematographer Floyd Crosby, whose credits included *High Noon* but who enjoyed just as much his B-movies like *Monster from the Ocean Floor* and the Rogert Corman-directed *Attack of the Crab Monster*, and Aliph Van Cortland Whitehead. David and his older brother Floyd (aka Ethan and Chip) grew up in Santa Barbara and became child multi-instrumentalists. Though David's musical interests were initially jazz and classical, he became drawn into the folk music revival at the start of the 1960s and started to travel around the US as a singer-songwriter after his parents' 1960 divorce. Both brothers briefly joined folkie group Les Baxter's Balladeers and while with them David met Cass Elliot and through her, later, Graham Nash, who in 1969 would manage to move up in the world from dull Manchester-based beat group the Hollies to join Crosby in Crosby, Stills & Nash (with Stephen Stills). In the interim, though, Crosby returned to live in LA in 1963 and the following year formed THE BYRDS with Jim (later ROGER) McGUINN, Gene Clark, Chris Hillman and Michael Clarke. Crosby was an excellent musician with a fine ear, and while McGuinn gave the group its defining electric 12-string sound, Crosby pioneered those high, ethereal harmonies that were taken up later by everyone from the GRATEFUL DEAD to the Eagles. His contribution was particularly strong on Byrds albums like *Younger Than Yesterday* and *Notorious Byrd Brothers*.

In August 1967 Crosby quit—he felt forced out—in the middle of the recording of their sixth album. He ran away to Florida and bought a 60-foot wooden schooner, *The Mayan*, and at a local club saw an unknown singer-songwriter, JONI MITCHELL.

Crosby told Wally Breese in 1997: 'I went looking for a sailboat to live on. I wanted to do something else. Find another way to be. I was pretty disillusioned. I walked into a coffee house and was just completely smitten. She was standing there singing all those songs—"Michael from Mountains", "Both Sides Now", and I was just floored. I couldn't believe that there was anybody that good. And I also fell . . . I loved her . . .' Crosby helped kickstart her career, and eventually produced her début album, protecting her from the record company's insistence on a folk-rock sound.

In 1968, Crosby began writing songs with Stephen Stills, then with NEIL YOUNG in Buffalo Springfield. Crosby and Stills brought in Nash, and in 1969 released *Crosby, Stills & Nash*, which topped the US charts and featured as a highlight Crosby's spacey-Elizabethan song 'Guinevere' and the co-written 'Wooden Ships'. Young joined that summer, they appeared as the biggest 'supergroup' since Cream at Woodstock and then in 1970 they released *Déjà Vu*. Off and on, Crosby, Stills, Nash & Young have kept on recording and touring for over 30 years. In 1970, Crosby also released his first solo album (though it was crammed with other star players), *If I Could Only Remember My Name*, a record widely rubbished at the time but now often considered a landmark record full of Crosby's progressive harmonic ideas and exploratory songwriting.

That same year, Crosby accompanied Bob and SARA DYLAN to Princeton and stood at his side (along with Dylan's music publisher Naomi Saltzman's husband Ben) giving moral support through the ceremony at which Dylan was presented with his honorary doctorate in music from this prestigious Ivy League university. As Dylan recalls almost 35 years later, in *Chronicles Volume One*, 'Somehow I had motivated David Crosby to come along' and in the end, after 'whispering and mumbling my way through the ceremony, I was handed the scroll. We piled back into the big Buick and drove away. It had been a strange day. "Bunch of dickheads on auto-stroke," Crosby said.' A succinct verdict, but less interesting than Dylan's, which was the *New Morning* song 'Day of the Locusts'.

Dylan also offers a thoughtful description of Crosby as he was at that time, still in his 20s, with the success of the Byrds behind him and now the first name in the mega-successful Crosby, Stills, Nash & Young, and yet already metamorphosing from an anonymous, shy, slim youth into a swelling but endearing mix of the Cheshire Cat and the Penguin:

> 'Crosby was a colorful and unpredictable character, wore a Mandrake the Magician cape, didn't get along with too many people and had a beautiful voice—an architect of harmony. He was tottering on the brink of death even then and could freak out a whole city block all by himself . . . I liked him a lot. . . . He could be an obstreperous companion.'

The catalysts, of course, were drugs and alcohol, a resultant paranoia and a fascination with firearms. As Crosby's official online biography states: 'for Crosby, success led to increasingly destructive habits, and eventual alienation from most of his friends and fellow musicians. As the 1980s began he found himself in the grips of a serious drug abuse problem. . . . The crash came in 1985, when a drug-related arrest in Dallas a few years earlier resulted in a prison term for Crosby. He spent a year in Texas jails before the court overturned his conviction on appeal . . .' On top of which, Crosby's father died in September 1985.

His drug years were supposed to be behind him when, in 1988, he published an autobiography, *Long Time Gone*, that described in painful detail his former degradations and slide. Yet, as the official online tale concedes (it doesn't mention *Long Time Gone*), 'Crosby endured a new series of personal disasters in the 1990s. These included a serious motorcycle accident, financial woes due to criminal mishandling of his business affairs, and severe earthquake damage to his . . . home, followed by its loss through foreclosure. . . . [And then] his liver, damaged by years of substance abuse and . . . Hepatitis "C," went into rapid deterioration.' In 1995 Crosby was taken into hospital and received a liver transplant.

The official story, still online in January 2006, then ends with a de-toxed, happily married Crosby having a new baby, Django, after being reunited with his 30-year-old professional musician son, James Raymond, who had traced his famous father the same year Crosby gained his new liver. The two of them, plus Jeff Pevar, formed the new group CPR (for Crosby, Pevar & Raymond) in 1998 and it is still going. Meanwhile CSN&Y undertook mega-successful US tours in 2000 and 2002 and issued the stubbornly titled *Looking Forward*, featuring Crosby's equally defiant song 'Stand and Be Counted'. He has also published a campaigning book of the same name, and as a result fronted a spin-off documentary TV series celebrating musicians' activism and social awareness on issues like human rights and the environment.

Unfortunately, this narrative omits the fact that in 2004, when Crosby left some luggage behind when leaving a New York hotel, the hotel staff found a quantity of marijuana, a 45-caliber handgun and a knife. Crosby was charged with illegal possession of a hunting knife and of a handgun and ammunition as well as possession of drugs.

All this lurid personal dysfunction gets in the way of the recognition of Crosby's achievement as a main player in the shaping of rock (and so popular consciousness) in the 1960s and 1970s. But time will tell. And in any case, even in the midst of all the mayhem, in the spring of 1990 Crosby was still able to meet up again with Bob Dylan, 20 years after their 'strange day' at Princeton, this time in the studio in LA, to lend his 'beautiful voice' to 'Born in Time' and '2 × 2' on Dylan's album *Under the Red Sky*.

Crosby says time will tell, too: and he thinks it will come down more favourably for Joni Mitchell than for Dylan: 'In a hundred years when they look back and say, "Who was the best?"—it's going to be her. . . . She's a better poet than Dylan and without question a far better musician. I don't think there's anybody who can touch her.'

[David Crosby, *If I Could Only Remember My Name*, US, 1970. David Crosby, *Long Time Gone*, New York: Doubleday, 1988. *Crosby, Stills & Nash*, US, 1969. Crosby quotes from 'A Conversation with David Crosby (Part One)' by Wally Breese, 15 Mar 1997, seen online 15 Jan 2006 at *www.jonimitchell.com/Croz97A.html*. Bryan Alsop's official biography on Crosby's website *http://crosbycpr.com*, seen ditto. Bob Dylan, *Chronicles Volume One*, 2004, pp.132 & 134.]

Cross, Billy [1946 -] William Cross was born on July 15, 1946 in New York City. He started playing music in local band the Esquires while still at high school in 1962. While a Columbia University student he launched his own band, the Walkers, and after graduating in 1968 joined Sha Na Na, the most prominent and least objectionable of the pastische-1950s revival bands that emerged at the end of the 1960s during that glorious but hip-snobbish period when the music of the 1950s felt much further away and less relevant than it has done since. Billy Cross appeared in this guise at Woodstock in 1969.

He left Sha Na Na for very brief 1970 stints with Cat Mother and the All Night Newsboys and joined the cast of the Broadway musical *Hair* (so switching from a rocker to a hippie pastiche). After Broadway, he joined the *Hair* national touring company and as its musical director toured with the group for a year, returning to New York in 1973. Here he scuffed around with club dates and small Broadway jobs (though these included some involvement with PAUL McCARTNEY on the 1974 show *Sgt. Pepper's Lonely Hearts Club Band*); but he also began working as a session guitarist, and at the Electric Ladyland studios in the early 1970s he worked with, and learnt engineering and studio production from, the late JIMI HENDRIX's engineer Eddie Kramer.

In 1974 he visited Denmark for the first time, which led to annual visits there until eventually he made it his home base. Between mid-1970s trips there, Cross played live dates in New York with Robert Gordon, Link Wray, MICK RONSON, Meat Loaf and others and in 1977 joined with ROB STONER and HOWIE WYETH to form the short-lived rock group Topaz.

This led to Billy Cross stepping into the Dylan world, and working alongside Stoner again he became the fake-blonde long-haired lead guitarist (and occasional backing vocalist) on Dylan's huge 1978 world tour: 114 concerts, starting in Tokyo on February 20 and finishing in Florida on December 16. Cross is therefore to be heard on the live double-LP *Bob Dylan at Budokan*, but he also went into the studios with Dylan for the sessions that yielded 1978's studio album *Street Legal*. These sessions began in late April 1978 in Santa Monica. There is a circulating rehearsal tape from an undated session that month at which ten songs were recorded; then on April 25 the album sessions began, yielding nothing that day but continuing on April 26 to 28 and concluding on May 1st. Billy Cross is the lead guitarist on all tracks.

Cross was not retained for the early 1979 sessions for *Slow Train Coming*, and returning to Denmark he played with the Delta Blues Band on their live recording *No Overdubs* in 1979, after which the two fused into the Delta-Cross Band. This toured and recorded in Europe until disbandment in 1983, by which time Cross had drawn himself to the attention of Dylan-watchers again by recording a rare Dylan song not copyrighted till 1981, 'Legionnaire's Disease', but learnt from a soundcheck during the 1978 tour. The song appears on *Up Front*, the second of the Delta-Cross Band's four albums, and as the B-side to their single 'Back on the Road Again'.

Since 1983, Billy Cross has been freelance producing and session playing and made an eponymously titled solo album in 1985. Today he teaches at the Rhythmic Conservatory of Music in Copenhagen, plays with both a rock group, Cross, Schack & Ostermann, and the acoustic trio Everybody's Talking (with Jimmy Colding and Lars Måsbøl), and nearly 20 years after the first, released a second solo album, *Life Is Good*, in 2004. He used to look like a TOM PETTY wannabe; now he sounds like one.

[Billy Cross: *Billy Cross*, 1985; *Life is Good*, Kick Music, Denmark, 2004. Delta Cross Band: 'Legionnaire's Disease' c/w 'Back on the Road Again', Medley MdS 176, Denmark, 1981; *Up Front*, Medley, Denmark, 1981.]

''Cross the Green Mountain' [song & video, 2003] Commissioned from Dylan to play over the closing titles of the 2003 film *Gods and Generals*, which is about the first half of the American Civil War, this long, dolorous ballad hovers between the portentous and the touching. It doesn't stand up on the page—it's full of awkwardnesses of word order such as 'I think of the souls in heaven who we'll meet'—but it has the virtues of sounding like a long, unwinding movie in itself, of a dark, stately vocal, and of Dylan compressing into the lyric much of what was felt and rumoured at different phases of the war: the early disorientation at its having broken out at all, the bravado and the glory, the capacity for grandiloquent declaration and the later onset of dread that the war would stretch out into a future of hopeless carnage. This jostling of conflicts within the conflict is embedded into a song of shifting voices and episodes, making for an historically informed meditation.

It's been suggested that he quotes on the quiet from W.B. Yeats' poem 'Lapis Lazuli', written in 1938 as Europe headed into World War II, and which includes the phrase 'Heaven blazing into the head'—in Dylan's opening stanza there is

'Heaven blazing in my head'. Others have identified tips of the hat to Civil War poems by Herman Melville ('brave blood to spill' comes from 'The Scout Toward Aldie', in *Battle-Pieces and Aspects of the War*, 1866) and to the less well-known Southern poet Henry Timrod, 1829–1867 (that 'dim Atlantic line' comes from his poem 'Charleston'). But beyond this period colouring Dylan has rightly minimised the scissors-and-paste assemblage technique so prevalent on the *"Love and Theft"* album, and the imported phrases are occasional, overtly quoted and extemporised upon with some finesse, as for instance when stanza ten begins with 'Stars fell over Alabama' only to add, at once, 'I saw each star', and to end that verse with the chiselled couplet 'Chilled are the skies, keen is the frost / The ground's froze hard and the morning is lost.'

The song marks a return to subject matter that has always been dear to him. He writes revealingly in *Chronicles Volume One* of his responses towards the American Civil War but had he not done so we would still have those two adjacent songs on the solo acoustic album of a decade earlier, *World Gone Wrong*, 'Two Soldiers' and 'Jack-a-Roe', which he sings with such intense empathy and such alert interest. (See **American Civil War in *World Gone Wrong*, the.**)

The video made to accompany ''Cross the Green Mountain' mixes footage from the movie with sequences shot in the vast Hollywood Cemetery for Confederate troops in Richmond, Virginia; these show us glimpses of TONY GARNIER and LARRY CAMPBELL, and longer shots of Dylan surveying an encampment's dead and wounded, and the cemetery itself, both from on horseback and on foot. Wearing the false beard and wig that he puzzled us all by wearing first at his NEWPORT FESTIVAL performance of July 2002 he looks, on the video, more like Fagin than a figure from the Civil War.

Gods and Generals, directed by Ronald F. Maxwell, who also wrote the screenplay, is based on the book by Jeffrey M. Shaara. It was not well received by the critics when released in 2003, but may be superior to Maxwell's 1993 film *Gettysburg* (it is a prequel to this), which was much derided for its glut of continuity errors and anachronisms (a plane flying over, for one). The *Gods and Generals* soundtrack album includes the full version of the Dylan song; a Limited Edition 'bonus' DVD contains the Dylan video plus a video for Mary Fahl's 'Going Home' and 'extra' movie scenes.

[''Cross the Green Mountain', Studio City, CA, late Jul 2002, *Gods and Generals Original Motion Picture Soundtrack*, Sony Classical / Sony Music Sountrax SK87891, US, 4 Feb 2003; special sequences for the video filmed Richmond, VA, 23 Nov 2002.]

Crow, Sheryl [1962 -] Sheryl Suzanne Crow was born on February 11, 1962 in the Missouri town of Kennett: 'It's a nice town, with nice people in it / . . . Kennett', as its official song has it. Her mother was a singer and music teacher and her father a trumpet playing lawyer (they had both been in swing bands) and she grew up hearing popular music and studying classical, moving on to take a degree in the latter at Missouri State University. While a student she sang with a college group named either Kashmir or Cashmere but after graduation she taught in an elementary school in suburban St. Louis before making more money on the side singing on jingles, including for McDonald's. (All these years later, in contrast, she's a celeb magazine fitness icon: yet another 40-something wonderwoman, and until recently engaged to the world's best cyclist, Lance Armstrong.)

Tapes of her jingle singing got her into session work when she moved to LA. She was a backing singer on Michael Jackson's *Bad* tour for 17 long months, and shared lead vocals with him on one song per night. She returned to session work after that, then made a very expensive solo album 'too polished to release', and then in 1993 released *Tuesday Night Music Club*, from which came two semi-successful singles before a third, 'All I Wanna Do', became a vast hit and propelled the previously sleeping album to multi-million sales and Crow into the big time. By August 1994 she was performing to 300,000 people at Woodstock II (at which Dylan also performed).

Crow is a spirited live performer whose strengths are open simplicity, acoustic singer-songwriterliness and modish pluck; yet in the studio she is a multi-instrumentalist, playing bass, Wurlitzer, percussion, organ, steel guitar, keyboards, harmonica, electric and acoustic guitar, electric and acoustic 12-string electric and clavinet.

Employing, not for the first time, the tactic of having as his support act that month's hot new young performer, Dylan opened his run of May 1995 Never-Ending Tour concerts in LA with Sheryl Crow on the bill. On the third and final night, she was brought on at the end of Dylan's set too, to share vocals on 'I Shall Be Released'. Five months later, in New Orleans (on October 16) Crow again came on stage at the end of his concert, playing accordion on 'Alabama Getaway', 'The Times They Are a-Changin'' and the so often unavoidable 'Rainy Day Women # 12 & 35', and singing on the chorus on the first of these three. That year Crow also headlined her own tour and was support to the Eagles at their enormous comeback concerts and, more modestly, to Joe Cocker.

After Bob Dylan tried out his then-new song 'Mississippi' at the sessions for *Time Out of Mind* in Miami in January 1997, and rejected the result, he revisited the song for *"Love and Theft"*, the next new studio album four years later (luckily for us, since it is without question a major highlight of that album). But in between, he gave the song to Sheryl Crow, none of whose virtues are apparent on her adenoidal, foggy, upbeat self-produced version (inside which, somewhere, lurks the keyboard work of BENMONT TENCH), which was released on her third solo album, *The Globe Sessions*, in 1998. Crow said at the time: 'I was so excited that he thought about me singing it. It's an undeniably brilliant song.' Perhaps he had given her the song around December 19, 1997, the night she appeared on stage with him once again at the fourth of his five LA concerts of December 1997 (part of that month's 'club tour', which had begun at the start of the month in Atlanta), when near the end of his set she played guitar and sang on 'Highway 61 Revisited' and played accordion and sang on 'Knockin' on Heaven's Door'.

In 1998 Crow played on a rather larger scale in New York's Central Park, with star guests including CLAPTON and KEITH RICHARDS, from which came 1999's *Sheryl Crow and Friends: Live–There Goes the Neighborhood*. In 2002 came *C'mon C'mon*, in 2003 a greatest hits collection, *The Very Best of Sheryl Crow* and in 2005 *Wildflower*. In 2004 she appeared, unadvisedly, wrestling with 'Begin the Beguine' in the Cole Porter biopic *De-Lovely*. She has continued to produce and devise hit-making remixes for other artists, and to write songs, though rarely with lines as courageous and memorable (and unlike Cole Porter's) as on the co-written 'Love Is a Good Thing', from her 1996 second album, *Sheryl Crow*: 'Watch out sister, watch out brother / Watch our children while they kill each other / With a gun they bought at Wal-Mart discount stores'.

When it came to selecting a Dylan track for the Starbucks album *Artist's Choice: Sheryl Crow–Music That Matters to Her* (2003)–tagline: 'Spend an hour with Sheryl Crow's record collection'–her choice was neither a protest song nor 'Mississippi' but 'Don't Think Twice, It's All Right' from *Freewheelin'*, recorded when Crow was nine months old.

[Sheryl Crow: *Tuesday Night Music Club*, A&M 126, US, 1993; *Sheryl Crow*, A&M 587, 1996; *The Globe Sessions*, A&M 540959, 1998; *Sheryl Crow and Friends: Live–There Goes the Neighborhood*, A&M, 1999; *C'mon C'mon*, Uniscope, US, 2002; *The Very Best of Sheryl Crow*, A&M, 2003; *Artist's Choice: Sheryl Crow–Music That Matters to Her*, Hear Music / Universal Music Special Markets 069493585-2, US, 2003; *Wildflower*, 2005. *De-Lovely*, dir. Irwin Winkler, written Jay Cocks; Winkler / Potboiler / UA, US, 2004.]

Crowe, Cameron [1957 -] Cameron Crowe was born in Palm Springs, California, on July 13, 1957 and grew up in San Diego, with rock'n'roll banned from the house. After a brief, defiant stint in the bad local group the Masked Hamster, he began writing for the underground *San Diego Door* (like LESTER BANGS before him). He joined the staff of *Rolling Stone* while still a teenager, but quit to stay on the West Coast when the magazine moved East in 1977, though he remained a contributor. At the end of the 1970s he published a hit book, *Fast Times at Ridgemont High*, and then wrote the screenplay for the 1982 movie version.

Thus began a successful life writing and later also directing movies, which have included the overrated *Jerry Maguire* (the soundtrack and soundtrack album of which offered a previously unissued take of Dylan's 'Shelter from the Storm') and the much better (and autobiographical) *Almost Famous*. He has also made music TV specials and videos with TOM PETTY, Pearl Jam and others. But in September 1985 Crowe conducted a series of interviews with Bob Dylan that were published within the box set *Biograph*: interviews that enabled Dylan to talk, sometimes with surprising candour, about his life, beliefs and views on contemporary culture–but also to offer explanations of how he came to write particular songs, and/or comments as to what particular songs were 'about' (often discussing this at some length), in a way that he had never done in public print before. Some credit for this valuable, energetic and beguiling material must go to Cameron Crowe, who was still in his 20s when he conducted these interviews and already a success in his own right, but who here put himself wholly and unobtrusively in the service of drawing out Dylan for Dylan's sake.

[Cameron Crowe: *Fast Times at Ridgemont High* (book), New York: Simon & Schuster, 1981; *Fast Times at Ridgemont High* (film), dir. Amy Heckerling, 1982; *Jerry Maguire*, dir. Cameron Crowe, 1996; *Almost Famous*, dir. Crowe, 2000. Bob Dylan: 'Shelter from the Storm', NY, 17 Sep 1974, *Jerry Maguire: Music from the Motion Picture*, Epic Soundtrax EK 67910, US, 10 Dec 1996.]

Crudup, Arthur 'Big Boy' [1905 - 1974] Arthur William Crudup was born into rural poverty in Forest, in southern Mississippi, on August 24, 1905 and was singing in church by the age of ten. He worked as a labourer before taking up the guitar at the unusually late age of 32 but was soon playing at local parties. In the depths of the Depression he struggled to stay in music but in 1940 joined gospel group the Harmonizing Four, moved to Chicago with them in 1941 (living, to begin with, in a wooden crate under the 'L' station) and then quit the group and turned back to the blues. Discovered by a Victor talent scout, he was asked to perform that same evening in front of towering figures like Tampa Red, BIG BILL BROONZY and LONNIE JOHNSON. His guitar playing was simple but he was a strong songwriter with a spare, field-holler voice, and after impressing this intimidating audience he was signed up. He recorded over 80 sides between 1941 and 1956, scoring 78rpm successes with a handful.

His fame in the wider world rests on the fact that ELVIS PRESLEY's first record, the immortal 'That's All Right', recorded in July 1954, was a revolutionary revival of an Arthur 'Big Boy' Crudup song. (When Presley moved from Sun to RCA at the beginning of 1956, he swiftly recorded another old Crudup 1940s record, 'So Glad You're Mine'.)

Yet it's an example of how timeless Elvis Presley's exciting new transmissions could be that the line 'That's alright, mama, that's alright for you' figures in a much earlier blues classic than the Crudup song. It's a stanza from BLIND LEMON JEFFERSON's seminal 'Black Snake Moan' (cut in Chicago as 'That Black Snake Moan' in 1926 and re-cut in Atlanta as 'Black Snake Moan' in 1927). The lines 'Mama that's alright, sugar that's alright for you / That's alright mama, that's alright for you / . . . just the way you do' then recurred the following year in one of the two takes of Ishman Bracey's terrific ''Fore Day Blues'. *Then*, on the early Crudup side 'If I Get Lucky', in 1941, he not only tried out the lines 'That's alright mama, that's alright for you / Treat me low-down and dirty, any old way you do' for the first time but did it with a style of hollering that admits a debt to Bracey as much as to Jefferson.

The connection makes sense: Crudup hung out in Jackson, Mississippi, in the 1940s, when Ishman Bracey was the city's most popular and active musician. In turn, it was 150 miles up Highway 55, in Memphis, that Elvis saw Crudup perform. Somewhere there's an interview with Elvis in which he's asked, when he's the ultimate star, if he had imagined that kind of fame and success for himself when he started out. Elvis replies: 'No. When I started out I just wanted to be as good as Arthur Crudup was when I saw him live in '49.'

One of the Crudup records Presley surprised Sam Phillips by knowing was 'Rock Me Mama', and this is the other Crudup song besides 'That's All Right' that Dylan recorded. He tried 'That's All Right' fairly early in his own career, at the session of October 26, 1962 that yielded both the *Freewheelin'* and the slightly different single-release version of 'Corrina Corrina', and again at the session of November 1; these have circulated but remain unissued. A little over ten years later Dylan tried Crudup's 'Rock Me Mama' at the sessions for *Pat Garrett & Billy the Kid* in 1973, to no especially significant avail. It's a simple song, anonymous in character and Dylan does nothing much with it—or at least, you'd say so until you find that in 2004 the group Old Crow Medicine Show include the song under the title 'Wagon Wheel' and credit this title partly to Dylan and his music publishing company. (And don't credit Crudup at all.) The two known Dylan takes have never been released but have circulated in rather poor quality.

Other Crudup records have Dylan connections. His 'Death Valley Blues' (see the entry on Dylan's song **'Dignity'**) tells a story that takes place out on Highway 61; his 'Mean Old Frisco Blues' is one of the very few pre-1950s records to use the phrase 'special rider', which Dylan took as the name of his most important music-publishing company; Crudup made a record called 'That's Your Red Wagon' in 1945; his 1941 revisit to CHARLEY PATTON territory on 'Black Pony Blues' includes the phrase 'she fox-trot and pace' which Dylan echoes in his own 'New Pony' blues on *Street Legal* in 1978; and Crudup recorded a 'Dirt Road Blues' in 1945.

Presley had always credited Crudup, both in interviews and on the record label; but royalties paid never reached the musician and he remained in poverty even while being labelled 'the father of rock'n'roll'; in response he liked to refer to his most famous fan as 'Elvin Preston'. He had returned to southern Mississippi by the end of the 1940s—like BLIND WILLIE McTELL, his sound had become passé in Chicago—and though he made the occasional foray into Memphis, he was back to playing rural juke joints by the early 1950s. It is a bellowing irony that the same year Elvis Presley shot to national prominence and that undreamt of fame, 1956, Arthur Crudup gave up music and returned to farm work.

However, he was still only 50 years old, and he survived long enough to receive an eventual $60,000 in back royalties when 'rediscovered' in 1965 by Dick Waterman, who pointed him towards the folk revival movement. He toured the US East Coast and Europe as a rightly valued survivor of the pre-war country blues world, recorded with British musicians on a UK trip in 1970 and back in the US even went out as the support act to Bonnie Raitt.

Arthur 'Big Boy' Crudup suffered a fatal stroke and died while still a working musician, in Nassawadox, Virginia, on March 28, 1974.

[Arthur Crudup: 'If I Get Lucky', 'Death Valley Blues' & 'Black Pony Blues', Chicago, 11 Sep 1941, the 1st on *King of the Blues Vol. 3* (EP), RCA RCX204, London, 1962; the others on *Bluebird Blues*, RCA LPV-518 (Vintage Series), NY, 1965; 'Mean Old Frisco Blues', Chicago, 15 Apr 1942, *The Rural Blues*, RBF FR-202, NY, 1964; 'That's Your Red Wagon' (unreleased till 1983) & 'Dirt Road Blues', Chicago, 22 Oct 1945, the latter on Victor 20-2757, NY, 1947; 'That's All Right', Chicago, 6 Sep 1946, known by Presley from the 78rpm Victor 20-2205 (c/w 'Crudup's After Hours'), NY, 1946.

Bob Dylan: 'That's All Right', NY, 26 Oct 1962; 'Rock Me Mama', Burbank, CA, Feb 1973; both unreleased. Elvis Presley: 'That's All Right', Memphis, 5–6 Jul 1954, Sun 209, Memphis, 1954. Blind Lemon Jefferson: 'That Black Snake Moan', Chicago, c.Nov 1926, *Black Snake Moan: Blind Lemon Jefferson*, Milestone MLP-2013, NY, 1970. 'Black Snake Moan', Atlanta, 14 Mar 1927, *Jazz Vol. 2: The Blues*, Folkways FP55 & FJ-2802, NY, 1950. Ishman Bracey: 'The 'Fore Day Blues' (alternate take), Memphis, 31 Aug 1928, *Jackson Blues 1928–1938*, Yazoo L-1007, NY, c.1968, CD-reissued YAZCD1007, NY, c.1988. (The lyric fragment quoted is not on the better-known take, issued on *The Famous 1928 Tommy Johnson-Ishman Bracey Session*, Roots RL-

330, Vienna, 1970; both takes are CD-reissued on *Ishman Bracey & Charley Taylor*, Document DOCD-5049, Vienna, c.1991.) Old Crow Medicine Show: 'Wagon Wheel', *Old Crow Medicine Show*, Nettwerk, US, 2004.

Main sources: Michael Gray, *Song & Dance Man III: The Art of Bob Dylan*; Rick Anderson, entry in *The Blues Encyclopedia*, New York: Routledge, 2005, pp. 240–243, and Tony Russell, *The Blues From Robert Johnson to Robert Cray*, London: Arum Press, 1997, p.105.]

Cruzados, the See the Plugz.

cummings, e.e. [1894 - 1962] Edward Estlin Cummings was born in Cambridge, Massachusetts, on October 14, 1894. He styled himself e.e. cummings right from the publication of his first poetry collection, *Tulips and Chimneys*, in 1924.

There's a superficial correspondence between cummings' long obtuse titles ('If Up's the Word; And a World Grows Greener', 1958) and Dylan's ('It Takes a Lot to Laugh, It Takes a Train to Cry', 1965) but each of cummings' is a title that is the opening line of the poem in question; with Dylan, such titles are wilfully gangling yet cryptic summaries of a mood contained within the song concerned. But Dylan's work itself acknowledges the notice he's taken of cummings' long titles. As noted in WISSOLIK & McGRATH's *Bob Dylan's Words* (1994) a Dylan phrase that occurs very early on in his 1960s novel *Tarantula*, i.e. 'a much of witchy', alludes to cummings' 'What if a Much of a Which of a Wind', from 1944.

Then there's the fact, so obvious as to have remained unstated, that Dylan's ostentatious refusal of capital letters all through the poetry of *11 Outlined Epitaphs*, 'Advice for Geraldine on Her Miscellaneous Birthday' (very much a modernist poet's title), 'Alternatives to College' and *Some Other Kinds of Songs*, and all through the *Bringing It All Back Home*, *Highway 61 Revisited* and *World Gone Wrong* sleevenotes, as well as in *Tarantula*, is all in the wake of e.e. cummings.

Wissolik & McGrath find three further tips of Dylan's hat to cummings' work in *Tarantula*: namely, an allusion to his title 'Your Sweet Old Etcetera' (1925) and two direct quotes from the poem 'Buffalo Bill's' (1920): 'Jesus he was a handsome man', and 'blueeyed boy', both taken from the poem's final lines 'Jesus / he was a handsome man / and what i want to know is / how do you like your blueeyed boy / Mister Death'. They note too that Dylan uses 'my blue-eyed son' recurrently in 'A Hard Rain's a-Gonna Fall'. We might add that the cummings passage is specifically echoed—the tone exactly seized and duplicated—in 'I Shall Be Free', where Dylan recites: 'What I want to know, Mr. Football Man, is / What do you do about Willy Mays . . . ?' and then again (with T.S. ELIOT thrown in too) in the 'Mouthful of Loving Choke' section of *Tarantula*: '"& i think i'm gonna do april or so is a cruel month & how do you like your blue eyed boy NOW mr octopus?"'. These are allusions he returns to in a fine passage of reminiscence, a decent piece of prose poetry itself, within the sleevenotes for *Biograph*. (See **Beats, the**.)

Finally (less attractively, but tellingly all the same) there's a tone of hectoring assertiveness that cummings often resorts to—as here: 'his flesh was flesh his blood was blood; / no hungry man but wished him food; / no cripple wouldn't creep one mile / uphill to only see him smile' (from 'My Father Moved Through Dooms of Love', 1940), and that Dylan debases further into those sentimentalized portraits of hobo-saints and friends in early songs like 'Only a Hobo' and 'He Was a Friend of Mine' and to which he returns for 'Hurricane' and 'Joey' on *Desire*.

e.e. cummings died in North Conway, New Hampshire, on September 3, 1962.

[e.e. cummings' *Complete Poems, 1913–1962* was published posthumously, in 1973. Wissolik & McGrath, *Bob Dylan's Words*, Greensburg, PA; Eadmer Press, 1994.]

D

Daniels, Charlie [1936 -] Charles Edward Daniels was born in Wilmington, North Carolina, on October 28, 1936 and grew up moving around somewhat–mostly living in Wilmington, Elizabethtown and Spartanburg, South Carolina, but always listening to Pentecostal gospel music live and R&B and country music on the radio. He learnt to play guitar, fiddle and mandolin and began performing and songwriting after graduating from high school in Goldston, North Carolina, in 1955. After forming bluegrass band the Misty Mountain Boys and playing guitar for female vocalist Little Jill in a Wilmington bar, he joined the Jaguars, a rock'-n'roll band. In Texas they bumped into singer, songwriter and then-tyro producer BOB JOHNSTON, who produced their instrumental single 'Jaguar'. Later, with Johnston, Daniels wrote an ELVIS PRESLEY side, 'It Hurts Me,' which was issued only as a B-side yet deserved better, securing from Presley one of the best, most heartfelt vocal performances for several years, on which he seemed to awake from the stupor induced by making all those vacuous 1960s films. It was at Johnston's urging, at the beginning of 1969, that Daniels moved to Tennessee and applied himself to session work in Nashville.

He was at once employed, via Johnston, on a run of Bob Dylan albums, beginning with *Nashville Skyline*. Daniels played guitar and dobro from the very first session (February 13, 1969). He returned in the spring for the first of the *Self Portrait* sessions, playing guitar on April 24–25 & 26 and on May 3, and then returned once more in mid-March 1970 and early that April to contribute to the overdubs recorded in Nashville on tracks Dylan had begun in New York earlier that month.

Charlie Daniels also played guitar on Dylan's JOHNNY CASH TV show appearance, filmed on May 1, 1969 and a year later to the day was playing at the session by Dylan and GEORGE HARRISON that yielded, among much else, the version of 'If Not for You' released on the *Bootleg Series Vols. 1–3* over 20 years later in 1991. Daniels also played on the New York Dylan sessions held on the first five days of June 1970, which yielded much that has never circulated but from which some of the tracks on the *Dylan* album were taken, and which, from June 3 onwards, started to provide material for the *New Morning* album too, on which the studio paperwork suggests Daniels was playing guitar and dobro again (as on 'Went to See the Gypsy'), though the album liner notes online at *bobdylan.com* credit him with playing electric bass.

By now, though, the session musician had his own first album deal, and that year released the first of what has become an astonishing number of albums, almost all of which have since been billed as by the Charlie Daniels Band. That first album, *Charlie Daniels*, contributed forcefully to the then-nascent genre, southern rock. He scored a hit as early as 1972 with the novelty song 'Uneasy Rider' on his third album, *Honey in the Rock* (since renamed after that hit single) and the next album, *Fire on the Mountain*, was the first of many to go platinum. Several have gone triple platinum. By the time of *Songs from the Longleaf Pines* in 2005—which sports a creepy recitation of the 91st Psalm, read as if he's pointing a gun at your head—there were a total of 45 such albums, an excess that included no less than three Christmas albums and an increasing tendency, in song and album titles, towards the combatively rightwing and redneck. 'The South's Gonna Do It', *America, I Believe in You*, '(What This World Needs Is) A Few More Rednecks' and the vigilante barbarism of 'Simple Man' were among the espousals of this good ole boy's repellant world view.

By 2003 Daniels was publishing 'An Open Letter to the Hollywood Bunch', a diatribe against everyone who was anti-war and in foaming defence of George W. Bush's illegal adventurism in Iraq. Sample: 'You people are some of the most disgusting examples of a waste of protoplasm I've ever had the displeasure to hear about. Sean Penn, you're a traitor to the United States of America.' (Worse, there's a misplaced apostrophe: '. . . disbanded it's horrible military . . .') This was collected in a book full of Daniels' political philosophising, *Ain't No Rag: Freedom, Family and the Flag* (of which surely no-one need read any more than the title). It was not his first book; in 1985, he had published a collection of short stories, *The Devil Went Down to Georgia*, named after one of his songs.

On the 4th of July 2005 his first DVD release was recorded live in front of 100,000 people in Nashville. That September, Daniels and the band toured US bases in Eastern Europe, Kuwait and Iraq. He cut a bizarre figure out there, resembling as he does these days a cross between a ZZ Top and Santa Claus–but at least he'd put himself where his loud mouth was.

[Charlie Daniels/Charlie Daniels Band: *Charlie Daniels*, Capitol 11414, US, 1970; 'Uneasy Rider', *Honey in the Rock* (aka *Uneasy Rider*), Kama Sutra 2071, US, 1972; 'The South's Gonna Do It', *Fire on the Mountain*, Kama Sutra 2603, 1974–5; *Simple Man*, Epic EK-45316, US, 1989; *America, I Believe in You*, Liberty 80477, US, 1993; '(What This World Needs Is) A Few More Rednecks', *Freedom & Justice for All*, Audium Entertainment, US, 2003; *Songs from the Longleaf Pines*, Koch, US, 2005; *CDB DVD Live*, Koch, 2005. Charlie Daniels, *The Devil Went Down to Georgia*, Atlanta: Peachtree,

1985; 'An Open Letter to the Hollywood Bunch', collected in *Ain't No Rag: Freedom, Family and the Flag*, Washington, D.C.: Regnery Publishing, 2003. The Jaguars: 'Jaguar' c/w 'Roundabout', Fort Worth, TX, 1959, Epic 5-9308, 1959.]

Danko, Rick [1942 - 1999] Richard Clare Danko was born at Walsh, near tiny Simcoe, Ontario, just south of the Six Nations Reservation (and just east of a small town named Woodstock, as it happens), on December 29, 1942. He grew up in a musical family, quit school at 14 to concentrate on music, joined RONNIE HAWKINS & the Hawks as rhythm guitarist at 17, and then learnt to play bass on the job—eventually developing his very distinctive style, 'percussive but sliding'. After the group quit Hawkins they went out on the road as LEVON & the Hawks, recorded under the additional name the Canadian Squires, and in 1965 met Bob Dylan.

That September the group rehearsed with Dylan in Woodstock, New York, ready for further live gigs beyond those already played with Levon & ROBBIE (and other, non-Hawk musicians) in the aftermath of 'going electric' at Newport that July. The first Dylan concert Danko played was probably October 1 at Carnegie Hall. Four days later the group went into the studio with Dylan for the first time, followed by more live concerts and on November 30 a second studio stint—two days after Helm had quit—from which comes the single 'Can *You* Please Crawl Out Your Window?'. This session has also now yielded the version of 'Visions of Johanna' released on the *Bootleg Series Vol. 7*, 2005.

Back in the studio in New York at Dylan's behest on January 21–22, 1966, the Helmless Hawks helped create that quintessential mid-60s Dylan record, 'She's Your Lover Now' (finally issued on the *Bootleg Series Vols. 1–3* in 1991). On January 25–28, Dylan got Robertson and Danko back into the studio without the others, added them to AL KOOPER on organ, Paul Griffin on piano, BOBBY GREGG on drums and, alongside Danko as a second bassist, Bill Lee. These sessions yielded 'Sooner or Later (One of Us Must Know)'—and therefore got Danko and Robertson onto *Blonde on Blonde* (though Danko's name is missing from the credits). They also yielded the rather inferior version of 'I'll Keep It with Mine' that was also issued on *Bootleg Series Vols. 1–3*.

Then came Dylan's 1966 tour, beginning in Louisville, Kentucky, on February 4 and going across the States, into Canada and Hawaii, over to Australia and then Europe, where they began in Stockholm, Sweden, on April 29 and ended at the Royal Albert Hall in London on May 27. Every musician was crucial to the consummate glory of those performances, but Danko's bass playing was especially dramatic on the intro to the hurled-out 'Like a Rolling Stone' that came at Manchester in response to the shout of 'Judas!' from someone in the crowd, with Dylan's retort of 'I don't believe you!' followed by the explosive challenge of that bass riff coming in, making Dylan's second sentence—'You're a liar!'—part of the song itself: part of the opening tumult.

After all that came the calm of Woodstock and West Saugherties, 1967, when the Hawks were working very differently with Bob Dylan, laying down the Basement Tapes and preparing to turn into THE BAND. Here Dylan began to seek out Danko as his vocalist of choice to harmonise with, whereas within the Hawks he had rarely been more than automatically backing vocalist to MANUEL and Helm.

The exceptions amount to little more than these: that Danko takes lead vocal on Robertson's 'song sketch' '(I Want to Be) The Rainmaker', 1965; he shares lead vocals with Helm & Manuel on the 1965 Levon & the Hawks single 'Go Go Liza Jane'; that he takes lead vocal on the Dylan-free *Basement Tapes* tracks 'Caledonia Mission' and 'Ferdinand the Imposter'; and that he shares lead vocal with Manuel on another such track, 'Will the Circle Be Unbroken'.

At any rate, it's sometimes been argued that herein lies one of the benefits Dylan derived from working with the Hawks: that harmonising with Danko's countrified wail freed Dylan up to sing out in a country style himself. Danko was the first person Dylan had sung with while fronting an electric group. And it was Danko to whom Dylan gave his dog Hamlet (allegedly after discovering that Hamlet's pedigree was suspect).

The Woodstock sessions saw Dylan and Danko in songwriting partnership too: the great 'This Wheel's on Fire' is a Dylan-Danko composition (though Danko again misses his credit on the original LP cover of The Band's *Music from Big Pink*) and it is Danko who has won the right to be lead vocalist on their début album recording of the song. Again he's lead singer on 'Caledonia Mission' too, and on 'Long Black Veil', and shares lead vocals on 'The Weight'. He also plays violin on 'Chest Fever'.

On the second album, Danko plays trombone on 'Across the Great Divide' and 'Unfaithful Servant', violin on 'Rag Mama Rag' and 'The Night They Drove Old Dixie Down', and he sings lead on 'When You Awake', 'Look Out Cleveland' and 'Unfaithful Servant'; on the third album, *Stage Fright*, he sings lead on the title song, and shares lead with Manuel on 'Time to Kill' and with Helm & Manuel on 'The Rumor' and 'W.S. Walcott Medicine Show'. And he plays violin on 'Daniel & the Sacred Harp'.

On *Cahoots* he co-wrote 'Life Is a Carnival' with Helm and Robertson. It was his first writing credit since *Music from Big Pink*. Things were falling apart within the group. On *Moondog Matinee* he played rhythm guitar on one track but only bass on everything else. His main contribution was his lead vocal on SAM COOKE's 'A Change Is Gonna Come'—a lead vocal that wasn't credited on the album sleeve and had many people, GREIL MARCUS included, assuming it was by Richard Manuel.

On *Islands* Danko managed a co-composer credit with Robertson on 'Street Walker' and with Robertson and HUDSON on the title track, but he wanted out. He, as much as Robertson, wanted to call a halt, and welcomed the grand bow-out that became *The Last Waltz*.

In a way Danko was the keenest of all to make solo albums, though he looks bereft at the prospect of an uncertain future when, in that film, SCORSESE asks him what his plans are; and in fact after the first solo album, in 1977, 14 years elapsed before the next. Danko's solo (and soloish) albums were: *Rick Danko* (1977), *Danko/Fjeld/Andersen* (1991), *Ridin' on the Blinds* (also an album of shared billing with Eric Andersen and Jonas Fjeld, 1994), *In Concert* (a poorly recorded return to solo billing, and also to the material of classic Band days, 1997) and *Live on Breeze Hill* (a better offering, with a larger band, 1999). These were followed by the posthumous *Times Like These* (a far worthier collection than either of its immediate predecessors, 2000), *One More Shot* (a live Danko/Fjeld/Andersen CD added to a re-release of their first album from ten years earlier, 2001) and the discountable rehash of *A Memorial Edition* (2002).

Many Band aficionados feel a special affection for that first solo album—not because it sounds like The Band but because it doesn't. It sounds like Danko in full bloom. Less is more here; his vocal work and his harmonies are tremendous; and the album's particular treats include his song 'New Mexicoe' (co-written with BOBBY CHARLES), which weirdly combines ERIC CLAPTON's electric guitar with Garth Hudson's ghostly hillbilly accordion.

So much promise. And yet . . . Nothing happened to the album at the time, and Danko seemed to disappear in the late 1970s to early '80s—though in fact he turned up on other artists' records, including EMMYLOU HARRIS' *Quarter Moon in a Ten Cent Town* and Joe Cocker's *Luxury You Can Afford*. In 1983 he retreated back into the reformed Band—and even then, when those 1990s Band albums finally arrived, it was only on the third and final one, *Jubilation*, that Danko co-wrote any of the material.

Outside of the group, however, he was not inactive. Encouraged by Levon Helm, Danko took an acting rôle, as the unnamed father of a kidnapped child, in the 1986 film *Man Outside* (as do Hudson, Helm and Manuel). He played live music with many people, including PAUL BUTTERFIELD and Jorma Kaukonen, and in 1987 released *Rick Danko's Electric Bass Techniques*, an instructional video. In 1990 (again with Helm and Hudson) he made a guest appearance in Roger Waters' 'The Wall' concert in Berlin (and so in the TV film of the concert, *The Wall: Live in Berlin*) and then in 1991, prompted by the success of a shared low-profile gig in Woodstock and a follow-up tour of Norway, came *Danko/Fjeld/Andersen*, which won Norway's equivalent of a Grammy, and is widely felt to capture some of Danko's best work. It was issued in the US in 1993.

By this time Danko and Dylan had combined again. Levon Helm and Rick Danko gigged at the Lone Star Café in New York City in February 1983, and on the 16th, Dylan joined them to sing and play guitar on 'Your Cheatin' Heart', 'Willie and the Hand Jive', 'Ain't No More Cane' and 'Going Down'. In 1992 Danko was a member of The Band that took part in the so-called 30th Anniversary Concert for Dylan at Madison Square Garden, at which they performed 'When I Paint My Masterpiece' and joined the ensemble for the penultimate song of the evening, 'Knockin' on Heaven's Door'; on January 17, 1993, he (and Garth and Levon) played with Dylan at President Bill Clinton's inauguration party, the so-called 'Absolutely Unofficial Blue Jeans Bash (For Arkansas)'. And then in 1997, Dylan's long-serving band member TONY GARNIER joined The Band to play stand-up bass on three numbers at their March 20 show in Carnegie Hall, and on August 18, 1997, at a Dylan Never-Ending Tour concert in Wallingford, Connecticut, Rick Danko joined Dylan on stage twice over—to sing with him and play guitar on 'This Wheel's on Fire' and, a few songs later, on 'I Shall Be Released'.

Rick Danko died in his sleep at his home in Woodstock on December 10, 1999. Steve Forbert wrote a tribute song for him, 'Wild as the Wind', which means well and doesn't avoid acknowledging the rôle cocaine played in his life and demise. But Danko's own posthumous album *Times Like These* is a more substantial tribute to his considerable talents. Everyone who knew him misses the sweet, good-humoured person that it's agreed he was. Everyone who knew the music of The Band misses his artistry.

[Rick Danko: *Rick Danko*, Arista AB-4141, US, 1977; *In Concert*, Foxborough, MA, 22 Feb & Clinton, NJ, 6 Mar, 1997, Woodstock Records, US, 1997; *Live on Breeze Hill*, Breeze Hill/Woodstock, US, 1999; *Times Like These*, Breeze Hill, US 2000 (different version issued Cora-Zong / Nordic 255034, 2003). Danko/Fjeld/Andersen: *Danko /Fjeld/Andersen*, *nia*, Norway, 1991 & Rykodisc, US, 1993; *Ridin' on the Blinds:* Grappa GRCD 4080, Norway, 1994 (Rykodisc 10371, US, 1997). *Man Outside*, dir. & written Mark Stouffer, US, 1986. Steve Forbert: 'Wild as the Wind', Neptune, NJ, *nia*, *Just Like There's Nothin' to It*, Koch KOC-CD-9534, NY, 2004. For a full Danko discography see *http://theband.hiof.no/albums/danko_index.html*.]

Darby & Tarlton See **'Columbus Stockade Blues' [1960]**.

Darby, Tom [1884 - 1971] See **'Columbus Stockade Blues' [1960]**.

Davis, Blind Gary [1896 - 1972] See Davis, Rev. Gary.

Davis, Jesse Ed [1944 - 1988] A full-blooded Kiowa Indian and teenage ELVIS PRESLEY fan, Jesse Ed Davis was born in Norman, Oklahoma, on September 21, 1944. He started his journey towards becoming a superbly versatile blues guitarist in his early teens by acquiring, like all those penurious pre-war blues guitarists who'd gone before him, a cheap Stella guitar. He formed his first band as a teenager (describing it later as 'an abortive Kingston Trio imitation'), acquired his first electric guitar in seventh grade (a Silvertone) and was taught to play the blues by 'the first really professional musician' he met, a 'black cat named Wallace Thompson' who played in the piano bar lounge of Uncle Tom's Hickory Pit Barbecue. Before launching into a music career he took a degree in literature at the University of Oklahoma; he came out the other end and started touring behind CONWAY TWITTY.

In 1964 he decided to call on his old acquaintanceship with LEVON HELM, who gave him a place to stay when he moved to California. He joined Taj Mahal's band, which included CHUCK BLACKWELL on drums, and played on his albums *Taj Mahal* (1967), *Giant Step* (1968–9) and *The Natch'l Blues* (1969). It was on their version of BLIND WILLIE McTELL's 'Statesboro Blues' that Jesse Ed Davis first added slide guitar to his repertoire. MICK JAGGER and KEITH RICHARDS, fans of Mahal and his band, brought them into the film *THE ROLLING STONES' Rock'n'Roll Circus*, made in December 1968 (as a TV Special), which brought Davis to the attention of JOHN LENNON, ERIC CLAPTON, GEORGE HARRISON and others.

Davis started doing session work in every area of music, eventually playing for B.B. King, Steve Miller, Helen Reddy, David Cassidy, Albert King, WILLIE NELSON, Rod Stewart, LEON RUSSELL, Wayne Newton, BOOKER T., Gary Lewis & the Playboys, John Lennon, JOHN LEE HOOKER, Jackson Browne, Donovan, NEIL DIAMOND, 5th Dimension, GEOFF MULDAUR, the Pointer Sisters, DAVID BLUE and Jackie de Shannon. That's quite some list. Davis' own musical taste was even broader; in 1974 he told interviewer Steven Rosen he felt that Charlie Parker was in his blood.

1971 seems to have been an especially happy year. Davis produced and played on Gene Clark's second solo album *White Light* and recorded his own début solo LP, *Jesse Davis*, on which he wrote most tracks, sang and played keyboards as well as guitars, and on which Leon Russell, Clapton and Gram Parsons all featured. He appeared at the Concert for Bangla Desh, clinched a warm working relationship with George Harrison—whose Native American cousin he somewhat suggested in appearance—by playing on his 'Bangla Desh' single; he did sessions for Leon Russell, Delaney & Bonnie, Buffy Sainte Marie, Ben Sidran and others; and he put onto Jackson Browne's début album (issued January 1972) the striking guitar solo on the track 'Doctor My Eyes'. In 1972 he also made his own second solo album, *Ululu*, on which he had written less but included MERLE HAGGARD's 'White Line Fever', George Harrison's 'Sue Me, Sue You Blues' and THE BAND's 'Strawberry Wine', and called in CLYDIE KING and Merry Clayton on background vocals. In 1973 came a label change and a third solo album, *Keep Me Comin'*, on which he returned to more self-penned numbers and featured a battalion of background vocalists and a seven-man horn section.

From the mid-1970s onwards life proved difficult for Davis, despite worldly success and the respect in which his playing was held. He played on John Lennon's *Walls and Bridges* and *Rock'n'Roll Songs*, contributed the poignant slide guitar to Clapton's *No Reason to Cry* track 'Hello Old Friend' and many other things besides—including singing on Bryan Ferry's album *These Foolish Things* (1973) and playing on Bert Jansch's *LA Turnaround* and Harry Nilsson's *Pussy Cats* (both 1974)—but he lived a life of LA-based excess, often hanging out with Lennon and Nilsson through binge drinking sessions and once fighting Lennon so hard while both were drunk that Davis' girlfriend called in the police.

Though drugs were as much a part of Davis' life as alcohol, he could continue to play and function on tour and in the studio (working with Van Dyke Parks, Keith Moon and RINGO STARR), and it was in this period that he and Bob Dylan came together, first on the LEONARD COHEN session that Dylan and ALLEN GINSBERG dropped in on in March 1977, all of them contributing to the track 'Don't Go Home With Your Hard-On', released on *Death of a Ladies' Man*. On the last two days of the same year, Davis rehearsed with Dylan in Santa Monica for a place in the 1978 World Tour band. In the event, he didn't get it or didn't take it.

In the mid-1980s Davis met up with fellow Native American performer John Trudell, and told him: 'I can make music for your words.' Trudell said later: 'With Jesse and me, we each came from our collective Indian experience, and had our individual experiences in the non-Indian world. We had both literally been to the last door of hell, opened it and saw what was inside.' Their first album together, *aka Graffiti Man*, comprising ten tracks of Trudell's spoken poetry fused with Davis' guitar and keyboards, was issued on Trudell's own small label Peace Company, and only on cassette; yet Dylan not only heard it but told *Rolling Stone* magazine it was 'the best album of 1986' and had it played over the PA system to the crowds in the intermission at his July 1987 concerts with THE GRATEFUL DEAD. Four months earlier, that March 5 in a Hollywood studio, Jesse Ed Davis and Dylan came together one last time. It was a Dylan session, and with four other musicians (on unspecified instruments) they recorded takes of four songs: 'Street People', 'Sidewalks', the ELIZABETH COTTEN song 'Shake Sugaree', and 'My Prayer' (possibly the old hit by the Platters). None was issued. None has circulated.

Davis and Trudell—who now barely mentions Davis on his own website's discography—made a second album together that year, called *Heart Jump Bouquet*, and a Tribal Voice series recording, *... But This Isn't El Salvador*. But Jesse Ed Davis died of a drug overdose on June 22, 1988 in a laundromat in Venice, California.

[Jesse Ed Davis: *Jesse Davis*, Atco SD33-346, US, 1971, CD-reissued Atlantic 7567-80772-2, 1999; *Ululu*, Atco, 1972; *Keep Me Comin'*, Epic KE32133, US, 1973. John Trudell & Jesse Ed Davis: *aka Graffiti Man*, Peace Company TPC5158 (cassette only), US, 1986; *Heart Jump Bouquet*, TPC-21587 (cassette only), US, 1978; *... But This Isn't El Salvador*, Tribal Voice, *nia*, US, 1987.

George Harrison, 'Bangla Desh', Apple R5912, US, 1971. Jackson Browne: *Jackson Browne*, Asylum 7E-5051, US, 1972. John Lennon: *Walls and Bridges*, Apple SW-3416, US, 1974; *Rock'n'Roll*, Apple 3419, US, 1975. Eric Clapton: 'Hello Old Friend', *No Reason to Cry*, RSO 2479179, US, 1976. *The Rolling Stones Rock'n'Roll Circus*, dir. Michael Lindsay-Hogg; ABKCO, US, 1968, re-released US, 1996. Steven Rosen interview, *Guitar Player*, US, Mar 1974. John Trudell quoted from profile seen online 19 Jan 2006 at *www.spitfiretour.org/trudell.html*. Some discographical detail from *www.geocities.jp/hideki_wtnb/jessedavis.html*; none from *www.johntrudell.com/discography.html*.]

Davis, Rev. Gary [1896 - 1972] Gary Davis, who was born in Laurens, South Carolina, on April 30, 1896, was one of those whose influence touched both other blues musicians of the pre-war era and the post-war folk and blues revivalists. Among the former, Davis' dexterous finger-picking guitar style especially affected BLIND BOY FULLER, whom he taught, and among the latter he was a dramatic presence whose repertoire and delivery pressed upon everyone from DAVE VAN RONK to Taj Mahal, though part of his armory was his attempted replication of the songs and style of BLIND WILLIE JOHNSON.

The Reverend Gary Davis (aka Blind Gary Davis) comes recommended by ROBERT SHELTON for a 'marvellously rough and penetrating voice' and for carrying on 'Blind Willie Johnson's tradition of "the holy blues"', deploying 'Heartfelt blues vocal and guitar language, dressed up in religious togs by a curbstone preacher.' The pioneering British blues critic Bruce Bastin calls him 'superb' and 'a superlative guitarist'. Other blues connoisseurs are less keen; while recognising his technical mastery it is very possible to be unmoved by his somewhat brusque, often overbearing style. And Blind Willie Johnson he ain't.

His first recordings were made in New York City over three days in 1935. He moved to New York in the early 1940s, recording next in 1945 and frequently thereafter. He was around to be heard and admired before the rush of 'rediscovered' pre-war greats arrived on the folk revival scene, was established within before Bob Dylan was first exploring Greenwich Village, and was thus a major figure on the Folk Festival and college circuit (appearing, for instance, at the Mariposa Festival of 1959 and at the NEWPORT FOLK FESTIVAL in 1963). Dylan lists him in *Chronicles Volume One* as one of the singers he'd heard on record before he reached New York City—one of those he had come there to find; later in the book he says he had followed him around in those early Greenwich Village days, seeing him as 'one of the wizards of modern music' and as someone who looked 'like he'd been raised upright and was watching over things, keeping constant vigilance over what was happening.' An eerie impression for a blind man to convey.

Items in Gary Davis' sets that have a connection with Dylan's own include 'You're Goin' Quit Me Baby' [sic], 'Jesus Met the Woman at the Well', 'Motherless Children', 'Cocaine Blues' and 'There Was a Time When I Was Blind'.

Dylan was taped singing this last item and Davis' 'Death Don't Have No Mercy' in Minneapolis back in May 1961. (Aeons later, in the psychedelic 60s, THE GRATEFUL DEAD made a near-endless version of the latter one of their standards). And though on his début-album track 'Baby Let Me Follow You Down', Dylan says he learnt the song from (E)RIC VON SCHMIDT 'in the green pastures of Harvard University', he was aware that it could be traced back to Davis' 'Baby, Let Me Lay It on You'—and further back beyond that all the way to MEMPHIS MINNIE and her second husband, Joe McCoy. Davis finally committed it to tape in 1968, his version predictably close to Blind Boy Fuller's, confirming that he had had it in his repertoire since the 1930s. (For a more detailed history, see separate entry on this song.)

At some point when Dylan was exploring out loud with SUZE ROTOLO the possibility of marrying her, he suggested, if more than half jokingly, that they could get Davis to perform the ceremony—or at least sing at it.

Dylan recalls Davis in these Greenwich Village years as switching—oddly, for someone who was ashamed of his blues side and was supposed to have renounced it—between religious and devil's music:

'Strange, he used to sing "Twelve Gates to the City", "Yonder at the Cross" and then "Baby, Let Me Lay It on You".' This typical piece of Dylan eloquence tells us with brevity something that's true in spirit and in its surprisingly specific detail too. The Davis discography confirms that Dylan's recollection is likely to be absolutely right. At a 1962 gig he sang 'Sally, Where You Get Your Liquor

From?' straight after 'If I Had My Way (I'd Tear the Building Down'), and when, later in the 1960s, he recorded at his music-publisher's office, Davis followed 'Oh Glory, How Happy I Am' with 'Cocaine Blues'.

Gary Davis, who remained secretive all his life about the details of when and how he had become blind, died in Hammonton, New Jersey, on May 5, 1972.

[Davis first recorded his 'Twelve Gates to the City' as by Blind Gary, NY, 26 Jul 1935, 1st vinyl-issued *Rev. Gary Davis 1935–1949*, Yazoo L-1023, NY, 1970. His first recordings of the Dylan-connection items were: Rev. Gary Davis: 'You're Goin' Quit Me Baby', 'Oh Glory, How Happy I Am' & 'Cocaine Blues', NY, 1963 or 1968, *Let Us Get Together*, Kicking Mule SNKF 103, London, 1973; Blind Gary Davis (with SONNY TERRY): 'Jesus Met the Woman at the Well' & 'Motherless Children', NY, Apr 1954, *Blind Gary Davis with Sonny Terry*, Stinson SLP 56, NY, 1954; Blind Gary Davis: 'There Was a Time When I Was Blind', NY, 29 Jan 1956, *Rev. Gary Davis & Pink Anderson Gospel, Blues and Street Songs*, Riverside LP 148, NY, prob. 1961; Rev. Gary Davis: 'Death Don't Have No Mercy', Englewood Cliffs, NJ, 24 Aug 1960, *Harlem Street Singer*, Prestige Bluesville BVLP 1015, Bergenfield, NJ, 1961; Blind Gary Davis: 'Baby, Let Me Lay It on You', Ann Arbor, MI, 1968, *Lo' I Be With You Always*, Kicking Mule LP1, London 1973. He never recorded the title 'Yonder at the Cross'. Rev. Gary Davis: 'If I Had My Way' and 'Sally, Where You Get Your Liquor From', Paoli, PA, 8 Sep 1962; *Philadelphia Folk Festival Vol.2*, Prestige International 13072, c.1963.

Bob Dylan: 'Death Don't Have No Mercy' & 'It's Hard to Be Blind', Minneapolis, May 1961, unissued. The Grateful Dead: 'Death Don't Have No Mercy', San Francisco, 2 Mar 1969, *Live/Dead*, Warner Bros. 2WS 1830, LA, 1969.

Bob Dylan 1st quote from the *Biograph* box set interview, 1985; *Chronicles Volume One* quote p.191 (& earlier listing p.9). Robert Shelton, *No Direction Home: The Life and Music of Bob Dylan*, 1986. Bruce Bastin, *Cryin' for the Carolines*, London: Studio Vista, 1971, p.26. For more on Davis see Robert Tilling's 1992 book *Oh! What a Beautiful City: A Tribute to Rev. Gary Davis 1896–1972*.]

Day, Aidan [1952 -] Aidan Day was born on April 19, 1952. An English Literature academic, he was at Edinburgh University from 1984 to 2001, becoming Professor of Nineteenth Century and Contemporary Literature in 1999; in 2001 he became Professor of British Literature and Culture at the University of Aarhus, Denmark. His books include *Romanticism*, 1995, *Angela Carter: The Rational Glass*, 1998, and *Tennyson's Scepticism*, 2005. He and CHRISTOPHER RICKS were joint editors of the 31-volume facsimile-edition hardback series *The Tennyson Archive* (1987–1993).

Aidan Day first listened to Dylan with interest in 1972. His first work on Dylan was no.3 in the Wanted Man Study Series edited by JOHN BAULDIE, *Bob Dylan: Escaping on the Run*, 1984, which had first been delivered as an undergraduate lecture at the West London Institute of Higher Education that February. His essay 'Reels of Rhyme: Mr. Tambourine Man' was published in *The Telegraph* in 1986, and, slightly revised, republished in *All Across the Telegraph* the following year. Most recently he contributed the essay 'Looking for Nothing: Dylan Now' to the book *Do You Mr. Jones?: Bob Dylan with the Poets and Professors*, 2002.

His most substantial scrutiny of Dylan's work, however, lies within his 1988 book *Jokerman: Reading the Lyrics of Bob Dylan*, which, three years ahead of STEPHEN SCOBIE's *Alias Bob Dyan*, was the first to pioneer a postmodernist approach to Dylan's work, the first to apply to him the preoccupations of post-structuralist criticism—in which the canon has crumbled, the 'authority' of the author has gone and the most interesting source for the work is the work itself.

This new criticism is based on ideas that had been hovering in the outside critical-intellectual world since late 1960s/early 1970s work by Roland Barthes, Jacques Derrida and other cultural studies guerrillas (though this slow momentum of ideas really began far earlier, perhaps with a book of radical linguistics by Ferdinand de Saussure published in 1916, which leads into the post-Saussurean linguistics of the 1970s of Jacques Lacan, Louis Hjelmslev and others; there is also the German Rezeptionsästhetik developed from Hans Robert Jauss by Wolfgang Iser and others).

Post-structuralist criticism is especially alert to questions of identity, its fragmentedness and open-endedness. This means a stress on who-and-what Bob Dylan is, and what his 'text' is, and a keen scrutiny of his 'self-referring' songs, his 'self-reflexive texts'—for instance those products of the Muse which are *about* seeking, chasing and needing the Muse (a prime example is 'Mr. Tambourine Man'); those songs which, as Day puts it so concisely, 'take as their immediate subject the creative processes by which they are themselves brought into being'.

Likewise postmodern questions about how we see the individual and the self fire Day's interest in Dylan's 'non-linear narratives': songs like 'Tangled Up in Blue' that don't have a fixed or clearly identifiable voice telling a clear sequential story—songs which, he argues, reflect the non-linear (tangled up) way the human brain is currently thought to perceive and interpret the world in front of it and the past behind it. His concern here is for 'lyrics which open out into an exploration of the workings of the psyche as a whole': including 'Shelter from the Storm', 'Isis' and (via 'I Shall Be Released') 'Tangled Up in Blue'.

This last excites Aidan Day also because of a fundamental effect that comes, he argues, from the way the lyric splits its 'I' into an 'I' and a 'he', and splits its 'she' into what may be a series of shes, and into 'she' and 'you'. The effect is this:

> 'Considerable inventive effort on the part of the reader is provoked whether the lyric is taken either as one story or as a series of stories. Co-operation in the making of the story may be demanded of the reader of any narrative. The specially modernist feature of "Tangled Up in Blue" is that the fragmentation of linear structure, together with the indeterminacy generated by that fragmentation about whether we are in the presence of one or more stories, encourages specific awareness of the creative role of the audience in reading or hearing narrative.'

That's at the heart of the new-critical claim, and it's followed up by an eloquent, admirably confident passage of Barthesian generalisation about our deep psyches:

> '. . . teasing us into generating story, "Tangled Up in Blue" also explores the extent to which the mind is fundamentally disposed to think in terms of story or narrative. The conscious self is inseparable from the stories of its own life that it ceaselessly recites, however silently, to itself. . . . in the same way cultures frame themselves through myths of origin, through histories and through fictions of the future . . . the subject of the lyric is in one sense the inescapability of the narrative impulse itself. But more than this, in its disturbance of narrative order the lyric simultaneously inquires into the possibility of something beyond such order.'

Day similarly looks at 'Brownsville Girl', and then slides back across the years to *Blonde on Blonde* to find Dylan's 'Visions of Johanna' again advancing a post-structuralist concern, by questioning the validity of 'the fixities of a classical canon'. Day is very good here on what's very good about 'Mona Lisa musta had the highway blues / you can tell by the way she smiles', noting that this frustration with canonised fixity 'is pictured acutely and comically as being experienced from within the canon. Established orders are not modified simply from without, but themselves contain the seeds of their own exhaustion. The colloquialism which here defines the Mona Lisa's unease—her boredom with her own status—itself constitutes an affront to and an erosion of the laws of approved respect that conventionally hem her in.'

There could be no better fusion than this between the critic's clear statement of his post-modernist idea and the equally clear summation of how Dylan's intuitive lines evoke the truth of it. It's at such moments, and there are many, that Day's seems a great book.

It seems a pity, therefore, that after many chapters admirably alert to language, and liberatingly adept at using it, Aidan Day ends up spending ten pages on the song his book is named after, 'Jokerman', as if it's a philosophy essay: you'd not think there was *poetry* there at all. Many lines of the song are quoted, but apart from the one phrase 'with fine ironic understatement' Day never says a word about how they work or what they achieve. They're just there on the page, shining out against prose like this: 'Recurrently imaged as occupying a position removed from ordinary reality he is at the same time never envisaged as fully transcending that reality. . . . But, more complexly, across the lyric as a whole, the principle of the Jokerman resists containment within a constant dualistic frame of reference.' It's a pity because Aidan Day himself wouldn't hone in on so brilliant a user of language as Bob Dylan at all if he didn't prefer language that's alive to language that isn't.

Day himself says now that while he is 'still happy with some of the ideas in the book' he is 'not happy with the manner in which' he wrote it. Nevertheless, the book stands up for itself, and thanks to it, Day's contribution has been a large one, both introducing post-structuralist ideas into the writings about Dylan and highlighting those areas of Dylan's art that seem to reflect such ideas right back at us.

[Aidan Day, *Romanticism*, London: Routledge, 1995; *Angela Carter: The Rational Glass*, Manchester: Manchester University Press, 1998; *Tennyson's Scepticism*, London: Palgrave Macmillan, 2005; *Bob Dylan: Escaping on the Run*, Bury, UK: Wanted Man Study Series no.3, 1984; 'Reels of Rhyme: Mr. Tambourine Man', *The Telegraph* no.24, Bury, summer 1986 & Michael Gray & John Bauldie, eds., *All Across the Telegraph: A Bob Dylan Handbook*, London: Sigwick & Jackson, 1977; 'Looking for Nothing: Dylan Now', *Do You Mr. Jones?: Bob Dylan with the Poets and Professors*, ed. Neil Corcoran, London: Chatto & Windus, 2002; *Jokerman: Reading the Lyrics of Bob Dylan*, Oxford: Blackwell, 1988 & (slightly amended) 1990. Quotation above is from the 1990 edition.]

Deevoy, Adrian [1964 -] It's generally forgotten that when the Never-Ending Tour started, in June 1988, it wasn't called that at all. It had no real name, official or otherwise, but was sometimes called 'Interstate 88', after the design on its back-stage passes. Adrian Deevoy, born in London on September 5, 1964 and first interested in Dylan's work at the age of five (his mother says), and who became a UK music journalist on *Q* magazine's staff in the 1980s, has the distinction of having invented the term 'the Never-Ending Tour'—a name he put to Dylan during a Rhode Island interview for *Q* in October 1989.

Oddly, when he wrote the interview up for the magazine, Deevoy put the phrase into Dylan's mouth (nothing odd about a journalist doing that, the artist mutters), like so: '[Deevoy:] "Tell me about the live thing. The last tour has gone virtually straight into this one." "Oh," he begins, establishing brief, cautious eye contact. "It's all the same tour. The Never-Ending Tour . . ."'

But when you listen to the recording, it goes like this:

AD: 'Tell me about the live thing. You've gone straight into this, into this tour again—one tour virtually straight into the next one.'
BD: 'Oh, it's all the same tour.'
AD: 'It's the Never-Ending Tour.'
BD [unenthusiastically]: 'Yeah. Yeah.'

So it was Deevoy, not Dylan, who coined this phrase we all use.

[Adrian Deevoy: Dylan interview, Narraganset, RI, Oct 22, 1989, published Q no.39, London, Dec 1989. Also author of 'The Untold Story of an Extraordinary Fax to Q Magazine, *The Telegraph* no.50, Romford, UK, winter 1994; & co-writer, with Kevin Godley, of screenplay *Where the Treetops Glisten*, due to go into production 2006.]

Dennis, Carolyn [1954 -] Carol Yvonne (aka Carolyn) Dennis, born in Compton, Greater Los Angeles, in April 1954, is a gospel singer and gospel/rock backing vocalist who has appeared on albums by, among others, the Carpenters, Harry Chapin, TRACY CHAPMAN, Art Garfunkel, Michael Jackson, Gladys Knight, Olivia Newton-John, SMOKEY ROBINSON, David Soul, BRUCE SPRINGSTEEN, Candi Staton, Donna Summer and STEVIE WONDER. She has also appeared on stage with Bob Dylan, as well as on a number of his albums. When first prompted to work with him, she is reputed to have asked 'Who is Bob Dylan?' She soon found out.

Carolyn Dennis married Bob Dylan on June 4, 1986 and they have a daughter, Desiree Gabrielle Dennis-Dylan, born January 31, 1986 in Canoga Park, California. She is mentioned in the long dedication list on the sleeve of that year's album, *Knocked Out Loaded*. Carolyn Dennis filed for divorce on August 7, 1990, and obtained it in October 1992. This information was first 'revealed' in the HOWARD SOUNES biography of Dylan, *Down the Highway: The Life of Bob Dylan*, 2001.

Carolyn Dennis joined Dylan's ensemble in 1978, starting after the February–April first leg of the tour, which had gone through Japan, New Zealand and Australia. First she was brought into the studios to sing back-up on the *Street Legal* sessions, and then when the North American leg of the tour began on June 1 in LA, JERRY SCHEFF replaced ROB STONER on bass and Carolyn Dennis replaced Debi Dye, joining Jo Ann Harris and HELENA SPRINGS on backing vocals.

She remained part of the group until the tour's last night, December 16 in Hollywood, Florida, and in the course of it sang SAM COOKE's 'A Change Is Gonna Come' solo at Nuremberg, Germany, on July 1 and in front of 300,000 people at Blackbushe, England, on July 15. At soundchecks she, Harris and Springs sang 'One More Cup of Coffee', 'To Ramona', 'Mr. Tambourine Man', 'Where Are You Tonight (Journey Through Dark Heat)?', 'Am I Your Stepchild?', 'True Love Tends to Forget' and 'Rainy Day Women # 12 & 35', and as from November 10 (in Seattle), most concerts' second halves began with the three of them singing 'Rainy Day Women'. She also brought her childhood friend REGINA McCRARY (aka Regina Havis) into Dylan's orbit by getting him to audition her when the tour arrived in Nashville on December 2.

Throughout the tour, Dylan gave playful onstage introductions of his backing group personnel. Examples, from September: at Portland, Maine on the 16th: 'My current girlfriend, Carolyn Dennis'; New Haven, Connecticut, on the 17th: 'my ex-girlfriend, Carolyn Dennis'; Springfield, Massachusetts, on the 26th: 'On the left my fiancée Carolyn Dennis; and in the middle, my current girlfriend, Helena Springs'; Uniondale, NY, on the 27th: 'my fiancée Carolyn Dennis—wishful thinking!' At Greensboro, North Carolina, on December 7 he introduced 'my ex-girlfriend Jo Ann Harris, my new girlfriend Helena Springs and my fiancée Carolyn Dennis.' For the last few gigs of the tour, he called her 'the true love of my life, my fiancée. Carolyn Dennis.'

Dennis, Springs and the newly recruited Regina McCrary then put backing-vocal overdubs onto the *Slow Train Coming* album in May 1979 in Sheffield, Alabama—and then Regina replaced Dennis for Dylan's first gospel tour, in November–December 1979.

She was then in the group that played the short second gospel tour, from January 11 (Portland, Oregon) to February 9 (Charleston, West Virginia); she was then absent from the recording sessions for the *Saved* album in February, and from the third and last gospel tour, from April 17 (Toronto) to May 21 (Dayton, Ohio); but returned to take part in the magnificent concerts that fall from November 9 at the Fox Warfield, San Francisco, to December 4 (Portland, Oregon again); on most nights of the tour she sang 'Walking Around Heaven All Day' as a solo mid-way through.

Next she took part in the concerts starting June 10, 1981 in Chicago and finishing July 25 in Avignon, France—in which she sang lead solo on 'Walking Around Heaven All Day', this time every night—but then there was a four-years-plus gap. Dennis next worked with Dylan when he made some demos in a Hollywood studio on Hallowe'en 1985 (we don't know what songs these were: they haven't circulated), and then in Topanga Park, California, in late April to early May 1986 she was among those recording 'You'll Never Walk Alone', 'Unchain My Heart', 'Lonely Avenue', 'Without Love', 'It's Too Late', 'Come Back Baby (One More Time)' and 'Wild and Wicked World' with Dylan—none of which has been released—as well as *Knocked Out Loaded* material, and overdubs on a couple of other unreleased tracks, 'So Good' and 'I Need Your Lovin''.

Two days after their marriage Dennis was back-up singing on stage with Dylan at the Amnesty International Benefit Concert in Inglewood, California, and for the rest of the second leg of the True Confessions Tour with Dylan and TOM PETTY & THE HEARTBREAKERS, finishing on August 6, 1986, at Paso Robles, CA. The other side of Dylan's subsequent dates with THE GRATEFUL DEAD, Dennis was part of the 1987 Temples in Flames tour beginning with Dylan's début in Israel on September 5 and ending at London's Wembley Arena on October 17.

On record, she was also on *Shot of Love*, *Empire Burlesque* and *Down in the Groove*. (She is sometimes wrongly listed as a participant on the albums *Dylan* and *Saved*.)

In *Chronicles Volume One* Dylan writes of Dennis many times, though referring to her only as 'my wife', and dealing with the period around the recording of *Oh Mercy* (on which there are no background vocals). Dylan describes her first as someone who 'could make me feel like I wasn't in some godforsaken hole.' She is also glimpsed announcing that she's 'going up to bed' rather than listen to BONO and Bob drone on for hours while drinking a case of Guinness. Then she's riding on the back of Dylan's 1966 Harley-Davidson Police Special motorcycle on the beautifully described trip they take around small parts of Louisiana (though again she prefers reading John Le Carré out on the patio of King Tut's Museum to the conversation inside between Dylan and the mysterious Sun Pie). The last thing he writes about her is that she has 'the ability to see a grain of truth in just about anything.' She leaves New Orleans to take part in a gospel play in Baltimore.

Carolyn Dennis is the daughter of MADELYN QUEBEC, who has also been a Dylan back-up singer.

[Website *http://home.cogeco.ca/~mansion1/carolyndennis.html* lists artists whose albums Dennis has appeared on, but re Dylan albums wrongly lists her as singing on *Dylan* and *Saved*; correct information re her concert and studio contributions is listed by Trevor Midgley at *www.geocities.com/trevormidgley/GiggingBands.html*, seen online 5 Aug 2005. Bob Dylan, *Chronicles Volume One*, pp.164, 175, 199–209 & 211.]

***Desire* [1976]** Dylan's 18th album and the next newly recorded studio work after *Blood on the Tracks*, it proved to be Dylan's biggest seller, finding him a new following among teenagers who would hardly have been toddlers when the mid-60s Dylan was so much in vogue. After such a predecessor it was bound to be a disappointment but it is an important album nonetheless—a work with its own distinctive unity yet with most of Dylan's traditional strengths: not least wit, warmth, energy and a beautiful disregard for finishing things off with professional songwriterly polish.

The downside is, in part, that the featherweight pop song is back in Dylan's repertoire with 'Mozambique' and the protest song is back in 'Hurricane', the weakness of which is shown by how much better the music is than the ideas behind the words; the hollowness of 'He could have bin the champion of the world' having been assured, years and years earlier, by Dylan's own youthful, sharper 'Davey Moore'.

Even on the more substantial songs on *Desire* there is a distinct falling-away from the incisiveness of the *Blood on the Tracks* collection, by virtue of Dylan's shift of preoccupation, away from an engaged concentration on the corrosions of time and failures of love, and towards a more mystical, religious focus.

'Oh Sister' thrusts this new emphasis at us, yet also suggests, with a plainness it's hard to understand how we could have ignored at the time, that part of Dylan's religious focus is on its way to the conventionally Christian: 'We grew up together from the cradle to the grave / We died and were reborn and then mysteriously saved.' (It also seemed to stand, back then, as a hopelessly clumsy attempt at dialogue with the new 1970s generation of liberated woman—clumsy not least in making bluntly clear, from lines like 'And is our purpose not the same on this earth / To love and follow His direction?' that he had not been listening to a word of the new politics of gender. It seemed important at the time.)

All of this sternness underrates the album, in some ways caused more by the fact of its coming after *Blood on the Tracks* than because of its own weaknesses—which are, after all, largely the result of its limitations of scope and intention. More importantly, *Desire* revealed a Dylan still wanting to experiment, still refusing to stand in one place.

One experiment was the songwriting collaboration with JACQUES LEVY, who co-wrote every song on the album except for 'One More Cup of Coffee' and 'Sara'. (For more on 'Sara' see **Poe, Edgar Allan**.)

The resulting album has exploratory strengths of its own that were easy to overlook when it was new and remain difficult to write about even now. Never before had Dylan so utterly made his word content the servant of his music. The precise, almost mathematical interlocking of the two is primarily what concerns him on this album. He is serving an apprenticeship here, at something new. Who else would have done that, after scoring so total a success as *Blood on the Tracks*?

The nature of this apprenticeship—of honed communication of feeling, emotion sparked off at the innate mystery of things and places and sounds—is well suggested in ALLEN GINSBERG's short sleevenotes to the album. They merit much re-reading and make a lot of unpindownable sense—in exactly the same way as the album itself.

Recorded in the summer lull before the first Rolling Thunder tour and released soon after it, the stand-out tracks are 'Isis', 'Romance in Durango' and 'Black Diamond Bay', but 'Hurricane', 'One More Cup of Coffee' and 'Oh Sister' are breathing down their necks.

[Recorded NY, 28 & 30–31 Jul and 24 Oct 1975, released as Columbia PC 33893 (CBS 86003 in UK), 5 or 16 Jan 1976.]

Desolation Row Information Service, the See **Baldwin, John**.

'Dharma & Greg' [1999] In August 1999 Dylan was filmed participating briefly in episode 51 of the TV sitcom 'Dharma & Greg', shown on ABC-TV that October 12. The episode was titled 'Play Lady Play' and Dylan is seen as himself yet as a bandleader sitting there as Dharma (Jenna Elfman) on drums says 'You count it in'. Dylan replies, 'I'll count it in, yeah. Yeah!' A short conversation follows, in which she casts doubt on his taste for funkiness. Dylan picks up a guitar, sketches some maralinga and polka-style riffs and laughs.

Dylan agreed to take part after being asked by one of the sitcom's writers, Eddie Gorodetsky, a Dylan acquaintance. Taping took an hour. Dylan appeared unbilled.

Diamond, Neil [1941 -] Neil Leslie Diamond was born in Brooklyn on January 24, 1941–making him exactly four months older than Bob Dylan. He is a singer-songwriter who has enjoyed a number of hits with records that manage to be both oleaginous and knowing, so fusing two unappealing qualities. His only known connection with Bob Dylan is that because ROBBIE ROBERTSON had produced a Neil Diamond album, Diamond was squeezed into the roster of artists performing at THE BAND's so-called Farewell Concert in San Francisco on November 25, 1976–squeezed in, ignominiously, by reducing MUDDY WATERS' performance time–and that reportedly when he came off stage he said to Dylan, 'Beat that!': to which Dylan replied, 'Waddaya want me to do–go on stage and fall asleep?'

Diaz, César [c.1952 - 2002] César Carillo-Diaz was the Puerto Rican guitar amplifier specialist, a technician and designer brought onto the Never-Ending Tour staff by G.E. SMITH, whom he'd known since 1970, to look after Dylan's and Smith's equipment. He was born in Old San Juan, Puerto Rico, around 1952, played guitar from the age of six and moved to the US mainland while playing in Johnny Nash's group in 1969.

When G.E. Smith was leaving Dylan's band, Diaz was promoted to temporary guitarist band member–a number of people were tried out in this period–first playing on stage on September 11, 1990 in Santa Fe, New Mexico, and the next night in Mesa, Arizona. There was then a one-month break, and when the tour resumed in Greenvale, New York, on October 11, Diaz was again a guitarist, remaining so for each concert from then until the last of the year, at Detroit on November 18. On stage he had a nifty slouch, wearing a variety of headgear and black leather trousers, and could have been a slimmer brother to bass player TONY GARNIER.

He remained a band member for the whole first leg of the 1991 tour, from Zurich on February 28 through to the fourth and final Mexican concert in Mexico City on March 2. He remained on the team as a techie and guitar tuner and was always available to come back up front when required, as for the last seven songs of Dylan's 18-song set in Wilkes-Barre, Pennsylvania, that November 15th.

On the last day of June 1992 he was brought on stage at Dylan's Dunkirk festival set to play guitar on the sixth song, 'What Good Am I?' and to play dobro on the tenth, 'A Hard Rain's a-Gonna Fall'. Twelve days later, in Antibes on the French Riviera, César played guitar on 'Highway 61 Revisited' in mid-set. In London on February 7, 1993, he played guitar on 'Mr. Tambourine Man', also in mid-set, and that July 13, in Cascais, Portugal, he played on a number of songs.

Diaz left later in 1993 to devote more time to his amplifier business and to be at home with his family more often, yet as late as December 1995, when the last leg of that year's Never-Ending Tour reached Philadelphia, he made a brief swansong appearance, playing on the last encore number of the night, 'Rainy Day Women # 12 & 35'. He had played at a total of around 50 concerts, and on the televised Grammy Awards Show of February 20, 1991.

He was a thoughtful interviewee on the subject of Bob Dylan's musicianship, not sharing the widely held view that it is mainly characterised by its dodginess. This 'outspoken advocate of tube amps and vintage guitars', as *Guitar Player* magazine described him in 1993, said of Dylan: 'Whoever he learned to play the guitar from must have been very old, because his chording and approach to melody is so old-fashioned. For example, he plays a first-position Dm [D minor] by fingering F on the D string, A on the G string and D on the B string. He has this formula worked out where he plays these triadic shapes all up and down the neck.' (Which we can now see corresponds closely to what Dylan, in *Chronicles Volume One*, says–in much less clear terms–that he was taught by the pre-war guitar great LONNIE JOHNSON.)

Diaz went on to tell the magazine: 'I've seen Bob do some amazing ragtime and Travis-style fingerpicking. Listen to his first album, and you'll hear some incredible shit! And the tone of those Gibson guitars! The recorded sound of the acoustic guitar was defined by him. Listen to that original version of "Don't Think Twice". When he starts doing that flatpicking thing on the low strings–my God, not even DOC WATSON had that kind of tone.'

It was Diaz's testimony too that gave us this example of Dylan's eccentricity on the road in the early 1990s: 'the crew stay at Hyatt Regency and all the nice hotels, and Bob and the band stay at

Motel 6 at the side of the road away from town. . . . he likes to see what the low life is like so he can get inspiration. So we would stay at all these places where you . . . would roll back the sheets to go to sleep and you could see that somebody had slept there the night before.'

César Diaz, who towards the end of his life became a great friend of DEREK & TRACY BARKER of *Isis* fanzine, died in the US while waiting for a second liver transplant on April 26, 2002 at age 50.

[César Diaz, 1st quote *Guitar Player*, *nia*, quoted from *Isis* no. 48, UK, 1993; 2nd quote interview by Derek Barker, Old San Juan, Puerto Rico, 23–25 Mar 1999, 'A Chat with César Diaz, part 2', *Isis* no. 84, UK, Apr–May 1999.]

Diddley, Bo [1928 -] Otha Ellas Bates, later known as Ellas or Elias McDaniel, aka Bo Diddley, was born near McComb, Mississippi, on December 30, 1928, was adopted by his mother's cousin in infancy and moved to Chicago in childhood. From 1946 to 1951 he played in the Washboard Trio but signed to Chess Records' Checker label in 1955, swiftly establishing his reputation and imposing his defiantly zany persona on the worlds of R&B and rock'n'roll with the eponymous hit 'Bo Diddley', which utilised a distinctive and 'primitive' shuffle beat and laid down a blueprint for much of his own subsequent work as well as for records by others, notably including BUDDY HOLLY's 'Not Fade Away' (which Bob Dylan began to perform in concert as from the first night of the opening leg of the 1999 part of the Never-Ending Tour). Bo Diddley employed an array of preposterously shaped electric guitars (mostly custom Gretsches) and was an early live exponent, long before JIMI HENDRIX, of playing his instrument behind his head and with his teeth.

In *Chronicles Volume One*, 2004, Dylan recalls that one of his Minnesota-based singer friends, DAVE RAY, was 'a high school kid who sang . . . Bo Diddley songs on a twelve-string guitar, probably the only twelve-string guitar in the entire Midwest'. Bob Dylan, Bo Diddley: spoken aloud, they're strangely similar names.

At the rehearsal for his unusual Supper Club gigs in New York City in 1993 Dylan played an instrumental version of 'Bo Diddley'. More significantly, George White's 1995 book *Bo Diddley—Living Legend* claims that the debt of Dylan's *Blonde on Blonde* track 'Obviously 5 Believers' is to a 1956 Bo Diddley track, 'She's Fine, She's Mine'. Certainly you could make a case that the Dylan arrangement owes something to the shuffle-beat, maracas and harmonica set-up that Diddley creates on that record, but White seems unaware of the earlier blues records upon which the Diddley song too is based.

If Bo Diddley and Bob Dylan both look back here to MEMPHIS MINNIE and her 'Me and My Chauffeur Blues', they also share the more unlikely repertoire item 'Some Enchanted Evening'. Diddley, appearing live on the Ed Sullivan TV Show after having been told at rehearsal by the irascible Sullivan to stop singing 'Bo Diddley' because it was wrong to sing a song mentioning his own name all the time, and to sing 'Some Enchanted Evening' instead, duly did so—but segued into 'Bo Diddley' in the middle. Bob Dylan recorded 'Some Enchanted Evening' at a Los Angeles session for the 1990 album *Under the Red Sky* during March–April 1990; it remains uncirculated.

Under the Red Sky was the album on which Dylan explored nursery rhyme in an intelligent, resourceful and poetic way, befitting someone who understands that it is not a dismissable, trivial genre but a legitimate, often highly valuable branch of folksong. One of the many African-American recording artists who preceded him with a more conventionally playful (and often rather suggestive) recycling of better-known nursery rhymes was our friend Bo Diddley. A song called 'Nursery Rhyme' is on one Diddley album, while 'Babes in the Woods' and 'Hey, Red Riding Hood' are on others—this last on an album titled *500% More Man*. RONNIE HAWKINS may or may not have known this when he made his immortal remark: 'Abraham Lincoln said all men were created equal, but he never saw Bo Diddley in the shower.'

[Bo Diddley: 'Bo Diddley', Chicago, 3 Mar 1955, Checker 814, Chicago, 1955; 'She's Fine, She's Mine', Chicago, 10 May 1955, Checker 819, Chicago, 1956; *Chuck & Bo, Volume 2*, Pye International 44012, London, c.1963; Bo Diddley: 'Nursery Rhyme', Chicago, Spring 1959, *Have Guitar—Will Travel*, Checker LP 2974, Chicago, 1960 (1st UK-issued *Bo Diddley Rides Again*, Pye International NPL 28029, 1963); 'Babes in the Woods', Chicago, Jul 1962, *Bo Diddley*, Checker LP 2984, Chicago, 1962 (Pye International NPL 28026, 1963); 'Hey, Red Riding Hood', Chicago, 25 Jul 1965, *500% More Man*, Checker LP(S) 2996, Chicago, 1965. Bob Dylan: 'Not Fade Away', 1st performed Fort Myers, FL, 26 Jan 1999; 'Bo Diddley', rehearsal, NY, 16 Nov 1993. Dylan quote from *Chronicles Volume One*, p.256. Bo Diddley & Ed Sullivan as described by Paul Gambaccini, undated interview with Spencer Leigh, *Baby, That Is Rock and Roll: American Pop 1954–1963*, p.75; Ronnie Hawkins quote, ditto p.132.]

Digby, Sir Everard [1578 - 1606] See 'Judas!' [shout].

'Dignity' [1989] The search for dignity is writ large all over *Oh Mercy*. It's therefore a pity that the album opens with as weak an upbeat track as 'Political World', when the *song* 'Dignity' would have been so much more germane. 'Political World', despite the multi-layering of the three guitars and dobro, and the double drumming (there are conga drums in there, credited as 'percussion'), and despite one or two isolated flashes of cutting edge, is exactly the kind of rockin' number that shouldn't have made it onto the album. There's no wildness, no clear sense of what Dylan is on about—and no heart in it, which is what makes it impossible to warm to. It's a bore, as so many of these things are. Dylan's account of wrestling with it, which he gives in *Chronicles Volume One*, is far more beguiling than the track itself.

At least as upbeat and rockin' as 'Political World' but an infinitely better piece of writing, with a far more appealing melody, with heartfelt energy and good humour, the great song 'Dignity', which describes so resourcefully the yearning for a more dignified world, would have been the album's ideal opening track. It scorches along musically, declaring its allegiance to the timeless appeal of the blues, while sounding, above all things, fresh. Its lyric, meanwhile, though 'Dylanesque' in that it sounds like no-one else's work and sounds like a restrained, mature revisit to a mode of writing you might otherwise call mid-1960s Dylan, is fully alert and freshly itself, admits of no leaning on laurels, and has the great virtue that while not every line can claim the workaday clarity of instructional prose, the song is accessible to anyone who cares to listen, and offers a clear theme, beautifully explored, with which anyone can readily identify.

'It fits in,' wrote Mel Gamble, 'with . . . an album . . . based on self-examination . . . [and] the attempt to separate the important from the distractions and irrelevancies that clog up day to day life.' The song is both one of those 'you know [is] going to be special' when you first hear the opening bars, and one of those where 'you never want the song to end.' For others, it is one of those like 'A Hard Rain's a-Gonna Fall', where every line might be the beginning of a separate song.

That would be a lot of separate songs—'Dignity' has 16 verses of four lines each, in which recurrently the singer describes a lengthy search for dignity in the turmoil of a fragmented world in which people jostle and hustle among themselves but show no sign of genuine community, and in which places are also described as lost, inhospitable and bleak. All this is achieved, however, at a rollicking pace, with dancing deftness and indomitable humour, so that the mood of the song is the opposite of bleak.

The verses divide between two different rhyme-schemes. The predominant one uses the attractive AAAB pattern, with the 'B' the same in every verse of this construction, because each ends on the title word 'dignity'—and how he loves to land on it! He rolls it around in his mouth, slowing it down, feeling its contours—'dig-ni-teeee!'—as if in the very act of saying it he can explore its elusive qualities. This core construction, and many of its lyric ground-rules, are established in the opening verse: 'Fat man lookin' in a blade of steel / Thin man lookin' at his last meal / Hollow man lookin' in a cottonfield / For dignity.'

Some of the song's characters are bumming and hustling, watching their backs or chancing their arm but many, though living in what seems insoluble isolation, are united with the narrator in a common yearning for the dignity missing in contemporary life. No moral superiority is being claimed here by the writer. This is the ballad of a thin man, fat man, hollow man, wise man, young man, poor man, blind man, drinkin' man, sick man and Englishman. Plus a couple of somebodies, the cops, Mary Lou, the maid, Prince Philip, the sons of darkness and the sons of light, another somebody and a someone, plus the tongues of angels and tongues of men in general.

There are 11 more verses of this construction, plus four that are built differently, in an AABC pattern, where the B and C may or may not half-rhyme. The first time around, they do (this is the third verse): 'Somebody got murdered on New Year's Eve / Somebody said dignity was the first to leave / I went into the city, went into the town / Went into the land of the midnight sun', in which there is a half-rhyme between 'sun' and 'town'. Next time around, in verse seven, there is a sort of semi-rhyming, if you will, between 'men' and 'me': 'I went down where the vultures feed / I would have gone deeper but there wasn't any need / I heard the tongues of angels and the tongues of men / And there wasn't any difference to me.' (That second line is a fine example of the song's freshness, with its apparent spontaneity of direct address—its undercutting of the declamatory by the unexpected straightforwardness of informal conversationality, its clipped modernity of tone.) But in the two verses of this pattern later in the song—verses 11 and 15—there is no such half-rhyming, and the unusual AABC pattern is strictly observed. The effect is not at all that you notice, in listening, an absence of resolving rhyme, but that combined with the unresolved fifth note of the scale on which the final word of each verse lands, your ear waits for what is to come: tells you that there is more to come, that the search for dignity is itself not resolved. Thus form becomes realised as content.

The difference of shape between the two kinds of verse is matched by quiet distinctions in their subject matter. The format of 'Fat man . . . Thin man . . . Englishman . . .' never occurs in the AABC verses, which tend to focus on places the narrator goes—great, sweeping places—rather than on characters: 'I went into the city, went into the town, / Went into the land of the midnight sun . . .'; 'I went down where the vultures feed . . .'; 'In the bordertowns of despair . . .'; 'Into the valley of dry bone dreams . . .' When he does encounter people in these sections of the song, they too are presented in vague or sweeping generalised terms: 'Footsteps runnin' cross the silver sand . . .'; 'Somebody got murdered . . .'; 'Somebody said . . .'; 'Someone showed me . . .'; 'I heard the tongues of angels and the tongues of men . . .'; 'I met the sons of darkness and the sons of light . . .'

However, these distinctions between the two sorts of verses are never stressed, and the entire song is repeatedly interwoven with threads of correspondence, sometimes of the most delicate and subtle kind and sometimes with robust, abrasive *mock*-correspondences that keep you stimulated and guessing. Thus there are phrases that echo each other in form but depart in content, for example as when that 'went into the city, went into the town' is slyly mismatched later by 'went into the red, went into the black', or when different kinds of metaphor are bumped together as if they are of the same order, or even as if they are not metaphors at all but actual physical actions, as with the splendid 'He bites the bullet and he looks within', where there is the added surreal implication that the one 'action' is consequent upon the other: that he bites the bullet and then looks within to see what damage the bullet has caused, or where it's landed, and whether he's still alive.

There are many such games played here, and played lightning-fast, in passing. Since Dignity is spoken of throughout as a missing character, as in detective fiction (as in a film), might not 'Somebody' be a character too—such that when Dylan sings that 'Somebody got murdered on New Year's Eve / Somebody said Dignity was the first to leave' this not only has the odd effect of making Dignity the prime suspect (rather than simply a Good Guy) but also makes it possible to see at this murder scene that it is Somebody's own dying testimony that fingers Dignity.

The opening couplet alone has weird comic resonances. 'Fat man lookin' in a blade of steel / Thin man lookin' at his last meal', which draws on the two meanings of 'his last meal', achieves by doing so a bizarre fleeting picture of the fat man wielding either a carving-knife or an executioner's blade: either way putting him into an uneasy relationship with the thin man. At the very least, you wonder if the thin man is looking at his own last meal or at the fat man's stomach, into which what should have been his own meal has just disappeared.

Then there is this quiet implied pun on thinning hair, almost at the end of the song (balancing the thin man at its beginning): 'Combin' his hair back, his future looks thin', and the adroit comic moment in this surreal one-line scene: 'Met Prince Philip at the home of the blues', very pleasingly augmented like this: 'He said he'd give me information if his name wasn't used / He wanted money up front, said he was abused / By Dignity.' It would be high comedy merely for a Dylan song to mention Prince Philip, but to place him in so unlikely a milieu as anywhere that might call itself 'the home of the blues' creates a glorious incongruity. It also creates a sort of namesake version of Prince Philip in the mind: putting him together with the idea of the blues conjures up a figure in that other destination-point of the black diaspora, the Caribbean, in which there are plenty of flamboyant singers and musicians with names like Prince Buster. Making you hear Prince Philip as a name of this sort is a fine bonus comic payoff.

As the lines pile up, of course, so does the preposterousness of the Prince Philip idea. Hence no sooner have we savoured the picture of this meeting, and its meeting-place, than we relish the notion of him acting the cheap con-artist, offering to sell suspect information right there on the street and then throwing in a hard-luck story for good measure—or else we picture it now as being someone else, someone who *is* a con-artist, with Dylan throwing in the extra joke that while he's claiming to be this extravagantly high-profile and notoriously indiscreet figure, he's also trying to do a deal that hinges upon protecting his anonymity.

And at the end of the verse, if we take it that this *is* Prince Philip, Dylan's 'said he was abused / by Dignity' works as a wonderfully compressed summation of how it might feel to be trapped inside the machinery of the Royal Family. To characterise a lifetime of dressing up and parading about in risible ritual and ceremonial show as 'abused by Dignity' is confident cutting to the bone indeed. And to put this complaint into the mouth of someone as brutishly insensitive and graceless as Prince Philip, whose name is a byword for the unthinking verbal abuse of others, is delicious. To achieve all this in 30 words is, well, Dylanesque.

The detail of the song is always careful; everything dovetails; everything is balanced; and where there is doubt, ambiguity or contradiction, it is intended. The list of who is looking where, for example, shows evidence of the kind of care absent in the listings in 'Everything Is Broken'. The young man looks 'in the shadows that pass'—a poetic ellipse of the idea that the young, impatient of history and precedent, are entranced by the illusions of the moment, believing that 'now' is the only worthwhile moment, while his opposite—not the old man but the wise man (the old not necessarily being wise at all)—looks 'in a blade of grass': that is, in something that sounds just as fragile and temporary as a passing shadow but is strong enough to hold several connotations. We might take it that, like every grain of sand, it is in such things as the blade of grass that the believer 'can see the master's hand'; or, like BLAKE, we might take it that in looking in the blade of grass, again as into a grain of sand, he is seeking a vision of the world. We can take it that unlike the young man in thrall to the temporarily fashionable, the wise man understands that the natural world is all that really matters. We can take it that by its very temporariness the blade of grass tells the essential truth that 'everything passes'—that everything 'comes to pass', to quote from Bob Dylan and to remember a fragment of a different poet's work (John Crowe Ransom's 'Spectral Lovers') quoted by CHRISTOPHER RICKS in the essay on Dylan's use of American and English English, 'Clichés That Come to Pass': '. . . swishing the jubilant grass / Beheading some field-flowers that had come to pass.'

At times, too, 'Dignity' offers unlooked-for extra tidiness, as when that 'blade of grass' in verse two echoes the 'blade of steel' in verse one, or when, in that first verse, there is the neat gradation in lines one-two-three of men who run fat-thin-hollow, while all through the song small surprises act as cumulative energy, a recurrent renewal of stimulus, as when we expect, after 'searching high, searching low' that 'searching everywhere I' will be completed by 'go' and isn't: it's 'searching everywhere I know' instead.

In the 12th verse, out of nowhere, and to most pleasing effect, we suddenly get, for the first and only time, an extra rhyme, by means of an internal rhyme, on one of the AAA lines: '. . . got no coat / . . . in a jerkin' boat / Tryin' to read a note somebody wrote / About dignity.' This both disrupts the pattern we've grown to know and at the same time of course is not mere surprise for it's own sake but to make the line enact the 'jerkin" motion he's ascribing to the boat. (Regrettably, he has always revised this line in concert to eliminate the internal rhyme, altering it to the inferior 'Tryin' to read a letter somebody wrote'.)

NIGEL HINTON declares it to be his favourite of all the 'big' songs of the last 25 years: more loved than 'Brownsville Girl', 'Angelina' or even 'Blind Willie McTell'. He writes:

> 'What I particularly like about it is the consistency of its conceit: Bob Dylan as Sam Spade, or any one of those hard-bitten, cynical LA-based private dicks, conducting his B-movie, film noir search through the corrupt world in search of the missing character, Dignity. I like the array of characters—all those sons of darkness and sons of light—typical of the wonderful supporting actors who people those films (Sidney Greenstreet as the Fat Man, Elisha Cook Jnr. as the Blind Man, and Thelma Ritter as the maid, perhaps?). And I love the little familiar scenes from those movies—the murder at the New Year's Eve party, the wedding of Mary Lou who, frightened and nervously looking over the singer's shoulder at the other guests, whispers that she could get killed if she told him what she knew (played by the young Lauren Bacall?), and the continual echo of films—the drinking man in a crowded room full of covered up mirrors could come straight from *Citizen Kane* (played by Joseph Cotten—drink, instead of cigarettes). The images come straight from a medley of dimly remembered movies: the chilly winds blowing the palms; the house on fire; looking out of a window from behind billowing net curtain while asking the maid for some hot poop on the case; the bordertowns of despair (Mexico, of course—perhaps *A Touch of Evil*, Orson Welles' Tijuana masterpiece); the blackheart wind sending those tumbleweeds rolling down the dusty street while the Englishman (Leslie Howard) stands there so incongruously, combing his hair back; the sick bed of the the man who lovingly fingers his books while praying for a cure; and the con artist pretending he's Prince Philip and trying to bum some money in exchange for dodgy information—'abused by dignity', him: ha!
>
> 'Dignity is also so perfectly what the Sam Spade persona would be looking for. Truth, Fame, Fortune, Hope, Faith and all the other rewards offered by the world or the illusions offered by the purveyors of the spiritual world have been seen through by this guy—he's heard the tongues of angels and the tongues of men and he can't see any difference. The most he can hope for is to live with dignity: but in this corrupt and deluded age, where and what is it? And in this topsy-turvy place the most you get by way of help is a note that somebody wrote—but of course you're trying to read it on a rolling river in a jerking boat: a wonderful metaphor for the struggle of trying to make sense of things. Such an alive and direct picture of us all, without comfort (no coat) and with nowhere to hide (fade), in our little craft being swept headlong towards the rapids, trying to find out why.
>
> 'And the language is so Chandleresque: "the valley of dry-bone dreams", "bites the bullet", wind "sharp as a razor blade". The song even ends in the kind of despairing, enigmatic way that the best films noirs do—standing at the edge of the lake, knowing that everywhere leads to dead ends and that the case won't get solved. It's a black and white masterpiece.'

As with so much of Dylan's finest writing, its credible possibilities are open, and the opposite of limiting. 'Dignity' makes perfect sense in that film noir context: it holds its own, as Hinton says, as that sustained conceit. Yet the song's fundamental quest for something both precious and elusive through a world of travail holds to a far more ancient archetype, and as such resonates on other levels. The archetype of this quest is also contained, for instance, in the search for the Holy Grail (medieval legend having it that the bowl used by Christ at the Last Supper was brought to Britain by Joseph of Arimathea, so that in the time of knights in silver armour, seeking its whereabouts was a physical *and* spiritual quest). It is there too in the *Pilgrim's Progress* of JOHN BUNYAN's hero, Christian (of which more shortly). While Bob Dylan summarises such questing in a single line of his 1970s song 'Dirge'—'In this age of fiberglass, I'm searching for a gem'—'Dignity' devotes itself to envisaging such a quest.

It succeeds at doing so in the genre of Hollywood film noir, but there's also more than a hint here of the ordeals of Job, when God has afflicted him and he wanders, seeking recognition and the restoration of dignity, and asking 'How long will ye vex my soul, and break me in pieces with words?' As he wanders, he asks the servant for recognition—in effect, 'have you not seen me?'—just as Dylan's narrator asks the maid has she not seen Dignity. As we know, Job's faith triumphs and he finds acceptance in the end, but not before being in the position Dylan parallels at the inconclusive end of 'Dignity', where there are 'So many dead ends, so much at stake.'

In Job's case he cries out that God 'hath fenced up my way that I cannot pass, and he hath set darkness in my paths.' As with Job, there is a strong mood of 'how long, Lord?' (or as Dylan expresses it elsewhere, 'How much longer? How much longer?') about the wanderings here in search of 'Dignity', which ends on 'Sometimes I wonder what it's gonna take / To find dignity.'

As Dylan does so magnificently well elsewhere, here too we have a case where he rides the parallel lines between biblical language and modern American speech. Nigel Hinton hears 'the valley of dry-bone dreams' as 'so Chandleresque'—yet this lovely phrase draws upon, but does not better, one wonderful sound-bumping line from blues artist ARTHUR CRUDUP, 'I went down in Death Valley, among the tombstones and dry bones': a line that Dylan might have written and been admired for. In turn, as Crudup's mention of 'Death Valley' hints, this is poetic ellipsing of biblical text. The 'valley of the shadow of death' resides in the Old Testament book that follows Job, in Psalm 23:4—through which its narrator, David, walks fearing no evil, knowing that God is with him; and many gospel lyrics have been founded upon this text. The splendid 1930 LONNIE JOHNSON title 'Death Valley Is Just Half Way to My Home' may hover in the back of Arthur Crudup's and Bob Dylan's mind. There's also 'You've Got to Walk That Lonesome Valley', a 'sermon with singing' by Rev. F.W. McGee. (The fusion of biblical with modern American speech is contained in the very name Death Valley, of course; it is a US National Monument in California-Nevada, serendipitously just west of Las Vegas and almost immediately south-west of Skull Mountain and the Nellis Air Force nuclear testing site.)

Among the 123 other verses of the King James Bible that contain a 'valley', many involve travail experienced as rather more arduous than David's, and these include 'the valley of slaughter' and 'the valley of the dead bodies' in Jeremiah, and in Ezekiel 'the valley which was full of bones.' The phrase 'dry bones' comes only from Ezekiel (37:3–4), in which the prophet, set down in a valley of human bones, is asked by God, 'Son of man, can these bones live?' to which Ezekiel replies 'O Lord God, thou knowest.' So God says '. . . say unto them, O ye dry bones, hear the word of the Lord.' Through Ezekiel's unlimited faith and willingness, and God's power, the whole valleyful of bones becomes fleshed out, and the people of Israel come alive again. This is not, in the end, the same place as Death Valley, and it is this vision that is the stimulus for further gospel songs called 'Dry Bones in the Valley' and even 'In the Valley of Dry Bones'. In turn, Dylan's 'In the valley of dry-bone dreams' draws upon these phrases.

The song holds other moments and phrases where Dylan bestrides such parallel lines. Nigel Hinton's 'Sam Spade persona' can quite well be described as having 'heard the tongues of angels and the tongues of men' and seen through both. You can hear the phrase on the tongue of Dylan's old favourite, Humphrey Bogart; yet as Dylan and Nigel Hinton both know, the phrase rearranges that in St. Paul's address to the Corinthians: 'Though I speak with the tongues of men and of angels, and have not charity, I am become as sounding brass, or a tinkling cymbal.' (I Corinthians 13:1.)

Dylan swaps this around doubly. First, either for the sake of cadence or the more neatly to make his point that there 'wasn't any difference' between them, he puts his angels before his men. Second, where Paul's illustration has him speaking with the two kinds of tongue, Dylan has his narrator listening to them instead. And in saying that there 'wasn't any difference', Dylan manages to emphasise the part of Paul's text that he doesn't actually cite at all: namely, that those he hears speaking are all 'as sounding brass, or a tinkling cymbal.'

There is one other extraordinary parallel that Dylan achieves inside his song. While Nigel Hinton hears the lines 'Drinkin' man listens to the voice he hears / In a crowded room full of covered-up mirrors' as part of 'the continual echo of films', in this case calling to mind Joseph Cotten in *Citizen Kane*, the same lines also depict a scene from Jewish religious ritual. To observe the practice of shiva, during the period of mourning after a funeral, the committed mourners must gather together in one of their houses and remain there a week. Inside the house, no music can be played and every mirror must be covered up.

Far more thoroughgoingly, however, 'Dignity' parallels Christian's journey of quest for the Celestial City in *The Pilgrim's Progress* (a quest presented as a dream in Bunyan's book). Christian too has to pass through the Valley of the Shadow of Death, as well as a river (the River of the Water of Life), somewhere on fire (the Burning Mount) and despair (the Giant Despair). Dylan's long geographical cataloguing of his wide-ranging journey ('searching high, searching low'), including travelling into the city, into the town, into the land of the midnight sun, down where the vultures feed, across the silver sand, down into—in a beautifully Dylanesque flash of existential truth—'Tattoo Land', as well as along so many roads and up against so many dead ends, is the equivalent of the geographical catalogue in *Pilgrim's Progress*, which takes in the Hill Difficulty, the Valley of Humiliation, By-path Meadow, Doubting Castle and, most famously, the Slough of Despond.

And just as Dylan's song presents the quality of Dignity as a character, so Bunyan gives us characters called Ignorance, Much-afraid and, yes, Mercy. The Dylan song is sly, quick-witted, darkly modern and full of Americana where Bunyan's work was pious, plodding and bursting with 17th century England; but Bunyan's work was written as an allegory of the Christian life and 'Dignity' too can withstand being seen, and even intended, as just such an allegory.

Nigel Hinton sees his movie ending 'at the edge of the lake, knowing that everywhere leads to dead ends and that the case won't get solved'; but does the song end so darkly? The last word is not of dead ends but with the 'How long, Lord?' question, the keep-on-keeping-on faith that holds on through all trials and tribulations, implying that the quest will be pursued and that eventual success is anticipated. It is only in the meantime, and sometimes, that resolve flags: 'Sometimes I wonder what it's gonna take / To find Dignity.' 'How long will ye vex my soul, and break me in pieces . . . ?', as Job puts it when times are tough in different times—and the point about Ezekiel's valley of dry bone dreams is that in the end, through faith, new life is given.

Dylan's commentary on the writing and recording of 'Dignity', given in *Chronicles*, is fascinating, not least for the background information that it came to him the day he heard the news of the death of the basketball player Pistol Pete Maravich, who collapsed and died on a Pasadena basketball court—'just fell over and never got up'—and for the energised description of how the song came about. 'It's like I saw the song up in front of me and overtook it,' he writes, before also explaining why, having written it, he was in no hurry to rush into recording it, and then, in due course, what a struggle the attempt to record it duly proved. (See **O'Brien, Brendan**.)

In spite of these difficulties, as a song it succeeds completely. What is so liberating and invigorating about 'Dignity' is that while it is free-spirited and ineffably relaxed, fluid as mercury and malleable as clay on the wheel, it is at the same time so meticulously assembled, beautifully thought-out and thrillingly well-crafted.

[Bob Dylan: commentary on 'Political World', *Chronicles Volume One*, pp.165, 166 & 183–185; commentary on 'Dignity', pp.168–169, 189–190, 191. Bob Dylan: 'Dignity', New Orleans, prob. 13 Mar 1989.

Mel Gamble: 'Dignity', *Homer, the slut* no.5, London, Jan 1992. John Crowe Ransom, 'Spectral Lovers', *nia*, quoted in Christopher Ricks, 'Clichés That Come to Pass', in Michael Gray & John Bauldie, eds., *All Across the Telegraph: A Bob Dylan Handbook*, London: W.H. Allen, 1987. Nigel Hinton: e-mails to this writer, 30 & 31 Mar 1999, reprinted with permission. *Citizen Kane*, dir. Orson Welles, written Herman J. Mankiewicz & Welles, starring Welles, Joseph Cotton, RKO, US, 1941 (in which when the Hearst-type newspaper mogul dies, 'a magazine reporter interviews his friends in an effort to discover the meaning of his last words': *Halliwell's Film Guide*, ed. John Walker, London: HarperCollins 11th edn., 1995); *A Touch of Evil*, dir. & written Orson Welles, U-I, US, 1958 (in which a 'Mexican narcotics investigator honeymooning in a border town clashes with the local police-chief over a murder': *Halliwell*, ditto).

John Bunyan: *The Pilgrim's Progress: From This World to That Which Is to Come*, Part I published 1678, Part II 1684. The first Job passage starts at 19:2, continues thru the dead-end dark paths (v11) & asking the servant's recognition (v16) thru to the terrific 'and I am escaped with the skin of my teeth' (from v20).

Arthur Crudup: 'Death Valley Blues', Chicago, 11 Sep 1941, *Bluebird Blues*, RCA Victor LPV-518, NY, 1965. Lonnie Johnson: 'Death Valley Is Half Way to My Home', NY, 23 Jan 1930. Rev. F.W. McGee: 'You've Got to Walk That Lonesome Valley', Chicago, 7 Jun 1927, CD-reissued *Rev. F.W. McGee Complete Recorded Works Volume 1 (1927–1929)*, RST Blues Documents BDCD-6031, Vienna, *nia*.

Jeremiah 7:32 & 21:13 contain 'the valley of slaughter', Jeremiah 21:40 'the valley of the dead bodies' & Ezekiel 37:1 'the valley which was full of bones'. (The Jubilee Gospel Team: 'Dry Bones in the Valley', NY, c.Sep 1928. Joe McCoy: 'Dry Bones in the Valley', Chicago, 15 May 1935. Rev. R. McFryar: 'In the Valley of Dry Bones', NY, 29 Aug 1928.) That 'room full of covered-up mirrors' corresponds to the practice of Shiva noted from Kevin Lawler & Steve Watson: 'The Importance of "Señor (Tales of Yankee Power)" When Considering Dylan's Conversion to Christianity (I'm Exiled. You Can't Convert Me)', *Dignity* no.16, Welwyn Garden City, UK, Jun 1998.]

***Dignity* fanzine** See **Baldwin, John.**

Domino, Fats [1928 -] Antoine 'Fats' Domino, born 26 February 1928, became the most successful New Orleans big-band R&B million-seller of the long era between 1955 and the early 1960s: a man who gave us hit after huge, endearing hit, with a fat, simple sound and a warm, much-imitated faux-naïve voice that built many memorable self-penned songs into mountains on the music landscape.

One of the creators of rock'n'roll, and by far the biggest-selling rhythm & blues artist of the 1950s, his originality was such that these labels don't quite fit him. Nor was he anything so flimsy as pop, yet his records often crossed onto the pop charts, so that while he was crucial in breaking down the musical colour barrier, he was too mainstream and popular to retain credibility as a blues singer. He brought a new, heavy back-beat to white

Photo by Henry Diltz

David Crosby

Publicity photo by James Shea

Charlie Daniels and his band

Fats Domino

Thomas A. Dorsey

ears, yet trailed old-fashioned jazz-band habits behind him. Out in his own uncategorisable stratosphere, Fats Domino sold astonishing quantities of records much loved by blacks and whites alike, until that point in the 1960s when a new black consciousness rejected all the pre-soul stars, and white consciousness shied away from hit-singles artists and the suddenly embarrassing, unhip simplicities of 1950s music. Fats seemed further away in 1970 than he does now.

In the classic photos, Fats Domino's head is a perfect cube, thanks in part to his trademark flattop haircut. This, unique to Domino in the 1950s, became fashionable among young black males in the US and UK 30 years later. (In *Chronicles Volume One*, Dylan, describing how he envisages some future rap star rising to artistic greatness, writes that it will be someone 'with a chopped topped head'.) In Guy Peellaert & Nik Cohn's book *Rock Dreams*, Domino is painted at home, in a pink stage suit but grinning into the casserole his tired wife Rose Mary is stirring. His eight smiling children surround him, and Fats is saying 'Clean living keeps me in shape . . . and New Orleans home cooking.'

He never was master of the bon mot, but he was one of the few true giants of post-war American popular music. No-one sounded like him, yet when you ask who he influenced, the answer is everyone.

The second number he ever recorded was 'The Fat Man' (named after a radio detective), which sold 800,000 in the black market and gave the 22-year-old the first of his many gold discs. In 1955 came 'Ain't It a Shame' (aka 'Ain't That a Shame'): and though Pat Boone's cover topped the pop charts, Fats' original chased it, the blackest sound that had ever hit the Hot 100, and the no.1 R&B side for 11 weeks.

So great was his reach that it was he who taught white pop fans about idiosyncratic flexibility in lyrics—particularly in rhymes—through odd emphasis (later a Dylan trick) and odd pronunciation. These were specific lessons Dylan must have picked up from Fats Domino.

In his 'Good Hearted Man' (1961) he manages, by his accent and his disregard for consonants, to make the word 'man' rhyme with 'ashamed': no mean feat. Dylan not only walks this forward so that in 1965's 'I Wanna Be Your Lover' he can rhyme 'hers' with a laughing 'yours!' but then runs with it to score a previously undreamt-of goal by rhyming 'January' with 'Buenos Aires' in 1981's 'The Groom's Still Waiting at the Altar'.

In 1961 Fats Domino issued a record called 'Rockin' Bicycle'—but, delightfully, he sang it as 'Rockin' Bi-*sic*-l', and its lyrics included nifty formulations like 'If we don't be in front we'll be right behind', and 'Let 'em take the bus / 'n' leave the 'sic-l to us.' There's plenty of evidence in Dylan's work of this Domino oddity of emphasis, too: as for instance, in 'Absolutely Sweet Marie', to achieve the rhyme of 'half-sick' with 'traffic'. In 'Jokerman', in the 1980s, when Dylan comes to rhyme 'scarlet' with 'harlot', well, any other white person would do it straight—would maximise the rhyme by sounding both as '-arlutt'. Dylan sings 'scarlett' and then snatches a full rhyme by singing 'harlett' to match!

Domino also comes up, maybe accidentally, with the pathetic use of bathos, which again is something that Dylan has used. 'Fell in Love on Monday' (1960) includes this hilarious couplet: 'Her hands, were soft, as cotton / Her face, could never, be forgotten.'

All these winsome characteristics can be found in abundance in this great artist's earlier work too: on the big hits like 'Blue Monday', 'Blueberry Hill' (which Domino didn't write but makes utterly his own), 'I Hear You Knockin'' and 'My Blue Heaven' (or as Fats has it, 'Mah, Blee-oo, Heav*on*'). Of course, all these things were in the great tradition of idiosyncratic pronunciation exemplified in black song from the beginning of time, but we encountered them first from Fats Domino.

GLEN DUNDAS' *Tangled Up in Tapes Revisited*, 1990, says that Fats Domino's early 'Please Don't Leave Me' (so early—the start of the 1950s—that his voice was an octave higher than later on) was among the songs Dylan rehearsed in Woodstock in September 1965. Decades later—August 3, 1988—Dylan ventured a very Fats Dominoid version of 'I'm in the Mood for Love' in concert in Hollywood. It also emerged in the 1990s that Dylan sang the same song on the Basement Tapes in 1967.

Then with Dylan's *Time Out of Mind*, which echoes many records of the period in which Fats Domino was in his pomp, it's natural that we should encounter Fats himself once more.

The first vocal remark of the album, 'I'm walkin'', is the title of one of Domino's greatest hits. Of course it's also a very anonymous remark, but that doesn't stop us remembering that Fats Domino whispers behind Bob Dylan many times down the years. It's impossible that Dylan should sing that phrase without being conscious of its Fats connection. Especially since one of the spiritual homes of Dylan's album is New Orleans, which would not be the same place without Fats Domino, the most famous epitomiser and greatest populariser of New Orleans R&B. Everyone knows too that all his classic and hit recordings were made there and he names this, his hometown, in his lyrics—not least in the case of his big 1960 hit 'Walking to New Orleans'. In Dylan's line 'I'm goin' down the river, down to New Orleans', then, it is hard not to hear an allusion to Domino's early classic 'Going to the River'. Elsewhere on *Time Out of Mind* we encounter the Domino title 'Sometimes I Wonder', and the allusion that seems the most subtle yet the most certain: namely, the line from ''Til I Fell in Love with You' where he sings that he's 'thinkin' about that girl who won't be back no' mo'.' This 'who won't be back no' mo'' echoes in every way—the attractively bouncy distribution of the syllables, the accent on that 'no' mo'', the mournful tone, as well as the words themselves: all these recreate Fats Domino's singing about the girl who 'won't be back no' mo''—and left a note to say so—in another 1960 hit song 'It Keeps Rainin''. One of the girls Dylan is thinkin' about who won't be back no' mo' cannot but be the one on Fats Domino's great record. And you can bet that her hands were soft as cotton.

[Fats Domino: 'The Fat Man', New Orleans, 10 Dec, 1949, Imperial 5058, LA, 1950; 'Ain't It a Shame', New Orleans, Feb 1955, Imperial 5348, 1955; 'Let the Four Winds Blow' c/w 'Good Hearted Man', New Orleans, May 1961, Imperial 5764 (London-American HLP 9415, London), 1961; 'What a Party' c/w 'Rockin' Bicycle', New Orleans, Aug 1961, Imperial 5779, (London-American HLP 9456), 1961; 'Fell in Love on Monday', New Orleans, Dec 1960, Imperial 5734, 1961; 'Blue Monday', New Orleans, Feb 1955, Imperial 5417, 1955; 'Blueberry Hill', LA, Jul 1956, Imperial 5407, 1956; 'I Hear You Knockin'', New Orleans, 4 Nov 1958, Imperial 5796; 'My Blue Heaven', New Orleans, Dec 1955, Imperial 5386, 1956; 'Please Don't Leave Me', New Orleans, 18 Apr 1953, Imperial 5240, 1953; 'I'm in the Mood for Love' c/w 'I'm Walking', both New Orleans, 3 Jan 1957, Imperial 5428, (London American HLP 8407), 1957; 'Walking to New Orleans', New Orleans, Apr 1960, Imperial 5675, 1960; 'Going to the River', New Orleans, Dec 1952, Imperial 5231, 1953; 'Sometimes I Wonder', New Orleans, Feb 1951, Imperial 5123, 1952; 'It Keeps Rainin'', New Orleans, Dec 1960, Imperial 5753, 1961. The Imperial sides are all CD-reissued in the $200 8-CD box set *Out of New Orleans*, Bear Family BCD 15541, Vollersode, Germany, 1993. Beware cheap imitations.

There is one fine post-Imperial Domino LP, the self-produced *Sleeping on the Job*, New Orleans, 1978, Conmedia, Germany (Sonet SNTF 793, London), 1979.

Dylan quoted from *Chronicles Volume One*, p.219.]

'Do Right to Me Baby (Do Unto Others)' [1979] On the final night of Dylan's great 1978 World Tour, he included in his repertoire the first live performance of a 'Born Again' song. It would turn up the year afterwards on the *Slow Train Coming* album. It was 'Do Right to Me Baby (Do Unto Others)'.

The phrase behind the sub-title and chorus of this song is taken not from the passage in Deuteronomy 19:20 that Dylan draws on in 'Wedding Song' and 'I and I': '. . . life shall go for life, eye for eye, tooth for tooth, hand for hand, foot for foot'—teaching drawn upon in the story of Samson, in which the Philistines say to the men of Judah: 'To bind Samson are we come up, to do to him as he hath done to us', after which Samson tells them, similarly: 'As they did unto me, so have I done unto them' (Judges 15:10–11).

Rather, Dylan is following Christ's *reversal* of the same passage of Deuteronomy preached within the Sermon on the Mount, in which he says: 'Therefore all things whatsoever ye would that men should do to you, do ye even so to them: for this is the law and the prophets.' (Matthew 7:12). This comes a few verses after his saying: 'Judge not, that ye be not judged'—which is the opening sentence of Matthew 7. (In Luke 6:37 Christ's words are given as 'Judge not, and ye shall not be judged . . .') Dylan echoes this directly in the opening line of his song: 'Don't wanna judge nobody, don't wanna be judged'.

A once-famous and still-interesting spin on this apparent clear choice between two contrasting ways of dealing with the world occurs in the children's book *The Water Babies*, 1863, by Charles Kingsley (1819–1875), himself the embodiment of muscular Christianity and a leading figure in the so-called Christian Socialist movement. In *The Water Babies* the hero meets the fairy who punishes those who ill-treat others, Mrs. Bedonebyasyoudid, and her sister, Mrs. Doasyouwouldbedoneby. The first explains that she is 'the ugliest fairy in the world; and I shall be, till people behave themselves as they ought to do. And then I shall grow as handsome as my sister, who is the loveliest fairy. . . . So she begins where I end, and I begin where she ends; and those who will not listen to her must listen to me . . .'

Christ's injunction '. . . all things whatsoever ye would that men should do to you, do ye even so to them . . .' is rendered in modern Bibles as 'do unto others as you would have them do unto you', which Dylan uses directly as the final (and summarising) chorus-line of 'Do Right to Me Baby (Do Unto Others)'.

(He also refers to this injunction indirectly in the companion song 'Gonna Change My Way of Thinking': it is 'the golden rule' to which he refers, when he complains preachily that 'You remember only about the brass ring, / You forget all about the golden rule.')

'Do Right to Me Baby' is not all dry sermonising. It includes the beautifully trademarked Dylan bite of 'Don't wanna amuse nobody, don't wanna be amused.'

On the three all-gospel tours (November–December 1979, January–February 1980 and April–May 1980), Dylan sang the song at every concert except one: the penultimate night of the third tour. That fall, when he reintroduced some secular songs into the set, and toured from November 9 until December 4, he sang 'Do Right to Me Baby' only once, on November 18 in San Francisco—and he has never played it since.

[Bob Dylan: 'Do Right to Me Baby (Do Unto Others)', débuted Hollywood, FL, 16 Dec 1978.]

Donne, John [1572 - 1631] Born in London, John Donne's maternal grandfather was the dramatist John Heywood. He was educated at Oxford but left without taking a degree. After forays in Cambridge, London and at sea, he became chief secretary to the Lord Keeper of the Great Seal and in 1601 a Member of Parliament, before a secret marriage to a minor brought him brief imprisonment, dismissal from office and social disgrace. After further travels, he took holy orders, ending up as Dean of St. Paul's Cathedral. Little of his poetry appeared in his lifetime but subsequently he has enjoyed universal recognition as one of the greats among the metaphysical poets.

Dylan's work sometimes calls John Donne to mind. Donne's modernity stems partly from the renowned directness of statement in the opening lines of his poems: 'For Godsake hold your tongue, and let me love'; 'Now thou hast lov'd me one whole day'; 'Oh do not die, for I shall hate / All women so when thou art gone'. One of Dylan's contributions has been to reintroduce such directness to white popular music. That Donne immediacy—directness balanced by intelligent discretion—is at work here: 'Go 'way from my window / Leave at your own chosen speed' (the song is 'It Ain't Me Babe'). And here: 'You got a lot o' nerve to say you are my friend' ('Positively 4th Street'). And here: 'I hate myself for loving you' (the opening line of 'Dirge', from *Planet Waves*).

These and others share with Donne more than plain directness and the conversational tone: more, even, than the measuredness both writers communicate, which takes its power from the sense that intellect is engaged in the communicating. Common to both is the bond between the passion and the rhythm. It was another poet, Coleridge, who pointed this out in Donne's case. He wrote: 'To read Dryden, Pope, etc, you need only count syllables; but to read Donne you must measure Time, and discover the time of each word by the sense of Passion.'

That must go down as an equally useful approach to Dylan's metre. Coleridge's point is proved by a song like 'The Lonesome Death of Hattie Carroll'—or, come to that, 'Like a Rolling Stone'. The vibrant and intricate changes of rhythm in each occur through the investment of different words with differing degrees of feeling.

Another point in relation to Donne is this. Donne's tricksiness appeals to our habit of expending the intellect on trivia—and Dylan is not exempt from this, as songs from 'I Shall Be Free No. 10' through to 'Million Dollar Bash' transparently show. Donne in this sense suits our times very well. It takes a serious man to be funny; it takes a sizeable mind to write satisfying minor love songs. Donne would have made a great songwriter for this reason. He could have done excellent, tricksy things for people like, say, Elvis Costello. A line from Donne's 'The Good-Morrow', for instance, would, adapted slightly, make a perfect Carole King title: 'You Make One Little Room an Everywhere'. And the phrase 'catch a falling star' originates with Donne, not Perry Como. The other John Donne opening that would work as intelligent, delicate, strong songwriting is that of his poem 'The Triple Foole': 'I am two fooles, I know, / For loving, and for saying so / In whining poetry . . .' That is the kind of conscious flirtation with ideas and nonsense that Dylan has exploited so well. The 1960s Dylan song most seeped in this kind of tricksiness is perhaps '4th Time Around', from *Blonde on Blonde*, with its stretched-out metaphors of sexual innuendo culminating in the rebounding pun on 'crutch', which Donne would have appreciated.

Finally, it is striking that Donne and Dylan both find it hard to subjugate intensity and passion into an appropriate devotional stance in their later religious work. Both artists exhibit a constant difficulty with the war of the flesh and the spirit. Donne's secular love poetry gets to pointing towards Christ (notably in 'The Canonization', where orgasm is likened to the death of Christ and the Resurrection) just as Dylan's does, on *Street Legal* and *Blood on the Tracks* in particular; and in the religious work of both men the passion they applied to lovers is no less lustily transferred to the Lord. At the same time, the religious work of both lacks general appeal, so that both artists end up with a substantial body of very popular secular work and a largely unheeded religious output.

[Donne's opening lines are from 'The Canonization', 'Woman's Constancy' and 'A Feaver', all c.1593–1601. Coleridge quoted from the Introduction in *John Donne: A Selection of His Poetry*, ed. John Hayward, 1950, which also quotes Coleridge's verse 'On Donne's Poetry', which begins with the splendid 'With Donne, whose muse on dromedary trots'. That last phrase, by chance, is paralleled (if parallels can be so bumpy) by Dylan's 'cemetery hips', from the opening song of the electric half of his 1966 concerts, 'Tell Me Momma' (a parallel more pronounced when, on the bootleg that was for many years the only way to hear this, it sounded like 'cemetery kicks').

Donne's 'For love, all love of other sights controules, / And makes one little roome, an every where' is from 'The Good-Morrow'; 'Goe, and catche a falling starre' is the opening line of one of the two Donne poems titled 'Song'. These, plus the other 'Song' and 'The Triple Foole', quoted above, all belong to the period c.1593–1601. Perry Como's record 'Catch a Falling Star' (NY, 9 Oct 1957) was, with 'Magic Moments' (NY, 3 Dec 1957), a double-sided hit in 1958 (RCA 20-7128).

Hayward quotes a 'friend' of Donne making a comment that many will feel rings an approximate bell in Dylan's case: that Donne wrote 'all his best pieces ere he was twenty-five years old'. Hayward notes too that 'Donne did not suddenly sober down when he took Holy Orders at the age of forty-three.']

'Don't Fall Apart on Me Tonight' [1983] By the time of *Infidels*, on which 'Don't Fall Apart on Me Tonight' appears, Bob Dylan had become the canonised fixity experiencing the very Mona Lisa syndrome he had sung about from the privileged position of flexible youth in 'Visions of Johanna'. By 1983, aged over 40, 'it's like I'm stuck inside a painting / That's hanging in the Louvre / My throat starts to tickle and my nose itches / But I know that I can't move.' Yet as so often with the revisits in newer songs to ideas and images from older ones, the newer version is less succinct, vivid and striking. 'Mona Lisa musta had the highway blues' is more audience-trusting, more humour-sharing, more quotable and far sharper than the expression of only some of what it contains in that clumsily catalogued, over-explained 'My throat starts to tickle and my nose itches / But I know that I can't move'. More is less.

This is not the only resonance within 'Don't Fall Apart on Me Tonight'. When, on the lines immediately preceding those above, Dylan sings 'But if I could I'd . . . build you a house made out of stainless steel', it is a 'found line' (in this case a fragment of conversation he overheard in the street, as he mentions somewhere in the course of discussing songwriting), but it surely got itself 'found' by Dylan—commended itself to his attention where very many others do not—because it had the resonance of echo. It echoes and contradicts his own earlier 'Build me a cabin in Utah', from 'Sign on the Window', which in turn echoes a common blues formula: the 'I'm-going-to-build-me-a . . .' stanza. When you hear, as unavoidably happens, those two Dylan lines together, their place in the cumulative life of this stanza is hard to disavow. It is a stanza that takes in MEMPHIS MINNIE's 'I'm going to build me a bungalow, just for me and my bumble bee', Pearl Dickson's 'I'm going to build me a castle, out of ice and snow', Clifford Gibson's identical 'I'm going to build me a castle, out of ice and snow', Will Weldon's 'I'm going to build me a castle, fifteen storey high' and Willie Brown's 'I had a notion, Lord and I believe I will / I'm going to build me a mansion, out on Decatur Hill'. Clamouring for house-room here too are Joe McCoy's 'That Will Be Alright', which begins: 'I'm going to build me a house, out on the sea' (also echoed by Dylan's 'Well, meet me in the middle of the ocean' on his 1962 blues 'Down the Highway') and even Dylan's own 1990 third-person variant, 'He's got that fortress on the mountain / With no doors, no windows, so no thieves can break in' (from 'Handy Dandy', on *Under the Red Sky*), which invokes a castle built out of ice and snow of the heart.

In this way, 'Don't Fall Apart on Me Tonight' is one of Dylan's non-blues songs in which his inwardness with blues consciousness shows through. It does too when the first verse of the lyric reaches this: 'You know, the streets are filled with vipers / Who've lost all ray of hope / You know, it ain't even safe no more / In the palace of the Pope.'

Used like this, 'vipers' passes by with just enough drawing of attention to itself for the listener to register where it's from. Which is here: 'O generation of vipers, who hath warned you to flee from the wrath to come?' (from both Matthew 3:7 and Luke 3:7); 'O generation of vipers, how can ye, being evil, speak good things?' (from Matthew 12:34) and 'Ye serpents, ye generation of vipers, how can ye escape the damnation of hell?' (Matthew 23:33.)

It's a pity that though Dylan doesn't quite manage here to pass off the biblical term as contemporary American speech, he succeeds with a secondary achievement (it's almost a private joke), punning on 'vipers' so as to meld the biblical with the jazz/blues patois of the 1920s–1940s. A 'viper' seems to arise around 1925 as a street term for a police informer (a spin on the phrase 'a snake in the grass', as is the modern term 'a grass' and the subsequent 'supergrass'); by the 1930s it is adopted, stigma-free, as a name for a dope-smoker or dealer. Hence the song 'If You'se [or You're] a Viper', recorded by many people from 1930s jazz violinist Stuff Smith to minor blues singers like Rosetta Howard and Lorraine Walton. These lines give the song's flavour: 'Dreamed about a reefer five foot long / The mighty mezz but not too strong / You'll be high but not for long / If you'se a viper.' There was another number called 'A Viper's Moan', there was Sidney Bechet's 'Viper Mad', and in 'Really the Blues', an unreliable but entertaining memoir by the indifferent jazz musician and consummate drug-dealer Mezz Mezzrow (a white man who lived as a black man), there is this splendid variation: 'Poppa, you never smacked your chops on anything sweeter in all your days of viping.' So Dylan's lines 'You know, the streets are full of vipers / Who've lost all ray of hope' work neatly enough on these two levels: as biblical and historical-streetwise allusion, and as biblical and old doper talk.

Unfortunately, by the time the matching lines have limped past us, we've lost more than we've gained. Dylan's 'vipers' get lost because the verse ends so bluntedly. The idea that 'the palace of the Pope' has traditionally been a 'safe' place seems exasperatingly dumb. It fits with the dumbness inherent in phrases like 'I just don't think that I could handle it', and indeed the phrase 'Don't Fall Apart on Me Tonight': both prime examples of nasty Californian therapy-speak.

[Bob Dylan, 'Don't Fall Apart on Me Tonight', NY, backing track prob. 12 Apr 1983, vocal overdubbed 5 Jun–Jul 1983; unissued but circulated take with original vocal, 12 Apr 1983; 10 further uncirculated outtake attempts (incl. fragments), 12 Apr 1983.

Memphis Minnie: 'Bumble Bee', Memphis, 20 Feb 1930; *Rare Blues of the Twenties* [sic], Historical HLP-2, Jersey City, NJ, c.1967. Pearl Dickson: 'Twelve Pound Daddy', Memphis, 12 Dec 1927; *Frank Stokes' Dream, 1927–1931 (The Memphis Blues)*, Yazoo L-1008, NY, 1968.

Clifford Gibson: 'Ice and Snow Blues', NY, 26 Nov 1929; *Clifford Gibson: Beat You Doing It*, Yazoo L-1027, NY, c.1971. Will Weldon (with the Memphis Jug Band): 'Peaches in the Springtime', Memphis, 13 Feb 1928; *Harmonicas, Washboards, Fiddles, Jugs*, Roots RL-311, Vienna, 1968. Willie Brown: 'M and O Blues', Grafton, WI, 28 May 1930; *The Mississippi Blues 1927–1940*, Origin Jazz Library OJL-5, Berkeley, CA, 1963. Joe McCoy: 'That Will Be Alright', NY, 18 Jun 1929; *Memphis Jamboree, 1927–1936*,Yazoo L-1021, NY, 1970.

Stuff Smith: 'If You'se a Viper', NY, 13 Mar 1936. Lorraine Walton: 'If You're a Viper', Chicago, 9 Feb 1929. Rosetta Howard (with the Harlem Hamfats): 'If You're a Viper', NY, 5 Oct 1937. Sidney Bechet with Noble Sissle's Swingers: 'Viper Mad', NY, 10 Feb 1938; *Sixteen Original Jazz Classics: Reefer Songs*, Stash ST100, Tenefly, NJ, c.1973. (This LP also offers Bob Howard & His Boys: 'If You're a Viper', *nia*, 7 Feb 1938.) Mezz Mezzrow with Bernard Wolfe, *Really the Blues*, New York: Random House, 1946 (re-pub'd London: HarperCollins 1993); quotations from this & from Stuff Smith's version of 'If You'se a Viper' appear in Andrew Kowl, ed, *The High Times Encyclopedia of Recreational Drugs*, New York: Stonehill, 1978.]

***Don't Look Back* [film, 1967]** This extraordinary black and white film of Bob Dylan's 1965 tour of Britain was the first film of any Dylan tour, and turned out to document the last solo acoustic tour of Dylan's career. The signs of what was to come were already there. The first electric album had already been made, and released in the US, by the time Dylan flew in to England at the end of April 1965 for a press conference followed by eight concerts, opening in Sheffield on April 30 and then playing Liverpool, Leicester, Birmingham, Newcastle and Manchester, and finishing at London's magnificent Victorian edifice, the Royal Abert Hall, on May 9 and 10. And while Dylan had charted for the first time in Britain in March with the single of 'The Times They Are a-Changin'', the following month it was being chased up by 'Subterranean Homesick Blues'. The film itself begins with what has been hailed as the first pop video, the film to accompany the 'Subterranean Homesick Blues' record, shot in the alley near the Savoy Hotel with ALLEN GINSBERG lurking in the background and a wondrously stylish Bob dropping big word-cards on the ground.

Besides, the Dylan who arrived in Britain trailing the *Don't Look Back* film crew behind him did not look like a folk singer: he was modishly thin, Chelsea-booted and black leather jacketed; his hair wasn't huge yet, but it made everyone else's look like they worked in a bank. (See also **1965–66: Dylan, pop & the UK charts**.) And he began as he meant to go on, talking hip and talking back, pioneering his daring reproaches to inane press-conference questions. He's asked why he's carrying a gigantic light bulb; he says a friend gave it to him. He's asked 'What is your real message?' He answers: 'My real message? Keep a good head and always carry a light bulb.'

Accounts differ sharply as to how the film came to be made. The most plausible seems to be that Dylan's manager ALBERT GROSSMAN wanted a film made but didn't want to have to pay for it. He brought in producer John Cort and the two of them then turned to Grossman's old friend HOWARD ALK and his wife Jones Alk (who had worked as a hat-check girl in Grossman's Chicago club, the Gate). Alk was a trustworthy, suitably hip character who had by this time also become a friend of Dylan's; he was also a film editor. They still needed a production company to take it on, and Alk approached Richard Leacock, a filmmaker he much admired and was on good terms with (good enough that he always called him Ricky). But Leacock's response was: 'I'm not going to make a film about a guy who sings "Malaguena".' He couldn't be dissuaded from the notion that Dylan was a folksinger of that bland, uninteresting ilk. So Leacock said no, but his partner, D.A. PENNEBAKER, said yes. Because of Grossman's financial approach, Pennebaker was able to make the film largely on his own terms.

Thus it was that the film came about with the Alks still on board but with little personal or artistic sympathy between Pennebaker and them—and no agreement, in retrospect, as to how valuable the contribution of each was. Pennebaker not only directed the film, but also 'authored' a book of the film, published by Ballantine in 1968. On the front cover it says 'Bob Dylan: *Don't Look Back*, a Film and Book by D.A. Pennebaker', even though the contents are a transcript of scenes from the film, plus over 200 stills taken from it. As Pennebaker's preface states: 'This is not the script from which *Don't Look Back* was made. The film was made without a script. This is simply a transcript of what happened and what was said.' At the back of the book it states: 'The film Produced by Albert Grossman, John Cort and Leacock Pennebaker Inc.'

Pennebaker thought the Alks were bohemian amateurs; they thought he was too plodding and straight. When you see concert footage shot from the front, it's by Pennebaker; that's how he liked to do it. When you see footage shot from the wings, it's by Alk. Pennebaker has consigned him to the wings because he thinks that's of less interest; but it often yields more interesting, and always more intimate, material. (This is even more striking in the following year's tour film, *Eat the Document*.) According to Jones, Pennebaker would also tell Alk things like 'Go and film some pigeons in Trafalgar Square'; and Pennebaker agrees that he only regarded Alk as operating a 'fallback camera'.

Dylan too probably felt that Pennebaker was a little unimaginative. Jones Alk remembers that Pennebaker always wanted to call his films by the name of the person who was its subject, and wanted to call this film *Dylan*. When he told Dylan this, Dylan pulled a face and said 'Why don't you call it *Pennebaker*?'

Nevertheless they all settled down to it. Pennebaker says that Bob Van Dyke 'recorded the concerts'; Jones Alk says that she was in charge of the sound on the film itself; Howard Alk filmed what he pleased. Pennebaker even ended up saying that he 'would really like to thank Jones and Howard Alk who helped make it work'. Dylan's early unease about the whole thing was banished by his deciding to just go with the flow and play the part of this person in this movie.

The result was an extraordinary document, capturing in an aptly fresh, cinema-vérité style an artist coming to the peak of his powers, intensely alive, intelligent and charismatic–and allowing unprecedented backstage rights to the cameras. It was a core part of the anti-showbiz stance Dylan was pioneering that you were allowed to see the very immediate moments before and after the artist was on stage. When it was new, *Don't Look Back* gave us an undreamt-of privileged access to its 23-year-old star. The only complaint people had was that it never showed much interest in, or gave any generous footage from, the song-performances from the concerts themselves.

As time has passed the film has become an ever more valuable historical document, too (though the use of the word 'man' in every sentence, man, has long seemed risibly quaint). It's also mordantly funny: never more so than when the soon to be High Sheriff of Nottingham comes to call on Bob backstage, or when Albert Grossman gets together with one of the pompous big-name hustlers of the British 'entertainment industry', Tito Burns, forces him to negotiate British TV appearances for Dylan right there in front of us all, and makes this wily bully-boy look a bumbling fraud alongside Grossman's genuine article.

The film premièred at the Presidio Theater in San Francisco on May 17, 1967; that September 6 it opened at the 34th Street East Theater in New York City. The book was published in April 1968. The film was released on DVD in 2000 with audio tracks in Dolby Digital 2.0 Stereo, a commentary by D.A. Pennebaker and 'tour manager' BOB NEUWIRTH, an alternate version of the 'Subterranean Homesick Blues' mini-movie and five uncut song performances: 'It Ain't Me Babe', 'It's All Over Now, Baby Blue', 'Love Minus Zero/No Limit', 'The Lonesome Death of Hattie Carroll' and 'To Ramona'.

In 2005, not long before the MARTIN SCORSESE film *No Direction Home* hit the screen (and probably not unconnected with its being announced), a bootleg 2-DVD set of raw outtake footage from *Don't Look Back* came into circulation, bulging with the complete concert performances that had only been glimpsed in tiny tantalising fragments in the film itself.

[*Don't Look Back*, dir. D.A. Pennebaker, Leacock-Pennebaker, US, 1967; DVD: New Video Group, US, Jan 2000. Quotes from Richard Leacock & Bob Dylan, plus other detail, from Jones Alk, phone-call with this writer 01 Nov 2005.]

Dorsey, Thomas A. [1899 - 1993] Thomas Andrew Dorsey was born in tiny Villa Rica, Georgia, on July 1, 1899, the son of a Baptist preacher. As a child he worked as a circus water boy, moved to Atlanta at age 11, started selling soda pop at the city's 81 Theatre and there encountered the likes of Bessie Smith 'doing those blues numbers and shaking everything they had.' He became a successful vaudeville pianist, moved to Chicago in 1916, kept his options open by joining the Pilgrim Baptist Church and studying at the Chicago School of Composition and Music. He was Ma Rainey's pianist and band leader–and travelled the south with her Rabbit Foot Minstrel show–from 1924 to 1928. He had begun to write songs, especially for Paramount and Brunswick/Vocalion Records, and was a staff arranger for the Chicago Music Publishing Company. As Georgia Tom, he and Tampa Red had the biggest hit of 1928 with the hokum'n' innuendo of 'It's Tight Like That', followed by more in the same vein both with Tampa Red and with BIG BILL BROONZY, and in the 1930s he worked with many others including MEMPHIS MINNIE.

At the same time, he was active in performing church music, and in 1930, in the middle of playing a church concert, Dorsey received a telegram reading 'Hurry home. Your wife is very sick. She is going to have the baby'; he telephoned back to be told that she was dead; the baby died shortly after. This made him turn away from his career as a bluesman to writing hymns, though only after resisting the impulse to do the opposite. He felt that 'God had been unfair' and wanted to plunge back fully into the secular blues; but his turmoil resolved itself the other way and he was able to say afterwards: 'I was doing alright for myself but the voice of God whispered, "You need to change a little".' Though influenced by composer C.H. Tindley (who founded the Tindley Methodist Church, Philadelphia, where Bessie Smith is buried), Dorsey brought to his sacred songs blues feeling and syncopation, and this powerful combination of styles created the musical revolution that was modern gospel music. He became the first black publisher as well as composer of songs in the genre, and a prolific writer who can be said to have been a shaping force in African-American consciousness.

In 1933 he founded the still-active National Convention of Gospel Choirs and Choruses. Dorsey composed over 500 published songs, among them the best-loved and most widely recorded in the entire gospel repertoire, including 'Precious Lord, Take My Hand' (aka 'Take My Hand Precious Lord') and 'Peace in the Valley', propelled to popularity partly by the new power of radio and partly by a working alliance with Mahalia Jackson, whom he'd first met in 1929. He became her musical advisor and accompanist from 1937 to 1946, and she sang his songs in church programmes and at conventions, promoting his compositions. Her signature song became 'Precious Lord Take My Hand' (which she would eventually sing at Martin Luther King's funeral in Atlanta in 1968).

The new style of Dorsey's religious songs was not without controversy, though. In ALAN LOMAX's *The Land Where the Blues Began*, he deplores these new me-me-me *gospel* songs of the 40s as against the old *spirituals* of an earlier era, and deplores Dorsey's 'Precious Lord Take My Hand' especially. He says the new songs elevated the preacher to a new primacy over the congregation that suppressed the previous democracy of worship (though it certainly wasn't every church that had an all-participating congregation before the Dorsey generation came along).

The pull between secular and religious music was ever-present in Dorsey's life, as for so many of the singers of the pre-war era, and it is unsurprising that his influence on the music world Bob Dylan inherited should be detectable on both sides of that divide. Today it would be impossible to read these four consecutive lines from Georgia Tom's 1928 'Grievin' Me Blues' without being reminded of Dylan's mid-1960s work; re-formulated, they infuse at least the chorus of 'Tombstone Blues', the opening of 'Subterranean Homesick Blues' and something of the spirit of both: 'Daddy's got the washboard, mama's got the tub / Sister's got the liquor and brother's got the jug / My water-pipe's all rusted, water's running cold / Someone's in the basement trying to find the hole.'

Of course, only *something* of the spirit of the Dylan lines is there—the upbeat rhythmic facility—because the innovative transformation Dylan makes is via the context in which he places his own so-similar lines. The context removes the tone of jolly family just-folksiness, replacing it with an opposite consciousness: that of the alienated loner at odds with, yet surrounded by, people obdurately going about their own incomprehensible business and, 'in the basement', communing with their own drug-paranoia.

In fact, though, the Dorsey of this period wasn't really 'just-folksy' at all but a cool, sly, city dude. There's a wonderful photograph of him, republished in Paul Oliver's book *The Story of the Blues*, in which, dressed sharper than we'll ever be, he's cupping his hands to light a cigarette. His eyes, feral and knowing, pierce the camera-lens: except for the fact that he's black, it's a shot the Hollywood of 40s film noir would have killed for.

On the religious side, no-one interested in popular or gospel music could have avoided the impact of Thomas A. Dorsey's work, and Dylan's own gospel compositions would have been different had Dorsey's not existed. More specifically, Dylan must have grown up knowing the early 1950s hit version of 'Peace in the Valley' by white artist Red Foley (which was a hit with black audiences too), and then the immaculate and gloweringly powerful ELVIS PRESLEY recordings of 'Peace in the Valley' *and* 'Take My Hand Precious Lord' from 1957. Presley's are classic soul-in-torment versions, and his 'Peace in the Valley' recognises the song's genius: indeed makes it a work of darker genius, emphasising the intense, gothic spookiness of the lyrics, in which, for instance, 'the night is as black as the sea'. Its pinnacle is this re-statement of the biblical vision of the peaceable kingdom: 'Well the bear will be gentle and the wolves will be tame / And the lion shall lay down with the lamb / And the beasts from the wild shall be led by a child / And I'll be changed, changed from this creature that I am.' (See also **'the lion lies down with the lamb'**.) The song was performed *much* less satisfactorily by Bob Dylan in concert in 1989 (Frejus, France, June 18).

Probably the last survivor of the key figures born around the turn of the century who were originally recording in the 1920s, Dorsey died in Chicago on January 23, 1993, aged 93.

[Georgia Tom: 'Grievin' Me Blues', Chicago, c.6 Sep 1928, *Rare Blues of the Twenties, No. 1*, Historical HLP-1, NY, 1966. Tampa Red & Georgia Tom: 'It's Tight Like That', Chicago, 24 Oct 1928. Dorsey photograph in Paul Oliver, *The Story of the Blues*, London: Penguin, 1969, p.99. Sources includes Michael W. Harris, *The Rise of Gospel Blues: The Music of Thomas Andrew Dorsey in the Urban Church*, New York: Oxford University Press, 1992 edn., Dorsey 2nd quote p.219, telegram p.217; Dorsey 1st & 3rd quote *www.honkytonks.org/showpages/tadorsey.htm*, seen online 29 Jul 2004.]

Douglas, Steve [1938 - 1993] Steven Douglas Kreisman was born in Hollywood on September 24, 1938, served in the US Navy Drum and Bugle Corps after leaving school and became one of rock-'n'roll's greatest sax players. He came to prominence playing on Duane Eddy's instrumental records of the late 1950s. Eddy used three other tenor sax players in this period (Jim Horn, Gil Bernal and Plas Johnson) but on many of them, Eddy's 'million dollar twang' guitar sound, shudderingly reverberative and deep, would concede half a verse or so to Douglas' gorgeously beefy, crucially *unjazz-like* solos—and between the two of them, on 'Cannonball' (1958), 'Yep!', 'Forty Miles of Bad Road' (1959), 'Peter Gunn' (1960) and others, they created one of the defining sounds of 1950s teenage rebellion, epitomes of the strutting toughness of teddy boys and rock'n'roll. And it has to be said that now, hearing these old records anew, it is Duane who sounds overly simple and seemly, mild and polite to a fault; the sax holds up far better.

Douglas, pianist Larry Knetchel and Al Casey went out on the road as the Rebels on Dick Clark

Bandstand package shows but Douglas also kept up session playing, and in this capacity worked on lots of PHIL SPECTOR wall-of-sound hit singles (those 'little symphonies for the kids', as Spector called them); his is the growling baritone blasting into the middle of the Crystals' 'Da Doo Ron Ron'. He made a solo album, *Twist*, in 1962 (of course it was in 1962) but also augmented a whole slew of the surf records of the early 1960s, among them hits by Jan & Dean and the Beach Boys, including 1965's masterwork *Pet Sounds*, as well as recording with everyone from the Lettermen to Lesley Gore.

In the 1970s Steve Douglas played with Mink DeVille, Ry Cooder, Mickey Hart and the Ramones, among others, and in 1978 he joined Bob Dylan's uniquely large line-up for the 1978 World Tour. Dylan made a point of stressing Douglas' rock'n' roll credentials, and used him not only for the 114 concerts that of that year, in Japan, Australia, Europe and the US, but also on the 1978 album *Street Legal*. He came back three years later for the *Shot of Love* sessions in late April and early May 1981. On the released album he plays the alto sax on 'Dead Man, Dead Man' and 'Every Grain of Sand'.

In the early 1980s Douglas also played with Duane Eddy again, along with the great Hal Blaine on drums and, at one point in 1983, Ry Cooder on second guitar. He reappeared in Dylan's professional life on some *Knocked Out Loaded* sessions exactly five years after his *Shot of Love* contributions, playing on the overdubs of April 28–29, 1986 onto the original recording of 'Driftin' Too Far from Shore' made on July 26, 1984, and on attempts at 'You'll Never Walk Alone', 'Unchain My Heart' and 'Without Love' made between April 29 and May 5, 1986, all in Topanga Park, California. More significantly, at the same sessions he plays on the *Knocked Out Loaded* tracks 'They Killed Him', 'You Wanna Ramble', 'Precious Memories', 'Maybe Someday' and 'Brownsville Girl'. Their association fizzled out in an unused session in Hollywood some time in April 1987, at which Douglas played on still-uncirculated versions of 'Look on Yonder Walls', 'Rollin' and Tumblin', 'Red Cadillac and a Black Mustache' and two takes of BILLY LEE RILEY's song 'Rock with Me Baby'.

Steve Douglas died of heart failure at the beginning of a session for Ry Cooder in LA on April 19, 1993.

***Down in the Groove* [1988]** Dylan's 33rd album (if you count the compilations), and bearing, like so many of the same era, a title determined to undercut any idea that inspired work might lie within. After a silence of nearly two years, here was a further devaluing of the whole notion of a new Bob Dylan album as something significant, and another refusal to offer new songs of his own. If it had been better recorded and Dylan had brought some creative alertness to his vocals, instead of rasping through on automatic, this could at least have been a *Self Portrait II*: there are interesting song selections here; but Dylan treats them maladroitly, fails to commend them as a purposive collection and throws in feeble makeweights: 'Had a Dream About You Baby', recycled from the soundtrack of the quaintly atrocious *Hearts of Fire* film of 1987; the risibly turgid 'Death Is Not the End', cut at the *Infidels* sessions and rightly rejected then; and two songs with lyrics by ROBERT HUNTER rejected even by the GRATEFUL DEAD as under-par: the tetchy, braggartly 'Silvio' and the shrivellingly dull-minded 'Ugliest Girl in the World'. This quality of work was so far below that of Dylan's albums of the 1960s that it just depressed the hell out of you. Continued silence would have been more dignified than this.

[Recorded London, 27–28 Aug 1986, Los Angeles, Apr 1987 and LA or Malibu, May 1987; released as Columbia OC 40957 (LP) & CK 40957 (CD), 19 or 31 May 1988.]

Drake, Pete [1932 - 1988] Roddis Franklin Drake was born in Atlanta, Georgia, on October 8, 1932. He grew up to be an innovative steel guitarist and eminent Nashville session musician, a producer and music publisher. In the mid-1950s, still based in Atlanta, he had his own group, full of players who were later big names: Jerry Reed, JOE SOUTH, DOUG KERSHAW, Roger Miller (playing fiddle) and country singer Jack Greene (playing drums). He said later: 'We kind of wore ourselves out, so I decided to move to Nashville.' But 'the steel guitar was kind of dead then, in 1959. Everybody was trying to go pop. They was putting strings and horns on Webb Pierce records, and nobody was using steel guitar. So I starved to death the first year and a half. Then I worked with DON GIBSON a while, then Marty Robbins.'

Eventually he played behind many artists, including THE EVERLY BROTHERS, ELVIS PRESLEY, GEORGE HARRISON (on *All Things Must Pass*, including the mega-hit 'My Sweet Lord'). He introduced the so-called 'talking steel', heard on his own hits 'Forever' (1964) and 'Talking Steel' (1965). It's also been claimed that he singlehandedly opened 'the entire pop and rock field to the sounds of the pedal steel': though Dylan's using him in 1967 surely had something to do with that.

Pete Drake first played steel guitar behind Dylan on the final two tracks of the 1968 *John Wesley Harding* album, 'Down Along the Cove' and 'I'll Be Your Baby Tonight', both recorded in Nashville on November 29, 1967, and then on all four sessions for the *Nashville Skyline* album, beginning on February 13, 1969 and concluding February 18. These included the large number of duets sung by Dylan and JOHNNY CASH, which not only included the issued take of 'Girl of the North Country' but also the 'One Too Many Mornings' filmed and included in the 1969 film *Johnny Cash: The Man and His Music* and a widely circulated tape of further duets.

Nashville Skyline was released on April 9, and just under two weeks later Pete Drake was back in the studios for Dylan to play on the earliest of the sessions that eventually yielded *Self Portrait* and *Dylan*. In the midst of these, on May 1, 1969, Drake backed Dylan and Cash on Bob's delightful appearance on ABC's 'Johnny Cash TV Show', broadcast on June 7. He seems to have stopped playing on the studio sessions after that of May 3: the final session of 1969. (The 1970 sessions for the same albums featured steel guitar from Lloyd Green and Norman Spicher.)

Pete Drake's health declined badly in the 1980s, from an accumulation of illnesses including emphysema, diabetes and heart trouble. He moved to Florida in 1987, but got bored, moved back to Nashville and tried to restart his business activities. He died there of lung failure on July 29, 1988.

[Pete Drake interview quotes online 9 Mar 2005 at *www.calsharp.com/music/Pete.html*; some other detail from *www.countryworks.com*.]

***Drawn Blank* [book, 1994]** This hardback book of Dylan's selected drawings, presented as being 'sketches for paintings', mostly done on the road 'from about 1989 to about 1991 or '92 in various locations mainly to relax and refocus a restless mind', as he put it in September 1994 in his short foreword to the book, was published in the US late that same year and comprises 124 unnumbered pages containing 92 sketches. It's a modest achievement, likely to have gained publication only because Bob Dylan's name can be attached to it, and it certainly lacks most of the fun and vigour of the drawings published decades earlier in the first official song lyrics book, *Writings & Drawings of Bob Dylan* (1973), which were clearly influenced by the sketches by WOODY GUTHRIE contained in his 1943 autobiography, *Bound for Glory*, though some of the feel for that old rough-and-tumble perspective remains. *Drawn Blank* reveals a Dylan still curious about outside life, still observing the real world and its ordinary detail: something his songwriting does not always show. The world observed here is sometimes the almost Van Goghian shaking vernacular chunkiness of chairs, kitchens, cupboards, balconies, feet, old wooden houses and vibrant individuals; at other times the view is bleak and featureless, the world glimpsed on tour outside a series of hotel-room windows, devoid of human activity or architectural interest, while inside, a few large-breasted women loll about looking bored. One way and another there's a lot of blank that gets drawn here, but much to notice too.

At the time of its publication there were many who sniffed that Dylan's 'restless mind' would have been better occupied 'refocusing' on writing songs. The book emerged when Dylan's most recent two albums had contained none of his compositions; but you can't reasonably tell creative people what they should concentrate on; and as so often with Dylan, to appraise this work now that it's now longer new and therefore no longer being taken to augur anything, its virtues come on stronger and its weaknesses recede.

[Bob Dylan, *Drawn Blank*, New York & Toronto: Random House, 1994.]

Drummond, Tim [1940 -] Timothy Lee Drummond was born in Bloomington, Illinois, on April 20, 1940 but spent a year of his adolescence in Charleston, South Carolina, where he began playing guitar, and on his return to Chicago joined local groups Wild Child Gibson and Eddie Cash & the Cashiers. He changed to playing bass when working for CONWAY TWITTY, but didn't care for Twitty's switch to country music and moved to Cincinnati, playing clubs with early 1960s minor pop star Troy Seals and Lonnie Mack and session playing behind Hank Ballard (composer of 'The Twist') and James Brown.

By 1968 Drummond was in James Brown's hardworking touring band—just as Black Power was in its pomp, and Brown was being criticized as an Uncle Tom for his single 'America Is My Home'. (The next single was to be 'Say it Loud—I'm Black and I'm Proud'.) It didn't go down well with Brown's audience that Drummond, his bassist, was a whitey. Drummond stuck it out; but these were dramatic days—so that when, at the end of the 1970s, he went out on the gospel tours with Dylan, playing to partially hostile audiences again, it must have all seemed pretty tame.

Drummond quit Brown's band exhausted, moved to Nashville and with such high-level credentials became a top session player for R&B performers like Margie Hendricks and Joe Simon, country artists like Ronnie Milsap and then for NEIL YOUNG. Drummond played on Young's *Harvest* (issued 1972), became one of his Stray Gators, toured with him and moved to California. In the end he played on Young's albums *Time Fades Away* (1973), *On the Beach* (1974), *Zuma* (1975), *American Stars 'n' Bars* (1977), *Comes a Time* (1978), *Hawks and Doves* (1980), *Everybody's Rockin'* (1983) and *Harvest Moon* (1992). He also played on most of the CROSBY & Nash album *Wind on the Water* and on *Crosby, Stills and Nash* (1977).

Drummond has also played on albums by Ry Cooder, J.J. Cale, the Beach Boys, RICK DANKO, Don Henley and many others—and in 1990 he was on the soundtrack of the Dennis Hopper film *The Hot Spot*, playing in a heavyweight ensemble led by Miles Davis, Taj Mahal and JOHN LEE HOOKER.

Drummond first played with Dylan at the SNACK Benefit on March 12, 1975 in San Francisco—on this occasion playing guitar, not bass.

Then, in the middle of his later session work and his involvement with Neil Young, Drummond became a key part of Bob Dylan's Born Again story. After California rehearsals, he was brought down to the Muscle Shoals studios in Sheffield, Alabama, to be the bass player on the *Slow Train Coming* sessions, starting on April 30, 1979 and completed on May 4—and then he went out on the road with that first gospel tour, beginning that November 1 in San Francisco and ending in Tucson, Arizona, on December 9. He played too on Dylan's 'Saturday Night Live' TV appearance that October 20 and then on the first gospel tour of 1980, from January 11 in Portland, Oregon, through to February 9 in Charleston, West Virginia.

On both of those tours, on the *Saved* album begun just three days after that last concert, and on the next tour, from April 17 in Toronto through to May 21 in Dayton, Ohio, the drummer was JIM KELTNER—and on that last day in Dayton, Bob Dylan told an interviewer: 'I think Jim Keltner and Tim Drummond are the best rhythm section that God ever invented.'

God's and Bob's dream team held together through the brief fall tour too, from San Francisco on November 9 on back to Portland, Oregon, on December 4, and for the *Shot of Love* sessions in Santa Monica and LA in March to May 1981. Tim Drummond seems to have missed only the final session, on May 15 in LA, at which 'Heart of Mine' was recorded—and on June 15 & 16 he and Keltner were brought in to overdub on this anyway. By this point, the first 1981 tour had begun (in Chicago on June 10) and Tim Drummond was still there, and stayed there for all the June–July dates (finishing on July 25 in Avignon, France) and was back for the fall tour from October 16 in Milwaukee through to November 21 in Lakeland, Florida.

This was to be his last date as part of Dylan's band, but it has not been the last time they worked together. Both were in the same studio, probably in New York, around the end of 1995 or early in 1996, playing on two songs for CAROLE KING's ex-songwriting partner Gerry Goffin—'Masquerade' and 'Tragedy of the Trade'—with Drummond on bass and Dylan on guitar. Both tracks were released on Goffin's album *Back Room Blood* in 1996.

Drummond also owns four music publishing companies—Barn Yard Music, Dragin River Music, Gamblin Heart Music and Tornado Alley Music—and with this hat on too he bumps into Bob Dylan. One of the outtakes from the *Shot of Love* sessions was a song called 'Fur Slippers' (a title unheard but much bandied about at the time in the world of Dylan aficionados because it sounded so, well, so unBorn Again: so WARHOL Factory, 1966ish). Like the title track of the *Saved* album, it proved to be a joint composition by Dylan and Drummond, but this one remained unreleased and uncovered until a version emerged on the soundtrack of the CBS-TV mini-series 'Shake Rattle and Roll' in 1999 by one of the few performers who still goes out on the road more relentlessly than Dylan—B.B. King.

[Tim Drummond with Miles Davis, Taj Mahal, John Lee Hooker & others: *The Hot Spot: Original Motion Picture Soundtrack*, Verve 46813, US, 1990; Tim Drummond with Northern Blues Gospel AllStars: *Northern Blues Gospel AllStars*, Northern Blues Music NBM 0013, 2002. Main source *www.timdrummond.net*; others include the James Brown biography at *www.soulexpress radio.com/soulbiob.htm*; both seen online 18 Jan 2006. B.B. King: 'Fur Slippers', *Shake Rattle and Roll*, Uni/MCA, US, 1999. Dylan quote, interview by Karen Hughes, Dayton, OH, 21 May 1980, *The Dominion*, New Zealand, 2 Aug 1980.]

Duluth, Minnesota As Dylan writes truthfully in his poem 'My Life in a Stolen Moment': 'Duluth's an iron ore shipping town in Minnesota / It's built up on a rocky cliff that runs into Lake Superior / I was born there—my father was born there—'. It was still called Zenith City in those days, but by the time Bob Dylan was born there on May 24, 1941, though still the third-largest city in Minnesota, its population of 100,000 was going down.

Duluth is a scruffy, tough little city full of whiskery geezers hitting the precipitous streets that tumble down to the industrial waterfront where the wind comes off the water. The lake is so huge it's like the sea, making Duluth feel like a seaport, with a constant wind, tough people, a slight sense of menace, or at least the sense that you better have your wits about you on these colourless and poverty-soaked streets.

The ore from Hibbing leaves Duluth by boat to Chicago and points east. In the opposite direction came the immigrants from Russia, the Ukraine and, like Dylan's maternal grandmother's family, Lithuania, coming in via Liverpool, New Brunswick, Montreal and Michigan and along the Great Lake to Superior, across the bay from Duluth. You can see it all from the upstairs windows of 519 3rd Avenue East, the fast-deteriorating house the Zimmermans lived in when Bob was a baby. The alley down the side is strewn with foul rubbish, including big lumps of raw meat that the rats haven't eaten yet. There's no blue plaque on the wall here, no commemoration at all.

Armed with DAVE ENGEL's excellent book *Just Like Bob Zimmerman's Blues: Dylan in Minnesota*, you can drive up and down the grid of shabby roads, looking for, and finding almost all of, the apartments and houses through which the Zimmerman family passed in stages when they arrived here, becoming Americans and struggling to chase the Dream. A tough place to start.

Hard for the very young Bob too. Here is St. Mary's Hospital, where Dylan was born, and the dour, forbidding Nettleton elementary school where Bob shamed his father by having to be dragged the two blocks to it kicking and screaming. It's so ordinary, so drab. The change when Bob moved to Hibbing High was quite some upgrade. For Dylan's father, there was another school. Dominating the heights of Duluth is the Victorian monstrosity that he attended as a child, Central High, looking as if it's been built out of dogshit, and with a ludicrous 300-foot tower.

On 'Something There Is About You', from *Planet Waves*, Dylan sings this: 'Thought I'd shaken the wonder and the phantoms of my youth / Rainy days on the Great Lakes, walkin' the hills of old Duluth . . .' But he also writes of Duluth again, 30 years later, in the vivid prose of *Chronicles Volume One*:

> 'Duluth, even though it's two thousand miles from the nearest ocean, was an international seaport. Ships from South America, Asia and Europe came and went all the time, and the heavy rumble of the foghorns dragged you out of your senses by the neck. Even though you couldn't see the ships through the fog, you knew they were there by the heavy outbursts of thunder. . . . Foghorns sounded like great announcements. The big boats came and went, iron monsters from the deep. . . . As a child, slight, introverted and asthma stricken, the sound was so loud, so enveloping, I could feel it in my whole body and it made me feel hollow. Something out there could swallow me up.'

[Bob Dylan: *Chronicles Volume One*, pp. 273–74. Dave Engel, *Just Like Bob Zimmerman's Blues: Dylan in Minnesota*, Rudolph, WI: River City Memoirs-Mesabi, 1997.]

Dunbar, Sly [1952 -] See **Sly & Robbie**.

Dundas, Glen [1941 -] Glen Thomas Dundas was born on September 7, 1941, in Port Arthur—which is now called Thunder Bay, and where Glen still lives—in Ontario, Canada, at the northern end of Highway 61 and the Mississippi River, just north of Dylan's birthplace of Duluth, Minnesota. He first took an interest in Dylan's work in 1965 and his first publication was *Tangled Up in Tapes*, the 1987 first edition of the invaluable reference work that he has now given us five editions of, the most recent titled *Tangled: A Recording History of Bob Dylan* and published in 2004.

This is a large-format, generously illustrated published database, comparable only to the work of MICHAEL KROGSGAARD, which lists, track by track and song by song, in chronological order, every extant recording of Bob Dylan, whether made officially in a studio (and whether issued officially or not) or recorded on an amateur tape, from the earliest known recordings (made in 1956) through to the last concert performance of 2003. In every case, Dundas also indicates whether the recording has been circulated amongst collectors and which live tracks are 'line recorded', i.e. have been taken from the sound mixer in the concert hall or some pre-mixed source or similar.

There is also a complete listing, with description, of every known extant professional film, TV and video appearance Dylan has ever made or been glimpsed in (though occasionally the Dundas judgment is wildly askew, as when he describes Dylan's feeble and near-impenetrable version of 'Chimes of Freedom' from the inauguration celebration for President Bill Clinton on January 17, 1993 as 'robust').

In the 2004 edition there is also an admittedly incomplete list of other people's songs covered by Dylan, listing who composed and wrote them, a chart of how many appearances Dylan is known to have made year by year since 1961 and a listing, for every track on every Dylan album, of how many times he has performed it live—from which, of course, it's also possible to see at a glance which songs have *never* been offered in concert—plus the total number of song performances derived from each album. (Thus for instance to the end of 2003 we can see that Dylan had given 3,112 song performances from *The Freewheelin' Bob Dylan* and only 418 from *Street Legal*, and that he has drawn more from *Bringing It All Back Home* than *Blonde on Blonde*.)

Glen Dundas has occasionally written a piece in a Dylan fanzine too, such as the lengthy 'Walk the Line' in the Winter 1999 issue of *The Bridge*, but his magnum opus is unquestionably the *Tangled* series. The present work has necessarily drawn extensively on Glen Dundas' own.

In November 1991, Dylan was handed a copy of Dundas' *Tangled Up in Tapes Revisited* on his tour-bus somewhere in the mid-west, and is reported to have handed it back remarking that it only showed where he'd been—and that he'd appreciate instead a book that showed him where he was going. But Dylan well understands that past and future are not two separate books, and that, as he put it in 1981's self-searching song 'Need a Woman' (a version of which was released on the *Bootleg Series Vols. 1–3*), 'whatever's waiting in the future could be what you're runnin' from in the past'.

[Glen Dundas, *Tangled Up in Tapes*, Thunder Bay: SMA Services, 1987; *Tangled Up in Tapes Revisited*, ditto 1990; *Tangled Up in Tapes: The Recordings of Bob Dylan* (3rd ed.; hardback), ditto, 1994; *Tangled Up in Tapes: A Recording History of Bob Dylan* (4th ed.) ditto, 1999; *Tangled: A Recording History of Bob Dylan*, ditto, 2004; 'Walk the Line', *The Bridge* no.4, Gateshead, UK, winter 1999.]

Dunn, Tim [1952 -] Timothy Dunn was born in Painesville, Ohio, on July 31, 1952. He first took an interest in Dylan's work in 1971, co-edited the fanzine *Look Back* from 1987 to 1992, was a contributing editor and staff researcher for fanzine *ON THE TRACKS* 1993–2004 and is a regular contributor to ALAN FRASER's extraordinary website 'Searching for a Gem'. His book *'I Just Write 'Em as*

They Come': An Annotated Guide to the Writings of Bob Dylan was published in 1990; in 1996 came *The Bob Dylan Copyright Files*, in 1998 *The Dylandex 1962–1997: An Index to Authorized and Unauthorized Bob Dylan Songbooks, Lyrics Collections & Sheet Music (And a Little More)* and in 2000 *The Bob Dylan Copyright Files Supplement 1*. In 2006 the books on Dylan copyrights were superceded by the much expanded *The Bob Dylan Copyright Files 1962–2005*.

The first of these attempted to log every known item of Dylan writing (song or not), including rumoured works, through to 1989, with lists of official releases, recording and publication dates and annotations. The second book, and the supplement, reproduced relevant US copyright registrations from the US Copyright Office *Catalog of Copyright Entries* and online database. *The Dylandex 1962–1997* has a self-explanatory sub-title, but it also covered *Broadside, Sing Out!* and other publications that included otherwise exclusive Dylan writings. The 2006 edition of the copyrights book broadens out to include annotations and a far wider variety of copyright registrations, such as for versions of Dylan songs on which he guests with other artists, songs by other people derived from Dylan songs and his *Broadside* magazine songs (copyrighted by publication rather than registration), with a chronology of initial copyrights and a composers index. Not everyone's idea of fun.

In his other life, Tim Dunn gained a Master of Library Science degree at Kent State University in 1976 (six years after 29 members of the US National Guard fired into a crowd of unarmed student protesters there, killing four and injuring others). He has worked for the Geauga County Public Library in Chardon, Ohio, since 1977 and is its current Head of Cataloging.

[Tim Dunn, all books, Grand Junction, CO: Rolling Tomes / Not-A-CES, except *The Bob Dylan Copyright Files 1962–2005*, Concord, OH: Not-A-CES, 2006.]

***Dylan* [album, 1973]** Unlucky 13th album—though it barely counts, since Dylan didn't intend its compilation or release. Essentially a malicious record company response to Dylan's signing with a new label, Asylum, in the US—a deliberate release of the worst tracks they could find in their vaults without going to the trouble of looking very far back: Dylan warming up before recording other things; Dylan messing about; outtakes largely from the *New Morning* sessions; and all compounded by a mix that brought the back-up vocals horrendously far forward. Two ironies: despite all this malice aforethought, the album isn't as bad as they meant it to be; and Dylan subsequently returned to Columbia/CBS because of Asylum's less effective sales-distribution system, not because of this shoddy bully-boy tactic of a release. Best tracks: 'Can't Help Falling in Love' (simultaneously witty and touching), 'Mr. Bojangles' and 'A Fool Such as I'.

[Recorded Nashville, TN, 24 & 26 Apr 1969 and NY, 1–4 Jun 1970; released as Columbia PC 32747 (CBS 69049 in UK), 16 Nov 1973. (Never CD-issued in US or UK, CD versions were released Japan 1990 & Europe 1991.)]

***Dylan & the Dead* [1989]** Yet another live album, in this case recordings from 1987 that you'd assume set out to humiliate Bob Dylan and prove how awful such joint concerts were: but in fact Dylan was given all the tapes and made these choices himself. He can't remember the words to any of the songs, the vocal sound is miserable and THE GRATEFUL DEAD are lumpenly uninspired. As ever with Dylan's live albums, it would have been possible to compile something distinctive and compelling instead, in this case from tapes that show Dylan and the Dead making sense as a unit blessed with the bounty of each partner's openness to the spontaneity of the moment. Richard Williams wrote of the 'wasted majesty' of this version of 'Queen Jane Approximately'; this was wishful thinking. (Wasted, yes; majesty, no.) Dylan's abject incompetence at groping for the words makes it rather a form of public self-abasement, excruciating and sad to witness. By the time this was released, Dylan was more than seven months into the Never-Ending Tour, and feeling rather better.

[Recorded in concert Foxboro, MA, 4 Jul, Eugene, OR, 19 Jul, Oakland, CA, 24 Jul and Anaheim, CA, 26 Jul 1987; released as Columbia OC 45056 (LP) & CK 45056 (CD), 6 or 9 Feb 1989.]

Dylan, Anna [1967 -] Anna Lea Dylan, only daughter of Bob and SARA DYLAN, was born in Woodstock, New York, on July 11, 1967. JAKOB DYLAN has said in interview that she is 'an artist'; she has chosen to have no public presence in that professional capacity. She is believed to be married and living in Santa Monica, California.

Dylan being 'bored' by his acoustic material 1965–66, the myth of The received wisdom seems to be that Dylan was so bored by the predictability of everything when he played his solo tour of Britain in 1965 that he had to go electric, and then, excited as he was by that, had to suffer the tedium of pushing his way through the acoustic first halves of all those 1965–66 'electric' shows. C. P. LEE's book *Like the Night* not only repeats this line but argues that Dylan's boredom was showing by the time he came to perform 'Mr. Tambourine Man' at Newport the previous year, 1964—offering as aural evidence that Dylan sounds stoned and his harmonica solo is 'lazy'.

Er, hang on a minute. First, the confident assertion that Dylan is stoned at Newport 1964 sits strangely with Lee's later description of Dylan at Manchester '66 as using only an 'almost stoned drawl'. Second, if Dylan is giving the harp on 'Mr. Tambourine Man' at Newport '64 less than his full attention, this is quite clearly because he's so enthralled by, so *unbored* by, the *song*. This performance of it is only two weeks after he recorded the duet version with RAMBLIN' JACK ELLIOTT—when the song is so unfinished that the chorus offers 'and there *ain't* no place I'm goin' to'. Even Bob Dylan hasn't tired of something so new-born, so much a wondrous new level of creation. And actually, you don't need to remember the chronology. You only have to hear the way he sings it back then to know that (stoned or not) he is far from bored.

The same surely seems true of the 1965 performances of which we see and hear such scandalously fleeting moments in *Don't Look Back*. You've only got to listen to them: part of their compelling, entrancing power is the never-known-to-make-a-foolish-move, living-on-instinct deftness of the man-I'm-not-even-25 Bob Dylan, who but rarely needs even to touch a toe down on the highwire he's tracing—but part of the entrancement too is the unremitting compulsion to communicate that fizzes out of every pore, out of each unfaltering syllable. The level of direct and pure communication given off here—just listen to that tape of Newcastle '65. This is not a man suffering from boredom on stage.

It's probably the filmmaker, D.A. PENNEBAKER, who was unengaged by these performances, which is why we're given so shockingly little of them, and so sacrilegiously chopped up, on his otherwise wonderful film. At the time people didn't protest because the off-stage material was and is so gripping, no-one had dared dream of getting such access, such private revelation, and the off-stage Dylan there on film was so stupendously cool and beautiful and, excepting a couple of minor callow moments, so intelligent and *wise*. But really, if anyone else—the BBC, say—had shot footage of Dylan 1965 in performance and only shown little fragments, it would have been trumpeted as proof of their outrageous insensitivity.

Pennebaker says Dylan was bored on stage because Pennebaker wasn't enthralled by it. The myth starts there. Dylan off-stage rivets Pennebaker, and us: not least for the spikiness born of his *off-stage* boredom.

All this could be said at any time—but in 2005 came the bootleg release of a 2-DVD set of outtakes from *Don't Look Back*, yielding the treasure of many complete song performances. Unsurprisingly, this blows away any lingering possibility of claiming that the Dylan captured in these concerts is 'bored' with his acoustic material.

Nor, surely, is Dylan bored with his acoustic set in Britain in May 1966. Those soft and slurred yet ice-clear enunciations, those thrillingly magical harmonica trips through unmapped synapse connections . . . every sound purrs out perfectly from an imperative core of calm and silence. This is not the sound of Bob Dylan being bored. (We know how that sounds: we hear it for at least part of almost every concert of the last twenty years.)

Dylan, Bob, family background of See **Stone/ Edelstein family, the**, and **Zimmerman family, the.**

Dylan in books of quotations General books of quotations sometimes include one or two, rarely more, from Bob Dylan, and they're always 'The answer my friend is blowing in the wind' or 'The times they are a-changin''. They should be offering a plethora of quotes, from 'Are you for sale or just on the shelf?' to 'He bought the American dream but it was all wet'; from 'i accept chaos. i am not sure whether it accepts me' to 'What looks large from a distance, close up ain't never that big' and 'To live outside the law you must be honest'.

In 1945, the Gnostic Gospels, known in Egypt as the Nag Hammadi Codices, were found near the town of Nag Hammadi, near Abydos, centre of the cult of Osiris and other death cults, and associated with Anubis, the jackal-headed god of embalming. These gospels are 4th century Coptic translations of 2nd century Greek originals, except that the Gospel of Thomas might date from about 50 AD, which would make it as old or older than the gospels of Matthew, Mark, Luke and John. The Gospel of Thomas contains 114 sayings of Christ, including some which inspired the early Greek mystics known as the Gnostics. This is one: 'If you bring forth what is within you, what you bring forth will save you. If you do not bring forth what is within you, what is within you will destroy you.'

Bob Dylan is with the Gnostics here: these remarks have always made fundamental sense to him, and he restates them, or builds upon them, in at least two songs from the early 1980s. He shares their assumptions in 'Need a Woman', when he observes that 'Whatever's waiting in the future / Could be what you're runnin' from in the past', and he re-states their message in that line from 'The Groom's Still Waiting at the Altar' in which he refers to '. . . the madness of becoming what one was never meant to be.'

You might also hear Christ's words as the impetus behind a compelling, quiet motto from the contemporaneous 'Angelina'. There are lines of Dylan's that tiptoe into the brain without the warning that obvious brilliance signals: sayings that settle in unobtrusively, and make themselves quietly useful about the place, until you find yourself calling on their services surprisingly often. The lovely last verse of 'Angelina' contains such a saying. To put it in context, you need this much of it: 'In God's truth, tell me what you want and you'll have it of course / Just step into the arena.'

This surely expresses a great truth: that to get what you want, you must be prepared to put the whole of yourself into contesting for it, must fully enter the world in which lies the prize you seek, no matter how the odds are stacked, or how ugly the howling crowd . . . and that it must be a prize you truly want, your choice informed by some self-knowledge. Which is why a decent round-up of Dylan quotations ought to include 'Just step into the arena'. It may be less catchy than 'To live outside the law you must be honest' but it holds as much truth, and one has more occasion to say it.

Dylan interpreters There is a common confusion between critics and interpreters of Dylan. The critic's function is a large and porous topic but 'Dylan interpreter' is a much narrower, clearer term and a far less useful creature, whose mutton-headed aim is to say what Dylan's songs are 'about'. The first 'interpreter' was A. J. WEBERMAN but prurient journalism, especially when Dylan was new and could be presented as a novelty item, also went in for much superficial message-hunting in his songs. It provokes, in the artist, an appropriate defensiveness: '. . . I do know what my songs are about.' 'And what's that?' 'Oh, some are about four minutes, some are about five minutes, and some, believe it or not, are about eleven or twelve.' (Dylan's *Playboy* interview, March 1966.)

He goes on to deplore 'interpreters' overtly nearly 20 years later, complaining on the sleeve-notes to *Biograph*: '"You're a Big Girl Now", well, I read that this was supposed to be about my wife. I wish somebody would ask me first before they go ahead and print stuff like that. I mean it couldn't be about anyone else but my wife, right? Stupid and misleading jerks sometimes these interpreters are . . .'

In fact this instance opens up a more nebulous area, because the 'interpreter' here (the present writer) *was* a critic: one who never mentioned Dylan's wife at all until after Dylan chose to issue the explicitly autobiographical song 'Sara', on *Desire*, and did so in the case of 'You're a Big Girl Now' feeling that if it wasn't about his wife, it ought to have been, because part of the song's sinewy strength is that it speaks to an experience widespread among those of Dylan's generation, who found in the 1970s that much-vaunted theories of principled non-monogamy were a source of anxiety in practice, especially when feminism had emboldened all those ex-Hippie Chicks. All the same, the song is alive independently of the 1970s, and of any other specific social conditions or cultural moment—which rather reiterates the point that 'interpretation' is unwise and militates in favour of reductiveness, as criticism ought not to do.

In the same passage, Dylan goes on to say: '. . . I don't write confessional songs . . . well, actually I did write one once and it wasn't very good—it was a mistake to record it and I regret it . . . back there somewhere on maybe my third or fourth album.' He means 'Ballad in Plain D', on *Another Side of Bob Dylan*.

GREIL MARCUS wrote eloquently on these issues—on reductive interpretations of what works of art are 'about'—back at the end of the 1960s, addressing himself to a 'rock' readership in 'Let the Record Play Itself', *San Francisco Express-Times*, February 11, 1969:

> 'The game is still going on . . . "As I Went Out One Morning", a song in which Tom Paine guest stars, is about a dinner Dylan attended years ago, at which he was presented with the Tom Paine Award by the Emergency Civil Liberties Committee. Dylan, during his acceptance speech, said something about how he might understand how Lee Harvey Oswald felt, and the audience booed. This interpretation makes Dylan a real interesting guy. He waits for years to get a chance to get back at an unfriendly audience, and all Tom Paine means to him is the bad memory of an award dinner. Poor Tom Paine. The fellow who came up with this job [Weberman] has said: "I consider Bob Dylan America's greatest poet." Well, naturally; why should such a mind waste his time on a lesser figure? It's not just that such terms are pointless . . . but is this sort of thing—the Tom Paine Award Dinner Revenge—is this what makes a great poet?
>
> 'Poetry, music, songs, stories, are all part of that realm of creation that deepens our lives and can endow our lives with a special kind of grace, tension, perhaps with beauty and splendor. Meaning has many levels—one might meet the artist himself on one of those levels, find friends on another, reach a fine solitude in the light of another man's creation on yet another level. That kind of power in art might be scary—it might be sure enough to survive interpretation and the enforcement of the particular. . . . Take these lines from "London" by WILLIAM BLAKE: "But most thro' midnight streets I hear / How the youthful Harlot's curse / Blasts the newborn infant's tear / And blights with plagues the Marriage hearse". Now what that "means", it was once explained to me, is that a prostitute got syphilis, gave birth to a deformed child, the father of which also died of the disease. . . . That can all be confirmed by balancing and referring the images in the verse—but is it necessary to grasp that . . . in order to feel the weight and power of Blake's vision of London? Blake's words transcend the situation about which he's writing.'

Likewise, says Marcus, with Dylan: 'One will never "understand" "Just Like a Woman" by proving, logically, that it is about transvestites or Britain (Queen Mary and the fog) even if, by some chance, the song really is "about" such things.'

Dylan himself argues this case neatly at the end of 'Gates of Eden' where he commends his lover for valuing her dreams 'With no attempts to shovel the glimpse / Into the ditch of what each one means.'

Dylan, Jakob [1969 -] Jakob Luke Dylan was born in New York City on December 9, 1969, the youngest child of Bob and SARA DYLAN. He is the child for whom Dylan is supposed to have written the *Planet Waves* song 'Forever Young'. When he was 12, in 1982, Bob took him to a gig by the Clash at the Hollywood Palladium. After attending art school, Jakob formed the band the Wallflowers, singing, playing lead guitar and writing all the songs. The band's début album, *The Wallflowers*, came out quietly in 1992 and though not a great commercial success (it sold 40–45,000 copies at the time: 'failure' is a relative term), it achieved in one fell swoop a complexity of resonance and a musical dignity that make it a remarkably fine rock album. Anyone who has since been captivated by Jakob Dylan's work on the subsequent albums by newer incarnations of the Wallflowers should go back to it. Its lead musician's character is already fully formed here: likeable and straightforward, intelligent and articulate, he's no-one's imitator and far too shrewd to strain for effect. The album cover, however, typified its excess of modesty, stemming from Jakob's determination not to use his father's name too readily: it shows only the lower halves of the musicians and the drummer's dog. Inside, the photo of their faces hides them behind the lettering of the credits. The back cover doesn't even mention their names. You could say that even the band's name suggests undue shyness.

The LA-based Wallflowers left Virgin after that one album, opened tours for the Spin Doctors, Cracker and 10,000 Maniacs, including supporting the Maniacs at Minneapolis' Historic Orpheum Theater, which Bob Dylan had long since owned by this point. Jakob's grandmother, Bob's mother Beatty, came to the concert. Jakob, who spent summers in Minnesota, remembers seeing the musical *Beatlemania* at the theater.

The band signed to a new label and recorded *Bringing Down the Horse* with veteran producer T-BONE BURNETT. (He wasn't called in as a Bob Dylan contact: Jakob sent a demo tape to Burnett and let it jump out of the pile on its own merits.) Issued in May 1996, *Bringing Down the Horse* made a slow start, reached the top 10 the following March and has now sold over six million, helped by its including the tracks 'One Headlight', '6th Avenue Heartache' and 'Three Marlenas', which became hit singles, but also helped by conforming more to the norms of mainstream rock. It's more à la SPRINGSTEEN and less quirkily à la Jakob Dylan than its predecessor, unfortunately.

The albums may have been few and far between but the Wallflowers worked, live, even harder than Jakob's father, playing 275 gigs in 1997 alone. Bob played an unrepresentatively meagre 97 that year, though it was the year of his hospitalisation with a heart infection. After he recovered, he and Jakob shared a bill for the first time, at a private concert for the employees of a Silicon Valley firm, Applied Materials, that November 14 in San Jose.

That year brought a further conjunction, far less welcome. A.J. WEBERMAN turned his attention on the son as well as the father. As *Rolling Stone*'s Gerry Hirshey reported it, having first summarised the Garbologist's hounding of Bob and Sara in Greenwich Village in 1970 when Jakob was a baby: 'And now, like some howling ancestral curse, he has descended, fangs dripping, upon the son. The Scavenger has boasted that he rooted through Jakob's soiled Pampers. And a quarter-century later, he tosses up more alleged flotsam of that infancy, online, offering photo negatives of Bob feeding his baby boy a bottle, pouring venomous supposition into tracts he calls "Analysis of Jakob Dylan's Poetry.'"

The third album, *Breach*, released after another gap in 2000, sold far less well but signalled a step forward in Jakob Dylan's preparedness to write less guardedly—to frisk himself less for untoward autobiographical confession in his lyrics, for contraband Dylanesque turns of phrase. Eventually he came out and said this: 'Every other songwriter in the world has been influenced by my dad. So why should I be any different?' The fourth Wallflowers album was 2002's *Red Letter Days*, and in 2005 came the much-praised *Rebel, Sweetheart*, produced by BRENDAN O'BRIEN. None has sold as well as the multi-platinum second album, but Jakob Dylan knows better than to care about that.

Jakob has often discussed his father in interviews, but never other than with a disarming mix of honesty and discretion. Meanwhile he keeps on keeping on with his own serious-minded but unsolemn, engaging and purposive work. As they say in Cockney soap operas, the boy done good.

[The Wallflowers: *The Wallflowers*, Virgin America CDVUS 54, US, 1992. Gerry Hirshey, 'Jakob's Ladder', *Rolling Stone* no.762, NY, 1997. Quote re being influenced by 'dad' as a songwriter, Nigel Williamson: *The Rough Guide to Bob Dylan*, London: Rough Guides, 2004, p.366. See also the useful website *www.the-wallflowers.net*.]

Dylan, Jesse [1966 -] Jesse Byron Dylan, Bob's eldest son, was born to SARA DYLAN and Bob on January 6, 1966 in New York City. He worked his way up from helping to film pop videos through TV commercials, including for Coca-Cola, Pepsi and MTV, to becoming a film director. He directed, among others, brother JAKOB's first Wallflowers video, 'Ashes to Ashes', Lenny Kravitz's 'It Ain't Over 'til It's Over' and TOM PETTY's 'A Face in the Crowd'. He also devised the album cover concept and photographs for Tom Waits' albums *Bone Machine* (1992) and *Blood Money* (2002).

In 1996 it was reported that he would make his directorial début with a Disney film to be called *The Deedles Down Under*; this didn't happen. Nor did he direct, as announced in 1998, the movie version of the Sega arcade game *The House of the Dead* (which Bob Dylan's office supremo JEFF ROSEN was going to produce). However, Jesse Dylan *was* given 'special thanks' in the credits of *The Matrix Revisited* in 2001, and that year also directed the comedy film *How High*, written by Dustin Abraham and starring rappers Method Man and Redman. In 2003 he directed the brash sex comedy *American Wedding*, written by Adam Herz, the third film in the *American Pie* series.

In 2005 Jesse Dylan directed the critically unacclaimed family comedy about sports, *Kicking & Screaming*, written by Leo Benvenuti & Steve Rudnick (which manages to include the great Robert Duvall), and was co-producer on the Michael Almereyda film *William Eggleston in the Real World*. Jesse Dylan is married to the actor Susan Traylor, whose credits include appearing as Mrs. Brown in Bob Dylan's *Masked and Anonymous*, 2003.

[*How High*, dir. Jersey Films / Native Pictures Productions, US, 2001; *American Wedding*, Universal, US, 2003; *William Eggleston in the Real World*, dir. & written Michael Almereyda, produced Almereyda, Jesse Dylan & Anthony Katagas, Keep Your Head / High Line Productions, US, 2005.]

Dylan Liberation Front See **Weberman, A. J.**

Dylan, Maria [1961 -] See **Himmelman, Maria.**

Dylan, Samuel [1968 -] Samuel Abram (or Abraham) Dylan was born in Woodstock, New York, on July 30, 1968, the second-youngest son of Bob and SARA DYLAN. Bar Mitzvahed in Israel in 1982, he later attended Hampshire College where he met his future wife, fellow student Stacy Hochheiser, and was, perhaps only briefly, a member of the band the Supreme Dicks. As blogger Jack Carneal recalls:

> 'A number of years ago we played some shows in California with a band called the Supreme Dicks. They'd gone to Hampshire College at the height of the 80s hippy revival and said they'd come up with the most obnoxious name possible mostly in order to tweak dorky earnest hippie sensibilities of their liberal Yankee counterparts. One of the Supreme Dicks looked familiar to all of us. . . . the familiar Dick [was] Sam Dylan, son of Bob and Sara . . .'

Hampshire College sat on 800 acres of orchard and farmland in South Amherst, Massachusetts, and admitted its first students in 1970. When Sam Dylan graduated in about 1990, his father arrived on the campus by helicopter. By the time the Supreme Dicks played a session for John Peel on BBC Radio in October 1995 Sam Dylan was no longer in the group, which by this point had already made two albums, *The Unexamined Life* (1993) and *Workingman's Dick* (1994)—though the latter was a compilation of 'archival recordings' from 1987–1989, and therefore may include Sam Dylan. This online review suggests the band's flavour (if the title of the album doesn't already point at one area of homage): 'Intentionally blasé, insomnia-soaked vocals and cryptically nonsensical lyrics intermingle with meandering guitar/rhythm section, stumbling through climaxes and decrescendos with muddled spontaneity and a penchant for subtle tongue-in-cheek absurdity; whereas others would fail miserably in their attempts to create anything of interest by following this treacherous path, this is the territory of the Supreme Dicks, and they comport themselves with aplomb.'

Samuel has been known to attend his father's concerts, as for instance at the Staples Center in Los Angeles in October 1991, when he and JAKOB were together in the audience. According to Jakob, his next-oldest sibling has become a photographer, though he has no online presence in this capacity. His wife Stacy Hochheiser co-edited the Hampshire College student paper *In Black and White*, which she and her two colleagues closed down in November 1986 'due to apathy and workload', but within a year she had become a founding co-editor of its replacement, then unnamed but running as *Name This Paper*, in October 1987. The paper becomes called *Legal Grafitti* and then *The Permanent Press*. One of her co-editors is called, er, Chris Dick.

[Jack Carneal quoted from 'The Lion in the Road', 9 Aug 2005, seen online 11 Nov 2005 at *http://altogether now.blogspot.com*. The Supreme Dicks: *Workingman's Dick*, Freek FRR002, UK, 1996; excerpt online at *www. apexonline.com/freek/catalogue.html*; review seen 12 Nov 2005 at *www.angelfire.com/ca/musicmix/faves/Faves Pre1996.html*.]

Dylan, Sara [1939 -] Shirley Marlin Noznisky was born in the large port of Wilmington, Delaware, on October 28, 1939, the daughter of a scrap-metal dealer shot not 'in a stickup', as alleged by AL ARONOWITZ, but by a drunken fellow Eastern European immigrant with whom he had been friendly and who believed, wrongly, that Isaac Noznisky was responsible for losing him his job. He was shot in the face with a .38 bullet in a neighbourhood sweetshop on the morning of Sunday, November 18, 1956, soon after the two men quarrelled in the street; the bullet severed a main artery to the brain and he died in the Delaware Hospital two days later. He was buried in the Workers Circle section of the Wilmington Jewish Community Cemetery that Thursday, November 22.

Isaac Noznisky had been born around 1894 in Poland (though he sometimes told officials he was from Russia) and had become a US citizen in 1912;

by 1920 he and two brothers, Israel and Charles, were in Chester, Pennsylvania, in the household of his sister and brother-in-law. Isaac was a blacksmith, but brother-in-law Abe was a junk dealer. Around 1924 Isaac married; by 1930 he, wife Bessie and six-year-old son Jules (the only one of the three who could read and write) were sharing another house in Port Chester and working in the mushroom industry. They moved to Wilmington around 1931.

There they set up in business as I. Noznisky & Son, Junk Dealers, at South Claymont Street and Christiana Avenue. Shirley was 16 when her father was killed. Jules continued to run the junk business after their father's death. By the end of the 1950s Bessie, daughter Shirley, Jules and his wife Adele were living on West 38th Street, a block away from their earlier family home. Shirley was a student. Her mother is said to have suffered a stroke many years earlier.

In 1960 Shirley moved to New York City and that same year became the third wife of a little-known magazine photographer, Hans Lownds, who was, reportedly, 25 years older than her (and thus more than twice her age). He persuaded her to change her first name too, declaring: 'I can't be married to a woman named Shirley'. Thus she became Sara Lownds, though the marriage did not last long and soon after daughter Maria was born in October 1961, she was working for the film production company Drew Associates as secretary to its founder, the American cinema verité and camera pioneer Robert Drew, who started the company in 1960. D.A. PENNEBAKER and his associate Richard Leacock were also working for Drew then, before they quit to start their own production company. Pennebaker says of Sara Lownds in this period: 'She was supposed to be a secretary but she ran the place.' Robert Drew says: 'I had a contract with Time Inc.: our office was in the *Time-Life* building, and when I needed a secretary they would send me one. They were devilish about sending me the most attractive young women and Sara Lownds was one of them. We do not have records going back that far but my recollection is that she worked at Drew Associates in 1961 and 1962. I know it couldn't have been '63. I knew nothing about her personal life, but she was extremely gracious and competent.'

By late 1964 she had met Bob Dylan, either while reportedly driving her little MG sports car around Greenwich Village or through her waitress friend Sally Bueler, who in 1964 married ALBERT GROSSMAN. It's been said that they met at this wedding. By the beginning of 1965 Sara was living with her daughter in the Chelsea Hotel; Dylan rented an apartment there in order to court her.

It's sometimes said that Hans Lownds had 'transformed her into a magazine cover girl' but there's no evidence that she was ever a successful model, though the Ford Agency commissioned JERRY SCHATZBERG to take test shots of her and at one stage she was briefly a *Playboy* bunny girl. This, together with Hans Lownds' own low career profile, led many people to put two and two together and make five: to assume that her ex-husband was Victor Lowndes (sic), the prominent *Playboy* executive who was in charge of the serious money of Hugh Hefner's casino operations, owned a London mansion called Stocks and in the 1970s persuaded Playboy Pictures to co-finance the Monty Python film *And Now for Something Completely Different*. Since it was known that Dylan's 'Sad-Eyed Lady of the Lowlands' was 'about' Sara, and that his 'Lowlands' played upon the name 'Lownd(e)s', the assumption was that his marvellously dismissive line 'And your magazine husband, who one day just had to go' was the clincher for this pairing.

In recent times it's been said that this merely got Victor Lowndes scratching his head and trying to recall which of his many bunnies people were linking him with; in fact he was so unamused that when ROBERT SHELTON made the mistake of linking Sara with Victor Lowndes in early drafts of his biography *No Direction Home*, Lowndes threatened to sue and Shelton had to eliminate the suggestion from his text.

Of course, 'your magazine husband' equally well fitted Hans Lownds, while one of the strengths of the line, taking it beyond mere sneering, is the lovely ambiguity of whether he 'one day just had to go' at his own behest or at hers. In the particular case, that isn't our business; and for the great majority of listeners, for whom the personal subtexts are meaningless and don't interfere, that ambiguity is part of the innate mystery of the song. Which doesn't stop the subtext being interesting: and the Nozniskys' junk-dealer background certainly adds an extra layer of resonance to the mysterious evocativeness of the song's previous line—'with your sheet-metal memory of Cannery Row'. Your ears are also likely to hear anew that innocuous line in 'From a Buick 6' that introduces his 'soulful mama' like this: 'She's a junkyard angel . . .'

Bob Dylan married Sara Lownds in a private ceremony in Mineola, Long Island, on November 22, 1965, either in the judge's chambers or outside under an oak tree, depending who you believe. (Outdoors on the East Coast in late November?) Dylan adopted Sara's daughter Maria, who grew up to marry singer-songwriter PETER HIMMELMAN. Sara and Bob Dylan had four children, JESSE Byron Abram, ANNA, SAMUEL and JAKOB, all born between 1966 and 1971.

Jakob has referred to the painful experience of hearing the *Blood on the Tracks* album: 'When I'm listening to "Subterranean Homesick Blues", I'm grooving along just like you. But when I'm listening to *Blood on the Tracks*, that's about my parents.' But he has also paid tribute to the upbringing both parents gave him, though he lived mostly with his mother. He said in 2005: 'My father said it himself in an interview many years ago: "Husband and wife failed, but mother and father didn't." I've got a life that really matters to me, and that's because of the way I was raised. My ethics are high because my parents did a great job.'

The parents' separation was indeed a main theme of *Blood on the Tracks*, but in 1975 they reconciled, after Sara Dylan, back from a holiday in Mexico, turned up for the very last summer session-day at the studios where Dylan was recording the next album of new material, *Desire*. JACQUES LEVY told HOWARD SOUNES that as she stood there in the control booth, he sang what would turn out to be the album's final song, 'Sara'. This song not only broke precedent by its outright personal naming, but enfolds the autobiographical-sounding claim of recalling 'staying up for days in the Chelsea Hotel / Writing "Sad-Eyed Lady of the Lowlands" for you', alludes to past family holidays and ends, plainly enough, by asking: 'Don't ever leave me, don't ever go.' Levy said: 'You could have heard a pin drop. She was absolutely stunned by it. And I think it was a turning point. . . . The two of them really did get back together.'

They were together that fall for the Rolling Thunder Revue tour and therefore the making of *Renaldo & Clara*, in which Sara features prominently, taking part in many of the improvised acting scenes, including the sequence where, coming up from under ALLEN GINSBERG's recitation from 'Kaddish', Dylan's funky piano-pounding audio track of 'She Belongs to Me' accompanies the prolonged footage of Sara walking rainy city streets.

It was a year on from this filming—in late 1976—before the Dylans moved into the Malibu house they'd been building, with its famous copper onion-dome roof; Sara filed for divorce mere months later, on March 1, 1977. She gained temporary custody of the children, hired Marvin M. Mitchelson to fight her cause, won custody, and in the June 29, 1977 divorce settlement gained an unspecified sum of money. Robert Shelton speculated in the 1980s that it may have been as much as $10 million. According to Ed Caesar in the *Independent* 20 years later, it was a great deal more than that: 'Lownds won $36m from the settlement, as well as half the royalties from songs Dylan had written during their marriage.' A condition of the settlement was that Sara would remain silent about her life with Dylan. She has done so.

Sara's mother had died many years earlier; her brother Jules died in 1990, and his wife Adele in June 1998.

Of course, Dylan fans still picture Sara as she was in *Renaldo & Clara*, because they haven't seen her since. But she'll be 70 years old in three years' time.

[Noznisky research by this writer & Sarah Beattie incl. 1920 & 1930 Census pages; Wilmington, DE, City Directories for 1955, 1959 & 1961; *Wilmington Morning News*, 19 Nov 1956, pp.1 & 2, 21 Nov, pp.1 & 5, 22 Nov p.19; *Journal Every Evening*, Wilmington, 19 Nov 1956, pp.1 & 6, 20 Nov, p.24, 21 Nov, pp.1 &4; *Sunday News Journal*, Wilmington, 7 Jun 1998, Sectn B4; special thanks to Rhonda Allende at Wilmington Public Library. Hans Lownds quote from Wikipedia, seen online 10 Nov 2005 at *http://en.wikipedia.org/wiki/Sara_Lownds*; quotes from Aronowitz & Pennebaker from Andy Gill & Kevin Odegard, *A Simple Twist of Fate: Bob Dylan and the Making of* Blood on the Tracks, New York: Da Capo, 2004, Ch.1. Robert Drew quoted from phone call with & e-mail to this writer, 17 Nov 2005. Jerry Schatzberg info e-mail to this writer 26 Dec 2005. *And Now for Something Completely Different*, dir. Ian MacNaughton, UK, 1971. Jakob Dylan quoted from Anthony de Curtis interview, *New York Times*, 10 May 2005. Jacques Levy quote in Howard Sounes, *Down the Highway*, New York: Grove Press, 2001; Sounes also first pioneered Noznisky background research. Ed Caesar, *Independent*, London, 23 Sep 2005.]

Sara Dylan

Photo by John Byrne Cooke

Ramblin' Jack Elliott at Club 47, Cambridge, Massachusetts, July 1963

Photography by Sherry Rayn Barnett

Mimi Fariña

Photo courtesy of Smokey Smith

Lefty Frizzell (centre) with Smokey Smith and Moon Mullican, KRNT, Des Moines, Iowa

Original cover of Robert Graves' *The White Goddes*, 1948

Photo courtesy of Lester Flatt & Earl Scruggs

Flatt & Scruggs

E

earliest blues & gospel recordings, Dylan's These are the earliest known recorded blues and gospel performances by Bob Dylan. Some songs in his very early repertoire are hard to categorise; but at the very least we can count the following:

St. Paul, Minnesota, May 1960: 'Delia' and 'Blue Yodel No. 8 [Muleskinner Blues]'. Minneapolis, August 1960: 'K.C. Moan'.

Minneapolis, May 1961: 'Death Don't Have No Mercy', 'Still a Fool', 'James Alley Blues'. Gerde's Folk City, NY, September 1961: 'Ain't No More Cane'.

NY, November 4, 1961: 'In the Pines', 'Gospel Plow', 'Back-water Blues', 'Fixin' to Die'. NY, November 20, 1961: 'Baby Let Me Follow You Down', 'In My Time of Dyin''. NY, November 32, 1961: 'See That My Grave Is Kept Clean', 'Highway 51'. NY, November 23, 1961: 'Worried Blues'.

Minneapolis, December 22, 1961: 'Baby Please Don't Go', 'Candy Man', 'Stealin', 'Dink's Song', 'Wade in the Water', 'In the Evening' and 'Cocaine'.

Where had these songs come from? 'Delia' was traditional, and a repertoire item of BLIND WILLIE McTELL (to be revisited by Dylan over 30 years later on his 1993 folk and blues album *World Gone Wrong*). 'Blue Yodel No.8' was a JIMMIE RODGERS song. 'K.C. Moan' by the MEMPHIS JUG BAND, from 1929, was one of the tracks on HARRY SMITH's seminal *AMERICAN FOLK MUSIC* anthology.

'Death Don't Have No Mercy' and 'Cocaine' were both from the REV. GARY DAVIS (aka Blind Gary Davis); 'Still a Fool' was from MUDDY WATERS; 'James Alley Blues', by RICHARD RABBIT BROWN, from 1927, was another *American Folk Music* track; 'Ain't No More Cane' and 'In the Pines' had been popularised by LEADBELLY (though the former title was also well-known in folkie circles by ALAN LOMAX himself: it was one of the tracks on his 1958 LP *Texas Folk Songs*). 'Gospel Plow' was rewritten by Dylan from a traditional song. 'Back-Water Blues' came from Bessie Smith, and 'Fixin' to Die' from BUKKA WHITE. 'Baby Let Me Follow You Down' has been claimed by many; see separate entry. The sleevenotes to Dylan's début album say that he had never performed 'In My Time of Dyin'' before he recorded it, and couldn't remember where he'd got it but in fact it was based on BLIND WILLIE JOHNSON's 'Jesus Make Up My Dying Bed' [Dallas, December 3, 1927]. (It's quite similar to 'Fixin' to Die'.) 'See That My Grave Is Kept Clean' comes from BLIND LEMON JEFFERSON, and had been collected on the *American Folk Music* anthology. 'Highway 51 Blues' came from CURTIS JONES, and 'Worried Blues', created from common-stock phrases, seems to have been assembled by Hally Wood, a white transcriber and annotator of folksong recorded by Alan Lomax.

'Baby Please Don't Go' was a 1935 hit by BIG JOE WILLIAMS that turned into a classic blues repertoire item. 'Candy Man' was such an item too, but unattributable to anyone in particular. The Memphis Jug Band had recorded 'Stealin', Stealin'' in the 1920s; 'Dink's Song' and 'Wade in the Water' were traditional, and 'In the Evening' (aka 'When the Sun Goes Down') was from Leroy Carr, perhaps via SONNY TERRY & BROWNIE McGHEE.

Two of these songs Dylan had picked up from what was, after Harry Smith's anthology, the next crucial vinyl issue of previously hard-to-obtain pre-war blues material, the 1959 LP *The Country Blues*, issued to accompany SAM CHARTERS' pioneering book of the same name—the book that spurred so many people to go down south, winkling out old blues singers from their anonymous penury and presenting them in northern coffee-houses.

This LP featured the Memphis Jug Band's 'Stealin', Stealin'', which Dylan sang onto the same 1961 tape as his own 'I Was Young When I Left home', and Bukka White's 'Fixin' to Die Blues', which Dylan put on his début album.

One way and another then (and see also **pre-war blues, Dylan's ways of accessing**), by the end of 1961, Dylan knew enough pre-war blues and gospel that he could confidently perform and record almost 25 such repertoire pieces, and this while also going through his GUTHRIE-fixation period.

[Blind Willie McTell: 'Delia', Atlanta, 5 Nov 1940. Jimmie Rodgers: 'Blue Yodel No. 8, Hollywood, CA, 11 Jul 1930. Memphis Jug Band: 'K.C. Moan', Memphis, 4 Oct 1929 & 'Stealin', Stealin'', Memphis, 15 Sep 1928. Rev. Gary Davis: 'Death Don't Have No Mercy', Englewood Cliffs, NJ, 24 Aug 1960 & later re-recordings, & 'Cocaine Blues', *nia* but mid-1960s. Muddy Waters: 'Still a Fool', Chicago, 11 Jul 1951, Chess 1480, Chicago, 1951. Richard Rabbit Brown: 'James Alley Blues', New Orleans, 11 Mar 1927. Bessie Smith: 'Back-Water Blues', NY, 17 Feb 1927. Bukka White: 'Fixin' to Die Blues', Chicago, 8 Mar 1940. Blind Willie Johnson: 'Jesus Make Up My Dying Bed', Dallas, 3 Dec 1927. Blind Lemon Jefferson: 'See That My Grave Is Kept Clean', Chicago, c.Feb 1928. Curtis Jones: 'Highway 51 Blues', Chicago, 25 Jan 1938. Big Joe Williams: 'Baby Please Don't Go', Chicago, 31 Oct 1935. Leroy Carr: 'When the Sun Goes Down', Chicago, 25 Feb 1935.]

earliest extant recordings, Dylan's It's an odd process, but as we have travelled further and further away from the 1950s, earlier and earlier recordings made by Bob Dylan in that decade have emerged, surprising us with their existence.

The first pre-1961 item to emerge—in 1978—was a fall 1960 tape of 11 songs, supposedly recorded at Dylan's Minneapolis apartment, which was partly of WOODY GUTHRIE songs but also included the Dylan-written 'Talking Hugh Brown' (Brown being a friend of his). The tape circulated but never created much excitement. In 2005 one track—now called 'Rambler, Gambler' though previously known as 'I'm a Gambler'—was issued on the *Bootleg Series Vol. 7—No Direction Home: the Soundtrack*; but the film itself contained not only a fragment of this song but fleeting moments too of 'Streets of Glory', described in the screen credits as 'Traditional, Arranged and Performed by Bob Dylan', and of a version of the MEMPHIS JUG BAND's 'K.C. Moan' from this tape, and the tape's enticing, very funny aural glimpse of Dylan's tremendous Irish accent on 'Johnny I Hardly Knew You'; all were credited as 'Courtesy of Cleve Pettersen and the Minnesota Historical Society,' and the tape was dated more specifically as from August 1960, and to have been recorded at the University of Minnesota in Minneapolis by Cleve Petterson, on a new tape-recorder. He is said to have recorded 'a dozen' songs, but this may still be an approximate description, rather than suggesting that there is a track never previously known about or circulated.

Next, and this emerged later in 1978, was a 27-song, 36-minute recording made even earlier, at the apartment of a Karen Wallace in St. Paul, Minnesota, in May 1960, featuring a sweet-voiced young Dylan (a comparison has often been made to the *Nashville Skyline* voice). But its authenticity remained in doubt for some time so far as a number of discographers were concerned. MICHAEL KROGSGAARD did not include it in the 1988 edition of his listings *Master of the Tracks: The Bob Dylan Reference Book*, and in GLEN DUNDAS' 1990 *Tangled Up in Tapes Revisited* 'doubt as to the authenticity of this tape' was mentioned. Only in the 1990s, then, were all the main specialists in Dylan recordings information convinced that it was genuine.

The power of television was illustrated in 1993 when a BBC-TV documentary team visited Minnesota and were offered something that not even ROBERT SHELTON's assiduous and privileged researches in the North Country had managed to discover—a tape made at Dylan's own boyhood home in 1958 (long before he was Bob Dylan) with one of Shelton's interviewees, Dylan's 'best buddy', John Bucklen.

This features Bob Zimmerman the rock'n'roller, playing piano and guitar and singing snatches of five songs (with some shared vocals by Bucklen) interspersed with conversation between the two. The songs are 'Little Richard' (composed by Dylan), 'Buzz Buzz Buzz' (a hit for the Hollywood Flames in late 1957 to early 1958), 'Jenny, Jenny' (a LITTLE RICHARD song), 'We Belong Together' (a minor chart hit in March that year for an adenoidal black harmony duo from the Bronx called Robert & Johnny, i.e. Robert Carr and Johnny Mitchell) and the unknown 'Betty Lou' (sometimes listed wrongly as 'Blue Moon'). Four were first heard, though incompletely, on BBC-TV's excellent 'Highway 61 Revisited', first broadcast in the UK on May 8, 1993.

Later still—indeed not until the 21st century had arrived—did we find that there was an even earlier extant recording of Bob Dylan, made in a custom recording facility in the Terlinde Music Shop in St. Paul, Minnesota, on Christmas Eve, *1956!* He and two friends from summer camp, LARRY KEGAN and HOWARD RUTMAN, are all aged 15; Dylan is on piano and shares vocals with the others as they race through incomplete versions of eight songs in little more than nine minutes.

The songs are: 'Let the Good Times Roll' (an R&B million-selling instant classic that year by Shirley & Lee: a record that's been giving pleasure ever since), 'Boppin' the Blues' (a small hit by CARL PERKINS, also 1956), an unidentified song with almost no lyric beyond the phrase 'Won't you be my girl?', 'Lawdy Miss Clawdy' (Lloyd Price's first record and first hit, and one of the earliest black R&B records to cross over into the white markets and so to help shape rock'n'roll), 'Ready Teddy' (a 1956 Little Richard hit), 'Confidential' (a hit by Sonny Knight—a song Dylan would revisit on the Basement Tapes in 1967, live in Helsinki on May 30, 1989 and in the first two of his unusual four-set gig at Toad's Place, New Haven, CT, on January 12, 1990), 'In the Still of the Night' (an R&B ballad by the Five Satins, also a hit the first time around in 1956, and often named as one of the most beautiful such records ever made) and 'Earth Angel' (a 2-million-seller by the Penguins from 1954). Clearly, one of Dylan's main musical enthusiasms at the time was for black doo-wop.

In June 1986, with TOM PETTY & THE HEARTBREAKERS, the night after he'd played Minneapolis, he performed 'Let the Good Times Roll' in East Troy, Wisconsin, introducing it thus: 'This is pretty old. I used to play this when I was twelve years old. And . . . this is a song that got me booed off my first stages. . . . It was a different band, but it sort of went the same way.'

Most recently, one further tape has emerged: a four-song tape stated to be from May 1959, recorded by another friend from Hibbing, RIC KANGAS, who appears in the film *No Direction Home* showing us the tape-recorder on which 'Bob Zimmerman', as he calls him, wanted to know how he sounded. One track mentioned and excerpted on the film, 'When I Got Troubles', is released complete on the *Bootleg Series Vol. 7—No Direction Home: the Soundtrack*, and the notes suggest that it is 'most likely the first original song recorded by Bob Dylan'—though this can't be true, granted that the *No Direction Home* film's credits claim/confirm that

'Little Richard', on the 1958 John Bucklen tape, was also composed by Dylan.

In any case, 'When I Got Troubles' is one of four songs on the Ric Kangas tape, the others being Kangas performing 'I Wish I Knew' with back-up by Dylan, plus Dylan performing 'Teen Love Serenade', aka 'I Got a New Girl', and 'The Frog Song', described as having a Clarence 'Frogman' Henry style vocal (meaning of the croaking voice on his first minor hit, the novelty song 'Ain't Got No Home' from 1956). A little bit of 'Teen Love Serenade' is also played on the film soundtrack, but—a neat juxtapositioning—underneath Dylan talking about his early girlfriends. On October 1, 2005, Ric Kangas put the original reel of tape containing these recordings up for sale on eBay with a starting price of $1.5 million. The auction ended with no bids.

(See also **earliest blues & gospel recordings, Dylan's.**)

[Dylan quote re John Bucklen, in Shelton, *No Direction Home: The Life and Music of Bob Dylan*, 1986, p.16. Hollywood Flames: 'Buzz Buzz Buzz', LA, 1957, Ebb 119, LA, 1957; CD-reissued *Buzz Buzz Buzz*, Specialty SPC-2166-4, *nia*. Robert & Johnny: 'We Belong Together', *nia*, Old Town Records, 1958; CD-reissued *The Very Best of Robert & Johnny: We Belong Together*, Collectable COL 6068, US, 2000 and *Robert & Johnny—We Belong Together*, Ace CDCHD384, UK, 2004. Shirley & Lee: 'Let the Good Times Roll', New Orleans, May 1956, Aladdin 45-3325, LA, 1956. Carl Perkins: 'Boppin' the Blues', Memphis, 1956, Sun 243, Memphis, 1956. Sonny Knight: 'Confidential', CD-reissued *The Golden Age of American Rock 'n' Roll Volume 7*, *nia*. The Five Satins: 'In the Still of the Night', New Haven, CT, 1956, Standard (& then Ember), US, 1956. The Penguins: 'Earth Angel', LA, Sep 1954, DooTone 348, LA, 1954. Clarence 'Frogman' Henry: 'Ain't Got No Home', New Orleans, Sep 1956, Argo 5259, Chicago, 1956.

Bob Dylan, Tom Petty & the Heartbreakers: 'Let the Good Times Roll', East Troy, WI, 27 Jun 1986.]

'Early Morning Rain' Song by the Canadian singer-songwriter GORDON LIGHTFOOT, which Dylan recorded for *Self Portrait*, on which it appeared as if it were one of the many oldies on that collection. But 'Early Morning Rain' was barely an oldie: its composer was 'discovered' by fellow-Canadian folkies IAN & SYLVIA, who had a near-hit single with the title track of their LP *Early Morning Rain* in 1965. It was then cut by JUDY COLLINS for her *5th Album*, also 1965. Lightfoot signed to United Artists that year (his first US public appearance was at the 1965 Newport Folk Festival) and included 'Early Morning Rain' on his LP *Lightfoot*, 1966.

Bob Dylan performed 'Early Morning Rain' at four concerts in 1989, two in 1990 and two in 1991, including a glorious version at South Bend, Indiana, November 6, 1991, on which the band keeps up a distinctive circular rolling beat and Dylan marries its spiky, garage-band compulsion to a delicately expressive vocal.

[Ian & Sylvia: 'Early Morning Rain', *nia*, also issued on *Early Morning Rain*, Vanguard VSD-79175, NY, 1965. Judy Collins: 'Early Morning Rain', NY, *nia*, issued *5th Album*, Elektra EKS 7300, NY, 1965. Gordon Lightfoot: 'Early Morning Rain', *nia*, on *Lightfoot*, United Artists, *nia*, Hollywood (UAS 6487, London), 1966.]

***Eat the Document* [film, 1971]** This was the film made by D.A. PENNEBAKER under Dylan's direction during his unsurpassable tour of Britain in May 1966, when he brought over the band for the first time. He turned 25 while he was there. It was a very different film from the previous year's black and white documentary, also filmed by Pennebaker. Then, the latter had been the auteur director; now he was Dylan's hired hand. HOWARD ALK was filming too, and the whole thing was supposed to be for an ABC-TV Special, for which Dylan had been paid up front. As with *Renaldo & Clara* a decade later, Dylan wasn't very interested in the concert footage, or even in what was going on in real life in between; he was mostly interested in set-up scenes full of visual jokes and surreal happenings, filmed in hotel rooms and the like, as in the shaky sequence of people pouring out of a wardrobe.

A burdensome amount of time is also spent with Dylan and ROBBIE ROBERTSON walking around sniggering at the unhipness of everyone they encounter. Robertson fulfils the same rôle here as BOB NEUWIRTH fulfilled in *Don't Look Back* the year before; he's the sidekick, the Robin to Dylan's Batman. One of the sequences used only very fleetingly indeed, but shot at length, shows Dylan and JOHN LENNON riding in the back of a limo, with Dylan so stoned that he's about to throw up and Lennon, nervous as a racehorse and compensating for his nerves and the moment's futility by keeping up a frenetic overly perky commentary. This largely omitted scene was transcribed and its dialogue first published by JOHN BAULDIE in the first issue of the British music magazine *Mojo* in 1993.

When it came to editing the film, Dylan struggled to make headway alone at first, but when he found that there was a great swathe of undeveloped footage shot by Alk in the middle of it all, he got Alk to come and help him edit it. They had no chance of finishing in time for the TV schedule, and in any case no chance of satisfying the TV executives with what they had to offer. Jones Alk remembers a screening of some hastily assembled early version of the film for the TV suits, at which she and ALBERT GROSSMAN's wife Sally had to go and sit in the screening theatre with the executives while Howard Alk and Dylan hid away in the projection room. No-one was happy and the film, though still shaped for television, has rarely been seen except in bootleg circulation in dire quality. (The bootleg DVD appeared in 2003, and included the Lennon-Dylan sequence.)

Despite the tiresome staged scenes and the excess of stoned hippie scenes, the film offers, of course, marvellous fragments of heart-stoppingly great performance footage, some backstage music too, and a now-incongruous glimpse back at the Dickensian Britain that Dylan, the original spider from Mars, had descended upon. There are also excellent examples, here, of Alk's flair as an editor, particularly in the way that he juxtaposes music and specific lines of lyric with conversation and images pulled from elsewhere, not least—and Alk's instinct for letting the disenfranchised speak plays to advantage here—when the blazing glory of the electric music is intercut with the vox-pop verdicts of young concert-goers who are passionately for and against this new Dylan.

D.A. Pennebaker is said to be planning to issue his own version of his own footage, to be titled *Something Is Happening*; but it isn't happening yet.

Eat the Document was premiéred at the New York Academy of Music and the Whitney Museum of American Art in 1971 and remains, another 35 years later, rarely seen in its own right. But if it can be regarded as in some ways a trial run for *Renaldo & Clara* (see entry **Alk, Howard** for more on this, and on the editing of the film), and as a film that didn't work, it must also be recognised as providing much of the best and most crucial archive footage in a film that does work, and has been very widely seen, MARTIN SCORSESE's *No Direction Home*.

Naturally, Bob Dylan's 2004 memoir *Chronicles Volume One* makes no mention of *Eat the Document*, *Don't Look Back*, *Renaldo & Clara*, Pennebaker or the Alks.

[Source for Pennebaker's changed status, his own interview given to Shelley Livson, NY, spring 1984, collected as '1966 and All That: D.A. Pennebaker, Filmmaker' in Michael Gray & John Bauldie, eds., *All Across The Telegraph: The Bob Dylan Handbook*, London: W.H. Allen, 1987. Further information from Jones Cullinan (then Jones Alk), phone call with this writer 1 Nov 2005.]

Ecclesiastes, Dylan's use of The Old Testament Book of Ecclesiastes is famously the one book in the Bible which gives space and a sympathetic airing to doubt. Ecclesiastes alone accommodates the idea of doubt not as a sin marking out the wicked and shameful, but as a problem that is bound to visit, probably recurrently, those of good will and a reflective temperament. It offers a forum for our inevitable feelings about the brevity of human life, and about whether, being so brief, it isn't also meaningless. This is where 'vanity of vanities; all is vanity' comes from (Ecclesiastes 1:2): 'Vanity of vanities, saith the Preacher, vanity of vanities; all is vanity.' This becomes the basis of what is almost an incantation, a repeated theme, as here (1:14): 'I have seen all the works that are done under the sun; and behold, all is vanity and vexation of spirit.'

'The Preacher' meditates aloud about exactly the kinds of contradiction and injustice in life that cause us to doubt either God's existence or his kindliness, and perhaps to lose hope for the future. As the *Good News Bible* notes: 'the fact that this book is in the Bible shows that biblical faith is broad enough to take into account such pessimism and doubt. Many have taken comfort in seeing themselves in the mirror of Ecclesiastes . . .'

When Dylan opens his great song 'Jokerman' (see separate entry) with a highly compressed, adroit balancing of allusions to both Christ's espousal of the power of *faith* and, by quotation, to Ecclesiastes' recognition of the legitimacy of *doubt*, he is exploring the themes of this book for by no means the first time. One of its themes is the difficult question of whether it is better to be alive, enduring and aware of the inevitable pain of the human lot, or to be dead and feeling nothing (the Preacher first looks at the question with pessimism, and later more hopefully): and Dylan addresses this dilemma in 1965's sleevenotes to *Bringing It All Back Home* and then with an explicit nod at the text of Ecclesiastes in a song contemporary with 'Jokerman', 1983's 'Tell Me', recorded at the *Infidels* sessions but released only on the 1991 box set *Bootleg Series Vols. 1–3*.

In the first he writes that it is better to be a live nobody than a dead hero: '. . . i would not want / t' be bach. mozart. tolstoy. joe hill. gertrude / stein or james dean / they are all dead'; but in the second he simply poses the question to the song's addressee: 'Which means more to you, a live dog or a dead lion?' This is a direct allusion to Ecclesiastes 9:4, a part of the text in which optimism prevails and the Preacher decides the issue the same way Dylan decided it back in 1965 when he wrote those sleevenotes: 'For to him that is joined to all the living there is hope: for a living dog is better than a dead lion.'

In 1965's 'It's Alright Ma (I'm Only Bleeding)' Dylan refers to two more of the main themes explored in Ecclesiastes—the hopeless limits of our understanding: 'To understand you know too soon / There is no sense in trying'; and the always-unsatisfying way that the foolish and the wise so often get the same deal: 'Although the masters make the rules / For the wise men and the fools / I got nothing, Ma, to live up to.'

This compares directly with Ecclesiastes 2:15–16: '. . . As it happeneth to the fool so it happeneth even to me; and why was I then more wise? Then I said in my heart, that this also is vanity. For there is no remembrance of the wise more than of the fool for ever; seeing that which now is in the days to come shall all be forgotten. And how dieth the wise man? as the fool.'

In 1967's 'Tears of Rage', Dylan echoes what is almost the first preoccupation of Ecclesiastes, the shortness of the human lifespan and the impossibility of leaving anything that lasts (though this is not to suggest that one *needs* Ecclesiastes to prompt this line of thought): '. . . you know we're so alone / And life is brief', while in the contemporaneous Basement Tapes song 'Too Much of Nothing' (a title that in itself summarises the gloomy end of the Ecclesiastes meditative spectrum) Dylan worries away at other parts of the Preacher's text. The song's opaque second verse seems to follow a line of thought prompted by the beginning of Ecclesiastes 8, which advises people to be circumspect and at least appear obedient in front of a king, to be safe: and goes on immediately to the thought that no-one knows anything about anything much, and certainly not about when they will die. Here is Ecclesiastes 8:2 & 5–9 in the ploddingly unmemorable *Good News* version: 'Do what the king says. . . . As long as you obey his commands, you are safe, and a wise man knows how and when to do it. There is a right time and a right way to do everything, but we know so little! None of us knows what is going to happen, and there is no one to tell us. No one can keep himself from dying or put off the day of his death . . .'

Dylan's meditation boils this down to 'Too much of nothing / Can make a man abuse a king. / He can walk the streets and boast like most / But he wouldn't know a thing.' ('Curse not the king . . .', as Ecclesiastes says again in 10:20)—after which Dylan adds at once, echoing Ecclesiastes far more plainly: 'Now, it's all been done before, / It's all been written in the book.'

This again is a main theme of Ecclesiastes, connecting with the idea of life's brevity and the impossibility of leaving anything behind. It's all been done before and it all disappears. Everything will be forgotten: so much so that we forget that everything in our own times has been around before, time and again. 'There is no remembrance of former things; neither shall there be any remembrance of things that are to come with those that shall come after' (1:11).

Dylan's 'Now, it's all been done before, / It's all been written in the book' is in one way an awkward fit here, of course: especially since there's a close parallel with what he offers immediately after '. . . i would not want / t' be bach. mozart. tolstoy. joe hill. gertrude / stein or james dean / they are all dead' in those *Bringing It All Back Home* sleevenotes, which is: 'the / Great books've been written. the Great sayings / have all been said.' The noticeable similarity of these passages suggests that 'It's all been written in the book' means that what has gone before gets preserved, whereas the point argued in Ecclesiastes is that everything's been done before and never gets remembered. It's all been written in the book of human history but nobody reads the book; no-one even remembers that if they did read the book they'd find that 'it's all been done before'. Nonetheless, Dylan continues to nudge the Ecclesiastes text around.

And, that text encourages us to ask, if the individual's life is so short, and what s/he tries to leave behind must sink without trace, then what can be the point? A key part of this is famously summarised in the first chapter (1:9): 'The thing that hath been, it is that which shall be; and that which is done is that which shall be done: and there is no new thing under the sun.'

In his Christian evangelical period, Dylan returns to these themes, usually drawing on more positive ways of looking at them—as does Ecclesiastes, in spite of all the doubts, in the course of its meditation—or else with every appearance of relishing the gloom they might induce. Hence we find 'That which hath been is now; and that which is to be hath already been' (3:15) transferred almost verbatim into the second of these lines from 'Pressing On', from the *Saved* album of 1980: 'What kind of sign they need when it all come from within, / When what's lost has been found, what's to come has already been?'; and in 'Ain't No Man Righteous, No Not One' the similarly near-verbatim 'God got the power, man has got his vanity . . . / Don't you know there's nothing new under the sun? / Well, there ain't no man righteous, no not one' while another song contemporaneous with 'Jokerman' (and 'Tell Me'), the rather less approachable 'I and I', manages to snatch some kind of solace from the jaws of gloom with its use of yet another near-verbatim Ecclesiastes quotation. That song, looking frantically on the bright side, declares: 'Took an untrodden path once, where the swift don't win the race. / It goes to the worthy, who can divide the word of truth', though in Ecclesiastes (9:11) the Preacher '. . . returned, and saw under the sun, that the race is not to the swift, nor the battle to the strong, neither yet bread to the wise, nor yet riches to men of understanding, nor yet favour to men of skill; but time and chance happeneth to them all.' (The non-Ecclesiastes reference, 'It goes to the worthy, who can divide the word of truth', which Dylan pairs with the Ecclesiastes-based 'the swift don't win the race', derives from Paul's Second Epistle to Timothy: 'Study to shew thyself approved unto God, a workman that needeth not to be ashamed, rightly dividing the word of truth' (2:15).

When we return to where we started—with 'Jokerman'—we can recognise that not only its opening line but also its second verse is, among other things, another venture among these themes of Ecclesiastes. That second verse marks a return to the book's notions of life's brevity: 'How swiftly the sun sets in the sky'; how we leave nothing behind: 'You rise up and say goodbye to no-one'; how the master makes the rules for the wise men and the fools, and both face the same void: 'Fools rush in where angels fear to tread / Both of their futures so full of dread, you don't show one.'

When Dylan cites Ecclesiastes in 'Jokerman', then, he is returning to biblical territory he has drawn on many times, and to know something of this book's special function as a forum for airing inherent problems to do with human purpose is to hear more fully this 1980s song's greatness of resonance—and to recognise that Dylan's work continues to draw upon the wide, humane resource of the book of Ecclesiastes.

[*Good News Bible: Today's English Version*, London: Bible Societies / Collins / Fontana, 1976.]

Eliot, T.S. [1888 - 1965] Thomas Stearns Eliot, was born in St. Louis, Missouri, on September 26, 1888. An Anglo-American poet, dramatist and literary critic, was the single most important poet of the 20th century.

The Love Song of J. Alfred Prufrock (a dramatic monologue) threw away 'the canons of the poetical' and made nonsense of the distinction between 'seriousness' and 'levity' in art. In 'Mr. Eliot and Milton' (*The Common Pursuit*, 1952), the critic F.R. Leavis describes Eliot as 'a poet confronted with the task of inventing the new ways of using words that were necessary if there was to be a contemporary poetry . . . when current poetic conventions and idioms afforded no starting point'.

Folk-rock was Dylan's *Prufrock*. With the Dylan songs that inspired this form, he—like Eliot 50 years earlier—was answering the demands of the times for a new poetry. It follows, more generally, that Dylan's finely chiselled language owes something emphatic to the tutoring of Eliot's early poetry.

As *Prufrock* broke the rules laid down by tradition as to what the language of poetry should be, so folk-rock broke the rules of song: of rock/pop music, what its lyrics could deal with and the language it could use, and achieved similar results (even to the early hostility of academics to Eliot being echoed in much of the initial response to 'electric Dylan').

Dylan used 'popular' as opposed to 'serious' music, and married it to fresh language, including much slang, street patois and the double-meanings and double-imagery of cult terms—especially drug terms. Perhaps this was Beat poetry set to music (as against Beat poetry intoned in front of modern jazz) but the result was a solid body of work, 'poetry that freely expresses a modern sensibility, the . . . modes of experience of one fully alive in his own age.' That description (it is Leavis again, from *New Bearings in English Poetry*, 1932) was written about Eliot's early work, but is every bit as accurate as commentary on *Highway 61 Revisited* and *Blonde on Blonde*.

The other affiliations between Dylan and Eliot stem from this. There is the attempt to turn formlessness into form itself. *The Waste Land* (1922) does this openly; Dylan's attempts are usually checked by his allegiance to regular verses—a musical check on his lyrics. But though they may be regular, they are often less regular than most: in many songs some verses have more lines than others; early songs like 'A Hard Rain's a-Gonna Fall' and 'The Lonesome Death of Hattie Carroll' slide nimbly away from the need to make lines rhyme; and the structure and language of a song like 'Subterranean Homesick Blues' (often now claimed to prefigure rap) attempt to interpret the formlessness of the age. 'I accept chaos,' Dylan wrote on the album cover of *Bringing It All Back Home*: 'I am not sure whether it accepts me.' A different brave attempt at 'formless' art from mid-1960s Dylan is the novel *Tarantula*: an often witty work of prose poetry thronging with schoolboy-smart playfulness with T.S. Eliot quotes—along with allusions to almost everyone whose name was ever dropped in class in Hibbing High.

Allied with the formlessness is the uprooting, urbanizing process of the age, and Dylan shares with Eliot the appropriately tough use of urban imagery and the expression of urban disillusion. Eliot first developed this in poems like 'Preludes' (from the *Prufrock* collection): 'The morning comes to consciousness / Of faint stale smells of beer / From the sawdust-trampled street / With all its muddy feet that press / To early coffee-stands'.

Dylan begins 'Visions of Johanna' with: 'Ain't it just like the night / To play tricks when you're tryin' to be so quiet / We sit here stranded / Though we're all doin' our best to deny it . . . / In this room the heat-pipes just cough / The country music station plays soft / But there's nothing / Really nothing to turn off.'

Reading another *Prufrock* poem, 'Rhapsody on a Windy Night', you might feel that Dylan could have written some of this: 'Along the reaches of the street . . . / Every street lamp that I pass / Beats like a fatalistic drum, / And through the spaces of the dark / Midnight shakes the memory / As a madman shakes a dead geranium. / . . . The street-lamp said, 'Regard that woman . . . / You see the border of her dress / Is torn and stained with sand . . .' Certainly it leaves no doubt about Eliot's influence on Dylan. It's plainly a source of direct strength, carrying the tutor's message: chisel your language. Eliot's voice sounds here, for instance: 'The vagabond who's rapping at your door / Is standing in the clothes that you once wore: / Strike another match, go start anew; / And it's all over now, Baby Blue.'

That the influence has been direct is in any case confirmed by Dylan's allusions to Eliot's phrases. That oddly presented 'geranium', plus nearby 'drum', reappear in 'Sad-Eyed Lady of the Lowlands'; 'Visions of Johanna' echoes *The Waste Land's* handful of dust: Louise holds a handful of rain. Eliot writes that 'In the room the women come and go / Talking of Michaelangelo'; Dylan's 'All Along the Watchtower' changes the tense: 'While all the women came and went.'

Allusion-making, including undeclared direct quotation, is a highly developed weapon in Eliot's armory, and has come to be a similarly powerful part of Dylan's own corpus. (See ***"Love and Theft"***.) Sometimes it seems a game: one that Eliot himself perfected. In the third section of *The Waste Land*, for instance, he writes: 'To Carthage then I came / Burning burning burning burning'—which, subtly enough for most of us, quotes from St. Augustine's *Confessions*: 'To Carthage then I came, where a cauldron of unholy loves sang all about mine ears . . .'. 'I Dreamed I Saw St. Augustine', sings Dylan, on the same album as 'All Along the Watchtower'.

Matthew Zuckerman points out an Eliot reference that comes between 'Visions of Johanna' and 'I Dreamed I Saw St. Augustine', in the Basement Tapes song 'Too Much of Nothing'. The song's chorus is 'Say hello to Valerie, say hello to Vivien / Send them all my salary on the waters of oblivion'; Vivien Haigh-Wood was Eliot's first wife, Valerie Fletcher his second. Zuckerman adds: 'Coincidence? Probably not . . . [and] "too much of nothing" is a fair précis of . . . [one theme of] *The Waste Land*'. These lines illustrate the point: 'What is that noise now? What is the wind doing? / Nothing again nothing. / You know nothing? Do you see nothing? Do you remember / "Nothing"?'

Peter C. Montgomery also finds a Dylan allusion or borrowing from Eliot's 'Sweeney Agonistes' (1932)—'But if you understand or if you don't / That's nothing to me and nothing to you'—in Dylan's sleevenote poetry *Some Other Kinds of Songs*: 'i hope you understand / but if you don't / it doesn't matter' and notes that the same Dylan work gives us 'holy hollowness . . . hollow holiness': a playing with Eliot's 'The Hollow Men' (1925).

Dylan's much later song 'Maybe Someday', from *Knocked Out Loaded* (1986), revisits Eliot's 'And the cities hostile and the towns unfriendly' ('Journey of the Magi', 1927) where the line becomes 'Through hostile cities and unfriendly towns'.

A more complex touching upon Eliot, in Dylan's 1980s song 'Jokerman'—in this case connecting with Eliot's 'at the still point, there the dance is', from 'Burnt Norton' (1935)—is argued by AIDAN DAY in his book *Jokerman: Reading the Lyrics of Bob Dylan*.

The clearest of Dylan's cross-references to Eliot occurs in the penultimate verse of 'Desolation Row' (a title, of course, that resembles *The Waste Land*). He does more than simply mention Eliot specifically. 'EZRA POUND and T.S. Eliot' are 'Fighting in the captain's tower . . . / Between the windows of the sea / Where lovely mermaids flow / And nobody has to think too much about / Desolation Row.' This deliberately parallels the ending of *Prufrock*, where 'We have lingered in the chambers of the sea / By sea-girls wreathed with seaweed red and brown / Till human voices wake us, and we drown.' Same imagery, same contrast, same argument.

In *Chronicles Volume One*, Dylan is dismissive of Pound but understatedly respectful of Eliot: 'I liked T.S. Eliot. He was worth reading.'

T.S. Eliot died in London on January 4, 1965.

[T.S. Eliot, *The Love Song of J. Alfred Prufrock*, published *Poetry* magazine, USA, Jun 1915; reprinted in Eliot, *Prufrock and Other Observations*, 1917. Other poems quoted above can be found in *Collected Poems, 1909–35* and *Collected Poems 1909–62*.

Matthew Zuckerman: 'If There's an Original Thought Out There I Could Use It Right Now: The Folk Roots of Bob Dylan', *Isis* no.84, Bedworth, Warwickshire, UK, Apr–May 1999. Peter C. Montgomery: 'Dylan in Ol' Possum's Diamond Mine', 1993, in *Bob Dylan's Words*, ed. WISSOLIK & McGRATH, Greensburg, PA; Eadmer Press, 1994. Bob Dylan: *Chronicles Volume One*, p.110.]

Elliott, Ramblin' Jack [1931 -] Elliott Adnopoz was a sucessful Brooklyn doctor's son, born there on August 1, 1931. He actually did run away out west and join the rodeo: a real Brooklyn cowboy.

Soon a disciple of WOODY GUTHRIE (in the early 1950s he lived in his house for several years, back in New York), as Ramblin' Jack Elliott he became the singer-guitarist of whom Guthrie famously remarked, 'He sounds more like me than I do.' Indeed in *Chronicles Volume One* Dylan implies that it was the fact that Elliott got there first as an imitation walking Woody that persuaded Dylan he'd better move beyond that ambition himself. He recounts how JON PAŇKAKE ('folk music purist enthusiast') gives him a good talking-to on the subject, and alerts Dylan to Elliott's existence and work in the first place, back in Minneapolis in 1959:

'The record he took out and played for me first was *Jack Takes the Floor*. . . . Damn, I'm thinking, this guy is really great. He sounds just like Woody Guthrie, only a leaner, meaner one. . . . I felt like I'd been cast into sudden hell.' He goes on to effuse more than a little about Elliott's talents, and concludes this: 'Elliott, who'd been born ten years before me, had actually traveled with Guthrie, learned his songs and style firsthand and had mastered it completely. Pankake was right. Elliott was far beyond me.'

(The songs on that 10-inch LP include both 'San Francisco Bay Blues' and 'Dink's Song', both of which Dylan was performing by 1961. Elliott was the first to popularise 'San Francisco Bay Blues' in folk revival circles. In *Chronicles* Dylan adds to his story that Pankake heard Dylan again later and told him 'that I used to be imitating Guthrie and now I was imitating Elliott . . .')

Elliott might have been a 'master', and a recording artist for the important British folk label Topic, but he mostly spent his London years busking on the street. There didn't seem to be a lot of money in being a folksinger (or in being Woody Guthrie). On the other hand Guthrie himself made a telling distinction between Elliott and Dylan—in a remark that Dylan himself must have taken as the greatest compliment on earth:

'PETE SEEGER's a singer of folk songs,' he said, 'Jack Elliott is a singer of folk songs. But Bobby Dylan is a folk singer. Oh, Christ, he's a folk singer all right.'

The young Dylan of 1961 was himself less respectful of Elliott than *Chronicles* suggests. IZZY YOUNG's journal for that October 20 transcribes these remarks, offered by Dylan when he dropped in on the Folklore Center to chat:

'I've been with Jack Elliott . . . Jack hasn't taught me any songs. Jack doesn't know that many songs. He's had his chances.'

In *Don't Look Back*, in London in 1965, when Bob Dylan is also becoming a very cool star and Elliott's old busking companion Derroll Adams certainly isn't, Dylan nonetheless recalls another record that was important for him, telling Adams: 'I got a record of yours and Jack's . . . *The Rambling Boys*'. He's referring to the joint album *Rambling Boys* made by Elliott and Adams in London in about 1956 and issued on another 10-inch LP on Topic Records in 1958—an album that includes the track 'Roll on Buddy': a song that picks up, a decade before Dylan uses it on 'Stuck Inside of Mobile With the Memphis Blues Again', the line from Bascom Lamar Lunsford's 1920s 'I Wish I Was a Mole in the Ground' about railroad men drinking your blood like wine. In *Chronicles*, Dylan says Adams 'played banjo like Bascom Lamar Lunsford' and that Derroll and Ramblin' Jack together 'sounded like horses galloping'.

Dylan and Elliott first met *very* early on in Dylan's time in New York City at the start of 1961: within two days of reaching Greenwich Village, according to the ANTHONY SCADUTO biography. And when Elliott saw Dylan performing in the Village, he liked him enormously—perhaps because he *was* imitating Jack at that point. He told Scaduto (with a brusque disregard for what we'd now call political correctness): 'I didn't know it was some of me, at first. I thought he was doing it Woody Guthrie style, in the Guthrie-CISCO HOUSTON school. I was tickled to see somebody doing it well 'cause I was really bored with all the other folk singers. There was not another son of a bitch in the country who could sing until Bob Dylan came along. Everybody else was singing like a damned faggot.'

It was soon after this that the Village crowd discovered that Elliott was, in truth, Mr. Adnopoz from Ocean Parkway, Brooklyn. DAVE VAN RONK told Scaduto: 'Bobby fell off his chair. He rolled under the table, laughing like a madman. . . . We all suspected that Bobby was Jewish, and that proved it. He'd be laying under the table and just recovering from his fit and every once in a while Barry [Kornfeld] or somebody would stick his head under the table and yell 'Adnopoz!' and that would start him off roaring again.'

At some point in the summer of 1963 in New York City, Dylan dropped in on Elliott's sessions for a new Vanguard album, and on 'Will the Circle Be Unbroken?' played harmonica behind Ramblin' Jack's guitar and vocals. When the album was released, in June 1964, under the title *Jack Elliott*, Dylan was credited under the rather more imaginative name of Tedham Porterhouse. The same month as this saw release, Jack Elliott was in the studio at a *Dylan* session—the great one-day stint that yielded *Another Side of Bob Dylan*—and sang behind him on a first tentative try-out of 'Mr. Tambourine Man'. (This halting version was first released on the *Highway 61 Interactive* CD Rom in 1995 and then again another ten years later on the 2-CD set the *Bootleg Series Vol. 7—No Direction Home: the Soundtrack*.) Elliott said later: 'I listened to it once, and I never want to hear it again. It was real bad singing. Amazingly bad.' It's true.

In 1975, Dylan popped up again with Elliott at a gig by the latter back at the Village's Other End Club—at which they duetted on Guthrie's 'Pretty Boy Floyd' and the old Leroy Carr blues 'How Long?', and then Dylan débuted, solo and sweetly, a brilliant new song, 'Abandoned Love', later studio-recorded with musicians at the *Desire* sessions but not released until *Biograph*, 1985.

It's telling that they alighted on 'Pretty Boy Floyd'—and this is the earliest extant version we have of Dylan performing it: 14 years after discovering Guthrie, whose well-known song it is—because when, later still, in around April 1987, Dylan studio-recorded it solo for the Woody Guthrie and LEADBELLY tribute album *Folkways: A Vision Shared*, his recording was clearly modelled on Elliott's own two classic recordings of the song (versions cut in England in 1956 and in the US in 1960: the latter on the classic album *Jack Elliott Sings the Songs of Woody Guthrie*).

Ramblin' Jack was subsequently one of Dylan's guests on the first Rolling Thunder Revue tour (he was dropped from the second one, and it hurt) and so can be seen in Dylan's film *Renaldo & Clara*, 1978, an amiable but uncharismatic figure. By this time, too, he had made brief appearances inside two Dylan songs: one from the 1960s and one from the 1970s. In the sublime *Blonde on Blonde* outtake 'She's Your Lover Now' a very Dylanesque persona swirling in some sumptuous druggy maelstrom pleads with comic desperation: 'You don't have to be *nice* to me / But will you *please* tell that / To your friend in the cowboy hat / You know he keeps on sayin' everything *twice to meeeee*'; and in 'Tough Mama', on *Planet Waves*, 'Jack the cowboy went up north / He's buried in your past.' Perhaps too, Dylan returns to thinking of Ramblin' Jack inside a song on his 1997 album *Time Out of Mind*. Alluding once more to 'Roll on Buddy' he sings: 'Buddy you'll roll no more.'

However, Elliott is still alive and interest in him has recently revived, thanks partly to the film *The Ballad of Ramblin' Jack*, directed by his daughter Aiyana, which won the Special Jury Prize for Artistic Achievement at the Sundance Film Festival 2000. Included on the soundtrack album is the much-bootlegged but never before officially released duet that Jack and Dylan performed back on July 21, 1961 at the Riverside Church Saturday of Folk Music in New York City (bootlegged because broadcast by radio station WRVR-FM eight days later). The song they duetted on was called 'Acne', and of no intrinsic merit. It was a song Dylan returned to a few months later when he was taped performing it (with an unidentified second vocalist) in CYNTHIA GOODING's New York City apartment.

Elliott has also been writing his autobiography, with help from a Rick Steber. *Ramblin'* is published 2006 by Da Capo Press of Cambridge, Massachusetts.

[Ramblin' Jack Elliott: *Jack Takes the Floor*, Topic 10T15 (10-inch LP), London, 1958; 'Talking Miner's Blues' c/w 'Pretty Boy Floyd', London, c.1956, Topic TRC98 (78 rpm), London, c.1956; & 'Pretty Boy Floyd', NY, June 1960, *Jack Elliott Sings the Songs of Woody Guthrie*, Prestige PR13016, Bergenfeld, NJ, 1960/61. Ramblin' Jack Elliott & Derroll Adams: 'Roll on Buddy', London, c.1956, *Rambling Boys*, Topic 10T14 (10-inch LP), London, 1958; reissued *Roll on Buddy*, Topic 12T105 (12-inch LP), London, c.1964; CD-reissued on *Ramblin' Jack*, Topic TSCD477, London, 1996. *Ramblin': The Autobiography of Ramblin' Jack Elliott*, with Rick Steber, Cambridge, MA: Da Capo, 2006.

Ramblin' Jack Elliott & Bob Dylan: 'Acne', NY, 21 Jul 1961, *The Ballad of Ramblin' Jack*, Vanguard 79575-2, NY, 2000; 'Will the Circle Be Unbroken', on *Jack Elliott*, Vanguard VSD 79151, NY, 1964; 'Mr. Tambourine Man', NY, 9 Jun 1964, *Highway 61 Interactive* CD Rom, NY, Feb 1995; the *Bootleg Series Vol. 7—No Direction Home: the Soundtrack*, Columbia/Legacy COL 520358 2, NY, 2005.

Bob Dylan: 'Abandoned Love', Other End, Greenwich Village, NY, 3 Jul 1975 and *Desire* sessions NY, 31 Jul 1975. 'Pretty Boy Floyd', LA, prob. Apr 1987, *Folkways: A Vision Shared*, Columbia OC 44034, NY (CBS 460905 1, London), 1988. *Chronicles Volume One*, 2004, pp.250–251, p.252. Quote noted down by Izzy Young, Folklore Center, NY, 20 Oct 1961, republished in *Younger Than That Now: The Collected Interviews with Bob Dylan*, ed. Jim Ellison, New York: Thunder's Mouth Press, 2004. Anthony Scaduto, *Bob Dylan: An Intimate Biography*, 1972; Abacus UK paperback edn.: swiftness of Dylan meeting Elliott p.53 + ; Guthrie on Seeger, Elliott & Dylan, p.56; Elliott on Dylan, p.58; Van Ronk quote, p.67.]

'Emotionally Yours' [1985] See 'Spanish Harlem Incident' [1964].

***Empire Burlesque* [1985]** Dylan was truly floundering in this period (it was the year of his appearance on *LIVE AID*, at which he finally blew his automatic right to headline at any international gathering of superstars), and though this studio album has a cohesion lacking in those either side of it—*Infidels* and *Knocked Out Loaded*—it features undistinguished pop songs, most of which anyone could have written, and an overwrought production made worse by a horrible, supposedly modish re-mix by the graceless ARTHUR BAKER.

Here is the shameful spectacle of a man whose early work avoids adroitly every pop dissimulation in work of unsurpassed, pioneering clarity of individual vision and vocal richness, now mewling his thin vocal way through a thick murk of formulaic riffs, licks and echo-laden AOR noises devised with a desperate eye on rock-radio formats. Here is the artist whose mature intelligence revolutionised the love song in popular music, now reduced to lines like 'You to me were true / You to me were the best' and titles like 'Emotionally Yours'. Ugh. Even the cover photograph signals how adrift the artist of *Empire Burlesque* is: it shows Dylan the perplexed fashion-victim in Bruce Willis jacket. Early Bob Dylan would have found the whole thing contemptible.

[Recorded NY, Jul & LA, Dec 1984, Hollywood, Jan 1985 and NY, Feb–Mar 1985; released as Columbia FC 40110 (LP), 30 May 1985; in UK as CBS 86313, 8 Jun 1985.]

Engel, Dave [1945 -] David Donald Engel was born in Wisconsin Rapids, Wisconsin, on August 12, 1945. He was first interested in Dylan's work in 1964 and first proposed writing a study of Dylan's hometown in 1968. Nothing came of it until many years later. Meanwhile he became an English teacher at the University of Wisconsin and then Western Illinois University from 1968 to 1980, when he switched to becoming a journalist on the *Wisconsin Rapids Daily Tribune*—he has been there for 25 years now—while also writing a series of regional history books, including several in the series *The Home Front: River City Memoirs* in the 1990s, and *Cranmoor: The Cranberry Eldorado*, 2004 (all on Wisconsin history) and, co-authored with Gerry Mantel, *Calumet: Copper Country Metropolis* in 2002 (on Michigan history). He has also co-edited, with Justin Isherwood, a poetry collection with a Dylan title: *Ring them bells : a Mid-State Poetry Towers Collection* (New Past Press, 2000).

While contributing various Dylan-history pieces to the now-defunct US fanzine *ON THE TRACKS*, Dave Engel's main contribution in this field, to which he brought his historian's skill as well as his depth of regional understanding, has been the magnificent *Just Like Bob Zimmerman's Blues: Dylan in Minnesota*, one of the four or five most valuable books on Bob Dylan ever published. Every subsequent biography has drawn heavily upon it, with differing degrees of acknowledgement. Engel was also consulted but unpaid by Dylan's office while the material for MARTIN SCORSESE's *No Direction Home* was being assembled.

Just Like Bob Zimmerman's Blues took four years to research and write, after a visit to Hibbing persuaded Engel that earlier Dylan biographers had 'got it all wrong'. The result is often hard to steer your way around because of its chosen pattern of short segments: the material about Dylan's ancestors, for example, is chopped into many different sections, interspersed with other material, rather than being set down as a sustained narrative in one place in the book. Nonetheless, though it therefore makes you work at its excavation, the book is filled with a most astonishing amount of gem-like detail, waiting more like diamonds than taconite for others to mine.

The tone of voice, laconic but shrewd, is a delight and well suits the material; the research itself phenomenal—not least in its pioneering, painstaking, detailed research into the world of the North Country's Jewish minority; and then there are the historic photographs, retrieving the past in two main layers. There are the pictures that document the old Duluth, the old Hibbing, the old Mesabi Iron Range way back when Hibbing was being built and re-built; and then there are the photos from the 1940s onwards, in which we can see the 40s sliding into the 50s, the world of men standing at a bar on Howard Street in their suits and black hats morphing into the quaint rock'n'roll world of Bob Dylan's adolescence—the world of all his friends, loitering around the driveways of their parents' homes, posing in bedrooms with guitars, sipping sodas.

This is a marvellous book, particularly as a history of Hibbing as well of Bob Dylan's early years: a Minnesota equivalent of *Pleasantville* rendered with tenderness but no sentimentality, and with vividness but no melodrama. This is also a book that has never been reprinted since its 1997 publication, straight to paperback, by the obscure regional publisher River City Memoirs-Mesabi, of Rudolph, Wisconsin. This is a book Bob Dylan should be grateful for, let alone the rest of us.

[Dave Engel, *Just Like Bob Zimmerman's Blues: Dylan in Minnesota*, Rudolph, WI: River City Memoirs-Mesabi, 1997. Dave Engel & Justin Isherwood, eds., *Ring them bells: a Mid-State Poetry Towers collection*, Friendship, WI: New Past Press, 2000. (*Pleasantville*, dir. & written Gary Ross, Larger Than Life / New Line, US, 1998.)]

Epstein, Howie [1955 - 2003] Howie Epstein was the odd one out within TOM PETTY & THE HEARTBREAKERS, managing not be born in Gainesville, Florida, but in Milwaukee, on July 21, 1955. He was also the last to join the group, only replacing original bass player Ron Blair in 1982, in time to be part of the fifth album, *Long After Dark*, and leaving again 20 years later at the rest of the band's request 'because of his ongoing personal problems,' as their spokesman said at the time.

He not only played bass but mandolin and his harmony vocals with Petty became a distinguishing feature of the band. Outside of this highly successful unit he wrote songs and produced albums, most notably for JOHN PRINE and his own long-term partner, the singer Carlene Carter. He played on sessions for a number of others, including Dylan.

His work with Dylan began on December 6, 1984, in a Hollywood studio when he, MIKE CAMPBELL and BENMONT TENCH backed Dylan's attempts at 'New Danville Girl' and other unreleased material. Further sessions followed for Epstein that month and in early 1985. (See entry **Campbell, Mike** for details.) That fall they were reunited with Dylan within Tom Petty & the Heartbreakers, backing him at Farm Aid. Then came the group's tours with Dylan in 1986 and 1987.

Epstein's last work with Dylan was not in the company of any of the others in the Heartbreakers. It took place in the studios at New Bloomington, Indiana, on November 20, 1989, a few days after Dylan had completed his second year's Never-Ending Tour concerts. With BARRY GOLDBERG producing and on keyboards, and with Carlene Carter among the backing vocalists, Epstein played bass and sang backing vocals on the rather subdued Dylan cut of 'People Get Ready' made for the film *Catchfire* (aka *Backtrack*) and issued on the soundtrack album in January 1990.

In 2001, Howie Epstein and Carlene Carter were arrested in New Mexico after three grams of heroin were found in their car; late on the evening of February 23, 2003 Epstein died in hospital in Santa Fe after being found with a suspected overdose. He was 47. The statement from Tom Petty & the Heartbreakers included this: 'The world has lost a great talent and a kind and gentle soul.'

[Bob Dylan (with Howie Epstein et al.): 'People Get Ready', New Bloomington, IN, 20 Nov 1989, *Backtrack* soundtrack album, WTG 46042, US, Jan 1990. *Catchfire*, dir. Dennis Hopper & Alan Smithee, Mack-Taylor / Precision / Vestron Pictures, US, 1990. Band quotes & some other details online 5 Jun 2005 in 'Tom Petty News' at *www.gonegator.com/news/tom_petty_news_022003.asp*.]

***Essential Bob Dylan, The* [2000]** Released a mere five months after *The Best of Bob Dylan Vol. 2*, this compilation duplicates enormous chunks of it, plus huge chunks of the first *Best of Bob Dylan* from just three years earlier. In fact of the 30 tracks on this double-CD set, only four tracks are not on one or other of those so-called best-of compilations: and of the four, two are different versions of songs that were *also* on those compilations.

You could also complain that there's nothing from the first album, a disproportionate amount from *Bringing It All Back Home*, that the Basement Tapes are hardly best represented by 'Quinn the Eskimo', there's nothing from *Street Legal*, *Shot of Love* (isn't 'Every Grain of Sand' more essential than 'If Not for You'?), and nothing from the two solo acoustic albums of the early 1990s. And so on. Yet of course you could complain whatever was chosen, because of what would have to be omitted.

To add to the confusion over Dylan compilation albums all available at the same time, a 36-track version of this album, with the same title, was released in the UK, France and Australia in 2001 (and in Germany as *The Ultimate Bob Dylan*). The extra tracks included the unmessed-up version of 'Dignity'. On its UK re-release in 2005, this was the album that saw a significant sales increase immediately after the TV showing of the *No Direction Home* film.

[Released as 30-track 2-CD set, Columbia C2K 85168, US, 31 Oct 2000; 36-track 2-CD version Sony Music TV STVCD 116, UK (Columbia 5031332, France), 2001 (Columbia 50313320000, Australia, 2002; re-released UK in Sep 2005 as Columbia 503133 2.]

Estes, Sleepy John [1904 - 1977] John Adam Estes was born outside Ripley, Tennessee on January 25, 1904, grew up in Brownsville, lost the sight in his right eye in a baseball accident in adolescence, learnt guitar, joined the great mandolin player Yank Rachell and harp and jug player Hammie Nixon, acquired his distinctive monicker in rather brutal reference to the narcolepsy from which he suffered, went to Memphis with Rachell & Nixon, played on the streets in a jug band and began his prolific recording career in Memphis in 1929. He was recorded there by Victor on eight separate days between his début session that September 17 and May 30, 1930, yielding 15 still-extant sides, of which 12 were issued. Moving to Chicago with Hammie Nixon in 1931, it took him some time to get back into a studio, but he did so in July 1935 (twice), on two consecutive days in August 1937 and once in April 1938 (these three in New York City), once in June 1940 and once in September 1941 (back in Chicago).

After World War II he made just two more Chicago sides, for the tiny Ora-Nelle label in 1948 but soon afterwards returned to Brownsville, Tennessee, and took labouring work, though occasionally performing on the streets of Memphis as he had done nearly 30 years earlier. In April 1952 the great Sam Phillips recorded him at the Sun Studios in Memphis. HOWLIN' WOLF's career was beginning there; Sleepy John's appeared to be ending. He made three sides at his first Sun session, all of them unissued; later that month he made four sides; none was issued until years afterwards.

He was back in Brownsville, almost 60 years old and close to penury when he was 'rediscovered' in 1962, made new records and worked the folk revival circuit of clubs, festivals (including NEWPORT 1964) and an American Folk Blues Festival tour of Europe. As Dylan said, 'there was a bunch of us . . . who got to see all these people close up—people like SON HOUSE, REVEREND GARY DAVIS or Sleepy John Estes. Just to sit there and be up close and watch them play, you could study what they were doing, plus a bit of their lives rubbed off on you. Those vibes will carry into you forever, really, so it's like those people, they're still here to me. They're not ghosts of the past or anything, they're continually here.'

There's nothing peripheral about what Dylan has taken and remodelled from Sleepy John Estes. Who does this sound like? An artist of great originality, whose work combines traditional and self-penned material, who went through a 'protest' phase, is '. . . not a particularly accomplished guitarist' and whose 'broken, fragmented song' is 'held in tension by the contrast between the tendency to disintegration and the rhythmic impetus of his strumming.' Well, yes, it is Sleepy John Estes but it might so easily be Touring Bob Dylan. (The quotes are from Paul Oliver's 1969 book *The Story of the Blues*.)

To listen to a sweep of Estes' pre-war recordings is to have confirmed what Dylan himself hints at by his own prominent naming of Estes in his *Bringing It All Back Home* sleevenotes: namely that Estes is a *seminal* figure in Bob Dylan's blues education. (Dylan mentions him again in the mid-60s: to JOHN LENNON in the limo-ride filmed for, but not used in, *Eat the Document*.) As so often, Dylan tells us something true but says it in so flip and casual a way that we tend to disregard it. In this case, his notes to his first 'rock' album begin by declaring (quietly): 'i'm standing there watching the parade / feeling combination of sleepy john estes. jayne mansfield. humphrey bogart'—and sure enough, it transpires that those distinctively 'Dylanesque' clunking blues from 1965 owe much to Sleepy John Estes' pioneering work and very individual style, while the clear resemblance between Paul Oliver's description of Estes and our own picture of the older Bob Dylan's artistry suggests aspects of Sleepy John's influence beyond those Dylan displayed back in 1965 that have remained and grown within him.

The evidence is everywhere. The very *title* of Estes' first hit, 'The Girl I Love, She Got Long Curly Hair' (1929), indicates by its distinctive jerky rhythmic strut, an Estes trademark, just how songs like 'California', 'Outlaw Blues', 'From a Buick 6' and 'Sitting on a Barbed-Wire Fence' are built to the Estes blueprint. You can hear it straight away in the special way the delivery of the line is chopped up to incorporate those odd, crucial pauses. Estes: 'Now the, girl I love she got, long curly hair'; Dylan: 'Well this, woman I got she's, killin' me alive.' The half-correspondence of the words that begin those two lines merely adds to the certainty already felt that the one song has inspired the other.

Nine months after cutting 'The Girl I Love', which was to prove Estes' most popular disc, he recorded a song he called 'Milk Cow Blues'. It bears no resemblance to anyone else's song of that name (and doesn't mention milk cows): but it bears a very striking resemblance to 'The Girl I Love, She Got Long Curly Hair'. It has the same knowing clunkiness, that hip manipulation of chunky pauses on the backbeat—a sort of sure-footed clog-dancing: and it is the clear model for 'From a Buick 6'. The special rhythm is the same. The tune is the same. Dylan's lyric even starts out in tribute to the Estes prototype. Where Dylan's 1965 song begins 'I got this, graveyard woman you know she, keeps my kid / But my soulful mama you know she, keeps me hid', Estes opens this way: 'Now, asked sweet mama let me, be her kid / She says I, might get 'bove you like to, keep it hid.' And the first vinyl release of this Estes recording was in 1964.

The same Estes song, as it happens, offers some common-stock blues lines which have Dylan connections from elsewhere in his repertoire. The line after the opening couplet just quoted is one we find Dylan singing in 'Blood in My Eyes': 'Well she looked at me, she begin to smile', and the line that ends the Estes 'Milk Cow Blues' is 'Now it's a, slow consumption an' it's, killin' you by degrees'. Dylan's matching line, with matching pauses, tune and strut, is 'Well if I, go down dyin' you know she, bound to put a blanket on my bed.'

The very first track Estes recorded was his own version of BLIND LEMON JEFFERSON's 'Broke and Hungry', which he either misheard or re-wrote, as 'broken-hearted', and which was given a characteristically lengthy Estes title, 'Broken-Hearted, Ragged and Dirty Too'. This was the début recording that went unissued; he had another go just nine days later, and this time achieved release. The version Dylan performs on *World Gone Wrong* is far more similar to the Sleepy John Estes than to the 1940s Willie Brown version cited in Dylan's sleevenotes.

'Someday Baby Blues' is Sleepy John Estes' particularly heartfelt and individual variant of 'Sittin' on Top of the World', which has in turn been revised and revisited in several guises. CHUCK BERRY's 'Worried Life Blues' uses the Estes chorus but thoroughly different verses; the Allman Brothers' version of the MUDDY WATERS version, 'Trouble No More', does the opposite, reinstating an approximation of Estes' verses while abandoning his chorus. When Bob Dylan sang it live at Toad's Place, New Haven, Connecticut, in 1990, it was recognised as the same song as Muddy Waters', and duly appears in the various listings of his performances as 'Trouble No More'—yet really Dylan brings it all home to Sleepy John, reinstating his chorus and imbuing it with the customary Estesian pauses ('Someday baby, you ain't gonna worry, my mind, anymore'). The only vocal moment worth speaking of in Dylan's befogged performance is the fair imitation of Estes' voice he achieves on the penultimate delivery of that line.

The Estes voice, on his slower numbers, also possesses a painful, crawling quality, always threatening to break down, always wavering between esoteric possibilities. He pulls himself along his vocal line like a snail over pebbles. On the slow songs, even the awkward lengthiness of his titles enacts this tortuous slow motion, matching the delivery, a fine example being 'Who's Been Tellin' You Buddy Brown Blues'. This is the very attenuation Dylan uses so effectively in the unreleased Basement Tapes song 'I'm Not There (1956)'.

Estes' 'Drop Down Mama', another 'From a Buick 6' prototype, has one of those 'It Ain't Me Babe' openings: 'Go, 'way from my window quit scratchin', on my screen' and a refrain which you have only to hear Estes deliver to connect with Dylan's jerky 1965 blues again. 'Now I may look like I'm crazy, poor John do know right from wrong' is clearly the eccentric piece of scaffolding on which Dylan builds 'Well I might, look like Robert Ford but I, feel just like a Jesse James.'

It could be added that the mild, unobtrusive element of social commentary implicit in Dylan's early blues 'Down the Highway' is less in the spirit of his own 'protest songs' than of Estes'. At any rate these are wholly Estesian lines: 'And your streets are gettin' empty / And your highway's gettin' filled'—and you have only to listen to four or five consecutive pre-war Estes recordings to hear how these apparently undistinguished phrases prove distinctively to belong to him.

'Special Agent (Railroad Police Blues)' is another jerky blues, the vocal delivery an object lesson in the inspired eccentricity that sets the few aside from the many: the sort of vocal eccentricity that we may have found first in FATS DOMINO or BUDDY HOLLY or Howlin' Wolf, in rock'n'roll or R&B, and which pulls us into this music when we're very young because it speaks to us from a strange, magic kingdom alluringly unlike school. Anyone who ever felt that way can recognise the authentic pull of Sleepy John Estes, as Bob Dylan must have done. He probably heard this Estes record before any other: it was included on SAM CHARTERS' crucial *The Country Blues* LP issued back in 1959.

This track also offers a salutary reminder that there's nothing exclusively postmodern about the self-reflexive text. More than 50 years before Dylan played with 'I'll be back in a minute. . . . You can tell me, I'm back' and 'now I'm back on the track' on his fine *Oh Mercy* recording 'What Was It You Wanted?', Estes was ending 'Special Agent (Railroad

Police Blues)' with this devilishly clever pay-off line: 'Now special agent, special agent, put me off close to some town / Special agent, special agent, put me off close to some town / Now I got to do some recording: an' I oughta be recordin' right now!'

John Estes went to his final sleep back home in Brownsville, Tennessee, on June 5, 1977.

[Sleepy John Estes: 'The Girl I Love, She Got Long Curly Hair', Memphis, 24 Sep 1929 & 'Milk Cow Blues', Memphis, 13 May 1930, both vinyl-issued on *Sleepy John Estes 1929–1940*, RBF RF-8, NY, 1964: the latter also on Sam Charters' 2-LP box set *The Rural Blues*, RBF RF-202, NY, 1964; 'Broken-Hearted, Ragged and Dirty Too', Memphis, 17 Sep 1929, unissued; 'Broken-Hearted, Ragged and Dirty Too', Memphis, 26 Sep 1929, RBF RF-8; 'Someday Baby Blues' & 'Who's Been Tellin' You Buddy Brown Blues', Chicago, 9 Jul 1935, *The Blues of Sleepy John Estes: Vol. 1*, Swaggie S-1219, Australia, 1967. 'Drop Down Mama', Chicago, 17 Jul 1935, issued ditto & on *The Blues in Memphis, 1927–39*, Origin Jazz Library OJL-21, Berkeley, c.1969; 'Special Agent (Railroad Police Blues)', NY, 22 Apr 1938, *The Country Blues*, RBF RF-1, NY, 1959; 'Little Laura Blues', Chicago, 24 Sep 1941, Treasury of Jazz No. 30 (EP), RCA Victor 75.752, Paris, 1963. A terrific selection of pre-war Estes material, including all the above, is *Sleepy John Estes: I Ain't Gonna Be Worried No More: 1929–1941*, Yazoo 2004, US, 1992.

Blind Lemon Jefferson: 'Broke and Hungry', Chicago, c.Nov 1926, *Blind Lemon Jefferson, Volume Two*, Milestone LP 2007, NY, 1968. Chuck Berry: 'Worried Life Blues', Chicago, 12 Feb 1960 (B-side of 'Bye Bye Johnny', same session), Chess 1754, Chicago, 1960. Allman Brothers: 'Trouble No More', NY, Sep 1969; *The Allman Brothers Band*, Capricorn ATCO SD-33-308, NY, 1969. Muddy Waters: 'Trouble No More', Chicago, Oct 1955, Chess 1612, Chicago, 1955. Bob Dylan: 'Trouble No More / Someday Baby Blues', live New Haven, CT, 12 Jan 1990.

Dylan quote re Estes & others 'continually present', interview San Diego, c.3 Oct 1993 by Gary Hill, Reuters, wired to US newspapers 13 Oct 1993; his *Eat the Document* outtake Estes mention transcribed by John Bauldie in *Mojo* no.1, London, 1993.]

Everly Brothers, the The Everly Brothers defined the rock'n'roll duet and the sound of adolescent angst. Their unmistakeable harmonies drew on 700 years of Scottish Borders' misery, transplanted via the Appalachians, to sing out late 1950s teenage confusion. Like ELVIS PRESLEY and CHUCK BERRY, the Everly Brothers blueprinted how things would be, and in later years were bitter at receiving less credit for this than rock'n'roll's solo giants. It typified their knack of snatching sourness from the jaws of sweetness.

Don, born in Brownie, Kentucky, in 1937, and Phil, born in Chicago in 1939, were duetting long before rock'n'roll, on parents Ike and Margaret's radio show on WKMA in Shenandoah, Ohio. They were seasoned professionals by the time they poured out their magic vocals onto a run of hits that married hillbilly harmonies and Nashville nouse, their full-chorded acoustic guitars embracing BO DIDDLEY's exotic rhythms to create the rock'n'roll end of country music's rich, commercial sounds.

They could not complain at their initial success. After one unsuccessful session for RCA, yielding the rare 1956 single 'Keep a Lovin' Me', they signed with New York label Cadence, later switching to the newly formed Warner Brothers Records. From 1957 to 1965 they had 28 hits in the British top 30, and comparable American success, first topping the US charts in 1957 (with 'Wake Up Little Susie'), and from then till some time in the earlyish 60s they were constantly having hits, it seemed. 'All I Have to Do Is Dream' was another US no.1, also topping the UK charts. 'Bye Bye Love', 'Bird Dog' and 'Problems' were US no.2s, and '('Til) I Kissed You' a UK no.2. Other hits included 'Let It Be Me', 'Take a Message to Mary', 'Like Strangers', 'Crying in the Rain' and the UK no.1 'Walk Right Back'. One of the great pop death-records, 'Ebony Eyes', was theirs too.

Many of their hits were written by another duo, Boudleaux and Felice Bryant, but the Bryants' claim that they schooled Don and Phil in their vocal parts was nonsense, and the brothers wrote plenty themselves. Both penned the phenomenally successful début single on Warner Brothers, 'Cathy's Clown', which was another US no.1 and achieved an almost unprecedented nine weeks at no.1 in Britain in 1960. Phil wrote 'When Will I Be Loved'; Don wrote 'Since You Broke My Heart', '('Til) I Kissed You' and 'So Sad (To Watch Good Love Go Bad)'.

They were very commercial and they were very good. At a time when most people found a sound by accident, they developed one deliberately and intelligently, bridging what gap there was between pop and modern country music. And at a time when pop's understanding of music was near-retarded, the Everlys were consistently alert and curious. They handled their own arrangements and they had taste.

They had the gravitas to cover other artists' crucial songs, including black ones, without apology, from LITTLE RICHARD's 'Lucille', given a keening slow-motion vocal fall, to blues classics like the immortal 'Trouble in Mind' and the cheerily inconsequential 'Step It Up and Go' (which Dylan recorded for *Good As I Been to You*, 1992) and Mickey & Sylvia's 'Love Is Strange'. Don, taken down Chicago's Maxwell Street as a young boy by his father, was ever after aware of gospel and blues. And in an era of pretty pop, the Everlys sought a tougher sound on records like 'The Price of Love' and their extraordinary revival of the standard 'Temptation', which pre-figured PHIL SPECTOR's 'wall of sound'. But like Spector's 'River Deep, Mountain High', the Everlys' 'Temptation' was (by their standards) a flop in the USA, and 'The

Price of Love' a bigger one. Don never forgave the American public.

Then there were THE BEATLES, whose 'new' harmonies made the Everlys old-fashioned overnight. Made redundant before they were 30, Don and Phil felt (wrongly) that the Beatles had stolen from them without acknowledgement. Sidelined further by progressive rock, Don & Phil tried first to sound like SIMON & Garfunkel (indeed like anyone but themselves), then responded with more dignity with their influential 1968 album *Roots*, which, with THE BYRDS' *Sweetheart of the Rodeo*, catalysed the creation of 'country rock' in 1969, the year they're said to have turned down Dylan's 'Lay, Lady, Lay'.

Everyone had loved Don & Phil except Phil & Don. Under pressure, they couldn't stand themselves or each other. The Everly Brothers split up in public acrimony, their last performance together on July 14, 1973.

It emerged eventually that even at the very height of Dylan's artistic genius and hipness, the tour of 1966, he could still (off stage) bear in mind work of the Everly Brothers from that most sneered-at period of pop, 1960–62: the semi-documentary film of his tour, *Eat the Document*—not screened until 1971 (and then but briefly)—catches him in May 1966 performing the Everlys' 1960 hit 'When Will I Be Loved?' in his Glasgow hotel-room. He 'went public' on his affection for the Everlys by recording their 'Let It Be Me' and 'Take a Message to Mary' on his 1970 album *Self Portrait* (something very badly received by a hip public). The inclusion of Everly Brothers songs was more striking at the time than it is now, since in recent years, through rock'n'roll revivals galore, they have been acknowledged as crucial figures in the pre-Dylan era; but when *Self Portrait* came out, you weren't supposed to still like or even remember that old stuff: you were supposed to be progressive and despise the three-minute single. But Dylan's 'Let It Be Me' is a perfectionist's re-drafting of the Everlys' version, in effect; Dylan stays very faithful to their wistful and solid pop world. With 'Take a Message to Mary', Dylan does something more, somehow returning the song (in Bill Damon's phrase) 'back to the Code of the West'.

By then, Dylan had also written the Everlys a song, 'The Fugitive', which the Everlys never recorded. (It turns up in Dylan's catalogue as 'Wanted Man', and has been recorded by JOHNNY CASH, who brings to it all the animation of a totem pole.) Later, after the Everlys had reluctantly re-formed, they did record the lovely Dylan song 'Abandoned Love', a *Desire* sessions outtake—and they could have done this song justice, expansively and warmly; unfortunately, and uncharacteristically, a rigid rhythm and uncommitted vocals throw it away.

Harking back not to the Everly Brothers' version but to the well-known later black cover by Jerry Butler and Betty Everett, Dylan re-recorded 'Let It Be Me', with CLYDIE KING as vocal duettist, in 1981, and sang it in three 1981 concerts, this time implying that the 'you' the song addresses is Christ rather than woman. He has not revisited 'Take a Message to Mary'. Yet, by coincidence or not, he does re-meet the Everlys on the long instrumental intro to his great 'Not Dark Yet' on 1997's album *Time Out of Mind*. Nineteen seconds in, presaged by a sketch of itself a few seconds earlier, a falling guitar-line arrives, laid across the top of the rest, that is straight out of the distinctive musical introduction to the revisit-version of that great early Everlys song 'I Wonder If I Care as Much'—the version we find on their influential *Roots* album of 1968.

For the Everlys themselves, meanwhile, it had been a further trauma to discover that separately, no-one cared about either of them. On September 23, 1983, with Don grown fat but retaining in spades the charisma he must have been born with, they staged an historic and moving Reunion Concert at the Royal Albert Hall. This they seem doomed to repeat forever. In the 1990s, at the age of 60, spurred to a fat-free diet, Don lost a lot of weight, just as Phil was belatedly gaining it: a coincidence typical of their sibling disharmony.

They still sing exquisitely, and a small segment of their shows offer songs learnt from father Ike, whom they worshipped, and mine-worker Mose Rager: authentic old-time country material. Don plays loving, intense guitar, though sparingly in latterday performances. Singing lead, he lives in the spontaneity of the moment, his phrasing inspired, warm and free. He is an artist. But they hardly dare stray now from their teenage hits, first offered to us almost half a century ago.

See also **Nashville c.1960, influence of**, and **country music, Dylan's early interest in**.

[The Everly Brothers: 'Keep a Lovin' Me', Nashville, Nov 1955, Columbia 1956; 'Wake Up Little Susie', Nashville, 1957, Cadence 1337, NY (London American HLA 8498, London), 1957; 'All I Have to Do Is Dream', Nashville, 6 Mar 1958, Cadence 1348, NY (London American HLA 8618, London), 1958; 'Bye Bye Love', Nashville, Apr 1957, Cadence 1315 (London American HLA 8440), 1957; 'When Will I Be Loved?', Nashville, 18 Feb 1960, Cadence 1380 (London American HLA 9157), 1960. 'Let It Be Me', Nashville, 15 Dec 1959, Cadence 1376 (London American HLA 9039), 1960; 'Take a Message to Mary', Nashville, 2 Mar 1959, Cadence 1364 (London American HLA 8863), 1959; both LP-issued *The Fabulous Style of the Everly Brothers*, Cadence CLP 3040, NY, 1960. 'Cathy's Clown', 18 Mar 1960, Warner Bros. 5151, NY (Warner Bros. WB 1, London), 1960. 'Temptation', Nashville 1 Nov 1960, c/w 'Stick With Me Baby', Nashville, 27 Jul 1960, Warner Bros. 5220 (WB 42), 1961. 'Step It Up & Go', Nashville, fall 1961, *Instant Party*, Warner Bros. W (WS) 1430, 1962. 'Abandoned Love', London, 1984/5, *Born Yesterday*, Mercury CD 826 142-2 (LP MERH 80), Holland &

London, 1985; 'I Wonder If I Care as Much', summer 1968, *Roots*, Warner Bros. W1752, 1968. *The Everly Brothers: Reunion Concert I*, London, 23 Sep 1983, Impression IMDP1, 1984.

Bob Dylan: 'When Will I Be Loved', Glasgow, 18–19 May 1966, fragment in *Eat the Document*, 1971; 'Let It Be Me' (with Clydie King), LA, 1 May 1981 (issued in Europe only, as B-side of 'Heart of Mine', CBS A-1406, 1981). Jerry Butler & Betty Everett: 'Let It Be Me', Chicago, 1964, Vee-Jay 613, Chicago, 1964. Bill Damon, 'Herewith, a Second Look at *Self Portrait*' in *Rolling Stone*, 3 Sep 1970.]

Evers, Medgar [1925 - 1963] Medgar Wiley Evers, born July 2, 1925 in Decatur, Mississippi, became prominent in the civil rights movement of the early 1960s and was field secretary of the National Association for the Advancement of Colored People in Mississippi. He had served in the US Army in World War II, married in 1951, and moved to Jackson to set up an NAACP office there. He was murdered on the lawn of his bungalow in a respectable black suburb in Jackson, June 12, 1963, causing a national outcry.

Two rigged trials of Ku Klux Klan member Byron de la Beckwith in the 1960s ended in hung juries. On February 5, 1994, in Jackson, de la Beckwith, now aged 73, was at last found guilty of Evers' murder and sentenced to life imprisonment. A statue of Evers stands outside the Medgar Evers Public Library on Medgar Evers Boulevard in today's Jackson. The bungalow is now a small museum.

De la Beckwith was from Greenwood, Mississippi, the town where ROBERT JOHNSON was lethally poisoned in 1938. Greenwood had 11,000 people, half of them black, when Johnson played and died there. Byron de la Beckwith, one of the town's 5,500 whites, would have been a 17-year-old then. Noticeably, the man who killed Evers was *not*, as in Dylan's 'Only a Pawn in Their Game', poor white trash. Nevertheless it was apt that when Dylan performed this brave political song for a black audience of farm workers on July 6, 1963 (within four weeks of Evers' death), the venue was a rural patch just outside Greenwood, Mississippi.

[Mystery of Evers' middle name (always stated as just initial W.) solved by Eric Oliver, NAACP Library, 31 Oct 2005. 1994 information: 'American Survey', the *Economist*, London, 12 Feb 1994. For a fuller account see Maryanne Vollers' book *Ghosts of Mississippi: The Murder of Medgar Evers, the Trials of Byron De La Beckwith, and the Haunting of the New South*, 1995.]

'Every Grain of Sand', non-Blake elements On the demo version Dylan made of this song, issued in 1991 on the *Bootleg Series Vols. 1–3*, the music seems uncertain of itself. FRED TACKETT's guitar work and Dylan's keyboards make for a muted turbulence that fails to support the regularity of the song's construction: and this produces not an expressive tension between the two (as, say, between ROBBIE ROBERTSON's guitar and Dylan's keyboards on 'Dirge') but an indeterminacy, while Dylan's voice strains unattractively in a key just out of reach. Far from carrying over into a suggestion of the hard struggle for faith, this merely sounds a failure of performance. And since JENNIFER WARNES' singing is so low in the mix as to be unjudgeable, we might say that the best vocal on the track belongs to the dog that barks in the middle. Its voice, unlike Dylan's here, has a rounded, bell-like tone, harmonically rich and in every way expressive, while the timing of its entrance is startling but immaculate. It strongly recalls, in tone *and* timing, the imitations of the bells achieved to such beguiling effect by the back-up singers on that religious potboiler of the 1950s 'The Three Bells (The Jimmy Brown Song)' by Les Compagnons de la Chanson. (The back-up singers on Dylan's recording of 'Copper Kettle' do much the same job.)

The religious potboiler that bubbles in the background of *all* versions of 'Every Grain of Sand', because it does touch on the words rather than the music, is 'I Believe', which Dylan will have known, if not from Frankie Laine, then certainly from ELVIS PRESLEY, whose 1957 recording was released on both *Elvis' Christmas Album* and alongside 'Peace in the Valley' (a song Dylan performed in concert in 1989) on the EP of that name. The short lyric of 'I Believe' lists things that seem ordered in the universe ('I believe for every drop of rain that falls, a flower grows') and in which the Master's hand can be discerned, including 'Every time I hear a new-born baby cry . . .' (where did these songwriters hang out: a maternity ward?) '. . . or touch a leaf, or see the sky / Then I know why, I, believe.'

The *Shot of Love* album version of 'Every Grain of Sand', recorded in May 1981, echoes another pop record also: it has the same intro as ROY ORBISON's great single 'Crawling Back' (from his otherwise fallow period at MGM, after the run of Monument hits), with exactly the same stately arpeggios. Since this is an obscure echo, however, the predominant effect of the arpeggio'd intro is to establish, by the hint of formal *musique* it carries, the ordered nature of the whole song. Then Dylan's voice comes in: direct, serious and without melodrama. It is a broad, steadfast voice, not straining but submitting to the discipline of the formal, careful structure of the song, *its* orderliness an enactment of that claimed by the title. We are served notice that here is a submission to order on every level of the song's being.

There is no distracting small-talk. We are at once into the narrator's confession of feeling prompted to confession (to his crawling back), and then 'onward' into the 'journey' of following this through. There is no evocation of turmoil or chaos here: the experience of turmoil undergone is logged objectively. The recounting of the journey is unemphatic about the narrator's personal anguish; though the faith and possible doubt experienced is necessarily of a personal nature, the song is concerned to emphasise the stages of the journey rather than the declamatory 'me! me! me!' of it: so much so that there is no other Dylan song so saturated in biblical text; all through, the personal sojourn scrupulously follows scriptural signposts.

Matthew 10:29–31, a passage that quotes Christ directly, is the founding text of the song's title theme: 'Are not two sparrows sold for a farthing? and one of them shall not fall on the ground without your Father. But the very hairs of your head are all numbered. Fear ye not therefore . . .' Or as Luke reports it: 'Are not five sparrows sold for two farthings, and not one of them is forgotten before God? But even the very hairs of your head are all numbered. Fear ye not therefore . . .' (Luke 12:6–7).

But what does this mean? And what does Dylan make it mean in his song? Christ's message here is not nearly so wide, liberal and all-inclusive as it sounds. What follows at once is: 'Fear ye not therefore, ye are of more value than many sparrows. Whosoever therefore shall confess me before men, him will I confess also before my Father which is in heaven. But whosoever shall deny me before men, him will I also deny before my Father which is in heaven. Think not that I am come to send peace on earth: I came not to send peace but a sword.' (Matthew 10:31–34; the equivalent passage of Luke, which omits the waving of the sword, is in 12:8–9.)

Far from throwing God's infinite care over every tiny creature in his universe, as the early part of his speech might imply, it's a severe and conditional vision: it mentions the sparrows only to devalue them in the comparison with men, and it excludes from God's care all but true Christian believers.

Christ's words 'the very hairs of your head are all numbered. Fear ye not therefore . . .' are reworked in a later address to the disciples, reported by Luke: 'But there shall not an hair of your head perish' (Luke 21:18), and this reassurance too occurs in a specific and exclusive context: that of Christ warning his disciples of the future destruction of the temple, accompanied by 'great signs . . . from heaven' (21:11), and of Jerusalem, prior to the Second Coming of Christ. He is telling them that as long as they keep their wits about them, *they* will be all right: that every genuine Christian shall be protected when desolation falls upon the Jewish state and everybody else.

Clearly there are occasions when Dylan takes up this narrowed meaning: for instance he takes up the very prophecy of Christ which contains the formulation 'there shall not an hair of your head perish', in the contemporaneous song 'Caribbean Wind'.

Moreover, though the context of the sparrows-and-numbered-hairs passage is not, like that of the later one, predicting the mass-destruction of all but the chosen few at the end of the world, Christ's words in the later prophecy as reported by Luke do make deliberate cross-reference to earlier rhetorics, thus binding the intent of the various passages firmly together. Telling the disciples that '. . . when ye see these things come to pass, know ye that the kingdom of God is nigh at hand', he cautions them: 'And take heed to yourselves, lest at any time your hearts be overcharged with surfeiting, and drunkenness, and *cares of this life* and so that day come upon you unawares. For *as a snare* shall it come on all them that dwell on the face of the whole earth. Watch ye therefore, and pray always, that ye may be accounted worthy to escape . . .' (emphases added).

That, then, is the scriptural basis for the *title* theme of 'Every Grain of Sand'. That Christ's narrow meaning as regards sparrows and numbered hairs has stimulated innumerable other, broader ideas drawing on the same metaphors, some of which may reverberate through Dylan's song, we can leave till a little later to consider. In following *all* the song's biblical signposts we had really reached only the end of the second verse. Dylan begins his third and final verse with 'I have gone from rags to riches in the sorrow of the night'. While the phrase 'rags to riches' is a secular commonplace, used less often as a material boast than as a metaphor for the transforming value of love—as in the song 'Rags to Riches', by Adler and Ross, recorded originally by Tony Bennett in 1953, covered in the UK by David Whitfield, an R&B hit by Billy Ward & the Dominoes in 1954, revived by Sunny & the Sunglows in 1963 and Lenny Welch in 1966, and a minor hit for Elvis Presley in 1971—and while the whole phrase 'rags to riches' is to be found nowhere in the Bible, nonetheless the Bible frequently applies the same metaphor to suggest the greater transforming power of God's love. Paul talks of 'the riches of his grace' in his Epistle to the Ephesians (1:7: compounded to 'the exceeding riches of his grace' a chapter later [2:7]).

This is surely Dylan's meaning here, and to complete his fusion of secular phrase with religious meaning (something he so often does with quiet panache) he invokes a passage aptly located in Isaiah: aptly because it catches Isaiah making *his* confession, and citing those metaphoric 'rags' while supplicating for the riches of being returned to God's favour:

'But we are all as an unclean thing, and all our righteousnesses are as filthy rags; and we all do fade as a leaf: and our iniquities, like the wind, have taken us away.' (Isaiah 64:6.) Of course this also gives us the 'leaf' that Dylan uses earlier, while another of his songs, 'Ain't No Man Righteous, No Not One', gives a clear explanatory précis of this exact same biblical verse: 'Put your goodness next to God's and it comes out like a filthy rag.'

Being appalling misogynists, what the ancients really mean by 'an unclean thing' and 'a filthy rag' is a cloth used to absorb menstrual blood. This was too much for the early Victorians. Adam Clarke's *Commentary* names the term only in Latin (pannus menstruatus) and adds: 'If preachers knew properly the meaning of this word, would they make such liberal use of it in their public ministry? . . . How many in the congregation blush for the incautious man and his "filthy rags!"' The same passage of Isaiah is translated in an Old English manuscript Bible as 'And we ben made as unclene alle we: and as the cloth of the woman rooten blode flowing, all our rigtwisnesses.' In contrast, the New Inclusive Anglican Version probably gives the passage as 'But at the end of the day we are all sort of at the wrong time of the month really, OK?'

Confirming the 'rags to riches' theme, and the context of confession in which it arises here, as in 'Every Grain of Sand'—confession not to a God whose existence is doubted but one whose mercy has been withheld—the biblical verses that follow immediately are: '. . . thou hast hid thy face from us, and hast consumed us, because of our iniquities. But now, O Lord, thou art our Father. . . . Be not wroth very sore, O Lord, neither remember iniquity for ever: behold, see, we beseech thee, we are all thy people' (Isaiah 64:7–10). This passage comes almost at the end of the Book of Isaiah, the prophet who comes immediately before Jeremiah, and who is giving here a confession on behalf of his people. (Prophet, *nabi*, derives from *naba*, which means not only to foretell future events but also to pray and supplicate; and before they were termed prophets they were called seers, which was the translation of both *haroeh*, the seeing person, and *chozeh*, the person who has visions or supernatural revelations.)

The confession relates to the period of the Babylonian captivity (which God had permitted the Jews to suffer to punish them for their great wickedness), as the prophecy of Jeremiah was to do also; and it was because of Jeremiah's prophecy as to when this should end that Daniel understood himself to be making *his* confession in the final days of that captivity. In the sequencing of this part of the Old Testament, the books run as follows: Isaiah, Jeremiah, [Jeremiah's] Lamentations, Ezekiel and Daniel. Ezekiel, interposed between Jeremiah and Daniel, lived under the Babylonian captivity too, and prophesied in Mesopotamia at the same time that Jeremiah prophesied in Jerusalem. Daniel prophesied in Babylon itself. Hence Dylan parallels his modern, idiomatically casual usage of 'I got to confess' with its numinous scriptural meaning, re-inhabiting the person of Daniel, in the wonderful understatement of 'I been to Babylon, I got to confess' in 'Someone's Got a Hold of My Heart'.

In 'Every Grain of Sand' it follows from the 'rags to riches' that with 'in the sorrow of the night' Dylan may have in mind Psalm 6, verse 6, a most poetic Psalm of David and one which also shares the supplicatory intent of the passages alluded to from Daniel and Isaiah: '. . . all the night make I my bed to swim; I water my couch with my tears.' The context is given in the first three verses of this Psalm: 'O Lord, rebuke me not in thine anger, neither chasten me in thy hot displeasure. Have mercy upon me, O Lord; for I am weak: O Lord, heal me; for my bones are vexed. My soul is also sore vexed: but thou, O Lord, how long?'

It is hardly possible to read those lines without being conscious that they reverberate through many fragments of Dylan's work, even if we did not know of Dylan's admiration for 'some righteous king who wrote psalms beside moonlit streams' ('I and I', 1983). Surely the earlier 'fury of the moment', the present 'sorrow of the night' and the imminent 'violence of a summer's dream' are all stirred up by that marvellous 'in thy hot displeasure'.

Dylan's line 'I am hanging in the balance of [either] the reality of man [or] a perfect finished plan' can carry a weight of meaning, and a breadth of implication, which is informed by the whole complexity of the title theme. But the King James Bible offers one more scriptural quotation that holds to notions of God's guardianship over us and that might be said to hover over Dylan's lyric. This too comes from a Psalm of David:

'How precious also are thy thoughts unto me, O God! how great is the sum of them! If I should count them, they are more in number than the sand' (Psalm 139:17–18), which occurs in the context of David's acknowledging that God is everywhere, and sees everything, and has guarded over him always, and that he is counted among the works of God, and that he cannot expect to understand all of his knowledge of God: '. . . the darkness and the light are both alike to thee. For thou hast possessed my reins: thou hast covered me in my mother's womb. I will praise thee; for I am fearfully and wonderfully made; and that my soul knoweth right well. . . . Such knowledge is too wonderful for me; it is high, and I cannot attain unto it' (Psalm 139:12–14 & 6). And that last is a conclusion Alexander Pope arrives at in his poem 'The Essay on Man', after *he* has contemplated the falling sparrow and God's regard. Which returns us to post-gospels extrapolations from this main theme of Dylan's song.

However narrowly Christ intended the significance of the Fatherly eye on the falling sparrow, a huge and broad sweep of ideas, including the liberal, the radical and the mystical, has been activated by the sheer poetry of possibility in Christ's *words*. Taken to embrace the idea that God cares for every sparrow, the implications are endless.

It has been possible to argue from this that the New Testament contradicts the speciesism of the Old (which appears to insist that the animal kingdom is ours to dispose of as we wish: 'dominion over the fish of the sea, and over the fowl of the air, and over the cattle, and over all the earth, and over every creeping thing that creepeth upon the earth' [Genesis 1:26]–though this too is open to debate as to the real implications of the word 'dominion', not to mention modern scepticism about the propriety of basing ideas about the relation of people to animals on those of a primitive farming community).

It was possible for the Victorians to take from Christ's remarks a means of reconciling Darwin's disturbing ideas of evolution, of natural selection, with that of God's providence. It was possible for Shakespeare to extrapolate from Christ's words a different set of considerations: to have Hamlet take from them, after the agonies of his inner struggles as depicted throughout the play (after 'toiling in the danger and in the morals of despair', in fact), something closer to a peaceful acceptance not only of the *idea* of death's inevitability but to the prospect that his own death might be imminent. It is at this juncture that Hamlet can say: '. . . There is special providence in the fall of a sparrow. If it be now, 'tis not to come; if it be not to come, it will be now; if it be not now, yet it will come. The readiness is all. Since no man of aught he leaves knows, what is't to leave betimes [i.e. early]? Let be.'

Hamlet, writes the critic E.M.W. Tillyard, 'is painfully aware of the baffling human predicament between the angels and the beasts, between the glory of having been made in God's image and the incrimination of being descended from Adam'; or, as Maynard Mack puts it: 'When we first see him . . . he is clearly a very young man . . . suffering the first shock of growing up. He has taken the garden at face value . . . , supposing mankind to be only a little lower than the angels . . . now he sees everywhere the general taint, taking from life its meaning . . . Hamlet . . . [has] felt the heavy and the weary weight of all this unintelligible world; and . . . in his young man's egocentricity, he will set it right. Hence he misjudges Ophelia . . . he misjudges himself . . . he takes it upon himself to be his mother's conscience, though the ghost has warned . . . "Leave her to heaven . . ." Even with the king, Hamlet has sought to play at God'. Later, Hamlet comes to understand that 'There is a divinity that shapes our ends / Rough hew them how we will'. Thus he comes round to feeling that 'Are You Ready?' is the question.

'"Readiness" here means both submitting to providence and being in a state of preparation. It is not that death does not matter . . . but [that] readiness matters more. Shakespeare's tragic heroes do not renounce the world. [For the] dying Hamlet . . . such values are never denied, but at the end . . . they are no longer primary,' as Edward Hubler explains it. As Robert Ornstein lists them, the irresolvable questions remain these: 'Are we to assume from Hamlet's references to heaven, divinity and providence that he is now convinced of the great moral design of creation? Or do we see a Hamlet bowing before a universe which defies man's intellectual attempts at comprehension?'

This last question also seems to have preoccupied the exemplar of 18th century man, Alexander Pope, though you would not know it by taking the relevant lines from his 1733–34 poem 'The Essay on Man' out of context: '[He] . . . sees with equal eye, as God of all / A hero perish, or a sparrow fall.'

For early Victorian believers, these lines were to suggest a shocking coldness of equality, an irreligious equalising of noble mankind and lowly sparrow: yet this is exactly what makes such a notion of God's guardianship over everything in the universe seem warm and benign to some more modern sensibilities. Pope's lines actually point up the contrast between the blindness of God's creatures ('Heaven from all creatures hides the book of fate. . . . O blindness to the future! kindly giv'n') and the clarity of God's all-seeing vision, and his 'equal' may embrace the sense of the Latin word (aequus): 'propitious' or 'benign'.

In any case, Pope is, as he says at the poem's beginning, simply rummaging around among these ideas himself: 'Let us (since life can little more supply / Than just to look about us and to die) / Expatiate free o'er all this scene of man; / A mighty maze! but not without a plan.'

Without suggesting that Bob Dylan has been trying to echo Pope (any more than that his song attempts to carry every other resonance or idea sparked off by Christ's words), we can be reminded, by these last-quoted two lines, one after the other, of Dylan's two alternative endings for his song. In the album version and the version published in the songbooks this is 'I am hanging in the balance of the reality of man / Like every sparrow falling, like every grain of sand.' In both the earlier demo version and the later concert version of 1984, it is 'I am hanging in the balance of a perfect finished plan / Like every sparrow falling, like every grain of sand.'

Which returns us to the overall *orderliness* of the song. It is not the quality one first looks to Dylan to supply; traditionally, we are likely to value him more for his incomparable acid derangement, the universe of sizzling, surreal, chaotic wit that he creates in work like 'She's Your Lover Now', in which an apt strength is his famous ability to fit into irregular lines however many syllables he likes, another is his panache with madly dislocated rhymes ('sadness' with 'Charles Atlas', for instance). To 'Every Grain of Sand', Dylan brings a concentrated purposiveness that draws on another side of his multiform talent. Instead of dislocated rhymes, this song demands, and gets, exact ones, and in the most orderly pattern possible: which is, within each four-line cluster, the AABB pattern rather than the easier and more common ABCB, or even ABAB.

AABB is better at establishing orderliness because in hearing the rhyme close on the heels of itself, we are made more aware of it, of its regularity: its mechanism constantly reaffirms that regularity. Yet it takes a skilful, judicious touch to achieve this effect without it toppling over into mechanistic intrusion—without our experiencing the rhyme as a clumping heaviness we await with fastidious dread, like corny rhymes that loom threateningly over the listener well in advance of their falling on the ears. It takes a restraint and a lightness of touch that involves resisting making any of those rhymes 'clever', to gain the effect required, so that each rhyme sounds to the listener as if it falls pleasingly into place. Dylan does this with such skill that the skill is inaudible. His AABB pattern never varies, and except for the last rhyme, at song's end, each rhyme is an exact one: 'need/seed'; '-where/-pair'; '-take/break'; 'hand/sand'; '-year/cheer'; 'the way/decay'; 'flame/name'; '-stand/sand'; 'night/light'; 'space/face'; 'sea/me'.

For the special occasion of the final, signing-off rhyme, there is purpose in the last-minute variation, to the less precise pairing of 'man' with 'sand' (exactly paralleled in the alternative ending by 'plan' and 'sand'). This slight demurring from formal precision is the appropriate complement to the sense: the narrator does not quite achieve that all-ends-tied-up perfect neatness; he must sign off hanging in the balance, not neatly at rest.

The structural orderliness is present in many other ways. The three lines that contain the title of the song themselves make a pattern (like a sandwich), rather than offering a rigid repetition. That is, in the line at the centre of the song, we get the solo narrative journey of 'That every hair is numbered like every grain of sand', whereas with the first and last of the song's title lines, each offers a neatly balanced pairing, while at the same time the grammar of each pairing differs. The first is 'In every leaf . . . in every grain . . .' while the counterbalance in the last line is 'Like every sparrow . . . like every grain . . .'.

For the song to live and breathe, there has to be more to it than the classicism of order, however resourcefully the theme-serving structure achieves the detail of that order. The humane personal character that shines through the song, so that the individual's narrative superimposes itself upon both the scriptural blueprint and the formal construct—the living and breathing of the song—is achieved mostly on levels that fuse performance with poetry. Since it *is* a song, and not a poem, it may be fortuitous as to whether it works on the page too. There is one instance, as it happens, when Dylan's poetry, the expression of the individuality, works better on the page than on the recording. 'The sun beat down upon the steps of time to light the way' can be read, as it should be, as an uninterrupted line from start to finish: to do so is the most effective way to 'get' the idea the line proposes, and, as the long insistent burn of the uninterrupted line enacts its own meaning in its rhythm, to get too the sense of that sun's remorseless beating-down. In performance, the pause after 'steps' dislocates the phrase 'the steps of time', and in doing so makes less accessible the sense of the line. The sun doesn't beat down right across time here, it gets switched off half-way across.

Elsewhere, though, such effects are perfectly achieved in the performance. Look at the individual muscularity of what Dylan does with the sixth line in each of the three verses. These are, respectively, 'Like Cain, I now behold this chain of events that I must break', 'And every time I pass that way I always hear my name' and 'Sometimes I turn, there's someone there, other times it's only me.' Quite what the first-verse line means (what chain of events?) may be unclear, but the dexterity and confidence of control by which he achieves that brilliantly placed and far from facile internal rhyme—'Cain' and 'chain' are marvellously held apart, held in a far more effective tension than any greater closeness would effect, by the equally emphasised 'behold', while the slight pause between 'chain' and 'of events' enacts the pulling effect required—make this one of the finest lines in the song. The shorter middle-verse line and the longer last-verse line each distribute their syllables quite differently, the one acting out the weary glide of guilty repetition and the other the fitful turning back and forth. Yet it is what Dylan does with the endings of these three lines that shows him, as poet-performer, so wholly on top of his material. As each line is delivered, particularity of form acts out perfectly his particularity of meaning. When he reaches 'I must break', word, delivery and music all make that break; when, called by temptation every time, he reaches 'hear my name', we get the opposite of a break: we get a lingering; and in the same place in the third verse, where there is neither the compunction of an 'I must', nor the clarity of an 'always', but only the shifting uncertainty of a 'sometimes . . . other times', what he manages at line-end this time, on that doubtful 'only me', is something halfway between a break and a lingering: it hangs in the balance.

Meanwhile, behind this living, necessarily irregular individuality, the imagery of the song holds to its own systematic structure too. Not only are there the immediately adjacent matchings-up of, for example, 'rags to riches' and 'a summer's dream' to 'a wintry light', but more deep-seatedly the 'pool' of the first verse is matched by the 'sea' of the last, the 'reaching out somewhere' of the first matched by the 'hanging in the balance' of the last; 'newborn' discourses with both 'dyin'' and 'ancient'; 'footsteps' echo 'the steps of time'; and though the moon is unmentioned, perhaps its presence is implicit 'in the sorrow of the night . . . in the chill of a wintry light, / In the bitter dance of loneliness fading into space', so that as the cold moon fades into that 'space', this has its own pull upon 'the motion of the sea'. Since the broad theme of the song is the problematic one of understanding where we stand in creation, it is right that with the single, dodgy exception of the 'mirror', all its imagery is that of birth and death; the earth and the heavens; time and space; motion and fixity; humans and the animal kingdom; conscience, temptation and crime; the onward journey of consciousness and the ebb and flow of the elements.

Most broadly of all, these 'eternals' interact with the repeated auguries of impermanence placed throughout the song: an interaction focussed so intensely by the title image of the grain of sand itself. This image, as WILLIAM BLAKE suggests, can be opened up from many angles. Crucially, the grain of sand is all that's left of solid rock, that classic symbol of dependable permanence, when the motions of the sea are through with it; the grain of sand is all that's left of nature's fecundity and 'the garden', when these have become desert wastes; and while Dylan sings of 'the steps of time', the phrase echoing softly behind that is 'the sands of time'. In all these ways, sand whispers of impermanence, its shifting quality at odds with the clear fixity of 'a perfect finished plan'. It embodies 'the memory of decay'.

The grain of sand is also the poetic embodiment of the idea of the fundamental tiny particle of matter: and now quantum physics shows, by its tracking and tracing of the tiniest such particles, new things about the universe: crucially that there really *are* no absolutes. Quantum physics can detect, and even explain, things coming into existence out of nothing. This is the end for nature as Newtonian machine, in which every particle of matter is locked into a pattern that has forever been predetermined. It is the beginning of genuine indeterminism, in which it's possible to argue that not even God can know what is going to happen in the future. It is precisely the study of 'every grain of sand', in other words, that has killed off the credibility of any perfect finished plan. It's interesting that in revising the song, Dylan draws back from that 'perfect finished plan' to the more circumspect 'hanging in the balance of the reality of man'—and then sometimes in performance reverts once more to the earlier line: forever hanging in the balance of conflicting claims, because though the earlier line is too pat as philosophy, it's better poetry.

Of course, not even quantum physics can abolish God that easily: it's just that we do seem to have to keep changing our idea of what God is like. It's been said that 'anyone not shocked by quantum physics has not understood it'; and the new cosmology makes it imaginable that space and time may simply have flickered into existence by the laws of physics, not dependent upon a God to start it all off. Then again, God can still be thought of as out there, the great auteur-director, presiding (like Robert Altman) over the chaos of the set. Meanwhile the new cosmology also tends to re-offer us the old story. Coming after the traditional position, that God created the whole universe for the benefit of mankind, and after the scientific reductionism that followed—which held that nature, life and the human spirit were all created randomly by the blind, mechanical interactions of impersonal forces—now nature is looking like an elegant unity again, and one in which we (the very elements of our bodies fashioned in the stars) have an inescapable rôle. We're brought back, perhaps, to that part of the Max Ehrmann prose-poem 'Desiderata', much derided for its hippiesque homilism though published in 1927 and widely loved and disseminated ever since, in which 'You are a child of the universe, as much as the trees and stars. You have a right to be here.' Seeing the Big Bang as the beginning of all space and time fits in with our old notions from the book of Genesis: of 'Time moving in one direction, of a particular process unfolding,' as theologian Rowan Williams says, that has 'put back into our understanding of the universe elements of narrative. . . . This is a story which moves forward, which accumulates.' It is possible, as for Brian Swimme, to find in all this 'a God working with recalcitrant materials.' Sometimes I turn, there's someone there . . .

All this, then, above and beyond the resonant effect of the line 'Sometimes I turn, there's someone there, other times it's only me', insinuates doubt into the claimed orderliness of the song, giving it a dynamic complexity that keeps it alive.

We find a sub-text of tension too in 'Every Grain of Sand' from the very fact of Dylan's offering a song of submission to the authority of 'the Master's hand' to a secular, postmodernist, post-feminist audience. Yet the song and the performance are alive and open enough to have a wide appeal to non-believers. As PAUL NELSON wrote in a review of the *Shot of Love* album, in this song 'he touches you, and the gates of heaven dissolve into a universality . . .'

This universality is one of meaning and feeling. Essentially, to say that every hair is numbered, and that every sparrow falling counts, is simply to say that what we take to be innumerability does not make for valuelessness. The uncountable still count. This addresses the very heart of the problem we know that we have, for example, in responding humanly to any vast human disaster in a faraway place. The impersonality of the sheer numbers of the starving, the suffering, the wronged: we know how the mega-figures of death disconnect our sense of connection. Yet we know too that if any one of us matters, the only humane logic possible is that everyone—every one—matters also.

The universality of feeling that complements this simple humanitarianism at, as it were, the heart of the song, is finally given flight in Dylan's lovely, inspired, humane harmonica solos: using the soft, rounded, *different* harmonica that he introduced on the *Saved* album, and which, typically, was widely resented at the time because it wasn't *the right one*! The first solo sketches out chunky, shuddering possibilities of frailty and resilience; the second, coming at the end of the song and fading into space, soars beyond it, spinning its disarming idiosyncracy around a beautiful melodic line and dancing with the freedom of acceptance, humility and grace.

Despite our preferring the modern intelligence and fractured sensibility—the non-submission to any traditional authority—of something like 'Visions of Johanna', so well does 'Every Grain of Sand' live and breathe, that when, on *Biograph*, the running-order gives us the full push-to-the-edge, follow-that! of a live 1966 'Visions of Johanna', and what has to follow it is 'Every Grain of Sand', the stately 1981 song holds its own. That's some achievement.

[Adam Clarke, *Commentary on the Bible*, 7 vols., London: Thomas Tegg, 1844 edn., is used because it represents the informed but traditional thinking of believers, not academic outsiders. Clarke (1762–1832) was a polymath and Methodist; his popular *Commentary* was informed by critical inquiry yet just predates the influence of the German scholarship that drove a wedge between the intellectual theological élite and churchgoers who accepted the Bible as the word of God. On *Hamlet* all quotations come from essays reprinted in the Signet Classic Shakespeare *Hamlet, Prince of Denmark*, London: New English Library 1963, except the Tillyard, which is cited in the Maynard Mack essay with no further attribution. Rowan Williams & Brian Swimme quoted from Part 1 of the series 'Soul' by Anthony Clare, BBC-TV, London, 1992. Paul Nelson: *Shot of Love* review, *Rolling Stone* no.354, NY, 15 Oct 1981.]

Ezekiel, Dylan's use of That great 1981 song 'Angelina' (see separate entry), with its 'angel with four faces', draws strongly upon Ezekiel, the Old Testament book that the writer of Revelation seems to have had continually in mind. But Dylan has been down this road before. Ezekiel is where we find the angels' 'wheels on fire' (though see also **'wheels of fire'**). The vision of the four-faced cherabims on the fiery wheels of the divine chariot revisits Ezekiel in chapters 10 and 11. The phrase 'fall by the sword', which Dylan uses so freshly in 'your fall-by-the-sword love affair with Errol Flynn', in 'Foot of Pride' (also 1981), is part of God's admonition to Ezekiel in his vision—'and a third part shall fall by the sword round about thee' (Ezekiel 5:12), with the phrase itself repeated in 6:11 & 12, as well as elsewhere in the Bible. Another phrase from Ezekiel (31:16) is 'the trees of Eden', the phrase with which Dylan ends the first verse of 'Gates of Eden', while his lovely line 'in the valley of dry bone dreams', in 'Dignity', arises from the vision of the 'valley of dry bones' in Ezekiel 37.

***Far from the Madding Crowd* [book & film]** For relevance to a Dylan song, see **Hinton, Nigel.**

'Farewell Angelina' [1965] Most of us first encountered that rare and elusive Dylan song 'Farewell Angelina' on a record by JOAN BAEZ. She recorded it in New York City in 1965, and made it the title song of her sixth album, released by Vanguard the same year. With no available recording, it seemed, by Dylan himself, either this had to do (and it's perfectly pleasant, though in stressing a dreaminess rather than a dream-like quality, she brings it close to whimsy) or else it had to be regarded as, really, a poem—as words-on-the-page. And indeed it was available in that form, in the several official books of lyrics, including *Lyrics 1962–1985*.

F

But Dylan, it turned out, had indeed recorded it (in January 1965, at the *Bringing It All Back Home* sessions), though, remarkably, no tape had ever circulated until shortly before its sudden, surprise release on the official box set the *Bootleg Series Vols. 1–3* in 1991.

'Farewell Angelina' seems to introduce surrealistic language with a bang, in a new way for Dylan, whereas by the time of *Blonde on Blonde* he has adjusted that language almost out of recognition. In this sense 'Farewell Angelina' stands alone. Where *Blonde on Blonde* works as a sort of contemporary technicolour surrealist movie, 'Farewell Angelina' seems like a black and white 1940s surrealist short—especially the lyric as we knew it for decades prior to 1991.

'Just a table standing empty by the edge of the sea': that is the line that encapsulates the song, its essential tone and its distinctive kind of image. A strange song: and the fact that there are still things in it that do seem characteristic of Dylan's other work does not make it, in overall effect, any the less strange—quite the opposite. The melody is typically Dylan: it has a similar expansive lightness and brightness to the near-contemporaneous 'Mr. Tambourine Man'. Some of the lines in the lyric add to this similarity: 'The triangle tingles and the trumpets play slow / . . . The sky is on fire, and I must go'; and 'In the space where the deuce and the ace once ran wild / Farewell Angelina, the sky is folding'. But 'Farewell Angelina' is emphatically and fundamentally visual: a series of pictures, sometimes switching suddenly on and off, sometimes sliding into each other: 'King Kong little elves / On the rooftops they dance / Valentino-type tangos / While the make-up man's hands / Shut the eyes of the dead, / Not to embarrass anyone: / Farewell Angelina, / The sky is embarrassed, / And I must be gone.'

Even that remarkable 'the sky is embarrassed' is an assertion we reach to visualise. We picture the sky, and picture it in relation to the narrative's other protagonists, throughout the song. This is all that is offered or required; if we receive all the visual glimpses, if we really can 'See the cross-eyed pirates / Sitting perched in the sun / Shooting tin cans / With a sawn-off shot-gun' then the song has worked.

That said, Dylan's own recording, as belatedly released, seems to capture an earlier draft of the song. Several of the respects in which it differs show a hesitancy about the words themselves and how to fit them into the melodic lines; and Dylan resorts to the same line twice in consecutive verses—'The sky is flooding over'. We lose several of the passages quoted above (the best passages): 'Just a table standing empty by the edge of the sea' is instead 'A table stands empty by the edge of the stream'; 'the music', rather than 'the trumpets', play slow; 'the night', rather than 'the sky', is on fire; the 'King Kong little elves' dance 'in' rather than 'on' the rooftops; we see the cross-eyed pirates 'sit' rather than 'sitting'; and 'the hero's clean hands', rather than the make-up man's, 'shut the eyes of the dead, not to embarrass anyone'—after which instead of the lovely Pathetic Fallacy of 'the sky is embarrassed', we get the first appearance of 'the sky is flooding over'. (There is also an extra verse, inserted between the published version's penultimate and last verses, and it is at the end of this extra verse that 'The sky is flooding over' again; by the time of the published version, this line has been dropped altogether.)

That 'hero's clean hands' prefigures Dylan's surprising formulation a few years later, in 'Lay Lady Lay', in which 'His clothes are dirty but his hands are clean'—which reverses the expected moral weighting. The Noble Workman has honourably *dirty* hands, and in the West of the cowboy (the terrain with a Nashville skyline), clean hands belong only to the no-good gamblin' man. In 'Farewell Angelina' there is no such location by genre, and 'clean hands' can simply suggest spotless honesty. But even in 'Lay Lady Lay' the image isn't deployed as a double-edged commentary, such as we have on the song 'John Wesley Harding': it is a plain statement of praise in both cases, with 'clean hands' taking its ethic not from the mid-west but from the Bible: from verses 2–3 of the 24th Psalm, which is a Psalm of David: 'Who shall ascend into the hill of the Lord? / Or who shall stand in his holy place? / He that hath clean hands, and a pure heart.'

The best line that Dylan's own early recording of 'Farewell Angelina' hasn't yet arrived at, 'the sky is embarrassed', may also have had a biblical prompting. Chapter 24, verse 23 of Isaiah envisages world's end as happening when 'the moon shall be confounded, and the sun ashamed . . .'

Dylan has never performed 'Farewell Angelina' in concert. He did, however, feel drawn to the name Angelina again at the beginning of the 1980s, when he recorded the more simply titled but longer, richer and more complex 'Angelina' at the sessions for the *Shot of Love* album (see separate entry for details).

[Joan Baez: 'Farewell Angelina', NY, *nia*, issued *Farewell Angelina*, Vanguard VRS-9200 (stereo VSD-79200), NY, 1965; CD-reissued Vanguard VRM 79200-2, NY & London, 1995. (The album contained 3 other Dylan songs, plus, among other things, 2 songs he has covered since: 'Will Ye Go, Laddie, Go' and 'Satisfied Mind'.) The UK hit single was Joan Baez: 'Farewell Angelina', Fontana TF 639, London, 1965.]

Fariña, Mimi [1945 - 2001] Margarita Mimi Baez, younger sister of JOAN, was born in Palo Alto, California, on April 30, 1945. The family spent a year in Baghdad when Mimi was age six to seven, returning to Redlands, California, in 1952. Two years later, the two sisters saw PETE SEEGER in concert and resolved to become folksingers, which they duly did, discovering and moving into the Cambridge, Massachusetts, folk scene when the family moved east in 1958.

Both played guitar and sang. Mimi was the prettier of the two, and the less talented. She remained in Joan's shadow, and was with her when the two first met Bob Dylan, which was at Gerde's Folk City in Greenwich Village on April 10, 1961—by which time Joan was a star and Mimi's future husband RICHARD FARIÑA was married to that other pretty young folk singer, CAROLYN HESTER. It was towards Mimi, not Joan, that Dylan directed his playful, flirtatious charm. She was not quite 16 years old.

A year later, Mimi met Hester and Fariña in France, sitting with the two of them in the back seat of a car on a scenic ride around the countryside. Early the following month (May 1962) Hester left France for her home state of Texas after quarrelling with Fariña in Paris, and he immediately wrote a poem for Mimi. At the beginning of that September, when Hester rejoined her husband for a shared booking at the Edinburgh Festival, she found the 17-year-old Mimi was there too, and at Richard's invitation.

They married after Hester obtained a Mexican divorce from Fariña, and he set out to inveigle himself into her career just as he had done with Carolyn Hester's. They became Richard and Mimi Fariña, folk duo. They collaborated on the albums *Celebrations for a Grey Day* and *Reflections in a Crystal Wind* (both 1965).

When Dylan's album *The Freewheelin' Bob Dylan* came out in 1963, it was Mimi who had played it to Richard Fariña, stimulating his ambitions to break new ground in writing himself. Mimi's copy of the album had been sent to her by Joan, with a cryptic note attached: 'My new boyfriend.'

This was her attempt to shut the door firmly upon the previously open question as to which of the two Dylan preferred. In truth, he found Mimi the more personally attractive, Joan the more useful professionally. There is a photo of him and Mimi by the hotel pool at the NEWPORT FOLK FESTIVAL in July 1964, in which they seem at least as relaxed together as Bob and Joan ever do. Mimi is all of 19 at that point. On her 20th birthday, at the Café Espresso up in Bearsville, NY, the two had a violent row after Dylan launched into a couple of his famous 'truth attacks' on a friend of Richard's and on Joan; Mimi pulled Dylan's hair until he wept.

By her 21st birthday, she'd already been married three years. She and Richard had married on August 24, 1963, at the Baez Seniors' rented house in Portola Valley, California. Mimi turned 21 two days after the publication of Richard's novel; he had a book signing and pretended he'd forgotten her birthday until after the signing, when she found he'd co-organised a surprise party with the other Baez sister, Pauline (the oldest). During the party Richard hopped on the pillion seat of another guest's Harley Davison and died when it came off the road on a bend. Bob Dylan was in Denmark on his 1966 tour with the Hawks. Sixty days later, back in upstate New York, he too met with a motorcycle crash.

In 1967 Mimi and Joan recorded some duets together. One was Donovan's song 'Catch the Wind'. Mimi moved to San Francisco and married record producer Milan Melvin, but she retained the name Fariña and separated from Melvin after two years. She continued to perform, sometimes recording and touring with Joan, and from 1970 to 1972 with the rather more obscure singer-songwriter Tom Jans. Like Baez, she signed to A&M Records in 1971, and that year she and Jans released *Take Heart*. In 1973 she abandoned a solo album for the same label.

In 1974, she founded Bread and Roses, a charity formed to deliver free live music shows to hospitals, nursing homes and prisons, and it was on this non-profit organization that she concentrated in her last years, though she released an album titled *Solo* in 1985 (by which time her voice had a pleasing timbre, reminiscent of Carly Simon's), gave performances with Baez in the mid-1990s and, in a last tangential brush with Dylan, appeared on Baez's 1995 album *Ring Them Bells*. Nevertheless, she found this side of her pallid career a struggle. 'I suffered from comparing my voice to my sister's,' she said in February 1999. 'In the end, it was a great relief to stop singing.'

Mimi became and remained a conscientious literary and audio executor of Richard Fariña's works. She also became, in DAVID HAJDU's biography *Positively 4th Street: The Life and Times of Joan*

Baez, Bob Dylan, Mimi Baez Fariña and Richard Fariña, an equal figure with the others (and the most likeable of them as a human being). Three months after its publication, looked after by her last partner, the journalist Paul Liberatore, Mimi Fariña died of lung cancer at her home in Mill Valley, California, on July 18, 2001.

[Mimi Fariña: *Solo*, Rounder, US, 1985, CD-reissued Philo, US, 1993. Mimi & Richard Fariña: *Celebrations for a Grey Day*, NY, Sep 1964, Vanguard VRS-9174 (mono VSD-79174), US, 1965; *Reflections in a Crystal Wind*, Vanguard 79204, US, 1965. Mimi Fariña & Tom Jans: *Take Heart*, A&M SP 4310, US, 1971.

The main source here is David Hajdu, *Positively 4th Street: The Life and Times of Joan Baez, Bob Dylan, Mimi Baez Fariña and Richard Fariña*, New York: Farrar, Strauss & Giroux, 2001; quoted note from Joan Baez from ditto, London: Bloomsbury, 2001, p.162. The Mimi quote re giving up singing is from the compilation of obituaries seen online 29 Dec 2005 at *http://lists.village.virginia.edu/lists_archive/sixties-l/3377.html*.]

Fariña, Richard [1937 - 1966] Richard George Fariña was born in Brooklyn, New York, on March 8, 1937, attended Brooklyn Technical High School and then took engineering at Cornell, switching to English Literature soon after arriving and befriending the writer Thomas Pynchon, whose classic 1970s novel *Gravity's Rainbow* was dedicated to Fariña's memory. While a student Fariña published short stories in literary journals but also in *The Transatlantic Review* and *Mademoiselle*. Suspended from Cornell, he eventually dropped out, to become a handsome hipster, folkie, novelist and pioneer of counter-cultural amorality: a self-congratulatory conman whose manipulation of those around him made Bob Dylan seem transparent in comparison.

For details of Fariña's marriages and folk-duo careers see the entries on **Hester, Carolyn** and **Fariña, Mimi**. (He met the former in 1960, marrying her 18 days later; he met the latter, JOAN BAEZ's younger sister, in 1962 and married her in August 1963, when she was 18.)

Aside from pushing his Svengaloid way into both these singers' careers, he also wrote songs and hung around with other male folksingers, most notably ERIC VON SCHMIDT and Bob Dylan, with both of whom he shared a giddy, brief skitter through the London folk scene at the beginning of 1963, during which, that January 15, the three recorded some of the album *Dick Fariña and Eric Von Schmidt*, on which Dylan sings backing vocals and plays harmonica (as detailed in the entry on **Von Schmidt, Eric**).

It is sometimes alleged, or at any rate implied, not least in DAVID HAJDU's biography *Positively 4th Street: The Life and Times of Joan Baez, Bob Dylan, Mimi Baez Fariña and Richard Fariña*, that Fariña actually invented folk-rock and was writing inspired multi-layered songs of a complexity to rival Dylan's ahead of the latter, and that if only he had lived he would have been able to rise to similar heights of artistry and fame, and might have been equally crucial in affecting the consciousness of the age. The Hajdu book, published in 2001, has certainly been the stimulus to a renewal of interest in Fariña's work—his recordings span the period 1963-65—from which it is perfectly clear that his talent was not equipped to travel any further than it did. His best-known song, 'Pack Up Your Sorrows', was co-written with the little-known, oldest Baez sister, Pauline Marden.

His best work was his novel *Been Down So Long It Seems Like Up to Me*, a work of energetic comedy and ferocious contemporaneity now inevitably termed 'a cult classic', which was published two days before his death on the back of a shiny red Harley Davison Sportster in Carmel, California. Crassly hurtful of others to the last, he managed to get himself killed on his wife's 21st birthday, April 30, 1966.

[Richard Fariña, *Been Down So Long It Seems Like Up to Me*, New York: Random House, 1966. Mimi & Richard Fariña: *Celebrations for a Grey Day* (incl. 'Pack Up Your Sorrows') NY, Sep 1964, Vanguard VRS-9174 (mono VSD-79174), US, 1965; *Reflections in a Crystal Wind*, Vanguard 79204, US, 1965.

David Hajdu, *Positively 4th Street: The Life and Times of Joan Baez, Bob Dylan, Mimi Baez Fariña and Richard Fariña*, New York: Farrar, Strauss & Giroux, 2001.]

Ferlinghetti, Lawrence [1919 -] Ferlinghetti, born in Yonkers, New York, on March 24, 1919, became one of the most influential figures of the Beat Generation. He was a publisher—and was arrested for publishing GINSBERG's *Howl* in 1955—as well as a poet: and not the usual self-taught poet—he studied at the University of North Carolina, Columbia University and the Sorbonne. He co-founded the City Lights Bookstore in San Francisco, where he moved in 1951 after working for *Time* in New York City. City Lights was an important rendezvous, talkshop and publishing house for experimental writers.

Unsurprisingly, then, he is the Beat poet whose work most noticeably includes constant allusions to others' texts and titles—a feature we recognise as characteristic in Dylan's 1960s poetry, in *Tarantula* and throughout his songs. Ferlinghetti's poem 'Autobiography' includes allusions to T.S. ELIOT, Matthew Arnold, Thomas Wolfe, ALLEN GINSBERG, WOODY GUTHRIE, Wordsworth, Thoreau and Melville.

Specific passages also prefigure Dylan: 'I got caught stealing pencils / from the Five and Ten Cent Store / the same month I made Eagle Scout' absolutely sets the tone for Dylan's 'My Life in a Stolen Moment'. 'Junkman's Obbligato' [sic] chimes similarly, updating Eliot's glamorously sordid city in very much a 'Dylanesque' way: 'Stagger befuddled into East River sunsets / Sleep in phone booths . . . / staggering blind after alleycats / under Brooklyn Bridge / blown statues in baggy pants / our tincan cries and garbage voices / trailing.' And you can't read, in 'The Long Street', the unmemorable lines 'where everything happens / sooner or later / if it happens at all' without hearing Bob Dylan's voice reciting a passage with that same rhythm and that same last line on the unreleased early version of 'Brownsville Girl', 'New Danville Girl' [Hollywood, December 1984]: 'Nothing happens on purpose / It's an accident / If it happens at all.' Another poem, 'Dog', with the recurrent line 'The dog trots freely in the street', might be the prompt for 'If Dogs Run Free'.

All these Ferlinghetti poems are from the group 'Oral Conversations' in *A Coney Island of the Mind*, 1958, which Dylan namechecks in the sleevenotes to *Biograph*—but Dylan also alludes to Ferlinghetti's collection *Pictures from the Gone World* in his interesting sleevenote prose poem for *Planet Waves*: 'Yeah the ole days Are gone forever And the new ones Aint fAR behind, the Laughter is fAding away, echos [sic] of a staR, of Energy Vampires in the Gone World going Wild!' (See also ***Planet Waves*, the disappearing sleevenotes**.)

Dylan is known to have written Ferlinghetti a long, not overly successful prose-poem-style letter, postmarked April 28, 1964, after calling on him that February 20, finding him not at home, and leaving him a short note. Despite this apparent friendliness, the following year, when Ferlinghetti attended one of Dylan's early electric concerts (Berkeley, November 3, 1965), his attitude was described like this by RALPH GLEASON:

> 'I thought Larry was a tragic figure that weekend, a shaken and embittered man. You know, "What is that stringy kid doing up there with his electric guitar?" I mean, "I am a major poet and this kid has thirty-five hundred kids in this hall." And Larry has been mumbling to himself ever since.'

He appeared to have reached an acceptance of the electric guitars by the time of *The Last Waltz* concert in 1976, at which, already looking ancient, he performed his ersatz version of the Lord's Prayer.

His 40+ poetry books also include *Endless Life: The Selected Poems*, 1981. At the time of writing, Ferlinghetti is still alive, aged 86. He has outlived all his major contemporaries among THE BEATS.

[Lawrence Ferlinghetti: *Pictures of the Gone World*, San Francisco: City Lights, 1955; *A Coney Island of the Mind*, New York: New Directions, 1958; *Endless Life: Selected Poems*, New Directions, 1981. Bob Dylan: note and letter to Ferlinghetti, 20 Feb & 28 Apr 1964, both in the City Lights archive deposited with the Bancroft Library at UC Berkeley; first published in *The Telegraph* no.36, Romford, UK, summer 1990; letter seen online 02 Sep 2005 in the 'Words Fill My Head' section of *www.bjorner.com* (though here it is laid out like a poem and not as on Dylan's typed sheet). Ralph Gleason quoted in Robert Shelton, *No Direction Home: The Life and Music of Bob Dylan*, 1986, Penguin edn. p.333.]

film dialogue in Dylan's lyrics The first critic to notice Dylan's sustained but stealthy sewing of Hollywood film dialogue into his lyrics (especially those of the mid-1980s), and to tease out some of the detail in print, was JOHN LINDLEY, in 1986; it lead to a flurry of further discoveries by Dylan-following insomniacs watching old films on late-night television. This was not hard. Filmic references are dotted throughout Dylan's writing from very early days.

In the mocking 'Talkin' John Birch Paranoid Blues' he says of George Lincoln Rockwell 'I know for a fact he hates commies cus he picketed the movie *Exodus*'. 'She got movies inside her head,' he sings in 'Hero Blues' (in one variant 'nail-movies'), while 'Motorpsycho Nitemare' offers a playful focus on the Hitchcock film *Psycho* and mentions *La Dolce Vita*. Perhaps he first *specifies* quoting from a film at the end of his unfailingly interesting '11 Outlined Epitaphs': 'there's a movie called / *Shoot the Piano Player* / the last line proclaimin' / "music, man, that's where it's at" / it is a religious line . . .' (Its original French title is *Tirez sur le pianiste*; the English-language title is often *Shoot the Pianist*. Years later, Dylan recalls this film, asking the playwright SAM SHEPARD if he had ever seen it. This is at their first meeting, prior to Shepard being subsumed into the Rolling Thunder Revue and the making of Dylan's own film *Renaldo & Clara*. Shepard says yes he has seen *Shoot the Piano Player* and asks if that's the kind of movie Dylan wants to make. Dylan replies, 'Something like that.')

We find *unacknowledged* fleeting quotation from film dialogue in his early work too. In the 1958 film of Tennessee Williams's play *Cat on a Hot Tin Roof*, Paul Newman says to Burl Ives: 'You don't know what love is. To you it's just another four-letter word.' 'Love Is Just a Four-Letter Word' is a pre-electric Dylan song. In Don Siegel's film of the same year, *The Lineup*, a drug trafficker says: 'When you live outside the law you have to eliminate dishonesty.' It's a very short step of elimination to Dylan's famous dictum from 'Absolutely Sweet Marie', 'To live outside the law you must be honest.' The *Self Portrait* instrumental title 'Woogie Boogie' is also a quote from film dialogue. In the Marx Brothers' 1941 film *The Big Store*, Chico, a piano teacher, tells his pupils: 'Keep practising while I'm away—but remember: NO woogie boogie!'

There is also the submerged presence of the singing-cowboy movies in Bob Dylan's consciousness. These were both a successful Hollywood genre and a part of the early history of commercial country music. The stars were Gene Autry, whose *Tumbling Tumbleweeds*, 1935, was one of the best of his 100+ films and provided a title song that has proved recurrently popular. (A majestic, spacey, superb version of 'Tumbling Tumbleweeds' is the opening track of Don EVERLY's flawed masterpiece *Don Everly*, 1971.) After Autry came Roy Rogers, and though Tex Ritter was never that big, he made 58 singing-cowboy films and became a star in the 1950s with the theme tune to *High Noon*. One of his film songs is 'Blood on the Saddle', a phrase Dylan alludes to ('blood on your saddle') in his 1970s song 'Idiot Wind', on *Blood on the Tracks*.

In the mid-1980s period covering the *Infidels*, *Empire Burlesque* and *Knocked Out Loaded* albums, this linkage with Hollywood spreads like a craze for a new game in Dylan's work. The title *Empire Burlesque* itself, of course, flags this preoccupation. It doesn't merely present itself as offering a 'burlesque' of the Hollywood 'empire', or allude to the chains of cinemas called Empires. It's a more detailed reference than that: there were moviehouses named Empire Burlesques. The Empire Burlesque in Newark, New Jersey, is mentioned in Philip Roth's *The Anatomy Lesson* (1983), notes David Hill in *Telegraph* 29 (Romford, Essex, spring 1988). In 'The Night Bob Came Round', Raymond Foye reports first-hand: '"What were you thinking of calling the album?" [ALLEN] GINSBERG asked at last. "*Empire Burlesque*", Dylan said. . . . "That was the name of a burlesque club I used to go to when I first came to New York, down on Delancey Street," Dylan volunteered. . . . How like him, I later thought, only volunteering information when it will mislead.'

Inside the album, quotations come thick and fast, and almost entirely from distinctive films of the 1940s and 1950s, or from undistinguished vehicles for distinguished stars of the same period. These are clearly Dylan favourites, and John Lindley quotes Dylan as saying: 'I can do a few other people's voices: Richard Widmark, Sidney Greenstreet, Peter Lorre. They really had distinctive voices in the early talkie films. Nowadays you go to a movie and you can't tell one voice from the other'; and in another note about the making of Dylan's own film *Renaldo & Clara*, Sam Shepard reports that in a kitsch gun museum in Connecticut or Vermont, the crew were 'trying to film a scene . . . with Dylan and [BOB] NEUWIRTH. Some kind of *Maltese Falcon* take-off.'

It's as easy to look at Dylan's use of movie dialogue film by film as song by song. As Lindley noted, *The Maltese Falcon* featured most of Dylan's Hollywood favourites and includes many fragments of dialogue magpied inside Dylan's songs. 'I don't mind a reasonable amount of trouble' is a Sam Spade line and becomes, verbatim, a line in the *Empire Burlesque* song 'Seeing the Real You at Last'. Spade growls 'I'll have some rotten nights after I've sent you over—but that'll pass.' In the same Dylan song this becomes 'Well I have had some rotten nights / Didn't think that they would pass.' Spade's partner says 'You don't have to look for me. I'll see you.' In 'When the Night Comes Falling from the Sky' Dylan sings 'Don't look for me, I'll see you.' The film gives us 'I don't care who loves who—maybe you love me and maybe I love you' and the song gives us 'It won't matter who loves who / You'll love me or I'll love you / When the night comes falling from the sky.' The film offers the exchange 'We wanna talk to you, Spade.' 'Well, go ahead and talk.' In 'Tight Connection to My Heart' Dylan offers 'You want to talk to me, / Go ahead and talk.'

Humphrey Bogart lines from several other films curl like his cigarette smoke into these Dylan lyrics too, though Dylan never attempts a Bogart delivery. Bogart's style makes numinous to the movie viewer lines that would otherwise have no special ring to them—which is what one can so often say of Dylan's delivery also. There are at least three snippets of Bogart movie dialogue in 'Tight Connection to My Heart' alone: two from *Sirocco* (1951) and one from *Tokyo Joe* (1949). The first of these comprises the line that Dylan uses as the starting-point of the song. Actress Marta Toren says 'I'm coming with you.' Bogart retorts: 'I've got to move fast: I can't with you around my neck.' Dylan sings 'Well I had to move fast / And I couldn't with you around my neck.' Later in the same verse Dylan sings 'I'll go along with the charade / Until I can think my way out.' This comes straight out of Bogart's mouth in *Tokyo Joe*. (This was recycled in a 'Star Trek' episode, 'The Squire of Gothos', in which Sulu asks: 'How far do we go along with this charade?' and Captain Kirk answers: 'Until we can think our way out.')

Further on in the Dylan lyric, we hear 'But I can't figure out if I'm too good for you / Or if you're too good for me', while Bogart says to Marta Toren, back in *Sirocco*, that 'I don't know whether I'm too good for you or you're too good for me.'

The song has another, more deeply buried filmic allusion. When Dylan sings 'Well they're not showing any light tonight / And there's no moon / There's just a hot-blooded singer / Singing "Memphis in June"', the figure who leaps to mind, not as hot-blooded singer but as composer of 'Memphis in June', is HOAGY CARMICHAEL, who himself launched that song in another movie, the 1945 George Raft film *Johnny Angel*.

In *The Big Sleep* (1946) Bogart mumbles that 'There's some people you don't forget, even if you've only seen them once.' Dylan sings this in the forgettable 'I'll Remember You' as 'There's some people that / You don't forget, / Even though you've only seen 'em / One time or two.' The film's closing exchange, which is between Bogart and Lauren Bacall, goes like this: 'What's wrong with you?' 'Nothing you can't fix.' Dylan intervenes more than usual with this one, making it, in 'Seeing the Real You at Last': 'At one time there was nothing wrong with me / That you could not fix.'

In the same studio-producer-director-and-writing team's *To Have and Have Not*, the first film to pair Bogart with Bacall, he tells her to 'stop that baby talk'. In 'Seeing the Real You at Last' Dylan sings that he's 'gonna quit this baby talk now', while the same song's opening line comes straight from the mouth of Bogart's co-star Edward G. Robinson in 1948's *Key Largo*, another John Huston film and again pairing Bogart with Bacall. Robinson says: 'Think this rain would cool things off, but it don't.' The Bob Dylan song begins with 'Well I thought that the rain would cool things down / But it looks like it don't.'

Indeed this song has so many film lines inside it that Dylan increases his hunting range into the 1960s—even into the 1980s—to find material. *The Hustler* (which *The Observer* called 'The supreme classic of that great American genre, the low-life movie') provides Dylan with these lines, almost verbatim: 'I got troubles, I think maybe you got troubles / I think we'd better leave each other alone', while the last two of the following four lines come out of the Clint Eastwood vehicle *Bronco Billy* (1980) and the first two, while they've not been identified, certainly sound as if we're back in one of Bogart's joints: 'When I met you baby / You didn't show no visible scars. / You could ride like Annie Oakley / You could shoot like Belle Starr.' In *Bronco Billy*, Eastwood, in the title rôle, asked what kind of woman he's looking for, replies: 'I'm looking for a woman who can ride like Annie Oakley and shoot like Belle Starr.' The pithiness of the simile is somewhat reduced by knowing that the real Belle Starr was in fact a hopeless shot. (For more on Belle Starr in films, see **Guthrie, Woody**.)

In Clint Eastwood's case, the compliment of lifting dialogue has been repaid. In his later film *Pale Rider* (1985) one of the characters says 'Well, I wish there was something I could do or say, to try and make you change your mind and stay': verbatim lines, of course, from Dylan's 1962 song 'Don't Think Twice, It's All Right'.

At any rate, it's small wonder that John Lindley was moved to write of 'Seeing the Real You at Last' (an ironic title, in this context) that so much appears to come from film dialogue that he 'would not be surprised to discover in time that the entire song . . . is constructed of lines from this medium'—though actually, not all its lines derive from Hollywood. The song ends with a re-statement of the words of Jesus to Judas at the Last Supper (giving an extra frisson to the petulant and self-aggrandising bitterness of Dylan's stance throughout): 'Whatever you gonna do / Please do it fast,' writes Dylan; in *John* 13:27, '. . .Satan entered into him [Judas]. Then said Jesus unto him, That thou doest, do quickly.' (It is a moment Dylan had used before, in 'Groom's Still Waiting at the Altar' and 'Man of Peace'.)

Yet we have not finished with Hollywood sources even for 'When the Night Comes Falling from the Sky'. Dylan sings, within it, the opaque 'I saw thousands who could have overcome the darkness, / For the love of a lousy buck, I've watched them die.' Is it, as the grammar insists, *his* love of a lousy buck that makes him watch them die where he might have intervened, or is it, as plain sense might more readily suggest, *their* love of a lousy buck that dooms them, the singer being mere witness to all this greed and come-uppance? In any case, in *On the Waterfront* Karl Malden as the streetwise priest says far more straightforwardly that what oils the wheels of society is 'the love of a lousy buck'. (This is also the film with the more widely quoted line 'I coulda bin a contender', which was perhaps in the back of Dylan's mind in 1975 when his lyrics for the chorus of 'Hurricane' include 'He coulda bin the champion of the world.') And while in *Twelve Angry Men*, one of the other jurors says to Henry Fonda, 'You thought you would gamble for support', in Dylan's song we get 'But you were gambling for support.'

Even that beautiful formulation of Dylan's in 'Tight Connection to My Heart' that 'What looks large from a distance / Close up ain't never that big' turns out, although its pithiness and concentrated impact is Dylan's, to be inspired by a film line. At the end of 1934's *Now and Forever*, Gary Cooper, about to be arrested, says of the cops: 'Close up they don't look as large as they do from a distance.'

Inevitably, a line from one of Dylan's favourite films, the classic western *Shane*, also reappears on *Empire Burlesque*. Shane says: 'I don't mind leaving, I'd just like it to be my idea.' And here it is in 'Never Gonna Be the Same Again' (not a claim this line can make): 'Don't worry, baby, I don't mind leaving / I'd just like it to be my idea.'

In 'Clean-Cut Kid'—written for the *Infidels* album but re-recorded for and released on *Empire Burlesque*—the source for a fragment of lyric seems to have been lifted from a vehicle for another Hollywood star whom Bob Dylan seems especially fond of, Elizabeth Taylor. In *The Sandpiper* (in which Taylor plays a bohemian artist living in a Monterey beach shack), headmaster Richard Burton says that her son should 'adjust' better. Taylor snaps: 'Adjust to what?' The Dylan song's opening rhetoric is 'Everybody's askin' why he couldn't adjust—/ Adjust to what? A dream that bust?'

To stray, temporarily, from *Empire Burlesque*, to round up filmic references from the surrounding albums, is to remember that a major song of the early 1980s, 'Caribbean Wind', deliberately alights in passing on another movie title, *The Cruel Sea*, and to look at another item that originated on *Infidels*. In 'Sweetheart Like You' Dylan asks ponderously, 'What's a sweetheart like you / Doin' in a dump like this?' You might think so undistinguished and recycled a line needs no hunt for any provenance, but it can't be helped: in *All Through the Night* (another Bogart film, and with Peter Lorre again too) he asks: 'What would a sweetheart like that Miss Hamilton dame be doing in a dump like this?'

There is a further flurry of dialogue raids on the album after *Empire Burlesque* too, Dylan's 1986 release *Knocked Out Loaded*. In *Bend of the River* (1952) someone says to James Stewart: 'I figure we're even. Maybe I'm one up on ya.' The opening verse of 'Driftin' Too Far from Shore' gives us 'I didn't know that you'd be leavin' / Or who you thought you were talkin' to. / I figure maybe we're even / Or maybe I'm one up on you.' Later in the same song we reach the curiously period touch of 'No gentleman likes makin' love to his servant / Specially when he's in his father's house.' This comes from yet another Bogart film, *Sabrina* (1954), in which actor Walter Hampden declares that 'No gentleman makes love to a servant in his mother's house.' Similarly, there are brief quotations from two more films in 'Maybe Someday', another *Knocked Out Loaded* song. 'Forgive me baby, for what I didn't do / For not breakin' down no bedroom door to get at you' comes across from *Separate Tables* (1958), in which Burt Lancaster says to his ex-wife, talking of her new lover: 'He didn't break any bedroom door down to get to you.' And the splendid 'Dylanesque' put-down 'I always liked San Francisco: I was there for a party once' turns out, more's the pity, to come straight from *Out of the Past* (indeed), a 1947 film in which Kirk Douglas asks: 'Do you know San Francisco?' and Robert Mitchum mumbles back: 'I've been there to a party once.'

On top of *Knocked Out Loaded* (or rather, quite a long way underneath it, which is saying something) 1986 gave us the single 'Band of the Hand', recorded with TOM PETTY & THE HEARTBREAKERS. This too looked back to Hollywood for a fragment of its lyric. In *I Wake Up Screaming* (1941) Laird Cregar says to the oleaginous Victor Mature: 'One day you'll be talking in your sleep, and when you do I wanna be around.' The song's last verse ends: 'I know your story is too painful to share. / One day, though, you'll be talkin' in your sleep / And when you do I wanna be there.' (It was a full circle of sorts that this wretchedly crude song was itself specially provided by Dylan as the title song for a film. His music had by then been used in many films but this was the first time he had specially recorded a song for a film in which he played no part himself.)

We encounter at least another couple of these small raids on movies within Dylan's 1989 release *Oh Mercy*, too. The title 'Man in the Long Black Coat' surely owes something to the Gregory Peck film title 'The Man in the Gray Flannel Suit' (1956), while the song's lines 'Somebody is out there / Beating on a dead horse', give a flashback to an equally momentary scene in *Catch-22*, when the hero Yossarian glimpses someone literally flogging a dead horse, as he stumbles through the Italian urban night seeing horror after phantasmagoric horror. In *The African Queen*—yet another 1950s Humphrey Bogart vehicle—there is the line 'Most of the time I know exactly what you're saying.' Dylan's song 'Most of the Time' adapts this, with a series of mock-defiant lines including 'Most of the time, I know exactly where it all went.' And at the closing moment of *Oh Mercy*'s closing song, 'Shooting Star', he chooses to say 'Saw a shooting star tonight / Slip away / Tomorrow will be another day . . .', which neatly parallels the closing moment in *Gone with the Wind*, in which 'After all, tomorrow is another day' is both heroine Scarlett O'Hara's last remark and, in the book on which the film is based, its final sentence.

It might be revealing to investigate how many of these reprocessed movie lines had in fact already been reprocessed by film scriptwriters from the books on which many of the films were based (and indeed from other books they happened to admire or have to hand). It might turn out that via this process many of Dylan's film lines are actually from literary or theatrical works. We know, after all, that *Cat on a Hot Tin Roof* reworks the Tennessee Williams play, that *The Maltese Falcon* began as Dashiell Hammett's novel, *The Big Sleep* as Raymond Chandler's and *To Have and Have Not* as Hemingway's, and that in the last two cases, novelist William Faulkner worked on the film scripts. *The African Queen* was scripted by the writer James Agee, *Separate Tables* by the distinguished, unfashionable British playwright Terence Rattigan, based upon his own play. *Sirocco* was adapted from *Le coup de grâce*, a novel by Joseph Kessel first published in Paris in 1931, and *The Cruel Sea* was scripted by novelist Eric Ambler from the novel by Nicholas Monsarrat. *Catch-22* is far more important as a novel than a movie, and *The Man in the Gray Flannel Suit* more so too (though in this case the author of this half-literary, half-pulp yet always beguiling novel, Sloan Wilson, confessed on his book jacket that its title, which is what Dylan echoes, was coined by his wife, Elise Pickhardt Wilson). And *Gone with the Wind* was a lengthily famous and best-selling novel before it was a mega-movie, though the movie has proved the more enduring. Given all this, surely at least some of those we recognise as movie lines in Dylan songs must actually have started their journey on the page, and could be found there, more or less verbatim.

Sometimes, though, the literary connection misleads, and a film connection is more at the heart of things. It's true that Truffaut's *Tirez sur le Pianiste* was based on a thriller by American writer David Goodis, *Down There*, but Goodis was primarily a screenplay writer. The same applies in many other cases. *Out of the Past*, scripted by Geoffrey Homes, was based upon his novel of the same name but Homes (a pseudonym for Daniel Mainwaring) was mainly a screenwriter. *Key Largo* was based upon Maxwell Anderson's play, but he too primarily wrote for movies. *Shane* was built from the novel by Jack Shaefer, but the same is true of him and of Steve Fisher (*I Wake Up Screaming* began as his novel), Budd Schulberg (*On the Waterfront* was scripted by him from his own novel) and Reginald Rose (who scripted *Twelve Angry Men* from his own play).

None of this alters the fact that the main and prominent conduit for these conversational titbits has been Hollywood and that it is the resonant, distinctive voices of movie stars who have set these phrases ringing in Bob Dylan's ears. Confirming this, it is one more noticeable feature of Dylan's mid-1980s songs that within them he mentions several stars by name.

In his early work, his approach is different. In 'Last Thoughts on Woody Guthrie' he says the sense of hope we all need 'ain't made in no Hollywood wheat germ'. Film luminaries are named inside his songs in the service of jokes—Brigitte Bardot, Anita Ekberg, Sophia Loren, Elizabeth Taylor and Richard Burton in 'I Shall Be Free', Tony Perkins in 'Motorpsycho Nitemare', Cecil B. de Mille in 'Tombstone Blues'.

In the mid-1960s prose-poems, the *Bringing It All Back Home* liner notes have throwaway mentions of 'jayne mansfield.humphrey bogart' sandwiched between 'SLEEPY JOHN ESTES' and the wonderful invention 'MORTIMER SNERD', and a list of people he doesn't want to be (because they are all dead) in which James Dean comes after 'bach. mozart. tolstoy. joe hill. gertrude stein'; and 'Alternatives to College' throws only Jerry Lewis into its huge babble of named characters. In '11 Outlined Epitaphs', in the rhapsodic list of people who are 'entrancin'' him, beginning with FRANCOIS VILLON and ending 17 names later, there is only one filmstar, Marlene Dietrich.

As shorthand descriptions, rather than as jokes, there are only two such names dropped into the first 15 years' worth of his recordings—right up to and including the *Desire* album: 'Bette Davis style' in 'Desolation Row' (1965) and 'He looked like Jimmy Cagney' in 'Joey' (1976).

In the 1980s, this suddenly changes. We get more than that in 1983 alone. 'Up pops Errol Flynn,' in John Lindley's happy phrase, in both the evangelical 'You Changed My Life' (1981) and in the extraordinary religious rant that is 'Foot of Pride' (1983), followed by Clark Gable in 'Don't Fall Apart on Me Tonight' (1983), Peter O'Toole in 'Clean-Cut Kid' (1983 and 1985) and then Gregory Peck, the insistent hero of the unreleased 'New Danville Girl' (1984) and the *Knocked Out Loaded* magnum opus 'Brownsville Girl' (1986): a song that, among the many things it does—see separate entry—also returns us full circle to the way Bob Dylan used *Shoot the Pianist* back in 1963. That is, it *tells* you about a film *and* then quotes from it. The film in this case is *The Gunfighter* (1950), from which Dylan manages to quote in consecutive songs. The title of the song that follows 'Brownsville Girl' on *Knocked Out Loaded* is 'Got My Mind Made Up' (co-written with Tom Petty). This is a line of dialogue spoken four times in *The Gunfighter*.

The same album quotes from another Gregory Peck western, 1958's *The Big Country*. In its minor way, the insertion of dialogue from this film is remarkable: for what he inserts it into is a song that isn't his own composition! The album's opening track, 'You Wanna Ramble', is a revival of an old R&B song by Junior Parker (the man who wrote and first recorded the ELVIS PRESLEY classic 'Mystery Train')—and in the middle of 'You Wanna Ramble', Dylan slips in his own addition, 'What happens tomorrow / Is on your head, not mine' . . . except that it isn't his own addition, it's taken from *The Big Country*, in which Burl Ives warns: 'What happens here tomorrow is on your head not mine.'

In the mid-1980s, one consequence of Dylan's continuing to be interested in scripture alongside his continued pursuit of movie dialogue is that he takes the extra step of trying to fuse the two. That is, we see in these songs several attempts to make a particular phrase, taken from film, serve also as scriptural allusion and as part of his work's religious themes.

Actually Dylan's first namecheck of Errol Flynn comes in an evangelical song, 'You Changed My Life' (1981)—in which Dylan makes this experiment with great audacity, choosing to sing, in the song's final verse, that he experienced his conversion to Christ not only as something sudden, and something elemental, but also with the heightened dramatic impact of Hollywood. It certainly makes for a surprising effect, though it's doubtful how far this escapes bathos and a damaging undercutting of the gravitas he wishes to retain, despite its audacity, when he sings: 'You came in like the wind, / Like Errol Flynn: / You changed my life.' Dylan's first co-option of dialogue from *The Maltese Falcon* is within an evangelical song too. In this much-utilised movie Sam Spade's last line is 'The stuff that dreams are made of.' (Itself a slight misquotation from Shakespeare's *The Tempest*.) In 'City of Gold', premièred in concert in San Francisco in 1980, Dylan makes this part of his armoury of preaching, as he sings 'There is a city of love / Far from this world / And the stuff dreams are made of.'

In 'Tight Connection to My Heart' this co-option may be apparent even in the reference to the singer being lulled to sleep 'In a town without pity / Where the water runs deep.' Dylan is certainly mindful here of the film title *Town Without Pity* (and no doubt remembers its overwrought title song, a hit for the overwrought Gene Pitney);

but the film's theme has no relevance to Dylan's, and commentator BERT CARTWRIGHT argues that this same passage is 'mindful of' Jeremiah 20:16 and Lamentations 2:17, which (though only in the Revised Standard Version) refer to 'the cities which the Lord overthrew without pity' and to the cities 'demolished without pity'. Similarly, to return to the lines in 1986's 'Maybe Someday' adapted by Dylan from the Bogart film *Sabrina* –where the film's 'No gentleman makes love to a servant in his mother's house' becomes the song's 'No gentleman likes makin' love to his servant / Specially when he's in his father's house'–NIGEL HINTON comments in an article on *Empire Burlesque* and *Knocked Out Loaded*: 'Put a capital letter on "Father", of course, and there are all kinds of other resonances here. . . . He makes his lines ring with mysterious possibilities: where one level works perfectly but where, if you care to switch contexts, the whole thing works on another level too. . . . it needs only a slight sideways step to see that each line carries a moral/spiritual implication.'

In all of the above, regardless of any such scriptural sub-text, it's likely to strike us that these film script snatches, barely if at all modified by Dylan, are so unmemorable and unarresting as content yet are mostly so attractive, tersely energetic and imitable as conversational rhythms, and offer cadences of heightened moment: they are great movie lines, in fact, and understandably appealing to the contemporary American poet. In other cases, Dylan's sub-editing, his tightening-up, gives them their radiance. You might feel that they're easy building blocks for writer's-block sufferers, or for singer-songwriters with nothing special to say. Or you might feel that Dylan has made himself inward with, and then re-expressed creatively, yet another branch of American popular culture: one that may have been handed down from above, from the on-highs of Hollywood, but one that has inhabited the shared minds of millions of ordinary people.

[John Lindley: 'Movies Inside His Head: *Empire Burlesque* and *The Maltese Falcon*', *The Telegraph* no.25, Bury, UK, autumn/winter 1986. Readers' further sightings from other films were then published in *Telegraph* nos. 26, 27, 28, 29 (all Romford, UK) and spasmodically later.

Exodus, dir. Otto Preminger, written Dalton Trumbo, starring Paul Newman, Eva Marie Saint, Ralph Richardson, Peter Lawford, Lee J. Cobb, Sal Mineo, Felix Aylmer, Uncle Tom Cobley & all; UA/Carlyle/Alpha, US, 1960. *Psycho*, dir. Hitchcock & Saul Bass, written Joseph Stefano, starring Anthony Perkins & Janet Leigh; Shamle/Alfred Hitchcock, US, 1960. *La Dolce Vita*, dir. Federico Fellini, written Fellini, Tullio Pinelli, Ennio Flaiano & Brunello Rondi, starring Marcello Mastroianni, Anita Ekberg & Anouk Aimée; Riama/Pathé, Italy/France, 1960. *Tirez sur le Pianiste*, dir. Francois Truffaut, written Marcel Moussy & Truffaut; Films de la Pléiade, France, 1960. Sam Shepard, *Rolling Thunder Logbook*, London: Penguin edn., 1977, p.13.

Cat on a Hot Tin Roof, dir. & written Richard Brooks, starring Elizabeth Taylor; MGM/Avon, US, 1958. *The Lineup*, dir. Don Siegel, written Stirling Silliphant; Columbia, US, 1958. *The Big Store*, dir. Charles Reisner, written Sid Kuller, Hal Fimberg & Ray Golden; MGM, US, 1941. (For this last connection, thanks to Christer Svensson, letter to this writer from Molkom, Sweden, c.1982.)

Tex Ritter: 'Blood on the Saddle', Hollywood, 1 May 1945, CD-reissued *High Noon*, Bear Family BCD 15634, Vollersode, Germany, 1991, which also includes 'Jingle Jangle Jingle', 'Wichita', 'The Chisolm Trail' and 'Billy the Kid', all cut for Capitol 1942–57. Vol. 4 of *Reprints from* Sing Out!, NY, *nia*, also includes 'Blood on the Saddle'. Don Everly: 'Tumbling Tumbleweeds', *Don Everly*, Ode SP-77005, LA (A&M AMLS 2007, London), 1971.

Empire Burlesque in Philip Roth, *The Anatomy Lesson*, New York: Farrar, Straus & Giroux, 1983, noted by David Hill, *The Telegraph* no.29, Romford, UK, spring 1988. Raymond Foye: 'The Night Bob Came Round', *Telegraph* no.36, Romford, summer 1990. *The Maltese Falcon*, dir. & written John Huston, also starring Mary Astor; Warner, US, 1941. *Sirocco*, dir. Curtis Bernhardt, written A.I. Bezzerides & Hans Jacoby; Columbia/Santana, US, 1951. *Tokyo Joe*, dir. Stuart Heisler, written Cyril Hume & Bertram Millhauser; Columbia/Santana, US, 1949. 'Star Trek', 'The Squire of Gothos', *nia*, noted by Clinton Heylin, *Telegraph* 29, op. cit. *Johnny Angel*, dir. Edwin L. Marin, written Steve Fisher; RKO, US, 1945.

The Big Sleep, dir. Howard Hawks, written William Faulkner, Leigh Brackett & Jules Furthman, starring Bogart & Lauren Bacall; Warner, US, 1946. (Bogart is again a private eye, this time Philip Marlowe. Based on the novel *The Big Sleep* by Raymond Chandler, 1939.) *To Have and Have Not*, dir. Howard Hawks, written Jules Furthman & William Faulkner, also starring Walter Brennan & Hoagy Carmichael; Warner, US, 1945; based on the novel of the same name by Ernest Hemingway, 1937, but just as obviously an imitation of the movie *Casablanca* (dir. Michael Curtiz; Warner, US, 1942). *Key Largo*, dir. John Huston, written Richard Brooks & Huston; Warner, US, 1948. *Bronco Billy*, dir. Eastwood, written Dennis Hackin; Warner/ Second Street, US, 1980. *Pale Rider*, dir. Eastwood, written Michael Butler & Dennis Shryack; Warner/ Malpaso, US, 1985.

Twelve Angry Men, dir. Sidney Lumet, written Reginald Rose, also starring Lee J. Cobb & E.G. Marshall; Orion-Nova, US, 1957. *Now and Forever*, dir. Henry Hathaway, written Vincent Lawrence, starring Gary Cooper, Carole Lombard & Shirley Temple; Paramount, US, 1934. *Shane*, dir. George Stevens, written A.B. Guthrie Jr., starring Alan Ladd, Jack Palance & Brandon de Wilde; Paramount, US, 1953. *The Sandpiper*, dir. Vincente Minelli, written Dalton Trumbo; MGM/Filmways, US, 1965. *The Cruel Sea*, dir. Charles Frend, written Eric Ambler, starring Jack Hawkins; Ealing, UK, 1953. *All Through the Night*, dir. Vincent Sherman, written Leonard Spigelgass & Edwin Gilbert; Warner, US, 1942. *Bend of the River* (in the UK

Where the River Bends) dir. Anthony Mann, written Borden Chase, starring James Stewart & Rock Hudson; U-I, US, 1952. *Sabrina* (in the UK *Sabrina Fair*), dir. & written (& produced) Billy Wilder, starring Bogart, William Holden & Audrey Hepburn; Paramount, US, 1954. *Separate Tables*, dir. Delbert Mann, written Terence Rattigan, starring Burt Lancaster, Rita Hayworth, David Niven, Deborah Kerr, Wendy Hiller, Gladys Cooper, Felix Aylmer & Rod Taylor; UA/Hecht-Hill-Lancaster, US, 1958. *Out of the Past* (in the UK *Build My Gallows High*), dir. Jacques Tourneur, written Geoffrey Homes, starring Mitchum, Douglas & Jane Greer; RKO, US, 1947.

I Wake Up Screaming (alternative and UK title *Hot Spot*), dir. H. Bruce Humberstone, written Dwight Taylor, also starring Betty Grable; 20th Century Fox, US, 1941. *Band of the Hand*, dir. Paul Michael Glaser; RCA/Columbia/Tri-Star, US, 1986. Bob Dylan, with Tom Petty & the Heartbreakers: 'Band of the Hand (It's Hell Time Man!)', Sydney, 8–10 Feb 1986, MCA 52811 (12-inch MCA 23633), US, 1986; soundtrack album *Band of the Hand*, MCA 6167, US, 1986 (Dylan, Petty & the Heartbreakers appear on no other track).

The Man in the Gray Flannel Suit, dir. & written Nunnally Johnson; 20th Century Fox/Darryl F. Zanuck, US, 1956; based on novel of same name by Sloan Wilson, New York: Simon & Schuster, 1955. *Catch-22*, dir. Mike Nichols, written Buck Henry, starring Alan Arkin; Paramount/Filmways, US, 1970; based on novel of same name by Joseph Heller, 1961. *The African Queen*, dir. John Huston, written James Agee, starring Bogart & Katherine Hepburn; IFD/Romulus-Horizon, UK, 1951. *Gone with the Wind*, dir. Victor Fleming, George Cukor & Sam Wood, written Sidney Howard & others, starring Vivien Leigh, Clark Gable & Leslie Howard; MGM/Selznick International, US, 1939; based on novel of same name by Margaret Mitchell, 1936. Tennessee Williams (1911–1983), *Cat on a Hot Tin Roof*, the play, 1955. Terence Rattigan (1911–1977), *Separate Tables*, the play, 1952. Joseph Kessel, *Le coup de grâce*, the novel, Paris: Les Éditions de France, 1931. Nicholas Monsarrat (1910–1979), *The Cruel Sea*, the novel, 1951. Dashiell Hammett (1894–1961, creator of private eye character Sam Spade), *The Maltese Falcon*, the novel, 1930.

The Gunfighter, dir. Henry King, written William Bowers & William Sellers; 20th Century Fox, US, 1950. (The detection of the recurring line 'Got my mind made up' in this film is in Stephen Scobie, *Alias Bob Dylan*, Red Deer, Alberta: Red Deer College Press, 1991, p.189.) *The Big Country*, dir. William Wyler, written James R. Webb, starring Peck, Jean Simmons, Charlton Heston, Carroll Baker, Burl Ives & Charles Bickford; UA/Anthony/Worldwide, US, 1958. *Town Without Pity*, dir. Gottried Reinhardt, starring Kirk Douglas; UA/Mirisch/Osweg/Gloria, US/Switzerland/Germany, 1961. Gene Pitney: 'Town Without Pity', 1961, Musicor 1009, US (HMV POP952, UK), 1961.

Bob Dylan: 'New Danville Girl', LA, Dec 1984, unreleased; 'City of Gold', Fox Warfield (itself a palace from the golden age of cinema), San Francisco, 10 Nov 1980. Dylan quote re the Bible in Bill Flanagan, *Written in My Soul*, Chicago: Contemporary Books, 1986. Bert Cartwright: 'The Bible in the Lyrics of Bob Dylan: 1985–1990', *Telegraph* no.38, Romford, UK, spring 1991. Nigel Hinton: 'Into the Future, Knocked Out and Loaded', *Telegraph* no.25, Bury, UK, autumn/winter 1986, but quoted here from the version collected in Michael Gray & John Bauldie, eds, *All Across the Telegraph: A Bob Dylan Handbook*, London: W.H. Allen, 1987.]

Finn, Julio [1936 -] See **Arnold, Jerome.**

first extant recordings, Dylan's See **earliest extant recordings, Dylan's.**

Flatt & Scruggs Lester Flatt [June 19, 1914–May 11, 1979] & Earl Scruggs [January 6, 1924–], bluegrass stars.

Four months before Dylan recorded *Nashville Skyline* in February 1969, Flatt & Scruggs issued an album called *Nashville Airplane*, using the same musicians, on the same label (Columbia) and featuring countrified versions of 'Like a Rolling Stone', 'Rainy Day Women # 12 & 35', 'I'll Be Your Baby Tonight' and 'The Times They Are a-Changin'', plus an instrumental, 'Freida Florentine', which Dylan's 'Nashville Skyline Rag' proved similar to in character. Scruggs and Dylan later recorded 'Nashville Skyline Rag' together for the LP *Earl Scruggs: His Family and Friends*, 1971.

But *Nashville Airplane* was a follow-up to Flatt & Scruggs' *Changin' Times*, 1967, which alongside 'Where Have All the Flowers Gone?' and 'Ode to Billie Jo' offered Dylan's 'Down in the Flood', 'Mr. Tambourine Man', 'Don't Think Twice, It's All Right', 'It Ain't Me Babe' and 'Blowin' in the Wind'.

All these might be explained by the fact of Dylan's producer BOB JOHNSTON becoming Flatt & Scruggs' producer as of September 1967—except that their first recording of a Dylan song (billed as by Lester Flatt, Earl Scruggs & the Foggy Mountain Boys) was in 1966: the rather good 'Mama You Been on My Mind', issued as a single.

In 1969—the year of *Nashville Skyline*, as it happens—Flatt & Scruggs split up, last performing together in public that February and then forming, respectively, Lester Flatt & the Nashville Grass, and the Earl Scruggs Revue. A main reason for the split was Lester Flatt's unhappiness at the way that, under pressure from Columbia Records, they had moved away from bluegrass towards an increasingly commercial kind of country music that flirted with the rock music of people like Bob Dylan. Indeed it's been said that for Flatt, 'Like a Rolling Stone' was the last straw. As Barry R. Willis puts it (with a nice spinsterliness): 'Flatt was very opposed to non-bluegrass music and associated those long-haired musicians with rock music and marijuana-smoking.' This answers the question as to why it was with Scruggs, not Flatt, that Dylan performed at the end of the 1960s.

[Flatt & Scruggs: 'Like a Rolling Stone', Nashville, 18 Jul 1968; 'Rainy Day Women # 12 & 35' & 'I'll Be Your

Baby Tonight', both Nashville, 9 Sep 1968; 'The Times They Are a-Changin'', 16 Sep; 'Freida Florentine', 17 Sep: *Nashville Airplane*, Columbia CS 9741, NY (CBS 63570, London), 1968. *Changin' Times*, Columbia 9596 (CBS 63251), 1967. Lester Flatt, Earl Scruggs & the Foggy Mountain Boys: 'Mama You Been on My Mind', Nashville, 16 May 1966, Columbia CO 43803, NY, 1966.

All these Flatt & Scruggs covers of Dylan material are CD-reissued on *Flatt & Scruggs 1964–1969, Plus*, Bear Family BCD 15879, Vollersode, Germany, 1995.

Earl Scruggs & Bob Dylan: 'Nashville Skyline Rag', Carmel, NY, Dec 1970; *Earl Scruggs: His Family and Friends*, Columbia KC 30584, NY (CBS 64777, London), 1971.

Barry R. Willis, quoted from the Scruggs biography seen online 9 Aug 2005 at *www.flatt-and-scruggs.com/earlbio.html*.]

folk and sophisticated culture, links between See **song in the history of English Literature**.

folk music, American, four main types American folk music is that day-to-day music created by the people and for the people. It gives form to the democratic ideal. It moves below the mainstream of culture, the flow of which is sustained and altered by small élites. In the 20th century, this music of the ordinary American people became radically less regionalized. The slump and dustbowl times provided a focus on this inevitable shift. As the people moved from the farms and small communities, folk music moved to the media.

On the other hand, though the way of life from which folk music flowed naturally has essentially disappeared, the changes of environment forced upon millions of Americans by an ailing capitalist system have acted as stimuli to self-expression (however defensive that impulse must be) and so as a regenerative influence on the creativity of ordinary people. Urbanized life still provokes a means of invention of music and song undreamt of in Cole Porter's philosophy.

ALAN LOMAX wrote (in noting the effects of such environmental changes) that 'there are aesthetic needs that Hollywood and Tin Pan Alley do not yet know how to satisfy. Tomorrow the Holy Rollers, the hillbillies, the blues shouters, the gospel singers—the Leadbellies, the Guthries . . . who have formed our twentieth-century folk-music, will be replaced by other folk artists . . . [who] will give voice to the deep feelings and unspoken needs of their own time, as have all the folk-singers of the past.'

Future or past, folk music must flow naturally from peoples' lives. When such lives were eked out traditionally, in country communities, the primary material—to shelter in and to work with—was wood. This was the simple reason for the centrality of the acoustic guitar in folk music. Now that people buy their environments in units of electric and electronic technology, folk culture has new material to work with. Serious contemporary artists cannot ignore the technology that surrounds them and shapes their lives, and they have every reason to utilize it not only for their art but also in the interests of the clear duty to reach an audience. The black folk artists of 20th century America always understood this.

Disputing the validity of 'going electric' in folk music disregards the responsible resources of artistic work; and the attempts of the 'purists' to 'preserve' folk music from such moves can only, where successful, act to the detriment of folk music's potential for growth. This is not to argue that the issue at stake is one of trendiness versus the old-fashioned; nor to deny that the borderline between folk art and art proper (between the subculture and the mainstream) is likely to be blurred.

When American life was wholly localized and regional, there were four main types of American folk music (apart from the traditions preserved by foreign-language immigrants). These four were: YANKEE, SOUTHERN POOR WHITE, COWBOY and BLACK. All four figure strongly in Dylan's art, if in very different guises as that art matured.

folk music, American, black One of the four main types of American folk music, and Dylan's engagement with it is at least as strong and clear as with any of the other three. Black folk music is a vast subject, especially given that it's impossible to say where that folk music elides into the commercial pre-war blues. Throughout this book there are further entries that touch on aspects of this music and on Dylan's resourceful use of it. What follows is the crudest possible preliminary summary.

Black folk music in America began by reflecting the basic dream of release—yet it first impinged upon white America as a novel, engaging entertainment (which is as telling an introduction to the history of race relations on that continent as the attempt to wipe out the Amerindian: the 'Red Indian', as we used to say). The distinctive, animated dancing of slaves won the attention and applause of their owners. Then enforced initiation into the prosaic mysteries of the Protestant tradition gave rise to spirituals which reflected a double burden: chains plus original sin. These spirituals were first studied and collected by campaigners for the abolition of slavery, whose aim was to prove that the black man had a soul and should therefore be set free.

Since then, the influence of white and black folk music on each other has been substantial. The black, while preserving African modes of tune and rhythm, has adopted many Celtic musical conventions even while retaining habits of improvisation and adaptation and the endless repetition of short, sharp phrases. Owing to African influence, correspondingly, white folk music has become increasingly more polyphonic and polyrhythmic. The blues, which emerged in the 20th century, relied on newly found African-American dialects, 'spoken' through the guitar as well as the voice, latterly (but not always) in a 3-line, 12-bar verse pattern. A song such as the old 'Blowin' Down the Road' illustrates the common ground that developed both musically and socially between blacks and poor whites. This was the seminal folk song of the Depression and New Deal period. In form and origin a blues number, it became of expressive importance to millions of displaced whites. The *Grapes of Wrath* people understood the blues.

WOODY GUTHRIE's autobiography *Bound for Glory* (1943) certainly describes the experience of those times in a noticeably duo-racial way. The box-car ride of the opening and closing chapters is one in which blacks and whites are so jumbled together as to disarm any racial distinctions: they are all men who share the same nomadic discomforts; they are all looking unsuccessfully for a living; they are all outside the cop-protected communities: '"And remember—take an old 'bo's word for it, and stay th' hell out of the city limits of Tucson." "What kind of a damn town is this, anyhow?" "Tucson—she's a rich man's bitch, that's what she is, and nothin' else but."'

Both white and black are hungry, poor, 'a problem', the pawns of an economic game that demands unemployment for flexibility of labour (and thereby high profits) yet attacks, economically and socially, the people who have to provide its unemployment pool. This common ground reduces the difference between black and white perception. So much so that Guthrie's pen-and-ink sketches, included in his autobiography, feature people not easily classifiable by race—indeed his sketches of himself make him look, if anything, more black than white. In the text he cites only one instance of racial prejudice amongst the hobo community.

Dylan, then, inherited black folk traditions not entirely from the outside—not as a separate form but as ever-present influences on other hybrid forms. This inheritance shows clearly right from the start. As WILFRID MELLERS expressed it: 'In the first phase of his career . . . (his) musical materials were primitive: modal white blues, hillbilly, shaker songs and hymns, with an interfusion of (pentatonic) black holler, relating the young white outcast to the Negro's alienation.'

The strands for Dylan are pulled together by his 'Only a Pawn in Their Game', a song written after the murder of MEDGAR EVERS. The poor white is the pawn, and so is the black. Both are used by the Southern politicians to maintain a corrupt status quo not just by keeping blacks disenfranchised in every area of life but by saying to poor whites, in Dylan's summary, 'You got more than the blacks, don't complain'. Dylan bravely follows all this to its logical conclusion, arguing that even when the poor white joins the lynchmob 'it ain't him to blame: / he's only a pawn in their game'. And this is the song Dylan has the courage to sing to black workers outside Greenwood, Mississippi, in July 1963. (See **Greenwood, MS, Dylan visit to**.)

Dylan, however, comes closer to black folk culture than is suggested by this 'holding hands'. When Paul Oliver sums up succinctly what the blues encompasses (in his pioneering book *Conversation with the Blues*, 1965) he describes those strands of black folk music and culture that the blues draws together: 'The narrative and folk tales, the telling of "lies" or competitive tall tales, the healthily obscene "putting in the dozens", the long and witty "toasts" and the epigrammatic rhyming couplets which enliven the conversation of folk negro and Harlem hipster alike, have their reflections in the blues. They are evident in the earthy vulgarity, the unexpected and paradoxical images, the appeal of unlikely metaphors, the endless story that makes all blues one.' For all this, Dylan's work shows an affinity that is often blatant and forceful. He has absorbed its characteristics into his thinking and thereby his vocabulary.

Oliver also writes: 'Song, speech and music are frequently one in the blues . . . the piano, guitar, even harmonica is a complement to the voice. Though he may play instrumental solos, the most characteristic blues artist sings through both voice and instrument(s).' How striking is the pertinence of that passage to Dylan's work. Dylan plays piano, guitar and harmonica—three of the commonest blues instruments—plays instrumental solos on each and emphatically uses each as a complement to his voice. This is evident even in such a 'white' protest song as 'The Lonesome Death of Hattie Carroll' (about a black woman, though it never has to say so, as CHRISTOPHER RICKS points out in his unsurpassable commentary on this song), where, in the final refrain, the irregular strum of the guitar rises and falls, quickens and slows again, conveying the heartbeats of the narrator, while the harmonica phrases between the vocal lines act as graphs of his anger, shame and sympathy.

A huge instance in Dylan's work where this fusion shows vividly its creative force is in his wide-ranging, flexible, recurrent treatment of the classic Railroad Theme; see **Railroads, a classic theme**.

In his early songs explicitly 'about' contemporary America—the protest songs, in the main—one of the aims is, as Mellers suggests, to express the relation of the spirit of the young white outcast to that of the alienated black. In Dylan's later work his encompassing of black traditions serves more subtly to enhance the expression of many different perceptions. Musically, of course, this is often obvious. Beyond examples like that of 'Hattie Carroll', in which part of the impact comes from a blues-derived feeling for voice, words and instruments as complements, there are plenty of examples in Dylan's work of songs with the conventional 3-line, 12-bar verse structure, including, from his 1970s work, the outstanding 'Buckets of Rain', 'Meet Me in the Morning', 'New Pony' and 'Gonna Change My Way of Thinking', and the more recent 'Lonesome Day Blues'.

Others use similar structures to similar effect–like the still underrated 'Pledging My Time', from *Blonde on Blonde*: 'Well they sent for the ambulance, and one was sent / Somebody got lucky, but it was an accident . . .' In that verse the black influence is especially strong. It goes beyond the music–the coiled insistence of guitar, harmonica, drums and voice–and beyond that characteristic bending of 'ambulance' in the pronunciation: there is also the curiously ominous quality of those first two lines. They recall those legends of Beale Street in the Memphis of the 1930s, where Saturday night razor fights between blind-drunk blacks were so frequent that a fleet of ambulances waited like taxis at one end of the street. Killer ambulances, apparently, with drivers who made sure that if you weren't dead when they got to you, you were before they'd finished their night's work.

As these stories have blown up into myth, they provide an odd corollary to the stories about hospitals and doctors, and particularly surgeons, widely current in 19th century England and passed into upper and middle-class consciousness by terrifying children's nannies. The subject is aired in George Orwell's grim essay, 'How the Poor Die' (1946). Here too, then, black folk culture is in symbiosis with white.

Actually it was the railways that succeeded, without intending it, at disseminating black song across the land and into mainstream American consciousness. When the railroad came through the Appalachian mountains in the mid-19th century, it was built by blacks. They kept up their spirits by singing, and the white mountain men listened. The black song 'John Henry the Steel-Driving Man' became a white ballad. There were also strong black influences on Appalachian music-making. In his 1990 TV documentary 'Appalachian Journey', ALAN LOMAX argues that in the case of fiddle playing it is black fluidity that gets the white performer's left hand sliding up and down the strings while the right hand is playing the bow, and sets his middle body jigging as he plays. One consequence is that when, now, you see these old Appalachian fiddlers–and indeed the younger dancers in their home-community audiences–you recognise that the flat-foot shuffle they insist on derives, just as CHUCK BERRY's duck-walk surely does, from the flat-foot shuffle that is the fundamental of black dance.

Paul Gilroy proceeds more circumspectly than Alan Lomax to the pros and cons of emphasising black performance strengths. He quotes from Eduoard Glissant's book *Caribbean Discourse*: 'It is nothing new to declare that for us music, gesture, dance are forms of communication just as important as the gift of speech. This is how we first managed to emerge from the plantation: aesthetic form in our cultures must be shaped from these oral structures.' But while Gilroy is concerned to avoid what he calls 'the pernicious metaphysical dualism that identifies blacks with the body and whites with the mind' he also wants to give due weight to 'the traditions of performance which continue to characterise the production and reception of diaspora musics'. He notes too that 'The pre-eminence of music within the diverse black communities of the Atlantic diaspora is itself an important element in their essential connectedness.' Yet the ever-shifting 'complexity of black expressive culture alone supplies powerful reasons to resist the idea that an untouched, pristine Africanity resides inside these forms', though he also writes of the long shadow of our enduring traditions–the African ones and the ones forged from the slave experience which the black vernacular so powerfully and actively remembers.

Lomax, untroubled by such PC notions, has this to say about the overall black influence: 'A note of unconflicted happy eroticism rings out . . . all the little double- and triple-entendre rhymes of the ring games, of black minstrely, of ragtime, jazz, the blues, and rock–have gradually chiselled away at the starchy standards of nineteenth-century propriety. . . . Nowadays the language of song employs the explicit argot of the streets. In all this, the driving force has been the sexually more permissive African cultural tradition, in which fertility rather than continence is a central value.' (Lomax, *The Land Where the Blues Began*, 1993. He argues the same points specifically of the influence of black culture on dance, too.)

James Baldwin is also untroubled by dangers of racial stereotyping when considering the question of black influence on music and language. The British photographer and jazz critic VAL WILMER writes of attending a public meeting at which Baldwin spoke in the early 1960s: 'One student asked him how he could explain to unsympathetic whites that black people had earned the right to equal treatment through the history of their presence in America. Baldwin mused, "Ask them how America would *sound* without us. How would the language sound? How would the music sound?" Everyone laughed. It was just so obvious, but exactly the kind of explanation that was resisted so strongly in England.'

Back in the Appalachian mountains, it was, too, blacks who first used the fiddle as a rhythm instrument, and who first put the fiddle and the banjo together. Later, there were the mountain communities where blacks and whites were neighbours, and, in Lomax's phrase, 'swapped favors, and stole each other's music'.

[Wilfrid Mellers, 'Reactionary Progressives', *New Statesman*, London, 11 Jul 1969. A revised version of Christopher Ricks on 'The Lonesome Death of Hattie Carroll' appears in his book *Dylan's Visions of Sin*, 2003. George Orwell, 'How the Poor Die', *Now* magazine, London, Nov 1946; collected in *Orwell: Shooting an Elephant and Other Essays*, 1950; reissued in *Collected Essays, Journalism & Letters*, ed. Sonia Orwell & Ian Angus, 1968 (4 volumes). Alan Lomax, 'Appalachian Journey', Dibbs Productions, Channel 4 TV, London, 1990. Val Wilmer, *Mama Said There'd Be Days Like This*, 1989 and 1991.]

folk music, American, Cowboy One of the four main types of American folk music, the Cowboy music tradition was, like the Southern Poor White, a hybrid: it was basically an amalgam of Southern and Yankee brands of folk. In ALAN LOMAX's phrase, 'the cowboy singer was a Yankee balladeer with a southern accent'.

As with the hillbilly genre, Dylan uses the cowboy tradition in two ways. He uses the structures and conventions, and he uses the atmospheric essence. This essence is the lyric magic that first takes its being from the 'noble' struggle of hard-living men in a hostile work environment (and later, much more famously, from the communion of the individual with his own loneliness in the environment of the great western plains).

A traditional sample of the hard-struggle song is this: 'Our hearts were made of iron, our souls were cased with steel, / The hardships of that winter could never make us yield, / Our food, the dogs would snarl at it, our beds were in the snow, / We suffered worse than murderers up in Michigan-i-o.' That recalls, in Dylan's output, more than his delighted use of that last rhyming device in his early recorded version of 'Pretty Peggy-O' ('He died somewheres in Loos-i-ana-o'. We can easily envisage Dylan singing—say, on *Self Portrait*—the lines just quoted. Phrases like 'our food, the dogs would snarl at it' are well within what we've come to know as Dylan's scope. And to think back to 'Song to Woody' is to recognize a rhythmic effect similar to that achieved in the above—lines very close to verse four of 'Range of the Buffalo' in Lomax's *Penguin Book of American Folk Songs* and very close to those of what is (according to Charles Darling's *The New American Songster: Traditional Ballads and Songs of North America*, 1992) the progenitor of 'Buffalo Skinners'/'Range of the Buffalo', i.e. 'Canaday-I-O', an 1854 re-working by Ephraim Braley of Maine of a British song 'Canada I.O.'. The same genre gives us 'Diamond Joe', on Dylan's 1992 album *Good as I Been to You*. (That album's 'Canadee-i-o' is a quite different song.)

This same flavour is prominent again in Dylan's 'Ballad of Hollis Brown', even though there the sense of community is taken outside the song's characters and exists solely between the narrator and his subjects (and is only a one-way awareness, for the narrator's sympathy cannot reach their loneliness): 'Way out in the wilderness a cold coyote calls / Your eyes fix on the shotgun that's hangin' on the wall.' A very different song from the same Dylan album, 'When the Ship Comes In', draws just as firmly on the idea of the hard struggle of decent men to overcome adversity, though taking it out of the realm of gritty realism and into that of visionary moral parable. (See separate entry on this song.) Here Dylan has taken us a long way beyond the cowboy tradition on which the song is based; and in any case its basis is in the less recognisable of the two cowboy types. What needs to be considered now is Dylan's relation to the other type: that which corresponds to our image of the cowboy hero, that which is bathed in the romantic lyricism of saddle-sore silent men set against lonesome prairies and plains.

The traditional song 'I'm a-Ridin' Old Paint' well represents the genre: 'Now when I die don't bury me at all / Just saddle my pony, lead him out of the stall / Tie my bones in the saddle, turn our faces to the west / And we'll ride the prairie that we love best.'

The cowboy nurtured an internal restlessness into something bigger than himself. His home became the Big Wide West—and he always felt compelled to be 'movin' on'. And how easy it was for this spirit to pass from the 19th century cowboy to the 20th century professional hobo. Dylan takes this up, sometimes comically, more often with a plausible earnestness. (It's worth remembering that the mid-west begins in Minnesota, Dylan's home state. 'The Twin Cities', where Dylan lived after leaving home, mark the divide, St. Paul being 'the last city of the East' and Minneapolis the first of the mid-west.)

The comical example that springs to mind is from 'Country Pie', on *Nashville Skyline*: 'Saddle me up a big white goose! / Tie me on her and turn her loose! / Oh! me, oh! my / Love that Country Pie!'

Dylan's expressions of this compulsion to move on, to not get entangled, are numerous. On *Self Portrait* he relaxes (as he does more conspicuously and perhaps less wholeheartedly on 'Country Pie') and handles PAUL CLAYTON's 'Gotta Travel On' as the archetypal statement it is: he lets the words remain as simple as they are and puts the song across as music—music that rides on beautifully. In contrast, he gives voice to the same roving compulsion in the disarming aphorism that brings his 'Ballad of Frankie Lee and Judas Priest' to a close on *John Wesley Harding*: 'And don't go mistaking Paradise / For that home across the road.'

In Dylan's more concentrated and sustained expressions of this same theme, of this negative-positive moral, their plausibility derives from their being always addressed to a particular woman or specific entanglements of which the narrator understands the full worth. It is never, in Dylan's hands, a merely boastful theme—never a Papa Hemingway conceit, an I'm-too-hot-to-hold bravado. The opposite impulse, the desire to stay and be entangled, is always felt to be present, though it cannot (until *Nashville Skyline*) win. Later still, on 'You're Gonna Make Me Lonesome When You Go', from 1975's *Blood on the Tracks*, things have progressed further—to the point where it is the woman who has the gotta-travel-on urge, and the male narrator who must accept this philosophically.

Later still, on *Street Legal*, the 1978 album that prepares us for the Born Again Christian albums *Slow Train Coming* and *Saved*, Dylan takes a further step—to the point where he again feels he has to move on and abandon love: but this time it is in order to embrace Jesus instead of 'the road'; to find a specific salvation rather than a nebulous, wandering 'freedom'.

We have one moving-on theme in 'Don't Think Twice, It's All Right', from the second Dylan album: 'I'm a-thinkin' and a-wond'rin', all the way down the road, / I once loved a woman—a child, I am told: / I gave her my heart but she wanted my soul / But don't think twice, it's all right.' The same integrity of spirit underlies the 1964 song 'It Ain't Me, Babe': 'You say you're looking for someone / Who'll pick you up each time you fall, / To gather flowers constantly / An' to come each time you call: / A lover for your life an' nothing more / But it ain't me, babe.'

There are many more instances of Dylan using the 'gotta travel on' spirit. Perhaps his most directly autobiographical statement of it comes in the hastily composed yet excellent 'Restless Farewell', with which he closes his third album, *The Times They Are a-Changin'*. Within the same collection, that word "restless" is taken up again in a song Dylan has revisited innumerable times since, the lovely 'One Too Many Mornings' (with its multiple negatives at the end of the first line—a direct inheritance from hillbilly traditions of grammatical construction): 'It's a restless, hungry feeling that don't mean no one no good / When ev'rything I'm sayin' you can say it just as good / You're right from your side and I am right from mine: / We're both just one too many mornings / An' a thousand miles / Behind.'

Often, then, this restlessness runs into what is for Dylan a search for the ideal, for nothing less than the perfect. It is only when we reach as far through his career as the *Nashville Skyline* album that we find this search largely discarded. Consciously, at last, an imperfect love can be accepted as salvation. The last song on the album brings this out most explicitly: 'Tonight I'll Be Staying Here With You'. As its title suggests, it's a deliberate announcement of the fall from restlessness. The habit of always moving on has been kicked and the impulse to stay has at last succeeded. The singer's 'should have left this town this morning', in the second verse, is a tip of the cowboy hat to the old traveling compunction now renounced, not to some particular journey's schedule, and the point of the title line is that it isn't just tonight; the narrator has come to rest. Not even the train whistle heard in the distance can lure him back to homeless sojourns now.

In 1964, when people first heard that line from 'It Ain't Me, Babe', 'A lover for your life and nothing more', it was radical: it rocked you back on your feet, because in pop songs there never had been anything more: to be 'a lover for your life' was the ultimate ideal. Five years of Dylan output later, 'Tonight I'll Be Staying Here with You' could make use of its own dramatic contrast to 'It Ain't Me, Babe'. It wasn't a step back, it was another step beyond. (It is in this same spirit of achievement that Dylan can reintroduce, on *Self Portrait*, that line 'I bless the day I found you' in 'Let It Be Me', so that despite its being an old pop song it too, under Dylan's auspices, shows the same progressive second step. It parallels 'Throw my ticket out the window'.)

Love doesn't always come Dylan's way on *Nashville Skyline*, but it does provide the focus of his desire. The second verse of the quiet 'I Threw It All Away'—the 'it' being love—echoes the cowboy ethos succinctly by using, as his image for the discarded love's value, the scenery the lonesome traveller has around him (though it acts also as sexual imagery): 'Once I had mountains in the palm of my hand / And rivers that ran through every day . . .' The choice made is bemoaned, but the choice propounded is again that between loving and moving on.

It may be said that there are much stronger influences in all this from more modern country music ('Country & Western', as it was once called in England) than from the older traditional material; but it is from the traditions that the modern amalgam derives, and in any case it is hardly possible to draw a line through some year in American history and say that behind the line stands virginal tradition, and in front the whore of Nashville. There is more in Dylan's country pie than cowboy classics revisited and more, equally, than the bland successors of HANK WILLIAMS can match.

As for a Dylan song that most clearly registers Williams himself—'One More Night', from *Nashville Skyline*—the tune of the verses is that of an old English popular song. Correspondingly, the lyric is not only consciously 'unoriginal' but actually recalls other lyrics: 'I will turn my head up high / To that dark an' rollin' sky / For tonight no light will shine on me. / I was so mistaken when I thought that she'd be true / I had no idea what a woman in love would do.' That couplet beginning 'I will turn my head up high' comes straight from 'Lonesome Prairie'—a traditional cowboy song.

See also **heroes, special cowboy fondness for**.

folk music, American, Southern Poor White

One of the four main types of American folk music, Southern Poor White folk music, hillbilly mountain music, the music of settlers, consisted of hybrids. Its songs fused Scots, Irish and English influences and yet expressed a new-world pioneer milieu. Songs like 'Come All You Virginia Girls', 'Old Blue', 'I Love My Love', 'Went Up on the Mountain' and 'Pretty Saro' reflected normal life all across the southern backwoods, and testified to the cultural bonds between poor whites as far west as Texas and Oklahoma.

It was a tradition linked fundamentally to Calvinist precepts: to the passionate belief in sin, the concern for individual salvation and the surety of a God on Our Side. Uncle John, from Oklahoma, in *Grapes of Wrath*, is in this sense the complete descendant of the pioneers who constructed the tradition.

With its vital mixing of ancient and fresh vocabulary and its truly pioneering grammatical freedom, this tradition offered what is the real core of folk song: a conserving process which is at the same time creative; and in his use today of that fundamental life-force, Dylan is the great white folk singer. He has drawn on this tradition in two ways: he has used its established characteristics for some of his song structures, and he has used its very lively inventiveness as a source of strength for his own.

His adaptation of the traditional Scottish song 'Pretty Peggy-O', on his first album, gives a Texas accent a central rhythmic purpose. The guitar-work and melodic structuring on 'Ballad of Hollis Brown' are straight from the Appalachians, where such forms and modes had evolved over almost 200 years. And a traditional song such as 'East Virginia' reflects the brooding about death which Dylan echoes throughout his first album (and sometimes in later work) and which is rooted as much in the orthodoxy of Calvinism as in black folk culture.

The Calvinist precepts are not, of course, taken up wholesale by Dylan: rather, he takes up the challenge, the encapsulating threat, of these ideas. In 'With God on Our Side', which appeared (on *The Times They Are a-Changin'*) towards the end of his flirtation with the protest movement, it is the early part of the song, and not the later homilies on world wars and atom bombs, that is of real and lasting interest. It gives us Dylan assessing the inroads of pioneer religiosity on his own sensibility: 'O my name it means nothing / My age it means less. / The country I come from / Is called the Mid-West. / I was taught an' brought up there / The laws to abide / And that the land that I live in / Has God On Its Side.'

There is an extraordinary sweep of implicit experience in those first four lines. The sense of the narrator's context—his sense of history and therefore of identity—makes itself felt quietly, with a truly compelling delicacy, yielding very finely the narrator's sense of the intellectual and moral pressure of his upbringing in terms of 'folk education'. Dylan is stating his awareness that the country he comes from has its claims upon him, and upon his art, for both good and bad.

He nowhere draws more on his background familiarity with Calvinistic folk life than in his beautifully poised, pinched delivery on the early 'Quit Your Low Down Ways'—a definitive cameo, as he does it—or the much later 'Gotta Serve Somebody'.

Dylan also returns to Appalachian music on his 1970 album *Self Portrait*, to give us an odd but effectively atmospheric version of the traditional song 'Copper Kettle'. As with all the music he touches on this collection, he brings back to life the spirit of the age that the song is all about, and does it immeasurably better than those purists to whom his version (it has violins and women on it) is anathema. And as if to emphasize further his ability to do this sort of thing, the same album offers 'Belle Isle' (see separate entry), which may reach back even further into the traditional folk past, invoking those purely Celtic origins which are part of the founding ingredients of America's Southern Poor White music.

folk music, American, Yankee One of the four main types of American folk music. The Yankee, who first sang on packet ships and there revived the sea-shanties that had dropped out of circulation in the British Navy, adapted his songs to the newer environment when working in the forests that stretch from Maine to Dylan's home state of Minnesota. The nature of this life and work produced a tradition of song in which the workman was a hard and grimly realistic hero. A less 'reflective' Hemingway ideal.

The Yankee backwoodsman sang in a hard, monotonous, high-pitched, nasal voice; his songs used decorated melodies in gapped scale structures; and words mattered more than tunes. Those familiar with Dylan's early work will recognise aspects of it, both of style and content, in that description. Indeed, the close relation much of the early Dylan output keeps with this Yankee tradition is what makes that output difficult for newcomers to it to attune to—not only for those accustomed to, say, Gilbert & Sullivan (in which the words are nonsense and a-tune-you-can-hum is the main ingredient) but also for the pop-orientated. There is perhaps little more in the Yankee tradition that claims Dylan as its modern voice. Although a song such as his magnicent 'Lonesome Death of Hattie Carroll' makes an ordinary worker into a kind of heroine, Dylan makes this happen as a device, not an end in itself: a device for strengthening an essentially political and social polemic. He does the same with MEDGAR EVERS and his killer in 'Only a Pawn in Their Game': the two men are just pawns in Dylan's 'game'.

Yet his tremendous 'North Country Blues' much more nearly exhibits a traditional Yankee perspective: it deals very consciously with a working community's suffering, treated through the story of one family's misfortunes, and that community's annihilation. The song provides a timely epitaph to the destruction of the folk culture such communities produced, while taking the dynamics of its construction from that kind of culture. When, on the later album *Self Portrait*, Dylan returns to a genuinely old Yankee song, 'Days of '49', he offers it quite rightly as a museum-piece even as he breathes new life into it.

Lasting, well-known traditional Yankee songs—many remaining quite close to their English antecedents—include 'The Erie Canal', 'The Bay of Mexico', 'The Foggy Dew', 'Weary of the Railway', 'Katy Cruel' and of course 'Yankee Doodle'.

Folkways Records See Asch, Moses.

Forryan, Robert [1945 -] Robert Forryan, born at Nuneaton, UK, on August 27, 1945, has listened to Dylan since 1964 and written about him since 1992. His work has appeared in *Homer, the slut*, *Dignity*, *Freewheelin'*, *Judas!* and *The Bridge* (and in the VAN MORRISON fanzine *Wavelength*). Forryan's hard-to-find 'Songs from Another World', published in *Homer, the slut* no.11, is *the* best description of a 1966 Dylan acoustic set: truly attentive and accurate, its admirable stance born of clear understanding: a brave, fine attempt to really *describe* a specific, indescribable performance (London, May 27, 1966). Another piece of his is cited in the entry on ROY KELLY: a piece which, in praising Kelly's writing on Dylan fandom, manages to be a terrific piece on that subject too.

[Robert Forryan: 'Songs from Another World', *Homer, the slut* no.11, London, May 1994; 'Roy Kelly's Blues', republished *Freewheelin' Quarterly*, Huntingdon, UK, vol. 21, Oct 2001, pp.13–21.]

Foster, Stephen [1826 - 1864] Stephen Foster was born near Pittsburgh on the 4th of July 1826 and wrote his pseudo-black southerner songs from the North. He never *saw* the South till late on in his life, and perhaps didn't much care for black music. (Posterity's southern revenge is that an area of south Georgia swamp is now named after him.) Yet Foster created a series of massively influential as well as popular songs, all written while their black protagonists in the South were still slaves. His hits included 'Oh Susannah' (1848), 'Campdown Races' (the song from which the world picked up the phrase 'all of a doodah', 1850), 'The Old Folks at Home' (1851), 'My Old Kentucky Home' (1853), 'Jeannie with the Light Brown Hair' (1854) and 'Old Black Joe' (1860). ('The Old Folks at Home' is the one that begins 'Way down upon the Swanee river'. This river would be less famous if Foster had stuck to his first draft, which used the Pee Wee river instead.)

Though his work was hugely successful in his lifetime, Foster received very little financial reward until late on. When he did make money, he spent it and failed to support his wife and children. In 1860 he moved to New York, where his debts increased and he started drinking heavily. His wife left him for the second and last time, after which he churned out many mediocre songs just for drinking money. Out of this period, however, came 'Beautiful Dreamer', written just a few days before his death.

President Lincoln had emancipated the slaves the year before; the Civil War was still raging. Segregation laws were tried in Mississippi immediately after the war in 1865 and after the period of Reconstruction were reinstated in 1888. By 1900 the Supreme Court had approved segregation laws and 14 states possessed them.

Foster's legacy is bound up in the history of the minstrel shows that were so popular in the 19th century and have never quite been killed off since. The name of the 1960s pseudo-folk group the New Christy Minstrels, through which the world was brought the modest talent of Gene Clark, Kenny Rogers and Barry McGuire, refers back to the most famous of the 19th century minstrel companies, Edwin P. Christy's. This was American, but it became internationally popular, and as it did so it came to rely less on the distinctive African-American input responsible for its initial appeal, and to embrace far more European 'drawing-room song' material. However dodgily, the minstrel-show movement brought black music and song to the ears of Europe and made it fashionable (so much so that at the turn of the century the future British King Edward VII, then the Prince of Wales, took banjo lessons) and probably speeded up the rise in interest in genuine black music.

Such was the context in which Stephen Foster's songs became popular and influential. His work encouraged the black songwriter James Bland, who was ten years old when Foster died, and who went on to write 'Carry Me Back to Old Virginny', and in 1871, seven years after Foster's death, the Fisk University Jubilee Singers conquered Britain with a repertoire that first popularised at least three other songs that have since become classics: 'Nobody Knows the Trouble I've Seen', 'Swing Low Sweet Chariot' and 'Deep River'. These and the songs of Stephen Foster in turn set the scene for later widely popularised songs like 'Old Man River' and 'That Lucky Old Sun': songs that cross many boundaries and political eras and slide into the repertoires of people from Paul Robeson to JERRY LEE LEWIS, the Isley Brothers to Frankie Laine, and RAY CHARLES to Bob Dylan.

Scott Joplin's compositions were also deeply influenced by Foster's melodies, though Joplin was born four years after Foster's death, and in this way too, when Joplin's work spearheaded the turn-of-the-century ragtime craze, Foster's melodic legacy passed across to the BLIND BLAKEs and Peg Leg Howells who inhabited the early blues world.

Foster's politically least embarrassing songs were still being revived–in the country-pop market, on the whole–in the 1960s. 'Old Black Joe' was revived resplendently, 100 years after its first publication, by Jerry Lee Lewis, who did not, as did so many at the time, alter the title to the vaguer and supposedly more polite 'Poor Old Joe'. Marty Robbins (whose 'cowboy' hit 'El Paso' Bob Dylan clearly knew: 'Romance in Durango' is on one level a parodic tribute to it) cut Foster's 'Beautiful Dreamer' in 1963 and ROY ORBISON cut the same song in the early 1960s also. SAM COOKE (who was nobody's Uncle Tom) recorded 'Jeannie with the Light Brown Hair' in the same period, and years later, prompted by hearing Cooke's record on the radio, JOAN BAEZ cut a version of the song that she fused with 'Danny Boy', making the two songs one track on her mid-1970s album *Diamonds and Rust*.

'Hard Times', about the only Stephen Foster song now politically acceptable, was revived hideously in 1981 by academic-revivalist Old Time Country Music outfit the Red Clay Ramblers, who once provided the soundtrack for a SAM SHEPARD film but on 'Hard Times' sound as if they've never had any. The song was also recorded in the 1980s by three acts with Dylan connections: AARON NEVILLE, EMMYLOU HARRIS and Syd Straw (one-time wife of T-BONE BURNETT). In 1992, Dylan released his own solo acoustic version on *Good as I Been to You*.

'Hard Times' is interesting for being a song-within-a-song–a splendid 19th century example of the self-reflexive text, announcing and singing itself and even predicting its own future: 'There's a song that will linger forever in our ears / Oh Hard Times Come Again No More' (except that 'Oh' is a sort of 'Aaow', as Dylan pronounces it, half-howling the pain of it to himself), and ''Tis the song, the sigh of the weary: / Hard Times, Hard Times, Come Again No More.' As an imprecation this compares with BUDDY HOLLY's immaculate blues 'Mailman Bring Me No More Blues', which, had it first been recorded in the 1930s, might well have appeared on the label as 'Mailman Bring Me No More Blues Blues'.

Dylan's version of 'Hard Times', though it's been said that it doesn't fully exploit the nobility of Foster's melody, is a thrilling achievement. The voice breathes his affection for Foster's craft and his respect for its capacity to evoke, regardless of political correctness, a mythic Old South that still has the power to shiver the imagination and to smoke its way inside the landscape we know from those writers and blues singers who inhabited the real terrain. The chorus of 'Hard Times' conjures up a world that ROBERT JOHNSON struggled to leave behind, and that the early HOWLIN' WOLF *lived*: it puts us right inside one of those cabins in the spooky backwoods where ghostly mists are in the trees, animals howl fitfully in the night and oppression too can seem a creature that might be creeping under the door. And as with Johnson's 'Hellhound on My Trail' ('all around my door, all around my door . . .') and Howlin' Wolf's solo acoustic 'Ain't Goin' Down the Backroads (By Myself)', in Dylan's handling of the 'Hard Times' refrain the resonating wood that is the sound-box of the acoustic guitar is the perfect medium for putting us inside the woods of the lyrics. (The benign side of nature outside the cabin door is represented in JIMMIE RODGERS' song 'Miss the Mississippi and You', which Dylan recorded late the same year, in which 'mockingbirds are singing around the cabin door'.)

At the same time another world hovers in the words of the verses of 'Hard Times', contemporaneous with Foster's American backwoods but a very different place: the England of the great Charles Dickens, with its waiflike victims of industrialism, its tattered urban poor. The two writers were near-contemporaries, Dickens being 14 when Foster was born, and touring America as a triumphantly successful novelist in 1841, while Foster was an educated, literate 15-year-old in middle-class Pittsburgh. When Dickens' novel *Hard Times* was published, Foster was at the height of his powers, and by the time of Foster's death ten years later, Dickens had published all of his work except *Our Mutual Friend* and *The Mystery of Edwin Drood*. No specific relationship is suggested between *Hard Times* the novel and 'Hard Times' the song (though both were published the same year, 1854), but on the evidence of this song alone, Foster has clearly been influenced by Dickens' compassionate vision and his concomitant reforming zeal. 'Let us . . . all sup sorrow with the poor' is both a characteristic sample of its Dickens-inspired expression and the stated theme of the song. Foster brings it to odd but vivid half-life, or after-life, showing us the hungry poor as 'frail forms fainting at the door'.

Foster obviously had a bit of a thing about these frail forms, this Victorian Gothic ghostliness that happens to suit the world he never knew, of cabins in the woods and mist on the bayou. A favourite word of his is 'vapors'. Even in 'Jeannie' we meet this ingredient right at the start of the song, where he dreams of Jeannie 'Borne like a vapor on the summer air.' In 'Beautiful Dreamer', very similarly, 'over the streamlets, vapors are borne' (or possibly 'born'). Later in 'Jeannie', he hears melodies 'like joys gone by. . . . Sighing like the night wind and sobbing like the rain'. In 'Old Black Joe' it is the voices of the singer's long-dead friends he hears calling him, and he is left 'grieving for forms now departed long ago.' In 'My Old Kentucky Home' 'They sing no more by the glimmer of the moon / On the bench by the old cabin door / The day goes by like a shadow o'er the heart . . . / By'n'by hard times comes a-knockin' at the door.'

It would be easy to find in all this only the unacceptable face of its of-its-time sentimentality: but just as Dylan maximises the vividness of that 'all around my cabin door' in the refrain, because he's more interested in being alert to its imaginative pull than to its shortcomings as eternal-truth poetics, so too in the verses of 'Hard Times' Dylan brings out marvellously the song's lurid Dickensian darkness. How he lingers in fretful fascination (far more than on the word 'linger') over that mad, ghostly line 'There are frail forms fainting at the door', singing the nebulous, Victorian Gothic word 'forms' as if test-pushing against it, as if endeavouring by sheer concentration of will to make it materialise into something more human, less supernatural. And it is the most human of touches that he brings, in a moment of lovely articulation, to the pale maiden's 'sighin' all the day', enacting the sigh not on the word 'sighin'' itself but right across the four syllables he makes of 'all' in that phrase.

With its majestic incantatory length and the marvellous voice Dylan gives us, concentrated and sustained throughout, this is one of the finest performances on the two 1990s acoustic solo albums: one of Dylan's best lead vocals of the last 20 years. The compelling vision of Stephen Foster, compressing so much into this great song, can take some credit, giving Dylan a work he could approach with such respect.

In the freezing bathroom of a cheap Bowery hotel, Stephen Foster hit his head on the edge of a sink, went into a coma and died in hospital next day, January 13, 1864.

['Way Down Upon the Pee Wee River' from William Least Heat-Moon, *Blue Highways*, US, 1983 (London: Picador, 1984). Frankie Laine, 'That Lucky Old Sun', *nia*, 1949. Jerry Lee Lewis: 'Old Black Joe', Memphis, 1959–60, Sun 337, Memphis (London-American HLS 9131, London), 1960; CD-reissued on the 8-CD set *Classic Jerry Lee Lewis*, Bear Family BCD 15420-HH, Vollersode, Germany, c.1991. Marty Robbins: 'Beautiful Dreamer', Nashville, 7 Aug 1963; reissued *Long Long Ago*, Columbia CBS 40-88649, NY, 1984. Roy Orbison: 'Beautiful Dreamer', prob. Nashville, 1963; CD-reissued *Roy Orbison: Best Loved Standards*, Monument 463419 2, NY, 1992. Sam Cooke: 'Jeannie with the Light Brown Hair', NY, 9 Sep 1960; *Swing Low*, RCA Victor LSP2293, NY (RD 27222, London), 1961 (an album that also includes 'You Belong to Me', *nia*, the standard Dylan covered so beautifully at the same sessions as the *Good as I Been to You* tracks [Malibu, Jul–Aug 1992] and contributed to the soundtrack of Oliver Stone's movie *Natural Born Killers*, UNV Interscope ITSC-92460, US, 1994). Joan Baez: 'I Dream of Jeannie/ Danny Boy', LA, 17–29 Jan 1975, *Diamonds and Rust*, A&M SP-3233, LA (AMLH 64527, London), 1975. Aaron Neville: 'Hard Times', *nia*. Emmylou Harris: 'Hard Times', May 1991, *nia*. Syd Straw: 'Hard Times', 1989, *Surprise*, Virgin America VUSLP6 (& CD 91266-2), 1989. Buddy Holly: 'Mailman Bring Me No More Blues', Clovis, NM, 8 Apr 1957, reissued on *The Complete Buddy Holly*, 6-LP box set, MCA CDSP 807, London, 1979. Robert Johnson: 'Hellhound on My Trail', Dallas, 20 Jun 1937, CD-reissued *Robert Johnson: The Complete Recordings*, Columbia Roots n' Blues Series CBS 467246, US, 1990s. Howlin' Wolf: 'Ain't Going Down That Dirt Road (By Myself)', Chicago, Nov 1968, unissued till the 3-CD *The Chess Box*, MCA CHD3-9332, US, 1992. Jimmie Rodgers: 'Miss the Mississippi and You', NY, 29 Aug 1932. Bob Dylan: 'Miss the Mississippi and You', Chicago 4–21 Jun 1992, unreleased.]

'4th Time Around' [1966], coarseness & innuendo '4th Time Around', a minor song on *Blonde on Blonde*, is more than just a parody of THE BEATLES' song from a few months earlier, 'Norwegian Wood', though there is certainly a strong parallel between that song's distinctive melody, sung by JOHN LENNON, and the melody Dylan uses. It says something about how these two were perceived that Dylan was suspected (not least by Lennon) of parodying, rather than copying, the Beatles. Years later, when GEORGE HARRISON was asked in an interview about the way that the Beatles and Dylan had influenced each other, he seemed to suggest that '4th Time Around' was *about* 'Norwegian Wood', and about how *that* song had been inspired by Dylan in the first place:

> 'To my mind, it was about how John and Paul, from listening to Bob's early stuff, had written "Norwegian Wood". Judging from the title, it seemed as though Bob had listened to that and wrote the same basic song again, calling it "4th Time Around". The title suggests that the same basic tune kept bouncing around over and over again.'

'4th Time Around' begins as a cold, mocking put-down of a woman and a relationship untouched by love. For extra sarcasm's sake, it is set against a backing of fawning, schmaltzy guitar-work. But the drumming hints from the start at something more urgent and compelling than cold mockery, so that by the time the lyric switches attention to a second, and love-tinged, relationship, the tone of the song has been switched over too.

The contrast between the two women is plain enough: 'She threw me outside' and 'You took me in'—but the perspective is not that simple. The vast majority of it focuses on the 'she' part, and so suggests the narrator's personal weakness and perhaps vulnerability; and in consequence this majority consists of language soaked in coarse sexual innuendo that brings out Dylan's skill in pursuing the suggestive.

The songs on the Basement Tapes, recorded the year after *Blonde on Blonde*, indulge in the suggestive to an unprecedented extent for Dylan, with lines like 'I bin hittin' it too hard / My stones won't take', 'that big dumb blonde with her wheel gorged', 'slap that drummer with a pipe that smells', and much of 'Please Mrs. Henry'. 1974's *Planet Waves* returned more heavy-handedly and so less comfortably to this coarseness. It is there in Dylan's sleevenotes: 'Back to the starting point! . . .

I dropped a double brandy and tried to recall the events . . . family outings with strangers–furious gals with garters and smeared lips on bar stools that stank from sweating pussy . . . space guys off duty with big dicks and duck tails all wired up and voting for Eisenhower . . .'; and it is there in the otherwise admirable 'Tough Mama', where Dylan lazily offers the awkward analogy 'Today on the countryside / It was hotter than a crotch'.

Dylan's technique for delivering sexual innuendo is more interesting in '4th Time Around'. It is almost like a parody of a schoolboy reading Shakespeare aloud in class; instead of the frequently required line overflow, there is a pause–encouraged, but not exaggeratedly, by the tune–at the end of odd lines in the lyric. Into each pause comes all the innuendo and ambiguity that Dylan can muster: 'I / Stood there and hummed / I tapped on her drum / I asked her how come / And she / Buttoned her boot / And straightened her suit / Then she said Don't Get Cute. / So I forced / My hands in my pockets and felt with my thumbs . . . / And after finding out I'd / Forgotten my shirt / I went back and knocked. / I waited in the hallway, as she went to get it / And I tried to make sense / Out of that picture of you in your wheelchair / That leaned up against / Her / Jamaican rum / And when she did come / I asked her for some.'

The pause Dylan creates at the end of 'And I tried to make sense' has a different purpose. (And after it, the lapse back for that pointed 'come' has an added force: it seems in every sense uncontrollable on the narrator's part.) With 'tried to make sense' the pause is to allow a change of mood to begin impinging. The tone is no longer jaundiced. From here on it is open and alert and more sensitive; for from the midst of the imagery appropriate to the narrator's sexual, loveless encounter, Dylan–and here is the touch of genius–produces a clear and striking counter-image: '. . . that picture of you in your wheelchair . . .' With that, he establishes the hint that here, in the offing, is something with a warmer potential, something for which it is worth the narrator's while to salvage his own sensibility. Yet having produced this counter-image, Dylan allows it to recede and settle at the back of the listener's mind. Only at the very end is it reintroduced, to fuse into one clear perspective all the different threads of feeling and of imagery which run through the song. It ends: 'And / When I was through / I filled up my shoe / And brought it to you; / And you, / You took me in / You loved me then / You didn't waste time / And I, / I never took much / I never asked for your crutch / Now don't ask for mine.'

That 'crutch' has all the complexity at work in a worthwhile pun. As we are presented with the mental cadence from 'wheelchair' down to that 'crutch' at the close, in the sweep of which the 'picture' is brought sharply to life, we have one of those fine, rare moments in poetry where although the technical device is seen functioning it does so with such supreme calculation and panache that its 'intrusion' enriches the finished work.

In form, the song is, like so many Dylan works, a dramatic monologue (see **Browning, Robert** for more on this), here broadened by there being two women, rather than the more usual one woman, portrayed in this extraordinary implicatory way.

Dylan performed '4th Time Around' in the solo half of his 1966 concerts, starting, as far as we know, at Hempstead, NY, on February 26 (twelve days after recording it for *Blonde on Blonde*) and keeping it in the repertoire every night. He next performed it as a one-off on the 1974 'comeback' tour, playing it only in Memphis, January 23. Likewise on the 1975 Rolling Thunder tour, he performed it only in Augusta, Maine (November 26), and he didn't play it at all on the 1976 tour.

When he revisited the song in concert in the 1990s the melody line he chose showed just how close to 'Norwegian Wood' the song really was. He gave an especially fine performance at the first of his two concerts in Portsmouth, England, on September 24, 2000.

See also ***Planet Waves*, the disappearing sleevenotes**.

[The Beatles: 'Norwegian Wood', London, 21 Oct 1965, *Rubber Soul*, Parlophone PCS 3075, London (Capitol ST 2442, LA), 1965 (it is the track on which George Harrison first plays the sitar). Harrison interview quote originally for *Guitar World*, unspecified issue, posted on the official Beatles Ireland website and seen online there 4 Mar 2005 at *www.iol.ie/~beatlesireland/harrison/interviews/georgeinterview3.htm*.]

Fraser, Alan [1945 -] Alan Fraser was born in Dorset, UK, in 1945 and has been a Dylan fan since buying *The Freewheelin' Bob Dylan* in 1963 when a student in Manchester. An independent IT security consultant, he has provided information to Columbia Records and various Dylan fanzines, but his major contribution is the website *www.searchingforagem.com*: a huge, painstaking and scrupulous documenting, in mind-boggling detail, of officially released Dylan rarities and more. You can have no idea how much of this material there is until you turn to Fraser's excellent and lavishly illustrated website.

Freedom Singers, the The Freedom Singers comprised Rutha Mae Harris, Charles Neblett and Cordell Hull Reagon, plus Bernice Johnson, who later married Reagon, thereafter calling herself BERNICE JOHNSON REAGON. The two women were from Albany in southwest Georgia, where they had always sung in church; Cordell Reagon was from Nashville, where as field secretary of the Student Nonviolent Coordinating Committee he had organised nonviolence training workshops and campaigned against segregation at the start of the 1960s.

The group was created in 1961 by the SNCC as the SNCC Freedom Singers, its mission to raise consciousness and campaigning funds. In an old red Buick station-wagon—at which bullets and other missiles were often fired—they traveled 50,000 miles through 40 states in nine months, bringing news and stories of the civil rights movement to the South and performing at colleges, universities and rallies and speaking in jails and at political meetings. The group's members were sometimes jailed themselves as they took part in registration drives, picketing and demonstrations. Their repertoire of 'freedom songs' mainly fitted political lyrics to traditional African-American choral music—hence 'Oh Mary, Oh Martha' became 'Oh Pritchett, Oh Kelley', directing itself at Albany's aggressively racist police chief, Laurie Pritchett, and mayor, Asa Kelley); other key songs were 'If You Miss Me at the Back of the Bus', 'We Shall Not Be Moved', 'Governor Wallace', 'Which Side Are You On?' (see separate entry) and the powerful 'Woke Up This Morning With My Mind on Freedom'. Sometimes they used acoustic rhythm-guitar backing but usually sang unaccompanied.

By 1963 they were appearing with many of the folk revival movement's stars, including Bob Dylan. He appeared with them, JOAN BAEZ and ODETTA on a no-longer extant 'Freedom Songs' television special in New York (on WNEW-TV; ROBERT SHELTON, acting as a consultant to the show, asked Dylan onto it) on an unknown date in the first half of 1963, and flew down to Mississippi to drop in on their voter-registration campaigning early that July, when they, PETE SEEGER and THEODORE BIKEL all performed for farm workers in a field outside GREENWOOD. Later that month, the Freedom Singers appeared, like Dylan, at the 1963 NEWPORT FOLK FESTIVAL. At the end of the final evening, Baez, PETER, PAUL & MARY and the Freedom Singers sang 'Blowin' in the Wind' behind Dylan, followed by an ensemble 'We Shall Overcome': one of the many songs the group recorded for Folkways. A month later they, like Dylan and LEN CHANDLER, appeared at the historic March on Washington at which Martin Luther King delivered his 'I Have a Dream' speech.

The group disbanded soon after this, re-forming in 1964 as an all-male vocal quartet.

[The Freedom Singers are well-represented on the Various Artists 2-CD retrospective set *Voices of the Civil Rights Movement: Black American Freedom Songs 1960–1966*, Smithsonian Folkways SFW40084, Washington, D.C., 1997, which includes the songs cited above. Sources include Rita Neubauer journal extract, seen online 23 Jan 2006 at *www.voicesofcivilrights.org/bus tour/journal_entry33.html* and a *Green Left Weekly* online edn., seen ditto at *www.greenleft.org.au/back/1992/65/65p21.htm*. WNEW-TV information from Robert Shelton, *No Direction Home: The Life and Music of Bob Dylan*, London: Penguin edn., p.167.]

Freeman, Denny [1944 -] Dennis Edward Freeman was born in Orange County, Florida, on August 7, 1944 but spent his adolescence in Dallas, Texas, where in the 1950s he thrilled to rock'n'roll and R&B and caught the live acts of many Chicago and Louisiana blues artists. By the late 1960s he had added Cream and JIMI HENDRIX to his list of special favourites and when he moved to Austin, Texas, in 1970 after attending college, he began playing music in earnest himself. Though mainly a guitarist he has always played piano too, including on records by JENNIFER WARNES, James Cotton and JIMMIE VAUGHAN, and was pianist on Vaughan's first solo tour. (He had first heard 16-year-old Vaughan play in Dallas, and later heard 17-year-old STEVIE RAY VAUGHAN in Austin, and fell in with them. 'We became friends, roommates, bandmates. Stevie still owes me $30 rent,' Freeman says on his website.)

Denny Freeman's first band was the Corals; around 1973 he was in the short-lived Southern Feeling and in 1976, with the Vaughans, the Cobras (who staged a reunion in 1982 and were back again by 2000, making a new album). For most of the 1970s and 1980s he was with the Vaughans in various combinations, including in the Fabulous Thunderbirds, which was the house band at Antones in Austin when it opened in 1975. Freeman had played with Freddie King as early as 1970 but now he was pitched in with many of the heroes of his youth—on one 1975 club night he was up there playing with the great Hubert Sumlin, JOHN LEE HOOKER, Walter Horton and others. In another house band, in the 1980s, he played—sometimes guitar, sometimes piano—with Otis Rush, Junior Wells, Albert Collins, Buddy Guy and other blues big names.

In 1986 he made *Blues Cruise*, the first of five 'solo' albums, all largely instrumentals which, despite that first title, ranged across rock'n'roll, soul, jazz and R&B as well as the blues, and featured many musicians, among them the Texan singer-songwriter Angela Strehli, with whom he had often worked. The others were *Out of the Blue* (1987), *Denny Freeman* (1991), *A Tone for My Sins* (1997: this last title a pun that drew on his Catholic upbringing—something he mentions himself when, recalling that he and the Vaughans had been influenced by Dallas-based group the Nightcaps, he describes them as 'young Catholic boys playing blues. It was their version of "Thunderbird" that Stevie liked to play') and *Twang Bang* (2002). In 2000 he released the album *Denny Freeman and the Cobras*, and played in Japan and elsewhere in Taj Mahal's Phantom Blues Band.

Freeman had moved to LA in 1992, and remained there until late 2004, by which time he had also appeared on a Percy Sledge album for which he co-wrote one track, 'Love Come and Rescue Me'. He also co-wrote (with Debbie Harry and three others) the postmodernist lounge jazz track 'Boom Boom in the Zoom Zoom Room', on her 1999 'Blondie comeback album' *No Exit*.

In 2005 he had something else to do: he joined Bob Dylan's Never-Ending Tour band, rehearsing in Seattle as from that March 1, and débuting in concert with Dylan on the first night of the 82-date spring US leg of the tour, which opened with three consecutive nights in Seattle, starting on March 7. Denny Freeman, these days balding and solid and tending to sport dark glasses (giving him 'a sort of Jack Nicholson look', according to one first-night fan's review), has remained in the band since, playing second guitar. By the end of 2005 he had played 113 Dylan concerts in all.

[Denny Freeman: *Blues Cruise*, *nia*, US, 1986; *Out of the Blue*, *nia*, US, 1987 (both CD-reissued on 1 CD, *Blues Cruise/Out of the Blue*, Amazing, *nia*, US, 1992); *Denny Freeman*, *nia*, US, 1991; *A Tone for My Sins*, Dallas Blues 8904, US, 1997; *Twang Bang*, V-8 V8-001, US, 2002. Denny Freeman & the Cobras: *Denny Freeman & the Cobras*, Crosscut 11028, US, 2000. Main sources *www.dennyfreeman.com*, Bill Pagel's Bob Links (incl. Dennis Lind's 'Nicholson look' quote) at *http://my.execpc.com/~billp61/030705r.html* (both seen online 7 Jan 2006), and e-mail from Denny Freeman to this writer, 21 Jan 2006.]

Freeman, Eddie [1939 - 1962] In one of the *11 Outlined Epitaphs* published in early 1964 on the sleeve of Dylan's third album, *The Times They Are a-Changin'*, Dylan rhapsodises about a series of people whirling around in his head in the vivid tumult of his youthful New York City days. Most of those he lists, from the first, FRANCOIS VILLON, through to the last, PETE SEEGER, are well-enough known names. Only one figure is that of a person with no public face; Dylan's sad line 'the dead poems of Eddie Freeman' has always stood out.

Edward Bromwell Freeman, Jr. was born in Maryland on July 6, 1939 and grew up in Towson, Maryland. He died on November 27, 1962 in a plane crash in the Peruvian Andes en route to Lima. In his Yale Class of '62 obituary he was called 'Ed Freeman, our Class Poet'.

He had been a talented all-rounder, a sportsman despite being only five foot seven and a scholar who graduated from Yale *magna cum laude* and had also studied at the Sorbonne in Paris. He died at the end of a period of some months in Brazil 'researching television scripts' and had intended to enrol for graduate study at the University of Copenhagen, in the rather different climate of Denmark, and then to become a professional writer.

His friend and classmate Toby Berger, now a Professor of Electrical Engineering at Cornell, remembers him at Yale as a vibrant young man with a round face and straight, glaringly blonde hair, rushing around 'laden with notebooks full of poems', and recalls that he organised a poetry reading in the men's room of Sterling Library (Yale's main library), and urinals were flushing as students came and went throughout the reading. Freeman also wrote an avant garde play 'in which people kept switching identities and even sexes from one scene to the next', which was performed twice at Silliman College (a Yale residential college, and all male) in April or May of 1962.

At weekends Freeman 'frequently disappeared to Greenwich Village where he befriended a young Bob Dylan.' Berger remembers Ed coming back and saying that 'There's this guy in New York that everyone is wild for. He plays guitar and harmonica both at once, and sings his poetry!'

Berger believes that Ed's poetry influenced Dylan's own, and that the line 'I met a white man who walked a black dog' in 'A Hard Rain's a-Gonna Fall' was either a line, or the reversal of a line, from a Freeman poem from 1958–59.

Berger recalls meeting Dylan backstage between sets at a concert in Cambridge; the online obituary places this wrongly as 'in the late 1960s'; in fact it was in 1964, possibly at his early April concert at Symphony Hall, Boston. Berger brought the bound typescript of Freeman's play to give to Dylan but he took it only momentarily before handing it back and saying something along the lines of 'No, it's yours: it should stay with you'; they 'exchanged a few words about how hard it was to think of Ed as dead when he'd been *so* much alive such a short time before.'

Freeman was 23 at the time of his death. Thus quite a lot is compressed into that one quiet line of Dylan's, 'the dead poems of Eddie Freeman'.

[Sources *www2.aya.yale.edu/classes/yc1962/obituaries/freeman.html*, augmented & corrected by e-mail correspondence with Toby Berger, 28, 29 & 31 Oct 2005.]

***Freewheelin' Bob Dylan, The* [1963]** Dylan's second album, this was his first opportunity to show how fast he was to develop from one album to the next. The first sessions for this album were held in April 1962, just five months after the first album was recorded—but in the end nothing from the April sessions was included on the album.

All the songs were his own, though many were based on older folk melodies. He was better known in 1963 as a new songwriter of weird promise than as a performer, though this album not only brought together an impressive group of songs that have since become classics—'Blowin' in the Wind', 'Girl of the North Country', 'Masters of War' and 'A Hard Rain's a-Gonna Fall' were all on one side of the original LP, while the other includes 'Don't Think Twice, It's All Right'—but also gained him an unstoppable cult following among people who preferred the harshness of Dylan's performances to the string-soaked or softer cover-versions other singers released.

See also ***Freewheelin' Bob Dylan, The*: withdrawn early version**.

[Recorded NY, 9 Jul, 26 Oct, 14 Nov, 6 Dec 1962 & 24 Apr 1963; released as Columbia CL 1986 (mono) & CS 8786 (stereo), in the UK as CBS BPG 62193 (mono) & SBPG 62193 (stereo), 27 May 1963.]

***Freewheelin' Bob Dylan, The*: withdrawn early version** Test pressings and promo copies of Dylan's second album featured four tracks that were replaced before the album's commercial release. The withdrawn tracks were 'Solid Road' [more commonly called 'Rocks & Gravel'] and 'Talkin' John Birch Society Blues' (both still unreleased), 'Let Me Die in My Footsteps' (released, but with one verse edited out, on the *Bootleg Series Vols. 1–3*, 1991) and 'Gamblin' Willie' [more commonly 'Ramblin' Gamblin' Willie'] (released complete on ditto). The tracks that replaced them on the standard version of the album were 'Girl of the North Country', 'Masters of War', 'Bob Dylan's Dream' and 'Talkin' World War III Blues'.

But there are many further permutations to the withdrawn release: copies where the stated tracklist does not match the tracks featured (both ways round), a Canadian version of the proper album that gave the wrong tracklist not just briefly but for many years, etc. etc. The rarest, most valuable collector's item is a correctly labeled (on sleeve and record label) stereo pressing of the withdrawn version.

The withdrawn *Freewheelin'* is listed here as being of special historical note, but there are always 'rare' and 'collector's item' versions of Dylan releases, and there is no scope in the present volume to detail others. The best source for such discographical minutiae, not of bootlegs but of errant and obscure officially released and misreleased records, is ALAN FRASER's vast and scrupulous website *www.searchingforagem.com*.

[Catalogue nos. for the withdrawn album are: Columbia CL 1986 (mono) and CS 8786 (stereo), April 1963.]

***Freewheelin'* [fanzine]** For most of its history the UK fanzine *Freewheelin'* was a privately circulated newsletter (to an extremely small list of subscribers), but one that gave significant amounts of support to other, bigger fanzines. Various columns reviewing books, videos and bootlegs and surveying newspaper sightings of Dylan were imported into *Isis* and others straight from *Freewheelin'*. It was, in the phrase he prefers, 'collated by' John R. Stokes. Latterly accessible online, it has also turned itself into a glossy full-colour quarterly, starting to call itself *Freewheelin' Quarterly* as from 'Volume 21', the October 2001 issue.

Fremerman, Elana [1970 -] Elana Jaime Fremerman, aka Elana James, who was born in Kansas City, Missouri, on October 21, 1970, has the distinction of being the shortest-serving member of Dylan's Never-Ending Tour Band. She guest-performed with him on the summer 2004 tour co-headlined by WILLIE NELSON, playing her wired-up 1962 Mittenwald violin on the first two songs of the concerts in Jackson, Tennessee, on August 20, Comstock Park, Michigan, on the 24th, Peoria on the 25th and Madison, Wisconsin, on the 27th. Then, seven months later, she joined the band, from March 7 to April 22, 2005 (after which that leg of the tour finished without her). Even within this brief period she was missing from the Boston concerts on April 15, 16 and 17.

Fremerman's mother is a professional violinist and her stepfather played in the Kansas City Symphony Orchestra. She learnt violin from the age of five, played on Kansas City streets for tips as a young teenager and went to college in New York to play viola and study classical music. After graduation, uncertain what she wanted, she went to India and studied North Indian dhrupad music, then worked in Nepal before returning to the US. After day jobs and playing in a band in Colorado she went back to New York where she placed an ad in the *Village Voice* for like-minded fans of 1930s-40s violinists, the upshot of which was eventually the Texas-based Hot Club of Cowtown, the band at the bottom of the bill on Dylan's summer 2004 tour, from which came her all-too-brief moments of professional connection with him.

Afterwards, she returned to Hot Club of Cowtown but almost immediately the band broke up (at the guitarist's behest, she says). Fremerman, who has since re-named herself Elana James, gave a phone interview from her Austin home to the *Berkshire Eagle* in Pittsfield, Massachusetts, in which she said: 'The past year was very strange. It had a lot of highs and lows. I have played with the upper edge of the industry and then I have also come home and played in tiny little hellholes for no money. I have spanned the gamut and what I have realized is that it doesn't really matter where I am playing: it is just important that I am playing and moving forward artistically.'

She can be heard on Dylan's recording of 'Tell Ol' Bill' (see ***Self Portrait***), on the soundtrack of the 2005 film *North Country*.

[Dave Madeloni, phone interview Jan 15, 2006, *Berkshire Eagle*, Pittsfield, MA, 20 Jan 2006; seen online 23 Jan at *www.berkshireeagle.com/fastsearch/ci_3420138*. Birthdate & full name info from Elana by e-mail via her agent, the Nancy Fly Agency.]

French symbolist poets, the Along with the verse of EDGAR ALLAN POE, the poetry of CHARLES BAUDELAIRE was an important precursor of the symbolist movement, initiated by PAUL VERLAINE and Mallarmé, which used symbols to explore and evoke cross-currents and 'illogical' affinities, especially between the senses. (The relationship between drugs and this sense-mingling is discussed briefly in the entry on Baudelaire.)

Dylan gives Verlaine and RIMBAUD playful namechecks in the *Blood on the Tracks* song 'You're Gonna Make Me Lonesome When You Go', and elsewhere quotes Rimbaud's dictum 'I is another'.

In his 1986 biography *No Direction Home: The Life and Music of Bob Dylan*, ROBERT SHELTON quotes DAVE VAN RONK on the subject of asking Dylan whether he was aware of the French symbolist poets:

> 'I did come on to Bob about Francois Villon. I also told him about Rimbaud and Apollinaire. I once asked Bobby: "Have you ever heard about Rimbaud?" He said: "Who?" I repeated: "Rimbaud—R-I-M-B-A-U-D. He's a French poet. You really ought to read him," I said. . . . Much later, I was up at his place. . . . On his shelf I discovered a book of translations of French symbolist poets that had obviously been thumbed through over a period of years! . . . I didn't mention Rimbaud to him again until I heard his "A Hard Rain's a-Gonna Fall". . . . I said to Bob: "You know, that song of yours is heavy in symbolism, don't you?" He said: "Huh?"'

[Robert Shelton: *No Direction Home: The Life and Music of Bob Dylan*, Penguin edn., pp.99–100.]

Fried, Hans [1944 -] Hans Rolf Fried was born in London on May 31, 1944, the eldest son of the poet Erich Fried (translator into German of the work of Dylan Thomas and Sylvia Plath). A London-based long-time folk, blues and jazz expert, now working for the UK office of the Mechanical Copyright Protection Society—Performing Rights Society Alliance, he has two specific Dylan connections: see **Graves, Robert** and ***Madhouse on Castle Street, The***.

Friedman, Kinky [1944 -] Richard F. Friedman was born in Chicago on Hallowe'en 1944 but moved to Texas as a child, where he developed an interest in chess and then music. He graduated from the University of Texas in Austin in 1966 and joined the Peace Corps, which sent him to Borneo. Unsurprisingly, he found this very different from Texas and became an admirer of its culture.

Back in the US, he formed the cod western swing band for which he became famous, Kinky Friedman & the Texas Jewboys, in the early 1970s and has always hovered between wanting to play good music and wanting to challenge anti-semitism and 'good taste' in equal measure in his ponderous, sub-'Springtime for Hitler' way. His first album was *Sold American* (1973), on which the musicians included Billy Swan, Tompall Glaser and DAVID MANSFIELD, followed by *Kinky Friedman* (1974), on which Waylon Jennings and WILLIE NELSON join him on 'They Ain't Makin' Jews Like Jesus Anymore'.

Friedman performed his signature song, 'Ride 'em Jewboy', at the one-off Rolling Thunder Revue concert on January 25, 1976 in Houston, which was a fundraiser for RUBIN HURRICANE CARTER; subsequently he was a guest performer on the second Rolling Thunder Revue proper, which kicked off that April 18, ran through till May 25 and incorporated the concert that yielded the 'Hard Rain' TV special from Fort Collins, Colorado, on May 23. When Friedman released his third album that November, *Lasso from El Paso*, the track 'Sold American', a live version recorded at Fort Collins, is credited as 'Recorded live with Bob Dylan and the Rolling Thunder Revue'. This was characteristic self-promotion; Dylan does not appear on this recording and wasn't on stage at the time. On the Revue shows, Friedman had also performed 'Rock and Roll Across the USA', 'Dear Abbie' and 'I'm Proud to Be an Asshole from El Paso'—which many were disappointed to find does not appear on the *Lasso from El Paso* album (because it was a pastiche of 'Okie from Muscogee' and Buck Owens withheld his consent). The album does, however, contain a version of Dylan's *Desire* outtakes song 'Catfish', which had not been released by Dylan at the time (it's on the *Bootleg Series Vols. 1–3*, 1991); it also features an astonishing parade of musicians, among them Dr. John, RONNIE HAWKINS, ROGER McGUINN (on banjo), RINGO STARR (on vocals), RON WOOD, RICK DANKO, MICK RONSON, ROB STONER, STEVEN SOLES, GARY BURKE, T-BONE BURNETT, ERIC CLAPTON (on dobro), LEVON HELM (on guitar), RICHARD MANUEL (on drums) and HOWIE WYETH.

Since those days Friedman has continued to make music but has also become a prolific writer of humourous detective fiction, starring himself—and regularly also starring LARRY SLOMAN, whose own book about the Rolling Thunder Revue, *On the Road with Bob Dylan: Rolling with the Thunder*, foregrounds Friedman. This genial mutual back-scratching went further in 2002, when a new edition of Sloman's book was augmented by a new preface by Kinky Friedman. There are at least 20 of Friedman's private-eye novels, starting with *Greenwich Killing Time* in 1986.

Fifteen years after the 1976 Rolling Thunder Revue, Dylan and Friedman connected again—and if it was a brief reunion, at least they were on stage together—as Dylan played guitar behind Friedman as he reprised 'Sold American' on the September 15, 1991 CHABAD TELETHON shown live from Hollywood.

Today Friedman lives at the family summer camp, Echo Hill Ranch, in deepest Texas, where he also founded his most worthwhile project, the Utopia Animal Rescue Ranch. In 2005 he launched a supposed campaign to become state governor and is running a repeat campaign in 2006, on a predictably jocular programme. In middle age, he has finally acquired the extra weight to look plausible in those photos in which he poses, inevitably, with John B. Stetson hat, large cigar and scarily expansive grin. He remains one of those confident, happy souls who always finds himself more amusing than anyone else does.

[Kinky Friedman: *Sold American*, Vanguard VSD79333, US, 1973; *Kinky Friedman*, ABC ABCD-829, US, 1974; *Lasso from El Paso*, Epic EPC 34304, US (Epic SEPC 81640, UK), 1976. *Greenwich Killing Time*, New York: Beech Tree Books, 1986. Larry Sloman: *On the Road with Bob Dylan: Rolling with the Thunder*, New York: Bantam, 1978, republished (with new introduction by Friedman), New York: Three Rivers Press & London: Helter Skelter Publishing, 2002.]

Frizzell, Lefty [1928 - 1975] William Orville Frizzell, born March 31, 1928 in Corsicana, TX, became a highly influential honky-tonk singer of the 1950s, an idiosyncratic vocalist whose mark can be detected on the work of MERLE HAGGARD and people like Randy Travis, and who must count among those who had a subliminal influence on Dylan. He came out of the dance-halls of Texas, and 'If You've Got the Money I've Got the Time' made him a star in 1950. (This song was in ROY ORBISON's early repertoire, across the other side of Texas from BUDDY HOLLY's Lubbock homebase).

He had about 30 subsequent smaller hits, and within weeks of Holly cutting the great 'Mailman, Bring Me No More Blues' in 1957, Frizzell covered it (though his cover remained unissued until 1992).

He was one of the first to record a song much associated with THE BAND and performed by Dylan, 'Long Black Veil'. Frizzell reached no.6 in the US country charts with it in 1959. Dylan débuted it in concert in Wheeling, West Virginia, on April 28, 1997. He also performed Frizzell's song 'You're Too Late' in concert on January 29, 1999, at Daytona Beach, Florida.

Lefty Frizzell more or less drank himself to death at 47, suffering a fatal alcohol-triggered stroke on July 19, 1975, in Nashville.

[Lefty Frizzell: 'If You've Got the Money I've Got the Time', Dallas, TX, 25 Jul 1950; 1950; 'Mailman, Bring Me No More Blues', Nashville, 10 May 1957; 'Long Black Veil', Nashville, 3 Mar 1959; all issued on the 12-CD box set *Lefty Frizzell: Life's Like Poetry*, Bear Family BCD 15550, Vollersode, Germany, 1992.]

'Froggie Went a-Courtin'' [1992] Bob Dylan's recording of 'Froggie Went a-Courtin'' is one of the stand-out tracks on his solo acoustic album of 1992 (his first since 1964), *Good as I Been to You*. Sung and played with real charm by Dylan, he keeps deftly away from both hammed-up comedy and song-archivist solemnity, enabling him to offer a version that is good-humoured and alert to the riches and full humanity of the song.

This is at base an ancient nursery rhyme/ballad, which also has a niche in the history of folksong recordings. The sleevenotes to HARRY SMITH's anthology *AMERICAN FOLK MUSIC* begin by remarking that the most famous recording of the early 1900s was Uncle Josh's unaccompanied 'Frog Went a-Courtin''. But one collector, Theodore Raph, believes that the song itself can be traced back to Wedderburn's book of 1549, *The Complaynt of Scotland*, in which it appears as 'The Frog Cam to the Myl Dur', a song he suggests was chiefly sung by shepherds. Bruno Bettelheim, giving the publication date of *The Complaynt of Scotland* as the slightly earlier 1540, says that it includes mention of a pre-Grimms version of their fairy tale 'The Frog King', called 'The Well of the World's End'. Since 'the well' is also the frog's location at the beginning of the earliest known versions of the 'Frog Went a Courtin'' song, this may suggest some conjunction between that 13th century version of this 'animal groom' story and the 'Frog Went a Courtin'' song-group. But nursery rhyme experts Peter & Iona Opie and Harry Smith both note that the earliest listing is the title 'A moste Strange weddinge of the ffrogge and the mowse', listed by Her Majesty's Stationery Office in England on November 21, 1580, and it seems generally agreed that the earliest extant version of the *song* is in Ravenscroft's *Melismata* of 1611.

This version is called 'The Marriage of the Frogge and the Movse' and is a 13-verse text with tune, beginning: 'It was the Frogge in the well . . . / And the merrie Movse in the Mill' and including 'The Frogge would a woing ride . . . / Sword and buckler by his side.' In this version the frog and mouse are married by the rat, and the wedding supper ('three beanes in a pound of butter') is interrupted by the cat catching the mouse, a drake catching the frog and the rat escaping up the wall.

The song grew widespread as a nursery rhyme in the 18th century, and by the time we get to Kirkpatrick's *Ballad Book* (1824) it begins 'There lived a puddy in a well', it has become 'Sword and pistol by his side' and they have to get Uncle Rotten's consent. (A variant that connects with other things, 'Squire Frog's Visit', has the chorus 'Heighho! says Brittle / With a namby pamby / Mannikin pannikin / Heigh! says Anthony Brittle.' The line pairing the sword and the pistol occurs in other folksongs and game-chants. The poet and Blake scholar Kathleen Raine writes of her father that during his childhood in the north of England he had been 'initiated, unawares, into a tradition older than Christianity, surviving in the "guiser's play", handed down by the older to the younger boys in secrecy and by word of mouth. . . . "Here comes in King George, / King George is my name, / With sword and pistol by my side / I hope to win the game."' A 'guiser' is a mummer, usually one performed at Christmas or Hallowe'en. The same 'guiser's play' verses also include the line 'Round the world and back again', which Dylan implants into 'Handy Dandy' on his nursery-rhyme-studded album *Under the Red Sky*.)

The Opies suggest that the nursery rhyme is best known in the comparatively recent version called 'A Frog He Would a-Wooing Go', 'popularised first by Grimaldi and then by the comedian John Liston in the early nineteenth century'; it was first published with a tune in about 1809 under the title 'The Love-Sick Frog'. Its repeated chorus line 'Heighho! says Anthony Rowley' is not found before the 19th century. Earlier versions tend to have 'Humble-dum, humble-dum, tweedle tweedle wino', which, representing the humming of the wheel and the twiddling and winding of the thread, suggests that it may have started as a spinning song. 'Yes kind sir I sit and spin.'

As a song, always popular in America in both white and black folksong, it holds several Dylan connections. His version, substantially that in Cecil Sharp's *Nursery Songs from the Appalachian Mountains* (1921), is also included in the 1927 *American Songbag* collection by CARL SANDBURG, whom Dylan went to visit in 1964. 'Froggie Went a-Courtin'' is also included in John A. Lomax and ALAN LOMAX's *American Ballads & Folk Songs* (1934) and in many others. (In 1926 the Texas Folklore Society alone knew of 40 versions, and the *American Folklore Bibliography* of 1939 listed 22 US variants.) One variant version is yet another song Dylan found on the 1952 Harry Smith anthology: the 1928 recording 'King Kong Kitchie Kitchie Ki-Me-O' by Chubby Parker & His Old Time Banjo ('vocal solo with 5-string banjo and whistling'). Parker was, in the blues and old country expert Tony Russell's phrase, 'up at the minstrel end of hillbilly' but his performance on this track has a pleasantly clean-cut, straightforward quality: a light touch and no ingratiation. It is not the version sung by Dylan, though it begins with the near-identical first line 'Frog went a-courtin' and he did ride', and does include 'With a sword and a pistol by his side', 'He rode till he came to Miss Mousie's door', 'He took Miss Mousie on his knee / And he said Miss Mousie will you marry me?'. However, it ends with the frog killing all comers (with his sword and his pistol) before honeymooning with his mousy wife.

The most authoritative study of the song in its American form is in *Ozark Folk Songs Volume 1: British Ballads and Songs*, by Vance Randolph, reissued 1982. Randolph was probably the last great southern folksong collector, and published huge amounts on the song and folklore of the Ozarks—and the very young Bob Dylan was acquainted with some of his work. In Minneapolis in 1959, reports biographer ROBERT SHELTON, Bob's friend SPIDER JOHN KOERNER had a room-mate called Harry Weber, 'a ballad scholar', who says: 'I did loan Bob a set of Randolph's *Folk Songs of Arkansas* [sic]. I wonder if he still has them.' As with 'Black Jack Davey', Dylan's friend TONY GLOVER is one of the people who has recorded 'Froggie Went a-Courtin'' in more recent decades. So has DOC WATSON (collected on *The Essential Doc Watson*, 1974), Wally Whyton (*50 Children's Songs*), and ex-Steeleye Span member Tim Hart (*The Drunken Sailor and Other Kids' Songs*, 1983).

While Cecil Sharp printed the first American version of 'Froggie' taken from oral tradition, the first version into print taken from black oral tradition was in Thomas W. Talley's classic collection of *Negro Folk Rhymes*, published in 1922. On disc, 'Frog Went a Courting' was field-recorded for the Library of Congress in Frederica, Georgia in June 1935, performed by Drusilla Davis and an accompanying 'group of little girls'.

Of course, 'Froggie' might be said to be a deeply conservative song: nature is destiny and nature will out. The socialist experiment collapses because cats will be cats and ducks will be ducks. Yet its theme runs far deeper, and less judgmentally, than that. The basic story-line, summarised in typical style by Harry Smith as 'ZOOLOGIC MISCEGENY ACHIEVED IN MOUSE FROG NUPTUALS, RELATIVES APPROVE', seems to be one European version of an archetypal human myth-wish. Colombian Indians have a ritual/ceremony 'wedding' of a condor to a bull: they strap an enormous condor on the back of a bull and set them running. In the nursery rhyme 'Hoddley, poddley, puddle and fogs / Cats are to marry the poodle dogs / Cats in blue jackets, and dogs in red hats / What will become of the mice and rats?' and in the fairy tale 'Thumbelina' the toad wants the heroine to marry her son, and the field-mouse tries to make her marry the mole (though in the case of the pseudo-human Thumbelina, the archetype of 'zoologic miscegeny' shifts over into another, the 'animal groom' archetype—in which the human protagonist's sexual partner is first experienced as an animal). Bruno Bettelheim writes that this motif 'is so popular worldwide that probably no other fairy-tale theme has so many variations.' His analysis is that these are tales 'which—without any reference to repression which causes a negative attitude to sex—simply teach that for love, a radical change in previously held attitudes about sex is absolutely necessary. What must happen is expressed, as always in fairy tales, through a most impressive image: a beast is turned into a magnificent person. . . . Some fairy stories emphasise the long and difficult development which alone permits gaining control over what seems animalistic in us, while conversely other tales center on the shock of recognition when that which seemed animal suddenly reveals itself as the source of human happiness. . . . "The Frog King" belongs to the latter category.'

A little of this might be felt to reverberate through 'Froggie Went a-Courtin'' (which may, as noted, share a common ancestry with that fairytale), in which we readily identify with the story, especially in the early parleying between prospective groom and bride and authoritative relative, so that on one level it doesn't matter whether they are given as animals or people, while on another we never quite forget the 'ugly' animal potency of the frog: so deeply has the image of the frog and the princess spoken to our psyches that it remains common currency between us all as subject matter for jokes–especially around the politics of gender–which surely confirms the gist of Bettelheim's analysis.

A different arc of psychological truth cuts through the song too. Behind the twinkling guitar that propels Dylan's version along like a rolling hoop, and via a melody line which parallels BLIND WILLIE McTELL's 'Hillbilly Willie's Blues' and at its centre also parallels ELVIS' 'Paralysed' (the deft lines of added detail like 'sword and pistol by his side' use the same tune as those like 'couldn't say a word for thinkin' of you' in 'Paralysed') we identify with the world in which the story's events unfold. We recognise the truth of the shadow falling over the initially ideal, the chain of events darkening as the wedding feast collapses from exquisite and generous communal celebration, on a tiny and delicate scale, first into the black comedy of the grotesque, monstrously overlarge and clumsy intrusion of Mrs. Cow (mere mention of whom suggests the accidental squashing of some of the smaller guests). This is followed by the intrusion of evil, in the symbolically loaded figure of the black snake, and finally the effectively wanton destruction of the main protagonists. This is a timeless human story. (It even has a certain biological accuracy, as with the wedding food 'fried mosquito'. Frogs' legs used to be an export from the port of Cochin, India, until conservationists succeeded in banning them. As an importer-exporter told travel writer Alexander Frater, this has been a blessing because 'you need a thriving frog population to keep the mosquitoes down.')

One way and another, therefore, 'Froggie Went a-Courtin'' is an extraordinary song, and one that proves–insists on–the indivisibility between adult and children's song. In this way, given the emphasis it enjoys by being the last song on *Good as I Been to You*, it is a fine postscript to the Dylan's previous album, *Under the Red Sky*. And like that collection, which bows out with 'Goodnight my love and may the Lord have mercy on us all', this one has a great sign-off, provided by 'Froggie Went a-Courtin''s' self-reflexive text of a last line: 'If you want any more you can sing it yourself.'

[Theodore Raph: *The Songs We Sang: A Treasury of American Popular Music*, New Jersey: A.S. Barnes, 1965. Bruno Bettelheim: *The Uses of Enchantment*, London: Thames & Hudson, 1976, footnote 111; later quotes also from *The Uses of Enchantment*.

'The Well of the World's End' is republished in Katherine M. Briggs, *A Dictionary of British Folk Tales* (4 vols), Bloomington: Indiana University Press, 1970. Peter & Iona Opie, *The Oxford Dictionary of Nursery Rhymes*, Oxford: OUP (rev'd edn.), 1951. Kathleen Raine, 'Farewell Happy Fields', 1973, collected in *Autobiographies*, London: Skoob Books, 1991. Carl Sandburg, *An American Songbag*, New York: Harcourt Brace, 1927. Tony Russell, conversation with this writer, 17 Sep 1996. Robert Shelton, *No Direction Home: The Life and Music of Bob Dylan*, New York: Beech Tree Books / William Morrow, 1986.

Tony Glover: 'Froggie Went a-Courtin'', *nia*. Doc Watson, *nia*, collected on *The Essential Doc Watson*, Vanguard VMLP5038, NY, 1974, now CD-reissued. Wally Whyton, *nia*, *50 Children's Songs*, *nia*. Tim Hart, *nia*, *The Drunken Sailor and Other Kids' Songs*, Music for Pleasure *nia*, London, 1983. Blind Willie McTell: 'Hillbilly Willie's Blues', Chicago, 25 Apr 1935, on Various Artists: *The East Coast States Vol. 2*, Roots RL-326, Vienna, 1969–70. Elvis Presley: 'Paralysed', Hollywood, 2 Sep 1956 (composed by Otis Blackwell, later co-producer of the title track of Dylan's 1981 album *Shot of Love*); first issued *Elvis Volume One* (RCA Gold EP) RCA EPA-992, NY, 1956; re-released on CD box set *The King of Rock'n'Roll–The Complete 50s Masters*, BMG / RCA PD90689(5), 1992.

Alexander Frater, *Chasing the Monsoon*, London: Penguin, 1991.]

frying an egg on stage, the prospect of In Japan in 1986 Dylan reportedly said this: 'Somebody comes to see you for two hours or one and a half hours, whatever it is . . . I mean, they've come to see *you*. You could be doing anything up on that stage. You could be frying an egg or hammering a nail into a piece of wood.'

Instead of blitzing truculently through his 700th 'Tangled Up in Blue' or his 1,500th 'All Along the Watchtower', how infinitely more magical it would be if he *did* come on stage and proceed to fry an egg. All that Chaplinesque panache! The comic possibilities! The *freshness* of such a performance! It would be so much more revealing, so much greater an artistic nakedness, a revisit to Highway Surrealism at once dramatic and intimate.

Fuller, Blind Boy [1907 - 1941] Fulton Allen was probably born on July 10, 1907, and certainly at Wadesboro, North Carolina. He was not blind at birth but his eyesight began to fail by the age of 20 when, already married to a 14-year-old bride, he moved to the important tobacco-trade town of Winston-Salem. He was a coal-yard labourer until forced to give up this job, after which he resorted to musicianship. By 1928 he had gone wholly blind and had begun to apply himself seriously to the guitar, which he had not begun to play till around 1925. (He played a big, steel-bodied National guitar.) He and his wife moved to Durham in 1929, playing to workers coming off shift in all the tobacco towns up and down Highway 70 and around Winston-Salem; he remained in penury, though in the end he became the south-east's best-selling and most prolific recording artist of the 1930s, characterised not by originality of material but by an ear for a catchy song, a deft finger-picking style and straightforward vocals.

He recorded only between 1935 and 1940, beginning with a New York City solo session on July 23, 1935 that included an attractive re-write of 'Sittin' on Top of the World', named 'I'm Climbin' on Top of the Hill'; two days later he was accompanied by Blind GARY DAVIS and Bull City Red and their three-song session included a title THE BAND would later borrow, 'Rag, Mama, Rag'. Next day came a further solo session before he returned to North Carolina. In 1936 he went back to New York for a longer two-day solo session (which included a version of 'Mama Let Me Lay It on You'), and in 1937 he made the journey no less than four times for further multi-day sessions, the last of these in freezing mid-December. He returned once again in April 1938 but that October was able to record more conveniently in Columbia, South Carolina, with SONNY TERRY and Bull City Red; in July 1939 they reconvened in Memphis but were back in New York on March 5, 6 and 7 for sessions that began with a take of what has become one of Fuller's signature songs, 'Step It Up and Go' (with Bull City Red on washboard but Sonny Terry not playing).

His final, long session, again with these two accompanists, augmented by BROWNIE McGHEE on at least one track ('Precious Lord', one of several issued as by Brother George & His Sanctified Singers, a name often used for religious sides by McGhee & Red) took place in New York on June 19, 1940. Twelve numbers were recorded. A month later he was in hospital and on February 13, 1941 he died in considerable pain, back in Durham, from restriction of the urethra and a bladder infection. He was 33 years old.

Such was his influence and popularity that Brownie McGhee not only recorded as 'Blind Boy Fuller No. 2' but made a record titled 'Death of Blind Boy Fuller'. In the 1960s-70s Fuller became a subject of great interest to those blues researchers who liked the Piedmont school (and liked to debate whether there was such a thing), as opposed to those more insistent voices who dismissed Fuller, BLIND WILLIE McTELL and others from the southeast as 'lightweight' and would only countenance the heavier, fiercer blues of the Mississippi Delta. It was the detailed research by one of the Piedmont-style enthusiasts, Briton Bruce Bastin, that overturned the myth that Fuller had been blinded by a girlfriend (as still relayed in Paul Oliver's classic work *The Story of the Blues* as late as 1969). Fuller and McTell—that other great performer who followed the tobacco season trail in the south-eastern states—listened to each other's work. Fuller's 'Log Cabin Blues' of 1935 is virtually a cover of McTell's 1929 'Come on Around to My House Mama'.

'Midnight Special', the LEADBELLY song recorded by HARRY BELAFONTE with Bob Dylan as harmonica accompanist in the early 1960s, had been, in between times, a key item in Blind Boy Fuller's repertoire. In 1937 Fuller recorded 'Weeping Willow' (one of those songs that includes the lovely common-stock couplet 'I lay down last night, tried to take my rest / My mind got to ramblin' like the wild geese in the west'), which Dylan performed at the Supper Club in New York in 1993. Fuller's 'Stealing Bo-Hog' is one of the cluster of songs that pre-figures Dylan's opening line of 'It Ain't Me Babe' (and LITTLE RICHARD's 'Keep a-Knockin'') with its 'Say you get away from my window, don't knock at my door'; his 'Pistol Snapper Blues', from 1938, is one of those to invoke that character the monkey man, which Dylan pairs with 'Tweeter' in the title of a TRAVELING WILBURYS song; and Fuller's 'Piccolo Rag' (from the same 1938 session) is one of the many blues using 'great big legs' as a term of approbation—in Fuller's case 'Got great big legs and a little bitty feet'—which gets reprocessed by Dylan into the 'great big hind legs' on his 'New Pony', on 1978's *Street Legal*.

In 1992 Dylan recorded and released his own version of Fuller's 'Step It Up and Go' on the *Good as I Been to You* album. It was a song that had rapidly become as much a hillbilly property as a blues dance number: it was performed by nearly every bluesman south of Chicago in the 1940s and 50s *and* became a standard repertoire item—one of those test numbers, like 'Foggy Mountain Breakdown'—that every self-respecting hillbilly blues guitarist had to be able to play. To look at the history of this comparatively recent song is to encounter yet again the extraordinary commonality of American grass-roots music, to see how shared a musical heritage there so often was between, as Tony Russell's book has it, *Blacks Whites and Blues*.

At the beginning of the 1960s, THE EVERLY BROTHERS recorded 'Step It Up and Go', and to look at their slim interweaving within the story is to see a representative illustration of how this music passes to and fro. Their 'Step It Up and Go' isn't on the album *Songs Our Daddy Taught Us*, but Ike Everly would have been their source. Ike had been taught guitar by Arnold Schultz, a black musician who also taught the Monroe Brothers; in turn Ike taught the 14-year-old Merle Travis thumb-pick style—a style Travis developed and showcased on 'Step It Up and Go'.

The song was also in the repertoire of populist cowboy outfit the Maddox Brothers & Rose, the pre-rockabilly artist Harmonica Frank Floyd (a figure championed by GREIL MARCUS in *Mystery Train*) and JOHN HAMMOND JR., who includes it on his album *Frogs for Snakes*. It's of a type that crops up over and over again. The building blocks of the lyric are common-stock, in some cases shared with those in that other frisky classic of inconsequence, Tampa Red's 'It's Tight Like That', which, as remembered by Eugene Powell, for instance (a 1930s Bluebird recording artist and veteran blues musician interviewed in ALAN LOMAX's *The Land Where the Blues Began*), includes 'Had a little dog, his name was Ball / Gave him a little taste and he want it all', which Dylan puts in as the fourth stanza of 'Step It Up and Go': 'Got a little girl, her name is Ball / Give a little bit, she took it all'.

At the same time we find the melody of 'Step It Up and Go' used everywhere from the Kansas City jazz-tinged boogie pianist-singer Julia Lee's 1946 'Gimme Watcha Got' to ELVIS PRESLEY's 1958 New Orleans pastiche 'Hard Headed Woman'. Another Blind Boy Fuller song, 'You've Got Something There', and Blind Willie McTell's 'Warm It Up to Me' are more or less the same, as is the MEMPHIS JUG BAND's 'Bottle It Up and Go' (cut in 1932 and 1934) and Tommy McClennan's 1939 'Bottle It Up and Go', later recorded by JOHN LEE HOOKER as 'Bundle Up and Go', 'Shake It Up and Go' and 'Bottle Up and Go'. Under that last title it was also recorded in the late 1950s by Snooks Eaglin (at that time a street musician). Then there's 'Got the Bottle Up and Gone', a début-session track by Sonny Boy Williamson I from 1937, and 'Touch It Up and Go', a track by Fuller associate SONNY TERRY & Jordan Webb, cut in New York a year after Fuller's death.

'Step It Up and Go' must owe its predominance to having the most accessible and familiar title. Like so many figures of speech, indeed like so much of the poetry of the blues, 'step it up and go' crossed over to the world of dancing from the world of work. It was what people said to their mules and horses. They still do, though it's now more common as an exhortation to the tourist trade horses drawing carriages in New Orleans than in the fields, where tractors now do the ploughing.

Bob Dylan's version is unambitious, as befits someone who understands the tradition in which the song sits. Conscious that a bravura performance is for the young and brash, and that there's a hundred voices capable of matching up to what is a simple dance number, Dylan settles quite rightly for something egolessly unexceptional. This is intelligent good-time, on which his robust and clumsy guitar-work is countered by an alert, true-to-the-genre vocal. As John Wesley Harding (aka WES STACE) notes, 'He screws up the riff at the end . . . so he goes through the whole sequence again, just for the hell of it.' It's true.

[Blind Boy Fuller: 'Weeping Willow', NY, 14 Jul 1937, *Blind Boy Fuller on Down—Vol. 1*, Saydisc SDR143, Badminton, UK, c.1967; 'Stealing Bo-Hog', NY, 7 Sep 1937, & 'Pistol Snapper Blues', NY, 5 Apr 1938, *Blind Boy Fuller with Sonny Terry and Bull City Red*, Blues Classics BC-11, Berkeley, CA, 1966; 'You've Got Something There', Memphis, 12 Jul 1939, CD-reissued *Blind Boy Fuller: East Coast Piedmont Style*, Columbia Roots n' Blues 467923, NY, 1991 (insert notes by Bruce Bastin), a representative sample of Fuller's work, incl. 'Log Cabin Blues', NY, 26 Jul 1935 (a previously unreleased take) but excluding 'Step It Up and Go'.

Bob Dylan: 'Weeping Willow', NY, 17 Nov 1993, unreleased. Everly Brothers: 'Step It Up and Go', Nashville, autumn 1961, *Instant Party*, Warner Brothers W (WS) 1430, US, 1962; *Songs Our Daddy Taught Us*, Nashville, Aug 1958, Cadence CLP 3016, NY, 1958 (reissued as *Folksongs by the Everly Brothers*, Cadence CLP 3059 / CLP 23059, NY, 1962; CD-reissued on Ace CDCHM 75, UK, 1990). Merle Travis: 'Step It Up and Go', *nia*, *Walking the Strings*, Capitol *nia*. (Travis used the refrain of another Fuller song, 1935's 'Ain't It a Cryin' Shame?', in his 1946 radio broadcasts.) Maddox Brothers & Rose: 'Step It Up and Go', *nia*, *Maddox Brothers and Rose 1946–1951 Vol. 2* (along with 'Dark as the Dungeon', *nia*), Arhoolie 5017, El Cerrito CA, 1976. Harmonica Frank: 'Step It Up and Go', *The Great Original Recordings of Harmonica Frank Lloyd 1951–1958*, Puritan 3003, Evanston, IL, 1973. John Hammond Jr: *Frogs For Snakes*, *nia*, Rounder *nia*, Somerville, MA, *nia*. Julia Lee & Her Boyfriends: 'Gimme Watcha Got', LA, Sep 1946, reissued *Tonight's the Night*, Charly CRB 1039, UK, 1982. Elvis Presley: 'Hard Headed Woman' (composed Claude Demetrius, whose 'Mean Woman Blues' also uses the same tune), Hollywood, 15 Jan 1958, *King Creole*, RCA LPM 1884, NY, 1958. Blind Willie McTell: 'Warm It Up to Me', NY, 14 Sep 1933.

Blind Willie McTell: 'Come on Around to My House Mama', Atlanta, 30 Oct 1929, *King of the Georgia Blues Singers: Blind Willie McTell*, Roots RL-324, Vienna, 1968.) The Memphis Jug Band (billed the first time around as Picaninny Jug Band, and then as by Charlie Burse with Memphis Jug Band): 'Bottle It Up and Go', Richmond, IN, 3 Aug 1932 & Chicago, 7 Nov 1934, both CD-reissued *Memphis Jug Band Complete Recorded Works 1932–1934*, RST Blues Documents BDCD-6002, Vienna, *nia*. Tommy McClennan: 'Bottle It Up and Go', Chicago, 22 Nov 1939, CD-reissued *Travelin' Highway Man*, Travelin' Man TM CD-06, *nia*. John Lee Hooker: 'Bundle Up and Go', Chicago, 10 Jun 1958, unissued, & Detroit, Apr 1959, *The Country Blues of John Lee Hooker*, Riverside LP 838, c.1960; 'Shake It Up and Go', Culver City, CA, c.1959, *John Lee Hooker's Detroit*, United Artists 3LP 127, US, 1973; 'Bottle Up and Go', Chicago, 1963, *On Campus*, VJ LP 1066, 1963, & NY, 23 Nov 1965, *It Serves You Right to Suffer*, Impulse LP 9103, *nia*. Snooks Eaglin: 'Bottle Up and Go', New Orleans, 1959, *Country Boy in New Orleans*, Arhoolie LP 2014, El Cerrito, CA, *nia*, CD-reissued Arhoolie CD348, El Cerrito, c.1990. Sonny Boy Williamson I: 'Got the Bottle Up and Gone', Aurora, IL, 5 May 1937, *Sonny Boy Williamson*, RCA 75.722 (Treasury of Jazz EP no.22), Paris, 1963, CD-reissued *Sonny Boy Williamson Complete Recorded Works, Volume 1 (1937–1938)*, Document DOCD-5055, Vienna, *nd*.. Sonny Terry & Jordan Webb: 'Touch It Up and Go', NY, 23 Oct 1941.

Alan Lomax, *The Land Where The Blues Began*, London; Methuen edn., p. 374. John Wesley Harding: 'Good as He's Been to Us', *Stereofile*, US, Feb 1993.]

Fuller, Jesse [1896 - 1976] Jesse 'Lone Cat' Fuller, best-known as a one-man band, inventor of that agreeably shambolic instrument the fotdella, and composer of 'San Francisco Bay Blues', was born at Jonesboro, Georgia, on March 12, 1896. He was another one-off performer whom Dylan had met, cross-examined and seen perform before he even reached the Village (Fuller was temporarily on the Denver folk scene when Dylan dropped into it in 1959) and it was from him that Dylan took the first track on his first album, 'You're No Good' on *Bob Dylan*.

Fuller endured a cruel childhood to become an eccentric, token-exotica figure in Hollywood who had a shoe-shine stand close to one of the film lots, got taken up by the stars and landed small uncredited rôles in Douglas Fairbanks' 1924 film *The Thief of Bagdad* and the 1925 Pola Negri vehicle *East of Suez*, both silent films directed by the extraordinary Raoul Walsh (who lost an eye to a jackrabbit and directed films for over 50 years).

Fuller had arrived in California at the start of the 1920s but moved back to Georgia in the mid-1930s and was an industrial worker for decades. He first tried to earn a living from music in 1950, playing 12-string guitar, harmonica and kazoo, and making himself a one-man band by adding a hi-hat cymbal played with one foot while operating the fotdella (an upright bass with pedals) with the other. His repertoire covered everything from rags to hymns and from 19th century popular songs to the blues.

He moved back west and first recorded in about 1954, making a crucial slow-burner of an album, a 10-inch LP that was the first (possibly the only) release on the tiny Californian label World Song, issued in 1955. From it, RAMBLIN' JACK ELLIOTT took, and was first to popularise in folk revival circles, 'San Francisco Bay Blues' itself: an immensely celebratory song that gave the city rather more than the city ever gave its composer.

Two 1958 Fuller LPs won critical plaudits—*Jazz, Folksongs, Spirituals & Blues* includes what critic Ken Smith called 'one of the best versions of "Stagolee" you'll ever hear'—and he performed successfully on TV and in Europe in 1960; yet he was back in California picking cauliflowers for a living in 1961 while Bob Dylan was first being recorded performing 'San Francisco Bay Blues' in New Jersey (in February or March 1961), Minneapolis (May) and at Gerde's Folk City in New York (sharing vocals with JIM KWESKIN on stage there that September). Dylan also included the song in his first concert, at Carnegie Chapter Hall that November 4, shortly before going into the studios and recording 'You're No Good'. This was not only the first track on the LP: it was also the first song recorded at the first day's session. Three days later, at the New York home of friends, he was recorded performing *both* these songs, and adjacently, in a 14-song set that begins with 'Hard Times in New York Town' and ends with 'This Land Is Your Land'.

Fuller's own first East Coast appearances were in 1962—by which time Dylan had issued 'You're No Good' on that début album and Fuller had made four and a half LPs of his own, though his very wide range of repertoire had him frowned on in some quarters during the strict revival period. The notes to *Bob Dylan* say that 'You're No Good' was 'learned from Jesse Fuller', and indeed it must have been learned in person, back in Denver, since Fuller didn't record the song himself until 1963. Dylan says in the *Biograph* notes in 1985 that his own song 'Baby I'm in the Mood for You' (recorded at the *Freewheelin'* session of July 9, 1962 but unreleased until on *Biograph*) was 'probably influenced by Jesse Fuller' too.

In 1988, after a quarter of a century's gap, Dylan played 'San Francisco Bay Blues' again, first at Berkeley, on what was the third concert of the Never-Ending Tour, then at Canandaigua, New York, two weeks later and then again at the Bridge School Benefit Concert, which took place in Fuller's adopted hometown of Oakland California, when Dylan opened his set with the song. In 1989, on stage at a GRATEFUL DEAD show in Los Angeles, Dylan played guitar on a performance of Jesse Fuller's 'The Monkey and the Engineer'.

All those years earlier, in his pre-Village days, Dylan may also have gained something very specific from the charmingly eccentric Fuller: something that has been a key part of his own equipment and image ever since. According to ROBERT SHELTON it was from Jesse Fuller that Dylan learnt how to use the harmonica holder around his neck. If true, this might be said to confirm usefully that Dylan didn't come across the crucial HARRY SMITH anthology *AMERICAN FOLK MUSIC* until after his 1959 Denver visit: because in the sleevenotes to the Harry Smith compilation we find a clear, comical drawing to show how to use what we think of as a 'Dylan-style' harmonica holder.

Jesse Fuller remained a distinctive figure on the folk and blues festival circuit into the 1970s. He died, aged almost 80, on January 29, 1976 at home in Oakland.

[Jesse Fuller: 'San Francisco Bay Blues', El Cerrito, CA, c.1954, *Working on the Railroad*, World Song LP 1, 1955 (issued on Topic, UK, 1957); 'Stagolee', *nia*, *Jazz, Folksongs, Spirituals & Blues*, Good Time Jazz LP 12031, *nia*, CD-reissued on Original Blues Classics OBCCD 564, US, 1994; 'The Monkey & the Engineer', San Francisco, 12 Apr 1958, *The Lone Cat*, Good Time Jazz LP 12039, US, 1958, CD-reissued Original Blues Classics OBCCD 526, US, c.1992; 'You're No Good', San Francisco, 13 May 1963, *San Francisco Bay Blues*, Folk Lore LP 14006, 1963. *The Thief of Bagdad*, dir. Raoul Walsh, co-written by & starring Douglas Fairbanks; Douglas Fairbanks Pictures Corp, US, 1924. *East of Suez*, dir. Raoul Walsh, co-written Somerset Maugham; Famous Players / Lasky, US, 1925.

Bob Dylan: 'You're No Good', NY, 20 Nov 1961; 'San Francisco Bay Blues', Berkeley, CA, 10 Jun 1988, Canandaigua, NY, 24 Jun 1988 & Oakland, 4 Dec 1988; guitar on 'Monkey & the Engineer', Grateful Dead concert, LA, 12 Feb 1989.]

'gal shaped just like a frog' See Smith, Warren.

Gant, Sandy [19?? -] Sandy Gant was a pioneering early Dylan session-discography researcher whose work in this area began in the 1960s, long before there was any kind of Dylan fan network, any home computers or internet; nor were there any fax machines, nor cheap international phone calls. He was an early source of information for ROBERT SHELTON and many others, and photocopied pages of his listings of unreleased Dylan recordings passed between many hands in that first era of research. He lives in North America. He declined to provide any information for this book.

G

Garcia, Jerry [1942 - 1995] Jerome John Garcia was born in the city he later came to embody, San Francisco, on the first day of 1942. Although his reputation essentially rests on his having been a founder member, and the leader, of THE GRATEFUL DEAD, as of the groups that preceded it and morphed into it, he nevertheless pursued a very large number of other projects, even forming a parallel band in the 1970s, the Jerry Garcia Band, which itself had an active life and recorded prolifically. He was an extraordinary guitarist and a fine banjo player, and another performing project of his was the short-lived bluegrass band Old and in the Way, in which he played banjo, teamed with mandolinist DAVID GRISMAN, plus Peter Rowan and the great veteran fiddle player Vassar Clements (who died in August 2005). In 1975 they produced what was until recently the biggest selling bluegrass album in history, *Old and in the Way*. (Garcia and Grisman had first met in 1964 at a Bill Monroe concert in Pennsylvania.)

Jerry Garcia was also sufficiently interested in film to study it briefly in college in the early 1960s. In 1970 he worked on the soundtrack of Antonioni's *Zabriskie Point*, playing an improvised guitar piece known as 'Love Scene'. Later he co-directed *The Grateful Dead Movie*, which mixed animation with concert footage. He also played banjo in the 1978 re-make of *Invasion of the Body Snatchers*. In 1990 he and David Grisman got back together, formed an acoustic duo and (of course) recorded a number of albums.

Jerry Garcia died of a heart attack in a drug-rehabilitation clinic in California on August 9, 1995, aged 53. Dylan paid him just about the most fulsome tribute he's ever paid anyone (and he tends towards the fulsome on these occasions, perhaps surprisingly):

> 'There's no way to measure his greatness or magnitude as a person or as a player. I don't think any eulogizing will do him justice. He was that great, much more than a superb musician, with an uncanny ear and dexterity. He's the very spirit personified of whatever is Muddy River country at its core and screams up into the spheres. He really had no equal. To me he wasn't only a musician and friend, he was more like a big brother who taught and showed me more than he'll ever know. There's a lot of spaces and advances between THE CARTER FAMILY, BUDDY HOLLY and, say, Ornette Coleman, a lot of universes, but he filled them all without being a member of any school. His playing was moody, awesome, sophisticated, hypnotic and subtle. There's no way to convey the loss. It just digs down really deep.'

Dylan was among the many who attended the funeral service for Garcia at St. Stephen's Episcopal Church in Belvedere, California, on August 11, 1995.

[The 6-CD box set *All Good Things: Jerry Garcia Studio Sessions*, 2005, includes a 'Simple Twist of Fate', a 'Tangled Up in Blue' and a 'Knockin' on Heaven's Door'; if bought direct from *www.jerrygarcia.com* a bonus 7th CD is included, which features a lengthy 'Visions of Johanna' (*www.bobdylan.com* says 16 minutes long, the Garcia site says 17).]

Garnier, Tony [1955/6 -] Tony Garnier was born in St. Paul, Minnesota, in 1955 or '56, the grandson of D'Jalma Thomas Garnier, the New Orleans bandleader, trumpet player, pianist and violinist rumoured to have taught Louis Armstrong at the New Orleans Boys Home for Colored Waifs.

Tony grew up mostly in California, attended university there but dropped out to join Asleep at the Wheel in 1971, which dithered between various places before basing itself firmly in Austin, Texas, in 1973. The band was successful on album and the road but Garnier quit in 1978, moved to New York City and tried to develop a career as a jazz musician. He was rescued from penury and depression by Robert Gordon, who phoned to ask him to join the Lounge Lizards, from which came work on movie soundtracks and TV jingle sessions. From here Garnier joined G.E. SMITH's band on the interminable TV show 'Saturday Night Live', which in turn led to Bob Dylan's Never-Ending Tour Band. By this time Tony had also played on albums by Roy Clark, Robert Gordon, Tom Waits, Marshall Crenshaw and others. Playing live for Dylan was something else again. He flew out to Europe to join the group at the beginning of June 1989, just a year after the tour had begun.

Garnier first arrived on stage with Dylan in Dublin that June 3, to replace original bass player KENNY AARONSON; but illness forced Aaronson to drop out again after June 8, so that Tony Garnier replaced him again on June 10 in the Hague and settled in as the band's regular bass player. By the time of that fall's run of concerts at the Beacon Theater in New York, he seemed confident of his position and amused by the whole experience he had found himself plunged into. Emerging onto the street outside the theatre one night just ahead of the evening's performance, he saw one Dylan aficionado holding her 14-month-old daughter in her arms. 'Ah look,' he said, smiling at her, 'they even bring him their babies to be blessed!'

Looking Cuban, placid, besuited and slightly pudgy, and standing on stage with his short legs planted well apart, as if braced for the unexceptional, Garnier was for most fans an unwelcome substitute for the model-thin, twitchy, punk contemporaneity of Aaronson, and his playing seemed unremarkable. Perhaps that has been the secret of his longevity with Dylan. Not only has he remained in the Never-Ending Tour Band ever since—that is to say, for *over 16 years* at the time of writing: far, far longer than anyone else except Bob—but he has long since become the longest-serving musician of Bob Dylan's entire career.

On stage, he's always the lieutenant, ready for anything, clocking everything with equanimity, passing on to other musicians his accurate interpretations of Dylan's often inscrutable nods and narrowings of the eyes, yet at the same time smiling at fans and giving every appearance of a contented man who still enjoys his work. By the end of 2005, quite apart from playing on the *MTV Unplugged* album, *Time Out of Mind*, *"Love and Theft"* and *Masked & Anonymous*, Tony Garnier had played at over 1,700 Bob Dylan concerts.

Geldof, Bob [1951 -] Robert Frederick Xenon Geldof was born on October 5, 1951 at Dún Laoghaire (pronounced Done Leery), in County Dublin, Ireland, the son of a cinema manageress who died before he 'was out of short trousers' and a hotel-manager father he only saw at weekends. He attended the same school as had the Irish Free State's first president Eamon De Valera—Blackrock College, Dublin—before going into 'freefall . . . in an endless round of useless jobs and self-abuse', spending 1972 in a London squat and then moving to Canada where he travelled and worked as a music journalist on a Vancouver weekly paper, the *Georgia Straight*.

On his return to Ireland he became the manager and then lead singer of the Nightlife Thugs, who began gigging in October 1975, changed their name to the Boomtown Rats, swiftly built a reputation in Ireland and in October 1976 moved to London. A successful first single, 'Lookin' After No. 1', released in 1977, was followed by 'Mary of the Fourth Form', 'She's So Modern' and 'Like Clockwork', all UK chart hits, and then by two no.1 UK singles, 1978's 'Rat Trap' and 1979's 'I Don't Like Mondays'. They had many further releases after this, but it says something about the group that 'I Don't Like Mondays' is now the only record of theirs anyone but an avid fan remembers. It is anthemic, catchy and very much of its time, or rather, slightly behind its time, being concurrent with the commercial height of British punk yet in sound and spirit closer to mid-1970s pub rock. In 1981 Geldof performed it solo at an Amnesty International benefit concert in London, which marked his first alignment with a cause of a charitable, campaigning and international character.

Geldof appeared in the 1982 Pink Floyd film *The Wall*, taking the lead rôle of Pink, which he managed creditably, but by 1984 his mind was on other things. He established the Band Aid Trust, co-ordinated the assemblage of UK pop stars who recorded the sanctimoniously vacuous fund-raising single 'Do They Know It's Christmas?' (surely subtitled 'Do they care?'), co-written with Midge Ure, and duly went on to organise the truly extraordinary two-continents mega-event that was LIVE AID—Geldof also sang on the chorus of the US equivalent to 'Do They Know It's Christmas?', the superstar-laden 'We Are the World'—and just as importantly, persuaded a large number of world leaders face-to-face, by sheer chutzpah and the force of his own impassioned eloquence, to significant action and to change in their aid policy rather than the usual lip-service. All this amounted to an unprecedented effort to alleviate first the 1984 famine in Ethiopia and then more generally hunger in Africa from 1985 onwards.

In the midst of this clamorous struggle against the system, Geldof was reduced to appalled rage to hear Bob Dylan, on the stage at Live Aid, ask whether some of the money being raised couldn't be diverted from the starving in Africa to give to American farmers. Afterwards, Geldof wrote that 'the biggest disappointment of the evening was Dylan. He sang three of his classics, including "Blowin' in the Wind", which ought to have been one of the greatest moments of the concert. Unfortunately, the performance was catastrophic. . . . Then he displayed a compete lack of understanding of the issues raised by Live Aid by saying, unforgivably, "It would be nice if some of this money went to the American farmers." . . . a crass, stupid and nationalistic thing to say. . . . Dylan left the stage and as he walked by his manager, he just looked up and said "Sorry".'

In 1986 Geldof was given a knighthood by the British, published his literate and energetic autobiography, *Is That It?*, which set a new standard of candour in rock literature, and married Paula Yates, beginning a new era in his life, largely of domestic pain and consequent tabloid celebrity, eventually leading Geldof to lend his aggressively articulate support not merely to campaigning for 'fathers' rights' in general but to Fathers for Justice, a particularly nasty activist movement he has called 'heroic'. It's not unreasonable to draw a parallel with Dylan's Live Aid wrongheadedness here; of course there are injustices when divorced fathers are unable to gain access to their children, but the more fundamental truth is that there remains an imbalance of power loaded in men's favour, and that it is women who carry an immensely greater burden of responsibility in caring for children and live on lower incomes as a result of those divorces.

By this point Geldof had produced, over a span of 18 years, four solo albums: *Deep in the Heart of Nowhere*, *Vegetarians of Love*, *The Happy Club* and, in 2001, *Sex, Age & Death*.

In 2005 Geldof was involved in the Live 8 campaign against globalisation, 20 years on from the achievement of Live Aid; and on December 27, 2005 it was announced that the new leader of the British Conservative Party, David Cameron, was launching 'a wide-ranging policy review on globalisation and global poverty' to which Bob Geldof had agreed to act as consultant. This was, in the words of the *Guardian*, 'another eyecatching repositioning of the Conservative party' but pleased noone. Those on the Left saw it as another step away from the side of the angels by Geldof; the traditionalists in the Tory party had no wish to be consulting a figure as disreputable, scruffy and foulmouthed as Sir Bob Geldof.

What everyone can agree on, including the man himself, is that whereas it's often been said of Bob Dylan, in Bob Geldof we have someone who *really* can't sing.

[Bob Geldof: *Deep in the Heart of Nowhere*, Mercury/Universal, 1986; *Vegetarians of Love*, Mercury/Universal, 1990; *The Happy Club*, 1992; *Sex, Age & Death*, Eagle Rock/Edsel, 2001. Bob Geldof, *Is That It?*, London: Sidgwick & Jackson, 1986; quotes from Penguin edn., 1986, pp.11, 12 & 390. *The Wall*, dir. Alan Parker; Goldcrest/MGM/Tin Blue, UK, 1982. Michael White, *The Guardian*, 28 Dec 2005. The Boomtown Rats: 'Lookin' After No. 1', Ensign ENY-4, UK, 1977; 'Mary of the Fourth Form' c/w 'Do the Rat', Ensign ENY-9, 1977; 'She's So Modern', Ensign ENY-13, 1978; 'Like Clockwork', Ensign ENY-14, 1978; 'Rat Trap', Ensign ENY-16, 1978; 'I Don't Like Mondays', Ensign ENY-30, 1978; *The Boomtown Rats*, Ensign ENVY-1, 1977; *A Tonic for the Troops*, Ensign ENVY-3, 1978.]

Genet, Jean [1910 - 1986] Jean Genet was born in Paris on December 19, 1910. This French playwright, novelist and poet became a convicted thief long before turning to writing in 1939, and was rescued from life imprisonment by being taken up by Sartre, Gide and Cocteau as from 1947. Sartre considered him important as the prototype of existentialist man: one who arrived at the distinction between good and evil by personal choice and decision.

Dylan's *New Morning* song 'Three Angels' echoes closely a short, striking passage from Genet's 1944 novel *Our Lady of the Flowers* (the original French-language title was the parallel *Notre dame des fleurs*): 'But neither of the two seemed to care whether Divine was absent or present. They heard the morning angelus, the rattle of a milk can. Three workmen went by on bicycles along the boulevard, their lamps lit, though it was day. A policeman on his way home . . . passed without looking at them.'

In WISSOLIK & McGRATH's *Bob Dylan's Words*, 1994, Dylan's use of the word 'flowerlady' in his novel *Tarantula* is cited as possibly also alluding to *Our Lady of the Flowers*. You might add his 'all of the flower ladies' in the *Highway 61 Revisited* song 'Queen Jane Approximately'.

At any rate, ROBERT SHELTON's Dylan biography, *No Direction Home*, 1986, quotes Dylan, interviewed by Shelton on a plane between Lincoln, Nebraska, and Denver, Colorado, in mid-March 1966, as saying: 'William Burroughs is a poet. I like all his old books and Jean Genet's old books.' Perhaps then, 'Absolutely Sweet Marie', recorded for *Blonde on Blonde* in the same period as this interview, offers those 'ruins of your balcony' in conscious reference to another Genet work, his 1957 play *Le Balcon/The Balcony*. (The Balcony is the name of the brothel in which the play is set.)

Dylan might be said to confirm some of the above in *Chronicles Volume One*, 2004, in which, discussing the orthodoxy of thought and behaviour that everyone was expected to follow in mainstream society at the end of the 1950s, he writes: 'Reality was not so simple and everybody had their own take on it. Jean Genet's play *The Balcony* was being performed in the Village and it portrayed the world as a mammoth cathouse where chaos rules the universe, where man is alone and abandoned in a meaningless cosmos. The play had a strong sense of focus, and . . . it could have been written one hundred years ago. The songs I'd write would be like that, too. They wouldn't conform to modern ideas.'

Genet died in Paris on April 15, 1986 but was buried in Larache, Morocco.

[Robert Shelton, *No Direction Home: The Life and Music of Bob Dylan*, 1986, Penguin edn., p.353. Bob Dylan, *Chronicles*, p.89. Wissolik & McGrath, *Bob Dylan's Words*, Greensburg, PA: Eadmer Press, 1994.]

'George Jackson' c/w 'George Jackson' [1971] See **Jackson, George.**

Georgia Tom See **Dorsey, Thomas A.**

Gershwin, George [1898 - 1937] & Ira [1896 - 1983] Jacob and Israel Gershovitz were born in Brooklyn on September 26, 1898 and December 6, 1896. They became towering figures in the history of 20th century American music, with the younger of the two the more exalted, thanks especially to his inspired jazz-classical 'Rhapsody in Blue' of

1924. This was also the year their songwriting partnership began, with George as composer and Ira as lyricist, by providing the songs for the Fred and Adele Astaire show *Lady, Be Good*. They moved to Hollywood in 1931.

This is no place to appraise their work, either individually or as a team, for while there can be few who have not been drawn at least to 'Summertime', from *Porgy and Bess*, a song that has lent itself readily to a variety of treatments from rock'n'roll, R&B and pop artists since the mid-1950s, there will always be those for whom the name Gershwin is synonymous with exactly the kind of complacent sophistication and middle-class dinner-dance ennui that rock'n'roll, and then Bob Dylan, were born to abolish.

Yet on March 11, 1987, at the Gershwin Gala held at the Brooklyn Academy of Music in New York, to the puzzlement of most of the predictably affluent, ageing and conservative audience, a nervous and tuxedoed Bob Dylan appeared as one of the performers, armed with acoustic guitar and harmonica, and gave a sweet, touching and unparalleled rendition of a nicely obscure item from the Gershwins' repertoire, the 1929 song 'Soon', a number with a melody that wanders diffidently across jazzy minor chords and a lyric of dull sentimental doggerel ('Soon my dear you'll never be lonely / Soon you'll find I live for you only', and much more in like vein) spiked by one audacious rhyme—'who cares what time it is / . . . or what the climate is'.

Dylan told friends that he'd been thinking of performing 'Swanee', the early George Gershwin song popularised by Al Jolson, but had then found 'Soon' instead. He and friend Ted Perlman, domestic partner of sometime Dylan session singer Peggi Blu, worked on an arrangement for the song. Perlman told biographer HOWARD SOUNES that Dylan asked, while practising the song, 'Do I sound stupid?' He certainly did not. The event was televised on July 7, 1987 by the West German channel ZDF-TV, and on PBS in the US later that year. By the customary Sod's Law, since this was, on the night, a fine and in every sense unique performance, naturally the only bootleg recording of it in circulation is in wantonly poor quality.

George Gershwin slipped into a coma on July 9, 1937 and died of a brain tumour two days later, in Hollywood, at the age of 39; Ira outlived him by a further 46 years, collaborating on songs with many other people, including Kurt Weill and Jerome Kern, and establishing the Gershwin Archive at the Library of Congress. Ira died at home in Beverly Hills on August 17, 1983, aged 86.

[Howard Sounes, *Down the Highway: A Life of Bob Dylan*, New York: Grove Press, 2001, quoted from manuscript p.447.]

Gibson, Don [1928 - 2003] Donald Eugene Gibson was born in Shelby, North Carolina, on April 3, 1928. He was one of Chet Atkins' protégés at RCA Victor in Nashville and a regular on the Tennessee Barn Dance (on WNOX Radio, Knoxville). He first recorded in 1949 and 1952, wrote 'Sweet Dreams' in 1955, and in 1957 recorded 'Oh Lonesome Me', on which he and Atkins omitted the usual steel guitar and fiddle, to offer a new sound featuring only guitars, piano, drums, upright bass and (rather obtrusive) backing singers. This pioneered what became known as the Nashville Sound (and gave Gibson a no.1 hit).

A prolific and affecting songwriter as well as a singer, his best-known, most-covered song is 'I Can't Stop Lovin' You' (recorded by over 700 people, among them RAY CHARLES, whose version topped the charts and sold a million). 'Sea of Heartbreak' was among several countrified pop hits he had himself in the US and UK charts 1959–1963. Others included 'It's Too Soon to Know', 'Lonesome Number One', 'Oh Lonesome Me' (revived by NEIL YOUNG), 'Sweet Dreams' (first a success by Patsy Cline but revived exquisitely by Don EVERLY in 1971 on the brilliant solo album *Don Everly*), and '(I'd Be a) Legend in My Time'. In 1989, Dylan performed '(I'd Be a) Legend in My Time' at three concerts.

Don Gibson died November 17, 2003, aged 75.

[Don Gibson: 'Oh Lonesome Me' c/w 'I Can't Stop Lovin' You', Nashville, *n/a*, RCA Victor 474-4133, 1957; 'Sea of Heartbreak', Nashville, *n/a*, RCA Victor 47-7890, 1961; 'It's Too Soon to Know', Nashville, *n/a*, RCA Victor 47-7010, 1957; 'Lonesome Number One', Nashville, *n/a*, 47-7959, 1961. Don Everly: *Don Everly*, Ode SP-77005, LA (A&M AMLS 2007, London), 1971. Bob Dylan: '(I'd Be a) Legend in My Time', Columbia, MD, 19 Jul; Atlantic City, 20 Jul; & Saratoga Springs, NY, 26 Jul 1989.]

Ginsberg, Allen [1926 - 1997] Irwin Allen Ginsberg was born in Newark, New Jersey, on June 3, 1926. It's invidious to separate out THE BEATS: they felt like a community, they influenced each other, they sometimes worked together, and in the sleevenotes interview for *Biograph* in 1985 Dylan speaks warmly of how the whole movement was part of an alternative culture that 'all left the rest of everything in the dust' (see separate entry). Yet it would be invidious too simply to corral all the Beats together as if they were not individual artists at all, or as if their work were somehow all interchangeable and none of them attained a distinctive voice.

Allen Ginsberg, perhaps more than any other individual writer of the Beat Generation, opens up for Dylan, and for *his* whole generation, a bright, babbling, surreal, self-indulgent, sleazy, intensely alert modern world no predecessor had visited. *Howl* (1956) might not have been possible without WHITMAN, but Dylan's debt to *Howl* (and the later *Kaddish*) is far more direct than Ginsberg's to *Leaves of Grass*.

This is from *Howl*: 'who jumped in limousines with the Chinaman of Oklahoma on the / impulse of winter midnight streetlight smalltown rain, / . . . who went out whoring through Colorado in myriad stolen nightcars . . . / . . . who faded out in vast sordid movies, were shifted in dreams, woke on a sudden / Manhattan, and picked themselves up out of basements hungover / with heartless Tokay and horrors of Third Avenue iron dreams . . .'

There is not one line from this huge, sprawling poem that cannot claim to be the deranged, inspired midwife of the Dylan of the mid-1960s, the Dylan of 'the motor cycle black madonna two-wheel gypsy queen' and the rest. Dylan's achievement has included the remarkable fact of his being able to turn right round and become a major influence on Allen Ginsberg, as Ginsberg's beautifully expressive sleevenotes to Dylan's *Desire* album, and his endearingly woolly-mammoth presence in Dylan's *Renaldo & Clara* film, both testify.

Sometimes these mutual influences are hard to disentangle—particularly since the forceful inspiration of WILLIAM BLAKE helps to shape the writing of both Ginsberg and Dylan. Not least, the Blakeian influence on Ginsberg is so strong that in some cases what seems Blakeian in Dylan may actually have come *via* Ginsberg.

For instance, the line in Dylan's 'Ring Them Bells' that uses Christ's shepherd-and-his-sheep analogy—'And the mountains are filled with lost sheep'—is likely to remind you of the harmonium song that Ginsberg sings in *Renaldo & Clara*, with its echoey last line 'And all the hills echoéd': but this is Ginsberg directly quoting Blake: it is the echoey last line of 'Nurse's Song', from *Songs of Innocence* (1789).

Ginsberg has twice recorded this Blake poem, set to his own music, and on the second occasion he was accompanied by Dylan, whose gift of a Uher tape-recorder in 1965 encouraged Ginsberg to improvise one-chord music. 'I kept hearing musical fragments of Blake's "Grey Monk" moaning through my brain', he wrote in 'Explanation of First Blues'. His album *Songs of Innocence and of Experience Tuned by Allen Ginsberg* was recorded in 1968. His 1971 recordings of Blake songs 'Nurse's Song' (accompanied by Dylan on guitar, piano and organ), and 'The Tyger', remained unissued.

Like Blake, Ginsberg can write both carefully simple verse and what he calls his 'long line' poetry (much influenced by Walt Whitman also). Indeed he writes in his 1973 poem 'On Reading Dylan's Writings' that he has 'to break [his] long line down' to write like Bob Dylan.

Dylan first mentions Ginsberg in an early poem: a section of the *11 Outlined Epitaphs* that made up Dylan's sleevenotes for his third album, *The Times They Are a-Changin'*. In some ways this prefigures that *Biograph* reminiscence. As Dylan memorialises his fond early influences, he delineates the way that poetry and music, painting and film—American and European—all rubbed shoulders in the process. Yet here it's noticeable that Ginsberg is the only big-name Beat writer in the list:

> 'with the sounds of Francois Villon / echoin' through my mad streets / as I stumble on lost cigars / of BERTOLT BRECHT / an' empty bottles / of Brendan Behan / the hypnotic words / of A.L. Lloyd / each one bendin' like its own song / an' the woven spell of PAUL CLAYTON / entrancin' me like China's plague / unescapable / drownin' in the lungs of Edith Piaf / and in the mystery of Marlene Dietrich / the dead poems of EDDIE FREEMAN / love songs of Allen Ginsberg / an' jail songs of RAY BREMSER / the narrow tunes of Modigliani / an' the singin' plains of Harry Jackson / the cries of Charles Aznavour / with melodies of Yevtushenko / through the quiet fire of Miles Davis / above the bells of William Blake / an' beat visions of JOHNNY CASH / an' the saintliness of PETE SEEGER'.

The two first meet in December 1963, introduced by AL ARONOWITZ. They get on well, talk poetry, and Dylan invites Ginsberg to a Chicago gig. He declines, partly because he's busy apartment hunting in New York but also out of pride. He says later: 'I thought he was just a folksinger, and I was also afraid I might become his slave or something, his mascot.' Ginsberg knew himself well.

Nevertheless he soon went with Dylan to another concert (Ginsberg's biographer specifies Princeton, and says the photos later used on the sleeve of *Bringing It All Back Home* were taken backstage here—but no Princeton concert has been logged in this period and it's generally believed that the photos were taken when Ginsberg was a fellow-guest with Dylan on the 'Les Crane Show' on US television in February 1965; the photos, of Ginsberg in top hat and tie, appear on the LP cover that March). At any rate, in 1964 Ginsberg attended the post-concert party after Dylan's Hallowe'en Concert at the Philharmonic Hall, NYC.

On May 8, 1965, he arrived in England to join Dylan again, partied with him and THE BEATLES and is to be seen loitering in the alley by the Savoy Hotel in the Strand, London, in the film footage that prefigures the modern pop video, with Dylan looking, and moving as, the embodiment of cool, while dropping the cards to the soundtrack of 'Subterranean Homesick Blues'; he can also be seen in a hotel suite in the film that begins with that 'video', D.A. PENNEBAKER's *Don't Look Back*. In June Ginsberg told British national newspaper the *Daily Mail* that he and Dylan were writing a film together (Dylan had told Les Crane that they aimed to make a film that summer).

At the end of the year Ginsberg was with Dylan again, this time in California, participating in the San Francisco press conference on the afternoon of December 3, asking Dylan: 'Do you ever think there will ever be a time when you'll be hung as a thief?', and pictured in the street with Dylan, ROBBIE ROBERTSON and poet Michael McClure. At Christmas Dylan gave him $600 to buy a professional-standard Uher tape recorder, and encouraged him to 'learn an instrument'. At around the same time JOAN BAEZ told Ginsberg and McClure that they should be 'Dylan's conscience' now that he was no longer involved in the civil rights movement.

Ginsberg gets a second name-check from Dylan on an unreleased moment during the Basement Tapes sessions in 1967, when THE BAND and Dylan turn Bill Haley's hit 'See You Later, Alligator' into 'See Ya Later, Allen Ginsberg'. Ginsberg also visited Dylan that August 19, saying later that he had brought Bob as a gift 'a box full of books of all kinds. All the modern poets I knew. Some ancient poets like Sir Thomas Wyatt, Campion, Dickinson, RIMBAUD, Lorca, Apollinaire, BLAKE, Whitman and so forth.'

Ginsberg was around when Dylan made his first post-accident appearance as a performer, at the Woody Guthrie Memorial Concerts in January 1968; he attended the party for the participants held at actor Robert Ryan's large apartment in the Dakota Building. That same year, Dylan was able to return to its author Ginsberg's old typescript of his *Gates of Wrath*: the first time he'd had a complete copy since the manuscript had been 'carried to London by lady friend early fifties' and had 'disappeared'.

If Ginsberg brought Dylan books of poetry–and indeed, as RALPH GLEASON puts it, had 'made Dylan and THE BEATLES respectable'–one of the ways that Dylan surely influenced Ginsberg was bringing the blues to his attention, by the extraordinary regenerative use of blues lyric poetry within his own work, which must have nudged Ginsberg towards this music–though in 1975 Ginsberg stresses a different route (again in 'Explanation of First Blues'): 'I had some kind of American Blues in my heart without knowing it–I could sing but didn't reckon it important poetically, until I met Krishna & remembered EZRA POUND's ken that poetry & music, song & chant (and dance) went together before the invention of the printing press and long after–forgotten by the same academies that forgot that the genre of American Black Blues & rags was as great a treasury of poetics as Bishop Percy's *Reliques* & Scottish Border Ballads & Elizabethan song books & Tom O'Bedlam folk treasuries.' At any rate, Ginsberg knew of BLIND BLAKE as well as William, and his [Ginsberg's] 'Tear Gas Rag', about an anti-Vietnam War demo in Colorado in 1972, is based on what he calls Blind Blake's 'Old Southern Rag'.

Dylan and Ginsberg first performed together on October 30, 1971, at a New York City television studio, where on a programme that also featured Peter Orlovsky and Gerard Malanga, Dylan played guitar behind Ginsberg's performances of seven items, including 'Nurse's Song', 'September on Jessore Road', 'A Dream', 'Mantra to Shiva' and 'John Sinclair'. This was shown on 'Freetime' on a PBS-TV station, WNET-TV, a few days later, with Dylan unbilled. Dylan also attended a Ginsberg poetry reading at this point, at New York University.

Ginsberg and Dylan first recorded together very soon after this (NY, November 1971). These were essentially Ginsberg sessions to which Dylan contributed. Ginsberg was the main voice, with Dylan on shared vocals, guitar, piano and organ on all tracks. On the 17th they cut 'Vomit Express', 'Going to San Diego' and 'Jimmy Berman Rag', and possibly 'Om My Soul Shalom', 'Nurse's Song', 'Many Loves', 'Prajnaparamitra Sutra' and 'A Dream' (though the last five may have been three days later). On the 20th they recorded two takes of 'September on Jessore Road' and 'The Tyger'.

'Vomit Express', 'Jimmy Berman Rag', 'September on Jessore Road' and 'Om My Soul Shalom' were co-written by Ginsberg and Dylan. 'Going to San Diego' and 'Prajnaparamitra Sutra' were Ginsberg compositions; 'Nurse's Song' and 'A Dream' were credited to Blake and Ginsberg. There was some interest in these tapes from Apple Records, according to ROBERT SHELTON, and the plan was to release them with Dylan billed as Egg O'Schmillson; but nothing came of this and Dylan wrote to Ginsberg in June 1973, saying: 'Don't worry, the energy has gone, save your songs for friends and go on and do something else.'

On February 13, 1982, in Santa Monica, however, the two of them got together again for a shorter session, this time with Dylan only playing bass, to lay down two Ginberg compositions, 'Do the Meditation' and two takes of 'Airplane Blues'. (For release details of all these, see below.)

In between these Ginsberg sessions, Dylan had recalled the poet's work when naming his 1974 album *Planet Waves*, echoing an anthology of Ginsberg's poetry published by City Lights in 1968 under the title *Planet News*; and when, in 1975, Ginsberg published his little book *First Blues, Rags, Ballads & Harmonium Songs 1971–74*, it was dedicated 'To Minstrel Guruji Bob Dylan', includes a photograph of the two together at KEROUAC's grave and includes a poem about Dylan written in 1972, 'Blue Gossip'. Other Ginsberg poems about Dylan include 'Postcard to D—', 1972, the aforementioned 'On Reading Dylan's Writing', 1973, and 'Bob Dylan (1941–)', 1986.

In addition, STEPHEN SCOBIE's *Alias Bob Dylan Revisited*, published in 2004, has a section drawing on Ginsberg's unpublished journals, which include fragments of verse written on Dylan-in-performance in 1975.

The two artists re-connected in person in the mid-1970s for the Rolling Thunder tours–Ginsberg is prominent in *Renaldo & Clara*, not least in the sequence where the two visit the Kerouac grave and the marvellous, long scene of Ginsberg intoning *Kaddish* to an audience of elderly ladies attending a mah-jongg championship—and Ginsberg worked hard with Dylan on the film's scenario; he also wrote warm, evocative sleevenotes for Dylan's 1976 album *Desire*. The following March they came together with others to take part (as background vocalists) in a LEONARD COHEN recording session in Los Angeles, the released result of which was their participation on the track 'Don't Go Home With Your Hard On' on the PHIL SPECTOR-produced Cohen album *Death of a Ladies' Man*. That October Ginsberg visited Dylan in Malibu and taped several interviews with him.

In 1985 Dylan called at Ginsberg's New York apartment to show him the lyrics to his forthcoming album, *Empire Burlesque*, and found to his delight that the legendary HARRY SMITH was there. (See the Smith entry for the end of this brief story.) Some might think Ginsberg shirked his responsibilities when he let Dylan run those lyrics past him without demurring at their quality.

The same year saw Dylan provide a blurb quote for the cover of Ginsberg's *Collected Poems 1947–1980*. This was provided as a favour for a friend, as a gesture of respect for a poet's work and at the time seemed to be a one-off (unhappily he would soon start endorsing far less deserving books: see **book endorsements, unfortunate**). Perhaps Dylan's blurb for Ginsberg held the attraction of offering him a modest writing exercise, as he tried out the language of conventional criticism: 'Ginsberg,' ran Dylan's wordbite, 'is both tragic and dynamic, a lyrical genius, con man extraordinaire, and probably the single greatest influence on the American poetical voice since Walt Whitman.' A splendidly unDylanesque composition: and fairly plausible stuff.

Allen Ginsberg died in his Lower East Side apartment in New York City at 2:39 am, Saturday, April 5, 1997, of a heart attack related to his terminal liver cancer, according to friend and archivist Bill Morgan. He was writing poems as late as the Thursday. On the evening after Ginsberg's death, Dylan was playing in concert at Moncton, New Brunswick, and after performing 'Desolation Row' told the audience that it was Ginsberg's 'favourite song: that was for Allen.'

[Ginsberg's 'Explanation of First Blues' is in his small book *First Blues, Rags, Ballads & Harmonium Songs 1971–74*, 1975. So is 'Tear Gas Rag'. His *Songs of Innocence and of Experience Tuned by Allen Ginsberg*, 1968, issued as Verve/Forecast FTS3083, USA, 1969, was reissued as *Allen Ginsberg*, MGM Archetypes M3F-4951, USA, 1974. Allen Ginsberg: 'September on Jessore Road' (edited version) released on a flexidisc given away with *Sing Out!* magazine vol.21, no.2, NY, 1972; 'Vomit Express' & 'Going to San Diego' on Ginsberg's LP *First Blues*, John Hammond Records W2X 37673, US 1973; 'Jimmy Berman Rag', on *Disconnected–The Dial-a-Poem Poets Double*, Giorno Poetry Systems, US, 1974. 'Vomit Express' re-issued Ginsberg's 4-CD box set *Holy Soul Jelly Roll: Poems And Songs 1949–1993*, Rhino Word Beat R2 71693, US, 1994; this also includes 'A Dream' & (a re-edited) 'September on Jessore Road', plus 2nd take of 'Airplane Blues'.

Blind Blake's 'Southern Rag' was recorded Chicago, c.Oct 1927; CD-reissued on *Blind Blake: Foremost Fingerpicker*, Yazoo 1068, 1984. Ginsberg & Dylan on the 'Les Crane Show', ABC-TV, 17 Feb 1965; Dylan's promo film for 'Subterranean Homesick Blues' was released within *Don't Look Back*, dir. D.A. PENNEBAKER, 1967; *Daily Mail* story in Robert Shelton, *No Direction Home: The Life and Music of Bob Dylan*, 1986, Penguin edn., p. 301, the Ralph Gleason quote p.333, and the Dylan letter of June 1973 p.424. Dylan's San Francisco press conference, 3 Dec 1965, shown on KQED-TV. *Gates of Wrath* story, 'Interviews and a Poem: Allen Ginsberg', in *All Across the Telegraph: A Bob Dylan Handbook*, ed. Michael Gray & John Bauldie, London: 1988 Futura edn., p.161–76, and poems list p.267–68.

The excellent *Ginsberg: A Biography*, by Barry Miles, New York: Simon & Schuster,1989, is drawn on in the above for the 'just a folksinger' quote & Princeton concert & photos suggestion (p.334), partying with the Beatles (p.369–70), Dylan to Les Crane re film (p.380), Dylan giving Uher gift as money, & Baez quote (p.381), date of Woodstock visit (p.391) and mah-jongg detail (p.460). Stephen Scobie: *Alias Bob Dylan Revisited*, Calgary, Canada: Red Deer College Press, 2004.

Leonard Cohen: *Death of a Ladies' Man*, LA, Mar 1977, Columbia PC 44286 (USA) & CBS 86042 (UK/West Germany), 1977.]

Gleason, Ralph J. [1917 - 1975] Ralph J. Gleason ('the "J" was for Joseph, although we often joked that it stood for "jazz"', said his son Toby) was an old-fashioned music enthusiast and journalist based in San Francisco, an influential American jazz and pop music critic in the 1950s who adjusted painfully to the decade that followed, but having done so, co-founded *Rolling Stone* magazine as an 'underground paper'. The name *Rolling Stone* came from Gleason; co-founder and editor Jann Wenner wanted to call it *Electric Newspaper*. There was little love lost between the two. (See **Wenner, Jann and unloading heads**.)

Gleason was born in New York City on March 1, 1917, attending Columbia University before moving to the West Coast in his early 30s. He began contributing to the *San Francisco Chronicle* in 1950, and there introduced the first regular coverage of jazz and popular music in US mainstream media. He interviewed, among others, HANK WILLIAMS, FATS DOMINO and ELVIS PRESLEY, helped bring about San Francisco's cultural flowering in the late 1950s and, as Joe Selvin notes: 'At a time when there were practically no books on the subject, he wrote the history of jazz on the back of album covers, writing literally hundreds of liner notes in the golden age of long-playing albums.' He was also a radical who spoke out in the McCarthy era, and later was named on Richard Nixon's Enemies List.

He became an earlyish supporter of, and copious commentator on, Dylan's work, having been an early champion of LENNY BRUCE and Miles Davis; later he was similarly enthusiastic about San Francisco's pioneering rock groups, and in 1966 wrote a paean to FRANK ZAPPA and the Mothers of Invention, 'Those Mothers Can Really Play', in the *San Francisco Chronicle*.

Gleason continued to contribute to *Rolling Stone* until his death in 1975. He was also an associate editor and critic on *Down Beat*, and his weekly columns in the *New York Post* were syndicated in the US and in Europe.

Gleason produced and hosted many TV documentaries, including a series of nearly 30 jazz and blues programs, 'Jazz Casual', featuring musicians from Dave Brubeck to B.B. King; a documentary on Duke Ellington; a series on the Monterey Jazz Festival; and several looks at San Francisco rock, notably *A Night at the Family Dog*, catching the Haight-Ashbury scene in one night's performances from the GRATEFUL DEAD, SANTANA and Jefferson Airplane (1970).

His books, compiled from articles and reviews, include *Jam Session* (1957), *The San Francisco Scene* (1968) and *Celebrating the Duke, and Louis, Bessie, Billie, Bird, Carmen, Miles, Dizzy & Other Heroes* (1975).

He was writing for the *San Francisco Chronicle* in 1963 when Dylan, then a rising star, performed at the Monterey Folk Festival. Gleason slated the concert, telling ROBERT SHELTON: 'It was an old Dylan concert and I didn't dig it. The talking blues stuff was poor imitation GUTHRIE. He looked wrong to me and I didn't like his voice. Although I didn't like "Hard Rain", I became haunted by it. Jesus, it was disturbing.' (PETE SEEGER, THEODORE BIKEL and others wrote a protest letter in response to this review, and Gleason recanted: 'I was deaf,' he wrote.)

From then on, Gleason's advocacy of Dylan never faltered. His was a useful voice, since he *was* of an older generation and could address its doubts from the inside, as here, in 1964: 'To the generations raised on solid Judeo-Christian principles, on the rock of moral values of our fathers, on the idea that cleanliness is next to Godliness, the deliberate sloppiness, the disdain for what we have thought of as perfect by Dylan's generation is shocking. But we are wrong. Look where our generation has gotten us . . . a hard core of reality connects the music of Dylan, the best of jazz, of contemporary poetry, painting, all the arts, in fact, with the social revolution that has resulted in CORE and SNCC, Dick Gregory, James Baldwin and the rest.'

An aeon later, after the unenthusiastic response to *Self Portrait* in 1970, it was Gleason, in *Rolling Stone*, who came out with the now almost notorious claim in response to hearing *New Morning*: 'We've got Bob Dylan back again!'

The Rex Foundation, a non-profit charity organization founded by the Grateful Dead and friends, established the Ralph J. Gleason Award in 1986, and 1989 saw the launching of the annual Ralph J. Gleason Music Book Awards, sponsored by *Rolling Stone*, BMI and New York University.

Gleason, who died aged 58, in Berkeley, California, on June 3, 1975, after suffering a massive heart attack, was a catalyst and an enthusiast—as his widow said in 2004: 'He was not a good writer. He wrote about interesting things.'

[Ralph J. Gleason: 1st two quotes taken from Robert Shelton, *No Direction Home: The Life and Music of Bob Dylan*, p.170 & p.250; 3rd quote *Rolling Stone* no.70, San Francisco, 12 Nov 1970. *A Night at the Family Dog*, Sep 1970, is DVD-issued by RED Distribution, 2005. Joe Selvin & Mrs. Gleason quotes, Steven Rubio's Online Life, 23 Dec 2004, seen 16 Aug 2005 at *http://begonias.typepad.com/srubio/2004/12/ralph_j_gleason.html*. Toby Gleason, e-mail to this writer, 3 Oct 2005.]

Glover, Tony [1936 -] David Curtis Glover was born in Minneapolis on October 7, 1939. His change of name from Dave to Tony was a switch about on a par with that of the British poet who changed his name from William Roberts to, er, Michael Roberts.

A close and influential friend of Dylan from the Dinkytown Minneapolis period, his fine essay on Dylan's progress through to 1966 was written for and published in the booklet for the 1998 official release the *Bootleg Series Vol. 4: Bob Dylan Live 1966*. (These sleevenotes won him the 1999 Deems Taylor award.)

Glover started playing 'professionally' with SPIDER JOHN KOERNER and DAVE RAY. Koerner, Ray and Glover—that was the name of their outfit—made many albums, starting with *Blues, Rags & Hollers*, issued first on the small Audiophile label in June 1963 but picked up by Elektra, who signed them, bought the rights, reissued the LP that November (with four tracks missing) and then several further albums.

Glover wrote three books on how to play blues harmonica, starting with *Blues Harp*, 1965. After the end of Koerner, Ray and Glover he moved to Berkeley, wrote articles for *Creem* and *Rolling Stone*, moved back to the Twin Cities and became a local 'underground' DJ, moved to New York and sat in with the Doors at Carnegie Hall and with the Allman Brothers at the Fillmore East. His best article from earlier days than the *Live 1966* essay is probably the very prescient 'A Wonderful New Group', written about THE BAND (one of the earliest pieces on their then-new incarnation) and published in November 1968. He might also be credited, with *Creem*, for 'discovering' PATTI SMITH.

In 1986 he wrote, produced and co-directed a video history of Koerner, Ray and Glover, which led to reunion gigs and eventually to their first new album in over 30 years, *One Foot in the Groove*,

1996. In 2002 he published (co-authored with Scott Dirks and Ward Gaines) the book *Blues With a Feeling: The Little Walter Story*.

He first met Dylan in mid-1960 on the Beat/folk scene in Dinkytown, near the University of Minnesota campus. 'We played at some parties here and there and traded a few harp riffs,' he wrote. After Dylan reached New York, he 'proudly sent back a flyer advertising him playing at Gerde's Folk City on a bill with JOHN LEE HOOKER.'

He was one of the few people Dylan kept in touch with after he went East. In 1963 Dylan described Glover as 'a friend to everything I am. Dave Glover, who I really love. Dave Glover, who feels and thinks and walks and talks just like I do.'

ROBERT SHELTON writes of him: 'Tony was tough and taciturn, yet gentle, cool as a bluesman, and passionate about his music and his friends. . . . His dark, laconic, James Dean-like manner made Bob feel Tony could be trusted. . . . Tony was one of the first to *know* that Bob was going somewhere. He liked Bob as much when he was a prophet without honor in Minneapolis as when he triumphed.'

Glover would prove that he 'could be trusted': in the early years he often recorded Dylan informally, and he is one of the very few people who never allowed his tapes to circulate among Dylan collectors (though just once he was tricked into it). Shelton says that Glover first taped Dylan in early 1961, when he was singing 'R&B-type Chuck Berry songs', and then again that May, when he was in his Guthrie phase. Dylan played Glover 'Song to Woody' and told him that JOAN BAEZ wanted to record it—and Tony tried to persuade Bob to keep it for himself, adding that he'd 'do a much better job on it'.

When Dylan returned to Minneapolis for the second time, in December 1961, and performed a large number of songs at his old friend BONNIE BEECHER's apartment (or possibly at DAVE WHITAKER's), this powerful informal session was recorded on two machines. The tape made on Beecher's art teacher's machine has long circulated, and in reasonable quality; the one Tony Glover recorded has not circulated, and is in better quality. Three songs taken from this 'master tape'—'Hard Times in New York Town', 'Dink's Song' and 'I Was Young When I Left Home'—have been issued officially; the first in 1991 on the *Bootleg Series Vols. 1–3*, the others in 2005 on the *Bootleg Series Vol. 7—No Direction Home: The Soundtrack*.

Shelton commissioned Dylan to write a piece for the 1963 NEWPORT FOLK FESTIVAL program (edited by Shelton as Stacey Williams). The result, 'typed single-spaced on tired yellow sheets. . . . Roughly one hundred fifty lines of free verse', was Dylan's key piece 'To Dave Glover', in which he urged people to understand why he had to move on from the old, traditional material and the old accompanying mindset.

Nine days before Dylan's first appearance at that festival, an informal recording was made at Dave Whitaker's home in Minneapolis, on which Glover plays harmonica behind Dylan on 'West Memphis' and 'Death Letter Blues'. (Koerner was there too, playing guitar on an instrumental jam.)

Glover also remembers playing informally with Dylan and BOB NEUWIRTH in the Viking Hotel during the 1964 Newport Folk Festival; they sang some HANK WILLIAMS, but also tried 'Tell Me' from the ROLLING STONES' first album. (At the festival itself, Koerner, Ray and Glover were performers.) It wasn't long before Glover was sitting in on nearly all the sessions for *Highway 61 Revisited* (which, in May 1998, he describes in pleasing detail in his sleevenotes to the *Live 1966* set).

In September 1992, when Dylan played the Orpheum Theater in Minneapolis, the support band was Ray and Glover. More recently, Tony Glover was one of the Back Porch Rockers, along with Dave Ray, Camile Baudoin and Reggie Scanlan (they issued a live album in 1999), but Dave Ray died on Thanksgiving 2002.

Glover is an interviewee in the SCORSESE film *No Direction Home*, remembering Dylan's first return to Minneapolis, only a couple of months after he'd left, as being the time Dylan's performing skills had improved out of all recognition; the evidence of the tapes suggests that when he returned in May 1961, he had improved a fair bit—but when he returned that December, *that's* when he'd made a quantum leap.

Dylan recalls Glover only briefly in *Chronicles Volume One*: but what he recalls is the time when 'Glover's playing was known and talked about around town, but nobody commented on mine'.

[1st Glover quotes from *Live 1966* essay; other detail, *www.island.net/~blues/tglover.htm*. Koerner, Ray and Glover: *Blues Rags and Hollers*, Audiophile AP-78, 1963; *One Foot in the Groove*, Tim/Kerr T/K 96CD137, US, 1996. Robert Shelton, *No Direction Home: The Life and Music of Bob Dylan*, 1986, Penguin edn., Dylan quote on Glover p.80; description of Glover p.81; on Glover taping Dylan, p.82; on 'To Dave Glover', p.210; Glover 'discovering' Patti Smith, p.439. Tony Glover, *Blues Harp*, New York: Oak Publications, 1965; 'A Wonderful New Group', *Eye* no.7, Nov 1968, available online at *http://theband.hiof.no/articles/eyes_7_november_1968.html*. Glover, Dirks and Gaines, *Blues With a Feeling: The Little Walter Story*, New York: Routledge, 2002. Bob Dylan, *Chronicles Volume One*, 2004, p.257. Minnesota Birth Index 1935–2002, file no. 1929-MN-014872.]

Gods and Generals **[2003]** See **''Cross the Green Mountain'**.

Goffin, Gerry [1939 -] Gerry Goffin was born in Brooklyn on February 11, 1939. He began writing song lyrics at the age of eight but had to wait many years before finding a music-writing partner. After high school he enlisted in the US Marine Corps Reserve and was duly admitted to the Annapolis Naval Academy in Maryland, from which he resigned after a year, returning to New York and majoring in chemistry at Queens College, where he met CAROLE KING.

For a few golden years as from 1959, when they married and started to dream up songs together, they enjoyed huge success as the prolific writers of pop hits, working out of the famous Brill Building at 1819 Broadway, New York City, for Nevins-Kirchner-Colgem from 1960 onwards. (For details of their joint songs, see under **King, Carole**.) While in this golden age, Goffin also co-wrote with Barry Mann (whose usual partner was Cynthia Weill), as in the case of 'Who Put the Bomp?', which Goffin himself recorded, scoring a top 10 US hit.

Just as Goffin and King did not write together exclusively while married, so too their professional collaboration did not end with their divorce (they co-wrote Blood Sweat & Tears' 'Hi-De-Ho'), though Gerry Goffin seemed to come out of this less well equipped than Ms. King, both as a songwriter and a performer. He made a 1973 solo album, *It Ain't Exactly Entertainment*, which was not a success (while King enjoyed spectacular solo success with her album *Tapestry*, albeit including the Goffin-King song 'Smackwater Jack') and he wrote only the occasional hit in the 1970s—notably Gladys Knight's 'I've Got to Use My Imagination' and Rod Stewart's 'It's Not the Spotlight', both co-written with BARRY GOLDBERG (who recorded the latter himself, with some minor assistance from Bob Dylan, on a 1973 album, while on Dylan's 1984 European tour, musician GREGG SUTTON was given a solo slot in which he regularly sang the former). In the 1980s Goffin managed to co-write, with Michael Masser, 'Tonight I Celebrate My Love', recorded by both Perry Como and Roberta Flack, Crystal Gayle's 'A Long and Lasting Love' and Whitney Houston's 'Savin' All My Love For You', released on her début album in 1985 (an album that eventually sold 24 million copies) and a no.1 hit single.

In late 1995 or early 1996 Gerry Goffin was working on a new solo album, his first for aeons, when Bob Dylan dropped into the studios, brought along by their mutual friend Barry Goldberg. Dylan duly played guitar (along with Goldberg on keyboards and TIM DRUMMOND on bass, plus various others) on two tracks that made it onto Goffin's album. The tracks are 'Masquerade' (on which Dylan is listed as co-producer with Goffin, and as co-writer) and 'Tragedy of the Trade' (co-written by Goffin, Dylan and Goldberg). A posting on Amazon's website suggests that Dylan can also be heard on background vocals on the track 'A Woman Can Be Like a Gangster'. The album, *Back Room Blood*, was released in July 1996. You might assume the title refers to the fact that Goffin's main career has been as backroom boy—songwriter rather than singer—but the long, bitter, foaming, 'Hurricane'-style lyric of 'Tragedy of the Trade' includes the opaque couplet 'The world's been run with backroom blood / Long before the time of the flood'. A third co-written song, 'Coast to Coast Blues', is covered by Anders Osborne on his 1999 album *Living Room*—on which FREDDY KOELLA plays guitar—but it isn't included on Goffin's.

Back Room Blood is not a great album, and Goffin's voice sometimes sounds like a poor imitation of Dylan, but these co-written songs have certainly been under-attended to by Dylan aficionados, and the album that contains them has, overall, a kind of floundering agitation that's rather endearing.

[Gerry Goffin: *It Ain't Exactly Entertainment*, *nia*, 1973, CD-reissued Airmail *nia*, 2001; *Back Room Blood*, Genes 4132, US, 1996. Anders Osborne: *Living Room*, Shanachie 5375, Newton, NJ, 1999.]

Goldberg, Barry [1941 -] Barry Goldberg was born in 1941 in Chicago, and long ago claimed the motto 'Born and raised in Chicago, born and raised to play the blues'. Like his friend and musical compadre the late MICHAEL BLOOMFIELD he was a teenage prodigy—in Goldberg's case on keyboards—and was sitting in on live club dates by the greats of the Southside by the late 1950s, including MUDDY WATERS. Like Bloomfield too, he decided at the start of his career, at a time when many musicians were changing their names to duck out of any obvious declaration of Jewishness, that he would go out there as Goldberg and be damned. He had a rôle model: he was the nephew of Supreme Court Justice Arthur Goldberg. 'It hurt me, not changing my name,' he told journalist Scott Benarde in 1998, but 'Bloomfield and I were really into our heritage and traditions and proud of our names and if people didn't like them it was tough shit. We were emphatic about keeping our real names. . . . I thought of my uncle Arthur using Goldberg and being proud of it. . . . He blazed through politics and the legal system and faced a lot of adversity. Every time he met with Lyndon Johnson, he went in there like a hero. When Kennedy needed advice, he would call my uncle. It made me feel proud.'

Goldberg and Bloomfield even made a 1969 album together titled *Two Jews Blues* (featuring the not especially Jewish Duane Allman on one track). For contractual reasons (the album was on Buddah, Bloomfield was contracted to Columbia), Bloomfield didn't appear on the cover, on which the credit in words went inanely to 'Barry Goldberg and Barry Goldberg' but in the illustration the second Jew depicted alongside Goldberg, who hadn't been consulted, was Jesus. When Bob Dylan saw the album, he said he 'thought I had an ego problem', Goldberg remembers. It didn't impair their long friendship, which had begun through Bloomfield and been forged in the flames of the NEWPORT FOLK FESTIVAL appearance in 1965, when Dylan went electric and Barry Goldberg was the pianist.

Goldberg later developed into a songwriter and producer, but his first strength was as a distinctive player of his Hammond B-3 organ. Soon after Newport '65 he formed the Goldberg/Miller Blues Band with Steve Miller and made one eponymously titled album; his concurrent session work included playing live with JIMI HENDRIX (at New York's Café Au Go Go) and in the studio for Mitch Ryder (along with Bloomfield and AL KOOPER). He moved to the West Coast, and after being in Charlie Musselwhite's first band—Charlie Musselwhite's South Side Band—long enough to play on their 1967 Vanguard album *Stand Back!*, he and Bloomfield co-founded the Electric Flag—which recorded the soundtrack to the film *The Trip* (1967) and the album *Long Time Comin'* (1968) before Goldberg quit to form the Barry Goldberg Reunion (with guitarist Harvey Mandel and drummer Eddie Hoh), which made two albums, *Barry Goldberg Reunion*, aka *There's No Hole in My Soul*, and *Blowin' My Mind*. This outfit was described in retrospect by *Billboard* as a 'lost gem, one of the real sleepers of the psychedelic pop era'. Goldberg, 30 years on, said of this period and its youth culture: 'It was a chaotic, crazy time. We were like guinea pigs for chemists and drug dealers. Some people went too far. I came through in one piece with a brain and mind fairly intact.'

In 1968 Goldberg played electric piano on the Bloomfield-Kooper-Stills *Supersession* and in 1969 made the 'solo' album *Barry Goldberg and Friends* and the aforementioned *Two Jews Blues* (apparently with no apostrophe). More solo work followed: *Streetman*, 1970, *Blasts from My Past*, 1971, and then, with no commercial success from any of these records, his record deal was over. He was at a loss. He looked up Bob Dylan.

ROBERT SHELTON reports that 'for two days running they jammed for hours. Later, Goldberg went to Dylan's place at Woodstock, jamming there with DOUG SAHM. . . . Goldberg got an offer to do a single for RCA, but Dylan told him to hold off. The next day Dylan rang him and said: "I'm on the phone with JERRY WEXLER from Atlantic Records and I think we can work out a deal, but I'm gonna have to produce you; that's cool, isn't it?"'

It was August 1973 when they went into the Muscle Shoals studios in Sheffield, Alabama, for five days of sessions for this album, co-produced, in the end, by Dylan and Wexler. Dylan can be heard on background vocals on 'Stormy Weather', 'Silver Moon', 'Minstrel Show' and 'Big City Woman', and he supplies percussion—as does Wexler—on 'It's Not the Spotlight', the album's one song Goldberg had co-written with GERRY GOFFIN (who was by now often the lyricist for his compositions). Goldberg played guitar as well as keyboards on the album, and sang the lead vocals; he had a horn section and a number of other musicians (including Muscle Shoals regular, BARRY BECKETT). The album, one of the many muted projects Dylan busied himself with in 1973, was released that December under a new deal Goldberg had with Atco, the subsidiary label of Atlantic Records.

Their professional paths crossed again in March 1977 when Goldberg was on piano on the sessions for LEONARD COHEN's album *Death of a Ladies' Man* in Los Angeles, produced by PHIL SPECTOR, which Dylan and ALLEN GINSBERG dropped in on, contributing backing vocals to the track 'Don't Go Home With Your Hard-On'. Eight years later, Goldberg played piano behind Dylan on a session in Hollywood on June 16, 1985 that yielded nothing Dylan has ever released but did include circulated takes of that sweet song by Allen Toussaint, 'Freedom for the Stallion', which Dylan sings with delicacy and feeling.

In November 1989, in New Bloomington, Indiana, Goldberg was again on piano (and this time shared vocals too) among the crowd of musicians backing Dylan on the subdued recording he made of 'People Get Ready' for use on the soundtrack of the film *Catchfire*, directed by and starring Dennis Hopper (in which Dylan appears unbilled as a 'chainsaw artist'). And finally, so far, Dylan and Goldberg met up when they both worked on Gerry Goffin's 1996 album *Back Room Blood*, which includes many Goldberg-Goffin compositions.

Goldberg, meanwhile, has worked on a number of film scores, including that other Dennis Hopper film with the confusingly similar title *Flashback* (1990), and the 1989 film *Pow Wow Highway* and has produced albums for, among others, Percy Sledge. With his Chicago bluesman's hat on, he has more recently been music supervisor to the PBS 'Muddy Waters Tribute Concert' at the Kennedy Center, and part of the group now called Chicago Blues Reunion, whose other veterans are Nick Gravenites, Harvey Mandel, Tracy Nelson, Corky Siegel and that other Newport '65 man, drummer SAM LAY. In 2005 they issued an odd but compelling two-disc set, one a CD and the other a DVD, covering their reunion concert plus documentary extras and interviews about their own history on Chicago's North Side blues scene. Twisting Goldberg's old motto but slightly, it's called *Buried Alive in the Blues*.

[Barry Goldberg: *Barry Goldberg and Friends*, Cherry Red CR-5105, US, 1969; *Streetman*, *nia*, US, 1970; *Blasts from My Past*, Buddah BDS-5081, 1971; *Barry Goldberg*, Sheffield, AL, Aug 1973, Atco SD 7040, US, 1973; *Barry Goldberg & Friends Live*, Buddah BDS-5684, 1976. Goldberg & Bloomfield: *Two Jews Blues*, Buddah BDS-5029, 1969. Electric Flag: *The Trip*, Sidewalk ST-5908, US, 1967; *Long Time Comin'*, Columbia 9597, US, 1968. Barry Goldberg Reunion: *Barry Goldberg Reunion*, Buddah 5012, *nia*; *Blowin' My Mind*, Epic 26199, *nia*. Various Artists soundtrack CD *Backtrack*, WTG 46042, US, 1990. Chicago Blues Reunion: *Buried Alive in the Blues*,

33rd Street (CD & DVD), US, 2005. Quotes from interview by Scott Benarde in 'Rock of Ages: Pop Stars Sing Out About Their Judaism', posted online Nov 16, 2000, seen 14 Jun 2005 at *www.jewhoo.com/editor/columns/rockofages5.html*; this has been incorporated into the book as by Scott R. Benarde, *Stars of David: Rock'n'Roll's Jewish Stories*, Lebanon, NH: University Press of New England, 2003. Robert Shelton, *No Direction Home: The Life and Music of Bob Dylan*, London: Penguin edn., 1987, p.426.]

Goldberg, Steven [1941 -] Steven Goldberg was born in New York City on October 14, 1941. His article 'Bob Dylan and the Poetry of Salvation' was one of the earliest essays to sweep aside as unimportant both Dylan's earlier work of social and political protest *and* much of his radical mid-1960s work, and to argue instead that only with the *John Wesley Harding* album ('Dylan's supreme work') did he become an 'artist in the Zen sense'. This article, which appeared when *Nashville Skyline* was Dylan's newest LP and shortly before the release of *Self Portrait*, seemed attuned to the contemporaneous move toward the countryside, towards setting up communes and growing your own crops of drugs, and dropping out of America's hideous 'Great Society'. Goldberg singled out the then-unissued track 'Lay Down Your Weary Tune' as signaling Dylan's change from politics to mysticism.

Goldberg's own incantatory, mystic prose flowed like this: he wrote that Dylan 'was searching for the courage to release his grasp on all the layers of distinctions that give us meaning, but, by virtue of their inevitably setting us apart from the life-flow, preclude our salvation. All such distinctions, from petty jealousies and arbitrary cultural values to the massive, but ultimately irrelevant, confusions engendered by psychological problems, all the endless repetitions that those without faith grasp in order to avoid their own existence—all of these had to be released.'

Sizeable chunks of this essay were drawn upon in the chapter 'Lay Down Your Weary Tune: Drugs and Mysticism' in MICHAEL GRAY's early study *Song & Dance Man: The Art of Bob Dylan* (1972), for which Dylan's office gave permission for the entire lyric of this unreleased song to be published.

Goldberg has published many books on popular social science and contemporary culture since his 1970 essay on Dylan and was until recently chairman of the Department of Sociology at City College, City University of New York. In his 2003 book *Fads and Fallacies in the Social Sciences* he republished the essay on Dylan—leading one reviewer, Berel Dov Lerner, to complain that the book 'could have been no less appropriately titled *All Kinds of Stuff That I Wrote That Has Not Yet Been Republished in a Book*.' This was churlish. Certainly the Dylan essay deserved to be republished—though this was not its first reappearance; it had been collected in CRAIG McGREGOR's round-up of Dylan writings in 1972 and again in 1990.

Goldberg also appears, though using the pseudonym S.J. Estes, as the compiler of the Dylan discography inside ROBERT SHELTON's long-gestated book *No Direction Home: The Life and Music of Bob Dylan* in 1986.

Steven Goldberg still lives and works in New York City.

[Steven Goldberg: 'Bob Dylan and the Poetry of Salvation', *Saturday Review* no.53, 30 May 1970, collected in Craig McGregor, ed., *Bob Dylan: A Retrospective*, 1972, reissued as *Bob Dylan, the Early Years: A Retrospective*, 1990; and extracted in Michael Gray, *Song & Dance Man: The Art of Bob Dylan*, 1972, revised & updated as *Song & Dance Man III: The Art of Bob Dylan*, 1999. Steven Goldberg, *When Wish Replaces Thought:* Why So Much of What You Believe Is False, Amherst, NY: Prometheus Books, 1992; *Why Men Rule: A Theory of Male Dominance*, Peru, IL: Open Court Books, 1993; *Culture Clash: Law and Science in America*, New York: New York University Press, 1994; *Fads and Fallacies in the Social Sciences*, Amherst, NY: Humanity Books, 2003. Berel Dov Lerner, review of this last, seen on *http://mentalhelp.net*, 12 Sep 2005. Further data from Steven Goldberg, phone call to this writer 27 Feb 2006.]

Goldstein, Harvey [1944 -] Harvey Goldstein was born on the 4th of July in New York City, and grew there up adept at guitar but keener on playing electric bass. At 19, rebelling against his conformist Jewish upbringing, he started using the stage name Harvey Brooks after he 'got into a Jew boy scenario', as he put it: he was attacked during a break at a gig in Michigan in the early 60s. 'I took that name to avoid conflicts. . . . I thought, "Just let me get a professional name without any connotations, the blandest name I can find." In those days you wanted to blend in. It was easier to blend in than fight your way in. . . . If I had to do it again, I wouldn't.'

Either way, his career took off in 1965. 'AL KOOPER called me and told me Dylan needed a bass player. I didn't even know who Dylan was.' He arrived at Columbia's New York Studio A next day, July 30, to find himself on the sessions for *Highway 61 Revisited*. Plunging straight in, he played that day on the album take of 'From a Buick 6', on the outtake version that somehow got issued on the Japanese LP instead, and on the 'Can You Please Crawl Out Your Window?' single that was issued mislabelled as 'Positively 4th Street'. Two mistakes out of three in the issuing but not in the playing. The next session, on August 2, wrapped up 'Highway 61 Revisited', 'Just Like Tom Thumb's Blues', 'Queen Jane Approximately' and 'Ballad of a Thin Man'; and finally, on August 4 (it is now believed), 'Desolation Row'. Goldstein knew who Bob Dylan was by then. 'That session,' he says, 'created a career in pop music for me.' And, you might say, a niche in history.

It wasn't quite over then, either. On the early electric gigs that followed NEWPORT '65, starting at Forest Hills, New York, that August 28, Goldstein played live in Dylan's band along with Al Kooper, LEVON HELM and ROBBIE ROBERTSON. This unit didn't last, and after a Hollywood Bowl concert on September 3, Goldstein departed.

He went on to play sessions and concerts with a wide range of people, from Miles Davis (he's on *Bitches Brew* and *Big Fun*) to PHIL OCHS, from JUDY COLLINS to the Fabulous Thunderbirds, from Richie Havens to the Doors, from Eric Andersen and DAVID BLUE to Graham Bond, John Martyn and John Cale, and from the BLOOMFIELD-Kooper-Stills *Supersession* to the 1968 Mama Cass solo album *Dream a Little Dream of Me*.

He was also a member of the short-lived first and second line-ups of the Electric Flag, remaining in it long enough to take part in its sessions for the soundtrack of the film *The Trip* (1967), the first 'proper' album, *Long Time Comin'* (1968) and the next, *Electric Flag*—on which Goldstein played not only bass and guitar but saxophone, and was co-producer. He left, in time to play on the long *Bitches Brew* sessions, which stretched from August 1969 to March 1970. Soon after that, and in quite some contrast, he played bass once again for Bob Dylan, on *New Morning*.

In the 1990s Goldstein moved to Arizona, to live a slower, cleaner life, but in 2001 he was in sighted in the suitably named group Raisins in the Sun, along with Jules Shear, Paul Q. Kolderie, Chuck Prophet and Jim Dickinson. The subtle *ffwd* ('Calgary's news & entertainment weekly') described them as 'a great fuckband: a bunch of seasoned vets who can play the hell out of their instruments and write songs in their sleep—which I think they might have here. The record as a whole falls right between Hater and THE TRAVELING WILBURYS . . .'

[Electric Flag: *The Trip*, Sidewalk ST-5908, US, 1967; *Long Time Comin'*, Columbia 9597, US, 1968; *Electric Flag*, Columbia 9714, US, 1968. Raisins in the Sun: *Raisins in the Sun*, Rounder, US, 2001. Goldstein quotes c/o interview by Scott Benarde in 'Rock of Ages: Pop Stars Sing Out About Their Judaism' posted online Nov 16, 2000, seen 14 Jun 2005 at *www.jewhoo.com/editor/columns/rockofages4.html*; this has been incorporated into the book as by Scott R. Benarde, *Stars of David: Rock'n'Roll's Jewish Stories*, Lebanon, NH: University Press of New England, 2003. *ffwd* review, 22 Mar 2001, seen online 14 Jun 2005 at *www.ffwdweekly.com/Issues/2001/0322/cd2.htm*.]

'Gonna Change My Way of Thinking' [2003 version] Dylan certainly changed 'Gonna Change My Way of Thinking' when he revisited his 1979 gospel song for the various-artists album *Gotta Serve Somebody: The Gospel Songs of Bob Dylan*, in a version that re-writes the lyrics so that they bring in, by allusion, JIMMIE RODGERS, THE CARTER FAMILY and Oscar Wilde, and as a recording offers a duet between Dylan and MAVIS STAPLES.

This ferocious version, which seems to pace menacingly between the spiritual and secular worlds, begins with a drum beat reminiscent of 'Like a Rolling Stone' and offers one stanza sung by Dylan at his most phlegmishly dreadful, before stopping for a spoken routine played out by Mavis Staples and Bob that is a very funny, twisted update of a hokum routine on a recording by Rodgers and the Carter Family from 1931, titled 'The Carter Family and Jimmie Rodgers in Texas'—or, on one of the six labels that issued it at the time, 'The Carter Family Visits Jimmie Rodgers'. (It was recorded straight after the unsurprisingly similar 'Jimmie Rodgers Visits the Carter Family'; both had also been attempted unsuccessfully, at the previous day's session.) In the 1931 version, after Rodgers sings one stanza, the Carters arrive and say what a nice place Jimmie has in Texas, and he says yes, and that from his porch you can see all the way to Mexico; the 2003 'update' has Mavis saying what a nice place Bob has in California, and he says yes, and that from his porch you can see all the way to Hawaii. Both dialogues include proposing to 'knock over' a couple of chickens and eat them fried without delay.

(They do not attempt to duplicate the part where A.P. Carter, not so impressed, declares of Texas that he's 'seen further and seen less' than anywhere else he's ever been. And indeed the exchange captured here, scripted though it is, actually encapsulates the classic clash that lies at the heart of this 'meeting': Jimmie Rodgers is relaxed, delivers his lines pretty well and speaks for the mischievous world of the honky-tonk, innovation, bluegrass and pleasure; the Carters, stiff and prim as boards, adopt the stance of deeply conservative backwoods religion—folks who'd have been preachers if their kin could have afforded it. If there's any faint parallel to this in the Dylan-Staples version, it's a mirror image, in which Bob sounds like the tormented, mad, backsliding Calvinist and Mavis is the relaxed soulful mama encouraging him to sing away his blues. A small extra point of difference: the Dylan-Staples track really was recorded in California, whereas the Rodgers-Carter track was cut not in Texas but Louisville, Kentucky.)

After their wondrous dialogue (the best thing Dylan's done since *"Love and Theft"*), Mavis and Bob duet on several more stanzas, utterly rewritten from the *Slow Train Coming* lyrics, yet pulling in lines and phrases from other Carter Family records. As Christopher Rollason has it:

'The "welcome table" in stanza 2 was already laid in "River of Jordan", while in stanza 6 "There are storms on the ocean / Storms out on the mountain too . . . / Oh Lord / You know I have no friend without you" combines elements from "The Storms Are on the Ocean" . . . and "Can't Feel at Home"

. . . the latter number has the Carters singing: "Oh Lord, you know I have no friend like you".' (Rollason adds that all these tracks are on a Carter Family 5-CD box set issued in 2001.)

Dylan's re-written lyric ends by alluding to a rather different source, a reversal of the well-known couplet that ends Oscar Wilde's 'The Ballad of Reading Gaol'. Wilde, elaborating on the theme that 'each man kills the thing he loves', writes that 'The coward does it with a kiss, / The brave man with a sword!'; Dylan and Mavis end the song with this: 'A brave man will kill you with a sword / A coward with a kiss.'

[Bob Dylan & Mavis Staples: 'Gonna Change My Way of Thinking', Malibu, CA, 4 Mar 2002 (with Dylan's tour band plus Mavis & Yvonne Staples), *Gotta Serve Somebody: The Gospel Songs of Bob Dylan*, Columbia/ Legacy CK 89015 (US) / Columbia COL 511126 2 (UK), 2003. Jimmie Rodgers & the Carter Family: 'The Carter Family and Jimmie Rodgers in Texas' (aka 'The Carter Family Visits Jimmie Rodgers'), Louisville, KY, 12 Jun 1931. The Carter Family: *The Carter Family 1927–1934* (5-CD box set), JSP JSPCD7701, UK, 2001. Christopher Rollason: "'It is only he who can reduce me to tears": Review of the tribute CD *Gotta Serve Somebody: The Gospel Songs of Bob Dylan*', Bob Dylan Critical Corner, *www.geocities.com/Athens/Oracle/6752*, 18 Aug 2003. Oscar Wilde: 'The Ballad of Reading Gaol', 1st published 1898.

NB. In 2006 came a DVD version of *Gotta Serve Somebody: The Gospel Songs of Bob Dylan*; it excludes Mavis & Bob's 'Gonna Change My Way of Thinking' but offers instead footage of Dylan's burning performance of 'When He Returns' from Toronto, 20 Apr 1980; dir. Michael B. Borofsky; Burning Rose Video/ Image Entertainment ID2894RBDVD, US, 2006 (officially dated 2005).]

Good as I Been to You **[1992]** Dylan's return to a solo acoustic album, 28 years after the last. Much maligned as being vocally impoverished and incompetently self-produced, and bemoaned for its lack of Dylan compositions, this endlessly rewarding demonstration of the strengths of traditional folksong and pre-war acoustic blues, the two forms used in flexible alternation, sets up all manner of resonance and dialogue, shifting and circling and forming a richly persuasive whole that works both as an impassioned treasury of folksong and an intimate revelation of how firmly some specifics of Dylan's own early styles and songs were founded upon this material.

There are striking changes of genre and oeuvre between one song and another—perhaps most spectacularly the wonderful switch of worlds between 'Tomorrow Night', that brilliant re-creation of the American 1940s radio-romance poor-white-trash world (the world of Vernon and Gladys Presley and their little boy ELVIS in their shack in Tupelo, Mississippi, in act), and the insouciant self-confident grace of the articulate working-class in 18th century Ireland evoked by 'Arthur McBride'. Yet these dramatic contrasts jostle inside a cohesive whole: for the unity of the collection is as marked as its contrasts.

There is, to begin with, that striking cavalcade of individual names: Frankie, Albert, Jim Jones, Blackjack Davey, Little Maggie, Arthur McBride, Diamond Joe and Froggie in the song-titles alone, and a comparable catalogue in the last song's narrative. Going far beyond this, however, is the songs' thematic unity.

Of course, we might demur at the idea that all their thematic common ingredients were significantly in Dylan's mind in compiling the album. Stephen Scobie, reviewing it when it was almost new, wrote: 'I am about to argue that the songs on *Good as I Been to You* appear to be obsessed with the themes of infidelity and revenge—but if, say, you were to pick at random *any* 13 songs out of the folk and blues tradition, wouldn't there be a good chance that you would come up with a fair number . . . about unfaithful lovers and avenging spouses?' Yet what Dylan assembles here involves the continual re-exploring of the same sets of themes and correspondences of expression—themes that range far wider than personal infidelity and revenge.

'I ain't gonna tell you no story', he sings in the opening track; 'If you want any more you can sing it yourself', he sings in the last. In between, we have more talk about talk: in the second song, 'Come and listen for a moment lads and hear me tell my tale'; in the seventh, 'There's a song that will linger forever in our ears'; in the tenth, 'Now mark what followed and what did betide . . . / And so to conclude and to finish this speech'; and in the fourth 'Well it's [i.e. my story is] all of a fair and handsome girl.'

The heroine of 'Blackjack Davey' is a 'pretty little miss' in her tender years; so too the heroine of the next is a girl is 'all in her tender years'. At the end of her story is a matching exhortation to Jim Jones' 'Come and listen for a moment lads and hear me tell my tale'—'Come all ye fair and tender girls, wheresoever you may be.' In this song, and also in songs one and three, the heroine pursues her own true love (though all with differing results). In the same three songs there is a love-triangle and a betrayal, while in the sixth there is a posited triangle and in the 12th a betrayal.

In the first there is a shooting, a judge and a hanging; in the second there's a judge, a threatened hanging and a threatened shooting. In the tenth, a threatened execution; in the 11th, a threatened killing. In the first there is 'a .44', in the sixth a rifle and a 'six-shooter'. In the first there is jail, in the 11th the threat of the jailhouse, in the second men in irons, and in the 11th again, the chain-gang. Each of the first three songs features a folk-hero baddie, while 'Diamond Joe' centres around a notorious baddie (though not a folk-hero).

Three songs feature the sea; the second involves exile, the third a sort of exile and the sixth a posited exile. The second, third and tenth emphasise a rejection of ruling class values, while the harsh oppression of a colonial power comes into song two and ten, and in 'Hard Times' there is social injustice and oppression all around. The fourth includes a captain and the wearing of a military (naval) uniform; the tenth includes a sergeant and the wearing of a military (army) uniform. In 'Blackjack Davey' fine clothes are sacrificed; in the adjacent 'Canadee-i-o' fine clothes are gained; in 'Arthur McBride' 'fine clothes' are offered and declined; in 'You Gonna Quit Me' shoes and clothes are bought in vain. In the third song there are horses and an implied blanket ('wrapped up with Blackjack Davey'), and there are horses and blankets too in 'Diamond Joe'.

There are even neat, small conjunctions in the use of children's descriptive phrases, from the opening song's 'rooty-toot-toot', through another's 'rowdy-dow-dow' to the closing song's 'bumble-y-bee'.

Dylan has always had a taste for narrative ballads that offer tales of horses and daughters and hangings, exile and injustice. The songs on *Good as I Been to You* fit this pattern pretty well. In the end, what is so clear from this collection is not merely that it has the thematic unity of a concept album without any of the potential self-importance, but that while Bob Dylan hasn't written a single one of these songs, the album could hardly be more Dylanesque.

There *is* a sad decline in Dylan's vocal range, including a dropping away of his once unerring ability to place and control each syllable and each breath, each guitar note and each telling pause, with absolute precision and optimum vividness of communication.

Yet this album, imprecise, errant, at times blurred and furry, is a singular creation that gains as well as loses by Dylan's loss of the effortless certainty of youth. Dark, complex, surreal and fractured, it is like an inspired, lost work from some opium-thralled folk archivist throwing his own torrid genius into celebrating the myriad strengths of anonymously created song: song from before there was a music industry to kill off its mystery and its purpose. Stand-out tracks: 'Hard Times', 'Arthur McBride', 'You're Gonna Quit Me', 'Diamond Joe' and 'Froggie Went a-Courtin''. The fine outtake 'You Belong to Me' was used on the soundtrack of Oliver Stone's film *Natural Born Killers*.

[Recorded Malibu, CA, Jul-Aug 1992; released as Columbia CK 53200, 3 Nov 1992 (in UK, Columbia 472710 1/2 (LP/CD), Dec 1992. Stephen Scobie: 'As Good as Who's Been to Who?', *On the Tracks* no. 1, Grand Junction, CO, summer 1993.]

Gooding, Cynthia [1924 - 1988] Cynthia Day Gooding was born in Rochester, Minnesota, on August 12, 1924, and grew up there and in Lake Forrest, Illinois. She also attended school in Toronto, before spending some time in the late 1940s in Mexico City, where she learned that she had a voice and how to play the guitar. A 'name' folk revivalist singer by the end of the 1950s, she was not an especially good one—in one critic's phrase, 'almost a paradigm for inauthenticity' (an American Julie Felix, perhaps), but it might be more reasonable to see her work as typifying the 1950s 'mainstream folk' style of people like THEODORE BIKEL (with whom she recorded) and Burl Ives.

She first met Dylan in 1959 in Minneapolis, where she gave a concert and he buttonholed her at a party afterwards and made her listen to him play—for half an hour, according to SPIDER JOHN KOERNER's roommate Harry Weber: 'Cynthia was amazed. It was quite a sight, because she was somebody then.' Later, when Dylan was fresh to New York, Cynthia saw him perform at Gerde's Folk City and bumped into him all over the place, and wrote to Harry Weber, describing him: 'People listen . . . he talks and he laughs and just when they are about to catch him in a lie, he takes out his harmonica and blows them down.'

Cynthia was clearly keen on him. You can hear it in her voice and in the whole flirtatious stance she took with him when he was a guest on her radio show 'Folksinger's Choice' in early 1962. He was 20; she was 37. Probably recorded that January 13 at WBAI Radio in New York, it consisted of Ms. Gooding coaxing from Dylan an entertaining version of his fictional biography and much further chat, in between his singing no less than 11 pieces. Very interestingly, they run a gamut of influences right from the off, which is a version of HANK WILLIAMS' 'I Heard That Lonesome Whistle Blow', running through BUKKA WHITE's 'Fixin' to Die' to HOWLIN' WOLF's 1956 hit 'Smokestack Lightnin'', treated as if it were a pre-war blues from the 1920s—which in a way it was, and certainly granted Dylan's early love of electric post-war blues and R&B it's especially fascinating here to hear him transmute this into the acceptable sound of acoustic folk blues. Then comes WOODY GUTHRIE's 'Hard Traveling', Dylan's own early 'protest song', 'The Death of Emmett Till', his early song 'Standing on the Highway', the traditional 'Roll On, John', THE MEMPHIS JUG BAND's 'Stealin'', 'It Makes a Long Time Man Feel Bad'—which Dylan says here that he learnt from RALPH RINZLER (of THE GREENBRIAR BOYS), BIG JOE WILLIAMS' 'Baby Please Don't Go' and finally his own adroit reworking of 'Penny's Farm' (a track on the seminal HARRY SMITH collection) into the charming 'Hard Times in New York Town'. The programme was broadcast on March 11 that year—eight days before the release of his débût album, which, on this show, he was already dismissing as no longer representative of him.

A second recording took place in Cynthia Gooding's apartment, probably that same March. This one comprises Dylan singing 'Ballad of Donald White', 'Wichita (Going to Louisiana)', 'Acne' (shared vocal with unknown other person), 'Rocks and Gravel' (with humming by an unknown other person), '(It Makes) A Long Time Man Feel Bad' and 'Ranger's Command'.

According to OLOF BJÖRNER, Dylan returned to Gooding's radio show that October, though no recording of such a performance seems to exist. Björner says Dylan performed with John Gibbons and that one song performed was 'TB Blues' which was also mentioned by Dylan a week later, when he appeared on the Billy Faier Show on the same station, WBAI.

Gooding's style of folk singing was never so challenged, never made to sound so enervated, as by the approach to folksong Bob Dylan embodied. Her Elektra producer, the prolific Jac Holzman, summed her up as a 'tall, beautiful, intelligent, multilingual Village folk singer'. It wasn't enough.

Cynthia Gooding died of ovarian cancer at Princeton Hospital, New Jersey, on February 10, 1988.

[Cynthia Gooding: *The Queen of Hearts—English Folksongs*, Elektra EKL 11 (mono 10-inch), US, 1953; *Italian Folk Songs*, Elektra EKL 17 (mono 10-inch), US, 1954; *Faithful Lovers and Other Phenomena*, Elektra EKL 107, 1956; *Turkish and Spanish Folk Songs*, EKLP 6, *nia*; *Mexican Folk Songs*, EKLP 8, *nia*; *Queen of Hearts—Early English Folk Songs* (mostly same as 1953 LP same title), EKL 131, 1958. Theodore Bikel and Cynthia Gooding: *A Young Man and a Maid (Love Songs of Many Lands)*, Elektra EKL 109, 1956. Cynthia Gooding and Yves Tessier: *French and Italian Folksongs*, Elektra EKL 221, c.1962. Various Artists, *Folk Festival*, Elektra SMP-2, 1956, incl. 'Bella Regazza' & 'The Derby Ram' by Cynthia Gooding, and 'Coplas' by Cynthia Gooding & Theodore Bikel. The 1957 Various Artists LP *Folk Pops 'n Jazz Sampler* (what a title!), Elektra SMP-3, incl. her 'Lass of the Low Countrie'. *Folk Sampler Five*, Elektra SMP-5, 1959, incl. her 'Ankaranin Tasina Bak'. *The Folk Scene*, Elektra SMP-6, 1962, incl. 'Lowlands of Holland'.

Dylan on Cynthia Gooding radio show broadcast WBAI, 11 Mar 1962; unreleased except for 'Roll on John', issued *There Is No Eye: Music for Photographs, recordings of musicians photographed by John Cohen*, Smithsonian Folkways SFW CD 40091, Washington, D.C., Oct 2001. Olof Bjorner claim at *www.bjorner.com/62.htm*. Jac Holzman quote from his book *Follow the Music: The Life and High Times of Elektra Records in the Great Years of American Pop Culture*, Santa Monica, CA: FirstMedia Books, 1998, as quoted online at *www.followthemusic.com/whobook.html*.]

Goodman, Steve [1948 - 1984] Steve Goodman was born on Chicago's North Side on July 25, 1948, the son of a used car salesman, about whom Steve eventually wrote the song 'My Old Man'. He started learning guitar and writing songs as a young teenager and while at Lake Forest College and the University of Illinois he began to perform in a local club, soon dropping out of college (in 1969) to make music his career. In this he was never financially successful, though he survived early on by writing and singing advertising jingles. He returned to Chicago after a short stint trying his luck in Greenwich Village and in 1971 was recorded performing live on a local album, *Gathering at the Earl of Old Town*. A support spot to KRIS KRISTOFFERSON that April led to a record deal with Buddah and a first album, *Steve Goodman*, in 1971. Typically, as soon as Goodman had Kristofferson's attention, he insisted he go and hear another performer who deserved to be discovered too—his friend JOHN PRINE, whose song 'Donald and Lydia' Goodman would cover on his own début album.

That album also offers Goodman's signature song, 'City of New Orleans', which was a hit not for Goodman but for ARLO GUTHRIE—and then again, the year of Goodman's death, for WILLIE NELSON. Also on Steve Goodman's first album is the good-natured parody of a country song 'You Never Even Call Me By My Name' (which Prine had co-written but wouldn't take credit for); this too would become a hit, a couple of years later and for David Allen Coe.

All this tells the Goodman story: he wrote songs others had hits with, and he was, as writer and performer too, much admired by big-name fellow performers. He was a fine guitarist (he plays on all Prine's early albums, just as Prine plays on his) and it's said that when, in solo performances, he broke a guitar string, which was often, he would keep singing while getting a new string out of his pocket, fitting and tuning it, and would then resume his playing unfazed—yet he never broke through as a performer himself. In September 1972, with Arif Mardin as producer, Goodman went into Atlantic's studios in New York to make his second album, *Somebody Else's Troubles*, and a single, 'Election Year Rag', and for that single, and for the album's title track, Bob Dylan was a participant. Supposedly Goodman was frustrated at Dylan's turning up hours and hours late, and perhaps this is why he doesn't appear on the rest of the material, but he plays piano and sings harmony vocals on these two tracks (both penned by Goodman), along with DAVID BROMBERG on dobro and mandolin, and Prine, among others. The album also included the song that Goodman would come nearest to having a hit with, 'The Dutchman'—the one song he didn't write. When the album was issued, in early 1973, Dylan was credited as Robert Milkwood Thomas.

Though Buddah issued *The Essential Steve Goodman* in 1974 (which also featured 'Election Year Rag'), it was 1975 before Goodman made his next album, when a label switch gave him greater encouragement and saw an increase in his output. The 1975 album was *Jessie's Jig & Other Favorites*; then came *Words We Can Dance To* (1976), *Say It in*

Private (1977) and *High and Outside* (1978), which included a duet with then-newcomer Nicolette Larson, and *Hot Spot* (1980). 'Chicago Shorty', as he was dubbed by friends, had also acted as a producer, notably of John Prine's 1978 album *Bruised Orange*, and formed his own label, Red Pajama Records, for which he duly recorded *Artistic Hair* and *Affordable Art* (both 1983) and his last album, *Santa Ana Winds*, which reached record stores the day after his death.

Goodman had been suffering from leukaemia all his adult life, and from Chicago made regular and frequent trips to New York for treatment. He moved to the West Coast (to Seal Beach, just below Long Beach, in Southern California) at the beginning of the 1980s, and received treatment in Seattle. The *Artistic Hair* album cover depicted him standing in front of a hairdressing salon of that name, his own head bald from the effects of chemotherapy. On August 31, 1984 he underwent a bone marrow transplant. Twenty days later he died of the liver and kidney failure brought on by his leukemia in hospital in Seattle. He was 36.

[Steve Goodman: 'Eight Ball', 'Chicago Bust Rag' & 'City of New Orleans', Chicago 1970–71, on Various Artists, *Gathering at the Earl of Old Town*, Dunwich 670, Chicago, 1971, CD-reissued Mountain Railroad, US, 1989; *Steve Goodman*, NY, 1971, Buddah BDS-5096, US, 1971–2; *Somebody Else's Troubles*, NY, Sep 1972, Buddah BDS-5121, US, 1973; 'Election Year Rag', Buddah BDA-326, 1973; *Artistic Hair*, Red Pajama 001, US, 1983; *Affordable Art*, Red Pajama 002, 1983; *Santa Ana Winds*, Red Pajama 003, 1984. Many posthumous recordings have been issued, and CD-reissues of the original LPs, some remastered and with extra tracks. There is also a video, *Steve Goodman Live From Austin City Limits . . . And More!*, including Prine, Guthrie & Kristofferson, *nia*, US, 2003.]

Gorgoni, Al [1939 -] Albert Gorgoni was born in Philadelphia on October 11, 1939 but moved to the Bronx at 14, took up the guitar and after early dinner-show gigs in Greenwich Village he played on his first demo session in 1959, falling in with the Brill Building crowd and playing on demos for all the pop songwriters of the period, including for GERRY GOFFIN and CAROLE KING, PHIL SPECTOR, Leiber & Stoller and PAUL SIMON. His rhythm guitarwork being youthfully vibrant he was soon asked to play on the real records too, duly playing on 'The Name Game' by Shirley Ellis, 'Sherry', 'Walk Like a Man' and 'Big Girls Don't Cry' by the Four Seasons, 'Leader of the Pack' by the Shangri-Las, 'Chapel of Love' by the Dixie Cups, 'Our Day Will Come' by Ruby & the Romantics and many others. From 1963 onwards, as the pop business changed, Gorgoni shifted into arranging, producing and songwriting (though this last was not his strong suit), while still playing on sessions of some note, among them VAN MORRISON's historic 1967 Bang sessions (including 'Brown-Eyed Girl'), the Monkees' 'I'm a Believer', '1-2-3' by Len Barry, 'At Seventeen' by Janis Ian (and three of her albums), Melanie's *Leftover Wine*, Simon & Garfunkel's 'The Sound of Silence' and, er, the Archies' 'Sugar Sugar'. He was also producer and/or arranger on the New Christy Minstrels' album *The New Christy Minstrels* and albums by B.J. Thomas and Astrud Gilberto and has played on albums by NEIL DIAMOND, CAROLE BAYER SAGER and the pioneering Blood, Sweat & Tears album *Child Is Father to the Man*. He has also recorded with Aretha Franklin, Laura Nyro, RICHARD & MIMI FARIÑA, JOAN BAEZ, Bobby Darin, Herbie Mann and Marvin Gaye & Tammi Terrell. All told, that's some track record.

Gorgoni has also written and played music for films and TV, but in the 1970s and since has more keenly worked on advertising jingles and other ad campaigns, including for Chevrolet and Frontier Airlines. The ad on which RAY CHARLES sings Gorgoni's 'It Couldn't Be Anything But Maxwell House' is one of those Bob Dylan deplored in the 1985 *Biograph* interview (before, of course, selling lingerie and Starbucks himself). Gorgoni's other clients have included the obesity-inducing triumvirate of McDonald's, Burger King and Colonel Sanders' Kentucky Fried Chicken. Naturally it would be churlish to suggest that this is amoral work and that Al Gorgoni is a fool if he eats at these places and a hypocrite if he doesn't.

Back in the much cleaner era of 1965, Gorgoni's career intersected with Dylan's directly. He was brought in to play on the sessions for *Bringing It All Back Home* that January, and is there on rhythm guitar on every track, and also the single of 'If You Gotta Go, Go Now' released in Europe and the alternate take of the same song later released on the *Bootleg Series Vols. 1–3* (on which his credit misspells him Gorgone).

However, his real place in history comes from the fact that he was there at the first of the *Highway 61 Revisited* sessions and not at the second one. That is, he was there on June 15, playing rhythm guitar while Dylan was on piano and AL KOOPER, on guitar, was chastened to find in MIKE BLOOMFIELD a player so much his superior. FRANK OWENS was on the organ and along with drums and bass that day they worked on the fast version of 'It Takes a Lot to Laugh, It Takes a Train to Cry' and on 'Sitting on a Barbed Wire Fence' and then they began to work, without success, on 'Like a Rolling Stone'. By the end of the session, then, Al Gorgoni had played on outtakes of all three numbers and they too appear (though he goes uncredited) on the *Bootleg Series Vols. 1–3* (and in the case of several 'Like a Rolling Stone's on the *Highway 61 Interactive* CD-rom also).

Next day, though, Al Gorgoni was absent—and as a result, Dylan moved over from piano to rhythm guitar, which meant that PAUL GRIFFIN, who had replaced Frank Owens as keyboards player, moved over from organ to piano, and *that* is why the organ was free for Al Kooper to play, resulting in the classic recording of 'Like a Rolling Stone'. He wasn't on it, but in this crucial sense, Al Gorgoni was the key–and unlocked that revolutionary door.

[Main sources: *www.gorgoni.net* and e-mail exchange with this writer 26 Jan 2006. Up-to-date details on personnel at the June 1965 sessions from Derek Barker, researched for & given in 'So You Want to Be a Rock & Roll Star: The Story of "Like a Rolling Stone"', *Isis* no.120, UK, May 2005, plus phone calls to this writer, 26 Jan 2006.]

'Gotta Serve Somebody' [1979] Recorded at the Muscle Shoals studios in Sheffield, Alabama, on May 4, 1979, this is one of the standout tracks on Dylan's first Born Again album, *Slow Train Coming*, and its rather vengeful-sounding chorus–'It might be the devil or it might be the Lord / But you gotta serve somebody' has both an Old and a New Testament basis. Joshua 24:15, in a passage dealing with the need to put away other idols and choose to serve God instead, begins: 'And if it seem evil unto you to serve the Lord, choose you this day whom ye will serve'. Like Dylan's song, this urges that vacillation and moral shiftiness be renounced in favour of clear-sightedness about a clear and unavoidable choice. (As Deuteronomy 30:19 makes clear: '. . . I have set before you life and death, blessing and cursing: therefore choose life . . .') This gotta-serve-somebody theme is taken up in Matthew 6:24: 'No man can serve two masters: for either he will hate the one, and love the other; or else he will hold to the one, and despise the other. Ye cannot serve God and mammon.'

Yet the chorus of this blues-structured song also reformulates blues lyric poetry and echoes aspects of the older genre of the Negro Spiritual. There is a formulation which, beginning with 'Ashes to ashes and dust to dust', then adds any one of a number of permutations of a clear-cut, no-middle-way choice, presented as 'if A don't get you then Z must'; these include 'New York don't get me, Chicago must' and 'The police don't get you, now the undertaker must'. One of these, from Joe Evans, prefigures Dylan's 'Gotta Serve Somebody' chorus: 'Ashes to ashes and dust to dust / And if God don't have me you know the devil must.'

This is not the Dylan song's only debt. Both MEMPHIS SLIM's song 'Mother Earth' and Dylan's 'Gotta Serve Somebody' owe a modest indebtedness to the old Negro Spiritual 'Ev'rybody Got to Die', which runs like this: 'Rich and poor, great and small / Got to meet in Judgment Hall / Ev'rybody who is living / Ev'rybody got to die . . . / Young and old, short and tall / Got to meet in Judgment Hall / Ev'rybody got to die.'

But the debt of Dylan's song to Memphis Slim's is more than a modest one. This is from the 1966 version of his 'Mother Earth': 'You may own a half a city, even diamonds and pearls . . . / You may play at racehorses, you may own a racetrack / You may have enough money baby to buy anything you like / Don't care how great you are, don't care what you're worth / When it all end up you got to go back to Mother Earth.'

The core idea, the structure of the verses as you-may-be-rich-or-poor listings, the specific ways these are expressed–not just the 'you may own x or you may own y' and the occasional judicious use of that 'even z', but the effective device of quantum-leaping what 'rich' might mean, from 'you may play at racehorses' to 'you may own a racetrack', which Dylan matches with his rather less neat 'you might be somebody's landlord, you might even own banks'–and the insistent 'ain't no escaping' that is the message of the chorus: *all* these, duplicated in Dylan's lyric, are there in Memphis Slim's.

An echo of this same formulation lingers in secular form in another song, one the teenage Bob Dylan would have been familiar with, ELVIS PRESLEY's fourth single, 'Baby Let's Play House': 'You may go to college, you may go to school / You may drive a pink Cadillac but don't you be nobody's fool / . . . Come back baby, I wanna play house with you.' This was written by Arthur Gunter (his version was an R&B hit earlier in 1955), though it was Elvis himself who threw in the line 'You may own a pink Cadillac': the one which, as it happens, best fits the pattern of the 'Mother Earth'/'Gotta Serve Somebody' lyrics. And the line Elvis dropped to accommodate his Cadillac was 'You may have religion . . .' Dylan's core contribution is that he picks that religious ingredient up again and re-entwines it with the secular formulations of Memphis Slim.

'Gotta Serve Somebody' has become one of his 30 most performed songs, with well over 400 concert appearances in the first 25 years of its life. And back in February 1980, at the televised Grammy Awards, it was this song's chastising burn that Dylan chose to hurl at a a glitzy audience which, having so clearly chosen to serve mammon, was satisfactorily discomfited by its lyric. Whether Dylan the man, as against the artist, was entitled to preach that gospel is another matter. But one of the 'you-may-be-rich' listings in his song seems to allude more to his own life than to Memphis Slim's lyric. Those who remember pictures of the Dylans' white-elephant Malibu home, with its ostentatious dome of copper at the top, will get a flash of recognition here: 'You might be living in a mansion / You might live in a dome . . .' In the midst of all this lip-smacking, it's a quietly slipped-in but honourable self-rebuke.

[Bob Dylan: 'Gotta Serve Somebody', Grammy Awards, LA, 27 Feb 1980, televised CBS-TV. Joe Evans: 'New Huntsville Jail', NY, 20 May 1931; *Early Country Music*, Historical HLP-8002, Jersey City, NJ, late 1960s. 'Ev'rybody Got to Die' reprinted (with the minstrelisation of the text removed) from H.A. Chambers, ed., *The Treasury of Negro Spirituals*, London: Blandford Press, 1964. Memphis Slim: 'Mother Earth', Chicago, 1951, Premium 867, Chicago 1951; 'Mother Earth', NY, 1961, *Memphis Slim: All Kinds of Blues*, Original Blues Classics OBC 507, US, 1961 CD-reissued OBCCD 507, *nia*. Arthur Gunter: 'Baby Let's Play House', Nashville, 1954, Excello 2047, US, 1955. Elvis Presley: 'Baby Let's Play House', Memphis, 5 Feb 1955, Sun 217, Memphis, 1955 (HMV POP 305, UK, 1957).]

Gover, Robert [1929 -] Robert Gover is the author of a cult bohemian novel of the end of the 1950s, *One Hundred Dollar Misunderstanding*, about a white college boy, a 14-year-old black prostitute and their 'riotous, crazy weekend' together. The book is largely forgotten and has not perhaps stood up well, yet by its very datedness and embarrassment quotient it says plenty about what was regarded as daring subject matter in the period when Bob Dylan was coming to young adulthood. It is eloquent by default about how uptight Eisenhower's America was about things in general and race in particular.

In an interview by Studs Terkel in May 1963, Dylan not only mentions the book as one that articulates contemporary consciousness, one that 'actually comes out and states something that's actually true, that everybody thinks about', but also claims friendship with the author. His first words on the subject are: 'I've got a friend who wrote a book called *One Hundred Dollar Misunderstanding*. I don't know if it's around Chicago. . . . This guy Robert Gover wrote it.'

Gover was born in Philadelphia on November 2, 1929. His book was published in 1961 by Grove Press, that great Greenwich Village-based progressive publishing house which first published, in the same era, Henry Miller's *Tropic of Cancer* (1961), William Burroughs' *Naked Lunch* (1962) and the first American edition of Lawrence's *Lady Chatterley* (1959). *One Hundred Dollar Misunderstanding* was published in this milieu and was duly a mildly scandalous success, a cult item, championed by Gore Vidal and others. It was also published in Britain in 1961 by a similarly 'minority' publishing house, Neville Spearman, and went quickly into UK paperback the same year. Gover's novel went on through many printings and by the 1964 third printing of a US mass-market paperback edition, its cover was trailering a forthcoming Broadway musical. This never happened.

In 1965 its author began studying astrology and by the mid-1970s had begun to focus on 'stock market astrology'. He has published seven novels, a number of short stories and the non-fiction study *Voodoo Contra*, and belongs to, among other bodies, the International Federation of Business Astrologers. Now in his late 70s he lives in Rehoboth Beach, Delaware, and keeps working.

In 2005 he published *Time and Money: The Economy and the Planets*. He also confirmed that he and Dylan had indeed known each other:

> 'Dylan and I met in a bar in Greenwich Village back when his first album first appeared. We were introduced by a journalist who was interviewing me about my first novel. Dylan and I sneaked off to a Spanish restaurant to have dinner and talk. We got along like long lost brothers. During the dinner, Bobby wanted to let me hear a song he had written not long before, so pulled out his guitar and began playing and singing. The restaurant management threatened to throw us out if we didn't quiet down, so we finished our meal and then went to a club where Bobby asked to be allowed to play this song, even though he was not on the program that evening. He appeared on stage and delivered the song. I think it was called "The Masters of War" then.
>
> 'Just so happened his manager had stopped by the club in the meantime and was upset by this unpaid appearance, and gave Bobby a scolding afterwards. We then went out drinking and talking till the wee hours and met the next day for brunch and continued our intense conversations. I then had to leave New York on other business and later wrote him a note, but never heard back from him. . . . I don't know if he ever got the note.
>
> 'So our friendship was brief but very intense . . . our brief encounter was a highlight for me. Over the years I've listened to his music and been sustained through rough times by it.'

[Robert Gover: *One Hundred Dollar Misunderstanding*, New York: Grove Press, & London: Neville Spearman, 1961; New York: Ballantine Books, 1964; testimony re knowing Dylan, e-mail to the present writer 19 Sep 2005. Bob Dylan interview by Studs Terkel, Radio WFMT, Chicago, May 1963; most recently reprinted *Granta* no.90, London, summer 2005, pp.243–54.]

grandma and Walpole's cat When, on 'Going, Going, Gone', from *Planet Waves*, grandma is recollected as saying 'Boy, go follow your heart / I know you'll be fine at the end of the line / All that's gold doesn't shine', her old, simple wisdom is deftly stressed by Dylan having her speak that last truism, that neat opposite of 'all that glisters is not gold'—a line that, while often held to be from Shakespeare, in fact conflates two other formulations. The proverb, taken from the Latin and taking in grandma's point as well as the converse, is 'All is not gold that glitters / All that glitters is not gold'. Then an allusion to this by the poet Thomas Gray (1716–1771) gives us the apparently more elevated but in fact merely archaic 'glisters', and not quite as expected: 'Not all that tempts your wand'ring eyes / And heedless hearts, is lawful prize; / Nor all, that glisters, gold.' This comes not from the one poem for which Gray is still remembered, 'Elegy Written in a Country Church-Yard' (published 1751), but from the odd source 'Ode on the Death of a Favourite Cat, Drowned in a Tub of Gold Fishes' (1747). And it wasn't his own cat, it was Horace Walpole's.

Grateful Dead, the In the 1960s, the Grateful Dead were hardly unique in being heavily influenced by Dylan's work, though they were unique. They seized on his material as from 1966, when they took up 'It's All Over Now, Baby Blue' and 'She Belongs to Me'. Yet their first album, *The Grateful Dead*, recorded in January 1967 and released that March, contained no Dylan songs and indeed few originals, the emphasis being on amphetamine-fast, ragged hippie versions of old blues material like 'Sittin' on Top of the World' and numbers by JESSE FULLER and Noah Lewis—material, apart from anything else, that Dylan would have known, and taken from the same folk revival period sources. And no wonder: JERRY GARCIA was an old folkie himself.

The band came into being from the starting point of an acoustic 1963 group, Mother McCree's Uptown Jug Champions, which comprised Garcia, Pigpen (Rod McKernan), John 'Marmaduke' Dawson (later in New Riders of the Purple Sage, which began as a Garcia Dead by-product), Bob Matthews (later a Dead recordings and equipment person) and BOB WEIR. They became the electric band the Warlocks, losing Dawson and Matthews and gaining Bill Kreutzmann (then called Bill Sommers) and, soon afterwards, PHIL LESH. This electric band played its début gig the same month Dylan 'went electric'—July 1965—and soon started dropping acid, tangling with Ken Kesey's Merry Pranksters and renaming themselves the Grateful Dead as their folk-rootsy rock'n'roll became elongated, experimental, stoned and strange, as they acquired an extended family—including second drummer Mickey Hart, lyricist ROBERT HUNTER and acid-manufacturer/sound-engineer/financial benefactor (this last only briefly) Owsley—and as the band became a formative part of the San Francisco psychedelic scene.

This first heyday saw two more studio albums before 1970's *Live/Dead*, which showed their strength as performers to a wide audience for the first time. Influenced by THE BAND, from whom they were so very different, they made *Workingman's Dead* and *American Beauty* in 1971 and then another live double-LP (their first gold album). By 1973, despite the drugs and Pigpen's death in March, and further personnel changes, they were organised enough to set up their own record companies, Grateful Dead Records and Round Records (the latter for less commercial projects). It was the beginning of a fiercely independent but highly competent business machinery that showed many other musicians and singer-songwriters that the record industry could be changed, subdued and made the servant of the music and of the lifestyle the artist required. The family was 150 strong by 1975 and ran, among much else, its own booking agency and its own travel company. They went on to be the exemplar of the permanent touring unit, retaining a 'people's park' consciousness even in the nasty new world of the 1980s. Instead of trying to prosecute bootleggers, they invented the idea of the special tapers' corner, which they provided at every venue (much to Dylan's shock-horror, it's said, the first time he encountered it).

Like a successful songwriter's catalogue, or like Bob Dylan himself, an outfit like the Dead that keeps on working and releases vast amounts of material eventually seems to acquire a momentum and a presence that becomes unstoppable, regardless of what's new or modish in the culture. Yet the underlying strength of the band necessarily remains its music, which has even survived the death of Jerry Garcia in 1995. Nevertheless, people will always disagree about whether the Grateful Dead is a sublime and visionary outfit playing the coolest bravest music in the universe (free form inside structure) or a bunch of self-indulgent white boys who couldn't play in sync for five minutes if they tried, playing to crowds too stoned to care.

These two once-counter-cultural institutions, Dylan and the Dead, first came together in person when Dylan stood side of stage at a five-hour Dead concert in a Jersey City stadium on July 18, 1972, generating false rumours that they were recording together then. They first appeared on the same bill at the SNACK Benefit in San Francisco on March 23, 1975—but while Dylan shared the stage with NEIL YOUNG, RICK DANKO, LEVON HELM, TIM DRUMMOND and Ben Keith, none of the Dead joined him; nor did he appear during their own set. However, when Dylan gave his thrilling run of *twelve* concerts at the Fox Warfield in San Francisco in November 1980, Jerry Garcia was among the guest guitarists there for one night each. He appeared in the middle of the November 16 concert, playing guitar on a run of four numbers, 'To Ramona', 'Ain't Gonna Go to Hell for Anybody', 'Girl of the North Country' and 'Slow Train'.

They were reunited on stage in 1986, when Dylan and the Dead staged two double-bill concerts: at Akron, Ohio, on July 2 (billed 'The Grateful Dead & Dylan') and at Washington, D.C., on July 7 (yep, 'Dylan & the Grateful Dead'). For Dylan, these were two dates among many on his own long tour with TOM PETTY & THE HEARTBREAKERS, but it was unusual for Petty and his band to be billed in such small print as they were for these Dylan/Dead nights. In each case, Dylan's own set was with Petty and band, but he also took the stage during the Dead's sets, at Akron to play guitar on 'Little Red Rooster'and then to take lead vocals (with backing vocals by Bob Weir) on 'Don't Think Twice, It's All Right' and 'It's All Over Now, Baby Blue', and in Washington to play guitar on 'Satisfaction' and sing on 'It's All Over Now, Baby Blue' and 'Desolation Row'.

Next came their brief joint tour of July 1987 (set up by Dylan's manager, Elliot Roberts). Dylan's comments about the rehearsals for these dates, as given in *Chronicles Volume One*, make it sound as if the Dead knew Dylan's repertoire a lot better than he felt he did, and describe quite disturbingly how distanced he was made to see that he was from his own songs, having approached the rehearsal in the first place assuming that they'd be 'as easy as jumping rope'. This section of his memoir then describes Dylan escaping onto San Rafael's Front Street, stumbling upon an old jazz bar band, having a (rather vaguely explained) eureka moment and then returning to the doubtless unfazed Dead, now feeling that he 'couldn't wait to get started'. He goes on to describe breezing through the shows knowing he could perform 'any of these songs without them having to be restricted to the world of words.' Certainly the evidence of the album is that he hardly had any grip on that world at all. (See also ***Dylan and the Dead***.)

The Dylan songs the Dead re-introduced him to were not all good ones. The wretched 'John Brown' was a mutton-headed, mawkish and crass anti-war song that Dylan himself didn't choose to try at the sessions for either *The Freewheelin' Bob Dylan* or *The Times They Are a-Changin'* (that is, at sessions stretching from April 1962 to October 1963), in spite of the prevalence of 'protest songs' on both albums, and by mid-1964 he had dropped the song from his concert repertoire. He disinterred it under the encouragement of the Dead, and after rehearsing it June 1987, they played it in 11 concerts that July. Dylan then re-introduced it on the Never-Ending Tour (1988 onwards) and eventually featured it on the abject *MTV Unplugged* album of 1995. He has continued to scrape away at it in concert since.

Another song of dubious quality from Dylan's repertoire and which he had never performed live before these Dylan & the Dead concerts was 'Joey', from the 1976 *Desire* album. It was débuted at the Foxboro concert on Independence Day 1987.

After these joint dates, Dylan wandered off into the fall 1987 tour of Israel and Europe with Tom Petty & the Heartbreakers, and then began the Never-Ending Tour—and surely that fall 1987 tour, with its deranged weirdness, random repertoire and dim lights (and its inclusion of 'Joey' on opening night and 'John Brown' at the second concert) showed Dylan at least as much influenced by the Dead as on the Never-Ending Tour: except that it was in the course of the latter that Dylan started performing, over and over again, some of the Dead's own dreariest songs: 'Alabama Getaway', 'Friend of the Devil' and 'West LA Fadeaway'—plus, less often, 'Touch of Gray' and 'Black Muddy River'. And that's not to mention the lamentable songs co-written by Dylan and Robert Hunter, 'Silvio'—not only a track on the wretched *Down in the Groove* but also performed live by Dylan a heart-sinking number of times: 592 by the end of 2003—and (though so far only on the album and never live), 'Ugliest Girl in the World'. And when 'Silvio' was recorded, at a session the same month as the Dylan & the Dead rehearsals, Jerry Garcia and Bob Weir both played guitar and sang backing vocals.

For their part, the Grateful Dead went back to music and business as usual—but increasingly they would use Dylan songs in nearly all their performances. Their album *Postcards of the Hanging* comprises ten such live renditions, cut over a period of almost two decades (plus a 'bonus track' from the Dylan & the Dead rehearsals, 'Man of Peace'), including an interesting 'When I Paint My Masterpiece'. Other Dead releases that include Dylan songs are: *Dick's Picks, Vol. 9*; *Terrapin Station (Limited Edition)*; *Fallout from the Phil Zone*; *Dick's Picks, Vol. 17*; *View from the Vault*; *Dick's Picks, Vol. 21*; *View from the Vault II*; *Nightfall of Diamonds*; *The Golden Road (1965–1973)*; *View from the Vault III*; *Dick's Picks, Vol. 27*; and *View from the Vault IV*. And taking one relatively recent year at random, 1993, in the course of 81 Grateful Dead concerts they performed (mostly a number of times each) 'Queen Jane Approximately', 'All Along the Watchtower', 'Just Like Tom Thumb's Blues', 'Desolation Row', 'Knockin' on Heaven's Door', 'Maggie's Farm' and 'When I Paint My Masterpiece'. (Five of the seven from the 1960s, and nothing later than 1973.)

Dylan and the Dead have come back together occasionally since that 1987 tour. Six days after the release of the *Dylan & the Dead* album—but over 18 months after the concerts themselves—Dylan joined the Dead on stage in Inglewood, CA (February 12, 1989), and played guitar on 'Iko Iko', 'Monkey and the Engineer', 'Alabama Getaway', 'Dire Wolf' and 'Cassidy', and offered guitar plus backing vocals on 'Stuck Inside of Mobile With the Memphis Blues Again', 'Not Fade Away' and 'Knockin' on Heaven's Door.' At a Dylan concert in San Francisco on May 5, 1992, Jerry Garcia came on stage to play guitar during 'Cat's in the Well' and 'Idiot Wind'. At a Dead concert at Madison Square Garden, New York City, on October 17, 1994, Dylan joined *them* to sing 'Rainy Day Women # 12 & 35' (with Garcia and Weir both on backing vocals). The following summer, Dylan played five concerts in enormous venues as the 'very special guest' of, i.e. the opening act for, the Grateful Dead. At the last of these, at a stadium in Washington, D.C., on June 25 (1995), Jerry Garcia played guitar on Dylan's encore numbers, 'It Takes a Lot to Laugh, It Takes a Train to Cry' and 'Rainy Day Women # 12 & 35'. Six weeks and three days later, Garcia died of a heart attack. After this, the word 'Grateful' was dropped from the band's name so that after first touring as the Other Ones, they really did become just the Dead.

Four more years on and, perhaps still surprisingly, Dylan's Never-Ending Tour incorporated a 1999 fall Tour on which the opening act was Phil

Lesh & Friends. There were 19 of these concerts, and though Dylan never strayed on stage during Lesh's sets, Lesh made an occasional appearance during Dylan's. The year after, nevertheless, they tried the combination again—though never appearing on stage together—in a series of 32 summer concerts running from June 16 in Portland, Oregon, to July 30 in Stanhope, New Jersey . . . this time giving Lesh the headliner's position. Many Dylan supporters found this bizarre.

Into the 21st century and from July 29 till August 8, 2003, Dylan opened for the Dead at a series of eight 'Summer Getaway' concerts, once more appearing during the band's sets as well as his own. In the course of these Dead sets Dylan shared vocals with Bob Weir on 'Alabama Getaway', 'Goin' Down the Road Feelin' Bad', 'Around and Around', 'Big River', 'Johnny B. Goode' and 'Good Morning Schoolgirl', and also performed (in some cases with Weir on back-up vocals) 'It's All Over Now, Baby Blue', 'West LA Fadeaway', 'Friend of the Devil', 'Gotta Serve Somebody', 'Like a Rolling Stone', 'Señor (Tales of Yankee Power)', 'Desolation Row', 'Ballad of a Thin Man', 'Oh Boy', 'Big Boss Man', 'Subterranean Homesick Blues', 'You Win Again', 'Tangled Up in Blue' and 'It Takes a Lot to Laugh, It Takes a Train to Cry'. This time, though, there was a soupçon of Dead participation in two of Dylan's sets too: Phil Lesh played bass and Mickey Hart tambourine on the last number ('Rainy Day Women') on August 5 in Noblesville, Indiana; and in Darien, New York, on August 8, the last of these double bills, Bob Weir played electric guitar on 'Highway 61 Revisited', 'Positively 4th Street', 'Honest With Me', 'Summer Days' and 'Rainy Day Women'.

Did the Grateful Dead re-awake Dylan's interest in traditional material—an interest he revealed in the early days of the Never-Ending Tour? Well, maybe, but the Dylan & the Dead tour rehearsals spend little time on such material, and infinitely more on Dylan's own back catalogue. Nor does he explore folk or old blues material when he goes back on the road after those dates with the Dead, later in 1987. Almost a year passes before he launches the Never-Ending Tour, with a stripped-down band much tighter than the Dead like to be; it's only here that he starts to revisit old ballads and old blues.

The impossibility of ascribing Dylan sources as between the Dead and the folk, blues and country music they themselves draw on is encountered again and again, necessarily. Look, for example, at some of his repertoire at the Bonnaroo 2004 Music Festival in Manchester, Tennessee, that June 9. He performed the traditional 'Samson and Delilah', popularised in the folk revival period by the REV. GARY DAVIS, plus HANK WILLIAMS' 'You Win Again' and MERLE HAGGARD's 'Sing Me Back Home'. You can point out that all these had been in the repertoire of the Grateful Dead—or you can say that Dylan knew all these songs by their original popularisers and composer-performers anyway. Another example: the Dead famously perform a near-endless version of another Rev. Gary Davis number, 'Death Don't Have No Mercy' (it's one of their standards); but aeons earlier, Dylan was recorded performing it himself, along with the further Davis song 'It's Hard to Be Blind', in Minnesota in May 1961. (See also **blues, inequality of reward in**.)

But did the Dead re-awaken Dylan's interest in playing live? Did they persuade him by example of the virtues of sticking at it, year in year out—of adopting, in other words, a Never-Ending Tour state of mind? Quite possibly. For better or worse.

[Grateful Dead: *The Grateful Dead*, LA (1 track SF), Jan 1967, Warner Bros. WS-1689, 1967; *Postcards of the Hanging: The Grateful Dead Perform the Songs of Bob Dylan*, Grateful Dead GDCD 1060, 2002. Bob Dylan, *Chronicles Volume One*, 2004, Dylan & the Dead rehearsals & tour comments pp.149–51. A handy source of information is Blair Jackson, *Goin' Down the Road: A Grateful Dead Traveling Companion*; New York: Harmony Books (paperback), 1992; so is Phil Lesh, *Searching for the Sound: My Life with the Grateful Dead*, New York: Little, Brown, 2005.]

Graves, Robert [1895 - 1985] Robert von Ranke Graves was born in Wimbledon, then a village outside London, on July 24, 1895. One of ten children, his father was Alfred Perceval Graves, a Gaelic scholar and a minor Irish poet. At Oxford University, to which he won a scholarship, he was rebuked about his English Literature essays in memorable terms: 'Mr. Graves,' he was told severely, 'it appears that you prefer some books to others.'

He enlisted in 1914, was seriously wounded, returned to Oxford, published some war poetry and a biography of his friend T.E. Lawrence (Lawrence of Arabia), and then in 1929 published the controversial memoir *Goodbye to All That*, which in part deals with the psychological repercussions of the horrors of World War I. It ends with his departure from the UK. He duly lived in Italy, France, the US and the Spanish island of Majorca.

Like T.S. ELIOT, he wrote critical books as well as poetry, though taking a very different stance, not least toward modernism. He also wrote 13 novels, most famously *I, Claudius* and *Claudius the God* (both 1934). In 1948 he published his major critical work *The White Goddess*, formulating his mythology of poetic inspiration, inspired by late 19th century studies of matriarchal societies and goddess cults; its sub-title is *A Historical Grammar of Poetic Myth*. Seven years later came his minor classic *The Greek Myths*.

By the 1950s his international reputation was assured; he became Oxford Professor of Poetry 1961–1966. He published, altogether, over 140 books before succumbing in his later years to 'silence and senility'.

Bob Dylan has often cited Graves, specifying *The White Goddess* as a significant influence upon his own work (which is to say, essentially on the development of his ideas about myth and poetic resources).

This is too large a subject to explore in detail here (it is scrutinised perhaps especially in WISSOLIK & McGRATH's *Bob Dylan's Words*, 1994) but, briefly, Graves' book is interested in motifs of apocalypse, and can therefore be suggested as a building block for Dylan's own subsequent similar interest. Significantly too, perhaps, the figure of the goddess herself, or Triple Goddess (mother, bride, hag), forms part of the so-called 'monomyth' of the hero figure's endeavours, and so can be said to impinge upon a number of Dylan songs–especially since it closely connects with the figure of the twin. It can be argued that the figure of the White Lady, in Dylan's 1970s film *Renaldo & Clara*, stands in some relation to that of the White Goddess elaborated by Graves, and that Dylan's work of prose poetry *Tarantula*, written in the mid-1960s but only published in the early 1970s, hints recurrently at a familiarity with Graves' ideas.

More particularly, it is within *The White Goddess* that Graves gives a translation of the 14th century apocalyptic Celtic poem 'Cad Goddeu', or 'Battle of the Trees' (part of the *Romance of Taliesin*), which, encountered now, cannot but recall 'A Hard Rain's a-Gonna Fall'. In a long incantation of line upon unrhymed line (it is a canto fable), we find these: 'I have been the string of a child's swaddling clout / I have been a sword in the hand / I have been a shield in the fight / . . . There shall be a black darkness / There shall be a shaking of the mountain / . . . I have slept in a hundred islands / I have dwelt in a hundred cities . . .'

Dylan the Welsh Hero-God, after whom Dylan Thomas was deliberately named (the word 'Dylan' meaning 'son of the sea-wave'), also figures in 'The Battle of the Trees'; he is a yellow-haired child. Bob Dylan's lengthy and mysterious 1980s song 'Angelina' comes to mind here too, with its 'Blood drying in my yellow hair as I go from shore to shore'.

According to RAMBLIN' JACK ELLIOTT, in ANTHONY SCADUTO's *Bob Dylan: An Intimate Biography*, Bob Dylan actually met Graves, in England in 1962. The young whippersnapper was rude, and the meeting an embarrassing failure. If the story is true, and the date right, it must have been very soon indeed after Dylan saw HANS FRIED (son of the German poet Erich Fried) standing in Collet's record shop in London with a copy of *The White Goddess* under his arm–which led to these two young Graves enthusiasts repairing to a not-very-Greek restaurant called the Star, on Old Compton Street in Soho, and discussing Graves, life and the universe for close on three hours in the cold winter of 1962–63, just before Dylan's appearance in the BBC drama *The Madhouse on Castle Street*.

According to Dylan's own account in *Chronicles Volume One*, he first read *The White Goddess* when 'invoking the poetic muse was something I didn't know about yet.' He adds, with his usual imprecision about dates and chronology: 'In a few years' time I would meet Robert Graves himself in London. We went out for a brisk walk around Paddington Square. I wanted to ask him about some of the things in his book, but I couldn't remember much about it.'

Robert Graves died in Majorca on December 7, 1985.

[Sources include *Cambridge Guide to Literature in English*, ed. Ian Ousby, 1995 edn., p.387; the biography posted online by the Academy of American Poets, seen 22 Aug 2005 at *www.poets.org/poet.php/prmPID/193* (including the phrase 'silence and senility'); Wissolik & McGrath's *Bob Dylan's Words–A Critical Dictionary and Commentary*, 1994, esp. pp.57–58, 67 & 218; and Hans Fried, phone conversation with the present writer 22 Aug 2005, re meeting with Dylan. *Chronicles Volume One*, 2004, p.45. The rebuke to Graves about literary preferences quoted from memory, from reading decades ago, source forgotten: possibly F.R. Leavis, or even Evelyn Waugh.]

Gray, Michael [1946 -] Michael John Gray was born on August 25, 1946 in Bromborough, Cheshire, UK ('the wrong side of the River Mersey', as Liverpudlians like to say). He wrote the first full-length critical study of Dylan's work, the pioneering if rather Leavisite *Song & Dance Man: The Art of Bob Dylan*, published in the UK in November 1972 and in the US in January 1973. A Japanese hardback edition was published on his 27th birthday and the UK paperback the same year. There was no US paperback of that first edition. Nevertheless he dropped his day-job when offered the original US deal for the book, becoming a freelance writer.

A revised and updated second edition, its title reversed to become *The Art of Bob Dylan: Song & Dance Man*, was published in simultaneous hardback and paperback in the UK in 1981 and US 1982. After this he wrote the occasional piece for the fanzine *The Telegraph*, and in 1987 came *All Across the Telegraph: A Bob Dylan Handbook*, the first best-of selection from the magazine, co-edited by Gray and JOHN BAULDIE. By then Gray had also written the rather less useful *Mother! The Frank Zappa Story*, and in 1996 co-authored *The Elvis Atlas: A Journey Through Elvis Presley's America*. He continued to write on music, and on travel, mostly for UK national newspapers, including obituaries of rock'n'roll stars for *The Guardian*.

However, he spent most of the 1990s writing a third and final edition of his Dylan litcrit study, this time titled *Song & Dance Man III: The Art of Bob Dylan*. This is over 900 pages long and includes a 112-page study of Dylan's use of the blues (especially of pre-war blues lyric poetry), and was published in the UK two weeks before the end of the

20th century and in the US in March 2000. The book's two strengths are felt to lie in the critical assessments of individual songs and the depth of research into Dylan's sources.

Gray then began giving talks on Dylan's work ('Bob Dylan and the History of Rock'n'Roll' and 'Bob Dylan and the Poetry of the Blues'), and in 2001 was invited to deliver one at Hibbing Public Library, where he told a variegated audience of Dylan's hometown citizens that they were wrong to keep ignoring and minimising Dylan's achievement, especially since their town had been so formative an influence upon him.

Michael Gray is also the author of the present volume, and of the first full biography of BLIND WILLIE McTELL, the forthcoming *Hand Me My Travelin' Shoes*.

[*Song & Dance Man: The Art of Bob Dylan*, London, Hart-Davis, MacGibbon, 1972 and Abacus Books (paperback), 1973; New York: E.P. Dutton, 1973; Tokyo: Shobun-Sha, 1973. *The Art of Bob Dylan: Song & Dance Man*, London: Hamlyn, 1981; New York: St. Martin's Press, 1982. *Mother! The Frank Zappa Story*, London: Proteus, 1985. *All Across the Telegraph: A Bob Dylan Handbook* (co-editor with John Bauldie), London: W.H. Allen, 1987 & Fontana Paperbacks 1988. *The Elvis Atlas: A Journey Through Elvis Presley's America* (co-author with Roger Osborne), New York: Henry Holt, 1996. *Song & Dance Man III: The Art of Bob Dylan*, London: Cassell, 1999 (reprints Continuum, 2000–2005); New York: Continuum, 2000. *Hand Me My Travelin' Shoes: In the Footsteps of Blind Willie McTell*, London: Bloomsbury, 2007.]

Green, Al [1946 -] Al Greene [sic] was born on a farm outside Forrest City, Arkansas, on April 13, 1946 but grew up in Grand Rapids, Michigan, 'raised on the sound of SAM COOKE and the Soul Stirrers' (Cook added an 'e'; Greene took one away) and singing from an early age with the Greene Brothers Quartet, then the Creations and the Soul Mates, who in 1967 had a top 5 R&B hit, 'Back Up Train'. Touring through Texas he met up with producer and songwriter Willie Mitchell, who pointed Greene to Memphis and the Hi label in 1969, and a collaboration that stretched over the next eight years and included co-writer and drummer Al Jackson Jr. A string of hit singles resulted, achieved by crossbreeding Stax with Barry White, sometimes hitting big in the US pop as well as R&B charts, as with the double no.1 'Let's Stay Together' in 1972.

On October 18, 1974 Al Green was taking a shower when his girlfriend came in and threw either boiling water or, with a more southern touch, boiling *grits* all over him before running to an adjacent room and shooting herself dead. This was a factor in turning Green's thoughts to God, in whose service he duly became a minister, acquiring the Pentecostal Hale Road Full Gospel Tabernacle Church in Memphis while continuing to record. For some time, starting with *The Belle Album* in 1977, he concentrated on religious material, and spent most of the period from then until the end of the 1990s singing and recording and preaching on Sundays; but he reverted to secular songs on July 24, 1984 when, at a brief session at the suitably named Intergalactic Studio in New York City, he and Bob Dylan came together to record three numbers, none of which has been released, though two have circulated amongst Dylan collectors. Backed by Al Green's band, along with RON WOOD on guitar and a Steve Potts on drums, and perhaps with CAROLYN DENNIS singing too, the three tracks were 'Honey Wait', 'Mountain of Love' and the Donny Fritts & Troy Seals songs 'We Had It All'. A thick fog surrounds the facts about this session but it seems that Dylan takes the lead vocal on 'Honey Wait', which may be his own composition, and that Al Green takes lead vocal on the others.

It was an unlikely partnership, except that Dylan had always been interested in soul music, and Green, who parlayed an insinuatingly slinky, ineffably 1970s sound, was undeniably a consequential figure on the Memphis scene. If Bishop Tutu could sing soul, and used the band behind Ruby & the Romantics on 'Our Day Will Come', he would sound like Al Green.

Perhaps even prompted by the encounter with Dylan, Al Green returned to the secular world soon afterwards, reuniting with Willie Mitchell in 1986, recording a top 40 duet with Annie Lennox in 1988 ('Put a Little Love in Your Heart') and in 2003 he signed to Blue Note and released a well-received secular soul comeback album, *I Can't Stop*, followed in 2005 by *Everything's OK*.

[Al Green: 'Let's Stay Together', Hi 2202, US, 1972; *The Belle Album*, Hi *nia*, US, 1977, CD-reissued re-mastered Hi 160, UK, 2000; *I Can't Stop*, Blue Note, US, 2003; *Everything's OK*, US, 2005.]

Green, Keith [1953 - 1982] Keith Green, born in Brooklyn, New York, on October 21, 1953, grew up in a religious Jewish family, learnt to play ukulele and piano, wrote songs from the age of nine, obtained a record deal from Decca at the age of 11, appeared on 'The Jack Benny Show' and got dubbed 'a pre-pubescent dreamboat' by *Time* magazine, became the youngest-ever member of ASCAP (the American Society of Composers, Authors and Publishers), played Kurt Von Trapp in a Broadway production of *The Sound of Music*, got displaced as media Boy Heartthrob by Donny Osmond, ran away from home at 15, pursued drugs, sex and Eastern mysticism, married at 20 and then at 21, through the evangelistic efforts of Christian singer-songwriter Randy Stonehill, became a Born Again Christian. As it says on his widow's website, in 1975 '. . . he proudly told the world, "I'm a Jewish Christian."'

Green's songwriting and musicianship took off in this new ardent direction and in 1977 he and his wife Melody were living in the suburbs in the San Fernando Valley, where they became involved with the Vineyard Fellowship. Greens' official website seems to have written the Fellowship out of the story. At any rate, Keith was soon 'discipling 70 believers' making a solo album, *For Him Who Has Ears to Hear*, which Dylan is said to have liked, and which prefigured what is now known as Contemporary Christian Rock. In 1979 Green and Dylan met through the Vineyard Fellowship, but later that year Green and his family, plus about 20 followers, moved their ministry base to 140 acres around Lindale, in East Texas ('where many martyrs fell,' as Dylan has it), and established the suitably apocalyptic-sounding Last Days Ministries.

In or around March 1980 Dylan went into Mama Jo's, a North Hollywood studio, to play harmonica on Green's track 'Pledge My Head to Heaven', on which REGINA McCRARY's sisters Linda and Charity are backing singers and on which Green sounds like a buoyant young ELTON JOHN. This was duly released even more obscurely than *For Him Who Has Ears*, on Green's album *So You Wanna Go Back to Egypt?* in December 1980, on Pretty Good Records ('a Division of Last Days Ministries'). This LP contains a booklet with song lyrics, notes by Green and a back cover drawing of the musicians, including Dylan. A remix, with Dylan's previously prominent harmonica almost suppressed by an electric guitar, was issued on Green's posthumous album *I Only Want to See You There* in 1983; the original mix was then reissued on *Keith Green: The Ministry Years Vol. 1: 1977–79* in 1987 (again an LP) and on CD two years later.

Green made two other albums in his own lifetime, *No Compromise* (1978) and *Songs for the Shepherd* (1982). Among his many songs 'You Put This Love in My Heart', 'Your Love Broke Through', 'O Lord You're Beautiful' and 'Grace by Which I Stand' are now said to be 'enduring classics that have been recorded by many of today's top artists.'

'In seven short years of knowing Jesus,' it says here, 'the Lord took Keith from concert crowds of 20 or less to stadiums of 12,000 people who came to hear only him. His recordings were chart topping [?] and when he began to give his recordings away for whatever people could afford, some misunderstood. His views were often controversial but never boring. Television and radio appearances became the norm. Still, Keith's heart was to please the Lord and build His kingdom, not his own.'

Green and two of his children—three-year-old Josiah David and two-year-old Bethany Grace—died when the heavily overloaded small plane leased to Last Days Ministries for his touring crashed just after sunset within a minute of take-off outside Lindale on July 28, 1982, also killing the Greens' friends the Smalleys and their six children, who were visiting, and the pilot. Melody Green now runs the ministry from Oceanside, California; the Texas site has been acquired by the Teen Mania Ministry. Only in America . . .

[Keith Green: *For Him Who Has Ears to Hear*, Sparrow, US, 1977; *So You Wanna Go Back to Egypt?*, Pretty Good PGR-1, US (Last Day Ministries BIRD 139, UK), Dec 1980; CD-reissued Sparrow PGD 5431, US, 1990; 'Pledge My Head to Heaven' (incl. Bob Dylan) re-mix reissued *I Only Want to See You There*, Sparrow SPR 1066, US, 1983; original mix reissued *Keith Green: The Ministry Years Vol. 1: 1977–79*, Sparrow SPD 1146, US, 1987 (LP) & Sparrow SPD 1558R, US (G2 7243 8515582 6, Holland), 1999; *No Compromise*, *nia*, CD-reissued Sparrow, 1990; *Songs for the Shepherd*, *nia*. Melody Green & David Hazard, *No Compromise: The Life Story of Keith Green*, Eugene, OR: Harvest House, 2000 (2nd edn.), available through the Last Days Ministries website, from which come all quotes above, seen online 3 Jan 2006 at *www.lastdaysministries.org*, except the 'prepubescent dreamboat', at *www.cbn.com/cbnmusic/artists/green_keith.asp*. Additional detail from Wikipedia & 'Searching for a Gem'.]

Greenbriar Boys, the The Greenbriar Boys were top of the bill and Dylan their support act at Gerde's Folk City when ROBERT SHELTON gave him that famous rave review in the *New York Times* in September 1961, helping to speed his being signed by JOHN HAMMOND to Columbia Records. As Dylan notes in *Chronicles Volume One*, 'It was unusual because I was the second act on the bill and The Greenbriar Boys were hardly mentioned.'

The Greenbriar Boys were a bluegrass group formed in 1958, their name taken from the song 'The Girl on the Greenbriar Shore'. They were semi-revivalists, much like THE NEW LOST CITY RAMBLERS, though with a more 'progressive' approach and less of an inclination towards replicating Old Timey records from the 1920s. (Bob Dylan once offered this jokey comparison: 'The Greenbriar Boys: the best country group in the city. The New Lost City Ramblers: the best city group in the country.')

With exceptional playing by JOHN HERALD on flat-pick guitar and sweet vocals, BOB YELLIN on banjo and RALPH RINZLER on mandolin, the Greenbriar Boys helped bridge the canyons between rural southern bluegrass and the early-1960s folk scene. (Buddy Pendleton also played violin with the Greenbriar Boys on some of their 1961 gigs.) They became the first touring bluegrass group comprised of north-easterners, but their repertoire was wider than that, and came from Library of Congress field recordings, minstrel shows, gospel, Nashville and even Tin Pan Alley.

With Yellin and Herald, ERIC WEISSBERG had also been, on violin, a founding member of the Greenbriar Boys (it was his mother who'd thought up their name), but he had defected to the Tarriers in 1959. He was replaced first by Paul Prestopino (who defected to the Chad Mitchell Trio) and then by Ralph Rinzler.

In 1962 the group accompanied JOAN BAEZ on two songs on her second LP ('Pal of Mine' and 'The Banks of the Ohio') and toured with her, signed to Vanguard Records and made their eponymously titled début album. Three further albums followed: *Ragged but Right!*, 1964, *Dian & the Greenbriar Boys*, 1965 (backing one Dian James, a singer in the Molly O'Day mountain singing tradition) and *Better Late Than Never* in 1966. But Rinzler left the group, replaced by bluegrass mandolinist and singer Frank Wakefield and fiddle player Jim Buchanan. Their arrangement of Mike Nesmith's 'Different Drum' became a hit by Linda Ronstadt in 1967, the year the Greenbriar Boys disbanded. In the 1980s there was a brief reunion for an appearance at the Philadelphia Folk Festival and a few concerts, including one at Carnegie Recital Hall.

Ralph Rinzler died in 1994; John Herald committed suicide in 2005. Bob Yellin, aged 70, is still around.

[Bob Dylan, *Chronicles Volume One*, p.278. The Greenbriar Boys: *Best of the Vanguard Years*, CD, Vanguard, US, 2002, well complemented by *Big Apple Bluegrass*, Vanguard 2003. Dylan on Greenbriars cf. Ramblers, quoted *Young Bob: John Cohen's Early Photographs of Bob Dylan*, powerHouse Books, 2003, p.7. Additional information from Bob Yellin, phone call from this writer 2 Nov 2005.]

Greenwood, MS, Dylan's visit to Dylan went to Mississippi at the beginning of July 1963, at the height of the civil rights struggle. He went with THEODORE BIKEL and PETE SEEGER for a rally organised by the Student Non-violent Co-ordinating Committee. On July 6, three miles outside Greenwood, they and THE FREEDOM SINGERS performed to around 250 black farm-workers and 25 young whites and media people. Dylan, bravely, sang 'Only a Pawn in Their Game'. A tantalising fragment is included in D.A. PENNEBAKER's film *Don't Look Back* (Leacock-Pennebaker, US, 1967). The visit was reported in the small news item 'Northern Folk Singers Help Out at Negro Festival in Mississippi', *New York Times*, July 7, 1963, in which 'Only a Pawn in Their Game' was singled out and cited for its theme. Yet Dylan was identified as 'Bobby Dillon', a 'local singer'. The event is well documented in ROBERT SHELTON's 1986 biography of Dylan, *No Direction Home*.

Gregg, Bobby [1929/30 -] Robert J. Gregg was born in Philadelphia in either 1929 or 1930. By 1955 he was the only white musician playing with an obscure and struggling black group called Steve Gibson & the Red Caps (an offshoot of the Romaines). He plays as second drummer alongside Henry Tucker Green on their September 23, 1955 RCA session and recording 'Free Hearted', 'Always', 'How I Cry' and 'Bobbin' with them, and remained with them through a label switch to ABC-Paramount and on through further sessions till 1959 or 1960. He seems to have become a house drummer for Cameo-Parkway in the very early 1960s too, playing behind hit acts of theirs like the Orlons, Dee Dee Sharp and Bobby Rydell (as did bass player Joe Macho Jr., who would also later do Dylan sessions) and fronting his own outfit, Bobby Gregg and His Friends, on at least two 1962 instrumental singles on their subsidiary Cotton label: 'The Jam', which reached the US top 30 (and was later re-issued on Columbia) and, including the then-unknown guitar wizard Roy Buchanan, 'Potato Peeler', the first item ever to capture Buchanan's developed innovative guitar-work. In 1963, on a major label, Columbia's sister imprint Epic, Gregg released his own album, *Let's Stomp and Wild Weekend*, which rather sounds as if it should have been two LPs rather than one. He was producing records in this period too, sometimes working with the jazz original Sun Ra to make R&Bish pop singles. One was 'Marlene' and 'Do You Still Care for Me?' by Richard Popcorn Wylie, which Gregg produced, with Sun Ra on piano; Gregg played drums on one of the two tracks. He was still making singles under his own name, playing with Sun Ra's musicians, in this period too: 'Any Number Can Win', 'MacDougal Street' and 'It's Good to Me' were all released on Epic around 1964, and in 1965, on Veep, came 'Charly Ba-Ba'.

There was a connection between Gregg, these jazzers and producer TOM WILSON, and with or without a parallel link through AL KOOPER, this led to Gregg playing for Dylan—and at an absolutely crucial period.

Bobby Gregg became the drummer on both Dylan's 1965 albums (*Bringing It All Back Home* and *Highway 61 Revisited*), and in concert took over from LEVON HELM when Helm quit the Hawks and the pressure of playing with Dylan that November. Gregg played on the ten Dylan concerts from December 1 in Seattle through to the 19th in Santa Monica. It's remarkable that Dylan, Gregg and the rest of the Hawks were recording in a New York studio on November 30—and the following night they were playing a concert 3,000 miles away in Seattle.

Gregg's first Dylan work was unfortunate, though. In Dylan's absence, in December 1964, Gregg was among those brought in by Tom Wilson to overdub backings onto Dylan's début album track 'House of the Rising Sun' (this unhappy amalgam was released in 1995 on the *Highway 61 Interactive* CD-ROM, with packaging that implied that the whole recording had been made back in 1961) and onto three tracks from the *Freewheelin'* sessions, 'Mixed Up Confusion', 'Rocks and Gravel' and 'Corrina Corrina', all of which had to have their original backing tracks removed for the benefit of this futile exercise.

Bobby Gregg first worked *with* Dylan, and more positively, on the afternoon session of January 14, 1965, the first session with an electric group—and it yielded 'Love Minus Zero/No Limit', 'Subterranean Homesick Blues', 'She Belongs to Me' and 'Bob Dylan's 115th Dream'. He didn't take part in the evening session (which was drummerless, used the odd combo of JOHN HAMMOND JR., JOHN SEBASTIAN and the shadowy 'John Boone'—who was probably Steve Boone, Sebastian's bassist—along with Dylan and BRUCE LANGHORNE, and provided nothing for the album) but Gregg was back the next day, January 15, for the session that produced, in addition to several solo tracks, the electric numbers 'Maggie's Farm' and 'On the Road Again' used on the album, plus various takes of that radical yet playful song 'If You Gotta Go, Go Now', one version of which was issued as a European single later that year and another issued on *Bootleg Series Vols. 1–3* in 1991. *Bringing It All Back Home* was issued on March 22, 1965.

When Dylan stepped out at the NEWPORT FOLK FESTIVAL that July, he used none of the musicians from the album. By then, though, he had already begun recording *Highway 61 Revisited*, and for this, beginning with two mid-June sessions produced by Tom Wilson, many of the *Bringing It All Back Home* session-men were back, including Gregg. He, therefore, is the man who provides that opening snare-drum shot indelibly marked on the brains of at least one generation as signalling the start of 'Like a Rolling Stone'. Not surprisingly he kept the gig for the rest of the sessions and is the only drummer on this seminal album.

At that November 30 session, when Gregg was back in the studios with Dylan, Al Kooper and the Helm-less Hawks, it was to play on the early, exploratory proto-*Blonde on Blonde* session that produced a number of fast versions of 'Visions of Johanna' (one of which was released 40 years later on *Bootleg Series Vol. 7—No Direction Home: The Soundtrack*), and a number of takes of 'Can You Please Crawl Out Your Window?', the last of which was issued as the follow-up single to 'Positively 4th Street'. (Gregg, like Kooper, also recorded with Tom Rush that year, on his album *Take a Little Walk with Me*; later Gregg would play on the 1967 hit by Keith, '98.6', and work with PAUL SIMON, John Cale and others.)

Gregg's last Dylan session was late into the night of January 27, 1966, at which he played alongside Dylan, Kooper, ROBBIE ROBERTSON and RICK DANKO and which yielded the version of 'I'll Keep It With Mine' on the *Bootleg Series Vols. 1–3*. They also made unsuccessful attempts at 'Leopard-Skin Pill Box Hat' and 'One of Us Must Know (Sooner or Later)'. When Dylan and the still Helm-less Hawks went back out on the road to start the long, gruelling and transcendent 1966 tour, Gregg had been replaced, first by SANDY KONIKOFF and later by MICKEY JONES.

Gregg had to content himself with playing on that year's *The Peter, Paul & Mary Album*, which was still offering songs like 'Kisses Sweeter Than Wine', and on which quite clearly he'd been asked to play the drums as quietly as humanly possible. It must have been one of the most mortifying comedowns in human experience.

[Bobby Gregg & His Friends: 'The Jam Pt 1' c/w 'The Jam Pt 2', Cotton 1003, US, 1962 & Columbia 4825, US 1963? ('The Jam Pt 1' reissued on the compilation *Cameo Parkway 1957–1967*, ABKCO, 2005); 'Potato Peeler' c/w 'Sweet Georgia Brown', Cotton 1006, 1962; *Let's Stomp and Wild Weekend*, Epic BN-26051, US, 1963; 'Charly Ba-Ba' c/w 'Hullabaloo', Veep 1207, 1965. Steve Gibson & the Red Caps: 'Bless You' c/w 'I Miss You So', Rose 5534, US, 1959. Steve Gibson & the Original Redcaps: 'Where Are You' c/w 'San Antone Rose', Casa Blanca 5505 & Hunt 330, US, 1959. Red Caps and Sun Ra/Epic singles data mostly from, respectively, Marv Goldberg: 'The Red Caps', at *http://home.att.net/~marvy42/Redcaps/redcaps.html* and Ed Bland (arranger-bandleader on the cited sessions): 'Personal Recollections of Sun Ra 1956–1967', 24 Aug 2005, *www.jazzinchicago.org/Internal/Articles/tabid/43/ctl/ArticleView/mid/522/articleId/410/PersonalRecollectionsofSunRa19561967.aspx*, both seen online 21 Nov 2005.]

Griffin, Paul [1937 - 2000] Paul Griffin was born on August 6, 1937 in Harlem, where he studied the local organist's work at Paradise Baptist Church and then classical music, gaining a place at New York's High School of Music and Art, from which he graduated in 1953, and playing first viola in the All-City Orchestra. Nonetheless, he found himself having to work as a cutter in the garment district and delivering groceries for a supermarket before getting an usher's job at the legendary Apollo Theater in Harlem, where he was allowed to play piano now and then, and was 'discovered' by sax player King Curtis, for whom he toured and recorded.

In 1960 he began playing on sessions, playing in the Scepter Records house band but also working with producers like Bert Berns, for whom he eventually played on the historic VAN MORRISON Bang sessions. He became a top keyboards player whose work on organ and piano spanned a vast number of recordings, including albums and singles by Aretha Franklin, the Shirelles, the Isley Brothers (he's on 'Twist and Shout'), Cissy Houston, Solomon Burke, Garnett Mimms, Irma Franklin, Dionne Warwick and many more; he plays that organ part on Chuck Jackson's 'Any Day Now', yet also plays the piano on B.J. Thomas' 'Raindrops Keep Falling on My Head'. Later he played on Don McLean's 'American Pie' and for PAUL SIMON, PETER, PAUL & MARY, IAN & SYLVIA, Eric Andersen, Tom Rush, Carly Simon and John Denver. In the 1970s he began a long association with Steely Dan, which included co-writing 'The Fez' and scat singing on 'Peg' and lasted right through to Donald Fagen's 1993 solo album *Kamkiriad*.

Of infinitely greater importance is that Paul Griffin plays on *Bringing It All Back Home*, *Highway 61 Revisited*, *Blonde on Blonde* and *Blood on the Tracks*.

On *Bringing It All Back Home*, on piano, he played only on the session of January 14, 1965, the first session with an electric group—but it was the session that yielded 'Love Minus Zero/No Limit', 'Subterranean Homesick Blues', 'She Belongs to Me' and 'Bob Dylan's 115th Dream'. Griffin was more audible on *Highway 61 Revisited*. He was brought in on the second session, on June 16, 1965: the one that delivered 'Like a Rolling Stone'—on which he moved across from organ to piano, thus letting AL KOOPER onto the organ, with historic results. Then Griffin was brought back in for the late July to early August 1965 sessions, when BOB JOHNSTON took over from TOM WILSON as the producer. Griffin plays piano on the morning session on July 29, and may play on the next day's session too. More certainly he plays again on the session of August 2 and August 4. On the first of these, therefore, he's the pianist on the album track 'Tombstone Blues' (and on the alternate takes of this and three other tracks issued 40 years later on the *Bootleg Series Vol. 7—No Direction Home: The Soundtrack*). Next day he plays on the album cut of 'From a Buick 6', the alternate take issued on the Japanese album, and on the version of 'Can You Please Crawl Out Your Window?' issued mislabelled as 'Positively 4th Street' that September.

On the marvellously productive August 2 session, Griffin again plays piano throughout, and so appears on the album on 'Highway 61 Revisited', 'Ballad of a Thin Man', 'Just Like Tom Thumb's Blues' and 'Queen Jane Approximately', contributing particularly lovely piano-work on these latter two. It's one of the eternal depths of the album that Dylan's radical songs and challenging voice are pitched against the lyrical warmth of the piano on these tracks: piano-work that is never soft but exudes a touching romantic optimism. This Dylan masterpiece would not sound the same without Paul Griffin.

He returned to the studios for just one day during the recording of *Blonde on Blonde*: on January 25, 1966 in New York City, when he joined ROBBIE ROBERTSON, RICK DANKO, Al Kooper, BOBBY GREGG and WILLIAM E. LEE to play the cascading, gospel-meets-Liszt piano part on 'One of Us Must Know (Sooner or Later)': a part whose audible presence has varied enormously in the various different mixes on Columbia's many attempts at re-releasing *Blonde on Blonde* properly since the original 1966 vinyl issue. Music journalist Jonathan Singer wrote this about the piano part you're supposed to be able to hear:

> 'Griffin gives the song its tragic depth—and height. He picks his way sensitively through the verses; but at other times, he prowls beneath the words with judgement and an ominous gospel lick that he stokes until he has climbed to the verse's peak. At the chorus, Griffin unleashes a symphony; hammering his way up and down the keyboard, half GERSHWIN, half gospel, all heart. The follow-up, a killer left hand figure that links the chorus to the verse, releases none of the song's tension. Then, on the last chorus, not content to repeat the same brilliant part, Griffin's playing . . . so completely embodies the lyric, that he enters into some other dimension. For several seconds, on one of Dylan's best songs, Griffin makes Dylan seem almost earthbound.'

He returned to the studios with Dylan almost ten years later to participate more briefly in the recording of that other masterwork, *Blood on the Tracks*, this time playing organ. On the second New York session, on September 17, 1974, he plays on the outtake of 'You're a Big Girl Now' later released on *Biograph* (1985) and on the album versions of 'Shelter from the Storm' and 'You're Gonna Make Me Lonesome When You Go'.

Session-work dried up for Griffin from the early 1980s onwards, and though he made a living from jingles and teaching, he lived the last years of his life modestly in the Bronx, one of the unsung true heroes of music history.

Paul Griffin, who suffered latterly from diabetes, died of a heart attack at home in New York while awaiting a liver transplant, on June 14, 2000.

[Sources include 'Paul Griffin' by Jonathan Singer, Mar 4, 1999, pub'd *New York Daily News* Mar 1999, online at *www.steelydan.com/griffin.html*, 27 Jan 2006; ditto *www.soulwalking.co.uk/Respect2.html* and *http://elvispelvis.com/paulgriffin.htm*.]

Griffith, Nanci [1954 -] Nanci Caroline Griffith was born in Seguin, Texas, on July 6, 1954, the daughter of a publisher who sang in barbershop quartets and a mother who was a real estate agent and amateur actress. She taught herself to play guitar by watching a PBS television series and started writing songs because she found it easier than learning other people's. Her first paid gig was at age 14, in Austin, Texas, where she later studied education at the university and then taught small children before committing herself to a career in music in 1977.

Her folkie 1978 début album, *There's a Light Beyond These Woods*, on a local label, was followed in 1982 by *Poet in My Window* (on another local label), on which one track featured her father and his barbershop quartet. In 1985 came her third album, *Once in a Very Blue Moon*, on a label with national distribution, and with the backing musicians who would duly form her Blue Moon Orchestra, with which she played for over a decade. In 1986 came *Last of the True Believers* (and the re-release of her first two albums) and she moved to Nashville. Another label upgrade brought *Lone Star State of Mind*, released in 1987, which included an early cover version of the Julie Gold song 'From a Distance', a song from which many people never feel at a sufficient distance yet which gave Nanci Griffith her first career breakthrough, since when she has built strong followings with further albums and widespread touring. She is especially popular in Ireland.

After featuring big-name guests on 1989's album *Storms*, duetting with Phil EVERLY, recording 'The Wexford Carol' for the Chieftains' 1991 album *The Bells of Dublin*, in 1993 came an album entirely comprised of other singer-songwriters' material, *Other Voices Other Rooms*, the artistic coup of which was that on 'Boots of Spanish Leather', she persuaded its composer to overdub a harmonica part onto her recording. Dylan added his undistinguished part at his home studio in Malibu at some time in the summer of 1992; the album was released the following March.

It was the second small professional connection between them; the first had been at the beginning of the same year—when Griffith had been among the many big-name backing singers bellowing along with the super-sized band ranged behind Dylan on his suitably bemused performance of 'Like a Rolling Stone' at the 'Late Night with David Letterman' 10th Anniversary Show, recorded that January 18 and televised February 6.

In 1998 Nanci Griffith released a follow-up album, *Other Voices, Too*, and published a 'companion' book, *Nanci Griffith's Other Voices: A Personal History of Folk Music*, since when she has continued her demure career.

[Nanci Griffith (with Bob Dylan): 'Boots of Spanish Leather', Malibu 1992, *Other Voices Other Rooms*, Elektra CD-61464, US, 1993. Nanci Griffith, *Nanci Griffith's Other Voices: A Personal History of Folk Music*, New York: Three Rivers Press, 1998.]

Grisman, David [1945 -] David Grisman was born in Hackensack, New Jersey, on March 23, 1945, the son of a professional trombonist. He learnt piano, loved rock'n'roll, discovered folk music, and at 15 met RALPH RINZLER: 'and that turned everything around.' He grew up to be the defining bluegrass mandolin player of his generation, playing in the Even Dozen Jug Band in the early 1960s (with MARIA MULDAUR, then Maria D'Amato, and JOHN SEBASTIAN, among others), and with them made his first record, in 1963. He played on a Folkways session by Red Allen & Frank Wakefield the same year, and in 1965–66 was briefly in Frank Wakefield & the Kentuckians. In the late 1960s he joined the rock group Earth Opera with Peter Rowan, and in 1973 both joined with JERRY GARCIA, John Kahn and Vassar Clements to form the short-lived but ultra-successful Old and in the Way, whose eponymously titled album remained for decades afterwards the biggest-selling bluegrass album ever made. From 1974 to 1975 Grisman was also in the all-instrumentals group the Great American Music Band, and in 1975 formed the David Grisman Quintet, which has kept going, in between other projects, ever since. Grisman's early fusions with Django Reinhart-style jazz led to the creation of the 'newgrass' genre, and in 1977 he made the solo album *Hot Dawg* ('Dawg' being the nickname given him by Garcia in 1973), which featured his jazz-violinist hero Stephane Grappelli, and which was followed in 1981 by *Stephane Grappelli and David Grisman Live*.

During Dylan's fall 1980 tour, Grisman came on stage in Portland, Oregon, on December 4, playing mandolin on 'To Ramona'—though Dylan had hoped he'd play on the traditional 'Mary from the Wild Moor' earlier in the set. Introducing that song, Dylan told the audience:

> 'We're gonna play a real old song here that I used to play before I wrote any songs. People always want to hear old songs: well this is real old. Anyway it's like when—there's a musician friend of mine here tonight, David Grisman. I don't know if you ever heard of him. Well he's playing in town someplace else: you go see him if you get a chance to. He's playing tomorrow night. We wanted him to play on this song but can't seem to find him. Anybody know where he is? But it'll be too late by that time. He can't play on the next one. Anyway, this is called "Mary from the Wild Moor".'

Six songs later, ahead of 'To Ramona', he announced: 'David Grisman actually did show up! So he's gonna play with us on this song.' After it, Dylan added: 'You go see his band now! I can't remember where he's playing but he is playing.'

He still is.

[David Grisman: *Hot Dawg*, A&M Horizon SP-731, US, 1979. Grisman & Grappelli: *Grappelli-Grisman Live* Warner Bros BSK-3550, US, 1981. Even Dozen Jug Band: *Jug Band Music and Rags*, Elektra EKS-7246, US, 1963. Red Allen and the Kentuckians: *Bluegrass Country*, Country 704, US, 1965; *Red Allen*, Country 710, 1966. Earth Opera: *Earth Opera* Elektra EKS-74016, US, 1968; *Great American Eagle Tragedy* Elektra EKS-75010, 1969. Old and in the Way: *Old and in the Way*, Round RX-103, US, 1975. David Grisman Quintet: *David Grisman Quintet*, Kaleidoscope F-5, US, 1977.]

'The Groom's Still Waiting at the Altar' [1981] 'The Groom's Still Waiting at the Altar' was recorded at the *Shot of Love* sessions of early May 1981 but issued initially only as the B-side of the 'Heart of Mine' single (and only in the US); it was later reissued on the *Biograph* box set in 1985 and subsequently built back into the *Shot of Love* album itself: the first instance of such a revision in Dylan's canon.

Written in 1980 and emerging in the later part of the Gospel Period, the song returns us towards the Dylanesque chaos of an earlier era, even though the fundamental structure of the song is a thoroughly conventional R&B/blues one, and even though the lyrics still keep the Bible close at hand. Christ is the bridegroom and the bride for whom he waits is the Church, representing the Christian faithful. The analogy is drawn by John the Baptist, who says in John 3:28–29: 'I am not the Christ, but that I am sent before him. He that hath the bride is the bridegroom: but the friend of the bridegroom, which standeth and heareth him, rejoiceth greatly . . .' Yet what's appealing and interesting here is not the scriptural bewailing of people's fecklessness, nor the declamatory global sweep of Dylan's customary 'look! the apocalypse is coming!', as given in the choruses of the song, but the chaotic absurdity both of the visions glimpsed and of the poetry that makes them, along with the directed energy of the performance: the pacing, shuddering expressiveness of the vocal, breathing in hot pursuit of the listener across the switchback longs and shorts of the verses and the punching ups and downs of the chorus melody. The hooks on which are hung both the craziness of vision and the tour-de-force performance are the song's extremes of variation in line length and its deranged, rule-breaking rhymes. Set against the conventional regularity of the music, these two delirious elasticities contract and expand the possibilities of structure like a mad concertina banging about inside an old, familiar cardboard box.

The only solidly inevitable rhyme is, aptly, that of 'altar' with 'Gibraltar'. All the others are unpredictable, switching between 'da *da* da' and '*da* da da' line endings ('to *want* me' and '*snob*bery', for instance), occasionally pushed to a '*da* da da da', as in '*ob*ligated') and ranging restlessly between the orderliness of 'order' and 'border' and the purring blur of 'to haunt me' and 'to want me'; between ragged half rhymes like 'humiliated' and 'obligated'—pushing snatched raggedness to the limit in putting 'cement' with 'innocent' and 'nauseated' with 'deteriorated'—and the jokingly precise and splendid 'temperature' and 'furniture'; and between the simplicity of 'to leap it' and 'to keep it', the tiny sneakiness of 'sent to me' and 'meant to be' and the take-a-bow outrageousness of the last verse's last rhyme—the incomparable pairing of 'January' and 'Buenos Aires'.

Matching these elastic contortions, the variations in line length, over which Dylan's ever-resourceful delivery triumphs, careen between the *nine* syllables of one verse's first line and the *18* syllables of another's.

These technical crimes and jokes of accomplishment fit the visions of the lyric. If the opening verse vividly evokes the bizarre grogginess of waking up, half-knowing where you are—'Prayed in the ghetto with my face in the cement / Heard the last moan of a boxer, seen the massacre of the innocent / Felt around for the light switch . . .'—this surreal uncertainty, as to how things are and how they feel, is not dispelled but intensified by waking to daytime consciousness. 'Put your hand on my head, baby, do I have a temperature?' is such a great, funny line: itself enacting feverishness in its hypochondriacal fretting rhythm; expressing such distance from the person it addresses yet doing so with the intimacy of wholly conversational cadences. It is a masterly line of conversational speech, in which 'baby' is for once used inspiredly, clinching the tone of easy familiarity while suggesting that the speaker may not actually know who he's talking to, while playing to the hilt the absurdity of being so out of touch with how you feel that you need someone else to feel your head to tell you (an absurdity not reduced by our recognition that we have all been there too). In doing these many things, the line also expresses the cry for help out of this chaos: a chaos of alienation that the speaker of the line knows he embodies as diseasedly as does the world around him.

It is, of course, a world of contradiction, polarity, violence and catastrophe, seething with nebulous omens and hopeless ambiguity. As so often, the modern locating detail is in bed with the timeless or ancient scene: in this case 'Cities on fire' (which might be of biblical antiquity) and 'phones out of order'. The same verse reverberates with the contemporary hell of South and Central American war zones in which the CIA funds the murder squads. As in Guatemala in June 1980, around the time of the song's creation, 'They're killing nuns'; yet any suggestion that this is a world rational enough to let us hope that socio-political protest might be effective is at once undercut by the adding of 'and soldiers', which topsy-turvies any inferred what-could-be-worse-than-killing-nuns? rhetoric. Meanwhile the timelessness of 'Cities on fire' also prises away from that 'killing nuns' any limiting contemporariness it may have, so that we find underneath its layer of modernity reminders of far older religious wars—indeed wars so old that they were inevitably religious ones.

Psychic doom and physical brutality collide into fused imperatives. 'There's a wall between you and what you want and you got to leap it', Dylan sings, and as he sings it he puts up that wall between 'between you' and 'and what you want' with a pause, a vocal silence so solid you can hear that fevered head crash into it. The exhortation to act, ostensibly an affirmation of things decisive and positive, withers at once into the accompanying prediction of imminent failure. Even if you read the signs aright, and 'leap it' and 'take it', seizing the moment of 'tonight', what you gain still can't be held onto 'tomorrow'.

Under conditions like these, it comes as a surprise to the narrator—as something worth remarking on—when something works, when something happens as it could be expected to in an ordered world: 'Got the message this morning, the one that was sent to me', and Dylan follows this with the lovely lucidity of 'About the madness of becomin' what one was never meant to be.' It's typical of Dylan's intuitive intelligence that the song's only mention of 'madness' is here in its most rationally styled line.

Aside from the centrality of chaos, there is something else from a bygone Dylan era that reappears in 'The Groom's Still Waiting at the Altar', albeit briefly: a specific area of poetic focus that was at one time wonderfully prevalent in his work, and which, until it reappeared, you might not have known you'd missed. It belonged to a particular period: that of his early post-hobo songs, as he reminded us when, at Radio City Music Hall in 1988, early on in the Never-Ending Tour, he revisited 'With God on Our Side' for the first time in decades, and sang again those small lines 'The words fill my head / And fall to the floor.' The early New York City songs were full of things bouncing off the walls and floors and ceilings: full of walls and floors and ceilings bouncing with noises, and air and light bouncing and splitting and pounding like noise; air like walls and walls like air. It was a way of seeing—a recognisable supra-realism of his, and it yielded much evocative poetry:

'The night aimed shadows / Through the crossbar windows, / And the wind punched hard / To make the wall-siding sing' ('Walls of Red Wing'); 'When all at once the silent air / Split open from her soundin voice' ('Joan Baez in Concert, Part 2'); 'And the silent night will shatter / From the sounds inside my mind' ('One Too Many Mornings'); 'The morning breeze like a bugle blew / Against the drums of dawn' ('Lay Down Your Weary Tune'); 'As her thoughts pounded hard / Like the pierce of an arrow' ('Eternal Circle'); '. . . midnight's broken toll' and '. . . while the walls were tightening' ('Chimes of Freedom'); 'Crimson flames tied through my ears' ('My Back Pages'); 'Though the night ran swirling and whirling' ('I Don't Believe You'); 'the breeze yawns food' ('Some Other Kinds of Songs'); 'the breath of its broken walls / being smothered' (*11 Outlined Epitaphs*); 'Beneath a bare lightbulb the plaster did pound' ('Ballad in Plain D'); and 'The wind howls like a hammer' ('Love Minus Zero/No Limit').

By the time of this last example, framed as a simple simile, it is also a more consciously BAUDELAIREan equivalent of earlier successes like 'your baby's eyes . . . are tuggin' at your sleeve' ('Ballad of Hollis Brown') and that special Dylan vividness with images of people's mouths: 'people cheered with bloodshot grins' ('Long Ago, Far Away') and 'but you're smilin' inside out' ('Denise').

Later, he doesn't usually stray this way, perhaps because on the whole it's a very New York City apartment block feeling: it belongs in an environment no longer at the centre of Dylan's consciousness. It is a minor pleasure, therefore, to find a fair example of this specific poetic focus revisiting Dylan in the midst of 1985's 'When the Night Comes Falling from the Sky'—'That icy wind that's howling in your eye'—and a greater pleasure to savour, in the version of 'The Groom's Still Waiting at the Altar' printed in *Lyrics 1962–1985*, the marvellous 'She was walking down the hallway while the walls deteriorated.'

This is so powerful because it has such, well, corrosive concreteness, at the same time as such a strong nightmare mood. It's one of Dylan's most filmic lines—in fact reminiscent of Roman Polanski's early film *Repulsion* (starring Catherine Deneuve as a maddened Belgian manicurist), in which, in a scene that prefigures *Alien*, as the heroine-victim runs down a long passageway the plaster erupts out of shape: hands of plaster burst from the living walls, thrusting out to grab at her as she runs.

Words like 'deteriorated' are notoriously hard to use without bathos: Dylan manages it perfectly here because he brings the word alive, allowing it to shake with its onomatopoeic aptness—the way it sounds so crumbly—by highlighting its sheer weirdness of meaning.

Of the two relatively important differences between the text of 'The Groom's Still Waiting at the Altar' as given in print and as we hear it on the studio recording, the first is that on the record we lose the whole of that 'deteriorated' line, along with its less happy mate, 'Felt around for the lightswitch, became nauseated'. We gain instead a couplet that starts with the improved line 'Felt around for the lightswitch, felt around for her face' (such plain speaking, such tactile contrast, so strong an evocation of *groping*) but Dylan follows the extra vividness of that with the unduly lumbering 'Been treated like a farm animal on a wild goose chase', which, against all odds, is less of a line than the one we lose to it.

The other significant difference between the two versions of the song, and by far the more damaging, consists in what has happened to the words of the choruses. The performed version's consistent 'East of the Jordan, west of the rock of Gibraltar' is so tinkered about with in print that in five choruses, the line is given in three ways: 'East of . . . hard as,' 'West of . . . east of', 'West of . . . west of', 'West of . . . east of' again, and 'West of . . . west of' again. The next line gets similarly silly revision, the consistent 'I see the turning of the page' of the recorded version replaced by 'I see the burning of the page', '. . . burning of the stage', '. . . burning of the cage', '. . . burning of the stage' again, and '. . . burning of the page' again. Even the 'Curtain risin' on a new age' is altered, in the third chorus, to 'Curtain risin' on a new stage'. Whatever switches between notions of text and performance ('page' and 'stage') may be embedded here, they remain fiddlesome alterations in which there's no pattern, but only a mess, making clear how little any of them mean.

After such wilful reductionism, it comes as a relief that the song's other changes are insignificant.

One, indeed, is surely only an error of transcription: the text gives 'Mistake your shyness for aloofness, your shyness for snobbery' but should read 'Mistake your shyness for aloofness, your silence for snobbery'. This is mistaken shyness indeed. Meanwhile if anything, the published text's 'I'd a-done anything for that woman if she didn't make me feel so obligated' seems truer than the studio version's 'I'd a-done anything for that woman if she'd only made me feel obligated': but not true enough to matter one way or the other to the success of this gloriously seething, restive song.

Dylan himself felt it sufficiently compelling to give it live performances well ahead of recording it in the studio, introducing it in concert on November 13, 1980 (with CARLOS SANTANA on lead guitar) and reprising it two nights later when he brought MIKE BLOOMFIELD on stage to blaze away on the song's second outing, in what proved the last drama of that great guitarist's life.

['The Groom's Still Waiting at the Altar', LA, May 1981, Columbia 18-02510, US, 1981; & on *Biograph*, 1985 & *Shot of Love* CD reissues. 'The Groom's Still Waiting at the Altar' (live), San Francisco, 13 & 15 Nov 1980. *Repulsion*, dir. Roman Polanski; Compton/Tekli, UK, 1965.]

Gross, Michael [1952 -] Michael Gross was born on July 16, 1952 in New York City, where he continues to live and work. A slick, prolific journalist with a string of lucrative appointments on glossy magazines, he also turns out strongly commercial non-fiction books with enviable speed. These include *Model: The Ugly Business of Beautiful Women* (1995), a 'generational biography of the baby boom', *My Generation* (2000), and *740 Park: The Story of the World's Richest Apartment Building* (2005). His next will be on 'another great institution of the American aristocracy, the Metropolitan Museum of Art.' But before he locked into all this Manhattan money, he 'produced' a book on Dylan, *Bob Dylan: An Illustrated History*, back in 1978 when Dylan books did not yet constitute an industry.

If 'produced' seems an odd word, it covered an odd arrangement: the title page declared that this was 'Produced by Michael Gross with a text by Robert Alexander'; yet poor Robert didn't get his name on the cover or the spine, the back-cover blurb attributes the 'sensitive, thorough text' to Gross himself and the whole thing was copyrighted *by* Gross. For most people, this didn't matter, because the striking feature of the book was its collection of photographs, some previously unseen and many rather beautiful.

Not to be confused with ALAN RINZLER's *Bob Dylan: The Illustrated Record*, Gross' book has not been republished and did not do much for this writer's subsequently Dylan-free career. Nor, of course, for Robert Alexander's.

[Michael Gross, *Bob Dylan: An Illustrated History*, New York: Grosset & Dunlap 1978; *Model: The Ugly Business of Beautiful Women*, New York: Morrow, 1995; *My Generation*, New York: Cliff Street Books/HarperCollins 2000; *740 Park: The Story of the World's Richest Apartment Building*, New York: Broadway, 2005. Quotes from *www.mgross.com*; birthdate information e-mail to this writer 16 Sep 2005.]

Grossman, Albert [1926 - 1986] Albert B. Grossman was born in Chicago on May 21, 1926, the son of Russian Jewish immigrants who worked as tailors. He attended Lane Technical High School and graduated from Roosevelt University, Chicago with a degree in economics, though he's also said to have studied child psychology under the great Bruno Bettelheim (later the author of the pioneering work *The Uses of Enchantment*, a 1970s study of the inherent psychological wisdom of the fairytale). Perhaps this helped Grossman to psych people out, which he was extremely good at, in his later business dealings in the music industry.

After university he worked for the Chicago Housing Authority, leaving in the late 1950s in unclear circumstances–it's often suggested that he was fired for misconduct–to go into the club business. Seeing folk star Bob Gibson perform at the Off Beat Room in 1956 prompted Grossman's idea of a 'listening room' to showcase Gibson and other talent, as the folk revival movement grew. The result was the Gate of Horn in the basement of the Rice Hotel, where Jim (later ROGER) McGUINN got his early inspiration and kicked off his career as a 12-string guitarist. Grossman moved into managing some of the acts who appeared at his club, and in 1959, with Boston-based club owner George Wein, who had founded the Newport Jazz Festival, Albert started up the NEWPORT FOLK FESTIVAL. 'The American public,' he told ROBERT SHELTON, 'is like Sleeping Beauty, waiting to be kissed awake by the prince of Folk Music.'

He was a pudgy man with derisive eyes, with a regular table at Gerde's Folk City from which he surveyed the scene in silence, and many people loathed him. In a milieu of New Left reformers and folkie idealists campaigning for a better world, Albert Grossman was a breadhead, seen to move serenely and with deadly purpose like a barracuda circling shoals of fish. Other people–among them Jones and HOWARD ALK–liked him, finding him loyal, flexible and tolerant, polite and considerate on a personal level and possessed of a dry sense of humour. Either way, he protected those whose careers he managed, building them up, gaining them far more of their dues and defending their interests more fiercely than the nicer, more amateurish managers in the Village. His clients included Bob Gibson and Hamilton Camp, ODETTA, PETER, PAUL & MARY, JOHN LEE HOOKER, IAN & SYLVIA, GORDON LIGHTFOOT, Richie Havens, Todd Rundgren, THE BAND, the Electric Flag, Janis Joplin and Bob Dylan. Sometimes he advertised that he was managing an act before they knew it themselves (as for instance in the 1965 Newport Folk Festival programme, when MIMI & RICHARD FARIÑA—and their manager—were surprised to find their names on Grossman's list of clients).

He moved in on Bob Dylan's career very early—secretly his manager by the time he encouraged IZZY YOUNG to lay out the money to hire Carnegie Chapter Hall for Dylan's launch there in November 1961, though not officially in place as manager until August 20, 1962—and who is to say that Dylan might not have taken a little longer to break through had Grossman not been wheeling and dealing for him? Nor can it be denied that he accommodated this most intelligent, difficult hustler of a client superbly—giving him space, not only figuratively but literally too, out at his house near Woodstock (where DANIEL KRAMER photographed him so memorably in early 1965), and never telling him, as others were quick to do, that he should stay where he was artistically, or stay sober, or play safe.

Grossman is to be seen in all his stealthy pomp, like the Cheshire cat without its grin, oozing in and out of the scenes of *Don't Look Back* as he guides Dylan through his 1965 British tour and out the other side into superstardom.

In 1969 he built the Bearsville Recording Studio near Woodstock, and in 1970 founded Bearsville Records. He had a pudgy finger in every possible pie, taking his percentage from venues and festivals his clients played, from their fees and royalties, from their music publishing, from the studios they recorded in, from the record labels that released their work, and sometimes from the houses they rented out of town.

By this time he was coming to the end of his association with Dylan. But he guarded Dylan's premium value to the end. At the Isle of Wight Music Festival in August 1969, by this time with his long hair in a ponytail (a rare sight on a man in his 40s), he was prowling around the hospitality tents ahead of Dylan's appearance. Asked if he'd heard the rumours that various members of THE BEATLES were going to join him on stage, he replied, sotto voce: 'Of course the Beatles would like to join Dylan on stage; *I* should like to fly to the moon.' Bob Dylan has never been given that level of guardianship since. The contracts between them were officially dissolved on July 17, 1970.

There are two interesting comments on Grossman in the SCORSESE film *No Direction Home*. One is Dylan's: 'He was kind of like a Colonel Tom Parker figure . . . you could smell him coming.' The other is JOHN COHEN's: 'I don't think Albert manipulated Bob, because Bob was weirder than Albert.'

Albert Grossman died of a heart attack while flying on Concorde to London on January 25, 1986. He is buried behind his own Bearsville Theater near Woodstock, New York. His widow Sally, née Bueler, an ex-New York City waitress whom he'd married in 1964, and who is the woman in red on the front cover of *Bringing It All Back Home*, continued to oversee his domain after his death. In 2004, reportedly, she began to sell off some of her late husband's holdings, including the theatre complex, the Bearsville restaurant and the studios.

[Albert Grossman to Robert Shelton, *No Direction Home: The Life and Music of Bob Dylan*, London: Penguin edn., 1987, p.88; Grossman on Dylan & the Beatles, remark to this writer, Isle of Wight, UK, 31 Aug 1969. Bruno Bettelheim, *The Uses of Enchantment*, London: Thames & Hudson, 1976.]

Guam [1975 - 1976] Guam was the band name informally given to the great assemblage of musicians Dylan took on the Rolling Thunder Revue tours of 1975 and 1976. Alternative names considered and/or given out in jest were the Budweiser Revue, Somebody & the Flaming Corks and MC & the Ushers. In 1975 Guam comprised: BOBBY NEUWIRTH, SCARLET RIVERA, T-BONE BURNETT, ROGER McGUINN, STEVE SOLES, MICK RONSON, DAVID MANSFIELD, ROB STONER, HOWIE WYETH and LUTHER RIX. For some reason JOAN BAEZ, RONNE BLAKLEY, RAMBLIN' JACK ELLIOTT and ALLEN GINSBERG were generally not considered part of Guam.

In his *Rolling Thunder Logbook*, SAM SHEPARD tags Guam as 'Neuwirth's miraculous band of street thugs.' In 1976 the line-up was unchanged except that Luther Rix was replaced on congas by GARY BURKE.

[Sam Shepard, *Rolling Thunder Logbook*, London & New York: Penguin, 1978, p.54.]

guitars, Bob Dylan's, acoustic Bob Dylan may have presented himself as a hoboing young freewheeler with nothing but the clothes he stood up in, but apart from the cheap and nasty acoustic guitar he may have owned before his electric guitars back in Hibbing, MN, he has actually owned nothing but good quality acoustic instruments ever since he first went folkie, back in Dinkytown in 1959. There he swapped his electric for a 1949 Martin 00-17, and plays it on the Minnesota tape of May 1961, before giving it to early manager Kevin Krown, who kept it until his death in 1992. It's now at the Experience Music Project in Seattle.

Next came the 1945 J50 Gibson Dylan is holding on the cover of *Bob Dylan*, and which he plays on that album and at some of the sessions for *Freewheelin'*, on which he also plays unspecified Martin guitars. This Gibson was 'lost in action' in late 1963, and was replaced by a 1930s 13-fret Gibson Nick Lucas Special, bought from Fretted Instruments store-owner Marc Silber (son of IRWIN SILBER), which became the acoustic guitar Dylan played on *Another Side of Bob Dylan* and *Bringing It All Back Home* and was his instrument of choice in

© Last Days Ministry

Keith Green

Woody Guthrie (left) and family

Photo by Elliott Landy

Producer John Simon, Robbie Robertson, Albert Grossman and promoter Bill Graham in a lift, San Francisco, CA 1969

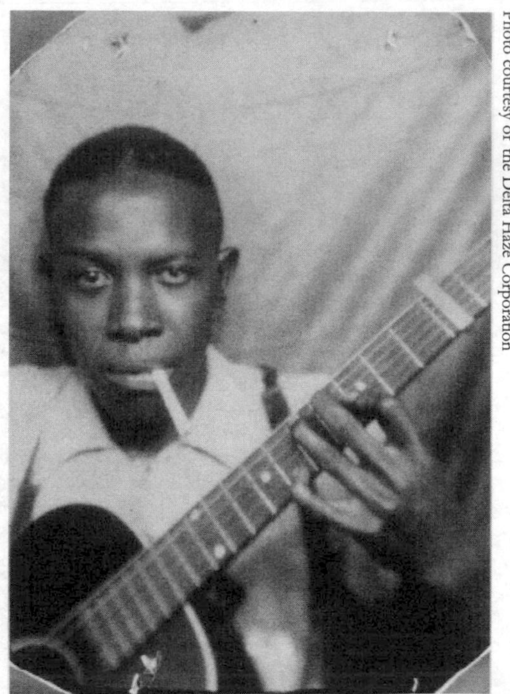
Photo courtesy of the Delta Haze Corporation

Robert Johnson

Franz Kafka

Photo by John Byrne Cooke

Tony Glover & Spider John Koerner, Newport Folk Festival

concert from late 1963 right through till he arrived in Melbourne from Sydney in mid-April 1966 and found that its front had caved in (because Dylan had piled harmonicas on top of it in its case and then rammed it shut). The Gibson can also be seen in *Don't Look Back*. Its seller, Silber, remembered that later, he went to sell Dylan another guitar, up in Woodstock, probably in the early 1970s: 'a really nice late-60s Martin. He was a tough guy to do business with, though, because he didn't have any idea what the guitars were worth.'

In Melbourne, Dylan had borrowed another guitar while the Gibson was being repaired. Local musician Phillip T. Pascoe recalls that afterwards, 'The one he borrowed went on sale in a little guitar shop in Melbourne for $500. I went by that store after school every day for a couple of weeks and dreamed up ways of coming up with that kind of money (impossible when you're 18 years old). He had only played four concerts but that sucker had flatpick scratches all across the face. I'd watched him play it and man, he flatpicked from the elbow not the wrist.'

By the time the 1966 tour reached Britain, Dylan was playing an acoustic Fender King, which can be seen in the hotel-room scenes in *Eat the Document* when Dylan is playing 'What Kind of Friend is This?' and 'On a Rainy Afternoon'. These electric-look Fenders, introduced in 1963, never caught on and were discontinued in 1971.

After the motorcycle crash, Dylan used a Gibson Dove on *John Wesley Harding*, recorded in late 1967, and when he reappeared in public for the first time, at the WOODY GUTHRIE Memorial Concert in January 1968, he was playing a Martin 0-18. On *Nashville Skyline* he plays GEORGE HARRISON's Gibson J-200 (as seen on the album cover), as he did at that year's Isle of Wight Festival. On the JOHNNY CASH television show that May he plays a Martin Triple-0 18, and he stuck with Martins all through the early 1970s, including on the Nashville *Self Portrait* sessions, at the Concert for Bangla Desh in August 1971 (a D-28) and at the Friends of Chile Benefit Concert in May 1974 (a 1943 00-21). This last was also used for much of the 1974 'comeback' tour and for the New York September 1974 sessions for *Blood on the Tracks*, for the 'World of JOHN HAMMOND' TV performance filmed in September 1975 and sometimes on Rolling Thunder Revue concerts. (At the Minnesota *Blood on the Tracks* sessions in December 1974 he had used a Martin 00-42, a similar model.) On the Rolling Thunder Revue in general he used a number of vintage guitars, both Martins and Gibsons, but in 1978 he was given two Yamahas which he used occasionally on that year's World Tour and again later, also using Washburns in the same period. He retained a sunburst Washburn Monterey right through to the 1984 tour of Europe. It can be seen on the cover of the *Real Live* album. In 1986 and 1987, a black Washburn EA-26 alternated with various Martins.

In 1988 when he embarked upon the Never-Ending Tour, and displayed such a renewed interest in acoustic material, his main instrument was a Martin D-28, but in the mid-90s he returned to favouring Gibsons, and except for the fall tour leg of 2001, when he often played a special Martin HD-28 that looked like a photo negative image of a 'normal' black and white guitar, since around 1998 he has concentrated on playing a sunburst Gibson J-45.

On record, you'd have to say that throughout a career of what would seem a privileged profligacy of acoustic instruments, he has never achieved a better sound than he had right back at the beginning, on those first two albums.

[This entry relied entirely on Eyolf Østrem's 'Dylan's Guitars' ('relying heavily on input from Peter Stone Brown & Paul Hostetter'), & Joel Gilbert's 'Highway 61' guitars pages, seen online 15 Jan 2006 at *www.dylanchords.com/professors/dylans_guitars.htm* & at *www.highway61revisited.com/guitars.htm*.]

guitars, Bob Dylan's, electric In a recently emerged photograph taken by Dylan's mother in Hibbing, and dated via rickety provenance as being from September 1958, 17-year-old Bob is shown with his second electric guitar. Most more youthful rock'n'roll moments seem to have him on piano. We can say for certain from the photograph that this electric instrument is not a Fender (it's sometimes been said that he owned a Fender in Hibbing)—and we can say with less certainty but reasonable conviction that it isn't his first electric, a $39 turquoise Silvertone bought mail-order from Sears Roebuck, but must be his second, a new Supro Ozark (a guitar JIMI HENDRIX also had as a lad), bought at Mr. Hautala's store in Hibbing at a knock-down $60 because Bob and his friend John Bucklen each bought one at the same time: and September 1958 is too late for him to be just acquiring the Silvertone. This is the picture of a boy who's proud of having upgraded. In Minneapolis, Dylan swaps his electric—whether the same one or a successor we don't know—for an acoustic. From there he emerges into the world as an acoustic-playing folkie, and remains so until July 1965.

In *Don't Look Back*, though, when Dylan is on his last acoustic solo tour, earlier in '65, we see him standing in a street in Newcastle-upon-Tyne, twitching about in his Chelsea boots, delighting at a display of electric guitars in a music-shop window. 'Look at this guitar, man,' he says excitedly, 'this one right here! Do you believe that guitar?! They don't have those guitars in the States, man. They're incredible!'

He's retained that relish for rare guitars ever since. Norman Harris, a Reseda, California, specialist dealer, told *Guitar Player* magazine: 'Dylan has a lot of strange things–though he's not really into guitars–just because of what they look like.'

Dylan bought two favourites from Harris: a 1959 cherry-sunburst Stratocaster, commonly used in concerts over a number of years, and a yellow vintage Fender Telecaster bought for the 1974 tour, and which had been acquired from an ex-musician car-dealer who had played it on a tour with the Three Stooges after being given it by Leo Fender in person.

Then there's the flamboyant white guitar on which Dylan surprised us by playing unprecedented slide, on 'Shelter from the Storm', in the 1976 'Hard Rain' TV Special. This was an early-1960s Glenwood 98 National, one of three Nationals bought that spring from Don Vargas, of Woodland Hills, California (the others were a lap-slide and a jazz model). The Glenwood was sometimes brought on stage during the 1978 World Tour (and features in the backstage photo used on a November 1978 *Rolling Stone* front cover) but was never played again in concert after 1976. It also appears on the back of the *Hard Rain* LP, and guitar technician Larry Cragg is seen working on it in a photo in that jolly book *Encounters with Bob Dylan: If You See Him Say Hello*, compiled by Tracy Johnson in 2000. This is the guitar that Dylan named 'Rimbaud', though collectively in the business this model is known as 'the map' because its body shape resembles that of the USA.

On the whole, however, the electric guitars Dylan has used most consistently down the years have been classic, rather than weird, models. When he went electric at the 1965 NEWPORT FOLK FESTIVAL he used a black and white 1962 Fender Stratocaster; on the 1966 tour he used a black and white 1958 Fender Telecaster; with TOM PETTY & THE HEARTBREAKERS in 1987 he used a 1959 sunburst Fender Strat–and in general, though there have been exceptions, including some Gibson Les Pauls, essentially ever since 1978, his guitar of choice has been the Fender Strat.

[Main sources: '1970s: Bob Dylan's Favourite Electric Guitars', author unstated but prob. John Bauldie, in Michael Gray & John Bauldie, *All Across the Telegraph: A Bob Dylan Handbook*, London: W.H. Allen, 1987 (but with corrections; that piece dated the Glenwood 98 as early 1950s; they weren't introduced till 1962); survey by Eyolf Østrem at *www.dylanchords.com/professors/dylans_guitars.htm*, seen online 15 Jan 2006; Derek Barker, guitars piece in *Isis* no.104, Aug–Sep 2002 & 'God Said to Abraham', *ISIS: A Bob Dylan Anthology*, London: Helter Skelter, 2001 & 2004 & conversations & e-mails with Derek Barker, Jan 2006; amendments to Hibbing guitars details thanks to Dave Engel, *Just Like Bob Zimmerman's Blues: Dylan in Minnesota*, Rudolph, WI: River City Memoirs–Mesabi, 1997, p.179.]

Guthrie, Arlo [1947 -] Arlo Guthrie, one of WOODY GUTHRIE's many children, was born at Coney Island, Brooklyn, on July 10, 1947 and grew up mostly in Queens with his mother Marjorie, his father having rarely been around while fit and having been moved to the Greystone Park New Jersey State Hospital when ill, when Arlo was eight years old. He first encountered Bob Dylan five years later, when Dylan was barely a grown-up himself but had arrived in New York at the start of 1961. The first meeting between Bob and Arlo has long possessed a mythic quality, but seems to be true:

'The story,' wrote Brian McCoy in the *Miami News*, 'goes like this: Shortly after arriving in New York . . . Dylan made a pilgrimage to the Guthrie home . . . looking for Arlo's famed father, Woody. He was greeted at the door by a baby-sitter who, not knowing what to make of the scruffy kid, called Arlo's mom at work. "Don't let him in," Mrs. Guthrie said. "Tell him to come back when I'll be home." The baby-sitter hung up the phone only to find Dylan showing Arlo a new way to play harmonica. "That happened," Guthrie said . . . in an interview from Taos, NM [in 1988].' Dylan gives his own account of the story in *Chronicles Volume One* in 2004, referring to Arlo's mother more familiarly as 'Margie' and forbearing to mention the harmonica lesson–saying rather that he 'stayed just long enough to warm up, said a quick goodbye and left' with his 'boots still waterlogged'.

Arlo had become a singer-songwriter himself by the time of his father's death in October 1967–and that year enjoyed the most prominent hit he would ever achieve, with what seemed at the time the oh-so-cool talking ramble of 'Alice's Restaurant Massacree', a tall stoned-hippie tale about avoiding the draft and being busted for littering, told with a relaxed if slightly nasal delivery, set to an acoustic guitar and a gentle rhythm-section shuffle, part of its joke being the way that it stretched itself counter-culturally over 18 minutes. His début album, *Alice's Restaurant* (1967) included his follow-up, the equally lengthy 'Motorcycle Song'.

Arlo performed his father's fiercesome 'Jesus Christ' at the two Memorial Concerts on January 20, 1968 (and stood in the ensemble with Dylan and everyone else to share vocals and play harmonica on 'This Land Is Your Land' at the end of one show and 'This Train Is Bound for Glory' at the end of the other); he appeared at Woodstock in the summer of 1969, singing an excited and affecting 'Coming Into Los Angeles', and enjoyed a hit single with STEVE GOODMAN's train song 'City of New Orleans' in 1972, after which he settled down to a more conventional folkie career.

In May 1974 Arlo Guthrie was on stage again with Bob Dylan, at the Friends of Chile Benefit Concert at Madison Square Garden's Felt Forum. Dylan sang backing vocal on Arlo's 'Deportees', and then after Dylan sang 'North Country Blues' he and Guthrie, plus PHIL OCHS, DAVE VAN RONK, Larry Estridge, Melanie and PETE SEEGER all battled their way through 'Spanish Is the Loving Tongue' and 'Blowin' in the Wind'.

In the late 1960s Arlo Guthrie had been one of those who, according to ROBERT SHELTON, strongly encouraged Dylan to go into films, aided by Harold Leventhal, who had been Woody's agent and was associate producer of Arlo's own film, a predictably vacuous and shallow Hollywood *Alice's Restaurant* in which Joseph Boley played Woody and Sylvia Davis played Arlo's mother. Despite being directed by Arthur Penn, who in 1966 had directed that great Marlon Brando film *The Chase* and in 1967 *Bonnie & Clyde*, Arlo's embarrassing film must have more than nullified his ability to point Dylan at Hollywood, and it would be a further four years until Dylan entrusted himself to SAM PECKINPAH.

Since the mid-1970s Arlo Guthrie has continued to perform, not least, in recent years, with more than 25 different symphony orchestras; since 1983 he has run his own record label, and throughout a long career of performing and recording, has continued to be active in fundraising and campaigning in the fight against Huntington's Chorea, the degenerative disease that killed his father. Like Dylan, he spends much of the year on the road. Weirdly, in 1996 he *re-recorded* the whole of the *Alice's Restaurant* album, replicating it right down to the cover, on which the middle-aged, silver-haired, naked Guthrie sits at the same table, in the same pose, as had the young man of nearly 30 years previously. This too parallels something Dylan has sometimes talked of doing—not, of course, posing naked at a restaurant table but re-recording some of his old records . . . which would be interesting to hear but also, as in Arlo's case, unnecessary.

On the subject of Dylan, Arlo told the *Miami News*: 'he's obviously somebody whose work I greatly admire'—and then summarised his impact shrewdly: 'he . . . succeeded in doing something that had never been done: making our music serious. Before he was a generation's hero, he was a folk singers' hero.'

[Arlo Guthrie: *Alice's Restaurant*, Reprise R-6267 (mono) / RS-6267, US, 1967; 'City of New Orleans', on *Hobo's Lullaby*, Reprise MS-2060, US, 1972; *Alice's Restaurant—The Massacree Revisited*, Rising Son RSR-0010, US, 1996. *Alice's Restaurant*, dir. Arthur Penn; Florin, US, 1969. Friends of Chile Benefit Concert, NY, 9 May 1974. Brian McCoy, 'Arlo Guthrie back in spotlight after album', *The Miami News*, 6 Dec 1988, online 14 Dec 2005 at *www.bobdylanroots.com/arlo.html*. Robert Shelton, *No Direction Home: The Life and Music of Bob Dylan*, London: Penguin edn., 1987, p.300. Bob Dylan, *Chronicles Volume One*, 2004, p.100.]

Guthrie, Woody [1912 - 1967] Guthrie travelled around with LEADBELLY, SONNY TERRY and CISCO HOUSTON during the Second World War. Their recordings include a Leadbelly song, 'We Shall Be Free', on which Dylan based his own 'I Shall Be Free' and 'I Shall Be Free No. 10'. The tune is the same in all three songs, all of which belong to an older song cluster (see **'I Shall Be Free'**) and to the talking-blues genre. This genre is generally acknowledged to have originated (on record, at least) with the white artist Chris Bouchillon but when we attribute Dylan's talking-blues style to Guthrie we tend to forget that black artists explored this form earlier than Guthrie did, and that Guthrie himself listened attentively to black music. (A particularly fine example is BLIND WILLIE McTELL's 'Travelin' Blues', recorded in Atlanta on October 30, 1929.)

Dylan's early work includes a Guthrie Period, of course, and while one of the two self-composed songs on his first album is the direct address 'Song to Woody', the other, 'Talkin' New York' also quotes from him, transcribing and reiterating his morality ('Now a very great man once said / Some people rob you with a fountain pen', which comes from Guthrie's 'Pretty Boy Floyd'): a morality that has remained crucial in Dylan's work ever since. We meet it close to the surface again in the interestingly political 1980s song 'Union Sundown': a genuine protest song in the Guthrie tradition, and an honourable addition to it because it is observant about a reality that wasn't there to be observed in the 1960s—a real and contemporary 'state of the union' survey, and with a title that carries among its many meanings one that echoes a far earlier Dylan sleevenote poem in its recognition that the Guthrie era of noble, simple pro-union sentiment is no longer an available option.

Guthrie Americanised the ancient ballad 'Gypsy Davey' (CHILD ballad no.200), abolishing its 'milk-white steed'; his was a version Dylan was recorded performing at the home of Sid & Bob Gleason in East Orange, NJ, February-March 1961, and Dylan clearly knew it like the back of his lily-white hand when he was writing his own 'Boots of Spanish Leather'.

Early Dylan can also use the tone of Guthrie's autobiographical writing unaltered, can capture it exactly, in song. The chaotic scurrying around of cram-jam-packed humanity, which Guthrie describes so well in his tremendous autobiography *Bound for Glory* (1943), which Dylan is believed to have read in 1958–particularly in the sequence about the box car ride that opens and closes the book—is done precisely in this way: 'Dogs a-barkin', cats a-meowin' / Women screamin', fists a-flyin', babies cryin' / Cops a-comin', me a-runnin' / Maybe we just better call off the picnic.' *That* is Woody Guthrie's voice. It's from Dylan's 1962 song 'Talking Bear Mountain Picnic Massacre Blues'.

Similarly, a line like 'In the misty crystal glitter' (from Guthrie's song 'Grand Coulee Dam') clearly has its influence even on the Dylan of 'Chimes of Freedom'—and you need only compare the writing and delivery of Guthrie's 'Talking About Songs' (1944) with particular passages of Dylan's 'Last

Thoughts on Woody Guthrie' (recorded in live recitative performance in 1963 and finally released on the *Bootleg Series Vols. 1–3* box set, 1991) to hear yet another side of Guthrie's voice: and it's surprising to find his influence still so strong at this point. Here's Woody Guthrie: 'I hate a song that makes you think that you're just / born to lose—bound to lose—no good to nobody, no / good fer nuthin' because yer either too old or too young / or too fat or too slim or too ugly or too this or too that: / songs that run you down or songs that poke fun at ya on / account of yr bad luck or yer [pause] hard travelin' . . . / I am out to sing songs that will prove to you that this is / *your* world, that if it has hit you pretty hard and / knocked you down for a dozen loops, no matter *how* hard it's run you / down or rolled you over, no matter what color, what size / y'are, how y're built . . .' and here's Bob Dylan's ambiguously titled 'Last Thoughts on Woody Guthrie': 'When yer head gets twisted and yer mind grows numb / When you think you're too old, too young, too smart or too dumb. . . . You need something to make it known / That it's you and no one else that owns / That spot that yer standing, that space that you're sitting / That the world aint got you beat / That it ain't got you licked / It can't get you crazy no matter how many times you might get kicked . . .'

Even Dylan's 1960s drawings and paintings owe a lot to the quirky pen-and-ink sketches in Guthrie's *Bound for Glory*. Look at the sketches published in *Writings and Drawings by Bob Dylan* in 1972 (a book dedicated to 'the magnificent Woodie [sic] Guthrie and Robert Johnson . . .') and the paintings on the covers of Dylan's album *Self Portrait* and THE BAND's first album *Music from Big Pink*.

Guthrie's work was not always from that mythical terrain, the pure oral-tradition land of the folk. He seems to have based his rather awful poem 'Belle Starr' (in *American Folksong*, 1947) on the equally awful film *Belle Starr* (directed Irving Cummings, 20th Century Fox, 1941)—a poem that PETE SEEGER and RAMBLIN' JACK ELLIOTT had no more sense than to put a tune to and record (*The Bad Men* [sic], Columbia L2L-1011, *nia*) and to publish in *Sing Out!* vol.15, no.5, November 1965.

Dylan also recorded some of Guthrie's children's songs in early 1961, and kept them in his repertoire while he was conquering New York. These included 'Car Car' (East Orange, NJ, February-March 1961, BONNIE BEECHER's Minneapolis apartment that May, and at the Gaslight, NY, Sep 1961) and 'Howdido' (Beecher's, May 1961). Who knows why? You have never met a child (or adult) who enjoys listening to Guthrie (or Dylan) singing these dreary songs, with their plodding, morose jollity. And since Guthrie spent as little time as possible with his own children, it's no wonder he misjudged his audience. (His son ARLO GUTHRIE and other relatives have apparently 'revived' these songs on a spooky 1990s album that mixes old Woody Guthrie vocal tracks with new recordings.)

In 1987 Dylan said that the first thing that struck him about Guthrie was his sound: not words but his sound—and interestingly, he added that he thought it quite close to THE CARTER FAMILY's sound. Then Dylan uses the phrase 'links in a chain' to describe how people pass on what has gone before to those who come after; this comes in answer to questions about Guthrie's influence upon him.

Dylan's first public appearance after the motorcycle crash of 1966 was at the January 1968 Woody Guthrie Memorial Concert at Carnegie Hall. At the afternoon show he and The Band performed vibrant, fresh versions of Guthrie's 'I Ain't Got No Home', 'Dear Mrs. Roosevelt' and 'Grand Coulee Dam', and, with the ensemble of other performers, joined in 'This Land Is Your Land'. At the evening show Dylan and The Band performed the same three songs and, ensemble, joined in 'This Train Is Bound for Glory'. And in 1987, for the album *A Vision Shared: A Tribute to Woody Guthrie and Leadbelly*, Dylan contributed a new recording of 'Pretty Boy Floyd'.

Nowhere in song does Dylan throw us back to Guthrie—to song titles he's written or performed, and to phrases associated with his work—more than within the multiple allusions, the deep soundings of meaning and memory that boom and rumble beneath the surface of the 1997 album *Time Out of Mind*.

In prose, Dylan has fully seized the opportunity, in *Chronicles Volume One*, 2004, to give Guthrie and his impact and influence a truly fulsome amount of careful yet warm attention. Woody is there on pages 9, 63, 83, 98–100, 227, 229, 243, 250, 251, 257, 270 and 283. Being 'knocked out' by Woody is on pages 243–46. Visiting his Coney Island house is on pages 99–100. His repertoire is discussed on pages 247, 248 and 252. Songs and records by Woody are considered on pages 49, 53–54, 63, 98, 243–44, 246–47 and 279. *Bound for Glory* is cited on page 245. As ever, Dylan's observations are as shrewd as they are romantic, as thoughtful as respectful. And the early period in which Dylan more or less tried to become Guthrie, and is tackled on the subject by JON PANKAKE, is candidly discussed.

The great folklorist ALAN LOMAX wrote of Guthrie that 'he inherited the folk tradition of the last American frontier (western Oklahoma) and during his incessant wandering across the US he has recomposed this tradition into contemporary folky ballads about the lives of the American working class. . . . No modern American poet or folk singer has made a more significant contribution to our culture.' Well, except one.

[*Woody Guthrie: The Library of Congress Recordings* is a 3-CD set, Rounder Reissue Series 1041–1043, 1993, comprising '3 hours of songs and conversations' incl. 22 monologues. For other recording details see *www.woodyguthrie.org*. Leadbelly: 'We Shall Be Free', NY, May 1944 (with Woody Guthrie & Sonny Terry); *Leadbelly Sings Folk Songs*, Folkways FA 2488, 1962, CD-reissued as FA 2488, 1995.

Dylan 1987 remarks re Guthrie: Questions from Robert Noakes, aka Rab Noakes, 1970s singer-songwriter turned Scotland-based radio producer; recorded answers sent by Dylan's office on a 9′ 27″ tape, 8 Jul 1987; parts broadcast in 4-program series *Woody Guthrie*, BBC Radio, and in *A Vision Shared: A Tribute to Woody Guthrie and Leadbelly*, CBS-TV, 1987. (The whole tape of Dylan's answers is in circulation.)

Dylan & The Band: 'I Ain't Got No Home', 'Dear Mrs. Roosevelt', 'Grand Coulee Dam' & 'This Train Is Bound for Glory' issued *Tribute to Woody Guthrie Vol. 1*, Columbia KC31171, 1972; 'This Land Is Your Land' issued *Tribute to Woody Guthrie Vol. 2*, Warner Bros. K46144, 1972. Bob Dylan: 'Pretty Boy Floyd', prob. LA, Apr 1987; *Folkways: A Vision Shared—A Tribute to Woody Guthrie & Leadbelly*, Columbia OC 44034, 24 Aug 1988.

The standard biography is *Woody Guthrie: A Life* by Joe Klein (New York: Random House, 1980) but the more recent *Ramblin' Man: The Life and Times of Woody Guthrie* by Ed Cray, 2005, is also absorbing. There is too a collection of other Guthrie writing, *Born to Win*, edited by ROBERT SHELTON (1965). But above all towers the autobiography, *Bound for Glory*: a great book, written when its author was 30. Dylan's copy was the 1st edition paperback, 1949.]

Haggard, Merle [1937 -] Merle Ronald Haggard was born on April 6, 1937 in Bakersfield, California, the son of Okie refugees from the Dust Bowl of the 1930s. He had a luridly dysfunctional childhood of truancy, general delinquency and crime—he was sentenced to 15 years in San Quentin at the age of 20—but he learnt to play outstanding guitar and after being released from prison in 1960 and subsequently pardoned, he became, encouraged first by LEFTY FRIZZELL and later by JOHNNY CASH, a big-name singer and songwriter in 1970s country music, looking wiry, dark and handsome, like a sort of Nashville Warren Beatty.

Granted his history, it was not surprising that he matched the lugubrious sentimentality of mainstream country with a notably tough and abrasive electric guitar sound, and at the end of the 1960s was a founding member of the so-called Outlaw Country movement. 1970's 'Okie from Muskogee' suggested a right-wing agenda but Haggard saw his own stance as merely blue-collar, and he declined to endorse the notorious Governor Wallace when invited to do so. Early songs that spread into the mainstream include 'Mama Tried' (covered memorably by THE EVERLY BROTHERS on their pioneering country rock album of 1968, *Roots*, and later by THE GRATEFUL DEAD) and 'Sing Me Back Home', both characteristic of Haggard's subject matter in dealing with crimes and regret, and the yearning of the hardened and the doomed for an idealised, irretrievable past. Between his 1965 début album, *Strangers*, and *Chicago Wind* 40 years later, he issued no less than 73 other newly recorded albums (some as by Merle Haggard and the Strangers), including, in 1969, the double album *Same Train, A Different Time: Merle Haggard Sings the Great Songs of JIMMIE RODGERS*.

In 2005, he shared most of a spring tour with Bob Dylan, beginning in Seattle on March 7 and ending in New York City with five nights at the Beacon Theater, the last of them on April 30. The opening act was Amos Lee, then Haggard and his band, and then Dylan. (Reno and Las Vegas, on March 18 and 19, and Mount Pleasant, Michigan, on April 11, were Dylan-only concerts.) Altogether, there were 36 Haggard-Dylan double bills. They never shared the stage, but Dylan did sing Haggard's 'Sing Me Back Home' in nine of his own concerts. (He had sung it once before, at his exceptional Bonnaroo Music Festival performance in Manchester, Tennessee, on June 11, 2004.)

Haggard's official website greets you with the branding 'Haggard: Poet of the Common Man'. The common man, of course, retires; like the common woman, the performer generally doesn't, and Merle, almost 70 and now grey-haired and—well, yes, haggard—keeps on keeping on.

[Merle Haggard: *Strangers*, Hollywood, 1965, Capitol, *nia*, US, 1965; *Sing Me Back Home & Mama Tried*, Capitol, 1968; *Same Train, A Different Time: Merle Haggard Sings the Great Songs of Jimmie Rodgers*, 1969; *Okie from Muscogee—Live*, 1969. *Chicago Wind*, EMI-Capitol CD 2005, US, 2005.]

H

Hajdu, David [1955 -] David Anthony Hajdu was born in Philipsburg, New Jersey, on March 8, 1955 and was introduced to the first Dylan album by a much older brother when the album was new (and when Hajdu was aged seven). He became Music Critic for the *Hollywood Reporter* 1985–90, Senior and then General Editor of *Entertainment Weekly* 1990–99 and has been Music Critic of *The New Republic* since 2003. He is also a contributor to the *New Yorker*, *New York Review of Books*, *Atlantic Monthly*, *New York Times*, *Rolling Stone* and *Vanity Fair*. His first book, *Lush Life*, was a biography of jazz musician Billy Strayhorn; his latest book is *The Ten-Cent Plague: The Great Comic-Book Scare and How It Changed Popular Culture*.

Hajdu first wrote on Dylan when reviewing him at the Beacon Theatre, NYC, in 1989 but his significant contribution to Dylan scrutiny is his book *Positively 4th Street: The Lives and Times of JOAN BAEZ, BOB DYLAN, MIMI BAEZ FARIÑA and RICHARD FARIÑA*, a fascinating, detailed account of the early career years of Dylan and key people around him. Instead of an account that sets the determinedly individualistic young Dylan up against the old hands of the folk revival movement and the purist guardians of traditional song, Hajdu's book hones in on four young, relatively privileged suburbanites—young lions using the folk revival / New Left world as their playground, and flitting back and forth not just between Greenwich Village and Boston but from East Coast to West and from the US to Europe.

If Hajdu has an axe to grind, it's the elevation of Richard Fariña to the status of both folk-rock inventor and brilliant novelist robbed of recognition only by tragic early death: but there's no glorification of Fariña as a person, any more than of the book's other spoiled, self-regarding protagonists—nor any crass attempt to suggest that such characteristics can't go hand in hand with fine work. Hajdu is scrupulously fair to all four, and he handles both copious amounts of generous personal detail—his research has been deep and thorough—and the broad drama of social change going on while these young lives fizz across the foreground.

Even at his most journalistic (and he is, after all, a writer for slick American mainstream journals) he's acute and economical, as for instance here: 'In folk circles . . . [amid] down-home characters groaning in and out of tune, Joan Baez seemed like the spirit of a child-queen, floating in off the moors.' More skilfully and valuably, he summarises beautifully what was at stake, ideologically, in the struggle between the folkies and mainstream America at the specific historical moment that Dylan, with his usual good timing, managed to catch with his arrival in New York:

> '. . . folk put a premium on naturalness and authenticity during a boom in man-made materials, especially plastics. . . . A music that gloried in the unique and the weird, folk challenged conformity and celebrated regionalism during the rise of mass media, national brands, and interstate travel. . . . A music historical by nature, it conjured distant times, often in archaic language, celebrating the past rather than the "new" and "improved". . . . It was small in scale . . . when American society, with its new supermarkets, V8 engines, and suburban sprawl, appeared to be physically ballooning. Folk music was down to earth when jet travel and space exploration were emerging; while FRANK SINATRA was flying to the moon, PETE SEEGER was waist deep in the Big Muddy.'

[David Hajdu: *Positively 4th Street: The Lives and Times of Joan Baez, Bob Dylan, Mimi Baez Fariña and Richard Fariña*, New York: Farrar, Straus & Giroux, 2001; quotation from pp.19 & 32–33.]

Hall, Bobbye [19?? -] Bobbye Jean Hall Porter was born in Detroit and by 17 was playing percussion on Motown Records; when the company moved to Los Angeles, she followed. She is one of the few women to succeed as a session player in what must be one of the most male-dominated professions in the world. She has played on a number of significant albums including TRACY CHAPMAN's *Crossroads*, Marvin Gaye's *Let's Get It On*, JONI MITCHELL's great *For the Roses* and *Hejira*, MARIA MULDAUR's *Waitress in a Donut Shop*, Randy Newman's *Good Old Boys* and albums by Greg Allman, the Allman Brothers Band, PAUL BUTTERFIELD, Lowell Fulson, JERRY GARCIA, Jefferson Starship, CAROLE KING, AL KOOPER, Lynyrd Skynyrd, Dave Mason, TOM PETTY, Poco, James Taylor, the Temptations, Sarah Vaughan, Mary Wells, STEVIE WONDER and *many* others. In 1977 she made her own album, *Body Language for Lovers* (with Dorothy Ashby, Chuck Rainey, Andy Belling and other jazz-funk people) and later the obscurely titled *No. 29*.

Bobbye Hall was the only female musician (as against backing singer) on Dylan's big 1978 World Tour, right through from the rehearsals in late 1977 in Santa Monica and throughout the tour itself, beginning in Japan in February and ending in mid-December in Florida. She therefore appears, of course, on the live album *At Budokan*, but she also plays percussion, congas and tambourine on all the April to May 1978 studio sessions back in Santa Monica which give us the *Street Legal* album of that year. She is sometimes listed as having played on the far earlier album *Dylan*, released by Columbia from outtakes recorded right at the beginning of the 1970s, which is hard to confirm or disprove—but it doesn't help that she is *also* listed as having played on *Bob Dylan*, his first and most definitely solo album, recorded in 1961. She has re-connected with Dylan professionally only once since the heady year of 1978, but not due to any cooling of enthusiasm on his part. As late as that November 28 in Jackson, Mississippi, he was introducing her to the audience as: 'On the conga drums, from Detroit, the most amazing Miss Bobbye Hall!' Her reappearance was at one Los Angeles studio session for the *Shot of Love* album on March 31, 1981, when she played on a number of unused takes of 'Caribbean Wind'.

[Bobbye Hall: *Body Language for Lovers*, 20th Century T534, US, 1977; *No. 29, nia*, 1989?]

Hammond, John [1910 - 1987] John Henry Hammond was born into a branch of the Vanderbilt family in New York City on December 15, 1910, attended Yale and the Juilliard school of music. He gave up classical music in order to pursue his enthusiasm for jazz (which he discovered in the city's clubs as an adolescent) and black popular music. He wrote music criticism and journalism for *Down Beat* and the British papers *Melody Maker* and *The Gramophone*, wrote widely on race relations in the US and even became a vice-president of the National Association for the Advancement of Colored People. His family money financed his further career as an impresario: he owned a theatre at which he presented black acts, and he pioneered integrated touring and recording sessions. (As PETE SEEGER once said, 'Jazz became integrated 10 years before baseball largely because of John Hammond.')

His career as a promoter of talent and as a record producer stretched from the 1930s to the 1980s and the list of greats he discovered or brought into the studio was phenomenal. He worked in executive positions for several labels, though most notably for Columbia Records, for whom he produced artists from Bessie Smith to Bob Dylan. He discovered and/or brought studio opportunities to Count Basie, Charlie Christian, Lionel Hampton, Billie Holiday, Meade Lux Lewis, Teddy Wilson and Lester Young and many other jazz artists, and in 1938 and 1939 Hammond financed and promoted the now-famous 'From Spirituals to Swing' concerts at Carnegie Hall—bringing a wide range of black music to Manhattan's swankiest venue—and featuring many of the above, plus Benny Goodman, BIG BILL BROONZY and SONNY TERRY. He wanted to include ROBERT JOHNSON at the first of these concerts and sent for him, not knowing that Johnson had been murdered shortly beforehand.

Hammond served in the US Army in World War II, returning to the musical fray as soon as possible. But when swing gave way to bebop, Hammond, who didn't understand the latter, switched his attention more towards blues and pop. Just as many of the earlier jazz names he had espoused were unknowns when he latched onto them, so too he followed only his own instincts in the postwar era, in which he signed, among others, the important Nigerian drummer Babatunde Olatunji (Hammond produced his ground-breaking first album, *Drums of Passion*, released in 1959 and still selling today), Big Joe Turner, Pete Seeger, Aretha Franklin, MICHAEL BLOOMFIELD, LEONARD COHEN and BRUCE SPRINGSTEEN, and had a significant hand in opening the careers of George Benson and STEVIE RAY VAUGHAN (his last signing).

Hammond had the decency and belief to produce the 1965 album by the fragile but giant figure SON HOUSE that yielded at least one invaluable addition to his canon, the exquisite 'Pearline', and in 1962 it was also Hammond who, returning his attention to one of House's pupils, compiled and released on Columbia the hugely influential LP of Robert Johnson's work *Robert Johnson, King of the Delta Blues Singers*.

In 1961 Hammond signed Bob Dylan to Columbia, and then produced his first and second albums. After the poor sales of the first album, Dylan was known around the Columbia building as 'Hammond's folly'. On September 10, 1975, it was in Hammond's presence at the recording of the tribute TV show 'The World of John Hammond' that Dylan delivered the first public performances of 'Hurricane', 'Oh Sister' and 'Simple Twist of Fate', from his then-forthcoming album *Desire*.

No-one except DAVE VAN RONK receives a more respectful write-up in Dylan's 2004 memoir *Chronicles Volume One* than John Hammond. Dylan appreciates not only the man's straightforwardness and seriousness of purpose, his depth of knowledge and his insight into the very young Dylan's potential, but also makes the specific point that when Hammond gave him a pre-release copy of *King of the Delta Blues Singers* this had ramifications for his own development as a writer: 'If I hadn't heard the Robert Johnson record when I did, there probably would have been hundreds of lines of mine that would have been shut down–that I wouldn't have felt free enough or upraised enough to write.'

Returning to the more general, Dylan says of Hammond that men like him 'came from an older world, a more ancient order. . . . They knew where they belonged and they had guts to back up whatever their beliefs were. You didn't want to let them down.'

John Hammond died, from complications following several strokes, on July 10, 1987, at the age of 76.

[Seeger quote seen online 5 Jan 2006 at *www.rockhall.com/hof/inductee.asp?id=117*. Bob Dylan: 'Hurricane' (1st take, uncirculated), 'Oh Sister', 'Simple Twist of Fate' & 'Hurricane', WTTW-TV, NY, 10 Sep 1975, broadcast 'The World of John Hammond', PBS-TV, 13 Dec 1975; Dylan quotes, *Chronicles Volume One*, pp.287–88 & 288–89.]

Hammond, John Jr. [1942 -] John Paul Hammond was born in New York City on November 13, 1942, the good-looking son of JOHN HAMMOND, the legendary record producer, with whom he did not grow up, though they remained in contact. He attended private school and then Antioch College, Ohio, but after seeing JIMMY REED at the Apollo Theater in New York he dropped out of college to become a blues singer and guitarist. But though he sometimes suggested to his father people he thought he ought to check out, he didn't seem to impress his father unduly as a performer himself, and signed to Vanguard in 1962. After Dylan signed to Columbia some months earlier, John is supposed to have been the first to tell Hammond Sr. that Dylan's real name was Zimmerman. A dedicated, rather solemn archivist of the blues, who more often imitated than created from it (see **prewar blues, Dylan's use of, an introduction**), he was always around the Village in Dylan's folkie period, and was perhaps a friend of Dylan's early on.

Along with BRUCE LANGHORNE, JOHN SEBASTIAN and the mysterious bassist 'John Boone', Hammond played on a Dylan session in New York on the evening of January 14, 1965 in the midst of the *Bringing It All Back Home* sessions, but it provided nothing used on the album; it did, however, provide the below-par version of 'I'll Keep It With Mine' released 20 years later on the *Biograph* box set.

John Hammond Jr. also claimed to have 'discovered' the Hawks in Toronto in 1964, and it was perhaps through him that Dylan picked up on them. Certainly some of them were featured on his 1965 album *So Many Roads*. This was so early, from the pre-nascent BAND point of view, that not only was ROBBIE ROBERTSON billed as Jaime R. Robertson but LEVON HELM was billed as Mark Levon Helm and GARTH HUDSON as Eric Hudson. (Charlie Musselwhite was billed as C.D. Musselwhite.) But as ROBERT SHELTON points out, 'Mary Martin, [ALBERT] GROSSMAN's executive secretary, had heard THE HAWKS on visits to Toronto and was ecstatic, possibly earlier than Hammond.'

It is rumoured that at some time after Hammond 'went electric', there was a giddy five-day residency at the Gaslight when both ERIC CLAPTON and JIMI HENDRIX played in Hammond's band. (It is more likely that this is a twisting of the known fact that in 1966 Hendrix was a sideman for many people who played at the Café Au Go Go, and that Clapton, already a star in Britain, was never involved.) In 2001, John Hammond Jr.'s album *Wicked Grin* entirely comprised Tom Waits songs, and featured Waits as producer, guitarist and backing vocalist. In 2004, Dylan wrote about Hammond fondly in *Chronicles Volume One*, and in doing so not only shone a light onto their early friendship but also exonerated Hammond from any lingering notion that he ever pulled any nepotistic strings in furthering his own career. Dylan wrote of going to sign his Columbia deal in fall 1961:

> 'I gazed around Mr. Hammond's office and saw a picture of a friend of mine, John Hammond Jr. John, or Jeep as we knew him on MacDougal Street, was about my age, a blues guitar player and singer. Later he'd become an acclaimed artist in his own right. When I met him he had just gotten back from college, and I think he had only been playing guitar for a short time. Sometimes we'd go over to his house, which was on MacDougal Street below Houston, where he'd grown up, and we listened to a lot of records out of an amazing record collection . . . mostly blues 78s and grassroots rock and roll. I never made the connection that he was the son of the legendary John Hammond until I saw the photograph and only then did I put it together. I don't think anybody knew who Jeep's father was. He never talked about it.'

Now based in northern New Jersey, Hammond continues to perform, and continues not to write songs of his own.

[John Hammond Jr.: *So Many Roads*, Vanguard VSD-79178, NY, 1965; CD-reissued Vanguard 79178, US, 1993; re-packaged with many extra tracks (mostly previously issued on other records, & not all including any Hawks) as *So Many Roads: The Complete Sessions*, Vanguard VMD 79178, US, 2001. Bob Dylan, *Chronicles Volume One*, 2004, p.280. Robert Shelton, *No Direction Home: The Life and Music of Bob Dylan*, London: Penguin edn., 1987, pp.315–16.]

'Handy Dandy' [1990] In 'Handy Dandy', one of the best tracks on *Under the Red Sky*, Dylan takes some of the inherently magical language deployed in a nursery rhyme riddle, to which the solution is merely 'an egg', and allows it freer rein on its mystical level. The riddle goes like this: 'In marble walls as white as milk / Lined with a skin as soft as silk / Within a fountain crystal clear / A golden apple doth appear. / No doors there are to this stronghold, / Yet thieves break in and steal the gold.'

Re-occupied by the lyric of 'Handy Dandy', the numinous charge of this language is retained and extended in Dylan's 'He got that clear crystal fountain / He got that soft silky skin / He got that fortress on the mountain / With no doors, no windows so no thieves can break in.'

He does a great thing here. It's the same side to Dylan's genius that we encounter when, time and again, he takes a phrase from the Bible, cuts to its core and colloquialises it. (In fact there is a biblical connection here: the nursery rhyme itself echoes a passage from Christ's Sermon on the Mount, as Dylan would certainly have known. In Matthew 6:19–22, Christ's words are given as these: 'Lay not up for yourselves treasures on earth, where moth and rust doth corrupt, and where thieves break through and steal: But lay up for yourselves treasures in heaven, where neither moth nor rust doth corrupt, and where thieves do not break through and steal: For where your treasure is, there will your heart be also.' This is reiterated more briefly in Luke 12.) Paring the nursery rhyme down from six lines to four, Dylan strips away the old Classical Greekery—the marble walls, the golden apple—and transforms what's left from florid or portentous Victorian formalism into a poetry that combines mystic potency with the rhythms and cadence of street-talk. So the vicarishly 19th century versifying tone of 'Within a fountain crystal clear' is turned around (literally, with the last three words) into the street-smart pretend-inarticulacy of 'He got that clear crystal fountain'; the purring poesy of 'Lined with a skin as soft as silk' is clipped to the conversational 'He got that soft silky skin'; and the conclusion 'No doors there are to this stronghold, / Yet thieves break in and steal the gold', with its over-supervising 'Yet' and its earthbound explanation for the break-in, is doubly transformed by Dylan. The stronghold/fortress soars into the mountains, magnifying the scale of the scene and intensifying our sense of the isolation of this unspecified 'He'. At the same time—by abolishing the 'gold', by making the break-in feared instead of fact, by increasing the check-list of security provisions and by the effect of that nervy rhythm in describing them ('he got that . . . he got that . . . he got that . . .', which had been street-easy before, now echoes as nervily as 'no doors, no windows . . . no thieves')—by all these touches, Dylan gives *his* conclusion a modern sensibility, evoking the paranoia at the heart of the re-written scenario, and without one supervisory word pointing up its lonely madness: 'He got that clear crystal fountain / He got that soft silky skin / He got that fortress on the mountain / With no doors, no windows so no thieves can break in.' While dismantling the riddle of the rhyme, Dylan has given it the mystery of art.

In the same song, he picks up 'a basket of flowers' from another nursery rhyme (quoted in discussing the album's title-song, **'Under the Red Sky'**: see separate entry) and he snatches a stick from another riddle, one of the nursery rhyme riddles beginning 'Riddle me riddle me ree': in this case 'Riddle me, riddle me ree / A little man in a tree / A stick in his hand / A stone in his throat' / (If you read me this riddle / I'll give you a groat).

The great nursery rhyme experts Iona and Peter Opie say that a number of riddles have been based on the imagery of 'a stick in his hand, a stone in his throat', the solution being either (as here) a cherry or the hawthorn berry. Dylan drops this in passing, as the marvellously dodgy hero 'Handy Dandy' is chatting someone up with '. . . a stick in his hand and a pocket full of money.' It's one of those admirable, quiet, intelligent achievements of Dylan's: he slips in this obscure, innocuous quotation; he re-writes it in such a way as to satisfy us by its twisted echo of the original–both catalogue 'a stick in his hand' and a something else, and both mention money; and he puts his quotation and his re-write in the service of inventive depiction. Handy Dandy, an utterly authentic Dylan character, as *Paris, Texas* as the narrator of 'Clothes Line Saga', as laconic as HOAGY CARMICHAEL, strolls through this wonderful, good-natured song both enigmatically and cinematically. As he finishes his drink, gets up from the table and says 'OK boys I'll see you tomorrow', we realise that there's a final parallel between the riddle-me-ree verse and what Dylan has done with it: the central figure in each demands to be explained. Dylan's is the better riddle.

The listener's 'Who *is* this?' goes unanswered, but dissatisfaction is counter-balanced by the sheer pleasure offered by this pay-off line: a fourfold pleasure, coming from savouring the image evoked, the words chosen, the demands these make so gleefully upon the singer's skill in timing their delivery *and* Dylan's absolute success in meeting those demands. All these points, about the pictures you get from the song and about the pleasures of the words and of their high-wire delivery, are met also in this one confidently invented, supremely free-form line: 'Sitting with a girl named Nancy in a garden feelin' kind of lazy'.

The song's rhythms writhe so enjoyably: the overall framework proceeds at so stately a pace, made the more ocean-linerish by the richness of sound of Dylan's voice and AL KOOPER's organwork; yet within this Dylan moves so restlessly, so variegatedly, as he surveys his chameleonic hero: one who seems a different person in every brief encounter, so that 'he', 'you', 'she' and 'Nancy' seem to multiply, giving us refracted passing glimpses of people and conversation, all sunlit for a moment and then gone again, all with their own daubs of obdurate disorder, vulnerability, darkness and hope.

Each fragment possesses a different rhythm of speech, to which Dylan's singing is superbly alert. Ray Davies or JOHN SEBASTIAN might have devised the line lauded earlier, the luxuriantly unfurling 'Handy Dandy, sitting with a girl named Nancy in a garden feeling kind of lazy' (either might be the unconscious influence behind it). No-one but Bob Dylan could paint this onto the same canvas as so many other cadences and contrasting modes of speech.

There's the intimate, inquisitorial brevity of the conversation which begins with the nursery rhyme about what little boys and little girls are made of (slugs and snails and puppy-dog tails . . . sugar and spice and all things nice . . .), adultising it into darker colloquialisms about inner being: 'You'll say "What are you made of?" / He'll say "Can you repeat what you say?" / You'll say "What are you afraid of?" / He'll say "Nuthin': neither 'live nor dead."' As we 'overhear' this drifting across to us on beguiling waves of music, we are not so charmed that we don't pick up the prevarication and bragging on our hero's part.

It is, furthermore, a moment at which Dylan uses a nursery rhyme from within a fairytale–and uses it brilliantly, to paint in the right psychic backdrop against which to pick out that hollow bragging. The rhyme, the one that begins 'Fee, fie, fo, fum / I smell the blood of an Englishman', is of course spoken by the giant in the fairytale 'Jack and the Beanstalk'. The giant's next line is the one Dylan so niftily puts into the mouth of Handy Dandy: 'Be he 'live or be he dead / I'll grind his bones to make my bread.' It too proves a hollow boast, of course: the giant loses in the fight with brave little everyman Jack. Dylan echoes that 'Be he 'live or be he dead' so closely in Handy Dandy's 'Nuthin': neither 'live nor dead' that he repeats the slight awkwardness of diction noticeable in the giant's remark, such that in each case you can't quite decide whether it's an overtly foreshortened ''live' or a more slippery half-swallowed 'alive'.

There is a further strength and harmony in Dylan's use of 'Jack and the Beanstalk', a tale Dylan alluded to in such a different way in 1964's 'I Shall Be Free No. 10' (and again, in passing, in the phrase 'swap that cow' in *Tarantula*). It contributes to a main theme of the album in being another powerful parable about the need to journey towards maturity, like the fairytale 'The Goose Girl' and the nursery rhyme 'My Mother Said', which Dylan draws on in his 'blind horse' image on the album's title song. Like them, 'Jack and the Beanstalk' deals with the child's dilemma caught between its early need for parental love and guidance ('instruction', in the terminology of the book of Proverbs) and the eventual desirability of trusting oneself and moving towards independence: Jack plays his hunch, charged with the task of taking his cow to market to get a good price; his mother ridicules his folly in swapping the cow for a supposedly magical bean; Jack faces the consequences, and in the end beats the giant. ('What looks large from a distance, close up ain't never that big', as Dylan sings elsewhere.) Jack proves wiser than his mother, arguably through faith, centred upon faith in himself. It's a fairytale Bruno Bettelheim scrutinises in detail along these lines in his pioneering book *The Uses of Enchantment*, and a classic example of the humane inner importance of the genre.

To return to Dylan's distinctive dexterity with rhythms and modes of speech, there's the switch from the calm and patience with which he spreads the child's comfort-food over the 11 syllables of 'Handy Dandy, just like sugar and candy' to the apparent clipped brevity of the line that follows—apparent because this line too is 11 syllables—in which the grown-up's comfort-food is cynically provided instead: 'Handy Dandy: pour 'im another brandy'. And there's the joyous, acrobatic horde of syllables that comes streaming past us at some point in every verse. As well as lazing around with Nancy (a 24-syllable line, since Dylan makes the word 'la-zy' into a lazy 'la-za-a-ay'), there's also the technical wizardry of the line in which we get a quick-fire narrative list of what the hero does, ending with the slow drawl of his remark: 'He finishes his drink, he gets up from the table, he says "OK boys, I'll see ya tamarro-o-ow"' (26 syllables as Dylan delivers it). Best of all, there is the playful self-reflexive joke of the singer having to hurry to fit in the preposterously long 'He'll say "Darlin' tell me the truth: how much time I got?" She'll say "You got all the time in the world, honey."' Imagine anyone but Bob Dylan achieving the necessary timing and phrasing here. Not possible.

For all this audacity, all its refreshing sunlit glimpses—for all its authenticity as a Bob Dylan song—it's one people don't altogether embrace. The chorus is to blame. No-one likes a line such as 'Handy Dandy, just like sugar and candy' (partly because of its tiresome tautology). It's there because it's part of the song's traditional baggage, and Dylan leaves it in because he's feelin' kind of lazy.

'Handy Dandy' is a game and a rhyme. The game is one in which a small object is juggled from hand to hand and then the rhyme is said as you're challenged to guess which hand it's in. The rhyme is one of those which, like 'Humpty Dumpty', has a Scandinavian equivalent and is of a type that has close equivalents all over north Europe. In some cases what seems a nonsense rhyme in one language ('Jeck og Jill' in Danish) makes sense in another. Some may result from long oral traditions, others from direct translations. This one is so old that it was already known before the creator of 'Piers Plowman', William Langland, wrote of 'his handidandi' in 1362. Variants include 'Handy dandy, riddledy ro / Which hand will you have, high or low?'; 'Handy pandy, Sugary candy / Which will you have?' and 'Handy-dandy, Jack-a-dandy / Which good hand will you have?'

(There is also a rhyme, not associated with the game, that Pope and Carey alluded to when attacking the syrupy poetry of their contemporary Ambrose Philips: 'Handy spandy, Jack-a-Dandy / Loves plum cake and sugar candy / He bought some at a grocer's shop / And out he came, hop, hop, hop, hop.' A variant begins 'Namby pamby Jack-a-Dandy', and 'Namby pamby' was Pope and Carey's nickname for Philips. Not that these antecedents improve Dylan's chorus one jot, jot, jot.)

The same rhyme was quoted by George Chapman (now best known for his great translation of Homer) in his play *The Blinde Begger of Alexandria* in 1598: 'handy dandy prickly prandy, which hand will you haue?', and is referred to in this crucial speech in *King Lear*, by Lear himself: 'Handy dandy, prickly prandy. . . . What, art mad? A man may see how this world goes without eyes . . .'—or, as someone once put it, 'you don't need a weatherman to know which way the wind blows'—'Look with thine ears: see how yond justice rails upon yond simple thief. Hark, in thine ear: change places, and, handy-dandy, which is the justice, which is the thief?' (Another 'Dylanesque' question, this.)

Lear's speech here is part of the scene described by Hugh Haughton in *The Chatto Book of Nonsense Poetry* as having 'as vivid a place in the history of nonsense as in that of madness. The dialogue is shot through with queer, garbled, oracular language, and shifts back and forth between reason and madness, pathos and absurdity. It's not only the most vivid representation of the fool in literature, but in its vision of violent social upheaval and broken authority suggests that through the language of madness and adopted madness the characters make touch with truths and feelings outside the pale of their normal language. What they say in their terrible crisis makes sense . . . but it takes a route that zigzags giddily across the border with nonsense . . .'

Stripped of the Shakespearean tragedy's pain, more Edward Lear than *King Lear*, Dylan's 'Handy Dandy' too gives us broken sound-bites that make no sense yet make perfect sense, and glimpses of characters who challenge each other with crazy truths, as it takes us on a route that zigzags giddily across the border with nonsense. The discomforting banality of its chorus aside, it is a sustained, successful work in which well-hewn writing interlocks with a bravura vocal performance, making for a warm, humourous—often black-humourous—hymn of celebration to human quirkiness and flexibility.

[Iona & Peter Opie: for details of their work & sources, see endnotes to **nursery rhyme, Dylan's use of, an introduction**. Bruno Bettelheim, *The Uses of Enchantment*, London: Thames & Hudson, 1976. Hugh Haughton, ed., *The Chatto Book of Nonsense Poetry*, London: Chatto & Windus, 1988. It was Andrew Muir, in *Homer, the slut* no.2, London, Jan 1991, who first linked the passage from Haughton to *Under the Red Sky*.]

'Hard Times' [1992] See **Foster, Stephen**.

***Hard Rain* [album, 1976]** Dylan's 19th album and his second live one, this once seemed a generally poor selection from two concerts that were far from his best. After *Dylan* and the 1967 *Greatest Hits* collection, this seemed, at the time, Dylan's least essential album. His voice even sounded oddly anonymous at first. Hindsight shows that this album introduces the ragged, postmodern Bob Dylan, right from the grungy instrumental ground-pawing ahead of the start of the first number. Moreover the running order now seems surprisingly well thought out. It represents, too, the late phase of the historic Rolling Thunder Revue tour and captures the distinctive, bare-wired sound of Dylan's existential gypsy band. Stand-out track is 'Idiot Wind', which, as Dylan grows ever more engaged, bursts open and pours out its brilliant venom. Some tracks are the same performances as on the 'Hard Rain' TV Special, filmed in concert at Colorado State University, Fort Collins, CO, on May 23, 1976, but 'You're a Big Girl Now', though recorded at that concert, is on this album but not in the TV film, and four album tracks were from an earlier concert.

[Recorded Fort Worth, TX, 16 May and Fort Collins, CO, 23 May 1976; released as LP Columbia PC 34349, 10 Sep 1976.]

'Hard Rain' [TV Special, 1976] Dylan's first made-for-TV filmed concert, filmed outdoors in the rain at Colorado State University, Fort Collins, CO, on May 23, 1976, this is a riveting, essential item and captures an extremely charismatic, energised Dylan, sounding harshly robust and looking uncannily like Jesus Christ—but more beautiful. The crowd is interesting to look at too, though it wasn't an aesthetically pleasing era. By the late 1980s young people coming to the film afresh tended to remark on the awfulness of 1970s clothes and all that hair.

Some song performances are the same as on the *Hard Rain* album, though six song performances in the film are not on the album, while 'You're a Big Girl Now', recorded at the concert and issued on the album, is not included in the film (and four album tracks were from an earlier concert).

Stand-out moments include an utterly transformed 'I Pity the Poor Immigrant', a fiery 'Idiot Wind' and a numinious 'Deportees'—the best duet JOAN BAEZ ever managed with Dylan.

This was the second attempt at making such a concert film, the first being a month earlier, when two Rolling Thunder concerts on the same day, April 22, 1976, were filmed in the Starlight Ballroom of the Bellevue Biltmore Hotel in Clearwater, Florida.

The later film was first shown on NBC-TV in September 1976 (the same week the album was released). Filmed and edited by HOWARD ALK, this was magnificent television, using the small screen imaginatively: not least by the recurrent, almost mesmeric device of keeping the camera close up on Dylan's unattended vocal microphone so as to make into visual drama the flair and split-second timing with which he would re-appear behind it. While *Renaldo & Clara* teased the audience with fragmentary concert footage from 1975's first Rolling Thunder Revue, strung out across a four-hour film, *Hard Rain* offers a very straightforward, gritty sampler of 1976's second Rolling Thunder Revue. This cries out for DVD release.

Not to be confused with the *Hard Rain* that *is* available on DVD, a wretchedly poor 1998 thriller directed by Mikael Salomon and starring Morgan Freeman.

[*Hard Rain*, dir. Howard Alk, NBC-TV, NY, aired 14 Sep 1976.]

Harding, John Wesley [1965 -] See Stace, Wes.

Hare, David [1947 -] See 'Keats v. Dylan'.

Harris, Emmylou [1947 -] Emmylou Harris was born in Birmingham, Alabama, on April 2, 1947, and being a military pilot's daughter, grew up moving around—in North Carolina and between Virginia and Washington, D.C. She won a scholarship in Dramatic Studies at the University of North Carolina but after local folkie performances in a duo with one Mike Williams, she moved to New York. An early marriage and record deal soon failed, and she returned to Washington, D.C., to raise her young daughter alone. In 1971 she met Gram Parsons, with whom she went to LA to work on his début solo album, *GP*—which wasn't, of course, solo at all, since for many people its highlights were the duets with Harris. The album was released shortly before Parsons' death from a drugs overdose, but not before they had assembled the Fallen Angels band and gone out on the road, starting disastrously but pulling itself together and during four nights in Houston including guest spots from Linda Ronstadt and NEIL YOUNG. The tour ended in New York City, playing live at Max's Kansas City and a Long Island radio station, WLIR.

In June 1973, Parsons and Emmylou Harris reunited for a country rock tour and then recorded the *Grievous Angel* album. Parsons' life was in chaos and his drug taking reckless, and he was declared dead half an hour into September 19, 1973 at the aptly name Hi-Desert Memorial Hospital in Yucca Valley, California. He was 26.

The work Harris and Parsons created together, outtakes and all, has been issued and reissued many times since *GP* and *Grievous Angel*, beginning with that fine 1976 album of scraps *Sleepless Nights*, billed as by Gram Parsons/Flying Burrito Brothers but including three duets by Parsons and Harris and sleevenotes by Harris too.

Their duets soar high above the ordinary, unencumbered by weary professional tricks; shimmering and numinous, full of integrity and space, held in a thrilling tension between abrasion and sweetness, they are the embodiment of duets between beauty and pain. For many, they remain Emmylou's most glorious moment, however much a subsequent three-decade piling up of achievement and success may clamour for plaudits.

Early on she had also sung on the JOHN SEBASTIAN album *Tarzana Kid*, Little Feat's *Feats Don't Fail Me Now* and Linda Ronstadt's *Heart Like a Wheel* (all 1974), Pure Prairie League's *Two Lane Highway*, Bonnie Raitt's *Homeplate*, Ronstadt's *Prisoner in Disguise*, Guy Clark's *Old #1* and DAVID BROMBERG's *Midnight on the Water* (all 1975), but it was from her work with Parsons that she gained a major-label deal with Reprise, and a début album, *Pieces of the Sky*, 1975, which included both a small hit single and her own strong composition memorialising Gram Parsons, 'Boulder to Birmingham'. *Elite Hotel* followed that December, the album for which her Hot Band was formed and which yielded two no.1 hits, 'Together Again' and 'Sweet Dreams', launching a long career in which she has enjoyed a special niche in country and country-rock, touring and recording prolifically. Notable albums have included *Quarter Moon in a Ten Cent Town*, the acoustic bluegrass of 1980's *Roses in the Snow* and the DANIEL LANOIS-produced rock of *Wrecking Ball* in 1994, on which Neil Young plays and sings, and on which Emmylou covered Dylan's 'Every Grain of Sand'.

She first connected with Bob Dylan himself in 1975, early on in her own solo career, when she was brought in on the New York sessions for *Desire*. Early on, the studio was full of people milling about wondering whether they'd be used, and then, when they'd done their best to play along with Dylan's wayward one-off song run-throughs, wondering whether they *had* been used. Harris' first day in this melée seems to have been July 28, 1975, when she had to jostle for space with at least 20 other people (including ERIC CLAPTON and Kokomo, a British jazz-rock group fronted by sax player Mel Collins). She was, as she told interviewer NIGEL WILLIAMSON years later, 'astonished' at the way Dylan was working. 'I'd never heard the songs before, and we did most of them in one or two takes. I just watched his mouth and watched was he was saying. That's where all that humming on the record comes from.'

She was unhappy with how this made her sound, and asked Dylan if she could 'fix' her vocals, but Dylan pressed ahead with the tracks they had. The first day she was there (which was the second session), they recorded the album version of 'Romance in Durango' and the take of 'Catfish' issued on the *Bootleg Series Vols. 1–3*, and made various attempts at other songs. The next day, July 29, yielded nothing; July 30 produced not only 'Golden Loom' (on *Bootleg*) and 'Rita May' (issued as the B-side of a single that November and on the Japanese-initiated *Masterpieces* compilation) but the *Desire* tracks 'Oh Sister', 'One More Cup of Coffee', 'Black Diamond Bay', 'Mozambique' and 'Joey'. Harris was not present on July 31 for 'Sara' and 'Isis' and the outtake 'Abandoned Love' issued on *Biograph* in 1985, nor at the hasty re-recording, with amended lyrics, of 'Hurricane' on October 24th.

Harris' main contributions were on 'Oh Sister' and 'Mozambique'. 'Oh Sister' features Harris particularly strongly, but both are in effect duets and add their own shades to the unique colouring of the album; and the way that Emmylou had to plunge in and try to read Dylan moment by moment to know what to sing at all, though a hard task at the time, and well survived, actually adds to the shaking chemistry of their duets, and in the case of 'Oh Sister' this out-on-a-limb quality tugs pleasingly against the exceptional conventionality and old-fashioned-values message the song evinces.

She and Dylan next connected nearly 17 years later, and far more trivially, if in more extravagant circumstances, when Harris was among the many big-name backing singers and over-excited all-star band ranged behind Dylan on his comically guarded 'Like a Rolling Stone' at the 'Late Night with David Letterman 10th Anniversary Show', recorded on January 18 and televised February 6, 1992.

In May 1994 Dylan was in the studios in Memphis recording a short but interesting session with his Never-Ending Tour band of the time, one item being a couple of different takes of the JIMMIE RODGERS song 'My Blue-Eyed Jane'. A short snatch of one take was thrown into the *Highway 61 Interactive* CD-ROM in 1995, but when the complete second take circulated in 1996, shared vocals by Emmylou Harris had been overdubbed in the interim. A third version, with Dylan's vocal re-recorded and Harris' removed, was then released on the Various Artists album *The Songs of Jimmie Rodgers—A Tribute*.

In October 1988, when Emmylou Harris released her compilation album *Duets*, she included 'Mozambique' from the *Desire* album. This has now become a very collectable item because a dispute with Dylan's management forced its withdrawal. *Duets* was reissued on vinyl in 1990 and on CD in 1993, minus the Dylan track.

All the collaborations between Harris and Dylan seem to have been subject to difficulty and disappointing excisions, and interviews Harris gave soon after the *Desire* collaboration appeared to suggest that she had never held too high an opinion of him. Yet one story tells a different truth. In the US Bible Belt, people throw around the acronym WWJD?—meaning that when you're uncertain how to behave, just ask 'What Would Jesus Do?' Emmylou Harris told interviewer Nigel Williamson that country singer-songwriter Gillian Welch had given her a bracelet engraved 'WWDD'. She asked what that meant, to be told it stood for 'What Would Dylan Do?'—not in life but in song-craft. Harris endorsed this message with enthusiasm: 'When you're writing a song, just ask yourself that question,' she said.

[Emmylou Harris: *Pieces of the Sky*, Reprise MS-2213, US, 1975; *Elite Hotel*, Reprise MS-2236, 1976; *Quarter Moon in a Ten Cent Town*, Warner Bros BSK-3141, US, 1978; *Roses in the Snow*, Warner Bros BSK-3422, US, 1980; *Duets*, Reprise 25791-1, US, 1988 (withdrawn); *Duets*, Warner Bros 25791, 1990 & CD, *nia*, 1993. *Wrecking Ball*, Elektra 61854, 1995. Gram Parsons & Emmylou Harris: *GP*, Reprise MS 2123, 1973; *Grievous Angel*, Reprise MS 2171, US, 1974; *Sleepless Nights*, A&M SP-4578, US, 1976; *Gram Parsons & the Fallen Angels: Live 1973*, Sierra GP 1973 & *More Gram Parsons & the Fallen Angels Live 1973*, Sierra GP/EP 104, both US 1982 (the latter an EP). Sources include the basic *www.divastation.com/emmylou_harris/eharris_bio.html*, the invaluable *http://ebni.com/byrds/memgrp5.html*, the online discography *www.luma-electronic.cz/lp/h/Harris/emmylou1.htm*, all online 8 Dec 2005, & that excellent small book, Nigel Williamson's *The Rough Guide to Bob Dylan*, London: Rough Guides 2004, pp.222 & iv.]

Harrison, George [1943 - 2001] George Harold Harrison was born in Wavertree, Liverpool, UK, on February 25, 1943. He grew up on Merseyside, joined the Quarrymen, who turned into THE BEATLES, and was their lead guitarist. For teeny fans of the pop group, George was 'the quiet one', very much in the background behind the main pin-ups and main songwriting team of JOHN LENNON and PAUL McCARTNEY; but for fans of musicianship and people who recognised a decent human being when they encountered one, George was a crucial Beatle, and the songs he contributed to the group's repertoire, never less than interesting, were sometimes milestones in their development and often important and much-loved. 'Here Comes the Sun' and 'Something' became instant classics, and the latter was the A-side of the penultimate Beatles single. Harrison had introduced the sitar to Beatles music, and so to western pop, and became the one Beatle deeply engaged by Indian culture, its music and its religious mysticism. Meditation, learnt in the late 1960s, anchored the rest of his life.

When the Beatles broke up in 1970, George was, to many people's surprise, the one who stepped most effectively into the solo artist's rôle. His triple-LP *All Things Must Pass* (co-produced by PHIL SPECTOR) was a rich and mature piece of quintessential 1960s work and yielded the single 'My Sweet Lord'. Both topped the UK charts. George Harrison was 27.

The next year, prompted by Ravi Shankar, Harrison organised the fundraising Concert for Bangla Desh, which sold out Madison Square Garden, New York, and yielded a best-selling triple-LP and a film, raising millions of dollars for UNICEF so that Bangladeshi refugees from Pakistan could be helped and protected. It was the first time that musicians had collaborated on a large scale in the name of a humanitarian cause, and thus it set the precedent that can be seen to have led to LIVE AID and Live8.

In 1974 Harrison formed the record company Dark Horse, and in 1978 began an important contribution in another cultural area, the British film industry, by forming Handmade Films, which backed and produced the Monty Python movies and more. After years of issuing no albums of his own in the 1980s, his hit album *Cloud Nine* in 1987, co-produced with JEFF LYNNE, gave him a top 3 single on both sides of the Atlantic ('Got My Mind Set on You'). Soon afterwards, he instigated the TRAVELING WILBURYS when he used Dylan's garage studio for a project of his own that turned into the Wilburys instead.

None of this 1980s work represented any kind of musical peak for Harrison, but he had always enjoyed his collaborations with Bob Dylan, and had offered the latter a dependable, solid partnership, calmly treating Dylan as a worthy musician and being content to put his own far more virtuoso playing skills encouragingly in the other's service.

Harrison and Dylan first met during the famous encounter at the Del Monico Hotel in August 1964 (see the entry on Harrison's acquaintance AL ARONOWITZ) and later encountered each other during Dylan's London visits of 1965 and 1966. By 1968 the two were getting together informally, and this resulted in a co-composition. As George told it:

'I was at Bob's house and we were trying to write a tune. And I remember saying, "How did you write all those amazing words?" And he shrugged and said, "Well, how about all those chords you use?" So I started playing and said it was just all these funny chords people showed me when I was a kid. Then I played two major sevenths in a row to demonstrate, and I suddenly thought, Ah, this sounds like a tune here. Then we finished the song together. It was called "I'd Have You Anytime," and it [became] the first track on *All Things Must Pass*.' A version was recorded at Dylan's Woodstock, NY, house in November 1968, with Dylan on guitar and Harrison on lead vocals; at the same session they shared vocals on two other numbers, one of which was another co-written song, 'Nowhere to Go', often known as 'Every Time Somebody Comes to Town'.

The Beatles attended Dylan's 1969 Isle of Wight Festival of Music appearance and got together privately while on the island but musically the next collaboration between Dylan and Harrison was in the studios in New York City on May 1, 1970 (running into the early hours of May 2). This was Dylan's first time in the studio since the *Self Portrait* sessions early that March, and before that album's release, but he was clearly trying out material that would later be re-recorded for *New Morning*. (Indeed both Harrison and AL KOOPER believed that the album version of 'Went to See the Gypsy' comes from this May 1–2 session, though the aural evidence is against it.)

What's not in dispute is that this session features Dylan and Harrison on guitars, Dylan on vocals, plus CHARLIE DANIELS on guitar, RUSS KUNKEL on drums and producer BOB JOHNSTON on piano, and that to hear it is to hear Bob and George working together. 'Working on a Guru' is another co-composition, 'If Not for You' is tried out (one take has been issued on the *Bootleg Series Vols. 1–3*) and other tracks that have circulated include hopeless attempts at 'Da Doo Ron Ron' and 'Yesterday', other pop hits including 'Cupid' and 'All I Have to Do Is Dream' but also lovely revisits to 'Song to Woody' and 'I Don't Believe You (She Acts Like We Never Have Met)' sung in Bob's best Nashville '69 voice, and much more. Some tracks, including the first attempts at 'Sign on the Window', remain uncirculated. From here Harrison picked up 'If Not for You' and released his own version on *All Things Must Pass* the same year. Dylan's August 12 recording of it was issued on *New Morning*.

At the Concert for Bangla Desh (actually two concerts: an afternoon and an evening performance) Dylan's performances—reaching their zenith with the glorious vocal, so high, melodious, penetrating and inspired, on the evening concert's 'Just Like a Woman'—feature Harrison on guitar, LEON RUSSELL on bass and RINGO STARR on tambourine. George's spoken introduction, 'I'd like to bring on a friend of us all, Mr. Bob Dylan', and the roar that greets this, form one of the warmest moments from a marvellous event. (And with the release of the audio on CD and the video on DVD, we now have extra material taken from that afternoon concert—the CD gives us that show's performances of 'Love Minus Zero/No Limit' and 'Mr. Tambourine Man'; the DVD gives us 'Love Minus Zero' and adds in Dylan and Harrison singing 'If Not for You', harmonising and strumming acoustic guitars, from the previous day's rehearsal, and the ROBERT JOHNSON song 'Come on in My Kitchen' by Leon Russell, ERIC CLAPTON and Harrison, from a soundtrack.)

In another lifetime, the twilight zone of Dylan's 1987 UK tour with TOM PETTY & THE HEARTBREAKERS, George Harrison turned up on the last of their four nights at London's vile Wembley Arena, but was only allowed to come on stage for the penultimate encore number, the long-since exhausted 'Rainy Day Women # 12 & 35', on which he shared vocals and played guitar. Less than six months later, in early April 1988, George brought 'Handle With Care' to Dylan's garage studio in Malibu, and the Traveling Wilburys were born. Further tracks that ended up on *Traveling Wilburys, Volume 1* were recorded at DAVE STEWART's home studio in LA that May—tracks taken away and overdubbed in England by Lynne and Harrison. Soon afterwards, in June 1988, Dylan released his own deeply unsuccessful *Down in the Groove* album, and began the Never-Ending Tour. That October, the Wilburys album was released. Harrison, aka Nelson Wilbury, had written 'Handle With Care' (on which he shared lead vocals with ROY ORBISON), 'Heading for the Light' and 'End of the Line'; Dylan (Lucky Wilbury) had written 'Dirty World', 'Congratulations' and 'Tweeter and the Monkey Man.'

Two months later, Orbison was dead. Harrison did not appear with Dylan at the tribute concert held in LA on February 24, 1990, but within a month they had come together at a recording studio in that city where Dylan was recording tracks for his album *Under the Red Sky*. Harrison played the unobtrusively perfect slide guitar on the title track. A month on from this session and after a phone-call from Bob to George, asking when they were going to do another Wilburys record, the surviving members reassembled at their 'Wilbury Mountain Studio' in Bel Air, where they recorded the tracks for *The Traveling Wilburys: Volume III* (the second album), plus 'Runaway', issued as B-side to the 'She's My Baby' single, and 'Nobody's Child', the latter for the Romanian Angel Appeal fund. Bob was now Boo Wilbury and George Harrison now Spike.

In October 1992 Harrison was one of those who participated in what was billed as 'Columbia Records Celebrates the Music of Bob Dylan', aka the 30th Anniversary Concert for Dylan at Madison Square Garden, New York City—21 years after being there together for the Concert for Bangla Desh. This time Harrison was among the small group of compadres sharing vocals on Dylan's 'My Back Pages' performance, as well as being in the ensemble for 'Knockin' on Heaven's Door', the penultimate number; earlier in the evening, in his own solo spot, he had gone for 'Absolutely Sweet Marie'.

George Harrison's life had been in jeopardy when he was stabbed by an intruder in his home in England in 1999. He survived, but died in Los Angeles on November 29, 2001, from complications arising from cancer of the throat.

Bob Dylan was unable to perform at the subsequent Concert for George, in 2002, but attempted a sweet version of 'Something' at his own concert in New York City on November 13, 2002. He also paid Harrison this tribute:

> 'George was a giant, a great, great soul, with all of the humanity, all of the wit and humor, all the wisdom, the spirituality, the common sense of a man and compassion for people. The world is a profoundly emptier place without him.'

[Harrison quote, *www.iol.ie/~beatlesireland/harrison/interviews/georgeinterview3.htm*. Both *All Things Must Pass* and *Concert for Bangla Desh* have been reissued remastered and with extra material; both have received lavish praise. *All Things Must Pass*, EMI, UK, 2001; *The Concert for Bangla Desh*, now called *The Concert for Bangladesh* (and with George Harrison on the cover instead of a starving child), 2-CD set, Sony BMG

82876729862, 2005; DVD on Apple/Warner Music Vision/Rhino R2 97048, US (R2 0349-70480-2, Europe), 2005; DVD De-Luxe limited edition (retaining child on cover) on Weasel Disc 970481, US (Apple/Warner Music Vision/Rhino 0349-70481-2, Europe, 2005. (Both sets have the extra footage, but the limited edition set also has postcards, a mini concert poster, hand-written lyrics, a 60-page booklet and a sticker. 'Limited edition' in Europe means limited to 100,000 copies!)]

Harvey, Todd [1965 -] Todd Dunham Harvey was born in Ohio on January 15, 1965, the day Dylan finished recording *Bringing It All Back Home* at a session that yielded 'Maggie's Farm', 'On the Road Again', 'It's Alright Ma (I'm Only Bleeding)', 'Gates of Eden', 'Mr. Tambourine Man' and 'It's All Over Now, Baby Blue'.

Todd Harvey first took an interest in Dylan's work when, aged 14 in 1979, he encountered the album *The Times They Are a-Changin'*. However, apart from contributing a few concert reviews to the BobLinks website, and a paper on the song 'Man of Constant Sorrow' delivered at the 'Bob Dylan's Performance Artistry' colloquium in Caen, France, March 10–12, 2005 (sponsored, interestingly, by the US Embassy in Paris), Harvey's work on Dylan has been confined to one book: the small but invaluable *The Formative Dylan: Transmissions and Stylistic Influences, 1961–1963*, published in 2001.

A scholarly examination and analysis of 70 of the earliest songs Dylan recorded (actually 69 songs plus the poem 'Last Thoughts on Woody Guthrie'), as known about at the time, it begins by discussing Dylan's knowledge of traditional music and literature and describes his stylistic influences and his developing aesthetics in this early period. The songs are listed and looked at alphabetically, in each case giving details on its historical and stylistic background, how Dylan arrived at its composition, a technical analysis of its musical components, and performance data. There is also a series of appendices, including references, set and session lists, a chronology of the songs studied and a table of data on over 275 versions of the 70 songs.

However, it isn't as dry as that sounds, and it is informed by a sharp intelligence and great fondness for Dylan's artistry. It offers much useful fresh thought and observation, and, crucially, when it was first published it offered significant new information, especially about Dylan's 1963 Newport Folk Festival song performances: information Harvey gained from his unique and unhindered access to the Library of Congress' archives, and which he had the knowledge and alertness to understand and evaluate fully.

Todd Harvey has also been a lecturer in music at Ohio State University and is now a Folklife Specialist at the American Folklife Center within the Library of Congress.

[Todd Harvey, *The Formative Dylan: Transmissions and Stylistic Influences, 1961–1963*, Lanham, MD: The Scarecrow Press, 2001 (7th volume in this publisher's American Folk Music and Musicians series).]

Havis, Regina See McCrary, Regina.

Hawkins, Ronnie [1935 -] Ronald Hawkins was born in Huntsville, Arkansas, on January 10, 1935—'two days after ELVIS PRESLEY', as he likes to say, though any other resemblance is hard to suggest, since Elvis became God and Hawkins became a third-rate, derivative perpetual rockabilly who couldn't make it in the US and on the wise recommendation of CONWAY TWITTY moved to Canada, where audiences had less opportunity to be fussy. Starting out in Hamilton, Ontario, at a club called the Grange, Hawkins formed a working bar band that toured and recorded under various names, the first of which was, quaintly, the Ronnie Hawkins Quartet. On record, starting as he meant to continue, by covering songs of other people, his first single, 'Hey BO DIDDLEY', was released (in Canada only) in 1958. A deal with US label Roulette in 1959 did not underwrite any return to the US, and in 1964 Hawkins took permanent Canadian residency.

He may not be significant as a musical figure himself, but he is a key figure in the history of Bob Dylan's music in that he assembled THE HAWKS, starting with fellow Arkansas boy LEVON HELM and duly adding the rest (all Canadians). Hawkins both recorded with them and led them around the gruelling small-club and honky-tonk circuits of Canada, fusing them into the unit that Dylan picked up, galvanised and made history with. (The details of which records by Ronnie Hawkins & the Hawks involve which members of what became THE BAND is traced in the endnotes to this entry.)

He's a key witness as to how much of a musical leap The Band made between leaving him and Toronto behind and emerging with their own albums after working with Dylan. Talking especially of the second album, he says: 'I was so surprised that Robbie wrote that stuff, because they were a rhythm'n'blues act. They played rhythm'n'blues great. And they didn't *like* country music. . . . I wanted to play that to people and they wouldn't play it. And then when their albums came out, man, I was shocked, because they were definitely country roots. So different.' And songwriting before they entered Dylan's orbit?: 'Nothing! I couldn't even get Robbie to sing or nothing!'

Hawkins says he first met 'Robert' through ALBERT GROSSMAN and through the Hawks: 'I didn't know too much about Bobby. I just knew he was one of those folk-singers that was supposed to be a hero. I'd never seen him and I'd never paid too much attention to any of his songs. Then ROBBIE ROBERTSON and them came down and said boy, he writes a lot of good stuff. So I started listening a little bit, you know? And so in Toronto, when they decided to go with Bob, the band was playing up there and Bob came up to, I think it was the Friars Tavern—and they rehearsed some songs. That was when they were gettin' ready to go on the road.'

Hawkins says that at this point he had already put another band together, because 'they had a chance to better themselves, and anytime somebody has a chance to better themselves, you just wish 'em well and hope they can make it. You've done all you can do. And I wouldn't travel in those days much. I was up there in the Coq D'Or Tavern in Toronto, because my kids were kids then. I wouldn't travel till they got grown up.'

A decade later, Hawkins was thrilled to be called in on the Rolling Thunder Revue and the *Renaldo & Clara* film (while the entourage was passing through Canada) in which he played the part of 'Bob Dylan'; but he was bemused by Dylan's approach to life and filming. Having always kept his wife and personal life very private, suddenly it was up on the screen, and Hawkins couldn't fathom that: 'Bob is so intelligent, y'know—and he's mysterious. He's hard to figure out. I can figure out people pretty quick, because I've been in the business so long, and I can judge an audience and all that. But Bob is like a—what's the word?—a *schizophreniac.* [Hawkins knows more than he makes out: one of his children, Ronnie Jr., was diagnosed with schizophrenia in his teens; the Hawkinses campaign and fundraise for the Schizophrenia Society of Ontario.] I'm not sure he's like that, but he has different personalities for different things. . . . It was kinda like the story of his life. He had his wife and he had his girlfriend, JOAN BAEZ—and they were both there. He lived with one of 'em and then he lived with the other one, and then he lived with both of them, and they were both there! I said, "Bob, howja ever did this, boy? It's amazing!" I told Bob, I said, "I don't know how you ever got this job done." But he managed to handle it somehow!'

And then there was the film's construction: 'Ha! There was no rehearsing, y'know. Bob was directing and producing and doing everything. I did three or four little skits, and he'd just call me up, three or four o'clock in the morning, and say "Come on, let's do somethin'". . . . All ad-libbed. All of it.'

Hawkins is prominent in a neat scene where MICK RONSON tries to stop him getting into the dressing-room; in a scene where he tries to seduce a young girl as the 'Moonlight Sonata' plays in the background; and the scene where he arrives in town at a hotel and is accosted by a local TV interviewer. 'She actually thought I was Bob Dylan. She knew nothing about Bob; she was just doin' her TV thing. So when I came in with the hat and a lot of people around me, she thought "Wow, must be Bob!" . . . And I think that's where Bob got the idea for me being Bob Dylan, because I'm answering questions, and when I saw that she didn't know any better, I started answering Bob's questions for him—just for fun, y'know. And he was laughing. He was standing alongside and he said "Go ahead, go ahead!" So I'm goin' ahead. It was somethin'! So she's askin' me all these questions about all the songs I'd written: "Blowin' in the Wind" and all that . . .'

And the end result? 'When I was down in California . . . Bob invited us down and . . . we watched about eight hours of film. And he had everybody in it: all the freaks, the greeks, the cripples, everything.' He never saw the four-hour finished film:

> 'Where did it play? It must be the art theaters or something. But it's going to have to be a classic, because no matter how bad the film stuff was, he had so many people on there that nobody else could have gotten on the film. I mean he had everybody. I think that film was mostly just about the 60s. I think you'd have to know that era. He had eskimos in there, and some of the old punch-drunk boxers; he had lots of different people in that booger. Bad photography, bad everything; but: he's got the people.'

Hawkins' involvement was only while the Revue rolled through Canada, but he was also around for The Band's Farewell Concert, and hence for *The Last Waltz*. Again, he was thrilled to sample the high life:

> 'I was out there for a month, before it was recorded. . . . I stayed out there at the Shangri-La. The Shangri-La was the studio that the Band and Dylan owned, y'know. And it was *reverse* shangri-la. That's the place I said you come in at 19 and you leave at 300—in about six months. So anyway, they were trying to get that together: and all these heroes of the world came in. And I had never seen a lot of them, y'know. I'd played in the bars of Ontario: I didn't know that much about what was going on, except that Rolling Thunder Revue. . . . This was my chance—I got to see all the heroes, and their lifestyles. Boy, it was fast! Ha! Fast pace! It was one hell of a party.'

Since that party, Hawkins has continued to make records, ventured into other movies, including the magnificent disaster of Michael Cimino's *Heaven's Gate* (1980), but has connected up with Dylan professionally only a couple of times. On the first occasion, when Dylan had temporarily stopped having 'one hell of a party' and was declaring 'I Ain't Going to Go to Hell for Anybody', his second gospel tour of 1980 hit Toronto and there in the midst of his fiery April 20 concert (which was filmed and recorded, though it remains officially unreleased), hearing that Hawkins was in the audience, Dylan said this from the stage just before a transcendently howling version of 'When He Returns': 'Well, I'm very happy to say we have Ronnie Hawkins here tonight. Yeah. I don't know where he is, I know he's here somewhere. Ronnie and I go back a long ways—in fact Ronnie's, I hear he's gonna be doing movies now, I think. Was it a movie a year now? Is that right, Ronnie? Well, remember, you know, actually I gave Ronnie his first part in the movies. That's right. Ronnie was in a little movie we made called *Renaldo & Clara*, about—a few years back; and Ronnie played the part of Bob Dylan. Interesting movie. Anyway, I guess there's no place to go but up now, hey Ron?'

Ten years later, when the Never-Ending Tour hit the same city, Hawkins came on stage in the middle of Dylan's set and took the lead vocal on 'One More Night', after an appropriate flourish of an intro from Dylan, who said this: 'A hero of mine—Ronnie Hawkins! Where is he? He said he would come up and sing a song: called "One More Night". It would be awfully nice if he would come up! If he doesn't want to come up, that's OK too! All right—Oh, here he comes now!' Hawkins, with his customary numbing jocularity, took the stage yelling 'Keep the women back! Keep the women back!'

Finally (so far) at 'the Absolutely Unofficial Blue Jeans Bash (for Arkansas)' in Washington, D.C., on January 17, 1993, Ronnie Hawkins was one of those on guitar alongside Dylan. He played behind Dylan on 'To Be Alone With You' and then they both played behind Stephen Stills on 'Key to the Highway' and the Cate Brothers on 'I Shall Be Released' and '(I Don't Want to) Hang Up My Rock'n'-Roll Shoes'. A fragment of 'To Be Alone With You' was televised on CBC-TV in Canada two nights later as part of a news item on Hawkins, and a fragment of 'I Shall Be Released' a further two nights on as part of a feature on The Band.

Things probably hadn't changed between them. 'You know what Bob is,' says Hawkins, 'he's mysterious. He's always been mysterious.' As he'd readily admit, what's equally true is that Ronnie Hawkins has never been mysterious.

[Ronnie Hawkins Quartet (incl. Levon Helm): 'Hey Bo Diddley' c/w 'Love Me Like You Can', Toronto, summer 1958, Quality 1827, Canada, 1958. Ronnie Hawkins & the Hawks (but only incl. Helm): 'Forty Days' c/w 'One of These Days', NY, 13 & 15 Apr 1959, Apex 76499, Canada (Roulette R4154, US), 1959; 'Mary Lou' c/w 'Need Your Lovin', NY, 29 Apr 1959, Apex 76561 (Roulette R4177, US; Columbia DB4345, UK), 1959; 'Southern Love' c/w 'Love Me Like You Can', NY, 26 Oct 1959, Apex 76623 (Roulette R4209, Columbia DB4412), 1960; 'Lonely Hours' c/w 'Clara', NY, Nov 1959, Roulette R4249, Canada (Roulette R4228, US; Columbia DB4442, UK), 1960. Ronnie Hawkins: 'Ballad of Caryl Chessman', NY, 22 Feb 1960 c/w 'Death of Floyd Collins', NY, 26 May 1959, Roulette R4231, Canada & US, 1960. Ronnie Hawkins & the Hawks (incl. Helm only): 'Ruby Baby', NY, 13 Apr 1959, c/w 'Hayride', NY, 26 Oct 1959, Roulette R4249, 1960. Ronnie Hawkins (w Helm, & Robertson on A-side only): 'Summertime' c/w 'Mister and Mississippi', Nashville, 28 Apr 1960, Roulette R4267, 1960; 'Cold Cold Heart' c/w 'Nobody's Lonesome for Me' (both w Helm only), Roulette R4311, 1961. Ronnie Hawkins & the Hawks (w Helm, Robertson & Danko): 'Come Love' c/w 'I Feel Good', NY, 13 & 18 Sep 1961, Roulette R4400, 1961. Ronnie Hawkins & the Hawks (with Helm, Robertson, Danko & Manuel): 'Bo Diddley' c/w 'Who Do You Love', NY, Jan 1963, Roulette R4483 (Columbia DB7036, UK), 1963. Ronnie Hawkins & the Hawks (with all 5): 'High Blood Pressure' c/w 'There's a Screw Loose', NY, 3 May 1964, Roulette R4502, 1964. *Heaven's Gate*, dir. & written Michael Cimino; Partisan Productions/UA, US, 1980. All Hawkins quotes from interview by this writer, St. Johns, Newfoundland, fall 1985, collected as '1976 & Other Times: Ronnie Hawkins, Rock'n'Roller' in Michael Gray & John Bauldie, *All Across the Telegraph: A Bob Dylan Handbook*, London: W.H. Allen, 1987.]

Hawks, the See Band, The.

Hayward, Richie [1946 -] Richard Hayward was born on February 6, 1946 at Clear Lake, Iowa, where, four days before Richie's 13th birthday, BUDDY HOLLY, RITCHIE VALENS and the Big Bopper played their final gig, before getting into the plane that flew off towards Fargo, North Dakota, crashing and killing them in the snow en route. Undeterred, Hayward played his first gig as a drummer in a local hall soon afterwards.

In the mid-1960s, by now a ferociously accomplished drummer, Hayward co-founded a group with Lowell George, and after its disbandment and a brief gap, co-founded another with him, Little Feat. Hayward remained with it until it collapsed after the June 1979 death of Lowell George; but he was back with the group when it reformed in 1988. Meanwhile Hayward has also performed and recorded with everyone from Joan Armatrading to WARREN ZEVON.

In 2004 he became a short-lived member of Dylan's Never-Ending Tour band, playing drums and percussion in a supporting rôle to GEORGE RECILE (who was having problems with one arm). Hayward played from the Tulsa, Oklahoma, concert of February 28 (not playing on the opening number or the encore songs this first night) through till the end of the April 4 concert in Washington, D.C.

***Hearts of Fire* [film, 1987]** In great contrast to those end-of-1965 press conferences, in which Dylan radiated good humour, unguarded spontaneity and optimism, when he consented to attend the press conference at the National Film Theatre in London to announce the making of *Hearts of Fire* in 1986, at a time of dull floundering around in his artistic life, he sat alongside his director and co-stars emanating boredom and a deeply cynical, self-lacerating dispiritedness. He broke out of it momentarily when journalist Philip Norman was brave enough to press him on why he wasn't writing songs instead of proposing to waste his time on the set of a movie that was obviously going to be awful. Warming to this theme, Norman invited Dylan to imagine how bored he was going to be in the making of it, and Dylan came out of his already-bored-shitless shell just long enough to murmur: 'Oh, I don't know—maybe *you'll* be around': a put-down to compete against any from his own past. But this was six seconds' worth of life and spirit in an hour of stultifying disaffection. The rest of the event just proved Philip Norman right. As did the film.

Before Dylan made *Masked & Anonymous*, this was the ELVIS movie in his limited list of celluloid credits. Though the style of the two films is very different—*Masked & Anonymous* determinedly unrealist and *Hearts of Fire* doggedly conventional—Dylan plays the same character in each: a has-been rock star who sings a bit and eventually knocks someone to the ground in a fight he's reluctant to enter but naturally wins. The director, RICHARD MARQUAND, had come to the film straight from the triumph of his powerful and successful thriller, *Jagged Edge* (1985), so a more than competent film might have been expected. But its co-stars were hopeless, and powerless to escape the yawning pit of tepid goo that was the storyline and script.

Hearts of Fire was written initially by Scott Richardson but rewritten by Joe Eszterhas because the studio regarded Richardson as too inexperienced to be writing a film for Dylan. Dylan is rumoured to have threatened legal action to retain the original Scott Richardson script, but to no avail.

'Fiona', as singer-actress Fiona Flanagan was calling herself at the time (which betrays no small misjudgement itself: it's one thing to launch yourself on the world as Madonna, or even Fabian, but *Fiona?*), embodied everything that was wrong with 1980s MTV showbiz, inflating a minor singing talent with pointless fiestiness, and mistaking declamatory postures for dramatic life. Rupert Everett, in parallel, embodied everything that was wrong with etiolated British acting. Set against these two, Dylan's performance, though erring on the soporific side, wasn't as bad as often suggested. The dyed blond hair didn't help, but he could still move with charismatic cool, wielding a mean pool cue and a sharp eyebrow.

Richie Havens and Ian Dury had small parts; RON WOOD appeared as himself. As did Bob Dylan—except of course that Bob Dylan has lots of selves, and this film only captured one of the less interesting. Far more beguiling were the interviews he gave to Christopher Sykes of BBC-TV while on the set of *Hearts of Fire* and shown in edited form in the 'Omnibus' arts series in September 1987. These showed a different Dylan, direct and playful, and well able to hold his own against the boredom Philip Norman had predicted. Whether he could sit through his own film is another matter.

[*Hearts of Fire*, dir. Richard Marquand, written Joe Eszterhas & Scott Richardson; Lorimar/Warner Bros., US/UK, 1987. Bob Dylan, press conferences San Francisco, 3 Dec 1965, telecast KQED-TV, US, 1965; LA, 16 Dec 12 1965 & London, 17 Aug 1986, excerpts broadcast Capital Radio and TV-AM, London, 18 Aug 1986; interviewed by Christopher Sykes, Bristol UK & Toronto, Sep-Oct 1986; telecast 'Omnibus', BBC-TV, UK, 18 Sep 1987.]

Helm, Levon [1940 -] Mark Lavon Helm was born on May 26, 1940 in the tiny town of Marvell, Arkansas, 20 miles west of the Mississippi River and 75 miles southwest of Memphis. He learnt to play guitar as a child but switched to drums after being taken to see that time-warp outfit, the F.S. Walcott Rabbits Foot Minstrel Show (slightly rechristened the 'W.S. Walcott Medicine Show' on a song written by Canadian BAND member ROBBIE ROBERTSON on the group's third album, *Stage Fright*).

Levon Helm was well placed to absorb country and blues music, R&B and early rock'n'roll, and after gigging locally with his sister on washtub he formed a high-school group, the Jungle Bush Beaters. Moving to Memphis he managed to sit in with CONWAY TWITTY and then got 'discovered' by RONNIE HAWKINS (another Arkansas good ole boy).

Helm joined the Hawks and they moved up into Canada, making Toronto their base. In 1959, signed to Roulette, Hawkins & the Hawks had two immediate hits with the derivative 'Forty Days' and its follow-up, 'Mary Lou'. From there the other members of what would eventually become The Band were brought into the group—Robbie Robertson (then known as Jaime) as guitarist, RICHARD MANUEL as pianist, RICK DANKO as bass player and GARTH HUDSON on organ.

Quitting Hawkins eventually (each side has its own version of how this came to pass) the group went out as Levon & the Hawks, then briefly as the Canadian Squires, and then as Levon & the Hawks again.

They met up with Bob Dylan in 1965 and Levon was the drummer on the early electric gigs that followed the NEWPORT FOLK FESTIVAL electric début—starting at Forest Hills, New York, that August 28. The rest of Dylan's band at this point were Robbie Robertson on guitar, AL KOOPER on organ and HARVEY BROOKS (aka Goldstein) on bass. This unit lasted only a short time, and after a Hollywood Bowl concert on September 3, Dylan got together with Helm, Robertson, Danko, Hudson and Manuel to rehearse in Woodstock, New York, for further live gigs.

On October 5 they went into the studio with Dylan for the first time, followed by more live concerts and a second studio stint on November 30 (from which comes the single 'Can You Please Crawl Out Your Window?')—but Levon wasn't with them for this session (though he's credited as drummer on the session in the sleevenotes to *Bootleg Series Vol. 7*). He'd quit, playing his last Dylan concert of the tour in Washington, D.C., on November 28. He couldn't stand all the booing that Dylan's electric performances were bringing down upon their heads. He went home to Arkansas, worked on oil rigs in the Gulf and felt like giving up, but played some dates around Memphis with the Cate Brothers Band. By December 4, at Dylan's Berkeley concert, the rest of the Hawks were still in there, but Levon had been replaced by BOBBY GREGG. The whole of the amazing 1966 tour took place without Levon Helm.

He returned to the fold only for the last part of the informal Basement Tapes sessions. Those sessions began without him in June 1967 at Dylan's house in Woodstock and continued over that summer and autumn, partly at Dylan's house but mostly at 'Big Pink', the group's house at nearby West Saugerties–in *the* basement. A total of 145 tracks plus seven further fragments were recorded, with the band members spreading themselves out into multi-instrumentalism, so that when Levon Helm rejoined them he was sometimes drumming but on other occasions played mandolin and bass. But he had only come back among them in October. Exactly when he arrived, what he missed and what he played on are impossible to say reliably.

When Dylan made his first public appearance for 20 months in January 1968 at the WOODY GUTHRIE Memorial Concerts, the Hawks (or the Crackers) played behind him, and Levon Helm was on stage with them for the first time in over two years. The group went on to become The Band, and it was Levon's lead vocal carving into us on 'The Weight', 'Rag Mama Rag', 'The Night They Drove Old Dixie Down', 'Up on Cripple Creek', 'Jemima Surrender' and later on 'Strawberry Wine', 'All La Glory', 'W.S. Walcott Medicine Show' and, on the rock'n'roll revival album *Moondog Matinee*, 'Ain't Got No Home', 'Mystery Train', 'Promised Land' and 'I'm Ready'.

The Band accompanied Dylan again at his Isle of Wight Festival appearance on August 31, 1969. In turn, at their 1971 New Year's Eve concert in New York City, Dylan came on in the early hours of January 1, 1972 and as well as singing 'Down in the Flood', 'When I Paint My Masterpiece' and 'Like a Rolling Stone', he also played guitar behind Levon Helm as Helm sang on 'Don't Ya Tell Henry'. (These performances were finally released in 2001 among the many extra tracks on a 2-CD reissue of The Band's *Rock of Ages* album.)

In 1974 The Band rejoined Dylan for his Come-Back Tour of North America, from which came *Before the Flood*, which followed their working together one more time in the studio, on Dylan's *Planet Waves*. In 1975 a SNACK Benefit gig in San Francisco featured Dylan, NEIL YOUNG, Rick Danko and Levon. And then came the end of The Band, with the concert at the Winterland Palace in San Francisco on November 25, 1976, filmed by MARTIN SCORSESE as *The Last Waltz*, and one last album, *Islands*.

Levon would make his feelings clear about the last years of The Band, and about the Scorsese-Robertson partnership, in many a subsequent interview and then in his 1993 autobiography *This Wheel's on Fire* (which carried this endorsement by Dylan: 'Torrid and timeless . . . wisdom and humor roaring off every page . . . you've got to read this').

After The Band split up, Helm made a series of solo albums, all calling on a huge cast of friends in the studio, beginning with *Levon Helm and the RCO All Stars* in 1977. Dylan sang 'Your Cheatin' Heart' as a guest at a Levon Helm & Rick Danko gig in New York City on February 16, 1983; Dylan & Helm performed 'Nadine' during Helm's Lone Star Café gig in NYC on May 29, 1988, and the two were reunited again on the ensemble finale song ('Only the Lonely') at the ROY ORBISON tribute concert in LA on February 24, 1990.

By this time The Band had reformed in a partial sort of way, with Earl Cate of the Cate Brothers and without Robbie Robertson (in 1983), but after Richard Manuel's suicide in 1986 the trio that was left took years more before they made a new Band album, *Jericho*, recorded in 1993 at the studio Helm now owned in Woodstock. It included a version of Dylan's 'Blind Willie McTell'; when Dylan subsequently took to performing it in concert, he followed their way of doing it rather than his own.

Ahead of making *Jericho*, a rather enfeebled version of The Band appeared at Dylan's so-called 30th Anniversary Concert in New York City in 1992, and on January 17, 1993 Levon (and Garth and Danko) played live with Dylan once again, at President Bill Clinton's inauguration party, the so-called 'Absolutely Unofficial Blue Jeans Bash (For Arkansas)'. More albums billed as by The Band followed, including *High on the Hog* in 1996, which included a cover of the Dylan-HELENA SPRINGS song 'I Must Love You Too Much'–but in the late 1990s Helm formed a new blues-based band of his own, Levon Helm & the Barn Burners (featuring his daughter Amy).

He and Dylan came to one more conjunction of sorts in 2003, when the Dixie Hummingbirds' recording of Dylan's 'City of Gold' was included on the *Masked & Anonymous* soundtrack. It came from their album *Diamond Jubilation*, on which Levon and Garth Hudson both played, as indeed did Dylan tour-band members LARRY CAMPBELL, TONY GARNIER and George Recile, and which Campbell produced.

Helm has also appeared in (and sometimes narrated) a number of TV profiles of other artists (including 'ELVIS '56', 1987, 'Legends: The Who', 1997, and 'JOHNNY CASH: Half a Mile a Day', 2000) but has also put in plenty of time as a movie actor. His 13 rôles to date have included playing Loretta

Lynn's father very creditably in the 1980 bio-pic *Coal Miner's Daughter* and a Bible salesman in *Feeling Minnesota*, 1996. (For Levon's rant about *The Last Waltz*, see **Scorsese, Martin**.)

Levon Helm may not be the intellectual of the group and he may not be a prolific songwriter—on the original Band albums he co-wrote only 'Jemima Surrender', 'Strawberry Wine' and 'Life Is a Carnival'—but his vocals were a crucial part of the classic sound of The Band, a sound that influenced so much music, and he has always been a superb rock'n'roll drummer.

[The SNACK Benefit Concert, San Francisco, 23 Mar 1975. Levon Helm: 'Don't Ya Tell Henry', NY, 1 Jan 1972, *Rock of Ages* (2-CD set reissue with bonus tracks), Capitol 72435-30181-2-2, US 2001; *Levon Helm and the RCO All Stars*, ABC AA-1017, NY, 1977, CD-reissued Edsel EDCD 494, 1996. The Band: *High on the Hog*, Rhino/Pyramid 72404, US (Transatlantic TRA CD 228, UK), 1996. Levon Helm: *This Wheel's on Fire: Levon Helm and the Story of The Band* (written with Stephen Davis), New York: Wm Morrow, 1993 & Chicago: A Capella Books, 2000. Dixie Hummingbirds: 'City of Gold', *nia, Diamond Jubilation*, Treasure TR0302, US 2003, & on *Masked & Anonymous*, Sony 90536 (ltd. edn. album with bonus CD: Sony 90618), NY, 2003. For full Helm discography see *http://theband.hiof.no/albums/helm_index.html*.]

Helstrom, Echo [1942 -] Marvel Echo Star Helstrom Shivers was born in Duluth, Minnesota, in 1942, by far the youngest child of mechanic, painter and welder Matt Helstrom and his wife Martha. Her brother (also named Matt) was 14 years older than her, and her sister (also named Martha) 15 years older. She was, as she said herself, 'from the other side of the tracks' from the middle-class Robert Zimmerman; and this was part of her fascination for him: 'he was rich folk and we were poor folk,' as she told ROBERT SHELTON. There was another difference too: 'he was Jewish and we were German, Swedish, Russian, and Irish, all mixed together.' In fact, Echo's mother was born in Ohio and her father in Minnesota, but all four of her grandparents were from Finland.

In the 2005 film *No Direction Home* Dylan says that before Echo there had been another girl, with, for him, an equally resonant name, 'Gloria Story'; but until he volunteered it, no such name had ever been mentioned in his biography, whereas Echo has long and famously been his 'Girl of the North Country'. It's sometimes been guessed—in the dark, either way—that Bonnie Beecher, aka JAHANARA ROMNEY, was the 'real' girl whose hair 'rolled and flowed all down her breast', but Echo has the better claim: she's the one from Hibbing rather than Minneapolis, and she came first.

She had taken accordion lessons, played the harmonium the Helstroms had at home and sang in the school choir. Like Dylan, though, she was into rock'n'roll and like him listened to R&B on the late-night radio station that beamed all the way up from Shreveport, Louisiana. They 'went steady' in 1957–58, when they were 16. In the 1958 High School Yearbook Bob wrote against Echo's name: 'Let me tell you that your beauty is second to none. . . . Love to the most beautiful girl in school.' On May 2, 1958, they went to the Junior Prom together, in the school's Boys Gymnasium, and both danced badly.

The Helstrom household was a wooden shack three miles southwest of Hibbing on Highway 73, to which Bob would often hitchhike out after school. Matt Helstrom didn't approve of his daughter's young man any more than the Zimmermans approved of Echo, but when he wasn't around, Bob would play Mr. Helstrom's three guitars, or listen to his JIMMIE RODGERS records, and sing her songs out on their porch. In *Chronicles*, Dylan describes Echo's father as 'The kind of guy that's always thinking that somebody's out to take advantage of him', whereas her mother 'was the kindest woman—Mother Earth.' Martha Helstrom (a name Shelton never gives, always calling her, irritatingly, 'Mrs. Helstrom') liked Bob, looked on the relationship with equanimity, and felt that Bob 'seemed much more humble than his family. Both Echo and Bob seemed so sorry for the working people.' Bob's brother, DAVID ZIMMERMAN, told Shelton: 'Bobby always went with the daughters of miners, farmers, and workers. . . . He just found them a lot more interesting.'

In 1968, working as a film-company secretary in Minneapolis to support a child from a failed marriage (cold rain can give you the Shivers), Echo looked back to the events that must have seemed lightyears ago. Without trying to claim more than her due in Dylan's story, she told Shelton that they had both felt outsiders together, both misfits in conventional, old-fashioned, narrow-minded Hibbing. 'We weren't like the other people at school in any way. I just couldn't stand being like the other girls. I had to be different.' Bob was going to be a pop star and Echo was going to be a movie star. Mrs. Helstrom remembered a time when they were going to get married and have a child. 'They planned to call their child Bob, whether it was a boy or a girl. You know how teenagers are.'

They were drifting apart by mid-1958, with Bob making it ever clearer that he was going with other girls, and they broke up in early summer. She saw him around, but after he left for New York the next time she saw him was at the Hibbing High School Class of '59 tenth reunion in 1969. Bob and SARA DYLAN turned up unexpectedly, and so did Echo. They spoke briefly; Echo was among the old friends who asked for, and received, an autograph. He signed it before he recognised her, then said 'Hey! It's you!' and said to his wife, 'This is Echo!', and signed her programme 'To Echo, Yours Truly, Bob Dylan'. That same year saw the release, on *Nashville Skyline*, of the re-recorded 'Girl of the North Country'.

They must either have met up or spoken on the phone again, after almost another decade's gap, some time in the late 1970s: Echo told biographer HOWARD SOUNES that it was 20 years after their schooldays relationship that Bob confessed to her new intimate detail about it.

Soon after talking to Shelton in 1968 (for a book that didn't emerge till 1986) and more than 30 years before talking to Sounes, she had also talked—some might feel excessively—to TOBY THOMPSON, the gawky young author of the first book to explore the subject of Hibbing in relation to Bob Dylan, *Positively Main Street: An Unorthodox View of Bob Dylan*, published in 1971. He had reached Echo first in October 1968, very soon after Shelton; she was still in her basement apartment in Minneapolis, and gave him the new information that once, when she'd been listening to one of Bob's Hibbing bands practising, when she'd deciphered his voice from within the over-amplified whole, he 'was *howling* over and over again, "I gotta girl and her name is Echo!" making up verses as he went along. I guess that was the first song I'd ever heard him sing that wasn't written by somebody else. And it was about me!'

It's always seemed likely that a song from aeons later, 'Hazel' on *Planet Waves*, was also, on one level, about Echo. The album is full of warm memorialising about the Minnesota years—'the phantoms of my youth', 'twilight on the frozen lake'—and to hear 'Hazel'—'dirty blonde hair / I wouldn't be ashamed to be seen with you anywhere'—is to feel a hunch that the song's tender tale recollects fragments of feeling from the days when Echo and Bob were riding around, coming together from different sides of the tracks, united in wanting to get out of Hibbing—'you're going somewhere / And so am I'. In 2004, in *Chronicles Volume One*, Dylan says that the last time he saw his 'old hometown girlfriend', 'she was heading West. Everybody said she looked like Brigitte Bardot, and she did.' And he memorialises her again: 'my Becky Thatcher', he calls her.

Now there's a group, from Portland, Oregon, who call themselves Echo Helstrom. But the real one is still around, and so does she.

[Quotes from Echo, her mother & David Zimmerman from Robert Shelton, *No Direction Home: The Life and Music of Bob Dylan*, London: Penguin, 1987 edn., pp.46–52 & 53, except quote from Toby Thompson, *Positively Main Street: An Unorthodox View of Bob Dylan*, London: New English Library edn., March 1972 reprint, p.63. Bob Dylan, *Chronicles Volume One*, 2004, pp.59–60. Echo's full name from the Minnesota Births Index; Junior Prom date & gym location from Dave Engel, *Just Like Bob Zimmerman's Blues: Dylan in Minnesota*, Rudolph, WI: River City Memoirs–Mesabi, 1997, p.178.]

Hendrix, Jimi [1942 - 1970] James Marshall Hendrix was born in Seattle, Washington, on November 27, 1942, taught himself guitar as a schoolboy, grew up listening to electric blues guitarists and in 1961 enlisted in the US Paratroopers. While serving he played in clubs and met bassist Billy Cox (whom he would call upon years later when he needed an old friend). Back in civilian life he was briefly in a group called the Flames and then toured as an unremarkable guitarist behind one of his heroes, B.B. King, and subsequently behind SAM COOKE, LITTLE RICHARD and Ike & Tina Turner. Moving to New York City he played behind the Isley Brothers, King Curtis and others, became lead guitarist for the indifferent but amiable Curtis Knight and finally came to the attention of Chas Chandler, the ex-ANIMALS bassist, who bought him out of a series of unfavourable contracts and brought him to England in 1966, rescuing 'Jimmy James' from routine work and routine indifference and allowing Jimi Hendrix to set London ablaze.

In Harlem, as the Only Ones' guitarist John Perry writes in his excellent small book *Electric Ladyland*, Jimi's friends 'didn't share his interests in the Greenwich Village scene, the new English guitar rock or Bob Dylan, and thought him far too flaky to succeed'; but the swinging London of 1966 recognised his guitar genius at once, and his physical beauty, and he was the talk of the town within a week. Driven by an incorrigible appetite for getting high and getting what were then called dolly birds, he was nonetheless ambitious: quietly so in ordinary life and ferociously so with a guitar in his hands. Jeff Beck, Pete Townshend and ERIC CLAPTON held a hasty meeting to decide how to cope; they chose, wisely, to surrender with relatively good grace. It's said that when Hendrix got on stage with super-cool, super-hot Cream, Clapton blocked off his amp and Jimi had to plug into JACK BRUCE's. It was Clapton's last finger in the dam. The torrent of Hendrix's opening notes settled the matter.

Hendrix also had a sharp if spacey wit. Asked about this Cream-conquering incident in advance, when it was in his mind's eye, Hendrix said: 'I can't wait to find out if he is as good as he really thinks I am.'

Yet Hendrix was not an arrogant man; no-one was more approachable by his fans or (often the same thing) other musicians. And when the Jimi Hendrix Experience was signed up for a series of low-fee college dates before 'Hey Joe' was released, and he found himself a national star by the time those dates came around, instead of blowing them out, Jimi fulfilled them all—even when, as with his £70 booking at the University of York on February 18, 1967, the van broke down and the group couldn't reach the hall till midnight. There, standing calmly in the group dressing-room, looking immaculate and relaxed, Hendrix talked warmly about his 'total admiration' for Bob Dylan—and then went on stage to include in his set an amp-assaulting, torridly original version of 'Like a Rolling Stone' that almost matched for vituperative power those Dylan and the Hawks had given in Britain eight months earlier and which displayed with a showman's bravado that supernatural non-delay between the brain's conception and the fingers' immediate and fluent execution.

No-one knew then that within a year, a new Dylan album would arrive, an album in stark contrast to that electric whirlwind—or that Hendrix would find a song within the stripped-down acoustics of *John Wesley Harding* and take it right back into that whirlwind: take it over so completely that ever since Dylan's return to touring afterwards, in 1974, he has been playing 'All Along the Watchtower' entirely in the spirit of the Jimi Hendrix interpretation.

That's the crucial conjunction between the two. Everything else is peripheral: that Dylan saw Hendrix play somewhere in the Village in 1965, and 'knew Jimi slightly before he became a big star . . . [when] he was basically a blues player . . . he was young and he was the real thing'; that they met, apparently, only once and briefly after Jimi was a star; that the *John Wesley Harding* track Hendrix had first picked out had been 'I Dreamed I Saw St. Augustine'; that he did record a marvellous 'The Drifter's Escape' too, though this was hidden inside one of the innumerable cheap first-wave posthumous releases; that when Dylan eventually débuted *this* song in concert, in 1992, this too was taken at a Hendrixian pace; and that when, that same year, Dylan opened his Australian tour on March 18 in Perth, he included an attempt at 'Dolly Dagger', and when he closed his summer tour of European festivals that July in Juan-les-Pins, his set opened with a one-off performance of 'Hey Joe'.

Dylan's tribute, then, has essentially been musical—and it isn't Jimi Hendrix's fault if Bob's fans have heard altogether too many revisits to 'All Along the Watchtower' down the years (by the end of 2003 Dylan had performed it in concert 1,393 times, and never once à la *John Wesley Harding*)—but he has also paid tribute in words:

'It can't be expected that a performer get under the song. . . . it's hard enough for me to do it sometimes. . . . He sang them exactly the way they were intended to be sung. . . . the way I would've done them if I was him.' (Though of course it wasn't how Hendrix *sang* but how he *played* that was the point.) And: 'Jimi was a great artist. I wish he would've lived. . . . It's not a wonder to me that he recorded my songs but rather that he recorded so few of them—because they were all his.'

As John Perry points out: 'Jimi Hendrix's recording career lasted less than four years. Had Bob Dylan's career been equally foreshortened it would have ended with 1965's *Highway 61 Revisited*. No *Blonde on Blonde*, no *John Wesley Harding*. No *Blood on the Tracks*.'

Jimi Hendrix died alone in London, at the height of his powers and still young and beautiful, choked by his own vomit, on September 18, 1970. He was 27 years old.

[Jimi Hendrix: *Electric Ladyland*, Track 613009, UK, 1968; 'The Drifter's Escape', *Loose Ends*, Polydor 2310301, UK, 1973. Bob Dylan: 'Hey Joe', Juan-les-Pins, France, 12 Jul 1992. John Perry, *Electric Ladyland*, New York: Continuum 33⅓ series, 2004; this contains a detailed analysis of how Hendrix built his 'Watchtower' from Dylan's. All Hendrix & Dylan quotes from ditto, except Hendrix re 'total admiration' for Dylan, conversation with this writer, York, UK, early hours of 19 Feb 1967.]

Herald, John [1939 - 2005] John Herald was born in Greenwich Village, NYC, on September 6, 1939. He discovered he could sing when PETE SEEGER visited a summer camp he was staying at and urged everyone to sing in chorus. Herald heard his own high voice soaring out above the rest. He attended the University of Wisconsin and there met ERIC WEISSBERG and Marshall Brickman, whom he'd heard perform together in the Village. He took up guitar and they started playing bluegrass together, and turned into THE GREENBRIAR BOYS. Signed to Vanguard Records, the group was headlining at Gerde's Folk City when Dylan was the support act—and received a rave review from ROBERT SHELTON in the *New York Times*: a review that barely mentioned Herald & co.

Herald said they were asked if it was OK to have Dylan on the bill. 'By this time Bob was a friend of mine, so I said fine. I wish he would return the favor now . . . [but] I liked Dylan quite a bit, so that's how it happened.' He also said: 'Dylan was one of those few people that happened to like traditional music as much as me. . . . We were both night owls and enjoyed café society, our girlfriends were also best friends, so he was one of the maybe ten scuffing partners that I had.'

Herald also seems to be the lone witness to a little-known phase of Dylan's early Greenwich Village days: Dylan as fiddle player. 'I actually first encountered him by seeing him when he was playing fiddle . . . he was noodling around on the fiddle, and it kind of surprised me because there weren't many fiddle players around. . . . Maybe he could have been a great fiddle player if he practised . . . but back then there was a lot of experimenting going on.'

In March 1963 Herald accompanied Dylan and SUZE ROTOLO when Dylan took an early acetate of *The Freewheelin' Bob Dylan* to play to Bob Fass at WBAI-FM radio station in New York City. Herald and Rotolo sat in on the Fass interview.

In 1972, after a few years in Woodstock, NY—to which he later returned to live, becoming a great amateur mycologist—he moved for a couple of years to California, where a reconstituted Greenbriar Boys briefly included JERRY GARCIA. Shortly before the move, Herald had made a solo album on which appeared HOWIE WYETH, ROB STONER, BOB NEUWIRTH and STEVE SOLES among the many musicians helping out. It was the first time these four had all met; later they came together again for Dylan's Rolling Thunder Revue. Herald moved to Philadelphia in 1976, formed a new bluegrass band, but then moved back to Woodstock the following year and there formed an electric bluegrass band that became the Woodstock Mountain Revue and included Artie and HAPPY TRAUM.

John Herald is associated with the song 'High Muddy Water' (a phrase Dylan incorporates into his *Time Out of Mind* song 'Tryin' to Get to Heaven'). Dylan once said, perhaps with more enthusiasm than clarity, that John Herald was 'the country STEVIE WONDER'. In the late 1990s Dylan paid a private visit to Herald in Woodstock, where they played songs together and to each other.

John Herald killed himself at his home, aged 65, on July 18, 2005.

Herdman, John John Macmillan Herdman is a Scottish novelist, short story writer and literary critic who has written rarely but well on Dylan's work. He was born in Edinburgh on July 20, 1941. He first took notice of Dylan's recordings in 1964; his first published work on Dylan was the article 'Attitudes to Bob Dylan', published in the journal *Akros* in 1976. For JOHN BAULDIE's *Telegraph* in 1985 he wrote an exemplary piece on the Dylan of the *Infidels* and *Empire Burlesque* period, 'The Truth in the Missing File', published three years after his book on Dylan's work, the excellent *Voice Without Restraint: Bob Dylan's Lyrics and Their Background*, which was published simultaneously in the US and the UK and was followed by a Japanese edition in 1983.

As a novelist and writer on other subjects he has published 15 books, including *A Truth Lover* (1973), *Pagan's Pilgrimage* (1978), *The Double in Nineteenth-Century Fiction* (1990), *Imelda* (1993), *Ghostwriting* (1996), *The Sinister Cabaret* (2001) and a French translation of his novel *Imelda* (2006).

[John Herdman: 'Attitudes to Bob Dylan', *Akros* no.30, Preston, UK, 1976; 'The Truth in the Missing File', *Telegraph* no.22, UK, winter 1985. *Voice Without Restraint: Bob Dylan's Lyrics and Their Background*, Edinburgh: Paul Harris Publishing, 1982; New York: Delilah Books, 1982; and Tokyo: CBS/Sony Publishing, 1983.]

heroes, special cowboy fondness for, and 'John Wesley Harding' [song] One aspect of American folk music's cowboy tradition is its special fondness for heroes, and Dylan comes to this on the *John Wesley Harding* album, as he reaches back into America's past for the secret strengths of her myths. The album is a 'retreat', a turning away, from the chaos of the modern urban burden; yet clearly it is a regenerative spirit that drives Dylan to search back as he does. He engages, in this album, in a desperately serious struggle to free himself, and so to free us, from the debilitating predicament our fragmented sensibility has placed us in: the predicament Dylan defined on his previous album, the druggy, urban, chaotic, compelling *Blonde on Blonde*. There, 'Visions of Johanna' sums up this mess: 'We sit here stranded / Though we're all doin' our best to deny it.' As Dylan comes, in *John Wesley Harding*, to the myths and extinct strengths of America, he explores the world of the cowboy as well as the pioneer. The man in the title song is a cowboy, and, indeed, a hero.

It is a modest exploration, in that the cowboy-outlaw is not an unusual subject for hero-treatment; but what a delicate, subtle portrait the song offers. It is all so simple, so straightforward (like the system of values we have come to associate with the cowboy world): a ballad that tells the story of its hero's exploits. Yet at the end we still have no idea what actually happened, nor any clear indication of the narrator's attitude. We get clues but no bearings. It was never like this when Tennessee Ernie Ford sang 'The Ballad of Davy Crockett'.

The song's economy of organization and language is noticeable at once. There is no use of simile and no reliance on images or symbolism. Following that, we notice a corresponding lack of what may be called 'moral centre'. Nine of the 12 lines provide what could be taken, at first glance, as testaments to the hero's worth and virtue: yet actually none is free from significant ambiguity—and these equivocations, collectively, have a piercing eloquence to offer. 'John Wesley Harding was a friend to the poor . . .' In what way? To what extent? The claim has, deliberately, no core behind its apparent bluntness. It refrains from contradicting the suspicion that Harding's name could be added to a long list of men whose lives and interests are spent in opposition, effectively, to the lives and interests of the poor but to whom it is advantageous to seem to appeal. Plenty of hero reputations depend upon this pretence. As for those two very reasonable questions raised by that first line: they are in no way answered by the rest of the song. 'All along this countryside he opened many a door.' We could put similar questions in response to that, and be met by a similar blank. The line opens no doors for us. It works, as intended, by yielding an echo which lingers throughout the song: the echo of a second empty claim. To it must be added the corresponding echoes of the other claims that confront us. As we meet them, the next is this: 'But he was never known to hurt an honest man.' Dylan chooses the negative form of expression; and the consciously reductive intention this reveals gets reinforcement from further negatives in the song; and it ends by giving us a pile-up of three of them: 'But no charge held against him could they prove / And there was no man around who could track or chain 'im down / He was never known to make a foolish move.' Not only is all this presented carefully in the negative, but it all serves to emphasise the deliberate vicariousness of the testimony we're given: 'He was never known to. . . . He was never known to . . .' Other lines are linked in such a way as to discredit any inference of virtue from them when they're considered together. He opened many a door but he was never known to hurt an honest man. That careful word 'but' gives the statements either side of it a cynical focus that the substitution of 'and' could have avoided had Dylan's intention been different (had Dylan's approach, for instance, been Hollywood's). And the following lines add nothing good to our picture of the hero's character: ''Twas down in Chaynee County, the time they talk about . . . / And soon the situation there was all but straightened out . . . / All across the telegraph his name it did resound.' The inferences to be made do not concern his heroism, his virtue or his good deeds. They concern the lesser strengths of his fame and reputation. There is, again, a consciously reductive intention on Dylan's part: to repeat, and give a collective weight to, the idea that Harding had a reputation for . . . and then the vague list: lending help, opening doors, refraining from injuring the honest, *almost* straightening out some utterly unspecified 'situation', not getting tracked down, and, lastly, looking after himself cleverly. This repeated insistence on Harding's reputation also casts a doubt on the veracity of what is being insisted upon. Thus Dylan trades on our methinks-he-doth-protest-too-much reaction, in order to increase further our sense of the empty centre of the story.

Two of the lines—but only two—work in a different way. 'With his lady by his side he took a stand' adds to those echoes of the unspecific in the way that other lines do, by that flamboyantly vague phrase 'he took a stand'; but it creates, with the other half of the line, an almost explicit condemnation. Within the cowboy ethic, the hero should neither have needed his lady by his side to give him his courage nor have placed her inside the danger-zone. The line 'He traveled with a gun in every hand' goes further. The wit of that phrase 'in every hand' serves quietly to highlight Harding's inadequacy. Such a reliance on his weapons suggests something discreditable. (As in that more recent folk saw: flash car, small dick.) In support of this, Dylan's sly phrase acts as a reference back to Dylan's earlier song 'With God on Our Side': 'And the names of the heroes / I's made to memorize / With guns in their hands / And God on their side.'

Yet it is not from these two lines of near-explicit criticism that 'John Wesley Harding' gets its power. This comes emphatically from Dylan's carefully constructed 'echoes of the unspecific': and these are indeed eloquent. In its three short verses, the song offers a keen critique of values pertinent not only to the 19th century cowboy's world but to the heirs of that bygone civilization in contemporary America. The clichés of thought exploded so precisely in the song are still in the way today; but Dylan has done battle with them. 'John Wesley Harding' joins with the rest of the album of that name to give us Dylan successfully engaged in the mature artistic attainment of reconstruction and revaluation: Dylan at his most seriously and intelligently creative. But of course even when he was far younger, and not being 'serious' at all, his irreverent, comic 'Hero Blues' questioned the motives of heroes and of those who wanted to construct them.

['John Wesley Harding' recorded Nashville, 6 Nov 1967; as of Apr 2005 Dylan has never sung it 'live'. 'Hero Blues' recorded 3 times (plus fragment), NY, 6 Dec 1962; performed at the New York Town Hall Concert, 12 Apr 1963 and re-recorded as a Witmark music-publishing demo, NY, May 1963. All these versions have circulated. So has a version recorded NY, 12 Aug 1963. So too, in extreme lo-fi, has the version privately recorded at the home of DAVE WHITAKER, Minneapolis, MN, 17 Jul 1963. Eleven years later, to everyone's surprise, Dylan chose it as the opening song of the opening concert of his huge 'come-back' tour of 1974 (Chicago, 3 Jan). And the next night (also Chicago). Then it disappeared again.]

Herron, Don [1962 -] Donald John Herron Jr. was born in Steubenville, Ohio, on September 23, 1962. A violinist, guitarist, steel-guitarist, dobro player, banjo player and mandolinist, he is currently a member of Dylan's Never-Ending Tour band.

He came out of the one of the key country bands of the 1990s, the Nashville-based BR5-49, named after an old phone number seen in a sketch on 'Hee Haw', signalling the unapologetic retro character of the band, which has been described as 'Gram Parsons-style country rock'. It was founded in early 1993 by Gary Bennett and Chuck Mead, guitarists and vocalists from the Pacific Northwest and Kansas respectively. They added upright bassist and ex-Hellbilly Smilin' Jay McDowell, drummer Shaw Wilson, also from Kansas, and Bennett's old friend Herron. They signed a record deal in 1995 and in 1996 issued an EP. Albums followed, as did tours; but after the release of a 2001 album, McDowell and Bennett left and the band broke up. Herron and others went back to Nashville and played with musical collective the Hillbilly All-Stars but re-formed BR5-49 (now reconfigured as BR549) in 2004 with a new bassist and singer-guitarist.

Then Bob Dylan asked Herron to join the Never-Ending Tour Band, and he became one of the several people brought in for the spring 2005 tour, beginning in Seattle on March 7.

Hester, Carolyn [1937 -] Carolyn June Hester was born in Waco, Texas, on January 28, 1937. Because she came from Texas, she gravitated to Norman Petty's legendary custom studio in Clovis, New Mexico, when she wanted to make a record—and, partly because she was very pretty, Norman decided to manage her. Her début album, *Scarlet Ribbons*, was recorded in July and August 1957, produced by Petty. Carolyn, on vocals and guitar, was 20 years old. She was accompanied by George Atwood on string bass and, on 'Wreck of the Old '97', by Jerry Allison on brushes and box.

Norman Petty's other act, BUDDY HOLLY, dropped in on the sessions and heard music that beckoned from a world beyond his own—the world of traditional folk music but also of inchoate New Left, civil rights, democratising and intellectual youthfulness. He followed her to Greenwich Village and moved into an apartment in what proved to be, unfortunately, the last few months of his life.

The musical influence was not just one way. Holly was a star and Hester a new kid on the musical block, and she appreciated rock'n'roll. When she and Bob Dylan met up on the folk scene in 1961, she was playing three sets a night at Gerde's Folk City, in the Village. Dylan was there listening one night, and as she told TERRY KELLY, 'I was down to my third set and . . . I'm saying "Buddy Holly taught me this song" and I start singing "Lonesome Tears" and the place had kinda thinned out and there were not many people, so Bob pulled his chair right up to the stage—that close—and said "Buddy *Holly* taught you that song?!"'

Accounts vary as to how Dylan came to play harmonica on tracks cut at the sessions for her third album, *Carolyn Hester*, made for JOHN HAMMOND and Columbia Records on September 29, 1961—i.e. before Dylan was signed to a record contract at all himself, and almost two full months before he went back into the same New York studios to make his own first album. (One account, possibly askew, is offered in Dylan's memoir *Chronicles Volume One*, 2004.)

What's certain is that the day of the Hester session was the very day ROBERT SHELTON's unprecedented rave review of Dylan's support-act performance at Gerde's Folk City was published in the *New York Times*, and in Hester's words, 'Hammond just went for it. He was trying to build a stable of folk singers at that time.' Hester had already been trying to help Dylan get gigs—she let him open for her at Club 47 in Boston not long after their Holly conversation—and out at Revere Beach she told him she had this Columbia session coming up, that she already had BRUCE LANGHORNE booked and was trying to get ODETTA's bass player, BILL LEE (father of Spike), and that Hammond was producing, and would he like to come along?

They rehearsed, with Hammond listening in, and then in the studio Dylan played harmonica on 'I'll Fly Away' (a gospel song performed by everyone from the Rev. J.M. Gates to ROY ACUFF, but written by ALBERT E. BRUMLEY, a white Oklahoman quartet singer and music teacher who became a professional gospel songwriter after this song's success), 'Swing and Turn Jubilee' ('a square-dance number associated with Jean Ritchie', according to DAVID HAJDU) and 'Come Back, Baby'. This last was a Walter Davis blues, cut in 1940, and became, post-war, the most covered of his records. Carolyn had asked Dylan to teach her some blues, he'd played her a large number of them on the spot, and this was the one she opted for. He taught it to her.

For some reason the resulting album, *Carolyn Hester*, was not released until mid-May 1962—two months later than Dylan's own début LP. (In 1961, however, she did see the release of her second album, also called *Carolyn Hester*, on the Tradition label.)

All three of the tracks recorded with Dylan on were included on the Columbia album. Thirty-three years after the sessions, when the album was issued on CD, an extra take each of 'I'll Fly Away' and of 'Come Back, Baby' were included as 'bonus tracks'. None of them have any merit beyond the historical one of having given Dylan his first chance in a professional recording studio.

At the time Dylan played on that Hester album, she was married to RICHARD FARIÑA. In David Hajdu's words, she was 'a womanly, voluptuous beauty with sculpted features' who was 'often asked if she was a movie star'. She had taken acting classes and even while performing in the Village was still taking voice and guitar lessons but by the time Dylan met her she was a widely liked and accepted performer. 'Carolyn was a contender, no doubt about it,' DAVE VAN RONK told Hajdu. When Gerde's had opened, on May 30, 1960, Hester had been its featured attraction. Fariña was merely a hustler and hanger-on. They'd been introduced by Robert Shelton (who was infatuated with Hester, according to her manager of the time, Charlie Rothschild) at the White Horse Tavern in the Village, and Fariña had aimed at her at once. Eighteen days after her Folk City appearance, she married him. By the time her Columbia album came out in 1962, he was aiming at JOAN BAEZ's 16-year-old sister MIMI instead. Hester arranged a Mexican divorce. In *Chronicles Volume One*, Dylan's own comments on the Carolyn Hester of this period are comically disingenuous. 'Carolyn was married to Richard Fariña, a part-time novelist and adventurer. . . . I thought he was the luckiest guy in the world to be married to Carolyn.'

In 1992, at the so-called 30th Anniversary Concert Celebration at Madison Square Garden, NYC,

Carolyn Hester was invited to appear. JEFF ROSEN, in Dylan's office, phoned and said that since Bob had recently played harmonica for NANCI GRIFFITH on her recording of 'Boots of Spanish Leather' maybe she and Carolyn Hester could perform together. On stage, Hester handed Dylan a bunch of flowers someone had thrown from the crowd and afterwards attended the party at TOMMY MAKEM's. Subsequently she was invited out to California to be interviewed for the documentary 'videography' that Jeff Rosen was making about Dylan's life.

[Carolyn Hester: *Scarlet Ribbons*, Clovis, NM, Jul–Aug 1957, Coral 57143, NY, 1958; *Carolyn Hester*, *nia*, Tradition 1043, NY, 1961; *Carolyn Hester*, NY, 29 Sep 1961, Columbia CL1796, NY, 1962, CD-reissued (with 'bonus tracks') Columbia Legacy CK57310, NY, 1994. Quotes re Holly, Hammond, 30th Anniversary & 'videography' from interview by Terry Kelly, *The Bridge* no.16, Gateshead, UK, summer 2003, pp.8, 10 & 12–14. David Hajdu quoted from his *Positively 4th Street: The Lives and Times of Joan Baez, Bob Dylan, Mimi Baez Fariña and Richard Fariña*, pp.32 & 99; Van Ronk quoted from Hajdu p.32; Shelton infatuation Hajdu p.37. Thanks to Ms. Hester for extra information by e-mail, Aug 2005.]

Heylin, Clinton [1960 -] Clinton Manson Heylin was born on April 8, 1960 in Urmston, Lancashire (Greater Manchester, UK). He is the Dylan biographer who started from the position of fan and collector. His interest in Dylan and his work long preceded the writing of his several books, and by the time the first of these was published, Heylin was a dominant figure in the world of Dylan fanzines and Dylan trainspotting. His knowledge is immense, his research formidable and his prose prolific. He has unearthed so much of the information we have about Dylan's recordings and his life, and has interpreted that information so forcefully, that had Heylin never interested himself in these subjects, the whole face of Dylanology would be different. It would also be less combative. Heylin's achievement as a Dylan researcher and biographer is such that his notorious belittling of, and quarrelling with, almost everyone else in the field is as unnecessary as it is crass.

Tracking Heylin's bibliography is made difficult by his giving every edition of every book a different or amended title. However, essentially the list is this:

His early work *Stolen Moments: The Ultimate Reference Book* set itself the blood-curdling task of documenting what Dylan had done on every day of his life up till Heylin's completion-date, and he followed up this triumph with *Behind the Shades*, which, unlike the previous big biography, *No Direction Home* by ROBERT SHELTON, has the virtue of paying Dylan's later years as much attention as the earlier ones. But as Robert Strachan notes in a scrupulously even-handed account (in *The Making of a Rock Biography: Authority And Critical Space*), 'Heylin deliberately misrepresents *No Direction Home* in order to undermine Shelton's biographical authority at the same time as establishing his own.'

The early *Stolen Moments* had been published, like most Dylan books in the 1980s and earlier, by a small non-mainstream publisher; but after editing *The Penguin Book of Rock & Roll Writing* in 1992, Heylin began a long term relationship with Viking, an imprint of Penguin Books. In 1995 his listings book *Bob Dylan, The Complete Recording Sessions: 1960–1994* (a hardback), was published by the mainstream but small US imprint St. Martin's Press, but in UK paperback by Penguin (in 1996, slightly amended and under the different title *Bob Dylan: Behind Closed Doors*). They also published the US hardback and the UK paperback of *Behind the Shades*, and the UK editions of the revised, updated version, *Behind the Shades—Take Two* (published in the US by Morrow).

Heylin's other Dylan books include the 44-page booklet *Rain Unravelled Tales*, the much larger *Rain Unravelled Tales (The Nightingale's Code Examined): A Rumourography*, 1982 and *To Live Outside the Law: A Guide to Dylan Bootlegs*, 1989 (all effectively self-published); *Saved: The Gospel Speeches of Bob Dylan*, published in India by Chelsea Hotel habitué and avant garde art publisher Raymond Foye, 1990; and *Dylan's Daemon Lover: The Tangled Tale of a 450-Year-Old Pop Ballad*, 1999.

Heylin's articles on Dylan are too numerous to list, but he contributed copiously to the best Dylan fanzine, *The Telegraph*, as well as co-founding the organisation that published it and acting as news editor in its early years. He has written for all the major Dylan fanzines and extracts from his biographies have been serialised in the popular national press. His 'Profile of HOWARD ALK' was republished in *All Across the Telegraph: A Bob Dylan Handbook* in 1987, as was his detailed survey of the inadequacies of *Bob Dylan Lyrics 1962–1985*.

Heylin has also published biographies of Sandy Denny, VAN MORRISON and, most recently, Orson Welles; in 1992 he edited *The Penguin Book of Rock & Roll Writing* and is the author of *From the Velvets to the Voidoids: The Birth of American Punk Rock* (2005) and the excellent *Bootleg! The Secret History of the Other Recording Industry*, aka *The Great White Wonders: A History of Rock Bootlegs* (1995).

[Clinton Heylin: *Rain Unravelled Tales*, Sale, UK: Ashes & Sand, *nia*; *Rain Unravelled Tales (The Nightingale's Code Examined): A Rumourography*, Sale: Ashes & Sand, 1982; *To Live Outside the Law: A Guide to Dylan Bootlegs*, Sale: Labour of Love, 1989; *Stolen Moments: The Ultimate Reference Book*, Romford, UK: Wanted Man, 1988; *Saved: The Gospel Speeches of Bob Dylan*, Madras & New York: Hanuman Books, 1990; *Bob Dylan, The Complete Recording Sessions: 1960–1994*, New York: St. Martin's Press, 1995, and as *Bob Dylan: Behind Closed Doors*, London: Penguin, 1996; *Behind the Shades*, London & New York: Summit Books, 1991; *Be-*

hind the Shades—Take Two, London: Viking/Penguin & New York: Morrow, 2001; *Behind the Shades Revisited*, London: Penguin, 2003; *Dylan's Daemon Lover: The Tangled Tale of a 450-Year-Old Pop Ballad*, London: Helter Skelter, 1999; *Bootleg! The Secret History of the Other Recording Industry*, New York: St. Martin's Press, 1995.

Robert Strachan, *The Making of a Rock Biography: Authority and Critical Space*, MA thesis in Popular Music Studies, University of Liverpool, 1997.]

Hibbing, Minnesota Bob Dylan: 'it's where I was raised an went t school . . . my youth was spent wildly among the snowy hills an sky blue lakes, willow fields an abandoned open pit mines. contrary t rumors, I am very proud of where I'm from . . .'

Hibbing is the least populous and the most important place in Dylan's Minnesota past. Up from St. Paul, old highway 65 is snowy by November. Flat, frozen fields, Dutch-roof barns, loblolly pines and stripped silver birch trees, Lutheran churches, dilapidated fencing, pick-up trucks more frequent than cars. A timeless scenery of telegraph poles and roadside mailboxes, the aluminium-grey road stretching out flat ahead; signs for Jumbo Leeches and Flathead Worms, snowmobiles for sale, 'MEAT RAFFLE every Saturday'. A hundred miles north of St. Paul you pass through McGrath, pop. 62, with its Catholic Church, Calvary Presbyterian Church and Pliny Graveyard. Then trailer-homes and more white clapboard than before, more and more picturesque old barns, grain-elevators like cocktail-shakers. The closer you come to the Iron Range towns, the narrower and emptier the road grows, and the taller the trees, and the more the banks of snow press in from the verges. The whole hushed place turns into Winter Wonderland, and cocooned inside it, Hibbing shines and twinkles like the set for an old Perry Como Christmas Special.

It would have been in Canada but for a mistake on an historic map. Deep in snow but easy to move around in, it epitomises pleasant, old-fashioned small-town life. It's not such a small town, either. At 186 square miles, its grid of leafy, spacious streets is the state's largest by area. The people are exceptionally equable, and make you welcome. It almost makes you wonder why Bob Dylan ever left.

He lived here from the age of six. To begin with, he slept on the floor in Grandma Florence's house; later, in the front room at 2425 7th Avenue East, his boyhood home, Bob practised in his first and nameless beat group, survived his Bar Mitzvah party and stared out of the window dreaming of escape. It was a mere couple of blocks' walk to Hibbing High School.

And what a school. You'd never know it from anything Dylan's let slip, but iron ore built Hibbing a school of palatial grandeur that cost four million dollars in 1920–23, with a sanitised medieval castle exterior in brick and Indiana limestone, hand-moulded ceilings, a 75-foot-long oil painting in the library, marble steps with solid brass handrails and, in the 1,825-seater auditorium, six Belgian crystal chandeliers now worth a quarter of a million each and a stage that can hold the Minnesota Symphony Orchestra.

In 1958, with his second group, the Golden Chords, Dylan stood hammering on Hibbing High School's 1922 Steinway Grand piano (breaking a pedal in the process) and shouting out rock'n'roll songs at the annual student concert . . . and got laughed at, up there on stage in an auditorium so lavish and ornate, and with such acoustic excellence, that it almost justifies STEPHEN SCOBIE's conceit that 'Every stage Bob Dylan has played on for the past thirty years has been, after Hibbing High School Auditorium, an anticlimax.' (See also next entry.)

Bob Dylan: 'A train line cuts the ground / showin' where the fathers an' mothers / of me an' my friends had picked / up an' moved from / north Hibbing / t'south Hibbing. / old north Hibbing . . . deserted / already dead / with its old stone courthouse / decayin' in the wind . . .'

Bobby often explored North Hibbing's ghost-town, where everyone lived before they moved them two miles south to dig out the ore they were sitting on. The whole place is just snow-covered ground, close to the edge of the vast, vast hole far down below, filled like a lake of iron-brown water. This is the world's largest open pit mine: 'the biggest hole dug by man' on the planet, as Hibbing loves to boast.

'Hibbing's got schools, churches, grocery stores an' a jail . . . high school football games and a movie house . . . corner bars with polka bands. . . . Hibbing's a good ol' town.'

Dylan's mixed feelings about Hibbing are expressed perfectly in that one last line from 'My Life in a Stolen Moment', and he and it have had a difficult relationship ever since he left. In fact Minnesota altogether has a problem with Dylan. They resent his having left: still resent his rudeness of 40 years ago. Minnesotans hear tell he was difficult despite being shown much tolerance; they feel he bit the hand that nurtured him and/or denied his roots. Invoking the stroppy teenager, they're determinedly unimpressed by the great artist.

In consequence, to the soul's delight and the professional eye's puzzlement, there is no exploitation of Dylan's incandescent name by the Heritage Industry. Look at how poor Liverpool exploits Beatledom: it's one of the city's biggest revenue sources. Yet until the last two or three years, Dylan remained conspicuously absent from Minnesota tourism bumph. Now there is an annual series of low-key events called 'Dylan Days', and the street he lived on has been renamed Dylan Drive (though East 7th Avenue still remains the official postal address).

Hibbing's 1990s coffee-table puffery 'On the Move Since 1893' managed only this: 'Some contemporary well-known natives include Rudy Perpich; Kevin McHale; Jeno Paulucci, founder of Jeno's Pizza; Bob Dylan, folk musician, songwriter; Roger Maris and Vincent Bugliosi, Charles Manson Trial prosecutor'. Thirty-five miles away, the Judy Garland Museum welcomes you to the Garland Birthplace Historic Home, Grand Rapids ('It's a swell state, Minnesota. . . . We lived in a white house with a garden. It's a beautiful, beautiful town', quoth Judy on the brochure in the Minnesota tourism press-pack); in Duluth, Dylan's birthplace home is disregarded; in Hibbing, the many pilgrims who come to the 7th Avenue house must simply decide whether to ring the bell and disturb the present owner or not.

When the Zimmerman house went on sale in 1989, the realtor had enquiries from all over the Dylan-fan world, and thought he'd make his fortune. This came to nothing, and Greg French paid $45,000 for the flat-roofed, two-storey 1940s property in Mediterranean Moderne style, not because it was Dylan's but because it was the best bargain in the neighbourhood at the time.

Once, a state tourism 'PR specialist' called, to ask Greg if he'd consider doing B&B. That was their big idea for the boyhood home of one of the 20th century's greatest artists. Meanwhile downtown there's only the bar-cafe called Zimmy's to cater to the swell of Dylan-visitors, a swell that cannot but increase.

This extraordinary non-exploitation might seem bizarrely nose-and-face syndrome: a collective sulking at least as immature as the Dylan who said 'You're boring, I'm off' four decades ago. Yet the communal hurt is quite misplaced. Those who actually knew him in the past—ex-classmates like Larry Furlong and Margaret Toivola—feel neither spurned nor uncomprehending of Dylan's quantum-leap away. More importantly, Dylan has written beautifully in poetry and song about these places and their wintry magic. In interviews too, he has often re-affirmed his pride in his formative Iron Range, North Country roots:

> 'I'm that color. I speak that way. . . . My brains and feelings have come from there. . . . The earth there is unusual, filled with ore. . . . There's a magnetic attraction there: maybe thousands of years ago some planet bumped into the land there. There is a great spiritual quality throughout the mid-West. Very subtle, very strong, and that is where I grew up'.

It seems a shame, a relapse into immaturity, that in the SCORSESE film *No Direction Home*, as emphasised by the title, Dylan appears to have returned to being as dismissive of the place as he was when he first got up and left—and certainly less balanced about its virtues than when he wrote those early poems quoted above. This relapse seems especially regrettable since, at least in one way, the gulf between his hometown's constraints and Dylan's restlessness was always illusory. For Hibbing was also the birthplace of Greyhound Buses, and the road from there to Duluth, where Dylan was born, was Greyhound's earliest route. It was from way up here that those routes spread out and beckoned. The far-off was part of the business of Hibbing.

[Dylan quoted from: 'A Message from Bob Dylan' (sent to the Emergency Civil Liberties Committee after his badly received Tom Paine Award Bill of Rights dinner speech of 13 Dec 1963); '11 Outlined Epitaphs'; 'My Life in a Stolen Moment'; 'The *Playboy* Interview: Bob Dylan—a candid conversation with the iconoclastic idol of the folk-rock set', *Playboy*, Chicago, Feb 1966.

By far the best and most detailed study of Dylan's Hibbing is Dave Engel, *Just Like Bob Zimmerman's Blues: Dylan in Minnesota*, Rudolph, WI: River City Memoirs—Mesabi, 1997. Also good are Stephen Scobie's *Alias Bob Dylan*, Calgary, Alberta, Canada: Red Deer College Press, 1991 & *Alias Bob Dylan Revisited*, Calgary: Red Deer College Press, 2003. For historical interest, see also Toby Thompson's *Positively Main Street: An Unorthodox View of Bob Dylan*, New York: Coward McCann & Geohegan Inc., 1971 (& London: New English Library, 1972).]

Hibbing rock'n'rollers Apart from John Bucklen and RIC KANGAS, Bob Zimmerman the aspiring Hibbing rock'n'roll star played with a number of other duck-tailed enthusiasts in various configurations—though perhaps his first outfit was formed with his St. Paul friends LARRY KEGAN and HOWARD RUTMAN from the summer camp he used to go to. They called themselves the Jokers, and though they aspired to rock'n'roll, they were basically just singing round the piano wherever they could find one. Rutman says their mothers made them sleeveless cardigans in red and grey, with JOKERS stitched across the fronts, and that they went on a Twin Cities Channel 9 TV talent show. Bob was only 14; it was early 1956. They played together off and on till spring 1958, but by then, up in Hibbing, Bob had more serious groups to encourage and boss about.

His first proto-rock'n'roll Hibbing ensemble never got as far as agreeing on a name (though HOWARD SOUNES says they were called the Shadow Blasters); they comprised Bob (on piano) plus Bill Marinac, Larry Fabbro and Charles (inevitably Chuck) Nara. DAVE ENGEL reports: 'Bob has known Bill Marinac, "always good for a laugh", since fifth grade.' He 'has learned string bass in a tamburitza band', and it is Bill who 'gets Bob together with Larry Fabbro, a trumpeter who is picking up guitar, and Chuck Nara, a clarinettist giving drums a try.' This is the group that steps out at the first of Dylan's school concert appearances—Bill on bass, Chuck on drums, Larry on guitar and Bob on the school's almighty 1922 Steinway Grand—and pounds out LITTLE RICHARD songs to a mixed response; it is April 5, 1957. In Larry Fabbro's yearbook, ECHO HELSTROM writes '. . . I really liked the way you played guitar . . .'

Then bad-boy school friend LeRoy Hoikkala (the only one still living in Hibbing), who played drums a little, got together with Monte Edwardson, who was 'a natural guitar player', and did some practising, and after a while Bob pushed in and said 'Hey, I'm playing piano, mouth-organ, harmonica and guitar; maybe we could get together'—and so they did, practising in the Zimmerman garage—and sometimes in the house because that's where the piano was—and this small unit became the Golden Chords.

This is the group Dylan played his second school concert with, on the afternoon of February 6, 1958, this time with everyone amplified, and extra mikes for his piano and vocals—and though they were on the bill, as a 'local rock'n'roll instrumental group', they were so loud and so indecorous—and Bob so vehement that in the middle of the second number he broke one of the Steinway's pedals—that Principal Pederson got Bob's English teacher, the splendidly named Boniface J. Rolfzen, to cut the power to the house mikes. This is the event that has passed into legend.

Undeterred, on Saturday March 1, 1958, they played and got paid for a one-off performance at the intermission of a Rock & Roll Hop for Teen-Agers at the National Guard Armory, billed as 'Hibbing's Own Golden Chords Featuring Monte Edwardson, Leroy Hoikkala, Bobby Zimmerman', and then played at the Winter Carnival Talent Contest, getting through to the final in the 'piano and song' category before losing to a tap dancer. They even got onto the Chmielewski Brothers' 'Polka Hour' on TV in Duluth. It didn't work out well—Bob was, well, too Bob—and the group began to fall apart.

The other Golden Chords wanted more work—wanted both to oblige the teenage hop audiences and 'to *get* somewhere'. They decided they'd be better off without the uncompromising Bobby Z., and then came an approach they couldn't resist. As Dave Engel writes, after the talent contest two junior college students, Jim Propotnick and Ron Taddei 'approach[ed] LeRoy and Monte. They recognize[d] in Monte Hibbing's best young guitarist, a versatile musician. . . . You can replace a singer easier than a good guitar player.' The four of them formed the Rockets, and earned terrific reviews in the local press.

Dylan turned to cousin Bill Morris, a drummer in Duluth, who brought along two others he'd been playing jazz with, Marsh Shamblott (piano) and Dennis Nylen (bass)—the Satin Tones, and they came up to Hibbing on weekends to practise at the Zimmerman house. Nothing came of it. Again, Bob was obdurate and wayward; he was 'just too wild'.

[Main sources: Dave Engel, *Just Like Bob Zimmerman's Blues: Dylan in Minnesota*, Rudolph, WI: River City Memoirs—Mesabi, 1997; interview with LeRoy Hoikkala, *On the Tracks* no.18, spring 2000; Howard Rutman testimony in Howard Sounes, *Down the Highway: A Life of Bob Dylan*, New York: Grove Press, 2001, manuscript p.44; 'The Shadow Blasters' p.45; 'The Satin Tones', p.55.]

'Highlands' [1997] Is the narrator of 'Highlands', the long final song on Dylan's 1997 album *Time Out of Mind*, a persona? GREIL MARCUS heard it that way, as speaking for a character living in some cruddy apartment building who doesn't get out much ('an older man who lives in one of Ed Kienholz's awful furnished rooms in the rotting downtown of some fading city—Cincinnati, Hollywood, the timeless, all-American Nowheresville you see in David Lynch's *Blue Velvet*—getting up and going for a walk, maybe for the first time in weeks. . . . The song is someone else's dream, but as Dylan sings it, you are dreaming it.') Or is 'Highlands', as for instance David Bowman hears it, the song in which we come closer than we've ever come before to walking around the world inside Bob Dylan's head: in which we hear Dylan 'finally share with us what it's like for Bob Dylan to be Bob Dylan . . .'? Is it persona or raw Bob Dylan? Even if you're with Bowman on this, that's not to say that 'raw' means artless. On the contrary, 'Highlands' is a most artfully wrought achievement and of a very high order.

Some say that 16½ minutes long is too long: more reasonable to say it's too short. The track never ends without sounding unfairly foreshortened, like an idyll snatched away. Bob Dylan has always been a talking blues maestro, to achieve which requires being in infinitely intelligent control of timing and phrasing; and he displays 99.9 per cent of that control on this tour de force (there are two tiny, minor fluffs, neither of which matters): and displays it with the crowning touch of the genuine maestro, that of making it sound easy, as he steers us through its twenty stanzas, alternating without a microsecond's hesitation between the 'otherly', aspirational 'My heart's in the highlands' chorus sections, with their magnificent recourse to formal poetic strengths, and the 'here and now' sections that seem—if they do—to walk you round Dylan's daily world as seen from inside his head, and which offer the perfect illusion of spontaneous composition.

The all-encompassing sweep of 'Highlands' is constructed with genius, fusing into one three-dimensional portrait the high and black comedy, the Dylanesque sarcasms and off-the-wall observations—all of which are plentiful, authentic and delivered as faultlessly as anything in his back-catalogue—and, set against all these, the recurrent expressions of yearning for a better version of himself and of the world, for a renewed sense of moral cleanliness as well as an unsullied terrain of natural grandeur, while all but confessing that what his eyes are raised to is never-neverland.

All this is performed with an unshakeable, wise, good-humoured authority that trusts the form even as it achieves a large expansion of its possibilities, that acts in good faith and addresses itself to an intelligent audience, creditably belying its writer-composer's claims to have lost his conscience and sense of humanity. In doing this, 'Highlands' acts as the best possible conclusion to the album, achieving, just as the final lines of the song do, a farewell bow of dignified, painfully gained, limited optimism, dragged back from the turbulent labyrinths of despair and decay.

'Highlands' begins by, well, setting the scene—the scene the singer envisages, yearns for, dreams of, aspires to. It does so exhilaratingly: 'Well my heart's in the Highlands, gentle and fair / Honeysuckle blooming in the wildwood air / Bluebells blazing where the Aberdeen waters flow / Well my heart's in the Highlands / I'm gonna go there when I feel good enough to go.'

One of the immediately striking things is how much better written it is than the Robert Burns poem it founds itself upon. ANDREW MUIR writes interestingly (in a 1997 fanzine piece, 'The Difference Between a Real Blonde on Blonde and a Fake') about the significance of 'My Heart's in the Highlands' (1790) for Burns' reputation, granted its 'triviality' yet its immense popularity, and about Burns having based his poem's beginning and end on 'a circulating folk source with a couple of stock traditional images thrown in'. Whatever the reasons, the Burns poem opens (and closes) with nothing better than 'My heart's in the Highlands, my heart is not here; / My heart's in the Highlands a-chasing the deer; / Chasing the wild deer and following the roe; / My heart's in the Highlands, wherever I go.' Its two middle verses offer nothing beyond a listing: 'Farewell to the' this 'and farewell to the' that—and the only imaginative or personal touch in the whole poem is the phrase 'wild-hanging' in 'Farewell to the forest and wild-hanging woods'.

Dylan takes the framework of Burns' poem (a frame that Andrew Muir argues is taken in turn from Scottish folk song). He also effects a reversal of Burns' implicit theme, which is of yearning to return to a real place, inhabited in the edenic past and in which he has left his heart—a heart formed by these known, loved, roamed-over, geographically specific as well as sentimentalised Scottish Highlands. Dylan instead yearns for are-they-aren't-they-Scottish? Highlands—his pseudo-geographic hints are contradictory—to which he makes no claim ever to have been, and which represent a dream-future in time and space, and not an idealised past.

The main thing Dylan does, though, is write of it imaginatively: that is, so that we see the idealised fantasy-place that calls to the contemporary, alienated, rootless citizen of today's urban/suburban USA, whose grasp of plant-life detail is shaky but whose ardour is real. Bluebells don't 'blaze'—especially in Scotland, where what are called bluebells are what the English call harebells: delicate meadow flowers, rather than the form of wild hyacinth that masses in the woods. But 'bluebells blazing' is not only a fine alliterative touch: 'blazing' sets the tone of how these Highlands are in the singer's mind. After the initial 'gentle and fair' the whole scene blazes with the singer's rapture (and perhaps with the restorative cleanliness that is next to Godliness). The energising 'Aberdeen waters' must flow sparklingly clean and bracingly cold. Lest this is getting too hiking-bootedly wholesome, the heady scent of honeysuckle blooms in the air.

Here again, botanical realism is not all it might be. As the British sculptor Andrew Darke writes: 'In selecting [English] bluebells and honeysuckle he has two of the most transporting scents that might come to you on a woodland walk. They are so powerful that is it like total immersion—for a first, brief moment (and the brevity is part of the power) they overwhelm and immobilise the mind and spread a balm of pure pleasure. But . . . in actuality it is unlikely that one could experience both on the same day . . . honeysuckle is later in the season.' Similarly, the fourth stanza's gaze is on the buckeye trees, but 'the buckeye—American for the horse chestnut—is not likely to be seen in the Scottish Highlands.'

Dylan's honeysuckle blooms inside that quintessential place of childhood mystery and exciting danger, the 'wildwood'. Impossible to have read Bruno Bettelheim on fairytales (*The Uses of Enchantment*, 1976) and not take the wildwood too as the emblem of inner confusion, lostness and unresolved desires. One way and another, it is not so much that the bluebells are blazing but that the singer's yearning blazes for the redemptive power of these imagined Highlands.

In accord with the aim of this opening stanza, the point about its last line—'I'm gonna go there when I feel good enough to go'—is not that it stumbles into unintended bathos, as the reader of the isolated stanza (A.S. BYATT, perhaps) might assume, but that its descent into this near-comic ungainliness, into this prosaic conversational mode both captures sympathetically the narrative tone of irresolution that makes clear how vague is his will actually to *go* to these Highlands, and guides us down into the unrarified air of the narrator's daily round, now introduced in the second stanza. Additionally, there is the neatly comic pun (a pun with a purpose, as good puns must have) that Dylan slips in with that 'when I feel good enough'. Behind the main meaning—'when I feel cheerier, or more energetically healthy'—loiters the alternative, that of 'when I feel I'm a good enough person to deserve to go', furthering our sense of the spiritual, redemptive nature of these yearned-for Highlands.

He starts with the problematic lines 'Windows were shakin' all night in my dreams / Everything was exactly the way that it seems / Woke up this mornin' and I looked at the same old page.' Are the windows shaking while he dreams, the noise intruding upon the dreaming, or are they shaking only in the dreams? Does everything seem the same in the dreams as in waking life (a fine touch) or does he, as the third line implies, wake more conventionally from twisted dreams to find tired normality restored? This latter is then expanded upon with the wrong kind of tiredness—not evoked by creative writing but enacted only by the tired writing of 'Same old rat-race, life in the same old cage'—and we move on to the second of the initial this-is-my-awful-life verses, which almost duplicates, but actually darkens, the 'Not Dark Yet' line about not looking for anything in anyone's eyes—'I don't want nothin' from anyone—ain't that much to take'—and then offers the precarious 'Wouldn't know the difference between a real blonde and a fake.'

This is a distinctly unpromising start to the grim story of the speaker's shrivelled husk of a life, with nothing to suggest the riches that are to come, and to prove wholly capable of counterbalancing the Highlands choruses. If it's hard to feel that some of this lazy sourness is not a fake, the feeling is soon dispelled. The hopeless, doomed plea 'I wish someone'd come and push back the clock for me' is said with a rueful quietness that is affecting, and then comes the second chorus, in which the Highlands are given one of their two most explicit heavenly touches, on the line 'That's where I'll be when I get called home' (a nice use of an old-fashioned gospel-song stock phrase—as indeed he also manages for his second such Christian allusion, which is to 'Big white clouds like chariots that swing down low').

Then we begin to enjoy the surprises and sly wit the song delivers, starting with the somehow innately comic prospect conjured by Bob Dylan singing 'I'm listening to NEIL YOUNG'. Part of the surprise here is a sort of stepping through the glass that normally divides the work from the person, or a breaking of some Dylan-imposed convention about what gets specified and what doesn't.

The last bad moment in the song's construction—and it only happens to British Empire ears—comes at the start of the next verse, when we get a disastrous pause after 'Insanity is smashing' and before 'up against my soul'. It's a poor line anyway, but only English jolly-hockey-stickism makes its first half comically incompetent. It gives way to the intentional sardonic comedy of the nicely put 'You could say I was on anything [pause] but a roll', with its funny, almost slapstick puns on drugs and bread rolls, and then the audacious lines about being so bereft of a conscience that all he can imagine he'd do with one if he had it would be to 'take it to the pawn shop'.

At that point the third Highlands chorus comes in, winging us with soothing, balm-giving grace from this gritty, dirty Los Angeles of the soul to the cleansing break of dawn and the deeply inviting 'beautiful lake of the black swan': a transformation that enacts exactly the sense of catharsis that we recognise from city-clogged experience as one of the rescuing powers of Wordsworthian nature and benign landscape.

So far the established pattern of the song has been to have a Highlands chorus, two verses, chorus, two verses, chorus. Now comes an extraordinary shift of pattern, which only reveals itself in retrospect. We now get seven verses, all spinning the vivid, ridiculous yarn of an encounter between him and a waitress in a Boston restaurant. This is so off-the-wall, so riveting, so sublimely told, so funny and at the same time so inspired an evocation of how it might feel to be the 'artist' being told peremptorily that you must come up with some 'art'; as Richard Harrington put it in a review of the album, their encounter is 'a caustic metaphor for the historically high expectations of critics.'

The tactical manoeuvring in their odd, shifting relationship is delineated step by conversational step, as they jockey for advantage in an encounter that is partly a flirtation, partly a tale about the narrator's myriad uncertainties having to gird themselves to repel the outsider's intrusions, and partly, as its setting of the forlornly empty restaurant on a public holiday so brilliantly evokes, a momentary, unhopeful effort by both people to wrest a little diversionary human contact while marooned by the emptiness of their lives.

It would be unpalatable to go through it phrase by phrase applying the butterfly-pins of critical exegesis, but its many, many highlights include his saying that *she* studies *him* closely as he sits down but immediately making clear that it's been mutual with the observation 'She got a pretty face and long white shiny legs'—those legs so comically described, as if she's either a horse or from another planet; and *his* choice of 'hardboiled eggs' as *her* choice of what he probably wants to eat—with its hint of a put-down, perhaps even an ageist put-down, and the silly follow-up of there not being any: or rather, of her claiming that there aren't any. Another hint of her contempt is subtly achieved too in the battle over whether he must draw her on the napkin, when she hands it to him and says 'You can do it on that', as if *he's* asked, and as if what he's asked is where he can relieve himself. Then there's the exquisitely made internal rhyme of 'napkin' and 'back an'' in 'Well she takes the napkin, and throws it back an' / Says "That don't look a thing like me".'

There's also the way that he brings in the language of the traditional white ballad to use as part of the elaborate push and pull of rudeness and politeness between them, when he contradicts her brusque dissatisfaction with his 'Oh kind miss'. This would be nothing special as mere surface sarcasm: what makes it delightful is that its smiling aside invites a comparison between their crude contemporary skirmishes and the elaborate courtship rituals of old.

There are also the quite brilliant detonations set off on his hilarious self-put-down of a retort to her challenge 'You don't read women authors do you?' (itself a refreshing, unpredictable capturing of the waitress' contemporary sensibility, 'made' in less than 'a few lines') and he says, like a reluctant schoolboy whose teacher has questioned his homework excuse: 'Read Erica Jong', pronouncing this 'Jong' instead of 'Yong' and still making for a long-suspended, joyously ludicrous half-rhyme with the other real name he threw into the song hours ago, 'Neil Young'. The whole gift of Bob Dylan giving us a cameo of feminist debate, and wholly free of any unpleasant reactionary sneering, is a delightful surprise, totally outside the range of subject matter we expect from him. There's also the uncanny fact that Erica Jong's terrible novel *Any Woman's Blues* (1990), actually includes the line 'he had scribbled a rough sketch on a napkin . . . Not my style at all.'

Then there's the slyly resourceful way that one of the many brushes with blues consciousness brought to this album occurs here, as he deploys, without the least elbow-nudging, one of the standard blues-song double-entendres, that of the pencil as the penis, with or without lead in it–which he takes into marvellous, surreal realms as the sparring moves from '. . . but I don't know where my pencil is at' (which also resonates with his hard-boiled-egg agedness) to 'She pulls one out from behind her ear.' A conjuring-trick indeed. (Of course 'lead in his pencil' belongs as much to English music-hall as to the blues world, but *Time Out of Mind* owes little to English music-hall and plenty to the blues, in which the image is used, for instance, by Bo Carter in his 1931 release 'My Pencil Won't Write No More'.)

Andrew Darke comments that the entire exchange 'is so silly and unlikely that it has a strong ring of truth about it.' The song takes us through it word for word, and we're so entranced by its clever and very contemporary, bleak dance of courtship–one with real adversarial edge–and so transfixed by what strongly suggests itself as this unprecedented tour of the world of yer actual Bob Dylan, that the time goes by and the story unfolds and we quite forget the existence of the other side of the song, and are taken by surprise when, after this six-minute spellbinding passage we're reintroduced to 'Well my heart's in the Highlands . . .' and we find ourselves transported once again, this time '. . . with the horses and hounds.'

As ever, the contrast of worlds is immense, wrought on this chorus specifically by the pre-20th century atmosphere, perhaps the medieval British atmosphere of twanging arrows and snapping bows and the 'sport of kings': one more fanciful version of the Highlands, to which is added a new geographical laxity, as he sings of being 'Way up in the border country'. The border country is not 'way up' but 'way down', below even the central lowlands, and thus as far from the Highlands as you can get without crossing the border and leaving Scotland altogether. (Dylan never claims that he is singing of Scotland. There are many places called the Highlands, from Kentucky to Kenya, and there are Aberdeens in Mississippi, Idaho and Washington.)

With a relapse into the cornered gloom of 'My heart's in the Highlands, can't see any other way to go' we're back to the remorseless sameness of daily life, except that he feels '. . . further away than ever before', an expression of disconnectedness echoed later still in 'I got new eyes: everything looks far away.' Before that, however, there is the surprising common-sense candour of 'Some things in life it just gets too late to learn', followed at once by one of those brief, affecting passages that it is impossible not to take autobiographically: 'Well I'm lost somewhere–I must have made a few bad turns'.

But the spiky black humour of 'Highlands' is not over. Lost, he sees, in a splendidly Dylanesque formulation, '. . . people in the park, forgettin' their troubles and woes / They're drinkin' and dancin', wearin' bright-colored clothes.' This is one of the great observations of this or any other Dylan album–the wonderful, strong-grain-of-truthful perception that our culture's garish predilection for brightly coloured clothes is just one long, pathetic attempt to escape our troubles. Playing further on this idiot vanity, as we trudge across the dreary street with him '. . . to get away from a mangy dog' he envisages saying to himself ('in a monologue': another clever small joke) the supremely withering 'I think what I need might be a full-length leather coat.' In a song that cascades with superlative vocal delivery, this is a high point of encapsulated contempt for the culture's emptiness. Adding a similarly clipped articulation of our common powerlessness, he gives comparable but sadder treatment to 'Somebody just asked me if I'm registered to vote.'

Four lines on and we swap it all, for the last time, for the metaphysical Highlands: 'Well, my heart's in the Highlands at the break of day / Over the hills and far away / There's a way to get there and I'll figure it out somehow / Well I'm already there in my mind and that's good enough for now.'

Dylan takes his bow of dignified yearning with one of the loveliest touches he has ever brought to anything. Throwing off the despairing 'further away than ever before', the deteriorated, stricken 'far away' of his 'new eyes' in the here and now, he regains the positive, glowing wonderment of that lovely line from English nursery rhyme and folksong, 'Over the hills and far away', singing *this* 'far away' incomparably beautifully: finding an infinitely delicate, fleeting tone that manages a rhapsodic regret, a momentary lyrical sigh of grace and adieu. It is the most beautifully understated thing.

Confessing to the never-neverland pull of these Highlands, it signals sad resignation that in truth he will never get there; but the warmth and tragic nobility that informs this sadness comes from its also being his loving farewell to the real, human world that once was ardently lovable and is now glimpsed again for a moment before receding, equally unreachable. To carry this admirable concentration of meaning so lightly and elegantly, he discards, briefly, the simple, relentless musical straight line that is so appropriate and right for the great unstoppable machine of the rest of the story, and with a fine enactment of ease gives this 'far away' a little rising and falling filigree of melody that floats off just a little way above the rest, like the curve of one of these faraway hills.

This nursery rhyme line is undeniably evocative by itself—you have only to use it without facetious knowingness to let its affectiveness come through. The British writer G.K. Chesterton described it as one of the most beautiful lines in all English poetry, and Peter and Iona Opie add, in their pioneering *Oxford Dictionary of Nursery Rhymes*, that 'as if in confirmation, Gay, Swift, Burns, Tennyson [and] Stevenson . . . thought well enough of the line to make it their own.' Aptly, for Dylan's purposes, its earliest printed use (1670, though possibly alluded to in 1549) comes from Scotland.

Its spell, its conjuring of a simple, peaceable, unattainable eden—its self-reflexive ability to transport us—comes partly from its having been, as the Opies put it, among the lines that form the 'first poetic memory' of childhood, so that *that* lost edenic rapture throws its softening golden light upon the one evoked by the line itself. Bob Dylan's use of it, therefore, goes to the heart of his song: it distils the unfailing yearning for what is lost, and catches the fleeting redemptive moment, a moment of contact with his better self, the self of loving, open hopefulness, which allows him—perhaps propels him—to end the song, and thus the album, on a note of good faith, albeit limited and fragile.

'Highlands' epitomises the best of *Time Out of Mind*: it deals with most of the album's prominent themes: endless, almost compulsive walking; desolation; lack of a sense of contact with other people; a suffocating sense of the hollowness of everything, and therefore the purposelessness of life; a looking forward to death, alternating with a wish that time was not running out; the conviction that long ago some crucial wrong turning was taken in life: one that meant the loss of true love; the conviction that there is little to say and ever less point to saying it; the exhaustion of feeling, mingled with a passionate sorrow for all this loss. It's not dark yet, but it's getting there. Yet 'Highlands' manages to draw the eye upwards to where the sky is still bright.

[Bob Dylan: 'Highlands', Miami, 13–28 Jan 1997. Greil Marcus: *Interview* magazine, Jul 1997; David Bowman, reviewing *Time Out of Mind* in *Salon* online magazine, US, 19 Sep 1997 (Bowman's novels include *Bunny Modern*, 1998). Andrew Muir: 'The Difference Between a Real Blonde on Blonde and a Fake', *Dignity* no.12, Welwyn Garden City, UK, Sep–Oct 1997. Robert Burns (1759–96), 'My Heart's in the Highlands', 1790, quoted from Muir, ibid. Andrew Darke, Gloucestershire, UK, 11 Apr 1999, letter to this writer; thanks to Sarah Beattie for bluebell information. Richard Harrington, 'This Dylan's No Wallflower', *Washington Post*, undated but c.Oct 1997. Erica Jong, *Any Woman's Blues: A Novel of Obsession*, New York: Harper & Row, 1990; napkin quote e-mailed to this writer by Andrew Muir, Jun 1999. Bo Carter: 'My Pencil Won't Write No More', NY, 4 Jun 1931. Peter & Iona Opie, *The Oxford Dictionary of Nursery Rhymes*, Oxford: Oxford University Press, 1945, revised edn., 1951, p.2.]

Highway 61 *Highway 61 Revisited* meant exactly that: it was revolutionary and new, but it was also, had we heeded it, a clear signal that Dylan had *revisited* the world of the blues. (Other comparable signposts are discussed in **blues, external signals of Dylan's interest in**.)

Many bluesmen had been there before him, all recording versions of a blues called 'Highway 61'—a blues in which, ironically, one of the things that varies, puzzlingly and fascinatingly, is the described route of the highway itself! It is, though, above all, a blues that exemplifies the shared, fluid, communal nature of blues composition.

Roosevelt Sykes' unusually loose 'Highway 61 Blues' was recorded in 1932. The Sparks Brothers cut '61 Highway' the following year, in which Jack Kelly & His South Memphis Jug Band also cut 'Highway No. 61 Blues' and 'Highway No. 61 Blues No. 2', and, two days later, with violinist member Will Batts taking the vocal, another 'Highway No. 61 Blues'. MEMPHIS MINNIE's Joe McCoy (though he never recorded under this, his own name) cut 'Highway 61' in 1935. The pre-war blues singer and pianist Jesse James' only session (in 1936) yielded four tracks, including the unissued 'Highway 61'. Then Charlie Pickett cut his brilliant 'Down the Highway'—a geographically inaccurate 'Highway 61 Blues' by another name—in 1937. And Sampson Pittman, a levee-camp worker and 'excellent guitarist' field-recorded by ALAN LOMAX for the Library of Congress, cut 'Highway 61 Blues' in 1938.

It's odd that both Will Batts and Charlie Pickett sing that Highway 61 runs from Atlanta, Georgia, to New Orleans, because it doesn't go anywhere near Georgia and runs several times as far as such a journey would be. Perhaps Batts never did get very far along it, and perhaps Pickett just copied Batts' stanza.

At any rate this is also a song that carries on drawing people in the post-war period too, and does so both sides of, and heedless of, Dylan's own 1965 recordings. Speckled Red (Rufus Perryman) cut a spirited post-war 'Highway 61 Blues' (with New York City at one end: which is especially surprising since he was a pianist who had hoboed, in Paul Oliver's phrase, 'from the Gulf to the Great Lakes'). Furry Lewis, performing the song in his twilight years, has the route running from Atlanta, Georgia. Fred McDowell cut '61 Highway Blues' in 1959 and Memphis Willie B cut 'Highway 61' in 1961, the same year that Smokey Babe cut 'I Went Down 61 Highway'.

David Honeyboy Edwards cut 'Highway 61' in 1964, the same year that Fred McDowell returned to '61 Highway' in a version with an especially interesting lyric. It incorporates a stanza neatly fusing the highway with part of CHARLEY PATTON's 'Pony Blues'—'I'm gonna buy me a pony can pace, foxtrot and run / Lord when you see me comin' pretty mama I'll be on Highway 61'—and includes a verse that offers a perfect summary of Bob Dylan's mythic position in all this: 'I started school one Monday morning, I throwed my books away / I wrote a note to my teacher: "I'm gonna try 61 today!"'.

Nathan Beauregard (born at Ashland, Mississippi, in about 1869; died in Memphis in 1970) performed it, and splendidly, at the age of 99 at the 1968 Country Blues Festival in Memphis. His version of the 'longest highway I ever knowed' stanza has it running 'from New York City to the Gulf of Mexico.' (These late-60s Memphis Blues Festivals are written about with much passion and splendid rhetoric by Stanley Booth in 'Even the Birds Were Blue', in *The Rolling Stone Rock'n'Roll Reader*, 1974: 'a moving, depressing account of black bluesmen suffering the good intentions of their white admirers', as the book's blurb has it.)

James 'Son' Thomas was recorded singing 'Highway 61 Blues' on film in 1974. Sunnyland Slim cut a geographically correct version of the song (his expansive piano-work beautifully recorded) in 1983. Of especial interest as well as luminosity is Charlie Pickett's 'Down the Highway'. It is brilliant for its torrential guitar-work, determinedly individual vocal delivery and its utterly successful, restless fusion of the two. This is a small masterpiece, from a man who made only four sides of his own in his life, this being the last of them, spread over two days in August 1937 (though as a musician he also enhanced sessions by SLEEPY JOHN ESTES). Dylan uses this title for a *Freewheelin'* song, a song that seems aware of Pickett's, but takes it no further than that, except that both use as an ingredient the format 'this highway runs from A to Z'. Charlie Pickett's runs 'from Atlanta in Georgie down to the Gulf of Mexico'; Dylan's has him 'a-walkin' down your highway. . . . From the Golden Gate Bridge / All the way to the Statue of Liberty'. What's interesting too about this early Dylan blues is that his awkwardness within the form is something he turns to advantage: he uses it, giving the song white layers, city-ironic layers, as well as black. In fact the route he describes is a white one, but only because he's heading west-east in this instance. Dylan is describing here the route of the Lincoln Highway, the USA's first transcontinental highway, which opened in 1923 running between New York and San Francisco. (Later in the 1920s names were abandoned in favour of numbers. North-south highways were given odd numbers and east-west highways evens.)

Heading east-west is often thought of as primarily a white route too—blues writer Bill Ferris, for instance, notes that Route 66 was the white escape route, while Highway 61, south-north, was the black escape route; and certainly Route 66 was the migration path for the displaced Okies of the dust-bowl 1930s, as personified by the Joads, who take this highway in Steinbeck's *The Grapes of Wrath*: 'Route 66 is the path of a people in flight . . .'—yet in 'Bright Lights, Big City: Urban Blues', Mark A. Humphrey writes that 'Industry was drawing blacks to the West Coast from the same Depression-ravaged states . . . that gave California its Okies. There were approximately seventy-five thousand black Los Angelenos in 1940. . . . By 1950 there were more than two hundred thousand . . .' (In 1985, as Bill Bryson notes in his fine book *Made in America*, 'the federal highway department removed all the Route 66 shield signs along its 2,200 miles. . . . Overnight this once great highway became a series of back highways and anonymous frontage roads.')

There is no mistaking, however, the significant route in Dylan's musical life. Jack Kelly's 'Highway No. 61 Blues No. 2' includes the affecting 'I am in dear love with 61, I say it from my heart'; ARTHUR CRUDUP's 1941 story of 'Death Valley Blues' also takes place out on Highway 61, while for Roosevelt Sykes '. . . it breaks my heart, to sing about Highway 61 / I felt so blue when I was out on that lonely highway.' But from among the many weary celebrations of this blues-soaked road two lines sum up its twin significance for Dylan. On the one hand 'That 61 Highway,' as Will Batts, among others, puts it, is the 'longest road I ever knowed'; yet as Charlie Pickett sings, 'Now the 61 Highway, you know an' it runs right by my door'. Bob Dylan's literal journey was, with a couple of diversions, east in stages to Greenwich Village. His existential journey was down Highway 61. He saw it run right past his door in Duluth, Minnesota: and the further he moved along it, the deeper he went into the world of the blues.

As it runs past Duluth, it is on its way from right up at the Canadian border, and it goes on down to St. Paul, through Red Wing along the Minnesota side of the Mississippi River, with Wisconsin on the other side. It drops down into Iowa, then into Missouri near Keokuk. Keeping south, always parallel to the Mississippi, Highway 61 passes St. Louis and then, skirting the corner at which the south-eastern tip of Missouri meets corners of Kentucky and Tennessee, it plunges down into the north-east tip of Arkansas, flowing on south till it meets that mythic city in the south-western toecap of Tennessee–Memphis, to reach which it finally has to cross the Mississippi River.

In Memphis it almost meets its sister-highway, Highway 51, which meets Beale Street and on which Graceland stands at no. 3764 in South Memphis. From there, while 51 runs due south, 61 first veers south-south-west, running down through the vast Mississippi Delta and eventually reaching Vicksburg, the first real town in 200 miles. Still running alongside the river, it crosses the state line into Louisiana south of Natchez, skirting round to the east of Baton Rouge and running on, past Lake Pontchatrain, into New Orleans and the Gulf of Mexico.

The young Bob Dylan's stretch of Highway 61, from Duluth down to St. Paul, is now a road so displaced by Interstate 35 that for most of its Minnesota stretch it's merely a county road today. It's a delight to drive down, therefore: it runs through real, scruffy towns, not strip cities, and now that it's so under-used except for local farmers' pick-ups, the constant eyesore of billboards has vanished. It runs through dolorous, fog-coloured forest, past little lakes with frozen edges and circles of ice around tiny islands of cliff and tree in the water, with small wooden jetties and tied-up boats: Coffee Lake, Moose Lake, Sand Lake. 'Twilight on the frozen lake / North wind about to break / On footprints in the snow / And silence down below,' as Dylan sings so beautifully on the best song on *Planet Waves*, 'Never Say Goodbye'. There are 10,000 of these frozen lakes in Minnesota.

Sometimes farmland asserts itself for a while and there are horses and big old barns and log-piles; more often the road is a dark, forlorn corridor with olive-green sides, such that it's always a surprise to find a clearing glimpsed beyond the trees. Inappropriately flimsy houses are camped from time to time along the road, their front-yard junk mixed up with their plastic decorative squirrels and fawns, lions and Santa Clauses. You have to dodge and weave and pay attention to keep a grip on 61 as its keeps getting entangled in interstates.

Across a pretty river lies Pine City, the least piney and largest place since Duluth. There's a whiff of the prairies here and on the other side of town there it is: prairie landscape instead of the Great North Woods. Easy to imagine Bob riding this highway; you can still find, on the Oldies Stations, the very music he would have had blasting out when he came down for weekends in the big city. And though you won't find some old bluesman's record of 'Highway 61', you might set the dial on your radio and chance upon Bob Dylan's old record of 'Highway 61 Revisited'.

Down in St. Paul, smart people hurry out of the street's icy wind into the warm Manhattan glamour of the Saint Paul Hotel, smiling as they adjust their overcoat collars. They're excited by winter: by its imminent, welcome drama. These people are proud that they endure this climate. Its heartland ruggedness, they like to think, puts its iron in their souls. 'I'm used to four seasons / California's got but one,' as the young Bob Dylan also sang, on the sessions for *Bringing It All Back Home*.

[Bob Dylan: 'California', NY, Jan 13, 1965; unreleased but circulated. Roosevelt Sykes: 'Highway 61 Blues', Richmond, IN, 22 Sep 1932, 1st vinyl-issued *Mr. Sykes Blues 1929–1932*, Riverside RLP 8819, Holland, 1960s. The Sparks Brothers: '61 Highway', Chicago, 2 Aug 1933. Jack Kelly & His South Memphis Jug Band: 'Highway No. 61 Blues' & 'Highway No. 61 Blues No. 2', NY, 1 Aug 1933 (*The Country Fiddlers*, Roots RL-316, Vienna, 1968 & *Memphis Blues (1927–1939)*, Vol.2, Roots RL-329, Vienna, c.1971) and, with Will Batts' vocal, 'Highway No. 61 Blues', NY, 3 Aug 1933, *Memphis Jamboree, 1927–1936*, Yazoo L-1021, NY, c.1970; all 3 CD-reissued *Jack Kelly & His South Memphis Jug Band Complete Recorded Works (1933–1939)*, RST Blues Documents BDCD-6005, Vienna, c.1991. Joe McCoy (as Hallelujah Joe & Congregation): 'Highway 61' Chicago, 15 May 1935, CD-reissued *Charlie & Joe McCoy Complete Recorded Works Volume 1 (1934–1936)*, RST Blues Documents BDCD-6019, Vienna, 1992.

Jesse James: 'Highway 61', Chicago, 3 Jun 1936. Charlie Pickett: 'Down the Highway', NY, 3 Aug 1937, *The Rural Blues: A Study of the Vocal and Instrumental Resources*, 2-LP set, RBF RF-202, NY, 1964. Sampson Pittman: 'Highway 61 Blues', Detroit, 1 Nov 1938, *I'm in the Highway Man*, Flyright FLYLP542, Bexhill-on-Sea UK, 1980, CD-reissued *The Devil Is Busy: Sampson Pittman*, Laurie LCD 7002, Norwood, NJ, 1992. (That odd LP title *I'm in the Highway Man* perpetuates a mishearing by Alan Lomax from the 1930s of another field-recorded item, being the title he ascribed to a Frazier Family song-performance fragment also on the LP.)

Speckled Red (Rufus Perryman): 'Highway 61 Blues', *nia*. Furry Lewis: *nia*. Fred McDowell: '61 Highway Blues', Como, MS, summer 1959, Prestige 25010, c.1961; & '61 Highway', Como, 13 Feb 1964, *Delta Blues*, Arhoolie F1021, Berkeley, CA, 1965, CD-reissued *Mississippi Delta Blues*, Arhoolie CD304, El Cerrito, CA, c.1991. (McDowell re-recorded the song again with white back-up musos in Jackson, MS, Sep 1969, LP-issued on *I Do Not Play Rock'n'Roll*, Capitol ST409, NY, 1969.) Memphis Willie B: 'Highway 61', Memphis, 12 Aug 1961; *Introducing Memphis Willie B.*, Bluesville LP 1034, US, c.1962. Smokey Babe: 'I Went Down 61 Highway', Scotlandville, LA, 18 Apr 1961, *The Country Blues*, Denmark, c.1962. David Honeyboy Edwards: 'Highway 61' Chicago, 17 Mar 1964, *Ramblin' On My*

Mind: A Collectin of Train and Travel Blues, Milestone LP 3002, NY, 1968.

Charley Patton: 'Pony Blues', Richmond, IN, 14 Jun 1929, *The Immortal Charlie Patton 1887–1934*, Origin Jazz Library OJL-7, Berkeley, c.1963. Nathan Beauregard: 'Highway 61', Memphis, 20 Jul 1968, *1968 Country Blues Festival*, Sire SES 97003, NY (Blue Horizon LP 7-63210, UK), *nia*. James 'Son' Thomas: 'Highway 61 Blues', Leland, MS, summer 1974, filmed for *Give My Poor Heart Ease*, Yale Media Design Studio & the Center for Southern Folklore, Memphis, directed Bill Ferris (ex-Director of the Center for the Study of Southern Culture, University of Mississippi, Oxford, MS), 1975. An extract was shown on BBC-2 TV's 'Arena' profile 'Highway 61 Revisited'. (Ferris re Route 66 said to the 'Arena' TV crew, as reported to this writer by programme researcher Debbie Roberts.) Sunnyland Slim: 'Highway 61 Blues', Chicago, 26 or 29 Jan 1983, *Sunnyland Train*, Red Bean 002, US, 1983/4. Arthur Crudup: 'Death Valley Blues', Chicago, 11 Sep 1941, *Bluebird Blues*, RCA Victor LPV-518, NY, 1965.

Stanley Booth: 'Even the Birds Were Blue', *The Rolling Stone Rock'n'Roll Reader*, ed. Ben Fong-Torres, San Francisco: Rolling Stone, 1974. Mark A. Humphrey: 'Bright Lights, Big City: Urban Blues', in *Nothing But the Blues: The Music & the Musicians*, ed. Lawrence Cohn, New York: Abbeville Press, 1993. Bill Bryson, *Made in America*, London: Secker & Warburg, 1994.]

***Highway 61 Revisited* [album, 1965]** Dylan's sixth album and his first fully fledged eagle-flight into rock. Revolutionary and stunning, not just for its energy, freshness and panache but in its vision: fusing radical electric music—electric music as the embodiment of our whole out-of-control, nervous-energy-fuelled, chaotic civilization—with lyrics that were light-years ahead of anyone else's, Dylan here unites the force of blues-based rock'n'roll with the power of poetry. The whole rock culture, the whole post-BEATLE pop-rock world, and so in an important sense the 1960s, started here. It isn't only 'Like a Rolling Stone' and the unprecedentedly long Armageddon epic 'Desolation Row': it's every song. It's the carving out of a new emotional correspondence with a new chaos-reality. There it all was in one bombshell of an album, for a generation who only recognized what world they were living in when Dylan illuminated it so piercingly.

[Recorded NY, 16 Jun, 29–30 Jul & 2 Aug 1965; released as Columbia CS 9189 (stereo) & CL 2389 (mono), 30 Aug 1965. In UK, CBS SBPG 62572 (stereo) & BPG 62572 (mono), Sep 1965.]

Himmelman, Maria [1961 -] Maria Himmelman was born Maria Lownds on October 21, 1961, the daughter of Hans and Sara Lownds. Divorced soon afterwards, Maria's mother married Bob Dylan in 1965 and Dylan adopted Maria, who thus took the surname Dylan and grew up as the older sister of their children JESSE, ANNA, SAMUEL and JAKOB. She married the singer-songwriter PETER HIMMELMAN in 1988. Under the name Maria Dylan she seems to have been production supervisor on the 1995 film *Panther*, directed and written by Mario Van Peebles, and line producer on the Whoopi Goldberg vehicle *Theodore Rex* (also 1995), directed and written by Jonathan R. Betuel. If this is not a case of mistaken identity, perhaps her production credits were essentially for legal work facilitating the films. Jakob Dylan has described Maria in interview as a 'part-time lawyer and full-time mom'.

[Jakob Dylan quote: 'Jakob's Ladder' by Gerry Hirshey, *Rolling Stone* no.762, NY, 12 Jun 1997.]

Himmelman, Peter [1960 -] Peter Himmelman was born in 1960 and raised in the St. Louis Park suburb of Minneapolis. Bob Dylan's son-in-law by being married to Dylan's adopted daughter MARIA (they married in 1988), he was a guitarist and vocalist first in high school band the Reflections and then, based on the West Coast (as he still is) in the group Sussman Lawrence in the early 1980s.

He left to become a singer-songwriter. 'There were some psychics in Minnesota,' he said, 'who told me that if I wasn't more true to my muse I would die . . . literally.' Under his own name he released his début album, *This Father's Day*, in 1986, followed by *Gematria* (1987) and *Synesthesia* (1989). A change of label resulted in *Strength to Strength* (1991), *Flown This Acid World* (1992) and *Skin* (1994). Then, on a different label each time, he issued *Stage Diving* (1996), *My Best Friend Is a Salamander* (1997) and *Love Thinketh No Evil* (1998). Since then he has released *The Himmel Vaults 1* through to *The Himmel Vaults 4*, plus *My Fabulous Plum*, *Unstoppable Forces*, *My Lemonade Stand* and *Imperfect World*. Himmelman has also created film scores for many undistinguished movies including *Dinner and Driving* (1997), *The Souler Opposite* (1998), *Liar's Poker* (1999), *Bill's Gun Shop* (2001), *Four Feet* (2002) and *Jews N the Hood* (2005) and for television series including Disney's 'Bug Juice' and CBS-TV's 'Judging Amy'.

Himmelman, ludicrously, has been compared to ELVIS COSTELLO and BRUCE SPRINGSTEEN, but is also notorious for a certain kind of crowd-pleaser improvisation. One of his many record labels imagined it was a recommendation to put it like this:

'His fans are used to him concocting songs on demand. He's a wiz at improv, they'll tell you—give him a subject, he'll give you a song. Just like that. Himmelman's devoted following has known for years that, his critically acclaimed catalog of studio albums notwithstanding, this is one guy you gotta see live.' The example of 'on demand' songwriting skill and wit they cite (presumably the best they could find) was this: 'This is a song about steak, maybe the only one you will ever hear. / This is a song about steak, the child of a cow—and a steer.'

Dylan fans can judge how Himmelman comports himself on the only known occasion when he and Dylan undertake a shared public performance, which took place live on the CHABAD TELETHON television programme 'L'Chaim—To Life' in LA on September 24, 1989. It's a hilarious ten minutes, in which Himmelman, Dylan and HARRY DEAN STANTON perform together on three songs: 'Einsleipt Mein Kind Dein Eigalach', 'Adelita' and 'Hava Negilah' (truly). On the first of these, Dylan surprises everyone, not least his fellow-performers, by choosing to play the flute. On the second, he plays the recorder and shares vocals with Stanton. On the third song, he plays harmonica. The entire event, bizarre enough merely for its line-up and song choice, is made the more so by Dylan's eccentricity and spontaneity, which is unusually out-on-a-limb even by his standards. All the while, Peter Himmelman is struggling to act normally, to play the guitar and sing as if everything is OK. He fails of course—who can blame him?—but it's the manner of his failure that is so charmless. There's no pleasurable response to the live vagaries of the moment, no rising to the occasion nor any good-humoured surrender in its place: there's nothing from Himmelman but a petulant clumsiness and a good deal of self-regard; he sulks at being upstaged instead of being honoured to be on stage at all. His slob-adenoidal singing, his indifferent playing, but most of all his personal comportment: all is gracelessness.

If you want to give him another chance, or test him in a fairer circumstance (and one that's easier to access), go to his website—there is, naturally, a flash intro—click on Audio and scroll down till you encounter the live performance that he has *chosen* to offer of 'Like a Rolling Stone'. It says it all.

[Peter Himmelman: quote re psychics from his official Six Degrees record-label bio; quote re steak from Plump Records at *www.plump.com*; 'Like a Rolling Stone' heard online 13 Nov 2005 at *www.peterhimmelman.com*.]

Hinchey, John [1947 -] The author of strong and thoughtful critical writing on Dylan's work, John Joseph Hinchey was born July 8, 1947 at the Chelsea Naval Hospital, Massachusetts. He first heard Dylan in 1963 when a radio DJ failed to identify the singer after playing Dylan's 'Don't Think Twice, It's All Right'. John and his brother agreed that it couldn't have been JOHNNY CASH, though they argued as to why; one felt it sounded too young for Cash, the other that it sounded too old. A proper process of listening to Dylan began in early 1965.

After gaining a PhD in English and American Literature and becoming assistant professor at Swarthmore College (1973–80), Hinchey began working for the *Ann Arbor Observer*; his first published work on Dylan was a blurb written in this ahead of Dylan's 1981 concert in Ann Arbor, Michigan. He is still this monthly news magazine's calendar editor and city government reporter.

A more substantial early piece formed the first of the booklets in JOHN BAULDIE's Wanted Man Study Series, written in 1980 and published (without any of the editing that Hinchey felt it needed) as *Bob Dylan's Slow Train*, 1983. He also published a provocative article about Dylan's *Shot of Love* album in the *Telegraph* fanzine in 1985, in which he appeared to argue that poor material had been deliberately included by Dylan as an artistically skilful way of communicating his angst. But then came his admirable self-published *Like a Complete Unknown: The Poetry of Bob Dylan's Songs 1961–1969* in 2002. It is especially strong on the much-neglected song 'North Country Blues'.

Album-by-album essays that will form a second volume (through to *Saved*) have begun to appear in the fanzine *Judas!*, notably including a fine, substantial scrutiny of the *Planet Waves* album.

His critical position, he writes, is this: 'What I have to say about Dylan's poetry is simply a report on what it looks like, and feels like, from where I stand. . . . The form of criticism I practise is Emersonian . . .'

[John Hinchey: *Bob Dylan's Slow Train*, Wanted Man Study Series Booklet no.1, Bury, UK, undated but 1983; 'Shot of Love: Some Other Kinds of Blues', *The Telegraph* no.22, Bury, UK, winter 1985; *Like a Complete Unknown: The Poetry of Bob Dylan's Songs 1961–1969*, Ann Arbor, MI: Stealing Home Press, 2002 (quote is on p.12); 'Planet Waves: Not Too Far Off', *Judas!* no.12, Huntingdon, UK, Jan 2005.]

Hinton, Nigel [1941 -] Nigel Hinton is a British writer of prize-winning children's and adults' fiction, born in London on September 28, 1941. His adult fiction includes *Heart of the Valley* (1986); his books for teenagers include *Collision Course* (1976), *Buddy* (1980) and *Time Bomb* (2004). His work for younger children includes the *Beaver Towers* series. He has also scripted the BBC-TV series 'Buddy' (starring Roger Daltrey, 1985) and written the screenplays for the movies *Buddy's Song* (1991) and, with novelist Peter Prince, *Blood Ties* (2007). He first listened to Dylan when given *Freewheelin'* in 1963 but 'didn't become passionate about him until 1969'. He has written little on Dylan (beyond his unpublished MA dissertation of 1975, University of Kent) but that little is passionate, sane, intelligent, fresh and alive. A letter to *The Telegraph* was reproduced in part on the cover of its first issue—'that's the odd thing about Dylan; he reduces me almost to the level of a screaming groupie, [I'm] anxious for details about what he eats for breakfast and for the latest photograph of him and, at the same time, [he] inspires me to a contemplation of the most crucial questions about Life and Art . . .' Later writing for *The Telegraph* included 'In Defence of "Joey"' and a pro-*Knocked Out Loaded* review, titled

'Into the Future, Knocked Out and Loaded', that also brought a keen analytic eye to *Empire Burlesque* (this essay was republished in *All Across the Telegraph* in 1987). More recently, for *Judas!*, he has written 'Lowdown and Disgusted: The Ballad of Jack Fate' and 'Angles and Triangles'—this last including a tracing of parallels and correspondences between the *Blood on the Tracks* song 'Buckets of Rain' and, surprisingly, the Thomas Hardy novel *Far from the Madding Crowd*.

(See also the entries ***Chronicles Volume One*** and **'Dignity'**.)

[Nigel Hinton: letter, *Telegraph* no.1, Bury, UK, Nov 1981; 'In Defence of "Joey"', *Telegraph* no.14, Nov 1983; 'Into the Future, Knocked Out and Loaded', *Telegraph* no.25, autumn 1986; 'Lowdown and Disgusted: The Ballad of Jack Fate', *Judas!* no.5, Huntingdon, UK, Apr 2003; 'Angles and Triangles', *Judas!* no.10, Jul 2004. Thomas Hardy: *Far From the Madding Crowd*, 1st published serially, *The Cornhill Magazine*, 1874 & in volume form same year; its title taken from Thomas Gray's 'Elegy Written in a Country Church-Yard', 1751; a hit film, *Far From the Madding Crowd*, dir. John Schlesinger, was released in 1967.]

Holly, Buddy [1936 - 1959] Charles Hardin Holley, aka Buddy Holly, created some of the territory of rock'n'roll, virtually inventing the guitars-bass-drums beat group with composer-vocalist leader. His large body of timeless, unpretentious work, achieved in a very few years (like bluesmen such as BLIND LEMON JEFFERSON and ROBERT JOHNSON) was first given properly documented reissue by John Beecher and Malcolm Jones, with the 6-LP box set *The Complete Buddy Holly* in 1979–20 years after Holly's death.

He had more personal talent, charisma and potential than anyone except ELVIS PRESLEY. Even on his very early recordings, where the studio sound, the arrangements and the type of song featured all drew heavily on Presley's earliest Sun cuts, you could not but be aware of a very different talent feeling its way and testing its strengths. By the time he was having hits, he not only had a distinctive sound but also an integrity and an inquiring interest in country music and city blues. The famous Holly sound is on songs like 'That'll Be the Day', 'Peggy Sue', 'Heartbeat', 'Every Day', 'Listen to Me', 'Tell Me How' and so on. His fine later ones, with their plumper sound, include 'Peggy Sue Got Married', 'That's What They Say', 'What to Do' and the immortal record that was his latest release at the time of his death, Paul Anka's composition 'It Doesn't Matter Anymore' coupled with 'Raining in My Heart.'

Holly had played Duluth on the so-called Summer Dance Party tour of the mid-west—Duluth was on July 11, 1958—but when Dylan saw Holly perform, it was on the Winter Dance Party tour that began in Milwaukee on January 23, 1959. Dylan was in the audience at the Duluth Armory eight days later, just three nights before Holly died with RITCHIE VALENS and the Big Bopper in a chartered single-engined plane that crashed in the snow in the early hours of February 3, on its way to North Dakota. This was *the* rock-star death of the 1950s, the first such death of huge significance to the rock'n'roll generation. Hence its memorialisation in Don McLean's 'American Pie' as 'the day the music died'. (The earlier death, by Russian roulette, of R&B artist JOHNNY ACE, backstage in Houston, Christmas Eve 1954, is better known now than at the time, and Ace a lesser artist than Holly.)

The last things studio-recorded before his death were 'True Love Ways' and 'Moondreams', and they were oddly, beguilingly mellow—one even used an aspidistra saxophone sound (a tenor sax by Sam 'The Man' Taylor). But the hint that Holly might have been slacking off into popular balladland is belied by the evidence of his musical interests. He cut the only white commercial blues that could even touch Presley's best: 'Mailman, Bring Me No More Blues'. Written for Holly, it remains superb: one of those magic combinations of song, pace, conviction, sound, vocals, guitar-work (all Holly's) and mood. An undiminished, shimmering achievement. He could handle BO DIDDLEY and CHUCK BERRY songs too, adding something of his own in a way that showed rare understanding. 'Bo Diddley' and 'Brown-Eyed Handsome Man' make the point with a kind of raw panache. (Cricket Sonny Curtis reveals that he and Holly used to listen to Stan's Record Rack on the radio beamed all the way from Shreveport, Lousiana: 'That was a real good program that played the black music of the day.' Dylan, up in Minnesota, was listening to the same powerful station in the same period.)

The music on Holly's own songs is riddled with the clichés of the time but handled with intelligence enough to show that had he lived he would have readily discarded them. People talk automatically about ERIC CLAPTON and his ilk as 'the great guitarists' but there's a sense in which Holly was a great guitarist, boxed in by the restrictions of convention in his time. His lyric writing not only touched a generation but could have a poet's compression and economy. As British singer-songwriter Harvey Andrews argues: 'All the great [modern] songwriters . . . were influenced by Holly. When rock'n'roll first started, there was something about Holly that got them. They all liked Elvis and LITTLE RICHARD but Holly is the one that they related to. He was the first singer-songwriter, but we didn't know it at the time. His lyrics are incredible. One verse of "I'm Lookin' for Someone to Love" goes "Drunk man, street car / Foot slipped, there you are." Well, that's a book, a novel, a play and a film. Nine words and it's lyric writing of the highest order.'

If he had lived . . . GREIL MARCUS said that Buddy Holly would have joined Dylan for a duet on, say, 'I Don't Believe You'. That rings true, and true in part because of the similarities that exist in any case between the two singers.

Control is a main point of resemblance. It went missing from rock when the British beat-group boom got going in 1963, and suddenly a loose, ramshackle sound was considered good enough and singers weren't sure where they were throwing their voices and didn't care which notes they were going to hit. Many of the solo stars had known exactly what their voices were doing—even when they were ripping it up. Little Richard was wild, but he was always in control. Presley always had this same sort of precision. So did the EVERLYS and Jackie Wilson. Buddy Holly had it too. Control in Holly was a special thing, tantamount to integrity: a precision demanded by artistic considerations, and part of his greatness.

Dylan surely learnt a lot about such considerations directly from Holly. There are times when in both of them flashes of phrasing sound on first hearing like mistakes but aren't. They turn out to be more right than the expected alternatives that don't appear, and in demonstrating it both artists have taught you something.

You can trace the effects of this teaching, as Holly gave it to Dylan, right down to similarities of timing, phrasing, emphasis, pronunciation. Greil Marcus dealt very well with this. 'Dylan and Holly', he wrote, 'share a clipped staccato delivery that communicates a sly sense of cool, almost teenage masculinity,' and he cited Holly's performance on 'Midnight Shift'. There, says Marcus, 'the phrasing is simply what we know as pure Dylan': 'If she tells you she wants to use the caahhh! / Never explains what she wants it faaahhh!'

Marcus makes another but a connected point, in discussing some of the home tape-recordings of Holly's voice that were released, after his death, with backing tracks added: 'Sometimes, these ancient cuts provide a real sense of what rock'n'roll might have become had Holly lived. The same shock of recognition that knocked out the audiences at the Fillmore West when THE BAND . . . lit into Little Richard, takes place, with the same song, when the ghost of Buddy Holly is joined by the Fireballs for "Slippin' and Slidin". . . . An agile, humorous vocal is carried by a band that knows all the tricks. They break it open with the Everly Brothers' own seductive intro, constantly switching, musically, from song to song, while Holly ties it together. The guitarist actually sounds like ROBBIE ROBERTSON, throwing in bright little patterns around the constant whoosh of the cymbals . . . it's certainly one of the best things Buddy Holly never did.'

There must be a good deal of similarity, albeit perhaps too intangible to document, for that idea to strike home so sharply. Obviously, the 'Midnight Shift' resemblance is tangible enough, and we have it on innumerable Dylan tracks from 'I Want You' to 'On the Road Again' and from 'Absolutely Sweet Marie' back to 'When the Ship Comes In'. The last of these may seem a strange choice, but Buddy Holly could have sung 'When the Ship Comes In'. It has all the right tensions, all the polarities of high and low notes, rushes and lapses, that Holly, alone among the pre-Dylan stars, could easily control. And Dylan's 'Odds and Ends', on the Basement Tapes, seems strikingly and wholly in the spirit of Buddy Holly & the Crickets records, while 'Maybe Someday', on *Knocked Out Loaded*, 1986, not only has that spirit and a very Holly title but some very adroit lines that Holly might have written if he'd been more daring in his lyrics.

Another commonality is an intangible additive in the voices. Holly's voice transcends the limits set by the words of his songs. On the page they may be trite, even fatuous but his voice lights them up, making them touching or thrillingly direct. Both Dylan and Holly suggest a level of emotion at work below the words, way out beyond the scope of the lyric. Holly shows it on, for example, 'True Love Ways'; Dylan shows it everywhere.

(For another potential connection between Holly and Dylan, see **Clayton, Paul** and **Hester, Carolyn**.)

In September or October 1980, when Dire Straits were playing some dates at the Roxy just after the release of their album *Making Movies*, Dylan was among those present at the Sunset Marquis hotel in Los Angeles, along with TIM DRUMMOND, MARK KNOPFLER, two members of BRUCE SPRINGSTEEN's E Street Band, the Dire Straits manager Ed Bicknell, two unidentified young women and music-journalist Mike Oldfield. This informal session, which has become referred to as 'the Knopfler Hotel Room Tape' included Dylan and Knopfler performing Buddy Holly's 'That'll Be the Day'. Unfortunately, Bicknell believes that no-one present taped this material. Dylan also performed 'That'll Be the Day' a number of times, sharing vocals with PAUL SIMON, on some of their double-bill concerts of 1999, beginning in Milwaukee on the 4th of July and finishing, many performances of the song later, in Dallas on December 18.

Recalling that tenor sax on Holly's 'True Love Ways', the pleasant surprise of a comparable saxophone at the end of Dylan's *Oh Mercy* track 'Where Teardrops Fall'—a pool of aural coloring encountered nowhere else on the album—acts as a fond tribute to the Holly recording.

Dylan acknowledged Holly's importance to him more specifically at his 1998 Grammy acceptance speech for Best Male Rock Vocal Performance and Best Contemporary Folk Album for *Time Out of Mind* (New York City, February 25), in which he also described having a sense of Holly's presence all through the recording of that album—almost 40 years after Holly's death. And within a year of this, Dylan also resumed performing Holly's great Bo Diddley-inspired song, the appropriately titled 'Not Fade Away', in concert, starting on the first night of the opening leg of the 1999 tour, at Fort

Myers, Florida, that January 26. (He'd first sung it as a surprise concert-opener at Hartford, CT, on April 19, 1997.)

In the end, perhaps the way to encompass what Dylan has done via Holly is to say that there's a strong positive level on which Dylan has effectively replaced him.

[Buddy Holly: the 6-LP box set *The Complete Buddy Holly*, MCA Coral CDSP 807, London, 1979; The Crickets: 'That'll Be the Day' (2nd, & hit, version), Clovis, NM, 25 Feb 1957, Brunswick 55009, NY (Coral Q 72279, London), 1957. Buddy Holly: 'Peggy Sue', Clovis, 29 Jun–1 Jul 1957, c/w 'Everyday', Clovis, 27 Jun 1957, Coral 61885, NY (Coral Q 72293, London), 1957; 'Heartbeat', Clovis, Jun–Aug 1958, Coral 62051 (Q 72346), 1958; 'Listen to Me', Clovis, 29 Jun–1 Jul 1957, Coral 61947 (Q 72288), 1958. The Crickets: 'Tell Me How', Clovis, May–Jul 1957, B-side of 'Maybe Baby', Oklahoma City, 27–28 Sep 1957, Brunswick 55053 (Coral Q 72307), 1958. Buddy Holly: 'Peggy Sue Got Married', NY, Jan 1959 (overdubs NY, June 1959), Coral 62134 (Q 72376), 1959; 'That's What They Say' and 'What to Do', NY, Jan 1959 (overdubs NY, Jan 1960), *The Buddy Holly Story Volume 2*, Coral LP 57326 (Coral LVA 9127), 1960 (and UK single Coral Q 72419, 1961); 'It Doesn't Matter Any More' c/w 'Raining in My Heart', NY, 21 Oct 1958, Coral 62074 (Q 72360), 1959; 'True Love Ways' and 'Moondreams' also NY, 21 Oct 1958; 'Mailman Bring Me No More Blues', Clovis, 8 Apr 1957, Coral 61852, 1957 (B-side of 'Words of Love', also Clovis, 8 Apr 1957), 1st UK issue on *Buddy Holly* LP, Coral C 57210, 1958, not a UK single until as B-side of 'Look At Me' (Clovis, May–Jul 1957), Coral 72445, 1961; 'Bo Diddley', Clovis, 1956 (overdubs by the Fireballs, Clovis, 1962), Coral C 62352 (Q 72463, London: different B-side), 1963; 'Brown-Eyed Handsome Man', Clovis, 1956 (overdubs Fireballs, Clovis, 1962), Coral C 62369 (Q 72459, London: different B-side), 1963; 'Midnight Shift', Nashville, 26 Jan 1956 c/w 'Rock Around with Ollie Vee', Nashville, 22 Jul 1956, Brunswick O 5800, London, 1959 (top 30); 'Slippin' and Slidin'', NY, Jan 1959 (overdubs Fireballs, Clovis, 1962), US B-side of 'What to Do', Coral C 62448, 1965 (UK B-side of 'Brown-Eyed Handsome Man', Coral Q 72459, 1963).

Tracks recorded Jan 1959 were solo demos by Holly, made in his Greenwich Village apartment, after he had broken with both the Crickets and Norman Petty, with 1959–60 overdubs by Jack Hansen, commissioned by Dick Jacobs (with whose 'Orchestra' Holly had recorded his last studio session, i.e. the NY, 21 Oct 1958 session). The Jan 1959 demo material was later re-acquired by Petty, who made different overdubs, using the Fireballs (Clovis, 1962–68) on this and other material. Through the 1960s and 1970s, therefore, with US & UK companies issuing different releases, the two different sets of overdubbed tracks were issued more or less haphazardly. The box set *The Complete Buddy Holly* contains both, plus Holly's undubbed original solo demo versions of some but not all these tracks. To the extent that some were not included—'What to Do' and 'That's What They Say' among them—the box set is mistitled.

Sonny Curtis and Harvey Andrews quoted from undated interviews by Spencer Leigh in *Baby, That Is Rock and Roll: American Pop 1954–1963*, p.88 & 90. Greil Marcus quoted from 'Records', *Rolling Stone* no. 35, San Francisco, 28 Jun 1969. Details re 'the Knopfler Hotel Room Tape' from Ed Bicknell in conversation with the present writer in c.Apr 1981 & 31 Aug 1995; the occasion is also described in Mike Oldfield's book *Dire Straits*, 1984.]

***Homer, the slut* [fanzine]** See Muir, Andrew.

'Honey Just Allow Me One More Chance' See Thomas, Henry.

Hooker, John Lee [1917 - 2001] John Lee Hooker was born a few miles south-east of Clarksdale, in the tiny community of Vance, Mississippi, on August 22, 1917. He became an influential, and very successful, post-war bluesman: a singer, guitarist and songwriter with a distinctive voice people either like or dislike strongly, and a shambling style that seemed as old as voodoo chants yet always managed to sound modern and knowing.

After an adolescence in Memphis, where he worked as a theatre usher, Hooker moved north to Detroit in 1943, played in the city's important black entertainment district around Hastings Street, and kept a home in Detroit until 1969, by which time he had achieved crossover hit singles in European hit parades as well as in the US. He first recorded in 1948, starting as he meant to continue with a sizeable hit, 'Boogie Chillen', and then between 1959 and 2000 released a staggering 77 albums. The titles of the earliest of these suggest his popularity with the folk-revival market: the first was *Folk Blues* and the next handful included *The Country Blues of John Lee Hooker* and *The Folk Lore of John Lee Hooker*. Ludicrously, granted his unmistakeably individual voice and style, many of these early records were made under pseudonyms for rival labels to Modern, the one that had signed him: pseudonyms like Delta John, Texas Slim, Birmingham Sam & His Magic Guitar and, as Tony Russell notes, 'flimsiest of all, John Lee Booker on Chess, a label for which he made some particularly compelling sides in 1950–51'. Nevertheless it was with Modern and under his own name that he followed up his first hit with 'Hobo Blues' and 'Crawlin' King Snake' (1949), and 'I'm in the Mood' (1951).

He has had no discernible impact on Dylan's style, yet he occupies a special place in his history: for it was a tangible step forward for Dylan when he was given support-act billing to Hooker for a two-week stint at Gerde's Folk City in April 1961 (the weeks of April 11–16 and 18–23), and named as such on the handbills. Dylan proudly sent copies of these back up to Minneapolis, to impress his friends. Dylan's friend Sybil Weinberger told the makers of BBC-TV's 1993 *Arena* Special 'Highway

61 Revisited' that in the early Village days, Dylan loved Hooker, and that whenever he was playing, Bob would be there.

In *Chronicles Volume One*, although Dylan makes no comment on Hooker, he does mention him in noting ruefully that his own harmonica playing was too basic to ever attract any comment, with the exception of one time 'a few years later in John Lee Hooker's hotel room on Lower Broadway . . . SONNY BOY WILLIAMSON was there and he heard me playing, said, "Boy, you play too fast."' That 'a few years later' probably means 'not long afterwards'. In 1985, Hooker said of Dylan: 'Bob is a beautiful person. A good, good man. Very sweet, very kind. I met him when I was playing in the coffee-houses. He wasn't famous then but he came to see me. We played some shows together and he'd come back to my place and we'd stay up all night playin' and drinkin' wine.'

Hooker went on to create band-backed 1960s R&B cross-over hits out of 'Dimples' (actually cut in 1956) and 'Boom Boom' (1962), and crossed too from the solo 'folk blues' of Dylan's Greenwich Village days to the electric blues mainstream of that decade's end. In the 1970s he was taken up by younger star names like Elvin Bishop and VAN MORRISON; for most of the 1980s he more or less disappeared, but turned up on stage for the encore of Dylan's concert with TOM PETTY & THE HEARTBREAKERS at Mountain View, California, on August 5, 1986 to perform 'Good Rockin' Mama' backed by all these rock musicians (augmented by AL KOOPER).

Not long after that Hooker made one of those unpromising albums that gathers up clusters of star guest performers, *The Healer*, in 1989—on this occasion CARLOS SANTANA, Robert Cray, Los Lobos, George Thorogood, Charlie Musselwhite and Bonnie Raitt (yielding, with her, a much-admired vocal duet revisit to his 1950 hit 'I'm in the Mood')—which turned out to become the biggest-selling blues album in history and was followed by the similarly stellar-supported *Mr. Lucky* (with Albert Collins, Ry Cooder, KEITH RICHARDS and Van Morrison).

John Lee Hooker died of natural causes at his home in Los Altos, near San Francisco, on Thursday, June 21, 2001. He was 83.

[John Lee Hooker: 'Boogie Chillen', Detroit, Sep 1948, Modern 20-627, US, 1948; 'Hobo Blues', Detroit, Sep 1948 or 18 Feb 1949, Modern 20-663; & 'Crawlin' King Snake', 18 Feb 1949, Modern 20-714, 1949; 'I'm in the Mood', Detroit, 7 Aug 1951, Modern 835, 1951; 'Dimples', Chicago, 17 Mar 1956, Vee-Jay VJ 205, US, 1956; 'Boom Boom', Chicago, late 1961, Vee-Jay VJ 438, 1962; *The Healer*, California, Jan 2 & Oct 1987 & Apr–May 1988, Chameleon LP 74808, US, 1989; *Mr. Lucky*, nia, Apr 1990–May 1991, Silvertone ORE CD 519. (There is a monumental Hooker discography online at *http://web.telia.com/~u19104970/johnnielee.html*, by Claus Röhnisch.) Hooker quote on Dylan: Brian Walden, 'Questionnaire: John Lee Hooker', *Q* no.85, London, Oct 1993. Bob Dylan: *Chronicles Volume One*, p.257. Tony Russell quote, *The Blues—From Robert Johnson to Robert Cray*, 1997, p.69.]

Hornby, Nick [1957 -] Nick Hornby, born in Redhill in England on April 17, 1957, is a madly successful lad-lit novelist whose million-selling books are about boyish obsessiveness, focused on collecting records, following football, whatever, interspersed with comic scenes about their heroes' failures to 'get girls' / 'understand women'. This work culminates in the hit movie *About a Boy*, starring, naturally, Hugh Grant. To raise money for UK charity the TreeHouse Trust and US charity 826 Valencia, Hornby then wrote the book *Songbook* (US title, 2002), aka *31 Songs* (UK title, 2003), which enthuses about 31 *records* rather than songs.

He is not a huge Dylan fan, and doesn't care much about the words, yet has a clearly authentic passion for music and an articulate intelligence, so his comments on Dylan's career and omnipresence in our consciousness are refreshing, the more so because he's too young to have been around when Dylan was young himself. The one Dylan track on his list is 'Can You Please Crawl Out Your Window', which he likes because it's 'mid-sixties, electric . . . but it's poppier and grungier than anything on *Blonde on Blonde*' and isn't over-familiar: 'If you can hear Dylan and THE BEATLES being unmistakeably themselves at their peak—but unmistakeably themselves in a way we haven't heard a thousand, a million times before—then suddenly you get a small but thrilling flash of their spirit, and it's as close as we'll ever get, those of us born in the wrong time, to knowing what it must have been like to have those great records burst out of the radio when you weren't expecting them, or anything like them.'

[Nick Hornby: *Songbook*, San Francisco: McSweeney's Books, 2002 & London: Viking, 2003. The film *About a Boy*, dir. Chris & Paul Weitz, screenplay Peter Hedges, 2002.]

Horowitz, David [1939 -] David Horowitz, born in Forest Hills, New York, on January 10, 1939, is a political analyst and journalist who wrote, among much else, the excellent book *Free World Colossus: From Yalta to Vietnam*, 1967, a compelling study of the Cold War and US imperialism.

He also wrote a pioneering early piece on Dylan's work—especially on its politics and on the song 'A Hard Rain's a-Gonna Fall'—in 1964. This article, 'Bob Dylan: Genius or Commodity?', was published in Britain in *Peace News*, which was a mouthpiece for the nuclear disarmament movement and was responsible, in the 1960s, for a mini-poster, handy for notice-boards and as a car-sticker, with the splendid motto 'Join the Army; travel to exotic, distant lands; meet exciting, unusual people and kill them.'

All this writing was done while Horowitz was a decent and scrupulous historian on the Left. However, he suffered a political conversion and now enjoys mega media coverage in the US as a combative campaigner on the Right. He has taken up the rôle of reactionary court jester, imagines that he is a useful and vibrant bête noir pestering the (now barely extant) American Left, partly by ranting away in his magazine *Front Page* and writing crassly populist books like *Hating Whitey*.

[David Horowitz, *Free World Colossus: From Yalta to Vietnam*, US: American, 1967, published UK as *From Yalta to Vietnam*, Harmondsworth: Penguin, 1967; *Hating Whitey*, Dallas, TX: Spence Publishing, 1999. 'Bob Dylan: Genius or Commodity?', *Peace News*, London, 11 Nov 1964, reprinted in Richard Mabey, *The Pop Process*, 1969.]

'Horseman & the Twist-up Gang' [1965] This was the original title of the 850-word prose-poetry piece ROBERT SHELTON asked Dylan to write for the 1965 NEWPORT FOLK FESTIVAL 'program book', and which Dylan sent on two neatly typed sheets (with minimal typed and handwritten changes), together with a handwritten note that included the incautious 'use it anyway you feel fit'.

Shelton duly 'corrected' some of Dylan's pronouns, replaced his characteristic ampersands with ands, broke the continuous piece into short paragraphs (his breaks not always keeping faith with the sense) and generally made it look both more readable and more conventional. His biggest intervention was to retitle it 'Off the Top of My Head'.

It duly appeared in the Festival 'program book', mostly on page 17 but with a small amount shoved back to page 59, where it sat incongruously alongside a photo of Julie Andrews playing her guitar in the mountains in *The Sound of Music*. The program was jointly edited by RALPH RINZLER and Shelton, using the same pseudonym, Stacey Williams, which he had used for his sleevenotes on the back of Dylan's first album.

[For a more detailed examination of the changes from 'Horseman & the Twist-up Gang' to 'Off the Top of My Head', see IAN WOODWARD's article 'Tracking Dylan 4', *Isis* no.122, Bedworth, UK, Sep–Oct 2005, pp.39–42.]

House, Son [1902 - 1988] Eddie James House, Jr. was born on March 21, 1902 on a Delta plantation at Riverton, Mississippi, grew up to become a Baptist pastor before the age of 20, initiating the drama of a lifetime's enacted pull between religious and secular passion. He learnt guitar only after returning to Mississippi from some years spent in Louisiana; in 1928 he was sent to Parchman Farm for mortally shooting a man, reportedly in self-defence, but was released within a year. He met up with the equally powerful CHARLEY PATTON and with Willie Brown, travelled with them to Grafton, Wisconsin, where on May 28, 1930 he recorded his classic début session—a session of ten tracks that proved him an originator of the dark and heavy Mississippi Delta blues style. He continued to play with Patton and without him, but never returned to the studios in the pre-war period. He was field-recorded in Mississippi by ALAN LOMAX in 1941 and 1942.

'The Jinx Blues Part One', one of his 1942 tracks, rages like this against the dying of delight: 'You know these blues ain't nothin but a low-down shakin', low-down shakin', achin' chill / I said the blues is a low-down old achin' chill / Well if you ain't had 'em honey I hope you never will. / Them blues, them blues is a worryin' heart, worryin' heart, heart disease / Just like a woman you be lovin', man, it's so doggone hard to please.'

It's typical of Son House (though also of Patton) that he should expand the lyric with these long, erupting, erratic surges of repetition. Another vocal effect he employs time and again, yet always effectively and without ever quite losing its element of surprise, is in *not* repeating or approximating the whole of the first line of a verse as the second line, but instead beginning that second line with an 'mmm-mmm-mmm' and then repeating only the end-portion of the first line, which often has a different resonance when divorced from its other half. Though he's by no means alone in doing it, this inspired, intelligent word-conjuring is one of the things that makes him great. He has a way, too, of using common-stock formulations yet always making his songs sound like works in progress, and he has a rare expressive intensity.

In 1943 House moved to the slums of Rochester, New York, where he gave up playing, sold his guitar and was eventually amazed to be 'rediscovered', let alone find that he was regarded by these strange young middle-class white people as a great artist. He recorded anew in Rochester in 1964, in Chicago later that year, in New York City in 1965 and a number of other times afterwards, the last being in London in July 1970. He played the NEWPORT FOLK FESTIVAL in 1964 and 1965.

He is a giant figure in 20th century American music, the single most potent stylistic influence on ROBERT JOHNSON—who as a boy used to hang around him, listening, before he could play a note himself—a model for MUDDY WATERS and a creative, forceful performer in his own right.

To be specific, Johnson's 'Walking Blues' recycles 'My Black Mama' by Son House, who was himself calling it 'Walking Blues' in the 1930s before Robert Johnson used the title for his own song (the title 'My Black Mama' was because the 'black mama' lyrics House took as his starting-point came from one of his mentors, James McCoy); and House's 1942 field-recorded 'Walking Blues' re-emphasises this lineage. But the story doesn't end there. Extraordinarily, in 1985 the collector Mike Kirsling found 42 Paramount test-pressings in the roof of a house in Illinois, and more left out in the snow. (As he took them home he prayed 'Please God, don't let them be by white singers!': some were, some weren't.) Among them—it's almost too good to be true—was a Son House recording of 'Walking Blues' itself from 1930—indeed recorded the same day as his 'My Black Mama'—a record not known to have existed, and confirming the song as an item in House's repertoire at least six years before Robert Johnson recorded it.

Specifically too, Muddy Waters' first recorded side, August 1941's 'Country Blues', is also founded upon House's 1930s 'Walking Blues'. The similarity between Waters' bottleneck playing on this and Robert Johnson's on *his* 'Walking Blues' has been widely noted—but both are extremely similar to that on Son House's 'My Black Mama', and the field-recorded interviews with Muddy Waters make it clear that it was Son House who taught him bottleneck guitar. (All this is detailed in a 1981 article 'Really the "Walking Blues": Son House, Muddy Waters, Robert Johnson and the Development of a Traditional Blues', by John Cowley.)

Even in old age, debilitated and at times distracted, he was a person of great dignity. Among the Columbia sides made in 1965 is the gorgeous, touching 'Pearline', on which House sounds infinitely older than his 63 years but turns his frailty to transcendently poignant advantage, his clawing, arthritic slide guitar glistening like tears across the track.

Interviewed in San Diego in autumn 1993, Bob Dylan said: 'The people who played that music were still around . . . [in the early 1960s], and so there was a bunch of us, me included, who got to see all these people close up—people like Son House, REVEREND GARY DAVIS or SLEEPY JOHN ESTES. Just to sit there and be up close and watch them play, you could study what they were doing, plus a bit of their lives rubbed off on you. Those vibes will carry into you forever, really, so it's like those people, they're still here to me. They're not ghosts of the past or anything, they're continually here.' Indeed.

Son House moved to Detroit in 1976 and though he outlived almost all the rest, including many of his successors, he died there on October 19, 1988, aged 86.

[Son House: 'My Black Mama Part 1', 'My Black Mama Part 2', Grafton, WI, 28 May 1930; 'Walking Blues', Grafton, 28 May 1930, unissued until *Delta Blues 1929–1930*, Document DLP 532, Vienna, 1988; 'Walking Blues', Robinsonville, MS, 17 Jul 1942, CD-reissued *Son House: The Complete Library of Congress Sessions 1941–1942*, Travelin' Man TM CD 02, Crawley, UK, 1990; 'Pearline', NY, 12–14 Apr 1965, *Son House—Father of Folk Blues*, Columbia CL 2417, NY, 1965; reissued on 2-CD set *Son House: Father of the Delta Blues: The Complete 1965 Sessions* (produced by John Hammond), Roots N' Blues Masters series, Columbia Legacy 4716622, NY, 1992 (incl. re-recordings of, among others, Blind Willie Johnson's 'John the Revelator' & Patton's 'Pony Blues').

Robert Johnson: 'Walking Blues', San Antonio, TX, 27 Nov 1936, *Robert Johnson: King of the Delta Blues Singers*, Columbia CL-1654, NY, 1961.Muddy Waters (as McKinley Morganfield): 'Country Blues', Stovall, MS, c.24–31 Aug 1941 (field-recorded for the Library of Congress), vinyl-issued on the compilation *Afro-American Blues and Game Songs*, AFS L-4, Washington, D.C., 1962 & Polydor UK 236.574, London, *n/a*, CD-reissued Rounder CD 1513, Cambridge, MA, 1999; also CD-reissued *The Complete Plantation Recordings: Muddy Waters: The Historic Library of Congress Recordings 1941–1942*, MCA CHD 9344, London, 1993.

For the 1985 Paramounts discovery story see Bob Hilbert: 'Paramounts in the Belfry', *78 Quarterly* no.4, Key West, FL, 1989. John Cowley: 'Really the "Walking Blues": Son House, Muddy Waters, Robert Johnson and the Development of a Traditional Blues', *Popular Music Vol. 1*, ed. Richard Middleton & David Horn, Cambridge: Cambridge University Press, 1981.]

Houston, Cisco [1918 - 1961] Gilbert Vandine Houston was born in Wilmington, Delaware, on August 18, 1918. He became a singer, guitarist and songwriter, and was a minor figure in and around the WOODY GUTHRIE circle. Guthrie describes first encountering 'the Cisco kid' in his autobiography *Bound for Glory* (1943). They traveled together before World War II, till Houston joined the merchant marines. Dylan, in *Chronicles Volume One*, says that Houston had also played with Burl Ives at migrant camps during the Depression, and that in the McCarthy era of the 1950s he had a CBS-TV show dropped because of political pressure on the network.

Houston's album *I Ain't Got No Home*, recorded in New York City in early 1961, includes two songs Dylan performs, Guthrie's 'I Ain't Got No Home' and the traditional 'Waggoner's Lad', plus two traditional songs of tangential import for Dylan in the 1980s, 'Danville Girl' (Dylan's early, unreleased version of 'Brownsville Girl' is called 'New Danville Girl') and 'Streets of Laredo' (one of the 'Unfortunate Rake' cycle of songs, which lies behind Dylan's 'Blind Willie McTell'). Around the same time, Houston recorded another version of 'Danville Girl', under its common alternative title, 'The Gambler'. He also includes a version of one of the songs later included on Dylan's 1992 album *Good as I Been to You*, 'Diamond Joe'. Houston's version, which may have been the one picked up by Boston-based folkie Tom Rush and indeed by RAMBLIN' JACK ELLIOTT, was included on his LP *Cowboy Ballads*, 1957, after being published in *Sing Out!* three years earlier. In 1965, Oak Publications issued the posthumous songbook entitled *900 Miles: The Ballads, Blues and Folksongs of Cisco Houston*.

In *Chronicles Volume One*, Dylan describes the Guthrie-Houston connections and their records very straightforwardly, and then gives a sketch of the Cisco Houston he saw for himself around Greenwich Village, including his final performances, at Folk City: 'I was there to hear him. . . . He was a perfect counterpart to Woody and had a soothing baritone voice. . . . Cisco, handsome and dashing with a pencil thin mustache, looked like a riverboat gambler, like Errol Flynn. People said he could have been a movie star, that he once turned down a starring role opposite Myrna Loy.' Introduced to him at a 'bon voyage party' on the eve of his departure for California (a party given an extraordinary 11-page description), Dylan found him 'gracious, with a dignified air, talked like he sang.'

By now he was, as Dylan notes, 'a hair's breadth from death', and indeed he died of cancer on the West Coast, in San Bernadino, California, on April 29, 1961. He was 42.

He was commemorated in the songs 'Fare Thee Well, Cisco' by Tom Paxton, 'Cisco Houston Passed This Way' by his protégé PETE LaFARGE, and the poem 'Blues for Cisco Houston' by Tom McGrath.

[Cisco Houston: *I Ain't Got No Home*, NY, 1961, Vanguard VRS-9107, 1962; 'The Gambler', NY, c.1961, *Railroad Songs*, Folkways FA2013, c.1961; 'Diamond Joe', NY, 1957?, *Cowboy Ballads*, Folkways FA 2022, 1957. 'Diamond Joe', *Sing Out!* vol.4, no.4, March 1954. Dylan, *Chronicles Volume One*, p.63. Thomas McGrath, 'Blues for Cisco Houston', collected in *Movie at the End of the World*, Swallow Press, 1972.]

'how be it?' In that fine *Slow Train Coming* track 'Precious Angel', Dylan sings a gentle rhetorical couplet that asks us to acknowledge that there's a susceptibility to religious belief inside all of us: '. . . how be it we're deceived / When the truth's in our hearts and we still don't believe?'

Regardless of how we may wish to respond to that, we can recognise that Dylan's use of the phrase 'How be it' here is a pleasing echo of the rich plain-speaking of the King James Bible, in which, especially in Paul's epistles, the phrase occurs with zen-like, majestic, repetitive effect. Though Dylan's official songbooks print it as a three-word phrase, as above, the Bible has it as a single word, 'Howbeit'.

Collins English Dictionary, 1994, says of this only that it is 'archaic' before mis-defining it as meaning either 'however' or 'although'. In fact, of course, it means exactly what it says, ellipsed from the longer 'How does it come to be that?' What we shorten to 'How come?', the King James Bible shortened to 'Howbeit?'.

It *is* archaic: meaning that it is language characteristic of an earlier period and not in common use. Yet its clarity and simplicity make it a model of effective rhetoric, and Dylan's use of it here—in exact accord with its use in the scriptures—sounds to have arisen naturally from his inevitably meeting the word within the Word. That's howbeit he's in tune with it.

Howlin' Wolf [1910 - 1976] Chester Arthur Burnett was born on June 10, 1910 in West Point, Mississippi: a small town 30 miles south of Tupelo, and from there another 75 miles to Memphis. He moved west with his parents to the heart of the Delta when he was 13, and farmed on a plantation at Ruleville, close to CHARLEY PATTON's home-base near Cleveland, Mississippi, on Highway 61, driving a plough pulled by mules. Except for a spell in the army, he continued to farm, while performing at fish fries and juke joints through the 1930s and early 40s, turning professional only in the late 1940s.

In the blues-structured 'Man of Peace' (1983), when Bob Dylan comes in the seventh stanza to invoke images of imminent annihilation, he draws on the blues to do so for him. The opening line, 'Well, the howling wolf will howl tonight, the king snake will crawl', fuses two creatures long since appropriated into blues poetry: the howling wolf—which refers both to the mythic creature from the backwoods feared by rural blacks when darkness fell, and the fierce blues singer who took its name for his own, the great Howlin' Wolf himself—and the king snake that will crawl, which Dylan twists around but slightly out of BIG JOE WILLIAMS' threatening 'Crawlin' King Snake', made in 1941. Or perhaps the snake too comes to Dylan via Howlin' Wolf, whose 'New Crawlin' King Snake' came out in 1966.

That Dylan's images here might have come directly from the old rural blues songs—balancing the Big Joe Williams 'Crawlin' King Snake' there are two J.T. Funny Papa Smith cuts of 'Howlin' Wolf Blues' from 1930, one of which was a hit—but might equally have come to Dylan via their more modern incarnations by Howlin' Wolf himself, tells us something about the special value of the latter, *and* about the myth that there is a sharp divide between the acoustic rural blues and the electric city 'Chicago' blues.

Though he was one of the four or five real giants of the tough, electric Chicago blues, and certainly the roughest and vocally most ferocious, he grew up in the pre-war country blues world, and was a prime conduit through which much of this older blues music passed across into the new. While he was taught harmonica by SONNY BOY WILLIAMSON II, Wolf learnt the guitar and much repertoire from one of the most influential figures in the history of the blues, CHARLEY PATTON, and even played some dates with ROBERT JOHNSON in 1930. His importance as a custodian, as much as a moderniser, of this pre-war material is in part explained by the fact that he didn't record at all until he was 41 years old. His early sides were made at Sun Records in Memphis, blues capital of the South in which he had lived his whole life.

Most rural blacks who migrated north did so either in their teens or early 20s. It was exceptional that a man who had lived so long in the South should then move to Chicago, blues capital of the North, but Howlin' Wolf did so within two years of Sun Records' Sam Phillips leasing some of his first sides to Chess Records in Chicago. (MUDDY WATERS, his great rival, and five years his junior, was recorded as early as 1941, and moved to Chicago in the 40s.) Accepting a cash advance from Chess Records, he *drove* to Chicago: 'the onliest one drove out of the South like a gentleman,' he is quoted as saying.

A southern gentleman he remained. Wolf's 1952 'Saddle My Pony' is based in detail on Patton's 1929 'Pony Blues', and Wolf's 'Spoonful' on Patton's 'A Spoonful Blues'; 1952's 'Color and Kind', its remake 'Just My Kind' and 1968's 'Ain't Goin' Down That Dirt Road' all build on Patton's 1929 'Down the Dirt Road Blues'. Even Howlin' Wolf's biggest hit, 1956's 'Smokestack Lightnin'', a remake of his own earlier 'Crying at Daybreak', was in turn a restatement of Patton's 1930 'Moon Going Down'. A later 1956 session yielded 'I Asked for Water', based on Tommy Johnson's 1928 'Cool Drink of Water Blues', and 'Natchez Burning', a remake of a song recorded earlier by Gene Gilmore and Baby Doo Caston about a dance-hall fire of 1940.

Wolf's 1952 'Bluebird (Blues)', which he re-recorded in 1957 and re-fashioned two years later as 'Mr. Airplane Man', is a 1938 Sonny Boy Williamson I song (quite possibly via nearby Yazoo City singer Tommy McClennan: a singer whose vocal fierceness prefigured Wolf's and whose personal fierceness greatly exceeded it); 1952's 'Decoration Day (Blues)' is also from Sonny Boy Williamson I (though written by CURTIS JONES). In 1957 Wolf cut a splendid version of the 1930 MISSISSIPPI SHEIKS standard 'Sittin' on Top of the World', which Bob Dylan was to record first with Big Joe Williams; in 1966, the same year Wolf turned Big Joe's 'Crawlin' King Snake' into his own 'New Crawlin' King Snake', he also recorded 'Poor Wind (That Never Change)', which, to the tune of W.C. Handy's classic 'Careless Love', incorporated elements of BLIND LEMON JEFFERSON's 1926 'See That My Grave Is Kept Clean', Papa Harvey Hull & Long Cleve Reed's 1927 'Hey! Lawdy Mama—The France Blues' and/or Fred McMullen's 1933 'Wait and Listen', and of the standard 'St. James Infirmary Blues'. The following year, Wolf cut 'Dust My Broom', which comes, via Elmore James or not, from Robert Johnson, who in turn had taken his title phrase from the lyric of Kokomo Arnold's 'I'll Be Up Someday'.

You get some sense of how 'country' Wolf looked in person too, through the eyes of these northern city record executives, when you read Marshall Chess recalling his sheer physical size: 'Whenever we shook hands, mine was a little nothing inside his huge hand. He could never buy shoes that were wide enough and he would cut the sides of his new shoes with a razor. You could see his socks sticking out.'

From 1959 or 1960 onwards, Chess was pressuring Wolf into recording not his own material but songs by the prolific Willie Dixon—but many of these, like the material Dixon had recorded as a member of the Big Three Trio in the 1940s, were also strongly based on country blues songs from the 1920s and 30s. While the label credits Dixon with having composed Wolf's 1961 hit 'The Red Rooster', Wolf himself said that the credit belonged to Patton.

When Howlin' Wolf's career and influence was at it peak, therefore, which was from the mid-1950s till the mid-1960s, he was as synonymous with Chicago as Muddy Waters—and yet he never really sounded like the city. The world he invoked, in his uniquely spooky, surreal way, was in essence that of the back roads, the Mississippi swamplands made mythic and primeval, not far from Robert Johnson's crossroads, in the nighttime of country soul. What he was bringing forward thunderously into the 1950s and 60s, and making accessible to the likes of ELVIS PRESLEY on through to THE ROLLING STONES, and thus to the pop-buying public, was a rich meld of country blues lyric poetry. Wolf's 1954 side 'Evil' was transmuted into Elvis' 'Trouble' just four years later. In 1964, 'Smokestack Lightnin'', reissued in Britain, reached the charts, and Wolf appeared on the TV series 'Ready Steady Go!' while he was over in Europe as part of the American Folk Blues Festival. In 1965, as special guest of the Rolling Stones, who performed 'Little Red Rooster', Wolf performed his early-1950s Sun record 'How Many More Years?' on the US 'Shindig' TV show.

By this time, Bob Dylan had already long been familiar with his work: which is why at times it is both impossible to tell, and perhaps unimportant to know, whether Dylan takes a line, or an image, or a flavour, from Howlin' Wolf himself or from somewhere in the earlier country blues, as Wolf had done in turn. In early 1962, on the unedited tape made for a New York radio, Dylan tells CYNTHIA GOODING that he knows the work of both Muddy Waters and Howlin' Wolf: and goes on to perform a country blues version of 'Smokestack Lightnin'' that sounds closer in style to Charley Patton than Wolf's does. This says much for Dylan's recognition that Wolf was essentially a country wolf in city clothing.

If Dylan had gained nothing from Howlin' Wolf except an early piece of repertoire, that would be interesting. However, it seems as clear as such things ever can be that there is some direct inspiration. First, it's unlikely that Dylan's absorption of the Charley Patton legacy was never through Wolf, his last great pupil. Second, there must have been a time in Dylan's youth when, as for so many, the comprehensible beat, electricity and audible recording quality of Wolf and Muddy Waters made for a far easier way into much of the blues than the 'old-fashioned', gruesomely lo-fi recordings of their pre-war country blues predecessors.

So, musically as well as lyrically, Wolf was a conduit. His early band included Ike Turner and JUNIOR PARKER—whose elegant, cool 'Mystery Train' was to be transformed in the same Sun studio, via Elvis, into a founding classic for rock'n'roll—while the main guitarist Wolf used from 1954 onwards was the consummate Hubert Sumlin, whose best work is amongst the finest electric guitar playing in the universe. He plays solos of divine, deranged descending notes, tense as steel cable, grungy as hot-rod cars crashing, and as piercing as God cracking open the sky. Howlin' Wolf brought Sumlin up to Chicago from the south. He hailed from the Delta too: from Greenwood, Mississippi (where Robert Johnson was murdered in 1937 and where Bob Dylan commemorated the murder of MEDGAR EVERS by singing 'Only a Pawn in Their Game' at a civil rights rally in 1963). Hubert Sumlin's influence is as plain as lightning on MIKE BLOOMFIELD—you can hear it on 'Maggie's Farm', Dylan's electric début performance at the Newport Folk Festival of 1965—and on ROBBIE ROBERTSON, as you can hear equally on the 1966 Dylan concert performances and the later album *Planet Waves*.

There is another Wolf-Dylan conjunction on *Planet Waves* too, and it inhabits the boundary between the written word and pronunciation. Early on in his sleevenotes to the album (long since vanished: see ***Planet Waves*, disappearing sleevenotes, the**), Dylan is recalling, with a careening and savage impressionism, what the 1950s had felt like; and he writes of '. . . priests in overhauls, glassy eyed, Insomnia! Space guys off duty with big dicks & ducktails all wired up & voting for Eisenhower . . .' That pun on overhauls/overalls—clever because to perform the one you put on the other—may have come to him directly from Howlin' Wolf. In his 'Sitting on Top of the World', instead of 'overalls', Wolf sings the line that should include it as 'Had to make Christmas in my overhauls.'

Of course it may *not* come directly from Wolf: as so often, Dylan could have picked it up from any one of a number of blues records or performances or white rural idiom. This poetic ellipse has become common-stock among whites as well as blacks. It is not a universal Americanism, however. Just down the hills in Georgia, BLIND WILLIE McTELL, for instance, sings in his version of BLIND BLAKE's 'That'll Never Happen No More': 'Well it's Chicago women in the fall / Got to make your days in your overalls'—and sings the word in the straight, unpunning, one might say middle class, way. That freedom, that ability to pun, to make one word do two jobs—which need not be for a humorous purpose—is of course characteristic of Dylan, who usually exercises it, as Howlin' Wolf and others do there, orally rather than on the page, but whose *Planet Waves* sleevenote shows that he can manage it on the page too.

The same was true for Shakespeare, as CHRISTOPHER RICKS pointed out in a 1980 Australian radio broadcast about Bob Dylan. (Of course Shakespeare could do this orally as well as via flexible spelling, since most of his work was for the stage rather than the page.) Ricks gave an example taken from Dylan's 'Shelter from the Storm': 'He'll use his voice to get back some of the freedom which a poet used to have in the old days before spelling got finally fixed. I'm thinking of the way in which Shakespeare could spell the word "travelled" so that it included "travailed" . . . included worked as well as journeyed. So Dylan will sing "moaning dove" and then print "morning" . . .'

This illustration is especially interesting because it too can be found in Howlin' Wolf's work. When Muddy Waters' 'Still a Fool' (which as we've noted, Dylan knew) was issued by Chess, it was part of a triple set that also included Wolf's 'Moanin' at Midnight'. But this also ended up on Chess' rival label Modern—and was released by them under the odd title 'Morning at Midnight': a mistake of transcription that occurred because of Wolf's ambiguity with the very same words as Dylan. And just as Ricks picked up on it from 'Shelter from the Storm' simply because he liked it—as a pun it has, after all, no significant *meaning* in the Dylan song: it just sounds good—so too it's likely that Bob Dylan picked this up from Howlin' Wolf simply because he liked it. At least as likely as that he invented it à la Shakespeare.

A related feature of the blues that Howlin' Wolf distils as well as anyone is the warping of pronunciation to make a rhyme. Dylan's relish of this has led him to surpass defiantly simple examples like rhyming 'hers' with 'yours' in 1965's 'I Wanna Be Your Lover' by the spectacular rhyming of 'January' and 'Buenos Aires' in 1981's great 'The Groom's Still Waiting at the Altar'. However, the pleasure of eccentric pronunciation in general and its use to make counterfeit rhymes in particular is a fundamental delight rock'n'roll picked up from the blues. If FATS DOMINO was good at it (as when rhyming 'man' with 'ashamed'), so was Howlin' Wolf. As with 'moaning/morning', in 1959's 'Howlin' for My Darlin'' he makes the verb and the noun of the title rhyme ('If you hear me howlin' / Callin' on my darlin'').

What this serves to remind us also is that Howlin' Wolf's records often built up the mythic, fairytale-beast connotations of the name itself. His song titles include 'Moaning at Midnight' and 'Crying at Daybreak'; 'Howlin' for My Darlin'' (a remake of 'Howlin' for My Baby' from seven years previously); 'The Red Rooster'; 'Tail Dragger'; 'I'm the Wolf'; 'Moanin' for My Baby'; 'Call Me the Wolf' and 'Howlin' Blues'. The last new album released in his lifetime was called *The Back Door Wolf*.

He had been given the name at the age of three, by his grandfather:

'He just sit down and tell me tall stories about what the wolf would do, you know,' he told an interviewer in 1968. 'Cause I was a bad boy, you know, and I was always in devilment. . . . So he told me the story 'bout how the wolf done the Little Red Rilin' [sic] Hood.' He goes on to recount a splendidly garbled version of the story, in which the fairytale and the existential reality of his own childhood—the woods and the backwoods—are bound up together:

'. . . the girl would ask him, "Mr. Wolf, what make your teeth so big?" He said "the better I can eat you, my dear." Then said "What make your eyes so red?" "The better I can see you, my dear." And so, you know, and then they finally killed the wolf and drove him up to the house, you know, and showed me the wolf. And I told him it was a dog. He said no, that's a wolf. I said well what do a wolf do? Say he howl: he say "ooh-wyooooh!", you know, and so I got afraid of this wolf.'

Granted Dylan's familiarity with Howlin' Wolf's records, and his own fusion of the singer's name with the beast-figure in 'Man of Peace', it isn't surprising that there should be special conjunctions between the Wolf and the album by Bob Dylan that is itself a glorious fusion of fairytale and nursery rhyme with the blues and the Bible, 1990's *Under the Red Sky*.

Specifically, we can recognise flashes of Dylan's '2 x 2' and '10,000 Men' in the chorus of Wolf's 'I Ain't Superstitious': 'Well I ain't superstitious, black cat just crossed my trail . . . / Don't sweep me with no broom, I might just get put in jail'; while another line from '10,000 Men', Dylan's joke-exaggeration of multiple negatives, 'None of them doing nothing that your mama wouldn't disapprove', goes far enough to be impenetrable in meaning but barely goes further in construction than the last line of Wolf's 1954 song 'Baby How Long': 'Ain't nobody never lived that didn't do somebody wrong.'

The Dylan song on *Under the Red Sky* that most successfully unifies children's song and folktale, intimations of Biblical retribution for our 'devilment' and the country blues world, is the sumptuously phantasmagoric 'Cat's in the Well'. This features the cat, the horse, the bull, the dogs and—dramatically, as the first omen that the innocent face imminent death—the wolf: 'The cat's in the well, the wolf is looking down / He got his big bushy tail dragging all over the ground.' Dylan doesn't say why his tail drags on the ground, but this is elucidated in one of Howlin' Wolf's best records, 1962's shudderingly powerful 'Tail Dragger'. Its chorus runs: 'I'm a tail dragger, I wipe out my tracks / When I get what I want, I don't come sneakin' back', and the first of its two irregular verses concludes with 'The hunters they can't find him / Stealin' chicks everywhere he go / Then draggin' his tail behind him.'

The other verse calls up some more inhabitants of the animal kingdom, as Dylan's song does: 'The 'cuda drags his tail in the sand / A fish wiggles his tail in the water / When the mighty wolf come along, draggin' his tail / He done stole somebody's dog.' So the wolf cannot be tracked, hunted down or stopped. The cat has no chance.

This is not the last of the lyric conjunctions between Dylan and Howlin' Wolf, but it is the greatest, as one piece of barnyard apocalypse draws strength and meaning from another, from 28 years earlier. And there's a general sense in which, because of Wolf's towering primitivism, the style he constructed, its psychic meld of electric power and old country darkness, if there had been no Howlin' Wolf, an album like *Under the Red Sky* would have been a different, thinner thing.

There's another general gift that Wolf and his contemporaries give to those like Dylan who come later and from another culture. To hear Wolf's massive voice singing 'Well, mama done died and left me, / Wooh, daddy done throwed me away' is to note the way that the *age* of the singer is so utterly unimportant to these bluesmen when it comes to the subject matter of their songs. They have no truck with our modern self-conscious ageism or apologism, and clearly when they sing about the lives of themselves and their peers, they experience those lives as unities. Furry Lewis as an old man, and Howlin' Wolf as a middle-aged one, still sing out about the childhood trauma of parental abandonment: they have no sense that they 'should have got over all that' in the contemporary way. At the same time, they still sing too about romantic love: they have no modern sense of the shame of being politically incorrect 'dirty old men'.

Likewise they can sing out clear and free about imminent death: they have no sense that this is aerobically incorrect, or 'not nice'. In 1961's 'Goin' Down Slow', which features what may be Hubert Sumlin's all-time *best* guitar solo, Howlin' Wolf proves himself a *great* singer about imminent death, which will certainly have recommended him to Bob Dylan.

Howlin' Wolf himself died in the Hines district of Chicago, on January 10, 1976. He was 65.

[Howlin' Wolf: 'New Crawlin' King Snake', Chicago, 11 Apr 1966, *Change My Way*, Chess LP 418, Chicago, 1977; 'Sittin' on Top of the World', Chicago, Dec 1957, Chess 1679, Chicago, 1958; *The Back Door Wolf*, Chicago 1973, Chess LP-50045, Chicago, 1973; 'Tail Dragger', Chicago, 28 Sep 1962, *The Real Folk Blues*, Chess LP-1502, Chicago, 1966, CD-reissued Chess MCA CHD 9273, US, 1987. Wolf's 'Red Rilin' Hood' story is on his spoken reminiscence re 'Ain't Goin' Down That Dirt Road (By Myself)', Chicago, Nov 1968, unissued till the 3-CD *The Chess Box*, MCA CHD3-9332, US, 1991.

Big Joe Williams: 'Crawlin' King Snake', Chicago, 27 Mar 1941, *Big Joe Williams: Crawlin' King Snake*,

RCA International INT-1087, London, 1970. J.T. Funny Papa Smith: 'Howlin' Wolf Blues No.1' & 'Howlin' Wolf Blues No.2', Chicago, 19 Sep 1930, *'Funny Papa' Smith: The Original Howling Wolf*, Yazoo L-1031, NY, 1972; there's also his 'Hungry Wolf', Chicago, c.Apr 1931, same LP. Blind Willie McTell: 'That'll Never Happen No More', Atlanta, Sep 1956; *Blind Willie McTell: Last Session*, Prestige Bluesville 1040, US, 1961. Marshall Chess quoted from undated interview by Spencer Leigh, *Baby, That Is Rock and Roll: American Pop, 1954–1963*, Folkestone, UK: Finbarr International, p.50.]

Hudson, Garth [1937 -] Eric Garth Hudson was born in Windsor, south-west Ontario, Canada, on August 2, 1937, grew up in nearby London and had a classical training in music. He was the last of the future BAND members to join RONNIE HAWKINS & THE HAWKS, but after they split from Hawkins, Garth was in the group in the studios in Toronto when they recorded the instrumental 'Bacon Fat' in 1964, which was that rare thing, a Hudson-ROBERTSON composition.

For the main story of The Band and how they became that seminal American band of the late 1960s, see separate entry. Aside from the fact that he didn't sing, Hudson was as crucial as any other member to the group's sound—and not only to *their* sound but also to the sound Bob Dylan achieved when the Hawks went out behind him on the just-gone-electric tour of late 1965 and then again, including in Australia and Europe, in 1966. Garth Hudson's swirling, wondrous organ, his brooding genius at the keyboards, his arranger's ear, his solidity combined with imagination, his willingness to improvise, to stay below and to soar above—all this was essential to the tumultuous majesty of Dylan's live performances in that period.

Hudson was just as crucial to the very different sounds made in the Basement the year afterwards: especially since in large part it was Garth who tape-recorded those unique, informal sessions, and had the sense to look after, afterwards, all the dozens of unknown-about extra ones beyond those of immediate interest to Dylan's music publisher, and which only began to circulate decades later.

Hudson was also the musicians' musician—and actually gave the other Hawks music lessons—and when the Hawks became the Crackers became The Band, he was the multi-instrumentalist supreme in a group of multi-instrumentalists. If The Band introduced a small orchestra's worth of olde worlde instruments to mainstream rock music, it was Hudson who had introduced many of them to The Band. On the credits to the second album, *The Band*, their 1969 masterwork, Garth Hudson's credits take up two lines to everyone else's one. He plays organ, clavinette, piano, accordion, soprano sax, tenor sax, baritone sax and slide trumpet. And alongside the old he brought the new: always experimenting, and building instruments and amps of his own.

His amazing technique on his trusty Lowrey organ was, though, the rock solid basis of what was so unique about the sound he brought to The Band—and just as it had been there for Dylan '66, so it was there for the different purposes of *Music from Big Pink*. So much so that his confrontational yet infinitely pained solo organ intro to 'Chest Fever' developed afterwards into the separately named 'Genetic Method', and in live performance the thrill of finding how Hudson might seize this improvisational opportunity was always a concert high-spot.

Garth Hudson added something else to The Band, too: visually, he was the one who most looked the part in those image-building photos with the Civil War flavour; he was the mountain man with the 19th century beard. He was the most genuinely old-fashioned, the most sombre in demeanour. He gave The Band much of its gravitas.

By the time these first two great Band albums were released, Hudson had also recorded, and played on, sessions by the Indian musicians pictured with Dylan on the front cover of the *John Wesley Harding* album: sessions that would be released in 1968 as *The Bengali Bauls at Big Pink*.

Hudson had worked with Bob Dylan in the studios by this point too. The first occasion was on October 5, 1965, with the whole group; this session gave us two tracks issued 20 years later on *Biograph*: 'I Wanna Be Your Lover' and 'Jet Pilot'. It also gave us one of the most widely circulated and earliest bootleg tracks, the instrumental known as 'Number One'. A second 1965 studio stint (minus HELM) on November 30 produced the single 'Can You Please Crawl Out Your Window?'—and has also now yielded the version of 'Visions of Johanna' released on the *Bootleg Series Vol. 7*, 2005. The now-Helmless Hawks went back in the studio with Dylan on January 21–22, 1966, when they helped create that quintessential mid-60s Dylan record, 'She's Your Lover Now' (finally issued on the *Bootleg Series Vols. 1–3* in 1991)—but when Dylan, Robertson and DANKO returned to the studio three days later, for *Blonde on Blonde* sessions held January 25–28, neither MANUEL nor Hudson were asked to attend.

After backing Dylan again on *Planet Waves* and the big 1974 comeback tour that yielded the double LP *Before the Flood*, Hudson didn't connect up with Dylan again in the studio. On stage they came close when the re-formed Band appeared at the so-called Dylan 30th Anniversary Concert in New York City in 1992, at which Garth played only the accordion on a disappointing rendition of 'When I Paint My Masterpiece', but then on January 17, 1993, he (and Helm and Danko) played with Dylan at President Bill Clinton's inauguration party, the so-called 'Absolutely Unofficial Blue Jeans Bash (For Arkansas)'.

The re-formed Band had been together nine years by then, but only started making albums the year afterwards. These served to confirm that Hudson had abandoned the Lowrey, and was interested instead in synths. Much of the other keyboards solo work seemed to go to Richard Bell. It seemed a shame.

By this time, Hudson also had another 20 years of credits on other people's albums behind him, including: Jesse Winchester's *Jesse Winchester*, 1971; BOBBY CHARLES' *Bobby Charles* and ERIC VON SCHMIDT's *2nd Right, 3rd Row*, 1972; PETER YARROW's *That's Enough for Me*, RINGO STARR's *Ringo* and MARIA MULDAUR's *Maria Muldaur*, 1973; MUDDY WATERS' *The Muddy Waters Woodstock Album* and Poco's *Head Over Heels*, 1975; CLAPTON's *No Reason to Cry*, 1976; EMMYLOU HARRIS' *Quarter Moon in a Ten Cent Town* and VAN MORRISON's *Wavelength*, 1978; Hoyt Axton's *Rusty Old Halo*, LEONARD COHEN's *Recent Songs* and DAVID BROMBERG's *You Should See the Rest of the Band*, 1979; Don Henley's *I Can't Stand Still*, 1982; Marianne Faithfull's *Strange Weather*, 1987; Robert Palmer's *Heavy Nova*, 1988; Camper Van Beethoven's *Key Lime Pie*, 1989; and Robbie Robertson's *Storyville* and Graham Parker's *Struck By Lightning*, 1991. In addition, he had worked on many soundtrack albums from movies.

Hudson had released a sort of solo album back in 1980, *Our Lady Queen of the Angels*: music he had written and recorded to accompany a one-off project by sculptor Tony Duquette at the LA Museum of Science and Industry. Hudson released this on *tape only* on his own label. It was a rarity then; it's certainly a rarity today. But his first 'proper' solo album came 21 years later, with *The Sea to the North*: and it proved sumptuous yet edgy, playful but dark, virtuoso but soulful, crossing genres and times in six highly disparate tracks that make up a cohesive, thrilling whole (five Garth compositions plus an outrageous version of THE GRATEFUL DEAD's signature song 'Dark Star' that you might think steals it away from them in one audacious raid). It's the great album everyone knew Garth Hudson could make.

Since then, in bathetic contrast, we've only had *Live at the Wolf*, an album from a low-key concert billed at the time as 'An Intimate Evening with Garth and Maud Hudson', recorded on September 8, 2002 back in London, Ontario—which only offers Garth's grand piano, sounding decoratively beautiful but an insufficient aural meal, plus, on most tracks, the indigestible dumpling of Maud Hudson playing the grande dame concert-hall artiste—as if rock'n'roll had never happened: as if *nothing* had ever happened since uptown New York 1938 or thereabouts—emoting around with her fine, self-conscious, insincere and thus uninteresting voice. What she does with 'Young Blood' and Dylan's 'Blind Willie McTell' makes for an unpleasant experience, as is having to hear her own hopeless song 'You'll Be Thinkin''. You'll be thinkin' no thanks.

At the premiere of the re-cut *Last Waltz* in 2002, Garth showed up with two of the Bengali Bauls. He was also photographed standing alongside Robbie Robertson, looking ancient but real, his beard greyish white, smiling innocently and showing up Robertson's dyed black hair look for the vain artifice it is.

Garth will continue working, at whatever pace he likes, never denying the past but always journeying onwards through music, equipped with eclectic talent, wide curiosity and a capacity for disciplined practice not commonly found in the world of rock music: a music that would not have been the same without him in the period when it was at the centre of our culture and mattered most.

[The Bengali Bauls: *Bengali Bauls at Big Pink*, Buddah BDS 5050, US, 1968. Garth Hudson: *Our Lady Queen of the Angels*, Buscador Music EGH 770, US, 1980; *The Sea to the North*, Breeze Hill 0011-2, US, 2001 (CoraZong 255039, Europe, 2003). Garth & Maud Hudson: *Live at the Wolf*, Make It Real MIR006, Canada/US, 2005. For a full Hudson discography see *http://theband.hiof.no/albums/hudson_index.html*.]

Humphries, Patrick [1952 -] Patrick Humphries was born in London on August 11, 1952. He first became aware of Dylan's work when he heard 'Mr. Tambourine Man' on a pirate radio station and thought it was Donovan. He has written 20 books, from a history of Fairport Convention, published in 1982, through biographies of Nick Drake, RICHARD THOMPSON, PAUL SIMON and BRUCE SPRINGSTEEN to *Tomfoolery: The Lives and Lies of Tom Waits* in 2006. His two books on Dylan are *Oh No! Not Another Bob Dylan Book*, co-authored with JOHN BAULDIE, published in 1991 (re-titled *Absolutely Dylan* in the US), and *A Complete Guide to the Music of Bob Dylan*, published in 1995. In 2001 he was commissioned by Dylan's office to write the sleevenotes for the compilation album *The Essential Bob Dylan*.

[Patrick Humphries & John Bauldie: *Oh No! Not Another Bob Dylan Book*, Brentwood, UK: Square One Books, 1991, aka *Absolutely Dylan: An Illustrated Biography*, New York: Viking Studio Books, 1991. Patrick Humphries: *A Complete Guide to the Music of Bob Dylan*, London: Omnibus Press, 1995.]

Hunstein, Don [1928–] Donald Robert Hunstein was born in St. Louis, Missouri, on November 19, 1928, studied liberal arts at Washington University there and then, fearful of army call-up to fight in Korea, enlisted in the US Air Force instead. His squadron was sent to England, and visiting Paris he discovered the work of Cartier-Bresson, which prompted his career in photography. Discharged in spring 1954, within months he moved to New York City, where he learnt the business as a Pagano studio gofer, after which work for another photographer led to a Columbia Records publicity department job in January 1956. So it came about that he was the staff photographer who took the cover shot for *Bob Dylan* and, more famously, the iconic cover of *The Freewheelin' Bob Dylan*. This was taken after an amiable session, mostly on black and white film, in Dylan's West 4th Street apartment with and without SUZE ROTOLO, arranged by publicist Billy James (who was also present), so as to build up Columbia's stock of photos of an artist rapidly becoming 'hot'. As the light was threatening to fade, Hunstein suggested trying some shots in the street, with happy results, taken on one roll of colour film on a Hasselblad. Hunstein is certain, despite other claims, that his back was to West 4th Street and Dylan's apartment as he took the shot, and that Bob and Suze are walking down Cornelia Street.

Don Hunstein took his last Dylan shots in 1965: lovely shots at the piano. He ran the photographic studio Columbia created in 1966, until it closed in 1982; after four years of corporate work for CBS he went freelance. He has not 'gone digital' and now, at 77, he is 'somewhat more than semi-retired'.

[Source: Don Hunstein, phone calls from & to this writer 13 Mar 2006.]

Hunter, Robert [1941 -] Born Robert Burns in San Luis Obispo, California, on June 23, 1941, Hunter was a guitar-playing folk-scene friend of JERRY GARCIA's in the early 1960s, and was an early volunteer guinea-pig in Stanford University's psychedelic research programme (secretly CIA-funded). Paid to take LSD, mescaline and psilocybin, and to log his experiences, he found them a creative release. Thus he was ready and available when Garcia needed a lyricist for THE GRATEFUL DEAD. Early lyrics like 'China Cat Sunflower' didn't just sound as if written on acid: they *were*. Hunter was, generally speaking, Garcia's lyricist for most of the band's original songs; he therefore wrote, among much else, almost all the words on the crucial early albums *Workingman's Dead* and *American Beauty*. His best-known lyric is probably 'Dark Star'. A collection of his lyrics, *A Box of Rain*, was published in 1993. When Jerry Garcia died, in 1995, Hunter wrote a super-competent, rhyming 'Elegy for Jerry', which he recited at the funeral service.

His work with Bob Dylan was far less inspired than any of the above. Two lyrics quite rightly rejected by Garcia and the Dead were inexplicably accepted and turned into songs by Dylan: 'Ugliest Girl in the World' (copyrighted Dylan-Hunter 1987 jointly to Dylan's Special Rider Music and to Hunter's Ice Nine Music), and 'Silvio' (ditto for 1988). Both songs appear on Dylan's desperately unnecessary, reluctantly offered album *Down in the Groove*, where they were absolutely par for its course. (For details of Dylan's copious live coverage of 'Silvio', see the entry **Grateful Dead, the**. Just as redundantly it has been collected, since *Down in the Groove*, on both *Bob Dylan's Greatest Hits Volume 3*, 1994, and *The Essential Bob Dylan*, 2000.)

Hunter and Dylan still keep in touch now and then. They chatted, for instance, at some point in 2003. Hunter wrote in his online journal in October 2004: 'Last year Dylan told me he was writing his autobiography before he forgot everything. Said he got down to reading some of his biographies, which he hadn't done before, to refresh his memory about his own life.' (Which seems the least truthful thing Dylan has said by way of explaining what gets said in *Chronicles Volume One*.) Hunter added: 'The only thing he thought they got right was dates and situations and the rest was pretty much bullshit and interpretation compounded on previous biographies that were pretty far off the mark in the first place.'

Joining the age of the internet, Robert Hunter was the first webmaster of the official Dead website *http://dead.net*, and still runs it.

[Robert Hunter: *A Box of Rain: Lyrics: 1965–1993*, New York: Penguin Poets, 1993. 'Elegy for Jerry' seen online 23 Aug 2005 at *http://hake.com/gordon/news.html*.]

Hurt, Mississippi John [1893 - 1966] John Hurt was born in Teoc, Mississippi (too small to be on the map), on July 3, 1893 and grew up farming in Avalon, Carroll County; but he also became a highly distinctive, inventive finger-picking guitarist and a singer of sometimes strikingly violent songs delivered with a trademark gentleness and placidity. He was one of those who recorded in the 1920s—cutting eight sides in Memphis in February 1928 and a further 12 in New York in two sessions that December, of which in total 12 were issued—and then disappearing back into farm-work, to be 'rediscovered' decades later. He made no attempt to become a professional singer and was unchanged as a performer when 'rediscovered'. Contacted by a record-collector from Washington, D.C., Tom Hoskins, only in March 1963, he was on at Newport that July, becoming an instant star of the folk revival movement: performing in coffeehouses and other festivals, recording again after a 35-year gap, and influencing almost every musician who heard him. Including Dylan. He learnt and assimilated experience from many of the older songs and the older singers, and Hurt was one of them.

Dylan already knew Mississippi John Hurt's début 78rpm release, his 1928 recording of 'Frankie', before ever he arrived in New York. He knew it from its reissue on HARRY SMITH's anthology *AMERICAN FOLK MUSIC*—it is one of that crucial set's 84 holy-relic tracks—and you might think that Dylan's own performance, decades later, namely 'Frankie & Albert' on the 1992 album *Good as I Been to You*, confirms that specific familiarity, recapturing something of Hurt's approach to the song, which differs somewhat from the general flavour of Hurt's work.

Mississippi John Hurt's last recording session was in 1966. He died in Grenada, Mississippi, that November 2. A deservedly well-known piece by the Georgia-based writer Stanley Booth, describing going to (and finding himself having to speak at) Hurt's funeral, includes this exchange about Hurt between Booth's girlfriend ('Christopher') and Furry Lewis:

> '"I loved him", Christopher said. "He was such a sweet little man, and he was a wonderful guitar player."
>
> "Yes," said Furry . . . "but he was sho ugly. I swear 'fore God he was."'

[Mississippi John Hurt: 'Frankie', Memphis, 14 Feb 1928, *American Folk Music*, Folkways FP 521-523, NY, 1952, later on, *Mississippi John Hurt: 1928 Sessions*, Yazoo 1065, US, CD-reissued 1990; this also contains his 'Stack O' Lee Blues', NY, 28 Dec 1928. Stanley Booth: 'Been Here and Gone: The Funeral of Mississippi John Hurt', republished in the collection *Rythm* [sic] *Oil*, London: Cape, 1992.]

Hutchison, Frank [1897 - 1945] Frank Hutchison was born in West Virginia in March 1897. He was the coalminer and singer whose hillbilly version of 'Stack a Lee' Dylan follows so closely—you might say recreates so affectionately—on the *World Gone Wrong* album of 1993. Dylan's sleevenote says with unDylanesque plainness: '"Stack a Lee" is Frank Hutchison's version', while his note about another song on the album, BLIND WILLIE McTELL's 'Broke Down Engine', manages to slip in allusions to several train songs, among them 'the train that carried my girl from town . . .' Hutchison's first record, cut in New York in the autumn of 1926, was indeed 'The Train That Carried the Girl from Town'.

Hutchison, a near contemporary of McTell, exemplifies the America of 'the invisible republic'. The 'first real white bluesman to record', in Charles K. Wolfe's words, he 'came from a rough, isolated community in Logan County, West Virginia . . . where miners both black and white found themselves living in company towns, fighting with company thugs when they tried to unionize. . . . In many ways, the miners led lives as desperate as sharecroppers in the Mississippi delta, and many . . . were drawn to the blues.'

Hutchison learnt his from two local blacks, railroad worker Henry Vaughn (from whom he learnt to play slide guitar with a knife) and one Bill Hunt, who was also able to pass on to him a wealth of 19th century songs. 'The Train That Carried the Girl from Town' alone influenced 'generations of hill country musicians'. Between 1926 and 1929 Hutchison cut 32 sides, concentrating on slide-based blues and offering white blues a grittily authoritative alternative seam to that so strongly hewn by JIMMIE RODGERS. Another Frank Hutchison song about a train, his 'Cannon Ball Blues', includes lines Bob Dylan uses on 'Caribbean Wind' and 'Man of Peace'.

Hutchison's own recordings of 'The Train That Carried the Girl from Town' and 'Cannon Ball Blues' are issued, along with the notes by Charles K. Wolfe, on the excellent 2-CD set *White Country Blues 1926–1938: A Lighter Shade of Blue* in the Columbia Roots n' Blues series. Not included, however, is Hutchison's version of 'Stack a Lee'. This is available, however, on—yes, you guessed it—the 1952 HARRY SMITH anthology *AMERICAN FOLK MUSIC*: and to hear this 1927 Hutchison side is to recognise just how closely Bob Dylan follows it, in lyrics, melody, guitar-part, harmonica and, most importantly, in spirit, almost 50 years later. When you hear the Hutchison, you come to appreciate what a resourceful, knowledgeable, live-wire thing the Dylan recording really is.

Frank Hutchison died in Ohio in November 1945.

[Frank Hutchison: 'The Train That Carried the Girl from Town', NY, 28 Sep 1926; 'Cannon Ball Blues' NY, 9 Jul 1929, both CD-reissued *White Country Blues 1926–1938: A Lighter Shade of Blue*, Columbia Roots n' Blues 01-472886-10, NY, 1993; 'Stack a Lee', NY, 28 Jan 1927, *American Folk Music*, Folkways FP 251–253, NY, 1952.]

'I Forgot More' 'I Forgot More (Than You'll Ever Know About Her)' is a country classic, written and composed by Cecil Null, and on *Self Portrait* Dylan sings it much like ROY ORBISON might have done. JOHNNY CASH had recorded 'I Forgot More Than You'll Ever Know' in Nashville in 1962, for the widely known LP *The Sound of Johnny Cash*; but Dylan was almost certainly aware of the song much earlier. Dylan revisited it live in 1986, as a duet with TOM PETTY, at 55 concerts. His introductory remarks about the song to the audience in Sydney, Australia, perhaps reveal why he chose to include it on *Self Portrait*. 'Very seldom,' he said, 'do you hear a real song anymore. But we were lucky enough to grow up when you could hear 'em all the time. All you had to do was just switch on your radio . . .'

I

[Bob Dylan remarks to Sydney, Australia, audience, 24 Feb 1986. Johnny Cash: 'I Forgot More Than You'll Ever Know', Nashville, 10 Feb 1962; *The Sound of Johnny Cash*, Columbia CS 8602, NY (CBS BPG 72073, London), 1962, reissued, as it happens, the same year Dylan issued *Self Portrait* on the compilation *Country Gold, Volume 2*, Harmony 30018, US, 1970.]

'I Shall Be Free' / 'I Shall Be Free No. 10' Dylan based these early compositions on a cluster of songs exemplified by LEADBELLY's 'We Shall Be Free', recorded with WOODY GUTHRIE and SONNY TERRY in 1944. But these songs go back much further, pre-dating the era of recordings: '. . . stanzas of "You Shall Be Free" have been traced to the mid-nineteenth century,' writes John H. Cowley in a fascinating essay, 'Don't Leave Me Here: Non-Commercial Blues: The Field Trips, 1924–1960'.

Splendid early versions on record include two versions of 'You Shall' by the Beale Street Sheiks (i.e. the great Memphis figure FRANK STOKES plus Dan Sane) made in 1927.

Stanzas from 'You Shall' occur too in an early recording by Stokes' Memphis colleague JIM JACKSON. His 1928 'What a Time' has verses close to the Leadbelly-Guthrie-Terry version—and more to the point, rendered in what is ear-poppingly close to the style we think of as Dylan's on 'I Shall Be Free': not only in vocal delivery and feel but with the very same guitar strumming. You can't hear the Jim Jackson version without wondering whether Dylan knew it back then, though it had never been released on vinyl when Dylan cut 'I Shall Be Free' *or* 'I Shall Be Free No. 10'.

Dylan recorded 'I Shall Be Free' in 1962 for release on *The Freewheelin' Bob Dylan* (and again for *Broadside* magazine and a third time as a music-publishing demo, both in 1963). He recorded 'I Shall Be Free No. 10' in 1964 for *Another Side of Bob Dylan* (though this version is an edit of two takes, the longer of which was later included on the official CD Rom *Highway 61 Interactive* in 1995). He has never performed either 'I Shall Be Free' or 'I Shall Be Free No. 10' in concert.

Of course, the very fact that he calls the latter 'I Shall Be Free No. 10' has him confessing his knowledge of the old songs: he knows that there are many antecedents and variants and versions of 'You Shall' or 'I Shall Be Free'. And again, it's an example of how at the time, when this was new, we thought its title a bit of Dylanesque quirkery, whereas now we can see that it's yet another example of him walking the hallways of the old blues.

[Dylan: 'I Shall Be Free', NY, 6 Dec 1962, *The Freewheelin' Bob Dylan*, 1963; NY, Mar 1963, *Broadside* Sessions; & NY, Apr 1963, Witmark demo (this version issued on the rare, untitled demo LP by Warner Bros. 7 Arts Music Inc., XTV221567, 1969); 'I Shall Be Free No. 10', NY, 9 Jun 1964, *Another Side of Bob Dylan*, 1964.

Leadbelly (with Woody Guthrie and Sonny Terry): 'We Shall Be Free', NY, May 1944; *Leadbelly Sings Folk Songs*, Folkways FA 2488, NY, 1962, CD-reissued as FA 2488, 1995. Beale Street Sheiks: 'You Shall', Chicago, c.Aug 1927, *Frank Stokes with Dan Sane and Will Batts (1927–1929)*, Roots RL-308, US, 1968, and 'You Shall', Chicago, c.Sep 1927, *Mississippi & Beale Street Sheiks, 1927–1932*, Biograph BLP-12041, US, 1972. Jim Jackson: 'What a Time' (2 takes), Memphis, 28 Aug 1928, *Kansas City Blues*, Agram AB2004, 1980 (take 2) and *Jim Jackson . . . Vol. 2*, Document DOCD-5115, 1992 (take 1).

John H. Cowley, 'Don't Leave Me Here: Non-Commercial Blues: The Field Trips, 1924–1960', in Lawrence Cohn, ed.: *Nothing But the Blues: The Music & the Musicians*, New York: Abbeville Press, 1993.]

'I Wanna Be Your Lover' [1965] Several takes of this venomously surreal early electric Dylan song were recorded with THE HAWKS on their first day in the studio with Dylan—New York City, October 5, 1965. The song wasn't copyrighted until 1971, and all takes remained unissued until the *Biograph* box set in 1985; but a different take from the one offered there had circulated widely years before on early bootlegs, notably on *Seems Like a Freeze Out* and *40 Red White and Blue Shoestrings*. These two takes have minor differences in the verses (in the use of words like 'and', 'but' and 'then') but the bootlegged version is the more assured in its vocal delivery.

As Paul Cable notes in *Bob Dylan: His Unreleased Recordings*, the chorus 'unashamedly rips off THE BEATLES' "I Wanna Be Your Man". . . . But it works because, whereas the lyrics of the first three lines are identical to the Beatles' song, the last line veers off at a tangent.' Indeed. The tangent has Dylan comically rhyming 'hers' with 'yours', as by an act of will, using his classic italicisation: 'I don't wanna be *hers*, I wanna be *yrrrs*!'

[Paul Cable: *Bob Dylan: His Unreleased Recordings*, UK: Scorpion/Dark Star, 1978, p.74.]

Ian & Sylvia Ian Tyson was born in British Columbia on September 25, 1933, and Sylvia Fricker in Chatham, Ontario, on September 19, 1940. Tyson turned to folk music and learnt to play guitar while recovering from injuries sustained as a professional rodeo rider, moved to Toronto in the late 1950s and there teamed up with Fricker. They moved to New York in 1960, played at the Mariposa Folk Festival in 1961 and were signed by ALBERT GROSSMAN and by Vanguard, releasing their début album (*Ian & Sylvia*) in 1962. They married in 1964.

Disparagement of all things Canadian is a tedious tack to take, and none is intended by saying that their becoming the best Canadian folk act of the time is not in itself an over-arching claim. They sang a mix of contemporary and traditional material, and with a detectably Canadian accent, which had its charm and differentiated them from a mass of other folk-revival acts. As Richie Unterberger puts it in the online All Music Guide, they 'helped expand the range of folk by adding bass . . . and mandolin to Ian's guitar and Sylvia's autoharp. Just as crucially, they ranged far afield for their repertoire, which encompassed not just traditional folk ballads, but bluegrass, country, spirituals, blues, hillbilly, gospel, and French-Canadian songs.'

As Mr. Unterberger also puts it, their albums 'can seem a tad earnest and dated today' but they have been 'overlooked influences upon early folk-rockers such as the Jefferson Airplane, the We Five, the Mamas and the Papas, and Fairport Convention, all of whom utilized similar blends of male/female lead/harmony vocals.'

Their stiff-backed, earnest delivery was of its time, and one of the things Bob Dylan arrived on the scene to abolish. In Ian's case it sometimes makes him sound like SEEGER of the Rockies, especially on a song like 'The Mighty Quinn', one of the many covers they made of work by singer-songwriters who seem to have admired them. (They had covered 'Tomorrow Is a Long Time' on their second album, *Four*, in 1963.) 'The Mighty Quinn' lends itself to fluidity, humour and a warm looseness, and doesn't accommodate the humourless declamatory manliness that Tyson brings to it, as he sings 'You'll not, see, nothing, like the, Mighty, Quinn' as if it's the national anthem. Indeed, it wouldn't be surprising to find that the Monty Python Lumberjack Song was inspired as much by Tyson as by an ensemble of the Mounties.

Beyond those influential harmonies, their strengths are Tyson's rich-sounding guitar picking, Fricker's resonant voice and their individual early songwriting. She wrote 'You Were on My Mind' (which the now-forgotten We Five turned into one of the first folk-rock hits) and he wrote 'Some Day Soon', which JUDY COLLINS has made a key piece of her repertoire. His best-known song, 'Four Strong Winds', was popularised first by Ian & Sylvia themselves, but later by a range of people, most notably fellow Canadian NEIL YOUNG.

Another Canadian, GORDON LIGHTFOOT, composer of 'Early Morning Rain', was 'discovered' by Ian & Sylvia, who had a near-hit single with the song, taken from their LP *Early Morning Rain* in 1965. They left Vanguard for MGM in 1967, after recording what might be thought a prefiguring of the late-60s interest in country music, the album *Nashville*, but their career declined, despite forming back-up band the Great Speckled Bird, which included Amos Garrett and BUDDY CAGE, and recording the album *Great Speckled Bird* with Todd Rundgren as producer. Their marriage and professional partnership ended in the 1970s. Ian Tyson moved into country music, returning to the subject matter of cowboys and rodeos and to Canada, where his work has continued to be popular. Sylvia made a number of less successful solo albums, including, in 1987, one titled *You Were on My Mind* (which the duo had already used as an LP title in 1972). The CD *Ian & Sylvia: Best of the Vanguard Years* includes 'The Mighty Quinn', 'Rocks and Gravel' and 'A Satisfied Mind' as well as 'Four Strong Winds', 'Some Day Soon' and 'You Were on My Mind'.

Dylan showed his fondness for Ian & Sylvia's repertoire just as their career was faltering, in 1967. Among the Basement Tapes recorded in upstate New York that year are warm versions of 'The French Girl' (a Fricker/Tyson composition), 'Song for Canada' (a Peter Gzowski & Ian Tyson song long listed mistakenly as 'One Single River' on Dylan discographies) and 'Four Strong Winds'. He revisited 'The French Girl' 20 years later when he and THE GRATEFUL DEAD rehearsed it–though they never went on to perform it in concert–in San Rafael, California, in May 1987.

In the summer of 1986, for a CBC-TV tribute to Ian & Sylvia for which the duo re-united and gave a live performance (televised that September) Bob Dylan filmed an extremely short speech (from an unknown location), which said, not exactly fulsomely: 'Ian & Sylvia, I wish I could be there where you are tonight, but I can't be, so I wish you good luck anyway and I hope to see you soon.'

[Ian & Sylvia: *Ian & Sylvia*, Vanguard, NY, 1962; *Four Strong Winds*, Vanguard VMD 2149, US, 1963; 'Early Morning Rain', *nia*, also issued on *Early Morning Rain*, Vanguard VSD-79175, NY, 1965; *Nashville* Vanguard 79284-2, US, 1967. *Ian & Sylvia: Best of the Vanguard*

Sandy Konikoff (right) in the Ravens

Photography by Sherry Rayn Barnett

Al Kooper

Bruce Langhorne advertising Brother Bru Bru's African Hot Sauce

Photo by John Byrne Cooke

The Jim Kweskin Jug Band (left to right): Mel Lyman, Maria D'Amato, Geoff Muldaur, Jim Kweskin, Bill Keith

Lomax Collection / Library of Congress

Leadbelly and his wife, Martha Promise, February 1935

© Ed Rhodes

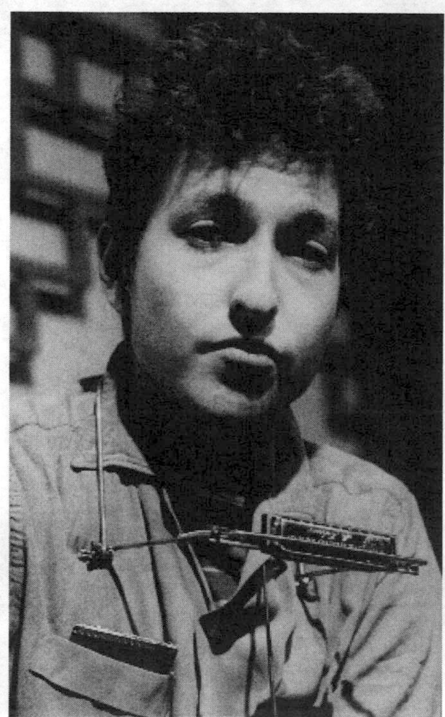

Bob Dylan in *Madhouse on Castle Street*

Blind Willie McTell, 1956

Years, Vanguard 79516, US, 1998. Richie Unterberger, 'Ian & Sylvia' at All Music Guide, seen online at *www.allmusic.com*, 22 Apr 2005.]

'If Dogs Run Free' [1970] The way in which Dylan has revisited, live, in the 2000s, 'If Dogs Run Free'—a song that for 30 years he had shown no evidence of remembering at all after its original inclusion on the 1970 *New Morning* album—suggests a pleasing connection between that work and the *"Love and Theft"* album, which would not otherwise have been obvious. The live 'If Dogs Run Free' sounds markedly similar to 'Bye and Bye'.

Dylan describes how the studio recording of 'If Dogs Run Free' was achieved in one improvised take, starting from his lyrics and some AL KOOPER keyboard riffs, and embracing the improvised scat singing of MAERETHA STEWART (elsewhere on the album a back-up singer), in 2004's *Chronicles Volume One* (p.138).

'I'm a-Ridin' Old Paint' For this traditional song's relevance to Dylan, see **folk music, American, Cowboy**. This song was 'found' by Margaret Larkin, popularised by poet and folksong collector CARL SANDBURG in his important anthology *The American Songbag*, 1927, and republished by ALAN LOMAX in the *Penguin Book of American Folk Song*, 1964. (Penguins have always loved American folksong.) 'Rake and Rambling Boy', a traditional ballad on the first JOAN BAEZ LP [*Joan Baez*, Vanguard VRS-9078, NY, 1960], has a final verse that shares the 'I'm a-Ridin' Old Paint' format: 'when I die, don't bury me at all / Place my bones in alcohol'.

'I'm a-Ridin' Old Paint' also shares common stock ingredients with black song. An almost identical verse occurs in the middle of the splendid early 'blues' record by Papa Harvey Hull and Long Cleve Reed, 'Hey! Lawdy Mama—The France Blues' [Chicago, c. April 8, 1927; *Really! The Country Blues*, Origin Jazz Library OJL-2, NY, c.1961]. This isn't really a blues at all, but an effervescent jostling of disparate verses from the rich memory-banks of largely 19th century repertoire by these songsters: men already of a certain age by the time they came to record.

'In Search of Little Sadie' / 'Little Sadie' These two *Self Portrait* interpretations are based on an older song, which JOHNNY CASH recorded as 'Transfusion Blues' when he was with the Tennessee Two and as 'Cocaine Blues' on later recordings (one studio, one live with a prison audience). The storyline has remained much the same—it tells of an escape, arrest, trial and jailing. But while Cash plods through a lifeless narrative, congealing in his artificial manliness, Dylan ditches the worst platitudes, transforms others, by his timing, into wit, and fills his narrative with creative idiosyncrasy. While Cash versions have 'overtook me down in Juarez, Mexico' (a place already associated with Dylan in song, from 'Just Like Tom Thumb's Blues'), Dylan returns it to the line in the 1962 CLARENCE ASHLEY & DOC WATSON version, 'They overtook me down in Jericho'. In literal terms this is in South Carolina, not that far from another town cited in the song, North Carolina's Thomasville, but in Dylan's mouth, 'Jericho' inevitably offers, as Geoffrey Cannon wrote, 'an echo of his persistent references to places of abstract myth.'

Dylan's re-use of 'Jericho' makes allusion to something else from the Golden Oldie past, too. One of the little witticisms in the performance is the way Dylan's voice goes up and up as he sings the word 'down': and this is exactly what ELVIS and the Jordanaires do with the same word on their version of 'Joshua Fit the Battle of Jericho' on Presley's *His Hand in Mine* album of 1960, with which Dylan must be familiar.

This is not the only example of Dylan putting two versions of a song back to back. He does the same on the single of 'George Jackson' in 1971 and with 'Forever Young' on the 1974 *Planet Waves* album—and on *Self Portrait* he does it all over again with 'Alberta', which he calls 'Alberta No.1' and 'Alberta No.2'.

[Johnny Cash: 'Transfusion Blues', Nashville, 17 Feb 1960, *Now There Was a Song*, Columbia CS 8254, NY (CBS 62028, London), 1960. (Columbia Records cannot now trace a 2nd Cash studio recording pre-1970.) 'Cocaine Blues', Sacramento, 13 Jan 1968, *Johnny Cash at Folsom Prison*, Columbia CS 9639 (CBS 63308), 1968. Cash re-recorded it Nashville, 24 Apr 1979, *Silver*, Columbia 36086 (CBS 83757), 1979. Clarence Ashley (with Doc Watson): '(In Search of) Little Sadie', Chicago, Feb 1962, *Old Time Music at Clarence Ashley's, Vol. 2*, Folkways FA 2359, NY, 1963.

Elvis Presley: 'Joshua Fit the Battle', Nashville, 30–31 Oct 1960, *His Hand in Mine*, RCA Victor LPM/LSP-2328, NY (RCA mono RD27211, stereo SF5094, London, 1961), 1960; CD-reissued *Amazing Grace: His Greatest Sacred Performances* (2-CD set), RCA 07863 66421 2, London, 1994.

The retrospective LP by Bill Clifton and Hedy West, *Getting Folk Out of the Country*, Bear Family BF 15008, Vollersode, Germany, 1975, also includes 'Little Sadie' (London, 1972) and 'Mary of the Wild Moor' (London, 1972), a traditional song Dylan performed in 16 concerts 1980–81.

Manfred Helfert's comments re the Ashley version, seen online 1 Sep 2005 at *www.bobdylanroots.com/sadie.html*, were helpful here; thanks too to Jim Clements, *The Bridge* no.22, UK, summer 2005, p.36.]

'In the Garden' [1980] By the time we reach the 'Born Again' albums, *Slow Train Coming* and *Saved*, there is a marked decrease in the Dylan-Christ identification that was so clear and prevalent on *Street Legal*. The only example of it, and it is implicit, occurs on the *Saved* track 'In the Garden': 'The multitude wanted to make Him king, put a crown upon His head / Why did He slip away to a quiet place instead?' Dylan, if drawing a parallel here, is suggesting that he at least knows exactly why Jesus should have 'slipped away'.

'In the Garden' (the phrase itself is from John 19:41) actually centres upon two gardens, and two compelling sections of Christ's story: the episode in which Judas betrays Him to the armed gang of high priests and elders and their henchmen in the garden of Gethsemane and He is arrested (leading to His crucifixion); and the episode in which, when He rises again from the sepulchre 'in the garden' at Calvary, Mary Magdalene and then the eleven remaining disciples meet Him one more time in Galilee.

Like the title phrase 'in the garden', Nicodemus, the named character in the song's second verse, also serves to link the stories either side of the crucifixion, since he is there beforehand, asking Christ why a man must be born again (John 3:1–7) and he is there again afterwards, helping Joseph of Arimathaea to place Christ's body in the garden sepulchre (John 19:39).

Dylan's first verse deals with His arrest, in the course of which Peter slices off a high priest's servant's ear and is all for further swashbuckling resistance. (He is over-keen to prove his ardour because Jesus has just told him he'll deny Him three times before that rooster crows at the break of dawn.) Jesus now tells him to put his sword away: '. . . Put up again thy sword into his place: for all they that take the sword shall perish with the sword' (Matthew 26:52) or 'Peter, put up thy sword into the sheath: the cup which my Father hath given me, shall I not drink it?' (from John 18:11). Dylan's next two verses follow and fuse texts respectively from Mark 2:9 & John 5:1–30 and from Luke 19:37–38 & John 6:15.

Dylan's last verse quotes from Christ's last words to the disciples after His resurrection (given in the final three verses of Matthew, i.e. 28:18–20): 'All power is given unto me in heaven and in earth. Go ye therefore, and teach all nations, baptizing them in the name of the Father, and of the Son, and of the Holy Ghost: Teaching them to observe all things whatsoever I have commanded you: and, lo, I am with you always, even unto the end of the world. Amen.'

'In the Garden' has remained one of the evangelical songs Dylan returns to in concert; it is by far the most-frequently performed song from *Saved*, and by the end of 2003 he had sung it live 331 times (more than twice as many as the second-most-played number, 'Solid Rock'). Its début came on the opening night of the first gospel tour, in November 1979, three months before the studio recording. In 1986, on the long tour with TOM PETTY & THE HEARTBREAKERS, 'In the Garden' was jointly most-played song of all (jointly with 'Ballad of a Thin Man' and 'Seeing the Real You at Last'), and on the first leg of the tour, in New Zealand and Australia, Dylan took to introducing the song with a variable rap that always ran roughly like this one (delivered in Sydney, Australia on February 11:

> 'For lots of people MUHAMMAD ALI's a hero, right? Yeah. And Albert Einstein, he sure was a hero. I guess you could say even Clark Gable was a hero. Michael Jackson, he's a hero, right? BRUCE SPRINGSTEEN. I care nothing about them people though. None of those people are my heroes, they don't mean nothing to me. I'm sorry but that's the truth. I wanna sing a song about my hero.'

(For a variant see **Jesus v. Springsteen**.)

The song's most audacious outing was in 1987, when, in his début concert in Israel, Dylan chose to deliver this very specifically Christian song to his Tel Aviv audience.

[Bob Dylan: 'In the Garden', San Francisco, 1 Nov 1979; Tel Aviv, 5 Sep 1987.]

***Infidels* [1983]** Another ragbag collection of insipid material, hailed in the US as a great return to form on Dylan's part. This is the sort of work that makes Dylan's earlier 'minor' albums sound like masterpieces. In depressing contrast to *Nashville Skyline*, *New Morning* or *Planet Waves*, there is on *Infidels* generally no warmth, no unity and no sense that real music is being created and played for pleasure by people who know what they want. There is instead the unwelcome return of the portentous quality of the evangelical albums of 1979–80, while the production is half-hearted and irresolute. It is Dylan beginning to say that he doesn't really want to write songs or make records any more, and to behave as if it hardly matters whether an album is any good or not. This is not a welcome stance from a great artist. As with *Shot of Love*, its predecessor, it needn't have been this way: the sessions yielded important work excluded from the release, including what is perhaps Dylan's greatest single recording of the 1980s, the lapidary 'Blind Willie McTell'. Best of the released tracks: 'I and I' (though this admonishes you into feeling it's important, rather than claiming a place in your heart) and the album's one incontestable major success, 'Jokerman'.

[Recorded (though session information is unclear) NY, Apr and Jun–Jul 1983; released as stereo LP Columbia QC-38819 (in UK CBS 25539), 27 Oct or 1 Nov 1983.]

Ingber, Ira [1950 -] Ira Beard Ingber is a composer and multi-instrumentalist musician, playing guitar, mandolin, bass, keyboards and percussion, and a producer and studio engineer. He was born on March 29, 1950 in Minneapolis but grew up in LA where at 15 he recorded his own first song, playing a guitar that belonged to Don EVERLY. At 16 he was playing in the group the New Generation and had a record deal, but he went on to study music at Los Angeles City College, at UCLA and under conductor Joseph Valenti.

Ira Ingber is the younger brother of the Mother of Invention and Captain Beefheart's Magic Band member Elliot Ingber, aka Winged Eel Fingerling. Way back in 1968 both brothers played on an eponymously titled Fraternity of Man album (Elliot had co-founded that band), the group's song 'Don't Bogart That Joint' featuring on the soundtrack of the film *Easy Rider*, and in 1974 on Beefheart's album *Bluejeans and Moonbeams*. On both these, Ira played bass. He went on to produce for Lowell George and others, and then got a new record deal as part of the band the Pets, which included GREGG SUTTON and Jo Ann Harris and made the album *Wet Behind the Ears* in 1978. He re-involved himself with the Motherworld around the start of the 1980s, playing on the Grandmothers' albums *Grandmothers* (1981) and *Lookin' Up Granny's Dress* (1982).

Ingber says that he was then 'asked to form a band for Bob Dylan that led to the recording of [the] two . . . albums *Empire Burlesque* and *Knocked Out Loaded*.' This is overstating it somewhat, given that various musicians came and went over long periods of sessions for these albums, and he was not at the first session at all—but certainly he is the guitarist whose caressingly expressive, taut but intuitive electric playing enriches the unreleased 'New Danville Girl'—playing which is displaced when Dylan records his masterly recording of the revised lyrics, by this point re-titled 'Brownsville Girl', over the backing track. It may be that as it comes in after the third chorus of 'New Danville Girl', at once soaring and dignified, impassioned and restrained, simple and imaginative, there is no better electric guitar solo on any studio recording in Bob Dylan's work—yet on the re-make that is 'Brownsville Girl' it has to go, because this better-realised version of the song must single-mindedly occupy the cowboy and western genre, not criss-cross in and out of rock music signifiers. On the sleevenotes for *Knocked Out Loaded*, Ingber still gets a credit for guitar on 'Brownsville Girl' (and on his own website claims to have produced that track).

This exemplary solo was almost certainly recorded at an early Hollywood session for *Empire Burlesque* on December 10 or 11, 1984—and Ingber had first participated on the 7th, helping to record an uncirculated take of a 'Look Yonder', followed two days later by a similarly unheard song logged as 'Gravity Song'. Then came 'New Danville Girl'. He's also credited with playing on the album version of 'Something's Burning, Baby', recorded on the 14th, as was another uncirculated track, of 'The Girl I Left Behind' (which may not be the same as the old ballad of that name Dylan had sung so rivetingly on the 'Oscar Brand's Folk Song Festival' radio programme 23 years earlier, on October 29, 1961). Ingber also plays on an April 17, 1985 session, again in Hollywood, which yielded only two further uncirculated tracks, 'Too Hot to Drive' and 'As Time Passes By'.

After these mixed-success Dylan sessions Ingber went on to play on, among many other albums, Bonnie Raitt's *Nine Lives* (1986) and BRIAN WILSON & Van Dyke Parks' *Orange Crate Art* (1990s). In 2005 he made a new solo album, *Here Is Where* (released 2006), and when not in his own studio, plays LA club dates with his band the New Corvairs.

He has also composed many film scores, including for *A River Runs Through It* and Robert Altman's *The Company*, has recorded with both FRANK SINATRA and Cheech & Chong (though not together) and, disappointingly, turned out a good deal of music for advertisements, for everything from Kelloggs to Gatorade and the Chicago Mercantile Exchange.

[Ira Ingber: *Here Is Where*, Colonel Muscletone (with no stated catalogue no.), US, 2006. Fraternity of Man: *Fraternity of Man*, ABC S 647, US, 1968. Captain Beefheart: *Bluejeans and Moonbeams*, Mercury SRM 1-1018, US (Virgin V2023, UK), 1974. The Pets: *Wet Behind the Ears*, Arista 4154, US, 1978. Bonnie Raitt: *Nine Lives*, Warner Bros. 25486, US, 1986. Brian Wilson & Van Dyke Parks: *Orange Crate Art*, *nia*. Ingber's website is *www.iraingber.com*. Birthdate & full name data, Ingber e-mail to this writer 2 Feb 2006.]

interviews and the myth of their rarity It's always been a myth that Dylan interviews are rare: they average about one a month for all four and a half decades of his career. That's something over 500 interviews and press conferences given, written up and published, and in many cases recorded and/or broadcast or telecast. And since the mid-1960s almost every one is published prefaced by the claim that it comes from a man who rarely gives interviews.

***Isis* [fanzine]** See **Barker, Derek & Tracy**.

J

'Jack-a-Roe' [1993] See **American Civil War in *World Gone Wrong*, the.**

Jackson, George [1941 - 1971] Born in Chicago, and four months younger than Bob Dylan, Jackson moved to LA with his family at age 14. In 1960, aged 18, he was jailed for one-year-to-life for driving the getaway car for a friend who stole $70 from a gas station. The friend was released in 1963; Jackson stayed in San Quentin till 1969, when he was moved to Soledad. He joined the Black Panther party (formed 1966) in 1969, and his book *Soledad Brother: The Prison Letters of George Jackson* was based on letters to his family on the brutality and racism of the prison system. He spent long periods in solitary confinement. In January 1970, in a new bi-racial exercise yard, guards fired on fighting prisoners, killing three blacks; when a 'justifiable homicide' verdict was returned, a white guard was killed in the prison; Jackson and two others were arrested and moved back to San Quentin. On August 17, when Jackson's trial was imminent, his 17-year-old brother Jonathan seized the judge and three jurors as hostages during another Black Panther trial in Marin County; in the ensuing shoot-out, Jonathan Jackson, the judge and two others were killed.

George Jackson's trial was postponed until August 1971; on August 21, two days before it was due to begin, Jackson was shot dead by a San Quentin guard, allegedly while attacking guards during an attempted escape. His two co-accused, John Cluchette and Fletta Drumgo, were later found not guilty of the murder of the guard.

That Bob Dylan could still be directly touched by something so much from the urban world, despite the rural terrain he had been exploring since *John Wesley Harding*, was demonstrated swiftly by the single that he issued near the end of 1971, 'George Jackson'. Recorded that November 4, it was issued eight days later. This rush-release may have indicated Dylan's urgency to get its 'message' across: his first acoustic-guitar solo single since the pre-electric period (1961–64), it marked a surprise (and brief) return to 'protest' material. Yet the rush-release perhaps also indicated the song's 'lateness' rather than its topicality: it was recorded two and a half months after its eponymous hero's death.

Two takes were released—the B-side was the so-called 'Big Band version' (Dylan on acoustic guitar, harmonica and lead vocal, Dan Keith on steel guitar, LEON RUSSELL on electric bass guitar and KENNY BUTTREY on drums, with Joshie Armstead and Rose Hicks on background vocals), and Dylan's solo version was the A-side.

He starts the song very simply by declaring his response to events, and using the classic blues opening line to say so: 'I woke up this morning', and then tightening up at once into the particular and the special—personalising it: 'There were tears in my bed / They killed the man I really loved / Shot him through the head.'

It is exactly like the pre-1964 protest songs—even down to the formula of a guitar backing till the end of the penultimate verse, then a harmonica solo laid on top, then guitar alone again through the last verse, then back with the harmonica for the fade-out. What is not like the pre-1964 protest material is this: 'They were frightened of his power / They were scared of his love.' This is the post-mystic Dylan, the post-acid Dylan; and in the light of STEVEN GOLDBERG arguing that after *Nashville Skyline* Dylan's post-mystic politics would be reactionary, it is interesting to find these mystic traces in the middle of this committedly radical song. It's also interesting to see the way the end of the song shows Dylan's most BLAKEian simple language deliberately echoing one of George Jackson's most spirited (and unBlakeian) remarks. Jackson says in one of his letters that from now on, he's just going to divide people into the innocent and the guilty. As Dylan re-states this, it is Us and Us, not Us and Them: 'Sometimes I think this whole world / Is one big prison yard / Some of us are prisoners / The rest of us are guards.'

The story circulated in the music industry in the early 1970s that when Columbia Records in New York received a telephone enquiry as to whether a part of the royalties on Dylan's record of 'George Jackson' would be going to the Soledad Brothers, the reply was: 'We don't think so. They're not on our label.'

In 1975 another George Jackson book was published: *Blood in My Eye* (from a manuscript completed 'just a few days' before his death, said Penguin Books). On Dylan's 1992 album *Good as I Been to You* he included a version of a MISSISSIPPI SHEIKS song, the title of which he shortened to 'Blood in My Eyes'. Long or shortened, the expression may be unusual but is not unique. Pre-war bluesman J.T. Funny Papa Smith's 'Hungry Wolf' includes the beautifully 'Dylanesque', brooding lines 'With blood in my eye, and malice in my heart / In places I used to go . . .' There's also a 1939 record by Bill Gaither titled 'Bloody Eyed Woman'. George Jackson's text never explains the use of this title, but his meaning is clearly that blood—physical violence, revenge—is what he has his eye on. The book's dedication is 'To the black Communist youth—To their fathers—We will now criticize the unjust with the weapon.' Between the Sheiks' song from the 30s, and Jackson's title from the 70s, therefore, it's clear that the phrase itself has had some currency in black America. Dylan uses the phrase rather more opaquely in *Chronicles Volume One*, in which he says of his old Greenwich Village friend Ray Gooch that 'there was something special about him. He had blood in his eyes, the face of a man who could do no wrong . . .'

(See also **radical political activity in 1960s-70s US, the strange disappearance of.**)

[George Jackson, *Soledad Brother: The Prison Letters of George Jackson*, 1970 (Preface by JEAN GENET); and *Blood in My Eye*, 1975. Most of the above information on Jackson is taken from Edmund White, *Jean Genet*, 1992. Bob Dylan: 'George Jackson' c/w 'George Jackson', NY, 4 Nov 1971, Columbia 4-45516, NY, 12 Nov 1971.

Steven Goldberg: 'Bob Dylan and the Poetry of Salvation', *Saturday Review* no.53, 30 May 1970, collected in Craig McGregor: *Bob Dylan: A Retrospective* (1972, reissued as *Bob Dylan, the Early Years: A Retrospective*, 1990).

The Mississippi Sheiks: 'I've Got Blood in My Eyes for You', Atlanta, 25 Oct 1931, first vinyl-issued *Stop and Listen Blues: The Mississippi Sheiks*, Mamlish S-3804, NY, 1974, CD-reissued *Stop and Listen*, Yazoo 2006, NY, 1992. J.T. Funny Papa Smith: 'Hungry Wolf', Chicago, c.Apr 1931; *'Funny Papa' Smith: The Original Howling Wolf*, Yazoo L-1031, NY, 1972. Bill Gaither: 'Bloody Eyed Woman', Chicago, 22 Oct 1939.]

Jackson, Jim [c.1884 - c.1937] Jim Jackson was born in Hernando, Mississippi, probably in 1884 (1890 used to be given), and probably died in the same tiny town 53 years later; but he lived, worked and recorded in Memphis in the 1920s and was famous for one of the biggest-selling blues hits of that decade, 'Kansas City Blues', which sold almost a million. In 1950s and 60s Memphis, when WDIA, the first all-black radio station, was championing the music of younger generations he wasn't remembered at all. Like his Memphis contemporaries FRANK STOKES and Furry Lewis, he isn't even mentioned in *Wheelin' on Beale*, Louis Cantor's history of WDIA: 230 pages on how this wonderful station gave blacks their own voice, abolished Perry Como in favour of B.B. King, and put the blues on the air—but no change for a bluesman of Jackson's generation: he was still excluded.

His musical sensibility was formed more fully than that of most blues singers by 19th century minstrelsy and ragtime, so that he was already sounding old-fashioned by the time he brought his very limited technical proficiency into the studios for the first time, in October 1927. It may be hard now to see quite where lay the appeal of his début recording (and biggest hit), 'Kansas City Blues': he has a vocal delivery so ponderous it borders on the comical, and a heavy, unvarying guitar strum to match, and you're likely to come to the end of listening to 'Part 1' with no great compunction to play 'Part 2'—and yet his voice has a resonance, a natural echo to its timbre, that fuses with his insistent mournfulness to create an unforgettable impression, an irresistible force.

Nothing is known of his later life; he is believed to have died in 1937 in Hernando and obscurity. For how he comes to dovetail into Bob Dylan's work, see **'I Shall Be Free'** and **'Lay Down Your Weary Tune'**.

[Jim Jackson: 'Jim Jackson's Kansas City Blues Part 1 & Part 2', Chicago, 10 Oct 1927, *Kansas City Blues*, Agram AB2004, Holland, 1980. Louis Cantor, *Wheelin' on Beale*, New York: Pharos Books, 1992.]

Jackson, John [1956 -] John Stigler Jackson was born in Nashville on October 23, 1956 and grew up to be a Nashville-based guitarist who stands six feet three inches tall. When he joined Dylan's touring band at the beginning of the first 1991 tour he was a virtual unknown—and was rumoured to have accepted a pay offer to match: allegedly offered, as a try-on, $500 a week, he accepted it, so placing all future Dylan musicians at a disadvantage before they started. Whatever the truth of that, Dylan had apparently seen him playing on stage with Joe-El Sonnier at the original Lone Star in New York, and knowing that G.E. SMITH was to leave, offered John Jackson the gig (though in the event there was a gap between Smith's departure and Jackson's arrival, filled by CÉSAR DIAZ and JOHN STAEHELY).

John Jackson had spent most of the 1980s playing in Nashville bands, the Practical Stylists and then his own John Jackson & the Rhythm Rockers, but Kathy Mattea also remembers that he had 'played with Sweethearts of the Rodeo when they were doing well, and before that for Terri Gibbs.' He was, says Ms. Mattea, her 'first real guitarist'. (Kathy Mattea is one of the artists who handles a duet with RALPH STANLEY on the same CD of special recordings as Dylan.)

In summer 1998 he was to be found playing guitar for the hugely successful Lucinda Williams, though a Dylan fan who saw one such concert reported that Jackson 'was quite overshadowed by her other lead guitarist . . . who is some kind of mad genius with a fat tone, incredible dexterity, and especially, excellent taste. J.J. stood out by playing a lot of slide.' (It's often reported that only Dylan, and thereafter Dylan fans, called him 'J.J.', but he'd been called that by Kathy Mattea too.) More recently he has played the music on the performance poet Minton Sparks' highly unusual album *Sin Sick*, and is currently playing in the Dylan-based musical *The Times They Are a-Changin'* by Twyla Tharp, which has sold out its three-month San Diego run and shows every sign of bringing Dylan's material to yet another large group of those weird people who say they like his songs but not his voice.

In his real Dylan years, Jackson stood out on stage by being very tall (and never taller than when alongside Bob Dylan) and, as many fans complained, by grinning a great deal. He arrived in the band just as Dylan was in his worst 1990s mode of being: January 1991 saw him appearing much the worse for wear many nights, and the new band itself wasn't great. As ANDREW MUIR wrote in *Razor's Edge: Bob Dylan & the Never-Ending Tour*: 'The opening show in Zurich on January 28th . . . featured "Bob Dylan's Dream" from his *Freewheelin'* days, which had not been performed for nearly 30 years–talk about whetting your appetite! . . . [but] for much of this early bout of 1991 touring . . . The band . . . were terrible. John Jackson did nothing but grin maniacally at the audience while playing the same thing on every song . . . and the drums sounded like a drum machine with a replay button that had got stuck.'

This was the band, and the Bob Dylan, who appeared at the Grammy Awards on February 20 in New York, playing an incomprehensible version of 'Masters of War' as Dylan accepted a Lifetime Achievement Award from JACK NICHOLSON. It was also the band Dylan left behind when he appeared at the Seville Guitar Legends festival that October. Yet at the end of that month, when another tour leg began, Dylan and the band went through a short golden period, when the drumming was rolling in a distinctive way, and the guitar-work was nicely grungy–and within this short sunlit phase came the really exceptional concert at South Bend, Indiana, on November 6, when Dylan even brought 'I'll Remember You' to life, so pressing his best expressive skills into the service of this empty and inauthentic song that he convinced you there really is something tangible inside it. That one night it was far better than it ought to have been. He shared with his audience a lovely unrestrained vocal searching; it was mannered but exploratory, his quick-witted good taste and instinct always in evidence. That night too, there was a fine 'Watching the River Flow' and a wondrous run of consecutive inspired performances on 'Shelter from the Storm', 'Early Morning Rain', 'Gotta Serve Somebody' and 'You Don't Know Me', this last managing to be both the ultimate prom band moment and an affecting tribute to RAY CHARLES.

Jackson can take a little credit for this, though overall he was not a strong contributor, and was easily intimidated by Dylan into never playing anything prominent or individual at all. Despite or because of this, he remained with the band all through 1992–96 and on until February 24, 1997, when he bowed out in Sapporo, Japan.

He is therefore in the band that played the four New York Supper Club sets on November 16 & 17, 1993, followed next day by the 'Late Show with David Letterman' performance of 'Forever Young'; for the wretched *MTV Unplugged* performance of exactly a year later; and for the fine European concerts of spring 1995, beginning with Dylan's Czech Republic début in Prague on March 11. He was also around to *not* be invited to play on the January 1997 sessions for *Time Out of Mind*, in contrast to his tour-band colleagues TONY GARNIER (bass) and WINSTON WATSON (drums).

Lagging behind only the phenomenally resilient Garnier, and steel guitarist BUCKY BAXTER (who joined only a few weeks after Jackson and outlasted him by more than two years), John Jackson has so far proved the Never-Ending Tour band's third-longest-serving musician. He had played a total of 590 Dylan concerts.

[Andrew Muir, *Razor's Edge: Bob Dylan & the Never-Ending Tour*, London: Helter Skelter, 1991, p.71. Quotes from Kathy Mattea, e-mail for this writer, 5 Feb 2006; re Lucinda Williams concert, unidentified posting dated 30 Aug 1998, online 9 Jul 2005 at *www.expectingrain.com/dok/who/j/jacksonjohn.shtml*; further detail from John Jackson, phone call from this writer 16 Feb 2006.]

Jagger, Mick [1943 -] Michael Philip Jagger was born in Dartford, Kent, England, on July 26, 1944 and dropped out of one of Britain's best universities, the London School of Economics, to become a ROLLING STONE in 1963. Though Jagger hung around a New York session for *Blood on the Tracks* in fall 1974, he and Dylan were never simpatico musicians or personalities, and played together without the rest of the Stones only once, at the concert to launch the Rock'n'Roll Hall of Fame in New York City's Waldorf-Astoria Grand Ballroom on January 20, 1988, when among other hopelessly artificial musical moments there came the one when Dylan played inaudible guitar behind Jagger and BRUCE SPRINGSTEEN as they sang '(I Can't Get No) Satisfaction'. This was ironic, granted that at an abrasive and fleeting encounter between the two men 20 years earlier, Dylan told Jagger, truthfully enough: 'The difference between us is that I could have written "Satisfaction" and you couldn't have written "Tambourine Man".'

[Jagger & Springsteen (with Dylan on guitar): '(I Can't Get No) Satisfaction', NY, 20 Jan 1988; Dylan comment to Jagger related by Jagger in a *Rolling Stone* interview, 1968, *nia*.]

'James Alley Blues' See **Brown, Richard Rabbit**.

James, Skip [1902 - 1969] Nehemiah James was born on a plantation at Bentonia, Mississippi, on June 9, 1902. He was unusual in playing guitar and piano, and unique among pre-war blues musicians in regarding himself as an artist, indeed as a great one, without being told that he was by white blues-revival enthusiasts. And he was right. Had he never survived to be 'rediscovered', his reputation would be secure from his sole pre-war recording session, made in about February 1931 in Grafton,

Wisconsin: a session that was prolific and of astonishing virtuosity.

One of the big cats of the genre, the unique Skip James made the crucial recording of a 'Special Rider Blues', after which Dylan named his primary music-publishing company. (Unlike the common blues term 'rider', the phrase '*special* rider' is more special: it seems to occur in only four pre-war songs and by implication in a fifth. One of these is Skip James'.) James is also one of those whose old records saw early vinyl release on the pioneering blues label Biograph, the name Dylan chooses for his 1985 retrospective box set. But Dylan's inwardness with the blues is such that he cannot help but have imbibed things from this highly distinctive figure, and we can glimpse them all over the place in Dylan's work.

The only appealing thing about the *Hearts of Fire* filler-song 'Had a Dream About You Baby' is the comic yet stylishly lazy 'Late last night you come rollin' across my mind,' with its pleasant evocation of someone feeling this image move across from one side of their head to the other: an image that recurs between Dylan's unmemorable verses, so that it enacts the in-between of 'in one ear and out the other' (it's a self-reflexive text, even)—but it's at least as pleasurable hearing the same main phrase in Skip James' '4 O'Clock Blues', in which: 'Brownskin girl, she rollin' across my mind.'

On Dylan's nigh-perfect *Blonde on Blonde* performance of 'Pledging My Time', the melody, the gulping movement of the melodic phrases *and* Dylan's mysteriously ominous line 'Somebody got lucky, but it was an accident' may all echo 'Come on in My Kitchen' by ROBERT JOHNSON, from 30 years earlier, but while the restless melodic phrasing is Johnson's, the melody that inspires it is the same as 'Sittin' on Top of the World', and the Johnson line that Dylan's echoes—'Some joker got lucky, stole her back again'—is itself an echo of a line from Skip James' brilliant 1931 début recording, 'Devil Got My Woman'.

This is not the whole story: BLIND WILLIE McTELL's 'Stole Rider Blues', recorded at *his* first session (1927) includes 'I stole my good gal from my bosom friend / That fool got lucky, he stole her back again', which anticipates Skip James' 1931 'Devil Got My Woman' *and* Robert Johnson's 1936 'Come on in My Kitchen', and it would be hard to say from whom Dylan picked up the line—as Dylan sings his matching line, his 'accident' rhymes neatly with the 'back again' offered by McTell, James *and* Johnson—except that James' line, 'Somebody got lucky, stoled her back again', is the closest to Dylan's. And certainly Robert Johnson's line comes down from Skip James rather than from McTell (who may have picked his up from listening to Ida Cox's 'Worried Mama Blues', which predates all of them with its 'I stole my man from my best friend / But she got lucky and stole him back again', from 1923). 'Devil Got My Woman' is also the *musical* basis of another Robert Johnson song, 'Hellhound on My Trail', while Johnson's '32-20' is an almost verbatim reworking of Skip James' '22-20 Blues'.

These songs came to Johnson via his Jackson, Mississippi, contemporary Johnny Temple, an ex-protégé of Skip James, whereas for Dylan, James was accessible more or less directly; that is, he was both a figure of legend from the 1930s and one of the most important of the 'rediscovered' bluesmen in the couple of years immediately before *Blonde on Blonde* was recorded.

Another part of the same Skip James lyric becomes entwined in a different Dylan song, 'When I Paint My Masterpiece'—which was recorded, coincidentally or not, within a year of the first release on vinyl of the original 1931 James recording of 'Devil Got My Woman'. The 'wild geese' Dylan recalls himself following on a hilltop in 'When I Paint My Masterpiece' fly straight out of a number of old blues songs, in which they feature as a common-stock formulation. Whenever you hear the line 'I lay down last night, tried to take my rest' you can more or less bet that the next line will be 'My mind got to ramblin' like the wild geese in the west.' It occurs, for example, in BLIND BOY FULLER's 'Weeping Willow', which Dylan performed at the Supper Club in New York in 1993.

Sometimes the 'wild geese', with engaging grammatic licence, is singular ('my mind got to rambling like a wild geese in the west'). There are also several songs called 'Wild Geese Blues', as for instance recorded by Barbecue Bob, Alberta Jones and the theatrically masculine Gladys Bentley. Yet because of Skip James' vocal intensity, and because of a tiny one-word change he makes to the couplet, these wild geese fly most vividly and particularly out of 'Devil Got My Woman', so that the image works as a most poignant lunge of the imagination suddenly arising out of his beautifully evoked restless yearning. James sings: 'I lay down last night, tried to take my rest / My mind got to ramblin' like the wild geese from the west.' The more common 'in the west' is less moving, in both senses, than James' 'from the west': 'in the west' abolishes movement, leaving these birds, and the image, hanging motionless. Skip James' tiny change sets them flying across the sky, wild geese indeed, making the image one of visitational loveliness.

James was taught guitar by the unrecorded singer Henry Stuckey, born in the 1890s. James first saw him play in a Bentonia, Mississippi, juke joint in about 1908, and learnt guitar from him after Stuckey's 1917 return from World War I, using pieces like 'Salty Dog' and 'Stack O'Lee'. James' own wonderful piano-accompanied recording 'If You Haven't Any Hay Get on Down the Road' is based on a ragtime number Stuckey played on guitar as 'All Night Long', fused with the traditional 'Alabama Bound', learnt in James' youth from local fiddle-player Green McCloud. Stuckey, tracked down in 1965 by the blues collector and critic Gayle Wardlow, still refused to record, and died in 1966.

Skip James concentrated primarily on his own compositions, and continued to make many of them out of songs that were not really blues at all, but which he alchemised into blues by the sheer ingenuity of his wayward style. He also found his own eccentric, intelligent ways of enriching his guitar-work from his experience as a pianist, and vice versa. The brilliant, distinctive delivery James uses at the end of his vocal lines—an ostentatious yet felicitous filigreeing around the note—finds a pale echo in Bob Dylan's delivery on 'North Country Blues'. In full, skittering flight, as achieved by Skip James, it prefigures, among other things, Robin Williamson's Incredible String Band vocals. There is just one occasion when the radiant wondrousness of Mr. James crashes badly. His 1931 performance of '4 O'Clock Blues' holds a disquieting moment for those familiar with 1950s–60s British culture. There you are, entranced by his precarious, eerie genius when all at once the phrase his perilous falsetto offers is 'Goodbye my darling—', and he sounds exactly like Charlie Drake.

James returned to Bentonia in the late 1940s, went on the road again with his wife in the early 1950s but wearied of traveling and retired. The drama of his recording career lies in the fact that he had only ever done one recording session, the substantial one from 1931 that had yielded so much. Then, 33 years later, 'rediscovered', he appeared like a ghost at the 1964 NEWPORT FOLK FESTIVAL, and was recorded there by Vanguard Records. The first of his four Newport songs was 'Devil Got My Woman' (and of the three others, two were also revisits to songs he had cut at his recording session of three decades earlier).

Peter Guralnick's 1971 book *Feel Like Going Home* is good on Skip James' 'rediscovery', and appears to give an eye-witness account of his triumphant performance at Newport. It is an account that recognises the agitation most of us can fall prey to in coping with the emergence of the much-loved, obscure artefact into clear accessibility:

> 'As the first notes floated across the field, as the voice soared over us, the piercing falsetto set against the harsh cross-tuning of the guitar, there was a note of almost breathless expectation in the air. It seemed inappropriate somehow that this strange haunting sound which had existed till now only as a barely audible dub from a scratched 78 should be reclaimed so casually on an overcast summer's day at Newport. As the song came to an end . . . the field exploded with cheers and whistles and some of the awful tension was dissipated.'

JON PANKAKE's colleague PAUL NELSON, reviewing Skip James' performance as issued on one of the festival LPs, wrote that "the rediscovered Skip James contributes four of the greatest blues performances . . . of recent years, his high, emotional falsetto singing and carefully considered guitar-playing setting a nearly impossible standard."'

James continued to record and perform after Newport—and not at all as a shadow of his former self, though it's expected that you should say so. To listen, for example, to his 1966 recordings for Vanguard's album *Skip James Today!* is to be astonished by the man's genius and chutzpah. He sounds like no-one else on the planet; he sounds ageless and in his prime; his singing is still eerily beautiful and his acoustic guitar-work is inventive and precise. Play *Skip James Today!* up against Bob Dylan's 1993 album *World Gone Wrong* and much as you might love the latter, the former rebuffs with shining energy the notion that blurred guitar-work or last-gasp vocalising is all you can expect from the over-50s; and the Skip James of 1966 was 15 years older than the Dylan of 1993. (James' album is also, you won't be surprised to learn, immensely better recorded than Dylan's.) Still, while one of these artists was recording *Skip James Today!*, the other was recording *Blonde on Blonde*. Can't complain.

His impact was felt widely in the blues-revival and 'rediscovery' period. Cream's 1966 début LP *Fresh Cream* included a version, albeit barely recognisable, of James' 'I'm So Glad' (said to have earned him only $6,000). Further James recording sessions followed in the 1960s, including a live concert recording from Bloomington as late as 1968, never released until it appeared on two separately issued CDs in 2002.

Skip James died of cancer in Philadelphia in early October 1969.

[Skip James: 'Special Rider Blues', Grafton, WI, c.Feb 1931, *Mississippi Blues 1927–1941*, Yazoo L-1001, NY, 1968 & *Skip James: King of the Delta Blues Singers 1928–1964*, Biograph BLP-12029, Canaan, NY, 1970; '4 O'Clock Blues', Grafton, c.Feb 1931, *Skip James: The Complete 1931 Session*, Yazoo 1072, Newton, NJ, 1988; 'Devil Got My Woman', 'Special Rider Blues' and '22-20', Grafton, c.Feb 1931, all on Biograph BLP-12029 (James' only pre-war recordings were c.Feb 1931; the Biograph album boasts the dates '1928–1964' because it includes a 1928 Chicago test pressing by someone else, wrongly attributed to James, and because it draws on a Falls Church, VA, session, 16 Dec 1964, at which James cut 22 sides. BLP-12029 uses just two: 'I'm So Glad' & 'Special Rider Blues'); 'Devil Got My Woman', 'Cherry Ball Blues', 'Sick Bed Blues' & 'Cypress Grove Blues', Newport, RI, 23–26 Jul 1964, *The Blues at Newport 1964, Part Two*, Vanguard VRS-9181 (mono) & VSD-79181, NY, 1965; *Skip James Today!*, NY, Jan 1966, Vanguard VLP 9219, NY, c.1967; *Skip James: The Complete Bloomington Indiana Concert March 30, 1968, Part 1* & *Part 2*, Document DOCD 5633 & 5634, Austria, 2002.

Blind Willie McTell: 'Stole Rider Blues', Atlanta, 18 Oct 1927; *Blind Willie McTell 1927–1935*, Yazoo L-1037,

NY, 1973 (issued in stereo!). Ida Cox: 'Worried Mama Blues', Chicago, Dec 1923. Robert Johnson: 'Hellhound on My Trail' (2 takes), Dallas, 20 Jun 1937; one issued *Robert Johnson: King of the Delta Blues Singers*, Columbia CL-1654, NY, 1961; '32-20 Blues' (2 takes), San Antonio, TX, 26 Nov 1936, ditto. (Another significant influence on Johnson, Kokomo Arnold, recorded 'Front Door Blues (32 20 Blues)', Chicago, 15 Jan 1935.) Blind Boy Fuller: 'Weeping Willow', NY, 14 Jul 1937; *Blind Boy Fuller on Down—Vol. 1*, Saydisc SDR143, Badminton, UK, c.1967. Bob Dylan: 'Weeping Willow', NY, 17 Jul 1993. Cream: 'I'm So Glad', *Fresh Cream*, Reaction, UK, 1966.

Peter Guralnick, *Feel Like Going Home*, New York: Outerbridge & Dienstfrey, 1971 (reissued London: Penguin, 1992). Paul Nelson, *Sing Out!* vol.15, no.5, NY, Nov 1965.]

Jean, Wyclef [1972 -] Nelust Wyclef Jean was born on October 17, 1972 in Croix-des-Bouquets, Haiti, moved with his family to the Marlborough Projects, Brooklyn, New York, at age nine and moved again, to northern New Jersey, where he attended high school, studied jazz and became proficient on the guitar. In 1987 he and a cousin and one of that cousin's classmates formed the group the Tranzlator Crew, but changed their name to the Fugees before signing to Ruffhouse Records in 1993. Their début album, 1994's *Blunted on Reality*, did nothing, but after that came *The Score*, in 1996, which included several hit singles and was in itself a phenomenal success, selling some 17 million copies. While its repertoire ranged widely, as Wyclef Jean's subsequent work has also done, it was firmly rooted in hip-hop and proved an unprecedented disperser of the genre.

While the Fugees didn't exactly fold after that, group activity was suspended while its individual members, starting with Jean, launched solo careers. His solo début, in 1997, was with *The Carnival* (full name *Wyclef Jean Presents the Carnival Featuring the Refugee All-Stars*), on which the guests included the other Fugees, Jean's back-up singing siblings the I Threes, the Neville Brothers and Celia Cruz. The album yielded two hit singles and itself went triple platinum.

One of the hit singles from the album was 'We Trying to Stay Alive', a riposte to the insufferable Bee Gees; the other, issued in 1998, was 'Gone Till November', on which Jean sings the line 'Gotta do some knockin' on heaven's door like Bob Dylan'; the album version doesn't mention Dylan. But in late 1997, for the promo video for the single, Jean is shown walking around inside Los Angeles International Airport and then sitting down in a row of seats and singing the 'Dylan' line, finding that Dylan himself is in the seat alongside him. It's a neat if brief moment, and an unusual one in Bob's career.

After various collaborations, including as a producer, with everyone from Michael Jackson to Sinéad O'Connor, Jean made a second, less well-received solo album in 2000, *The Ecleftic: 2 Sides II a Book* (on which the guests included Youssou N'Dour and Kenny Rogers, and the material pulled in Pink Floyd's 'Wish You Were Here': all in all an eclefticism too far, many felt), which was followed in 2002 by *Masquerade*, on which he *did* sing 'Knockin' on Heaven's Door', giving it a pleasant reggae treatment.

The Wyclef Jean Foundation uses some of this unusual hip-hop star's money to help children living in poverty and crime-ridden conditions in the US and Haiti.

[Wyclef Jean: *Carnival*, Ruffhouse/Sony 67974, US, 1997; *The Ecleftic: 2 Sides II a Book*, Sony 62180, US, 2000; *Masquerade*, Sony, *nia*, US, 2002; 'Gone Till November', Columbia 665323 2, US, 1998. Main sources: *www.askmen.com/men/entertainment_100/124c_wyclef_jean.html*, *http://en.wikipedia.org/wiki/Wyclef_Jean*, *www.amazon.com* &, as so often, Glen Dundas, *Tangled*, Thunder Bay, Ontario: SMA Services, 2004.]

Jefferson, Blind Lemon [1894 - 1929] A great blues singer, also a guitarist and composer, born on October 26, 1894 (given until recently as September 26, 1893) in Wortham, Texas, about 60 miles south of Dallas. Hugely influential because he shaped the Texas blues and put it on record, though his recording career was, typically, very short (1926–29). He was the main blues influence on LEADBELLY and, through Leadbelly, an important tutor to many, many others. It is said that BLIND WILLIE McTELL was encouraged to take up the 12-string guitar thanks to a personal encounter with Jefferson (though Jefferson was a 6-string guitarist). His records were also a significant influence on hillbillies, who heard them on the radio. This is clear in the marvellous work of Roscoe Holcomb in the 1950s–60s.

There is only one extant known photograph of Lemon. He sits against a photo-studio backdrop, besuited, with his guitar across his lap. He's a young man and looks a Bunterish outsider, a goody-goody deacon, plump and polished-skinned, his hair too neat. He has the thinnest possible pencil moustache, though this utterly fails to lend him a dandyish air. His spotted silk tie has been drawn onto the picture afterwards. Contradicting the sharp creases of the suit trousers, the guitar strap around his neck is of crude white string. Most oddly, he is *wearing glasses*—and written across the foot of the picture in a large, confident, regular hand is the comically formal message 'Cordially Yours Blind Lemon Jefferson'.

More reliably, Jefferson wrote the line 'I'm standin' here wonderin' will a matchbox hold my clothes', which crops up 25 years after his death in CARL PERKINS' 'Matchbox' and, around the same time as Dylan's first album was released, in SAM COOKE's 'Somebody Have Mercy'. (It's odd that Cooke should be wondering will a matchbox hold his clothes, because earlier in the same lyric he's standing at the bus-station with a suitcase in his hand.)

Jefferson first recorded the song that Dylan includes on his début album, 'See That My Grave Is Kept Clean', as 'See That My Grave's Kept Clean' in Chicago in about October 1927; this was never available on vinyl until 1968. Jefferson's re-recording, as 'See That My Grave Is Kept Clean', again cut in Chicago but in about February 1928, was the one Dylan knew: it had been included on the seminal HARRY SMITH compilation *AMERICAN FOLK MUSIC* in 1952, which was crucial to Bob Dylan from very early in his career, as to everyone in the folk revival movement of the late 1950s to early 1960s.

Dylan records 'See That My Grave Is Kept Clean' for that first album on November 22, 1961; he is then taped singing it at the home of Eve & Mac Mackenzie in New York in September 1962, and performing it live at the Gaslight the following month—and then revisits it, trying out a proto-*Nashville Skyline* voice, during the Basement Tapes sessions years later.

He also alludes to it elsewhere. In the opening line of 'Call Letter Blues' (recorded at the *Blood on the Tracks* sessions but left off the album and issued, in the end, on *Bootleg Series Vols. 1–3* in the 1990s) when Dylan sings that he is 'hearin' them church bells tone', one of the things we might recognise him as hearing is the church bell tone that Blind Lemon imitates on the guitar in his performance of 'Grave'. And though there are horses galloping all over balladry and the blues, white horses are rare in the latter—but having whinnied their way into the Jefferson song, they play a cameo role in Dylan's 'Absolutely Sweet Marie' and his terrific (unreleased) later song 'Yonder Comes Sin'.

After Harry Smith's anthology, the most significant compilation was a crucial LP issue of previously hard-to-obtain pre-war blues material, *The Country Blues*, 1959, which included Blind Lemon Jefferson's 'Match Box Blues', recorded in Chicago in about March 1927. Jefferson re-recorded it twice, a month later, but the original recording is best: it was made for OKeh and exists in pretty good quality; the re-recordings were for Paramount, a label synonymous with cheap equipment, and hence with atrocious sound quality. Unfortunately almost all Jefferson's sides were on Paramount. Dylan played around with a version of 'Matchbox' during his studio session with GEORGE HARRISON in New York in May 1970.

Dylan's extraordinary regenerative use of the blues—and especially of pre-war blues lyric poetry—is a huge subject and Jefferson's presence is widespread within it; but Dylan's usage isn't always resourceful, and the presence of Jefferson's 'Lonesome House Blues' is a case in point. You might say that the weakest lines in that bluesy *Blonde on Blonde* song 'Temporary Like Achilles' are in the bridge section between the second and third verses, where he sings 'But is your heart made out of stone, or is it lime / Or is it just solid rock?' The unrock-like limpness of that repetition, that tautology, long seemed puzzlingly poor. It's just as poor but no longer a puzzle, when we learn that Dylan has extrapolated it from Blind Lemon's song, in which we get the more economical 'If your heart ain't rock, sugar it must be marble stone.'

Blind Lemon Jefferson is reputed to have frozen to death in the streets in a snowstorm in Chicago in December 1929, but by his producer J. Mayo Williams' account, he collapsed in his car and died after his chauffeur abandoned him. No death certificate has ever been found.

[Blind Lemon Jefferson: 'See That My Grave's Kept Clean', Chicago, c.Oct 1927, *Blind Lemon Jefferson Volume 2*, Roots RL-306, Vienna, 1968; 'See That My Grave Is Kept Clean', Chicago, c.Feb 1928, *American Folk Music* (3 double-LPs), Folkways FP 251-253, NY, 1952, CD-reissued Smithsonian Folkways SRW 40090, Washington, D.C., 1997 (the Jefferson track CD-reissued earlier on *King of the Country Blues*, Yazoo CD-1069, US, c.1990); 'Lonesome House Blues', Chicago, c.Oct 1927; 'Match Box Blues', Chicago, c.Mar 1927, *The Country Blues*, RBF RF-1, NY, 1959.

Bob Dylan: 'See That My Grave Is Kept Clean', NY, 22 Nov 1961, *Bob Dylan*; Mackenzies, NY, Sep 1962 (unreleased); Gaslight, NY, Mar 1962 (unreleased); West Saugherties, NY, Oct–Nov 1967 (unreleased).

Carl Perkins: 'Matchbox', Memphis, 30 Jan 1957; Sun 261, Memphis, 1957. (An earlier cut, 'Matchbox', Memphis, 4 Apr 1956, remained unissued until the box set *Carl Perkins: The Sun Years*, Charley Records, London, c.1980.) Sam Cooke: 'Somebody Have Mercy', Hollywood, 15 Feb 1962, RCA Victor (and RCA 1310, London), 1962.

Source for birthdate: his WWI draft registration card, online at *www.ancestry.com*, as reported to pre-war blues e-mail discussion group *pre-war-blues@yahoogroups.com*, 5 Dec 2005.]

Jesus v. Springsteen On the 1986 tours with TOM PETTY & THE HEARTBREAKERS, beginning in Australia and Japan in February and March, Dylan would nightly regale his audiences with garrulous, slightly mad raps before a number of songs. Disappointingly, these were always roughly the same (i.e. descending to showbiz routine, rather than the spontaneous one-off communications of earlier eras—or at least of those when he spoke at all).

The most effective was the rap that introduced 'In the Garden', from the *Saved* album: a song about Christ. The rap always begins with a short list of other people's heroes, and those on the list varied nightly—except that they always seemed to include BRUCE SPRINGSTEEN. The list was particularly nifty in Tokyo on March 10, at his last concert in the Far East. Dylan says:

> 'This song here's about my hero. Everybody's got a hero. Where I come from heroes are . . . John Wayne, Boris Karloff, Henry Winkler, Michael Jackson, Bruce Springsteen, Ronald Reagan, Richard Nixon. Anyway, I don't care nothing about any of those people. I have my own hero.'

(For a variant see **'In the Garden'**.)

'Jim Jones' [1992] The melody of 'Jim Jones', on Dylan's solo acoustic album of 1992, *Good as I Been to You*, might in a general way seem echoed by that of 'If You See Her Say Hello', from *Blood on the Tracks*, though it is said to be that of the song 'Irish Molly-O'. It was Mick Slocum, then of the group the Bushwackers, who set the old convict song to the melody Dylan used, and first released it on the Bushwackers' album *The Shearer's Dream* in 1974. His new melody was copyrighted in Australia in 1977, but apparently not in Washington, D.C.; Dylan's version is copyrighted to his own Special Rider Music company as 'arranged by Bob Dylan.'

Regardless of its provenance, though, the more interesting point is how intensely well Dylan performs 'Jim Jones', despite—not because of—the broke-down engine of his voice. The way he sings the phrase 'New South Wales' is as disarmingly particular, as yearningly expressive of the romance of a place-name as he has ever been (when he's been paying attention). He sings 'New South Wales' more under-statedly but as beautifully as in 'Boots of Spanish Leather' he sings 'Barcelona'—and anyone who knows the studio version of the latter, recorded in August 1963 and issued on *The Times They Are a-Changin'*, will know that this is high praise indeed. His purpose this time, however, is not to stress romance, but to turn that level of poignancy to different effect.

In singing so savouringly of 'New South Wales' Dylan manages to bring out something of the extremity of aloneness of those sentenced to deportation: and something of the bitter irony of naming a place so far away after somewhere on the home side of the sea. As Gail Smith writes: 'In 1788 the first convicts arrived on the "fatal shore". Another world away, it might have been the moon—but as Robert Hughes so aptly observed, you could see the moon; you could not see Botany Bay. "It was 12,000 miles away, a desolate wilderness whose limits nobody knew, perched on the edge of a hypothetical map."'

In evoking such desolation by vocal caress as well as by stark and wayward strain, Dylan fully inhabits the song's world of a savage penal code in the old land, and of exile across a huge sea to further chains and cruelty, scrubland and thwarted desire.

Dylan's first live performance of 'Jim Jones' was in Dublin on February 5, 1993, after which he performed it nightly through his run of London Hammersmith concerts and the European dates that followed.

[Bob Dylan: 'Jim Jones', Malibu, Jul–Aug 1992; 'Boots of Spanish Leather', NY, Aug 1963. The Bushwackers, 'Jim Jones', *The Shearer's Dream*, Larrikin, *nia*, Australia, 1974, reissued Larrikin LRF 019, 1980. Gail Smith, 'Bob Dylan on Botany Bay', *Who Threw the Glass?* (Dylan fanzine) no.1, Sydney, fall 1993; her quotation is from Robert Hughes, *The Art of Australia*, Sydney: Penguin, 1966. Bushwackers LP & Slocum copyright data from A.J. Iriarte, e-mailed comments to this writer, 2000, based on Mick Slocum interview by J. Lattanzio & S. Wynands, *The Telegraph* no.47, UK, winter 1993, pp.44–46.]

John, Elton [1947 -] Reginald Kenneth Dwight, aka Elton John, was born on March 25, 1947, in Pinner, Middlesex, England. A pop singer and pianist who has outsold Dylan innumerable times over, he plays piano on '2 x 2', one of the less than memorable songs on Dylan's 1990 album *Under the Red Sky*. This track was recorded in LA in February or March 1990.

***John Wesley Harding* [album, 1968]** The eighth album, not counting greatest-hits compilations. This quiet masterpiece, which manages to sound both authoritative and tentative (a mix that gave it a highly contemporary feel), is neither a rock nor a folk album—and certainly isn't folk-rock. It isn't categorisable at all. The back-up musicians are pared down to three: bass, drums and, on two tracks only, pedal steel. Plus Dylan on guitar, harmonica and piano. Economy, in fact, is the key to this huge change of direction. There could be no greater contrast between consecutive albums than that between *Blonde on Blonde*'s richness and the taut asceticism of *John Wesley Harding*. This album is no cheap thrill. It is, though, a most serious, darkly visionary exploration of the myths and extinct strengths of America; its Calvinist spirit gives it an eerie power in mixing the severely biblical with a surreal 19th century, American-pioneer ethos. Dylan comes across like a man who has arisen from armageddon unscathed but sobered, to walk across an allegorical American landscape of small, poor communities working a dusty, fierce terrain. The masterpieces within the masterpiece are 'I Dreamed I Saw St. Augustine', 'All Along the Watchtower' and 'I Pity the Poor Immigrant'. Then there are the last two tracks of the album: the à la JERRY LEE LEWIS 'Down Along the Cove' and the brilliant country-pastiche song 'I'll Be Your Baby Tonight'. With these, Dylan was serving notice of the next sharp shift in direction that was to come from him. *John Wesley Harding* was to be Dylan's last masterpiece of the 1960s—and in spirit it was most markedly not a part of the 1960s world at all.

It is the most underrated of Dylan's *great* albums: a record that everyone puts in the pantheon but few embrace. Yet how especially pleasurable it is to revisit now that so many years have passed since it was new: to bathe in the relief of remembering that Dylan is not just the flailing old bruiser of the Never-Ending Tour, whose patchy virtues must be snatched from rough, loud, swirling chaos and carelessness, his intermittent inspiration lobbing out of the aural fog as he stumbles down his road. It's salutary to be pulled away from picking through concert bootlegs for these rare and shaky treats and re-directed towards the Bob Dylan who gave us *John Wesley Harding*, throughout which he insists upon the virtues of calm and silence, of less-is-more, of exquisite precision and particularity, carved out with blade-sharp, unwavering certainty. Here, there is no floundering search for some intangible juiced-up mystic rock'n'roll moment: there is instead the artist standing naked, with a very particular vision in his sights, and illuminating it with the intuitive alertness of his genius.

[Recorded Nashville, TN, 17 Oct, 6 & 29 Nov 1967; released as stereo LP, Columbia CS 9604 & mono LP Columbia CL 2804; in the UK CBS SBPG 63252 (stereo) & BPG 63252 (mono). This was the last Dylan LP to be offered in a separate mono mix. Theoretically the US release-date was 27 Dec 1967; in fact it was released Jan 1968, and the UK release-date was 23 Feb 1968.]

'John Wesley Harding' [song] See heroes, special cowboy fondness for.

Johnnie & Jack Johnnie Robert Wright was born on May 13, 1914 in Mount Juliet, Tennessee; Jack Anglin was born exactly two years later in Franklin, Tennessee; both were within 20 miles of Nashville. The two men met in 1936 and became brothers-in-law a year later, when Jack married Johnnie's sister Louise.

A youthful Jack Anglin and his older brothers Van Buren ('Red') and Jim had met the Delmore Brothers, been influenced immediately and had formed the Anglin Brothers in 1933. (Red sang, Jim wrote songs, sang and played string bass and Jack wrote songs, sang and played guitar.) After years of playing on radio, they recorded in 1937 and 1938 but disbanded in 1940 when Red was drafted, and subsequently injured in France. Jim wrote a number of songs which he sold to ROY ACUFF (which is why Acuff is often given the composer credit for them) before going off to war in the Pacific. Jack teamed up with Johnnie, then in a part-time outfit of no special merit. Together they became the Tennessee Hillbillies, the Tennessee Mountain Boys and eventually Johnnie & Jack. Hence two of the lesser country acts of the 1930s ended up as one of the better country duos of the 1940s and 50s.

Johnnie & Jack were distinctive for blending traditional country instrumentation and vocal harmonies (often bringing in a third voice, Eddie Hill) with a Latin beat. Late in their career, therefore, they were more open than most country acts to the black rhythms of rock'n'roll, though it wasn't always a comfortable or persuasive integration.

After early studio attempts for Apollo in New York and King in Cincinnati, they signed to RCA Victor in 1949 and had a big hit two years later with the song 'Poison Love' (which becomes one of the songs on the DOUG SAHM album *Doug Sahm and Friends*: a track Bob Dylan plays guitar on).

This was the first of a run of country hits on the label, many of them written by Jack's brother Jim. Johnnie, meanwhile, had married country star Kitty Wells, who also enjoyed country hits from the early 1950s onwards. In 1961 Johnnie & Jack moved to Decca, where they met with far less success, scraping into the country charts only once (with 'Slow Poison') and attempting things like a revival of the EVERLY BROTHERS' 1957 hit 'Bye Bye, Love' in 1963, the year their act came to an end.

In the world away of 1976, one of the joyous moments onstage at THE BAND's farewell concert at the Winterland in San Francisco (filmed and recorded as *The Last Waltz*) comes when BOBBY CHARLES performs the Wright, Anglin & Anglin song 'Down South in New Orleans.'

Among the items in Johnnie & Jack's repertoire penned with Jim Anglin were the timorously delivered yet in its lyrics severely fire-and-brimstone gospel 'This World Can't Stand Long', which they recorded for King back in 1947, a train song, 'Humming Bird', recorded for RCA in 1951, and 'Searching for a Soldier's Grave', which they never got around to recording under their own name. The Bailes Brothers recorded it for Columbia in 1945, but then Kitty Wells recorded it accompanied by an unbilled Johnnie & Jack in 1952, though it was released only as an LP track in 1955; the Louvin Brothers revived it in 1962. Sweetly redolent of what sounds misleadingly like an innocent age, none features a Latin beat. All three songs were introduced into Dylan's concert repertoire during the Never-Ending Tour.

'This World Can't Stand Long' was first performed in Delaware on November 20, 1999, Dylan's last concert of the year. It was the fourth item in a show that had opened with THE STANLEY BROTHERS' similarly gospel-country song 'I Am the Man, Thomas'. When Dylan returned to touring in 2000, starting in Anaheim, California, on March 10, 'This World Can't Stand Long' was back in there, receiving 15 performances in the course of the year. In amongst these, on June 15 in Portland, Oregon, Dylan introduced 'Searching for a Soldier's Grave' in the same slot in the set-list. This latter song was given a further 51 performances before the end of 2000 and 39 more in 2001. 'This World Can't Stand Long' was again played 15 times in 2001, while 'Humming Bird' suddenly opened Dylan's concert in Langesund, Norway, that June 28, the first of what turned out to be 13 renditions by year's end. In 2002 there were ten more 'Humming Bird's, 20 further 'Searching for a Soldier's Grave's and 7 'This World Can't Stand Long's. All three songs then vanished from Dylan's repertoire.

A far more dramatic Dylan connection centres on the duo's 1961 Decca record 'Uncle John's Bongos' (on which they're billed as Johnny & Jack). Dylan's *"Love and Theft"* track 'Tweedle Dum & Tweedle Dee' steals this dreadful record's music so completely that the backing on the one might almost be sampled from the other. And yet Dylan makes into a decent record, with a lyric rich in sly delights, what was gruesomely clunky, unmusical and vacuous: audio proof, in fact, of how much better Johnnie & Jack were when they stuck to country music and didn't try to be hep rock'n' rollers.

It has been suggested (by OLIVER TRAGER) that their 'fluid mélange' of bluegrass, religious music and even R&B 'stretched the boundaries' of the country sound of the day, and that their penchant for the Latin beat 'brought a new rhythmic consciousness to country music'; but, Latin beat aside perhaps, all this could be said about almost any country group in the 1940s, when Western Swing and bluegrass were driving the genre forward, and when religious music was, as ever, a normal part of the repertoire pushed out by country radio all the time. Johnnie & Jack were not exceptional pioneers; they were resourceful participants.

Red Anglin died in 1975, Jim in 1987. Johnnie Wright is still alive; Jack Anglin met his death in tragi-comic circumstances: he was killed in a car crash on his way to a memorial service for Patsy Cline, on March 8, 1963.

[Johnny (sic) & Jack: 'This World Can't Stand Long', Cincinnati, 8 Aug 1947, King 674, 1947. Johnnie & Jack: 'Humming Bird': Atlanta, GA, 6 May 1951, RCA 20-4251 (78rpm) & RCA 47-4251 (45rpm); 'Uncle John's Bongos', *n/a*, Decca 31289, NY, 1961, CD-reissued on *MCA Rockabillies, Vol. 3*, Big Tone BT 5707, London, 1993; 'Bye Bye, Love', Decca 31472, NY, 1963. Kitty Wells: 'Searching for a Soldier's Grave', Nashville, 3 May 1952, *Country Hit Parade*, Decca DL. 8293 (LP) & Decca ED. 2361 (45rpm EP). Oliver Trager, *Keys to the Rain: The Definitive Bob Dylan Encyclopedia*, New York: Billboard Books, 2004, p.264.]

Johnson, Blind Willie [1897 - 1945] Willie Johnson was born on a farm in the tiny community of Independence, Texas (halfway between Austin and Houston), on January 22, 1897. He is said to have been blinded by his stepmother at the age of seven, but grew up to become one of the finest bottleneck guitarists ever recorded, and therefore an influence on everyone from those who knew him to Duane Allman, Jimmy Page, Ry Cooder, ERIC CLAPTON and all the usual suspects. He was also a singer of thrilling, controlled power and great dignity. Indeed he could produce two distinctly different singing voices (as mentioned in the entry **Simon, Paul**, as it happens).

Johnson recorded 30 sides between 1927 and 1930, some with his first wife, Willie B. Harris, and then never recorded again, though his first release, 'If I Had My Way I'd Tear the Building Down', coupled with 'Mother's [a mis-transcription of 'Motherless'] Children Have a Hard Time', sold 15,000 copies, and he continued to travel, preach and sing all the way 'from Maine to the Mobile Bay', to quote his old friend BLIND WILLIE McTELL, and he was a regular broadcaster on KTEM in Temple and in church services broadcast on KPLC in Lake Charles.

By the early 1960s he had become one of the best-known pre-war gospel bluesmen, because he had made an appearance on both the crucial vinyl compilations of the 1950s. First, HARRY SMITH's *AMERICAN FOLK MUSIC* reissued Johnson's 'John the Revelator' in 1952; then SAM CHARTERS' 1959 LP *The Country Blues* included his 'You're Gonna Need Somebody on Your Bond'. Both tracks had been recorded in Atlanta in 1930.

Johnson's 'Jesus Make Up My Dying Bed', cut in Dallas three years earlier, duly became 'In My Time of Dyin'' on Dylan's début album. 'Jesus Make Up My Dying Bed'—often spelt as 'Dying-Bed': a compound noun like 'praying-ground' and 'cooling-board'—was an old spiritual that had been recorded by a large number of jubilee and gospel groups, sermons-with-singing preachers and many individual singers, among them CHARLEY PATTON, a figure as early and as eminent as Blind Willie Johnson, though not so early onto disc with this particular song. (His 'Jesus Is a Dying-Bed Maker' was cut in 1929.) At the Gaslight Café in Greenwich Village in October 1962, Dylan performed 'Motherless Children'.

In late 1980, approaching Christian songs from a changed perspective, Dylan brought MARIA MULDAUR on stage at one of his San Francisco concerts, to sing 'It's Nobody's Fault But Mine'; in 1992, in a studio in Chicago, Dylan recorded it himself (a recording that remains unreleased and uncirculated). Twelve years later, at the Bonnaroo 2004 Music Festival in Manchester, Tennessee, he gave a worthy performance of 'If I Had My Way I Would Tear the Building Down' (aka 'Samson and Delilah').

Johnson remains a mysterious figure, though his second wife Angeline was interviewed by Sam Charters at her shack in Beaumont, Texas, in 1955 (from which Charters concluded mistakenly that she had been the singer who had accompanied him on some of his sides). The interview was issued on a Folkways album, *Blind Willie Johnson: His Story*, in 1963 (and is transcribed in the notes to the 1993 CD set *The Complete Blind Willie Johnson*). His last known address was in Beaumont, Texas, where he ran a House of Prayer. He died in Beaumont of malarial fever, exacerbated by syphilis, on September 18, 1945.

In 1977 Johnson's 'Dark Was the Night (Cold Was the Ground)', a compelling synthesis of guitar-work plus wordless humming and moaning cut at his début session in early December 50 years earlier, was included in the 'Sounds of Earth' compilation sent into space aboard Voyager One.

[Blind Willie Johnson: 'John the Revelator' & 'You're Gonna Need Somebody on Your Bond', Atlanta, 20 Apr 1930; 'It's Nobody's Fault But Mine', 'Mother's Children Have a Hard Time', 'If I Had My Way I'd Tear the Building Down' & 'Dark Was the Night (Cold Was the Ground)', Dallas, 3 Dec 1927; all tracks CD-reissued *The Complete Blind Willie Johnson*, Columbia Legacy Roots N' Blues Series 472190 2, NY, 1993. *Blind Willie Johnson: His Story*, Folkways FG3585, NY, 1963. Charley Patton: 'Jesus Is a Dying-Bed Maker', Grafton, WI, c.Oct 1929. Bob Dylan: 'Motherless Children', NY, Oct 1962, unissued; 'It's Nobody's Fault But Mine', Chicago, Apr 1992, unissued; 'If I Had My Way I'd Tear the Building Down', Manchester, TN, 6 Nov 2004. Maria Muldaur with Dylan & band: 'It's Nobody's Fault But Mine', live, San Francisco, 19 Nov 1980. Thanks to Michael Corcoran for new information researched & published in 'The Soul of Blind Willie Johnson: Retracing the life of the Texas music icon', *Austin American-Statesman*, Austin, TX, *nia*, & e-mail to this writer, 7 Aug 2003.]

Johnson, Lonnie [1889 - 1970] Alonzo Johnson was born in New Orleans, probably on February 8, 1889, and grew up to be one of the most important of all blues guitarists. He had a formidable technique and influenced everyone, from ROBERT JOHNSON (no relation) to JIMI HENDRIX.

He is one of the artists whose pre-war work was heard early in the revival period because he was represented (by his 1928 recording of 'Careless Love') on Sam Charters' highly influential 1959 *Country Blues* LP, though he was a city-dwelling, sophisticated man and artist who also swapped solos with Louis Armstrong on the latter's crucial 1927 jazz recordings, featured on Duke Ellington's early classic 'The Mooche' and made classic duet recordings with white jazz guitarist Eddie Lang. He was also well travelled: he had visited London, for instance, as early as 1917.

He enjoyed an unexpected hit at the age of almost 60 with his 1947 recording of 'Tomorrow Night', written by Sam Coslow and Will Grosz in 1939 and recorded that year by sickly outfits like Horace Heidt & His Orchestra (vocal by the Heidt-Lights). The song began its real life as a black-market ballad hit when Johnson released it in 1948. He sold a million, and it kept him going for years.

ELVIS PRESLEY was 13 years old at the time. It's been suggested that he would have been reminded of 'Tomorrow Night' by LaVern Baker, who put it on the B-side of her 1954 hit 'Tweedle-Dee' (which we know Elvis covered in live performance, as soon as it was a hit: a performance live at the Louisiana Hayride in Shreveport in 1955 is available on the misleadingly titled *Elvis: The First Live Recordings*). But in fact Elvis' 'Tomorrow Night', backed only by Scotty Moore's guitar, was cut at Sun on September 10, 1954, before LaVern Baker's was recorded, let alone issued. Elvis' version is in any case markedly similar to Lonnie Johnson's in sound, feel and delivery.

It remained unissued till 1965, when it was doctored—a bridge cut out, many things overdubbed—and put out on a ragbag album called *Elvis for Everyone*. In 1985 the proper version was issued on the *Reconsider Baby* album, and reappeared on the Elvis 1950s box set, issued the same year Bob Dylan issued his own version—which showed very little Lonnie Johnson influence—on *Good as I Been to You*.

When Dylan performed this live in his exemplary concerts of early 1993, he varied his acoustic guitar intro enormously from one night to another; at least once he was using the guitar intro from *another* Lonnie Johnson ballad track, 'No Love for Sale', recorded by Johnson as late as 1960—the very period in which Dylan was able to catch Johnson in and around Greenwich Village.

This was when Dylan had encountered Johnson first: for Johnson was one of those treasures of the pre-war world who was still around in the 1960s, when Dylan arrived in New York—and for VICTORIA SPIVEY's label the two men even appeared on the same album, *Three Kings & the Queen* (recorded in early 1962 and released in late 1964). Dylan had watched Lonnie Johnson's fingers at work on the guitar—Johnson had introduced and/or popularised a number of techniques as a younger man, and still knew his way around the strings in a super-professional, individual way, and Dylan was acutely aware of his value as a guitar mentor. In *Chronicles Volume One*, in 2004, Dylan gives what appears to be a deliberately mystifying account—an account that purports to be a detailed explanation but in fact explains nothing that any other musician has been able to claim to understand—of significant things Johnson taught him in person: indeed a whole new style of playing, apparently, 'something more active with more definition of presence', that Dylan says rescued him when he felt marooned by an inability to relate to his own repertoire in the second half of the 1980s:

> 'I didn't invent this style. It had been shown to me in the early '60s by Lonnie Johnson. . . . [He] took me aside one night and showed me a style of playing based on an odd- instead of an even-number system. . . . He said, "This might help you," and I had the idea that he was showing me something secretive, though it didn't make sense to me at the time. . . . It's a highly controlled system of playing and relates to the notes of a scale, how they combine numerically, how they form melodies out of triplets and are axiomatic to the rhythm and the chord changes. . . . now all of a sudden it came back to me, and I

realized that this way of playing would revitalize my world.'

Johnson's last recordings, singing and playing guitar alone, were made for Folkways in New York City in 1967 and yielded two albums: *Tears Don't Fall No More* and *Mr. Trouble*. Lonnie Johnson died from his injuries on June 16, 1970, after being hit by a car in Toronto. He was 81 years old.

[Lonnie Johnson: 'Careless Love', NY, 16 Nov 1928, *The Country Blues*, RBF RF-1, NY, 1959; 'Tomorrow Night', Cincinnati, 10 Dec 1947, LP-issued *Lonesome Road*, King LP 520, Cincinnati, 1956, CD-reissued *Lonnie Johnson 1946–1963: Tomorrow Night*, Blues Encore CD 52016, Italy, 1991 (Johnson re-recorded the song a few months later, Detroit, 1948, for the Paradise label, issued with a cut by George Dawson's Chocolateers on the B-side, Paradise 110, Detroit, *nia*; this excursion to Paradise seems odd, because it came in the midst of the many sessions Johnson did for King 1947 to 1952); 'No Love for Sale' & 'I Don't Hurt Anymore', Englewood Cliffs, NJ, 8 Mar 1960, *Blues By Lonnie Johnson*, Bluesville LP 1007 & Original Blues Classics OBC 502, *nia*; CD-reissued Original Blues Classics OBCCD 502, *nia* (the same Johnson session included 'I Don't Hurt Anymore', which Dylan recorded on the Basement Tapes in Woodstock, NY, Jun 1967); *Tears Don't Fall No More*, NY, 1967, Folkways LP 3577, NY, *nia* & *Mr. Trouble*, NY, 1967, Folkways LP 3578, NY, *nia*. Louis Armstrong (with Lonnie Johnson): 'Savoy Blues', I'm Not Rough' and 'Hotter Than That', *The Hot Fives & Hot Sevens, Vol. II*, Columbia CK44422, NY, c.1953. Bob Dylan: 'Tomorrow Night', London, 8 & 12 Feb 1993. (The latter is the better performance.)]

Johnson, Robert [1911 - 1938] Robert Leroy Johnson was born in Hazelhurst, Mississippi, on May 8, 1911, the son of a labourer and a partner who had been abandoned by her first husband, but with whom she left Robert when he was very young. Moving in with a Robinsonville, MS, sharecropper in 1916, she resumed responsibility for young Robert in 1918. He grew up playing harmonica before taking up the guitar around 1929–not, in other words, fired by any precociously youthful fervour. He was fortunate enough to have, in the Robinsonville of 1930, that giant of the blues SON HOUSE as an exemplar (along with Son's fellow musician Willie Brown), from whom he picked up some repertoire and some aspects of style. He has become, posthumously, the single most widely revered figure in the entire history of the blues. Only two photographs of him are known to exist, and he was dead within months of turning 27.

Between the playing Son House heard as from a tyro in 1930 to the dazzling mastery with which he astonished the older man a year later, Johnson travelled and studied with an Alabama guitarist, Ike Zinnerman. He travelled again throughout the Delta in 1932–33, picking up further repertoire, via Johnny Temple, from SKIP JAMES, and by 1934 was including Helena, Arkansas, in his orbit of places to land up, play and find domestic obligement in.

In October 1936 he went to see the great white talent scout H.C. Speir in his shop in Jackson, MS, auditioned for him and as a result recorded 16 titles over three days that November for ARC (the American Recording Corporation) in San Antonio, Texas. From these sessions came Johnson's only successful record, 'Kind-Hearted Woman Blues' coupled with 'Terraplane Blues', a celebration of the Hudson automobile company's unusually light, and therefore speedy, stylish car, introduced in 1932, not without a drawing of erotic metaphors about oil, spark plugs and a rival driver.

This success was never repeated, and after a long trip north with Johnny Shines and his fugitive cousin Calvin, taking in St. Louis, Chicago, New York and Windsor, Ontario, Robert Johnson returned to Texas for a fourth and fifth ARC session, this time in Dallas, at which he recorded 13 more songs over two days in July 1937. Of these, few were issued and none was a commercial success. He left the studios, travelled, womanised and performed, and outside Greenwood, Mississippi, in circumstances that remain of alluring mystery, he died in great pain, officially of syphilis but probably after being poisoned, on August 16, 1938.

It was outside Greenwood, just 25 years later, that the young Bob Dylan was singing to black farm-workers–and singing 'Only a Pawn in Their Game', a brave song about politics and the manipulation of race relations but also memorialising another slain young black man, MEDGAR EVERS. His killer too came from Greenwood.

As blues researchers Stephen Calt and Gayle Dean Wardlow have emphasised, Robert Johnson's reputation is almost wholly retrospective: 'Between January and October of 1937 Johnson's commercial sponsors issued nine of his records, averaging one new release every month. Its [sic] first offering, "Terraplane Blues" and "Kind-Hearted Woman", proved to be his most successful work and probably served as the justification of his return session in Dallas seven months after the first. . . . The session produced no commercially successful sides, and when his ARC contract expired in June of 1938, he was not returned to the studio. At the age of 26, Johnson was a record industry has-been.'

You could add that even in retrospect, Johnson has only become a giant of 20th century music among white aficionados. The overwhelming majority of African-American music enthusiasts in the United States today who are familiar with the names MUDDY WATERS and B.B. King have still never heard of Robert Johnson. Veteran blues field-recordist Peter B. Lowry, whose 1970s work contributed greatly to our knowledge of the Piedmont Blues and of figures within it like Buddy Moss and BLIND WILLIE McTELL, puts it most strongly: 'Writing a history of the blues by focusing on Robert

Johnson,' he argues, 'is like writing a history of the automobile and focusing on the Edsel. Both failures in their intended marketplace.'

Nevertheless, Robert Johnson is not to be knocked off the pedestal on which an appreciation of his incomparable improvisational strengths as a wordsmith and as a guitarist of near-incomprehensible dexterity have placed him. His sound is fluid, sexy, volatile; his songs, which are mostly conjured up from other people's material (but then, the blues was a communal process), run a dazzling gamut from lone despair to delirious flirtation and intimate communion, and his voice is agile, elastic, light-stepping and yet heartfelt, in touch with both the ancient field holler and trembling, youthful heat.

If his work represents the glorious triumph of lasting artistic value over short-term commercial worth, it also illustrates the impact of vinyl reissues in the blues revival years. Collectors could pass around old 78s, and reel-to-reel tape copies, but in Robert Johnson's case it was the compilation and issue by JOHN HAMMOND (who had sat up and taken notice of Johnson's first 78, back in 1936) on a Columbia LP, *Robert Johnson: King of the Delta Blues Singers*, in 1961, which rocketed Johnson up there among the stars.

This would soon enough bring Johnson into the orb of the young Brits who were re-fashioning the blues and re-exporting it to the States—an LP by JOHN MAYALL & the Bluesbreakers featuring ERIC CLAPTON included Johnson's 'Ramblin' on My Mind' in 1966, the same year Cream's début LP *Fresh Cream* included his 'From Four Until Late'. But before that, Johnson's recordings established themselves at the heart of the Greenwich Village repertoire. Hammond gave Dylan an advance copy of Johnson's album in late summer 1961, and he reacted with a strength of feeling and wonderment only equalled by his earlier response to hearing WOODY GUTHRIE. Dylan writes in *Chronicles Volume One*: 'I'd never heard of Robert Johnson, never heard the name, *never seen it on any of the compilation blues records* [emphasis added]. . . . I immediately differentiated between him and anyone else I had ever heard. The songs weren't customary blues pieces. They were perfected pieces. . . . utterly fluid. . . . They jumped all over the place in range and subject matter, short punchy verses that resulted in some panoramic story. . . . Johnson's voice and guitar were ringing the room and I was mixed up in it.'

Dylan describes the discussion he has with DAVE VAN RONK, in which Van Ronk very reasonably hears what Johnson has taken from elsewhere—from Skip James and Leroy Carr and so on (elsewhere in the book Dylan himself says how much Robert learnt from LONNIE JOHNSON)—and Dylan just as reasonably hears the man's originality, and explains it by offering the parallel with Guthrie, conceding that he had taken a lot from THE CARTER FAMILY but so put his own spin on it that he became a great original. You could say the same about Dylan, of course, in time. You can say it of any great artist. Originality comes from what you do with what's there, not by devising some ungrounded novelty: that kind of 'originality' never lasts or adds to the great chain that stretches link by link from the art of the deep past to the combustible present.

Dylan spends several more pages describing Johnson's 'elemental' strengths and the effect of this 'fearsome apparition' who 'had come into the room'—and most especially he is interested in describing how the 'highly sophisticated business' of Johnson's song structures, his freedom and his 'startling economy of lines'—and he concludes that if he hadn't heard the Hammond compilation when he did, 'there probably would have been hundreds of lines of mine that would have been shut down—that I wouldn't have felt free enough or upraised enough to write.'

In smaller, more specific ways, we can look back and hear Robert Johnson's work beating like a heart inside Dylan's own songs—so that it's entirely appropriate that the cover of that crucial Johnson LP is shown within the cover photograph on Dylan's first electric album, the one with the equally apt title, *Bringing It All Back Home*. By this time he had long since passed an early phase of including Johnson songs in his own folkie repertoire—as at the Gaslight in October 1962 when he performs 'Kind Hearted Woman Blues' that he segues into '32-20 Blues' (unfortunately a track omitted from the *Live at the Gaslight* album) and as when that same year he recorded a version of 'Milk Cow Blues' (also unreleased) that used part of Kokomo Arnold's lyric, part of PRESLEY's, part of LEADBELLY's 'Good Morning Blues' and part of Robert Johnson's 'Milkcow's Calf Blues', shuffling these elements around in the course of two takes.

On the great *Highway 61 Revisited* blues 'It Takes a Lot to Laugh, It Takes a Train to Cry', Dylan's last verse begins with 'Wintertime is coming'; on Johnson's 'Come on in My Kitchen', his last verse begins 'Wintertime's coming'; it isn't far from the opening line of Johnson's 'Honeymoon Blues'—'Betty Mae, Betty Mae, you shall be my wife someday'—to Dylan's opening line on that *Desire* outtake: 'Rita May, Rita May, you got your body in the way.' Nor is it far from Johnson's 'Little Queen of Spades' line 'Everybody says she got a mojo' (not original to Johnson, but there all the same) to Dylan's 'New Pony' line, 'Everybody says you're using voodoo'. And on Dylan's *Slow Train Coming* outtake 'Trouble in Mind', a 1979 neo-blues with a classic blues title, he may have taken his 'Miss So-and-so' directly from Robert Johnson's 'Ramblin' on My Mind'. Even the 'all-night girls' of 'Visions of Johanna' echo the 'Saturday-night women' of Johnson's 'Stop Breaking Down Blues'. Then there's Robert Johnson's 'I Believe I'll Dust My Broom'

(1936), in which 'I don't want no woman wants any downtown man she meet / She's a no-good donay, they shouldn't allow her on the street.' This couplet—retained word for word by Elmore James in his 1950s hit versions of 'Dust My Broom'—is interesting for being, as it were, at once Johnsonian and Dylanesque. It begins with a back-echo of that line in Dylan's 'Need a Woman' about wanting a woman '. . . who don't make herself up to make every man her friend' (Johnson's doubling of 'want' replaced neatly by Dylan's doubling of 'make'), and ends with the comic 'they shouldn't allow her on the street': which, both as idea and cadence, Dylan might easily have used verbatim. You can hear him muttering that one very well, italicising 'street' as he goes.

When Dylan published his own selected *Writings and Drawings* in 1972, no wonder it was dedicated in part 'To the magnificent Woodie [sic] Guthrie and Robert Johnson who sparked it off'. In 1978, a year during which Dylan draws especially deeply and recurrently from the waters of the blues, as evidenced by that year's world tour—on which within 114 concerts he gave a total of 109 performances of six different blues songs by people from Tampa Red to Willie Dixon, as well as a remarkable re-write of his own 'Going Going Gone', riddled with Johnson's words: cascading Johnson's lines out to 69 different audiences.

That year's album, *Street Legal*, too, which is at least as soaked in the blues as any work of his before or since, is one within which Dylan seems to cut a wrist to mingle his own work-blood with that of Robert Johnson—though in every case, as usual, Johnson's is not the only presence on this busy street. How inward Dylan is with this predecessor's work: again and again he tends to put the direct blues phrases into his non-blues songs. A line from 'Changing of the Guards' that arguably sums up that song, 'my last deal gone down', is an elision from Johnson's title 'Last Fair Deal Gone Down'. In 'Where Are You Tonight (Journey Through Dark Heat)', 'horseplay and disease are killing me by degrees'; in Johnson's 'Preachin' Blues' it is *the blues itself* which is 'a low-down achin' heart disease / Like consumption, killing me by degrees', though this is but a variation on a widely mobilised pair of lines, on any of which Bob Dylan's might be drawing. The same Dylan song gives us 'he should have stayed where his money was green', a phrase he might be picking up from, or have been reminded of its existence by, Johnson's 'Little Queen of Spades', whose eighth line runs 'Let's put we/us heads together, ooh fair brown then we can make our money green'.

Another line in Dylan's 'journey through dark heat' is this: 'I bit into the root of forbidden fruit with the juice running down my leg.' Though this numinous evocation of sinful sex is built up from a common-stock base, it makes compelling sense that Dylan should be quoting here from Johnson's 'Traveling Riverside Blues'. Elsewhere we can find, as in Joe Williams' 'I Want It Awful Bad', 'You squeezed my lemon, caused my juice to run', or as in Charlie Pickett's 'Let Me Squeeze Your Lemon', 'Now let me squeeze your lemon baby until my love comes down' (repeated without significant variation by Bo Chatman's 'Let Me Roll Your Lemon' and Sonny Boy Williamson I's 'Until My Love Comes Down') but Robert Johnson's lyric, offering this—'Now you can squeeze my lemon till the juice run down my leg' is the only one that, like Dylan, specifies the *leg*.

Another non-blues song on *Street Legal* is 'Is Your Love in Vain?', a title that enfolds within it Johnson's title 'Love in Vain'. But Dylan also seems to have one ear on Sonny Boy Williamson in 1978. Dylan's title might carry its echo of Robert Johnson both directly and by relay from WILLIAMSON II's 'All My Love in Vain' (not the same song), which was cut at the same splendid session as the Williamson song Bob Dylan performed with THE PLUGZ on US TV in 1984, 'Don't Start Me (to) Talkin''. It could be from either, and so could the echo in that other *Street Legal* title, 'Baby, Stop Crying'. Of course Dylan could have arrived at this without any back-echoes, as it were: it's no big deal as a phrase or as a notion. On the other hand you can't but notice that Robert Johnson's 'Stop Breakin' Down Blues' is a song with several Dylan connections, and that one is its baby-stop-crying imprecation, repeated many times: 'Stop breakin' down, please, stop breakin' down'. Sonny Boy Williamson's 'Stop Crying', recorded several times, presses the same plea: 'baby please, please stop crying'.

A very different Dylan creation that certainly hides a Robert Johnson line within it, and just where you wouldn't expect one, is in his 1963 'Last Thoughts on Woody Guthrie'. It's a poem almost as far from the blues as you can get; but when you've been listening to a lot of Robert Johnson, and then you hear Dylan reach for the conclusion of this lengthy poem with the simple and anonymous yet insistent, didactic line 'And though it's only my opinion, I may be right or wrong', you're bound to hear behind it Johnson's 'Baby it's your opinion, oh I may be right or wrong' and 'It's your opinion, friend-girl, I may be right or wrong', which come from the two recordings of Johnson's 'When You Got a Good Friend', one of which was on that seminal 1961 LP, issued 16 months before Dylan's performance of his poem at New York Town Hall in April 1963.

As the 1960s and 1970s progressed, and Robert Johnson's posthumous reputation grew, he also became an industry—though one that was slow to start. Columbia's *Robert Johnson: King of the Delta Blues Singers, Volume 2* was issued only in 1970; and as late as 1969, when Paul Oliver first published his pioneering book *The Story of the Blues*, it was still thought that no photo of Johnson existed. The excellent one we know today—no mere snapshot but a studio portrait—was 'discovered' but sat on by putative biographer Mack McCormick in 1971, and then in 1973 it was acquired and sat on instead, as was the other extant shot found later, by researcher Stephen C. LaVere, who duly acquired the copyrights not only on these two photographs but also on Robert Johnson's songs—and by 1991 was already hundreds of thousands of dollars the richer as a result: not least because Columbia Records decided that to pay LaVere was cheaper than contesting the case through the courts. The full scandal of this was examined in Robert Gordon's excellent piece 'The Devil's Work: The Plundering of Robert Johnson' in *LA Weekly* in July 1991.

Quite apart from the illegitimacy of LaVere's claim on Johnson's copyright, granted the communal nature of such songs in general, and the many clear specific debts owed by Johnson's songs to specific songs associated with other people—on which subjects see **ridin' the blinds without Robert Johnson** (and the interesting Yazoo album *The Roots of Robert Johnson*, which compiles related recordings by others that predate his)—the LaVere coup seemed laughably unjustifiable on every level from legal nicety to natural justice. It's also a measure of the scale of the Robert Johnson industry that all this happened, and that a number of legal actions and counter-actions have taken place more recently so that the current situation—Johnson's septuagenarian son Claud established as rightful heir, LaVere out of the picture—may not be the end of the story.

The artistic battle has surely been permanently won. The digitally re-mastered 2-CD set *Robert Johnson: The Complete Recordings* was issued in 1990. In May 1993, at Bob Dylan's solo acoustic sessions for his *World Gone Wrong* album, one of the songs he recorded but didn't release was, 30 years on from the Gaslight performance, Robert Johnson's '32–20 Blues'.

[Robert Johnson: 'Kind Hearted Woman Blues' (2 takes), 'I Believe I'll Dust My Broom', 'Sweet Home Chicago' (2 takes), 'Ramblin' on My Mind' (3 takes), 'When You Got a Good Friend', 'Come on in My Kitchen' (2 takes), 'Terraplane Blues', 'Phonograph Blues' (2 takes), San Antonio, TX, 23 Nov 1936; '32-20 Blues' (2 takes), San Antonio, 26 Nov 1936; 'They're Red Hot', 'Dead Shrimp Blues', 'Cross Road Blues' (2 takes), 'Walkin' Blues', 'Last Fair Deal Gone Down' (2 takes), 'Preachin' Blues' (2 takes), 'If I Had Possession Over Judgment Day', San Antonio, 27 Nov 1936; 'Stones in My Passway', 'I'm a Steady Rollin' Man', 'From Four Till Late', Dallas, TX, 19 Jun 1937; 'Hell Hound on My Trail', 'Little Queen of Spades' (2 takes), 'Malted Milk', 'Drunken Hearted Man' (2 takes), 'Me and the Devil Blues' (2 takes), 'Stop Breakin' Down Blues' (2 takes), 'Traveling Riverside Blues', 'Honeymoon Blues', 'Love in Vain' (2 takes), 'Milkcow's Calf Blues' (2 takes), Dallas, 20 Jun 1937. *Robert Johnson: King of the Delta Blues Singers*, Columbia CL-1654, NY, 1961; *Robert Johnson: King of the Delta Blues Singers, Volume 2*, Columbia C-30034, NY, 1970; *Robert Johnson: The Complete Recordings*, Columbia/Legacy Roots N' Blues 46222, US, 1990.

Various Artists: *The Roots of Robert Johnson*, Yazoo L1073, US, 1986, CD-reissued Yazoo CD1073, 1991. Kokomo Arnold: 'Milk Cow Blues', Chicago, 10 Sep 1934; Peetie *Wheatstraw and Kokomo Arnold*, Blues Classics BC-4, Berkeley, CA, 1960. Leadbelly: 'Good Morning Blues', NY, 15 Jun 1940, or NY, summer 1943.

Bob Dylan, *Chronicles Volume One*, 2004, pp.281–288; *Writings and Drawings*, New York: Knopf, 1972. Stephen Calt & Gayle Dean Wardlow, 'Robert Johnson', *78 Quarterly* vol.1 no.4, Key West, FL, 1989. Peter B. Lowry, Australia, phone interview by this writer, 14 Sep 2004. Robert Gordon: 'The Devil's Work: The Plundering of Robert Johnson' (with research assistance by Tara McAdams), *LA Weekly*, 5–11 Jul 1991.]

Johnston, Bob [1932 -]. Donald William Johnston was born in Hillsboro, Texas (about 50 miles south of Dallas-Fort Worth), on May 14, 1932, into a family of songwriting women. His grandmother co-wrote 'When Irish Eyes Are Smiling', his mother wrote for singing-cowboy star Gene Autry and in the 1950s she and Bob co-wrote material for rockabilly artist Mac Curtis. Johnston tried to make it as a singer too, putting out a début single, 'Born to Love One Woman', as by Don Johnston, in late 1956—a bog-standard rockabilly record but with a clever way of making one verse's end slide along to become the start of the next—and he followed it up with the rather less appealing 'Whistle Bait', issued on two different labels in 1957, and finally, in 1958, 'I'm Hypnotized' (as by Don Johnson); but he quit after feeling humiliated on a Los Angeles package-tour date 'sandwiched between Tommy Sands and RICKY NELSON . . . with all the little girls hollering "We want Ricky! We want Ricky!" . . . It was embarrassing. I looked like shit 'cause I didn't have any money, and he looked like four million dollars. I thought, "This isn't a good way to earn a living."'

He turned back to writing and took up producing and arranging. With Joy Byers, his future wife, he co-wrote (uncredited for contractual reasons) the great Timi Yuro's 'What's a Matter Baby?', surely one of the best, most shudderingly ferocious pop records ever made, and, rather harder to feel proud about, a slew of songs for 1960s ELVIS PRESLEY movies. Then, at this point working in New York, he happened to produce a comeback hit for Patti Page, which gained him access to bigger, newer stars. He was working under JOHN HAMMOND ('my mentor all the way down the line') and told Hammond that above all else, he wanted to produce Bob Dylan.

How that turned into reality, starting with *Highway 61 Revisited*, he doesn't know, beyond hearing rumours that Dylan and ALBERT GROSSMAN were tired of using TOM WILSON. Dylan reportedly didn't know how the change was effected either: he's supposed to have said 'I don't know. One night

Wilson was there and the next night Johnston was there.' In fact, Wilson produced the first two sessions, the June 15 & 16, 1965 sessions; Johnston produced the three later sessions, on July 29 & 30 and August 2. It was Wilson, therefore, who produced 'Like a Rolling Stone' but Johnson who produced all the rest.

Wilson might have gone because he questioned Dylan's decision to turn up the organ in the mix on 'Like a Rolling Stone', though as AL KOOPER testifies, he had been 'gracious' enough to let Kooper play it in the first place. But with Johnston there was no questioning. His policy, at least with Dylan, was always that not dictating from behind the desk could yield richer rewards, via happenstance. 'I never cared what he did and I never cared what he did in the studio. I was trying to get down *anything* he was doing next, so we could have a *record* of it. . . . I told everybody . . . "Just keep playing: don't stop–we can always overdub somebody else but you can't make him go back and do that song again." . . . I thought Dylan's music was so important, what he was doing and what he was putting down. It was *joyous* to me. . . . Whenever he'd ask me, "What do you think?" I'd say, "What possible difference could it make, what I think?"'

When Johnston did make a suggestion–that Dylan should try recording down in Nashville, Tennessee, some time–'They got no clocks down there, and they've got a really great bunch of musicians: everybody really cares', Dylan was noncommittal but Grossman and company president Bill Gallagher pulled him aside and said if he *ever* mentioned Nashville to Dylan again, he'd be fired. In due course, Dylan decided to try it: which is why half of that ultra-modern city album *Blonde on Blonde* comes from the deeply conservative heart of the country music industry.

Johnston went on to produce *John Wesley Harding*, *Nashville Skyline*, *Self Portrait* and *New Morning* (plus the sessions from which Columbia constructed the *Dylan* album). Compared to this towering list of credits, it is bathetic to add that his own songs have been recorded by Bill Haley, JOAN BAEZ, Ricky Nelson and Aretha Franklin, or that he also produced FLATT & SCRUGGS' *Nashville Airplane*, SIMON & Garfunkel's *Bookends* and JOHNNY CASH's *Live at San Quentin*.

[Don Johnston: 'Born to Love One Woman' c/w 'How Many', Mercury 70991X45, US, 1956; 'Whistle Bait' c/w 'The Whisperer', Algonquin AR-717, NY, 1957 & Chic 1014, Thomasville, GA, 1957. Don Johnson: 'I'm Hypnotized' c/w 'Luigi', Dot 45-15812, US, 1958. Timi Yuro: 'What's a Matter Baby', Liberty, US, 1962.

Bob Johnston quotes and much background detail from the interview by Richard Younger, *On the Tracks* no.20, Grand Junction, CO, *nia*. (Richard Younger is the author of *Get a Shot of Rhythm & Blues: The Arthur Alexander Story*, Tuscaloosa, AL: University of Alabama Press, 2000.)]

'Jokerman' [song, 1983] 'Jokerman' is the magnum opus of the *Infidels* album: a song you can inhabit, as you can so much of Bob Dylan's earlier work. It isn't a sermon or a pop song but a real creation, a work you can wander inside, explore, breathe in, pass through, wrap around you. It looks different in different lights. It's always shifting, but this is because it's alive, not because it's nebulous (though it may be that too). Its complexity isn't off-putting, nor distancing. On the contrary, Dylan sings you through the complexity with almost as much generosity of expression, almost as much bestowing of concentrated warmth, as he gives out on, say, 'Sad-Eyed Lady of the Lowlands', a nebulous and complicated song from another lifetime.

It is as much the warmth as the substance of 'Jokerman' that makes it such a welcome item in Dylan's corpus. The two qualities cohere in Dylan's openness towards the listener in confessing his fondness for the song itself, and in his palpable desire to communicate it (a desire often absent in 1980s Dylan).

You wouldn't necessarily use the word 'substance' of 'Jokerman' when you first hear the recording. On the contrary you might find it a curiously skeletal thing, as if it were the piece of paper with the dots on from which you might construct and colour in a Bob Dylan Song By Numbers. This effect is owing partly to the sparsity of its sound (an attractive sparsity, but an undeniable one) and partly to the way in which the song's title and the words of its chorus seem like pale, thin shadows of that great prototypical Dylan song, 'Mr. Tambourine Man': 'Jokerman dance to the nightingale tune, / Bird fly high by the light of the moon, / Oh— Jokerman.' Not only does this remind us of 'Mr. Tambourine Man', but it reads more like somebody's notes, a hasty summary of a lyric heard fleetingly, than like a finished lyric. Strip it down by only two or three more words (the definite articles) and it could be one of HARRY SMITH's celebrated summaries–'JOKERMAN DANCE TO NIGHTINGALE TUNE. BIRD FLY HIGH BY LIGHT OF MOON. OH OH JOKERMAN'–directly comparable, for instance, to his summary of the song 'Present Joys': 'PRAISE LORD OF HEAVEN AND EARTH PRESENTS JOYS PASSING FAST. HEAVEN AT LAST.'

The chorus of 'Jokerman' may be skeletal and derivative, fleshed out only by Dylan's extraordinary vocal resourcefulness (naturally he never sings it the same way twice), but the verses are richly textured and freely imaginative–carefully, densely structured yet rhapsodically fluent blocks of writing that glow with inspiration, recognisably of Bob Dylan's making without ever being 'Dylanesque'. There are many lightly thrown out biblical allusions, but the lightness makes clear that these are valued more for their relishable poetics than for any sermonising usefulness. Starry-eyed and laughing with deft, acute touches only

Bob Dylan could alchemise, in the writing and performance, 'Jokerman' is essentially a song like no other.

Sometimes Dylan seems to be singing about himself and sometimes about Jesus, but the whole is too fluid to need from the listener any analytic effort at separation. The intertwining of the two is, in any case, part of what the song evokes, one theme of 'Jokerman' being a recurring self-mockery that laughs at the superficial parallels between Dylan, mythic public figure and Artist-Creator, and Christ, mythic public figure and Son of the Creator. The post-Evangelical Period Dylan seems ruefully to acknowledge here that there had been foolish moments when he had taken such parallels solemnly. Yet Dylan also seems sceptical of the idea that Christ's powers are wholly a good thing—and this in turn suggests both another rueful parallel (a real resemblance between two questionable heroes) and one further opportunity to instance the singer's own failings; for to admit to such scepticism is to confess another failure: to confess that even in his much-vaunted embrace of Christ, he is now faltering.

Thus the song begins with a nice mockery of superheroes and the singer's own mythic pretensions, in an opening verse that at once reveals that here is a work of a high order—chiselled, clever, complex, compressed and unapologetically articulate, yet carrying itself lightly, with likeable grace and poise, entirely free of solemnity or the didactic, and delivered with unguarded generosity of spirit: 'Standing on the waters casting your bread / While the eyes of the idol with the iron head are glowing. / Distant ships sailing into the mist / You were born with a snake in both of your fists while a hurricane was blowing.'

There is so much here, and so adroitly put together. The opening line neatly combines Christ's walking on the water, a New Testament story emphasising his Godly power, with the well-known proverb 'Cast your bread upon the waters: for thou shalt find it after many days', an Old Testament injunction to humankind from Ecclesiastes and the textual basis for the Jewish Passover ritual, in which people take bags of breadcrumbs and throw them into the river to symbolise the casting out of their sins—hence Dylan's lovely 'breadcrumb sins' in 'Gates of Eden'.

The combining of these two biblical moments in one modest line is one of Dylan's skilful and intelligent achievements, quietly acerbic and inspired, like one of his bumpings-together of two clichés. It makes for a splendid piece of self-mockery, since it evokes so simply yet vividly the picture of the pretender, the 'Jokerman'. Christ is not only Godlike but *purposive*: He 'went unto them, walking on the sea'; but Dylan refuses '*Walking* on the water', despite the tempting alliterative appeal of that phrase for use in a song sewn through with alliteration and internal rhyming. He chooses instead to show himself caught in the comically functionless, dithering position of 'Standing on the waters'. The implication is of 'standing around'; its effect is to stress the physical impossibility of the act. You can almost credit that by a swift and light enough stepping forward, a not staying in one place long enough to put your weight on it, you might briefly walk across water; you cannot but picture that standing still will make you sink. That the self Dylan is addressing here is standing there casting his bread emphasises that his real position, far from being God-like, is that of the humble sinner quite rightly in the act of contrition. The contrast between that hopeless bravado and this humility makes the situation still more comic.

The conjunction of the two biblical allusions in 'Jokerman's' opening line achieves a further compression of meaning, deepening the import of the song. What Dylan bumps together here are two texts that are associated with opposite notions: faith and doubt. Christ's walking on water shows him urging upon his followers one of his favourite messages, namely that anything can be achieved if you have sufficient faith. Peter tries walking on the water immediately after Christ, and fails, we're told, only through lack of wholehearted faith. (This insistence on the power of faith—on its superhuman physical power: power like a mythic hero's—is alluded to again in at least two other lines of 'Jokerman'.) But Dylan bumps his allusion to this into his allusion to a proverb from Ecclesiastes—famously the one book in the Bible which gives space and patience, a sympathetic airing, to Doubt. (See also **Ecclesiastes, Dylan's use of**.)

It is only after the lovely opening verse that we come to the song's 'skeletal' chorus, and in context it becomes possible to hear the ellipsed simplicity of its words as a balm, a plunge into the unjudgemental natural world after the verse's crowding of ideas and doubt, perfectly matching the way that the musical tension resolves itself as *it* plunges from the end of the verse into the chorus. Let the mind rest. Let the body and the intuition dance. Give inspiration a chance: 'Jokerman dance to the nightingale tune / Bird fly high by the light of the moon / Oh—Jokerman.'

This is not Bob Dylan's first use of the nightingale in his compositions, nor the first to encourage a sense of the presence of Keats behind the lines: a sense that Dylan is consciously re-using Keats' association of the nightingale with the muse, the inspirational power of nature and mystery. There is an early draft of 'Visions of Johanna'—a song that details a particular kind of life in the contemporary city and speaks of the haunting visions that float above it—a draft which Dylan records on two occasions ahead of the main *Blonde on Blonde* sessions (yielding one uneasy, fast version and one sumptuous, slower one), in which Dylan begins the final verse like this: 'The peddler he [now] steps to the road / [Knowing] everything's gone which was owed / He examines the nightingale's code / Still left on [written on] the fishtruck that loads. / My conscience explodes.'

Bill King, in 'The Artist in the Marketplace', hears this song as 'constantly [seeking] to transcend the physical world, to reach the ideal where the visions of Johanna become real. That can never be, and yet life without the quest is worthless: this is the paradox at the heart of "Visions", the same paradox that Keats explored in his "Ode on a Grecian Urn".'

That key Dylan phrase 'the nightingale's code', a lovely and wonderfully short encapsulation of the core idea of how unknowable is the mystery of nature's music, is founded upon a familiarity with another of Keats' four great odes, the 'Ode to a Nightingale': a poem about both poetic inspiration and the fear of its loss. Dylan addresses this theme himself, of course, in 'Mr. Tambourine Man', and it is the correspondences between the Keats poem and 'Mr. Tambourine Man' that are drawn out as far as they will stretch in Nigel Brooks' essay 'The Nightingale's Code: The Influence of John Keats on Bob Dylan', but Brooks also pays some attention to 'Jokerman' in this context. He writes: 'Here is a further song where Dylan is, at least on one level, addressing himself as artist in the guise of the jokerman, the trickster figure, the Fool. . . . responding, in the chorus, to the music of nature as represented by the nightingale. . . . In addition, the nightingale is associated with the moon, just as in Keats' "Ode" where the poet declares of the bird: "Already with thee! tender is the night, / And haply the Queen-Moon is on her throne."'

The moon too is the muse: and always has been. Keats' long work 'Endymion', written shortly before the odes, is based on a legend of the Greek moon goddess; the heroine of Dylan's song 'Isis' is a moon goddess; and the main thrust of ROBERT GRAVES' book *The White Goddess*, the importance of which as an influence on Bob Dylan has been widely stressed, is that the moon goddess inspires poetry endowed with a magical quality.

While the chorus of 'Jokerman' surrenders to the intuition and the dance, invoking the muse of nightingale and moon, the very term 'Jokerman', which it introduces, perpetuates as well as summarises the song's arguments: it is a name that in itself mocks and deflates the idea of the 'superman'—and indeed, as well as its abundant yet shrewdly deployed scriptural allusions, the song holds within it much contemplation of Carl Jung's ideas about the hero myth, and perhaps hints at the similarity between the Jungian idea of 'the shadow' and the Judeao-Christian idea of 'original sin' (as between 'the dragon' and 'the snake').

The core of both is to define the human being as containing within both the light and the dark: insisting that 'evil' is not 'out there', among 'the others', but is inside us all, and that all progress, individual and societal, must be built upon coming to terms with this literally inescapable, fundamental truth. The other way lies war and bloodshed, Hitler and fatwah, hatred and racism across the globe and a stunting immaturity in the heart. 'Jokerman', like so much of Bob Dylan's pre- and post-evangelical work, is written in acute awareness that we cannot just kill the dragons, and, as with most of the post-evangelical songs, sobered by his knowledge that in the evangelical period he did sometimes give way unwisely to that enemy within in the instant that he preached.

The whole song seems to enact the need to grapple with the many-sided: to express, in poetry rather than argument, the uncomfortable truth that there *can* be no choosing anything as straightforward as one position or the other. There is no one or the other. The song is fundamentally an expression of both celebration *and* something more negative: not despair but a rigorous scepticism.

The song flows on, through its dexterous, complex verses and choruses, and we are carried along to the end of verse five, which offers what CHRISTOPHER RICKS calls 'one of the loveliest lines on *Infidels*': 'Only a matter of time 'til night comes stepping in.' So naturally does this quietly emphatic line announce itself, a line so apparently simple and so loaded, that on first hearing you're almost certain to expect that this is to be one of Dylan's 'final ends': it sounds so apt as last line of a last verse.

The finishing end proves not quite at hand. Not only does 'Jokerman' move on through another chorus and on into what really is the song's last verse, its sixth, but Dylan begins this with a line that manages to make that previous 'last line of a last verse' seem no finished thing at all: makes it seem instead to have been only the first half of a rumination about omens in the sky, the second half of which now comes through to us: 'It's a shadowy world, skies are slippery gray.'

Dylan isn't afraid here to open with the most basic of generalisations, one that summarises with the utmost simplicity the song's core argument—and indeed what might be allowed as the core conclusion of human experience, the core truth about human nature, its inherent goodness and badness: the core truth as expressed in the Bible (sin and potential transcendence) and by psychoanalysis (the shadow and the transcendent self) and at the same time expressive of the modern sensibility, the Dylanesque insistence, that unfixity is everywhere, that 'there are no truths outside the gates of Eden'.

Context is all, though. If we encountered 'Eh up, it's a shadowy world' in a song by the Housemartins, or 'It a shadowy world, mon' in a rap from Benjamin Zephaniah, we wouldn't seize on it as a numinous summary of the human predicament. That it can register in this way in 'Jokerman' is because of what has gone before and what comes after.

The before is five verses of a sustained work exploring these themes in poetry of focussed imagination. The after is the remainder of the line itself—and this gives us a phrase as quietly distinctive as the earlier one is quietly anonymous: 'skies are slippery gray'. That 'slippery' is itself slippery, almost by onomatopoeic enactment: the perfect word to fix the particular look of a certain sort of grey sky, and to summarise the imperfect, ungraspable unfixity we live under.

At the end, this last verse prefigures the chorus—more precisely the *end* of the verse prefigures the *end* of the chorus—in reiterating that rueful self-addressed remonstrance 'Oh Jokerman . . . / Oh Jokerman . . .', and these lines end with something close to an explicit lamenting that the singer, most certainly the Jokerman of the title now, knows that wholehearted commitment to Godliness is what Christ requires of each of us (is *all* Christ requires of each of us) yet cannot let go and give it. Rather he must respond in keeping with his troublesome vision of all-prevalent unfixity—in which even Christ is perceived ambiguously. 'Oh Jokerman, you know what he wants, / Oh Jokerman, you don't show any response.'

That is, he must respond with what seems no response at all, though the use of the word 'show' there itself refuses any such neat simplicity. The whole weight of the song, as well as the remonstrative 'Oh Jokerman' in the line itself, presses us to feel here that while Jokerman doesn't 'show' any response, the turmoil within is strong and inescapable. The importation of part of the *chorus*, that 'Oh Jokerman . . . / Oh Jokerman . . .', into the *verse*, is also a technical indication that we are reaching the end of the song. It's exactly what Dylan does at the end of that neglected 1978 song 'No Time to Think', in which the title-phrase occurs only in the chorus—until we reach the last verse, when the bulk of it takes over as the repeated opening phrase: 'No time to . . . / No time to . . . / No time to . . . / No time to . . .'

In both songs, repeating a key phrase from the chorus in a verse has the same function: it signals that the end is imminent. It does this by way of suggesting that a summing-up is being offered—and a summing-up is of course the beginning of the end.

'Jokerman' does indeed then end, with one last chorus: one last dropping of the argument in favour of the dance. Yet this cannot be fully entered into either: the finishing end is one last stepping-back, one last compunction to qualify (one foot drawing back while the other advances), in the renewed self-deprecation of that very last 'Oh—— Jokerman!'

Nor is the invocation of the dance free of the process of argument: it is after all an assertion of the *idea* of renewal, of the *concept* of submission to the muse. And it insists, as the verses do, on the impossibility of unconditional surrender to any fixed position. AIDAN DAY writes: 'It's a dance invested with paradox in that it is both a dance of death and a dance of life: a dance simultaneously of matter and spirit.' He also describes it as 'at once a dance of death and a flight of the soul by a light that governs both creativity and waste.' Day points out how trenchantly T.S. ELIOT analyses such dance within the poem 'Burnt Norton', and quotes this Eliot passage: 'Neither flesh nor fleshless; / Neither from nor towards; at the still point, there the dance is, / But neither arrest nor movement. And do not call it fixity . . .'

Clearly this is argument as well as poetry. 'And do not call it fixity . . .' brings us full circle back to the central argument of the verses of 'Jokerman': that there can be no fixity. 'Neither flesh nor fleshless . . .': we're back in the unfixed terrain between the flesh and the spirit, between death and re-birth, between the Trickster and the transcendent self, and in the unfixed terrain which is unfixed because nothing, not even the figure of Christ, can be singularly anything.

Nor, in the end, can the song settle for, in Aidan Day's words, 'containment within [even] a dualistic frame of reference . . . even the usableness of the opposition between time and non-time, life and death, is called into question. . . . Generating questions which it does not resolve, the lyric itself is presented to its audience in the form of a question or riddle. In its refusal to close lies its strength, its commitment to confront and challenge. And in that refusal it epitomizes the most distinctive perspective of Dylan's lyrical career: a continually renewed scepticism regarding the possibility of attaining absolutely final positions and a protest at the paralysing intolerance of such as settle for closed and fixed points of view. The work neither simply despairs nor simply celebrates. Recognising a "hateful siege / Of contraries" it simultaneously exults in that siege.'

It is Day's final point here that most needs stressing: that there is throughout the song not only an *acceptance* of unresolvability—not only some kind of resolute commitment to the notion that no position can command one's resolute commitment—but exultation too.

Part of this exultant spirit, the celebratory, dancing beneficence that pours off the recording even more vividly and recurrently than off the page, seems surely to flow from the sense Dylan has, as it goes along, of what the song is achieving by its sheer concentratedness of application, its sheer wholeness and openness of engagement, its unguarded addressing of big themes resourcefully, maturely and anew. As with 'Mr. Tambourine Man' there is a self-reflexive motor here. The song seems to celebrate inspiration by the sheer display of it. It enjoys itself. It is a pleasurable irony that, as with 'Mr. Tambourine Man', a song that is partly about standing in need of the muse succeeds in possessing it.

At the same time, another part of what 'Jokerman' enjoys about itself is a quite different quality from its handling of large themes. For all the attention given to these themes, the song tends to be at its best when dealing not with the cataclysmic and the Significant but with the quiet and the everyday: the human in the tangible world.

Not that the one order of things doesn't invade the other. Many of the best lines in the song are, you might say, about the weather. Now that weather may be intended as more symbolic than real—it might be brought into play merely to augur this or that—yet somehow in 'Jokerman' real weather seeps in through the constructs of symbolism. Something happens which is in interesting opposition to what the critic John Carey claims when writing about Charles Dickens' use of the weather in his novels: namely that 'In Elizabethan drama the turmoil in the elements which accompanies human misdeeds like the murder of Duncan relates to a system of belief binding man to his universe. By the nineteenth century this kind of sympathetic weather has dwindled to a poetic convenience.'

In 'Jokerman' what lingers, rather, is a sense of how interested in real weather the song is: and how interested in the human compunction to observe it *and* read auguries into it. Spread through the song is a series of notes about the weather in which Dylan is as focussed upon the detail of reality, as intent upon accurate observation of the actual, as upon its correlative symbolic value. This comes through, as implied earlier, in the 'slippery' of 'skies are slippery gray'; in the 'smoke', which is another specifying of a kind of grey, in 'In the smoke of the twilight . . .'; and in the way that these skies are continually looked up at. The song is pervaded by awareness that its events take place out in the elements all the time. Through the mist. Under slippery grey skies. In the smoke of the twilight. The sun sets in the sky. Night comes stepping in. And we remain, even then, out under those skies: 'half-asleep 'neath the stars', and 'by the light of the moon'.

Even the obvious symbolic 'meaning' of the near-detail-free line 'So swiftly the sun sets in the sky' incorporates our mutual recognition (Dylan's and the listener's) that the analogy between the brevity of the day and of human life is not only enriched by being a part of the shared experience of all of humankind but by its being continually renewed with the days themselves.

The rhythm of ever-affecting poignancy is necessarily that of the ever-setting and returning sun itself. The recognition of the analogy, and of its poignancy, is itself part of the quiet, everyday reality of human life: you cannot pass a certain age without your every experience of an actual sunset incorporating, somewhere between the eye and the brain and the heart, its symbolic import also. What Dylan's line communicates, then, is as much humanity and reality as theory and debate. And what clinches this is that its rhythms are entirely devoted to expressing not force of argument but feeling: they give voice to exactly the simple human poignancy of observing the sun set and being touched anew by regret at life's brevity. The line's rhythms enact this brevity and regret. 'So swiftly the sun sets in the sky' is the briefest opening line of any verse in 'Jokerman': nine syllables, delivered as two simple, falling phrases—the one following and repeating the path of the other, but yet more briefly, in a perfectly distilled replication of our experience—with the soft alliteration of its repeated 's' sounds acting as a sighing and a slippage.

Dylan's alertness in these matters has him switching at once from feelings and rhythms of quiet acceptance at the sun's setting to stubbornly resistant corollaries. The sun sets, but 'You rise up and say goodbye to no one'. Against this, however, the elements must inevitably prevail. It's 'Only a matter of time 'til night comes steppin' in': another line in which the symbolic import is founded upon the common human feeling which enriches it, and which is disarmingly expressed. The song also has an eye on the weather and the elements when we arrive at one of the most attractive moments in all of 'Jokerman', the affectionately rendered and lovely scene in which the 'you' of the song is found 'Resting in the fields, far from the turbulent space, / Half asleep 'neath the stars with a small dog licking your face.'

These lines have replaced those of the early-draft version, in which the 'you' of the song is instead 'So drunk, standing in the middle of the street, / Directing traffic with a small dog at your feet.' The re-write is for the better, but what is best is that Dylan makes such a change at all. He's often berated for withholding good work and offering less good, and for re-writing material that could profitably be left untouched. Here is a re-write that improves on every level a couplet that was 'good enough', and so providing an example of Dylan having sufficient incentive to say that 'good enough' wasn't good enough. (That early draft is in circulation among collectors in the form of an outtake from the *Infidels* sessions, and though the singing is yet more lithe on the earlier version, the later re-writes in the lyric are generally improvements.)

Both versions carry Dylan's consciousness that chaos is everywhere, that each of us comes close to barking. It's a compassionate song and a very open one, with Dylan not just mocking himself for the preaching phase but, far more courageously, examining how the things inside which drive us can drive us to the wrong places. This is strong, complex, intelligent writing—in some ways quite beyond what he could have handled in the 1960s. It comes from the Dylan who is unafraid to stand inside the chaos of passion and vulnerability, unafraid of risk and contradiction, prepared to acknowledge the fragility of each individual's hold on sanity and strength. It is, despite the difficult themes and the scriptural foundations, a fluid and imaginative, humane work.

Both studio performances (though more especially the unreleased take) are bathed with the radiance of the song's quintessential warmth, its generosity of heart and spontaneity of spirit. Dylan's voice is marvellously expressive and celebratory as he winds his ever-alert and flexible way through verses as richly baroque as any of his earlier work and a chorus as airy and light-footed as Fred Astaire.

'Jokerman' is always compelling, however its author treats it. Its melody, the long lines of writing, the bounty of its variety, its space—it's always attractive. After spacey studio performances, on which foreboding bass-riffs brood behind vocals of shimmering reverie, there is the glorious amphetamine anarchy of the version performed with THE PLUGZ (aka the Cruzados) on TV in March 1984. In concert in Europe that summer, the song glowers along very differently again, rising above the corporeal and musical torpor of guitarist MICK TAYLOR, impelled by a churning, magnificent grandeur.

Even in Japan a decade later, when Dylan is taking the song fast again and it would demand much energy and precision to deliver the full lines and stay on top of them, and Dylan, regrettably, can't be bothered, choosing instead to dispense with the first 50 per cent of the long fourth lines of the verses (reducing that of the opening verse to 'Born with a snake in your fists, hurricane blowing', for example)—even then, with him slurring the lines and hitting only their endings, the song still enriches every concert. Even though the same laziness has him prune it down from six verses to four (not always the same four) in *every* concert performance, 'Jokerman' is always welcome, always alive and benign, always rich and complex, always habitable, always ready to open up its labyrinthine possibilities.

[Bob Dylan: 'Jokerman', NY, 13 or 14 Apr 1983, unreleased; 'Jokerman', ditto but new vocal overdubbed Jun-Jul 1983, *Infidels*, 1983; 'Jokerman' with the Plugz/Cruzados, 'The David Letterman Show', NBC-TV, NY, 22 Mar 1984; 'Visions of Johanna', LA, 30 Nov 1965 (the fast one), issued the *Bootleg Series Vol. 7—No Direction Home: The Soundtrack*, Columbia Legacy 520358 2, US, 2005 and NY, 21 Jan 1966 (the slow), still unreleased. These early versions were long known as 'Seems Like a Freeze-Out' or 'Freeze-Out'.

Harry Smith, notes re Alabama Sacred Harp Singers: 'Present Joys', Atlanta, 16 Apr 1928 (mis-ascribed to Birmingham, AL, by Smith), issued on *American Folk Music*, Folkways FP251–253, NY, 1952, CD-reissued as *Anthology of American Folk Music*, Smithsonian Folkways SRW 40090, Washington, D.C., 1997. Bill King, 'The Artist in the Marketplace', doctoral thesis, University of North Carolina, 1975; quoted from Robert Shelton, *No Direction Home: The Life And Music of Bob Dylan*, New York: Beech Tree Books / William Morrow, 1986.

John Keats: 'Ode on a Grecian Urn' and 'Ode to a Nightingale' written 1818–19 and published in *Lamia and Other Poems*, 1820. The other two 'great odes' are 'To Psyche' and 'To Autumn', same details. John Keats: 'Endymion', 1818. Nigel Brooks, 'The Nightingale's Code: The Influence of John Keats on Bob Dylan', 1993, in Richard David Wissolik & Scott McGrath, eds., *Bob Dylan's Words: A Critical Dictionary and Commentary*, Greensburg, PA: Eadmer Press, 1994. Robert Graves, *The White Goddess: A Historical Grammar of Poetic Myth*, 1948 (revised 1952), London: Faber, 1952 (3rd edn.). Christopher Ricks, 'Clichés That Come to Pass', in Michael Gray & John Bauldie, *All Across the Telegraph: A Bob Dylan Handbook*, London: W.H. Allen, 1987.

Aidan Day quoted 1st from his essay 'Bob Dylan: Escaping on the Run', The Wanted Man Study Series no.3, Bury, Lancashire, UK, 1984, & 2nd from *Jokerman: Reading the Lyrics of Bob Dylan*, Oxford: Blackwell, 1989. T.S. Eliot: 'Burnt Norton', 1935, collected in *The Four Quartets*, 1943. (The 'hateful siege / Of contraries' is Milton, *Paradise Lost*, Book 9.) John Carey, *The Violent Effigy: A Study of Dickens' Imagination*, London: Faber, 1979.]

'Jokerman' [video, 1984] For the US fanzine *On The Tracks*, LARRY SLOMAN told Mitch Blank about the making of the exceptional promo video for 'Jokerman', the best track on the 1983 album *Infidels*, which was co-produced by Sloman, author of *On the Road with Bob Dylan*, and George Lois, a hot Manhattan adman who had met Dylan during the fund-raising concerts for RUBIN 'HURRICANE' CARTER in the mid-1970s:

> 'I played the song for George Lois. He and I sat down and George says, "Oh yeah, but Michelangelo this and that . . ." and he starts doing storyboards and stuff. . . . We were set to shoot, and I got a call the night before that Bob wants to have dinner with me in Chinatown. . . . I walk into this restaurant . . . Bob is wearing a green parka with the hood up and I think it's summer time. Bob is saying, "Do you think I should do this? What do you think of this video?" I'm saying, "It's great!" So the next day we shoot him . . . this guy is one of the greatest poets that we have working in contemporary music, so we were going to take his words and put them in your face. The second thing was we would use great artworks to illuminate his art. And third, we would shoot Bob and make him look as heroic as these artworks . . . and the whole time Bob was lip-synching the chorus, "Jokerman dance to the nightingale tune . . ." For the whole shoot he kept his eyes *closed*. After every take George would plead with him, "Bob, please open your eyes." Bob would say, "I'm trying." Finally, on the last take, and to me this is the ultimate Dylan video, we got him to open his eyes and he looks cagily at the camera. We had captured that

Dylan mystique, I think. So Columbia flips out, they think it's the greatest video ever done, and it's about to go on the air and Bob wants to kill it. Well . . . not kill it, he likes everything except what was shot of him. He wants to go to Malibu and to take an 8mm handheld thing and do some shots of him on the beach instead. George says, "Fuck him, I know better, I don't want him to do that." Columbia, who had paid for the video, said they agreed with Lois. So we finished the video over Bob's objections.'

In the end, the works of art paraded in front of the viewer's eyes along with Dylan's lyric, were these:

'Self Portrait as the Redeemer' (Durer, 1500)
Sumerian idol (2700 BC)
'The Slave Ship' (Turner, 1840)
Minoan snake goddess (1500 BC)
Bob Dylan poster (Glaser, 1966)
'Moses' (Michelangelo indeed, 1514)
'Man in Bondage', from *The Book of Urizen* (Blake, 1795)
'Dead Christ' (Mantegna, 1490)
The Delphi Charioteer (Greece, 5th Century BC)
'Weeping Woman' (Picasso, 1937)
'Woman and Man' (Lindner, 1971)
'The Musicians' Hell' (Bosch, 1510)
Jewish illuminated manuscript (Germany, 1300)
Island Man of New Guinea (Kirk, 1970)
'The Battle of San Romano' (Uccello 1435–50)
'David' (Michelangelo again, 1504)
'Cow's Skull—Red White and Blue' (O'Keefe, 1931)
'Chief Joseph of the Nez Perce' (Curtis, 1903)
'The Third of May 1808' (Goya, 1814)
The armour of Henry VIII (1520)
'Muhammed Ali as St. Sebastian' (Lois, 1969)
Colossal Head (from the Palazzo Orsini, Bomarzo, Italy)
'Slain Heroes at Arlington' (Lois, 1969)
The Joker (DC Comics)
'The Scream' (Munch, 1893) and
Goddess of Earth and Procreation (Aztec, 1400).

['Jokerman' video, filmed Mar 1984, released by Columbia, NY, with single, Apr 1984. Larry Sloman interview *On the Tracks* no.2, Grand Junction, CO, fall/winter 1993, pp.30–35; list of artworks taken from 'Some Bob Dylan Lists' in Michael Gray & John Bauldie, eds., *All Across the Telegraph: A Bob Dylan Handbook*, London: Futura Paperbacks edn., p. 264.]

Jones, Curtis [1906 - 1971] Curtis Jones was born in Naples, Texas, on August 18, 1906. Learning guitar and living in Dallas as a teenager, he became a blues pianist long resident in Chicago, where he moved in 1936, and he recorded prolifically in the years 1937–41. Jones was, in his low-key way 'the bluesman's blues singer', in Paul Oliver's phrase, and his piano-work was equally unassuming yet accomplished.

His 'Lonesome Bedroom Blues', a pre-war classic composed after his wife left him, and which Dylan performed live in Japan in 1978—indeed it was the opening number on the opening night of the entire 1978 World Tour—was recorded at Curtis Jones' début session in September 1937. 'Highway 51 Blues', which Dylan included on his first album, was cut at Jones' fourth session, in 1938. It often surprises blues aficionados to learn that he was also the composer of Sonny Boy Williamson I's pre-war hit 'Decoration Day Blues', later revived by HOWLIN' WOLF and MUDDY WATERS. (Indeed Jones' very first recorded track was his own version of the song, though this remained unissued, as did another attempt, made at his third session.) Other material he cut showed an unusual variety of song title, including such items as 'Schoolmate Blues', 'Down in the Slums', 'Mistakes in Life', 'Reefer Hound Blues', 'War Broke Out in Hell' and 'Glamour and Glory Blues'. Other songs he wrote included 'Bull and Cow Blues', 'Morocco Blues', 'Skid Row' and 'Suicide Blues'.

His first post-war recording—and as it turned out, his only one of the 1950s—came from two brief sessions in 1953, but then, 'discovered' in a fleabag Chicago hotel room in 1958 by three blues enthusiasts, he cut an album in New York City in 1960, performed at universities and clubs in Chicago in 1961–62 (including the Gate of Horn, a seminal place in ROGER McGUINN's folk music education) and cut another album in 1962, *Lonesome Bedroom Blues*.

Re-recordings of both the title track and 'Highway 51' (and of 'Stackolee') are on this album, but this was made *after* Bob Dylan recorded 'Highway 51'; nor could Dylan have picked up the song from Jones' 1960 LP because 'Highway 51' wasn't included on that album. Nor had there been any vinyl reissue of the original pre-war track before Dylan recorded the song in November 1961. How Dylan came by Curtis Jones's 'Highway 51 Blues', used on his first album, is thus a puzzle usefully illustrative of how variegated sources of such material could be. The likelihood is, in this case, that he had access either to Jones' pre-war recording on 78rpm or to somebody's private tape of that record (reel-to-reel tape recordings of old records circulated widely among folk and blues enthusiasts and musicians around Greenwich Village and so on—but also in enclaves of folk revivalist activity like Dinkytown in Minneapolis).

Jones emigrated to Europe in 1962, recorded with Alexis Korner in London in 1963, and subsequently spent some time in Morocco. His last recordings were again in London, for Blue Horizon in 1968. The last track he ever cut was 'Born in Naples Texas'. He died in Munich, then in West Germany, on September 11, 1971 and was buried in a pauper's grave.

[Curtis Jones: 'Lonesome Bedroom Blues', Chicago, 28 Sep 1937; 'Highway 51 Blues', Chicago, 25 Jan 1938; *Cool Playing Blues*, Chicago, 19 May & 10 Aug 1953,

Parrot 782, Chicago, 1953 (unissed tracks from 2nd session incl. on a Various Artists compilation, *Chicago Blues After Midnight*, Delta Swing LP 379, Chicago, c.1955); *Trouble Blues*, NY, 9 Nov 1960, Bluesville 1022, NY, 1961; *Lonesome Bedroom Blues*, Chicago, 12 & 27 Jan 1962, Delmark LP 605, Chicago, 1965. Bob Dylan: 'Lonesome Bedroom Blues', Tokyo, Feb 20, 21, 23 & 25, 1978.]

Jones, Evan [1927 -] See *Madhouse on Castle Street, The.*

Jones, Mickey [1941 -] Michael Jones was born in Houston, Texas, on June 10, 1941, but grew up in Dallas, learning to play drums early in life and dropping out of high school to play on tour with Trini Lopez, whom he followed Los Angeles, where Lopez had a regular gig at PJ's nightclub. When Lopez was signed to Reprise, they wanted an album *Live at PJ's*, and this, released in 1963, launched Lopez's career. From it came his big hit single of 'If I Had a Hammer', which he had learnt from a PETER, PAUL & MARY records. Hence even Mickey Jones' first recording success had a tenuous Dylan connection—and yes, that finger-snappy, thin, echoey drum sound on Lopez's irksomely chirpy 'If I Had a Hammer' is Mr. Jones.

From Lopez he went to work for smoothed-out-rock'n'roll hit-maker Johnny Rivers (an act Bob Dylan seems to have been inordinately fond of, and whose 1968 version of 'Positively 4th Street' Dylan says he liked better than his own, even calling it his favourite cover version). Mickey Jones stayed with Johnny Rivers for three years, playing on seven of his albums and including in his touring a March 1966 trip to Vietnam with Ann-Margret.

Before that trip, Dylan caught Johnny Rivers at the Whiskey-A-Go-Go in LA, called Jones over to his table, told him he loved his playing and offered him a job. The job began straight after the Vietnam trip: it was playing live on the Hawaii-Australia-Europe tour of 1966 with Dylan and THE HAWKS, after LEVON HELM had earlier dropped out and been replaced by SANDY KONIKOFF, who had played the February–March 1966 US dates. Mickey Jones made his début with the group on April 9 in Honolulu. He rode it out right through till after the London Royal Albert Hall concert of May 27–and he was up for the further North American dates he'd been led to expect, including New York's Shea Stadium, till Dylan had his motorcycle crash and cancelled everything. Except, apparently, Jones' paychecks. 'I had a two-year deal, and Bob never tried to renege,' said Jones. 'He's a man of his word.'

Opinions vary as to the quality of Jones' contribution. Barney Hoskyns writes scathingly about him, as musician and personality, in his biography of THE BAND, *Across the Great Divide* (1993), calling him 'the overweight Texan' with a 'penchant for collecting Nazi regalia', whose 'sensibility was as different from that of the Hawks as his ham-fisted drumming technique was from the rangy, loose-limbed style of Levon Helm.' And he quotes D.A. PENNEBAKER as saying: 'The Hawks' hearts were down in the swamps of Lousiana. . . . Mickey's wasn't, I'll tell you that. He'd gotten out of Texas as fast as he could, and he wanted the bright lights.'

It's true that Levon Helm's playing was more subtle and flexible, but for many, Mickey Jones' drumming was *perfect* for the radical, incendiary electric music that Dylan and the Hawks were hurling out at their audiences. The uncompromising defiance of his snare-drum attacks, like volleys of machine-gun fire, cranking up the pitch of excitement unfurled by this most glorious music, propelled the sound and the spirit of the whole fiery ship on through hostile oceans. It was the surely the best rock drumming since its obvious precursor, D.J. Fontana's thrilling, galvanising rat-a-tat-a-tat-a-tat on ELVIS PRESLEY's 'Hound Dog' ten years earlier.

Even the 'overweight' jibe seems slightly unfair. Alongside the Bob Dylan of 1966 nearly everyone else in North America looked overweight. None of which lessens the pleasing witticism of the editing on a fleeting moment of the concert footage of 'Ballad of a Thin Man' put together by Pennebaker as a promo for *Eat the Document* (back when he thought Dylan would co-operate with *his* version of that project). Before the extraordinary riches of extant 1966 concert film were glimpsed more generously in SCORSESE's *No Direction Home* in 2005, bootleg copies of this would-be promo film, centred upon a Scandinavian concert's 'Ballad of a Thin Man', offered the only complete song-performance to be seen—and there's a neat moment within it where Dylan sings that chorus line 'You know something is happening but you don't know what it is, do you, Mr. Jones?' and as he completes the question, the film cuts to Mickey Jones, pudgy and blonde, in the dark behind his drumkit.

It isn't a fair connection, and isn't meant to be—plenty of people were in the dark at the time, while Mickey Jones understood the thrust of the music and helped make it—but it was a gem of editing (and it was surely HOWARD ALK who devised it).

After the tour, Jones' moment of glory, his contribution to history, was over. It was straight downhill into Kenny Rogers & the First Edition after that, and 'I Just Dropped in to See What Condition My Condition Was In'. When Kenny Rogers went solo in 1976, to become rich as Croesus in the multi-platinum late-1970s country superstar stakes, Mickey Jones concentrated on acting, encouraged by a small part alongside Rogers (and with music supplied by the First Edition) in the TV film *The Dream Makers* in 1975. As he grew larger, hairier and more piggy-eyed he became increasingly suited to rôles as the menacing biker, the creepy backwoodsman, 'man at pizza joint' and 'burly miner'. He enjoyed a starring rôle as the Ice Man in *Misfits of Science* (supported by Courteney Cox), played the character Peter Bilker in the TV series 'Home Improvement' throughout the 1990s, and according to Edna Gundersen in *USA Today*, 'he became a household face as the burly biker in a long-running Breath Savers commercial.'

In 2002 he released the video/DVD *Bob Dylan—World Tour 1966: The Home Movies—Through the Camera of Dylan's Drummer Mickey Jones*. Its anecdotes, told by Jones with some verve, are inevitably interesting, though as one punter-review on Amazon noted, the overall package was 'heavily criticised by fans, who felt that a DVD with the words "World Tour 1966" in the title should contain at least some concert footage. (It does, but without sound.) . . . It is a collection of primitive silent home movie clips, some of which actually include Bob Dylan in the frame.'

[Barney Hoskyns, *Across the Great Divide: The Band and America*, London: Viking / Penguin, 1993 & New York: Hyperion, 1993; 2nd edn., London: Vintage/Ebury, 2003. Edna Gundersen, *USA Today*, 16–18 Oct 1998; this is also the source of the Jones quote re his salary from Dylan. DVD review by 'Docendo Discimus', seen online 4 Feb 2006 at *www.amazon.com*.]

Jones, Norah [1979 -] Geetali Norah Jones Shankar, a daughter of the distinguished Indian musician Ravi Shankar and of music enthusiast Sue Jones, was born in New York City on March 30, 1979 but, brought up by her mother, moved to Dallas, Texas, at the age of four. She attended a performing arts high school and studied jazz piano at the University of North Texas, by which time she had changed her name to Norah Jones (at age 16), had already won various contests and awards and was clearly headed for professional success as a musician and singer-songwriter.

Her first album, *Come Away with Me*, begun at ALBERT GROSSMAN's studio in Bearsville, NY, in May 2001 and completed under Arif Mardin in New York City, was released in 2002, sold 20 million copies world-wide and won almost everything at the 2003 Grammies.

It duly became the most over-played album in music history, so that whatever the merits and dollar-power of her follow-up album, the less jazz-tinged and more countrified *Feels Like Home*, Norah Jones went straight from sounding like *the* most exciting new wave in years to being elevator music you couldn't get away from, and of course spawning bevies of other 'new' young female singers with vaguely soft-jazz albums madly over-hyped to an increasingly indifferent public.

At a private concert for the employees of Amazon.com in Seattle on July 16, 2005, she and Bob Dylan both performed short sets. In the course of Dylan's, the two of them duetted on a version of 'I Shall Be Released' (first recorded by Dylan 12 years before Norah Jones was born). Dylan's performance (including the duet) has circulated on bootleg DVD.

[Norah Jones: *Come Away with Me*, Bearsville, NY & NY, 2001, Blue Note, US, 2002; *Feels Like Home*, *n/a*, Blue Note, US, 2004.]

***Judas!* [fanzine]** See **Muir, Andrew.**

'Judas!' [shout] The most dramatic moment of Dylan's spectacularly confrontational 1966 tour—aside from the high drama of the brave, numinous music itself—took place in Manchester on May 17, where, at the Free Trade Hall, a voice from the crowd called out 'Judas!' and Bob Dylan responded, 'I don't believe you. You're a liar!'

This exchange was a curious re-enactment, though in circumstances less lethal, of that between the British Public Executioner and the Gunpowder Plot conspirator Sir Everard Digby 360 years earlier. As John Aubrey's 17th century *Brief Lives* reports it, 'When [Digby's] heart was pluct out by the Executioner (who . . . cryed, "Here is the heart of a Traytor!"), it is credibly reported, he replied, "Thou liest!"'

In the more modern case, it is almost as surreal, and certainly Dylanesque, that the identity of the man who shouted 'the world's most famous heckle' should be mired in dispute, and largely between two equally plausible contenders, both now dead.

For several decades, no-one claimed to know who had created this powerful moment (and it was sometimes rumoured that Dylan's manager ALBERT GROSSMAN had paid someone to do it). Then, in 1998, as English radio front-man and Dylan fan Andy Kershaw wrote later about the process of fulfilling a desire he'd nursed for 20 years to make a radio documentary about the night in question: 'With fellow Dylanologist, Dr C.P. LEE—who had been at the Manchester show as a 15-year-old schoolboy—we assembled in the spooky, derelict Free Trade Hall about 20 veterans of that infamous night. Among them was a chap called Keith Butler, who'd come all the way from Canada, claiming to be the celebrated heckler.'

News that the heckler had finally been unveiled duly roared around the world of Dylan-watchers (to use a polite term). But after the Kershaw & Lee documentary was broadcast, in January 1999, 'something strange happened. . . . I received an e-mail from a guy in Cumbria, John Cordwell, who'd heard the programme. The tone of his message was . . . plaintive and plausible: "What puzzles me is why someone should falsely claim that it was they who produced the notorious 'one-worder'. How do I know the claim is false? Simple; I was the one who stood up on the second balcony of the Free Trade Hall all those years ago and felt betrayed enough to give voice to my feelings."' When Kershaw met this second claimant, he was 'a small, wiry 55-year-old with white hair and a short beard, wearing a denim jacket and round spectacles. He looked every inch the liberal child of the 1960s who might now be lecturing at a Manchester teacher training college. Which is exactly what he did.'

John Cordwell told Kershaw: 'I think most of all I was angry that Dylan . . . not that he'd played electric, but that he'd played electric with a really poor sound system. It was not like it is on the record. It was a wall of mush.' Which is true.

C.P. Lee has always accepted that Keith Butler, the first claimant, *believed* that he had been the shouter, but he too finds Cordwell the firmer candidate. Butler, born on December 10, 1945 in Tamworth, in the English Midlands, had been a student at Keele University at the time of Dylan's concerts, had later emigrated to Canada and by the time he was 'found' he was a 53-year-old living in Toronto, working in a bank and feeling that his life was falling apart. C.P. Lee says: 'I met him . . . when we recorded the BBC documentary about the gig and he was likeable, open and honest and was believable.'

But Lee adds this: 'When Keith rose from his Canadian exile claiming to be the "Judas" shouter he certainly appeared to fit the profile–and without a doubt he's the earnest young man in *Eat the Document* who goes on about "Pop groups produce better rubbish than that!" I think when he read about it all those years later, in the middle of the night in Toronto, suffering from an asthma attack, a chord rang deep inside him and he recognised himself. I think there's no doubt that he booed and there's no doubt that he shouted and walked out. However: Keith was a man in crisis. I suspect that he really believed he was the shouter, but as to whether he actually was or not. . . . [When] John Cordwell stepped forward after Andy Kershaw's documentary had been broadcast . . . Andy and I met up with him and he was equally as convincing and convinced. If pushed to make a decision I would fall on the side of John. He had two people prepared to be witness; Keith had one, who was prepared to say that he remembered Keith shouting "something".'

Lee concludes: 'The consternation caused by another claimant . . . never diminished Keith's assertion and, as both contenders have now sadly passed on all we can say for certain is they were both there, they both heckled Dylan and both saw the errors of their ways eventually and became firm fans.'

Andy Kershaw says the timing of the shout of 'Judas!' couldn't have been better. 'What it unleashed from Dylan was something so subversive, so angry and contemptuous, that what followed was punk rock, 10 years before Johnny Rotten. Rather better played.' C.P. Lee says: 'I was aware even then that I would never see anything like it again.' And as Keith Butler said, 'What made it different was that Dylan shouted back and that the concert was recorded and the bootleg went around the world.'

The 'Judas!' shout dramatised Dylan's centrality to music when music itself was at the core of everything. It was an incomparable moment in music history.

John Cordwell (born 1944) died in England on July 11, 2001, from severe allergic shock, possibly in reaction to being stung by the bees he had started to keep. Keith Butler died of cancer in Toronto on October 25, 2002.

[Sir Everard Digby, 16 May 1578–30 Jan 1606. Keith Butler, 1946–2002. John Cordwell, 1944–11 Jul 2001. Andy Kershaw: 'Bob Dylan: How I found the man who shouted "Judas"', *Independent*, UK, 23 Sep 2005; last Kershaw quote, Butler quote & last C.P. Lee quote all from piece by Andy Gill, *Independent*, 23 Jan 1999. First C.P. Lee quote, e-mail 28 Oct 2002 to the *rec.music.dylan* discussion group, seen online 14 Oct 2005 at *www.expectingrain.com/dok/who/who.html*. Longer C.P. Lee quote e-mail to this writer, 10 Jan 2006. Thanks also to Craig Jamieson and to Jane Butler for Keith Butler date & place of birth, e-mail to this writer 9 Jan 2006.]

'Jumpin' Judy' Dylan's inwardness with the world of the blues is modestly revealed in his enrolment of 'Jumpin' Judy' into 1965's 'I Wanna Be Your Lover' (released on *Biograph* 20 years later). She is not, contrary to most people's assumption, one of those 'made-up' quirky names, so many of which throng the populous world of mid-1960s Dylan songs.

Jumpin' Judy was one of the heroines of the Southern convict farms, where, among the savagery of the régime, was the allowing in of 'wives' at weekends. She was celebrated in many a blues song, as in this common-stock stanza: 'It's Jumpin' Jumpin' Judy / She was a mighty fine girl / Oh well she brought that jumpin' / Baby to the whole round world.'

There is a commercial recording, by Wiley and Wiley [Arnold and Irene], titled 'Jumpin' Judy Blues' from 1931; Allen Prothro's performance of 'Jumpin' Judy' was field-recorded by John and ALAN LOMAX for the Library of Congress at the Nashville State Penitentiary in 1933; an unidentified group of convicts was field-recorded singing the same song at the Shelby County Workhouse, Memphis, a couple of days earlier; and Kelly Pace's 'Jumpin' Judy' was field-recorded by John Lomax at Cumins State Farm, Gould, Arkansas in 1934. Another version, by prisoners known as Tangle Eye, Fuzzy Red, Hard Hair & group were field-recorded singing it on Parchman Farm, probably in 1947. A version by RICHARD FARIÑA and ERIC VON SCHMIDT (with lead vocal by von Schmidt) was recorded in London in 1963.

The verse quoted above can be found incorporated into other songs too: for instance, as Dylan would have been aware, into LEADBELLY's 1940 version of 'Midnight Special'.

This mythic heroine is 'immortalized in song for her innovations', as Alan Lomax puts it. Or as Dylan puts it in 'I Wanna Be Your Lover', 'Jumpin' Judy can't go no higher'. This line, so casual and unemphasised, thus manages a three-layer play on 'higher', acknowledging Jumpin' Judy as a figure who has achieved immortality in blues folklore, like Stagolee or John Henry, as well as punning on being stoned and alluding to literal jumping.

[Bob Dylan: 'I Wanna Be Your Lover', NY, 5 Oct 1965, *Biograph*, 1985. Wiley & Wiley [Arnold & Irene]: 'Jumpin' Judy Blues', NY, 23 Jul 1931. Allen Prothro: 'Jumpin' Judy', Nashville State Penitentiary, c.15 Aug 1933, *Afro-American Spirituals Worksongs & Ballads*, Archive of Folk Song LP AFS L3, Washington, D.C., 1956, CD-reissued Rounder CD1510, Cambridge, MA, 1998. Kelly Pace: 'Jumpin' Judy', Gould, AR, c.5 Oct 1934, also vinyl-issued AFS L3 (detailed above) & extracted on *The Ballad Hunter: John A. Lomax Lectures on American Folk Music, Parts III and IV*, Archive of Folk Song LP AFS L50, Washington, D.C., c.mid-1950s. Tangle Eye, Fuzzy Red, Hard Hair & group: 'Jumpin' Judy', Parchman Farm, MS, prob. 1947; *Negro Prison Songs from the Mississippi Penitentiary*, Tradition TLP 1020, Salem, MA, c.1959, CD-reissued as *Prison Songs V. 1: Murderous Home*, Rounder ROUN1714, Cambridge, MA, 1997. Dick Fariña & Eric von Schmidt: 'Jumping Judy', London, Jan/Feb 1963, *Dick Farina & Eric von Schmidt*, Folklore F-LEUT-7, US, 1964. Leadbelly: 'Midnight Special', NY, 15 Jun 1940, CD-reissued *Leadbelly: Midnight Special*, The Blues Collection (magazine + CD) BLU NC 030, Editions Atlas, Paris, 1993 (Orbis, London, 1994).]

Junior Parker [1932 - 1971] Herman Parker was born on the wrong side of the river in West Memphis, Arkansas, on March 27, 1932. He was the harmonica player, bandleader and rather smoothie vocalist who wrote and first recorded 'Mystery Train', making it elegant, cool and not especially striking. ELVIS PRESLEY then made it into a far more numinous, restless and primeval creature, one of his most influential early sides and thereby one of the founding classics of rock'n'roll.

By then Parker had played behind SONNY BOY WILLIAMSON II, whose musicianship influenced him; in HOWLIN' WOLF's early band, alongside Ike Turner; and in B.B. King & the Beale Street Boys, alongside Bobby Bland and Roscoe Gordon. In 1951 he had formed the Blue Flames (a name stolen in England a decade afterwards by Georgie Fame), and later Blues Consolidated, which toured widely in the late 1950s and early 1960s. He had first recorded for Modern, then been pinched by rival Memphis label Sun and in 1954 switched to the Texas-based Duke records, enjoying a number of R&B hits before moving on again to Minit, Mercury, United Artists and Capitol. He continued working and recording throughout the 1960s, an underrated figure, though not when resorting to covering THE BEATLES' 'Lady Madonna' with the Jimmy McGriff Orchestra; but a late studio work was the all-blues, harmonica-driven 1970 album *You Don't Have to Be Black to Love the Blues* (alluding playfully to a high-profile ad campaign of the day with the slogan 'You don't have to be Jewish to love Levy's [rye bread]'). The album was reissued posthumously in Britain as *Blues Shadows Falling*, and then in the US as the CD *Way Back Home: The Groove Merchant Years* in 2000. But Parker has not sold well since the 1950s, so that all his releases are swiftly deleted.

Dylan told CAMERON CROWE, for the *Biograph* notes in 1985 that as far as his harmonica playing went, '. . . well, I'd always liked WAYNE RANEY and JIMMY REED, SONNY TERRY . . . Li'l Junior Parker . . .'

On *Knocked Out Loaded* in 1986, Dylan released a rewritten version of Parker's 'I Wanna Ramble' (one of Parker's earliest Duke sides), re-titling it 'You Wanna Ramble'. It's the album's first track, and in the middle Dylan slips in his own addition, 'What happens tomorrow / Is on your head, not mine' . . . except that it isn't his own addition, it's taken almost exactly from that Dylan film favourite *The Big Country*, in which Burl Ives warns: 'What happens here tomorrow is on your head not mine'.

Parker died at the age of 39 while undergoing surgery for a brain tumour in Blue Island, Illinois, on November 18, 1971.

[Junior Parker: 'Mystery Train', Memphis, c.Oct 1953, Sun 192, Memphis, TN, 1954. 'I Wanna Ramble', Houston, TX, 10 Jun 1954, Duke 137, Houston, 1954; *You Don't Have to Be Black to Love the Blues*, Groove Merchant, US, 1970; *Way Back Home: The Groove Merchant Years, VSOP CD 2901*, 2000. Elvis Presley: 'Mystery Train', Memphis, 11 Jul 1955, Sun 223, Memphis, 1955. *The Big Country*, dir. William Wyler, written James R. Webb, starring Gregory Peck, Jean Simmons, Charlton Heston, Carroll Baker, Burl Ives & Charles Bickford; UA/Anthony/Worldwide, US, 1958. Sources include Tom Fisher, entry in *The Routledge Blues Encyclopedia*, New York: Routledge, 2005 & Tony Russell, *The Blues from Robert Johnson to Robert Cray*, London: Aurum Press, 1997.]

Kafka, Franz [1883 - 1924] 'Kafka' means 'jackdaw' in Czech. Franz Kafka was born in Prague, July 3, 1883, into a middle class German-speaking Jewish family. He also learned Czech as a child, and some French. (He was keen on Napoleon and Flaubert.) He graduated in law at the University of Prague in 1906 and while holding down a day-job, began to write. He caught tuberculosis in 1917, and also suffered from insomnia, constipation, migraine, boils and (perhaps no wonder) clinical depression. He was painfully diffident—except, oddly, when insisting on promoting Yiddish theatrical productions against the advice of friends and family—and felt enormous self-loathing, even while others found him likeable and highly intelligent, with a quirky sense of humour and boyish good looks. In 1923 he moved to Berlin to concentrate on his writing, but his TB grew worse, and after returning to Prague he entered a sanatorium at Kierling, near Vienna, and died there—in part from voluntary starvation—on June 3, 1924.

K

Kafka published only a few short stories during his lifetime, and attracted little attention until after his death. Famously he instructed his friend and literary executor Max Brod to destroy his manuscripts when he died, but Brod could not, instead ensuring that the work saw proper publication. Critical attention and acclaim soon followed, and he became acknowledged as one of the great modernist writers of the 20th century, crucially for his depiction of contemporary individual powerlessness in the face of omnipotent, bizarrely irrational, unfathomable bureaucracy. He is, thereby, one of the founding figures of modern consciousness—the father, if you will, of alienation.

Hence the ready and widespread use, not least among people who have never read his work, of the term 'Kafkaesque', to describe any personal experience of protracted struggle against obdurate authority, and by extension any sensation of being caught up in rules, regulations or institutional customs you don't understand or don't agree with. Kafka himself is generally envisaged as the haplessly lonely writer enveloped in anguished alienation. This rather detracts from his superb craftsmanship, and fails to pay attention to his subversive good humour and energy.

Dylan's mid-1960s work is inevitably informed by Kafka's work, and without naming him, Dylan brings intimations of his vision into 'Desolation Row'. The eighth verse indicts the education system, depicting it as organised to enforce and perpetuate ignorance, a nightmarish machinery for bringing into line the potential enemies of the state—which is to say, of the status quo—the independent thinkers: 'Now at midnight all the agents / And the superhuman crew / Come out an' round up everyone / That knows more than they do.' That 'crew' suggests, along with the opening phrase 'At midnight . . .', the whole sinister morass of collective vandalism, political purges and press gangs. Those lines insist, equally acutely, on an overriding presence of violence; it is conjured up in the first two lines of that verse, so that we are primed for the imminent appearance of the 'heart-attack machine' that will be 'strapped across his shoulders', and for the near impossibility of escape. Dylan urges upon us anew a sense of the powerlessness of the individual, who is 'brought down from the castles / By insurance men who go / Check to see that nobody is escaping / To Desolation Row.'

The allusion to Kafka's visions, clinched by that 'castles', and perhaps by that 'insurance men' too, makes this pessimism clear. *The Castle*, 1926, like *The Trial*, 1925, is one of Kafka's (posthumous) novels, and it was at the Workers Accident Insurance Institute that Kafka worked, and which formed for him a model 'kingdom of the absurd', in Alan Bennett's phrase. (Bennett, in an excellent and modest essay, makes the same allusion as Dylan—assumes, like Dylan, that the very word 'castle', in a certain context, connotes Kafka's work: 'His work has been garrisoned by armies of critics, with some fifteen thousand books about him at the last count. As there is a Fortress Freud so there is a Fortress Kafka, Kafka his own castle.') Kafka's other important work is the short story 'Metamorphosis', in which the narrator wakes up to find himself not merely in Desolation Row but in 'Kafkaesque' extremis: trapped inside a new body, that of a gigantic beetle. 'Right now I don't feel too good' indeed.

In 'Desolation Row', Dylan leaves us with the insistence that all any individual can do is hold to some integrity of personal perspective. And that, in the end, deepened by its emanations of Kafka, is exactly what 'Desolation Row' itself offers.

[Some biographical detail taken from *www.nationmaster.com/encyclopedia/Franz-Kafka*, online 8 Jun 2005. Alan Bennett: 'Kafka in Las Vegas', *London Review of Books* no.14/87, London, 23 Jul 1987, collected in Bennett: *Writing Home*, 1994.]

Kalb, Danny [1942 -] Danny Kalb was born on September 19, 1942 in Mount Vernon, New York. He grew up listening to folk music and learning to play guitar, then caught rock'n'roll shows in Manhattan and joined a high school rockabilly band that rejoiced in the name the Gay Notes. By 16 he had discovered Greenwich Village, where he met and was bowled over by the playing and singing of DAVE VAN RONK, who became at once a crucial influence.

He started as a history student at the University of Wisconsin in fall 1960, which had its own coffeehouse scene, and when Dylan lingered there in Madison, Wisconsin, on his way between Minneapolis and New York City, the two met and formed what Kalb claims has been 'a lifelong friendship'. Certainly the two hung around together a bit when they were both very young, not only in Madison but in Greenwich Village too, to which Kalb was still making forays.

Kalb says that it was from him that Dylan learned the song 'Poor Lazarus', while admitting that he himself had taken it from Dave Van Ronk. And at the Riverside Church Folk Music Hootenanny, uptown in New York City on July 29, 1961, Dylan performed that song (after playing 'Handsome Molly' and 'Naomi Wise, aka 'Omie Wise')—and then played harmonica behind Kalb's guitar and vocals on the traditional song 'Mean Old Southern Railroad'. (After which Dylan sang 'Acne' with RAMBLIN' JACK ELLIOTT and spent the evening with SUZE ROTOLO for the first time.)

Kalb moved to New York City in 1962 and soon after joined two revival jug bands, Van Ronk's short-lived Ragtime Jug Stompers and then the True Endeavor Jug Band with Artie Traum and Van Ronk's one-time roommate SAMUEL B. CHARTERS, the pioneering blues field-recorder and researcher whose 1959 book *The Country Blues* had inspired the blues revival. The True Endeavor Jug Band made one album, *The Art of the Jug Band*, in 1963. Kalb and Charters also functioned as a piano and guitar duo, the New Strangers (an LP came out of this too), while Kalb *also* worked with Barry Kornfeld and Artie Rose in a trio called the, er, Folk Stringers. (Another group, another LP.)

He was one of the featured artists on the specially recorded Various Artists album *The Blues Project*, on which Dylan played piano on a GEOFF MULDAUR track. Kalb had a track on each side of the LP, with renditions of 'I'm Troubled' and his own song 'Hello Baby Blues'. The other featured artists were DAVE RAY, ERIC VON SCHMIDT, Dave Van Ronk, Ian Buchanan and MARK SPOELSTRA.

This album sold well and gave Kalb the name for his group of a year later, formed from the ashes of the Danny Kalb Quartette (in which, influenced by Tim Hardin, Kalb 'went electric') plus AL KOOPER and Tommy Flanders. The Blues Project issued two albums, the second of which, 1966's *Projections*, influenced the folk-rock and blues-rock of the period. In 1967 Kooper and Steve Katz left to form Blood, Sweat and Tears. Kalb kept on going, and in 1973 the Blues Project held a first series of summer reunion concerts.

After years on the West Coast, Danny Kalb returned to live in New York City in 1990. He is said to have been an influence on BRUCE SPRINGSTEEN; Al Kooper says he's 'the equivalent of a JOHN LEE HOOKER'. He released a new solo album, *Livin' With the Blues*, in 1995, his first for 20 years. (One of its tracks was a revival of BLIND WILLIE McTELL's 'Statesboro Blues'—the very McTell track Kalb's old partner Samuel Charters issued on the LP released alongside his book *The Country Blues* 36 years earlier: the track that first brought McTell's name to the attention of Greenwich Village and of Bob Dylan). *Livin' With the Blues* proved Kalb to be, as ever, a mediocre singer but a very fine guitarist.

[Danny Kalb: 'I'm Troubled' & 'Hello Baby Blues', NY, early 1964, *The Blues Project*, Elektra EKL 264, NY, Jun 1964; *Livin' With the Blues*, *nia*, Legend CD R LR 103, France, 1995. The Blues Project: *Projections*, Verve/Folkways FTS-3008, NY, 1966. Samuel B. Charters, *The Country Blues*, New York: Reinhart, 1959. The True Endeavor Jug Band: *The Art of the Jug Band*, Prestige/Folklore 14022, US, 1963. The New Strangers: *Meet the New Strangers*, Prestige/Folklore 14027, US, 1964. The Folk Stringers: *The Folk Stringers*, Prestige PR 7371, US, 1964. Blind Willie McTell: 'Statesboro Blues', Atlanta, 17 Oct 1928; *The Country Blues*, RBF Records RBF 1, NY, 1959. (Al Kooper quote from sleevenotes to *Soul of a Man: Al Kooper Live*, *nia*, Music Masters Jazz 65113, US, 1995, on which Kalb also appears.)]

Kangas, Ric [1939 -] Richard Kangas was born in Hibbing, Minnesota, on October 20, 1939. (As he grew up he was known as Dick but today gives his name as Ric.) His mother was a housewife, his father a miner in the Hull Rust iron-ore mines who had previously been a copper and silver miner (and in his youth a lumberjack in the Northern Minnesota Woods).

Two years ahead of Bob Zimmerman at Hibbing High School, Ric left in summer 1957, before the two had ever knowingly met. Bob would come to put as his 'Ambition' in the 1959 school yearbook 'To join LITTLE RICHARD'. Kangas wrote the parallel 'to be another ELVIS'. Like Bob, he too belaboured the gorgeous auditorium of Hibbing High School with early rock'n'roll at a school concert, singing and playing the brand-new 'All Shook Up' with a borrowed guitar and amp.

Ric and Bob met around town in Hibbing sometime in 1958. 'I hear you're a songwriter. So am I,' Bob said. Ric says the two played together at town hall talent contents and house parties, and auditioned (without success) for the Hibbing Winter Frolic, a big annual pageant, fair and festive event in the town that drew people in from all over the Great North Woods.

Their most significant musical collusion occurred in May 1959. Kangas had bought a reel-to-reel tape recorder, and the two of them got together in his bedroom, set it up and recorded four songs. (Detailed in **earliest extant recordings, Dylan's**.)

Back then, beyond their musical bond was the fact that Kangas had a 1953 Ford (after 'totaling' his 1950 Oldsmobile). It's easy to see why the younger boy would want them to hang out together–and Kangas says they'd cruise around on summer nights drinking gin and orange juice, picking up girls and driving out to necking spots like Snowball Lake; it's not so clear why Kangas wanted to have Bob in tow. Ric was driving a truck for Kelly Furniture from 1957 till 1960 (a truck that was parked in a warehouse across the alley from the Zimmerman home); for most of that time Bob was still at school. At any rate, Bob would get Ric to drive him around, and one day their destination was local radio station WMFG. It was the start of their destinies dividing. Dylan played some material to DJ Ron Marinelli and was given some airtime on the strength of it; Kangas' tapes were rejected.

They drifted apart when Dylan went off to the University of Minnesota and Ric Kangas got a steady girlfriend out in Eveleth, another taconite mining town some 20 miles away. He'd traded in his Ford for a Harley Davison too, and wouldn't let anyone else drive *that*. He says Dylan would sit on the gleaming bike in the Kangas driveway, pretending to be Marlon Brando in *The Wild One*.

Dylan went off to New York City; Kangas got a gig as lead singer for a group from Superior, Wisconsin, the Sonics. This didn't last, and he was drafted into the US Army, serving from January 18, 1962 till December 17, 1963, stationed in Fort Carson, Colorado. He moved to Tennessee around 1966. The last time Kangas and Dylan met was in 1974, backstage at Dylan's concert at the Memphis Mid-South Coliseum when Bob introduced him to the members of THE BAND.

About a year later, Kangas moved again, this time to Southern California. He's since moved around within the Golden State but lives there still. He's been a Hollywood extra, a stuntman, a magician, a photographer, a portrait sketcher and a wildlife painter. He never quite gives up–even after writing, he says, 900 songs without ever releasing an album. Dryly he calls himself 'Hibbing's other songwriter.'

In the late 1990s, Kangas was living in Acton, just south of Lancaster, when he mentioned his 1959 Dylan tape to a banking acquaintance who happened to know JEFF ROSEN, who runs Dylan's office and archive. Rosen phoned, got to hear the tape and eventually brought a film crew out to film a four-hour interview with Ric. About seven years later Rosen called again to say that he and the tape were going to feature in the MARTIN SCORSESE movie, and that one of the songs would be on the soundtrack CD set too.

Kangas told the Minnesota newspaper the *Ventura County Star* that he was paid 'a guitar, a small royalty cut from the CD and some up-front cash'. He 'declined to discuss monetary specifics.' On October 1, 2005, soon after the movie opened, he offered the original reel of tape for auction on eBay (item #7550832002) with an ill-advised reserve price of $1.5 millon. The auction ended October 11 with no bids.

Quoting Ric's schooldays ambition 'to be another Elvis', the *Star* reporter notes that in a way he's made it: these days Ric Kangas is an active performing member of the Professional Elvis Impersonators Association.

Kangas remembers another declaration from Hibbing days too: 'Bob always used to tell us, "When I make it, I'll send for you. We'll all walk down Hollywood Boulevard and we'll be stars."' Kangas, deadpan, adds: 'I'm still waiting for that call.'

[Sources include Dave Engel's *Dylan in Minnesota: Just Like Bob Zimmerman's Blues*, Amherst, WI: Amherst Press, 1997; Brett Johnson's profiles, *Ventura County Star*, MN, Sep 2005; & Ric Kangas, e-mails to this writer 31 Oct & 1 Nov 2005.]

Karlin, Danny [1953 -] Daniel Karlin was born in London on December 4, 1953. He is a Cambridge (UK)-educated literary critic and editor specialising in 19th century British poetry but with a particular interest in American literature and popular music. He held a Junior Research Fellowship at Merton College, Oxford, and is a Founding Fellow of the English Association. He joined the faculty of University College London in 1980 and left in 2004 to become a Professor of English in the College of Arts and Sciences at Boston University. He also accepts agreeable bookings such as chairing a session at a BROWNING Society conference in Vallombrosa, Italy, 2005. His first book was *The Courtship of Robert Browning and Elizabeth Barrett* (1985); his others include *Proust's English* (2005), to be followed by a book on the figure of the singer in English poetry. He is *not* the Daniel Karlin who made the documentary film *And if one spoke about love*, a graphic film about wheelchair sex.

His essay 'Bob Dylan's Names' is included in the collection *Do You Mr. Jones?: Bob Dylan Among the Poets and Professors* edited by Neil Corcoran and published in 2002, and at a Shakespeare & Co. Literary Festival in Paris in summer 2004 he delivered a paper on Bob Dylan and ALLEN GINSBERG which he hopes to publish. But notably, back in 1987, the rigorous *London Review of Books* published Karlin's 'It ain't him, babe', a review of ROBERT SHELTON's biography *No Direction Home* that included this fine rant:

> 'I have to confess to an unreasoning impatience with those who profess not to respect or understand Dylan's work. In 1600 the same people were going around saying that the drama was not a serious medium, that the theatre was frequented by riffraff and that guys like Shakespeare stole their plots and were only in it for the money. . . . I know I ought to explain, patiently, that Dylan is the practitioner of an original art . . . that his skills of composition and expression are indivisible, and provide him with

a resource of extraordinary range, power and intensity; that he uses this resource to sing about things that matter . . . that, like all great artists, he tells some of the truth.'

[Daniel Karlin: 'Bob Dylan's Names', *Do You Mr. Jones?: Bob Dylan Among the Poets and Professors*, ed. Neil Corcoran, London, Chatto & Windus 2002, pp.27–49; 'It ain't him, babe', *LRB*, London, 5 Feb 1987.]

'Keats v. Dylan' As late as 1992 'radical' English playwright David Hare imagined he was summing up the battle-lines between civilised culture and its enemy, a cheap and destructive pop culture, in the phrase 'Keats versus Dylan'. Never mind that Bob Dylan had spent the previous three decades with his face set firmly against the vulgar and the cheap, or indeed that JOHN KEATS had been a cockney upstart himself.

Hare's comically inaccurate personifying of the divide caught on like a pop craze itself. Within minutes, that doyenne of the literary clerisy, A.S. BYATT, could go on BBC Television's all-purpose arts programme, 'The Late Show' (BBC-2-TV, London, February 25, 1992) and pronounce that the qualitative difference between Keats and Dylan is that with Keats, she could take you through one of his poems and reveal many layers . . . She couldn't take you through a Dylan lyric because she wouldn't know where to begin. What's disgraceful is not the preference for Keats nor the ignorance about Dylan but the malappropriate self-confidence that has her thinking it reasonable to hand down these uninformed but lofty judgements. As if, indeed, her very unfamiliarity with Dylan's work affirms the loftiness that justifies dismissing that work. Anyone not under the moonie spell of this clerisy might feel that if they were as uninformed about Keats as A.S. Byatt (or David Hare) was about Dylan, they wouldn't rush onto TV to discuss his work.

Keenan, Larry [1943 -] Larry Keenan was born in San Francisco on November 20, 1943 and grew up photographing the last of that city's BEATS scene and then its hippie inheritors. A professional photographer since 1970, he has become eminent in his field with works in many major galleries. Some of his documentation of the Beats is in the permanent collection of the Archives of American Artists in the Smithsonian in Washington, D.C., and in 1999 FERLINGHETTI's City Lights Books published his *Postcards from the Underground*. Since 1985 he has experimented with creating images using computers.

When Keenan was 22, ALLEN GINSBERG introduced him to Dylan at the party after Dylan's high-profile electric Berkeley concert of December 4, 1965 (at which, without permission, he managed to take a couple of photos). He *did* get permission for a session with Dylan to get potential *Blonde on Blonde* pictures the next day, which was supposed to be a 'last day of the Beats' gathering at the City Lights bookstore at North Beach, San Francisco. Dylan and entourage, plus Keenan, were hiding from fans in the basement, and when people tried to break the door down they climbed out of a window and ran along the alley just outside, where Keenan then took what proved to be the classic shots of Dylan in his polkadot shirt with Michael McClure, Ginsberg and ROBBIE ROBERTSON. Keenan's friend Dale Smith was also there taking shots in the alley, one of which—a close-up of McClure, Dylan and Ginsberg—is used full-page in the *Biograph* box set (p.13).

In the end none of Larry's pictures were used on *Blonde on Blonde*, but they were used in *Biograph* (1985) and the *Bootleg Series Vol. 4: Bob Dylan Live 1966* (1998): including one of the shots he wasn't supposed to take at the Berkeley concert. Larry Keenan was still a college student, and still living at home, when these photos were taken. He had to mow the lawn before he could borrow the car to drive to his rendezvous with Dylan and do the shoot.

Kegan, Larry [1942 - 2001] In the sleevenotes to the *Street Legal* album of 1978, Larry Kegan gets an affectionate if opaque namecheck: 'Champion of all Causes—Larry Kegan'. In fact Dylan's friendship with Kegan—born in St. Paul on April 16, 1942—stretched all the way back to August 1954, when they met at a Jewish summer camp, the co-educational Camp Herzl, near Webster, Wisconsin. As DAVE ENGEL documents in *Just Like Bob Zimmerman's Blues: Dylan in Minnesota*: 'With other Jewish boys and girls, mostly from Duluth and the Twin Cities' they go swimming and rowing, play tennis, listen to ghost stories, play jokes on counsellors and cook outdoors. They 'must speak Hebrew in the dining hall, call buildings by Hebrew names and dress in white for the Sabbath. The campers play at Zionism. It's Arab versus Jew, just like cowboys and Indians. . . . Some see Bobby sitting on the bathroom roof with *those guys*, LOUIS KEMP, Steve Friedman, Stevie Goldberg, Larry Keegan [sic].' (Dylan biographer CLINTON HEYLIN also misspells him as 'Keegan'.)

As HOWARD SOUNES tells it in *Down the Highway*: 'Bob was playing piano when twelve-year-old Larry Kegan walked into the lodge. "How do you know this song?" asked Kegan, recognizing a bluesy tune from the radio. "Well, late at night up north where I live you get this [radio] station," said Bob. "Well, I've been listenin' to the same stuff."' Kegan did indeed know 'the same stuff', and he and Bob started performing together at the camp, which they continued to attend for two weeks each August up until 1958.

Sounes reports that Kegan grew up in St. Paul, 'was an accomplished singer' and 'had a high school doo-wop group, including three African-American boys whom he introduced to Bob. . . .

This was something new.' As with HOWARD RUTMAN, also from St. Paul, Kegan's friendship with Dylan gave him somewhere to stay on visits to the city. They'd turn up at parties, sing and play rock'n' roll piano and make themselves unpopular. According to Paul Spindle's profile of Kegan's fellow University of Minnesotan Gene, aka Geno, LaFond (with whom he wrote songs and performed—they called themselves the Mere Mortals), when Larry was in hospital after the accident that made him a paraplegic at age 15, Bob 'would come in and wheel Larry into the day room on a gurney, where they would sing together. . . . the nurses, doctors and patients had no idea what was going on.'

The accident has variously been described as a diving accident, a motorbike crash and an auto accident, and has been said to have happened at age 15, age 16 and age 17. Certainly it was an auto accident a decade later that made Kegan a quadriplegic and put him in the wheelchair in which he spent the rest of his life. 'If he could have stood up he would have been tall,' wrote Billy Golfus, director & writer of *When Billy Broke His Head*, a 1995 TV film about the disabled in which Larry Kegan featured, adding: 'and he wasn't any wider than a beer truck.' Kegan disliked the weight he put on in the last years of his life.

Kegan gained a masters degree in Speech Communication; managed a Florida orange grove and citrus farm for a while; pioneered (with a Dr. Ted Cole) a programme for 'attitude reassessment about disability and sexuality' that has long since become a student requirement at the University of Minnesota's Medical School; and ran a resort for disabled Vietnam veterans in Mexico, where he lived for some time, originally 'because it was cheap'. He is reputed to have been the 'model' for the character of Charlie, played by William Defoe, in Oliver Stone's film *Born on the Fourth of July*.

Larry Kegan returned to Minnesota in the mid-1970s. He never mentioned his friendship with Dylan to outsiders, except when singing with the Mere Mortals, when he might say 'Here's a song by a friend of mine', yet from the mid-1970s onwards he would spend sustained periods on tour with Dylan, every touring year when his health permitted. The first time Gene LaFond went along was the Rolling Thunder Revue in 1975: 'Sometimes I would fly out and meet up with them, hang for a few days and then fly home. Larry would go for weeks sometimes and different people would meet up with him and help him.' He would phone Dylan up and say 'Where are you? We're coming out!'

Billy Golfus describes how they 'would load up Larry's handicapped equipped van and catch up with the tour and hang out as long as they could. Sometimes they'd stay for weeks as Bob's personal guests. Bob put the word out to the crew that these were his friends and they were to be treated right and "make sure they don't get in the way or arrested." The routine was that at the end of the show, during Dylan's encore, they would get in Larry's van and get in line behind Bob's tour bus and roll into the night to the next gig. As they moved through the night, Bob and Larry would talk on the CB until Larry would drift off to sleep in the back of the van.'

Memorably, Kegan was brought on stage at two consecutive concerts in 1981: at Merrillville, Indiana, on October 19, and at Boston two nights later (not, as per Sounes, 'the next night'). These appearances marked Kegan's début professional performances with Dylan, almost three decades on from their first get-togethers. At Merrillville, Kegan came on at the end of the encore, and Dylan introduced him: 'You wanna, you wanna hear something really strange? I got a friend of mine who's gonna sing a song now. Gonna bring him on stage. I wonder if he's gonna sing? This is a friend of mine named Larry!' What was 'really strange' was that as Larry sang CHUCK BERRY's 'No Money Down' as the concert's final number, Dylan picked up a tenor sax at the same time (another first) and made honking noises in appropriate places. At Boston, Kegan came on before the encore and played harmonica on the concert's 23rd song, 'When You Gonna Wake Up?', and then again the evening ended with 'No Money Down', with Dylan honking away on the sax for the second and (so far) last time. This was all caught on (unissued) filmed by HOWARD ALK.

In the course of these various tours—and as a friend Kegan came to Europe with Dylan at least four times too—he met and befriended other stellar artists, including NEIL YOUNG, who invited the Mere Mortals to play at two of his annual Bridge Benefit concerts. Reportedly Kegan and LaFond were flown in 'like the stars that they were. Picked up at the airport in a long black Cadillac, the two were treated just like the "rest of the hotshots."' (So that's what some of the money goes on: limos for the stars . . .) As Paul Spindle noted, 'The Bridge School being for disabled kids, well; it just seem[ed] natural to have a performer in a wheelchair at this event.' In 1991, they preceded JOHN LEE HOOKER in the line-up. Another time, on stage at a Hannukah Festival in San Francisco, Larry seemed to stop singing in mid-song. 'The plug had falled out of the hole in his throat; his jaw was moving but nothing was coming out. Geno reached over and jammed it back in. Kegan didn't miss a beat.'

In summer 1992, when Dylan did a run of five nights at the Orpheum Theater in Minneapolis, the Mere Mortals were asked to perform a support set on September 2, the fourth night. Soul Asylum, the official support act, an up and coming local-heroes punk band, were not happy to have to start the show with only a 15-minute set. Then, for the same amount of time, on came the Mere Mortals—on this occasion Kegan, LaFond, Sid Gasner and George Palmer, augmented on their last two numbers by Dylan's long-serving bass player TONY GARNIER.

In 1999, Kegan sang at Minnesota Governor Jesse Ventura's inauguration bash. But by now his health was draining away. He needed frequent dialysis treatment and more. Billy Golfus also reports that by this point Kegan 'had embraced Orthodox Judaism and become a Lubavi(t)cher. . . . I couldn't make that scene. Larry was a praying Jew; I'm a lox and brisket Jew.' Above Kegan's bed there were two photos of him with Dylan and their friend LOUIS KEMP: one of them at age 13 and another at age 50. There was also a photo of Kegan with MUDDY WATERS. 'It's like the old joke,' says Golfus, 'where the Pope comes out with Kegan at St. Peter's Square, huge crowds cheering. Somebody pulls your coat and asks, "Who's the guy with Larry Kegan?"'

As with the earlier accidents that had so marked his life, reports of his death vary: he 'died of a heart attack while driving his van' (the 'Bob Dylan Who's Who' web page), or he 'quietly died in bed in Minnesota'. The latter is the more likely; either way, he died of heart failure, and on September 11, 2001. His was not the only music-biz death that day. David Skepner, 63-year-old longtime manager of Loretta Lynn, also suffered a fatal heart attack; Carolyn Mayer Beug, a 48-year-old filmmaker who had made videos for DWIGHT YOAKAM, was a passenger on American Airlines flight 11 and died when the plane crashed into the World Trade Center. On that particular day, few people paid attention to Larry Kegan's passing.

[Dave Engel, *Just Like Bob Zimmerman's Blues: Dylan in Minnesota*, Rudolph, WI: River City Memoirs-Mesabi, 1997, pp.135–36. Clinton Heylin, e.g. *Behind the Shades*, p.32 & *A Life in Stolen Moments*, p.234. Howard Sounes, *Down the Highway: A Life of Bob Dylan*, New York: Grove Press, 2001, Ch.1.

Paul Spindle, 'Gene LaFond—A Musician for the Ages', *All About Surf*, Jul 2005, online 16 Sep 2005 at *www.allaboutsurf.com / 0507 / articles / lafond / index.php*. *When Billy Broke His Head . . . and Other Tales of Wonder*, dir. Billy Golfus, ITVS, US, 1995. Billy Golfus: 'Life and Death of a Mere Mortal', seen online 16 Nov 2005 at *www.mouthmag.com/issues/69/no69pg28.htm*. *Born on the Fourth of July*, dir. Oliver Stone, Ixtlan, US, 1989. 'Bob Dylan Who's Who' webpage *www.expectingrain.com/dok/who/k/keeganlarry.html* (sic).]

Kelly, Roy [1949 -] Roy Kelly, British poet, librarian and Dylan commentator, was born in Walsall, England, on March 5, 1949. He first encountered Dylan as a name mentioned by PETER, PAUL & MARY on a TV appearance on 'Sunday Night at the London Palladium', probably in 1964. This was followed by a chance acquisition of two copies of the short-lived magazine *Hootenanny*, edited by ROBERT SHELTON, in which Dylan wrote a column 'whose style I loved'. By this time Kelly 'co-owned but did not possess (Bart Simpson style) a copy of *The Freewheelin' Bob Dylan*.'

Though Kelly has never written a book on Dylan he has certainly written enough on the subject to fill one. He was a subscriber right from the beginning of the life of the great UK fanzine *The Telegraph*, a regular letter writer within it from early on and his first piece, a review of *Infidels*, was published in it in the summer of 1984. Editor JOHN BAULDIE asked him to write more and he did. His review 'Find Out What It Means to Me: Fans, Collectors and *Biograph*', from *Telegraph* no.23, was republished in the collection *All Across the Telegraph: A Bob Dylan Handbook* in 1987.

His Dylan assessments grew and shifted from reviews to lengthy meditations on themes such as Dylan, change and the embedded 1960s consciousness within long-term fans. His best pieces include 'Big Apple Bobbing', an account of a 1989 trip to NYC to see a run of three Dylan concerts at the Beacon Theatre, and the excellent 'A Bunch of Basement Noise in G', published in 1992: an extended musing on the then recently revealed much-expanded Basement Tapes material, some years before GREIL MARCUS colonized this terrain. His last *Telegraph* essay was a 14,000-word fictional feature about Dylan fandom and 1966 and all that, 'Now and Again: The Ballad of a Then Man'. This piece, which could have appeared in no other publication, emerged in 1996 in the last issue before John Bauldie's death and thus became 'an involuntary memorial to him'. (A posthumous final issue of the magazine was edited by JOHN LINDLEY.) It was a great and affecting, sad and funny piece.

Afterwards Roy opted for a period of silence, followed by Dylan commentary for *On The Tracks* and then for the British Dylan quarterly *THE BRIDGE*, for which he still writes—and still writes, in particular, about the strange pain of being a Dylan fan, and being a Dylan fan of a certain age now: about the complex turmoil of reacting to Dylan. This is territory *he* has colonized, though unambitiously, and with a modesty that is part of what's involved in the reacting. As another fine writer who has never written a Dylan book, ROBERT FORRYAN, puts it in another fanzine: 'Roy Kelly is the best Dylan writer who has never produced a book on Dylan.'

Roy Kelly's other work includes stories and plays broadcast on BBC radio, and a book of poems, *Drugstore Fiction*, 1987.

[Roy Kelly: review of *Infidels*, *Telegraph* no.15, Bury, UK, summer 1984; 'Fans, Collectors and *Biograph*', *Telegraph* no.23, 1986, republished in shorter form in *All Across the Telegraph: A Bob Dylan Handbook*, UK, 1987 & 1988; 'Big Apple Bobbing', *Telegraph* no.34, Romford, UK, Winter 1989; 'A Bunch of Basement Noise in G', *Telegraph* no.43, Autumn 1992; 'Now and Again: The Ballad of a Then Man', *Telegraph* no.55, summer 1996; and *Drugstore Fiction* (poetry), Calstock, UK, Peterloo Poets, 1987. Robert Forryan, in his

'Roy Kelly's Blues—Part Two', republished *Freewheelin'-Quarterly*, Huntingdon, UK, vol.21, Oct 2001, pp.17–21.]

Kelly, Terry [1958 -] Terence Kelly was born in Jarrow, Tyne & Wear, in the north-east of England, on March 9, 1958. He first developed a serious interest in Dylan's work as a teenager in 1972, after borrowing copies of *Bringing It All Back Home* and *Bob Dylan's Greatest Hits*. His first piece of published Dylan commentary was a review of *Shot of Love* in a Northumberland weekly local newspaper, the *News Post-Leader*, in 1981. He began writing for the UK Dylan fanzine *THE BRIDGE* from its launch issue in 1998 and has written recurrently for it since, writing features, book and record reviews and conducting interviews as well as looking after its interests more generally—not least in arranging some of the interviews it runs (including with CHRISTOPHER RICKS, NEIL CORCORAN, CAROLYN HESTER and TOBY THOMPSON), securing pieces by others through his own contacts and suggesting other ideas.

His own contributions include 'Thin Wild Mercury Sounds on Tyneside: Bob Dylan in Newcastle 1965 & 1966'; 'Sixty Ways of Looking at Bob Dylan'; 'Bob Dylan's Songs of Innocence and Experience'—a long, brave early plunge into print with an assessment of *"Love and Theft"*; 'A Long-Forgotten Truth: An Exploration of *Planet Waves*'; and 'A Million Shards of Meaning: The 1984 Letterman Show Revisited'.

Terry Kelly continues to work as a journalist in the north-east of England, mainly for the *South Shields Gazette*.

[Terry Kelly: 'Thin Wild Mercury Sounds on Tyneside: Bob Dylan in Newcastle 1965 & 1966', *The Bridge* no.1, Gateshead, UK, summer 1998; 'Sixty Ways of Looking at Bob Dylan', *The Bridge* no.10, summer 2001; 'Bob Dylan's Songs of Innocence and Experience', *The Bridge* no.11, autumn 2001; 'A Long-Forgotten Truth: An Exploration of *Planet Waves*', *The Bridge* no.12, summer 2002; 'A Million Shards of Meaning: The 1984 Letterman Show Revisited', *The Bridge* no.18, spring 2004.]

kelp In 'Sara', on *Desire*, when Dylan sings that the beach was deserted 'except for some kelp' he is cheating in the same way as George Eliot in *Middlemarch*, 1871 (Chapter 42): 'But there were none to stare at him except the long-weaned calves, and none to show dislike of his appearance except the little water-rats which rustled away at his approach.' Each attempts to modify an absence of people by dragging in wantonly upgraded lower life forms—rather lower in Dylan's case than in Eliot's.

Keltner, Jim [1942 -] James Keltner was born in Tulsa, Oklahoma, on April 27, 1942 and began his drumming career in the 1960s. He became one of the most sought-after of session players, and has worked live and in the studio with an absurdly all-star list of artists, from Barbra Streisand to JOHN LENNON, B.B. King to JONI MITCHELL, ERIC CLAPTON to Martha Reeves, Charlie Watts to Rickie Lee Jones and DAVID CROSBY to the Bee Gees. He can add Manhattan Transfer, ARLO GUTHRIE, Pink Floyd, BRIAN WILSON, Freddie Hubbard, Randy Newman, JOHN LEE HOOKER, Jackson Browne, WILLIE NELSON, the Indigo Girls, ELVIS COSTELLO, Joe Cocker and a good few more. He can also add the TRAVELING WILBURYS and, more important, Bob Dylan.

Perhaps he first played with Dylan in the studio, in March 1971, pulled in by LEON RUSSELL, who produced the session. As Keltner recalls it, 'We did "Watching the River Flow" and "When I Paint My Masterpiece" on that same day. And then I didn't see him again until we did "Knockin' on Heaven's Door" in Los Angeles. That was a monumental session for me because it was such a touching song. It was the first time I actually cried when I was playing. When I hear that on the radio now, it's very special to me. . . . because it's a frozen moment in my life that will always be there.'

Two possible demurrals here. First, it wasn't literally true that Keltner hadn't *seen* Dylan again till 'Knockin' on Heaven's Door', because Keltner played behind Eric Clapton at the Concert for Bangla Desh, four months after the 'Watching the River Flow' studio session. Far more importantly, the drummer on that March 1971 session is more usually said to have been CHUCK BLACKWELL; Blackwell certainly thinks so.

Either way, Jim Keltner certainly appeared on 'Knockin' on Heaven's Door', and therefore on the album *Pat Garrett & Billy the Kid* (1973); the next Dylan album he played on was *Saved* (1980), but this began a run of three 1980s albums on which Dylan used this highly reliable drummer, the others being *Shot of Love* (1981) and *Empire Burlesque* (1985). But by this time Keltner had also toured behind Dylan too, and played on the 1979 'Saturday Night Live' and the 1980 Grammy Awards TV shows. The live concerts began for Keltner with the first gospel tour, from November 1 to December 9, 1979, and continued with the 1980 tours (January 11 to February 9, April 17 to May 21 and November 9 to December 4). He remained for the 1981 tours too (June 10 to July 25, mostly in Europe, and then October 16 to November 21 in North America), though on the latter he found that Dylan was adding a second drummer.

After these tours and the 1980s albums, Keltner's next Dylan assignment was in the studio in May 1988 to play on the album *The Traveling Wilburys Volume 1*. Next came the 'Late Night with David Letterman' TV show on January 18, 1992, with a bemused Bob Dylan singing 'Like a Rolling Stone', backed by a calm, solid Keltner plus a horder of others comically hyped up to the point of rabidity. That October 16, Keltner was the drummer in the house band at the so-called 30th Anniversary Concert Celebration, playing behind most of that night's performers—including Dylan. Less than two years later, in Japan, Keltner was Dylan's drummer alongside the Tokyo New Philharmonic Orchestra at the self-proclaimed 'Great Music Experience' at the Todaiji Temple in Nara, as Dylan sang 'A Hard Rain's a-Gonna Fall', 'I Shall Be Released', 'Ring Them Bells' and an ensemble reprise of 'I Shall Be Released' three nights running (May 20–22, 1994).

In 1997 Keltner was called down to Miami to play drums on seven of the 11 tracks on *Time Out of Mind* (he's absent on 'Dirt Road Blues', 'Cold Irons Bound', 'Make You Feel My Love' and 'Highlands')—and then after another gap of years, he found himself called up again, more surprisingly, to become one of the Never-Ending Tour musicians. Twenty-one years after his previous concert-tour job with Dylan, he came back to replace GEORGE RECELI. He 'shadowed' Receli, who was having a problem with an arm, on the Milan concert of April 20, 2002, took over for the first ten numbers of the following night's concert in Zurich and then replaced Receli altogether as from Innsbruck on April 23, through to the last nights of that tour leg, in London on May 11 & 12. In Brussels, on April 28, in Cardiff on May 6 and on the last night in London, he got to play 'Knockin' on Heaven's Door' again.

[Jim Keltner quoted from interview by Don Zulaica, seen online 6 Jan 2006 on the Drummerworld website at *www.drummerworld.com/drummers/Jim_Keltner.html*.]

Kemp, Louis [1941? -] Louis Kemp has been an almost life-long friend of Bob Dylan's, since first meeting him at a Jewish co-educational summer camp, Camp Herzl, which they both attended annually in the mid-1950s.

Louis inherited the long-established family business of A. Kemp Fisheries Inc., based at 4832 West Superior Street, Duluth, which had been founded in 1930 by Aron and Abe Kemp, who started taking Lake Superior fish to the Chicago markets. It's a company whose relationship with Swedish and Finnish fishermen goes back a long way. There's a statue to the memory of these men on the shore at Green Point, just north of Thunder Bay, erected in 1990 on the 100th anniversary of their trading. 'The Finns of Green Point would sell their fish to Kemp Fisheries located in Duluth,' noted Mike Roinila in a 1997 article, 'and over the years a trusting and lasting association was formed between the fishermen and the American seller. . . . [And] when an unexpected thaw one winter left the fishermen with no way to keep their harvest frozen, Kemp Fisheries rented out the Port Arthur arena to freeze the fish and preserve them for market.'

Today's marine traffic is mostly boats used by the owners of the shoreline cottages—Green Point's last commercial fisherman retired in 1990—but A. Kemp Fisheries survived. Louis Kemp took over in 1967, expanded into Alaska and re-named it Louis Kemp Fisheries in 1986, and has since seen it taken over and moved. It was taken over first by Tyson Seafood (1992) and then by Bumble Bee (1999). Bumble Bee is a subsidiary of International Home Foods, which was itself taken over in 2000 by ConAgra Foods, which moved production from Duluth to Motley, Minnesota. Its official address is now in Downer's Grove, Illinois. They mostly turn North Pacific white fish pulp into imitation shellfish (surimi), and Louis Kemp has become a registered trade mark; you can buy Louis Kemp® Crab Delights® in Chunk Style, Flake Style, Leg Style or Easy Shreds; Lobster Delights® Salad Style, and Scallop Delights® Bay Style. Mmm.

Kemp was among the entourage on Dylan and THE BAND's 1974 'comeback' tour, and with Barry Imhoff was tour manager on the Rolling Thunder Revues—on which, SAM SHEPARD noted, he showed 'a remarkable gift for being able to speak words without moving his mouth,' and also 'managed to buy a 1934 Packard coupé'. At The Band's so-called 'Farewell Concert' dinner in San Francisco on November 25, 1976, Kemp Fisheries supplied the smoked salmon. It was even through his fisheries that he became a friend of Marlon Brando's, and duly brought Brando and Dylan together for a very different kind of meal. As his own account of 2005 explains it:

> 'I got to know Marlon about thirty years ago through a mutual friend. His son, Christian, came to work for me in fisheries I owned in Alaska and Minnesota. . . . One of my visits to Los Angeles coincided with Passover. I was not yet Orthodox and made plans to attend a seder at a local synagogue with my sister. Marlon called me that very day and invited me out to dinner. I graciously declined, explaining that it was Passover and I was going to a seder. Marlon became audibly excited over the phone and said, "Passover—I've always wanted to attend a seder. Can I come with?" He had made me an offer I couldn't refuse. . . . A short time later, Marlon called me back and asked if he could bring a friend. I said, yes, by all means. . . . I called the shul again. They were a little less patient this time and begrudgingly told me that they could squeeze one more person in, but this was absolutely the last one as they were now officially sold out.
>
> 'Still later that day, I received a phone call from a childhood friend of mine who had become a well-known singer/songwriter. . . . he asked if he and his wife could go along. The shul was unhappy . . . but somehow I softened the heart of the receptionist and she agreed to let my people go—to the seder.
>
> 'I will never forget the sight of our table in the synagogue, Marlon Brando was to my left and

sitting next to him was his guest. This was during the height of Marlon's involvement with Native American causes and he had brought with him noted Indian activist Dennis Banks of Wounded Knee fame. Banks was dressed in full Indian regalia: buckskin tassles on his clothes and long braids hanging down from a headband, which sported a feather. My childhood friend Bob Dylan sat to my right, joined by his wife, my sister Sharon, and other friends. . . . After about forty-five minutes, the rabbi figured out that ours was not your average seder table. "Mr. Brando, would you please do us the honor of reading the next passage from the hagaddah," he said. Marlon said, "It would be my pleasure."

'He smiled broadly, stood up and delivered the passage from the hagaddah as if he were reading Shakespeare on Broadway. Mouths fell open and eyes focused on the speaker with an intensity any rabbi would covet. When he was done I think people actually paused, wondering if they should applaud.

'Somewhat later the rabbi approached another member of our table. "Mr. Dylan, would you do us the honor of singing us a song?" The rabbi pulled out an acoustic guitar. . . . Much to my surprise Bob said yes and performed an impromptu rendition of "Blowin' in the Wind" to the stunned shul of about 300 seder guests. . . . Needless to say, everyone was both shocked and thrilled by this unusual Hollywood-style Passover miracle.'

But Louis Kemp seems always to have remained important at least in part because of his pre-showbiz credentials with Dylan. ROBERT SHELTON reported that it was with Kemp, in September 1974, that Dylan 'revisited Highway 61, touring the North Country . . . [and] showing his oldest children where he'd grown up'.

[Mike Roinila: 'Finnish Fishermen of Lake Superior', *The Finnish American Reporter*, Jan 1997, seen online 12 May 2005 at *http://sfhs.eget.net/P_articles/Pelo112.html*. Sam Shepard, *Rolling Thunder Logbook*, London: Penguin edn., p.8. Louis Kemp memoir extracted from *www.expectingrain.com/dok/who/who.html*. Robert Shelton, *No Direction Home: The Life and Music of Bob Dylan*, London: Penguin edn. p.446.]

Kemper, David [1947/48 -] David Law Kemper was born in Chicago in 1947–48 but attended high school in Ogden, Utah, where in his senior year he was drumming in contest-winning local band the Groobies; when he was 17, his father's job transferred the family to Sedalia, Missouri, but David was allowed to stay behind to remain in the band. He had already been drumming for a decade by this time, and never had any other ambition. When he managed to avoid the draft in 1966 by faking insanity, he said he realised his good luck. 'It all lay before me, no more detours.' A friend encouraged him to move to LA and start session playing, which he did that same year, getting into it by helping the friend build a studio in which he then watched others, including JIM KELTNER, at work. He made a slow start but once he got going, Kemper was working non-stop, and in the 1970s played on a huge number of albums including for Joan Armatrading, GEOFF MULDAUR, Dion, Glen Campbell and Manhattan Transfer and touring with many others.

He'd first seen THE GRATEFUL DEAD in 1968, but thought that compared to people like Miles Davis, 'they lumbered along. They weren't agile. . . . [They] were like a big clunky old machine. Boy, they got the ball rolling, though, and it was just like a locomotive.' Decades later, he joined the JERRY GARCIA Band, playing with them from 1983 to 1993, and not only on drums but percussion, tambourine, congas and even slide guitar and vocals. He's on Garcia's 1988 solo album *Almost Acoustic* too, and in the 1980s–90s also played sessions for T-BONE BURNETT, John Hiatt and even David Cassidy. After being abruptly fired from the Garcia Band (for reasons he was never given and never understood) he plunged back into session-work, including for PHIL SPECTOR. And despite the avowal of single-mindedness ('no detours'), he also developed his hobby of painting into something closer to a professional activity, with work on display at Ghengis Cohen in LA and a 1996 one-man show in Germany.

1996 was also the year he joined Bob Dylan's Never-Ending Tour band, replacing WINSTON WATSON and playing his first concert at San Luis Obispo, California, that October 17. He remained the band's drummer—a still-slight, balding, intense-looking figure, often in dark glasses—all the way through till the last date of 2001, on November 24 in Boston. That's a total of 569 concerts, making him one of the longest-serving of Dylan's musicians, behind only TONY GARNIER, BUCKY BAXTER and JOHN JACKSON. David Kemper also plays on both *Time Out of Mind* and *"Love and Theft"*.

Since leaving the band, he has returned to session-work, and in 2005 worked on the soundtrack for the JOHNNY CASH biopic *Walk the Line*.

[Quotes from the engaging article by Barry Smolin, 'Drumming at the Edge of Jerry: an Interview with David Kemper', *Dupree's Diamond News* no.36, US, 1997 (interview done in 1996 just before Kemper joined Dylan's band), seen online 13 Dec 2005 at *www.well.com/user/shmo/kemper.html* (in which he talks fondly & interestingly about Jerry Garcia's warmth & intelligence).]

Kerouac, Jack [1922 - 1969] Jean-Louis Lebris de Kerouac was born in Lowell, Massachusetts, on March 12, 1922 to French-Canadian parents. He became the quintessential BEAT figure yet a highly individual and influential voice. He is primarily a novelist, albeit with a prose style that can rightly be called prose poetry, as his masterpiece *On the Road*, 1957, shows.

Dylan paid his work close, continuing attention. Kerouac's poetry book, *Mexico City Blues*, 1959, as ALLEN GINSBERG told WES STACE, was a specific influence on Dylan: 'He read that in '58–9. . . . Somebody gave it him and . . . as he said . . . it [was] the first book of poetry which talked the American language to *him* . . .' Dylan uses this title in 'Something's Burning, Baby' on the 1985 album *Empire Burlesque* ('I got the Mexico City blues . . .').

While the impact of Kerouac's work has been, like Dylan's, unquantifiably wide, Dylan makes specific use of Kerouac's titles, commonly recycling them into his own. Thus *On the Road*–'On the Road Again'; *The Subterraneans*, 1958–'Subterranean Homesick Blues'; *Visions of Gerard*, 1963–'Visions of Johanna'; *Desolation Angels*, 1965–'Desolation Row'.

In the case of this last work, the borrowing happened fast and ran deeper. In 'Desolation Row' Dylan recycles a phrase direct from the Kerouac book: 'in the perfect image of a priest'; the book also yields the phrase 'housing project hill', which Dylan throws into the same album's 'Just Like Tom Thumb's Blues'. Kerouac's book was first published in March 1965; the songs were recorded that August.

Kerouac died of alcohol and despair at St. Petersburg, Florida, on October 21, 1969. He was 47.

[Ginsberg interviewed by Stace, Cambridge, UK, 27 Apr 1985, from 'Interviews and a Poem: Allen Ginsberg, Poet', in *All Across the Telegraph: A Bob Dylan Handbook*, ed. Michael Gray & John Bauldie, 1987.]

Kershaw, Doug [1936 -] Douglas James Kershaw was born in Tiel Ridge, Louisiana, on January 24, 1936, the seventh child in a family of nine, whose mother played guitar and whose father was an alligator hunter who committed suicide when Doug was seven years old. The three youngest boys first formed a band as children in 1948; two of the three (Rusty and Doug) stuck with it and had a top 5 country hit in 1955 with their first single, 'So Lovely, Baby' on ROY ACUFF's Hickory label. But if the Kershaws' ambition was indicated by their childhood band's original name, the Continental Playboys, it proved to be with the more geographically limited name 'Lousiana Man' that they first went even bigger than continental. A huge hit in 1961, it was eventually covered by around 800 other artists, and in 1969 it became the first song broadcast back to earth from the moon by the Apollo 12 astronauts.

1969 had already been, by then, the year Doug Kershaw was 'rediscovered' with a 'JOHNNY CASH TV Show' appearance in June, and he ended it as opening act for ERIC CLAPTON's Derek & the Dominos band at the Fillmore East. (Rusty and Doug had split up professionally in 1964.) More pertinently for us, a month before Kershaw's Cash TV appearance he had played a May 3, 1969 *Self Portrait* session for Bob Dylan in Nashville, where he played violin on 'Take a Message to Mary'—and then came his gorgeously gear-grinding, down-home fiddle solo which dominates Dylan's 'Blue Moon'.

By early August he had been interviewed and splashed large across *Rolling Stone* magazine, in which he made interesting comments about perceived differences between Dylan's old hip milieu and his current country explorations, assuming it to be all of a piece with a Dylan rejection of foul-mouthed 'underground' language. Kershaw, clearly a man who, in the spotlight for the first time in years, was determined to seize his moment and speak on behalf of the by-passed, conservative world, said:

> 'You wonder why Dylan's down here? You saw his little boy, didn't you?—Well then I think that you should know why he's here. He's grown up. Just what is this big difference between here and San Francisco? Do you really think the people are that different between here and there? You think people aren't poor here? You think people don't go out on their wives here?'

A revered musician who claimed to play 28 different instruments, Kershaw himself spent the 1970s and early 1980s in a doldrums of career failure, drug and alcohol abuse, except for a brief shake-up in 1975 when he re-married and in 1981 when he returned to the country top 40 with 'Hello Woman'. After 1984 he re-emerged as a musician with a career, made a hit duet with Hank Williams Jr. ('Cajun Baby', 1988) and in 1998 released his first French-language material since the early 1950s. In 2001 he made a new solo album, *Still Cajun After All These Years*.

[Rusty & Doug: *Rusty & Doug Sing Louisiana Man and Other Favorites*, Hickory LPM-103, 1961 includes 'So Lovely, Baby', their 1958 hit 'Hello Sheriff' & 'Louisiana Man'; the 2-CD set *Louisiana Men* contains their complete Hickory sessions. Patrick Thomas: 'Doug Kershaw' (interview), *Rolling Stone* no.39, San Francisco, 9 Aug 1969.]

Kibbutz Ein Dor, Dylan visit to See **Yellin, Bob.**

Kimball, Stuart [1956 -] Stuart Morse Kimball was born in Massachusetts on December 21, 1956, and grew up in Hopkinton, New Hampshire, before basing himself in Boston in the early 1980s, when he played guitar in a band called Face to Face. He had been playing self-taught guitar from the age of ten. Apart from playing with Carly Simon he has spent most of the last quarter-century as a Boston local hero, a 'comrade in arms' of that other local hero, Peter Wolf, whose solo albums *Long Line* and *Sleepless* he has worked on.

He played on two Dylan sessions for *Empire Burlesque* in 1985 (on February 21 & 23), and therefore gets a credit on the album cut of 'When the Night

Comes Falling from the Sky', and then re-appeared almost 20 years later, with dark glasses, pork pie hat and a stolid, weary, middle-aged look, as the replacement for the great FREDDY KOELLA in the Never-Ending Tour band of 2004, playing his first concert in Gilford, New Hampshire, on June 4.

As of early 2006 he remains in the band, a competent team player who has never contributed the slightest musical personality of his own to the rest.

[Quote & background data from 'Kimball's career is a-changin" by Steve Morse, *Boston Globe*, 6 Aug 2004.]

King, Carole [1942 -] Carol(e) Klein was born in Brooklyn on February 9, 1942 and swiftly became a gifted child pianist. As a teenager she was already a keen songwriter, recording demos, backup singing, arranging sessions, and recording some early unsuccessful singles while attending Queens College.

Neil Sedaka wrote 'Oh Carol' for Carole King but she opted instead for lyricist GERRY GOFFIN, and for a few golden years as from 1959, when they were married and dreaming up songs together, they were the prolific writers of major pop hits, working out of the famous Brill Building at 1819 Broadway, New York, for Nevins-Kirchner-Colgem from 1960 onwards. It was far less Goffin's inconsequential words than Carole King's strong, confident, catchy melody lines that made memorable and even exciting records that would otherwise have been workaday milk-white pop.

Not all their hits were for white artists—the first to serve notice that here was a composer of distinctive zing and a youthful, humane optimism, regardless of subject matter, was the Shirelles' tremendous 'Will You Still Love Me Tomorrow?', with its inexorable lyric thrust propelled along by thin, remorseless voices and shuddering strings. Goffin & King also turned their African-American babysitter, Little Eva, into a pop star with 'The Locomotion' and its equally cheery follow-up, 'Keep Your Hands Off My Baby' (which had nothing to do with the babysitting) and wrote the Cookies' hit 'Chains', later covered by THE BEATLES, the Chiffons' 'One Fine Day' (later accidentally plagiarised by GEORGE HARRISON) and the Drifters' 'Up on the Roof'.

But Goffin & King also gave big stars like BOBBY VEE their biggest hits, Vee's 'Take Good Care of My Baby', a no.1, epitomising the unstoppable hit quality of their output. When these records were new, and you first heard them on the radio, it was obvious in a moment that they were bound to be big hits. When Carole King was allowed to record one of these teeny-bop songs herself, 'It Might As Well Rain Until September', it was clear that this too would be a transatlantic hit: and it was. The hits continued even after the impact of the Beatles, the 'British invasion', mid-1960s Bob Dylan and the liberating explosion into more complex songs. The plaintive 'Goin' Back' was a hit for Dusty Springfield in 1966 and covered by THE BYRDS. (It was later revived to good effect by King herself and later still to bad effect by Queen.) Even in the summer of love, there were plenty of clients for songwriters, and it was Goffin & King who wrote the Monkees' 1967 smash 'Pleasant Valley Sunday'. Aretha Franklin's '(You Make Me Feel Like) A Natural Woman' was theirs too, though a third credit went to producer JERRY WEXLER. (And of course there had always been a middle of the road market: the unspeakably awful Steve Lawrence and Edie Gormé topped the charts in 1963 with another Goffin-King song, 'Go Away Little Girl'—a title Bob Dylan would mirror some decades later with his own less successful 'Go Away Little Boy'.)

Just as Goffin and King did not write together exclusively while married, so too their professional collaboration didn't quite end with their 1968 divorce—they co-wrote Blood, Sweat & Tears' 'Hi-De-Ho'—but it was King who emerged the more strongly, both as a songwriter and a performer, moving to LA, adapting to the changed music world of the late 1960s and of the hip singer-songwriter, and enjoying slow-burning but spectacular solo success with her album *Tapestry*, which was released in 1971 after a lack of success first with Danny Kortchmar and her second husband Charles Larkey in their trio The City and with a first solo album, *Writer*, in 1970.

Tapestry was effectively an album of reinterpretations of her own work, including a couple of Goffin-King hits, on which King signalled that she could ease up on the bouncy-bounciness and allow her pop compositions to breathe more maturely in the freer air of a new age. Her own songs here included 'I Feel the Earth Move' (which duly became a no.1 single), 'So Far Away' (a no.3) and 'You've Got a Friend' (a huge hit by James Taylor) as well as 'It's Too Late' (another no.1, co-written with Toni Stern) and versions of the Goffin-King hits by Aretha Franklin and the Shirelles. Aided by a posse of top musicians, including JONI MITCHELL on backing vocals and James Taylor on guitar, vocals and, er, grandfalloon, King herself not only sang in her newly mournful, clear-eyed, frail but resonant voice but also played synthesiser, guitar, piano and other keyboards and contributed background vocals. She seemed to have been around forever, yet she was still in her 20s.

Tapestry was an album you couldn't get away from, not only in 1971, but on for several years afterwards as it continued to colonise the charts and sell more and more millions of copies. Further albums followed, including *Thoroughbred* (1975), featuring DAVID CROSBY and Graham Nash as well as James Taylor, and *Simple Things* (1977), after which she made a third unhappy marriage, again to a songwriting partner, Rick Evers, who died of a heroin overdose a year later. Becoming more and more of an environmental activist, she released the album *Speeding Time* in 1983 and dropped out to live and campaign in Idaho, but returned to recording in 1989 with the album *City Streets*, followed in 1993 by *Color of Your Dreams* (with two songs co-written by Slash).

The year before that she had made a first professional connection with Bob Dylan, when she could be seen at the piano, still looking youthful in well-cut dark jacket and blue jeans, jumping up and down on the pedals, waving a mane of golden hair and smiling in unrestrained delight, the most prominent musician in the swollen, surreal band ranged behind Dylan on his wary performance of 'Like a Rolling Stone' at the 'Late Night With David Letterman 10th Anniversary Show', recorded that January 18 and televised February 6. Three years later, on March 30, 1995, she popped up at one of Dylan's Never-Ending Tour concerts in Brixton, London, sharing backing vocals on 'Rainy Day Women # 12 & 35' with Chrissie Hynde and ELVIS COSTELLO; and then on March 11, at the Dublin concert, she came on stage after the first nine songs and played piano on the remaining eight (for the last three of which VAN MORRISON was sharing vocals, as was Costello on the last two). So it was that in the unexpected setting of a vile stadium in Dublin, Carole King, now a woman of 53 and only Bob's junior by nine months, joined that far greater singer-songwriter than herself to play on 'Highway 61 Revisited', 'In the Garden', 'Ballad of a Thin Man', 'Like a Rolling Stone', 'The Times They Are a-Changin', 'Real, Real Gone', 'I Shall Be Released' and another 'Rainy Day Women'.

In 2003 Carole King, an active Democrat, picked the wrong man yet again, actively campaigning for John Kerry in the Democratic primaries. On July 29, 2004, she spoke and sang at the Democratic National Convention. Two hours later, Kerry made his acceptance speech as Presidential nominee and marched off down the long road to oblivion.

Carole, however, has marched off to Stars Hollow, Connecticut, fictional hometown of the TV show 'Gilmore Girls', in which she appears now and then as Sophie Bloom, the sharp-tongued owner of Sophie's Music Shop.

[Carole King: 'It Might as Well Rain Until September', Companion 2000, US (London-American HLU 9591, UK), 1962; *Writer*, Ode SP 77006, US, 1970; *Tapestry*, LA, Jan 1971, Ode SP 77009, 1971; *Thoroughbred*, Ode SP 77034, 1975; *Simple Things*, Capitol SMAS 11667, US, 1977; *Speeding Time*, Atlantic ATL 80118, US, 1983; *City Streets*, Capitol CAP 90885, 1989; *Color of Your Dreams*, Priority/Scarface SCA 57197, US, 1993. The City: *Now That Everything's Been Said*, Ode Z 12-44012, US, 1969. 'Gilmore Girls', Warner Bros, US; King débuted in Season 2, episode 20 ('Help Wanted', 2002). Sources include *http://carole-king.biography.ms/* & the Ode discography at *www.bsnpubs.com/aandm/ode.html*, both seen online 5 Feb 2006.]

King, Clydie [1943 -] Clydie May Crittendon (daughter of a Curtis Crittendon and a Lula Mae King) was born in Dallas, Texas, on August 21, 1943. She is generally thought a backing singer, but in fact has made many records of her own, some of them a surprisingly long time ago. She made her first, 'A Casual Look' c/w 'Oh Me', in the *mid-1950s* in Memphis, for the Bihari Brothers' label RPM, billed as by Little Clydie King & the Teens. Soon afterwards, credited as Clydie King, she made two singles on Speciality: 'Our Romance' c/w 'Written on the Wall' (1956–57) and 'I'm Invited to Your Party' c/w 'Young Fool in Love' (1957). She made two further singles for Philips in the early 1960s (as Clydie King & the Sweet Things) plus one as by Mel Carter & Clydie King; three more in 1965 for Imperial, a 1968 duet with Jimmy Holiday and four more 1968–69 solo singles, all on Minit. In 1972 or 1976 came a shoddily packaged solo album on Lizard, *Direct Me*. One more single, a version of Sly & the Family Stone's 'Dance to the Music', credited to Clydie King & Brown Sugar, came out on Chelsea Records in 1973, as did the album *Brown Sugar Featuring Clydie King* (with a heavy reliance on songs penned by Donna Weiss). As one of the vocal group the Blackberries she also made a mysteriously never-released album for Motown at the end of the 60s, followed by several Blackberries singles in 1973 and 1974.

Her prodigious back-up singing career included being a one-time member of RAY CHARLES' Raelettes, singing on many of PHIL SPECTOR's girl-group records of the very early 1960s, being among Joe Cocker's Mad Dogs & Englishmen, singing on JESSE ED DAVIS' second solo album, on Steppenwolf's hit 'Born to be Wild', on the 1973 SONNY TERRY & BROWNIE McGHEE album *Sonny & Brownie*, tracks by Lynyrd Skynyrd and Tim Rose and, while romantically linked to MICK JAGGER, on THE ROLLING STONES' album *Exile on Main Street*. In 1972, backed by a 31-piece Quincy Jones orchestra, Clydie followed the double-act of CAROLE KING & James Taylor and preceded Barbra Streisand at a lavish, star-packed 'Four for McGovern' fundraiser at the LA Forum, the nature of which is indicated by the fact that Warren Beattie and Goldie Hawn acted as ushers. Four years later King worked with Streisand again, as one of the Oreos in her movie with KRIS KRISTOFFERSON, *A Star Is Born*. In 1977 she sang behind another diva, BETTE MIDLER, on her *Broken Blossom* album.

Clydie King first joined the Dylan world in 1970, when at a session of overdubbing held in LA under producer BOB JOHNSTON's supervision, Clydie King and fellow Blackberries Venetta Fields and Genger Blake Schackne (plus Johnston himself) sang backup vocals on a session with various musicians. Dylan himself wasn't there. It isn't known what tracks were worked on but the date (overnight on March 26) falls in the middle of sessions for *New Morning*. It was another decade before Clydie King and Dylan actually worked together. A committed Christian, she seems to have arrived in the picture in February 1980, and is thought to have become a valued singer, a moral support and a girlfriend, first working on most of the *Saved* sessions at Muscle Shoals in Sheffield, Alabama, and then joining the backing singers on the second 1980 gospel tour, starting in Toronto that April 17 and finishing in Dayton, Ohio, on May 21. In general, she sang a solo number, 'Calvary', in the middle of alternate shows. (The backing singers also began most concerts with several jointly sung gospel numbers before Bob Dylan came on stage, so that King was in the group singing five songs, sometimes as many as seven, most evenings.)

In October 1980, she was among those in the studio with Dylan in Santa Monica for a long session, at which 13 tracks were cut, though only six have circulated, among them a fascinating 'Caribbean Wind' and that great unreleased number 'Yonder Comes Sin'. On the semi-gospel fall tour (the 'Musical Retrospective Tour') that followed, from November 9 in San Francisco to December 4 in Portland, Oregon, Clydie was there again. A few of these concerts also began with several songs from the backing singers, King included, but this time she and Dylan also sang vocal duets on two numbers—'Abraham Martin and John' (with Dylan on piano) and 'Rise Again'. From November 19, both were being performed in the same concert. King was thus afforded a rare prominence on this tour, and the mutual respect and affection between her and Dylan was obvious.

From late March to early May of 1981 Clydie King pitched into almost all of the sessions for *Shot of Love*, though one of the few she missed was the last one, on May 15 in LA, at which 'Heart of Mine' was recorded.

The 1981 tour—sometimes called the 'Shot of Love Tour'—comprised four warm-up shows in the US in June, a leg in Europe in June–July and another in North America in October–November. Concerts during the first two legs were structured much like the previous one, starting with four songs by the backing singers plus TERRY YOUNG on piano; Dylan and the band would then perform ten to 12 numbers, followed by one song from a backing singer (with the band) and then came a further ten to 14 songs by Bob Dylan and the band and an encore of one or two more songs with the band and one or two more by Dylan alone. The fall concerts omitted the backing-singer section at the start, and ended with the encores reversed so that Dylan's solo songs came before one or two final numbers with the group. Within all this, Clydie King took no solo slots on the US warm-up dates, but duetted with Dylan on 'Abraham Martin and John' or 'Rise Again' each night, and, on the last concert (Columbia, Maryland, June 14), on 'Dead Man, Dead Man' also.

For some reason, King missed the first European concert, in Toulouse, France, on June 21, but she was there for the rest, and on her first night, in Colombe on June 23, she and Dylan débuted their duet of the old EVERLY BROTHERS song 'Let It Be Me', sung now as if a devotional song addressed to God, yet not without a frisson of something between the two singers. This proved a one-off, and on subsequent nights in London it was back to 'Abraham, Martin and John', then the Jim Webb song 'Let's Begin', then no duet at all, then 'Let's Begin', 'Abraham' and 'Let's Begin'. In Birmingham there was no duet either night, and after that it settled down to a routine nightly 'Let's Begin', all the way through from Stockholm on July 8 to Avignon on the 25th. On the fall tour of North America, though the backing singers didn't start the show they did perform one number in the middle each night; Clydie and Bob started the tour by continuing to sing 'Let's Begin' but soon introduced the old Tommy Edwards hit 'It's All in the Game' (débuted in Merrillville, Indiana, October 19, 1981), in turn replacing this with 'I'll Be Your Baby Tonight' in Bethlehem, Pennsylvania, on October 25, throwing in an extra 'Let's Begin' at the concert after that and then reintroducing 'Let It Be Me' in Toronto on October 29, retaining it in Montreal and then, dropping both this and the 'I'll Be Your Baby Tonight' duet, returned to 'It's All in the Game' in Kitchener, Ontario, on Hallowe'en. After that it was mostly back to 'I'll Be Your Baby Tonight', though there was no duet in Atlanta on November 15.

There was no 1982 tour, but at Dylan's Rundown Studios in Santa Monica, on June 1 that year, Dylan and Clydie King recorded a series of duets together, with Dylan on organ, guitar and bass and Jimmie Haskell on piano. None has circulated, though four songs are known to be extant: 'Standing in the Light', three takes of 'Average People', 'In the Heat of the Night' and 'Dream a Little Dream of Me'. Some years later Dylan said in an interview: 'I've also got a record with just me and Clydie King singing together and it's great, but it doesn't fall into any category that the record company knows how to deal with.' The nearest they came to any such Dylan-King release was with the studio version of their duet on 'Let It Be Me', recorded at a *Shot of Love* session on May 1, 1981, which was released, though in Europe only and billed as solely by Bob Dylan, on the B-side of 'Heart of Mine', in September 1981.

Clydie King reappeared on the promo video for the *Infidels* single 'Sweetheart Like You' and contributed to the album sessions of April 27 & 29 and May 2, 1983, this last yielding the 'Death Is Not the End' released on the 1988 album *Down in the Groove*. Her last day of action in Dylan's professional life seems to have been at Dylan's home studio in the garage at the Malibu house in March 1984, when she sometimes joined Bob and THE PLUGZ at their rehearsal sessions for the 'Late Night with David Letterman' TV show that month, though she didn't take part in the show itself.

HOWARD ALK filmed King, Dylan and the band both backstage and on stage on the fall 1981 tour, and also took copious pictures of Clydie and Bob together in 1980–81, several of which are published in the large-format booklet with the 5-LP box set *Biograph* in 1985, one of which, reproduced full page, has a quiet air of intimacy about it, at least on Ms. King's part. HOWARD SOUNES' *Down the Highway: A Life of Bob Dylan*, published in 2001, claimed that at some point Bob Dylan even bought her a house. Perhaps she's still in that house today.

[Clydie King: 'Our Romance' c/w 'Writing on the Wall', Specialty 605, (78 rpm), US, 1956–7, reissued on the 5-CD box set *The Specialty Story*, Specialty 4412, US, 1994; 'I'm Invited to Your Party' c/w 'Young Fool in Love', Specialty 642, US, 1957; *Direct Me*, Lizard Ampex A-20104, US, 1972/76. Clydie King & Brown Sugar, 'Dance to the Music', Chelsea 0239, US, 1973. *Brown Sugar Featuring Clydie King*, Chelsea BCL1-0368, US, 1973. Little Clydie King & the Teens: 'A Casual Look' c/w 'Oh Me', RPM RPM 462, mid-1950s, reissued on *Modern Vocal Groups Volume 4*, Ace, CDCHD 764, UK, *nia*.]

King of Sweden, the See **Carl XVI Gustav of Sweden.**

Kirkland, Sally [1944 -] Sally Kirkland was born in New York City on Hallowe'en, 1944. The daughter of a *Vogue* fashion editor, she became an actor via off-Broadway (1962), the WARHOL Factory and Lee Strasberg's Actors' Studio. She has subsequently appeared in an astonishing number of bad movies and failed to land significant rôles in many successful ones, including *The Sting*, *The Way We Were* and *A Star Is Born*. Her finest hour is generally agreed to have been playing an unsuccessful Czech actor in the 1987 film *Anna*. She is reputed to have had an affair with Bob Dylan in 1976 and returned within his orb some years later. In 1990 she played the man-eating other woman in the promo video for 'Unbelievable', a hopeless piece of rockist sludge plucked from the obscurity of the album *Under the Red Sky* and issued as a single. Almost any other track would have fared better. The video was filmed in the Mojave Desert on June 24, 1990; co-stars were Rob Bogue and MOLLY RINGWALD. Bob played a guitar-doodling chauffeur. At one point he chauffeurs a pig with a ring in its nose; the two act equally well.

Undeterred, Sally Kirkland remains an ordained minister in the Church of the Movement of Spiritual Inner Awareness. That'll be in California.

kisses and silver In 'With God on Our Side', on the *Times They Are a-Changin'* album of 1964, Dylan sings: 'I've been thinkin' about this / That Jesus Christ / Was betrayed by a kiss.' In 'No Time to Think', on 1978's *Street Legal*, he sings of being 'Betrayed by a kiss on a cool night of bliss'. On 'What Was It You Wanted', on *Oh Mercy*, 1989, he sings: 'What was it you wanted / When you were kissin' my cheek?'.

The biblical texts behind these references to the betrayal of Christ by his disciple Judas Escariot include Matthew 17: 22: 'And while they abode in Galilee, Jesus said unto them, The Son of man shall be betrayed into the hands of men'; Matthew 26: 20–21: 'Now when the even was come, he sat down with the twelve. And as they did eat, he said, Verily I say unto you, that one of you shall betray me'; and Matthew 26: 45–49: 'Then cometh he to his disciples, and saith unto them, Sleep on now, and take your rest: behold, the hour is at hand, and the Son of man is betrayed into the hands of sinners. Rise, let us be going: behold, he is at hand that doth betray me. And while he yet spake, lo, Judas, one of the twelve, came, and with him a great multitude with swords and staves, from the chief priests and elders of the people. Now he that betrayed him gave them a sign, saying, Whomsoever I shall kiss, that same is he: hold him fast. And forthwith he came to Jesus, and said, Hail, master; and kissed him.' There are equivalent passages in Mark 14:18 and 14:41–45, Luke 22:14 & 21–22 and 22:47–48, John 13:1–2 & 21 and (without mention of the betrayal being 'by a kiss') John 18:3–9.

An earlier line in 'No Time to Think'—'One secret for pieces of change'—resonates with the same theme, and so does the more specific 'thirty pieces of silver' in Dylan's 1986 song 'Maybe Someday', on *Knocked Out Loaded*. The biblical text here is Matthew 26:14–16: '. . . Judas Iscariot, went unto the chief priests, And said unto them, What will ye give me, and I will deliver him unto you? And they covenanted with him for thirty pieces of silver. And from that time he sought opportunity to betray him.' Equivalent texts, without specifying the amount of money, are in Mark 14:10–11 and Luke 22:3–6.

These 'thirty pieces of silver' are paid many centuries on from the 'twenty pieces of silver' for which Joseph was sold into Egypt by his brothers (Genesis 37:28), which suggests a remarkably low level of inflation. (More remarkably, the lords of the Philistines each paid Delilah 'eleven hundred pieces of silver' to betray Samson: to 'Entice him, and see wherein his great strength lieth, and by what means we may prevail against him' (Judges 16:5).

***Knocked Out Loaded* [1986]** An album title suggesting that its contents were thrown together when Dylan was drunk bodes ill by its very defensiveness. Nevertheless after the overblown robotic coldness of *Empire Burlesque* this third-rate assemblage of studio scrapings, taken from various sessions 1984–86, has a warmth and human frailty that at least lets you in. Tired R&B ('You Wanna Ramble') and rockism ('Got My Mind Made Up'); immaculately sung but shifty pop ('Under Your Spell'); a cover of KRIS KRISTOFFERSON's wretched 'They Killed Him'; and Dylan's fine 'Maybe Someday' so badly produced that it is incomprehensible and could be sung by one of the Chipmunks. There's a tender rendition, well-produced and refreshingly arranged, of the gospel standard 'Precious Memories', a robust cut of the good minor Dylan song 'Driftin' Too Far from Shore' (with mad drumming), and, hidden among the dross, 'Brownsville Girl', co-written with SAM SHEPARD: a wonderful and innovative major work, intelligent and subtle, from a Bob Dylan out from behind his 1980s wall of self-contempt and wholly in command of his incomparable vocal resources.

[Recorded NY, Jul 1984, LA, Dec 1984, London, 19–22 Nov 1985, LA, Jan–Feb 1985, Topanga, CA, Apr–May 1986 and Van Nuys, CA, May 1986; released as Columbia OC 40439 (LP), 14 Jul or 8 Aug 1986.]

Knopfler, Mark [1949 -] Mark Knopfler was born in Glasgow, Scotland, on August 12, 1949 but from age seven lived in Newcastle-upon-Tyne in north-east England, learnt guitar and at 16 appeared on local TV in a harmony duo with a Sue Hercombe. After a year studying journalism in Harlow, Essex, and a junior reporter's job on the *Yorkshire Evening Post*, he took a BA in English Literature at Leeds University. It was an odd, and endearing, route to superstardom, which Knopfler duly achieved as the leader of what became, in the early 1980s, the world's most successful, though far from its most interesting, band. Knopfler had got there via the Duolian String Pickers, a record made in somebody's home studio in Pudsey, West Yorkshire ('Summer's Coming My Way'), a move to London after graduation in 1973, to join the unpleasantly named group Brewer's Droop, whose drummer PICK WITHERS would join him again in Dire Straits, and a lecturer's job for two years at Loughton College, Essex, where he stayed for two years, supplementing his income by giving guitar lessons at a local school.

On another planet some light-years away, Bob Dylan first heard Mark Knopfler when assistant and engineer Arthur Rosato played him the Dire Straits single, 'Sultans of Swing'. Of course he liked it: it was a clear homage to himself, though only a krafty cheese slice boiled down from the St. Agur of *Blonde on Blonde*, the album Knopfler somewhere remembers as having listened to over 'a million cups of coffee' back in the 1960s. Decades later, Dylan would throw back a mischievous imitation at Knopfler, on the bridge section of 'Most of the Time', on the 1989 album *Oh Mercy* (the section where Dylan sings 'Most of the time / She ain't even in my mind, / I wouldn't know her if I saw her / She's that far behind'), on which not the lyric but the melodic line, sound and vocal delivery all seem to echo trademark 'Sultans of Swing' era Straitsery.

On March 29, 1979, Dylan caught the last of Dire Straits' Roxy shows in LA, approached Knopfler afterwards and asked him to play on the sessions for his new album. Later, Knopfler was disconcerted to find, as he said to his manager, that 'all these songs are about God.' The album was *Slow Train Coming*. They 'prepped it' in California, with co-producer JERRY WEXLER, and with Knopfler. 'Bob and I ran down a lot of those songs beforehand', Knopfler said, 'and they might be in a very different form when he's just hittin' the piano, and maybe I'd make suggestions about the tempo or whatever. Or I'd say, "What about a twelve-string?"'

On April 30, 1979, they started recording at Muscle Shoals, in Sheffield, Alabama, with Dylan and Knopfler, his Dire Straits drummer Pick Withers, co-producer BARRY BECKETT on piano and organ, and bass player TIM DRUMMOND. The whole album was completed by the end of May 4, apart from some overdubs added from then until May 11. It was released that August 18. Knopler's one incontestably decent contribution was his guitar solo on 'Precious Angel', on which Dylan goads him, provokes him into playing with real bite.

Dylan and Knopfler got together again, with various other musicians, playing on what has become referred to as 'the Knopfler Hotel Room session' at the Sunset Marquis hotel in LA in fall 1980, when Dire Straits were back at the Roxy soon after the release of their album *Making Movies*. Present were Dylan, Knopfler, Tim Drummond, two members of BRUCE SPRINGSTEEN's E Street Band, Dire Straits manager Ed Bicknell, two unidentified young women and music journalist Mike Oldfield. (The occasion is described in Oldfield's 1984 biography *Dire Straits*.) Bicknell, no Dylan enthusiast, described an early version of 'Caribbean Wind' heard on this occasion as 'one of the most beautiful songs I ever heard'. It was a solo guitar-and-vocals performance by Dylan, and proved the only sustained performance of anything in the course of the usual jamming process of trying 12 bars of this, switching to something else, finding you don't know it and trying another doomed fragment of something else again. Other songs tried included BUDDY HOLLY items like 'That'll Be the Day'. Unfortunately, Bicknell believes, no-one there taped any of this material.

Knopfler had no involvement in the rest of Dylan's gospel period work, but re-surfaced with him in 1983 to co-produce and play on the *Infidels* album, the sessions for which were, even by the usual standards, logged unreliably, resulting in much dispute among the Dylan discographers trying to catalogue all these things later—but essentially the sessions began on April 11, 1983 and ran through (though not daily) till May 5, and were followed by some overdubbing of Dylan vocals June to July. Dylan took the tapes away and had them remixed in Knopfler's absence, and the resulting finished album was, when Knopfler heard it, shockingly less than it might have been, in his opinion—and certainly it was a remix that tends towards the lumpen and lacklustre. On the released version of 'License to Kill', for example, the riff in between the chorus lines is played only on the bass; on the unreleased mix in circulation just ahead of the album's issue, the same riff is carried by a light, almost whimsical guitar, which lends it extra colour and, paradoxically, strength, and a welcome counter-pointing optimism to the doomy prognostications of the lyric. Even 'Sweetheart Like You' sounds less stodgy and laboured on the early-circulated outtake than on the version Dylan chose for release. On 'Jokerman', it is noticeable that the outtake version, while offering lyrics Dylan was right to revise, offers a vocal performance and a music track more alive and lithe and open, and with a fuller exploration of melodic line.

The more unfortunate *Infidels* misjudgements, though, exactly as in the case of *Shot of Love* before it, concerned which songs were included on, and which excluded from, the album rather than as between Knopfler and Dylan mixes. For Knopfler can be heard too on all those terrific rejected recordings like 'Julius and Ethel', 'Someone's Got a Hold of My Heart', 'Lord Protect My Child', 'Foot of Pride', 'Tell Me' and, most especially, 'Blind Willie McTell' (of which there remains, unreleased but circulated, a more interesting take than that eventually released on the *Bootleg Series Vols. 1–3*, a take on which again Knopfler proves able to rise to an exceptional occasion). He can also be heard, therefore, on the far from terrific *Infidels* outtake 'Death Is Not the End', released out of desperation to help Dylan fill up *Down in the Groove* in 1988.

Next, nearly two years later, came a couple of sessions just as Dylan was finishing off *Empire Burlesque*, when on February 24 and March 4, 1985, Knopfler and his keyboards player ALAN CLARK played on unknown, uncirculated material along with Ted Perlman on guitar and SLY & ROBBIE as rhythm section. The following year, Mark and Bob bumped into each other again, this time in Australia in February 1986, and for the first time Knopfler came on stage during a Dylan concert, playing guitar behind him on the encore songs 'Blowin' in the Wind', 'Uranium Rock' and 'Knockin' on Heaven's Door' alongside TOM PETTY & THE HEARTBREAKERS. Nine nights later, in Melbourne on February 19, Dylan reciprocated at a Dire Straits concert in Melbourne, singing 'All Along the Watchtower', 'Leopard-Skin Pill-Box Hat', 'License to Kill' and 'Knockin' on Heaven's Door' backed by the whole group. And so far, that occasion, now 20 years ago, is the last time, at least professionally, that Dylan and Knopfler met.

Back in the spring of 1984, when aficionados learnt more or less simultaneously of Dylan's exciting live appearance on US TV with the splendidly punky outfit THE PLUGZ and of the fact that his new album, *Infidels*, had been made with such major assistance from the ploddingly unpunky Dire Strait, Mark Knopfler, a widespread reaction was to feel 'Oh kno, knot Knopfler!'—but it worked out OK in the end.

All the same, he was a significant absentee from the '30th Anniversary Concert Celebration' and (albeit like many a significant figure) he goes unmentioned in Dylan's memoir *Chronicles Volume One*.

[Knopler background from *www.mark-knopfler-news.co.uk/biogs/mark.html*, quotes from *www.answers.com/topic/slow-train-coming*, seen online 12 May 2005. Ed Bicknell, conversations with this writer c.Apr 1981 & 31 Aug 1995.]

Koella, Freddy [1958 -] Frederic Koella was born on October 16, 1958 in Mulhouse, France, where he grew up. He first started listening to Bob Dylan when in his 20s. He was a crucial guitarist on three albums by the Cajun singer-songwriter Zachary Richard—*Snake Bite Love* (1992), *Cap Enragé* (1996) and *Couer Fidèle* (1999), the first of these recorded in New Orleans and the others in Paris. In 1996 he had two tracks ('Back to New Orleans' and 'A Man's Gotta Do') on the Various Artists album *Everybody Slides, Vol. 2.*

Playing both guitar and violin, he has also toured with Doctor John and Willy DeVille, in whose band he played from 1990 to 2002; he has played on numerous albums (including DeVille's 1996 album *Loup Garou*) and produced the Richard Gilly album *Le Nouveau Monde* (2000), the eponymously titled *Kenny Edwards* (2002) and *Miracle Mule* by the Subdudes (2004). Koella also plays featured guitar on Bjorn Schaller's 'Mandarin' on the soundtrack of Eric Byler's 2002 movie *Charlotte Sometimes*. In 2005 he rejoined Willy DeVille but also produced his own début album, the instrumental *Minimal*, which, surprisingly, is all acoustic guitar. But more important than any of that, he was, from 2003–4, a member of Bob Dylan's Never-Ending Tour band.

And how. Freddy (as he prefers to spell it) was Dylan's best-ever lead electric guitarist (and just might be the best electric guitarist altogether since the heyday of Hubert Sumlin). ROBBIE ROBERTSON was near sublime—the next best, a very close second—but Freddy *was* better. And in THE BAND all the other musicians were crucial too, whereas in Dylan's band Freddy had to carry the whole front line.

Of course you could say MIKE BLOOMFIELD was right up there, but he was, though a virtuoso, essentially more limited (Dylan had to tell him, for 'Like a Rolling Stone', to play 'none of that B.B.

King shit'); and G.E. SMITH was terrific, but *safe*. You never wondered excitedly what he might do next. Whereas Freddy played by living on the edge, like Bob, fusing Django Reinhart and CARL PERKINS and playing as if it were 1957 *now*. He was the electric lead guitarist Dylan himself would have been, had Dylan ever bothered to master the instrument.

Tragically, Koella's stint with the Never-Ending Tour Band was all too brief. In February 2003, the band was rehearsing in Los Angeles and looking for a guitarist to replace CHARLIE SEXTON. Koella says he 'was lucky enough to get invited to one of the rehearsals, and that's how it started.' He first played with them in Dallas, Texas, on April 18, 2003–it was the opening night of the first US leg of that year's touring—and his last performance was just under a year later, on April 14, 2004 in Atlanta, Georgia. He played a total of 121 Dylan concerts and—like bass player KENNY AARONSON before him—was forced out through illness. He has recovered fully now.

If you can, listen to 'Watching the River Flow' and 'Memphis Blues Again' from the concert in Graz, Austria, on October 26, 2003. There is Freddy Koella's genius.

[Freddy Koella: *Minimal, nia*, Minimal, US, 2005. Zachary Richard: *Snake Bite Love*, New Orleans, 1992, A&M 75021 5387 2, 1992; *Cap Enragé*, Paris, 1995, Initial ADCD 10093, 1996; *Couer Fidèle*, Paris, 1999, *nia*, 1999. Willy DeVille: *Loup Garou*, Discovery 77040, US (East-West 24562, Germany), 1996. Various Artists: *Everybody Slides, Vol. 2*, Rykodisc, 1996.]

Koerner, Spider John [1938 -] John Koerner was born on August 31, 1938 in Rochester, New York, where he grew up (as it happens, the town the great SON HOUSE was living in when 'rediscovered'). Koerner gained a glider pilot's license at age 15, joined the marines (briefly) and enrolled as an engineering student at the University of Minnesota in 1956. By the time Bob Dylan met him in Dinkytown, he was living in Minneapolis with a young wife, in an apartment stocked with folk music records.

Dylan writes about Koerner the musician in some detail in *Chronicles Volume One*, and says of the person that he 'was tall and thin with a look of perpetual amusement on his face. We hit it off right away.'

Dylan says he was 'The first guy I met in Minneapolis like me', that they met in the 10 O'Clock Scholar coffee-house, that Koerner was an acoustic guitarist and an exciting singer, that they already knew a few of the same songs and that they sat around together learning more. It was Koerner who first played him the NEW LOST CITY RAMBLERS, and many other key records, including a compilation called *Foc'sle Songs and Shanties* (Dylan slightly mistitles this as *Foc'sle Songs and Sea Shanties*), and another, an Elektra sampler album, which he says first introduced him to the voices of DAVE VAN RONK and Peggy Seeger, and included ALAN LOMAX (one of those folklorists who always fancied himself a bit of a performer) singing 'Doney Gal'—which, as Dylan mentions, he added to his repertoire. (It's one of the songs on the tape made at Karen Wallace's apartment in St. Paul in May 1960.) And in the interview given to CAMERON CROWE for *Biograph* in 1985, Dylan specified other songs he'd learned from Koerner: 'He knew more songs than I did. "Whoa Boys Can't Ya Line 'M", "John Hardy", "Golden Vanity", I learned all those from him. We sounded great; not unlike the Delmore Brothers.'

Koerner and Dylan hung around together, going off to see performers who were passing through town and to seek out rumoured rare records. And while each continued to perform by himself, the two of them began to perform together as well—'playing and singing a lot together as a duo', as Dylan reports. They played 'at house parties, in the coffee-houses, street singing', and after Dylan plunged into his WOODY GUTHRIE phase, Dylan and Koerner would play Guthrie together too. Sometimes Dave Glover (aka TONY GLOVER) would play harmonica with them too.

At some point after Dylan left for New York City, Koerner started playing 'professionally' with Tony Glover and DAVE RAY. Koerner, Ray and Glover—that was the name of their outfit—made many albums, starting with *Blues, Rags & Hollers*, issued first on the small Audiophile label in June 1963 but picked up by Elektra, who signed them, bought the rights, reissued the LP that November (with four tracks missing) and then several further albums.

John Koerner was also one of the artists on the 1964 compilation album *The Blues Project*, on which Bob Dylan appeared on Side 2, Track 4 of the original LP, billed as Bob Landy, playing a piano duet with ERIC VON SCHMIDT behind GEOFF MULDAUR on the latter's song 'Downtown Blues'. Koerner was featured artist on the previous track, performing BIG BILL BROONZY's 'Southbound Train', and on Side 1 of the album he performs 'My Little Woman'. Soon after this compilation LP was issued, Koerner Ray & Glover were fellow performers at the 1964 NEWPORT FOLK FESTIVAL.

Koerner continued to record after the group split up, and made albums in the 1970s, 1980s and 1990s, while continuing to perform and write from his Minneapolis base. One of the albums he made in the mid-1960s, with Glover as his harmonica player, received a memorably savage review from Albert McCarthy, the stalwart critic of *Jazz Monthly*: 'Each country has its own way of finding room for the talentless, in Britain the traditional escape-route for many years being the church or the army. It appears that the outlet in the US . . . is for them to become folk singers. . . . This is, without any doubt, one of the worst records I have had to review for many a long day . . .

a passably competent guitarist, a poor harmonica player and a quite dreadful singer. . . . the butchery of inoffensive blues verses is spread out remarkably evenly throughout . . . this grotesque blues kitsch.'

Koerner ventured into filmmaking in the 1970s, and developed his hobby of building and rebuilding telescopes. He reunited with Ray and Glover in 1996 for *One Foot in the Groove*, the trio's first recording together in 30 years. Dylan gave it this sound-bite: 'Exactly like you'd think it would be, stunning. Koerner, Ray and Glover haven't lost a step. Every time they play the lights shine.'

In 1998 Koerner had, and fully recovered from, triple by-pass heart surgery. By 2005 he was back playing a long string of summer dates, from June's Minnesota Folk Festival onwards.

[John Koerner: 'My Little Woman' & 'Southbound Train', *nia*, 1964, *The Blues Project*, Elektra EKL 264, NY, Jun 1964; *Spider Blues*, *nia*, Elektra EKL-290 (mono) / EKS-7290, NY, 1965. Koerner Ray & Glover: *Blues Rags and Hollers*, Audiophile AP-78, 1963; *One Foot in the Groove*, Tim/Kerr T/K 96CD137, US, 1996. Albert McCarthy, *Jazz Monthly*, UK, Jul 1965. Bob Dylan, *Chronicles Volume One*, 2004, pp.237–239, 241.]

Köhler, Robert [1953 -] Robert Köhler was born in Vienna, Austria, on July 28, 1953. After leaving school and spending nine months in the army, Köhler started working as an accountant, first for the Phonodisc division of PolyGram and later for General Motors. He dropped out of this to start up his own small computer company in the mid-1990s. He first took an interest in Dylan's work in 1967, and first saw him live in 1981. In 1984 he attended a small Bob Dylan Festival in Michelstetten, a village north of Vienna. The Michelstetten events finished in 1991, and Köhler and two others (Karl Ossberger and Michael Lohse) determined to organise a bigger and better alternative. This became the annual AUSTRIAN BOB DYLAN CONVENTION. As the years went by, Köhler's cohorts dropped out and he took sole responsibility for organising this popular event.

Konikoff, Sandy [1943 -] Sanford Konikoff was born in Buffalo, New York, in 1943, grew up there and in the early 1960s played in local beat groups including the clean-cut, besuited Stan & the Ravens. He was temporarily imported into Canada in RONNIE HAWKINS' Rolls-Royce to play drums while LEVON HELM was otherwise engaged, and there was a period when he'd be playing two sets in a club in Buffalo and then rushing up north to play two more in Canada on the same night. 'I always felt I subbed for Levon,' Konikoff says: 'There was no way I could match him.' The connection eventually secured him a place with the rest of THE HAWKS on the January 21, 1966 Dylan session, cutting that tremendous early *Blonde on Blonde* outtake 'She's Your Lover Now' (which emerged officially 25 years later on the *Bootleg Series Vols. 1–3*).

Then ROBBIE ROBERTSON asked him to do the live 1966 tour with Dylan. 'Ronnie Hawkins said I had to give him two weeks' notice or he'd break my legs,' says Konikoff, 'but Robbie told me he wouldn't really do anything.' So, starting on February 4 in Louisville, Kentucky, and running through till March 26 in Vancouver, Canada, Sandy Konikoff was the drummer out there every night being shouted at and booed on the North American leg of the 1966 world tour.

He says he wasn't much aware of the booing, but he felt swamped by the whole experience. 'I was like the baby of the group. I was in a top 40 band in Michigan and I heard "Subterranean Homesick Blues" on the radio and it just stopped me in my tracks—and a year later I was playing with them! And I was just struggling from the pressure and the mystique and the frustration of it all. I arrived in my mohair suit, you know, pretending I knew what "acid" meant, and so on. Bob was a really great guy but he never hung out with us much, and I lacked the courage to ask questions. And the sets were so short: things were going so fast.' So when the tour moved on to Hawaii, Australia and Europe in April to July, Konikoff stayed behind, replaced by the louder, more volatile MICKEY JONES. 'I'll regret it to my grave that I prematurely left,' says Sandy now.

He stayed in California, though, and plunged into the golden years of semi-communal life among great musicians, bankrolled by record companies hitting undreamt of peaks of power and affluence. In 1967 he was in a group produced by THE BYRDS' Terry Melcher, the Gentle Soul: they got nowhere but they were living high (in every way) in a house on Sunset Boulevard right by the Chateau Marmont.

Konikoff, who was small and slight and at this point looked not unlike the young PAUL SIMON, soon found his feet in a hip milieu, becoming gregarious, eccentric and covering early hints of baldness with a trademark series of groovy hand-sewn skullcaps from the 'Benin of Africa' shop. He started to play on sessions, too, including for DAVID BLUE. He played on a number of tracks on the first Taj Mahal album, and after Levon Helm introduced him to LEON RUSSELL he played with Joe Cocker on his Mad Dogs & Englishmen tour (who didn't?). In New York he played in Grinderswitch with the talented laid-back-soul singer-songwriter Garland Jeffreys, and on other sessions fixed for VAN MORRISON's *Astral Weeks* producer (Konikoff had played some gigs in the Village with Morrison earlier). At some point he also played on a recording of a SPIDER JOHN KOERNER song in an odd time-signature, 'Magazine Lady', with Ry Cooder on bass and Van Dyke Parks on piano, and on the John Cale album *Village Violence*.

Konikoff was described cryptically by Elektra producer Jac Holzman as 'Sal Mineo as Gene

Krupa' and as 'Purveyor of the Sphincterphone' (which sounds alarming, but let's not investigate). He was among the musicians at Bruce Botnick's house, along with Duane Allman, Gram Parsons, JIM KELTNER, Carl Radle, Buddy Miles, Uncle Joe Cocker and all, at the sessions for Bonnie & Delaney's *Motel Shot* album in 1971. (There weren't any drums: only a suitcase for all those drummers to fight over. Konikoff played tambourine, using a technique, he says, taught him by the great Sandra Crouch.)

Around the mid-1970s he moved back to Buffalo, touring with the great harmonica player King Biscuit Boy and others. By 2000 he was to be found in the 'Americana roots music' group LeeRon Zydeco and the Hot Tamales, and he is about to work with the Rockin' Rebels. He's swapped the skullcaps for berets and baseball caps now.

Sandy Konikoff is close to being the forgotten man in the Bob Dylan 1966 story. He shouldn't be.

[Jac Holzman quoted from the online blurb at *www.followthemusic.com/whobook.html*, seen online 23 Nov 2005, for Jac Holzman & Gavan Daws, *Follow the Music: The Life and High Times of Elektra Records in the Great Years of American Pop Culture*, US: First Media, 1998. Quotes & main source Sandy Konikoff, phone interview with this writer 7 Feb 2006.]

Kooper, Al [1944 -] The ubiquitous Al Kooper was born Alan Peter Kuperschmidt in Brooklyn, New York, on February 5, 1944; his family moved to Queens, NY, when he was four. At age 14 he was a guitarist with pop group the Royal Teens soon after they'd had a top 10 hit with 'Short Shorts' in 1958. A session guitarist by the age of 19, he dropped out of college to train as a studio engineer and then teamed up with songwriters Irwin Levine and Bob Brass, with whom in 1964 he wrote the Gary Lewis & the Playboys hit 'This Diamond Ring' and Gene Pitney's minor hit 'I Must Be Seeing Things', which became the title track of a Pitney album (and EP) and in French, as 'Mes yeux sont fous', a single by Johnny Hallyday.

After a brief first Manhattan stay on W. 77th Street, Kooper moved into Greenwich Village and involved himself in a wide range of musical activity. At the 1965 NEWPORT FOLK FESTIVAL he performed with RICHARD & MIMI FARIÑA (plus BRUCE LANGHORNE) and the same year joined the group the Blues Project with DANNY KALB, Steve Katz, Tommy Flanders, Andy Kulberg and Ray Blumenfeld. Kooper, invited to join the group after playing first as a session-man for them, stayed with the group for its first three albums (two of which were live) and for a performance at the Monterey Pop Festival of 1967, but then quit, moved to the West Coast and formed Blood, Sweat & Tears, largely in order to create a rock band with a horn section. After one interesting album, *The Child Is Father to the Man*, Kooper left and the group became highly successful plying jazz-rock of the nastiest possible kind.

Kooper then recorded his solo album *I Stand Alone* and the album *Supersession* with MIKE BLOOMFIELD and Stephen Stills (both 1968), followed by live work with Bloomfield and the albums *The Live Adventures of Al Kooper and Mike Bloomfield* and the solo *You Never Know Who Your Friends Are* (both 1969). In the early 1970s he made several more extravagantly funded solo albums, among them the gate-fold sleeve LP *Naked Songs* (1972) in which what was naked was Kooper's lack of having anything to say and lack of a voice to say it with. Nonetheless, sheer chutzpah gets him through songs like SAM COOKE's 'Touch the Hem of His Garment' where any comparison of Kooper's voice to Cooke's would be ludicrous. In 1976 came *Act Like Nothing's Wrong*, co-produced (like *Child Is Father to the Man*) by THE BAND's producer John Simon, on which Kooper revives 'This Diamond Ring' with a mix of ironic superiority and obvious fondness.

In 1977 he published the first edition of his book *Backstage Passes* and the following year produced RICKY NELSON's still-unreleased album *Back to Vienna*. He was a veteran producer by this point, having enjoyed a late-1960s stint as a Columbia Records A&R man, during which he had signed the long-uncommercial British cult band the Zombies, who promptly delivered the significant album *Odessey & Oracle* and a major hit single, 'Time of the Season'. In 1972, as his time with Columbia ended and he set up, courtesy of MCA, his own Sounds of the South studio in Atlanta, Georgia, he discovered the admirable Florida band Lynyrd Skynyrd (they were playing local bars) and duly produced their first three albums—including, on their début album, their great anthemic 'Free Bird'. He sang back-up vocals and played on this album too (bass and mellotron), and, as on piano on the Tom Rush album *Take a Little Walk with Me*, he is billed here as Roosevelt Gook. Yes, the ubiquitous Al Kooper, *not* Bob Dylan, was Roosevelt Gook.

Lynyrd Skynyrd was a long way from the sound of the Zombies, and another demonstration of Kooper's eclectic musical tastes and openness. He went on to produce albums by NILS LOFGREN, the Tubes, Joe Ely and B.B. King. He also wrote the music for the 1969 Jim McBride documentary film *My Girlfriend's Wedding*, the 1970 Hal Ashby film *The Landlord*, various TV series and, after a long gap, the Peter Riegert short *By Courier* (2000) and the same director's movie *King of the Corner* (2004).

As a session musician Al Kooper has played on records by a vast swathe of big-name artists, including Cream, JIMI HENDRIX (on 'Long Hot Summer Nights') the Who ('Rael'), the ROLLING STONES ('You Can't Always Get What You Want') and GEORGE HARRISON's *Somewhere in England* album. But his most significant contribution, by quite some way, has been to the work of Bob Dylan. Al Kooper is the hero who on June 16, 1965 in New

York City inveigled his way into playing the organ part on 'Like a Rolling Stone', and was lucky enough to have Bob Dylan say 'turn it up!' and thus to help make history. He has told the story of how this happened many times, never more weirdly than as a hologram on the CD Rom *Highway 61 Interactive* and never more endearingly than as a cool and genial interviewee in the film *No Direction Home*, released 40 years after the making of that record. He also provides a detailed memoir of the sessions for *Highway 61 Revisited* and *Blonde on Blonde* inside the booklet issued with its audio partner, the *Bootleg Series Vol. 7—No Direction Home: The Soundtrack Album* (2005).

Al Kooper helped to make history at Newport 1965 too, not because he played with the Fariñas but because he played 'Maggie's Farm', 'Like a Rolling Stone' and 'It Takes a Lot to Laugh, It Takes a Train to Cry' with Bob Dylan on that tumultuous, historic electric début—since when his involvement with Dylan's work has been plentiful. He attended and played organ on the later *Highway 61 Revisited* sessions (July 30 and August 2, 1965 in New York) and then saw action at the first electric concerts Dylan gave—at Forest Hills, New York, that August 28 and the Hollywood Bowl on September 3rd. After that, Dylan's band became the Hawks and Kooper returned to New York.

That November 30, he was back in the studios for the first of the sessions that yielded *Blonde on Blonde*, and was there again on January 25–26 and 27–28, 1966. When Dylan finished the album in Nashville, in mid-February (between tour dates) and March (between tour dates again), only Al Kooper and ROBBIE ROBERTSON were still with Dylan from the New York sessions (apart from producer BOB JOHNSTON, who was Nashville-based in any case), and Kooper is interesting on the cultural gulf between this long-haired East Coast triumvirate and the country musicians and downtown Nashville. The last session took place in the early hours of March 10th.

Next time Kooper came to a Dylan session, it was in back in New York and in the very different musical universe of the *Self Portrait* recordings. He and DAVID BROMBERG and others laid down basic tracks for 'Little Sadie', 'In Search of Little Sadie', 'Belle Isle', 'Copper Kettle', 'It Hurts Me Too', 'The Boxer' and 'Woogie Boogie' on March 3, 1970, though all but 'It Hurts Me Too' were overdubbed later without Kooper (and indeed without Dylan). The following days Kooper played again, contributing, altogether, organ, piano and guitar, though again there was much subsequent overdubbing on most tracks. He was also there at the June sessions (on organ) which yielded some of the tracks on the *Dylan* album and, more importantly, most of *New Morning*. Indeed Kooper claims to have produced *New Morning*, though Bob Johnston disagrees. (Al was also present on June 30, again in New York, playing guitar and organ when Dylan attempted at least 15 takes of 'Blowin' in the Wind' with a small group of musicians: takes which have never circulated.)

A long gap in the Kooper-Dylan professional relationship followed. Al next turned up with Bob in 1981, when he replaced WILLIE SMITH as the keyboards player on the third leg of that year's semi-gospel, semi-secular tour, starting on October 16 in Milwaukee and ending on November 21 in Lakeland, Florida: a total of 27 concerts. At one of them—at East Rutherford, New Jersey, that October 27—he had the unusual experience of hearing Bob Dylan introduce his parents, Mr. & Mrs. Kooper Senior (Sam and Natalie), to the audience from the stage of the Meadowlands Arena. The private recording of this surreal moment later circulated among Al's friends on a custom-made LP. According to the description provided by someone selling a copy of this album on eBay decades later, for several years in the late 1970s and early 80s 'Kooper put out an annual Christmas album filled with novelty and strange music and dialogue for his friends only. . . . the third, features a track with Bob Dylan in concert introducing Al's parents . . . from the stage. Here's what the notes say: "In 1981, I toured for three months with BD and my parents came to see us play in New Jersey. I mentioned to Bob that my folks were there before we went onstage, and this is what happened. Thanks Bob." Bob introduces them, goofs around telling the audience they are the parents of a friend, but he's not gonna tell the audience who. Then after a bit, he says "OK, I'll tell you". And introduces Al. No music, but a rare bit of Bob humour. . . . With a great cover and Al's funny liner notes. Very very rare.' This LP did indeed exist: it was titled *The Third Annual Kapusta Kristmas Album*, billed as by Al Kooper & Friends, privately distributed on Partners in Crime NL-109 that December. (The eBay store of the seller, Nethollywood, has since been closed and the result of the item auction is not known.)

A little over four years later, Kooper was back in the New York studios for a couple of the sessions for the *Empire Burlesque* album, playing rhythm guitar on a rejected (but circulated) cut of 'Something's Burning, Baby' (February 21, 1985) and two days later again played rhythm guitar on a number of attempts at 'When the Night Comes Falling from the Sky', one of which became the album track. Kooper is credited with playing on this, but so much was overdubbed later that it's not certain his most minor contribution survives.

Quirkier and more interesting are his participations the following year. On April 28, 1986, in Topanga Park, California, along with other musicians and back-up singers, Al Kooper played keyboards on never-circulated attempts at 'You'll Never Walk Alone', 'Without Love' and a song logged as 'The Beautiful Life'; the following day they re-attempted 'You'll Never Walk Alone' and

'Unchain My Heart' (also uncirculated); and the day after that they laid down further never-heard versions of 'You'll Never Walk Alone', 'Unchain My Heart' and 'Lonely Avenue'. On May 1 they tried 'Without Love' and 'Unchain My Heart' again, and on May 2 yet another 'Unchain My Heart'—but they also managed, across these two sessions, to overdub the backing to 'Brownsville Girl' that we hear on *Knocked Out Loaded*—a backing they dubbed onto the Dylan vocal he had in turn dubbed onto the original 1984 backing track just one day earlier (at the April 30 session). Again, Kooper played keyboards.

Later that month he was among those overdubbing onto a May 5 take of the KRIS KRISTOFFERSON song 'They Killed Him', a take of JUNIOR PARKER's 'You Wanna Ramble' from the same day and a take of the old gospel favourite 'Precious Memories', and to record from scratch Dylan's own song 'Maybe Someday'. All these were duly released on the *Knocked Out Loaded* album that June—the same month that Kooper surfaced playing organ on 'Like a Rolling Stone' on stage with Dylan at a Cosa Mesa, California, concert by Dylan and TOM PETTY & THE HEARTBREAKERS. A month later (on July 21, 1986) the audience at Dylan's East Rutherford, New Jersey, concert had the bonus of Kooper on organ for the last five numbers of the night: 'Like a Rolling Stone', 'In the Garden', 'Blowin' in the Wind', 'Union Sundown' and 'Knockin' on Heaven's Door'; on August 3, at Inglewood, California, Kooper repeated the process, this time squeezed on stage with DAVE STEWART and Annie Lennox, and this time with 'Uranium Rock' instead of 'Union Sundown'. Two nights later Stewart and Lennox were out of the way and Kooper played on the last 11 of the set's 26 songs: 'Rainy Day Women # 12 & 35', 'Gotta Serve Somebody', 'Seeing the Real You at Last', 'Across the Borderline', 'I and I', 'Good Rockin' Mama' (with Dylan also joined on this one song by JOHN LEE HOOKER) and then the same five final songs as at the previous concert.

Another hiatus followed, but Al was back in the studios in Hollywood to lay down overdubs on various tracks for *Under the Red Sky* in 1990. He overdubbed organ on 'Handy Dandy' (originally recorded on January 6) and keyboards on 'Unbelievable' and 'Under the Red Sky' (both originally cut in LA in February or March), on May 3 and 4.

The two men had an odd semi-conjunction at the so-called 30th Anniversary Concert Celebration in New York on October 16, 1992–because Kooper came on and played organ on 'Like a Rolling Stone' and 'Leopard-Skin Pill Box Hat' . . . not behind Dylan but behind John Cougar Mellencamp. But they were bound to come together again under more normal concert circumstances, and in 1996 they did. On Dylan's first revisit to the city of Liverpool in 30 years—the city that he astonished when, with THE HAWKS in May 1966, he played electric rock infinitely more complex and radical than the city had ever heard from its beat groups when it had supposedly been the centre of the music universe just two or three years earlier—Dylan now came back in the middle of his Never-Ending Tour's latest European leg (which had begun on June 15, 1996 at a festival in Denmark), and played two nights in Liverpool, June 26 & 27: and his band was augmented by Al Kooper on keyboards throughout the first concert and on all but two numbers of the second (Al disappeared for 'To Ramona' and 'It Ain't Me Babe'). Two nights later, at the Prince's Trust concert in London's Hyde Park, Al was there again (alongside RON WOOD too, this time) for the short nine-song Dylan set.

So far, apart from the *No Direction Home* contributions mentioned above, that's been the last instance of a partnership that began with so triumphant a bang over 40 years ago.

In July 2005, Kooper released his first solo album in almost 25 years, the well-received *Black Coffee*. He had been playing, meanwhile, with the awkwardly named ReKooperation, from whom there was an eponymously titled album in 1994, and with a bunch of Boston academics (Kooper has honorary degrees and taught at Berklee School of Music in the late 1990s) just as uncomfortably named the Funky Faculty. A second, much-expanded edition of his book, now entitled *Backstage Passes and Backstabbing Bastards* and dealing with the first 54 years of Al's life, was published in 1998. By 2002, unfortunately, it had been remaindered.

Al Kooper lives in Boston these days, and though he's lost most of his eyesight he's lost none of his acumen, and if anything has gained in self-deprecating grace down the years. Usually. 2001 saw the release of a retrospective 2-CD box set, *Rare & Well Done*, going all the way back to previously unreleased material from 1964 and his first solo single from 1965, the deeply obscure 'New York's My Home.' It further includes an outtake of 'Went to See the Gypsy' from a *New Morning* overdubbing session on June 30, 1970. Dylan is absent from the track, which Kooper describes in the accompanying notes as 'a conception I had for Dylan to sing over'. This may or may not be a Dylan claim too far.

[Al Kooper: *Naked Songs*, Columbia KC 31723, US, 1972, CD-reissued Sony SRCS 6201, Japan, *nia*; *Act Like Nothing's Wrong*, Liberty US (United Artists UAG 30020, UK, 1976), CD-reissued One Way CD S21-18565, US, *nia*; *Rare and Well Done*, Columbia/Legacy AC2K 62153 US, 2001; *Black Coffee*, Favored Nations FN25202, US, 2005. Al Kooper & Ben Edmonds, *Backstage Passes: Rock'n'Roll Life in the Sixties*, Lanham, MD: Rowman & Littlefield, 1977; Al Kooper, *Backstage Passes and Backstabbing Bastards*, New York: Watson-Guptill Publications, 1998. Al Kooper with Dylan, Tom Petty & the Heartbreakers: 'Like a Rolling Stone', Costa Mesa, CA, 17 Jun 1986. The Blues Project: *Live at the Café au Go-Go*, NY, 1965, US, 1966; *Projections*, NY, 1966, Elektra US, 1966; *Live at Town Hall*, NY, May

1967, Elektra US, 1968. Blood, Sweat & Tears: *Child Is Father to the Man*, Columbia CS 9619, US, 1968.

The Royal Teens: 'Short Shorts', US, 1958. Gary Lewis & the Playboys: 'This Diamond Ring', US, 1964. Gene Pitney: 'I Must Be Seeing Things', US (& on EP Stateside SE1030, UK), 1964. Johnny Hallyday: 'Mes yeux sont fous', France, 1965. Tom Rush: *Take a Little Walk with Me*, Elektra EKL-308 & EKS-7308, 1966. Lynyrd Skynyrd: *Lynyrd Skynyrd (pronounced "leh-'nérd 'skin-'nérd")*, Doraville, GA, 1972, MCA MCL 1798, US, 1973.]

Kramer, Daniel [1932 -] Daniel Kramer was born in Brooklyn, New York, in 1932. He is the veteran New York-based photographer who, having trained in his profession by working as an assistant to Allan and Diane Arbus and to Philipe Halsman, was first given exceptional access to Bob Dylan in 1964 and whose images of Bob Dylan the following year have become iconic. You might say that Kramer's pictures *define* Bob Dylan 1965 as a look: black and white, extremely cool, in dark clothes and Chelsea boots, utterly differentiated from both the earlier folkie and the wild-haired amphetamine-wired full-colour figure of 1966. His photos include Dylan up a tree, in the street with top hat, in the studios, on stage acoustic and electric, with and without JOAN BAEZ, ironing Baez's hair, playing pool, rehearsing for the 1965 NEWPORT FOLK FESTIVAL, playing chess with Victor Maymudes, posing with SARA DYLAN—and many, many shots where you say 'Oh *that* one! Is that Kramer too?!': and it is.

When Kramer ventured into colour with Dylan it was to create the front cover of *Bringing It All Back Home*, one of the all-time great LP covers, taken at ALBERT GROSSMAN's house in Bearsville in January 1965, with his wife Sally Grossman in the red dress. The front cover of *Highway 61 Revisited* is Kramer's too (and that's his Nikon SP being dangled by BOB NEUWIRTH, whose legs are behind Dylan's in the shot). Kramer's work has also been used on *Biograph* and generously within the *Bootleg Series Vol. 7—No Direction Home: The Soundtrack*, respectively 20 and 40 years on from when the work was done.

Kramer's *Bob Dylan*, published in 1967, was the first major book of photographs of the artist, and had a well-written, thoughtful text to match. As PAUL WILLIAMS notes, 'Kramer was given the unique opportunity to photograph Bob Dylan in private and in performance . . . August 1964 to August 1965, as Dylan progressed from "It Ain't Me Babe" and being a folk hero to "Mr. Tambourine Man" and "Like a Rolling Stone" . . .' Pictures and words were recurrently revealing but never prurient or obtrusive. Kramer was respectful but clear-sighted.

Kramer's wife Arline Cunningham was active in the 1960s music business, worked with Harold Leventhal when he presented Dylan's Carnegie Hall concert of October 1963, helped work on Kramer's book *Bob Dylan* and was at the time of its publication Albert Grossman's management office 'executive assistant'. In association with Ms. Cunningham, Daniel Kramer is still at work, and has his own studio.

[Daniel Kramer: *Bob Dylan*, New York: Citadel, 1967; Pocket Books edn., 1968; large-format republication as *Bob Dylan: A Portrait of the Artist's Early Years*, with short new introduction by Kramer, New York: Citadel Underground/Carol Publishing, 1991. Paul Williams quoted from back cover, 1991 edn. Information in part via e-mails to this writer from Kramer & Cunningham, 8 & 9 Feb 2006.]

Kristofferson, Kris [1936 -] Kristoffer Kristofferson was born in Brownsville, Texas, on June 22, 1936, went to high school in San Mateo, California, went on to Pomona College (where FRANK ZAPPA used to sneak into composition classes) and then won a Rhodes Scholarship to Merton College, Oxford (UK), where he obtained a master's in English Literature in 1960. He also tried to be one of Larry Parnes' pop stars. Parnes was a British svengali-manager figure who groomed UK pop idols of the late 1950s to early 60s, including Britain's first rock'n'roller, Tommy Steele, Billy Fury, Marty Wilde, Georgie Fame and Duffy Power. Clearly there was a pattern to these surnames, and Kristofferson's pseudonym was Kris Carson, which didn't fit and didn't work. Returning to the States he joined both the US Army and, stationed (like ELVIS) in Germany, a group. From here he began songwriting, mailed songs back to a Nashville contact, and moved there himself in 1965. He was the janitor in the CBS Nashville studios when Dylan was there recording some of *Blonde on Blonde* in 1966.

Kristofferson was able to give up this day-job as country stars began having hits with his songs, beginning with Dave Dudley's cut of his pro-war 'Viet Nam Blues' in 1966, getting JOHNNY CASH's attention by landing a helicopter on his lawn (he'd been a pilot when in the Army) and then signing as a recording artist himself in 1967. In the latter capacity he was unsuccessful and for most of his career has remained so, though with the occasional blip of good fortune (especially, decades later, when teamed with WILLIE NELSON, Johnny Cash and Waylon Jennings in the WILBURYish country super-group the Highwaymen—not to be confused with the folkie-style vocal harmony group of the 1950s–60s).

However, as a songwriter, Kristofferson was not only successful but influential, as songs like 'Me and Bobby McGee', 'Sunday Morning Coming Down' and 'Help Me Make It Through the Night' let a whisper of hip looseness into the rigid factory of Nashville song production. In 1970, uniquely, he won the year's two most prestigious country music association awards, each with a different song, making him the talk of the town he was now sweeping with a different sort of broom. In 1971 Janis Joplin had a posthumous no.1 hit with 'Me and Bobby McGee', Kristofferson had his first taste of success with his own second album, *The Silver Tongued Devil and I*, and he launched another lucrative career with his film-acting début in the Dennis Hopper-directed *The Last Movie*. Various permutations of these three careers have continued ever since, and his films have included *Cisco Pike*, *Blume in Love*, *Bring Me the Head of Alfredo Garcia*, *Alice Doesn't Live Here Anymore*, *A Star Is Born* (with Barbra Streisand) and the financial mega-disaster *Heaven's Gate*.

As for connections with Bob Dylan, their first was through film. Kristofferson played convincingly and with charm the rôle of Billy the Kid, opposite James Coburn, in PECKINPAH's *Pat Garrett & Billy the Kid*, in which Dylan took the minor but beguiling part of Alias, and in which RITA COOLIDGE, then Kristofferson's real-life wife, provided the pallid love interest. Dylan reportedly got the part through Kristofferson's manager, Bert Block, an old associate of ALBERT GROSSMAN (they had co-managed Janis Joplin) who had once been Billie Holiday's manager too.

A decade later, in that desperate mid-1980s patch of his, Dylan was so keen to avoid writing songs that he even included one of Kristofferson's, the abjectly sanctimonious 'They Killed Him', on his 1986 album *Knocked Out Loaded*: a track recorded at Topanga Park, California, on May 5, 1986, and on which there's a terrific bass guitar part (by Vito San Filippo), some lovely singing and a children's vocal chorus. In 1991 Monument Records issued a 2-CD set, *Kris Kristofferson: Singer/Songwriter*, with Kristofferson performing his own songs on one CD and other people's records of mostly the same songs on the other. The final track on each was 'They Killed Him', by its composer and by Dylan.

After that, they were reunited for the so-called 30th Anniversary Celebration Concert at Madison Square Garden on October 16, 1992, at which they didn't play together but Kristofferson not only performed—singing 'I'll Be Your Baby Tonight' helped by Willie Nelson on guitar and vocals—but also acted as the evening's MC, introducing other acts and mopping up Sinead O'Connor after the crowd booed her arrival on stage.

In June of 1999 Kristofferson underwent heart bypass surgery, since when he has continued, looking more grizzled than anyone but KEITH RICHARDS, to make indifferent movies. He once said, with nice self-deprecation: 'I think between us, Bill Clinton and I have settled any lingering myths about the brilliance of Rhodes scholars.'

[Kris Kristofferson: *Kris Kristofferson: Singer/Songwriter*, Monument A2K-48621, US, 1991. Quote at movie database *http://us.imdb.com/name/nm0001434/bio*, online, 6 Dec 2005.]

Krogsgaard, Michael [1953 -] Michael Rindom Krogsgaard was born in Copenhagen, Denmark, on July 18, 1953. He became interested in Dylan's work in 1965, and started collecting tapes and information after meeting JOHN BAULDIE in 1969 or 1970. He contributed to *The Telegraph* fanzine 'a little, over the years'. Since *The Telegraph* folded, he has contributed similarly to *THE BRIDGE* fanzine, and from 1996 to 1999 he wrote a number of pieces on Dylan's live recordings for the fanzine *Look Back*. His first book, *Twenty Years of Recording: The Bob Dylan Reference Book*, was self-published in February 1981, though as by the grandly named Scandinavian Institute for Rock Research, and had a print run of 2,000. Its aim was to rectify the fact that all previous discographies of Dylan's work had 'lacked the strict systematic organization that would make them a valuable instrument for collectors.' It aimed to list all the material in circulation among collectors but with the safeguard of including 'nothing we haven't listened to ourselves'. This included tapes of concert performances. It also included official releases, but 'limited to American releases, plus non-American releases containing different or never available material'.

It was a huge and pioneering undertaking and came six years before the similar hard labour of GLEN DUNDAS' first edition of *Tangled Up in Tapes*. As Michael Krogsgaard recognised from the start, such work is almost immediately out of date, and needs updating. This happens not only because Dylan continues to work and his record company continues to release material, but also because more and more information comes to light unofficially, which contradicts previous 'facts' and adds to the unreleased material in circulation. Some of Dylan's sessions remain far less well-documented than others, and some leak outtakes far less readily than most. Michael Krogsgaard therefore published updated editions of his work as *Master of the Tracks* in 1988 and as *Positively Bob Dylan: A Thirty-Year Discography, Concert & Record Session Guide 1960–1991*, in 1991. This last finally gained Krogsgaard a 'proper publisher', and in the USA.

Such was the scrupulous quality of his work and the obvious conscientiousness he brought to the daunting task he had set himself that in 1995 Bob Dylan's office finally granted him access to the files of Dylan's recording sessions—'to all the structured information in connection with the recordings. A great experience!', as he puts it.

He is now working, therefore, on an electronic discography, and on another updated printed version ('more or less in the form of an encyclopedia in several volumes'), and on a more limited but very thorough discographical book, *Bob Dylan's Columbia Studio Recordings*, which should see publication by the end of 2006.

In his other life Michael Krogsgaard is an orthopaedic surgeon at Copenhagen University Hospital

Bispebjerg and Assistant Professor in orthopaedic surgery at the University of Copenhagen. He has specialized in arthroscopic surgery and sports traumatology, and on bone loss caused by treatment with corticosteroid drugs. In his spare time he takes a special interest in the silversmith Georg Jensen, is chairman of the Georg Jensen Society and in 2004 co-authored the book *The Unknown Georg Jensen.*

[Michael Krogsgaard: *Twenty Years of Recording: The Bob Dylan Reference Book*, Copenhagen: SIRR, 1981; *Master of the Tracks: The Bob Dylan Reference Book of Recording*, ditto, 1988; *Positively Bob Dylan: A Thirty-Year Discography, Concert & Record Session Guide 1960–1991*, Ann Arbor, MI: Popular Culture Ink, 1991. Michael Krogsgaard & Liv Carøe: *The Unknown Georg Jensen*, Copenhagen: The Georg Jensen Society, 2004.]

Kunkel, Russ [1948 -] Russell Kunkel was born in Pittsburgh in 1948 but from age 11–12 grew up in Long Beach, California, drummed in various local groups before forming the Things to Come, which became a house band at the Whiskey-A-Go-Go for five months, opening for Cream, Traffic, THE BYRDS and others, and in Kunkel's case also playing on song-publishing demos. Apple Records head Peter Asher (previously in the notoriously wet Brit duo Peter & Gordon) offered Kunkel a gig on James Taylor's début album.

From there, often partnered by bass player Lee Sklar, Kunkel became one of the pre-eminent players in rock session work in the 1970s and 80s. (With guitarist Danny Kortchmar and keyboardist Craig Doerge, Kunkel and Sklar became known as 'the Section' and made three albums as such, in 1972 and 1977.) Kunkel has drummed and/or produced for everyone from Jackson Browne to Barbra Streisand and from TRACY CHAPMAN and JONI MITCHELL to B.B. King, Lyle Lovett, NEIL YOUNG and WARREN ZEVON. Carly Simon once claimed that he was 'every singer's favorite drummer' and that she'd heard he was LEVON HELM's favourite drummer too.

His association with Dylan came early in Kunkel's career. He was brought in to play the all-night session with GEORGE HARRISON and Dylan (plus CHARLIE DANIELS and producer BOB JOHNSTON) on May 1, 1970 in New York: a session at which Bob and George ran through previews of several of the songs about to be recorded for *New Morning*, including the version of 'If Not for You' issued 21 years later on the *Bootleg Series Vols. 1–3*, plus much-circulated unreleased minor gems like 'Working on a Guru', lovely Dylan 'country voice' treatments of 'Song to Woody' and 'I Don't Believe You' and much else. This led to further Dylan sessions for Kunkel a month later, which yielded four *Dylan* sides, 'The Ballad of Ira Hayes' and 'Sara Jane' (June 1) and 'Mr. Bojangles' and 'Mary Ann' (June 2) plus the group version of 'Spanish Is the Loving Tongue' issued on *Masterpieces*. These proved mere warm-ups for *New Morning* proper, and Kunkel played on the whole album. He played with Dylan one more time, on a Burbank session for the *Pat Garrett & Billy the Kid* soundtrack in February 1973, this time playing tambourine and bongos.

[Carly Simon quoted on *www.drummerworld.com/drummers/Russ_Kunkel.html*, seen online 6 Feb 2006.]

Kweskin, Jim [1940 -] James Kweskin was born on July 18, 1940 in New England and attended Boston University, where he was inspired by local folk group the Hoppers, centred upon John 'Fritz' Richmond. After Fritz was drafted Kweskin began to perform himself, cultivating a lightly humourous stage presence and a large moustache. Looking much like Dennis Weaver, in fact, he linked up with GEOFF MULDAUR and in 1963, together with harmonica and banjo player Mel Lyman and a returned Fritz Richmond, he formed the Kweskin Jug Band. A mix of energetic playing, pre-war repertoire and comedy made them an immediately popular live act and earned a Vanguard Records contract. Augmented by Maria D'Amato (who swiftly became MARIA MULDAUR), the Kweskin Jug Band remained Cambridge-based.

Mel Lyman left the group in 1964 and was replaced by ex-Bill Monroe Blue Grass Boy Bill Keith—but Lyman still played on 'solo' Kweskin albums like 1966's *Relax Your Mind* and his malign influence over Kweskin was ever more ascendant. Soon after the band signed to Reprise and made various national TV appearances, Jim Kweskin disbanded it and moved into Lyman's monomaniacal religious commune 'family' in Boston's scuzzy Fort Hill, where he remained for some years. In 1971 came the album *Jim Kweskin's America co-starring Mel Lyman & the Lyman Family*, which had been recorded in San Francisco with Lyman on harp and vocals, Kweskin on guitar and vocals and Jim's wife Marilyn Kweskin on further vocals. The tracks were familiar old songs like the MEMPHIS JUG BAND's 'Stealin", Stephen Foster's 'Old Black Joe' plus 'The Old Rugged Cross' and 'Dark as a Dungeon', but the sleevenotes included a long, myopic declaration by Kweskin about the soul of America, ending with this: 'I am singing America to you and it is Mel Lyman. He is the new soul of the world.'

Lyman eventually disappeared, in still-mysterious circumstances, and Kweskin re-emerged, making further records, forming the 1980s group the U & I Band and remaining in Boston. He was among those who turned up and played at the celebration reunion held in 2000 in the old Club 47 premises soon after ERIC VON SCHMIDT had been given an ASCAP Lifetime Achievement Award for Folk Music.

Dylan first met Jim Kweskin when both appeared at the Indian Neck Folk Festival in Bransford, Connecticut, in May 1961. That September, at Gerde's Folk City, Dylan and Kweskin were performing together when someone taped the two sharing vocals on JESSE FULLER's 'San Francisco Bay Blues' and WOODY GUTHRIE's 'The Great Divide'; and at some point that fall, according to CLINTON HEYLIN, Kweskin and Dylan shared a Gaslight residency. Peter Stampel of the Holy Modal Rounders, interviewed on Bob Fass' radio show on WBAI in New York in about 1970, recalled seeing Kweskin and Dylan together at the Gaslight back then:

> 'He's very easy to play with, Dylan is, and, uh, we did a couple of things. He did a lot of things with Jim Kweskin. . . . somebody must have tapes of him and Kweskin singing together, man. They were doing . . . folk-hippie 1961 tunes like "Long Black Veil" and "San Francisco Bay Blues" when hardly anybody was doing it, and they did like the best of that I've ever heard. . . . I play kazoo. Wow, it was just mind blowing. Dylan would flatpick and Jim would fingerpick, and they'd play like in . . . they'd use capos so that they would both play in different configurations so they wouldn't get on each other. They were so gas . . .'

Gas or not, Dylan and Kweskin don't seem to have played music together again since 1961. Nor has any tape of the two of them ever surfaced, except for those two songs from Gerde's.

[Jim Kweskin & Bob Dylan: 'San Francisco Bay Blues' & 'The Great Divide', Gerde's, NY, Sep 1961. Jim Kweskin: *Relax Your Mind, nia*, Vanguard VRS-9188/VSD-79188, NY, 1966, CD-reissued Universe CDKWESKRELA, US, 2003; *Jump For Joy, nia*, Vanguard VRS-9243/VSD-79243, NY, 1967; *Whatever Happened to those Good Old Days . . . , nia*, Vanguard VSD-779278, NY, 1968; *Jim Kweskin's America co-starring Mel Lyman & the Lyman Family*, SF, *nia*, Reprise RS6464, US, 1971. Jim Kweskin Jug Band: *Unblushing Brassiness*, Vanguard VRS 9139/VSD-2158, NY, 1963; *Jug Band Music*, Vanguard VRS-9163/VSD-79163, NY, 1965; *See Reverse Side for Title*, Vanguard VRS-9234/VSD-79234, NY, 1966; *Garden of Joy*, Reprise R-6266/RS-6266, US, 1967. Stampfel interview as transcribed by Harvey Bojarsky, seen online 2 Oct 2005 at 'Bob Dylan Roots', at *www.bobdylanroots.com/stampfel.html#kweskin*.]

L

LaFarge, Pete [1931 - 1965] Oliver Albee LaFarge was born on April 30, 1931, in New York City but, unlike the hero of his most famous song, 'The Ballad of Ira Hayes', he was not, as often stated, of Pima Indian descent. He was part French and part Narragansett Indian, the son of heiress Wanden Mathews LaFarge and Indian activist and author Oliver LaFarge, who won a Pulitzer Prize in 1930 for the novel *Laughing Boy*, a pioneering positive scrutiny of the Navajo achieved through its portrayal of an Indian youth caught between traditional tribal life and the forces of modern society. MOSES ASCH's sleevenotes to Pete LaFarge's 1963 Folkways album *As Long as the Grass Shall Grow* claimed that the singer came 'from Fountain Colorado, where he was raised as a cowboy on the Kane Ranch. His second home is in Santa Fe, New Mexico, where his father resides. . . . Peter left school when he was sixteen, to sing and rodeo. . . . [He] was adopted . . . by the Tewa Tribe of the Hopi nation. . . . In 1946 Josh White came through Pete's country, and stopped off to work with him. Much work with Josh, BIG BILL BROONZY and a close friendship with CISCO HOUSTON followed . . .'

Some of this can now be amended and augmented. Pete LaFarge moved to Fountain when he was five years old, after his parents divorced. His mother then married rancher Andy Kane in 1940 and he was raised on their ranch. It was here that he started to call himself Pete. His father Oliver duly moved to Santa Fe, and Pete spent time at both parents' homes, though his relationship with his father was apparently strained. Pete was adopted by the Tewa as a gesture of thanks for his father's contribution to native studies and culture in Santa Fe; he never lived on the reservation there. And though he did go off singing and rodeoing after leaving school at 16, he also joined the US Navy at 19, at the start of the Korean War.

For much of his three wartime Navy years he was aboard the aircraft carrier Boxer, which duly sustained a major hit, which, though not wounding him physically, caused LaFarge recurrent psychological torment. After his discharge he studied acting for two years in Chicago and married a young fellow actor, Susan Becker, in 1958. In the late 1950s, after working with touring companies, LaFarge got a part on Broadway and moved back to New York, and, with parts hard to come by, also returned to singing.

A decade older than Bob Dylan, and with his young wife locked away in a mental hospital, LaFarge was already installed on the Greenwich Village scene when Dylan arrived from Minnesota. Mother figure Sidsel Gleason told ANTHONY SCADUTO, Dylan's first real biographer, that when she got worried about Dylan's pot-smoking, she 'asked Peter LaFarge to keep an eye on him, and he did. . . . Pete would walk into a party where Bob was and stand with his arms crossed, not saying a word, just watching.' Eventually Dylan phoned her, saying 'Mom, please get that Indian off my back.' But LaFarge was the last person to play the responsible adult, and in time he and Bob arrived at an equitable relationship. In *Chronicles Volume One* Dylan recalls that this 'folksinger friend' gave him 'a couple of Colt single-shot repeater pistols . . .'

'The Ballad of Ira Hayes' was the first track on his first album, *Ira Hayes and Other Ballads*, produced by JOHN HAMMOND and released on Columbia in 1962. After this Columbia dropped him, allegedly because of his drunkenness, and he went to Folkways, releasing *Iron Mountain and Other Songs* in 1962, *As Long as the Grass Shall Grow* in 1963, *Sings of the Cowboys and Sings Women's Blues* in 1964. Lastly in his lifetime case *On the Warpath*, 1965, which also had 'Ira Hayes' as its opening track and included too the song 'Move Over, Grab a Holt', which namechecks both Dylan and BAEZ: 'With Bobby and Joanie singin' so bright / Who needs a compass with all that light?'

JOHNNY CASH recorded not only 'Ira Hayes' (in 1964) but almost a whole album's worth of LaFarge pro-Indian protest songs (*Bitter Tears: Ballads of the American Indian*, 1964) including 'Custer', from LaFarge's second LP, which labelled this hero a racist killer, prompting a black-listing of Cash by country radio stations.

LaFarge's father died in early August 1963, and was buried in the Santa Fe National Cemetery. Another son, John Pendaries LaFarge, a child from Oliver's second marriage, still lives in the Santa Fe house their father owned.

LaFarge brought the topic of Native American suffering and oppression into the folk revival world, encouraging those like Buffy Sainte-Marie to sing out and campaign in the years after LaFarge's death. He is the subject of the forthcoming book *The Ballad of Peter LaFarge: Native America's Protest Pioneer* by Nashville-based writer Sandra Hale Schulman, and of her short documentary film *The Ballad of Peter LaFarge*. At the time of this writing, Ms. Schulman was also most of the way through putting together a tribute CD, originally planned to include Dylan's 1970 studio recording of 'The Ballad of Ira Hayes' but now possibly to include a newly recorded track by Dylan made specially for this project.

Meanwhile Clint Eastwood is reportedly directing *Flags of Our Fathers* for fall 2006 release: a film following the story of Ira Hayes and the two other soldiers who also raised the flag at Iwo Jima in 1945 and survived but were then used as pawns in the game of the American government to sell war bonds.

For Dylan, though, 'The Ballad of Ira Hayes' was not a political diatribe but, as usual, a human story and to see brief archive footage in SCORSESE's *No Direction Home* (2005) of a disturbed LaFarge singing the song as if with wacky throwaway self-consciousness is to recognise how warmly and with what magisterial grace Dylan's 1970 recording restores the song.

In the interview in the *Biograph* box set of 1985, Dylan said this about his old friend: 'Actually, Peter is one of the unsung heroes of the day. His style was just a little bit too erratic. But it wasn't his fault, he was always hurting and having to overcome it. . . . We were pretty tight for a while. We had the same girlfriend. When I think of a guitar poet or protest singer, I always think of Peter, but he was a love song writer too.'

The shared girlfriend was almost certainly 'Avril the dancer', as JOHN BAULDIE calls her in a brief biographical sketch in *All Across the Telegraph: A Bob Dylan Handbook* (1987): 'New York girlfriend: dancer & actress who saw Dylan perform at a Gerde's Folk City Monday night Hootenanny, perhaps as early as mid-February 1961. Dylan lived with Avril on East 4th St. for the last weeks of his first stay in NYC, March–April of that year.' Pete LaFarge wrote a song called 'Avril Blues', released on *Iron Mountain and Other Songs*, which is laden with references to dancing.

LaFarge and ex-*Playboy* bunny and singer Inger Neilsen had a daughter, Karen, in August 1965; they were both incapable of looking after her, and when she was two weeks old, Pete's mother took her away. Two months later, on October 27, 1965 (*not* 1964, as sometimes given), Pete LaFarge died of a drugs overdose.

It's impossible to know whether he meant to kill himself. He had long been in bad shape: rodeo riding had given him broken bones and a broken nose, he'd almost lost a leg and wore a leg brace; he'd been diagnosed as schizophrenic, though he was more likely a manic depressive; he was on various unsuitable prescribed medicines, including, thanks to a US navy experiment, cobra venom (to paralyse and thereby calm his nerves . . .), on top of which he was a heavy drinker and recreational drug user. There's also no doubt that he regarded his career as a complete failure and knew that his personal life was in tragic chaos.

It's bandied about on the internet that 'officially' he'd been stated to have died from a stroke, but in fact his death certificate gives under 'cause of death' only 'pending further study'. He was 34 years old. His daughter Karen Wanden was assaulted and sustained severe head injuries in Colorado Springs in summer 2005.

[Pete LaFarge: *Ira Hayes and Other Ballads*, Columbia CL 1795, US, 1962; *Iron Mountain and Other Songs*, Folkways FN 2531, 1962; *As Long as the Grass Shall Grow*, Folkways FN 2532, 1963; *Peter LaFarge Sings of the Cowboys*, Folkways FA 2533, 1964; *Peter LaFarge Sings Women's Blues*, Folkways 2534, 1964 & Verve FVS 9004, *nia*; *On the Warpath*, Folkways FN 2535, NY, 1965; CD reissues *On The Warpath / As Long as the Grass Shall Grow*, Bear Family BCD 15626 AH & *Sings of the Cowboys / Iron Mountain and Other Songs*, BCD 15627 AH, Vollersode, Germany, 1992. Bob Dylan, *Chronicles Volume One*, 2004, pp.116–17. Anthony Scaduto, *Bob Dylan, An Intimate Biography*, London: Abacus revised edn., 1973, p.64. Sandra Hale Schulman, *The Ballad of Peter LaFarge: Native America's Protest Pioneer*, forthcoming 2007. *Rare Breed: The Songs of Peter LaFarge* (tribute album), ESP Disk *nia*, expected release US, 2006. *The Ballad of Peter LaFarge* (film), dir. Sandra Hale Schulman; Slink Productions/String Theory Media, US, 2005. Sources: comments by 'Mark' at *http://maninblack.net/Mhic/folk.htm*, seen online 6 Feb 2006 (though these are very unreliable), the compilation of relevant snippets at *www.bobdylanroots.com/laf.html* (also very unreliable) and, reliably, information from Sandra Hale Schulman at *www.peterlafarge.com* & e-mails & phone conversation with this writer 7 Feb 2006; discographical information from Stefan Wirz's LaFarge discography, online 4 April 2006 at *www.wirz.de/music/lafarge.htm*.]

Landau, Jon [1947 -] Jon Landau was born in Brooklyn, New York, on May 14, 1947. In the late 1960s, some years before he became the record producer of that 'new Dylan' BRUCE SPRINGSTEEN, Landau was a rock journalist. He wrote for the American magazine *Crawdaddy*, and in a review of *John Wesley Harding* in May 1968 he pinned down something crucial about what Dylan was doing and not doing with this album: and his comments, usefully, still give a sense of how it was when Dylan's dramatic chameleon changes were occurring contemporaneously. He wrote:

> '*John Wesley Harding* is a profoundly egotistical album. For an album of this kind to be released amidst *Sgt. Pepper*, *Their Satanic Majesties Request*, *Strange Days* and *After Bathing at Baxter's*, somebody must have had a lot of confidence in what he was doing. . . . Dylan seems to feel no need to respond to the predominate trends in pop music at all. And he is the only major pop artist about whom this can be said. The Dylan of *John Wesley Harding* is a truly independent artist who doesn't feel responsible to anyone else, whether they be fans or his contemporaries.'

(The florid albums referred to here were by, respectively, THE BEATLES, THE ROLLING STONES, the Doors and Jefferson Airplane.)

By 1973—which is to say the last year existentially of the 1960s—Landau had become a rock critic of powerful position. As Simon Frith noted, reviewing Landau's book *It's Too Late to Stop Now* (a collection of reviews and essays previously published in journals): 'Landau has genuine claims to importance. He may not be the best (?) rock critic around but he is the most influential . . . on the tastes and attitudes of the average rock writer. Partly this is a result of his position as record editor of *Rolling Stone* but mostly it's because he has pioneered the approach to music that other rock critics find most suited to their self-conscious seriousness . . . it was Landau who helped to forge this critical consensus . . .'

[Jon Landau: 'John Wesley Harding', *Crawdaddy* no.15, May 1968, reprinted in Craig MacGregor, *Bob Dylan: A Retrospective*, 1972; *It's Too Late to Stop Now: A Rock and Roll Journal*, San Francisco, Straight Arrow, 1972. The Beatles: *Sergeant Pepper's Lonely Heart's Club Band*, London, 1967, Parlophone PCS 7027 (PMC 7027 mono), London (Capitol SMAS 2653, LA), 1967; the Rolling Stones: *Their Satanic Majesties' Request*, Decca TXS 103, London (London NPS 2, NY), 1967; the Doors: *Strange Days*, Elektra 74014, LA (& London), 1967; and Jefferson Airplane: *After Bathing at Baxter's*, RCA Victor LSP 4545, NY (RCA SF/RD 7926, London), 1968. Simon Frith on Landau in *Let It Rock*, London, May 1973, now online at *www.rocksbackpages.com*.]

Langhorne, Bruce [1938 -] Joseph Bruce Langhorne was born in Tallahassee, Florida, on May 11, 1938. Despite the loss of several fingers in a childhood accident, he became *the* session guitarist of the folk-rock era, after moving to New York City, getting his Greenwich Village start playing behind BROTHER JOHN SELLERS at Gerde's Folk City and so being asked to play with others on the contemporary folk scene. After Dylan's album *Bringing It All Back Home*, on which Langhorne was prominent, he was called upon to help almost everybody else 'go electric' too, though he continued to support acoustic sessions in his unique way.

Richie Unterberger explains his style and special import concisely:

> 'Langhorne developed a distinctive economic style that acted as the response half of a call-and-response with singer/songwriters' vocals, often using rapid triplets. . . . When folk-rock came in, Langhorne used an acoustic guitar with a pickup, running it through a Fender Twin Reverb amp that he borrowed from guitarist (and fellow multi-instrumentalist) Sandy Bull. Influenced by Roebuck Staples of THE STAPLE SINGERS, he would set up a tremolo effect in time with the song. The result was a sound, both acoustic and electric in color, well-suited to the period in which rock and folk music were combining.'

Thus from the mid-1960s onwards Bruce Langhorne recorded with JOAN BAEZ, RICHARD & MIMI FARIÑA, GORDON LIGHTFOOT, Buffy Sainte-Marie, Tom Rush, Hugh Masekela and others, arranged the 1967 Richie Havens LP *Mixed Bag*, produced RAMBLIN' JACK ELLIOTT's 1968 album *Young Brigham* and played live with JUDY COLLINS and many more besides.

Bruce Langhorne's first studio encounter with Dylan's repertoire came in July 1962, when he was brought in to play on the album *The Chad Mitchell Trio in Action!*, on which the group included an early cover of 'Blowin' in the Wind'. (The LP was later re-titled *Blowin' in the Wind*—see entry on the song for detail.) But Langhorne first played on a session with Bob Dylan himself in September 1961, before Dylan even had a record deal; both played on CAROLYN HESTER's third album: Langhorne on guitar and Dylan on harmonica.

A year later, on October 26 and November 1 and 14, 1962, Langhorne played behind the still-unsuccessful Dylan on sessions for *The Freewheelin' Bob Dylan*. These particular sessions were the first on which Dylan was sometimes backed by an assemblage of other musicians—a drummer, pianist, bass guitarist and another guitarist besides Langhorne—and they yielded 'Corrina Corrina' (the album version and the single version), the always-underrated 'Mixed-Up Confusion' (one take on the B-side of the single, another issued later on *Masterpieces* and, 'speed-corrected', on *Biograph*) plus the album version of 'Don't Think Twice, It's All Right' and the lovely outtake of 'Kingsport Town' eventually issued on the *Bootleg Series Vols. 1–3* in 1991. (The liner notes for this track say 'second guitarist unknown'.)

Dylan and Langhorne next met up professionally at the beginning of 1965. The first session day for *Bringing It All Back Home*, January 13, seems to have been by Dylan alone, but the following afternoon and evening, Langhorne played on various takes of 'Love Minus Zero / No Limit', 'Subterranean Homesick Blues', 'Outlaw Blues', 'She Belongs to Me' and 'Bob Dylan's 115th Dream', including, in each case, the take that made it onto the album, plus takes of 'On the Road Again' and 'I'll Keep It With Mine' that didn't. This last was issued on the *Biograph* box set 20 years later.

Next day, January 15, Langhorne played on 'Maggie's Farm' (which seems to have been achieved in one take, and the first take of the day at that), 'On the Road Again', 'It's Alright Ma (I'm Only Bleeding)', 'Gates of Eden', 'Mr. Tambourine Man' and 'It's All Over Now, Baby Blue', plus the take of 'If You Gotta Go, Go Now' issued as a single in some territories and the take of the same song issued on the *Bootleg Series Vols. 1–3*.

Langhorne was especially thrilled with 'Maggie's Farm' because by default he ended up playing lead guitar instead of just an accompanying rôle:

> 'There was a stellar crop of musicians in the studio that day . . . but somehow no one stepped up

to fill the lead rôle. I sort of filled in the gaps, waiting for someone to take over. The result was a guitar lead part that never got in the way of anything or stepped forward to say "Look at Me!". In retrospect, I feel that it was just what the song needed. Since then, I have always hoped to find myself in a similar circumstance, with a strong, inspired vocal part like Dylan's to follow and a room full of great musicians playing only what the music dictates.'

In addition to which, not only did Bruce Langhorne play on 'Mr. Tambourine Man', but perhaps he *was* Mr. Tambourine Man. As Dylan says on the *Biograph* interview: 'Bruce was playing guitar with me on a bunch of the early records. On one session TOM WILSON [the producer] had asked him to play tambourine. And he had this gigantic tambourine. . . . It was as big as a wagon-wheel. He was playing, and this vision of him playing this tambourine just stuck in my mind. . . . I don't know if I've ever told him that.'

This is problematical as an explanation, since the song certainly wasn't written at these sessions but almost a year earlier (Dylan performed it at his Royal Festival Hall concert in London on May 17, 1964), and while Tom Wilson had been Dylan's producer since 1963, Langhorne had not been on any of the 1963–64 sessions. On the other hand, Langhorne's tambourine *was* enormous, and looked most unusual, like something ancient and tribal imported from the Horn of Africa; he had bought it from IZZY YOUNG's Folklore Center.

In any case, the *Bringing It All Back Home* sessions also included the outtakes of 'It's All Over Now, Baby Blue' and 'She Belongs to Me' that saw release 40 years later on the *Bootleg Series Vol. 7—No Direction Home: The Soundtrack*, the booklet for which refers to 'She Belongs to Me' as notable for 'the beautifully liquid guitar of Bruce Langhorn' (slightly reducing the compliment by misspelling his name).

A month after the sessions, Langhorne accompanied Dylan for a rare TV performance, on 'The Les Crane Show' on WABC-TV in New York, on 'It's All Over Now, Baby Blue' and 'It's Alright Ma (I'm Only Bleeding)'. This was in February 1965. Dylan moved on to using 'harder' musicians, and though he played tambourine on 'Like a Rolling Stone' Langhorne wasn't used again as a guitarist until his 'beautifully liquid guitar' was called upon for Dylan's still-underrated soundtrack to *Pat Garrett & Billy the Kid*, recorded and released in 1973, on which he plays with his customary, admirable mix of feeling and restraint on 'Main Title Theme', 'Cantina Theme', 'Billy 1' and 'River Theme', and with the necessary gusto on 'Turkey Chase'.

Langhorne had himself composed and recorded a 'western' film soundtrack just a couple of years earlier—for the 'lost' 1971 Peter Fonda film *The Hired Hand*: a film often described as a 'masterpiece', and finally re-released in a '30th Anniversary edition'. Langhorne's score too has often been singled out as haunting, and this music was at last issued on CD in 2004, to further highly favourable notice (described in *Mojo* magazine as 'unbearably lovely' and 'ever-so-gently psychedelicised Americana' in which hillbilly musical figures 'morph into modular rags and echoes of gamelan ring hypnotically').

Since the early 1970s Bruce Langhorne has pursued his career quietly, part-owning a recording studio, working as a film composer again on the Jonathan Demme film *Melvin and Howard* (1980) and a number of others, writing music for a couple of TV ads and taking an active part recently in the loosely structured band the Venice Beach Marching Society, 'a mobile tribute to New Orleans' with the motto 'We march for fun and other good causes'. He is about to release a new CD of previously unreleased 'very danceable' compositions of his own on which he plays all instruments and handles all vocals, though in fact while continuing to play fiddle and other things (including, naturally, tambourine) he has now stopped playing guitar.

His website divides between profiling his musical activities and Brother Bru-Bru's African Hot Sauce, to the efficacy of which his own indecently youthful appearance is a tribute. Praising hot sauce online, or praising Bob Dylan in the film *No Direction Home*, Bruce Langhorne may have greying hair but looks by far the younger man. He will be 70 in two years' time.

[Bruce Langhorne: *The Hired Hand Score*, Blast First Petite, US, 2004. With Bob Dylan: 'Corrina Corrina', NY, 26 Oct c/w 'Mixed-Up Confusion', NY, 14 Nov 1962, Columbia 4-42656, US, 1962; 'The Les Crane Show', WABC-TV, NY, 17 Feb 1965. 'Ramblin' Jack Elliott, *Young Brigham*, Reprise RS-6284, US, 1968. *The Hired Hand*, dir. Peter Fonda, Pando/Tartan/Universal, US, 1971. Sources include e-mails to this writer from Bruce Langhorne (incl. 'Maggie's Farm' quote), 27 Sep 2005; Richie Unterberger quote & hot sauce online 21 Sep 2005 at *www.brobrubru.com*.]

Lanois, Daniel [1951 -] Daniel Lanois is a French Canadian, born in Hull, Québec, on September 19, 1951. Though he is a musician—he plays guitar and dobro, sings and writes songs—and since 1989 has released half a dozen albums of his own (three of them, oddly, in 1996), he is primarily valued as a highly distinctive record producer, though the very ease with which his style can be recognised is a mixed blessing for the artists around whom he wraps his plangent ambience (like, it sometimes seems, a spider's silk around a fly).

He started his career as a producer by setting up his own studio and engineering records for local groups in Hamilton, just 30 miles southwest of Toronto (and 30 miles west of Niagara Falls and New York State). His first relative success was with Canada's new wave synth-pop group Martha and the

Muffins. Their 1979 album *Metro Music* gave the band its one big international hit single, the toweringly vacuous 'Echo Beach', but in 1981, various personnel changes included the arrival of Daniel's bass-playing sister Jocelyne Lanois; thus he produced their albums *This Is the Ice Age* (1981) and *Danseparc* (1982), and, after their name change to M + M, the 1984 album *Mystery Walk*.

By then, however, Lanois had been 'discovered' by Brian Eno, and after they'd worked together (including on Eno's 1982 album *Ambient 4/On Land* and the following year's *Apollo: Atmospheres and Soundtracks*) Eno and Lanois co-produced U2's 1984 album *The Unforgettable Fire*, shooting Lanois into the music-biz hot-producer seat in his early 30s. After various further Eno albums, a couple by Peter Gabriel and U2's insanely mega-selling *The Joshua Tree* (1987), Lanois then produced ROBBIE ROBERTSON's much-delayed début solo album, *Robbie Robertson*, in 1988. The year after came the Neville Brothers' *Yellow Moon* and Bob Dylan's *Oh Mercy*, the latter's one near-great album of the 1980s, released in the nick of time on September 22, 1989, and recorded in New Orleans that March and April.

Dylan describes in *Chronicles Volume One* how, after BONO's enthusiastic suggestion of Lanois to Dylan, the two men first met in the humid courtyard of the Marie Antoinette Hotel in New Orleans. Lanois, no doubt painfully aware of how tentative and generally below par Dylan's 1980s albums had been by his own earlier standards, said a brave, direct yet supportive thing to Dylan at this first meeting. He said: 'You can make a great record, you know, if you really want to.' That's what more or less every Dylan aficionado would have wanted to say to him.

Dylan's memoir devotes the fourth of its five sections to the making of this album and the period surrounding it, offering an immense amount of detail. Most unexpectedly, it's a highly specific account of the process the artist goes through–the artist in general and this artist in particular–from not knowing 'what kind of record I had in mind', through the struggles and pitfalls of songwriting, testing out sounds, trying to hang onto fleeting ideas and elusive successes of 'feel', drifting in and out of the resolve to concentrate and care, the push and pull of personalities, including Lanois', the nebulous or not-so nebulous influence of New Orleans itself on the proceedings, the ungraspable things that escape along the way, the compromises that are all too clear but cannot always be subverted or dodged. It's an invaluable, highly absorbing account that takes us all the way through to the completion of what turned out to be *Oh Mercy*. In the course of its recording, Lanois himself had played electric guitar, 12-string guitar, steel guitar, dobro, harpsichord, omnichord, bass, drums and tom-tom. And he pushed Bob Dylan to be more hands-on himself than he was inclined to be: to play guitars, dobro, piano, harmonium, bass and harmonica.

After *Oh Mercy* Lanois went back to his work with Peter Gabriel and U2 (he produced *Achtung Baby* in 1991) and for others, including EMMYLOU HARRIS, whose *Wrecking Ball* he produced in 1995. And then in 1997, who should call upon Lanois again but the Bob Dylan whose albums of the 1990s so far had been the badly received *Under the Red Sky* at the beginning of the decade and the two solo acoustic albums of traditional ballads and pre-war blues, 1992's *Good as I Been to You* and 1993's *World Gone Wrong*. Dylan had also rejected outright the sessions in Chicago in between these two albums, which had been an attempt to combine the repertoire of these records with a return to the use of other musicians. Since 1993 there had been nothing: just more years of the Never-Ending Tour.

This time it was January instead of the fall. They met up in Miami–another Southern city, another late-in-the-decade attempt at a major album. Lanois played only guitars this time; Dylan played guitars, piano and harmonica. And this time it was almost billed as a co-production: it is 'produced by: Daniel Lanois . . . in association with Jack Frost Productions.' Again, the album was widely hailed as Dylan's best in a long time: for many, it was his best since *Oh Mercy*, and Lanois was given plenty of the credit.

In retrospect, his contribution had been a mixed blessing. The production, for all Lanois' alchemical skills, sometimes accentuates a sense of cheap fabrication. On 'Love Sick', the opening track, his aural theatricality is unhelpful, for example, when this frail question hobbles into the frame: 'Did I hear someone's distant cry?' The accompaniment here ought to lend a steadying hand, a bit of solid, unobtrusive support, allowing the lyric to pass on quickly. Instead, an immediate musical 'cry'–a dweepling electronic ooh-ooh, ooh-ooh–comes up behind the singer's querulous wobble toward portentousness and kicks away any hope of it not sounding risible. Its less processed prototype may sound fine on steel guitar on Santo & Johnny's 'classic' 1959 instrumental hit 'Sleep Walk' (the supposedly dream-like plangent echo in which this semi-Canadian no.1 hit single was saturated may well be the core inspiration behind the entire Lanois sound) but in its 'Love Sick' context, it's so crass you can hardly believe you're hearing it.

The sound is elsewhere unhelpful too on *Time Out of Mind*. Some tracks have Dylan so buried in echo that there is no hope of hearing the detailing in his voice that was once so central and diamond-like a part of his genius. 'Dirt Road Blues', which might under normal production circumstances be a heartening, even dexterous little rockabilly number, puts Dylan so far away and so tiny you just despair. It's as if the microphone were an audio telescope and he's using the wrong end of it. The voice on 'Cold Irons Bound' is so badly down in the mix that without clamping headphones to your ears the lyric comes and goes, recurrently offering indecipherable passages, while the contrived voodoo galumph of the music clatters across the foreground like donkeys on a tepid tin roof.

Some of the tracks that aren't so distancing are perversely reductive in a different way, bringing his voice forward with a crude excess of echo, as on 'Million Miles' and ''Til I Fell in Love With You', 'recorded in Lanois' proverbial echo-laden cyber-bunker', as the novelist David Bowman puts it. A bunker is where you retreat when you're desperate. Was Dylan's voice really so weak, so pitiful a husk of its former self (of any of its former selves) that instead of recording it straightforwardly, up close, alertly, as on the very first albums he ever made, Dylan's implausibly reconstituted voice had to puff forward in a swollen simulated intimacy that robs it of all its truly distinctive power? No. It wasn't.

Despite the ill-judged production of the voice on these musically unattractive tracks, the overall sound of the music on *Time Out of Mind*, as with *Oh Mercy*, still offers cohesion. One of its distinctive ingredients is AUGIE MEYERS' Farfisa organ, which David Bowman hears as coming 'from the soundtrack of some 1950s saucers-from-Mars drive-in movie' (he says he means this as a compliment) but which also throws us straight back to the eerie magic of the first Country Joe & the Fish album, the indispensable *Electric Music for the Mind and Body*, which used exactly the organ sound we confront at once on *Time Out of Mind*. All these elements are stirred into Daniel Lanois' digital soup, which nourishes everything in an enveloping way: and in doing *that* it may remind us of nothing so much as the very different music on *Blonde on Blonde*. As that does, this too sweeps you along all through the album, as if the songs were one; and as that does, it binds together the weaker tracks with the strong.

What of the strongest? 'Standing in the Doorway', 'Trying to Get to Heaven', 'Not Dark Yet' and 'Highlands' are surely great, and Lanois surely helps them to be so. On these four, the vocals are not drenched in echo: not swollen forward artificially as in the Buddy Grecoland of 'Million Miles', nor ill-judged as on 'Dirt Road Blues' (on which the parping organ provides quite the wrong touch, if recreating the Sun Sound was the aim, the result more Joe Meek than Sam Phillips). On the album's Big Four, the voice is beautifully attended to, permitting the listener to attend to it too: in such a way that, whatever has actually been done technically in the studio, it is experienced as if directly, matching absolutely aptly the directness with which Dylan sings.

That was the second and last time Dylan used Lanois: and the argument that while he might have had a place, he certainly wasn't necessary, was made best in 2001, when Dylan produced his own next album, *"Love and Theft"*, and gave himself an impeccable, unobtrusive production just as technically professional as, and less me-me-me than, anything Daniel Lanois can offer.

In 2005 he offered a new solo album of his own, the instrumental *Belladonna*, on which he returns to the ambient sound-pictures of old, and decides that no vocals shall get in the way, freeing listeners to 'use their imagination and build their own scenario'. If they like that sort of thing.

[Daniel Lanois: *Acadie* 1989; *For the Beauty of Wynona*, 1993; *Sweet Angel Mine*, 1996; *Lost in Mississippi*, 1996; *Sling Blade*, 1996; *Shine*, 2003; *Belladonna*, 2005.

Bob Dylan, *Chronicles Volume One*, 2004, p.177. David Bowman, reviewing *Time Out of Mind*, *Salon* on-line magazine, US, 19 Sep 1997 (Bowman's novels include *Bunny Modern*, 1998.)

Santo & Johnny: 'Sleep Walk', NY, 1959, Canadian-American Records 103, Winnipeg & NY, 1959; CD-reissued *The Golden Age of American Rock'n'Roll Volume 5*, Ace CDCHD 600, London, 1995. Country Joe & The Fish: *Electric Music For The Mind & Body*, Berkeley, CA, *nia*, Vanguard SVRL 19026, NY (Fontana TFL 6081, London), 1967, CD-reissued Vanguard VMD 79244-2, NY, c.1990 (London, c.1994).]

'Lay Down Your Weary Tune' [1963] 'Lay Down Your Weary Tune' is an outtake from the sessions for Dylan's third LP, *The Times They Are a-Changin'* (and recorded in New York City the same day as its title track, October 24, 1963). Two days later Dylan performed it, for the only known time, at his Carnegie Hall concert, which was also recorded by Columbia for a planned but never issued album, *Bob Dylan in Concert*.

The studio version, long thought to be an outtake from *Another Side of Bob Dylan*, 1964, remained unreleased not only at the time but for years, though the track could be found on the early bootlegs *Seems Like a Freeze-Out*, *The Villager* and *A Rare Batch of Little White Wonder Volume 3*. It was at last officially released on the Bob Dylan box set *Biograph*, 1985. The wonderful live recording remains officially unreleased, except on a sampler issued by Sony in 2005.

'Lay Down Your Weary Tune' is perhaps Dylan's first acid song: his first concentrated attempt, at any rate, to give a hint of the unfiltered world, and a supremely successful *creation*. STEVEN GOLDBERG refers in an article to Dylan's having 'heard the universal melody'. Nothing could better substantiate the spirit of such a claim than 'Lay Down Your Weary Tune'—one of Dylan's very greatest and most haunting creations.

The tune, in A Major, runs through a simple 14-bar structure which, after its initial chorus statement, is repeated nine times, always with delicate variation. By the device of having one self-renewing tune to serve both chorus and verses, Dylan doubles the sense of unity which covers the whole song, and its images. We find an impression of perfect balance not only between verse and chorus but between the opposites focused by the words: between the night that has gone and the morning announced by its breeze; between the trees and the earth to which their leaves descend; between the ocean and the shore; between the rain that sings and the listening winds.

The melody seems to entwine itself around us, in allegiance to the associations of 'wove', 'strands', 'waves', 'unwound', 'unbound' and 'winding strum' in the lyric. And by its very impingement it urges the felicity of Dylan's analogies between nature's effects and the sounds of musical instruments. As it flows through each line, with a graceful and liquid precision, the melody nurtures and sustains in us an awareness of how involving and creative such analogies are made to be. The tune offers itself as an embodiment of 'the river's mirror'; its water smooth does indeed run like a hymn.

In contrast, the solo guitar accompaniment involves itself less with the verses than with the chorus. Based on the three simple chords of A, D and E, it does offer a strength in its strings. Paradoxically, it achieves this strength through strumming: and this maintains a rhythm that is at once flexible–responsive to Dylan's voice–and insistent–almost marching (as on a pilgrimage)–in its beat. Dylan's voice is as expressive as ever of distilled, unspecified experience and a fine sensibility, totally engaged. Handled by anyone else, it would not be the same song: which also means that the words of the song have a complexity that demands such a voice as Dylan's. Words, music *and* performance are all central.

Never before or since has Dylan created a pantheistic vision–a vision of the world, that is, in which nature appears not as a manifestation of God but as containing God within its every aspect.

Underlying an exhilaration so intense as to be saddening, there is a profound composure in the face of a world in which all elements of beauty are infused with the light of God. Rejecting, here, the Wordsworthian habit of mixing poetry with explicit philosophising, so that it is explained, in a prose sense, that the divine light shines through everything, Dylan registers the same conviction with true poetic genius, making that dissembled light a felt presence throughout the song.

The words not only work as images but also as symbols: 'Struck by the sounds before the sun / I knew the night had gone.' That night is both real and metaphorical: and so is the morning that follows. Dylan uses the same symbolism in 'When the Ship Comes In', which looks forward to the triumph of righteousness when '. . . the mornin' will be a-breakin''. This in turn relates closely to the chorus of 'I Shall Be Released': 'I see my life come shinin' / From the west unto the east' [where morning breaks] 'Any day now, any day now / I shall be released.'

It is, of course, a conventional metaphor, but its very conventionality prevents it from obtruding *as* a metaphor. The song would be much less powerful if the symbols were not contained within their corresponding realities–the symbolic within the real night, and so on.

The morning Dylan sings of in 'Lay Down Your Weary Tune' is heralded by a breeze: and again, Dylan accommodates the conventional associations of freshness and change. The 'bugle' at once alters the complexion of the line. It places the morning more specifically–because the bugle is not commonly a secular instrument–within a context of salvation.

In the following verse, this religious complexion is supported by the 'organ', with its obvious associations with worship, and later confirmed by the 'trumpet', by 'like a hymn' and 'like a harp'.

The pantheistic idea is also implicit in the rejection of all distinctions. Each part of nature is given equal weight: to no part is any directly qualitative adjective or adjectival phrase ascribed. The nearest Dylan comes to such ascription is with the 'clouds unbound by laws' and the rain that 'asked for no applause'–and these confirm the idea of God as an evenly distributed presence by suggesting a moral gulf between divinity in nature and the reductive inadequacy of man. The perception of this gulf is upheld by the last line of the chorus, which, were the implicit made explicit, would read 'No *human* voice can hope to hum.' The song also rejects evaluative distinction between the various facets of nature by uniting them all in the central motif of the orchestra: each 'instrument' contributes towards an overall sound; each is concerned with the one divine melody.

This unity is substantiated by a wealth of onomatopoeic words within the song: strum, hum, bugle, drums, crashin', clashed, moaned and smooth. It is further developed, becomes multidimensional, because in response to this enchanted world the singer's senses (and therefore ours also) mix and mingle. An open acceptance of BAUDELAIREan *correspondances* is involved. There is a huge tracery of this sense-mingling in the song. What constitutes the strength of strings? Their sound? Their physical vibration? Their vertical parallel lines? Their tautness? Their recalling of classical Greece (the lute of Orpheus, the melodious divinity of Pan's music)? The *emotion* experienced as dawn appears corresponds to the *sound* of drums: and mingling such as this helps give the verse its haunting pull on the listener–an effect far beyond the simple dynamics of alliteration in that 'breeze like a bugle blew / Against the drums of dawn.'

Part of the sense-mingling achieved by 'the cryin' rain like a trumpet sang' is surrealistic. Fleetingly, we get a visual image of the rain becoming a trumpet. This belies the effect of that 'cryin'' because to transform itself (from silver-grey to gold) into a singing trumpet, the rain must pour out, if not upwards, horizontally, like musical notes on a sheet of manuscript. It is a tribute to Dylan's achievement that we can accept, in passing, this strangeness of effect without finding it a distraction.

Again, the cadence of the melody works perfectly: the notes that carry the words 'rain like a' ascend so that they enact the pressing down of consecutive trumpet stops. Not only that, but the 'a' is held, extended, so that the 'trumpet' emerges on resolving notes; and we accept the image readily because the music that presents it returns us to base. To produce the 'trumpet' image on home-coming notes lends it a certain familiarity. The image remains striking, but not incongruous.

The cadence is equally cooperative in the first line of that same verse, where again it enacts what the words describe: it allows a graceful unwinding of the voice from the cushioning effect of that 'unwound', where the second syllable lingers, in the air, and dissembles into the cascading fall of 'beneath the skies'.

In fact not one phrase in the lyric fails to gain an extra power from the cadence—which shows how delicate and responsive Dylan's variations are within his 'simple' and economical 14-bar melody.

None of these devices, or course, depends for its effectiveness on the kind of identification-parade attempted above. Being poetic devices, they work inwardly and unseen. The song only needs its listener to have an open responsiveness to nuance.

The song is enriched in another small way: it echoes the Elven songs that celebrate Lothlorien in TOLKIEN's *Lord of the Rings*.

Like Dylan's world in 'Lay Down Your Weary Tune' Lothlorien is pastoral. ('Pastoral', of course, is most pointedly applicable to the Dylan song in that conceit which opens the fourth verse. The idea of leaves forsaking the branches—arms—of their first love for the welcoming breast of the earth is a surprising one for Dylan: surprisingly traditional. It seems to have escaped from a poem by, say, Wordsworth, or Thomas Hardy, or even Matthew Arnold.)

Like Dylan's world, too, Lothlorien is a paradise, spiritual because real. Colours and sounds are ennobled and enhanced; and that there is an ethereal quality which caresses everything is no denial of the intense reality. It is an extra quality, endowed by the light—which Dylan manages to suggest in his world also.

That 'Lay Down Your Weary Tune' echoes Tolkien is first apparent when Legolas sings 'a song of the maiden Nimrodel, who bore the same name as the stream beside which she lived long ago. . . . In a soft voice hardly to be heard amid the rustle of the leaves above . . . he began: "An Elven-maid there was of old / . . . And fair she was and free; / And in the wind she went as light / As leaf of linden-tree. / Beside the falls of Nimrodel, / By water clear and cool / Her voice as falling silver fell / Into the shining pool."'

You can at once hear Dylan's voice breathing the right kind of delicate life into those lines—and beyond that, it's clear that the whole of the Legolas song fits Dylan's tune. There are (less precise) connections too, between the Dylan song and this: 'I sang of leaves, of leaves of gold, and leaves of gold there grew: / Of wind I sang, a wind there came and in the branches blew. / Beyond the Sun, beyond the Moon, the foam was on the Sea . . .'

(Again, the Dylan tune fits exactly.) That is a part of the song of 'Galadriel, tall and white; a circlet of golden flowers . . . in her hair, and in her hand . . . a harp.' And there we come across a similarity even between Dylan's song and Tolkien's prose. And just as Dylan's vision in 'Lay Down Your Weary Tune' corresponds to Frodo's perception of the land of Lorien, both correspond, in turn, to an aspect of what an LSD vision can offer, by transforming an ordinary world into an earthly paradise. Anyone who ever dropped acid will recognize this:

> '. . . Frodo stood awhile still lost in wonder. It seemed to him that he had stepped through a high window that looked on a vanished world. A light was upon it for which his language had no name . . . the shapes seemed at once clear cut, as if they had been first conceived and drawn at the uncovering of his eyes, and ancient as if they had endured for ever. He saw no colour but those he knew, gold and white and blue and green, but they were fresh and poignant, as if he had at that moment first perceived them and made for them names new and wonderful. In winter here no heart could mourn for summer or for spring. No blemish or sickness or deformity could be seen in anything that grew upon the earth. On the land of Lorien there was no stain. He turned and saw that Sam was now standing beside him, looking round with a puzzled expression. . . . "It's sunlight and bright day, right enough," he said. "I thought that Elves were all for moon and stars; but this is more Elvish than anything I ever hear tell of. I feel as if I was inside a song, if you take my meaning." . . . Frodo felt that he was in a timeless land that did not fade or change or fall into forgetfulness . . . he laid his hand upon the tree beside the ladder; never before had he been so suddenly and so keenly aware of the feel and texture of a tree's skin and of the life within it. He felt . . . the delight of the living tree itself. . . . Frodo looked and saw, still at some distance, a hill of many mighty trees, or a city of green towers; which it was he could not tell. Out of it, it seemed to him that the power and light came that held all the land in sway. He longed suddenly to fly like a bird to rest in the green city.'

Frodo, like Dylan, stood unwound beneath the skies and clouds unbound by laws: without confusion, in the discovery of release, attuned to the holy chord.

Yet Dylan's song owes different, less mystical debts too: one for its melody, another for its lyrics. Dylan says in the *Biograph* box set interview that the melody comes from a (traditional) Scottish ballad: 'I wrote [that] on the West Coast, at JOAN BAEZ's house. She had a place outside Big Sur. I had heard a Scottish ballad on an old 78 record that I was trying to really capture the feeling of, that was haunting me. I couldn't get it out of my head. There were no lyrics or anything, it was just a melody—had bagpipes and a lot of stuff in it. I wanted lyrics that would feel the same way. I don't remember what the original record was, but ['Lay Down Your Weary Tune'] was pretty similar to that—the melody anyway.'

As for the lyrics, it is impossible not to hear Dylan's arresting opening lines when you hear these gospel song lines: 'Lay down thy weary one lay down / Your head upon his breast'—and impossible for the Dylan who wrote the one not to have known the other: for it is (like so many things Dylan used) on the HARRY SMITH anthology *AMERICAN FOLK MUSIC*—where the lines leap out at you, as presumably they did at Dylan, from the 'lining hymn' at the end of the sermon 'Oh Death, Where Is Thy Sting' by the Rev. J.M. Gates.

In turn these lines come verbatim—except for that odd 'thy'—from the hymn by Havergal and Bonar, 'I Heard the Voice of Jesus Say'. Known throughout the English-speaking world, it is commonly described as 'the English hymn', but its words are by a Scotsman. (The gospel version was recorded by several pre-war outfits, including the Biddleville Quintette and the Norfolk Jubilee Quartette.)

This hymn begins: 'I heard the voice of Jesus say / Come Unto Me and Rest / Lay down thou weary one, lay down / Thy head upon his breast.'

When we look at these four lines together, and then at the four lines of Dylan's chorus, we find much shared vocabulary as well as the close correspondence of Dylan's title line to the third line of the hymn cum gospel song. The Dylan song even alludes to the finding of a different restful breast, as it replaces Christian with pantheist worship.

But long before Dylan's 'Lay Down Your Weary Tune', 'I Heard the Voice of Jesus Say' yielded another spin-off: Memphis blues songster JIM JACKSON's parody 'I Heard the Voice of a Pork Chop'. Jackson's is the (albeit pleasantly) ridiculous spin-off, Dylan's the truly sublime.

[Steven Goldberg: 'Bob Dylan and the Poetry of Salvation', *Saturday Review* no.53, New York, 30 May 1970; collected in *Bob Dylan: A Retrospective*, ed. Craig McGregor, 1972 (reissued as *Bob Dylan, The Early Years: A Retrospective*, 1990). J.R.R. Tolkien, *The Lord of the Rings* (3 vols.), London: Allen & Unwin, 1954–55.

Rev. J.M. Gates (with three singers): 'Oh Death, Where Is Thy Sting', Camden, NJ, 11 Sep 1926, excerpted on *American Folk Music*, Folkways FP251-253, NY, 1952; CD-reissued *Anthology of American Folk Music* (6-CD box set) with copious notes by many hands and a CD-ROM of extras, Smithsonian Folkways SRW 40090, Washington, D.C., 1997. 'I Heard the Voice of Jesus Say', words Horatius Bonar (1808–1889), music Frances Ridley Havergal (1836–79), collected in *Hymns Ancient & Modern Revised*, 1972.

Biddleville Quintette: 'I Heard the Voice of Jesus Say Come Unto Me and Rest', Chicago, Oct 1928 and 'I Heard the Voice of Jesus Say', Long Island City, NY, c.Apr 1929; Norfolk Jubilee Quartette: 'I Heard the Voice of Jesus Say', prob. NY, c.Feb 1929. Jim Jackson: 'I Heard the Voice of a Pork Chop', (2 takes), Memphis, 30 Jan 1928; take 1 on *Jim Jackson* (EP), RCA Victor RCX 7182, UK, 1966 (an 'early' vinyl release in a series from Victor's vaults devised by British blues baron Mike Vernon), reissued on the 2-CD set *Good for What Ails You: Music of the Medicine Shows, 1926–1937*, Old Hat OLCD 1005, Raleigh, NC, 2005. This cheerily Dickensian song was covered, some months after the Jim Jackson session, by Blind Bogus Ben Covington: 'I Heard the Voice of a Pork Chop', Chicago, c.Sep 1928.]

Lay, Sam [1935 -] Samuel Lay was born in Birmingham, Alabama, on March 20, 1935 and took up drumming at age 14. He moved to Cleveland, Ohio, and joined his first band in 1956, moved over to the Thunderbirds in 1957, moved to Chicago, played in Little Walter's band in 1959 and the following year joined HOWLIN' WOLF's. At one point he was shot, sustaining a bullet wound that continued to give him problems. He remained with Wolf until 1963, when he and bassist JEROME ARNOLD were lured away by the promise of better pay to become founder members of the PAUL BUTTERFIELD Blues Band. Fond of garish clothes and extraordinary shoes, he wore a towering pompadour above his handsome face, and in the words of Charles Sawyer in a potted online biography of the Butterfield Band, Lay 'played drums with weight-lifter's arms'. When ALBERT GROSSMAN had a physical fight with ALAN LOMAX after Lomax had given the Paul Butterfield Blues Band's own set at the 1965 NEWPORT FOLK FESTIVAL some patronising introduction that no-one can quite remember but was along the lines of 'let's see if these white boys can play the blues', Sam Lay pitched in to separate them.

Like Jerome Arnold, he is a member of the group Dylan chose to back him at his début electric gig at the festival that July 25; unlike Arnold, he was also in the studios in New York on the August 2 session for the *Highway 61 Revisited* album. Many takes of the title track, 'Just Like Tom Thumb's Blues', 'Queen Jane Approximately' and 'Ballad of a Thin Man' and were attempted that day, including the take of each issued on the album, but what

Sam Lay played on is doubtful; he is uncredited on the album and the official Dylan website listing for the album, and BOBBY GREGG was also in the studio that day and *is* credited.

Sam Lay was in poor health by this point, despite his robust appearance and his youth (he only turned 30 that year), and had to leave the Paul Butterfield Blues Band before they recorded their second album.

He recovered, however, was the original drummer for the James Cotton Blues Band and in 1969 played on MUDDY WATERS' *Fathers and Sons* album (along with Butterfield and Bloomfield). Later he formed the Sam Lay Blues Revival Band, and subsequently the Sam Lay Blues Band. He has released albums like *Shuffle Master*, *Sam Lay Live*, *Stone Blues* and *Rush Hour Blues*, followed by *Live on Beale Street* in 2000 and *I Get Evil* in 2003. That year he also appeared as himself in the movie *The Howlin' Wolf Story*, in which his silent home movies were a highlight, showing Wolf and the great Hubert Sumlin on stage and SONNY BOY WILLIAMSON and Little Walter in the audience.

[Bob Dylan with Sam Lay et al: 'Maggie's Farm', 'Like a Rolling Stone' & 'It Takes a Lot to Laugh, It Takes a Train to Cry', Newport, RI, 25 Jul 1965. Charles Sawyer quote from 'Blues With a Feeling: A Biography of the Paul Butterfield Blues Band', 1994, online 2 Jul 2005 at *www.people.fas.harvard.edu/~sawyer/bwf.html*.]

Leadbelly [1888 - 1949] Huddie Ledbetter was born at Mooringsport, near Shiloh, Louisiana, on January 21, 1888 and learnt to play accordion, piano, harmonica and then guitar. By the age of 15 he was a father of two with a police record after his involvement in a shooting, and was singing in the red-light district of Shreveport. Moving to Dallas, Texas, he met and learnt songs from BLIND LEMON JEFFERSON and moved onto the 12-string guitar, of which he became an almost incomparable master (perhaps only equalled by BLIND WILLIE McTELL) with a distinctively strong rhythmic style.

He spent nearly as much time in prison as busking on the streets, and when the folklorist John A. Lomax and his then-teenage son ALAN LOMAX encountered him in the Louisiana State Penitentiary in Angola in July 1933, he already had two pardons behind him (he had killed a man in Texas in 1917) and was now serving what was supposed to be another 30-year sentence, but after proving an incomparable source of black folksong and 19th century repertoire on the field recordings he made for the Lomaxes for the Library of Congress, they obtained his pardon once again and this time set him to work as their chauffeur and recording assistant. After this, he travelled with them on many field trips but was also presented as a performer to folksong societies and in progressive East Coast establishment society, becoming in the 1940s part of a circle of Left-Wing folk enthusiasts and musicians (as you can tell by the very title 'The Bourgeois Blues') that included WOODY GUTHRIE, SONNY TERRY & BROWNIE McGHEE, Alan Lomax and PETE SEEGER. In Tony Russell's words, 'Leadbelly the performer and the Leadbelly songbook are twin peaks on the map of American music. His enormous repertoire has no parallel in black folksong. He sang everything, ballads and blues-ballads, dance songs and children's rhymes, memories of minstrelsy and freshly made songs about his own rapidly changing circumstances. To his white audiences he seemed a mythic figure, a lone carrier of all-but-lost messages from black worlds of field and prison farm.'

As this implies, little of his repertoire was really the blues, though 'Good Morning Blues' and 'The Bourgeois Blues' are prized items. In the mid-1940s he tried to 'make it' in Hollywood but was unsuccessful and returned to live in New York by 1947, making his one foreign trip in 1949—to Paris—before dying in New York City that December 6, of a form of motor neurone disease termed Lou Gehrig's disease. No sooner was he dead than Pete Seeger's goody-goody group the Weavers had a no.1 hit single with a revoltingly twee version of a song he'd refashioned from a 19th century minstrel number, 'Goodnight Irene'. (The other Weavers were Ronnie Gilbert, Lee Hays and Fred Hellerman; Lee Hays is the one who looked, back then, exactly like the 2005 British Home Secretary, Charles Clarke.)

By the end of the 1950s we were all familiar with Leadbelly songs: the UK's father of skiffle, Lonnie Donegan, signalled his 1956 shift from 'jazz' to 'rock'n'roll' with a hit version of 'Rock Island Line', while between them, skiffle and the folk revival ensured the continued circulation of 'Boll Weevil' (of which Leadbelly's own recording is soaringly the best), 'Midnight Special', 'Pick a Bale O' Cotton', 'Bring Me a Li'l Water Silvy', 'Take a Whiff on Me' (as 'Have a Drink on Me' by Mr. Donegan) and 'Cotton Fields'.

'Midnight Special' was the song on which Dylan had played harmonica behind HARRY BELAFONTE in February 1962, shortly ahead of the release of his own début album; but there is a longer connecting thread between Leadbelly and Dylan's work than that, and beyond the fact of Leadbelly's repertoire having both informed the understanding of, and permeated so thoroughly into, the common currency of the folk revival—such that, for instance, Dylan was performing 'Ain't No More Cane on the Brazos (Go Down Old Hannah)' at the Gaslight Café in October 1962; that when Dylan recorded a version of 'Milk Cow Blues' in 1962, he used part of Kokomo Arnold's lyric, part of ELVIS PRESLEY's, part of ROBERT JOHNSON's 'Milkcow's Calf Blues' and part of Leadbelly's 'Good Morning Blues'; and that he and HAPPY TRAUM were performing 'Keep Your Hands Off Her' in February 1963.

First, it was a set of Leadbelly 78rpm records, given to Dylan as a gift before he left Hibbing, that proved his first revelatory direct initiation into the pre-war black repertoire. He might well have proved the first person Dylan heard who 'talked his way into a song', in ROBERT SHELTON's phrase, as he duly did himself on his first album.

The Leadbelly favourite 'Pig Meat Mama' offers a vivacious demonstration of something we're likely to think still more Dylanesque. That is, given an ostentatious rhyme, he delivers it with a sly knowingness which, far from downplaying it, milks its comic extravagance to the full, by throwing in a pause just long enough to draw attention to itself immediately ahead of the clamorous rhyme. In this song from 1935, Leadbelly gives us '. . . Louisiana / . . . Texacana / . . . a girl named *[pause]* Silvana!' This is a way of writing and delivering lines that we know well from many Dylan recordings, such as the 'Angelina' rhymes in the 1981 song of that name, the risky comedy of 'subpoena' being the one that pushes this furthest. It's the same glee that tops 'the castle honey' with 'El *[pause]* Paso honey' in the superb 1966 outtake 'She's Your Lover Now'. (Actually, Silvana might not have struck Leadbelly as an especially attention-grabbing name: he had an adopted sister called Australia.)

Leadbelly's breadth of repertoire is used by Dylan in a quite different way, too. In a speech on stage at the Fox-Warfield Theatre in San Francisco in 1980, Dylan tells the audience this, about Leadbelly switching from prison songs to children's songs—offering it as a parable about his own switch from secular to Christian songs: 'He made lots of records there [in New York]. At first he was just doing prison songs, and stuff like that. . . . He'd been out of prison for some time when he decided to do children's songs. And people said "Oh my! Did Leadbelly change?" . . . But he didn't change. He was *the same man.*'

[Leadbelly: 'Good Morning Blues', NY, 15 Jun 1940 or summer 1943; 'The Bourgeois Blues', NY, 1 Apr 1939; 'Irene', Angola, LA, 16–20 Jul 1933 & 1 Jul 1934, & Wilton, CT, 20 Jan 1935; 'Rock Island Line', Washington, D.C., 22 Jun 1937, NY, Jan 1942 & (with the Golden Gate Quartet) NY, 15 Jun 1940; 'Boll Weevil', Shreveport, LA, prob. Oct 1934, Wilton, Feb 1935 & NY, 19 Jun 1940; 'The Boll Weevil', NY, 1 Apr 1939; 'Midnight Special', Angola, 1 Jul 1934, Wilton, Feb 1935 & (w Golden Gate Quartet) NY, 15 Jun 1940; 'Pick a Bale a'Cotton', NY, 25 Jan 1935; 'Pick a Bale O' Cotton', Wilton, Mar 1935; 'Pick a Bale of Cotton' (w Golden Gate Quartet), NY, 15 Jun 1940; 'Bring Me a Li'l Water Silvy', Wilton, Mar 1935; 'Bring Me Lil Water Silvy', NY, late 1943; 'Honey Take a Whiff on Me', Angola, 16–20 Jul 1933; 'Take a Whiff on Me', Angola, prob. 1 Jul 1934 & Wilton, 1 Feb 1935; 'Baby Take a Whiff on Me', NY, 25 Jan 1935; 'Go Down, Old Hannah', Wilton, Mar 1935; 'Ain't Goin' Down to the Well No Mo'/'Go Down Old Hannah', NY, 1 Apr 1939; 'Pig Meat Mama', NY, 25 Mar 1935; *Negro Folk Songs for Young People*, Folkways FC 7533, NY, c.1962; a good general selection of his work is CD-reissued *Leadbelly: King of the Twelve-String Guitar*, Columbia Roots N' Blues Series 467893 4, NY, 1991.

Dylan on Leadbelly & children's songs, San Francisco, 12 Nov 1980, quoted from 'Bob Dylan's Leadbelly Parable', in Michael Gray & John Bauldie, eds., *All Across the Telegraph: A Bob Dylan Handbook*, London: W.H. Allen, 1987. Tony Russell, 'Leadbelly', *From Robert Johnson to Robert Cray*, London: Aurum Press, 1997, p.38. Robert Shelton, *No Direction Home: The Life and Music of Bob Dylan*, London: Penguin edn., 1987, p.119.]

Ledbetter, Huddie [1888 - 1949] See **Leadbelly**.

Lee, Bill [1928 -] William J. E. Lee was born in Atlanta, Georgia, on July 23, 1928, and grew up there. At the city's all-black Morehouse College he attended classes alongside Martin Luther King. He moved to Brooklyn in the late 1950s and though essentially a jazz musician he had become a well-known bass player on the New York folk scene by the beginning of the 1960s, playing behind Bob Gibson at the first NEWPORT FOLK FESTIVAL in 1959, on ODETTA sessions and many others, and enjoying an especially good working relationship with Columbia producer JOHN HAMMOND. Lee therefore played on the sessions Aretha Franklin recorded for the label before she went to Atlantic and found her own genre; he and guitarist BRUCE LANGHORNE (who often worked together) played on the CAROLYN HESTER sessions in September 1961 on which the young Bob Dylan played harmonica, and by April 1962 Lee was playing on sessions for *The Freewheelin' Bob Dylan*, including the April 14 session that yielded the 'Ramblin' Gamblin' Willie' released in 1991 on the *Bootleg Series Vols. 1–3*. Dylan writes in *Chronicles Volume One* of Lee and Langhorne that if you 'had them playing with you, that's pretty much all you would need to do just about anything.'

Lee, like Langhorne, returned for some of the 1965 sessions for *Bringing It All Back Home*, though since there were two other bass players on the same sessions it's hard to know who played on which tracks from among the successful January 14 recordings of 'Love Minus Zero/No Limit', 'Subterranean Homesick Blues', 'Outlaw Blues', 'She Belongs to Me' and 'Bob Dylan's 115th Dream'; on 'Maggie's Farm', 'On the Road Again', 'Mr. Tambourine Man' and 'It's All Over Now Baby Blue' the following day; and on that day's cuts of 'If You Gotta Go, Go Now', released as a European single and on the *Bootleg Series Vols. 1–3*. Bill Lee never played with Dylan live.

It may irk him that he is mostly famous today for being the father of film director Spike Lee (though he is also the father of three other people with film industry careers: Joie Lee, David Lee and Cinqué Lee), and that in about 1995 the *New York Post* made his own arrest for marijuana possession a cover story because of the Spike Lee connection. On the other hand Bill Lee has been musical director and film score composer for many of son Spike's films: namely, *Joe's Bed-Stuy Barbershop: We Cut Heads* (1983), *She's Gotta Have It* (1986), *School Daze* (1988), *Do the Right Thing* (1989) and *Mo' Better Blues* (1990). He also played bass in *She's Gotta Have It*, conducted the Natural Spiritual Orchestra on *Do the Right Thing* and was 'technical consultant' on *Mo' Better Blues*. He also took acting parts in *She's Gotta Have It* and *Mo' Better Blues*. His film work for directors other than his own son runs from taking part in 1965's art documentary *George Dumpston's Place*, filmed by Ed Emshwiller, playing a restaurant owner in Serge Rodnunsky's 1993 film *Rage of Revenge* and composing the score for Stephen Kijak's 1996 film *Never Met Picasso*.

[Bob Dylan, *Chronicles Volume One*, 2004, p.278. *New York Post* story cited on a 1998 e-mail posting seen online at 'Bob Dylan Who's Who' 2 Jun 2005.]

Lee, C.P. [1950 -] Christopher Paul Lee is a British academic, film buff, musician and critic who has written two books on Dylan—one about the Manchester 1966 concert and one on Dylan's films. The former is the more significant work, and two editions of it have been published.

Lee was born in Manchester, England, on January 19, 1950. He first became interested in Dylan's work in 1964. He wrote an essay on Dylan while still at school in September 1966, and first published work about him in *Grass Eye*, an 'underground paper', in August 1969. Finding himself with a rekindled interest in Dylan in the mid-1990s he started writing in *Isis*, joined the *FREEWHEELIN'* co-operative and has been publishing articles online in recent years.

Once a founder member of Alberto Y Lost Trios Paranoias (the group lasted 1972–82), Lee now teaches cultural studies at the University of Salford, near Manchester. He writes and presents BBC radio documentaries and is published in academic journals and elsewhere on Manchester music, folk music and film history. His book *Shake, Rattle and Rain: Popular Music in Manchester, 1955–1995* was published in 2002. He is now especially involved with researching and archiving the history of the Mancunian Film Studios (see *www.itsahotun.com*). His book on the celluloid Dylan, *A Bullet of Light: The Films of Bob Dylan*, was published by music-books specialist company Helter Skelter in 2000.

Like the Night: Bob Dylan and the Road to the Manchester Free Trade Hall was published in 1998, and despite its many carelessnesses it is an important work that adds greatly to our knowledge of that unsurpassable concert's context. The revised and updated second edition, *Like the Night Revisited*, is even better. The book begins with an excellent initiation into Manchester and England circa 1964. Then there's a fine, mordant chapter on how it was back then, on the post-war, post-rationing feel that persisted right into to the Britain of the 1960s, and, tellingly, on the Stalinism of the folk movement, and in particular the rôle of the Communist Party of Great Britain in keeping the post-World War II folk scene purist and traditional. He offers particularly fine material on the state of British folk clubs, the ideologies of different sorts of jazz, and how all this rubbed up against, but still managed to bully, post-adolescent consciousness circa 1966. His pursuit of the mind-set of the old left, including the communists and the folk scene's star practitioners, is excellent. (See also **MacColl, Ewan**.)

Then there's the main enterprise of the book, the exploration of this pivotal moment in Dylan's career—all this is inevitably fascinating, and handled well, and Lee's research and insistence on connecting detail is admirable. It may be suspect to claim to tell us what Dylan and ALBERT GROSSMAN notice and don't notice as they take their taxi-ride to Didsbury in May 1964, but what they *might* have noticed is nicely drawn, and so are they. The richly comic way that they're seen as mesmerising exotica by a young Mancunian, Neville, whose task is to look after them at the TV studio: this is beautifully rendered, and with great vividness, from Bob's spidery shyness to Grossman's fleshy coldness to Neville's dilemmas and delight. (C.P. has more than a soft spot for Albert. He speaks ruefully here and there in the book of how we all wished in vain for Dylan's mid-60s cool, but actually C.P. would settle for Grossman's.)

And of course, to go from the specific to the very general, the whole thing is just such a *good* idea for a Bob Dylan book. We all wish we'd written it.

[C.P. Lee, *Like the Night: Bob Dylan and the Road to the Manchester Free Trade Hall*, London: Helter Skelter Publishing, 1998; updated edition, *Like the Night Revisited*, Helter Skelter, 2004. *A Bullet of Light: The Films of Bob Dylan*, Helter Skelter, 2000. *Shake, Rattle and Rain: Popular Music in Manchester, 1955–1995*, Aylesbeare, Devon, UK: Harding Simpole, 2002.]

'Legionnaire's Disease' [1981] This little-known Dylan song was copyrighted in 1981, when it was recorded by BILLY CROSS and his band. No Dylan recording has surfaced.

See also **blues, external signals of Dylan's interest in**.

Lennon, John [1940 - 1980] John Winston Lennon was born in Liverpool on October 9, 1940 and, incredibly, had already formed his first group, the Quarrymen, while still at school in *1955*! That's before anyone outside the southern states had ever heard of ELVIS PRESLEY! It emphasises the weird way that though the Beatles came along a full musical generation after rock'n'roll, and even after the pop that replaced it, Lennon, like Dylan, was at least as old as many of those who had shaped the music years before they came into the public eye. Lennon was older than RITCHIE VALENS, who was dead by early 1959; he was older than BOBBY VEE, Brian Hyland, Shelley Fabares and Fabian, Danny of Danny & the Juniors, Frankie Ford and Freddie Cannon, older than Paul Anka, Chubby Checker and Brenda Lee; he was the same age as Cliff Richard and RICKY NELSON.

Lennon's first encounter with Dylan was when all four Beatles met Dylan in New York City in 1964 (see **Aronowitz, Al**), the same year Lennon saw his father for the first time in close on two decades. As the most acerbic Beatle, John was the one regarded as most similar to Dylan. He was, like Dylan, the one who had ambitions in art forms other than music, and had published two books of surreal prose, albeit of a very English kind, *In His Own Write* (1964) and *A Spaniard in the Works* (1965), before Dylan completed, let alone published, *Tarantula*. Like Dylan, he had a penchant for travelling under pseudonyms, as when he and Yoko booked into hotels as Fred and Ada Gherkin.

Lennon and Dylan were always wary of each other, precisely because of their similar verbal gifts, though in their songwriting Lennon never created lyrics comparable to Dylan's, and indeed the non-Beatles song for which he's most famous, 'Imagine', is of a disingenuous soppiness Dylan has never managed. Nevertheless they were sometimes companions in the other's land in the mid-1960s.

Lennon called on Dylan at the Savoy Hotel in London in 1965 and brought him down to his own house in Weybridge, Surrey—exactly the sort of stuffy stockbroker-belt mansion the earlier mop-top Beatles had laughed at and the later New York City street-wise Lennon would have considered bourgeois death. Dylan told ROBERT SHELTON: 'I dug his situation where he lived. It was a twenty-two-room house. Do you know what I did when I got back from England, man? I bought me a thirty-one room house. . . . And it turned into a *nightmare*.' And Lennon told Shelton: 'We swapped addresses and said we'd exchange ideas for songs, but it never happened.'

One shared lyric did *begin* to happen the year after, however, when Lennon and McCARTNEY called on Dylan in his London hotel room in May 1966 (see the entry **McCartney, Paul** for details). That aside, though, the enthusiasm of the Lennon-Dylan meeting in Surrey never led to anything. 'Maybe that's why we get on well', Lennon told Shelton, 'we're both pretty disorganised blokes.' Events, of course, have proved that Dylan never was one iota as disorganised as he made out.

Dylan and Lennon shared a far-from-sober limo journey during that 1966 Dylan concert tour, and though Dylan and HOWARD ALK let through only a moment of the film footage in *Eat the Document*, D.A. PENNEBAKER had filmed it at some length, and this footage has circulated. (See the entry ***Eat the Document*** for detail.)

Lennon would turn up at Dylan concerts too. He and other Beatles saw Dylan at the Royal Albert Hall in 1965 and 1966 and on August 31, 1969, they were there to see Dylan and THE BAND at the second Isle of Wight Music Festival. Lennon damned with faint praise when asked by the press to defend Dylan's brief performance (an hour was brief granted that the audience, though not of course John Lennon, had been sitting in the mud for three days to await it). Lennon allegedly told the *Daily Express*: 'He gave a reasonable, albeit slightly flat, performance, but everyone was expecting Godot, a Jesus, to appear.'

Lennon had not been pleased to hear Dylan's song '4th Time Around' at the Royal Albert Hall in 1966, taking it to be a mocking parody of the Beatles' 'Norwegian Wood'; in later years there were a number of times when Lennon felt hostile to some turn Dylan's work was taking, or to some imagined slight. He and McCartney must have seen that on one level the *John Wesley Harding* album was a cutting reproach to the overblown production values of *Sgt. Pepper's Lonely Hearts Club Band*. It's been suggested that the Beatles' 'Rocky Racoon' was in turn a parody of that Dylan album. In 1970, in his big post-Beatles interview recorded by JANN WENNER for *Rolling Stone*, Lennon was denigrating everyone (especially GEORGE HARRISON) and sounding less like the 'genius' he claimed to be than just another whingeing Liverpudlian. 1970 was also the year of the Lennon/Plastic Ono Band track 'God', on which he sings 'I don't believe in Zimmerman'. Some posthumously issued material took less innocuous potshots than this. It may be that these emerged in 1990 on the syndicated radio series 'The Lost Lennon Tapes', hosted by a publicist Lennon and Dylan had both used, Elliot 'Chewy' Mintz. And it's said that when Lennon saw Dylan perform 'Gotta Serve Somebody' on 'Saturday Night Live' he was so annoyed that he retorted with 'You Gotta Serve Yourself', which was released posthumously on *The John Lennon Anthology* in 1998.

Other mentions of Dylan in the work of the Beatles and Lennon include the line 'I feel so suicidal, just like Dylan's Mr. Jones' in 'Yer Blues' (1968) and 'Everybody's talking about John and Yoko, Timmy Leary, Rosemary, Tommy Smothers, Bobby Dylan . . .' in 'Give Peace a Chance'.

Lennon was among those who wrote a letter to the *Village Voice* in December 1971 protesting on Dylan's behalf about his hounding by A.J. WEBERMAN, who, they wrote, 'is to Dylan as Manson is to The Beatles—and uses what he interprets from Dylan's music to try and kill Dylan . . .'

Nine years later Lennon was the artist killed by the mad fan; he was fatally shot with four bullets at close range from a .38 outside the venerable Dakota Building on West 72nd Street, New York City, his home, on December 8, 1980.

[Dylan quoted by Robert Shelton, *No Direction Home: The Music and Life of Bob Dylan*, London: Penguin edn., p.294; Lennon's *Daily Express* quote Shelton p.409; *Village Voice* letter excerpt quoted from Shelton p.411. May 1966 Lennon-McCartney-Dylan meeting detailed very journalistically in Mark Shipper, *Paperback Writer*, London: New English Library/Times Mirror, 1978, Ch.12. Lennon-Dylan limo ride transcript available online at *www.recmusicbeatles.com/public/files/bbs/etd.html*.]

'Leopard-Skin Pill-Box Hat' [1966] The *Blonde on Blonde* song 'Leopard-Skin Pill-Box Hat' is neatly revealing about the way that even in his hippest, most radical and risky period, Dylan stood upon the bedrock of the blues. In one way, this song is utterly Dylanesque, and wholly redolent of that WARHOL Factory New York City milieu: so 1960s, so chic and fey, so knowing and druggy and poised, and engaging for its weird mix of energy and high comedy with an elaborate and ostentatious stance of ennui. Yet at the same time it is coach-built upon the chassis of a LIGHTNIN' HOPKINS song from 1949, his 'Automobile (Blues)'.

It is not just a melodic parallel. Hopkins begins: 'I saw you ridin' round, you was ridin' in your brand-new automobile / Yes, I saw you ridin' round, you was ridin' round in your brand-new automobile / Yes, you was sittin' there happy with your handsome driver at the wheel / In your brand-new automobeeeeel'—and as Hopkins sings that extra last line, his voice takes that familiar downward curve, ending on that 'Dylanesque' long, sliding 'beeeel' that is a slippery mixture of a knowing sneer and some malicious envy. Dylan makes sly acknowledgement of his source in the last verse of his own song, with the in-joke admonition that 'you forgot to close the garage door.'

In taking from Lightnin' Hopkins, Dylan was driving down a very old road. Hopkins' label, Gold Star, was typical of the new wave of independent labels being created in the early post-war period, after the ending of the Petrillo ban on recording but with shellac still hard to get hold of. As Paul and Beth Garon write in their excellent biography of MEMPHIS MINNIE, 'When shellac was scarce, record producers like Gold Star's Bill Quinn recycled thousands of old 78s (and no doubt many treasures among them) to provide the raw material for their new releases, giving a bizarre literalism to the notion of one style developing out of another. Many of Lightnin' Hopkins' early records were literally *made* out of melted down Minnie's and Big Bill's!'

When outtakes of some of the *Blonde on Blonde* songs were heard for the first time in 2005—they had never circulated before their release on the *Bootleg Series Vol. 7—No Direction Home: The Soundtrack*—the most interesting was a boyishly playful yet slow and slinky 'Leopard-Skin Pill-Box Hat'. It was a far more avowedly straight blues song at this early point, and when it runs on beyond the 'garage door', *its* last verse implores: 'Well can I be your chauffeur, honey can I be your chauffeur? / You can ride with me, honey I'll be your chauffeur . . .' This is a dazzling touch: not only does it match the 'garage' allusion to Hopkins with an equally deft automobile-centred allusion to Memphis Minnie herself (her 'Me and My Chauffeur Blues' being an instant association for anyone who knows much about the blues) but in conflating these two car songs, he is re-enacting in art the way that Hopkins' and Minnie's work was fused on shellac.

[Lightnin' Hopkins': 'Automobile (Blues)', Houston, TX, 1949, Gold Star 666, Houston, 1949; *Early Recordings*, Arhoolie 2007, El Cerrito, CA, 1965 (i.e. first vinyl-released the year before Dylan composed 'Leopard-Skin Pill-Box Hat'), CD-reissued *The Gold Star Sessions Vol. 1*, Arhoolie CD 330, El Cerrito, c.1991, & *Vol. 2*, Arhoolie CD 337, ditto. Hopkins re-recorded the song as 'Automobile Blues', NY, 9 Nov 1960, *The Blues of Lightnin' Hopkins*, Bluesville 1019, Bergenfield, NJ, c.1960. Paul & Beth Garon, *Woman with Guitar: Memphis Minnie's Blues*, New York: Da Capo, 1992.]

Lesh, Phil [1940 -] The official GRATEFUL DEAD website describes member Phil Lesh as 'the most creative and inventive bass player in the history of rock and roll—in fact, he is a distinctive bottom-end guitar player. He began his musical career playing classical violin, moved on to trumpet (both classical and then big-band jazz), and then to avant-garde composition, studying with the great Luciano Berio at Mills College. Then he went to see his buddy Jerry's rock band at a pizza joint called Magoo's in 1965 . . . and neither he nor rock have ever been the same.'

Putting it less rhapsodically, Phillip Chapman Lesh was born in Berkeley, California, on March 15, 1940, became a founding member of the Grateful Dead and played bass guitar in the band from its inception. In 2005 he published a memoir of the 1960s and his involvement with the band. For his connections with Bob Dylan, see the entry on the Grateful Dead.

[Phil Lesh, *Searching for the Sound: My Life with the Grateful Dead*, New York: Little, Brown, 2005.]

'Let's Keep It Between Us' [1980] The little-known Dylan song 'Let's Keep It Between Us'—the lyric of which, in the songbooks, has been subjected to unfortunate text-revisions that make it inferior to the song as performed—is given in those songbooks as belonging among the songs excluded from, or arising in the aftermath of, the 1981 album *Shot of Love* album, and it is copyrighted 1982. Yet Dylan was performing the song in concert in 1980—and not once but in 19 consecutive concerts!

Most of us would understand such public performance to be an act of publication, and so would a dictionary. The first meaning of 'publication' in *Cassell's New English Dictionary* is 'the act of making publicly known'. Moreover, in Britain at least, if the song was deemed to be published by these performances, Dylan would have collected monies on them, via the Performing Right Society, as for every other published song performed in a public place. However, Dylan's office recognises a nicety lost on most here, arguing that public performance is *not* in fact publication, and copyrighting 'Let's Keep It Between Us' only in 1982 when the singer Bonnie Raitt pressed her intention to record the song.

So there sits 'Let's Keep It Between Us', in *Lyrics 1962–1985* and *Lyrics 1962–2001*, alongside 'The Groom's Still Waiting at the Altar', copyrighted 1981 (because it was on the B-side of a Dylan single then), alongside 'Need a Woman', copyrighted 1982 (because that's when Ry Cooder put his inferior version of the song on record), and alongside 'Caribbean Wind', copyrighted 1985 (because only then did Dylan's version emerge, on *Biograph*, though this song too was performed in concert in 1980). The last consideration in this sequencing of the songs in the songbooks is thus the one anyone outside 'the business' or anyone interested in scholarship might assume would come first: a concern to order the songs to reflect accurately their order of composition.

In the case of trying to establish when 'Let's Keep It Between Us' might have been composed, there is an added puzzle. Even if you didn't know that it had been performed in fall 1980—as one of the secular songs insinuated amongst the evangelical material that had alone comprised the previous tours' uncompromising repertoire—and even if you didn't care to notice the tardy copyright date, it would still be likely to strike you as curious, coming upon it where it is within the songbooks, which is to say smothered by the press of religious songs that surrounds it, when it is itself so obdurately a secular song: a song which, if it is to have any meaning at all outside Bob Dylan's private codification, must surely be about trying to preserve a long-term human relationship in danger of falling apart.

This also makes it a most unusual, and valued, part of Dylan's work, so little of which addresses the realities of *maintaining* relationships, even though this is, for Dylan's contemporaries, an area of experience likely to be more pressing and central than the relatively easy romantic angst of regretting yet another break-up. Indeed one reason why so many people feel that while Dylan used to reveal the world to them, now he just plays concerts, is precisely because one of his main areas of address is splitting up and moving on, while they themselves are working through the harder, more complex business of sticking together, with or without raising children, at a time when shifting sexual roles continually affect how things are between individuals. They are, thereby, coping with a far more 'contemporary' life than the old one Dylan speaks to with all his stoic leaving-or-left-alone songs cocooned in romantic images of dusty roads and lonesome oceans.

Nevertheless 'Let's Keep It Between Us' touches upon travel, at least as metaphor. In performances, though not in the garbled and nondescript version of the lyric in the songbooks, Dylan avows: 'Let's just move to the back of the back of the bus.' This phrase is a classic Dylanism: it's like 'in the final end', in 'I Pity the Poor Immigrant' (a phrase he re-uses in 'Idiot Wind', having also warped it into the variant 'it's the top of the end' in 'Going Going Gone'). It's creative and interesting because it serves a similar purpose, which is partly to be emphatic but partly to acknowledge an existential or qualitative distinction between the ordinary and the emphasised meaning. 'Let's just move to the back of the back of the bus' stresses a solidarity with the oppressed—stresses that, as with Desolation Row, it is morally cleaner to be there—by drawing on the resonance the phrase 'the back of the bus' must have for anyone who grew up around or before the civil rights struggle in America: before, in fact, the changes triggered by the bravery of Rosa Parks by her *refusal* to keep on moving to the back of the bus. (THE FREEDOM SINGERS, who appeared with Dylan at the 1963 NEWPORT FOLK FESTIVAL, used to feature a song called 'If You Miss Me at the Back of the Bus'.)

In fact Dylan's back-reference in 'Let's Keep It Between Us' to this example of racial inequality represents a return to the subject on his part. He refers to it first in one of the barbed jokes he puts into 'I Shall Be Free', on *The Freewheelin' Bob Dylan*: '. . . a can a black paint it fell on my head. / I went down to scrub and rub / But I had to sit in the back of the tub.'

Choosing the back of the bus still involves taking a *stance*. It's where the surreptitious drinkers, the so-what youth sits, on the Greyhounds that cross the country. This contemporary back-of-the-bus milieu is pinned down excellently in Irma Kurtz's 1993 book *The Great American Bus Ride*.

'Let's Keep It Between Us' has a further black resonance: it is noticeably similar to Jimmy Witherspoon versions (and thence to Otis Spann's version) of 'Nobody's Business', a traditional song that goes back at least to the beginning of the century and has been recorded very many times. As sung by, for instance, MISSISSIPPI JOHN HURT, or FRANK STOKES (both of whom made Memphis versions in 1928), you wouldn't see any resemblance at all to the Dylan song—not even in theme, since what is nobody's business but the singer's includes killing his woman, so making it a me-against-everyone song rather than, as 'Let's Keep It Between Us' so eloquently is, an us-against-them song. But as Jimmy Witherspoon and Otis Spann perform it, as 'Ain't Nobody's Business' and ''Tain't Nobody's Biz-ness If I Do', the rich and stately musical progression, the mood and the theme are likely to strike you at once as the inspiration for Dylan's own rich and stately song. Witherspoon-Spann's friendlier version of the lyric says: 'Me and my baby, you know we fuss and fight / Just the next morning, baby we's all right / Now ain't nobody's business, have mercy!, what I do'—from which you might say that Dylan has more or less reversed that 'fuss and fight' to get to end a line of his own with 'fuss', putting it among his 'us' rhymes.

Inasmuch as 'Let's Keep It Between Us' belongs neither with the romance-of-moving-on oeuvre nor with the evangelical one in which it's located in the songbooks, where might it belong? When Dylan performed it in those 1980 concerts, its secular companions ranged from 1962's 'Blowin' in the Wind' to 1978's 'Señor'. No help there. It would have been unusual had Dylan been introducing a song written two or three years beforehand, yet the years immediately preceding 1979's *Slow Train Coming* do seem the most likely to have yielded such a lyric, while its music is especially lacking in clues, since it too is unusual in Dylan's repertoire for luxuriating in such a rich swathe of sumptuous chords. In fact it's exactly the kind of music most musicians will tell you Bob Dylan cannot write.

[Bob Dylan: 'Let's Keep It Between Us' from San Francisco, 9 Nov through to Portland, Oregon, 4 Dec 1980. Bonnie Raitt: 'Let's Keep It Between Us', *nia*, *The Green Light*, Warner Bros. 3630-2, US, 1982. The Freedom Singers: 'If You Miss Me at the Back of the Bus', published in *Broadside* no.17, NY, 1963. Irma Kurtz, *The Great American Bus Ride*, New York: Simon & Schuster, 1993 (& London: Fourth Estate, 1994).

Jimmy Witherspoon: 'Ain't Nobody's Business', LA, 20 Nov 1947, Supreme 1506 & Swingtime 263, LA, c.1948; *Spoon Calls Hootie (Polydor Jazz Masters Vol. 5)*, Polydor Special 545 105, London, 1966. Jimmy Witherspoon: 'Ain't Nobody's Business', Chicago, 15 Aug 1956, unreleased till *Spoon So Easy*, Chess MCA CH93003, USA, c.1989. Otis Spann, with the Muddy Waters Band: ''Tain't Nobody's Biz-ness If I Do', Chicago, 30 Aug 1966; *The Blues Is Where It's At*, Bluesway 6003, NY, 1967. Mississippi John Hurt: 'Nobody's Dirty Business', Memphis, 14 Feb 1928; *Mississippi John Hurt Complete 1928 Recordings*, Yazoo L-1065, Newton, NJ, 1988, CD-reissued Yazoo CD-1065, NY, *nia*. Frank Stokes: 'Ain't Nobody's Business If I Do Part 2', Memphis, 30 Aug 1928; *Memphis Blues 1928–1930*, RCA 2-LP set NL89276, Paris, 1984.]

Levy, Dan [1958 -] Daniel Levy was born in Los Angeles on April 12, 1958, was introduced to Dylan's work at age eight by his guitar teacher and so was playing and singing 'Mr. Tambourine Man' before he ever heard a recording of it. He heard Dylan records for the first time at age nine and was first able to see him live at age 15 on February 14, 1974 (the early show) in Inglewood, California, the penultimate concert of that year's big 'comeback' tour.

Levy became a book editor and management consultant and via his consultancy company produces websites for a number of major musical artists. His first work on Dylan was a short piece in *Newsday* on the occasion of Dylan's 50th birthday in May 1991, but his main contribution has been the running of the official Dylan website, *www.bobdylan.com*. After meetings with members of Dylan's management and record label beginning in 1994 he began to work with them to plan the site, which was launched in fall 1997 around the time of the release of the *Time Out of Mind* album.

In its early days the website was much criticised by fans for its limitations and was in danger of becoming one of those sites people fail to revisit because of how seldom it changed. It still errs in this direction—there's little point having tour setlists posted if the current tour isn't included—but in other ways it has become almost exemplary: simple to use and easy on the eye (there are no unpleasant 'artistic' flash intros), it offers a vast amount of information, a search facility for words within Dylan lyrics—not every Dylan composition is up there but the exceptions are few—and even a changing page of 'Performances' from which you can hear recordings of quirkily selected particular songs from recent concerts, plus in some cases the original, often obscure recordings of songs Dylan has covered by other artists. The site even includes critical essays and has, in SEAN WILENTZ, a 'resident historian'. In several ways, therefore, Dan Levy's website has encouraged a Dylan online presence that has moved away from attitudes he and/or his management long espoused (anti-outside 'products', anti-bootleg recordings, anti-critics, anti-pinning things down). Levy has also made it possible to get a sense from the site that real people, not just a corporate face, are behind it.

Levy, Jacques [1935 - 2004] Jacques Levy was born in New York City on July 29, 1935. After attending City College he gained his PhD in Clinical Pyschology at Michigan State University and practised at the Meninger Foundation Clinic in Topeka, Kansas, where he was drawn into producing amateur dramatics. Returning to New York City in 1965 he concentrated on a theatrical career and that year, Off-Off Broadway, directed SAM SHEPARD's early play *Red Cross*. He joined the Open Theatre Group and the New Dramatists Committee, and directed at the La MaMa experimental theatre and the Judson Poets Theater. He became the second director of Jean-Claude Van Italie's pioneering 'protest theatre' play *Motel* (which featured big grotesque puppets, designed by the then-unknown Robert Wilson and prefiguring those in FRANK ZAPPA's 1984 production *Thing Fish*) and in 1967 directed Van Italie's *America Hurrah*, an Off-Broadway success that ran to 640 performances in New York and was brought over to London.

There the aging enfant terrible of British theatre criticism, Kenneth Tynan, brought Jacques Levy the bones of an idea for 'an evening of Victorian esoteric pornography', which Levy turned into an amalgam of sketches he commissioned from Shepard, JOHN LENNON and others, including the great Samuel Beckett (whose own Off-Broadway play *Happy Days* had starred Ruth White, a main puppet's voice in *Motel*). The result was the tediously controversial *O Calcutta!*, which opened in 1969 under Levy's direction.

This in turn brought Levy to ROGER McGUINN's attention as he sought a librettist for a project of his, namely to turn Henrik Ibsen's classic play *Peer Gynt* into a country-rock musical, *Gene Tryp*. Levy and McGuinn duly wrote songs for this doomed musical, and McGuinn rescued them by their inclusion on subsequent BYRDS albums. One, the ludicrous but appealing 'Chestnut Mare' became one of the group's best-known songs and biggest hits. Levy and McGuinn continued to collaborate on songs for McGuinn's solo albums of the early 1970s, and when Dylan put a harmonica part on one such track in 1972 ('I'm So Restless' on *Roger McGuinn*), Levy's work as a lyricist came to his attention.

They only met, however, by chance, in the street, in 1974, when Levy seized the chance to introduce himself and, according to his own testimony, spent the evening with Dylan in Levy's La Guardia Place loft. It was another year before they met again, when at some point in the first half of 1975 they bumped into each other on Bleecker Street in the Village. Though Dylan 'had no specific plans at that time to do anything . . . he said something like, "I really like the stuff you do with Roger, how about if you and I do something together?" Which was slightly strange, right? Because he knew *I* did lyrics and I knew *he* did lyrics. But I said, "Sure, let's give it a shot."'

Beginning back at Levy's loft that same evening with an unformed piece Dylan played on piano, with lines thrown around between the two of them, they emerged with a major song: 'Isis'. Encouraged, they worked together again for about a week, found too many distractions, went out to Dylan's house at East Hampton, Long Island, and spent a further three weeks writing together. 'The pressure was tremendous,' said Levy.

The result was the great majority of the *Desire* album. Of its nine songs, seven were Dylan-Levy collaborations: 'Hurricane', 'Isis', 'Mozambique', 'Oh Sister', 'Joey', 'Black Diamond Bay' and 'Romance in Durango'. Only 'One More Cup of Coffee' and 'Sara' were by Dylan alone. Outtakes from the sessions, also co-written with Levy, were 'Rita May', 'Catfish' and 'Money Blues'; and there on the back cover of the original LP is a photo of the bearded Levy, alongside Dylan at the microphone.

Such collaboration was a major surprise: Dylan had never worked like this before. *Desire* proved a distinctive, significant work in Dylan's canon. It was overshadowed, artistically, by the previous year's *Blood on the Tracks*, but it was Dylan's fastest-selling album. In turn, Levy's other work has been overshadowed by his contribution to *Desire*.

After it, Dylan brought him in to 'direct' the Rolling Thunder Revue concerts, asking: 'Can you figure out a way of doing it—a presentation? What would it be like?' So the staging, the idea of the running order to accommodate the different performers, the lighting ('this little jewel box all lit up', as Levy described it afterwards): all this was sorted out by Levy. Crucially, as Dylan required, he staged it so that it didn't look staged.

Roger McGuinn says that on the tour itself, Levy was also 'camp counsellor', arguing naively that 'Because he was a practising psychologist, he knows how to work with people.' (For suggestions of Levy's training coming into the lyrics of 'Romance in Durango', see entry on that song.)

Levy returned to the theatre, directing the musical comedy *Doonesbury* (which was about as funny as the cartoon strip) in 1983, and writing the lyrics for the stage musical spin-off from the film *Fame* in 1988. In 1993 he accepted the post of English Professor and Director of Theatre at Colgate University, New York, while continuing to work on theatre projects, including *Marat/Sade* in 1994, a 1997 revival of William Inge's 1950s drama *Bus Stop*, and *BRECHT on Brecht* in 2000.

Jacques Levy died of cancer on September 30, 2004.

[Jacques Levy quotes from John Bauldie, 'Jacques Levy and the *Desire* Collaboration', *Telegraph* no.11, UK, Apr 1983, republished in Michael Gray & John Bauldie, *All Across the Telegraph*, London: W.H. Allen, 1987. (This piece details the process of the collaboration on the songs.) Other sources include theatre review feature on Jean-Claude Van Italie in *Gay City News* vol.3, no.340, NY, 30 Sep–6 Oct 2004.]

Lewis, Furry [1893 - 1981] See **blues, inequality of reward in**.

Lewis, Jerry Lee [1935 -] Jerry Lee Lewis, a creator of rock'n'roll, is still alive in 2005, in defiance of medical science. For 50 years he has soaked up drugs and drink—mostly designer-speed, downers and whiskey—while living in perpetual, often violent struggle against his loved ones and the world.

This long strife followed bedazzling early success as a defining hero of rock'n'roll, when he muscled in amongst ELVIS PRESLEY, LITTLE RICHARD and CHUCK BERRY, creating rock'n'roll piano from honky-tonk and hymn, as if doing so were as natural as breathing, and commandeering R&B with a casual authority achieved by no other white performer except Presley. With 'Whole Lotta Shakin' Goin' On', 'Great Balls of Fire' and 'High School Confidential' he made three of rock'n'roll's indispensable classics.

He was born in Ferriday, Louisiana, on September 29, 1935, to Mary Ethel, who spoke in tongues, and Elmo, a labourer. Jerry had two sisters, Frankie Jean and Linda Gail. His elder brother, Elmo Jr., was killed by a drunk driver when they were boys. His father, imprisoned for bootlegging, was brought to the funeral in chains.

Jerry Lee was raised in the Pentecostal church, on family gospel singing and country music by JIMMIE RODGERS, Gene Autry, HANK WILLIAMS and the state's singing governor, Jimmie Davis. He taught himself guitar, drums and fiddle as well as piano, and hung around local club Haney's, where he claimed he heard top black performers from Duke Ellington to MUDDY WATERS.

At 12 he made his first paid appearance, moved onto Radio WNAT in Natchez, Mississippi, and at 13 played clubs there, while his splendidly named cousin Betty Jo Slamper taught him to 'smooch'.

Hired as pianist by a travelling preacher, in 1952 Lewis married the preacher's 16-year-old daughter, Dorothy Barton. Jerry Lee too was 16. The following year he attended the Pentecostal Bible Institute in Waxahatchie, Texas. Expelled for playing gospel music 'like colored people', he told them, rightly, that they 'might as well accept it, 'cause some day that's how it's gonna be.' Back home, he bigamously married pregnant Jane Mitcham, after three days' jail for store-breaking and stealing a gun.

In Shreveport he made two country-music demos, and in Nashville sought work from Slim Whitman. But rock'n'roll was erupting across the South, and like others drawn to Sun Studios, Memphis, by Presley's success, Lewis auditioned there. In December 1956 Sun issued 'Crazy Arms', which sold well despite Ray Price's version having long been on the charts and despite Lewis sounding almost diffident (not something that would recur). The B-side, 'End of the Road', one of Lewis's few compositions, was an authentic dark howl, a perfect expression of its time and place.

At year's end Lewis played on several other artists' rockabilly cuts, among them CARL PERKINS' 'Matchbox' and BILLY LEE RILEY's 'Flyin' Saucers Rock'n'Roll'. Days later, ROY ORBISON asked him to play. Lewis replied: 'I don't do sessions anymore.' Later, pressed by a discographer as to who had played on Jerry Lee's own records, he offered one of the all-time great ripostes to the collector-mentality: '*I* played on 'em: what the hell else d'you need to know?'

'Whole Lotta Shakin' Goin' On' was his second single. Widely banned for lewdness, it sold poorly until Lewis shook up Steve Allen's national TV show in July 1957, after which he was a star, undertaking nationwide tours while the record sold over a million. The glorious 'Great Balls of Fire' followed (and riveted Great Britain when Lewis' rendition in the film *Disc Jockey Jamboree* was shown on TV), then 'Breathless' and the title-song of the film *High School Confidential*, in which Lewis performed. All stormed the pop, country *and* R&B charts.

These hits, plus unbeatable versions of 'Mean Woman Blues', Chuck Berry's 'Little Queenie' and many more, shared an immediately identifiable style, an alchemy of the 'Sun sound', fluid vocal brio and a pounding yet lyrical piano. Both hands were crucial in his playing, his striding left-hand the foundation of the rhythm, even with a bass guitarist behind him. Live, and as captured on film, he was an explosive performer in the early years, genuinely close to the edge. And uninhibitedly competitive. Resenting lower billing than Chuck Berry, he once ended his act by setting the piano on fire. As they met in the wings, Lewis challenged Berry: 'Follow that!'

In May 1958 Jerry Lee arrived in Britain. The press discovered that the 13-year-old with him was his wife. Jerry confessed his whole hillbilly history: 'I was a bigamist at 16. . . . My wife Myra and I are very happy.' The nation was not. His tour cancelled, Lewis was deported, ammunition given to America's anti-rock'n'roll campaigners and his career shattered.

Lewis remained at Sun, its heaviest star, making rock'n'roll A-sides and wonderful country B-sides of the immaculate Hank Williams kind, years before country became an established new career for ex-rockers. Lewis would be a main player in opening up this route. (These B-sides are detailed in the entry **Williams, Hank**.) He regained the UK top 10 once, in 1961, with a superb version of RAY CHARLES' 'What'd I Say', its sumptuous thunder Sun Records' last golden moment. Lewis left the label in 1962.

On record he lost direction for a time, but toured with an arrogance burnished into art, wilfully infuriating audiences of Teds by dwelling on slow country songs while provoking country crowds with unabashed rock'n'roll. In mid-song he would order a musician to 'play it, son!' only to prevent his doing so with a piano solo no-one would interrupt.

Two 1963–64 live recordings show his genius. On a tawdry, humdrum date at the Star Club, Hamburg, playing to what sounds like about 50 people, and using, in the tradition of visiting American stars, an English backing-group met mere minutes before show-time (the Nashville Teens), Lewis gave a marvellously ferocious masterclass, and rose to a transcendent 'Your Cheatin' Heart', with exquisite vocal phrasing, and unsurpassable piano, coursing with understatement and grace. And then in contrast, in front of 50,000 seething fellow-peckerwoods in Birmingham, Alabama, he threw down a 'Hi Heel Sneakers' of shuddering, majestic excitement, stealing the song from all previous wearers.

For a while he joined the rock festivals circuit, including, implausibly, the Toronto Peace Festival, but by the 1970s he had cracked the mainstream country market with a succession of hits like 'What's Made Milwaukee Famous (Has Made a Loser Out of Me)' and the impeccably wily 'She Still Comes Around (To Love What's Left of Me)'. A rangey, muttering 'Me and Bobby McGee' in 1971 was made 'to show that damn *woman* [Janis Joplin] how it should be done.'

Ten years later, his skin waxy and his gait old, he combed his greased hair for the Wembley Country Festival crowd, put on filthy glasses and delivered a consummate 'Over the Rainbow': the mike still placed to show off how stylishly his right hand could steer around it, his vocal control sublime.

He proclaimed himself forever a rock'n'roller, through decades of turmoil, lurid tragedy and farce. Three-year-old son Steve Allen Lewis drowned in their swimming-pool in 1962; drug-ridden Jerry Lee Jr. died at 19 in 1973; Myra divorced him citing mental cruelty and physical abuse; in 1983 fifth wife Shawn Stephens took a fatal overdose ten weeks into their marriage—fatal because he failed to get help—a year after fourth wife Jaren Pate drowned in another swimming-pool. *Rolling Stone* published 'The Mysterious Death of Mrs. Jerry Lee Lewis', accusing him of murdering one wife and abusing and/or hounding to death several others.

In 1975 his plane was seized with cocaine and 11 kinds of amphetamine on board; in 1976 he was arrested outside the gates of Graceland, drunk in possession of a gun; the IRS seized his property in 1979 and 1983, and he filed for bankruptcy even as Dennis Quaid was making the Hollywood film of his life, *Great Balls of Fire!*. (A short, tax-avoiding emigration to Eire with sixth wife Kerrie and young son Lee followed in 1992.) Meanwhile there was a collapsed lung, gall-bladder removal, bleeding stomach ulcers and car-crash injuries. In 1984 he was twice brought back to life in an ambulance, and had half his stomach removed in 1985, a year his wife said he also spent shooting up methadone, tranquillisers and speed.

Perhaps no disparagement of the redneck is unfair to Lewis. He embodies pinched obduracy, brooding, malevolent ignorance, violent unreliability and borderline madness. A cousin of disgraced TV evangelist Jimmy Swaggart, he founded his own deranged and volatile religious guilt on the commie-hating protestant fundamentalism that gives the Bible Belt its bad name. He abused women, played with guns and shot at men; he drove the highways of the South blind drunk with his loaded pistol on the dashboard. He claimed plain-speaking as his compensating virtue, but where honesty is wielded with such self-regard, who needs hypocrisy?

Yet in the vivid contrast between the meanness of the man and the grandeur of the artist, the common denominators are his phenomenal energy and admirable, all-conquering self-belief. Jerry Lee Lewis will be remembered for his lifetime of hillbilly delirium, but he will be remembered best for his seizure of the musical moment at the dawn of rock'n'roll, when an incomparable talent was his intoxicant and ours: when he shot up the old order and played out his defiant dramas on the keyboard, in the studio and on the stage.

Dylan benefited as much from this legacy as the rest of us (and perhaps became acquainted with some of Hank Williams' work via Jerry Lee), but part of his debt is also more specifiable. The two songs that relent and relax at the end of the *John Wesley Harding* album, 'Down Along the Cove' and 'I'll Be Your Baby Tonight', would not have been possible without Jerry Lee; nor would that lovely minor song 'Living the Blues', which Dylan released on *Self Portrait* and performed on the 'JOHNNY CASH TV Show' on May 1, 1969. Not only is its style Jerry Lee Lewis', but its melody is said to be taken straight from a specific Lewis record, 'I'm Feeling Sorry', from 1957 (a Claud Demetrius composition, as was the great 'Mean Woman Blues'). And more modestly, when birds become 'birdies' on 'If Not for You', this jolly word trills through to us from its earlier appearance inside Lewis' 'Livin' Lovin' Wreck'.

There are other small conjunctions too. The 1961 A-side of Lewis' cover of Hank Williams' 'Cold, Cold Heart', a song called 'It Won't Happen with Me' (which name-checks Elvis) features guitarist WAYNE MOSS; five years later he plays on *Blonde on Blonde*. Bob may have had Jerry Lee's consummate, glowing version of 'What'd I Say' in mind at least as much as the Ray Charles original when performing the song at the rehearsals for Farm Aid in 1986. (Jerry Lee was also one of those who preceded Dylan in recording versions of 'Frankie and Johnny', 'That Lucky Old Sun' and 'Tomorrow Night'.)

Jerry Lee was also perhaps the egotist most prone to put his own name into the lyrics he sang—something Dylan eventually does himself (to more subtle, indeed to more or less opposite effect, since it signals his mooted obliteration) in a live version of that fine 1980s song 'Caribbean Wind', in which he sings of 'Flies on my balcony buzzin' my head / Slayin' Bob Dylan [here] in my bed'. (Jerry Lee was always the Killer, never the slain.)

In the end, though, like so many others before him, Jerry Lee came visiting Bob, recording the *Desire* outtake song 'Rita May'—which sounds, when you hear Dylan's version, as if it had been written for Lewis, and sounds, when you hear Jerry Lee's, as if he isn't quite so sure.

A story that may or may not be felt to illuminate this emerged in the book by Jimmy Guterman, *Rockin' My Life Away: Listening to Jerry Lee Lewis*. Producer Bones Howe gave Lewis the song and he recorded it. Afterwards he asked, 'Who wrote that song?' 'Bob Dylan,' Bones Howe replied, smiling. Jerry Lee showed no recognition. 'That boy's good,' Jerry Lee said. 'I'll do anything by him.'

[Jerry Lee Lewis: 'I'm Feeling Sorry', Memphis, 10 Sep 1957, *Jerry Lee Lewis—The Great Ball of Fire* (EP), Sun EPA 107, 1957 (in UK issued as B-side of 'You Win Again', London American HLS 8559, 1958); 'Livin' Lovin' Wreck', Memphis, 9 Feb 1961 c/w 'What'd I Say', Memphis, 9 Feb 1961, Sun 356, 1961; 'Cold, Cold Heart', Memphis, 9 Feb 1961, c/w 'It Won't Happen with Me', 12 Jun 1961, Sun 364, Memphis (London American HLS 9414, London), 1961; 'Frankie and Johnny', Memphis, Mar 1958, *Jerry Lee's Greatest*, Sun 1265 (London American HAS 2440), 1961; 'That Lucky Old Sun', Memphis, prob. Dec 1956, Mule 201, *nia* ; 'Tomorrow Night', Memphis, 1956, *Rockin' and Free*, Phonogram 6467.029, London, 1974. 'Rita May', *nia*, Elektra E-46067 LC, NY (c/w a re-make of 'Who Will the Next Fool Be?'), 1979; CD-reissued *Rockin' My Life Away*, Newsound 2000 NSTD209, 2002.

Bob Dylan: 'Caribbean Wind', live in San Francisco, 12 Nov 1980.

Jimmy Guterman, *Rockin' My Life Away: Listening to Jerry Lee Lewis*, Nashville: Rutledge Hill Press, 1991.]

Lightfoot, Gordon [1938 -] Gordon Lightfoot, Canadian singer-songwriter, was born November 17, 1938, in Orillia, Ontario. He performed in public from the age of five, making custom records and appearing on radio, including within a barbershop quartet. He wrote his first song in 1956 and dropped out of the no-longer-extant Westlake College of Music in Los Angeles in 1959. He became a choral singer and dancer on CBC's 'Country Hoedown' 1960–62, learnt various instruments and became drawn to folk music by hearing Bob Gibson (an early singing partner of PAUL CLAYTON) and, incredible as it may seem, by hearing the *Weavers at Carnegie Hall* LP. He and Terry Whelan became the Two Tones, and enjoyed a Canadian hit with 'Remember Me (I'm the One)' in 1962. The following year he hosted some BBC-TV shows called 'Country and Western'. In 1964 he fell under the spell of Bob Dylan, which served to focus his own songwriting. He wrote 'Early Morning Rain' that summer.

On November 10, 1986, Bob Dylan presented Lightfoot with a Juno Lifetime Achievement Award at a ceremony in Toronto, shown live on CBC-TV. Dylan looked fragile but extraordinarily cool and charismatic (not often the case in the mid-1980s) and said this: 'Pleased for me to be here to give this award to Gordon. I've known Gordon for a long time and I know he's been offered this award before but he has never accepted it because he wanted me to come and give it to him. Anyway, he's somebody of rare talent and all that . . .'

Lightfoot suffered from serious illness in 2002 but recovered and resumed concert appearances.

Beware his book of wretched poetry and feel-good homilies, *I Wish You Good Spaces*, 1977 (a belated artefact of an earlier era, as its title hints), one of a series from Blue Mountain Arts of Boulder, Colorado, also offering the improbable *My Life and Love Are One* by Vincent van Gogh and *We Are All Children Searching for Love* by Leonard Nimoy.

See also **'Early Morning Rain'**.

Lightnin' Hopkins [1912 - 1982] Samuel Hopkins, a country blues man with an electric guitar, was born in Centreville, Texas, on March 15, 1912 and 'raised in the piney woods of East Texas' (as Chris Strachwitz puts it). Lightnin' Hopkins was a confident writer of autobiographical songs, much influenced by his cousin Texas Alexander, by LONNIE JOHNSON (who frequently accompanied Alexander on record) and by the somewhat oppositely named SLEEPY JOHN ESTES.

Hopkins is, in turn, a weighty influence. His in-your-face 1947 record '(Let Me) Play with Your Poodle'—one of those where the euphemism sounds at least as rude as the sexual term it replaces—is hardly original by most criteria: it's a Tampa Red number from 1942, and just a 'Step It Up & Go' kind of song in any case, but it's innovative because with Hopkins' electric guitar, piano by Thunder Smith and a drummer too, it sounds like rock'n'roll years ahead of its time—which indicates one way in which, though he only lived to be 69, he was one of those important, extraordinary figures who spans so many eras of 20th century popular music. Starting with a head full of 19th century repertoire learnt as a child and as an acquaintance of Texas' great BLIND LEMON JEFFERSON, Hopkins ended up singing his distinctive story-songs about the Vietnam War and, with the charming 'Happy Blues for John Glenn', the space race.

As for the impact of his work on Dylan's, not only did his 'Automobile (Blues)' give Dylan the chassis for 'Leopard-Skin Pill-Box Hat' (see entry on that song), but with 'Brownsville Girl' too, Dylan rides a trail already explored by Hopkins. His 'I Would If I Could', one of the best (which is to say, least self-indulgent) of Lightnin' Hopkins' 1960s sides, is not only a song about going to see a cowboy movie, in this case about Jesse James, but it too has a narrator who drifts between 'real-life' and on-screen events awash with rumour and shooting.

More generally, Hopkins can be said to prefigure Dylan in having sung 'protest' songs like 'Tim Moore's Farm (Tom Moore Blues)', which he recorded in Houston in 1948 and which is part of what Dylan draws on for his own 'Maggie's Farm', and in more characteristically delivering self-composed, often lengthy stories, half sung and half spoken, a fiercely independent artist and, as noted by a folklorist and blues critic who knew him well, Mack McCormick, 'the embodiment of the jazz-and-poetry spirit, representing its ancient form in the single creator whose words and music are one act.' Though Hopkins' work first came to prominence when he was 'discovered' by SAM CHARTERS, who recorded the album *Lightnin' Hopkins* in January 1959, it was McCormick who contemporaneously re-branded Hopkins as a folk-blues artist and therefore gave his career a new life on the coffee-house circuits from the early 1960s onwards. In 1968 Les Blank made an acclaimed short film, *The Blues According to Lightnin' Hopkins*, which captures the music and personality of the older man.

Hopkins, who continued to record prolifically, died of cancer in Houston, the town in which he had been poet in residence for most of his adult life, on January 30, 1982.

[Lightnin' Hopkins: 1st sessions & subsequent Aladdin sessions, incl. '(Let Me) Play with Your Poodle', LA, 15 Jul 1947, LP-issued *Lightnin' Hopkins and the Blues*, Imperial 9211, US, 1950s, CD-reissued *The Complete Aladdin Recordings*, Aladdin CDP 7968442, Holland, 1991; 'I Would If I Could', Houston, TX, 18 Dec 1967, *Lightnin' Hopkins: Texas Blues*, Arhoolie CD 302, US, 1989; 'Tim Moore's Farm (Tom Moore Blues)', Houston, 1948; *Fast Life Woman*, Dart LP 8000, Houston, early 1960s, CD-reissued *The Gold Star Sessions Vol. 1*, Arhoolie CD 330, US, c.1991; *Lightnin' Hopkins*, Folkways US, 1959; 'Happy Blues for John Glenn', Houston, Feb 1962, *Walkin' This Road By Myself*, Bluesville BVLP1057, c.1962. Tampa Red: 'Let Me Play with Your Poodle', Chicago, 6 Feb 1942. *The Blues According to Lightnin' Hopkins*, dir. Les Blank; Flower Films/Blank, US, 1970.

Chris Strachwitz, notes to Arhoolie CD 302, above (which mention Hopkins' original 'late 1940s' recordings for Gold Star though the album itself contains instead a 1967 re-recording). Mack McCormick quoted from 'Lightnin' Hopkins' in Tony Russell, *The Blues from Robert Johnson to Robert Cray*, London: Arum Press, 1997, p.64.]

'Like a Rolling Stone' [1965] 'The first time I heard Bob Dylan,' BRUCE SPRINGSTEEN said, inducting Dylan into the ludicrous Rock'n'Roll Hall of Fame at the Grand Ballroom of the Waldorf Astoria Hotel in New York City (though the Hall itself is in Cleveland, Ohio), on January 20, 1988, 'I was in the car with my mother listening to WMCA, and on came that snare shot that sounded like somebody had kicked open the door to your mind.'

'Like a Rolling Stone', from the *Highway 61 Revisited* album, was recorded June 16, 1965 and released on July 20, over a month ahead of the album, split between the two sides of a 45rpm record. It entered the American charts four days later. It was hurriedly re-issued complete on one side because of listener-demand to radio stations that they play it all. Thus this record also kicked open the doors of radio. When FRANK ZAPPA heard it, he said later: 'I wanted to quit the music business, because I felt: "If this wins and it does what it's supposed to do, I don't need to do anything else."'

If the length was subversive of all the rules, and the music announced itself as unique and enormous—it wasn't only the opening drum sound that was thrilling, but the beautifully expressive guitar licks, the interaction, the torrid, clever flow of it all, while the voice was at once so young and so snarling, so energetic and so cynical. And then there were the words. They too were a jolting, glorious assault: a chaotic amalgam of blues vernacular, impressionism, allegory and an intense directness: 'How does it feel?'

The opening verse is straightforward, almost monosyllabic slang: 'Once upon a time you dressed so fine / Threw the bums a dime in your prime, didn' you? / People'd call, say "Beware, doll, you're bound t' fall" / You thought they were all kiddin' you . . .'

The brevity and crispness of the language—city language, straight from the streets—combines with the pile-up effect of all those internal rhymes, fired past the listener as from a repeater-rifle, establishing at once the tone of stinging recrimination.

The tone is modified as the language changes, becoming softer and less monosyllabic as it accommodates a broader theme, a heightened appreciation on the narrator's part of Miss Lonely's fall to 'homelessness': 'You said you'd never compromise / With the mystery tramp, but now you realize / He's not selling any alibis / As you stare into the vacuum of his eyes / And say, do you want to, make a deal? / How does it feel?! Ah! How does it feel?!'

Here the words are longer, those '-ise' sounds slow-fading, the phrasing much less colloquial, the 'meaning', in prose terms, vaguer. This change of language keeps its momentum, and paradoxically, as the language gets vaguer so the meeting of eyes between narrator and Miss Lonely intensifies: they reach the point where understanding is searching and personal, and communication can be achieved at this pitch: 'You never turned around to see the frowns on the jugglers an' the clowns / When they all came down to do tricks for you . . . / You used to ride the chrome horse with your diplomat . . . / You used to be so amused / At Napoleon in rags and the language that he used / Go to him now, he calls you, you can't refuse . . .'

This calculated lack of specificity becomes, in Dylan's hands, a positive entity grown out of and beyond the specific; it unfolds a complex tale that works on many a level, and never quite lets go. 'How does it feel?'—well, liberating. It felt liberating for him too. He said in 1966 that until 'Like a Rolling Stone' he was 'singing words I didn't really want to sing. I don't mean words like "God" and "mother" and "President" and "suicide" and "meat-cleaver". I mean simple little words like "if" and "hope" and "you".'

The single never did top the charts, though: not on either side of the Atlantic. Bob Dylan never has had a no.1 hit single. Like CHUCK BERRY a decade earlier, his influence has always been stratospherically greater than his sales.

'Like a Rolling Stone' was among the songs attempted live at the NEWPORT FOLK FESTIVAL the day after it entered the pop charts, using members of the Paul Butterfield Blues Band, including MICHAEL BLOOMFIELD, who had earlier been flown in for the recording session—Dylan choosing, in other words, a blues lead guitarist for this most radical of records, while reputedly instructing him to play 'none of that B.B. King shit'. The other musicians on the studio recording are Dylan himself plus AL KOOPER on organ, BRUCE LANGHORNE on tambourine, PAUL GRIFFIN on piano, Joseph Macho Jr. on bass and BOBBY GREGG on drums. TOM WILSON was the producer.

After Newport, 'Like a Rolling Stone' then became the last song of the night on Dylan's August-onwards 1965 concerts, and for the unsurpassable firestorm concerts of 1966, where it is used as a retaliatory weapon against those in the audience who shout and slow handclap and boo at him. In Manchester that May 17th, the shout of 'JUDAS!' is met first with a spoken retort from Dylan and then by the most sustained howl of articulate vituperation ever hurled at an audience. That opening snare shot comes into its own yet again. The very last performances of the tour, in London on May 26 and 27, may be still more majestically fiery.

GREIL MARCUS' book *Like a Rolling Stone: Bob Dylan at the Crossroads*, 2005, reports Dylan's producer BOB JOHNSON as saying that after these gruelling, confrontational concerts, 'Like a Rolling Stone' was never the same afterwards (and, Marcus adds, neither was Bob Dylan). But when was Dylan ever the same after anything?

The song, the quintessential rock anthem, inevitably became a warhorse in Dylan's later performance decades, after a diffident rendition at the Isle of Wight Festival with THE BAND in August 1969—where the hoarse way he delivers the shouted last chorus lines as a melodic descent makes it a cry of defeat, like a rattling of chains—and after determinedly high-energy performances (usually as the penultimate song of the night) on the 'come-back' tour of North America in early 1974. It is one of Dylan's most-often performed songs, and usually used just before or during the encore: a certain crowd-pleaser, whatever the standard of performance. Only occasionally has Dylan himself subverted its iconic power and confounded his public's expectations by placing it in a less significant slot—third, for instance, and placed between 'I Believe in You' and 'Man Gave Names to All the Animals' when he re-introduced secular material to his repertoire in the concerts of November–December 1980 on the US West Coast.

Sometimes, too, there has been real re-interpretation. In a run of 1990s renditions, starting with his third and final night in Prague in March 1995, Dylan has sung the song not as vituperation, not a snarl or a sneer 'out there' at someone else, but as a reflective, Hamlet-style soliloquy, in soft tones and contemplative mood, in a spirit of 'This is so, isn't it?' addressed to himself: 'Once upon a time you dressed so fine . . . didn't you?'

There was, though, all along, one way in which this radical anthem was not a creature of snarling newness, but rather was leaning upon old truths and old formulations: those of nursery rhyme and fairytale. Dylan's lyric's much-quoted aphorism, 'When you ain't got nothin' you got nothin' to lose', had been said before, in the same direct way, in a pre-19th century nursery rhyme, in which 'There was an old woman / And nothing she had . . . / She'd nothing to eat / She'd nothing to fear / She'd nothing to lose' (and indeed Dylan repeats 'you got nothin' to lose' after the words 'wiggle wiggle wiggle' in the song of almost that name on his 1990 album of nursery rhyme re-workings, *Under the Red Sky*). It's also so obvious a thing that we're likely to miss it that 'Like a Rolling Stone' is the only classic rock record whose opening words are those of every classic fairytale: 'Once upon a time . . .'

In April 1998, in South America for concerts in Argentina, Brazil and Chile, Dylan several times found himself on shared bills with THE ROLLING STONES. Thus on four nights in three different cities in two different countries, Dylan appeared to share vocals with MICK JAGGER on renditions of 'Like a Rolling Stone'. The Stones subsequently issued their own studio-recorded version of the song as a single—and it would be hard to explain just how the reputed world's-greatest-rock-band managed to make such a stultifyingly tedious, profoundly unexciting record out of so quintessential a hot rock anthem, and one with which Dylan had changed popular music so radically.

When Dylan receives Lifetime Achievement awards and the like, they are because of that six-minute single from 1965. The insignificant 1997 *Time Out of Mind* recording 'Cold Irons Bound' won a Grammy because 'Like a Rolling Stone' never did.

(See also **1965–66: Dylan, pop & the UK charts**.)

[Springsteen & Zappa quotes from Greil Marcus book extract, *The Guardian*, London, 13 May 2005; Dylan quote from 1966: 'The *Playboy* interview: a candid conversation with the iconoclastic idol of the folk-rock set', *Playboy*, Chicago, Mar 1966; Dylan quote re B.B. King from Mike Bloomfield, article in *Hit Parader*, Jun 1968, republished (but quoting it as 'stuff'), as 'Impressions of Bob Dylan', *On the Tracks* no.10, Grand Junction, CO, 1997. Nursery rhyme quoted from Michael Gray: *Song & Dance Man III: The Art of Bob Dylan*,

1999. Dylan's 1990s soliloquy versions of 'Like a Rolling Stone' e.g. Prague, 13 Mar 1995.

Dylan & the Stones live 'Like a Rolling Stone': Buenos Aires, 4 & 5 Apr 1998; Rio de Janeiro, 11 Apr 1998; and Sao Paulo, 13 Apr 1988. The Rolling Stones: 'Like a Rolling Stone' (single): oh, whenever.]

Lindley, John [1952 -] John Francis Lindley was born in Stockport, Cheshire, UK, on February 16, 1952. He is a creative writing tutor, a poet and a veteran poetry performer in pubs, clubs, theatres and literary festivals. Five of his poetry collections have been published, including *Stills from November Campaigns* (1998) and *Scarecrow Crimes* (2002). He was winner of a Words of Silk Open Poetry Competition and was Cheshire Poet Laureate for 2004.

Though he has not published a book about Dylan, he has an honourable history of commentating, and enabling commentary by others, on Dylan's work and was the first critic to notice Dylan's sustained but stealthy sewing of Hollywood film dialogue into his lyrics (especially those of the mid-1980s), and to tease out some of the detail in print, in his 1986 article 'Movies Inside His Head: *Empire Burlesque* and *The Maltese Falcon*'.

Lindley was a founder member of Wanted Man, in 1981, the organisation that devised and launched the pioneering UK fanzine *The Telegraph* under the editorship of JOHN BAULDIE, and became a frequent contributor. His work included 'Reels of Rhyme', 1990, an acute essay on the way that in concert Dylan has frequently applied himself to the finding of extra internal rhymes within the lines of his songs (for instance securing the extra half-rhyme of 'do yer' with 'Mister' in 'Ballad of a Thin Man'). In the immediate aftermath of John Bauldie's sudden death, John Lindley agreed to take on the editorship of the issue left half-completed, which it was felt it would be wrong just to abandon, and so oversaw that final *Telegraph*, no.56, published in late 1996.

Lindley wrote too for that other early UK fan publication, *Endless Road* (his first published piece was in issue 3, in 1982: it dealt with Dylan's singing voice and was titled 'A Dead Man's Last Pistol Shot: A defence for the dog in the barbed wire'). He has also written on Dylan for *Isis* and *Look Back*, and wrote a self-published booklet, '7 Days', about Dylan's 1987 UK concerts.

[John Lindley, *Stills from November Campaigns*, Salford, UK: Tarantula Publications (no Dylan connection but a poetry press), 1998; *Scarecrow Crimes*, Gee Cross Hyde, UK: New Hope International, 2002; 'Movies Inside His Head: *Empire Burlesque* and *The Maltese Falcon*', *Telegraph* no.25, UK, autumn/winter 1986; 'Reels of Rhyme', *Telegraph* no.36, Romford, UK, summer 1990; 'A Dead Man's Last Pistol Shot: A defence for the dog in the barbed wire', *Endless Road* no.3, Hull, UK, 1982; *Telegraph* no.56, Congleton, UK, late 1996.]

'lion lies down with the lamb, the' In that remarkable *Street Legal* song 'No Time to Think', 1978, Dylan offers the lines 'Your conscience betrayed you when some tyrant waylaid you / Where the lion lies down with the lamb. / I'd have paid off the traitor and killed him much later / But that's just the way that I am.'

The lion lies down with the lamb in the Old Testament book of Isaiah—or rather, it doesn't quite: it lies down with the calf and the fatling; it's the wolf who lies down with the lamb (though possibly they're all cheek by jowl). The Christian understanding of this passage is that it envisions Christ's peaceable kingdom-to-come:

'For unto us a child is born, unto us a son is given: and the government shall be upon his shoulder: and his name shall be called Wonderful, Counseller [sic], The mighty God, The everlasting Father, The Prince of Peace' (Isaiah 9:6); '. . . with righteousness shall he judge the poor, and reprove with equity for the meek of the earth: and he shall smite the earth with the rod of his mouth, and with the breath of his lips shall he slay the wicked. And righteousness shall be the girdle of his loins, and faithfulness the girdle of his reins. The wolf also shall dwell with the lamb, and the leopard shall lie down with the kid; and the calf and the young lion and the fatling together; and a little child shall lead them. . . . They shall not hurt nor destroy in all my holy mountain: for the earth shall be full of the knowledge of the Lord, as the waters cover the sea' (Isaiah 11:1–6 & 9).

Dylan may have this passage in mind again in that moving song of 1983 'Lord Protect My Child' (released only on the *Bootleg Series Vols. 1–3* box set in 1991), with its 'Till men lose their chains and righteousness reigns / Lord protect my child.'

The lion lies down with the lamb in WILLIAM BLAKE, when he extemporises on the same biblical passage in the last of the *Songs of Innocence*, the exquisite 'Night', 1789—in which the rhythms of the rhyming and half-rhyming couplets forming each verse's second half (italicised here) are likely to remind us of those in 'No Time to Think': 'When wolves and tygers howl for prey, / They [i.e. angels] pitying stand and weep; / Seeking to drive their thirst away, / And keep them from the sheep. / *But if they rush dreadful, / The angels, most heedful, / Receive each mild spirit, / New worlds to inherit.* // And there the lion's ruddy eyes / Shall flow with tears of gold, / And pitying the tender cries, / And walking round the fold, / *Saying "Wrath, by his meekness, / And, by his health, sickness / Is driven away / From our immortal day."* // "And now beside thee, bleating lamb, / I can lie down and sleep; / Or think on him who bore thy name, / Graze after thee and weep. / *For, wash'd in life's river, / My bright mane for ever / Shall shine like the gold / As I guard o'er the fold.*"'

The same scriptural text is also the basis for one of the best-known paintings in all of Naïve Art, 'The Peaceable Kingdom', by Edward Hicks, who was born nine years before Blake's poem was first published. He Americanises the theme by including, in the background, Penn making his treaty with the Indians in 1681. What is great in Hicks' painting (as in Dylan's song), is the sense of inner warring required to attain, or even believe possible, the promised peaceable kingdom. The anguished eyes of the lion, glaring in mute appeal at the viewer, make the painting, once seen, unforgettable. As James Thomas Flexner comments:

> 'Hicks painted no relaxed allegories in which wild animals find it easy to be tame. He shows, instead, "man's cruel, selfish nature," as symbolized in the carnivores, controlled by will rather than completely routed. The wolf, the leopard, and the lion do not, it is true, hurt the domestic animals, and those helpless creatures are not afraid of them, yet the great beasts, who were once infected with the lust for meat, are afraid of themselves. They stare . . . ahead with strained eyes that reflect inner conflict. The war against savagery has moved back into its primeval seat, the individual mind. It is never altogether won.'

[James Thomas Flexner, 'The Peaceable Kingdom' in *Man Through His Art: War and Peace*, ed. de Silva & von Simson, East Ardsley, UK: Educational Productions, 1963.]

Lipscomb, Mance [1895 - 1976] In his 1965 book *Conversation With the Blues*, Paul Oliver makes the point that 'if the blues, like any folk art or indeed almost any art form, is illuminating in terms of a whole group it is still sung and played by individuals . . . the individual tends to become submerged . . . and even when the assessment of the major figures is made, the minor blues singer is forgotten.'

To listen to much of Dylan's work—which at least between his break with 'protest' and his conversion to Christianity in every sense put a consistent emphasis on the importance of the individual rather than the mass—is to feel that Dylan has not forgotten the minor blues singer at all. He has listened to the minor figures wherever the somewhat random process of recording folk artists has allowed. We know it from listening to his work.

(Where Dylan heard what; the influence of 'minor figures' and unknown ones; the communal nature of much blues composition and how this gells with post-structuralist ideas of the unfixed text and the death of the author: all these are big questions, much discussed throughout this book. They are also central preoccupations of MICHAEL GRAY's *Song & Dance Man III: The Art of Bob Dylan*, Chapter 9, 'Even Post-Structuralists Oughta Have the Pre-War Blues'.)

Dylan learnt and assimilated experience from the older songs and the older singers—singers who, in some cases, were 'discovered' or 're-discovered' in the 1960s. MISSISSIPPI JOHN HURT is one example, the stylish and dapper Mance Lipscomb another.

Lipscomb was born April 9, 1895, in Navasota, Texas—and eventually died there (on January 30, 1976). He was 'discovered' in July 1960 by Mack McCormick and Chris Strachwitz and recorded—for the first time—a few weeks later in his two-room cabin, by which time he was in his 60s, though still with a strikingly youthful way of moving around in performance. He had almost a thousand songs he could perform.

Dylan met Lipscomb, and we can get an idea of the aura of the man, and thus a hint of the insights he could have given Dylan, from the description of him, and a transcribed conversational fragment, in Paul Oliver's book. He was a 'Texas sharecropper and songster with a reputation that extends widely in Grimes, Washington and Brazos counties. . . . A man of great dignity and natural culture . . . a veritable storehouse of blues, ballads and songs of more than half a century . . .' This is Lipscomb talking (the spelling is as in Oliver's transcript):

> 'I been playin' the git-tar now 'bout forty-nine years, and then I started out by myself, just heard it and learned it. Ear music. . . . My pa was a fiddler; he was an old perfessional fiddler. All my people can play some kind of music. Well, my daddy . . . he played way back in olden days. You know, he played at breakdowns, waltzes, shottishes and all like that and music just come from me. . . . Papa were playing for dances out, for white folks and coloured. He played Missouri Waltz, Casey Jones, just anything you name he played it like I'm playin'. He was just a self player until I was big enough to play behind him, then we played together. . . . "Sugar Babe" was the first piece I learned, when I was a li'l boy about thirteen years old. Reason I know this so good, I got a whippin' about it. Come out of the cotton-patch to get some water and I was up at the house playin' the git-tar and my mother came in; whopped me n'cause I didn't come back—I was playin' the git-tar: "Sugar babe I'm tired of you, / Ain't your honey but the way you do, / Sugar babe, it's all over now . . ."'

In Glen Alyn's *I Say Me for a Parable: The Oral Autobiography of Mance Lipscomb*, 1993, Lipscomb talks of encountering Dylan (and of RAMBLIN' JACK ELLIOTT first hearing of Lipscomb when Dylan played him a Lipscomb record) but specifies no dates. Lipscomb says Dylan followed him to 'Berkeley University' and then 'from Berkeley to the UCLA. . . . And when I went off a duty he was settin round me, an hear what I was sayin, an pick up a lot of songs. He could imitate. But he wadna playin no gittah. Then. Takin you know, learnin from his head.' On May 18, 1963, Dylan appeared on the same bill as Lipscomb at the first Monterey Folk Festival.

Lipscomb must have been an invaluable contact for Dylan—the one a black Texan with a personal repertoire stretching back to 1908 and incorporating songs a generation or two older than that, the other a white Minnesotan would-be artist of the whole American people born in 1941. Not only could Dylan have gained a knowledge ready to work for him but also, in a specific and personalised testimony, a feeling for the intimacy of connection of words and music in the expression of a spirit and a theme.

Lipscomb's repertoire included 'Jack O'Diamonds Is a Hard Card to Play' (he was field-recorded performing it in his hometown area the first time he ever recorded), which is a title-phrase picked up wholesale and retailed by Bob Dylan inside a piece of his own work that is not a blues. It is, in fact, from one of those poems he calls *Some Other Kinds of Songs . . .*, published on the back sleeve of the album *Another Side of Bob Dylan*. This long and generally inferior poem repeats several times, and then ends with, 'jack o' diamonds / is a hard card t' play.'

Other songs Lipscomb recorded include 'Baby Please Don't Go', 'You Gonna Quit Me' (the BLIND BLAKE song on Dylan's *Good as I Been to You*, retitled 'You Ain't Gonna Quit Me' by Lipscomb), 'Corrina Corrina', 'Mama, Let Me Lay It on You', a song called 'When Death Comes Creeping in Your Room'—a title that strongly suggests it may prefigure Dylan's 'Watcha Gonna Do'—and 'Night Time Is the Right Time'. In the section called 'Playing for the White Folks' in the Glen Alyn book, Lipscomb claims that Dylan took 'Baby Let Me Follow You Down' from 'his' 'Mama, Let Me Lay It on You'.

[Mance Lipscomb: 'Jack O' Diamonds Is a Hard Card to Play', Navasota, TX, summer 1960; *Mance Lipscomb Texas Sharecropper & Songster*, Arhoolie LP 1001, El Cerrito, CA, 1960. 'Night Time Is the Right Time', *nia*; *Mance Lipscomb Vol. 4*, Arhoolie LP 1033, El Cerrito, CA, *nia*.]

Little Richard [1932 -] Richard Penniman, the self-styled King of Rock'n'Roll, was born in Macon, Georgia, on December 5, 1932. Such was his explosive impact in late 1955 that many baby boomers remember better where they were when they first heard Little Richard than when they heard that Kennedy was killed—the assassination of 'melody' being more vividly felt.

To comprehend his impact, picture yourself stuck in the mid-1950s as puberty strikes. Life has been drab. The grown-ups talk about 'before the war' all the time; it has cast a long shadow over your childhood. In Britain, ration-books have only just disappeared. Few people have TV. School is like the army. Everybody's house is cold and you must eat up your liver and rice-pudding. Your parents listen to awful, syrupy music on their radiogram by people like Bing Crosby and FRANK SINATRA, who think they're so smooth and sophisticated and who imagine that these are virtues.

AWOPBOPALOOBOPALOPBAMBOOM!

By the time you're halfway through hearing Little Richard's first hit, 'Tutti Frutti', your mind has been mangled by this mad, wild, delicious gibberish from a human voice like no other, roaring and blathering above a band cranking along like a fire truck running amok in the night. By the time the record finishes, you have glimpsed the possibilities of a whole new universe. All those sophisticats defeated at a stroke. Enter glorious barbarity, chaos and sex.

With only half a dozen others (FATS, Bill Haley, ELVIS, CHUCK, JERRY LEE, BUDDY), Little Richard laid down the blueprint for what the whole of rock'n'roll was going to be like. And among that few, he stood out as the blackest, the hottest, the most exhibitionist, the loudest.

Richard Penniman was one of 12 children. His father made bootleg whiskey and his uncles were preachers. He was raised in the Seventh Day Adventist Church, where he learnt piano and sang in the choir. But he became a hooligan, claimed to have been thrown out of the house at 13, and played medicine shows and a club in Fitzgerald, Georgia, before hitching the country road from Macon through peach-trees and Spanish moss and black-water swamps to the big city, Atlanta, where he signed to RCA Records in 1951. He sounded like blues shouter Roy Brown, and his first record, 'Taxi Blues' c/w 'Every Hour', issued 1952, epitomises the dreary music that jazz people scorn for its crudeness and everyone else dislikes for its jazziness. After six more sides he was dropped from the label.

His optimism undimmed but his style still unformed, he moved across to Houston, to Don Robey's indy label, Peacock. Here, backed by the Tempo Toppers and the Johnny Otis Band, his sides included an unsuccessful first go at his own fine blues composition 'Directly from My Heart to You', and a 'Maybe I'm Right' built upon the delicate, elaborately filigreed vocal style he would reveal again years later on slow gospel numbers but that would sometimes augment his rock sides too, as on the hit 'She's Got It', where that word 'got' is twiddled into ten syllables.

The Peacock deal failed, and at the beginning of the year that was to end in triumph for him, Little Richard went back to Macon and took a day-job washing dishes. He sent a new demo to Art Rupe, a white entrepreneur who'd set up another of the South's indy labels, Specialty Records, in 1945: an outfit that, like Sun in Memphis, would come to concentrate on rock'n'roll, instead of assuming, like the majors, that this would soon pass. Indeed Rupe would become so convinced that Little Richard's raw, driving style defined the future that he would turn down SAM COOKE as too pallid.

Brought to New Orleans and put together with almost the same hot R&B band that backed Fats Domino, Penniman and producer Bumps Blackwell went into J&M Studios on September 14, 1955, and came out with 'Tutti Frutti', its obscene lyric reworked into acceptable nonsense in the studio by local writer Dot La Bostrie. Selling 500,000 despite being covered by Pat Boone, it made no.21 on the US pop chart as well as no.2 on the R&B list.

A cascade of hits, all frantic but tight, established Little Richard as a prime creative force in rock'n'roll. His piano-work, crucial to his sound, was limited to hammered chords and skitterish riffing (he didn't even play it himself on 'Tutti Frutti') but with that megaphone voice and falsetto squeal, the bursting energy and powerhouse band, his records fast became classics: songs every local group in the West had to play every Saturday night long into the future; songs the other rock giants made versions of; songs that also fired the ambition of those whose own music would change the 1960s, the Beatles and Bob Dylan.

'Long Tall Sally', 'Slippin' and Slidin'', 'Rip It Up', 'Ready Teddy' and 'She's Got It' were all 1956. 1957 gave us the title song of the film *The Girl Can't Help It*, 'Lucille', 'Send Me Some Lovin'', 'Jenny Jenny Jenny', 'Miss Ann' and 'Keep a Knockin''. 1958 produced the last great batch: 'Good Golly Miss Molly', 'True Fine Mama' and a glorious pillage of the music-hall oldie 'Baby Face'.

It's obvious now from the titles alone that something formularised soon set in with these records. Back then it was just how Little Richard was: an unstoppable force. Within the flailing combustion of 'True Fine Mama' we now recognise a conventional 12-bar blues; at the time we heard formless galactic meltdown.

Similarly, it might seem obvious now that Little Richard's presentation was partly that of outrageous queen, and his catchphrase 'Ooh ma soul!' pure camp. But these were clichés from the future. When rock'n'roll and Little Richard were new, his preening and boasting and benign lasciviousness seemed highly individual to him.

Besides, his sexuality was no simple thing. As his innovatively candid autobiography revealed (*The Life & Times of Little Richard the Quasar of Rock*, as told to Charles White, 1984), he fancied men and women but most of all himself. Here we learnt of Buddy Holly's enormous penis, and of an unforgettable incident backstage with Buddy, Richard and his girlfriend Angel: 'Buddy was having sex with Angel, I was jacking off . . . when they introduced his name on stage. He was trying to rush. . . . He made it too. . . . He came and he went!'

It's impossible to overestimate the beneficial effect back then of such open sexual flexibility: with this characteristic off-the-wall daring, Little Richard made a contribution to sexual politics as well as rock'n'roll.

The combination prefigured the styles of later black heroes with white audiences. JIMI HENDRIX learnt a lot from playing guitar behind Penniman all across the USA. And as Richard noted, 'You saw Prince on stage and you saw Little Richard, right? The little moustache, the moves, the physicality. He's a genius but he learnt it from me. I was wearing purple before he was born. I was wearing make-up before anyone else.'

But touring Australia in 1957, the unbelievable happened. The papers said he'd stood on Sydney Harbour Bridge and thrown his gold and diamond rings into the water, renouncing rock'n'roll and the Devil and going over to God.

For a few years he did. The man who'd once said of gospel music that 'I knew there had to be something louder than that, and I found it was me' now divided his time between Bible-school in Huntsville, Alabama, and the Seventh Day Adventist Church in Times Square, New York. Specialty kept the hits going through to 1959, when the last of a long line was reached with a game 'By the Light of the Silvery Moon', but it was the end of an era.

Elvis was away, Holly was dead, and black and white tastes in music were moving apart again, the one toward a new R&B that would soon turn into soul, the other toward teeny-clean pop. Richard Penniman went back into the studio with God and Quincy Jones on his side. He made religious records, starting with the LP *It's Real* for Mercury (including a shimmering bravura version of 'Peace in the Valley', which Dylan would perform rather less well in concert in 1989); but he kept the old egomania: he now billed himself 'King of the Gospel Singers'. 1962 saw one supreme meeting of the old and new: a single called 'He Got What He Wanted (But He Lost What He Had)', a sermon but delivered in utterly vintage style: a churning, steaming, bellowing, funny, irreverent tour de force to equal 'Long Tall Sally'.

Soon after, he returned to rock'n'roll, went back briefly to Specialty Records, cut a single called 'Bama Lama Bama Loo' (!), and revisited Britain in 1963 on a package with BO DIDDLEY, THE EVERLY BROTHERS and this new group called THE ROLLING STONES. As the British style writer Nik Cohn testified, 'he cut them all to shreds'. When he stood on top of the piano, took a ring off his finger and threw it into the audience, even those at the back dived forward, hypnotised by this consummate artist and frothing lunatic.

But fashions had moved on and it was to be downhill for two decades of failed comebacks, indifferent re-recordings and embarrassing live theatrics in place of solid rock. The exceptions were fine, lasting versions of 'Lawdy Miss Clawdy' in 1964 and 'Bring It on Home to Me' in 1966, and 1970s covers of THE BEATLES' 'I Saw Her Standing There' and the Stones' 'Brown Sugar' that served to remind us that he had inspired those songs and their writers in the first place. Attempts to update himself brought little success and involved much compromise, and in 1976 he went back to the Lord.

In the 1980s, however, the world and Little Richard were ready for each other again, and in 1985 the unstable rocker without a record deal appeared, briefly but with presence, all smiles and Hollywood good health, in the hit film *Down and Out in Beverly Hills*, to which he also contributed the awkwardly titled song 'Great Gosh a Mighty'. It says much for his unquenchable charm that at the same time as publishing his upfront autobiography he could remake himself into a thriving Disney favourite, with an album of children's songs and a TV series to match, on which a revisited 'Keep a-Knockin'' incorporated the swapping of knock-knock jokes with his new young audience.

He never resolved his unstable contradictions, even though he regained the showbiz mainstream. After Hollywood and Disney he appeared at rock revival festivals and refused to sing his hits; in 1993 it was announced that the 60-year-old gospeler and rocker had 'become Jewish' and could not fulfil engagements on Fridays. In 1996, still gloriously incongruous, he appeared in 'Baywatch', performing on the boardwalk with grand piano to an adoring audience of the beswimsuited, his eerily plastic-smooth face looking that of a 35-year-old from a different planet.

Like so many others, Bob Dylan gave him a special hero's place in his adolescent heart. In the second extant recording we have of Dylan, made informally in his home in 1958, the first song of the four recorded, and the only one to capture such an early Robert Zimmerman composition, was called 'Hey Little Richard'; the third song was Richard's 'Jenny Jenny'. In the Hibbing High School yearbook for 1959, Dylan wrote against the interrogative word 'Ambition': 'To join Little Richard'.

Eventually, Little Richard joined him, being persuaded, somewhat out of character, to be one of the many back-up singers at Bob's Rock'n'Roll Hall of Fame Induction in 1988. When Dylan made his acceptance speech, he was quick to say this: 'I'd like to thank a couple of people who are here tonight who helped me out a great deal coming up. Little Richard, who's sitting over there. I don't think I'd have even started without listening to Little Richard.'

Seven years earlier, Dylan had been recording the *Shot of Love* album. The title track was co-produced by Chuck Plotkin, Bob Dylan and . . . Bumps Blackwell, the producer and band-leader on 'Tutti Frutti' and the rest.

If the opening words of Dylan's 'It Ain't Me Babe'—'Go 'way from my window / Leave at your own chosen speed'—peculiarly resemble Little Richard's 'Keep a-Knockin'' ('but you can't come in') that's because both are built, in their very different ways, upon phrases or fragments from a host of half-remembered as well as well-remembered songs, from the traditional 'Go Way from My Window', collected by folklorist John Jacob Niles and sung by Dylan on the May 1960 St. Paul, Minnesota, tape, through to a cluster of blues songs that use this formulaic blues pattern: 'Get away from my window, honey babe get away from my door . . . / Say you get away from my window, don't knock at my door . . . / Said get away from my window mama, don't knock at my back door . . . / Get away from my window, stop knockin' on my door . . . / Go away from my window, stop knocking at my door.' Little Richard was the first to appropriate this for rock'n'roll, Bob the first to reappropriate it for 1960s modernism. Likewise, perhaps, Bob followed Little Richard into nursery rhyme. The ring-game song 'Sally Water', with its 'Shake it to the east, Sally shake it to the west, Sally / Shake it to the very one that you love the best, Sally'—lies very recognisably behind 1955's 'Tutti Frutti'; Dylan's flabby equivalent, on his very interesting nursery-rhyme-based album *Under the Red Sky*, is 'Wiggle Wiggle', while Sally becomes the 'back-alley Sally' who can 'do the American Jump' on the same album's closing track, 'Cat's in the Well'.

(*Under the Red Sky* co-producer DON WAS claimed in an interview that 'Wiggle Wiggle' *is* Dylan writing 'Tutti Frutti'; but the Dylan song is retro, stale, guarded *and* uninventive where Little Richard's invented something exciting that was radical, fresh and open. 'Wiggle Wiggle' is to 'Tutti Frutti' as Kenny Ball is to Louis Armstrong.)

Few people can shock a whole new world into existence by sheer creative conviction. Little Richard came close. He placed his unique persona at the service of sexual freedom, black pride and anti-stereotyping, way back in the drab Dwight Eisenhower world, before these were even known concepts, and in this way he dragged us forwards into the future. By shaping rock'n'roll, he shaped us all.

[Little Richard: 'Long Tall Sally', New Orleans, 7 Feb 1956, Specialty 572, Hollywood, 1956. The 'go n'way from my window' blues cluster quoted respectively from Papa Charlie Jackson: 'Papa's Lawdy Lawdy Blues', Chicago, c.Aug 1924; Blind Boy Fuller: 'Stealing Bo-Hog', NY, 7 Sep 1937; 'Memphis Jug Blues', Memphis, 24 Feb 1927; Anna Bell: 'Every Woman Blues', Long Island City, NY, c.Sep 1928; and Noah Lewis (with Gus Cannon): 'Going to Germany', Chicago, 1 Oct 1929. Don Was interview: LA, 15 Oct 1990, the *Telegraph* no.37, Romford, Essex, UK, winter 1990.]

'Little Sadie' See **'In Search of Little Sadie' / 'Little Sadie'** and **Ashley, Clarence**.

Live Aid [1985] An enormous co-ordinated series of pop music events—recordings and concerts—prompted, and in the latter case organised, by BOB GELDOF, in response to the 1984 famine in Ethiopia, which had been brought to the western world's attention by gruelling TV news coverage, primarily by a BBC team fronted by reporter Michael Buerk.

The recording of the US-based charity-fundraising single 'We Are the World' (written by Michael Jackson and Lionel Richie) took place on January 28 at A&M Studios, Hollywood, under producer Quincy Jones. Dylan is one of many vocalists contributing a line or two individually as well as ensemble singing. A tape with 21 takes circulated, several of which are included in the officially released video *The Making of We Are the World*, issued February 1986. The single itself (spliced together from four takes) was released March 11, 1985 and included on the album *USA for Africa: We Are the World* in April. For a detailed account of the recording, at once funny and dispiriting, see JOHN BAULDIE's 'We Are the World' in *The Telegraph* no.20.

The main US concert took place at the John F. Kennedy Stadium in Philadelphia on July 13, 1985, at which a cavalcade of stars appeared in an international bill topped by Bob Dylan. The concert was televised live, so that untold millions of viewers around the world watched Dylan come on, flanked by (you couldn't say 'supported by') RON WOOD and KEITH RICHARDS, and saw him give one of the most dishevelled, debilitatingly drunken performances of his career.

They had rehearsed together—all playing acoustic guitars—at Wood's New York home the previous day (running through 'Ballad of Hollis Brown', 'Girl of the North Country', 'Trouble' and 'Blowin' in the Wind'). In the event, the songs Dylan offered, apt choices in theory but distressingly mauled in practise, were 'Ballad of Hollis Brown', 'When the Ship Comes In' and 'Blowin' in the Wind'. He then joined the ensemble cast for the final number of the event, 'We Are the World', though it was noticeable that he left the stage early and abruptly, before the song's end.

Dylan further fell from grace on this occasion by delivering a short speech, as follows, after his 'Ballad of Hollis Brown' (and sending Bob Geldof into incandescent rage):

> 'Thank you. I thought that was a fitting song for this important occasion. You know while I'm here, I just hope that some of the money that's raised for the people in Africa, maybe they could just take just a little bit of it, one or two million maybe, and use it to, maybe use it to pay the mortgages on some of the farms, that the farmers here owe to the banks.'

Calling for millions of dollars to be diverted from starving Africans and given to Americans did not go down well—except apparently with WILLIE NELSON, who, watching at home, was inspired to move towards organising Farm Aid. Some good, therefore, came from Dylan's befuddled, breathtakingly insensitive, well-meaning remarks. In his further defence it might be added that there was nothing dishonourable in Dylan's being, as he visibly was, desperately embarrassed by the whole spectacle of these superstars patting themselves on the back while advancing their global profiles in the name of charity—so that one might not wish to rush to judgment on Dylan's failure to 'behave himself'. Perhaps it was also to his credit that he, and he alone, chose 'this important occasion' to mention the rôle of American banks in the rich-poor divide.

Nevertheless, with the sorry sight and sound of Dylan's performance, he finally blew his automatic right to be the headline name at any gathering of international superstars.

(For a fuller discussion of these topics, see Clive Wilshire, 'Charity Is Supposed to Cover Up a Multitude of Sins', reprinted in *All Across the Telegraph: A Bob Dylan Handbook*, ed. MICHAEL GRAY & John Bauldie, 1987.)

20 years later, when Bob Geldof returned to the African fray and organised Live 8, Dylan was conspicuous by his absence. He had not been invited to appear.

[Various Artists: 'We Are the World', single, Columbia US7-04839, NY; album, Columbia 40 043, NY; both 1985. John Bauldie: 'We Are the World', *The Telegraph* no.20, Bury, UK, summer 1985.]

***Live at the Gaslight 1962* [2005]** This CD, originally available only from the Starbucks Corporation's US coffee-shops, but produced by Sony BMG, comes in a digipak with a 12-page booklet with liner notes by SEAN WILENTZ.

The album's ten tracks are 'A Hard Rain's a-Gonna Fall', 'Rocks and Gravel', 'Don't Think Twice, It's All Right', 'The Cuckoo Is a Pretty Bird', 'Moonshiner', 'Handsome Molly' (previously released on the Japan-only CD *Bob Dylan Live 1961–2000: Thirty-Nine Years of Great Concert Performances* in February 2001), 'Cocaine', 'John Brown', 'Barbara Allen' and 'West Texas'.

These give us in better quality ten out of the 17 previously circulating song performances—though Wilentz's booklet states that the 17 come from two separate sets. The seven omitted are: 'No More Auction Block' (already issued on the *Bootleg Series Vols. 1–3* box set), 'Black Cross' (long ago issued on the *Great White Wonder* bootleg but never issued officially), 'Ballad of Hollis Brown', 'Motherless Children', 'Kind-Hearted Woman Blues' (the ROBERT JOHNSON song) and 'See That My Grave Is Kept Clean'.

It seems a missed opportunity not to include these other Gaslight performances, both for completeness' sake and because some of the omitted tracks are among the best: 'Black Cross' is one of Dylan's finest early works, with an absolute mastery of timing and of assumed accents.

A version of the same CD, but with different artwork, was also available for a limited time in

Belgium—in Belgium only—through the weekly magazine *Humo*, in which two October 2005 editions included exclusive vouchers that, with the addition of 12 Euros, could be exchanged for the album in branches of the Standaard Boekhandel bookstore chain's stores. This digipak version of the CD, in a brown slipcase, reads '*Humo* presenteert Bob Dylan Live at the Gaslight 1962'.

[Bob Dylan: *Live at the Gaslight 1962*, NY, Oct 1962, Columbia/Legacy A 96016, US (COL 82876728622, Belgium), 2005.]

Lofgren, Nils [1951 -] Nils Lofgren was born in Chicago on June 21, 1951 and became a highly distinctive rock singer and electric lead guitarist, whose high, light voice is full of warmth and an expressive generosity and shakes as if with sheer delirious energy—sometimes shown physically on stage when he was young by the back-flips for which he was famous. Now that he's in his 50s these may no longer happen. After first learning to play accordion and then joining NEIL YOUNG's band at 17, playing piano on the album *After the Gold Rush* and others, he became a member of Crazy Horse just long enough to appear on the band's 1971 album. He then formed his own band, Grin, which made four albums—the first work on which Nils Lofgren's own spirit and songwriting skills were set free. These were virtually indistinguishable from the post-Grin solo albums of the mid-1970s: *Nils Lofgren* (1975), *Cry Tough* (1976), *I Came to Dance* (1977) and *Night After Night* (1978).

These albums also yielded some hit singles and much radio airplay, and it was a shock to many of those who regarded him as a consequential star in his own right when in 1984 he subsumed himself into the very secondary rôle of playing guitar in BRUCE SPRINGSTEEN's band, which seemed a backflip of the wrong kind, and surely an unprecedented move for a so big-name an artist.

He did continue to make solo albums, and to tour; he twice became a member of RINGO STARR's All-Starr Band. Lofgren's very confident solo album of 1991, *Silver Lining*, put some of these people behind *him*: Springsteen, Ringo Starr, LEVON HELM (who sang on three tracks), Billy Preston and Clarence Clemons among them. But in 1999 he rejoined the newly re-formed E Street Band behind Springsteen once again.

He has only done Bob Dylan the favour of playing on stage with him three times. On October 20, 1996, at the Amphitheater in Mesa, Arizona, Lofgren came on for the last four numbers of Dylan's concert, playing guitar on 'Highway 61 Revisited', 'Alabama Getaway', 'Girl of the North Country' and the unavoidable 'Rainy Day Women #12 & 35'. In 1999 he and STEVIE VAN ZANDT (who also rejoined the Springsteen band that year) appeared on stage together at Dylan's April 25 concert in Zurich, playing on the rather fresher final encore number 'Not Fade Away'.

In New York City on August 12, 2003, Nils Lofgren appeared on Dylan's stage again, this time very early on—after the fourth number—and for the rest of the set not only played guitar and slide guitar but lit up the whole concert. As JOHN BALDWIN summarised a punter's report of proceedings: 'This was a show where the set-list didn't matter, the songs didn't matter. It was all about the performance. Lofgren was beyond phenomenal, but his presence reminded the band what it was all about and most important of all he inspired Dylan to give what was quite possibly his best performance this year.'

Nils Lofgren's 'I Came to Dance' includes the line 'I'm not Bob Dylan but I never miss a beat'.

[Nils Lofgren: 'I Came to Dance', *nia*, *I Came to Dance*, US, 1977; *Silver Lining*, Rykodisc RCD-10170, US, 1991. John Baldwin, Desolation Row Information Service e-mail, 14 Aug 2003.]

Lomax, Alan [1915 - 2002] Alan Lomax was born in Austin, Texas, on January 31, 1915, the son of the indefatigable folklorist John A. Lomax. He was driven all his life by the need to prove himself to his father in the same field—which he more than managed. It is not possible here to list or delineate his unparalleled success as a collector of folksongs and blues in many lands; it must be enough to note that had he not chosen the path he did, our entire understanding of American music would be immeasurably the poorer and our troves of recorded sound vastly less. Everything would have developed differently without him: the Library of Congress would be smaller, its archive of pre-war field-recordings less extensive and less valued; the Folk Revival movement would have supped on a far thinner gruel and the conditions that nurtured Bob Dylan's career so different that Dylan's own creative canon could not have been the same.

Lomax was—to mention merely a couple of ways his work concretely affected Dylan's—a great advocate of WOODY GUTHRIE's importance ('No modern American poet or folk singer has made a more significant contribution to our culture'), and a tireless field-recorder, like his father, of men on prison farms (not least in father and son thus first recording LEADBELLY), so retrieving exactly the kind of magical material HARVEY ABRAMS said that the young Bob Dylan was a purist about ('He had to get the oldest record and, if possible, the Library of Congress record').

Dylan refers to Lomax directly a number of times in *Chronicles Volume One*, introducing him first as 'the great folk archivist' and a few pages on describing a tangible feature of the Village's musical topography, 'Alan Lomax's loft on 3rd Street. Lomax used to have parties twice a month where he'd bring folksingers to play. . . . You might see Roscoe Holcomb or CLARENCE ASHLEY or Dock Boggs, MISSISSIPPI JOHN HURT, Robert Pete Williams or even Don Stover and The Lilly Brothers—sometimes, even real live section gang convicts that Lomax would get out of state penitentiaries on passes and bring to New York to do field hollers in his loft. The invitees to these gatherings would most likely be local doctors, city dignitaries, anthropologists, but there'd always be some regular folk there too. I'd been there once or twice . . .'

On January 20, 1988 Alan Lomax was, bizarrely, in the audience during Dylan's acceptance speech at his induction into the Rock'n'Roll Hall of Fame; Dylan included Lomax in his thanks, adding: 'I spent many nights at his apartment house listening to and meeting all kinds of folk music people which I never would have come in contact with.'

Dylan was also taped by Lomax at this apartment, in early 1963 (the tape is undated but has to have been made after Dylan returned from England that January and before the assassination of Kennedy on November 22). The result consists of Dylan singing a rather beautiful version of 'Masters of War', Lomax asking him where he wrote it and Dylan going into a somewhat drunken-sounding monologue about having written it in England where people don't like Kennedy and then about General de Gaulle and Russian Premier Khruschev. Altogether the tape lasts around eight minutes, with the singing running to four and a half.

This item was unlogged by Dylan discographers until very recently. The Alan Lomax Archive keeps adding to its online lists, and this item only appeared in fall 2005, though it had been offered to Dylan's office as an item for inclusion in the *No Direction Home* movie some time earlier (but not used).

By the time he made this tape, Dylan had also known some of Alan Lomax's own performing of folksong. The album of sea-shanties he was introduced to by SPIDER JOHN KOERNER back in Minneapolis included, he remembers, 'Alan Lomax himself singing the cowboy song "Doney Gal", which I added to my repertoire.' Indeed he did: he was recorded performing it in his sweetest pre-New York voice as early as May 1960 in a St. Paul apartment. Later, at the NEWPORT FOLK FESTIVAL of 1965, it was Alan Lomax who introduced the PAUL BUTTERFIELD blues band with some disparaging comment that no-one can quite remember (it is quoted differently in every account), prompting Dylan's manager ALBERT GROSSMAN to wrestle him to the ground. Lomax was 50 years old at the time; he had decades of work still to achieve.

As it happened, by this point Lomax had long since impinged upon Dylan's personal life too: in 1961, Lomax's personal assistant was one Carla Rotolo, and through her, Dylan was introduced to her younger sister, SUZE ROTOLO.

Lomax's biggest book, *The Land Where the Blues Began*, was published in 1993, when he was 78 years old. He had become an eloquent writer about the geography of the Delta, as well as about its music, and equally good on the work song as the main source of the poetry of the blues. By now he was, too, unafraid to make the broadest kind of statement, as here: 'Singing and making music are a kind of dreaming out loud, pulling the listener into the dream and thus taking care of his deep needs and feelings.'

Alan Lomax was no saint—but since this has not been the place to list his achievements, nor should it be the place to list his faults. He died at age 87, on July 19, 2002.

[Alan Lomax, quote on Guthrie from *The Penguin Book of American Folk Songs*, Harmondsworth, UK: 1964. Other works include many co-written with his father, plus *The Folk Songs of North America*, Garden City, NY: Doubleday, 1960 and *The Land Where the Blues Began*, New York: Pantheon, 1993. Lomax taped interview with Dylan listed at *www.lomaxarchive.com/guide-audio.jsp*, foot of page, seen online 9 Oct 2005; the tape is Alan Lomax Collection aggregate no.AFC 200404, tape no.T1248. Bob Dylan, *Chronicles Volume One*, pp.55, 70 & 239.]

Lone Justice An over-hyped early 1980s pioneering cow-punk group, Lone Justice was fronted by country-rock Tammy'n'Dolly singer and songwriter Maria McKee, who soon went solo and among much else co-wrote a song called 'Nobody's Child' with ROBBIE ROBERTSON on her début solo album. Lone Justice's eponymously titled first album, released in 1985, was produced by Jimmy Iovine and featured 'special guests Annie Lennox and STEVE VAN ZANDT'.

It might have included Bob Dylan too, since he dropped in on one of their New York sessions for the album, probably in November 1984, and played rhythm guitar on their recording of his own obscure *Empire Burlesque* outtake song 'Go 'Way Little Boy'. This was excluded from their album and issued only as one of the two tracks on the UK B-side of their 12-inch single 'Sweet Sweet Baby (I'm Falling)', a song co-written by McKee, Van Zandt and BENMONT TENCH.

Dylan was rumoured to have played harmonica on 'Go 'Way Little Boy' too. Both the 1999 and the 2003 retrospective collection releases of the track state that the harmonica is by Maria McKee, but these versions are re-mixes, so the truth remains, as so often, unclear. The original mix from the 1985 B-side has not been reissued. It is also rumoured that Lone Justice recorded 'Clean Cut Kid' at the same session, again accompanied by Dylan; if so this remains uncirculated as well as unissued.

Maria McKee was interviewed about the Dylan connection in 1987, and asked how come Dylan had given the group a song. She answered:

'That came about through Carole Childs, who was the woman who originally signed me to Geffen Records. She was very close to Dylan–very, very close–and she brought him to a gig or something. A long time ago. She said, "Why don't you write Maria a song?" He said, "OK." How she talked him into it I don't know but he *did* it. And–and it was real cool. He came down to the studio when we were recording our first album and taught us the song. And he stayed around. He brought RON WOOD with him and they played on it. . . . And we ended up hanging out 'til like two in the morning in the studio. . . . We ended up working on it a very long time because he didn't like the way that I sang it–until I sang it like him! It got to the point where finally I just did my best Bob Dylan imitation–and he said, "Ah, *now* you're doin' some *real singing!*" That's exactly what he said: "Now you're doin' some real singing."'

Lone Justice's second album, *Shelter*, 1986, was its last, except for *Lone Justice in Concert*, recorded for and released by the BBC in Britain in 1987.

[Lone Justice: 'Sweet Sweet Baby (I'm Falling)' (re-mix) c/w 'Stay 'Way Little Boy' & 'Pass It On', Geffen TX 6426, UK, 1985; *Lone Justice*, Geffen/CBS GHS 24060, US, 1985; *Shelter*, Geffen/WEA GHS 24122-1, 1986; *Lone Justice in Concert*, BBC CN4885S (LP), UK, 1987, CD-reissued Windsong WIND048, UK, 1993. Remixed 'Go 'Way Little Boy' on *The World Is Not My Home*, Geffen/BMG GEFD 25304, US, 1999 & *20th Century Masters: The Millennium Collection*, Geffen/Universal 860985, US, 2003. Maria McKee quote from interview by Thomas Lasarzik, Munich, 10 Mar 1987, in *The Telegraph* no. 27, Romford, UK, summer 1987, p.30.]

'Lone Pilgrim' [1993] This is the song of spectral calm with which Dylan closes his solo acoustic album of 1993 (his last such album), *World Gone Wrong*. He writes in his liner-notes that it 'is from an old DOC WATSON record.' But long before Doc Watson recorded it, 'Lone Pilgrim' was a piece of core repertoire of the always unaccompanied and now legendary Aunt Molly Jackson. In 1939 a Jackson performance of this song was field-recorded by the omnipresent ALAN LOMAX for the Library of Congress (and issued 22 years later).

Aunt Molly Jackson begins her performance by remarking that the song was always a favourite of her grandfather's as well as of her own. It might be assumed that, as with 'St. James' Hospital', Doc Watson has been fed this repertoire directly by Alan Lomax: except that the sleevenotes to Watson's record say that it was his father's favourite hymn. In any case, the lyric Doc Watson sings, and that Bob Dylan uses word for word, is both more poetic than Aunt Molly Jackson's and at moments dangerously close to being more 'poetic' instead, and it has four lines that simply aren't there in the version Aunt Molly Jackson performed for Lomax.

Jackson's version veers between creditable straightforwardness and the dully prosaic; the Watson-Dylan version just manages to avoid the faults of leaning the other way. This is surely a very old song either tampered with, or more likely written by, one of those 19th century men of the church who so much enjoyed re-writing folksongs by a process of empurplement. When this is done to a very good, robust old ballad, as happened to so many of the songs of 19th century Ireland, the new version gets put into print, played in the drawing-room for a few faddish years and soon dropped as dated, mannered and artificial. If we're lucky, the people who can't read go on singing the older, unempurpled version and it survives down the generations, oblivious to drawing-room tastes that come and go. But when a song that isn't so good in the first place gets set upon by a Victorian man of letters or hobbyist-poet of above-average instinct, or originates with such a person, it may be that versions of differing degrees of gentrification can co-exist more equably. 'Lone Pilgrim' is surely such a song, and the gentleman in question may have been a John Ellis, a William Walker or a B.F. White.

White, a 19th century folksong collector, singer and teacher from Georgia still given a composer credit on the Doc Watson and Bob Dylan albums, is first credited with its authorship in the 1911 edition of an anthology he had edited and first published back in 1844; but the song had not been included in the 1844 edition, and first saw publication three years after this, in the second edition of another anthology, *Southern Harmony*, a collection of hymns edited by White's brother-in-law, William Walker, a popular figure known as Singin' Billy. *Southern Harmony* sold 600,000 copies in the South between 1835 and the Civil War. 'The Lone Pilgrim' wasn't in that 1835 edition; it makes its first appearance in print in the edition of 1847, with Walker crediting the song to himself. (Watson and Dylan both attribute 'Lone Pilgrim' to B.F. White and J.M. Pace; but Pace's is in fact only an arranger's credit, and B.F. White is claimed to be the sole composer.)

In fact the song's origins are older than this. Gavin Selerie (in 'Tricks and Training: Some Dylan Sources and Analogues Part Two', in a 1995 *Telegraph*) suggests that aside from 'Jack-a-Roe' and 'Love Henry', 'Lone Pilgrim' is the oldest song on the album. He notes that its tune has been identified as that of the Scottish melody 'The Braes O' Ballquhidder', which may itself duplicate a still older tune, the Gaelic 'Brochun Buirn'. He notes too that folklorist D.K. Wilgus argues that 'Lone Pilgrim' is a variant of 'The White Pilgrim', whose text was written in 1838 by John Ellis, a preacher, after visiting the New Jersey grave of an evangelist, Joseph Thomas, who had been converted to the preaching life by meeting a 'believing Jew' who wandered moneyless, dressed in a long robe and preaching. Thomas began to do the same in 1815, travelling throughout the East and South on foot, dressed in white. Ellis visited his grave when it was 'fresh made' and wrote 'The White Pilgrim' afterwards.

John Ellis' text seems to have been revised by Singin' Billy Walker, making it, argues Selerie, 'more universal in reference and richer in imagery'. Did B.F. White then revise it again? Whoever fashioned which verses, all three of these men were of exactly the kind described earlier: teacherly amateur collectors of a religious bent and with literary aspirations.

The pen that has replaced the pinched and desiccated 'came to the spot' (Aunt Molly Jackson) with the rich nebulousness of 'came to the place' (Watson-Dylan), has done the song a favour in its very opening line, banishing the inevitability of things earth-bound, and coming out at once in recognition of ethereal, weirder dimensions. It readies us for the delight, in the third line, of 'I heard something say'—not 'someone' but the occult 'something'—and so deepens our own receptivity as listeners to hearing from the realm of the dead: a prevalent possibility in the most moving kinds of folk ballad: in songs like 'Love Henry', in fact.

Similarly, Aunt Molly Jackson's final line—'Has quietly conducted me home'—has been improved in the Watson-Dylan version by the change to 'kindly assisted me home'. The former makes God sound like a tight-lipped male nurse, escorting you back to the ward whether you like it or not: certainly a process requiring no uplift or desire by the soul concerned. Changed to 'kindly assisted' instead, it evokes the narrator's own ardour and effort, while at the same time, paradoxically, it makes the Master's hand much more akin to the human, with its hint of a journey in which one old soul leans upon the other and they make their slow way together.

The lines immediately before this last are also less effective in the Jackson version. Her 'The same hand that brought me / Through all dangers and fears' is replaced in Watson-Dylan by 'The same hand that led me / Through scenes most severe.' Again 'brought me' is less participatory, more automated, than 'led me'—the one has no resonance of any kind, the other suggests being taken childlike by the hand: it's more humane and gives the imagination something to see; and although both 'dangers and fears' and 'scenes most severe' avoid specifics, the former has a hint of sermonly rhetoric about it that the latter avoids. That word 'scenes', suggesting distance, gives an apt hint of the inviolability the speaker believes that God-given protection affords, while the phrase taken as a whole is simply the less tired of the two options.

One tiny change seems preferable on Aunt Molly's version. Her pilgrim's body asks that the narrator tell her 'companions' and children not to weep; Dylan sings 'companion', which achieves a jarring dislocation of period, making it sound like a present-day politically correct term like 'significant other' or 'partner'.

Ms. Jackson's version omits a verse that Watson uses, and therefore that Dylan uses too, that is actually a compression of *two* verses from the song as published in the 1950s in G.P. Jackson's [no relation] *Spiritual Folk Songs of Early America*. These two are: 'The cause of my master compelled me from home, / I bade my companions farewell; / I blessed my dear children who now for me mourn,— / In far distant regions they dwell. / I wandered an exile and stranger from home / No kindred or relative nigh; / I met the contagion and sank to the tomb, / My soul flew to mansions on high.' [Punctuation as given.]

The compression that drops all but the opening line from the first of these verses and the first line from the second seems entirely meet. It clears away a good deal of the purple in the drawing-room curtains of such songs. The only line that Dylan might have been tempted to retain, had he known of its availability, is that 'I wandered an exile and stranger from home'—a sentiment he so often expresses in his own songs, takes up in songs by others and appreciates for its biblical import.

All three recordings also avoid the glutinous gilding of the religious lily offered by the extra final verse offered in G.P. Jackson's published text: 'And there is a crown that doth glitter and shine, / That I shall for evermore wear; / Then turn to the Savior, his love's all divine, / All you that would dwell with me there.' Again, well worth avoiding. (In any case, how many people's notion of heaven would involve dwelling with Aunt Molly Jackson, especially with a crown forever on her head?)

That Jackson sings none of these verses gives her version, for all its lyric inferiority to Watson's, a stripped-down quality, a narrative reticence, that matches her unaccompanied, uncompromising and inelegant delivery. As Selerie comments, 'her stark delivery, slow and stretched out, gives us a sense of a fiercely independent and unbroken tradition. Whatever consolation is offered through the words, there remains a fidelity to the tough circumstances of life.'

Bob Dylan's interest is more in the question of fidelity to self. He is uncharacteristically straightforward in writing of the song's appeal: 'what attracts me to the song is how the lunacy of trying to fool the self is set aside at some given point. salvation & the needs of mankind are prominent & hegemony takes a breathing spell. "my soul flew to mansions on high".'

This re-states a core position Dylan has long, probably always, held. He expressed it on an earlier occasion like this: 'if you try to be anyone but yourself, you will fail; if you are not true to your own heart, you will fail,' just as in 'Groom's Still Waiting at the Altar' he sings of 'the madness of becoming what one was never meant to be.' Among other things, the songs on these two albums amount to an investigation on Dylan's part as to how far he can remain true to, as it were, this folksong part of himself.

These rich, difficult 1990s acoustic albums, teeming as they are with the history of North America and her immigrants and exiles, from Europe and from Africa, take their leave too soon. 'Lone Pilgrim' takes *its* leave too soon, like the person who speaks from the tomb. But it provides yet another fine farewell from Bob Dylan, who is so very good at farewells at the ends of albums, and who has here provided us with so many pathways back into the ever-present past. As the song's conclusion has it, 'The same hand that led me through scenes most severe / Has kindly assisted me home.'

[Aunt Molly Jackson: 'The Lone Pilgrim', *nia*, 1939; *Aunt Molly Jackson: Library of Congress Recordings Vol. 7 no. 4*, Rounder 1002, Somerville, MA, 1961. B.F. White, *The Sacred Harp*, 1844; song 1st credited to him in the 1911 edn. William Walker, *Southern Harmony and Musical Companion*, 1835; 2nd edn., 1847, gave 1st publication to the song; a reprint of the 1854 3rd edn. was published LA c.1966. Gavin Selerie: 'Tricks and Training: Some Dylan Sources and Analogues (Part Two)', *Telegraph* no.51, UK, spring 1995. Details re the tune via Selerie from G.P. Jackson, ed., *Spiritual Folk Songs of Early America*, 1953, pp.47–48 & re the texts via Selerie from D.K. Wilgus: ' "The White Pilgrim": Song, Legend, and Fact', *Southern Folklore Quarterly* Vol.14, no.3 (pp.177–84), Florida, 1950. Buell Kazee recorded a version of 'The White Pilgrim', Kentucky, c.1956; *Buell Kazee Sings & Plays*, Folkways FS3810, NY, 1958. Bob Dylan, interview by Ron Rosenbaum, Burbank, CA, Nov 1977, 'The *Playboy* Interview', *Playboy*, Chicago, Mar 1978.]

***Lonely Crowd, The* [1950]** *The Times*' obituary of American sociologist David Riesman (1909–2002) included this: 'Riesman was the author of *The Lonely Crowd*, a book which wielded a huge influence on an increasingly self-scrutinising American middle class. . . . *The Lonely Crowd* sold more than a million copies, an astonishing number for a work of sociology at that time. It formed the subject of heated debate at the dinner parties of the 1950s, as well as in school classrooms and lecture theatres. Among other things it is credited with having influenced Bob Dylan to write the lines: "Standing next to me in this lonely crowd / Is a man who swears he's not to blame," in the song "I Shall Be Released".'

[Obituary of David Riesman, unsigned, *The Times*, London, 30 May 2002. NB: this gives the date of publication as 1951; 1950 is correct. David Riesman, *The Lonely Crowd*, New Haven, CT: Yale University Press, 1950.]

'loon, crazy as a . . .' 'Bob Dylan's 115th Dream' includes 'Just then this cop comes down the street / Crazy as a loon'. In most places, this 'loon' is assumed to be an abbreviation from 'lunatic', but not in Dylan's home state of Minnesota, where the Common Loon (aka Great Northern Diver), is the state bird. It can be found in many parts of the US, however, and in Europe and Asia. John James Audubon wrote: 'There is an absurd notion, entertained by persons unacquainted with the nature of this bird, that its plaintive cries are a sure indication of violent storms. Sailors, in particular, are ever apt to consider these call-notes as portentous.' This is interesting in light of the suggestion that the iridescent keening sound Dylan makes on harmonica in solo performances on the 1966 UK tour—most noticeably on the officially released 'Mr. Tambourine Man' from Manchester—is strongly reminiscent of the distinctive cry of the loon.

[John James Audubon quoted from *Audubon's Birds of America*, 1840, 1st Octavo Edition, online 3 Jul 2005 at *www.flyingmobiles.com/html/statebirds/common_loon.htm*. The resemblance between Dylan's harmonica and the cry of the loon suggested by Ruth Williams, Fellow of Girton College, Cambridge, UK, 30 Jun 2005.]

Lord Buckley [1906 - 1960] Richard Myrle Buckley was born 15 miles west of Yosemite in the miserable mining and lumber town of Tuolumne, California, on April 5, 1906, to English immigrant parents. He was a talented mimic who grew up to pursue an edgy, perilous career as a unique vaudeville, radio and nightclub stand-up act, an iconoclastic hip raconteur. As Klas Gustafson puts it (courtesy of a translation from the Swedish—'under duress'—by IZZY YOUNG), Lord Buckley 'came on as a British aristocrat and sounded like black jazz.'

It was rumoured that, like Henry VIII, he had six wives—and there is a 1956 transcript of him being teased about this by Groucho Marx, who asks: 'Well, are you planning on fighting any more preliminaries or is this current one the main bout?' Much in Buckley's life was a matter of rumour, though, and like the young Bob Dylan who came to admire him (but who never saw him live: he was just too late), he manufactured many of the rumours about himself. He was also a practical joker, and is said to have had himself driven through city streets in a coffin so that he could open the lid and sit up en route, to shock passers-by and publicise his act. It's also said that FRANK SINATRA was a Buckley fan who would come to see him perform—till Buckley and an entourage reciprocated, turning up entirely naked to see Sinatra.

He launched his career in the 1920s, performing with travelling tent shows and marathon dances, and somehow thrived in the Depression of 1930s Chicago, where he owned a club, the Suzie Q, and learnt the jazz patois that he admired, adopted and adapted: it was, he said, 'a magical way of speaking. . . . a language of such power, purity and beauty that I found it irresistible.'

As someone else said, before LENNY BRUCE there was Lord Buckley–and he was, as Dylan said of Lenny, 'always on the outside of whatever side there was'. He was the inventor of the long, improvised hip comic narrative, his speech flowing with jazz rhythms and surreal elaboration, sometimes with scat singing thrown in.

His style continued to develop, hitting its peak in the late 1940s, when he began to be 'a name', enchanting audiences with endlessly inventive spiels based on stories from 'Willie the Shake' (Shakespeare), current events and the Bible, as in his ever-varying tour-de-force routine 'The Nazz' (i.e. the Nazarene). He often shared the stage with black musicians, and had long running battles against police harassment as a result. They often closed him down, and in the end they confiscated his cabaret card, making it illegal for him to work in any club.

Not all his work had been cod-sophisticated satire. 'Black Cross', a Lord Buckley monologue written by Joseph S. Newman, the actor Paul Newman's uncle, was a straightforward reading of Newman's anti-racist poem–and it was with this that Dylan started to prove his own skills as a mimic. He comes to 'Black Cross' very early on, performing it at his first concert–at the Carnegie Chapter Hall in New York City on November 4, 1961; recording it on the December 22, 1961 tape made privately back in Minnesota a month after he'd recorded his début album in New York, and performing the song again in 1962 at the Gaslight–it is, unfortunately, one of the numbers omitted from the official release *Live at the Gaslight* (2005), though it has circulated.

The Minnesota recording is simply great. He took it from Lord Buckley, but incontestably he made it his own. No-one in the world can deliver a talking song or a half-talking song as Bob Dylan can. It's a facet of his genius that he has remained in full control of, and it's certainly evident when he produces the perfect mimickry of the white voices and the black voice on 'Black Cross'. And what you hear there is not just mastery but Dylan's joy in exercising it: a generous, sharing joy.

Lord Buckley's recording of this piece, made in LA in February 1959, is on his album *Way Out Humor*, while Buckley's 1959 and early 1960 recordings of the Robert Service poem 'The Shooting of Dan McGrew', which Buckley titles 'The Ballad of Dan McGroo' (both posthumous releases, on *Lord Buckley Blowing His Mind (And Yours Too)* and *Bad-Rapping the Marquis de Sade*), have been suggested as influences on Dylan's 'Lily, Rosemary & the Jack of Hearts'. More certainly his posthumous release *The Best of Lord Buckley* (1963) stands on the mantelpiece on the front cover photograph of Dylan's *Bringing It All Back Home*. And Dylan once called him, rather grandly, 'the fuel to my success'.

Lord Buckley died in Columbus Hospital, New York, on November 12, 1960, probably from a stroke. He sounded about a hundred years old but he was only 54. His death certificate nonetheless read 'natural causes'. His ashes were scattered in Red Rock Canyon, just west of Las Vegas.

[Lord Buckley: 'Black Cross', LA, 12 Feb 1959, *Way Out Humor*, World Pacific WP-1279, LA, 1959; 'The Ballad of Dan McGroo', LA, 12 Feb 1959, *Lord Buckley Blowing His Mind (And Yours Too)*, World Pacific WP-1849, LA, 1966; 'The Ballad of Dan McGroo', Oakland, CA, 1960, *Bad-Rapping the Marquis de Sade*, World Pacific WPS-21889, 1969; *The Best of Lord Buckley*, Crestview CRU-801 & CRU7-801, US, 1963.

Sources: *www.lordbuckley.com*, incl. Klas Gustafson, 'The Lord Who Became a Performer's Performer' (translation by Izzy Young); the very good entry on 'Black Cross' in Oliver Trager: *Keys to the Rain: The Definitive Bob Dylan Encyclopedia*, New York: Billboard, 2004, pp.41–44; the *Salon* interview (dated 26 Jun 2002, online at *www.salon.com/people/feature/2002/06/26/buckley/index.html*) by Douglas Cruikshank re Trager's book *Dig Infinity!: The Life and Art of Lord Buckley* New York: Welcome Rain, 2002; & discographical detail from Michael Gray, *Song & Dance Man III: The Art of Bob Dylan*, London: Cassell Academic, 1999 & Continuum, 2000, p.591.]

***"Love and Theft"* [2001]** This is Dylan's 30th studio album, not counting compilations, and had the unfortunate release date of September 11, 2001. It was his first new studio album since *Time Out of Mind* four years earlier. The Dylan world seemed at once to divide into those finding it much less substantial and those taking to it far more wholeheartedly. All agreed that the two albums differ in nearly every respect.

DANIEL LANOIS' fingerprints are nowhere on *"Love and Theft"*; the musicians used are, for the first time, Dylan's Never-Ending Tour Band of the day, augmented by AUGIE MEYERS and his son; there are no obviously *great* songs–no equivalent of 'Not Dark Yet' or 'Highlands'. But on *"Love and Theft"* a tumult of generously packed minor songs bump up boisterously against each other, like tuba players in a charabanc bouncing off on the excursion of a lifetime, calling to and fro amongst themselves in excited dialogue about everything under the sun. Dylan's voice is almost completely shot here, yet what he does with it is most subtlely nuanced and shrewdly judged. And he is in such a good mood! This is the warmest, most outgoing, most good-humoured Bob Dylan album since *Nashville Skyline*, if not *The Basement Tapes*.

On *Time Out of Mind* he finds himself singing something that may be a brave thing to say but a terrible one to feel: 'My sense of humanity has gone down the drain.' On *"Love and Theft"* he has recovered it and is looking at that humanity fondly, through Damon Runyon eyes. His multiplicity of characters is created with warmth and wit and a sense of fun, as if Dylan himself has thrown off a great weight of portentousness and remembered a better self, in hock to neither the obligation to be profound nor the sour defensiveness brought on by fame.

On *Time Out of Mind* the onset of old age is fretted away at, as when on 'Highlands' he looks at these young people in the park and would swap lives 'with any of them / In a minute' if he could —and it's dealt with head on in 'Not Dark Yet'. It isn't everyone who wants a song about there being nothing to look forward to but decay and the diminution of one's powers, of course: but if you do, 'Not Dark Yet' is *it*. But on *"Love and Theft"*, old age is dealt with very differently: not as a theme, and not simplistically as a problem, but far more creatively, by Dylan's *enacting* a series of older persona, all with their own takes on life, their own quirks and absurdities and cares. As the songs jostle together, these enactments form an almost phantasmagoric throng, energised by a senior-citizen version of the surreal world Dylan gave us in *Tarantula* and the 'Clothes Line Saga', Mrs. Henry and the crazy people from 1965.

Old age is created in 3D on *"Love and Theft"*. Here, as old people do, the songs' narrators are always mentioning their relatives: 'my mother', 'my father', 'my uncle', 'my grandmother', 'my cousin', my 'Aunt Sally / But you know she's not really my aunt'. Here 'my brother got killed in the war' and 'My sister she ran off and got married / Never was heard of any more'. Here too, throughout this body of song, Dylan creates, again as old people do, sudden conversational non sequiturs, sometimes of embarrassing directness—never more touchingly than on 'Lonesome Day Blues' when (combining the non sequitur with the citing of your relatives), he sings that he is '. . . forty miles from the mill—I'm droppin' it into overdrive / Settin' my dial on the radio—I wish my mother was still alive.'

As with older people too, you can't always be sure whether they're talking of yesterday or a hundred years ago, or sometime in between, or even further back. Different time-frames slide across in front of each other, frequently in mid-sentence. The album is soaked in hypersensitivity to the atmosphere of period. We know, hearing those lines about being 'forty miles from the mill' and 'droppin' it into overdrive' that we are in some patch of the 20th century, a time relatively recent yet infinitely long gone. It's recent enough that there are automobiles with radios and overdrive, yet it certainly isn't the present: no-one measures where they are by their distance from the mill anymore; the mills have all closed down. This is like driving through Georgia in the 1940s. At other moments, clearly we're in the time of the American Civil War, as when 'They went down the Ohio, the Cumberland, the Tennessee / All the rest of them rebel rivers'—and a fine example, that, of the undimmed expressiveness Dylan can bring to his maimed voice (when he bothers, as he so rarely does now in concert).

At other moments on the album, we are in the present, or comparing the present with the past—as when, for instance, immediately before those Civil War rivers flow, Dylan gives us that contemporary equivalent to the romantic dialogue of Romeo and Juliet, sketching so deftly the gracelessness of today's spotty teenagers' talk, not with scorn but warm understanding and comic relish: 'Romeo, he said to Juliet, "You got a poor complexion. / It doesn't give your appearance a very youthful touch!" / Juliet, she said back to Romeo / "Why don't you just shove off if it bothers you so much?"' (See also **Shakespeare in *"Love and Theft"*.**)

Other comic moments on the album are those created by the corny jokes that are yet another imaginative device for inhabiting the older person's world. The songs are dotted with just the kind of creaking joke you groan at and laugh at when your old uncle comes out with it, yet they tend to carry other resonances too as when Dylan fleetingly conjures a whole era from the sheer Groucho Marxism of that joke in 'Po' Boy', 'Poor boy, in the hotel called the Palace of Gloom / Calls down to room service, says, "Send up a room".' A different resonance is called up by the same song's equally creaky joking pun: 'Knockin' on the door, I say, "Who is it and where are you from?" / Man says, "Freddy!" I say, "Freddy who?" He says, "Freddy or not here I come."' In tandem with its silly joke is the knocking on another door, opening with one of those 'shocks of recognition' onto a particular fragment of the past, one of those old records that helped to midwife the birth of rock'n'roll. On 'The House of Blue Lights', by Ella Mae Morse with Freddie Slack & His Orchestra, which JERRY LEE LEWIS named one of the favourites of his youth and which LITTLE RICHARD mentions in the lyric of 'Good Golly Miss Molly', the male voice pronounces: 'Well what you say, baby? You look ready as Mr. Freddie!'

The fused intimations of mortality and mid-60s Dylan do not take the form of easy self-imitation: rather, the writing on this album—and there is writing in abundance—is always placed in the service of faithful character creation, so that we find in 'Floater (Too Much to Ask)', the song in which we've found those rivers and those adolescents, a line so unDylanesque as to be striking: namely, when the narrator sings that you 'Gotta get up near the teacher if you can / If you wanna learn anything'.

In one key respect, *"Love and Theft"* does not differ from, but rather goes further than, *Time Out of Mind*, and that is in its use of verbatim quotation from a multiplicity of sources. Like the traditional women's work of 'heritage' quilting, Dylan here makes a huge aural patchwork bedspread out of rags and snippets torn from other people's work: from other voices. It is a crucial part of the album's multi-layering–a multi-layering of time as well as place. Thus we have not only rock'n'roll, Shakespeare, Mark Twain and Tennessee Williams allusions, plus, as ever with Dylan, lines from old blues records, but a raid on a Civil War general's speech, a piece of dialogue from F. Scott Fitzgerald (from *The Great Gatsby*), at least 12 phrases lifted from the English translation of the Japanese writer Junichi Saga's book *Confessions of a Yakuza* and a great deal more besides. (Saga's book is in turn an oral history itself, told to him by the gangster of the title.)

The album title *"Love and Theft"* is itself thieved (which is why, uniquely in Dylan's canon, it comes with quotation marks around it), from the 1990s academic book by Eric Lott, *Love and Theft: Blackface Minstrelsy and the American Working Class*–itself a multi-faceted work on a swathe of topics of special interest to Dylan: to the Dylan who speaks, in GREIL MARCUS' phrases, for 'the old, weird America', for 'the invisible republic' but a book that also re-examines the earliest forms of American music, the first major artistic relationship between black and white cultures, and thus the connections between the minstrel show and American literature (as when Lott writes, for example, that 'Without the minstrel show there would have been . . . no *Adventures of Huckleberry Finn*'). But Lott's title itself, as he said in an interview, is 'a riff on one of Leslie Fiedler's; he wrote a famous book of literary criticism called *Love and Death in the American Novel*.' (He added, in jest: 'I think I'm going to call my next book *Time Out of Mind*.')

Dylan himself once said that *"Love and Theft"* is based on the 12-bar delta blues, and the old blues work much like the album, by assembling common-stock phrases, common-stock verses, and by recombining them, with tweaks and mis-hearings and spontaneous alteration, making something new. There is a specific homage to CHARLEY PATTON on the album, and Patton himself was a master of this process of reconfiguration, using borrowed lines and floating verses–'floaters', in a word–to create something singular and personal. Dylan's sources are in part more self-consciously chosen, and deliberately range wider and deeper through era and location, but only partly. It's in the very nature of those old blues that memory cannot log it all; he surely knows, for instance, that the *"Love and Theft"* song 'Lonesome Day Blues', the album's most overtly blues-structured song, has a title that was used long ago by BLIND WILLIE McTELL and others; he didn't *necessarily* recall consciously, though, that his own opening line, 'Well today has been a long old lonesome day' is taken almost verbatim (Dylan's alert use of that opening 'Well' replacing the original's 'Yes') from the very first recording made by Texas Alexander, his 'Long Lonesome Day Blues' of 1927.

Yet if the process can never be wholly conscious, by the nature of the process *and* of human memory, the conscious part of the work Dylan has constructed takes this archaeology of shard and fragment much further even than did *Time Out of Mind*; and via the imaginative persona Dylan has chosen to make dominant–via the strategy of his creative enactments of old age–he makes all this scrutiny of memory and rehabilitation of history that much more vividly human, more poignant, more richly layered.

At the same time, as with that worn-out old tobacco-worker narrator in 'Floater', these old geezers Dylan creates so freshly here, with their fitful, sometimes fruit-machining memories, they are *today's* old people (and thereby the relatives, for better or worse, of today's young people): they are true to the spirit of Bob Dylan's generation of oldies–they haven't renounced rock'n'roll or had the loyalties of the 1950s or 60s removed from their souls, nor lost the acute awareness that we stand hearing all these voices of the fractured past in the dark world of today.

Has there ever been another such album? Absolutely not. It is, deliberately and liberatingly, the album of an old bloke in his garden shed–but it is incontestably *Bob Dylan*'s album. It is *Highway 61 Revisited* on a bus pass. The turbulent whole is unquestionably a real Dylan album: one of the ten or 12 you'd have to rescue if God were determined to destroy all the rest.

[Recorded NY, 9–25 May 2001, released as Columbia 504364 2 (& as 2-LP vinyl set Columbia 504364 1), US & Europe, 11 Sep 2001.

Ella Mae Morse with Freddie Slack & His Orchestra: 'The House of Blue Lights' c/w 'Hey Mr. Postman', Capitol 251 (78rpm), US, 1946. Blind Willie McTell & 'Ruby Glaze' (as Ruby Glaze–Hot Shot Willie): 'Lonesome Day Blues', Atlanta, 22 Feb 1932. Texas Alexander: 'Long Lonesome Day Blues', NY, 11 Aug 1927.

Eric Lott, *Love and Theft: Blackface Minstrelsy and the American Working Class*, New York: OUP, 1993, & quoted from interview by David McNair & Jayson Whitehead, Gadfly Online, seen at *www.gadflyonline.com/12-10-01/book-ericlott.html*, 5 Dec 2005. For good detailed scrutinies of the album, see Andrew Muir, *Troubadour: Early and Late Songs of Bob Dylan*, Bluntisham, UK: Woodstock Publications, 2003; Stephen Scobie, *Alias Bob Dylan Revisited*, Calgary, Canada: Red Deer College Press, 2003; and the article '*"Love and Theft"*, or How Dylan's Mind Multipies the Smallest Matter', by Chris Rollaston, *The Bridge* no.14, Gateshead, UK, winter 2002, pp.34–64.]

'Love Henry' [1993] On *World Gone Wrong* this ancient song becomes one of the most beautiful recordings Dylan has ever made, and its ancientness does not make it, in Dylan's consciousness, a relic. The sleevenotes to the album are part of his armoury of insistence on the contemporary relevance of such material: the continuing value and pertinence of both the poetry of the old blues world and that of medieval balladry. The title-character in 'Love Henry' is presented immediately in Dylan's sleevenote as 'Henry—modern corporate man . . .' and his adversary as a tough mama: a 'fairy queen exploiter'.

This thrilling CHILD ballad is essentially Child no.68, 'Young Hunting', of which he gives 11 versions, all from Scotland, but which is offered with over 40 variants in Bronson's standard work *The Traditional Tunes of the Child Ballads—Vol. II*. Dylan sings Bronson Variant 19 almost word for word with the addition of one verse from elsewhere. Bronson comments that this begins as a Scottish ballad, or that if it began in England it has left no trace there (which is odd, granted that one of the variants he includes is set firmly in Yorkshire), and seems to have passed straight from Scotland to the US, 'where it has enjoyed a great vogue in our own century—at least in the Appalachians.' Its early history remains murky, as is its relationship to the ballads 'Lady Isabel' and 'The Elfin Knight'. However, we do know that versions called 'Young Redin' and 'Earl Richard' were in collections published as far back as 1827.

Dylan's treatment is dark, serious and fully committed to the mystery of traditional song, but it doesn't detract from this to enjoy surveying the song's variants, which is an informal process of deconstruction. You see the elements retained and lost along the way, those distorted by design and accident: perhaps misheard and then passed on as in a game of Chinese Whispers. You see how common-stock ingredients drift in and out of the core narrative, and the relishable, comic ways in which the incandescent poetry of some versions collapses into ungainly, fatuous bathos in others.

This is the one Dylan sings so immaculately: 'Get down get down Love Henry she cried / And stay all night with me / I have gold chains and the finest I have / I'll apply them all to thee. / I can't get down an' I shan't get down / Or stay all night with thee / Some pretty little girl in Cornersville / I love far better than thee. / He laid his head on a pillow of down / Kisses she gave him three / With a penny knife that she held in her hand / She murdered mortal he. / Get well, get well Love Henry she cried / Get well get well said she / Oh don't you see my own heart's blood / A-flowing down so free? / She took him by his long yellow hair / And also by his feet / She plunged him into well water where / It runs both cold and deep. / Lie there lie there Love Henry she cried / Till the flesh rots off your bones / Some pretty little girl in Cornersville / Will mourn for your return. / Hush up hush up my parrot she cried / Don't tell no news on me / Oh these costly beads around my neck / I'll apply them all to thee. / Fly down fly down pretty parrot she cried / And light on my right knee / The doors to your cage shall be decked with gold / And hung on a willow tree. / I won't fly down and I can't fly down / And light on your right knee / A girl who would murder her own true love / Would kill a little bird like me.'

There are three moments where Dylan's voice allows a hint of variation from this version. As Dylan sings the second verse, it isn't clear whether he has Love Henry sing 'I won't fly down and I shan't fly down' or 'I won't fly down and I shouldn't fly down'—which would suggest his immediate wavering, preparing the way for his laying his head on her pillow. Then, Dylan sings 'She plunged him into well water where' as if singing 'water wet', which ought to sound unhelpfully obvious, a clumsy tautology; yet it somehow has a rightness that appeals, by elucidating further her heightened instability of mind: she's so intensely aware of the feel and look and sound of everything at this point, that a suggestion of her awareness of the water's wetness is all of a piece with her awareness of its coldness. Thirdly, Dylan sings her plea to the parrot such that you cannot tell for certain whether he sings 'Don't tell no news on me' or whether he makes it the even better 'Don't trill no news on me'.

At any rate, this version is a taut ellipse—taut even though it uses all those echoing repetitions that bounce back and forth within its dialogues: 'Get down, get down. . . . I can't get down and I shan't get down'; 'Fly down, fly down. . . . I won't fly down and I can't fly down'. But in omitting part of the story and simplifying a further part, it gives us a particular take on the motives and characters that fuller versions do not bear out.

These begin with the hero going hunting, and then returning to his lover, usually named as Lady Margaret. When she welcomes him back and invites him to her bed, he tells her he prefers another—the usual phrase here the blunt one that he loves her 'far better than thee'—or even his wife: 'For I have a far better bride than you / To enjoy when I go home.' In any case, this already shifts the moral picture, showing the hero as faithless to the one rather than faithful to the other. And exceptionally tactless too. Then, adding arrogance to his other qualities, he no sooner tells her how much less attractive she is than the third party he's never mentioned before, than he bends down from on high on his horse—a 'milk-white steed' in some variants—and kisses her. (Bob Dylan's brilliant updating of this is his sleevenote description of Love Henry as 'career minded, limousine double parked'.) Enraged, she stabs him, and he realises he is mortally wounded. Filled with remorse, she sobs out her imprecations that he should live. ('Get well, get well, Love Henry, she cried . . .')

At this point two common-stock ingredients drift through the picture like character-actor stalwarts whose faces you recognise from a hundred films but whose names you don't feel a need to know. First, the heroine promises that if he'll just hold on she'll summon a doctor and he will heal the hero. This is exactly the formula met in songs like 'Jack-a-Roe', 'Across the Rocky Mountains' and even 'The Unfortunate Rake', and the same words too, with 'town' rhymed with 'wound': 'For there's a doctor in yonder town / Can cure your mortal wound' or 'You shall have all the doctors in the whole round town / For to heal and cure your wounds'–to which the stabbed lover replies along the lines of 'There hain't a doctor but God alone / Can cure those wounded wounds.' Second, in many versions the dead man is strapped back on his horse and sent riding off again, so that the body will be found elsewhere, though somehow it always end up deep in water. (In rare instances, she sends him off not to place the crime elsewhere but in the forlorn hope that he'll reach the doctor in time.) Within these stanzas it sometimes happens that when he's tied back on his steed and sent off, his murderess makes sure that, like Froggie, he goes 'with a sword and pistol by his side'.

These stalwarts having made their brief appearances, the narrative continues with the disposal of the body, usually down a well. This is often achieved with the help of the heroine's servants. Thus Dylan's version's one touch of bathos–when she picks him up by his hair 'and also by his feet'–has been inherited from older formulations in which there are staff to attend to these matters, so that 'Some took him by the golden hair / Some took him by the feet' (a more seemly phrasing).

Two main alternative resolutions follow this. In one, as with Dylan's, the heroine realises that the crime has been observed by the bird and either attempts to buy its silence or else, soon abandoning this ploy, tries to lure it within killing distance by crude coaxing and lavish promises. The bird is not that bird-brained, and states its suspicions and refusal with varying degrees of bluntness. When, as with the Dylan variant, the song ends there, it leaves the bird's power hovering over the heroine, and this might be thought a refined, unending punishment; but this is a foreshortened ending, omitting a further exchange between woman and bird, in which, just as suddenly as she switched with the hero from loving invitation to murder, so she drops her politesse towards Polly, switching abruptly to shouting straightforwardly at it that 'If I had a bow all in my hand / And an arrow to a string / I'd shoot you through the very heart / Among the leaves so green . . .' This merely brings the bird more plainly to blackmail as it retorts along these lines: 'If you had your bow arrow / Your bow arrow and string / I'd fly away to yonder green / And tell what I have seen.'

This is usually the end of the song, so that it might be said Dylan's variant merely says the same in fewer stanzas. Occasionally, though, this is still not the end, for the heroine then dies too. In Child's variant B8, ungainliness of form and content become one, as we come to the comic awkwardness of the penultimate line: 'With her heart like a stone / She stood there alone / Then she walked to the side of the well / Soon she fainted and fell over sideways / And down she fell, fell, fell.' One or two examples have the heroine so filled with remorse that she commits suicide. Yet this is only one of two main endings. The other may or may not include a bird, but nemesis comes not by feathers but by blood and fire. The body being discovered by the authorities, the murderess then seeks to blame the servants. However, the victim's body remains inactive in their presence, his wounds by now 'As white as a linen clout / But as the traitor she cam near / His wounds they gushéd out!' When they try to burn the servant, the flames don't take. Trial by fire finally proves the guilt of the heroine. Verdict and punishment are one. In Child's first example, which gives us the full tale, the 'wylie' parrot's refusal to 'come doun, come doun' occurs in verse 14. It takes a further ten verses to reach the end of the song.

There is altogether between these variants a great clamouring of elements wanting to be in the song. The Scots version just quoted begins with Young Redin out hunting. When he reaches 'his true-love's' home, with 33 lords accompanying him, the heroine tells him 'Ye're welcome here, my young Redin / For coal and candle licht / And sae are ye, my young Redin / To bide wi' me the nicht.' That is to say, the woman is offering the civilities of shelter and accommodation to the hunting party, and extends her lover the politeness of asking, instead of assuming, if he will spend the night with her. He, with the sensitivity of the boar he's been hunting, accepts the warming and lighting of the guest-rooms but tells her he's no intention of sleeping in *her* bed because '. . . thrice as fair a ladie as thee / Meets me at Brandie's well.' Having told her that, they go to their separate chambers, and then he comes sneaking along the corridor to her room (again it's stressed here that she is his 'true-love'), finds her crying and lies in her arms. He's stabbed with the penknife; she asks her chamber-maid Meggy (her 'bouer-woman') to take away the body and is told to sort it out herself. The heroine pleads: 'O heal this deed on me, Meggy / O heal this deed on me', and promises her a reward of silken finery. So they put his boots back on and throw him in the deepest part of the river Clyde. The parrot then causes its usual trouble and eventually the fire burns the bouer-woman's hands and then burns '. . . the fause, fause arms, / That young Redin lay in.'

But in time and North America, the elements that introduce themselves include what may be seen as a sort of 'poetic' neatening-up: the heroine offers not hospitality but a bribe to lure the hero to her bed, in exactly similar terms to the bribe she then offers the servants and the third set of bribes she offers to the parrot. Form being inseparable from content, this change in the structural pattern of the song reverses our perception of who is the goodie and who the baddie in the tale. The Dylan version omits the hunting and the servants but retains the parallel bribing of man and bird, so that it loses both the heroine's civility and ill-treatment from the beginning and the bribing of the servant in the middle, and therefore ends up retaining two bribings (making another of the many doublings contained within the song).

Despite the disappearance of the chamber-maid, an echo of the conversation between lady and servant is retained in Dylan's version. The lady's plea to the servant has become a plea to the parrot (a plea not there in 'Young Redin'), changing from 'Oh heal this deed on me' to 'Don't trill no news on me'. As we've seen, Dylan's version also retains the phrases that used to describe the help in moving the hero's body by the now-abolished servants. It retains too a vestige of the dialogue about whether the now-abolished doctors can make him well again when she is immediately sorry for what she's done and begs him to get well, as he responds with 'Oh don't you see my own heart's blood A-flowing down so free' but has dropped the elaboration that only God can save him now.

In all probability, though, in dropping the doctors, the Dylan variant removes an ingredient that was never there in the first place and was introduced in North America only by mistake. Tristram P. Coffin points out that the sending for doctors 'is entirely absent from the Scots tradition that supplied all the texts in Child. It is distinctly possible, therefore, that it is derived from the "send for the king's duckers" episode that does appear in Child. . . . Thus may the searching of the waters for the body—the duckers' function—have been transformed . . .'

Yet mishearing or transforming the by-then-meaningless 'duckers' may not be how the doctors got summoned into the song: as noted, sending for the doctors (with the 'town' / 'wound' pairing) is a common-stock ingredient. At any rate, by the time of Dylan's 'Love Henry', it has been introduced and dropped again. Meanwhile the other sweetheart, who shifts from 'Brandie's well' to 'the girl that I've left on the Arkansas line' to 'a girl in Yorkshire land' to 'in the Eden land' to 'that pretty little girl in Gospel Land' to 'a bonny lass in a merry green land', has become an inhabitant of Cornersville, Tennessee, due south of Nashville and 20 miles north of the Alabama border. This makes perfect sense, granted that the version Dylan sings is, with an extra verse added at the end, the one collected by Byron Arnold in his *Folksongs of Alabama*, published in 1950, from the singing of one Lena Hill of Lexington, Alabama, five years earlier. Lexington is only *just* below the Tennessee state line, and the old highway runs north-east from there to Cornersville, less than 40 miles away.

It's curious, then, that while these antiquated 'duckers' are amended, and knights and Lords become nicknamed lads called Henry, and ladies and maidens become girls from Arkansas, and the parrot sits up in anything from a willow to a vine, or becomes a bird in the street outside a bar-room, or doesn't appear in the song at all, through all this the weapon remains unchanged (except for that one Spanish dart), and this in spite of the array of weaponry available in North America. (Whether Dylan is singing the corruption 'penny-knife' is impossible to decide.)

We're left with none of the comic clumsiness of other variants—variants that yield, between them, such mishandlings of the power of words as these: 'She called her housemaids three / Saying Lord Bonnie he has died in my lap; I think it's time he was taken away' (this from 'Lord Bonnie', collected in North Carolina: a version that has no parrot —no bird at all—and specifically has her say to the dead body 'Lie there, lie there, you false-hearted man'); 'I can't shut up and I won't shut up' and 'She picked him up all in her arms / Being very active and strong / And she throwed him into an old dry well / About sixty feet.'

Leaving the depth unspecified is doubly wise. It allows the creation of yet another of the song's neat pairings: the penknife plunges 'deep' into his heart, and the body plunges 'deep' into the water. And it avoids bathos. Once you start specifying how deep the well is, you're asking for risible variation, and this we get. 'About sixty feet' is the depth of the dry well. Most are full of water—in Yorkshire, aptly, the well is 'Where it rained so cold and deep'—and sometimes so deep that it is measured in fathoms, like the ocean: 'Sixteen fathoms deep'; 'Full thirty fathoms deep'; 'Some sixty fathoms deep'; plus the comically cautious 'Just about eighteen feet' and the splendidly incredible 'dew drop well' that is 'About forty-thousand feet deep.'

It may be that this Scottish dialect imprecation is seductively melodious, when sung, but seeing it on the page it's hard to imagine, even when the addressee is the parrot: 'Come doon, come doon, my pretty parrot / An pickle wheat aff my glue' (text V in Child); and the equally Scottish version collected by CARL SANDBURG, 'Little Scotch-ee' (which is also in Bronson), has the unwise addition of chickens: 'Are the chickens a-crowing for the middle of the night / Or are they a-crowing for day?'

While avoiding these dullard sore thumbs, Dylan's version inevitably dispenses too with a few attractive phrases. A usage that ties in with a blues phrase Dylan uses of his own 'Tough Mama'—'meat shakin' on your bones'—gives the apt, murderous toughness of one version of 'Young Hunting' in which 'till the flesh rots off your bones' is replaced by 'till the meat drops off your bones'. Nor is anything wrong with the Dylan version's description of the hero's blood 'A-flowing down so free"—yet the more unusual expressions chosen by others, though a risible list if stacked up alongside each other, offer an affecting poetic appeal considered singly, as in 'For don't you see my own heart's blood / Come twinkling down me knee?' and '. . . don't you see my own heart's blood / Is trinkling to my knees?', while in one version a chic and nifty pun is achieved, as the lady uses her knife, with the simple phrase 'She pierced him heartilee'. All in all, though, the version Dylan uses is as fine and sinuous a recreation of the song as could be wished for: a version full of mystery and poetry, loaded with menace and grace, and retaining vivid vestiges of ancientness–including, if you will, what Bronson calls 'a relic of belief in metempsychosis, the bird being the soul of the dead lover.'

Dylan will have selected his version from among the several or more he must know. One of these is a recording on–you'll never guess–the HARRY SMITH anthology. It is in fact the opening track of the entire 84-track set, Dick Justice's 1929 recording 'Henry Lee': a version with a different melody, a plodding, dull strum for its guitar accompaniment and a voice of now-touching naivété. The song is summarised in Smith's unmistakeable, endearing style as 'SCORNING OFFER OF COSTLY TRAPPINGS, BIRD REFUSES AID TO KNIGHT THROWN IN WELL BY LADY'. This is an unusual twist on the customary narrative and suggests a reading that is eccentric even by Harry Smith's standards. Why would he think it is the dead 'Lovin' Henry Lee' who requests the bird's help (or then threatens to shoot it from a hundred feet down in the well), especially since the bird's response is the standard one, that 'A girl would murder her own true love / Would kill a little bird like me'? Despite the yokel charm of the vocal, and touches such as 'the girl I have in that merry green land', this is in essence an urban version, bringing into the action 'you ladies in the town' and with phrasing delightfully more redolent of the cruel .44 than the ladylike weapon cited: 'With the little penknife held in her hand / She plugged him through and through.'

Other recordings include Peggy Seeger's 'Henry Lee' (probably learnt from the Dick Justice version); John Jacob Niles' 'Lady Margot and Love Henry'; 'Lowe Bonnie' by JIMMIE TARLTON (its text and melody the final, 43rd version in Bronson, which starts with 'a hunting young man' who is offered 'white chocolate tea' but declines, saying endearingly, and rather like the White Rabbit, 'But I haven't got a moment to spare'; this version includes doctors but avoids parrots: a very different lyric from Dylan's) and even a 'Henry Lee' by P.J. Harvey, Nick Cave & the Bad Seeds. June Tabor's and Hedy West's versions (both the untitled Bronson Variant 22) treat the song as a maypole-tripping throwaway to be pranced through unthinkingly, instead of treating it with respect and allowing its mystical depths to work on them. Dylan will have heard more than one of these, but implies in his sleevenotes that he takes his version from performances or a recording he remembers by TOM PALEY.

Paley in turn took it from the Byron Arnold book of Alabama folk songs, and Arnold field-recorded it from a woman in a tiny Alabama town in 1945 who says that she arrived at *her* version 'when a girl'. What a brilliant poetic instinct she had, this unschooled girl. As noted, there are many looser versions of less power and resonance, and many with no special faults but no distinction either. While paying tribute to the middle-aged Bob Dylan for picking out a version of the ballad that compresses it into so rich and taut a form, let's also admire the intelligence of judgement and the poetic maturity of Lena Hill of Lexington, Alabama.

Dylan all along recognised the power of traditional song itself. He has said so many times, reasserting warmly (in the *Biograph* interview) the thrall in which he stands to traditional music: 'The thing about rock'n'roll is that for me anyway it wasn't enough. . . . I knew that when I got into folk music it was more of a serious type of thing. The songs are filled with more despair, more sadness, more triumph, more faith in the supernatural, much deeper feelings . . .' You could hardly look for a more exact summary of his approach to, and his valuing of, a song like his chosen version of 'Love Henry'. It explains the seriousness he brings to it.

He begins with a guitar part that doesn't announce at once whether this is going to be a black song or a white: it doesn't trailer 'ballad', 'blues' or recognisable genre. It just pulls you into its musical well. Then the vocal comes in, more muttered than sung and yet most beautifully sung: a sustained and concentrated whole, nuzzlingly intimate, smouldering yet fastidious. And without anything so obtrusive as a vocal mannerism, he gives us the best breathing and dyings-away of any Bob Dylan vocal for many years, soaked in regret and consternation, mortal fear and supernatural dread. The unexpected extra two musical notes he adds at the end of the word 'deep', to make it 'dee-ee-eep', is done not only long after you assume that the first note and syllable will continue its long dying-out, but is effected with the most understated discretion you will ever hear: at light-years' remove from easy pop cliché; the slightest possible pause on 'mourn' is likewise an irreproachable gesture, so subtly done as to be barely discernible, such that what we're offered is a performance that demands, and amply rewards, the closest possible attention.

This is itself the optimum matching of subject matter to approach: Dylan inhabits the character of the murderous heroine so well that it's as if her secret pathology, her suppressed jealousies and seething, quiet derangement have been kept so tightly clutched in her heart that the listener must put an ear close to the singer's chest to hear at all the rangey, fitful ebb and flow of an infantile anger, dark despair and spectral desperation.

[Francis James Child, *The English and Scottish Popular Ballads, 1882–98*: a standard work. Bertrand Harris Bronson, *The Traditional Tunes of the Child Ballads—Vol. II*, Princeton, NJ: Princeton University Press, 1962, pp.60–82. Tristram Potter Coffin, *The British Traditional Ballad in North America*, Austin, TX: University of Texas Press, 1950 & 1977. Carl Sandburg, *An American Songbag*, New York: Harcourt Brace, 1927.

Harry Smith's *American Folk Music*, Folkways FP251–253, NY, 1952, CD-reissued Smithsonian Folkways SFW 40090, Washington, D.C., 1997; Dick Justice: 'Henry Lee', Chicago, 20 May 1929, issued ditto. Peggy Seeger: 'Henry Lee', *nia*, Prestige PRS 13005, *nia*. John Jacob Niles: 'Lady Margot and Love Henry', *nia*, Tradition TRD 1046, *nia*. Darby & Tarlton (but this track is only Tarlton): 'Lowe Bonnie', Atlanta, 3 Dec 1930; Folksong Society of Minnesota LP KB3796, Minneapolis-St. Paul, 1960 (very rare: but Dylan was in the right place at the right time to hear it), 1st widely circulated on *Darby and Tarlton*, Old Timey OT112, El Cerrito, CA, 1970s, CD-reissued *On the Banks of the Lonely River*, County CTY 3503, Floyd, VA, 1994. P.J. Harvey, Nick Cave & the Bad Seeds: 'Henry Lee', *nia*, REP 46195, *nia*. June Tabor: 'Love Henry' (demo), UK, Mar 1990, *Circle Dance*, Hokey Pokey cassette, London, 1990. Hedy West: 'Love Henry' *nia*, *Ballads*, *nia*, 1967.

Tom Paley: 'Love Henry', Beckenham, UK, 1964, on Peggy Seeger & Tom Paley: *Who's Gonna Shoe Your Pretty Little Feet?*, Topic 12T113, London, 1964. Information that Paley took 'Love Henry' from *Folksongs of Alabama* is from Paley (London, phone-conversation with this writer, 22 Apr 1999).]

'Love Sick' [1997] One of the immediate responses to *Time Out of Mind*, on which 'Love Sick' is the opening track, was disappointment at Dylan's automatic concentration on Lurve as subject matter (though concentration seemed not much in evidence). Across most of the album this apparently exhausted topic demanded our attention without offering one tangible feeling, evocative moment or observant sentence. All this croaking phlegm about lost love, all this cocooned preoccupation with it, this trying to sound tragic about vanished impossible perfect loves: was there nothing else to engage the intelligent adult's interest, or to be written about?

He *promises* something else, in the opening song, summing up the situation with admirable terseness: 'I'm sick of love / I hear the clock tick / This kind of love—/ I'm love sick', yet for much of the album 'this kind of love' seems the only topic, and an awareness of time running out does not seem to concentrate its singer's mind on other matters. Far from sounding like the mature work of a major artist in middle-age, dealing with the serious questions of life, or even with its small pleasures, all this crying in the doorway, calling out his baby's name, enchained and haunted by the ghost of an old love, all this wondering if you'll be true—it sounded more like the posturing of a spoilt celebrity hamming up gravitas.

The production, for all DANIEL LANOIS' alchemical skills, sometimes accentuates this sense of a sham. Lanois explained exactly the *intention* behind the distorted vocal sound on 'Love Sick': 'We treated the voice almost like a harmonica when you over-drive it through a small guitar amplifier.' That's spot on: the track's distorted sound is familiar because it does recreate the harmonica sound on things like the King Biscuit radio shows of the early 1950s. But does it work? If it gives 'Love Sick', and therefore the album's opening moments, a sort of stark drama, it comes very close to contrived starkness and melodrama.

'I'm walkin' . . .', announces this sepulchral voice, 'through streets that are dead': and if Boris Karloff isn't lurking behind a lamp-post, LEONARD COHEN surely is.

['Love Sick', Miami, FL, 13–28 Jan 1997, *Time Out of Mind*, 30 Sep 1997. Two 4-track 'Love Sick' CD singles were issued: 'CD1' comprised a live 'Love Sick' (Grammy Awards performance, NY, 25 Feb 1998) + live cuts of 'Cold Irons Bound' & 'Cocaine Blues' (both LA, 16 Dec 1997) & 'Born in Time' (Newark, NJ, 1 Feb 1998), Columbia COL 665997 5, US, 1998. 'CD2' comprised the album version of 'Love Sick' + live cuts of 'Can't Wait' (LA, 20 Dec 1997) & 'Roving Gambler' (LA, 17 Dec 1997) & 'Blind Willie McTell' (Wantaugh, NY, 17 Aug 1997, & not as stated on the sleevenote), Columbia COL 665997 2, US, 1998. The song's live début was at Bournemouth, UK, 1 Oct 1997 (the day after its album release); since then it has become one of his 30 most performed songs.]

Lovelle, Herb [1924 -] Herbert E. Lovelle was born in New York on June 1, 1924. A jazz drummer, he lowered himself to play on a number of rock'n' roll, folk and rock records in the 1950s and 60s, including playing for LaVern Baker on 'Tweedle Dee' and for (or against) Bob Dylan on the *Freewheelin'* sessions of November 1 and 14, 1962. The results can be heard on 'Mixed-Up Confusion' and 'Rocks and Gravel', neither of which made it to the album.

Jazz musicians generally regarded the blues, too, as beneath them, and thereby disqualified themselves from performing any of it well. A splendid tirade from BIG BILL BROONZY against these people is quoted in ALAN LOMAX's *The Land Where the Blues Began*: 'Got they dark glasses on. Some of um wearin' their little bebop goatees . . .'

Since 1988 Herb Lovelle has moved into acting, starting as a hospital clerk in Sidney Lumet's *Running on Empty*. He has a moustache but no little bebop goatee.

[Alan Lomax, *The Land Where the Blues Began*, London: Methuen edn., p.455.]

***Lovesick* [album, 2004]** See **co-option of real music by advertising, the.**

lowlands, the In Dylan's song 'Sad-Eyed Lady of the Lowlands', his metaphoric reference is surely to the lowlands of the Mississippi Delta: the lowlands which imperilled people down in the floods, where all those crashes on the levee happened, where all that high water was everywhere, and which have in turn flooded American folk consciousness. These are the lowlands that spread across *Blonde on Blonde*, an album saturated in the blues.

The flooding of the delta only became a problem when agriculture intensified, so that instead of the annual flood replenishing the land naturally, it threatened the new inhabitants–imported Chinese as well as black labour–and infrastructure. Levees had not been needed before this intensification. Indeed the *forests* of the Delta were still being cleared in the years just before the 1920s. In *A Turn in the South*, 1989, V.S. Naipaul tells of meeting Louise, a woman of 80, in Jackson in 1987, who remembers the wilderness: 'The land hadn't been cleared and travel was hard. . . . *And it was beautiful country* . . . great oaks that had not been harvested. This was before the plantations. . . . It was a land of flowers, all kinds of wild iris and wild violets, water lilies and alligators. . . . I had malaria every summer when I was a child. It took a while to clear the Delta. It flooded every spring. When I was a little girl–say in 1915–they were still clearing it. They would go and chop around these mighty oaks and they would let them die and then they would cut them. . . . I took it for granted. I played in the woods. . . . It was a privilege to live in the Delta. At night we would hear animals in the forest. A panther. It sounded like a woman crying.' (Naipaul comments: 'There is no landscape like the landscape of our childhood. For Louise . . . the "big cotton patch" that the planters had created in the Delta was a disfiguring of the forest . . . [but] for Mary, born in the Delta forty years later, there would be no landscape like the flat, stripped land she had grown up in. She said: "I think there is nothing more beautiful than the flat, flat land and the big, big sky."') ALAN LOMAX's *The Land Where the Blues Began*, 1993, has a good description of the clearing of the jungle to create the cotton wealth of the Delta, and argues that African agricultural know-how created the Delta farmland from the wilderness.

Though the Delta flooded annually, 1927 brought a spectacularly big flood, over an area the size of Scotland; workers were kept in camps at gunpoint to make them repair the levees; and blues-singers were called in to help in the propaganda effort to get people to come to do flood-relief work. As BIG BILL BROONZY once explained to a European audience, 'They sent for a lot of musicians. They didn't have to send for me 'cos I was already there . . . and whoever wrote the best song got 500 dollars. So Bessie [Smith] got the 500 dollars, so we always played hers . . . "Back-Water Blues".' (Not that it matters in this context, but folklorist David Evans has recently established that Bessie Smith's song was originally composed in response to a different flood altogether: a Christmas Day flood that struck Nashville in 1926.)

Dylan himself performed her song at his first real concert, at New York City's Carnegie Chapter Hall on November 4, 1961. It opens like this: 'It rained five days and the clouds turned as dark as night / It rained five days and the clouds turned as dark as night / Lotta trouble takin' place, Lord in the lowlands that night'–which is interesting for its conventional prefiguring of Dylan's unconventional 'She can take the dark out of the nighttime and paint the daytime black' (a perfect blues line) and for that specific citing (and siting) of 'the lowlands'.

Forty years later he returns to the subject in the *"Love and Theft"* song 'High Water (For CHARLEY PATTON)', which consciously builds from the levee of Patton's own 'High Water Everywhere Part 1' and 'Part 2'. Patton is remembering the 1927 flood, and his opening phrase is 'Well, backwater done rose . . .' He doesn't use the phrase 'the lowlands', but he catalogues where they're under water all through the song, as he aspires to their opposite: 'I would go to the hilly country but they got me barred', he sings halfway through 'Part 1', and then ends with a renewed resolve: 'I'm goin' back to the hilly country, won't be worried no more.'

[V.S. Naipaul: *A Turn in the South*, New York: Knopf, 1989. Alan Lomax: *The Land Where the Blues Began*, New York: Pantheon, 1993. Bill Broonzy quote: introducing his own 'Backwater Blues' [sic], 12–13 Jul 1957, *The Bill Broonzy Story*, Verve MGM-3000-5 (5-LP box set), US, *nia*. Bessie Smith: 'Back-Water Blues', NY, 17 Feb 1927. Charley Patton: 'High Water Everywhere Part I' and 'High Water Everywhere Part II', Grafton, WI, c.Oct 1929.]

Lynch, Stan [1955 -] Stanley Lynch was born in Gainesville, Florida, home of almost all the members of TOM PETTY & THE HEARTBREAKERS, on May 21, 1955. He learnt to play drums, moved to Los Angeles and became a founding member of that group, remaining with it from its beginning in 1975 until he quit with some acrimony in 1994 (though he and the others seemed cordial later, and he took part in their Rock'n'Roll Hall of Fame induction, MC'd by JAKOB DYLAN, in 2002).

In 1985, Lynch began a regular writing and producing partnership with Don Henley; he collaborated on the Eagles' 10-million-selling album *Hell Freezes Over* and co-produced tracks on Henley's *The End of the Innocence* (the title track of which Bob Dylan has sung in concert). Lynch has also co-written songs with THE BYRDS, RINGO STARR, Toto, the Fabulous Thunderbirds and many more. As a session player he has worked with Jackson Browne, Aretha Franklin, the Eurythmics, T-BONE BURNETT, WARREN ZEVON and others.

His contribution to Dylan's work, however, was solely from within Tom Petty & the Heartbreakers.

[Source: mainly *www.gonegator.com/news/tom_petty_news_022003.asp*, seen online 5 Jun 2005.]

Lynne, Jeff [1947 -] Born in Birmingham, England, on December 30, 1947, Lynne came to prominence playing second fiddle to Roy Wood in the Move (actually, Wood played his own fiddle, Lynne played guitar), when the original line-up changed after the group's disastrous excursion into cabaret in the late 1960s. The first Move album with Lynne on it was *Looking On*, 1970. Lynne later formed the Electric Light Orchestra (originally intended as a Roy and Jeff collaboration), an increasingly successful, florid, corporate-rock outfit designed to reveal Lynne as the ultimate wannaBeatle. (The BEATLE he wanted to be was PAUL.)

Exactly the sort of person who can't see the point of Bob Dylan, Lynne became the least interesting TRAVELING WILBURY (the Graham Nash of that particular super-group), his heavy hand deleteriously present in the group's songwriting and production values.

MacColl, Ewan [1915 - 1989] There is no better introduction to the significance of two British communists, MacColl and A.L. Lloyd, to the folk scene that preceded 'the denim-clad and Dylanesque' than the second chapter of C.P. LEE's 1998 book *Like the Night: Bob Dylan and the Road to the Manchester Free Trade Hall*, which stresses the role of the Communist Party of Great Britain (CPGB) in keeping the post-World War II folk scene purist and traditional, and looks at the figures of MacColl and Lloyd within it.

(Lloyd—whose mid-1960s book *Folk Song in England* attempted to chart its subject's development in Marxist terms—is the large man with the menacing grimace sitting high up behind Dylan in those pictures from the latter's early British gig at the Singers Club party at the Pindar of Wakefield pub in Gray's Inn Road, London, on December 22, 1962. The Singers Club was run by MacColl and his wife Peggy Seeger, sister of PETE.)

MacColl, as C.P. Lee notes, typified 'all that was good and all that was bad about the Folk Revival'. The good is that he wrote fierce pro-proletarian songs of quality in the immediate post-war period, the best of which was 'Dirty Old Town' (opening line: 'I met my love by the gas works wall', and a song covered to great effect by the Pogues on their 1985 album *Rum, Sodomy & the Lash*); and, put together with Lloyd by ALAN LOMAX in England in 1951, MacColl and Lloyd produced a radical series of now-legendary radio programmes, 'Ballads and Blues', which placed alongside each other previously separate styles of music including British jazz, Calypso music and American blues. Later, with Seeger and Charles Parker, he pioneered the yet more radical so-called 'radio-ballad', an audio documentary format that looked at the lives of railway workers, fishermen, teenagers and so on, by combining songs and instrumental music with sound effects and, crucially, the recorded voices of 'ordinary people', the subjects of the documentaries. Earlier radio documentaries had always hired professional actors to do all the speaking.

What was bad was that MacColl was a hypocritical old Stalinist who was against anything innovative or non-CPGB yet whose own purity and uncommerciality were in doubt from the start. MacColl wasn't even his real name; it was a showbiz name. He was born James Miller, on January 25, 1915—and not in Scotland but in Salford, just outside Manchester, where he grew up. He was married three times, first to the distinguished British theatre figure Joan Littlewood (he was an actor and dramatist on the London stage before becoming a folksinger and man of the people) and then to a Jean Newlove, whom he left in 1956 to take up with the much younger Ms. Seeger (for whom he wrote the maudlin 'The First Time Ever I Saw Your Face').

Unsurprisingly, MacColl was famously quick to declare of Dylan that he was 'unable to see in him anything other than a youth of mediocre talent', and that 'Dylan to me is the perfect symbol of the anti-artist in society—the last resort of somebody who doesn't want to change the world. . . . I think his poetry is punk.' And on the other hand: 'Poetry? What poetry? . . . embarrassing fourth-grade schoolboy attempts . . .'

Within the fecund group of traditional songs known as the 'Unfortunate Rake' cycle, one version is 'The Trooper Cut Down in His Prime', which MacColl learnt from the Norfolk (UK) traditional singer Harry Cox and recorded. It ends with these lines: 'Then beat the drum slowly and play your fife lowly / And sound the Dead March as you carry me along . . .', which Dylan folds into his *Oh Mercy* song 'Where Teardrops Fall' as 'We've banged the drum slowly and played the fife lowly / You know the song in my heart', so neatly suggesting within his own song that the song in his heart is the Dead March.

Four years after *Oh Mercy*, when Dylan issued his sublime recording of the far more ancient ballad 'Love Henry' (on *World Gone Wrong*, 1993), he says he took the song from TOM PALEY. He doesn't specify that he took it from a recording, and certainly he watched live performances by Paley in the early 1960s, but nevertheless there is a Paley recording of the song—and Paley says that this, cut in 1964, was made at the home of Ewan MacColl and Peggy Seeger.

MacColl died on October 22, 1989. The contemporary singer Kirsty MacColl was his daughter. She died in a boating accident in December 2000, off the coast of Mexico.

[Ewan MacColl, 'A Symposium', *Sing Out!*, NY, Sep 1965; as quoted in *Broken Arrow*, the Neil Young Appreciation Society quarterly, Scotland, no.93, Feb 2004, p.54; and *Sing Out!* again. Ewan MacColl: 'The Trooper Cut Down in His Prime', 1958; issued on *Bless 'Em All*, Riverside RLP 12-642, NY, 1958; collected on *The Unfortunate Rake: A Study in the Evolution of a Ballad*, various artists, compiled by Kenneth Goldstein, Folkways FS3805, NY, 1960.

C.P. Lee, *Like the Night: Bob Dylan and the Road to the Manchester Free Trade Hall*, London: Helter Skelter, 1998; updated edition, *Like the Night Revisited*, London: Helter Skelter, 2004. Tom Paley: 'Love Henry', Beckenham, Kent, UK, 1964, issued on *Peggy Seeger & Tom Paley: Who's Gonna Shoe Your Pretty Little Feet?*, Topic 12T113, London, 1964. Paley recording info from Michael Gray: *Song & Dance Man III: The Art of Bob Dylan*, p.774, footnote.]

MacLeish, Archibald [1892 - 1982] Archibald MacLeish was born in Glencoe, Illinois, on May 7, 1892, graduated from Yale in 1915, served in World War I, took a Harvard law degree, edited *The New Republic*, practised law for a short period and in time became a distinguished poet, though too much influenced by T.S. ELIOT and EZRA POUND for many tastes. He was also a playwright and, as it were, an official appointee, active in academic and public life, not least in becoming the US Government's Librarian of Congress from 1939–44, an Assistant Secretary of State for Cultural Affairs the following year, a US representative at UNESCO and Boylston Professor of Rhetoric and Oratory at Harvard from 1949 to 1962. He achieved these appointments despite earning the antipathy of the FBI and Senator Joe McCarthy and espousing Left Wing and anti-war causes, and after having been, in the 1920s, one of those poetry-writing Americans in Paris (1923–28).

His early poetry collections were *Tower of Ivory* (1917), *The Happy Marriage* (1924), *The Pot of Earth* (1925), *Streets in the Moon* (1926) and *The Hamlet of A. MacLeish* (1928). After returning from France he published *New Found Land* (1930), *Conquistador* (1932) and *Frescoes for Mr. Rockefeller's City* (1933). His best-known short poem, taking Horace's title, is *Ars Poetica*, and very neatly gives voice to the main tenets of the modernist poetics; it begins 'A poem should be palpable and mute / As a globed fruit' and ends 'A poem should not mean / But be.'

His verse plays include *Nobodaddy* (1926, *its* title taken from WILLIAM BLAKE's term for the unwise God stumbling around creating the flawed universe, 'Nobadaddy' being an ellipse of 'nobody's Daddy'), *Panic* (1935), *J.B.* (1958) and *Herakles* (1967). He also wrote striking plays for radio, including *The Fall of the City* (1937) and *The Trojan Horse* (1952). Many of these works had socio-political themes: in the latter two cases totalitarianism and the 1950s US fear of Communism respectively. It was to write songs for another such play that MacLeish asked Bob Dylan to go and see him at his home outside Conway, Massachusetts, at the end of the 1960s.

In *Chronicles Volume One*, Dylan describes these visits in great detail—he specifies the kinds of flowers in the room, the names of many poets MacLeish asked Dylan if he had read, and a good deal of fragments of their conversations—perhaps not least because unlike CARL SANDBURG, who in 1964 wouldn't let Dylan any further than his pig-farm porch, MacLeish invited Dylan into his inner sanctum. They got on well (Dylan soon refers to him as 'Archie') but there was no real chance of their working together as MacLeish hoped: his notion of Bob Dylan was of the protest singer, the socio-political poet of 1963—even specifying that he liked Dylan's song 'John Brown' (it would be interesting to know how MacLeish knew this); he didn't realise how much Dylan's artistic interests had shifted and developed. 'After hearing a few lines from the script,' Dylan wrote, 'I didn't see how our destinies could be intermixed.'

Nonetheless at their first meeting MacLeish gave Dylan some suggestions for song titles, and Dylan says that 'a few of them' were 'Red Hands', 'Lower World' and 'Father of Night': this last being a title Dylan duly used. It became the last track on the album *New Morning*. Dylan also says that he wrote that album's title track as a song for MacLeish's play. But the old poet-playwright—he was in his late 70s when they met—wondered 'why the songs weren't darker than they were'.

As Dylan writes at the end of this section of his memoir (it is the last sentence of the section titled 'New Morning'): 'The MacLeish play *Scratch* opened on Broadway at the St. James Theatre on May 6, 1971, and closed two days later on May 8.'

The middle night of *Scratch*'s humiliatingly short run was MacLeish's 79th birthday. He had another 11 years to go, and died in Boston on April 20, 1982.

[Archibald MacLeish, *Collected Poems, 1917–1982*, Boston: Houghton Mifflin, 1985. Bob Dylan, *Chronicles Volume One*, 2004, pp.113, 129 &141.]

McCartney, Paul [1942] James Paul McCartney was born in Liverpool, UK, on June 18, 1942. As the other main songwriter in THE BEATLES besides JOHN LENNON—and not always the less avant-garde of the two: he was interested in Yoko Ono's work before Lennon (and it was Lennon, after all, who famously said that 'avant garde is French for bullshit')—McCartney has affected Dylan's output just as Dylan's own work influenced that of the Beatles. Dylan first met all four Beatles in New York City in 1964 (see **Aronowitz, Al**). A subsequent meeting when McCartney and Lennon called at the London Hilton during Dylan's May 1966 visit resulted in a typed unfinished lyric jointly produced (in both senses) by Lennon-McCartney-Dylan, known now as 'Pneumonia Ceilings'. It went like this:

'Words and phrases right / Cigarette ash keeps me up all night / How come your mama types so fast? / Is daddy's flag flyin' at half mast? / Pneumonia ceilings, pneumonia floors / Daddy ain't gonna take it no more / Elephant guns blazing in my ears / I'm sick & tired of your applesauce tears! / Thermometers donat tell time no more / Since aunt mimi pushed them off the 20th floor / So say goodby to skyscrapers / You'll read about it in the evening paper/ I picked my nose & I'm glad i did'. It's said that in a cultural act prefiguring A.J. WEBERMAN, a hotel maid rescued it from the waste-bin in Dylan's room (but then sold it to a Beatles fan for next to nothing).

The two bumped into each other from time to time—as for instance at the wedding of Chick Edwards, drummer with the group Bittersweet, in San Francisco in 1974. But as to real work, ex-

Quarryman and ex-Silver Beatle Paul became the only ex-Beatle with whom Bob Dylan has had no professional dealings.

McCoy, Charlie [1941 -] Charles Ray McCoy was born in Oak Ridge, West Virginia, on March 28, 1941, making him an almost exact contemporary of Bob Dylan, for whom he played on that crucial run of albums from *Blonde on Blonde* to *Self Portrait*. He grew up in Miami and played harmonica from the age of eight, adding guitar in his teens. He became a Nashville-based multi-instrumentalist session musician of resourceful versatility, though primarily a master harmonica player, and at different times he played harmonica, harpsichord, bass and trumpet behind Dylan. It's also possible that he played the lovely acoustic guitar part overdubbed onto the last track to be recorded on *Highway 61 Revisited*, 'Desolation Row'. (This is something no-one seems to agree about. CLINTON HEYLIN suggests that BRUCE LANGHORNE played that guitar, though Langhorne has no recollection of being at the session; AL KOOPER maintains that it was Charlie McCoy; TONY GLOVER, who was probably at the sessions, denies that McCoy was there; MICHAEL KROGSGAARD and GLEN DUNDAS merely report these warring claims. The liner notes to the album itself, as given online at *www.bobdylan.com*, credit McCoy as a guitarist, and since he played on no other track this credit must be for 'Desolation Row'. But then, the official musician credits on Dylan tracks are not always reliable.)

At any rate, certainly Charlie McCoy plays the harmonica that sounds like a 'normal' harmonica, as opposed to Dylan's harmonica work, on that minor *Blonde on Blonde* song 'Obviously 5 Believers'. Elsewhere on the album he plays guitar and bass, and on '4th Time Around' he plays harpsichord, a part overdubbed in June 1966 (as were some KENNY BUTTREY drums), four months after the rest of the track. Al Kooper writes that when Dylan, ROBBIE ROBERTSON and himself first arrived in Nashville for the sessions, though they were harassed in town because of their appearance, in the studio things were fine: 'The cast was mighty: Charlie McCoy, ersatz leader, played bass, trumpet, guitar and harmonica—no mean feat on a Dylan session.' Kooper writes too of how that trumpet got onto 'Most Like You Go Your Way (And I'll Go Mine)':

'I came up with this little organ lick after each phrase. . . . Charlie McCoy was playing bass and said to me that he'd like to overdub a trumpet playing that lick with me. "Bob is not a big fan of overdubbing", I reminded Charlie. . . . Bob had gone out of his way to *not* overdub anything on this album and play everything live. . . . [So] Charlie . . . said to us "I can actually play both at the same time . . ."' And he did.

On the pared-down *John Wesley Harding* album, McCoy was the bass player throughout, and was so again on the more musically expansive *Nashville Skyline*. He also played bass for Dylan's 'JOHNNY CASH TV Show' appearance of late spring 1969, and played further studio sessions for *Self Portrait*. He therefore appears too on the *Dylan* album, which pulled together outtakes from these and *New Morning* sessions.

In 1992 there was a curious *Record Collector* interview with McCoy, which throws an odd light onto how some of these sessions worked. The interviewer put it to McCoy: 'The last album you did with Dylan was *Self Portrait*. Do you have any idea what he was trying to create out of that strange mixture of covers and new songs?' McCoy replied: 'In my estimation, Bob had already decided by that point that he wasn't going to work with BOB JOHNSTON any more—for what reason, I don't know. Bob Johnston brought us a tape full of demos that Dylan had done—just guitar or piano and vocals—and on a lot of the songs, Kenny Buttrey and I simply overdubbed drums and bass. Dylan did do a couple of sessions here [i.e. in Nashville] for that album, but he wasn't here for the whole thing, by any means. I'm not sure, actually, that *Self Portrait* was a "mutual agreement" project. Either Dylan told Bob [Johnston] to just go ahead and finish it up, by taking those demos and patching them up; or else maybe Bob Johnston still had to come up with some more tracks to complete his production contract with Dylan, and he just did them off his own bat. We never knew what the deal was.'

McCoy had played vibes, too, on an overdub session that April, and in New York as late as July 23, 1970 he was overdubbing bass onto attempts at 'Went to See the Gypsy', 'Spanish Is the Loving Tongue' and 'If Not for You'—songs that would end up, recorded again without McCoy, on *New Morning*. It was the end of their association.

McCoy had also played on ELVIS PRESLEY sessions and in the late 1960s and 1970s performed with many other big names in rock, folk and country. It's said that in his prime he was playing on 400 sessions a year (more than one a day!) but he was a live performer too and in 1969 joined Area Code 615. He made a solo album the same year, inevitably titled *The Real McCoy*, but though it did nothing at the time, a track played on radio two years later gained such audience response that 'I Started Loving Her Again' became a top 20 hit single in 1972. McCoy wisely retained his session-work, and also moved across from Area Code 615 into its mutated successor Barefoot Jerry. In the 1980s he toured Europe and in the 1990s semi-retired. In 1994 he released an instructional video, *Beginning Country Harp*—though how he remembered his way back to being a novice is surely a mystery. In 1996 he and HARGUS ROBBINS, another *Blonde on Blonde* musician, played with the Jordanaires and others in an all-veterans combo behind a cult deconstructionist duo called Ween. He is still touring in 2006, in North America and Europe, and in 2005 released a CD of country standards played as instrumentals highlighting his harmonica, *Classic Country*.

[Charlie McCoy: *Beginning Country Harp*, OV11128, video, US, & *Classic Country* CD, *nia*, from *www.charliemccoy.com*. 'In the Studio: Charlie McCoy on Dylan', *Record Collector*, UK, Sep 1992. Data too from the entry by Jason Ankeny in the online All Music Guide. Bruce Langhorne non-recollection, e-mail to this writer, 9 Feb 2006.]

McCrary, Regina [1958 -] Regina McCrary (sometimes billed under her previous married names Regina Havis and Regina McCrary Brown) was born on May 22, 1958 in Nashville, the daughter of the late Rev. Samuel Brown, who as Sam McCrary was lead singer of the Fairfield Four gospel group in the 1940s (the group had been formed in the 1920s; re-formed in the 1980s, the Fairfield Four performs 'Lonesome Valley' on the soundtrack of the film *O Brother, Where Art Thou?*). The younger sister of gospel-singer Ann McCrary, she was encouraged to audition for a place in Dylan's back-up singers' group by her friend CAROLYN DENNIS, whom she had known since they were small children.

She auditioned when the 1978 World Tour hit Nashville on December 2, almost at the end of its long run—and she was brought in for the sessions for *Slow Train Coming* in spring 1979, beginning with vocal overdubs in the Muscle Shoals studio in Sheffield, Alabama, that May 5 and continuing on May 7, 10 & 11. Next, the very beautiful Ms. McCrary formed part of the back-up singing outfit on Dylan's 'Saturday Night Live' appearance on October 20, 1979 and then embarked on the first Dylan gospel tour, starting with the long run of sold-out dates at the Fox Warfield in San Francisco that November 1 and finishing on December 9 in Tucson, Arizona. She had no idea how 'big' Bob Dylan was when she signed up with him: it was only when confronted with these audiences that she registered how important a figure he was to so many people.

Carolyn Dennis was not in the group on this tour: Regina's vocal colleagues were Mona Lisa Young and HELENA SPRINGS. The group sang some opening numbers each night before Dylan himself came on, but he plunged Regina in at the deep end by making her deliver as a monologue a particular 'Christian homily' story she'd known all her life and been heard retailing backstage.

In 1980 McCrary stayed on the Dylan payroll, remaining all through the year's touring—from snowy Portland, Oregon, on January 11 through to Charleston, West Virginia, on February 9, and from Toronto on April 17 through to Dayton, Ohio, on May 21. She was there too for the recording of the *Saved* album in between the two tours, beginning in the studio on February 13, along with Mona Lisa Young and CLYDIE KING, and she sang behind Dylan on 'Gotta Serve Somebody' at the Grammy awards show on CBS-TV in LA that February 27. (In March, when Dylan played harmonica on KEITH GREEN's track 'Pledge My Head to Heaven', two other McCrary sisters, Charity and Linda, were the back-up singers.)

On the second 1980 tour, she duetted with Dylan on his little-known song 'Ain't No Man Righteous, No Not One' at Hartford, Connecticut, on May 7, and two weeks later sang it solo on the tour's last night. Again, this tour did not include Carolyn Dennis.

In 1981 Regina McCrary was still with Dylan when he went into the studios in Santa Monica on March 11 to start work on the *Shot of Love* sessions, and towards the end of that month during one day's session she not only sang back-up vocals but was recorded singing solo lead vocals on 'Please Be Patient With Me' and (as she had done live the year before) 'Ain't No Man Righteous, No Not One'. She and Dylan even co-wrote a song at these sessions, 'Got to Give Him My All' (though it has never circulated, by either singer). She remained at the sessions until May, though she seems to have left before the last session, at which were Carolyn Dennis and MADELYN QUEBEC but no Regina.

On the June–July 1981 tour, Regina was there again, and sang solo lead vocal on 'Till I Get It Right' in an early slot at each concert, and duetted with Dylan on 'Mary from the Wild Moor' at the third London performance on June 28.

In all, she had been with Bob Dylan on three albums and over 150 concerts. By 1999, when interviewed for the US Dylan fanzine *ON THE TRACKS*, McCrary was working 'as a drug counselor in a Christian ministry' and singing on 'The Bobby Jones Gospel Show', then the largest gospel TV show in the country, which went out twice each Sunday via cable TV channel BET from Nashville, her home base. By 2004 she had become the Rev. Regina McCrary and was billed as a guest speaker at the Surviving Heartbreak Hotel Women's Retreat, again in Nashville.

In 2003, a circle of sorts was completed with the release of the various-artists compilation album *Gotta Serve Somebody: The Gospel Songs of Bob Dylan*, which features two relevant items (alongside Dylan's own duet with MAVIS STAPLES): here we find an a cappella 'Are You Ready?' by the newest incarnation of the all-male Fairfield Four—and a version of 'Pressing On' billed as by the Chicago Mass Choir on which the lead vocalist is . . . Regina McCrary.

McGhee, Brownie [1915 - 1996] Walter Brown McGhee was born in Knoxville, Tennessee, on November 30, 1915. He was the older and smoother brother of Granville Sticks McGhee, composer of 'Drinkin' Wine Spo-Dee-O-Dee', with whom Brownie played in New York in the early 1940s, and on whose brother's huge hit record of 1949 Brownie too played and sang. He learnt ukelele, five-string banjo, piano and guitar but concentrated on guitar, met harmonica player SONNY TERRY in 1939 and off and on worked with him for 40 years thereafter.

McGhee first recorded in August 1940 in Chicago (his début track was 'Pickin' My Tomatoes'), and being an exemplar of the Piedmont blues school (if, in fact, there ever was such a thing) he was promoted as *the* successor to BLIND BOY FULLER, with whom he and Sonny Terry had both worked shortly before Fuller's death. He made one gospel session in 1941—as it happens, the day before Bob Dylan was born—billed as Brother George and his Sanctified Singers and he was recorded for the Library of Congress in 1942.

With and without Sonny, Brownie recorded for Folkways from the mid-1940s till the late 1950s (though moonlighting under pseudonyms for many other labels) and the two became an omnipresent part of the folk revival and blues revival scene in New York City (McGhee had even played on the soundtrack of Elia Kazan's 1957 film *A Face in the Crowd*, and both would do more film-work later).

By the time Bob Dylan arrived in Greenwich Village they were perhaps the world's best-known still-active blues artists. McGhee's Leroy Carr-inspired 'In the Evening' was in Dylan's repertoire by the time he went back to Minneapolis in December 1961 to show his old friends there his greatly improved skills and knowledge.

Dylan mentions Sonny & Brownie alongside THE BEATS and the jazz musicians when listing, in the *Biograph* box set interview of 1985, the constituent parts of the underground, bohemian scene that he found and tagged onto just before it was too late. But as Tony Russell sums it up, 'They were around for so long that they began to be overlooked or underestimated. Their blues stories, once new and fascinating, were still worth listening to but they had told them too often and like pub bores they . . . lost their audience. Still, for a generation they had been despatch riders of the blues . . .'

Sonny & Brownie, as it was sufficient to call them, played all through the 1960s and survived beyond them, recording, in 1973, a 'contemporary' album (itself just called *Sonny & Brownie*) on which they were joined by CLYDIE KING, Don 'Sugarcane' Harris, JOHN MAYALL and even (on a cover of Randy Newman's splendid song 'Sail Away') ARLO GUTHRIE, and which included versions of 'People Get Ready' and SAM COOKE's 'Bring It on Home to Me'.

By this point, the two could hardly stand each other though their duo continued until 1982, after which McGhee recorded with the inferior harp player Sugar Blue. He long outlived his ex-partner and died of cancer in Oakland, California, on February 16, 1996, aged 80.

[Brownie McGhee: 'Pickin' My Tomatoes' (& 3 others), Chicago, 6 Aug 1940; Sonny Terry & Brownie McGhee: *Sonny & Brownie*, A&M 64379, US, 1973, CD-reissued A&M 210-829, 1989 & Mobile Fidelity 641, US, 1995. *A Face in the Crowd*, dir. Elia Kazan; Newtown Productions, US, 1957.

Bob Dylan: 'In the Evening', Minneapolis, MN, 22 Dec 1961, unreleased. Tony Russell, *The Blues From Robert Johnson to Robert Cray*, London: Aurum Press, 1997, pp.62–63. Also used: *The Blues Encyclopedia* vol. 2, New York: Routledge, 2005, pp.670–71.]

McGrath, Scott [1969 -] Scott McGrath was co-editor with RICHARD DAVID WISSOLIK of the book *Bob Dylan's Words—A Critical Dictionary and Commentary*, 1994. McGrath, born in the USA in 1969, was a graduate student in English Literature at Duquesne University, Pittsburgh, when he helped Wissolik compile and write this book; a published poet, artist and illustrator, McGrath dropped out of graduate school, taught in South Korea and cannot currently be traced. For his main contribution to Dylan matters, see ***Tarantula***.

[Wissolik & McGrath: *Bob Dylan's Words—A Critical Dictionary and Commentary*, Greensburg, PA: Eadmer Press, 1994.]

McGregor, Craig [1933 -] Craig Rob-Roy McGregor was born in Jamberoo, New South Wales, Australia, on October 12, 1933. He is the author of 23 books, several of them on popular culture, including *Pop Goes the Culture*; *People, Politics and Pop*; and *The History of Surfing*. He has also written political biography and studies like his well-regarded analysis of the class structure of Australian society, very reasonably titled *Class in Australia*. From 1988 to 2000 he was Associate Professor and then Emeritus Professor of Visual Communication at the University of Technology, Sydney (which has 24,000 students).

He first became interested in Dylan in 1963, when he was writing on pop, jazz and folk for the *Sydney Morning Herald* and heard PETE SEEGER sing 'Who Killed Davey Moore?'; then he got to know WILFRID MELLERS, who visited Australia and lectured on Western pop music. Dylan's records only arrived in Australia later.

However, McGregor achieved an unusual access to Dylan when he and THE HAWKS arrived in Australia in April 1966 (accompanied by their manager, ALBERT GROSSMAN). At a time when the rest of the Australian press seemed determined to be offended and offensive, to trivialise and deride, McGregor knew what he was talking about, took Dylan seriously but wasn't intimidated, and wrote with flair. Still working for the *Herald*, he attended the hostile press conference held at the airport on Dylan's arrival, listened in on the separate interview given to some hopeless, pathetic TV smoothie,

Ken Regan / Camera 5

Bob Dylan & Muhammad Ali

Photo by Allen Tannenbaum

Sonny Terry & Brownie McGhee

Photo by Rayburn Flerlage, courtesy of James Fraher

Memphis Slim

Library of Congress

Odetta

Courtesy RoyOrbison.com

Roy Orbison

and didn't leave when the rest of the press did. He was there to see Dylan mobbed by fans when he emerged too, and wrote up what he'd seen. In a surprising break with tradition, his piece, though cut in half, was published on the front page of this staid and haughty paper.

In response, Dylan's road manager phoned to say he wanted to meet him that night at the concert–and when he arrived, he was told Dylan wanted to see him *during the interval*. Naturally, this was a difficult encounter, but McGregor returned the following night and then went to Dylan's hotel room, talked very briefly to a more relaxed Dylan but then in front of everyone had to pass the test of having some *Blonde on Blonde* acetates played to him. This went badly but when, later, McGregor was charged with inviting Dylan to a party laid on for him by local folkies, Dylan said he'd come if McGregor came too.

Later he wrote all this up in his very honest, absorbing introduction to the book of early, important writings about Dylan that he edited. This book, one of the first of any kind on Dylan, was published as *Bob Dylan: A Retrospective* in 1972, and collected together for the first time such historically significant pieces as ROBERT SHELTON's *New York Times* review of Dylan from September 1961, a number of items from IZZY YOUNG, PAUL NELSON, IRWIN SILBER, RALPH J. GLEASON and others, through to a testy review of *Tarantula* by Robert Christgau in the *New York Times* in 1971. The book ended with a specially commissioned piece by Wilfrid Mellers, which ended by expressing the wish that he might still be alive in 2000 to find out whether Dylan would 'preserve his folk-like integrity from youth through the middle years and even into a venerable old age'.

On Dylan's return visit to Australia in 1978, Craig McGregor was given a long interview, later incorporated into the 1980 edition of *Bob Dylan: A Retrospective* published in Australia. In the US the book was republished in 1990 as *Bob Dylan, the Early Years: A Retrospective* but excluded the 1978 interview.

[Craig McGregor, 'Bob Dylan's Anti-Interview', *Sydney Morning Herald*, 13 Apr 1966; *Bob Dylan: A Retrospective*, New York: William Morrow, 1972; also published in Australia (Sydney: Angus & Robertson, 1980), the UK and Sweden; reprinted as *Bob Dylan, the Early Years: A Retrospective*, New York: Da Capo, 1990; *Pop Goes the Culture*, London: Pluto Press, 1984; *People, Politics and Pop*, Sydney: Ure Smith, 1968; *The History of Surfing*, Sydney: Palm Beach Press, 1983; *Class in Australia*, Sydney: Penguin, 1997.]

McGuinn, Roger [1942 -] James Joseph McGuinn III was born in a Chicago suburb on July 13, 1942, the son of James and Dorothy McGuinn, whose book *Parents Can't Win*, a comic parody of the Dr. Spock genre, became a bestseller in 1947, and whose house was full of artistic friends as young Jim was growing up. Musically, his first inspiration was ELVIS PRESLEY, but he claimed that this was a short-lived interest (more fool him) and that rock'n'roll was displaced in his affections by folk when he saw Bob Gibson play, after which he wanted to get a banjo and a 12-string guitar and learn play folk songs, and absorbed the records of PETE SEEGER, ODETTA, BIG BILL BROONZY, LEADBELLY and FLATT & SCRUGGS. However, he has given other accounts that stress the Elvis phase rather more, suggesting that it led him to acquiring his first guitar at age 14, and to GENE VINCENT, CARL PERKINS, THE EVERLY BROTHERS and the rockabilly era of JOHNNY CASH before the Bob Gibson encounter. At any rate he was then one of the first pupils to enrol at the new Old Town School of Folk Music in Chicago, where he remained from 1957 to 1960, learning guitar, banjo and 12-string and an extensive folksong repertoire.

McGuinn started to play acoustic guitar in local clubs while still at school, was recruited into the Limelighters, brought to LA to play live and on their 1960 LP *Tonight in Person* and then fired within weeks as an economy drive by the core of the group. He stayed on in LA, met DAVID CROSBY, then moved to San Francisco, found himself recruited into the Chad Mitchell Trio and taken to Greenwich Village, where he played on their albums *Mighty Day on Campus* and *Live at the Bitter End* (1961 and '62), toured South as well as North America with them and then was just about to defect to the New Christy Minstrels when the excellent teen idol turned SINATRA wannabe Bobby Darin offered him a back-up guitar rôle in his new move into supper-club folk music. He never played on any Darin records but he became a writer in Darin's Don Kirscher-run Brill Building publishing company, where with co-writer Frank Gari he turned out surf songs, several of which turned into records as by the City Surfers (a quietly candid name) on which Gari sang, McGuinn played guitar and Darin drummed: 'Beach Ball' c/w 'Sun Tan Baby' and 'Powder Puff' c/w '50 Miles to Go' were 1963 singles.

At the same time, McGuinn was playing down in the Village again, and on sessions, including for Hoyt Axton and on *JUDY COLLINS #3* (1963), which included the Seeger song 'Turn! Turn! Turn!' that McGuinn would later recreate with THE BYRDS. After all this came a return to LA, a gig at the Troubadour and before too long, the Byrds. (For Dylan's relationship with the Byrds and the McGuinn of those years–the period during which he switched from being Jim to being Roger–see separate entry on the group.)

After the end of 1965, when Dylan appeared on stage and sang fleetingly with the Byrds at Ciro's in LA, he and McGuinn never worked together again until Bob gave Roger a line or two informally for his song 'The Ballad of Easy Rider', written for the *Easy Rider* soundtrack in the late 1968;

McGuinn tried to give Dylan a co-writer's credit; Dylan was furious and made him remove it. (The film was released in 1969.) Dylan also appeared to rebuke McGuinn when, with HAPPY TRAUM, he re-recorded his own 'You Ain't Goin' Nowhere' in 1971 and sang 'Pack up your money, pull up your tent, McGuinn', as if correcting the Byrds' version of the line.

The two didn't try again until after McGuinn 'went solo' in 1972, at which point Dylan dropped in on the sessions for his début album in LA that August or September, and played harmonica on the song 'I'm So Restless', which duly became the opening track on 1973's *Roger McGuinn*. This album contained no Dylan songs, but the McGuinn solo albums that followed reverted to the Byrds-style habit of covering Dylan's catalogue; so *Roger McGuinn & Band* (1975) covered 'Knockin' on Heaven's Door', *Cardiff Rose* (1976) included the *Blood on the Tracks* outtake song 'Up to Me' and *Thunderbyrd* (1977) included the *Desire* outtake 'Golden Loom'.

After the unexciting collaboration on 'I'm So Restless', McGuinn recurs in the Dylan story innumerable times, all equally insignificantly. It's always been intriguing that someone with McGuinn's heavyweight credentials *and*, as leader of the Byrds, a seminal place in the shaping of the 1960s—and someone who, face to face, has an almost intimidatingly powerful aura—should always come over, placed alongside Bob Dylan, as a conspicuous drip and so awkwardly unnecessary an appendage.

He plays anonymous guitar and adds backing vocals on the LA sessions for *Pat Garrett & Billy the Kid* (and so is in there somewhere on 'Knockin' on Heaven's Door') and he and Dylan share a sometime producer in Don DeVito and a sometime songwriting partner in JACQUES LEVY. He becomes one of the name artists on the Rolling Thunder Revues in 1975 and 1976, with his own short slot in each concert, inevitably centred around 'Mr. Tambourine Man' and his electric 12-string, plus a sharing of vocals with Dylan on 'Knockin' on Heaven's Door'. There he is, therefore, in *Renaldo & Clara*, and there he is in SAM SHEPARD's *Rolling Thunder Logbook*, looking a twit in every photograph and sounding one in Shepard's polite description: 'Roger has a portable telephone'—he's always been into boys' toys and sci-fi techno-fantasy, and here he is in 1975, projecting himself into the cell-phone future years before the rest of us—'that he carries everywhere, contained in a black attaché case. . . . He usually dresses in a black silk top hat, brown hunting jacket, beige jodhpurs, riding boots and a whip.' Shepard adds (surely superfluously): 'The whip is more for show than anything else.' When he comes on stage, the audience has no idea who he is till JOAN BAEZ introduces him. Then, with his big guitar and his curiously sheep-like voice, he performs 'Chestnut Mare' or 'Eight Miles High' and the crowd goes apeshit.

It is on these tours that Dylan develops, even more slapstick-aggressively with McGuinn than with Baez, his habit of treating a duet as a duel: of goading and torturing the adversary at the microphone by singing as waywardly as possible and thrusting his face disconcertingly close to theirs. Some people hold their own; some wilt away; some, like Roger, stand there with a wan and feeble grin, being a victim but coming back for more, over and over again. In McGuinn's case this can be seen on film to high comic effect years later when they come together to sing 'Mr. Tambourine Man' at the ROY ORBISON tribute concert in LA on February 24, 1990 (a song with no connection to Roy Orbison at all, and sung less competently than Orbison ever sang anything).

In between the Rolling Thunder years and the Orbison occasion, McGuinn had first reappeared as a guest at the last of the 12 tremendous San Francisco concerts in 1980. That November 22, Dylan brought him on and introduced him with his customary mix of apparent enthusiasm and barely disguised belittlement: 'All right. We been here for 12 nights I think, and different people have been stopping down. I wanna thank them all. JERRY GARCIA was here, let's see: ELTON JOHN, BRUCE SPRINGSTEEN, Captain Beefheart. They all went through here one time or another. Anyway got another special guest, ha ha, tonight. Can't get away, we know so many people you know. Anyway I first met this next man I think about, almost 20 years ago if not that. Probably was, and he was playing in a group. I don't remember the name of the group actually, but he went on and started a group called the Byrds: I'm sure you heard of them. Anyway we've played together before, been on tours together and all that kind of stuff. I'll bring him out here now, you know who he is: Roger McGuinn!'

Next McGuinn was the opening act on the 1987 European tour by Dylan with TOM PETTY & THE HEARTBREAKERS—inevitably coming on stage for a Dylan encore more nights than not, and standing there at the dread shared microphone like a medieval peasant in the stocks. He was there again in 1989, at a Dylan Never-Ending Tour concert in Tampa, Florida, duetting on, ho hum, 'Knockin' on Heaven's Door' and retiring to guitar only for 'Maggie's Farm'. In 1992 he was one of the guests at the so-called 30th Anniversary Concert Celebration event for Dylan at Madison Square Garden, where he secured the penultimate slot, just ahead of Dylan himself, inevitably occupying it with 'Mr. Tambourine Man' (backed by Petty, the Heartbreakers, JIM KELTNER and Anton Fig), and then joining in, one of the chosen few, alongside Dylan once again for 'My Back Pages'. In 1996, McGuinn came on stage yet again, at yet another Never-Ending Tour concert, this time in Cleveland, singing backing vocals on 'My Back Pages' and playing guitar on that and 'Rainy Day Women # 12 & 35'. He'll be along again any minute.

[Roger McGuinn: *Roger McGuinn*, Columbia C-31946, US 1973; *Peace on You*, Columbia KC-32956, 1974; *Roger McGuinn & Band*, Columbia PC-33541, 1975; *Cardiff Rose*, Columbia PC-34154, 1976; *Thunderbyrd*, Columbia PC-34656, 1977. The Limeliters: *Tonight in Person*, RCA RD7237, US, 1960. The Chad Mitchell Trio: *Mighty Day on Campus*, Kapp KS 3262, US, 1961 & *At the Bitter End*, Kapp KS 3281, 1962. The City Surfers: 'Beach Ball' c/w 'Sun Tan Baby', Capitol 5002 & 'Powder Puff' c/w '50 Miles to Go', Capitol 5052, both US, 1963. James & Dorothy McGuinn, *Parents Can't Win*, New York: Farrar, Straus & Giroux, c.1947.

Background data sources incl. 'Jim McGuinn the Early Years 1956–1964' & 'The Roger McGuinn Discography', both at *http://ebni.com/byrds/memrm1.html* & interview in Tower Records' *epulse* July 2, 1999, all online 19 Jan 2006; & interview by this writer, Birmingham, UK, 1974.]

McLagan, Ian [1945 -] Ian 'Mac' McLagan was born on May 12, 1945 in Hounslow, Middlesex, England (that is, neither in London nor the countryside out beyond it), grew up playing piano, acquiring a Hammond organ and, in an early band, the Muleskinners, backing HOWLIN' WOLF, Little Walter and other scary figures on their quick, cheap tours of Britain in the early 1960s. In 1965 he joined the Small Faces, which turned into the Faces in 1969. The Faces broke up when RON WOOD joined THE ROLLING STONES; McLagan joined them as a sideman later. In 1984 he was the keyboards player on Bob Dylan's European tour (Dylan's first since the semi-gospel tour of 1981), playing from May 28 in Verona, Italy, through to Slane, Ireland, on July 8: a total of 27 concerts. Thirteen years later, though the detail is murky, he says he was on a session for *Time Out of Mind*—including on the song 'Love Sick'—but that the versions he played on were not used.

Near the end of the 1990s, McLagan published a well-received memoir, *All the Rage*, and though the original hardback edition is out of print, the paperback is advertised online with this nicely judged short blurb: 'The book covers pre-Small Faces days with the Muleskinners, the great days with the Small Faces and the Faces. After that Mac plays with a number of bands including the Rolling Stones, Bonnie Raitt and the ever-cheerful Bob Dylan. He talks about both sides of the Moon (Keith, that is), the losses of Ronnie [Lane] and Steve [Marriott], his fight with drugs and drinks and what Rod Stewart is really like. Furthermore, he gets royalties on this so buy it now.'

The great British music critic Charles Shaar Murray elaborates on this in the review he gave the book in *Mojo* in January 1999: '*All the Rage* contains an unfeasibly large helping of unforgettable vignettes of the rich and famous at work and play. . . . Here's KEITH RICHARDS, back in his druggy period [?], shooting himself up in the arse straight through his jeans, and then walking around with syringe still protruding from his butt. Or Bob Dylan replying to a large man introducing himself as "Hello, Bob, I'm Peter Grant. I manage Led Zeppelin", with a terse "I don't come to you with my problems."'

Long since married to Kim, the former Mrs. Keith Moon (a man much loved by McLagan even though Moon once paid someone to break his fingers—Pete Townshend paid the same man the same amount again not to), Ian McLagan has lived in Austin, Texas, for some years. It is a very different place from Hounslow, Middlesex.

[Ian McLagan, *All the Rage: A Rock'n'Roll Odyssey*, London: Sidgwick & Jackson, 1998; republished as *All the Rage: My High Life with the Small Faces, the Faces and the Rolling Stones*, London: Pan, 2000. *Time Out of Mind* session claim in interview by Kent H. Benjamin, 5 Dec 1997 for *Pop Culture Press* no.44, US, 1998.]

McLuhan, Marshall [1911 - 1980] A Canadian academic who became a cultural guru of the 1960s–70s, McLuhan coined or made famous the phrases 'the medium is the message' and 'the global village'. His works include *The Gutenberg Galaxy: The Making of Typographic Man*, 1962; *Understanding the Media*, 1964; and *The Medium Is the Massage* [sic], 1967.

Dylan told Scott Cohen (*Spin* vol.1, no.8, USA, December 1985): 'I say, if you want to know about the '60s, read *Armies of the Night* by Norman Mailer, or read Marshall McLuhan. . . . A lot of people have written about the '60s in an exciting way and have told the truth. The singers were just a part of it.'

McLuhan's first name was Herbert.

McTell, Blind Willie [1903 - 1959] William Samuel McTell was born in the Happy Valley area south of the small town of Thomson, Georgia, in 1903. May 5 has long been rumoured the specific date, but this is impossible to confirm. (Until very recently it was thought that his birth was in either 1898 or 1901; it was also assumed that his first name was Willie, rather than William.) Before he reached adolescence, he and his young mother moved to Statesboro, Georgia, a far larger and more progressive town, and he thrived within it.

McTell grew up to be the most important Georgia bluesman to be recorded. He was a songster of wide repertoire and as fine a 12-string guitarist as ever lived. The dexterity of his playing was extraordinary, and his voice was an unusually smooth tenor. The interplay between voice and guitar also brought into the equation McTell's intelligence and wit, and it was the fusion of all these elements that led Bob Dylan to write in his 1983 tribute song that 'no-one can sing the blues like Blind Willie McTell.'

McTell explodes every archetype about blues musicians. He is no roaring primitive, no ROBERT JOHNSONesque devil-dealing womaniser. He didn't lose his sight in a juke-joint brawl, or hopping a freight-train. He didn't escape into music from behind a mule in the Delta. He didn't die violently or young. Instead, blind from birth but never behaving as if handicapped, this resourceful, articulate man became an adept professional musician who travelled widely and talked his way into an array of recording sessions.

He never achieved a hit record, but he became one of the most widely known and well-loved figures in Georgia. Working clubs and car-parks, playing to blacks and whites, tobacco workers and college kids, Blind Willie McTell, human juke-box and local hero, enjoyed a modest career and an independent life.

He recorded prolifically from the early days of blues recording and laid down a masterpiece on his first day in a studio, in 1927. In the mid-30s, as the Depression gripped, he dropped from sight. In 1940 John Lomax's wife spotted him playing in Atlanta, and he was recorded singing and talking for the Library of Congress. He was paid a dollar and his taxi-fare and dropped from sight once more: just another blind singer, and now turning 40.

He survived, and managed a return to commercial recording in 1949–50, with sessions for Atlantic Records and Fred Mendelson's small label Regal. By now there was no market for his pre-war acoustic blues style. MUDDY WATERS had already electrified Chicago. McTell disappeared once again. He was recorded, privately, one more time, in 1956 (by which time rock'n'roll was shaking up the blues in yet another way) and he died in obscurity in 1959—the very year his 'Statesboro Blues' became a 'discovery' of the new folk and blues revival movement. It would become a million-selling hit by the Allman Brothers Band (also from Georgia) in the 1970s.

No inferior shellac crackle dooms Blind Willie McTell to the ranks of the almost unlistenable. His pre-war recordings, like his diction, are clear, while the best of his lyrics show him to be an inspired individual composer within a milieu of shared, communal composition. Even where his lyrics are common-stock, the early voice is quietly pained and intimate.

This is evident on 'Mama 'Tain't Long fo' Day', the gem from McTell's début day in the studio, October 18, 1927. Early on, McTell tended to make songs more by putting together stock couplets of blues lyric poetry than by conscious composition. Yet here, though the great opening lines of verses 1, 3 and 4 ('Wake up mama, don't you sleep so hard', 'Blues grabbed me at midnight, didn't turn me loose till day' and 'The big star falling, mama 'tain't long 'fore day') derive from early vaudeville women performers and BLIND LEMON JEFFERSON, he reworks them into a song of real individuality, made unforgettable by his voice and playing. A universe of communication seems held in tension between the exquisite keening of his bottleneck guitar and the vulnerable, edgy hope in his voice.

It's easy to hear too why 'Statesboro Blues' became much loved: this 1928 recording is so rock'n' roll. The lyrics are full of expressions baby boomers will recognise from JERRY LEE LEWIS records and the like: 'Sister got 'em . . . brother got 'em . . .' and 'hand me my travelin' shoes'. In truth these come from old hokum songs and gospel, but McTell propels them forward with fresh exuberance. The record's abrupt start signals its restlessness. It's as if McTell had begun before the machinery was ready and the first notes of the tumbling opening phrase are missing.

Woody Mann wrote of McTell's idiosyncratic genius on the 12-string: 'He treats each phrase of his music as a separate entity with its own rhythmical and melodic nuances. . . . As McTell's musical stream-of-consciousness wanders, so do his bar structures; he may follow a verse of ten bars with another of fourteen.' It's debatable whether McTell represents a Piedmont 'school' of guitarists, but there's no doubting his distinctive mastery of a difficult instrument. His is always uncannily well tuned, evincing a great sense of pitch, and he can make it do anything—on 'Atlanta Strut' he has it imitate mandolin, bass, cornet and trombone. He also played other instruments: harmonica and accordion. Later he experimented with electric guitar, and still owned one at the time of his death.

McTell mastered a number of styles and he could adopt a different accent for a particular recording. When he cut 'Motherless Children Have a Hard Time' for Atlantic Records in 1949, he made it a memorial to his long-dead friend BLIND WILLIE JOHNSON by a sustained imitation of both Johnson's voice and the distinctive atmosphere of Johnson's recordings. On 'Hillbilly Willie's Blues' in 1935 he indulged his penchant for wry impersonations of the hillbilly singers who lived in the Appalachian hills above his native Georgia plains: a talent first glimpsed on his début session's 'Stole Rider Blues', the finest record JIMMIE RODGERS never made.

McTell attended to white musicians as well as singers. 'Warm It Up to Me', 1933, may have been a re-write of any one of a number of similar songs, but noticeably it resembles white veteran guitarist JIMMIE TARLTON's 'Ooze Up to Me', cut in Atlanta 18 months earlier.

As well as being a friend of Blind Willie Johnson and good friends over a long period with fellow-Georgians Curley Weaver and Buddy Moss, with whom he recorded, McTell reportedly knew LEADBELLY, BLIND BLAKE, Lemon Jefferson, GEORGIA TOM and Tom's sometime partner Tampa Red. Their hit 'It's Tight Like That' was adapted on record by McTell and Weaver as 'It's a Good Little Thing', as was 'You Can't Get Stuff No More', while their 'Beedle Um Bum' was remembered by McTell nearly 30 years later at his 'last session'. He also knew and heard many performers who never recorded–among them the guitarist brothers Jonas and Hollis Brown (yes) from Atlanta.

For McTell it paid to be able to perform different sorts of material at different sorts of gigs, but he took pride in being a songster, knew all about the history of his material and felt deep affection for many kinds of song. Equally, he felt entitled to reshape them. As he says of 'Dyin' Crapshooter's Blues', 'I had to steal music from every which way to get it to fit.' He also said, of others' songs he performed, like Blind Blake's 'That Will Never Happen No More', 'I jump 'em from other writers but I arrange 'em my way.'

Few documents exist about McTell, and some that do, such as his marriage and death certificates, contain false or misleading information. His very surname dissolves and re-forms as it is scrutinised. His father's name was McTear or McTier, and members of his family swapped between these spellings. His professional pseudonyms included Pig'n'Whistle Red, Hot Shot Willie, Georgia Bill, Barrelhouse Sammy and Blind Sammie. Among friends he seems to have been known as Willie in Atlanta but in Thomson and Statesboro as Doog or Doogie.

Early on, he ran away from home: 'I run away and went everywhere, everywhere I could go without any money. I followed shows all around till I begin to get grown . . . medicine shows, carnivals, and all different types of funny little shows.' His recorded songs mention seven towns in Georgia plus Baltimore, Birmingham, Boston, East St. Louis, Florida, Lookout Mountain, Memphis, Newport News, Niagara Falls, New York, Ohio, Tennessee and Virginia. He also knew New Orleans, Kate McTell says he once took her to Oakland, California, and in 1935 the two of them recorded in Chicago.

Willie told Kate: 'Baby, I was born a rambler. I'm gonna ramble till I die.' However, McTell's romantic rambling spirit has probably been over-stressed, and it seems clear now that McTell spent the great majority of his time within Georgia, and that his traveling was mainly following the tobacco markets–Statesboro was an important tobacco town–and playing to winter tourists in Florida. Late in life his travelling routine centered around church concerts in the patches of Georgia he knew best and where he had relatives with whom he stayed recurrently throughout his life. He was a member of churches in Atlanta, Statesboro and Happy Valley, and often performed at church concerts, sometimes with gospel quartets. At WGST in Atlanta he sang spirituals on the air in the early 1950s, as he did for WEAS in nearby Decatur.

His country-gospel sides can delight: 'Pearly Gates' (Atlantic), 'Hide Me in Thy Bosom' and 'Sending Up My Timber' (Regal) make a thrilling trio. McTell was alive with conviction for these performances, while his Library of Congress session gives us a fond reminiscence about 'those old-fashioned hymns' his parents used to sing around the house before going out to work in the fields. McTell sings material like 'I Got to Cross the River Jordan' without melodrama and with great simplicity.

For all his efforts, and the extraordinary quality of his talent, Blind Willie McTell's career was doomed. By the time he was 50, to the extent that he was known at all, it was as an old Atlanta street-musician. McTell does not seem to have become embittered, though he drank, at times heavily, and suffered health problems.

Helen Edwards, with whom McTell had lived for at least 14 years–far longer than with Kate, who has received all the attention by having survived to be interviewed in the 1970s–died in November, 1958. The following spring McTell had a stroke, and moved back to Thomson to live with relatives. For a while his health improved and he played guitar once more. But suddenly in summer his health deteriorated again and he was admitted to Milledgeville State Hospital (a mental hospital). He died there one week later, on August 19, 1959, of 'cerebral hemorrhages'.

He was buried at Jones Grove Baptist Church, in Happy Valley, south of Thomson. Kate McTell learnt of the funeral too late to fulfil his request that one of his guitars be buried with him. This was not the only slip-up. The stonemason mixed up the name of the person who'd commissioned it with that of the person it was to commemorate, so Blind Willie's gravestone offered us one last pseudonym. It read EDDIE MCTIER 1898–AUG 19 1959 AT REST.

The white clapboard church has now been rebuilt in concrete, and David Fulmer, who directed the documentary film 'Blind Willie's Blues', has replaced McTell's gravestone with a new one, with a large picture of a guitar below the inscription BLUES LEGEND 'BLIND WILLIE MCTELL' BORN WILLIE SAMUEL MCTIER MAY 5, 1901 DIED AUGUST 19, 1959.

Since his death the re-emergence of his many recordings has shown that McTell was one of the blues world's consummate artists. Little of his influence shows in contemporary music. Unlike some of the Delta stars, he is not a father of rock'n' roll, but points backwards into an earlier world. Nevertheless, a well-kept secret among blues and folk fans in Britain and America since the 1950s, Blind Willie McTell is the last unrecognised superstar of the blues.

Not unrecognised by Bob Dylan, however, who, like his fellow Greenwich Village folkies, knew McTell's work from the inclusion of 'Statesboro Blues' on the compilation album *The Country Blues* issued to accompany the pioneering book of the same name by SAM CHARTERS. And Dylan not only respects and learns from that distinctive McTell interplay of music and quick intelligence, but deploys particulars of the older man's work resourcefully, and sometimes unexpectedly, in his own.

A very secular Blind Willie McTell line gets quoted in the 1979 album version of Dylan's Christian song 'Gonna Change My Way of Thinking'. The song is full of the one 'authority on high', waved over us in all his Jehovah-severity, and verse six opens with the narrator on his way to following what he's earlier called 'a different set of rules': he's now 'got a God-fearing woman'. Yet, concerned to insist that she's a multi-dimensional character, he effects the surprise of slipping in a bit of raunchy approbation—letting into his evangelical, flagellant mansion the fresh air of an outside world. He sings ambitiously of a woman who is both the queen of his flesh and the lamp of his soul: a woman so well-balanced that 'She can do the Georgia crawl / She can walk in the spirit of the Lord.'

That 'Do the Georgia crawl' doesn't come straight from McTell, but it arises in Dylan's work because McTell used it. It's odds on that Dylan himself knew the earlier song, Henry Williams' and Eddie Anthony's 1928 'Georgia Crawl' (in which the singer's 'Aunt Sally . . . Do the Georgia Crawl till she died away'). It was an influential recording in its own right, by a popular local string band, and McTell certainly knew it, and took up its title phrase, making it his own by using it *often*, primarily on several versions of the song Bob Dylan finally puts on record himself on *World Gone Wrong* in 1993, 'Broke Down Engine [Blues]': a song Dylan suggests he came upon 'second-hand' yet which he calls 'a Blind Willie McTell masterpiece.' On McTell's first, and best, version of this song, 'Broke Down Engine Blues' from 1931, he sings 'What makes me love my woman: / She can really do the Georgia crawl', which he repeats on a 1933 re-recording, 'Broke Down Engine'. He sings the variant line 'What make me love little Sara, she can do the Georgia crawl' (that 'Sara' an odd little coincidence) on the 1933 remake 'Broke Down Engine No. 2'.

Three days later, McTell also puts a passing reference to 'that old Georgia crawl' into his version of 'East St. Louis Blues'—on which he also anticipates Bob Dylan by pulling in from elsewhere the folk refrain 'fare you well': 'Fare ye, honey, fare ye well. / You can shake like a cannonball / Get out and learn that old Georgia Crawl. / Fare ye, honey, fare ye well.' Bob Dylan recorded 'Fare Thee Well' in Minnesota back in May 1960, and then on another early, privately recorded performance of the wonderful 'Dink's Song', he quotes roughly the same line from 'Fare Thee Well' that McTell quotes in 'East St. Louis Blues', using it, like McTell, as a repeated refrain: 'Fare thee well my honey, fare thee well.' He even throws in, right next to it, as McTell does, the phrase 'like a cannonball'.

Just as Dylan puts that old Georgia Crawl to use in 1979 and 1993, so he uses other fragments from McTell recordings at different widely spaced points in his work. McTell's 'Southern Can Is Mine', recorded the same day as his first 'Broke Down Engine Blues', includes these lines: 'Ashes to ashes and sand to sand' and 'You might wiggle like a tadpole, let it jump like a frog', which Dylan utilises on two occasions over 20 years apart. When it was announced that he would found his own record label in the late 1960s, it was to be called Ashes & Sand; in 1990, on the album *Under the Red Sky*, the other line from the same McTell song gets tweaked into service for the lyric (such as it is) of Dylan's 'Wiggle Wiggle'. More interestingly, 'Rough Alley Blues', sung by Ruth Willis but with McTell providing the guitar-work, chorus singing and spoken commentary, includes the line 'Lay across my big brass bed.'

Then there is the talking blues 'Travelin' Blues', the stand-out track from McTell's session of autumn 1929. When we attribute Bob Dylan's talking blues style to WOODY GUTHRIE, we forget that black artists also explored this form, and that Guthrie himself listened attentively to black music. Specifically, we forget that Blind Willie McTell's 'Travelin' Blues' is a renowned example of the genre. His artistry and quick intelligence combine here to produce a talking blues of great good humour and poise, deftly quoting snatches of older popular songs ('Poor Boy' and 'Red River Blues'), imitating train noises on the guitar, recounting a long dialogue between the speaker trying to bum a ride and the railroad man refusing and tormenting him, and sewing together all these elements and more into a quirky, playful, sardonic whole.

Passages of its lyric, as well as quirks of McTell's delivery, cannot but put us in mind of Bob Dylan. What could be more 'Dylanesque' than McTell's insouciant spoken opening?: 'I was travelin' through South Americus / Walked up to a lady's house / *[pause]* Called her Grandma / *[pause]* Didn't know 'er name / *[pause]* She give me someth'n' to eat. / Walked on down the road.' Strongly reminiscent of 'I Shall Be Free No. 10' and with something akin to the flavour of 'Motorpsycho Nitemare', the McTell song also anticipates not only Dylan's mood and delivery but even, with that 'Walked on down the road', a line of lyric, from 'Talkin' World War III Blues', while the memorable way Dylan mumble-jerks the line 'Well I asked for something to eat', on 1965's 'On the Road Again', is a direct echo of the way Blind Willie McTell delivers the same little phrase in 'Travelin' Blues'.

On top of all this there is the parallel between McTell's switch to religious recordings and Dylan's. As noted, McTell's gospel sides of 1949–50 catch him performing with a renewed vigour. Similarly, Dylan's gospel tours of 1979–80 show *him* remarkably fired-up, while his newfound conviction inspired an explosion of songwriting more prolific than any since the mid-1960s. McTell's great 'Hide Me in Thy Bosom' sounds recorded behind fibreglass, yet at almost 50 he can still make you think of PRESLEY's 'That's All Right', his fluid vocal rides and swoops with such unloosed passion. There is also a particular, inspired piece of singing, early in the track, that one can imagine Dylan coming up with. On repeats of the line later in the song McTell is content with the conventional 'feed me, feed me, feed me', which follows the rhythm and gets its excitement from sheer insistent repetition, but the first time around he hits instead a long, sustained, utterly unpredictable 'feeeeeeeeeeeeeeeed me', cutting across the rhythm and holding a note between the expected two. Dylan has done much the same in concert with the chorus of 'Knockin' on Heaven's Door', turning 'knock knock knocking' into 'kno——ckin'', and you can imagine him doing the same in the course of a live performance of something from *Slow Train Coming* or *Saved*.

The two shared evangelically Christian interests at this point in their lives are. 'Sending Up My Timber' states the 'Are You Ready?' theme, performed with the same crusading spirit as the 'Saved' sessions generally: 'It may be morn or night or noon / But I do not know just how soon . . .' while McTell's Library of Congress session gives us a reminiscence about 'those old-fashioned hymns' his parents used to sing around the house before going out to work in the fields, one of which carried the same message: 'Are you just well to get ready?: You got to die, you got to die / Just well to get ready, you got to die / It may be tomorrow, you can't tell the minute or the hour / Just well to get ready, you got to die, you got to die.'

Most interesting here is the switch from the righteous 'you' in 'Just As Well Get Ready, You Got to Die' to the affecting 'I', in 'I Got to Cross the River Jordan': 'I got to face my dear Saviour, / I got to face Him for myself . . . / I got to lie in some old lonesome graveyard / I've got to lie there by myself / There's nobody there can lie there for me / Lord, I got to lie there for myself.' McTell sings this such that we feel his faith to be a struggle: a summoning of courage a hair's breadth from the bereft. It clinches the case for Blind Willie McTell's ability to lament for us—to be the artist onto whose shoulders Bob Dylan can place the weight of his visionary requiem for America's past and everybody's future.

So does 'The Dyin' Crapshooter's Blues'. This is Willie's personalised version, one among a whole sequence of songs, based on the traditional English ballad 'The Unfortunate Rake' and which also becomes the black standard 'St. James Infirmary'. 'The Unfortunate Rake', 'St. James Infirmary' and 'The Dyin' Crapshooter's Blues' all end up wondrously transmuted—see separate entry on this—into 'Blind Willie McTell'.

[Blind Willie McTell (all tracks listed here under this name, regardless of pseudonym on 78rpm records at the time): 'Mama 'Tain't Long Fo' Day' & 'Stole Rider Blues', Atlanta, 18 Oct 1927; 'Statesboro Blues', Atlanta, 17 Oct 1928, *The Country Blues*, RBF RF-1, NY, 1959 (issued alongside Sam Charters, *The Country Blues*, NY: Reinhart, 1959); CD-reissued *Blind Willie McTell: The Early Years (1927–1933)*, Yazoo CD-1005, NY, 1990; 'Atlanta Strut' & 'Travelin' Blues', Atlanta, 30 Oct 1929; 'Motherless Children Have a Hard Time' & 'Pearly Gates', Atlanta, Oct 1949, *Blind Willie McTell: Atlanta Twelve String*, Atlantic SD 7224, NY, 1972; CD-reissued Atlantic 7 82366-2, 1992; 'Hillbilly Willie's Blues', Chicago, 25 Apr 1935; 'Warm It Up to Me', NY, 14 Sep 1933; 'Beedle Um Bum' & 'Dyin' Crapshooter's Blues', Sep 1956, *Blind Willie McTell: Last Session*, Prestige Bluesville 1040, Bergenfield, NJ, 1961, CD-reissued Prestige Bluesville Original Blues Classics OBCCD-517-2 (BV-1040), Berkeley, CA, 1992; 'Hide Me in Thy Bosom' & 'Sending Up My Timber', Atlanta, May 1950; 'I Got to Cross the River Jordan' & 'Just as Well Get Ready, You Got to Die', Atlanta, 5 Nov 1940; 'Broke Down Engine Blues' & 'Southern Can Is Mine', 23 Oct 1931; 'Broke Down Engine' & 'Broke Down Engine No. 2', NY, 18 Sep 1933; 'East St. Louis Blues', NY, 21 Sep 1933;. Ruth Willis (with McTell): 'Rough Alley Blues', Atlanta, 23 Oct 1931.

Woody Mann quote from sleevenotes by Stephen Calt & John Miller for *Blind Willie McTell 1927–1935*, Yazoo L-1037, NY, 1973. McTell quotes Atlanta, GA, Sep 1956, recorded by Ed Rhodes, issued *Blind Willie McTell: Last Session*. Kate McTell quote from interview with Kate McTell Seabrooks by Anne M. Evans, *Blues Unlimited* no.125, Sussex, UK, Jul/Aug 1977, p.6. David Fulmer, *Blind Willie's Blues*, Missing Lenk [sic] Video, Lawrenceville, GA, 1996; DVD-reissue within a *Blind Willie McTell* limited-edition box set due late 2005, details tba, still unreleased as of Apr 2006.

McTell's biography—Michael Gray, *Hand Me My Travelin' Shoes: In the Footsteps of Blind Willie McTell*, London: Bloomsbury—is due out in 2007, represents the first new research into his life since work by David Evans and his family in the 1970s, and will yield new information about McTell's life.]

Madhouse on Castle Street, The [1962 - 1963]

This was a BBC Television Drama (at the time there was only one BBC channel), filmed in London on December 30, 1962 and January 4, 1963, and transmitted in the UK that January 13. It was a consciously modernist play, written by the contemporary white Jamaican playwright Evan Jones, directed by Philip Saville—a young man of 28 at the time (he was born in London in October 1934)—and starring the young and relatively unknown ex-RADA (Royal Academy of Dramatic Arts) and Royal Shakespeare Company actor David Warner, and the still more unknown Bob Dylan.

The plot centres around a man who locks himself in a room in a boarding house—the 'madhouse' of the title—leaving a note announcing that he has decided to 'retire from the world'. His sister and the other residents try to find out why.

Philip Saville had seen Dylan perform in Greenwich Village and had managed to get the BBC to bring him over, paying a fee of 500 Guineas (at the time a couple of thousand US dollars) plus expenses; Saville also spent some time with Dylan in

London in this period, Dylan staying as a guest at his home in affluent Hampstead, entertaining his two Spanish au pair girls late into the night and asking why he wanted to live the family life: why didn't he abandon it for the life of the road?

Saville wanted to incorporate Dylan's striking way with a folksong within the body of a play he much admired, but when it came to it, the play had to be altered at the last minute, separating the singing and acting rôles and bringing in David Warner for the latter (as Lennie) because Dylan flunked it when it came to the pre-performance readings. (This solution to the problem was the playwright's idea.)

Dylan (as Bobby) sat on the stairs and sang four songs (though as broadcast they were shown in often fleeting sections, never as whole-song performances): the traditional 'Hang Me Oh Hang Me' (aka 'I've Been All Around This World') and 'Cuckoo Bird' (aka 'The Cuckoo Is a Pretty Bird'), plus 'Blowin' in the Wind'—which had been recorded but not yet released, which Dylan had been performing in the Village for some time and which Philip Saville particularly wanted to include—and a song written in folksong style by Evan Jones, 'The Ballad of the Gliding Swan', which Dylan amended on the spot and never performed again.

After the broadcast, David Warner rapidly became a star. He was acclaimed for his role in *Morgan, A Suitable Case for Treatment* and for his playing of Hamlet at the RSC, both in 1966, and since then has appeared in almost 150 films including *Straw Dogs*, *The Omen* and *Titanic*. The tapes and film of *Madhouse on Castle Street* were retained by the BBC until these participants were huge stars, and then, in *1968*, they destroyed the footage.

For over 40 years this unusual early moment in Dylan's career was thought to have been irretrievably lost—no footage of the play has yet come to light—until in 2005 Anthony Wall, a director of the BBC-TV arts series *Arena*, made an appeal for rare Dylan treasures while planning some extra material to augment the first British TV showing of MARTIN SCORSESE's documentary *No Direction Home* in September 2005.

Pete Read, a schoolboy at the time, had made a recording, and so had HANS FRIED, a young music enthusiast who had met Dylan, by chance, in a London jazz record shop very soon beforehand (see **Graves, Robert**), and who achieved a reasonably good sound on his tape, using a Baird reel-to-reel machine. For some time, this copy's existence had been known to IAN WOODWARD, a British Dylan expert and acquaintance of Fried's, and Woodward passed the recording to the BBC. (This was the second time the BBC's *Arena* series had unearthed early Dylan recordings: see also **earliest extant recordings**.) Later, but in the nick of time, a third and much superior tape-recording came to light, made by a Ray Jenkins from Esher in Surrey.

Until these tapes were gathered in, the lyrics of 'The Ballad of the Gliding Swan', as improved by Dylan, were lost to posterity. They begin memorably, yet in the style of an ancient ballad: 'Tenderly William kissed his wife / Then he opened her head with a butcher's knife / And the swan on the river went gliding by. / The swan on the river went gliding by. / Lady Margaret's pillow was wet with tears . . .'

These recordings were supposed to be publicly transmitted at long last in September 2005, within Anthony Wall's *Arena: Dylan in the Madhouse*, part of a short BBC4 'Dylan season'. In the event, not only did the programme spend most of its time on old news footage of Britain going through the exceptionally cold winter of 1962–63 (such that had the winter been mild, *Arena*'s programme would have lasted about 15 minutes), and not only did it fail to press David Warner for detail on his recollection of meeting up with Dylan years afterwards (Dylan recalled 'You played *me*!' and astonished Warner by remembering the names of all the other actors), but these much-trumpeted recordings were treated in a most dilatory way, with no attempt to play them straightforwardly for all those who had turned their TVs on especially to hear them: and indeed the fragments that *were* played were from the inferior recordings, right until the closing moments of this hopelessly spun-out yet careless programme, when a few seconds of the superior version was played, as if deliberately to taunt the disappointed viewer.

Evan Jones, who had been born in Portland, Jamaica, in 1927, was most highly thought of in exactly the period of *Madhouse on Castle Street*. Film director Joseph Losey, given the chance to direct *The Damned* (1962), threw away the script, used a better one written by Jones, and delivered an uncompromising, bleak thriller. Jones went on to write screenplays for *King and Country*, *Modesty Blaise*, *Funeral in Berlin* and many later films. In 1976 his play *The Man with the Power* was commissioned and screened within the BBC's TV drama series *Playhouse: The Mind Beyond*, which looked at paranormal phenomena. The year before that, he had co-written the BBC's TV documentary series *The Fight Against Slavery*. In 1999 his memoir 'A Cushion for My Dreams' was collected in *A Tapestry of Jamaica—The Best of SkyWritings*, published by Macmillan Caribbean.

Philip Saville, who had started out his media life as an actor (he played a teenage dinner guest in the would-be surreal 1948 film *A Piece of Cake*) went on to direct, among much else, the film *Stop the World I Want to Get Off* in 1966, the TV series 'The Boys from the Blackstuff', written by Alan Bleasdale, which was the critical and commercial success of 1982, *Life and Loves of a She-Devil* in 1985, and the film *Metroland* in 1997.

It should be counted another of his successes that he brought Dylan over to London in 1962—that he brought him over to Europe for the first time in his life—and thereby introduced him to the English folk scene, to its clubs and prejudices and personnel, to Martin Carthy and so to 'Scarborough Fair' and 'Lord Franklin', and more: not to mention that Philip Saville gave Dylan his first experience of high-production-value broadcasting: network TV that was rife with the sense of its own importance; and all this at the very moment when the 1960s were beginning to dawn.

Mansfield, David [c1956 -] David Mansfield is very coy about his birth date but he was born around 1956 in Leonia, New Jersey, where he grew up to be a multi-instrumentalist, playing mostly violin, mandolin and guitar. His first band is said to have enjoyed the name Quacky Duck and His Barnyard Friends, which, as if that weren't bad enough, also included two of Tony Bennett's children.

He arrived, out of nowhere, in GUAM, not the unfortunate US dependency but the band put together for the 1975 Rolling Thunder Revue tour, and unlike most of the Revue musicians, he continued to play not only through the second Rolling Thunder tour of 1976 but rejoined Dylan for the entire 1978 World Tour. (STEVEN SOLES and ROB STONER were the only others to do so.) All through this period, he looked about 12 years old, and not necessarily in a good way. 'Genius kid. Played everything but the kitchen sink,' wrote SAM SHEPARD, observing Mansfield in action on the first Rolling Thunder tour, without any hint that he found him likeable. Shepard watched him play, 'looking like Little Lord Fauntleroy, and impressing everyone with his classical violin technique.' Shepard noted too that Mansfield was 'often referred to' by ALLEN GINSBERG, also on the tour, as 'the boy with the Botticelli face'—a propos of which RONNIE HAWKINS would later tell this endearingly *Hawkins* story:

> 'Darlin' Doug was beautiful, but he wasn't gay. But he wanted to be a hero. He couldn't figure out why he wasn't on top of the world, he was so goodlookin' and this and that. And so I played a little joke on him. I was over talking to Allen, and Allen said "Who's that good-lookin' kid over there?" I said, "Oh, that's my rhythm-guitar player", I said, "But he's a little mixed-up." I said, "He thinks he wants to be gay." Of course Allen, the sweat broke out on him! Then I went over there and told Darlin' Doug, I said: "Now listen, see that guy over there? His name is Allen Ginsberg. He's the one that made Bob Dylan. He's worth *billions*. If he likes you, he'll buy a record company for you!" So Darlin' Doug goes over, and they sit down with each other, and meanwhile I'm hid in a corner watching the play! Oh man, it was a classic! Should have filmed that one.'

The main Rolling Thunder violinist was SCARLET RIVERA, but Mansfield played violin too, plus dobro, steel guitar and mandolin. Between the end of the Revue and the start of the '78 tour, Mansfield and Soles plus T-BONE BURNETT formed the Alpha Band, which released three albums. On the 1978 tour, while still ornamenting the sound with mandolin and guitar, Mansfield came into his own as sole violinist. He also played on the *Street Legal* album (violin and mandolin) as well as on the two live albums *Hard Rain* (his credit here is for guitar) and *At Budokan*.

Mansfield was also, like Soles and Burnett, a committed Born Again Christian, and therefore one of those quizzed about his faith by Dylan in 1978 as he tottered towards Jesus himself.

In 1986 Mansfield was in Bruce Hornsby and the Range just long enough to play on their hit 'Mandolin Rain' (guess what instrument he plays on that), but not long enough to go on tour with them. Both sides of the Hornsby job, he continued session-work, including for Edie Brickell, JOHNNY CASH, NANCI GRIFFITH, ROGER McGUINN, the Roches, Spinal Tap, Lucinda Williams and DWIGHT YOAKAM. He had also begun film work in 1980; perhaps it was ironic that after *Renaldo & Clara*, he and Ronnie Hawkins should both find themselves appearing next in *Heaven's Gate*, Michael Cimino's famously studio-busting commercial flop in 1980, in Mansfield's case playing the violin on roller skates as a member of the Heaven's Gate Band (along with T-Bone Burnett); but he also wrote the film's original music, after which he composed for many other films, including, more recently, co-writing the score for the 2002 film of *Divine Secrets of the Ya-Ya Sisterhood*, to which Dylan contributed the indifferent 'Waitin' on You'. And in 1996, when Ginsberg was giving early readings, set to music, of the last poem in his *Collected Poems 1947–1995*, 'The Ballad of the Skeletons', which grew into a collaboration with PAUL McCARTNEY, Philip Glass, Lenny Kaye and eventually the four-minute video directed by Gus Van Sant (1997), it was the no longer quite so Botticelli-faced David Mansfield who played guitar behind him.

[Sam Shepard quoted from *Rolling Thunder Logbook*, London: Penguin edn., 1978, pp.17 & 31. Ronnie Hawkins' story, told to this writer, St. Johns, Newfoundland, fall 1985, in '1976 & Other Times: Ronnie Hawkins, Rock'n'Roller', collected in Michael Gray & John Bauldie, *All Across the Telegraph: A Bob Dylan Handbook*, London: W.H. Allen, 1987.]

Manuel, Richard [1943 - 1986] Richard Manuel was born in the small town of Stratford, Ontario, Canada, a few miles southwest of Toronto, where he joined RONNIE HAWKINS & THE HAWKS in the summer of 1961, aged 18, as the group's pianist. He had learnt to play as a young teenager, 'brought in gospel music from his church upbringing,' as RICK DANKO noted, and could sing in conscious imitation of RAY CHARLES—though later, in THE BAND, he found his own style without ever abandoning the Charles resemblance. A highlight of this fusion, caught on the album *Islands* yet even better on the unissued alternate take, is his 1977 recording of 'Georgia on My Mind'.

However, first came touring and recording with Ronnie Hawkins & the Hawks, then with LEVON & the Hawks and then with Bob Dylan. The Hawks met Dylan in 1965 and that September got together with him to rehearse in Woodstock, New York (with Manuel on piano), for further live gigs beyond those already played with Levon & Robbie and other, non-Hawk musicians in the aftermath of 'going electric' at Newport that July. The first Dylan concert Richard Manuel played was probably October 1 at Carnegie Hall. Quite some initiation.

On October 5 the group went into the studio with Dylan for the first time, followed by more live concerts and a second studio stint—minus Helm—on November 30 (from which comes the single 'Can You Please Crawl Out Your Window?'). This session has also now yielded the version of 'Visions of Johanna' released on the *Bootleg Series Vol. 7*, 2005.

The now-Helmless Hawks were back in the studio in New York at Dylan's behest on January 21–22, 1966, where they helped create that quintessential mid-60s Dylan record, 'She's Your Lover Now' (finally issued on the *Bootleg Series Vols. 1–3* in 1991), but when Dylan, Robertson and Rick Danko returned to the studio three days later, for sessions held January 25–28, Richard Manuel and GARTH HUDSON were not with them.

Manuel and Hudson certainly were there, however, for the madness and the glory of Dylan's 1966 so-called World Tour, beginning in Louisville, Kentucky, on February 4 and going across the States, into Canada and Hawaii, across to Australia and then to Europe, where they began in Stockholm, Sweden, on April 29 and ended at the Royal Albert Hall in London on May 27.

After all that came the calm of Woodstock and West Saugherties, 1967, when the Hawks were working very differently with Bob Dylan, laying down the Basement Tapes and preparing to turn into The Band.

Now, Richard Manuel came more fully into his own. He was, aside from ROBBIE ROBERTSON, the songwriter of the group. This side of his gift was previewed during the Basement Tapes sessions (when he was also, in Levon Helm's continued absence, playing drums). From here came the all-too-brief 'Beautiful Thing', the co-written 'Ruben Remus' and (co-written with Dylan) 'Tears of Rage'.

And this is the song that opens the great *Music from Big Pink*. As Barney Hoskyns writes: 'Richard Manuel's is the first voice you hear on the first Band album . . . his aching baritone launches into the first reproachful line of "Tears of Rage". . . . And by the end of the first chorus you realize why . . . fellow Band vocalists Levon Helm and Rick Danko always looked upon him as the group's "lead" singer.'

Manuel also wrote the painful yet shimmering 'In a Station', 'We Can Talk' and the exquisite, anguished 'Lonesome Suzie' on that album, and after 'Tears of Rage' he shared lead vocals with Robertson on 'To Kingdom Come', sang lead again on 'In a Station' and on 'We Can Talk' and 'Chest Fever', 'Lonesome Suzie' and the closing song, his lovely rendition of Dylan's 'I Shall Be Released'. He also sang back-up vocals and played keyboards.

On the even better second album, *The Band*, Richard Manuel was already starting to slide away from a prominence as great as Robbie Robertson's. While Robertson co-wrote or wrote everything on the album, Manuel this time merely co-wrote three songs: 'When You Awake', 'Whispering Pines' and 'Jawbone', though he was still very present as a multi-instrumentalist (he's credited with playing piano, drums, baritone sax and harmonica) and as lead vocalist on 'Across the Great Divide' and 'Jawbone', and shares lead vocals too on 'Whispering Pines', 'Rockin' Chair' and 'King Harvest (Will Surely Come)'.

Subsequent albums came, so much less wondrous than those first two. Manuel's contribution to their composition diminished till it disappeared. Many people would say that these two things were directly related. The group that had started out as so effective a demonstration of the rich fruits of collaborative labour now seemed increasingly led by Robertson's ego. On the third album, *Stage Fright*, Manuel co-wrote just one song, 'Just Another Whistle Stop'. On the fourth, *Cahoots*, nothing. On 1975's *Northern Lights—Southern Cross*, nothing. (Meanwhile Dylan, at Madison Square Garden on December 8, 1975, the last night of the first Rolling Thunder Revue, says when introducing 'I Shall Be Released': 'Gonna dedicate this song to Mr. Richard Manuel, who does it so well.')

On the original 3-LP set of *The Last Waltz*, even though this is supposed to take us back through classic Band repertoire, not one track—not one! —is either a Manuel composition or even co-composition.

He's there as musician, of course, and he's the lead vocalist on, aptly, 'The Shape I'm In' and co-lead singer with VAN MORRISON on 'Tura Lura Lura' and with Dylan on 'I Shall Be Released'. Shamefully, however, Richard Manuel's wonderful 'Georgia on My Mind' is *still* missing, even on the new 4-CD set of *The Last Waltz*. He really does get squeezed out.

And then, with The Band disbanded, Manuel was the one to suffer most. Raddled with addiction, to both alcohol and cocaine, he was the one who couldn't make it on his own. He made no solo albums; he joined no other band.

Somehow, when The Band itself re-formed, in 1983, Manuel was there, addiction free and functioning well, though some of the spine-tingling ethereal quality was now missing from his still-soulful voice. One of the great oldies he performed at this point was the Eddy Arnold song that had given Ray Charles a big hit in 1962, and which Dylan started performing some years later on the Never-Ending Tour: 'You Don't Know Me'.

Encouraged by Levon Helm, in 1985 Manuel was filmed in a small acting rôle, as Vigilante no.1, in the film *Man Outside* (Hudson, Helm and Danko appeared too), released in 1986 to no particular success.

In January 1986, disaster came swiftly. The old Band (and Dylan) manager ALBERT GROSSMAN died. Richard Manuel lost a man he'd come to depend upon to keep him relatively straight. He plunged back into addiction. Levon Helm's book *This Wheel's on Fire* claims that he was drinking as much as 12 bottles of Jack Daniels a day—possibly the heaviest consumption ever attributed to anyone, and scarcely credible. Whatever the details, it was an addiction that took a lethal toll. In the early hours of Tuesday, March 4, 1986, after a Band gig at the Cheek to Cheek Lounge in Winter Park, Florida, Richard Manuel hanged himself from his Quality Inn motel room's bathroom curtain rod, leaving his wife to find him.

He never played in public with Bob Dylan after 1976, and never made a solo album, though he did make, weirdly, posthumous appearances on a couple of albums by The Band. More significantly, in 2002 the Japanese label Dreamsville released a CD *Whispering Pines: Live at the Getaway*, taken from two intimate shows Richard Manuel gave at a club back in Saugherties, New York, on October 12, 1985, on which many tracks are solo but a few feature Rick Danko, Jim Weider and harmonica player Sredni Vollmer: 18 tracks, including two versions of 'Georgia on My Mind' and two of 'Across the Great Divide'.

'For me,' said ERIC CLAPTON, 'he was the true *light* of The Band.'

[Band album details see **The Band**. Richard Manuel: *Whispering Pines: Live at the Getaway*, Dreamsville YDCD-0082, Japan, 2002 (Other Peoples Music CD-OPM-6603, US), 2005. *Man Outside*, dir. & written Mark Stouffer, US, 1986. For a full Manuel discography see *http://theband.hiof.no/albums/manuel_index.html*.]

Marcus, Greil [1945 -] Greil Marcus was born in San Francisco on June 19, 1945. He became one of the writers who created rock criticism. Taking an interest in Dylan's work in 1963, he later started writing as a music critic for the 1960s Underground Press, penning eloquent, influential pieces on Dylan such as 'Let the record play itself', in early 1969, which derided A.J. WEBERMAN's crude 'interpretations' of Dylan's lyrics and used WILLIAM BLAKE to argue a point. His first piece of published writing on Dylan had been shortly before this: 'The Legend of Blind Steamer Trunk', *San Francisco Express-Times*, December 24, 1968.

His *Rolling Stone* review of *Self Portrait* in 1970 famously began by demanding: 'What is this shit?'; yet Marcus was invited to write the sleeve-notes to the officially released double-LP *The Basement Tapes* in 1975. The same year saw publication of his fine and impassioned book *Mystery Train*. Later he moved on to works on punk and other subjects, and to speaking engagements, magazine columns, appointments such as being a Director of the National Book Critics Circle (1983–88) and academic posts.

Marcus then contributed to the positive sea change in Dylan's critical and popular esteem that suddenly occurred from 1996 onwards when he published a critical study centered upon one aspect of Dylan's work, *Invisible Republic: Bob Dylan's Basement Tapes* (1997), soon republished under the title he had wanted all along, *The Old, Weird America: The World of Bob Dylan's Basement Tapes* (2001): a book that was accorded a huge amount of reviewing attention in the press on both sides of the Atlantic, breaking down barriers thanks to Marcus' stature in cultural studies criticism, and even earning a mention in Dylan's own *Chronicles Volume One*. In 2005 Marcus published the book *Like a Rolling Stone: Bob Dylan at the Crossroads*, centered around Dylan's recording of that song. The book was written hurriedly, contains various errors of fact and has received rather more mixed reviews than he is accustomed to.

Marcus has, in other words, made a very significant contribution, and been well rewarded for it, but there is always a detectable groundswell of muttered resistance to the charms of his prose and the weight of his eminence. He sometimes comes close to self-parody, and sometimes may not actually be saying anything. Here he is, for example, in an essay published with the compilation album *And the Times They Were a-Changin'* in 1998: 'Bob Dylan's "All Along the Watchtower" takes place outside of time; JIMI HENDRIX's accepts time, and then unravels it.' It's a great technique, used sparingly, and his writing seems to pluck these verdicts from the air—verdicts with all the cryptic power of a guru up a pole, so that the hapless reader feels he can argue with neither the supreme self-confidence of the delivery nor with the content, since this is as ungraspable as it is forcefully done.

A good test is to put them the other way round and see if it makes any difference: 'Hendrix's "Watchtower" takes place outside of time; Dylan's accepts time, and then unravels it.' Hmm. Nonetheless, Marcus is a major figure, and, to his eternal credit, one of those who first insisted to the critics and guardians of mainstream culture that rock'n'roll music mattered and that figures like Bob Dylan mattered a lot.

[Greil Marcus, 'The Legend of Blind Steamer Trunk', *San Francisco Express-Times*, 24 Dec 1968 (revised version collected in *Rock and Roll Will Stand*, ed. Marcus, San Francisco: Beacon Press, 1969); 'Let the record play itself', *San Francisco Express-Times*, 11 Feb 1969; 'Album Review: Self Portrait', *Rolling Stone* no.25, San Francisco, 23 Jul 1970; *Mystery Train: Images of America in Rock 'N' Roll Music*, 1975; essay with album *And the Times They Were a-Changin'* (Various Artists, Débutante DeLuxe 555 431-2, PolyGram, London), 1998.]

Marquand, Richard [1938 - 1987] Richard Marquand was born in Cardiff, Wales, on April 17, 1938. After an education in England and France, he worked first as a television newscaster in Hong Kong (when this was still a British colony), getting into films via BBC documentaries and in 1979 making the dramatised TV film *The Birth of THE BEATLES*. From here his career took off, with 1981's post-war spy story *Eye of the Needle*, despite its mixed reviews, leading directly to his being hired by George Lucas to direct the third Star Wars movie, *Return of the Jedi*. In 1984 he directed a less successful love story, *Until September*, before his 1985 thriller *Jagged Edge* proved another high-quality work within its chosen genre, and enough of a commercial success that he could try to realise, next, a personal ambition to make a film with Bob Dylan: and not just *a* film, but Dylan's first mainstream rôle since *Pat Garrett & Billy the Kid* more than a decade earlier.

Unfortunately for him, Dylan and the rest of us, Marquand seemed to become curiously paralysed by being granted his wish, and never arrived at any clear idea of what film to create with Dylan or how to gain anything more from this artist than his signature on a contract. Though sharing the same writer (Joe Eszterhas) as well as director, none of the flair, freshness or intelligently devised drama of *Jagged Edge* was even hinted at in *Hearts of Fire*.

The film was barely finished when Richard Marquand died from a stroke in Los Angeles on September 4, 1987, at the age of 49. At least he didn't have to read the reviews. On the other hand, as WOODY ALLEN once remarked: 'Life is scarier than art. If you fail in life it can be dangerous. If you fail in art it's only embarrassing.'

[*Birth of the Beatles*, ABC, UK, 1979; *Eye of the Needle*, Juniper/King's Road, UK, 1981; *Star Wars: Episode VI—Return of the Jedi*, LucasFilms, US, 1983; *Until September*, MGM, US, 1984; *Jagged Edge*, Columbia, US, 1985; *Hearts of Fire*, written Joe Eszterhas & Scott Richardson, Lorimar/Warner Bros., US/UK, 1987. Woody Allen, BBC-TV interview, 1992.]

Marqusee, Mike [1953 -] An American left-wing writer and political activist, Marqusee was born in New York City in 1953, grew up in Scarsdale, NY, moved to Britain in 1971, spent three years at Sussex University and then settled in London, his base ever since. He is the author of the award-winning 1999 MUHAMMAD ALI biography *Muhammad Ali and the Spirit of the Sixties* (updated 2nd edition 2005), *Anyone But England* (on race, class and nationality in cricket, 1994) and *War Minus the Shooting* (on the Cricket World Cup in South Asia, 1996).

In 2003 he published the excellent study *Chimes of Freedom: The Politics of Bob Dylan's Art*. This refocusing of attention upon Dylan's early political songs—the so-called Protest Songs—was a timely and useful counterweight to the long general pull of Dylan studies and of opinion among Dylan aficionados that these songs are his least interesting. At the same time, Marqusee is eloquent on Dylan's abandonment of such overt political writing, and acute on the difference between that and an abandoning of political consciousness itself. Here he is on 'My Back Pages':

> 'Here he sneers at "corpse evangelists" who use "ideas" as "maps", who spout "lies that life is black and white" and who fail to understand that "I become my enemy in the instant that I preach." Alarmed by the discovery of authoritarianism at the heart of the movement for liberation (and within himself), he rebels against the left's self-righteousness. . . . [The song's] refrain—a recantation in every sense of the word—must be one of the most lyrical expressions of political apostasy ever penned. Ex-radicals usually ascribe their evolution to the inevitable giving-way of rebellious youth to responsible maturity. Dylan reversed the polarity. For him, the retreat from politics was a retreat from stale categories and second-hand attitudes. The refrain encapsulates the movement from the pretence of knowing it all to the confession of knowing nothing.'

And on the work that follows:

> 'Dylan's break with politics and the movement that had been his first inspiration unleashed his poetic and musical genius; it freed him to explore an inner landscape. His lyrics became more obscure; coherent narrative was jettisoned in favour of carnivalesque surrealism; the austerity of the acoustic folk troubadour was replaced by the hedonistic extravagance of an electrified rock'n'roll ensemble. The songs depicted a private universe—but one forged in response to tumultuous public events. It's remarkable that so many of Dylan's left critics failed to see the politics that infuse his masterworks of the mid-sixties.'

Ironically, given his comments on 'My Back Pages', Marqusee was involved that same year (2003) in classic left-wing internecine squabbles. Having left the Labour Party unable to stomach any more Blairism, he worked with, but was not a member of, the Socialist Workers Party, in the short-lived Socialist Alliance and in the Stop the

War Coalition but found this an entirely negative experience: 'corpse evangelists'.

An updated, revised edition of *Chimes of Freedom*, re-titled *Wicked Messenger: Bob Dylan and the 1960s*, was published in late 2005, to include assessments of Dylan's film *Masked and Anonymous* and of his book of memoirs, *Chronicles Volume One*.

As well as an author and activist, Marqusee is also a prolific, pithy journalist and reviewer: see, for instance, his sharp, clear-eyed review of *Like a Rolling Stone: Bob Dylan at the Crossroads* by GREIL MARCUS in *The Guardian*, May 28, 2005, which includes a fine brief description of the Dylan song itself. Finally, he is unique among authors of books on Dylan in having given a series of public talks about Dylan in India (2005).

[Mike Marqusee, *Chimes of Freedom: The Politics of Bob Dylan's Art*, New Press, 2003; revised edition published as *Wicked Messenger: Bob Dylan and the 1960s—Chimes of Freedom, Revised and Expanded*, New York: Seven Stories Press, 2005. For the political squabbles referred to, see the *Morning Star*, London, 13 Aug 2003 and Marqusee's own website, *www.mikemarqusee.com*, which also posts the review of Marcus' book on 'Like a Rolling Stone'.]

Marsalis, Wynton [1961 -] Born October 18, 1961 in New Orleans, Marsalis studied trumpet from age 12 and in high school performed in marching bands, jazz bands, funk bands (it says here) and classical orchestras. He attended the Juilliard School of Music at 18, and the year after became a member of Art Blakey's Jazz Messengers and signed with Columbia Records. Since his début LP in 1982, he has sold millions of jazz and classical albums, co-founded Jazz at Lincoln Center, won the first Pulitzer Prize for Music, been more fêted by the American cultural establishment than any other black person in history . . . and generally serves to remind us that Bob Dylan is still an outsider.

The first time Wynton Marsalis and Dylan performed 'together' it was at a distance of 650 miles, when Marsalis was part of the Atlanta, GA, ensemble singing a posthumous 'Happy Birthday' to Martin Luther King while Dylan was part of the ensemble singing it simultaneously at the main event venue in Washington, D.C., on January 20, 1986. (King's birthday is now officially celebrated in the US on the *19th*; his real birth date was neither the 19th nor 20th but January 15; he was born in Atlanta in 1929.)

Dylan and Marsalis worked together properly, if very briefly, on June 7, 2004, at the Apollo Theater, NYC, when on a mixed bill of performing artists—Dylan, James Taylor, Al Jarreau, Branford Marsalis, Renee Olstead and the Wynton Marsalis Septet—Dylan sang and played harmonica on 'It Takes a Lot to Laugh, It Takes a Train to Cry' and 'Don't Think Twice, It's All Right', backed by the Septet: surely a most interesting combination, likely to have discomfited Dylan more than somewhat. No tape has emerged. This may be connected to the fact that the 800 tickets on sale for this event cost $1,000 and $2,500 each. (Tables of ten were available from $10,000 to $35,000.) It was a benefit concert for the Jazz at Lincoln Center Benefit Concerts fund.

***Masked & Anonymous* [film & soundtrack, 2003]** This large-scale film marked Dylan's first ambitious movie project since the badly received four-hour *Renaldo & Clara*, released in 1978. This time the acolytes surrounding Dylan are Hollywood rather than rock and poetry stars: Jeff Bridges, Penelope Cruz, John Goodman and Jessica Lange instead of ALLEN GINSBERG, JOAN BAEZ, RONNIE HAWKINS and SCARLET RIVERA. The production companies behind the making of *Masked & Anonymous*, however, are comparable not to those of *Renaldo & Clara* but of *No Direction Home* (2005). Dylan's chief factotum JEFF ROSEN, plus film man Nigel Sinclair, co-produced both.

When the forthcoming project of *Masked & Anonymous* first made the papers, in February 2002, it was said to be based on a short story called 'Los Vientos del Destino' ('The Winds of Destiny'); in April this was said to be by an Enrique Morales and there was speculation that perhaps this was a Dylan pseudonym; on July 2 Morales was said to be 'an obscure Argentinean writer'; ten days later Morales, who was indeed both a real person and an Argentinean writer, and living in Paris, denied all knowledge of any such short story. By this point it was strongly suspected that the movie's credited writers, Sergei Petrov and Rene Fontaine, were Bob Dylan and the director, LARRY CHARLES. The pseudonym Sergei Petrov was taken from the name of an actor from the silent-movie era, who had appeared as a soldier in the weird 1928 Russian film *Arsenal* and had survived to take a final rôle in 1960 in the much-admired *Roman i Francheska*, directed by Vladimir Denisenko. (Another Sergei Petrov is a contemporary photographer working out of Arlington, Virginia; another is a distinguished Russian architect.) At any rate, this pseudonym sounded a better name that than of the character Dylan was to play in the film: Jack Fate. That did sound bad.

Filming took place in Los Angeles from June 17 to July 21, 2002, in the period between that year's Never-Ending Tour spring leg, which ended with two exceptionally good concerts at London's Docklands Arena on May 11 and 12, and the start of the next leg, in August in the USA.

Those who like the result use terms like 'an imaginative allegory' that 'overturns expectations' with 'a barrage of wit', 'energy and spirit' and 'creative vision'. *Salon.com* declared it 'an exhilarating jumble' and a 'brilliant must-see film'.

Well. First, it's only two hours long but like *Renaldo & Clara* it is partly a film about Bob Dylan's mystique, which dooms us to watching much fore-lock-tugging to the maestro while little more is required of him than that he stand there looking unimpressed.

The finest moment in the entire two hours of *Masked & Anonymous* occurs in the caravan of tiresome scuzzy-manager character Uncle Sweetheart, as Bob Dylan sits sideways and drapes his contrastingly bony, bony legs over one arm of the chair (naturally, he is placing himself obliquely). The enormous John Goodman protests that he is only human, and Bob responds: 'I know. It ain't easy bein' human.' Dylan delivers the line disarmingly, sounding, for almost the only time in the film, well, human, yet contriving to look, while saying it, uncannily like a monkey.

What seems welcome in this perplexing, vexing, lavishly tatterdemalion movie is its preparedness to say things like that. To hold out lines that are not from Hollywood; to offer a script that plays by a different set of rules. This is not 'realistic' dialogue. Everyone is constantly discussing the meaning of life. If they are speaking at all. It is all as stylised as can be, and its cadences are familiar to anyone who has ever heard Dylan's songs or even read his album sleevenotes or interview answers.

To hear Goodman cascading on about Alexander the Great and crankcase oil is to remember the mutterings about soldiers in the mud in Dylan's notes to the *World Gone Wrong* album. To listen to Jessica Lange holding forth about Muslims, Buddhists, Hindus and war is to recall the long harangues on the inner sleeves of *Biograph*. But sometimes to listen is to squirm, and to watch this film tensed against those moments when the script is so Dylanesque it's just dismal. There are less stressful (and funnier) moments, when these pronouncements veer towards the Donald Rumsfeld cliff-edge of cleverness, as when the Jack Fate character (Dylan) intones that 'Sometimes it's not enough to know the meaning of things: sometimes we have to know what things don't mean as well.'

As recurrent as the lengthy preacher-like pronouncements is the opposite stylistic tic, the dialogue built of extra-compressed monosyllables. Often the two forms meet: the Jeff Bridges character, or the Val Kilmer madman, rap on at wizened, silent Bob for minutes on end, only to elicit a grunt in response. Bob's facial expressions are so enigmatic they're often motionless. Sometimes he's so gnomic he's garden-gnomic.

But constant discussion of the meaning of life makes a pleasant change from soap-opera atavism and piety, and it's by no means always portentous. When the two idle members of the road crew are talking, their earnestness is nicely comic. The always-compelling Bruce Dern, though here distressingly shrunken and almost as simian as Bob in that chair, has a nice line: 'What am I drinking? I'm drinking my life away.'

The postmodern discussions of the meaning of Dylan's songs are comic too—at one point Penelope Cruz discusses their open-endedness with the Pope and Gandhi—except that this is a running joke that rests on knowingness, which is never as attractive as sincerity. Throw-ins like the wall of song titles that includes 'I Hate You' as well as 'I Want You'—these are the jokes that wear thinnest quickest.

Best is when the dialogue brings an unexpected moment of human warmth into the verbal play—as when Jeff Bridges, the loathsome journalist (and in Bobland there is no other sort) is grinding out his weary cynical take at Penelope Cruz, belabouring her with the standard orator's trick of three-point argument, that 'It's an overcrowded world. It's hard to get to the top. There's a long line at the elevator,' and she undercuts him with humane simplicity, saying: 'It doesn't matter. We'll take the stairs.'

This is Bobland in other ways too. Here is the same world he sings of in 'Angelina' (whose melody, uncredited, plays at the film's final end) and 'Groom's Still Waiting at the Altar': the world of interminable war and corruption, greed and meaninglessness, the America that is not merely North America but teems with the poor and the enslaved, the third world, the world that speaks in Spanish and knows that everything is broken. But unlike the songs, the film works so hard and so clumsily to say so. And though, as he wanders through his fallen world, there's a sense of Dylan the Sam Spade fan behind it, terse one-liners are not enough, and Bob looks more David Niven than Humphrey Bogart.

The big downside of characters who are archetypes instead of individuals is that they're doomed to be cardboard, managing therefore to be both flimsy and stiff. (Blame Dylan's lifelong fondness for Francois Truffaut's film *Shoot the Piano Player*.) It's no triumph of form that you never for a moment watch a single scene and forget that it isn't real. You watch Bob on the bus and he's keeping up a ponderous rocking from side to side that is clearly false in itself and shown to be the more so by the fact that none of the other passengers moves remotely like this. And there's an awful lot of watching Bob riding in vehicles to be got through, just as there's a great deal of watching him walk a hat around the place.

Worse, several key ingredients found only in truly bad films that *are* conventional Hollywood are here too. One: war backdrop or not, the whole plot rests upon people saying 'Hey! Let's put on a concert!' Two: we're asked to take at face value, solemnly, that the main character and a suitably subservient buddy (Bob and Luke Wilson) are Firm Friends who'll do anything for each other. Three: there's a random moment when, for no reason (there's not even a lame attempt to convey one) our main character walks out on things, and has to be begged to remain—and this is imagined to be a moment of drama. Four: there's a gruellingly pathetic fight scene, in which our hero is pushed reluctantly into Man of Action.

Scenes like these force you to concede with shame and sadness that for all its strenuous efforts to be art, and all its good intentions, at bottom Dylan's *Masked & Anonymous* is just an ELVIS movie. The music's better though.

Other artists on the soundtrack album include Swedish vocalist Sophie Zelman muttering 'Most of the Time' (in English) and Turkish pop star Sertab Erener singing 'One More Cup of Coffee'. (Sertab, born in Istanbul in 1964, had made her début album in 1992, and the same year as she appeared on the *Masked & Anonymous* soundtrack she won the Eurovision Song Contest for Turkey.) The more interestingly 'foreign' soundtrack items were Japanese duo the Magokoro Brothers with a cover of 'My Back Pages' sung in Japanese, taken from their 1995 album *King of Rock* (their début single had been in 1989; they'd disbanded by the time the Dylan film came out) and two contrasting Italian items: Francesco de Gregori (born in Rome in 1950, whose début album had been made in 1970) singing a translation of 'If You See Her, Say Hello' titled 'Non Dirle Che Non E' Cosi', and the 'spaghetti funk' rap duo Articolo 31 with their splendid rapping-in-Italian 'Like a Rolling Stone', 'Come Una Pietra Scalciata', which incorporated fragments of Dylan's original studio version. This comes from their 1998 album *Nessuno*, recorded in New York City. (The duo, J. Ax, aka Alessandro Aleotti, and DJ Jad, aka Luca Perrini, named their act after the article of the Italian Constitution that guarantees the freedom of the press, and made their début album in 1993.)

Dylan's own Jack Fate 'concert sequence' was filmed at Canoga Park, California, on July 18, 2002 and comprised 11 numbers, nine of which are featured in the film, with a tenth ('Standing in the Doorway') shown as a 'deleted scene' in the 'extras' on the commercially issued DVD. The nine are 'Down in the Flood', 'Amazing Grace', 'Diamond Joe' (not the same song as on the solo acoustic album of 1992, *Good as I Been to You*), 'Dixie', 'I'll Remember You', 'Drifter's Escape', 'Watching the River Flow', 'Cold Irons Bound' and 'Dirt Road Blues'. The 11th number, recorded but unreleased, was 'If You See Her, Say Hello'. On the soundtrack album the four 'concert sequence' tracks included are 'Down in the Flood', 'Diamond Joe', 'Dixie' and 'Cold Irons Bound'. Again, opinions vary from how thrilling this music is and how great to see Dylan and his excellent band playing at such close range, through to how embarrassingly bad Dylan's vocal is on this version of 'Dixie', how tediously raucous 'Down in the Flood' and 'Cold Irons Bound' are, and how aesthetically displeasing it is to see Dylan in his overly tight, urine-yellow suit.

Dylan's band at the time, and therefore in the film, comprised guitarists LARRY CAMPBELL and CHARLIE SEXTON, bass player TONY GARNIER and drummer GEORGE RECELI. In late July Dylan and a Biff Dawes mixed the 'concert sequence' recordings in Studio City, California.

The film was premiered on January 22, 2003 at the Sundance Film Festival in Park City, Utah; various editing changes (shortenings) were then made; it was released in movie theatres that July 24. The DVD was issued on February 17, 2004.

[*Masked & Anonymous*, dir. Larry Charles, written by Bob Dylan & Larry Charles as Sergei Petrov & Rene Fontaine, prod. BBC Films / Destiny Productions / Grey Water Park Productions / Intermedia Films / Marching Band Productions / Spitfire Pictures, US, 2003. The DVD release (Columbia TriStar Home Entertainment, US, 2003) also includes the 16-minute 'making-of' feature *'Masked & Anonymous' Exposed*, dir. & written (it says here) by Alexander Yves Brunner & Matt Radecki, Spitfire Pictures, US, 2003, with movie main participants interviewed by co-producer Jeff Rosen. *Shoot the Piano Player*, dir. Francois Truffaut, Les Films de la Pléiade, France, 1960.]

***Masterpieces* [1978]** A distinctive compilation album, this was a Japanese triple-LP set later released elsewhere. A lavish compilation, mostly of obvious selections from other albums but also collecting for the first time on album versions of 'Mixed-Up Confusion' (an alternative take from that on the 1962 single) and 'Can You Please Crawl Out Your Window?' (the single) from 1965; the live-in-Liverpool '66 cut of 'Just Like Tom Thumb's Blues' (surely the greatest track in recorded history), the magnificent solo version of 'Spanish Is the Loving Tongue' and 'George Jackson (Big Band Version)' from 1971 (all previously only issued as B-sides of singles) plus an inconsequential outtake from the *Desire* sessions, 'Rita May'. An expensive way of acquiring these.

[Released as 3-LP set, CBS/Sony 57AP-875/6/7 (Japan), Mar 1978.]

Mayall, John [1933 -] John Mayall was born in Macclesfield, near Manchester, in north-west England, on November 29, 1933. He was a multi-instrumentalist, playing harmonica, organ, piano and guitar and having trained on the London clubs circuit under the wing of Alexis Korner, he formed his group the Bluesbreakers, from within which emerged, as if conjured into being by morose magician Mayall, a troop of individual players who all became stars: ERIC CLAPTON, Peter Green (who with founding Bluesbreaker bass player John McVie duly formed Fleetwood Mac), MICK TAYLOR, Aynsley Dunbar, Keef Hartley, JACK BRUCE . . .

The only times Dylan and Mayall met up were in London in 1965. It was in the middle of this weird American folkie protest singer's last solo tour, and to oblige his record company back home, which wanted him to record a sales convention message, he stuck his head into the lion's mouth of a small London studio where Mayall was ringmaster (though TOM WILSON had been flown over as producer). Dylan's attempt to lay down a cut of 'just one verse' of his novel song 'If You Gotta Go, Go Now', backed by John Mayall's Bluesbreakers, soon collapsed, since Dylan proved himself too embarrassed to count the others in competently and they were too perplexed to follow him. Eric Clapton, a recent recruit to the group, was in the room at the time, but did not play. Mayall and the others were unimpressed. 'Do it in *time!*' someone said, as if to an idiot. 'You haven't worked much with bands, have you?' asked someone else. Yet this was on May 12, 1965, by which time Dylan had already recorded *Bringing It All Back Home*, with a slew of musicians in New York (and, as it happens, versions of 'If You Gotta Go, Go Now' at the same sessions), the album had been released, and 'Subterranean Homesick Blues' had arrived in the British top 20 twelve days earlier, and had just jumped to no.6 that very week. The Bluesbreakers didn't even have a record deal at the time.

Mayall later called the session a two-hour-long 'fiasco', and claimed that he himself hadn't played behind Dylan anyway. Drummer Hughie Flint said: 'It was just messing around. I don't think we played a complete number. It was a real mess. There was a lot of booze there. . . . I'd never seen so much wine, and everybody got very pissed very quickly.' (A couple of years later the band McGuinness-Flint would make an album of Dylan covers, *Lo and Behold*.)

Despite all this, Mayall makes a brief appearance in *Don't Look Back*, seated in between Dylan and JOAN BAEZ in the back of the limo as they're driven from London to Birmingham exactly a week before their studio 'fiasco'. In the film scene, Baez is singing (as usual) and eating a banana. Dylan is writing down the words to a song (also as usual). He asks: 'Do you have some more paper where I can write out these things here?' Mayall gives the stolid reply, 'I'm afraid you'll have to make the most of that.'

Mayall went on to make jazz-blues fusion albums in the early 1970s, moved to Laurel Canyon in 1974, came back, reformed the Bluesbreakers in 1982 and was awarded the Order of the British Empire (even though there isn't one) in 2005.

Mellers, Wilfrid [1914 -] Wilfrid Howard Mellers was born in Leamington (pronounced Lemming-ton) Spa, in the English Midlands, on April 26, 1914. Educated at Cambridge, he fell under the rigorous influence of the pre-eminent and now deeply unfashionable literary critic F.R. Leavis, becoming a literary critic himself and writing for Leavis' defiant journal *Scrutiny* before turning towards music, publishing his book *Music and Society: England and the European Tradition* in 1946 and becoming, by the mid-1960s, the new University of York's first Professor of Music and a composer of distinction. He continued to straddle the rôles of critic and creative artist, and the genres of popular and classical music. His book *Music in a New Found Land*, written in the early 1960s and published in 1964, has held up creditably, and is remarkable for, among other things, its early (as it were) critical appraisal of ROBERT JOHNSON.

If it seemed an oblique comment when in 1967, in a news magazine survey titled 'Sixties', Mellers wrote that *Blonde on Blonde* was 'concerned more with incantation than communication', this may have been because at that point, like so many other musically sophisticated people, his interest in 'pop' was almost entirely taken up with an entrancement by THE BEATLES. He was among those who found the blandishments of *Sgt. Pepper's Lonely Hearts Club Band* more beguiling than Dylan's work, and his book *Twilight of the Gods* was an early professorial rush into print with a Beatles study.

However, he never stopped paying attention to Dylan's output, and he was extremely well informed as to many of its antecedents–and while in 1980 he could produce the detailed, part-Freudian, part-musicological study *Bach and the Dance of God*, and three years later *Beethoven and the Voice of God*, a year after that he could offer *A Darker Shade of Pale: A Backdrop to Bob Dylan*. Awkwardly titled, and more backdrop than Dylan, it has proved more and more interesting and relevant since its publication in 1984. When it was new, it was received without enthusiasm by many of us who still, as the 1980s dawned, preferred to insist upon the blazingly unerring individuality of Dylan's art rather than concede that he stood in a tradition occupied by wrinkly old people with fiddles and banjos and obdurately conservative faces. In retrospect we can be grateful for, and a little impressed by, the sharp but serious attention it pays to the CARTER FAMILY, Nimrod Stoneman, Aunt Molly Jackson, Roscoe Holcomb, JIMMIE RODGERS and others from among the souls who have haunted Dylan's imagination and suffused his own art.

In 2004 the York Late Music Festival opened with a weekend's tribute to Mellers, and that October (not April) a tribute concert was held at Downing College, Cambridge, to mark Mellers' 90th birthday.

[Wilfrid Mellers, *Music and Society: England and the European Tradition*, London: Dennis Dobson, 1946; *Music in a New Found Land: Themes and Developments in the History of American Music*, London: Stonehill, 1964 (New York: Alfred A. Knopf, 1965); 'Sixties', *New Statesman*, London, 24 Feb 1967; *Bach and the Dance of God*, London: Faber & Faber, 1980; *Beethoven and the Voice of God*, London, Faber & Faber, 1983; *A Darker Shade of Pale: A Backdrop to Bob Dylan*, London: Faber & Faber, 1984.]

'Memphis Blues Again' [1966] See 'Stuck Inside of Mobile With the Memphis Blues Again'.

Memphis Jug Band, the The Memphis Jug Band was one of the most popular and important outfits of its kind in the late 1920s and early 1930s. It was formed by Will Shade in the mid-1920s and many different musicians passed through its ranks; those who performed with the group (rather than in it) included MEMPHIS MINNIE and Furry Lewis. They recorded prolifically between February 1927 and November 1934 and they performed live in greatly varied settings, from country clubs to street corners and from political rallies to fish fries. Their success created a craze for jug bands in Memphis, among them GUS CANNON's Jug Stompers and Jack Kelly's South Memphis Jug Band.

What makes a jug band unique is explained in an excellent short passage from Robert Gordon's *It Came from Memphis*, 1995: 'It creates a sound where there should be none, from instruments intended for other purposes. . . . The handmade equipment—a guitar from a cigar-box, a harmonica from a corn-cob—conveyed an egalitarianism that reached into the guts of their audience . . . [while] the jug blowers made keeping the beat into a touch of God. Their *whoomp whoomp* filled with character, the musicians themselves responding to the audience's disbelief of their capabilities, pushing their talents to new heights while their heads floated off their shoulders from hyperventilating.'

While Bob Dylan's 1965 song title 'On the Road Again' might be taken as a direct reference to JACK KEROUAC's novel *On the Road*, it is also a well-known track from 1928 by the Memphis Jug Band, whose records 'Bob Lee Junior Blues' (1927) and 'K.C. Moan' (1929) had been among the tracks on the crucial 1952 HARRY SMITH anthology *AMERICAN FOLK MUSIC*—making them well-known items in the folk-revival repertoire—while their 'Stealin' Stealin' (1928) was one of the young Bob Dylan's early favourites.

The Memphis Jug Band's 'Bottle It Up and Go' (1932 and 1934) is one of those that led to BLIND BOY FULLER's big hit 'Step It Up and Go', revisited by Dylan on *Good as I Been to You* in 1992 but he had sung both 'K.C. Moan' and 'Stealin' Stealin' at the other end of his career—'K.C. Moan' as early as August 1960 in Minneapolis, and 'Stealin' on the December 22, 1961 taping done in Minneapolis, on the CYNTHIA GOODING 'Folksinger's Choice' WBAI radio programme in early 1962, live at the Finjan Club, Montreal, that July and in February 1963 on the so-called Banjo Tape with GIL TURNER on backing vocals. It's a song he loved, and performed extremely well.

The Memphis Jug Band couldn't get into a record studio again after 1934, though individual members continued to thrive. Will Shade survived until 1966, by which time the Greenwich Village and Cambridge, Massachusetts, folkie crowds had formed a whole new generation of jug bands, whose members included, at one time or another, JOHN SEBASTIAN, MARIA MULDAUR, SAM CHARTERS and many others with links to the Bob Dylan story.

[Memphis Jug Band: 'Bob Lee Junior Blues', Atlanta, GA, 19 Oct 1927; 'On the Road Again', Memphis, TN, 11 Sep 1928; issued on a soon-withdrawn British EP, HMV 7EG8073, London, *nia*, under the wrong title—i.e. as 'Overseas Stomp', another Memphis Jug Band track, itself more usually called 'Lindberg Hop', recorded the same day as 'On the Road Again'; 'Lindberg Hop', 2 takes, take 1 issued X, RCA Victor LVA3009, NY, *nia* (as it happens, Dylan, as Blind Boy Grunt, contributed to a version of 'Overseas Stomp' cut by Dick Farina & Eric von Schmidt, London, 10–11 Jan 1963, issued *Dick Farina & Eric Von Schmidt*, Folklore F-LEUT-7, UK, 1963); 'Stealin' Stealin'', Memphis, 15 Sep 1928; 'K.C. Moan', Memphis, 4 Oct 1929; Memphis Jug Band (as by the Picaninny [sic] Jug Band): 'Bottle It Up and Go', Richmond, IN, 3 Aug 1932 & (as by Will Shade & the Memphis Jug Band): 'Bottle It Up and Go', Chicago, 7 Nov 1934.

Robert Gordon, *It Came From Memphis*, Winchester, MA: Faber, 1995, p.42.]

Memphis Minnie [1897 - 1973] Lizzie Douglas was born in Algiers, Louisiana, on June 3, 1897, but moved to just south of Memphis as a child. She may have run away and joined Ringling Brothers Circus for a period, but certainly she was discovered (by Columbia Records) on Beale Street in 1929. She is an important artist in the history of the blues: an assertive singer, a very able lead guitarist and the confident composer of several classics. The country blues milieu was a male one, but she had great command of her material and a strong, confident voice; yet it was a voice full of subtle nuance as well as great directness. She brought women's blues forward, breaking free of the 'classic' style by bringing to her work less theatre and more musicianship. Lawrence Cohn calls her one of BIG BILL BROONZY's 'many gifted protégés', but the track of his that most resembles Memphis Minnie's style, his 1937 side 'Come Home Early', is strongly reminiscent of her *mature* work, suggesting another side to the question of who taught whom.

One of her husbands was Joe McCoy; they married in 1929, moved to Chicago in 1930 and recorded many sides together, some with great guitar duets, before they split up in 1935. (Wilber 'Joe' McCoy, an excellent guitarist, recorded between 1929 and 1937, using names from Mississippi Mudder to Kansas Joe to Hallelulah Joe, and joining the Harlem Hamfats in 1936 with his brother Charlie; both were influenced by Tommy Johnson. Joe also secured a reluctant Kokomo Arnold his record deal, and wrote 'Oh Red', a big record for BLIND BOY FULLER. McCoy was one of the earliest on record with the phrase 'shake, rattle and roll', which he built into his 'Shake Mattie': 'Shake shake Mattie, shake rattle 'n' roll / I can't get enough now, satisfy my soul.')

Playboy asked Dylan in 1977 what music he listened to—by implication wanting to see whether he would confess to keeping an ear on what was contemporary and popular. Dylan replied: 'I listen to Memphis Minnie a lot.' In 1985, when *Spin* magazine asked him to list his all-time top 10 favourite records, Minnie's classic 'Me and My Chauffeur Blues' was in there.

You can also hear it on that blues-soaked album, *Blonde on Blonde*. 'Obviously 5 Believers' is a filler track on the album, with a repetitive and undistinguished lyric; yet it stands in a distinguished tradition, its melody and structure and riff taken wholesale from 'Me and My Chauffeur Blues': a song with a history that is complicated to unravel but is a useful indication of how communal composition can work inside the blues.

Minnie was performing the song years before her 1941 recording. In 1933, Big Bill Broonzy lost a blues-playing contest to Memphis Minnie in a Chicago club, when he played 'Just a Dream' and she played 'Me and My Chauffeur Blues'. The judges were SLEEPY JOHN ESTES, Tampa Red and the man who wrote the lovely classic blues 'Trouble in Mind', Richard Jones. The prize was two bottles of whiskey. Broonzy, who must have had mixed feelings about losing to someone who might be called a protégé of his, says he lost the contest but ran off with the whiskey.

The story of the contest is especially interesting because if Broonzy is right about the date then Memphis Minnie was performing 'Me and My Chauffeur Blues' before Sonny Boy Williamson I put out his record of 'Good Morning, School Girl' and before competition judge Sleepy John Estes' 'Airplane Blues', though both are built on the same frame. Minnie's song even pre-dates the 1934 recording called 'Back and Side Blues' by Estes' pal from Brownsville, Tennessee, Son Bonds, cut at his début session, which 'Good Morning School Girl' also uncannily resembles. If Broonzy is *wrong* about the date of his story, then the contest probably took place in 1938—still three years ahead of Minnie putting her song on record—in which case Son Bonds would seem to have been the first into the studio with a song using this strongly distinctive structure and tune. Either way, it surely wasn't Sonny Boy Williamson's 'Good Morning, School Girl' that used this melody and structure first.

Memphis Minnie finally recorded 'Me and My Chauffeur Blues' in May 1941, three days before Bob Dylan was born. Within a year the now-forgotten Mabel Robinson went into the studios in New York and cut that rare thing, a worthy jazz version: one that doesn't patronise or apologise for the blues simplicity of the song but seizes joyfully on its strengths and retails it again, in this case sizzling with panache from the trumpet, tenor sax, piano, guitar, bass and drums of Sam Price's Blusicians (more or less the US Decca house-band, and featured on very many sides of the period).

In roaring contrast, in 1965, came a version by Big Mama Thornton which, more even than 'Ball and Chain', shows what a Thorntonnabe Janis Joplin was. Big Mama's 'Me and My Chauffeur' is not only uncannily Joplinesque, to put it the wrong way round, but offers the sort of grunge-rock that pterodactyls might have used as mating-calls. Less than a year later, Bob Dylan was disguising the song as 'Obviously 5 Believers'. (Jefferson Airplane put 'Me and My Chauffeur' on their second LP, *Surrealistic Pillow*, in 1967.) In 2005 the release of the *Bootleg Series Vol. 7—No Direction Home: the Soundtrack* included an outtake of 'Leopard-Skin Pill-Box Hat', another blues from the *Blonde on Blonde* sessions (and essentially based on a LIGHTNIN' HOPKINS record): but Dylan, here taking the song much slower than on the album version, sings a previously unknown verse, possibly improvised, that almost gives the Memphis Minnie song its due name-check. Making a funny rhyme of it too, and giving us an outrageously overlong third line, he sings: 'Well can I be your chauffeur, honey can I be your chauffeur? / Well you can ride with me, honey I'll be a chauffeur / Just as long as you stay in the car: if you get out and start to walk you just might topple over / In your brand-new leopard-skin pill-box hat.' Sublime.

Memphis Minnie survived the Depression and the war years, and recorded again post-war. She recorded four numbers for a session in Chicago in 1952 for the Chess company's Checker label, re-recording 'Me and My Chauffeur' with Little Walter on harmonica. It was released as a single, but it first came out, as it happens, the same year that Dylan made and issued *Blonde on Blonde*.

Linda Dahl, in *Stormy Weather*, writes that '. . . she moved back down to Memphis in the mid-fifties in poor health. She spent the last years of her life in a nursing home and died in 1963,' but this date is wrong. In Paul Oliver's *Story of the Blues*, 1969, there is a photo of Minnie captioned 'at her Memphis home after a recent stroke'. She died there on August 6, 1973.

[Memphis Minnie: 'Me and My Chauffeur Blues', Chicago, 21 May 1941, issued on Paul Oliver's compilation *The Story of the Blues*, CBS (M) 66218, London, 1969, 2-CD reissue Columbia 468992 2, NY, 1991; session for Checker, incl. re-recorded 'Me and My Chauffeur', Chicago, 11 Jul 1952, *The Blues Volume 5*, Cadet LP 4051, Chicago, 1966. Joe McCoy: 'Shake Mattie', Chicago, c.Feb 1931; *Memphis Minnie Vol. 2: With Kansas Joe, 1930–31*, Blues Classics BC-13, Berkeley, CA, 1967. Big Bill Broonzy: 'Come Home Early', Chicago, 16 Aug 1937, *Good Time Tonight*, Columbia Legacy Roots N' Blues 467247-10, NY, 1990. Lawrence Cohn, notes to ditto. Sonny Boy Williamson: 'Good Morning, School Girl', Aurora, IL, 5 May 1937. Sleepy John Estes: 'Airplane Blues', NY, 3 Aug 1937. Son Bonds: 'Back and Side Blues', Chicago, 6 Sep 1934. Mabel Robinson: 'Me and My Chauffeur', NY, 20 Jan 1942. Big Mama Thornton: 'Me and My Chauffeur', LA, 1965, Kent 424, 1965.

Dylan quote, interview by Ron Rosenbaum, Burbank, Nov 1977, *Playboy*, Chicago, Mar 1978. Top 10 records list, *Spin* vol.1, no.8, US, Dec 1985. Minnie v. Bill song contest information from Big Bill Broonzy's book *Big Bill Blues* (as told to Yannick Bruynoghe), London: Cassell, 1955, retold in Linda Dahl's *Stormy Weather: The Music and Lives of a Century of Jazz Women*, 1984, and discussed at length in the chapter 'Me and My Chauffeur' in Paul & Beth Garon, *Woman With Guitar: Memphis Minnie's Blues*, New York: Da Capo, 1992.]

Memphis Slim [1915 - 1988] John Peter Chatman, son of a juke joint operator, singer, guitarist and boogie-woogie pianist, was born in Memphis on September 3, 1915 and grew up to spend the 1930s playing piano and singing in dance halls, sporting houses and honky-tonks mostly in and around Memphis. In 1940, having moved to Chicago, he made his recording début as Peter Chapman, but later that year used the name Memphis Slim on further 78rpm releases. He became a session player for Bluebird and as such cut many tracks with BIG BILL BROONZY, but from the mid-1940s went out on his own and became a long-term success not only as a singer and pianist but as a songwriter and a bandleader with a shrewd ear for modern trends. His predilection for jump-band arrangements, strong rhythm sections and ensemble saxes did not stop him spotting a white 'folk' market in the late 1950s and consequently working with the world's least jump-band-minded person, PETE SEEGER. In 1960 he débuted in Europe, touring with Willie Dixon. In late 1961 he emigrated to Paris and for nearly 30 more years enjoyed an agreeable and graciously handled eminence among expat musicians, making return visits to the US now and then, acting in French films—including, curiously, a small part in a 1963 French TV drama based on Harriet Beecher Stowe's 19th century novel *Uncle Tom's Cabin*, namely *Le Théâtre de la jeunesse: La case de l'oncle Tom*—and being awarded (some years ahead of Bob Dylan) the title of Commandeur de L'Ordre des Arts et Lettres.

For Dylan's strong reliance upon Memphis Slim's song 'Mother Earth', first recorded in 1954, see **'Gotta Serve Somebody'**. He died in Paris on February 24, 1988.

[*Le Théâtre de la jeunesse: La case de l'oncle Tom*, dir. Jean-Christophe Averty, Paris, 1963.]

Meyers, Augie [1940 -] Augie Meyers, born in San Antonio, Texas, on May 31, 1940, contracted polio as a child, and is reputed to have taught himself to play piano when, to constrain the walking he found difficult, he was tied by a rope to the upright instrument owned by the grandparents who raised him. Later he played the Vox organ and accordion, and from local San Antonio bands of the late 1950s moved into a musical partnership with DOUG SAHM that enjoyed early success with the Sir Douglas Quintet but lasted, more on than off, until Sahm's death in 1999.

Bob Dylan first played alongside Meyers on the sessions for *Doug Sahm and Band* in New York in October 1972. Photos taken informally at the sessions show Dylan, a youthful 31, looking sexily radiant, at ease and in his prime; a few feet away, just as relaxed, there's Augie Meyers in a check shirt, overhauls and what might be a Davy Crockett hat, with a big black beard and a grin on his face, looking as if he just stepped out from behind a tree to exchange pleasantries with bears. Meyers plays guitar, organ and piano on the sessions (release details in the entry **Sahm, Doug**).

Twenty-five years later, Dylan brings him to Miami to play on the sessions for *Time Out of Mind*, on which he plays his Vox Continental—'your magic Vox', as Dylan calls it—supplying the sound that made the Sir Douglas Quintet so instantly recognisable on hits like 'Mendocino'. In 2001, Meyers comes back and plays it all over again on *"Love and Theft"*, while son Clay contributes bongos. Dylan is quoted as declaring:

> 'Augie's my man. . . . the shining example of a musician, Vox player or otherwise, who can break the code. His playing speaks volumes. Speaks in tongues actually. He can bring a song, certainly any one of mine, into the real world. I've loved his playing going all the way back to the Sir Doug days when he was featured and dominant. What makes him so great is that internally speaking, he's the master of syncopation and timing. And this is something that cannot be taught. If you need someone to get you through the shipping lanes and there's no detours, Augie will get you right straight through.'

The most recent of a string of Augie Meyers solo albums, which began with *Augie Meyers Western Head Music Co.* in 1971, is *Blame It on Love*, in 2002.

[Augie Meyers: *Augie Meyers Western Head Music Co.*, Polydor 24-4069, US, 1971; *Blame It on Love*, Texas World, US, 2002. Dylan quote from *www.augiemeyers.com*.]

Midler, Bette [1945 -] Bette Midler was born on December 1, 1945, in New Jersey, but grew up in Honolulu, Hawaii, where she majored in drama at university. Moving to New York City in the second half of the 1960s she soon made Broadway (in *Fiddler on the Roof*), but really made her name as a hyper-cabaret artiste in a gay bathhouse. She slid over to the mainstream via records (her first album went platinum, and in 1989 she had a no.1 hit single, 'Wind Beneath My Wings'), theatre and eventually film (among many others, she starred in *Down and Out in Beverly Hills*, *Ruthless People* and *Outrageous Fortune* in the second half of the 1980s, worked with WOODY ALLEN in the early 1990s and appeared in the remake of *The Stepford Wives* in 2004).

When Dylan was first asked to duet with Midler, he wanted them to record a version of 'Friends', a song she'd put two versions of on her début album, *The Divine Miss M* in 1973. After rehearsing it, they swapped to 'Buckets of Rain' instead, giving it a pleasing, relaxed but rollicking pace and an appealing melody line–it would be country if Midler's arranger and producer had been less mainstream showbiz–and with an altered lyric far more flirtatiously throwaway than the original, not least in singing of 'nuggets' instead of 'buckets', and ending with this spoken exchange:

Bob: 'Hum, meany.'

Bette: 'Oooh, you don't even know. You have no idea.'

Bob: 'I don't want to know. . . . You and PAUL SIMON should have done this one.'

This was not the last flirtation between the two, though it seems to have been very one-sided. Ms. Midler was quoted in British tabloid newspaper *The Sun* in 1982 as saying that she has tried and failed to seduce Bob: 'I got close . . . a couple of first bases in the front of his Cadillac.' At the end of the 1985 recording of 'We Are the World', the charity fund-raising single in response to famine in Ethiopia, Dylan avoids the embrace of many an over-excited fellow star, but cannot 'evade a block tackle by linebacker Bette Midler. . . . This time her determination proves irresistible.' She hugs him and tells him 'Goodnight, dearest.'

An earlier take of their duet on 'Buckets of Rain', with more conversation, has circulated among collectors. For more on Dylan's original lyric, see separate entry on the song.

[Bette Midler (with Bob Dylan): 'Buckets of Rain', NY, Oct 1975, *Songs for the New Depression*, Atlantic SD 18155, US (Atlantic K50212, UK), 1976; CD-reissued Atlantic 82784-2, US, 1997. Bette Midler: *The Divine Miss M*, Atlantic SD 7238, US, 1973. 'We Are the World' hug: breakfast time, 29 Jan 1985; quote from JOHN BAULDIE: '1980s: Dylan and the Making of USA-for-Africa', Michael Gray & John Bauldie, eds., *All Across the Telegraph: A Bob Dylan Handbook*, London: Futura edition, p.214.]

'Midnight Special' A traditional prison song about a train, associated with LEADBELLY. One of Dylan's earliest professional studio jobs was as harmonica player on a HARRY BELAFONTE version of the song, recorded at Webster Hall, NYC, February 2, 1962. At least 20 takes were attempted; one was released on Belafonte's album *Midnight Special* (RCA LMP 2449, NY), March 1962. Dylan, discounting his work on a CAROLYN HESTER album and indeed his own first LP, describes his Belafonte studio session as 'my professional recording début'; and then he adds, 'Strangely enough, this was the only one memorable recording date that would stand out in my mind for years to come. . . . With Belafonte I felt like I'd become anointed in some kind of way.'

Pop singer and writer Paul Evans notes re its 'shine your light on me' lyric that 'there was a legend in the southern states of America that if the light from the Midnight Special shone into your cell, you would be pardoned.'

[Bob Dylan, *Chronicles Volume One*, 2004, p.69. Paul Evans, undated interview by Spencer Leigh in *Baby, That Is Rock and Roll: American Pop 1954–1963*, p.132.]

Mississippi Sheiks, the The Sheiks comprised, on record, fiddle player Lonnie Chatmon and singer-guitarist Walter Vincson (aka Walter Vinson, Walter Vincent and Walter Jacobs), plus, sometimes, Chatmon's brothers Sam and Bo (aka Bo Carter). In live performance they were often augmented by yet more Chatmons and the great Jackson Mississippi mandolinist Charlie McCoy (not to be confused with the harmonica player and multi-instrumentalist on Dylan's late-60s albums). Live, too, Lonnie Chatmon played tremendous waltz and hoedown fiddle music within the duo/group; on record, they were more constrained by record company demands for the blues. This made them the most successful black string band of the pre-war period, and they started their prolific recording career with a bang, not only enjoying a hit from their first session with their own 'Sitting on Top of the World' but hearing it become a standard that crossed over swiftly to country, Western swing and bluegrass, and remained almost compulsory in the repertoires of innumerable musicians in these and later genres, as well as prompting plentiful covers and wide recognition within the blues.

Among those to cover the song pre-war were the Beale Street Rounders, Sam Collins and Joe Evans & Arthur McClain. ALAN LOMAX calls it 'the Delta favourite'. Post-war it continued to thrive, recorded by everyone from HOWLIN' WOLF to Bill Monroe & His Blue Grass Boys in the 1950s (with composer credits given to 'Henderson-Young-Lewis'), by DOC WATSON in the 1960s and by the hobo-white-blues-pre-rockabilly artist Harmonica Frank Floyd in 1974. (*Sittin' on Top of the World* was also the title track of the Johnny Shines collection issued by Biograph in the 1960s.)

There's an interesting variant on 'Sittin on Top of the World' by Bumble Bee Slim, 'Climbing on Top of the Hill' (1934), covered within a year by the man who popularised 'Step It Up & Go', BLIND BOY FULLER. Other songs using the melody and theme of 'Sittin' on Top of the World' are BIG BILL

BROONZY's 'Worrying You Off My Mind' (1932), Black Ace's lovely 'You Gonna Need My Help Someday' (1937) and SONNY TERRY's 'One Monkey Don't Stop the Show' (1960).

The very next song the Sheiks cut back at that début session (which was in Shreveport, Louisiana, in February 1930) was their next biggest hit, 'Stop and Listen Blues', which came from the great Tommy Johnson's own classic, 'Big Road Blues'. Their last session was over 100 sides but only five years later—some recordings were made under names like the Blacksnakes and the Mississippi Mud Steppers—after which, musically, Lonnie Chatmon left the building. Walter Vincson continued to record till 1941 and again post-war, reappearing in the 1960s and making sides under the name Mississippi Sheiks, but without its old sound, as late as the 1970s.

For details on Dylan's early recording of 'Sitting on Top of the World' see **Williams, Big Joe**. He revisited the song 30 years down the line on his return to a solo acoustic album, 1992's *Good as I Been to You*, and then relied on two further old Sheiks records, again both original compositions of theirs (probably Vincson's), on the album after that, 1993's *World Gone Wrong*. By the time he came back to 'Sitting on Top of the World', he could draw upon it, granted the history of its fortunes, to help build his album as a fusion of black and white repertoire. Yet the 1990s Dylan version surely fails. Of all the songs on these two solo acoustic albums, this is the one that Bob Dylan could most definitely do far better on another day. There's a strange rigidity to the rhythm, something Dylan is virtually never guilty of, and what explains this is to be found by listening to the Mississippi Sheiks version. Dylan replicates it—at the same pace, and word for careful word! Everyone has sung this song, and everyone has personalised it; the lyric variations are boundless . . . and Bob Dylan stands aside from all that, and reproduces the Sheiks' 1930 version! It's too scrupulous, too carefully exact; and its failure is compounded by the way that while Dylan adds harmonica accompaniment—and the harp suffers from the tentativeness that has been its fatal main characteristic for so long now—he offers no equivalent to the bluegrass flavour that makes the Sheiks' version attractive. The Sheiks have each other to raggedy it up, and give it internal movement. Dylan, on his own, lacks this. The flaccid ending is like a giving up, an admission of failure.

Not so—very much the opposite—when he turns his attention to the two Sheiks songs he uses on *World Gone Wrong*, though describing the group perhaps surprisingly straightforwardly in his liner notes, he still seems concerned to stress that their work needs no alteration:

> '. . . the Mississippi Sheiks, a little known de facto group whom in their former glory mustve been something to behold. rebellion against routine seems to be their strong theme. all their songs are raw to the bone & are faultlessly made for these modern times (the New Dark Ages) nothing effete about the Mississippi Sheiks.'

Throughout, these liner notes are part of Dylan's armoury of insistence on the contemporary relevance of such material: the continuing value and pertinence of both the poetry of the old blues world and that of medieval balladry. The title-character in 'Love Henry' is presented immediately by Dylan as 'Henry—modern corporate man . . .' He writes of the Civil War song 'Two Soldiers' something he clearly applies to all: that they're about 'learning to go forward by turning back the clock, stopping the mind from thinking in hours, firing a few random shots at the face of time.'

So too he changes the Mississippi Sheiks' title 'The World Is Going Wrong' into 'World Gone Wrong', deploying the past tense for present pertinence. In making this small, deft change, despite the insistence that all the Sheiks' songs are 'faultlessly made for these modern times', Dylan is updating. For the Mississippi Sheiks, 'The World Is Going Wrong'; for Dylan it's already a 'World Gone Wrong' (though he retains their present-tense version of the line in the repeated refrain—in fact singing it so that it's almost impossible to distinguish between the two). And here, as with 'Delia' on the same album, Dylan takes something jaunty and close to throwaway, something recorded in a few minutes back in 1931, and, as it were, restores it to a greatness it never knew it had.

The song's first phrase, too, makes such a good Bob Dylan opening statement: 'Strange things have happened . . .' is decidedly Dylanesque. It has a flash of mischief about it too, as well as its mordancy—the mischief of following up an album called *Good as I Been to You* with a similar album that begins 'I can't be good no more . . .' And as he occupies the song, it is far more poignant, far less preachy, than the rumours preceding its release had suggested—and he sings it so aptly, with a lovely, wriggling, burrowing delivery.

When Dylan comes to 'Blood in My Eyes', which they call 'I've Got Blood in My Eyes for You', here too he deepens it: he reaches higher than the Sheiks did. Again, he abbreviates their title and extends their contents. He has gained, by gaining middle-age, the ability to sing so sour and 'adult' a love song without it either ringing false or glamourising the unglamourously cynical, as a more youthful performer, a more youthful Dylan, would surely do. His version stalks along with predatory, loping menace, its quiet unhurried unstoppability sinister and brooding, the terrible calm of the guitar-work enacting some old, twisted animal's implacable pace. Early on, it even halts altogether for a moment—a moment in which anything might happen: and then it simply resumes its hunt.

The words are just lies, snares, hooks, traps. The singer is asked 'Hey hey man, can't you wait a while?' and he answers 'No, no, babe . . .' and even this is a lie. The long guitar-break comes in at this point, as if he can wait, and will wait, because waiting is part of the pleasure of the kill. He's like the treacherous judge in 'Seven Curses', whose 'old eyes deepened in his head'. And at the end, what is the last noise on the track? A cough! He coughs, like an old man. Like an old lion who has choked on his food. It is a vividly imagined, powerful performance, and as a reading of the Sheiks' song, indisputably up at the creative end of song-interpretation.

Dylan has never performed 'World Gone Wrong' live, but he has twice performed 'Blood in My Eyes': at the New York Supper Club early shows on November 16 & 17, 1993. He also made a terrific promo video of the track, filmed by DAVE STEWART, wandering round the streets of Camden, London, in July 1993. It's one of the few Dylan videos that's any good. Aptly for the era of the song, it's shot in black and white, and Dylan walks around like a New Orleans undertaker, complete with black top hat.

NB: It's fairly certain that Dylan knew all three of these Mississippi Sheiks recordings in the 1960s, but it's striking too that all three used on these two Bob Dylan albums were reissued on one Yazoo CD in 1992.

[Mississippi Sheiks: 'Sittin' on Top of the World', Shreveport, LA, 17 Feb 1930; 'The World Is Going Wrong', Atlanta, GA, 24 Oct 1931; 'I've Got Blood in My Eyes for You', Atlanta, 25 Oct 1931, all on *Stop and Listen Blues: The Mississippi Sheiks*, Mamlish S-3804, NY, 1974; CD-reissued on *Stop And Listen*, Yazoo 2006, NY 1992. Bob Dylan, 'Blood in My Eyes' promo video, London, 21 Jul 1993.

Beale Street Rounders: 'I'm Sittin' on Top of the World', Chicago, c.13 Oct 1930, CD-reissued *Memphis Harp & Jug Blowers (1927–1939)*, RST Blues Documents BDCD-6028, Vienna, 1992. Sam Collins: 'I'm Still Sitting on Top of the World', NY, 8 Oct 1931. Joe Evans & Arthur McClain as the Two Poor Boys: 'Sittin' on Top of the World', NY, 21 May 1931, *Early Country Music*, Historical HLP-8002, Jersey City, NJ, *nia*, CD-reissued *The Two Poor Boys*, Document DOCD-5044, Vienna, 1991. Johnny Shines: *Sittin' on Top of the World*, Biograph, *nia*, 1960s, reissued Biograph BLP 12044, Canaan, NY, 1973. Bill Monroe & His Blue Grass Boys: 'Sittin' on Top of the World', *nia*, *Knee Deep in Bluegrass*, Stetson, US, 1958, reissued Stetson HATC 3002, *nia*. Doc Watson: 'Sitting on Top of the World', NY, 25/26 Jan 1963, *Doc Watson*, Vanguard VRS-9152 (mono) & VSD-79152, NY, 1964. Harmonica Frank: 'Sittin on Top of the World', *Blues That Made the Rooster Dance*, Barrelhouse BH 05, US, 1974.

Bumble Bee Slim: 'Climbing on Top of the Hill', Chicago, 10 Sep 1934. Blind Boy Fuller: 'I'm Climbing on Top of the Hill', NY, 23 Jul 1935, CD-issued *Blind Boy Fuller: East Coast Piedmont Style*, Columbia Roots N' Blues Series 467923 2, NY, 1991.

Big Bill Broonzy: 'Worrying You Off My Mind', NY, 29 Mar 1932, CD-reissued *Big Bill Broonzy: Good Time Tonight*, Columbia Roots N' Blues 467247-10, NY, 1990. Black Ace: 'You Gonna Need My Help Someday', Dallas, TX, 15 Feb 1937, *New Deal Blues (1933–1939)*, Mamlish S-3801, NY (& on the EP *Black Ace*, XX Min701, UK), 1971, CD-reissued *Black Ace: I'm the Boss Card in Your Hand*, Arhoolie CD 374, El Cerrito, CA, c.1990. Sonny Terry: 'One Monkey Don't Stop the Show', Englewood Cliffs, NJ, 26 Oct 1960, *Sonny's Story*, Bluesville BV-1025, *nia*.

Alan Lomax quoted from *The Land Where the Blues Began*, New York: Pantheon, 1993.]

Mitchell, Joni [1943 -] Roberta Joan Anderson was born on November 7, 1943 in the tiny town of Macleod (now Fort Macleod), Alberta, Canada. She grew up teaching herself guitar and piano, both of which she plays like no-one else, so that these unique styles have themselves been the shaping forces behind many of her highly personal songs, along with lyrics of great intelligence and emotional directness mediated by acute self-observation and lightness of touch, all of which qualities were clear even on her début album, *Joni Mitchell*, produced by DAVID CROSBY in 1968, on which, despite its occasional immature gush, she was already evidently an original writer, capable of complexity of form and content. She also has a highly distinctive voice of great range (if with a tendency, unchecked early on, to shriek off at the top end).

The result is that she has been absolutely the most important female singer-songwriter of Bob Dylan's generation, and the greatest such figure alive today. It is a reflection of our culture's continued disinclination to take women as seriously as men that her work is not more commonly mentioned in the same breath as, if not Dylan's then at least VAN MORRISON's and NEIL YOUNG's. Like Dylan she has never been content to stay in one place artistically, and has created a large body of variegated, honourable work achieved over several decades. She has become too a figure of dignity and gravitas, a rôle model for women through her skilled, unpreachy delineation of the predicaments and inconsistencies of *being* a contemporary woman in the modern world as well as through her insistence on high standards for her artistry.

She began her career in the folk clubs of Toronto before belatedly joining the New York City folk scene in the mid-1960s and finding her first success as the writer of 'Urge for Going', recorded by Tom Rush and George Hamilton IV, and 'Michael from Mountains', recorded by JUDY COLLINS, who enjoyed a hit with Mitchell's 'Both Sides Now', one of the songs on her second album, *Clouds*, in 1969, along with the widely covered 'Chelsea Morning'. All these songs were picked up by other artists before Joni Mitchell landed her record deal. (Judy Collins' version of 'Both Sides

Now', for example, started out as a track on her 1967 album *Wildflowers*.)

In 1970 Mitchell had her own first hit single with 'Big Yellow Taxi', from her third album, *Ladies of the Canyon*, which also included the song 'Woodstock', covered by Crosby, Stills, Nash & Young, and 'The Circle Game'. Next came the lovely albums *Blue* and, even better, 1972's *For the Roses*, an album not far short of, and preceding, Dylan's *Blood on the Tracks* as a superb, contemporary yet timeless work of mature intelligence, fully achieved. 'Woman of Heart and Mind' is sublime, and is followed by the closing track of this masterwork, the dark and glorious 'Judgement of the Moon and Stars (Ludwig's Tune)'. The album also contained the hit single 'You Turn Me on, I'm a Radio'.

Sometimes, following this, Joni Mitchell would veer off into unwelcome jazz explorations, but she always came back, sometimes bringing something useful with her. There isn't the space here to do justice to her long, subsequent career, though any list of her other finest albums would have to include *Hejira* (1976), *Night Ride Home* (1991) and *Turbulent Indigo* (1994).

Bob Dylan first came to her attention back in 1965, when she was a struggling and unknown folkie with songwriting ambitions—and heard 'Positively 4th Street' on the radio: 'When I heard Bob Dylan sing, "You got a lotta nerve", I thought "Hallelujah!, man, the American pop song has grown up. It's wide open. Now you can write about anything that literature can write about." Up until that time rock & roll songs were pretty much limited to, "I'm a fool for ya, baby".'

Oddly, in the light of that, when it came to the Starbucks album *Artist's Choice: Joni Mitchell—Music That Matters to Her*, 2005, the Dylan track she includes is 'Sweetheart Like You', from the *Infidels* album of 1983. (She also chooses a track of her own, 'Harlem in Havana'.)

Dylan recorded a delightfully casual but convincing version of her 'Big Yellow Taxi' in the studios in New York on June 4, 1970, at one of the sessions for the *New Morning* album; it was issued not on that LP but on the subsequent compilation *Dylan* issued in late 1973. Mitchell and Dylan first worked together two years after that, when she dropped in on the Rolling Thunder Revue tour of 1975—by which time she was a major star in her own right. SAM SHEPARD reports DAVID BLUE as eagerly awaiting the psychic catfight in prospect when SARA DYLAN was due to arrive: 'Just wait,' said Blue, 'till her and Joni get around each other. You'll get some shit on camera then. . . . Sara's a very regal, powerful chick, and Joni's gettin' into her empress bag now. I mean Joni's a real queen now. She's really getting' up there.'

And she was. However, though no clash between her and Sara Dylan occurred, she did find the whole business of supporting RUBIN HURRICANE CARTER rather difficult. She never believed he was innocent (and she was probably right); nor did she enjoy the concert held in his presence at the Correctional Institute for Women in Clinton, New Jersey on December 7, 1975—on the eve of the 'Night of the Hurricane' concert at Madison Square Garden. *Rolling Stone* reported that the 'mostly black audience of prisoners . . . loved Dylan, Roberta Flack and ALLEN GINSBERG, but Joni Mitchell's supercilious songs were booed and she shrilly lectured Carter and the rest of the inmates: "We came here to give you love; if you can't handle it that's your problem."'

In Austin, Texas, on January 28, 1976, three days after the second and final fund-raising Rolling Thunder gig for Carter (staged in Houston), Dylan made a surprise guest appearance at a Mitchell concert, coming on stage to duet with her on 'Both Sides Now' and then to sing 'Girl of the North Country' by himself.

They next appeared on stage together at the Farewell Concert by THE BAND later that year (and consequently in the film *The Last Waltz*), but after that there seems to have been no conjunction till both performed, separately and together, in Japan in May 1994, at the so-called Great Music Experience at the Todaiji Temple, Nara, when for the finale of the third and final night's concert, on May 22, Joni shared vocals with Dylan on 'I Shall Be Released', backed by the Tokyo New Symphony Orchestra, conducted by Michael Kamen. This was televised around the world and caught Joni Mitchell looking askance at Dylan throughout this duet. Afterwards she complained that he never cleaned his teeth.

Undaunted, she reappeared on a triple bill with him and Van Morrison at a series of six West Coast concerts in May 1998, beginning in Vancouver on May 14. On the opening night she stood at the side of the stage for Dylan's set after completing her own. In the town of George, in Washington State, on May 16, she shared vocals with Bob and Van on the tenth song of Dylan's set, 'I Shall Be Released'. It was alleged that on the second of two dates at UCLA in Los Angeles, on May 22, Dylan came on during Joni's set to share vocals with her on 'Big Yellow Taxi'—but this didn't happen: Joni just imitated his voice on one verse. The last night of the six was at Anaheim on May 23.

Like Dylan, she has slowed down her output in middle age. She released only three albums of new material in the 1980s and a further three in the 1990s. But her career proceeds, recurrently beset by fights with the music-biz, which she has often roundly condemned, in tandem with her life-long interest in painting. She has painted not only a number of her own album covers but also for example the cartoonish front of the 1974 Crosby, Stills, Nash & Young album *So Far*.

Nor has she lost her sense of humour. The cover of *Turbulent Indigo* is a self-portrait of Joni as Van Gogh, complete with bandaged ear. And in 1996 she released two compilation albums. One was called *Hits*: the other, *Misses*.

NB: the 2005 *Joni Mitchell—Collector's Edition* 2-DVD set, combining the unmissable 2003 documentary *A Woman of Heart and Mind* with a 1998 live show previously released as *Painting With Words and Music*, is advertised as having a duet with Joni and Dylan on 'Positively 4th Street': but this is actually a clip of Joni singing along to the Dylan record. A bit of a swizz as a duet but belated proof of that special fondness for 'Positively 4th Street'.

[Joni Mitchell: *Joni Mitchell* (later re-titled *Song of a Seagull*), Reprise, US, 1968; *Clouds*, Reprise, 1969; *Ladies of the Canyon*, Reprise, 1970; *Blue*, Reprise, 1971; *For the Roses*, Asylum, US, 1972; *Hejira*, Asylum, 1976; *Night Ride Home*, Geffen 24302, US, 1991; *Turbulent Indigo*, Reprise / WEA 45786, US, 1994. *Artist's Choice: Joni Mitchell—Music That Matters to Her*, Starbucks / Hear Music / Rhino Special Products OPCD-7699 LMM-286, US, 2005. *Joni Mitchell—Collector's Edition* 2-DVD set, Eagle Eye Media EE 39072-9, US, 2005 (the 1st DVD includes brief footage of Dylan at Newport Folk Festival and from *Don't Look Back*). Quote re 'Positively 4th Street' from Bill Flanagan, *Written in My Soul*, Chicago: Contemporary Books, 1986; *Rolling Stone* quoted from online review of movie *Hurricane*, posted 2000, *nia*.]

'money doesn't talk' One of Dylan's best-remembered lines of the 1960s is that snarl from 'It's Alright Ma (I'm Only Bleeding)', that 'Money doesn't talk, it swears.' But while this spin on the phrase 'money talks' is Dylan's, the notion of making such a spin comes down through the blues from even further back, in black-face vaudeville. A Victor catalogue of 'Darky ditties' from around 1903 contains, in the category 'Comic and Coon Songs by Arthur Collins', one called 'If Money Talks, It Ain't on Speaking Terms with Me'; years later the same idea had migrated into an early blues that begins 'I can't make a nickel, I'm flat as I can be / Some people say money is talking, but it won't say a word to me.'

[Victor catalogue reproduced in Tony Russell, *Blacks Whites and Blues*, London: Studio Vista, 1970. Early blues song source unknown.]

More Bob Dylan Greatest Hits* [1971]** UK title for ***Bob Dylan's Greatest Hits Vol. II.

Morrison, Van [1945 -] George Ivan Morrison was born in Belfast, Northern Ireland, on August 31, 1945, and grew up in that harshly divided sectarian city. At 12 he joined the skiffle group Deannie Sands and the Javelins, later touring Germany's clubs in the Monarchs before returning to Belfast to become the lead singer of Them, one of the funkiest of the British beat groups reviving Chicago blues and rock'n'roll for teenage Saturday night dances in the early 1960s. All these groups attacked their material with crude simplicity—guitar, bass and drums all playing three-chord numbers in a home-made style—but Them's special funkiness was due in large part to the exceptional, almost venomous devotion to soul singing on the part of Morrison himself.

Them, a five-piece group, were signed to a major UK label, Decca—the one that had rejected THE BEATLES—and achieved hits first with a revamp of BIG JOE WILLIAMS' 'Baby Please Don't Go' and then with two songs that swiftly became anthemic classics, 'Here Comes the Night' and the Morrison-penned 'Gloria', though their studio work ranged more widely than this perfect pop and the group, at Morrison's prompting, was quick to make an audacious 'cover' of Dylan's 'It's All Over Now, Baby Blue'—the first overt indication that Dylan's work had in any way impinged upon this very different artist.

Tiring of the lumpen limitations of the rest of the group, and never especially skilled at intra-personal relations, Van Morrison went solo, signing a new deal with Bert Berns, who had been the group's manager and producer. Berns, an ex-Juilliard School of Music pupil but also one of the era's bumptious entrepreneurs, who might have sold frozen foods as easily as popular music, had enjoyed great success with various other R&B-style singles acts, and who, with the Erteguns and JERRY WEXLER, had recently formed Bang Records in New York.

Using session musicians just as capable as Them of dragging down Morrison's already extraordinary emergent talent, as both composer and vocalist, Berns produced the now-legendary Bang sessions in 1967 that included prototypes of 'Beside You' and 'Madame George', songs destined to re-emerge in transcendent form on *Astral Weeks* astonishingly soon afterwards; but the Bang sessions also included the lyrical and catchy 'Brown-Eyed Girl', a Morrison composition that revealed his rapturous muse and again became a 'classic', and a US top 10 hit.

Bert Berns died suddenly of a heart attack on December 30, 1967 and Morrison, freed to sign elsewhere, made *Astral Weeks* for Warner Brothers in 1968. This was a jaw-dropping quantum leap in Morrison's work, an album utterly unlike any ever made before and achieved by an artist who was 22 years old at the time of its recording. It is the most radiant weave of sounds and feelings, of words and music, of timing and phrasing, its exquisite yearning expressed in a soaringly imaginative, emotionally truthful way, and all achieved with immense dexterity and delicacy yet such shimmering ardour, in which every note played is vibrant with physicality and every vocal line a gloriously inspired solo. It is, in the words of the All Music Guide, 'not only Morrison's masterpiece, but one of the greatest records ever made'—to say which still seems to pay scant tribute to its unfathomable genius.

It was not immediately a successful album in commercial terms, yet somehow everyone came to know it, it touched people's lives deeply, it expanded the possibilities of the medium for everyone, and no-one doubted its artistic achievement. Unarguably, there were now two vast mountains on the musical planet, utterly different from each other yet of comparable mass: Bob Dylan and Van Morrison.

Like Dylan's 'She Belongs to Me', the *Astral Weeks* song 'Slim Slow Slider' was an utterly modern, hip evocation of things fleeting and beguiling, a track so markedly contemporary that you might never notice it was structured as an old-fashioned 12-bar blues. Like Dylan, Van Morrison made no attempt to make a follow-up album, and his next works led us through mostly very different staging-posts on the Morrison journey of exploration.

After two albums strikingly unlike *Astral Weeks* yet similar to each other, *Moondance* and *His Band & the Street Choir* (both 1970), came the mellower *Tupelo Honey* (1971), the majestic *Saint Dominic's Preview* (1972), the thinner *Hard Nose the Highway* (1973) and *Veedon Fleece* (1974), this last coming after Morrison's first return in eight years from the soft California hippie US universe to the embittered streets of Belfast. After much dithering came the uptight *A Period of Transition* (1977), the more rhapsodic if oddly produced *Wavelength* (1978), *Into the Music* (1979) and then *Common One* (1980), the first of a long run of albums hard to distinguish from each other.

Unlike Dylan, Morrison was intensely demanding musically, as the exquisite jazz-virtuoso playing on *Astral Weeks* had suggested, and soon afterwards he was prepared to form, rehearse and maintain a large unit of players, his Caledonia Soul Orchestra; one result was the 1974 double-LP *It's Too Late to Stop Now*, one of the most glorious, and most attentively recorded, live albums of all time. It also showed that Morrison, however difficult and prone to erratic behaviour on as well as off stage, could rise to the most intense demands of his own talent and deliver live performances of blazing charismatic power, volatile excitement and immense resourcefulness, calling up that golden voice and some of the timeless catalogue of work he had already dreamed into existence, and on other occasions taking solos himself with authority yet entirely without flash on guitar, harmonica and saxophone.

Despite the fact that Morrison was utterly undependent upon Bob Dylan's work for his own, it was perhaps inevitable that these two very different northerners would meet up professionally in the long run. It didn't happen easily, however. Morrison's ex-wife Janet Planet paints this picture of how things stood in the *Astral Weeks* period, when, she claims, she and Van moved to Woodstock largely to be near Bob Dylan: 'Van fully intended to become Dylan's best friend, but the whole time we were there they never met. Every time we'd drive past Dylan's house—Van didn't drive, I did—Van would just stare wistfully out the window at the gravel road leading to Dylan's place. He thought Dylan was the only contemporary worthy of his attention. But back then, Bob just wasn't interested in him.'

Their first encounter was nevertheless thanks to Woodstock residents THE BAND, on whose 1971 album *Cahoots* Morrison had performed, so that he was rightly a guest at their so-called Farewell Concert in 1976, filmed as *The Last Waltz* by MARTIN SCORSESE. There is Van, already beginning to put on weight and dressed inadvisedly in a purple jumpsuit, kicking his little legs in the air and reprising the incandescent melodrama of his long-drawn-out live 'Caravan'. Van also joins in the vocal chorus on Dylan's performance of 'I Shall Be Released'.

Since then, Dylan and Morrison have come together on stage many times, starting on Dylan's 1984 tour of Europe, when Van popped up in Paris and London to share vocals and play guitar on 'It's All Over Now, Baby Blue' (July 1 and 7); and for the tour's last concert, at Slane, Ireland, on July 8, they followed 'It's All Over Now, Baby Blue' with a 'Tupelo Honey' on which Van took lead vocals and Dylan joined in on the choruses.

Their next rendezvous, in June 1989, was for the filming of the BBC-TV arts documentary 'Arena: One Irish Rover', on which they sat together on the Hill of the Muses in sight of the Parthenon in Athens and were filmed performing 'Crazy Love', '(And) It Stoned Me', 'Foreign Window' and 'One Irish Rover', with Dylan contributing guitar and vocal accompaniment, and on 'Foreign Window' playing harmonica. Omitting '(And) It Stoned Me', this odd, nicely quiet collaboration was first broadcast in March 1991 on British television. Watching it, it was striking (and funny) that while Van was the avowed subject of the programme, the camera just couldn't help but keep swinging around to linger on the infinitely more charismatic, aesthetically pleasing Bob.

The night after the filming, Morrison came on stage near the end of Dylan's Never-Ending Tour set in the city and took lead vocals on 'Crazy Love' and '(And) It Stoned Me'. Dylan flew back to the US straight after this for a concert in Peoria, Illinois, three nights later, and in it ventured a version of 'One Irish Rover' himself.

When Dylan's Never-Ending Tour arrived in Belfast on February 6, 1991, Van joined him on stage for one song-performance towards the end of his set, on which 'Tupelo Honey' segued into 'Why Must I Always Explain?' and in Milan, Italy, that June 8, Dylan reciprocated, joining Van on stage to play harmonica on 'Whenever God Shines His Light' and 'Enlightenment'. In Dublin on February 6, 1993, Dylan joined Van on stage again, this time to play harmonica on a Morrison version of 'It's All Over Now, Baby Blue'—with a line-up that included Chrissie Hynde and KRIS KRISTOFFERSON on backing vocals. Four months after that, it was tit for tat again as Van joined Bob to share vocals on 'One Irish Rover' in the middle of Dylan's performance at the Fleadh (pronounced Flah) in London's Finsbury Park on June 12, 1993.

In LA in January 1994, Dylan filmed a televised message for Morrison for a UK awards ceremony, broadcast as 'The Brit Awards' on BBC-TV that February 15. Playing the game but wanting to show a cynical cool about the whole charade at the same time, Dylan somewhat gracelessly said this: 'Congratulations, Van, on this very prestigious award. "The Brit Award." No-one's more deserving of it than you for writing all those fine songs and giving us all that inspiration through the years. Thanks a lot. God bless you, Van. Blah, blah, blah, blah, blah, blah.'

In the spring of 1995, on the latest leg of the Never-Ending Tour—the leg that had begun with Dylan's début concerts in Prague, in the recently formed Czech Republic (as opposed to the old Czechoslovakia), and then wended its way through Germany, the Netherlands, France, Belgium, England, Wales, Scotland and Northern Ireland—when Dylan and his band then moved down to Dublin, Van Morrison joined them on stage that April 11, as did CAROLE KING and ELVIS COSTELLO. Van's contribution was to share vocals with Bob on Van's song 'Real Real Gone' (from his 1990 album *Enlightenment*) and to share vocals with Bob and Elvis on 'I Shall Be Released' and 'Rainy Day Women # 12 & 35'. (Carole King played piano on the two Dylan songs but not on 'Real Real Gone'.)

In July 1996, they both found themselves on the bill of a jazz festival in Molde, Norway (Morrison surely the better qualified to offer anything that might reasonably be called jazz), and here again Van joined Bob on stage to share vocals on 'I Shall Be Released' and 'Real Real Gone'. Two years later, they finally co-headlined some tour-dates together, which might be said to have been small parts of Dylan's long 1998 tour. For Dylan its first leg started in the US on January 13, in New London, Connecticut, and ran through till February 22 in Fairfax, Virginia. The concerts in New York City and in Boston—five nights at Madison Square Garden, no less, plus two at the Boston Fleet Center—were co-headlined with Morrison. During Van's set on the third consecutive concert night, January 18, Dylan came on stage and shared vocals on 'More and More', and on the last New York night, January 21, he came on in Van's set to share vocals on 'Blue Suede Shoes', two days after CARL PERKINS' death. They repeated this tribute at the second of the Boston dates, January 24, but this time Van also came on stage towards the end of Dylan's set to share vocals on 'Knockin' on Heaven's Door'.

In May came a short series of West Coast dates co-starring not only Dylan and Morrison but JONI MITCHELL too. On May 16 at George, Washington (yes), both Van and Joni joined Dylan to share vocals on 'I Shall Be Released', on which Van also played harmonica (rather better than Dylan might have done). By June 15, Dylan and Morrison were both in Europe in amongst the summer festivals circuit, and that night co-headlined in Rotterdam just ahead of a further series of co-headline concerts in the UK, starting in Belfast on June 19 and playing at Newcastle (June 20), Glasgow (21), Sheffield (23), Birmingham (24), Manchester (25) and London (27). But the only night that saw any collaboration was at Birmingham, when Morrison played harmonica and shared vocals on Dylan's 'Knockin' on Heaven's Door'. Finally, three months later, there was another short West Coast series of shared dates, from September 22 in Puyallup, Washington to the 27th in Reno, Nevada. On this leg, there was no on stage collaboration at all. Nor has there been any professional connection between the two artists in the eight years since.

Van Morrison flirts with the postmodernism of the self-reflexive text with 'I'd Love to Write Another Song', from 1989's *Avalon Sunset* album, a song which, far from offering insight into the elusiveness of the muse, is only a declaration of its absence, necessarily portentous and uninteresting. (This particular cul-de-sac was perhaps first explored by that renowned avant-gardeist Tommy Steele, with his 1962 'Hit Record', the lyric of which affects to put together a list of the ingredients you need to put together to have a hit record: thereby, and with cockney cheeriness too, taking as its immediate subject the commercial processes by which it is itself brought into being. Or not, since the record was a deserved flop. This did not discourage others, and by 1974 we started to get knowing album titles such as *I Thought Terry Dene Was Dead*, a compilation of tracks by another early British rock'n'roller.) Such items have never been popular, and Van Morrison's 'I'd Love to Write Another Song' was no exception.

In general, though, Morrison's work from the 1980s onwards has been characterised not by postmodernism but conservative sameness. With two or three exceptions (most appealingly *Irish Heartbeat*, with the Chieftains, in 1988 and, for its consummate 'Georgia on My Mind', 2002's *Down the Road*), all his albums since *Common One* have blurred into each other, expanding only in quantity. They form one big generic work, within which there is a heavy reprocessing of titles, phrases and lines from earlier songs, while the voice too has settled into a never-changing instrument: a fatter, infinitely less expressive older cousin to the marvellously fluid, vivaciously imaginative, lithe vocalist so sublimely present on *Astral Weeks*. Van has become the SINATRA of 'My Way' rather than of 'Come Fly with Me'.

Yet in concert he can still offer more. He can still give a vocal performance more felt and delicate live than in the studio, and can make all that reprocessing seem a richer thing—can make you feel, in concert, that one of the glories of his 1980s-onwards repertoire has become its threading-through with strands of earlier songs: not only from his own back-catalogue but from the whole canvas of other people's works that he has learnt from and loved. He can sing 'Cleaning Windows' (a directly autobiographical song from *Beautiful Vision*) so as to offer more than the lyric's inbuilt allusions to LEADBELLY, BLIND LEMON JEFFERSON, MUDDY WATERS and others (not forgetting the poetic inspiration from KEROUAC): he can also invoke that aeons-earlier autobiographical work 'The Story of Them Parts 1 & 2' and, in a playful, inspired flash, pop George Formby into the picture simply by switching pronunciation from 'windows' to 'winders'.

To defer to the judgement of the All Music Guide again: 'Equal parts blue-eyed soul shouter and wild-eyed poet-sorcerer, Van Morrison [has been] among popular music's true innovators, a restless seeker whose incantatory vocals and alchemical fusion of R&B, jazz, blues, and Celtic folk [has] produced perhaps the most spiritually transcendent body of work in the rock & roll canon.'

Here is a man who has made large journeys—from the long-gone dance-halls of the early 60s, where all such wannabe soul singers found themselves on the wrong side of the Atlantic with the wrong colour skin, through the unimaginable post-*Astral Weeks* hipness of California dreaming and back: back to self-knowledge and unapologetic middle-aged Irish blokeness, with a little 'Enlightenment' and WILLIAM BLAKEness thrown in. The man is grumpy, belligerent and spoilt; the artist is invaluable. And he is much loved because in journeying, he has summoned up more and more will-power for holding true to two vast diversities: the tumultuous embrace of the world of JOHN LEE HOOKER blues clubs, alongside the magic pantheism of the natural world with its rivers and green valleys, ancient lanes and timeless rapture.

There are very few great artists. Van Morrison is one of them.

[Van Morrison: 'Brown-Eyed Girl', NY, 1967 Bang, US, 1967; the Bang Sessions, NY, 1967, released retrospectively on *The Complete Bang Sessions*, Purple Pyramid/Cleopatra CD, UK, 2002; 'Slim Slow Slider' and the rest of *Astral Weeks*, NY, 1968, Warner Bros WS 1768, UK, 1968; *It's Too Late to Stop Now*, London, summer 1973, Warner Bros K86007, UK, 1974; 'I'd Love To Write Another Song', UK, prob. late 1988, *Avalon Sunset*, Polydor 839 262-4, London, 1989; 'Cleaning Windows', *Beautiful Vision*, 1982; 'Enlightenment' & 'Real Real Gone', UK, 1990, *Enlightenment*, Polydor 847 100-1, UK, 1990; *Down the Road*, Exile/Polydor 589 177-2, UK, 2002. Them: 'Baby Please Don't Go', London, 1965, Decca, UK, 1965; 'Here Comes the Night', ditto; 'Gloria'; 'It's All Over Now, Baby Blue', London, prob. 1966; 'The Story of Them Parts 1 & 2'. Van Morrison & the Chieftains: *Irish Heartbeat*, Dublin, Sep 1987–Jan 1988, Mercury MERH 124, UK, 1988. Van Morrison & Bob Dylan: 'Arena: One Irish Rover', filmed Athens, 27 Jun 1989, broadcast UK, 16 Mar 1991; 'Crazy Love' & '(And) It Stoned Me', Athens, 28 Jun 1989. Bob Dylan: 'One Irish Rover', Peoria, IL, 1 Jul 1989. Tommy Steele: 'Hit Record', Decca, London, 1962; The Happy World of Tommy Steele, Decca Records [S]PA 24, London, 1969. Terry Dene: *I Thought Terry Dene Was Dead*, Decca SPA 368, London, 1974.

Quotes on Morrison from Jason Ankeny, All Music Guide, seen online 31 Dec 2005 at *www.vh1.com/artists/az/morrison_van/bio.jhtml*. Quote from Janet Planet, *Los Angeles Times*, 17 Nov 1998, seen excerpted online 31 Dec 2005 at Bob Dylan Who's Who, *www.expectingrain.com/dok/who/who.html*.]

Morton, Dave [1939 -] David Morton, one of Dylan's Dinkytown and Minneapolis friends, was born in Salt Lake City, Utah, on November 14, 1939. At age three, he moved with his family to Berkeley, California, and then to upstate New York, arriving finally in St. Paul, Minnesota, in 1947 or '48. He grew up with folksong. 'We knew those folk songs when we were five,' he says.

He spent one year at the high school run by the University of Minnesota and there met the others in the Dylan Minneapolis crowd. He's lost touch now with HARVEY ABRAMS, though he heard not long ago that he was still alive, and still remembers him playing Dylan 'a bunch of records'. Dave was one of the bohemians, though only 18 months older than Dylan. He played guitar himself, wrote songs and collected records. He also gave DAVE RAY guitar lessons, and with his musical partner Vic Kantowski was the first act ever at the 10 O'Clock Scholar.

Asked what Dylan might have gained from him, Dave says modestly: 'Really nothing, except I encouraged him to stop singing those glitzy BELAFONTE songs. I said "If I can write songs, you can write songs." And then he did pretty good at that, didn't he?'

In summer 1963 Morton founded a small literary magazine, entitled *region*, which ran throughout the 1960s and published political material, poetry and fiction. Dave wrote poetry, and gave readings 'from coast to coast' in that decade. He got to know a lot of rock music people, including Janis Joplin: 'the nicest rock'n'roller I ever met: just a sweetheart'.

Dave Morton lives up in northern Minnesota these days: he moved out to Grand Rapids in 1970, and then settled in Angora in 1971. 'I dropped out of college for 30 years,' he says. 'Moved up north and went into cement work. Did OK: I have a big house with 40 acres and I've put my two daughters through college. One of them got a PhD: works for the Audubon Society nowadays.'

Dave is rumoured to leave Angora only to attend and perform at the annual Jug Band Festivals, principally those in Minneapolis and Duluth, the town of Dylan's birth. He and a friend founded these, by starting up the Minneapolis one, and then re-starting it in 1980.

After Duluth's '8th Annual Battle of the Jug Bands', in 2004, he was written up as follows online: 'Next, The Jook Savages, aka The Duke Sandwiches Jugband, from days of yore, 1964 to be exact. Down from Angora, on the Iron Range of Northern Minnesota. David Morton, chief instigator Buffalo Nickel, was among those few white boys who revived jugband music in the early sixties. SALUTE! Mort always seems to delight in walking the line between chaos and confusion and bringing harmony out of it in a remarkable way. We love it when he pulls off his "Poor Man's Jazz". Never one to play by the rules, or fair, he doesn't wait for applause, but just keeps on singing and playing, and even tuning without stopping. Changing tempo? No problem. He just keeps on playing and lets others catch up. We are honored to have him each year.'

That sounds spot on for an old compadre of Dylan's. The wordplay with the group name the Jook Savages seems a tradition. At the 23rd Annual Minneapolis Battle of the Bands, that same year, when the schedule of who was to play was posted up, someone changed 'Savages' so that it read 'Sausages'.

[Dave Morton Duluth jug band festival performance report: seen online 4 Oct 2005 at *www.elliotbrothers.com/8thbattlreview.html*. Literary magazine: *region* #1, MN, summer 1963. All quotes & biographical information phone call with this writer, 11 Oct 2005.]

Moss, Wayne [1938 -] Wayne Moss is the Nashville session player who created that 16th-note guitar lick that recurs all through 'I Want You', on *Blonde on Blonde*, the only Dylan album he contributes to. AL KOOPER remembers: 'The first time he came up with that, my jaw dropped—not only for the lick but for the effortlessness he played it with.'

Bradley Wayne Moss was born February 9, 1938 in South Charleston, West Virginia, where he grew up learning FLATT & SCRUGGS licks with a banjoist friend, then discovering Chet Atkins. He first came to Nashville in 1959 to work in Brenda Lee's backing band, and in 1962 set up his Cinderella Studios in Madison, Tennessee, and learnt to be a producer, eventually becoming one of the many regular Nashville cats, so many of whom gathered for those *Blonde on Blonde* sessions. It was HARGUS 'PIG' ROBBINS who first got him a session gig, but Wayne and CHARLIE McCOY had been playing together earlier in the 60s, in Charlie McCoy & the Escorts (along with KENNY BUTTREY, BILL AIKINS and others), back in the days of pencil-sharp suits hung on bony young bodies that tottered under the weight of huge greased quiffs—and Moss' rollmop style, was the best in the group. His retrospective album *Wayne's World* has a great shot of him from those days, a cheery reminder of what CARL PERKINS once said about this generation of young hopefuls: 'ELVIS,' he said, 'was the only one of us who didn't look like Mister Ed.'

After Dylan, Moss was one of those who joined Area Code 615 and when they mutated into Barefoot Jerry, he was the longest lasting, remaining in place till the end. The group went through several labels and many line-ups, the last of which, recruited by Moss, made the final Barefoot Jerry album, *Barefootin'*, in 1977. The group had worked and travelled for 11 years; 25 people had passed through its ranks. They once played 31 dates at the Paris Olympia theatre with 'the Elvis of France', er, Eddie Mitchell.

By this time Moss had also played on hundreds of other people's sessions, including on ROY ORBISON's 'Pretty Woman', a Ray Price album produced by veteran Columbia A&R man Don Law in 1967, *Danny Boy*, Waylon Jennings' album *Waylon* in 1970, and on work by everyone else from Nancy Sinatra to Mike Nesmith and from the Steve Miller Band's 1970 album *Number 5* to the Robert Mitchum single 'Little Ole Wine Drinker Me'.

In recent years, Moss has reformed a Barefoot Jerry/Area Code 615 band that is *very* big in Japan. And unlike most of these good ole boys, he's still so thin he could still wear that Escorts suit.

[Some data from Moss' website *www.barefootjerry.com*; more from Moss, phone call to this writer, 5 Apr 2006.]

Motion, Andrew [1952 -] Born in London, October 26, 1952, Motion is a prolific poet, biographer and anthologist, and a keen public advocate for poetry. Well-positioned in the contemporary British literary establishment, he read English at Oxford, taught at the University of Hull (where he met Philip Larkin), edited *Poetry Review*, was Poetry Editor and Editorial Director at Chatto & Windus publishing house (1983–89), succeeded Malcolm Bradbury as Professor of Creative Writing at the University of East Anglia, has been Chairman of the Arts Council's Literature Panel and is a Fellow of the Royal Society of Literature.

Like GREIL MARCUS, Motion contributed to the 1996+ positive sea-change in Dylan's critical and popular esteem when in late 1998, a few months before being appointed the United Kingdom's new Poet Laureate, Motion discussed the newly released 1966 concert recording from Manchester Free Trade Hall in terms of 'the tremendous beauty and subtlety of the songs and the matchless voice that sings them.'

[Andrew Motion: *Daily Telegraph*, London, 10 Oct 1998.]

***MTV Unplugged*™ [album, 1995]** The dreariest, most contemptible, phony, tawdry piece of *product* ever issued by a great artist, which manages to omit the TV concert's one fresh and fine performance, 'I Want You', but is otherwise an accurate record of the awfulness of the concert itself, in which the performer who had been so numinously 'unplugged' in the first place ducked the opportunity to use television to perform, solo, some of the ballad and country-blues material from his most recent studio albums, *Good as I Been to You* and *World Gone Wrong*. That could have been magical. Instead–instead of seizing this moment and really stepping into the arena–we got the usual greatest hits, wretchedly performed in a phoney construct of a 'live' concert. This is what happens when Bob Dylan capitulates and lets overpaid coke-head executives, lawyers and PRseholes from the Entertainment Industry tell him what to do.

[Recorded NY, 17 & 18 Nov 1994; released US as Columbia CK 67000, 30 Jun 1995 but in Europe & UK as Columbia 478374 2, 25 Apr 1995. In UK also released as 2-LP set, Simply Vinyl SVLP 100/Columbia 478374-1.]

***MTV Unplugged*™ [video, 1995]** See ***MTV Unplugged* [album]** for main details. The video release includes 'Love Minus Zero/No Limit', which is omitted from the album. Both omit 'I Want You', which was included in the version televised on PBS-TV stations in the US in 1995. The original TV airing, on MTV, December 14, 1994, was as on the subsequent video.

[Recorded NY, 17 & 18 Nov 1994; released as Columbia Music Video 19V-50113 (US) and SMV 50113 2 (UK & Europe), 25 Apr 1995.]

Muddy Waters [1915 - 1983] McKinley Morganfield was born at Jug Corner, Issaquena County, just across the county line from Sharkey County's little town of Rolling Fork, Mississippi, on April 14, 1915. He grew up on Stovall Plantation, near Clarksdale, was 'discovered' by ALAN LOMAX and was thus more or less literally field recorded before the end of World War II. These titles included 'Country Blues' and 'I Be's Troubled', both smouldering blues in the spirit of SON HOUSE. However, moving to Chicago and encouraged by BIG BILL BROONZY and Sonny Boy Williamson I, he soon created for that great city the template for its barband music, its post-war blues by–in Tony Russell's phrase–'reenergizing Chicago's formula-bound music with a waft of soul from the Mississippi bottomlands.'

His 1948 record 'I Can't Be Satisfied' was innovative, and in the 1950s he was in his prime, with a number of his songs becoming Chicago anthems (and later passing into the repertoire of every British beat group), as with 'I'm Your Hoochie Coochie Man' and 'I Just Want to Make Love to You' (both 1954) and 'Got My Mojo Working' (1956). He was a strong singer, a deft slide guitarist and a ready composer and re-composer of the blues. On top of which, he had gravitas–in his case an authoritative mix of shrewdness and dignity of carriage. A long list of great musicians played in his band and benefited from the experience and the exposure.

Eleven years on from 'I Can't Be Satisfied', Muddy Waters performed at the NEWPORT FOLK FESTIVAL of 1960, though VAL WILMER recalls that he caused 'controversy by playing the electric guitar in Britain' as early as 1958. In this respect, then–in producing an electric guitar in front of an audience expecting a 'folk' performance–the Bob Dylan of 1965 found himself re-enacting a scene already lived through by the great Mississippian bluesman.

Waters' 1960 Newport appearance was, as the late Mike Leadbitter put it, 'Muddy's first real crack at the white market'. Waters performed again with his band at the 1964 Festival, and, though his playing time was encroached upon by the addition of NEIL DIAMOND to the bill, he also performed at the Farewell Concert for THE BAND in San Francisco in November 1976, and thus appears in the SCORSESE film *The Last Waltz*. By this time Muddy Waters had quit Chess and become a regular on the campus circuit and the annual round of blues festivals. His 1969 Vogue album *Fathers and Sons* paired Waters and Otis Spann with PAUL BUTTERFIELD and MIKE BLOOMFIELD; and between 1977 and 1981 he made four albums for Columbia/Blue Sky produced by Johnny Winter.

Bob Dylan hadn't been at Newport 1960 but a couple of years earlier, back in high school in Minnesota, he had already expressed admiration for Waters and for JIMMY REED. In May 1961 in Minneapolis he was recorded performing Muddy's 1950s number 'Still a Fool'. In January 1962, on the unedited tape made for a New York radio programme (it first emerged, on a bootleg CD, 30 years later), Dylan tells CYNTHIA GOODING that he knows the work of Muddy Waters; that July, at the Finjan Club in Montreal, Dylan again performs 'Still a Fool' (sometimes known as 'Two Trains Runnin'). Of Muddy Waters' three verses, Dylan's version here uses two and then adds two more, of which one shows a personalised contribution by Dylan himself and both show his familiarity with common-stock blues lyric poetry.

A couple of years later, he makes subtle use of this song again inside his own work. In 'Bob Dylan's 115th Dream', while 'I saw three ships a-sailin'' is (vernacular dropped 'g' apart) a verbatim quote from the Christmas carol, when you add in the line Dylan adds, you find it is also a turnaround of a blues song's re-statement of the common folkloric commuter's lament about waiting for buses and trains and the wrong ones always turning up first. Dylan's 'I saw three ships a-sailin' / They were all heading my way' neatly reverses a blues line from 1927, 'They's two trains runnin', none of them going my way', from 'Frisco Whistle Blues' by Alabama's splendid blues artist Ed Bell (tagged in the Paramount catalogue as the Weird Guitar Player), from his début session. But you might approach the same putative traffic-jam from a later vantage-point, and conclude that the line Dylan attaches to the carol's 'I saw three ships a-sailin'' makes a darting imaginative connexion with–perhaps deliberately echoes–the Muddy Waters song. Waters' 'Well now two, there's two trains runnin' / Well they aint never goin' my way' becomes Dylan's 'I saw three ships a-sailin' / They were all headin' my way.'

The Muddy Waters song derives either from Robert Petway's pre-war classic 'Catfish Blues' or from his friend and performing partner Tommy McClennan's copy of it, 'Deep Blue Sea Blues', which both re-work a traditional Mississippi blues. Tommy Johnson's 1928 'Bye Bye Blues' has the similar line 'Well, two trains runnin', runnin' side by side' and the same tune as 'Still a Fool'. These things are hard to pin down but Dylan probably got it from Muddy Waters and Waters primarily from McClennan.

Aside from converging at The Band's Farewell Concert, Dylan and Muddy Waters met on stage just once. On June 30, 1975, Muddy and his band were playing the first of three consecutive nights at the Bottom Line, New York City, doing two sets per night. Dylan was in the audience, with SCARLET RIVERA and others, wandering among the tables dressed in a black leather jacket over a striped t-shirt and pale brown flared trousers. Muddy was up on stage in a loud red shirt, big-check golfer's trousers and matching waistcoat. Muddy brought on VICTORIA SPIVEY, and later his ex-harp player Paul Oscher, and later still Dylan. Oscher gave him a microphone and a harmonica, and Muddy asked him: 'Fast or slow?' Bob said: 'Fast', and off they went, beginning with a long harp solo from Dylan from which Muddy turned it into a 1930 MEMPHIS MINNIE number he'd just been recording, 'What's the Matter With the Mill?'. Mid-way through they were joined on stage by a cornet player and by Dylan's companions, Scarlet Rivera on violin and another woman on tambourine. The resultant jam lasted at least 15 minutes. Dylan and friends disappeared with Waters, heading for Victoria Spivey's place in Brooklyn. Two nights later, he was again in the audience for Muddy's set, this time accompanied by PATTI SMITH, but didn't return to the stage. This might have been because of Waters' announcement to the crowd: 'John Dylan is in the house!' Bob soon wasn't.

In 1990, when Dylan played his remarkable four-set gig at Toad's Place in New Haven, Connecticut, he performed a one-off of a song that was partly Muddy Waters'. 'Someday Baby Blues' is SLEEPY JOHN ESTES' particularly heartfelt and individual variant of 'Sittin' on Top of the World', which has in turn been revised and revisited in several guises. CHUCK BERRY's 'Worried Life Blues' uses the Estes chorus but thoroughly different verses; the Allman Brothers' version of the Muddy Waters version, 'Trouble No More', does the opposite, reinstating an approximation of Estes' verses while abandoning his chorus. When Dylan sang it at Toad's Place, it was recognised as the same song as Muddy Waters', and duly appears in the various listings of his performances as 'Trouble No More', though really Dylan brings it all home to Sleepy John Estes.

There was no such mixed parentage to sort out when Dylan alighted on another piece of Muddy Waters' repertoire and performed it in concert in a series of US concerts in late 1992. Starting on October 24 in Storrs, Connecticut, Dylan opened with 'I Can't Be Satisfied', and kept it as the opening number for a further four consecutive concerts; and after dropping it on November 1, he restored it at once, opening a further five consecutive concerts with it. On November 11, 1999, in Augusta, Maine, he sang a one-off 'Hoochie Coochie Man'.

In late 1997 (we think), Dylan was asked for a quote on Waters for a tribute show on PBS, aired in 1999. His brief comments at once cut to the core of what made Muddy's Chicago blues so powerful: 'He had that "dark woods" he brought up there with him. He was able to keep that in the city.'

Not everyone likes his particular kind of boastful insistence upon a voodoo masculinity. All that 'seventh son of the seventh son', that 'mojo' magic, that incantatory swagger, that 'I'm a MAN!': some people would rather drink muddy water than listen to much of him strutting that particular stuff. Yet there is hardly a more important figure in the history of the blues.

Muddy Waters died in Westmont, a Chicago suburb, on April 30, 1983. He had just turned 68.

[McKinley Morganfield: 'Country Blues', Stovall, MS, c.24–31 Aug 1941 (field-recorded for the Library of Congress), 1st vinyl-issued on *Afro-American Blues and Game Songs*, AFS L-4, Washington, D.C., 1962 and *Muddy Waters: Blues Man*, Polydor UK 236.574, London, 1969, the former CD-reissued Rounder CD 1513, Cambridge, MA, 1999; also CD-reissued *The Complete Plantation Recordings: Muddy Waters: The Historic Library of Congress Recordings 1941–1942*, MCA CHD 9344, London, 1993. Muddy Waters: 'Still a Fool', Chicago, 1951; 'Trouble No More', Chicago, Oct 1955, Chess 1612, Chicago, 1955.

Bob Dylan: 'Still a Fool', Minneapolis, May 1961 & Montreal, 2 Jul 1962; 'Trouble No More', New Haven, CT, 12 Jan 1990; all unreleased. Dylan's quote on Waters aired PBS, 27 Jan 1999. Memphis Minnie: 'What's the Matter With the Mill?', Chicago, 11 Oct 1930. Val Wilmer, *Mama Said There'd Be Days Like This*, London: Women's Press, 1989 & 1991. Mike Leadbitter, reviewing *Muddy Waters at Newport*, Checker 6467 416, UK, 1973, in *Blues Unlimited* no.103, Bexhill-on-Sea, UK, Aug/Sep 1973. For more detail (and photos) of Dylan & Waters at the Bottom Line, see *Isis* no.115, Bedworth, UK, Jun–Jul 2004.]

Muhammad Ali [1942 -] Cassius Marcellus Clay Jr. was born in Louisville, Kentucky, on January 17, 1942. He grew up to be one of the greatest athletes in history: a boxer so talented, handsome and lithe that he made a whole generation of people who didn't like boxing watch the sport; a pioneering

African-American celebrity who, in the civil rights era, lent his name to the cause by changing it, from Cassius Clay to Muhammad Ali–throwing off the heritage of slavery at the height of his initial fame, and so scandalising the forces of reaction in white America; a commoner who refused to bow down before the machine–refusing to fight in the unjust war in Vietnam and facing gaol, death threats and persecution instead; an intelligent, witty, charming, immensely gifted man who brought a new style of outrageous boastfulness, undercut by sly self-mockery, to the promotion of his fights and the discomfiture of his opponents, and who ran rings around the standard expectation that, well, OK, you could escape the ghetto by becoming a fighter but only if you minded your p's & q's and played by a set of rules stacked high against you.

In 'I Shall Be Free No.10' on *Another Side of Bob Dylan* in 1964, Dylan gives him a playful name-check as Cassius Clay–the name under which he was a Gold Medallist at the Rome Olympics of 1960, only to return to a segregated Louisville that failed to welcome him home as an American hero; the name under which he won his next 19 fights, 15 by knockouts; under which the brash 22-year-old knocked out the supposedly invincible Sonny Liston in the 7th round on February 25, 1964.

Dylan's song, recorded on June 9 the same year, says this: 'I was shadow-boxing earlier in the day / I figured I was ready for Cassius Clay / I said "Fee, fie, fo, fum, / Cassius Clay, here I come / 26, 27, 28, 29, I'm gonna make your face look just like mine / 5, 4, 3, 2, 1, Cassius Clay you'd better run / 99, 100, 101, 102, your ma won't even recognize you / 14, 15, 16, 17, 18, 19, gonna knock him clean right out of his spleen."'

Clay announced his conversion to Islam and his taking of the name Muhammad Ali shortly afterwards. His title was revoked in 1967 when, citing his faith, he refused induction into the US military and was fined $10,000 and sentenced to a five-year prison term (which he didn't, in the end, have to serve). The US Supreme Court did not officially reverse his conviction for draft evasion until 1971 but Ali resumed fighting in 1970, knocking out Jerry Quarry and Oscar Bonaven to earn a chance to regain his heavyweight crown. On March 8, 1971, Ali suffered the first loss of his career, losing to Joe Frazier in 15 rounds, but regained the heavyweight championship on October 30, 1974, in Kinshasa, Zaire (now the so-called Democratic Republic of Congo), knocking out George Foreman in 'the rumble in the jungle'. Ali defended his title ten times in the following four years, including victory over Joe Frazier in 1975 in the Philippines. In 1977 he played himself in a competent bio-pic based on his own book, *The Greatest*. He lost his crown again to Leon Spinks in Las Vegas in early 1978 but, unbelievably, regained it one more time that September at their rematch in New Orleans. He was the only fighter ever to win the heavyweight crown three times. He announced his retirement from boxing in June 1979, but within a year challenged champion Larry Holmes for the crown. On October 2, 1980, in Las Vegas, Nevada, Ali suffered the worst, most punishing loss of his career and retired permanently at the end of 1981.

When he was reigning heavyweight champion of the world, he appeared at Bob Dylan's fund-raising benefit concert for RUBIN 'HURRICANE' CARTER at the end of the first Rolling Thunder Revue, at Madison Square Garden, New York City, on December 8, 1975: the 'Night of the Hurricane'. Addressing the overwhelmingly white crowd, Ali declared: 'You've got the connections, and the complexion, to get the protection!' Backstage, Ali and Dylan posed together for photographer KEN REGAN, for what turned out to include an utterly charming, evocative, funny, touching picture of the two, standing like brothers in arms, looking right into the camera.

MIKE MARQUSEE's book *Redemption Song: Muhammad Ali and the Spirit of the Sixties* makes articulate and telling comparisons between the two figures, who are a mere eight months apart in age.

[Michael Marqusee: *Redemption Song: Muhammad Ali and the Spirit of the Sixties*, London: Verso, 1999. Ken Regan photo of Dylan &Ali republished in Michael Gray & John Bauldie, *All Across the Telegraph: The Bob Dylan Handbook*, London: W.H. Allen, 1987.]

Muir, Andrew [1958 -] Andrew Muir was born in Cowdenbeath, Fife, Scotland, on August 16, 1958. He first took an interest in Dylan's work in 1973, and in 1990 set up the first of the two UK fanzines he has edited, the crudely produced *Homer, the slut* (named after a character in Dylan's novel *Tarantula*). This ran to 11 issues, plus four 'specials', starting in May 1990 and ceasing publication with the final 'special' at Christmas 1995.

In 2000 he published his first book, *Razor's Edge: Bob Dylan & the Never Ending Tour*, a book characteristic of Muir's work in its straddling of the divide between critical assessment and factual reportage. It looks in great detail at specific concerts, year by year from the tour's beginning in 1988 through to 2000, but also succeeds in its aim of putting the Never-Ending Tour into perspective and assessing its significance within Dylan's career as a whole. At the same time, Muir also worries away with self-deprecating humour at the ever-knotty problems of experiencing from the inside levels of fandom that most people in the world regard as crazy. Hence the great Chapter 8 of the book, '21st July, 1993', which logs Muir's own thoroughly unexpected encounter with the man himself: a terrific, affecting piece of comic writing.

In 2003 came Muir's second book, *Troubadour: Early & Late Songs of Bob Dylan*, a thoughtful elaboration of his critical stance that scrutiny should be jargon-free and range widely, in a study of specific songs from the early 1960s right through to work on the *Time Out of Mind* and *"Love and Theft"* albums. The book begins with an extremely good, substantial introduction discussing the thorny questions of performance versus words in Dylan's art, which he covers very thoroughly and with great alertness of judgement. And does so in a fresh tone of voice, which is quite an achievement.

That hugely valuable freshness steps up a whole other level when he looks anew at 'Blowin' in the Wind'. It's a main strength of the book that Muir refocusses on exactly the songs we most take for granted and so largely fail to hear. Indeed he has tackled 'Blowin' in the Wind' better than anyone has ever done: bringing out, and with genuine vigour, not only the whys and hows of its original impact but equally well the enduring subtleties and intelligence of the song. At the other end of *Troubadour* is a very substantial scrutiny of the *"Love and Theft"* album, with some invaluable tracking of what has been loved and thieved from where, assiduously footnoted yet assembled with all the enthusiasm prompted by the newness and excellence of the album.

This book was a mix of new writing and some revised selected pieces from the fanzines to which Muir had contributed—and by this point the range of these, taking in *ON THE TRACKS*, *Isis*, *Dignity* and *FREEWHEELIN'*, included his own new journal, the good-looking and generally rigorous *Judas!*, which began publication in April 2002 and has, above all other fanzines, generally held out for critical writing of quality as well as of passion: sometimes achieving this in the face of strong deadline pressures to react swiftly.

Issue 15 was a case in point, arriving with subscribers on October 19, 2005 and containing, among much else, a considered and recurrently observant long piece by Nick Hawthorne, productively attentive to small significant detail, about *Bootleg Series Vol. 7—No Direction Home: The Soundtrack* and an essay by Peter Stone Brown on *No Direction Home*, the film, which opens with three pages of marvellously vivid, elegiac prose almost wholly derived from paying close, scene-by-scene attention to the movie's structure.

Behind the scenes Andrew Muir is also one of the great communicators within the Dylan world, constructively in touch with almost everyone, including those who will not speak to each other. In outside life he is a teacher of business and academic English in Cambridge, UK, and a vociferous supporter of Rangers, a Scottish football team.

[Andrew Muir, *Razor's Edge: Bob Dylan & the Never Ending Tour*, London: Helter Skelter Publishing, 2001; *Troubadour: Early & Late Songs of Bob Dylan*, Huntingdon, UK: Woodstock Publications, 2003. *Judas!*, ditto, and *www.judasmagazine.com*.]

Muldaur, Geoff [1943 -] Geoffrey Dayton Muldaur was born in Brooklyn, New York, on August 12, 1943. He moved almost at once to Pennsylvania, then to Connecticut and had moved again, to Pelham, New York, by the age of three. He grew up there listening to New Orleans jazz and doo-wop, and became a highly regarded singer in and around Greenwich Village, making his first solo album in 1963. Years later RICHARD THOMPSON would proclaim: 'There are only three white blues singers, and Geoff Muldaur is at least two of them.'

He was one of the featured artists on the Various Artists album *The Blues Project*, put out by Elektra in 1964—and he was the one who brought Bob Dylan into it. The other featured artists were DAVE RAY, ERIC VON SCHMIDT, DAVE VAN RONK, Ian Buchanan, DANNY KALB and MARK SPOELSTRA.

Muldaur, known to his friends as Mole, brought Bob Dylan along to a New York City session for this project early that year and had him and Von Schmidt both play piano on 'Downtown Blues' (a song Muldaur had earlier performed and recorded with the JIM KWESKIN Jug Band, one of whose other members was Maria D'Amato; when they married she continued her career as MARIA MULDAUR). The other musicians on 'Downtown Blues' were John 'Fritz' Richmond (bass) and JOHN SEBASTIAN (harmonica). When the album was issued, Dylan was credited under the anagramous name Bob Landy. It isn't very good.

Muldaur appeared soon afterwards with his jug band at that year's NEWPORT FOLK FESTIVAL, and the year after performed alongside Maria Muldaur and Eric von Schmidt. The Kweskin Jug Band collapsed in 1968; he and Maria moved to Woodstock and made two albums together before they too split up and he and PAUL BUTTERFIELD formed Paul Butterfield's Better Days in 1972. He 'took a sabbatical' for the 1980s and most of the 1990s, but has been active again as a songwriter and recording artist since the fall of '97, when BOB NEUWIRTH said to him: 'I'm going to play Italy . . . want to join me and find out what it feels like'? A year later he released his first new album in 17 years, *The Secret Handshake*, and followed it with *Password* in 2004. He lives in Venice, California, now.

[Geoff Muldaur: 'Downtown Blues', NY, early 1964, *The Blues Project*, Elektra EKL 264, NY, Jun 1964; *The Secret Handshake*, Hightone HCD8097, US, 1998; *Password*, Hightone HCD8125, US, 2004.]

Muldaur, Maria [1943 -] Maria Grazia Rosa Domenica D'Amato was born in New York City on September 2, 1942 or September 12, 1943, and grew up close to Greenwich Village—where she can be glimpsed in black and white footage in the Dylan film *No Direction Home*, looking about 15 years old, all puppy-fat and pigtails, singing with one of the jug band revival groups of the early 1960s. These groups, a quirky ingredient in the

Folk Revival mix, harked back to the recorded black outfits of the 1920s like the MEMPHIS JUG BAND and Cannon's Jug Stompers.

After a childhood enthusiasm for country music, and membership of a high school pop group, the Cashmeres, and after being one of those young white enthusiasts who went down to the Deep South to 'rediscover' old black bluesmen during the early 1960s' blues revival, Maria was a performer in *two* revivalist jug bands: the Even Dozen Jug Band, which played old-timey folk, blues and jazz, and then the similar JIM KWESKIN Jug Band, which was based in Cambridge, Massachusetts.

In the Even Dozen Jug Band, the line-up was D'Amato on vocals (though she also played fiddle), Stefan Grossman, Steve Katz, Joshua Rifkin, JOHN SEBASTIAN, DAVID GRISMAN and Peter Siegel. They signed to VICTORIA SPIVEY's label, Spivey Records (for which Dylan recorded as harmonica player and back-up vocalist for BIG JOE WILLIAMS and Spivey herself in March 1962), but Elektra bought out their contract and issued their eponymously titled and only album before they disbanded.

Maria D'Amato then joined the Jim Kweskin Jug Band, in which Kweskin was joined by Maria's future husband GEOFF MULDAUR (lead guitar and vocals), plus Bill Keith, the future religious cult-leader Mel Lyman on harmonica, John 'Fritz' Richmond, Richard Greene and, on vocals and kazoo, Maria.

This outfit lasted longer and recorded more, including the comic piece 'Never Swat a Fly', which has remained in Maria Muldaur's repertoire. After moving to Cambridge, she duly married Geoff, and after the disbanding of the Jim Kweskin Jug Band in 1968 they moved to Woodstock, NY, and performed and recorded as Geoff & Maria Muldaur, issuing two LPs, *Pottery Pie* (1970, which included a cover of 'I'll Be Your Baby Tonight') and *Sweet Potatoes* (1971). In 1972 the two split up, and Maria Muldaur launched an immediately successful solo career. Her first album, *Maria Muldaur*, included 'Midnight at the Oasis', which became a huge hit single. Her second album, *Waitress in a Donut Shop*, was also well-received.

Subsequent albums were not so successful and in 1979 Muldaur had to cope with her daughter's involvement in a near-fatal car crash. 'My whole life was severely jolted,' she explained later—at which point she heard Dylan's new album, *Slow Train Coming*, and 'realized that, no matter how successful your life, without a relationship with God or a higher power, there was something very big missing. It wasn't even a conscious intellectual decision. At that moment, I surrendered . . .'

During Dylan's run of dates at the Fox-Warfield in San Francisco in November 1980—the 12 dates that opened the short tour on which he reintroduced secular material—Maria Muldaur made a guest appearance on November 19, coming on stage and singing 'Nobody's Fault But Mine' as the evening's tenth song.

It was Maria Muldaur who told Dylan biographer HOWARD SOUNES that she thought Dylan 'dated some of these black girls because they didn't idolize him. They were real down to earth, and they didn't worship him. They are strong women who would just say, cut your bullshit.' (Sounes elaborated: 'While women from his own, white middle-class background often saw him as an over-awing presence, he was just another guy to African-American women and this was refreshing to him.')

Maria Muldaur also appears in colour in *No Direction Home* as a middle-aged interviewee, speaking especially as a witness to the furore when Dylan went electric at the 1965 NEWPORT FOLK FESTIVAL. She reports that later that night, when she asked Bob if he'd like to dance, he replied, 'I'd dance with you, Maria, but my hands are on fire.' She seems impressed with the profundity of this remark, but only succeeds in making it sound empty.

It seems an unfairness of the film that while it shows her in unformed youth and in blowsy middle age, it doesn't show footage of her as a solo artist in her prime in the early 1970s, when she looked absolutely gorgeous and sang with shimmering, poignant beauty.

She continues to perform and record, and many people claim that her voice now is even better than in her younger days, having deepened and broadened, making it more able to handle material drawn from the repertoires of the women blues singers she always admired—especially that favourite of hers who was always a favourite of Dylan's too, MEMPHIS MINNIE, in tribute to whom (among others) Muldaur recorded her 2001 album *Richland Woman Blues*.

She credits Dylan with having brought her back to this music, too. The sleevenotes refer to hearing him give a 'stunning performance' in Memphis and then reading his own 'wonderfully written liner notes' to *World Gone Wrong* and being inspired by his warning: 'Look out! There won't be songs like these anymore—factually there aren't any now.' Muldaur comments: 'I realized he was right. . . . Right then and there, I got the idea and inspiration for this musical tribute to all the blues legends who so deeply inspired and influenced me early on to follow my own path both musically and spiritually.' Guest players and singers on the album, which was released four months ahead of Dylan's own *"Love and Theft"*, include Bonnie Raitt, John Sebastian, Taj Mahal and that other great bluesy survivor, Tracy Nelson. The title track is a song by MISSISSIPPI JOHN HURT; other tracks include BLIND WILLIE JOHNSON's 'Soul of a Man' and, naturally, Memphis Minnie's 'Me and My Chauffeur Blues'.

On the front cover of the album, Maria Muldaur stands at the side of the road, leaning on a marker that reads 'Old Hwy. 61'.

[The Jim Kweskin Jug Band: *Jim Kweskin & the Jug Band: Greatest Hits*, CD-reissued Vanguard, NY, 1991. The Even Dozen Jug Band: *The Even Dozen Jug Band*, Elektra 7246, NY, 1964, CD-reissued Collector's Choice, 2002. Maria Muldaur: *Richland Woman Blues*, Stony Plain Music 1270, US, 2001.]

Murphy, Elliott [1949 -] Elliott James Murphy Jr. was born at Rockville Center, New York, on March 16, 1949, grew up in Garden City and started playing the guitar at age 12. His band the Rapscallions won the 1966 New York State Battle of the Bands. He began writing songs while busking in Europe in 1971, returned to the States and issued his first album, *Aquashow*, in 1973. Its critical success had him declared one of the 'new Dylans' (awful category), along with BRUCE SPRINGSTEEN, JOHN PRINE and others. More albums followed, first on major labels and then independents. By the late 1980s he was mostly touring Europe; he moved to Paris in 1989 and lives there still. He records and keeps touring, playing well over 100 shows a year in Europe. The vinyl limited-edition issue of his 2002 album *Soul Surfing* included as a 'bonus track' a version of 'If You See Her, Say Hello'.

As well as performing, Murphy has written for *Rolling Stone*, *Spin* and several European publications. His semi-autobiographical novel *Cold and Electric* has been published in France, Germany and Spain, and he has published two short story collections, *The Lion Sleeps Tonight* and *Where the Women Are Naked and the Men Are Rich*, and the book *Café Notes*.

Murphy first listened to Bob Dylan at Christmas 1962 or '63, when his sister gave him the first Dylan album. He was about 13 years old, and knew at once that here was something beyond the clean-cut America of the Kingston Trio and John F. Kennedy. Forty years later he wrote an articulate and respectfully affectionate essay on Dylan, 'The Picasso of Rock and Roll', published as the Foreword to an Italian Dylan-for-beginners book by PAOLO VITES. It is also posted on the official Elliott Murphy website. It includes this simple truth, with which so many of us can identify:

> 'I was born at the right time, I know that, because I fell in love with the guitar and rock and roll and I have walked on this planet in the shadow of ELVIS PRESLEY and the footsteps of Bob Dylan.'

[Elliott Murphy, 'The Picasso of Rock and Roll', Foreword to Paolo Vites, *Bob Dylan—1962–2002: 40 anni di canzoni* (with appendix by Alessandro Cavazzuti), Rome: Editori Riuniti, 2002; and online at *www.elliottmurphy.com/writings/picassorockroll.htm*.]

musical accompanists to Dylan, other Space prevents giving an entry to every musician and backing singer who has ever played or sung with Dylan on stage or in the studio. No slight is intended to any of those listed communally here instead. Nor is any judgemental distinction implied between those with an explanatory description and those simply namechecked. Apologies for omissions.

Tawatha Agee on the *Feeling Minnesota* soundtrack version of 'Ring of Fire'; *Butch Amiott*, on the unreleased Chicago 1992 sessions: see **Bromberg, David**; *Joshie Armstead*, on *Self Portrait* and a July 1975 session; *Kenny Aranoff*, on *Under the Red Sky*, a 1993 WILLIE NELSON TV show and the 1994 Dylan-TRISHA YEARWOOD TV duet; *Hilliard Atkinson*, on *Under the Red Sky*. *Byron T. Bach* and *Brenton Banks*, on *Self Portrait*; *Stan Barrons* in November 1989.

George Barnes (1921–77) was one of the great jazz guitarists of the 1940s–50s but he began backing blues singers at the age of 14—and if it is true that he played on a couple of Bob Dylan's *Freewheelin'* sessions, on November 1 & 14, 1962 (yielding the 'Rocks and Gravel' issued on early withdrawn copies of the album and reissued on the *Highway 61 Interactive* CD-Rom, and yielding 'Mixed-Up Confusion', an early single reissued on *Biograph* and *Masterpieces*) then he gave the young Bob Dylan a direct link back to his pre-war blues heroine MEMPHIS MINNIE: the teenage George Barnes played behind Minnie in 1935. Playing alongside Barnes (if it really was him) behind Dylan were drummer HERB LOVELLE, bassist *Gene Ramey* and *Dick Wellstood*, the New York-based jazz pianist who played on a couple of Dylan's *Freewheelin'* sessions in 1962 and on *ODETTA and the Blues* the same year.

Richard Bell, at the 'Absolutely Unofficial Blue Jeans Bash for Arkansas', 1993: see *Stephen Stills*, below, for details; *Vincent Bell* on a July 1975 session; *Ray Benson*, October 1996 and spring 2000; *Bill Berg* on the December 1974 sessions for *Blood on the Tracks* in Minneapolis; *Byron Berline* on the *Pat Garrett & Billy the Kid* sessions, 1973; *Rayse Biggs* on *Under the Red Sky*; *George Binkley* on *Self Portrait*; *Dyan Birch*, July 1975; *Roy Bitten*, February 1985.

Brady Blade Jr. was the percussionist who played bongos, tambourine and shaker at Dylan's Frankfurt concert of April 15, 2002. Based in Stockholm, he was flown in as a replacement drummer when GEORGE RECELI was having arm and shoulder problems. He is the older brother of BRIAN BLADE (a drummer on much of *Time Out of Mind*).

Peggi Blu on *Infidels*, plus May 1986 and June 1987; *'John Boone'*, supposedly the bass player on one session for *Bringing It All Back Home*. He played (with BRUCE LANGHORNE, JOHN HAMMOND JR. and JOHN SEBASTIAN) on the evening of January 14, 1965, from which nothing was issued on the album, though the session's less-than-best version of 'I'll Keep It With Mine' was released on *Biograph* 20 years later. Boone seems to have disappeared from public sight. Maybe he never existed, and the bassist on the session was in fact *Steve Boone*, who played bass in John Sebastian's band the Lovin' Spoonful and co-wrote songs with Sebastian.

Mary Elizabeth Bridges, 1980 tour; *Robert Britt* on *Time Out of Mind*; *Alexandra Brown*, June 1987; *Charles Brown III* and *Tony Brown*, in ERIC WEISS-

BERG's Deliverance, on the New York September 1974 *Blood on the Tracks* sessions; *Mickey Bucklins* on *Slow Train Coming*; *Malcolm Burn*, a session player who often works with DANIEL LANOIS, played guitar and bass on *Oh Mercy*. *Albert W. Butler*, on *Self Portrait*; *Debra Byrd* in February 1985.

Jorge Calderon in June 1985; *Chris Cameron* on the Chicago sessions, 1992; *Fred Carter Jr.*, April 24, 1969 and *Self Portrait*; *Cindy Cashdollar* on *Time Out of Mind*; *Lenny Castro* in March 1994; *The Cate Brothers*, closely associated with, and sometimes in, reformed versions of THE BAND, for whom Dylan played guitar at the 'Absolutely Unofficial Blue Jeans Bash for Arkansas' in 1993. *Fred Catz* on *Pat Garrett & Billy the Kid*; *Marvin D. Chantry* on *Self Portrait*; *Robin Clark* and *Dennis Collins* in February 1996; *Frances Collins* and *Mel Collins* on a July 1975 *Desire* session. Mel was a top UK sax player, old colleague of IAN WALLACE and member of Kokomo at the time of the session.

Ron Cornelius was the young Nashville producer who often worked with PETE DRAKE and played guitar with BOB JOHNSTON behind LEONARD COHEN when Cohen played in London in 1972; but it was in New York studios that he played guitar overdubs on *Self Portrait* (on March 13, 1970). On June 1 he was a guitarist in the group of musicians playing behind Dylan on a session that yielded the *Dylan* album takes of 'The Ballad of Ira Hayes' and 'Sara Jane', and on the next day's session, which gave us the *Masterpieces* version of 'Spanish Is the Loving Tongue' and the *Dylan* cuts of 'Mr. Bojangles' and 'Mary Ann'. Over the next three consecutive days he was playing on 'Can't Help Falling in Love' and 'Lily of the West' (*Dylan*) and the *New Morning* track 'One More Weekend', all recorded June 3; on 'Three Angels' and 'New Morning' (both *New Morning*) and 'Big Yellow Taxi' (*Dylan*), June 4; and the six *New Morning* tracks achieved on June 5: 'If Dogs Run Free', 'Went to See the Gypsy', 'Sign on the Window', 'The Man in Me', 'Father of Night' and 'Winterlude'.

Roddy Colona, March 1989; *Joey Cooper*, March 1971; *Dominic Cortese*, July 1975; *Thomas Cosgrove*, on *New Morning*; *Sammy Creason*, the January 20, 1973 *Pat Garrett & Billy the Kid* session; *Steve Cropper* at 'Guitar Legends', Seville, October 1991; *Paulino da Costa*, on *Under the Red Sky*.

Marvin Daniels on *Infidels* and February 1985; *Karl Denson* on October 19, 1990; *Jim Dickinson* is the Memphis-based pianist who says he'd been a Dylan fan for 35 years before finally getting to play on *Time Out of Mind*. He plays piano, Wurlitzer electric piano and pump organ and appears on all tracks except 'Standing in the Doorway', 'Cold Irons Bound' and 'Make You Feel My Love'.

Dottie Dillard on *Self Portrait*; *Daryl Dixon* on *Infidels* and February 1985; *Leslie Dowdell* on stage at Slane, Ireland, on July 8, 1984; *Charlie Drayton* at 'Guitar Legends', Seville, 1991; *Debi Dye*, December 1977.

Peter Ecklund, Chicago 1992; *Dolores Edgin* on *Self Portrait*; *Bernard Edwards* in February 1996; *Larry Estridge* in May 1974; *Robin Eubanks* on *Infidels* and February 1985; *Gwen Evans*, 1980 tour.

Andy Fairweather-Low, not a name you'd expect to find linked to Dylan's, played on stage with him on June 30, 1999 during ERIC CLAPTON's Benefit for the Crossroads Concert at Madison Square Garden. British ex-mod and founding member of late-1960s group Amen Corner, Fairweather-Low (born in Cardiff, Wales, on August 2, 1948) played guitar as Dylan performed on a handful of numbers.

The oddly named *Fick Fegy* was on the Chicago 1992 sessions and the delightfully named *Buzzy Feiten* was a guitarist on *New Morning*.

Anton Fig, born in 1952 in Cape Town, where he grew up, learning drums by the age of eight, moved to the US in 1970 and became a prominent drummer, playing for many years with the CBS Orchestra for 'The Late Show with David Letterman' and others, and on sessions. He has worked with, among others, Joan Armatrading, James Brown, Robert Gordon, PAUL SIMON and BRUCE SPRINGSTEEN, and first encountering Bob Dylan in July 1984, when he played on sessions that turned out to be for *Empire Burlesque* and *Knocked Out Loaded*—including one session that yielded a circulated take each of 'Driftin' Too Far from Shore' and 'Go 'Way Little Boy' on which RON WOOD plays guitar, and another session that gave Dylan the *Empire Burlesque* track 'Clean-Cut Kid' and the *Knocked Out Loaded* track 'Driftin' Too Far from Shore'; this was later radically overdubbed but Fig still gets a sleevenote credit. Next he plays on the Rock'n'Roll Hall of Fame event in New York on January 20, 1988, alongside Dylan on guitar behind everyone from Billy Joel and Ben E. King to MICK JAGGER, Springsteen and BRIAN WILSON; and he plays behind a number of people including Dylan at the so-called 30th Anniversary Concert Celebration in New York City on October 16, 1992.

Sammy Figueroa on April 19 and May 2, 1983; *Carl Fortina* and *Gary Foster* on *Pat Garrett & Billy the Kid*; *Solie J. Fott* on *Self Portrait*; *Bubba Fowler* on *Self Portrait*; *Eric Frandsen*, July 1975; *Robben Ford* on *Under the Red Sky*; *Glen Fukunaga*, March 1989. *Full Force* (Lucien & Paul & Brian George, Curtis Bedeau and Gerard Charles) provided backing vocals overdubs on Dylan's 'Tell Me' (cut New York City, April 21, 1983 and issued on *Bootleg Series Vols. 1–3* in 1991) and on 'Death Is Not the End' (cut New York City May 2, 1983 and issued on the 1988 album *Down in the Groove*). Their overdubs for both were done in New York City on May 18, 1983.

Jimmie Dale Gilmore, October 25, 1991; *Mat Glaser*, violin on November 10, 2000; *Andrew Gold*, who on May 31, 1981 overdubbed some guitar onto four *Shot of Love* tracks: 'Watered-Down Love', 'Property of Jesus', 'Shot of Love' and 'Every Grain of Sand'; *Dennis A. Good* on *Self Portrait*; *Emmanuel Green* in March 1970; *Lloyd Green* on *New Morning*;

Willie Green on *Down in the Groove* and *Oh Mercy*; *Myron Grombacher* on *Down in the Groove*.

Omar Hakim in February 1996; *Tony Hall* on *Oh Mercy*; *Hilda Harris* on *Self Portrait*; *Jo Ann Harris*, a backing singer throughout the 1978 World Tour and on *Street Legal*. *John Hart*, described by Dylan as 'the spitting image of Blind GARY DAVIS', is the sax player with *Rockin' Dopsie & His Cajun Band* who adds the lovely sax part to 'Where Teardrops Fall' on *Oh Mercy*. The rest of the band were brought in by Daniel Lanois to play on 'Dignity' after Dylan felt (rightly) that it was OK the way it was. The re-make didn't work well, and 'Dopsie got almost as frustrated as me,' Dylan says in *Chronicles Volume One*; but afterwards, 'playing any old stuff . . . like we were on a party boat', they all recorded 'Where Teardrops Fall'—which is when John Hart's 'sobbing solo' arrived. Later, Dylan overdubbed new vocals, Lanois got Malcolm Burn to overdub bass and later still overdubbed a guitar himself. The credits on the album don't mention Burn but do credit the members of the Dopsie band.

Warren Haynes, lead guitarist of Gov't Mule and the Allman Brothers Band, but also a longtime member of PHIL LESH & Friends, played on stage with Dylan on the fall 1999 leg of the Never-Ending Tour, which was shared with Lesh's group. During Dylan's set on November 18 in Amherst, Massachusetts, Haynes played guitar on 'All Along the Watchtower', 'Highway 61 Revisited', 'Not Fade Away' and 'Alabama Getaway'. *Jorma Kaukonen*, also a Lesh guitarist but with a longer pedigree, being 20 years older and having co-founded Jefferson Airplane and Hot Tuna, played on the same Dylan songs the same night (except for the first of the four). *Don Heffington* in December 1984 and February 1985; *Sharon Hendrix*, aka *Muffy* (don't ask), on *Infidels*.

John Hiatt, a singer but primarily a songwriter, came from Indiana, moved to Nashville, worked in music publishing, got two brief record deals in the 1970s and another in the 80s, became an alcoholic, formed Little Village with Ry Cooder, JIM KELTNER and Nick Lowe and had a big hit in 1987 when Bonnie Raitt covered 'Thing Called Love'. By then Dylan had covered 'Across the Borderline' (which Hiatt co-wrote with Cooder and Jim Dickinson) in 1986 concerts with TOM PETTY & THE HEARTBREAKERS (and would revisit at the Guitar Legends Festival in Seville in 1991) and had been so desperate for a song while filming *Hearts of Fire* that in August 1986 he recorded Hiatt's tedious, posturing 'The Usual' for its soundtrack, also releasing it as a single, in 1987 (and in a vile picture sleeve): the first time Dylan had offered someone else's composition as an A-side. Hiatt has continued to plough his grunge-country furrow.

Rosie Hicks on the 'George Jackson' single, 1971; *Frederick Hill* on *Self Portrait*; *Beau Hills* in August 1986; *Hilton*, February 1996; *Karl T. Himmel* on *Self Portrait*. *Jim Horn*, top LA-born sax player, first with Duane Eddy, King Curtis and PHIL SPECTOR (his sax is on the Righteous Brothers' 'You've Lost That Lovin' Feeling'), worked with LEON RUSSELL and Joe Cocker in the 1970s, played at the Concert for Bangla Desh and since then with everyone from the Beach Boys to WARREN ZEVON; he has also made solo albums. He played on *Traveling Wilburys Volume 1* and *Volume 3*, and was in the massed army of musicians behind Dylan on the 'Late Night with David Letterman' 10th Anniversary Show, recorded January 18 and televised February 6, 1992.

Bruce Hornsby, the interesting Virginia-born singer-songwriter, pianist and accordionist, who in 1984 formed Bruce Hornsby & the Range (one of whom was DAVID MANSFIELD), who from 1988 onwards made over a hundred concert appearances with the Grateful Dead and in 1989 co-wrote and played piano on Don Henley's hit 'The End of the Innocence' (sung in concert by Dylan in the 2000s), then played piano on two tracks on Dylan's 1990 album *Under the Red Sky*, 'Born in Time' and 'TV Talkin' Song', and on May 8, 2003 played piano on the encore number 'Rainy Day Women # 12 & 35' at Dylan's Portsmouth, Virginia, concert.

Neil Hubbard in July 1975; *Carol Hunter* on *Pat Garrett & Billy the Kid*. *Chrissie Hynde*, from Akron, Ohio, was at Kent State University in 1970 when the US National Guard shot four students dead and injured many more (for general information see **radical political activity in 1960s–70s US, the strange disappearance of**), moved to London, reviewed for the *NME*, and formed the Pretenders in the late 1970s. On Dylan's 1984 European tour, Hynde played harmonica and sang back-up behind Dylan (and alongside Eric Clapton) on 'Leopard-Skin Pill-Box Hat', 'It's All Over Now Baby Blue', 'The Times They Are a-Changin'', 'Blowin' in the Wind' and 'Knockin' on Heaven's Door' at the London Wembley Stadium concert of July 7. She reappeared singing behind Dylan in New York on the 'Late Night with David Letterman' 10th Anniversary Show in early 1992 and was back in London to sing backing vocals alongside CAROLE KING at Dylan's Brixton concert of March 31, 1995.

Greg Inhofer in Minneapolis for the December 1974 *Blood on the Tracks* sessions; *Randy Jackson*; *Randy Jacobs* in March 1994; *James Jamerson Jr.*; *Paul James*; *the JB Horns* on the 'Late Night with David Letterman' 10th Anniversary 'Like a Rolling Stone'; *Flaco Jiminez*; *Alphonso Johnson* on June 24, 1984; *Bashiri Johnson* on *Infidels*; *Darryl Johnson* on *New Morning*; *Don Johnson* on the 'Blue Jeans Bash'; *Philip Jones*, congas in May 1986; *Steve Jones* on *Down in the Groove*; *Steve Jordan* in May 1987 and at 'Guitar Legends' in Seville 1991.

Miles Joseph replaced Gary Richrath as REO Speedwagon's lead guitarist, and then Dave Amato replaced Miles Joseph, both in 1989. In 2004 he was a guitarist on the album *Scrape*, by AARON

NEVILLE's son Ivan. Miles Joseph played guitar with Dylan's band on August 31, 1990 in Lincoln, Nebraska, on September 1 in Lampe, Missouri, on September 2 in Hannibal, Missouri, and in Tulsa, Oklahoma, on September 4.

Mindy Jostyn rehearsed with Dylan and his touring band, playing violin generally and singing vocals on the non-Dylan songs 'Both Sides Now', 'Too Far Gone' and 'California Blues' at a New York studio in mid-May 1989, but never did tour with him.

Dennis Karmazin played cello on *Shot of Love*; *Martin Katahn* on *Self Portrait*; *Ben Keith* at the S.N.A.C.K. Benefit on March 23, 1975; *Dan Keith* on the 'George Jackson' single; *Jerry Kennedy* on a *Blonde on Blonde* session in February 1966; *Jewel Kilcher* in April 1996. *Bobby King* contributed background vocals to three tracks on *Down in the Groove*: 'Sally Sue Brown', 'Death Is Not the End' and 'Ninety Miles an Hour (Down a Dead-End Street').

Millie Kirkham on *Self Portrait*; *Larry Klein* on *Down in the Groove*; *Danny Kortchmar* in March 1981 and again in 1987; *Alison Krauss*, September 1995; *Lenny Kravitz* on October 19, 1990; *Greg Kuenn* in the 'Sweetheart Like You' promo video; *Sheldon Kurland* on *Self Portrait*.

Dickie Landry, on sax on April 26, 2003; *Michael Lawrence* in July 1975; *Bernie Leadon* in March 1994; *Chuck Leavell* at 'Guitar Legends' 1991; *Perry Lederman* in July 1975; *John Leventhal* in April 1993; *David Lindley* on *Under the Red Sky*; *Curtis Linberg* on the 1992 Chicago sessions; *Claudia Linnear* on the March 1971 'Watching the River Flow' and 'When I Paint My Masterpiece' session; *Jody Linscott*, July 1975; *Chuck Loeb*, August 20, 2003; *Mike Love* at the Rock'n'Roll Hall of Fame gala in January 1988; *Glenn Lowe* in Chicago, 1992; *Stan Lynch* at the 30th Anniversary Concert Celebration in New York in October 1992.

Hugh McCracken in July 1975; *Martha McCrory* and *Barry McDonald* on *Self Portrait*; *Kathie McDonald* in 1971; *Paddy McHugh*, July 1975; *David McMurray* on *Under the Red Sky*; *Joseph Macho Jr.* played bass on the 'Like a Rolling Stone' sessions, 1965; *Steve Madaio* on *Street Legal* and *Infidels*; *Gary Mallabar*; *Tony Mangurian* on *Time Out of Mind*; *Ed Manion* at 'Guitar Legends' 1991. *Aimee Mann*, a singer-songwriter who emerged out of the group Til Tuesday in the 1980s, and who on May 17, 1996 played acoustic guitar on stage with Dylan on 'Rainy Day Women # 12 & 35', his encore in Cleveland, Ohio, that night.

Phil Manzanera at 'Guitar Legends'; *Rick Marotta* in June 1970; *Queen Esther Marrow* on *Empire Burlesque* and *Knocked Out Loaded* and in the QUEENS OF RHYTHM backing group. *Vince Melamed*, rock, country and R&B musician and songwriter who played organ and synthesiser on one or two tracks on *Empire Burlesque* and *Knocked Out Loaded*, including on 'Something's Burning Baby' and 'Brownsville Girl'. Melamed also played on the *Eagles Live* album and on tours and sessions for Bobby Womack, Jimmy Buffett and many others, and has written, among much else, Trisha Yearwood's big hit 'Walkaway Joe' and the alt country smash 'Tell Me What You Dream' by Restless Heart.

Clay Meyers, son of AUGIE MEYERS, bongos on *"Love and Theft"*; *Brian Mitchell*, accordion December 17, 2000; *Donald Mitchell* on *Under the Red Sky*; *Oliver Mitchell* on *Self Portrait*; *Ted Michel/Mitchell* on *Pat Garrett & Billy the Kid*; *Carol Montgomery* and *Bob Moore* on *Self Portrait*; *Gary Moore*; *Ian Moore* in November 1995; *Leroy Moore* in July 1996; *Tommy 'Mad Dog' Morrongiello*, mostly Dylan's guitar technician but played guitar at some 2004 concerts; *Benjamin Muhoberac* on *Under the Red Sky*; *James Mullen*, July 1975; *Gene A. Mullins* on *Self Portrait*; *Charlie Musselwhite* in March 1994; *Larry Myers* in May 1986.

Cyril Neville on *Oh Mercy*; *the New West Horns* in August 1986; *Henry Newmark* in November 1989; *Stevie Nicks* several times, including February 6 and 12, 1986, the end of 1993 and November 1995.

Tony O'Malley in July 1975; *Kevin Odegard* at the December 1974 Minneapolis *Blood on the Tracks* sessions; *Carla Olsen* on the 'Sweetheart Like You' video.

Joan Osborne, a singer who was one of the Dead associates, was the opening act for Dylan for part of 1997, and sang 'Man in the Long Black Coat' in her set. In New York that December 8, in a small venue, she was at the bar while Dylan was performing, and suddenly she heard him say: 'And I'd also like to thank Joan Osborne. Joan and I are gonna sing a song'—so she leapt to her feet to come to forward, when Dylan added: 'but not tonight.' But the following Hallowe'en, backed by Dylan's touring band but in a studio, they did sing together: on 'Chimes of Freedom', 'A Hard Rain's a-Gonna Fall' and 'Forever Young'. The first of these was released on the compilation album *'The 60s'—the TV Soundtrack* in early 1999. They also came together during some Dylan-Dead double-bill concerts in 2003: she shared vocals on 'Friend of the Devil' (July 30, Tampa, FL), 'Tears of Rage' (August 5, Noblesville, IN, and August 6 in Columbus, OH), and sang backing vocals behind Dylan and Phil Lesh on 'Oh Boy' (August 5 again), and on 'Tangled Up in Blue' and 'It Takes a Lot to Laugh, It Takes a Train to Cry' in New York State on August 8.

Peter Ostrouchko at the December 1974 Minneapolis *Blood on the Tracks* sessions.

June Page on *Self Portrait*; *Pino Palladino* and *Phil Palmer* in May 1994; *John Paris*, July 1984; *Brenda Patterson* and *Terry Paul* on *Pat Garrett & Billy the Kid*; *Rex Peer* on *Self Portrait*; *Shawn Pelton* on drums on December 17, 2000; *Albert Perkins* in May 1986. *Ted Perlman*, husband of Peggi Blu and guitarist friend of Dylan's: on February 24 and March 4 1985 and May 1986 sessions; *Bill Peterson* at the Minneapolis *Blood on the Tracks* sessions; *Simon Phillips* at 'Guitar Legends'; *Carl Pickhardt* in March

1981; *Raymond Lee Pounds* on *Infidels*, October 31, 1985 and April 1987; *Billy Preston* on *Blood on the Tracks*.

Don Preston, the guitarist from Leon Russell's band who played on the Dylan session of March 16–19, 1971 in New York, which Russell produced and from which came 'When I Paint My Masterpiece' (on *Bob Dylan's Greatest Hits Vol. II*) and the 'Watching the River Flow' single. He is *not* the same person as Mother of Invention Don Preston, FRANK ZAPPA's brilliant keyboards player (who once received one of guitarist Preston's royalty checks by mistake and cashed it; meeting Leon Russell years later, he apologised).

Bill Pursell on *Self Portrait*.

Carl Radle on the March 1971 'Watching the River Flow' and 'When I Paint My Masterpiece' session; *Mickey Raphael* in April 1993; *Duke Robillard* on *Time Out of Mind*; *Nile Rodgers* in February 1996; *Alvin Rogers* on *Self Portrait*.

Arthur Rosato, long-term Dylan technician and general factotum who in 1981 became his second drummer on the first 18 October–November North American dates, from October 16 to November 8 and on the last night of the tour, November 21. Rosato was replaced by *Bruce Gary* for the November 10–20 dates; Jim Keltner was main drummer. (NB: some sources don't mention Bruce Gary and say Rosato played all dates.)

Mason Ruffner on *Oh Mercy* and on October 13, 2003.

Katey Sagal, real name Catherine Louise Sagal (born LA, January 19, 1956) rehearsed as a backing singer for Dylan's 1978 tour, and thus can be heard along with Debi Dye on the circulating rehearsal recording from Santa Monica, December 30, 1977; but Dylan allegedly fired her after one day (she reportedly claims to have rehearsed with him for six weeks) because she behaved too much like a fan. She went on to fame of her own as Margaret 'Peggy' Bundy, wife of Ed, in the successful American sitcom 'Married with Children' and more recently in 'Eight Simple Rules'. Her father Boris Sagal had directed ELVIS PRESLEY's dreadful 1965 film *Girl Happy*.

Vito San Filipo on *Infidels* and October 31, 1985; *Kevin Savigar* on *Down in the Groove*; *Richard Scher* on *Infidels* and February 1985. The attractively named *Carl Sealove* (born in August 1952 in Hempstead, New York, and who was therefore a 13-year-old when Dylan and THE HAWKS played an early electric concert there on February 26, 1966), played bass in December 1984 on some rehearsals and sessions for *Empire Burlesque* and on 'New Danville Girl', and therefore on 'Brownsville Girl'.

Sheena Seidenberg and *John Sessewell* in July 1975; *Brian Setzer* in February 1999; *Doc Severinson* on the 'Late Night with David Letterman' 10th Anniversary 'Like a Rolling Stone' in 1992; *Paul Shaffer* ditto, plus December 1993 and October 20, 1994; *Jack Sherman* on *Infidels*, June 1985, April 1987, November 1989 and on the GERRY GOFFIN session of 1995–96; *Michelle Shocked* on the Letterman 1992 'Like a Rolling Stone'; *Ralph Shuckett* on the Goffin session; *Denny Siewell* in December 1977; *Paul Simonon* on *Down in the Groove*; *Vikki & Donna Simpson* on May 13, 2003; *Frank C. Smith* on *Self Portrait*; *Jo-El Sonnier* on April 19, 1991; *Alan Spenner* in July 1975; *Norman Spicher* on *New Morning*; *Henry Spinetti* in August 1986; *Richard Stevenson* in February 1985.

Stephen Stills, who was on stage with Dylan at the 'Absolutely Unofficial Blue Jeans Bash for Arkansas' in Washington, D.C., on January 17, 1993, playing guitar behind Dylan on 'To Be Alone with You' and alongside Dylan behind the Cate Brothers on 'I Shall Be Released' and '(I Don't Want to) Hang Up My Rock'n'Roll Shoes', and behind whom, in turn, Dylan played guitar while Stills sang lead vocal on 'Key to the Highway'.

Brian Stoltz on *New Morning*. *Marty Stuart*, country music guitarist who played with WILLIE NELSON on the TV show 'Willie Nelson: The Big Six-O' recorded in Austin, Texas, on April 28, 1993, backing Dylan and Nelson as they shared vocals on 'Pancho & Lefty'; Stuart re-appeared on stage with Dylan for his concert at Antioch, Tennessee, on September 8, 1999, playing guitar and mandolin throughout (though only one at a time) and adding backing vocals to 'Like a Rolling Stone'. On the second number of the set, 'Mr. Tambourine Man', Stuart's presence seemed to enliven Dylan, who played a comparatively melodic harmonica solo right in the guitarist's face.

Jody Taylor in November 1989. *Susan Tedeschi*, contemporary youngish blues singer-songwriter, came on stage at Dylan's November 20, 1999 concert in Newark, Delaware, and played guitar in the melée on 'It Takes a Lot to Laugh, It Takes a Train to Cry' and 'Rainy Day Women # 12 & 35', and in between these two played guitar and shared vocals on 'Not Fade Away', after being the opening act for that concert: a slot she was offered after Dylan saw her jam with Phil Lesh, who'd been touring with Dylan that summer.

Anthony Terron on *Self Portrait*; *Annette May Thomas* on *Infidels*; *Boyd Tinsley* in July 1996; *the Tokyo Philharmonic Orchestra*, conducted by Michael Kamen (1948–2003), accompanied Dylan's performances at the so-called Great Music Experience, Nara, Japan, in May 1994; *Derek Trucks*, November 11, 1992; *Robby Turner*, March 1994; *Ricky Turpin* on fiddle on March 17, 2000; *Mike Utley* on *Pat Garrett & Billy the Kid*.

Steve Vai, star heavy metal guitarist recruited into Frank Zappa's band first as a music transcriber in 1980, and who in 1992 was one of the musicians in the general thrash behind Dylan at the 'Late Night with David Letterman' 10th Anniversary Show performance of 'Like a Rolling Stone' (invited on by house band leader and general irritant Paul Schaffer). Vai recalled that at the rehearsal Dylan 'was standing right in front of my amp . . . his head was directly in line with my amp. When we finished. . . . He made a comment about the way I was playing, that it was too soft, it was like an acoustic guitar, you know. So during the show I turned up really loud and put distortion on and really played hard and a lot. It was really like drilling him right in the head. And after the performance, on national television, he walked up to me and shook my hand. So I was very thrilled about that.'

Bobby Valentino on October 14, 1987; *Gary Van Osdale* on *Self Portrait*.

Waddy Wachtel on *Under the Red Sky*. *Joe Walsh*, guitarist and singer from the James Gang, who made successful solo albums, then replaced Bernie Leadon in the Eagles (he's on *Hotel Califonia*) and then went solo again, joined Dylan on stage at the second of two consecutive nights' concerts in Atlanta, Georgia, on July 25, 1988 (just seven weeks into the Never-Ending Tour) to augment Dylan's band with his guitar on the final two numbers, 'Forever Young' and 'Maggie's Farm'.

Mike Wanchic in November 1989; *David Watson* on *Infidels*; *Kenny Wayne* on November 23, 1996; *Chris Weber* on the December 1974 *Blood on the Tracks* sessions; *David Weiss* on *Under the Red Sky*; *Donna Weiss* on *Pat Garrett & Billy the Kid*; *Kevin Welch* in early 1993; *Steve Wickham* on violin at Slane, Ireland, on July 8, 1984.

Jack White of the White Stripes, a popular duo of the early 2000s, came on stage for the second encore of Dylan's Detroit concert of March 17, 2004 and helped out on guitar and vocals on Dylan's performance of the Stripes' own song 'Ball and Biscuit'. Dylan mumbled through the first verse, Jack took the second and they shared the choruses. 'There's no topping that,' said White afterwards, 'I can go on for an hour-and-a-half talking about it, or I can just say: It was splendid.' Stripes fans were touched that Dylan, the old, should embrace the new.

James Whiting aka *Sugar Blue*, harmonica at a July 1975 *Desire* session; *Willie Murphy & the Bees* in Minneapolis in August or September 1975; *Bob Wilson* on *Self Portrait*; *Carl Wilson* and *Mary Wilson* at the Rock'n'Roll Hall of Fame Gala in January 1988; *Robert Wilson* on February 13, 1969; *Kip Winger* in August 1986; *Edgar Winter* on the 'Letterman' 1992 'Like a Rolling Stone'; *Stu Woods* on *Self Portrait* and *New Morning*; *Elisecia Wright* at Farm Aid and on Hallowe'en 1985; *Jeff Wysor* on the 1992 Chicago sessions.

Andy York on August 20, 2003. *Mona Lisa Young* sang in Dylan's backing group on both his 1980 gospel tours and on the *Saved* album. She has been a back-up singer for many people, including Joe Cocker, Tom Scott (she's on his 1995 album *Night Creatures*) and AARON NEVILLE. She recorded one long-deleted solo album, *Knife*, released at the beginning of 1983; it was mostly cover versions performed in a funk'n'synth style; the session players included TERRY YOUNG on backing vocals, from whom she is divorced. *Reggie Young* in April 1993 and March 1994.

[Dylan's Dopsie & John Hart quotes, *Chronicles Volume One*, 2004, p.190. Steve Vai quote from undated mini-interview by Masato Kato, *The Bridge* no.17, winter 2003, p.75.]

musicians' enthusiasm for latest Dylan album, perennial No-one should ever believe what session musicians say about the imminent new Dylan album they've been working on. They always come out saying it's Bob's best since *Blonde on Blonde* and then it turns out to be *Down in the Groove*. It's natural that they should be so deluded. First, they're working in the presence of a genius, so they're bound to be dazzled, even if his genius isn't present; second, they've been hearing the playbacks on monumentally expensive speakers and very high-quality drugs; and thirdly, they have in mind the best tracks and the best mixes, which Dylan then deletes before the rest of us are offered the album. Normally. But next time . . . well, you just can't help but get your hopes up.

'Naomi Wise' [song] This old ballad, also known as 'Omie Wise', was briefly an item in Bob Dylan's early folksong repertoire, having been recorded in the 1920s by CLARENCE ASHLEY. He performed it on July 29, 1961 for the New York Riverside Church 'Saturday of Folk Music' (see also **Rotolo, Suze** and **Kalb, Danny**) and on the tape made in Minneapolis that December 22, from which it became one of the earliest tracks by Dylan in bootleg circulation, in appalling sound quality. He seems to have dropped it by 1962.

Anyone interested in the historicity of violent murder songs should enjoy reading about the lyrical development of 'Naomi Wise' in Eleanor R. Long-Wilgus' book *Naomi Wise: Creation, Re-creation, and Continuity in an American Ballad Tradition*, published by University of North Carolina, Chapel Hill, in 2003.

N

Nashville c.1960, the influence of Counterbalancing developments in R&B at the start of the 1960s, the commercial country pop coming out of Nashville at the same time had become a strong part of the mainstream popular music of the day, and therefore a major influence on Dylan's pop education.

Nashville lay behind most of the period's rock revival records; RAY CHARLES mixed it with soul, and so did other black artists. 'Blue Moon' and 'You Always Hurt the One You Love' are sort of country songs. 'Blue Moon' was a 1961 US and UK no.1 by black vocal group the Marcels, though in the late 1950s the song was associated in the rock'n' roll world with ELVIS PRESLEY, whose recording was an eerie, surreal hillbilly interpretation. Dylan included a version on *Self Portrait*, 1970. 'You Always Hurt the One You Love' was a big hit for Clarence Frogman Henry in 1961, the follow-up to his huge hit 'But I Do'.

The EVERLY BROTHERS were Nashville. ROY ORBISON had emerged, like ELVIS PRESLEY and JOHNNY CASH before him, after a less successful start on the Memphis label, Sun, and long after the move to Monument Records and 'Only the Lonely' he was still singing Nashville pop-country songs on albums, including the much-recorded 'All I Have to Do Is Dream' (an Everly Brothers US no.1 in 1958, which, it was discovered in 1994, had been recorded by Dylan with GEORGE HARRISON in 1970).

Dylan owes a lot to this Nashville. Dylan hears DON GIBSON bring something close to perfection, in its own small way, with 'Sea of Heartbreak'; Dylan hears JERRY LEE LEWIS break into extraordinary lyrical piano-work on beautifully poised performances of songs like 'Cold Cold Heart', 'Your Cheating Heart', 'Together Again' and 'How's My Ex Treating You?'; Dylan hears and befriends Johnny Cash; Dylan hears FLATT & SCRUGGS, Patsy Cline, JACK SCOTT (not Nashville-based but sounding it), Marty Robbins and a hundred others, with and without international 'names'—all exploring different paths but from the same prolific headquarters. And then when all this music has become deeply passé and reviled by the hip, in the late 1960s, Dylan decides to commit himself to a country music album and the result, *Nashville Skyline*, is stunning because he sees through to the basics in whatever he tackles. He turns out an album unrivalled in country music, an album so precisely right, so faithfully lifelike and yet so alive, that it almost makes the rest of Nashville redundant. And then he records and releases *Self Portrait:* an album far more directly Nashville 1960 in style, which, ironically, proves far less of an artistic success.

See also **country music, Dylan's early interest in**.

[For relevant Ray Charles, Don Gibson and Jerry Lee Lewis records, see their entries. Elvis Presley: 'Blue Moon', Memphis, 19 Aug 1954, RCA Victor 20/47-6640, 1956. Clarence Frogman Henry: 'You Always Hurt the One You Love', New Orleans, c.Mar 1961, Argo 5388 (Pye International 7N 25089), 1961. Roy Orbison: 'All I Have to Do Is Dream', Monument MSP-003 2, 1963. The Everly Brothers: 'All I Have to Do Is Dream', Nashville, 6 Mar 1958, Cadence 1348, NY (London American HLA 8618, London), 1958. Bob Dylan & George Harrison: 'All I Have to Do Is Dream', NY, 1–2 May 1970.]

***Nashville Skyline* [1969]** The ninth album, and though not Dylan's first from Nashville—much of *Blonde on Blonde* had, amazingly, been recorded there—this was his first sustained leap into country music. Again a massive contrast to the previous album, *John Wesley Harding*: down-home instead of visionary, warm instead of severely ascetic, optimistic instead of dark, and more under the influence of sunshine and the big sky than of catechism and nemesis. It also offered a complete change of language: away from the impressionistic and the allegorical—away from the distinctive complexity of his previous work, using a language of extreme simplicity.

It was quite a shock, on a first playing of *Nashville Skyline*, back in 1969, to hear Dylan singing lines like 'For your love comes on so strong'; and then in the middle section of the same song ('Tonight I'll Be Staying Here With You') coming on even stronger with this 'new' language: 'Is it really any wonder / The love that a stranger might receive? / You cast your spell and I went under / I find it so difficult to leave.' This compares closely with the middle section of the later song 'Hazel', from *Planet Waves*: 'Oh no I don't need any reminder / To show how much I really care / But it's just making me blinder and blinder . . .' The joke-rhyming of 'wonder' and 'under', and even more so of 'reminder' and 'blinder and blinder', combined with the playful vacuousness of the melodies of both those sections, suggest the milieu of the Broadway musical more than anything. They'd go comfortably inside 'ON THE STREET WHERE YOU LIVE' from *My Fair Lady*. Not exactly Dylan terrain.

So what was he playing at? A useful comment was soon offered by a review of *Self Portrait* by Geoffrey Cannon, in the *Guardian* (June 26, 1970): '. . . the coup of *Nashville Skyline* [was] to demonstrate that proverbs are aphorisms when used (as they always are, except in books) by a particular person to a particular person, in a place and a time. It's human context, not verbal dexterity, that lets words, especially words of love, work.'

That account is a little dangerous, of course but it does illuminate Dylan's work on *Nashville Skyline*. When Dylan sings 'For your love comes on so strong', he is effectively saying that that phrase will do as well as any to cover the part of his feelings that can be put into words. And in saying that, he was rejecting a self-image of Dylan the brilliant poet in favour of a concept of himself as an ordinary man coping with love. That is how such phrases work. This is not Dylan patronizing the ordinary mind; it is a confession, candid and accepting, that he is, in ways that it matters to be honest about, an ordinary man himself.

There is something else to be said in relation to the kind of language Dylan deals in here and on *Self Portrait*—and it's a point that relates also to Dylan's consistent independence of rock modishness. *John Wesley Harding* was a dramatic gesture of distancing; so too was *Nashville Skyline* (and *Self Portrait* even more so). They are very much out on their own, and one main way this was emphasized was in Dylan's rejection of the *language* of a modish rock-culture here.

Before *John Wesley Harding*, Dylan's language had been scattered with the old familiar phrases: hung up, where it's at and so on, along with much hip drugs terminology. From *John Wesley Harding* through to *Self Portrait*, this disappears.

Patrick Thomas, commenting on this shift as evidenced on *Nashville Skyline*, wrote: '. . . the "new" Bob Dylan lyrics, which wring out responses from words like "suitcase" and "rumors", are simply recognition of the fact that not all Americans feel the dead-weight of thrice-throttled, TV-choked English.' And he contrasts this 'new' Dylan language to the 'constant overstatement of urban vernacular'. And indeed on *Nashville Skyline* Dylan is using his 'ordinary language' with a dignity of expression which involves much of that weapon of the great artist, understatement.

As Dylan suddenly embraced the simplicity and clichés that are the currency of ordinary Americans' speech, he used a new singing voice to go with it. Gone were the various husky, grating Dylans and on came a light, melodic, almost Orbisonian tenor.

This was all an off-loading of the Dylan Myth—which he was to do again from a different direction with *Slow Train Coming* and *Saved* a decade later. In *Chronicles Volume One*, 2004, he argues that the album was indeed an attempt to get people off his back—but methinks he doth protest too much, and this dubious claim takes no account of the obvious respect he has for the genre and the musicians (including JOHNNY CASH), some of whom, encountering this version of history, might rightly feel insulted.

In the end, *Nashville Skyline* is a lovely album but not a heavyweight contender, though its effects were major ones. Country music was despised, hick music when Dylan took it up. People were divided into the hip and the non-hip. The counterculture was in full swing and riddled with its own self-importance and snobbery. *Nashville Skyline* was a hard pill to swallow: but it did 'em good.

See also **Flatt & Scruggs**.

[Recorded Nashville, TN, 13–14 & 17–18 Feb 1969; released as stereo LP, Columbia KCS 9825 (in UK CBS SPBG 63601), 9 Apr 1969. Patrick Thomas: 'DOUG KERSHAW', *Rolling Stone* no. 39, San Francisco, 9 Aug 1969. Dylan, *Chronicles Volume One*, p.113ff.]

Nelson, Paul [1936 - 2006] Paul Clifford Nelson was born on January 21, 1936 in Warren, Minnesota ('60 miles from Canada'), though he didn't like giving out his birthdate. 'I was born just after the Civil War,' he preferred to say. Though his early interests as a critic and consumer were films and detective fiction, in 1959 he discovered the HARRY SMITH anthology of *AMERICAN FOLK MUSIC* (a 6-LP set of pre-war recordings issued in 1952), introduced it excitedly to his friend and fellow University of Minnesota student JON PANKAKE, became with him in 1961 the co-founder of the small but influential critical journal *Little Sandy Review*, and was one of those who knew Bob Dylan in his Twin Cities Dinkytown days (1959–60), seeing him perform—and watching him develop as a performer—and meeting up with him again on subsequent Dylan revisits to the North Country (1961–63).

Early on in this acquaintanceship he was a witness to Dylan's being chased down for the return of a shrewdly judged bunch of LPs he had removed from Pankake's apartment—a tale he told when he appeared, looking every inch the weather-beaten but still amused old hippie, quirky cap on head, eyes crinkling with ironic would-be-detached humour, on the filmed interview included in MARTIN SCORSESE's *No Direction Home* (though see the entry **Pankake, Jon** for a denial of the latter's participation in this escapade).

Paul Nelson's pre-traditional folk music listening was to HANK WILLIAMS and to jazz of the Gerry Mulligan kind, and he maintained a lifelong habit of collecting Chet Baker releases. But by the early 1960s, Nelson had become one of the pioneers of rock writing (and may even have a claim to being one of the creators of 'the New Journalism' too). He reached New York City 'around 1963', long before *Little Sandy Review*'s 30 issues were completed—it had started with three subscribers and peaked at 1,000—and started writing for *Sing Out!*. He became a loud opponent of the NEWPORT FOLK FESTIVAL policy of packing in, indiscriminately, as many traditional and revivalist performers as possible (as in his 1965 Festival Program article 'A Voice of Dissent: How I Started Worrying and Learned to Bomb Newport': a scathing piece about the shortcomings of the 1964 event and its 'babyish, namby-pamby, goody-goody, totally phony atmosphere'); he was also one of the earliest supporters in print of Dylan's 'going electric'. But he didn't stick around long at *Sing Out!* to defend Dylan or not: indeed he quit because he 'knew they were going to nail him to the wall for not writing protest songs' and he 'didn't want any part of it'; he 'resigned out of protest' [as it were], because he 'knew what they would do to Dylan.' Nelson 'kept on watching Dylan's shows, like at Forest Hills [the first post-Newport 'electric' concert, August 28, 1965]. One *Sing Out!* critic left after the acoustic section. . . . A lot of people left . . . it was quite scary.' Nelson 'made it a point to applaud Dylan.' He said: 'People would come up to me and say, "JOAN BAEZ would never sell out." And I would say, "What does she have to sell out?"'

After *Sing Out!*, Nelson worked 'twice' at both teeny-bopper-to-rock magazine *Circus* and at *Rolling Stone* as a New York reporter ('or something like that') when it was San Francisco based. In 1970 he came in from the cold of freelance rock writing and took a press-office job at Mercury Records in New York, in which capacity he first met other critics like Robert Christgau, Dave Marsh and Richard Meltzer. He got fired because he signed and pushed the New York Dolls but had continued to write for *Rolling Stone* in any case. In the late 1970s he took over from Marsh as its Record Reviews Editor and stayed with it till 1983. In that period he gave Dylan's *Shot of Love* album an embittered-sounding mauling, excepting 'Every Grain of Sand', about which he rhapsodised that in this song Dylan 'touches you, and the gates of heaven dissolve into a universality.'

Since returning to freelancing in the 1980s Nelson was, among other things, a copy editor at *Jewish Week* (partly to avoid writing). He failed to create 'the hard-boiled detective novel' of his ambition, and gave up reading rock criticism—and *Rolling Stone*. 'A lot of us who worked there used to pose the question . . . if we didn't work there, would we buy the magazine, and my answer turned out to be no.'

By 2000, he was writing a screenplay he felt had no prospect of interesting Hollywood, and until July 2005 worked at the Evergreen video store in Greenwich Village. 'I don't really want a job anymore where you have to think,' he said. Paul Nelson was found dead at his home on July 5, 2006.

[Quote from *Shot of Love* review, *Rolling Stone* no. 354, US, 15 Oct 1981; other quotes & background from 'What Ever Happened to Rock Critic Paul Nelson?' by Steven Ward, seen online 9 Oct 2005 at *www.rockcritics.com/interview/paulnelson.html*. Minnesota birth index 1935–2002, file no. 1936-MN-021393.]

Nelson, Ricky [1940 - 1985] Eric Hilliard Nelson was born in Teaneck, New Jersey, on May 8, 1940, the younger son of radio stars Ozzie & Harriet Nelson, on whose TV series 'The Adventures of Ozzie and Harriet' he featured as from its inception in 1952; by 1953 he had appeared in the musical film *The Story of Three Loves*, playing an 11-year-old musician, in amongst Kirk Douglas, Zsa Zsa Gabor, James Mason, Agnes Moorhead, Farley Granger, Ethel Barrymore, Leslie Caron and the lovely Pier Angeli. In 1954 his parents quit radio to concentrate on their TV success, and Ricky became the first young music star promoted via this medium.

He made the first of the quality pop records that made him a teenage idol when he was 16, signed to Verve, where he had a double-sided smash hit with 'A Teenager's Romance' and his white cover of FATS DOMINO's 'I'm Walkin' before signing to the same Hollywood label as Fats himself, where he began a run of hits with 'Be-Bop Baby' c/w 'Have I Told You Lately That I Love You'. In 1959, though, he made a very creditable appearance as the young gun in the major Hollywood western *Rio Bravo*, directed by Howard Hawks and co-starring John Wayne and Dean Martin. JOHNNY CASH wrote him a song for the film, 'The Restless Kid', but Dmitri Tiomkin would have none of it and it appeared on Ricky's third album, the insipidly titled *Ricky Sings Again*.

At their best, his records were superior to the milk-white pap they so closely resembled, thanks to Ricky's immaculate vocal delivery, JAMES BURTON's beautifully understated guitar and a glistening, warm production only achievable using the large, glowing valve amps of the day (soon to be vanquished by transistors in the name of convenience and cheapness: not, God knows, in the name of sound quality). His hits included 'Poor Little Fool' (his first US no.1, in 1958: he was 18 years old), 'Lonesome Town', 'It's Late' c/w 'There'll Never Be Anyone Else But You', 'Travelin' Man' c/w 'Hello Mary Lou' and 'It's Up to You'. Altogether he released 21 singles and 12 albums before switching labels to US Decca in 1963. Ten minutes later he was one of the many made to sound instantly passé by the emergence of the more harmonically adventurous, more energetic and more working-class BEATLES.

Ricky, however, was more interested in the arrival of Bob Dylan than of the Beatles, and he shifted his name to the more mature and purposive Rick, grew his hair, re-presented himself as a singer-songwriter, issued a 1966 album named *Bright Lights & Country Music* and formed a country-rock group, the Stone Canyon Band, with which he performed and recorded a fair number of mid-1960s Dylan songs, some released as A-sides: 'Walkin' Down the Line', 'She Belongs to Me', 'If You Gotta Go, Go Now', 'I Shall Be Released', 'Love Minus Zero/No Limit', 'Just Like a Woman' and (though this last went unreleased) 'Mama You Been on My Mind'.

When Rick appeared in his newer guise at a 'rock revival night' at New York's Madison Square Garden in 1971, he was booed by the crowd for not being Ricky. In response, he wrote the song 'Garden Party'—with which, ironically perhaps, he enjoyed his first top 10 hit single (and gold record) in many years, and within which he mentioned Dylan somewhat à la Don McLean's 'American Pie' (singing 'Mr. Hughes hid in Dylan's shoes wearing his disguise') but primarily asserted his right to look how he liked and, while happy to sing some of the old songs, to refuse to be frozen in rock'n'roll aspic, making his stance with this nice line in defiance: 'But if memories were all I sang I'd rather drive a truck.'

Clearly this was a sequence of events Bob Dylan could identify with, and in the fullness of time, he acknowledged it—but not in 1972, when 'Garden Party', a protest record of sorts, was a hit. Nelson continued to work live, on record and on TV and film, including a 'Streets of San Francisco' appearance in 1973, a 'Tales of the Unexpected' in 1977 and a hosting of 'Saturday Night Live' in February 1979.

On August 22, 1985, in Los Angeles, he and Fats Domino got back together—or rather, nearer to together than in the segregated 1950s when he had pinched 'I'm Walkin''—for the TV Special 'Ricky [sic] Nelson & Fats Domino: Live at the Universal Amphitheatre', accompanied by ELVIS PRESLEY's old backing-vocals group the Jordanaires. Rick must have decided not to drive that truck after all. However, on a flight with his band and new fiancée over De Kalb, Texas, four months later, their plane caught fire and crashed, killing them all, on New Year's Eve 1985.

Barely over a month later, on February 5, 1986, in Wellington, New Zealand, at the opening night of his first concert tour of the year (the first concerts on which he was backed by TOM PETTY & THE HEARTBREAKERS), Dylan débuted a performance of 'Lonesome Town', one of the most crafted and memorable of Nelson's teen-idol hits—and duly performed it on all but two of the concerts that followed in New Zealand, Australia and Japan, its 15th performance being on the tour's last night in Tokyo that March 10. When the tour's US leg began in June, 'Lonesome Town' was still on the set-list, and was played every night but one.

Usually Dylan introduced it simply by saying that Ricky Nelson had sung a lot of his songs and he was going to sing one of Ricky's; but on the first night the tour arrived at Madison Square Garden itself (July 15, 1986) this was slightly augmented: 'Actually,' he added, 'I heard this song when I was about oh, say I dunno, two years old. It really had an impression on me.' At the same venue two nights later, Dylan offered his audience a dopily garbled version of the story of Nelson's unhappy 1971 appearance there, confusing the song Nelson wrote afterwards about the event with the repertoire for which he was booed on the night: 'I wanna play a real special song here in this special place. This is the very stage where Ricky Nelson got booed off for singing "Garden Party": this is the one, the very one. Anyway, it gives me a real great pleasure to sing one of Ricky's songs in this place. This is . . . called "Lonesome Town".'

Altogether on that US tour leg, the song was given 40 performances in the course of the 41 concerts—a total of 55 during the year—and then dropped. Ricky Nelson's version could be heard again in 1994 on the soundtrack of the movie *Pulp Fiction*, and ten years after that came Dylan's surprising homage to the former teen idol in the pages of *Chronicles Volume One*. Here, very early on in the book, we find the young folksinger who is trying to sound as gritty and 'authentic' and as far away from the world of late-50s commercial pop singles as possible, sitting in the kitchen of the Café Wha?, when he hears on the radio Nelson's 'new song, "Travelin' Man" [issued April 1961, and destined to be another US no.1]. . . . He was different than the rest of the teen idols. . . . Nelson had never been a bold innovator like the early singers who sang like they were navigating burning ships. He didn't sing desperately, do a lot of damage, and you'd never mistake him for a shaman. It didn't feel like his endurance was ever being tested to the utmost, but it didn't matter. He sang his songs calm and steady. . . . His voice was sort of mysterious and made you fall into a certain mood. I had been a big fan of Ricky's and still liked him, but that type of music was on its way out.'

After elaborating further on all this, Dylan produces one of the most adroit and cleverly used metaphors in the book. It's one of those moments when his sharp and literate mind darts out and surprises you, not by its intelligence (that's no surprise) but by its deft pinning-down of something not at all easy to describe: the area of affinity that he himself feels for Ricky Nelson—a figure most of us would assume he didn't much resemble at all:

'I'd always felt kin to him, though. We were about the same age, probably liked the same things, from the same generation although our life experience had been so dissimilar, him being brought up out West on a family TV show. It was like he'd been born and raised on Walden Pond where everything was hunky-dory, and I'd come out of the dark, demonic woods, same forest, just a different way of looking at things.'

[Ricky Nelson: 'A Teenager's Romance' c/w 'I'm Walkin'', *nia*, Verve 10047, US 1957; 'Be-Bop Baby' c/w 'Have I Told You Lately That I Love You', *nia*, Imperial 5463, US, 1957; 'Poor Little Fool', *nia*, Imperial 5528, US, 1958; 'Lonesome Town', *nia*, Imperial 5545, US, 1958; *Rick Sings Again*, Imperial LP-9061 (mono), US, 1959; 'It's Late' c/w 'There'll Never Be Anyone Else But You', *nia*, Imperial 5565, 1959; 'Travelin' Man' c/w 'Hello Mary Lou', Imperial 5741, 1961; 'It's Up to You', Imperial 5901, 1962; *Bright Lights & Country Music*, Decca DL 74779 (stereo), US, 1966; 'Walkin' Down the Line', *nia*, on *Country Fever*, Decca DL 74827, 1967; 'She Belongs to Me', *nia*, Decca 32550, 1969; 'She Belongs to Me', 'If You Gotta Go, Go Now' & 'I Shall Be Released', LA, 1969, *Rick Nelson in Concert*, Decca DL75162, 1970 (re-issued as *Rick Nelson in Concert (The Troubadour, 1969)*, MCA MCA-25983, 1987); 'I Shall Be Released' c/w 'If You Gotta Go, Go Now', Decca 32676, 1970; 'Just Like a Woman' & 'Love Minus Zero/No Limit', *nia*, *Rudy the Fifth*, Decca DL 75297, 1971; 'Garden Party', *nia*, Decca 32980, 1972; 'Mama You Been on My Mind', spring 1978, unreleased. *The Story of Three Loves*, dir. Vincent Minelli, MGM, US, 1953. *Rio Bravo*, dir. Howard Hawks, Armada, US, 1959. 'Ricky Nelson & Fats Domino: Live at the Universal Amphitheatre', dir. Thomas V. Grasso; LaBuick & Associates Media Inc., LA, 1985.

Bob Dylan, *Chronicles Volume One*, 2004, pp. 13–14. Most discographical detail from *www.ricknelson.com/discogc.html*, seen online 16 Dec 2005.]

Nelson, Willie [1933 -] William Hugh Nelson was born on April 30, 1933, in Abbot, Texas, was raised by his maternal grandparents, joined John Raycjeck's Bohemian Polka Band at the age of ten, joined the US Air Force after high school but left because of back problems and after a series of odd jobs, including selling encyclopedias, became a Fort Worth DJ while trying to launch his singing career. His inauspicious recording début was made with a cover of a Leon Payne song while he made the mistake of selling the rights in his own first successful composition, 'Family Bible', for $50.

After a short-lived move to Vancouver, Washington, he tried his luck in Nashville, arriving in the spring of 1960 and becoming Ray Price's bass player after Price recorded Nelson's song 'Nite Life' (later titled 'Night Life'), to which Nelson, still driven by family penury, again sold the rights. But for the support of others, especially friend Hank Cochran, he would have sold other songs without ever seeing the royalties they earned. He soon wrote the Faron Young hit 'Hello Walls' and ROY ORBISON's indifferent early record 'Pretty Paper'. His own first country hits, 'Willingly' and 'Touch Me' were both duets with his second wife, Shirley Collie, in 1962 (at which point he was dressed in a suit and tie, with brilliantined hair). He joined the Grand Old Opry and became a regular performer in 1964, though to little avail.

He has had a fitful career ever since, festooned about with lurid personal and professional problems, dramatic shifts as when he quit Nashville in the mid-1960s and 'retired' to Austin, Texas, yet also with mega-successes—platinum albums and no.1 country best-sellers galore—and the extravagant acquisition of resorts, golf courses, aeroplanes and, in 1990, a $16.7 million IRS bill. In 2005, with NEIL YOUNG and two business partners, his latest venture was to launch the energy company Willie Nelson's BioDiesel (or BioWillie, for short), selling this new-fangled fuel to truckers who might otherwise be the last to try it.

What matters, however, is that Charles Dickens look-alike Nelson is surely the most important figure in country music since HANK WILLIAMS, and just as effectively the father of that music today. Like anyone else remotely interested in or connected to it, Bob Dylan cannot help but have been touched by Nelson's influence. Blessed with a beautifully timbred voice and a concomitant sense of timing, such that as a singer he communicates, with the illusion of great ease, an affecting cocktail of emotion and intelligence, managing to sound both open and judicious, he is also the incomparable songwriter of the genre, whose songs have set the standards for others, whose catalogue stretches back further than Bob Dylan's and whose classics began with the unarguable fully formed achievement of Patsy Cline's sublime 1961 hit 'Crazy' (reputedly the most played record in jukebox history) and, cutting to the quick with a superb economy of line in both words and music, that numinous small masterpiece 'Funny How Time Slips Away', which has enriched many a singer's records since it was first a hit for Billy Walker: not least as by ELVIS PRESLEY and (better still, despite its cheap pop production values) by ARTHUR ALEXANDER.

Presley also covered Nelson's 'Always on My Mind' and perhaps it was this song Dylan had in mind when he paid this tribute on the TV show 'Willie Nelson: The Big Six-0: An All-Star Birthday Celebration' in 1993: 'He takes whatever thing he's singing and makes it his own, you know, and there's not many people who can do that. Even with something like an Elvis tune. You know, once Elvis has done a tune, it's pretty much done. But Willie's the only one in my recollection that has even taken something associated with Elvis and made it his.'

As a composer, of course, it already was 'his', and Dylan's tribute to Nelson's songwriting was as fulsome as to his performing skills: 'He's like a philosopher-poet. You know, he gets to the heart of it and in a quick way, gets it out and it's over. And it just leaves the listener to think about it.'

Nelson's other compositions include 'Mammas Don't Let Your Babies Grow Up to Be Cowboys', 'Bloody Mary Morning' and 'Blue Eyes Cryin' in the Rain'. As a performer he has sold millions of albums over a 40-year period, including albums of duets with others (most notably *Waylon and Willie* in 1978 and with different guests per track on *Across the Borderline* in 1993) and in the mid-1980s as one of the Highwaymen with Waylon Jennings, KRIS KRISTOFFERSON and JOHNNY CASH. He has also written music for, and appeared in, a number of Hollywood films, from *The Electric Horseman* (1979) to *The Dukes of Hazzard* (2005) and including a lead rôle in JERRY SCHATZBERG's 1980 film *Honeysuckle Rose*. And all this has been achieved with the public image of exactly the sort of weed-imbibing, long-haired, bandana'd old hippie that Nashville's country-music fraternity used to hate and fear.

It was in the 1980s that Nelson and Dylan began to work together, starting when Dylan's impolitic words at Live Aid about American farmers prompted Willie Nelson to organise the first Farm Aid, which took place in Champaign, Illinois, in September 1985, two months after Dylan's comments from the stage in Philadelphia. Dylan's own Farm Aid performance, backed by TOM PETTY & THE HEARTBREAKERS, took place on September 22, and for the last three numbers of the six-song set, they were augmented by Nelson playing guitar (on 'Trust Yourself', 'That Lucky Old Sun' and 'Maggie's Farm'). The following January, Dylan broadcast a TV message of congratulations to Nelson on his winning of a humanitarian award for that Farm Aid work, in which Dylan said this: 'It's not a bad thing to have a good idea, but it's an even better thing to take a good idea and do something about it. That's just what you did, Willie. You took time out from a busy career, you put in a lot of energy and money, you asked a lot of friends to help out and they did. You made Farm Aid a reality. For this, the music business thanks you, I thank you, the American farmer thanks you.'

Seven years on from Farm Aid, on October 16, 1992, Nelson was one of the many who participated in the so-called 30th Anniversary Concert Celebration for Dylan at Madison Square Garden, where Nelson, one of the oldest people present, chose to perform the newest song, the near-great, and in context savagely apt, 'What Was It You Wanted?', from the album of just three years earlier, *Oh Mercy*.

Three days after this concert, Willie and Bob went into the studio together in New York City to record their joint composition 'Heartland', on which they both played guitar and sang, and which was duly released on Nelson's album of duets *Across the Borderline*, in early 1993. This song, a return to the theme of Farm Aid in that it depicts a forgotten Heartland USA in which youth, hope and the natural world are blighted by economic neglect and by the rapacious greed of the moneymen and politicians who run things from the East. As with Eddie Arnold's contribution to that great song 'You Don't Know Me' (co-written with Cindy Walker), it's alleged that Dylan wrote only the title of 'Heartland', and that Nelson wrote all the rest. Vocally, it's a surprise that Dylan sounds the less shaky and the more reliable of the two.

In any case, to date it remains the only instance of their collaboration in the studio and as songwriters, though they do appear on adjacent tracks on the specially made 1997 album on Dylan's own Egyptian Records label, *The Songs of Jimmie Rodgers—A Tribute*, on which Dylan's tentative vocal on the comparatively obscure 'My Blue-Eyed Jane' is followed by a rather more spicey and alert Nelson rendition of 'Peach-Picking Time Down in Georgia'. Dylan had also recorded—and even released on the B-side of four different non-US singles—an appropriately wistful version of Nelson's song 'Angel Flying Too Close to the Ground', though not in Nelson's presence, at the sessions for the *Infidels* album of 1983.

In performance, however, Dylan and Nelson have come together on many other occasions. The two sang and played guitars on 'Heartland' on the TV show 'A County Music Celebration' recorded in Nashville on January 13, 1993 and broadcast by CBS-TV that February 6, and in late April, along with the televised tribute to Nelson's talents cited above, Dylan also gave three song performances for that 60th birthday programme: two of the STEPHEN FOSTER song 'Hard Times' and then one of Townes Van Zandt's 'Pancho & Lefty', a song much associated with Nelson, and on which, on this occasion, he contributed guitar and shared vocals.

A decade later, the two grizzled old contenders finally embarked upon a tour together. The summer 2004 leg of Dylan's Never-Ending Tour (though Nelson may not have accepted that he was standing under any such umbrella) saw the two sharing the billing on a tour that began for Dylan at an 800-capacity venue in Poughkeepsie, New York, on August 4 and for Nelson two nights later at an 11,500-capacity field in Cooperstown, New York, and ended for both on September 4 in Kansas City.

On May 5, 2004 they performed Hank Williams' song 'You Win Again' together for the TV show 'Willie Nelson & Friends: Outlaws and Angels', broadcast on the USA Network that May 31. Dylan's was an unannounced guest appearance, and greeted with wild enthusiasm. They had also duetted on 'I Shall Be Released' at some of the 2004 concerts, but not until August 27 at Madison Wisconsin did they début a live shared performance of 'Heartland'.

The following year they toured together again, this time opening in Fort Myers on May 25, 2005 and running through to July 12 in St. Paul, Minnesota—and including an appearance by Dylan at

'Willie Nelson's 32nd Annual 4th of July Picnic' in Fort Worth, Texas, at which the two again shared the microphone for a performance of 'You Win Again' midway through Dylan's set.

Not counting that one-off, the two had given a total of 52 shared-bill concerts in large-capacity sports parks and stadiums: 22 in 2004 and 30 in 2005. By the time these concerts ended, the combined age of their co-headliners was 136.

Three decades earlier, there had been a less amicable scene involving the two men, though in Nelson's case only indirectly. RONNIE HAWKINS remembers a post-Rolling Thunder Revue party at RONEE BLAKLEY's when Nelson's notoriously violent bodyguard was becoming belligerent towards Dylan:

> 'I got in a little trouble, because somebody was there knockin' Bob. . . . He and LEVON [HELM] got a little high, and they were singing, and cutting up, and this and that, and Bob was kinda nodding out . . . [and] Elliott Gould and the bodyguard for Willie Nelson, they were there, and they were drunk, and they were mouthing off at Bob and Levon. And I was a little drunk myself. I was gonna whip their ass right there at the damn party. . . . They were knockin' things, sayin' "Look in there—Bob's drunk and he's doin' this and ain't it awful?" I said, "Yes it is awful: he can draw more people drunk than all of you boys could if you were straight as a damn string." I was a little bit high, y'know. And this cat was supposed to be so rough and tough—had whipped three or four hundred people in Texas, and broke people's backs and stuff—Willie Nelson's bodyguard, that is. Well, I was gettin' ready to hit him in the head with a poker! They had a fireplace and I grabbed the poker and I was ready to whip him and that Elliott Ghoul real easy. I could have done it real easy; but they apologised and left.'

Since those days, Nelson has also been, allegedly, the man who started Bob Dylan playing golf. Ain't it funny how time slips away.

[Willie Nelson: 'Funny How Time Slips Away', Nashville, 14 Jun 1962, *And Then I Wrote*, Liberty LST-7239, US, 1962; 'What Was It You Wanted?', NY, 16 Oct 1992, *Bob Dylan the 30th Anniversary Concert Celebration*, Columbia 474000 2, US, 1993; 'Peach Pickin' Time Down in Georgia', Hollywood, *nia*, *The Songs of Jimmie Rodgers—A Tribute*, Egyptian/Columbia 485189 2, US, 1997. Willie Nelson & Bob Dylan: 'Heartland', NY, 19 Oct 1992, on Nelson: *Across the Borderline*, Columbia 472942 2, US (CK 52752, UK) 1993. Patsy Cline: 'Crazy', *nia*, Decca 31317, US, 1961. Elvis Presley: 'Funny How Time Slips Away', Nashville, 7 Jun 1970, *Elvis Country*, RCA 4460, US, 1971. Arthur Alexander: 'Funny How Time Slips Away', Nashville, Mar 1962, *You Better Move On*, Dot LP3434, US (London-American HA-D 2457, UK) 1962.

Bob Dylan: 'Angel Flying Too Close to the Ground', NY, 2 May, 1983, c/w 'I And I', CBS A 3904, Netherlands & Italy, 1983; c/w 'Union Sundown', CBS A 3916, UK & Spain, 1983; c/w 'Sweetheart Like You', CBS/Sony 07SP 765, Japan & CBS BA 223121, Australia & New Zealand; and c/w 'Jokerman', CBS 43560, Brazil, 1983. Dylan quotes, 'Willie Nelson: The Big Six-0: An All-Star Birthday Celebration', KRLU-TV, Austin, TX, 27 or 28 Apr 1993, broadcast CBS-TV, US, May 22, 1993 (& incl. in video release of same name, Columbia House 11141, Jun 1993); LA, Jan 1986, broadcast ABC-TV, US, 27 Jan 1986. Ronnie Hawkins quote, interview by Michael Gray, St. John's, Newfoundland, Canada, 30 Sep 1985, 1st published as 'The Wanted Man Interview: Ronnie Hawkins', *The Telegraph* no.22, UK, winter 1985, pp.72–86, collected in Michael Gray & John Bauldie, *All Across the Telegraph: A Bob Dylan Handbook*, London: W.H. Allen, 1987.]

Neuwirth, Bobby [1939 -] Robert Neuwirth was born on June 20, 1939 in Akron, Ohio, attended art school in Boston and was a minor figure in the Cambridge folk scene; part of his time was spent in California, to which he hitchhiked in order to visit the bohemian bars of North Beach, San Francisco and the folk clubs of Berkeley. Dylan biographer CLINTON HEYLIN says that he and Dylan first met at the Indian Neck folk festival in May 1961 (Dylan performed there on the 6th), but Dylan's memoir *Chronicles Volume One* describes first encountering him at the Gaslight, earlier than that. He gives a vivid description of Neuwirth's spiky character, without managing to explain what he liked about a man who seems to so many the archetypal snivelling sidekick, stroking Dylan's ego all through *Don't Look Back* while kicking and belittling everyone else around—as when he says of JOAN BAEZ, right in front of her, 'Hey, she has one of those see-through blouses that you don't even wanna'—and generally game-playing, suffused with the vicarious power of being Bob's friend, a position he first assumed in February 1964, when he replaced Pete Karman after Dylan's Berkeley concert.

It was from this position that he got into a relationship with EDIE SEDGWICK, whom he and Dylan first met that December in New York City. By the time she quit ANDY WARHOL's Factory in February 1966, declaring that Bobby Dylan was going to give her a starring film rôle, she and Neuwirth (not Dylan) were having an affair. She said of it: 'It was really sad. . . . The only true, passionate, and lasting love scene, and I practically ended up in the psychopathic ward.' Neuwirth ended their relationship in early 1967, helping D.A. PENNEBAKER with the filming of that summer's Monterey Pop Festival and two years later attending the Woodstock festival before going to Nashville with the then-unknown KRIS KRISTOFFERSON, whose song 'Me and Bobby McGee' Neuwirth would soon afterwards teach to Janis Joplin, with whom he wrote her well-known song 'Mercedes Benz'.

Perhaps its mix of the clever and facile was characteristically Neuwirthian; but he was not only a songwriter and film scene person: he was also a painter. His now absurdly quaint in-your-face-modern-art pictures, like brazen parodies of Picasso, with their proud creator stood beside them looking defiantly mod and moody in Cambridge in November 1964, can be seen in a photograph by John Cooke in ROBERT SHELTON's biography *No Direction Home*, re-used in MARTIN SCORSESE's film of the same name. A photograph with more importance in which Neuwirth also appears is the front cover of the *Highway 61 Revisited* album. His are the legs standing behind motorbike-persona Dylan, his black-jeaned crotch just off to one side of Dylan's head, while his fist, thumb in pocket, holds a dangling camera on a strap. Those legs have always contributed a very, very slight hint of Warholian arty eroticism to the photo: they're part of what gives the cover its cutting-edge modernity and cool.

Bob Neuwirth continued to perform as a countryish singer, and a few months after Janis Joplin's death, when he played the Gaslight in Greenwich Village in March 1971, Dylan turned up to catch his set, and at the select second party to celebrate the end of Dylan and THE BAND's 1974 'comeback' tour, Neuwirth was one of the inner-circle guests.

After bringing Dylan on stage as his 'surprise backup guitarist' at the Other End (formerly the Bitter End) on July 2, 1975—the month that Dylan was, as in the old days, around in the Village all the time—Neuwirth duly reappeared in his Dylan-sidekick rôle when Dylan decided to go back on the road with what became the Rolling Thunder Revue. It was Neuwirth who organised 'the house-band' for the tour, GUAM, in which he included himself on vocals and guitar. That's him on the *awful* harmony vocals when Dylan opens his set wearing his Bob Dylan mask and singing 'When I Paint My Masterpiece'. (When the *Bootleg Series Vol. 5: Bob Dylan Live 1975* was released, taken from five different concerts but put together to represent a complete Dylan set, it was decided to omit 'When I Paint My Masterpiece'. Some aficionados complained; very few people's ears did.)

But of course there was no getting away from Bob Neuwirth in the film *Renaldo & Clara*, and in the concert footage, he's the one mugging the bulbous-eyed faces and, in David Faciane's happy phrase, 'jumping around like he had to go to the bathroom'. On the second Rolling Thunder Revue, in 1976, Neuwirth shared vocals with Dylan not only on 'When I Paint My Masterpiece' but also on '(Where Did) Vincent Van Gogh?' He is therefore also to be seen in the TV Special 'Hard Rain', and is present on the album of that name.

In the 1980s Neuwirth recorded two albums of his own, *Back to the Front* and *99 Monkeys*, and had songs recorded by k.d. lang and others; in the 1990s he and John Cale collaborated on the album *Last Day on Earth*, his 1996 album *Look Up* included a contribution from PATTI SMITH that was her first time on record in over a decade, and he toured with WARREN ZEVON and others.

In the 2000s he has co-produced *Down from the Mountain*, the D.A. Pennebaker film about the musicians who contributed to the hit movie *O Brother, Where Art Thou?*, and performed Bascom Lamar Lunsford's trademark song 'I Wish I Was a Mole in the Ground' at the 'HARRY SMITH Concerts' in New York and London in 2004.

Yet whatever else he does, Bob Neuwirth will always be Robin to Dylan's Batman (or to put it another way, always batman to Bob). He is therefore also an interviewee in Scorsese's *No Direction Home*; by the time of this filming he had grown quieter, desiccated and slightly camp; but he remained articulate and gave illuminating testimony, as for instance when recalling that on the Village scene in the early 1960s, a key question always asked about any performer, even a musician who never used words, was 'Does he have anything to say?' In Dylan's case, of course, the answer had been an emphatic 'Yes'. In Neuwirth's case, it had probably been 'Neu'.

[Bob Neuwirth: *Bob Neuwirth*, Asylum 7E-1008, US, 1974; *Back to the Front*, Gold Castle 171015, 1988; *99 Monkeys*, Gold Castle 71347, 1990; *Look Up*, Watermelon 1050, 1996. Bob Neuwirth & John Cale: *Last Day on Earth*, MCA 11307, 1994. Bob Dylan's Neuwirth portrait in *Chronicles Volume One*, 2004, pp. 47–8. Edie Sedgwick quote on Neuwirth: Jean Stein, *Edie: An American Biography*, ed. George Plimpton, New York: Knopf, 1982, p.315. David Faciane, e-mail posting seen online 30 Nov 2005 at *www.expectingrain.com/dok/who/n/neuwirthbobby.html*.]

Neville, Aaron [1941 -] Aaron Neville was born in New Orleans on January 24, 1941 and grew up in the city to become one of the Neville Brothers, a soul singing group formed with siblings Art (a founder of the Meters, and a keyboards player), Charles (sometime saxophonist for B.B. King) and Cyril (percussionist on Dylan's *Oh Mercy* album and operator of the 'talking drum' on the outtake 'Series of Dreams', released on the *Bootleg Series Vols. 1–3* in 1991).

The Neville Brothers' albums began to be released in the 1970s but they were most successful with *Yellow Moon*, in 1989, for which Aaron Neville wrote the title song. He has also recorded in a range of styles on 12 solo albums, though whether he is singing gospel, country, rock or blues he always throws over everything the same unmistakeable shimmering vibrato, which divides people sharply into those who consider it exquisite, delicate and beautiful and those who hear it as repulsively exaggerated and able only to besmirch every song it smothers.

Bob Dylan attended the 1988 session for the *Yellow Moon* album, produced by DANIEL LANOIS, at which Aaron Neville sang a version of 'With God on Our Side' that included his own extra, 'updating' verse: 'In the 1960s came the Vietnam War: / Can somebody tell me / What we were fightin' for? / Too many young men died, / Too many young mothers cried; / So I ask the question, / Was God on our side?'

Though he had never himself written anything so bald about the Vietnam War (indeed had only mentioned it twice in songs, and then only in the obscure 'Legionnaire's Disease' and 'Band of the Hand'), Dylan in turn promptly 'covered' the Aaron Neville version at a run of October 1988 concerts, débuting it in Upper Darby, Pennsylvania, on October 13, repeating it at the same venue the following night and then giving it the greater prominence of performances at all four consecutive nights' concerts at New York's Radio City Music Hall on October 16 to 19. After including it in his six-song set at the Bridge Benefit concert in Oakland that December 4, he dropped it again, and when he next revived the song, six years later for *MTV Unplugged*™, he had abandoned the Aaron Neville augmentation.

(Once, many years earlier, Dylan had given a one-off performance of 'With God on Our Side'—at the afternoon concert at Providence, Rhode Island, November 4, 1975, near the start of the first Rolling Thunder Revue—at which he'd added a last verse of his own, and actually it offered another mention of Vietnam: 'I've learned to hate Russia and China and Korea and Vietnam and Bulgaria and Poland and South America and Cuba, all of my whole life.' That 'Bulgaria' name-check was nicely comic.)

Neville has since contributed to two Various Artists albums with a Dylan connection: *The Songs of Jimmie Rodgers—A Tribute* (1997), on which he sings 'Why Should I Be Lonely?' comparatively robustly, and *Gotta Serve Somebody: The Gospel Songs of Bob Dylan* (2003), on which, depending on the viewpoint, he sings 'Saving Grace' in his more usual sensitive style, or palpitates over it like an agitated hover-fly.

[Aaron Neville: 'Why Should I Be Lonely?', *nia*, *The Songs of Jimmie Rodgers—A Tribute*, Egyptian/Columbia 485189 2, US, 1997. 'Saving Grace', *Gotta Serve Somebody: The Gospel Songs of Bob Dylan*, Columbia/Legacy CK 89015 (US) / Columbia COL 511126 2 (UK), 2003. Neville Brothers: 'With God on Our Side', 1988, *Yellow Moon*, A&M, US, Mar 1989. Bob Dylan: 1st performance of 'With God on Our Side' after 1988: NY, 17 & 18 Nov 1994, released on *MTV Unplugged*™, Columbia CK 67000, US (Columbia 478374 2, Europe & UK) 1995; 'Legionnaire's Disease', *nia*; 'Band of the Hand (It's Hell Time Man!)', Sydney, 8–10 Feb 1986, MCA 52811 (12-inch MCA 23633), US, Apr 1986 & on soundtrack album *Band of the Hand*, MCA 6167, US, May 1986.]

New Lost City Ramblers, the A revivalist string band (in the musically, not the religiously, evangelical sense) the New Lost City Ramblers, formed in 1958, played old-time Appalachian music in New York City, swiftly gaining a high profile in Greenwich Village. The group is still a working unit, though more as a hobby for its members than as a full-time act. The original group comprised JOHN COHEN (guitar), TOM PALEY (banjo, guitar & autoharp) and MIKE SEEGER (fiddle & mandolin). Paley left in 1962, to be replaced by Tracy Schwarz. They faltered in later decades but in 1997 they re-formed, made the album *There Ain't No Way Out* and in 1998 held a 40th Anniversary concert.

Original guitarist John Cohen sums up the New Lost City Ramblers like this:

> 'We've pointed to down-home sounds and authentic performance styles. Although we never had a hit record, we've influenced the shape of folk music and affected the work of musicians like Bob Dylan and JERRY GARCIA. We introduced the notion that it was okay for city singers to play roots music in traditional styles. Other musicians have taken up our ideas. Now there are many old-time fiddle bands playing better than we do. Some are as good as the old-timers we learned from.'

ROBERT SHELTON notes that in reviving the prebluegrass music of the 1920s and 30s, 'this proselytizing work . . . helped the rural musicians to come to the fore, while the city trio slid to the back of the stage. This selfless form of activity is one of the little-known aspects of the folk revival that, in its strange irony, gave the whole interchange between city and country a glow of beauty, ethics and honour.'

In *Chronicles Volume One* Dylan says that he had heard records by the New Lost City Ramblers before he arrived in New York; they were part of why he held Folkways Records in esteem. He writes of 'the Ramblers':

> 'I took to them immediately. Everything about them appealed to me—their style, their singing, their sound. I liked the way they looked, the way they dressed'—this is hard to credit, seeing the besuited bank clerks cavorting with their instruments on the group's early LP covers—'and I especially liked their name. . . . All their songs vibrated with some dizzy, portentous truth. . . . At the time, I didn't know that they were replicating everything they did off of old 78 records, but what would it have mattered anyway? . . . For me, they had originality in spades, were men of mystery on all counts. I couldn't listen to them enough.'

[*The New Lost City Ramblers: The Early Years 1958–1962*, Smithsonian Folkways 40036, 1991, CD-reissued 1992; *There Ain't No Way Out*, Smithsonian Folkways 40098, 1997. John Cohen quote from his *There Is No Eye: John Cohen Photographs*, New York: powerHouse Books,

2001, p.15. Robert Shelton, 'Something Happened in America', in Dave Laing, Karl Dallas, Robin Denselow & Robert Shelton, *The Electric Muse: The Story of Folk Into Rock*, London: Methuen, 1975. Bob Dylan, *Chronicles Volume One*, p.238.]

***New Morning* [1970]** This 11th album came a bit hastily after the tenth, *Self Portrait*, and seemed at the time a capitulation to the huge Dylan audience's demand that he return to the milieu of *Blonde on Blonde*. Lines like 'The man standin' next to me / His head was explodin' / I was hopin' the pieces / Wouldn't fall on me' (from 'Day of the Locusts') seemed a bit written-to-order. And Dylan, despite all the changes he'd gone through, had never done that before.

There's much more going on here than this, though. Throughout the album there is a subtle but sustained falsification of the rural/patriarchal ideas suggested here (and on *Nashville Skyline*): a persistent kind of Midas touch that deliberately makes the picture here an idealised and therefore not a real one.

It shows in his going not to 'the hills' at the end of 'Day of the Locusts' but to the American hills most artificialised by Tin Pan Alley, 'the black hills of Dakota'. It suggests Dylan rushing off to Doris Day; it makes his escape to the hills just a story, by making it just a joke—mere fictional allusion. (Dylan mentions Doris Day twice in *Tarantula*.)

Dylan's allusion is defter than that, though, for the Black Hills of (South) Dakota are 'Indian country' (as Doris sings): in fact the state's best-known 'great men' include Crazy Horse and Sitting Bull and its major towns include Sioux Falls. Thus Dylan might be said, as so often on this album, to be invoking a two-headed image, both unreal and real: the latter a terrain associated with an ancient American culture—and one offering a starkly different milieu and set of values from those of the honourary-degree ceremony at Princeton from which Dylan is escaping at the end of 'Day of the Locusts'. In 2004, *Chronicles Volume One* implied that there had been an extra level of allusion at work here too: he refers to the importance, in the Minnesota of his childhood, of the *Black Hills Passion Play of South Dakota*, which 'always came to town during the Christmas season', and in which his own 'first performances' were seen; he also says that at around the time of the making of *New Morning*, the feeling of invincibility that he remembered from those performances 'seemed a million years ago . . . a million private struggles and difficulties ago.' To know which is to hear a more heartfelt yearning in the lines of 'Day of the Locusts' about wanting to head for those 'black hills of Dakota'.

Just as the next song, 'Time Passes Slowly', takes up the story in the hills, so also it takes up the unreality suggested earlier: 'Time passes slowly up here in the mountains / We sit beside bridges and walk beside fountains', warbles Dylan—and plainly, as he's testing whether we'll notice, there aren't any fountains up mountains. The very word suggests the ideal, not the real. It offers a kind of exquisite, ethereal, pastoral conceit: a sort of Greek mythology-land, an Elysium. Something not there.

In 'Winterlude' the unreal becomes dominant and explicit. The title itself implies that the album is all a show, like, in this sense, *A Midsummer Night's Dream*. The rhythm is waltz-time; the clichés focus on a dream-world of romance, denying any corresponding 'real life' romance—the kind that sparkles through the Dixie Cups' record 'Chapel of Love' ('. . . my little apple / Winterlude let's go down to the chapel'). And it's not only a waltz: it's a skating song. Dylan On Ice. This carries a further suggestion of the unreal: the ice-top as merely a precarious covering, a sheet hiding and transforming something else. We can see this urged unreality too in the song 'New Morning' itself, with its intentional things-aren't-what-they-seem touch of 'a country mile, or two', while 'The Man in Me' has as its theme the message keep-it-all-hid. Then there is, beyond the obvious theatrical mystique of the title 'Sign on the Window', a beautifully achieved confession that even the wife-and-children may merely be a possible formula to try out: 'Build me a cabin in Utah / Marry me a wife, catch rainbow trout / Have a bunch of kids who call me Pa . . .' To clinch it, this is followed not only by a patently unconfident remark (made less positive still by its being repeated, as if for self-persuasion): 'That must be what it's all about / That must be what it's all about' but then by the capping touch of genius—that intentionally ingenuous little 'Oh-oh-oh-oh!' which Dylan puts over the end of the riff that follows. As for 'Three Angels', it is a song of many facets, but what impresses straight away is its being not only surreal (a different kind of challenge to reality) but as echoing that pop classic of false religiosity, Wink Martindale's 'Deck of Cards'. The 'real world' in Dylan's song passes like a pageant below the gaze of the narrator and his rather ungainly angels. Dylan's making them ungainly—keeping them perched up on poles wearing 'green robes, with wings that stick out'—is another wry confession of his intent.

The cumulative effect of all this carefully established unreality is to make *New Morning* very different, in its vision, from any other Dylan album. It begins to express a new optimism-through-doubt. He may have little to say but he has the courage to know it: and to make, to pass his time, an intelligent critique of what he doesn't believe in any more. *New Morning* says for his country persona what 'My Back Pages' said about his protest persona. And in fact there is a great deal of interesting comment from Dylan himself, in *Chronicles Volume One*, about the making of this album, and about the ways in which it was shaped by the keenness of ARCHIBALD MacLEISH to have Dylan write some songs for a play of his (the title 'Father of Night', for instance, Dylan says was suggested by MacLeish); but primarily Dylan's straightforward comments explain why he couldn't, in the end, collaborate with MacLeish—and much of the reason for being unable to do so was because, as Dylan is careful to describe, he felt that he had so little to say, and no sense of any burning urgency about new songs.

In retrospect, then, *New Morning* is a very individual album, a brave attempt to fuse the old surreal richness of feeling of the *Blonde on Blonde* era with a new desire to test the striving for stability through rural-based concerns. This is all felt by Dylan in a hesitant, pessimistic, confidence-lost way, which comes out too in the strange hesitancy with which the album attempts its musical fusion of a sort of grown-up acid-rock with both country picking and gospel.

We must have come a long way downhill since the album, when new, could sound over-produced and too professional. Now it sounds almost recorded round the camp-fire in the woods, with smokey acoustic playing, ample space and a sense of music played from love, with much individual extemporising towards a collective whole, and with Dylan's lovely untutored gospel piano as if miked up from inside some nearby clapboard church. There is a considerable gospel feel throughout the album, created not only by Dylan's own terrific piano-work but by the use of an old-church-type 'girl' chorus, topped off with the is-it-or-isn't-it-Christian? closing song 'Father of Night'.

This is a quirky album, from a Dylan not pointing a way for anyone, but from a great artist remaining at his work knowingly in the face of not being creatively on top form in the phenomenal way he had been in the period 1964–68. Warm and abiding, it sounds better and better as the years go by.

[Recorded NY, 3–5 Jun & 12 Aug 1970; released as stereo LP, Columbia KC 30290 (US) and CBS S 69001 (UK), 21 Oct 1970. Comments in *Chronicles Volume One*, 2004, pp.105–41.

Doris Day: 'The Black Hills of Dakota', Hollywood, 16 Jul 1953, Columbia 40095, NY (Philips PB 287, London), 1954. This was a top 10 hit in Britain. The song, by Paul Francis Webster & Sammy Fain, comes from the soundtrack of the film *Calamity Jane*, Warner Brothers, US, directed David Butler, 1953. The soundtrack album (10-inch LP) is *Calamity Jane*, Columbia CL6273, NY, 1953.

The Dixie Cups: 'Chapel of Love', NY, *nia*, the first release on the George Goldner-Jerry Leiber-Mike Stoller label Red Bird (Red Bird 10 001), NY (Pye International 7N 25245, London), 1964. It was a US no.1. The Dixie Cups were a New Orleans act. Wink Martindale: 'Deck of Cards', *nia*, Dot 15968, Hollywood (London American HLD 8962, London), 1959. In the UK this was a recurrent hit: first charting in December 1959 (top 20), re-charting in 1963 (top 5) and, reissued on Dot Records DOT 109, re-charting again in 1973 (top 30). This last time around, even more of the UK public bought the cover version by Max Bygraves (Pye Records 7N 45276). It was on Wink Martindale's local TV show on WHBQ in the early months of 1957 that Elvis Presley first saw 19-year-old beauty-contest winner Anita Wood (he was watching the show, she was appearing on it), who would become his principal girlfriend 1957–60. While Presley was in the army, Wood recorded 'I'll Wait Forever' (Memphis, 28 Dec 1960, Sun 361, Memphis, 1961).]

New World Singers, the See **Traum, Happy** and **Turner, Gil**.

Newport Folk Festival, the It's easy to assume that by the time Dylan débuted at the Newport Folk Festival in 1963, it was a venerable institution. But the first Newport Folk Festival had been in 1959 (JOAN BAEZ, already a folk star, had appeared); and after the 1960 event, no festival took place in 1961 *or* 1962, so that the extraordinary coming-together in July 1963 was only the third such event. The founders of the festival, in 1959, were George Wein (of the already established annual Newport Jazz Festival) and his partner, one ALBERT GROSSMAN.

In retrospect the real significance of the 1959 and 1960 festivals was probably the inclusion of a number of bluegrass artists, which brought this music right to the centre of the folk revival movement. RALPH RINZLER's placing of Bill Monroe on the 1960 festival bill turned his career around, restoring him to some of the recognition he richly merited and reflecting credit on the festival for its full-on inclusion of bluegrass.

Wein restarted the festival in 1963, forming a committee to organise the event, which took place over the three days of July 26–28. The committee comprised THEODORE BIKEL, Bill Clifton, Clarence Cooper, Erik Darling, Jean Ritchie, PETE SEEGER and Pete Yarrow of PETER, PAUL & MARY. Yarrow, particularly, pushed the policy that 'the young singer-songwriters were really important', insisting that the Festival board recognise these people as well as the traditional singers. Hence the festival, at Freebody Park, included Tom Paxton, IAN & SYLVIA, PHIL OCHS, PETE LaFARGE as well as the big names (Peter, Paul & Mary and Joan Baez), older mainstream folk acts like Seeger and RAMBLIN' JACK ELLIOTT, gospel-oriented acts like the FREEDOM SINGERS, 'folk blues' performers like MISSISSIPPI JOHN HURT and ODETTA and the truly 'traditional' white performers no-one had ever heard of. Arriving within this mix as one of the 1963 newcomers, Bob Dylan left as its star. The final evening ended with Baez, Peter, Paul & Mary and the Freedom Singers singing behind him on 'Blowin' in the Wind' and an ensemble 'We Shall Overcome'. A month later came the March on Washington. Everything seemed transcendent with hope, warmed by communal consensus and the politics of change.

By the time of the 1964 festival, John F. Kennedy had been assassinated and Bob Dylan had begun to 'defect' from the commune, from his rôle as the figurehead for the singer-songwriter New Left and the politics of protest. (As he would sing, looking back on it all a decade later, on the *Planet Waves* album's 'Wedding Song': 'It's never been my duty to remake the world at large / Nor is it my intention to sound the battle charge.') More generally, the 1964 Festival 'overreached' itself: too many performers, too many different genres: in Theodore Bikel's words, 'giving both the individual performer and listener too little chance for expression or absorption.' PAUL NELSON wrote tetchily that it had left him 'unmoved to the point of paralysis. Under the misguided conception that a couple of regiments of folk singers were preferable to a hand-picked two or three squads, the Newport Committee enlisted what looked to be every folk singer, or reasonable facsimile, on the North American continent, and proceeded to attempt to have them all perform in the space of a single weekend. Even God himself needed six days. Further, Newport proved to be less of a folk festival than a spectacular three-ring morality play of cult worship. The scores of traditional artists remained virtually unnoticed in the back pew, while the hungry throng of worshippers craved a blood sacrifice to mount on a pedestal, another golden saint to add to their socio-religious trilogy of Pete Seeger, Bob Dylan and Joan Baez. I find it far easier to believe in God than in the mythical heroes of Newport and the aspiring Christs who, in cowboy hats and motorcycle boots, pierce their sides and cry "I am the Way!" to the cheers and hoopla of the fraternity folklorists and record-company desperadoes.'

This was hardly the whole story. To look back now at the Newport 1964 performers' list is to realise what a golden age it managed to capture. If you had wanted to concentrate on the blues alone, and been a bit quieter about your grievances than Paul Nelson, you could have sat at the feet of SLEEPY JOHN ESTES, Mississippi Fred McDowell, Robert Pete Williams, Hammy Nixon and Yank Rachell, ELIZABETH COTTEN, SKIP JAMES, JESSE FULLER, Mississippi John Hurt and more besides. The Festival Board supported other, smaller festivals too, at which traditional performers continued to be able to play to their own local crowds.

By 1965, everything was in restless flux. The Festival Board of Directors was now Bikel, Ronnie Gilbert, ALAN LOMAX, Ralph Rinzler, Pete Seeger, MIKE SEEGER and Pete Yarrow. Mike Seeger, ignoring Paul Nelson, was arguing that 'there is fortunately room for as many different types of festivals as there are songs and styles.' Newport, he felt, 'being the largest and relatively free from the usual commercial pressures, can not only explore the many isolated and individualistic areas of folk song but also the elements of the three principal streams of folk song', which he designated as 'mountain or country music, from Eck Robertson and Horton Barker to Bill Monroe and Roger Miller; Negro tradition from Joe Petterson, the Moving Star Hall Singers, and MANCE LIPSCOMB to CHUCK BERRY; urban singers and composers of folk and folk-based songs, from THE NEW LOST CITY RAMBLERS and the KWESKIN Jug Band to Bob Dylan and Joan Baez.'

Excitement, anticipation of big change, of the vanquishing of the Old Guard New Left (Pete Seeger, Alan Lomax, A.L. Lloyd), was tangible all through the crowd at the 1965 event, which was now spread over four days, July 22–25. Dylan wasn't the only person to play electric music at this event, but his playing it proved the incendiary moment. Accounts have been extremely various as to how key people behaved—among them Pete Seeger, who did try to cut the power during Dylan's set, albeit not actually with his axe, and Alan Lomax, who got into a physical fight with Albert Grossman for the contemptuous way he introduced the PAUL BUTTERFIELD blues band (though no-one can agree on what he actually said)—and equally about how the crowd reacted to Dylan's 'going electric' and how Dylan reacted in response.

There is, though, a certain plausibility to what ERIC VON SCHMIDT told ANTHONY SCADUTO; what he felt he witnessed was that 'whoever was controlling the mikes messed it up. You couldn't hear Dylan. It looked like he was singing with the volume off. . . . the whole thing [was] sounding like a Butterfield boogie and no Dylan. We were sitting in the press section, maybe thirty yards back, and yelling "Can't hear ya!" and "Cut the band down!" Only about four or five people were hollering. Then they went into the next song. . . . same thing, no voice coming through at all. . . . more people began shouting.'

By this analysis, people weren't anti-electric. As on the tour with THE HAWKS that followed, a lot of people were just anti bad sound. It's ironic, then, that there is no better single account of this most eventful weekend than that of the culprit sound engineer himself, insider Joe Boyd, the man who had already introduced MIKE BLOOMFIELD to the Paul Butterfield Blues Band and was later to be the manager and producer of the Incredible String Band and producer of the first Pink Floyd record, of Fairport Convention, of the first Kate & Anna McGarrigle album and of MARIA MULDAUR's *Midnight at the Oasis*, among other achievements. Joe Boyd's account is given in an interview by Jonathan Morley for *The Telegraph* in 1988, and republished in that fanzine's second anthology of pieces, *Wanted Man: In Search of Bob Dylan*. There may be an interesting revising of his account in the first volume of his autobiography, *White Bicycles: Making Music in the 1960s*, to be published in 2006.

In the end, though, whichever account or accounts you believe, the upshot of Dylan at Newport 1965 was a timely controversy that did his career nothing but good. As Scaduto summed it up, 'Although he may have lost a few folk fans, the publicity helped him gain an even wider audience among the young disaffected. His album began to sell at a quickened pace, and "Rolling Stone" shot up the charts.' It's a simplistic summary but fits the broad pattern of what people *think* happened, which is just as important as the minutiae of what actually did.

The institution of the Festival rolled on after 1965, though it folded again after the 1969 event and was only revived in 1985. The official recordings from Newport itself continued to flow from Vanguard Records. Dylan himself revisited the event in 2002.

[Bob Dylan: 'Talkin' World War III Blues', 'With God on Our Side', 'Only a Pawn in Their Game', 'Talkin' John Birch Paranoid Blues', 'A Hard Rain's a-Gonna Fall', Newport, RI, 26 Jul 1963, unreleased; 'Blowin' in the Wind' (with Peter, Paul & Mary and the Freedom Singers), Newport, 26 Jul 1963, *Evening Concerts at Newport*, Vanguard VRS9148, NY, 1964; 'North Country Blues' & 'With God on Our Side' (latter with Joan Baez), 27 Jul 1963, unreleased; 'Who Killed Davey Moore?', 'Masters of War', 28 Jul 1963, unreleased; 'Playboys & Playgirls' (with Pete Seeger) & 'With God on Our Side' (with Joan Baez), 28 Jul 1963, *Newport Broadside*, Vanguard VRS9144, NY, 1964. 'It Ain't Me Babe', 'Mr. Tambourine Man', Newport, 24 Jul 1964, unreleased; 'It Ain't Me Babe' (with Joan Baez), 24 Jul 1964, *Joan Baez Live at Newport*, Vanguard VAN0077015-2, NY, 1998; 'All I Really Want to Do', 'To Ramona', 'Mr. Tambourine Man', 26 Jul 1964, unreleased; 'Chimes of Freedom', 25 Jul 1964, *Bootleg Series Vol. 7—No Direction Home: The Soundtrack*, Sony BMG Columbia Legacy 5203582001, NY, 2005. 'All I Really Want to Do', 'Mr. Tambourine Man', Newport, 24 Jul 1965, unreleased; 'Maggie's Farm', 25 Jul 1965, *Bootleg Series Vol. 7*, op.cit.; 'Like a Rolling Stone', 'It Takes a Lot to Laugh, It Takes a Train to Cry', 'It's All Over Now, Baby Blue' & 'Mr. Tambourine Man', 25 Jul 1965, unreleased; 19-song performance, Newport, 3 Aug 2002, unreleased. Some footage from various Newport 1964–65 Dylan song performances is included in the Murray Lerner film *Festival*, US, 1967, and further Lerner footage is included in the Martin Scorsese film *No Direction Home*, US, 2005.

General information sources include William Ruhlman's account excerpted on *www.peterpaulmary.com* and, for Bikel and Paul Nelson quotes, the 1965 Festival Program, ed. Ralph Rinzler & Robert Shelton (as Stacey Williams). Eric Von Schmidt & Anthony Scaduto in Scaduto, *Bob Dylan*, London: Abacus edn., p.215. Jonathan Morley, 'The Wanted Man Interview: Joe Boyd', *Telegraph* no.31, UK, winter 1988 & John Bauldie, ed., *Wanted Man: In Search of Bob Dylan*, London: Black Spring, 1990. Joe Boyd, *White Bicycles: Making Music in the 1960s*, London: Serpent's Tail, 2006.]

Nicholson, Jack [1937 -] John Joseph Nicholson was born in Neptune, New Jersey, on April 22, 1937, grew up thinking his mother was his sister, attended Manasquan High School, NJ—and turned up at his class' 50th reunion event in 2004—and worked as a gopher in MGM's cartoon department before getting his start in movies with Roger Corman. It was *Easy Rider* in 1969 that made him, and it was he who made *Easy Rider*, rescuing this smudged counter-cultural movie with the fresh air and bite of his performance as the dodgy lawyer. It was obvious in a trice that here was one of the full-on irresistible charmers of the age, a fine actor licenced to settle for hamming it up as much as he liked, as a boyish Hollywood life of pranks, womanising and mega-million dollar success inevitably fell into his lap.

By the late 1970s, an established star, he was unusual in Hollywood in making public avowals of his unbounded admiration for Bob Dylan, and in 1978 was to be seen backstage on Dylan's World Tour, at least in London that June, wearing the most benign version possible of his patented playful-devil grin, happy simply to be in the presence of what he had no doubt at all was Dylan's genius. In July 1985, it was Nicholson who stepped out in front of the huge live Philadelphia crowd and a worldwide TV audience of 1,500 million people to introduce Dylan at LIVE AID with bad grammar, suspect logic and absolutely dewy-eyed anticipation and respect. He said, to rising cheers: 'Some artists' work speaks for itself; some artists' work speaks for his generation. It's my deep personal pleasure to present to you one of America's great voices of freedom. It can only be one man! The transcendent Bob Dylan!' The transcendent Bob Dylan immediately stepped forward to fall spectacularly from grace.

Undeterred, six years on, it was Nicholson who, a little more nervously but with no diminution of willingness for the job, introduced Dylan on another reasonably large occasion, that of offering him a Grammy Lifetime Achievement Award at Radio City Music Hall, New York, on February 20, 1991, again broadcast live on international TV. Having reportedly spent two of the previous three days in Dylan's company, possibly having a drink or two, Nicholson now took a deep breath and began:

'For the constant state of restlessness that has enabled you to seek newer and better means of expressing the human condition with words and music; for living your creative life fearlessly and without apology, and leading the way no matter how the times change—the National Academy of Recording Arts and Sciences joins a worldwide network of grateful fans in presenting you this Grammy Lifetime Achievement Award. Congratulations!' Then, steeled for anything, Nicholson had to stand there and witness Dylan's extraordinary out-on-the-edge response: a madly inspired acceptance 'speech' that was absolutely classic Dylan, pushing to the farthest limits of the occasion, starting out perilously enough, only to crank up the ante by making people sweat over an astonishingly long mid-speech tour de force of a pause: forcing the TV people, and Nicholson too, to wonder whether some awful puncturing of the whole ceremonial game wasn't happening or about to happen. And after the pause, what a route out: what a choice of topic, what a dark vibe Dylan reached for to end his deranged moment in the glittering lights. From start to finish, it went like this:

> 'Thank you. Well, um—alright. Yeah. Well my daddy he didn't leave me too much, you know: he was a very simple man and he didn't leave me a lot. But what he told me was this. He did say, "Son—" [*long, long* pause]—oh well he said so *many* things, you know?! [short pause] He said, "You know, it's possible to become so defiled in this world that your own mother and father will abandon you. And if that happens, God will always believe in your own ability to mend your own ways." Thank you.'

On March 3, 1994, Dylan was in the audience at the Beverly Hilton Hotel in LA to see Jack Nicholson given his own Lifetime Achievement Award for acting. Despite the undimmed incorrigibility of the recipient, it was not such a high-wire occasion.

1964 car ride through America, the By the beginning of 1964, Dylan was sufficiently famous that he needed his own 'staff', or 'protection': a road manager. He appointed Victor Maymudes (it has often been spelt Maimudes), a tall, beaky-nosed, saturnine, chess-playing ex-actor from LA, the son of Left-Wing activists and a man who, with Herb Cohen, FRANK ZAPPA's future manager, had opened LA's first coffee-house, the Unicorn on Sunset Boulevard, back in 1955. ROBERT SHELTON described him as having 'penetrating dark eyes, turbulent hair, and . . . an uncanny ability to keep his mouth shut.'

Opening it to HOWARD SOUNES more than 30 years down the line, Maymudes declared, in Sounes' summary, 'that Bob was not a very nice man at all, but a sociopath who, in his songs, became ten times the man he was in real life.' Dylan may have met first him in 1962 through mutual acquaintance RAMBLIN' JACK ELLIOTT. In 1964 he was happy to take on the rôle of Dylan's batman: companion, chauffeur, bodyguard, bag-carrier.

With Maymudes to rely on, Dylan decided on an epic journey across America; a scheme impossible not to think of in terms of KEROUAC and *On the Road*. Along with Dylan and Maymudes came two companions paid for through one of Dylan's businesses created and part-owned by ALBERT GROSSMAN. One was folksinger PAUL CLAYTON, already fragile and burdened, reportedly, by being at least half in love with Dylan at the time, who brought with him a suitcase full of amphetamines and other drugs (well somebody had to . . .). The fourth member of the party was an old friend of SUZE ROTOLO and her family, Pete Karman, theoretically *Suze's* 'protection', somehow supposed to prevent Dylan's womanising in general and connecting up with JOAN BAEZ in particular. Karman, who had knocked around a bit despite his youth (he was a year older than Dylan but had been to Cuba and been a newspaper reporter) went along for the ride, literally, 'not as a spy but as a chaperone.' Dylan told Shelton later: 'We had to kick Pete out and send him home on a plane.'

Two days after Dylan filmed his TV performance on the CBC show 'Quest' in Toronto, he was back in upstate New York and they set out from Grossman's, in Bob's blue Ford station wagon, on February 3rd—though not till dusk—aiming to drive all the way west to California in time for his Berkeley concert, fixed for the 22nd. Mostly Maymudes drove, and Dylan wrote songs, sometimes with a portable typewriter on his knees but more often in a notepad. These conditions suited both equally. Maymudes is said to have appreciated above all things music, a well-turned phrase and a good joint; Dylan, in turn, appreciated Maymudes' dependability and silence. The trip yielded, among other things, 'Chimes of Freedom' and the first part of 'Mr. Tambourine Man'.

Their route was more direct existentially than geographically. They stopped the first night in Charlottesville, Virginia, where Clayton had been a student and still owned an old cabin out in the woods, picking up two dozen copies of *The Times They Are a-Changin'*, which had been released only on January 13th, so that Dylan could hand them out to the deserving en route, as to the hitchhiker they picked up next day on the way to Harlan County, Kentucky, where they wanted to visit striking miners—representatives, for Dylan, of the world of several of his musical heroes: FRANK HUTCHISON and Roscoe Holcomb among them—and bring them some clothes and blankets collected by union supporters and activists in New York. Pineville, Kentucky; a motel. Then Asheville, North Carolina, their first step into the segregated south and, as Shelton noted, 'birthplace of novelist Thomas Wolfe, who wrote *You Can't Go Home Again*' (though in truth that powerfully epigrammatic title was posthumously given). From there they drove on to Hendersonville, to seek a still-living literary figure, CARL SANDBURG. (See separate entry for their encounter.)

When they left the Sandburgs' pig farm, they crossed into South Carolina, then Athens, Georgia (one of the regular haunts of BLIND WILLIE McTELL), home of the venerable University of Georgia, where on the streets Dylan was widely recognised by students. Next day, Atlanta, where Dylan gave a concert at Emory University; the day after, still in

Atlanta, he met the civil rights activists Cordell Reagon and 21-year-old Bernice Johnson (soon to be BERNICE JOHNSON REAGON). On from there, south and west into Mississippi, a land of green valleys, gentle hills and lakes and a panorama of segregation signage—WHITES ONLY, COLOREDS . . .

Shelton says they'd half promised 'to join SNICK [the Student Nonviolent Coordinating Committee] at Tougaloo College', but New Orleans and the Mardi Gras beckoned. They headed for the birthplace of jazz after a night in Meridian, Mississippi, birthplace of JIMMIE RODGERS—and the place where H.C. Speir, the pre-war Sam Phillips, brought CHARLEY PATTON after springing him from Belzoni Jail, to catch the train to New York so that Patton, 'the leadingest musicianer in Mississippi,' could record. Dylan & co. had no rooms booked in Mardi Gras-filled New Orleans, so all four shared one. They were woken by an ex-New York stripper who'd bumped into Pete Karman and been promised some grass; she showed up at three AM not knowing who his companions were. They were not pleased, but from next morning onwards, New Orleans was the delight and the festival of heightened sensations and serendipitous chaos it was supposed to be. Robert Shelton's biography describes it well, and in detail.

Moving on, they made a brief stop back at Tougaloo, and then had to drive west fast to get to Denver for another of Dylan's concerts scheduled beforehand. They went via Dallas, where President John F. Kennedy had been shot only three months earlier. Anxious but curious, they retraced Kennedy's route past the Book Depository.

They just made Denver for the concert. Pete Karman tutted that the whole jaunt was hopelessly disorganised, but the promoter was pleased with how it all went. Dylan wanted to look up JUDY COLLINS, but she was away, and his old Central City haunt, the Gilded Garter, but it was closed for the winter. Next day, as they left Denver, the car sustained its own BEATLES invasion, as the group's new hit 'I Want to Hold Your Hand' came on the radio. The group was in the States; they had been on 'The Ed Sullivan Show' and creating showbiz havoc while Bob and his old-style wannabohemians were driving cross-country.

Onward the compadres pressed, over the Rockies in a snowstorm; a night in Grand Junction, Colorado; a hairy moment when stopped by the police for speeding past a funeral: a delay but a lucky escape from a drugs bust; an all-night drive afterwards, through to Reno. On from there across the Sierra Madres into California and San Francisco.

It was over. For Dylan, maybe a last fling of youthful freedom was over with it. Artistically, as personally, it had been a memorable episode. En route, Dylan had undergone an epiphany of sorts, hearing the Beatles' boisterous rejuvenation of pop. He'd been struck at once by their freshness, their potency, their ability to resuscitate something close to the music that had been his first love, rock'n'roll. Yet while LENNON-McCARTNEY had been writing 'I Want to Hold Your Hand', a happy display of their ability with flyaway chords and harmonies, set to laughably shallow and simplistic words, Bob Dylan had been travelling across America several light-years ahead of them, writing 'Mr. Tambourine Man'.

Afterword: Victor Maymudes died, aged 65, in UCLA Hospital, Santa Monica, on January 26, 2001. From 1986 to 1996 he had returned to working as Dylan's personal manager but then, bitterly estranged from him, he retired to travel and write his memoirs. The result, *The Joker and the Thief*, was supposed to be published by St. Martins Press in 2002. It has never emerged.

[Maymudes data partly from *www.sierrabravo.co.uk/victor/*, online 10 Feb 2006; Howard Sounes, *Down the Highway: A Life of Bob Dylan*, New York: Grove Press, 2001, ms pp.182–85. Robert Shelton, *No Direction Home: The Life and Music of Bob Dylan*, London: Penguin edn., pp.240–49. Detail on Meridian: Michael Gray, 'Ghost Trains of Mississippi', unhappily renamed 'Rail Good Lesson in the Blues' by the *Weekend Telegraph*, London, 25 Sep 2004.]

1965 electric concerts, the A month and three days after re-launching himself with electric guitar at the NEWPORT FOLK FESTIVAL on July 25, 1965, Dylan began playing concerts with the same format that the British would find ourselves faced with in the golden maelstrom of May 1966—concerts at which he would play an acoustic first half and then after an intermission would bring out a bunch of unidentified musicians and blast through a second half that was the loudest experience his audiences had ever had.

What a curious itinerary these 1965 US concerts seem to have had, and how strange that the first ones were in places that presented particularly difficult acoustics problems. The first one was at America's most famous tennis stadium, a vast open-air venue adapted to accommodate a 15,000-seater concert. There was a five-night gap before he played again. The venue was another extremely famous, large out-door arena, the Hollywood Bowl, on September 3rd. Then—unless there are many undocumented (and unrecorded) extra ones, ones that have left no trace—there was a gap of a further three weeks before Dylan played two consecutive nights in Texas (at Austin and Dallas, on the 24th and 25th). Then there was another five-night space and then, only then, at the beginning of October, did something that looks like a tour itinerary kick in.

Even this was patterned strangely: two dates, six free nights, a third date, another five-night break, three more dates, a four-night break, three dates, a three-night gap, one date, one night off, one more date, five more nights off . . . and so on. The tour sprawled from October 1st to December 19th.

In all that time Dylan only once played more than three nights running, and appears to have given a total of 27 concerts over 80 days. In the literal sense, at the very least, it was certainly spaced out.

Not that he wasn't busy—he got married, recorded, did the original Nat Hentoff *Playboy* interview, the wonderful San Francisco and LA press conferences and more besides in this period—but as a Dylan tour itinerary goes, it's a curiously leisurely creature, especially since it was the focus of such fundamental controversy over his 'going electric': it was an oddly uncompressed start to this electric touring.

At any rate, these earliest electric concerts are not only a crucial part of the Dylan story but, because we have so little taped evidence of them, also deeply mysterious. The shows were necessarily experimental, with Dylan himself very new to fronting a professional rock band (or beat group, as we called them then), but beyond that, and over and above the way that everything Bob Dylan did in the mid-1960s was just absolutely *it*, there's the fact that these shows lie along the road that leads to Britain, May 1966, at which point the music being hurled out at us by Bob and his musicians, though still experimental in being a radical journey through an unknown universe, was nevertheless fully formed, was at its transcendent peak, was utterly and exactly what Bob Dylan wanted it to be. It's because what we got on that British tour is so immortally magnificent that we peer back so intently at the concerts that came before it. They may be invaluable in their own right, but they're the more so because they helped him achieve the impossible: helped him leap his dream of the music out into the world.

Until 1998, there was little on tape from these 1965 concerts to go on: an audience tape of the historic first show, Forest Hills, August 28th, but in very poor quality; bits of two or three others; another audience audiomurk through Berkeley, December 4th (almost unlistenable); and then a couple of lo-fi tapes of shows from February '66. Then, after a gap of almost 33 years, in the strange way that these things continue to happen, a pretty good quality tape came into circulation from the second electric concert ever, Hollywood Bowl, September 3, 1965. This clips off the beginning of the first electric number—an unfortunate moment to miss—but gives us the whole of the rest of the concert, acoustic and electric, and, in some ways just as importantly, the uninterrupted noises from the crowd at the end of each song.

The acoustic half starts with a 'She Belongs to Me' that has him singing wearily 'for Hallowe'en get her a trumpet', yet the harmonica flutters around proto-'66ishly but like a trapped butterfly. Then we get a mostly impatient 'To Ramona' and then a 'Gates of Eden' sung oddly straight, with such a plodding strummed guitar and nothing but a full-stop on the harp at the end. Yet this initial apparent boredom (see **Dylan being 'bored' by his acoustic material 1965–66, the myth of**) proves a fleeting mood, and it comes and goes, just like in concerts all through his career. Between the first two numbers somebody in the audience toots on what does sound like a trumpet, and Dylan, open and friendly and ready for anything, for any kind of spontaneous dialogue, asks 'What *is* that *thing* out there, man? What are you trying to *say*?!'—and in the middle of 'To Ramona' he finds himself again, beguiling himself anew with the song, or recalling its original range of feelings.

After 'Gates of Eden' there's no looking back. On comes 'It's All Over Now, Baby Blue' with every harmonica phrase intense, fresh and exquisite—and totally focussed: a solo any jazz musician would understand—even while he sounds oddly gauche as a vocalist. The furry quality so redolent of 1966 and *Blonde on Blonde*—a quality already present a couple of months later when he records 'Freeze Out' in New York in November—is completely missing here, and the voice sounds more *Bringing It All Back Home* than anything. Then someone shouts something and Dylan says 'I'm sorry, I can't hear you,' and then, 'This is called "Desolation Row"' and sings this very new, long song. He sings it so fast that it's well under ten minutes, and the audience laughs aloud at the jokey bits, and though the harmonica just replicates the recording (made just a month earlier and released four days before the show) and the guitar part here is just a rough strum, the vocal is light, fluid and warm, and he's warmed up transformingly by this point.

We're used to the song now, of course, but at the time, only two years on from 'The Times They Are a-Changin'', it was a modern poetry performance, very Left Bank, yet full of a unique Dylan frisson, the mind-blowing, mind-expanding world he introduced us to in 1965. Here it is, audibly arriving. And sure enough, the audience, which sounds to have a predominance of females in it, because this is the Dylan-the-pop-star period too, responds. At the end of the song two or three of them, obviously having resolved to do so, shout out in unison 'It's *so groovy*!!', and it is, and this moment recaptures touchingly the feel of that period at its pure and well-intentioned beginning; and Dylan laughs a 'yeah' that's half question, half concurrence.

'Love Minus Zero' is so generously tender, and with such a great Buddy Hollyish riff on the guitar, that it tops 'Desolation Row'. The voice is so utterly commanding, and so utterly without swagger or bluff: he's always on the microphone, there's never any danger of a fluffed word or a cheap trick. And then comes 'Mr. Tambourine Man', with another strange combining of the unmistakeably 1965 vocal quality—including 1965's rapturous vigour, as if he's running along that beach with his arms windmilling—and a harmonica solo that, while a long way short of, say, the wondrous Dublin '66 one that echoes as in a cathedral, is, all the same, heading that 1966 way, all spacey and dreamy and pioneering and great.

Then it's the electric half. No wonder this is different from the British dates seven months later. Only one of Dylan's musicians is the same, ROBBIE ROBERTSON. 'Tombstone Blues' comes on with such a great riff, so perky, so 1965, and there are times when, as this tape happens to catch the mix at any rate, there's virtually just drums and voice. Then there's a great guitar solo—Robbie was perfect back then, before he grew post-BAND sulky and modish and funky—and Dylan comes back in after it in his trademark weird place, and it works. But it's ironic that here he is with his rockin' white pop/blues band and yet his own performance is shouted, not sung: it's a poetry recitation.

It's all more like the studio sound of 'From a Buick 6' than the whirlwind of 1966 in concert, and there's so much pop music still in there among the rock'n'roll—mostly, it must be said, courtesy of AL KOOPER, who doesn't seem to know quite what he's in amongst here. He keeps putting these tinkly, twinkly noises in everywhere, while the guitar bass and drums and Bob are taking a far heavier road—but the upshot is a reminder of the pretty melodic touch that Dylan was not averse to in this period: the touch that makes 'Positively 4th Street' such a hit record, for instance. It's here, in concert, on 'I Don't Believe You', which sounds so light, so lilting, so provisional on Bob's part, at least until he hits his long-drawn out lines like 'Am I still, dreaming ye——t!' At the end, after the applause, a bit of the crowd starts caterwauling, and this recurs, but not menacingly, never threatening to gain the momentum to derail it all.

Then it *is* 'From a Buick 6'—in which 'she walks like RIMBAUD' but Bob and the band still rock like BO DIDDLEY. He seems a big influence all through this part of the evening, with a tangible touch of the Sir Douglas Quintet thrown in, but a great guitar sound, great drumming, great bass. Howls of 'Get off!' at the end, and then they're into 'Just Like Tom Thumb's Blues', light-years away from Liverpool '66, all twinkles and tinkles and catchy riffs, yet growing as it progresses, gaining from that heavy drumming and the cutting guitar and the occasional sustained howl from Bob, all culminating in a magnificent instrumental break, like a great dark liner, prow bearing down upon you, majestic but threatening.

This is 1965 and Dylan and the group are reshaping it in front of our ears so that THE BEATLES never existed. You just have to hear it. You wouldn't swap it for 1966, but it's part of the story of how 1966 came into being.

1965–66: Dylan, pop & the UK charts Bob Dylan began 1966 at the soaring peak of his inestimable genius, leaping from crag to lofty crag at giddying, undreamt of heights of incandescent inspiration, shaking his curls above the clouds, hearing that wild mercury sound in a rarified wind. He was to become 25 that year—which seemed, at the time, rather old for anyone to keep on being the hippest person in the universe.

His newest album was *Highway 61 Revisited*, and his revolutionary hit single 'Like a Rolling Stone', the longest thing you'd ever heard on the radio, had been released in the summer of 1965. In Britain Bob had charted for the first time in March 1965, with 'The Times They Are a-Changin'', which was still climbing when 'Subterranean Homesick Blues' entered the charts a month later; both reached the top 10 while an immaculately cool, Carnaby Street Bob toured England with his giant lightbulb, dark glasses, Chelsea boots and acoustic guitar.

Two months after that, 'Maggie's Farm' arrived in the lower reaches of the chart, and on August 19 'Like a Rolling Stone', soon giving Dylan his first top 5 hit record in the UK. (It would be his only one, excepting 'Lay Lady Lay'.) At the end of October, the scathing lilt of 'Positively 4th Street' charted, soon becoming another top 10 hit. Within four weeks of New Year's Day 1966, Bob's next single, 'Can You Please Crawl Out Your Window?', would join the hit parade too.

It was all go for Bob, the folk-singer who'd 'gone pop'. Except that it was obvious he hadn't. He was on his way somewhere else. Pop was all the others. THE BEATLES in 1965 were still moptops; their hit singles in Britain that year were 'I Feel Fine', 'Ticket to Ride', 'Help!' and 'Day Tripper' c/w 'We Can Work It Out': all no.1 smash hits and only just beginning to hint at something less vacuous than 'she loves you yeah yeah yeah' and 'I Want to Hold Your Hand'.

It took many people a while to get used to his voice, but once they could hear that within it lay such riches of expressive thought and feeling, such resources of intelligence, such clear-sighted, uncompromising purpose, they were hooked. He was crucial, the authentic contemporary heavyweight, an agent of the radical future, not as now a guardian of the past. He had cultural clout, not mere celebrity. He was also popular. You could play his albums without apology. (On the other hand he wasn't *that* popular: most of his records in circulation were still the pre-electric ones, you couldn't dance to him, and he was thought too doomy and intellectual for parties.)

Yet Dylan was becoming an ever-present, formative influence. From 1965 onwards, people's diaries and letters (people still wrote letters) began to alight more and more on moments and incidents for which a Dylan aphorism came as the natural bon mot—and they were all the more bon for their freshness. It was sparky then to throw off a line from 'Desolation Row' or 'To Ramona'. These records were almost new. Student newspapers too began to feature Dylanisms, sewn among their headlines and sub-heads.

Mostly, eager clusters of people just played the records. MARK KNOPFLER talks somewhere about listening to *Blonde on Blonde* over a million cups of coffee. That was exactly what people did. But it was like sitting round camp fires, waiting for smoke signals. There were no Bob Dylan networks then, nor any such concept, and things came through slowly. There was often a gap between when a record was released in America and in Britain, and often another gap between when it might be available in London and in the small provincial record-shops of the North. In most towns, you could only buy records at antiquated, infuriating hardware/electrical goods shops with a small record-section somewhere behind the vacuum-cleaners, refrigerators and lampshades; and the manager would be a tweed-jacketed, middle-aged man barely familiar with the name ELVIS PRESLEY, let alone Bob Dylan. The upshot was, for years, that if a record was in the top 10 they'd sold out of it and if it wasn't, they'd never heard of it. Under these conditions, news was a matter of leisurely-paced rumour rather than fanzined, hotlined, internetted instant dispersal.

Why didn't people go to all the 1966 British concerts? Because nobody did. Back then, *nobody* conceived of that level of fandom. You went to the one concert nearest your hometown, and you greeted this superlative genius, this pinnacle of 20th century art-in-action, with restrained applause from your seat.

Where Bob Dylan was going, nobody knew. Where the 1960s were going, nobody knew. It's as the original generation of rock'n'rollers always said decades later, it wasn't experienced as history-in-the-making at the time: at the time it was just how-things-are. But the feel of the period was upbeat: however fitfully or apparently randomly, we were escaping from 1950s drabness, its caution, predominant snobberies, poverty and grime. A boom economy meant that to be young then was to be allowed to be young: you no longer had to go down the mine, or work in that factory, or go to college solely to launch a sensible career along traditional lines. You could be fussy about which job you chose. You could go to university to postpone going to work. You could feel there was all the time in the world—unless they dropped The Bomb—before you condescended to write that great novel, or direct those films. The corollary was a freeing-up of the whole culture.

***No Direction Home* [film, 2005]** For this three and a half hour special (made for the *American Masters* PBS series, and first shown split into two parts on TV in the US and the UK), Dylan allowed MARTIN SCORSESE to draw from his and other people's priceless vaults of previously unseen, unheard material from the key years up to 1966: including, almost unbelievably, footage of the 'JUDAS!' moment from Manchester Free Trade Hall. Dylan also submitted, reportedly in 2000, to a ten-hour interview, given not to Scorsese himself but to Dylan's office manager and resident film producer JEFF ROSEN, as were the further interviews, excerpted in the film, with JOAN BAEZ, ALLEN GINSBERG, MARIA MULDAUR, SUZE ROTOLO, PETE SEEGER, DAVE VAN RONK and many others, all of which are interwoven with great imaginative skill with archive footage of telling contemporaneous events and quintessential items of popular culture from the years in which Robert Zimmerman grew up and became a series of Bob Dylans.

The film cost $4.5 million, of which Dylan took either $1m or $1.5m, and Scorsese took $1m, essentially for the use of his name. The BBC put in $500,000.

Scorsese's input to the film was very part-time; most of the real editing work was done by DAVID TEDESCHI—which is why his name is so prominent when the credits roll. On the other hand Scorsese has spoken thoughtfully in interviews about the challenges of the film: of how to make a narrative out of so many stories and so much material, about how to show footage of the civil rights struggle that people wouldn't already be inured to, and about how to set the scene, especially for younger viewers, as to what Greenwich Village, and the wider world it differed from, was all about.

There are, though, odd key misjudgments. The lack of attention paid to the impact of the blues on Dylan's formative years and on his own creative work is scandalous: we get less than ten seconds of HOWLIN' WOLF and of MUDDY WATERS, no mention of the impact of the pre-war blues greats who stood behind these men and no acknowledgement that a crucial part of what was going on in Dylan's Greenwich Village years was a *blues* revival as well as a (white) folk revival. Dylan himself has never underplayed this; Scorsese and Tedeschi obviously do. Which is odd, granted that they had worked together to produce a film about the blues for the PBS-TV series *The Blues* in 2003.

And though when the film first hits you, its enormous riches of Dylan concert footage leap out and thrill the viewer, as time passes it will surely come to frustrate the Dylan aficionado—just as it does in *Don't Look Back*, *Eat the Document* and *Renaldo & Clara*—that the music footage comes in snatches: that even in a seriously long film, over and over again we're denied complete song performances. Though the DVD release offers the Newcastle 'Like a Rolling Stone' complete, it doesn't offer the full Manchester version, and neither does the movie: even though this is the central drama, the culminating moment of the whole film. In this sense, *No Direction Home* is Dylan for beginners—palatable hors d'oeuvres of Dylan: a large number of them, of every variety, but always small samples and snatched away again too soon.

There is one clear moment where Scorsese's brilliant touch as an editor fails him, thanks to this distrust of the viewer's appetite. Marvellously plain-speaking young people are interviewed coming out of the 1966 British concerts—and this footage by D.A. PENNEBAKER, shot for what turned out to be *Eat the Document*, plunges us back magically into the vanished world of the still-industrial north of England that Dylan was visiting (as if from Mars)—but Scorsese, in general using this footage deftly, cuts from one young man deriding Dylan's harmonica playing to Dylan, on stage, just reaching the start of one of the two transcendental harmonica solos in 'Mr. Tambourine Man' . . . and cuts away from it immediately, where *anyone* attentive would have screened it: especially granted the gift in his lap of the *highly* attentive, heart-stopping close-up scrutiny that the 1966 camera had paid it.

Yet overall *No Direction Home* rises admirably to telling an impossibly large story, and does something remarkable: it tells that story so as to legitimise Dylan as an American golden boy. Untold numbers of people have said for decades now that Bob Dylan has been the most important this, the most influential that, the most significant the other—yet until now, his mysterious greatness has always been in the side tents of public acknowledgement. *No Direction Home* puts him up there with James Dean or Marilyn Monroe as a mainstream American hero. This is new.

[*No Direction Home: Bob Dylan*, dir. Martin Scorsese, BBC/Cappa Productions/Grey Water Park Productions/ Spitfire Pictures/WNET-Channel 13 NY/PBS/Vulcan Productions/Box TV, US, 2005; *No Direction Home: Bob Dylan*, 2-DVD set, Paramount Home Video 0973603 10542, US, 20 Sep (UK, 5 Oct) 2005. Scorsese interview online 16 Oct 2005 at *www.pbs.org/wnet/american masters/dylan/interview.html*.]

Nobel Prize for Literature, Dylan and the See **Ball, Gordon**.

North Country* [film, 2005]** See ***Self Portrait.

'Not Dark Yet' [1997] This sombre song, this dark recording, is surely one of the *Time Out of Mind* album's four great tracks—the others being 'Standing in the Doorway', 'Tryin' to Get to Heaven' and 'Highlands'; and DANIEL LANOIS, it must be said, helps them to be so. There's plenty of artfulness here, but it stands in the service of direct communication. There isn't a moment on any of these four when you think 'Ah, if only Dylan were younger, or still in his prime, he could sing that line beautifully.' He does sing it all beautifully.

Listen to how Dylan sings 'Not Dark Yet' from start to finish. The fit between every element in the song seems perfect, including Dylan's immaculately felicitous vocal. This is surely one of Bob Dylan's first-rate achievements: a song that can hold its own with those of earlier eras, in that it confronts a theme and pioneers a concentrated treatment of it.

If you were to ask for a work that expresses with dignity and fortitude the conviction that only decline lies ahead—decline of your powers and your capacity for openness to the world of colour and feeling—you could hardly ask for a better attempt than this: a better fusion of scrupulously concentrated singing, fittingly contemplative melody and resonant words.

The song's complex sombreness is constructed first by a slow, smouldering musical intro—an intro described by Richard Harrington as establishing 'a soft-spun martial cadence (the muffled drums evoke a funeral cortege)' complete with 'churchy organ'. Nineteen seconds in, presaged by a sketch of itself a few seconds earlier, a falling guitar line comes in, laid across the top of the rest, that is straight out of the musical introduction to the revisit-version of that great early EVERLY BROTHERS song 'I Wonder If I Care as Much': the version included on their influential *Roots* album of 1968.

This invoking of other songs is of course another of the album's most distinctive strengths; but of the many such sub-texts that Dylan calls upon in the course of *Time Out of Mind*, none is more apposite or cleverly placed than this. It is especially beguiling that he should let the thought be whispered 'I wonder if I care as much / As I did before' in the introduction to a song that explores the depths of Dylan's desolation and dares to say 'My sense of humanity has gone down the drain.'

This, the opening of the second verse, is so brave, clear and striking, and so attentively sung, that it combines with the stately pace and the stone steps of the descending chords in such a way as to seem like a sobered revisit to 'Like a Rolling Stone'. I wonder if I care as much. How does it feel?

What makes the words so resonant is that they mix powerful directness with subtle circuitousness. Balancing the clear-sighted confessional bluntness of 'My sense of humanity has gone down the drain' is the subtle complexity of feeling, two lines later, inside the couplet 'She wrote me a letter and she wrote it so kind. / She put down in writing what was in her mind.' Dylan's delivery of these edgy lines rises above guiding us as to their moral weighting. He remains magnificently inscrutable here. Is he recognising that her intention was 'kind' in setting down her feelings in a letter (something the narrator himself does to the 'you' in 'When the Night Comes Falling from the Sky'), or is 'she wrote it so kind' gallows sarcasm? Is there a barb here to the effect that ending a relationship—if that is what she's doing—would be kinder in person than by letter? More interesting, is the matter-of-fact 'She put down in writing what was in her mind' to be taken as honesty or, on principle, extreme foolhardiness? Is he condemning it as rash and dangerous? Should we? Is it an open question? This is writing of subtlety and strength, stripped of all adjectival elaboration. It can bear the weight of the conjecture it prompts from the listener, because it is thought out, and all its ambivalence is plausible.

Working out the balance of probability of meaning in this way is demanded of us at several other points in the song. In the first verse 'Feel like my soul has turned into steel': is this good or bad—toughened or dehumanised? If the latter, the truth of the lament is challenged in the line that follows: 'I've still got the scars . . .' is something only flesh or the psyche can claim.

When the third verse opens with 'Well I been to London and I been to Gay Paree', the effect is the opposite. Here the intensely expressive delivery belies the apparent neutrality of the line. This one is sung with shrivelling mordancy, conjuring a world of bleakness from this ostensible recitation of glamorous experience. It isn't as simple a snarl, on that long-drawn-out 'Gay—— Paree', as to suggest mere seen-it-all ennui—is it? What does it express? Murderous contempt for the vacuousness of the ooh-la-la, can-can Paris? Sullen resentment at having arrived too late to catch any of this except the seedy huckster version, a crumbling Moulin wearing too much Rouge? Despair at being unmoved even by this great chic European capital or by the contemplation of its immense and variegated cultural past?

Dylan's use of the word 'gay' is doubly insistent here—insistent because he holds the word on the note for so long, rolling it around in his mouth like a pretty poor sort of a toffee and then spitting it out into the waiting napkin of 'Paree', and because this is the second time he has used the word in the course of the album. It has been offered earlier, and in a phrase sufficiently surprising to draw attention to it, in the second verse of 'Standing in the Doorway', which finds him strumming on his 'gay guitar'. Does he do it to annoy, because he knows it teases? Yes. And the more purposive gesture that underlies this one is stubborn defiance of its appropriation by the thrash of sexual politics, and more generally as an insistence upon not submitting to the thought-police of political correctness.

This defiance draws on several different weapons. In 'Standing in the Doorway' the first weapon is comedy: 'I'm strummin' on my gay guitar, / Smokin' a cheap cigar' is inherently comic, partly for the joke of conceiving of such a thing as a homosexual guitar, partly by the notion of Dylan playing one and partly because, while retrieving the word 'gay' so as to have it mean 'cheery' again, he sings these cheery lines about pleasure with all the glumness of a great comedian, a Max Wall. In 'Not Dark Yet' the first weapon is licence. 'Gay Paree' is a phrase of unarguable familiarity: what, therefore, can possibly be wrong with using it?

But Dylan's underlying weapon in both these cases is the weapon of song. If he has asserted anything as strongly in the course of creating radical song-forms as in the course of re-stating the strengths of old ones, it is that the language of popular song can embrace an unconstrained vocabulary, drawing at will on the phrases and cadences of the Bible, the blues, folk balladry, high-brow poetry and the street—vocabulary that can be crude *and* sophisticated, simple and complex, modish and ancient. This is what he taught us in the first place, on the pioneering work of the 1960s. This unconstrained, resourceful flexibility is one of the main things he brought to rock'n'roll. On *Time Out of Mind* Dylan is asserting his defiant guardianship of the right—of everybody's right—to use and re-use an old word. Fighting with him he has all the old songs in which the word 'gay' means light-hearted or jolly, just as he has blues lyric poetry behind him when he wants to explore some other phrase that no-one else might dream of deploying inside their contemporary composition. To see this as an especially reactionary foray would be a mistake. The fact that many deeply conservative people are always moaning about the appropriation of the word 'gay' doesn't make Bob Dylan one of them. He isn't moaning; he isn't trying to stop its PC usage. He's just insisting on its revivable capacity to say something else. Were he to succeed in sparking off this renewed usage among the rest of us, he would rescue ELVIS PRESLEY's smouldering and macho song 'Paralyzed' from the unintended high comedy attendant upon its line 'I'm gay every morning, at night I'm still the same.' An uphill task.

In any case, Dylan's citing of 'Gay Paree' in 'Not Dark Yet' is one of those parts of the recording in which the subtleties of what is conveyed by Dylan's undimmed expressiveness of delivery get no clarification from the ostensible neutrality, or undirectingness, of the line itself. As we pass on through the lyrics, we return to writing that offers none of these complex weighings-up but offers instead a bleak straightforwardness—a plain-speaking this is how it is when things inside disintegrate: 'I ain't lookin' for nothin' in anybody's eyes.' 'I was born here and I'll die here against my will.' 'Don't even hear the murmur of a prayer.'

The metaphoric title line itself, of course, is also plain and unmistakeable in its import, even though we hear it first, as it closes the first verse, as a neat extension of the *non*-metaphor that ushers in the song's very first line. The first duty of 'It's not dark yet but it's getting there' is to round off a description of a particular day's end: to observe that dusk is drawing the curtains on a particular hot afternoon. The song's first lines are 'Shadows are falling, and I been here all day / It's too hot to sleep and time is running away.'

Only as that introductory particularity is, as it were, put to bed, should we accept the declared onset of darkness as the closing down of a life or a consciousness. As the line comes around again to conclude the other three verses, this metaphoric meaning is re-emphasised, of course, though whether the singer is looking forward to death as a release from this lingering, crepuscular shutdown, in which every nerve is 'vacant and numb', is again for the listener to try to put his or her finger on.

Whether the line announces an omnipresent consciousness of the comparative imminence of actual death or a consciousness that everything once worth savouring in life is losing its meaning, one of the things on offer here, as on 'Tryin' to Get to Heaven', is the sojourn of defeat. It is never more perfectly rendered than in the quiet achievement, in the song's concluding verse, of the line 'I can't even remember what it was I came here to get away from', on which Dylan achieves some extraordinary equivalence to onomatopoeia, enacting as he sings the line the long weary journeying, physical and emotional, away from something and somewhere. This is perfect singing and inventiveness, and quietly done.

[Bob Dylan: 'Not Dark Yet', Miami, FL, 13–28 Jan 1997. Richard Harrington: 'This Dylan's No Wallflower', *Washington Post*, c.Oct 1997. Everly Brothers: *Roots*, Nashville, summer 1968, Warner Bros. W 1752, US, 1968. Elvis Presley: 'Paralyzed', Hollywood, 2 Sep 1956, 1st issued *Elvis Volume One* EP, RCA Victor EPA-992, NY, 1956; re-issued on the CD box set *The King of Rock'n'Roll: The Complete 50s Masters*, BMG/RCA PD90689(5), 1992.]

nursery rhyme, Dylan's use of, an introduction No-one writing last century seems to link nursery rhyme and fairytale, nor even mention the one while discursing upon the other. Iona and Peter Opie's massive standard work, *The Oxford Dictionary of Nursery Rhymes*, published in 1945, ignores fairytales, though the Opies later published their own book of 'The Classic Fairy Tales'. Bruno Bettelheim's landmark study of fairytales, *The Uses of Enchantment*, ignores nursery rhymes. Vance Randolph, perhaps America's last great southern folksong collector, has written on and collected both fairytales and children's songs, yet separates the one wholly from the other. He collected folktales in the Ozarks, Arkansas, publishing them in *The Devil's Daughter & Other Folk Tales* in 1955; 25 years later much information on the songs and nursery rhymes behind 'Froggie Went a-Courtin'' was included in his *Ozark Folk Songs Vol. 1: British Ballads & Songs*.

This rigid division does not obtain in the stories offered by fairytales and nursery rhymes themselves, nor in the minds of the children they appeal to, nor in earlier collections. Wedderburn's 16th century *The Complaynt of Scotland* includes fairytales and songs, and so do Halliwell's 19th century collections. Nor is there any rigid separation of the two forms in the work by Bob Dylan that draws upon them.

It may even be that each has its roots in an internationally common form, the canto-fable: that is, a work that switches back and forth between verse and prose. The late-19th century collector Joseph Jacobs wrote in 1898 that in addition to the well-known canto-fables of France, the same form can be detected in the Arabian Nights' tales, the folktales of Zanzibar and parts of the Old Testament (as in the stories of Lamech and Balaam), and that in the Grimms' collection, verses occur in nos. 1, 5, 11, 12, 13, 15, 19, 21, 24, 28, 30, 36, 38, 39, 40, 45, 46 and 47: that is, in 36 of the first 50 tales.

The distinction between adult song, nursery rhyme and fairytale is therefore not clear-cut, as at least three conjunctions on Dylan's 1992 album *Good as I Been to You* make clear. 'Yes kind sir I sit and spin', sings Miss Mousie in 'Froggie Went a-Courtin'', describing just what princesses locked in the towers of fairytales must do. In the traditional 'adult' song that bears his name, Arthur McBride is told that he'll 'sup on thin gruel in the morning', a phrase offering the language and food of fairytales. 'Like a diamond in the sky', sings the hard-bitten narrator of 'Little Maggie', describing her eyes in the language of 'Twinkle Twinkle Little Star'.

F.J. CHILD (a happy name, in this context) writes that children's game songs are 'the last stage of many old ballads', and for ROBERT GRAVES 'The best of the older ones are nearer to poetry than the greater part of the *Oxford Book of English Verse*.' A specific example to back up such a claim is reiterated by the drama critic Ivor Brown: 'G.K. Chesterton,' he wrote, 'observed that so simple a line from the nursery as "Over the hills and far away" is one of the most beautiful in all English poetry'. Bob Dylan finally uses this very line—so knowingly yet so delicately—in his wonderful song of 1997, 'Highlands'.

The Opies emphasise that the adult-child distinction is not a clear one when they add that 'Chesterton would have been more exact if he had said "preserved by the nursery" rather than coming 'from the nursery' . . . the farther one goes back into the history of the rhymes, the farther one finds oneself being led from the cot-side. . . . the overwhelming majority . . . were not in the first place composed for children. . . . They are fragments of ballads or of folk songs . . . remnants of ancient custom and ritual . . . and may hold the last echoes of long-forgotten evil. . . . Some are memories of street cry and mummers' play. . . . Others are based on proverbs. . . . They have come out of taverns. . . . They are the legacy of war and rebellion. . . . They have poked fun at religious practices . . . and laughed at the rulers of the day. . . . They were the diversions of the scholarly, the erudite, and the wits.' (In a later period, the limerick form was lifted from a nursery rhyme, 'There Was a Sick Man of Tobago'.)

The age of the extant nursery rhyme varies enormously: many are ancient, but many others arise in the 19th century. 'We can say almost without hesitation that, of those pieces which date from before 1800, the only true nursery rhymes (that is, rhymes composed especially for the nursery) are the rhyming alphabets, the infant amusements (verses which accompany a game), and the lullabies.'

Yet 'At least a quarter, and very likely over half of the rhymes are more than 200 years old. . . . nearly one in four of all the rhymes are believed to have been known while Shakespeare was still a young man.' Lullabies and the counting-out rhymes are millennia old, and the 'infant amusements' can be ancient too. These include 'How Many Miles to Babylon?' and 'Handy Dandy', both of which Dylan draws upon in *Under the Red Sky*.

It is also in the nature of children to join in oral tradition very strongly: which makes them useful curators of folksong. So much so that there are instances of verses that make one chance written appearance and then no other till they reappear intact six or more generations later. A classic example relates to Dylan's work. Of the ballad 'Lord Randal', on which Dylan imposed his brilliant, visionary 'A Hard Rain's a-Gonna Fall', there is a nursery rhyme version—with as many variants as the adult ballad, the best-known in England being 'Where have you been today, Billy, my son?'. Robert Jamieson wrote in *Illustrations of the Northern Antiquities* in 1814 that 'Lord Randal' 'has had the good fortune in every country to get possession of the nursery, a circumstance which, from the enthusiasm and curiosity of young imaginations, and the communicative volubility of little tongues, has insured its preservation.'

Cecil Sharp, rigid old-school folklorist that he was, nonetheless recognised the validity of nursery rhymes as a branch of folksong, collecting such material for his 1923 book *Nursery Songs from the Appalachian Mountains*. The Opies also note that '. . . most English nursery rhymes are better known in the States, and in the case of the older ones, often known in versions nearer the original, than they are in their home country.'

Another reason for an unclear distinction between child and adult song is that in many periods there has been an unclear distinction between child and adult altogether. As the Opies note, 'in the seventeenth and eighteenth centuries children were treated as "grown-ups in miniature". . . . Many parents saw nothing unusual in their children hearing strong language or savouring strong drink. And behaviour was not as abashed as it is today.' Or rather, yesterday.

However, a residue of 'adult' ingredient is far from being what we need to find in order to imbue the nursery rhyme with value or interest: in fact a consideration of the triviality or worth of nursery rhymes must begin by dispelling such assumptions.

First, we were misled in being taught that the characters who populate the nursery rhyme world are all specific historical figures being attacked, lampooned or celebrated in verse—that Little Jack Horner is 'really' the Pope, or King James I, or whoever. This is a widely held belief, to hold which we often experience as a sign of our sophistication in early adolescence. It is quite unfounded. It arises from a clutch of wholly fraudulent 19th century books. There have been times when it has proved happily apt to mock kings, queens and politicians by comparing them to nursery rhyme characters; this continues to be apt, on occasion. But in almost every case ever cited, the nursery rhyme character arises before the real life satire victim is born. Similarly, the Opies do well to write of the Europe-wide ring-game song 'Ring a Ring o' Roses' in these robust terms:

> '. . . in satisfaction of the adult requirement that anything seemingly innocent should have a hidden meaning of exceptional unpleasantness, the game has been tainted by the legend that the song is a relic of the Great Plague of 1665; that the ring of roses was the purpuric sore that betokened the plague, that the posies were the herbs carried as protection against infection, that sneezing . . . was the final fatal symptom of the disease, and that "all fall down" was precisely what happened. This story has obtained such circulation . . . it can itself be said to be epidemic. . . . Those infected with the belief seem unperturbed that no reference to "Ring a Ring o' Roses" appears in Pepys' careful record of hearsay during the long months of the Plague, nor that Defoe's *Journal of the Plague Year* indicates no contemporary concern with either sneezing or redness of spots; nor by the fact that the song can be found, unassociated with sneezing and falling down, in America and all over Europe; nor by the fact that the linking of the song and the plague seems not to pre-date World War II.'

(This myth is kept in circulation in *Bob Dylan's Words: A Critical Dictionary & Commentary* edited by the American academics WISSOLIK & McGRATH, 1994, in a reference to Dylan's using the phrase 'ring around the rosey' in his novel *Tarantula*.)

The real value of nursery rhymes lies not in all this dodgy historical de-coding but in their poetry, their vivacity, their energy of character, story and language, and in the democratic, communal process (the oral tradition) that invents them and keeps them alive. As the Opies note, '. . . these trivial verses have endured where newer and more ambitious compositions have become dated and forgotten.'

As mentioned in discussing the *Under the Red Sky* song 'Cat's in the Well' in relation to HOWLIN' WOLF's blues, nursery rhyme has its value as a venerable yet living, expressive form of folklore—

one with its own internal logic and integrity, celebrating the vibrancy of direct yet magical language. When Dylan comes to use it so thorough-goingly on *Under the Red Sky*, he is exploring one more form of Anglo-American folk culture, and another part of his roots.

As the power and popularity of fairytales also attest, children are often more in touch with their deepest psychic geography than grown-ups are. The child's verse is father to the man's poetry, and it is a superficial mind that automatically dismisses it. Indeed it's hard to understand how anyone who much appreciates Bob Dylan's genius can discount a song as reverberative, warm and true as 'Under the Red Sky' because it is 'kiddie-stuff' any more than they can validate a song as dead and untrue as 'Trust Yourself' or 'Never Gonna Be the Same Again' (both on 1985's *Empire Burlesque*) on grounds of their supposed 'grown-upness'.

Dylan has gone some way to specifying some of this himself. He chose for the inner sleeve to *Shot of Love* this well-known passage from Matthew (11:25): 'I thank thee, O Father, Lord of heaven and earth, because thou hast hidden these things from the wise and prudent, and hast revealed them unto babes.' And even those so hip and intellectual, and so divorced from the world of children that they're intolerant of the nursery rhyme's 'simplicity', might, before responding to *Under the Red Sky* from 1990 heed part of the hip young Dylan's 'Advice to Geraldine on Her Miscellaneous Birthday' from 1964: '. . . if his terms / are old-fashioned an' you've / passed that stage all the more easier / t'get back there.'

The proper dividing line between adult stories and fairytales is at least as blurred as that between grown-up song and nursery rhyme. Bruno Bettelheim finds this unsurprising:

> 'Like Biblical stories and myths, fairy tales were the literature that edified everybody–children and adults alike–for nearly all of man's existence. . . . nothing can be as enriching and satisfying to child and adult alike as the folk fairy tale. . . . Through the centuries (if not millenia) . . . they came to convey at the same time overt and covert meanings–came to speak simultaneously to all levels of the human personality, communicating in a manner which reaches the uneducated mind of the child as well as that of the sophisticated adult. Applying the psychoanalytic model of the human personality, fairy tales carry important messages to the conscious, the preconscious, and the unconscious mind, on whatever level each is functioning at the time. . . . When the unconscious is repressed and its content denied entrance into awareness, then eventually the person's conscious mind will be overwhelmed by derivatives of these unconscious elements, or else he is forced to keep such rigid, compulsive control over them that his personality may become severely crippled. . . . However, the prevalent parental belief is that a child must be diverted from what troubles him most. . . . There is a widespread refusal to let children know that the source of what goes wrong in life is due to our own natures. . . . Instead, we want our children to believe that, inherently, all men are good. But children know that *they* are not always good; and often, even when they are, they would prefer not to be. This contradicts what they are told by their parents, and therefore makes the child a monster in his own eyes. . . . The fairy tale . . . confronts the child squarely with the basic human predicaments. . . . evil is as omnipresent as virtue.'

All this, of course, is very recognisable as Bob Dylan thematic territory.

Bettelheim finds it natural, therefore, that '. . . our common cultural heritage finds expression in fairy tales, [which] . . . also abound in religious motifs; many Biblical stories are of the same nature as fairy tales. Most . . . originated in periods when religion was a most important part of life; thus, they deal, directly or by inference, with religious themes.'

The same connection is made by a different route in Roger Shattuck's description of the 1880s adolescent Erik Satie: '. . . at about the age of sixteen he . . . [became] deeply drawn to the mystic doctrine and ritual of the Catholic faith. In literature he turned to Flaubert and Hans Christian Andersen, an unusual combination of tastes which suggests that he discerned in both writers their veiled yet deep-seated religious preoccupation. It is what makes Flaubert at his most earnest often read like an author of fairy tales, and Andersen like an author of stories not at all for children but for unbelieving adults.'

Bettelheim adds that 'since polarization dominates the child's mind, it also dominates fairy tales. A person is either good or bad, nothing in between.' At the same time, he also perceives that 'The question for the child is not "Do I want to be good?" but "Who do I want to be like?"' Yet he does not lose sight of the fact that the fairytale 'could not have its psychological impact on the child were it not first and foremost a work of art.'

It is, in the end, as works of art and imagination that fairytales and nursery rhymes survive and hold their interest. Nothing could show this more clearly than the way a creative artist as resourceful as Bob Dylan has used them in his own vast body of work.

[Main sources: Bruno Bettelheim, *The Uses Of Enchantment*, London: Thames & Husdon, 1976; Iona & Peter Opie, *Oxford Dictionary of Nursery Rhymes*, Oxford: Oxford University Press, 1945 (revised & reprinted 1951); *The Singing Game*, ditto, 1985 (Peter Opie died 1982; Iona completed the work, a companion volume to their *Children's Games in Street and Playground*, 1969); *The Oxford Nursery Rhyme Book*, ditto, 1955; & Jean Harrowven, *Origins of Rhymes, Songs & Sayings*, London: Kaye & Ward, 1977. The main early collections used by the Opies & mentioned here & in related main texts are: Joseph Ritson, ed., *Gammer Gurton's Garland or The Nursery Parnassus*, 1784; James Orchard Halliwell, *The Nursery Rhymes of England*, 1842-c.1860 & *Popular Rhymes and Nursery Tales*, 1849 & c.1860 (Bettelheim too cites Halliwell); & Alice Bertha Gomme, *The Traditional Games of England, Scotland and Ireland*, 2 vols., 1894–1898; their other sources include the *Gesta Romanorum* (stories & attached moralisations, prob. compiled England, late 13th century, & printed in Latin) & Wedderburn, *The Complaynt of Scotland*, 1549, plus the usual folksong source materials such as the works by F.J. Child.

Roger Shattuck: *The Banquet Years: The Origins of the Avant-Garde in France 1885 to World War I*, New York: Vintage, revised edn., 1968.]

nursery rhyme, Dylan's use of, pre-1990 Dylan has alluded to nursery rhymes and children's song, and used nursery rhyme formulae, all through his career. This includes performing, and referring to, songs by others either specifically written for children or where it is the child's penchant for oral repetition that has preserved parts of ancient folksongs as songs we've come to call 'nursery rhymes'. (Before 1824 'nursery rhymes' were simply called songs.)

As it happens, even the coffee-house in which Dylan made his début, the 10 O'Clock Scholar in Dinkytown, was named after an ancient nursery rhyme (one in print as early as 1784): 'A diller, a dollar / A ten o'clock scholar / What makes you come so soon? / You used to come at ten o'clock / But now you come at noon.' Since 'diller' and 'dollar' are thought to be dialect terms for 'dullard' this suggests that coffee-house owner David Lee held sardonic views about the students who spent their time on his premises instead of studying. It gives an extra fillip of sub-text, too, to Dylan's position then as university drop-out and his launching of a career ever since replete with disparagement of academia.

A traditional ballad Dylan performed at the start of his career, 'Barbara Allen', is linked to a children's circle-game song 'Old Roger', which begins: 'Old Roger is dead and laid in his grave . . . / They planted an apple-tree over his head . . .' In the game, one child plays dead in the middle of the circle until the time comes to jump up and counter-attack the apple-stealer. That it may have been a song before it turned into an acted-out game is suggested partly by the ancientness of these opening lines; as song or drama it shares with 'Barbara Allen' its expression of the ancient belief that the soul can pass into a plant or tree, and the plant or tree can then embody the person. A parallel children's game is called 'Dead Man Arise'. In many versions of 'Cinderella', including the Grimms', the lonely heroine is looked after by a tree that grows out of her mother's grave. In Greek mythology, when Adonis is killed by a wild boar, an anemone grows from his heart. This shared belief is one of the examples of the unkillable 'mystery' of traditional song that Dylan mentions specifically in the 1966 *Playboy* interview, when, giving it his inimitable twist, he refers to 'all these songs about roses growing out of people's brains . . .' It is a strong enough idea that it appeals equally to adults as the resolution of the tragedy of the 'Barbara Allen' story, in which the plants grow from the lovers' breasts and intertwine above their graves, and to children who love the drama of the dead person becoming the tree that can arise and hit back. ('Old Roger' was field-recorded in Glasgow in 1961, not so very long after Dylan was learning 'Barbara Allen'.)

The nursery rhyme 'The cuckoo is a merry bird' was said in 1796 to have already appeared in a children's book that had been published for years, if not for generations. Dylan was performing it, as 'The Cuckoo Is a Pretty Bird' at the Gaslight in October 1962. 'The Bells of Rhymney', an Idris Davies poem set to music by PETE SEEGER, is another song Dylan knew and performed early on: he was taped playing it on guitar back in 1961 and then singing it on the Basement Tapes in 1967 (by this time in a lovely version that seems to suggest Dylan's familiarity with the version THE BYRDS put on their first album, 1965's *Mr. Tambourine Man*). A protest song about industrial misery and exploitation in Wales, its majestic poignancy is achieved by its open re-writing of the children's game-song 'Oranges and Lemons'. (Its audacious couplet 'Even God is uneasy / Say the moist bells of Swansea' is omitted by the Byrds.)

It is a use of children's song Dylan mirrored exactly in his own work when he used 'Who Killed Cock Robin?' to build 'Who Killed Davey Moore?', while he also mirrored 'Oranges and Lemons' in mirroring 'The Bells of Rhymney' in a short, rather fine section of his fourth album's sleevenote poetry '11 Outlined Epitaphs': 'the underground's gone deeper / says the old chimney sweeper / the underground's outa work / sing the bells of New York / the underground's more dangerous / ring the bells of Los Angeles / the underground's gone / cry the bells of San Juan / but where has it gone to / ring the bells of Toronto.'

Dylan was also recorded performing some of WOODY GUTHRIE's childrens's songs in early 1961, including 'Car Car' and 'Howdido'. (There was a bout of interest in children's songs among the folk revival crowd in the early 1960s. A round-up of available LPs published in just one issue of *Sing Out!* in summer 1963 included the following: *Rhythms of Childhood with Ella Jenkins*, Jean Ritchie's *Children's Songs and Games from the Southern Mountains*, Pete Seeger's *Children's Concert at Town Hall*, *American Game and Activity Songs for Children* and *Song and Play-Time*, and the LEADBELLY album *Negro Folk Songs for Young People*. Almost 20 years later, in a speech on stage at the Fox-Warfield Theatre in San Francisco on November 12, 1980, Dylan talks of Leadbelly switching from prison songs to children's songs, using this as a parable about his own switch from street-legal to Christian songs.)

Dylan has been just as unapologetic about resting on nursery rhyme material. 1961's 'Man on the Street' shares its opening line, 'I'll sing you a song, ain't very long', with the nursery rhyme that runs 'I'll sing you a song / Though not very long / Yet I think it's as pretty as any / Put your hand in your purse / You'll never be worse / And give the poor singer a penny'. 1962's 'Ramblin Gamblin Willie' is prefigured by Scotland's 'Rattlin Roarin Willie', and both 'A Hard Rain's a-Gonna Fall' and 'Girl of the North Country' have significant nursery rhyme connections. Not only was the folksong on which the former is based, 'Lord Randal', one preserved in oral tradition by its nursery rhyme version; not only does Dylan's version still have room for nursery rhyme topography like the 'six crooked highways', rebuilt in the footsteps of the crooked man who walked a crooked mile—which Dylan echoes more audibly still in 'Ballad of Hollis Brown', with its 'walked a rugged mile'—but the apocalyptic heart of Dylan's version may itself have been midwifed into existence in some chamber of his imagination by a tradition of ostensibly visionary nursery rhymes. (This one, widely known in the mid-17th century and still popular with London schoolchildren 200 years later, has been preserved in American nursery rhyme collections—and might certainly be called Dylanesque: 'I saw a peacock with a fiery tail / I saw a blazing comet drop down hail / I saw a cloud with ivy circled round / I saw a sturdy oak creep on the ground / I saw a pismire swallow up a whale / I saw a raging sea . . .') It is 'ostensibly' visionary, because it belongs to a corpus of riddle or trick nursery rhymes which rely for their effects on layout and punctuation, the re-ordering of which reduces them to the mundane. As Walter de la Mare commented, 'So may the omission of a few commas effect a wonder of the imagination.'

The entanglement of 'Girl of the North Country' in traditional child-lore is of a different order, and brings together both nursery rhyme and fairytale. Dylan's song is clearly based upon the traditional or broadside song 'Scarborough Fair'—which does not necessarily include the repeated line 'Parsley sage rosemary and thyme' taken up by PAUL SIMON. Dylan's lyric hopes his ex is wrapped up warm against the howling wind; the Scottish borders version also moves on to questions of clothing, yet sticks closer to the key part of a far older story: one which is the basis for both a fairytale set down by the Grimms and the nursery rhyme which (published at least as early as 1784) preserves in its most common and accessible form the folksong cycle that lies behind both Dylan's and Paul Simon's recordings.

The nursery rhyme is 'Can You Make Me a Cambric Shirt?', which, like so many folksongs, has two narrators and comprises their dialogue. The fairytale version concerns a rich king; both involve setting tests for the 'true love', and the core of the story is so strong that in every extant version, in prose and verse, one of the tasks set is always the making of a shirt. This, as F.J. CHILD writes, is because 'A man asking a maid to sew him a shirt is equivalent to asking for her love, and her consent to sew the shirt is equivalent to an acceptance of the suitor'. Thus nursery rhyme and fairytale carry the deepest reverberations of the narrative that Dylan's song picks up on, and predate the folksong variants in which it is an old love who is challenged or, as in 'Girl of the North Country', merely remembered. But Dylan's 1960s song still holds in its invoking of the coat the vestigial traces of the pre-medieval tale: and it is the surviving nursery rhyme that shows the links between the two.

1963's 'Percy's Song' (issued on *Biograph*, 1985) begins and ends in the shadows of nursery rhyme. It opens with 'Bad news, bad news, / Came to me where I sleep', in which the repetition, for dramatic emphasis' sake, of the words 'bad news', echoes the 1690s broadside ballad 'The Unconstant Maiden': 'Bad news is come to town / Bad news is carried / Bad news is come to town / My love is marry'd'—which is itself in parodic echo of the nursery rhyme 'Brave news is come to town / Brave news is carried / Brave news is come to town / Jemmy Dawson's married', while the ending of the Dylan song, the lovely but formulaic 'And the only tune / My guitar could play / Was, "Oh the Cruel Rain / And the Wind" ' leans on a construct from the nursery rhyme 'Tom He Was a Piper's Son', with its repeated 'And all the tune that he could play / Was "Over the hills and far away"'.

The immediate echo behind the opening of 'With God on Our Side'—'Oh my name it ain't nothin' / My age it means less', derives from a Dominic Behan song, but behind that reverberates the many echoes of a children's game-song variously called 'Queen Mary', 'Sweet Dolly', 'Sweet Mary' and having many a relation with no name at all. The game, dating back centuries, is an Ur ring game—a simple, fast dancing game with one child in the middle of a ring—and the common factor in the lyric is that the song always starts, as Dylan's does, with the formula 'My name is X, my age is Y'. Hence 'My name is Queen Mary, my age is sixteen, / My father's a farmer on yonder green', or 'My name it is Jean, and my age is fifteen; / My father's a farmer, he lives on the plain', or 'My name is sweet Dolly, my age twenty three, / My father's a farmer over the Red Sea.' The Dylan song not only twists the formula of the opening line but shares with these far-flung children's versions the same rhyming pattern—each verse rhymes lines one with two and lines three with four—and shares the time signature of the tune, which is in 6/8.

Boots of Spanish leather were celebrated in song as the finest—as objects of desire—in nursery rhyme and singing-game in the 19th century. In *Sons and Lovers*, published in 1913 and set in Nottinghamshire, D.H. Lawrence has Mrs. Morel hearing children sing this in the street as the day is getting dark: 'My shoes are made of Spanish leather / My socks are made of silk / I wear a ring on every finger / I wash myself in milk', and variants collected earlier include 'Our boots are made of Spanish' and 'My boots are made of Spanish leather'.

That so much meaning is encapsulated as Dylan settles for these expensive boots at the end of the dialogue with his departed lover proves it one of the most deft, economical lines of writing in his whole repertoire. Yet it carries more than the young man's hiss of embittered rebuke. Underneath this literal pay-off, other reverberations rumble. If, like Mrs. Morel, we can hear the children singing the same words in the background, this adds an extra poignancy to the way the hurt scorn of Dylan's title-line both confesses the 'rejected' lover's immaturity, and tacitly acknowledges that the other has grown away from him. It's a further irony that the lines the children sing express aspiration towards such a grandiose, unreal idea of adulthood.

That there has not been, traditionally, any clear distinction between the two states is made very clear by the other song invoked in the background by Dylan's title 'Boots of Spanish Leather'—the omni-present 'Gypsy Davey' or 'Blackjack Davey', in which many versions bring us either boots or gloves of Spanish leather. Both, of course, carry similar strong sexual import, as is emphasised in almost every variant of the narrative. The ballad's heroine, at the same time as dealing in this symbolism of sex and power—and in doing so accepting responsibility for the momentous decision to abandon her baby—is a girl of only 15 herself. Yet 15 was the optimum age for a girl to marry in the Middle Ages, the period to which this ballad harks back. It is the marriageable age in fairytales too, including 'Cinderella', in which the shoe holds an equally strong sex-symbol rôle as the object of desire around which true love is measured by testing who fits, physically. (Here lies another example of fairytale and nursery rhyme coinciding—in the shared sexual significance of the shoe in 'Cinderella' and in the rhyme 'Cock a Doodle Do!': 'Cock a doodle do! / My dame has lost her shoe; / My master's lost his fiddle stick / And they don't know what to do!')

In his inimitable, gently off-kilter way, Bob Dylan sets 'Cinderella' humming in the background of another song of his a couple of years later, as he finishes '4th Time Around' (another love-triangle song) with these confusing signals of sexual symbolism: 'And when I was through' (which is to say, through with *her*: the other woman) 'I filled up my shoe / And brought it to you. / And you, you took me in . . . / And I, I never took much, / I never asked for your crutch, / Now don't ask for mine.' Similarly, 'Boots of Spanish Leather', especially the loaded potency of its ending, would be less complex if it did not offer all these reverberations from children's song, fairytale and an ancient ballad with a child-woman heroine.

1963's 'Seven Curses', as its title implies and its dénouement makes clear, deals in spell-like invocations of numbers modelled on the stuff of fairytales, while in 'Motorpsycho Nitemare', when the psychotic farmer asks 'What do doctors / Know about farms, pray tell?' the narrator's enigmatic response picks up on the fairytale milieu underlying that 'pray tell', so that he answers 'I was born / At the bottom of a wishing well.'

The last verse of 1964's 'Ballad in Plain D'—'Ah, my friends from the prison, they ask unto me / "How good, how good does it feel to be free?" / And I answer them most mysteriously / "Are birds free from the chains of the skyway?"'—echoes the nursery rhyme 'The Man in The Wilderness' plainly and simply (sufficiently that you can sing this nursery rhyme verse to his tune): 'The man in the wilderness askéd of me / How many strawberries grew in the sea? / I answered him, as I thought good, / "As many red herrings as grow in the wood"', and in 'Restless Farewell', the regular way that each verse begins—'Oh all the money that in my whole life I did spend'; 'Oh ev'ry girl that ever I've touched', 'Oh ev'ry foe that ever I faced', and so on—is modelled so closely upon a nursery rhyme (one collected by Halliwell in 1844, and which preserves the opening lines of a far older song) that as with the example above, you can envisage Dylan singing the nursery rhyme lines to his 'Restless Farewell' melody: 'Of all the gay birds that e'er I did see / The owl is the fairest by far to me / For all day long she sits on a tree / And when the night comes, away flies she.'

Dylan didn't appear to know, when asked to supply a rhyme for the word 'orange' at a 1965 press-conference, that the question was based on a nursery rhyme that expresses (and answers) much the same challenge: 'What is the rhyme for porringer? / The king he had a daughter fair / And he gave the prince of Orange her', but he was alive to much of the nursery rhyme and fairytale world at that time: alive to its innate surreality and its capacity for holding fundamental truths, as well as being quick to revivify its characters and bend them to his own requirements.

'Desolation Row' creates a world of mermaids and poisoning and of reciting the alphabet, of figures from the circus and from melodramas of fairytale proportions (doesn't 'The Phantom of the Opera' rewrite 'Beauty and the Beast'?) and children's folk heroes (Einstein wants to be Robin Hood). Cinderella is the cool, knowing star of a whole verse: a heroine identified with the narrator, one of the sane figures in the song's phantasmagoric pageant, one of those who has a hold on reality, because she lives *on* Desolation Row. In the prose-poem 'Alternatives to College' (1965) Dylan mentions, or rather tags other people as, 'little bo peep' and 'simple simon' and refers twice to 'crippled mermaid', an allusion to the Hans Christian Andersen fairytale 'The Little Mermaid', in which the heroine's fishtail is swapped, on account of love for a prince, for legs too painful to walk on. In *Tarantula*, written 1965–66, Dylan alludes to the nursery rhymes 'Jack and Jill went up the hill' (with 'would you like to buy a pail? jack,'), 'Ring a Ring O'Roses' ('ring around the rosey') and 'The butcher, the baker, the candle-stick maker' (the unaltered 'candle stick maker').

In 'Visions of Johanna' the ladies play a version of the children's game blind man's buff (nicely punned into 'blind man's bluff') and we meet Little Boy Blue's cousin 'little boy lost'. Another of Dylan's white-heat hip period songs is called 'Just Like Tom Thumb's Blues' (in the 18th century, nursery rhymes were called 'Tommy Thumb's songs'). 1969's 'Country Pie' parallels this identification of song narrator with nursery rhyme hero in the line 'Little Jack Horner's got nothing on me', and the same song's 'Saddle me up a big white goose / Tie me on 'er and turn me loose' is in effect the song of Old Mother Goose: 'Old Mother Goose / When she wanted to wander / Would ride through the air / On a very fine gander.' And after the goose has laid the golden egg and this has been lost and recovered, the rhyme ends: 'And Old Mother Goose / The goose saddled soon / And mounting its back / Flew up to the moon.' (Nursery rhymes are still called 'Mother Goose's songs' in the US.)

And then there are the Basement Tapes, which often hover knowingly around the nursery (Dylan says so explicitly of 'Quinn the Eskimo', telling interviewer CAMERON CROWE that 'I guess it was some kind of a nursery rhyme'), while 'See Ya Later Alligator' mutating into 'See Ya Later ALLEN GINSBERG' is an excellent example, caught on tape, of the spontaneous wordplay process common to the playground. Likewise ROY KELLY writes (in a long, excellent essay, 'Bunch of Basement Noise', 1992) that 'Apple Suckling Tree' is 'nonsense lyrically . . . What, after all, is an apple suckling tree?' and that the song seems 'like a twisted kind of nursery rhyme with a floppy rock beat, a children's chant with a knowing, surrealist nod'—perhaps forgetting that plenty of nursery rhymes are of 'a twisted kind' anyway, and often have knowing, 'surreal' qualities of their own.

Kelly's main point is that 'musically it sounds . . . like Bob and THE BAND were plugging into some subterranean source, a common flow of American music.' This is close to reiterating what GREIL MARCUS wrote in the sleevenotes to the teasing sampler of the same 1967 material issued as the album *The Basement Tapes* in 1975: '. . . they seem to leap out of a kaleidoscope of American music no less immediate for its venerability. Just below the surface . . . are the strange adventures and poker-face insanities chronicled in such standards as 'Froggy Went a Courtin'' . . . 'Cock Robin' . . . or a song called 'I Wish I Was a Mole in the Ground' . . . one side of *The Basement Tapes* casts the shadow of such things and in turn is shadowed by them.'

The name of the music-publishing company Dylan formed in the early 1970s, Ram's Horn Music, recalls at least two different nursery rhymes: 'Can You Make Me a Cambric Shirt?', discussed above, and another quite separate nursery rhyme with many local British and American place-name variants, of which this is one example: 'Little lad, little lad, where were you born? / Far off in Lancashire under a thorn / Where they sup buttermilk with a ram's horn.' (Not that these nursery rhymes are the main associations with the name 'Ram's Horn' for Dylan: it has its religious significance too. The Shofah, or Shophar, is the ceremonial ram's horn sounded daily in the synagogue during the month of Elul and repeatedly on Rosh Hoshanah. It was used by the ancient Israelites as a warning or summons. When Joshua fit the battle of Jericho and the walls came tumbling down, the trumpets were, as the song says, ram's horns. Then of course there's the MEMPHIS MINNIE song that's a special favourite of Bob Dylan's, the well-known 'Me and My Shofar'.)

The centre of that tantalising 1973 song 'Nobody 'Cept You' (an outtake from *Planet Waves*, released first on the *Bootleg Series Vols. 1–3* in 1991) concerns childhood play and dance and song: 'Used to play in the cemetery / Dance and sing and run when I was a child'; and in adding that '. . . it never seemed strange' to be playing, singing and dancing in 'That place where the bones of life are piled', Dylan is not making himself out to be individually interesting or quirky but speaking for all children. Graveyard play among children and young adults is so ancient a custom as to merge back into the ring-dances of antiquity. Such dancing and singing—called 'caroling', and not necessarily in a circle, but as likely by the early Middle Ages to be in a sort of wild, snaking procession (we see a sort of caroling, with Dylan holding a trumpet, in *Renaldo & Clara*)—grew to be both a main activity on feast days and the bane of the church authorities. The church always opposed secular dancing—the ecclesiastical councils tried for over a thousand years to ban it—not only because such dancing was pagan and sexy (like the ring-games of the black children in 1930s–40s Mississippi described by ALAN LOMAX in *The Land Where the Blues Began*) but because of the widespread habit of using graveyards to dance in. Etienne de Bourbon, made Inquisitor in about 1235, fulminated against 'those most sacrilegious persons who tread down the bodies of holy Christian folk in the churchyards . . .'

The ghostly presence hovers here of the ancient legend of 'The Devil at the Dance', in which a young girl disobeys her parents by attending such a graveyard dance. The Devil makes off with her. In one version they fly off leaving hoofprints on the rocks by the sea; in another version, to which Bob Dylan might be referring in 'Idiot Wind', they take off through the roof of a burning church: 'The priest wore black on the seventh day / And sat stone-faced while the building burned.'

On the 1976 album *Desire*, 'Sara' has Dylan recollecting wistfully a time when his own children were playing games and being told one of the Grimms' fairytales: 'playin' leapfrog and hearin' about Snow White'. You could add that in the line 'I left town at dawn, with Marcel and St. John . . .' on 1978's 'Where Are You Tonight (Journey Thru Dark Heat)?' there lingers vestigially the idea of setting out on one's journey protected by the apostles, which is articulated in one of the two main nursery rhymes called 'Matthew Mark Luke and John' (the lovely Scottish version of which then runs 'Hau the horse till I loup on / Hau it fast an hau it sure / Till I get owre the misty muir').

You might feel too that the chorus of 1986's 'Brownsville Girl', rhyming 'Brownsville girl' with 'Brownsville curl', is asking to be a reminder of the nursery rhyme attributed to Longfellow—'There was a little girl and she had a little curl / Right in the middle of her forehead'—and that in the mid-1980s song 'When the Night Comes Falling from the Sky', Dylan's line 'For the love of a lousy buck I've watched them die' offers an inflation-linked twist on the nursery rhyme confession 'I love sixpence better than my life.' Or you may not. But there is nothing tenuous about the (mis)quoting of the nursery rhyme 'The rose is red, the violet blue' in the dark last verse of 'Where Teardrops Fall' on 1989's *Oh Mercy*.

[Bob Dylan: 'Car Car', East Orange, NJ, Feb–Mar 1961, Minneapolis, MN, May 1961 & at the Gaslight, Sep 1961; 'Howdido', Minneapolis, May 1961; 'The Bells of Rhymney', 2nd MacKenzies Tape, NY, c.4 Dec 1961, unissued, & West Saugerties/Woodstock, NY, Jun–Aug 1967, unissued. Press-conference, San Francisco, 3 Dec 1965, telecast KQED-TV.

Idris Davies' poem 'The Bells of Rhymney', collected in Dylan Thomas, ed., *So Early One Morning*, a selection of Welsh poetry (in English), 1954. (Davies was born in Rhymney, Wales, in 1905, went down the mines at 14 and died of cancer 1953, the same year Dylan Thomas died of alcoholic poisoning.) Pete Seeger: 'The Bells of Rhymney', NY, 27 Dec 1957, *Pete Seeger & Sonny Terry at Carnegie Hall*, Folkways FA 2412, NY, 1958, & 'The Bells of Rhymney', Newport, RI, Jul 1959, *Folk Festival at Newport (Vol. 1)*, Vanguard VRS-9062 & VSD-2053, NY, 1960. The song was published in *Sing Out!* vol.8, no.2, NY, 1958 (& included in *Reprints from Sing Out! Vol. 3*, New York: Sing Out! c.1962).

The Byrds: 'The Bells of Rhymney', Hollywood, 14 Apr 1965, *Mr. Tambourine Man*, Columbia, US (CBS 62571, UK), 1965. *Rhythms of Childhood with Ella Jenkins, nia*, Folkways FC 7653, NY, *nia*; Jean Ritchie: *Children's Songs and Games from the Southern Mountains, nia*, Folkways FC 754, NY, *nia*; Pete Seeger: *Children's Concert at Town Hall*, NY, *nia*, Columbia CS 8747 (mono CL 1947), NY, *nia*, *American Game and Activity Songs for Children, nia*, Folkways FC 7003 (10" LP), NY, *nia* and *Song and Play-Time, nia*, Folkways FC 7526, NY, *nia*, & Leadbelly: *Negro Folk Songs for Young People*, Folkways FC 7533, NY, c.1962. *Sing Out!* vol.13, no.3, NY, summer 1963.

Walter de la Mare, *Come Hither*, 1923; quoted by Peter & Iona Opie (for details of their work & sources, see endnotes to **nursery rhyme, Dylan's use of, an introduction**). An Ur ring game song is quoted in Wolfgang Schmeltzel, *Quodlibet*, 1544. 'Queen Mary' published in the *Journal of the English Folk Dance and Song Society*, Jun 1915 (but a variant still heard in Harrogate, UK, 1959); 'Sweet Dolly' heard in Soho, London, 1907; unnamed 3rd song quoted collected (by T.G. Stevenson) in *Scottish Ballads and Songs*, James Maidment, Edinburgh, 1859, but these lines and six others from same song also collected from a Newfoundland fisherman in 1929, published in *Ballads and Sea Songs of Newfoundland*, Elisabeth Greenleaf & Grace Mansfield, 1933, reprinted 1968.]

nursery rhyme on *Under the Red Sky* It is unsurprising that it's the middle-aged Dylan who creates an album like *Under the Red Sky*, which steps so merrily and resourcefully into the fairytale and nursery rhyme arena: unafraid to use its 'simple' language straightfowardly but far more often releasing it into new shapes and scenes and resonance from his own intelligent imagination. This isn't a case of throwing in a few obvious references to, and quotes from, nursery rhymes as well and widely known as 'Mary Had a Little Lamb' and 'Sing a Song of Sixpence', as he does when he gives 'Jack Frost' a co-producer's credit for the album. Bob Dylan is either inwardly familiar with, or has researched energetically into, a huge number of nursery rhymes and children's game-songs. He seems to have poked into as many corner-cupboards of the genre as he has in the pre-war acoustic blues. The evidence is scattered like a paper-chase all across the lyrics of *Under the Red Sky*.

Both the most innocuous and the most striking phrases Bob Dylan sings here, the most modestly slipped-in and the most 'Dylanesque', very often prove verbatim quotations from nursery rhymes and game-songs most of us don't know. These run from 'there was a man who had no eyes' to 'thank you for my tea' and from 'a stick in his hand' to 'eat off his head'. Other allusions prove non-verbatim only because Dylan has deftly reversed them, as with 'that soft silky skin' and 'the barn is full of the bull'.

This would be all well and good, but not especially valuable, if it were no more than a game, though the element of play involved–even the suspicion that it might have started out as a game on Dylan's part–is attractive, and of course accords with the spirit of the genre itself. What makes *Under the Red Sky* more satisfying than that is that Dylan goes beyond *knowing* a great deal of nursery rhyme. He respects its capacity to be numinous, and he gives the poet within him free rein to explore it.

The power and poetry of nursery rhyme language is often put to the service of trickery, the solving of which has a strongly bathetic effect, as the poetic evaporates into the mundane. One of the things Dylan does so marvellously on this album is to reoccupy the innate poetry, freeing it from its servitude to cheap trickery, letting it fly off as it might in directions suggested by Dylan's own feeling for it.

This is most evident on 'Handy Dandy', one of the album's best songs–see separate entry–but even 'Unbelievable' raids two different tricksy nursery rhymes, one a riddle and the other a hand game (like handy dandy). Dylan jettisons the 'puzzles' and sets free the characters. The riddle is 'There Was a Man Who Had No Eyes', which begins with that line and then continues: 'He went abroad to view the skies / He saw a tree with apples on it / He took no apples off, yet left no apples on it'–the solution is that he has one eye, the tree has two apples and he takes one off–while 'Lady, Lady in the Land' is 'an infant amusement' or playground game, one of an almost infinite number of variants stretching back probably for millennia and listed in print at least as early as 1534 (by Rabelais), the object of which is explained by the rhyme itself: 'Lady, Lady in the land / Can you bear a tickly hand? / If you laugh or if you smile / You'll ne'er be lady in the land.'

Dylan marries these two up, so that 'Once there was a man who had no eyes / Every lady in the land told him lies'. The best small thing he does here is to take the second line from the riddle about the man with no eyes–'He went abroad to view the skies' and rewrite it. As we know, the man in the riddle actually has one eye, so he *can* go out and 'view the skies'; the man in Dylan's song really has no eyes, and Dylan evokes his greater helplessness in the re-write, in which 'He stood beneath the silver skies': to which Dylan adds a rewritten fragment from yet another nursery rhyme, changing Little Bo Peep's empathetic pain felt for her regained but wounded sheep–'She found them indeed but it made her heart bleed / For they'd left their tails behind them'–into the pain the man with no eyes feels for his wounded self: 'He stood beneath the silver skies / And his heart began to bleed.'

Dylan's 'You go north and you go south / Just like bait in the fish's mouth', from earlier in the song, is a twisted twisting of another game, 'King William', a kissing game in which the person who is 'it' must 'Choose to the east and choose to the west / Choose the one that you love best'. (This is strikingly similar to 'Little Sally Walker', the game played by young black girls in the Mississippi Delta as witnessed by ALAN LOMAX in the 1940s, and about which he writes in his expansive 1993 book *The Land Where the Blues Began*.)

'Wiggle Wiggle', a title about as alluring as 'Woogie Boogie' or 'Emotionally Yours', incorporates fleeting moments from several different variants of a similar singing game called 'Kentucky' that, while retaining some mention of the early 1920s dance the Shimmy, inexplicably 'swept the country [Britain] with the speed of a pop song in the mid-1960s', and enjoyed similar transatlantic success, according to the nusery rhyme and children's game songs experts Iona and Peter Opie. This singing game, stripped down melodically almost to a one-note chant, includes the lines 'Rumble to the bottom, rumble to the top . . . / Twisty twisty twisty, twisty all around . . . / Oh shake it, baby shake it, shake it if you can', followed by the splendid 'Shake it like a milkshake and drink it like a man.' This might indicate that the SAM COOKE song 'Shake', from which 'Wiggle Wiggle' has taken the line 'Shakin' like a bowl of soup', itself owes something to this piece of communal juvenilia. Then there's a Hank Ballard & the Midnighters single from 1954, 'Sexy Ways', that seems to embrace the singing-game song and prefigure 'Wiggle Wiggle' rather more: 'Wiggle wiggle wiggle wiggle / I just love your sexy ways / Upside down, all around / Any old way, just pound pound pound.'

(Dylan's exact title first belonged to an obscure 'commercial' pop-rock single by unfamous vocal group the Accents, dating from 1958, itself a tired and nondescript copy of the pop classic 'Little Bitty Pretty One' and stressing the primacy of womanly wiggling over beauty and fine clothes–'so wiggle wiggle wiggle for me'. Written by group member Robert Draper Jr., the record scraped up to no.51 in the US hot 100.)

These resemblances don't stop 'Wiggle Wiggle' being, like 'Unbelievable', off-the-shelf rockism. *Under the Red Sky* co-producer DON WAS claimed in an interview that 'Wiggle Wiggle' is Dylan writing 'Tutti Frutti'. This is stoned dithyrambling. The Dylan song is retro, stale, guarded *and* uninventive where Little Richard's invented something radical, fresh, exciting and open. Nor is 'Wiggle Wiggle' much improved by its nod towards one of several nursery rhymes called 'Little Robin Redbreast', who 'Sat upon a rail / Niddle noddle went his head / Wiggle waggle went his tail', which survives from older, ruder versions.

Dylan also gives a nod to his own earlier 'children's song', 'Man Gave Names to All the Animals'. Where that song ends by forbearing to name the last animal as the snake, 'Wiggle Wiggle', having a snake at the end too, hisses the word out loud, its final line being 'Wiggle like a big fat sssnake.'

'2 x 2', with its refreshingy unDylanish, post-Beatleish instrumental intro, is also perfectly at home on *Under the Red Sky* in being a simple counting-song (of the sort Dylan parodies in 'I Shall Be Free No. 10'). Its very title is a clear echo of the well-known children's song 'The Animals Went in Two By Two' which is in turn the story of Noah's ark, told in Genesis (6:19 to 7:9), a connection Dylan re-articulates in the darker couplet 'Two by two they step into the ark / Two by two they step in the dark.' The most flaccid line in the song is 'Six by six, they were playing for tricks'; the best is the funny, truthful 'Nine by nine they drank the wine / Ten by ten, they drank it again'. The song is inevitably reminiscent too of the nursery rhyme counting-song 'This Old Man', which Dylan went on to record the year after *Under the Red Sky*, for an album in support of the Pediatric AIDS Foundation.

That patchy song '10,000 Men' also contains two lines taken straight from the poetry of nursery rhyme, the one as quiet and nondescript as the other is grotesque and bizarre—though only in the context Dylan gives it. The quiet-as-anonymous 'thank you for my tea' at the end—'Baby, thank you for my tea / It's really so sweet of you to be so nice to me'—may not be much of a line in itself but it's a quietly clever fusion of blues and nursery rhyme worlds. There's a common-stock blues couplet, found for instance in Dylan's old friend HENRY THOMAS' beautiful, affecting 'Don't Ease Me In' (recorded at the same session as his 'Fishing Blues'), in which 'She brings me coffee and she brings me tea / She brings me everything but the jailhouse key' (the same first line and an almost identical matching line can also be found for example on Sam Collins' 1927 'The Jail House Blues'), so that for the blues afficionado 'Thank you for my tea' is a recognisably apt remark to hear addressed to the visitor in a blues song—especially one about 10,000 men who are 'just out of jail', sung by a narrator who has women standing at his window and sweeping his room—while in a 'Little Robin Redbreast' nursery rhyme that is apparently quite separate from the one Dylan almost quotes from in 'Wiggle Wiggle', we find another visitor and the 'Dylan line' verbatim: 'Little Robin Redbreast / Came to visit me / This is what he whistled / "Thank you for my tea."'

In strong contrast, Dylan imports into an earlier part of his song a phrase that is also straight from a nursery rhyme—within which it is explicable, mild and unexceptional but becomes, plucked out of context by Dylan and released like a wild card into the realms of free play, so bizarre that people commenting on the album tend to pick it out as one of Bob Dylan's truly weirdest moments. The phrase is 'eat off his head', and here it is in its nursery rhyme context: 'A long-tail'd pig / Or a short-tail'd pig / Or a pig without any tail / A boar-pig or a sow-pig / Or a pig with a curly tail / Take hold of the tail and eat off his head / And then you'll be sure the pig hog is dead.'

This nursery rhyme is actually a street-vendor's cry from the 18th century, when sellers with trays of little sweetmeat pigs were common. The clinching salesman's couplet at the end there is designed to charm, not frighten, the children. When Tom Tom the piper's son stole a pig and away he run, it was this sort of pig he stole, not a real one. Dylan steals it too—he takes it and runs it right inside the madness of a luridly jealous mind: 'Hey! Who could your lover be? / Let me eat off his head so you can really see.'

It's a reversal as neat as it is bizarre to shift eating off his head so you can 'be sure the pig hog is dead' to eating off his head 'so you can really see' who he is underneath, which, as it were, turns on its head the most basic notion of how to tell one person from another. (Dylan makes a different reversal from the same nursery rhyme decades earlier, in *Tarantula*, in which 'the pig jumps on him [the good samaritan] & starts eating his face'.) Why someone with 10,000 women in his room should be jealous of his visitor's lover is as unexplained as everything else in this disjunctive narrative.

Inasmuch as the women are 'Spilling my buttermilk, sweeping it up with a broom' they are also brushing the nursery rhyme world, in which 'Milkman, milkman, where have you been? / In Buttermilk Channel up to my chin / I spilt my milk and I spoilt my clothes.' That last line is almost replicated, in its phrasing and its rhythmic thrust, in the *Oh Mercy* song 'Where Teardrops Fall': 'I've torn my clothes and I've drained the cup', while that 'Buttermilk Channel' might remind us too of 'the Buttermilk Hills', whose silence sounds like 'a voice cryin' "Daddy"' in 'Caribbean Wind', an earlier 1980s Dylan song. A woman sweeping a room with a broom also occurs in the long nursery rhyme 'Two Little Kittens', in which 'The old woman seized her sweeping broom / And swept the two kittens right out of the room.' These brooms occur in other Bob Dylan songs too, as it happens: songs before and after *Under the Red Sky*. In the Basement Tapes song 'Please Mrs. Henry' (1967) the singer declares himself 'ready for the broom' and in 'Million Miles', on *Time Out of Mind* (1997) a metaphoric broom is implicit in 'Gonna find me a janitor to sweep me off my feet'.

And so too 'Cat's in the Well' (mentioned as a song of barnyard apocalypse in the entry on **Howlin' Wolf**). More substantially than '10,000 Men', and in amongst its end-of-the-world material, this eloquent song uses nursery rhyme aplenty, and a little fairytale too, starting with the obvious founding of Dylan's title upon the well-known 'Ding dong bell, pussy's in the well' and/or on a more obscure nursery rhyme featuring a more exactly equivalent feline: 'Dingle dingle doosey / The cat's in the well / The dog's away to Bellingen / To buy the bairn a bell.'

Wells themselves, of course, for the modern western urban listener, are objects of another age. 'Jesus Met the Woman at the Well' evokes one of the ages they represent; in the blues, they are resonant of a life of hand-drawn water in the southern pre-war rural backwoods, and they can evoke equally the life of medieval Europe in folksong *and* the magic wishing-well that is an essential prop in fairytale.

This is not the only moment in 'Cat's in the Well' where nursery rhyme and blues lyric poetry fuse into one. 'Bumpity Bump' is the title of a Joe Turner-style early record by Smiley Lewis, a vaguely farmyardish piece of nonsense in which instead of cat and wolf 'the dog jumped the rabbit' (the chant 'hop, skip and jump' exactly replaces Turner's own 'Flip, Flop and Fly' on the song of that name) and as for the dog, 'his heart went bumpity bump.' But Dylan's horse going bumpety-bump has a much earlier and more direct ancestry, and one in which, as in the Dylan song, there is father-daughter difficulty, a wild creature invading the domestic scene and much falling down. This is the nursery rhyme 'A Farmer Went Trotting': 'A farmer went trotting upon his grey mare / Bumpety bumpety bump / With his daughter behind him so rosy and fair / Lumpety lumpety lump / A raven cried "Croak!" and they all tumbled down / Bumpety bumpety bump / The mare broke her knees and the farmer his crown / Lumpety lumpety lump.'

Meanwhile in 'Cat's in the Well' Back Alley Sally is doing the 'American Jump'—yet another game with a rhyme to go with it, and one in which the theme of falling down recurs: 'American jump, American jump / One—two—three! / Under the water, under the sea / Catching fishes for my tea / Dead or alive?' The game, like the farmer's grey mare, holds together child and grown-up. The grown-up holds the child's hands and jumps her up and down till the word 'three', at which there's an extra-big jump so that the child's legs twist around the grown-up's waist; while saying 'under the water' the child is held but falls slowly backwards; when asked 'Dead or alive?' if the child answers 'alive' she's pulled up again, if 'dead' is allowed to fall down and if 'around the world' is whirled round and round.

This is an appealing fantasy-version of how we face life, death and the world around us: a version in which, improbably, we choose our own fate and determine our own future. It's an ironic reference on Dylan's part, in a song which, like so much of his recent work, seems preoccupied with less rosy views of how we face life, death and the world around us. It's a further irony that Back Alley Sally—an appellation that could equally suit a child or an adult—appears to be playing this game by herself.

Like 'Cat's in the Well', many nursery rhymes are set around farmyards, and it is no surprise that a number of their dramas take place in barns. There's the English 'There was a little boy went into a barn' and the American 'Jemmy Jed went into a shed', and there's the muted drama of this better-known nursery rhyme, in which well-being within the ordered domain of the farmyard is threatened not by the unpredictable swooping down of wolf or raven but by that regular enemy, the winter, against which the barn offers some (limited) protection: 'The north wind shall blow / And we shall have snow / And what will poor robin do then, poor thing? / He'll sit in a barn / And keep himself warm / And hide his head under his wing, poor thing.' Before winter comes, the typical 'picture-book farm' scene, which Dylan's song parallels, is as laid out for us in this nursery rhyme: 'The cock's on the woodpile a-blowing his horn / The bull's in the barn a-threshing of corn / The maids in the meadows are making of hay / The ducks in the river are swimming away.' (Is the widespread popularity of such formulaic verses perhaps the explanation for the term 'a cock and bull story'? Were these verses in such common currency that their opening lines recognisably ushered in a particular kind of fiction: that is, a children's story in which things are idealised and simplistic?) In any case, Dylan parallels the nursery rhyme's 'a-blowing' and 'a-threshing' with his own 'a-sticking' as well as assembling his parallel menagerie, with cat, wolf, lady, horse, bull, servant and dogs in place of cock, bull, maids and ducks.

The line about the bull in the barn has proved popular: it is retained in a 1740 manuscript from Wiltshire published in the British journal *Folk-lore* in 1901, while a chant collected by Alice Bertha Gomme in the 1890s in her *Traditional Games of England, Scotland and Ireland* is even called 'The Bull's in the Barn'. Dylan's expressing this in reverse, in that lovely line 'The barn is full o' the bull', is one of his funny, graphic touches, not only punning playfully—his reversal of words letting the contemporary Americanism of 'you're so full of bull[shit]' chime alongside the old nursery rhyme language—but more arrestingly conjuring up such a swift comic picture, yet drawing on our sense of the bull's fundamental character: its bulging muscularity, its hugeness, its bull-at-a-gate, bull-in-a-china-shop unwillingness to be contained (its *bullishness*), and the equally vivid picture of the story-book or comic-strip barn's propensity to be so full that it strains and creaks and bulges.

Dylan is not finished with nursery rhyme and story there. The 'Dylanesque' couplet 'The cat's in the well and Papa is reading the news / His hair's falling out and all of his daughters need shoes' brings together a handful of such antecedents. It is a North African belief that ancient stories—myths and fairytales—that revolve around the breaking of a taboo (such as the opening of a forbidden door) should never be told out loud in the daytime. To do so (to be heard 'reading the news') is to risk having your hair fall out. 'The Shoes That Were Danced to Pieces', sometimes called 'The Twelve Dancing Princesses', is a Brothers Grimm fairytale in which the king is tearing his hair out because despite locking them up in their room every night, every morning all of his daughters need new shoes, having danced the old ones to pieces. The pairing of 'news' and 'shoes' occurs in a rhyme for the paring of finger-nails ('Cut them on Wednesday, you cut them for news / Cut them on Thursday, a new pair of shoes') while one of the 11 verses of 'Old Mother Hubbard' goes 'She went to the cobbler's to buy him some shoes / But when she came back he was reading the news.'

Shoes and alleys figure too in the album's purposive, dignified and beautifully performed title-song—see separate entry. With great originality it pleaches the poetry of nursery rhyme and folklore, fairytale and the Bible into a 'simple', memorable whole. It is the song that sets the tone and establishes the territory for the better-intentioned, serious-minded, parts of the album.

There is, in addition to its unique and creative use of nursery rhyme, some fine, fresh writing and some sumptuous vocal performance, on *Under the Red Sky*: an album that offers, in particular, three wholly worthy additions to Bob Dylan's body of work in 'Under the Red Sky', 'Handy Dandy' and 'Cat's in the Well'. This last, on top of its already-catalogued virtues, contains one of the best lines of writing on the album, the deft, sharp stab of the second line of this couplet: '. . . the gentle lady is asleep / . . . silence is a-stickin' her deep.' This image, vivid and surprising, sudden and steely, in which silence is evoked as a pinioning visitation, a compressive staunch, seems to draw its blade of intensity from traditional ballads like 'Love Henry' without losing the good-humoured patoiserie of contemporary American street-talk.

Any listener ever exhilarated by what Philip Larkin called that 'cawing, derisive voice' and BRUCE SPRINGSTEEN called 'the toughest voice I had ever heard . . . somehow simultaneously young and adult', and drawn into the churning worlds Dylan has evoked—any such listener to *Under the Red Sky* is going to hear within its nursery rhymes and fairytale landscapes many echoing shouts of joy and rejuvenation all the way from Highway 61 and the Basement. The distinctive achievement of this album and no other, is the tugging dynamics that come from combining *this* voice with *that* sensibility.

In all, alongside the innumerable quotes from and reminders of blues, R&B and rock'n'roll songs and the many allusions to biblical text, *Under the Red Sky* (a very short album) makes direct raids on 32 nursery rhymes and game-songs, and offers demonstrable correspondence with three fairytales and a further 15 nursery rhymes, not counting variants.

The first review Dylan's work ever attracted, back in the *New York Times* in September 1961, alluded to his Chaplinesque quality. It is a quality that phases of ennui, bitterness and portentousness have occasionally suggested has vanished; but here it is again, rocking back on its heels, nimble and light. When your heels are nimble and light is, in any case, the best time to be serious, as the language of rhyme and song for children reminds us. Dylan uses this nursery rhyme and fairytale with an imaginative adult intelligence, to re-walk the corridors of the childhood psyche, to liberate some vivid imagery from under the bushel of superficial riddle, and to give his songs the same underpinning in eternal verities that he gets from folk and blues. 'Strap yourself to a tree with roots', he sang, so long ago that at the time those for whom he embodied the integrity of restlessness thought he was joking. He wasn't, of course.

[Bob Dylan: 'This Old Man', Malibu, CA, early 1991, issued on the Various Artists album *Disney for Children*, Disney 60616-2, LA, 1991. Sam Cooke: 'Shake', *nia*, RCA Victor 47-8486, NY (RCA 1436, UK), 1965. Hank Ballard & the Midnighters: 'Sexy Ways', Cincinnati, 24 Apr 1954, Federal 12185, Cincinnati, 1954. The Accents: 'Wiggle Wiggle', NY, 1958, Brunswick 55100, US (Coral Q 72351, UK), 1958; CD-reissued *The Golden Age of American Rock'n'Roll Volume 5*, Ace CDCHD 600, London, 1995. Henry Thomas: 'Don't Ease Me In', Chicago, 13 Jun 1928 & Sam Collins: 'The Jailhouse Blues', Richmond, IN, or Chicago, c.25 Apr 1927; *Really! The Country Blues*, Origin Jazz Library OJL-2, NY, c.1961. Smiley Lewis (with the Dave Bartholomew band): 'Bumpity Bump', New Orleans, Mar 1955, Imperial 5356, US, 1955.

For details re Iona & Peter Opie's work, and their sources, see the endnotes to **nursery rhyme, Dylan's use of, an introduction**. Don Was, LA, 15 Oct 1990, published *The Telegraph* no.37, UK, winter 1990. Philip Larkin, in 'Jazz Review', *Daily Telegraph*, London, 10 Nov 1965, quoted in E. Thomson & D. Gutman, eds., *The Dylan Companion*, London: Macmillan, 1990. Bruce Springsteen: speech at Dylan's induction into the so-called Rock and Roll Hall of Fame, NY, 20 Jan 1988. Robert Shelton: 'Bob Dylan: A Distinctive Folk Song Stylist: 20 Year Old Singer is Bright New Face at Gerde's Club', *New York Times*, 29 Sep 1961.]

O

O'Brien, Brendan [1960 -] Brendan O'Brien was born in Atlanta, Georgia, on June 30, 1960. His production credits include the 2005 album by JAKOB DYLAN's band the Wallflowers, *Rebel, Sweetheart*.

He has also worked with BRUCE SPRINGSTEEN, first on the album *The Rising*, released in 2002 and again on the 2005 album *Devils & Dust*. Springsteen says he tried recording the latter's title track as a rock song and as an acoustic ballad, but that it took producer O'Brien to bridge the gap. 'Brendan found something that put it in the middle,' Springsteen testified, 'where it picks up a little instrumental beef as it goes.' The same goes for the rest of the album, reportedly, on which O'Brien also plays bass; Springsteen thanks O'Brien for helping to rescue it from being another *Ghost of Tom Joad* (1995), giving *Devils & Dust* 'a more fleshed-out approach'.

If true, he has more to thank O'Brien for than Dylan has. All he did for 'Dignity' was ruin it. This outtake from the *Oh Mercy* sessions, suiting our times, is quick-on-the-ear, in effect quick-on-the-eye, and dancingly alert. It rollicks along, as 'on a rolling river': not cheap rockism 'n' roaring but real lithe Bob Dylan. It would have made a terrific opening track on *Oh Mercy*. Or rather, it would if they'd left it alone. When the unfinished outtake circulated among collectors, it sounded *great*. You could play it not only to non-Dylan-fans but even to people who thought they actively disliked him and *they'd* say it was great, and how come Dylan didn't release it, it would be a hit, you could just hear it on the radio . . . and you'd say, well, that's par for the course.

All it needed was an instrumental solo in the middle. It had an emphatic, compulsive rhythm that everybody loved, Dylan's vocals were strong and high in the mix, and his piano was Dylanesquely spiffing. One solo was *all* it needed . . . In *Chronicles Volume One*, Dylan acknowledges all this and more, as he describes the attempts to re-record it at the album sessions, bringing in Rockin' Dopsie and His Cajun Band:

> 'Once we started trying to capture it, the song seemed to get caught in a stranglehold. All the chugging rhythms began imprisoning the lyrics. . . . Every performance was stealing more energy. We recorded it a lot, varying the tempos and even the keys, but it was like being cast into sudden hell. The demo with just me and Willie [Green, drums] and Brian [Stoltz, guitar] had sounded effortless and it flowed smooth. Certainly, as DANNY [LANOIS] said, it didn't sound finished, but what recording ever does?'

So in the end, Dylan left it off the album, took it away from Daniel Lanois and in late 1994 gave it to that month's guru, Brendan O'Brien, then best-known as producer of Pearl Jam: and the first thing Brendan did was abolish its stand-out rhythm. Then he put all these silly 'modern' noises on. Then he pushed Dylan down in the mix so you hardly notice any piano at all and so that this long, immensely entertaining lyric, delivered with great panache by a Bob Dylan firing on something like all cylinders, is no longer accessible or ready to jump straight out of the radio at you but instead needs painful attending-to. O'Brien even made some small edits to Dylan's vocal, in his absence. Sometimes you wonder what it's gonna take . . .

That wasn't the last of it, either. Once they'd made sure it couldn't possibly be a hit, they released it on *Greatest Hits Volume 3*, in 1994—shortly before putting out another version, the limp live version on the *MTV Unplugged™* album, in 1995. There, with Brendan O'Brien playing an organ that wouldn't have worked at all if it *had* been 'unplugged', *and* getting 'very special thanks' on the sleevenotes, the song emerges little better than the ruined studio version.

Three years later, the Brendan O'Brien version was dumped in favour of a mix of the original recording; weirdly, this was issued first on a compilation album for a TV series, 'Touched By an Angel', having apparently been heard fleetingly in the 100th episode of this inconsequential goo. After its inclusion on *Touched By an Angel: The Album*, this more dignified 'Dignity' was issued on the 2000 Dylan compilation *The Best of Bob Dylan Vol. 2*.

'Dignity' has never yet become a song Dylan cares to perform often in concert, though it isn't a rarity in his repertoire either; and when he does perform it, he's perfectly capable of turning it into dreary jobs-worthiness, like any other 'fast' song that he doesn't bother to know his own lyric for. Yet when he performs it feeling fully alive and happy with it as a vehicle of wide-ranging expressiveness, as he did in London in 1995, then it comes into its own again, leaving Brendan O'Brien light-years behind and re-attaining accessible eloquence, excitement and, yes, dignity.

(For more on the song itself, see also the entry **'Dignity'**.)

[Bob Dylan: 'Dignity', New Orleans, prob. 13 Mar 1989. Dylan's comments on the song, *Chronicles Volume One*, pp.169, 189–90 & 191. The album sleeve credits for the *Greatest Hits Vol. 3* mix of 'Dignity' are: Bob Dylan, vocals & piano; Brendan O'Brien, guitar, bass & keyboards; plus Steve Gorman on drums & Rick Taylor on banjo; production credit goes to O'Brien and Daniel Lanois (in that order). *Touched By an Angel: The Album*, 550 Music/Sony Music Soundtrax

BK 68971, US (Epic/550 Music/Sony Music Soundtrax 491828 2 (France/NL), 1998. Bob Dylan: 'Dignity', live in Brixton, London, 29 Mar 1995. 1st live performance was Bielefeld, Germany, 16 Mar 1995; after 10 performances that year, it wasn't rebooted till 2000.

Springsteen quotes seen online 15 Nov 2005 at *www.brucespringsteen.net/news.]*

Ochs, Phil [1940 - 1976] Philip David Ochs (older brother of the photographer and photo-archive owner Michael Ochs) was born December 19, 1940 in El Paso, Texas, lived in a number of places while growing up (including, for six months, in Scotland), became a fine classical clarinet player, graduated from the Staunton Military Academy, Virginia (high school), in 1958, majored in journalism at Kent State University in Ohio (later the scene of the slaughter of four unarmed students by the National Guard on May 4, 1970) and there discovered WOODY GUTHRIE's balladry and realised that he could use music to express his own ideas. He arrived in Greenwich Village in 1962. Always a political radical—such that his attendance at Kent State seemed almost prescient—he came to, and continued to write, 'protest songs' long after Bob Dylan, who once told him: 'You're not a folksinger, you're a journalist.'

Ochs' first album was the musically minimal *All The News That's Fit to Sing* (1964), and it was followed by *I Ain't Marching Anymore* (1965), which includes the dreadful 'Draft Dodger Rag' (sample line: 'I'm only eighteen, I got a ruptured spleen') but whose title track would become one of his signature songs, along with 'There But for Fortune', which became a hit for JOAN BAEZ. This was featured first, along with his much-covered and lovely ballad 'Changes', on Ochs' 1966 album *Phil Ochs in Concert*, an album of all-new material generally considered the high point of his recorded work, though given a close run by the following year's studio album *Pleasures of the Harbor*, recorded in California and orchestrated mostly by an outside arranger whose forté was working with Liza Minelli. This, the first album from a new record deal (A&M in place of Elektra), demonstrated Ochs' hopeless unsaleability: outselling his earlier records, it reached no.168 in the *Billboard* charts. Nonetheless, dated as it is, and created in response to hearing *Sgt. Pepper's Lonely Hearts Club Band* and *Pet Sounds*, it is a poignant demonstration of Ochs' raw honesty and his determination to experiment.

By this point, most of his folkie contemporaries had become stars, in many cases major stars, and Ochs found it difficult to continue being so under-regarded and unrewarded himself. He and Bob Dylan had always had an uneasy relationship, characterised by being ferociously acerbic with each other. ('You ought to find a new line of work,' Dylan once told him, and another time asked: 'Why don't you just become a stand-up comic?') The imbalance in this vitriolic discourse between the two came from Dylan's stratospheric rise in the world, exacerbated by the way that Dylan looked more and more beautiful and cool as time went by, while Ochs gradually exchanged the grace of youth for the pudginess of the drinker.

Early on, Dylan was nervous of Ochs' apparently burgeoning talent; later, Ochs was determinedly, heroically unsyncophantic about Dylan's mid-1960s success, famously telling him that compared to 'Positively 4th Street' Dylan's new single 'Can You Please Crawl Out Your Window?' wasn't particularly good—a verdict delivered while driving around with Dylan in a taxi, which Dylan, enraged, stopped and threw Ochs out of. Silly boys.

If Ochs and Dylan ever performed together in the Village, there is no record of it. They are known to have appeared together only once, at the Friends of Chile Benefit Concert that Ochs had organised at Madison Square Garden, New York, on May 4, 1974, at which Dylan sang 'Spanish Is the Loving Tongue' and 'Blowin' in the Wind' with Ochs, DAVE VAN RONK, ARLO GUTHRIE, Melanie, PETE SEEGER and Larry Estridge behind him.

Ochs was far gone into schizophrenia and manic depression by this time. He had made a run of further albums in the period 1968–70—*Tape from California*, *Rehearsals for Retirement*, *Phil Ochs' Greatest Hits* (a sarcastically titled album of new material) and *Gunfight at Carnegie Hall*, which remained unreleased until 1974. In 1975, Ochs seemed to become swallowed up by a violent alter ego he named John Butler Train, and combined with his heavy drinking and a long-felt despair over the value of his own work, this damaging development left Ochs with few friends and little hope for the future. He desperately wanted to be included on Dylan's first Rolling Thunder Revue but Dylan wouldn't have him.

Their last encounter may have been at a birthday party for Gerde's Folk City owner Mike Porco on October 23, 1975, at which many of those being assembled for the Revue performed in front of HOWARD ALK's cameras. Late on, Ochs did a short set, which he concluded with a version of Dylan's largely ignored masterpiece 'Lay Down Your Weary Tune'. ROBERT SHELTON reported: 'Everyone at Dylan's table stood gaping at Phil' but 'Dylan praised Phil when he finished.'

Train insisted in an interview that he had murdered Phil Ochs—'he needed to be gotten rid of'—and on April 9, 1976, Ochs hanged himself in his sister Sonny's home in Far Rockaway, New York (also leaving a wife and small daughter). He was 35.

There have been two posthumous biographies: Marc Eliot's *Death of a Rebel* in 1979 and Michael Schumacher's *There But for Fortune: The Life of Phil Ochs* in 1996. Ochs' own works of prose include *The War Is Over*, a collections of articles published in 1968; the short essay 'The Art of Bob Dylan's "Hattie Carroll"', published in *Broadside* back in

1964; and his 'Open Letter from Phil Ochs to IRWIN SILBER, Paul Wolfe and Joseph E. Levine', again published in *Broadside* and again defending Dylan's art, in January 1965. He was acute too about the Dylan he saw live in White Plains, New York, on February 5, 1966, remarking: 'Dylan is like LSD on stage.'

Unlike many of his peers, Ochs himself has yet to be 'rediscovered'; thus lack of recognition the first time around remains compounded by neglect today. He isn't even mentioned in either Dylan's 2004 memoir *Chronicles Volume One* or in the great historic sweep of the *No Direction Home* film of 2005. It's almost adding insult to injury to note that he *has* been memorialised by Billy Bragg (the singing Neil Kinnock) in his song 'I Dreamed I Saw Phil Ochs Last Night'.

[Phil Ochs: *All the News That's Fit to Sing*, Elektra EKL-269, US, 1964; *I Ain't Marching Anymore*, Elektra EKL-287 & EKL-7287, US, 1965; *In Concert*, Elektra EKS-7310(S), US, 1966; *Pleasures of the Harbor*, A&M SP4133, US, 1967; *Tape from California*, A&M SP4148, US, 1968; *Rehearsals for Retirement*, A&M SP4181(S), US, 1969; *Phil Ochs' Greatest Hits*, A&M SP3125, US, 1970; *Gunfight at Carnegie Hall*, A&M, SP-9010, Canada, 1974.

Phil Ochs, *The War Is Over*, New York: Collier Books, 1968; 'The Art of Bob Dylan's "Hattie Carroll"', *Broadside* no. 48, NY, 20 Jul 1964, p.2; 'An Open Letter from Phil Ochs to Irwin Silber, Paul Wolfe and Joseph E. Levine', *Broadside* no. 54, 20 Jan 1965. Billy Bragg: 'I Dreamed I Saw Phil Ochs Last Night', *nia, Internationale, nia*.

Sources include Sandy Carter's fine piece 'The Legacy of Phil Ochs', seen online 5 Jan 2006 at *www.zmag.org/zmag/articles/nov97carter.htm*; the discography at *www.warr.org/ochs.html* & the bibliography at *www.cs.pdx.edu/~trent/ochs/books.html*, both online ditto; the anonymous profile on the Cosmic Baseball website seen online at *www.cs.pdx.edu/~trent/ochs/books.html* 14 Nov 2005 & the piece 'Phil Ochs 1940–1976', online ditto at *http://folkfanlcb89.tripod.com/id53.html*. Marc Eliot, *Death of a Rebel*, Garden City, NY: Anchor Press, 1979. Michael Schumacher, *There But for Fortune: The Life of Phil Ochs*, New York: Hyperion Press, 1996. Robert Shelton, *No Direction Home: The Life and Music of Bob Dylan*, London: Penguin 1987 edn., pp. 451–52.]

Odetta [1930 -] Odetta Holmes Felious Gordon was born on the last day of 1930, in Birmingham, Alabama, but she grew up from the age of six in LA with her mother and a sister, took singing lessons at 13 studying music at City College and became an actress, teacher and songwriter but more significantly a singer, at first hovering between musical shows and folksong but soon plumping for the folk. She had appeared in *Finian's Rainbow* through summer 1949, during which she first encountered the blues in the form of SONNY TERRY; in 1950 she was in San Francisco playing in *Guys and Dolls*, and there discovered the local folk scene. Her first concert, in San Francisco in 1952, co-produced by folksinger Rolf Kahn and the 18-year-old LYNN CASTNER (at whose Minneapolis apartment Dylan would first hear WOODY GUTHRIE's records) had people queuing round the block; her New York début, achieved only by taking time off from her work as an LA housekeeper, was in 1953 at the Blue Angel. Then came a short-lived duo, Odetta & Larry, yielding her début album, *The Tin Angel* (the name of a Philadelphia club), recorded in 1953 and '54, on which it's clear that the competent Larry Mohr, on banjo and vocals, was utterly superfluous. Less was Mohr, she must have decided. In 1956 came the solo *Odetta Sings Ballads & Blues*, and the next year *At the Gate of Horn*, recorded not live at the Chicago club but in the studio, and with BILL LEE on bass.

She was encouraged through the 1950s by many in the music business, especially HARRY BELAFONTE, on whose 1959 TV Special she appeared to great effect. This can be readily imagined by anyone who saw the vintage footage of Odetta performing 'Water Boy' shown within SCORSESE's *No Direction Home* in 2005, on which the stark, ferocious power of her field-holler delivery and explosive use of the sound-box on her guitar were matched only by her terrifying teeth. This all leapt out at the viewer across a 50-year divide to explain instantaneously why Bob Dylan had found her so revelatory and important to his early entrancement with folk—and when it was new, such a performance must have exploded into Eisenhower America's living rooms as the nightmare embodiment of the nation's oppressed ex-slaves rising up as if to start a slaughter of revenge.

But Odetta was no field-hand, as made clear when, appearing at Belafonte's Carnegie Hall concert of May 1960—billed above Miriam Makeba and the Chad Mitchell Trio—she followed a medley of 'I've Been Driving on Bald Mountain' and 'Water Boy' with a double act with Belafonte on that tiresome old LEADBELLY song 'There's a Hole in the Bucket', on which the timing and delivery of her spoken lines is that of a professional actress. To track back through her 1950s recordings is to recognise that despite the marvellous ferocity of 'Water Boy', the great majority are understandably invaded by the well-spoken gentility and concert-platform formality of musicianship that were prevalent in 1950s folk music, despite the way that both the blues and rock'n'roll had demonstrated the artistic glory to be had from abolishing these aspirations.

In Minneapolis at the start of the 1960s, JAHANARA ROMNEY (aka Bonnie Beecher) told *The Telegraph* 30 years later, 'Odetta was coming to town . . . so me and Cynthia Fisher were plotting as to how we could get Dylan to meet Odetta and play for her. . . . And in fact he did meet her. . . . Cynthia Fisher came running over to my house . . . saying

"She said that Dylan had real talent and he can make it!"'

This thrilled Dylan, keeping his determination fully charged, and encouraging his inclusion of Odetta repertoire items in his own. Years later, Dylan would specify that he had devoured *Odetta Sings Ballads and Blues*, her 1956 album: 'I learned all the songs on that record,' he said: '. . . "Mule Skinner", "Jack of Diamonds", "Water Boy", " 'Buked and Scorned".' He may also have learnt 'Devilish Mary', 'Ain't No More Cane' and 'No More Auction Block' from early Odetta recordings.

In 1960 she appeared at the NEWPORT FOLK FESTIVAL, made a flurry of albums, including *Odetta at Carnegie Hall*, and was an acceptable guest on Ed Sullivan's TV show 'Toast of the Town' that Christmas Day—but was criticised for 1962's *Odetta and the Blues* because it was 'closer to jazz than folk', as *Time* put it. This LP featured a combo of jazz musicians, including pianist Dick Wellstood, who that year also played on a couple of *The Freewheelin' Bob Dylan* sessions. Switching labels again she made two albums for the heavyweight RCA (Belafonte's label), the second of which, *Odetta Sings Folk Songs*, in 1963, made the top 75 album charts. It included her 'Blowin' in the Wind'—and by 1965 she had recorded *Odetta Sings Dylan*.

BRUCE LANGHORNE plays guitar and tambourine, and the tracks are 'Baby, I'm in the Mood for You', 'Long Ago, Far Away', 'Don't Think Twice, It's All Right', 'Tomorrow Is a Long Time', 'Masters of War', 'Walkin' Down the Line', 'The Times They Are a-Changing', 'With God on Our Side', 'Long Time Gone' and 'Mr. Tambourine Man': a mix of the obvious with the far from obvious, revealing that she had paid Dylan's work, including unreleased material, close attention.

Odetta has also written songs, appeared in films—including Tony Richardson's film of the William Faulkner novel *Sanctuary* in 1961 and, uncredited, in Paul Newman's extravagantly titled *The Effects of Gamma Rays on Man-in-the-Moon Marigolds* (1972). In late September 2005 she was one of the more effective performers at the London Royal Albert Hall's 'Talking Bob Dylan Blues: A Tribute Concert', no longer subduing the audience with 'Water Boy' but by taking 'Mr. Tambourine Man' at a punishingly funereal pace.

[Odetta: *The Tin Angel*, US, 1954; *Odetta Sings Ballads and Blues*, Tradition TLP1010, US, 1956; *Odetta at the Gate of Horn*, Tradition TLP1025, 1957; *Odetta at Carnegie Hall*, Amadeo Vanguard AVRS9027, US, 1960; *Odetta and the Blues*, Riverside RLP-9417, US, 1962; *Odetta Sings Folk Songs*, RCA LSP2643, 1963; *Odetta Sings Dylan*, RCA LSP3324, 1965. 'Talking Bob Dylan Blues: A Tribute Concert', London, 26 Sep 2005. Harry Belafonte: *Returns to Carnegie Hall*, NY, 2 May, 1960, RCA LOC-6007 (mono) & LSO-6007, US, 1962. *Time*, US, 23 Nov 1962, quoted from *www.bobdylanroots.com/odetta.html*; special thanks to Åke Holm's amazing discography at *www.akh.se/odetta/index.htm*; both seen online 10 Feb 2006.]

'Off the Top of My Head' [1965] See 'Horseman & the Twist-up Gang'.

***Oh Mercy* [1989]** A confident staunching of the flow, with an album that is accessible, authoritative and substantial. Attentively written, vocally distinctive, musically warm and produced with uncompromising professionalism, this cohesive whole is the nearest thing there is to a great Bob Dylan album of the 1980s. DANIEL LANOIS' determination to wrest such an album out of Dylan, and the plangent panache his production spreads across a variable collection of material, made for something overrated at the time (understandably, after what had gone before); but it remains a singular, welcome item in Dylan's huge back-catalogue. An honourable minor work, well-received by the public and reviewers, and marred only by the feeling that Dylan has one eye on that public approbation: that he is asking if this is the sort of album people want from him. It's all just a little too careful, guarded and stiff to be great Bob Dylan. Standout tracks: 'Where Teardrops Fall', 'Ring Them Bells', 'Most of the Time', 'What Was It You Wanted?' Tracks recorded but not selected: 'Dignity' and 'Series of Dreams'.

The making of the album is the subject of the fourth of the five main sections in Dylan's vivid memoirs, *Chronicles Volume One*, including thoughts on how the album turned out and on what he might have done differently if making the album again.

[Recorded New Orleans, Mar–Apr, 1989; released US as Columbia OC 45281 (LP) & CK 45281 (CD), and UK as CBS 465800 2 (CD), 12 or 22 Sep 1989. *Chronicles Volume One*, pp.143–221.]

Oldham, Spooner [1943 -] Dewey Lindon Oldham was born in Alabama on June 14, 1943. He rose to prominence as a keyboards session player, first at Rick Hall's Fame studios and then at the Muscle Shoals Sound studio in Sheffield, Alabama. He also formed a songwriting partnership with Dan Penn, yielding hits by Percy Sledge, Clarence Carter and James & Bobby Purify. Like almost every other session musician with any sort of 'name', in the madly extravagant music-biz milieu of the early 1970s, he got to make a disappointing solo album—in his case 1972's *Pot Luck*, on the Family Enterprises label (and with player support from Emory Gordy Jr., among others), on which Oldham sang and played organ and piano. The songs were mostly self-penned and fitted his profile as one of the creators of that particular 'soul country' R&B sound associated with Muscle Shoals. Ten years later, but in Japan only, came a truly solo album,

Spare Change, on which he revisited some of the same material.

As a session man, his 1960s track record begins with Wilson Pickett and takes in Aretha Franklin, Etta James, the Purifys and Bobby Gross—and possibly ARTHUR ALEXANDER. (He claims to have played on the classic 'You Better Move On' but Alexander's biographer Richard Younger is not so sure.) In the 1970s he played on albums by RITA COOLIDGE, Duane Allman, ARLO GUTHRIE, MARIA MULDAUR, ROGER McGUINN, THE EVERLY BROTHERS, the Flying Burrito Brothers, NEIL YOUNG and more. Since then he has been on records by many of the same again, plus works by JOHN PRINE, J.J. Cale and definitely Arthur Alexander.

Spooner Oldham's unofficial website (detail below) claims that his first connection with Bob Dylan occurred at the sessions from which Columbia Records created the 1973 release *Dylan* and while no Dylan discographers list him, all concede that the session information for these dates is far from complete. Thus he may indeed have participated in the Nashville sessions of April 24–26, 1969, or even those in New York City in June 1970.

More certainly he was recruited to play keyboards (as was TERRY YOUNG) behind Dylan on the first gospel tour (San Francisco, November 1 to Tucson, December 9, 1979); on 'Saturday Night Live' that October 20; on the second gospel tour (Portland, Oregon, January 11 to Charleston, West Virginia, February 9, 1980); at the sessions for the *Saved* album back on Spooner's home turf at Muscle Shoals Sound Studio from February 11 to 15, 1980; at the Grammy Awards TV show that February 27; and on the third gospel tour (Toronto, April 17 through to Dayton, Ohio, May 21, 1980). He did not play on the subsequent, blazing tour of November–December 1980, in which secular material was re-introduced amid the evangelising songs. In total he played at 79 Bob Dylan concerts.

Now looking thin and frail, resembling in profile a cartoon poondog, Spooner Oldham lives around Rogersville, in north-west Alabama: a tiny town on the road east to Huntsville, on the other side of the big Wilson Lake from Muscle Shoals.

[Spooner Oldham: *Pot Luck*, Family Enterprises FPS-2703, US, 1972; *Spare Change*, AVI AVI-6120, Japan, 1982. *www.geocities.jp/hideki_wtnb/spooneroldham.html* gives discographical & other detail.]

'Omie Wise' [song] See **'Naomi Wise'**.

omissions Time has naturally prevented the provision of an entry on many of those who have connected with Dylan in one way or another outside of those in categories deliberately excluded (background business people; album-cover designers; most photographers, journalists and editors; people whose only connection is having covered Dylan songs). Some of those who might have received an entry are rounded up here instead. No offence has been intended by this secondary listing:

Jerry Allison & Norman Petty, who with BUDDY HOLLY wrote 'That'll Be the Day'.

Joe Allison & Milton Estes, writers of '20/20 Vision', a nifty rock song Dylan has performed only once (more's the pity): in Austin, Texas, on October 25, 1991.

Emry Arthur (c.1900–1966), the rural Kentuckian who first popularised 'Man of Constant Sorrow' on record—a song included on Dylan's début album and deployed to immense effect in the film *O Brother, Where Art Thou?* nearly 40 years later. Emry Arthur first recorded it in Chicago on January 18, 1928 for Vocalion and re-recorded it for Paramount in Grafton, Wisconsin, around September 1931 (on which it may be that the banjo is by Dock Boggs). Not only did he sign to Paramount as a recording artist but as a labourer in their factory.

Charles Aznavour, the French megastar chanteur, songwriter and film actor who wrote 'Les Bon Moments', which Dylan sang once in concert, on November 1, 1998 in New York City, in its English language version, 'The Times We've Known'; Aznavour is also the star of one of Dylan's favourite films, *Shoot the Pianist* (see **film dialogue in Dylan's lyrics**), and gets a namecheck in '11 Outlined Epitaphs' on the back sleeve of *The Times They Are a-Changin'*. In a 1987 interview in *Rolling Stone*, Dylan said: 'I like Charles Aznavour a lot. I saw him in 60-something at Carnegie Hall, and he just blew my brains out.'

Bill Monroe & the Blue Grass Boys, an influence on everyone remotely interested in country music, and an acknowledged influence on Dylan. But see **Acuff, Roy**. Monroe and Bessie Lee Maudlin co-wrote 'A Voice from on High', which Dylan performed as a concert opener six times in 2002, starting on August 15 in Hamburg, New York. Monroe also wrote 'Blue Moon of Kentucky', performed by Dylan in a version that segued out of 'I Walk the Line' as an encore duet with PAUL SIMON during 11 of their co-headlined concerts of summer 1999.

Bumps Blackwell, producer of LITTLE RICHARD's great 1950s records, dropped in on one of Dylan's *Shot of Love* sessions in April 1981 and gets a co-producer credit for the album's title track.

Otis Blackwell, composer of 'Don't Be Cruel' but also of 'Fever', which Dylan performed in San Francisco on November 22, 1980, in Seattle eight nights later and at Clarkston, Michigan, on June 12, 1981.

The Blue Sky Boys made a significant recording of the traditional 'Mary of the Wild Moor' (aka 'Mary from the Wild Moor') on February 5, 1940 for Victor Records; it's a song Dylan sang very beautifully at 16 concerts in late 1980 through to June 1981.

Michael Bolton, the multi-platinum-selling embodiment of plastic 1980s man with whom Dylan co-wrote 'Steel Bars', a song so numbingly mediocre that you can't imagine what Dylan contributed, and which probably earned him more than the whole of *Oh Mercy*; the recording, on Bolton's 1990 album *Time Love & Tenderness*, perfectly demonstrates how the death-grip of the music industry sounds.

Boudleaux Bryant, composer of 'Take Me as I Am (Or Let Me Go)', recorded by Dylan on *Self Portrait*, and co-writer with his wife *Felice* of many EVERLY BROTHERS hits: among them 'Take a Message to Mary', also on *Self Portrait*.

Richard Bullock & Richard Whiting, composers of 'When Did You Leave Heaven?' (see **Broonzy, Big Bill**), which Dylan included on *Down in the Groove* and performed live seven times in 1989, once in 1990 and twice in 1991.

Paul Cable, an early Dylan discographer, author of *Bob Dylan: His Unreleased Recordings*, UK: Scorpion/Dark Star, 1978. *Sammy Cahn & Jimmy Van Heusen* were responsible for the awful 'All My Tomorrows', performed by FRANK SINATRA in the 1959 film *Hole in the Head* and which Dylan performed very badly just once, in Clarkston, Michigan, on June 30, 1986. *Leroy Carr*, one of the great pre-war blues artists, a pianist partnered by guitarist Scrapper Blackwell, and writer of the classic 'In the Evening (When the Sun Goes Down)', recorded beautifully by the 20-year-old Bob Dylan in Minneapolis on December 22, 1961 (see **Romney, Jahanara**). *Carlene Carter*, on whose version of Dylan's song 'Trust Yourself', recorded in LA in early 1993, Dylan contributed backing vocals. *Ry Cooder*, who co-wrote (with John Hiatt and Jim Dickinson) the song 'Across the Borderline', which Dylan performed in concert in 1986 with TOM PETTY & THE HEARTBREAKERS and revisited at the Guitar Legends Festival in Seville on October 17, 1991 backed by RICHARD THOMPSON on guitar. *Sam Coslow & Will Grosz*, composers of 'Tomorrow Night', the LONNIE JOHNSON million-seller from 1948, recorded by ELVIS PRESLEY in 1954 and by Dylan on his first acoustic album of the 1990s, *Good as I Been to You* in 1992. *Frances J. Crosby & William H. Doane*, writer and composer of 'Pass Me Not, O Gentle Savior', which Dylan sang five times in 1999. OLIVER TRAGER writes that his version of this 19th century hymn was 'eerily reminiscent' of the way the creepy Robert Mitchum character sang it in *Night of the Hunter*. Co-editor of *Broadsheet* magazine *Sis Cunningham*, a strong early New York supporter of Dylan, who died in a nursing home on 27 June 2004, aged 95.

Danny Dill & Marijohn Wilkin, writers of 'Long Black Veil', which Dylan knew from way back when (see **Frizzell, Lefty** and **The Band**) but which he sang in concert once in 1997—at Wheeling, West Virginia, on April 27—and four times in 1990. Dill also co-wrote, with *Mel Tillis*, 'Detroit City', performed in nearby East Lansing, Michigan, by Dylan on November 12, 1990, as the opening number of his concert. *Danny DiMinno & Carmen Lombardo*, composers of 'Return to Me' (see **'The Sopranos'**). *Dion DiMucci*, whose song 'Abraham, Martin and John' (the composer credit goes to the pseudonymous-sounding Dick Holler) Bob Dylan and CLYDIE KING performed together with fine felicity in concert in 1980–81 (a total of 23 times, with Dylan on piano, beginning in San Francisco on November 9, 1980 and last performing it in London on June 30, 1981), and for whose retrospective CD collection *Dion: King of the New York Streets* (2000) Dylan contributes eloquent sleevenotes. Dylan also sang the Dion hit 'The Wanderer' as an encore duet with Paul Simon 11 times in July and September 1999 (a song written by *Ernie Maresca*). In the UK Dion hit twice over with this record—in early 1962 and again in 1976. *Don & Dewey*, who wrote and had a big 1957 hit with 'Justine', which Dylan used as the murky opening number at ten concerts in 1986, starting on February 15 in Adelaide, Australia. *Donovan*. *Max Dyer*, 1970s Christian folkie composer of the obscure 'I Will Sing', performed by Dylan in Akron, Ohio, on one of his gospel tours (May 18, 1980).

Steve Earle, the country singer who opened for Dylan at some 1989 concerts, and whose song 'Nothin' But You' Dylan performed a couple of times in his own set on the same tour leg. *Tommy Edwards*, 1950s hit recording artist of, and *Carl Sigman & Charles Gates Dawes*, composers of, 'It's All in the Game': see **King, Clydie**. (Sigman also co-wrote 'Answer Me', aka 'Answer Me My Love', which Dylan sang at seven 1991 concerts.) *Rohusuke Ei & Hachidai Nakamura*, composers of the pop hit 'Sukiyaki', which Dylan attempted to perform in March 1986 in Osaka, Nagoya and Tokyo. Terry Ellis, the 'science student' in *Don't Look Back*.

Dorothy Fields & Jimmy McHugh, writers of 'I'm in the Mood for Love'; see **Domino, Fats**. *Bill Flanagan*, whose 1986 book *Written in My Soul*, a series of interviews with singer-songwriters, included a long and fascinating section on Dylan. *John Fogerty*, prominent as lead vocalist and front-man of Credence Clearwater Revival before going solo in 1973, behind whom Dylan played at a jam session in February 1987 (see *Taj Mahal*, below) and for whom at the Rock'n'Roll Hall of Fame inaugural concert in New York on January 20, 1988, Dylan played guitar as Fogerty performed the old Clearwater favourite 'Born on the Bayou'.

Robert Friemark, BOB NEUWIRTH's art teacher, who is supposed to have written 'Vincent Van Gogh?', performed by Dylan, Neuwirth & GUAM 18 times on the 1976 Rolling Thunder Revue.

Donnie Fritts & Troy Seals, composers of 'We Had It All', performed 32 times by Dylan on the 1986 US tour with Tom Petty & the Heartbreakers. *Seals* also co-wrote, but with *Dave Kirby*, 'No More One More Time', which Dylan performed at four concerts in 1990 and one in 1994.

Joseph Gallo (1929–72), gangster, subject of Dylan's *Desire* song 'Joey'. *Lowell George*, late lamented star of 1970s southern rock band Little Feat and writer of the truck-driving anthem 'Willin'', which Dylan has performed nine times in concert: in 1990 in Dallas, San Antonio and Austin, Texas, on September 6, 8 & 9 respectively; in Mesa, Arizona, that September 12; in Springfield, Massachusetts, exactly one month later; in New York City that October 17; in Wichita, Kansas, on Hallowe'en, 1991; in Sunrise, Florida, on November 13, 1992; and at Fort Lauderdale on September 23, 1995. *Haven Gillespie & Beasley Smith*, who wrote the instant classic 'That Lucky Old Sun' in 1949. (See **Charles, Ray** and **Foster, Stephen**.)

Bob and Sidsel Gleason, friends of Dylan at whose home in East Orange, New Jersey, he often stayed in the early New York period, and where he was recorded performing ten songs in February or March 1961, on a tape that has circulated but never seen official release and contains the only extant version we have by Dylan of the *Scott Wiseman* song 'Remember Me (When Candlelights Are Gleaming)', sung sweetly; the Gleasons also provide the location cited by Dylan in another private recording, 'The Story of East Orange, New Jersey', a creaking tall story about chess fanaticism, that was released retrospectively on the CD-Rom *Highway 61 Interactive* but had been a track, years beforehand, on one of the earliest Dylan bootleg LPs. The Gleasons were already middle-aged when Dylan first met them, which was when they organised excursions by WOODY GUTHRIE from the New Jersey State Hospital in Greystone Park to the Village during Guthrie's first years as an in-patient (1956–60).

Glen Glenn, writer of the rockabilly song 'Everybody's Movin'' which he recorded himself in 1958—it was a small hit—and which Dylan performed in concert twice in 1988, twice in 1989 and once in 1990. *Ellie Greenwich*, songwriting partner of Barry Mann in the early-1960s pop years, at whose New York City house Dylan played some guitar instrumentals in the summer of 1984, perhaps as they tried to write a song together. The Mann & Weill team, 'workhorses in the Brill Building. . . . cranked out the home-run hits', as Dylan puts it in *Chronicles Volume One*, bumping his metaphors together.

Tim Hardin, whose 'Lady Came from Baltimore' Dylan performed three times in concert in 1994, after recording it at the June 1992 Chicago sessions produced by DAVID BROMBERG. *Wilbert Harrison*, minor R&B star whose 'Let's Stick Together' Dylan included on *Down in the Groove*. *Red Hayes & Jack Rhodes*, composers of the gospel standard 'A Satisfied Mind', included on Dylan's *Saved* album of 1980. *Freddie Hart*, composer and hit performer of the 1970s country song 'Easy Lovin'', performed once by Dylan in 2003. *Nat Hentoff*, veteran jazz journalist who wrote the sleevenotes to Dylan's second album and with whom Dylan concocted the 1966 *Playboy* interview. *Dallas Holm*, fellow Minnesotan songwriter, whose signature song 'Rise Again' Dylan sang as a duet with CLYDIE KING at 11 concerts on the 'Musical Retrospective Tour' of late 1980, once, at Clarkston, MI, on June 12, 1981 and on the 1992 Chicago studio sessions. *Jim 'Catfish' Hunter*, baseball star hero of the *Desire* outtake 'Catfish', issued in 1991 on the *Bootleg Series Vols. 1–3*.

Michael Jackson & Lionel Richie, composers of the USA for Africa single 'We Are the World', recorded by the world and his wife in 1985. *Michael Kamen*, long-term Pink Floyd collaborator and musical director of David Bowie's 'Diamond Dogs' tour, conducted the Tokyo New Philharmonic Orchestra at the Todaiji Temple, Nara, Japan, in 1994, backing Dylan on his 'Great Music Experience' performances of 'A Hard Rain's a-Gonna Fall, 'I Shall Be Released' and 'Ring Them Bells' on May 20–22, from the final performance of which came a single release of 'A Hard Rain's a-Gonna Fall'. Two years later he was diagnosed as having multiple sclerosis, and he died at the age of 55 on November 18, 2003. *Pee Wee King*, *Redd Stewart* and *Chilton Price*, who wrote 'You Belong to Me' (see **Vincent, Gene**).

Baker Knight, writer of 'Lonesome Town': see **Nelson, Ricky**. *Jim Krueger*, composer of 'We Just Disagree', a hit for *Dave Mason* in the 1970s which Dylan sang 16 times in concert between November 1980 and October 1981. *Red Lane & Larry Henley*, composers of ''Til I Get It Right', performed 27 times in concert by Dylan in 1981.

Greg Lake, ex-member of British psychedelia-to-prog rock band Emerson, Lake & Palmer and co-writer of 'Love You Too Much' with Dylan and HELENA SPRINGS. *Leiber & Stoller*, whose 'Kansas City' Dylan sang *in* Kansas City in concert with Tom Petty & the Heartbreakers in 1986; their names are mentioned many times elsewhere in this book, since they wrote many of Elvis Presley's biggest hits. *Murray Lerner*, director of the film *Festival*, released in 1967, which included Dylan footage, some of which shows up in SCORSESE's *No Direction Home* in 2005. *Noah Lewis*, the great jug band harmonica player, who sometimes gets a composer credit for 'Viola Lee Blues', performed as a one-off by Dylan in Sapporo, Japan, on February 24, 1997, and who wrote 'Minglewood Blues', which Dylan sang live twice in Europe in 1996. (See **blues, inequality of reward in**.) *George Lois*, co-director of Dylan's 'Jokerman' promo video. *Eric Lott*, author of *Love and Theft*, the 1993 book whose title Dylan loved and thieved for his 2001 album.

Eve & Mac MacKenzie, patrons, supporters and friends of Dylan in his early days in New York at whose house on 28th Street he often stayed and where three known Dylan home recordings were made (14 songs on November 23, 1961: the day after he completed recording his début album); ten songs surmised to be on December 4, 1961; and six more in September 1962; of this total of 30 numbers, six are instrumentals and on several others Dylan only plays guitar. They are sketched in briefly in *Chronicles Volume One*, in which Dylan says that 'Mack' had been a Brooklyn waterfront union organiser and that Eve had been a Martha Graham dancer. They are survived by their son Peter, who has recently been selling Dylan artefacts, including an original reel-to-reel tape of some of these recordings, at Christie's auctions in New York.

The McPeake Family, the Northern Ireland singing group, on whom Dylan was keen and from whom he may have learnt 'Wild Mountain Thyme', which he sang way back on the May 1961 Minneapolis tape, again (and most beautifully) at the Isle of Wight in 1969, four times on the 1975 Rolling Thunder Revue and four more on the 1976 (duetting with JOAN BAEZ), and again in the first month of the Never-Ending Tour, in Cincinnati on June 22, 1988. The McPeakes reunited for a one-off concert at the Opera House in their home city of Belfast in early April 2005.

Ray Marcum & Ray Pennington, composers of 'Stone Walls and Steel Bars', the STANLEY BROTHERS song. The great contemporary blues interpreter *Taj Mahal*, for whom Dylan played back-up guitar, as he did for GEORGE HARRISON and John Fogerty, at a long jam session at the Palomino Club in Hollywood on February 19, 1987. *Henry Mancini & Johnny Mercer*, co-writers of 'Moon River': see **Vaughan, Stevie Ray** and **Carmichael, Hoagy**. *Moon Martin*, writer of 'Paid the Price', a one-off from Dylan in his second set at Toad's Place, New Haven, CT, on January 12, 1990. *William May & Lillian Bea Thompson*, composers of 'Red Cadillac and a Black Mustache'; see **Smith, Warren.** *John Cougar Mellencamp*, who produced Dylan's video for 'Political World', an unsuccessful single taken from *Oh Mercy*. *Dorinda Morgan*, composer of 'Confidential to Me' (aka 'Confidential'), which Dylan first performs, fragmentarily, way back in *1956*—when it was still a hot hit by *Sonny Knight*—playing piano and sharing vocals with his teenage friends LARRY KEGAN and HOWARD RUTMAN (see **earliest extant recordings, Dylan's**), and which he returns to over a third of a century later at the remarkable Toad's Place evening in New Haven, CT, in January 1990. *James Meredith*, the subject of Dylan's song 'Oxford Town'; see endnotes to ***Time Out of Mind***. *Joe Morris*, composer of the R&B classic 'Shake a Hand', which Dylan performed 22 times on the US tour of 1986 with Tom Petty & the Heartbreakers.

Cecil Null, writer of 'I Forgot More Than You'll Ever Know', which Dylan includes on *Self Portrait* in 1970 and sang in concert in 1986. *Webb Pierce & Merle Kilgore*, who wrote 'More and More', a 1954 hit for Pierce which Dylan sang in concert in Houston, TX, on August 26, 1989 and with VAN MORRISON on January 18, 1998 in New York City. *Chuck Plotkin*, co-producer with Dylan of the *Shot of Love* album. *Teddy Powell & Bobby Sharp*, composers of 'Unchain My Heart' (see **Charles, Ray**.)

Otis Redding & Steve Cropper, joint composers of Redding's great record 'Dock of the Bay', which Dylan sang as a one-off in George, Washington State, on August 18, 1990. Dylan offered Redding the *Blonde on Blonde* song 'Just Like a Woman', and it's said Redding was keen to record it, but died too soon—though in fact that was on December 10, 1967. That could have been a great record too.

Marty Robbins, huge country-pop star whose biggest international hit was 'El Paso', performed as an instrumental by Dylan at two 1990 concerts; see also **'Romance in Durango'**. *Dick Robertson, Nelson Cogane & Sammy Mysels*, writers of the old Ink Spots hit 'We Three (My Echo, My Shadow and Me)', which Dylan performed many times in the 1980s, mostly with Tom Petty & the Heartbreakers in 1986. *Don Robertson & Hal Blair*, composers of 'Ninety Miles àn Hour (Down a Dead End Street)': see **Snow, Hank**. *Rodgers & Hart* wrote 'Blue Moon', which Dylan sings on *Self Portrait*. *B. J. Rolfzen*, Dylan's high school English teacher. *Fred Rose*, composer of 'Wait for the Light to Shine', sung as a concert opener 31 times by Dylan between October 2001 and May 2002.

Joseph Scott, writer of 'Never Let Me Go': see **Ace, Johnny**. *Glen Spencer*, writer of 'Blue Bonnet Girl', a 1936 song by the Sons of the Pioneers, which Dylan performed as a one-off in Bloomington, IN, on November 1, 2000. *Janine Smith*, a surprise onstage guest in the middle of Dylan's Munich concert on July 20, 1981, at which she sang 'You Light Up My Life'; Dylan introduced her with this explanation: 'We just met somebody in the last town who's a real good singer. She's gonna come on here. . . . She's a young girl 16 years old. Her name's Janine Smith. I think she'd gonna be a big star someday. I don't know for sure of that, but she might be. Right now she don't have a record contract, but if there's any record producers out there looking for somebody to sign she's be good to sign. . . . She lives in Holland now. Give her a nice hand.' *Shirley & Lee*, big R&B stars of the 1950s, and never better than on the sexy (Shirley) and joyous (Lee) 'Let the Good Times Roll', performed five times in concert by Dylan with Tom Petty & the Heartbreakers in June–July 1986, in a version neither joyous nor sexy. *Shel Silverstein & Dennis Locorriere* wrote 'A Couple More Years', which Dylan sang at four 'Musical Retrospective Tour' concerts in fall 1980 and then reprised, singing it with great tenderness, for the *Hearts of Fire* film in 1987. *Jesse Stone*, aka Charles Calhoun, a man born in 1901 yet who wrote the nihilistic rock'n'roll classic 'Money Honey', which Dylan performed in Ithaca, New York, on November 15, 1999, six months after Stone died at the age of 97.

Tampa Red, one of the great pre-war blues artists, whose songs 'She's Love Crazy', 'Love With a Feeling' and 'But I Forgive You' Dylan sang in concert all through his 1978 World Tour (49 times and 31 times in the first two cases) and whose 'It Hurts Me Too' he includes on *Self Portrait*.

Elizabeth Taylor, whom Dylan mentions playfully in song in 1963 when he was a young would-be bohemian and she was a glamorous Hollywood film star (he envisages in jest that he might 'make love to Elizabeth Taylor . . . / Catch hell from Richard Burton!', in 'I Shall Be Free').

Emmett Till, the subject of an early Dylan 'protest' song, 'The Death of Emmett Till', and the 14-year-old Chicago victim of an especially repulsive race murder, which was followed by a 1955 charade of a trial, the transcript of which has now mysteriously gone missing, and at which Roy Bryant and J.W. Milam were acquitted by an all-white jury. Both are now dead, but the FBI finally re-opened the case in 2004.

Charles A. Tindley, the composer of spirituals who was a formative influence on THOMAS A. DORSEY and who among much else wrote 'Stand By Me' (not the Ben E. King song), a song almost as big in gospel circles as Dorsey's 'Precious Lord, Take My Hand'. Dylan performed the Tindley song in Merrillville, Indiana, on August 28, 1990. *Bill Trader*, composer of 'A Fool Such as I'; see **Presley, Elvis**. *Merle Travis*, significant guitar picker, taught to thumb-pick by the Everly Brothers' father Ike, and author of the marvellous 'Dark as a Dungeon', which he first recorded on August 8, 1946 in Hollywood and which Dylan performed marvellously, duetting with Joan Baez, 14 times on the 1975 Rolling Thunder Revue, and which he has revisited seven times since: twice in 1989, twice in 1990, once in 1998 and twice in 2000.

Townes Van Zandt, a figure who almost brushes the Dylan story a number of times, but who was, specifically, composer of 'Pancho & Lefty', a song Dylan has sung a number of times, with and without WILLIE NELSON.

Jerry Jeff Walker, the country rock singer (actually named Paul Crosby, and from New York State), composer of 'Mr. Bojangles', a crafty, dodgy song that Walker had a hit with in 1968 but to which, on the *Dylan* album of 1973, Bob Dylan affords the best possible treatment, full of rich humane sound, through which he makes the lyric not just palatable but appealing, freeing the song to be better than it was: softly gritty, smudged images on a grand canvas instead of a pinched sermon in a mean tract. *Karen Wallace*, at whose apartment in St. Paul, Minnesota, Bob Dylan was first recorded as a tyro folksinger, back in May 1960; it hasn't been possible to trace her. *Jim Webb*, singer-songwriter who wrote 'Let's Begin', a song on which Dylan and Clydie King duetted many times on the 1981 tour.

George Weiss, Hugo Peretti & Luigi Creatore (great name, Luigi's), writers of Elvis Presley's *Blue Hawaii* movie hit 'Can't Help Falling in Love', which Dylan performs so funnily, fondly and terrifically on the 1970s *Dylan* collection. *Donald White*, subject of a very early Dylan 'protest song'; see **Turner, Gil**. *Jimmy Work, Roscoe Reid & Joe Hobson*, composers of the mid-1950s country hit 'Making Believe', which Dylan sang as a one-off at his Istanbul concert of June 24, 1990. *J.B.F. Wright*, composer of 'Precious Memories', which Dylan included on *Knocked Out Loaded* in 1986 and performed live three times: twice in October 1989 and once at Toad's Place, New Haven, CT, in January 1990.

William Zantzinger [sic], real life villain of the factually inaccurate but socially truthful and artistically inspired Dylan song 'The Lonesome Death of Hattie Carroll'. *Paul Zollo*, who secured an illuminating interview with Dylan about songwriting, for *Songtalk* magazine in 1991, despite the disquieting circumstances in which, it turns out, it was conducted. (In 1992, when the interviewer became the interviewed, we learnt that Dylan's publicist, Elliot 'Chewy' Mintz, had not only sat in on the Dylan interview but had tried to proscribe it beforehand and censor it afterwards. Beforehand, Mintz told Zollo 'not to ask [Dylan] about songs that were so old that he would have to wrack his brain'. During the interview, Dylan made unexceptionable allusions to HENDRIX, the songs 'People' and 'Feelings' and NEIL YOUNG, and Chewy wanted them all cut out, in case they were 'offensive'. Zollo said: '. . . he was in control of the whole scene.' Do you often read anything quite so depressing? Does it occur to Chewy that his interventions and proprietism are 'offensive'? There ought to be a special hell for people like Mintz, who sanitise and demean the very personality of the artist they are supposed to look after. Eternal fire is too good for them. Eternal tape-loops of 'Feelings' and 'People', maybe.)

ZZ Top, men with Rip Van Winkle beards whose song 'My Head's in Mississippi' Dylan sang three times in 1990, the first time being *in* Mississippi, in Oxford Town (where he sang that song too, for the first time in three decades) but with whom he arrived at the ASCAP award ceremony in LA on March 31, 1986.

[Bob Dylan on Aznavour, *Rolling Stone*, US, Nov/Dec 1987; on Mann & Weill, *Chronicles Volume One*, 2004, p.227; on the MacKenzies, p.66. Paul Zollo interview, Beverly Hills, 14 Apr 1991, *Songtalk* vol. 2, no.16, US, 1991; Zollo interviewed *The Telegraph* no.42, UK, summer 1992. This entry has drawn more than a little, and gratefully, on Oliver Trager, *Keys to the Rain: The Definitive Bob Dylan Encyclopedia*, New York: Billboard, 2004.]

'On the Street Where You Live' [1956] Dylan has shown a penchant for this Broadway musical number, from Alan J. Lerner & Frederick Loewe's *My Fair Lady*, in at least three songs of his own, all written in the period 1969–74: 'Tonight I'll Be Staying Here with You', from *Nashville Skyline*, 'Hazel', from *Planet Waves*, and most especially 'The Man in Me', from *New Morning*. For the lesser resemblances in the first two cases, see ***Nashville Skyline***; but within 'The Man in Me', Dylan comes so close to the show-tune that he quotes it almost exactly, in words and melody. This is Dylan: 'But oh! what a wonderful feelin' / Just to know that you are near.' These are the lines from 'On the

Street Where You Live', sung to Eliza Doolittle by the chinless wannabe boyfriend (lines which, like Dylan's, are placed at the start of the 'bridge' or 'middle eight' of the song): 'And oh! the towering feeling / Just to know somehow you are near' (to which is paired 'The overpowering feeling / That any second you may suddenly appear').

Most parents of people of Bob Dylan's generation owned a copy of a *My Fair Lady* album: either the Original Cast Recording or the film soundtrack LP; and in 1958 'On the Street Where You Live' was also a huge pop hit, not least a no.1 in the UK, by crooner Vic Damone.

[John Michael King: 'On the Street Where You Live', Original Cast Recording LP *My Fair Lady*, Philips RBL 1000, London, 1958; the show had premiered 4 Feb 1956, New Haven, CT, and opened 15 Mar 1956, NY; the LP was issued to coincide with the show's London opening, 30 Apr 1958. Both productions starred Rex Harrison, Julie Andrews & Stanley Holloway. Vic Damone: Columbia 40654, NY (Philips PB 819, London), 1958.]

***On the Tracks* [fanzine]** For whatever reason, the most significant Dylan fanzines have always been British, though *Talkin' Bob Zimmerman Blues* (see **Styble, Bryan**) was an early US pioneer, as was *Look Back*, though this was always obscure and underwent more management changes than was good for it. Both were soon dwarfed by the long-term, serious British contenders *The Telegraph* (see **Bauldie, John**) and *Isis* (see **Barker, Derek & Tracy**). But in 1993 came a new US publication, *On the Tracks*, from an outfit calling itself Rolling Tomes, based in Grand Junction, Colorado.

The format of *On the Tracks* was slim, large-page, and with plenty of photographs: and it looked so glossy and slick that it needed the counter-balance of the legend THE UNAUTHORIZED BOB DYLAN MAGAZINE printed under the title on its front cover. Issue no.1 was dated 'Summer 1993', included interviews with ROGER McGUINN, CAROLYN HESTER and JAKOB DYLAN, and seemed to have signed up a posse of prominent 'Dylan writers', including Edna Gundersen, David Hinckley, PAUL WILLIAMS, BERT CARTWRIGHT and STEPHEN SCOBIE. It was edited by Mick McCuistion with crucial assistance from his wife Laurie.

This didn't come cheap. The cover price was $8.50 (and that's 13 years ago). Perhaps no-one would have minded this had the fanzine gone on to establish itself as driven by some editorial imperative, some strong individual take on Dylan, some genuine *stance*; but no such virtue ever came out from between the lines. Yes, it allowed various writers to publish interesting material; it provided an outlet for a large number of interviews with highly relevant people; and its large shiny pages accommodated much photography—but it was not alone in any of that, and unlike others it had no personality, and to pick it up and browse around it was always to feel that it was less a magazine than a merchandising catalogue. The editorial content always felt like the smoke and mirrors behind which lay the serious business of disseminating a vast For Sale list of overpriced items like t-shirts, singles, badges and general collectibles.

On the Tracks may or may not return—its editor has long been said to suffer from debilitating bad health, which might explain the long periods when its editorial staff is incommunicado (see the representative experience of Jonathan D. Lauer, detailed in the entry **Cartwright, Bert**). The quarterly magazine itself seems to have been in limbo for quite some time; the Rolling Tomes website is still up there, inviting people to send in their money.

'Open the Door, Homer' [1967] 'Open the door, Richard', a line Bob Dylan uses repeatedly in his Basement Tapes song 'Open the Door, Homer' (a phrase he *never* uses in the song) comes straight from an R&B novelty item first recorded in the 1940s, revived in the 1950s by Ernie Barton & BILLY LEE RILEY (one of Dylan's favourite rockabillies) and in the 1960s by Pigmeat Markham and Bill Doggett. Hence how Dylan completes that chorus line: 'Open the door, Richard—I've heard it said before.'

Based on the catchphrase of a Des Moines vaudeville act by Dusty Fletcher (who took it from 1920s comic John 'Spider Bruce' Mason, Mason's lawsuit later claimed), it was written by Jack McVea, first recorded by Jack McVea & His All-Stars in 1946 and became a huge R&B and pop charts hit of 1947, the catchphrase itself something of a national craze on the back of it. The record also has a niche in popular music history in being the first with a fade-out ending in its own right.

The record was covered by, and a huge hit on the same two charts for, Count Basie, black vocal group the Three Flames, Dusty Fletcher himself and the influential Louis Jordan & His Tympany Five (all 1947), engendering other pop chart hit versions, 'answer records' and more.

Dylan's Basement Tapes song was recorded at 'Big Pink' in West Saugherties, New York, in September or October 1967, first circulating as a music publishing demo from his UK music publishing outfit Big Ben Music, so becoming one of the first tracks floating around when bootleg records were new and thrilling. It was released on the official *Basement Tapes* album in 1975. He has never performed 'Open the Door, Homer' live.

Despite not singing 'Homer' in the song even in the studio, Dylan has always been keen on the name. Not only does he get a namecheck in this song title but he pops up as a character in *Tarantula*—'Homer, *the slut*': hence ANDREW MUIR's fanzine of that name—but he ends Dylan's prose poem 'Alternatives to College' too, and aptly:

> 'Homer on the gallows—his feet swollen & you wondering why there is no eternity & that you

make your own eternity & why there is no music & that you make your own music & where there are no alternatives & that you make your own alternatives.'

[Bob Dylan: 'Alternatives to College', dating from 1965 but first published officially in *Lyrics 1962–1985*, in which is it copyrighted 1985. Recordings of 'Open the Door, Richard': Jack McVea & His All-Stars, Hollywood, Sep 1946, Black & White 792, LA, 1946; Count Basie, *nia*, RCA Victor *nia*, NY, 1947; the Three Flames, *nia*, Columbia *nia*, NY, 1947; Dusty Fletcher, *nia*, National *nia*, 1947; Louis Jordan & His Tympany Five, LA, 23 Jan 1947, Decca 23841, NY, 1947; Ernie Barton with Billy Riley, Memphis, 25 Feb 1959, *nia*; Pigmeat Markham, *nia*, Chess 1891, Chicago, 1964; Bill Doggett, *nia*, 1965. Detail from Jim Dawson & Steve Propes, *What Was the First Rock'n'Roll Record?*, Winchester, MD: Faber & Faber, 1992: but their source was 'Open the Door, Richard' by Tony Burke & Dave Penny, *Blues & Rhythm* no.17, Cheadle, UK, Mar 1985 & update in no.19, May 1986 & (by Jim O'Neill) no.21, Sep 1986.]

Orbison, Roy [1936 - 1988] Roy Orbison was born in Vernon, Texas, on April 23, 1936. He first recorded in 1956 ('Ooby Dooby') and wrote THE EVERLY BROTHERS hit 'Claudette'. He and his early group the Wink Westerners regarded one side of Texas as their terrain, enjoying a rivalry with BUDDY HOLLY & the Crickets from the other side. Orbison had his own local TV show sponsored by a local furniture store, on which an early guest was ELVIS PRESLEY. But it was after signing to Monument Records that Roy began to have his long run of huge hit singles, beginning with 'Only the Lonely' and taking in 'Blue Angel', 'Runnin' Scared', 'Cryin'', 'Blue Bayou', 'Pretty Woman', 'Dream Baby', 'In Dreams', 'It's Over' and 'The Crowd'.

When hip snobbery was rife in the late 1960s and 1970s, not one music paper or magazine would publish such a thing as a Roy Orbison interview, despite the fact that, uniquely, he had worked both at the Sun studio in Memphis *and* at Norman Petty's in Clovis, New Mexico, in the crucial mid-1950s. And despite the further credentials of his voice and those early-1960s singles, Orbison's mid-70s live appearances were perforce in cabaret clubs. No-one was listening or respectful of his artistry then. He was widely dismissed as a clapped-out, tawdry pop star, as passé as haircream and condoms, neither of which we thought we'd see again. When he died (of a heart attack in Hendersonville, TN, December 6, 1988), everyone said how they'd always loved him.

By then he had enjoyed a second wave of success, winning a Grammy for a duet with EMMYLOU HARRIS ('That Loving You Feeling Again'), his re-recording of 'In Dreams' becoming pivotal to David Lynch's 1986 film *Blue Velvet*, re-recording his masterpiece of soaring heartache, 'Cryin'', as a duet with k.d. lang, having an album of new material produced by ELVIS COSTELLO (which Orbison unfortunately died before the release of, and which gave him a posthumous hit single, 'You Got It' and became his highest-charting album), and standing alongside Dylan, GEORGE HARRISON, TOM PETTY and JEFF LYNNE as one of the TRAVELING WILBURYS (Lefty Wilbury, in fact).

He was the oldest Wilbury, with the best rock'n' roll credentials, and his lovely voice gave an invaluable counterweight to the gruff touch of the others. On the first Wilburys album it was the major track on which Orbison took lead vocals, 'Not Alone Anymore', that brought Bob Dylan back into the hit-singles chart for the first time in two decades.

Dylan paid him a less than fulsome tribute after his death (especially in contrast to how grandiloquent he waxed in tribute to JERRY GARCIA and JOHNNY CASH). Dylan said of Orbison only this: 'Roy was an opera singer. He had the greatest voice.' He made up for it in sheer garrulousness in his comments in *Chronicles Volume One*, where he takes a series of fumbled lunges towards pinning Orbison down. In the course of them he includes this: '[He] transcended all the genres. . . . His stuff mixed all the styles and some that hadn't been invented yet. . . . With Roy you didn't know if you were listening to mariachi or opera. He kept you on your toes. . . . He sounded like he was singing from some Olympian mountaintop and he meant business . . . singing his compositions in three or four octaves that made you want to drive your car over a cliff. He sang like a professional criminal.'

Perhaps Dylan had paid him a more proper tribute at his appearance at the second Isle of Wight Festival of Music on August 31, 1969—for the versions he sang that night of the traditional 'Wild Mountain Thyme' and his own 'To Ramona' and 'It Ain't Me Babe' were all strongly redolent of Roy Orbison's distinctive vocals—and all exquisite.

[Roy Orbison: 'Cryin'', Monument 447, 1961; *Mystery Girl*, *nia*, 1988, Virgin 791058 1, 1989. Roy Orbison & k.d. lang: 'Cryin'', *nia*, Bob Dylan: 'Wild Mountain Thyme', 'To Ramona' & 'It Ain't Me Babe', Isle of Wight, 31 Aug 1969, all unreleased and only ever circulated in particularly poor quality, despite many attempts to 'upgrade' them. Bob Dylan quoted from *Chronicles Volume One*, p.33.]

Østrem, Eyolf [1967 -] Born in Stavanger, Norway, on February 15, 1967, prolific Dylan-commentator and guitar tutor Eyolf Østrem first wondered about Dylan in 1980, bought *Slow Train Coming* (with no foreknowledge of its context or contents) in 1984 and became hooked in 1989.

Enjoying the wealth of tabs (tablature = the Renaissance-devised notation system for playing plucked instruments, showing which fingers press down on which strings where) and chord files available online, he decided to bring together some competent tabbers to put an authoritative chord & text representation of every Bob Dylan song online; not knowing who to contact, he started doing it himself. It has grown from that. But for Østrem, a vital part of *www.dylanchords.com* is the 'Self-Ordained Professors' section, a collection of writings (mostly his own) on Dylan's *music*, since this is so little written about compared to the words.

Owens, Frank [19?? -] Frank Owens is a widely respected jazz and popular music session man, and one of the pianists on *Bringing It All Back Home* and *Highway 61 Revisited*. He played on the June 15, 1965 session–the one that attempted, but did not clinch, 'It Takes a Lot to Laugh, It Takes a Train to Cry', 'Sitting on a Barbed Wire Fence' and 'Like a Rolling Stone', but he was absent next day when 'Like a Rolling Stone' *was* achieved. The pianist on that second, fateful day was PAUL GRIFFIN. This is often disputed–but DEREK BARKER finally separated myth from fact 40 years later in his scrutiny of the sessions for *ISIS* no.120 in May 2005, in an incontestable analysis, helped crucially by a Don Hunstein photograph from the sessions which had emerged only in the booklet issued with the *Bootleg Series Vol. 4: Bob Dylan Live 1966–The "Royal Albert Hall" Concert* in 1998 (it's on page 19).

Owens was then the pianist on the afternoon session of July 29, replacing Griffin, who had played in the morning; he *may* have been the pianist at the July 30 session, while he and Griffin were *both* at the session on August 2nd. Therefore he can be heard, on official releases, on the versions of 'It Takes a Lot to Laugh, It Takes a Train to Cry' and 'Sitting on a Barbed Wire Fence', plus a 'Like a Rolling Stone' fragment, on *Bootleg Series Vols. 1–3* in 1991; on the *Highway 61 Interactive* CD-ROM of 1995; the version of 'It Takes a Lot to Laugh' on the *Bootleg Series Vol. 7–No Direction Home: The Soundtrack* (2005), and possibly on the 'Just Like Tom Thumb's Blues' on the same collection (though Paul Griffin is the one credited in the booklet). More importantly, Frank Owens is on *Bringing It All Back Home* and *Highway 61 Revisited* themselves, and on the hit single 'Positively 4th Street'.

Owens also earns this tribute from Paul Griffin himself. Here was a sideman, he said, so classy and so good that one time on stage at the Apollo in Harlem, he unwittingly stole the gig from the headliner. Who that was, he wouldn't say. On September 15, 2005, Frank Owens played at what would have been a celebration of Fats Waller's rhythm guitarist Al Casey's 90th birthday, at Saint Peter's Church in midtown Manhattan, alongside the Harlem Blues and Jazz Band and other pianists. Casey died four days too soon to be able to attend.

Pagel, Bill [1942 -] William Pagel was born in Chicago on May 15, 1942. He first became interested in Dylan's work back in 1962, after hearing *Bob Dylan*, his first album. A *serious* collector and archivist, Bill Pagel is the man behind the invaluable website BobLinks, which provides uncannily up-to-date information on Dylan's concert performances (and has concert archive pages going back to the fall 1995 leg of the Never-Ending Tour) as well as carrying a megalist of links to other Dylan-related web resources.

P

When Dylan is touring—as he so often is—you can go to BobLinks within hours of each concert and find, already posted, a reliable song-by-song set-list and running-order, plus the list of musicians who played that night. (You can often also find a punter's hopelessly over-enthusiastic 'review' of the concert too.) All this information can also be accessed as lists of songs performed by year—including how many times each has been performed and on what dates, each date hyperlinked to that whole concert's set-list. Set-lists can also be accessed by date or by country, this last acting also, therefore, as a list of every country Dylan has performed in since 1995 (and when), from Argentina to Wales, each one broken down into towns played. Hence you can see at a glance, for instance, that Dylan played in 14 different Spanish locations in the years 1995–99, and in 21 Italians locations between 1996 and 2001.

The megalist of links is divided into three main sections: 'Pages Dedicated to Bob', 'Pages with Some Dylan Content' and 'Friends Along the Way'. As of September 2005 the first list has links to 119 Dylan-devoted sites, 17 sites with some Dylan material included, and 50 sites about people with Dylan connections. There are also listings of Dylan sites arranged by category—'Music & Writings', 'CDs, Records, Books, Tapes etc.', 'Images', 'News and Interviews', 'Miscellaneous Resources' and 'Market Place'.

Bill Pagel founded this site in 1995; within ten years it had been accessed over 11,000,000 times. Bill lives in the town of Dylan's birth, Duluth, Minnesota.

[BobLinks is at *www.boblinks.org, or http://my.execpc.com/~billp61/boblink.html.*]

Paley, Tom [1928 -] Thomas Paley was born in New York City on March 19, 1928. After undergraduate study he took a Master's degree in Mathematics and became a maths teacher before choosing a career as a musician (and photographer). He performed in a duo with WOODY GUTHRIE before co-founding the NEW LOST CITY RAMBLERS, in which he played banjo, guitar and autoharp and sang. He left in 1962, formed the short-lived Old Reliable String Band but moved to Sweden from 1963 to 1965 before moving to England, which has remained his base. He has toured frequently in America and Europe, including as part of the New Deal String Band.

Bob Dylan's *World Gone Wrong* sleevenotes credit Tom Paley with having been the conduit for 'Jack-a-Roe' and 'Love Henry', but he doesn't specify (as he does re FRANK HUTCHISON and DOC WATSON) that he is referring to *recordings*. Nevertheless there are Paley recordings of both songs. (And, almost inevitably, a Paley recording of 'Little Maggie', which Dylan had singled out decades earlier but then recorded himself on *Good as I Been to You* in 1992.)

What Dylan says in the opening sentence of his liner-note on 'Love Henry' is that it is 'a "traditionalist" ballad. Tom Paley used to do it.' Not, that is, a traditional so much as a traditionalist ballad: one of those taken up by the traditionalist faction in the Great Folk Revival Wars of the 1950s and early 1960s.

'Folk music was a strict and rigid establishment,' Dylan says in the *Biograph* interview. 'If you sang Southern Mountain Blues, you didn't sing Southern Mountain Ballads and you didn't sing city blues. If you sang Texas cowboy songs, you didn't play English ballads. . . . You just didn't. If you sang folk songs from the thirties, you didn't do bluegrass tunes or Appalachian ballads. It was very strict.'

This gives the atmosphere but exaggerates the divisions. Apart from anything else, the songs cannot be divided that rigidly, since the same ones crop up inside different genres, as Sharp's very title *English Folk Songs of the Southern Appalachians* confirms. In the case of Tom Paley, while Dylan says that it is Paley from whom he took the traditional British ballad 'Love Henry' *and* the American broadside ballad 'Jack-a-Roe', Paley himself took 'Love Henry' from a book of folksongs field-recorded in Alabama, recorded it at the English home of EWAN MacCOLL and Peggy Seeger, and is also an enthusiast for music akin to the world of Frank Hutchison and pre-bluegrass.

What Karl Dallas calls 'the first and . . . most sensational folk-based pop music of the electric age, the American "hillbilly" string bands of the twenties whose records sold by the million', is, he says, regarded 'with peculiar reverence by American revivalists like MIKE SEEGER and Tom Paley', though he adds that they 'appear to treat it as a kind of musical fossil rather than as a fertile and creative source . . .' To which Dylan responds, in effect, in *Chronicles Volume One*, by saying this of

Paley & Seeger's group the New Lost City Ramblers: 'I didn't know that they were replicating everything they did off of old 78 records, but what would it have mattered anyway? . . . For me, they had originality in spades, were men of mystery on all counts. I couldn't listen to them enough.'

Within the group itself, there developed a less roseate glow. Paley, a stickler for detail, didn't like starting a number until his guitar was precisely tuned. It came to be said that the group broke up because the others got tired of waiting. (In fact, Paley left the group in 1962, to be replaced by Tracy Schwarz. When they re-formed, made the album *There Ain't No Way Out* and in 1998 held a 40th Anniversary concert, Paley was not involved.) When writer Tony Russell found himself reuniting Paley and John Cohen some 20 years after the group's demise, he reports that instead of the warm embrace he'd expected between the two, Paley greeted his long-lost musical brother by asking for the return of a book of songs lent out to Cohen two decades beforehand.

Paley now lives in London in circumstances as modest as himself (he has never boasted of, nor cashed in on, his own credentials—which include having shared bills with LEADBELLY) and has done for very many years. He is a member of the Friends of American Old Time Music and Dance in England, and of the Swedish Fiddlers' Association (Sveriges Spelmans Riksförbund), having rejected violin lessons as a child but returned to the instrument and learnt it at the age of 47. His son, Ben Paley Gould, is a folk-circuit performer and plays with his father in the re-formed New Deal String Band.

[Tom Paley: 'Jack-a-Roe' & 'Little Maggie', NY, 1952, *Folk Songs from the Southern Appalachian Mountains* (10-inch LP), Elektra EKL12, NY, 1953; 'Love Henry', Beckenham, UK, 1964, on Peggy Seeger & Tom Paley: *Who's Gonna Shoe Your Pretty Little Feet?*, Topic 12T113, London, 1964. Information that Paley took 'Love Henry' from *Folksongs of Alabama*, & recorded it at the home of Ewan MacColl & Peggy Seeger, is from Paley (London, phone conversation with this writer, 22 Apr 1999).

Karl Dallas: 'The Roots of Tradition' in *The Electric Muse: The Story of Folk into Rock*, London: Methuen, 1975. Bob Dylan: *Chronicles Volume One*, p.238. Tony Russell, conversation with this writer, London, 1993.]

Pankake, Jon [1938 -] Jon Alan Pankake was born in Meeker County, Minnesota, on April 20, 1938. It was long assumed that one reason why Dylan did not have to rely upon LP reissues for hearing old blues in his early Minnesota years was that he had access to 78s owned by record-collectors like Jon Pankake. Yet when the CD box-set reissue of *AMERICAN FOLK MUSIC* emerged in 1997, it included Pankake's essay 'The Brotherhood of the Anthology', detailing his own discovery of this music: and stating that he was introduced to, and epiphanously excited by, the anthology itself *in 1959* by his friend and University of Minnesota classmate PAUL NELSON—and that before this encounter their knowledge of folk music hardly ran further than a few records by PETE SEEGER and the other usual suspects (and that they couldn't even find GUTHRIE or LEADBELLY records locally).

Pankake's essay goes on to suggest that only after discovering SMITH (staying up 'late that night listening with astonishment to [its] strange music . . . so utterly unlike the "folk-music" we had heard') did he himself begin journeying into this 'music emotionally shattering yet culturally incomprehensible'. By inference, then, this must downplay the Pankake connection as a source for Dylan's Minnesota self-education in the mysteries of the pre-war blues, since it suggests that Pankake was hardly familiar with them much earlier than Dylan himself.

He and Nelson must have responded very fast. Pankake says that it was because they were unable to 'put aside the excitement of discovery' instilled in them by the anthology that they decided to found the small but fierce 'fanzine' *The Little Sandy Review*, 'devoted to discussing the difference between the "folk music" on the *Anthology* and the "folk music" represented by the artists and albums of the recording industry.'

Delving 'into a netherworld of collector's newsletters, record auction lists, jazz and blues scholarship, mimeographed ephemera and cranky antiquarian collectors', Jon Pankake must have responded fast too, to build up a collection of all kinds: fast enough that by some point in 1960 he could be, for Bob Dylan, a rich source of folk music on record, and of advice in person.

The music he played Dylan from his own collection included, according to ROBERT SHELTON, 'a Texas chain-gang song from an ALAN LOMAX album'. Asked, 40 years after the event, which record this was, Pankake could 'no longer recall exactly . . . I strongly suspect that the album in question was Alan Lomax's *Texas Folk Songs*. . . . It was a favorite of mine at the time and I would have been trying to introduce it to those who were interested in performing songs from the Library of Congress field-recordings. . . . I thought then—and still do—that Lomax was one of the best interpreters of the music he collected.'

Dylan 'borrowed' some of these records from Jon Pankake, and he showed great taste and shrewd judgement as to what was valuable in the items he took. The records included the début LP by ELIZABETH COTTEN (whose 'Oh Babe It Ain't No Lie' Dylan started to perform in concert over 30 years later, followed more recently still by a re-working of another of her songs, 'Shake Sugaree') and an important compilation LP titled *Mountain Music—Bluegrass Style*. The story of Pankake and Paul Nelson tracking Dylan down and recovering these records has been variously told, notably by Nelson in the MARTIN SCORSESE film *No Direction Home*, in which he's interviewed. Pankake, however, now denies that Nelson is referring to him at all: 'Dylan never mentions my name in the film. Paul Nelson never states a surname and describes his companion as a man of 6′ 4″. That's not me.'

In the film, Dylan comes close to still special-pleading a justification for his stealing of records, but in *Chronicles Volume One* he avoids the subject. He recalls, though, that it was Jon Pankake who 'had all the incredible records, ones you never saw and wouldn't know where to get . . . it was amazing that he had so many.'

As for advice, Dylan concedes in *Chronicles* that it was Pankake who derided his pressing on as a Woody Guthrie imitator, introduced him to the records of RAMBLIN' JACK ELLIOTT to reinforce the point (these would duly be among the items Dylan lifted), and urged him to find his own voice and style. Dylan didn't want to hear this, at first: 'Pankake was no fun to be around'. Indeed Pankake is one of the very few people in Dylan's book to receive any adverse criticism. Much of Dylan's suspicion is based on the wrong assumption that Pankake was no musician (eventually, by his own account, he could play banjo, fiddle, harmonica, mandolin, autoharp and Hawaiian guitar, and has recorded with Uncle Willie & the Brandy Snifters). Hence Dylan fiercely resents Pankake being able to tell him anything much, and feels talked down to. Nonetheless, as he concedes, 'Pankake was right'.

Pankake now refutes Dylan's account. 'I regard *Chronicles* as largely a work of fiction.' He suggests that Dylan has 'confused' him with others. 'Dylan says I lived above McCosh's bookstore. I never did.'

Started in 1960, *The Little Sandy Review* was not only swift to scorn the kind of folk music offered by groups like the Weavers but was also first to break the news that Dylan had changed his name and given himself a fanciful biography. Yet it did so while running a very enthusiastic critique of his début album and a piece by Pankake on how radically Dylan had improved as a performer between leaving for New York City in the first place and returning to Minneapolis in late May 1961. What galled Dylan in particular was the description of how his appearance had changed from when he had first appeared in 1959 'well-groomed and neat in the standard campus costume of slacks, sweater, white oxford sneakers, poplin raincoat and dark glasses . . .' (How interesting to see from *Chronicles Volume One* the way that after all these years, Pankake's judgements continue to rankle with Bob Dylan.)

More generally Pankake and Nelson's magazine was a focus of debate about the value of traditional song versus social reform campaigning song–a debate Dylan joined on return visits to Minneapolis right through till 1963, when he visited TONY GLOVER and friends yet again. *The Little Sandy Review* folded after 30 issues in 1964, the year after Paul Nelson had moved to New York City and started writing for *Sing Out!* magazine.

Jon Pankake also contributed to *Sing Out!*, including, for example, a feature on TOM PALEY in an issue in July 1964. He has written sleevenotes for numerous albums and programme notes for concerts, and in recent years has written for *The Old-Time Herald*, notably a short piece about the value of reviewing, which included this paragraph:

> 'In my 38 years of writing reviews I have written some of the most negative reviews of folk music albums ever published. In them, I jeered the credibility of the performers, mocked their intentions, parodied their efforts, and questioned their integrity. What brought forth these torrents of bile? Two things: pretentiousness and ripoffs. In the days of *The Little Sandy Review* and the Great Folk Scare there was plenty of both in the market for recorded folk music, afloat as it was in major-label money and hustlers from every seedy corner of show business crowding onto the folk stage and snatching for their share of the loot.'

The Old-Time Herald also published Pankake's essay 'Dock Boggs: Memories & Appreciations' in 1998: the same year he won a Grammy for his essay in the *Anthology of American Folk Music*.

With Marcia Pankake (a professor and bibliographer at the University of Minnesota) he is author of *The Prairie Home Companion Folk Song Book*, 1988, republished two years later as *Joe's Got a Head Like a Ping-Pong Ball*. He remains a student advisor at the University of Minnesota, and for the year 1994–95 he won the John Tate Award for Excellence in Undergraduate Advising.

[Jon Pankake: 'The Brotherhood of the Anthology', *Anthology of American Folk Music* 6-CD box set (with copious notes by many hands and a CD-ROM of extras), Smithsonian Folkways SRW 40090, Washington, D.C., 1997; feature on Tom Paley, *Sing Out!* vol.14, no.3, NY, Jul 1964; 'Dock Boggs: Memories & Appreciations', *Old-Time Herald* vol.6. no.6, Durham, NC, winter 1998–99; contributor to 'Issues in Old-Time Music—The Art of the Critique', *Old-Time Herald* vol.6, no.5, fall 1998; quote on Dylan on campus in *The Little Sandy Review*, in Shelton, *No Direction Home: The Life and Music of Bob Dylan*, Penguin edn., p.84; quote on Lomax & *Texas Folk Songs*, e-mail from Minneapolis to this writer, 17 May 1999; quotes re *No Direction Home* testimony & *Chronicles Volume One*, by phone to this writer, 24 Oct 2005. Minnesota Birth Index 1935–2002, file no. 1938-MN-015153.

Elizabeth Cotten: *Negro Folk Songs and Tunes*, Washington, D.C, 1957, Folkways FG3526, NY, 1957. Alan Lomax: *Texas Folk Songs*, Tradition TLP 1029, London, 1958 (CD-reissued Arion, France, 1991). Bob Dylan: *Chronicles Volume One*, pp.248–49, 250–52, 253, 254.]

Parker, Christopher [1950 -] Christopher Parker was born in Chicago on November 23, 1950, into a family that moved around a lot, including to Mobile, Alabama, Seattle, Forth Worth and eventually

New York City. He played drums at age three and played his first professional gigs at age 11, backing strippers at Nino's Cocktail Lounge in Brookfield, Connecticut. Still in his teens he started recording and touring with PAUL BUTTERFIELD, and at 20 became a regular New York studio session drummer, including on film-score soundtracks and on the 'Saturday Night Live' TV series. He has played for everyone from Miles Davis to Cher and from Aretha Franklin to Michael Bolton (i.e. from the sublime to the ridiculous).

In 1988 Parker became the very first drummer on what would become known as the Never-Ending Tour, which was launched on June 7 in Concord, California (and launched with the first live version of 'Subterranean Homesick Blues', followed immediately by the first live version of 'Absolutely Sweet Marie'). Parker played all that year's concerts, and all the following year's, adjusting to the departure of fellow rhythm section player KENNY AARONSON and his replacement by TONY GARNIER on bass. Parker continued in the band until the end of the last concert of 1990, in Detroit that November 18th. He'd notched up a total of 263 Dylan concerts. He asked to leave because he had missed most of the first 19 months of his new baby's life, and 'it felt wrong'. Dylan was supportive and their parting was entirely amicable.

Parker's nickname Toph (toe-ff rather than toff), may account for why the group he formed in 2000 is named Toph-E & the Pussy Cats. He still plays sessions and television and tours Japan. He lives in Sherman, Connecticut. That baby is now a 17-year-old musician.

[Data from *www.parkerdrum.com* & phone interview with this writer, both 11 Feb 2006.]

Parking Meter Rainer Vesely and Burkhard Schleser co-founded the Austria-based *Parking Meter* ('the German-language Dylan magazine'), which operated from 1997 to 2001, publishing its first issue in May 1997 in Vienna and launching its website that August. This was an important, witty and rare continental European fanzine, founded with the straightforward aim of 'publishing thoughts on the work of Bob Dylan', which not only succeeded to a high standard but built up a lasting means of communication between some knowledgeable and intelligent writers, music-lovers and Dylan fans within the German-speaking countries and beyond.

Burkhard Schleser was born in Vienna on September 18, 1960. He first listened to Dylan's work in 1977 and attended his first Dylan concert when he was 17 years old (at Nuremberg, July 1, 1978). From the 1980s onwards he began subscribing to fanzines, beginning with *The Telegraph* and then *Isis*, *Dignity* and *THE BRIDGE*, and occasionally read the US publication *ON THE TRACKS*. Nowadays he checks various websites daily instead. His other work in the world is in 'quality and information management'.

Rainer Vesely was born in Vienna on February 8, 1956. His interest in Dylan began in 1972 and his first published work on him was a review of *Empire Burlesque* in *Falter*, the Vienna City magazine, in 1985. He holds a PhD, was a freelance journalist 1984–95, is the editor and/or author of several books in the fields of cultural studies, poetry and literature and now works as a librarian in Vienna. His best non-Dylan work is probably *Querungen—Literarische Texte zu beiden Amerikas*, co-edited with Bernhard Widder (Vienna: Ritter-Verlag, 2001).

Parking Meter closed down as a published magazine after issue no. 16, in July 2001, but it continues to function as an online enterprise, at *www.parkingmeter.at*.

Pasqua, Alan [1952 -] Alan Pasqua was born in Elizabeth, New Jersey, on June 28, 1952. He learnt the piano at age seven, studied the classics and jazz, attended Indiana University and then gained a BA in Jazz Studies from the New England Conservatory. In New York he struck up a life-long friendship with guitarist Allan Holdsworth, and both joined drummer Tony Williams in his New Tony Williams Lifetime. After two albums, he moved to the West Coast and started to play sessions and tour with rock and pop artists, starting in Eddie Money's band and then, at age 25, becoming the keyboards player on Bob Dylan's 1978 World Tour. He therefore played a total of 114 Dylan concerts, and appears on the *Bob Dylan at Budokan* album. He also plays organ and piano throughout *Street Legal*.

After that he rejoined the ordinary world and Santana. In the late 1980s he and guitarist Danny Huff were responsible for the rock band Giant, from whose début album *Last of the Runaways* came a popular single, 'I'll See You in My Dreams', which Pasqua composed. He has also played with RAY CHARLES, Aretha Franklin, the Temptations, PHIL SPECTOR, Tom Scott, Dionne Warwick, Rod Stewart, Graham Nash, Pat Benatar, Quincy Jones, Henry Mancini, Stan Kenton . . . the list could go down and down. He co-composed the theme music for CBS-TV's 'Evening News' programme, heard nightly since 1987; topped the jazz charts with CDs called *Milagro* and *Dedications*; and wrote the score for the 1998 film *The Waterboy*. These days he plays with the Pasqua/Erskine Trio, fronts the Alan Pasqua Jazz Collective, accepts private pupils for piano tuition and is Assistant Professor of Jazz Studies at the Thornton School of Music at UCLA in Los Angeles. No doubt it's all finger-snappingly good, but it's not like playing with the Bob Dylan of 1978.

[Alan Pasqua: *Milangro*, Postcards POST1002, US, 1993; *Dedications*, Postcards POST1012, 1995. Pasqua/

Erskine Trio: *Live at Rocco*, Fuzzy Music PEPCD007, 2000; *Badlands*, Fuzzy Music PEPCD011, US, 2002. Giant: *Last of the Runaways*, A&M 75021-5272-4 (CD) & A&M 5272 (LP), US, 1989. *The Waterboy*, dir. Frank Coraci; Touchstone, US (very US) 1998. Some biographical data from *www.alanpasqua.com* & from Alan Pasqua, e-mail to this writer, 11 Feb 2006.]

***Pat Garrett & Billy the Kid* [album, 1973]** Dylan's 12th album of new work, but his first since 1970, was 'only' a film-soundtrack album (though, in the way of these things, it isn't the same thing as the soundtrack you hear on the movie: one of SAM PECKINPAH's best). It is a largely instrumental album, with all the characteristic roughness and lack of polish that has kept Bob Dylan less palatable to mass easy-listening taste than infinitely less talented contemporaries such as PAUL SIMON or PAUL McCARTNEY. Though a very minor item in Dylan's catalogue, it is a finely atmospheric work, engaging in its own right and effective as a part of the movie it was written for. It also includes the original hit recording of the perennially popular 'Knockin' on Heaven's Door'.

[Recorded Mexico City, 20 Jan 1973 and Burbank, CA, Feb 1973; released as stereo LP, Columbia KC 32460 (US) & CBS 69042 (UK), 13 Jul 1973.]

***Pat Garrett & Billy the Kid* [film, 1973]** By the time this film was made, in the last months of 1972, the genre of the western movie was almost extinct at the box office, hit by decades of safe films full of Alan Ladd and John Wayne and the same one-horse-town stage sets: decades in which white middle-class American life had become so prudish, sanitised and conformist that cowboy films easily satisfied a whimpering need to identify with a simpler, more manly life full of the great outdoors, goodies and baddies, cowboys and Indians, action and guns. By the mid-1960s the counter-culture was getting a hearing and the complexities and experiments of 'now', its tangle of new dress codes, music, openness and cultural excitation all made contemporary American life infinitely more interesting than all those uptight cowboys with their short hair and short fuses, their cornball campfire philosophising, sexual repression and racism. The western was almost wiped out. It was saved only by the exceptions of *Butch Cassidy & the Sundance Kid* (1969), for its genre-stretching modernist amorality, and *The Wild Bunch* (also 1969), for its trend-setting extravagance of modernist graphic violence.

In autumn 1972, therefore, SAM PECKINPAH, encouraged by the defiant success of *The Wild Bunch*, was ready to make another western: *Pat Garrett & Billy the Kid*. The screenwriter was Rudy Wurlitzer, author of three novels, one of which, *Nog*, had been a cult success. (In 1999, he and PATTI SMITH would share supplying the text to Lynn Davis' book of photographs, *Monument*.) The producer was Gordon Carroll, who would prove to be the one industry heavyweight to fight for Dylan's soundtrack against all those—from Peckinpah to music supervisor Jerry Fielding—who hoped to slick it up and smother it in 'professionalism'. KRIS KRISTOFFERSON was signed to co-star as Billy to James Coburn's Pat Garrett. Filming was to take place in the desert around Durango, Mexico.

Kristofferson's manager, Bert Block, who had handled business arrangements for Dylan's Isle of Wight Festival appearance back in 1969, enticed Dylan into the film: a casual mention that it was happening, and that Kristofferson was in it, was followed by a meeting between Dylan and Wurlitzer, and then a private screening of *The Wild Bunch*. Dylan, who had been mooching around doing very little all year, decided to go for it. A real film! Why not?! He moved down to Durango with his wife and five children on November 23, 1972.

Peckinpah didn't offer him a part till the second day Dylan was there. The part, when it came to it, was small but arguably crucial. Chris Whithouse noted that in the film as originally released 'we are left with 106 minutes of footage, in which there are only six scenes where Alias actually speaks. The part of Alias was always going to be relatively minor, even if Dylan's presence in the filming was major. Yet the first Alias appearance on screen implies, by recurrent cutting to him, that while he is only a spectator and takes no active part in the drama, he is to be significant nonetheless.' The rôle of Alias is indeed surely that of the human, humane everyman, the observer: the only male character of any import in the film who doesn't carry a gun. Film critic Gordon Gow wrote: 'To Alias, in fact, is assigned much of the film's neat recognition of fate. He broods silently, he worships and follows a hero but in time his left eye squints towards the camera, towards awareness of a hollow splendour.'

It's striking, too, that two key lines of film dialogue in the film, spoken in an exchange between the film's two main characters before the opening credits roll, come straight out of two crucial songs from Dylan's own history. Billy: 'How does it feel?' Garrett: 'It feels like times have changed.'

To achieve this Hollywood début, Dylan spent two months in the desert down in Mexico, either in the trailer he shared with Kristofferson on set or in a nearby rented house with SARA, the children and a dog called Rover. By the beginning of January, mostly thanks to technical problems, the film was two weeks behind schedule and $1 million over budget. It doesn't sound much now, but it was then—the total budget was meant to be $4m and went to $5m—and Peckinpah was continually harrassed by MGM executives. Dylan wanted to quit, but stayed on, making Kristofferson feel it was essentially for his sake. In the end, as a cost-cutting exercise, Peckinpah had to hand over the making of the final cut to the studio.

When the film came out, it was savaged by the *New York Times* and others. William S. Pechter dubbed it 'A rash adventure in inadvertent self-parody'; the great Stanley Kauffmann declared: 'Shows what Peckinpah can do when he doesn't put his mind to it.' The soundtrack album, too, was sniffily received. Nevertheless, Dylan came away from the experience wanting more: 'I want now to *make* movies,' he said. 'I've never been this close to movies before. I'll make a hell of a movie after this.' But he didn't.

Years later, the 'director's cut' of *Pat Garrett & Billy the Kid* was released. It was tremendous. This 'restored' film was first shown on US Cable TV in 1988, in UK cinemas in 1989 and on BBC-TV in January 1990. James Coburn had always said, 'Bobby Dylan's score too was cut up,' and the same proved true of film and music: that the restored version not only makes vastly more imaginative sense but, revealed after 15 years of familiarity with the MGM version, shows vividly just what mortifying butchery the corporation imposes upon its artists. That's no surprise, but *Pat Garrett & Billy the Kid* is a forceful demonstration of the process. There are, essentially, two versions of the film and so two versions of the music soundtrack, and without a doubt the restored version is in each case much superior.

[*Pat Garrett & Billy the Kid*, dir. Sam Peckinpah, written Rudy Wurlitzer; MGM, US, 1973; 'restored version', 1988; DVD 2-disc Special Edition, Warner Home Video, US, 2006. *Butch Cassidy & the Sundance Kid*, dir. George Roy Hill; TCF/Campanile, US, 1969. *The Wild Bunch*, dir. Sam Peckinpah; Warner Seven Arts/Phil Feldman, US, 1970. Rudy Wurlitzer: *Nog*, New York: Random House, 1968 (Pocket Books mass paperback, 1970). Gordon Gow, *Films & Filming*, UK, Aug 1973 & James Coburn, quoted in Chris Whithouse, 'Alias, Pat Garrett & Billy the Kid', revised from *The Telegraph* no.19, Bury, UK, autumn 1985 & collected in Michael Gray & John Bauldie, eds, *All Across the Telegraph: A Bob Dylan Handbook*, London: W.H. Allen, 1987. William S. Pechter & Stanley Kauffmann quoted from John Walker, ed, *Halliwell's Film Guide, 11th edition*, London: HarperCollins, 1995.]

Patchen, Kenneth [1911 - 1972] Kenneth Patchen was born in Niles, Ohio, on December 13, 1911. He was absorbed by literature from the age of 12 and read widely.

To alight on his work is to move away from the kind of American poetry that is taught in schools to the kind of poetry that you find for yourself after you've left school. Patchen's work was done in the 1930s-50s and beyond, and he was, if such a thing is possible, typical of the jazz-influenced, jazz-culture-influenced generation of writers who ended up being called the Beat Generation.

In 1942 he collaborated with John Cage on a radio play, *The City Wears a Slouch Hat*, and ten years later was pioneering a combination of poetry recitation with jazz accompaniment. Charles Mingus was one of his co-pioneers in this work.

For Folkways Records, MOSES ASCH recorded Patchen reading some of his poetry, and recorded him (in Patchen's own home) reading excerpts from his novel *The Journal of Albion Moonlight*, 1941 (a title in turn acknowledging BLAKE).

Patchen's influence on Dylan is first of all evident throughout Dylan's novel *Tarantula*. The first person to note this was Gabrielle Goodchild, in her essay '*Tarantula*: Tangled Up in a Web', 1979—in which she argues the specific relevance of *The Journal of Albion Moonlight* to Dylan's novel.

But Dylan is inspired by more of Patchen than that one work, as we can see even within *Tarantula*. This, for example, from Patchen's 'I Don't Want to Startle You' (1939), would fit well anywhere inside it, and typifies one of the tones of voice Dylan adopts in the sections styled as personal letters and messages from various self-regarding, belligerent, callow people to their friends or enemies:

'I knew the General only by name of course. / I said Wartface what have you done with her? / I said You Dirtylouse tell me where is she now? / His duck-eyes shifted to the guard. All right, Sam. / . . . Who is that fat turd I said—he hit me with his jewelled fist. / While his man held me he put a lighted cigarette on my eyelid. / I smelt the burning flesh through his excellent perfume. On the wall it said "Democracy must be saved at all costs." / The floor was littered with letters of endorsement from liberals.' (There's even that direct cigarette-eyelid connection, which Dylan resuscitates in 'Memphis Blues Again'.)

This, too, would pass for Dylan's work in *Tarantula*: 'When they fitted the black cap over his head / He knew that he'd never have another chance to be president.' It is from Patchen's 'All The Bright Foam Of Talk', 1939.

Then there is the Patchen influence upon Dylan's songs. A phrase of Patchen's, 'Cathedral evening', which opens his 1950s poem 'Beautiful You Are', is used unaltered in Dylan's 'Chimes of Freedom'. Patchen's title 'Nice Day for a Lynching', 1939, echoes behind Dylan's line from 'Talking World War III Blues': 'Good car to drive, after a war.' Perhaps another Patchen title, 'Red Wine and Yellow Hair', 1949, resonates under Dylan's line from 'Angelina': 'Blood dryin' in my yellow hair . . .' More surely the poem '23rd Street Runs into Heaven', 1939, brushes Patchen's wings across Dylan's 'Three Angels'. Patchen's lines include '. . . lights wink / On along the street. Somewhere a trolley, taking / Shop-girls and clerks home, clatters through / This before-supper Sabbath. An alley cat cries / To find the garbage cans sealed; newsboys / Begin . . .'; Dylan's narrator observes 'The Tenth Avenue bus going west. / The dogs and pigeons fly up and they flutter around, / A man with a badge skips by, / Three fellas crawlin' on their way back to work / . . . The bakery truck stops . . .' (In fact both sets of lines also resemble a short but striking passage from JEAN GENET's *Our Lady of the Flowers*.)

Dylan inherits ideas from Patchen too—or at least from the milieu that Patchen helped to create. The poem 'The Rites of Darkness' (1942) encompasses a lot of Dylan's oft-expressed Gemini-schizoid feelings about the glamour of urban wickedness and decadence felt contemporaneously with the ever-visible presence of God, and about the nature of truth and beauty. When Patchen writes: 'But no one sees the giant horse / That climbs the steps which stretch forth / Between the calling lights and that hill / Straight up to the throne of God', he offers a notion that becomes a second layer of input into Dylan's 'Three Angels', in which 'The angels play on their horns all day . . . / But does anyone hear the music they play?' And this, from the same Patchen poem—'We can't believe in anything / Because nothing is pure enough. / Because nothing will ever happen / To make us good in our own sight'—encapsulates succinctly attitudes Dylan has veered towards in many works, from the poem about JOAN BAEZ through to 'Dirge' and from 'Shelter from the Storm' to 'Highlands', in 1997, in which 'Well, my heart's in the highlands: / I'm gonna go there / When I feel good enough to go.'

As it claims on the dust-jacket of *The Selected Poems of Kenneth Patchen*, his work focuses on 'his direct and passionate concern with the most essential elements in the tragic, comic, blundering and at rare moments glorious world around us. He wrote about the things we can feel with our whole being—the senselessness of war, the need for love among men on earth, the presence of God in man, the love for a beloved woman, social injustice, and the continual resurgence of the beautiful in life.' Which is what you might reasonably say (though you might not choose to express it quite like that) about the recurrent concerns of Dylan's work.

All the above can be—has been—adduced from the work, rather than from biographical information. But then ROBERT SHELTON's Dylan biography, *No Direction Home*, published in 1986, revealed that Patchen was a favourite writer of TONY GLOVER, Dylan's close and influential friend from his Dinkytown Minneapolis period—the period when he first left home and attended, briefly, the University of Minnesota; and then in 1989, in BOB SPITZ's repellent *Bob Dylan: A Biography*, Dylan's other intimate of the period, DAVE WHITAKER, stated specifically that in the winter of 1960 he introduced Dylan to Kenneth Patchen's 'experimental verse'.

Patchen died of a heart-attack in Palo Alto, California, on January 8, 1972.

[Kenneth Patchen: *The Selected Poems of Kenneth Patchen*, 1957. Patchen recordings: *Kenneth Patchen Reads with Jazz in Canada*, Folkways 1959; *Selected Poems of Kenneth Patchen*, Folkways, 1960; *Kenneth Patchen Reads His Love Poems*, Folkways, 1961; and *From Albion Moonlight*, Folkways, 1972.

Gabrielle Goodchild: '*Tarantula*: Tangled Up in a Web', unpublished essay, 1979, available for reference in the Robert Shelton Collection at the Experience Music Project archive, Seattle. An extract was published under the title (not the author's) '*Tarantula*: The Web Untangled', in *Conclusions on the Wall*, ed. Elizabeth M. Thomson, 1980. The essay was originally commissioned by Shelton as background material for his Dylan biography.]

Patton, Charley [1891 - 1934] Charles or Charlie Patton (the spelling Charley derives from his record labels, and has recently been moved away from by some blues devotees) was born at Edwards, Mississippi, probably in April 1891. As the writer and critic Tony Russell puts it, with his usual elegant succinctness: 'Among Mississippi singers of the first blues generation . . . Patton was far and away the most celebrated in his own community. Perhaps as a reaction to the idolatry surrounding ROBERT JOHNSON, he has inspired a uniquely fierce devotion in many blues-lovers. His singing—gruff, barking, extraordinarily resonant—and his richly accented, percussive guitar-playing put him among the most influential blues artists . . .'

While Bob Dylan was entranced early on by Johnson (who was still a boy when Patton first entered a studio), he has come more and more to find solace in, as well as admiration for, Charley Patton's recordings: most of which were made for Paramount and are therefore as scratchy and aurally inhospitable as possible—a factor that of itself means that only the determinedly devoted ever really arrive at the creative rich heart of this powerful figure's music. Even his vocal delivery makes him harder than almost any other figure to decipher—much easier to pick up the urgency, the evocation of the geographically rooted hard life, the 'voice as thick as molasses' and the boisterous, rebarbative showmanship of the guitar-work, and catch the words when you can.

His first session was in Richmond, Indiana, on June 14, 1929–he laid down 14 sides, and Paramount made them into seven singles: not a take wasted. One single, 'Prayer of Death—Part 1' and 'Part 2', was released as by Elder J.J. Hadley; another, 'Mississippi Boweavil Blues' c/w 'Screamin' and Hollerin' the Blues', as by the Masked Marauder (on most but not all copies). When HARRY SMITH issued 'Mississippi Boweavil Blues' on vinyl in his *AMERICAN FOLK MUSIC* collection of 1952, such was the mysteriousness of Patton's life that Smith did not know that the Masked Marauder was Patton. Even today, only one photograph of him exists. Very recently, a full-length version of the same shot may have emerged: but people have dug deep to find more, and entirely failed.

Patton had three further sessions for Paramount, all 1929–30, playing behind Henry Sims on two sides and cutting 28 more sides of his own. Again not a single one went unissued. Then in early 1934 the indefatigable H.C. Speir got him out of jail in Belzoni and took him to New York City by train to record for Vocalion, for whom, at three sessions on three consecutive days, he played behind Bertha Lee (his last wife) and cut another 26 sides of his own; but this time 16 of them went unissued. His last session was on the first day of February 1934. He died from a general combination of poverty, drink and congenital heart disease on the Heathman plantation near Indianola, Mississippi, on April 28, 1934.

The world he describes in his blues is localised and particular–he names individual policemen, trains, flood effects ('Backwater at Blytheville done struck Joiner town / It was 50 families and their children . . .'), but he was the decisive influence on other musicians who heard him, Tommy Johnson included, and in a number of cases he was a literal tutor as well. People from HOWLIN' WOLF to Pops Roebuck of THE STAPLE SINGERS learnt to play guitar from Patton (as well as picking up, especially in Wolf's case, much repertoire). Most of his own life was lived on the Dockery plantation near Ruleville, Mississippi. His impact, like a meteor hitting earth in one spot, was immensely wide. Russell again: 'Apart from "Pony Blues", the songs of Patton's time and place that have become standards belong rather to Tommy Johnson or to BIG JOE WILLIAMS. His music survived less as a repertoire than as a grandiose sound effect, echoing through the years not only in the South but in the new Chicago blues of the post-war Mississippi migrants.'

In *Chronicles Volume One*, Dylan writes that he first heard Patton on Arhoolie blues compilation LPs owned by SPIDER JOHN KOERNER. That unreliable testimony aside, the book doesn't mention Patton–yet not only does Dylan follow the implicit homage of his *Street Legal* song 'New Pony' in 1978 with the explicit homage of the *"Love and Theft"* song 'High Water (For Charley Patton)', but he has also said in interview in recent years both that the guitar riff underneath his great 'Highlands' on *Time Out of Mind* is taken from an old Charley Patton record–he doesn't say which and it's hard to pin down, though the likely contender is 'Dry Well Blues'–and more sweepingly that if it were up to him, he wouldn't write songs at all any more: he'd just record songs by Patton. This would surely only be worthwhile if he could in some way match the originals–not by duplication, but rather by imaginative re-creation–and to try to do that would be to set himself an impossible task. Up to the end of 2005, Dylan had performed 'High Water (For Charley Patton)' 165 times in concert, starting in LA on October 19, 2001 and steaming through to Dublin on November 27, 2005. Many of his April 2006 US concerts have continued to feature the song.

See also **the lowlands**.

[Charley Patton: 'Pony Blues', Richmond, IN, 14 Jun 1929; 'High Water Everywhere', Grafton, WI, c.Oct 1929; 'Dry Well Blues', Grafton, c.28 May 1930; 'Stone Pony Blues', NY, 30 Jan 1934. Bob Dylan, *Chronicles Volume One*, 2004, p.239. Tony Russell, *The Blues from Robert Johnson to Robert Cray*, London: Aurum Press, 1997, pp.42–43. Birth date & death information from Dick Spottswood, Patton entry in *The Encyclopedia of the Blues*, New York: Routledge, 2006, 2 vols., pp.748–50.]

'Peace in the Valley' See **Dorsey, Thomas A.**

Peckinpah, Sam [1925 - 1984] David Samuel Peckinpah was born on February 21, 1925 in Fresno, California, growing up there when it was, in Walter Melnyk's phrase, 'still a sleepy town surrounded by pine forests.' He was strongly influenced by an uncle who was a judge, congressman and excellent shot. He enlisted in the Marine Corps in 1943, was sent to China in 1945 to disarm Japanese soldiers and send them home. He never saw combat and returned to the US at the end of 1946. He earned a Drama BA at Fresno State College in 1949 and an MA at the University of Southern California in 1950. Early jobs in the entertainment industry included floor sweeping for 'The Liberace Show' in 1952; two years later he got a job as gopher and dialogue coach to Don Siegel, and in 1956 had a small part in Siegel's *Invasion of the Body-Snatchers*. Via Siegel he came to write episodes of the TV series 'Gunsmoke'; other series followed, his first work as director being a 1958 episode of 'Broken Arrow' titled 'The Knife Fighter'. Further work directing TV western series led to a first film chance; he was assigned the 1961 Maureen O'Hara vehicle *Deadly Companions*, about a dance hall hostess. He was happier about his second film, *Ride the High Country* (1962), which won a series of international film prizes but was more or less killed off at the box office by MGM's lack of enthusiasm. Filming *Major Dundee* with Charlton Heston (1965) involved much location time in the Mexican desert, and ended up with Peckinpah losing control of an over-long film that was then cut by the studio before its release. In these ways prefiguring *Pat Garrett & Billy the Kid*, it was also the film that established Peckinpah's image as an erratic and dangerous man, and always at odds with both his stars and his studio.

As a result, the director spent three years unable to work, except on a quietly acclaimed ABC-TV Special, 'Noon Wine' (1966): but after the huge success of *The Wild Bunch* in 1969 came a flurry of films in quick succession–*The Ballad of Cable Hogue*, *Straw Dogs*, *Junior Bonner* and *The Getaway* (all 1970–72). And then *Pat Garrett & Billy the Kid*.

Peckinpah and Dylan didn't meet until they were already on location around Durango, Mexico, in late November 1972–and Peckinpah had only the vaguest idea of who Bob Dylan was. Co-star James Coburn describes how they came together:

'Sam says, "Who's Bob Dylan? Oh yeah, the kids used to listen to his stuff." And we all said, "What!! You gotta see Dylan." He said, "Okay, bring Dylan down." And Dylan had been in hiding . . . and he came down with his tall Indian hat and his little moustache. Very strange cat. Wonderful guy. He was like quicksilver. You could never put your finger on Bobby. So the night we were over at Sam's house and we were all drinking tequila and carrying on and halfway through dinner, Sam says, "Okay kid, see what you got. You bring your guitar with you?" They went in this little alcove. Sam had a rocking chair. Bobby sat down on a stool in front of this rocking chair. There was just the two of them in there. And Bobby played three or four tunes. And Sam came out with his handkerchief in his eye. "Goddamn kid! Who the hell is he? Who is that kid? Sign him up!" He was very moved.'

He didn't stay moved. As others saw it, he became increasingly jealous of Dylan's implacable charisma and the pull it gave him, despite the small size of his part in *Peckinpah*'s film, and in the end the two of them were clearly locked in competitive struggle. When Dylan had a recording session at Columbia's Mexico City studio, on January 20, 1973, Peckinpah tried to stop everyone flying off there by announcing a special screening of *The Getaway*. Everyone got away to the recording session instead.

Dylan nonetheless felt that Peckinpah still wanted him around. As he told CAMERON CROWE in the *Biograph* interview:

'Actually, I was just one of Peckinpah's pawns. There wasn't a part for me and Sam just liked me around. . . . Rudy Wurlitzer . . . invented a part for me but there wasn't any dimension to it and I was very uncomfortable in this non-rôle. . . . there I was trapped deep in the heart of Mexico with some madman, ordering people around like a little king. You had to play the dummy all day. . . . It was crazy, all these generals making you jump into hot ants, setting up turkey shoots and whatever . . . I was too beat to take it personal . . . I was sleep-walking most of the time and had no real reason to be there. I'd gotten my family out of New York, that was the important thing, there was a lot of pressure back there. But even so, my wife got fed up almost immediately. She'd say to me, "What the hell are we doing here?" It was not an easy question to answer.'

There is one terrible-quality circulating copy of a recording made of Dylan singing at that 'audition' at Peckinpah's Durango house: a single solo performance of 'Billy'. (The whole of the Mexico City session has circulated, and it includes the 'Billy 4' released on the soundtrack album, the rest of which was recorded in Burbank the following month.)

Altogether Peckinpah directed 14 films, and his reputation has not yet settled. He's not exactly a feminist favourite; but at their best, his films, even the much-stressed violence of his films, bring an elegiac quality, a largeness of vision—a poetry—to the screen. Peckinpah died of heart failure in California, aged 59, three days after Christmas, 1984.

[Sources: Gabrielle Murray, 'Sam Peckinpah', at *www.sensesofcinema.com/contents/directors/02/peckinpah.html*; Walter Melnyk from the IMDb at *http://us.imdb.com/name/nm0001603/bio*; James Coburn quoted from *http://frontpage.simnet.is/bobdylan/friends.htm*; all online 2 Oct 2005; Chris Whithouse, 'Alias, Pat Garrett & Billy the Kid', revised from *The Telegraph* no.19, Bury, UK, autumn 1985 & collected in Michael Gray & John Bauldie, eds, *All Across the Telegraph: A Bob Dylan Handbook*, London: W.H. Allen, 1987.]

Pelto, Gretel [1940 -] Gretel Hoffman was born in Minneapolis on May 6, 1940, into a left-wing intellectual Jewish family; her mother was a photographer and her father a sociologist. She left high school a year early and enrolled in Bennington College, Vermont, in September 1957 to study dance and choreography. Here she met East Coast arts students who played folk music, hung out in Greenwich Village and 'adored ODETTA'. But she dropped out in January 1960, at the end of the winter holiday, full of doubt about her dancing, got a part-time job and started hanging out in Dinkytown. 'This was very familiar territory because I had gone to high school on the University of Minnesota campus,' she told TERRY KELLY.

She and the bohemian DAVE WHITAKER met Bob Dylan in January 1960. She has no memory of any specific first encounter but she liked him enormously, straight away. 'He was obviously highly intelligent and had a wonderful sense of humor; he had a great smile. . . . Of all the folks who hung around the Scholar, he was by far the most interesting.' Right from their first meeting with Dylan, she and Dave knew him well, getting together with him every day at the 10 O'Clock Scholar for those first three months.

That June, she married Dave; she had just turned 20. Outside the Scholar soon afterwards, when she and Dylan bumped into each other, he didn't return her greeting but shouted back across the street, 'When you get divorced, come and let me know!' For a while Gretel and Dave lived in the boarding house above McCosh's bookstore along with another of Bob's friends, HARVEY ABRAMS. She said of Dylan's own accommodation at the time: 'He was living in a horrible green room that had a bed, a chair, a desk, a refrigerator with moldy food in it, some beer. . . . I was struck by his being just a sweet guy. There was something very gentle about him, something a little bit sad too. He used to say frequently that he would be dead before he was twenty-one. . . . It was clear that he wouldn't do it, that he wasn't suicidal, but he just felt that was the way his life was mapped out.'

It was at a party for Gretel in May 1960 that TONY GLOVER first met Dylan, and a year on, Gretel was generally around but doesn't remember being there when the Dylan tapes were made in BONNIE BEECHER's apartment in May and December 1961 (she was a close friend of Bonnie's). She always felt that Minneapolis was a very good place for someone to develop in music. She also confirmed that it was Dave Whitaker—'David' as she preferred to call him—who had 'turned Bob on to *Bound for Glory*'. Bob was living in the small back room of their apartment at the time.

Gretel thinks it 'very likely' that it was she who introduced Dylan to Odetta's work. She had bought the first album in fall 1959, 'virtually memorized the songs' and since she doesn't think she lent him the record, 'more likely I sang them for him'.

She continued to know Dylan, when he was around, until some time in 1963. She and Dave split up that November, 'a couple of days before the Kennedy assassination', as she puts it. She remarried, becoming Gretel Pelto, in July 1967, left Minneapolis in 1969, moved to Connecticut and completed her PhD in Medical Anthropology in 1970. From then till 1992 she was on the faculty at the University of Connecticut, where her primary appointment was in the Department of Nutritional Sciences but with joint appointments in the Medical School and the Department of Anthropology. In 1992 she moved to Switzerland to head up a behavioural research programme at Geneva, in the Division of Child Health within the World Health Organisation. She returned to the US in 1999 where she is now a professor in the Division of Nutritional Sciences at Cornell. She has taken, in other words, a very different route through the world from that of her ex-husband Dave.

She has had little contact with Bob Dylan since 1963. The last performance of his that she remembers is from his brief appearance on the annual *Sing Out!* Hootenanny at Carnegie Hall, on September 22, 1962. He performed 'Sally Gal', 'Highway 51' and a version of his 'Talkin' John Birch Paranoid Blues' but then finished with two major new songs, both as-yet unrecorded, 'Ballad of Hollis Brown' and 'A Hard Rain's a-Gonna Fall'. For Gretel, the entire experience was moving and numinous. 'It was an extraordinary evening,' she told Terry Kelly. 'When Bob was introduced, a huge roar went through the hall. We couldn't believe our ears. Bobby? Earlier in the day we thought he was just playing games when he said he didn't want to eat in a restaurant because he would be accosted by fans and he wore sunglasses. . . . His singing was superb. It was a moment of truth. It was wonderful.'

She'd no longer be able to say that of a Dylan concert today—but while Gretel Pelto hasn't read *Chronicles Volume One*, she was pleasantly surprised by the near-contemporary Bob seen in the interview sections in SCORSESE's *No Direction Home*: 'The fundamental honesty and straightness, his humor, his basic artist integrity all came through fully.' There was much else she liked about the film too; but she didn't care for its implicit claim—Dylan's implicit claim—that his artistic life began in, and was only formed by, New York City. As she knows, that's simply not the case.

[Gretel Pelto quoted in: Robert Shelton, *No Direction Home: The Life and Music of Bob Dylan*, London: Penguin edn., pp.72, 75; e-mail to this writer 13 Nov 2005; & written answers to Terry Kelly, for feature, *The Bridge* no. 24, Gateshead, UK, spring 2006.]

Pennebaker, D.A. [1925 -] Donn Alan Pennebaker was born in Evanston, Illinois, on July 15, 1925. A designer of power stations and owner of an electronics company, he worked through films for the YMCA and the Boy Scouts, and shorts like *Daybreak Express* (1953) to become a pioneer of cinéma vérité and 'direct cinema', making films that characteristically avoid voice-overs and interviews but merely 'watch' their subjects—in Pennebaker's case mostly musicians—with a hand-held camera and available light. In other words, he pioneered the kind of fly-on-the-wall documentary now so commonplace on television.

When Robert Drew, another pioneer, founded Drew Associates in 1960, Pennebaker and Richard Leacock were among his select group of filmmakers, but in 1963 they left to form their own film production company, Leacock Pennebaker Inc. Accounts vary greatly as to how Pennebaker came to be commissioned to film Bob Dylan's 1965 tour of Britain (see ***Don't Look Back*** and **Alk, Howard**) but film it he did, in black and white, and achieving an unprecedented intimacy of access to an artist who has always maintained his mystery. Pennebaker was almost 40 when he was filming, and Dylan was just turning 24; there must have been some misalignment of communication, but this may have kept everyone on their toes and helped to make Pennebaker's film the great achievement it is. He was not so lucky the following year when, no longer the auteur director but clearly the hired hand, he filmed in colour footage of Dylan's 1966 UK tour, and then had to hand it over to Dylan and Howard Alk, who had been an assistant on *Don't Look Back*, in whose hands the film turned into *Eat the Document*.

Pennebaker never worked with Dylan again, but moved on to make other films, including what turned out to be the historically invaluable *Monterey Pop* (filmed in 1967 and released in 1968), *Sweet Toronto* (filmed 1969, released 1971) and the 26-minute documentary *Keep on Rockin'* (released 1972), which featured performances by LITTLE RICHARD, CHUCK BERRY, BO DIDDLEY, JERRY LEE LEWIS, JIMI HENDRIX and Janis Joplin (and would have featured JOHN LENNON and Yoko Ono had their scenes not been deleted), and *Ziggy Stardust and the Spiders from Mars* (1973).

From 1977 onwards, Pennebaker has worked with the much younger Chris Hegedus, whom he married in 1982 (and who calls him Penny). Their collaboration began with a five-hour, three-part documentary, *The Energy War* (1977) and then with her discovering his old discarded 1971 footage of a stormy evening's confrontation that April between Norman Mailer and various eminent feminists at a public meeting in New York. She reworked this material into *Town Bloody Hall*, 1979, by which time it already seemed to document a bygone age and, for some commentators, in an equally dated style. Subsequent Pennebaker Hegedus Films' documentaries have included 1993's *The War Room*, following two of Bill Clinton's advisors around during his first presidential campaign, and *Down from the Mountain* (2000), about the musicians who performed in the film *O Brother, Where Art Thou?*. Co-directed by Pennebaker, Hegedus and Nick Doob, this documentary is co-produced by BOB NEUWIRTH—whom Pennebaker first came across as Dylan's 1965 sidekick (but who had also helped with lighting, filming and even editing on *Don't Look Back*)—and Donn's son Frazer Pennebaker.

D.A. Pennebaker, now 80 years old, still lives in New York City.

'People Get Ready' Dylan has recorded 'People Get Ready' three times, always obscurely: at the Basement Tapes sessions in Woodstock in June 1967, unreleased; in New York City in late 1975, not released officially but present on the *Renaldo & Clara* film soundtrack, 1978; and at New Bloomington, Indiana, in late 1989, for use on the soundtrack of the film *Catchfire*, directed by and starring Dennis Hopper, in which Dylan makes a brief appearance as a 'chainsaw artist'. (This film is also known as *Backtrack*, and has often been confused in accounts of Dylan's work with the different film *Flashback*, which also stars Hopper.) Dylan has performed 'People Get Ready' live only once—and, naturally, at a concert it's particularly difficult to find a recording of: in Buenos Aires, Argentina, on August 8, 1991.

THE STAPLE SINGERS may have popularised 'People Get Ready' but only Pops (Roebuck) Staples seems to have recorded it. His version, along with a revival of Dylan's 'Gotta Serve Somebody' is on his 1994 album *Father, Father*. But the song was first a hit by the Impressions, fronted by Curtis Mayfield, its composer, in 1965. We know that Dylan was familiar with this more or less immediately after its release, for the Impressions album containing it, *The Big Sixteen*, is pictured on the cover of his own album *Bringing It All Back Home*, which was issued in March 1965. Mayfield re-recorded the song on *Curtis Live*, for his own label, in 1971.

Dylan was probably familiar, too, with the rough, bluesy version cut by the Chambers Brothers as title track of their 1966 début album. They were a hit at 1965's NEWPORT FOLK FESTIVAL; Dylan brought them in on backing vocals on a rejected take of 'Tombstone Blues' in 1965; and he praises them in the 1985 *Biograph* box-set interview.

'People Get Ready', based in part on the gospel stalwart 'THIS TRAIN', remains one of the most potent songs inspired by the sufferings and hopes of black Americans in the civil rights era (Mayfield is said to have been moved to compose it by the March on Washington of August 1963).

[Bob Dylan: 'People Get Ready': Woodstock, Jun 1967; NY, c.28 Oct 1975; and New Bloomington, IN, 20 Nov 1989. Film: *Catchfire*, aka *Backtrack*, dir. Dennis Hopper, Vestron Pictures, US, 1989; soundtrack CD, *Backtrack*, WTG Records 46042, USA, 1990. *Flashback*, dir. Franco Amurri, Paramount, US, 1990.

Pops (Roebuck) Staples: 'People Get Ready' & 'Gotta Serve Somebody', LA, c.1994, *Father, Father*, Point Blank VPBCD 19, LA (Point Blank 7243 8 39638, London), 1994. The Impressions: 'People Get Ready', Chicago, 26 Oct 1964, ABC-Paramount 10622, Hollywood (HMV POP 1408, London), 1965; and *The Big Sixteen*, ABC-Paramount, Hollywood (HMV CLP 1935, London), 1965. Curtis Mayfield: 'People Get Ready', *Curtis Live*, NYC 1970–71, Curtom CRS 8008, Chicago, 1971. The Chambers Brothers: 'People Get Ready', *People Get Ready*, LA, 1966, Vault 9003, LA (Vocalion SVAL 8058, London), 1966.]

Perkins, Carl [1932 - 1998] Carl Perkins was born in Lake County, Tennessee, on April 9, 1932. Hearing ELVIS PRESLEY for the first time at the age of 22 meant recognising the same mad amalgam of styles he was already fooling with himself. 'When I heard Elvis singing "Blue Moon of Kentucky",' said Perkins, 'I knew I had a future in music. It was the same sound my band was making.'

The band comprised Carl on electric guitar and vocals, and his brothers Jay (on acoustic guitar) and Clayton (stand-up bass). They'd grown up in a largely black community, in which the division wasn't black or white but rich or poor. 'You either worked the dirt or you owned it,' said Carl, 'and we worked it.' Thus he was raised on country music and the blues, and as it happened the man who taught him guitar was black. 'He wasn't no great guitarist, but he could play these little blues licks, bending the notes like I hadn't heard them doing on the Grand Ole Opry.'

Like so many, Perkins was drawn to Sam Phillips' Sun Studios in Memphis, and Phillips signed him up. In late 1955 he was a support act to Presley on the Western Swing Jamboree Tour, and subsequently one of the so-called Million Dollar Quartet.

Unlike Presley, Perkins was as much lead-guitarist as singer, and composed his own material (though often by the brazen refashioning of older songs). He made only seven singles before being lured away from the Sun 'family' to the corporate graveyard of Columbia Records, Nashville, and alcohol-

Jon Pankake

Kenneth Patchen

Bob Dylan being filmed by D.A. Pennebaker, 1965

Photography by Sherry Rayn Barnett

Mary, Paul & Peter

Library of Congress

Doc Pomus

© Roger Marshutz

Elvis Presley, 1956, Tupelo, Mississippi

ism. Yet these few early recordings established Perkins as an influential guitarist—influential on how rock'n'roll guitar-work would be—whose playing was distinctive, creative, often exploratory and always interesting. These sessions yielded three Perkins songs that immediately became rock'n' roll standards: 'Matchbox', 'Honey Don't!' and, pre-eminently, 'Blue Suede Shoes', the first, and possibly only, rockabilly million-seller, and the perfect expression of a restless generation's innocent embrace of the new 1950s boom economy, the escape from post-war drear, and the fresh discovery of clothes, music, language and leisure-habits distinct from parental ones. Recorded and released in January 1956, it immediately became Sun Records' biggest single, outselling all their Elvis records just as Elvis had moved to RCA Victor, where the A&R men were set to wondering if they'd 'signed the wrong one'. But in March 1956 Carl and brother Jay were badly injured (Jay died two years later) when their driver fell asleep at the wheel en route to New York where they were to perform their smash hit on Perry Como's nationwide TV show. Carl lay in hospital while his big-time moment passed.

Myth had Perkins feeling that if it hadn't been for that accident, he might have become *the* hot phenomenon of rock in place of Elvis. He never suffered this delusion, which would have meant misunderstanding completely the importance of sex in music. On the contrary, he summed up the situation with self-deprecation and wit: 'Elvis,' he said, 'was the only one of us who didn't look like Mister Ed.'

If Carl would never have broken out of the world that fed his inspiration, this was as much his strength as his limitation. 'Put Your Cat Clothes On' was another call to sartorial Saturday night action, while his unusually tough 'Dixie Fried' gave a glimpse of how wild that action could be in the roadhouses Perkins and his band had started out playing. The genial Perkins word-play was strangely at odds with his voice, which only erratically carried authenticating energy, and was, when not fired up, as lacking in sharpness as in sexiness. Perhaps the essential dullness of his voice is what kept him the perfect rockabilly icon: he never stopped sounding candidly hick.

In 1964 Carl toured Britain as support to CHUCK BERRY, and found himself revered, not least by THE BEATLES, who recorded several of his songs. But with little tangible career left, he joined JOHNNY CASH's live show. He claimed that he helped Cash off drugs while Cash got him off booze. He stayed with him for over ten years.

That's how he came to play guitar on the 1969 Dylan-Cash duet of 'Girl of the North Country' on Dylan's *Nashville Skyline*—and on the many other Dylan-Cash duets recorded at the same day's session. Around 14 takes from this session have circulated, including an attractive version of the Jack Clement song 'Guess Things Happen That Way', but none has been released. The song 'Champaign, Illinois', jointly written by Dylan and Perkins, and which Perkins duly recorded and released, comes from 1970.

Splitting with Cash in 1976, Perkins tried to restart his own career, using his sons as his rhythm section, but though he held the respect of other musicians for his place in rock history, he had nothing but a handful of ever-tamer oldies to offer. Back in Britain in the late 1970s, he was easily upstaged by BO DIDDLEY, as he was by JERRY LEE LEWIS at 1981's Wembley Country Festival. His decision to wear powder-blue Elvis-in-Vegas stage clothes, bouffanty hair and a fake tan did not help.

Late in life he composed a no.1 country hit by the Judds, 'Let Me Tell You About Love', and 'Restless'. In 1986 came a TV Special filmed in London, 'A Rockabilly Session—Carl Perkins and Friends', the friends including GEORGE and RINGO, the inevitable ERIC CLAPTON and others. After ROY ORBISON's death, Perkins was mooted as his replacement in THE TRAVELING WILBURYS, but it never happened.

In Jackson, Tennessee, however, on November 10, 1994, he was brought on stage at the end of a Dylan concert, and sang his classic, 'Matchbox', backed by Dylan and the Never-Ending Tour band plus his own guitar. (Dylan had also played around with a version of 'Matchbox' during his studio session with George Harrison in New York City on May 1, 1970.)

Carl Perkins was the only rockabilly hero to write a song as big-selling and as famous as those of the seminal giants like LITTLE RICHARD or Chuck Berry. That's why, within the rockabilly genre, he has no equal in stature. But that is another way of saying that when rockabilly grew into rock'n'roll, and later into rock, Perkins stayed behind.

Despite the suicide of his brother Clayton in the 1970s, and his own throat cancer some years later, he continued to perform and record right up till his own death, which was on January 19, 1998 in Jackson, Tennessee. He was 65.

Two days after his death, at one of those shared-bill concerts by Dylan and VAN MORRISON, the two of them sang 'Blue Suede Shoes' in tribute at Madison Square Garden, during Morrison's set. They repeated this tribute three nights later in Boston. At Perkins' funeral that same day—at which George Harrison played an early Perkins song on guitar—Bob Dylan sent a note, which was read out. 'He really stood for freedom. That whole sound stood for all the degrees of freedom. It would just jump right off the turntable. We wanted to go where that was happening.'

And it was true that Dylan had wanted to go there very early on. One of the bits of song on the recently discovered 1956 recording of Dylan and his friends singing was of another Carl Perkins record from that very year: his minor hit 'Boppin' the Blues'.

[Carl Perkins: 'Blue Suede Shoes' c/w 'Honey Don't!', Memphis, TN, Jan 1956, Sun 234, Memphis, 1956; 'Matchbox', Memphis, 30 Jan 1957, Sun 261, Memphis, 1957 (an earlier cut, Memphis, 4 Dec 1956, remained unissued until the box set *Carl Perkins: The Sun Years*, Charley, London, c.1980); 'Champaign, Illinois', *nia*, 1970; 'Boppin' the Blues', Memphis, 1956, Sun 243, Memphis, 1956. Perkins on the Dylan-Cash duets, Nashville, 18 Feb 1969.]

Peter, Paul & Mary Commercially packaged 'folk' trio created and managed by shrewd bruiser ALBERT GROSSMAN, who also became Dylan's manager. When Dylan first went east and arrived in New York, at the start of the 1960s, the repertoire and styles of delivery he developed provided a culture-shock not only to SINATRA-tuned popular-music audiences but also to many of the patrons (and bookers) in the Greenwich Village 'folk clubs'. As he recalls the latter's reaction, it ran as follows: 'You sound like a hillbilly: we want folk-singers here . . .' The point, made here with a characteristic lightness of irony, is of course that Dylan *was* a folk singer; and to learn how variably his early work was received is to understand the various misconceptions that obtained in New York at that time and which, from New York, spread (though not back into the Appalachians) via college circuits and out across the Atlantic.

One version of how to sound like a 'folk singer' was to be smoothly ingenuous, angry and above all, sensitive. Peter, Paul & Mary fitted the bill. With a name like that how could they fail? They were ideal—pale white, middle-class and clean to the point of cultivated preciousness.

Even when the protest phase was rampant, most of its fans preferred the sweeter version of the 'Blowin' in the Wind' kind of song, as by Peter, Paul & Mary. See and hear archive footage of them and the level of sanctimonious earnestness, the tone of self-important, hushed preaching, is preposterous, and made worse by those overly careful harmonies they're clearly so pleased with. And what could be more repulsively cutesy than the chart hit still current when their version of 'Blowin' in the Wind' was released, 'Puff the Magic Dragon'?

Yet Dylan was not averse to the smoothie sounds of groups like the Kingston Trio, and when it came to Peter, Paul & Mary, he didn't spurn writing the sleevenote poem 'In the Wind' for their album of that name (Warner Bros. WS1507, 1963), especially since they were bringing him much success. He also sang 'Blowin' in the Wind' and 'We Shall Overcome' with them at the end of the NEWPORT FOLK FESTIVAL on July 26, 1963 (the latter included on *Evening Concerts at Newport Vol. 1*, Vanguard VRS9148, 1964)—and, 23 years later, he sang 'Blowin' in the Wind' with them again at the Martin Luther King Birthday celebration in Washington, D.C., on January 20, 1986.

One of them, Pete Yarrow, had also pleaded with the crowd on Dylan's behalf at the end of his defiant electric set at Newport 1965, explaining later: 'I gave him my guitar, and I said "Go back on," which he did.' He gives a variant explanation in the interview with him in the movie *No Direction Home* in 2005.

Mary Travers comes back into the Dylan story in the 1970s. She fronted a radio series back then, *Mary and Friend*, and on March 10, 1975 in Oakland, California, she recorded an interview with Dylan, a 20-minute version of which was broadcast by KNX-FM on April 26, 1975, and syndicated to other stations the following month. It is from this interview that Dylan's much-quoted remark about *Blood on the Tracks* derives: 'A lot of people tell me they enjoyed that album. It's hard for me to relate to that: I mean, people enjoying that type of pain.'

As for Noel (Paul) Stookey, in *Chronicles Volume One*, in 2004, Dylan recalls a side of his personality that you would never suspect from Peter, Paul & Mary's image: 'He could imitate just about anything. . . . He could imitate singers imitating other singers. He was very funny. One of his more outrageous imitations was Dean Martin imitating LITTLE RICHARD.'

[Peter Yarrow, b. 31 May 1938, NY. Noel ('Paul') Stookey, b. 30 Dec 1937 (other commonly given dates are wrong), Baltimore, Maryland. Mary Allin Travers, b. 9 Nov 1936, Louisville, Kentucky. There is an excellent history of the group by William Ruhlman, *Goldmine*, 12 Apr 1996, excerpted at length on *www.peterpaulmary.com*. Bob Dylan, *Chronicles Volume One*, p.259. Mary Travers is currently fighting leukemia and underwent a 'bone marrow transplant procedure' in 2005.]

Petty, Tom [1950 -] Thomas Earl Petty was born on October 20, 1950 in Gainesville, Florida. His earliest groups were the Sundowners, the Epics and Mudcrunch. This last also contained BENMONT TENCH and MIKE CAMPBELL. They formed TOM PETTY & THE HEARTBREAKERS in 1975. Petty always felt free, as did the others in the band, to pursue other projects too, and in 1981 one of these, a collaboration with Stevie Nicks (of Fleetwood Mac) on the single 'Stop Draggin' My Heart Around' proved especially fruitful commercially.

While the band toured with Dylan in 1986 and 1987, Petty's involvement with Dylan extended to sharing vocals with him on several songs performed nightly on the 1986 tour, producing Dylan's single 'Band of the Hand (It's Hell Time Man!)' for the film of the same name, co-writing a track on the *Knocked Out Loaded* album, 'Got My Mind Made Up', co-writing with Dylan and Mike Campbell the song 'Jammin' Me', which became one in a long line of Tom Petty & the Heartbreakers hit singles (in 1987), and then becoming, in 1988, one of THE TRAVELING WILBURYS.

From 1987 onwards, Petty also started making occasional appearances in episodes of the US TV series 'The Garry Shandling Show'; in 1989 he released a solo album, *Full Moon Fever*, augmented by several Heartbreakers and all the other Wilburys but Dylan, which went triple platinum and yielded several hit singles; five years later came a second, *Wildflowers*, which managed to include five hit singles including the especially successful 'You Don't Know How It Feels'; in summer 2001 he re-married, wedding a long-term girlfriend whose child from a former marriage is named Dylan. The ceremony was conducted by LITTLE RICHARD!

In 2002 Tom Petty appeared in the 'Simpsons' episode 'What I Did in My Strummer Vacation', and collected a Distinguished Achievement Award from the University of Florida; in 2004 he provided the voice for the character Lucky in the TV animation series 'King of the Hill'; and in 2005 he started hosting his own radio series on XM, 'Buried Treasure'.

Reportedly, Petty has said that his interest in music was first created at age 11 by the visit of ELVIS PRESLEY to his hometown: which is odd, really, since Presley never did play a concert in Gainesville, Florida, and played no concerts at all in 1961–62. But Petty has also said, asked about *Dylan's* influence: 'Bob Dylan influenced absolutely everything'.

[Tom Petty quote on Italian Dylan website *www.maggiesfarm.it*, 30 Aug 2005.]

Pichaske, David [1943 -] David Richard Pichaske, an academic in a backwoods check shirt, was born in Kenmore, New York, on September 2, 1943. He has a PhD in medieval literature and some of his early publications were on Spenser and Chaucer. Since then he has refocussed his scholarship onto contemporary Midwest American writers, especially rural writers, with a special interest in how place shapes thought, language and writing, and most of his own work examines these relationships. His newest book, *Rooted: Seven Midwest Writers of Place*, incorporates most of what he's wanted to say about the literature of the Midwest. His interest in Bob Dylan, which was first aroused in the mid-1960s, fits with all this.

He has taught at universities since 1965, and for the past quarter-century has been based in Dylan's home state of Minnesota. Currently he teaches in the English Department at Southwest Minnesota State University out at Marshall, MN, in the extreme flatness (or 'horizontal grandeur') of that part of the state where the great prairies begin. He has also had senior Fulbright lectureships in Poland, Latvia and Mongolia and has frequently revisited these places. His other published works include chapbooks, books of poetry, a novel, short stories and further non-fiction.

There has not been one semester in the last 35 years when a Pichaske book has not been used as a textbook in a university other than his own. These books have included *A Generation In Motion: Popular Music and Culture in the Sixties* (1979) and the earlier (but now out of print) *Beowulf to BEATLES: Approaches to Poetry*, which was his first published work involving Dylan, back in 1972. The same year came his first article bringing in Dylan, 'Towards an Aesthetics of Rock' in the *Illinois English Journal*, and a year later 'Rock and the Literary Mainstream' in the *Connecticut English Journal*. His book *The Poetry of Rock*—including an extended scrutiny of the *John Wesley Harding* album—was published in 1981, as was an update of *Beowulf to Beatles*.

His articles specifically on Dylan have been 'Bob Dylan and the Search for a Usable Past', in a 1983 *Telegraph* (collected in *All Across the Telegraph*, 1987); 'Bob Dylan's North Country: A Twenty-Five Year Report' in *Endless Road* in 1984; 'Bob Dylan's Publications in *Broadside Magazine*, 1962–65', *Telegraph*, 1985; the excellent 'The Prophet and the Prisoner: Bob Dylan and the American Dream', *Telegraph*, 1987; 'Bob Dylan' in the collection *American Popular Music: Annotated Readings in Popular Music from Colonial America to Kent State*, 1994; 'Poetry, Pedagogy and Popular Music: Renegade Reflections' in *Popular Music and Society* in 1999; and the two-parter 'Bob Dylan "And the Language That He Used"' in *Judas!* in 2003.

[David Pichaske, *Beowulf to Beatles: Approaches to Poetry*, New York: Free Press, 1972, revised as *Beowulf to Beatles and Beyond: The Varieties of Poetry*, New York: Macmillan, 1981; *A Generation in Motion: Popular Music and Culture in the Sixties*, New York: Schirmer Press, 1979 and Ellis Press, 1988; *The Poetry of Rock*, New York: Ellis Press, 1981; *Rooted: Seven Midwest Writers of Place*, Iowa City, IA: University of Iowa Press, 2006; and 'Bob Dylan' in Anderson, ed., *American Popular Music: Annotated Readings in Popular Music from Colonial America to Kent State*, New York: Simon & Schuster, 1994. 'Bob Dylan and the Search for a Usable Past, *Telegraph* no.14, UK, Nov 1983; 'Bob Dylan's North Country: A Twenty-Five Year Report', *Endless Road* no.6, Hull, UK, fall 1984; 'Bob Dylan's Publications in *Broadside Magazine*, 1962–65', *Telegraph* no.20, summer 1985; 'The Prophet and the Prisoner: Bob Dylan and the American Dream', *Telegraph* no.26, spring 1987; 'Poetry, Pedagogy and Popular Music: Renegade Reflections' *Popular Music and Society* no.23.4, US, winter 1999; and 'Bob Dylan "And the Language That He Used"', *Judas!*, Huntingdon, UK, nos.5 & 6, Apr & Jul 2003.]

Pickering, Stephen [19?? -] Chofetz Chaim ben-Avraham, aka Stephen Pickering, is the author and editor of (now highly collectible) early self-published Dylan booklets, the large-format *Dylan: A Commemoration*, 1969, and the more substantial

Praxis: One, 1972. The latter contains an exemplary selected listing of articles about Dylan published 1961–71 as well as articles by a number of writers but mostly by Pickering; both booklets are largely ill-written and always unpleasant about other Dylan authors—it's typical of both traits that he writes of TOBY THOMPSON that his 'purpose is to edify himself' and that 'he is neither genuinely interested in Dylan's work, nor is his book any kind of unbiased or useful reference.'

However, these large booklets offer generous numbers of fine and rare Dylan photographs, mostly freely donated to Pickering from the collection of the Swiss underground figure Urban Gwerder, founder of the FRANK ZAPPA fanzine *Hot Ratz Times*.

In 1975 came Pickering's *Bob Dylan Approximately: A Portrait of the Jewish Poet in Search of God—A Midrash*, which looked at the 1974 tour and Dylan as Jewish mystic.

Pickering was the first to assert, not always convincingly but with an aggressive torrent of opaque argument, the centrality of the Jewish faith and Jewish teachings to Dylan's work—a stance he had already developed by the time of *Praxis: One*. He wrote from what he called the Center for the Study of Bob Dylan & Torah Judaism.

[Stephen Pickering, *Dylan: A Commemoration*, 1969, Santa Cruz, CA: 2nd edn., 1971. *Praxis: One*, Santa Cruz: No Limit, 1972 (it is often dated as 1971 but since it lists published articles up to Dec 1971, this is unlikely). Stephen Pickering, aka Chofetz Chaim ben-Avraham, *Bob Dylan Approximately: A Portrait of the Jewish Poet in Search of God—A Midrash*, New York: David McKay/Acorn Books, 1975. Urban Gwerder: *Hot Ratz Times*, Zurich, 11 issues, 1973–1975. An A4-sized reproduction of *Dylan: A Commemoration* was published by Desolation Row Promotions, UK, 1995; ditto *Praxis: One*, 1996.]

***Planet Waves* [1974]** For the first ten minutes after it came out, this 14th Dylan album was hailed—as *New Morning* had been—as 'the best thing he's done since *Blonde on Blonde*'. Like *New Morning*, it then suffered a disappointment backlash from which it never fully recovered. Put in the long back-projection of Dylan's recording career it now seems a potent, open album. Warm, musically sumptuous yet tense, and emotionally rich, it points down no new road; asserting the artist's right to prefer minor work on old canvasses to doing no work at all, it is drawn from the inner resources of memory and a determination to record faithfully the artist's current state of mind in spite of tiredness, an unpopular grown-upness and some lack of self-confidence.

It is demonstrably a Dylan album of the 1970s in managing to bind together elements of the city-surreal-intellectual world from which *Blonde on Blonde*'s language derived, with a new willingness to re-embrace older, folksier, rural strengths. 'Going, Going, Gone' shows this binding together admirably. Here is the city language: 'I bin livin' on the edge . . .' and here is the urging of an older, simpler wisdom: 'Grandma said "Boy, go follow your heart / I know you'll be fine at the end of the line / All that's gold doesn't shine / Don't you and your one true love ever part."' Back on 'Memphis Blues Again' (on *Blonde on Blonde*), grandpa was just a joke; in 'Going, Going, Gone', grandma has insights to offer. She represents something stable, reliable and, by the implication of her age, something resilient. Through the rest of the song, Dylan presses this alliance of the two different worlds he'd previously walked through separately. He brings in an echo of his old folksinger days with a near-quote from 'Don't Think Twice, It's All Right'—'I bin walkin' the road'—and he binds a rural image with vaguer, mid-60s-Dylan language in the opening verse: 'I've just reached a place / Where the willow don't bend . . . / It's the top of the end / I'm going, I'm going, I'm gone.'

The whole album devotes itself to revisiting, as the adult with the mid-60s surreal achievement behind him, the Minnesota landscapes and feelings from which he had emerged in the first place—and recalls these Minnesota years largely for the first time (except for 'Winterlude' and 'Went to See the Gypsy' on *New Morning*). There is a strange tension created by the contrast between recollected childhood and adolescence and current father-figure weariness. The result is nostalgia-soaked but genuinely beautiful, with an eerie, compelling quality that marks this album as unique in Dylan's output.

'Hazel' deals with a girlfriend he'd had long before he first set out for New York City; and in 'Something There Is About You' he says it carefully and clearly: 'Thought I'd shaken the wonder / And the phantoms of my youth / Rainy days on the Great Lakes / Walkin' the hills of old Duluth . . . / Somethin' there is about you / That brings back a long-forgotten truth . . . / I was in a whirlwind / Now I'm in some better place.'

This same theme, of the inexorable tug of the past and the struggle to wed it to the present, runs throughout. It is there in 'Wedding Song', and, coming at the end of the album, these lines, with their chilling full-stop, emphasize the desperation the whole song examines: 'I love you more than ever / Now that the past is gone.'

An earlier image in the same song echoes across the years from 1965's 'Farewell Angelina': 'I've said goodbye to haunted rooms / And faces in the street / To the courtyard of the jester / Which is hidden from the sun . . .', and 'Dirge' similarly says goodbye to old haunts—to the old folk days of Greenwich Village, such that the song acts as a re-write of 'Positively 4th Street': 'Heard your songs of freedom / And man forever stripped / Acting out his folly / While his back is being whipped . . . / I can't recall a useful thing / You ever did for me /

'Cept pat me on the back one time / While I was on my knees . . . / No use to apologize / What difference would it make?'

All the tension explored here stems from the contradictory ways in which the past reacts upon the present. The chill desperation of 'Wedding Song' and the distanced vitriol of 'Dirge' show one side of the process; the enriching feelings of revisiting on 'Something There Is About You', 'Hazel' and 'Never Say Goodbye' show the other side.

As well as these stand-out tracks, there are also two versions of what became a perennial concert anthem, 'Forever Young'. And like *New Morning*, the album sounds far better now than then. The musicians were THE BAND.

See also ***Planet Waves*, disappearing sleevenotes, the**, and **grandma and Walpole's cat**.

[Recorded Santa Monica, CA, 2, 5–6, 8, 10 & 14 Nov 1973; released as stereo LP, Asylum 7E 1003 (US) & Island ILPS 9261 (UK), 17 Jan 1974.]

***Planet Waves*, disappearing sleevenotes, the** Sleevenotes in the form of a (roughly 300-word) prose poem by Dylan, which appeared, reproduced in his handwriting, on the back covers of the original Asylum Records (Island Records in the UK) issues of the *Planet Waves* LP, disappeared from the subsequent Columbia Records (and CBS) reissues, on vinyl and CD. Nor were they included in the book *Lyrics 1962–1985*. This is a pity, because despite some uncharacteristic coarseness (see **'4th Time Around'**) they amount to an inspired and vivid evocation of the 1950s, and how it felt to live through the Eisenhower years.

[Ex-General Dwight D. (David) Eisenhower (1890–1969) was US President 1953–1960.]

Plugz, the Rumoured at the time to have been the name of the band backing Dylan on his March 1984 David Letterman TV show appearance, they seemed to shift from being the Plugz to being the Cruzados at some weird undetectable moment in the middle of working with Dylan. They *had* been the Plugz, when they formed on the US West Coast in 1978 as perhaps the first Latino punk band—with Tito Larriva on guitar and vocals, the not very Latino-sounding Barry McBride on bass and vocals, then replaced by Tony Marsico, and with Chalo (aka CHARLIE) QUINTANA on drums. They made a three-track vinyl single, 'Move', 'Let Go' and 'Mindless Contentment' on Slash Records in 1978, an album called *Electrify Me* in 1979, and then in 1981 another single, 'Achin'' c/w their superfast version of RITCHIE VALENS' 'La Bamba', and another album, *Better Luck*, both on their own label, Fatima Records. In 1983 they featured on the compilation album *Los Angelinos* and in 1984 managed to get themselves on the soundtrack (and soundtrack album) of the movie *Repo Man*, performing 'El Clavo y la Cruz', 'Hombre Secreto' (aka 'Secret Agent Man') and 'Reel Ten'. By this time they had a fourth member, Steve Hufsteter.

In late 1983, before *Repo Man* was released, Bob Dylan played harmonica for them on their studio track 'Rising Sun' at Cherokee Studios, Hollywood (exact date unknown). This was unreleased at the time, and then came out on a catalogue-numberless cassette issued by the group in spring 2000, by which time they were calling themselves the Cruzados, and their guitarist was calling himself Justin Jesting. In 2003 the track with Dylan's harp on it was included on the German compilation *May Your Song Always Be Sung: The Songs of Bob Dylan Vol. 3* (which was, this track aside, a set of covers of Dylan songs by various artists) and in 2005 reissued on the CD *The Cruzados: Unreleased Early Recordings*, though this too is a home-made record and only available from their website (*www.thecruzados.com*). In the meantime they had released two official albums, *Cruzados* and *After Dark*, the first of which included a version of 'Rising Sun' without Bob Dylan on it.

More interestingly, soon afterwards the group—by this time Jesting, Marsico and Quintana—rehearsed with Dylan at his Malibu garage studio for a remarkable appearance on the NBC-TV show 'Late Night with David Letterman' on March 22, 1984. They had rehearsed dozens of songs, but in the usual Dylan way: that is, he had played through dozens of songs once or twice and then passed on to some more. At the TV-studio rehearsal, the video shows them performing 'I Once Knew a Man', 'Jokerman', 'License to Kill', 'Treat Her Right' and 'My Guy'. When it came to the performance itself, Letterman waved the cover of Dylan's new album *Infidels* in front of the camera, giving it a patronising but enthusiastic introductory spiel—and at the last minute Dylan sprang on them a gloriously grungy version of a 1955 SONNY BOY WILLIAMSON II song 'Don't Start Me to Talkin''. Dylan revelled in the punk sound of the band—and was dressed accordingly, not in Latino mode but in the hip thin dark suit and superthin tie of UK punks like the members of, say, the Jam or ELVIS COSTELLO à la 1980. Then came 'License to Kill' (not as good as at the TV-studio rehearsal, as it happened) and then a furiously fast, wondrous version of 'Jokerman', in the middle of which Dylan spent quite some time searching for a particular harmonica.

No-one else in the world would treat coast-to-coast high-ratings TV that way, and as a sampler of the album it was splendidly misleading. The version of 'Jokerman' on *Infidels* is magnificent—by far the album's best work—but this live version with the Plugz re-created it as an impassioned, howling anthem on the very edge of chaos, yet knowing and lither, as snarlingly fey and postmodern, as Television's album *Marquee Moon*—which was Tom Verlaine updating, via the Velvet Underground, the city-hipster-in-the-storm figure Dylan had first invented for himself back in 1966. Thanks more or less equally to the Plugz/Cruzados and Dylan, it was a transcendent mainstream television moment—made the more gloriously surreal when Letterman came on, looking like a lost Bible salesman at the end of the first number, clasping his hands and telling the musicians it had been 'very nice'. Very nice!

The Cruzados heyday began that same year. According to bass player Tony Marsico (not Marisco, as on a number of Dylan listings):

> 'From 1984 to 1988 the Cruzados toured non-stop throughout Europe and the US playing everywhere from your local dive bar to your over-the-top stadium show. Countless memories stick in my mind. . . . Praises from Bob Dylan, John Fogerty, David Byrne, Brian Setzer and Billy Joel hailing us as the "next big thing". Sorry if we let you down. We had fun trying! . . . Fleetwood Mac inviting us to play with them on a three-month incredible tour. Sitting on a bed at three in the morning in Florida with STEVIE RAY VAUGHAN showing us the right way to play "Tightrope". Playing to a hundred thousand plus crowd at Farm Aid and standing between NEIL YOUNG and ARLO GUTHRIE singing "This Land Is Your Land" while the sun set. Wow! Did I dream that?'

Apparently not. And perhaps all that activity explains why when Dylan himself embarked on a big European tour later in 1984, instead of using the Cruzados and delivering more of that alive and exciting stripped-down punkish music, he hired instead the usual bunch of seasoned players, including MICK TAYLOR, by then a lead guitarist of dependable mediocrity.

[The Cruzados: *Cruzados*, Arista, US, 1985, CD-reissued as Arista 8383, US, *nia*. Various Artists: *Repo Man*, San Andreas SAR 39019, US, 1984. Various Artists: *May Your Song Always Be Sung: The Songs of Bob Dylan Vol. 3* (2-CD set), BMG 82876 50567-2, Germany, 2003. Television: *Marquee Moon*, NY, fall 1976, Elektra 7E-1098, US, 1977.]

'Pneumonia Ceilings' [1966] See **McCartney, Paul.**

Poe, Edgar Allan [1809 - 1849] Edgar Allan Poe, born to actor parents, had little success in his own lifetime but gained posthumous recognition as a major figure in 19th century American literature. Critic, short-story (including ghost-story) writer and poet, he was also a promising athlete in his youth, impressing his teachers in Richmond, VA, 'by swimming six miles against the tide in a river during a heatwave'. His best-known works are the story 'The Fall of the House of Usher' (1839), 'The Murders in the Rue Morgue' (1841)—sometimes claimed to be the first detective story—and the poems 'The Raven' (1845) and 'The Bells' (1849). One of those who made Greenwich Village into Bohemia a century and more before Dylan arrived in it, Poe died in Baltimore, October 7, 1849.

Christopher Rollason has suggested Poe as the prompt for Dylan's wild 1960s book *Tarantula* being so-called. He points out that Poe's story 'The Gold-Bug' is prefaced by the epigraph 'What ho! what ho! this fellow is dancing mad! He hath been bitten by the Tarantula.' Poe credits these lines to *All in the Wrong*, a play of 1761 by Arthur Murphy, but Poe editor Thomas Ollive Mabbott says this is untrue; Poe may have made them up. Either way, as Mabbott comments: 'The bite of the tarantula spider was held responsible for a wild hysterical impulse to dance—tarantism—that affected great numbers of people, especially in Italy, during the later Middle Ages. In Frederick Reynolds' play *The Dramatist* (1789) . . . a character . . . says, "I'm afraid you have been bitten by a tarantula—you'll excuse me, but the symptoms are wonderfully alarming. There is a blazing fury in your eye—a wild emotion in your countenance."' The point being that the protagonist appears to be mad but eventually his actions are revealed as based on a hidden chain of logical reasoning. Rollason adds: 'the theme of Hamlet-like apparent madness would seem to make sense in the general context of *Tarantula*, a tragi-comic voyage across a world that refuses to make sense, a crazy extension of the carnival on Desolation Row.' This seems somewhat less speculative when we note that Poe himself features inside *Tarantula*: in the section 'The Horse Race', 'edgar allan poe steps out from beside a burning bush', while in 'Al Aaraaf & the Forcing Committee', Dylan writes of 'New York neath spells of Poe'. The phrase 'Al Aaraaf', which refers to a passage in the Koran about a kind of limbo poised between heaven and hell, is itself the title poem of a volume published by Poe in 1829.

These mid-1960s allusions to Poe follow those from the Dylan songs of 1965, in which 'some raven' appears in 'Love Minus Zero/No Limit', 'rue Morgue Avenue' is part of the geography of 'Just Like Tom Thumb's Blues' and Captain Kidd, having appeared in Poe's 'The Gold-Bug', reappears in 'Bob Dylan's 115th Dream'.

Poe's literary spirit also loiters behind some of Dylan's 1970s work, for good and ill. Poe's short poem 'To Helen', of which everyone knows two lines, usually without knowing where or whom they come from, removes the puzzle of all those embarrassingly florid pseudo-classical phrases of Dylan's that sit so uneasily in the choruses of 'Sara', on *Desire*. Where Helen is addressed in terms of 'Thy hyacinth hair, thy classic face / Thy Naiad airs . . .', which Poe says have brought him home 'To the glory that was Greece / And the grandeur that was Rome' (the lines everyone knows, of course), and adds: 'How statue-like I see thee stand . . . / Ah, Psyche, from the regions which / Are Holy Land!', so 'Sara' is bombarded with: 'Sweet Virgin Angel. . . . Radiant jewel, mystical wife / . . . Scorpio

Sphinx in a calico dress' and 'Glamorous nymph with an arrow and bow.'

Poe's influence has also been to the good. Dylan inherits the heart of Poe's quirky confidence with rhymes, and particularly internal rhymes. The tour-de-force example of Dylan's 'No Time to Think' (1978): 'I've seen all these decoys through a set of deep turquoise / Eyes and I feel so depressed . . . / The bridge that you travel on goes to the Babylon / Girl with the rose in her hair . . . / Stripped of all virtue as you crawl through the dirt / You can give but you cannot receive' is prefigured by that of Poe's scintillating 'The Raven' (1845): 'And the silken sad uncertain rustling of each purple curtain / Thrilled me—filled me with fantastic terrors never felt before / So that now, to still the beating of my heart, I stood repeating / 'Tis some visitor entreating entrance at my chamber door'.

In December 2004, interviewed on US TV by Ed Bradley, when Dylan says that the burden of being perceived as a 'prophet' in the late 1960s made him feel like an imposter, he elaborates: 'It was like being in an Edgar Allan Poe story and you're just not that person everybody thinks you are, though they call you that all the time.'

[*The Complete Poems and Stories of Edgar Allan Poe*, 2 vols, ed. A.H. Quinn & E.H. O'Neill, first published 1946, has been reprinted through to at least the 1970s. The quote re Poe's swimming prowess comes from Martin Wainwright, *The Guardian*, London, 25 May 2005, p.4, while reporting Sylvester Stallone's intention to direct a Poe film bio. Thomas Ollive Mabbott, *Collected Works of Edgar Allan Poe, Vol. 3, Tales and Sketches 1843–1849*, Cambridge, MA: The Belknap Press of Harvard University Press, 1978, pp.844–845. Dylan, *Tarantula*, New York: St. Martin's Press reprint, 1994, p.39 & 136. Christopher Rollason's comments posted on the online discussion group *http://rec.music.dylan*, 5 May 2001. Dylan to Ed Bradley: '60 Minutes', CBS-TV, 5 Dec 2004.]

poems on Bob Dylan Poems about Dylan, or inspired by him, probably remain the rarest form of tribute: or at least, published, professional ones probably are. They are also, as A.J. Iríarte notes, 'harder to keep track of than most other writings on Dylan', partly because 'poetry by its very nature [is] elusive'. However, published poems about Bob Dylan do include these (all cited by Iríarte in a short piece in 2003):

A number of poems by ALLEN GINSBERG (see separate entry); the 1978 poem 'Dog Dream' by PATTI SMITH; the 1999 collection by critic, academic and poet STEPHEN SCOBIE, *And Forget My Name: A Speculative Biography of Bob Dylan*; the excellent Irish poet Paul Muldoon's 'Bob Dylan at Princeton, November 2000'—eight couplets centered around comparing two Dylan visits to Princeton 30 years apart, the first being to receive his Honorary Degree and the second to play a concert—from the poet who had earlier written a poem he said had been inspired by Dylan's 1989 album *Oh Mercy*; the American Norbert Krapf's 'Song for Bob Dylan (1971)'—in a collection titled after a Dylan line, *The Country I Come From: Poems*; a poem called 'Bob Dylan's Harmonica Sound' (is there but one?) by Scottish poet, literary reviewer and school teacher Lachlan Mackinnon, in his third verse collection, *The Jupiter Collisions* (2003); and the Spanish poet and novelist Benjamín Prado's poem 'Mi vida se llama Bob Dylan' ('My life's name is Bob Dylan'), from his 2002 collection *Iceberg*. An earlier Prado book of poems, from 1995, translates Dylan's song title 'Shelter from the Storm' into Spanish to provide its own title, *Cobijo contra la tormenta*.

A less wholly professional but far larger collection of Dylan poems (including the Lachlan Mackinnon) can be found—or rather, could be when still in print—in the 1993 book *Jewels and Binoculars—Fifty Poets Celebrate Bob Dylan*, edited by Phil Bowen, who has also written the short play *A Handful of Rain*, centered upon an imagined meeting between Bob Dylan and Dylan Thomas. And going back to 1975, Michael McClure includes 'For Bob Dylan' in his collection *Jaguar Skies*.

[A.J. Iriarte, 'I Could Write You Poems', *The Bridge* no.16, Gateshead, UK, summer 2003. Patti Smith, 'Dog Dream', *Babel*, New York: G.P. Putnam & Sons, 1978; re-collected in *Early Work 1970–1979*, New York: W.W. Norton, 1994. Stephen Scobie, *And Forget My Name: A Speculative Biography of Bob Dylan*, Victoria, B.C., Canada: Ekstasis Editions, 1999. Paul Muldoon, 'Bob Dylan at Princeton, November 2000' in Neil Corcoran, ed., *Do You, Mr. Jones: Bob Dylan with the Poets and Professors*, London: Chatto & Windus, 2002. Norbert Krapf: *The Country I Come From: Poems*, Santa Maria, CA: Archer Books, 2002. Lachlan Mackinnon, *The Jupiter Collisions*, London: Faber & Faber, 2003. Benjamín Prado, *Iceberg*, Madrid: Visor Libros, 2002. Phil Bowen & John Cornelius, *Jewels and Binoculars—Fifty Poets celebrate Bob Dylan*, Exeter, UK: Stride Books, 1993. Michael McClure, *Jaguar Skies*, New York: New Directions, 1975.]

poetry, American, pre-20th century There are two difficulties in looking at the influence of pre-20th century US poetry on Dylan's work. The first is that so much of it echoes English literature anyway. Edward Taylor, often regarded as America's first great poet, was born in England. Emerson didn't begin writing poetry until after he had travelled abroad, touring Italy and meeting Coleridge, Carlyle and Wordsworth in England. Longfellow was a professor of modern languages and literature, spent a lot of time in foreign travel and pursuing an absorption with European literature, and as a poet offers obvious resemblances to Tennyson. EDGAR ALLAN POE went to school in England and worked outside the sphere of the reigning Boston-New York literati of his day. It was among British poets and critics that WHITMAN found his first admirers, and after the long period of disfavour into which his work fell after his death, it was in response to D.H. Lawrence's marvellous book *Studies in Classic American Literature* (1923) that Whitman was readmitted to the American Poetic pantheon of greats. After Whitman, it is true, there is a large amount of truly American poetry, but then come POUND and ELIOT and the Lost Generation, all trying to be unAmerican in Europe.

The other difficulty is that the balladry of American poetry is so close to the traditions of folksong as to make it impossible to say where Dylan derives from the one or from the other.

Let's begin where the echo is clearer–with Emerson. The English automatically link the pantheism of Dylan's 'Lay Down Your Weary Tune' with Wordsworth; but looking at the equivalent 19th century poetry written by Americans and today learnt by American middle-class children in schools, it is the pantheism of Ralph Waldo Emerson (1803–1882) that shines out just as brightly–revealing at once a source of inspiration and tradition for that excellent Dylan song. This is Emerson's 'Each and All', first published 1839: 'I inhaled the violet's breath, / Around me stood the oaks and firs / . . . Again I say, again I heard, / The rolling river, the morning bird; / Beauty through my senses stole; / I yielded myself to the perfect whole.' And here is Dylan: 'I stood unwound beneath the skies / And clouds unbound by laws . . . / I gazed into the river's mirror / And watched its winding strum . . . / The last of leaves fell from the trees / And clung to a new love's breast.' (A separate entry treats the song in more detail.)

A keen correspondence occurs between Emerson's 'Goodbye', written in 1823 and published sixteen years later: 'Goodbye to Flattery's fawning face . . . / To crowded halls, to court and street / To frozen hearts and hasting feet', and Dylan's 'Wedding Song', 1974: 'I've said goodbye to haunted rooms / And faces in the street / To the courtyards of the Jester / Which are hidden from the sun.'

Then there is Emerson's contemporary, Henry Wadsworth Longfellow (1807–1882), and his reputation's millstone, 'Hiawatha' (1855), which jingles in the memory as rhythm: the rhythm that is the basis of so much American song. It is a rhythm that suggests the music-and-words art; it does not stubbornly insist on its words-on-the-page lineage. Not only 'Hiawatha'. Poems like 'Hymn to the Night', 'The Day Is Done', 'My Lost Youth', 'The Fire of Driftwood', 'The Bells of San Blas', 'The Arrow and the Song', 'The Ropewalk'–all have their primacy in jingling rhythms that wield assured, consistent drum-beats. Drummed into the memory from school days, this tradition of words as parts of song–of words as music–must act as a momentum of inspiration, however unconscious it may be, for Dylan. Longfellow's is the literary voice that murmurs underneath, just as, from the oral tradition, the old folksong patterns do.

It isn't odd, therefore, that specific snatches of Longfellow can be read in Dylan's voice, nor that it is less conscious technique that matches than ease of tone (derived from the rhythmic familiarity) and ease of vocabulary (derived from the familiarity of the voice that Longfellow gave to American writing). Here is such a snatch, from Longfellow's 'The Day Is Done' (collected 1906): 'I see the lights of the village / Gleam through the rain and the mist / And a feeling of sadness comes o'er me / That my soul cannot resist.' That ease of tone and of vocabulary match so strongly the same qualities in Dylan's writing that no-one would be surprised if Dylan had himself written those lines anywhere on *New Morning*, *Planet Waves*, *Blood on the Tracks*, *Oh Mercy* or *Time Out of Mind*.

It is the same milieu–the same operation of ease of tone and vocabulary upon the careful straightforwardness of what is being said–that Dylan gives us in the better parts of 'Sara', on *Desire*: 'Now the beach is deserted except for some kelp / And the wreck of an old ship that lies on the shore / You always responded when I needed your help / You gave me a map and a key to your door.' The rhythmic melody of that song, moreover, is itself an exact echo of Longfellow's 'Curfew' (1870): 'No voice in the chambers / No sound in the hall! / Sleep and oblivion / Reign over all! / The book is completed / And closed, like the day / And the hand that has written it / Lays it away.'

Of all this material it would be plausible to ask, well, what could be more quintessentially Dylanesque?

What of Walt Whitman (1819–1892)? His influence, like that of balladry, seems so deeply woven inside the body of modern American poetry as to be unmeasurable. It is his use of workaday experience and colloquial expression that represents the fundamental turning-point in American poetry from the drawing-room towards the street. And certainly it is Whitman's voice that makes possible ALLEN GINSBERG's *Howl*, itself a major influence on Dylan's mid-60s work as on so much that came after it.

Perhaps Whitman's insistence on the interminable-list-as-poetry even made possible Dylan's 'A Hard Rain's a-Gonna Fall', 'Chimes of Freedom' and the whole idea of the 12-minute rock song, which seems suddenly to arrive out of nowhere (or out of the longer old folk-ballads) in the world of the two-and-a-half-minute pop song. Alongside a conventional poem, *Leaves of Grass* (a collection that grew and grew, from 12 poems in the self-published first edition of 1855 to 293 poems in the 1881 edition and more yet in the so-called 'Deathbed edition') parallels 'Desolation Row' or 'Highlands' alongside a normal popular song.

[The work of Emerson and Longfellow is well represented in *The Penguin Book of American Verse*, ed. Geoffrey Moore, 1979, and *The Mentor Book of Major*

American Poets, ed. Oscar Williams & Edwin Honig, 1962. For Walt Whitman there is *The Complete Poems*, 1977.]

poets on Bob Dylan Poets tend to be more circumspect than critics, and far more so than people in the music business, when it comes to expressing opinions on Dylan's work. When they do say something, it's usually been provoked by being asked outright whether they think his work is poetry. Not always, though. The British poet Philip Larkin, a pre-bebop jazz fan, wrote in a *Jazz Review* of late 1965 (so that he wasn't late coming to this at all):

> 'I'm afraid I poached Bob Dylan's *Highway 61 Revisited* out of curiosity and found myself well rewarded. Dylan's cawing, derisive voice is probably well suited to his material–I say probably, because much of it was unintelligible to me–and his guitar adapts itself to rock ("Highway 61") and ballad ("Queen Jane") admirably. There is a marathon "Desolation Row", which has an enchanting tune and mysterious, possibly half-baked words.'

Robert Lowell, writing in an issue of *The Review* in summer 1971, managed to touch on a number of points rather compressedly in asserting that 'Bob Dylan is alloy; he is true folk and fake folk, and has the Caruso voice. He has lines, but I doubt if he has written whole poems. He leans on the crutch of his guitar.'

Less interestingly, but representing, in his view, the feelings of many in the generation immediately preceding the post-WWII babyboomers, here's John Berryman in an exchange quoted from the authorised biography by John Haffenden:

> '"I can never forgive that young upstart for stealing my friend Dylan's name," he roared about Bob Dylan. "Yes, but don't you agree he's a poet?" "Yes, if only he'd learn to sing!"'

[Philip Larkin: *Jazz Review*, London, 10 Nov 1985. John Berryman quoted in John Haffenden, *The Life of John Berryman*, Boston: Routledge & Kegan Paul, 1982. Robert Lowell, *The Review*, *nia*, summer 1971. These comments were collected in 'Three Other Poets on Bob Dylan' in Michael Gray & John Bauldie, eds., *All Across The Telegraph: A Bob Dylan Handbook*, London: Futura Paperbacks edn., p.177 (though here Haffenden was given as Hoffenden).]

Pomarède, Michel [1952 -] Michel Pomarède runs the invaluable website 'Come Writers and Critics', which offers the most comprehensive listing of books about Dylan (including, of course, those by Dylan) with scans of the front covers of as many editions from around the world as possible, plus scans of large numbers of magazine covers featuring Dylan, songbook covers, tour programmes and more. Pomarède was born in Paris on March 24, 1952 and took an interest in Dylan's work from 1966 onwards. He decided to create his website after discovering computers and the internet in 1995. In his other life he is a pharmacist and owns a pharmacy near Paris.

['Come Writers and Critics', *http://perso.wanadoo.fr/michel.pomarede/CW&C/*.]

Pomus, Doc [1925 - 1991] Jerome Solon Felder was born in Brooklyn on June 27, 1925, and in childhood was struck down by polio, learnt the saxophone and was turned on to the blues by hearing Joe Turner on the radio. He performed, standing on crutches, as a white blues singer from the late 1940s to the mid-1950s before concentrating on songwriting. He wrote the words and with pianist Mort Shuman writing the music they became, from 1958–65, one of the greatest of all the songwriting partnerships of the era. If you thought 'Leiber & Stoller' first, you certainly thought 'Pomus & Shuman' second, and that went for ELVIS songs and songs in general.

By the time of this partnership Pomus had already written 'Boogie Woogie Country Girl' for Joe Turner, RAY CHARLES' smash hit 'Lonely Avenue' and the Coasters' 'Youngblood' with Leiber & Stoller (a song revived to gothic effect by LEON RUSSELL and performed by him at the Concert for Bangla Desh in 1971). With Shuman, Pomus wrote 'A Mess of Blues', 'Surrender', 'Little Sister', 'His Latest Flame', 'Viva Las Vegas', 'Suspicion' and others for Presley, and for others 'Teenager in Love' (Dion & the Belmonts), 'I'm a Tiger' (Fabian), 'Go, Jimmy, Go' (Jimmy Clanton), and for the Drifters 'Sweets for My Sweet', 'I Count the Tears' and the much-covered 'Save the Last Dance for Me'.

The two of them visited England in 1964; Shuman started composing with other people, and Pomus, back home in 1965, had a serious fall that confined him to a wheelchair for the rest of his days. There's something especially poignant about a man crippled by polio writing 'Save the Last Dance for Me'.

He stopped writing altogether, and spent ten years as a professional gambler until squeezed out by the mob, who sent two masked gunmen round to his 72nd Street apartment. He returned to songwriting, collaborating mostly with Dr. John on songs for B.B. King and many others.

At Pomus' posthumous induction into the Rock-'n'Roll Hall of Fame, the distinguished blues folklorist Dick Waterman said this of him: 'He never felt that he was creating High Art. It was his gig. He got up in the morning and went to work writing songs just as if he was delivering mail, driving a cab or practicing medicine.'

His son, Geoffrey J. Felder, e-mailed a Dylan discussion group in 1997 to say that he remembered 'the time Dylan came over to my dad's apartment to discuss life, songwriting, etc. My dad was very impressed with Dylan and always thought highly of him.'

It was mutual, and for the 1995 tribute album *Till the Night Is Gone,* a compilation of specially made recordings by Roseanne Cash, John Hiatt, LOU REED and others of 14 Doc Pomus songs, mostly co-written with Shuman, Bob Dylan went right back to the start of the story and recorded a version of 'Boogie Woogie Country Girl', in Memphis in May 1994, backed by his touring band of the day. It wasn't, of course, a patch on the great Joe Turner version, but it was meant well.

Doc Pomus died of lung cancer in New York on March 14, 1991.

[Bob Dylan: 'Boogie Woogie Country Girl', 9–11 May, 1994, *Till the Night Is Gone: A Tribute to Doc Pomus*, Rhino R2 71878, US, 1995. Geoffrey J. Felder e-mail, 22 May 1997, quoted from *www.expectingrain.com/dok/who/who.html*, online 13 Oct 2005.]

pop 1960–62: not all hopeless The myth has been created that 1960 was an all-time low in pop, which would suggest that there was nothing much for Dylan to gather from it; this is untrue. 1960 wasn't the best year ever but it introduced some beautiful sounds—a situation that held all through 1961–62 as well. The only thing missing was a genuine trend. All the good things were disconnected: separate end-products of the earlier rock years. This very disconnectedness made for unprecedented variety. What were the things that invalidate the myth of pre-BEATLES infertility?

The first thing to say is that this was actually a time when some rock came back: GENE VINCENT with 'Pistol Packin' Mama'; Eddie Cochran with 'Cut Across Shorty'; and Brenda Lee with 'Sweet Nuthins'. RICKY NELSON tried it, with blaring saxes, on 'I Got My Eyes on You (And I Like What I See)'. The Piltdown Men arrived; Gary US Bonds came along with 'New Orleans' and 'Quarter to Three'; and Freddie Cannon did 'The Urge'. THE EVERLY BROTHERS did 'Lucille'; JERRY LEE LEWIS came back with a classic version of 'What'd I Say'; PRESLEY himself made 'A Mess of Blues', 'I Feel So Bad' and 'Little Sister', and they issued a great but doctored BUDDY HOLLY rocker, 'Baby I Don't Care'. (Part of what was happening was that while rock'n'roll heroes Vincent, Cochran, Lewis and Holly all enjoyed short-lived popularity in the US, they all attained great longevity in Britain.)

Apart from this unchristened rock revival, on came a super-abundance of sounds that were newer, maybe cleverer, and which certainly stick in the mind. Blues singer Billy Bland made it with 'Let the Little Girl Dance'. Floyd Cramer started something with 'On the Rebound'—something Dylan's *Nashville Skyline* track 'Tell Me That It Isn't True' acknowledges. Clarence Frogman Henry was around, making delightful concert appearances as well as the records 'But I Do', 'You Always Hurt the One You Love', 'Ain't Got No Home', 'Lonely Street' and a great, great flop called 'A Little Too Much'. ROY ORBISON arrived, with grace, elegance of style and a voice that could not fail—the prototype voice for Dylan's Isle of Wight Festival 'Wild Mountain Thyme', for 'I Forgot More' on *Self Portrait* and part at least of 'Lay Lady Lay'. RAY CHARLES balanced nicely between soul and country. The Marcels did 'Blue Moon' and Ernie K. Doe did 'Mother-in-Law'. Dion found his 'Runaround Sue' sound and Neil Sedaka found 'Breakin' Up Is Hard to Do'. The Everly Brothers were better than ever, with 'Cathy's Clown', 'Nashville Blues', 'Stick With Me Baby' and 'Temptation'.

Tamla-Motown was young enough to be refreshing, as on 'Please Mr. Postman' by the Marvelettes and 'Shop Around' by the Miracles. (See also **Robinson, Smokey**.) PHIL SPECTOR came along like Armageddon with the Crystals, Bob B. Soxx & the Blue Jeans and later the Ronettes. The Tokens did 'The Lion Sleeps Tonight', and 'B'Wa Nina' and Bruce Channel made 'Hey! Baby'. Presley made his beautiful 'Surrender', and SAM COOKE sang 'Nothing Can Change This Love'. There was 'Monster Mash' by Bobby Boris Pickett & the Crypt-Kickers. Add to all that the Shirelles' 'Will You Love Me Tomorrow' and 'Tell Him' by the Exciters. Then add 'I Sold My Heart to the Junkman' by the Blue-Belles, and 'I'm Blue' by the Ikettes. 'Letter Full of Tears' by Gladys Knight & the Pips. 'Snap Your Fingers' by (the American) Joe Henderson. The Contours' 'Do You Love Me' and the Isleys' 'Twist and Shout'. Ketty Lester's 'Love Letters' and Claude King's wonderful 'Wolverton Mountain'. 'What's a Matter Baby?' by a resplendently vengeful Timi Yuro; and perhaps the very greatest of the lot, one minute twenty-eight seconds' worth of 'Stay', by Maurice Williams & the Zodiacs.

Far from being bad years, 1960–62 were very rich, and very diversified. The dominant influence, if there was one, was the search for a new bi-racial R&B, but there was a corresponding country strength. Altogether there was plenty happening for Dylan to notice, react to, pick up on: his pop education didn't need to have finished—couldn't have finished—in the 1950s.

[Gene Vincent (musical arrangement by Eddie Cochran): 'Pistol Packin' Mama', London, 11 May 1960, Capitol F4442, LA (and Capitol CL 15136, London), 1960; this reached the UK top 20 in Jun 1960. Eddie Cochran: 'Cut Across Shorty' [B-side of British top 3 hit 'Three Steps to Heaven'], LA, Jan 1960, Liberty 55242, Hollywood (London American HLG 9115, London), 1960.Jerry Lee Lewis: 'What'd I Say', Nashville, 9 Feb 1961; Sun 356, Memphis (London American HLS 9335, London), 1961: a British top 10 hit in May 1961; the original version by its composer, Ray Charles ('What'd I Say Part 1' c/w 'What'd I Say Part 2)', NY, 18 Feb 1959, Atlantic 2031, NY, 1959, was not released in the UK at the time. Lewis also scored minor UK top

40 hits with rock'n'roll records in 1962–'Sweet Little 16', Memphis, 5 Jun 1962, Sun 379, Memphis (London American HLS 9584, London) and 1963–'Good Golly Miss Molly', Nashville, 11 Sep 1962, Sun 382 (London American HLS9688). Dylan performed 'What'd I Say' at Farm Aid rehearsals, LA, 19 Sep 1985.

Elvis Presley: 'A Mess of Blues', Nashville, 20–21 Mar 1960, RCA Victor, NY, 1960; 'I Feel So Bad', Nashville, 12–13 Mar 1961, RCA Victor, 1961; 'Little Sister', Nashville, 25–6 Jun 1961, RCA Victor, 1961. 'I Feel So Bad' revived what had been a 1954 R&B hit for its composer, Chuck Willis ('I Feel So Bad', NY, 17 Sep 1953, OKeh 7029, NY); other Willis hits included 'It's Too Late' (NY, 13 Apr 1956, Atlantic 1098, NY, 1956): a song Dylan might also have known from the recording of it by Buddy Holly (the Crickets: 'It's Too Late', Clovis, NM, May–Jul 1957, issued on their first LP, *The Chirping Crickets*, Brunswick 54038, NY, 1957 and Coral LVA 9081, London, 1958). Dylan performed 'It's Too Late' live in Buenos Aires, 10 Aug 1991 and at the 'free rehearsal' in Fort Lauderdale, 23 Sep 1995.

Buddy Holly: '(You're So Square) Baby I Don't Care', Clovis, NM, Dec 1957, Coral Q 72432, London, 1961 (not issued as a USA single). Holly had further British posthumous chart successes with rock'n'roll records in this period as follows: 'Midnight Shift', Nashville, 26 Jan 1956 c/w 'Rock Around with Ollie Vee', Nashville, 22 Jul 1956, Brunswick O 5800, London, 1959 (top 30); 'Brown-Eyed Handsome Man' (a Chuck Berry song), Clovis, 1956 (overdubs by the Fireballs, Clovis, 1962), Coral C 62369, NY (Q 72459, London: different B-side), 1963 (top 3); and 'Bo Diddley' (a BO DIDDLEY song), Clovis, 1956 (overdubs Fireballs, Clovis, 1962), Coral C 62352, NY (Coral Q 72463, London: different B-side), 1963 (top 10).

Clarence Frogman Henry: 'Ain't Got No Home', New Orleans, Sep 1956; Argo 5259, Chicago, 1956. 'But I Do' c/w 'Just My Baby and Me', New Orleans, c.Aug 1960; Argo 5378 (Pye International 7N 25078, London), 1961. 'You Always Hurt the One You Love', New Orleans, c.Mar 1961; Argo 5388 (Pye Intnl 7N 25089), 1961. 'Lonely Street' c/w 'Why Can't You', New Orleans, c.Mar 1961; Argo 5395 (Pye Intnl 7N 25108), 1961. 'On Bended Knees' c/w 'Standing in the Need of Love' (a secular re-write of gospel song 'Standing in the Need of Prayer'), Memphis, c.Jul 1961; Argo 5401 (Pye Intnl 7N 25115), 1961. 'A Little Too Much' c/w 'I Wish I Could Say the Same', Memphis, c.Jul 1961; Argo 5408, (Pye Intnl 7N 25123), 1962. Excepting 'On Bended Knees' and 'I Wish I Could Say the Same', all these are on the CD *The Best of Clarence Frogman Henry*, MCA 19226, London, 1993 (unissued USA). Beware cheap re-recordings on cheap re-releases.

Re Clarence Henry, see also **Charles, Bobby**.

Everly Brothers: 'Cathy's Clown', Nashville, 18 Mar 1960, Warner Brothers 5151, NY (Warner Brothers WB 1, London), 1960; 'Temptation', Nashville, 1 Nov 1960 c/w 'Stick With Me Baby', Nashville, 27 Jul 1960, Warner Bros. 5220 (WB 42), 1961.]

post-war blues, Dylan's ways of accessing In general, Dylan's routes of access to the postwar electric blues and R&B were much the same as those of anyone else growing up in the 1950s a long way from any cities with sizeable black populations; but two specific sources are worth a mention.

Fifteen miles from Hibbing, in the small town of Virginia, MN, there was a DJ on station WHLB called Jim Dandy (real name James Reese), and in the summer of 1957 Dylan and his friend John Bucklen went over to find 'the man behind the voice', as ROBERT SHELTON puts it. Bucklen told Shelton that after they found him, they visited him often. 'He was a Negro, involved with the blues. He had a lot of records we like.' Dandy's was the only black family in town, and on radio he used a 'white' voice, which he dropped when he saw that Dylan and Bucklen were keen on black music. They spent many visits listening to R&B and blues records. As Shelton comments: 'Through Jim Dandy, Bob discovered a new Iron Range that his family scarcely knew. That is why Dylan could say: "Where I lived . . . there's no poor section and there's no rich section. . . . There's no wrong side of the tracks . . ."'

The other source for the music was the far more powerful, big-time radio stations you could pick up even in the North Country. Dylan's early girlfriend ECHO HELSTROM remembers listening to DJ Gatemouth Page, beamed up from Shreveport, Louisiana, in 1957, and Dylan was buying blues and post-war R&B records he'd heard on the radio from the age of 13, according to Stan Lewis, the legendary Shreveport record-store owner, plugger and radio-show packager, recollecting this in 1996:

'DJs like Wolfman Jack . . . had shows on other independent stations willing to work R&B into their formats. One of those clear-channel stations had a 250,000-watt transmitter in Mexico. On certain nights its signal could be heard all over the country, even in Europe and South America. I couldn't believe some of the places I started getting orders from.' One place was Hibbing, Minnesota. 'He used to call me at night, to order the records he'd just heard on the air. I thought to myself, Who is this rich kid, calling long-distance from the Midwest to order records? We'd chat and talk about the blues . . .'

See also **pre-war blues, Dylan's ways of accessing**.

[Echo Helstrom in Robert Shelton, *No Direction Home: The Life and Music of Bob Dylan*, Penguin edn., p.48. Stan Lewis: 'With the Record Man: A Half Century of Stan Lewis Memories', Willard Manus, *Blues Access* no.26, Boulder, CO, summer 1996.]

Pound, Ezra [1885 - 1972] American poet, musician and critic Ezra Weston Loomis Pound (October 30, 1885–November 1, 1972) was, with T. S. ELIOT, a major figure of the modernist movement in early 20th century poetry and was central to Imagism and Vorticism (the latter a termed he devised). He also edited Eliot's *The Waste Land* and wrote the important 1920 poem 'Hugh Selwyn Mauberley'.

He is given a namecheck in 'Desolation Row', where he and Eliot are envisaged as 'fighting in the captain's tower / While calypso singers laugh at them / And fishermen hold flowers', and another namecheck in the interviews for the sleeve-notes to *Biograph* two decades later.

Additionally, Pound's major work, *The Cantos*, a long never-finished poem mostly written between 1915 and 1962, was an influence on much modern poetry, especially for its pioneering use of the collage form. The British poet Lee Harwood explains this influence upon himself in terms that hint at what many of THE BEATS (and, via them, Dylan) might have gained from Pound: 'The collage technique seems to provide a so much more accurate picture of how the world works—a weave of conversations and ideas and history and all the interruptions and half-said bits . . .'—which is, perhaps as proof of the Pound-Dylan pudding, a description that seems to apply readily to *"Love and Theft"*. However, in *Chronicles Volume One* Dylan says bluntly: 'Pound . . . was a Nazi sympathiser in World War II and did anti-American broadcasts from Italy. I never did read him.'

Pound heard Dylan, though: ALLEN GINSBERG met the 81-year-old Pound in Italy, and in Venice sat him down and made him listen to THE BEATLES' 'Eleanor Rigby' and 'Yellow Submarine', followed by Dylan's 'Sad-Eyed Lady of the Lowlands' and 'Gates of Eden'. Pound said nothing.

[The first US *Collected Poems of Ezra Pound* was published in New York: New Directions, 1926. Lee Harwood, *Collected Poems*, 2004; quoted in a review of this by August Kleinzahler, 'Toss the monkey wrench', *London Review of Books* vol. 27, no.10, p.29. Dylan quote from *Chronicles Volume One*, p.110. Pound in Venice story from Barry Miles, *Ginsberg: A Biography*, New York: Simon & Schuster, 1989, p.401.]

'Precious Angel' See **angels** and **Artes, Mary Alice**.

Presley, Elvis [1935 - 1977] 'When I first heard Elvis' voice I just knew that I wasn't going to work for anybody; and nobody was going to be my boss. . . . Hearing him for the first time was like busting out of jail': Bob Dylan.

As everyone must know, Presley came from Tupelo, Mississippi, where he was born poor in the 1930s (January 8, 1935), and moved to Memphis with his mother and unemployed father at age 13; later he got a job driving a truck. (There's a neat Dylan allusion to this, delivered in a tough, Presley voice, on the Basement Tapes song 'Lo and Behold': 'Goin' down t' Tennessee! get me a truck or somethin".) Very much a southerner, Presley said Yes Ma'am, No Sir to hostile press reporters, was inward with a simple gospelly religion (via the First Assembly Church of God) and loved the voice of Mahalia Jackson.

Presley had the formula for rock'n'roll within him: a natural upbringing on blues and country music in its living environment. Through his extraordinary fusion of hillbilly, country, blues and rhythm & blues, he changed everything. He gave youth its separate presence; he gave white adolescence its sexual freedom; he gave black music its rightful place at the forefront of American consciousness.

All this with the direct help of four other people and a recording less than two minutes long, in the summer of 1954. That first record, issued by Sun for distribution only in the South, was ARTHUR 'Big Boy' CRUDUP's blues 'That's All Right', sung with a kind of subdued freneticism that sounds hillbilly, amateurish and absolutely genuine. Elvis neither prettied up nor replicated a hot blues record that day. What he started into with his restless but sensitive rhythm guitar and his gloriously fluid, expressive voice was an astonishing and complete re-working of a blues record of no particular distinction released back in 1946, when Elvis Presley was an 11-year-old school boy still living in a home-made shack in East Tupelo.

When Elvis lit into the song, Sam Phillips knew it but was amazed that Elvis did, and taken aback at how freely he was refashioning it. Scotty Moore and Bill Black (lead guitarist and bass player with the Starlite Wranglers) didn't know the song—they'd never heard anything like this from one of their contemporaries—but they joined in readily with a perfect musical match. They'd never have dreamt of it yet it made sense to them at once. Whole generations soon responded the same way.

How inward, how fundamental a strength, his understanding of the blues. He went into that studio already knowing *lots* of blues: 'We talked about the Crudup records I knew—"Cool Disposition", "Rock Me Mama", "Hey Mama", "Everything's All Right" and others, but settled for "That's All Right", one of my top favorites', he said in a 1957 interview. Blues came to him naturally. 'A Mess of Blues'; 'One Night'; 'That's All Right'; 'Reconsider Baby' (the Lowell Fulson classic); 'Blueberry Hill'; 'Anyplace Is Paradise'; 'Lawdy Miss Clawdy'; 'It Feels So Right'; 'Heartbreak Hotel'; listen to any of these today and the claim that Presley is a great white blues singer is hard to deny. Listen to Sun 209 now and it still shimmers and bounces off the walls with the sheer delight the musicians and singer are feeling at having found themselves and at the cathartic release this brings. You're hearing the tingling air in the room at the moment of bold, inspired creation.

He makes it his own. As he does with the bluegrass classic on the other side, Bill Monroe's 'Blue Moon of Kentucky', a parallel re-invention. His later 'Shake Rattle & Roll' makes Big Joe Turner's a different animal without compromising its animal nature, disproving the charge of making a cleaned-up product for whites. Elvis doesn't flinch from the sexual raunch of 'I bin over the hill and way down underneath / You make me roll my eyes and then you make me grit my teeth.' In other words, Presley trusts himself absolutely to stick to lyrics that are low-down and dirty and, equally, to abandon verses that do nothing for him, often substituting lines from elsewhere or of his own invention. All his Sun sides do this. So much for Presley being 'just' a singer of other people's songs.

He makes this then under-attended music his own, and in doing so makes it everybody's: most especially letting it speak straight to the souls of the young. For the truth is, when we were that young, we couldn't identify sexually with these older black singers: not because of their colour but because we thought they sounded, well, elderly. At the very least they were clearly grown-ups. Even when they were exuding innuendo, they sounded like comfortable uncles. To young ears, Wynonie Harris makes 'Meet me in the alley' sound sedate, and Arthur Gunter sings 'Baby Let's Play House' as if they'll be choosing the curtains. Elvis transforms its mood, reclaiming gleefully the forbidden thrill of its suggestive propositioning for teenagers still trapped in their parents' houses.

With an artistic self-knowledge beyond his years, he seized a music that thrilled him and made perfect sense to him as a vehicle for expressing his own vision, in such a way that it liberated millions. The upshot is a 'copy' or a 'cover' more original than the original.

Of course 'originality' wasn't the point of the blues. It began as a communal music, and the great body of blues lyric poetry mainly comprises moveable stanzas shared between everybody from the city street-corner guitarist to the men in their 40s before ever they recorded, who then found, like BLIND LEMON JEFFERSON, that banjo-picking Appalachian hillbillies were hearing them too.

Elvis' fusion was therefore the inspired articulation of something long in the air. His originality lay partly in coming out with it, and partly in his brilliant perception that the mysterious music of middle-aged black men, sung in a patois largely shared by crackers like the Presleys, could be the perfect expressive form for pent-up white youth.

There need be no divides, he realised. And he changed the world when he opened his mouth and let out that uniquely yearning voice—that voice in which inner nobility is as audible as the need to bust free of a stultifying, gentility-filled future.

From 1956 to 1960, his music was golden and he was the untouchable and inaccessible prototype superstar. What, after that, went out of Presley's world? All the sex; all that curious amalgam of insinuation and bluntness he had introduced; all the radiant and thrilling charisma that had more than compensated for the false posturing of everything in the pre-Dylan years; all the therapeutic, rôle-distancing humour; an impeccable control in a strong voice that understood (rare thing then) nuance; and an avowing, ever-present nobility.

When he started, the two striking things in his music were lack of inhibition, and sex. Adolescents admired him because he could be socially unacceptable and get away with it, on stage and on record and in the mind, even if not more than once on the Ed Sullivan TV show. Sullivan was right, by his own lights, to take Presley's hips out of camera-range: they were being rude. And certainly a lot of teen-singers who came after him were to discover that getting up on stage and yelling *Waaaaahhhh!!!* is like exposing yourself in public without being stigmatized.

Sexually, Presley offered a new world, at any rate to whites, and offered it with a blunt statement of interests. There was none of the sycophantic 'dating' appeal that was the context of the most of the 50s stars' records. 'At the Hop', 'Teenager in Love', 'Lonely Boy': these were the typical titles of the time—but not for Elvis. His titles suited the black labels that announced them. Presley's titles were 'Trouble', 'I Got Stung', 'Jailhouse Rock', 'Paralysed', 'King Creole'—these all fitted the various significant elements that made Presley a unique, thrusting and ominous force. He embodied an untapped violence (it lurks in that prophetic, pre-Pete Townshend line 'He don't stop playin' till his guitar breaks') that a song like 'Trouble' made explicit and the kind of hard bravado that 'Jailhouse Rock' merged with ecstasy. 'Jailhouse Rock' is a direct descendant of 'Hound Dog', where the voice seems to rage like King Kong in chains.

Most rock'n'roll stars tried to be aggressive and masculine, and made love to the stage microphone (GENE VINCENT most endearingly): but only Elvis Presley projected himself so well that he seemed often to be bearing down sexually on the listener. In the love songs he offered to the young and virginal a constant implication of prior sexual experience and a corresponding cynicism others could never bring off: 'Hey baby—I ain't askin' much o' you / No n-no n-no n-no no baby—ain't askin' much o' you: / Just a big-uh big-uh big-uh hunk of love will do.' In 1959 that came across as freshly candid, its message the forerunner of that line from Dylan's 'If You Gotta Go, Go Now', 'It's not that I'm askin' for anything you never gave before'. The two share the same ambiguity, the same ostensible politeness.

It was a unique stance at the time: unique, at least, in reaching the mass of white middle-class adolescents. Elvis was having sex with you while RICKY NELSON was singing 'I hate to face your dad / Too bad / I know he's gonna be mad / It's late . . . / Hope this won't be our last date' and in the mournful, sexless world of Eddie Cochran (despite his macho posturing), 'Six hot-dogs oughta be just right / After such a wonderful night.' Presley, in contrast, got down to the eternal verities of passion underlying the middle-class Saturday night: 'If you wanna be loved, baby you gotta love me too / Cos I ain't for no one-sided love affair: / Well a fair exchange ain't no robbery / An' the whole world knows that it's true'. And 'Why make me plead / For something you need?'

Presley's cynicism had such pungency that it provided, over the years, a sharp, concerted attack on the two-faced conventions imposed on the children of the 50s. His delivery gave a stylishness and authority to these open, soliciting songs that was utterly lacking in the other rock artists. Not just by sneers but by his pent-up tremble in the bass notes, the sudden, full-throated rasps and the almost confessional, mellow country moans. Presley was saying 'Let's fuck' years before John and Paul were wanting to hold your hand. Millions of eager teenagers, weary of the pudge next door, could respond a good deal more honestly when Elvis sang 'Stuck on You', 'Treat Me Nice' and 'Baby Let's Play House'. Even at his most melodic (which he was never afraid to be, and which he always carried off without false delicacy) there was a saving power.

A final point on Presley's sexuality. It is true that the pre-rock chart-toppers and radio-favourites, the night-club stars whose idea of perfection was a Cole Porter song and the Nelson Riddle Orchestra, dealt with sex too—but never, never with passion. Physical contact, desire, sexual aspiration always come across From SINATRA, Tormé, Tony Bennett and the rest as a kind of world-weary joke that goes with old age. The standard it's-one-in-the-morning-and-we're-pretty-smooth treatments of 'I've Got You Under My Skin', 'Night and Day', etc, could as easily be addressed to the bottle as to the babe.

Against this lifeless background, Presley's initial impact coast-to-coast in America, and in Britain also, was cataclysmic. Yet lack of inhibition, sex and the voice to carry it was not all that he offered. He also gave out a fair share of the vital humour that goes with the best hard-line rock and that FATS DOMINO, CHUCK BERRY and LITTLE RICHARD all used very well: as humour that shows itself aware of outside values and of the inextricable mixture of the important and the trivial, the real and the stylised in the pop medium. And if you go back now to the original Presley recordings, the pungency and freshness of this humour can still hit home.

Where to begin, on how Presley influenced Dylan? It's almost too all-embracing to bear delineation. But in the first place, Dylan would have heard at least part of his old blues material second-hand through Presley—to whom it seemed an entirely natural, fluid medium in which to express, well, everything. Elvis was a living demonstration of how this could be done. When we acknowledge that Dylan has worked the blues so strongly and resourcefully that he has given it something back, the nearest comparison must be to Presley.

You can see the extent of Dylan's drawing on the poetry of pre-war blues in a song as 'new' as 'It Takes a Lot to Laugh, It Takes a Train to Cry' (and in a couple of earlier songs), from looking at just one such old blues, Leroy Carr's 'Alabama Woman Blues': 'Did you ever go down on the Mobile and K.C. Line / I just want to ask you, did you ever see that girl of mine / I rode the central and I hustled the L&N / The Alabama women, they live like section men . . . / Don't the clouds look lonesome across the deep blue sea / Don't my gal look good when she's coming after me.' But additionally, though by the nature of the process inseparably, Dylan's lines draw in the couplet Presley sings *so* beautifully in the cathartic, lulled middle of his stormy Sun recording of 'Milk Cow Blues Boogie': 'Don't that sun look good goin' down / Well don't that old moon look lonesome when your baby's not around?'

Here, in one revelatory musical moment, we glimpse how electrifyingly such stuff passes along. To hear Presley sing these lines is to hear it all: to hear the graceful, rueing heart of the old country blues—never better voiced than in the brilliant ellipse of the opening line of BLIND BLAKE's 'One Time Blues' in 1927: 'Ah the rising sun going down'—yet to hear at the same moment the liberation of the soul that Elvis found in the blues almost 30 years later, a liberation he passed on to all of us whiteys when he first sang out—*and* in that same moment to hear too a sound that travels forward another 30-odd years to illuminate what Dylan has swirling around him when, on 1990's *Under the Red Sky* song '10,000 Men', he comes to sing its second line not as a full repeat of the first ('Ten thousand men on a hill', which might be thought abrupt and spare enough) but honed to the absolute minimalism of 'Ten thousand men, hill,' so that Dylan, sounding old as the hills himself (and pronouncing 'he-yi-ull' exactly as Elvis always did), stands shoulder to shoulder across the 60-year gap with Blind Blake. Sure has been a long hard climb; yet it has been a shared journey, and the terrain is constantly replenished.

(When Dylan recorded 'Milk Cow Blues' in 1962, he used part of Kokomo Arnold's lyric, part of Presley's, part of ROBERT JOHNSON's 'Milkcow's Calf Blues' and part of LEADBELLY's 'Good Morning Blues', shuffling these elements around in the course of two still-unreleased takes.)

Yet Dylan's debt to Presley reaches beyond the blues. We find Elvis in many corners of Dylan's canon. Perhaps it was even hearing Elvis' belatedly issued version of LONNIE JOHNSON's hit 'Tomorrow Night' that reminded Dylan of the song, and prompted its inclusion on his 1992 album *Good as I Been to You*. More certainly, Dylan's lyric and tune on 'One More Night', on *Nashville Skyline*, are heavily reminiscent of Elvis' 'Blue Moon of Kentucky'. 'That's All Right' is down there in the Bob Dylan songbook. The clear allusion to Floyd Cramer's piano style on the end of 'Tell Me That It Isn't True' is an allusion to a style much associated with Elvis and his RCA Victor studios at Nashville. The opening lines of 'Lay Lady Lay' do what Presley did all along—it's the same kind of ennobled overture that comes across in a hundred Elvis songs—while the immaculate soulfulness of 'I Threw It All Away' is like Presley's great 'Is It So Strange?'. Elvis' 'Milk Cow Blues Boogie' and 'Bob Dylan's 115th Dream' both begin and then stop and start again. Elvis says 'Hold it fellas!' and Dylan's producer echoes this with 'Hey, wait a minute fellas!' It may have been Dylan who, recognising the parallel, insisted on retaining it on the released version of the track. If so, it is not the only Dylan amendment of a Presley line. In the much later Elvis song 'Cotton Candy Land' there is the line 'We'll ride upon a big white swan'; Dylan's knowingly gauche 'Country Pie' amends it to 'Saddle me up a big white goose!' And it is impossible, when Dylan was recording his countrified version of 'Blue Moon' for the 1970 album *Self Portrait*, that he could have forgotten the eerie cowboy version—complete with the clip-clop of horses' hooves—that Elvis had recorded in the 1950s.

There are also many take-offs of Elvis slipped into Dylan's work—but they are never so much take-offs as tributes. Presley is melodramatic, and Dylan mocks that, mocks the exaggeration; but always he does it with a smile that confesses he can't help falling for Presley, that he notices the good things just as keenly. These take-offs/tributes include the end, musically, of 'Peggy Day'. Elvis' songs often end like this, right from his very early 'I Got a Woman' through to 'Beach Boy Blues', 'Steppin' Out of Line' and 'Rock-a-Hula Baby'. On the Basement Tapes version of 'Quinn the Eskimo (The Mighty Quinn)', Dylan's voice is deliberately near to the Presley voice of 'Trouble'. And two versions of 'Nothing Was Delivered' from those sessions evoke the Presley world. The one with the heavy piano backing is a finely measured acknowledgement of Elvis' handling of Domino's 'Blueberry Hill'; the version with Dylan's monologue is a wide-open laugh at Presley's posturing monologues on 'That's When Your Heartaches Begin', 'I'm Yours', 'Are You Lonesome Tonight?' and, again, 'Trouble'. On the last of these especially, Elvis 'talks tough', like a young Lee Marvin; Dylan simply makes the hollowness transparent by using the same bravado on weaker lines. Elvis stands there as if all-powerful, delivering the goods; Dylan comes on like a swindled consumer to talk from positions of weakness in the same posturing voice: 'Now you must, you must provide some answers / For what you sell has not bin received / And the sooner you come up with those answers / You know the sooner you can leave.' On the *Pat Garrett & Billy the Kid* soundtrack album, Dylan does three versions of a song called 'Billy', the last of which, 'Billy 7', is actually a beautiful imitation of how that Lee Marvin imitator James Coburn would sound if he were singing it. And the effect of this—as he sings with an astonishingly deep voice set against sleazy, smoky guitar lines and even sound effects of ominous thunder—is to give us a Dylan parodying exactly the kind of toughness that belongs to Presley.

Dylan also began to come clean, at the end of the 1960s, in acknowledging the special place Elvis Presley occupies in his canon of influences. First, when *Rolling Stone* asked whether there were any particular artists he liked to have record his songs, he replied (and was widely assumed to be joking at the time), 'Yeah, Elvis Presley. I liked Elvis Presley. Elvis Presley recorded a song of mine. That's the one recording I treasure the most . . . it was called "Tomorrow Is a Long Time".'

The *New Morning* song 'Went to See the Gypsy' seems to be about going to see Presley, and when Dylan's record company issued their ragbag album of warm-ups and reject tracks, *Dylan* (1973), it contained Bob Dylan versions of two Presley hits. Just as Elvis made versions of Dylan's 'Don't Think Twice, It's All Right' and 'Tomorrow Is a Long Time' (and, it was eventually revealed, a 'Blowin' in the Wind'), so Dylan had recorded Elvis' 'A Fool Such as I' (on the Basement Tapes and then again at the first of the *Self Portrait* sessions) and a most lovely, fond, humorous version of 'Can't Help Falling in Love' (a warm-up for an early *New Morning* session), plus, on the Basement Tapes, a version of another song much associated with Elvis' Sun recording of it, 'I Forgot to Remember to Forget'. Two decades later, accepting an American Society of Composers, Authors and Publishers Founders Award in a Los Angeles restaurant, Dylan even reached for the cornier side of Elvis, saying: 'I would like to quote, like Elvis Presley, when he accepted some award, and he said: "Without a song, the day would never end / Without a song, the road would never bend / When things go wrong, man ain't got a friend / Without a song."' (Presley had never recorded 'Without a Song', but had, as Dylan suggests, read out part of the lyrics during his acceptance speech when presented with an award as one of the Ten Outstanding Young Men of America by the Jaycees in 1971, the day after this 'young man' turned 36.)

The spirit of Presley's last year as a great artist, 1960, glides around the edges of Dylan's *Oh Mercy* album and then on the next album, 1990's *Under the Red Sky*, Dylan gives Presley a sympathetic namecheck, in 'TV Talkin' Song', when a snarl against the intrusiveness of television ends with 'sometimes you gotta do like Elvis did and shoot the damn thing out'. (Elvis had done this in Asheville, NC, while watching TV after a concert, July 22, 1975.) And after Dylan's recovery from illness in 1997, Dylan commented: 'I really thought I'd be seeing Elvis soon.'

On September 30, 1994, Dylan went into a New York City studio and recorded multiple takes of three songs associated with Elvis, 'Lawdy Miss Clawdy', 'Money Honey' and the glorious 'Any Way You Want Me (That's How I Will Be)'. None has been released, and only a take of the third song has circulated—and it's the sort of performance only a Dylan fan would appreciate, but it's a lovely thing. The opening electric guitar noise replicates 1957 so beautifully it's heartstopping; then Dylan's voice comes in weakly on the very phrase 'I'll be strong', but while he can't throw his head back and let out those orgasmic sobbing moans like Elvis, he finds a way to sing it that is at once a truly touching tribute and a re-invention: a way of translating those moans into his own expressive cadences, calling back across time to convey the numinousness of the 1950s moment anew. It's absurd that this recording remains unreleased.

In June 1972 Bob Dylan was 'spotted' attending one of Presley's four concerts at Madison Square Garden, NYC. The idea, suggested by 'Went to See the Gypsy', that Dylan might have met Presley in Minnesota (a) when both were famous, (b) after a Presley Las Vegas stint and (c) ahead of the *New Morning* songs being recorded, is impossible, though they might have met elsewhere. That Dylan might have seen Presley in concert in Minnesota is another matter: Presley first performed in Minnesota in St. Paul, May 13, 1956; next, 15 years later, was Minneapolis, November 5, 1971; then St. Paul, October 2 & 3, 1974; Duluth, October 16, 1976 and Minneapolis the following night; Duluth, April 29, 1977; and lastly St. Paul, April 30, 1977.

Presley also recorded a very foreshortened version of one further Dylan song, 'I Shall Be Released': he sings the chorus twice, unaccompanied, and then stops, adding the single word 'Dylan!', as if to identify the composer for the benefit of others in the studio. It is impossible to interpret Presley's attitude to Dylan from the tone of voice with which he speaks his name. On stage, however, in one of the 1970 Las Vegas concerts, he suggests an attitude towards Dylan's voice when he says to the audience: 'My mouth is so dry it feels like Bob Dylan spent the night in it.'

Elvis didn't need to listen to Dylan himself to pick up his material. As Peter Guralnick writes, about an Elvis session of April 1966: '. . . before going to the studio, they listened to *Peter, Paul & Mary in Concert* or the trio's latest, *See What Tomorrow Brings*, and *Odetta Sings Dylan* was never far from the turntable. Elvis showed a keen interest in IAN & SYLVIA as well, along with his usual gospel, blues and rhythm and blues favourites, and when they all got together to sing, he was as likely to suggest Bob Dylan's "Blowin' in the Wind" as a Statesmen number . . .' (*Odetta Sings Dylan* included 'Don't Think Twice It's All Right' and 'Tomorrow Is a Long Time', and *Peter, Paul & Mary in Concert* unsurprisingly included 'Blowin' in the Wind'. 'I Shall Be Released', of course, came later.)

Years ago, when Dylan was held to be the absolute opposite, the antithesis, of Presley, it would have been, if not actually heretical, at least controversial to argue that Dylan could owe Elvis anything. Now, recognition has grown for what Presley has achieved, even though the clichés and artifice that are a discountable part of it for those of us who heard his early work when it was new, must surely be too obtrusive for new listeners except on a few early classic tracks. But Dylan grew up with it, and would have grown up a different person, and a different artist—perhaps not an artist at all—if not for Elvis.

[Elvis Presley: 'That's All Right', Memphis, 5–6 Jul, 1954, Sun 209, Memphis, 1954; 'A Mess of Blues', Nashville, 20–21 Mar 1960, RCA Victor, NY, 1960; 'One Night', Hollywood, 23 Feb 1957, RCA Victor 47-7410, 1958 (RCA 1100, London, 1959); 'Reconsider Baby', Nashville, 3–4 Apr 1960, issued *Elvis Is Back*, RCA Victor LPM/LSP 2231 (RCA RD27171 & SF 5060—mono & stereo—London), 1960; 'Blueberry Hill', Hollywood, 19 Jan 1957, *Just For You* (EP), RCA Victor EPA 4041 (*Elvis Presley*, RCX 104, London), 1957; 'Anyplace Is Paradise', Hollywood, 2 Sep 1956, *Elvis*, RCA Victor LPM 1382, 1956 (*Elvis (Rock 'N' Roll no. 2)*, HMV CLP 1105, London, 1957); 'Lawdy Miss Clawdy', NY, 3 Feb 1956, RCA Victor 20/47-6642, 1956 (HMV POP 408, 1957: B-side of different single); 'It Feels So Right', 20–21 Mar 1960, *Elvis Is Back*; 'Heartbreak Hotel', Nashville, 10–11 Jan 1956, RCA Victor 20-6420 & 47-6420 (78rpm & 45rpm), NY (HMV Records POP 182, London), 1956; 'Tomorrow Night', Memphis, 10 Sep 1954, first on *Elvis For Everyone*, RCA Victor LPM-3450, 1965, but first issued properly on *Reconsider Baby*, RCA Victor AFL1-5418, 1985 & CD-reissued on the essential *The King of Rock'n'Roll—The Complete 50s Masters*, BMG/RCA PD90689(5), 1992. 'Blue Moon of Kentucky', as 'That's All Right'; 'Shake Rattle & Roll'; 'Baby Let's Play House', Memphis, 5 Feb 1955, Sun 217, Memphis, 1955 (HMV POP 305, 1957). 'Trouble', Hollywood, 15 Jan 1958, & 'King Creole', Hollywood, 23 Jan 1958, were both written and recorded for the film *King Creole*, Paramount Studios, US, directed Michael Curtiz, 1958 (based on Harold Robbins' novel *A Stone for Danny Fisher*, 1952); *King Creole*, RCA Victor LPM 1884, NY (RCA Victor RD 27088, London), 1958. 'I Got Stung', Nashville, 11 Jun 1958, RCA Victor 47-7410, 1958 (RCA 1100, London, 1959). 'Jailhouse Rock', Hollywood, 30 Apr 1957 (title song from the MGM film, US, directed Richard Thorpe, 1957), RCA Victor 20/47-7035 (RCA 1028), 1957: a no.1 hit single USA & UK, and also title-track of a no.1 EP, RCA Victor EPA 4114, 1957 (RCX 106, 1958). 'Paralyzed', Hollywood, 2 Sep 1956, on *Elvis*, 1956 and EP *Elvis Vol. 1*, EPA 992, 1956 (UK single on HMV POP 378, 1957); 'Hound Dog', NY, 2 Jul 1956, RCA Victor 20/47-6604 (HMV POP 249), 1956; 'A Big Hunk o' Love', Nashville, 10 Jun 1958, RCA Victor 47-7600, (RCA 1136), 1959;

'One Sided Love Affair', NY, 30 Jan 1956, on *Elvis Presley*, RCA Victor LPM 1254 (*Elvis Presley (Rock 'N' Roll)*, HMV CLP 1093), 1956 (his first LP, & a US no.1); 'Give Me the Right', Nashville, 12–13 Mar 1961, *Something for Everybody*, RCA Victor LPM/LSP-2370 (RD-27224 / SF 5106, London), 1961; 'Stuck on You', Nashville, 20–21 Mar 1960, RCA Victor (RCA 1187), 1960; 'Treat Me Nice', Hollywood, 5 Sep 1957, B-side of 'Jailhouse Rock'; 'Milkcow Blues Boogie', Memphis, prob. 15 Nov or 20 Dec 1954; Sun 215, Memphis, 1955 (1st issued UK on EP *Good Rockin' Tonight*, HMV 7EG8256, 1957); 'Is It So Strange?', Hollywood, 19 Jan 1957, on the EP *Just for You* (Presley had earlier sung the song at the legendary 'million dollar quartet' jam-session at Sun Studios with Carl Perkins, Jerry Lee Lewis and, briefly, Johnny Cash: Memphis, 4 or 11 Dec 1956); 'Cotton Candy Land', Hollywood, Aug 1962, *It Happened at the World's Fair*, RCA Victor LPM/LSP-2697 (RD/SF 7565, London), 1963; 'Blue Moon', Memphis, 19 Aug 1954, RCA Victor 20/47-6640, NY, 1956; 'I Got a Woman', Nashville, 10 Jan 1956, *Elvis Presley*; 'Beach Boy Blues' & 'Rock-a-Hula Baby', Hollywood, 23 Mar 1961, *Blue Hawaii*, RCA Victor LPM/LSP-2426 (RCA RD27238 / SF 5115), 1961 ('Rock-a-Hula Baby' was also a single); 'Steppin' Out of Line', Hollywood, 22 Mar 1961, *Pot Luck*, LPM/LSP-2523 (RD 27265 / SF 5135), 1962; 'That's When Your Heartaches Begin', Hollywood, 13 Jan 1957, B-side of 'All Shook Up', RCA 20-6870 (78rpm) & 47-6870 (45rpm), March 1957; 'I'm Yours', Nashville, 25–26 Jun 1961, *Pot Luck*; 'Are You Lonesome Tonight?', Nashville, 3–4 Apr 1960, RCA Victor 47-7810 ('living stereo' version 61-7810), (RCA 1216, London), 1960; 'Tomorrow Is a Long Time', Nashville, 25–28 May 1966 (the sessions include musicians Floyd Cramer, Pete Drake & Charlie McCoy), *Spinout*, RCA Victor LPM/LSP-3702 (*California Holiday*, RCA SF 7820, London), 1966; 'Don't Think Twice, It's All Right', Nashville, 16–17 May 1971, *Elvis* (nb. not 2nd LP, which had same title, 1956), RCA Victor APL1-0283 (SF 8378, London), 1973; 'Blowin' in the Wind', Feb 1966—early 1967, Hollywood, *Platinum: A Life in Music*, RCA/BMG 07863 67469-2, 1997; 'I Shall Be Released', Nashville, May 20, 1971, *Elvis—Walk a Mile in My Shoes—The Essential 70's Masters*, RCA/BMG 7432130331-2, 1995. *NB:* The great first post-Army album, *Elvis Is Back*, has been reissued complete with many outtakes and the singles recorded at the same sessions, plus outtakes from these, as a highly praised 2-CD set, *Elvis Is Back!*, Follow That Dream 8287 667968-2, US 2005.

The 1957 interview quoted from Charlie Gillett: *Sound of the City*, 1971. The 1970 Las Vegas quote, and details re Elvis shooting the TV, from *The Elvis Atlas: A Journey Through Elvis Presley's America*, Michael Gray & Roger Osborne, New York: Henry Holt, 1996. Presley's Madison Square Garden concerts, one of which Dylan attended, 9–11 Jun 1972. Dylan quoted from *Rolling Stone* no.47, San Francisco, Jun 1969. Peter Guralnick, *Careless Love: The Unmaking of Elvis Presley*, New York: Little Brown, 1999, p.223.

Arthur Crudup: 'That's All Right', Chicago, 6 Sep 1946, known by Elvis Presley from its issue on 78rpm on Victor 20-2205 (c/w 'Crudup's After Hours'), NY, 1946–47; 'Cool Disposition' & 'Rock Me Mama', Chicago, 15 Dec 1944, Bluebird 34-0738, NY, 1945;'Hey Mama, Everything's All Right', Chicago 7 Oct 1947, Victor 20-3261, 1947–48; 'If I Get Lucky', Chicago, 11 Sep 1941, Bluebird B8858, NY, 1941.

Arthur Gunter (1926–1976) cut 'Baby Let's Play House' at his first session, Nashville, 1954, Excello 2047, Nashville, 1955; Bob Dylan: 'If You Gotta Go, Go Now', live NY, 31 Oct 1964, *Bootleg Series Vol. 6*; 'Milk Cow Blues', NY, 25 Apr 1962, unreleased; Ricky Nelson: 'It's Late', Hollywood, 21 Oct 1958, Imperial 5565, LA (London American HLP 8817, London), 1959; Eddie Cochran: 'Drive-In Show', LA, 1957, Liberty Records 55087, Hollywood, 1957; Leroy Carr: 'Alabama Women Blues', Chicago, 9 Sep 1930; Kokomo Arnold: 'Milk Cow Blues', Chicago, 10 Sep 1934; Robert Johnson: 'Milkcow's Calf Blues', Dallas, 20 Jun 1937, 2 takes; Leadbelly: 'Good Morning Blues', NY, 15 Jun 1940 or summer 1943. Blind Lemon Jefferson: 'That Black Snake Moan', Chicago, c.Nov 1926; 'Black Snake Moan', Atlanta, 14 Mar 1927; Ishman Bracey: 'The 'Fore Day Blues' (alternate take), Memphis, 31 Aug 1928; Lonnie Johnson: 'Tomorrow Night', Cincinatti, 10 Dec 1947. Fats Domino: 'Blueberry Hill', LA, Jul 1956, Imperial 5407, 1956. Odetta: *Odetta Sings Dylan*, *nia*, RCA LSP-3324, NY, 1965 (the CD reissue of which does include 'Blowin' in the Wind', plus 'Paths of Victory', each taken from earlier Odetta albums); *Peter, Paul & Mary in Concert*, Warner Bros. 1555, NY, 1964.]

pre-war blues & post-structuralism See **'Call Letter Blues' & 'the shock of recognition'.**

pre-war blues, Dylan's use of, an introduction Because it's so crackly on record, so lo-fi, so immured behind a white-noise wall, the black noise that is the pre-war blues can seem inaccessible, unreachable. To be put off by this would be to lose great riches. Sometimes it's best to play it really *loud* (and maybe go into the next room): then you'll hear all the joys and mysteries of esoteric vocals, guitar magic, sheer moody weirdnesses: all the synapse-crinkling giddy-hop that rock'n'roll gave you when you were 13.

Garfield Akers' 'Cottonfield Blues', especially the transcendent 'Part 2', comes across as the birth of rock'n'roll . . . from 1929! It's also as incantatory as buddhist chanting or as VAN MORRISON's 'Madame George'. (Yet Garfield Akers recorded only four tracks.) Or there's BLIND WILLIE JOHNSON's 'Motherless Children Have a Hard Time': a record from 1927 that you hear and say of the guitar—if this was achieved then, how come it took 30 years to get to rock'n'roll (or 40 years to get to ERIC CLAPTON)?

Yet it isn't that the pre-war blues is proto-rock'n' roll that makes it so uplifting, exciting and vivid. The experience of the encounter is comparable; and the music may hold some of the main ingredients that rock'n'roll returned us to using—but the pre-war blues is a liberation and an enrichment because it's different, not merely more of the same. These old blues are at once thrillingly exotic and our common heritage.

Garfield Akers—a deeply obscure but compelling, intense and distinctive artist who reputedly played around Memphis in the 1920s–30s and again in the 1950s—should have been a tremendous star. His shockingly small number of recordings, or, say, Furry Lewis' 'I Will Turn Your Money Green', are whole new rich seams of their own, a fresh and revelatory 3D world, as glorious as ever LITTLE RICHARD and BUDDY HOLLY were. This blues world burns with its own heroic energy and vision, and across a musical spectrum of concentrated emotional expression from the utmost in delicacy and finesse to the most searing invocations of cacophonous rapture and pain, while the language of the blues—blues lyric poetry—is one of the great streams of consciousness of 20th century America: a rich and alertly resourceful African-American fusion and reinvention of the language of the Bible and the dirt road, plantation and medicine show, of the Deep South countryside and the city streets, of 19th century children's games, folktales and family lore and African folk-memory: above all the language of the oppressed community and the individual human heart.

For Bob Dylan then, as listener and as writer-composer, the specifics of an old record by JIM JACKSON, BLIND BLAKE or MEMPHIS MINNIE yield far richer pleasures than a Johnny Winters or an Eric Clapton performance.

This is not a matter of being politically correct about authenticity. The whole question of 'authenticity' in black music is highly complex and contentious, and involves matters far more consequential than whether Eric Clapton plays the blues. Paul Gilroy's riveting, if sometimes barely penetrable, essay 'Sounds Authentic' cites a number of these issues, across which white-boy debates about authenticity in the blues are bound to stumble rather clumsily, and from which, as Gilroy writes, authenticity 'emerges as a highly charged and bitterly contested issue.' It's an issue too large to detail here.

Rather than argue, therefore, as to whether the blues can really be called the blues when purveyed by the Claptons who speed 'black cultural creation on its passage into international pop commodification', it seems more useful to suggest, as Bob Dylan probably would, that *that* sort of blues is simply no longer interesting. It can't be: such is its shopping-mall forgetfulness that it's no longer interest*ed*—in either the specifics of where it's come from or of what it's thrown away.

Dylan stands in a very different relation to the blues from that of the white frontmen of the trans-global blues industry. He occupies a position as near to that of the poet or composer (even to the critic) as to the rock'n'roll performer. This difference arises from how he feels about the potency and the eloquence of the old blues records and the expressive vernacular of the world they inhabit. This is why what Dylan wants to do with this immense, rich body of work is experiment in how he might utilise its poetry, its codes and its integrity—to see how these may stand up as building blocks for new creative work—just as he (and just as the blues) uses the language and lore of the King James Bible. He is not concerned with translating a few lowest-common-denominator dynamics of the blues into some MTVable product.

First, he claims no blues-singer specialism like a JOHN HAMMOND JR.: it isn't, for him, his trademark. His stance does not downgrade blackness per se, therefore: does not carry the inherent subtext that blues is essentially a matter of 'style'. It's telling that on those rare occasions when Dylan performed to specifically black audiences, as in GREENWOOD, Mississippi, in 1963 and at the women's penitentiary in New Jersey during the Rolling Thunder Revue of 1975, he didn't hesitate to sing about racial politics but chose to do so via his white 'protest' songs—'Only a Pawn in Their Game' and 'Hurricane' respectively—rather than via blues songs. In contrast, witness the spectacle of John Hammond Jr. imposing his fussy impersonation of an old blues-singer upon the embarrassed black occupants of a Mississippi bar-room for his TV documentary 'In Search of Robert Johnson'.

Second, Bob Dylan's interest and special dexterity is in exploring the innards of the blues, taking from the blues the strengths of its vernacular language (to some extent musically as well as lyrically) and building them into the core of his own work—into the machinery of his own creative intelligence. As, in this spirit, he raids the Bible, traditional white folksong and nursery rhyme, so he raids the poetry of the pre-war blues.

To do this to such creative profit would be impossible without a mix of curiosity towards and respect for the original contexts from which these things are seized and reworked. This guarantees that, unlike many of those in the global blues industry, Dylan has no interest in seeing the blues 'deprived of its historical base' (to quote a *Living Blues* magazine editorial condemning 'white blues' as 'not blues').

Then there's a question folklorist Peter Narváez raises when he contends that 'While historically many forms of downhome blues were played by soloists, and urban blues have always featured individual entertainers . . . blues fans today recognise blues as a collective activity, that is, a music played by groups who interact among themselves and with audiences.'

We can at once picture Bob Dylan's response. On the one hand, he too interacts with groups and with audiences. More than ever before, in fact, live audiences seem indispensable to him. Yet he has always believed in the power of the artist with the lone guitar and a point of view. As he said in 1985:

'I always like to think that there's a real person talking to me, just one voice you know, that's all I can handle—Cliff Carlisle . . . ROBERT JOHNSON. For me this is a deep reality: someone who's telling me where he's been that I haven't, and what it's like there—somebody whose life I can feel.'

At the same time, he knows that the music and the poetry of the blues, its fundamental assumptions, are founded in an Africanness that is itself characterised by 'groups who interact among themselves and with audiences'—a theme that the great blues field-recordist and collector ALAN LOMAX, for instance, repeatedly stresses in his 1993 book *The Land Where the Blues Began*.

In other words, the lone blues guitarist would have a different point of view, a different way of expressing him or herself, if the culture from which the blues arose had not been a communal, democratically interactive one—one in which there is almost no hierarchical Artist Up Here and Audience Down There, but, rather, a collaborative performance in which the singer/musician takes cues moment by moment from the dancers/spectators and mingles physically among them, his or her repertoire as much a reaction as an imposition.

This is a very different kind of participation from mass-marketed blues performances in which big-name entertainers and high-energy tyro groups please hyper crowds with the most easily magnified clichés of the genre transmitted through flashy guitar solos and greatest-hits repertoire.

Dylan himself talks about the crucialness of old blues couplets (though if he hadn't, we would know their importance to him from the vast extent to which he has drawn from their wells of material and added to them) in 1985:

> 'You can't say things any better than that, really. You can say it in a different way, you can say it with more words, but you can't say anything better than what they said. And they covered everything.'

That the young Bob Dylan could insinuate his creative imagination into the world of the older white and black folk artists to enrich even very early songs of his own is not in doubt. What is still more interesting is to look far beyond his very early work to the period from 1964 onwards, when increasingly he freed himself from writing within borrowed folk formats: and to see the huge extent to which, having found the blues powerful and real, and having come to know it so intimately and inwardly, Dylan has drawn deeply from its poetry in creating his own.

In the end, it isn't the main point whether Bob Dylan discovered these people in or around Dinkytown or Greenwich Village, on the radio or via the incredible diverse riches of the blues records avalanching onto vinyl in the 1950s and 60s. Engaging though it is to retrace his routes to these discoveries (see **pre-war blues, Dylan's ways of accessing**), in the end, the point is that he made them.

And he uses, *so singularly*, the huge amount he learnt, in the construction of his own extraordinary work. No-one else has used the blues in anything like the way Bob Dylan has. Most people who are 'into' the blues take a few standard numbers and riffs from it, and run with them in ever more amplified, clichéd, unrooted ways, or else, at the other extreme, bore us to death with their pedantic archival reproductions of obscurer-than-thou acoustic repertoire. The far smaller number of people whose work is genuinely enriched by the blues are usually musicians, rather than singer-songwriter musicians.

But Dylan takes myriad complex treasures from the pre-war country blues, both passionately and quietly, paying them at least as much loving attention as he pays to the vibrant strengths of those 1940s-to-50s electric blues that made possible, more than we knew at the time, all the taken-as-givens of rock'n'roll. And he draws all this cultural richness, the music and the lyric poetry of it, into the very core of his own work. Dylan has worked the blues so strongly and resourcefully that he has given it something back.

He inhabits the blues as the best of the old bluesmen themselves did, fusing traditional and personal material into fresh, expressive work of their own, layered with the resonance of familiarity, the subconscious edits of memory and the pleasures of unexpected recognition, sharing the energy that flows between the old and the new, and between the individual and the common culture. He has used the blues with such insistent individuality, yet never in bad faith to the gravitas he found within it, or to the world in which its people had moved.

Interviewed in San Diego in autumn 1993, Dylan said:

> 'The people who played that music were still around . . . [in the early 1960s], and so there was a bunch of us, me included, who got to see all these people close up—people like SON HOUSE, REVEREND GARY DAVIS or SLEEPY JOHN ESTES. Just to sit there and be up close and watch them play, you could study what they were doing, plus a bit of their lives rubbed off on you. Those vibes will carry into you forever, really, so it's like those people, they're still here to me. They're not ghosts of the past or anything, they're continually here.'

It should be no surprise, therefore, to find that blues lyric poetry is everywhere in Dylan's work: in amongst the New York City hip culture of Dylan 1965 and the radical acid-rock of *Blonde on Blonde*, in the evangelism at the start of the 1980s and work of more modest, mellowed knowingness right on through to the darkness of *Time Out of*

Mind and the teeming good cheer of *"Love and Theft"*.

Blues lyric poetry runs into the mainstream of Dylan's work, while he in turn makes a clear creative contribution to this major form of American music. It follows, then, that the more you know of the blues corpus, the more you'll appreciate Bob Dylan's extraordinary regenerative use of it; and the better you know Dylan's output, the better placed you'll be to hear the blues coursing through it.

(See also **'Call Letter Blues' & 'the shock of recognition'**.)

[Garfield Akers (c.1900–c.1960): 'Cottonfield Blues—Part 1' & 'Cottonfield Blues—Part 2', Memphis, c.23 Sep 1929, 'Dough Roller Blues' & 'Jumpin' and Shoutin' Blues', Memphis, c.21 Feb 1930, all CD-reissued on *Son House and the Great Delta Blues Singers (1928–1930)*, Document DOCD-5002, Vienna, 1990. Van Morrison: 'Madame George', NY, 1968, *Astral Weeks*, Warner Bros WS1768, US (K46024, UK), 1968. Blind Willie Johnson: 'Mother's Children Have a Hard Time' (sic: a mistranscription), Dallas, 3 Dec 1927, *Blind Willie Johnson*, RBF Records RF-10, NY, 1965. Furry Lewis: 'I Will Turn Your Money Green' (2 takes), Memphis, 28 Aug 1928; take 1 issued *In His Prime 1927–1928*, Yazoo L1050, NY, c.1973; take 2 (the version originally issued on 78) issued *Frank Stokes' Dream . . . 1927–1931*, Yazoo L1008, NY, 1968.

Paul Gilroy, 'Sounds Authentic: Black Music, Ethnicity and the Challenge of a *Changing* Same'; London: unpublished, 1991, later incorporated into Gilroy's *The Black Atlantic: Modernity and Double Consciousness*, London: Verso, 1993.

Bob Dylan: 'Only a Pawn in Their Game', Greenwood, MS (civil rights rally), 6 Jul 1963 & 'Hurricane', Clinton, NJ, 7 Dec 1975. John Hammond Jr.: 'In Search of Robert Johnson'; Iambic Production for Channel Four TV, London, 1991. (Greenwood is where Robert Johnson played his last gig, and died.) Paul Garon, 'Editorial', *Living Blues, nia*, & Peter Narváez: both quoted from Narváez's essay '*Living Blues* Journal: The Paradoxical Aesthetics of the Blues Revival', collected in *Transforming Tradition: Folk Music Revivals Examined*, ed. Neil V. Rosenberg, Urbana, IL: University of Illinois Press 1993. Dylan 1st quote, *Biograph* notes, 1985; 2nd quote in Bill Flanagan: *Written in My Soul: Rock's Great Songwriters Talk About Creating Their Music*, Chicago: Contemporary Books, 1986; 3rd quote, interview by Gary Hill, San Diego, c.3 Oct 1993 for Reuters, wired to US newspapers 13 Oct 1993.]

pre-war blues, Dylan's ways of accessing Back in Hibbing, at the High School graduation party thrown by his parents, Robert Zimmerman was given a number of LEADBELLY 78s—and found them revelatory. Thrilled as he was by rock'n'roll, he rang up his friend John Bucklen and yelled down the phone: '*This* is the real thing! You gotta hear this!'

Soon afterwards he was in the Twin Cities, where his bohemian friend DAVE WHITAKER claims to have had a large collection of blues records that he and Dylan used to listen to all the time; and HARVEY ABRAMS, a student who knew Dylan then, says that by that point Dylan was already keen on the pre-war blues, and busy trying to get at it: that he was one of those who 'had to get the oldest record and, if possible, the Library of Congress record, or go find the original people who knew the original song.'

Perhaps Harvey Abrams was that way inclined too, because Bonnie Beecher, an important Minnesota friend of Dylan's later known as JAHANARA ROMNEY, recalls that she first met the two of them when they sat around in the 10 O'Clock Scholar in Dinkytown dropping obscure singers' names, and got talking to them because, to their surprise, she was able to join in. She used to go to Sam Goodys in New York to buy records, choosing 'any old record that looked like it had some kind of funky singer or blues singer . . .' Those she mentioned included the great RICHARD RABBIT BROWN, a deeply obscure figure to anyone not seeped in the pre-war blues. Very unusually for a young Minnesotan, she had a large blues record collection, and Dylan listened to it and borrowed from it.

As this suggests, some of these old, elusive recordings were being reissued on vinyl for the first time—and two *crucial* releases happened well before Dylan left Minnesota: the *AMERICAN FOLK MUSIC* anthology in 1952 and *The Country Blues*, the album that accompanied SAMUEL B. CHARTERS' ground-breaking book of the same name, in 1959. (See separate entries for these albums' contents.)

At the same time, we know that in Minnesota Dylan did not have to rely upon LP reissues for hearing old blues: he had access to 78s owned by record collectors like JON PANKAKE, co-founder with PAUL NELSON of the small but fierce magazine *Little Sandy Review*. (See entry on Pankake for detail.) There were also the Minnesota-based revivalist performers, like Dylan's friend TONY GLOVER and DAVE RAY, dedicated to performances that amounted to a lively advocacy of the old blues.

At some point in summer 1959 or 1960, Dylan the nascent folksinger also went to Colorado, possibly played piano in a strip club called 'The Gilded Garter' in Central City and then certainly hung around 20 miles east of there in Denver (particularly at 'The Exodus' coffee-house), where he had access to at least three live performers, plus the record collection of one of them. One was JUDY COLLINS, but another was the unique JESSE FULLER, who was temporarily on the Denver folk scene when Dylan dropped into it.

The third Denver performer, who let Dylan stay at his house, and from whom Dylan stole some records (just as he did from Jon Pankake in Minneapolis) was the black folksinger WALT CONLEY, 'founder of the Denver folk scene', as he was dubbed by locals.

When Dylan reached Greenwich Village, at the very beginning of 1961, he had access to a whole slew of revivalist performers, 'an urban school of musicians dedicated to re-creating the country blues', as Dave Laing put it—amongst whom was the man Dylan expends so many words on praising in *Chronicles Volume One*, DAVE VAN RONK, 'a walking museum of the blues', plus the resources of IZZY YOUNG's Folklore Center, plus the record collections of more blues collectors than ever before, plus the priceless additional presence as live performers of a number of the great pre-war blues artists themselves: the ones who had been 'rediscovered'.

Van Ronk was at one time roommates with Sam Charters, a serious collector who had been a field-recorder of blues singers all over the South since 1955. Dylan also got on well with Len Kunstadt, a major collector of 78s, whom he knew through VICTORIA SPIVEY, whose record label Kunstadt helped manage and who would turn out to be the last of her husbands. (A sweetly youthful Dylan of this period is pictured with Spivey on the back cover of *New Morning*, and the original art-print photograph was owned by Kunstadt.) In March 1962 Dylan recorded with Spivey and BIG JOE WILLIAMS, whose three-week stint at Folk City in February 1962 was attended by Dylan many nights, while of Spivey herself Dylan said: '. . . oh man, I loved her . . . I learned so much from her I could never put into words.'

The other old blues performers who were around to have their repertoires, and in most cases guitar styles, mopped up by the sponge-like young Bob Dylan included BROTHER JOHN SELLERS, REV. GARY DAVIS, JOHN LEE HOOKER, LIGHTNIN' HOPKINS, ELIZABETH COTTEN, MISSISSIPPI JOHN HURT, BUKKA WHITE, SON HOUSE, Roosevelt Sykes, SONNY TERRY & BROWNIE McGHEE, SLEEPY JOHN ESTES, Furry Lewis, Mississippi Fred McDowell, Gus Cannon, SKIP JAMES, Tampa Red and LONNIE JOHNSON. Indeed there were so many of these people that the whole folk audience became highly knowledgeable about country blues.

[For the Hibbing, Harvey Abrams & Jon Pankake information, and quote re Van Ronk as 'museum' see Robert Shelton's *No Direction Home: The Life and Music of Bob Dylan*, 1986. For Dave Whittaker's testimony see Bob Spitz's *Dylan: A Biography*, 1989. Jahanara Romney, see 'The Wanted Man Interview: Jahanara Romney', by Markus Wittman, *Telegraph* no. 36, Romford, UK, summer 1990. Dave Laing quoted from 'Troubadours & Stars', in Laing, D., Dallas, K., Denselow, R. & Shelton, R., *The Electric Muse: The Story of Folk Into Rock*, London: Methuen, 1975. Kunstadt photo ownership: VAL WILMER, photographer, to this writer, phone call c.1994. Dylan on Spivey: interview published in *Biograph* box set, 1985. Dylan on old bluesmen seen in person: interview San Diego c.3 Oct 1993, by Gary Hill, for Reuters News Agency, wired to US newspapers 13 Oct 1993.]

Price, Alan [1941 -] Alan Price was born in the delightfully named Fatfield, on Tyneside in the north-east of England, on April 19, 1941. He was in various local Newcastle-based groups before personnel from several mutated into THE ANIMALS. Price was the organist on, and the credited arranger for, their second single, a fine electric version of 'House of the Rising Sun'. The credit 'Traditional, arranged Price' was the source of much discontentment in the group, since they felt that the arrangement had been collaboratively arrived at. Nonetheless, Alan Price has always taken 100 per cent of the writing royalties on this international no.1 record.

Price quit the Animals in 1965, reportedly because of his fear of flying, and became a hanger-on during Dylan's visit to Britain that year, filmed by D.A. PENNEBAKER as *Don't Look Back*. He therefore appears in the film. Indeed he disappears in the film too: we see Dylan at his least appealing, shouting and throwing his weight around in his hotel because someone had dropped a wine glass out of the window and into the street; and when a drunken Price finally confesses, Dylan kicks him out.

Price made an immediately successful solo career, beginning by copying an American record, as UK artists were still wont to do even in the mid-1960s. In this case Price took Randy Newman's savagely sarcastic 'Simon Smith and his Amazing Dancing Bear' and made a jolly hit single out of it, renouncing his marvellously grungy organ sound for a twinkling piano and clinching his image as a professional Geordie.

Prine, John [1946 -] John Prine, born in Maywood, Illinois, on October 10, 1946, a singer-songwriter guitarist who emerged from local fame in Chicago at the beginning of the 1970s (as did his friend STEVE GOODMAN, though to lesser effect). Immediately saddled with the 'new Bob Dylan' label, partly for a strikingly similar—but also strikingly different—generic vocal gruffness, he was a compelling singer and a beguiling live performer of stripped-down simplicity and a backwoods charm that was intriguing, after a Chicago upbringing: you might more readily have guessed Kentucky.

The extra factor, though, was a perfectly matched major talent for songwriting: and at a time when Dylan's subject matter had long been other-worldly or somewhat generalised, Prine burst through with a début album full of detail and specificity. *John Prine* contained a song about the Vietnam War and its spill-over into US domestic life, 'Sam Stone'; a song about the environment, 'Paradise'; about patriotism and religion, 'Your Flag Decal Won't Get You into Heaven Anymore'; but most of all, he sang about *small* detail and ordinary people—people like 'Donald and Lydia', with names not the least bit counter-culturally cool, and people stuck in domestic drudgery and dead-end jobs in places like Montgomery, Alabama.

The point, however, was not the subject matter of Prine's songs per se, but the fact that they were such *fine* songs, not at all preachy (though 'Sam Stone' comes close) and suffused with their matured creator's refreshing personality, so that what most had in common was a quirky minimalism, a trusting of the listener to pick up from the tiniest detail a whole world portrayed. With a warm, shrewd voice and subtle delivery, John Prine sang from a perspective almost akin to gallows humour, but nobler, and owing something to a WOODY GUTHRIE defiance: as if the world were so bleak you could only cheer up and find solace where you might, but that no solace was possible without a clear-sighted compassion that seemed to come naturally to Prine, and which he seemed to expect of the rest of us too.

He was influenced by Dylan, and there was that superficial similarity of voice, but Prine was never Dylanesque: he was his own man and his own artist, and his second album, *Diamonds in the Rough*, was masterly. For those who bought it, it often became more of a soundtrack to the 1970s than his first had ever been; and it's no belittlement to say that sometimes when you want something less demanding than *Blood on the Tracks* but just as acoustic and somehow winding through similar terrain, John Prine's *Diamonds in the Rough*, with tracks like 'Clocks and Spoons', 'Rocky Mountain Time' and 'The Late John Garfield Blues', is the perfect album to play.

The third, *Sweet Revenge*, found him appearing to struggle to keep up the song quality, and perhaps in danger of imitating himself, but 'Mexican Home' was a churning, DOUG SAHMish delight. It was a signal, though, that Prine was not going to become, like SPRINGSTEEN, a megastar, but would settle down in time to a large, quiet constituency, and that if he was lucky and survived, he would serve it well down the decades. And he has.

Bob Dylan's direct connection with Prine came in 1972, when Dylan was scuffing around avoiding doing anything much in his own right. Prine was playing a solo gig at the Bitter End in the Village that September 9th and Dylan came quietly on stage, unannounced—and from Prine's point of view, somewhat disconcertingly, perhaps—and played harmonica and sang back-up vocals on three numbers. There is no circulating tape (perhaps none extant) of this performance, and the first song Dylan augmented remains unidentified; then came 'Donald and Lydia' and finally 'Sam Stone'. What a gig to have caught.

[John Prine: *John Prine*, Atlantic 8296, US, 1971; *Diamonds in the Rough*, Atlantic 7240, 1972; *Sweet Revenge*, Atlantic 7274, 1973.]

pseudonyms used by Dylan These include the following: Justin Case, Jack Frost, Blind Boy Grunt, Elston Gunnn [sic], Elmer Johnson, Bob Landy, Jim Nasium, Egg O'Schmillson, Sergei Petrov, Tedham Porterhouse and Robert Milkwood Thomas. He has never used Roosevelt Gook (see **Kooper, Al**).

Elston Gunnn was the name he gave to BOBBY VEE's brother Bill when he asked to join Vee's band as a pianist. As Vee recalls: 'He was in the Fargo/Moorhead area. He was working as a busboy at a place called the Red Apple Cafe. We didn't know that at the time. Bill was in a record shop in Fargo, Sam's Record Land, and this guy came up to him and introduced himself as Elston Gunnn—with three n's, G-U-N-N-N.'

Blind Boy Grunt was used on the album *Broadside Ballads*, released in September 1963, on which Dylan performs 'Talkin' Devil', 'Only a Hobo' and 'John Brown' and plays guitar behind HAPPY TRAUM on 'I Will Not Go Down Under the Ground' (later re-titled by Dylan 'Let Me Die in My Footsteps'), recorded in New York City that January and February. Dylan also recorded 'Farewell' and 'Masters of War' at these sessions but these remained unreleased. At a further session in March, he cut 'I Shall Be Free', 'Train-a-Travelin'' and 'Cuban Missile Crisis'; only the second of these was released, on the somewhat laggardly follow-up album *Broadside Reunion* in 1971, and also contained 'I'd Hate to Be You on That Dreadful Day', cut for *Broadside* magazine in November 1962, and 'The Death of Emmett Till' and 'The Ballad of Donald White', both from 'The *Broadside* Show' on WBAI-FM radio, NYC, in May 1962. Again, Dylan was billed as Blind Boy Grunt—as he was too, on the album *DICK FARIÑA* and *ERIC VON SCHMIDT*, recorded in London in January 1963 and in the UK later that year, on which Dylan played harmonica and contributed backing vocals on 'Glory, Glory', 'Xmas Island', 'Cocaine', 'You Can Always Tell', 'Overseas Stomp' & 'London Waltz'.

Tedham Porterhouse was used on the RAMBLIN' JACK ELLIOTT album *Jack Elliott*, released in 1964, to credit Dylan's harmonica playing behind Ramblin' Jack's guitar and vocals on 'Will the Circle Be Unbroken?'; this was recorded in summer 1963 in New York City, during Elliott's sessions for a new album.

Bob Landy was Dylan's credit on the various artists album *The Blues Project* in 1964, on which he and Eric Von Schmidt played piano behind GEOFF MULDAUR on 'Downtown Blues'.

Elmer Johnson was the name under which Dylan stayed while in Edwardsville, Illinois, where he performed with THE BAND during their set on July 14, 1969, singing 'I Ain't Got No Home', 'Slippin' and Slidin' and 'In the Pines'. (This material has not circulated.) Egg O'Schmillson was the pseudonym planned for Dylan for the mooted but abandoned Apple Records release of ALLEN GINSBERG recordings from November 1971 to which Dylan donated shared vocals, guitar, piano and organ.

Robert Milkwood Thomas was Dylan's billing as backing musician on the title track of the album *Somebody Else's Troubles*, by STEVE GOODMAN, recorded in New York in September 1972, when it was released on Buddah in 1973 (an album Dylan co-produced).

Jack Frost was first used for the co-producer credit on the 1990 album *Under the Red Sky* (and was apt, given that this is an album full of nursery rhyme); and was used again as co-producer of *Time Out of Mind* in 1997 and for the sole producer credit on *"Love and Theft"*.

Lucky Wilbury was Dylan's name on the first TRAVELING WILBURYS album, Boo Wilbury on the second. Sergei Petrov was the name Dylan hid behind as co-writer of the 2003 film *Masked & Anonymous* (with LARRY CHARLES, billed as Rene Fontaine), when the project was first announced.

Justin Case and Jim Nasium are among the names Dylan has used when checking into hotels.

[Bobby Vee quote from interview in *Goldmine, nia*, 1999, quoted from 'The Bob Dylan Who's Who', seen online 9 Jan 2006 at *www.expectingrain.com/dok/who/who.html*. Blind Boy Grunt: 'Talkin' Devil', NY, 19 Jan, 'I Will Not Go Down Under the Ground' (with Happy Traum), 24 Jan, 'Only a Hobo' & 'John Brown', Feb 1963, all on *Broadside Ballads*, Broadside BR301, NY, Sep 1963; 'The Death of Emmett Till' & 'The Ballad of Donald White', NY, May 1962, 'I'd Hate to Be You on That Dreadful Day', Nov 1962 & 'Train-a-Travelin'', Mar 1963, all on *Broadside Reunion*, Folkways FR 5315, NY, Nov 1971. 'Glory, Glory', 'Xmas Island', 'Cocaine', 'You Can Always Tell', 'Overseas Stomp' & 'London Waltz', London, Jan 14–15, 1963, *Dick Fariña and Eric Von Schmidt*, Folklore F-LEUT-7, UK, 1964. Tedham Porterhouse: 'Will the Circle Be Unbroken', on *Jack Elliott*, Vanguard VSD 79151, NY, 1964. Bob Landy: 'Downtown Blues', NY, early 1964, *The Blues Project*, Elektra EKL 264, NY, Jun 1964. Robert Milkwood Thomas: on 'Somebody Else's Troubles', on Steve Goodman's *Somebody Else's Troubles*, NY, Sep 1972, Buddah BDS-5121, US, 1973.]

Quebec, Madelyn [1935 -] Madelyn R. Quebec was born June 12, 1935. She served as one of the Raelettes until the early 1980s, along with Estella Yarbrough, Trudy Cohran-Hunter, Pat Peterson and Avis Harrell, before starting to work with Dylan. She was still in the Raelettes when a RAY CHARLES concert using the Edmonton Symphony Orchestra was filmed in Canada on January 27, 1981 (so she can now be glimpsed in the DVD reissue of this rather short concert), yet her first collaboration with Dylan was in the studios in Santa Monica three months later, for the last couple of sessions for *Shot of Love*, starting on April 29, 1981, when she joined her daughter CAROLYN DENNIS among the backing singers.

The first time Quebec toured with Dylan was in June 1981, when he began another semi-secular tour, this time warming up with four US dates before traveling round Europe, beginning in Toulouse, France, on June 21 and finishing in Avignon on July 25. Mother and daughter were both back-up singers, along with CLYDIE KING and REGINA McCRARY. When Dylan finished his summer break and resumed concerts in the States that fall, Quebec stayed with the tour though Carolyn Dennis dropped out.

In the course of that tour, the back-up group sang (without Dylan) a song called 'The Rose' at two concerts in October, and from October 18 onwards they sang 'Gamblin' Man' at every concert. The live 'Heart of Mine' issued later on *Biograph* was recorded at the New Orleans concert of November 10.

Dylan didn't tour again till 1984, and used no back-up singers then. But that July, in New York, when Dylan was back in the studios, recording tracks that would end up on both *Empire Burlesque* and *Knocked Out Loaded*, Quebec, Dennis and other back-up singers were participants again, though when overdub sessions were done in early 1985, Madelyn Quebec was not involved.

She was brought back in for the Farm Aid rehearsals, beginning on September 19, 1985 in LA, and duly performed behind Dylan on 'Clean-Cut Kid', 'Shake', 'Trust Yourself', 'That Lucky Old Sun' and 'Maggie's Farm' on the night itself, September 22 in Champaign, Illinois. She sang back-up in a Hollywood studio that Hallowe'en (though nothing from this session has circulated, or even been named), and when Dylan began to tour in 1986, with TOM PETTY & THE HEARTBREAKERS, beginning in New Zealand of February 5, Madelyn Quebec was amongst the backing singers, who were now being billed as the Queens of Rhythm. She therefore appears in the officially released video *Hard to Handle*, first broadcast by HBO in the US on June 20, 1986. And while they were all in New Zealand in February, they went into a studio in Wellington and recorded the song 'Band of the Hand', for the movie of the same name, so Quebec is on that too.

She remained in the group for the whole of the long second leg of the tour, which ran from June 9 in San Diego through to August 6 in Paso Robles, California. And when Dylan went back into the studios in March 1987, to begin cobbling together tracks for *Down in the Groove*, Quebec was back—and this time, not only did she contribute back-up vocals, but on 'When Did You Leave Heaven?' and 'Ninety Miles an Hour (Down a Dead-End Street)' she both duetted with Dylan (she's mixed low, but is not inaudible, on the finished release) *and* played keyboards. It was their last professional collaboration.

Being Carolyn Dennis' mother, Madelyn Quebec was also Dylan's mother-in-law from 1986 to 1992, and is the grandmother of Desiree Gabrielle Dennis-Dylan. On June 12, 1986, eight days after marrying her daughter, Dylan sang 'Happy Birthday' to her in the encore of the concert in Sacramento.

[Quebec, King & McCrary: 'The Rose', Milwaukee, WI, 16 & 17 Oct 1981; 'Gamblin' Man', Madison, WI, 18 Oct, Lakeland, FL, 21 Nov 1981. Madelyn Quebec duet vocals & keyboards: 'When Did You Leave Heaven?', Hollywoods, prob. Jun 1987; 'Ninety Miles an Hour (Down a Dead-End Street)', Hollywood, Apr & Jun 1987.]

Queens of Rhythm, the 'The Queens of Rhythm' was the collective name given by Dylan to the group of backing singers on his 1986 and 1987 tours with TOM PETTY & THE HEARTBREAKERS. For the first 1986 tour, from February 5 to March 10, they were MADELYN QUEBEC, Debra Byrd, Elisecia Wright and Queen Esther Marrow; for the second 1986, from June 9 to August 6, Debra Byrd and Elisecia Wright were replaced by Louise Bethune and CAROLYN DENNIS. For the 1987 European tour, from September 5 to October 17, the Queens of Rhythm were Madelyn Quebec, Carolyn Dennis and Queen Esther Marrow.

Quintana, Charlie Charles Edward ('Chalo') Quintana was born in the Tex-Mex border town of El Paso on March 25, 1963 and raised there in some poverty. He grew up drumming and in 1977, aged only 14, moved to LA to join THE PLUGZ (later the Cruzados), a pioneering early West Coast punk band. He stuck at it right through till the mid-1980s. He also started up the Havalinas, which made one album (on Elektra).

For Quintana's main 1983–84 Dylan connections (Dylan playing harmonica on one group track, and then the 'Late Night with David Letterman' TV show) see the entry **Plugz, the**; but he worked with Dylan individually too, both in that period and again almost a decade later.

First he featured in Dylan's promo video for the *Infidels* track 'Sweetheart Like You', filmed in LA in October 1983, in which he's glimpsed behind the drums, though he hadn't played on the recording itself. And then in 1992, when the Never-Ending Tour came back from Australia, New Zealand and Hawaii, and opened a mainland US West Coast leg in Seattle on April 27, Charlie Quintana played as second drummer in the band (second to IAN WALLACE). He stayed in the band through the June 26 to July 12 European leg and then through most of the August-September North American leg, up to and including September 5 in Omaha, Nebraska. Quintana left, replaced for the last six September dates by WINSTON WATSON.

Aside from this Dylan work, his post-Cruzados, post-Havalinas work has drawn him in an arc through playing with Izzy Stradlin and the Ju Ju Hounds, Cracker, Joan Osborne, Soul Asylum and then in 2000 a tour that punk band Social Distortion's front man Mike Ness was doing to promote a solo album (*Cheating at Solitaire*). At the end, he was asked to join the band. It was a full circle. Quintana said yes.

'Quit Your Low-Down Ways' [1962] Copyrighted in 1963 and 1964 as a Dylan song, 'Quit Your Low-Down Ways' may derive ultimately from an old gospel song; Dylan's verse 'You can read out your Bible / You can fall down on your knees / Pretty mama and pray to the Lord / But it ain't gonna do no good' is lifted directly from the great Kokomo Arnold's recording of his own 'Milk Cow Blues', made in Chicago on September 10, 1934.

Dylan cut 'Quit Your Low-Down Ways' at the *Freewheelin' Bob Dylan* session of July 9, 1962 and as a Witmark demo that December 1962 (both in New York City). A week before first recording it he performed it at the Finjan Club, Montreal, introducing it with 'Here's a funny one . . .'. It was introduced to a far wider audience when PETER, PAUL & MARY included it, along with 'Blowin' in the Wind', on their *In the Wind* album of 1963, for which Dylan wrote the sleevenote piece 'In the Wind'.

The *Freewheelin'* outtake version was released on the *Bootleg Series Vols. 1–3* box set in 1991.

Rabbit Brown See **Brown, Richard Rabbit.**

radical political activity in 1960s–70s US, the strange disappearance of The history of radical political activity in the 1960s–70s in the USA (in Amerika, as we styled it then, taking the 'k' from the initials of the Ku Klux Klan, to suggest its political complexion) seems to have fallen from sight as from the 1990s. When *Soledad Brother: The Prison Letters of George Jackson* was published in 1970, the British *Sunday Times* called GEORGE JACKSON 'one of the great voices of the American Left'. Now you look him up in vain in almost all the major encyclopedias and in the reference works on who's who in recent political and public life. He's become an unperson. Even on Google he's the hardest George Jackson to find. (The information on him given in the present volume is taken mostly from Edmund White's book *Jean Genet*, 1992. GENET had written the Introduction to Jackson's book.)

R

Yet at the time of Jackson's death, Amerika, waging war in Vietnam and Cambodia, was hugely in turmoil, and the Left was a real presence, with 'revolutionary action' called for among whites as well as within the Black Power movement. Malcolm X, the first modern black revolutionary leader, was assassinated January 21, 1965; Martin Luther King was shot in Memphis, April 4, 1968, provoking riots in 22 city ghettoes. 1968 also saw the Presidio Mutiny, San Francisco; a bloody conflict with students at Columbia University in April; and mayhem during the Democratic Party National Convention in Chicago (including a Yippie plot to dump LSD in a reservoir). One student was shot dead at 'People's Park', May 20, 1969, as 2000 National Guardsmen occupied Berkeley, California, in order to regain an empty parking-lot; protesters invaded Fort Dix, New Jersey, in October 1969; there was a student occupation of Harvard in 1969 and a strike at Berkeley in May 1970; four students were shot dead at Kent State University in Ohio on May 4, 1970; the Santa Barbara branch of Bank of America was firebombed by the Left in 1970; the Atlanta office of the South's biggest underground newspaper, *The Great Speckled Bird*, was firebombed in 1972 by the Right. Governor Ronald Reagan of California was quoted as saying 'If it takes a bloodbath, let's get it over with. No more appeasement.'

Even rock concerts were considered to constitute political defiance in Amerika, as in the Soviet Bloc. Over 100 people were badly injured at THE ROLLING STONES' first Iron Curtain concert, April 3, 1967, as police used tear-gas and batons against 2,000 fans storming the Warsaw Palace of Culture, Poland; likewise Jethro Tull and their audience were tear-gassed by police in Denver, Colorado, June 10, 1971, putting 25 grown-ups and three babies into hospital.

Dylan's 'George Jackson' suggests his tacit acknowledgement, at the time, of this violent struggle between revolutionary and reactionary activists. A good contemporary account of the period is Roger Lewis' *Outlaws of America*, 1972. The chapter 'Gimme Some of That Rock and Roll Music' includes what was at the time the best short summary of Bob Dylan's social significance in the 1960s. The best recent work on this subject is MIKE MARQUSEE's *Chimes of Freedom: The Politics of Bob Dylan's Art*, 2003.

[Sources: *Shots: Photographs from the Underground Press*, ed. David Fenton, 1971; Michael Horowitz (not the British poet) & Dana Reemes: 'Historic Sites of Psychedelic Culture and Research', 1977, in *High Times Encyclopedia of Recreational Drugs*, ed. Andrew Kowl, 1978; and Michael Gray: 'The Let It Rot Calendar of Death', *Let It Rock* no.28, London, Apr 1975 (republished *Creem* no.10, Birmingham, MI, Jul 1976 & *Record Mirror*, London, 29 Oct 1977).]

Raeben, Norman [1901 - 1978] Norman Raeben was the youngest son of Shalom Aleichem (1859–1916), the Ukrainian-born author and humorist known as 'the Mark Twain of Yiddish literature' and creator of the character Tvye (around whom the musical *Fiddler on the Roof* is centered), whose real name was Shalom Rabinovitz.

Norman was born in Russia on March 21, 1901 and emigrated to the USA as a teenager. He became Dylan's art teacher in the spring of 1974, when Dylan started attending group art-classes at his 11th-floor studio in Carnegie Hall, New York City, after hearing of his clear-sighted ability to define 'truth and love and beauty and all these words I had heard for years' from friends of his wife SARA DYLAN. 'Five days a week I used to go up there,' Dylan recalled later, 'and I'd just think about it the other two days of the week. I used to be up there from eight o'clock to four. That's all I did for two months . . .'

Raeben had studied with the artists George Luks, Robert Henri and John Sloan. He conducted his own classes for over 40 years, and over the same period lived with another painter, Viki Lipper.

Raeben's habitual exclamatory use of the word 'idiot' prompted Dylan's use of it in the *Blood on the Tracks* song 'Idiot Wind'. More generally, Raeben was, as Dylan himself testified in a series of interviews, a strong, perhaps profound, influence on that whole album and on how Dylan approached his work in this period of creative renewal.

> 'He put my mind and my hand and my eye together, in a way that allowed me to do consciously what I unconsciously felt . . . *Blood on the Tracks* did consciously what I used to do unconsciously. I didn't perform it well. I didn't have the power to perform it well. But I did write the songs . . . the ones that have the break-up of time, where there is no time, trying to make the focus as strong as a magnifying glass under the sun. To do that consciously is a trick, and I did it on *Blood on the Tracks* for the first time. I knew how to do it because of the technique I learned—I actually had a teacher for it . . .'

Norman Raeben is believed to have died in December 1978.

[Dylan quotes taken from 'The Mysterious Norman Raeben' by BERT CARTWRIGHT, online 7 Jun 2005 at *www.geocities.com/Athens/Forum/2667/raeben.htm.*]

railroads, a classic theme The use of the railroad theme, as of the highway theme, is the province very largely of the folk artist. Dylan is more than a folk artist—his social class, its literacy and education and his own creative insight and integrity all set him beyond that sphere—but his work has been gorged on the folk culture of America. It has literally been fundamental. In both senses, folk music is behind him. His wide-ranging, flexible, recurrent treatment of the classic railroad theme is an ample case in point. It's also a huge instance in Dylan's work where the fusion of black and white folk strengths shows vividly as a creative force.

Just as the heroic-outlaw-of-the-West myth was, despite its European antecedents, significantly the product of the frontier social situation, so too the railroadmen, the hobo and the railroad itself became folk heroes as a result of environmental circumstances. The railroad meant, or was at least seen to mean, freedom, opportunity, rebirth. It became, as in WOODY GUTHRIE's autobiography *Bound for Glory*, 1943, a duo-racial symbol and experience. It is only natural and appropriate that a duo-racial consciousness is required to deal with such a theme in modern folk art. Dylan applies just such a consciousness to this focus.

If it is a standard American symbol of freedom, the railroad also represents 'home' for the professional tramp of the dust-bowl years. The railroad symbolises other things too, from the real as well as from the dream world. 'When a woman blue, she hang her little head an' cry, / When a man get blue, he grab that train an' ride': the traditional black folk song that includes these lines makes the railroad a symbol of masculine social virility. Dylan, singing in the 1960s, emancipates contemporary woman. In 'It Takes a Lot to Laugh, It Takes a Train to Cry': 'Don't the moon look good, mama, shinin' through the trees? / Don't the brakeman look good, mama, flagging down the double-E's! / Don't the sun look good goin' down over the sea / Don't my gal look fine when she's comin' after me! . . .' These lines are an adaptation of several things, including parts of PRESLEY's version of 'Milk Cow Blues Boogie' and from an older blues song that runs: 'Don't the clouds look lonesome 'cross the deep blue sea / Don't the clouds look lonesome 'cross the deep blue sea / Don't my gal look good when she's comin' after me?' (Dylan had already used them once, in his unissued recording of the traditional song 'Rocks and Gravel'. And ten years after 'It Takes a Lot to Laugh', Dylan gives us another variant on those same lines, in 'Meet Me in the Morning', from *Blood on the Tracks*.)

It is, paradoxically, the repetitive framework that helps a notable economy in the evocation of railroad feeling in the original studio issue of 'It Takes a Lot to Laugh, It Takes a Train to Cry' (on *Highway 61 Revisited*). In the music—of which the vocal tone and phrasing are parts—the drums and piano suggest not only the rattle of the train, and, as such, a measure of its speed and mechanic vitality, but also the elation of the traveller who identifies with the locomotive's performance. The lyric's economy on adjectives and its emphasis of nouns—the moon, the sun, the brakeman, the trees, the sea, 'my gal'—makes for an exciting balance between the romantic and the concrete. Symbol and reality are fused.

This fusion, in context, recalls a passage from one of those autobiographical Dylan poems that got into print from time to time on the back of LP covers and in old underground magazines (in this case the sleevenote poem for *JOAN BAEZ in Concert Part 2*): 'An' my first idol was HANK WILLIAMS / For he sang about the railroad lines / An' the iron bars an' rattlin' wheels / Left no doubt that they were real . . . / An' I'll walk my road somewhere between / The unseen green an' the jet black train.' Dylan can not only give the railroad the importance a hard-travelin' hobo might give it but can also use it as an axis round which to spin ideas of what is real and so pursue his quest for the concrete.

The railroad appears in many other early songs—'Freight Train Blues' among them—and in several an essential ingredient is the railroad's importance where some fundamental choice is involved, related to the real or the true. In the poem just quoted from, the 'iron bars an' rattlin' wheels' provide a yardstick, albeit simplistic, of reality, against which are contrasted smoother kinds of beauty—the nightingale sound of Joan Baez's voice is an instance he gives—and against which is balanced Dylan's consciousness of 'the unseen green'. In *Nashville Skyline*'s 'Tonight I'll Be Staying Here with You' the choice is between two lifestyles, with the railroad as the symbol of the one Dylan at last renounces. It calls to him on behalf of the 'keep traveling' spirit and it loses to new-found love: 'I find it so difficult to leave / I can hear that whistle blowin' / I see that station-master too . . . / . . .

tonight I'll be staying here with you.' He hears, but this time, at last, he doesn't follow.

In direct contrast is Dylan's first-album adaptation of the traditional 'Man of Constant Sorrow', which equally relates to this particular choice. In this song, he wants the girl but cannot have her. He has traveled a long way to make the attempt to win her, and so the railroad becomes the symbol of a nomadic no-man's-land: 'Through this open world I'm bound to ramble / Through ice and snow, sleet and rain / I'm bound to ride that mornin' railroad / P'raps I'll die on that train.'

Here Dylan has come away from the concrete—despite the 'realism' of that wintry weather—and into the realms of romance. What could be more splendid, granted the imagined death-wish, than dying on that train? Even though 'Bob Dylan's Dream', with all its ponderous nostalgia, is launched with the lines 'While riding on a train goin' west / I fell asleep for to take my rest / I dreamed a dream . . .' Dylan never quite returns to the dream mood given us by the 'Man of Constant Sorrow' railroad.

There is a parallel of sorts on *Blonde on Blonde*, in the surrealistic symbolism of 'Absolutely Sweet Marie', but the mood is very different. The solemnity is replaced by a good-natured if double-edged mockery: 'Well your railroad gate, you know I just can't jump it / Sometimes it gets so hard, you see / I'm just sitting here beating on my trumpet / With all these promises you left for me / But where are you tonight, sweet Marie? / . . . And now I stand here lookin' at your yellow railroad / In the ruins of your balcony . . .' but the symbol there, though used at both the beginning and the end of the song, is incidental. It is not a song that has much to do with trains.

The romance returns, but more respectably than in 'Bob Dylan's Dream', or even 'Man of Constant Sorrow', in another part of 'It Takes a Lot to Laugh, It Takes a Train to Cry', where the narrator grows lyrically expansive: 'Well I ride on the mail-train baby; can't buy a thrill / Well I've been up all night, leanin' on the windowsill / Well if I die on top of the hill / Well if I don't make it, you know my baby will.' That last line provides the ballast, taking the railroad romance away from narcissism and into a wider context, that of a more selfless and universal celebration of life. The goal here is to 'make it', to survive, not to die in glory on the train (although paradoxically, that conjectured dying 'on top of the hill' brings in by allusion a picture of history's most celebrated martyrdom, that of Christ on the cross on Calvary).

Guthrie's autobiography itself takes its title from a song that uses this train-as-salvation symbol: the phrase 'Bound for Glory' comes from the song 'This Train', the chorus of which declares that 'This train is bound for glory, this train'. And of course it is precisely this use of the train symbol that Dylan finally comes to on the *Slow Train Coming* album, and in a couple of instances just prior to it—he sings Curtis Mayfield's 'People Get Ready' on the *Renaldo & Clara* soundtrack, and the glory-train image runs through that, while the last track on the album leading up to *Slow Train Coming*, *Street Legal*, opens by forewarning us: 'There's a long-distance train rolling through the rain', and has Dylan riding that train to his own new-found salvation.

[*Joan Baez in Concert Part 2*, Vanguard VRS-9113, New York, 1964 (on which Baez sings the traditional 'Jack-aroe' with the same set of lyrics Dylan uses 30 years later for the version on *World Gone Wrong*). Dylan's sleevenote poem appeared in *Circuit* magazine no.6, London, c.1967, one of the small arts journals inspired by Michael Horovitz's pioneering poetry magazine *New Departures*, founded South Hinksey, nr. Oxford, summer 1959. With no other title than 'Joan Baez in Concert, Part 2', the poem was collected in Bob Dylan: *Writings & Drawings*, 1972, and is also in *Lyrics 1962–85* where, improbably, it is copyrighted 1973: almost a decade after its publication on the back of the Baez album.

Elvis Presley: 'Milk Cow Blues Boogie', Memphis, probably 15 Nov or 20 Dec 1954; Sun 215, Memphis, 1955 (1st issued UK on the EP *Good Rockin' Tonight*, HMV Records 7EG8256, London, 1957). Bob Dylan: 'Rocks and Gravel (Solid Road)', Cynthia Gooding's apartment, NY, probably Mar 1962. 'Rocks and Gravel (Solid Road)', Finjan Club, Montreal, 2 Jul 1962. 'Rocks and Gravel (Solid Road)': NY, 9 Jul and 13 Nov 1962 (outtakes from *The Freewheelin' Bob Dylan*). 'Rocks and Gravel (Solid Road)': Gaslight Café, NY, Oct 1962. 'Freight Train Blues' is on *Bob Dylan*.

'People Get Ready' probably recorded Quebec City, 28 Nov 1975; released only on a 12-inch 4-track promotional EP, *4 Songs From Renaldo & Clara*, CBS XSM 164035, 25 Jan 1978.]

Raney, Wayne [1921 - 1993] Bob Dylan told CAMERON CROWE, for the *Biograph* notes in 1985, that as far as influences on his harmonica playing went, '. . . well, I'd always liked Wayne Raney and JIMMY REED, SONNY TERRY . . . Li'l JUNIOR PARKER . . .'

Wayne Raney is the obscure name here (and the only white man), and he was not a part of the folk-revival scene. He was born in the luridly named Wolf Bayou, Arkansas, on August 17, 1921, avoided agricultural labour by having a crippled foot, and was already determined to be a harmonica player by the time he met fellow player Lonnie Glosson at Radio Station KMOX in St. Louis, with whom he formed a double act on radio stations in Little Rock, several Mexican border towns and then in Cincinnati. You could send off for their harmonicas by mail order, and at one time they claimed to be selling a million a year.

Raney signed a record deal with the Cincinnati label King in the mid-1940s, and Raney-Glosson was the composing team behind Raney's hit 'Why Don't You Haul Off and Love Me', a song revived by Johnny Burnette (a post-rockabilly side: lots of strings, but real vocal energy). On Raney's version, he says he's '43'; Burnette amends this to '17'.

Most of Raney's songs, co-written with a number of different people, are demure love songs with an old-fashioned 'good-humoured' novelty element, in melody and lyrics. He has a penchant for terrible, occasionally repulsive, rhymes, such as '. . . sloggin' / . . . on my noggin'; on his more guitar-based rockabilly items you can hear exactly why he influenced Johnny and Dorsey Burnette. 'Jack and Jill Boogie' is one of his best, and with a more prominent harmonica than usual, and 'Gone with the Wind This Morning' is, to put it the wrong way round, another Burnetteish track.

Raney also played on post-war Delmore Brothers records (such as 'Blues Stay Away from Me', a song he co-wrote, which Dylan recorded with DOUG SAHM & his band in 1972) and on various suitably obscure rockabilly sides. He toured with LEFTY FRIZZELL and spent one year as a Grand Ole Opry regular, went back to tiny Concord, Arkansas, in 1960, and there set up a chicken farm and a record label, Rimrock, which included a custom studio and a pressing plant.

He is also remembered for a dreadful single of his own called 'We Need a Whole Lot More of Jesus and a Lot Less Rock'n'Roll'. And while Sun Records supremo Sam Phillips is often quoted as having said of blues music 'This is where the soul of man never dies', it's less well-known that this poetic turn of phrase is itself a quote from a song title, 'Where the Soul of Man Never Dies', recorded pre-war by the Anglin Brothers and Jack & Leslie, and post-war by HANK WILLIAMS . . . and composed by our Mr. Raney. In 1990 he published a very short autobiography, more booklet than book, with the delightfully scratchety, peckerwoods title *Life Has Not Been a Bed of Roses*.

The funny thing about Dylan's citing of Raney as a harp player who influenced him is that his harmonica playing never really resembles Raney's at all. Still alive and living in Arkansas when Dylan's tribute was published, Wayne Raney sold Rimrock, lost his voicebox, retired five miles down the road to Drasco, Arkansas, and died there on January 23, 1993.

[Wayne Raney: 'Why Don't You Haul Off and Love Me', Cincinnati, OH, 6 May 1949; *Wayne Raney: Songs from the Hills*, King LP 588, Cincinnati, reissued Dearborn, MI, 1987; 'sloggin . . . noggin' is on 'I Was There', Cincinnati, Mar–Apr 1955; 'Jack and Jill Boogie', prob. Cincinnati, prob. late 1948 & 'Gone with the Wind This Morning', Cincinnati, Mar–Apr 1955; all on *Songs from the Hills*; 'We Need a Whole Lot More of Jesus and a Lot Less Rock'n'Roll', *nia*, *16 Radio Gospel Favorites*, Starday SLP-124, Madison, TN, 1961.

Bob Dylan and others: 'Blues Stay Away from Me', NY, Oct 1972, on *Doug Sahm & Band*, Atlantic SD-7254, NY, 1972. Delmore Brothers: 'Blues Stay Away from Me', Cincinnati, 6 May 1949. (A selection of Delmore Brothers material, though excluding 'Blues Stay Away from Me', is CD-reissued on Delmore Brothers & Wayne Raney: *When They Let the Hammer Down*, Bear Family BFX 15167, Vollersode, Germany, c.1990.) Johnny Burnette: 'Why Don't You Haul Off and Love Me", *nia*, *Dreaming*, Liberty *nia*, LA, 1960, reissued *Johnny Burnette Tenth Anniversary Album*, Sunset SLS 50413, UK, 1974. Hank Williams: 'Where the Soul of Man Never Dies', Nashville, Oct 1949; *Hank Williams On Stage!*, MGM B3999, LA (MGM-C-893, London), 1962.]

Ray, Dave [1943 - 2002] David Ray was born on August 17, 1943 in Minneapolis, MN. He was a keen white blues singer and guitarist before he even left school, and he continued to be one, and to be anchored in Minnesota, throughout his life.

In *Chronicles Volume One*, Dylan remembers him as part of the Dinkytown scene. 'As far as other singers around town, there were some but not many. There was Dave Ray, a high school kid who sang LEADBELLY and BO DIDDLEY songs on a 12-string guitar, probably the only twelve-string guitar in the entire Midwest . . .' He could have added that they moved in the same circles, and that he used to listen to records at Ray's place.

Ray started playing 'professionally' with SPIDER JOHN KOERNER and TONY GLOVER. Koerner, Ray & Glover—that was the name of their outfit—made many albums, starting with *Blues, Rags & Hollers*, issued first on the small Audiophile label in June 1963 but picked up by Elektra, who signed them, bought the rights, reissued the LP that November (with four tracks missing) and then several further albums.

Dave Ray was one of the artists on the 1964 compilation album *The Blues Project*, on which Bob Dylan appeared on side 2, track 4 of the original LP, billed as Bob Landy, playing a piano duet with ERIC VON SCHMIDT behind GEOFF MULDAUR on the latter's song 'Downtown Blues'. Dave Ray was featured artist on the next track, his own composition 'Leavin' Here Blues' and on the last track, 'Slappin' on My Black Cat Bone'. Side 1 of the album began with Ray performing a song Dylan had put on his own début album, 'Fixin' go Die'. Soon after this compilation LP was issued, Koerner, Ray & Glover were fellow performers at the 1964 NEWPORT FOLK FESTIVAL.

In 1967 he released a well-regarded solo album, *Fine Soft Land*, that showed more of his range than do the Koerner, Ray & Glover albums. Thirty years later, he made the equally well-regarded *Snake Eyes*. (He performs 'One-Room Country Shack' on both, making for an absorbing comparison.) Among his other achievements, Dave Ray helped engineer, with his first wife Sylvia, the 1971 album that launched Bonnie Raitt's career.

It's said that Dylan and Dave Ray remained friends. In September 1992, when Dylan played the Orpheum Theater in Minneapolis, the support band was Ray and Glover. He reunited with Koerner and Glover in 1996 for *One Foot in the Groove*, the trio's first recording together in 30 years. Later, Dave Ray was one of the Back Porch Rockers, along with Glover, Camile Baudoin and Reggie Scanlan (they issued a live album in 1999). Dave Ray died of cancer on Thanksgiving 2002, aged 59.

[Bob Dylan: *Chronicles Volume One*, 2004, p.256. Koerner, Ray & Glover: *Blues Rags and Hollers*, Audiophile AP-78, 1963; *One Foot in the Groove*, Tim/Kerr T/K 96CD137, US, 1996. Dave Ray: 'Fixin' to Die', 'Leavin' Here Blues' & 'Slappin' on My Black Cat Bone', NY, Mar 1964, *Blues Project*, Elektra EKL 264, NY, Jun 1964. Dave Ray: *Fine Soft Landing*, 1966, Elektra EKL 319 (mono) / EKS 7319 (stereo), NY, 1967; *Snake Eyes*, MN, 1997, Tim/Kerr T/K 172-2, US, 1998.]

Reagon, Bernice Johnson [1942 -] Bernice Johnson, daughter of a Baptist minister, was born in the south-west Georgia town of Albany—50 miles east of the Alabama border and 60 miles north of Florida—on October 4, 1942. At age 16 she entered Albany State College, where she studied music and first became involved in the political activities for which the college expelled her. She became a civil rights activist and in 1961 a founder member of the vocal quartet THE FREEDOM SINGERS (originally created by the Student Nonviolent Coordinating Committee as the SNCC Freedom Singers), along with three others, one of whom, Cordell Hull Reagon, she later married.

In 1962 she and the rest of the group met Dylan through a leading SNCC activist whom Dylan already knew, James Forman. ROBERT SHELTON says this initiated a period in which Dylan 'began to think their topical songs were more relevant than *Broadside*: "They are singing about themselves and the kind of lives they're leading."' Shelton goes on to say: 'The New Yorkers embraced Bernice Johnson as a young ODETTA. At eighteen [actually she'd be 20 in October 1962], she had a gentle demeanor, yet could uncork a huge, beautiful voice.' In contrast, she told Shelton later that Dylan at this point seemed 'embarrassed' at his own voice: 'He seemed to think then that it was really bad. When he came up with a new song he always said that I should sing it, or GIL TURNER, because we had better voices.' She added: 'We all thought, those of us in the movement and those of us in the Freedom Singers, that Dylan was fantastic as a songwriter and as a person.' When Dylan started exploring more personal subject matter, Bernice Johnson was, perhaps surprisingly, disinclined to join the criticism, and made a point not much discussed or even acknowledged in all the retrospective scrutiny of his history:

'I felt he was going through some fantastic emotional things and I didn't want to make any judgment. . . . When he simply drifted away from the movement, it was the whites in SNICK [i.e. SNCC] who were resentful. The blacks in SNICK didn't think that, or say that. We only heard the phrase "sell-out" from the whites, not from the blacks.' She added: 'I've always just regarded Bob as a friend. He's never been a star to me, just a friend.'

Soon after the August 1963 March on Washington, at which Martin Luther King delivered his 'I Have a Dream' speech, the Freedom Singers disbanded. Dylan and his cohorts visited the Reagons in Atlanta a day or two after they'd dropped in on CARL SANDBURG in February 1964. As late as 1976 Dylan was telling Shelton: 'I love Cordell. He's a madman. He's the only faithful madman . . . that can wipe you out with pure strength who I could trust to go anywhere with.'

That wouldn't have stopped him pursuing or at least harbouring a romantic interest in Bernice—and it has always been rumoured (though no-one seems to know on what authority) that she was the addressee of the lovely song 'To Ramona': the young woman whose 'cracked country lips' he still wished to kiss, 'as to be by the strength of [her] skin.'

Johnson Reagon went back to college in the late 1960s, gained a BA in History from Spellman College in 1970 and a doctorate in History from Howard University in 1975. She joined the Smithsonian Institution in 1974, founded its Program in Black American Culture (later re-named the Program in African American Culture) and was appointed a curator specialising in the National Museum of American History, where she created, among much else, the National Public Radio series 'Wade in the Water: African American Sacred Music Traditions'. In 1992 she published *We'll Understand It Better By and By: African American Pioneering Gospel Composers*, and in 2001 *If You Don't Go, Don't Hinder Me: The African American Sacred Song Tradition*.

In 1973, while busy in academia and at the same time Vocal Director for the Washington, D.C., Black Repertory Theatre, she formed a new a cappella singing group, Sweet Honey in the Rock, whose members included herself. Sixteen years later, on the album *A Vision Shared: A Tribute to WOODY GUTHRIE and LEADBELLY* (on which Dylan offers a solo version of Guthrie's 'Pretty Boy Floyd'), the group's tracks—'Sylvie' and 'Gray Goose'—are almost the only ones tipping a hat to Leadbelly rather than Guthrie. The dull but worthy group's history is written up from the inside in her lengthily titled 1993 book *We Who Believe in Freedom: Sweet Honey in the Rock . . . Still on the Journey*.

Johnson Reagon retired from the group in 2004; she still lives in Washington, D.C., where she remains Distinguished Professor of History at the American University and Curator Emeritus at the Smithsonian. Bob Dylan still sings 'To Ramona'.

[Bernice Johnson Reagon, *We'll Understand It Better By and By: African American Pioneering Gospel Composers*,

Washington, D.C.: Smithsonian Press, 1992; *We Who Believe in Freedom: Sweet Honey in the Rock . . . Still on the Journey*, New York: Doubleday, 1993; *If You Don't Go, Don't Hinder Me: The African American Sacred Song Tradition*, Lincoln, NE: University of Nebraska Press, 2001. Various Artists: *A Vision Shared: A Tribute to Woody Guthrie and Leadbelly*, Columbia OC44034, NY (CBS 460905, UK), 1988. Sources include Robert Shelton, *No Direction Home: The Life and Music of Bob Dylan*, London: Penguin edn., 1987, pp.149–50 & 359, &, seen online 23 Jan 2006: *Green Left Weekly* online edn., *www.greenleft.org.au/back/1992/65/65p21.htm*, Rita Neubauer journal extract at *www.voicesofcivilrights.org/bus tour/journal_entry33.html* & Eve M. Ferguson's profile of & interview with Reagon, *Washington Examiner*, Washington, D.C., online at *http://dcexaminer.com/articles/2006/01/11/features/profiles/35profile1reagon*.]

***Real Live* [1984]** Dylan's fourth live album—all four having been made in the foregoing decade. Quite apart from the overload (especially granted that what everyone really wanted, the incomparable live 1966 Dylan, remained glaringly withheld), how was it that such poor stuff could be chosen, time and again, from among such riches? You could easily compile a better live album from the Rolling Thunder Revue than *Hard Rain* and a much better one from the 1978 tour than *Bob Dylan at Budokan*. And you could hardly offer a worse live album from Dylan's 1984 tour of Europe than this. The choice of songs is hopeless, the choice of performances injudicious, the production inexcusably murky. How did the supposed ace-producer Glyn Johns manage this? At the very least, Dylan's expensive, classy guitar should have a good sound. Dylan's major re-write of 'Tangled Up in Blue', featured prominently and exclusively on this tour, is included—but represented by a swaggering, mannered, unfelt performance. There were far finer moments than this. The Barcelona concert is generally judged outstanding. The album waywardly misrepresents this tour in particular and the whole glory of Bob Dylan in live performance generally.

[Recorded Newcastle, 5 Jul, London, Wembley, 7 Jul and (God help us) Slane, Ireland, 8 Jul (though at least narrowly avoiding Bono's inept intrusion into an encore performance of 'Blowin' in the Wind'); released as stereo LP, Columbia FC 39944 (US) & CBS 26334 (UK), 29 or 30 Nov or 3 Dec 1984.]

Receli, George [19?? -] George Receli, born in New Orleans but now living in Hartford, Connecticut, is currently the drummer in Dylan's Never-Ending Tour band. He is a multi-instrumentalist, singer, songwriter and producer who has also played with HOWLIN' WOLF's great guitarist Hubert Sumlin (along with LEVON HELM and KEITH RICHARDS), with MAVIS STAPLES, James Brown, Etta James, and a number of the less venerable.

He began working with Dylan on January 31, 2002, that year's first concert, in Orlando, Florida, but by that April he was having problems with one arm, and after JIM KELTNER played the first half the April 21 concert for him in Zurich, he dropped out temporarily, replaced by Keltner for the rest of that leg of the tour. Receli returned at the start of the next, on August 2 in Worcester, Massachusetts, and has remained in place ever since. This means he has also played on Dylan's re-make of 'Gonna Change My Way of Thinking', made with Mavis Staples; on Dylan's *Divine Secrets of the Ya-Ya Sisterhood* soundtrack song 'Waitin' on You', on his *Gods and Generals* soundtrack song ''Cross the Green Mountain', on the film *Masked & Anonymous*, on the *North Country* soundtrack song 'Tell Ol' Bill' and, it is assumed, on the new studio album Dylan was reportedly recording in New York in February 2006.

[Receli, Helm & Richards all play on Hubert Sumlin's 2003 CD *About Them Shoes*, *nia*, 2003.]

recording quality and cynicism The 1980s was a hard period to get through, and Dylan managed it without turning into one of the Stepford Wives of the American entertainment industry like so many other public figures. Not for him the renouncing of the bohemian hard rains of the 60s; not for him any joining of the Cher-style born again body worshippers (Look at us! We came through all that counter-cultural nonsense unscathed!, and great is our reward in the garden of showbiz: we have cleaned up in both senses). Bob Dylan, the old spoilsport, showed no interest in aerobics, looked his age, was liable to sing about what will happen when we die, and generally made himself far from the ideal guest on glitzy chat shows or for opening that new shopping mall; you couldn't even trust him not to mention the rôle of American banks at a charity event for the starving of the third world. Not for him the making of music that sounds like a Pepsi ad even before it got turned into one.

Yet Dylan has grown a more cynical outer shell, from which part of the cynicism, in the corrosive form of some kind of self-contempt, some denigration of his own artistry, has seeped inside. It damages the very integrity it was meant to protect. It makes for a whole series of ways in which he appears to give less, care less and respect his own talent less, and it delivers him into demeaning situations and tawdry dullnesses his best self would avoid. Indeed it was *by* his avoidance of shabbiness and ennui that his best self taught us in the beginning what unfaltering nimble grace was possible for the popular artist in the marketplace.

Among the ways this decline manifests itself most damagingly for his art is in the matter of the sheer technical quality of his recordings. Bob Dylan tells Bill Flanagan (in *Written in My Soul*) that 'When I hear my old stuff I just think of how badly it was recorded.' Yet this is the opposite of the truth. Almost without exception, the work Dylan has recorded since the start of the 1980s is markedly inferior, technically, not only to what is and should be possible but to what was achieved on his own earliest work.

The deleterious effect applies all round but especially in what happens to his vocals. Listen to the way the voice is recorded on any track on the first four albums, and it's right *there*: you hear the detail of the voice vividly, as it chisels out each crystalline syllable; you hear every intake of breath, and you hear how each exhalation is distributed along the lines he sings. You register every nuance, feel every surface, receive all that close-up intelligence of communication, the infinitely variable, fluid expressiveness of it. This is how it should be. This is how to bring out the genius of his singing, in which these intakes of breath, these chiselled inflections that change moment by moment, these almost silent sighs, are all integral: all alive, interdependent dynamics in his uniquely intensive vocal detailing. He wasn't joking when he famously described his songs as 'exercises in tonal breath control'. There's an equivalence here to what's meant in a remark about blues guitar playing that Stanley Booth recounts in *Rythm Oil*: 'An old black Memphis musician stood one night in an alley beside a young white guitarist, pointed to the stars, and said, "You don't plays de notes—you plays de molecules."' This is how Dylan's voice is when it gives you goosebumps. To capture it demands close attention from the vocal mike, like a diamond under a magnifying glass: and on the early albums it gets it. It more or less gets it too on the solo 'Spanish Is the Loving Tongue', the *Folkways: A Vision Shared* track 'Pretty Boy Floyd', on *Oh Mercy* tracks like 'Ring Them Bells' ('we've recaptured some of the quality that the early records had; you can really hear him in the foreground', said LANOIS) and some of *"Love and Theft"*; but on the whole it's absent and there's no such care and attention on the work of the 1980s onwards. Listen to the 3-D vividness, the shining, buoyant (pre-transistorised?) *presence* of the voice either in the studio on, say, 'To Ramona' or 'North Country Blues' (to cite two vocals that are in other ways stylistically quite different) or in concert on 1963's 'Tomorrow Is a Long Time'. And then listen to the dry, flattened out, wrong-end-of-a-megaphone recording the vocals get (incompetently tricked out with phony echo) on *Empire Burlesque*.

Or listen to 'Maybe Someday', a song that would be terrific if the voice weren't half-way to sounding like a Chipmunks parody of Dylan recorded from the far side of a football field. The difference in recording quality between the vocal on a track like this (recorded in 1986) and on, say, 'Black Crow Blues' (1964) is simply pathetic. Or listen to the disparity between the recording quality of ARTHUR ALEXANDER's 1959, *one*-track-tape-deck cut of 'Sally Sue Brown' and Bob Dylan's 1987, 24-or-48-track cut of the same song. Alexander's voice is, as Dylan's once was, right *there*; Dylan's seems to be flailing around inside the dishwasher.

Dylan elsewhere acknowledges this deterioration himself, according to U2's axeman the Edge: 'Talking to Dylan, he was saying that the technology has improved but the recordings were still better in the Sixties, when they had more of whatever they had; and whatever they had is essential.' And interviewed by Bono, Dylan elaborated:

> 'You know the studios in the old days were all much better, and the equipment so much better, there's no question about it in my mind. . . . they were just big rooms, you just sang, you know, you just made records; and they sounded like the way they sounded there. . . . You go into a studio now and they got rugs on the floor, settees and pinball machines and videos and sandwiches coming every ten minutes. It's a big expensive party and you're lucky if you come out with anything that sounds decent.'

Even the tape used in the 1950s and early 1960s was better. In 1992 *Q* magazine quoted Rhino Records re-mastering engineer Bill Inglot as saying that modern tape deteriorates more in storage than older tape: 'Most things from 1954 are in better condition than masters from 1974.'

Then there's the shift to digital recording, which swiftly dominated the marketplace *and* proved a disappointment. NEIL YOUNG says we're living in the dark ages of audio because of CDs and digital recordings. He told Bob Colbourn's 'Rock Line' listeners on the Global Network Satellite that digital recording meant

> 'people started hearing much less of the original sound, and all of . . . the universe of sounds available to the ear and to the brain to analyse and to feel were all gone. . . . and those are the very things that stimulate the . . . body into reacting and feeling and enjoying music and . . . its therapeutic effects. . . . it's all reduced, it's a surface sham, it's not the real thing. It's like . . . digital cameras, when you take a picture of a field full of cows. . . . you take the same picture with a Kodachrome camera with a film in it and you look at the film picture . . . take a magnifying glass and . . . go way in and you look at the cows and it still looks like a cow. . . . and you go to the digital picture and you go in with a magnifying glass and all you see is like three or four little black squares where the cow was. And that's what's happening to your ears and your heart and your brain when you listen to digital music.'

There are those who feel we had a loss imposed upon us long before digitalisation, when transistors took over from valves. When Jackie Wilson's dazzlingly sung 1957 hit 'Reet Petite' was a hit all over again in the UK in the 1980s, one generation bought it on 12-inch; another already owned it on 78rpm. Playing the reissue on modern equipment and then playing the 78 on an old electric valve-driven radiogram, there was no doubting the extra warmth and beefiness of the older system. In the early 1980s valve-driven recording consoles started to be resuscitated, to cater for those who've felt there is this difference. A number of top quality hi-fi companies make valve-driven amps. Bob Dylan could afford to check into all this.

There are only occasional signs that he's interested. The main studio used on *Under the Red Sky* was Oceanway, which was dedicated to achieving an old ambient warmth and recognised the need to strive for one to compensate for digital, transistorised coldness—but the resulting production on *Under the Red Sky* was as criticised as any other Dylan album of recent decades; then again, *"Love and Theft"* stands out as a production that *does* pay the closest of attention to the minutiae of Dylan's voice—to hear 'Mississippi' is to feel returned to a model demonstration of how that voice should be recorded: and the producer was Dylan himself.

This seems the exception, and certainly you can't blame all the deficiencies of recordings like 'Maybe Someday' or 'Sally Sue Brown' on tape-storage, transistors or digits: they're inept productions by the standards of any audio regime.

In any case Dylan is never going to become an equipment-expert; and granted his capacity for shooting himself in the foot from boredom, it seems hard to expect that if we stand on the threshold of a new recording era, Dylan will step across it. Look at the cheapness of his equipment for touring through most of the 1990s; his not seeming to care that he was paying a technical crew uninterested in the new generation of mikes, DAT recorders and so on: uninterested even in keeping the heads clean on the cassette machine on the mixing desk. As Paul D. Lehrman wrote of a 1996 concert, in the recording-sound magazine *Mix*: '. . . he was only playing medium-size theaters, with a small band. How could the sound be bad there? . . . The guy at the mixing board, even though he had a clear path to the aisles, never moved, never walked away to see what it sounded like anywhere else.'

It doesn't have to *be* like this. It's all of a piece with Dylan telling the Never-Ending Tour's fine original bass player KENNY AARONSON 'I don't give a shit who plays bass' when Aaronson, recovered from illness, asked in vain for his job back. It's all of a piece with Dylan referring, in the *Biograph* interview, to 'my little voice'. With him telling AL KOOPER with a shrug that *Knocked Out Loaded* didn't turn out right because it got handed over to producers and what can you do? With his saying something about how any one album is only an album, and there'll always be another one: a dispiriting way of replacing the previously held Dylan view, which was that each album was a unique step along an unknown road: a deliberate creation under the control of the artist, however much the chaos of the moment was allowed to feed into it. (*Blonde on Blonde* is exemplary in this respect, as in so many others.)

Dylan seems usually to have given up fighting to maintain that control—perhaps given up on that responsibility to his art. It may be a sign of this that even his judgement about the running-order of the tracks seems to have slipped. It would be absurd to say that the running-order of any of the albums of the 1960s or 1970s was 'wrong' or ill-judged; yet even without going into such perversities as *Shot of Love*'s including 'Trouble' and excluding 'The Groom's Still Waiting at the Altar' (now 'restored'), or *Oh Mercy*'s choosing 'Political World' as an opener instead of 'Dignity', it seems self-evidently wrong that on the second side of *Knocked Out Loaded* the running-order does its best to minimise the impact of 'Brownsville Girl' by putting it before the humdrum 'Got My Mind Made Up' and the superfluous 'Under Your Spell', instead of allowing 'Brownsville Girl' to be the long, impressive conclusion to the record, as 'Sad-Eyed Lady of the Lowlands' and 'Every Grain of Sand' had been on earlier collections.

Even the album cover-art seemed to get given up on in the 1980s. It hardly matters what's on the cover of a CD, of course: it's such a squitty little artefact it can't possibly hold any power; but the big bold covers of Dylan LPs used to give a clear, imaginative signal as to what sort of world was within. What a surprise it was to find that the five inner-sleeve photos on the vinyl version of the *Bootleg Series Vols. 1–3*, and the front cover photograph of *Good as I Been to You*, reverted to this skilled panache, this intelligent accuracy of signalling. It was a surprise because of the opportunities flabbily squandered with such covers as *Shot of Love*, *Real Live* and *Down in the Groove*, and more recently on *Time Out of Mind* and *"Love and Theft"*.

Not caring to secure a decent vocal sound; accepting crepuscular artwork; excluding the best tracks; minimising the impact of the best of the rest—these are part of the new defensiveness, the 1980s-onwards posture of 'if I don't really try I don't really fail' that may seem inoffensively low-key, even charmingly fallible, but surely signals an aggressive distrust of the audience and of himself. A parallel stance has become more and more commonplace in concerts latterly too; by 2004 it was possible to be in the front row at one of these and *still* feel that Bob Dylan was a long way away, since he couldn't be bothered to project any further than to the front of the electric piano he was standing behind and playing so inconsequentially.

In personal terms, this encrusted defensiveness can't be criticised: if it's how he feels, it's how he feels—but in terms of his work, it is damaging, regrettable, self-destructive, 'and if you can't speak out against this kind of thing . . .'

[Stanley Booth: *Rythm Oil*, London: Cape, 1991. 'Tomorrow Is a Long Time', live NY, 12 Apr 1963, *Bob Dylan Greatest Hits Vol. II* & *Masterpieces*. Arthur Alexander: 'Sally Sue Brown', Sheffield, AL, 1959; Judd 1020, US, 1960: his début single. Jackie Wilson: 'Reet Petite', NY, Jul 1957, Brunswick 55024, NY (Coral Q 72290, London), 1957; SMP SKM 3, UK, 1986. The Edge quote, *Melody Maker* Dylan supplement, London, 3 Feb 1990; Bono interview with Dylan, Slane, Ireland, 8 Jul 1984, *Hot Press* no.26, Dublin, 1984. Bill Inglot, Q no.70, UK, Jul 1992. Neil Young, quoted *Broken Arrow* no.46, Bridgend, Wales, *nia*. Paul D. Lehrman: 'Sounding Off: What Happened to the FOH Mix?', *Mix*, Emeryville, CA, May 1996.]

Reed, Jimmy [1925 - 1976] Jimmy Reed was born on September 6, 1925 on a plantation at Dunleith, Mississippi. He was a hugely influential, popular artist. His hits, on which he played guitar and harmonica and sang, began in 1955 with 'You Don't Have to Go' and 'Ain't That Lovin' You Baby'; his many others include 'Baby What You Want Me to Do' (1960), 'Big Boss Man', 'Bright Lights, Big City' and his biggest US crossover (into pop) hit, 'Honest I Do' (1955), all made for Vee Jay Records. His only scrape into the British charts was with 'Shame Shame Shame', which peaked at no.45 in 1964. THE ROLLING STONES revived 'Honest I Do' on their first album, *The Rolling Stones*, the same year.

Dylan's Basement Tapes rock song 'Odds and Ends' is the title of a prominent 1957 JIMMY REED record—prominent for the splendidly named Remo Biondi 'playing the electric violin', and for Jimmy Reed's harp. Indeed his relentless, pulsating, slow harmonica-work on this moody alligator of an instrumental record is surely the model for Bob Dylan's on that masterly *Blonde on Blonde* blues, 'Pledging My Time'.

The figures Reed relied on more than Remo Biondi were his long-time guitarist partner Eddie Taylor, whose distinctive riffs often 'make' Reed's records, and his wife, Mary Lee Mama Reed, who wrote much of his material. An epileptic with an alcohol problem, Jimmy Reed died from respiratory failure on August 29, 1976 in Oakland, California. He was 50.

[Jimmy Reed: 'Odds and Ends', Chicago, 3/4/57, Vee Jay 298, Chicago, 1957. 'Shame Shame Shame', Stateside SS 330, London, 1964. The Rolling Stones, 'Honest I Do', London, Feb 1964, *The Rolling Stones*, Decca LK 4605, London (London PS 375, NY), 1964.]

Reed, Lou [1942 -] Lewis Allen Reed was born on March 2, 1942 in Brooklyn, New York, and became with John Cale (with whom he had played in the Primitives) a founder member of the iconic WARHOL-patronised group the Velvet Underground in 1965, in which he was guitarist, singer and principal songwriter, responsible equally for grunge classics like 'Waiting for the Man' and those eerily pretty songs like 'All Tomorrow's Parties'. The group was the prototype for all US punk music, and Reed the formative influence behind the group. He quit in 1970 to pursue a solo career that peaked early, in commercial terms, with 1972's 'Walk on the Wild Side'.

Dylan told interviewer Bill Flanagan that his own 'Brownsville Girl' was written partly in response to a song by Lou Reed, 'Doin' the Thing That We Want To', which starts by referring to going to see a play—the SAM SHEPARD play *Fool for Love*—and describing its impact on the singer. Reed presents this in the most vague and lackadaisical terms, and the song is of no great complexity or depth. 'Brownsville Girl' owes it nothing at all in structure, complexity of concept or use of language. But Reed's song advances a simple message, which might be said to be a rather obvious assumption underlying the Dylan song: that certain films and plays are 'very inspirational'.

Reed shocked many in the 1980s when he made TV ads for that most wretched of corporate banking brands, American Express; it was bizarre, but essentially disappointing, to see the Godfather of Punk earnestly recommending this symbol of the Fat Suit Universe. The soundtrack might have been, but for some reason wasn't, 'I'm waiting for my man / American Express card in my hand.'

Lou Reed was, almost as surprisingly—considering his absolute lack of career connection with Dylan—one of those who appeared at the 30th Anniversary Celebration Concert for Dylan in New York City on October 16, 1992—and chose very creditably not to perform some obvious 1960s anthem but a particularly difficult song that was an outtake from the *Infidels* sessions of 1983, the lengthy and fairly incomprehensible 'Foot of Pride'. Reed needed an autocue, but still, he did it.

[Lou Reed: 'Doin' the Thing That We Want To', NY, Dec 1983–Jan 1984, *New Sensations*, RCA PL84998, NY, 1984. Referred to by Dylan in his Mar 1985 interview for Bill Flanagan, *Written in My Soul*, Chicago: Contemporary Books, 1986. Sam Shepard: *Fool for Love*, the play, premiered San Francisco, 8 Feb 1983, dir. Shepard & NY, May 1983, again dir. Shepard.]

Regan, Ken [1950s -] Ken Regan was born in the Bronx in the 1950s, grew up there, studied journalism at Columbia and then attended New York University's Film School. His first photography work was in sports, selling a wide range of pictures including of tennis, boxing, athletics, basketball, auto racing, hockey and football to the usual heavyweight suspects: *Time*, *Life*, *Newsweek* and *Sports Illustrated*.

In the 1970s, he founded the Camera 5 photo agency, to represent himself and 14 others. Since then he has specialised in politics and hard news all over the world—riots, demonstrations, wars, Vietnam vets, gold mining in Brazil, famine in Ethiopia, the Kennedy family—but also in stills for Hollywood movies. In 1971 he was the principal official photographer at GEORGE HARRISON's Concert for Bangla Desh and, 14 years on, at LIVE AID.

All Regan's work in music, he says, came from promoter Bill Graham having taken him under his wing, including meeting Dylan. The two first met informally at JOHNNY CASH's house in 1972–73, but the meeting that clinched his work with Dylan came during the 1974 comeback tour with THE BAND.

It was a fruitful meeting—for it was Regan's photographs of the 1970s Bob Dylan that have, more than anyone else's, created the quintessential image most people have of him in that decade. All those utterly beautiful shots of him from the 1975 Rolling Thunder Revue and on the sets, therefore, of *Renaldo & Clara*: the shot with BRUCE SPRINGSTEEN, the shots with ALLEN GINSBERG, with JONI MITCHELL, with MUHAMMAD ALI, the covers of the *Desire* and *Hard Rain* albums, almost all the generous sweep of pictures in SAM SHEPARD's *Rolling Thunder Logbook*, every picture in the lavish booklet with the *Bootleg Series Vol. 5: Bob Dylan Live 1975* (2002) . . . all Ken Regan's. And you can buy a gelatin print of any one of them for an average of only $1,700.

re-interpretation and renewal in Dylan's work The main cliché of Dylanology from the 1980s onwards lies in insisting that Dylan's constant 're-interpretation' of his work in performance shows—and itself *argues*—that there is no finished text of any individual song. This has become so orthodox a mantra that you cannot demur without coming under attack. Dylan does indeed re-interpret his songs in performance—but the notion that therefore there is no finished text seems rather too convenient for the Bob Dylan who might have writer's block or lost his way. How much nicer to go round saying that the song is a text in permanent revision, like Trotsky's revolution, than to say that yes, this important song was actually written in 1964 or 1965, and so was this one *and* this one *and* this one . . . It's no small irony that while the never-ending-text theory is radical and post-modern and *now*, it's also a great one to cling to for those who have lost the muse and written comparatively little since *back then*. Where are the new songs the Bob Dylan of the future might want to keep on re-interpreting?

In any case, if all these live concerts are authentically about the high-minded quest for 're-interpretation', how come the unfinished texts Dylan revisits the most are so often the easy rockist numbers, like 'Rainy Day Women # 12 & 35'—which by the end of 2003 had received nearly 800 performances. That's not re-interpretation, it's settling for the lowest-common-denominator easy option.

It is equally clear to all but the most blinkered that in around 95 per cent of cases, the best interpretation of the work, if you had to choose just one, would turn out to be the original Dylan recording. Listen to the syllable-by-syllable care and precision and on-the-ball acuteness of his delivery on almost every studio recording—not just the early ones but on, say, *Time Out of Mind* and *"Love and Theft"* too—and then hear how much these qualities are purposelessly lacking in every rough and careless live 're-interpretation'.

Yet of course you *don't* have to choose just one interpretation, and there have been many instances when a particular live performance—or even a whole particular year's or tour's re-invention—has offered invaluable, revelatory re-interpretation that no-one would wish to be without. On top of which, while the Bob Dylan of the 1980s onwards is no longer, measured by his own earlier standards, prolific, and often loses sight of the meticulous standards he himself laid down as writer and performer, his artistic struggle to survive and to be renewed has given us new work that, at its best, still offers unparalleled variety, an admirable insistence on exploration, and a continued authentic uniqueness.

He might fail more often than he succeeds over these decades, and he might seem marooned inside an 'entertainment industry' that has lost, in this period, its last shreds of tolerance for unformatted openness—the very condition that once allowed such major creative leaps as PRESLEY's fusion of hillbilly music with rhythm'n'blues or Dylan's own fusion of poetry with rock'n'roll. Yet he has continued to strive to explore, and has mostly refused, to his great credit, the easier option of being Dylanesque.

***Renaldo & Clara* [film, 1978]** A film based around Dylan's first Rolling Thunder Revue tour of 1975, which began as a series of surprise concerts in small towns and small halls, with a bright gyspy band of other performers including ROGER McGUINN, JOAN BAEZ, RAMBLIN' JACK ELLIOTT, MICK RONSON, RONEE BLAKLEY and ALLEN GINSBERG. To help make the film, Dylan also brought in SAM SHEPARD, who was supposed to script non-concert scenes in and around the hotels and quirky places alighted upon en route. This didn't work out, and the scenes ended up mostly as improvisations, but Shepard stayed to act in some of them—there's an embarrassingly awkward scene between him and Dylan's wife SARA—and afterwards wrote the underrated *Rolling Thunder Logbook*, which is blessed by a rich supply of beautiful photographs taken on the tour, mostly by KEN REGAN.

Ginsberg witnessed Dylan's editing and organisational method for the film:

> '. . . he shot about 110 hours of film, or more, and he looked at it all. Then he put it all on index cards, according to some preconceptions he had when he was directing and shooting.

Namely, themes: God, rock & roll, art, poetry, marriage, women, sex, Bob Dylan, poets, death—maybe eighteen or twenty thematic preoccupations. Then he also put on index cards all the different characters, all the scenes. He also marked on index cards the dominant color–blue or red . . . and certain other images that go through the movie, like the rose and the hat, and Indians–American Indian–so that he finally had an index of all that. And then he went through it all again and began composing it, thematically, weaving in and out of those specific compositional references. So it's compositional, and the idea was not to have a plot, but to have a composition of those themes.'

The result, cut down to four hours, was over-long, self-indulgent, ego-centric and to watch it is to alternate between being riveted and bored rigid. Like the 1966 documentary film that followed Dylan's tour around, *Eat the Document*, here is a film that could have given us sustained concert footage of marvellous intensity, joy and high-flying creative foment but that gives, instead, cruelly foreshortened concert performance glimpses and tantalising backstage glimpses and concentrates, wrong-headedly, on the tiresome amateur improvised dramas devised by Dylan and some of his cohorts. As in *Eat the Document*, these flaccid scenes are what interest Dylan and therefore what he gives us.

Nevertheless, there are riches within the film beyond the shaking wonder of the concert footage. There is the clever way that Dylan somehow manages to use the downtown Montréal of the mid-1970s as a kind of stand-in for the Greenwich Village of the early 1960s; this is never spelt out but you get a strong sense that the one is observed so as to reminisce about the other. More straightforwardly, and almost certainly thanks to HOWARD ALK, there's the long sequence of wonderfully vivid, plainly observed interviews with randomly encountered people in the litter-blown, hard streets of Harlem, which let the disenfranchised speak for themselves: even the mad ones. This is all of a piece with the film's general insistence on keeping one eye open for the non-WASP North America.

In the end, *Renaldo & Clara* is a failure, but it's a grand failure. You might argue for it, as did a commentator to the IMDb online movie database, that what 'makes it such a valuable cinematic document is that it bridges the gap in American cultural history between the "Beat Generation" and the emerging post-modern movement.' And alongside *Masked and Anonymous* it's a radical masterpiece.

The credits give Dylan as director, Dylan and Alk as editors, and Alk, David Mayers and Paul Goldsmith as cinematographers. It has never been officially released on video or DVD.

[*Renaldo & Clara*, directed Bob Dylan, Circuit Films, US, 1978. Allen Ginsberg quoted from a transcript by John Hinchey of discussion between Ginsberg and students at Swarthmore College, PA, 4 Nov 1978, *Telegraph* no.12, Bury, UK, Jun 1983 (a transcript re-used almost word for word but uncredited in Clinton Heylin: *Bob Dylan: Behind the Shades. Take Two*, Penguin Books edn., p.460.) Quote from movie database seen online 14 Aug 2005 at *http://us.imdb.com/title/tt0078151/*.]

repertoire, Dylan's early, unsuited to commercial radio In *Chronicles Volume One* Dylan offers this list of topics occupying the songs of his early repertoire, noting that these songs 'weren't for radiophiles': 'debauched bootleggers, mothers that drowned their own children, Cadillacs that got only five miles to the gallon, floods, union hall fires, darkness and cadavers at the bottom of rivers' (p.34).

Ribakove, Sy [1928 -] & Barbara [1932 -] Sy Ribakove and Barbara Joan Mayer, now Barbara Ribakove Gordon, were born in New York on February 28, 1928 and November 21, 1932 respectively. They wrote the first book on Bob Dylan, the 'quickie' *Folk Rock: The Bob Dylan Story*, in 1966.

It may seem odd now that 1966 was the first year to see such a thing in print, but this was an era in which neither publishers nor the mainstream media were much concerned with 'pop music'. In 1964 Douglas R. Gilbert's photographs of a fresh-faced young Dylan, looking, in retrospect, rather neat and short-haired, were rejected by the heavyweight New York magazine *Look*, which had commissioned them, on the grounds that Dylan was 'too scruffy for a family magazine'.

Barbara recalls: 'Sy and I were given . . . four weeks in which to write the Bob Dylan book. We had never heard of him, but immediately bought all his records and played them night and day while researching and writing the book. Sy's musicianship was very important to this work; he holds two degrees from Juilliard. We made the deadline.' Sy adds: 'We were forbidden to contact Bob Dylan or quote his lyrics . . . [and] couldn't have done the book without the generous material in . . . the daybook provided us by IZZY YOUNG.'

The book was published by Dell as a small-size 124-page paperback with 16 pages of photographs; it mixed biography with a rudimentary discography and a semi-musicological description of the transitional albums from folk to rock. A Japanese translation continued to sell in Japan for some years.

The Ribakoves, who enjoyed a 23-year marriage and collaboration on writing magazine articles, and in 1974 wrote one other 'quickie' book (Sy's own term), *The Nifty Fifties: The Happy Years*, went their separate ways in the late 1970s.

Sy, now aged 78 and long retired, has played and taught piano professionally, been President of the Rockland Music Teachers Guild and President of the Hospice of Rockland in New City, NY.

Barbara was Senior Editor of the now-defunct *Health Magazine* and won an award for journalistic writing on hypertension in 1985. In 1981 she went to Ethiopia with the first American mission to Jewish villages, defying the Ethiopian government's order not to make contacts with villagers; in 1982 she co-founded the North American Conference on Ethiopian Jewry and in 1991, during a temporary armistice between warring factions, she took part in Operation Solomon, airlifting over 14,000 Ethiopian Jews to Israel.

[Sy & Barbara Ribakove, *Folk Rock: The Bob Dylan Story*, New York: Dell, 1966; *The Nifty Fifties: The Happy Years*, New York: Award Books, 1974. Quotes, e-mails to this writer from Barbara Ribakove Gordon and from Sy Ribakove, 1 Feb 2006.]

Richards, Keith [1943 -] Keith Richards was born in Dartford, Kent, on December 18, 1943 and grew up to be one of THE ROLLING STONES, co-writer with MICK JAGGER of the Stones' self-penned hits (credited on record labels, early on, to Nanker-Phelge, a sort of obtuse riposte to the formula 'LENNON-McCARTNEY'), a great guitarist and inventor of riffs, and over time shifting from an amiable-looking mod with the street-cred cool of a bewildered pet rabbit, through the long heroin-happy years as Britain's licenced bad boy, to the extraordinary figure he cuts today as everybody's favourite cadaver.

What's remarkable is how long his dark, hip makeover took him. Look at any photograph right up to 1975—right on past the time when RON WOOD joined the group—and Keith is still nowhere close to Jagger, as a persona. Mick's right in your face with his cold green eyes and his drain-unblocker lips, pouting away with consummate ease: and Keith's there with his spiky hairdresser's hair gone all tufty and uncertain, and underneath it the ill-advised eyeliner and the stance of a provincial adolescent trying to look tough, as if he's just been caught smoking in school.

Their early manager, Andrew Loog Oldham, had made Keith change his surname to the singular Richard (though it wasn't, of course, singular at all, and merely made Britons wonder if perhaps he were related to Cliff: not an ideal image for a Rolling Stone)—and he didn't assert himself and change it back until *the early 1980s*.

He and Bob Dylan have had, aside from Dylan-Stones conjunctions, two memorable professional encounters: using the word 'professional' loosely, especially in the case of LIVE AID, the first of the two—except that though you wouldn't know it, they had rehearsed beforehand, on July 10–12, 1985, at Ron Wood's New York home, with Keith and Bob sharing vocals on 'Girl of the North Country' and Keith playing guitar throughout.

They reconvened at the Guitar Legends Festival in Seville, Spain, on October 17, 1991. After Dylan had played with others—primarily RICHARD THOMPSON—on 'All Along the Watchtower', 'Boots of Spanish Leather', 'Across the Borderline' and 'Answer Me (My Love)', then he and Keith, backed by a posse of musicians, performed the early R&B/rock'n'roll classic 'Shake, Rattle & Roll', sharing vocals.

It was a gift to Dylan: he went into one of his classic guesting-on-stage routines, a masterly piece of theatre that can be savoured on the film footage, on which he mimes faultlessly the high comedy of making out that he's woken to find himself on stage with certifiable lunatics it might be best to humour (Keith & co.) and has never heard anything as mystifying as 'Shake, Rattle & Roll' in his life.

Ricks, Christopher [1933 -] Christopher Bruce Ricks was born in Beckenham, Kent ('the Garden of England'), on September 18, 1933. His parents divorced (unusually for the time) when he was three. He was sent to King Alfred's School, Wantage, where he 'discovered Milton', and in 1952 served briefly in Egypt as a junior officer in the British Army's Green Howards regiment. He graduated from Balliol College, Oxford, in 1956, became an academic and eventually Professor of English at Bristol (1968–75) and then at Cambridge (UK) from 1975 to 1986. By the end of his time at Bristol he had already established his reputation as one of the great literary critics of the day. His first book was *Milton's Grand Style*, 1963; among others there has also been *Keats and Embarrassment*, 1974; *T.S. Eliot and Prejudice*, 1988; *Tennyson*, 1989; and in 1996 *Inventions of the March Hare: Poems 1909–1917*, described by the *New Yorker* as 'the best book ever written on T.S. ELIOT'.

Ricks never visited the United States until 1964, and then came only to look at the Tennyson manuscripts, but being entranced, wanted to live and work there, and duly became a visiting professor at Berkeley, Stanford, Smith College, Harvard, Wesleyan and Brandeis, and in 1986 left England to become Professor of English at Boston University. There, the *Boston Magazine* dubbed him 'the greatest teacher in the post-Socrates era', though he generally felt less appreciated than that would suggest, regarding himself as 'the lone champion of dead white male European writers' in an 'anglophobic English Department'. He once said: 'I sometimes think there is a specific prejudice against English people in English Departments.' Nevertheless, asked if he envisaged a return to England, he replied, 'Yes, but perhaps only in a coffin.' Despite that, he was elected Professor of Poetry at Oxford in 2004 and now lectures there several times a year.

He also feels, in old age, vindicated in having been, on the whole, an enemy of the virulent literary theorists whose ideas were for many years far more modish than his own. He told *The Guardian* in 2005 that 'a lot of people who were looking for a certain sort of salvation from literary theory—political and perhaps personal salvation—have been a little bit disappointed. There have been quite a lot of defections from the theory ranks and a lot of people have found out, to their mild surprise, that they were really liberal humanists all along. One shouldn't be complacent that fashions are sure to disappear without doing much harm. But it does seem to me that a great deal of good sense has prevailed and almost everyone now teaches, at least at undergraduate level, in a rather valuably old-fashioned way.'

Christopher Ricks was an early academic advocate of the idea of Bob Dylan as a serious artist. He delivered talks on Dylan at least from the mid-1970s, including on radio in Australia (and his occasional lectures on Dylan have always been exhilarating *performances*); he first published his fine Dylan essay 'Clichés That Come to Pass' in an early issue of the fanzine *The Telegraph* (later revising the material for publication within his book *The Force of Poetry*) and his 'What He Can Do for You' was written specially for *The Telegraph*. That he was contracted to write a book on Dylan was first rumoured in the early 1980s. At long last, and after almost as many delays as with ROBERT SHELTON's Dylan biography *No Direction Home*, the 69-year-old Christopher Ricks finally published *Dylan's Visions of Sin* in 2003.

The surprise was that this is Ricks' fattest critical work. A slimmer volume than he had accorded Tennyson, Milton or T.S.Eliot had been expected. Yet the book's amplitude is not entirely a blessing. Ricks indulges as never before in his remorseless, grinding word-play. You can hardly read beyond the first two pages without wishing he'd ease up on the compulsive punning: and after an hour's immersion you find yourself having to resist the same bad habit of mind. In this sense it's like reading Oscar Wilde: before long you find yourself reaching for aphorisms every time you open your mouth. The difference being that Oscar's aphorisms beguile and last, and Ricks' puns tend to besmirch and aggravate:

'"True Love Tends to Forget", aware that rhyming depends on memory, has "forget" begin in the arms of regret, and end, far out, in "Tibet". The Dylai Lama.' Later, Bob is 'Dyligent'. Discussing whether Dylan's songs end, as Bob once claimed, by wishing you good luck, Ricks writes of 'Positively 4th Street' that it does not end 'with "Good Luck" to its interluckitor.' On 'Lay Lady Lay' word-play on OED definitions of 'lalia' runs via 'erotolalia' into 'Try erotolayladylaylia. The chatter might be just the thing for a chatter-up of someone.' Not.

There is much else similarly ill-judged. Quoting another's adverse comment on him, Ricks retorts: 'I bridle slightly at that "fetishizing-a-recording" bit. (What, me? All the world knows that it is women's shoes that I am into.)' Another bad ego moment, followed by a particularly wearisome bout of punning, consumes 'Country Pie'. Where is the restraint with words that Ricks so admires in Dylan?

In the middle of discussing, brilliantly, 'Like a Rolling Stone', Ricks can't resist snatching 'pawn' from the lyric and, regurgitating its use in another song, writing 'That word "pawn" may hold a grudge, yes, but then if you were a grudge, wouldn't you like to be held?' Or, using 'Highlands' as his platform: 'if you fail to recognize that you are in Robert Burns country you must be a sad-eared laddy of the lowlands.'

It's also easy to tire of prose *about* Dylan that reprocesses his own lines and phrases. Anyone can resort to it, yet what could be more subject to the law of diminishing returns? In *Dylan's Visions of Sin* it has already become wearying by the time you reach, not far in: 'Nor do I think of myself as at all denying Dylan's license to expand his songs. (Who's going to take away his license to expand?)' Certainly no Penguin editor took away Ricks'.

Further, there is the false note sounded sometimes when Ricks aims to express in prose what he believes is the thrust of a Dylan lyric. Here is Ricks' imaginary blokeish chat, supposedly relaying the sentiments of 'All the Tired Horses': '. . . the second line . . . is nothing but a fatigued remonstration. "How'm I s'posed to get any riding done". I ask you. Not that you need take the trouble to answer. It is in vain for any of us to kick against the pricks—and anyway kicking would be more of an effort than I'm prepared to make, I don't mind telling you. Forget it. But don't forget the song, even though *Lyrics* does.'

Claiming to echo the lyric's meaning, he wholly misrepresents its tone—and since we know from another eminent professor that style is inseparable from content, this is to misrepresent the song's meaning too. Yet this is offered as the culminating flash bang wallop of four pages of this most catherine-wheel-minded critic's radiant rap about two and a half lines of lyric. At times like these, and there are many, you feel that here is a book about an English critic and his compulsive brainy word-games, and while it vividly evokes his distinguished yet intellectually playful milieu—Cambridge, Boston, Eng. Lit. student precocity—it barely seems to be looking at Bob Dylan at all.

All this is trebly wasteful. First, Ricks is better qualified than most to know how valuable—how economical and revealing—an alert, apposite pun can be; he knows, similarly, how serious, useful and concentrating can be the sparing use of word-play. In writing about Dylan, the same goes for throwing in reprocessed quotes from the songs. Second, Ricks pins down his own ailment. In the section on 'Like a Rolling Stone' he refers to 'the vacuum that is flippancy' and later gives his own verdict on extravagance of self-regard: 'This is like kissing yourself in the mirror, full on the lips, the only place you can kiss yourself in the mirror, and yet somehow not as satisfying as one had hoped, don't you find?' Since he asks, you might find yourself remembering what F.R. Leavis said of C.P. Snow's lecture on 'the Two Cultures': 'The peculiar quality of [his] assurance expresses itself in a pervasive tone: a tone of which one can say that, while only genius could justify it, one cannot readily think of genius adopting it.'

But the most provoking, the most damaging, upshot of Ricks' self-indulgence is that it so gets in the way of the incomparable light his gifts can and sometimes still do shine on the work of the incomparable Bob Dylan.

How bright a light *can* he shine, and on what aspects of Dylan's work? It has been suggested, in several quarters, that Ricks concentrates too exclusively on the lyrics and says virtually nothing about music, performance, politics or the times Dylan has been writing about. This is untrue. Early on, he contributes cogently to the weighing of 'straight' literary criticism as against 'say, music criticism or art criticism', and of the artist and how conscious he is of 'all the subtle effects of wording and timing'; the citing of Philip Larkin's feelings about the merits of reading poetry on the page and the inherent faults with reading it aloud leads into a fine discussion of Dylan's re-performances and what is gained and lost.

Similarly a very attentive critique of Larkin's poem 'Love Songs in Age' returns us, over several pages, to the discussion of print v. performance. Ricks often mentions the effects achieved by the voice; he mentions, if not regularly, effects too made by specifics on guitar or harmonica. (Anyhow, isn't it refreshing to find for once that songs from *Oh Mercy* and *Time Out of Mind* can be discussed without mention of DANIEL LANOIS or his atmospherics?) In any case, the book ends not with some summation of the literary side of life but with rumination on Dylan's dilemmas as a performer.

Ricks also has the courage and curiosity to raise the rarely discussed but significant question of 'Faith in Dylan. . . . Was that weird wording of his a slip of the lip or was it his speaking in tongues? Did he make a dexterous move, or am I—when I exclaim at how intriguing some turn of phrase is—just going through the critical motions? The choice can be stark.'

But it *is* the words that Ricks can best illuminate, and there is plenty here to stimulate and to teach. There's some terrific scrutiny of 'Blind Willie McTell', delivered with direct enthusiasm, and within which allusions are real bricks on the path, not distractions or confessions of distractedness: perhaps especially in the discussion of blindness that takes us from McTell, via Dylan Thomas, and ends up illuminating specifics in 'Under the Red Sky' and 'High Water (For CHARLEY PATTON)'.

He's good on putting 'Lay Down Your Weary Tune' and 'Mr. Tambourine Man' alongside each other, and at his most alert best in pinning down, here, what we may never quite have noticed for ourselves but immediately recognise that we have felt: that the 'Yes,' in 'Yes, to dance beneath the diamond sky . . .' is in itself exultant. Similarly, he's very acute on 'Boots of Spanish Leather', and never more so than showing how Dylan's repeated 'No' is affirmative—is hanging on to the ideals of love—while only at the end, when he sings that 'yes' ('And yes, there's something you can send back to me') is he being negative, negating something larger.

Ricks on 'The Lonesome Death of Hattie Carroll' remains wondrously good—this may be the single finest piece of critical writing on Dylan, and raises itself above the rest much as Ricks argues that Dylan's song itself does. He's riveting, unbeatable, on 'Seven Curses' (where the pun about the judge's eyes, 'Bed-rheumy eyes', works—there's a point to it—and where it is almost the only pun in the essay, which is all the better for its plain speaking).

He achieves elegant, thoughtful writing about songs to God, the eye and the ear, the achievement of humility without falsity or archness, while scrutinising 'Saving Grace', starting with a most rewarding scrutiny of the phrase 'saving grace' itself. There's a fine, very different piece on the darkness of 'What Was It You Wanted?' and, ironically, he's very human, within it, on the power of wordlessness, as against Dylan's getting in, with this song, 'the first word, the last word, and every word along the way.' He's excellent too on 'One Too Many Mornings' and (when he gets down to it) on 'Only a Pawn in Their Game'.

He's better still on 'Like a Rolling Stone': a major piece to fit a major song, from micro to macro comment. Giving us a savvy observation in a pungent phrase, he quotes 'Threw the bums a dime, in your prime' and notes 'its evocation of small-minded largesse', while in dealing with the song's whole sweep he argues adeptly that it is the lyric's 'misgivings' that save it from being '—in all its vituperative exhilaration—even more damnably proud than the person it damns.' And his exposition of why it is exultant, not gloating, and how it carries, by its end, greater recognition of 'her' feelings than it seemed aware of at its outset, its recognition that there are *mixed* feelings as well as *more* feelings at stake: all this is great critical work.

It is, too, attractive that Ricks seems so at ease with the entire Dylan oeuvre, not least by bringing in frequently (surprisingly so for a critic so insistent on the artist being unbeholden to the man) many interview answers from Dylan from across the whole stretch of decades, from 2001 as well as 1966, quotes from 1963 and 1997 alike, and a healthy drawing upon *Tarantula*.

Equally attractive is the readiness to bring in Gerard Manley Hopkins, Tennyson, Eliot, Milton, Matthew Arnold, Keats and Larkin (à la Ricks, there's an awful lot of Larkin about), and his capacious readiness to do so is one of his great strengths *when writing about Dylan*. Not because it elevates Dylan when he's put in their company—for the truth is that he puts himself there, by his work—but because their proximity recurrently rubs the reader up against pithy, rigorous-minded comment and eloquence (pertinently, too: his quoting of Eliot on Goldsmith, allowing another's critical light to shine on Bob, helps say something of what's fine about 'One Too Many Mornings'). This rigour, this assemblage of great minds, does Dylan more favours than he usually gets within the narrow walls of rock writing, where perspectives on his work rarely roam further than from WOODY GUTHRIE to THE ROLLING STONES.

It's a further attraction of the book that he rarely makes those value-judgements most of us so easily slip into as to how great an artist A is, or how much better than B. So there's no 'Dylan is better than BROWNING' (nor any 'Browning is better than Dylan'). There's only the playful Ricksian reference to Shakespeare as Dylanesque.

[Quote re Boston, interview by A.M. Chambers, 2000, seen online 17 May 2005 at *www.britishinamerica.com/cricks.html*; quote re theorists, interview by Nicholas Wroe, *The Guardian*, London, 29 Jan 2005; some background material from both; more, and most Dylan-oriented material, revised from Michael Gray: 'Christopher Ricks: Dylan's Visions of Sin', *Judas!* no. 7, Bluntisham, UK, Oct 2003, pp.56–60.]

ridin' the blinds without Robert Johnson 'I Was Young When I Left Home' is an early Dylan song, recorded in a Minneapolis apartment in 1961 but only released officially 44 years later, on the *Bootleg Series Vol. 7—No Direction Home: The Soundtrack*. In writing about it in the interim, CLINTON HEYLIN conceded that though deriving its tune and some lyric phrases from the traditional '900 Miles', some 'aspects of the lyrics seem wholly Dylanesque'. He quoted these lines: 'Used to tell my ma sometimes / When I'd see them ridin' blinds / Gonna make me a home out in the wind', but then backtracked that 'even here, the second line hints of [sic] ROBERT JOHNSON's "Walkin' Blues": "Leavin' this morning, I have to ride the blinds".'

The 'Dylanesque' lines are acutely chosen, but Heylin's conclusions mislead. First, the opening line, not derivative of any specific body of song, is the least individual of the three. Secondly, what makes the *last* line 'Dylanesque', his taking a common-stock phrase and tweaking it into something fresh—in this case taking the western folkloric 'gonna make me a home out in the west', and fusing it with the anonymous 'in the wind'—is also what's Dylanesque about the *middle* line. And we can recognise this by seeing that the point about that middle line is not that it echoes a Robert Johnson song but that it *doesn't*.

Johnson's song contains 'ride the blinds', but so do many, many other pre-war blues songs which, like Johnson's, were subsequently collected onto the re-issue albums that largely determined which of the pre-war blues-singers became known to the enthusiasts and revivalists Dylan moved among when he was young and when he left home. Indeed *at least 16* other such artists used 'Robert Johnson's' phrase on record before Johnson ever entered a studio. A 1929 harmonica instrumental record by Eddie Mapp, offering one of the great virtuoso train-imitating harmonica performances, was *titled* 'Ridin' the Blinds'. The phrase was so widespread by 1935—still before Robert Johnson recorded—that two singers could be found using it in different recordings cut in the same town on the same day: Chasey Collins (a 'Walking Blues' too) and Otto Virgial, in Chicago on Hallowe'en. And among those who had already put the expression on record before Johnson were a number of other artists Dylan has cited or sung songs by (in one case even worked with) down the years: THE MEMPHIS JUG BAND, MEMPHIS MINNIE, BLIND WILLIE McTELL, SLEEPY JOHN ESTES and BIG JOE WILLIAMS (with whom Dylan was to record three months later).

Dylan would certainly have heard the phrase on the Jenny Clayton & the Memphis Jug Band's 1927 track, 'Bob Lee Junior Blues': because this was one of the tracks reissued on HARRY SMITH's extraordinary anthology *AMERICAN FOLK MUSIC*, which came out back in 1952—and what indicates that Dylan already knew the collection by the time he put 'I Was Young When I Left Home' on tape is that the same tape and even earlier tapes by Dylan contain his versions of eight of the songs on the set. (Detailed in **earliest blues & gospel recordings, Dylan's**.)

Dylan, then, may just possibly have first heard the phrase 'ride the blinds' from Robert Johnson, but the strong likelihood is that he heard it elsewhere first. Either way, he had certainly heard enough pre-war blues by the end of 1961 to know that the phrase was recurrent—to know that he was quoting a common-stock phrase from the great body of pre-war blues lyric poetry. (See also **pre-war blues, Dylan's ways of accessing**.)

In any case, Robert Johnson's 'Walking Blues' recycles 'My Black Mama' by SON HOUSE, who was calling it 'Walking Blues' in the 1930s before Robert Johnson used the title for his own song; House's 1942 field-recorded 'Walking Blues' re-emphasises this lineage. And then, decades later, in one of those magic moments in music history, an unreleased test acetate was discovered, of House performing 'Walkin' Blues' itself, recorded at his début 1930 session. Clearly the song had been central to his repertoire in that period, when

Robert Johnson had been hanging around him listening and learning.

It does not undervalue Robert Johnson's importance as a giant figure in the history of the blues, or as an influence on Dylan, to remember that he was still a boy when Son House, CHARLEY PATTON and their contemporaries first recorded—his own recordings were *all* made in Texas in five days in 1936–37—or to stress that the phrase being traced does not originate with that great originator. On the contrary, the danger is that since we've had Dylan's word, several times over, that Johnson was a such a key figure, we may see him in Dylan's work where he does not belong—which does no service to either artist, or to understanding the blues.

Dylan touches on this himself in the 1963 poem 'My Life in a Stolen Moment': 'WOODY GUTHRIE, sure / Big Joe Williams, yeah / It's easy to remember those names / . . . What about the records you hear but one time . . . ?'

If we know, therefore, as Dylan knew, how *commonplace* a formulation is the phrase 'ride the blinds', we are then (only then) in a position to appreciate that what he does with it is the *most* original thing in the whole three-line sequence quoted from 'I Was Young When I Left Home'.

The blinds were the spaces behind the tender and between baggage-cars on the train, where, if you could jump on undetected, you could travel free. Even if you evaded assault by the railroad-man's club, it was dangerous: even more so under the carriages where, in essence, if you rolled over you killed yourself. This is why, immediately after 'Leaving this morning, I have to ride the blinds', the other half of Robert Johnson's couplet is 'Babe I been mistreated, baby and I don't mind dying.'

The very young Bob Dylan understood this, especially since the two themes in the blues that appealed to him most were death and travel, the two things that come together in 'riding the blinds'.

What's certain is that while the blues yields a score of 'ride the blinds' and 'riding the blinds', there is *no* occurrence of 'them ridin' blinds'. Dylan has invented this designation. It is not a small thing. His phrase compresses their lethal promise of opportunity, and the desperation of those needing to travel in such a way. To refer to 'them ridin' blinds' is to express foreboding anew. And in being a different formulation, in standing out, it confesses the young man's later-generation outsiderism (which Dylan makes explicit in the even earlier 'Song to Woody', concluding with 'The very last thing that I'd want to do / Is to say I been hittin' some hard travelin' too.') On 'I Was Young When I Left Home', that '*When I'd see* them' adds the confirming touch: he'd see them but he'd not say he'd 'ride the blinds' himself.

[Bob Dylan: 'I Was Young When I Left Home', Minneapolis, 22 Dec 1961, the *Bootleg Series Vol. 7—No Direction Home: The Soundtrack*, Columbia Legacy 520358 2, NY, 2005.

Eddie Mapp & His Harmonica: 'Riding the Blinds', Long Island City, NY, c.May 1929. Memphis Jug Band: 'Bob Lee Junior Blues', Atlanta, 19 Oct 1927, *American Folk Music*, Folkways FP 251-3, NY, 1952. Sleepy John Estes: 'Broken-Hearted, Ragged and Dirty Too', Memphis, 26 Sep 1929, *The Memphis Area, 1927–1932*, Roots RL-307, Vienna, c.1968. Blind Willie McTell: 'Travelin' Blues' & 'Come On Around To My House Mama', Atlanta, 30 Oct 1929. Son House: 'My Black Mama Part 1', 'My Black Mama Part 2' & 'Walking Blues', Grafton, WI, 28 May 1930; 'Walking Blues', Robinsonville, Mississippi, 17 Jul 1942, CD-reissued *Son House: The Complete Library of Congress Sessions 1941–1942, Travelin' Man TM CD 02*, Crawley, UK, 1990. Memphis Minnie: 'Chickasaw Train Blues', Chicago, 24 Aug 1934, *Out Came the Blues*, Coral CP-58, London, 1970. Big Joe Williams: 'Little Leg Woman', Chicago, 25 Feb 1935, *Lonesome Road Blues: 15 Years in the Mississippi Delta*, Yazoo L-1038, NY, 1973. Chasey Collins: 'Walking Blues', Chicago, 31 Oct 1935, *The Country Fiddlers*, Roots RL-316, Vienna, c.1968; Otto Virgial: 'Little Girl in Rome', Chicago, 31 Oct 1935, Mississippi Bottom Blues, Mamlish Records S-3802, NY, c.1973.

Then comes Robert Johnson: 'Walking Blues', San Antonio, 27 Nov 1936, *Robert Johnson: King of the Delta Blues Singers*, Columbia Records CL-1654, NY, 1961.

After him, among many others, come Tampa Red: 'Seminole Blues': Aurora, IL, 11 Oct 1937, *Tampa Red: Bottleneck Guitar, 1928–1937*, Yazoo L-1039, NY, 1973. Blind Boy Fuller: 'Step It Up and Go', NY, 5 Mar 1940, *Blind Boy Fuller with Sonny Terry and Bull City Red*, Blues Classics BC-11, Berkeley, CA, 1966.

(NB. The *first* to record these hard travel blues had been women: Trixie Smith: 'Freight Train Blues', NY, c.May 1924, Trixie Smith: *Masters of the Blues, Vol. 5*, Collectors Classics CC-29, Copenhagen, c.1971, & Clara Smith: 'Freight Train Blues', NY, 30 Sep 1924, Clara Smith: *Volume Three*, VJM VLP-17, London, 1969.)

Clinton Heylin: 'Them Ridin' Blinds', *Telegraph* no. 27, Romford, UK, summer 1987.]

Riley, Billy Lee [1933 -] William Lee Riley was born into a family of sharecroppers in Pocohontas, Arkansas, on October 5, 1933. He was a country singer who wanted to be a blues singer but ended up in Memphis doing rockabilly for Sam Phillips at Sun from late 1956 until he left to form his own label, Rita, in 1960. He was a session-man and multi-instrumentalist (quite good on bluesy harmonica); JERRY LEE LEWIS and Charlie Rich played piano on Riley's records, the best-known being his 1957 titles 'Red Hot' and (as by Billy Lee Riley and his Little Green Men) 'Flyin' Saucers Rock'n'Roll'. He also revived the 1940s hit 'Open the Door, Richard', a title Dylan makes into the refrain of his own 1967 song 'Open the Door, Homer' (see separate entry).

More importantly, Riley is the man who had the gumption to turn on the tape recorder when Sam Phillips and fundamentalist Bible-study boy Jerry Lee were discussing the evils of secular music at the Sun session that later yielded Lewis' 'Great Balls of Fire' (a discussion first issued on a Dutch bootleg in the 1970s), and more than a decade later he was a guest performer at ELVIS and Priscilla Presley's New Year's Eve Party at the Thunderbird Lounge, Memphis, in 1968.

In the end he was able to cut records in every genre he liked: as one rock historian catalogued it, he 'recorded country for Sun, Mojo, Pen, Hip, Sun International, Entrance, backwoods blues for Rita, R&B for Dodge, Checker and Hip, rock for Brunswick and Home of the Blues, and soul for Smash, Fire, Fury, Mojo and Myrl.' He cut many of his blues sides, including 'Repossession Blues', under the pseudonym Lightnin' Leon. In the 1960s he moved to LA and did session-work and in the 1970s-80s toured Europe many times.

Bob Dylan sang 'Repossession Blues' at a rehearsal for the 1978 World Tour in Santa Monica (February 1, 1978) and subsequently twice in concert (in Osaka, February 24 and Tokyo four nights later), and he performed Riley's 'Rock with Me Baby' at six US concerts in 1986.

On September 8, 1992, when Dylan's Never-Ending Tour hit Riley's home patch of Little Rock, Arkansas, Bob brought Billy on stage as a guest. He was introduced fulsomely by Dylan, who stayed on stage to play back-up guitar as Riley sang 'Red Hot'. Riley went on from this heartening evening's encounter to re-activate his own performing career. The Smithsonian interviewed him for their archives and he released his first all-blues CD, *Blue Collar Blues*, that same year. Now based in Newport, Arkansas, he gives combination lecture-concerts about the blues, the Mississippi Delta and his childhood as a sharecropper. He disappoints everyone who admired his work by revealing that he regards working with Sammy Davis Jr. in the 1960s as a high point of his career.

[Billy Lee Riley: 'Flyin' Saucers Rock'n'Roll', Memphis, TN, 11 Dec 1956 (w Jerry Lee Lewis), Sun 260, Memphis, 1957, reissued *The Sun Story 1952–1968*, Sun 6641 180, London, 1974; 'Red Hot', Memphis, 1957, Sun 277, Memphis, 1957; 2-CD set *Classic Recordings 1956–1960, Including the Complete Sun Recordings*, Bear Family BCD 15444-BH, Vollersode, Germany, c.1990; *Blue Collar Blues*, Hightone HCD 8040, US, 1992; 'Repossession Blues', *nia*, Rita 1005, US, 1960. Lewis-Phillips discussion 1st issued *Good Rocking Tonight*, Bopcat LP-100, Holland, 1970s.]

Rimbaud, Arthur [1854 - 1891] Jean-Nicholas-Arthur Rimbaud, the most original French symbolist poet and a romantic tragic hero, was born in Charleville, in the Ardennes, France, on October 20, 1854. He became 'the bad boy of 19th century poetry', lured PAUL VERLAINE away from his wife and baby at the age of 16, published groundbreaking poetry, lived a life of alcoholic and druggy excess, got shot in the hand by Verlaine and by the age of 21 had given up literature to explore the world and go gun-running.

The year he initiated meeting Verlaine, 1871, he published his best-known single poem, 'Le Bâteau Ivre' ('The Drunken Boat'), and after running away from their wild and stormy relationship he assembled a collection of poetry and prose pieces, *Une Saison en Enfer* (*A Season in Hell*), in 1873. Later, in England, he completed the prose-poems collections *Illuminations* before burning his remaining manuscripts and abandoning writing.

It was, touchingly, Verlaine who kept trying to bring Rimbaud's poetry to the world's attention. In 1884 he included a Rimbaud selection plus an essay about the younger poet in his collection *Les Poètes Maudits* (*The Accursed Poets*); in 1886 he published Rimbaud's *Illuminations*; and in 1895 it was Verlaine who published the posthumous *Poésies Complètes*. This was selfless not only because Rimbaud had ended their personal relationship (granted, Verlaine shot and injured the teenage Rimbaud during their quarrels) but because Rimbaud's work was the more original of the two, and for Verlaine to publish it was to make his own poetry seem old-fashioned and pedestrian.

Dylan mentions the relationship between Rimbaud and Verlaine in the *Blood on the Tracks* song 'You're Gonna Make Me Lonesome When You Go'. Perhaps there's a glancing allusion to Rimbaud's 'Le Bâteau Ivre' in Dylan's line from 'Dignity', 'I'm on the rollin' river in a jerkin' boat', and perhaps a similar echo discernible behind those quietly great two lines from 1978's *Street Legal* song 'True Love Tends to Forget', where he sings that 'This weekend in hell / Is makin' me sweat'. In his liner notes to the *Desire* album, Dylan writes: 'Where do I begin . . . on the heels of Rimbaud . . .' and Rimbaud gets a 'thanks' on the credits of the 'Hard Rain' TV film. He even called one of his guitars Rimbaud (a white National electric).

Dylan has famously quoted Rimbaud's motto 'I is another'—'It's like Rimbaud said, "I is another"'—and in *Chronicles Volume One* he refers to first encountering this early in his New York years, courtesy of SUZE ROTOLO: '. . . someplace along the line Suze had also introduced me to the poetry of French symbolist poet Arthur Rimbaud. That was a big deal . . . I came across one of his letters called "Je est un autre," which translates into "I is someone else." When I read those words the bells went off. It made perfect sense.'

More fundamentally, Rimbaud can be said to have created the very idea of the modern poet—personifying the kind of poet that all THE BEATS, and following on from them, Dylan, wanted to be. Rimbaud's stance includes a recognisably modern insistence on the validity of low culture, of subcultures, as well as high. Rimbaud wrote this, and it's easy to see how readily it is taken forward into the consciousness of the Bob Dylan of both *Tarantula* and of *"Love and Theft"*:

'For a long time I found the celebrities of modern painting and poetry ridiculous. I loved absurd pictures, fanlights, stage scenery, mountebanks backcloths, inn-signs, cheap colored prints; unfashionable literature, church Latin, pornographic books badly spelt, grandmothers novels, fairy stories, little books for children, old operas, empty refrains, simple rhythms.'

Other contemporary figures on the rock/poetry edge who have declared their allegiance to Rimbaud include Jim Morrison, PATTI SMITH and VAN MORRISON (who namechecks him in the splendid 'Tore Down à la Rimbaud'). Less interestingly, Christopher Hampton's play *Total Eclipse*, first produced in 1968, became the panting Hollywood movie of the same name in 1995—tagline 'Touched by Genius. Cursed by Madness. Blinded by Love.'—starring David Thewlis as Verlaine and Leonardo di Caprio as Rimbaud.

At first, having abandoned literature, Rimbaud became, rather unromatically, a teacher in Germany, but after that he worked on the docks in Marseilles, joined the Dutch army but deserted in Sumatra, traveled through Java, today's Yemen, Ethiopia, Egypt and elsewhere, becoming the first European to enter part of what is now Somalia, and leading traders' caravans trekking through dangerous places. Mostly he was working for French import-export companies, trading in everything from household objects to guns and ammunition. It's quite possible that he was dealing in slaves, too.

Rimbaud had a cancerous leg amputated in early 1891 and died in Marseilles that November 10. He was barely 37.

(See also **French symbolist poets, the**.)

[Arthur Rimbaud, *Complete Works*, 1976; *Rimbaud Complete Works: Selected Letters*, 1987. The 'bad boy' quote is from Judy Stone, *San Francisco Chronicle, nia*, seen online 12 Sep 2005 at *www.rimbaud.freeserve.co.uk/page14.htm*. Van Morrison, 'Tore Down à la Rimbaud', *A Sense of Wonder*, 1984. *Total Eclipse*, dir. Agnieszka Holland, US, 1995. Bob Dylan, quote from *Biograph* box set interview, 1985; *Chronicles Volume One*, p.288. Rimbaud guitar name, Joel Bernstein interviewed by John Bauldie, *The Telegraph* no.35, Romford, UK, spring 1995.]

Ringwald, Molly [1968 -] Molly Ringwald was born on February 18, 1968 in Roseville, California. A Hollywood actor who appeared on stage at age five as the dormouse in *Alice in Wonderland*, she made an album at six, came to fame as one of the so-called Brat-Pack via her starring rôle in *Pretty in Pink* and turned down the lead rôle in *Pretty Woman*.

In 1990 she played the female romantic lead—and Dylan had the grace not to try to play the male romantic lead—in the ludicrous piece of froth that was the promo video for the doomed single 'Unbelievable', taken from the album *Under the Red Sky*. The video was filmed in the Mojave Desert on June 24, 1990, with Molly looking pale and uninteresting; co-stars were Rob Bogue (now a regular on soap opera *Guiding Light*) and SALLY KIRKLAND.

['Unbelievable', dir. Paris Barclay, US, 1990.]

Rinzler, Alan [1938 -] Alan Rinzler was born in New York City on October 26, 1938, a cousin of the great folklorist RALPH RINZLER. Alan went into publishing and has been a book editor since 1962, the year he first took an interest in Dylan's work. One of his earliest projects was to edit the *Young Folk Song Book*, which came out in 1963 and which he believes marked Dylan's first appearance in any book. The book had sections on JOAN BAEZ, Dylan, RAMBLIN' JACK ELLIOTT, THE GREENBRIAR BOYS, THE NEW LOST CITY RAMBLERS and Peggy Seeger. There was also 'An Appreciation' by Rinzler's cousin Ralph and an 'Introduction' by PETE SEEGER. Curiously, the book was copyrighted to 'The Society for Traditional Music, Inc., friends of old time music'. The book gave lyrics and musical notation (all arrangements by Earl Robinson) to a handful of songs by each of the artists, plus a short prose introduction. In Dylan's case the intro was by ROBERT SHELTON and the songs were 'Song to Woody', 'Fare Thee Well', 'The Ballad of Hollis Brown', 'Boots of Spanish Leather' and 'Masters of War'.

Rinzler has also published books by WOODY GUTHRIE, Pete Seeger, ANDY WARHOL, HUNTER S. THOMPSON, Toni Morrison, Robert Ludlum and many others. In 1978 he wrote and published the large-format paperback *Bob Dylan: The Illustrated Record*, which was indeed lavishly illustrated. The text was scissors-and-paste, and its song analysis brutish, but the idea was highly appealing and simple: to tell the Dylan career story album by album, reproducing not only the front cover of every LP—up to and including 1978's *Street Legal*—but augmenting it with beautifully chosen and in some cases previously unseen photographs of what was going on in the artist's life at the time. Spread across glossy pages that were 11 inches by 11, the book was a visual feast that must have been extremely expensive to publish. An Italian hardback was published in 1980, with a translated text, but the English-language edition has never been reissued. Not to be confused with the similarly titled *Bob Dylan: An Illustrated History* by Michael Gross.

[Alan Rinzler, *Young Folk Song Book*, New York: Simon & Schuster, 1963; *Bob Dylan: The Illustrated Record*, New York: Harmony Books, 1978. Italian hardback edition *Bob Dylan: Profeta, poeta, musicista e mito*, trans. Massimo Villa, Milan: Sonzogno, 1980.]

Rinzler, Ralph [1934 - 1994] Ralph Carter Rinzler was born in New York City on July 20, 1934. By the age of seven he was listening to Library of Congress field recordings and as a Swarthmore

College freshman he was inspired to teach himself the banjo after hearing PETE SEEGER play. Like many others in the folk revival movement, he leaned for some of his own early repertoire on HARRY SMITH's *AMERICAN FOLK MUSIC* anthology, and later catalogued the 1,500 items in the Harry Smith collection of recordings, which was held by the New York City Public Library.

Rinzler became a significant North American folklorist who made important field recordings of DOC WATSON, CLARENCE ASHLEY, Bill Monroe and others, was instrumental in bringing Ashley's traditional musicians, including Watson, into the folk revival scene as live performers in 1961, and ran their management from his base on West 3rd Street in Greenwich Village. He became the man who interpreted bluegrass for college intellectual types. He was also a field collector for Folkways Records and eventually the founding director of the Office of Folklife Programs at the Smithsonian Institution, where he co-founded its annual summer Festival of American Folklife on the Mall in Washington, D.C.

He was also a musician in his own right, and a well-known figure around the Village when Dylan first arrived there in the very early 1960s. Though for some time he retained his day-job handling complaints at Pan American, he was a member, with JOHN HERALD and BOB YELLIN, of THE GREENBRIAR BOYS, in which he played mandolin, when Dylan was their support act at Gerde's Folk City in September 1961. There is a widely used, slightly blurry photograph by JOHN COHEN, taken at the Gaslight in 1962, that shows Rinzler, Dylan and Herald on stage together. Rinzler looks like a Depression-era Texas store-owner, while Dylan is doing his Huck Finn act and Herald looks like a Buster Keaton imitator in a 1920s minstrel show.

Dylan liked the Greenbriar Boys but he singles out Ralph Rinzler as having been the source of the song 'Roll on John', which he performs in early 1962 for radio station WBAI in New York. Within a performance of 11 songs, plus much talk in between them, most of which has Dylan mythologizing himself with good-humoured chutzpah, his respectful citing of Rinzler is unusually straightforward.

In 1961 Rinzler was, with JOHN COHEN and IZZY YOUNG, a founder of the Friends of Old Time Music, formed to bring traditional performers to New York audiences. Rinzler was also one of the directors of the NEWPORT FOLK FESTIVAL Foundation, and hence one of the team selecting the artists for the festival—including the 1965 festival (for which, with ROBERT SHELTON, he co-edited the Festival Program book that featured Dylan's prose-poem 'Off the Top of My Head'), though as its Director of Field Research Programs he was mainly responsible for the traditional music side of things; he was funded by the Foundation to make field recording trips, and often brought back tapes he'd made of unknown performers to play to the rest of the selection board.

Rinzler was not, however, against electric music, and that same year appeared as a musician on JOAN BAEZ's album *Farewell Angelina* alongside BRUCE LANGHORNE and RUSS SAVAKUS, who each played on Dylan's pioneering electric albums that year too (Langhorne on *Bringing It All Back Home* and Savakus on *Highway 61 Revisited*).

Nor was his Washington Festival of Folk Life free from adverse criticism in the second half of the 1960s, but BERNICE REAGON JOHNSON pays him this tribute, while explaining that festival's raison d'être:

> 'He was a brilliant organizer. . . . The Smithsonian Festival of American Folklife, actually, was an effort to put something on the Mall in Washington so American tourists could walk through America, and in their minds everything on the mall would be American. No matter what it looked like, no matter what the language was, you would walk from this area to that area, to the other area . . . and everywhere you went, everybody was from America. . . . You could go back to your all-white neighborhood, and you would not be taking all of these different kind of people. But maybe, you would actually remember you had a good time. . . . Some white people are so anxiety-ridden when faced with the truth about this country as a home to many cultures and races and ethnic groups. They cling to a mythology of a white America. . . . Rinzler tried to combat that mentality . . .
>
> 'On the other hand, this festival was considered "artificial" by some people. The folklorists at that time (and we are talking about the late sixties), were saying: "festivals that you study should come up out of the culture." They didn't like academically-trained people creating "artificial" festivals.'

(Johnson and Rinzler both ended up as heads of department at the Smithsonian.)

Ralph Rinzler died in Washington, D.C., on July 2, 1994, aged 59. At the time of his death he was still working with MIKE SEEGER on the project to reissue the Harry Smith anthology. This came to fruition later. In his memory, the Smithsonian created the vast Ralph Rinzler Folklife Archives and Collections at the Center for Folklife and Cultural Heritage.

[Bob Dylan: 'Roll on, John', NY, prob. 13 Jan 1962, broadcast WBAI, NY, 11 Mar 1962. Bernice Reagon Johnson, interview in *Radical History Review* no.68, NY, date not given, seen online 25 Sep 2005 at *http://chnm.gmu.edu/rhr/interview.htm*.]

Ripley, Steve [1950 -] Paul Steven Ripley was born in Boise, Idaho, on January 1, 1950, but went to high school in Glencoe, Oklahoma. His group the Tractors' website claims him as an 'Oklahoma native', and that he grew up on the family farm before studio-engineering for LEON RUSSELL.

Also a singer, songwriter and self-proclaimed inventor as well as a guitarist, he has produced records for Freddy Fender, Johnny Lee Wills and Gatemouth Brown, and played with J.J. Cale. Though he often plays a 1954 Martin guitar himself, he has designed a range of custom-made instruments for other people—including Ry Cooder and John Hiatt.

Introduced to Dylan by drummer JIM KELTNER, a friend, he first played guitar with Dylan as a session musician for what became the *Shot of Love* album (starting in Santa Monica on March 11, 1981—at which Dylan performed early versions of 'Shot of Love' and 'You Changed My Life': versions that have not circulated). He plays on the recordings of 'Angelina' and 'You Changed My Life' issued on the *Bootleg Series Vols. 1–3* in 1991 (but probably not on that collection's 'Need a Woman'), on the circulated outtake of 'Caribbean Wind' from March 31 and the version issued on *Biograph* in 1985, on the circulated but unreleased tracks cut in April and May 1981 (plus more uncirculated tracks from these sessions), on the 'Let It Be Me' single recorded on May 1 and released only in Europe, on 'Groom's Still Waiting at the Altar' and on some but not all of the issued album tracks.

He then joined Dylan's 1981 tour band, playing second guitar to FRED TACKETT (who'd been with Dylan's earlier gospel bands) from the year's first concert, in Chicago on June 10, right through to the last, on November 21 in Lakeland, Florida: and on October 16, in Milwaukee, he sang 'Gypsy Blood', backed by Dylan & the rest of the band.

Nine years later he reappeared, joining the band when G.E. SMITH was in the process of leaving it, and played four 1990 concerts: Oklahoma City on September 4, two nights later in Dallas, two nights later in San Antonio, Texas, and finally the concert on September 9 in Austin. (The first two of these four opened with instrumental performances of 'Old MacDonald Had a Farm' and the last two with instrumental versions of the 'Marine Hymn'.) The following year he was back again, augmenting the band at Dylan's Tulsa, Oklahoma, concert on October 30, 1991.

[*www.thetractors.com*; birthplace & birthdate from *www.wikipedia.com*.]

Rivera, Scarlet [19?? -] Bob Dylan picked Scarlet Rivera up on 13th Street, in New York City. He stopped his car to speak to her, because she was so striking. Manhattan is full of determined-looking, skinny-limbed young women striding along carrying violins or saxophones, but they don't usually have hair three foot long swinging down behind them. Dylan asked if she could play her fiddle, and she proved she could, auditioning on the spot and later that evening. She was working in a salsa band in the city, but she'd come from Chicago. Next day she was plunged into the early chaotic sessions for *Desire*. It was her first time in a studio.

Scarlet stayed the course, not only playing on *Desire* but on both the Rolling Thunder Revue tours, and adding, live and in the studio, tremendous texture to the sound. She was capable of duetting with Dylan's harmonica as few other players of any instrument have, so that these two thin, vibrant, scrapey sounds sparked spontaneous dancing lines off each other, mimicked each other, flirting in quick flashes, to a degree that is all too utterly absent from any Dylan on stage performance in the 21st century. By virtue of her mid-1970s sessions and touring with him, she also appears on tracks on the *Biograph* box set of 1985, the *Bootleg Series Vols. 1–3* (1991) and the *Bootleg Series Vol. 5: Bob Dylan Live 1975* (2002), on the *Hard Rain* album and the *Renaldo & Clara* film, not least when she's running down the ghastly brick-work hallways backstage somewhere, like a whippet in a little black dress, trying to find the stage, anxious that she's going to be late on.

Scarlet was also one of the smaller group with Dylan for the 'Tribute to JOHN HAMMOND' TV Special at WTTW's National Educational Television Studios in Chicago on September 10, 1975 (for transmission that December 13), at which, ROBERT SHELTON reports, 'Observers were fascinated with the violinist in a long dress, with dark gypsy eyes and flowing hair. Some believed her to be a real gypsy Dylan had discovered walking along Second Avenue with her violin case. Some Chicagoans recognized her as Donna Shea, who had been on their local rock scene in the late 1960s.'

RONNIE HAWKINS used to claim that Rivera 'ran off with Darlin' Doug [DAVID MANSFIELD].' He must have meant temporarily, in the course of the Rolling Thunder Revues; Mansfield stayed on with Dylan through the entire 1978 World Tour, and Rivera wasn't around then.

In 1978, following up her eponymously titled 1977 début solo album, she released a second, *Scarlet Fever*, on Warner Brothers. In due course she played on TRACY CHAPMAN's *Crossroads*, Keb Mo's *The Door* and Stanley Clarke's *Just Family*, among others. In 1993, by now married to the Sheffield-born British keyboards session player Tommy Eyre, whom she'd met at the Montreux Festival in 1988, they both played on the Melanie Harrold & Olly Blanchflower album *Instinctive behaviour*. Scarlet's own album *Magical Christmas*, produced by Eyre, came out in 1997, followed by the New Age music of *Behind the Crimson Veil*, 1998, credited to Eyre & Rivera, and played by the two of them plus percussionist BOBBYE HALL. The same year saw two more double-billed CDs, *Celtic Myst*, with Lesa MacEwan on vocals, and *Celtic Dreams*, with Richard Cook on uilean pipes. Two further Christmas albums followed. In November 1999 Scarlet Rivera was among the performers at the Baked Potato 1999 Angel Award ceremony for Miles Davis and Santana lead vocalist Alex Ligertwood.

Tommy Eyre, diagnosed with cancer, died on May 23, 2001. In 2002 the following was posted as part of an event in Malibu on August 30: 'GO-VEGAN-FOR-THE-ENVIRONMENT ALL-STAR BAND—FEATURING—SCARLET RIVERA [YES, THE SCARLET RIVERA PLAYING VIOLIN ON THE BOB DYLAN ALBUMS . . . TOURING . . . WITH THE INDIGO GIRLS, AND THE DUKE ELLINGTON ORCHESTRA . . . AND HEADLINING THE 50TH ANNIVERSARY OF THE UN IN GENEVA].'

In 2006 Scarlet Rivera appeared as a 'special guest' on the Dylan tribute band Highway 61 Revisited's misleadingly titled CD *Bob Dylan 1975–1981, Rolling Thunder and the Gospel Years*—which contains neither Bob Dylan nor any of his songs.

[Scarlet Rivera: *Scarlet Rivera*, US, 1977; *Scarlet Fever*, Warner Bros BSK 3174, US, 1978; *Magical Christmas*, BCI, 1997. Scarlet Rivera & Tommy Eyre: *Behind the Crimson Veil*, BCI, 1998; *Celtic Myst*, BCI, 1998; *Celtic Dreams*, BCI, 1998. *Highway 61 Revisited*, Highway 61 Entertainment BD0503, US, 2006. Robert Shelton, *No Direction Home: The Life and Music of Bob Dylan*, London: Penguin edn., 1987, p.449. Ronnie Hawkins quote from interview by this writer, St. Johns, Newfoundland, fall 1985, collected as '1976 & Other Times: Ronnie Hawkins, Rock'n'Roller' in Michael Gray & John Bauldie, *All Across the Telegraph: A Bob Dylan Handbook*, London: W.H. Allen, 1987.]

Rix, Luther [1942 -] Luther Rix was born in Lansing, Michigan, on February 11, 1942, took Music Business Studies at Indiana University, a post-graduate degree at the Jordan Conservatory of Music (renamed the Jordan College of Fine Arts in 1978) at Butler University, Indiana, and then worked as a percussionist and timpanist first for the Indianapolis Symphony Orchestra and then the Winter Consort in New York City. He broke into session-work as a drummer and composer, and has played with everyone from ELVIS COSTELLO to Manhattan Transfer and from Lonnie Mack to BETTE MIDLER.

Rix was the percussionist and conga player on the first Rolling Thunder Revue, in 1975. SAM SHEPARD noted in his *Rolling Thunder Logbook* that Rix meditated before every set, and seemed very much a 'jazz soul'. He was unavailable for the 1976 Rolling Thunder Revue because of a prior booking to play with LEONARD COHEN in Europe.

[Source re prior engagement: Gary Burke, e-mail to this writer, 12 Jan 2006.]

Robbins, Hargus 'Pig' [1938 -] Hargus Melvin Robbins was born on January 18, 1938 at Spring City, Tennessee, in a house without electricity. At age two or three, he stabbed himself in the eye with a pocket knife and despite specialist treatment in Chattanooga, not only was that eye removed but he became blind in the other by the age of four. He has said that he remembers only the colour green, the colour of his parents' car. He took piano lessons at the Tennessee School for the Blind in Nashville from the age of seven, abandoning his lessons at 15 to play clubs instead, breaking into recording in 1959 with country star George Jones and in time becoming one of that city's top session players. He's made a number of albums under his own name too, starting with *A Bit of Country Piano* in 1963. His list of credits is absurdly long and really does cover everyone, including JOAN BAEZ (*Any Day Now*, 1968), Country Joe MacDonald (*Thinking of WOODY GUTHRIE*, 1969) and THE EVERLY BROTHERS (*Pass the Chicken*, 1973), and in the mid-1980s he toured with NEIL YOUNG—but his career really kicked off when Bob Dylan descended on Nashville in 1966.

Robbins is the pianist on the Nashville sessions for *Blonde on Blonde*, recorded that February and March. AL KOOPER writes in the booklet inside the *Bootleg Series Vol. 7—No Direction Home: The Soundtrack* (2005) that Dylan had to speak to him through an intermediary—Kooper, generally—saying: 'You do it. I can't call that guy "pig".'

[Main source: 'Century of Country: the Definitive Country Music Encyclopedia', seen online 4 Jun 2005 at *www.countryworks.com/artist_full.asp?KEY=ROBBINS*.]

Robertson, Robbie [1943 -] Jaime Robert Robertson was born on July 5, 1943 in Toronto, but since his mother was a Mohawk Indian, he also spent time south of the city at the Six Nations Reservation, where she had grown up. He learnt guitar as a child, attracted first to country music. He quit school to try for a career in music, and is supposed to have joined RONNIE HAWKINS & THE HAWKS in 1958, aged only 15.

Soon he was the prolific writer of the group, and remained so as LEVON & the Hawks, freed from Hawkins' narrow track, made their own records and kept working. The main story of how this talented but undistinguished unit turned into THE BAND is told in the main entry on the group. But Robertson's was a special rôle: his was the ambition, the facility on guitar, the heart-throb good looks, the manipulative capacity, the songwriter's gift. At first these were all placed in the service of a band that was the exemplar of the co-operative unit, and the results were spectacular.

They were also spectacular when Robertson's talents as a guitarist, and as a sort of vice-captain, were put to work for Bob Dylan, whom he and the rest of the Hawks met in 1965. A few weeks after Dylan had 'gone electric' at the NEWPORT FOLK FESTIVAL, Robertson was on stage with him (along with AL KOOPER, Harvey Brooks (aka HARVEY GOLDSTEIN) and Levon Helm) for the first of the half-acoustic-solo, half-electric concerts Dylan undertook, at Forest Hills on August 28. It's uncertain how many such concerts took place in this initial period, but it's known that after rehearsals with them in Woodstock, NY, in September, Dylan's group became all five of the Hawks from September 24, in Austin, Texas, till November 28 in Washington, D.C. After that night, Levon Helm quit: quit Dylan and the group, and went back home to Arkansas. He was replaced by BOBBY GREGG at the next gig, which was right across the other side of the country in Seattle, Washington, at the beginning of December.

By this time, Robertson and the others had also been in the studio with Dylan, beginning with a session in New York City on October 5th. This session produced nothing that was released at the time, but retrospectively they have yielded 'I Wanna Be Your Lover' and the tiny 'Jet Pilot' on *Biograph* (1985) and 'Medicine Sunday', issued on the still relatively obscure *Highway 61 Interactive* CD-Rom (1995). They returned to the studios (minus Helm) on November 30 and cut the single 'Can *You* Please Crawl Out Your Window?' (and, almost 40 years later, the version of 'Visions of Johanna' released on *Bootleg Series Vol. 7: No Direction Home*).

Robertson had already gained a relationship to Dylan that none of the other Hawks enjoyed (and that not all would have wanted). He had become the right-hand man, assuming the rôle BOBBY NEUWIRTH had filled on Dylan's tour of Britain earlier that year (captured in D.A. PENNEBAKER's film *Don't Look Back*). So it is that it is Robbie standing with Dylan, Michael McClure and ALLEN GINSBERG in Larry Keenan's telling shot taken in the alley behind City Lights Books in San Francisco when Dylan is there for his press-conference that December 3.

So it is too that in January 1966 Robertson is back in the studio with Dylan even when the other Hawks aren't. DANKO, MANUEL and HUDSON are there too on January 21–22, recording the great 'She's Your Lover Now' (issued on *Bootleg Series Vols. 1–3*, 1991); but on January 25–26, when the *Blonde on Blonde* track 'Sooner or Later (One of Us Must Know)' is recorded, along with the early outtake of 'Leopard-Skin Pill-Box Hat' that surfaces on *Bootleg Series Vol. 7* in 2005, the Hawks present are down to Robertson and Danko, and it's the same on January 27–28.

Robertson has not been included in the names listed for the next *Blonde on Blonde* sessions (February 12–17), but Al Kooper, who was there, says he was present and so does CLINTON HEYLIN (who wasn't there but always has firm opinions). Thus the lead guitarist on the album version of 'Visions of Johanna' is Robbie Robertson, as he is on 'Obviously 5 Believers'; and despite what it said on the original album, the lead guitarist on 'Leopard-Skin Pill-Box Hat'—meaning the one who takes the guitar solo—is Robertson again. Dylan plays only the opening notes at the start of the track (Band guest book, June 16, 2000).

Then comes Dylan's 1966 tour, and while all the Hawks except Levon Helm are on stage, the rest of the time, as we see in the elusive movie covering the European leg of this tour, *Eat the Document*, it's Robbie Robertson who is the crony at Dylan's side as they walk around the world throwing their weight about. And in March, when Dylan is in Nashville, Tennessee, for further *Blonde on Blonde* sessions, Robertson is, like Al Kooper but unlike any of the rest of the Hawks, in there amongst the Nashville session musicians, contributing to the laying down of 'Absolutely Sweet Marie' on the 7th, 'Pledging My Time' and 'Just Like a Woman' on the 8th, and six further tracks on the 9th-to-10th: 'Most Likely You Go Your Way (And I'll Go Mine)', 'Temporary Like Achilles', 'Rainy Day Women # 12 & 35', 'Leopard-Skin Pill-Box Hat' and 'I Want You'. According to Kooper, Dylan had insisted that if he were to go down to Nashville to record (which was producer BOB JOHNSTON's idea), Robertson and Kooper had to come too.

A couple of days later, running into the early hours of March 13, ROBERT SHELTON tape-records Dylan and Robertson in a Denver hotel room, going through songs together and working out guitar arrangements; and though one of the songs, 'Sad-Eyed Lady of the Lowlands', had already been recorded for *Blonde on Blonde* in the middle of the previous month (without Robertson), here Dylan seems to be teaching Robertson the song.

On stage, through the wild last months of this most out-on-the-edge, unprecedented tour, the Helmless Hawks plus drummer MICKEY JONES makes for a magnificent cohesive unit, yet there's no doubting that Robbie Robertson's lead electric guitar lines set a blazing high standard, catching and matching all Dylan's demands.

In the contrasting backwoods calm of Woodstock in 1967, when, with and without Dylan, the Basement Tapes were being laid down, Robertson was both solidifying his guitar-work (often bringing much to a track without trying to attract any particular attention) and maturing as a songwriter at the same time as the group was turning inexorably into The Band. Songs composed by Robertson and tried out at this time included 'Caledonia Mission' and 'Ferdinand the Imposter'—but there were also joint compositions with Richard Manuel, 'Ruben Remus' and 'Katie's Been Gone', and back then it looked as if the group's great strength as a co-operative unit was going to include its songwriting too. At the time of the first sessions for The Band's début album, *Music from Big Pink*, it still looked as if Robertson's greater facility for turning out songs might have been something cyclical, something that came and went, and that maybe in a few months' time, Manuel or even Danko and Helm might be just as strongly on-stream as writers. It also seemed, perhaps, as though if Robertson's writing was a particular strength of his, singing was a corresponding weakness, so that things still seemed well-balanced all round between the five members of this ultra-talented group.

And all-round balance did indeed characterise the first two—the great—Band albums. The songs on *Big Pink* included a Dylan song, a Dylan-Manuel song, a Dylan-Danko song, an outsider song (the wonderful 'Long Black Veil'), three songs by Manuel alone and four by Robertson: 'To Kingdom Come', 'Caledonia Mission', 'The Weight' and 'Chest Fever'. For the second album, *The Band*, Robertson as writer was more omni-present—seven songs were composed by him alone, and they included the superb 'The Night They Drove Old Dixie Down'—but the co-operative spirit still seemed intact: he had also co-written several songs with Richard Manuel and one with Levon Helm, while as a musician his contribution seemed counter-balancingly modest; he was the only one to stick to a single instrument, and his voice wasn't on the album at all.

Yet something was happening here: as The Band became a mega-successful group, Robbie Robertson's ambition was setting him apart; his business sense did the same, and the more he came to dominate the group, especially in becoming its prime, virtually its sole, songwriter, the less democratic the ethos became—and the more his royalties exceeded those of the other musicians. Levon Helm's book *This Wheel's on Fire*, 1993, expresses vast amounts of pain and unforgiving anger on this whole subject: a subject that is inextricably linked with the demise of the group's ability to keep on making crucial albums. From the third album, in 1970, it's downhill. *Stage Fright* disappoints everyone; and from *Stage Fright* onwards, more or less every song recorded by The Band is a J.R. Robertson composition.

Despite the ego and ambition, Robertson remains willing to return to a back-up rôle when Dylan calls. Thus the Hawks are there at the WOODY GUTHRIE Memorial Concert in January 1968, and they're there at the Isle of Wight Festival in August 1969 (two weeks after starring in their own right at Woodstock). More significantly, they go back into the studios with Dylan in November 1973 to give him the music, the sound, on his underrated album *Planet Waves*, a bright strength of which is Robbie Robertson's never-faltering, intelligent, beguiling guitar-work, a unique noise yet still retaining his gutsy homage to the 1950s work of Hubert Sumlin behind HOWLIN' WOLF. And to listen to the shimmering, edgy, perfectly attuned duet between Dylan's piano and Robertson's guitar, out there alone on an aural high-wire on 'Dirge' is to hear what long-term musical togetherness can yield between two engaged musicians.

After the album, the tour: the huge Dylan & The Band comeback tour of 1974 through North America, and the double-LP that came from it, *Before the Flood*. Then in 1975 we get the release of the official double-LP version of *The Basement Tapes*, an unhappy mixing up of tracks with and without Dylan that reveals (though only later) an almost compulsive, and a slightly shocking, lack of respect on Robbie Robertson's part for the truth about how things had been. For it is Robertson who makes the track selection, apparently, and Robertson who insinuates onto the album tracks by the group that are not from the Basement Tapes sessions at all! One of these, 'Bessie Smith', is in the end admitted to be an outtake from the *fourth* Band album, *Cahoots*!

As Band expert Peter Viney comments: 'Robbie Robertson is notoriously untruthful about dates and times. . . . The remaster of *Cahoots* finally admits that "Bessie Smith" was a 1971 outtake . . . and we now know that much of *Live at Watkins Glen*, remastered by Robertson and released in 1994, isn't from Watkins Glen at all.'

At year's end, on the last date of the 1975 Rolling Thunder Revue, at Madison Square Garden, NYC, Robbie Robertson joins Dylan to play guitar on the fifth number of his set, 'It Takes a Lot to Laugh, It Takes a Train to Cry'. Three months later, in Dylan's studio in Malibu, Bob and Robbie find themselves re-united by ERIC CLAPTON, on the track 'Sign Language', later released on Clapton's album *No Reason to Cry*. Recorded in March 1976, Robertson plays guitar while Clapton and Dylan share vocals.

After that, it's back to The Band on its own again, and it's Robertson who calls a halt. He gets together with MARTIN SCORSESE and orchestrates The Band's last concert as a drama on a grand scale; Winterland, San Francisco, November 25, 1976 becomes an always-extant great rock movie, 1978's *The Last Waltz*. Again, it's Robertson separated from the rest: Robertson the Scorsese crony, Robertson the producer of the 3-LP set, Robertson the composer of *all* the extra material in the so-called 'Last Waltz Suite' and Robertson the sole composer of every featured Band song but one. More, Robertson was also, alone amongst the members of The Band, co-producer of the movie. Levon complains that after playing to the cameras instead of the audience all through the live event, Robbie then 'placed himself and director Martin Scorsese, and all their flunkies and yes men, on huge salaries. And so began their year and a half love story of buying houses and apartments on both coasts, taping up all the windows with aluminum foil (like ELVIS did) and spending all night and all day "cutting" the movie.'

When *The Last Waltz* was reissued digitally, years later on DVD, Robertson had re-mastered the music, made all the choices about what extras went in and what didn't, added a scene-by-scene commentary by himself and Scorsese, and written the eight-page accompanying booklet.

After the demise of The Band, and the release of *The Last Waltz* in 1978, Robbie Robertson appears to have concentrated on film rather than music. Perhaps, as Colonel Parker seemed to feel about Elvis Presley, movies were a safer bet than rock'n' roll. Instead of producing the solo album most people expected, he developed his affiliation with Scorsese and tried to become a film star. In 1980 he composed the music for Scorsese's great film *Raging Bull*, and both produced and took a lead rôle in the rather less great *Carny*, directed by Robert Kaylor (making his first film since a documentary nine years earlier) and co-starring Jodie Foster and Gary Busey. The posters for the movie show Robertson exuding every possible morsel of his rather self-aware good looks, glamorous hat on head and cigarette in side of mouth, shirt unbuttoned half-way to navel, insouciant slouch, insolent stare to camera, Foster's arm round his shoulder—all under the strap-line 'When you're young and going nowhere, the Carny looks like a good way out.' Robertson was 37 years old at the time. That sounds like his line, though. It has the same sententious self-pity and special pleading, the same style of bullshit, as his famous *Last Waltz* line, offered on camera to Scorsese to explain the termination of The Band, 'The road. . . . It's a goddam impossible way of life.'

It wasn't only Levon or the other Hawks who demurred at this. Stephen Thomas Erlewine, appraising *The Last Waltz* on the All Music Guide website, tackles Robertson head on:

> 'Perhaps Robbie Robertson's greatest gift is how he can spin a myth, making the mundane into majestic fables. Outside of his songs, his greatest achievement in myth-making was *The Last Waltz* . . . the people who sound the best here—Dylan, Van Morrison, Dr. John, Levon Helm himself—are the ones who didn't treat the road as a goddam impossible way of life, but as what a working musician *does*. *The Last Waltz* teeters between these two schools of thought, wanting to celebrate the end while blithely ignoring that musicians make music for a living . . .'

But Robertson was making a living from his corpus of songs, and from Hollywood. He was music producer on *The King of Comedy* (1983) and was involved with *The Color of Money* (1986). He was 'creative consultant' on 1987's lovely *Chuck Berry: Hail! Hail! Rock 'n' Roll!*, music consultant on *Casino* (1995), executive soundtrack producer on *Phenomenon* (1996) and *Gangs of New York* (2002) and executive producer of *Jenifa* (2004), acted in *The Crossing Guard* (1995), acted as 'host' for the video *The Allman Brothers Band: Live at Great Woods* (1992) and as narrator on *Dakota Exile* (1996) and *Wolves* (1999). And so on.

Not until 1987 did he release his first, and eponymously titled, solo album. Using DANIEL LANOIS as producer, bringing in guests like U2, Peter Gabriel and jazzman Gil Evans—but also Danko and Hudson—this was so far removed from the sound of The Band as to seem like a brutal rejection of the past. Some people found that its sound painting and ghostliness, interwoven with Robertson's small voice and experimental drum programmes, amounted to an impressively ultra-modern success; others found in it only self-conscious artifice and a tiresome excess of dweedling.

The concept album *Storyville* followed, to much the same responses, three years later. In 1994 Robertson composed a song collection for a TV documentary series titled (patronisingly, you might think) *Music for the Native Americans*, on which he performed with Native American group the Red Road Ensemble. It was a kind of homecoming for the son of the Mohawk. He followed it up in 1998 with *Contact from the Underworld of Redboy*, and in 2002 a compilation album of solo tracks, re-mastered and in some cases remixed.

In 2004 he wrote and recorded music for the movie *Ladder 49* and appeared in an advert for the clothing company GAP, sitting with a woolly jumper on and a guitar across his knee, looking like a creepy Perry Como or Val Doonican. In June 2005 he accepted an Honorary Law degree from York University, Toronto, two years after receiving one from Queen's University in nearby London, Ontario. And in 2005 he saw the release of another of his rewritings of history, a 5-CD plus one DVD set titled *The Band: A Musical History*, in which he re-mastered his own choices of material from Ronnie Hawkins & the Hawks' 1963 single 'Who Do You Love' through to the combined Band and STAPLE SINGERS performing Robertson's 'The Weight' in a studio in 1977 for inclusion in the *Last Waltz* movie—the notes to which fudge over the date and place of recording for quite a number of those items once claimed as coming from the Basement Tapes sessions. The re-masters include various tracks with Dylan: the 'Can *You* Please Crawl Out Your Window?' single from 1965, 'Tell Me Mama' and 'Just Like Tom Thumb's Blues' live from Liverpool May 1966, 'Odds and Ends' from the Basement Tapes 1967, 'I Ain't Got No Home' from the Guthrie Memorial Concert in 1968, 'Forever Young' from *Planet Waves* recorded in 1973, and 'Rainy Day Women #12 & 35' and 'Highway 61 Revisited' from the 1974 come-back tour.

How he feels about these collaborations of the past is hard to say. But in 1992 he had been conspicuous by his absence from the so-called Bob Dylan 30th Anniversary Concert Celebration in New York City. Thirteen years later, in his good friend Martin Scorsese's film about Dylan, *No Direction Home*, Robbie Robertson is conspicuously absent again. And in *Chronicles Volume One*, he is almost the only musician adversely criticised. Dylan effectively repudiates all that Bob & Robbie cronyism of the mid-60s years:

> 'Once in the midsummer madness I was riding in a car with Robbie Robertson . . . I felt like I

might as well have been living in another part of the solar system. He says to me, "Where do you think you're gonna take it?"

'I said, "Take what?"

'"You know, the whole music scene." The whole music scene! The car window was rolled down about an inch. I rolled it down the rest of the way, felt a gust of wind blow into my face and waited for what he said to die away . . .'

[Robbie Robertson & Bob Dylan: 'Positively Van Gogh (?)', 'Don't Tell Him (?)', If You Want My Love (?)', 'Just Like a Woman' & 'Sad-Eyed Lady of the Lowlands', privately recorded Denver, CO, 12–13 Mar 1966, unreleased but circulating; 'It Takes a Lot to Laugh, It Takes a Train to Cry', NY, 8 Dec 1975. Eric Clapton, Robbie Robertson & Bob Dylan: 'Sign Language', Malibu, Mar 1976, issued Eric Clapton, *No Reason to Cry*, Polydor RSO RS1-3004, 1976. The Band: concert at Winterland, San Francisco, CA, 25 Nov 1976, filmed as *The Last Waltz*, dir. Martin Scorsese, US, 1978; *The Last Waltz—Special Edition* DVD, MGM Home Video 1003426, US, 7 May 2002 (17332DVD, UK, Oct 2002); soundtrack first issued as *The Last Waltz*, Warner 3 WS 3146, 7 Apr 1978; 4-CD box set version *The Last Waltz*, Warner Bros/Rhino R2 78278, US, Apr 2002. *Carny*, dir. Robert Kaylor, Lorimar, US, 1980. Robbie Robertson: *Robbie Robertson*, Geffen WX-133, NY, 1987; *Storyville*, New Orleans, *nia*, Geffen GEC 24303, NY, 1991; *Music for the Native Americans*, Cema/Capitol 28295, NY, 1994; *Contact from the Underworld of Red Boy*, Cema/Capitol 54243, NY, 1998; *Classic Masters*, EMI/ Capitol 39858, NY, 2002.

Peter Viney: e-mails to present writer 8 Aug & 28 Oct 2005. Levon Helm, *This Wheel's on Fire: Levon Helm and the Story of The Band* (written with Stephen Davis), New York: Wm Morrow, 1993 & Chicago: A Capella Books, 2000. Bob Dylan, *Chronicles Volume One*, 2004, p.117. Stephen Thomas Erlewine, All Music Guide, seen online 19 Sep 2005 at *http://theband.hiof.no/albums/last_waltz.html*. Al Kooper testimony re Feb 1966 sessions, e-mail to Peter Stone Brown, reported to the online Band Guestbook 16 Jun 2000.]

Robinson, Edwin Arlington [1869 - 1935] Robinson's is not a name bandied about much these days, but, like POE and WHITMAN, he was a self-taught poet (and a Pulitzer prize-winning one at that) and might be considered a small influence on Dylan's work. The bulk of his own was achieved between 1910 and 1935, after an earlier career on the New York subways.

His poems forge the way, either directly or via his influence on modern ballads, for something in Dylan's early songwriting. Short, sharp, quirky poems like 'Richard Cory', 'Reuben Bright' and 'Charles Carville's Eyes' contain those little detonations of observation that Dylan echoes in the better flashes of his hobo-hero, old-friend-hero songs. This is from 'Richard Cory': 'And he was always quietly arrayed / And he was always human when he talked; / But still he fluttered pulses when he said / "Good morning", and he glittered when he walked.'

(Hopelessly corrupted but recognisable by its title and crude narrative parallels, the poem re-emerges as a PAUL SIMON song on *The Sounds of Silence*. The album sleeve offers 'apologies to E.A. Robinson' . . . rather than royalties. The poet died only in 1935; under European law, his copyright would have been protected until 75 years after his death; lucky for Paul Simon that US law required active renewals every 28 years to keep copyrights protected. He could therefore not only misrepresent and ruin the poem but steal the proceeds too—including those from its recording by VAN MORRISON'S early group Them.)

The echo of Robinson in Dylan is perhaps not a point to insist upon. It is more in the nature of a hunch, a suggestion of a link there somehow, and offering it is simply to go along with F.R. Leavis' definition of the critic's task—that of saying/asking: 'This is so, is it not?'

['Richard Cory', 'Reuben Bright' and 'Charles Carville's Eyes' are in Robinson: *The Torrent and the Night Before*, 1896, re-published as *The Children of the Night*, 1897. Robinson's *Collected Poems*, 1921, 1929 & 1937. Simon & Garfunkel: 'Richard Cory', nd., 1965; *The Sounds of Silence*, Columbia CS 9269, New York (CBS SBPG 62690, London), 1966. Them: 'Richard Cory', nd., Apr 1966; *The World of Them*, Decca (S)PA 86, London, 1970. F.R. Leavis' assertion that 'A judgment . . . aspires to be more than personal. Essentially it has the form: "This is so, is it not?" . . . a collaborative exchange.' is in the essay 'Mr. Pryce-Jones, the British Council and British Culture', 1951, *Scrutiny* vol. XVIII, Cambridge, UK, 1951–52; collected in *A Selection from Scrutiny* vol. 1, 1968.]

Robinson, Smokey [1940 -] William Robinson Jr. was born on February 19, 1940 in the Brewster ghetto of Detroit, where he grew up. Inspired to turn to music by his mother's record collection, he became one of the greatest commercial soul singer-songwriters, a great promoter of other people's talent and almost as crucial to the phenomenal rise of Motown Records as its founder, Berry Gordy. From 1961 to 1988 he was company vice-president, but far more importantly, he was the writer of a huge number of its hit songs, including 70 top 40 hits for Motown between 1959 and 1990 as a recording artist, some solo but more as the lead singer of the label's most magical group, the Miracles. This witty, light-footed, blazingly optimistic outfit, with an unmistakeable sound that appealed across all boundaries of race and class (and across many of nationality), released a torrent of hit singles, including the great 'Shop Around', 'What's So Good About Goodbye?', 'You've Really Got a Hold on Me', 'The Tracks of My Tears', 'Going to a Go Go', 'I Second That Emotion' and 'The Tears of a Clown'. Robinson's hit compositions for others included the Mary Wells classic 'My Guy',

Marvin Gaye's 'Ain't That Peculiar' and 'I'll Be Doggone' and the Contours' 'First I Look at the Purse'. At their best, and many were at that level, his fusion of words and melody made it sound as if the two sprung unbounded and without effort from one clear fountain of adept and sassy inspiration. At the end of 1965, just when such music, and indeed the whole notion of the hit single, was starting to be scoffed at and held in contempt by a burgeoning hip snobbery, Bob Dylan was asked at his San Francisco press conference whom he considered his favourite poets and answered, among others: 'Smokey Robinson'.

This answer was not especially noted at the time—but by 1967 it was being said in an interview in which Dylan had been asked to name *the greatest living poet*, and had answered 'Smokey Robinson'. This reply, with no source given, was widely quoted, very often as an example of Dylan's wit. But search back now for the quote and you won't find it: you will only find the much less specific, much less definite 1965 press conference mention of Robinson in a list of other people.

You won't find the 'greatest living poet' reply because in fact Dylan never said it: Al Abrams, a PR man for Tamla Motown, made it up, as he revealed in an interview in 2005, discussing his first moves after setting up Al Abrams Associates in April 1967:

> 'I wrote the bios. . . . Along the way, I created some legends that I made up on the spur of the moment. Smokey Robinson—the Bob Dylan quote about him being America's greatest living poet—I made that up. Now, it's been around so much that if you asked Dylan, he'd probably say he said it.'

It's true that in the very funny interview with JANN WENNER published in *Rolling Stone* on November 29, 1969, when Wenner says, 'What about the poets? You once said something about Smokey Robinson . . .' Dylan responds with 'I didn't mean Smokey Robinson, I meant ARTHUR RIMBAUD.' But he wasn't really retracting; he was simply teasing Jann Wenner. It was easily done.

Robinson and Dylan came together decades later for the recording of the 'We Are the World' single in Hollywood on January 28–29, 1985. How much better that song might have been if Bob and Smokey had written it between them.

[Dylan press conference, KQED-TV studios, San Francisco, 3 Dec 1965. Al Abrams, phone interview 22 Jul 2005 for 'Living Music', seen online 21 Feb 2006 at *http://sitemaker.umich.edu/lmadmin/browse_subjects&mode=single&recordID=595398*, website of the University of Michigan School of Music's American Music Institute.]

rock'n'roll Rock'n'roll happened as a strange, appealing mixture of 'race' and country music. Mix FATS DOMINO with HANK WILLIAMS and you get the beginning of rock'n'roll. (This very combination eventually occurs. 'Jambalaya' uses Creole patois but was written by Hank Williams; Fats Domino's version is a classic.) But rock took off en masse for whites because of ELVIS PRESLEY. Without Presley, Bill Haley would have been a nine-day blunder, like the Twist; without Haley, Elvis would still have been a massive original talent. It simply wasn't Haley in 1955 that mattered, it was Presley in 1956, as even the *Billboard* charts bear out. (*Billboard* was the Cincinnati-based weekly trade-paper, rivalled by New York's *Cashbox*.) Haley's 'Rock Around the Clock' topped the US Hot 100 in 1955 only to be followed for the rest of that year by the appalling Mitch Miller, the Four Aces, the saccharine piano of Roger Williams and the saccharine gravel of Tennessee Ernie Ford. 1956 began just as comfortably, with Dean Martin. Then—the false craze exposed—Kay Starr climbed up there with her peekaboo 'Rock and Roll Waltz', just as FRANK SINATRA and Ella Fitzgerald were to yawn in on the Twist craze in 1962, crooning in its coffin nails. After Kay Starr, it was back to dinner-suits with the Nelson Riddle Orchestra and Les Baxter. And that would have been that, but for 'Heartbreak Hotel', Presley's first nation-wide no.1 hit record. It owed as much to Bill Haley as Dylan owes to RINGO STARR, and on its own it transformed the US charts and more besides. (The no.1s that succeeded it that year were Gogi Grant's 'The Wayward Wind' and then 'Hound Dog' and 'Don't Be Cruel', both by Presley, the Platters' 'My Prayer' and back to Elvis for 'Love Me Tender'.) The give me-the-moonlight regime was vanquished. Presley became the prototype: rock'n'roll was made in his image.

One of the changes—and it was part of the sudden flow of black modes of speech and song into the white mainstream—was that before rock'n'roll you had to enunciate. Every word had to be heard (even though the words so carefully delivered weren't generally worth any attention). With rock'n'roll the meaning of words, as a general rule, mattered less than their sounds, and the voice became an instrument. The grown-ups who laughed at Presley's 'mumbling' didn't understand. It was actually exciting to have part of the record where you didn't know what you were singing when you sang along with it. (On Bill Haley's records, you *can* hear every word, from 'one o'clock' right through to 'twelve o'clock rock'. Perhaps this is partly to be blamed on his being half English. Maude, his mother, was a music teacher from Ulverston, Lancashire, and emigrated to the US as a child.)

The best of the American stars had music that grew out of their own local roots. They picked up genuine skills and techniques unself-consciously. So Presley was not a suffocating influence—he got a lot of people started on things that weren't just copies. Duane Eddy said that 'none of us would have got anywhere without Elvis', and Duane Eddy didn't sound at all like Elvis Presley.

People were independent-minded, partly because they had vital popular music to draw on, and partly because music in America was never handled through a monopolistic institution. (In Britain, everything was obstructed, diluted, mishandled and misdispensed by BBC Radio, which had no idea what rock'n'roll or pop music was, didn't know how long it would last, didn't like or approve of it and so hardly bothered to adapt to its demands. Radio Luxembourg, the only alternative life-line, was little better. Reception was terrible, it was evenings only, and the DJs were mostly old men.)

American radio, in contrast, was infinitely variegated. In any one town, a single DJ with gumption and enthusiasm could tap undiscovered markets, shape tastes—could play what s/he liked!—free from the dictates of play-lists. Dewey Phillips in Memphis in the 1950s was one example out of many. It took a couple of decades before US radio completely ossified, becoming over-formularized through sheer greed. (The future loomed early, though: the first fixed play-list based on the national pop charts was introduced on Todd Storz's chain of Midwest stations in 1955.) Which goes to show that 'free enterprise' can stifle anything as fully as a nationalized industry if it tries.

Variety was also inbuilt in the US because of the record company situation. There were myriad small companies attuned to local communities and able to breathe because of local radio. By 1961, there were over 6,000 independent labels in America. Today, uniformity has crept across America too but in the 50s and early 60s, American rock'n'roll and pop was boundlessly healthy.

One of many good things offered by Peter Guralnick's *Last Train to Memphis: The Rise of Elvis Presley*, 1994, is his re-creation of the way that, when Elvis went into the studio to make not only that first record but the ones that followed, no-one knew what a record should be like. No formulae, no rules, no norms existed. That anything might be possible and no-one could know what: this was the essence of the moment, the fundamental artistic condition—one that is today virtually inconceivable, let alone attainable. Elvis, the musicians, producer Sam Phillips: they didn't say 'let's make a rockabilly record', or 'let's aim for a crossover'. The categories were unformed. All they knew was that they were reaching for a new, exciting noise to express the volatile moment.

Presley's very success created categories, including rockabilly, a genre that has enjoyed cult status ever since the early 1960s. GREIL MARCUS' *Mystery Train*, 1975, is good on its essential mediocrity: '. . . most rockabilly singers weren't even imitating blacks, they were imitating "All Shook Up". Collectors call the likes of Alvis Wayne and Johnny Burnette geniuses, but their aggressive stance is never convincing and the flash is always forced.' The only snag with this existentially accurate analysis is that most 'authentic' rockabilly was recorded before the release of Presley's 'All Shook Up' (in March 1957). Any connoisseur will tell you that if it's after 1957, it's suspect.

Bob Dylan's interest in rockabilly was as unadvertised as his love of early Presley. His mid-60s electric rock music paid clear tribute, for example, to the work of CHUCK BERRY, yet we lived out the second half of the 1960s in a counter-cultural climate in which all of rock'n'roll, the simplicities and crude brevity of its 'singles' and the naively consumerist, pre-druggy world it represented, seemed to have been outgrown. Rock'n'roll was regarded as so laughably 'unprogressive' and irrelevant that it was felt that Dylan's writing 'Ambition: To join LITTLE RICHARD' in his Hibbing High School yearbook (1959) had been youthful misjudgement, pre-dating a damascene conversion to the integrity of folk music and then to the values of the new counter-culture.

The complexity of Dylan's own work, of course, had begun our journey into these delusions. He radically expanded the possibilities of song; that didn't make him responsible for the hip snobbery of the Progressive Rock era. Nonetheless Dylan himself deliberately made no further public acknowledgement of the pioneers of rock'n'roll or of the two and a half-minute single until in 1969, in a *Rolling Stone* interview, he mentioned Presley's having recorded his own 'Tomorrow Is a Long Time' and then put versions of THE EVERLY BROTHERS' 'Let It Be Me' and 'Take a Message to Mary' on *Self Portrait* (1970): something very badly received by a hip public. (It emerged later that even at the very height of Dylan's artistic genius and hipness, the tour of 1966, he could still—off-stage—bear in mind the Everly Brothers of the much sneered-at 1960–62 period: the film *Eat the Document* shows him performing their 1960 hit 'When Will I Be Loved?' in his Glasgow hotel-room, May 18–19, 1966. *Eat the Document* was first screened only in 1971—and only twice then—and remains, another 35 years later, rarely seen.)

These debts to rock'n'roll and the pop it ushered in should perhaps have been admitted readily by everyone: they were surely undeniable. No-one was owning up to any of it back then. No-one talked about Elvis as a great artist except Greil Marcus in *Mystery Train*. The furtiveness about liking Elvis that was felt necessary among the hip was eventually confirmed by Dylan himself. He told ROBERT SHELTON (*No Direction Home*, 1986): 'The thing SUZE [ROTOLO] could tell you . . . [is] that I played, back in 1961 and 1962, when nobody was around, all those old Elvis Presley records.'

(There *was* an oldies-revivalism in the mid-1970s but it was mere kitsch, like Sha Na Na, or merely naff, like Britain's Showaddywaddy, or it was unconvincing attempts to revisit Chuck Berry, as with the Electric Light Orchestra's 1973 top 10 hit with 'Roll Over Beethoven' and Presley's 1975 top 10 hit with 'The Promised Land'.)

At any rate, this period was not the first era to assume that rock'n'roll had died. Its initial flowering had been brief (though it didn't seem so if you were young at the time). Its first year of international impact was 1956—when Dylan was 15: the perfect age to feel transformed by music—and 'the day the music died', with the death of BUDDY HOLLY, was in 1959. Indeed along with the pressure on radio stations from advertisers trying to squeeze out this anti-social oeuvre, a series of personal disasters befell the greats of rock'n'roll, and by the time Dylan came out of school and discovered the small bohemian world of Dinkytown and the Twin Cities of Minneapolis-St. Paul, Little Richard was no longer there to be joined, and the pop mainstream was (unfairly: see **pop 1960–62: not all hopeless**) felt to have returned to dull, safe platitudes placed in the teen-clean mouths of the boy and girl next door by music-industry men with cigars in their own mouths. Rock'n'roll was dead. Bob Dylan went into Folk.

[Fats Domino: 'Jambalaya (On the Bayou)', Philadelphia, PA, 6 Nov 1961; Imperial 5796, LA (in the UK London American 9520), 1961. Re Bill Haley: in 1953 'Crazy, Man, Crazy' by Bill Haley and His Comets became the first rock'n'roll song to make the best-selling lists. 'Shake, Rattle and Roll' was top 10 for 12 weeks from Sep 1954; 'Rock Around the Clock' was top 10 for 19 weeks, including 8 at no.1, from May 1955. Elvis Presley: 'All Shook Up', Hollywood, 12 Jan 1957; RCA 20-6870 (78rpm) and 47-6870 (45rpm), New York, March 1957. Everly Brothers: 'Let It Be Me', Nashville, TN, 15 Dec 1959, Cadence 1376, NY (London American HLA 9039, London), 1960; 'Take a Message to Mary', Nashville, 2 Mar 1959, Cadence 1364 (London American HLA 8863), 1959; both LP-issued *The Fabulous Style of the Everly Brothers*, Cadence CLP 3040, NY, 1960; 'When Will I Be Loved?', Nashville, 18 Feb 1960, Cadence 1380 (London American HLA 9157), 1960.]

Rodgers, Jimmie [1897 - 1933] Jimmie Rodgers was born in Meridian, Mississippi, on September 8, 1897, disproving General Sherman's post-march announcement of the 1860s that 'Meridian no longer exists!' Rodgers, looking in his publicity pictures like a cross between Bing Crosby and Stan Laurel, was 'the father of country music' yet he was mesmerised by the blues, a genre to which he contributed, and with which he became familiar from working alongside black railroad labourers. Hence his other appellation, 'the Singing Brakeman'.

(The railroad line, and even the train, still runs through Meridian, which is built on a rise. The track crosses a wide street that climbs to tall, elderly buildings, some of which must have gone up during Jimmie's childhood.)

Rodgers, the inventor of the Blue Yodel, had a short life and a brief career. He had already contracted tuberculosis and had to give up his day-job by the time he was discovered and first recorded by Ralph Peer in 1927, and his last session was 36 hours before his death, which was in New York on May 26, 1933. In the five and a half years in which he recorded he cut 110 sides. You can get them all on a 6-CD set.

At least he enjoyed stardom while he lived, as well as posthumously. Recognised in his own lifetime as having initiated an important idiom, it has proved enduring since. His records were astoundingly popular, selling in huge numbers, and he became the first rural artist to match the commercial success of northern popular singers.

His fame in segregated Mississippi sometimes had surprising results. At the huge and swanky King Edward Hotel in downtown Jackson, Rodgers, hearing marvellous Tommy Johnson and Ishman Bracey on the street, brought them up to the hotel roof to perform for his own audience. This black ragamuffin act, plucked off the street, bemused the supper-club crowd, but Rodgers knew talent when he heard it.

This is what Bob Dylan said of him in the *Biograph* interview of 1985: 'The most inspiring type of entertainer for me has always been somebody like Jimmie Rodgers, somebody who could do it alone and was totally original. He was combining elements of blues and hillbilly sounds before anyone else had thought of it. He recorded at the same time as BLIND WILLIE McTELL but he wasn't just another white boy singing black. That was his great genius and he was there first . . . he played on the same stage with big bands, girly choruses and follies burlesque and he sang in a plaintive voice and style and he's outlasted them all.'

As early as May 1960, and again that fall, Dylan was recorded performing Rodgers' 'Blue Yodel No. 8 (Muleskinner's Blues)' in Minneapolis, and 'Southern Cannonball' in East Orange, New Jersey, in February or March 1961. The Rodgers influence on the young Dylan was perhaps not wholly beneficial. The repulsively maudlin 'Hobo Bill's Last Ride' (written by West Texas farm boy Waldo O'Neal, and, at his sister's urging, submitted cold to Rodgers in 1928) influenced Dylan's deservedly obscure 'Only a Hobo'. Both lyrics make the same crude attempt at rhetoric, in protest-singer-saintly style: 'just another railroad bum . . .', whines Rodgers; 'Only a hobo . . .', whines Dylan. As Rodgers sings it, though, the melody for 'Hobo Bill's Last Ride' shares quite a bit with that of 'I Dreamed I Saw Joe Hill Last Night', which is, in turn, the song behind Dylan's own 'I Dreamed I Saw St. Augustine'—in which altogether more complex issues of saintliness, and guilt, come in for a fine, detached scrutiny, light-years ahead of either 'Only a Hobo' or 'Hobo Bill's Last Ride'.

Dylan and JOHNNY CASH's duets, recorded in Nashville on February 19, 1969, included 'Blue Yodel No.1' and 'Blue Yodel No.5', and it may have been from their presence in 'Blue Yodel No.12', recorded a week before Rodgers' last session, that Dylan took the essentially common-stock couplet 'I got that achin' heart disease / It works just like a cancer, it's killin' me by degrees' and re-processed it into his own line 'Horseplay and disease are killin' me by degrees' on 'Where Are You Tonight (Journey Through Dark Heat)?' on *Street Legal*.

Mules' years later, Dylan went into the studios in Chicago in June 1992 and recorded, among other things, Rodgers' 'Miss the Mississippi and You' (see **Bromberg, David**). In Memphis, two years later, he recorded Rodgers' 'My Blue-Eyed Jane' for a tribute album that was, reportedly, a project Dylan initiated. We first heard a tantalising snatch of one take on the CD-ROM *Highway 61 Interactive* in 1995, its woodsmoke guitars making it sound almost like an outtake from *New Morning*; a second complete take circulated among collectors in 1996, on which shared vocals by EMMYLOU HARRIS had been overdubbed in the interim; and then later that year a third version, with Dylan's vocals re-recorded and Harris' removed supplanted both and saw release on what turned out to be the first release on Dylan's own Egyptian Records label, in the collection finally issued as *The Songs of Jimmie Rodgers—A Tribute*.

More recently still, Dylan pays Rodgers the further tribute of impersonating him, in jest, on a re-recording of a *Slow Train Coming* song with MAVIS STAPLES (see the entry **'Gonna Change My Way of Thinking' [2003 version]**); and in 2004, in *Chronicles Volume One*, Dylan returns us to the beginning of Rodgers' impact upon him, which he says was back in Hibbing, in the days before his earliest performances of the material:

> 'One of the reasons I liked going there [to ECHO HELSTROM's house], besides puppy love, was that they had Jimmie Rodgers records, old 78s in the house. I used to sit there mesmerized, listening to the Blue Yodeler, singing, "I'm a Tennessee hustler, I don't have to work." I didn't want to have to work, either.'

[Jimmie Rodgers: complete recorded works, from 'The Soldier's Sweetheart', Bristol, TN, 4 Aug 1927, to 'Years Ago', NY, 24 May 1933, on *The Singing Brakeman*, Bear Family BCD 15540-FH, Germany, 1992. Bob Dylan: 'My Blue-Eyed Jane', Memphis, TN, 9 May 1994, vocals re-recorded unknown location early May 1997, *The Songs of Jimmie Rodgers—A Tribute*, Various Artists, Egyptian/Columbia Records 485189 2, NY, 1997. Bob Dylan, *Chronicles Volume One*, 2004, p.59.

The book on Rodgers is Nolan Porterfield's *Jimmie Rodgers: The Life and Times of America's Blue Yodeler*, Champaign, IL: University of Illinois Press, 1979.]

Rogers, Weldon [1927 -] The bass riff used on the *Oh Mercy* track 'Everything Is Broken', and relied upon far more heavily in live performance of the same song, is taken from the Weldon Rogers song Dylan often used, perversely, to *greet* his 1986 US tour audiences: 'So Long, Good Luck & Goodbye'. Rogers cut his own record of it at Norman Petty's legendary custom-studio in Clovis, New Mexico, some time in the first half of that marvellous music year, 1957.

He is an impressively obscure rockabilly (or old-fashioned country wannabille) artist for even Bob Dylan to have picked up on. Born in Marietta, Oklahoma, on October 30, 1927, he learnt to play guitar while serving in Italy in World War II. Returning to the States, he drifted around for many years but then, in Texas with his accordion-playing girlfriend Jean, founded Jewel Records ('Je' from Jean, 'wel' from Weldon), which used Norman Petty's studios and issued ROY ORBISON & the Teen Kings' 'Ooby Dooby' before the far larger Sun Records (no giant itself) stepped in when the record was beginning to do well, signed Orbison and halted sales of the Jewel label pressing.

Rogers, who had previously been a Seminole, Texas, DJ and cut two 1955 sides for the Quenn label in San Antonio, then cut a duet with his brother Willie on Jewel, before persuading Lew Chudd of Imperial Records to sign him up by pretending that Orbison's 'Ooby Dooby' B-side, 'Trying to Get to You', was his own. Chudd paid for Rogers, now backed by the Teen Kings (whom Orbison had dumped), to go back into the Clovis studios. On the way there, Weldon wrote 'So Long, Good Luck & Goodbye'. It was issued with Orbison's version of 'Trying to Get to You' on the B-side. Consequent ructions meant that despite the A-side's moderate success, it was the end of Weldon Rogers' Imperial Records career.

Later, with his wife Wanda Wolfe duetting, he made records (back on Jewel), such as 'Everybody Wants You', as by Weldon Rogers & Wanda Wolfe, with the then-unknown Glen Campbell on lead guitar. From 1961, he started moving around again, taking day-jobs as a radio DJ and making records now and then—in Farmington, NM; Pueblo, Colorado, and Medford, Oregon. His last recordings were in 1972, and in the 1980s the radio-station jobs became as station manager instead of DJ. He retired in 1989, the same year Bob Dylan recorded 'Everything Is Broken', finally settling back in the Texas panhandle in 1991.

When Dylan picked up Rogers' 'So Long, Good Luck & Goodbye' and re-used its riff over 30 years on, he was suggesting that even one-hit rockabilly stars are not forgotten—and that not everything is broken.

[Weldon Rogers: 'So Long, Good Luck & Goodbye', Clovis, NM, Jun? 1957, Imperial X5451, 1957. Weldon Rogers & Wanda Wolfe: 'Everybody Wants You', Jewel 45-103, late 1958-early 1959. Bob Dylan: 'So Long, Good Luck & Goodbye', débuted as his set-opened San Diego, 9 Jun 1986, and used as such at 17 further 1986 concerts; 'Everything Is Broken' débuted 'live' 1st night at the Beacon, NY, 10 Oct 1989. The same riff is also the basis of 'Melo Melo' (1978), written by Serge Gainsbourg, on the LP *Ex-Fan des Sixties—Baby*

Alone in Babylone (pardon?) by Jane Birkin, CD-reissued Phonogram 514124-2, UK, 1992.]

***Rolling Stone*, London office of** See **Wenner, Jann and unloading heads.**

Rolling Stones, the In middle age, decades after their prime, the once-incomparable rock band the Rolling Stones toured with Bob Dylan, rather briefly, in South America, in April 1998. On the 4th & 5th, during the Stones' sets in the River Plate Stadium in Buenos Aires, Argentina, Dylan came on stage and shared vocals with MICK JAGGER as the Stones played Dylan's 'Like a Rolling Stone'. The on stage collaboration was repeated in Brazil, on April 11 in Rio de Janiero and two nights later in Sao Paolo.

Three years earlier, on July 27, 1995, they had tried this out at a Rolling Stones' concert in Montpellier, France, though on this occasion Dylan had sung only the second verse of the song and Jagger all the rest. This was eight days after the Stones had studio-recorded the song themselves with stupefying dullness.

In 2004, when *Rolling Stone* magazine announced its poll results for the 'Top 500 Songs of All Time', Dylan's 'Like a Rolling Stone' was no.1; the Stones' '(I Can't Get No) Satisfaction' was no.2.

(See also **Jagger, Mick; Richards, Keith; Wood, Ron;** and **Taylor, Mick.**)

[The Rolling Stones: 'Like a Rolling Stone', 19 Jul 1995, *Stripped*, Virgin CDV2801, 1995; also issued on 4-track single VSCDT 1562, Virgin, 1995.]

'Romance in Durango' [1976] 'Romance in Durango', one of the songs on *Desire* co-written with JACQUES LEVY, is a kind of pop song—it is splendidly the heir of Marty Robbins' 'El Paso', and parodies that 1959 hit single's death-scene magnificently—but it is utterly marvellous, right from its flinty, glistening opening line: 'Hot chili peppers in the blistering sun', which gets a supercharged impact from the minimal melody, the stabbed bunching of the syllables and the desert-burn of Dylan's voice.

Hence it raised the pop song onto an undreamt-of high plane (or in this case high plain), through its skilful concentration of language. It has a strange dynamism, derived from alternating the travail of long, syllable-crammed lines—'We'll drink tequila where our grandfathers stayed'—with sudden oases of more spacious lines, in which, as often before, Dylan says more with less: 'The dogs are barking and what's done is done.'

While it's impossible to trace accurately those parts of the Bob Dylan-Jacques Levy lyrics which have been contributed by Levy, it seems a plausible hunch that, overall, Levy's input, like SAM SHEPARD's in the Dylan-Shepard lyric 'Brownsville Girl' in the mid-1980s, has been by way of additional *detailing*: that the co-writer encourages an attention to concrete objects and a tendency to insert or retain adjectives where Dylan's own bent is more for 'keeping things vague', as JOAN BAEZ puts it in her own excellent song about Dylan, 'Diamonds and Rust'.

Perhaps without Levy the opening line of 'Romance in Durango' would have been 'Chili peppers in the sun'. Or perhaps not. There is, however, one specific touch in the song which must surely have come from Levy—from his knowledge of psychotherapy, a subject in which Dylan has never expressed sympathetic interest (rather the opposite) but in which Levy trained. Levy would have known the subject matter described here in Eric Berne's popularising book of the early 1970s, *What Do You Say After You Say Hello?*; he may well have known the book and thus this passage itself:

> 'Amenhotep-haq-Uast's other name (besides Ikhnaton) was Nefer-kheperu-Ra-ua-en-Ra, whose hieroglyphs roughly translate as "Take your lute and your scarab and enjoy the sun", while according to the Ikhnaton cartouche, he has traded this in for a cake and a feather. . . . This is like a modern, hippie script switch, either way: people with guitars get a yen for cake, or people with cake turn it in for a guitar.'

So it proves to be in 'Romance in Durango', in which Dylan sings: 'Sold my guitar to the baker's son / For a few crumbs and a place to hide / But I can get another one . . .'

Berne's most famous and successful book was the earlier *Games People Play*, 1964, which injected copious amounts of psychobabble into everyday language and preceded the JOE SOUTH record of the same name, a hit in 1969—and unfortunately for the neatness of the lute/cake, guitar/crumbs parallel, Berne's assertions about Ikhnaton's name are equally unreliable, even if Levy took them on trust. As Egyptologists transliterate the hieroglyphs, they mean 'Beautiful are Ra's transformations, the only one in Ra, glory in the Aten [the solar disk].' (Ikhnaton is a variant spelling of Akhenaten/Akhenaton, the original name of Amenhotep IV, a king of the 18th Dynasty of Ancient Egypt, who died in 1358 BC.)

Dylan began performing 'Romance in Durango' on the very first night of the first Rolling Thunder Revue—before the release of *Desire*. Indeed it was the first of *six* songs from the album that were previewed ahead of its release that night; the others were 'Isis', 'Oh Sister', 'Hurricane', 'One More Cup of Coffee', and 'Sara'. He continued to perform it early on in every 1975 Rolling Thunder Revue concert. The version from Cambridge, Massachusetts, on November 20 has since been released on the *Bootleg Series Vol. 5*, while that from Montreal on December 4 was featured in the *Renaldo & Clara* movie and on the 1985 *Biograph* box set.

On the 1976 leg of the Rolling Thunder Revue, 'Romance in Durango' was performed far less regularly and was not among the songs on the 'Hard Rain' television special. Its last performance that year was on May 11 in San Antonio, Texas—and then Dylan never revisited the song until, to the amazement of everyone lucky enough to be there, he suddenly embarked upon it, and rather magnificently, on the penultimate night of a 33-concert tour of Europe in 2003, at the Hammersmith Apollo, London.

In Las Cruces, New Mexico, on August 29, 1989, Dylan began his concert with an instrumental performance of, yes, Marty Robbins' 'El Paso'.

[Bob Dylan: 'Romance in Durango', NY, 28 Jul 1975; live début Plymouth, MA, 30 Oct 1975; surprise live performance London, 24 Nov 2003.

Marty Robbins: 'El Paso', Nashville, 7 Apr 1959, Columbia 4-41511, NY (in the UK, Fontana Records H 233, London), 1959. Joan Baez: 'Diamonds and Rust', Los Angeles, 17–29 Jan 1975, *Diamonds and Rust*, A&M SP 3233, LA (AMLH 64527, London), 1975. Eric Berne, *What Do You Say After You Say Hello?*, c.1972. The contradictory transliteration of the hieroglyphs has been supplied by A.J. Iriarte.]

Romney, Jahanara [1941 -] Bonnie Jean Beecher was born in Minneapolis on April 25, 1941, the daughter of people who owned the well-to-do Beecher's Resort in Annandale, MN, west-northwest of Minneapolis. So she had money, and used to go on shopping trips to New York City, where she bought a number of LPs on each trip. She would go to Sam Goodys, choosing 'any old record that looked like it had some kind of funky singer or blues singer . . . records by CAT IRON, RABBIT BROWN . . .' So it was that when she first met Dylan in Dinkytown in 1959 or 1960, he and HARVEY ABRAMS were sitting around in the 10 O'Clock Scholar, mentioning obscure singers' names, and she was able to join in.

They got on well, had enough of a relationship for some commentators to suspect that she, rather than ECHO HELSTROM, was the 'Girl of the North Country'. This is unlikely, but certainly Dylan was keen on Bonnie, and she seems to have been the subject of a passing reference in his early poem 'My Life in a Stolen Moment', in which he writes: 'I fell hard for an actress girl who kneed me in the guts / an' I ended up on the East Side a the Mississippi River / with about ten friends in a condemned house / underneath the Washington Avenue Bridge just south a Seven Corners / That's pretty well my college life . . .'

They remained close throughout Dylan's Minneapolis days and they stayed in touch all through his rise to New York City fame. He would see her on each revisit to Minnesota during 1961, and she (as well as TONY GLOVER) recorded Dylan performing at her apartment that May and December. The December tape is particularly important, and had they not been friends, and her apartment thus not available, we would be the poorer for its non-existence. Her recording of this magical early Dylan performance, made on her art teacher's reel-to-reel machine, has long circulated, and in reasonable quality; the one Tony Glover recorded did not circulate, is in better quality and has been drawn upon for three officially issued tracks (so far). The May tape, catching a far less confident performance and in far poorer sound quality, is nonetheless interesting for its choice of material, which reveals how deeply Dylan had already sunk himself into blues material (including pre-war blues) as well as into Guthrie's and traditional white folksong.

Not all its material was old. Bonnie gave a delightful interview to Markus Wittman, for fanzine *The Telegraph*, in 1990, in which she gave a vivid and fond picture of the endearing, advantage-taking, hustling, shambolic young Dylan. Asked if he wrote songs back then, she revealed that he had written 'a couple of fooling around songs', including the one on the tape called 'Bonnie Why'd You Cut My Hair?'—which collectors were familiar with but had always assumed was an obscure traditional song.

She said: 'He wrote one when I cut his hair, which made me so angry! He came to my apartment and said, "It's an emergency! I need your help! I gotta go home an' see my mother!" He was talking in the strangest WOODY GUTHRIE-Oklahoma accent. I don't know if she was sick, but it was an unexpected trip he had to make up to Hibbing and he wanted me to cut his hair. He kept saying, "Shorter! Shorter! Get rid of the sideburns!" So I did my very best to do what he wanted and then in the door come DAVE MORTON, JOHNNY KOERNER and Harvey Abrams. They looked at him and said, "Oh my God, you look terrible! What did you do?" And Dylan immediately said, "She did it! I told her just to trim it up a little bit but she cut it all off. I wasn't looking in a mirror!" And then he went and wrote that song, "Bonnie, why'd you cut my hair? / Now I can't go nowhere!" He played it that night in a coffee-house and somebody told me recently that they had been to Minnesota and somebody was still playing that song, "Bonnie, Why'd You Cut My Hair?" It's like a Minnesota classic! And so I've gone down in history!'

Bonnie also said she was grateful to Dylan for his example:

> 'When I lived in the sorority house we had a music room with a piano that no-one ever used and Dylan would come and learn how to play piano there and the harmonica. I got him his first harmonica holder at Schmidt's Music Shop. So he would come over to the sorority house and play the piano, horribly! And he'd play this harmonica, which he didn't know how to play! And my friends would come in and they would just go, Uurgh! Who is this geek? I wanted him to play the guitar, which he could play well and which I knew would impress them, but he wasn't

having any of it. He was saying, Naw. I wanna get this—Hwang! Whwaongg! Hahaha! I was mortified but he didn't give a shit. It's been a big lesson to me in life—don't give a damn what people think, just go for what you are!'

Of course, this wouldn't work if everyone were equally selfish; in her own case, this bright, quick-minded, talented girl understood him, picked him out of the gutter, cleaned him up, lent him money and so on—and did so as if it were her vocation, even though she was ambitious herself, to be an actor.

By the time of that interview Bonnie Beecher had long been calling herself Jahanara Romney—Jahanara was a Sufi name she took in 1975—having moved to the West Coast 'probably in 1962 or 1963' and acted in television from 1964 to 1968. She was running a Hollywood restaurant, the Fred C. Dobbs, when she met Hugh Romney, aka Wavy Gravy, and settled for a life of hippiedom on the California avant garde art scene.

'Together,' said Wavy later, 'we survived L.A. Acid Tests and in 1965 we married each other. We also married the Hog Farm. The Hog Farm is the name still associated with our expanded family. We acquired it while living rent free on a mountaintop in Sunland, California, in exchange for the caretaking of forty actual hogs. Within a year of moving there, the people engaged in our bizarre communal experiment began to outnumber the pigs. At first we all had separate jobs. I had a grant to teach brain-damaged children improvisation while teaching a similar class to contract players at Columbia Pictures. Harrison Ford was one of my students. My wife Bonnie was a successful television actress. . . . Bonnie Jean gave birth to Howdy Do-Good Gravy at the Tomahawk Truckstop in Boulder, Colorado.' In 1976 she gave Wavy another child, Birthday Party Gravy. (On *his* 13th birthday, Howdy legally changed his name to Jordan Romney, and he's now a computer programmer.) Wavy and Jahanara run Winnarainbow, a performing arts summer camp—so Bonnie has ended up in a version of her parents' business after all. Its website (designed by Jordan) shows a photo of Jaharana and Wavy together, and reports that she has been the camp's administrative director since 1983, and that she also serves on the board of the Berkeley-based Seva Foundation, helping to develop its Central American projects.

Dylan says in *Chronicles Volume One* that it was Bonnie—described only as 'A girl I used to know in Minneapolis' who 'had become an actress'—who introduced him to John Wayne when he went to visit her in Hawaii on the set of *In Harm's Way* (where she 'was playing a supporting role')—but she says that is *not* how it happened: 'No. I drove him to the airport when he was going to Hawaii, and ended up going there with him. Brandon de Wilde, an actor in that film, and his wife were friends of mine, so I took Bob and Victor [Maymudes] to the filming at Brandon's invitation. We all got to hang out on the set and with the cast, for several days. They were all interested in meeting Bob. At one point I was invited to join a group of extras creating a crowd scene, but I was not officially cast in any rôle whatsoever!'

Like Dylan, she got away from Minnesota; like him, she comes back to have another look around from time to time on the quiet. Last time was in 1997 for a memorial service for her mother. She doesn't recall when she last saw Bob Dylan. 'It has been a long time.'

[Jahanara Romney, aka Bonnie Beecher, interview by Markus Wittman, 'The Wanted Man Interview: Jahanara Romney', *Telegraph* no.36, Romford, UK, summer 1990, reprinted John Bauldie, ed., *Wanted Man, in Search of Bob Dylan*, London: Black Spring Press, 1992, pp.26–27, and by the present writer, by e-mail, 29 Nov 2005. Bob Dylan, *Chronicles Volume One*, 2004, p.249. Gravy quotes from 'A Sketch of my Thumbnail', seen online 25 Oct 2005 at *www.cleartest.com/testinfo/gravy.htm*. More detail Paul Krassner, 'Wavy Gravy: Salute to a Good-humored Humanitarian', online 5 Oct 2005 at *www.earthisland.org/project/newsPage2.cfm?newsID=600&pageID=177&subSiteID=44*. Relevant Winnarainbow website page is *www.campwinnarainbow.org/staff/staff.html*. *In Harm's Way*, dir. Otto Preminger, 1965.]

Ronson, Mick [1946 - 1993] Michael Ronson was born in what is now claimed to be the obesity capital of Britain, the north-east port of Hull, more fully named Kingston-upon-Hull, on May 26, 1946. He grew up to be the opposite of obese himself, and donated his considerable lead guitar talents primarily to another artificial stick-insect blonde with a penchant for make-up and repulsive 1970s clothes, David Bowie, starting with his early band the Hype and then *The Man Who Sold the World*, though he also collaborated a good deal with Ian Hunter and his group Mott the Hoople, co-produced (with Bowie) LOU REED's significant album *Transformer*, playing piano on its track 'Perfect Day', and in the early 1990s produced the album *Your Arsenal* by the great Morrissey, giving him a heavier sound and less emphasis on the lyrics but making for a compelling whole. He worked with many other people and released three solo albums, the last, *Heaven and Hull*, issued posthumously and featuring Bowie as guest on Ronson's cover of 'Like a Rolling Stone'.

It was a surprise to Dylan followers when Ronson became a lead guitarist on the Rolling Thunder Revues of 1975 and 1976, since those who find Bob Dylan interesting and those who find David Bowie interesting are almost wholly different groups of people. Stylistically, however, his expansive white lines of electric guitar-work proved an inspired blend with Dylan and threw an authoritative rock-star hauteur in amongst the munchkin collective of STONER, SOLES and NEUWIRTH. He can be seen to fine effect in *Renaldo & Clara* and the 'Hard Rain' TV Special as well as blazing his way across the *Hard Rain* album. The lead guitar part he brought to Dylan's very different Rolling Thunder version of 'It Ain't Me, Babe', mournful but resourceful, alive but elegiac, is a fine instance of how much he contributed. He was also particularly good in the improvised playlets within *Renaldo & Clara*, inhabiting the rôle of jobsworth-on-the-door perfectly, blocking the RONNIE HAWKINS character and refusing to countenance any reasoning or plea with the stolid implacability that in real life only the stupid can fully muster. A nice irony, then, as well as appealing humour, that when asked by RONEE BLAKLEY at some point on the tour, 'Isn't Bob wonderful?', Ronson replied: 'I don't know—he's never spoken to me.'

Oddly, Ronson was a member of the Church of Jesus Christ of Latter-day Saints (the Mormons), though reportedly he became disillusioned with it late in life. He died of cancer of the liver on April 29, 1993.

Rosen, Jeff [1950s -] Jeffrey Rosen was born in Brooklyn in the 1950s and would prefer to leave it at that. He has been running Bob Dylan's music publishing empire and general office since the retirement of his mentor Naomi Salzman (who with her husband Ben was still being thanked on the sleevenotes of *Knocked Out Loaded* in 1986; Ben's name gave rise to Big Ben Music, the UK branch of Dylan's music publishing in the 1960s which circulated the initial 14 Basement Tapes songs as demos, from which came early bootlegs). If Jeff Rosen were merely a business executive he wouldn't require an entry here but he has not only transformed Dylan's publishing from a commercially modest enterprise into an exponentially larger one but along the way he has been proactive in creating the *Biograph* box set ('Produced for reissue by Jeff Rosen', as the back-cover credit has it) and creating the whole *Bootleg Series*, devising and overseeing its production and its compilations. He was also co-producer with Don DeVito of the so-called 30th Anniversary Concert Celebration of 1992 and of its 2-CD live album set.

Rosen has supervised the introduction of the website *www.bobdylan.com* and led the systematised accumulation of Dylan's invaluable archives, including taking the active rôle of conducting most of the interviews filmed over the past decade—among them the interview with Dylan himself that we see in SCORSESE's *No Direction Home* film in 2005: a film he gets a 'producer' credit on. He was active too when Dylan performed JOHNNY CASH's 'Train of Love' on film in March 1999, for playing at the Cash Tribute he was unable to attend in person; it was Jeff Rosen who made that single-camera film. He is also the interviewer in, and co-producer of, the extra feature in the *Masked & Anonymous* DVD package, the 16-minute feature *'Masked & Anonymous' Exposed*, in which the movie's stars talk to him about making the film—and he was, with Nigel Sinclair, the producer of the film itself. Look at the production credits for the film, and there's a swathe of people down as 'executive producer'—Marie Cantin, Joseph Newton Cohen, Vladimir Dostal, Guy East, Anatoly Fradis, Pietro Scalia, David M. Thompson—and there are 'co-producer' credits for David Gaines and Nikolai Makarov; but only Sinclair and Rosen are tagged 'producer'.

Through all this runs a main theme: that Jeff Rosen has, while optimising Dylan's business potency dramatically, also effected a sea-change in the Dylan-office culture as it affects the ordinary aficionado, fundamentally improving and making more productive the level of contact and exchange between the business guardianship of Dylan's art and the constituency out there that has long been interested in the art itself.

Rotolo, Suze [1943 -] Susan Elizabeth Rotolo was born in Queens, New York, on November 20, 1943, the younger sister of Carla Rotolo. ('Of the two sisters, I loved the young,' as Dylan sang in his immaturely personal yet majestically delivered 'Ballad in Plain D' on 1964's *Another Side of Bob Dylan*.) They were the nieces of the Boston-based painter Petro Pezzati, and their parents were political Lefties and friends of Charles Flato (aka Floto), a member of the American Communist Party who acted as a Soviet agent while working for the US Government (though he was never prosecuted). Not long before his death in 1984 he gave Suze (pronounced 'Suzy') his car.

Suze and Carla's father died when Suze was 14, after which, deciding college wasn't going to be possible, she was free to come and go as she pleased, crossing the bridge into Manhattan and finding in Greenwich Village a place that made sense to a teenager whose idols were Edna St. Vincent Millay and Lord Byron.

'I grew up as an outsider, having politically Left parents,' she has said. 'Having a sense of social consciousness in the 1950s was very, very, very unusual . . . people were very wary of speaking out, of saying anything. And folk music was a place to hear other voices and people who were like you, who were socially conscious . . . and it was through music that I found people . . . who had the same interests I had.'

Suze was a teenage activist. Already involved at school in SANE (which was somehow the acronym for the National Committee for a Sane Nuclear Policy), Suze picketed Woolworths stores in New York City in parallel with those picketing for the integration of lunch counters in the South, and by the time she met Bob Dylan in the first half of 1961, she was already a seasoned attendee of hootenannies at Gerde's Folk City, performances in Washington Square Park and concerts at Carnegie Hall. Though it's often said by Dylan commentators that she first saw Dylan at his first paid gig, which was that April 5, at the Loeb Music Center for the University of New York Folk Society, which she attended, *she* says she first saw Dylan while he was playing at a hootenanny with MARK SPOELSTRA, and though she was more attracted physically to the latter (he 'had lovely shoulders'), Dylan's harmonica playing had 'an earthiness that was wonderful' and she was 'a sucker for anyone who plays a good harp'. The two began a flirtation at the end of an all-day hootenanny to launch Riverside Church's radio station that July 29, at which Dylan performed 'Handsome Molly', 'Naomi Wise' (aka 'Omie Wise') and 'Poor Lazarus' before playing harp for DANNY KALB on 'Mean Old Railroad' and then joining RAMBLIN' JACK ELLIOTT for a song that scoffed at teen pop culture, 'Acne'.

As Dylan recalls in *Chronicles Volume One*, they were introduced by Carla, whom Dylan knew slightly because she was at this point ALAN LOMAX's assistant: Suze was 'the most erotic thing I'd ever seen.' They were soon 'going steady'—so that Suze was a witness to almost the entire transition from Dylan the hustling unknown to Dylan the Columbia Records recording artist, Dylan the writer of a PETER, PAUL & MARY hit single, Dylan the star. At the same time, Suze was doing day-time odd jobs and took an extra job painting scenery for off-Broadway productions—most significantly for *Brecht on Brecht*, a sort of theatrical compilation sampler of BERTOLDT BRECHT's work, staged at the Circle on Sheridan Square, in the Village.

Dylan, remembering the production as having been at the Theatre de Lys on Christopher Street, says that going there 'to wait for Suze' he 'was aroused straight away by the raw intensity of the songs.'

To the dismay of Carla and of Suze's mother, who saw Dylan as a fairly harmless young phoney and nicknamed him Twerp, Suze moved into Bob's apartment above Bruno's Spaghetti Shop at 161 West 4th Street, and they became, in her own phrase, increasingly 'huddled together'. Yet she also took a job with CORE (the Congress for Racial Equality)—an office job, but in an office where news constantly poured in about the freedom rides in Birmingham, Alabama, and other campaigning demonstrations CORE was involved with as part of the civil rights battles of the day.

'The time of the early 1960s,' Suze wrote recently, 'was a protest time and an eventful time and an event-filled time and the time leading up to and out of the release of Dylan's *Freewheelin'* album in 1963—and talk made the music and music made the talk, and action was already in the making with Civil Rights marches and marches against the Bomb, and THE BEATS had already cracked the rigid morality of the 1950s. So we were ready to roll. And it was my personal story but . . . it's become history.'

Rotolo did indeed occupy at once a typical and a very untypical position at this time. It was, as she says, her 'personal story', just as it was the story of all those who fought and campaigned, all those who were rejecting America's mainstream 1950s culture, all those who were part of the Folk Revival and the Blues Revival, the coffee-house scene in Greenwich Village and equivalent places in Boston, Philadelphia and Washington, D.C. Yet at the same time, as Bob Dylan's girlfriend as he was shooting to fame, she was at once being singled out, pointed at and set apart from her chosen life.

For a start, she was there with Dylan on the cover of that *Freewheelin'* album, still a teenage girl yet looking far more mature than the Gallup, New Mexico, tale-spinning Huck Finn-faced youth she's arm in arm with, walking down that snowy street. And at the March on Washington in August 1963, when Martin Luther King made his 'I have a dream' speech, Suze was bound to be there—how would she not have been, given her background and interests and her involvement with CORE: and she remembers, in that context, 'listening to King and looking around. . . . It was wall to wall people; no longer were we a small group of protesters. . . . This was definitely a turning point, a special time.' Yet it must also have been special to witness Bob stand up in front of those wall to wall people, one of those who had earned the right to be there as a performer—to be there, as it were, on the same bill as Martin Luther King.

But before either the release of *Freewheelin'* or the March on Washington, their relationship had changed; it was finishing. Her mother had remarried in 1962, and that year Suze had the chance to sail to Italy with her mother and stepfather and to live in Perugia, the lovely and ancient hill town that is the capital of Umbria. She agonised about going, but she went—and didn't regret it: 'I felt I didn't want to be a string on his guitar, because I wasn't ready to retire. I hadn't even started out yet.' In sunny Italy, a million miles from the dark clubs of dark New York, she felt 'let loose to be young again'.

Thus Suze, by escaping Dylan, became the prompt for some of his finest early songs: in particular 'Don't Think Twice, It's All Right'—its line 'I once loved a woman, a child I'm told' re-uses a remark of ROBERT SHELTON's to Dylan, telling him how young Suze still was—and the magnificent 'Boots of Spanish Leather'. (There are also the lines Dylan puts inside his minor *Freewheelin'* song 'Down the Highway': 'the ocean took my baby, / My baby took my heart from me. / She packed it all up in a suitcase, / Lord, she took it away to Italy. Italy.'

Suze stayed away about seven months, and returned to much hostility in the Village (including from JOHNNY CASH), from those who thought it their business to tell her how she'd hurt Bob. 'He mooned in public. He created this image of himself as the abandoned, wounded lover. I'm sure he was having a fine time also. Classic.' They got back together for a while, and it's generally held to have been in February 1963 that the *Freewheelin'* cover shot was taken (by DON HUNSTEIN, a Columbia Records staff photographer).

In the years after their demise as an item, Rotolo retained Dylan's respect by her determined silence and her absolute refusal to give interviews. The first interviews she gave were for Victoria Balfour's misleadingly titled book *Rock Wives*, and for Robbie Woliver's book *Hoot! A 25-Year History of the Greenwich Village Music Scene*, both published in 1986: and in neither did she break her silence on the private side of her life with Dylan.

For his part, in *Chronicles Volume One* he remembers her warmly and in the sort of detail that surprises the reader all the way through that book: 'Suze was seventeen years old. . . . She was involved in the New York art scene, painted and made drawings for various publications, worked in graphic design and in off-Broadway theatrical productions, also worked on civil rights committees—she could do a lot of things. Meeting her was like stepping into the tales of 1,001 Arabian nights. She had a smile that could light up a street full of people and was extremely lively, had a particular kind of voluptuousness—a Rodin sculpture come to life.'

In the 1970s, Suze Rotolo married an Italian film editor whom she'd first met on that early trip to Perugia, Enzo Bartoccioli. Their son Craig Rotolo plays rhythm guitar in Cleanser, a pop rock band in New York that includes a violinist. In late 2004, Suze made a surprise appearance on a discussion panel as part of the Experience Music Project's exhibition in Seattle, 'Bob Dylan: An American Journey 1956–1966'; and in 2005 a small part of the interview she had given to Dylan's office was used in MARTIN SCORSESE's film *No Direction Home*. (A typed letter written by Suze to her mother on July 10, 1962, which begins with the rebuke 'Mother, I have lost all faith in being honest to you because you never give Bob a chance', was auctioned in 2005: but Rotolo insists this was a fake.)

Dylan attributes his beginning to draw to Suze's example: 'I actually picked up the habit from Suze, who drew a lot.' And 'someplace along the line Suze had also introduced me to the poetry of French Symbolist poet ARTHUR RIMBAUD. That was a big deal too.' More generally, 'I began to broaden my horizons, see a lot of what her world was like, especially the off-Broadway scene . . . [and] I went with her to where the artists and painters hung out. . . . A new world of art was opening up in my mind . . .' Finally, as Dylan acknowledges, it was also through Suze Rotolo that he encountered the work of Brecht—work that would strongly influence his own early writing.

Suze told Robbie Woliver: 'It was always sincere on his part. He saw something. The guy saw things. He was definitely way, way ahead. His radar was flying. He had an incredible ability to see and *sponge*—there was a genius in that. The ability to create out of everything that's flying around. To synthesize it. To put it in words and music. It was not an intellectual approach that he had to research something—he did it on his own.'

But with a little help from Ms. Rotolo.

[Main sources for the above are Rotolo's comments at the EMP panel discussion Nov 2004, online at *www.emplive.org/visit/galleries/dylanPanel.asp*, incl. part 'she wrote recently'; Victoria Balfour, *Rock Wives*, New York: Beech Tree Books & London: Virgin Books, 1986; Robbie Woliver, *Hoot! A 25-Year History of the Greenwich Village Music Scene*, New York: St. Martin's Press, 1986; Wikipedia, online 23 Sep 2005 at *http://en.wikipedia.org/wiki/Suze_Rotolo*; and *Chronicles Volume One*, pp.272, 264–65, 288, 268–70. Link between 'Don't Think Twice' line and Shelton remark claimed by Shelton to the present writer, date unremembered.]

'Royal Canal, the' Dylan may have been inspired in respect of the seagulls smilin' in his 'When the Ship Comes In' by the pseudo-folksong 'The Royal Canal', aka 'The Old Triangle', by Brendan Behan—which, it later emerged, Dylan and THE CRACKERS/THE BAND included among the rich assortment of material recorded on the Basement Tapes (Woodstock/West Saugerties, June–October 1967). One verse runs: 'On a fine spring evening / The lag lay dreaming / The seagulls beaming / High above the wall.'

It may also have influenced Dylan's 'I Shall Be Released', also on the Basement Tapes. In *Invisible Republic*, 1997, GREIL MARCUS calls 'The Royal Canal' '. . . "I Shall Be Released" without any hope for freedom'; he might also have noted the particularity of Dylan's song repeating that phrase 'High above the wall' from within Behan's.

It is possible too that Dylan's phrase 'the jingle jangle morning', in 'Mr. Tambourine Man', was inspired by 'The Royal Canal', the chorus of which runs 'And that old triangle / Goes a jingle jangle / All along the banks / Of the Royal Canal.' However, there are other possible sources for this. In *Chronicles Volume One* Dylan mentions Tex Ritter's 'Jingle, Jangle, Jingle' as something heard on the radio late at night in his youth. 'Jingle Jangle' is also a record by the Penguins, whose hit 'Earth Angel' was known to Dylan and friends in Minnesota back in 1956.

'The Royal Canal' is a key element in Behan's first play, *The Quare Fellow* (first produced Dublin, 1954, with Behan singing the song off-stage). It was familiar repertoire in early 1960s Greenwich Village.

['Jingle, Jangle, Jingle', Bob Dylan, *Chronicles Volume One*, p.188. Tex Ritter: 'Jingle, Jangle, Jingle', Hollywood, 11 Jun 1942, CD-reissued (adjacent to his 'Blood on the Saddle', Hollywood, 1 May 1945), on the Ritter compilation *High Noon*, Bear Family BCD 15634, Vollersode, Germany, 1991. The Penguins: 'Jingle Jangle', Hollywood, 12 Nov 1955; CD-reissued *Earth Angel*, Bear Family BFX 15222, c.1991).]

Russell, Leon [1942 -] Claude Russell Bridges was born in Lawton, Oklahoma, on April 2, 1942, attended Lawton's Will Rogers High School and went out into the music world after playing in a club with RONNIE HAWKINS behind JERRY LEE LEWIS at age 14 and moving to LA at 16, where he started work in PHIL SPECTOR's wall-of-sound factory in time to appear on many of those classic girl-group hit singles.

Later, Russell played on THE BYRDS' 'Mr. Tambourine Man'–the only member of the group to do so being McGuinn. His first hit as a songwriter was Joe Cocker's 'Delta Lady', after which he was the organiser of Cocker's Mad Dogs and Englishmen tour–something he achieved in two weeks, to the astonishment of A&M bosses Herb Alpert (on whose own records Russell had also played piano) and Jerry Moss.

He came into Dylan's orb by producing, as well as playing piano on, the Dylan session of March 16–19, 1971 in New York from which came 'When I Paint My Masterpiece' (on *Bob Dylan's Greatest Hits Vol. II*) and the 'Watching the River Flow' single. The session also yielded a set of still-uncirculated recordings that sound very alluring indeed: 'Spanish Harlem', 'That Lucky Old Sun', 'Alabama Bound' and 'Blood Red River'. Russell also played on the recording of 'George Jackson (Big Band Version)', but this time on bass, on November 4, 1971.

Appearing at the Concert for Bangla Desh that August seemed to make Russell an instant superstar–or for those who had followed Joe Cocker's Mad Dogs & Englishmen tour perhaps confirmed him in that rôle: he came on all-powerful, utterly in your face, musically supra-vivid, his lurid gothic vocals allied to a laconic confidence at the piano only ever surpassed by that of Jerry Lee himself. And then within a couple of years he became, like Melanie and Donovan, one of the showbiz disappeared. He kept on working, playing, producing, writing and recording–but he had vanished from the land of the giants.

Rutman, Howard [1941 -] Howard Irving Rutman was born in St. Paul, Minnesota, on February 13, 1941 and met Bob Dylan when they were both adolescents at the co-educational Jewish summer camp they and LARRY KEGAN were all sent to, Camp Herzl in Webster, Wisconsin–sent to, in Bob's case, as Rutman told biographer HOWARD SOUNES, because his mother wanted him to 'meet Jewish kids and maybe some Jewish girls'.

Bob Dylan made his earliest known extant recording with Rutman and Kegan, at a custom recording facility in the Terlinde Music Shop in St. Paul, Minnesota, on Christmas Eve *1956!* The three 15-year-olds share vocals along with Bob's piano as they race through incomplete versions of eight songs in little more than nine minutes. (See **earliest extant recordings, Dylan's.**) This trio, formed first at summer camp, called itself the Jokers. Though these aspiring rock'n'rollers never really got beyond singing round the piano, Rutman says their mothers made them sleeveless cardigans in red and grey, with JOKERS stitched across the fronts, and that they once went on a Twin Cities Channel 9 TV talent show, even earlier than their début recording. He says it was early 1956, when they were all 14. They played together off and on till spring 1958, when Bob had Hibbing groups–groups with real instruments–to concentrate on.

Dylan often stayed overnight at the Rutman family home in St. Paul, and they would listen to radio programmes like 'Lucretia the Werewolf' and Bob would play the piano in the basement. 'He would bang the shit of the piano,' Howard told Sounes. 'He would get up there and dance on the damn thing. . . . Ah God, he just ruined it.'

Rutman left Minnesota around the same time as Dylan, but headed in the opposite direction, taking dentistry at Arizona State before settling in LA and hoping to become an actor. He worked in television a little but didn't give up the dentistry, and he says that Dylan's mother Beatty came into his office one time, around 1978, to say she wanted to make an appointment for her son to have his teeth looked at. Her son? Yes, she said, Bobby Zimmerman. Howard said he could see him right away. He didn't realise it but Bob was waiting in the car-park. Howard was just phoning his wife of the time to say guess what: Bob Dylan is coming in here to get his teeth fixed, when he felt a tap on his shoulder. Bob was already in the room. It takes a very old friend to get away with making that kind of phone call in Dylan's hearing, but he did.

Since 1990 Rutman has worked in films, mainly as a driver and 'transportation coordinator'–on films including *Killer Tomatoes Eat France!* and *Captain Nuke and the Bomber Boys*–though his credits also include second unit director on 1995's *Criminal Hearts* and 'additional photography' on 1997's *Campfire Tales*.

Howard Rutman's father Harvey was first cousin to, and best friend of, the Joseph Rutman who eventually married Beatty Zimmerman, many many years after their first spouses had died. So Howard and Bob, decades down the road from their teenage comradeship, have ended up related by marriage.

[Quote from Howard Sounes, *Down the Highway: A Life of Bob Dylan*, New York: Grove Press, 2001, Ch.1; post-Minnesota, dentistry and Rutman family detail, Howard Rutman phone call from this writer, 13 Feb 2006.]

S

Sager, Carole Bayer [1947 -] See **Bayer Sager, Carole.**

Sahm, Doug [1941 - 1999] Douglas Wayne Sahm was born on November 6, 1941 in a predominantly black section of San Antonio, Texas, where he grew up. He was of German and Irish descent, not, as often reported, of Lebanese. A steel-guitar, mandolin and fiddle prodigy he sang on radio at age five and by eight he was a regular on the Louisiana Hayride radio show, billed as Little Doug Sahm. Just weeks before HANK WILLIAMS' death, he brought Doug on stage with him in Austin.

He heard many live blues and country musicians as he grew up and by 13 knew the records of HOWLIN' WOLF, FATS DOMINO and JIMMY REED. His mother wouldn't let him accept an offer to join the Grand Ole Opry but he did start making records for local labels, starting with the 78rpm as well as 45rpm release 'A Real American Joe' c/w 'Rollin', Rollin'', made when he was 11 but released in 1955, and fronting local bands while still in high school.

It was the British invasion and the BEATLES that led to producer Huey P. Meaux, with whom Sahm had been pushing to record, to commission Sahm to get a group together, write a song with a Cajun two-step beat (Meaux thought the Beatles' hits had the same on-the-beat formula), grow his hair long and come back to the studio. Hence the supposedly British-sounding name the Sir Douglas Quintet, and hence 'She's About a Mover', recorded in January 1965 and an immediate massive hit, which Bob Dylan was quick to praise.

In March 1966, arrested in Texas for possession of marijuana, Sahm moved to San Francisco for five years, there recording the album *Mendocino* and others, to increasingly little effect; but in 1972 Sahm and the group appeared in the movie *Cisco Pike* with KRIS KRISTOFFERSON (its soundtrack featuring his 'Michoacán') and that October JERRY WEXLER bought him out of his record deal, brought him to Atlantic and to New York, rescuing him from the doldrums and producing the album *Doug Sahm & Band*, one of the most charming albums ever made, Sahm's lazy but perky voice one ingredient in a fond fusion of loose yet sinewy Tex-Mex country-rock music on which Bob Dylan appeared on a number of tracks in a variety of mostly self-effacing minor rôles. The whole thing sounded as if it were being played in your parlour, yet also sounded the unarguable laid-back prototype for the Austin Sound that was so successful later that decade.

Doug Sahm himself plays guitar, piano and bajo sexto on the album; other players include Dr. John, DAVID BROMBERG, Flaco Jiminez, AUGIE MEYERS and Dave 'Fathead' Newman. On the expansive, chunky opening track '(Is Anybody Going to) San Antone' Dylan sings harmony vocals and plays guitar; on 'It's Gonna Be Easy' and 'Faded Love' he plays organ and on 'Poison Love' guitar; on his own composition 'Wallflower' he sings lead vocals and plays guitar, on 'Blues Stay Away from Me' he shares vocals and plays guitar, and on 'Me and Paul' he plays guitar and harmonica. The outtakes—some released in 1992 on *Doug Sahm & Friends*, and all released in 2003 on the set *The Genuine Texas Groover*—were 'On the Banks of the Old Pontchartrain', 'Hey Good Lookin', 'Mr. Sandman' and 'I'll Be There' (all with Dylan on guitar), 'COLUMBUS STOCKADE BLUES' and 'The Blues Walked In' (Dylan on piano and organ) and 'Tennessee Blues', with Dylan on harmonica.

Nothing much happened for Doug Sahm as a result of the original album release, in December 1972, and Atlantic persevered with his career no more than Mercury before it, though his fan-base in Texas remained ardent. He drifted through the rest of the 1970s, playing guitar on RICK DANKO's eponymously titled solo album of 1977 and appearing in the film *More American Graffiti* in 1979. In 1983, with long-time musical compadre Augie Meyers, he signed to Swedish label Sonet, enjoying one of the biggest hit singles in Scandinavian history with 'Meet Me in Stockholm', from their album *Midnight Sun*, and touring Europe recurrently until in 1985 he moved to Canada, where he formed a new band with Amos Garrett. Three years later he finally returned to Texas, recording for a small Austin label and after various touring configurations with others, he joined the Texas Tornados—intended as a Tex-Mex TRAVELING WILBURYS—along with Meyers, Flaco Jiminez and Freddie Fender. They made seven albums plus *The Best of Texas Tornados*, the last being a live album made in Austin 11 months before his death. However, in tandem with the Texas Tornados (also the name of a Houston volleyball team), Sahm reformed the Sir Douglas Quintet in 1994 with two sons.

On August 24, 1988, shortly before Sahm quit Canada, Bob Dylan's Never-Ending Tour, then only ten weeks old, played Edmonton, Alberta. TRACY CHAPMAN came on for the encore number 'Knockin' on Heaven's Door' and that must have seemed to the audience the end-of-evening surprise. But topping that, Doug Sahm was brought on stage and, backed by Dylan and his band, finally got to sing 'She's About a Mover' to its prominent admirer, 23 years after he'd first heard it. The two men's final conjunction came another seven years on, when the Never-Ending Tour was back in Texas and on their second and final night in Austin, on November 5, 1995, Doug Sahm graced the stage one more time, playing guitar on 'Maggie's Farm', 'Just Like Tom Thumb's Blues', 'Never Gonna Be the Same Again', 'Highway 61 Revisited', 'Alabama Getaway', and the final number of the night, 'Rainy Day Women # 12 & 35'. At the end of 'Just Like Tom Thumb's Blues', on which Sahm also shared vocals, he said to the audience: 'Austin, Texas, do we love this dude or what! He's the greatest! I'm telling you man, I've got to say it. And tomorrow's my birthday and tomorrow this year will be thirty years this man's been a beautiful friend of mine and I love him. I wish everybody in the world could know him like I do. I love this dude. Thank you, Austin, Texas! Thank you Bob Dylan!'

It was indeed Sahm's 55th birthday next day. Soon after his 58th, Doug Sahm died of a heart attack while on holiday in Taos, New Mexico, on November 18, 1999.

[Little Doug: 'Real American Joe' b/w 'Rollin, Rollin'', *nia*, Sarg 113, US, 1955. The Sir Douglas Quintet: 'She's About a Mover', Texas, 15 Jan 1965, Tribe 8308, US, 1965. Doug Sahm: *Doug Sahm & Band*, NY, Oct 1972, Atlantic SD-7254, US, 1972; *Doug Sahm & Friends*, Rhino R2 71032, US, 1992; *The Genuine Texas Groover*, Atlantic/Rhino RHM2 7845, US, 2003. The Texas Tornados: *The Best of Texas Tornados*, Reprise 45511-2, US, 1994. Career rundown based largely on Joseph Levy's 'Doug Sahm and the Sir Douglas Quintet: A Brief History', online 3 Dec 2005 at *www.laventure.net/tourist/sdq_hist.htm*.]

'Sally Sue Brown' See Alexander, Arthur.

Sandburg, Carl [1878 - 1967] Carl August Sandburg was born in Galesburg, Illinois, on January 6, 1878, the son of Swedish immigrants. Leaving school at 13, he worked as a newsboy, milk delivery boy, barbershop shoeshine boy and milkman, and at 19 rode a boxcar to Missouri, Kansas, Nebraska, Colorado and Iowa, and worked on a railroad section gang, as a farmhand and a dishwasher. He volunteered for the Army and served in Puerto Rico in the Spanish-American war, and then, back in the US, worked as a journalist and copywriter. He wanted to become a poet of the Midwestern American people and began his poetry career with the privately printed *Reckless Ecstasy* in 1904.

This got him nowhere and he continued in journalism until he became the secretary to Emil Seidel, Milwaukee's first socialist mayor, from his election in 1910 till his defeat in 1912. Sandburg's experiences had made him a sometime Wobbly, sometime anarchist and lifelong man of the Left. In 1914 some of his work was published in *Poetry* magazine, followed by the free-verse volume that made his reputation as a major poet of the Midwest, *Chicago Poems* (1916), followed by *Cornhuskers* (1918), *Smoke and Steel* (1920) and *Slabs of the Sunburnt West* (1922). After that he wrote the first part of a huge biography of Lincoln–*Abraham Lincoln: The Prairie Years* (2 volumes, 1926)–and published *The American Songbag* (1927), the collection of folksongs for which he is valued by generations of folksong students and musicians who have never read his poetry.

By this point he had also published his first two collections of stories for children, *Rootabaga Stories* (1922) and *Rootabaga Pigeons* (1923), followed by a third, *Potato Face* in 1930. After *The American Songbag* he produced the further volumes of his own poetry, *Good Morning, America* (1928) and *The People, Yes* (1936) and the second part of the Lincoln biography, *Abraham Lincoln: The War Years*, published in four volumes in 1939. In 1948 he published a novel, *Remembrance Rock*, in 1950 his *Complete Poems* plus a second folksong collection, *The New American Songbag*, and in 1952 his autobiography, *Always the Young Strangers*.

He was now 74 years old–and he was a man of 86 by the time Bob Dylan and his road-trip companions made their stoned way to his house to meet him in February 1964. They were directed to the 240-acre ranch at Hendersonville, North Carolina, where Sandburg and his family had lived since 1945, and found his wife Lillian–an internationally recognised goat breeder–sitting out on the porch. 'I am a poet,' Dylan announced. 'My name is Robert Dylan and I would like to see Mr. Sandburg.' Mrs. Sandburg duly took this message indoors. There was an extremely long wait. When Sandburg eventually emerged, unshaven and shambling but sharp-eyed, he surveyed the group of four and immediately honed in on Dylan. 'You look like you are ready for anything: I would like to ask you about 40 good questions,' he told him. Sandburg had never heard of Dylan nor listened to his work. Dylan handed him a copy of *The Times They Are a-Changin'*, and PAUL CLAYTON proffered one of his own albums too. Sandburg expressed interest, they in turn enthused about *The American Songbag*, Dylan reiterated that he was a poet and a singer, and Sandburg said he'd always regarded poetry and songs as related arts. After 20 minutes, the old man announced that he must get on with his work. His visitors left disappointed. ROBERT SHELTON writes that 'Dylan had wanted this great writer to "open up" and take them into his study to see his books, his piles of manuscripts.'

Afterwards, Dylan told Shelton that Sandburg had said to him: 'You certainly look like an intense young man.'

'I'm a-Ridin' Old Paint' (see separate entry), having been 'found' by Margaret Larkin, was one of the songs popularised by its publication in *The American Songbag*; the collection of some 280 ballads and songs also contained, among those with a subsequent Dylan connection, 'Frankie & Albert' and 'Froggie Went a-Courtin''.

The Dylan news-item collector IAN WOODWARD thinks that Dylan went to call on Sandburg because of his folksong collecting rather than because he was a poet: 'There were plenty of poets he didn't go and see.' This seems wilfully at odds with accounts of the visit itself, and ignores the fact that Dylan often *did* call on other poets. We know that by the time he went to see Carl Sandburg he had long since been drawn into friendships with aspiring poets like EDDIE FREEMAN, had initiated a disappointing meeting with ROBERT GRAVES and had struck up a friendship with ALLEN GINSBERG; he would go on to hang out in California with FERLINGHETTI and many others; and in *Chronicles Volume One* we get a highly engaged Dylan's detailed account of his visits to, and attempts to work with, ARCHIBALD MacLEISH. For Dylan, Carl Sandburg was at least as much a poet, and a symbol of fellow Midwestern heroism, as a folksong collector. It has always been the creative writer, not the documentarist, that Dylan has admired. There were plenty of folklorists he didn't go and see.

Carl Sandburg died at the home Bob Dylan had visited, on July 22, 1967. He was 89. His ashes were returned to Galesburg, Illinois, as he'd wished, and buried behind the three-room cottage in which he'd been born. Ten years later, his wife's ashes were placed there too.

[Carl Sandburg's poetry now available as *Complete Poems*, New York: Harcourt, revised edn., 1970; *The American Songbag*, New York: Harvest Books, 1990. Sources: for poetry career: Ian Ousby, ed., *The Cambridge Guide to Literature in English*, Cambridge, UK: Cambridge University Press, 1995; for early labour, *www.uncp.edu/home/canada/work/canam/sandburg.htm timeline*, seen online 13 Oct 2005; Robert Shelton's account of the Dylan-Sandburg meeting, *No Direction Home: The Life and Music of Bob Dylan*, London: Penguin edn., pp.242–43. Ian Woodward quote, phone call to this writer, 1994.]

Santana, Carlos [1947 -] Carlos Augusto Alves Santana was born in Autlán de Navarro, Mexico, on July 20, 1947, the son of a mariachi violinist. Carlos swapped violin for guitar by the age of eight, later playing in dangerous border-town clubs in Tijuana before moving to San Francisco in 1961. Five years later he formed the Santana Blues Band, a jazz-rock fusion outfit with African and Latin elements (but not enough), which went down well at Fillmore West. By the time they played Woodstock in 1969, leading to their mega-success and a major record deal, the name had been pruned to Santana.

The first time Carlos Santana played with Dylan was as one of those nightly guests during Dylan's half-gospel, half-secular 'Musical Retrospective' tour in the fall of 1980. On November 13 in San Francisco he came on and played guitar alongside Dylan and the band on a run of four songs in mid-set: 'Covenant Woman', Solid Rock', 'What Can I Do for You?' and the live début of 'Groom's Still Waiting at the Altar'. Dylan seemed to hope he'd play more, because after the four he told the audience: 'Carlos is gonna be up here and he can play anytime he wants. He may, he may just be walking by'; and he did walk on by. However, when Dylan launched into his big-venue European tour of 1984—his first European dates for three years—Carlos' mega-selling group Santana co-headlined. Carlos Santana attended the press conference Dylan gave in Verona, Italy, before the tour began there on May 28, and the tour itself continued through to July 8 in Slane, Ireland. On their 27 shared dates, Carlos generally appeared on stage in Dylan's set to play electric guitar on the encores, and sometimes accompanied Dylan on acoustic guitar during his otherwise-solo acoustic numbers.

On these, he could decorate around Dylan attractively, but he was not popular with Dylan's crowd, because before these Dylan performances you had to stand through the almost interminable vulgar tedium of the group Santana's own sets.

Savakus, Russ [1925 - 1984] Russell A. Savakus, a bass player, was born in Reading, Pennsylvania, on May 13, 1925. Thirty years later he replaced Joseph Macho Jr. on bass for the afternoon Dylan session of July 29, 1965, and therefore plays on the 'Positively 4th Street' single. He returned for the next day's *Highway 61 Revisited* session, at which the album cut of 'From a Buick 6' and the alternative Japanese album cut of the same song were recorded, and which also yielded the early version of 'Can You Please Crawl Out Your Window?' mistakenly released by Columbia under the title 'Positively 4th Street'. Savakus did not play on any other Dylan sessions.

Though he worked a good deal with jazz musician Chet Baker, he was a more widely used bass player among folk-rock people, has toured and recorded with Don MacLean and has played on albums by Jean Ritchie, IAN & SYLVIA, JUDY COLLINS, RICHARD & MIMI FARIÑA, JOAN BAEZ, Buffy Sainte-Marie, THE CLANCY BROTHERS, NEIL DIAMOND, Phoebe Snow, Donny Hathaway, THE GREENBRIAR BOYS, John Denver, PETER, PAUL & MARY and DOC WATSON.

Russ Savakus died in Bangor, Pennsylvania, on June 25, 1984, aged 59.

***Saved* [album, 1980]** The nearest thing to a follow-up album Dylan has ever made: a *Slow Train Coming II*, and inferior. Two stand-out tracks, nonetheless: the turbulent 'Pressing On' (Dylan creating convincing hot gospel) and the intelligently submissive, courageous address (including a lovely, aptly devotional harmonica) that is 'What Can I Do for You?'

[Recorded Sheffield, AL, 12–15 Feb 1980, released as stereo LP Columbia PC 36553 (in UK CBS 86113), 19 or 20 Jun 1980.]

Saville, Philip [1934 -] See ***Madhouse on Castle Street, The***.

Scaduto, Anthony [19?? -] Anthony Scaduto was Dylan's first biographer. He became a police reporter for the *New York Post*, specializing in organized crime stories. He also wrote showbiz biographies, including, in 1968, one called *The Beatles*. It was because he was an 'outsider' and a 'hack journalist' rather than a Dylan fan, that he wasn't too awed to go after his subject nor to expect, and receive, a series of interviews with Dylan in 1971 for his book, which was published in 1972. There was a commensurate amount of hostility among Dylan aficionados, who felt that someone more sensitive and knowledgeable should have done the book instead—yet Dylan undoubtedly prefers 'outsiders', and might have been less co-operative with the 'sensitive and knowledgeable' type. At any rate, retrospectively, most Dylan enthusiasts concede that Scaduto did a decent job: including an intelligent exploration of the *John Wesley Harding* album. As NIGEL WILLIAMSON noted, it was 'not only the first Dylan biography, but one of the first serious rock biographies' but 'has become very much a period piece.'

His other books include *Mick Jagger*, 1974, *FRANK SINATRA* in 1976 (looking at Sinatra's alleged Mafia connections), and, the same year, *Scapegoat: The Lonesome Death of Bruno Richard Hauptmann* (interesting sub-title), a contentious re-investigation of the Lindbergh case, which had engaged his interest in 1973, shortly after the modest success of his Dylan biography. He continued on his two-track career, writing, for instance, a lurid piece titled 'How the Mafia is Destroying the FBI' for *Gallery* magazine, a *Playboy*-type US monthly, in 1979, and interviewing Suzanne Vega, for *New York Newsday* in 1997.

[Anthony Scaduto, *Bob Dylan, An Intimate Biography*, New York: Grosset & Dunlap, 1971, and London, W.H. Allen, 1972; paperback: London: Abacus, 1972, revised edn., 1973; New American Library edn., US 1979; republished London: Helter Skelter Publishing, 1997 and 2001. *Mick Jagger*, Mayflower paperback edn., London, 1975. *Frank Sinatra*, New York: Putnam Books, 1976. *Scapegoat: The Lonesome Death of Bruno Richard Hauptmann*, Putnam Books, 1976. 'How the Mafia is Destroying the FBI', *Gallery*, Feb 1979. Interview with Suzanne Vega, *New York Newsday*, 18 Oct 1997. Nigel Williamson, *The Rough Guide to Bob Dylan*, London: Rough Guides, 2004, p.368.]

Schatzberg, Jerry [1927 -] Jerrold Schatzberg was born in the Bronx on June 26, 1927. He attended the University of Miami and from 1954 to 1956 served an apprenticeship as a photographer under Bill Helburn before becoming a freelance fashion and portrait photographer. By the late 1960s he was directing TV commercials and in 1970 made his film director's début with, aptly, a movie about the fantasy reminiscences of a fashion model, *Puzzle of a Downfall Child* written by Adrien Joyce (aka Carol Eastman), starring Faye Dunaway and described by *Halliwell's Film Guide* as a 'Pretentious, fashionable, seemingly interminable collage of sex and high living.' Schatzberg's second film was the more widely noticed and better-regarded *The Panic in Needle Park* (1971), partly written by Joan Didion and starring Al Pacino, who also starred in Schatzberg's *Scarecrow* (alongside Gene Hackman). This very 1970s film about two confused drifter-victims of the alienation of the day was, according to the veteran critic Stanley Kauffmann 'a picture that manages to abuse two American myths at once—the Road and the Male Pair.'

These scrutinies of modish losers had a suggestion of autobiography about them, since Schatzberg was an independent both as photographer and film-maker, coming into movies at the start of a renaissance decade for Hollywood yet belonging to no 'school', and often attracting more admirers in Europe than the States. Nonetheless Schatzberg attempted more commercial films too, including *Honeysuckle Rose* (1980), starring WILLIE NELSON, Dyan Cannon and Slim Pickens, and *The Seduction of Joe Tynan* (1979), the latter probably his best-known and certainly most conventional work. A decade after it came *Reunion*, scripted by Harold Pinter from the novel of the same name by Fred Uhlman, filmed and produced in Europe in 1989 and starring Jason Robards. His last film was *The Day the Ponies Came Back* (2000), in which, coming full circle, the action takes place in the Bronx as a man wanders alone in search of his long-lost father, and thus his own past.

Jerry Schatzberg's photographic portrait subjects make for a fine list of odd bedfellows, including as they do Fidel Castro and FRANK ZAPPA, Milos Foreman and THE ROLLING STONES, Roman Polanski and JIMI HENDRIX, Francis Ford Coppola and ARLO GUTHRIE. More to the point, they include Bob Dylan, to whom Schatzberg was introduced by SARA DYLAN. He had known Sara since 1962 or '63, when, he recalls: 'she was modeling. The [Ford] agency asked me to do test shots of her. I did and we subsequently became friends. She was the first person to make me aware of Bob Dylan's music.' It was two or three years later before Schatzberg told Sara that he wanted to photograph Dylan. The most striking result was the iconic gatefold cover of *Blonde on Blonde*, showing Dylan blurred and golden, as if so hip that you couldn't even see or capture him in clear focus.

This Schatzberg shot was, at the time, the single most crucial visual signal that Dylan had changed again from the clear-cut sharp hipness of 1965 and

Highway 61 Revisited to the warmer, softer, fuzzier, still-more-far-out Dylan of 1966 and that expansive, purring double-album. Schatzberg also took the black and white pictures on the inner sleeve (including a shot of himself), selected by Dylan from among shots he saw in Schatzberg's studio as well as some taken specially. Hence the self-portrait and the photograph of Claudia Cardinale, which was later withdrawn because of a dispute over clearance.

The Dylans, ALBERT GROSSMAN and Schatzberg all kept in touch afterwards: 'We went out socially. I was a fashion photographer and I would host big parties . . . they'd show up at the parties for a while. I also was part-owner in a couple of discotheques at different times and he used to hang out at them.' Schatzberg took many photographs of Dylan and his entourage in this period, most of which remain unpublished. Another of his studio shots from 1966 was used 32 years later for the slipcase front cover of the *Bootleg Series Vol. 4: Bob Dylan Live 1966*. This seems the inevitable choice. Many photographers took fine photographs of the volatile Dylan of 1966—but it was Jerry Schatzberg who, in creating the *Blonde on Blonde* cover shot, implanted that one shimmering image in a generation's mind.

[*Puzzle of a Downfall Child*, Universal/Newman-Foreman, US, 1970. *The Panic in Needle Park*, Gadd, US, 1971. *Scarecrow*, Warners, US, 1973. *The Seduction of Joe Tynan*, Universal, US, 1979. *Honeysuckle Rose*, Warners, US, 1980. *Reunion*, Rank/Les Films Ariane/FR3/NEF/GLC/TAG, UK-France-Germany, 1989. *The Day the Ponies Came Back*, Mondo Films, France, 2000.

First quote from Jerry Schatzberg, e-mail to this writer 26 Dec 2005; 2nd quote from interview in *On the Tracks* no.18, Grand Junction, CO, *nia*, seen online 21 Aug 2005 at *www.b-dylan.com/pages/samples/jerry schatzberg.html* (in which Ms. Cardinale is given as Claudia Cartinelli & Sara Lownds as Sara Lowndes). Quote from *Halliwell's Film Guide*, 11th edn., London: HarperCollins, 1995, p.926; quote from Stanley Kauffmann ditto p.998.]

Scheff, Jerry [19?? -] Jerry Scheff was born in Vallejo, northern California, grew up there in a housing project, took up the tuba in the school orchestra, swapped to bass violin in his teens and later to electric bass, after moving to Sacramento at age 14, where a supportive mother encouraged his interests by taking him to jazz and classical concerts, while he was also paying attention to R&B on the radio. By 16 he was playing clubs in San Francisco, preferring East Coast jazz to the 'cool' West Coast scene. Playing too much to do well in school, he was nudged into the military, joining the US Navy but landing in its music school in Washington, D.C. He quit the Navy for San Diego State College, then after some bad patches found work with the 16-year-old Billy Preston, which led to sessions in LA, but as a horn player initially. After the Watts riots of 1964 he felt prevented, to his great regret, from working within the black music scene again. He played on hits by the Association, with jazz guitarist Barney Kessel, on bubble-gum hits and with album artists from Johnny Mathis to the Nitty Gritty Dirt Band and from JUDY COLLINS to Leonard Nimoy, and he played on the Doors' album *L.A. Woman*.

After working with JAMES BURTON, he was invited (by Burton) to join the band he was assembling to play on ELVIS PRESLEY's return to live performance. He wasn't a fan, but was converted within minutes of meeting him, and took the gig. Scheff can be heard to advantage on June 1972's *Elvis as Recorded at Madison Square Garden* performances. He continued to work with him off and on until his death.

In late 1977, he reports: 'I got a call from saxophonist Steve Douglas telling me that Bob Dylan was rehearsing and had fired his bass player [ROB STONER]. I went down to play with him and all of a sudden we were on our way to Europe . . .' He omits to mention that before that he played bass in the studios on the whole of the *Street Legal* album. But he does mention that they toured 'on a private train. It was a wonderful tour. We had a private dining car complete with private chef and an extensive wine collection. When we left, say, Paris for Berlin, our cars were added to a train heading for Berlin, and away we went. . . . The last concert . . . was at Blackbush Aerodrome in England for 250,000 people: the largest crowd I have ever played for live.'

After that he settled for John Denver ('a very gracious and generous person in material ways') until T-BONE BURNETT recruited him for ELVIS COSTELLO's *King of America*. After years of further session-work, Scheff returned to working with the other Elvis—the dead one. The band and the vocal group and so on now tour around the world playing 'Elvis the Concert', playing live along with footage from early 1970s shows from which all the music except Presley's vocals has been removed. A backing musician's dream:

> 'For us, the only differences between the shows we did with Elvis and this present show are that the present show is twice as long as the old shows and we are twice as old. The intensity is just the same, and if anything . . . the band is playing even better today. Also, in the old days, we never knew what Elvis was going to do from one second to the next. That is understandably not the case now.'

Not perhaps the ideal attitude to have brought to playing with Bob Dylan.

[Quotes & background detail *www.scheff.com/jerry/index.html*. Elvis Presley: *Elvis as Recorded at Madison Square Garden*, RCA LSP-4776 (LP), 1972.]

Schleser, Burkhard [1960 -] See ***Parking Meter***.

Scobie, Stephen [1943 -] Stephen Arthur Cross Scobie was born in Carnoustie, Scotland, on the last day of 1943. He first took an interest in Dylan's work in 1963, and his first published writing about him was a letter in the *Glasgow Herald* in summer 1965, protesting against 'a dumb "Dylan's gone electric" review'. Moving to Canada, he pursued an academic career at the University of Alberta and then the University of Victoria, publishing work on Canadian literature, Paris, literary theory and more, while also becoming a poet with over 20 books published. He was the 1981 winner of Canada's most prestigious literary prize, the Governor-General's Award, and has an entry in the *Oxford Companion to Canadian Literature*.

He has written a number of essays on Dylan's work in the fanzines *ON THE TRACKS* (US) and *Judas!* (UK) and used to be a regular contributor to the online newsgroup *rec.music.dylan*. He has sometimes fused his interest in Dylan and his work as a poet, as with *And Forget My Name: A Speculative Biography of Bob Dylan*, 1999. However, his major work on Dylan is *Alias Bob Dylan*, which, like AIDAN DAY's *Jokerman: Reading the Lyrics of Bob Dylan* (1984), pioneered a post-structuralist critical approach to its subject. Published in 1991, it was republished, updated, revised and much expanded, as *Alias Bob Dylan Revisited* in 2003. It is one of the critical works of consequence about Bob Dylan's art.

Scobie specifies patiently some of the new critical notions: that 'the very idea of "canon" itself is now in question', that 'What dies in "the death of the Author" is . . . his authority: . . . the position of the author as the final criterion by which every reading of a work is to be measured and judged', and that rather than being 'concerned with Bob Dylan as biography', the aim is to deal 'with the alias Bob Dylan: "Bob Dylan" as text . . . multiple and shifting . . .' Yet his book begins boldly with a preface about Robert Zimmerman's childhood in the odd milieu of Hibbing, Minnesota: an upbringing to give any artist-to-be a formative sense of the double, if not multiple, identity of everything ('Reality has always had too many heads', Dylan sings on 1997's 'Cold Irons Bound'), and this first part of the book is inspired, well-written and a better slice of biography than we get in the biographies (not least for a wonderful description of why 'Every stage that Bob Dylan has played on for the last thirty years has been, after Hibbing High School Auditorium, an anticlimax'). Indeed, despite his disclaimers, Scobie is actually very interested in Bob Dylan's biography and his book is none the worse for that.

Crucially, though, Scobie argues that 'the notion that we are not singular entities but variable and multiple personalities' is a major concern of Dylan's work itself, and that in this sense, 'far from being opposed to critical theory, Dylan's work thematizes one of its central questions.'

[Stephen Scobie: *Alias Bob Dylan*, Calgary, Alberta, Canada: Red Deer College Press, 1991; *And Forget My Name: A Speculative Biography of Bob Dylan*, Victoria, B.C., Canada: Ekstasis Editions, 1999; *Alias Bob Dylan Revisited*, Calgary: Red Deer College Press, 2003.]

Scorsese, Martin [1942 -] Martin Scorsese was born on November 17, 1942 in Flushing, Queens, New York. After wanting so strongly to enter the priesthood that he was entered a seminary in 1956, he turned instead to films, graduating in film studies at NYU in 1964. (He also went on to have five wives.) He co-edited *Woodstock*, 1970, and then directed *Boxcar Bertha*, 1972, followed by the film that defined his style, made his name and showed his talent, *Mean Streets*, 1973. After other work came *Taxi Driver*, in 1976, *New York, New York*, 1977, and *Raging Bull*, 1980. Subsequent films include *The King of Comedy*, 1983, *The Color of Money*, 1986, *The Last Temptation of Christ*, 1988, *Goodfellas*, 1990, and *The Aviator*, 2004.

From *Mean Streets* onwards, Scorsese deployed the rock music that so entrances him, foregrounding it to what was then a pioneering extent. But he has also made rock music the subject of films, beginning with his filming of THE BAND's farewell concert as *The Last Waltz* in 1978, for which ROBBIE ROBERTSON was a producer. This partnership didn't please everyone involved: LEVON HELM's autobiography has this to say, first about the concert event and its filming:

> 'As the evening progressed, I couldn't figure out what was wrong with Robbie. Instead of taking care of business and getting the guitar parts solid and in pitch, Robbie was running up to the microphone and pretending to sing the lead vocals on all the songs: my songs, RICK [DANKO]'s songs, even RICHARD [MANUEL]'s songs. . . . After the show, it became obvious what had happened: As we tried to play the best concert of our lives, it was picture-taking time for Scorsese and Robertson . . .
>
> 'We had just fought our way through five-plus hours of backing every "big star" who happened to live in California at the time, doing their songs. All we had accomplished was the same old thing we had worked our asses off to avoid—being another backup house band. Congratulations boys, you are once again relegated to the old "sideman" position. This means that GARTH [HUDSON], Rick, Richard and I get to enjoy billing underneath and below all the big names on the marquis.
>
> 'When *Music from Big Pink* was released, we made a point of emphasizing the collective, egoless nature of The Band—no individual outranked the other in importance. Now our group was being portrayed as Robbie Robertson and his back-up musicians. Years of history and hard work were corrupted in one fell swoop.'

Helm's criticism didn't stop there; he alleges that Scorsese and Robertson also had the whole project sewn up financially too:

'It was going to be a grand celebration of our legacy with the promise that it would generate huge profits and financial security for Rick, Richard, Garth and I. To say that it fell short of our expectations would be the understatement of the century. Robbie made himself executive producer of the project and placed himself and director Martin Scorsese, and all their flunkies and yes men, on huge salaries. And so began their year and a half love story of buying houses and apartments on both coasts, taping up all the windows with aluminum foil (like ELVIS did) and spending all night and all day "cutting" the movie. Scorsese said of the new partnership, he "just loved being around all that energy." That "energy" was referred to as coke and blow by most people . . . I'd hate to see that part of the budget. Better still, I'd like to see a real accountant and find out if they hid it in the travel, marketing, advertising or entertainment portions of the budget. I'm a patient man, but it's been almost 30 years and Garth and I are still waiting for our "financial security" to materialize. The sad thing is there's no more waiting for Rick and Richard.'

Scorsese and ROBBIE ROBERTSON are certainly long-time friends, even ex-housemates, and in the 1980s Robertson composed and produced the soundtrack for *The Color of Money*.

Helm's criticisms of *The Last Waltz* may be as valid as they are heartfelt, and it was obvious all along that the guest appearance of NEIL DIAMOND was incongruous (and could only be explained by Robertson's having produced a Diamond album), but in most respects, for the average viewer, the film was a masterly documenting of a great event.

Dylan was among those taking part, and though it was far from his best performance, he was sympathetically filmed, as were The Band when they were on stage with him—perhaps especially Levon Helm, in fact, whose keen relish of Dylan's unpredictability is captured beautifully. The film has recently been released on DVD, with extra material, colour correction, and re-mastering (by Robertson), but also with omissions and much rewriting of history; there is also now a 4-CD audio version, which is different again. And look up the DVD online and you'll soon find it billed as 'starring Robbie Robertson', rather than The Band.

The amount of Bob Dylan on offer varies between all these different issues. The original movie version showed his 'Forever Young', the reprise version of 'Baby Let Me Follow You Down' and (sharing vocals with Richard Manuel) 'I Shall Be Released'; the original audio gave us the same, omitted the second verse of 'Forever Young' but also included Dylan's first rendition of 'Baby Let Me Follow You Down' and his 'I Don't Believe You'. The 4-CD box set adds 'Hazel' and a complete 'Forever Young'. (And then in February 2003 Rhino also reissued the original 1978 audio release but as a 30-track Limited Edition 3-LP box set, reproducing the original album, but using the 2002 remasters.)

Scorsese returned to music in 1987 when he directed Michael Jackson's 'Bad' video, and in 2003 directed the program 'Feel Like Going Home' in the acclaimed PBS series 'The Blues'. In 2005 he returned both to music and to Bob Dylan, making the extraordinary documentary *No Direction Home: Bob Dylan* ('A Martin Scorsese Picture'): an absolutely unprecedented Bobfest.

[The Band: concert at Winterland, San Francisco, CA, 25 Nov 1976, filmed as *The Last Waltz*, dir. Martin Scorsese, US, 1978; *The Last Waltz—Special Edition* DVD: MGM Home Video 1003426, US, 7 May 2002 (17332DVD, UK, Oct 2002); soundtrack first issued as *The Last Waltz*, Warner 3 WS 3146, 7 Apr 1978; 4-CD box set version *The Last Waltz*, Warner Bros/Rhino R2 78278, US, Apr 2002. *No Direction Home: Bob Dylan*, 2-DVD set, Paramount Home Video 097360310542, US, 20 Sep 2005 (UK, 5 Oct 2005).

Levon Helm: *This Wheel's on Fire: Levon Helm and the Story of The Band* (written with Stephen Davis), New York: Wm Morrow, 1993 & Chicago: A Capella Books, 2000; quotes taken from *www.razormagazine.com/feature0204c.php*.]

Scott, Jack [1936 -] Jack Scott was a rocker who found, after many a label switch, that the country-pop market was larger. He was born Giovanni Scafone, Jr. on January 24, 1936 in Windsor, Ontario, Canada, but when he was ten his family moved close to Detroit. He might have been an Italian Canadian, but he soon sounded like Nashville. His biggest successes were the US top 3 record 'My True Love' and the transatlantic hit 'What in the World's Come Over You', a hit in the UK alongside Jim Reeves' more lugubrious but comparable 'He'll Have to Go'.

Scott hasn't had a hit since 1960 and rarely performs live, though he does appear from time to time with the Starlight Drifters back in his hometown of Hazel Park, Michigan.

Dylan performed Scott's 'Let's Learn to Live & Love Again' at two concerts in 1990—in Berlin on July 5 and in Des Moines, Iowa, on August 26.

Sebastian, John [1944 -] John B. Sebastian Jr. was born in Greenwich Village on March 17, 1944, the son of a classical harmonica player and a radio script writer. Growing up in the city, he absorbed its music, learnt harmonica from his father, saw many musical greats in person—some of them as visitors to his parents' house, including WOODY GUTHRIE—and became a member of the Even Dozen Jug Band (with MARIA D'Amato—later MULDAUR—Stefan Grossman, Steve Katz, Joshua Rifkin, DAVID GRISMAN and Peter Siegel).

After that he joined the Mugwumps and then, with the Canadian ex-Mugwump Zal Yanovsky on

Photo by John Byrne Cooke

Dave Ray at Club 47, Cambridge, Massachusetts, 1965

Library of Congress

Carl Sandburg, 1955

Photo by Leo Kulinski, Jr.

Carlos Santana

Photography by Sherry Rayn Barnett

John Sebastian

From Jazz Hot magazine, 1958

Brother John Sellers, 1958

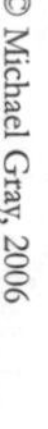

© Michael Gray, 2006

Robert Shelton in Great Malvern, England, 1974

Ken Regan / Camera 5

Bob Dylan & Bruce Springsteen

guitar, bassist Steve Boone and drummer Joe Butler, he formed the Lovin' Spoonful. A regular act at the Nite Owl Café in the Village, they cut four unsuccessful sides for Elektra (for whom Sebastian had been a session musician) but then, perhaps to their surprise, found themselves a pop hit act with their next release. Turning down an offer from PHIL SPECTOR, they signed to Kama Sutra and in August 1965 released 'Do You Believe in Magic?', giving them a top 10 hit single and a top 40 album. This success was sustained over a period of several years, as the band produced albums full of catchy songs and hit singles that somehow managed to be happy without causing offence, among them 'Daydream', 'Nashville Cats', 'Summer in the City', 'Did You Ever Have to Make Up Your Mind?' and 'Darling Be Home Soon', mostly written by Sebastian. In 1967 a drug bust turned sour, and in 1968 the group collapsed.

By this time, Dylan and Sebastian had long been acquainted. They can be seen together in 1964 in photographs by Douglas R. Gilbert in the book *Forever Young*, to which Sebastian contributes an Introductory Note. One photo shows Dylan falling backwards onto an alarmingly candlewick bedspread, swamped by the entire Paturel family, owners of the Café Espresso in Woodstock, plus John Sebastian. (Dylan used to write in the studio apartment above the café.) Another shot, inside the café, shows Sebastian playing an acoustic guitar and looking hesitant, faced with the puzzlement of how to fit in with Dylan, cigarette-in-mouth cool, who is plunking an electric guitar.

On January 14, 1965, in New York City, Sebastian was one of those who played on that evening's session for the *Bringing It All Back Home* album (along with BRUCE LANGHORNE and others). Nothing performed that day made it onto the album, but 'I'll Keep It With Mine' was issued 20 years later on *Biograph*. That evening's versions of 'Love Minus Zero/No Limit', 'It's All Over Now, Baby Blue', 'Bob Dylan's 115th Dream', 'She Belongs to Me' and 'Subterranean Homesick Blues' have not circulated.

(According to DAVID HAJDU's *Positively 4th Street*, Sebastian had also been there on the *first* day of *Bringing It All Back Home* sessions, January 13, playing bass as Dylan 'sang and played acoustic versions of eleven new songs'. This was the day that yielded the versions of 'Subterranean Homesick Blues' and 'Farewell Angelina' that emerged on the *Bootleg Series Vols. 1–3*, but on which Sebastian receives no credit.)

In 1969 the still-youthful John Sebastian appeared, very tie-dyed, at the Woodstock Festival, babbling away but singing exquisitely, including on the lovely 'Sporting Life'. Various solo albums were followed by another unexpected huge hit, 'Welcome Back', a no.1 record in April 1976 (a TV-series theme song). His solo career has continued since, embracing TV and film appearances (including in the TV series 'Married with Children' and the 1980 PAUL SIMON movie *One Trick Pony*). He has played harmonica behind Willie Dixon, MISSISSIPPI JOHN HURT, the Doors, JUDY COLLINS, CROSBY, Stills, Nash & YOUNG and many others.

In the 1990s he returned to the idea of the jug band, playing live as John Sebastian & the J-Band, which included Fritz Richmond (who died in 2005), the great Yank Rachell (who died in 1997) and GEOFF MULDAUR. In 2004, on a PBS special, he described in detail how he felt that 'Daydream' and 'Do You Believe in Magic' had influenced the music of THE BEATLES, while the same year saw 'Welcome Back' sampled on a hit by Mase (a rapper), also titled 'Welcome Back'. Sebastian still lives in Woodstock, New York.

[Douglas R. Gilbert, *Forever Young: Photographs of Bob Dylan*, New York: Da Capo, 2005. David Hajdu, *Positively 4th Street: The Life and Times of Joan Baez, Bob Dylan, Mimi Baez Fariña and Richard Fariña*, London: Bloomsbury edn., p.232.]

Sedgwick, Edie [1943 - 1971] Edith Minturn Sedgwick was born in Santa Barbara, California, on April 20, 1943, into an etiolated, mentally unstable Old Boston Family. She grew up on the family ranch in California, attended private school and had already suffered two breakdowns by the time she met BOB NEUWIRTH, Bob Dylan's mid-1960s sidekick, in December 1964. Neuwirth told her biographer:

> 'Bobby Dylan and I occasionally ventured out into the poppy nightlife world. I think somebody who had met Edie said, "You have to meet this terrific girl." Dylan called her, and she chartered a limousine and came to see us. We spent an hour or two, all laughing and giggling, having a terrific time. I think we met upstairs at the Kettle of Fish on MacDougal Street, which was one of the great places of the Sixties. It was just before the Christmas holidays; it was snowing, and I remember we went to look at the display on Houston Street in front of the Catholic church. . . . Edie was fantastic. She was always fantastic.'

They met, that is to say, a month before Edie Sedgwick met ANDY WARHOL, and three months before she starred in her first Factory film, *Vinyl*, shot in March 1965. That year she also appeared in *Space*, *Restaurant*, *Poor Little Rich Girl* (which is what Warhol always called her, while spending her money), *Kitchen*, *Horse* and *Beauty #2*. In 1966 she was to have been the star of *Chelsea Girls*, but Warhol supposedly edited her out after she quit the Factory.

The Warhol people–Andy, Paul Morrissey and Gerard Malanga–all felt that she quit because she'd been misled by Neuwirth into believing both that Warhol was exploiting her and that 'Dylan's people' were going to make her a real star. Perhaps in this case, without his knowledge, this meant

D.A. PENNEBAKER, since he was involved in Dylan's mid-1960s films, and Neuwirth had been an assistant on the first of them, *Don't Look Back*. Pennebaker shot 'a lot' of footage of Edie Sedgwick, he said later, simply because she often came round to his studio.

The non-Warhol people tended to feel that Sedgwick quit the Factory because she was provoked, in a row with Warhol in a restaurant in February 1966, when she had announced that she was going to star in a film with Dylan, and Warhol, out of spite, had asked her if she knew that Dylan was married. She left the room, made a phone call (to Dylan, Paul Morrissey assumed) and then left, never to return.

Either way, there's no evidence—and no real grounds to suppose—that Dylan and Edie had any personal relationship at all, let alone a significant one. She comes into the Dylan equation only because people used to believe that she is the girl whispering in Dylan's ear in a photograph on the foldout sleeve of the original *Blonde on Blonde* double-LP, and because of a persistent hunch by many people that, with however light a prompt, she *was* the 'blonde on blonde'. PATTI SMITH said so, in her poem 'Edie Sedgwick (1943–1971)': 'Everyone / knew she was the real heroine of / Blonde on Blonde. . . . / she was white on white / so blonde on blonde'. Smith's poem goes on to hint, and again this was widely whispered, that Edie Sedgwick was a subject of the album's song 'Just Like a Woman': 'she broke down / like a little girl / like a baby girl / like a lady.' It's also been claimed that she was the woman who wore the 'Leopard-Skin Pill-Box Hat', that she's the 'débutante' in 'Stuck Inside of Mobile with the Memphis Blues Again'. This may all or mostly be untrue; but even if it is *all* true, it doesn't signify Sedgwick was a significant person in Dylan's life—only that she was an interesting spectacle or personality, visually memorable and made more so by the air of tragedy she carried around with her: the fog, perhaps, in 'her fog, her amphetamines and her pearls'.

It's also been suggested that she and Warhol were both the subject of an earlier Dylan song, 'Like a Rolling Stone'—she the addressee who 'went to the finest school', he the 'Napoleon in rags'. Well, to go there is only possible 'if you're looking to get silly'. But there's no doubting that the ghost of Edie Sedgwick hangs around *Blonde on Blonde*.

Edie's last film was *Ciao! Manhattan*, which was filmed partly in 1967 in black and white, and partly in colour very soon before her death. Alternating between the two sets of footage, it alternates between 'now' and 'then', between 'fact' and fiction, between Edie looking the gorgeous young model and Edie the near-comatose self-abasement queen. She died of 'acute barbituate intoxication' in bed on the West Coast in the early hours of November 16, 1971. She was 28.

The film *Factory Girl*, in production in 2005, was going to include the supposed Sedgwick-Dylan 'affair', but he threatened legal action unless this theme was dropped. The film is going ahead, starring Sienna Miller as Edie and Guy Pearce as Warhol, but with no 'Bob Dylan'. According to *The Times* (October 28, 2005): 'To fill the void, producers have cast Hayden Christensen and given him messy hair, and sunglasses. "They aren't allowed to call him Bob Dylan," says Meredith Ostrom, who plays Velvet Underground collaborator Nico. "But he is absolutely the young Dylan. It's obvious."'

[*Ciao! Manhattan*, dir. John Palmer & David Weisman, US, 1972; DVD '30th Anniversary edition' with outtakes, US, 2002. Bob Neuwirth & Pennebaker quotes, Jean Stein, *Edie: An American Biography*, George Plimpton, ed., New York: Knopf, 1982, p.166 & *nia*. Patti Smith: 'Edie Sedgwick (1943–1971)', *Seventh Heaven*, Boston: Telegraph Books, 1972. *Factory Girl*, dir. George Hickenlooper, written Captain Mauzner (aka Josh Klausner) & Simon Monjack, Bob Yari Productions, US, 2006.]

Seeger, Mike [1933 -] Michael Seeger was born in New York City on August 15, 1933 into, yes, *that* Seeger family. His father was the academic musicologist Charles Seeger, his mother the avant-garde composer Ruth Crawford Seeger, his half-brother PETE SEEGER and his sisters Peggy, Barbara and Penny Seeger.

Mike grew up in Maryland, close to Washington, D.C., on a heavy diet of folk music. He learnt to play a large number of instruments: guitar, banjo, auto-harp, harmonica, fiddle, mandolin, dulcimer, dobro, jew's harp and pan pipes (quills). He began making recordings of traditional musicians on his own tape recorder at age 20, and later field-recorded for MOSES ASCH's Folkways label, including making the first recordings of ELIZABETH COTTEN (she was closest to hand, being the family maid), and field-recording the Stoneman Family, the Lilly Brothers, Doc Boggs, Don Stover and many more. In 1958, with JOHN COHEN and TOM PALEY he co-founded the seminal folk-revivalist group THE NEW LOST CITY RAMBLERS. He has also performed, and toured the world, as a solo artist and in duos with various of his romantic partners. He has been the director of a number of folk festivals, the producer of instrument instruction books and videos, worked with innumerable other musicians and even won a GRATEFUL DEAD Rex Foundation award. In 1960, with Pete, he co-wrote and performed the original music for the fiction film *Indian Summer*, in which 'an old farmer on New York's Delaware River is displaced by the construction of a reservoir', and 20 years later was the sole subject of Yasha Aginsky's 42-minute documentary film 'Homemade American Music'.

Every so often in recent years he has rounded up musicians from his past and recorded with them to produce a series of 'reunion albums'. Dylan was drawn in to one of these. In the same month that we believe Dylan recorded *World Gone Wrong*, May 1993, he got together with Mike Seeger for a re-recording of his own 'Ballad of Hollis Brown', with Seeger on banjo, in Los Angeles. Alongside tracks Seeger shared with MARIA MULDAUR, DAVID GRISMAN, RALPH STANLEY and the inevitable scattering of other Seegers, the Bob Dylan/Mike Seeger track duly appeared in 1995 on the *Third Annual Farewell Reunion* album.

'Mike Seeger's really real', wrote Bob Dylan in the *poem* 'Blowin' in the Wind', published in *Hootenanny* magazine in December 1963. In *Chronicles Volume One*, 40 years later, he elaborated at some length. The gist of it comes here, when he explains that Mike Seeger struck him as *so* good that it pushed him into truly deciding, for the first time, that he would have to *write* songs: 'He . . . played in all the genres and had the idioms mastered—Delta blues, ragtime, minstrel songs, buck-and-wing, dance reels, play party, hymns and gospel—being there and seeing him up close, something hit me. It's not as if he just played everything well, he played these songs as good as it was possible to play them. . . . The thought occurred to me that maybe I'd have to write my own folk songs, ones that Mike didn't know. That was a startling thought. Up 'til then, I'd gone some places and thought I knew my way around. And then it struck me that I'd never been there before.'

[Bob Dylan with Mike Seeger: 'Ballad of Hollis Brown', LA, 19 May 1993, on the Various Artists compilation album *Third Annual Farewell Reunion*, Rounder ROU-0000313, Somerville, MA, 1995. Bob Dylan: *Chronicles Volume One*, 2004, pp.70–71.]

Seeger, Pete [1919 -] The youngest of three sons of ethnomusicologist Charles Seeger, an academic grandee, and his first wife Constance, Seeger was born on May 3, 1919, in Paterson, New Jersey. His parents divorced in 1927, when Peter was eight. Five years later, his father married Ruth Crawford, and moved the expanding family to Washington in 1935. Pete's half-siblings by this marriage included MIKE and Peggy Seeger, both of whom grew up to be folksingers too, the latter marrying the British communist folksinger EWAN MacCOLL.

A comrade of WOODY GUTHRIE, blues giant LEADBELLY, the great folklorist ALAN LOMAX and other formative figures in the history of 20th century musical America, Seeger spent decades touring the world, adapting songs and passing them along, while preaching ceaselessly the primacy of the common people and democratic politics, and the power of song to inspire, uplift and persuade people into paths of political righteousness.

He and two others formed the pioneering folk group the Almanac Singers, setting up a Greenwich Village commune in 1940. Guthrie joined the group in 1941, and Seeger encouraged him to write his great autobiography, *Bound for Glory*. Seeger was a tireless internationalist, a leading light of *Sing Out!* and a founder of *Broadside* magazines and, in 1948, of the Weavers, the group that was, in popularising folksong and songs that copied folksong instead of Tin Pan Alley, the precursor of such later popularisers as the Kingston Trio and PETER, PAUL & MARY.

Seeger was also a brave man blacklisted in the McCarthy era after standing up to the House Un-American Activities Committee under threat of a gaol-sentence (and was long blacklisted by ABC-Television's 'Hootenanny' folk showcase). He was a lifelong advocate of universal brotherhood—if, like most of us, a rather shorter-term enthusiast for sisterhood—and a campaigning supporter of black rights long before the movement was widespread or fashionable. You'll find him standing alongside Martin Luther King in photographs back in 1957.

Nor was Seeger closed to later manifestations of 'the struggle'. In his late 70s, admirably, Seeger ensured that a 2-CD collection of his songs—by various artists, but with notes by Seeger himself—made room to detail current campaigning organisations from Peace Action and Honor the Earth to World Hunger Year and the Center for Defense Information, and to remind us that 1998 was the 25th anniversary of the murder of Victor Jara in Chile. (All rather more admirable than advocating the attractions of Victoria's Secret underwear.)

As well as an uncountable number of recordings, Seeger has published at least 27 books and songbooks, from the self-published *How to Play the Five-String Banjo* (1948), *Bantu Choral Folk Songs* (1959) and a Moscow State Publishers edition of *Pete Seeger Sings Songs of the American People* (1965) through to 1991's *Everybody Says Freedom* and beyond.

He became, inevitably, a star of the anti-star folk revival movement of the late 1950s and early 1960s, and a father-figure to more than one generation. He was also the first established performer to be influenced by Bob Dylan. By the end of 1962 Seeger was performing Dylan songs and, presciently, calling him the most important new songwriter of the time—though in writing 'Where Have All the Flowers Gone?' in the mid-1950s, Seeger can himself be said to have created the modern Protest Song. It isn't far from this anthem to 'Blowin' in the Wind'. At the 1963 NEWPORT FOLK FESTIVAL, very soon after the two had visited GREENWOOD, Mississippi, together, Seeger and Dylan sang Dylan's tedious and self-righteous song 'Ye Playboys & Playgirls' at one of the afternoon workshops. It is their only officially released duet performance.

Yet Seeger's songwriting might be said to have reached full bloom with 'Where Have All the Flowers Gone?', whereas Dylan's had barely begun to peep up from the compost of the folk-revival movement with 'Blowin' in the Wind'. For all his international wandering and co-operative cross-fertilisation, Seeger's writing has never really developed in the 60 years or so that he has been at work. Indeed Seeger has written and composed remarkably little. Of the 200 songs on *Where Have All the Flowers Gone: The Songbook*, Pete was creditably quick to point out that most were other people's, or everybody's, and he is associated with them only because he tinkered with them slightly or sang them a lot. Solo invention was rare. The words of his best song, 'Turn, Turn, Turn', are, with one line's exception, from Ecclesiastes. Overall, his well-meant quilt-making is not so much the folk process as creative paucity.

If the Seeger muse is a meagre muse, it is partly political correctness that stifles it. His compulsion to be Goody Two-Shoes also overrides the critical faculties most people turn upon themselves as well as on others. There is no abrasion or anti-pomposity-alarm at work with Seeger. When Dylan called him 'saintly' it was a two-edged, sly critique: exactly the kind of subtle barb Seeger is incapable of. The main feature of his persona is an overarching piety. Even when you're in solid agreement with his politics, it's hard not to want to hit him.

His 'saintliness' also embraces a suspect just-folksiness. In the stimulating and professorial Washington home of his teenage years, Pete learnt the songs of the people, not least from family servant and folksinger ELIZABETH COTTEN, the writer of 'Freight Train'. When he grew up, he went to folksy old Harvard (and in due course dropped out).

Alongside the earnestness and working-man style sits an uneasy 'sense of humour', not coursing naturally through everything but offered as a special, separate segment in his work. Just as there are earnest songs, so there are humorous songs. These have a fatal, fey whimsy once widespread on the folk scene. To listen to the insufferably cutesy 'All Mixed Up', or to be jollied through 'Get Up and Go' ('How do I know my youth is all spent? / My get-up-and-go just got up and went / But in spite of it all I'm able to grin / And think of the places my get-up has bin'—he found these words on a diner-menu and *liked* them) is to be plunged back to the excruciating sing-along folk-world in which Julie Felix was always going to the zoo, zoo, zoo.

This sense of fun did not extend to tolerance of other people's ideas of 'folk'. When Dylan 'went electric' at the 1965 Newport Folk Festival (where blues artists had been 'electric' many years earlier), Seeger wanted to cut the cables with the woodsman's axe with which he had been conducting a work-song workshop.

Even if you knew nothing of his history of antagonism to rock'n'roll, you could tell that Seeger carried this disapproval right next to the heart on his sleeve from hearing him perform. He has exactly the sort of wooden unmusicality that white banjo playing is heir to. Considering the people among whom he has moved as a performer and those he has identified with politically throughout a long career and life, it's quite remarkable, and sadly ironic, how little impact black music had upon his musicality.

'Pete showed us all that caring about people is the music. We follow the path he has blazed—with gratitude and pride,' declared Peter Yarrow of Peter, Paul & Mary in the 1990s. These people still believe that well-meaningness makes good music, and, like Seeger, still prove that it doesn't.

[Bob Dylan & Pete Seeger: 'Ye Playboys & Playgirls', Newport, RI, 27 Jul 1963, *Newport Broadside (Topical Songs)* Vanguard VRS-9144 (mono) / 79144, NY, 1964; CD reissued Vanguard VCD 770003-2, NY, 1997.]

Seger, Bob [1945 -] Robert Clark Seger was born on May 6, 1945 in Dearborn, Michigan, a town long since sprawled in upon by Detroit. He was a pre-SPRINGSTEEN 'Heartland rocker', a blue-collar guitar star who started out with Bob Seger & the Last Heard and the Bob Seger System before settling for the group he steered to mega-sales, Bob Seger & the Silver Bullet Band. His first album, *Ramblin' Gamblin' Man* (by the Bob Seger System) came out in 1969, the first of four made for Capitol; after one oldies album on a smaller label (*Smokin' O.P.'s* on Palladium) he switched to Reprise, released his sixth album under his own name and with a title that seems to have been prescient about the phenomenon of instant nostalgia—issued in 1973 it was called *Back in '72*. The seventh album, reasonably enough, was called *Seven*, and its opening track was Seger's signature song 'Get Out of Denver'. Issued as a single, it was not the huge hit it's assumed to have been: it reached only no.80 on the *Billboard* Hot 100, but in the decades since its 1974 release it has become regarded as some kind of classic. Certainly its remorselessly simple upbeat churn—pop made rock only by being guitar-led—typified the Seger style. After *Beautiful Loser* (which marked his return to Capitol) he made the first albums with the Silver Bullet Band, *Live Bullet* and *Night Moves*, both 1976, the latter his real breakthrough album, making the top 10 album charts and giving him a top 5 single with the LP's title track. He might have looked like Roy Wood and sounded like Status Quo, but he typified a certain sort of 1970s Americana. After 1995's album *It's a Mystery* there was a ten-year gap before the next new album, announced for 2004 as *Face the Promise* but still unreleased as of November 2005.

His slender connections with Bob Dylan are these: when Dylan and TOM PETTY & THE HEARTBREAKERS played Clarkston, Michigan, on July 1, 1986, Seger came on stage for the last encore number and shared vocals on 'Knockin' on Heaven's

Door'; and 18 years later, when Dylan's Never-Ending Tour spent three nights at the small, old-fashioned State Theater in Detroit, Dylan paid Seger the tribute of a one-off performance of 'Get Out of Denver' as the last encore song in his second-night set, on March 16, 2004.

***Self Portrait* [1970]** The tenth album, and misjudged on Dylan's part. You could have made a good minor album out of it if you'd cut it down from the overblown double-LP set that it was. There was no reason why Dylan shouldn't have made this new departure–largely into pop songs and Tin Pan Alley country material written by other people–but it just wasn't that good. It was the cue for large numbers of Dylan's followers to give up on him. In *Chronicles* Dylan claims that this was what he'd set out to do: that the album's vapidness was deliberate. That's rather an insult to the musicians who worked on it with him, and to whom he was perfectly respectful at the time. Either way, he had deconstructed himself.

Now, seen in the long back-projection of his work, it isn't gruellingly important that the album was so second-rate–but when it was new, in 1970, the adjustments necessary to come to terms with *Self Portrait* seemed enormous. Dylan was demanding more and giving less with this album. At first hearing, much of the work was trite, rutted and simplistic: and that, in itself, had huge and perplexing impact. Here was an apparently mediocre collection of work from a man who, rightly or wrongly, had become accepted as the genius of our generation.

There were, of course, people who didn't face these difficulties–those who simply listened and enjoyed; and Dylan has always been on their side, against classification, with those who, in his view, know 'too much to argue or to judge'. All the same, the question 'How should we respond to this album?' was a common one among those whose concern isn't disproportionately with Dylan's music at the expense of a concern with the words.

First, there is a blandness of defeat about it, which comes across most clearly through Dylan's voice. It conveys, especially in the 'happy' songs, a sort of choking caution (listen, for instance, to 'I Forgot More')–an impression that Dylan has walked, Godlessly, close to the valley of the shadow of death and dare not now explore beyond the simplistic verities adhered to by Nashville, Tennessee. It is not so much mental plumpness as an exhaustion of courage–as if the Dylan of *Self Portrait* has placed himself under house-arrest because the old Insanity Factory is too close to his gates. And while this kind of rest/retreat is understandable enough in the man, it doesn't do much for his art.

The parallel with the Born Again Christian albums *Slow Train Coming* and especially *Saved* is very strong: on these, Dylan s panic at Godlessness has him clinging not to Nashville's country verities and simplicities but to the gospel ones of the Bible Belt. The main virtue of 'Saving Grace' is that it confesses this need-to-cling, just as 'Watching the River Flow' was to do not long after *Self Portrait*. Yet just as *Slow Train Coming* and *Saved* are good enough to repay countless plays, so too *Self Portrait*, albeit a very minor Dylan work, has its own riches; and now that the album is well into the past, it is easier to enjoy them.

First, the album does not lack warmth; and second, its self-deprecation can be seen as showing an egolessness which is, now and then, a welcome ingredient in Dylan's largely ego-emphatic output. As Bill Damon put it (*Rolling Stone*, September 3, 1970): 'With all of its unity and inclusiveness, *Self Portrait* is too complex to have a point of view. . . . It is Eastern in its egolessness. . . . Dylan does remind us on this album of all the ways we have known him . . . but Dylan's image serves only his music.'

Even the cover painting has its virtues: its childlike technique and colouring are a relief from image-building ad-man photography, and interesting also because, like the painting Dylan did for THE BAND's *Music from Big Pink* album, it owes a lot to the pen-and-ink sketches of WOODY GUTHRIE.

Quite a throwback–and on one level, the whole album is a throwback: a deliberate package of Golden Oldies, from folk to country to chart-climbing pop. Best tracks are 'Days of '49', 'Early Morning Rain', 'Let It Be Me', 'Belle Isle', 'Copper Kettle' and 'Wigwam'.

In September 2005 it was reported that an out-take from the *Self Portrait* sessions, Dylan's recording of the traditional song 'Tell Ol' Bill', never previously circulated even among collectors, was lined up for imminent release on the soundtrack album to the film *North Country*. By October 2005 this had been contradicted and we were told that Dylan had recorded the song anew for the film, and that the backing musicians included Elana Fremerman, fiddle player from the group Hot Club of Cowtown; and then it transpired that this recording was not only new but of a *new* song: that Dylan had taken the title 'Tell Ol' Bill' but written a song entirely different in melody and words from the traditional song. (A novelty in itself, in the age of *"Love and Theft"*.)

The film is the real-life-based story of one woman's struggle in the 1980s against discrimination by Eveleth Mines of Minnesota–a taconite mining and processing company (owned by Oglebay Norton Co. of Cleveland, Ohio) that opened in 1965 and is based in Eveleth, a very small town less than 20 miles east of that other taconite town, Hibbing.

Thus an apparent resourceful redirecting of attention to the *Self Portrait* sessions proved to be no such thing.

[Recorded Nashville, TN, 24 & 26 Apr & 3 May 1969; Isle of Wight Festival, UK, 31 Aug 1969; and NY, 3–6

Mar 1970; released as stereo 2-LP set, Columbia C2X 30050 (in UK CBS 66250/S 64085-86), 8 Jun 1970.

The Band: *Music from Big Pink*, NY & LA, Jan–Feb 1968, Capitol SKAO 2955, LA (Capitol ST 2955, London), 1968. Bob Dylan: 'Tell Ol' Bill', NY, 4 Mar 1970, unissued. Bob Dylan: 'Tell Ol' Bill', *nia*, 2005, *Music from the Motion Picture 'North Country'*, Columbia/Sony Music Soundtrax 1CK 97777, NY, 11 Oct 2005 (which also includes previously released Dylan tracks). *North Country*, dir. Niki Caro, US, 2005.]

Sellers, Brother John [1924 - 1999] John Sellers was born in Clarksdale, Mississippi, on May 27, 1924. Abandoned by his parents in a flood at the age of four, he was performing in tent shows at five, removed from a bordello at the age of ten by Mahalia Jackson (but what was she doing there?), taken to live with her in Chicago and encouraged to sing with her and with BIG BILL BROONZY. From 1945 to 1951 he stuck with gospel but then went secular and in London sang with a jazz group that included the famous British cartoonist Trog. He recorded blues and gospel from the 1940s onwards, billed as Reverend John Sellers on Miracle in 1948 and as Johnny Sellers on some 1952 blues sides. He moved to New York City and fell in with the Greenwich Village world, recording 'folk blues' in the predictable way. He was not a great singer or an especially dexterous tambourine-shaker, but according to Studs Terkel, whose talks he helped illustrate with song around the end of the 1950s, he had 'a clarity and a sense of urgency. . . . Brother John had a way of making things come alive.' He was best on material like 'Wade in the Water'.

In 1961 in the Village, Dylan and MARK SPOELSTRA were 'the Dungarees' in Brother John & the Dungarees, playing back-up guitars and harmonicas behind Sellers at hoot nights at Folk City, where he was an MC and a regular performer. Dylan played at his birthday party there in August 1961.

In 1963 Sellers appeared in the first Broadway production of the black playwright-poet-novelist Langston Hughes' *Tambourines to Glory* (first published as a novel in 1958). He also collaborated with choreographer Alvin Ailey on the latter's *Blues Suite* and *Revelations* and continued to perform as a musician in Ailey's American Dance Theatre until 1997. Sellers died in New York City on March 27, 1999, in the middle of suing Ailey over royalties and copyright.

[Main sources include the *Independent*'s obituary, *nia*, seen reproduced without author byline 13 Feb 2006 online at *http://elvispelvis.com/johnsellers.html*.]

Sexton, Charlie [1968 -] Charles Wayne Sexton was born in San Antonio, Texas, on August 11, 1968, and like his younger brother Will, became a guitarist prodigiously young. He was taken under Joe Ely's wing, became a friend of STEVIE RAY VAUGHAN and was already famous on Austin's music scene by the time he signed a record deal and made his first album at the age of 16. *Pictures for Pleasures* was released in 1985. He toured with David Bowie in 1987, joined the Arc Angels in the early 1990s (appearing on their ferociously good 1992 album), formed the Charlie Sexton Sextet in 1995, produced and played on an Edie Brickell album, and played on albums by Don Henley, Lucinda Williams and the excellent Shawn Colvin.

He has also appeared in, and /or written and played music for, a small number of films, including *Beverly Hills Cop II* (1987) and *Air America* (1990). In *Thelma & Louise* (1991) he played a bar-band singer, and in *F.T.W.* (1994) a cowboy called, er, Slim. In 2003 he also appeared in *Masked & Anonymous*—because by that time his career path had crossed with Bob Dylan's.

It has been rumoured that he was first involved with Dylan when contributing to some demos with him in 1983–85, but no such material has been logged, let alone circulated. A more reliable first sighting is when Dylan's Never-Ending Tour hit Austin on October 25, 1991 and Charlie Sexton and Jimmie Dale Gilmore both came on stage to play guitars with Bob and the band on 'Everything Is Broken'. Five years went by, almost to the day, and Dylan was back in town, this time for two nights at the Austin Music Hall, and Charlie Sexton appeared both nights. That October 26 (1996)—allegedly brought on in instant response to Dylan's visible falling out in mid-set with his longstanding lead guitarist JOHN JACKSON—Sexton played on 'Man of Peace', 'Where Teardrops Fall', 'Maggie's Farm', 'Like a Rolling Stone' and 'Rainy Day Women # 12 & 35'; the following night he was back at exactly the same point in the set, and played on 'Seeing the Real You at Last', 'Positively 4th Street', 'Cat's in the Well' and again on 'Like a Rolling Stone' and 'Rainy Day Women # 12 & 35'.

After a further couple of years, he was called into the Never-Ending Tour band itself, replacing BUCKY BAXTER as from June 5, 1999 in Denver, Colorado (the first of the shared tour with PAUL SIMON), and remaining in place until after the last concert of 2002, on November 22 in Fairfax, Virginia (except for a couple of numbers in the middle of the set that August 31, in Grand Junction, Colorado, when, early on, he was replaced for 'To Be Alone with You' and 'Lay Lady Lay' by DAVE ALVIN). When the tour resumed in 2003, Sexton had been replaced by BILLY BURNETTE.

Altogether, Sexton played in 396 Bob Dylan concerts. He also took part in the recording of the *"Love and Theft"* album and, as noted, the filming of *Masked & Anonymous*. He's also to be glimpsed in the video of ''Cross the Green Mountain'. For all that he was a guitar prodigy in his youth, he never took—and would not have been allowed to take—a virtuoso rôle in Dylan's band. He augmented rather than led. He worked co-operatively with LARRY

CAMPBELL, the other main guitarist with the band throughout Charlie Sexton's time in it, and aside from the horrible vocal choruses they added to 'Blowin' in the Wind' and 'Knockin' on Heaven's Door', he was a pleasure to listen to. For many, he was more of a pleasure to watch; it was widely felt that his cheekbones put the sex in Sexton.

Surprisingly for someone who made such an early start, he has still made only four solo albums. After 1985's *Pictures for Pleasures* came *Charlie Sexton* in 1989; then, with Charlie Sexton & Sextet, he released *Under the Wishing Tree* in 1995. After that his devotees had to wait a decade for *Cruel and Gentle Things*. Such a spare tally of releases is especially odd granted that he feels, as he told the *Rocky Mountain News*: 'Touring is fine, but for me records are the thing. That's the legacy everyone leaves behind.' There's probably nothing like touring with the Dylan of the late 1990s and beyond to urge that conclusion upon you.

Meanwhile Sexton is back in Austin, Texas. He might be perplexed, despite his good looks, to read this postscript to his online movie database biography: 'Trivia—he is a guitar player.'

[Charlie Sexton: *Pictures for Pleasures*, MCA 31163, US, 1985; *Charlie Sexton*, MCA 6280, 1989; *Under the Wishing Tree*, MCA 11208, 1995; *Cruel and Gentle Things*, Back Porch, *nia*, 2005. The Arc Angels: *Arc Angels*, Geffen 24465, 1992. Movie Database bio: *www.imdb.com/name/nm0786644/bio*, seen online 22 Nov 2005.]

Shakespeare, Robbie [1953 -] See **Sly & Robbie**.

Shakespeare in *"Love and Theft"* Eric Lott's book about minstrelsy, *Love and Theft*, from which Dylan thieves his 2001 album title, establishes that the minstrel shows incorporated cod-Shakespeare recitals: snatches of speeches like Hamlet's 'to be or not to be', treated with varying degrees of competence, melodrama and comedy.

In parallel, Dylan offers his own comic Shakespeare touches on the *"Love and Theft"* album. In 'Po' Boy' we have this wittily rhyming, sly extrapolation from *Othello*: 'Othello told Desdemona "I'm cold, cover me with a blanket / By the way, what happened to that poisoned wine?" / She said "I gave it to you, you drank it"', delivered with all Dylan's unimpaired capacity for squeezing whatever number of syllables he cares to into a line and for catching conversation with authentic casualness. And in 'Floater (Too Much to Ask)', he gives us this marvellous comic compression of a contemporary adolescent conversation which, by calling the speakers Romeo and Juliet, he contrasts so good-humouredly with the language of their Shakespearean equivalents: 'Romeo, he said to Juliet, "You got a poor complexion, / It doesn't give your appearance a very youthful touch!" / Juliet said right back to Romeo, "Why don't you just shove off / If it bothers you so much?"'

But there is a third Shakespeare presence on *"Love and Theft"*, and not, as it happens, comic in character. As so very often, Dylan's skill with literary allusion is such that if you don't happen to pick up on the echo, it doesn't obtrude, distract or bother you; but if you do pick up on it, it deepens the resonance of the song. In this instance, it occurs in 'Bye and Bye', when Dylan sings that lovely line 'I'm not even acquainted with my own desires'. The delivery, on the track, is modest, reflective, personally confessional, but at the same time the language itself is of Shakespearean eloquence. It comes from Rosalind, the heroine of *As You Like It*, in Act One, Scene 3, when she has been exiled and accused of treason by the duke, and she replies: 'I do beseech your grace, / Let me the knowledge of my fault bear with me: / If with myself I hold intelligence / Or have acquaintance with mine own desires . . .'

[Eric Lott, *Love and Theft: Blackface Minstrelsy and the American Working Class*, New York: Oxford University Press, 1993.]

Shelton, Robert [1926 - 1995] Robert Shelton, who was born Robert Shapiro on June 28, 1926 in Chicago, was one of the very few arts journalists whose work had a tangible influence on the shape of the 1960s.

At age 13, still in Chicago, Shelton discovered jazz and blues; drafted into the US Army in France at 18 in 1944, he developed there another lifelong passion, becoming a Europhile with a special abiding love of France, French culture and cinema. After World War II, he attended the School of Journalism at Northwestern University, gaining an early BSc in journalism and moving in the early 1950s to New York City, where he soon joined the *New York Times*.

His political allegiance, which was to a passionate, perhaps naive, liberalism—he always looked for the best in individuals and in humanity—was tested when the Eastland Committee (part of the McCarthyite machinery of the times) subpoenaed him in a case of mistaken identity. He could have corrected their error and escaped their attentions, but he refused to dignify their questions by answering at all; thus he paid his dues in siding with the angels.

From 1958 to 1968 he was the paper's folk, pop and country-music critic, and with a rare commitment and gusto, rightly recognised at the outset that what was beginning to happen in and around Greenwich Village would catalyse a musical and cultural revolution around half the world.

Instead of descending from his prestigious newspaper to turn in adequate reviews of whatever headline acts were in town, he entered fully into the milieu of coffee-bars, folk festivals and bohemian basements, urging the creation of Gerde's Folk City, co-editing the annual NEWPORT FOLK FESTIVAL programmes and above all befriending and encouraging new talent. While knowledgeable about the history of a wide range of American music, he was actively responsive to the young and fresh.

At the first Newport Folk Festival, in 1959, he 'discovered' 18-year-old JOAN BAEZ, and over the next decade aided the careers of many others including PHIL OCHS, Janis Ian and JUDY COLLINS. Catching the very different talent of FRANK ZAPPA at his first East Coast shows, Shelton's review on Christmas Day 1966 recognised presciently 'the first pop group to successfully amalgamate rock'n' roll with the serious music of Stravinsky and others.' But it was Shelton's write-up of the 20-year-old support-act to THE GREENBRIAR BOYS at Gerde's, one Bob Dylan, on September 29, 1961 which, kick-starting Dylan's career, made both of them famous.

Shelton's prose could suffer from an old-fashioned 'professionalism' and glib metaphor, but more often and more importantly it was acute, accurate and thoughtful beyond the call of journalistic duty, and it says much for these qualities that that first write-up of Dylan still captures the essence of this most chameleonic star, 45 years later: not least in its description of Dylan's voice and its understanding of how much this drew upon the pre-war country blues tradition. Under the pseudonym Stacey Williams, he also wrote the début album's sleevenotes. He continued to write essays about and reviews of Dylan's work for many years, including a review of the New York Town Hall concert of April 1963, in which he called Dylan a 'young giant', a review of Dylan & the Hawks' Forest Hills concert of August 1965, and a piece on the 'Born Again' period in 1980.

In writing his main work, the critical biography *No Direction Home: The Life and Music of Bob Dylan*, 1986—a project which took almost 20 years—Shelton was cruelly messed-about by succeeding publishing editors, so that after years writing and re-writing 300,000 words, he then had the dispiriting, time-demanding task of pruning 100,000 off (with Dylan, of course, inconveniently active all the while).

Shelton chose to move out of New York City to get the book written, and moved to a tiny cottage up a dirt track off Sydenham Hill in south-east London, where he also found himself grappling with an isolation worse than the interference he foresaw himself suffering if he stayed in New York. Fêted by the music industry as well as valued in the Village, he was disdainful of the bribes constantly offered, yet resentful of others' profiting from the very integrity that kept him poor: bitter, for instance, that Dylan's manager ALBERT GROSSMAN could use his Janis Joplin review to land her a huge Columbia Records contract (making Grossman mega-bucks overnight) precisely because Columbia knew Shelton's rave-review could not have been bought.

So Shelton escaped all that, and from the pressures he felt would rain down on him from Dylan's office if he were in town—and landed up in a miserable, philistine part of London where there was no music in the cafés at night (there were no cafés at night), it could take 90 minutes to get in or out of the city center, and there was certainly no equivalent to the camaraderie and street-life of the Greenwich Village in which Shelton had been a star. In Sydenham he was just a middle-aged American: a small fish in no pond at all but rather, out of water. And getting divorced, from Carol, his third wife (there had been two short-lived marriages in his youth), who had hoped in vain that he might turn her into a country-music star.

Shelton soon ran out of money too, and had to keep breaking off from the book to write bits of journalism, not least to pay storage on 2,000 albums acquired from reviewing in New York (there's no such thing as a free platter). There was no room for them all in the cottage, where the book alone took up a room full of filing cabinets. He generally wouldn't let people even peep into this room, perhaps because the paper-work was a lot less, or a lot less ordered, than he wanted to maintain, or perhaps because the extreme guardedness he derided in Bob Dylan he came close to himself. While trying to surround himself with bright young things, essentially he worked alone.

Out of touch with any thriving arts scene of the kind he had helped to shape before his emigration, he was also out of touch with Dylan collectors. Wary because he had uncirculated tapes he feared having stolen, he was nonetheless given to tantalising others by describing some of these treasures—'I've got a tape of Dylan teaching ROBBIE ROBERTSON "Sad-Eyed Lady of the Lowlands" in a hotel-room in March '66: I have it because I was in the room at the time', he might say: or more rarely, might play fragments of one or two of these things. At the same time he needed to keep all this to himself to avoid dishonouring or losing Dylan's trust: a hard fear to live and work under since Dylan's trust was bound to be, in any circumstances, fitful.

They continued to see each other on occasion. When Dylan toured Europe for the first time in 12 years in 1978, and his tour reached London, a number of people were brought out into the deep black backstage area in small groups to meet Dylan; Shelton was amongst the few who also went out to dinner with Dylan that week. Nevertheless the two long maintained an uneasy relationship, since Shelton felt due some credit for having helped Dylan's career and Dylan resented the slight hint of a proprietorial air.

Shelton's book was too long in the making for its own good, and disappointing, tainted by a haste that usually betrays a too-quick project, not one so very long in the making. When it emerged at last, the reviews were mixed. But it was a triumph against many demons that he published the book at all, and despite its scars it will remain important for its solidity, wide-ranging interests and the many gems that come from Shelton having been an influential intimate of Dylan himself in the vital early years.

Shelton did many interviews to promote the publication of the book in 1986, but none more thorough than the one he gave to the fanzine *The Telegraph*, published in 1987. A further interview was published in *The Telegraph* posthumously in 1996 (and featured Shelton on its cover), though this was a slightly abbreviated version of an interview he had given in November 1987 to the very short-lived literary magazine *Words International*, reprinted 'as *The Telegraph*'s memorial to' its subject.

Shelton's other books include: a songbook-cum-biography of Josh White; *The Face of Folk Music* with photographer David Gahr; *The Country Music Story* with illustrator Burt Goldblatt in 1966 (an early history of a genre Shelton championed far ahead of its revival); and, with Karl Dallas, Dave Laing and Robin Denselow, the fine *Electric Muse: The Story of Folk into Rock*. He also edited *Born to Win*, 1965, a collection of WOODY GUTHRIE's prose and poems.

In 1982 Shelton moved to Brighton, reviewing for the *Evening Argus* and specialising in films—a specialism he maintained, as film critic for the *Birmingham Post* and reviewer for the international newspaper *The European*, until his death. When Dylan and his partners in the crime of the film *Hearts of Fire* held a press conference at the National Film Theatre in London, on August 17, 1986, Shelton was there as a film critic, casting an understandably baleful eye on this non-event.

A founder-member of the UK's Guild of Regional Film Writers, he displayed in this final phase of his life the same rare qualities as in his New York City heyday: he was gregarious, warm, a good listener, secretive to a fault about his own distinguished past, and whole-heartedly committed to the humane arts.

Robert Shelton died, aged 69, in his adopted hometown of Brighton, England, on December 11, 1995. His papers were divided between the Music Experience Project in Seattle, Washington, and the University of Liverpool's Institute of Pop Music. The latter shocked visitors by cellotaping some of this material when displaying it, but it also honoured its donor's memory by founding the annual Robert Shelton Memorial Conference in 1999.

Meanwhile that tape of Dylan and Robbie Robertson (including more than a moment of Dylan in truth-attack mode sneering unpleasantly at Shelton), which was recorded on the night of March 12–13, 1966, in a Denver, Colorado, hotel-room, has passed into general circulation. The 221-minute tape of the interview with Dylan that Shelton recorded earlier the same day, during their flight together from Lincoln, Nebraska to Denver, has not circulated.

[Robert Shelton: 'Bob Dylan: A Distinctive Folk Song Stylist: 20-Year-Old Singer is Bright New Face at Gerde's Club', *New York Times*, 29 Sep 1961; 'Bob Dylan Sings His Compositions: Folk Musician, 21, Displays Originality at Town Hall', *New York Times*, 14 Apr 1963; 'Dylan's Godspell', *Melody Maker*, UK, 21 Jun 1980; *No Direction Home: The Life and Music of Bob Dylan*, New York: Beech Tree Books/Wm Morrow, 1986; republished New York: Da Capo Press, 2003. Interviews with Shelton: *The Telegraph* no.27, UK, summer 1987 & no.54, UK, spring 1996.]

Shepard, Sam [1943 -] Samuel Shepard Rogers was born in Fort Sheridan, Illinois, on November 5, 1943, grew up in Calfornia, moved to New York City as an actor in 1963 and starting writing plays that year, seeing the first two, *Cowboys* and *Rock Garden*, staged in a double bill in 1964. He has written prolifically ever since: he wrote over 40 plays between 1963 and 1993, his work has been staged in many countries and by the 1970s he was being dubbed 'the most influential young playwright in America'. He also played drums for a while in the 1960s with Pete Stampfel's Holy Modal Rounders, lived with PATTI SMITH and co-wrote a play with her, *Cowboy Mouth* (a phrase from Dylan's song 'Sad-Eyed Lady of the Lowlands').

He published an early collection of other work, *Hawk Moon: A Book of Short Stories, Poems and Monologues* (1971) and *Rolling Thunder Logbook* (1977), his underrated account of being commissioned to come along on Dylan's 1975 Rolling Thunder Revue to help write mini-scripts for the *Renaldo & Clara* film. Though any idea of scripts was soon forgotten, Shepard proved a refreshing observer of the Rolling Thunder process in action, as well as bringing a disinterested eye to bear on its individual musicians. He is best in the *Logbook* when grappling with the largest talents, giving acute and sympathetic accounts of seeing both Dylan and ALLEN GINSBERG in action, especially in front of audiences. His account 'Kaddish on the Mah-Jong Circuit' is tremendous writing, which acts out what it describes in cranking up many notches when it reaches Dylan's arrival on stage, energizing everyone 'until every molecule of air in the place is bursting. This is Dylan's true magic. Leave aside his lyrical genius for a second and just watch this transformation of energy which he carries. . . . he can do it here, in the dead of winter, at an off-season seaside resort full of menopause . . .' The book ends with a self-effacing account of the excruciating experience of having Bob and SARA DYLAN attend an off-Broadway production of his play *Geography of a Horse Dreamer*.

The major Dylan-Shepard collaboration came a decade later, on the jointly written 'Brownsville Girl'. It's an oddity perhaps that while Dylan told Bill Flanagan that 'Brownsville Girl' was written partly in response to a LOU REED song, in turn that Lou Reed song starts by referring to going to see Sam Shepard's play *Fool for Love*. But for their collaboration on the song, see the see separate entry on the song itself.

They collaborated again in a more minor way the year after 'Brownsville Girl' was released, in that Dylan allowed himself to be interviewed by Shepard, and this turned into a Shepard piece in *Esquire* (July 1987), presented as the script of a short play called 'True Dylan'. This is discussed at length in STEPHEN SCOBIE's book *Alias Bob Dylan*, though perhaps with a flawed determination to feed a particular bee in his critical bonnet. Scobie's theme is the death of patriarchy, a theme he finds everywhere in Dylan's work. He cites the key features of the 'play' as including the eccentricities of the soundtrack on the intermittently played cassette machine, the noises off and so on, but he doesn't notice that the talk between Dylan and Shepard - the talk that Scobie insists is grounded in the death of patriarchy—is repeatedly interrupted by Dylan going off to talk on the telephone *to his daughter*.

More simply, it might be concluded from all of this that 'True Dylan' is a more than usually oblique work, and certainly not a play. But Shepard has certainly written plenty more of those since, and has continued his film careers as actor and writer. Like that other SAM, PECKINPAH, though in very different style, his work has always pushed away at the theme of the myth of the West and the betrayal and death of the American dream. His major plays include *La Turista* (1966), *Operation Sidewinder* (1967), *The Tooth of Crime* (1972), *Buried Child* (1978), *True West* (1980), *Fool for Love* (1983), *A Life of the Mind* (1985), *The State of Shock* (1991), *Simpatico* (1994), *The Late Henry Moss* (2000) and *The God of Hell* (2004). A further short stories collection, *Great Dream of Heaven*, was published in 2002.

In film, he wrote the acclaimed screenplay for *Paris, Texas* (1984) and acted in *Days of Heaven* (1978), *Resurrection* (1980), *Frances* (1982), *The Right Stuff* (1983), *Paris, Texas*, *Fool for Love* (1985), *Crimes of the Heart* (1986), *Baby Boom* (1987), *Voyager* (1991), *The Pelican Brief* (1993) and more besides. So while you might think from the content of his work that he spends a lot of time staring off into the desert from behind the dusty curtains of a seedy motel room, the sheer listing of his work tells a different story. Like Bob Dylan, he works almost incessantly.

[Sam Shepard: *Rolling Thunder Logbook*, New York: Viking Press, 1977; 2nd ed., New York: Da Capo, 2005 with new preface by Shepard, new foreword by T-Bone Burnett but less than half the photos in the original edition; *Fool for Love*, play, premiered San Francisco, 8 Feb 1983, dir. Shepard & NY, May 1983, again dir. Shepard; *Fool for Love*, film, dir. Robert Altman, written Shepard, starred Shepard, Kim Basinger, Randy Quaid & Harry Dean Stanton; Cannon/Golan-Globus, US, 1985. Shepard's 'play'/interview 'True Dylan', *Esquire*, US, Jul 1987. Bill Flanagan, *Written in My Soul*, Chicago: Contemporary Books, 1986.]

***Shot of Love* [1981]** The first post-evangelising album, a ramshackle collection of generally second-rate tracks with Dylan's voice often petulant and querulous, the music tired and the production thin. It excludes some of the best songs cut at the relevant sessions: a snatching of mediocrity from the jaws of distinction that Dylan was to manage again and again with his 1980s albums. Even the cover was careless and tawdry (as those of *Saved*, *Slow Train Coming* and *Bob Dylan at Budokan* had been before it), whereas before the late 1970s a Dylan cover was rightly used to help define an album's distinctive character, and had to be devised with care and imaginative precision. Time has not transformed *Shot of Love* into a first-rate collection, but has made more engaging the interest in 1950s music on Dylan's part which suffuses its atmosphere. Best of the minor songs on the album is the shimmering Motownesquerie of 'Watered-Down Love'. 'Lenny Bruce' is an endearing bad song. The stand-out track, and free of all these vocal, instrumental and production faults, is the defiantly classic 'Every Grain of Sand'. Subsequent reissue of the album on CD has added as track 6 one of the good initial rejects, 'The Groom's Still Waiting at the Altar' (a song interesting for its vibrantly creative, ferocious words—new Dylan writing—fused to a music that re-uses SONNY BOY WILLIAMSON II's 1955 song 'Don't Start Me Talking', which Dylan would perform on US TV three years later).

[Recorded (though the documentation on this is confused) LA, May 1981; released as stereo LP Columbia TC-37496 (in UK CBS 85178), 12 Aug 1981.]

Silber, Irwin [1925 -] Irwin Silber was born in New York City on October 17, 1925. He was editor of *Sing Out!* magazine from 1951 to 1967, writer and executive editor for the US weekly radical newspaper *The Guardian* from 1968 to 1979, associate editor of *CrossRoads* (another left-wing US journal, formed from the merging of two others, *Front Line* and *North Star Review*) from 1990 to 1995 (it died after issue no.62 in August 1996), and author of books including *Songs of the Civil War*, *Songs of the Great American West* and *Socialism: What Went Wrong?* He also founded a self-proclaimed Marxist-Leninist party called Line of March.

With his brother Fred, he also edited, in 1973, the 1,000-song collection *Folksinger's Wordbook*, while his son Marc Silber was a folk performer at one time in a group with Artie and HAPPY TRAUM (but also ran, with IZZY YOUNG, a Greenwich Village guitar shop called Fretted Instruments; he describes his encounters with Dylan very graciously in Tracy Johnson's book *Encounters with Bob Dylan: If You See Him, Say Hello*).

In the November 1964 issue of *Sing Out!* Irwin Silber published his rebuke 'An Open Letter to Bob Dylan', written 'because some of what has happened is troubling me. And not me alone. Many other good friends of yours as well. . . . Your new songs seem to be all inner-directed now . . . maybe even a little maudlin or a little cruel on occasion. And it's happening on stage, too. You seem to be relating to a handful of cronies behind the scenes now—rather than to the rest of us out front. Now that's all OK—if that's the way you want it, Bob. But then you're a different Bob Dylan from the one we knew. The old one never wasted our precious time.'

Dylan offers his own thoughts on this, recollected in tranquility, in *Chronicles Volume One*:

> 'Irwin Silber, the editor of the folk magazine *Sing Out!* . . . would castigate me publicly in his magazine for turning my back on the folk community. It was an angry letter. I liked Irwin, but I couldn't relate to it. Miles Davis would be accused of something similar when he made the album *Bitches Brew*, a piece of music that didn't follow the rules of modern jazz, which had been on the verge of breaking into the popular marketplace, until Miles's record came along and killed its chances. Miles was put down by the jazz community. I couldn't imagine Miles being too upset. Latin artists were breaking rules, too. . . . As for me, what I did to break away was to take simple folk changes and put new imagery and attitude to them, use catchphrases and metaphor combined with a new set of ordinances that evolved into something different that had not been heard before. Silber scolded me in his letter for doing this, as if he alone and a few others had the keys to the real world. I knew what I was doing, though, and wasn't going to take a step back or retreat for anybody.'

Dylan, of course, was right—right from his side, and from art's; and it takes a sly mendaciousness to write such a letter, tugging the 'good friend' string yet publishing it for all to see; Dylan was outraged at this, and stopped making his songs available in *Sing Out!* in response. On the other hand Silber was, as he claimed, writing what many others on the folk scene were feeling. In addition to which, while his 'Open Letter' is notorious, it's less well-known that Silber later retracted. In *The Guardian* in 1968 he wrote: 'Many of us who did not fully understand the dynamics of the political changes . . . in America . . . felt deserted by a poet. . . . And Dylan did desert—not us, but an outmoded style of values which had become unequal to the task of reclaiming America. "This land is *not* your land", Dylan told us in 1965. But some of us . . . inheritors of a superficial "Marxism" based on diluted Leninism and rationalized Stalinism were not ready . . .'

Silber is still going—still playing tennis after two knee and one hip replacements (he wrote a book about that too)—and though living on the West Coast now, he's still slogging away in the endless internecine warfare of the American Left. Here he is in September 2001, opening a book review: 'The great virtue of *Commies*, Ronald Radosh's self-serving *Journey Through the Old Left, the New Left and the Leftover Left*, is that it clears up any remaining ambiguity as to his niche in the political spectrum. It also manages to demolish the dubious notion that his work is that of a "distinguished conservative scholar and historian." Radosh's politics were always paper-thin and had more to do with his acknowledged ambition "to become a leader in the American Communist movement" than with any readily apparent interest in their substance.' Just the sort of talk Bob Dylan has always enjoyed.

[Irwin Silber: *Songs of the Civil War*, New York: Columbia University Press, 1960; *Songs of the Great American West*, New York: Macmillan, 1967; *Socialism: What Went Wrong?*, London: Pluto Press, 1994; *A Patient's Guide to Knee and Hip Replacement*, New York: Simon & Schuster, 1999; 'An Open Letter to Bob Dylan', *Sing Out!*, New York, Nov 1964, reprinted in CRAIG McGREGOR: *Bob Dylan, the Early Years: A Retrospective*, New York: Da Capo, 1990; retraction in *The Guardian*, *nia*, 1968, quoted from ROBERT SHELTON, *No Direction Home: The Life and Music of Bob Dylan*, London: Penguin edn., p.314; review of Radosh's *Commies* in Z magazine, Sep 2001, online 23 Oct 2005 at *www.zmag.org/ZMag/articles/sept01silber.htm*. Fred & Irwin Silber, *Folksinger's Wordbook*, New York: Oak Publications, 1973, reissued Music Sales Corp., 2000. Bob Dylan: *Chronicles Volume One*, 2004, p.66–67. Tracy Johnson, ed., *Encounters with Bob Dylan: If You See Him, Say Hello*, Santa Cruz, CA: Humble Press, 2000. Ronald Radosh, *Journey Through the Old Left, the New Left and the Leftover Left*, San Francisco: Encounter Books, 2001.]

Simmons, Gene [1949 -] Gene Simmons was born Chaim Witz in Haifa, Israel, on August 25, 1949, moved to Brooklyn, NY, at age nine and grew up to be the bassist and vocalist with the successful American 1970s glam-punk group Kiss.

Simmons and Bob Dylan have co-written two songs: 'Laughing When You Want to Cry' in 1991 and the ballad 'Waiting for the Morning Light'; they came out of a day spent together at Simmons' LA home. The latter was recorded by Simmons and released in June 2004 on his first solo album for 25 years, understatedly titled *A**hole*.

Simmons said of the collaboration with Dylan: 'We understood each other right away. He picked up an acoustic guitar, and we just tossed it back and forth, "How 'bout this, how 'bout that?" And he started to strum, because he—at least with me—tended to talk and strum guitar at the same time.

And as soon as I heard the first three or four chords, I went, "Wait, wait, what's that? Do that again." So I went and started to write a lyric around that.' About the later co-composition, and why it emerged some years after the first, Simmons said: 'Bob came up with the chords, most of them, and then I took it and wrote lyrics, melody, the rest of it. I'd see him on tour, and I'd say, "Bob, you wanna write the song?" And he would say, "No, man, you write it, Mr. Kiss."' In this 1996 interview, he added that a demo had been made of the song; no other detail was given, and none has emerged. It might be thought comical that in a collaboration between these two talents, it was Simmons who wrote the words.

[Gene Simmons: 'Waiting for the Morning Light', *nia*, *A**hole*, Sanctuary, US, 2004. Simmons quote & background information thanks to the 'Starlight in the East' section of Alan Fraser's website *www.searchingforagem*.]

Simon, Paul [1941 -] Paul Frederic Simon was born in Newark, New Jersey, on October 13, 1941 and grew up in Queens, New York. He and Art Garfunkel had a pop hit as Tom & Jerry with 'Hey Schoolgirl' at age 16; Simon had a minor hit in 1962 with the group Tico & the Triumphs ('Motorcycle') and as Jerry Landis with 'The Lone Teen Ranger' in 1963.

The precocious pop singer became, with and without Art Garfunkel, one of the key folk-rock singers and composers of the 1960s, with a popularity that saw him remain a star ever afterwards. Always more accessible, more melodic and less substantial than Dylan, Simon (and Simon & Garfunkel) outsold Dylan many times over.

Dylan's first acknowledgement that Paul Simon existed was his revisit to Simon's 'The Boxer' on the 1970 *Self Portrait* album. Dylan's minimal rewrite of the lyric is very telling–and typical of Dylan's ability to say more with less. He simply changes one word, shifting it from 'And he carries a reminder / Of every glove that's laid him down' to 'Of every blow that's laid him down.' That 'blow' means we actually see the boxer better: we comprehend that outside the ring as well as inside it, his life is a series of defeats.

The inspiration for Dylan's use of two different voices on 'The Boxer' may well be a pre-war gospel record, BLIND WILLIE JOHNSON's marvellous 'Let Your Light Shine on Me', which in its chorus strongly prefigures that of Dylan's 'Precious Angel' and in using two voices on one track certainly shines a new light on 'The Boxer'. Johnson didn't have the technology to double-track his two voices, as Dylan does, but in switching suddenly from the one to the other (in mid-line, even, at the end) he makes the difference between them so stark that this becomes the central point of the recording, as with Dylan's double-tracking on 'The Boxer'. (For Dylan's familiarity with, and debt to, **Blind Willie Johnson** see separate entry).

Dylan never performed 'The Boxer' live but did perform Simon's earlier songs 'Hazy Shade of Winter' (two concerts, 1992) and 'Homeward Bound' (three concerts, 1991) and he contributed harmonica & back-up vocals behind the GRATEFUL DEAD on a rehearsal of Simon's later 'Boy in the Bubble' (San Rafael, CA, March–April 1987). In spring 1999 it was announced that Dylan and Simon would tour together that June in North America. And they did, despite their well-known mutual dislike.

They began in Denver, Colorado, on June 5, giving 38 high-priced, large-venue concerts between then and the last day of July. They alternated who headlined and whose set came first, and mostly the one whose set was first would come back on to share the stage for four numbers at the end of the headliner's set. Dylan headlined on the opening night (as he had doubtless insisted on doing), performing 13 songs with his band. Paul Simon came on at the end to share vocals and guitar on 'The Sound of Silence', 'I Walk the Line', 'Blue Moon of Kentucky' and 'Forever Young'. And this was the way it continued, except that they dropped 'Forever Young' after that first attempt and substituted 'Knockin' on Heaven's Door' thereafter. As from July 4 (in Milwaukee), 'That'll Be the Day' and 'The Wanderer' replaced the middle two songs, until they reverted to their earlier choices as of July 23 in Mansfield, Massachusetts. For the last few nights, the middle songs switched about between the four, but introduced nothing new. The tour ended with two nights at Wantagh, New York.

In September, however, Dylan & Simon went out on the road together again, for a brief (ten-date) tour through Florida, Georgia, North Carolina, Tennessee, Indiana, Louisiana and Texas. This time their duets began with . . . 'The Boxer'.

When they duetted, it was a very rare experience for Dylan: he was the taller one.

[Paul Simon: 'The Boxer', *nia*, issued on Simon & Garfunkel's *Bridge Over Troubled Water*, Columbia KCS 9914, NY (CBS 63699, London), 1970. Blind Willie Johnson: 'Let Your Light Shine on Me', New Orleans, 10 Dec 1929, *Blind Willie Johnson*, RBF RF-10, NY, 1965; 'John the Revelator', Atlanta, GA, 20 Apr 1930, *American Folk Music*; 'Jesus Make Up My Dying Bed', Dallas, TX, 3 Dec 1927; all CD-reissued *The Complete Blind Willie Johnson*, Columbia Roots N' Blues Series COL 472190 2, NY, 1993.]

Sinatra, Frank [1915 - 1998] Francis Albert Sinatra was born to Italian parents in Hoboken, New Jersey, on December 12, 1915 and became a fine actor, a controversial celebrity with a series of glamorous actress wives and with Mafia connections, but more importantly the finest male singer of his generation. (A certain sort of singer, that is.) At his peak, in the early 1950s, his attractive voice combined with a unique instinct for timing and phrasing to give him a primacy comparable to that of Bing Crosby in an earlier age. This is not the place for a summary of his career, though it is the place to note that his musical world was the one rock'n'roll was born to abolish—that of the jazz-tinged crooner who emerged from the era of the Big Band and whose performances relied upon the supposedly sophisticated songs of Cole Porter and his ilk (typically replete with lines like 'Use your mentality, wake up to reality', as in the awful 'I've Got You Under My Skin') and the notated orchestral arrangements of Nelson Riddle, Billy May and the like.

Two and a half years before his death, at the so-called 80th Birthday concert held in his presence at the Shrine Auditorium in Los Angeles several weeks before he turned 80, one of the guest artists was Bob Dylan. With his Never-Ending Tour band of the day, he performed just one song, an inspired choice from his 1964 album *Another Side of Bob Dylan*, 'Restless Farewell', which he had never performed live in the 34-year interim. (He first sang it live in Chicago in December 1963, and then twice in 1964.)

By the time Dylan came to sing it for Sinatra, he was looking almost equally old, and holding himself so stiffly and defensively that to watch the performance on TV detracted from the experience of hearing it. To attend to the audio alone was to recognise that Dylan's greatness was still present. He offers a near-wholly sustained, considered performance, blotched only once, on the title phrase at the end of the first verse, by that posturing gargle he gives us sometimes—that short tour of the phlegm in his throat, which never fails to coarsen things—and its twin assassin, the silly sob. Throughout the rest, he's controlled, careful, discreet, alert to what he's on about: so much so that it makes you conjecture as to how it might have seemed if it were a new song, and on *Time Out of Mind*. Many's the person who would have rushed to say what a major work it was: a major work of retrospection, looking back down the long hallways of his life. Ironic, since it was not only a work of his youth but always regarded as a very minor work back then. One of the penalties he pays for our over-enthusiasm and under-discrimination these days is that when we step back, in this case, we're likely to re-stress that it *is* a minor and youthful work, rather than recognising that what he achieves with this revisit is a refashioning that is expressive for the middle-aged artist. One or two of the lines do betray an immaturity, but in general his 1995 performance re-occupies and renews the material. Whoever would have guessed?

'Happy birthday, Mr. Frank!' said Dylan eccentrically and shyly at the end. Frank Sinatra died of a heart attack in Los Angeles on May 14, 1998. He was 82. Dylan reprised 'Restless Farewell' in his LA concert one week later, and has never sung it again since.

[Bob Dylan: 'Restless Farewell', LA, 19 Nov 1995; complete song performance televised in Europe, first on Swedish TV, 12 Dec 2005; only 3 verses televised on ABC-TV, US, 14 Dec 1995. Other live performances Chicago, 27 Dec 1963; Berkeley, CA, 22 Feb 1964; London, 17 May 1964 & LA, 21 May 1998.]

Sloman, Larry [1950 -] Larry 'Ratso' Sloman is the author of one of the few great books about Bob Dylan, the essential and very funny *On the Road with Bob Dylan*, written about the 1975 Rolling Thunder Revue. Sloman was born on July 9, 1950 in New York City, growing up in Queens. He was first struck by Dylan's work hearing 'Like a Rolling Stone' in the summer of 1965; his first act of Dylan publication was putting him on the cover of a special music issue of the University of Wisconsin newspaper *The Daily Cardinal* that Sloman edited in 1971. Next came a preview article about *Blood on the Tracks* in *Rolling Stone*.

On the Road with Bob Dylan was his first book and its strength was its outsider's pitch: it's a classic account of scrabbling for access to the star—though in fact he became a halfway-insider pretty early on. He features in the cast list of *Renaldo & Clara* as 'Newspaper Man', but the name 'Ratso' was appended by JOAN BAEZ; by the time of the 11th concert, at Waterbury, Connecticut, Dylan was dedicating a song to Sloman from the stage, and when they reached Montreal it was Sloman whom Dylan delegated to go and collect LEONARD COHEN, to make sure he came to the concert.

Years later, brought much further inside, Sloman found himself co-producing, with George Lois, the crudely splendid video for 'Jokerman', the best track on 1983's *Infidels* album. Insider or not, his account of how this video came into being—and how easily it might have fallen by the wayside—is also entertaining. (See **'Jokerman' video, the**.)

Being around the Rolling Thunder Revue also inspired Sloman to write song lyrics, and after the tour he collaborated on many songs with Rick Derringer and then with John Cale. The latter turned into a collaboration over several albums.

Larry Sloman has also written books about professional ice hockey, the history of marijuana in the USA, and on Abbie Hoffman and the 1960s' radical movement. He has also collaborated on books with Howard Stern, Anthony Kiedis of the Red Hot Chili Peppers, and on David Blaine's *Mysterious Stranger*—in which Blaine says that thanks to Sloman's background research he became 'much more knowledgeable about the art than most magicians'. Sloman's most recent book, on Houdini, will be published on Hallowe'en 2006. Meanwhile he also appears as a character in another author's fiction: in the 16 or more detective novels by Kinky Friedman, 'editor Larry "Ratso" Sloman' makes many an appearance.

He has been involved in other films besides *Renaldo & Clara*. He is credited as a 'developer' on the John Waters movie *Hairspray* (1988), plays a reporter character based on himself (but called Charlie Phelps) in the 1992 movie *Primary Motive*, and, uncredited, plays a town mayor who goes to a Hallowe'en party dressed as Bob Dylan in the 2004 horror film *Santa's Little Helper* 'from genre master Jeff Lieberman'.

In 2002, when the 2-CD set the *Bootleg Series Vol. 5: Bob Dylan Live 1975, The Rolling Thunder Revue* came out, the text of its lavish booklet was dominated by a long retrospective essay, full of unexpected detail, specially written by Larry 'Ratso' Sloman.

[Larry Sloman: *On the Road with Bob Dylan: Rolling with the Thunder*, New York: Bantam Books, 1978, republished (with new introduction by Kinky Friedman), New York: Three Rivers Press and London: Helter Skelter Publishing, 2002; *Reefer Madness, Marijuana in America*, New York: Bobs-Merril/Grove Press, 1979; *Steal This Dream: Abbie Hoffman and the Countercultural Revolution in America*, New York: Doubleday, 1998. David Blaine: *Mysterious Stranger*, New York: Villard and London: Channel 4 Books, 2002.]

***Slow Train Coming* [1979]** Anyone else, riding as high as Dylan was in 1978, would have stuck with the same band and produced another *Street Legal*-type album. Dylan did no such thing. Converted to Born Again Christianity, he gathered different musicians around him and produced an album destined to be profoundly unpopular amongst almost everyone who'd ever valued him as a writer. It is not, however, an album that can be ignored, and in some ways now seems a logical direction for Dylan to have taken. No-one should have been surprised at Dylan choosing to add gospel to the many different modes of American popular music he has covered (and so well) on his artistic travels over the decades. Musically it's strong, and strikingly well produced in Alabama's Muscle Shoals Sound Studio under the supervision of veteran Atlantic Records producer JERRY WEXLER. Stand-out tracks are 'Gotta Serve Somebody', 'Precious Angel', 'Slow Train' and 'When He Returns'.

[Recorded Sheffield, AL, 1–4 May 1979 (with later overdubs), released as stereo LP Columbia FC 36120 (in UK CBS 86095), 18 or 20 Aug 1979.]

Sly & Robbie Sly & Robbie—Sly Dunbar and Robbie Shakespeare—make up the longstanding and innovative Jamaican rhythm section used by Dylan for the *Infidels* sessions of 1983 in New York.

Lowell Charles Dunbar was born on May 10, 1952 and Robert Shakespeare on September 27, 1953, both in Kingston, Jamaica. They were first brought together as live performers by Bunny Lee in the Revolutionaries and as studio players for the Hoo Kim Brothers' Channel One label. This is not the place for an informed appraisal of the changes they contributed to in the history of reggae and related musics (nor to any listing of the astonishingly large number of recordings on which they have appeared) but their three main innovations were: the harder beat of the Rockers style, which displaced the previously ubiquitous One Drop style when Sly & Robbie brought it onto the Mighty Diamonds' début album *Right Time* in 1976; the Rub a Dub sound they created at the start of the 1980s; and the Bam Bam style—so called because introduced on the huge hit 'Bam Bam' by Chaka Demus & Pliers (and on their 'Murder She Wrote'), which pushed sweet and rough vocals into a novel partnership. Since then Sly & Robbie have explored the use of computers in music, fused Latin and other sounds and launched an experimental melding of R&B with Hip Hop.

They have performed live and in the studio with more or less everyone in Jamaica, including Peter Tosh, Black Uhuru, the Upsetters, Gregory Isaacs, Dennis Brown and the great, mad Lee Perry. (Check out his emphatically rewritten 1988 version of 'That Lucky Old Sun', which he titles 'Show Me That River' and claims sole composer credit for.) They set up their own Taxi label in 1980, on which many reggae stars' albums have seen release.

At the same time, Sly & Robbie have always been fans of a wide range of other music, from country to Tamla Motown. They have worked with Grace Jones, Joan Armatrading, Joe Cocker, MICK JAGGER, THE ROLLING STONES and many others from Sting to Serge Gainsbourg. Their album *La Trenggae* includes versions of JONI MITCHELL's 'Big Yellow Taxi' and of that late-1950s Italian pop hit 'Volare', while Sly had chosen that nickname in the first place in tribute to a favourite black American star, Sly of Sly & the Family Stone. When Sly & Robbie were brought in to provide the rhythm section for Bob Dylan in 1983, therefore, they were fully aware of who he was and were open to whatever music was required.

He was open too, and they found him easy to work with. Sly told HOWARD SOUNES: 'He would just come into the studio with his 'armonica and his guitar, and he start play the song, and we just fall into the groove. He would take different takes of a song in different keys and he would change words on the fly. . . . He would look at us and say, "That's the take." . . . We couldn't believe how smooth it went.' They in turn were able to slip in a little reggae ('so quietly that you wouldn't realise that's what we're doing'): and on 'I and I' they did. Perhaps this smooth way of flowing together in the studio works best of all on 'Jokerman', on which the Sly & Robbie rhythm section is a prominent and distinctive backbone to a spare sound counterbalanced by Dylan's lovely vocal and his superlative words. Sly told Howard Sounes that this was achieved before they'd realised the tape was running.

They began on April 11, 1983 and worked six consecutive days, had one day off before resuming on April 18 for a further nine consecutive days and after two days' break resumed for several scattered days in May. Robbie Shakespeare's bass and Sly Dunbar's drums therefore pin down everything on *Infidels* and also the transcendental still-unreleased version of 'Blind Willie McTell' as well as the released version, 'Foot of Pride', 'Tell Me', 'Lord Protect My Child' and 'Someone's Got a Hold of My Heart' (all on *Bootleg Series Vols. 1–3*, 1991), 'Death Is Not the End' (on *Down in the Groove*, 1988) and 'Angel Flying Too Close to the Ground', which was released on the B-side of the 'Union Sundown' single in Europe.

In 1985 Sly & Robbie returned to the same New York studios to play on February 19 on at least one attempt at 'Never Gonna Be the Same Again' and various early tries at 'When the Night Comes Falling from the Sky', including the one later released on the *Bootleg Series Vols. 1–3*; next day they returned to trying out 'Never Gonna Be the Same Again' and achieved the take used on *Empire Burlesque*; over the days that followed they were joined by AL KOOPER and others and achieved the *Empire Burlesque* cut of 'When the Night Comes Falling from the Sky', an unreleased but circulated attempt at 'Something's Burning Baby' and further unknown and uncirculated tracks.

The last of these sessions took place on March 4, 1985 and in April, Dylan reciprocated, going into another New York City studio to overdub a harmonica part onto Sly & Robbie's 'No Name on the Bullet', which was released that August as one of the six tracks on their electronics-oriented album *Language Barrier*.

[Sly & Robbie: *Language Barrier*, Island 90286-2, US, 1985. *La Trenggae*, Taxi *nia*, Jamaica, 2001. Mighty Diamonds: 'Right Time', *Right Time*, nia, 1976. Chaka Demus & Pliers: 'Bam Bam' & 'Murder She Wrote', *nia*. Lee 'Scratch' Perry: 'Show Me That River', *Battle of Armagideon (Millionaire Liquidator)*, Trojan, *nia*, 1988. Bob Dylan: 'Blind Willie McTell', NY, 5 May 1983, unreleased; 'Angel Flying Too Close to the Ground', NY, May 2, 1983, CBS A 3916, Europe, 1983. Howard Sounes, *Down the Highway: A Life of Bob Dylan*, New York: Grove Press, 2001, manuscript p.421.]

Smith, G.E. [1952 -] George Edward Smith was born in Stroudsburg, Pennsylvania, on January 27, 1952, learnt the guitar at four, 'started getting good at seven' and by 11, when he was given his first electric guitar (a 1952 Fender Telecaster), he was playing in high school bands and for vacationers in resorts in Pennsylvania's Pocono Mountains. In his teens, he switched musical base to New Haven, Connecticut, and in the second half of the 1970s was a member of the Scratch Band, which was considered hot. Then he was hired by Dan Hartman and toured Europe and the US with him, moved to Manhattan and played guitar for the 1979 Broadway show *Gilda Live* (starring Gilda Radner, whom he married).

From Broadway he went back into rock music, hired by Hall & Oates in 1979 and remaining with them a surely purgatorial six years. In his last year with them came LIVE AID, at which the Hall & Oates band, fronted by G.E., served as house-band, backing MICK JAGGER and Tina Turner. In consequence he duly appeared on two Jagger solo albums, *She's the Boss* and *Primitive Cool*; but 1985 also saw Smith appointed as band frontman and lead guitarist on the long-running TV series 'Saturday Night Live'. Again, he served a long sentence: ten years this time, and thus played with many a star.

In November 1987, when Dylan was putting together the original band for the first legs of what became known as the Never-Ending Tour, he auditioned and/or rehearsed G.E. Smith—this was just five weeks after the end of that year's touring with TOM PETTY & THE HEARTBREAKERS. The upshot was that he brought Smith in as the centrepiece of his newly stripped-down unit, and from the tour's opening night, June 7, 1988 in Concord, California, it was clear that the tall, slim man with the flat, cadaverous face under lustrous blond ponytailed hair was a powerful electric guitarist whom Dylan could lean on.

For many long-term fans, here was Bob Dylan's best lead guitarist since ROBBIE ROBERTSON. And the pattern of the concerts was such that after a run of seven electric numbers—kicking off to general amazement with the first-ever live renditions of the 1965 classic 'Subterranean Homesick Blues'—there would be a patch of acoustic songs, and for these segments, during which Dylan revealed a renewed interest in traditional folk songs, G.E. Smith provided acoustic guitar support. This allowed Dylan to go noodling away, clawing at the strings anyoldhow, in the knowledge that Smith would throw him melodic lifelines to keep it going and to make it alright in the end. Over time, though Smith was always fluid, many people grew to wish that Dylan would take on the burden of the acoustic playing alone, and ask Smith to take a break. At the end of 1988, when Dylan played NEIL YOUNG's Bridge Benefit concert in Oakland, he performed six songs, all acoustic, without his band, but again he brought G.E. Smith along to play second guitar.

All too soon, as it now seems in retrospect, the Smith years came to an end: October 19, 1990, the last of that year's run of concerts at New York City's Beacon Theater, was his final concert as a member of Dylan's band. He had been there three years—only half the time he'd spent with Hall & Oates, and less than a third of the time he'd given to 'Saturday Night Live'.

It wasn't the last time they shared the stage, though. Smith found himself in another house-band supporting a string of stars for the so-called Bob Dylan 30th Anniversary Celebration Concert at Madison Square Garden on October 16, 1992. Moreover, he was the event's musical director. He remembers that 'The rehearsals for that concert you wouldn't believe. I was rehearsing with GEORGE HARRISON in the morning, ERIC CLAPTON in the afternoon, and LOU REED at night. One afternoon, rehearsing the finale, I had Harrison, Tom Petty, Clapton, Neil Young, Dylan and ROGER McGUINN all lined up and I'm saying, "OK, George you sing here, Eric you play now, Bob you come in here" . . .'

Three years on, and back at the Beacon Theater on December 14, 1995, the familiar figure of G.E. came on stage to play guitar with Dylan once again, though only on 'Rainy Day Women # 12 & 35', the gruesome final encore number. A further five years down the line and there he was again, on November 5, 2000, at Dylan's Ann Arbor, Michigan, concert, coming on to play in mid-set on a 'Leopard-Skin Pill-Box Hat' and reappearing at the end, including on the encore, for 'All Along the Watchtower', 'Highway 61 Revisited' and a final acoustic rendition of 'Blowin' in the Wind'.

Altogether he had played at well over 200 Dylan concerts.

[G.E. Smith quote from his Green Mirror record-label website, seen online 25 Jun 2005 at *www.greenmirror.com/gebio.html.*]

Smith, Harry [1923 - 1991] Harold Everett Smith was born in Portland, Oregon, on May 29, 1923, the son of a salmon cannery night-watchman and a teacher, both followers of theosophist Madame Blavatsky, and as a child he spent time on the Native American reservation where his mother taught. He duly studied Anthropology at the University of Washington but dropped out into an early West Coast bohemia, started into abstract painting, made abstract animated films by applying paint straight onto the film itself, and began large collections of many esoteric things; those usually mentioned are Ukranian Easter eggs, Mayan codices, tarot cards, rare books, Seminole patchwork dresses, the mounted string figures he wrote a vast treatise on, found paper airplanes and above all the 78rpm hillbilly and 'race' records from the 1920s from amongst which he would eventually assemble his masterpiece, the 1952 6-LP vinyl anthology *AMERICAN FOLK MUSIC*, the importance of which is stressed in the present work not only in its separate entry but necessarily in myriad others.

Smith's work in avant garde film, painting and off-the-wall anthropology has been avidly studied by different enthusiasts but what matters most surely remains the unequalled impact of his work in music. Perhaps music mattered most to Smith too. One of the contributors to the box set CD-reissue of *American Folk Music* in 1997, Luis Kemnitzer, wrote that 'He would lend out books that he thought you might want, gave away paintings and collages, but once a record came into his room it never left.' He loved 'the records themselves as well as the music encoded in them'.

His polymath talent was remarkable even within music. Another contributor to the 1997 box set's booklet, Luc Sante, tells an especially pleasing small story about him late in his life, when he was staying in ALLEN GINSBERG's 'tenement on East 12th Street'. Smith and Sante both attended a nearby party, and Sante recalls: 'He was rude in that preemptive way that small men sometimes assume, and he helped himself to a great deal of cake and bogarted all the reefers. Then he proposed a challenge: if we'd sing a verse of "Barbara Allen," he'd tell us what county we were born in. As it happened, the only person present who remembered the words was my then-girlfriend. After she sang, Harry instantly said, "Bennington County, Vermont." And he was right. It was news to me—I'd always thought she was born in Massachusetts.'

Another pleasing story about Smith is also set in his Ginsberg-apartment days. On a visit to New York from Colorado in 1985 he was sleeping in Ginsberg's spare room when Bob Dylan called round to show Ginsberg the lyrics to his brand new album, *Empire Burlesque*. Dylan was thrilled to learn that the legendary Smith was there, and asked to meet him. Ginsberg went through to tell Smith who their visitor was. Smith refused to get up.

In his New York days a long-term resident of the Chelsea Hotel, Smith had moved to Colorado in the 1970s; he moved back to New York City to die, which he did six months later, checking out of the Chelsea Hotel for good on November 27, 1991.

[Smith-Dylan story reported fully in 'The Night Bob Came Round', by Raymond Foye, *Telegraph* no.36, Romford, UK, summer 1990.]

Smith, Patti [1946 -] Patricia Lee Smith, born in Chicago on December 30, 1946 but raised in Woodbury, New Jersey, near Philadelphia, grew up to be one of those essential and endearing New York punk bohemians who keeps on keeping on, wearing her art on her sleeve, living, at least in our imaginations, an endlessly erratic life in the world of Chelsea Hotel grot-chic, with a string of liaisons with the famous behind her, from Robert Mapplethorpe to SAM SHEPARD and from poet Jim Carroll to Tom Verlaine. A singer, songwriter and poet, she began to record in the mid-1970s, beginning with a single 'Piss Factory' c/w 'Hey Joe', made with Lenny Kaye and underwritten by Mapplethorpe. Both sides had strong spoken word elements, one citing ARTHUR RIMBAUD and the other Pattie Hearst.

The Patti Smith Group then signed to a major label deal and the result was the 1975 classic *Horses*—a stark Mapplethorpe cover enclosing a clamorous début, with punk, poetry and rock'n'roll fighting among themselves, and right from the outset: a seizing of VAN MORRISON's 'Gloria' for her own argumentative purposes. After the less well received *Radio Ethiopia*, a fairly serious fall from the stage and a period of quiet, she came back in 1978 with the far more accessible *Easter*, the album with her great anthemic hit 'Because the Night', co-written with BRUCE SPRINGSTEEN.

For Patti, though, Bob Dylan has always been more special—she has never been afraid to be a fan, whether he likes it or not—and her poem 'Dog Dream', in her 1978 collection *Babel*, is about him. (Her first collection, *Seventh Heaven*, was a slim volume published in Boston in 1972). She had 'hung out' with him in 1975 when he was back in New York and starting to dream up the Rolling Thunder Revue. There's a particular photograph of the two of them together at this point: black and white, as it would have to be, and it's one of those examples of Dylan's great chameleon talent for looking like the person he's alongside: he and Patti look almost mirror images of each other, both black shocks of hair above thin white striking faces. A shot of them embracing in the *Village Voice* was captioned TARANTULA MEETS MUSTANG. Smith said later:

> 'It was so intense, like, when you have a crush on a guy in high school and after a year he finally talks to you and you have nothing to say . . . it was so adolescent . . . very sexy. . . . He has levels completely untapped. . . . He just needs to be sprung loose again. He's got all this stuff just waiting to come gushing out. . . . The electricity coming from his face, his eyes, is real!'

It was many years after that before they worked together, but in late 1995 they did, at a run of seven consecutive concerts on that leg of his Never-Ending Tour, starting in Boston on December 10, followed by New York City (11), Bethlehem, Pennsylvania (13), New York City (14) and then three nights in Philadelphia (December 15–17). Every night Patti Smith would come on in the middle for the tenth song of the set and they would share vocals on 'Dark Eyes', the acoustic song from the end of the *Empire Burlesque* album of ten years earlier, and which he had never sung live before.

The routine might have been the same every night but there was nothing routine about it. It's a song about which NIGEL HINTON said, in assessing the album version, 'I'm slightly suspicious of people who declare that they ". . . live in another world / Where life and death are memorised"'—but without question live performance brought it alive, and it was Patti Smith who made it happen. Here, in the tingling electricity between them as they traded verses and duetted on the choruses, the song was the conduit of a beauty and excitement it had never possessed.

Many Dylan followers believed that he felt challenged by Patti Smith's still possessing a fierce anti-showbiz, anti-bullshit credibility that had in his own case been compromised by then: that she therefore kept him on his toes as no performance with his own band alone would have done. As it was, he rose higher than his toes.

Patti Smith's career seems to have become reactivated since, reaching a crescendo of international activity in 2005, including curating the London Meltdown Festival that June, within which Smith performed the whole of *Horses*; being made, as Dylan had been 15 years earlier (and MEMPHIS SLIM earlier still), a French Commandeur de L'Ordre des Arts et Lettres; and in August performing twice at the German RuhrTriennale, delivering Pattified versions of songs by Dylan, HENDRIX and PHIL SPECTOR—and then next morning delivering a lecture on the poetry of BLAKE and Rimbaud. It's not very punk but it's certainly pitching in—and it's certainly still toiling in the fields of poetry and music.

[Patti Smith: *Seventh Heaven*, Boston, MA: Telegraph Books, 1972; *Horses*, Arista LP 4066, US, 1975; *Radio Ethiopia*, Arista LP 4097, 1976; 'Dog Dream', *Babel*, New York: G.P. Putnam & Sons, 1978, re-collected in *Early Work 1970–1979*, New York: W.W. Norton, 1994; *Easter*, Arista LP 4171, US, 1978. *Village Voice*, 7 Jul 1975 & Smith on Dylan 1975 from Robert Shelton, *No Direction Home: The Life and Music of Bob Dylan*, London: Penguin edn., 1987, p.439. Nigel Hinton: 'Into the Future, Knocked Out and Loaded', 1st published *Telegraph* no.25, Bury, UK, autumn/winter 1986, but quoted here from the version collected in Michael Gray & John Bauldie, eds, *All Across the Telegraph: A Bob Dylan Handbook*, London: W.H. Allen, 1987.]

Smith, Warren [1932 - 1981] The extravagant 'thanks' list in the liner notes to *Knocked Out Loaded* includes thanks to 'gal shaped just like a frog'. Though the 'gal' in Washboard Sam's post-war 'Soap and Water Blues' is claimed to be 'shaped like a frog', Dylan's allusion is more likely to be to (and is more exactly a quote from) Warren Smith's rockingest record, 'Miss Froggie', which has the opening line 'Well I got a gal shaped just like a frog'. Smith's recordings, first for Sun in Memphis and then 2,000 miles west in Hollywood, for Liberty, ring other Bob Dylan bells too.

Warren Smith was born near Yazoo City, Mississippi, on February 7, 1932. He served in the US Air Force before heading for Memphis and a career in music. He became one of Sam Phillips' rockabilly legends, but reluctantly: he wanted to be a country singer and, oddly, was allowed to become one in Hollywood.

He was the vocalist with the quaintly named Snearly Ranch Boys (also featuring the great Stan Kesler) when he went into the studios with a song

JOHNNY CASH wrote (or bought from George Jones), 'Rock'n'Roll Ruby'. A rockabilly classic that was also an instant regional hit. Smith dumped his aggrieved band and went solo.

His next single was a rockabilly version of a song Dylan includes on *Good as I Been to You*, 'Black Jack David': in Smith's case a version that teeters on the edge of being comically terrible—a foreshortened, moralising version on which Smith sounds as if he's pretending to be Johnny Horton. Smith's Sun recordings also give us 'Red Cadillac and a Black Moustache' (the spelling of 'moustache'/'mustache' varies between record labels) and 'Uranium Rock', both unreleased by Sun at the time but soon prized items on many compilation albums. Dylan has covered both. And it might even have been the Smith version of Slim Harpo's 'Got Love If You Want It' that Dylan remembered when he recorded and nearly released the song on his *Down in the Groove* LP in 1988 (it is on the version issued in Argentina).

Neglected by Phillips, who was busy trying to cope with JERRY LEE LEWIS' far bigger success, Smith went west, cut some morose sides for Warner Brothers under the pseudonym Warren Baker and then signed with Liberty, where he was produced by ex-Cricket Jerry Allison. At his second Liberty session, Smith, like JIMMY REED before him, recorded a number with the title 'Odds and Ends', a title Dylan recycles for a song of his own on the Basement Tapes.

Amphetamine addiction and a serious car smash in 1965 ended that phase of his career. Drink and drugs prevented much happening on the other labels he signed to after this. He spent 18 months in gaol in Huntsville, Alabama, and then took a day job as, er, Safety Director for a company in Longview, Texas. In April 1977 Britain's rockabilly fanatics brought him over to the UK and, to his amazement, gave him the kind of adoring reception he'd always thought his due. He died of a massive heart attack at age 47 on January 31, 1981.

Dylan's 1986 tours found him especially interested in revisiting the rockabilly era. At the third concert of the tour, in Sydney on February 10, he débuted Smith's song 'Uranium Rock', playing it a further 26 times on subsequent nights—if not 29, since there are three Perth concerts mid-February for which no tape or set-list is known (what's wrong with these people?) and no reason to feel that Dylan would have stopped singing the song nightly, as before and afterwards. Perhaps 'Uranium Rock', with the repeat line 'rock 'em dead', wasn't his most tactful song choice for the concerts in Japan (where he took to performing it just ahead of a hummed version of 'Sukiyaki').

When the next leg began, in the US, on June 9 in San Diego, Dylan opened the concert with another rockabilly artist's hit, WELDON ROGERS' 'So Long, Good Luck and Goodbye', but retained 'Uranium Rock' for the first two nights. After that Dylan dropped the Smith song temporarily but reintroduced it in Chicago on June 29, the concert after he'd débuted 'Red Cadillac and a Black Mustache' (at East Troy, Wisconsin, June 27). At the Chicago concert he performed *both* Warren Smith songs. Altogether 'Uranium Rock' was used 13 times on this leg of the tour, but 'Cadillac' was dropped after a third performance (July 2, Akron, Ohio).

However, Dylan later set about recording 'Red Cadillac and a Black Mustache': first in Hollywood in April 1987 (an uncirculated version featuring DAVE ALVIN on guitar, STEVE DOUGLAS on sax, James Jamerson on bass and MADELYN QUEBEC and CAROLYN DENNIS on backing vocals) and then more purposively in early May 2000 (this time with his tour-band members CHARLIE SEXTON, LARRY CAMPBELL, TONY GARNIER and DAVID KEMPER). This pleasant, fond version, from quite a sweet-voiced Dylan, was made for, and released on, the various-artists album *Good Rockin' Tonight: The Legacy of Sun Records*, issued 18 months later.

Finally, and perhaps inspired by his visit to Sun Studios the previous month, Dylan also got around to recording 'Rock'n'Roll Ruby': on May 1, 1987 in Hollywood, a *Down in the Groove* session. This remains uncirculated.

[Warren Smith: 'Miss Froggie', Memphis, 1957, Sun 268, Memphis 1957; 'Rock'n'Roll Ruby', Memphis, 5 Feb 1956, Sun 239, 1956; 'Black Jack David', Memphis, Aug 1956, Sun 250, 1956; 'Got Love If You Want It', Oct 1957, Sun 286, 1957; 'Red Cadillac and a Black Moustache', Memphis, 1957, unissued by Sun; 'Uranium Rock', Memphis, 23 Feb 1958, unissued by Sun; all CD-reissued on *Warren Smith: Classic Sun Recordings*, Bear Family BCD 15514-AH, Vollersode, Germany, c.1991. 'Odds and Ends', Hollywood, 17 Nov 1960, Liberty LRP 3199, Hollywood 1961, CD-reissued (with all his Liberty and later Slick recordings) on *Call of the Wild* Bear Family BCD 15495-AH. Some of the info on Smith above comes from the splendid British rockabilly website Rockabilly Hall of Fame, *www.rockabillyhall.com*.

Bob Dylan: 'Red Cadillac and a Black Mustache': Hollywood, Apr 1987, unissued, and *nia*, early May 2000, *Good Rockin' Tonight: The Legacy of Sun Records*, London, Sire 31165-2, US 1991.]

Smith, Willie [1944 - 1997] William Daniel 'Smitty' Smith was born on August 30, 1944. He played keyboards on the 1980 semi-gospel 'Musical Retrospective' tour (November 9 to December 4), on some of the April 1981 sessions and the May 15 session for the *Shot of Love* album and on the spring 1981 tour (June 10 to July 25).

On the 1980 tour he opened the concerts, playing sole musical accompaniment, on piano, while the gospel group sang four numbers, and in the middle of each show there was a slot where Dylan and Smith played alone, Dylan on acoustic guitar and Smith again on piano. On the 1981 tour, these duets were dropped. The four-song gospel set at the start of each concert continued to include a song co-written by Smith, 'Saved By the Grace of Your Love'. On one occasion—July 14—Smith sang the song himself. On *Shot of Love* his only credit is for organ on 'Heart of Mine'.

Smith, a widely used session player, died in Los Angeles on November 28 (not the 26th, as reported), 1997.

Snerd, Mortimer J. Dylan's untitled prose-poem on the back cover of the 1965 *Bringing It All Back Home* LP sandwiches 'jayne mansfield.humphrey bogart' between 'SLEEPY JOHN ESTES' and 'mortimer snerd'.

Mortimer J. Snerd is one of the inventions of ventriloquist Edgar Bergen (1903–78). Bergen was on US radio as from December 1936 but long remained less famous than his first major creation, the top-hatted, monocle-wearing, quick-witted dummy Charlie McCarthy ('the funny wooden dummy . . . we all knew and loved so well', as Dylan mentions in passing in *Chronicles Volume One*). In 1937, given his own series on NBC (he switched to CBS in 1949), Bergen added a hayseed with six toes on one foot and a favourite cow named Bessie, who grew up on his grandfather's farm in Snerdville—the outrageously slow-witted Mortimer J. Snerd. Except that the dumbness of this dummy was allowed to be penetrating too, as when appearing on 'The Muppets' TV show in 1977 (Jim Henson had been a Bergen fan). Bergen says 'Our act is easy' and Snerd says, 'Yeah. I sit on the stage and talk and Bergen stands next to me and moves his lips.'

Edgar Bergen died before completion of *The Muppet Movie*, in which he, Charlie McCarthy and Mortimer Snerd also appeared. Snerd's film début had been in 1938 (in *Letter of Introduction*). On April 29, 1956 he was a mystery guest on the TV series 'What's My Line'.

A further Ed Bergen creation (1946) was his daughter, Candice Bergen.

['The Chase & Sanborn Show' (named for sponsors but starring Bergen etc.), NBC; 'The New Edgar Bergen Hour', CBS. *Letter of Introduction*, dir. John M. Stahl; Universal, US, 1938. 'The Muppet Show', 13 Jul 1977. Main source: *www.snerdville.com*. Bob Dylan, *Chronicles Volume One*, 2004, p.269.]

Snow, Hank [1914 - 1999] Clarence Eugene Snow was born in a Nova Scotia fishing village on May 9, 1914. He ran away from an abusive stepfather by going to sea as a cabin-boy at age 12. Here he first heard JIMMIE RODGERS (on the radio) and determined to become a country singer. He had a Canadian radio show in 1933, first recorded October 1936 (in Montréal), and after years of trying to break into the US market—years that included performing with his trained horse Shawnee and working at a radio-station in Wheeling, West Virginia, in the mid-1940s—he finally appeared on the Grand Ole Opry on January 7, 1950. He became a regular for over 40 years. He wrote and recorded 'I'm Movin' On', which became the top country song of 1950; 'I Don't Hurt Any More' repeated this feat in 1954.

ROBERT SHELTON's Dylan biography *No Direction Home*, 1986, notes that Dylan 'often alluded to Hank Snow' and that in Bob's boyhood home in 1968, the old records left behind in his bedroom included the LP *Hank Snow Sings Jimmie Rodgers*.

This last contains no material Dylan has yet utilised; but this was neither the first nor last Snow LP of Rodgers material, nor the only evidence of Dylan's familiarity with Snow's work. In 1953 the 10-inch LP *Hank Snow Salutes Jimmie Rodgers* had included 'My Blue-Eyed Jane' and 'Southern Cannonball'. Dylan recorded the former in 1994 for a Various Artists' JIMMIE RODGERS 'tribute album'; 33 years earlier Dylan was taped performing 'Southern Cannonball' at the Gleasons' home in East Orange, New Jersey, in February or March 1961. *Hank Snow Sings in Memory of Jimmie Rodgers (America's Blue Yodeler)*, 1970, containing no material utilised by Dylan except 'Frankie and Johnny', was followed by *The Jimmie Rodgers Story*, 1972, on which Snow sings Rodgers songs interspersed with narrations by one Albert Fullam. This too includes a Snow version of 'My Blue-Eyed Jane', and on the sleevenotes Ernest Tubb remarks that Hank's special favourite in this collection is 'My Blue-Eyed Jane'.

But Hank Snow served more of a function for Dylan than as a purveyor of Jimmie Rodgers repertoire. First, Dylan would certainly have heard him on the radio. Second, Dylan performed 'I'm Movin' On' at 16 1986 concerts, a 1988 sound-check and three 1993 concerts. Snow also recorded, ahead of ELVIS PRESLEY, '(Now and Then There's) A Fool Such as I', which Dylan performed on the Basement Tapes in June 1967 and recorded again at the *Self Portrait* sessions—a version released instead on the 1973 LP *Dylan*.

(Snow helped Presley's early career: star of the Opry when Elvis made his bottom-of-the-bill appearance on it in October 1954, Snow soon had Presley on tour with him, and the first gigs booked by Col. Tom Parker were for Hank Snow Enterprises. It was also Snow who first told RCA Nashville, and his own music publishers, Hill & Range, about Presley. But when Snow's 'I Don't Hurt Anymore'—another song Dylan cut on the Basement Tapes—was at no.2 on the Country & Western charts for August 18, 1954, Presley's 'Blue Moon of Kentucky' was at no.3.)

Snow also made the single 'Ninety Miles an Hour', which Dylan recorded on the largely abject *Down in the Groove* in the 1980s. Dylan also performed Snow's song 'I'm Glad I Got to See You Once Again' as a one-off during the very first leg of the Never-Ending Tour (in Hollywood on August 4, 1988).

But the most interesting instance of a direct influence of Hank Snow upon the young Bob Dylan came to light only in 1993, courtesy of the Dylan fanzine *Isis*. One issue had published the text of a 'poem', written in Bob Zimmerman's own hand, the original of which had been posted by an unnamed hand to the fanzine's editor, DEREK BARKER. This 'poem' was a mournful tale narrated as if by a scared boy in hiding to avoid being beaten by his drunkard father. Five issues later, reader John Roberts wrote in to say that he had found an album on the cheap RCA Camden label, dated 1962, titled *The One and Only Hank Snow*, and risked wasting his 75p (then about $1) on this unknown music because of its inclusion of a song, credited to Clarence E. Snow, titled 'The Drunkard's Son' and handily summarised in the sleevenotes as 'the mournful tale of a scared boy in hiding to avoid being beaten by his drunkard father.' Yes indeed. As Roberts nicely observes, if the 'Zimmerman Transcript' is authentic, which now seems established, it is a 'truly unique document—the first evidence we have of Bob's plagiarism!'

Ironically, it's an example of Snow's plagiarism, too. Look back at the Jimmie Rodgers catalogue, and there, recorded in Atlanta in 1929, is Rodgers' 'A Drunkard's Child'.

Perhaps it was still in Hank Snow's repertoire when Dylan, in his youth, was in the audience for his show at the Veterans Memorial Building, Hibbing. Dylan mentions this in *Chronicles Volume One*—and a few pages later writes that before he encountered WOODY GUTHRIE, when HANK WILLIAMS had been his 'favorite songwriter', Hank Snow had been 'a close second'.

Snow died at home in Madison, TN, December 20, 1999, aged 85.

[*Hank Snow Sings Jimmie Rodgers' Songs*, RCA Victor LSP/LPM-2043, NY, 1959; 'My Blue-Eyed Jane' & 'Southern Cannonball', Nashville, TN, 12 Feb 1953, *Hank Snow Salutes Jimmie Rodgers* (10-inch LP) RCA Victor LPM-3131, NY, 1953; 'Frankie and Johnny', Nashville, 9 Dec 1969, *Hank Snow Sings in Memory of Jimmie Rodgers (America's Blue Yodeler)*, RCA Victor LSP/LPM-4306, NY, 1970; 'My Blue-Eyed Jane', Nashville, 27 Dec 1971, *The Jimmie Rodgers Story*, RCA LSP-4708, NY (RCA LSA 3107, London), 1972 (this LP was re-issued as RCA Victor ANL1-2194, 1977, though without Tubb's sleevenotes); 'I'm Movin' On', Nashville, 28 Mar 1950, 10-inch LP-issued *Country Classics*, RCA Victor LPM-3026, 1952 (reissued as 12-inch with extra tracks as LPM-1233, 1955) & on *The Best of Hank Snow*, RCA Victor LSP-3478, 1966; '(Now and Then There's) A Fool Such as I', Nashville, 19 Feb 1952, LP-issued *Country Classics* (above), LPM-1233, 1955 and *The Best of Hank Snow* (ditto); 'I Don't Hurt Anymore', Nashville, 1954, RCA Victor 5698, 1954; 'Ninety Miles an Hour (Down a Dead-End Street)', RCA Victor 8239, 1963. (Snow is billed as 'The Singing Ranger' on two 4-CD sets of his RCA Victor work issued on Bear Family BCD 15426-DH and 15476-DH, Vollersode, Germany, 1988 & 1990, which include 'I'm Movin' On' & '(Now and Then There's) A Fool Such as I'. 1954–1958 sides Snow recorded for radio play only are on a 5-CD set *The Thesaurus Transcriptions*, Bear Family BCD 15488-EH, 1991, including another 'Frankie and Johnny'.) 'The Drunkard's Son', *nia*, 1st issue Canada 1943–49, *nia*; 1st US issue as a single, RCA 21-0303, NY, 1950; LP-issued on *The One and Only Hank Snow*, Camden CAL-722, NY (RCA Camden CDN5102, London), 1962 (sleevenotes by Roy Horton). The song appears on various other Snow releases, variously titled 'The Drunkard's Son', 'The Drunkard's Child' and 'A Drunkard's Child'.

Bob Dylan: 'My Blue-Eyed Jane', details see entry on **Rodgers, Jimmie**; 'Southern Cannonball', East Orange, NJ, Feb/Mar 1961, unreleased; 'A Fool Such as I' & 'I Don't Hurt Anymore', Woodstock, NY, June 1967. Bob Dylan, *Chronicles*, 2004, p.43 & 49. *Isis* no.44, Aug–Sep 1992, & no.49, Jun–Jul 1993, Coventry, UK.]

Soles, Steven [1948 -] John Steven Soles, born October 26, 1948, became a guitarist, harmony vocalist and sometime record producer and was the first husband of actress and *Penthouse* model P.J. Soles (the husband before Denis Quaid). They married in 1971 and divorced in 1975.

Soles, who is a vintage car fan, was one of the few who played in Guam on both the Rolling Thunder Revue tours *and* throughout the 1978 World Tour (guitar and vocals each time), and who was also called in to work on both the studio albums recorded in that period, *Desire* and *Street Legal*, as well as, of course, appearing on the two live albums *Hard Rain* and *At Budokan* and in both the 'Hard Rain' TV Special and *Renaldo & Clara*.

On *Desire*, his only session was the October 24, 1975 session, almost two full months after the last of the rest, and necessitated by Dylan's need to avoid litigation by re-cutting 'Hurricane' with amended lyrics. Soles plays guitar; on *Street Legal* he contributes vocals as well as guitar, and plays on all tracks. On the first Rolling Thunder tour, the opening set by Guam each night generally included Soles singing his own song 'Don't Blame Me'; on the second tour, this changed to 'Mad Man'.

DEREK BARKER reports another Dylan-Soles connection: 'Dylan band member Steven Soles says Dylan came to his apartment one afternoon in 1977 and played him and T-BONE BURNETT ten or twelve ". . . Very dark, very intense" songs. Soles could only recall one title, "I'm Cold".'

Like Burnett, Soles was a Born Again Christian and thought Bob would be happier (and presumably write cheerier songs) if he joined the march of onward Christian soldiers too. Soles told CLINTON HEYLIN: 'I kept telling him that I was so glad that I didn't have to place my faith in man any longer.' Clearly, since he said this more than once, he can have had little idea how repulsive it sounds.

Despite his long service and his proselytising, or possibly because of them, he was not asked to be part of any of Dylan's own Born Again or gospel recording or touring in the period immediately following the 1978 World Tour. He was a co-founder of the Alpha Band (for details see the entry **Burnett, T-Bone**), and after it folded released two solo albums, *Promise* (1980), and *Walk By Love* (1982). In 1988 Soles was among those on the 'ROY ORBISON and Friends: Black & White Night' TV Special, and in the early 1990s played in ELVIS COSTELLO's band—on acoustic guitar and harmony vocals. He has also composed for a handful of films, including, in 1996, for an action thriller titled *Don't Look Back*.

[Derek Barker, '1978 and All That', collected in *20 Years of Isis: Bob Dylan Anthology Volume 2*, New Malden, UK: Chrome Dreams, 2005, p.220 but taken from Sounes, p.210. Clinton Heylin, *Behind the Shades Revisited*, London: Penguin, 2003.]

'Solid Rock' [1980] Dylan recorded this on the second day of the sessions for the *Saved* album (though some percussions and back-up vocals were overdubbed a day later). Like the title track, this is at the least skilfully written end of Dylan's evangelical work. The sound strives for power but achieves only bombast, while the lyrics foam with generalised scriptural rebuke. The only moment of Dylan's creative flash comes here: 'It's the ways of the flesh to war against the spirit / Twenty-four hours a day you can feel it and you can hear it', where he wakes us up briefly by inserting into this deadening biblical fulmination that playfully modern phrase 'Twenty-four hours a day'. It's a small blob of jam on a large pill.

Dylan's text here is taken from Galatians 5:17: 'For the flesh lusteth against the Spirit, and the Spirit against the flesh: and these are contrary the one to the other . . .' But this theme doesn't have to be expressed with such dead preachiness. The Bible itself makes the same point elsewhere in far more human, attractive and poetic terms. In Romans, for example, Paul speaks, neatly, of those who 'served the creature more than the Creator' (1:25) and, not to exclude himself, admits that 'I see another law in my members, warring against the law of my mind' (7:23); while in his Second Epistle to the Corinthians he says that '. . . while we are at home in the body, we are absent from the Lord' (5:6).

The founding texts, as it were, behind the title and chorus of 'Solid Rock' (behind 'Well I'm hangin' on to a solid rock / Made before the foundation of the world') are from John 10:4 ('. . . and that Rock was Christ') and the verbatim 'before the foundation of the world'—one of those nondescript phrases which hook the attention by incantatory repetition throughout the New Testament. It is in John 17:24, Ephesians 1:4 and I Peter 1:20 (with the lesser 'from the foundation of the world' in Matthew 13:35, Luke 11:50 and Hebrews 4:3 and 'since the foundation of the world' in Hebrews 9:26).

In the so-called *Good News Bible*, 1966–76, the full phrase has become so much *more* nondescript that the effect of repetition is nil, since it passes entirely unnoticed, being merely 'before the world was made'. This, of course, killing all figurative possibility, obviates the connection with 'solid rock'.

The full phrase, as Dylan uses it, allies most clearly with the idea of Christ as the Rock in I Peter 1:20, which describes him so: 'Who verily was fore-ordained before the foundation of the world, but was manifest in these last times for you.' In this way Christian orthodoxy solves the problem of how Christ can be such a late-comer yet can have been around all along: God, forseeing the fall of humankind, pre-prepared the remedy that was to cure the disease. (Even in Jewish orthodoxy, seven things existed before the creation of the world, and one was the Messiah.)

Dylan débuted 'Solid Rock' live in concert on the opening night of the first gospel tour (on November 1, 1979, in San Francisco), long before he recorded it. He performed it every night of that tour, and every night of the follow-up tour in January–February 1980. It remained in place for the third and last all-gospel tour, with Dylan still playing the preacherman. Introducing the song on the fourth night in Toronto that April, as the music twitches restlessly behind him, ready to burst through, Dylan declaims from memory another text by Paul, from I Timothy 3:16. The text is this: 'God was manifest in the flesh, justified in the Spirit, seen of angels, preached unto the Gentiles, believed on in the world, received up into glory.' Whether deliberate editing or faulty recollection prompts Dylan's changes, they work well enough, as he declares: 'It [the solid rock] was manifest in the flesh! an' justified in the Spirit! an' seen by angels! an' preached on in the world!' Had his audience been black church, you would have heard the 'Yes, Lord!'s' and 'A-men!'s' coming back at him between each ascending, clamorous phrase. As it was, his gospel back-up vocalists supply these responses with mellifluous but authentic 'Oh yea-ea-eah!'s'.

[Bob Dylan: 'Solid Rock', Sheffield, AL, 12 Feb 1980; Toronto, 20 Apr 1980.]

song in the history of English Literature WILFRID MELLERS, professor of music and former *Scrutiny* literary critic: 'We talk nowadays as though the relationship between . . . [words and music] . . . constituted a problem; even as though there were a natural antipathy between them which composer and poet must overcome as best they may. Yet the separation of the two arts is comparatively recent, and the link between them would seem to be rooted deep in human nature.'

Dylan has chosen a medium we are still unused to taking seriously: an inseparable mixture of music and words. We grew up finding this a cheap and trivial formula but if we look back beyond the Elizabethan age we find a very long period in which troubadours were an important part of our culture, when that culture was orally dominated and when sophisticated art was the same in kind as the heritage 'of the people'.

It is only comparatively recently that folk and sophisticated culture have been separate. The gulf was not complete in England until the emergence of the Augustans, with their classicists and coffee-house smart-sets, although it had started with Chaucer, who brought to dominance an East Midlands dialect which became what we call 'standard English'.

With only a few exceptions, pre-Elizabethan poetry was 'of the people'. Pre-Aelfredian poetry was all vernacular and all, in essence, orally disciplined, including 'Beowulf', the longest surviving poem in Old English, and written about a thousand years ago. It was sung, and its development was the responsibility of its singers; and so, roughly, things continued until the Norman Conquest. And in the long run, the English absorbed the Normans and the English language rose in importance.

The poetical literature that grew with it was again emphatically 'of the people' from Langland's 'Vision of Piers Plowman' in 1362 to Orm's 'Ormulum' (early 13th century verse homilies by an Augustinian canon). 'Piers Plowman' might now be the province of university English departments, but in its own time it appealed to everyone. Written in the Old English manner, in alliterative verse, it had an equal impact on those who wanted a reform of the Church and those labourers and serfs to whom Wat Tyler offered himself as a symbol of progress and hope.

Throughout the entire 15th century the divisive power of Chaucer's influence was fought by those ingredients of English life which worked towards keeping up the old cultural unity. In this transitional period, ballads, lays and so on blossomed alongside a renewed concern with classical literature. So the Elizabethan age that followed grew out of a cultural turmoil never equalled before or since, until our own times. Folk culture was intimately and creatively linked with literary culture in the age that has given us an unmatched richness of artistic achievement.

If 1960s guru MARSHALL McLUHAN was right, if our technology is pushing us forward into another orally dominated age, then it shouldn't be surprising to find a serious artist once again at work in the medium Dylan has chosen. Nor should it astonish us that such an artist can have re-forged the links between folk and sophisticated culture.

Everywhere in the West, minority cultures are being tossed together and mixed with, on the one hand, lumpen uniformity and on the other, what passes as the *haute culture* of the age (and the process accelerates all the time), so that whatever our class or geographic centre, we have more in common with one another, more shared experience, than the men and women of any period since the heyday of the Elizabethan age in England. Full circle. And this wheel's on fire—we are caught up in a kind of vulgar, neurotic renaissance. Hail the return, as McLuhan insists, to oral primacy.

Small wonder that Dylan should select, or rather, find himself at home in, an artistic medium not merely literary but involving a return to a medieval interdependence of words and music. 'Popular songs,' he said in 1965, 'are the only form that describes the temper of the times. . . . That's where the people hang out. It's not in books; it's not on the stage; it's not in the galleries.'

See also **Bunyan, John**.

[Mellers: source unknown; quoted from Michael Gray, *Song & Dance Man III: The Art of Bob Dylan*, p.45. Dylan re-quoted in 'The *Playboy* Interview: Bob Dylan: a candid conversation with the iconoclastic idol of the folk-rock set', *Playboy*, Mar 1966.]

'Song to Woody' [1962] The only self-composed songs on Dylan's first album were 'Talkin' New York' and the reflective 'Song to Woody'. Here, irony closes the lyric: after he salutes CISCO HOUSTON, SONNY TERRY and LEADBELLY and the unnamed other 'good people' who had traveled with WOODY GUTHRIE, Dylan ends by saying 'the very last thing that I'd want to do / Is to say I bin hittin' some hard travelin' too.' Clearly, to say he'd been hitting some hard travelling too is not the last thing Dylan would like to be *able* to do. It is with those final lines—which get their special strength not just from the understatement but from the carefully clipped reluctance of the cadence—that we get a fresh focus on the whole theme of the song. At the same time, we still hear the echoes of all those delicate rushes of confidentiality which, throughout the lyric, establish its tone. Other aspects of the song also contribute to its appeal. There is the frank if implicit statement of what is, on Dylan's part, a plea for an innocent drop-out and the concern to find a new allegiance in the 'hard travelin'' ethos. Again there is a delicacy in handling this: a balance struck in perceiving both the harsh reality and its romantic flavour. The song not only reflects Guthrie faithfully but assesses his real but disappearing America from Dylan's, the young man's, perspective. We are offered a highly intelligent understanding of the subject.

This comes over too in the rhythmic balance of the lyric: look at the third and fourth lines, the seventh and eighth, and so on; and likewise, the wind and the dust are there in the song's construction. Lines and syllables take the form of a list:

the suggestion is one of restless movement within a preordained pattern of repetition. The sharecropper's life rhythm. In Guthrie's triumphant autobiography, *Bound for Glory* (1943), we see him travelling around with the homeless families who are also the heroes of Steinbeck's *Grapes of Wrath* (1939); and while recalling one particular encounter, Guthrie quotes one of his own songs, 'Pastures of Plenty'. Dylan's tribute reworks this, changing the last verb in Guthrie's 'We come with the dust and we go with the wind' from 'go' to 'are gone', showing his awareness that the era which produced such men was all but over.

If Dylan's debt to Guthrie is, as he admits, substantial, it is not in essence just derivative. Few people can have gained so much from Guthrie's work, even though that work is among the best of the American folk-art accessible to us from the pre-1960s. When Dylan sings in 'Song to Woody' that 'I'm seein' y'r world of people and things' he is too modest: he has not so much seen as re-created.

[Recorded NY, 20 Nov 1961, but Dylan is known to have performed the song 'live' at the Gaslight Café in Greenwich Village on 6 Sep that year (there's an extant unreleased recording). By the end of 1998 Dylan had only performed the song 'live' 24 times. A version recorded NY, 1–2 May 1970 with GEORGE HARRISON has also circulated.]

'Soon' [1987] See **Gershwin, George & Ira**.

'The Sopranos' [TV series] Created by David Chase, 'The Sopranos' occupies the world of the New Jersey mob as if it were Ancient Greece. First aired in 1999 on cable TV, it has proved one of those drama series not only popular but cool to admire. Dylan recorded a song specially for it. On December 17, 2000, at the New York session at which he recorded 'I Can't Get You Off of My Mind' for the HANK WILLIAMS tribute album *Timeless*, he also recorded 'Return to Me', a song co-written by Guy Lombardo's brother Carmen and a big 1958 hit by Dean Martin, for 'The Sopranos'. Dylan's version, a fond and fumbling recreation of the Martin version, complete with a verse in Italian, cut with TONY GARNIER on bass and LARRY CAMPBELL on guitar but augmented by Shawn Pelton on drums and Brian Mitchell on accordion, was for the slot at the end of each episode when the credits roll to a different slice of music each time. It ran in the 2001 series—Episode 38, 'Amour Fou'—and was released on the compilation soundtrack album *The Sopranos—Pepper & Eggs: Music from the HBO Original Series*, released in 2001. (Episode 24 in the first series had used part of the *Slow Train Coming* cut of 'Gotta Serve Somebody' and included it in the first compilation album.)

[Bob Dylan: 'Return to Me', NY, 17 Dec 2000, *The Sopranos—Pepper & Eggs: Music from the HBO Original Series*, Columbia/Sony Music Soundtrax C2K 85453, May 2001.]

Sounes, Howard [1965 -] Howard Guy Sounes was born in Welling, Kent, UK, on January 3, 1965. He first took an interest in Dylan's work in about 1979 when he started to explore an older sister's record collection and found within it, among an abundance of Rod Stewart, Roxy Music, *Tommy* and the like, the quiet jewel of *Blood on the Tracks*. An acoustic-guitarist best friend at school, and the friend's dad, were both Dylan fans; the friend worked his way through Dylan songbooks while Howard smoked cigarettes and listened. At age 16, the two of them went to see Dylan live at Earl's Court, London, in June 1981.

Apart from writing the highly praised biography *Locked in the Arms of a Crazy Life: Charles Bukowski*, published in 1998, *Bukowski in Pictures* (2000), *The Wicked Game* (i.e. golf, 2004) and *Fred & Rose: The Full Story of Fred and Rose West and the Gloucester House of Horrors* ('by a journalist who covered the story from day one', 1995), Howard Sounes became one of Bob Dylan's many biographers, interviewing 250 people to produce *Down the Highway: A Life of Bob Dylan* in 2001. Its particular achievement, beyond its competence at handling detail, was the revelation of Dylan's having been married to CAROLYN DENNIS and their having a daughter.

Since the golf book he has turned his attention to a history of the arts in the 1970s, to be published by Simon & Schuster in 2006. Its working title is *Seventies*. Dylan is touched upon.

[Howard Sounes, *Down the Highway: A Life of Bob Dylan*, New York: Grove Press, 2001; *Fred & Rose: The Full Story of Fred and Rose West and the Gloucester House of Horrors*, London: Warner Books, 1995; *Locked in the Arms of a Crazy Life: Charles Bukowski*, New York: Grove Press, 1998; *Bukowski in Pictures*, Edinburgh: Rebel Inc., 2000; *The Wicked Game*, New York: HarperCollins, 2004.]

South, Joe [1940 -] Joseph Alfred Souter was born on February 28, 1940 in Atlanta, Georgia, and grew up to be a briefly famous hit-making performer in his own right, the writer of a cluster of big hit songs that have been recurrently covered, and a fine session-playing guitarist with a distinctive biting sound. His first work was playing in R&B groups in Atlanta, as a staff guitarist for National Recording Corporation in Atlanta (as were Ray Stevens and Jerry Reed) and on country radio. In 1957 he joined PETE DRAKE's group, recorded the 1958 novelty single 'The Purple People Eater Meets the Witch Doctor' and became a session player both in Nashville and at Muscle Shoals in Sheffield, Alabama. He played on records by Marty Robbins and Eddy Arnold but also on tracks by Wilson Pickett and Aretha Franklin (his is the stand-out guitar part on her 'Chain of Fools'). He creates the distinctive sound on Tommy Roe's wannabe-BUDDY HOLLY hit 'Sheila' and plays the lead electric guitar part that producer TOM WILSON overdubbed onto SIMON & Garfunkel's 'The Sound of Silence'.

In his own right he had a transatlantic top 10 hit in 1969 with his fearsomely catchy and swamp-like 'Games People Play', proving himself a fine co-ordinator of words and music. He scored again with 'Walk a Mile in My Shoes' after a more minor success with 'Don't It Make You Want to Go Home'. His first hit as a writer was in 1962, with the Atlanta-based group the Tams' hit 'Untie Me'. He went on to write the Deep Purple hit 'Hush' (a UK hit all over again by the short-lived but mega-successful Kula Shaker in 1997), Billy Joe Royal's splendid 'Down in the Boondocks' and 'I Knew You When' (both 1965; the latter revived by Linda Ronstadt) and Lynn Anderson's huge 1971 hit '(I Never Promised You a) Rose Garden'.

His own version of 'Rose Garden', like 'Games People Play', was on his début solo album, *Introspect* (1968)—a pioneering classic of soul country which was quickly withdrawn and then reissued as *Games People Play*. It also includes his 'Birds of a Feather', the melody of which rather resembles that of VAN MORRISON's 'Brown-Eyed Girl'. South's follow up, *Don't It Make You Want to Go Home* (1969), included 'Walk a Mile in My Shoes'. Two further albums followed, *A Look Inside* and *So the Seeds Are Growing*. South also produced Billy Joe Royal, Sandy Posey and others.

'Walk a Mile in My Shoes' became a personally applied theme song in ELVIS PRESLEY's live repertoire of the 1970s, and was the first of the 50 songs Bob Dylan performed at his four-set night at Toad's Place, New Haven, CT, on January 12–13, 1990.

Joe South, however, had earlier Dylan connections. He played guitar on the November 30, 1965 Dylan session, at which first attempts at *Blonde on Blonde* material were made, using as musicians a blend of Hawks and session men: RICK DANKO, ROBBIE ROBERTSON, RICHARD MANUEL and GARTH HUDSON, plus AL KOOPER, BRUCE LANGHORNE, PAUL GRIFFIN, BOBBY GREGG and South. It was the session that produced circulated first outtakes of 'Visions of Johanna' (though he goes uncredited when one is released on the 2005 set the *Bootleg Series Vol. 7—No Direction Home: The Soundtrack*) plus the properly issued version of the single 'Can You Please Crawl Out Your Window?' On this occasion, the session log has South down under his real name, Joseph Souter. Not so for the February 14–16, 1966 sessions, on which he plays both bass and guitar, or the March 7–9 sessions, on which he plays guitar. Al Kooper credits him with 'playing the soul guitar on "Stuck Inside of Mobile". . . . [and] the great bass line of "Visions of Johanna".'

South was derailed by the 1971 suicide of his brother Tommy, who had also been the drummer in his studio and touring band. Joe suffered severe clinical depression and vanished to live in the jungle on the Hawaiian island of Maui. He made a brief return in 1975 with a solid new solo album, *Midnight Rainbows*, but though two more albums followed in 1976, *You're the Reason* and *Look Inside*, South promptly retired again, emerging only in 1994, when he took part in a multi-artist London concert showcasing southern musicians and then settled down to work in music publishing.

[Joe South: *Introspect*, Capitol ST108, US, 1968; *Don't It Want to Make You Go Home*, Capitol ST392, 1969; *A Look Inside*, Capitol ST-11074, 1972; *So the Seeds Are Growing*, Capitol ST637, *nia*; *Midnight Rainbows*, Island LPS 9328, US, 1975. Al Kooper quoted from booklet inside Dylan's *Bootleg Series Vol.7—No Direction Home: The Soundtrack*, 2005.]

'Spanish Harlem Incident' [1964] On the fourth album, *Another Side of Bob Dylan*, perhaps the most historically interesting song is 'Spanish Harlem Incident', because here we find the really substantial beginnings of Dylan's famous complexity, the beginnings of what 1965 brought out so explosively.

'Spanish Harlem Incident' begins with this: 'Gypsy Gal, the hands of Harlem / Cannot hold you to its heat'—which is a stylish and immediately impressive declaration of independence on Dylan's part: a marker in the development of his figurative language.

'I am homeless, come and take me / Into the reach of your rattling drums. / Let me know, babe, all about my fortune / Down along my restless palms.' There, strikingly, is that individual style of impressionism that Dylan was to cultivate (and which attracted so many unfortunate imitations—including much from the Beatles, with their 'plasticine porters' and 'marmalade skies'). Dylan's has work to do. He begins simply enough with that non-literal, non-physical 'homeless'; and while he moves to that apparently vaguer 'rattling drums' yet the adjective there has a precision of its own: we're shown how appropriate the phrase is to the spirit of the Gypsy Gal as Dylan sees her. Next, there is a precise function in the uniting of two ideas in 'my restless palms'—the validity of the fortune-telling allusion being sympathetically strengthened by its connection to the singer's admitted desire for hand-in-hand contact, while the wish implicit there harks back to that 'come and take me' in the earlier line. It is as part of the evocation of this particular Gypsy Gal that this near-Gothic effect works also: 'The night is pitch black, come an' make my / Pale face fit into place, ah! please!' For such a girl, the night would make itself dramatic. Again, we feel that her individual personality draws out this, in the final verse: 'On the cliffs of your wildcat charms I'm riding, / I know I'm round you but I don't know where.'

The first of those lines gives a perfect summary of how the writer stands for the creation of the song. His language, throughout, is intent on eliciting a captivating vision of those 'wildcat charms'—a nice phrase, jostling the untamed with the traditionally genteel so freshly—and his singleness of purpose places Dylan's impressionistic imagery a long way from the random hit-and-miss version of his imitators. Theirs is exhibited for its own sake and is its own reason for being; Dylan's is there to assist the communication of specific and personally realised themes.

It's instructive to take this 'minor' song from 1964 and compare it to a minor song from the wretched *Empire Burlesque* album of 1985: say, 'Emotionally Yours'. The differences in vocal performances on such early and such later recordings are discussed elsewhere. Here let's consider the songs themselves.

Whatever aspect of the two you choose, there's simply no contest. Compare the titles. 'Spanish Harlem Incident' has a deft particularity, even after all these years: in its cultural allusiveness—the playfully used mock movie title or mock headline it conjures—it carries the spark of an alert mind, not taking itself too seriously but on the ball, while as a comment on its contents—a making light of the feelings expressed with such energy in the song, it contributes to the expression of those feelings, signalling the singer's wistful regret that such affairs must pass. What does the title 'Emotionally Yours' signify? Bullshit and sludge. There's nothing alert, sparky or culturally allusive here, no deft particularity—no particularity at all. It makes no comment, other than by default, since anyone with a modicum of alertness to language themselves will be warned off by the clumsy untruth at its ponderous core.

Compare the repeating line that ends the verses—the device that is as near to having a chorus as either song comes. In 'Spanish Harlem Incident' we get 'I got to know babe . . .' (yes, there's one 'babe' in each of the three verses); then that 'Let me know babe, all about my fortune / Down along my restless palms'; then 'Let me know, babe—I'm nearly drowning—If it's you my lifelines trace'; and then 'I got to know babe, will you surround me / So I can know if I am really real.' (These lines were subjected to stupid twiddles of alteration in the version published in *Writings and Drawings*, 1972, and perpetuated in later songbooks.)

What we have here, then, is a sustained conceit—'gypsy gal' = fortune-teller—deftly used, to say that in the *moment* evoked in the song, the singer feels that his future is in her hands; this is sustained for the conclusions of the first two verses—and without a pop cliché in sight: not with 'your heart is in my hands', but rather in language new to popular song, and with a particularity that convinces you there's a specific person envisaged here, and a particular moment experienced: these are 'restless palms'. This also allow the verse's end to balance its beginning, in which 'the hands of Harlem / Cannot hold you to its heat.'

This conceit, this calculation and planning, if you will, in the composing of the lyric, far from having the effect of making it seem a construct of artifice, enables the song's authenticity to flow. Its last verse ends with just the necessary minimal difference to signal that it *is* the song's end, and to finish with a renewal of ardour and urgency, acting as a protestation at coming to the end of the affair it describes. Where the other verses both end with 'Let me know', in the last this becomes 'I got to know'. What of the repeated line at each verse end in 'Emotionally Yours'?: 'And I will always be emotionally yours.' 'And I will always be emotionally yours.' 'But I will always be emotionally yours.' The 'And' becomes 'But' to signal song's end. Nothing else moves, in any sense.

Compare strikingness of openings. 'Spanish Harlem Incident' opens vividly, with a clear-sighted placement of person and cityscape that yet leaves the listener to fill that picture in—trusts the listener to do so—while beginning as it means to go on, with a poetic conceit, and one that coheres with what will follow. 'Emotionally Yours' also begins as it means to go on: 'Come baby, find me, come baby remind me, of where I once begun. / Come baby, show me, show me you know me, tell me you're the one.' On this evidence the writer is sorely in need of reminding of where he once begun.

Further, the one song has vivid imagery, the other virtually none. Does 'come baby, lock me into the shadows of your heart' do anything but palely loiter in the shadows of 'come and take me / Into the reach of your rattling drums'? Something is *happening* in the specific moment, something is being visualised in the Harlem night, when the Dylan of 1964 sings 'The night is pitch black, come an' make my / Pale face fit into place, ah please!'—not least because something is happening to *enact* it in the dynamics of the line itself. Dylan expresses his awkward fit with the marvellous awkward fit of the word distribution and the inspired onomatopoeic stuttering of those alliterative ps and fs along that insistent, urging second line. Nothing is happening when the Dylan of 1985 sings 'Come baby, shake me, come baby, take me, I would be satisfied. / Come baby, hold me, come baby, enfold me, my arms are open wide.' The verbs of imprecation hold no urgency here: they're there because they rhyme; there's no enactment of any of the demanded shaking or taking—and nothing for the visual imagination to get a grip on, except for the stiff cliché of 'my arms are open wide'. Where the earlier minor song is personal and fresh and fired by particularity, the later one is tired before it starts, and its only stuffing is the dullest of pop cotton-wool.

You'd think it should be the other way around. In 1964 Bob Dylan had good reason to be drawn to pop. Pop was exciting right at that point, not least to Dylan. This was the era when he was freeing himself from the constraints of 'folk', taking his car trip around America and hearing, inevitably, THE BEATLES on the radio all the time. The 1960s was really beginning. Yet the young Bob Dylan, absorbing all this, was nevertheless writing songs that benefited from his saturation in all the richness of folksong. By 1985 what had been fresh was stale, what had been youthfully alive was encrusted in weary detritus. Weird time for Bob Dylan to join the pop party, and for his writing to benefit only from saturation in the shallow histrionics of corporate rock. (See also **co-option of real music by advertising, the**.)

Yet despite all this, Dylan himself seems never to have cared much for 'Spanish Harlem Incident'. He performed it live only once, so far as we know: having recorded the studio version on June 9, 1964 (along with all the other tracks on *Another Side of Bob Dylan)*, he ignored it at the NEWPORT FOLK FESTIVAL that July, didn't play it at the JOAN BAEZ concert at Forest Hills in August (at which he sang three songs), and ignored it at his Philadelphia Town Hall concert in September. Then he performed it as the second song at his important New York Philharmonic Hall concert that Hallowe'en (issued 40 years later on the CD the *Bootleg Series Vol. 6*), and has never played it again since. One live performance of this tremendous song!

[Bob Dylan: 'Spanish Harlem Incident', NY, 9 Jun 1964 & NY, 31 Oct 1964; 'Emotionally Yours', Hollywood, 14 Feb 1985 (+ overdubs Feb 25 & beyond). The Beatles' phrases are from 'Lucy in the Sky With Diamonds', London, 2 Mar 1967, *Sgt. Pepper's Lonely Hearts' Club Band*, Parlophone PCS 7027 (PMC 7027 mono), London (Capitol SMAS 2653, LA), 1967.]

Spector, Phil [1940 -] Phil Spector, the world's oldest boy genius, was born Harvey Phillip Spector in the Bronx on Boxing Day, 1940. He and his mother Bertha moved to Los Angeles when he was 12, three years after his father Ben's suicide: an event that, more than any other, 'explains' Spector's lifetime of disturbed behaviour. Mad, inspired record-producer; seven-stone weakling; gun-toting paranoiac; teen tantrum king; abusive husband and father: this is Phil Spector on a good day.

He achieved immortality in the world of pre-BEATLES pop, making what he dubbed as 'little symphonies for the kids'—a lava flow of hit singles by the Crystals, the Ronettes, Darlene Love, the Righteous Brothers, Bob B. Soxx & the Blue Jeans and more besides—and spent the next 40 years or so in dark and stormy decline.

He learnt piano, french horn, drums and guitar at school, and began writing songs with school friend Marshall Lieb. With the splendidly named Annette Bard (really Kleinbard), another school friend, they formed vocal trio the Teddy Bears, and in 1958 recorded Spector's composition 'To Know Him Is to Love Him', its title taken from his father's tombstone. It hit the US top 10 and sold a million. Spector was 17 years old. Unforgettably catchy, it is an artfully naïve record, very sweet and very 'white'. Even the upbeat B-side has a timid sensitivity, summed up in the comically solicitous couplet 'Don't you worry my little pet, don't you worry and don't you fret'.

All this was totally out of character for its creator. Spector's own musical taste ran to jazz and rhythm'n'blues; as his later records would soon prove, he preferred thunderous bedlam to tender timidity and he was about as solicitous as a crocodile.

Four Teddy Bears follow-ups were flops, and so were records by the so-called Spectors Three. This was the first of many career reverses, and the ambitious singer and songwriter didn't take it well. A murky period in Spector's history followed. It's said that he took advantage of a job-offer as interpreter in French at UN headquarters in New York to get his airfare paid but never showed up for work, instead meeting his backroom-boy heroes, Leiber & Stoller, who had written hits for ELVIS and for many black acts like the Coasters. More likely, he stayed in LA, worked as a typist while studying at UCLA and then at 18 re-entered the record-business, working under guitarist Duane Eddy's producers, Lester Sill and Lee Hazelwood in Phoenix, Arizona, learning studio production before persuading Sill to send him to New York in 1960.

There he not only met Leiber & Stoller but co-wrote, with Leiber, Ben E. King's classic 'Spanish Harlem'. He also met Ray Peterson, star of the death record 'Tell Laura I Love Her', and produced his follow-up, 'Corrina Corrina', Spector's first hit as a producer. He was soon back in the charts with the Paris Sisters' 'I Love How You Love Me', Gene Pitney's 'Every Breath I Take' and Curtis Lee's 'Pretty Little Angel Eyes', and doing freelance A&R for Atlantic Records. These conventional slices of pop gave no hint of the distinctive vision Spector was about to unleash.

The famous Wall of Sound arrived in 1962, by which time Spector had bought out his partner and at 21 was sole owner of the record-label Philles. He brought together a team of session players, many of whom, like pianist LEON RUSSELL and guitarist Glen Campbell, would later be famous themselves. Spector bullied and hectored these people into a phenomenon—a hit-making machine that, under his dictatorial direction, turned out around 15 timeless classics, including 'He's a Rebel', 'Da Doo Ron Ron' and 'Then He Kissed Me' by the Crystals, 'Be My Baby' and 'Baby I Love You' by the Ronettes, 'Zip-a-Dee-Doo-Dah' by Bob B. Soxx & the Blue Jeans and '(Today I Met) The Boy I'm Gonna Marry' and 'Christmas (Baby Please Come Home)' by Darlene Love. Spector was a millionaire before he was 22. Tom Wolfe called him 'the first tycoon of teen'.

These records changed the rules. Instead of the music being mere 'backing' behind the vocals, it became exponentially multiplied, so that the mix of teenage angst and howling sexuality offered by the singers had to make itself heard above a torrid cacophony in which no distinction was possible between percussion and other instrumentation. Instead of the producer being an anonymous figure whose job was to transmit without interference the individual singer and song, Spector invented, at a stroke, the auteur director of sound, dreaming up and hurling out three-minute Wagnerian operas in which the youthful and raunchy vocalists were almost as interchangeable as back-row violinists. So thoroughly were all these other talents mere tools in the fiery workshop of the maestro that to this day everyone knows the 1963 LP *A Christmas Gift for You* as *Phil Spector's Christmas Album*. As Darlene Love recalls, 'He wanted to build an empire for himself and be bigger than his artists. And it worked.' More generous than Spector ever was, she adds: 'You don't know how some of those singers sounded without him. Phil made everyone sound good.'

He also revitalised the early-60s pop record, replacing the thin, exhausted platitudes of a hundred Bobbies and Johnnies with the tumult of musical armageddon and the erotic exotica of nubile girl groups with very short skirts and towering, sticky beehive hair-dos. For many fans, their first glimpse of the sultry Ronettes and first hearing of that up-front demand 'Be my baby NOW!' was a sexual awakening.

Yet at the same time, just as black Americans were beginning to march and stand up for their civil rights, Spector had the nerve to make records that were often racially androgynous. You couldn't tell if the Righteous Brothers were black or white; you couldn't tell the male-female mix of Bob B. Soxx & the Blue Jeans.

Spector's unique mastery of the sound-desk meant that his songwriting skill went unnoticed. Yet if he hadn't been a producer, he'd still have been a rich, significant figure in pop as a writer or co-writer of classics, from his very first attempt, on across his Wall of Sound smashes (he co-wrote most of them), through 'You've Lost That Lovin' Feelin'' to Ike & Tina Turner's 'River Deep Mountain High'. In later years he co-wrote with Harry Nilsson, GEORGE HARRISON and LEONARD COHEN.

Spector was one of four pop figures customarily called a genius, and influenced at least one of the others, Beach Boy BRIAN WILSON. While Spector himself 'retired' at 25, furious that 'River Deep Mountain High' was a flop in America (it was a smash in Britain), the Beach Boys' complex mid-60s recordings like *Pet Sounds* and 'Good Vibrations' owed much to Wilson's admiration for Spector.

His influence was everywhere. THE ROLLING STONES' early manager/producer, Andrew Loog Oldham, was a Spector wannabe. And if the Beatles and Stones made Spector seem old-fashioned, and the girl-group hits dried up, he bounced back when notorious music mogul Allen Klein put Spector and the Beatles together. By this point a legend and still only 30 years old, Spector was hired by Klein to remix *Let It Be*. McCARTNEY hated Klein issuing the re-mixed 'Long and Winding Road' as a single. Beatle publicist Derek Taylor says when Paul heard what Spector had done, he thought it was 'the shittiest thing anyone had ever done to him, and that was saying something.'

After the Beatles split, LENNON used Spector on his first solo LP and then Phil produced the ex-Beatle solo album that wiped the floor with everyone else's, George Harrison's triple-LP *All Things Must Pass*. Spector-produced hits from these albums included 'Instant Karma' and 'My Sweet Lord', and in 1971 he produced the Concert for Bangla Desh organised by Harrison that brought together everyone from Ravi Shankar to CLAPTON and Dylan. (Dylan and Harrison, getting together in the studio the previous May, had tipped their hats to Spector with a fond but daft, Dylanised version of 'Da Doo Ron Ron', on which 90 per cent of the lyric remained out of his grasp.)

This was the first of only two real Spector-Dylan encounters, though between the two has come the famous hoax of a rumoured 1965 Bob Dylan Christmas album, supposedly part-produced by Spector and titled *Snow Over Interstate 80*: a hoax perpetrated by UK music paper *New Musical Express* in 1975. (One of the tracks they claimed as included, 'Silent Night', *was* later recorded by Dylan: at an *Infidels* session in New York on April 22, 1983; this has never circulated, but, unlike *Snow Over Insterstate 80*, did exist.)

The other actual Spector-Dylan encounter was in 1977 when, on Leonard Cohen's Spector-produced album *Death of a Ladies' Man*, Bob Dylan and ALLEN GINSBERG were back-up vocalists on one song, 'Don't Go Home with Your Hard-On'. This album was not a success, and nor were Spector-produced mid-1970s records by Dion and Cher.

People never gave up on Spector, though. In 1980 New York punk group the Ramones got him to produce their album *End of the Century*, and as late as 1996 he was warring with Celine Dion's team over an abortive collaboration, declaring: 'You don't tell Shakespeare what plays to write, or how to write them, and you certainly don't tell Phil Spector.'

Rather, he gave up on himself. He stayed locked inside the most wired, guard-dog infested mansion in all of Hollywood, and wore, as well as the obligatory dark glasses, a huge cross around his neck and a gun on his hip. Drug stories and arrests, bodyguard beatings and dangerous tantrums became commonplace around him, culminating in his indictment on a murder charge in 2004, after 40-year-old actor Lana Clarkson was found dead in early 2003, shot through the mouth at his home. Spector was freed on $1 million bail. At the time of writing (January 2006), he has withdrawn a $1 million suit against his own first trial attorney, lost his bid to rule out police testimony that he first claimed he'd shot Ms. Clarkson by accident before claiming she'd killed herself, and announced that if acquitted he will, at age 65, marry 25-year-old fiancée Rachelle Short.

As writer Mary Harron put it, 'He had one perfect moment in the early 60s, and never recovered.'

[The Teddy Bears: 'To Know Him Is to Love Him', LA, 1958, Doré 503, US & Canada (London-American HL 8733, UK), 1958. Various Artists: *A Christmas Gift for You, nia*, Philles PHLP-4005, US, 1963. Bob Dylan & George Harrison: 'Da Doo Ron Ron', NY, 1–2 May 1970, unreleased. The *NME* hoax article, dated only as 1975, is reproduced online (seen 6 Jan 2006) at *www.searchingforagem.com/snowover.htm*.]

Spitz, Bob [1950 -] Robert Spitz was born in Reading, Pennsylvania, on January 29, 1950. He is an American writer who claims to have once 'represented' BRUCE SPRINGSTEEN and ELTON JOHN, and whose books include the malevolent *Dylan: A Biography* (1988), which *Publishers Weekly* described as '526 cliché-ridden pages' on Dylan up to 1978 followed by 25 pages on the Born Again period and after. 'Spitz (by name and spits by nature)', as Andrew Ford noted, 'is the sort of writer who wants to grow up to be Albert Goldman . . . not much of an ambition.' In 2005 Spitz published *The Beatles: The Biography*. Enjoy.

[Bob Spitz, *Dylan: A Biography*, New York: McGraw-Hill, 1988; *The Beatles: The Biography*, New York: Little Brown, 2005. Andrew Ford on Spitz, in 'Wagner v. a man named Zimmerman', *Sydney Morning Herald*, 26 Aug 1989.]

Spivey, Victoria [1906 - 1976] Victoria Spivey was born in Houston, Texas, on October 15, 1906, and turned out to be one of the few 'classic women blues singers'–the women who mainly came out of vaudeville and jazz and were earliest on record with the blues–who survived and continued to perform all the way through to the folk and blues revival period at the beginning of the 1960s, though her career declined in the 1940s and in the 1950s she temporarily quit secular showbiz for church-based performing. She survived not least because she was a talented songwriter as well as a singer and pianist, she had a good head for business, knew her market and aimed straight at it. Many of her songs 'dwelt on disease, crime and outré sexual images', sung in a 'small, acrid voice', as blues critic Tony Russell puts it (with quiet relish).

After providing the musical entertainment in Houston whorehouses, she began recording in 1926, and her first song, 'Black Snake Blues', was a big success. By mid-1929 she had seen 21 of her records released on the OKeh label, and in the same year she appeared as Missy Rose in King Vidor's first sound movie, the black musical *Hallelujah* (at one point playing Wagner's 'Here Comes the Bride' on harmonium). At her peak she could command accompaniment by Louis Armstrong and LONNIE JOHNSON, and she continued to record copiously for major labels in the 1930s. Two of her sisters, Addie and Elton, who performed as Sweet Peas (sometimes spelt Pease) Spivey and Za-Zu, were less successful.

The photograph by Len Siegler on the back cover of the 1970 album *New Morning*, of a sweetly youthful Dylan pictured with a mumsy Victoria Spivey, is a memento of the sessions Dylan charmed his way into with Spivey and BIG JOE WILLIAMS for her newly formed, Brooklyn-based label Spivey Records in March 1962. (For these sessions' recording and release details see the Williams entry.) Dylan writes in *Chronicles* that when it came to the *New Morning* album, he 'knew that this photo would be on the cover before I recorded the songs. Maybe I was even making this record because I had the cover in mind and needed something to go into the sleeve.' A few pages later he calls it 'the photo of me and Vickie'.

The original art-print photograph was owned for many years afterwards by Len Kunstadt, a record collector, artists' manager and blues magazine editor whom Dylan knew and who was also the last of Spivey's husbands. Kunstadt edited *Record Research*, in which Spivey wrote a regular column, 'Blues Is My Business'.

In her column for December 1964 she wrote an utterly unreliable, highly entertaining piece, 'Just thinking about the original "Corinne, Corrina"', which tells us in passing a little about Ms. Spivey and her family too:

> 'Corrina was actually a Creole girl, the most beautiful thing you ever saw in your life, with such gorgeous clothes, who came from New Orleans to Houston, Texas, before the first World War. Her mother was called Miss Marie Green who had a small mansion in the first ward in Houston. The door was open to anybody nice who wanted to have a good time and pay for it. Corrina was about 16 and I was eight, and through my oldest sister, Leona, I met Corrina and her mother. At their home I learned to do the Ball The Jack. My musical inspiration, the great pianist Robert Calvin also used to drop by to peep sweetly at my sister, Leona, when I was there. Corrina was a well-preserved girl with her mother giving her all the motherly protection in every walk of life. Corrina had very wavy red hair, was very light skinned (you couldn't tell her from white), had blue eyes and had a beauti-

ful mole on her face. Her speech was soft-spoken and educated-like. I believe that this was the Corrina that they immortalized with that great all-time blues standard, Corrine, Corrina.'

The April 1965 issue ran an ad for her label—'Spivey Means High Blues Fidelity: A Class Product for Today's and Tomorrow's Generation'—and Ms. Spivey's column turned to describing Dylan. Under the heading 'Luck Is a Fortune!' she wrote:

'If you live long enough your luck is bound to change. I was just thinking about little BOB DYLAN. The years flashed back to 1961 when I first met him at Gerde's Folk City in Greenwich Village, New York City. He was the sweetest kid you would ever want to meet. Just a bundle of nervous energy. He would say Moms, this Moms, that Moms, always trying to get my attention, He was a doll. I was so proud of him then because he really had some talent which was just ready to explode. And did it! Just a couple of years later he was on his way to becoming a world idol in his field.

'Speaking about idols! Bob used to tell us all about his childhood and how he used to get next to the Chicago blues people. He had an idol too, among others, and he was none other than the great country blues singer, Big Joe Williams. A dream came true for Bob when Big Joe was here in New York for a Gerde's engagement. Bob knew about my little record company SPIVEY and my plans to record Big Joe, and he wanted "in" too. What a sight as little Bob was carrying Big Joe's unusual guitar to the studio! And did they play well together! Like they were together for 50 years! "Come on Big Joe Little Junior, Play your harp." That's the way Big Joe proudly gave Bob the cue to "take off" on one of the titles. Yes, this was Bob before Dame fortune was to reward him for his great talent.

'When I see him now he still gives me that big baby kiss and hug. He's still the same Little boy to me and I am so happy for him. On a recent Les Crane TV show Bob was simply great. I believe he could become a great comedian in addition to his writing and singing.

'So Bob! keep up the good work and stay the same young man you were in 1961, and you won't have to look back.'

In 1985 Dylan said of Spivey herself: 'oh man, I loved her . . . I learned so much from her I could never put into words.'

Victoria Spivey died in Brooklyn on October 3, 1976.

[Victoria Spivey: 'Black Snake Blues', St. Louis, MO, 11 May 1926. *Hallelujah*, dir. King Vidor, MGM, 1929. The first three Spivey releases, just prior to that with Dylan on it, were: Lucille Hegamin, Hannah Sylvester, Victoria Spivey with Buddy Tate, Eddie Barefield, Dick Vance: *Basket of Blues*, Spivey LP 1001; Victoria Spivey: *Victoria and Her Blues*, LP 1002; & Willie Dixon, Sunnyland Slim, St. Louis Jimmy, Homesick James, John Henry Barbee, Cocoa (sic) Taylor, Evans Spencer & Washboard Sam: *Chicago Blues*, LP 1003.

Victoria Spivey: 'Blues Is My Business', *Record Research* no. 65, NY, Dec 1964 & no.67, NY, Apr 1965, p.11. Bob Dylan: *Chronicles Volume One* quote, p.139; 1985 quote, the *Biograph* box set. Tony Russell, *The Blues—From Robert Johnson to Robert Cray*, London: Aurum Press, p.168. For an entertaining read on Spivey and others, see the chapter 'Billie and Bessie' in David Widgery, *Preserving Disorder*, London: Pluto Press, 1989.]

Spoelstra, Mark [1940 -] Mark Spoelstra was born on June 30, 1940 in Kansas City, Missouri, but grew up in El Monte, California, where he was playing guitar by age 11. His third gig was opening act for SONNY TERRY & BROWNIE McGHEE. He moved to New York City (via Berkeley) and joined the folk revival scene, playing a big B-45 Gibson 12-string guitar.

According to his own breezy account, 'A friend of mine ran into me on the street one day and said there was a guy he thought I should meet. He was sitting alone in a joint, having just come to town. So I was one of the first acquaintances Bob Dylan met when he came to the big city. We hung out together a lot, because at the time we had a lot in common. One night we were playing at the Café Wha?, and JOHN COHEN, who was with THE NEW LOST CITY RAMBLERS, came in and was blown away by my JOHN HURT style guitar and Bob's blues harp . . .'

A couple of months after they met, as an extant photograph confirms, Dylan and Spoelstra performed together at the Indian Neck Folk Festival in Branford, Connecticut, in May 1961; the corollary tape catches Dylan singing 'Talking Columbia', 'Hangknot, Slipknot' and 'Talking Fish Blues': all WOODY GUTHRIE songs. Spoelstra's main influences, Mississippi John Hurt aside, were JESSE FULLER, PETE SEEGER and Skip James.

That summer, the two often appeared behind BROTHER JOHN SELLERS at Gerde's Folk City hootenannies, backing up his gospel shouts and tambourine with guitars and harmonica (and were even announced as Brother John & the Dungarees). Spoelstra says in the film *No Direction Home* that in these early years, Dylan shared with him and so many others the belief that song could help to abolish racial segregation and change the world for the better: that they talked about these things with enthusiasm.

In *Chronicles Volume One* Dylan describes Spoelstra as 'a singing pal of mine', recalls their playing with Brother John Sellers and recalls the day when, having arranged to meet up with Mark at 'a creepy but convenient little coffeehouse . . . run by a character called the Dutchman', who 'resembled Rasputin', he arrived to find Mark Spoelstra there waiting for him and the Dutchman lying dead in the doorway with a knife in him, killed by the old man who was his landlord.

Spoelstra got a record deal with Folkways that same year, and recorded two albums for them, *The Songs of Mark Spoelstra with Twelve-String Guitar* and *Mark Spoelstra Recorded at Club 47 Inc.*, which were both released a bit belatedly in 1963.

He was one of the featured artists on two different albums on which Dylan appeared as Blind Boy Grunt. On the Various Artists album *Broadside Ballads*, released in October 1963 (on which Dylan performed 'John Brown', 'Only a Hobo' and 'Talkin' Devil'), Mark Spoelstra performed his own topical song 'The Civil Defense Sign'; and on the Various Artists album *The Blues Project* in 1964, on which Dylan played on a GEOFF MULDAUR track, Spoelstra had a track on each side of the LP, with renditions of 'France Blues' and 'She's Gone'. The other featured artists were DAVE RAY, ERIC VON SCHMIDT, DAVE VAN RONK, Ian Buchanan and DANNY KALB.

Like Dylan, Spoelstra also became an occasional contributor to *Broadside* magazine, and appeared at the 1965 NEWPORT FOLK FESTIVAL. Unlike Dylan, his career never took off, despite having an early hit single in Canada ('Walkin' 'Round Town' by Mark & the Two Timers), despite signing to Elektra and making another two albums, released in 1965 and '66, despite a couple of his pieces being used on the soundtrack of that great film *Electra Glide in Blue*, and despite Janis Joplin covering one of his songs. In part, but only in part, this was because he was a conscientious objector placed in 'alternative service' instead of being called up, and so he was prevented from touring to promote those mid-60s albums.

In San Francisco he formed a rock band; it got nowhere. In 1969 Columbia signed him as a solo artist again, and released one album, *Hobo Poet* (from which the *Electra Glide in Blue* tracks are taken) but by this time Spoelstra and his family were 'almost starving'. He gave up trying to find music-industry success and found God and a series of day-jobs instead.

Mark Spoelstra still has a day-job, driving a shuttle bus at a northern California Indian Casino. He's stayed with God, too; but in 2001, after a gap of more than 20 years, he released a new album, *Out of My Hands*, for the distinguished blues-revival company Origin Jazz Library, with a cover-painting by ERIC VON SCHMIDT and a sound-bite from Tom Paxton: 'I always wanted to play guitar like Mark Spoelstra. I still do and I still can't.'

[Mark Spoelstra quoted in Eric von Schmidt & Jim Rooney, *Baby, Let Me Follow You Down*, Garden City: Anchor Books, 1979, p.204 and précis'd from *No Direction Home*, dir. Martin Scorsese, 2005; *The Songs of Mark Spoelstra with Twelve-String Guitar*, NY, 1961, Folkways FA 2444, NY, 1963; *Mark Spoelstra Recorded at Club 47 Inc.*, Boston MA, 1961, Folkways FG 3572, 1963; 'The Civil Defense Sign', NY, Feb-Mar? 1963, *Broadside Ballads*, Broadside BR301, NY, Oct 1963; 'France Blues' & 'She's Gone', NY, early 1964, *The Blues Project*, Elektra EKL 264, NY, Jun 1964; *Five & Twenty Questions*, *nia*, Elektra EKL-283 / EKS-7283, NY, 1965; *State of Mind*, *nia*, Elektra EKL-307 / EKS-7307, NY, 1966; *Hobo Poet*, San Francisco, *nia*, Columbia CS 9793, 1969; 'Meadow Mountain Top' & 'Song of Sad Bottles' also on *Electra Glide in Blue* (dir. James William Guercio) soundtrack album, United Artists UA-LA062-H, US, 1973; *Out of My Hands*, *nia*, Origin Jazz Library OJL 2001, Thousand Oaks, CA, 2001. Mark & the Two Timers: 'Walking Around Town' c/w 'Corinna Folkways', *nia*, F45001, NY, 1964. Bob Dylan, *Chronicles Volume One*, pp.74–75.]

Springs, Helena [1961? -] Helena Lisandrello, professional name Helena Springs, worked with Dylan both as a back-up singer and songwriting partner. As the former, she was the only one there throughout the entire 1978 World Tour—from Japan in February through to the American end in December—and to remain with him for the gospel tours of 1979. She may have acted as a small preparatory catalyst for the change in nature between the two. She says she and Dylan had a conversation about prayer: 'He was having some problems once and he called me and asked me questions that no one could possibly help with, and I just said, "Don't you ever pray?" And he said, "Pray?" . . . I said, "When I have trouble, I pray." He asked me more questions about it, he started inquiring: he's a very inquisitive person which is one good thing about him—he's always searching for truth, truth in anything he can find.' Springs may therefore have helped to prepare the way, ahead of MARY ALICE ARTES. (See **'Born Again' period, a slow train coming to the**.)

As a co-songwriter with Dylan, in the same period, Helena Springs had mixed success. On the one hand she co-wrote a larger number of songs with him than any other collaborator in his career; on the other hand, most of them remained barely recorded and unreleased. The titles copyrighted (to Dylan-Springs except where otherwise stated) were as follows:

'Baby Give It Up', 'Coming from the Heart (The Road Is Long)', 'Her Memory' (Dylan-Springs-Ken Moore), 'I Must Love You Too Much' aka 'Love You Too Much' (Dylan-Springs-Greg Lake)', 'If I Don't Be There By Morning', 'More Than Flesh and Blood', 'One More Time' (though this one now seems not to have been part of the list, but rather a song by Shel Silverstein titled 'Daddy's Going on One More Ride'), 'Responsibility', 'Someone Else's Arms' 'Stop Now', 'Take It or Leave It', 'Tell Me the Truth One Time', 'Walk Out in the Rain', 'The Wandering Kind', 'What's the Matter', 'Without You' and 'Your Rockin' Chair'.

Though the most appealing lyric is probably that of the patchy but often adroit 'The Wandering Kind', the nearest to significant from among these songs are 'Coming from the Heart (The Road Is

Long)', 'I Must Love You Too Much', 'Walk Out in the Rain' and 'If I Don't Be There By Morning'. The first of these was rehearsed with the tour band in Santa Monica in April 1978 (this tape has circulated) and recorded at the *Street Legal* sessions on May 1 (this has not circulated, though another Dylan-Springs song recorded the same day has: the unremarkable 'Stop Now', as has another performance of this latter from a rehearsal on June 8) and performed once on the tour itself: at St. Paul, Minnesota, on Hallowe'en 1978. The circulated recordings show it to have a catchy, almost anthemic chorus melody. It was covered in 1979 by those survivors of the 1960s Merseybeat scene, the Searchers, who had been offered a comeback opportunity by Sire Records and included the song on the first of the two albums that resulted (though only on the US version).

'Love You Too Much', with messed-about lyrics, was recorded and released as a 1981 single by Greg Lake (formerly of Emerson, Lake and Palmer, who in an earlier era had made a magnificently, perversely different extravaganza out of Dylan's 'She Belongs to Me'). The lyrics as published subsequently in the *Bob Dylan Lyrics 1962–1985* and *Bob Dylan Lyrics 1962–2001* both determinedly preserve Lake's rewrites instead of the Dylan-Springs words as performed in concert by Dylan when he came to sing the song, which was twice: in Binghampton, NY, on September 24 and at Madison Square Garden on September 29, 1978. (Dylan and the band had sound-checked it in New Haven, CT, on the 17th.) Years later, the re-constituted version of THE BAND included a version on their *High on the Hog* album of 1996.

'Walk Out in the Rain' and 'If I Don't Be There By Morning' were both covered by ERIC CLAPTON on his *Backless* album of late 1978, and he makes both mournfully appealing. Helena Springs must have gained more royalties income from this album than from any other professional source. The album went platinum immediately upon release, and remains, via CD reissue, part of the mega-selling industry that is the Clapton catalogue. In 1997 'Walk Out in the Rain' was a bluegrass hit single for Robbie & Ron McCoury, two years after its inclusion on their eponymously titled début album.

As with 'Coming from the Heart', Dylan recorded his own 'Walk Out in the Rain' on May 1, 1978, at the *Street Legal* sessions, but this hasn't circulated; ditto with 'If I Don't Be There By Morning', recorded sometime that same month. He never performed either in concert, nor 'Your Rockin' Chair', though this was sound-checked in Omaha, Nebraska, that November 4th.

'The Wandering Kind' was covered by PAUL BUTTERFIELD on the album *The Legendary Paul Butterfield Rides Again* in 1986. 'More Than Flesh or Blood' and 'Take It or Leave It' got as far as being sound-checked in mid-September 1978 (and a tape has circulated); otherwise, that seems to have been the end of the co-written material—except that Helena Springs herself made demos of 'Responsibility', 'Tell Me the Truth One Time' and 'The Wandering Kind' (and possibly 'What's the Matter' and 'Without You') in Santa Monica in September 1979. Bob Dylan may play piano on these tracks. Dylan recorded 'Her Memory' in Santa Monica on September 23, 1980, playing piano himself, with FRED TACKETT on guitar and JENNIFER WARNES sharing vocals (this tape has not circulated) and again, along with another co-written song, 'Brown Skin Girl', at a longer session that October.

Helena Springs hung on in Dylan's backing group till the after the last date of 1979, in Santa Monica on November 21, sometimes taking lead vocals, mid-set, on the gospel song 'What Are You Doing with Your Heart?'—but she did not re-appear with Dylan for the 1980 dates—or ever again.

She met actor Robert De Niro in 1979 and began what she told the papers was a three-year affair with him. She told the *New York Post* she became pregnant by De Niro 'at Chateau Marmont. . . . But I knew he didn't love me so I didn't tell him. I aborted. He never knew.' However, she gave birth to a daughter on July 1, 1982, and both believed De Niro to be the father. (Ten years later she hired Marvin Mitchelson to file a paternity suit against him, and pursued this even after blood tests proved he was not the child's father—because, said Mitchelson, De Niro 'had accepted the girl as his daughter and supported her for a long time.')

By May 1983 she had joined BETTE MIDLER's troupe, as one of the Harlettes, for the second leg of her touring show 'De Tour', which began in Philadelphia on June 16 and ran through till early September in Minneapolis. Springs can therefore be glimpsed in the video release of Midler's HBO-TV Special *Art or Bust*, taken from the show.

After going back in the studios with David Bowie and MICK JAGGER—she's on their terrible 1985 hit single 'Dancing in the Street' (as is Dylan's first Never-Ending Tour lead guitarist G.E. SMITH)—she was on tour with ELTON JOHN in 1986. That year too she co-wrote a song with the Pet Shop Boys, variously called 'New Life, New Love', 'A New Life' and 'New Love', which they recorded. (She had also sung on their records 'West End Girls' and 'You Know Where You Went Wrong'.)

Helena Springs also recorded 'New Love' herself, for an album of the same name made for Arista UK that summer. She had made some demos in London for popster and songwriter BA Robertson ('BA' put like that is how he likes it), and used one of these, of 'The Other Side of the World', co-written with Mike Rutherford of Genesis, to get her own record deal.

Her track 'New Love' was also issued as a UK single, following up the earlier single 'I Want You' from the same album—for which a video was made, directed by Brian Grant (who has apparently directed 175 pop videos . . .). Other titles included 'Paper Money', 'Midnight Lady' and, er, 'Be Soft with Me Tonight'. The album was also issued in Germany, but never released in the US.

Helena Springs has continued to work in cabaret (her lawyer was describing her as 'a cabaret singer' by 1992); in 2001, living in New York City, she reportedly moved home 'from near the World Trade Center shortly before 9/11'.

[Helena Springs: 'Responsibility', 'Tell Me the Truth One Time & 'The Wandering Kind', Santa Monica, CA, Oct 1979, unissued; 'What Are You Doing with Your Heart?' live during Dylan concerts, e.g. San Francisco, 10 Nov 1979; *New Love*, US & UK, summer 1986, Arista 208 119, London, 1986. Quote re prayer from 'Bob Dylan's Unshakeable Monotheism—Part II: The 1970s', by Scott Marshall, seen online at *www.jewsweek.com*, 11 Oct 2005; *New York Post* quote from Andy Dougan, *Untouchable: A Biography of Robert De Niro*, New York: Thunder's Mouth Press, 1996, p.136; paternity suit details from headline article, *AmeriCast.com*, 1 Nov 1992, seen online 11 Oct 2005 at *www.mit.edu/afs/net.mit.edu/user/tytso/usenet/americast/twt/news/338*; quote re home online ditto *http://216.127.80.118/~admin27/adf/messages/1019/1978.html?1084070847* but posted May 2004.

Greg Lake: 'Love You Too Much', *nia*, Chrysalis 103634, US (Chrysalis CHR1357, UK), 1981, & on the LP *Greg*, CD-reissued as *The Greg Lake Solo CD*, GL-CD 0115, *nia*. Eric Clapton: 'Walk Out in the Rain' & 'If I Don't Be There By Morning', *nia*, *Backless*, RSO 3039, 1981. Robbie & Ron McCoury: *Robbie & Ron McCoury*, Rounder CD 0353, US, 1995. Paul Butterfield: 'The Wandering Kind', *nia*, *The Legendary Paul Butterfield Rides Again*, Amherst AMH 3305, 1986. Dylan & tour band: 'More Than Flesh or Blood' & 'Take It or Leave It', sound-check, New Haven, CT, 17 Sep 1978. Bette Midler: *Art or Bust*, Lion's Gate Video, US, 1983. David Bowie & Mick Jagger: 'Dancing in the Street', London, 29 Jun 1985, EMI America B-8288, US (EA 204, UK), 1985. BA Robertson detail, e-mail to this writer 16 Oct 2005.]

Springsteen, Bruce [1949 -] Bruce Frederick Springsteen was born in Long Branch, New Jersey, on September 23, 1949, grew up in Freehold Borough, New Jersey, bought his first guitar at 13, joined local group the Castilles (they recorded two tracks in a custom studio in Bricktown, NJ), then joined Virginia's Richmond-based group Steel Mill before returning to New Jersey and becoming a local hero in Asbury Park and other waterfront towns. JOHN HAMMOND signed him to a Columbia solo contract in 1972 and at the start of 1973—effectively at the existential start of the 1970s—he was 'launched' with the début album *Greetings from Asbury Park, NJ* and with a magnificent, edgy, sweaty performance for music journalists at Max's Kansas City in New York. After a slow start and a re-launch, based upon journalist JON LANDAU's May 1974 review quote 'I have seen the future of rock'n'roll, and it's name is Bruce Springsteen' and the third album, *Born to Run*, he became the most important rock artist of the decade and of his generation.

As NIGEL WILLIAMSON reminds us in *The Rough Guide to Bob Dylan*, Springsteen was, early on in his Columbia career, one of several new artists given the tag 'the new Bob Dylan' but proved 'the one who transcended the tag the most effortlessly'. Indeed he swiftly overshadowed Dylan by music-biz standards: 'At the time Dylan hadn't toured in seven years, and the throne appeared to be vacant. Bruce was enthusiastically awarded the crown by critics . . .' (Speak for yourself.) *Born to Run* paralleled this conquest in sales terms. Williamson notes that *Born to Run* sold 'six million copies, while *Blood on the Tracks*, released in the same year, sold two million.' He was also a thrilling, grandstanding live performer, his E Street Band a unit of extravagant pizzazz, and as he jumped about in his tight building-worker t-shirts and delivered three-hour-long high-energy shows, he couldn't help but emphasise that he was the fittest young lion in the pack.

The side of Bob Dylan that cared about all these things was wounded, without doubt. Springsteen's prowess, his sales figures, the critical plaudits he had achieved in what seemed from the outside a rocketing to fame: all this gave Dylan's pride a knock. You could sometimes detect this in oblique remarks Dylan made later in the 1970s, as for instance when he said of his own 1978 World Tour sax player STEVE DOUGLAS that it was unreasonable to put anyone else (meaning the E Street Band's Clarence Clemons) in the same league. Perhaps even the decision to front such a large band himself, and give such long performances with it on that 1978 tour, was in part a response to the phenomenon of Springsteen. It was noticeable too, at the so-called Dylan 30th Anniversary Concert in New York City in 1992, Springsteen was not a guest.

But if he was a mega-success, and a phenomenon, Springsteen was also palpably a likeable, straightforward man, and one who never showed anything but ardent respect for Dylan's work. The two first met in that crucial year for both, 1975. Bruce has famously paid Bob tributes and given great sound-bites about him, for instance describing the impact of first hearing of 'Like a Rolling Stone' at least as articulately as anyone else, and saying in January 1988, as he inducted Dylan into the Rock'n'Roll Hall of Fame, that 'ELVIS freed our bodies, and Dylan freed our minds.' Dylan, in response, paid tribute, as so often, to earlier pioneers, going out of his way to thank ALAN LOMAX and LITTLE RICHARD (and MUHAMMAD ALI). The occasion also gave us Dylan and Springsteen performing together, notably as Springsteen shared backing vocals on 'Like a Rolling Stone' and as Dylan played guitar for MICK JAGGER and Springsteen on '(I Can't Get No) Satisfaction'.

It was not their only on-stage meeting. Two years later, at a TOM PETTY & THE HEARTBREAKERS concert in Los Angeles on March 1, 1990, after Dylan came on and sang 'Rainy Day Women # 12 & 35' and then sang with Petty on 'Everybody's Movin', Bruce Springsteen arrived on stage and Dylan played guitar behind him while Springsteen sang 'Travelin Band' and 'I'm Crying'. Then in October 1994, at the last of Dylan's three Never-Ending Tour concerts at the old Roseland Ballroom in New York, Springsteen—plus NEIL YOUNG—played guitar on the encore numbers, 'Rainy Day Women # 12 & 35' and 'Highway 61 Revisited'. As ANDREW MUIR, who was there, commented: 'Musically forgettable it might have been but the sight of the three together was one not to be missed.'

A year later, at a Rock'n'Roll Hall of Fame Gala Concert in Cleveland, Ohio, on September 2, 1995, Dylan sang 'All Along the Watchtower', 'Just Like a Woman', 'Seeing the Real You at Last' and 'Highway 61 Revisited'—and then Bruce Springsteen came on and shared vocals with Dylan on 'Forever Young'. (Only Dylan's 'All Along the Watchtower' was included on the album *The Concert for the Rock'n'Roll Hall of Fame*, but all of it was shown on HBO on September 26, 1995). Most recently, Dylan sang 'Highway 61 Revisited' with the E Street Band in a brief guest appearance at the end of a Springsteen show at Shea Stadium on October 4, 2003. It was the first time the band had played the song but they seemed to know it better than Dylan.

The two singers have not performed together in public since, but one final conjunction is that Dylan's lyric for 'Tweeter and the Monkey Man', on the first Travelin' Wilburys album, is riddled with good-natured comic references to the words of Springsteen songs. That's the nearest he's come to any paying of tributes in reverse.

In the end, of course, to concentrate on Springsteen's greater music-biz success, or even his once great critical modishness, is to miss the essential point in any comparison. Dylan knows, and so do we, that though commercially Bruce Springsteen might have been far more successful, as an artist Dylan's achievement has been incomparably greater.

[Rock'n'Roll Hall of Fame induction: NY, 20 Jan 1988; Dylan Roseland concert, NY, 20 Oct 1994. Various Artists: *The Concert for the Rock'n'Roll Hall of Fame*, Columbia 483 793 2, US, 1997. Nigel Williamson: *The Rough Guide to Bob Dylan*, London: Rough Guides, 2004, p.362. Andrew Muir, *Razor's Edge: Bob Dylan & the Never-Ending Tour*, London: Helter Skelter, 2001, p.119.]

St. Andrews University Honorary Degree ceremony [2004] The University of St. Andrews, Scotland's oldest, awarded Dylan an honorary doctorate (in Music) on the afternoon of Wednesday, June 23, 2004. It was the first time he had agreed to accept an honorary degree since Princeton had awarded him one in 1970.

Much credit for St. Andrews' success (and it says something about Dylan's status and behaviour in the world that it should be counted more the ancient university's success than the degree recipient's) belongs to NEIL CORCORAN, with the support of Brian Lang, the University's Principal. For the speech Corcoran delivered at the ceremony, see separate entry. For a good eye-witness account of the proceedings, see ANDREW MUIR's 'Went to Find a Doctor', *Judas!* no.10, Bluntisham, UK, July 2004.

A fine parody of all this appeared in *Private Eye* no.1,110, London, July 9–22, 2004, which, below a photograph of a be-robed Dylan looking outrageously put-upon and vexed, offered a mock version of the citation in cod-Latin, rendering the title 'Blowin' in the Wind' as 'Responsus Est, Amicus Meus, Pufferandum in Vento', and finishing with '© University of St Andrews (formerly the Glen Miller Distillery and Polytechnic, "A wee dram afore ye graduate")'.

Stace, Wes [1965 -] Wesley Stace was born in Hastings, England, on October 22, 1965. He first took an interest in Dylan's work at the age of 12, and first wrote about him in a fanzine review of *Infidels*. He became a contributor to *The Telegraph*, conducting its interviews with ALLEN GINSBERG and RAMBLIN' JACK ELLIOTT and supplying anecdotes and photos. He also wrote on Dylan in *LA Style*, *Stereophile*, *The Stranger* and elsewhere. His first encounters with *The Telegraph* also served notice of his other career, as a singer-songwriter. As Dave Dingle recalled years later: 'A youngster called Wes came visiting JOHN [BAULDIE] and they both sat playing and singing. Wes was still at school talking about becoming a star whilst us older guys sat humoring him, little knowing he would go on to a successful career as John Wesley Harding.' After playing in the Accelerators, Wes did indeed become John Wesley Harding, and since 1989 has released 15 albums, starting with *It Happened One Night* (produced by, er, Wes Stace). He has also toured the world (performing duets with SPRINGSTEEN, JOHN PRINE and others along the way), and had his songs featured in movies and covered by many other artists. As Wesley Stace he published a very well-received first novel, *Misfortune*, in 2005.

[Wes Stace: 'Interview: Allen Ginsberg', *The Telegraph* no.20, Bury, UK, summer 1985 & in *All Across the Telegraph: A Bob Dylan Handbook*, ed. Gray & Bauldie, London: Sigwick & Jackson, 1987; 'Interview with Ramblin' Jack Elliott', *Telegraph* no.50, Romford, winter 1994; *Misfortune*, New York: Little, Brown & London: Cape, 2005. John Wesley Harding: *It Happened One Night*, Demon L-Fiend 137 (CD & vinyl), London, and Rhino 70764, US, 1989; Dave Dingle quote from 'Wherever You Might Look Tonight, You Might See This Wanted

Man', seen online 24 Aug 2005 at *www.interferenza.com/bcs/frnpage1.htm.*]

Staehely, John [1952 -] John Staehely was born in Austin, Texas, on January 25, 1952. A guitarist and vocalist who, with his bassist & guitarist brother Al, joined the fourth line-up of Spirit in 1972. After their disbandment in 1973, the Staehely brothers went out on the road *as* Spirit, and in 1974 sold the name back to the original members at great profit, the same year John joined Jo Jo Gunne, in which he remained until 1975, the same year both brothers played on Keith Moon's album *Two Sides of the Moon*. In 1976 John Staehely returned to the status of minor local hero, supporting the band Gypsee Eyes at the World Armadillo Headquarters back in Austin. When Dylan was including a series of extra guitarists on stage in the summer of 1990, John Staehely was the first, augmenting the Never-Ending Tour band in Edmonton, Alberta, Canada, on August 13, in Calgary on the 15th and 16th, and at George, in Washington State, on the 18th. That fall, when G.E. SMITH was leaving the band and Dylan was virtually auditioning replacements in concert as he went along, John Staehely played in the band from the third night at the Beacon Theater in New York City on October 17 through to the last concert of the year, in Detroit on November 18.

[Keith Moon: *Two Sides of the Moon*, MCA 2136, US (Polydor 2442 134, UK), 1975, CD-reissued Pet Rock KBD 60038, US, 1997.]

Stanley Brothers, the Carter Stanley was born on August 27, 1925, two years ahead of brother RALPH, in Big Spraddle Creek, western Virginia, and they grew up influenced by THE CARTER FAMILY, the folk culture of their rural surroundings, the Primitive Baptist Church they belonged to and their parents' amateur performing. Their father wasn't a musician but sang a repertoire that included 'Man of Constant Sorrow' and 'Pretty Polly', and their mother played old-timey claw-hammer banjo. With Ralph on banjo and a high tenor voice, and Carter on guitar and lead vocals, they formed the Stanley Brothers in 1946, made their radio début on 'Farm and Fun Time', on WCYB in Bristol Tennessee that December 26, and their first recordings in 1947, on the small label Rich-R-Tone, before signing to Columbia and then Mercury and, in the end, the King of Cincinnati. Carter was the more usual songwriter for the act, including songs like 'The Lonesome River', 'I Just Got Wise', 'She's More to Be Pitied' and 'The White Dove'. They also sang ALBERT E. BRUMLEY's 'Rank Stranger to Me'.

They temporarily in 1948 to take day-jobs working at the Ford car factory in Detroit, and disbanded briefly again in 1951, when after another Detroit stint, Carter Stanley became one of Bill Monroe's Blue Grass Boys (and in five months with them managed two recording sessions) and Ralph helped Monroe out when his own banjoist was called up—until Ralph was in a car crash. This was an odd blip, given Bill Monroe's antipathy to the Stanleys, which was strong enough that he had quit Columbia Records when the label signed them in 1949; but brief disbandments aside, the Stanley Brothers performed and toured together for 20 years—till Carter Stanley's death at 41 from liver cancer on December 1, 1966.

In the early days of the Folk Revival, ROBERT SHELTON remembers, the Stanley Brothers were 'sponsored by MIKE SEEGER', just as 'RALPH RINZLER squired about Bill Monroe and DOC WATSON, and JOHN COHEN became Roscoe Holcomb's "discoverer" and good friend': this was at a time (Shelton specifies no dates) when 'it was as if each active city performer "adopted" a country performer to escort, tout and make popular'.

When the Stanley Brothers couldn't get a record deal in the early 1960s they cut sessions for a radio station, returning to their traditional repertoire after years of trying to be more modern. These were pressed and put into private circulation (on Wango), after which three LPs were 'commercially' released from this material in the early 1970s on County Records of Virginia. One of these, *The Stanley Brothers of Virginia Vol. 2: Long Journey Home*, includes 'Pretty Polly' and 'East Virginia Blues'.

WILFRID MELLERS uses the Stanley Brothers as a springboard for some interesting comments on the relationship between country and other kinds of music in his A Darker *Shade of Pale: A Backdrop to Bob Dylan* (1984). Hearing their recording 'Daniel Prayed' on the collection *Hills and Home: 30 Years of Bluegrass*, he terms it 'bluegrass euphoria' and says that it 'is similar in principle to the antiphony of black gospel music, which in turn relates to the improvised dialogue of jazz. As with solo singers, country music groups grow up when their country manners come to terms with the reality of black jazz . . .'

The Stanley Brothers have been increasingly acknowledged as an important influence by Dylan in the 1990s. He chose to open a 1997 charity performance in aid of the Simon Wiesenthal Center by singing the Stanley Brothers' 'Stone Walls and Steel Bars'. Three months and one day later he reintroduced it into his repertoire when the Never-Ending Tour hit the Stanleys' home turf of Virginia on August 23, 1997, after that performing it a further 11 times between that year, 13 times in 1998, seven times in 1999, four times in 2000, giving it a rest throughout 2001 and bidding it farewell with a reprise in Baltimore on August 18, 2002.

[Stanley Brothers: *The Stanley Brothers of Virginia Vol. 2: Long Journey Home*, County 739, Floyd, VA, c.1973; 'Man of Constant Sorrow' & 'Rank Stranger to Me', CD-reissued on *Stanley Brothers & The Clinch Mountain Boys 1949–1952*, Bear Family BCD 15564-AH, Vollersode, Germany, c.1990. Bob Dylan: 'Stone Walls and Steel Bars': Beverly Hills, 22 May 1997.

Robert Shelton, in Laing, D., Dallas, K., Denselow R. & Shelton, R., *The Electric Muse: The Story of Folk Into Rock*, London: Methuen, 1975. Wilfrid Mellers, *A* Darker *Shade of Pale: A Backdrop to Bob Dylan*, London: Faber & Faber, 1984, p.83. Other background detail mainly from John Wright, *Traveling the High Way Home: Ralph Stanley & the World of Traditional Bluegrass Music*, Urbana, IL & Chicago: University of Illinois Press, 1993.]

Stanley, Ralph [1927 -] Ralph Stanley, younger brother of Carter, with whom he formed THE STANLEY BROTHERS, was born in Big Straddle Creek, in south-western Virginia, on February 25, 1927. After Carter Stanley's premature death in 1966, bluegrass claw-hammer banjoist and high tenor singer Ralph continued to play, and after a gap revived the CLINCH MOUNTAIN BOYS, who had backed the Brothers. In 1997, still playing and singing extremely well, Ralph Stanley made a follow-up to his 2-CD set *Saturday Night and Sunday Morning*, not a retrospective soundtrack to the British 1950s Angry Young Men novel by Alan Sillitoe or the spin-off Albert Finney film (1960), but a mix of secular and gospel material with guest performers from Bill Monroe to EMMYLOU HARRIS.

The 1997 follow-up 2-CD set was billed as by 'Ralph Stanley & Friends' and titled *Clinch Mountain Country*, on which he performed on a total of 36 tracks, each one with a different partner or partners. The first person signed up for the project was Bob Dylan, who plays guitar and sings lead on the verses alongside Ralph's banjo (and shared chorus vocals) on a Stanley Brothers classic, 'The Lonesome River'.

Dylan's vocal is precarious but avoids the easy rasp, and when they sing together on the choruses it works extremely well. They recorded it in Nashville on November 30, 1997, along with an uncirculated attempt at 'Riding the Midnight Train' and an earlier take of 'The Lonesome River'. Dylan overdubbed guitar onto the finished take later, and the set was released the following May on Rebel Records: the label Stanley had been on since the early 1970s. At the time of its release, this rebel was 70 years old and the sleevenotes claimed he was still performing 200 dates per year—which was more than Bob Dylan (who in 1998 played a mere 111).

The night after the recording, and the night after that, Dylan tried 'The Lonesome River' and the Stanley Brothers' 'The White Dove' at his sound-checks in Atlanta, but didn't play 'The Lonesome River' when it came to his performances. He did, however, play 'The White Dove' both nights and on a further four on that leg of the Never-Ending Tour.

Ralph Stanley was, inevitably, one of those turned to by T-BONE BURNETT when assembling the music for the film *O Brother, Where Art Thou* (2000); it includes his recording of 'O Death'.

[Ralph Stanley: *Saturday Night and Sunday Morning*, Freeland 9001, US, 1993. Ralph Stanley & Friends: *Clinch Mountain Country*, Rebel RBL 0005001, US, 1998.]

Stanton, Harry Dean [1926 -] Harold Dean Stanton was born in West Irvine, Kentucky, on July 14, 1926, grew up in Lexington, graduated high school in 1944 and served briefly in World War II before acting on stage first at the University of Kentucky and then at the Pasadena Playhouse. A musician as well as an actor, he toured the US with a male voice choir and worked in children's theatre before heading for Hollywood, appearing first under the name Dean Stanton in a 1957 cowboy film, *Tomahawk Trail*. He continued to use this name till the start of the 1970s, and worked prolifically, but always in minor rôles in film and in TV series, right through till the 1980s.

He has been the classic case of a character actor whose wonderful face you see a hundred times before you ever become aware of his name, and whose rôles improve only as he comes close to retirement age in other industries. In Harry Dean Stanton's case the face has been splendidly long and miserable, exuding a kind of life-battered meanness that pulls in your sympathy, a parched, fish-eyed lugubriousness and a dry, deadpan humour. It's said that his rôles went up a grade in films like *Cool Hand Luke* (1967), *Kelly's Heroes* (1970), *Dillinger* (1973) and *The Godfather: Part II* (1974), but he still wasn't exactly one of the star faces on the posters for those movies, and in the last of them had only got as far as playing 'FBI man #1'. He fared a little better in *Alien* and far better in John Huston's *Wise Blood* (both 1979), based on the Flannery O'Connor novel, in which he played Asa Hawks. Stardom, however, arrived only with the release of two stand-out films of 1984, *Repo Man* and *Paris, Texas*—by which time Stanton was 58 years old. Only from 1984 onwards does he ever appear as 'himself' on TV shows by David Letterman types. These two key rôles make him a star.

They also enabled him to form a sort of Tex-Mex mariachi jazz-rock band, Harry Dean Stanton & the Repo Men, later known as just the Harry Dean Stanton Band, featuring his lead vocals and guitar (though he made no contribution to the music in *Repo Man* itself).

His connection with Bob Dylan is not simply that both appear in the 1973 SAM PECKINPAH film *PAT GARRETT & BILLY THE KID*—in which Stanton plays the minor rôle of Luke—nor even that during the filming, it was Dylan and Stanton who ruined a second day's attempt at a crucial shot, so that Harry nearly got knifed by Peckinpah, as explained by KRIS KRISTOFFERSON in Garner Simmons' book *Peckinpah—A Portrait in Montage*:

'Well, Bobby wasn't in the shot, and he and Harry . . . decided they were goin' on a health campaign and run five miles. Only the first part of the five miles was right through the shot. I came out on the set, and it was like a tomb. I asked what happened and I hear "The Dylan boys just ran through the shot." And everybody is sittin' around not sayin' a word as Harry Dean Stanton comes walkin' in. . . . sayin' "Hi, Sam!" And everybody is sayin' to themselves, "Oh shit," and Sam growls, "You just cost me $25,000." And Harry Dean says, "Sam, I knew it was wrong, and I was runnin' after him to tell him to stop." Now Sam throws a pretty mean knife. . . . he's got this knife in his hand, and he lets 'er fly, and it sticks in the wood next to old Harry Dean, who flies through the door like nothin' flat shoutin' behind him, "I promise, Sam, it'll never happen again." And when Dylan heard about it, he just said, "Well, let's have a concert and pay him back."'

Stanton was also among those on set who flew up to Mexico City for Dylan's recording session there on January 20, 1973, though he didn't take part as a musician or singer. However, he did drop in on a session for *Planet Waves* later that same year in Santa Monica, and plays guitar on outtakes of 'Forever Young' and an uncirculated cut of the traditional song 'Adelita'; there are two attempts at this, with Stanton also on shared vocals.

After this, he makes a nice beanpole appearance in Dylan's own film *Renaldo & Clara*, filmed in 1975 and released 1978, as Lafkezio. This is still the 1970s: it's another very minor rôle.

The two reconvene after Stanton has become a star; along with Dylan's son-in-law PETER HIMMELMAN, they appear together, in a splendidly bizarre TV performance for that year's CHABAD TELETHON, with Stanton on harmonica on the traditional 'Einsleipt Mein Kind Dein Eigalach', on vocals and harmonica on 'Adelita' (16 years down the line from their first attempts) and on guitar and vocals for 'Hava Nagilah'. The informal group name was said to be Chopped Liver.

Finally, at the ROY ORBISON tribute concert in LA on February 24, 1990, Harry Dean Stanton and Bob Dylan found themselves jostling in the crowd of back-up singers on an ensemble rendition of 'Only the Lonely' fronted by ROGER McGUINN and DAVID CROSBY.

Harry Dean Stanton is still making films and his band still plays around the LA area. He's 80 years old.

[Harry Dean Stanton at *Planet Waves* session, Santa Monica, CA, 10 Nov 1973. Garner Simmons, *Sam Peckinpah—A Portrait in Montage*, *nia*, quoted from Chris Whithouse, 'Alias, Pat Garrett & Billy the Kid', collected in Michael Gray & John Bauldie, eds, *All Across the Telegraph: A Bob Dylan Handbook*, London: Futura edn., 1988, pp.114–15.]

Staple Singers, the This American musical institution was formed in 1948 in Chicago by the Mississippi-born Roebuck 'Pops' Staples (1915–2000) and his family. It was known in the plural as the Staples Singers for many years, till Roebuck Staples (who had been taught guitar by CHARLEY PATTON and been a member of the Golden Trumpets and the Trumpet Jubilees) decided to change it in 1965. The family's recording career began in 1953 with a series of gospel singles, mostly on Vee-Jay Records. Their last Vee-Jay single, in 1962, was 'Sit Down Servant', which Bob Dylan misremembered as one of the songs of theirs he heard earliest. That year they switched to Riverside, and in 1963 released a version of 'Blowin' in the Wind', their first real non-gospel A-side. Their commercial success began in the 1960s on Epic, then Stax and later on Curtis Mayfield's Curtom label, as they explored different kinds of secular soul music, made albums with BOOKER T. & the MGs, and a no.1 US single with 'I'll Take You There' in 1972. They appeared with THE BAND in a studio-filmed 1977 performance of 'The Weight' included in the film *The Last Waltz*, and returned to the song in 1994 to record a minor hit version with Mary Stuart.

Dylan has specified the Staple Singers as a strong influence on his musical development, and gave a surprising amount of detail when interviewed for the Chicago TV station WTTW's 'Chicago Stories' programme in 2001: '. . . when we met for the first time . . . I was probably about 20 . . . but I'd heard them since I was about 12. . . . I couldn't have been more than 12 years old, listening to the radio. . . . we used to pick up this station out of Shreveport. . . . at midnight the gospel stuff would start . . .' He said that what struck him in the Staple Singers was the two different voices. Pops had, he remembered, 'a sweet, gentle kind of approach to it, but even back then . . . he sounded more to me like a blues singer singing gospel.' (Re MAVIS' voice see separate entry.) 'And,' he added, 'they had the other stuff, the more rhythmic things and different combinations of rhythm that I later found out was just Pops playing that tremolo guitar. . . . Pops' sound not only made the listener tremble and shake where other peoples' seemed very conventional to me, and also very professional. . . . the Staple Singers they were just more way off the road, and there was no telling which way they were gonna go. . . . every song was different. It had combinations of rhythmic pulse but then it could go down to no pulse, which would go like a Greek drama . . . some Armageddon type thing which I could relate to where that was at the time.'

[The Staples Singers: 'Sit Down Servant', Vee-Jay 912, US, 1962; 'Blowin' in the Wind', Riverside 4568, US, 1963. Bob Dylan's quotes, Staple Singers tribute show, Chicago, 27 Oct 2001, fragments shown on 'Chicago Stories', WTTW-TV, Chicago, 25 Feb 2002;

taken here from Glen Dundas' transcription in *Tangled*, Thunder Bay, Ontario: SMA Services, 2004.]

Staples, Mavis [1939 -] Mavis Staples was born in Chicago on July 10, 1939 (though her birth year is very often given as 1940), into the singing family THE STAPLE SINGERS, headed by her father Roebuck and her mother Oceola. She began to sing with the group as a child from around 1948 onwards and became a full member in 1950 and in 1953 started recording, her strong deep voice combining with her father's higher, thinner singing. A record of theirs that got nowhere but which the young Bob Dylan found compelling, 'Sit Down Servant', was not one of their earliest–indeed its release date was 1962, so he may well have been conflating it with another when in a television tribute to the Staple Singers in October 2001, he described hearing the group as a teenager and specified the effect achieved by Mavis' voice on this material:

> '. . . then this other voice came on, which was . . . Mavis. And one of the first songs I heard . . . was a song called "Sit Down Servant". And that just made me stay up for about a week after I heard that song. Mavis was singing stuff like "Yonder comes little David with his rock and his sling, I don't want to meet him, he's a dangerous man". And oh my goodness, you know, I mean that just made my hair stand up listening to that. I mean, that just seemed like "that's the way the world is".'

The astonishment worked the other way around when Mavis and family heard 'Blowin' in the Wind'. As the same interviewer expressed it: 'In our talks with Mavis, she explained how she reached greater understanding through talking to you. And I'll read you a quote . . . : "We just wondered how with him being a little white boy, how he could feel all those things we felt, you know? All this pain and the hurt, you know. How could he write these songs? He saw things and he wrote about them."'

The two met that same year, introduced by ROBERT SHELTON, then still Folk Critic on the *New York Times*. According to HOWARD SOUNES' Dylan biography, young Bob 'developed a platonic crush' (whatever that means) on Mavis Staples, as soon as they were introduced. 'During SUZE [ROTOLO]'s absence,' he writes, 'Bob became so besotted he went to the patriarch of the family, Roebuck "Pops" Staples, and asked: "Pops, can I marry Mavis?" "Don't ask me, ask Mavis," replied Pops, not best pleased. . . . She did not accept his proposal, although she and Bob remained friends.'

Thirty years later, Mavis Staples' redoubtable presence was to be seen and heard at the performance of 'Like a Rolling Stone' at the 'Late Night with David Letterman' 10th Anniversary Special, recorded in New York on January 18, 1992 and aired that February 6. She was the heartiest of the backing singers–the others being Roseanne Cash, NANCI GRIFFITH, EMMYLOU HARRIS and Michelle Shocked.

Forty years after 'Blowin' in the Wind', Bob and Mavis recorded together: they sing a duet, and talk their talk, on the re-make of Dylan's *Slow Train Coming* song 'Gonna Change My Way of Thinking'–see separate entry–made specially for the album *Gotta Serve Somebody: The Gospel Songs of Bob Dylan*.

Mavis continues to sing powerfully. She has spent most of her career as the group's lead singer but starting in 1969 with *Mavis Staples* she has also made a number of solo albums, including two produced by Prince–1987's *Time Waits for No One* and 1993's *Voice*. After the latter there was a gap of more than a decade before her most recent CD, *Have a Little Faith*, released in 2004.

[Mavis Staples: *Mavis Staples*, *nia*, 1969, CD-reissue Hdh 300, 1995; *Only for the Lonely*, *nia*, 1970, CD-reissue Stax 88012, 1993; *Don't Change Me Now*, *nia*, Stax, *nia*; *Time Waits for No One*, *nia*, 1987; *Voice*, Slash *nia*, 1993; *Have a Little Faith*, *nia*, Alligator *nia*, 2004. The Staples Singers: 'Sit Down Servant', Vee-Jay 912, US, 1962. Bob Dylan's interview re Mavis Staples, Staple Singers tribute show, Chicago, 27 Oct 2001, fragments shown on 'Chicago Stories', WTTW-TV, Chicago, 25 Feb 2002; Mavis Staples' quote re Dylan, recording date unknown, other details same; both taken here from Glen Dundas' transcription in *Tangled*, Thunder Bay, Ontario: SMA Services, 2004. Howard Sounes, *Down the Highway: A Life of Bob Dylan*, New York: Grove Press, 2001, manuscript p.161.]

Starr, Ringo [1940 -] Richard Starkey was born in the Toxteth district of Liverpool on July 7, 1940, in a terraced house the city council is now determined to demolish. Ringo moved out of it at age four and grew up across the city in Dingle. Ill health scarred his childhood, consigning him to much time in hospital and leaving him semi-literate (though not unable, in later life, to narrate many UK children's TV series of 'Thomas the Tank-Engine'). He learnt drums and played in his first group, the Eddie Clayton Skiffle Group, in 1957. Following a stint in the Raving Texans, he joined Rory Storm & the Hurricanes and while playing with this well-known Liverpool beat group in Hamburg, West Germany, in 1960, first met the rest of the Beatles. When they sacked Pete Best in August 1962, Ringo replaced him. When the Beatles met Dylan in 1964 and Dylan handed JOHN LENNON the first joint any of them had encountered, John immediately passed it to Ringo (as a king to his taster); Ringo, not knowing the etiquette, smoked the whole thing himself.

Never the brightest starr in the firmament, and one of its dullest vocalists, the point about Ringo has always been that he is one of rock's greatest drummers. After the Beatles disbanded in 1970, he was surprisingly quick off the blocks with his solo albums: *Sentimental Journey* and the better-received *Beaucoups of Blues* both came out that year, followed by hit singles like 'It Don't Come Easy' (1971) 'Back Off Boogaloo' (1972) and later the US no.1 hits 'Photograph' and a remake of Johnny Burnette's 'You're Sixteen', both from 'his first rock album', *Ringo*, in 1973.

By this time he had already also starred in the movie version of Terry Southern's *Candy* (1968), in *The Magic Christian* (1969) and *That'll Be the Day* (1973) and played both FRANK ZAPPA and Larry the Dwarf in Zappa's *200 Motels* (1971). He had also been a participant in the August 1971 Concert for Bangla Desh, at which he played tambourine behind Dylan. Later film rôles included being the Pope in the Ken Russell film *Lizstomania* (1975) and the Mock Turtle in a US TV film of *Alice in Wonderland* ten years later. He has been married twice, detoxed after becoming an alcoholic in the 1980s, has suffered the further ignominy of TV-advertising Pizza Hut, has inevitably voiced himself in 'The Simpsons' (1991) and in 2005 agreed to work with comic-books legend Stan Lee on the creation of an animated musical featuring an unlikely, Starr-based new superhero.

His work with Dylan did not stop at the Concert for Bangla Desh, however. At THE BAND's Farewell Concert in San Francisco on November 25, 1976, Ringo made a surprise appearance to share drumming duties on the Dylan-plus-ensemble version of 'I Shall Be Released'. Five years later, on May 15, 1981, Ringo was in the studios in LA with Bob recording a session for the *Shot of Love* album, from which one track, 'Heart of Mine', made it onto the album and became a single. Though the liner notes for the album credit Ringo with playing drums on an unspecified track, in fact he plays tom tom on this track, and on this track only.

On April 14, 1987 (Beatle people say April 29, but they're less reliable), Dylan repaid the favour, dropping in on a Starr session at Chips Moman's studio in Memphis to share vocals on 'I Wish I Knew Now (What I Knew Then)'—a session it's reported that Starr had videotaped. This entire album, blighted by Starr's alcoholism at time of the prolonged sessions (they'd begun that February), never came out except on bootlegs; Moman tried to issue it but Starr blocked its release, which was to have been in 1989.

That was also the year Ringo turned up again with Dylan, this time at a Never-Ending Tour concert in Frejus, France, during the summer festivals season, when Starr was back in action and touring the first of his Ringo Starr & His All-Starr Band line-ups (in which at different times various members of The Band, among others, took part). Coinciding geographically, Starr came on stage during Dylan's June 13 concert to play drums on the last two pre-encore numbers, 'Highway 61 Revisited' and 'Like a Rolling Stone'.

In LA on December 17, 1997, Ringo was in the audience for another Dylan concert. At one point Dylan said from the stage: 'One of the great drummers on this kind of music is in the audience tonight—Ringo Starr! Where are you, Ringo?' Pause. 'I guess we don't want to put the spotlight on him.' Ringo was up in the balcony's VIP section. He gave a cheery wave, as in the long-gone moptop days.

[Joint-smoking, see **Aronowitz, Al.** Ringo Starr: *Sentimental Journey*; *Beaucoups of Blues*; *Ringo*. *Candy*, dir. Christian Marquand, ABC/Corona, France-Italy-US, 1968. *The Magic Christian*, dir. Joseph McGrath, Commonwealth United/Grand Films, UK, 1969. *200 Motels*, dir. Tony Palmer & Charles Swenson, Bizarre/Murakami-Wolf, US, 1971. *That'll Be the Day*, dir. Claude Whatham, EMI Films, UK, 1973. *Lisztomania*, dir. Ken Russell, Goodtimes/VPS/Warner, UK, 1975. *Alice in Wonderland*, dir. Harry Harris, CBS-TV, US, 1985. 'The Simpsons' series 2, no.18, 'Brush with Greatness', 11 Apr 1991.]

Stewart, Dave [1952 -] David Allen Stewart was born in Sunderland, Tyne & Wear, in the northeast of England, on September 9, 1952. Diverted by injury from football to music and the guitar, his early band Longdancer signed to ELTON JOHN's Rocket label but broke up in 1977 when Stewart met Annie Lennox, forming the Catch with her and a Peet Coombes. After the single 'Borderline' the Catch mutated into the Tourists (1978–80), a new waveish group that enjoyed two UK top 10 hits, 'I Only Want to Be With You' and 'So Good to Be Back Home Again.' In mid-tour in Bangkok the Tourists disbanded, to be superceded by Lennox and Stewart's new group the Eurythmics. They rose slowly but inexorably, their first hit 1983's plaintive and catchy 'Sweet Dreams (Are Made of This)', to become the most successful male-female duo in pop history (it says here).

It was clear that Annie Lennox was a gifted singer, though with an irritating inability to vary her phrasing, as for instance on the title line of their hit 'There Must Be an Angel', which she sings identically over and over again as if she were a tape-loop or a singing parrot; but it was never clear what Dave Stewart's talent was. The PR aura surrounding them attempted to portray him as a musical genius and inspired Svengali, though to most reasonable people he looked like a self-regarding and affected twit with a gift for wide-ranging mediocrity.

The Eurythmics split in 1990, Lennox to a successful solo career and Stewart not, though he produced other people's albums, worked with Alison Moyet, MICK JAGGER, Shakespear's Sister, BOB GELDOF and others. His own band the Spiritual Cowboys (well, quite) released two indifferently received albums and in 1993 he joined Terry Hall of the Specials to form a new group, Vegas, releasing one album ahead of Stewart's 1994 solo album

Greetings from the Gutter. He has also worked in film, his biggest project being *Honest*, a very badly reviewed film directed and co-written by him and starring some of the group All Saints. He has been a session musician on albums by Aretha Franklin (1985), Daryl Hall (1986), Hall and Oates (1990 and 1997), Steve Hillage (1991), Carly Simon (1994), Joe Strummer and the Mescaleros (1999), Sinéad O'Connor (2000), Bryan Ferry and Marianne Faithfull (both 2002), Jimmy Cliff (2004) and many others.

The number of professional connections Dave Stewart has managed to make with Bob Dylan is absurdly large (and even one or two might seem excessive). On August 22, 1985, in the gymnasium of the First Methodist Church in Hollywood, Stewart directs the hopeless videos for Dylan's 'When the Night Comes Falling from the Sky' and 'Emotionally Yours'—and while he's at it records himself singing 'I Shall Be Released'. Three months later to the day, in his own London studio, he's on guitar (with three other musicians) backing Dylan on two instrumental rambles televised on *The Old Grey Whistle Test* on BBC-2 that November 26, and on a backing track for the song 'Under Your Spell', co-written by Dylan and CAROLE BAYER SAGER, onto which Dylan later dubs vocals; with backing vocals also added, this becomes the last track on the 1986 album *Knocked Out Loaded*.

From this visit to Stewart's London home turf of Crouch End comes the delightful story of Dylan being directed to Dave's house, knocking on the door and having it answered by a young woman who doesn't recognise her visitor. 'Is Dave in?' Bob asks. 'No, but he shouldn't be long: come in and wait,' comes the reply. Bob spends an hour or more at the kitchen table before the householder, a plumber called Dave, duly returns to find Bob Dylan in his house.

Stewart joins Bob onstage near the end of the 1986 tour with TOM PETTY & THE HEARTBREAKERS, at Inglewood, CA that August 3, playing guitar on nine songs (Annie Lennox, there too, shares vocals on the last of these). Six years later Stewart arrives onstage in the middle of Dylan's Never-Ending Tour set at the festival at Antibes (July 12, 1992) to play guitar on a thrash through 'Highway 61 Revisited', and does exactly the same thing again near the end of two of the London dates in early 1993 (February 9 and 13). Four more years and there he is with Dylan in Japan—February 10 and 11, 1997 in Tokyo—filming him from onstage the first night and playing guitar the second night, this time on the almost unavoidable encore number 'Rainy Day Women # 12 & 35'. A fragment of his film of 'Like a Rolling Stone' was later made available from Stewart's website.

Before these last two sightings, Stewart had been occupied more usefully on Dylan's behalf behind the camera (the preferable placement, you might think), filming another video, this time for 'Blood in my Eyes' from Dylan's *World Gone Wrong* album. This was filmed in Camden Town, London, on July 21, 1993 (see the entry **the Mississippi Sheiks**) and is Dave Stewart's only valuable contribution.

Stewart, Maeretha [19?? -] Maeretha A. Stewart is a gospel, soul and general session singer who has recorded with a wide range of people and in many genres, from Cyndi Lauper's 'Girls Just Want to Have Fun' to Philip Glass' *The Photographer: A Music-Drama in Three Acts* (both 1983), HARRY BELAFONTE's *Turn the World Around* (unreleased in the US, and which as it happens featured Dylan's friend Ted Perlman on guitar) and Nina Simone's fine 1978 album *Baltimore* (1978), with its majestic non pareil version of JUDY COLLINS' great song 'My Father'. Maeretha Stewart is also one of the backing singers on Dylan's *Self Portrait* and *New Morning* albums of 1970—and hers is the scat singing on the latter's track 'If Dogs Run Free'. In *Chronicles Volume One*, Dylan says that this was done in one take; he also makes it sound as if he hadn't a clue who she was. He writes: 'There were three girl singers in the room, who sounded like they'd been plucked from a choir and one of them did some improvisational scat singing.'

[Bob Dylan, *Chronicles Volume One*, 2004, p.138.]

Stibal, Brian [1954 -] See **Styble, Bryan**.

Stokes, Frank [1888 - 1955] The stupendous black Memphis artist Frank Stokes was born in Whitehaven, Tennessee (now a section of South Memphis), on New Year's Day 1888, and became both a blacksmith and a founding father of the Memphis blues, making solo records, remarkable duets with fellow guitarist Dan Sane as the Beale Street Sheiks and lovely creations with violinist Will Batts (including his 'South Memphis Blues' of 1929). He was particularly good at anti-preacher and anti-deacon rants. His recording career was over by the end of 1929 but he continued to perform through to the 1940s, sometimes working with BUKKA WHITE in that decade. He retired but continued to hold memorable house parties full of guests we might now term celebs. He died in Memphis on September 12, 1955.

His specific relevance to Dylan resides in his successful début recording from 1927, 'You Shall', which strongly prefigured Dylan's 'I Shall Be Free': see separate entry. See also **blues, inequality of reward in**.

Frank Stokes' grandson, Nathaniel Kent, runs a reggae band in Memphis, and his granddaughter is the librarian at the Memphis *Commercial Appeal* newspaper.

[Frank Stokes: 'South Memphis Blues', Memphis, 23 Sep 1929.]

Stone/Edelstein family, the The maternal side of Robert Allen Zimmerman's family. Dylan's mother was born Beatrice R. Stone in 1915, and had an older brother, Vernon. Two younger siblings followed, Lewis and Irene. All born in the US, they were the children of Lithuanian Jewish immigrants Benjamin David Solemovitz (born 1883), who changed Solemovitz to Stone, and his wife Florence Sara née Edelstein, herself one of ten children.

Taking Florence Sara first: the Florence who would become Bob Dylan's grandmother–she and the other nine Edelstein children were in turn the sons and daughters of Benjamin Harold Edelstein (born 1870) and Lybba née Jaffe, from Korno in Lithuania. (Benjamin Harold's parents were David and Ida Edelstein; Ida's parents were Yehada Aren and Rachel née Berkovitz. Lybba Jaffe's parents were Aaron Jaffe and Fannie.)

Benjamin Harold and wife Lybba, plus the first four of their ten children, left their village of Vilkomir, Russia, in 1902, on the ship *Tunisia*, arriving into the US at Sault St. Marie, Michigan, by way of Liverpool, St. John, New Brunswick and Montréal. They arrived on Christmas Eve 1902 and settled with relatives at Superior, Wisconsin, across Lake Superior from Duluth. The four children who came with them were Bob Dylan's grandmother-to-be, Florence Sara (born 1892), Goldie and Julius (1896) and Rose (1899). In Superior, Wisconsin, came Samuel (1903) and Jennie (1905). Their father moved to Hibbing in 1904, brought the rest along in the second half of 1905 and in Hibbing they had their last four children, Max (1906), Mike (1908), Ethel (1911) and Sylvia (1912). These siblings all duly became Beatty's maternal aunts and uncles. Their father, in partnership with one of his immigrant brothers, Julius, starting with tent shows, set up a chain of Iron Range movie theatres. In Hibbing they acquired the Garden Theater in 1925, renamed it the Gopher and sold it to another chain in 1928. In the 1940s they built a new Hibbing movie house, naming it the Lybba after Benjamin Harold's wife.

On Beatty's father's side of the family were the Stones, previously known as the Solemovitzes, again a family of Lithuanian Jewish immigrants. Her father Benjamin David Stone was one of four children, his siblings being Rosy, Eddy and Ida, all the children of Robert aka Samuel Solemovitz (aka Solomawitch aka Salamovitz) and Bessie née Kaner. Robert, the son of Abraham and Mary Solemovitz, arrived in Superior from Lithuania in 1888 or 1889, and five years later Bessie and the children arrived. In 1906 Ben's younger sister Ida was murdered by a Scot named John Young, who had wanted to marry her. Within a year, her mother Bessie had died 'of a broken heart'. Her husband remarried in 1909, to another immigrant from Russia, May Levinson, who had three children of her own, Roy, Bennie and Sam.

That same year–three years after his sister's murder–Ben, then aged 26, started work in Hibbing. There he met Florence Sara Edelstein; they married in 1911 and set up a store at Stevenson Location, 12 miles west of Hibbing, supplying clothing to iron ore miners' families; when the mine was used up, they opened their store in downtown Hibbing instead. Florence's grandparents–Benjamin Harold Edelstein's parents–were still alive when Florence and Ben's first three children, were born: Vernon in 1910, Beatty on June 16, 1915 and Lewis in 1918. But Florence's grandmother, Ida Edelstein, died at 69 in Superior in 1922, the year before Ben and Florence's youngest child, Irene, arrived. Florence's grandfather, David Edelstein, died aged 73 in 1924.

Beatty married Abe Zimmerman at her mother's house on June 10, 1934. He was 22; she was six days short of her 19th birthday. Six years and 11 months later, she had her first child, Robert Allen, on May 24, 1941. Her grandmother Lybba died the year after, on September 5, 1942. Five years after Robert came Beatty's second child, DAVID. Her father, Ben Stone, died in 1952; her grandfather, Benjamin Harold Edelstein, survived till January 24, 1961, dying in the same Duluth hospital Bob had been born in almost 20 years earlier. Beatty's mother Florence, the grandmother who then lived in the Zimmerman house when Bob and David were growing up–the grandmother much praised in *Chronicles Volume One*–died in March 1964.

Some years after the boys' father's death in 1968, Beatty married again, to a Joseph Rutman of St. Paul, Minnesota. (See **Rutman, Howard**.)

Beatty appeared on stage with Bob Dylan, clapping along to the music during the finale of one of the 1975 Rolling Thunder Revue concerts in Toronto, as shown in the photo on page 40 of the booklet inside the 2-CD set *Bootleg Series Vol. 5: Bob Dylan Live 1975, The Rolling Thunder Revue*, released in 2002. She died in St.Paul, Minnesota, on January 27, 2000. She was 84. She was survived by her younger brother Lewis, Bob Dylan's uncle, who died at home in Hibbing at the age of 86 on January 24, 2005. Their youngest sister Irene, now Irene Goldfine, is still alive and living in Arizona.

[Main source: Dave Engel, *Just Like Bob Zimmerman's Blues: Dylan in Minnesota*, Rudolph, WI: River City Memoirs-Mesabi, 1997 + the 1900 & 1920 US censuses; special thanks to Sarah Beattie.]

Stoner, Rob [1948 -] Robert David Rothstein was born in New York City on April 20, 1948. He grew up in Manhattan and New Rochelle, New York, and formed a rockabilly band, Rockin' Rob & the Rebels, at the age of 11 in 1959, and could play guitar, bass and keyboards. Before attending Columbia College, New York, from which he graduated in 1969, he'd also played in a high school band signed to a music publishing deal with the once-great Leiber and Stoller (themselves songwriters who wrote many of ELVIS PRESLEY's greatest 1950s hits but who seem to have felt nothing but contempt for rock'n'roll and felt that their best work was achieved later writing for 'real song stylists' like Peggy Lee). In 1973 Stoner signed to the Nashville division of Epic as a solo recording artist and songwriter. His songs have been recorded by Shirley Bassey and Johnny Winter (a pleasingly rare linkage of artists).

In 1975 Bob Dylan appointed him his bass player and the informal leader of GUAM, the band that played the 1975 and 1976 Rolling Thunder Revues. In the group slot at the start of each concert, Stoner sang lead on his own song 'Too Good to Be Wasted', which SAM SHEPARD called a 'great song'. Stoner also played bass on all but the first of the *Desire* sessions: he started on July 28, 1975 (the session that yielded the album cut of 'Romance in Durango' and the outtake 'Catfish', released in 1991 on the *Bootleg Series Vols. 1–3*), and was there on July 29–31 and October 24. Stoner also played on the televised 'World of John Hammond' performance Dylan gave in Chicago that September 10—technically September 11, since it was 1:30AM before he came on—at which the stripped-down unit of Dylan, Stoner, SCARLET RIVERA and HOWIE WYETH played 'Oh Sister', 'Simple Twist of Fate' and 'Hurricane' (televised on PBS-TV that December 13). Stoner features quite prominently in the movie *Renaldo & Clara* and in the 'Hard Rain' TV Special, and is also on the *Hard Rain* album. Since he was the band leader, he can take a great deal of credit for the way that Guam delivered for Dylan exactly the kind of ragged gyspy band he'd wanted; as a bassist, his work achieved an admirable mix of nervy precision and melodic freedom. He brought his adolescent admiration for rock'n'roller GENE VINCENT's band into his own New York punk style (and even spent the 1975 tour with a teddy boy look and a 1950s greaser haircut created for him by MICK RONSON, a man whose own hair was irremediably of the 1970s Rod Stewart persuasion).

Stoner, along with DAVID MANSFIELD and STEVE SOLES, made the transition to Dylan's 1978 World Tour Band—and at one of the December 1977 rehearsals, on Boxing Day in Santa Monica, Dylan performed an otherwise unknown composition, 'First to Say Goodbye', specifically for Rob Stoner. As it turned out, Stoner *was* first to say goodbye. He survived only to the end of the first leg, the Far East section of the tour, starting on February 20 in Tokyo and ending on April 1 in Sydney: a total of 23 concerts. According to the 'Dylan Who's Who' webpage on Stoner, Dylan biographer CLINTON HEYLIN says that Stoner quit; but his replacement, JERRY SCHEFF, reports being recruited by a phone call from sax player STEVE DOUGLAS, saying that Dylan had just fired his bass player.

At any rate, no special animosity can have been involved, because when the subsequent European leg of the tour reached London, for a run of six nights at the huge Earls Court hall, DEREK BARKER reports that one night (June 14), Dylan and his London record-company press officer, Elly Smith, went out late to a number of uninspiring clubs, ending up at the Music Machine in Finchley, where Dylan was attacked with a knife by Sid Vicious backstage—and that Dylan had gone there to see Robert Gordon, 'whose band then featured Link Wray and Bob's recently departed bandleader Rob Stoner.'

After that band, Stoner made a solo album, *Patriotic Duty* (1980), and became the first non-southerner to record for Sun Records in Memphis—fulfilling a fantasy that every old rockabilly must have entertained.

Rob Stoner played on sessions and/or in live performance with a large number of interesting artists, among them Hank Ballard (writer of 'The Twist'), CHUCK BERRY, Don Covay, JERRY GARCIA, LEVON HELM, JOHN HERALD, Garland Jeffreys (with whom Dylan drummer SANDY KONIKOFF also worked), LOU REED, ROBBIE ROBERTSON and BRUCE SPRINGSTEEN.

In 2006 Stoner appeared as a 'special guest' on the Dylan tribute band Highway 61 Revisited's misleadingly titled CD *Bob Dylan 1975–1981, Rolling Thunder and the Gospel Years*—which contains neither Bob Dylan nor any of his songs. Based in West Nyack, New York State, today Rob Stoner offers private lessons in songwriting, singing, bass and guitar, specialising in beginners.

[Background data in part from Rob Stoner, e-mail to this writer, 18 Feb 2006. Derek Barker, '1978 and All That', collected in *20 Years of Isis: Bob Dylan Anthology Volume 2*, New Malden: Chrome Dreams, 2005, p.231]

Stookey, Noel [1937 -] See **Peter, Paul & Mary.**

***Street Legal* [1978]** Released around the time of Dylan's first London concerts for 12 years, this is Dylan's 20th album and for a minority it is, after *Blood on the Tracks*, arguably Dylan's best record of the 1970s: a crucial album documenting a crucial period in Dylan's own life.

Every song deals with love's betrayal, with Dylan's being betrayed like Christ, and, head on, with the need to abandon woman's love. *Street Legal* is one of Dylan's most important, cohesive albums: and it warns us, as pointedly as art ever should, of what is to come. It prepares us for Dylan's conversion to Christianity just as plainly as the end of *John Wesley Harding* prepares us for the country music of *Nashville Skyline*, and just as plainly as *Bringing It All Back Home* signals what is just around the corner on *Highway 61 Revisited*.

It is of astonishing complexity and confidence, delivered in one of Dylan's most authoritative voices, and extremely badly produced. The 1999 and 2003–4 attempts at re-mastering for CD reissue (after a first CD reissue, which wasn't re-mastered and is now a rarity) have failed to make aural amends. The other fault might be said to be the title. After the overblown swagger of titles like *Planet Waves* and *Masterpieces* here we have another dodgy claim, this time cloaked in modesty; but there is nothing modest about claiming cool status. Such virtues shouldn't be self-proclaimed.

[Recorded Santa Monica, CA, 26–28 Apr & 1 May 1978, released as stereo LP Columbia JC 35453 (in UK CBS 86067), 15 Jun 1978; re-mastered, re-mixed CD release, Columbia CK 65974, 1999; further re-mastered CD reissue, taken from the specialist 2003 hybrid SACD released, Columbia CK 92403, 1 Jun 2004 (in Europe Columbia 512355 2), 29 Mar 2004.]

Strzelecki, Henry [1939 -] Henry Strzelecki—the name is Polish, and more famously belongs to Count Paul Edmond de Strzelecki, an early explorer of Australia—was born in Birmingham, Alabama, on August 8, 1939. He became one of *the* session bass players in the Nashville of the late 1950s onwards, playing on records by everyone from Homer & Jethro through to Reba McEntire. Between the two he's played for Patsy Cline and k.d. lang, for Narvel Felts and CONWAY TWITTY, Hazel Dickens and David Allan Coe, Chet Atkins and Joe-El Sonnier, RAY CHARLES and MEMPHIS SLIM, JOHNNY CASH and GORDON LIGHTFOOT, FLATT & SCRUGGS and JOAN BAEZ, Sleepy LaBeef and Tom T. Hall, WILLIE NELSON and ELVIS PRESLEY, Waylon Jennings and Box-Car Willie, Hank Locklin and Hank Williams Jr., DON GIBSON and Marty Robbins.

Among these sessions he played on two different albums considered a humiliation by the artists themselves. In February 1965 Henry Strzelecki joined the old Elvis team of Scotty Moore and D.J. Fontana, plus further guitarists Grady Martin and CHARLIE McCOY and further drummer KENNY BUTTREY, along with keyboards veteran Floyd Cramer, to play the contemptible songs that formed the soundtrack album for what may be the nadir of Elvis' film career—imagine that!—namely the thrown-together *Harum Scarum*, in which Elvis dressed up in old Rudolph Valentino costumes and sulked about on a 1925 Cecil B. de Mille set. And in late 1968, Strzelecki played on the Flatt & Scruggs album *Nashville Airplane*, on which they made pleasant country covers of songs like 'Like a Rolling Stone': a process so unpalatable to Lester Flatt that he broke up the duo shortly afterwards.

Between those two albums, the Nashville sessions Henry Strzelecki contributed to included those for *Blonde on Blonde* held on February 16–17, March 7, 8 & 9, 1966. He therefore plays bass on 'Absolutely Sweet Marie', 'Pledging My Time', 'Just Like a Woman' and 'Stuck Inside of Mobile with the Memphis Blues Again'. (He's also on the earlier outtake from the same session, released on the *Bootleg Series Vol. 7—No Direction Home: The Soundtrack*, 2005). The only mystery seems to be why Charlie McCoy had to play bass and trumpet simultaneously on 'Most Likely You Go Your Way (And I'll Go Mine'), granted that Henry Strzelecki and his bass was on hand at that session too. Maybe he just clocked off early that day, feeling he'd done enough. And all told, he certainly had.

'Stuck Inside of Mobile with the Memphis Blues Again' [1966] 'Memphis Blues Again' (nowadays officially listed as 'Stuck Inside of Mobile with the Memphis Blues Again' on the *www.bobdylan.com* website) goes beyond being an exciting rock-music performance. It shares with those slower *Blonde on Blonde* songs 'Visions of Johanna' and 'Sad-Eyed Lady of the Lowlands' a greater-than-average duration and a general high seriousness of intention. The narrator is someone just trying to get by in modern America: someone trying to get by, that is, without shutting off or closing up; someone who sees a lot happening around him but can't discern any pattern to it nor any constant but meaninglessness; someone who, in this situation, stays more outwardly vulnerable than he needs to because he retains a yearning, however vague, for some better kind of world.

All this comes through to the listener from disconnected visual glimpses. The song begins with this: 'Oh the ragman draws circles / Up an' down the block / I'd ask him what the matter was / But I know that he don't talk'—and the visual dominance is such that we get a picture to cover the third and fourth lines, they don't just pass over as abstract reflection. We see the singer standing disconsolate, aware that there is no point in trying to communicate. The same applies throughout the song. The narrator is there in front of us, avoiding 'some French girl who says she knows me well', confronting Mona, believing the railroad men, thinking about Grandpa, hiding under the truck, winning his argument with the teen preacher, staggering around stoned and telling us that we just get uglier, smiling at Ruthie, and sitting patiently on Grand Street ('where the neon madmen climb'). It is only with the heartfelt cry of the chorus, 'Oh! Mama! Can this really be the end?! / To be stuck inside of Mobile with the Memphis Blues again!' that the visual predominance dies away. We only picture Dylan saying 'Oh! Mama!': we don't picture Memphis, Tennessee, or Mobile, Alabama, at all. They are not part of the visual language; they are symbols, words that stand for other things—hope and despondency, potential and restraint, energy and somnambulence. They are, except in the special sense touched upon later, abstract ideas.

The song is interesting too in the way that Dylan handles his moral point. He bestows an implicit blessing on some things and frowns on others, drawing to the listener's attention that some things strike the artist as enhancing and others as restrictive. The narrator himself is also made to represent certain values, certain virtues–a frank and sensitive openness to life, even at the expense of sophistication and propriety: 'An' I said Oh! I didn't know that! . . . / . . . Ev'rybody still talks about / How badly they were shocked; / But me I expected it to happen, / I knew he'd lost control! . . .', which is contrasted with the machinations of the senator 'Showing everyone his gun, / Handing out free tickets / To the wedding of his son' and to the neon madmen of the modern city, the ones who have settled into it all, and to the claustrophobic 'ladies' who 'furnish' him with tape, and so on.

In this stance, in its whole sensibility, 'Memphis Blues Again' very much anticipates the influential HUNTER S. THOMPSON book *Fear and Loathing in Las Vegas*, 1972. This formative and unequalled work of the New, or Gonzo, Journalism, takes exactly the position expressed so cogently in the Dylan song. His line 'And people just get uglier and I have no sense of time' especially prefigures the prose of Thompson's book–a book sub-titled 'A Savage Journey to the Heart of the American Dream', in which 'Every now and then when your life gets complicated and the weasels start closing in, the only real cure is to load up on heinous chemicals and then drive like a bastard from Hollywood to Las Vegas . . . not a good town for psychedelic drugs. Reality itself is too twisted. . . . The TV news was about the Laos Invasion . . . Pentagon generals babbling insane lies. . . . The man was getting ugly, but suddenly his eyes switched away. . . . The frog-eyed woman clawed feverishly at his belt. . . . I turned away. It was too horrible.' Towards the end, Thompson acknowledges his debt: 'I listened for a moment, but my nerve ends were no longer receptive. The only song I might have been able to relate to, at that point, was "Mister Tambourine Man". Or maybe "Memphis Blues Again". . .' (The book is dedicated 'To Bob Geiger, for reasons that need not be explained here–and to Bob Dylan, for "Mister Tambourine Man".')

The humour that breaks out in the song, beyond the histrionics of hamming up 'Oh! I didn't know that!', also aids the moral evaluation. The narrator only adds to our awareness of his virtue when he raps out 'Y'see, you're just like me. / I hope you're satisfied.' Who wouldn't have been back then?

Dylan ends the song–calming down here into a patient acceptance that Hunter S. Thompson does not replicate–with a disarming, memorable summary of the predicament he's been showing us that we are all in: 'And here I sit so patiently / Waiting to find out what price / Ya have to pay to get out of / Going through all these things twice.'

The one way in which Memphis and Mobile are not, in the song, mere abstract ideas is this: Dylan's title, 'Memphis Blues Again', includes implicit acknowledgement that there is another 'Memphis Blues'–and indeed there are several. The classic W.C. Handy song 'Memphis Blues' (he wrote the melody, published in 1912; George A. Norton wrote the lyrics in 1913) was cut by Esther Bigeou at her début session as early as 1921. Ma Rainey sang 'Memphis Bound Blues' in 1925; FRANK STOKES (with Will Batts on violin) cut a 'South Memphis Blues' in Memphis in 1929; MEMPHIS MINNIE's 'North Memphis Blues' was cut in Chicago in 1930.

Influence is often hard to trace. It just could be that Dylan picked up his own song's Mobile-Memphis contrast from something he must have seen in print many times: HARRY SMITH's summary of the Uncle Dave Macon track 'Way Down the Old Plank Road' (NY, April 14, 1926). While the recording itself would hardly suggest it, Smith's typically comic, pithy ellipse summarises the song as giving us 'WENT MOBILE, GET GRAVEL TRAIN, NEXT I KNEW: BALL AND CHAIN . . . NASHVILLE PRETTY, MEMPHIS BEAUTY.'

As for the *format* 'stuck inside of Mobile with the Memphis Blues again', it parallels exactly that we associate with BUKKA WHITE's powerful 1940 track 'Aberdeen Mississippi Blues', with its simple 'Sittin' down in Aberdeen with New Orleans on my mind.'

[Bob Dylan: 'Stuck Inside of Mobile with the Memphis Blues Again', performed live hundreds of times, usually with several verses deleted. Hunter S. Thompson's *Fear & Loathing in Las Vegas* began life as a sprawling serialisation: 'Fear and Loathing In Las Vegas', by 'Raoul Duke', *Rolling Stone* nos.95 & 96, San Francisco, 11 & 25 Nov 1971.

Esther Bigeou: 'Memphis Blues', NY, c.5 Oct 1921; Ma Rainey: Chicago, c.Aug 1925; Frank Stokes: 'South Memphis Blues', Memphis, 23 Sep 1929; Memphis Minnie: 'North Memphis Blues', Chicago, 11 Oct 1930. Harry Smith, notes on Uncle Dave Macon: 'Way Down the Old Plank Road', NY, 14 Apr 1926, on *American Folk Music*, Folkways FP 251–3, NY, 1952. Bukka White: 'Aberdeen Mississippi Blues', Chicago, 8 Mar 1940, issued on *The Male Blues Singers*, Collectors Classics CC3, Denmark, c.1965; CD-reissued *Parchman Farm Blues*, Blues Collection CD 23 (magazine + CD), London, 1994.]

Styble, Bryan [1954 -] Brian Stibal was born on October 12, 1954 in St. Louis, Missouri, where he grew up. He attended Boston University and as a sophomore founded and edited the very early Dylan fanzine *Talkin' Bob Zimmerman Blues*, which under three different names ran from early 1975 till late 1979, by which time its editor was pursuing a media career and found himself in Houston, Texas.

For the first five issues, the name was as above. These were dated February 1975, March 1975, July 1975, March 1976 and August 1976. Then he shortened its name and lengthened the gap yet further between issues; *Zimmerman Blues* was the title for issues 6–9 (respectively dated August 1976, winter 1977, fall 1977, fall 1978, winter 1979). For issue

10, summer 1979, he changed the name again, to *Changin'*, because when he met his hero, 'Dylan personally asked if perhaps a new title couldn't be found, one that concentrated more on looking ahead . . .' This seemed to be the kiss of death; that turned out to be the last issue. He handed it over to one Carol Weissbein for a projected issue 11, but this never came out. The last published issue came out just ahead of the first Bob Dylan Convention, which Stibal helped organise and which he attended.

'The impetus was simple: I saw the need for a clearing-house for information and ideas regarding the figure I recognised as the most important recording artist of the 20th century. Since no-one else was doing it, "I knew it was up to me."' The fanzine quickly gained 'a circulation in the low thousands throughout North America, Europe, Australia and Japan after only a few tiny classifieds in *Rolling Stone*.'

Its editor couldn't sustain it:

> '*Zimmerman Blues* ended because it was more or less a one-man operation. While I had people contributing things from all over, there was no-one else around to assist me, and I just didn't have the energy to pull it off myself. The other folks I credited each issue were all over the country, and of course never around to assist in the editing, layout, printing considerations, etc. . . . Besides, by the end I felt I'd started the ball rolling and I figured folks like JOHN BAULDIE would be able to do a vastly better job than I ever had, and sure enough he and others did. I was happy to step aside.'

His first interest in Dylan had been when, as a teenage BEATLES fan, he heard the *Concert for Bangla Desh* and was surprised to find Dylan's set 'vastly more interesting than anything GEORGE or RINGO did' that first Sunday in August 1971. He says now that in truth, even in 1975, 'through at least the first three issues' of *Talkin' Bob Zimmerman Blues*, he still 'didn't understand the first thing about the artist's import'.

In the course of editing the fanzine, he suffered a political conversion to what is now the Neo-Con Right, having voted for Gerald Ford in 1976 and being, by 1978, 'a solid conservative' who found Ronald Reagan 'a thoughtful thinker on a wide range of national and international issues'. Stibal was 'a bona fide Reaganite by 1980'.

So now he's a sometimes deliberately obnoxious radio talk-show host, mostly on small stations—he was recently based on the no.2 talk radio station in Albuquerque, New Mexico, the no.71 sized radio market in the US—but he held a slot on the big-league WJR/Detroit from 1993 to 1996 and at present he's back in the big-time on 710 KIRO in Seattle, Washington, 'the most prestigious newstalk radio operation in the Pacific Northwest', heard across a good portion of western Canada, down to Oregon and east to Idaho.

He has changed his name to Bryan Styble—which, as he likes to say on air, 'rhymes with Bible'. He says the surname change was not, 'contrary to a persistent and annoying rumor in the Dylan fan community, to emulate the spelling of Dylan's name; it was because, as a broadcast journalist, I was tired of people familiar with my print work routinely mispronouncing it; the simultaneous first-name adjustment was for symmetry's sake.'

Styble is not always aggressively right-wing on air: he's capable of talking uncontroversially about sports for eight or nine minutes straight without ever stopping and without ever *saying* anything. But clearly he manages to provoke some listeners. Here's a representative blog posted in August 2005:

> 'His big selling point is "I'll talk to just about anyone about just about anything—from Astronomy to Zoology" . . . and he's obsessed with talking about himself . . . where he stands on the political spectrum (and how "independent" he thinks he is, etc) and moving from random topic to random topic . . . puffing his chest and "propagating conversation at the speed of light" (his god-awful catchphrase). . . . Very sad.'

Perhaps the last testimony to rely on is that of someone with nothing better to do than listen to talk radio in the middle of the night, but it gives a flavour of what seems to have happened to a man who once pioneered Dylan fanzines.

[Bryan Styble: quote re Dylan asking for fanzine name change from issue no.10 itself; all other quotes from e-mails to this writer, 24 Nov & 2 Dec 2005. He can be heard live on *www.710kiro.com*. Some *TBZB* detail is online at *www.geocities.com/soho/hall/8988*. Blogger Willis, *http://willisreed.blogspot.com/2005_08_01_willisreed_archive.html*, online 31 Oct 2005.]

Sutton, Gregg [1949 -] Gregg William Sutton was born on July 1, 1949 in New York City, where he grew up. A bass player, he formed his first group, the Horizons, in 1963, and joined his first 'bigtime group', KGB, in 1976, before moving into what IRA INGBER calls 'a pop band', with Ingber and Vince Malamed, the Pets, who made one album for Arista. He was also the bass player and the only American on Dylan's 1984 European tour. ('That made me feel proud', he told a *Telegraph* fanzine subscriber.)

He got the gig through CHARLIE QUINTANA, a friend, who brought him in to rehearse with Dylan before dropping out himself—though Sutton says Dylan was hard to pin down about it right to the last: 'He was very mysterious about it, you know? I sort of had to say, "Well, do I have the gig? I have to make certain arrangements if I'm going to Europe." He said, "Oh well, somebody'll call you later." That kind of thing. The same was true with

IAN McLAGAN. He told Ian McLagan about three days before the tour!'

Sutton says that the final line-up rehearsed for 'maybe five days', but that he'd listened to Dylan's records all his life, but he 'spent a week listening to all kinds of stuff, and playing along with it just to brush up.'

In the end, Gregg Sutton not only had the gig but, bizarrely from the audience point of view, was given a solo slot in the middle of each concert: 'Bob likes to take a break in the middle of the show,' he said by way of explanation later,

> 'so he can recover his voice, and it's like a transition. He would do seven songs with the band and then I'd sing and then he'd come out and do three or four acoustic numbers. So he just wanted to have five minutes to shift gears and everything. So he sort of asked me the day before the first gig, "You can sing, can't you?" So for a while we did "I've Got My Mojo Working", because it was the easiest thing to do without rehearsing! And then after we got a chance to rehearse it became "I've Got to Use My Imagination", which is an old song by Gladys Knight and the Pips [and written by GERRY GOFFIN and BARRY GOLDBERG] . . . so that was fun. It was a real thrill for me to do it. I never sang for 50–80,000 people before, so I got off on it. People usually liked it . . .'

Ian McLagan describes the day of the opening gig, and how Dylan swapped jackets with Gregg Sutton:

> '. . . the first night . . . we played Verona, in this huge coliseum. It's bigger than the one in Rome: it's the biggest the Romans ever built. And it poured with rain. And we asked to see Him. We hadn't played, and we asked for a set list, 'cause we were nervous. It was only MICK TAYLOR, Greg[g] Sutton, another guy, and me. A very small band, and we had rehearsed, but you knew Dylan could play any one of a thousand songs. And a set list came back to us from his room, with like five songs here, another three over here, and four over here, and we were like, fuck!, well, I guess this is a set list. So the promoter, Bill Graham, brought him into the dressing room for like a bit of solidarity, and the first thing he says is: "Hey, Ian, what are they wearing?" And I said to him, "Bob, it's raining, so they're wearing raincoats. I dunno, black ones, blue ones, red ones, yellow ones . . .". So then he says: "Hey Ian, I like your shirt . . ." So I took it off and I gave it to him. And he turned to Greg[g] and said, "I like your jacket . . ." And Dylan was wearing a beautiful old Harley jacket that he'd been wearing for weeks while we rehearsed, and he hadn't taken it off. It was really old and beaten up, fabulous! And he took it off and gave it to him and took his jacket. It's just ridiculous—for him he was just making conversation, and we were trying to read in hidden meanings.'

It wasn't all a question of staring at each other from across an abyss of non-communication, at least between Dylan and Sutton, as writer Bill Zehme testifies, discussing the death of Andy Kaufman, the edgy multi-personality conceptual comedian who had starred in the hit TV series 'Taxi', who died of cancer aged 35 on May 16, 1984:

> 'Gregg Sutton, Andy's childhood friend and bandleader, was on the road in Europe with Dylan when he heard Andy had died. . . . he was crushed when he heard the news. He knew it was coming but it still devastated him, as it would, but Dylan was so respectful, apparently, of Sutton's mourning that he would sit with him. They'd ride together to and from gigs and he would talk about Andy with him and how much he dug Andy. Andy's rebellion was not lost on any genius.'

Gregg Sutton's professional connections with Kaufman had been as the comic's bandleader and musical director; he played with him at Carnegie Hall, the Huntington Hartford Theatre and on lots of Kaufman's television work.

After the Dylan tour Sutton joined LONE JUSTICE, the first new member when their line-up shifted; replacing Marvin Etzioni, he arrived too late to be involved in the sessions Dylan dropped in on (see entry on the band) but played bass for them from the time of their second album, *Shelter*, in 1986, until the group's demise. By 2003 Sutton was writing songs and running his own music publishing company, and recently, perhaps encouraged by the example of his old compadre Ian McLagan, he has published a book of memoirs, *Here's Your Hat, What's Your Hurry?* which includes chapters on Andy Kaufman and on Bob Dylan.

[Gregg Sutton, *Here's Your Hat, What's Your Hurry?*, Conroe, TX: Stone River Press, 2006. Sutton 'bigtime' quote and much background detail, e-mail to this writer 22 Feb 2006; other Sutton quotes from 'Brief Encounter: Greg[g] Sutton', an interview by Thomas Lasarzik, Munich, 9 Mar 1987, in *The Telegraph* no.27, Romford, UK, summer 1987, pp.26–29. Ian McLagan quote, interview by Kent H. Benjamin, 5 Dec 1997 for *Pop Culture Press* no.44. US, 1998, at *www.makingtime.co.uk/rfr/macint2.htm*; Bill Zehme, author of *Lost in the Funhouse—The Life and Mind of Andy Kaufman*, New York: Delacorte Press, *nia*, quoted from *www.randomhouse.com/boldtype/1299/zehme/interview.html*, both seen online 18 Feb 2006.]

Svensson, Christer [1946 -] Christer Svensson, born in Lund, Sweden, on February 16, 1946, brought a deep knowledge of the blues to bear on Dylan's work, shared it in correspondence with many others, and drew on it himself in a brief but important early piece, 'Stealin', Stealin'', in the short-lived UK fanzine *Endless Road* in 1983, having also written a series of three pieces on Dylan's harmonica playing for the same publication. Today, Christer's much-expanded Dylan harp-keys listing is on the huge musicianly website run by EYOLF ØSTREM, *www.dylanchords.com*.

In the 1980s Svensson had also been an entertaining correspondent to *The Telegraph*, writing this about Dylan fandom: 'Every now and then something happens which puts the whole business into perspective. When I played the KEITH GREEN album, with Dylan's brief harmonica solo on one track, to a fellow collector, we laughed ourselves silly. Ten dollars for a few seconds' worth of harp playing! We realised we must both be mad! Then he sent away for it too.'

[Christer Svensson: 'Inside Out and Upside Down' (3-part series), *Endless Road* no.2, Hull, UK, Mar 1982, no.3, Oct 1982 & no.4, Jun 1983; 'Stealin', Stealin'' also *Endless Road* no.4, Hull, UK Jun 1983; letter to *The Telegraph* republished in *All Across the Telegraph: A Bob Dylan Handbook*, London: Futura Paperbacks edn., 1988, p.243.]

Sweden, the King of See **Carl XVI Gustav of Sweden.**

symbolist poets, French, the See **French symbolists poets, the.**

Tackett, Fred [1945 -] Frederick Tackett was born in Little Rock, Arkansas, on August 4, 1945, into a family in which, he says, everyone played the trumpet ''cept Mom'. He had been writing songs for Little Feat, and playing on their recordings, ever since 1972 and finally became a member of the group in 1987, just in time to play on their album *Let It Roll*. In 1967 he moved to LA to link up with Jimmy Webb, an old friend of his, and duly became an LA session guitarist, mandolinist and, yes, trumpet player.

T

He went out on the road with Boz Scaggs to promote the *Silk Degrees* album (infinitely inferior to, and more popular than, Scaggs' début album on Atlantic), and spent a year on the road with BOB SEGER. He spent a lot longer than that with Bob Dylan, working on the road and in the studio, starting with the late 1979 first gospel tour: 26 concerts, starting in San Francisco on November 1 and finishing in Tucson, Arizona, on December 5. He didn't play trumpet or mandolin, but he was the lead guitarist. He also played on the NBC 'Saturday Night Live' TV show just ahead of the tour, that October 20 and on the Grammy Awards TV show on February 27, 1980 live in LA and shown live coast-to-coast on CBS-TV—by which time Tackett and the rest of the group had played the first 1980 gospel tour leg (January 11 in Portland, Oregon, through to February 9 in Charleston, West Virginia) *and* recorded the *Saved* album at Muscle Shoals in Sheffield, Alabama.

That spring, the next gospel tour began, with Tackett still in place, running from Toronto on April 17 through to Dayton, Ohio, on May 21: another 29 concerts. The *Saved* album was released that June 20, and three months later, on September 23, Fred Tackett joined Dylan, JENNIFER WARNES and a dog to record an early attempt at 'Every Grain of Sand'—a track issued ten years later on the *Bootleg Series Vols. 1–3*—and a still-uncirculated try at a song called 'Her Memory'. Immediately after that came rehearsals for the last 1980 tour, the 'Musical Retrospective' tour, including a recorded rehearsal that captures several of Dylan's great unreleased 1980s songs—'Yonder Comes Sin' (this cut used as a Special Rider music publishing demo), 'Caribbean Wind' and 'Let's Keep It Between Us'—as well as further new songs and try-outs of 'Mr. Tambourine Man' and 'Blowin' in the Wind'. The tour itself, with Tackett now on mandolin as well as lead guitar, began on November 9 with 12 nights in San Francisco followed by a further seven concerts in five cities: Tucson, San Diego, Seattle, and Salem and Portland, Oregon, ending there on December 4.

Fred Tackett seems to have missed the first studio sessions for *Shot of Love*, held in Santa Monica in March 1981 and yielding the recording of 'Angelina' released ten years later, but he arrived at the sessions of April 1 & 2, and reappeared on April 28 & 29 (none of these yielded anything that has been released), and then during the first half of May, from which the finished album's tracks all derive, along with the 'Let It Be Me' sung by Dylan and CLYDIE KING and released as a European B-side, and the cut of 'Groom's Still Waiting at the Altar' released as a US B-side and later incorporated into the CD reissue of the album itself. It may be that Dylan was unhappy with Tackett's guitar-work on some of these tracks: in mid-May David Campbell put guitar overdubs onto 'Lenny Bruce' and on May 31 guitarist Andrew Gold put overdubs onto 'Watered-Down Love', 'Property of Jesus', 'Shot of Love' and 'Every Grain of Sand'.

Fred Tackett played live with Dylan throughout the 1981 tours, all the same: the US warm-up dates in early June, the European dates in June and July, and the fall dates in North America, starting in Milwaukee on October 16 and finishing in Lakeland, Florida, on November 21. That was his last Dylan concert; he'd played a total of 152.

Today he and guitarist-singer Paul Barrere work together as an acoustic duo.

[Fred Tackett, quote on trumpets & Mom from PR blurb for Barrere & Tackett, seen online 11 Nov 2005 at *www.skylineonline.com*.]

Talkin' Bob Zimmerman Blues See **Styble, Bryan.**

'Tangled Up in Blue' [1975] This opening song from *Blood on the Tracks* deals with the way in which many forces—past upon present, public upon privacy, distance upon friendship, disintegration upon love—are further tangled and reprocessed by time. It's a scintillating account of a career and a love affair and of how they intertwine. It becomes a viable history of 15 years through one man's eyes, and in its realism and mental alertness it offers a vigorous challenge to all the poses of wasted decay that most 'intelligent' rock has been marketing since the fall from grace of 1960s optimism.

As it would need to be, Dylan's writing here is chiseled by the full concentration of his artistry. He can coin a new mode of expression with an almost in-passing agility—'Later on when the crowd thinned out / I was about to do the same'—and there is the wit, tossed out as if it were easy, and there too is the bubbling spontaneity that Dylan achieves within the disciplined limits of a strikingly precise verse-structure.

(The deft trick of Dylan's formulation here is reminiscent of something that Colin Wilson, in *The Outsider*, 1956, picks out of Jean-Paul Sartre's first novel *La Nausée* [*Nausea*], 1937, in which the narrator says of a café patron that 'When his place empties, his head empties also.')

Dylan makes the exacting verse structure work for him so well. There is, for instance, a rhyming spill-over towards the end of each verse, like this: 'I was standin' on the side of the road / Rain fallin' on my shoes / Headin' out for the east coast / Lord knows I paid some dues / Getting through / Tangled up in blue.' It is there as that fourth line (rhyming with the second) spills over into the short fifth line (which rhymes with the sixth). As we listen to the song, these short spill-overs become more and more stabbing in their emotional effect as they become at the same time more and more agile and clever as rhymes. As here: 'She studied the lines of my face / I must admit I felt a little uneasy / When she bent down to tie the lace- / -s of my shoe—/ Tangled up in blue'; and finally, triumphantly, here in the last verse: 'But me I'm still on the road / Headin' for another joint / We always did feel the same / We just saw it from a different point / Of view—/ Tangled up in blue.'

Beyond that wonderful use of a formal, limiting shape and structure to yield scintillating leaps of feeling and expression, 'Tangled Up in Blue' contains a whole assortment of verbal spikes and explosions that all operate not as distractions from the main body of *feeling* in the song but as ways of evoking the emotional complexity and urgency of it all. That Dylan can make time, in the course of what is delivered as a fast, breathless narrative, for flashes like this—'I had a job in the Great North Woods . . . / But I never did like it all that much / And one day the axe just fell'—shows an alertness and mental dexterity that augments the emotional seriousness and depth of the song. And there is an accompanying dexterity of sketching in, quick as a flash, a whole range of universally recognizable moments in fresh, intensely accurate strokes of language, from the evoked dialogue with inbuilt self-mockery here—'She lit a burner on the stove / And offered me a pipe / "I thought you'd never say hello," she said / "You look like the silent type"'—to the very funny sureness of touch in this summary of that common feeling of whatever-happened-to-*those* people: 'Some are mathematicians / Some are carpenters' wives / Dunno how it all got started / I dunno what they're doin' with their lives', where that last line communicates the inevitable ambiguity of feeling—sadness at time's destruction of friendships and at the same time, truly, an indifference to where or what those people are now.

The song is also highly valued by post-structuralist critics, because, more than any other single Dylan song, it is not a single Dylan song. It is a living demonstration of how unfixed 'the text' is. It occupies a special position among Dylan's many 'non-linear narratives' (in AIDAN DAY's phrase), firing up postmodern questions about how we see the individual and the self. It doesn't have a fixed or clearly identifiable voice telling a clear sequential story, and so it reflects, Day argues, the non-linear (tangled up) way the human brain is currently thought to perceive and interpret the world in front of it and the past behind it. Day's concern here is for 'lyrics which open out into an exploration of the workings of the psyche as a whole'.

One of the song's indeterminacies is the shifting between 'I', 'he' and 'you'; and Day argues that as the lyric splits its 'I' into an 'I' and a 'he', and splits its 'she' into what may be a series of shes and into 'she' and 'you', this creates an important effect:

> 'Considerable inventive effort on the part of the reader is provoked whether the lyric is taken either as one story or as a series of stories. Co-operation in the making of the story may be demanded of the reader of any narrative. The specially modernist feature of "Tangled Up in Blue" is that the fragmentation of linear structure, together with the indeterminacy generated by that fragmentation about whether we are in the presence of one or more stories, encourages specific awareness of the creative role of the audience in reading or hearing narrative . . . teasing us into generating story, "Tangled Up in Blue" also explores the extent to which the mind is fundamentally disposed to think in terms of story or narrative. The conscious self is inseparable from the stories of its own life that it ceaselessly recites, however silently, to itself. . . . in the same way cultures frame themselves through myths of origin, through histories and through fictions of the future . . . the subject of the lyric is in one sense the inescapability of the narrative impulse itself. But more than this, in its disturbance of narrative order the lyric simultaneously inquires into the possibility of something beyond such order.'

Comparably, the song excites NEIL CORCORAN because it explicitly declares its own open-endedness (making it a self-referring, or self-reflexive, text). He writes that the song 'encodes an account of itself in its own variations; it becomes an allegory of its own procedures. Keeping on keeping on, getting on the train and riding, staying on the road and heading towards the sun become not only the activities recommended by the song, but what the song . . . does; it changes, it adapts, it refuses the consolations of the finished in favour of a poetics of process, of constant renewal, of performance rather than publication. Recommending the provisional as an ethic, it also embodies it as an aesthetic.'

Dylan re-wrote the 'She opened up a book of poems' verse towards the end of his 1978 world tour, changing it to 'She opened up the Bible and started quotin' it to me', so that it became, thereby, one of his first public suggestions of having converted to Christ; then he re-wrote the song wholesale for the 1984 tour of Europe, not merely re-writing lines of lyric but restructuring the whole song (a braggadocio version of the re-write is on the album *Real Live*); but ever afterwards Dylan reverted to the earlier structure and the original lyric (with minor variations), and devoted himself to making it one of his most over-performed repertoire items.

By the end of 1998 it was his most-performed post-1960s song, and his sixth most-performed number altogether, behind five songs from the previous decade, 'All Along the Watchtower', 'Like a Rolling Stone', 'Maggie's Farm', 'It Ain't Me, Babe' and 'Mr. Tambourine Man'. It far out-stripped renditions of even so over-visited a 1970s song as 'Forever Young'. To that point, Dylan had sung 'Tangled Up in Blue' 634 times in the 23 years of its existence—and, not surprisingly, sung it so unfeelingly so often that it has spoiled, for many admirers of his work, even the early studio versions of what was once a major work of consequence and delight. As the *Monthly Film Bulletin* comments somewhere in a different context, 'It's not the familiar which breeds contempt but the debasement of the familiar.'

[Aidan Day: *Jokerman: Reading the Lyrics of Bob Dylan*, 1989. Neil Corcoran, 'Going Barefoot: Thinking About Bob Dylan's Lyrics', *The Telegraph* no.27, Romford, UK, summer 1987. Bob Dylan: 'Tangled Up in Blue' containing 'She opened up the Bible' first performed Houston, TX, 26 Nov 1978. Performance statistics from Glen Dundas: *Tangled Up in Tapes*, 4th edn., 1999.]

***Tarantula* [1971]** Dylan's first published book (not counting songbooks issued by music publishers), this 'novel' was written during the tumult of 1965–66 but unpublished until 1971. In the interim Dylan tended to suggest, when asked, that *Tarantula* had only ever been cynically thrown together scraps of nonsense. This was untrue, as shown by the careful revisions Dylan made to an earlier manuscript version of his book, *Tarantula Meets Rex Paste*, which, dated 1965, was never published but was circulated on primitive roneo'd sheets. The finished version was first published by the New York office of Macmillan's, which had long trumpeted the book and pained Dylan in advance by floating absurd PR comparisons between him and James Joyce.

A singular item in, but an honourable part of, Bob Dylan's work, *Tarantula* combines lengthy prose-poem sections broken up by shorter, more readily comprehensible passages in the form of comic letters written by, and addressed to, different sharply drawn, vividly recognisable kinds of contemporary people: mostly risibly shallow young ones (Dylan has an excellent ear for their voices).

Both parts of the book draw heavily upon the oeuvre of THE BEATS—the 'letters' perhaps especially seeming to echo some of the work of KENNETH PATCHEN and GREGORY CORSO. But the long prose-poem sections are also awash in slick, playful allusions to, and puns upon, a vast range of books, films and other items sucked inside the knowing maw of Anglo-American culture, from the blues to nursery rhymes ('would you like to buy a pail, jack?', 'ring around the rosey', 'the candle-stick maker', 'swap that cow') to Davy Crockett's hat and from T.S. ELIOT to the *I Ching*. The book is fitfully, exhilaratingly acute about greed, corruption, manipulation, ugliness and threats to the social fabric.

Tarantula has been more than somewhat unattended by critics. Exceptions to this neglect include Elia Katz' interesting 1969 article 'Dylan's unpublished novel' (reprinted as '*Tarantula*: A Perspective' in 1972) and Gabrielle Goodchild's unpublished essay '*Tarantula*: Tangled Up in a Web', 1979, which was written as background material for ROBERT SHELTON's *No Direction Home: The Life and Music of Bob Dylan* but published in cut-down form as '*Tarantula*: The Web Untangled' in the slim volume *Conclusions on the Wall* in 1980, long before Shelton's book appeared.

Perhaps appropriately, fragments of some previously unpublished parts of Goodchild's original essay then emerged inside Shelton's book, in which he also ventures the claim that while 'the Left was vexed with Dylan for not having made more overt comments on the Vietnam War, we find a great deal of that war in the book. Goodchild holds it as a surrealist sort of "war" going on "beyond our control and yet poisoning our lives."'

Dylan's novel is also well-attended to, though in note form, in '*Tarantula*: Commentary and Textual Allusions', in *Bob Dylan's Words*, edited by RICHARD DAVID WISSOLIK & SCOTT McGRATH—except that it is blind to the many blues references in the book, and you must put up with this sort of thing: 'complete appreciation of *Tarantula* and the rest of Dylan's work is not possible without knowledge of the *I Ching*, Tarot symbolism and Robert Graves' *White Goddess*'—at which you have to laugh, especially since one of the typically funny fragments inside *Tarantula* itself is this: 'to my students: I take it for granted that youve all read & understand freud—dostoevsky—st. michael—confucius—coco joe—einstein—melville—porgy snaker—john zulu . . . the exam will be in two weeks—everybody has to bring their own eraser. your professor herold the professor').

This last book includes too Scott McGrath's essay 'Only a Matter of Time 'Til Night Comes Stepping In', 1993, which 'finds' in *Tarantula* a previously 'unknown poem', titled by McGrath 'To Maria'. That is: 'Seemingly incidental Spanish phrases are peppered throughout Dylan's novel. . . . Put together and translated into English, the individual hidden phrases, all of which appear in chapters with the name "Maria" in the title, form the . . . poem.' This enterprising exercise seems justified by a plausible result.

In 1994 came *The Cracked Bells: A Guide to 'Tarantula'*, by ROBIN WITTING, which attempts an annotating of the text similar to that by Wissolik & McGrath but taking the text section by section (rather than listing text-fragments alphabetically), and, naturally, honing in on different words, phrases and names for elucidation. Self-published from Scunthorpe in South Humberside, UK, the revised edition of 1995 is a large-format book of almost 200 pages.

In 1999 a Swedish edition of *Tarantula* was published, with an afterword in English as well as Swedish: 'The Art of Reading *Tarantula*', by one Peter Glas. This schoolmasterly six-page piece never fears to state the obvious and to explain it to the beginner, but in doing so it reminds us usefully that, at base, '*Tarantula* is Dylan's most thorough description of chaos. It is the same chaos that he describes in songs like "Subterranean Homesick Blues" . . . but *Tarantula* is the magnum opus of Dylan's chaos vision.' He goes on to argue that the book is rich, cliché-free, tough-minded and original, and that it is distinguished from the works of Joyce and of the absurdists and Beats by its hopefulness—and that Dylan's vividly rendered chaos, as captured in *Tarantula*, 'marks the starting point of Dylan's dynamic quest, spanning decades, for . . . structure . . . for truth and meaning in life.'

Most recently, Robin Witting has returned to the *Tarantula* fray by offering the 80-page book/booklet *'Tarantula': The Falcon's Mouthbook*, arguing that Dylan's novel is, from first to last, concerned with the religious and spiritual ramifications of 'oral obsession': from which it follows that Witting too refutes by exegesis any claim that the text of *Tarantula* was uncalculatingly assembled or thoughtless. More generally, Witting also points up, and protests at, the way that this unique piece of Dylan's work has been neglected. Witting writes: '*Tarantula* cannot be ignored forever; all these years on and still hardly anyone seems to have a good word for it . . . I still believe that [it] is a beautiful, dazzling creation; an orphan sonnet disinherited by its author.'

Certainly, granted that *Tarantula* comes from the very period in Dylan's creative life that most people value the most—the era of *Highway 61 Revisited* and *Blonde on Blonde*, the voice of 'She's Your Lover Now'—it's remarkable how much his audience too has neglected this orphan.

[Bob Dylan: *Tarantula*, New York: Macmillan & London: MacGibbon & Kee, 1971; newest paperback edn., London: Harper Perennial, 2005. Elia Katz: 'Dylan's unpublished novel', *Carolina Quarterly* no.21, fall 1969, reprinted as '*Tarantula*: A Perspective' in Stephen Pickering: *Praxis: One*, Santa Cruz, CA: No Limit, 1972. Gabrielle Goodchild: '*Tarantula*: Tangled Up in a Web', London, unpublished, 1979, published (cut down) as '*Tarantula*: The Web Untangled', *Conclusions on the Wall*, ed. Elizabeth M. Thomson, Prestwich, UK: Thin Man, 1980. Goodchild quotes within Shelton, London: Penguin Books edn., pp.236–38; Shelton quote, ditto p.236. (Shelton mentions too a Stephen Pickering essay, 'The Two Tarantulas: A Textual Comparison', but this writer has been unable to trace it.) Wissolik & McGrath, *Bob Dylan's Words*, Greensburg, PA: Eadmer Press, 1994. Peter Glas: 'The Art of Reading *Tarantula*', in *Tarantula*, Lund, Sweden: Bakhåll, 1999. Robin Witting: *The Cracked Bells: A Guide to 'Tarantula'*, Scunthorpe, UK: Exploding Rooster Books, 1994, revised edn., 1995; *'Tarantula': The Falcon's Mouthbook*, ditto, 2005.]

Tarlton, Jimmie [1892 - 1979] See **'Columbus Stockade Blues' [1960]**.

Taylor, Mick [1949 -] Michael Kevin Taylor was born in Welwyn Garden City, southern England, on January 17, 1949, and grew up in the nearby and equally benighted Hatfield to become, except for a brief patch around 1972, one of the world's most boring lead guitarists. Perhaps it was because THE ROLLING STONES wanted somebody pliant after the nightmare that was Brian Jones left the group in June 1969 that they replaced him with Mick Taylor, who left JOHN MAYALL's Bluesbreakers in order to join. (Jones left with the quaint understatement to the press: 'I no longer see eye to eye with the others over the discs we are cutting', and added that he was to form a new group of his own; on July 3, he was found drowned in Winnie the Pooh's swimming pool.) Taylor stood around not letting the madness and superstardom of the world's greatest rock band get him too excited—though he played on the studio albums *Sticky Fingers* (for which he woke up, contributing beautiful, resonant, indelible lines to this, their best album), *Exile on Main Street*, *Goats Head Soup* and *It's Only Rock and Roll*—and remained in place until the end of 1974, when he quit. Expecting, like ERIC CLAPTON perhaps, to become a solo star afterwards, Taylor was surprised to find this not happening. His solo albums have been *Mick Taylor* (1979), the live *Stranger in This Town* (1990), *A Stone's Throw* (2000, which includes a version of 'Blind Willie McTell') and *14 Below* (2003). He and Carla Olson made a live album together in 1991, *Too Hot for Snakes*.

In 1983 Taylor was called in to work on Dylan's *Infidels* album as another guitarist alongside MARK KNOPFLER, and he not only sleepwalked through all the April sessions but in May overdubbed further guitar-work onto several tracks. He is also credited with playing at the *Empire Burlesque* session, probably in December 1984, that gave us 'Tight Connection to My Heart'.

Earlier that year, just after Dylan had been playing with edgy stripped-down punk group THE PLUGZ, he disappointed everyone by chickening out of taking them on the road for his 1984 European tour but resorting to a safe concoction of mostly music biz veteran players, in the midst of which was Mick Taylor, who, blonde, supercilious, pudgy faced and stolid as blancmange, strolled through the tour's 27 concerts as bored as he deserved to be.

[Mick Taylor: *Mick Taylor*, CBS 82600, UK, 1979; *Stranger in This Town*, Maze, *nia*, 1990; *A Stone's Throw*, Cannonball, *nia*, 2000; *14 Below*, Pilot PLO0000175, US, 2003. Carla Olson & Mick Taylor: *Too Hot for Snakes*, Razor & Tie, *nia*, 1991.]

Tedeschi, David [1962 -] David Tedeschi was born in 1962 in Chicago. He is the film editor whose work resulted in the brilliant 2005 MARTIN SCORSESE film release *No Direction Home*. Scorsese's input as regards the editing was far less intensive than Tedeschi's, which is why Tedeschi's name is so prominent on the credits. He had worked with Scorsese before, on the 'Feel Like Going Home' episode of the TV series 'The Blues' in 2003.

David Tedeschi has worked as a writer in films as well as an editor; the 1993 film *8-A*, directed by Orlando Jiménez Leal, a documentary reconstruction of the 1989 trial and execution of Cuba's General Arnaldo Ochoa Sanchez (one of Castro's original revolutionary heroes), was co-written by Tedeschi, Jose Hugez and the director. Tedeschi also co-wrote the 1999 film *My Friend Paul* with independent film-maker and director Jonathan Berman. As an editor Tedeschi's credits start with the 1994 Guatemalan film *El Silencio de Neto*, directed by Luis Argueta, and include the 'TV Nation' television series in 1996. Since *No Direction Home* he has worked on *El Cantante*, directed by Leon Ichaso (and co-starring Jennifer Lopez), a drama based on the life Hector Lavoe, who launched the salsa movement in 1975 and brought it to the United States.

Interviewed online by the *Washington Post* about his work on *No Direction Home*, he said of it: 'The editing is all intuitive. The editing is emotional.' Asked if he had been a Dylan fan before he worked on the film, and if so how that affected the editing, Tedeschi replied: 'I was a big Bob Dylan fan and I was also a big fan of GINSBERG and KEROUAC. I'm not sure it affected the editing process except that I know we all felt like it was important to do a good job on the film because of how great an artist Bob Dylan is.'

His co-interviewee, the film's producer Susan Lacy, when asked if there were plans for a follow-up documentary, focussing on Dylan's later career, replied: 'We are having preliminary discussions about that.'

[*Washington Post* interview online 28 Sep 2005, transcript seen online 1 Feb 2006. Main source the IMDb film database & David Tedeschi, e-mails to this writer, 4 & 7 Feb 2006.]

***Telegraph, The* [fanzine]** See **Bauldie, John [1981–1996]**.

telegraphy and the religious imagination On the ponderous, musically monotonous *Empire Burlesque* track 'Something's Burning, Baby' (1985), a song that on the record and the page seems like Dylan on Mogadon, one of the more mysterious, compelling lines is the penultimate one: 'Ring down when you're ready, baby, I'm waiting for you'.

That 'ring down' implies 'from up above', which is to say from heaven, yet 'baby' is too familiar a form of address to be directed at God, even for Dylan. Is the song addressing someone who has died? Was it a funeral pyre right in front of his eyes?

Yet 'ring down when you're ready, baby, I'm waiting for you' is not a vague image alone in the world of song but one that echoes blues and gospel songs that have gone before it. In context, then, Dylan's line is not strange at all. In 1927, Papa Harvey Hull & Long Cleve Reed recorded 'Hey! Lawdy Mama—The France Blues', which assembled many traditional song-fragments and collided them together, and includes this couplet: 'Hello heaven, daddy want to give you a telephone / So you can talk to your daddy any time when he's gone.' The same year, 1927, also offered the Rev. Sister Mary Nelson's 'The Royal Telephone' (recalled and recorded nearly 40 years later for the Library of Congress by MISSISSIPPI JOHN HURT); in 1929 came Blind Roosevelt Graves' recording of 'Telephone to Glory'. (These telephone-to-heaven images were not restricted to black performance. In the early 1950s HANK SNOW cut the religious song 'I Just Telephone Upstairs'.)

One of the most remarkable uses of this image occurs in a 'Negro Spiritual' text called 'Tone the Bell Easy', which is a version of one of the songs from Bob Dylan's first album, 'In My Time of Dyin'', more usually called 'Jesus Make Up My Dyin' Bed' and associated with CHARLEY PATTON, BLIND WILLIE JOHNSON and many gospel groups. The chorus of the 'Tone the Bell Easy' text runs 'Well well well / Tone the bell easy' (repeated twice) 'Jesus gonna make up my dyin' bed', the second verse brings in Mary and Martha (as 'Ring Them Bells' does, of course) and then, in amongst this timeless scene, verse eight picks up the telephone: 'Ever since me and Jesus been married / We haven't been a minute apart / He put the receiver in my hand / And the Holy Ghost in my heart / Well well well, so I can call up Jesus . . .'

This is all part of what seems a rather naff kind of standard God-bothering rhetoric: part of the familiar recruiting ploy of 'it's-hip-to-be-Christian-cos-we're-jolly-modern'. 'Telephone to Glory', and the still more gruesome 'Ain't Gonna Lay My Receiver Down', are all of a piece with preposterous songs like 'Jesus Is My Air-O-Plane' by Mother McCollum (1930). Yet it isn't only Christians who go in for this sort of thing. In Martyrs Square, Damascus, a black bronze colonnade offers a massive and splendidly pompous commemoration of the opening of the Middle East's first telegraph link: a hotline from Damascus to Medina, home of God's prophet Mohammed. The colonnade rises up 20 feet above its tall plinth, festooned in sculpted wires and loops of sculpted cable, topped by a model of a mosque. There is, then, something about telegraphy that excites the religious imagination east and west alike.

In the end, its plausibility is all in the fine-tuning of words. There's nothing risible about 'People get ready, there's a train a-coming', or 'This Train Is Bound for Glory', or *Slow Train Coming*, yet a title like 'Life's Railway to Heaven' invites immediate mockery. (This song was recorded in the 1920s by the extraordinarily named black artist Hermes Zimmerman.)

There are, on other subjects, many entertaining titles provided by pre-war gospel songs and records of hot-shot preachers' sermons with accompaniments by their congregations. Among them you'll find 'Christ Was Born on Christmas Morn', 'Hell Is God's Chain Gang', 'Smoking Woman in the Street', 'The Black Camel of Death', 'The Fat Life Will Bring You Down', 'Must I Be Carried to the Sky on Flowered Beds of Ease' and, a favourite from 1931, 'He Came to Town Riding on His Ass'.

[Papa Harvey Hull & Long Cleve Rede: 'Hey! Lawdy Mama—The France Blues', Chicago, c.8 Apr 1927; *Really! The Country Blues*, Origin Jazz Library OJL-2, NY, c.1961. Rev. Sister Mary M. Nelson: 'The Royal Telephone', Chicago, 25 Feb 1927 (& poss. NY, 21 Apr 1927); CD-reissued *Memphis Gospel: Complete Recorded Works (1927–1929)*, Document DOCD-5072, Vienna, c.1991. Mississippi John Hurt: 'Royal Telephone', Washington, D.C., 23 Jul 1963, unissued. Blind Roosevelt Graves & Brother (Uaroy Graves): 'Telephone to Glory', Richmond, IN, 20 Sep 1929. This song was also cut as 'I'm Going to Telephone to Glory' by, for example, the Heavenly Gospel Singers, Charlotte, NC, 13 Feb 1936. Hank Snow: 'I Just Telephone Upstairs', *nia*; CD-reissued *The Singing Ranger—I'm Movin' On'* (4-CD set), Bear Family BCD 15426-DH, Vollersode, Germany, c.1990.

'Tone the Bell Easy' text taken (& de-minstrelised) from H.A. Chambers, ed, *The Treasury of Negro Spirituals*, London: Blandford Press, 1964.

Mitchell's Christian Singers: 'Ain't Gonna Lay My Receiver Down', NY, 28 Dec 1938. Mother McCollum: 'Jesus Is My Air-O-Plane', Chicago, c.Jun 1930; CD-reissued *Guitar Evangelists: Complete Recorded Works (1928–1951)*, Document DOCD-5101, Vienna, c.1989. Hermes Zimmerman (no relation): 'Life's Railway to Heaven', prob. NY, c.Apr 1926; prob. vinyl unissued.

Cotton Top Mountain Sanctified Singers: 'Christ Was Born on Christmas Morn', Chicago, 29 Aug 1929. Rev. J.M. Gates: 'Smoking Woman in the Street', Atlanta, GA, 23 Aug 1939; Rev. J.M. Milton: 'The Black Camel of Death', Atlanta, 5 Nov 1929. Rev. A.W. Nix: 'The Fat Life Will Bring You Down', Chicago, Jan 1930. Leadbelly: 'Must I Be Carried to the Sky on Flowered Beds of Ease', field-recorded for the Library of Congress in Washington, D.C., 23 Aug 1940. Rev. Emmett Dickinson & His Congregation: 'He Came to Town Riding on His Ass', NY, 10 Oct 1931.]

Tench, Benmont [1953 -] Benjamin Montmorency Tench III was born in Gainesville, Florida, on September 7, 1953. Like fellow-Gainesvillean TOM PETTY, he was a member of the band Mudhutch, and was responsible for bringing MIKE CAMPBELL into that precursor outfit to TOM PETTY & THE HEARTBREAKERS. His keyboard-work has not only been crucial to that mega-platinum rock group but has also contributed to a staggering number of albums by other artists, including work by ELVIS COSTELLO, THE ROLLING STONES, BRIAN WILSON, Crosby, Stills & Nash, the Ramones, ROY ORBISON and Aretha Franklin.

More to the point, he has done session work for Dylan, and like Mike Campbell, his time in the studio with Dylan long preceded the touring with Tom Petty & the Heartbreakers. In fact Benmont Tench was the *first* of the Heartbreakers to do sessions for Dylan, for the album that became *Shot of Love*. His first seems to have been on April 23, 1981, when on a long Los Angeles session with some of the musicians from Dylan's just-completed gospel tours, Tench was brought in to play keyboards on a number of tracks including three never issued but since circulated, namely 'Magic', 'Don't Ever Take Yourself Away' and 'Mystery Train', plus a number of uncirculated takes of 'Don't Ever Take Yourself Away', 'Trouble', 'Shot of Love', 'Half as Much', 'Groom's Still Waiting at the Altar', 'Dead Man, Dead Man', 'Heart of Mine' and 'You Changed My Life', plus a further take of 'You Changed My Life' which, though omitted from the album as released later that year, was issued a decade later on the *Bootleg Series Vols. 1–3*. The following day the same musicians tried 'Magic' and other material again; nothing from this session has emerged.

Benmont Tench was back in the studio on April 27, 1981, and this time Mike Campbell was there too. For details see the entry on the latter. Ditto for the Hollywood sessions of December 1984 at which Dylan attempted 'New Danville Girl' and others. On May 1, 1981, however, Tench alone from among the Heartbreakers was in the studio again with Dylan playing on various uncirculated numbers—'Caribbean Wind', 'Dead Man, Dead Man', 'It's All Dangerous to Me', 'My Oriental Home',

'Ah, Ah, Ah' and 'Don't Let Her Know' (some titles are speculative)—but also on the successful takes of the fine Motownesque 'Watered-Down Love' and the churning 'Property of Jesus' released on the *Shot of Love* album and on the lovely devotional version of 'Let It Be Me', sung by Dylan and CLYDIE KING and released as a single in Europe. Next day Benmont Tench was also there, this time playing on four successful *Shot of Love* album tracks, 'Dead Man, Dead Man', 'Lenny Bruce' (on which he plays organ), 'Trouble' and 'In the Summertime'. He is also credited on *www.bobdylan.com* with having played organ on the album cut of 'Every Grain of Sand'.

Tench was absent from the sessions Campbell and HOWIE EPSTEIN attended in January and February 1985, so that his next work with Dylan was rehearsing for, and then performing at, the Farm Aid Benefit Concert in Champaign, Illinois, that September. After that came the 1986 tour, the 'Band of the Hand' recording session in Australia and the 1987 tour, all accomplished within Tom Petty & the Heartbreakers.

In *Chronicles Volume One*, Dylan remembers that on the 1986 tour it was Benmont Tench in particular who tried to encourage him to broaden the concert repertoire he had settled on: '[He] . . . would always be asking me, almost pleadingly, about including different numbers in the show. "Chimes of Freedom"—can we try that? Or what about "My Back Pages"? Or "Spanish Harlem Incident"? And I'd always be making some lame excuse.' Tench felt far less jaundiced about it all, saying once: 'He's been great to play with. Great fun as well, mostly because you can never let your mind drift. He'll give the most familiar song an odd twist; a change of rhythm or a peculiar delivery. Playing with Bob Dylan certainly gives you a good kick up the arse.'

The last shared concerts the band and Dylan gave were 16 years after this, at Holmdel, New Jersey, in August 2003; but in Benmont Tench's case, there was one extra conjunction with Dylan, a decade earlier. When Dylan appeared as a guest on the TV Special 'WILLIE NELSON: The Big Six O' recorded in Austin, Texas, on April 28, 1993, after Dylan had performed 'Hard Times' with his own Never-Ending Tour band, he and Nelson together performed the Townes Van Zandt song 'Pancho & Lefty' using Nelson's band of the day—and these musicians included the irrepressible Benmont Tench on keyboards.

[Bob Dylan: *Chronicles Volume One*, pp.148–49. 'Willie Nelson: The Big Six O: An All-Star Birthday Celebration', Austin, TX, Apr 28, 1993, shown CBS-TV, 22 May 1993; video release Columbia House 11141, Jun 1993. Tench on Dylan quote seen online 25 Oct 2005 at *http://frontpage.simnet.is/bobdylan/friends.htm*.]

Terry, Sonny [1911 - 1986] Saunders Terrell was born on October 24, 1911 in Greensboro, North Carolina. He went blind in one eye at the age of 5, and in the other at 18. He played harmonica on the streets for money, and met and recorded with BLIND BOY FULLER in 1937. He appeared at JOHN HAMMOND's 1938 Spirituals to Swing Concert at Carnegie Hall, singing and playing harp accompanied by Bull City Red; his solo studio début was the following day, Christmas Eve, in New York, for the Library of Congress, at which he recorded several takes of that harmonica-showcase piece 'Lost John' (which Dylan tried to approximate with 'Long John' on the privately-recorded December 22 1961 performance in Minneapolis). Four days later came a commercial session for Columbia, on which he was billed as Sanders Terry. He met the Tennessee-born guitarist BROWNIE McGHEE in North Carolina in 1939 and off and on they worked together for 40 years thereafter. (For relevant information on the duo and its relevance to Bob Dylan, see the entry on **McGhee**.)

Terry was the cruder singer of the two but his harp playing was dazzling: always a virtuoso display of explosive effects, surprises and agility. After moving to New York City in the early 1940s and mixing in the same musical and political circles as WOODY GUTHRIE and LEADBELLY, Terry played in the New York production of *Finian's Rainbow* and, with McGhee, both appeared in Tennessee Williams' *Cat on a Hot Tin Roof*. The duo split up after years of acrimony (sometimes displayed onstage in the midst of their act), after which Terry's career was the shorter-lived but the more successful. He even collaborated with, and held his own against, Johnny Winter, on the 1981 album *Whoopin'*, on which the two (plus Willie Dixon) went for an ostentatiously more abrasive sound that was, as Tony Russell puts it, 'not like Terry & McGhee but Little Walter & MUDDY WATERS.'

Sonny Terry died in Mineola, New York on March 11, 1986.

[Sonny Terry: 'Mountain Blues' & 'The New John Henry', NY 23 Dec 1938, *Spirituals to Swing Concert at Carnegie Hall*, Vanguard VRS8524, *nia*; 'Lost John', NY, 24 Dec 1938. Sonny Terry & Johnny Winter, *Whoopin'*, NY Jul 1981, Albino MA501, *nia*; CD-reissued Alligator 4734, US, 1990. Bob Dylan: 'Long John', Minneapolis, 22 Dec 1961, unreleased. Tony Russell, *The Blues From Robert Johnson to Robert Cray*, London: Aurum Press, 1997, p.63.]

Them See **Morrison, Van**.

'Things Have Changed' [2000] This may be the only popular song that alludes to the work of both Percy Bysshe Shelley and Duane Eddy.

When the lyric refers to walking 'forty miles of bad road', it is yet another ready-made phrase from the pre-Dylan era of popular music. It was the title of one of Duane Eddy's biggest hit singles, so named after Eddy and his producer, Lee Hazlewood, overheard the phrase used in an argument between two Texans while standing in line to see a movie. 'Your girl had a face like forty miles of bad road,' said one. Hazlewood immediately recognised the phrase as a perfect title for one of Eddy's trademark tough but simple instrumentals.

[Duane Eddy title information from undated interview with Eddy by Spencer Leigh in *Baby, That Is Rock and Roll: American Pop 1954–1963*, p.166–67.]

'This Train (Is Bound for Glory)' The title of WOODY GUTHRIE's autobiography, *Bound for Glory*, is a quote from the old gospel song that runs 'This train is bound for glory / This train.' The song was a standard performance item for pre-war black gospel quartets, recorded by, among others, the catchily named Florida Normal & Industrial Institute Quartette (as 'Dis Train', NY, early September 1922), Bryants Jubilee Quartet (NY, March 20, 1931, as by the [Famous] Garland Jubilee Singers) and, prominently, by Sister Rosetta Tharpe (originally NY, January 10, 1939), who re-cut it several times post-war. Her 1947 version was a hit on the 'race' charts. Post-Guthrie it has been recorded by everyone from PETER, PAUL & MARY to Bunny Wailer. It is also one of the songs to which Bob Dylan refers so poignantly within his own lyrics on 1997's *Time Out of Mind*. 'Tryin' to Get to Heaven' incorporates the wistful lines 'Some trains don't pull no gamblers / No midnight ramblers, like they used to do.'

'This Train' became secularised into the Little Walter hit 'My Babe', 'written' by Willie Dixon, and is also the basis for Curtis Mayfield's 'PEOPLE GET READY', which uses the same train image to stand for the coming of the Lord.

[Sister Rosetta Tharpe: 'This Train', NY, 1 Jul 1947, Decca 48043 (78rpm), NY, 1947. Little Walter: 'My Babe', Chicago, 25 Jan 1955, Checker 811, Chicago, 1955.]

'This Wheel's on Fire' [1967] See 'wheels of fire'.

Thomas, Henry [c.1874 - c.1930?] The biography of Henry 'Ragtime Texas' Thomas remains shadowy, though the once-general suggestion that he was born around 1874 seems to have firmed up into a definite date. A birthplace of Big Sandy, East Texas (a small town about 40 miles west of Shreveport, Louisiana), has also been claimed less and less tentatively, and that he was one of nine children and ran away from home to avoid farm-work.

The date 1874 fits well with his 19th century repertoire. He would have been in his early 50s by the time he recorded (which was always in Chicago), and one of his last recordings, 'Railroadin' Some', does offer a travel itinerary that is likely to be based on his own experience; in Dave Oliphant's words it 'includes Texas towns like Rockwall, Greenville (with its infamous sign, "Land of the Blackest Earth and the Whitest People"), Denison, Grand Saline, Silver Lake, Mineola, Tyler . . . Longview, Jefferson, Marshall, Little Sandy, and his birthplace of Big Sandy.'

Tony Russell's finely sculpted paragraph on Henry Thomas in *The Blues—From Robert Johnson to Robert Cray*, 1997, says that his 'springy guitar-playing, probably inspired by banjo-picking styles, implies that he was used to catering for dancers. Practically uniquely among Southern musicians of his time, he also played the quill, or panpipes, which lent his music a fairy lilt.' Russell adds that 'LEADBELLY's apart, no recordings are more revealing about black recreational music in the late 19th century than the couple of dozen reels, rags, minstrel songs and blues' he left. The musician John Fahey has said in passing that Thomas also 'apparently used to play a lot of kids' birthday parties'.

The crucial 1952 anthology *AMERICAN FOLK MUSIC* includes two tracks by Henry Thomas—the last track of the whole collection is his 'Fishing Blues' from 1928—but neither of these is 'Honey Just Allow Me One More Chance', which Dylan includes on *Freewheelin'*—'first heard from a recording by a now-dead Texas blues singer', as Nat Hentoff's 1963 sleevenotes reported.

That Thomas recording, made in Chicago in 1927, may have been heard by Dylan on the original 78 issued by Vocalion but the likelihood is that he heard it on *Henry Thomas Sings the Texas Blues*, issued by the Origin Jazz Library, for a while the most important of the reissue labels, and active at the beginning of the 1960s. This album was issued in 1961 (in a limited edition of 500 copies). Dylan was performing 'Honey Just Allow Me One More Chance' by April 1962.

Paul Oliver, investigating the origins of both songs in *Songsters and Saints*, 1984, reports that 'Honey' was field-collected for folk-song collector Dorothy Scarborough by Mrs. Tom Bartlett from Marlin, Texas, that her transcription 'corresponded closely' to the Henry Thomas version, that possibly Mrs. Bartlett got it from Thomas himself, and that it was also recorded by (the far more obscure) Archie Lewis.

Folksong collectors seem to have been onto Henry Thomas for 'Fishing Blues' too. Oliver writes: 'Another Texas collector, the historian Walter Prescott Webb, published a number of song fragments "obtained from a Gatesville negro named 'Rags'." They included a verse of "If You Go Fishing" which was virtually identical to Henry Thomas's "Fishing Blues". Gatesville lies some fifty miles to the west of Marlin and it is tempting to think that "Rags" was none other than "Ragtime Texas"—Henry Thomas.'

(Oliver suggests that Thomas toned down the sexual suggestiveness of the lyric for his recording. HARRY SMITH, commenting on the Henry Thomas song in his sleevenotes to the *American Folk Music* anthology, cites 'Fishing Blues' by MEMPHIS MIN-

NIE as being an allied composition, and notes that 'references to fishing, other than as sexual symbolism, are rare in American folk music'. Dylan introduced his *Under the Red Sky* song 'Wiggle Wiggle' as a song about fishing at several European concerts in 1991. In Ljubljana, in what was then Yugoslavia, on June 10, he said: 'This song is off my last record. It's all about fish. In a pond.' Next night in Belgrade: 'Here's one of my fishing songs'. And three nights later in Linz, Austria: 'Here's a song about going fishing.')

A neat postscript to the matter of Dylan's knowledge of these songs emerged in 1994, with the first circulation of a fragment of studio session with GEORGE HARRISON from the beginning of May 1970, soon after Dylan has been recording some of *Self Portrait*. It's interesting because Dylan recalls *both* songs. A voice that sounds like producer BOB JOHNSTON prompts Dylan, saying he wants to hear 'a song that had "Mama" in it, or something, that you did . . .' and Dylan starts singing, country style, 'I'm a-goin' fishin' all the time . . . I'm a-goin' fishin', you're a-goin' fishin', I'm a-goin' fishin' too'. The tune is so reminiscent of 'Honey' that at this point Johnston says 'No—"one kind of favour I'll ask a-you"!' and Dylan retorts 'Oh, yeah. . . . Same guy!'—and then sings a pleasant country version of 'Honey Just Allow Me One More Chance'.

'Fishing Blues' was revived by the Holy Modal Rounders, Lovin' Spoonful and Taj Mahal. Canned Heat's asthmatic 'Goin' Up the Country' was a clumsy imitation of Thomas' sound.

The place, date and circumstances of Henry Thomas' death are all unknown, though the year 1930 has been suggested. The claim that he was seen still playing on the streets of Tyler, Texas, in the 1950s is also being retailed with increasing confidence, though it seems highly unlikely. Thomas would have been in his late 70s or even older by then.

The CD *Henry Thomas: Texas Worried Blues* collects all 23 of his recordings, and offers extensive notes by blues expert Stephen Calt. Oliphant quotes blues historian William Barlow's judgement that 'Railroadin' Some' is the most 'vivid and intense recollection of railroading' in all the early blues recorded in the 1920s. Certainly his anxious, warm voice on the incantatory 'Don't Ease Me In', which has one of the world's catchiest melodies, makes this one of history's indispensable records.

[Henry Thomas: 'Honey, Won't You Allow Me Just One More Chance?' Chicago, 7 Oct 1927, *Henry Thomas Sings the Texas Blues*, Origin Jazz Library OJL-3, NY, 1961; 'Fishing Blues', Chicago, 13 Jun 1928, *American Folk Music*, Folkways FP 251–253, NY, 1952, CD-reissued *Anthology of American Folk Music*, Smithsonian Folkways SRW 40090, Washington, D.C., 1997 (incl. booklet with John Fahey quote p.11); 'Don't Ease Me In', Chicago, 13 Jun 1928; all on *Henry Thomas: Texas Worried Blues*, Yazoo 1080–81, US, 1990.

Bob Dylan: 'Honey Just Allow Me One More Chance', NY, Apr 1962 (album version NY, 9 Jul 1962). Archie Lewis: 'Honey, 'Low Me One More Chance', Richmond, IN, 30 Mar 1933. Memphis Minnie: 'Fishin' Blues', NY, 3 Feb 1932. Bob Dylan: 'Fishing Blues' (fragment) and 'Honey Just Allow Me One More Chance', NY, 1–2 May 1970, unreleased; tape circulated 1994.

Dave Oliphant, *Handbook of Texas Online*, s.v. 'Thomas, Henry (Ragtime Texas)', *www.tsha.utexas.edu/handbook/online/articles/TT/fthxc.html*, seen online 8 Oct 2005.]

Thompson, Hunter S. [1937 - 2005] Born in Louisville, Kentucky, on July 18, 1937, Hunter Stockton Thompson was the rock'n'roller's Tom Wolfe, the first and best Gonzo Journalist. Beginning as an irreverent and wildly articulate sports journalist after a brief spell in gaol, service in the US Air Force and attendance at Columbia University, he published a de-mythologising book about the Hell's Angels, based on first-hand encounters (in some cases with those to whom he introduced LSD).

In his 30s he began to have his work published in *Rolling Stone*, and in the course of a long association with that paper, beginning and thriving when it was San Francisco-based and its heart still counter-cultural, he invented and developed the outrageous yet essentially morally outraged alter ego, Raoul Duke. Appointed *Rolling Stone*'s Political Correspondent, he reported the Nixon versus McGovern 1972 election from the heart of the McGovern campaign, and his immensely lengthy pieces thrust himself into the centre of his reportage.

By his style, passion, humour and vividly conveyed sense of horror, he captured and magnified, perhaps even helped to develop, a hip public's sense of rabid disgust at the politics and politicians of Amerika. Watergate was made for him, and he declared that Richard Nixon represented 'that dark, venal and incurably violent side of the American character.' (Actually, he almost had a soft spot for Richard Nixon, though Nixon is unlikely to have discerned inside the coruscating vitriol poured over him by Thompson's prose).

His reports turned into books, as with *Fear and Loathing: On the Campaign Trail '72* and later, sometimes collaborating with British cartoonist Ralph Steadman, came books that were mostly collections of articles, letters and essays, among them *The Great Shark Hunt*, *Generation of Swine*, *Songs of the Doomed*, *Better Than Sex*, *The Fear and Loathing Letters, Vol. 1: The Proud Highway* and his last work, *Hey Rube: Blood Sport, the Bush Doctrine, and the Downward Spiral of Dumbness*.

His masterpiece, though, and the work that preceded *On the Campaign Trail*, was *Fear and Loathing in Las Vegas*, published in book form at the end of 1971, which charmed and captivated a generation right from its combative and seductive opening sentence: 'We were somewhere around Barstow on the edge of the desert when the drugs began to take hold.'

There are striking connections and correspondences between this great early 1970s prose work and the Bob Dylan of 1966—especially the Dylan of 'Stuck Inside of Mobile with the Memphis Blues Again'. See separate entry for these.

Two attempts were made to film the unfilmable: *Where the Buffalo Roam* in 1980, starring Bill Murray, and the far less wretched *Fear and Loathing in Las Vegas*, 1998, Johnny Depp as the hero narrator. It's often mentioned that he appears in Gary Trudeau's tedious Doonesbury comic strip; more interesting is his being the model for actor/cartoonist Scott Shaw's anthropomorphic dog, Pointer X. Toxin, and for Spider Jerusalem in the comic series 'Transmetropolitan' by Warren Ellis and Darik Robertson.

Hunter Thompson produced little in his later years, and perhaps succumbed more fully to the gun-toting, paranoid drug-soaked nightmares than was useful, even to the man whose motto (the tagline for the film *Where the Buffalo Roam*) was 'I hate to advocate weird chemicals, alcohol, violence or insanity to anyone, but they've always worked for me.' He accidentally shot his assistant Deborah Fuller while chasing a bear on his property in 2000. In 1998, long reliant on his past work, he even published his (previously unpublished) first novel, *The Rum Diary*, written almost 40 years earlier in 1959 (also being turned into a film starring Johnny Depp).

He had long been an unreconstructed (and non-counter-cultural) member of the National Rifle Association and using one of his guns on February 20, 2005, he committed suicide at his fortified compound of a home near Aspen, Colorado. He was 67. Exactly six months later, in accordance with his wishes and at a cost of $2.5 million, met by Depp, his ashes were fired into the night sky from a cannon on his farm.

Dylan was rumoured to be going to attend, but didn't (of course). Nonetheless he was present through his work. It's said that after the ceremony's participants played the 1969 Norman Greenbaum anthem 'Spirit in the Sky' very loudly ('When they lay me down to die / Going on up to the spirit in the sky') and listened to Japanese ceremonial drummers and Buddhist readings in Tibetan, the rocket launch and fireworks display was followed by a Dylan recording of 'Mr. Tambourine Man', the song Hunter Thompson had said prompted him to co-dedicate *Fear and Loathing in Las Vegas* to Bob Dylan.

[Hunter S. Thompson: *Hell's Angels: A Strange and Terrible Saga*, New York: Ballantine, 1966. *Fear and Loathing in Las Vegas* began as a sprawling serialisation: 'Fear and Loathing in Las Vegas', by 'Raoul Duke', *Rolling Stone* nos.95 & 96, San Francisco, 11 & 25 Nov 1971; in book form *Fear and Loathing in Las Vegas: A Savage Journey to the Heart of the American Dream*, New York: Random House, 1971. *Fear and Loathing: On the Campaign Trail '72*, San Francisco: Straight Arrow Books, 1973. *Gonzo Papers, Vol. 1: The Great Shark Hunt: Strange Tales from a Strange Time*, New York: Summit Books, 1979. *Gonzo Papers, Vol. 2: Generation of Swine: Tales of Shame and Degradation in the '80s*, New York: Summit Books, 1988. *Gonzo Papers, Vol. 3: Songs of the Doomed: More Notes on the Death of the American Dream*, New York: Summit Books, 1990. *Gonzo Papers, Vol. 4: Better Than Sex: Confessions of a Political Junkie*, New York: Random House, 1994. *The Fear and Loathing Letters, Vol. 1: The Proud Highway: The Saga of a Desperate Southern Gentleman 1955–1967*, New York: Random House, 1997. *The Rum Diary: The Long Lost Novel (1959)*, New York: Simon & Schuster, 1999. Films: *Where the Buffalo Roam*, dir. Art Linson (with tiny appearances from NEIL YOUNG and David Briggs), Universal Pictures, US, 1980; and *Fear and Loathing in Las Vegas*, dir. Terry Gilliam, Fear and Loathing LLC/Rhino Films/Shark Productions/Summit Entertainment/Universal Pictures, 1998.]

Thompson, Richard [1949 -] Richard John Thompson was born in London on April 3, 1949, learnt the guitar and became a co-founder of Fairport Convention, whose members had left school only at the beginning of the magical summer of 1967. They comprised Simon Nicol, Ashley 'Tyger' Hutchings and Thompson, whose day-job was making stained glass windows (thus adding an aura of William Morrisonian arts-and-craftsmanship to his persona); their repertoire was not folk but folk-rock—contemporary West Coast and Dylan-inspired music—and at their first gig, in a church hall in Golders Green, North London, Martin Lamble got up from the audience to ask to be their drummer. They added not just him but vocalist Judy Dyble, a local librarian, went on to play in the city's new underground club scene and, spotted there by Joe Boyd, signed to a record deal and began to make a series of landmark albums and undergo a series of convulsive line-up changes.

Richard Thompson stayed through a number of both, his first composition to be recorded being 'Meet on the Ledge', issued as a single and included on *What We Did on Our Holidays*. He was therefore part of their important albums *Unhalfbricking*, *Liege and Lief* and 1970's *Full House*. Scattered through these albums were several Dylan songs, chosen in part for their relative obscurity as well as for their intrinsic appeal. Notably they cut Brit versions of 'Percy's Song' and 'I'll Keep It With Mine', and 'Si Tu Dois Partir', a French language version of 'If You Gotta Go, Go Now', which, also issued as a single, gave them a hit.

Thompson left the group at the height of their fame, prompted by Joe Boyd's re-location to the US West Coast, making a shrewd but surprise move into doing the rounds of folk clubs, grounding his improving songwriting in this grittier world without in any way renouncing his interest in rock but rather continuing his insistence that folk and rock went perfectly well together. Not everyone, of course, agreed, and there was a quiet English equivalent of the confrontational drama of Dylan's 'going electric' shortly after midnight on New Year's Eve 1972, when Thompson had temporarily joined the second line-up of the fairly informal grouping the Albion Country Band and they were playing in a London club, the Howff. This electric guitar, bass and drums group was joined on stage by some Morris dancers, a surprising but mutually congenial alliance that anticipated by 30 years the contemporary British folk emphasis on re-exploring folk *dance*, and so the rehabilitating of that much-maligned and long-scorned figure, the Morris dancer. *But*, inspired by this, Thompson then cranked up his electric guitar and lit into a bit of CHUCK BERRY—only to find Ashley Hutchings pulling out the plugs in a rage and vanishing into the New Year's night with them.

Thompson went back to playing solo—except that after his début solo album, *Henry the Human Fly*, he toured and made six albums with his vocalist wife Linda (née Peters), beginning with what many still regard as the best of all Richard Thompson's albums, *I Want to See the Bright Lights Tonight*, and typifying the way that he can alchemise into a unique whole the disparate elements of narrative coherence, intangible darkness and a guitar built of iron. Energised by the album's success, Thompson returned to the rock circuit. Since the Thompsons' divorce, Richard has continued to write and record, and to build his formidable career and reputation.

This is sufficiently heavyweight that it tends to elbow aside the prolific work that Thompson also achieved as a sideman on other people's albums. In more recent decades this may have been less significant but in the late 1960s and 1970s, he played on many landmark records, among them the Incredible String Band's *The Hangman's Beautiful Daughter* (1968), Nick Drake's *Five Leaves Left* (1969), Al Stewart's *Love Chronicles* (1970) and John Martyn's *Solid Air* (1972).

Thompson has clearly been influenced by Dylan's work, as he has readily acknowledged, though he has been, for three decades now, so much his own man and artist—so distinctive and authoritative and English a figure, and with his own mix of diffidence and haughty gravitas—that it's unproductive to make comparisons after the early 1970s. And before then, the comparisons can only be invidious. That is, you can pluck 'Dylanesque' lines out of Thompson's earlyish songs, but only to see in them the sort of embarrassing imitations that so many people came up with once upon a time. In Thompson's 'Genesis Hall', on the 1969 Fairport Convention album *Unhalfbricking*, for example, we find this pallid and portentous 'It's All Over Now, Baby Blue' imitation shivering in its own embarrassment: 'The gipsy who begs for your presents / He will laugh in your face when you're old'; but it's ill-mannered even to remember such things in the face of the immensely strong body of obdurately individual work carved out since by one of Britain's greatest musical figures.

It's easy to form the impression, indeed, that the matured Richard Thompson finds Dylan far too unskilled a musician to be regarded with much interest or respect: an impression not altogether contradicted by his comments in an interview included in a box set of his own work. 'Dylan', he says carefully, 'was an influence on everyone. It was obvious that some of his music was very traditional in its source, so there is a link there. Fairport recorded a lot of obscure Dylan songs.' The interviewer says: 'You played with him in Seville'—which indeed they did: at the Guitar Legends Festival on October 17, 1991—and Thompson answers, more in guarded self-defence than with any detectable enthusiasm: 'That came about because we were both part of something called The Night of the Guitar. I was asked if I'd play guitar with him. I knew the songs we were going to do though we hadn't really rehearsed. But he was a bit out of tune; his guitar was about a tone flat or something. So I spent the first number retuning.'

[Richard Thompson: *Henry the Human Fly*, Island ILPS 9197, UK, 1972. Richard & Linda Thompson: *I Want to See the Bright Lights Tonight*, Island ILPS 9266, 1974. Fairport Convention: *Fairport Convention*, Polydor 583 035, UK, 1968; 'Meet on the Ledge', Island WIP 6047, UK, 1968; *What We Did on Our Holidays*, Island ILPS 9092, 1969; 'Si Tu Dois Partir' c/w 'Genesis Hall', Island WIP 6064, 1969; *Unhalfbricking*, Island ILPS 9102, 1969; *Liege and Lief*, Island ILPS 9115, 1969; *Full House*, Island ILPS 9130, 1970. Bob Dylan backed by Thompson: 'Boots of Spanish Leather', 'Across the Borderline' and 'Answer Me (My Love)'; Dylan backed by Thompson & others: 'All Along the Watchtower'; all Seville, 17 Oct 1991.

Richard Thompson quoted from Nigel Schofield's interview inside the Thompson box set. Discographical detail from David Suff's 1997 listing seen online 1 Dec 2005 at *www.thebeesknees.com/bk-rt-d1.html*. Thompson is also the subject of a detailed biography by Patrick Humphries, *Richard Thompson: Strange Affair—the Biography*, London: Virgin, 1996.]

Thompson, Toby [1944 -] Toby Thompson was born in Washington, D.C., on September 15, 1944 (but 'conceived in New York City in war time'), the son of a Washington physician and a Manhattan ex-model whose brother, William Nicholls, wrote and produced 'Your Hit Parade', the MTV of its day but aired live from Manhattan, visiting the set for which gave young Toby a whiff of the possibilities of glamour, though not his first. His parents' house was open to many artists and show-biz people. 'As an infant I crawled beneath the piano while Aaron Copland polished his symphonies.... Boris Karloff tickled my toes.... When I was five, the painter Max Ernst took one of my watercolors, "Girl with Sunburnt Lips", and refused to give it back.'

Thompson is talking here from within the comfortable, sophisticated milieu of an associate professor of English at Penn State University, where he now teaches non-fiction writing, while retaining an apartment in New York City. It is a tone of voice he certainly managed to throw off in 1971 in his invaluable drongo paperback *Positively Main Street: An Unorthodox View of Bob Dylan*, about visiting Hibbing and interviewing Bob Dylan's relatives and friends.

For most people, it came out of nowhere—a breathless cavalcade of slightly off-kilter but delirious revelation back when most of Dylan's background and family history was an almost total mystery thanks largely to a good ten years' worth of myth-making and bare-faced lying on the part of the artist himself. Thompson's style at the time was a kind of juvenile version of the new journalism: if Tom Wolfe was this school's headmaster and HUNTER S. THOMPSON its boisterous head boy, Toby Thompson was the milk monitor.

In fact, Thompson's material had not come out of nowhere. The material he'd gathered from his first trip up to Hibbing, Minnesota, was published initially as series of articles in the *Village Voice*, starting in March 1969, and when this was fresh on the newsstands, he made a second trip, on which he collected ECHO HELSTROM from Minneapolis and they drove back up to Hibbing together in his red Volkswagen. En route they pulled over and she showed him Big Sandy Lake, where she and Bob had often parked. They went on up into Hibbing, went to the bar that is now named Zimmy's, heard live music, danced ...

The book was intrusive, audacious, fumbling and as subtle as a Woodstock Nation burger. Written as if on Kleenex by its author's adenoids, it was endearingly clumsy and gauche and essential reading. Thompson, unprecedentedly, managed to interview not only Echo Helstrom, almost certainly the 'Girl of the North Country', but Dylan's mother and brother, his uncle, his friends ... and to publish them 15 years before ROBERT SHELTON was ready. Dylan himself read the *Village Voice* pieces in early 1969 and told *Rolling Stone* that November: 'That boy—this fellow Toby—has got some lessons to learn.'

Thompson, you would not have guessed from his prose, had actually taken his lessons alongside Al Gore and John Kerry at St. Albans Episcopal school in Washington, D.C., made frequent pilgrimages to the graveside of F. Scott Fitzgerald at Rockville, Maryland, and later gained a BA in English Literature from the University of Delaware and an MA from the University of Virginia—all this before writing *Positively Main Street*. Since then he's written *Saloon* (1976) and *The 60's Report* (1979), and though he's published no further books in the last quarter century he's written for a slew of magazines and journals and is a long-term contributing editor to *Big Sky Journal*, in Bozeman, Montana.

Today's sophisticat version of Thompson manages to claim both that there was no assumed gulf, and that there was, between the suave man of letters and the Toby T who visits Hibbing and reports back:

> 'I like the book. It's got a smart-alecky tone that fits its time and the age of its author and protagonist, who'd just turned 24. It's also cannier than it seems. It's a meta-book. I'd studied modern literature ... and was aware of both the postmodern tradition, where experimentation rules, and that of the 19th century Bildungsroman, or novel of initiation—where a young hero set out against impossible odds, acts foolishly or ineptly, but confronts his enemies or the dragon, then returns home sadder, wiser. I'd studied Freud and I'd studied ROBERT GRAVES' complicated poetic theory in *The White Goddess*. . . . I knew that in literature and psychology, one had to slay one's hero to become the hero. There was an oedipal tinge to this. To win the queen, and sleep with her, one must kill the king.'

Thirty-five years on and he still wants us all to know that he slept with Echo Helstrom.

A harmonica playing friend introduced Thompson to Dylan's music in 1962, he says: a John Kerkam with whom Toby played blues 'at a club called the Zen Den, in Rehoboth Beach, Delaware. He'd hung out in Greenwich Village, had a friend who'd studied guitar with REVEREND GARY DAVIS and was in the know. "You ought to hear this cat, Bob Dylan," Kerkam said. . . . Dylan's first album was out and. . . . I was impressed with the roughness of his blues arrangements. . . . I didn't notice his writing until the second album, *Freewheelin'*. There it was unavoidable. It's hard now to reconstruct the power those lyrics held.'

Reminded that before *Positively Main Street* the only Dylan book had been *Folk Rock: The Bob Dylan Story* by SY & BARBARA RIBAKOVE, which was, in TERRY KELLY's phrase, 'mainly drawn from the cuttings file', Thompson responds: 'There were also DANIEL KRAMER's photography book, and the insights provided by the film *Don't Look Back*. I'd read Bob's *Playboy* interview, and Nat Hentoff's early *New Yorker* profile of him. But there was this gap in Dylanology, to use a term that did not exist. He was in seclusion in Woodstock and writers were intimidated by his disdain for the press. And by his power.'

Toby the dragon-slayer soon sorted that out. He even got Echo's father to be nicer to him than he'd ever been to the original Bob: 'They enjoyed me, particularly the father. "He likes you 'cause you're fair," Echo said. Meaning blond. They held a Sunday cookout for me and I played and sang a lot of Bob's songs. Including "Girl of the North Country". It was confusing for them, I think.' And the more so for Toby, it begins to sound. 'My theatricality and boyish enthusiasm made them feel as if Bob had come home, in some way. To use Graves' terminology, I seemed Bob's "blood brother, his other self, his weird." Everybody's feelings on that were decidedly mixed.' Yes indeed.

[Toby Thompson, *Positively Main Street: An Unorthodox View of Bob Dylan*, New York: Coward McCann & Geoghegan, 1971; London: New English Library, Jan 1972, reprint Mar 1972; but first trip material (first 13 sections of the book) published as series of articles, *Village Voice*, starting 20 Mar 1969; *Saloon*, New York: Viking/Grossman, 1976; *The 60's Report*, New York: Rawson Wade, 1979. All quotes from interview by Terry Kelly, conducted Jan 2005, published in *The Bridge* no.21, Tyne & Wear, UK, spring 2005.]

***Time Out of Mind* [1997]** It seemed astonishing that the general media world took *Time Out of Mind* to its fickle bosom so fulsomely. The whole public mood of the 1980s and 90s had been smile-smile-smile, never admit to gloom or despondency, never complain, and if you want to get ahead, be remorselessly *upbeat*! The Tina Turner Syndrome, in fact. In this climate, people were regarded as from the lunatic fringe if they insisted on saying that Bob Dylan was a seminal artist of the times and absolutely invaluable as a bulwark against Shopping Mall culture. Those of 'balanced' views and 'living in the contemporary world' spoke of Dylan with dismissive contempt as 1960s Man, a hopeless old has-been of no relevance whatever and whose talents, it went without saying, had vanished a good 20 years ago.

Then along came *Time Out of Mind*, the gloomiest, most desolate, least Tina-Turner-Princess-Di-David-Letterman-ELTON-JOHN record in human history . . . and suddenly it was 'Well of course we've known all along that Bob Dylan was a genius and a Great American Institution who could come back at any time with a work that would snuggle straight into that special place in our hearts we've always kept open for him: and here it is!'

It was a pleasure to see Dylan on the front of *Newsweek* and giving such relaxed, honest and interesting interviews, standing behind this new work with unaccustomed straightforwardness—even with that cover photo by Richard Avedon (whose pictures GREIL MARCUS once called 'the curse of rock') making Dylan look like a hairy LEONARD COHEN—but it was exasperating to be preached at by the *Sunday Times* in 1997 about how important an artist Dylan is, after exactly that kind of broadsheet had spent the previous two decades deriding him and anyone who had kept faith with him.

It was especially exasperating when this unusually lengthy album first arrived and the decade's most important collection of new Bob Dylan compositions (almost its only one) seemed riddled with lazy writing and lumpen music bordering on the kind of nightclub jazz that, almost four decades earlier, many of us had looked to Bob Dylan to vanquish ('Million Miles', ''Til I Fell in Love With You', 'Can't Wait'), plus the kind of rock that wins Grammies but makes you wish he'd stick to ballads ('Cold Irons Bound') and the kind of ballad that makes you wish he wouldn't ('Make You Feel My Love').

The album marked a return to the multi-layered production techniques of DANIEL LANOIS, giving it a cohesive sound (disrupted only by the mediocre rockabilly of 'Dirt Road Blues') which complemented Dylan's dour elegy, epitomised by 'Not Dark Yet'. What made all this compelling was not its sententious claims to shrivelled pessimism but its very human confessional quality and its intimate flashes of humour. The album was also experimental in its then-unprecedented use of lines from other songs, a usage much extended on *"Love and Theft"*, the studio album that followed.

Time Out of Mind brings out more variation in response than almost any other Dylan album. For many, many people, it is one of his *great* works, and held, for instance, to be far superior to *"Love and Theft"*. For others, anyone who *really* appreciates Dylan must see that the true assessment is the other way around. What achieves more general agreement is that *Time Out of Mind* offers no less than four major songs: 'Standing in the Doorway', 'Tryin' to Get to Heaven', 'Not Dark Yet' and the magnificent 'Highlands', an audacious 16½ minutes long and the inspired creative high on which the album ends: a song that is an inventive mix of splendidly off-the-wall talking blues and visionary rhapsody.

[Recorded Miami, 13–27 Jan 1997; released on CD as Columbia CK 68556, 27 or 30 Sep 1997 (UK vinyl version 2-LP set Columbia COL 486936 1, 1998).

Newsweek, NY, 6 Oct 1997; the same issue contained an interview with James Meredith, the first black student at the University of Mississippi, whose riot-causing enrolment in 1962 was the subject of Dylan's early song 'Oxford Town'; 35 years on he was working for Right-Wing Republican Senator Jesse Helms, and a Fellow at the Leadership Institute, Washington, D.C., *Sunday Times*, London, 28 Sep 1997.]

***Times They Are a-Changin', The* [album, 1964]** This third album was less of a leap forward, but was again a solo album, this time mainly of stark 'protest' songs, all written by Dylan, though often with adapted folk melodies. Like his second album, it contained songs that have achieved classic status: particularly the title track and 'With God on Our Side'. It also includes the love song 'One Too Many Mornings', a song that should have served notice on Dylan's early cult followers (most of whom were students and liberals who considered themselves radicals, hated pop music and wore Dylan on their sleeves like a political armband) that Dylan was not just going to be a graphic protest-singer. But many seemed not to notice, so that the next album came as a shock to them.

[Recorded NY, 6–7 Aug, 23–24 & 31 Oct 1963; released as LP Columbia CL 2105 (mono) & CS 8905 (stereo), (in UK CBS BPG 62251 mono, and SBPG 62251 stereo), 13 Jan or 10 Feb 1964; CD released Jan 1989.]

'Times They Are a-Changin', The' [song, 1963] The first time a lot of pop fans noticed Dylan was when the 'The Times They Are a-Changin'' came out as a single in 1964. To pop-trained ears, it was a laughable record. The singer had a voice that made Johnny Duncan and the Blue Grass Boys sound like Mario Lanza—and plainly, he hadn't even the most elementary sense of timing. He brought in the second syllable of that title word 'Changin'' far too soon: at a quite ridiculous point. What was the record company playing at? Just because Bob Dylan was the writer of an interesting song called 'Blowin' in the Wind' didn't mean he could expect to start singing all his other songs himself . . . To others, the striking thing was that here was someone who wasn't just pop-singing, but truly communicating.

But communicating what? 'The Times They Are a-Changin'' was the archetypal protest song. Dylan's aim was to ride upon the unvoiced sentiment of a mass public—to give that inchoate sentiment an anthem and give its clamour an outlet. He succeeded, but the language of the song is nevertheless imprecisely and very generally directed. It offers four extended metaphors, and makes no more than an easy politician's use of any of them. The four are: change as a rising tide; change dependent on the wheel of fate; the Establishment as an edifice; and yesterday and tomorrow as roads to be opted for. People enjoy the song to the extent that they approve of its theory. It has none of the warmth and personal impetus, and its metaphors deploy none of the fresh and vivid detail, that we find in that other Dylan song of the same period and much the same thrust, the lovely 'When the Ship Comes In'—a song so under-attended by its writer.

It's perhaps a surprise, looking back, to see how late on in Dylan's political songwriting 'The Times They Are a-Changin'' occurs. There is no extant recording or performance of it before he offered it as a Witmark music-publishing demo in October 1963, and the earliest attempts in the Columbia studios were on the 23rd and 24th of that month (the latter yielding the version that became the title song of the third album, and the hit single). In other words, 'The Times They Are a-Changin'' came not only long after 'Blowin' in the Wind' but also later than 'A Hard Rain's a-Gonna Fall', 'Oxford Town', 'Masters of War', 'Let Me Die in My Footsteps', 'The Death of Emmett Till', 'Paths of Victory', 'North Country Blues', 'Ballad of Hollis Brown', 'Playboys and Playgirls', 'Talkin' John Birch Paranoid Blues', 'Who Killed Davey Moore?', 'Only a Pawn in Their Game', 'When the Ship Comes In', 'John Brown', 'Only a Hobo', 'With God on Our Side' and more besides.

'The Times They Are a-Changin'' was prophetic of the imminent future—but it has been outdated by the very changes the song itself gleefully threatened. Its message is politically out of date. 'Mothers and fathers throughout the land' are as ready as ever to criticise what they don't understand, though no-one any longer listens; meanwhile people who want change have rightly lost the optimism of expecting senators and congressmen to heed their political calls, and the revolution has been lost.

The Bob Dylan of the late 1970s fully acknowledged that the changing of the times had dated his song about them. When he sang it, for the first time in 13 years, on his 1978 tour, he re-interpreted it as a sad, slow admission of his generation's failure. This version appears on the 'live' album *Bob Dylan at Budokan*, where there is even the inspired touch of a Duane Eddy guitar-sound to emphasise the song's anachrony. Better still is the acoustic version performed on the 1981 tour, as heard for example on the widely circulated bootleg *Hanging in the Balance*, which captures the arresting performance Dylan gives in Bad Segeberg, (West) Germany, on July 14. Without altering a word but with a divergent set of chords, Dylan effectively reverses the song's meaning, making it a sad memorial to vanished hopes.

Unfortunately he hasn't left it at that, but has performed it without end in the years since, and though occasional renditions have had their own minor attractions (at Houston in 1981, the mangling of words produced the irrational but splendid 'you'll be drenched like a bone'), the song has essentially become a meaningless Greatest Hit. This process reaches its demeaning nadir on Dylan's *MTV Unplugged™*, where the audience whoops and hollers its indiscriminate keenness as Dylan sings 'The Times They Are a-Changin'' so badly that, as Andy Gill comments, it's 'as if he's tried to do so many different versions he's simply lost track of how best to sing it, accenting words and phrases almost randomly, as if successive words were set in different typefaces and font sizes,' while those in the crowd 'applaud each successive indignity as a brilliant new interpretation'.

Dropping it would show more integrity. Leasing its use for finance and banking industry TV adverts shows none (see **Coopers & Lybrand**), and leads to the further indignity of advertising women's underwear. Not for this were the old and indecisive to get out of the doorway and unblock the hall for the times to be a-changed.

[Bob Dylan: 'The Times They Are a-Changin'', Witmark demo NY, Oct 1963, issued *Bootleg Series Vols. 1–3*, 1991; version NY, 23 Oct 1963 unissued; version at Houston, TX, 12 Nov 1981. Andy Gill: review of Dylan's *MTV Unplugged* in *Q* magazine, no.105, London, Jun 1995.]

***Titanic*, the** The most immediately vivid of the many evocations of impending catastrophe given in the lyric of the final song on *Highway 61 Revisited*, 'Desolation Row', is achieved very simply, in the one arresting line 'The *Titanic* sails at dawn.' Dylan takes the *Titanic* to represent contemporary America: for *RMS Titanic* was the ship of the future, the 'proof' of man's civilisation and progress, the unsinkable ship which, on her maiden voyage, sank. And, according to the best stories, when the ship began to sink the passengers refused to believe it was happening. The palm-court orchestra kept playing and the people in the ballroom danced obliviously on. Using the doomed ship's symbolic clout, Dylan explores the different kinds of oblivion and denial in America—the various ways in which the dancing continues.

The facts are slightly different. Sailing from Southampton on April 10, 1912 (not at dawn), bound for New York, the *Titanic* sank after hitting an iceberg off Newfoundland on the night of 14–15, with the loss of probably 1,513 lives out of 2,207 (exact figures are still disputed). The 'orchestra' was in fact a quintet that played everything from Offenbach to ragtime; as the ship sank, it did not remain below but played up on deck. The last number was almost certainly not 'Nearer My God to Thee', as in myth, but the hymn 'Autumn'. (Third class had to provide their own music, and mustered an Irish piper and a fiddler.)

'God Himself could not sink this ship,' a woman passenger had been told. It took ten seconds' contact with the iceberg to start disproving this claim, but two hours 40 minutes to sink the ship. As Michael Davie notes (in *The Titanic: The Full Story of a Tragedy*, 1986), the tragedy 'was also man-made, the result of a state of mind—grandiose, avaricious and self-confident'. Tellingly, too, '34 per cent of male first-class passengers [were] saved . . . 8 per cent of second-class . . . 12 per cent in third . . . death and disaster were not such great levellers after all.' On the other hand, 354 crew survived, compared to 351 passengers.

It was not just Dylan who used the ship as a symbol of an America headed for a fall. The *Titanic*'s extra significance is expressed in a number of blues songs exactly because black Americans relished it as a symbol of whitey's come-uppance—and Dylan, knowing this, is able to re-use the *Titanic* in a later song of his own that is enriched by the resonance of these blues songs that long pre-date his own work: indeed to draw on them so deftly and subtlely that he has no need actually to *name* the ship at all this second time around. The song is 1981's 'Caribbean Wind' (issued on *Biograph*, 1985), and some of the auguries of its 'tearin' down of the walls' are alluded to when Dylan sings that outside the narrator's window the 'Street band [is] playing "Nearer My God to Thee".' This line offers not only an allusion to the meaning-loaded *event* of the sinking of the *Titanic*, but also to the group of blues songs that arose to celebrate or commemorate it. We see this at once upon encountering one such blues, Hi Henry Brown's 'Titanic Blues', wherein Brown summarises the mythic moment that still lives in the popular imagination: 'Titanic sinking in the deep blue sea / And the band all playing "Nearer My God to Thee".'

Others to record songs about the *Titanic* include RICHARD RABBIT BROWN, whose 'Sinking of the Titanic' was recorded in a New Orleans garage on the same day as his immortal 'James Alley Blues', and shares with Dylan's 'Caribbean Wind' the citing of the hymn-title within its own lyric. Brown sings: 'The music played as they went down / On that dark blue sea / And you could hear the sound of that familiar hymn / Singin' "Nearer My God to Thee'".

(This myth was still being perpetuated as recently as the 1980s. In *The Lion Book of Favourite Hymns*, 1980, for instance, Christopher Idle claims as fact that as the *Titanic* began to tilt, 'Baptist minister John Harper asked the band to play "Nearer, my God, to thee." It was the last hymn in the lives of hundreds of people.')

Delight at the sinking of the Titanic, because it signified the come-uppance of human vanity and of the powerful, was not restricted to black Americans. The Russian symbolist poet Alexander Blok wrote: 'The sinking of the *Titanic* has made me indescribably happy; there is, after all, an ocean.'

Finally, in one of the lyric variations within the recorded 'live' version of 'Caribbean Wind', the shadowy presence of the *Titanic* story is reconfirmed by the line 'And like they say, the ship will sail at dawn': with which Dylan brings us full circle. We recognise that not only do 'they say' so but that we've heard Dylan himself say, back on 'Desolation Row', that 'The Titanic sails at dawn.'

[Hi Henry Brown: 'Titanic Blues', NY, 14 Mar 1932, 1st vinyl issue *St. Louis Blues, 1929–1935: The Depression*, Yazoo L-1030, New York, c.1972; Richard Rabbit Brown: 'Sinking of the Titanic', New Orleans, 11 Mar 1927, *Nearer My God to Thee*, Roots RL-304, Vienna, 1968, CD-reissued *The Greatest Songsters: Complete Recorded Works (1927–1929)*, Document DOCD-5003, Vienna, 1990. Alexander Blok quoted in Peter Vansittart: *Voices 1870–1914*, 1984, p.xix. Bob Dylan: 'Caribbean Wind' ('live' version), San Francisco, 12 Nov 1980.]

Tolkien, J.R.R. [1892 - 1973] John Ronald Reuel Tolkien was born in Bloemfontein, South Africa, on January 3, 1892. His *Lord of the Rings* was first published in three volumes, 1954–55. Longer and more ambitious than *The Hobbit*, 1937, it is a work of fantasy fiction but grounded in Tolkien's huge knowledge of medieval languages, Anglo-Saxon literature and folklore. Its portrayal of an idealised rural England threatened with destruction by evil forces found favour in the 1960s among those who had grown up threatened by nuclear and environmental disaster. In consequence there was in subsequent years much modish derision (the easy sneer persists that it is hippie twaddle) of this vivid, absorbing work (one of those long books that you wish were longer still), which is of an imaginative quality far beyond the reach of most 'fantasy' novels. More recently, *Lord of the Rings* has been made into a series of three Hollywood blockbuster movies, and thus into an industry with its own proliferation of merchandising, which only removes us further from the shimmering work itself.

UnDylanesque though *Lord of the Rings* would seem to be, there are resonances between parts of the Tolkien trilogy and Dylan's remarkable song 'Lay Down Your Weary Tune' (see separate entry).

Tolkien spent the last years of his life at Oxford University, where he died on September 2, 1973.

Tom Petty & the Heartbreakers TOM PETTY & the Heartbreakers was formed in the mid-1970s. The group recorded their eponymously titled début album in 1976. It was a slow burner but eventually a hit, helped by 'Breakdown', which became a top 40 hit on its 1977 re-release. The highly successful albums *You're Gonna Get It!* and *Damn the Torpedoes* (triple platinum), plus further hit singles, preceded the less commercial *Hard Promises* and *Long After Dark* (1982). A long taking stock followed, after which they came back firing on all cylinders with *Southern Accents* in 1985 (produced by DAVE STEWART), then with *Pack Up the Plantation—Live!*

In September 1985 they also played six songs behind Bob Dylan at the Farm Aid benefit concert in Champaign, Illinois (augmented by WILLIE NELSON playing guitar on the last three), as a result of which in 1986 Tom Petty & the Heartbreakers partnered Dylan on two separate legs of his True Confessions Tour of New Zealand, Australia, Japan and North America. After rehearsing over 60 songs in California in January, the first leg of the tour, the non-American shows, began in Wellington, New Zealand, on February 5, 1986 (it was the summer down there) and finished on March 10 in Tokyo.

In this phase they played only 19 concerts, distributed through three countries, but they were also filmed for the official concert video *Hard to Handle*, filmed by GILLIAN ARMSTRONG, and in Sydney they stopped into a recording studio to cut the dreadful song 'Band of the Hand (It's Hell Time Man!)', which Tom Petty produced and which Dylan had written for the soundtrack of the worthless movie of the same name. The song was of interest not in itself—it was a hopelessly crude piece of vigilante bombast—but because, aside from with the even more obscure Dylan work 'Legionnaire's Disease', it is the only mention of the Vietnam War in his entire canon. (In the earlier song, 'Granddad fought in the Revolutionary War, father in the War of 1812 / Uncle fought in Vietnam and then he fought a war all by himself'; in 'Band of the Hand' we have 'For all of my brothers from Vietnam / And my uncles from World War Two . . . / We're gonna do what the law should do.') It was also the first time Dylan had specially written a song for a film in which he played no part himself. The B-side of the single was not by Dylan.

Hard to Handle was filmed at the Sydney, Australia, concerts of February 24 and 25, two thirds of the footage used coming from the earlier night.

In April Petty had to join Dylan for a press conference in LA to promote the forthcoming American leg of the tour, which was preceded by a brief appearance at an Amnesty International benefit concert in the city on June 6, at which Dylan and the band (plus Philip Lyn Jones on congas) performed 'Band of the Hand', the *Infidels* song 'License to Kill' and the R&B classic 'Shake a Hand'. The second leg proper began at a sports arena in San Diego on June 9, and ran through a total of 41 concerts to finish on August 6 in Paso Robles, California.

The first of these concerts saw the début performance of a song Dylan and Tom Petty had co-written, 'Got My Mind Made Up', which Dylan, Petty and the Heartbreakers had studio-recorded a month earlier for inclusion on Dylan's *Knocked Out Loaded* album. The final concert, at the Mid-State Fairground, featured the only live attempt Dylan ever made at that album's masterpiece, 'Brownsville Girl'; and even then, he only sang the chorus. Nevertheless a fragment was shown on ABC-TV the next night, the eve of the release of the album. There was another brief TV duty the group performed with Dylan too; at some point that August in San Francisco they were filmed playing the Fred Rose song 'Thank God' for the CHABAD TELETHON shown that September 14.

The punishing thing, for Tom Petty & the Heartbreakers, was that at each of these concerts—a total of 60—they played their own set *and* then came back on as Dylan's backing band for his set. In effect, then, the band played the equivalent of 120 concerts. And Dylan's sets were *long* that year: most nights he performed 26 songs, and sometimes nearer 30. Petty himself also shared vocals with Dylan on the regularly performed 'I Forgot More Than You'll Ever Know', 'Blowin' in the Wind' and 'Knockin' on Heaven's Door' (and once, on July 1 in Clarkston, Michigan, JOHNNY CASH's 'I Still Miss Someone').

The significance of the tour for Dylan followers was considerable. First, it was his first tour since 1984, but that had been in Europe; this was his first North American tour for almost five years. It was also his first fully post-evangelical-period tour of the States, and the alliance with—and reliance on—Tom Petty & the Heartbreakers was interesting as to the way this Bob Dylan was defining himself. He was, in OLOF BJORNER's words, 'the rejuvenated legend', placing the emphasis very much on rock 'n'roll, including the rock'n'roll of the 1950s. As with SANTANA in Europe on the 1984 tour, he was trading on the commercial pull of another act; but this time it was an act that could be seen as making some kind of musical sense.

Not everyone liked the group, though Petty's louche sexiness and the group's mix of tight street-cred musicianship with outrageously catchy hit singles like their classics 'American Girl' and 'Refugee' meant that they appealed to plenty, combining the spirit of fey punkery Tom Verlaine's group Television had embodied with something of the magisterial rock'n'roll loyalty exemplified by the ROLLING STONES.

Dylan has always had an uncanny ability physically to resemble the person he's chosen to stand alongside; with Petty, therefore, he came on 'rather punkish, in sleeveless shirts and leather vests, lots of amulets and one eardrop', looking fit and lean, showing off sinewy bare arms and wearing fingerless gloves. Yet the 1986 tour is no Dylan fan's favourite. The music seemed monolithic and belaboured, and the retention of a gospel-style backing group an over-egging of the pudding. Everything sounded the same, all the time: echoey, muffled, overbearing, and Dylan himself nuance-free.

Oddly, because it wasn't done calculatedly on the band's part, their playing always sounded fresher, tighter, more resourceful and original in their own sets than in Dylan's. One or two of the musicians, individually, may have enjoyed the recurrent uncertainty of playing behind him, but as a unit they didn't give him their modernity or flair. Rather, he made them sound rockist and formulaic. There was also the inherent awkwardness that in 1986 Tom Petty & the Heartbreakers were *huge*; their records were immensely bigger-selling than Dylan's, and it became clear at the concerts that more than half the audiences were really there for the group and not for the 'legend' at all. It seemed to Dylan, as he remembers in *Chronicles Volume One*, that 'Tom was at the top of his game and I was at the bottom of mine'.

A further song co-written by Dylan and Petty, but with MIKE CAMPBELL too, the inconsequential 'Jammin' Me', was recorded by Tom Petty & the Heartbreakers, included on their April 1987 album release *Let Me Up (I've Had Enough)*; the song made it into the US top 20 when issued as a single.

Clearly Tom Petty & the Heartbreakers *hadn't* had enough; on September 5, 1987, they were back with Dylan for a so-called European tour, though it actually began in the Middle East, with two dates in Israel (officially Dylan's first performances in the country). These were remarkable for the fact that Dylan included songs from his overtly Christian repertoire at each: 'In the Garden' from *Saved* (and the less overt 'Dead Man, Dead Man', from *Shot of Love*) in Tel Aviv and 'Gotta Serve Somebody' and 'Slow Train', both from *Slow Train Coming*, in Jerusalem. They were more remarkable for the fact that not a single song sung in Tel Aviv on the first night was repeated in Jerusalem on the second. In *Chronicles Volume One*, after writing about how stuck he felt, how incapable of singing more than about 20 of his songs until he had done a few dates with THE GRATEFUL DEAD that July, Dylan writes that at these opening concerts and the two that followed, in Switzerland and Italy, he 'sang eighty different songs, never repeating one, just to see if I could do it. It seemed easy.' This is only a mild exaggeration; he repeated only two songs out of 44 in the course of the first three concerts, but didn't keep up this extraordinary pace for the fourth; its 15 songs included only four more non-repeats.

The tour moved on to West Germany, East Germany, the Netherlands, Denmark, Finland, Sweden, France, Belgium and England, finishing with three consecutive nights at London's vile Wembley Arena in mid-October: a total of 30 concerts, on which Dylan must have been especially difficult to play for. In contrast to the previous year, he was *not* now looking fit, but wearing some sort of back brace that made him look stiff and a little hapless. He insisted on the stage remaining almost in darkness for his sets, he was extremely erratic and for many people this tour tested their patience beyond the limit. You could say that after this, people came to see him either because they were ardent aficionados or living-legend shoppers, coming to see him to tick him off their list; but 1987 marked the last year for more than a decade in which people came to see him in droves simply because he was a mainstream rock draw.

It was almost the end, too, of the long collaboration with Tom Petty & the Heartbreakers. The group itself became a less active unit subsequently. Their first album since 1987 was 1991's *Into the Great Wide Open*, produced by JEFF LYNNE, though Petty's own 1989 album *Full Moon Fever* had included Heartbreakers' input. Two hit singles came from *Into the Great Wide Open*. Ten years later the group received a Hollywood Walk of Fame star at 7018 Hollywood Boulevard. In March 2002 they were inducted into the Rock and Roll Hall of Fame. Such marketing-led fluff, such after-the-event officialising of what ought to be wild and unofficial, wouldn't normally be worth a mention; but on this occasion the induction was MC'd by JAKOB DYLAN.

In 2003, on August 9 & 10, at Holmdel, New Jersey, Tom Petty & the Heartbreakers met up with Jakob's father Bob once again for two shared concerts. At the first, Petty, Mike Campbell and Benmont Tench came on at the end of the Dylan set, and with Petty on shared vocals too, they played on Dylan's encore numbers, 'Rainy Day Women # 12 & 35' and 'All Along the Watchtower'. On August 10, at the end of the Heartbreakers' set and ahead of his own, Dylan surprised the crowd by appearing for *their* encore. It wasn't altogether a surprise for longtime Dylan fan and commentator Peter Stone Brown, whose internet-posted review painted this picture:

> 'Okay, so Tom Petty and the Heartbreakers are done . . . and you know something's gonna happen because in the darkness you can see an extra mic has been set up on stage and extra amp which when the lights come up turns out to be an old tan Fender Bassman; and the Heartbreakers file back out and there's this guy in white, white cowboy, white shirt and off-white pants and white snakeskin cowboy boots . . . the white is glistening and this roar erupts from the crowd and whoever he is he's got this thing that's been missing from the stage for the past 90 minutes or so and that thing is presence. So a roadie plugs this guy's Fender Stratocaster into that tan amp and the band starts to play "Knockin' on Heaven's Door" and this cowboy dude, well he don't care if Mike Campbell's on the stage or not, he's gonna play that Strat and take one of his raunchy maybe I'll find maybe I won't solos . . . it was kinda like old times.'

[Bob Dylan (with Tom Petty & the Hearbreakers): Farm Aid: rehearsals, LA, 19 Sep, soundcheck Champaign, IL, 21 Sep & performance 22 Sep 1985; 'Band of the Hand (It's Hell Time Man!)', Sydney, 8–10 Feb 1986, MCA 52811 (12-inch MCA 23633), US, Apr 1986 & on soundtrack album *Band of the Hand*, MCA 6167, US, May 1986; *Band of the Hand*, dir. Paul Michael Glaser, film & video release RCA/Columbia Pictures, Apr 1986. Film & video of *Hard to Handle*, dir. Gillian Armstrong, US, 1986, broadcast HBO, US, 20 Jun 1986; video release CBS/FOX 3502, US, Oct 1986. Bob Dylan: *Chronicles Volume One*, pp.148 & 152. Olof Bjorner quoted from *www.bjorner.com/86-1.htm#Intro*, seen online 28 Jun 2005; Peter Stone Brown quoted from *http://my.execpc.com/~billp61/081003r.html*, seen online 6 Nov 2005.]

'Tomorrow Is a Long Time' There is a widely reprinted poem Dylan seems to have come across 'from the fifteenth century', not in this case Italian but English, and anonymous, which has been given the title 'Western Wind' (though in its own day poems weren't titled). Dylan has taken heed of this 'Western Wind' in his early song 'Tomorrow Is a Long Time'. Each of his three verses ends 'Only if she was lyin' by me / Would I lie in my bed once again.' The poem from 500 years earlier, in its entirety, runs like this: 'Western wind, when will thou blow / The small rain down can rain? / Christ, if my love were in my arms / And I in my bed again!'

The poem has been disseminated orally, like a folksong, for most of its history (in fact it's a fine example of the lack of separation between folk and literary culture), but it exists as a manuscript (British Museum MS. Royal Appendix 58) and has been collected repeatedly in 20th century anthologies, including both the Arthur Quiller-Couch *Oxford Book of English Verse* (1900–1930, 1939 and 1943, in which it has been titled 'The Lover in Winter Plaineth for the Spring') and the Helen Gardner *New Oxford Book of English Verse*, 1972.

Known Dylan performances and recordings of 'Tomorrow Is a Long Time' are as follows: private recording at the home of DAVE WHITAKER, Minnesota, August 11, 1962 (circulated only in very poor quality); as a Witmark music-publishing demo NY, December 1962; as one of three songs performed on WBAI Radio, NYC (on the Skip Weshner Show 'Wireless Waves') February 1963 and, exquisitely, 'live' at the New York Town Hall Concert, April 12, 1963; this version was released on *Greatest Hits Volume II*. It was also recorded, again privately at Dave Whitaker's in Minneapolis, on July 17, 1963 (uncirculated).

Dylan rehearsed the song nearly 15 years later, in Santa Monica, CA, January 27 & 30, 1978, and reintroduced it to concerts on the first night of the 1978 world tour, in Tokyo, February 20. He also sang it in Auckland, New Zealand, March 9, but by the time the tour reached Australia (March 12 to April 1) he had dropped it.

He reintroduced the song in concert again another nine years later, in Gothenburg, Sweden, on September 25, 1987, performing it 11 times during his fall tour of Europe that year. He played it just once in the first year of the Never-Ending Tour, 1988 (at Saratoga Springs, June 26), twice in 1989 and half a dozen times in 1990 before dropping it altogether again for another five years straight. One performance in 1997, but six in 1998, seven in 1999 and a positive flurry of 11 in 2000; then three in 2001, five in 2002 and none in the two years that followed. It received one performance—in Boston on April 15—in 2005.

ELVIS PRESLEY recorded 'Tomorrow Is a Long Time' in Nashville in 1966 (the sessions include musicians Floyd Cramer, PETE DRAKE & CHARLIE McCOY). In June 1969 *Rolling Stone* asked Dylan whether there were any particular artists he liked to do versions of his songs; he replied (and was widely assumed to be joking at the time), 'Yeah, Elvis Presley. I liked Elvis Presley. Elvis Presley recorded a song of mine. That's the one recording I treasure the most . . . it was called "Tomorrow Is a Long Time". I wrote it but never recorded it.'

Asked which Presley album this track was on, Dylan replied, '*Kismet*'. This was existentially correct: it was released as a 'bonus track' filling out the 'soundtrack album' for the awful mid-60s film *Spinout*, in Europe titled *California Holiday*. 'Kismet' was a song on the soundtrack LP of an even worse mid-60s Presley film, MGM's 1965 *Harum Scarum*, in Europe titled *Harem Holiday*.

[Elvis Presley: 'Tomorrow Is a Long Time', Nashville, 25–28 May 1966, *Spinout*, Victor LPM/LSP-3702, NY (*California Holiday*, RCA SF 7820, London), 1966. Film *Spinout*, aka *California Holiday*, MGM, dir. Norman Taurog, 1966. Elvis Presley: 'Kismet', Nashville, 24–25 Feb 1965, *Harum Scarum*, RCA Victor LPM/LSP-3468, NY (*Harem Holiday*, RCA RD/SF 7767, London), 1965.]

Trager, Oliver [1957 -] Oliver Trager was born in 1957. After art school, hitching and riding freight trains (it says here) to Alaska and back, 'seeing the other side of life, seeking the quicksilver in the great American starry dynamo night', 'Tripping the night fantastic of the sidewalks of New York' and graduating from college with a BA in English Literature, Trager worked in publishing for some years and 'eventually scored a job at Facts on File, Inc.' He is also the author of *The American Book of the Dead: The Definitive GRATEFUL DEAD Encyclopedia* (1997) and of the invaluable *Dig Infinity!: The Life and Art of LORD BUCKLEY* (2002). In 2004 came *Keys to the Rain: The Definitive Bob Dylan Encyclopedia*—a title that seems oblique ('keys *to* the rain'?) and serves to smother the uppity subtitle. The book is, naturally enough, far from definitive: why claim any different? It received very mixed reviews, and here is another, starting with the down wing.

Inevitably there are errors. There may be more in the present work than in Trager's. Facts are sometimes slippery by nature, at other times so small as to make it pedantic to poke at them, and any wide-ranging book will offer as facts generalisations or ellipses that the lifelong specialist in one sub-zone of it will regard as not quite accurate enough. But there's a sliding scale of these things, and works of reference shouldn't slide too far. It may not matter that 'I Can't Get You Off of My Mind' by HANK WILLIAMS was recorded on November 6, 1947, not in December 1948: but ELVIS PRESLEY certainly did not record 'Mystery Train' on Sun in *1953*, and errors of that order make the reader distrustful.

The book proceeds song by song, which, while fine it itself, means that without an index it's often hard to locate the information on a particular person, unless you already know which song their details will be lurking within. Each entry is augmented by utterly meaningless, useless lists of who else has covered each song. There is also an absurd amount of reliance, albeit acknowledged, on one book, Dorothy Horstman's *Sing Your Heart Out, Country Boy* (1975), and a tendency towards some rather obvious—and unacknowledged—paraphrasing. Here is MICHAEL GRAY's *Song & Dance Man III: The Art of Bob Dylan*, on a 1979 outtake from *Slow Train Coming*: '. . . the nuggety little "Trouble in Mind", which alone would be sufficient to prove that Christian faith, despite one's fears to the contrary, did not dull Dylan's cutting edge.' And here's Trager on the same song: '. . . this edgy little nugget of evangelical Dylan blues . . . further confirms that the euphoric rush ccompanying Dylan's salvation did not dull his creative flame.'

Some of the omissions seem rather obvious too. There's plenty of material about JOHNNIE & JACK, and an unhurried entry on the *"Love and Theft"* track 'Tweedle Dee & Tweedle Dum', but no mention that the music on Dylan's recording is *very* closely based on Johnnie & Jack's 1961 record 'Uncle John's Bongos'.

The book is also scarred by the revolting prose of the 'Introduction: Something Is Happening' (e.g.: 'You stop in the St. James Hotel for a beer to find LENNY BRUCE and Lord Buckley sharing a bill with SKIP JAMES, ROBERT JOHNSON, and Moondog. Outside, the Fortune Telling Lady hands you the Jack of Hearts and points to Desolation Row . . .'), while Trager's comments on Dylan's own songs are more or less completely useless: and always offered as if any old observation will do—as if a bank manager can turn his hand to art criticism just as casually. This is, to adopt Mark Dery's phrase, drive-by cultural criticism.

Sometimes the Intro prose and the comments on Dylan songs are the same. This is the start of the entry on 'Get Your Rocks Off!' (p.204): 'At once menacing and ribald, "Get Your Rocks Off!" as performed by Dylan and THE HAWKS picks up where every old-maid-theme limerick leaves off and takes a stroll down every back lane in Appalachia before stopping for some ale at a burlesque house featuring a Brothers Grimm playlet.'

And yet there's certainly an up wing. There is, to start with, the generous and above all resourceful use of photographs and illustrations, which consistently present the unusual without ever straining for relevance. Now and then, too, an entry on a Dylan-related subject is uncharacteristically lucid and useful: for example on Dylan's book *Drawn Blank*. Then there is the sheer amount of ground covered, the sheer number of text entries, which even if those on Dylan's own canon were dashed off as speedily as they indicate, still must have involved great labour and result in a considerable achievement, if not of original research then at least of assemblage: particularly since the great value of the book lies not in what is has to say about Dylan or rock music but in its portraits of the whiskery, tragic eccentrics, renegade old rounders, baby-faced boys and implacable peckerwoods who have composed and written the *other* songs Dylan has brought within his repertoire. Here Trager opens up another window onto what GREIL MARCUS has called 'the old, weird America', 'the invisible republic'. As JOHN

HINCHEY has noted: 'blurbs on the book ignore this element in it—but it's fascinating in itself and it does bear on the artistic and cultural milieu that has fed Dylan's art. . . . to my mind, it's the best thing about this book.'

This is true, and it's enough to make it one of the Dylan books you need.

[Oliver Trager: *The American Book of the Dead*, Fireside, 1997; *Dig Infinity!: The Life and Art of Lord Buckley*, New York: Welcome Rain, 2002; *Keys to the Rain: The Definitive Bob Dylan Encyclopedia*, New York: Billboard, 2004. Quotes in the 1st para are from Trager, 'Examining the Nightingale's Code', *The Bridge* no.22, Tyne & Wear, UK, summer 2005. John Hinchey, e-mail to this writer, 14 Aug 2005.]

Traum, Happy [1938 -] Harry Peter Traum was born in the Bronx, New York, on May 9, 1938. He became a singer, songwriter, guitarist and banjo player, and met Dylan in 1961, the year the latter arrived in New York.

Traum joined THE NEW WORLD SINGERS (the other members, already forming the group, were GIL TURNER, Bob Cohen and Delores Dixon) after they'd returned from Mississippi with 'new freedom songs' in 1962. These were published in the new street-cred folk magazine *Broadside*, which Gil Turner co-edited while also working at Gerde's Folk City. In *Chronicles Volume One* Dylan calls the New World Singers 'a group I was pretty close with' and says that Delores Dixon was the 'sort of part-time girl-friend' with whom he attended the farewell party for CISCO HOUSTON that he describes so vividly in the book's first section. Dixon, he says, 'was from Alabama, an ex-reporter and an ex-dancer.'

Dylan played at the *Broadside* Show of May 1962, performing 'Ballad of Donald White', 'The Death of Emmett Till' and an early 'Blowin' in the Wind', this last with back-up vocals by Turner, Sis Cunningham and PETE SEEGER. He is supposed to have taken the melody for 'Blowin' in the Wind' from the version of 'No More Auction Block' that he had heard sung by the New World Singers, with lead vocal by Delores Dixon. They, in turn, claimed to be first to record it (though in fact the Chad Mitchell Trio beat them to it).

Happy Traum and Dylan first recorded together on January 24, 1963, almost certainly at the Folkways studio at 147 West 46th Street, New York City. The New World Singers were recording material for *Broadside* magazine's benefit. When they finished, Dylan recorded 'Masters of War' (it was this new song's first studio outing, and three months to the day before he would cut it at Columbia's studios for *The Freewheelin' Bob Dylan*). Then, to Traum's surprise, Dylan wanted him to record 'I Will Not Go Down Under the Ground', later re-named 'Let Me Die in My Footsteps'. He'd never encountered the song before, but Dylan had the words written down and they went through it a couple of times and in the end recorded it together, with Traum singing lead and Dylan on harmony vocals and guitar. This first recording partnership was released as a track on the obscure various-artists compilation *Broadside Ballads, Vol. 1*, that September, with Dylan billed as Blind Boy Grunt.

Dylan allowed the magazine to publish 'Let Me Die in My Footsteps' in its third issue, and it's generally been stated in Dylan annals that this recording was made at *Broadside*'s office: but 'office' was basically a grand term for what was actually a corner of Sis Cunningham's apartment. Traum is certain that this is not where the recording took place: that the venue was the Folkways studio. (Others, though, remember other recordings being made in that 'office' on a tape-recorder there: Josh Dunson describes such a session in *Broadside* no.20, which ROBERT SHELTON quotes at length in his Dylan biography *No Direction Home*: a session at which Gil Turner and Dylan both sang onto the tape. So one person's certainty is another person's misremembrance. These things are rarely indisputable facts.)

At any rate, Dylan probably knew from Gil Turner that 'I Will Not Go Down Under the Ground' was a song that would have special resonance for Traum, because while both Turner and Traum had been arrested at a protest at City Hall Park against the mandatory civil defence drills in the City in 1961—you had to go down into the subway when the alarm sirens wailed—Turner had merely been fined but Traum had served a month on a work farm (an unusually close brush with the kind of oppression so much sung about in the revivalist repertoire). From May to June 1961 he was doing the shocking and unpleasant work of disinterring bodies and reburying them in bigger piles at the New York City Workhouse, on Hart Island, off the Bronx, which was the City Cemetery for unclaimed corpses known then and now as 'Potter's Field'. (Though no longer a work-house, the Department of Correction still runs the 101-acre island's cemetery site, and burials are still conducted using prison-inmate labour. Hart Island is closed to the public.)

Around the same time as recording 'Let Me Die in My Footsteps' together there was a longer informal get-together at which Dylan was taped performing 12 songs, backed by Traum and Turner. The date is uncertain but it was in January or February 1963. Again the venue has been the subject of dispute. It has often been claimed that it was recorded in the basement at Gerde's Folk City, but in a 1996 e-mail interview Traum was unapologetically vague about many a detail but quite certain that the venue had been Gil Turner's apartment in the East Village. He reconfirmed this in October 2005.

At any rate, while Dylan performs on all 12 songs, Traum sings back-up vocals on 'Masters of

Photo by Gerard Malanga

Sam Shepard & Patti Smith in *Cowboy Mouth*

Rob Stoner with Roy Rogers

Hank Snow

Photography by Sherry Rayn Barnett

Richard Thompson

that tambourine

Library of Congress

J.R.R. Tolkien

Courtesy Smothsonian/Folkways

Happy Traum

War' and the LEADBELLY song 'Keep Your Hands Off Her', and Turner sings behind Dylan on the last song, the MEMPHIS JUG BAND's 'Stealin', Stealin''. Traum also plays banjo on five songs. The tape of this session was one of the earliest to circulate among collectors, and was known as *The Banjo Tape*.

Dylan used to turn up at Gerde's Folk City when the New World Singers had week-long stints there, and would sometimes perform with the group during their late sets in those weeks. In late 1963, when the group released its eponymously titled début album (on, weirdly, Atlantic Records) its sleevenotes were specially written by Dylan, who had offered to do them. These notes emerged in his then-familiar Guthriesque prose-poem style, starting with the ingenuous lines 'I aint a record note writer–I never was, never will be an never wanna be / but that's ok tho cause the New World Singers ain't record note writer's subjects', and running through sideswipes at PETER, PAUL & MARY and his own manager, ALBERT GROSSMAN ('they ain't no tin pan alley put together group'), but also reminiscing about his early encounters with Gil Turner, Bob Cohen and Happy Traum, of whom he writes: 'I met "Happy Traum" an' his wife . . . an' I can remember when their baby girl Merry was born an' now she's over a year old an' with one laugh out a beautiful Merry you'd know why Happy wants a new an' better world . . . Happy's got the reason right there in his eyeview . . . closer to it than a lot of us are.'

That New World Singers album included one of the first covers of 'Don't Think Twice, It's All Right', and this was also issued as a single (coupled with their version of the JOHN HERALD song 'Stewball'). It wasn't a hit, and the group disbanded in 1964.

Though Traum and Dylan didn't record together again until the start of the 1970s, it was in the period from summer 1966 until Dylan's move to the West Coast that they knew each other best. Both were living in Woodstock, New York, with their families, and saw a fair amount of each other. (The Traums spent summer 1966 in nearby Bearsville, got reacquainted with Dylan then and there, spent a second summer there in 1967 and decided to move to Woodstock permanently that fall.)

Between 1967 and 1970 Traum was the editor of *Sing Out!* magazine (following the resignation of IRWIN SILBER), and at some point in spring 1968, Dylan approached Traum to ask if they would like to run an interview with him. He said he was being hounded by the big papers, the rock papers, and pressed by the record company, but would prefer to give any interview to *Sing Out!* In June and July 1968, Happy Traum and JOHN COHEN duly conducted the three interviews with Dylan that appeared in the magazine as one feature, 'Conversations with Bob Dylan', that October. Its appearance surprised many Dylan followers, who had never expected to see him again in the pages of this New York folk magazine.

Happy Traum, and his presumably less happy younger brother Artie, signed to Albert Grossman's management company as a guitar duo and issued their début album, *Happy & Artie Traum* in 1970, followed by *Double Back* in 1971, *Hard Times in the Country* in 1975 (with sleevenotes by ALLEN GINSBERG: the same year he wrote some for Dylan's *Desire* album) and, decades later, *The Test of Time* in 1994.

Early on in this partnership they were able to access large live audiences by being a support act to THE BAND and other headline acts. Later they were both also in the Woodstock Mountains Revue, which issued the cassette-only release *Mud Acres: Music Among Friends* in 1972, the album *More Music from Mud Acres* in 1977, *Pretty Lucky* in 1978 and finally *Back to Mud Acres* in 1981.

But whereas Artie had played banjo before taking up acoustic guitar, and had come up first through the True Endeavor Jug Band (which included DANNY KALB, and made the 1963 album *The Art of the Jug Band*), and then been in a group called Bear (which included STEVE SOLES, and issued the 1968 album *Greetings, Children of Paradise*: the perfect 1968 title!), Happy had taken other musical trails, all keeping closer to the main highways of folk. These had included going over to Harlem to take guitar lessons from BROWNIE McGHEE from 1958 to 1960 and then, as noted, joining the New World Singers. His subsequent solo albums include *Relax Your Mind*, which came out in 1975 and featured entirely traditional material except for the title track, a LEADBELLY song, and on which he played 12-string as well as 6-string guitar (but no banjo); *American Stranger* (1977, and including Dylan's 'Buckets of Rain'), *Bright Morning Stars* (1979, including Dylan's 'I Shall Be Released' and RICHARD MANUEL) and *Friends and Neighbors* (1982, and including LARRY CAMPBELL), plus the compilation CD *Buckets of Songs*.

In 1971 Happy Traum was, with Dylan, among the back-up musicians for Ginsberg when he performed on the PBS-TV show 'Allen Ginsberg & Friends' late that October, and again at the Record Plant in November (this time with Artie too), backing Ginsberg on nine audio tracks.

More significantly, Traum and Dylan had been back together in the studios that September, yielding very relaxed—some would say sloppy—revisits to Dylan's awful early song 'Only a Hobo' (four takes and an incomplete one, all still uncirculated), plus three of the 1967 Basement Tapes songs, 'You Ain't Goin' Nowhere', 'Down in the Flood' and 'I Shall Be Released', with Traum on bass, banjo, second guitar and vocal harmony. These were issued on *Bob Dylan's Greatest Hits Vol. II* in November 1971, and the sleevenotes say they were recorded that October; the date has been revised by discographers to September 24, 1971.

These days, though Happy Traum still performs, mostly he and his wife run Homespun Tapes, which they founded in 1967: a mail-order company with a catalogue of 400 music-instruction lessons on audio cassette, CD and video, all taught by performing musicians and produced by Happy Traum. Dylan was prescient, then, in his sleeve-note poem, glimpsing that Traum had a home life of value not attained by 'a lot of us': not many folk or rock musicians have been with the same marital partner for over 40 years.

In 2005 Traum also recorded and released a new CD, his first for over 20 years, produced by brother Artie, again featuring Larry Campbell, an old friend of many years' standing, and including Dylan's *Nashville Skyline* song 'Tonight I'll Be Staying Here with You'. He last met up with Dylan backstage at Madison Square Garden when the Never-Ending Tour came through there (with Larry Campbell in Bob's band at the time) on November 19, 2001.

[Happy Traum: *Relax Your Mind*, Kicking Mule SNKF 111, US, 1975; *American Stranger*, Kicking Mule SNKF 142, US, 1977; *Bright Morning Stars*, Greenhays GR703, US, 1979; *Friends and Neighbors*, Vest Pocket VP-001, US, 1982; *Buckets of Songs*, Shanachie *nia*, US, 1987; Roaring Steam IW01, US, 2005. Happy & Artie Traum: *Happy & Artie Traum*, Capitol 586, US, 1970; *Double Back*, Capitol 799, 1971; *Hard Times in the Country*, Rounder 3007, US, 1975; CD *The Test of Time*, Roaring Steam 201, US, 1994. The Woodstock Mountains Revue: *Mud Acres: Music Among Friends*, Rounder 3001 (cassette), US, 1972; *More Music from Mud Acres*, Rounder 3018, US, 1977; *Pretty Lucky*, Rounder 3025, 1978; *Back to Mud Acres*, Rounder 3065, 1981; CD compilation from these 4 is *Woodstock Mountains: Music from Mud Acres*, Rounder 11520, 1995.

Happy Traum & Bob Dylan: 'I Will Not Go Down Under the Ground', NY, 24 Jan 1963, *Broadside Ballads, Vol. 1*, Broadside BR 301, NY, Sep 1963, reissued 5-CD box set *The Best of Broadside 1962–1988*, Smithsonian/Folkways SFW CD 40130, Washington, D.C., 2000. New World Singers (with Dylan liner notes): *The New World Singers*, Atlantic 8087, NY, 1963; 'Don't Think Twice, It's All Right' c/w 'Stewball', NY, 1963, Atlantic 2190, NY, 1963. John Cohen & Happy Traum: 'Conversations with Bob Dylan', *Sing Out!* no.18, Oct-Nov 1968, New York, pp.6–23, 27. Bob Dylan: *Chronicles Volume One*, 2004, p.64. E-mail interview with Traum by Manfred Helfert, Feb 1996; seen online 21 Oct 2005 at *www.bobdylanroots.com/traum.html*. Josh Dunson in *Broadside* no.20, quoted from Robert Shelton, *No Direction Home: The Life & Music of Bob Dylan*, Penguin edn., pp.139–40. Most information, much of it contradicting assertions within the Smithsonian Folkways online biographies for Traum and the New World Singers, by e-mails & phone call between Traum & this writer 21, 22 & 24 Oct 2005.]

Traveling Wilburys, the [1988 - 1990] A jovial and unexpected grouping of superstars—originally Bob Dylan, GEORGE HARRISON, the rather less super JEFF LYNNE, the great ROY ORBISON and, bringing down the group's average age a little, TOM PETTY—who combined to make a few warm, likeable tracks together, added a few filler tracks and made an album which, to everyone's surprise, went platinum. George created the group by accident, in early April 1988. Over lunch, he happened to ask Lynne if he knew of a studio available quickly for recording a bonus track for a European 12-inch single track to go with his just-completed solo album *Cloud Nine*; Lynne suggested Dylan's Malibu studio; en route there George retrieved a guitar from Tom Petty, who came along too. Lynne was producing Orbison's *Mystery Girl* album at the time, and Roy came too. They ended up with the jointly composed 'Handle with Care' (with added drums and guitar from IAN WALLACE and MIKE CAMPBELL), and instead of this turning out to be the bonus track on Harrison's 12-inch singe, it became the first track on *Traveling Wilburys Volume 1*. The rest of the album was put together in LA that May, at DAVE STEWART's home studio, and released on October 18. Lynne and Harrison, the producers, did some overdubbing later, in England. JIM KELTNER played the drums; RAY COOPER added percussion; Jim Horn played saxophone.

If it came as a relief to everyone involved that they weren't required to deliver anything sensational within the group, it certainly came as a relief to Dylan, who was, at the time, going through a particularly bad patch. The album of his own on which work was just completed when the Wilburys sprang into being, and which would be released two weeks after the Wilburys album was cut, was *Down in the Groove*. Lumbering along behind, and released in February 1989, was *Dylan & the Dead*. As Dylan notes in *Chronicles Volume One*, while complaining of the struggle to make *Oh Mercy* and the poor sales it would attract: 'Although the record wouldn't put me back on the map in radio land, ironically I had two records in the charts, even one in the top ten, *The Traveling Wilburys*. The other one was the *Dylan & the Dead* album.'

If Dylan was free, as Lucky Wilbury, to chip in uncommittedly with minor bits of singing, guitar-work and composing—'Give us some lyrics, you famous lyricist,' George had said on day one—this freedom paid off. He played an easy, warm rhythm guitar throughout; he shared lead vocals on, and co-wrote, 'Handle with Care'; he took lead vocals on, and mostly wrote, 'Dirty World', 'Congratulations' (see separate entry) and 'Tweeter & the Monkey Man'. He lent a hand with the rest—and in doing so helped propel Roy Orbison (Lefty Wilbury) to the Indian summer of success he deserved, not least with the album's one fine Orbisonian vehicle, 'Not Alone Anymore'. In October, in LA, they all made a promo video for 'Handle with Care', and two months later, thanks to the album's success, they needed another, choosing to go with the far less charming 'End of the Line'. It should have been. It already was for Orbison. He died on December 6.

The next single, in June 1990, was the old Cy Coben and Mel Foree song 'Nobody's Child', recorded during the album sessions but as a one-off charity fundraiser for the Romanian Angel Appeal, in which the wives of George and RINGO STARR were involved, to help in some tiny way to relieve the horrendous suffering, physical and mental, of orphans locked inside inhumane institutions in an especially neglected, dictatorship-pillaged corner of eastern Europe. The B-side of the record was by Dave Stewart. It wasn't a great success. 'She's My Baby', the next single, was also the opening track of the follow-up album, wittily titled *Traveling Wilburys Volume 3*, recorded at Bel Air, California, in April 1990, with overdubs in July, again done in England, and released that October. Jim Keltner again plays drums, Ray Cooper percussion and Jim Horn sax; this time Gary Moore adds guitar. Again, Harrison and Lynne produced.

Dylan—this time Boo Wilbury—is as prominent on 'She's My Baby' and 'Inside Out' as he gets anywhere on this album, but there's nothing here anyone but a completist could need. Outtakes from both albums have circulated, with more Dylan vocals and less clutter, including a mix of 'She's My Baby' on which he takes lead vocal throughout; but these still suggest themselves as items fairly near the bottom of any bootlegs shopping list.

The cliché about the Traveling Wilburys is that it was all such good fun, and so much better than if its members had tried to make an important record; but test this argument by imagining the prospect of six, or nine, or 12 Wilburys albums. OLIVER TRAGER articulates this 'Hey, whatever!' approach very handily: he calls the first album 'a down-to-earth, everyman collection even your stodgy great aunt might find herself tapping her toes to.' That's exactly what's wrong with it. And what kind of yard-stick would Trager's improbable great aunt be? She'd tap her toes to the Archies.

The cheerily inconsequential only gets you so far, and even a second album, especially without Orbison, was pushing things—as their promo videos proved. There are few things more depressing than watching, back to back, the wretched descent of these items from the inoffensive novelty of 'Handle with Care' down past 'End of the Line', 'She's My Baby' and 'Inside Out' (both 1990) to the abject desperation of 'The Wilbury Twist' in early 1991—a desperation confessed by their having paid John Candy to make a cameo appearance. He stands there and twists, under his customary delusion that merely being a fat person makes him funny. You sit there and squirm, wondering what this flaccid, bleary concoction can possibly have to do with a great artist. 'Hey, whatever!' doesn't answer that.

[The Traveling Wilburys: *Traveling Wilburys Volume 1*, Wilburys Warner Bros. 9 25796, US, 1988; 'Nobody's Child', Warner Bros. 9 26280-2, US, 1990; *Traveling Wilburys Volume 3*, Wilburys Warner Bros. 9 26324, US, 1990. Bob Dylan, *Chronicles Volume One*, 2004, p.218. Oliver Trager: *Keys to the Rain: The Definitive Bob Dylan Encyclopedia*, New York: Billboard, 2004, p.639.]

Travers, Mary [1936 -] See **Peter, Paul & Mary**.

'Trouble in Mind' [1979] This Dylan song was recorded on the first day of the *Slow Train Coming* sessions but released only as the B-side of the single of 'Gotta Serve Somebody'. It suggested at once that Christian faith, despite one's fears to the contrary, did not dull Dylan's cutting edge. This is gospel with a real blues slouch to it, and the Dylan burn is here, delivered with as much italicized sarcasm as anything from the mid-60s repertoire: 'Well the deeds that you do don't add up to zero / It's what's inside that counts, ask any war-hero / You think you can hide but you're never alone / Ask Lot what he thought when his wife turned to stone.'

The mention of Lot's wife is a nicely achieved double reference. Primarily, it refers to the story in Genesis in which God says He will spare Lot, his wife and two daughters when He destroys the depraved cities of Sodom and Gomorrah with a hard rain of brimstone and fire: 'And it came to pass, when they [angels] had brought them forth abroad, that he said, Escape for thy life; look not behind thee . . . lest thou be consumed. . . . But his wife looked back from behind him, and she became a pillar of salt' (Genesis 19:17 & 26).

Yet when Dylan remembers Lot and his wife in 'Trouble in Mind', to illustrate the assertion 'You think you can hide but you're never alone', he is also, consciously and with good humour, paralleling Luke, who famously exhorts us, and with memorable brevity (it's one of the Bible's shortest verses) to 'Remember Lot's wife' (Luke 17:32).

'Trouble in Mind' quotes much scripture verbatim too: in calling Satan 'prince of the power of the air', it quotes directly Ephesians 2:2; in singing that Satan will make you 'worship the work of your own hands' Dylan echoes one of God's frequent, basic litanies against idolatry, expressed specifically in parallel in Isaiah 2:8: '. . . they worship the work of their own hands', and in Jeremiah 1:16: 'And I will utter my judgments against them . . . who have . . . worshipped the work of their own hands.'

In listing what else Satan will bring upon you, Dylan also has in mind (from the book of Leviticus) a text he uses with a contrasting calm and compassion in 'I Pity the Poor Immigrant'. In 'Trouble in Mind' Dylan sings that Satan will condemn you to 'serving strangers in a strange and forsaken land'.

Becoming an 'immigrant' like this is one of God's punishments for those who disregard his commandments: '. . . and I will make your heaven as iron, and your earth as brass. . . . And your strength shall be spent in vain . . . and ye shall eat, and not be satisfied. . . . And I will scatter you among the heathen. . . . And ye shall perish among the heathen, and the land of your enemies shall eat you up.'

The phrase 'a stranger in a strange land' itself comes from Exodus 2:22.

(For God's recurrent exhortation to His people to treat such strangers with kindness, see **'Covenant Woman' and 'Pretty Boy Floyd'**.)

The final verse of the recording of 'Trouble in Mind' is edited out of the issued single, but its lyric appears in *Bob Dylan Lyrics 1962–1985* and *Bob Dylan Lyrics 1962–2001*. The penultimate verse would have been the better omission, since, unlike the rest, the preaching is not sculpted by poetry and wit, but comes spluttering out in gobs of ugly prose ('They can't relate to the Lord's kingdom, they can't relate to the cross. / They self-inflict punishment on their own broken lives'). This track could usefully have been reissued on 1985's *Biograph* box set, but wasn't. Dylan has never performed the song in concert.

[Bob Dylan: 'Trouble in Mind', Sheffield, AL, 30 Apr 1979 (+ overdubs 5 & 6 May), c/w 'Gotta Serve Somebody', Columbia 1-11072, NY (CBS S CBS 7828, London), 1979. Quotations from *Leviticus*: 26:19, 20, 26, 33 & 38.]

Turner, Gil [1933 - 1974] Gilbert Strunk was born in Bridgeport, Connecticut, on May 6, 1933. He majored in Political Science at the University of Bridgeport and later wrote papers on the use of music in treating autism in children and on rheumatoid arthritis, from which he suffered himself. A singer, banjoist and guitarist–indeed a 'player of anything with string on it', as a promo leaflet for him once said–who learnt guitar partly from the REV. GARY DAVIS, he was an early member of *Broadside* magazine's editorial board (its founding main editors were Agnes 'Sis' Cunningham and Gordon Friesen), helped to organise the initial *Broadside* album and was responsible for bringing on board artists like MARK SPOELSTRA, Bonnie Dobson, PHIL OCHS and LEN CHANDLER, and young writers like Julius Lester and Josh Dunson as well as Dylan, who was a friend early on in his Greenwich Village days.

ROBERT SHELTON says that Turner was one of those Dylan turned to in particular after SUZE ROTOLO left for Italy, but that they had been good friends since late 1961 and remained so 'for two years'. Shelton portrays Turner as a 'portly, open-faced, wholesome-looking man . . . son of a former opera singer' who had been a Baptist preacher before PETE SEEGER showed him a 'wider pastorate'. He was 'an experienced congregational singing leader' with 'a large, warm baritone'. It was with Shelton and Dylan that Turner would, several times a week, hang out at the White Horse Tavern or elsewhere after Gerde's closed at around midnight. Shelton also recalls that it was to the same comrades that in 1963 Dylan said that if he made any money he'd fly them over to Italy: 'We'll drink red wine, night and day, until we explode', Dylan told Shelton and Turner.

Actively involved in civil rights marches in the South during the early 1960s, a member of SNCC and the War Resisters League, Turner helped to organize the Mississippi Freedom Caravan of Music and the New York Council of Performing Arts. He was, with Bob Cohen, Dolores Dixon and, slightly later, HAPPY TRAUM, a member of the New World Singers. He composed the anthemic 'Carry It On' (which was widely covered: it is, for example, on JUDY COLLINS' *Fifth Album* from 1965 and is used as the title of a JOAN BAEZ movie); he also wrote 'Benny Kid Paret', a song contemporaneous with Dylan's 'Who Killed Davey Moore?' about another boxer (the world welterweight champion) who died from wounds to the head sustained in a knock-out in the ring in March 1962. (It was ironic that the professional name he had himself chosen had also belonged to a boxer.) It was, too, Turner who discovered and recorded (within the New World Singers) a previously unnoticed WOODY GUTHRIE song, 'Bizzness Ain't Dead'.

At the same time as working at *Broadside*, Gil Turner was hosting the Monday night hootenannies at Gerde's Folk City when, on April 16, 1962, Dylan, accompanied by DAVID BLUE, brought him a song he'd just written, called 'Blowin' in the Wind'. Turner was thus the first person to sing it in front of an audience. (See separate entry on the song.) That fall, he wrote an article in *Sing Out!*, 'Bob Dylan–a new voice singing new songs', which was the issue's cover story; the front shows a photo of young Bob drawing on a cigarette and looking Guthriesquely cool. Turner's article begins by quoting lines from Dylan's 'Let Me Die in My Footsteps' and goes on to stress that for him, beyond Dylan's talents as 'a noteworthy folk performer with a bright future', his real significance is as a songwriter. And in the recorded discussion between Dylan, Seeger, Turner and Sis Cunningham at the *Broadside* show that May, Turner tries to explain one of that songwriting's special strengths–one of its innovations–as he saw it. Speaking of 'The Ballad of Donald White', Turner says: 'I feel about Bob Dylan's songs very often that Bob is actually a kind of folk mind that he represents to all the people around. And all the ideas current are just filtered down and come out in poetry. For example, one song he wrote about the fellow that asked to be put into an institution, what was his name–White?'

Dylan says yes, and that White is dead now, and Turner, addressing Dylan directly now, says: 'For example, you put in one line, you say the institutions were overcrowded. And I just couldn't see that appearing in a traditional ballad stanza before you sang it. And it's actually the first song I could think of, a modern song, that uses the ideas of the 20th century Freudian psychology, the ideas of people being afraid of life, in actually a folk song.' Seeger interrupts, to say, 'Instead of talking about it, let's hear it,' but Turner finishes his point, saying: 'Well, I think this particular song is historical in the sense that it's the first psychological song of the modern generation I've heard.'

After Dylan goes ahead and sings 'The Ballad of Donald White' he sings 'The Death of Emmett Till' and then Turner, along with Seeger and Cunningham, add back-up vocals as Dylan performs 'Blowin' in the Wind'. In January or February 1963, Dylan and Turner got together again, along with Happy Traum, to record what became known as *The Banjo Tape*. (See **Traum, Happy**; Turner gets several further mentions in this entry.)

Turner moved to California, probably in 1965 (the year his daughter was born in New York), appeared in the National Shakespeare Festival in San Diego in 1966, toured with the company, and worked with many different musicians in this period, including the great ragtime pianist and guitarist Hoyle Osborne. He was scheduled to play Lee Hays in a film biography of WOODY GUTHRIE, and told Kate Wolf (a bit of a feminist icon and a much-loved West Coast folkie, whom Turner had met through friends in Big Sur in 1970) that Will Geer wanted to write him into *The Waltons* as a singing mountain man. Turner, Wolf and Lionel Kilberg sang and played a concert together, and an album Kilberg and Wolf were recording was subsequently dedicated to Turner. A live version of Turner's 'Carry It On' by Wolf was released in 1996 on a posthumous album (Wolf died in 1986). As Kilberg tells it, in his execrably punctuated sleevenotes to the earlier album:

> 'At Kirby Cove . . . I met that jovial mountain of song Gil (Jellyroll) Turner, whom I hadn't seen in 10 years and after a half hour of lying, swearing and making music, he signed me for two appearances with him. The group "Gil (Jellyroll) Turner and the Donut Holes." I, as you have probably guessed was one of the holes. Two others were Don Coffin and Kate Wolf.'

As this implies, by now Turner had become strikingly overweight; he was also an alcoholic. In the middle of playing on a Shel Silverstein album in 1971 he had to quit session-work after contracting infectious hepatitis. That fall he moved from Marin County to San Francisco to be nearer comprehensive medical facilities. Faith Petric, Godmother of the San Francisco folk scene, remembers that he was living in a room on the 'Frisco waterfront with a small part-dachshund dog that he'd probably rescued when it was dumped off a boat from Australia. When Turner was hospitalized, Petric took in Willie the dog, thinking it would be a short-term visitor; but Turner never came out of hospital, and on September 23, 1974, he died. He was 41. Willie the dog lived on with Faith Petric for 17 more years.

[Gil Turner: 'Bob Dylan—a new voice singing new songs', *Sing Out!*, NY, Oct–Nov 1962; remarks at *Broadside* show, NY, May 1962, quoted from transcription seen online 19 Aug 2005 at *www.edlis.org/twice/threads/donald_white.html*. Lionel Kilberg & Kate Wolf with Don Coffin: *We Walked By the Water: Sociologically Singing Vol. 6*, Shoestryng Records, 1973. Other information from *Folk Music: More Than a Song*, Kristin Baggelaar & Donald Milton, New York: Thomas Y. Crowell, 1976; from Faith Petric, e-mail to this writer 26 Oct 2005 & from her newsletter *the folknik* vol.10, no.6, Nov–Dec 1974, pp.3&5.]

Twitty, Conway [1933 - 1993] Conway Twitty, born Harold Lloyd Jenkins in Friars Point, Mississippi, on September 1, 1933, began as an ELVIS wannabe—sounding like the Elvis of the Sun years—and must have been very badly managed, because after the move into the mainstream and after his first hit, the darkly magnificent million-seller 'It's Only Make-Believe', a no.1 hit in the US and UK on which he managed to sound both tormented and magisterial, he went into a rapid decline in popularity until his resuscitation in the US country market of the 1970s. Yet he cut many fine rock records and ballads, among them the masterly 'I Hope I Think I Wish'. This, released in 1963, was a clever pop lyric with an innovative use of sub-text, vividly evoking lovelorn gloom and wishful thinking, and it was given perfect performance by Twitty. The arrangement featured a distinctive piano part on very high notes which prefigures that on Dylan's 1989 *Oh Mercy* recording 'What Good Am I?'.

Conway Twitty died from an abdominal aneurysm en route to Nashville from a concert in Branson, Missouri, on June 5, 1993.

[Conway Twitty: 'It's Only Make-Believe', Nashville, TN, 7 May 1958, MGM E/SE 4217, Hollywood (MGM 992, London), 1958; 'I Hope I Think I Wish', Nashville, 11 Oct 1962, MGM SE 4709 (MGM 1187, London), 1963. Both Twitty tracks are on the 8-LP box set *Conway Twitty—The Rock'N'Roll Years (1956–1963)*, Bear Family BFX 15174 (9), Vollersode, Germany, 1985.]

'Two Soldiers' [1993] See **American Civil War in *World Gone Wrong*, the.**

U2 Inexplicably successful Irish rock group formed in 1980, fronted by one of the world's most self-important and vain celebrities, Bono (rhymes with con-oh, rather than with oh-no).

By the time Dylan was touring in 1984, more or less anyone could join him on stage, and at the open-air concert at Slane Castle, Ireland, on July 8, 1984, even Bono did, appearing during the encore to offer some shared vocals on 'Blowin' in the Wind', undeterred by not knowing any of the words. (Leslie Dowdell also shared the vocals with Dylan and our friend.) This was the last song on the last night of the 1984 European tour. Thus it finished, you might say if you were very rude, not with a bang but with a wanker.

U

Dylan met U2's guitarist the Edge at this time too, and the Edge sat in on the interview that Bono conducted with Dylan at Slane published in *Hot Press* no. 26, Dublin, 1984.

On April 20, 1987, Dylan was a guest at a U2 concert in LA, and shared vocals with Bono on 'I Shall Be Released' and 'Knockin' on Heaven's Door', and at some point the following month, for a U2 recording session, went into Sun Studios in Memphis to play harmonica and lend background vocals to 'Love Rescue Me', which he co-wrote; a year later he returned to the studios (this time in Hollywood) to play Hammond organ for U2 on the track 'Hawkmoon 269'. Both were released on their album *Rattle and Hum*, Island Records 7 91003-1, US, in October 1988.

When you deplore Dylan's increasing recent resort to tacky showbiz tricks of delivery in live performance, one quick listen to U2's live version of 'All Along the Watchtower', from the same album, reminds you that there are all kinds of cheap posturings and vulgarities that are stock in trade to stadium-rock in general and Bono in particular, and to which Dylan has yet to sink.

Dylan also allowed Bono on stage to play guitar and add (if that's the right word) backing vocals at his second 1989 Dublin concert (June 4) for the last two numbers, 'Knockin' on Heaven's Door' and 'Maggie's Farm' (you can imagine); almost ten years later Bono bounced back on stage during Dylan's encore in Las Vegas (March 2, 1999), again sharing vocals and playing guitar on 'Knockin' on Heaven's Door'.

In *Chronicles Volume One*, Dylan refers to Bono as a friend and says extravagantly positive things about his soul, knowledge, conversation and presence. He also credits Bono with having been the first to put him together with DANIEL LANOIS.

In fall 2005 Bono contributed a foreword to a UK book published in association with *Mojo* magazine, *Dylan: Visions, Portraits and Back Pages*, though by this point he was generally busy on bigger things. By 2005 Bono had gained the ear of world statesmen and European Union leaders, and could be heard pronouncing on every issue of global politics worthy of his attention. Another Irishman with a dodgy voice, he had become, in fact, the charmless man's BOB GELDOF.

[Dylan on Bono in *Chronicles Volume One*, pp.172–174. Mark Blake, ed., *Dylan: Visions, Portraits and Back Pages*, London: Dorling Kindersley/ Penguin, 2005.]

'Uncle John's Bongos' [1961] The record Dylan stole to make 'Tweedle Dee and Tweedle Dum' on *"Love and Theft"*. *See* **Johnnie & Jack**.

***Under the Red Sky* [1990]** The first Dylan album after *Oh Mercy* shows Dylan characteristically retreating from that album's mainstream production values and safe terrain, and refusing to offer a follow-up. Nevertheless his penchant for recently modish producers has him turn this time to DAVID & DON WAS of Was Not Was, who offer a rougher and less unified sound. It's a pity Dylan pads out the album with some sub-standard rockism ('Wiggle Wiggle' and 'Unbelievable') and the ill-fitting, foggy pop of 'Born in Time', because the core of the album is an adventure into the poetic possibilities of nursery rhyme that is alert, fresh and imaginative, and an achievement that has gone largely unrecognised.

The way Bob Dylan ends the album reflects his continued interest in challenging dividing lines between the song and the recording. This was in evidence on *Oh Mercy* in 'What was it you wanted? / You can tell me, I'm back' when his vocal returned after an instrumental break, followed by the punning 'let's get it back on the track'. It is in evidence here too. A reminder to the listener that it *is* a recording is built into the whole structuring of *Under the Red Sky*. The original vinyl Side 2 begins like a live recording: beginning before the song's beginning, by offering on the tape the ground-pawing noises musicians make just before they start to play, but without allowing you to feel certain if you've overheard genuine pawing or not. At the same time this sense of 'liveness' is undermined by the way that it begins with the smearing sound of this pre-song recording actually being switched on: to remind you that your LP, CD or tape is itself a copy of a tape. As that Side 2 begins, so it ends: like a live recording. For emphasis, every track on the album fades out except the last one. (The best thing about 'God Knows' being the way the shape of the song mocks the sermonising inside it, perhaps unintentionally, the singer has to rant more and more to squeeze the lines in as it works itself up like a sermon: and as soon as he starts to rant, they start fading him out. For the listener, it's as if you're slowly but surely closing the door on a Jehovah's Witness.) Only the last song on the album comes to a final end.

It's a challenge, though, a messy business: because while any pointing at *form* must distance the listener from *content*, Dylan's drawing attention to *this* form, this recording, stresses that the track has been done 'live': which is to make it, by rock's conventions, more 'real'. In turn the irony of this is that, unlike Dylan's early records, none of *Under the Red Sky* was done live: Dylan's vocals not only include drop-ins and overdubs but these are made as onto one big basic overdub: Dylan was still re-writing till the last possible moment, so that his vocals were added at the mixing stage of the album. Dylan challenges every divide here. All the same, the device of coming to a 'live' finish on the last track of an album on which every other song fades out also dramatises the outrageous last-minute call across another such divide that is, in the lyric, the album's final end: 'Cat's in the Well' has been entirely a third-person narrative, yet its last line is 'Goodnight my love, and may the Lord have mercy on us all.'

That 'Goodnight my love' is so personal it leaps out at you, cutting not only clean through the recording but jumping right out through the song itself. It is the most inspired, simple leave-taking on any of the albums of the artist who has always been incomparable at such leave-takings.

Stand-outs: 'Under the Red Sky' and 'Handy Dandy' (see separate entries), and 'Cat's in the Well'. See also **nursery rhyme on *Under the Red Sky*.**

[Recorded LA, 6 Jan & Mar–Apr 1990; released on CD as Columbia CK 46794 (in Europe as CBS 467188 2 & UK vinyl as Columbia 467188 1), 11 Sep 1990.]

'Under the Red Sky' [song, 1990] With great originality the *Under the Red Sky* album's purposive, dignified and beautifully performed title song pleaches the poetry of nursery rhyme and folklore, fairytale and the Bible into a 'simple', memorable whole:

> 'There was a little boy and there was a little girl / And they lived in an alley under the red sky. . . . / There was an old man and he lived in the moon / One summer's day he came passing by. . . . / Someday little girl everything for you is gonna be new / Someday little girl you'll have a diamond as big as your shoe. / Let the wind blow low, let the wind blow high / One day the little boy and the little girl were both baked in a pie. . . . / This is the key to the kingdom and this is the town / This is the blind horse that leads you around. / Let the bird sing, let the bird fly / One day the man in the moon went home and the river went dry. . . .'

'There was a little this and there was / he had a little that' is a common formula. Nursery rhymes that begin with it include 'There was a little boy and a little girl', 'There was a little girl, and she had a little curl', 'There was a little hare, and he ate his pasture bare', 'There was a little man, and he had a little gun', 'There was a little man, and he wooed a little maid', 'There was a little maid, and she was afraid', plus the comparable 'Shoe a little horse, shoe a little mare', 'There was a crooked man, and he walked a crooked mile', 'There was an old woman who had a little pig', 'There was a king met a king' and 'There was a mad man and he had a mad wife'. The one that resonates most clearly through 'Under the Red Sky' is 'There was a little boy and a little girl', collected in 1810: 'There was a little boy and a little girl / Lived in an alley. / Says the little boy to the little girl / Shall I, oh shall I? / Says the little girl to the little boy / What shall we do? / Says the little boy to the little girl / I will kiss you!'

In the nursery rhyme, there is time enough for playful romance. Not so today, Dylan seems to suggest, living 'Under the Red Sky': the alley is a narrower, darker place, nearer to the oppressive, narrow habitat of the old American underclass widely described in the blues than the airy playground of the children's clapping song 'Here comes Sally down the alley'. In the blues the alley is even more lowdown than the street, with 'doin' the alley boogie' a Lucille 'Shave 'Em Dry' Bogan speciality. She also sings that 'They call me Pig Iron Sally because I live in Slag Iron Alley: / And I'm evil and mean as I can be.' No place for children; yet of course children also play here, and it's an environment in which boys and girls grow up fast, one kind of game quickly becoming another, as in the fluid BLIND WILLIE McTELL song 'Georgia Rag', where 'Down in Atlanta, on Harris Street / That's where the boys and gals do meet / Out in the alley, out in the street / Every little kid that you meet / Buzz all around like a bee / Shake it like a ship on the sea.'

In 'Under the Red Sky' we are never invited to consider questions of romance between the little boy and the little girl: we are concerned with their very survival—and by extension, our own. All through the song survival is in doubt, with Dylan carefully handing us symbols that may or may not bode ill. As we've seen, the alley is of ambiguous import, and as we shall see too, even being baked in a pie may not be fatal.

In Matthew (16:2–4), Christ invokes the dual symbolism of the red sky when he's berating the corrupt sects of his day and telling them that the only 'sign' they can expect is the Resurrection: 'When it is evening, ye say, It will be fair weather: for the sky is red. And in the morning, It will be foul weather today: for the sky is red and lowring. O ye hypocrites, ye can discern the face of the sky; but can ye not discern the signs of the times?'

This might be said to be the key text, and a markedly 'Dylanesque' one, that Dylan is seeking to press home on 'Under the Red Sky' the song and *Under the Red Sky* the album. Christ's speech continues: 'A wicked and adulterous generation seeketh after a sign; and there shall no sign be given unto it, but the sign of the prophet Jonas.' (Christ is here responding not to his own followers but to the Pharisees and the Saducees, who try to get him to show them a sign from heaven, to prove himself, as if they're wanting to join him. This speech is his retort.)

Nursery rhyme, being sometimes more rational than we credit, takes the practical experience related here and boils it down to 'Red sky at night, shepherd's delight / Red sky at morning, shepherd's warning.' A peculiarly apt Indian equivalent is reported by Alexander Frater in his book *Chasing the Monsoon*. He reports that in the era of the British Empire, officials published a collection of almost 2000 peasants' proverbs (about 25 per cent were monsoon proverbs). Frater meets an antiquarian bookseller who knows this rare book and who tells him that 'the one that best sums it up is, "If the sky fails, the earth will surely fail too."' Bob Dylan's sentiments exactly.

Then there's the moon, and the old man in it. Is he a malign visitor, an incidental player, or the keeper of a benevolent eye upon the little boy and the little girl? STEPHEN SCOBIE's argument, in *Alias Bob Dylan*, that the moon symbolises some kind of evil intent, seems almost wholly unsupported. From earliest times the moon was beneficial: it was what we measured time by (the sanskrit root *me-*, to measure, is at the back of the word for moon in all the teutonic languages). In classical mythology the moon is several different heroines, all of them romantic: Hecate before she has risen and after setting, Astarte when crescent, Diana or Cynthia, she who 'hunts the clouds', when in the open vault of heaven (alluded to by Dylan in 'Sara': 'Glamorous nymph with an arrow and bow'), Phoebe the sister of the sun and Selene, or Luna, lover of the sleeping Endymion, when seen as moonlight on the fields.

In the villages of West Africa, as Chinua Achebe's pioneering 1958 novel *Things Fall Apart* reports, instead of the silence imposed by fear on a dark night, 'a moonlight night . . . would be different. The happy voices of children playing in open fields would then be heard.' The moon is regarded positively in the blues world too. 'Don't the moon look pretty' is recurrent, while in Michael Taft's *Blues Lyric Poetry* there isn't a single instance of the moon auguring bad news or evil in any of the 2,000 blues records transcribed.

In nursery rhyme too, the moon is contemplated with perfect equanimity, the classics of the genre being 'Boys and girls come out to play / The moon doth shine as bright as day' and 'I see the moon and the moon sees me / God bless the moon and God bless me.' Far from being sinister, or even cold, the moon is a companion for the child. Variants include the British 'I see the moon and the moon sees me / God bless the sailors on the sea,' said like a prayer when moonlight shines in through the child's bedroom window, and the American all's-well avowal of 'I see the moon, the moon sees me / The moon sees somebody I want to see.' Bob Dylan throws his own allusion to this into 'Wiggle Wiggle': its opening verse ends with 'Wiggle till the moon sees you.'

The moon is a friend and a familiar. The expression 'to cry for the moon' began as an allusion not to unreasonable ambition or greed but to children wanting the moon as a plaything. The French equivalent translates as 'He wants to take the moon between his teeth.' The moon is also benign in the legend that everything was saved and treasured there that was wasted and squandered on earth: misspent time, broken vows, unanswered prayers, fruitless tears, unfulfilled desires . . .

As for the man in the moon, he may have an ignominious biblical history but today we might consider him more sinned against than sinning. He's discernible when the moon is eight days old: a figure leaning on a fork, on which he carries a bundle of sticks gathered, sacrilegiously, on a sabbath. Some people also discern a small dog at his feet (which is why, in the Prologue to *A Midsummer Night's Dream*, 'This man, with lantern, dog and bush of thorn, / Presenteth moonshine'). Another tradition says the man is Cain, his dog and bush being respectively the 'foul fiend' and the thorns and briars of the Fall. Later legend claims that he was banished to the moon for trying to stop people attending mass by throwing his sticks across their path.

He comes from the Old Testament book of Numbers (15:32–36): 'And while the children of Israel were in the wilderness, they found a man that gathered sticks upon the sabbath day. And they . . . brought him unto Moses and Aaron, and unto all the congregation. And they put him in ward, because it was not declared what should be done to him. And the Lord said unto Moses, The man shall be surely put to death; all the congregation shall stone him . . .' And they did.

In nursery rhyme, the man in the moon's past is not held against him and at worst he takes on the moon's 'lunatic' influence, becoming an inspired simpleton, as in the English folksong (printed 1660 and reprinted as a broadside soon after) of which the nursery rhyme 'The man in the moon drinks claret' is the first few lines. In other nursery rhymes, when he is not receiving food, as in 'As I Went Up the Apple Tree', in which 'All the apples fell on me / Bake a pudding, bake a pie / Send it up to John MacKay / John MacKay is not in / Send it up to the man in the moon' he is providing it, as in 'There was a man lived in the moon', the chorus of which Dylan comes pretty close to quoting—his

'There was an old man and he lived in the moon . . . / There was an old man and he lived in the moon' being prefigured by its 'There was a man lived in the moon, lived in the moon, lived in the moon / There was a man lived in the moon / And his name was Aiken Drum.'

Here the man in the moon is a figure of bounty, clothed in provisions, satisfying primitive needs: 'he played upon a ladle . . . his hat was made of good cream cheese . . . his coat was made of good roast beef. . . . And his name,' far from being Cain, was the nonsensically jolly 'Aiken Drum'. Most of his clothes get eaten by Willy Wood, who then chokes to death on Drum's haggis breeches. This man in the moon, then, a mugger's victim, is hero not villain of his story.

So might it be with the old man who lives in the moon in Dylan's song. You might conclude, granted that it's when he goes home that the river runs dry, that it's not his visit that parches it—that his 'summer's day' visit has no discernible effect for good or ill: that at worst the man in the moon is being neutral, as in that exquisite blues couplet by Whistlin' Alex Moore, in which 'The wolves howled at midnight, wild ox moaned till day / The man in the moon looked down on us but had nothing to say.'

And yet . . . Dylan makes you work through conflicting implications here. Just as in the Moore verse, you're left feeling that this 'neutrality' means an unwillingness to be helpful or protective. There's a leaving-them-to-their-fate coldness at the end of both songs. Even on his first appearance in 'Under the Red Sky' he comes 'passing by'. If he passes right on by, he doesn't really visit the little girl and the little boy at all. On the other hand the very same phrase might equally well mean that he arrives on the scene, bestows his presence, makes his presence felt, becomes a figure in the action. Isn't it also implied that the man in the moon is the speaker of the soothing and benign lines that follow directly upon his 'passing by'?: 'Someday little girl everything for you is gonna be new / Someday little girl you'll have a diamond as big as your shoe.'

So we are left, as by every other image in the song, with some dynamic tension as to whether the man in the moon is a force for good or ill. This is, of course, the arena in which fairytales take place, since their fundamental message to the child is that good and ill are both within.

Dylan has taken 'Someday little girl you'll have a diamond as big as your shoe' from the nursery rhyme 'Little girl, little girl, where have you been? / Gathering roses to give to the queen. / Little girl, little girl, what gave she you? / She gave me a diamond as big as a shoe', and he strays from the strictly verbatim only in order to improve the slightly vague 'big as a shoe' to the more specific, and so more vivid, 'big as your shoe'.

Next comes 'Let the wind blow low, let the wind blow high'; inevitably this reminds us of lullabies ('When the wind blows, the cradle will rock'), if not also of the nursery rhyme in which when the wind blows the robin must shelter in the barn. But there is also a children's singing game, collected by nursery rhyme authorities Peter & Iona Opie, called 'The Wind Blows High'. Like so many others, it has numerous British and American variants. Each opening couplet is a variant of this one, to which Dylan's song alludes. It was collected in Washington, D.C., in 1886: 'The wind blows low, the wind blows high / The stars are dropping from the sky.' English versions tend to offer a lesser opening line but a lovely second one: 'The wind, the wind, the wind blows high / The rain comes scattering down the sky.' Both these variants fit neatly 'Under the Red Sky' in pointing to the sky as an imminent source of bad tidings.

On the face of it, what happens next is bad news indeed for our protagonists: 'One day the little boy and the little girl were both baked in a pie.' Pies are of course quintessential prized objects in the nursery rhyme world: things to savour and gobble, things to conceal other things, things to threaten to put people in, things to put people in. They occur everywhere: in 'Simple Simon', 'Georgie Porgie', 'Round about, round about, Maggotty pie / My father loves good ale and so do I'; 'Dame Get Up and Bake Your Pies'; 'There was an old woman / Sold puddings and pies'; 'Sing a Song of Sixpence'; 'Punch and Judy / Fought for a pie / Punch gave Judy / A knock in the eye'; 'Little Jack Horner' and many more. The man in the moon's waistcoat is made of piecrust. Yet the same worlds that savour all these pies allow their inhabitants to survive being baked in them. In his pioneering study of fairy tales, *The Uses of Enchantment*, Bruno Bettelheim writes that 'one of the most widely spread mythical incidents in the world [is] the reappearance of living people out of the monster that has devoured them.' When Christ cites the red sky he proceeds to allude to Jonah's survival in, and escape from, the belly of the whale as a prefiguring of his own Resurrection. In nursery rhyme this is a reassuring sub-text in 'Sing a Song of Sixpence'—the rhyme we all recognise as Dylan's source for the exact phrase 'baked in a pie'—in which 'When the pie was opened / The birds began to sing' (as Dylan has it, 'let the bird sing . . .'), and it is openly the cheery theme of another nursery rhyme, less familiar but also giving us the phrase 'baked in a pie', first published in 1843 (and which Bob Dylan seems to have known in an earlier age, when he borrowed its 'Baby and I' to make his 'Lady and I' in 'Desolation Row'): 'Baby and I / Were baked in a pie / The gravy was wonderful hot / We had nothing to pay / To the baker that day / And so we crept out of the pot.' One way and another, then, you can find implicit reason to hope that in 'Under the

Red Sky' the hero and heroine do not perish when baked.

With or without them, the song continues, extending its extraordinary tapestry of nursery rhyme, fairytale and biblical threads: 'This is the key to the kingdom / And this is the town / This is the blind horse / That leads you around . . .' It is just 14 verses after his red sky speech, in the same chapter of Matthew, that Christ tells Peter he is the rock upon which 'I will build my church; and the gates of hell shall not prevail against it. And I will give unto thee the keys of the kingdom of heaven'—bestowing not the means of entering but the power to admit or not admit others. Simultaneously the keys are the true knowledge of the doctrine of the kingdom of heaven. (The word 'church' here means assembly or congregation; it does not mean an institution. This text, including the passage that follows it immediately, is understood very differently by Protestants and Catholics.) The words that follow directly on from 'the keys of the kingdom of heaven' are 'and whatsoever thou shalt bind on earth, shall be bound in heaven, and whatsoever thou shalt loose on earth shall be loosed in heaven' (repeated in 18:18, and, in different words, in John 20:23), part of the meaning of which refers back to the belief held by the Jews that every thing that was done on earth according to the order of God was at the same time done in heaven. In Adam Clarke's *Commentary on the Bible* he says that for instance 'when the priest, on the day of atonement, offered the two goats upon earth, the same were offered in heaven. As one goat therefore is permitted to escape on earth, one is permitted to escape in heaven.' This compares nicely with the pagan belief, mentioned above, that every thing wasted on earth is saved and cherished on the moon.

The phrase 'key to the kingdom' occurs first in Dylan's work on the unreleased Basement Tapes song 'Sign on the Cross': 'Well, it's that old sign on the cross / Well, it's that old key to the kingdom, / Well, it's that old sign on the cross . . . / That worries me'; and as the context here makes unsurprising, 'Key to the Kingdom' is an old gospel song. It has a plain-speaking chorus that makes it clear that to be given the key to the kingdom is no small thing—and is just the sort of special power which protects many a fairytale hero/ine: 'I got the key to the kingdom / And my enemies can't do me no harm.' (It was recorded in 1929, for example, by both Bessie Johnson & Her Sanctified Singers and by Washington Phillips.)

However, the phrase is the title-line of a palindromic nursery rhyme too: 'This is the key of the kingdom: / In that kingdom there is a city. / In that city there is a town. / In that town there is a street. / In that street there is a lane. / In that lane there is a yard. / In that yard there is a house. / In that house there is a room. / In that room there is a bed. / On that bed there is a basket. / In that basket there are some flowers. / Flowers in the basket. / Basket in the bed. / Bed in the room. / Room in the house. / House in the yard. / Yard in the lane. / Lane in the street. / Street in the town. / Town in the city. / City in the kingdom. / Of the kingdom this is the key.' (The item around which pivots this jingle with two faces, the basket of flowers, is one that Dylan uses in 'Handy Dandy', in which the line 'he got a stick in his hand and a pocket full of money' is balanced in the last verse by 'he got a basket of flowers and a bag full of sorrow'.)

As Dylan uses the nursery rhyme's 'This is the key of the kingdom' for the second bridge of 'Under the Red Sky', he makes it sound like a song to accompany a winding-through-the-streets game (a 'Chains and Captives' game, to use the 19th century classification), like 'Thread the Needle', 'How Many Miles to Babylon?', 'The Big Ship Sails' and 'Oranges and Lemons': 'This is the key to the kingdom / And this is the town / This is the blind horse / That leads you around.'

It is easy to hear these lines that way, since they end by nominating (almost self-reflexively) something that 'leads you around', but by this point we've already picked up some sense of a game being chanted, thanks to its back-echoes of old familiars like the finger-rhyme 'Here's the church and here's the steeple / Open the doors and here's all the people'.

Like all the rest, the blind horse is, as it were, a symbol that looks both ways. The blind leading the blind is Not Good; why should the blind leading the baked be any better? On the other hand the blind horse suggests itself as Falada, a sort of equine fairy godmother, the benign guardian to the little girl in the fairytale 'The Goose Girl'. Falada may be a 'blind' horse (in fact decapitated rather than blinded) but it holds the key to the regaining of her rightful kingdom, and guides the little girl towards it not by explicit instruction but by the enigmatic hints of a repeated spoken rhyme, to prompt the heroine towards worthier, more mature action. Here is a rare and relishable instance of fairytale and adult folksong coming together: for the rhyme spoken by the horse in the story is echoed by the words of the folksong 'Pretty Peggy-O' (as sung by Bob Dylan, for instance at London Hammersmith on February 3, 1990): 'If this your mother knew / Her heart would break in two.'

In the fairytale the repeated rhyme eventually nudges the Goose Girl, who is really a dispossessed princess, into breaking out of the Goose Girl rôle in which a servant's duplicity has trapped her. Let the bird sing, let the bird fly. There is, moreover, a nursery rhyme dealing with a directly comparable theme: the eventual compunction not to stay safely in a rôle someone else has assigned you but to break out to chase fulfilment, and possible danger, in a wider world. And it is a nursery rhyme in which a blind horse is the agent for the plunge into the unknown. We all know its beginning; it is 'My mother said I never should / Play with the gypsies in the wood.' It ends like this: 'The wood was dark, the grass was green / Up comes Sally with a tambourine / . . . I went to the river, no ship to get across / I paid ten shillings for an old blind horse / I up on his back and off in a crack / Sally tell my mother I shall never come back.' Like 'the key to the kingdom', then, the blind horse can be a means to salvation, making Dylan's stanza, against all initial expectation, positive from start to finish.

This theme, that breaking free of one's inner constraints is an imperative, tallies with something Dylan has said about the song, according to the *Under the Red Sky* album's co-producer, DON WAS, who claimed: 'It's actually about people who got trapped in his hometown. I think it's about Hibbing and about people who never left. . . . He said, "It's about my hometown."'

It is almost unprecedented for Dylan to let out this kind of explanation as to what a song is 'about'. This doesn't mean he didn't say it, any more than it means he's right, or that he'd have offered the same 'explanation' 24 hours later: but it sits well enough alongside the song.

There is even a precedent for this sort of scenario in nursery rhyme. Instead of it being the little girl and little boy trapped in the alley under the red sky who eventually get baked in a pie (fatally or not), there is 'A little cock sparrow', who only avoids ending up in a pie by fleeing: 'A little cock sparrow sat on a tree / Looking as happy as happy can be / Till a boy came by with his bow and arrow / Says he, "I will shoot the little cock sparrow / His body will make me a nice little stew / His giblets will make me a little pie too." / Says the cock sparrow, "I'll be shot if I stay" / So he clapped his wings and flew away.'

Let the bird sing, let the bird fly.

[Lucille Bogan (as Bessie Jackson): 'Down in Boogie Alley', NY, 1 Aug 1934 & 'Pig Iron Sally', NY, 31 Jul 1934, both on *Lucille Bogan & Walter Roland (1930–1935)*, Roots RL-317, Vienna, 1968. Blind Willie McTell, 'Georgia Rag', Atlanta, 31 Oct 1931, *Blind Willie McTell: The Early Years (1927–1933)*, Yazoo L-1005, NY, 1968. Whistlin' Alex Moore: 'West Texas Woman', Dallas, 5 Dec 1929; *I'm Wild About My Lovin', 1928–1930*, Historical HLP-32, Jersey City, NJ, 1969. Bessie Johnson & Her Sanctified Singers: 'Key to the Kingdom', Atlanta, 21 Mar 1929, CD-reissued *Memphis Gospel*, Document DOCD-5072, Vienna, 1991. Washington Phillips: 'I've Got the Key to the Kingdom', Dallas, 2 Dec 1929, CD-reissued *Storefront & Streetcorner Gospel (1927–1929)*, Document DOCD-5054, Vienna, *nia*.

Alexander Frater, *Chasing the Monsoon*, London: Penguin, 1991. Stephen Scobie, *Alias Bob Dylan*, Red Deer, Alberta: Red Deer College Press, 1991. Chinua Achebe, *Things Fall Apart*, Oxford: Heinemann African Writers Series, 3rd UK edn., 1986. Michael Taft, *Blues Lyric Poetry: An Anthology*, New York: Garland, 1983; republished as *Talkin' to Myself: Blues Lyrics, 1921–1942*, New York: Routledge, 2005. Iona & Peter Opie: for details of their work & sources, see endnotes to **nursery rhyme, Dylan's use of, an introduction**. Bruno Bettelheim, *The Uses of Enchantment*, London: Thames & Hudson, 1976. Adam Clarke, *Commentary on the Bible*, London: Thomas Tegg, 7 vols., 1844 (not the 1st edn.). Don Was quote, LA, 15 Oct 1990, *The Telegraph* no.37, UK, winter 1990.]

Updike, John [1932 -] Eminent American writer, born March 18, 1932, Shillington, PA; he reviewed concerts in Ipswich, Massachussetts, 1961–1965. Of a JOAN BAEZ concert of 1964, he wrote: '[in] the unkindest cut of all, Miss Baez yielded the stage, with a delight all too evident, to a young man, Bob Dylan, in tattered jeans and a black jacket, three months on the far side of a haircut, whose voice you could scour a skillet with. Miss Baez, this admirer was pained to observe, visibly lit up with love-light when he came onto the stage, and even tried to force her way, in duet, through some of the impenetrable lyrics that Dylan composes as abundantly as poison ivy puts forth leaves.' This (in contrast to Dylan's impenetrable lyrics) was the consummate word-craft of America's great novelist, short-story writer and poet, a Pulitzer prize-winner with a reputation as 'a keen observer of modern American life' in fiction 'assured, urbane and ironic' and 'as versatile as it is prolific.' Before Baez started having Dylan perform at her concerts (after his success at the NEWPORT FOLK FESTIVAL of 1963) she had given a similar guest-slot to FLATT & SCRUGGS and to the GREENBRIAR BOYS. How were their haircuts, John?

[Updike quoted from the anthology of his concert reviews *Concerts at Castle Hill*, 1993. Quotes re his literary reputation are from Ian Ousby's excellent *Cambridge Guide to Literature in English*, 1993 (corrected reprint 1995).]

'Vacillation' Poem by W.B. Yeats (1865–1939) that may have given Dylan a phrase he uses on the 1964 song 'Chimes of Freedom', from *Another Side of Bob Dylan*, and may have given him rather more.

Dylan speaks in the mid-1960s about behaviour in the face of the certainty of death. In the course of a remarkable interview with Horace Judson, from *Time* magazine, given at the Royal Albert Hall, London, May 9, 1965, Dylan, wired up with youth's impatience (at least), and moving among lumpen dullards like some beautiful alien from superior space, can say to the 40-something reporter:

V

'I'm saying that you're going to die, and you're gonna go off the earth, you're gonna be dead. Man, it could be, you know, twenty years, it could be tomorrow, any time. So am I. I mean, we're just gonna be gone. The world's going to go on without us. All right now. You do your job in the face of that and how seriously you take yourself, you decide for yourself.' This is captured in the film *Don't Look Back*, and transcribed in the book of the film, D.A. PENNEBAKER's *Bob Dylan / Don't Look Back*, 1968. (Here the *Time* reporter is not identified, but he is named as Horace Judson in Peter Marshall's 'Hotel Blues', in the fanzine *The Telegraph* no.54, Richmond, Surrey, spring 1996.)

Although Dylan sounded prepared for death earlier than this (e.g. back on 1962's 'Let Me Die in My Footsteps'), perhaps it was reading Yeats in 1964 that gave him the conviction he expresses in that interview. Dylan's 'starry-eyed and laughing' echoes Yeats' 'open eyed and laughing'—the one describing the stance of youth, the other the resolve of middle age. Yeats' line is from 'Vacillation':

> 'No longer in Lethean foliage caught / Begin the preparation for your death / And from the fortieth winter by that thought / Test every work of intellect or faith, / And everything that your own hands have wrought, / And call those works extravagance of breath / That are not suited for such men as come / Proud, open eyed and laughing to the tomb.'

The precociously wise young Dylan of 1964–65 seems to have taken this teaching to heart. Perhaps 'Vacillation' both fired up this resolve to do what you do in the knowledge that you're going to die *and* gave him the phrase he revises in 'Chimes of Freedom'.

[W.B. Yeats: 'Vacillation' taken from *The* New *Natural Death Handbook*, ed. Albery, UK: Elliot & Elliot, 1997, p.11.]

Valens, Ritchie [1941 - 1959] Ritchie Valens was born the same month as Bob Dylan (on May 13, 1941, in LA) but died before Dylan ever made a record. Ritchie too formed a rock'n'roll band in high school (the Silhouettes, at San Fernando High), and was heavily influenced by LITTLE RICHARD. Signed to Bob Keene's Del-Fi label, his first hit was his own song 'Come on Let's Go'—which, defying all the rules of the known universe, was inferior to the British cover version by Tommy Steele. But the big Valens hit was the double-sided 'Donna' c/w 'La Bamba'. The latter has proved one of those immortal classics capable of being a hit time and again. No-one tried to cover this track when it was new, and no-one has since succeeded in covering it with half the appeal and energy of the original. Valens also had time to appear in one film: the Alan Freed let's-hold-a-talent-contest! movie *Go Johnny Go*, in which he performs his Little Richard-inspired 'Ooh My Head'.

Valens died, along with the Big Bopper, in the single-engine plane crash that killed BUDDY HOLLY in the early hours of February 3, 1959, en route to North Dakota in the snow. Holly's lead guitarist Tommy Allsup should have been on the plane, and Valens on the bus, but as Allsup recalls: 'I was the one who chartered the plane, but I flipped a coin with Ritchie Valens—he kept bugging me all night that he'd never flown in a little plane. He won the toss.'

Dylan saw them perform at the Duluth Armory just three nights before the crash. In 1987, Dylan was filmed driving near Malibu, CA, paying tribute to Ritchie Valens; a one-minute-long piece of footage of this was used within the promotional trailer for the film *La Bamba*, a Valens biopic.

[Ritchie Valens: 'Come on Let's Go', Del-Fi 4106, US (Pye International 7N 25000, London), 1958; 'Donna' c/w 'La Bamba', Del-Fi 4110, 1958 (London American HL 8803, 1959; all released (with more than enough other Valens tracks for anyone, and including 'Ooh My Head') on the CD *Ritchie Valens / Ritchie*, Ace CDCHD 953, London, 1990. *Go Johnny Go*, dir. Paul Landres, Hal Roach Studios Inc. / Valiant, US, 1959. Bob Dylan: spoken comments on Valens, spring-summer 1987, nr. Malibu; released in trailer for *La Bamba*, dir. & written Louis Valdez, Columbia Pictures / New Visions, US, 1987.]

Van Ronk, Dave [1936 - 2002] David Ritz Van Ronk was born in Brooklyn, New York, on June 30, 1936, grew up partly in Queens, attended Richmond Hill High School, sang in a barbershop quartet at 13, dropped out of high school at 15, joined the Merchant Marines, learnt the ukelele, loved jazz, moved to Greenwich Village and became a professional musician in 1956. He discovered prewar blues via 'a chance encounter with a recording of "Stackolee" made by Furry Lewis', as Van

Ronk said himself: 'Taking it to be a form of Jazz, in which I was primarily interested, I made some further investigations and discovered a whole field of music. . . . and so, having only such singers as Furry Lewis, King Solomon Hill and LEADBELLY for models, when I tried to sing these songs I naturally imitated what I heard and, if I couldn't understand a word here or there, I just slurred right along with the singer. At that time, nobody listened to me anyway.'

They soon did. He became a Washington Square regular and an established figure in the Village, recording, performing and keeping an open house several years before the young Bob Dylan came to town, slept on Dave's couch, got Dave's future wife Terri Thal to be his first manager, learnt some of Dave's repertoire, stole some of Dave's repertoire and generally looked up to him as the singer who 'reigned supreme'. Except of course financially. He was almost always on small, worthy record labels. Hence his famous wry remark: 'Other entertainers record for money; I record for Prestige.'

This is his friend Elijah Wald's summary: 'Dave Van Ronk was a founding father of the 1960s folk and blues revivals, but he was far more than that. For one thing, he was a marvelous raconteur, one of the funniest and most quotable figures on the Village scene. . . . Dave honed his tales along with his music, while holding court in cafes, bars, and from his apartment on Sheridan Square. As a musician, mentor, and barroom philosopher, his influence was so great that the block he lived on was recently renamed Dave Van Ronk Street. This is an honor that would have made him particularly happy, because much as he loved music, he loved the Village almost as deeply. From the time he moved there in the early 1950s until his death . . . he never considered living anywhere else.'

(He lived on MacDougal in the late 1950s, moved to 15th for a while after getting together with Terri, then ran back to the Village, specifically to Waverly Place, holding court there through the 1960s; he moved to Sheridan Place when he broke up with Terri, and lived there for the rest of his life. The 'Dylan' apartment was the one on Waverly Place.)

Van Ronk more or less invented the milieu of the young white city folk-blues, and though he wrote little material of his own, the entire East Coast singer-songwriter oeuvre would have been different without him. He set very high standards of guitar playing, not least in demonstrating what richness of instrumentation could be achieved on the lone guitar. His own guitar mentor had been REV. GARY DAVIS but Van Ronk made what he learnt his own, bringing a more modern consciousness to finger-picking without any loss of complexity or imaginative dexterity.

When people write, as they often do, of what tender guitar-work he puts alongside his 'rough voice', they are half right: they're right about the guitar. But the voice is not merely 'rough'—often there's nothing rough about it at all. To listen to Van Ronk is to hear is one of the most resourceful, subtle, *alive* voices ever put on record. Hear his early cover of Dylan's 'He Was a Friend of Mine'—here is a great artist, communicating as directly as Dylan himself, his tone a unique mix of keening and shimmer. It's only very rarely indeed that someone cuts through as strongly and exhilaratingly as he can. DANNY KALB wrote that 'Dave Van Ronk's sound was unafraid, funky and a joyous challenge. . . . The challenge was, I think, to go for it all the way, and don't look back.' Tom Waits said: 'In the engine room of the NY Folk Scene shoveling coal into the furnace, one Big Man rules. Dog faced roustabout songster. Bluesman, Dave Van Ronk. Long may he howl.'

Kalb's 'unafraid, funky . . . joyous' describes the voice far better than Waits' 'howl'; but Waits' affectionate portrait suggests the large man's energy and impact around town while also putting his finger on one of the reasons why Bob Dylan 'made it' in a way that Van Ronk never could. Look at photos of the two of them together in the early 60s and, a decade on, at the Friends of Chile Benefit Concert. Dylan is the lithe, sexy, charismatic one; Van Ronk is the awkward, fat-faced one with sweaty armpits and a beer gut. But if he didn't have the right image for national celebrity, nor the songwriting ability, nor the killer instinct, no matter: he had everything else. He was an unforgettable live performer, a stratospherically gifted guitarist, an all-time great singer, a shrewd observer of other people (including of Dylan), a generous host whose place was where everyone came for all-night poker games, abrasive talk and good cheer, and with all this, he was also a figure of gravitas—a great man. In *Chronicles Volume One*, Dylan's vivid, detailed portrait of Greenwich Village when it was new to him contains no other portrait half as long, half as warm, half as fulsome or half as respectful as of Dave Van Ronk.

Van Ronk was always shrewd and honest about Dylan. They fell out in a major way just once, and he said so: 'We had a terrible falling out about "House of the Rising Sun". He was always a sponge, picking up whatever was around him, and he copped my arrangement of the song. Before going into the studio he asked, "Hey Dave, mind if I record your version of Rising Sun?" I said, "Well, Bobby, I'm going into the studio soon and I'd like to record it." And later he asked me again and I told him I wanted to record it myself, and he said, "Oops, I already recorded it myself and I can't do anything about it because Columbia wants it." For a period of about two months, we didn't speak to each other. He never apologized, and I give him credit for it.'

Van Ronk was just as transparent about the younger musician's stories and myth-making (or lies, as some call it), again stepping back and seeing it in the round, and speaking for others as if all were as generous-minded: 'We accepted him not because of the things he had said he'd done but because we respected him as a performer. The attitude of the community was that it was all right, it was cool. He gets on stage and delivers, and that's fine. His pose didn't bother us. Nobody was turned off by it. Whatever he said offstage, onstage he told the truth as best he knew it.'

Van Ronk's perspective was wide enough, too, that he could see sides of Dylan beyond the folk-clubs. This, for instance, is accurate and at the same time very much his own judgement, independently arrived at: 'Bobby is very much a product of the Beat Generation. Dylan really does belong in a rack with KEROUAC. You are not going to see any more like him. Bobby came into Beat poetry just at the very tail end. He towers above all of them, except perhaps GINSBERG. But Bob was a latecomer and will have no successors, just as his namesake had no successors.' Every bit of that is extremely shrewd, and there are few who have dared venture, in plain terms like that, that Dylan 'towers above' all those revered BEATS.

There is precious little recorded evidence of Van Ronk and Dylan together, and what there is, as it happens, is pitifully unrepresentative of how they might have performed on the same stage. There's an amateur recording of a short Dylan set made at the Gaslight on September 6, 1961, when Dylan sings 'Man on the Street', 'He Was a Friend of Mine', 'Talking Bear Mountain Picnic Massacre Blues', 'Song to Woody' and 'Pretty Polly', after which Dave Van Ronk joins him and they share vocals on that arch GUTHRIE children's song 'Car, Car'. If only they had shared out 'He Was a Friend of Mine' instead! And apart from Van Ronk's voice lost in the general drunken haze of an ensemble 'Blowin' in the Wind' at that Friends of Chile Benefit Concert at the Felt Forum, New York City, on May 9, 1974, that's all there is! The only time they appeared on the same record—and then not on the same track—was that 1965 Elektra compilation LP *The Blues Project*, on which Dylan plays piano behind GEOFF MULDAUR on 'Downtown Blues' (billed as Bob Landy) and Dave Van Ronk performs 'Bad Dream Blues' on one side and opens the other with 'Don't You Leave Me Here'.

Fortunately, though, we do at least have not only Dylan's 'cover' of Van Ronk's 'House of the Rising Sun': we also have several tremendous Van Ronk covers of Dylan songs, including a lively version of 'If I Had to Do It All Over' (as he calls it), recorded with the Red Onion Jazz Band in 1962 and released on a 1964 single as well as the album *In the Tradition*, that very early 'He Was a Friend of Mine' (first on the 1963 album *Dave Van Ronk Folksinger*) through a 1979 'Song to Woody' on *Somebody Else, Not Me*, a 1994 'Subterranean Homesick Blues' on *To All My Friends in Far-Flung Places*, and a touching, almost consciously farewell-bidding solo version of 'Buckets of Rain', recorded at what turned out to be Van Ronk's last concert, in October 2001, and released on a posthumous album, the crummily titled . . . *and the tin pan bended and the story ended*. . . .

In the filmed interview with Van Ronk given to JEFF ROSEN of Dylan's office for the archives, and made available for use in SCORSESE's *No Direction Home*, the big bear-like figure, the Mayor of MacDougal Street, has become the mellow, shy, silver-stubbled, bronchitic, self-deprecating man with a laugh that makes the viewer laugh, a vulnerability that is touching (again, a strong contrast to that most steely interviewee, Dylan himself) and a generosity of spirit, a fondness for Dylan and an appreciation of his contribution to a whole musical community—all of which makes him one of the film's most fragile yet valuable contributors: still, after all these years, giving out and being *real*.

'Even now,' wrote Danny Kalb, 'I can almost hear him laughing freely and deeply, unfortunately still smoking those damn cigarettes, even as we, his friends left behind, weep and celebrate him at the same time.'

His many recordings cover a long, long period and vary enormously. If a 'best' has to be specified, then it is probably the work of the early 1960s that captures it most powerfully: yet whatever you pick out you'll find yourself more than amply rewarded.

Dave Van Ronk died of complications arising from his cancer, in hospital in New York City, on February 10, 2002.

[Dave Van Ronk: 'If I Had to Do It All Over' (with the Red Onion Jazz Band), Prestige PR 45-288, US, 1964 & on *In the Tradition*, Prestige 14001, US, 1964; *Dave Van Ronk Folksinger*, Prestige 14012, 1963 (CD-reissued Fantasy CD 24710, US, *n/a*); *Somebody Else, Not Me*, Philo PH 1065, US, 1980 (carelessly CD-reissued as *Someone Else, Not Me*, Rounder CD PHIL 1065, US, 1990); *To All My Friends in Far-Flung Places* (2-CD set), Gazell GPCD 2011/12, US, 1994; . . . *and the tin pan bended and the story ended* . . . , Adelphi, MD, 22 Oct 2001, Smithsonian Folkways SFW40156, Washington, D.C., 2004.

Van Ronk quotes from various unfootnoted sources. 'Dave Remembered', Danny Kalb, 2002, online 14 Sep 2005 at *http://members.aol.com/silvastr/danny/danny.htm*. Elijah Wald (to whom thanks for some information) quoted from the website page promoting Van Ronk's memoir, edited with Wald & completed by him after Van Ronk's death, *The Mayor of MacDougal Street, a Memoir*, New York: Da Capo, 2005; quote seen online 14 Sep 2005 at *http://elijahwald.com/vanronk.html#whiff*.]

Van Zandt, Steve [1950 -] Steven Lento was born in Boston on November 22, 1950 and grew up to be a lean-machine guitarist, mandolin player and extravagant showman in BRUCE SPRINGSTEEN's E Street Band, though he quit acrimoniously in 1982, returning fleetingly in 1995 and more permanently in 1999. He has also been the Miami Steve (aka Little Steven) songwriting, producing and arranging, most notably for Southside Johnny & the Asbury Dukes, which he co-founded in 1974 but also working with Dion, Gary Bonds, Ronnie Spector and others; disparate further projects have included five solo albums, part-time fronting of the group the Disciples of Soul, the hosting of the syndicated radio series 'Little Steven's Underground Garage' and, since 1999, acting impressively (despite a risible hairpiece) in the TV series 'THE SOPRANOS' as mobster and strip-club owner Silvio Dante.

In 1985 he created both the Solidarity Foundation, to support the sovereignty and protection of indigenous peoples, and Artists United Against Apartheid, to lead a campaigning boycott against the white-supremacist South African régime's most lavish and brazen tourist entertainment resort, Sun City. For this he pulled in 49 recording-artist collaborators to help create the echo-soaked, heavily rhymic semi-rap single release 'Sun City', recorded that summer in Hollywood, which was an effective publicity success. The participants, who pledged never to play the resort themselves, included Springsteen, Run DMC and Bob Dylan—who contributes shared vocals, dubbed over the basic music track, and was probably very grateful to be offered a chance to be seen on the side of the angels as regards Africa within weeks of his very unpopular remarks at LIVE AID that July 13.

By this point, Dylan and Van Zandt had already worked together. That February 19 (1985) Little Steven had dropped into the New York studios where Dylan was recording tracks for *Empire Burlesque* and played guitar on at least one attempt at 'Never Gonna Be the Same Again' (still uncirculated) and a number of attempts at 'When the Night Comes Falling from the Sky', one of which became the version subsequently released on the *Bootleg Series Vols. 1–3* in 1991.

Fourteen years on from that session, and at a Never-Ending Tour concert in Zurich on April 25, 1999, Steve Van Zandt (and NILS LOFGREN) came on stage for the last encore number of Dylan's set, playing guitar on the old Buddy Holly number 'Not Fade Away'.

That same year, Van Zandt released his fifth solo album, *Born Again Savage*, and a *Greatest Hits* collection, the former on his own label, Renegade Nation. He remains a bandana-wearing, biceps-flexing, Right On activist musician.

[Steve Van Zandt, Bob Dylan & others: 'Sun City', *Artists United Against Apartheid*, Manhattan ST 53019, US & UK, 1985.]

Vaughan, Jimmie [1951 -] Jimmie Vaughan was born in Dallas, Texas, on March 21, 1951. A blues guitarist and singer, he is the older brother of the late STEVIE RAY VAUGHAN. Jimmie's playing was much influenced by the three blues guitar Kings (Albert, B.B. but especially Freddie, whom he knew). He learnt guitar at 13, started his first band at 15, and at age 16 opened for JIMI HENDRIX at a live show in Dallas.

Like his younger brother, Vaughan moved to Austin in the early 1970s and in 1974 he and Californian vocalist & harmonica player Kim Wilson formed the Fabulous Thunderbirds, whose early albums (1979–83) are considered significant. Dropped from their record deal because of disappointing sales, they soldiered on but made themselves 'more commercial', got a new deal and made less interesting new albums. Vaughan quit the band in 1989, and early the following year recorded the album *Family Style* with brother Stevie, which was released after the latter's death in a 1990 helicopter crash. His first solo album, *Strange Pleasures*, came out in 1994 and contained a memorial to his brother, 'Six Strings Down'.

In 2004, Jimmie Vaughan headlined a benefit concert for the Libertarian Party's presidential candidate, Michael Badnarik, in Austin and performed at a 'Red, Rock and Blues' concert at the party's national convention in Atlanta.

Both brothers played on Dylan's 1990 album *Under the Red Sky*. Both featured on '10,000 Men', 'God Knows' and 'Cat's in the Well', with Jimmie playing lead on the lattermost; he alone also played on 'Handy Dandy'. And then on October 25, 1991, when the Never-Ending Tour came through Austin, Texas, Jimmie came on stage and played on 'Maggie's Farm'.

[Jimmie Vaughan: *Strange Pleasure*, Sony 57202, US, 1994.]

Vaughan, Stevie Ray [1954 - 1990] Stevie Ray Vaughan was born in Dallas, Texas, on October 3, 1954, learnt guitar after growing to love his older brother JIMMIE's blues-based record collection, dropped out of high school in 1972 and moved to Austin, where there was a vast student population and a burgeoning live music scene. He became a defining figure in 1980s Texas rock'n'roll (a kind of benign redneck R&B). A master of the Fender Stratocaster, with a unique tone and technique, he led the group Double Trouble. You might blame Stevie Ray Vaughan for the irritating riff on the only weak track on *"Love and Theft"*, 'Honest with Me'.

Prior to Double Trouble Vaughan had played with local Austin groups the Nightcrawlers and Paul Ray &the Cobras. In 1976, Vaughan formed his own band, the Triple Threat Revue, first renamed Triple Threat and then, when the vocalist quit in 1981, Double Trouble (though actually this remained a trio). In 1982 they played the Montreux Festival, Switzerland, where David Bowie asked Vaughan to play on what became his *Let's Dance* album. This led to other stints as a sideman with the ROLLING STONES and Jackson Browne.

Double Trouble's 1983 début album *Texas Flood* was a critical success and sold half a million; they followed it with the far greater commercial successes of *Couldn't Stand the Weather* (1984) and *Soul to Soul* (1985). These records were on Epic, but another album, *Blues Explosion*, on Atlantic, won a Grammy as Best Traditional Blues Record of the Year in 1984.

In 1986, after collapsing on stage in Germany, he checked into an Atlanta rehabilitation clinic. Two years later he seemed to be fully functioning again, performing an unplugged set on MTV and in 1989 touring with Jeff Beck and releasing the fifth Double Trouble album, *In Step*, which also gave him a no.1 radio hit, 'Crossfire'.

In 1990 Vaughan recorded *Family Style*, an album made with brother Jimmie, co-headlined another tour, this time with Joe Cocker, and embarked on a headlining Double Trouble tour. That April 30 he laid down some guitar overdubs on tracks for Dylan's *Under the Red Sky* album that Dylan had recorded that January 6th. He played on 'Cat's in the Well' and '10,000 Men', and played lead guitar on 'God Knows'.

Stevie Ray Vaughan died in a helicopter crash near East Troy, Wisconsin, on August 27, 1990 (having just performed as a guest at an ERIC CLAPTON concert in Alpine Valley). Bob Dylan first responded with appropriate restraint: 'He was a sweet guy. Something else was coming through him besides his guitar playing and singing.' Later, unfortunately, before a concert in Merrillville, Indiana, he added the vacuously inaccurate: 'It's almost like having to play the night that Kennedy died. He'll probably be revered as much as and in the same way as HANK WILLIAMS'. More sweetly, he dedicated a performance of 'Moon River' to Vaughan that night.

Posthumous record releases are plentiful. One of the earliest was that recorded with brother Jimmie that same year; *Family Style* was released as by 'the Vaughan Brothers'. There is now a ludicrous statue of Stevie Ray at Riverside Drive and South 1st Street in Austin.

[Double Trouble: *Texas Flood*, Epic FET/EK 38734, US, 1983; *Blues Explosion*, Atlantic 7 80149-1, US, 1984; *Couldn't Stand the Weather*, Epic FET/EK 39304, US, 1984; *Soul to Soul*, Epic FET/EK 40036, US, 1985; *Live Alive!*, Epic, EGK/EGT 40511, US, 1986; *In Step*, Epic OET/EK 45024, US, 1989. The Vaughan Brothers: *Family Style*, Epic ZT/ZK 46225, US, 1990.]

Vee, Bobby [1943 -] Robert Thomas Velline was born in Fargo, North Dakota, on April 30, 1943, and grew up via rockabilly to be a teenage pop star. By the time Bob Dylan was 'making it' in 1963, Vee, two years younger, was already struggling to hold onto pop stardom.

Dylan played piano in Bobby Vee's band for a very brief period in 1959. Vee has told the story many times, as here: 'After we recorded "Suzie Baby", we started getting out and we were a rhythm band with guitar, bass and drums. My brother Bill played lead guitar and I played rhythm guitar and we would switch round from time to time. We were looking for a piano player . . . as we had seen JERRY LEE LEWIS as the opening act on a country show and he just tore it up. . . . Bill was in a record shop called Sam's Record Land in Fargo and this guy approached him and introduced himself as Elston Gunn [but see the entry **pseudonyms used by Dylan**] and said that he had got off the road with CONWAY TWITTY as his piano player. Bill was blown away. He took him to the radio station where there was a piano and he rocked out pretty good in the key of C and we thought we would give him a try. He hadn't played with Conway Twitty. Conway Twitty had been in the area and Dylan had seen him in Duluth a couple of nights earlier and then he came down to Fargo and was working as a busboy at the Red Apple Café. It was not meant to be, he didn't have a piano and we didn't have enough money to buy him one. He stuck around a couple of days and then he headed off to Minneapolis and then went to Greenwich Village where he became Bob Dylan. He came through my hometown about five years ago and I saw him then. I was amazed at how much he remembered as that was such a small slice of his life. He even remembered where my dad worked.'

Dylan's comments on Vee in *Chronicles Volume One* add little to this account, but he recalls that he used the great pseudonym Elston Gunn at the time, says that he and this 'old friend and fellow performer . . . had a lot in common, even though our paths would take such different directions', and acknowledges that 'he was a great rockabilly singer' before he 'crossed over' to become a pop star. But though Dylan recalls that they saw each other when Bob was singing in folk clubs and Vee was 'on the top of the heap' at the Paramount in Brooklyn with an array of other stars, he gives no account of the more recent visit that so impressed Vee.

[Bobby Vee quoted from undated interview by Spencer Leigh in *Baby, That Is Rock and Roll: American Pop 1954–1963*, p.137. Bob Dylan: *Chronicles Volume One*, pp.78–80.]

Verlaine, Paul [1844 - 1896] Paul Verlaine, born in Metz, France, on March 30, 1844, became a critic as well as a poet, but his lasting importance lies in his poetry. One of the French symbolists, his stylistic innovations gave his nation's poetry a new musicality, prefiguring free verse and other characteristics of modernity. In 1867 he published *Les Amies*, a collection of poems promptly banned in France. Verlaine's poetry plus a wild life entwined with a questing after salvation provided a 19th century model for the 20th century avant garde and THE BEATS.

Verlaine met the 16-year-old ARTHUR RIMBAUD in 1871, and drama followed. As Evan Goodwin summarises it:

'Verlaine and Rimbaud became extremely close very quickly . . . and it was not long before the two men began a homosexual relationship that soon became known to the public. Two months after the birth of Paul's son in October, Verlaine and Rimbaud ran off to Brussels together. The two men spent the better part of the next two years traveling around northern France and Belgium. The relationship between the two unstable poets was extremely stormy; they fought and broke up often. Eventually, they wound up in London where they found plenty of bohemian amusements and a group of admirers who helped Verlaine publish *Romance Without Words* in 1874, a daring collection of poems composed during his travels with Rimbaud. However, before the book was published, Verlaine shot and lightly wounded Rimbaud during a heated argument, an event that ended their relationship and started Verlaine on the road to faith. Verlaine spent two years in a Belgian prison for the shooting. After he received news that his wife had filed for divorce, Verlaine underwent a religious crisis and converted to Catholicism.'

This makes still more interesting than it might otherwise be the reference to the two poets in Dylan's *Blood on the Tracks* song 'You're Gonna Make Me Lonesome When You Go': 'Relationships have all been bad / Mine have been like Verlaine's and Rimbaud.'

Paul Verlaine died in Paris on January 8, 1896. He was 51.

(See also **French symbolist poets, the.**)

[*Selected poems / Paul Verlaine*, translated with introduction & notes by Martin Sorrell, Oxford: OUP, 1999. Evan Goodwin, 'Little Blue Light—Paul Verlaine', seen online 10 Sep 2005 at *www.littlebluelight.com/lblphp/intro.php?ikey=29*.]

Vesely, Rainer [1956 -] See ***Parking Meter***.

Victoria's Secret See **co-option of real music by advertising, the.**

Villon, Francois [1431 - c.1465?] France's first great poet became popular in the 19th century and again in the 20th, not least when EZRA POUND translated some of his work. His 'Petit Testament', 1456, was followed by his 'Grand Testament', 1461, which includes his best-known work, 'Ballade des dames du temps jadis' ('Ballad of the Ladies of Former Times'), containing the line 'Mais où sont les nièges d'antan?'—'But where are the snows of yesteryear?'—which Dylan consciously echoes in *11 Outlined Epitaphs*, beginning a section with 'ah where are those forces of yesteryear?' In a later section he writes: 'with the sounds of Francois Villon / echoin' through my mad streets / as I stumble . . .'

Vincent, Gene [1935 - 1971] Vincent Eugene Craddock was born in Norfolk, Virginia, on February 11, 1935 and died from a bleeding ulcer in Newhall, California, on October 12, 1971, aged 36. He was in a motorcycle crash in July 1955, the year before his first and greatest hit, 'Be-Bop-a-Lula', and his left leg was permanently damaged. On stage he made much of this, limping around melodramatically in black leather. No wonder Ian Dury found him appealing. He also survived the car crash that killed Eddie Cochran in England in 1960, and lived there for many of his sunset years. He had a lovely voice but his career was all downhill.

Vincent, like Eddie Cochran, JERRY LEE LEWIS and BUDDY HOLLY, enjoyed short-lived popularity in the USA but great career longevity in Britain (including posthumously in all cases except that of Lewis, who both survived and had some success in the USA as a country singer from the 1970s onwards).

In 1987 Dylan recorded two takes of Vincent's 'Important Words' during the *Down in the Groove* sessions, though they remained unreleased; and in 1992 when he recorded an exquisitely sung version of the old Jo Stafford hit 'You Belong to Me' (1952) for the soundtrack of Oliver Stone's film *Natural Born Killers*, Dylan's version was in clear remembrance of, though didn't copy, the version Gene Vincent includes on his best-known album, *Gene Vincent Rocks! & the Blue Caps Roll*. This LP also included a Vincent version of 'Frankie and Johnny', a traditional song that Dylan recorded for *Good as I Been to You* as 'Frankie and Albert' at the same sessions that yielded 'You Belong to Me'.

[Gene Vincent: 'Important Words', Nashville, 18 Oct 1956, Capitol 3617, LA (Capitol CL 14693, London), 1957; 'You Belong to Me', Hollywood, prob. 5 Dec 1957, and 'Frankie and Johnny', 9 Dec 1957, both on *Gene Vincent Rocks! & the Blue Caps Roll*, Capitol T970, LA & London, 1958. ('You Belong to Me' was also a US top 20 hit in 1962 by the Duprees, *nia*, Coed 569, NY, 1962.)

Bob Dylan: 'Important Words', LA, Apr 1987; 'You Belong to Me', Malibu, CA, Jul–Aug 1992 (at the *Good as I Been to You* sessions), issued on *Natural Born Killers*, UNV Interscope ITSC-92460, USA, 1994.]

Vineyard Christian Fellowship, the The Vineyard Christian Fellowship of Churches was the outfit that formalised Dylan's conversion to Christianity, receiving him into its congregation and providing his Bible-study classes.

It was formed as an offshoot from the Calvary Chapel, started in Costa Mesa, California, by one Chuck Smith in 1965; this offshoot, a Bible study group led by Kenn (sic) and Joanie Gulliksen, began in West LA in 1974. Its early members were mainly ex-hippie 1960s Californian types, many of them musicians, and meetings were held at the home of the founder of a 'Christian rock' band, Lovesong.

Offering an alternative to normal structures of worship and denominational liturgy, the group expanded rapidly, splitting from the Calvary Chapel because of the latter's opposition to its emphasis on spontaneous healing through faith, trances and other informal demonstrations of supposed possession by the Holy Spirit. Early members included Debbie Boone, Bernie Leadon and KEITH GREEN. As fellow-member Dave Whiting-Smith comments: 'The Vineyard was, back then, a very music-oriented church. It was chock full of talented people, many of whom had record contracts.'

Despite vicious disputes within the organisation, as one pastor denounced another, the Vineyard movement spread all over California and beyond. It now claims to run 600 churches in the US and a similar number abroad.

See also **'Born Again' period, the**.

[Dave Whiting-Smith: 'Bob Dylan and the Vineyard Christian Fellowship: A View From the Inside', *Isis* no.121, Bedworth, UK, Jun–Jul 2005, pp.26–27.]

vipers See **'Don't Fall Apart on Me Tonight'**.

Vites, Paolo [1962 -] Paolo Vites was born in Lavanga, Italy, on June 27, 1962. He was first interested by Dylan's work when he heard the *Desire* album in 1976, at the age of 14. A rock journalist, he now works for the Italian monthly rock magazine *JAM* and has published slim volumes on the Clash, PATTI SMITH, SPRINGSTEEN, Jim Morrison and others, and in October 2005 published *Le canzoni di Cat Stevens*.

He founded and published an Italian Dylan fanzine, *Rolling Thunder*, from spring 1990 to fall 1992, contributed interviews with RAMBLIN' JACK ELLIOTT and others to US fanzine *ON THE TRACKS* and now contributes to the Italian Dylan website 'Maggie's Farm' (*www.maggiesfarm.it*). His first Dylan book was *Bob Dylan—Stories from a Never-Ending Concert*, looking at the first six years of the Never-Ending Tour. His more recent book, with a foreword by ELLIOTT MURPHY, is *Bob Dylan 1962–2002: 40 anni di canzoni* (*40 Years of Song*), an album-by-album commentary.

[Paolo Vites: *Bob Dylan—Stories from a Never-Ending Concert*, Italy: Penguin, 1994; *Bob Dylan 1962–2002: 40 anni di canzoni*, Italy: Editori Riuniti, 2002.]

Von Schmidt, Eric [1931 -] Eric Von Schmidt was born in Bridgeport, Connecticut, on May 28, 1931. He grew up listening to late-night radio and watching his father, Harold Von Schmidt, painting pictures of the old American West, most lucratively for the *Saturday Evening Post*. Thus he imbibed both music and art, and learnt the 6-string guitar in the 1940s. A big LEADBELLY fan when he first heard him on radio in 1948, he nevertheless stuck to the 6-string guitar himself when he began performing. He served in the US Army from 1952 to 1954, read Huxley's *The Doors of Perception*, started eating peyote mushrooms and left the army to paint. He studied art in Florence and then in Florida, where he taught at the Sarasota School of Art but in 1957 moved to Cambridge, Massachusetts, where he became prominent in the city's folk scene, centered upon Club 47, befriended RICHARD FARIÑA and in 1961 recorded an album with Folkways artist Rolf Kahn. His paintings now extended to album covers and concert posters.

He was there in Cambridge, therefore, in the June of that same year when Bob Dylan first encountered him, slept on his couch, heard him perform and filched several song arrangements from him. One of these was 'He Was a Friend of Mine', and another was 'Baby Let Me Follow You Down'. When Dylan recorded the latter that November for his début album, *Bob Dylan*, he delivered, with his ever-immaculate timing, a spoken intro over his guitar-work, admitting his debt and giving Von Schmidt a name-check: 'I first heard this from, uh, Ric Von Schmidt,' he said: 'I met him one day in the green pastures of, uh, Harvard University'—and then lit into the song, delivering it so beautifully that he made it his own. (See separate entry on the song's provenance.)

Eric von Schmidt responded after an almost 35-year delay, recording the variant 'Baby, Let Me Lay It on You' in a version that included the line 'Now Bobby Dylan, he put me in a song'.

The two first came together as performers in London in January 1963, when Dylan contributed backing vocals and harmonica to several tracks on the sessions for the album *Dick Fariña and Eric Von Schmidt*, which was released, in the UK only, in May 1963, with Dylan billed as Blind Boy Grunt. (The story of Von Schmidt and Fariña's time in Britain that year, with and without Dylan, is told in some detail in DAVID HAJDU's *Positively 4th Street*: a book in which there is much additional material on Von Schmidt and his rôle in the Cambridge folk scene—and for which Von Schmidt was an interviewee.) Later in 1963 Von Schmidt released his well-known album *The Folk Blues of Eric Von Schmidt*, which became more well-known after Dylan included its front cover among the records scattered around the room on *his* front cover for the album *Bringing It All Back Home*. In a later, further self-reflexive gesture, the cover Dylan chose for his *Nashville Skyline* album catches him in a pose that is itself a visual echo of the Von Schmidt cover.

In 1964 came *Eric Sings von Schmidt* (with GEOFF MULDAUR and creepy Mel Lyman). Though he appeared at the 1965 NEWPORT FOLK FESTIVAL, Eric didn't issue another album until his foray into psychedelia in 1969, *Who Knocked the Brains Out of the Sky?*, for which Dylan contributed sub-hokum liner notes in the declamatory style you might associate with MUHAMMAD ALI or LITTLE RICHARD. (These included—and there was plenty more of the same—'He can separate the men from the boys and the note from the noise. The bridle from the saddle and the cow from the cattle. He can play the tune of the moon. The why of the sky and the commotion of the ocean.' It certainly managed to avoid saying anything in particular, which for *Who Knocked the Brains Out of the Sky?* was probably best.)

Back in the pre-psychedelic 60s (peyote mushrooms notwithstanding) however, Von Schmidt had also contributed to that various-artists album *The Blues Project*, on which Dylan had played piano on one Geoff Muldaur track. Eric had played piano alongside Dylan on that track, and had one further track on the LP himself, 'Blow Whistle Blow', the second track on Side 1; he also painted the front cover. A month or two after these sessions, Dylan had visited Von Schmidt at the home he had retained in Sarasota, Florida, and one day in early May 1964 the two of them home-taped themselves on a total of 20 songs and song fragments.

As well as playing guitars, they shared vocals on two improvised songs, one 'Black Betty' and three attempts at 'Stoned on the Mountain'. Dylan took the lead vocal on 'Come All Ye Fair and Tender Ladies', 'Money Honey', 'More and More', 'Mr. Tambourine Man' (probably the earliest extant recording), 'Susie Q', 'I Want to Hold Your Hand' (oh yes) and 'Walkin' Down the Line'. Dylan also took lead vocal *and* played harmonica on two tries at 'Long Johnny CooCoo'; he played harmonica behind Von Schmidt on a further blues improvisation, a further instrumental and a revisit to 'Glory, Glory'; and he played harmonica and sang backing vocals on their final number, Von Schmidt's best-known composition, 'Joshua Gone Barbados'. This tape has never circulated, but 'Joshua Gone Barbados', quite new at the time, was on Eric's latest album (*Eric Sings von Schmidt*) and quickly became a widely covered song. Dylan himself attempted the song on the Basement Tapes sessions in 1967 (circulated but officially unreleased) but it remained unreleased. But the lyric includes, after the title phrase, the line 'staying in a big hotel', which Dylan liked enough to use verbatim after *his* title phrase at the beginning of 'Went to See the Gypsy' on the 1970 album *New Morning*.

Von Schmidt never gave up painting, and in more recent years has come to regard it as his prime purpose in the world, despite making further albums with the participation of many well-known musicians, including GARTH HUDSON. In 1979, with Jim Rooney, he published the book *Baby, Let Me Follow You Down: The Illustrated Story of the Cambridge Folk Years*. In the 1980s Von Schmidt returned from Provo, Utah, where he liked to paint, to his parents' home in Westport, Connecticut, and in December 1985 participated in the 25th Anniversary Reunion Concert of Club 47 performers (along with BAEZ, MIMI FARIÑA, Richie Havens and many others) at Boston Symphony Hall. In more recent times, Eric Von Schmidt has been fighting throat cancer, and though he is reported to have recovered, his days as a singer are over. He remains committed to painting, and has launched a website devoted to his own and his late father's art.

[Eric Von Schmidt: *The Folk Blues of Eric Von Schmidt*, Prestige/Folklore 14005, US, 1963; *Eric Sings von Schmidt*, Prestige 7384, 1964; *Who Knocked the Brains Out of the Sky?*, Smash SRS 67124, US, 1969; 'Baby, Let Me Lay It on You', *nia*, *Baby, Let Me Lay It on You*, Gazell GPCD2013, US, 1995. Dick Fariña, Eric Von Schmidt & Blind Boy Grunt: 'Glory, Glory', 'Xmas Island', 'Cocaine', London, 15 Jan 1963, *Dick Fariña and Eric Von Schmidt*, Folklore F-LEUT-7, UK, 1964; 'Overseas Stomp' (several takes), London, 15 Jan 1963, unreleased (the LP version excludes Dylan). 'Blow Whistle Blow', NY, early 1964, *The Blues Project*, Elektra EKL-7264, 1964. Eric Von Schmidt & Jim Rooney, *Baby, Let Me Follow You Down: The Illustrated Story of the Cambridge Folk Years*, New York: Anchor Books, 1979; 2nd edn., Amherst: University of Massachusetts Press, 1994. The Eric & Harold Von Schmidt website: *www.vonsworks.com*.

David Hajdu, *Positively 4th Street: The Lives and Times of Joan Baez, Bob Dylan, Mimi Baez Fariña and Richard Fariña*, New York: Farar, Straus & Giroux, 2001. Thanks too to the unreliable, interesting profile of Von Schmidt by John Kruth, seen online 4 Sep 2005 at *www.richardandmimi.com/eric-linernotes.html*.]

W

Wallace, Ian [1946 -] Ian Wallace was born in Bury, Lancashire, north-west England, on September 26, 1946, learnt to play drums as a child and in 1963, aged 16, had a school-friends band called the Jaguars before joining his first pro outfit, the Warriors, whose vocalist was the future co-founder of Yes, Jon Anderson. The Warriors lasted right up to the end of 1967: longer than any line-up Wallace has been in since. A few months in Copenhagen and couple of years backing other people on tours was followed by involvement in the complicated last days of the Bonzo Dog Doo-Dah Band and its leader Vivian Stanshall (who announced the Bonzos' breakup at a gig in London in January 1970) and then in the World, which was dominated by ex-Bonzo Neil Innes. The World made one album, *Lucky Planet*, but split up before its release. The band had lasted six months.

In spring 1971 Ian Wallace joined the almost equally volatile but rather more successful King Crimson, a defiantly jazz avant-garde unit of Real Musicians—and for most people, this is what Ian Wallace's work is all about: his era and his genre. On the group's extensive touring, Wallace's drumming was subjected to experimental processing with synthesisers, devised by lyricist and pioneering computer boffin Pete Sinfield. Off stage, internecine warfare was the norm, and less than a year after joining, Wallace was one of several who quit together to play with British R&B grandad Alexis Korner instead. He stayed with Korner for four albums, then worked with Steve Marriott's All Stars and Alvin Lee and emigrated to the US in 1976—in good time to be taken on by Bob Dylan to play on the 1978 World Tour. He played all that year's 114 concerts, and on the album recorded in Santa Monica that April, *Street Legal*.

After 1978 he was not retained for the work of the Born Again period, but worked instead with his old mate Jon Anderson, Jackson Browne, Don Henley, David Lindley, Graham Nash, Stevie Nicks, ROY ORBISON, Bonnie Raitt and RON WOOD. He was almost brought back into the Dylan orb by being called in to play on THE TRAVELING WILBURYS' first track, 'Handle with Care':

> 'JEFF LYNNE called me one morning to ask if I was available to do a session. Seems that he, TOM PETTY, Roy Orbison and GEORGE HARRISON were all hanging out at Bob Dylan's house in Point Dume and had written a song. . . . It had a drum machine on it but it needed spicing up with some drum fills and could I go over that afternoon to Quincy Jones' studio to play said fills. Of course I said yes and did that exact thing, playing tom fills. . . . MIKE CAMPBELL was also there adding guitar parts. The only person that wasn't there was Dylan.'

Wallace adds: 'I never did get paid for that session. At least, in cash. But I had spent part of my honeymoon at George's place in Maui and I do have a Traveling Wilburys platinum album on my studio wall, so I think that's payment enough!'

Then he joined Dylan's Never-Ending Tour band at the beginning of 1991—at, that is, one of its lowest points—playing his first gig that January 28 in Zurich, taking in the two dreadful gigs in Glasgow and the eight London concerts (of which only one was really any good), and finishing on March 2 in Mexico City; resuming on April 19 in New Orleans and running through till May 12 in Amherst, Massachusetts; resuming again on June 6 in Rome and including, after a short break in late July to early August, the South American concerts from August 8 in Buenos Aires through to August 21 in Rio de Janeiro—and then playing the far, far better autumn 1991 dates, from Corpus Christi, Texas, on October 24 through to Charlottesville, Virginia, on November 20: a tour leg that included that golden period that gave us concerts like Ames, Iowa; Madison, Wisconsin; South Bend, Indiana and Louisville, Kentucky (November 2, 5, 6 & 8), on which Wallace's drumming had a wonderfully rolling propulsion that liberated and transformed performances of 'Watching the River Flow', 'Shelter from the Storm', 'Early Morning Rain' and 'Gotta Serve Somebody'.

Wallace remained with the band for 1992. There was an unusually long first leg, from March 18 in Perth, Australia, through to May 23 in Las Vegas—and though Wallace remained in place, a second drummer, CHARLIE QUINTANA, was added as from April 27. Several further legs followed, and in early September Quintana went, but WINSTON WATSON was brought in to replace him, so there was still a second drummer alongside Wallace. This meant that he was able to miss, for some reason, the Binghampton, New York, date on October 12. The year's last date was November 15 in West Palm Beach, Florida. It was Ian Wallace's last date too. Add together his stint in 1978 and his two years in the Never-Ending Tour band, and his Dylan concerts total is 307.

He thought there were going to be more. He was all ready for the first leg of 1993: his drums had been shipped and he was to fly to Dublin two days later when Dylan's office phoned him and told him plans had changed. As he told HOWARD SOUNES: 'I don't hold any grudges . . . [but] the way that it was done was a little upsetting. . . . I think I'm the only person he's fired twice.'

[The World: *Lucky Planet*, Liberty LBG 83419, UK, Nov 1970. Wallace quotes re the Wilburys seen online 18

Feb 2006 at *http://dmme.net/interviews/wallace.html*; final quote from Howard Sounes, *Down the Highway: A Life of Bob Dylan*, New York: Grove Press, 2001, ms p.478.]

Wallflowers, the See **Dylan, Jakob**.

Warhol, Andy [1928 - 1987] Andrew Warhola was born to blue-collar Slovak immigrant parents in Pittbsurgh on August 6, 1928. After an early career in commercial illustration in New York City he became the best-publicised innovator in the pop art movement, mostly with quintessentially 1960s silk-screening and, in partnership with others, made a large number of 'underground' movies of deliberate technical amateurishness and interminable length (starting with the silent, black and white, 321-minute *Sleep* in 1963). He was also the 'designer' and producer of some of the Velvet Underground's début album in 1967 (TOM WILSON also worked on it) and might be considered, with the 1973 launch of his journal *Interview*, the inventor of the celeb magazine.

Warhol's career was dedicated to a nihilism that was timely and useful as a deflator of old pomposities that had lingered into the post-war world. He also coined a number of sayings, pre-eminently 'In the future everyone will be famous for 15 minutes': it is one of the things for which he remains famous.

One of those who became briefly famous on his slender coat-tails was Valerie Solanas of the one-woman SCUM (Society for Cutting Up Men), who shot Warhol on June 3, 1968, putting him in hospital for two months and herself in prison for three years.

For his main connections to Bob Dylan see the entry **Sedgwick, Edie**; but in the mid-1960s, when both men were so iconic and cool that it was painful to see them together, Dylan was briefly one of the subjects of Warhol's movie camera. He sits there in the Warhol Factory trying to be as immobile as the Empire State building (for, it is said, 15 minutes). A little of this footage is used in SCORSESE's *No Direction Home* and Warhol gets a 'special thanks' in the credits.

Their less mesmerising but more comic connection is that in payment, Warhol gave Dylan a painting—one of his ELVIS series (based on a publicity still from the decent 1960 Presley film *Flaming Star*)—and Dylan *swapped it for a sofa* belonging to his manager ALBERT GROSSMAN.

Andy Warhol died of complications following gallbladder surgery in a New York hospital in the early morning of February 22, 1987, aged 58. Valerie Solanas but barely outlived him; she died of pneumonia in 1988.

Warnes, Jennifer [1947 -] Singer, songwriter and keyboards player Jennifer Jean Warnes was born in Seattle on March 3, 1947; her father turned down a recording deal for her when she was seven years old. Aged nine, and in the swaddling band of the American flag, she sang 'The Star Spangled Banner' at the Shrine Auditorium in LA above the noise of 300 ensemble accordions. Rejecting opera for folk music, and trying to make it under the name Jennifer Warren, she made her eclectic first album, *I Can Remember Everything*, in 1968, followed up by 1969's *See Me, Feel Me, Touch Me, Heal Me* (an off-puttingly clamorous title, perhaps; its contents included 'Just Like Tom Thumb's Blues'). In 1970 she fell in with LEONARD COHEN, with whom, down the years, she would record guest vocals (and sing back-up) on a series of Cohen studio albums after touring Europe with him and featuring on his *Live Songs* album of 1973.

She was still calling herself Jennifer Warren when in 1972 she released *Jennifer*, the only album of her own between meeting Cohen in 1970 and her breakthrough seven years later with the album *Jennifer Warnes* and the hit single 'Right Time of the Night'. Her 1979 album *Shot Through the Heart* included a decent cover of Dylan's *New Morning* song 'Sign on the Window'. Her career highlights include 'It Goes Like It Goes' for the film *Norma Rae* (1980), duetting with Joe Cocker on the 1982 no.1 hit single 'Up Where We Belong' (written for *An Officer and a Gentleman*), and duetting with ex-Righteous Brother Bill Medley on another no.1 hit single, '(I've Had) The Time of My Life' in 1987. That January she also released her album *Famous Blue Raincoat: Songs of Leonard Cohen* and, from it, a single of 'Bird on the Wire'. She has also sung on recordings by HARRY BELAFONTE, Jackson Browne, Sam & Dave, James Taylor, Tina Turner, Bobby Womack, WARREN ZEVON and others; her own records have become few and far between; her last solo album—itself the first for nine years—was *The Well*, in 2001.

Twenty-one years earlier, she and Bob Dylan and FRED TACKETT and a dog had got together in Bob's garage studio in Santa Monica and recorded the early, try-out version of 'Every Grain of Sand'. It wasn't a happy conjunction, artistically, and Jennifer Warnes ended up barely there at all in the mix, but it was released in 1991 on the *Bootleg Series Vols. 1–3*. She was better off with Leonard. (See **'Every Grain of Sand', non-Blake elements** for details.)

[Jennifer Warnes: *I Can Remember Everything*, Parrot PAS 71020, US, 1968; *See Me, Feel Me, Touch Me, Heal Me*, Parrot PAS 71034, 1969; *Jennifer*, Reprise 2065, US, 1972; *Jennifer Warnes*, Arista 4062, US, 1977; *Shot Through the Heart*, Arista 4127, 1979; *Famous Blue Raincoat: Songs of Leonard Cohen*, Cypress 661-111, US, 1987; *The Hunter*, Private Music 82089, US, 1992; *The Well*, Music Force SD8960, US, 2001. Bob Dylan, Jennifer Warnes, Fred Tackett & dog: 'Every Grain of Sand', Santa Monica, 23 Sep 1980.]

Was, David [1952 -] David Weiss was born in Detroit on October 26, 1952, the son of Soupy

Sales' sidekick Shoutin' Shorty Hogan, and grew up to be a jazz critic for the *L.A. Herald-Examiner* as well as a songwriter, musician and, with his childhood friend DON WAS—with whom he'd had a dalliance in the White Panther Party and attended the University of Michigan at Ann Arbor—co-founded the wacky but modish pop group Was (Not Was), a sort of 1980s American 10cc meets the Pet Shop Boys but with an increasing fixation for lounge music. Featuring vocalists Sir Harry Bowen and Sweet Pea Atkinson, ex-MC5 guitarist Wayne Kramer, Don on bass and David on keyboards, they began making what became a small number of eclectic smarty-pants albums, starting with the electronic disco of *Was (Not Was)* in 1981. David must have had problems in the taste department; not only was he fixated on golf but he even gave that life-long enemy of rock'n'roll Mel Tormé a good review for an early 1980s concert performance. The punishment for the latter was Tormé singing on a silly Was (Not Was) song called 'Zaz Turned Blue' on the second Was (Not Was) album, *Born to Laugh at Tornadoes*. He and his pianist recorded a version that gave it, said Was, 'something of the wry poignancy of "Send in the Clowns".' Yes, it was as bad as that.

David Was was also a multi-instrumentalist himself; that album featured him on lead and background vocals, flute, trumpet, Korg organ, vibes and harmonica. Their record label Geffen refused to issue their third album, *Lost in Prehistoric Detroit* but after changing labels came *What's Up Dog?* in 1988, in the midst of a torrent of 12-inch singles, CD-singles and re-mixes, often with titles sometimes rather more interesting than the music—though not in the case of their top dance hits 'Tell Me That I'm Dreaming', 'Spy in the House of Love' and 'Walk the Dinosaur'. The 1990 album *Are You Okay?* and a hit revival of the Temptations' song 'Papa Was a Rolling Stone' followed.

In 1990 David and Don Was also co-produced Dylan's album *Under the Red Sky*. They began at Oceanway Studios in Hollywood on January 6, and that month recorded '10,000 Men', 'God Knows', 'Handy Dandy' and 'Cat's in the Well'. Overdubs were done in May, including some vocals by David—and by Sir Harry Bowens and Sweat Pea Atkinson—but at the January session(s) Dylan played piano, JIMMY VAUGHAN played guitar, Kenny Aronoff played drums and Don Was played bass. Further sessions in March–April completed the basic tracks.

In some quarters the Was production was much criticised for being so unlike that by DANIEL LANOIS on the previous Dylan album, *Oh Mercy*. In other quarters, this was what made people grateful.

David split off from the rather more successful Don after recording the unreleased album *Boo* in 1992 and touring Europe supporting Dire Straits. He worked on a number of film projects (after appearing as the keyboard player of the Gourmet Club Party Band in *Freshman* in 1990; Don appeared as a guitarist), including writing lyrics for the unremarkable Lenny Henry TV film *In Dreams* (1992), being the music supervisor on *An American Werewolf in Paris* (aka *An American Werewolf II*; 1997), *The X-Files* movie (1998) and *The Big Tease* (1999) and writing—as did Don—music for the TV series 'The Education of Max Bickford' (2001), which starred the splendid Richard Dreyfuss, and 'That Was Then', a comedy ABC cancelled after one series (2002).

In 2004 David and Don got back together to work towards a possible new CD and, reuniting with many Was (Not Was) members, they toured into 2005.

[Was (Not Was): *Was (Not Was)*, Island ILPS 9666, US, 1981; *Born to Laugh at Tornadoes*, Geffen LP 24251, US, 1983; *What's Up Dog?*, Capitol, *nia*, 1988. Tormé data from *www.npr.org/templates/story/story.php?storyId=5062814*; some further background info from *www.andwedanced.com/artists/wnw.htm*, both online 19 Feb 2006.]

Was, Don [1952 -] Don Fagenson was born in Detroit on September 13, 1952 and by junior high school was friends with the future DAVID WAS, his partner-to-be in the group Was (Not Was). They stayed in tandem right through to their attendance at the University of Michigan but Don dropped out after a year and when David went off to LA to write jazz reviews, Don stayed in Detroit taking whatever bass guitar gigs he could find until at the end of the 1970s, tiring of insolvency, he told his old friend that unless they got back together and *made it* in the music biz, he was going to go into the crime biz instead. Was (Not Was) was the result.

In the wake of the group's popularity, Don became, in the second half of the 1980s, an increasingly successful producer of other people's records. In 1989 Don produced both Bonnie Raitt's 'comeback album' and the B-52s' second mainstream breakthrough album *Cosmic Thing*, co-produced with Nile Rodgers (the group's 1980 album *Wild Planet* had also made the top 20 in the US and UK, but *Cosmic Thing* made both top 10s), and in 1993 he was among the many who produced ELTON JOHN's album *Duets*. Don Was also co-produced—and continues to co-produce—albums by THE ROLLING STONES: he and 'the Glimmer Twins' co-produced *Voodoo Lounge* (1994), the live album *Stripped* (1995), *Bridges to Babylon* (1997), the newer material on the greatest hits collection *Forty Licks* (2002), *Live Licks* (2004) and *A Bigger Bang* (2005). In 1995 Don Was directed that wonderful, touching TV film about BRIAN WILSON's struggle to return from the abyss, *Brian Wilson: I Just Wasn't Made for These Times*.

In 1990, however, and in tandem with David Was, Don produced Bob Dylan's album *Under the Red Sky*. He was impressed (even if the public wasn't), perhaps especially by Dylan's detailed and wide grip on the nuts and bolts of music history. Interviewed in LA that fall, he reported: '. . . he's a great authority on older rock'n'roll and blues forms. You can't stump him on a record—the most obscure Sun sides, the most obscure rockabilly stuff, the most obscure blues, he can sit down and play them and sing them for you. He really knows his stuff.' It was also Don Was who said of the album's title track: 'It's actually about people who got trapped in his hometown. I think it's about Hibbing and about people who never left. . . . He said, "It's about my hometown."'

Such an indiscretion might have been expected to spell the end of their association, but in fact a few years further down the road Don Was and Dylan re-connected. First, on January 13, 1993 they found themselves together in CBS' Nashville studios when Dylan and WILLIE NELSON shared vocals on a performance of their joint composition 'Heartland' for the TV programme 'A Country Music Celebration', shown that February 6. Don Was played bass (and JIM KELTNER drums) behind them. On April 28, at the KRLU-TV studios in Austin, Texas, it was much the same situation. It was for the TV special 'Willie Nelson: The Big Six-O' and after Dylan sang 'Hard Times' backed by his own band, he and Willie sang 'Pancho & Lefty' together, backed by a unit that included Don Was on bass (and included BENMONT TENCH on keyboards). Finally, when Dylan and TRISHA YEARWOOD tried to sing 'Tomorrow Night' together on 'Rhythm, Country & Blues: The Concert' in LA on March 23, 1994, there were the old Was (Not Was) vocalists Sir Harry Bowen and Sweet Pea Atkinson on backing vocals, and there was Don again on bass.

Don Was has returned to Motor City in a better money-earning capacity than when he still lived there. Beginning in 2004, he's been working on TV ads and campaigns for Lincoln and Mercury cars. When asked by *The Wall Street Journal* about the notion of rock stars selling out by either making music for TV commercials or appearing in them, such as Bob Dylan did in that 2004 Victoria's Secret commercial (see **co-option of real music by advertising, the**), Was said: 'The first thing I thought was "Love Sick" is one of the greatest songs ever recorded. It won a Grammy. They don't play it on the radio, but if Victoria's Secret has the good taste to want to associate their thing with that song, I think, "Good for him." Now, in the end, I'm trying to put myself in Bob's head—did you see the girl in that ad? If you get to spend two days on the set with her, and they pay you, you basically have landed on the dream scenario of rock and roll.'

Was not was that shallow or what?

[Don Was, quotes re Dylan: interview by Reid Kopel, LA, 15 Oct 1990, *The Telegraph* no.37, UK, winter 1990. *Brian Wilson: I Just Wasn't Made for These Times*, dir. Don Was; Cro Magnon/Palomar, US, 1995. Was (Not Was) data: see the David Was entry. *Wall Street Journal, nia*, quoted in *mph* magazine, undated but seen online 20 Feb 2006 at *http://mph-online.com/web/pr translated/00502*.]

Watson, Doc [1923 -] Arthel Lane Watson was born in Stoney Fork Township, near Deep Gap, North Carolina, on March 3, 1923. He could play the guitar by 16, but was married with two children by the time landed a gig playing electric lead guitar in a country and western swing band led by Jack Williams. Doc was then 'discovered' by RALPH RINZLER in North Carolina when Rinzler arrived there in 1960 to record CLARENCE ASHLEY. The following year Doc, Ashley and others (Fred Price, Clint Howard and Gaither Carlton) travelled to New York to perform a concert sponsored by Friends of Old Time Music. Watson made his first solo appearance, at Gerde's Folk City in Greenwich Village—playing to a very different crowd from those around Deep Gap, North Carolina—in 1962.

As well as proving an exceptional flat-pick guitarist, with an especially clear, crisp tone and an instinct for felicitous understatement, he became, despite a limited range of expression as a vocalist, a significant conduit of repertoire for the Folk Revivalists when Dylan was in amongst them.

'Alberta', which Dylan sings twice on his 1970 double-LP *Self Portrait*, is a song associated with Doc Watson. He also recorded one of the 'Unfortunate Rake' cycle of songs, calling his variant 'St. James Hospital'; he learnt it from ALAN LOMAX, who'd picked it up from James 'Iron Head' Baker (and Watson does give Baker the composer credit). The chapter 'Bob Dylan, BLIND WILLIE McTELL and "Blind Willie McTell"' in MICHAEL GRAY's *Song & Dance Man III: The Art of Bob Dylan* traces the ways that 'The Unfortunate Rake' and its variants become transmuted into McTell's 'The Dyin' Crapshooter's Blues' and eventually into Dylan's 'Blind Willie McTell' too, and it's reasonable to assume that one of the versions of the 'Rake' cycle Dylan knew was Doc Watson's. It re-appears on *The Essential Doc Watson Vol. 1*, first issued in 1973, which also contains a dreadful, cutesy version of 'Froggie Went a-Courtin'' and an excellent version—a remake: he had first recorded it for Folkways—of the early Frank Hutchison song 'The Train That Carried My Girl from Town' (in Hutchison's title he called her 'the girl', not 'my girl'), which Watson made into a standard repertoire item. In the 1960s he also recorded one of the many versions of 'Sitting on Top of the World', which, like his 'St. James Hospital' was on his 1964 album *Doc Watson*.

And so was 'The Lone Pilgrim', the song with which Dylan takes his leave of this *World Gone Wrong* in 1993: and doing so with a performance of spectral calm, and one that, aptly, requires you to put your ear close in order to hear a lyric that presents itself as from the death-bed and beyond. Dylan specifies in his liner notes to the album that this song was taken 'from an old Doc Watson record'. (But see separate entry on the song.)

Doc Watson's son Merle, who had started playing back-up guitar behind his father at the Berkeley Festival of 1964, died in a tractor accident on October 23, 1985. Merle keeps on keeping on. No-one has had a deeper influence on the way the acoustic flat top guitar has come to be played as a lead instrument in folk, traditional and bluegrass music.

[Doc Watson: 'Alberta', *nia*, *Southbound*, Vanguard VSD-79213, US (Fontana RFL 6074, UK), 1966, CD-reissued Vanguard VMD 79213-2, US, 1988 (UK 1995); 'Froggie Went a-Courtin" & 'The Train That Carried My Girl to Town', all *nia*, reissed *The Essential Doc Watson Vol. 1*, Vanguard 5308, US, CD-reissued Vanguard VMCD 7308, US, 1987; 'Sitting on Top of the World', NY, 25/26 Nov 1963 & 'St. James Hospital', *nia*, *Doc Watson*, Vanguard VRS-9152 (mono) & VSD-79152, US, 1964; 1st version of 'The Train That Carried My Girl to Town', *nia*, *The Doc Watson Family*, Folkways FA2366, NY, 1963.]

Watson, Winston A. [1961 -] Young, gifted and black Winston Augustus Watson was born in Columbus, Ohio, on September 16, 1961; his father is of African/Scots and Native American origin, and his mother is Dutch Indonesian. The first music he loved was country—'country '55 to '77'—and he knows 'more about Lynyrd Skynyrd than LL Cool J.'

He grew up in Tuscon, Arizona, to be a drummer and percussionist, starting to play in bars and clubs at age 17 and eventually joining the city's cult band Giant Sand. He first played on their 1985 album *Valley of Rain* and then on 1986's *Ballad of a Thin Line Man* and thus appears briefly on their later compilation album, 1989's *Giant Sandwich*. He has also played on solo albums by Giant Sand's Howe Gelb (*Hisser* and *Confluence*), on the 1990 Was (Not Was) album *What's Up, Dog?* [sic], on WARREN ZEVON's *Life'll Kill Ya* and for Robyn Hitchcock, Stevie Salas and others. He is not to be confused (as per the 'Bob Dylan's Who's Who' website and Itsuko Nishimura in Japan) with the older and more heavy-set Winston Watson from the Jamaican Trenchtown reggae band the Meditations, formed in the early 1970s.

Our Winston became a member of Dylan's Never-Ending Tour band in September 1992, débuting in Kansas City, Missouri, on the 6th, under a peculiar but effective arrangement under which for the first few concerts the serving drummer, IAN WALLACE, remained in place and Winston replaced temporary second drummer CHARLIE QUINTANA. Winston recalls that 'Chalo [Charlie] told me to fly out while Dylan was carrying two drummers. I arrived, Chalo left and the next day I played my first show with the man. 80,000 people, no rehearsal, no meeting, nothing!'

These two-drummers-at-once performances were terrific, but didn't last. The last one was on September 13, in Lafayette, Louisiana, after which there was a short break and when the tour resumed on October 9 in Pittsburgh, Winston Watson was, for the first time, the band's sole drummer.

He was popular at once. As Dylan-watcher John Howells noted, 'The late '92 shows were truly incredible, mostly thanks to the new drummer Winston Watson.' He was a joy to see, especially in the early period. His drumming was energetic and wholehearted without any undue obtruding; and his enthusiasm was a delight. He didn't know that you're supposed to keep your head down, so time and again when Dylan turned towards him to call a halt to whatever number they were on, Watson would grin at him in undisguised pleasure simply at being there playing. To start with, Dylan seemed as charmed as the audience. As Winston says, 'He thought I had something at the right time: that's why I was lucky enough to be there for as long as I was'; and for a long time it was an oddly pleasing sight to see this shining high-energy youth and the gnarled old master interacting. He was doomed.

This was, Winston is certain, at least in part thanks to VAN MORRISON, who told Dylan he thought his drummer 'couldn't play. Van hated me, my playing, my clothes, even my hair! He said so at dinner one night in Molde, Norway.' This would have been when they played the Molde Jazz Festival on July 19, 1996 or the following evening (a night off). Winston's last concert with the band was in Atlanta, Georgia, that August 4—though he was also in the studio in January 1997 in Miami to play on the recording of 'Dirt Road Blues' for the *Time Out of Mind* album.

Because of the period he was in the tour band, we also find him on the New York Supper Club appearances in November 1993 (two song-performances from which are included on the 1995 *Highway 61 Interactive* CD Rom), at 'WOODSTOCK II' in August 1994, on the wretched *MTV Unplugged™* album and video recorded that November and released in 1995 and on the November 1995 'FRANK SINATRA 80th Birthday' concert, in Sinatra's presence, at which Dylan performed 'Restless Farewell'.

In retrospect, Watson has, understandably, mixed feelings: 'To this day I love Van's music: the man is another story. I was crushed. I had to face a festival crowd the next day after having my ego snapped in two. Everything I did afterward failed to connect. I knew that I had stayed in Mississippi a day too long. There was nothing left and Bob knew it. They were already looking [for a new drummer]. In Atlanta, at the Olympics, I resigned to Jeff Kramer, Bob's manager. I told Jeff that I was just taking the man's money at that point. They told me there was work in the fall, and I said I'd go if he couldn't find someone else. The day before I was supposed to leave, they hired DAVID KEMPER. The first show of the tour was in my home town of Tucson. I got my gear from the venue and sent my friends to the show. I couldn't bring myself to go. But Bob's gift keeps giving. He brought me closer to music than anyone, and he took a chance on me. And it changed my existence. It follows me to this day.'

Since leaving Dylan's band, he has been a member of the Arizona band the Low Watts (an offshoot of the Gin Blossoms) and from September 1998 toured with Alice Cooper. In a way, this too brought him full circle: in the early 1980s, in his youth, he had played in a ('kind of Psychedelic Furs sounding') Phoenix-based band called Gentlemen After Dark. They released a 4-track EP, *Gentlemen After Dark*. Alice Cooper co-produced it.

[Gentlemen After Dark: *Gentlemen After Dark*, *nia*, US, c.1983. Giant Sand: *Valley of Rain*, New Rose ROSE84, France & Enigma 72050, US, 1985; *Ballad of a Thin Line Man*, Zippo ZONG 013, UK, 1986; *Giant Sandwich*, What Goes On GOES ON 33, UK & Homestead HMS 134-2, US, 1989. John Howells quote online 1 Jun 2005 at *www.punkhart.com/dylan/reviews/tours.html*. Alice Cooper & Gentlemen After Dark source: *www.alicecoopertrivia.pwp.blueyonder.co.uk/musicians/m-winstonwatso.php*, seen online 19 Nov 2005. Biographical detail, quotes and stories behind his time with Dylan, Winston Watson's e-mails to this writer, 11 Dec 2005.]

Weberman, A. J. [1945 -] Alan Jules Weberman, born in Brooklyn, New York on April 26, 1945, called himself the world's only living Dylanologist, and gave up college to be so. He was sitting there in college and suddenly it came to him. 'Well fuck this shit, man,' he claims to have said to himself. 'Interpreting Dylan is a hundred times more interesting than going to school so I dropped out of school and became a Dylanologist full time. . . . I really pushed my brain and I began to get some insight into Dylan' [source untraced]. Weberman played detective. He sniffed through files, kept an ear to the ground for useful rumours and combed Dylan's output for coded messages. Example: when Dylan uses the word 'lady' he means 'oligarchy'. So pushing our brains and letting insight dawn, we have 'Lay, Oligarchy, Lay', 'Sad-Eyed Oligarchy of the Lowlands' and so on.

Weberman's fame rested on his much-mooted but never-seen *Dylan Concordance*, his founding of the Dylan Liberation Front (he held a street-party outside Dylan's Greenwich Village home at 94 MacDougal Street on Dylan's 30th birthday), his taped phone-conversations with Dylan ('Dylan Meets Weberman', *East Village Other*, New York, January 19, 1971), his claim to have been beaten up in the street by Dylan, and his raids on Dylan's garbage can.

This last—thinking to investigate the artist's dustbin—was Weberman's real contribution: an innovation he called garbology. Psychically suited to the times we live in, it has been widely taken up by others, though Weberman's term has been ignored and he has rarely been credited as the innovator of this intrusive but resourceful investigative method. Weberman's book *My Life in Garbology*, 1980, devotes its main chapter to Dylan and his dustbins, and today he presides rather menacingly over the websites *www.dylanology.com* and *www.ajweberman.com*. He has also investigated and written about the Kennedy assassination.

The taped phone conversations with Dylan are now CD-released ('licensed personally by AJ', it says on the blurb!) on *Bob Dylan: The Classic Interview Vol 2 The Weberman Tapes*, Chrome Dreams/Isis CIS2005, UK, 2004, and include 'an introductory note' by Weberman. The best thing that came out of these ludicrous exchanges was surely the joking lines Dylan made up to tease Weberman with (and he succeeded: Weberman took them seriously and was therefore exasperated more than somewhat by their inadequacy as political commentary). These were: 'Down in Progresso / A bracero / Lived in a sombrero / Full of espresso.'

An affectionate account by JOHN BAULDIE of 'A Meeting with Weberman, Summer of '82', is in *All Across the Telegraph: A Bob Dylan Handbook*, ed. Michael Gray & John Bauldie, 1987. Weberman finally published a version of his 'Dylan concordance' as the *Dylan to English Dictionary* in late 2005.

See also **Dylan interpreters**.

[A.J. Weberman: *Dylan to English Dictionary*, North Charleston, SC: BookSurge Publishing, 2005.]

Weir, Bob [1947 -] Bob Weir was a member of the Warlocks, which became THE GRATEFUL DEAD; he was its first rhythm guitarist (often described as an idiosyncratic one) as well as one of its singers (sometimes described as a fine one). He was born Robert Hall Weir on October 16, 1947 in San Francisco and grew up in the suburb of Atherton. Because of his undiagnosed dyslexia, his school years were troublesome and he spent part of his adolescence away from home at a school in Colorado, where he first met John Perry Barlow, who would become, like ROBERT HUNTER, a regular lyricist for the Grateful Dead. Weir began playing guitar at age 13, after first trying the piano and trumpet.

As was normal for members of the Dead, Weir also pursued a solo career (albums like *Ace* and *Heaven Help the Fool*) and played in 'sidebands' Kingfish, and Bobby and he and the bassist Rob Wasserman formed a duo, though this soon became RatDog. (In 2003 Wasserman quit RatDog but retained a duo partnership with Weir outside it. In the group he was replaced by Robin Sylvester, known for a long, close association with saxophonist STEVE DOUGLAS, which is how Sylvester got to record with Bob Dylan, among others—though just after he joined RatDog it came to a long halt because Bob Weir was suffering from exhaustion.)

RatDog has always included Grateful Dead and Dylan numbers in its repertoire, as illustrated on its 2001 album *Live at Roseland*. On April 1, 2005, to take a recent example, the band played two sets that opened with a medley of the Champs' 'Tequila', Dylan's 'Silvio' and James Crawford Jr.'s 'Iko Iko'. Later they played, as the Dead often have, both 'Sugaree' and Dylan's 'When I Paint My Masterpiece'.

Dylan's direct musical collaborations with Weir, courtesy of the Grateful Dead (Weir and Bob sometimes shared on stage vocals), are detailed in the entry on the band.

[RatDog: *Live at Roseland*, Portland, OR, 25 & 26 Apr 2001, *nia*. 2005 concert repertoire details seen online 22 Aug 2005 at *www.musicbox-online.com/rd04-05.html*.]

Weissberg, Eric [1939 -] Eric Weissberg was born in New York City on August 16, 1939. With BOB YELLIN and JOHN HERALD, he had been, on violin, a founding member of THE GREENBRIAR BOYS in 1958. Herald, Marshall Brickman and Weissberg had met at the University of Wisconsin (though Weissberg also studied at the Juilliard School of Music). They'd started playing bluegrass together, and this had turned into the group. It was Eric's mother who had thought up their name. Though he had defected to the Tarriers in 1959 (originally as their bass player), he had sufficient loyalty to his group to feel outraged when ROBERT SHELTON wrote his subsequently famous, and admirably percipient, review of the group's support act, Bob Dylan, published in *The New York Times* on September 29, 1961. Some people, as Shelton wrote later, were pleased for Bob; others were not: 'VAN RONK, cool but gulping hard, told me I had done "a very, very fine thing." Pat CLANCY and his brother Tom said, "Bobby has a lot of talent. He deserves to go places." IZZY YOUNG said he had discovered Dylan months earlier than anyone. And much of the Village music coterie reacted with jealousy, contempt, and ridicule. Eric Weissberg, and Marshall Brickman, two of the ablest instrumentalists about, told me I needed a hearing aid.'

Weissberg was in the line-up of the Tarriers that made the well-received Atlantic album *Tell the World About This* (which included versions of 'John Hardy', 'Little Maggie' and 'Dark as the Dungeon'), but disbanded the group in April 1964 so as to spend an obligatory six months in the National Guard. They re-formed afterwards and in summer 1965 toured Eastern Europe with JUDY COLLINS. But in 1967, while Bob Dylan was making the Basement Tapes, Weissberg was the soloist at the world première of Earl Robinson's *Concerto for Five-string Banjo*, with Arthur Fiedler and the Boston Symphony Orchestra.

Seven years later, Weissberg was a session guitarist on the first day in the studio for Dylan's masterpiece *Blood on the Tracks*. It was the only day he participated; he was only there because he was recording an advertising jingle in an adjacent studio and bumped into Phil Ramone, who was Dylan's engineer on the album, who asked him if he could help bring some musicians along.

Weissberg brought in bass player Tony Brown, drummer RICHARD CROOKS, Charlie Brown III and Barry Kornfeld on guitars. Only that day's 'Meet Me in the Morning' survived though to the album—and even then, overdubs later in the month by BUDDY CAGE on steel guitar pushed Weissberg's contribution further back in the mix. However, Weissberg also plays on the cut of 'If You See Her, Say Hello', and may play on that of 'Tangled Up in Blue', released many years later on the *Bootleg Series Vols. 1–3*. When *Blood on the Tracks* came out, Eric Weissberg & Deliverance received a non-specific credit.

That band name derives from the one moment when Weissberg, an outstanding banjo player, had stepped from the relative shadows of folk revival groups and session-work and enjoyed a little fame and success. This had come in 1972 when he and Steve Mandel provided the memorable bluegrass instrumental track 'Duelling Banjos' for a scene of heightened drama within the powerful backwoods rape and survivalism movie *Deliverance*, directed by the Briton John Boorman but starring Jon Voight, Burt Reynolds, Ned Beatty and Ronny Cox. The Cox character, Atlanta suburbanite Drew, starts playing chords on his guitar. A twisted young albino hillbilly with learning difficulties (Billy Redden) appears on the porch and plays answering lines on the banjo. Their culture clash is acted out in the music.

As this suggests, it was not duelling banjos but a guitar-banjo duel; and in truth the tune was an arrangement by Weissberg and Mandel of 'Feudin' Banjos', composed by Arthur 'Guitar Boogie' Smith in the 1950s (whose over-echoed and meretricious recording *did* pitch banjo against banjo: 4-string against 5-string, in fact). The spirit and milieu of the Weissberg and Mandel was more that of FLATT & SCRUGGS but it had an extra energetic bite, and the way that it was used as a pivot within the film lifted it out of its genre rut, bringing, in effect, bluegrass music to a new audience. The soundtrack album became a hit, and 'Duelling Banjos', credited to Deliverance Soundtrack/Eric Weissberg & Steve Mandel, became a top 20 hit in the UK and a no.1 hit in the US in early 1973.

Weissberg has now played on over 8,000 other sessions, if you include jingles (which he certainly does). For many years he did no live performing but returned to it latterly, solo and with the New Blue Velvet Band ('The Blue Velvet Band' was a song written and recorded by HANK SNOW, after which was named a folk band of the late 1960s that made one album, *Sweet Moments with the Blue*

Velvet Band, in 1969). Since 2001 Eric Weissberg has toured widely as Art Garfunkel's lead guitarist.

[Eric Weissberg & Steve Mandel: 'Duelling Banjos', *nia*, in *Deliverance*, dir. John Boorman; Elmer Productions/Warner Bros, US, 1972; *"Duelling Banjos": From the Original Deliverance Soundtrack*, CD-reissued Warner Bros/WEA 2683, US, 1990. The Tarriers: *Tell the World About This*, Atlantic 8042/SD-8042, US, 1960. The Blue Velvet Band: *Sweet Moments with the Blue Velvet Band*, Warner Bros W 1802, US, 1969. Robert Shelton, *No Direction Home: The Life and Music of Bob Dylan*, London: Penguin edn., p.112.]

Wenner, Jann and unloading heads Jann Wenner, born in New York on January 7, 1946, worked in news media including NBC News and *Ramparts* magazine before stepping out into the counter-culture. He has published and edited the American pop music bi-weekly magazine *Rolling Stone* since co-founding it with RALPH J. GLEASON as a San Francisco-based 'underground music paper' in 1967: the year of going to San Francisco with some flowers in your hair. In this spirit he was also a co-author of the book *Got a Revolution!: The Turbulent Flight of Jefferson Airplane* by Paul Kantner and Jeff Tamarkin, though Wenner disliked the amateurish, sloppy look of the underground press and made *Rolling Stone* look far neater and more professionally designed. In 1971 Wenner turned his magazine interviews with John Lennon into the book *Lennon Remembers*, and the following year co-authored *Garcia: A Signpost to New Space* with Jerry Garcia and Charles A. Reich.

In *Rolling Stone*'s 1969 interview with Dylan, published that November, editor-interviewer Jann Wenner uses the phrase 'unload my head' and Dylan, who had used that phrase in 1965 on *Highway 61 Revisited* (in 'From a Buick 6'), remarks on how good it sounds and says he'll have to write a song with that phrase in it. This interview is greatly entertaining, with Dylan impersonating the amiable, unassuming, rather slow, solid citizen and prefacing his comments with 'Boy . . .' and 'My gosh . . .' and 'Well, Jann, I'll tell ya . . .'

After the present writer's *Song & Dance Man: The Art of Bob Dylan* came out in the USA in 1973, it was pleasing to learn that only when Jann Wenner saw the book's comments about this interview of four years beforehand did he realise Dylan had been 'putting him on'. *Rolling Stone* co-founder, the late RALPH J. GLEASON, wrote: 'I told Wenner at the time that Dylan was putting him on. . . . But it wasn't until you pointed out that bit about unloading his head and Dylan's reply that he ought to use that in a song, that Wenner caught on.'

Gleason added delightful background information on Wenner and the workings of *Rolling Stone* at that time: 'Wenner . . . said he had to have the book's editor at arm's length to him. I never found out why, since he does not read books.' And: 'In order to understand Wenner's attitude towards Dylan, you first have to know that Wenner never saw him in the 12 or more concerts he gave in the San Francisco-Berkeley area over a three year period. Never once! . . . Wenner did not cop to any of this until after we got *Rolling Stone* started. . . . Wenner['s] aim in those days was less to take over American publishing than to meet THE BEATLES . . .'

As it happened it was the second time this author had displeased Wenner. The first had been with a report that the short-lived *Rolling Stone* London office commissioned on the second Isle of Wight Music Festival, at which Dylan appeared, in August 1969. Wenner disliked this report so much that he didn't run it in the US edition, preferring the magazine to appear to have forgotten the entire event. '"Wenner," recalls [London advertising manager Alan] Marcuson, "was fuming at the bit."' Wenner hated the London office anyway, and the last proper British issue was October 18, 1969; when Wenner's interview with Dylan appeared a month later, London retained only an 'Acting Manager' (Jon Ratner), though copies sold in Britain were still printed in England.

In the US the magazine continued to flourish, moving to New York City (HQ of the 'real' American publishing industry) in the mid-1970s, multiplying its revenue with advertisements for mainstream items pitched at its baby-boomer readership and replacing its early hippie idealism with an enthusiastic endorsement of 'the American way of life', treating music as just so much corporately produced consumer product—which had, of course, always been the perspective of the music industry—and sliding its pitch towards a younger and younger audience. Paintings featured in *Rolling Stone: The Illustrated Portraits* (Chronicle Books, 2000) are now part of 'the Jann Wenner art collection'.

Wenner also publishes *Us*, a celebrity magazine, *Men's Journal* and *Outside*. In 2005, he was inducted into his spiritual home, the Rock 'n' Roll Hall of Fame in its 'Lifetime Achievement' category. His finest achievement, though this wasn't mentioned, might be said to have been using his position to secure a first US solo recording deal for Boz Scaggs (with Atlantic Records), who gave them one of the greatest début albums in rock history, 1968's *Boz Scaggs*.

[Paul Kantner, Jeff Tamarkin & Jann Wenner, *Got a Revolution!: The Turbulent Flight of Jefferson Airplane*, US: Atria Books, *nia*. John Lennon & Jann Wenner, *Lennon Remembers*, 1971; expanded edn., New York: Verso Books, 2000. Jerry Garcia, Charles A. Reich & Jann Wenner, *Garcia: A Signpost to New Space*, *nia*, 1972; republished New York: Da Capo, 2003. Bob Dylan interview, *Rolling Stone* no. 47, San Francisco, 29 Nov 1969; collected in Craig MacGregor, *Bob Dylan: A Retrospective*, 1972, reprinted as *Bob Dylan, The Early Years: A Retrospective*, 1990. Ralph J. Gleason: letter to this writer, Berkeley, CA, 14 Mar 1974. Michael Gray: 'That Million Dollar Serenade', *Rolling Stone* no. 42,

London edn., 20 Sep 1969. Alan Marcuson quote and information: Nigel Fountain, *Underground: The London Alternative Press 1966–74*, 1988. *Rolling Stone: The Illustrated Portraits*, San Francisco: Chronicle Books, 2000.]

Wexler, Jerry [1917 -] Jerome Wexler was born in Brooklyn, New York, on January 10, 1917, and was already into black music when he left high school at 15. He hung out in Harlem and 52nd Street clubs, studied in New York, served in the US Army and then majored in industrial journalism at Kansas State University, discovering much music in Kansas City. He is credited with having invented the term 'rhythm & blues', to replace the term 'race records', which was becoming a little difficult by the 1950s. He was a *Billboard* journalist at the time. He joined Atlantic in 1953 as a senior partner, promotion man and A&R man. The artists whose records he signed or produced in his time with the label are legion and include RAY CHARLES, Wilson Pickett, Aretha Franklin, the Coasters, the Drifters, Bobby Darin and LaVern Baker, and Wexler stuck with it all the way through to the overblown 1970s, when the label celebrated its 25th birthday with an enormous rack-jobbers' April in Paris (1973), at which the 'new product' played was almost entirely white. Wexler quit in 1975, but set up 'Atlantic South' in Miami, where he continued as a producer.

In December 1995 the Blues Foundation honoured him with its first Lifetime Achievement Award, and the Jerry Wexler Collection, 1967–2004, is now Collection Number 20393 within the Manuscripts Department at the Library of the University of North Carolina at Chapel Hill. He wasn't always so respectable. As AL ARONOWITZ remembered fondly, he 'learned every trick in the book just as well as the next music business crook and he takes no prisoners. He knows how to shave points off a beginner artist's royalties and he knows when to steal a piece of the songwriter's end. . . . [Yet] has emerged as a recording industry holy man, with a discography of hits big enough to keep the world listening for eons.' In 1993 (with David Ritz) he wrote his autobiography: *Rhythm and the Blues: A Life in American Music* (Knopf, 1993).

Along the way, he also produced Dusty Springfield, Dr. John, WILLIE NELSON, Dire Straits and Etta James, and he encountered Bob Dylan first in October 1972 in New York City, when he produced the DOUG SAHM album *Doug Sahm & Band*, on which Wexler proved himself commendably flexible, willing to go with the amiably shambolic spirit of the gathering rather than play the imperious star producer. It was Wexler who'd brought Sahm to Atlantic, rescuing him from years in the doldrums. (Tracks left off the album at the time have been issued on the CD version of 1992, and still more on *The Genuine Texas Groover* in 2003.) In August 1973, Dylan and Wexler actually co-produced an album: the début LP by BARRY GOLDBERG, at the Muscle Shoals Studio in Sheffield, Alabama.

Primarily, however, Wexler and regular co-producer BARRY BECKETT were called in by Dylan in 1979—and called back to Muscle Shoals—for his first Born Again album, *Slow Train Coming* (though they 'prepped it' in California first). Dylan knew that if the album was to work at all, it had to *sound* great, which meant that it had to be a tremendous production, and that the job had to go to someone with scorching R&B credentials. Jerry Wexler had 'em. It didn't help, however, to save *Saved*, the follow-up album also co-produced by Wexler and Beckett, again recorded in Sheffield, Alabama, in February 1980. This latter production was a less successful collaboration: Wexler wanted more precision; Dylan wanted it raw. Nor was Wexler impressed with the Born Again message. As he told CLINTON HEYLIN: 'I liked the irony of Bob coming to me, the Wandering Jew, to get the Jesus feel. . . . I had no idea he was on this born-again Christian trip until he started to evangelize me. I said, "Bob, you're dealing with a sixty-two-year-old confirmed Jewish atheist. I'm hopeless. Let's just make an album."'

[Jerry Wexler (with David Ritz), *Rhythm and the Blues: A Life in American Music*, New York: Knopf, 1993. Al Aronowitz quote 'Honoring Jerry Wexler', May 1996, seen online 12 Sep 2005 at *www.bigmagic.com/pages/blackj/column9.htm*. Clinton Heylin, *Behind the Shades Revisited*, London: Penguin, 2003, p.502.]

'What Can I Do for You?' [1980] An audacious instance of Dylan's using his old secular skills in a new devotional context is offered by 'What Can I Do for You?', on the *Saved* album. This not only gives us, out of nowhere, the most eerie, magnificent harmonica-work Dylan has done since the stoned, majestic concerts of 1966 but also applies all Dylan's enviable seductive gifts. The same knowingly disarming tone of voice that yielded 'Lay Lady Lay' back in 1969 is turned on here to disarm Jesus. Listen to the voice that sings these lines: 'I know all about poison, I know all about fiery darts / I don't care how rough the road is, show me where it starts.'

This audacity of delivery, the seductive intimacy of the voice as it handles these sumptuous, tactile syllables, is matched by the intimately personal, conversational nature of Dylan's highly attentive, judicious lyric, where every small word is carefully chosen and the whole adds up to a most beautiful act of articulate devotional humility. Within the lyric too we're offered a rich, seamlessly woven array of scriptural threads.

The central question asked in the song's title echoes the *only* question contained in the brief but lovely, devotional Psalm 116: 'What shall I render unto the Lord for all his benefits toward me?' (Psalms 116:12). Dylan's song retains some of the tone and import of this Passover Psalm while taking nothing else specifically from it. While Dylan might be said to echo its 'thou hast loosed my bonds' (in verse 16) in his '[You] Pulled me out of bondage', in fact his phrase more closely duplicates one found recurrently all through the Bible, being 'sold into bondage' and then brought 'out from bondage' being not only the core of the story of Exodus but by extension one of the central metaphors of Judaeo-Christian belief. Thus we can recognise Psalm 116 as providing here inspiration rather than further text.

Those 'fiery darts', meanwhile, are taken from Ephesians 6:11–16, in which Paul exhorts us: 'Put on the whole armour of God. . . . Above all, taking the shield of faith, wherewith ye shall be able to quench all the fiery darts of the wicked.'

'What Can I Do for You?' also offers, full of impact and panache, the line 'Soon as a man is born you know the sparks begin to fly.' This is a fine example of one of Dylan's greatest strengths: his capacity for modernising and colloquialising an archaic and formal line or phrase from biblical text: for rescuing and re-charging it. Dylan does this all through his work, sometimes at the most unexpected yet felicitous moments, often playfully.

For instance: in 'Joey', from the 1976 album *Desire*, Dylan's movie-like funeral scene has people weeping, immediately followed by Joey Gallo's old mafiosi friend Frankie muttering 'He ain't dead, he's just asleep', which is plausibly colloquial yet an exact re-statement of Christ's words at the death-bed of a young girl he then brings back to life: 'He said unto them, Give place: for the maid is not dead but sleepeth' (from Matthew 9:24). And: 'Why make ye this ado, and weep? the damsel is not dead, but sleepeth' (from Mark 5:39). And: 'Weep not; she is not dead, but sleepeth' (from Luke 8:52).

This updating and re-charging, with a surge which both brings out the essentials of the old and adds new layers of meaning, is especially powerful and generous on the 'Born Again' albums, since they offer such a concentration of biblical text and allusion.

Here in 'What Can I Do for You?' Dylan gives this intelligent creative treatment to the words of Job 5:7: 'Yet man is born unto trouble, as the sparks fly upward.' His re-write, 'Soon as a man is born you know the sparks begin to fly', gives it a sparky, edgy, threatening contemporaneity (which is the essence of contemporaneity), implying trouble without needing to keep the word 'trouble' in the line.

CHRISTOPHER RICKS noted this back in 1981, saying in a radio interview broadcast on Dylan's 40th birthday that he loved 'the adaptation of biblical quotations and allusions so that they become at once entirely modern and straightforward and simple while nevertheless having a lot of ancient feeling in them. Now that feeling that sparks *can't* but fly up into the sky, and that's like our trouble . . . [he] turns that into a modern world of aggression and punch-up . . .'

The corollary Dylan argues for in his next line—that 'He gets wise in his own eyes'—takes its scriptural cue from the Old Testament book of (Solomon's) Proverbs: 'Be not wise in thine own eyes' (3:7), reiterated by the prophet Isaiah: 'Woe unto them that are wise in their own eyes, and prudent in their own sight!' (Isaiah 5:21). Again Dylan's re-processing involves a telling shift. As Ricks said in the same interview, 'to "get wise" is different. . . . [Again it's] . . . that rather ugly, threatening American idiom: "Don't you get wise with me." It's not the same as *being* wise . . . the lyrics are full of these very beautiful turns with old sayings.' (Ricks gives the song further exemplary, alert attention to detail, in his essay 'What He Can Do for You'.)

A nice irony, as regards the trouble and the sparks, is that both arise only in the King James Bible's translation—a case, as Jorge Luis Borges said of others' endeavours, where 'The original is unfaithful to the translation'. In the Greek and the Hebrew, 'trouble' is probably 'labour', and 'the sparks fly upward' is given as 'the sons of the coal lift up their flight' or 'dart upward', or in the Hebrew as 'the sons of the burning coal lift up to fly.' In the magnificent translation in Miles Coverdale's Cologne Bible of 1535, and for the Great Bible of 1539, edited by Coverdale (c.1488–1569), Job's words are different again: 'It is man that is borne unto mysery, like as the byrde for to fle.' This in turn rubs up against a well-known verse of *The Book of Common Prayer* (Coverdale once more), from the service for the burial of the dead: 'Man that is born of woman hath but a short time to live, and is full of misery.' If this plays subliminally behind Dylan's lines, it helps along his message: he not busy being re-born is busy dying.

Another whisper of inspiration lurks behind 'What Can I Do for You?' too. The fifth and final verse of Christina Rossetti's lyric for the Christmas carol 'In the Bleak Mid-Winter' may have provided the prompt for the distinctively intimate, nuzzling series of questions Dylan assembles in this song. The Rossetti verse is intrinsically less intimate, because it speaks of God in the third person rather than the second, and of that manifestation of God that was the baby Jesus, but it journeys ever nearer to intimacy as it proceeds, and it proceeds by means of posited questions, intoned in crucial humility, just as the Dylan song does: 'What can I give him, poor as I am? / If I were a shepherd I would bring a lamb; / If I were a wise man I would do my part; / Yet what I can I give him—give my heart.' Dylan's song, in parallel, ends by imploring: 'Whatever pleases You, tell it to my heart. / . . . What can I do for You?'

Dylan débuted 'What Can I Do for You?' in concert on the opening night of the first gospel tour, in November 1979, long before he recorded it, and he retained it in his repertoire all through that tour and the next (January–February 1980), recorded it in Sheffield, Alabama, on February 12, played it again every night on the third and final all-gospel tour (April–May 1980) and then performed it at a further ten of the 19 concerts on the semi-gospel fall tour at the end of that year. He revisited the song 12 more times in 1981 but has never played it since.

[Christopher Ricks: radio interview, Cambridge, UK, Apr 1981, in '1961 Revisited: Bob Dylan's Back Pages', BBC Radio Wales, Cardiff, 1981, broadcast 24 May 1981; 'What He Can Do for You', *Telegraph* no.22, Bury, UK, winter 1985, collected in Michael Gray & John Bauldie, eds., *All Across the Telegraph: A Bob Dylan Handbook*, 1987.

Christina Rossetti (1830–94): 'Christmas Carol', aka 'In the Bleak Mid-Winter', first published in book form in the first collected edition of her work, *Goblin Market, The Prince's Progress and Other Poems*, 1875.]

'Whatcha Gonna Do?' [1962] Dylan cut three versions of 'Whatcha Gonna Do?' (all unreleased): two at the *Freewheelin' Bob Dylan* sessions in New York City on November 14 & December 6, 1962 and another as a songwriter's demo for Witmark in August 1963. This last is the version published in the official Dylan lyrics collections. The song was copyrighted in 1963 and 1966 as by Bob Dylan.

Yet 'Whatcha Gonna Do?' rests heavily on an old black church song, variously titled, and recorded for instance in the 1930s as 'When Death Comes Creeping in Your Room' by the Golden Eagle Gospel Singers, Chicago, May 11, 1937. Dylan did little more than tweak one or two lines for the lyric he publishes as his own.

The line 'When death comes slippin' in your room' also occurs in the chorus of the otherwise dissimilar gospel song 'You're Gonna Need Somebody on Your Bond', recorded twice by the great BLIND WILLIE JOHNSON ('You'll Need Somebody on Your Bond', New Orleans, December 11, 1929, and the last side he ever recorded, the superior 'You're Gonna Need Somebody on Your Bond', Atlanta, April 20, 1930) and subsequently a standard repertoire item (often performed by BIG JOE WILLIAMS as 'You're Gonna Need King Jesus' and by SONNY TERRY & BROWNIE McGHEE as 'I've Been 'Buked and I've Been Scorned') and which moved across into the Folk Revivalist repertoire, not least because the superior take by Johnson was one of the tracks on *The Country Blues*, the 1959 compilation LP by Sam Charters that was the most important & influential early vinyl issue of old blues after HARRY SMITH's anthology of 1952, *AMERICAN FOLK MUSIC*, a set of three double-LPs.

[Blind Willie Johnson: 'You'll Need Somebody on Your Bond' & 'You're Gonna Need Somebody on Your Bond'; both reissued on 2-CD set *The Complete Blind Willie Johnson*, Columbia Legacy Roots N' Blues Series 472190 2, NY, 1993. Various Artists: *The Country Blues*, RBF RF-1, NY, 1959. Various Artists: *American Folk Music*, set of 3 double-LPs (Vol.1: Ballads; Vol.2: Social Music; Vol.3: Songs), Folkways FP251–253, NY, 1952; CD-reissued as *Anthology of American Folk Music* (6-CD box set) with copious notes by many hands and a CD-ROM of extras, Smithsonian Folkways SRW 40090, Washington, D.C., 1997.]

'wheels of fire' Eleven years after the major Basement Tapes song 'This Wheel's on Fire' (1967) comes *Street Legal*, on which, in the opening song, the wonderful 'Changing of the Guards', Dylan sings: 'Peace will come / With tranquility and splendor on the wheels of fire'. These images correspond to the Old Testament prophet Daniel's vision of the Day of Judgment:

'I beheld till the thrones were cast down, and the Ancient of days did sit, whose garment was white as snow, and the hair of his head was like the pure wool: his throne was like the fiery flame, and his wheels as burning fire' (Daniel 7:9). Soon afterwards: '. . . behold, one like the Son of man came with the clouds of heaven, and came to the Ancient of days, and they brought him near before him. And there was given him dominion, and glory, and a kingdom, that all peoples, all nations, and languages, should serve him: his dominion is an everlasting dominion, which shall not pass away, and his kingdom that which shall not be destroyed' (Daniel 7:13–14).

'When He Returns' [1979] This is the final track on *Slow Train Coming*, the first of Dylan's 'Born Again' albums, and one of the strongest of the period. Not an especially attractive place to be, nevertheless the world of this song is fiercely, abrasively impassioned and Dylan gives it a tour de force, self-flagellant performance, demanding to know: 'How long can I listen to the lies of prejudice? / How long can I stay drunk on fear out in the wilderness?'

There's a vengeful tone here that sits ill with its declaimed obeisance to the will of Christ: a tone that suggests that there'll be a great deal of slaughter and pain when things come right in the end—when '. . . like a thief in the night / He'll replace wrong with right / When He returns.'

The analogy is of, course, Christ's own idea. According to Matthew 24:42–44, Christ tells the disciples: 'Watch therefore: for ye know not what hour your Lord doth come. But know this, that if the goodman of the house had known in what watch the thief would come, he would have watched, and would not have suffered his house to be broken up. Therefore be ye also ready: for in such an hour as ye think not the Son of man cometh.' (The same speech is reported also in Luke 12:39–40.) This message is later relayed in two further passages. In Paul's First Epistle to the Thessalonians, he writes: 'For yourselves know perfectly that the day of the Lord so cometh as a thief in the night' (I Thessalonians 5:2); and in the Second Epistle of Peter the Apostle, he too writes: 'But the day of the Lord will come as a thief in the night' (from II Peter 3:10).

The pleasingly quirky oxymoron of 'day' and 'night' here naturally so worries the writers of the *Good News Bible* that they abolish it, so reducing the resonant poetry of 'like a thief in the night' to the dully unmemorable 'like a thief.' Bob Dylan, in creditable contrast, not only uses the whole line but, in making it 'Like a thief in the night / He'll replace wrong with right', offers a matching oxymoron, emphasising the odd ostensible contradiction at the heart of Christ's analogy, while accurately summarising the import of His message.

'When He Returns' enfolds an extravagance of further scriptural reference. Verse 1 alludes (by 'the iron rod') both to God's giving His rod to Moses—the rod by means of which Moses eventually effects the Israelites' escape from 'the iron hand' of the Egyptians—and to Isaiah's prophecy of Christ's coming, in which 'there shall come forth a rod out of the stem of Jesse, and a Branch shall grow out of his roots: And the spirit of the Lord shall rest upon him . . . the spirit of the knowledge and the fear of the Lord . . . with righteousness shall he judge the poor, and reprove with equity for the meek of the earth: and he shall smite the earth with the rod of his mouth, and with the breath of his lips shall he slay the wicked' (Isaiah 11:1–2 & 4; and there is the tone of vengeful relish Dylan imports from the Old Testament into his own song).

Aptly, Dylan's opening couplet matches 'the iron rod' with 'a mighty God'—aptly because this latter is not the anonymous phrase we might assume but is also drawn from, and so alludes to, a passage of Isaiah, the nearby 9:6, which again envisages Christ's coming: 'For unto us a child is born . . . and his name shall be called. . . . The mighty God . . .'

Dylan's next line, 'For all those who have eyes and all those who have ears', uses a particular piece of rhetoric deployed time and again in the New Testament and founded upon a text from the Old Testament book of Ezekiel (12:1–2): 'The word of the Lord also came unto me, saying, Son of man, thou dwellest in the midst of a rebellious house, which have eyes to see, and see not; they have ears to hear, and hear not . . .'

('When He Returns' is not, of course, Dylan's first use of this: it's there as rhetoric in 'Blowin' in the Wind': 'Yes 'n' how many ears must one man have . . . ?'; 'Yes 'n' how many times must a man turn his head / Pretending he just doesn't see?')

In the New Testament we find the founding passage of Ezekiel cited by Christ Himself in Matthew 13:43 ('. . . Who hath ears to hear, let him hear') and repeatedly by Christ and others in Mark and Revelation: 'And he said unto them, He that hath ears to hear, let him hear' (Mark 4:9); 'If any man have ears to hear, let him hear' (Mark 4:23); 'If any man have ears to hear, let him hear' (Mark 7:16); 'Having eyes, see ye not? and having ears, hear ye not? . . .' (Mark 8:18); and 'He that hath an ear, let him hear . . .' (Revelation 2:7, 11 & 29; 3:6, 13 & 22).

And all that's just in the first verse of 'When He Returns'! The second begins from the text of Matthew 7:14: 'Because strait is the gate, and narrow is the way, which leadeth unto life, and few there be that find it.' Dylan echoes delicately the rhythms and the half-rhyming repetitions of this line with his own 'Truth is an arrow, and the gate is narrow, that it passes through'.

Indeed he uses this pattern for most lines in his song, including each verse's opening line: all three incorporate internally rhyming or half-rhyming pairings: 'The iron hand, it ain't no match, for the iron rod'; 'Truth is an arrow, and the gate is narrow, that it passes through'; 'Surrender your crown, on this blood-stained ground, take off your mask.' And this last, the opening line of Dylan's third and final verse, builds its balancing half-rhymes, whether by accident or design, from the balancing bookends of the Bible: 'Surrender your crown' cites Revelation (4:10), while 'this blood-stained ground' cites Genesis (also 4:10). The former describes the end days: 'The four and twenty elders fall down before him that sat on the throne, and worship him that liveth for ever and ever, and cast their crowns before the throne . . .'; the passage from Genesis is in the account of the first murder after the Fall, when Cain has slain Abel and God asks: 'What hast thou done? the voice of thy brother's blood crieth unto me from the ground.' (Dylan uses this again in the fascinating unissued 1980 song 'Yonder Comes Sin'.)

Finally, Dylan's 'He knows your needs even before you ask' is taken from the Sermon on the Mount: '. . . your Father knoweth what things ye have need of, before ye ask him' (from Matthew 6:8, immediately before the passage we call 'The Lord's Prayer').

It's admirable that 'When He Returns' shoulders so much biblical text without ever groaning under its weight or losing its own strong identity.

When Dylan came to the gospel tours of 1979–80, 'When He Returns' was a highlight of his performances, as he pushed his voice to experimental levels of expressive pain and ardour. Tapes of these performances are not the sort you can play to those who are less than keen on Dylan in the first place; but in concerts on which he was ablaze with the freshness of his evangelical fervour, 'When He Returns' was always a most powerful vehicle for it.

On the first tour of the period, from November 1 to December 9, 1979, Dylan sang 'When He Returns' early on in every concert, and kept it in the same slot for the second tour, from January 11 to February 9, 1980. For the third tour, from April 17 to May 21, 1980, its appearances began and ended on the fourth and final night in Toronto, on April 20: a night on which Dylan was especially fired up and turned in an almost embarrassingly extreme, thrilling rendition. (This has been issued on the *Highway 61 Interactive* CD-ROM of 1995.)

Unexpectedly, on November 4, 1981, he played it for the only time since then, towards the end of a concert in Cincinnati, Ohio, during which he told the audience: 'I don't think I sang one song in tune all night.' But tunefulness had never been the point of 'When He Returns'.

Postscript: in 2006 came a DVD version of the Various Artists compilation album *Gotta Serve Somebody: The Gospel Songs of Bob Dylan*, though it was not quite a full duplication; it excludes MAVIS STAPLES' & Bob's 'Gonna Change My Way of Thinking' (see separate entry) but *does* include the first official release of the film footage of Dylan performing that burning 'When He Returns' from the Toronto concert of April 20, 1980.

[Various Artists: *Gotta Serve Somebody: The Gospel Songs of Bob Dylan*, DVD, dir. Michael B. Borofsky; Burning Rose Video / Image Entertainment ID2894RBDVD, US, 2006 (officially dated 2005).]

'When the Ship Comes In' [1964] Recorded first as a Witmark music-publishing demo in New York City in August 1963 (a version released for the first time 28 years later on *Bootleg Series Vols. 1–3*), the song was recorded again that October 23. This is the version on the third Dylan album, *The Times They Are a-Changin'*. Three days later he performed it at his first Carnegie Hall concert. After a 22-year gap it resurfaced (and sank) at Live Aid, Philadelphia, July 13, 1985.

'When the Ship Comes In' draws just as firmly on the idea of the hard struggle of good-hearted men to overcome adversity as anything in traditional folk song; yet here Dylan's intelligence and artistry uses the strengths of this theme in the utterly different context of a moral struggle, and does it without faltering. It is a much-underrated song.

'When the Ship Comes In' prophesies a sociopolitical ideal future as strongly as does 'The Times They Are a-Changin'', and offers us Dylan singing of the coming change in terms of an arriving ship—which might seem as unsurprising as the use of roads, tides and so on in that other anthem. Yet unlike 'The Times They Are a-Changin'', 'When the Ship Comes In' has not been outdated by events. It survives because it is wisely unspecific—not out of vagueness, nor from an attempt to provide a common-to-everyone account. Necessarily and rightly, its references to coming changes are figurative to the point of allegory because the important thing is (by contrast) the personal responses of the writer towards the anticipated future. The details, figurative, metaphorical, allegorical and symbolic as they are, define and illustrate these responses. Where 'The Times They Are a-Changin'' gives us no sense of proximity to any individual's sensibility, 'When the Ship Comes In' plainly offers a sincere vision. It puts us in contact with a real and fine sensibility. It doesn't lean on mass sentiment at any point; mass sentiment can, if it likes, lean on it.

Part of its appeal comes from its anthemic tune and Dylan's impassioned yet light-footed performance. These two elements combine, and combine with the words, to sustain a maximum effect and energy (as, for instance, when we come to that simple word 'shout' in the last verse: the voice does indeed break into a shout, a celebratory exclamation, and hits the word as the tune hits the highest note in the verse).

It is partly the language of the Bible that propels this ship. Here is Matthew Chapter 24, verse 29, in which Christ says he is quoting the prophet Daniel's prophecy of the last days (though in fact these words don't occur in Daniel): 'Immediately after the tribulation of those days shall the sun be darkened, and the moon shall not give her light, and the stars shall fall from heaven, *and the powers of the heavens shall be shaken*'. This last sounds like a line of the song. (This part of the biblical text precedes a passage Dylan alludes to over 25 years later in 'Ring Them Bells': Matthew 24:31.)

Even as words on the page, though, the song has a charm very much its own—like a glimpse into a world both real and unreal: morally mature (if severe) yet child-like in conception. The internal rhyming is so effective, driving the vision along in the rhythm of the oncoming ship as it meets, again and again, relentlessly, the swell of the sea: 'And the song, will, lift, as the main, sail, shifts / And the boat, drifts . . .' and this internal rhyming collaborates perfectly with the alliterative effects (as well, of course, as with the tune): 'Then the sands will roll out a carpet of gold / For your weary toes to be a-touchin'. . .' The child-like allegory comes over as a quite unexceptionable moral cleanliness—a convincing wisdom. This not only redresses anger; it yields a positive and spirited apprehension of the new age's possibilities: 'Oh the fishes will laugh as they swim out of the path / And the seagulls, they'll be smiling . . . / And the sun will respect every face on the deck'.

Political yearnings do not sweep aside more ordinary joys: to talk of having sand between your toes, to feel glad of the imagined sympathy of fishes and to call up, in the midst of a mood of general anticipation, such a particular image as that of a smiling seagull face—this is to encompass a wise and salutary statement of hope. It accords with this achievement, this sustained control, that Dylan avoids painting 'the foes' as demons or fools. They are big enough to hold on to a certain

Dave Van Ronk & Bob Dylan

© Michael Gray, 1981

Bob Dylan at the Mariposa Folk Festival

Library of Congress

Paul Verlaine

VICTORIA'S SECRET EXCLUSIVE

FREE CD

WITH ANY PURCHASE NOW

Limited time offer ends at 3AM EST on April 11, 2004 while supplies last. Enter offer code DYLANCD Details below.

She Belongs To Me
Don't Think Twice, It's All Right
To Ramona
Boots of Spanish Leather
It's All Over Now, Baby Blue
Love Sick (remix)
Make You Feel My Love
Things Have Changed
Sugar Baby

BOB DYLAN'S *LOVE SICK* A collector's edition must-have, this extraordinary CD features an exclusive selection of Bob Dylan's most seductive love songs, including a never-heard-before remix of *Love Sick*. See Bob Dylan as you've never seen him before in a TV commercial for our new Angels bra.

► TV COMMERCIAL ► CD COVER

Simply place an order and enter offer code DYLANCD at checkout. Limited time offer ends at 3AM EST on April 11, 2004. Offer is valid in stores, catalogue and web site while supplies last.

Jennifer Warnes album cover

Library of Congress

Walt Whitman

Photo by Steve Rhodes

Dave Whitaker

dignity where the allegory goes biblical; yet, beyond this, the apparently child-like vision applies to them too, humanising them even as it condemns: 'Oh the foes will rise with the sleep still in their eyes / And they'll jerk from their beds and think they re dreamin' / But they'll pinch themselves and squeal and they'll know that its for real / The hour when the ship comes in.'

It was unfortunate that this deft, bright song of fresh and optimistic youth, so long ignored in Dylan's 'live' repertoire, was finally re-stumbled upon by the 1985 Bob Dylan and his rock-star friends KEITH RICHARDS and RON WOOD at Live Aid, doused in the embarrassingly undeft, tired inebriation of the world-weary middle-aged.

Re the smiling seagulls: see also **'Royal Canal, the'**.

'Which Side Are You On?' The lines in 'Desolation Row' which immediately follow 'The Titanic sails at dawn' are 'Everybody is shouting / "Which Side Are You On?".' It is a question Bob Dylan has usually resisted on principle ('Lies that life is black and white . . .', as he protests in 'My Back Pages'), though he swaps sides and asks much the same question in the Born Again period ('You either got faith or you got unbelief / And there ain't no neutral ground').

'Which Side Are You On?' was an intensely political song composed by Florence Reece (then aged 12), the daughter of Kentucky miner. (The tune, as ALAN LOMAX explains it, was a variant on the English 'Jack Munroe', the title phrase replacing 'lay the lily-o'). It later became a national union song and favourite in the repertoire of THE FREEDOM SINGERS in the civil rights struggle. It is cited also in Martin B. Duberman's political play *In White America* (1964). Dylan, interviewed in 1966 ('The Playboy Interview: Bob Dylan: A Candid Conversation with the Iconoclastic Idol of the Folk-Rock Set', *Playboy*, Chicago, March 1966), made his attitude clear: 'Songs like "Which Side Are You On?" and "I Love You Porgy", they're not folk music songs: they're political songs. They're already dead.'

Whitaker, Dave [1937 -] 'Dave Whittaker [sic], one of the Svengali-type BEATS on the scene happened to have WOODY's autobiography, *Bound for Glory*, and he lent it to me,' Dylan confirms in *Chronicles Volume One*. He also says that it was Whitaker who told him that Guthrie was still alive but 'in ill health somewhere in the East'.

Dave Whitaker was one of Dylan's earliest Dinkytown friends, and one of the most vociferously Bohemian in lifestyle and politics. He and his wife Gretel (now GRETEL PELTO), used to meet up with Dylan at the Ten O'Clock Scholar every day through the first three months of 1960. They shared an enthusiasm for traditional music and new music but Whitaker was mostly a mentor when it came to contemporary literature (and would have mentored Dylan about politics too, had Dylan not turned a deaf ear). And according to photographer LARRY KEENAN, it was Dave who first 'turned Dylan on to pot'. Whitaker remembers that the apartment he and Gretel shared in a house on 14th Avenue and 10th Street, right across the street from Dave (aka TONY) GLOVER, was a gathering place for all-night music playing and pot smoking, and that it was here that Glover made his recordings of Dylan—recordings made in 1961, 1962 and even 1963.

David Allen Whitaker was born on November 12, 1937 in Cleveland, Ohio, but his parents came from Minnesota and they moved back to Minneapolis when Dave was very young. He went to the same high school as BONNIE BEECHER and others. But in the February 26, 1957 issue of *The Nation*, Whitaker read an article by Kenneth Rexroth about the Beat scene in San Francisco, and promptly dropped out to join it.

He met KEROUAC, GINSBERG and others, and 'was in seventh heaven'. Later he went to Europe and Israel, stopping off in London in 1959 ('during the skiffle days') on his way back home. From London he went to New York City, found Greenwich Village and met DAVE VAN RONK, and then returned to Minneapolis.

This, then, was the Dave Whitaker Dylan met in Dinkytown: someone who had already been to these places, met these people, paid some dues. And Whitaker was 22 when Dylan was 18: it was a significant difference in age and experience. So when the Dylan of *Chronicles* says that Whitaker was 'one of the Svengali-type Beats on the scene' who 'happened to have Woody's autobiography', that's a little on the begrudging side and underplays his old friend's qualifications.

By 1966, when ROBERT SHELTON interviewed him, Dave had split up from Gretel and was back in San Francisco, a 'dropout living hand to mouth. A gentle, somewhat defeated man in his late twenties' who 'seemed prematurely old.' He'd moved back there in 1963 or 1964, and didn't feel 'somewhat defeated'.

He remained in San Francisco, trying to make a living as a poet and being an activist. In the 1970s he started hosting a radio show on KPOO-FM, a black station with a Black Panthers history, and they started calling him Diamond Dave, a name he's still known by all over the city. He became part of 'the Rainbow Family' and lived out the communal dream, having little money but needing little too. He used to talk to Dylan on the phone from time to time, and at the beginning of the 1980s, his oldest son, now known as Ubi Dube, asked Dave to ask Bob if he could send him a guitar. A very fine Stratocaster duly arrived, stickered with quotations from the Bible.

The last time Whitaker and Dylan met was around 1991, somewhere out in Wisconsin. The

Rainbow Family bus Dave was traveling in pulled up behind the far shinier Dylan tour bus by the side of the Mississippi River, and when Whitaker identified himself, the circle of security opened up and he, Dylan and LARRY KEGAN spent a couple of hours talking.

In 1999 Whitaker gave this poem to the San Francisco Coalition on Homelessness: 'take what you need / give what you can / where you can / when you can / however you can / in other words / lend a hand / And what happens then? / strangers become friends / friends become family / family becomes community / and community on the move / that's the movement / . . . we were brought together / for a reason / and that reason is / that we complement one another / like / yin and yang / left and right / up and down / man and woman / ROCK AND ROLL.'

Today Dave Whitaker still lives in Haight Ashbury, and has a radio series you can hear via *www.indybay.org*. He's involved with the 'Reclaim the Commons' movement, the 'Food Not Bombs' campaign and much else. In September 2005 he and the Rainbow Family were down in Waveland, Mississippi, opening the 'New Waveland Café' to help give out food to victims of Hurricane Katrina.

When you look at how Whitaker lives, freely and gregariously, and at how Dylan lives, super-rich but isolated, not even talking to his own musicians, who can say that Dave Whitaker hasn't chosen the healthier path? At any rate, he remains an activist, a defiant but mellow old bohemian, and proud of it.

[Bob Dylan, *Chronicles Volume One*, 2004, pp.245–46. Larry Keenan statement on his website at *www.emptymirrorbooks.com/keenan/m1996-4.html*. Robert Shelton, *No Direction Home: The Life and Music of Bob Dylan*, London: Penguin edn., p.72. Diamond Dave Whitaker: 'take what you need', Coalition for Homelessness, San Francisco, 1999, seen online 3 Oct 2005 at *http://aspin.asu.edu/hpn/archives/Dec99/0057.html*. Other Whitaker quotes and most information above from phone-call from San Francisco to this writer 4 Oct 2005.]

White, Bukka [1909 - 1977] Booker T. Washington White was born in Houston, Mississippi, on November 12, 1909, but moved down into the Delta as a child. His railroad-worker father taught him guitar and the music he produced was what he heard all around him. He played local gigs but also worked as a field-hand (most unusually for a musician) before moving around and settling in Memphis, where again he combined jobs, working partly as a musician, partly as a pro baseball player and partly as a fighter.

His first session was in 1930, in Memphis, when as Washington White he cut 14 titles for Victor on one May day, though ten remained unissued and have never been found. The other four sides became one blues record ('The New 'Frisco Train' c/w 'The Panama Limited') and one gospel record ('I Am in the Heavenly Way' c/w 'Promise True and Grand'). It's very possible that MEMPHIS MINNIE is the background voice on the gospel sides.

White didn't get back into a studio for over seven years, and then was able to cut only two numbers, 'Pinebluff Arkansas' and 'Shake 'Em on Down' (one of his best-known tracks), issued on Vocalion as by Bukka White. These sides were recorded in Chicago where White was hiding out, having jumped bail after being arrested for shooting a man in a fight in the South. He was soon captured and sent to the notorious hard-labour camp of Parchman Farm, which proved another recording opportunity, since naturally he was soon field-recorded by ALAN LOMAX. The two sides cut here (at Camp No.10, State Penitentiary, Parchman, Mississippi) were his first solo recordings.

Freed in 1940, Bukka White returned to Chicago and on two March days that year made the 12 tracks for which he is most valued, and which best display his beguiling mix of artistic precision and emotional ferocity, of dark pain and dexterous playing. (It helps too that the recordings are technically so fine: they glisten with acoustic clarity.) Accompanied this time by Washboard Sam on, er, washboard, Bukka White begins as he means to go on, with 'Black Train Blues', a smouldering prototype for ELVIS train songs, and on the second day nailing an old gospel song into his own distinctive 'Fixin' to Die Blues'.

This is the one that SAMUEL CHARTERS picks up on and includes on his ground-breaking compilation *The Country Blues* in 1959—the most important album since HARRY SMITH's 1952 anthology. This is therefore the song the young Bob Dylan picks up on and pulls into his repertoire at least as early as his Carnegie Chapter Hall concert of November 4, 1961—and which, three weeks later, he records for his début album. He is recorded playing it again at the home of the MacKenzies early that December, and again the following month for the CYNTHIA GOODING radio show 'Folksinger's Choice', broadcast in March 1963, the month the album came out. That seems to have been the end of the line for Dylan's 'Fixin' to Die'.

Bukka White, meanwhile, had settled back in Memphis at some point in the 1940s, his sumptuous old Delta blues too unfashionable for Chicago; but Memphis too proved hard to survive in and though he played sometimes with the veteran FRANK STOKES, he mainly reverted to labouring work. But Sam Charters had prompted a spate of 're-discoveries', and in 1963 White became one of them, 'found' and recorded by enthusiasts. Given a record deal, White worked the campus and folk club circuits, played the 1966 NEWPORT FOLK FESTIVAL, toured Europe and made further albums.

Though on the whole the later work is less economical, includes long and diffuse narratives and lacks the torrential fluidity of his earlier playing and the intensity of commitment, nonetheless he had by no means lost all his powers, and it's almost a fairy-tale ending that his Biograph album *Big Daddy*, recorded in 1973, is considered by some to be at least on a par with his best earlier work.

Bukka White died of cancer in Memphis on February 26, 1977.

[Bukka White: 'The New 'Frisco Train' c/w 'The Panama Limited' (as by Washington White & Napoleon Hairiston) & 'I Am in the Heavenly Way' c/w 'Promise True and Grand' (as by Washington White), Memphis, TN, 26 May 1930; 'Pinebluff Arkansas' c/w 'Shake 'Em on Down', Chicago, 2 Sep 1937; 'Sic n'Em Dogs On' & 'Po Boy' (as by Washington Barrelhouse White), Parchman, MS, 23 May 1939, recorded/released wrong speed; 'Fixin' to Die Blues', Chicago, 8 Mar 1940, *The Country Blues*, RBF RF-1, NY, 1959; 'Black Train Blues', Chicago, 7 Mar 40, *Mississippi Blues Vol. 1*, Roots RL-302, Vienna, 1968, CD-reissued *Parchman Farm Blues*, Blues Collection CD 23 (magazine + CD), London, 1994; *Big Daddy*, Biograph BLP-12049, US, 1973.]

Whitman, Walt [1819 - 1892] See **poetry, American, pre-20th century.**

Wilentz, Sean [1951 -] Robert Sean Wilentz was born on February 20, 1951 in New York City, where his family ran the 8th Street Bookstore, above which, in his uncle's apartment, in December 1963, AL ARONOWITZ introduced Bob Dylan to ALLEN GINSBERG (who, just back from India, was staying there temporarily). Sean's father, Elias Wilentz, edited *The Beat Scene*, one of the earliest anthologies of BEAT poetry, and was a friend of IZZY YOUNG, in and around whose Folklore Center on MacDougal Street Wilentz says he has 'dim boyhood memories of Bob Dylan'. He first saw Dylan live when, aged 13, he attended 1964's Hallowe'en concert at New York's Philharmonic Hall: a concert he duly writes about most eloquently in an essay commissioned for the liner notes for the concert's official release as a 2-CD set, the *Bootleg Series Vol. 6: Bob Dylan Live 1964*.

An historian and writer, Wilentz received his PhD in history from Yale in 1980 after BAs from Columbia University and Balliol College, Oxford. He teaches history at Princeton University now (he's Dayton-Stockton professor of history and director of the program in American studies), and is the author of, among other books, *Chants Democratic* (1984 and 2004), a study of the emergence of the working class in New York City, and *The Rise of American Democracy: Jefferson to Lincoln* (2005). His latest book is *Andrew Jackson* (2006).

In 2004 he co-edited, with GREIL MARCUS, *The Rose and the Briar*, a collection of historical essays and artistic creations inspired by American ballads—with a parallel CD that includes Bob Dylan's 'Lily, Rosemary and the Jack of Hearts' from the *Blood on the Tracks* album.

In his spare time Sean Wilentz also writes for, among others, the *New York Times*, *Los Angeles Times*, the *New York Review of Books*, the *London Review of Books* and *New Republic*. On *www.bobdylan.com* he is described as the website's 'historian-in-residence'. In the section titled 'Etc.' you'll find Wilentz's long article 'The Roving Gambler at Scenic Newport', described as 'Some notes on Bob Dylan, the 2002 Newport Folk Festival, and the modern folk process', and the first piece he wrote for the site, 'American Recordings: On *"Love and Theft"* and the Minstrel Boy'. Explaining how this came about, he wrote (in the *Chronicle of Higher Education*):

'. . . I published a few articles about Dylan and his work. Somebody, possibly from the old days, must have noticed, because in 2001 a phone call came from out of the blue asking if I would like to write something about a forthcoming album, called *"Love and Theft"*, for the official Dylan Web site. I agreed, with the provision that if I didn't like the album I wouldn't do it. Fortunately I loved what I heard, the people who had contacted me liked what they read, and it was the beginning of a beautiful set of friendships . . .' This essay was reprinted in slightly longer form in *'Do You Mr. Jones?': Bob Dylan with the Poets and the Professors*, edited by NEIL CORCORAN, 2002.

More recently Wilentz wrote those sleevenotes for the official release, four decades on, of the concert he had seen as a 13-year-old and then, in summer 2005, the notes to the Starbucks album *Bob Dylan Live at the Gaslight, 1962*.

[Sean Wilentz, *Chants Democratic: New York City & the Rise of the American Working Class. 1788–1850*, New York: Oxford University Press, 1984 & 2004; *The Rise of American Democracy: Jefferson to Lincoln*, New York: W.W. Norton, 2005; *Andrew Jackson*, New York: Time Books/Henry Holt, 2006. Greil Marcus & Sean Wilentz, eds., *The Rose & the Briar: Death, Love and Liberty in the American Ballad*, New York: W.W. Norton, 2004; CD of same name, Columbia/Legacy CK 92866, Sep 2004; 'Writing for Bob Dylan', *Chronicle of Higher Education*, 3 Mar 2005. Elias Wilentz, ed., *The Beat Scene*, New York: Corinth, 1960.]

Williams, Big Joe [1903 - 1982] Big Joe Williams, not to be confused with Joe Williams, singer with the Count Basie Band in the 1950s, was born in Crawford, Mississippi, on October 16, 1903 but began traveling beyond Mississippi in his youth, playing guitar and singing in lumber camps, and settled to an unsettled life—the classic roaming blues musician. He first recorded in 1935, gaining what was, in the Depression, an unusual ten-year contract with Bluebird.

Linda Dahl, author of *Stormy Weather*, 1984, a book of profiles of women (mostly jazz) singers, claims that Mary Williams Johnson, not husband Big Joe, wrote his classic 'Baby Please Don't Go', but Dahl's source is almost certainly careless assumption from the sleevenotes of a series of LPs on the Rosetta label, which were, like Dahl, trying to raise the profile of women's contributions to music. This admirable aim is not served by dodgy assertions. (At another point the same Mary Williams was the wife of LONNIE JOHNSON. No claim seems to have been made for her as the composer of his material.)

In any case, 'Baby Please Don't Go' is strongly based on the older common-stock number known as 'Don't You Leave Me Here', which was at least 30 years old by the time Big Joe recorded 'Baby Please Don't Go'. It was recorded in its traditional form by Papa Harvey Hull & Long Cleve Rede, as by Sunny Boy and His Pals, in Chicago, on about April 8, 1927 (the same session that yielded the wonderful 'Hey! Lawdy Mama—The France Blues', which became one of the treasures of the blues revival era, covered, for instance, by MARK SPOELSTRA on that compilation album *The Blues Project* in 1964.)

Either way, 'Baby Please Don't Go' was a big hit for Williams, and he had a lesser success with a 1941 version of 'Crawlin' King Snake'. Well-known for his unique 9-string guitar and his erratic delivery, he performed with many of the greats of his day and, unlike so many, continued as a working musician all the way through till the blues revival movement occurred. He didn't need to be 'rediscovered': he was already around.

When Dylan paid his return visit to Minnesota in December 1961, and was recorded in a Minneapolis apartment, one of his best song-performances was of 'Baby Please Don't Go.' (Dylan has rarely performed this song since those early days; its most recent rendition was when Dylan came on stage and performed it during the encore of a TOM PETTY set in Holmdel, New Jersey, on August 10, 2003.)

At some point, Dylan sought Williams out and played with him. According to *Blues Revue* magazine, the Chicago-based Delmark Records founder Bob Koester (pronounced Chester) got Williams booked into Gerde's Folk City in fall 1961, and over a two-week period Dylan sat in with him: and before the end of the run, they were being billed as Big Bill and Little Joe. But according to ROBERT SHELTON's Dylan biography *No Direction Home*, 1986, it was in early 1962 that Mike Porco was considering booking Williams, and Dylan pressed him on it, saying 'He's the greatest old bluesman. You gotta put him in here.' Shelton says that he was given a three-week booking that February and that Dylan showed up each night and jammed with him on stage several times. This would seem the more likely version, especially since the album *Big Joe Williams at Folk City* was recorded there on February 26, according to its own sleevenotes.

(Extra confusion is added by the Koester camp by his claim that Dylan first showed up at a Big Joe gig in Chicago back in 1957 and befriended him then; Williams makes it worse by claiming that he first met Dylan in the 1940s, when 'he was very very young, probably no more than six.' Dylan himself compounds the confusion by writing, as an aside in *Chronicles*—and it is the book's only mention of Williams—that 'I'd played with Big Joe Williams when I was just a kid.')

At any rate, soon after the Gerde's Folk City booking, in March 1962, Big Joe was in Brooklyn recording for VICTORIA SPIVEY's small label Spivey Records when Dylan asked her if she could use a little white boy on one of her records. She put him back with the almost 60-year-old Williams (not an easy man to play with), and the result was a tremendous version of 'Sittin' on Top of the World' on which Dylan, aged 20, plays very convincing blues harmonica and is also allowed to sing back-up vocals on the title line—and indeed more than back-up, since twice in the course of the performance Big Joe is generous enough to keep silent and let Dylan sing the line alone.

Since Williams was trying to sound still in his prime, and Dylan was trying to sound as ancient as the hills, it's a comical moot point here as to who sounds the older of the two. Dylan also plays harp behind Williams on a less striking 'Wichita', and on a formless jam later titled 'Big Joe, Dylan and Victoria' and behind Spivey's vocals and piano on 'It's Dangerous'.

In 1980 MIKE BLOOMFIELD published a short memoir, *Me and Big Joe*, which not only portrayed the difficulties of their relationship very honestly but also, in Peter Narváez' phrase, illustrated 'the cross-cultural triumph of the blues tradition'. Bloomfield wrote: 'Joe's world wasn't my world, but his music was. It was my life; it would be my life. So playing on was all I could do, and I did it the best that I was able. And the music I played, I knew where it came from; and there was not any way I'd forget.'

As it turned out, Mike Bloomfield died before his mentor, in February 1981. Big Joe Williams died in Macon, Georgia, on December 17, 1982.

[Big Joe Williams: 'Baby Please Don't Go', Chicago, 31 Oct 1935; Big Joe Williams: 'Crawlin' King Snake', Chicago, 27 Mar 1941, 1st vinyl-issued *Big Joe Williams: Crawlin' King Snake, RCA International INT-1087*, London, 1970; *Big Joe Williams at Folk City*, 26 Feb 1962, Bluesville BVLP 1067, US, 1962. Papa Harvey Hull & Long Cleve Rede, c.8 Apr 1927, 1st vinyl-issued *Really! The Country Blues*, Origin Jazz Library OJL-2, NY, c.1961. Sunny Boy and His Pals: 'Don't You Leave Me Here', Chicago, c.8 Apr 1927. Big Joe Williams & Bob Dylan: NY, 2 Mar 1962, 'Sittin' on Top of the World' & 'Wichita', *Three Kings & A Queen*, Spivey LP 1004, NY, 1964; Big Joe Williams, Victoria Spivey & Bob Dylan, NY, 2 Mar 1962, 'Big Joe, Dylan & Victoria' and Victoria Spivey & Bob Dylan, ditto, 'It's Dangerous', *Three Kings & A Queen Vol. 2*, Spivey LP 1014, NY, 1972. Bob Dylan: 'Baby Please Don't Go', Minneapolis, MN, 22 Dec 1961.

Bob Dylan *Chronicles* quote, p.182. 'Big Joe Williams: Memory of the Road', *Blues Revue*, Mar–Apr 1995, no further details given, précis seen online 5 Oct 2005 at *www.expectingrain.com/dok/who/w/williams bigjoe.html*. Shelton ditto. Peter Narváez: '*Living Blues* Journal: The Paradoxical Aesthetics of the Blues Revival', collected in *Transforming Tradition: Folk Music Revivals Examined*, ed. Neil V. Rosenberg, Urbana: University of Illinois Press, 1993. Mike Bloomfield, with S. Summerfield: *Me and Big Joe*, San Francisco: Re/ Search Productions, 1980.]

Williams, William Carlos [1883 - 1963] William Carlos Williams was born in Rutherford, near Paterson, New Jersey, on September 17, 1883. There are figures who need a mention in that they have, as it were, significantly influenced those who influenced Dylan—and Williams is one of them. Himself influenced by POUND, RIMBAUD, BAUDELAIRE, WHITMAN and the D.H. Lawrence of *Studies in Classic American Literature*, he prefigures THE BEATS in his openness to mundane, traditionally 'unpoetic' language and in his metric inventiveness. His impact, though, was long delayed: he was first published in 1909 and his ironically titled *The Great American Novel* saw him reach artistic maturity by 1923 but it was post-war publication of *Paterson* Book I, 1946, *Collected Later Poems*, 1950 and *Collected Earlier Poems*, 1951 which thrust him into prominence. *Paterson* (Books II–V appeared in 1948, 1949, 1951 and 1958) is his masterpiece, a huge scrutiny of Paterson, New Jersey: the town in which, as it happens, ALLEN GINSBERG grew up and of which Dylan gives us a swift nocturnal portrait in his 1970s song 'Hurricane', on *Desire*.

There is at least one clear, significant instance of how Williams' work reached down through Ginsberg and became part of what Dylan absorbed. 'I saw the best minds of my generation destroyed by madness' is the most frequently quoted line (it is the main part of the opening line) from Ginsberg's *Howl*—but this leaps out from William Carlos Williams' earlier work: 'the pure products of America go crazy'.

(Williams' novel *The Greater Trumps*, 1932, inspired T.S. ELIOT—a point first made by Helen Gardner in her pioneering critical book *The Composition of 'Four Quartets'*, 1978: namely that Eliot's image of the dance around the 'still point' in 'Burnt Norton', 1935, was suggested by his reading Williams's novel, in which 'in a magical model of the universe the figures of the Tarot pack dance around the Fool at the still centre.' This is relayed by AIDAN DAY—author of that last quotation—in his book *Jokerman: Reading the Lyrics of Bob Dylan*, 1989.)

William Carlos Williams died after a prolonged series of strokes at his home, back in Rutherford, New Jersey, on March 4, 1963.

[William Carlos Williams' 'the pure products of America go crazy', exact source unspecified, quoted from epigraph used in *The Secret Goldfish* by David Means, London: 4th Estate, 2005.]

Williams, Hank [1923 - 1953] Born in Mount Olive West, Alabama, on September 17, 1923, Hiram King Williams conquered the handicaps of spina bifida, poverty and an Alabama upbringing to become, defiantly, 'the first superstar of country music', a prolific composer of direct and heartfelt songs, mostly of unrequited love, a singer of unmistakeable emotional penetration, a big seller with a string of huge hits, and a modern, self-destructive, punk personality. At age 29, at some point after midnight on New Year's Day 1953, chronically addicted to alcohol and pills, he slipped from sleep into death in the back seat of his Cadillac en route to another show. Next day, Marvin Rainwater rushed into the studio to make a tribute record.

Hank Williams has been a specific influence on Dylan, though a broad and founding one rather than one relied upon particularly for Dylan's 1968–70 country music. As Dylan himself said all along: 'An' my first idol was Hank Williams / For he sang about the railroad lines / An' the iron bars an' rattlin' wheels / Left no doubt that they were real' (from the wonderful *JOAN BAEZ in Concert, Part 2* sleevenote poem, 1964).

Dylan has recorded and/or performed at least eleven Hank Williams songs, widely distributed through the decades of his career, as follows: 'Hey Good Lookin'', live in Tuscaloosa, Alabama, October 26, 1990. 'House of Gold', live in Madrid, June 15, 1989 and Athens, the 28th. '(I Heard That) Lonesome Whistle', at the home of Eve & Mac MacKenzie, NY, December 23, 1961; for WBAI Radio, NY, recorded on about January 13, 1962 and probably broadcast that March 11; at the *Freewheelin' Bob Dylan* sessions in NY, April 24–25, 1962; live at Toad's Place, New Haven, Connecticut, January 12, 1990 and live at Penn State University two days later. 'Lost Highway' and 'I'm So Lonesome I Could Cry' backstage in London, May 3–4, 1965 (a fragment is included in the film *Don't Look Back*, auteured by D.A. PENNEBAKER, 1967). 'Kaw Liga', NY, October 28, 1975 for the soundtrack to the film *Renaldo & Clara* (an extract is used), 1978. 'Lost on the River', Malibu, probably March 1984, during rehearsals for his defiantly splendid 'Late Night with David Letterman' NBC-TV appearance that month (though he didn't, in the event, perform this song). 'Weary Blues From Waitin'', live at Lakeland, Florida, April 18, 1976. 'You Win Again', during the Basement Tapes sessions at West Saugerties, June–August 1967; in a drunken private jam with Etta James & her band at Providence, Rhode Island, July 9-10, 1986; taking lead vocal during a set by the Dead in Columbus, Ohio, on August 3, 2003; with WILLIE NELSON in a surprise appearance at a Nelson concert in LA on May 4, 2004; at the Bonnaroo Music Festival in Manchester, Tennessee, that June 11; and again with Willie Nelson (but this time during Dylan's set) in concert at Forth Worth, TX, July 4, 2005. 'Your Cheatin' Heart', live during his guest performance at a LEVON HELM & RICK DANKO club gig in NYC on February 16, 1983. 'Honky Tonk Blues' in six concerts in February 1999, beginning in Tallahassee on the 1st of the month. His most recent Williams rendition, the recording of 'I Can't Get You Off of My Mind' for *Timeless*, a 2001 various-artists tribute album to the composer, is as disappointingly mannered as the early-1960s versions of '(I Heard That) Lonesome Whistle' were direct and heartfelt.

Probably most of these songs were known to Dylan from the Hank Williams 78rpm records he had back in his boyhood home in Hibbing, MN, which are referred to several times, though not itemised, in ROBERT SHELTON's biography *No Direction Home*. In *Chronicles Volume One*, Dylan specifies 'Baby, We're Really in Love', 'Honky Tonkin'' and 'Lost Highway' as being among them.

But in any case Dylan will also have known many of Williams' songs via the work of JERRY LEE LEWIS, who habitually put country songs on the B-sides of his late-1950s-to-early-60s rock'n'roll A-sides for the Sun label, and performed them, often to taunt his rocker fans, at concerts. Dylan will have heard Jerry Lee break into extraordinary lyrical piano-work on beautifully poised performances of Hank Williams songs like 'You Win Again', 'Cold Cold Heart', 'Your Cheatin' Heart' and 'I'm So Lonesome I Could Cry'.

Dylan has always utilised other song titles within his own work, and two neat examples occur from with Hank Williams' canon. His country gospel warhorse of a song 'Mansion on the Hill' trots across the landscape of the 1980s Dylan song 'Sweetheart Like You', and it's odds on that Dylan knew quite well when he wrote 'Just Like Tom Thumb's Blues' in the 1960s that there is a Williams song called 'Howlin' at the Moon'. Such cases crop up with differing degrees of obviousness, of course, and when they're not obvious, you're left to wonder not so much whether they are intended but rather, whether they are intended to be recognised. There is at least a fascination, an opening up of playful ironic possibilities, to hearing the end of the third verse like this: 'And she steals your voice / And leaves you "Howlin' at the Moon".'

In *Chronicles Volume One* Dylan stresses Williams' influence upon him: 'Even at a young age,' he writes, 'I identified fully with him. . . . In time, I became aware that in Hank's recorded songs were the archetype rules of poetic songwriting. . . . You can learn a lot about the structure of songwriting by listening to his records, and I listened to them a lot and had them internalized.'

Influence works in many ways. Elsewhere it's noted how struck Dylan was by the particular mode of address **e.e. cummings** used in his poem 'Buffalo Bill's': 'and what i want to know is / how do you like your blueeyed boy / Mister Death'—struck by its directness—and in the light of this, it's noticeable that two of Dylan's earliest songs, though three years apart and very different in style, share another particular mode of address: 'Hey, so-and-so . . .' The songs are 'Little Richard', aka 'Hey Little Richard' (a very early extant item on tape by Bob Dylan, recorded in Hibbing in 1958), and 'Song to Woody', from the first album, which begins its second verse 'Hey, hey, Woody Guthrie . . .' and its third verse 'Hey, Woody Guthrie . . .' Isn't it quite likely that Dylan was first struck by *this* mode of address in song when he heard it on Hank Williams' 'Hey, Good Lookin''?

[Hank Williams: 'Hey, Good Lookin'', Nashville, TN, 16 Mar 1951, MGM 11000, 1951; 'A House of Gold', *nia*, 1948–49, MGM 11707, 1954; '(I Heard That) Lonesome Whistle', Nashville, 25 Jul 1951, MGM 11054, 1951; 'Lost Highway', Nashville, 1 Mar 1949, MGM 10506, 1949; 'I'm So Lonesome I Could Cry', Cincinnati, OH, 30 Aug 1949, MGM 10560, 1949; 'Lost on the River', Cincinnati, 22 Dec 1948, MGM 10434, c.1949; 'Weary Blues from Waitin'', *nia*, 1948–49, MGM 11574, 1953; 'You Win Again', Nashville, 11 Jul 1952, MGM 11318, 1952; 'Your Cheatin' Heart' c/w 'Kaw-Liga', Nashville, 23 Sep 1952, MGM 11416, 1952; 'Honky Tonk Blues', Nashville, 11 Dec 1951, MGM 11160, 1952; 'Howlin' at the Moon', Nashville, 16 Mar 1951, MGM 10961, 1951 and on *Honky Tonkin'*, MGM E242 (10" LP), 1954; 'Mansion on the Hill', *nia*, MGM 10328, 1948; 'I Can't Get You Off of My Mind', Nashville, 6 Nov 1947, MGM 10328, 1948.

Bob Dylan: *Joan Baez in Concert, Part 2* sleevenote poem, Vanguard VRS-9113, NY, 1964; 'I Can't Get You Off of My Mind', NY, 17 Dec 2000, *Timeless: Hank Waillliams Tribute*, Lost Highway 088 170 239-2/170 239-2, 2001; 'Hey Little Richard', Hibbing, MN, 1958, unreleased. Dylan quotes from *Chronicles Volume One* pp.95–96.

Jerry Lee Lewis: 'You Win Again', Memphis, TN, 5 Sep 1957 (B-side of 'Great Balls of Fire'), Sun 281, Memphis, 1957; 'Cold Cold Heart', Memphis, 9 Feb 1961, Sun 364, Memphis (London-American HLS 9414, London), 1961; 'Your Cheatin' Heart', Hamburg, Germany, 5 Apr 1964, *Live at the Star Club, Hamburg*, Philips 842 945, Germany (BL 7646, London), 1964; 'I'm So Lonesome I Could Cry', *nia*, *Sings the Country Music Hall of Fame Hits Vol. 1*, Smash SRS 67117, NYC 1969.

e.e. cummings: 'Buffalo Bill's', 1920, included in *Complete Poems, 1913–1962*, 1973.]

Williams, Paul [1948 -] Paul Williams was born in Boston, Massachusetts, on May 19, 1948. He founded a sci-fi fanzine, *Within*, in 1962, and at the start of 1966 the music magazine *Crawdaddy*, which pioneered 'serious' rock criticism. In early 1967 he co-organised the first New York City 'be in' and 18 months later quit *Crawdaddy* to move to a 'cabin in the woods' in Mendocino, CA. His first book, *Outlaw Blues*, was published March 1969, two months later he sang with JOHN, Yoko & the Plastic Ono Band on 'Give Peace a Chance' and the following year moved briefly to a 'wilderness commune' at Galley Bay, BC, Canada. His output, on sci-fi, music and more, continued to be prolific. His 'practical philosophy' book *Das Energi* was published 1973.

In the last months of 1979, responding to Dylan's Born Again conversion, Williams swiftly wrote and self-published the 128-page book *Dylan—What Happened?*, followed quickly by the 12-page booklet 'What Happened? One Year Later'.

In 1986 he began writing what became a significant series of books on Dylan the performer, which have made his one of the most prominent names among Dylan writers. The series was published as *Performing Artist: The Music of Bob Dylan, Volume One, 1960–1973* in May 1990, followed by *Bob Dylan: Performing Artist, The Middle Years, 1972–1986* (1992), *Bob Dylan: Mind Out of Time, Performing Artist Volume 3, 1987–2000* (2004) and *Bob Dylan: Volume 4 (The Genius of a Performing Artist, 2003–1990 and back again)*, forthcoming. The third of these was self-published by means of Williams obtaining donations from prospective readers (Subscribers paid $60, Sponsors $100 or more, Patrons $200 or more, and Benefactors $5,000 or more; their names appear 'in a Roll of Honor at the back of the book') and the fourth is to be achieved by the same means.

In the middle of the *Performing Artist* series, in 1996, Williams self-published *Watching the River Flow: Observations on Bob Dylan's Art-in-Progress, 1966–1995*, a collection of articles, from a review of *Blonde on Blonde* to some notes on Dylan's 1995 touring. He has also self-published books on Neil Young and Brian Wilson, namely *Heart of Gold, Neil Young: Love to Burn*, and *Brian Wilson & the Beach Boys, How Deep Is the Ocean?*, in 1983 he launched and edited the *Philip K. Dick Society Newsletter* and in 1993 he revived *Crawdaddy* as a quarterly.

For many Dylan aficionados, Williams' eternally boyish style is hopelessly gushing and somewhat *Californian* (as suggested, perhaps, by a relatively moderate sentence on his website after he's thanked his different grades of donor: 'This community is truly as wonderful as the genius of a performing artist whose work brings us together'), while the unbounded enthusiasm of his descriptions of Dylan on stage often assumes he is privy to, and must explain for us, Dylan's thoughts and feelings as he stands there. On the other hand, for a wide range of readers, other Dylan writers and hip celebrities, Williams is the best possible explicator of the performing side of Dylan's art, and writes with a breadth of knowledge matched by percipience as well as passion.

[Paul Williams, *Performing Artist: The Music of Bob Dylan, Volume One, 1960–1973*, Novato, CA: Underwood-Miller, 1990. *Bob Dylan: Performing Artist, The Middle Years, 1972–1986*, Novato, CA: Underwood-Miller, 1992. *Watching the River Flow: Observations on Bob Dylan's Art-in-Progress, 1966–1995*, Encinitas, CA: Entwhistle Books, 1996. *Bob Dylan: Mind Out of Time, Performing Artist Volume 3, 1987–2000*, Encinitas, CA: Entwhistle Books, 2004, and *Bob Dylan: Volume 4 (The Genius of a Performing Artist, 2003–1990 and back again)*, forthcoming. All Williams' work has also been published in foreign editions. His website is *www.paulwilliams.com*.]

Williamson, Nigel [1954 -] Nigel Williamson was born in Saltburn, on the north-east coast of England on July 4, 1954. He first heard Dylan at age 11 ('Like a Rolling Stone') and later stole the first eight albums from a record shop in Kent. His earliest published Dylan articles were pieces of journalism in *The Times* and *Uncut* in the 1990s, and in 2003 he edited the fine one-shot magazine *Uncut Legends: Bob Dylan*. His well-received book *The Rough Guide to Bob Dylan* was published in 2004, with a revised and expanded edition in 2006. Though the first edition has many inconsequential errors of fact (BLIND WILLIE McTELL's 'Statesboro Blues' was 1928, not 1929; ALBERT GROSSMAN's wife's name is Sally, not Sarah), lacks any documenting of its sources (for its many quotations and for the less well-known facts it asserts) and is vague on recording-session detail, it's nonetheless a most attractive little volume, packed with far more information than you'd imagine it could hold, and its whole organisational scheme, with sections on the life, the albums, stories behind '50 Great Dylan Songs', 'New Bobs', fanzines and more, are clearly the work of a real fan with a judicious eye. It's a far, far better guide to its subject than the *Rough Guide to Paris*.

In his non-Dylan life Nigel Williamson has been a researcher for the great campaigning socialist politician Tony Benn, editor of *Tribune*, a diary editor and political correspondent for *The Times*, and has also written *Journey Through the Past: The Stories Behind the Songs of Neil Young*.

[Nigel Williamson, ed., *Uncut Legends: Bob Dylan* Vol.1, no.1, IPC Media, London, 2003; *The Rough Guide to Bob Dylan*, London: Rough Guides, 2004 & 2006; *Journey Through the Past: The Stories Behind the Songs of Neil Young*, London: Backbeat Books, 2002.]

Williamson, Sonny Boy II [1899 - 1965] Alec Ford Miller was probably born on December 5, 1899, and at Glendora, Mississippi; by the 1920s he was known as Rice Miller, Little Boy Blue, Willie Williams, Willie Williamson and Willie Miller, and was working his way around the Mississippi Delta as a singer and harmonica player. By the end of the 1930s, or soon afterwards, he was an act on the 'King Biscuit Flour Time' radio show on KFFA in Helena, Arkansas, and was calling himself Sonny Boy Williamson, either to honour or cash in on the confusion with (or both) the singer and harmonica wizard now known as Sonny Boy Williamson I, who had found success in Chicago in the mid 1930s and made his first recordings in 1937 (including 'Good Morning Schoolgirl', the classic that would later pass into the repertoire of every British beat group and be sold back to the US during the British Invasion).

Confusingly perhaps, Sonny Boy Williamson II was about 15 years older than Williamson I, but he found fame much later on and didn't make his first recordings till 1951—by which time Williamson I had been murdered, like Leon Trotsky, with an ice pick. The surviving Williamson II cut his first sides for Lillian McMurry's Trumpet label in Jackson, Mississippi: sides that included his widely known 'Crazy About You Baby' and 'Stop Crying', and showed his harmonica-work already at its exquisitely expressive peak. As well it might have been, granted that he was already in his 50s when making his studio début. He may have started late, but he got there: he became a towering, ever-influential figure in the world of the blues.

Williamson moved to Detroit and then Chicago in 1954 and the following year started recording for Checker, the sister label to Chess Records. His first session, in August 1955, yielded 'Don't Start Me to Talkin'', which typified his endearing blend of loud but super-casual Chicago blues, bluff vocal charm, vaguely menacing lyrics and superb harmonica work. At the same session he cut 'You Killing Me (On My Feet)', on which the harmonica solo is so physically direct yet of such delicate finesse that it could explain the soul of the blues and R&B to Jane Austen.

In Europe, which he visited for the first time in 1963 as part of the touring American Folk Blues Festival, he lingered in England and recorded with the Yardbirds, whose teenage guitarist was ERIC CLAPTON, and with THE ANIMALS.

Bob Dylan, as well as inevitably being influenced in general by the impact of Sonny Boy Williamson upon the whole timbre of the post-war blues, has cherry-picked small particulars from within it. His *Street Legal* song 'Baby Stop Crying'—a UK top 10 hit in 1978—may owe something to ROBERT JOHNSON's 'Stop Breakin' Down Blues', with its repeated imprecation 'Stop breakin' down, please, stop breakin' down', but it draws at least as directly from Williamson's 'Stop Crying', which presses the more exactly similar plea: 'baby please, please stop crying'. Dylan also takes the striking title of one of Williamson's best-known harmonica showcase songs, 'Nine Below Zero' and embeds it into the lyric of his 1965 song 'Outlaw Blues', which is part of, as its title says, *Bringing It All Back Home*.

In 1981, when Dylan is emerging from the evangelising burn of the Born Again period, his terrific song 'The Groom's Still Waiting at the Altar' uses the melody of Sonny Boy's 'Don't Start Me to Talking', and three years later, when he goes on the 'Late Night with David Letterman' TV show for the first time, backed by THE PLUGZ, supposedly to promote his new album *Infidels*, the first number he pulls out, right there live on high profile national television, is not a track from the album at all, nor even one of the songs warmed up with at the NBC studio rehearsal, but 'Don't Start Me to Talking' itself—from Sonny Boy Williamson's 1955 Chicago début session.

Sonny Boy Williamson II died of a heart attack asleep in a boarding house back in Helena, Arkansas, on May 25, 1965.

[Sonny Boy Williamson: 'Stop Crying', Jackson, MS, 4 Jan 1951 & 10 Jul 1951, both unissued, then 5 Aug 1951, issued as 78rpm single Trumpet 140, US, c.1951, vinyl-issued on *The Original Sonny Boy Williamson*, Blues Classics BC-9, Berkeley, CA, c.1967, re-recorded for Chess as 'Stop Cryin'', Chicago, 30 Apr 1964, *This Is My Story*, Chess 2CH-50027 (2 LPs), US, 1972; 'You Killing Me (On My Feet)', Chicago, 12 Aug 1955, *Sonny Boy Williamson—One Way Out*, Chess CHV 417, US, 1975; 'Don't Start Me to Talkin'' & 'All My Love in Vain', Chicago, 12 Aug 1955, both on 78rpm single Checker 824, US, 1955 & on *Sonny Boy Williamson Sings Down and Out Blues*, Checker LP 1437, US, 1960.]

Willis, Chuck [1928 - 1958] Harold Willis was born in Atlanta on the last day of January 1928. Singing professionally first with Red McAllister's band, he was signed to OKeh, Columbia's 'race' label, in 1951, and signed to management by Atlanta's R&B big-shot DJ Zenas Sears (on WAOK). A fine songwriter as well as a robust singer, and with a penchant for wearing a sort of 1,001 Nights turban on his head, pinned at the front with what would now be called bling, he had a series of R&B-chart top ten hits between 1952 and '54—'My Story', 'Going to the River' (a remake of the early FATS DOMINO classic), 'Don't Deceive Me' and 'I Feel So Bad'—before signing to Atlantic in 1956 and finding far greater success there, crossing him over into rock'n'roll stardom with 'It's Too Late', 'Whatcha Gonna Do When Your Baby Leaves You', 'CC Rider', 'Betty and Dupree' and the great double-sider '(I Don't Want to) Hang Up My Rock and Roll Shoes' and 'What Am I Living For?' Several of these became much-covered classics, remain in the memory and still get revived from time to time. Among others, ELVIS PRESLEY, on fine, torrid form, covered 'I Feel So Bad': and paid Willis the compliment of coming much nearer to a copy than was usual with his revisits to black hit songs; JERRY LEE LEWIS covered 'Hang Up My Rock and Roll Shoes'; Percy Sledge and CONWAY TWITTY covered 'What Am I Living For?'; and those who covered 'It's Too Late' included BUDDY HOLLY, ROY ORBISON, Otis Redding, JOHN HAMMOND Jr. and Derek & the Dominoes.

Willis stayed in Atlanta, a big name in a comparatively small city, often hanging around the Central Record Shop on Decatur Street, near the infamous 81 Theatre where LITTLE RICHARD and others got their break (and which comes into the BLIND WILLIE McTELL story too), and drinking far too much cheap wine in the basement of the shop. At the age of 30, Chuck Willis did have to hang up his rock'n'roll shoes: he died in Atlanta's Grady Hospital, after collapsing with a stomach ulcer, on April 10, 1958.

Bob Dylan made an attempt at Willis' 'It's Too Late' in the studios on May 6, 1986 at Topanga Park, California, during a session for *Knocked Out Loaded*—the same session that provided the album track 'Precious Memories'. Five years later, on August 10, 1991, he performed the same Chuck Willis song in concert, in Buenos Aires, Argentina, and at the 'Absolutely Unofficial Blue Jeans Bash (for Arkansas)' on January 17, 1993, Dylan played guitar behind the Cate Brothers as they performed '(I Don't Want to) Hang Up My Rock and Roll Shoes'. And finally—so far—he returned to 'It's Too Late' at two 1995 concerts: Fort Lauderdale on September 23 and Las Vegas on November 11. In *Chronicles Volume One*, Dylan includes Chuck Willis among 'the greats'.

[Chuck Willis: the OKeh hit sides CD-reissued on *Chuck Willis: Let's Jump Tonight*, Jump-O-Rama Jump 1021, US, 1993; all 51 OKeh sides CD-issued on *Chuck Willis Wails the Blues*, Sundazed *nia*, 2003; 'It's Too Late' c/w 'Kansas City Woman', Atlantic 1098, US, 1956; 'Juanita' c/w 'Whatcha Gonna Do When Your Baby Leaves You', Atlantic 1112, 1957; 'C.C. Rider' c/w 'Ease the Pain', Atlantic 1130, 1957; 'Betty and Dupree' c/w 'My Crying Eyes', Atlantic 1168, US, 1958; 'What Am I Living For' / '(I Don't Want to) Hang Up My Rock and Roll Shoes', Atlantic 1179, 1958; all CD-reissued.

Bob Dylan, *Chronicles Volume One*, 2004, p.187. Sources: discographical detail from Pete Hoppula's Roy Gaines listing at the excellent *www.wangdangdula.com*, seen online 20 Feb 2006; *The Encyclopaedia of Rock Vol.1: The Age of Rock'n'Roll*, eds. Phil Hardy & Dave Laing, London: Aquarius Books, 1976, p.84 and Jan Cox, friend of Willis, e-mail to this writer, Dec 2004.]

Wilmer, Val [1941 -] Valerie Sybil Wilmer was born in Harrogate, Yorkshire, on the day Pearl Harbor was bombed—December 7, 1941— but her family returned to living in London as soon as World War II was over.

Wilmer is a photographer and writer particularly interested in jazz and black music, and is the author of the autobiography *Mama Said There'd Be Days Like This*, an invaluable social document not least for its first-hand reportage of the visits to Britain by American and Caribbean jazz and blues musicians in the 1950s and 1960s, when her mother took in paying guests. Her other books include *Jazz People*, *The Face of Black Music*, *As Serious as Your Life: John Coltrane and Beyond* and (with Paul Trynka) *Portrait of the Blues*.

Best known for her photographs of musicians, Wilmer's pioneering exhibition *Jazz Seen: The Face of Black Music* was held at London's Victoria and Albert Museum back in 1973. A Wilmer photograph of Dusty Springfield, taken in 1964, is owned by the National Portrait Gallery, she has exhibited internationally and has work in the Musée d'Arte Moderne in Paris. She serves on the advisory panel of the *New Grove Dictionary of Jazz* and is an authority on the work of Ken Snakehips Johnson.

She photographed Louis Armstrong when she was still at school in 1956, was soon making superior informal portraits ('Mum takes tea with HERBIE LOVELLE', 1959, and 'JESSE FULLER cooks breakfast', 1960), and began taking photographs at Ronnie Scott's Jazz Club in Soho, London, in 1960, while also contributing jazz reviews to *Melody Maker* and jazz journals. She photographed a number of rock stars in the 1960s, including Screaming Jay Hawkins, GEORGE HARRISON and JIMI HENDRIX.

When Bob Dylan telerecorded his last-ever solo concert, namely 12 songs performed specially for BBC Television in London on June 1, 1965—just two weeks before he began recording the *Highway 61 Revisited* album—Val Wilmer was the photographer asked to shoot stills for the occasion. And since the BBC saw fit to dump their telerecording of the concert, Wilmer's photographs are, visually, all that remain.

[Val Wilmer, *Mama Said There'd Be Days Like This: My Life in the Jazz World*, London: Women's Press, 1989 & 1991; *Jazz People*, New York: Da Capo, 1977 (1st pub'd 1970). *As Serious as Your Life: John Coltrane and Beyond*, London: Serpent's Tail, 1999; *The Face of Black Music*, New York: Da Capo, 1976. Paul Trynka & Valerie Wilmer: *Portrait of the Blues*, London: Hamlyn, 1996.]

Wilson, Brian [1942 -] Brian Wilson, born in Los Angeles on June 20, 1942, became the founder of the Beach Boys, and one of four figures in popular music customarily called a genius. (The others are RAY CHARLES, PHIL SPECTOR and Bob Dylan.) Brian was the oldest of three brothers, the children of Audree and Murray Wilson, the latter a failed songwriter. They grew up in Hawthorne, a Los Angeles suburb, rubbing along with cousin Mike Love and friend Al Jardine. Brian and Dennis were often beaten for tiny transgressions, the worst being to better Murray Wilson. Enraged, he would pluck out his glass eye at the table, ordering his sons to stare into its socket.

This dysfunctional family bequeathed Brian a fundamental insecurity and incapacitating self-doubt that led to a life-long struggle, involving many lost years and intimacies, between floundering in sloughs of American despond and a rarefied level of creative expression and musicality. The Beach Boys' inception had to happen behind the parental back. When Mr. and Mrs. Wilson took a Mexican holiday in September 1961, the five teenagers rented instruments and started the group in their living-room.

They performed as the Pendletons (a surfers' shirt-brand), Carl & the Passions and Kenny & the Cadets before seizing on the Beach Boys, a name débuted at the RITCHIE VALENS Memorial Concert at Long Beach on New Year's Eve 1961.

Father Murray took the song 'Surfin'' (written by Brian and Mike Love) to his music-publisher, who recorded it, issued it on local labels and saw it touch the US Hot 100. In early 1962 Murray took 'Surfin' Safari' to Capitol and the record went top 20. The follow-up, 'Ten Little Indians', flopped but 'Surfin' USA' was a top 3 smash in summer 1963.

Surf Music was not their invention: Dick Dale ('King of the Surf Guitar') had ridden the wave of guitar-instrumental records that were a major hit genre of the era, devising a guitar sound that supposedly simulated the feel of bestriding a surfboard. Nor did the Beach Boys pioneer 'their' vocal sound. They stood in a tradition of close-harmony groups and were influenced by its modernisation on Jan & Dean's 1959 'Baby Talk', which launched a California falsetto style embracing doo-wop nonsense syllables. But because Dennis Wilson was obsessed with surfing, the Beach Boys were first with songs that named and celebrated it, making it a universal metaphor for being young while giving them ownership of a particular Americana, as evocative as THE BAND's backwoods Civil War dreamscapes at the other end of the 1960s. 'When you're talking states of mind,' wrote Bill Holdship, 'Brian Wilson *invented* California'.

For some time Brian Wilson thrived and grew artistically in this land of surf and honey. 'Surfer Girl' confirmed his talent for luxuriant harmonies above which his yearning falsetto steered a wistful course. These years gave us 'Fun Fun Fun' and the no.1s 'I Get Around' and 'Help Me Rhonda', the exquisite 'Don't Worry Baby', 'In My Room' and more. Terrific hit singles also included 'When I Grow Up', 'Sloop John B.', 'Barbara Ann' and 'God Only Knows'. Who'd have thought Charles Atlas could receive so sumptuously cool a makeover? (No wonder Dylan gave him a namecheck on 'She's Your Lover Now'.)

Brian Wilson and Mike Love wrote most of the early lyrics, and Bruce Johnson, who also contributed songs, joined in 1965. But Brian's music and input distinguished the group, and his Spector-influenced production was crucial to their increasingly complex recordings, hailed as 'the perfect blend of teen consciousness and musical innovation.' Bob Dylan said of Wilson in 1997, 'That ear! Jesus, he's got to will that to the Smithsonian.' He must have meant his right ear, for Brian is deaf in his left.

Wilson's first crack-up began on a tour of Texas, starting a long slide into stupor and derangement. Wilson quit stage performances in late 1964, though he hung around on the road with the others till 1967. In the studio his admiration for Phil Spector turned into obsessive one-sided rivalry. Bruce Johnston complained, 'He used to play "Be My Baby" to us over and over and we're going "Hey, Brian, we heard it already, so what?" Spector should have been bowing down in front of Brian, not the other way around.'

At home Wilson grew 'very paranoid,' said Marilyn, the wife who had to swap from student at his feet to grown-up taking care of him, and of business, surrounded by axe-grinding brothers, cousins and hangers-on, while Brian asked for drugs and the house filled with people to supply them.

What was remarkable was that he did so much in these years, rather than that he managed so little later. So strong was his work and its popularity that THE BEATLES' 1964 conquest of America hardly touched the Beach Boys at the time. Their 1965 LPs *Beach Boys Today!* and *Summer Days (And Summer Nights!!)* fired on all their distinctive cylinders, and Wilson triumphed creatively with the seminal *Pet Sounds* (cut 1965, issued 1966) and the single 'Good Vibrations' a massive hit (not least a UK no.1) in summer 1966 (part-written by Mike Love, who went uncredited, creating a resentment that would smoulder for decades and end in court).

Things collapsed suddenly. *Pet Sounds* was upstaged by *Sgt. Pepper's* and a comparative flop in the US. Brian forced the others into many months of studio-work on *Smile*, an album that was to outshine the Beatles and the Beach Boys' own past, but which Brian then abandoned. Ironically, while few could have been ingesting more LSD than Wilson, the West Coast 'psychedelic revolution' now made the Beach Boys passé. The ghost of *Smile*, issued as *Smiley Smile*, further damaged their reputation. It was the last Beach Boys album Brian Wilson would produce until 1976.

The group continued, and still had hits, survived an unsuccessful college tour with the Maharishi and abandoned short, hit-based sets for Progressive Rock. At home, meanwhile, Brian Wilson's renewed breakdown, in 1967, left him swallowing drugs and junk-food, hearing lost chords and growing obese, stranded at the grand piano inside a box of sand that was intended to inspire but attracted more dog-mess than muse. His daughter Carnie was born in 1968, and Wendy in 1969, into a family as dysfunctional as the previous generation's. As Marilyn struggled to cope, Murray Wilson sold his son's songwriting catalogue for a mere $700,000. (In the 1990s Wilson won it back, plus $10 million in recompense.)

In 1976, Marilyn brought in controversial therapist Dr. Eugene Landy, whose intensive '24-hour therapy' rescued Wilson from himself but not from Dr. Landy. First results were positive. Wilson shook off the torpor of his drugs habits and proved capable of work, giving interviews, performing on 'Saturday Night Live' and producing the albums

15 Big Ones and *Beach Boys Love You*, both huge American hits.

He relapsed. Marilyn and the children left in 1979 and the other Beach Boys, who had fired the overbearing Landy, whom they saw as a rival, were driven to recall him in 1980. More lost years of mayhem and madness followed, as brothers and cousins sued over business betrayals, Landy kept Wilson in sinister thrall and Marilyn divorced him. The Beach Boys stumbled on, but their 1980s were awful too, and in 1983, Dennis drowned while drunk.

In 1987, Brian re-emerged quietly on the WOODY GUTHRIE-LEADBELLY tribute album *A Vision Shared* with an affectionate, witty Black Pop 'Goodnight Irene'; but when he finally made a solo album, in 1988, five of its mediocre songs were co-written by 'executive producer' Landy. 1991's crassly titled *Sweet Insanity*, also co-produced by Landy, was refused release by the record company, though most people prefer it.

By the mid-1990s, a more precarious but plausible rehabilitation seemed in place. Dr. Landy had been banned by law from any contact with Wilson, who was trying to build a relationship with his daughters and resumed work with the Beach Boys after regaining his song publishing and an amicable settlement of the Mike Love court case. Then came 'I Just Wasn't Made for These Times', a brilliant, affecting TV documentary portrait of Wilson the musician and his struggle against his own mental instability, filmed by musician-producer DON WAS.

Was explained: 'People have heard the phrase "Brian Wilson is a genius" for years. I wanted someone who's not a musician to walk away with some understanding of why. Everything regarding his personal life in the movie relates to the music. Everyone has some sort of emotional stake in Brian's music. This is the important thing, not the sordid details and the gossip.'

The film succeeded so well, capturing so intimately Wilson's extraordinary talent and tragedy, that it stands now as a part of his legacy as valuable as anything from his golden past. Since this return to the heights, Wilson's resumption of touring has been a remarkable, sustained achievement, as he has gone around with a large set of accompanying musicians, recreating note for note entire studio albums live: something that in theory seems pointless and far less exciting than the spontaneity of free musical interaction, yet which has proved thrilling to huge crowds; and not merely thrilling but very moving too, just to witness so fragile a figure pulling off such triumphs with such sustained musicianship and such command of himself and his master works.

His connections with Bob Dylan have been brief but the more recent of the two proved interesting. First, on January 20, 1988, at the thrash for the Rock'n'Roll Hall of Fame's third annual round of inductions, Dylan played guitar behind a number of people (safely surrounded by hordes of other musicians), and this included playing behind Brian and Carl Wilson and Mike Love on a performance of 'Barbara Ann'. Three years later, in a Los Angeles studio, Dylan dropped in on one of Wilson's sessions for the doomed (unreleased) *Sweet Insanity* album; Bob shared the vocals with him on Brian's pastiche song 'Spirit of Rock'n' Roll'. Wilson commented afterwards: 'Now he *is* crazy. He couldn't even find the microphone!'

[Brian Wilson (with Bob Dylan): 'The Spirit of Rock'n' Roll': LA, early 1991; unreleased. Bill Holdship: 'Lost in Music: Brian Wilson', *Mojo*, London, Aug 1995.]

Wilson, Tom [1931 - 1978] Thomas Blanchard Wilson Jr. was born on March 25, 1931 in Waco, Texas, where he attended the A.J. Moore High School—'the first school in Waco designed to educate the Negro youth', as its Historical Marker now notes. Founded in 1881, its third Principal was Tom Wilson's grandfather, Prof. B.T. Wilson; its fourth was Tom's father, who took over in 1934. The school's inspiration was Booker T. Washington and his maxim 'Take what you have and make what you want'; the school's motto was 'A better Moore High through better behavior'; and though its list of what it aimed to instil in its pupils included 'To refrain from excessive theatre going', in general Tom Wilson became an exemplar of the school's positive stance, however old-fashioned and ameliorative it seems today.

Wilson, tall, dark and handsome and an affable young man with a throaty Texan drawl, became a Republican and, as 1970s friend Coral Browning said bluntly: 'Tom felt let down by blacks. He felt that after the civil rights successes of the 50s and 60s, blacks should stop complaining and get on with it. He felt they caused many of their own problems by carrying such large chips on their shoulders.'

Wilson thus occupies an interesting position in the history of those decades from the voteless 1930s to the civil rights struggle and beyond: the son and grandson of educated middle-class blacks inside the segregated school system of the South, he gained a place at Harvard, becoming President of the Young Republican Club and graduating cum laude in 1954. On the other hand he also helped run the Harvard New Jazz Society, got involved with radio station WHRB, moved to New York, founded the jazz record label Transition in 1955, produced radio programmes as from 1958, became jazz A&R director for Savoy, then worked for United Artists and Audio Fidelity before being hired as a staff producer for Columbia in 1963—the first black producer in the history of the company—by which time he was also executive assistant to the New York State Commission for Human Rights.

Not only did he become Bob Dylan's producer from *Freewheelin'* to *Highway 61 Revisited*—which is to say, the producer of many of Dylan's 'protest' anthems, the work that saw him go electric *and* of 'Like a Rolling Stone'—but then when he moved over to MGM he signed FRANK ZAPPA's Mothers of Invention and put his own career on the line to let them make an extravagant double-LP as their début release, throughout which they were articulating the kind of anarchic bohemian 'filth' that was anathema to Wilson himself (though in truth, of course, Zappa himself was an obsessively hard-working disciplinarian, very anti drugs and alcoholic excess). Zappa said years later: 'Tom Wilson was a great guy. He had vision, you know? And he really stood by us . . .'

While producing the second Mothers album, *Absolutely Free*, Wilson was also supervising the Velvet Underground's début album *The Velvet Underground and Nico*. Wilson was, too, the hands-on producer of its track 'Sunday Morning', and (albeit against the band's wishes) edited and re-mixed the album's other most important tracks: 'Heroin', 'Venus in Furs', 'All Tomorrow's Parties' and the especially brilliant 'I'm Waiting for the Man'.

Sometimes his interventionism paid off and sometimes it didn't. It paid off on *The Velvet Underground and Nico*; it paid off when after producing the acoustic SIMON & Garfunkel début album *Wednesday Morning 3 A.M.* he took its track 'The Sound of Silence', added a rhythm section and some electric guitar and then issued it as a single, without consulting them at all, and gave them a no.1 hit.

It didn't work with Bob Dylan when Wilson tried the same thing on him first; nor did it work, in the end, when Wilson tried to make decisions over Dylan's head in Dylan's presence in the studio. To start with, though, they got on fine. Wilson replaced JOHN HAMMOND for the final *Freewheelin' Bob Dylan* session on April 24, 1963—a year to the day after the first session—because ALBERT GROSSMAN tried playing games about Dylan's Columbia contract and Hammond rightly felt that Dylan himself was not trying to walk out on him or the label, that a producer switch would be diplomatic and maybe that a young black producer would be harder to reject. Even if that were a factor in the mix, it would not have weighed heavily: one thing Hammond, Dylan *and* Tom Wilson had in common was an absolutely undeflected view that people were individuals, not race representatives. When Dylan 'dropped out of' supporting civil rights and singing 'protest' songs, he always explained this in exactly these terms: that he knew, and wanted to keep on knowing, black people as people, not blacks; and Wilson felt the same. 'He lived his life unapologetically as a human being, not as a black man,' said his friend, the cookie magnate Wally 'Famous' Amos.

That first session yielded 'Girl of the North Country', 'Masters of War', 'Talkin' World War III Blues' and 'Bob Dylan's Dream'—plus the lovely 'Walls of Red Wing', given to Witmark as a music publishing demo, circulated widely many years ago and finally released on the *Bootleg Series Vols. 1–3* in 1991. (Hammond is credited as the producer of this track on the box set liner notes.)

When they worked together on Dylan's third album, *The Times They Are a-Changin'*, beginning on August 6, 1963, Wilson rightly allowed Dylan full control. That first day yielded the great, much-neglected 'North Country Blues' and attempted several other things, among them the stellar 'Seven Curses': another recording that circulated in bootleg form many years ago and saw official release in 1991. The next day's session yielded four album tracks: 'Ballad of Hollis Brown', 'With God on Our Side', 'Only a Pawn in Their Game' and the glorious 'Boots of Spanish Leather'. What a day's work. Further sessions on August 12 and October 23 were separated by momentous events: Dylan's star-making appearance at the NEWPORT FOLK FESTIVAL that August 17, the appearance at the historic March on Washington, D.C., on the 28th, and the less career-important but artistically significant writing of 'Lay Down Your Weary Tune' at JOAN BAEZ's house in California, followed by a performance that no-one appears to have taped of the two of them sharing vocals on a début outing for that song when Dylan made a guest appearance at her Hollywood Bowl concert on October 9.

The August 12 session had yielded various further outtakes for retrospective issue nearly 30 years later—the turgid 'Paths of Victory', the worse 'Only a Hobo' and the magnificent 'Moonshiner' (among the greatest vocal performances in Bob Dylan's entire canon)—but nothing for *The Times They Are a-Changin'*; but October 24, while adding 'Eternal Circle' and 'Suze (The Cough Song)' to the list of material held back till 1991, also gave them the album title track plus the lovely 'One Too Many Mornings'. A further session on Hallowe'en finished off the album with 'Restless Farewell'. A few days earlier, Wilson had been in charge of the recording of Dylan's concert at Carnegie Hall (October 26, 1963) from which, as from his New York Town Hall concert of April 12, it had been planned to make a live album, *Bob Dylan in Concert*, which got as far as a tracks selection and a Columbia job number (77110) but never did see release. No producer credit is given on the tracks issued retrospectively.

The fourth album, *Another Side of Bob Dylan*, was recorded entirely in one day, June 9, 1964, again with Wilson producing. They also came out with a long-since circulated take of 'Denise', the magnificent 'Mama You Been on My Mind' and early attempts at 'Mr. Tambourine Man'. The album was released to a mixed response in August, and on Hallowe'en Wilson supervised another live recording, Dylan's New York Philharmonic Hall concert, which was released 30 years later as the *Bootleg Series Vol. 6—Bob Dylan Live 1964*.

Things between them changed after that. In December 1964, Wilson got drummer BOBBY GREGG and others to overdub backings onto the *Bob Dylan* track 'House of the Rising Sun' (released in 1995 on the *Highway 61 Interactive* CD-ROM, with packaging that implied that the whole recording had been made back in 1961) and onto three tracks from the *Freewheelin'* sessions, 'Mixed Up Confusion', 'Rocks and Gravel' and 'Corrina Corrina', all of which had to have their original backing tracks removed for the benefit of this futile exercise. In an otherwise entertaining and acute article on its subject, 'The Amazing Tom Wilson', blogger Eric Olsen makes the absurd claim that it was Wilson's electric overdubs on 'House of the Rising Sun' that planted the seed for Dylan's electric flowering ('The folk spell was broken'). Wilson doesn't need his achievements augmented by that sort of claim; it's enough that he was the producer of *Bringing It All Back Home*—achieved in two days of sessions in mid-January 1965—and of the first sessions for *Highway 61 Revisited*, that June 15 & 16.

The first of these two days yielded the fast version of 'It Takes a Lot to Laugh, It Takes a Train to Cry', one take of which—the wrong take, it might be argued—was released in 1991 on the *Bootleg Series Vols. 1–3*, as was the same day's 'Sitting on a Barbed Wire Fence' and a fragment of an early try at 'Like a Rolling Stone'. (Other outtakes of this were issued in 1995 on the *Highway 61 Interactive* CD-Rom.) Far more importantly, the second day's session produced—and Tom Wilson produced—the classic take of 'Like a Rolling Stone'.

It was Wilson who brought in AL KOOPER, to watch and play a bit of subsidiary guitar. The story of how Kooper switched to organ, Wilson tolerated this, Bob Dylan liked the organ part and got it turned up in the mix and it led to the perfect take of the song—all this is well known: but a key exchange between Wilson and Dylan in the course of all this has usually been played down. When Dylan says 'Turn the organ up' and Wilson replies 'But he's not an organ player' Dylan is often quoted as merely saying, 'I don't care: turn it up'—but in fact what Dylan says is 'Hey, now don't tell me who's an organ player and who's not. Just turn the organ up.' The difference is small but telling; in that Dylan response is contained all his resentment, perhaps going back a considerable time, at what he perceived as Wilson's high-handedness: an attitude on Wilson's part that means he's always going to under-attend the artist's instincts and is likely to fail to catch the moment as it flies.

Fair and reasonable or not, that was the end between them. When the sessions for *Highway 61 Revisited* resumed on July 29, Wilson had been replaced by BOB JOHNSTON.

Among many other distinctions in a relatively short life, Tom Wilson also produced the Blues Project and 'discovered' and signed Hugh Masekela, went into music publishing and was a founding co-owner of the Record Plant studios in New York. At 47, he died of a heart attack at home in LA on September 6, 1978.

[Main sources: Eric Olsen, 'The Amazing Tom Wilson', posted 23 Oct 2003 on the *Blogcritics.Org* web page *http://blogcritics.org/archives/2003/10/23/154347.php*, incl. for the quotes from Coral Browning, Frank Zappa & Wally Amos; Waco City Directory 1934; Social Security Deaths Index; Moore High School data from its alumni reunion web pages seen online 21 Feb 2006 at *www.wacoisd.org/ajmoore/alumni/history.htm*; other sources include Al Kooper, *Backstage Passes & Backstabbing Bastards*, New York: Billboard, 1998 and Robert Shelton, *No Direction Home: The Life and Music of Bob Dylan*, New York: Beech Tree Books/ William Morrow, 1986.]

Wissolik, Richard David [1938 -] Richard David Wissolik, who was born May 7, 1938, is the co-editor with SCOTT McGRATH of *Bob Dylan's Words—A Critical Dictionary and Commentary*, 1994, which is partly a collection of commissioned articles but mostly an extraordinary assemblage of miscellaneous entries about literary allusions, people's names, places and objects in Dylan's work (rather like an encyclopedia, in fact), divided into the general categories 'Dictionary of Archetypes, Motifs and Symbols', 'Dictionary of Proper Names, Terms and Allusions', 'Selected Songs, Poems and Writings: Commentary and Textual Allusions', and '*Tarantula*: Commentary and Textual Allusions'. (This last remains one of the few real scrutinies of this neglected—many would say because impenetrable—Dylan work.)

Wissolik had earlier been the General Editor of the slimmer volume *Bob Dylan—American Poet and Singer: An Annotated Bibliography and Study Guide of Sources and Background Materials 1961–1991* (plus, its title page added under this fulsome sub-title, 'a Supplemental Checklist of Studies on the 1960s and the Folk Revival').

As might be suspected from all this, Wissolik is an American academic: in fact a Professor of English at St. Vincent College, a Catholic, Benedictine liberal arts and sciences college at Latrobe, Pennsylvania, founded in 1846. He is also Director of its Center for Northern Appalachian Studies. He has been general editor of a number of books on widely differing subjects and has also specialised in scrutiny of the Bayeux Tapestry.

Wissolik's first year of interest in Dylan was 1967, when he returned from five years as Program Director of Catholic Relief Services in Nairobi, Kenya. *Bob Dylan—American Poet and Singer* was his first published Dylan work. He has been involved with the Colorado outfit Rolling Tomes, which publishes the US fanzine *ON THE TRACKS*, and uses Dylan's lyrics in his classes on American Literature, Myth and Faces of Battle.

His *Bob Dylan's Words—A Critical Dictionary and Commentary* was reissued in an electronic edition in 1996 and a second print edition, revised and expanded, came out in 1997. An updated volume combining both his books is due in 2007; the title is yet to be decided but will certainly include the phrase 'Bob Dylan's Words'.

[Richard David Wissolik, gen. ed., *Bob Dylan—American Poet and Singer*, Greenburg, PA: Eadmer Press, 1992; Wissolik & McGrath, *Bob Dylan's Words—A Critical Dictionary and Commentary*, Greenburg, PA: Eadmer Press, 1994 & 1997.]

'With God on Our Side', extra verses to See Neville, Aaron.

Withers, Pick [1948 -] David Withers was born on April 4, 1948 in Glasgow, Scotland, and became a pro drummer at the age of 17. He played with a number of people, including Ian Anderson, Dave Edmunds' Rockpile, that other Welsh band the Neutrons (he plays hand drums only, on their 1974 album *Black Hole Star*) and Scottish singer-songwriter Rab Noakes—with whom he has worked again more recently—and he was in the British 'progressive rock' bands Magna Carta and Spring, calling himself Pique Withers before resigning himself to Pick and joining up with MARK KNOPFLER in Café Racers, which duly became Dire Straits. Withers was their drummer from the group's inception through till 1982, and in the middle of that period worked with Mark Knopfler on Dylan's first Born Again gospel album, *Slow Train Coming*, recorded between April 30 & May 4, 1979 at the Muscle Shoals studio in Sheffield, Alabama. He is the only drummer on the album—and therefore also on the single 'Trouble in Mind' and the outtake song 'Ye Shall Be Changed', released on the *Bootleg Series Vols. 1–3* in 1991—but has not worked with Dylan again since.

[The Neutrons: *Black Hole Star*, United Artists UAG 29652, UK, 1974. Spring: *Spring*, *nia*, UK, 1971.]

Witting, Robin [1953 -] Robin Witting, born in England on October 11, 1953, is author of a short book first called *Isaiah on Guitar* (1991) and later called *Isaiah for Guitar* (1998), this second edition revised and expanded, not from London or LA but from Scunthorpe, UK, and self-published. It looks amateurish, is expensive for its size and has no index. Nor does the layout always make clear who or where a quotation is from. He misquotes Dylan lines, he often fails to write in sentences and there's a lack of information just when it's most needed (e.g. re Zen teachings). Yet this is an absorbing, quirky, worthy piece of work that is often acute and extremely readable, his resourceful research is based on what genuinely interests him and his apparent detours—into the work of John Wesley, BUNYAN and Paine—turn out to inform and illuminate. Most of all, Witting maintains his own critical voice.

He has also self-published works on his real specialist subject, *Tarantula*, the largest being *The Cracked Bells: A Guide to 'Tarantula'*, which in its revised edition of 1995 is a large-format book of almost 200 pages offering a richly researched annotated guide to its text. More recently has come the energetic and often persuasive 80-page *'Tarantula': The Falcon's Mouthbook*, arguing that Dylan's novel is, from first to last, concerned with the religious and spiritual ramifications of 'oral obsession' and appetite.

[Robin Witting: *Isaiah for Guitar*, Scunthorpe, UK: Exploding Rooster Books, 1998; *The Cracked Bells: A Guide to 'Tarantula'*, ditto 1994, revised edn., 1995; *The Meaning of an Orange: the Pocket 'Tarantula'*, ditto 1996; *'Tarantula': The Falcon's Mouthbook*, ditto 2005.]

Wonder, Stevie [1950 -] Steveland Morris Judkins was born blind in Saginaw, Michigan, on May 3, 1950, grew up in Detroit, came to fame as Little Steve Wonder at age 13 as a harmonica prodigy on a tremendous hit single, the live and extremely lively 'Fingertips Part 2', on which, inimitably, you can hear one of the musicians shouting 'What key?! what key?!' (the first live recording ever to top the pop charts, it was made at the Chicago Regal Theater in 1963), and duly grew up to be an African American cross-over superstar, with a vast number of hits, though these have veered between the experimental and the saccharine.

Wonder recorded a high-profile version of 'Blowin' in the Wind' in 1966—he was still only 15 years old when he recorded it—and he and Dylan have bumped into each other several times since. In 1982 they both performed, but separately, at the Peace Sunday rally (Dylan duetting with JOAN BAEZ) at the Rose Bowl in Pasadena. Three years later they were contributors to the 'We Are the World' USA for Africa single (for which it's rumoured that Wonder had to cajole Dylan into sounding more Dylanesque on his small contribution), and in 1992 Wonder was a surprise guest among the celebrants at the so-called 30th Anniversary Bob Dylan Concert Celebration at Madison Square Garden, New York. Revisiting 'Blowin' in the Wind', he used his moment in this particular spotlight to give a long piano-led introductory speech about the continued relevance of the song, proving in the middle that he could still play a sublime harmonica but making an embarrassing, doomed attempt at the end to make the audience sing along with him. (This was not a peacenik, activist crowd: it was there to shop for legends and to boo Sinéad O'Connor.) Towards the evening's end, he took his place in the ensemble for 'Knockin' on Heaven's Door'.

But nearly seven years before that, at the Martin Luther King Birthday Celebration in Washington, D.C., on January 20, 1986 (though that was not his birthday), the two of them had sung together, on the Wonder song 'The Bells of Freedom': a title close to 'Chimes of Freedom', of course. Then, backed by Wonder and his whole band Wonderlove, Dylan sang a very jaunty re-written 'I Shall Be Released' before Bob, Stevie, PETER, PAUL & MARY all shared vocals on a 'Blowin' in the Wind'. The evening finished with an ensemble performance of 'Happy Birthday', sung simultaneously by people in New York and Atlanta as well as Washington, D.C.

Perhaps more interestingly, they had stood alongside each other to introduce the Grammies at the award ceremony in LA on February 28, 1984—a surprise because Dylan had never gone in for such glitz before, as he acknowledged, disarming any possible criticism when he told an interviewer: 'I know going on the Grammies is not my type of thing, but with Stevie it seemed like an interesting idea. I wasn't doing anything that night. I didn't feel I was making any great statement. For me, it was just going down to the place and changing my clothes.'

[Little Stevie Wonder: 'Fingertips (Part 2)', Chicago 1963, Tamla 54080, US, 1963. Dylan quote re Grammies, interview by Scott Cohen, *Spin* vol.1, no.8, US, Dec 1985.]

Wood, Ron [1947 -] Ronald David Wood was born in the outer reaches of London (Hillingdon, Middlesex, in fact) on June 1, 1947, began his music career with West London band the Birds, later joined Creation and then, with Rod Stewart, the Jeff Beck Group, in which he was the bass player. Next, again with Stewart, Ron joined that important, very British rock group the Small Faces, the idols of the Mod sub-culture, to which his quintessential cheery-cockney persona seemed ideally suited. Renamed the Faces soon after Wood joined, they disbanded in 1975.

Wood then collaborated with fellow-Face, the late lamented Ronnie Lane, on the 1976 album *Mahoney's Last Stand*, but was brought into the ROLLING STONES that same year (the year of their *Black and Blue* album), somehow managing to slide across from mod to rocker with ease. His invitation to join seemed inevitable and overdue.

Contemporaneously, Wood continued his solo career, pursued his interest in painting (which would, had he been a less famous person, have been his hobby) and worked with other artists—not least BO DIDDLEY, Aretha Franklin and ERIC CLAPTON. More to the point here, his collaborations with Bob Dylan have been perhaps surprisingly frequent. The two have bumped into each other professionally in 1976, 1981, 1983, 1984, 1985, 1986, 1987, 1991, 1996 and 2004.

In 1976 they were both on the sessions for Clapton's *No Reason to Cry* album; on May 15, 1981, Wood played guitar on the Los Angeles session that yielded 'Heart of Mine' for the *Shot of Love* album (and was also issued as a single); two years and two days later, Wood was one of those at a Dylan *Infidels* session in New York (along with Mark Rivera, Robert Funk and Laurence Etkin), playing guitar on an unissued (and uncirculated) attempt at 'Neighborhood Bully'. The following July, in New York again, they met up twice: Wood played guitar alongside the AL GREEN band behind Dylan's recording of 'Honey Wait', and at Dylan's own sessions played guitar alongside Anton Fig on drums and John Paris on bass, on unissued (but circulated) versions of Dylan's 'Driftin' Too Far from Shore' and 'Go 'Way Little Boy', and on the 26th of the month Wood played guitar on both the version of 'Clean-Cut Kid' released on *Empire Burlesque* in 1985 and on the 'Driftin' Too Far from Shore' that *was* released, on 1986's *Knocked Out Loaded*.

Then, yes, in Philadelphia, on July 13, 1985, in front of countless millions of television viewers and a packed crowd in the John F. Kennedy Stadium, having shared with Dylan and KEITH RICHARDS a number of bottles earlier in the day, Ron Wood now shared the humiliation of their LIVE AID appearance, after hosting the rehearsals for this débacle at his New York home a day or two earlier.

From June 15 to 17, 1986, Wood was back live at three consecutive concerts with Dylan and TOM PETTY & THE HEARTBREAKERS, playing guitar for the last nine songs of each concert, and in London that August 28–29, he played bass behind Bob at the recording of the miserably inadequate 'Had a Dream About You Baby', one take of which was issued on *Down in the Groove* and another on the soundtrack of the film *Hearts of Fire* (in which he appears as himself).

When the 1987 version of the tour with Tom Petty & the Heartbreakers reached London for four October nights, Ron popped up on the third night, to play guitar on the final encore number, 'Rainy Day Women # 12 & 35'. Much the same happened in 1991, when Dylan's Never-Ending Tour Band played a series of notably poor concerts at London, Hammersmith, and Wood came along on guitar on the penultimate night, February 16, playing on 'Everything Is Broken', 'Man in the Long Black Coat' and 'Like a Rolling Stone'.

In early 1996, it was Dylan contributing to some of Wood's work. He visited Ron at home at Sandymount, County Kildare, Ireland, and played guitar on two tracks, 'Interfere' and 'King of Kings'. The first of these, which had Dylan playing alongside Wood, IAN McLAGAN and bass player Willie Weeks, was later overdubbed by the legendary Scotty Moore on guitar and D.J. Fontana on drums (plus an Ian Jennings), so it's not certain Dylan's contribution survived; either way it's expensive to find out, since the result was issued only on a 4-track CD sold as part of the limited-edition book *Wood on Canvas: Every Picture Tells a Story*, published by the upmarket specialist company Genesis Publications in 1998. 'King of Kings', on the other hand, with Dylan also on guitar—and not overdubbed later—appeared as the final track on Wood's solo album *Not for Beginners* in 2002. It's nothing to rush out and buy: it's a short informal acoustic jam of no particular merit. A few months later, Wood came along again behind Dylan, this time at his London Hyde Park charity concert for the Prince's Trust (Prince Charles, that is: heir to the throne of the United Kingdom)—but this time Wood's contribution included not only guitar on all songs (alongside AL KOOPER on organ) but shared vocals on 'Seven Days', a Dylan song Wood had recorded himself, with odd insipidity, on his *Gimme Some Neck* album of 1979 and had performed at the 30th Anniversary Celebration Concert in New York in 1992. Since Dylan has rarely performed 'Seven Days' live, you might assume that on this occasion Ron Wood was the prompt for its inclusion, but no: having never played it in concert since 1976, Dylan had suddenly reintroduced it 20 years later, in April 1996, and had sung it 12 times between then and the June charity concert.

After that, there was an eight-year gap before Ron Wood reappeared on stage with Dylan one more time—so far the only time in the 21st century, at the Fleadh (pronounced Flar), again in London and again in a park (Finsbury Park this time), on June 20, 2004. Ron came on and played electric guitar on all 15 numbers.

Meanwhile in 1993 Ron Wood and Rod Stewart reunited on an *MTV Unplugged*™, giving them a sizeable hit album. Ron also continues to issue solo albums and remains a member of the Rolling Stones—in which capacity he has stood on the same stage as Dylan a further handful of times. His contribution to Dylan's work has never been significant (except negatively, at Live Aid, and that was probably more Keith's fault). But Ron and Bob keep getting together because they like each other. Ron likes Bob because he's Bob—unpredictable and unfathomable; and Bob likes Ron because he's undemanding, easy-going and as fathomable as a duck pond.

[Ron Wood: *Gimme Some Neck*, CBS 35702, UK, 1979; *Not for Beginners*, Steamhammer, US, 2002. Ron Wood, *Wood on Canvas: Every Picture Tells a Story*, Guildford UK: Genesis Publications, 1998.]

'Woodstock II' [1994] In the 25th anniversary year of the iconic Woodstock Festival of 1969, which Bob Dylan famously didn't attend (though THE BAND did), the large but infinitely less important 'Woodstock II' was held at Saugerties, New York (a stone's throw from the immortalised 'Big Pink'), in mid-August 1994. The rest of the event is immaterial; the point is that this time Bob Dylan *did* perform, with his Never-Ending Tour band of the day—BUCKY BAXTER on pedal steel and electric slide guitar, JOHN JACKSON on lead guitar, the inevitable TONY GARNIER on electric and stand-up bass and WINSTON WATSON on drums and percussion. Not only performed but reached a rare and special plane.

From the opening number, which was 'Jokerman', right through till the end of 'It's All Over Now, Baby Blue' this was magnificent Dylan, incontestably a set you wouldn't want to be without—and it has an extraordinary highlight in 'Just Like a Woman': a song normally rather the worse for wear in concert. Against all expectation, we get here one of his very most engaged, inspired, gloriously unloosed yet focused vocal performances in many years. And by far his best harp solo—almost *Blonde on Blonde*ish, no less. (Indeed when, before this, did Dylan last play three harmonica solos running, as here on 'Just Like a Woman', 'It Takes a Lot to Laugh, It Takes a Train to Cry' and 'Don't Think Twice, It's All Right'?)

The whole performance, with the sound so well-mixed and the band so good that night, argues that the mid-1990s Bob Dylan can stand in the same room with the Dylans of the past. He is alive, alert, fully into his jazz-improvisational vocals and making some wonderful noises: and not imitating himself but singing—phrasing—afresh. Woodstock II is a *real* performance.

The punkish, grungy music is good, complex, Tom Verlaineish, real: not remotely MTV/AOR, and surprisingly resourceful. How interesting the rendition of 'Masters of War'—so very different from the brave, scrupulous version at Hiroshima earlier the same year, yet so fine, with the double-bass ominous but not overplayed; the splendid bluegrass-folk of 'Don't Think Twice, It's All Right'; and yielding so fresh a milieu for 'It's All Over Now, Baby Blue' that Dylan rises fully to the occasion, creating a whole that is concentrated and time-stopping—this last for the first time since live 1966—and even, to hone in on a specific detail, devising something special for the repeated sound of the word 'home' in the 'seasick sailors' verse, just as he did so unerringly in 1966.

Here, then, is an example of mid-1990s Bob Dylan offering brave singing, braver harp playing and, yes, love.

[Bob Dylan: 'Jokerman', 'Just Like a Woman', 'All Along the Watchtower', 'It Takes a Lot to Laugh, It Takes a Train to Cry', 'Don't Think Twice, It's All Right', 'Masters of War', 'It's All Over Now, Baby Blue', 'God Knows' (an unhappy lapse here; everyone loses interest, starting with its composer), 'I Shall Be Released', 'Highway 61 Revisited', 'Rainy Day Women # 12 & 35' and 'It Ain't Me Babe', Saugerties, NY, 14 Aug 1994. Televised live on pay-per-view cable. 'Highway 61 Revisited' released on the various artists video *Woodstock 94*, Polygram Video 800 632 3510-3, US, 1994 & the CD *Woodstock 94*, A&M 289, US, 1994–95.]

Woodward, Ian [1946 -] Ian Woodward, who was born in Brentford, UK, in 1946, wishes to keep his date of birth a secret and says that the rest of his Dylan-centred career is a matter of public record. Within the Dylan fanzines world, this is true: for several decades he has run *The Wicked Messenger*, an itemised near-daily log of every Dylan news snippet, rumour and reported sighting that comes to his attention. Once an independent newsletter, later inserted into *The Telegraph*, it is now published inside *Isis*.

words and music, the relationship of Dylan has sometimes suggested that words come first and music afterwards, but he has just as often suggested that it happens the other way round or that the two come into his head together. Clearly there have been times when he took a folk melody and put new words to it. Then again, he's often said that with 'Like a Rolling Stone', for example, what he had first was screeds of words that weren't necessarily going to become part of a song at all. And for one example of the third way, see *Chronicles Volume One*, in which he says of writing 'What Was It You Wanted?': 'I heard the lyric and melody together in my head and it played itself in a minor key. . . . The song almost wrote itself. It just descended upon my head.'

Many people will have experienced the arrival of words and music together, starting perhaps with just a phrase or a line. Mort Shuman, songwriting partner of DOC POMUS, comments interestingly on how the separation of words and music was changed by rock'n'roll: 'It wasn't like the old, more established songwriting teams of the pre-rock'n'roll [era] where you would have "Words by . . ." and "Music by . . ." With a lot of rock'n'roll teams . . . it was "Words and music by . . ." because we didn't know where one process started and the other stopped.'

Dylan has also said contradictory things about the primacy of words over music and vice versa and/or the indissolubility of their importance. In *Chronicles Volume One*, he comments: '. . . if my songs were just about words, then what was Duane Eddy, the great rock-and-roll guitarist, doing recording an album full of instrumental melodies of my songs? Musicians have always known that my songs were about more than just words, but most people are not musicians.'

A reasonable rejoinder might be that many musicians consider Dylan's music rather less distinctive than his lyrics, that at the same time many musicians never listen to the words when they hear a record, and finally that actually *Duane Eddy Does Bob Dylan* manages only seven Dylan compositions, adds P.F. Sloan's 'Eve of Destruction' and refers in its sleevenotes to songs 'from the pen of Bob Dylan, the poet laureate of the 1960s', concluding that 'What Bob Dylan is capable of saying with his magical way with words, Duane Eddy is capable of saying instrumentally.'

[Quotes from *Chronicles Volume One*, p.172 & 119–20. Mort Shuman: undated quote in interview by Spencer Leigh, *Baby, That Is Rock and Roll: American Pop, 1954–1963*, p.183–84. Duane Eddy: *Duane Eddy Does Bob Dylan*, Colpix CPL-494 and SCP-494, US, 1965.]

***World Gone Wrong* [1993]** A follow-up of sorts: the album after *Good as I Been to You* was another solo acoustic one, though more focused, more clean-cut, less gothic. Again the recordings are self-produced (and it does seem lamentable that when Dylan owns the finest of acoustic guitars, and after 30 years of supposed progress in recording technology, he cannot produce a guitar-sound as clear, vivid, biting, exuberant or controlled as he achieves on his earliest forays into the studio). Again, vocal decline is evident too. Yet this is a fine album, at least as good as its predecessor (most people prefer it), and again asserting with inward intelligence and formidable interpretative skill the richly humane values and poetic power of communally created song, even as he commands this material so trenchantly that it can seem as if he had written it all himself.

With serious-mindedness and a strong sense of mystery, he insists on the continued relevance of these voices from the past, and takes us so deeply among them that he frees us from the tyranny of the present. Both these 1990s solo albums signal Dylan's regaining of the sense that his new recorded work matters: there's no comparison to the hapless flailing around so evident on the albums from *Empire Burlesque* to *Down in the Groove*. Even the titles, symptomatically, have regained focus. And with *World Gone Wrong* we are also offered, for the first time in decades and to our considerable surprise, Bob Dylan liner notes. Stand-out tracks: 'World Gone Wrong', 'Love Henry', 'Ragged & Dirty', 'Delia', 'Two Soldiers', 'Lone Pilgrim'. The next Dylan studio album, *Time Out of Mind*, would be four years later.

[Probably recorded Malibu, CA, May 1993; released as Columbia CK 57590 (in UK as CD Columbia 474857 2), 26 Oct 1993, and in UK on LP as Columbia 474857 1, Dec 1993.]

Wraith, John & Wyvill, Mike [1949 -] John Wraith was born in Felling, UK, on November 8, 1949 and Michael Wyvill on Tyneside, UK, on September 24, 1949. Both first took an interest in Dylan's work in 1963, contributed to *The Telegraph* from 1991 and the privately circulated *FREEWHEELIN'* from 1992; they have jointly published a number of slim listings volumes on Dylan's tours, starting with *Still on the* Road, 1992, and are both now academics at Sunderland University, UK. They are jointly editors of the handsome-looking fanzine *THE BRIDGE*.

Wyeth, Howie [1944 - 1996] Howard Pyle Wyeth was born in Jersey City, NJ, on April 22, 1944, into a family that was distinguished in the arts, technology and 'society'. His father, Nathaniel Wyeth, was an inventor and a DuPont Corporation Engineering Fellow; his mother was Caroline Pyle of Wilmington, Delaware (where she is unlikely to have known SARA DYLAN's parents, the scrap-dealing Noznisky). One of Howie's grandparents was the once-famous illustrator N.C. Wyeth; another was Ellen Pyle, illustrator of book jackets and magazine covers, including no less than 40 paintings used on the front of the *Saturday Evening Post*. In case this weren't enough illustrators in the family, Howie's great-uncle Howard was once known as 'the Dean of American Illustrators', while his uncle was the internationally famous painter Andrew Wyeth.

During his childhood Howie's family moved to Chadd's Ford, Pennsylvania, then Hockessin, Delaware, and then Hamorton, back in Pennsylvania. Howie survived the polio that struck him at age eight. (His older brother Howell died in a car crash, and his only sister, Caroline, died in childhood too.) In the early 1960s he moved to Syracuse, New York, where he formed an R&B band called the Sidewinders (which later became the Jam Factory) but he also studied music at Syracuse University, studied percussion under the Philadelphia Orchestra's Alan Abel and graduated in 1966. Three years later he made New York City his base.

He was a jazz pianist as well as a rock drummer and his studio session-work contributed to albums by Robert Gordon, Kinky Friedman, ROGER McGUINN, Link Wray and Don McLean (not to mention Joey Miserable & the Worms).

Howie Wyeth joined Bob Dylan in the studio on the last two days of July 1975 as drummer on sessions for the *Desire* album. These two days put him on the album tracks 'One More Cup of Coffee (Valley Below)', 'Black Diamond Bay', 'Mozambique', 'Joey', 'Isis' and 'Sara'. It also put him on 'Rita May' on *Masterpieces* (1978), 'Abandoned Love' on *Biograph* (1985) and 'Golden Loom' on the *Bootleg Series Vols. 1–3* (1991). It also meant that when Dylan performed on the 'World of JOHN HAMMOND' TV tribute, in Hammond's presence, in Chicago two months after the sessions, Wyeth was drummer on 'Oh Sister', 'Simple Twist of Fate' and 'Hurricane'. And that October 24, it meant that Wyeth went back into the studio to re-record Hurricane with its legally necessary amended lyrics.

Wyeth then joined Dylan on tour, in the line-up known informally as GUAM, on both Rolling Thunder Revues, playing drums and piano (though not at the same time), starting from its launch on October 30, 1975 in Plymouth, Massachusetts, finishing the first tour that December 8 at Madison Square Garden, New York ('The Night of the Hurricane'), playing the second fund-raiser for RUBIN 'HURRICANE' CARTER in Houston on January 25, 1976, starting the second Rolling Thunder Revue in Lakeland, Florida, that April 18 and arriving at the final end on May 25 in Salt Lake City, Utah (by which time he had also been featured on the live recordings and video that made up the *Hard Rain* album and the semi-aligned 'Hard Rain' TV Special). Wyeth subsequently rehearsed for Dylan's 1978 World Tour but dropped out before it began.

He had, of course, been captured in the footage for *Renaldo & Clara* shot on the first Rolling Thunder Revue, revealing a soppy grin that often drew people to him, and he was described economically by SAM SHEPARD in his *Rolling Thunder Logbook* as 'The mellowest fellow I ever laid eyes on. A slouched wool cap that seemed to be growing onto his head. I never saw him without it. . . . Black tennis shoes. Enjoyed playing music like nobody's business.' Shepard said of that music: 'Smooth drums. Holy ancient American piano. . . . Upside-down Chinese splash cymbal.'

As this hints, Wyeth was always drawn to jazz as well as rock, and later in life he decided to turn his attention more fully to the piano, playing in Barbecue Bob & the Spare Ribs and in the Dharma Bums, and leading informal combos that played in New York jazz clubs but roamed in the musical hinterland of early jazz, ragtime and blues, albeit with a touch of zydeco.

He died of heart failure in hospital in Manhattan on the night of March 27, 1996. He was 51. In 2003 came a 2-CD set of his solo piano-playing, *Chadds Ford Getaway*, its grand piano sound gorgeously recorded and its title returning Wyeth posthumously to the haunts of his grandfather and his childhood.

[Howie Wyeth: *Chadds Ford Getaway*, *nia*, Stand Clear Music, US, 2003.]

Wynton Marsalis Septet, the See Marsalis, Wynton.

XM satellite radio series hosted by Dylan On December 12, 2005 it was announced that the subscribers-only satellite radio giant XM had signed up Bob Dylan to host a series of weekly programmes on what it calls its 'deep album rock channel Deep Tracks', XM Channel 40, starting in March 2006, on which he would play records 'hand-selected' (huh?) from his 'personal music collections', interview other artists and read e-mails from fans. The company announcement, headed 'Music Icon Becomes First-Time DJ to Spin Records . . .', quoted Dylan saying in suspiciously plausible PRspeak: 'A lot of my own songs have been played on the radio, but this is the first time I've ever been on the other side of the mic. It'll be as exciting for me as it is for XM.' The date later shifted to May 3, 1 am Eastern time.

X

XM is a large and burgeoning corporate player in the entertainment industry, with 160 coast-to-coast digital channels, 71 of them specialist music channels, studios in Washington, D.C., New York and Nashville, 'additional offices' in Boca Raton, Florida, Southfield, Michigan, and Yokohama, Japan, and over five million subscribers getting these channels beamed to their cars. The company has 'partnerships' with most leading auto manufacturers. A main attraction for customers is that many channels exclude advertising. The cheapest subscription as of February 2006 is $12.95 per month. XM is a wholly owned subsidiary of XM Satellite Radio Holdings Inc. and has traded on the NASDAQ exchange since October 5, 1999.

Dylan's radio series proved a delight. He used his slot to recreate exactly the kind of 1950s radio that was so formative and fond a musical lifeline for the Bobby Zimmerman who was listening to it in Hibbing, Minnesota—a radio era he has expressed his fondness for in more recent years (see **'I Forgot More'**). Tom Palaima, an Austin, Texas, professor, sums up Dylan's intent and achievement here with what he calls Dylan's 'warm evocations of old-timey radio':

> 'In each hour, Dylan covers a chosen theme: mothers, fathers, baseball, coffee, weddings, divorce, showing how the common musical traditions of the United States shaped our lives in song and lyric. Dylan's succinct commentary makes the music shine. He is witty, gently humorous, erudite and always reverent about the music he is playing.
>
> We hear the sounds of big band, country swing, rockabilly, blues, rhythm and blues, rock'n'roll, Nashville, Motown, Sun Records, Frank Sinatra, the Ink Spots, Bob Wills and Kitty Wells. Interspersed, he gives plainly spoken information about the artists, where they came from, where they went, who influenced them and what influence they had. He recites lyrics, painting pictures of our lives in sound.
>
> Dylan doesn't peddle himself or anything else. No product placement here. Period commercials are spliced in to set the mood. A listener asks on Theme Time Coffee: "Why do you play so much old music? Do you have something against new music?" Dylan replies, "I like new music. But there's more old music than new music."
>
> . . . Theme Time Radio is hip, but not Tarantino's jaded hip, or William Shatner's self-mocking hip. Dylan respects the music we and he loved. He respects the artists who created it, even lived it.
>
> These shows are so humane, so out of time. . . . Dylan is still protesting. He is protesting our fast-paced, dehumanized present by calling us to gather round the hearth of old-time radio and remember life as it used to be and could be again, if we stop and really listen to it, and to each other.'

[Tom Palaima, 'The times they are a-changin' but Dylan's still protesting through music', *Austin American-Statesman*, 15 Jul 2006.]

Yarrow, Pete [1938 -] See **Peter, Paul & Mary**.

years Dylan didn't tour In the earliest years of his career Dylan wasn't 'touring', though he was playing live, mostly in clubs; but as from 1965 he can be said to have been touring. Since then, he has toured each year except these: 1967–73; 1977; 1982–83; 1985. The Never-Ending Tour began in June 1988 and, whatever names may be given to its constituent portions, is still going on.

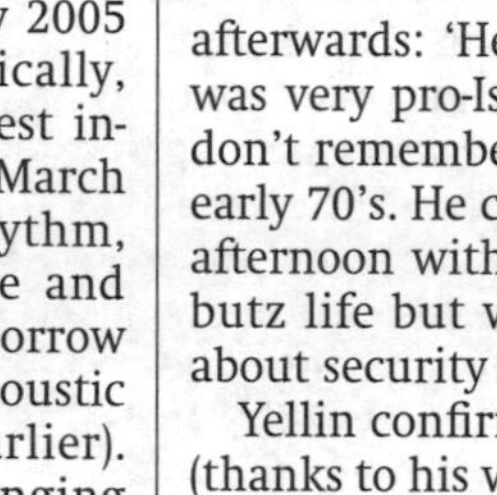

Yearwood, Trisha [1964 -] Trisha Yearwood was born in the pretty town of Monticello, Georgia, on September 19, 1964, grew up on her father's farm, attended Belmont University in Nashville, became a country music singer there and scored a no.1 country hit in 1991 with 'She's in Love With the Boy', one of three singles taken from her début album, *Trisha Yearwood*. It was a great start, and in chart terms she has rarely stumbled since.

Initially a protégé of Garth Brooks, she became engaged to him in May 2005 after two previous failed marriages. Musically, Yearwood cites Linda Ronstadt as her biggest influence, but she's really not that bad. On March 23, 1994 at the partly televised event 'Rhythm, Country & Blues: The Concert' in LA, she and Dylan attempted a duet on the song 'Tomorrow Night' (which he had recorded on his solo acoustic album *Good as I Been to You* two years earlier). Though Dylan has always enjoyed challenging those with whom he shares a vocal mike, it was generally felt in this instance that it might have worked better had he sung in the same key as Ms. Yearwood.

[Trisha Yearwood: *Trisha Yearwood*, MCA, US, 1991; *Hearts in Armor*, MCA, 1992; *The Song Remembers When*, 1993; *Inside Out*, MCA, 1994; *Thinkin' About You*, MCA, 1995; *Everybody Knows*, MCA 11477, 1996; *Songbook*, MCA, 1997; *Where Your Road Leads*, MCA, 1998; *Real Live Woman*, MCA, 2000; *Jasper County*, MCA, 2005.]

Yellin, Bob [1936 -] Anton Robert Yellin was born in New York City on June 10, 1936. He was a founder member of THE GREENBRIAR BOYS, to whom Dylan was support act when he was given the key review by ROBERT SHELTON in the *New York Times* in September 1961.

At some point earlier that year, while Yellin was sharing an apartment at 127 MacDougal Street, he recorded Dylan there on his Magnacorder tape machine. Yellin took the tape, which was of about six songs, to Maynard Solomon at Vanguard Records, feeling that the label really should sign him up. Every few days, Yellin would ask Solomon if he'd listened to the tape yet, and the answer would be no. Eventually Solomon said that he had listened but that he felt 'it's really not for us'. Yellin never retrieved the tape.

Yellin was the Greenbriar Boys' banjoist from its 1958 inception until 1969, when he moved with his family to Israel for what turned out to be 13 years, to live and work on Kibbutz Ein Dor, which is between Afula and Tiberias, below Mount Tabor: a settlement surrounded by Arab and Bedouin villages, with whom it has always been on friendly terms.

On his first night in the country, his 'greeter' told him there was no-one named Robert in the Old Testament so would he choose another name; he chose David (pronounced da-*veed*), but this got bastardised into the not particularly biblical Dave.

Larry Yudelson's website 'Bob Dylan: Tangled Up in Jews' reported that in the early 1970s Dylan paid a private visit to the kibbutz, as Yellin's guest; that Yellin showed him around and said afterwards: 'He was feeling his Jewish roots and was very pro-Israeli at that point in his life . . . I don't remember the date but I think it was in the early 70's. He came to see me and spent a Shabbat afternoon with me. . . . He was impressed by kibbutz life but was mostly concerned, in general, about security issues in Israel.'

Yellin confirms all this, and pins down the date (thanks to his wife) as Saturday, May 29, 1971, adding that Dylan came down from another kibbutz further north, probably Kibbutz Ein Gev, where he had reportedly given a concert the previous evening. That such a thing happened has never been mentioned within the world of Dylan loggers, and if he had given a concert in the middle of his private visit to the country, without other musicians, this would have been his only solo concert since 1965—an amazing thing to have remained unlogged. Yet Yellin says he only knew Dylan was in the country because he read of the concert in a local news report or heard of it on radio, and this is what prompted him to phone Dylan and invite him to Kibbutz Ein Dor. What *is* known is that Dylan was already in Israel on May 24, his 30th birthday, and was photographed at the Wailing Wall in Jerusalem with his wife SARA. It's also reported that both visited the Kibbutz Givat Haim, perhaps to investigate the possibility of moving there, though in fact this kibbutz already had an almost 50-year history of schism between the two factions that had been allocated its land, and the bitter politics that kept the two sides divided would have been the last possible milieu to attract Bob Dylan.

When Dylan arrived at Kibbutz Ein Dor to see Yellin, he was accompanied only by a tour guide cum driver. His interest in 'security issues', Yellin recalls, centred particularly on planes. 'He was interested in planes: what aircraft Israel had, that kind of thing.' He has the impression that Dylan's interest in Israel was short-lived. The visit was brief and that was the last time they met. His abiding memories of Dylan are from the early Greenwich Village days, when 'his leg would always be bobbing up and down, and he would always be sitting there writing.'

Yellin came back to the States, and back to being Bob instead of David, in 1982. He took part in the reunion performances of the Greenbriar Boys, and from the stage of the Philadelphia Folk Festival asked if people knew of any bluegrass players in Vermont; the result was meeting up with Mark Greenberg and three others and the formation of Bob Yellin & the Joint Chiefs of Bluegrass, which lasted right through to the mid-1990s.

Now 70, and still living up in 'the boonies' of northern Vermont, Yellin has more or less retired, though he still owns a folk-music store in Burlington, Vermont.

[Larry Yudelson's website is at *www.radiohazak.com/Dylan.html*. Most information from Bob Yellin, phone call with present writer, 2 Nov 2005.]

Yoakam, Dwight [1956 -] Dwight David Yoakam was born in Pikesville, Kentucky, but grew up in Columbus, Ohio, learning to play the guitar as a child, forming his first band while in high school and growing up to be an eccentric country singer, a quirky, nominally country songwriter and a fine actor, not only in Hollywood but also on stage. He first moved to Nashville in the late 1970s, and released a first EP (yes, an *EP!*) in 1984, *A Town Near Bakersfield*, and the début album *Guitars, Cadillacs, Etc., Etc.* in 1986. He began acting in TV and film at the beginning of the 1990s and made his theatrical début in 1993, in the two-act play *Southern Rapture*, written by Joseph G. Tidwell III and directed by Peter Fonda—in which he co-starred with SALLY KIRKLAND and Vanessa Marcil ('Brenda Barrett' on, er, 'General Hospital'), and in which one of the other characters is named 'Mr. Zimmerman'.

Yoakam connects with Dylan only briefly. In early 1993 in Los Angeles, Dwight backed Carlene Carter, along with HOWIE EPSTEIN, Joe Romersh and Kevin Welch, while Bob provided backing vocals as she recorded a version of Dylan's *Empire Burlesque* song 'Trust Yourself', later released on a CD single that accompanied her 1993 album *Little Love Letters*.

In 1997, Dwight Yoakam contributed the final track, a very choppy, wilfully contrived 'T for Texas', on the compilation album *The Songs of Jimmie Rodgers: A Tribute*, which Dylan and his office assembled and which was issued on Dylan's fitfully extant label Egyptian Records. And then on September 2, 1999, in the West Palm Beach, Florida, opening concert of Dylan's brief tour that month—squeezed between the June-July tour with PAUL SIMON and the October-November tour with PHIL LESH—Dylan delivered a one-off performance of Yoakam's 'The Heart That You Own'. Yoakam's immaculately sung studio version is on his 1990 album *If There Was a Way*: a performance that belies his image as 'hardly country at all', or 'cowpunk', and delivers a relaxed but nuanced and attentive vocal with a timbre that reminds you at once of George Jones and a panache with little filigrees that takes you straight back to LEFTY FRIZZELL.

[Dwight Yoakam: 'The Heart That You Own', *nia*, *If There Was a Way*, Reprise, US, 1990; 'T for Texas', Burbank, CA, *nia*, *The Songs of Jimmie Rodgers: A Tribute*, Egyptian/Columbia 485189 2, US, 1997. Carlene Carter: 'Trust Yourself', Giant 74321 17682, with *Little Love Letters*, US, 1993.]

Young, Izzy [1928 -] Israel Goodman Young was born in New York City on March 26, 1928. He grew up working in his parents' Brooklyn bakery and first encountered folk music in 1945 when on impulse he joined Margaret Mayo's American Square Dance Group. He attended LEADBELLY's last concert in New York City in 1949, and the concert at his funeral a few months later. He dropped out of Brooklyn College in 1950 and in the mid-1950s met the eminent folklorist Kenneth S. Goldstein, whose encouragement steered him towards folk revival activity, starting by compiling a 15-page listing of rare publications.

He was the founder of the Folklore Center, at 110 MacDougal Street, Greenwich Village, which he opened in March 1957 after cashing in a $1000 insurance policy to pay for the lease. 'I had about $50 in the bank,' he said later, 'and I had a batch of books I put up on the shelves and a few records, and I started doing business from the first minute.' The idea of the place was to supply the would-be folk musician's needs: records, sheet music, second-hand guitars, strings, capos, *Sing Out!* magazine and more. It was also, perhaps inevitably, a place for like-minded Villagers bump into each other and hang out, especially in a back room 'with a pot-bellied stove, crooked pictures and rickety chairs', as Dylan describes it in *Chronicles*. 'Some people,' he recalls, 'picked up their mail there.'

Dylan's descriptions of Young and his Folklore Center are, in a book of great vivacity and detail, especially vivid. He begins by hinting at its importance to him, saying that he started avoiding the Café Wha in the afternoons and hanging out at the Center instead. 'The small store was up a flight of stairs and the place had an antique grace. It was like an ancient chapel, like a shoebox sized institution.' The back room with the stove, he says, had 'old patriots and heroes on the wall, pottery with crossed-stitch design, lacquered black candles' and 'was filled with American records and a phonograph. Izzy would let me stay back there and listen to them' and even thumb 'through a lot of his antediluvian folk scrolls. . . . Extinct song folios of every type—sea shanties, Civil War songs, cowboy songs, songs of lament, church house songs, anti-Jim Crow songs, union songs—archaic books of folk tales, Wobbly journals, propaganda pamphlets . . .' (Young gave him pamphlets on Joe Hill to read, after Dylan asked who Hill was.) The Center was 'the citadel of Americana folk music . . . a crossroads junction for all the folk activity you could name and you might at any time see real hard-line folksingers in there. . . . I saw CLARENCE ASHLEY, Gus Cannon, MANCE LIPSCOMB, TOM PALEY, Erik Darling hanging around in the place.' It was here that Dylan first encountered DAVE VAN RONK, stepping in off the snowy street to look at a Gibson guitar.

Young himself was 'an old-line folk enthusiast, very sardonic and wore heavy horn-rimmed glasses, spoke in a thick Brooklyn dialect, wore wool slacks, skinny belt and work boots, tie at a careless slant. His voice . . . always seemed too loud for the little room. Izzy was always a little rattled over something or other. He was sloppily good natured. In reality, a romantic. To him, folk music glittered like a mound of gold.' Not everyone found him so good-natured: he often showed a short temper, occasionally a physically violent one, and could be intractable in nursing small imagined slights.

At some point Young started writing a news-snippets and gossip column for *Sing Out!*, called 'Frets and Frails', and kept a journal in which, invaluably in retrospect, he logged the comings and goings of his musician-customers—including Bob Dylan.

(Examples: 'September 23, 1961: Met Bob Dylan 3am this morning on the way to a JACK ELLIOTT party at 1 Sheridan Square . . . Terry Thal now a manager. Tom Paxton, Bob Dylan and someone else.' 'January 26, 1962: Passed Dylan on the street, he said to me that he "didn't know why so many things are happening to me." I said that he did.')

JOHN BAULDIE described him as 'a loud, disorganised, big-hearted folk enthusiast' at whose Center Dylan spent a lot of time, 'looking at records, music, trying out instruments, meeting people and, later, writing songs in the back room on Izzy's old typewriter. One of them, the unreleased "Talkin' Folklore Center", was specially composed on March 19, 1962 as a fund-raiser.' The previous October, when Young was interviewing Dylan for his journal, Dylan mentioned another composition, 'California Brown Eyed Baby', which he said he was performing at the time.

Dylan credits Young with fighting city hall to allow music in Washington Square Park, and in general fighting against 'injustice, hunger and homelessness'. More personally, though, he credits Young with having played him particular records as suggested pieces of repertoire for him, and even being so trustworthy that Dylan told him truths about his own family (a rare thing indeed).

It was also Young who, at ALBERT GROSSMAN's prompting, promoted Dylan's first real concert, at the Carnegie Chapter Hall on November 4, 1961—at which Bob performed 21 songs, finishing with the two of his own he would record later that month for his début album, 'Song to Woody' and 'Talkin' New York' . . . to an audience of 52. Young was not a great businessman, as Dylan comments: 'Young was beseiged with bill collectors and dictates from the landlord. People were always chasing him down for money, but it didn't seem to faze him.'

He's likely to have been one of those Dylan hit out against later, in 'Positively 4th Street'. By 1965 Young was highly critical of Dylan's move away from overt political songs, and he wrote a piece in the first issue of the radically underground *East Village Other*, published that October, after being angered by the absence, at an anti-war rally, of all Albert Grossman's artists. Looking back over Dylan's earlier years he saw them anew: '. . . everyone conveniently forgot that he allowed Columbia Records to delete "John Birch Society Talking Blues" from his second album. This was soon after he swore that Columbia would have its way over his dead body. (I was hoodwinked . . . into arranging an abortive protest march . . . Dylan and management pulled a no-show on our six brave marchers.)' He added that Dylan copyrighted work that 'reflected accurately' that of 'poets from PATCHEN to GINSBERG' and 'no-one complained'; that he went to England, 'picked up marvelous morsels' and then 'left the poets and England behind.' He added: 'There seemed no heights to which Dylan could not attain. He had only to meet the right person. If he could only meet Malraux he could write treatises on civilization'. And so on. Young said in 1992 that he sent this article to Dylan before it was published, and that Dylan 'always said it was the best single article ever written on him'.

In the fullness of time, Young was back on board the Dylan bus, giving a warm and generous interview to JEFF ROSEN for the MARTIN SCORSESE film *No Direction Home*, in which he appears. One story he tells in the film, however, is untrue. It was not Young but BOB YELLIN of THE GREENBRIAR BOYS who tried to get Maynard Solomon to sign Dylan to Vanguard—he took him a tape—and the remark Young has Solomon making about not signing 'freaks' does not ring true as the speech of the gently spoken, good-humoured Solomon.

When *Chronicles* appeared, Young was thrilled and gratified by Dylan's detailed, affectionate recall. 'No matter what else Dylan has done his starting point has always been folk music. He never leaves folk music and he never will.' And: 'The book he promised to write, with a chapter on me, in July 1962 has finally come true!'

Young handed over the Folklore Center to Rick Altman in 1973, moved to Sweden and there opened the Folklore Centrum in Stockholm. He and it are still going.

[Bob Dylan: *Chronicles*, 2004, pp.18–22; Joe Hill pamphlets p.52. Izzy Young background detail in part from Ronnie D. Lankford Jr., All Music Guide, seen online 5 Oct 2005 at *www.icebergradio.com/artist/499028/izzy_young.html*. Izzy Young journal extracts *Judas!* no.12, Huntingdon, UK, Jan 2005, p.53; article 'Bob Dylantaunt', *East Village Other* vol.1, no.1, NY, Oct 1965, republished *Judas!* no.10, Jul 2004, pp. 87–88; response to *Chronicles*, written 20 Jun 2005, *Judas!* no.14, Jul 2005, p.34. John Bauldie, 'Village Walking Tour', online 5 Oct 2005 *www.interferenze.com/bcs/villagesights.htm*.]

Young, Neil [1945 -] Neil Young was born November 12, 1945 in Toronto, Ontario, his father a sports-writer on the *Toronto Sun*. He survived many childhood illnesses and his parents' divorce, after which he lived with his mother in Winnipeg, Manitoba, and took up music. His early groups included the Jades, the Esquires, the Classics, Neil Young & the Squires and the Mynah Birds; his later groups have included Buffalo Springfield, the Bluenotes, the Stray Gators, the Ducks, Crazy Horse and CROSBY, Stills, Nash & Young.

There's always an interestingly edgy relationship between Dylan and Neil Young, especially since Young came along just late enough to be formatively influenced by Dylan, yet has grown into a music mountain many people believe to be of near-equal size and significance in the landscape of post-1950s rock. The only two possible other contenders would be JONI MITCHELL and VAN MORRISON. Dylan himself puts Young first when, in a 1991 interview with Paul Zollo for *Songtalk* magazine, he refers to other singer-songwriters. Young begins almost as a disciple, and ends with a near-matching prophet's gravitas himself. The two have often if fitfully come together, sometimes uneasily.

By 1965, while still in Yorkville, Toronto, Neil Young was playing Dylan songs; he performed 'Just Like Tom Thumb's Blues' at a Killington, Vermont, ski resort that September; and instead of fitting in with Stephen Stills in pop group the Squires, Young decided to become a folk troubadour. 'He wanted to be Bob Dylan and I wanted to be THE BEATLES,' said Stills.

Dylan saw Crosby, Stills, Nash & Young at the Fillmore East in New York in early June 1970 and attended the party at the end of their week's residency there. Young's song 'Last Trip to Tulsa', on his eponymous first album (January 1969), is the first of several Young tracks that either imitate or pay marked tribute to Dylan—these include 'Days That Used to Be' and 'Ragged Glory' (both cf. 'My Back Pages'), 'Sixty to Zero' and 'Ordinary People'—and when Dylan heard 'Heart of Gold' (from *Harvest*, 1972), he thought it sounded like him. (He also told Young that the same album's 'A Man Needs a Maid' was one of his favourites.) The following year, Dylan was in the audience for a Young set at the opening of the Roxy Theatre in LA; invited backstage to meet Young, Dylan reputedly replied 'No thanks, we've just eaten.'

Young was also impressed with Dylan's approach to live performing in the 1970s, declaring in 1976 that 'Dylan . . . has shown so many of us, especially with the *Before the Flood* album tour with THE BAND, that a major performer can live with his people'—and, inspired by the early small-hall ethos of the Rolling Thunder Revue, Young promptly organised his own Northern California Coastal Bar Tour (aka the Rolling Zuma Revue). Young fans often suggest, perhaps rightly, that influence moved in the opposite direction when Dylan, untypically, put sleevenotes about each song on his 1985 collection *Biograph*: they note that Young had done the same on his earlier retrospective collection *Decade* (1977). Possibly too, Dylan's intimate performances at the Supper Club in New York in 1993 were a belated paralleling of Young's five acoustic nights at the 150-seater Boarding House in San Francisco 15 years earlier.

The two first appeared on stage together at the SNACK Benefit Concert in San Francisco on March 23, 1975. (The acronym covers the revoltingly named Students Need Athletics, Culture and Kicks.) They performed a 35-minute set with backing musos TIM DRUMMOND and Ben Keith plus The Band's RICK DANKO, GARTH HUDSON and LEVON HELM, playing 'Are You Ready for the Country', 'Ain't That a Lot of Love', 'Lookin' for a Love', 'Loving You Is Sweeter Than Ever', 'I Want You', 'The Weight', 'Helpless', 'Knockin' on Heaven's Door' and 'Will the Circle Be Unbroken'—yet managed to share vocals only on the last two songs. Officially unreleased, though bootlegged from a radio broadcast, Dylan's vocals are barely audible.

The following year, both took part in The Band's farewell concert at the Winterland, San Francisco (filmed by MARTIN SCORSESE as *The Last Waltz*). Young, looking magnificently wasted, performed two of his own songs watched from backstage by Dylan, and they joined with others for an encore of 'I Shall Be Released'. Nine years later, both appeared at LIVE AID, again performing together only during the ensemble encore (from which Dylan sloped off early). But it was Young whose phone call persuaded Dylan to take part in Farm Aid, after the latter's ill-judged remarks at Live Aid had galvanised WILLIE NELSON into organising the Farm Aid event. Dylan and Young both performed at this, but met up only privately backstage. Another six years on and Young was one of the best performers at the 30th Anniversary Concert for Dylan at Madison Square Garden, NYC, on October 16, 1992, giving a ferocious, blazing performance of 'All Along the Watchtower', adding backing vocals (with ROGER McGUINN, TOM PETTY, GEORGE HARRISON and ERIC CLAPTON) on Dylan's performance of 'My Back Pages', and contributing to the ensemble rendition of 'Knockin' on Heaven's Door'. (An edited version of this concert was released as *The 30th Anniversary Concert Celebration* on album and video in 1993.)

By this time, Dylan was some years into the Never-Ending Tour—it began in June 1988—and Neil Young dropped in on this several times over. Indeed Young was in on the start of it, lending Dylan and his band his ranch for pre-tour rehearsals, and then took part in the first, third and fourth concerts, playing electric guitar. It was also Young and his wife Pegi who founded the Bridge School for Handicapped Children near San Francisco, which holds an annual benefit concert, and for which Dylan appeared on December 4 in that first year of the Never-Ending Tour, performing six songs with G.E. SMITH on lead guitar.

In 1993 Young revisited Dylan's tour (October 9, Mountain View, CA), playing guitar on one number, and then one year and 11 days later he and BRUCE SPRINGSTEEN both played guitar behind Dylan on two encore numbers at the Roseland, New York City. In 1996, weirdly, Dylan and his band were second on the bill below Young & Crazy Horse at a July 13 concert in Hamburg; there was no collaboration that night. When Young toured in the summer of 2000, and the support act was the Pretenders, he returned to 'All Along the Watchtower', with Chrissie Hynde on guitar and support vocals, one such performance being included on the live album *Road Rock Vol. 1*—but then he had also revisited this Dylan song in 1993 when he'd played in concert with Booker T & the MGs. (Dylan had played harmonica on a BOOKER T album track in 1973—an album called *Chronicles*.)

Perhaps the gentlest, best conjunction comes late on—when Dylan namechecks Young on the *Time Out of Mind* song 'Highlands' in 1997—'I'm listenin' to Neil Young / I got to turn up the sound / Someone's always yelling / "Turn it down!"'—and then Young namechecks Dylan on the *Greendale* album's song 'Bandit' (2003), and in such a way that it takes us back to two 1960s Dylan songs ('Talking World War III Blues' as well as 'Like a Rolling Stone')—'No-one can touch you now / But I can touch you now / You're invisible / You got too many secrets / Bob Dylan said that / Somethin' like that.'

There are other, more superficial conjunctions: from 1982–89 Dylan's personal manager was Elliot Roberts, Young's long-time manager; both artists have owned boats in the Caribbean; both have songs entitled 'Hurricane'.

In 2002 Dylan sang Young's early classic 'Old Man' over 30 times in concert, beginning at Sacramento on October 8. Dylan/Young/'Old': we seem to be forever tangled up in both's back pages.

[This entry has been informed by issue no.93 of the Neil Young fanzine *Broken Arrow*, Falkland, Scotland, edited by Scott Sandie; by the online 'Neil Young Biography: The Godfather of Grunge' by Dave Zimmer (author of *4 Way Street: The Crosby, Stills, Nash & Young Reader*) at *http://www.thrasherswheat.org/nybiozimmer.htm*, 1 Jun 2005; & by the anonymous *http://www.angelfire.com/ny4/heartofgold/neilyoungbio.htm* online 31 May 2005.]

Young, Terry [19?? -] Terry Young was the keyboards player playing behind Dylan on the fall 1979 gospel tour, the 'Saturday Night Live' TV appearance, both the 1980 gospel tours and the *Saved* album, recorded in February 1980 in Sheffield, Alabama. On the compilation album *Gotta Serve Somebody: The Gospel Songs of Bob Dylan*, 2003, Young was reunited with other members of that Dylan gospel-tour band, including bass player TIM DRUMMOND, guitarist FRED TACKETT and drummer JIM KELTNER, to play on the version of 'Solid Rock' by the Minnesota choir Sounds of Blackness.

Terry Young is a gospel songwriter himself, and penned five of the songs on the former Raelette and session singer Merry Clayton's 1994 album *Miracles*, for example: namely the title track plus 'He Touched My Life', 'Say Yes to the Spirit', 'What About You?' and 'I Know He'll Be There'. He has also contributed his voice to animation movies like 2003's *Brother Bear*, *The Lion King* and, with Mona Lisa Young, to *The Lion King II: Simba's Pride*. Together the two made the single 'So Good So Right' c/w 'Reflections', and he sings backing vocals on her long-deleted 1983 solo album *Knife*.

Terry and Mona Lisa Young are now divorced but remain friends.

[Terry Young & Mona Lisa Young: 'So Good So Right' c/w 'Reflections', *nia*, Encore ENC 100347, US, *nia*. Various Artists: *The Gospel Songs of Bob Dylan*, Columbia/Legacy CK 89015, US (Columbia COL 511126 2, UK), 2003.]

Z

Zappa, Frank [1940 - 1993] Frank Vincent Zappa was born in Baltimore on December 21, 1940 and lived in Edgewood, Maryland, before being uprooted to the no-man's-land of the Californian Mojave Desert in 1950. He became a key figure in the culture of the second half of the 1960s, and a composer and musician whose work ranged far wider than 'rock' suggests.

For many, he will remain the man who gave the world the Mothers of Invention, and albums called *Lumpy Gravy*, *Weasels Ripped My Flesh* and *We're Only in It for the Money* (this last a savage parody of THE BEATLES' *Sgt. Pepper's* artwork). His breakthrough came on the West Coast as a bohemian avant garde was becoming the mass 'hippie' movement, and with splendid early songs like 'Call Any Vegetable', 'Who Needs the Peace Corps?' and 'The Brain Police', Zappa made himself famous with equally savage satirical attacks on both the gullible hippie young and their parents, while appearing in early publicity shots sporting a flowery dress along with a distinctively swarthy moustache and imperial beard, and with his long hair up in bunches.

Having gained an entrée into the world of rock celebrity, however, Zappa put himself at the cutting edge of studio technology and was a pioneer at integrating modern 'classical' music, jazz and rock in complex, witty ways. In the end, he offered 30 years' worth of music across what was an unprecedented, and remains an unrivalled, breadth of musical terrain.

An artist of the most demanding musical sensibility, Zappa never outgrew a taste for smut songs, always missing the critical point by defending them for their 'humour' and 'sexual honesty', while those around him found them wretchedly unfunny and about as sexually honest as Benny Hill. But then he didn't much like people. His 1989 autobiography reported: 'A normal day for me is spent working by myself and not talking to anybody. . . . I have to work the night shift and [my wife] has to work the day shift. . . . Every three or four weeks I'm back on daylight—and I dread it. . . . All those questions Gail was dealing with when I was sleeping on the day shift, now *I have to answer—live, in person*. I can't edit . . .'

He was specially wary of musicians, rock and classical types equally, though occasionally both met amicably. In 1981, Frank contacted Nicolas Slonimsky, who had conducted the 1933 world première of Edgard Varèse's *Ionisation*, and soon afterwards the pianist-conductor appeared at a Zappa rock concert. Slonimsky was given earplugs (which he discarded), Zappa introduced him as 'our national treasure', he played electric piano, the band joined in, the audience whooped and Slominsky took a bow. He was 87 years old.

Zappa's life and work always displayed dramatic contradictions. A talented self-publicist with a trademark flair for grotesque-joke titles, he was always committedly serious about his work; a workaholic disciplinarian who despised the use of drink and drugs, he chose for his early image that of laid-back leader of an anarchic drug-fuelled hippie band. A loud champion of 'groupies', he was one of the very few men in rock to stay married (to Gail Sloatman) for over 25 years; an effective political campaigner against the New Right televangelists in Reagan's America, and a vociferous opponent of Tipper Gore's campaign to sticker albums with lyric-content warnings (he would have laughed loud and hollow had he lived to see Tipper's husband Al present himself as the good-guy presidential candidate in the 2000 US election), he never considered himself a liberal or a supporter of the Left. A fine rock guitarist, he was a steadfast enemy of mainstream rock music; a 'classical' composer, he was always quick to bring into his band jazz musicians of promise and talent, including George Duke and Jean-Luc Ponty.

In the end, perhaps, Zappa came to see musicians as purchaseable units, like editing suites or amps: part of the baggage the composer needs to finance and deploy. Or not, in the case of rock musicians. His 1986 release *Jazz from Hell* was made, one track excepted, entirely on the computer-keyboard instrument the Synclavier: dispensing with musicians yet sounding like lots of them.

The crunch came in 1988, when the rock tour that would be his last collapsed after 81 shows, Zappa sacking most of the musicians because they were all in dispute. As the me-decade ended, Zappa made trips to Russia and (as it was then) Czechoslovakia. He got caught up in 'facilitating American finance' (unsuccessfully) for a Russian horror film, and trying to help sell frozen muffins to the USSR. Zappa said: 'I met all these very interesting people who wanted to do a wide range of business things with people from the West. . . . [I was] kind of like a dating service.'

In 1990, Zappa revisited Prague, President Havel urging him to be a cultural liaison officer for the new régime in its approaches to the West. In 1991 he returned to Czechoslovakia and Hungary to celebrate the departure of their Soviet troops, and at a Prague concert gave his only guitar performance since the rock-tour collapse. In London he told BBC Radio 4 that he was still doing 'a feasibility study' on standing for the US Presidency in '92, by getting US radio listener-response. By the autumn, no decision had been announced, and then his prostate cancer was announced instead.

Despite myriad other activity, including the making and sponsoring of pioneering animation videos, serious composition had long been Zappa's main concern. The vegetable fetishist with the dope-head rock group and the aesthetically challenged publicity (older readers may recall the 'Zappa the Crapper' poster) had become a serious composer, his work performed in concert halls alongside Cage, Stravinsky and other moderns.

In 1983, overseeing a Barbican performance of his orchestral works with the London Symphony Orchestra and the young American conductor Kent Nagano, Zappa was unhappy at the orchestra's apparent drinking in the interval, and said that on the subsequent recording sessions, repairing trumpet-section faults needed 40 edits in seven minutes' music. These are undetectable because, as Nagano conceded, 'Frank was such a superb editor.'

Zappa also worked with Pierre Boulez, but felt that his Ensemble InterContemporain, too, was under-rehearsed, for its 1984 performance of his work in Paris. 'I hated that première,' he wrote. 'Boulez virtually had to drag me onto the stage to take a bow.'

No-one could have been more different in their approach from Bob Dylan. Indeed when Dylan went on tour in 1981, for example, he made his musicians rehearse for five days; when Zappa went on tour in 1988 he made his musicians rehearse ten hours a day, five days a week, for four and a half months. Yet not only had it been Dylan's revolutionising of the possibilities of song that had made it possible for people to make records as different as were the early Mothers of Invention albums, but when Zappa had heard 'Like a Rolling Stone' on radio in 1965 he'd felt like quitting the music business almost before he'd joined it: 'I felt: "If this wins and it does what it's supposed to do, I don't need to do anything else."' It seemed to Zappa that for a six-minute rock song with surreal and political lyrics to win AM airplay and reach the charts was a major breakthrough: that the old, straight pop scene might be destroyed and replaced by socially, politically *and* musically good rock music. He decided not to quit, partly because AM radio didn't transform itself overnight after all, but mostly because if 'Like a Rolling Stone' signalled the moment when music was going to break boundaries in what it said and how it said it, Zappa too wanted to contribute to that destruction and renewal.

Their careers never coincided directly until 1982. That December, a scruffy-looking figure turned up unannounced at the gate of Zappa's house claiming to be Bob Dylan. Zappa reported to the veteran British music-journalist Karl Dallas: 'I get a lot of weird calls here, and someone suddenly called up saying "This is Bob Dylan. I want to play you my new songs." Now I'd never met him and I don't know his voice but I looked at the video-screen to see who was at the gate, and there, in the freezing cold, was a figure with no coat and an open shirt. I sent someone down to check, to make sure it wasn't a Charles Manson, but it was him.' Dylan was asking if Zappa would be interested in producing his next album. Zappa: 'He played me his eleven new songs and I thought they were good songs. He seemed like a nice guy. Didn't look like it would be too hard to work with him.'

Apart from the general polarities between the two—Zappa's insistence on technical super-proficiency, Dylan's unconcern for it; Zappa's contempt for three-chord songs, Dylan's reliance on them; Zappa's studio perfectionism, Dylan's preference for one-take 'feel'—there was, for Zappa, one specific area of difficulty. At this point, the end of 1982, Frank had a fair head of steam going against the Born Again Christian New Right, as his recent work had stressed; Dylan had only made one album since the evangelising *Slow Train Coming* and *Saved*: and even that one subsequent work, 1981's *Shot of Love*, had certainly not repudiated that evangelising, and had included 'Every Grain of Sand' and 'Property of Jesus'.

Faced, therefore, with Dylan playing him a new collection of songs ('He basically just hummed 'em and played 'em on the piano'), Zappa said afterwards: 'I asked him if it had any Jesus in it. I said: "Do these songs have the Big J in?" and he said no; [but] when I took him upstairs to give him a sandwich, my dog barked at him. I told him to watch out, my dog doesn't like Christians. And he didn't laugh.'

This Zappa-produced Bob Dylan album never happened, unfortunately. Hard as it might have been to envisage, it's possible that the very different strengths of these two major artists might both have flourished within a partnership. Dylan could have done with a perfectionist production, and Zappa could have done with spending some time listening to an artist whose intelligence was so acutely in the service of heartfelt instinct instead of mechanistic boys' toys. As it was, the album Dylan eventually made in part from some of the songs he had played to Zappa, *Infidels* (1983), was an indifferent and peculiarly anonymous production that left the songs seeming an ill-assorted ragbag rather than a cohesive collection. It was also a collection on which, though he got no explicit namecheck, 'the Big J' was certainly still around. The two artists never came together again.

In 1989, asked to identify his 'primary goal', Zappa answered: 'That's easy. I'm still waiting for an accurate performance!' In the event, he lived to hear something he probably felt came close. Since his illness, Zappa had cancelled many public appearances and new works. His last completed major project was *The Yellow Shark*, a collection of work commissioned by the Ensemble Modern and premiered at the Frankfurt Music Festival in September 1992. Zappa had planned to conduct part of each evening's performance but in the event could manage the baton only for small portions of the first performance. The work was nevertheless an immediate success, and under Zappa's own supervision yielded a CD recording, released only a month before his death: one last release from one of the major creative figures of modern music.

Frank Zappa died of prostate cancer, incurable because diagnosed too late, at his home in Los Angeles on December 4, 1993. He was 52.

[Frank Zappa & the Mothers of Invention: *Lumpy Gravy*, Verve V(6)8741, US (Verve SVLP9223, UK), 1968, CD-reissued Ryko RCD40024, US; *Weasels Ripped My Flesh*, Bizarre RSLP2028, US (Reprise K44019, UK), 1970, CD-reissued Ryko RCD10163 (Zappa CDZAP24); *We're Only in It for the Money*, Verve V(6)5045, US (Verve SVLP 9199, UK), 1968; *Jazz from Hell*, Barking Pumpkin ST74205, US (EMI EMC3521, UK), 1st CD version Ryko RCD10030, US (Zappa CDZAP32, UK), 1986; *The Yellow Shark*, Barking Pumpkin, US (Zappa CDZAP57, UK), 1993. Frank Zappa (with Peter Occhiogrosso), *The Real Frank Zappa Book!*, New York: Simon & Schuster, 1989.

Zappa quote from Greil Marcus, *The Guardian*, London, 13 May 2005, extracted from his *Like a Rolling Stone: Bob Dylan at the Crossroads*, 2005. Zappa quotes to Karl Dallas from Michael Gray, *Mother! The Frank Zappa Story*, London: Plexus, 1993, pp.185–86.]

Zevon, Warren [1947 - 2003] Warren William Zevon was born in Chicago on January 24, 1947, the son of a Russian Jewish father and a Celtic Mormon mother. They moved to Arizona and then LA when Warren was a child, and though he dropped out of high school, he learnt classical piano and became acquainted with Stravinsky and the conductor Robert Craft.

His first successes in music were mostly as a songwriter; the Turtles recorded his song 'Like the Seasons' in 1967, and when his début album was released in 1969 (*Wanted Dead or Alive*) the track 'She Quit Me' was used in the iconic hit film *Midnight Cowboy*. After the album flopped he served THE EVERLY BROTHERS as pianist-bandleader during their sour last pre-split years and wrote jingles for Boone's Farm wine and Chevrolets (not necessarily combined). He sang in California and Colorado clubs, and moved to Spain to bum around, just as Jackson Browne was pushing Zevon's songs to the music biz. Hence the return to the US, the release of the Browne-produced *Warren Zevon* (1976), and *Excitable Boy* (1978) which brought him to public acclaim and success, not least thanks to the top 10 hit 'Werewolves of London'. A spindly blonde figure in a tight t-shirt and grannie glasses, he looked, in these early years, like an air-guitarist who had somehow got hold of a real instrument.

Excitable Boy kicked off his long career as a successful, distinctive lyricist of hedonistic celebration undercut by sharp mockery of that countercultural hedonism and of himself. His titles alone had a beguiling and quirky ring to them, from 'Desperadoes Under the Eaves' and 'Detox Mansion' to 'Lawyers, Guns and Money' and 'Things to Do in Denver When You're Dead' (this last written as part of his music for the 1996 film of the same name). One of his album titles was *Sentimental Hygiene*.

His songs were covered by many others, and in later life he collaborated with NEIL YOUNG and Bruce Hornsby but also with jazzmen like Chick Corea and with more youthful musicians, not least for an album of (mostly) blues standards made with three quarters of R.E.M. under the group name Hindu Love Gods (*Hindu Love Gods*, 1990).

It was on *Sentimental Hygiene*, in 1987, that Warren Zevon and Dylan connected. One of the songs Zevon recorded was 'The Factory'; Dylan was asked to overdub a harmonica part onto the track, which he duly did in an LA studio in February or March 1987. The track, a not especially outstanding example of Zevon's trademark twitchy energy and mordant relish, was included when the album was issued that August.

'Detox Mansion' had been written from personal experience; it came to seem that the same was true for his obsessive songs about death. His 2000 album was titled *Life'll Kill Ya*. He continued to work and record after being diagnosed with terminal cancer in 2002, and managed to make a final album in this period, *The Wind*, to which a parade of other stars contributed.

Bob Dylan was not among them, but a rather fine Zevon version of 'Knockin' on Heaven's Door' was one of its tracks, while it was at this point that Dylan introduced several Zevon songs to his set. It was unusual to give another writer's work such prominence within his own repertoire, but at the first concert of the 2002 Never-Ending Tour's last leg, on October 4 in Seattle, Washington, he performed three Zevon songs, the sinuously expansive 'Accidentally Like a Martyr', 'Boom Boom Mancini' and the lovely 'Mutineer'. The next night 'Lawyers, Guns and Money' replaced 'Boom Boom Mancini', which was never repeated, but the others were retained. Altogether between October 4 and November 22, he performed 'Mutineer' 31 times, 'Accidentally Like a Martyr' 22 times and 'Lawyers, Guns and Money' four times. The various-artists posthumous tribute album *Enjoy Every Sandwich: The Songs of Warren Zevon*, released in 2004, included one of Dylan's rough but ineffably tender live versions of 'Mutineer'—not, as it says on the album insert, 'live in Australia' but from his Red Bluff, California, concert of October 7, 2002. (JAKOB DYLAN's band THE WALLFLOWERS recorded 'Lawyers, Guns and Money' for the same album.)

Warren Zevon once said: 'Bob Dylan is the greatest. He was the greatest influence on every singer/songwriter. On everyone with any job remotely like this. Anyone who denies it is lying. There is only Dylan.'

Zevon's own final album, *The Wind*, was issued the month before he died, and was widely regarded as a strong addition to his canon. 'If you're lucky,' he once said, 'people like something you do early and something you do just before you drop dead. That's as many pats on the back as you can expect.'He died of mesothelioma, a rare and inoperable cancer in his lungs and liver, in LA on September 7, 2003. He was 56.

[Warren Zevon albums: *Wanted Dead or Alive*, US, 1969; *Warren Zevon*, 1976; *Excitable Boy*, 1978; *Bad Luck Streak in Dancing School*, 1980; *Stand in the Fire*, 1981; *The Envoy*, 1982; *A Quiet Normal Life: The Best of Warren Zevon*, 1986; *Sentimental Hygiene*, Virgin America 7-90603-1, 1987 (CD-reissue V21Y-86012-2); *Transverse City*, 1989; *Mr. Bad Example*, 1991; *Learning to Flinch*, 1993; *Mutineer*, 1995; *I'll Sleep When I'm Dead (An Anthology)*, 1996; *Life'll Kill Ya*, 2000; *My Ride's Here*, 2002; *Genius: The Best of Warren Zevon* (a Rhino anthology), 2002; *The Wind*, Artemis 51156, 2003. Hindu Love Gods: *Hindu Love Gods*, Warner Bros. 24406-2, US, 1990. Quote re pats on back, interview in *Entertainment Weekly*, *nia*, US, 1993. Various Artists: *Enjoy Every Sandwich: The Songs of Warren Zevon*, Artemis 51581, 2004. Zevon quote on Dylan online 4 Oct 2005 at *http://frontpage.simnet.is/bobdylan/friends.htm*.]

***Zimmerman Blues* [fanzine]** See **Styble, Bryan**.

Zimmerman, David [1946 -] David Benjamin Zimmerman, Bob Dylan's younger brother, was born in February 1946 in Duluth, Minnesota, two years before the family moved to Hibbing. When David was six and Bob 11, their cousin Harriet Rutstein started to give both boys piano lessons on the Gulbranson upright their parents had bought. Their uncle, Lewis Stone, told Dylan biographer HOWARD SOUNES that David was the better player: 'David . . . was a very, very smart boy [who] took it all in . . . he could play better than Bob. He was very musically inclined.' (Six years later, Les Rutstein became general manager of Hibbing radio station WMFG, and got a very hard time about its 'square' programming from the less musical Bob.)

Sounes tries to make a small mountain out of the fact that as children Bob and David weren't close—that David would be excluded when Bob's friends were around; that they didn't walk around town together—but of course that's how it was: look at the age gap. Who *does* want their kid sibling around when their friends come over? It would have been weird if they *had* been close. All the same, David was relied on to take the Polaroid shots of Bob that he started to pose for—practising for stardom—around 1956. And after that stardom had arrived, in the spring of 1964 Bob made a return visit to Hibbing to attend the kid brother's high school graduation. On June 6, 1968, the day after their father died of a heart attack, it was David who collected Bob from the tiny Hibbing-Chisolm Airport and drove him back to a house full of relatives and neighbours. After the funeral, David drove Bob round Hibbing on a rainy afternoon, and thought him 'So calm, so reserved, so clean . . . almost so saintly!' he told ROBERT SHELTON.

A few days before his important Carnegie Hall concert on October 26, 1963, attended by his parents, Dylan had told a *Newsweek* reporter: 'I don't know my parents. They don't know me. I've lost contact with them . . .' The journalist found him out, and got a quote from David, then 17, as well. 'We were kind of close,' David told *Newsweek*. 'We're both kind of ambitious. When we set out to do something, we usually get it done,' to which he added this clipped but truthful insight: 'He set out to become what he is.'

TOBY THOMPSON interviewed David Zimmerman around five years later. They met in a bar in Minneapolis one weekend in 1968–69: 'David was short like Bob, but stocky. Close to fat. He wore glasses; and well-tailored sports clothes—stylish—jodhpur boots, mod English jacket, cuffless tapered trousers—the whole trip.' Zimmerman wouldn't say much, reacting with frosty silence to Thompson's prattle, but he couldn't resist rubbishing the motorcycle crash:

'Know how Bob hurt himself on that motorcycle? He was riding around the backyard on the *grass* and slipped. That's all.' So he didn't really break his neck? 'Sure, if a cracked vertebra is a broken neck.'

Wife Gail was a Catholic, and when David had wanted to marry her, in the spring of 1968 (when he was only 22), this was a big deal in the Zimmerman family, and caused so much agitation to his father, who was unwell, that the wedding was postponed from its planned date of May 30. Abe Zimmerman told Robert Shelton: 'When my boys make mistakes, they make big ones.' On June 5, Abe died. The wedding went ahead later.

David Zimmerman was the culprit who persuaded Dylan that the tapes from the New York *Blood on the Tracks* sessions of September 1974 weren't good enough, and to take them up to Minnesota where he gathered together a new group of musicians for Bob to rework them with—overseeing all this because at the time he managed some local groups, was au fait with studio availability and so on. In the case of 'Lily, Rosemary and the Jack of Hearts' this brought about an improvement, mostly in Dylan's own re-writing and telling of the tale, but in other cases, especially that of 'Idiot Wind', the change was not for the better.

Nonetheless, David and Bob continue to have business connections: joint ownership of an old theatre in Minneapolis, and even an association in Circuit Films, the distributor of *Renaldo & Clara*.

On September 25, 2004, Bob returned to Hibbing to attend the funeral of David's mother-in-law, Myrtle Jurenes, spoke for a few minutes to his own English teacher, B.J. Rolfzen, and then left in a pick-up truck, not staying for the lunch laid on for relatives and friends.

David's sons Seth and Luke Zimmerman are both musicians, Seth leading the alt-country outfit Tangletown. Asked in December 2005 about his father's activities these days, Luke replied: 'My dad is retired from the music scene right now.'

[Robert Shelton, *No Direction Home: The Life and Music of Bob Dylan*, London: Penguin 1987 edn., quote p.61. Toby Thompson, *Positively Main Street: An Unorthodox View of Bob Dylan*, London: New English Library edn., March 1972 reprint, pp.72–74. Howard Sounes, *Down the Highway: A Life of Bob Dylan*, New York: Grove Press, 2001, Lewis Stone quote ms p.34, David 1963 quote ms p.178. Paolo Vites, 'Oh no! Not another Zimmerman!: An interview with Luke Zimmerman', *Rock 'n'Roll Circus*, Italy, 9 Dec 2005, seen online 13 Feb 2006 at *www.lukezimmerman.com/press.htm*.]

Zimmerman family, the Robert Allen Zimmerman and his younger brother, DAVID ZIMMERMAN, are the children of Abe and Beatty Zimmerman. For Beatty's side of the family, see **the Stone/Edelstein family**.

Abram H. Zimmerman, Bob's father, was born in America, in Duluth, Minnesota, on October 19, 1911, into a family of four other children. If you believe the 1920 census details, Abe was the first of the family born in the USA: but that would mean that the brother a year or two older than him, Jack/Jake, must have been born quite soon before their mother's arrival, which was definitely in 1910: which in turn is problematic since their father had arrived in 1907. It's more reasonable to believe the 1930 census, which says that Jack/Jake was born in the US a year ahead of Abe.

Abe's father—Bob's paternal grandfather—is Zigman Zimmerman; his Hebrew name is Zisel. 'I don't know how they got a German name,' said Dylan in the 1978 *Playboy* interview. Zigman was born in the thrusting Russian port of Odessa on Christmas Day 1875, and grew up in an atmosphere of active, vicious anti-Semitism. He seems to have run a shoe-making sweatshop before he fled Tzar Nicholas II's pogroms in 1906. His brother Wolfe not only stayed behind but became a soldier in the Russian army.

Zigman arrived into the US in 1907, through Ellis Island to New York City, like so many others. From there he moved north-west until he arrived in Duluth. He worked as a peddler and sent for his family soon afterwards: by 1910 they had arrived. His wife Anna, formerly Chana Greenstein, born in Odessa on March 16, 1878, had given birth to three children before their emigration: Maurice, aged eight on arrival; Minnie, aged six; and Paul, four. They squeezed into a small apartment at 22½ West 1st Street, where we presume the fourth child, Jake, was born (though the 1930 census says he was born in Wisconsin). Either way, before the next brother, Max, came along in 1914, the Zimmermans had moved to a house: 221 Lake Avenue North, Duluth. It is the only one of the homes Bob Dylan's father lived in as a child and as a young adult that does not still exist.

Zigman was still a peddler when Abe was born, but by 1917, Zigman, now styling himself Zigmond H. Zimmerman, was a 'solicitor' working for the Prudential Life Insurance Co. He had obtained his naturalisation papers in 1916, but when the US entered the Great War in 1918, the Zimmermans were forced to register as aliens. His wife Anna told the registrar she was a dressmaker, and that she spoke 'a little English'. Zigmond could speak it but not read it. By 1920 he was a dry goods salesman; later that decade he opened his shoe store but it failed, and by 1930 he was a salesman in someone else's. All the same, in 1925 they moved again, to a two-storey house at 725 East 3rd Street.

By 1930 the oldest children, Maurice and Minnie had left home, Maurice first working on railway equipment repairs and then as a railway ticket inspector, while Minnie worked as a typist at the *Duluth Herald* newspaper. Still living at home, 24-year-old Paul had become packer, clerk and then salesman for the Manhattan Woolen Mills. Abe, who by the age of seven had been shining shoes and delivering newspapers, had graduated from the repulsive looking Central High School in 1929, was now 18 and working for the Standard Oil company, first as messenger boy and then as clerk. As Dylan commented in 1978: '. . . my father never had time to go to college.'

When Abe, aged 22, married 18-year-old Beatty, whom he'd met on one of her weekend trips to Duluth, on June 10, 1934 at her parents' house in Hibbing, his older brother Paul was best man. They honeymooned in Chicago and then came back to live in Duluth, with Abe's mother and the three youngest brothers at 402 East 5th Street. Abe's father, Zigman, had moved out and had an apartment in the Kinsley Apartments on West 1st Street. On July 6, 1936, he died of a heart attack in the street on 2nd Avenue West, in a heat wave, at the age of 60.

Abe duly became a senior manager at Standard Oil, and ran the company union; he and Beatty moved house several more times, finally escaping Abe's siblings by moving into the upstairs of a duplex at 519 3rd Avenue East, high up on the hillside overlooking the port and Lake Superior. Their first child, Robert Allen Zimmerman, was born at the nearby St. Mary's Hospital on May 24, 1941, weighing in at 7lb 13oz: 'about as big as a good-sized lake trout,' writes DAVE ENGEL, in his invaluable *Just Like Bob Zimmerman's Blues—Dylan in Minnesota*. Robert Allen's Hebrew name is Shabtai Zisel ben Avraham.

In 1947 the family moved to Hibbing, where Abe's brothers Maurice and Paul had set up Micka Electric Co. the year Bob was born. Abe became an appliance salesman. When Bob's little brother David was a bit older, Beatty started working as a clerk at Feldman's clothing shop in the main street, Howard Street.

Abe contracted polio and suffered its debilitating physical consequences all through Bob's childhood. 'My father,' Dylan told the French paper *L'Expresse* in 1978, 'was a very active man, but he was stricken very early by an attack of polio. The illness put an end to all his dreams, I believe. He could hardly walk . . .' But others reported that he walked with a slight limp, not always noticeable. His mother, Anna, who had also moved to Hibbing, and lived for some years with Bob's Uncle Maurice, moved into a nursing home way down in St. Paul and died there of arteriosclerosis on April 20, 1955. She had outlived her husband by almost 20 years.

Her death certificate, with the information supplied by Uncle Maurice, confirmed that she'd been born in Odessa. Dylan contradicts this, writing in *Chronicles Volume One* of visiting her when she still lived in Duluth: she 'had only one leg and had been a seamstress. She was a dark lady, smoked a pipe. . . . [Her] voice possessed a haunting accent—face always set in a half-despairing expression. . . . She'd come to America from Odessa. . . . [but] Originally she'd come from Turkey, sailed from Trabzon, a port town, across the Black Sea. . . . Her family was from Kagizman, a town in Turkey near the Armenian border, and the family name had been Kirghiz. My grandfather's parents had also come from that area. . . . My grandmother's ancestors had been from Constantinople.'

Abe Zimmerman had a heart attack in summer 1966. On June 5, 1968, soon after 5 PM, he died of a second heart attack. He was buried in Duluth.

[Main sources: predominantly Dave Engel, *Just Like Bob Zimmerman's Blues—Dylan in Minnesota*, Rudolph, WI: River City Memoirs—Mesabi, 1977, incl. Abe's 'slight limp' (p.109); plus: Engel, emails to this writer 19 Nov 2005 & 22 Feb 2006; 1920 & 1930 US Censuses, Duluth City; Robert Shelton, *No Direction Home: The Life and Music of Bob Dylan*, London: Penguin edn., 1987, pp.59–60. Bob Dylan in *L'Expresse*, Paris, *nia*, 1978, quoted in Engel; *Chronicles Volume One* pp.92–93.]

Bob Dylan's parents, Beatty & Abe Zimmerman

Index